BECOMING AMERICA IS A 21ST-CENTURY APPROACH TO LEARNING HISTORY

SMARTBOOK™

STUDY SMARTER WITH SMARTBOOK

The first and only adaptive reading experience, SmartBook is changing the way students read and learn. As a student engages with SmartBook, the reading experience continually adapts by highlighting content based on what that student knows and doesn't know. This capability ensures that the student is focused on the content needed to close specific knowledge gaps, while it simultaneously promotes long-term learning.

LEARNSMART®

LEARN BETTER WITH LEARNSMART

The premier learning system, LearnSmart is designed to effectively assess a student's knowledge of course content through a series of adaptive questions. LearnSmart intelligently pinpoints concepts the student does not understand and maps out a personalized study plan for success. LearnSmart prepares students for class, thereby allowing instructors to focus on higher-level learning.

Which of the following statements best describes the Freedmen's Bureau?

It was an agency created by southern states to help provide jobs for emancipated African Americans.

It was a federal agency charged with helping former slaves make the transition to freedom.

It was a charity established by northern churches to help former slaves.

It was an agency created by southern states to monitor working conditions on former plantations.

Click one of the buttons below.

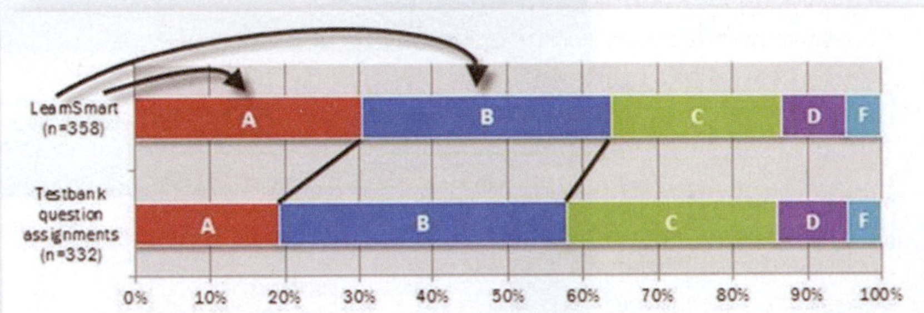

The distribution shows the aggregate of letter grades assigned by instructors. A Chi Square test was performed to determine if final course grades were distributed differently across the two groups (control and experimental). The test indicated a significant difference, X2 (4) = 11.667, p = .020 (an alpha level of .05 was adopted for this statistical test).

THINK CRITICALLY WITH CRITICAL MISSIONS

Critical Missions immerse students as active participants in a series of transformative moments in history. As advisors to key historical figures, students read and analyze sources, interpret maps and timelines, and write recommendations. In the process, students learn to think like a historian, conducting a retrospective analysis from a contemporary perspective.

Critical Mission | Experience History | **Truman and the Atomic Bomb**

learn about your mission

I have been president for only a few months, assuming the position of Commander-in-Chief for a nation involved a long, global war. New technology has provided me with an atomic bomb-the world's first nuclear weapon-which could forever change the face of warfare. Now, I must decide whether to use this devastating new weapon to end the war with Japan. One group of advisors, including my chief advisor and long-time mentor, Secretary of State James F. Byrnes, is encouraging me to approve the plan. Another group, including the Under-Secretary of State and expert on Japa[n] Grew, advises against it. Here is wha[t]

1. Review the information on t[he] pages-the timeline, the maps
2. Identify important themes a[nd] advisors have considered in opinions;
3. Write your recommendation should use the atomic bomb the themes and evidence to s[upport] conclusion.

This is a decision that will shape the consider it well!

President Harry S Truman

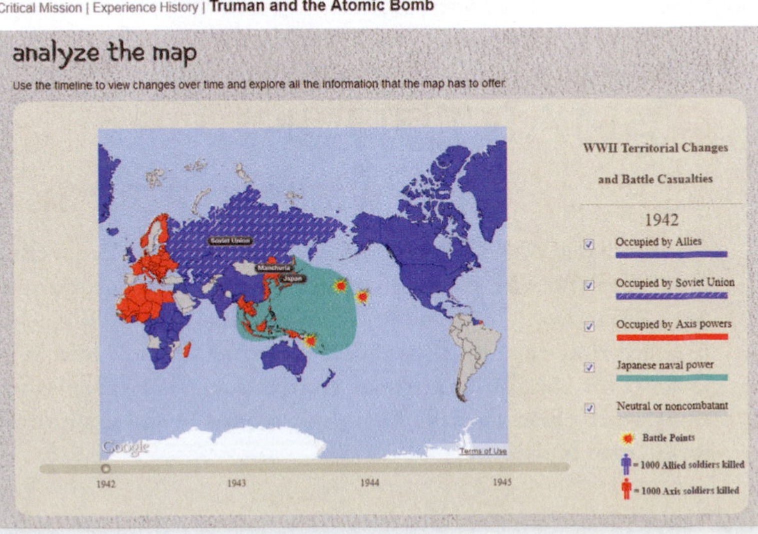

SUCCEED FASTER WITH CONNECT HISTORY

Connect History strengthens the links among faculty, students, and coursework. Innovative, adaptive technology aligns the goals of students and faculty, allowing them to work together to accomplish more in less time. Connect History engages students in the course content so they are better prepared, take a more active part in discussions, and achieve better course performance.

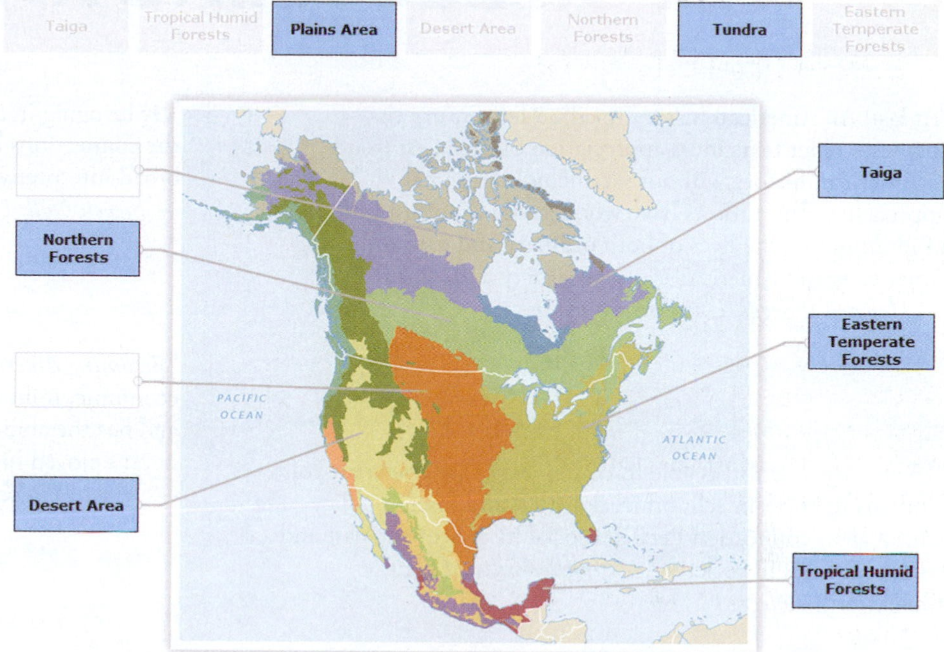

EASY ACCESS WITH MHCAMPUS

Becoming America integrates into school learning management systems, providing single sign-on access for students and a comprehensive grade book for instructors. With MHCampus, instructors can track students' progress, monitor and remediate on challenging topics, and ensure that students master the learning outcomes and core objectives of their U.S. history course.

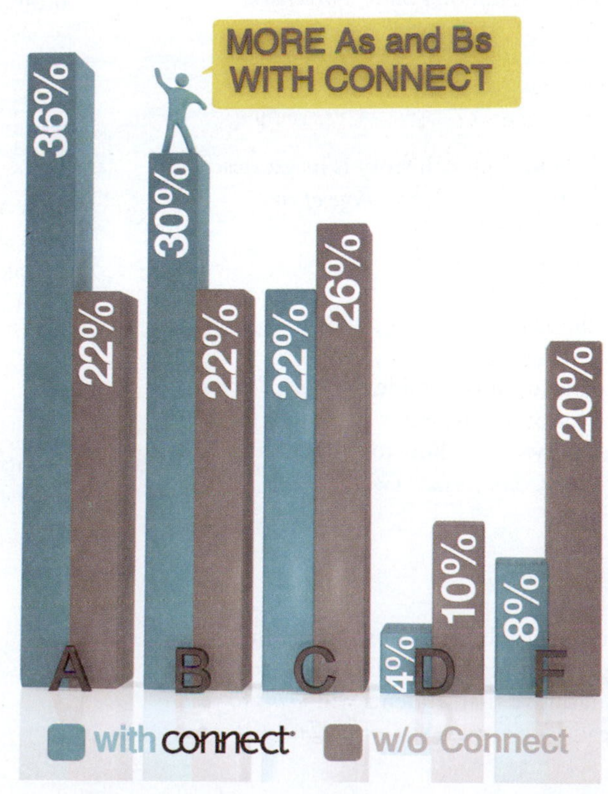

PRAISE FOR BECOMING AMERICA

"At last! An American history for the 21st century that surpasses older texts in its appreciation of the latest trends in American history without sacrificing traditional approaches. The authors have wonderfully innovative means of illuminating the lives of both ordinary and extraordinary Americans and America's evolving society and culture." — *Howard P. Segal, University of Maine*

"[*Becoming America*] is able to combine all that you want your students to cover in economic, political, and foreign policy with a great connection between social history of the past and current themes in society." — *Manfred Silva, El Paso Community College*

"This is an innovative text that offers a coherent, intelligent, and manageable survey of U.S. history. I think students will love it." — *Katherine Hijar, California State University, San Marcos*

"The use of various media to explore history is its greatest strength." — *Roger Rawlings, Savannah College of Art and Design*

"The authors' approach is to think outside the box: *Becoming America* is written not for other historians but rather for students, in a way that shows them how to think as historians think." — *Stephen F. Lopez, San Jacinto College*

"This is a well-written history that uses popular culture of the time periods to engage the student and tell the story of the United States. It is a narrative that students will *want* to read rather than *have* to read." — *Carole N. Lester, University of Texas, Dallas*

"By bringing in aspects of daily life, the book shows students the connections between seemingly mundane 'things' and the broad interpretive framework of American history." — *Steven Noll, University of Florida*

"*Becoming America* enthusiastically recounts the political, economic, military, and social history of the United States and has the ability to draw in students who may claim to have never enjoyed history. This might change their minds." — *Wyatt Moulds, Jones County Junior College*

"I think the authors did a fantastic job bringing together current scholarship, finding so many fascinating anecdotes and stories, and accurately explaining the broad scope of American history.... My older colleagues who like political history will not be disappointed, but the younger and women professors will be pleased with the focus on culture." — *Mike Young, Trinity Valley Community College*

"The authors are able to tell the story of men and women who shaped and led this nation and the millions of ordinary people who collectively created the American character." — *Walter Miszczenko, College of Western Idaho*

"In its goals, I'd definitely rate *Becoming America* at the top of the heap." — *Devan Bissonette, Northern Arizona University*

BECOMING AMERICA

A HISTORY FOR THE 21ST CENTURY

DAVID HENKIN **REBECCA McLENNAN**

The University of California, Berkeley

BECOMING AMERICA: A HISTORY FOR THE 21ST CENTURY

Some ancillaries, including electronic and print components, may not be available to customers outside the United States.

This book is printed on acid-free paper.

1 2 3 4 5 6 7 8 9 0 DOW/DOW 1 0 9 8 7 6 5 4

ISBN: 978-0-07-338563-1 (complete)
MHID: 0-07-338563-8 (complete)
ISBN: 978-0-07-727560-0 (volume 1)
MHID: 0-07-727560-8 (volume 1)
ISBN: 978-0-07-727561-7 (volume 2)
MHID: 0-07-727561-6 (volume 2)

Senior Vice President, Products & Markets: *Kurt L. Strand*
Vice President, General Manager, Products & Markets: *Michael J. Ryan*
Vice President, Content Production & Technology Services: *Kimberly Meriwether David*
Managing Director: *Gina Boedeker*
Director: *Matt Busbridge*
Brand Manager: *Laura Wilk*
Director of Development: *Rhona Robbin*
Content Development Editors: *Sylvia Mallory, Cynthia Ward*
Managing Development Editor: *Nancy Crochiere*
Maps: *Robin Mouat and Mapping Specialists*
Brand Coordinator: *Kaelyn Schulz*
Digital Product Analyst: *John Brady*
Digital Development Editor: *Denise Wright, Southern Editorial*
Executive Marketing Manager: *Stacy Best Ruel*
Director, Content Production: *Terri Schiesl*
Content Project Manager: *Emily Kline*
Senior Buyer: *Carol A. Bielski*
Design: *Trevor Goodman*
Cover Image: *Flight Patterns by Aaron Koblin*
Content Licensing Specialist: *Shawntel Schmitt*
Typeface: *10/12 Adobe Garamond Regular*
Compositor: *Aptara®, Inc.*
Printer: *R. R. Donnelley*

Library of Congress Cataloging-in-Publication Data

Henkin, David M.
Becoming America : a history for the 21st century / David Henkin, Rebecca McLennan, The University of California, Berkeley.
pages cm
Includes bibliographical references and index.
ISBN 978-0-07-338563-1 (complete : alk. paper)—ISBN 0-07-338563-8 (complete : alk. paper)—ISBN 978-0-07-727560-0 (volume 1 : alk. paper)—ISBN 0-07-727560-8 (volume 1 : alk. paper)—ISBN 978-0-07-727561-7 (volume 2 : alk. paper)—ISBN 0-07-727561-6 (volume 2 : alk. paper)
1. United States—History—Textbooks. I. McLennan, Rebecca M., 1967- II. Title.
E178.1.H485 2015
973—dc23
2013032368

www.mhhe.com

ABOUT THE AUTHORS

DAVID HENKIN

Since David Henkin joined the history faculty at the University of California, Berkeley, in 1997, he has taught and written about the sorts of subjects that rarely make it into traditional textbooks. He has offered entire courses on baseball, Broadway, consumption, time, leisure, newspapers, world cities, and urban literature, while publishing books and essays about street signs, paper money, junk mail, and intimate correspondence in the nineteenth century. The task of integrating that kind of material into the traditional narrative of the American past has been the singular challenge of his professional life. David holds a BA from Yale University and a PhD from U.C. Berkeley, and he was awarded Berkeley's Distinguished Teaching Award in the Social Sciences. Beyond the Berkeley campus, David teaches classes on the Bible, plays cards, eats lots of fish and berries, roots passionately for the St. Louis Cardinals, and accumulates frequent-flyer miles at a frenetic pace. Raised in New York, where his family still lives, he makes his home with friends and community in San Francisco.

REBECCA McLENNAN

Rebecca McLennan is associate professor of history at the University of California, Berkeley. Her research focuses on America since 1607, with an emphasis on post-revolutionary U.S. legal, political, and cultural history. She received her PhD from Columbia University and was on the faculty at Harvard University before joining Berkeley's history department. She has taught a diverse range of undergraduate courses, including classes on American and global foodways and agriculture since 1491; modern consumer culture; land, law, and property; and crime and punishment from colonial times to the present. Rebecca has published widely in American history and is currently writing a cultural history of courts in the early republic. Her most recent book, *The Crisis of Imprisonment: Protest, Politics, and the Making of the American Penal State, 1776–1941* (Cambridge University Press, 2008), won several major book awards, including the American Historical Association's Littleton-Griswold Prize for best book in U.S. legal history.

DEDICATION

To Mr. Hand, U.S. history teacher at Ridgemont High School, for his faith in our generation.

BRIEF CONTENTS

CONTENTS

5

1700–1765

CHAPTER 5. EMPIRES, WAR, & THE TRANSFORMATION OF INDIAN COUNTRY 102

6

1765–1781

CHAPTER 6. CRISIS & WAR 128

7

1776–1792

CHAPTER 7. MAKING A NEW NATION 158

12

1831–1848

13

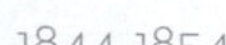

1844–1854

14

1848–1860

19

1878–1896

CHAPTER 19. POLITICS & DISCONTENT IN THE GILDED AGE 500

1896–1914

CHAPTER 20. THE PROGRESSIVE ERA 532

21

1880–1914

CHAPTER 21. BIRTH OF A GREAT POWER: THE UNITED STATES & THE WORLD 564

22

1914–1920

CHAPTER 22. WAR & PEACE 596

1920–1929

CHAPTER 23. AMERICA IN THE JAZZ AGE 628

24

1929–1939

CHAPTER 24. AMERICA REMADE: THE GREAT DEPRESSION & THE NEW DEAL 660

25

1939–1945

CHAPTER 25. AMERICA GOES TO WAR 692

26

1945–1953

CHAPTER 26. POSTWAR AMERICA 724

27

1953–1960

CHAPTER 27. AGE OF AFFLUENCE 756

McDonald's

INTERVIEW WITH THE AUTHORS

Rebecca McLennan and David Henkin

Q. Why a new U.S. history survey—and why now?

A. We wrote *Becoming America* in and for a new century, inspired by recent shifts in historical scholarship and the interests and learning styles of a new generation of students. Today's students live in a world where cultural, technological, and environmental transformation are palpably experienced and keenly debated. Paralleling this reorientation, the topics of environmental change, religious ritual, mass communications, technological innovation, and popular entertainment have become central and compelling subjects of historians' research and teaching. *Becoming America* seamlessly weaves these fascinating dimensions of the past into the core narrative of American history to produce an account that we believe students will find exciting, memorable, and relevant.

Q. What's different about your approach?

A. Key to our approach is an appreciation for how much the study of the past entails learning about the beliefs, attitudes, and mentalities of historical actors and about the worlds of communication and information exchange within which historical events acquired meaning. When we study a war, for example, we need to know more than its political causes and practical course; we also need to understand how different groups of participants, observers, and victims experienced the conflict. How long did it take military leaders in one part of the world to receive messages from civilian authorities in another? How did soldiers experience and make sense of war and demobilization? Did city dwellers read war news in newspapers reporting telegraphed messages from the front? Did voters watch live broadcasts of artillery fire while sitting in their living rooms? How were the dead commemorated? And in what ways did war and the memory of war change American culture, politics, and the economy?

Q. Where does the incorporation of the history of culture, media, technology, and the environment leave the political, social, and economic narrative that is essential to understanding the American past?

A. We have neither thrown out political, social, and economic history nor simply tacked on new subjects. Instead, we have innovated in a way that respects the need for chronology, narrative unity, social inclusiveness, and canonical coverage. For instance, the evolution of the British colonies after the Stuart Restoration, which many surveys identify narrowly as a project of imperial regulation or a pattern of demographic movement, emerges in these pages through broader shifts in folkways, foodways, sexual ethics, consumption, home design, and religious outlook (Chapter 4). Instead of isolating southern plantation slavery in a single chapter on the Old South spanning multiple periods, we spread the discussion of slavery across several chapters, showing how human bondage infused and influenced economic, political, and cultural developments in multiple regions through many different eras. We broaden the conventional treatment of southern Reconstruction as the story of political and economic struggle by exploring the parades, conventions, and "grapevine telegraphs" through which African Americans formulated and relayed their demands for full and meaningful freedom (Chapter 16). Our discussion of the political functions of saloons, urban machines, and women's clubs enlivens the story of Gilded Age government and helps students understand the roots and significance of mass politics (Chapter 19). And rather than painting a picture of the affluent 1950s solely as a period of conservative consensus punctuated by an increasingly assertive civil rights movement, we also explore the cultural and intellectual ferment that preceded and primed the upheavals of the 1960s (Chapter 27). Every chapter weaves new scholarship of this nature into the narrative.

Q. How does integrating old and new approaches enhance students' learning experience?

A. The new synthesis offers distinct advantages. First, students are excited by history that connects to their experience of contemporary life. Mass media, popular entertainment, technological innovation, religious ritual, material culture, and environmental change all capture their imagination, and consequently they come to class engaged and ready to learn more. *Becoming America* shows them how those subjects have developed over time and how earlier patterns of living have informed or differed from the pleasures, frustrations, dangers, and mysteries that students encounter in their own worlds.

Second, our updated survey of the American past helps students relate imaginatively to this rich history by actively drawing upon their interests, passions, and skills as both readers and creators of contemporary culture. We show for instance how nineteenth-century Americans experienced new kinds of connection through the postal service, cheaper newspapers, telegraph wires, sales catalogs, networks of religious instruction, and commercial entertainment. We encourage readers to grasp

the historical significance of slang, fashion trends, marketing strategies, spectator sports, and news scandals. Throughout the narrative, our visual program asks students to analyze the way in which engravers, photographers, cartoonists, advertisers, and other visual artists in both early and later eras created, affirmed, or disrupted public perceptions.

Finally, our approach teaches students to understand and ask questions about the cultural, political, and economic circumstances under which certain new media and technologies find—or fail to find—traction. Why did printing play such a prominent role in the politics of the American Revolution? Why, in the 1920s, did radio quite suddenly becoming a mass medium after years of relative obscurity? By demonstrating how to analyze these phenomena as historians do, we give students new critical tools with which to recognize and analyze the deep connections that bound—and still bind—culture, politics, and economics. Questions probing these connections are included in our Connect History program.

Q. History is more than a grand narrative. How do you incorporate fine-grained details of the sort that enliven the story for students?

A. Boxed essays throughout the text show students in detail how historians analyze the past, while also creating a vivid image of different periods in American history. Every chapter includes features entitled *Hot Commodities* and *Singular Lives,* as well as either a *States of Emergency* or a *Spaces and Places* selection. A set of questions encouraging students to analyze and contextualize the selection rounds out each essay. In addition, the Hot Commodities feature is included in Connect History as a gradable exercise. Descriptions of these learning features appear in the visual walk-through of the text that follows this interview.

Q. These features take the narrative deeper, but how do you guide students through the process of interpreting and analyzing primary sources?

A. Each chapter offers students the opportunity to examine historical evidence through an *Interpreting the Sources* selection. The primary sources in these boxed features include public and private documents, visual sources, material artifacts, and transcripts of oral traditions and stories. A headnote puts the source in context, and a series of questions after the source challenges students to think deeply and analytically about its significance. The *Interpreting the Sources* feature is included in our Connect History program; students can complete the exercise and submit it online for grading.

Q. What will students take away from *Becoming America?*

A. For all of our readers, whether *Becoming America* is their gateway to further studies in history or the only account they will read on the subject, our goals are the same. Our attention to the connections and discontinuities between past and present make it easier for students to grasp both the distinctiveness and the familiarity of bygone eras and to recognize themselves and our own time in the great sweep of American history. Students should come away with a contextualized understanding of the deep cultural changes that have characterized the American past; an appreciation for the interconnections among culture, technology, society, politics, economics, and the environment; and the analytical skills associated with rigorous interpretation of diverse sources. We want them to look with different eyes at the design of their own homes and neighborhoods, to actively interpret the meaning of mass spectacle and social media, and to think in a historically informed way about the urgent questions of our times. We hope that both our narrative and its lessons in critical thinking will help students participate fully and creatively in our diverse and culturally vital democracy.

Q: Is *Becoming America* available as an e-book?

A. Yes, in fact, it's available as a Smartbook, which means that students not only can read it online but can quiz themselves after every section. The Smartbook then adapts to their response, highlighting areas in the narrative that they need to study more.

BECOMING AMERICA:

A new way to learn U.S. history

Becoming America **weaves the latest research on culture, technology, and the environment into the traditional core of the U.S. history survey.**

HOT COMMODITIES offers a detailed study of consumer goods, food, paintings, recordings, and performances that were tellingly popular at a given point in time. These boxes—with topics ranging from beavers and Bibles to cigarettes and garbage—reinforce the importance of material artifacts to the study of the past. The point is that consumption patterns are not new phenomena (though they have changed radically) and that they offer valuable insight into past societies, much as they do in the present day.

HOT COMMODITIES

Whiskey

Early National Grain Surplus. George Washington's whiskey distillery, reconstructed at Mount Vernon.

In an effort to raise revenues, Congress acted in 1791 on Hamilton's plan to tax whiskey and other spirits. Unlike tariffs, which could be collected by customs officials at the ports, the whiskey tax applied to a range of distilleries, large and small, across the country. When government officials tried to collect the tax in 1794 from farmers in western Pennsylvania, an area chronically short on currency and generally hostile to taxation, they met stiff resistance. Whiskey rebels intimidated tax collectors, mobilized their militias, and invoked the spirit of the tax protests against Britain that had launched the revolutionary struggle. As many as seven thousand rebels gathered outside Pittsburgh, but took no immediate action. Still, the Whiskey Rebellion was the first major act of resistance to federal authority under the Constitution. Eager to make a show of strength for the new national government, Hamilton and Washington personally rode out with thirteen thousand militiamen, and the rebellion crumbled without a fight.

Behind this famous political crisis lurked a larger development in American life: an explosive growth in the production and consumption of whiskey. Congress might have targeted distilled spirits as luxurious vices, but whiskey drinking was becoming deeply ingrained in the daily habits of Americans across the socioeconomic spectrum. The late-eighteenth and early-nineteenth centuries marked a high point in alcohol consumption generally, and whiskey drinking in particular. The best evidence suggests that during the first third of the nineteenth century the typical American drank more alcohol than at any time before or after. In 1810, American distilleries were producing more than three gallons of distilled liquors—whiskey, rum, gin, and brandy, typically about 90 proof—for every man, woman, and child, and that figure does not include beer, wine, or cider. Overall, Americans consumed about twice as much alcohol per person in 1810 as they do now. Consumption levels would peak in the 1830s and then drop precipitously (see Chapter 12).

Whiskey flowed freely throughout American society during the early decades of the nineteenth century, though certain portions of the population drank more heavily. Women drank less frequently than men and tended to prefer sweetened rum, hard cider, or alcohol-heavy patent medicines. In the South, blacks drank less than whites. Whereas in white homes a julep before breakfast and whiskey at all meals was quite common, slaves (who in some places faced legal obstacles to buying liquor) typically restricted their serious drinking to special occasions and their everyday intake to a shot of whiskey during the cold season. Despite these variations, alcohol was a basic feature of everyday life in this period. Even religious folk drank heartily by later standards. A southern planter who wished to join the Methodist Church had to restrict his intake—within the acceptable daily quota of a quart of peach brandy. Aspiring ministers at the prestigious New England Andover Seminary would regularly and unabashedly down brandy toddies at the local tavern. Drinking was an important social activity, an indispensable form of hospitality and camaraderie. To refuse a drink was to refuse to enter a world of equality and solidarity.

Historians have offered several explanations for the rise of drinking around the turn of the century, but the most important factor was the growth of whiskey production, which made liquor cheap and plentiful. American farmers were producing large surpluses of grain, especially corn, and for those living in the western part of the country, whiskey was an especially efficient way to deliver corn to distant markets. A horse could carry six times the volume of corn in whiskey form, which was easier to store and far less likely to rot. Shipping grain in this form became even more profitable with technological improvements in the distilling process. Between 1802 and 1815, the federal government issued over one hundred patents for new devices to distill whiskey, which encouraged more farmers to become distillers. Once the Republicans repealed Hamilton's whiskey tax in 1802, the price dropped further. The result was a widespread drinking habit that would form a major part of American economy and culture.

Think About It

1. What does the Whiskey Rebellion suggest about federal power under the new Constitution? How did its outcome compare to that of Shays' Rebellion?
2. How did technological innovations affect whiskey consumption?
3. How have attitudes toward alcoholic beverages changed in the United States since the era of the early republic?

193

SINGULAR LIVES

Ehrich Weiss (Harry Houdini), Escape Artist

For talented new immigrants, the vaudeville stage provided a rare opportunity to gain security and prosperity in their new home. For Ehrich Weiss, born a Hungarian Jew in Budapest in 1874, it was the launch pad for a career as Harry Houdini, the most famous escape artist of all time.

Weiss's family immigrated to the United States in 1876, first living in Wisconsin, where Ehrich Weiss (as Houdini) would later claim to have been born. In 1887, when Ehrich was thirteen, his father, a rabbi, moved the family to New York and became a garment worker. At seventeen, Ehrich began doing magic shows at Coney Island, and a couple of years later, he and his younger brother, Theo, performed at the 1893 World Exposition in Chicago. The duo achieved some renown as part of a magic act dubbed "the Brothers Houdini," a name that evoked the great French illusionist Jean-Eugène Robert-Houdin. From there, "Harry Houdini," as Erich now called himself, started appearing in cheap New York theaters and then in more respectable vaudeville houses, perfecting an act that featured needle-swallowing tricks, handcuff escapes, and other remarkable displays of strength, ingenuity, or deception that captivated audiences. Houdini toured the country, generating publicity for his act by announcing in each new town that he could escape from any handcuffs provided by the local police. Then, at the beginning of the new century, Harry Houdini and his stage partner (and wife) Bess took their show abroad. America's great escape artist quickly became an international celebrity.

Harry Houdini Wows a Crowd. A handcuffed and chained Houdini prepares to plunge into the river below—and miraculously escape his bonds.

Houdini's act had several appeals. For some spectators, his ability to free himself from handcuffs or a straitjacket was truly supernatural, suggesting some link with mysterious powers and unseen worlds. (Houdini went on, in the 1920s, to debunk psychics and spiritualism, but much of his audience continued to believe that he himself had supernatural power.) Others may have been drawn by the challenge of uncovering his secrets, which often involved tools or keys hidden on his person, the athleticism of his acrobatic maneuvers, or the sheer spectacle of his mostly naked body. For Weiss, the role of Houdini the escape artist fit the experience of an immigrant who had left his home, discarded the religious tradition of his father, and made his own way in a new land, without having to endure the constraints of factory labor or office work.

Think About It

1. What traditional values did Houdini's act flaunt? What did his performances celebrate?
2. How would you explain the name Harry Houdini? Why would a Jew from Hungary have taken a stage name that sounded neither Jewish nor Hungarian?

SINGULAR LIVES spotlights unusual women and men whose experience, perspective, or mythological status captures some broader point about the period. These case studies reinforce the notion that individuals as well as larger social forces shape history.

Each chapter offers students the opportunity to examine historical evidence through an **INTERPRETING THE SOURCES** selection. The primary sources in these boxed features include public and private documents, visual sources, material artifacts, and transcripts of oral traditions and stories. A headnote puts the source in context, and a series of questions after the source challenges students to think deeply and analytically about its significance.

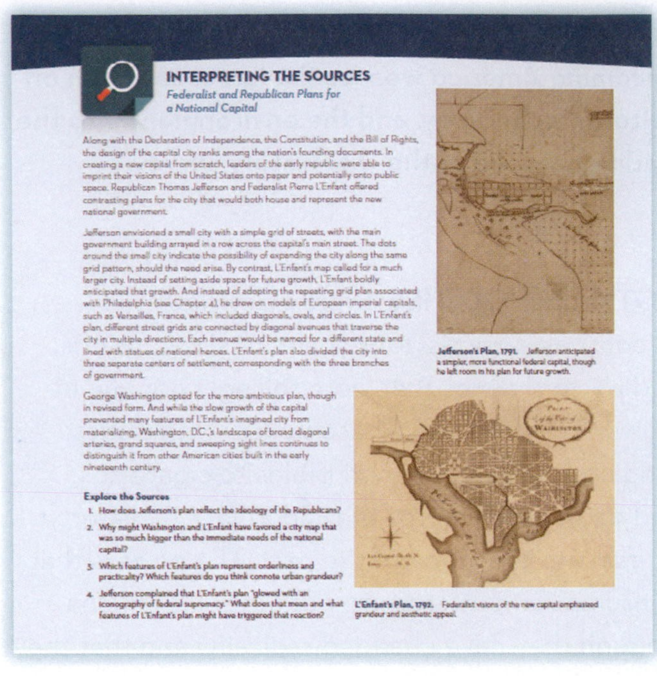

INTERPRETING THE SOURCES

Federalist and Republican Plans for a National Capital

Along with the Declaration of Independence, the Constitution, and the Bill of Rights, the design of the capital city ranks among the nation's founding documents. In creating a new capital from scratch, leaders of the early republic were able to imprint their visions of the United States onto paper and potentially onto public space. Republican Thomas Jefferson and Federalist Pierre L'Enfant offered contrasting plans for the city that would both house and represent the new national government.

Jefferson envisioned a small city with a simple grid of streets, with the main government building arrayed in a row across the capital's main street. The dots around the small city indicate the possibility of expanding the city along the same grid pattern, should the need arise. By contrast, L'Enfant's map called for a much larger city. Instead of setting aside space for future growth, L'Enfant boldly anticipated that growth. And instead of adopting the repeating grid plan associated with Philadelphia (see Chapter 4), he drew on models of European imperial capitals, such as Versailles, France, which included diagonals, ovals, and circles. In L'Enfant's plan, different street grids are connected by diagonal avenues that traverse the city in multiple directions. Each avenue would be named for a different state and lined with statues of national heroes. L'Enfant's plan also divided the city into three separate centers of settlement, corresponding with the three branches of government.

George Washington opted for the more ambitious plan, though in revised form. And while the slow growth of the capital prevented many features of L'Enfant's imagined city from materializing, Washington, D.C.,'s landscape of broad diagonal arteries, grand squares, and sweeping sight lines continues to distinguish it from other American cities built in the early nineteenth century.

Jefferson's Plan, 1791. Jefferson anticipated a simpler, more functional federal capital, though he left room in his plan for future growth.

L'Enfant's Plan, 1792. Federalist visions of the new capital emphasized grandeur and aesthetic appeal.

Explore the Sources

1. How does Jefferson's plan reflect the ideology of the Republicans?
2. Why might Washington and L'Enfant have favored a city map that was so much bigger than the immediate needs of the national capital?
3. Which features of L'Enfant's plan represent orderliness and practicality? Which features do you think connote urban grandeur?
4. Jefferson complained that L'Enfant's plan "glowed with an iconography of federal supremacy." What does that mean and what features of L'Enfant's plan might have triggered that reaction?

STATES OF EMERGENCY

The New York City Blackout of 1977

Through much of the twentieth century, New York City's bright electric lights distinguished nighttime in the United States' largest city, enhancing the city's claims to metropolitan grandeur and captivating the national imagination. On the evening of July 13, 1977, however, the city went suddenly and frighteningly dark. This was not the first time the lights went out in New York. Twelve years earlier, a regional blackout had shut down power through much of the Northeast. But the 1977 blackout was limited to New York City, and it struck during an economic downturn, at the end of a scorching summer day, when New Yorkers were reeling from the unsolved and ongoing crimes of a notorious serial killer. Unlike the 1965 blackout, whose occurrence at dusk gave residents some daylight time to prepare for the night ahead, the 1977 outage had an immediate visual impact.

Dark Skyline. Against this backdrop, a prolonged riot of looting and arson engulfed much of the city unlike anything that New York had experienced since the draft riots of the Civil War—which coincidentally had begun on the exact same date 114 years earlier.

The blackout was triggered by lightning strikes that tripped breakers and downed transmission lines at the plants of Con Edison, New York's power provider. Defective equipment and inadequate responses by the power company exacerbated the situation, and by 9:37 p.m. almost the entire city was without electricity, which was not restored until late the next day. What caused the crime spree that ensued is harder to determine. Looting erupted in thirty-one different neighborhoods throughout the city but Brooklyn, New York's most populous borough, felt the heaviest impact. In Brooklyn's Bushwick neighborhood, fires consumed whole blocks. Bushwick had been a middle-class area in the 1950s, but white flight, the decline of the Brooklyn Navy Yard, and the razing of single-family housing to make room for new housing projects had turned it into one of the city's poorest districts. By 1977, 80 percent of Bushwick residents were unemployed and the neighborhood had the highest infant mortality rate in the city. With the power down and police and firefighting services strained, desperate and angry residents found both an opportunity to steal and an outlet for their rage.

When the lights finally came back on, New Yorkers tallied up the heavy toll: stores destroyed, buildings burned to the ground, 4,500 individuals arrested (most of them in a single mass sweep), and more than $300 million in damage. City officials blamed Con Edison officials, who in turn called the outage an act of God and blamed the city for the poverty that lay at the root of the rioting. New York voters rejected incumbent mayor Abe Beame four months later, electing tough-on-crime candidate Ed Koch. To the rest of the country, viewing darkened skylines and burning houses on the evening news, the events of July 13–14, 1977, seemed to confirm what so many headlines, television shows, and movies had suggested. The great metropolis had declined.

Think About It

1. Why might a power outage have encouraged angry residents to riot and loot?
2. How did the fact that the 1977 blackout affected New York alone, rather than the larger region, contribute to the meaning of the event?

STATES OF EMERGENCY dramatizes scenes and moments of destruction, violence, epidemic, and natural disaster, from the Stono Rebellion and the New Madrid Earthquake to the Great Chicago Fire and the New York blackout of 1977. These extraordinary events often had far-reaching social and political consequences for the story we tell in the main narrative, but they also gripped the popular imagination and became the focus of fears and fantasies that help us understand larger historical forces.

BECOMING AMERICA

is a Program for the 21st Century

The Connect History digital program that accompanies *Becoming America* includes

- map activities using key maps from the text
- image analysis activities that ask students to examine artifacts and images
- primary source activities built around the documents in *Becoming America*
- key terms quizzes
- multiple-choice, short-answer, and essay questions

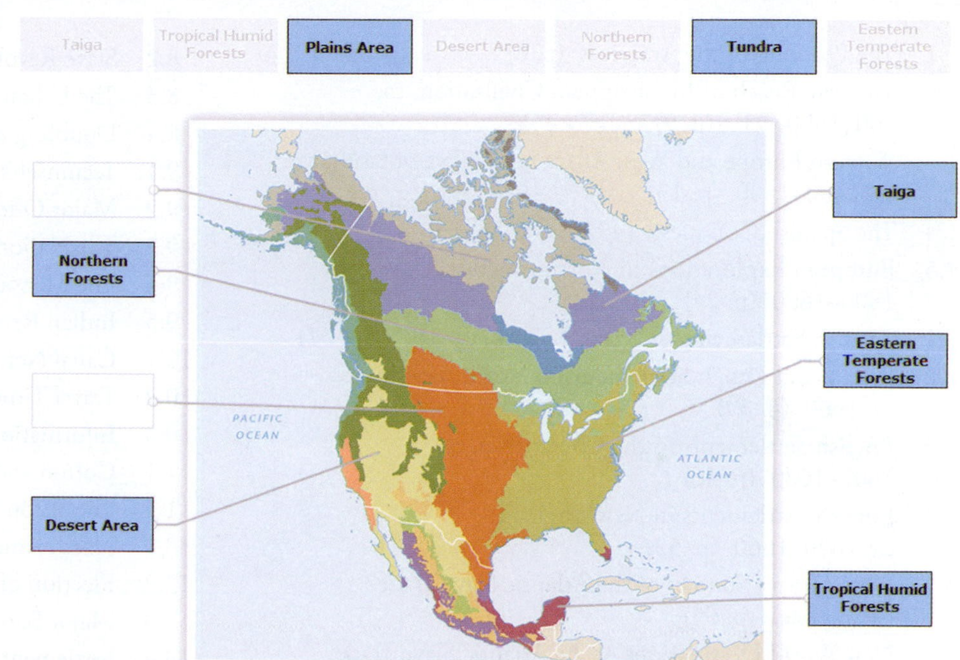

SPACES & PLACES

Cahokia, Hub City

Long before Europeans settled the region, a great city stood on a stretch of bottomland on the eastern side of the Mississippi River. For several centuries (longer than the United States has been a nation), the place historians call Cahokia was North America's largest city and the center of an extensive political and cultural empire. A thousand years ago, all roads led to Cahokia. And then it seems to have vanished.

After the urban settlement dispersed around the 1300s, the only traces of this once-mighty civilization were about two hundred pyramids of packed earth, spread out over 3,200 acres. In later centuries, French, Spanish, English, and eventually American travelers encountered these mound-like structures, but they did not see them as evidence of an American Indian city. Nineteenth-century Americans proposed theories of a lost race of pre-Indian moundbuilders, and in the early twentieth century, leading geologists regarded the mounds as natural phenomena. While Americans studied the scrolls, paintings, and hieroglyphs of distant civilizations, they had no idea that a major city had stood on the Illinois side of the Mississippi River.

Cahokia as It May Have Appeared in Its Heyday. The flat-topped pyramid at the center, later called Monks Mound, towered one hundred feet high and spanned sixteen acres at its base.

The history of that forgotten city lay buried deep in the ground, beneath layers of human activity. Even the mysterious earthen monuments themselves had begun to disappear. By the time of the Civil War many of the great mounds had been leveled. Since the 1960s, however, archaeologists have excavated evidence of a large housing development from the eleventh century. They reconstructed a circle of upright posts that were the basis of a large astronomical observatory. They found burial pits used to honor the city's great chiefs. They identified artifacts, such as distinctive chunkey stones (see p. 9), that established the city's central place in a far-flung culture. And they established a map of the city's earthworks projects, which included a central plaza the size of thirty-five football fields—the biggest planned public space built up to that point in the lands that would become the United States.

Prior to Cahokia's rediscovery, French and then American settlers had established a city, St. Louis, in the same area. As the St. Louis metropolitan region grew, many traces of the ancient ruins were destroyed. By the second half of the twentieth century, rental subdivisions in the Illinois suburbs of St. Louis covered the Grand Plaza where Mississippians had once regularly gathered to observe the stars and pay homage to the forces that controlled the universe. Ironically, however, the fact that St. Louis became a bustling U.S. transportation hub may have helped preserve Cahokia's history. In the late 1950s, when the federal government introduced a new interstate highway system, St. Louis was chosen as a gateway city. Once again all roads led to Cahokia, as five different interstate highway routes ribboned through the site that several archaeologists had recently begun to excavate. The possibility that the final remains of the mounds would be leveled to make room for off-ramps galvanized the archaeological community, and the fact that the land now passed into public control prompted a massive study of the site's history. By 1963, as construction began on St. Louis's Gateway Arch monument, scholars pieced together a picture of a forgotten Indian city just across the river.

Cahokia Today. Monk's Mound, Cahokia Mounds State Historic Site. Monk's Mound, shown here in aerial view, is flanked by two small strands of the vast network of paved roads streaming in and out of St. Louis, Cahokia's modern counterpart.

Think About It

1. Why might Americans in the nineteenth and twentieth centuries have been reluctant to believe that the enormous earthen mounds were once part of an American Indian city?
2. How would you explain the fact that a large city emerged on this location, so close to where St. Louis would be built many centuries later?

SPACES & PLACES features buildings, landscapes, monuments, and virtual spaces as sources for exploring the country's built and natural environments. U.S. history is partly a story of how human beings have continually reshaped and reimagined the landscapes that we now take for granted. With rich pictorial detail, we show how the spaces and places in which history unfolds have transformed over time.

LIST OF MAPS

MORE PRIMARY SOURCES IN CREATE

The American History Document Collection in McGraw-Hill's Create (www.mcgrawhillcreate.com) allows you to choose from over 300 primary sources, each with a headnote and questions, that can be added to your print text. Create also allows you to rearrange or omit chapters, combine material from other sources, and/or upload your syllabus or any other content you have written to make the perfect resources for your students. You can search thousands of leading McGraw-Hill textbooks to find the best content for your students, then arrange it to fit your teaching style. When you order a Create book, you receive a complimentary review copy in three to five business days or an electronic copy (eComp) via e-mail in about an hour. Register today at www.mcgrawhillcreate.com and craft your course resources to match the way you teach.

INSTRUCTOR RESOURCES ON THE ONLINE LEARNING CENTER

Online Learning Center for *Becoming America* at www.mhhe.com/becomingamerica1e contains a wealth of instructor resources, including an Instructor's Manual, Test Bank, and PowerPoint presentations for each chapter. All maps and most images from the print text are included. A computerized test bank powered by McGraw-Hill's EZ Test allows you to quickly create a customized exam using the publisher's supplied test questions or add your own. You decide the number, type, and order of test questions with a few simple clicks. EZ Test runs on your computer without a connection to the Internet.

CourseSmart

COURSESMART E-BOOKS

CourseSmart offers thousands of the most commonly adopted textbooks across hundreds of courses from a wide variety of higher education publishers. It is the only place for faculty to review and compare the full text of a textbook online, providing immediate access without the environmental impact of requesting a printed exam copy. At CourseSmart, students can save up to 50 percent off the cost of a printed book, reduce their impact on the environment, and gain access to powerful web tools for learning, including full text search, notes and highlighting, and e-mail tools for sharing notes among classmates. Learn more at www.coursesmart.com.

MCGRAW-HILL CAMPUS

McGraw-Hill Campus is the first-of-its-kind institutional service providing faculty with true single sign-on access to all of McGraw-Hill's course content, digital tools, and other high-quality learning resources from any learning management system (LMS). This innovative offering allows for secure and deep integration and seamless access to any of our course solutions such as McGraw-Hill Connect, McGraw-Hill Create, McGraw-Hill LearnSmart, or Tegrity. McGraw-Hill Campus includes access to our entire content library, including e-books, assessment tools, presentation slides, and multimedia content, among other resources, providing faculty open and unlimited access to prepare for class, create tests/quizzes, develop lecture material, integrate interactive content, and much more.

AUTHOR ACKNOWLEDGMENTS

The authors take great pleasure in thanking the many students, colleagues, friends, family members, teachers, reviewers, and collaborators who climbed aboard for one stage or another of the epic journey that was the making of this book. Over the years, countless and diverse U.C. Berkeley undergraduates have inspired us, enlightened us, and enduringly shaped the content and method of *Becoming America*. Corey Brooks, Adrianne Francisco, Bobby Lee, Erica Lee, Sarah Gold McBride, Giuliana Perrone, and Jacqueline Shine conducted indispensable research along the way and left a powerful imprint on the final product. Mark Peterson, Robin Einhorn, and Ray Raphael reviewed and commented on specific chapters and rescued us from errors of both judgment and fact. Jennifer Elias read many, many versions of many, many chapters and has now forgotten more about U.S. History than most professionals. Many thanks also to Rebecca Groves, who offered invaluable insights throughout, researched and contributed hundreds of extraordinary images to Volume 1, and made the creative process even more exhilarating.

A few longer-term acknowledgments are also in order. Adam Reingold, who sat near one of the authors at a wedding almost a decade ago, made the crucial introduction to Jon-David Hague, whose early vision of a new kind of textbook brought this project into our lives. Mark Kishlansky's sage and timely advice is the proverbial gift that keeps on giving. The team at McGraw-Hill, especially Cynthia Ward, Matthew Busbridge, Rhona Robbin, Nancy Crochiere, Sylvia Mallory, Robin Mouat, Laura Wilk, Kaelyn Schulz, and Stacy Best Ruel, expertly shepherded the book through to completion. Finally, our respective mentors, both undergraduate and graduate, bear more responsibility for the way we think about the American past than they might wish. But we would remind David Brion Davis, Mary P. Ryan, Roberto Rabel, Eric Foner, and Barbara Fields that such are the hazards of the profession.

REVIEWERS AND ADVISORS FOR *BECOMING AMERICA*

The authors and publisher would like to express their deepest gratitude to all those faculty members who read the manuscript, consulted on the digital program, did detailed fact-checking, and provided advice on content, images, maps, design, and cover concepts.

BOARD OF ADVISORS

Gene Barnett
Calhoun Community College
Jeff Carlisle
Oklahoma City Community College
Stephanie Cole
University of Texas, Arlington
Holly Fisher
Santa Fe College
Derek Hoff
Kansas State University
Marilyn Howard
Columbus State Community College
Phil Martin
San Jacinto College, South
Dave Tegeder
University of Florida, Gainsville
Michael Young
Trinity Valley Community College

REVIEWERS

Jeffery S. Adler
University of Florida
Termaine Anderson
Tarrant County College
Adam Arenson
University of Texas at El Paso
Jan Bailey McCauley
Tyler Junior College
Brett Barker
University of Wisconsin, Marathon City
Gene Barnett
Calhoun Community College
Leland Barrows
Voorhees College
Randal Beeman
Bakersfield College
Melissa Biegert
Temple College
Brian Birdnow
Harris Stowe State University
Devan Bissonette
Northern Arizona University
Jacob M. Blosser
Texas Women's University, Denton
Mark Boulton
University of Wisconsin, Whitewater
Wayne Bowen
Missouri State University
Michael Bowen
Westminster College
Bob Brennan
Cape Fear Community College
Blanche Brick
Blinn College
Robert Bromber
University of Maryland
Amy Canfield
Lewis-Clark State College
Jeff Carlisle
Oklahoma City Community College
Roger Carpenter
University of Louisiana at Monroe
Patrice Carter
Wharton County Junior College
Derek Catsam
University of Texas of the Permian Basin

Annette Chamberlin
Virginia Western Community College

Marisa Chappell
Oregon State University

Mark Cheathem
Cumberland University

Kenneth Cohen
St. Mary's College of Maryland

Stephanie Cole
University of Texas, Arlington

Yvonne Cornelius-Thompson
Nashville State Community College

Cynthia Counsil
Florida State College at Jacksonville

Lee Cowan
Tarrant County College

David Cullen
Collin College

Heather Davidson
Indian Hills Community College

Dominic DeBrincat
Southern Connecticut State University

Dawn Dennis
Los Angeles Mission College

Barbara Dunsheath
East Los Angeles College

Cassandra Farrell
Thomas Nelson Community College

William Feipel
Illinois Central College

John Fielding
Mount Wachusett Community College

Holly Fisher
Santa Fe College

John Flanagan
Weatherford College

Cheryl Foote
Central New Mexico Community College

Merle Funk
Front Range Community College

Jessica Gerard
Ozarks Technical Community College

Jason Godin
Blinn College

Donna Godwin
Trinity Valley Community College

David Golland
Governors State University

Aram Goudsouzian
University of Memphis

Bill Grose
Wytheville Community College

Thomas Gubbels
Lincoln University

Lawrence Guillow
CSULA

Sayrui Guthrie-Shimizu
Michigan State University

Mitchell Hall
Central Michigan University

Jennifer Hanley
Western Kentucky University

Deborah Hargis
Odessa College

Aimee Harris
El Paso Community College

Jay Hester
Sierra College

Scott Hickle
Blinn College

Katherine Hijar
California State University, San Marcos

Derek Hoff
Kansas State University

Justin Hoggard
Three Rivers Community College

Andrew Hollinger
Tarrant County College

Justin Horton
Thomas Nelson Community College

Marilyn K. Howard
Columbus State Community College

Johanna Hume
Alvin College

BT Huntley
Front Range Community College and Campbell University

Samuel C. Hyde, Jr.
Southeastern Louisiana University

Fran Jacobson
Tidewater Community College

Jeff Janowick
Lansing Community College

Andrew Johns
Brigham Young University

Stephen Julias
Rockland Community College

Lesley Kauffman
San Jacinto College

Christopher Kinsella
Cuyahoga Community College

Janilyn Kocher
Richland Community College

Laura Larque
Santa Rosa Junior College

Mitchell Lerner
Ohio State University, Newark

James Leslie
Lincoln University

Carole Lester
University of Texas, Dallas

Miguel Levario
Texas Tech University

Mary Lineham
University of Texas at Tyler

Stephen Lopez
San Jacinto College

Rodney Madison
Oregon State University

RobertMangrum
Howard Payne University

Michael S. Mangus
Ohio State University

Padma Manian
San Jose City College

Philbert Martin
San Jacinto College

Richard McCaslin
University of North Texas

Nina McCune
Baton Rouge Community College

Susan McFadden
Austin Community College

Sheila McIntyre
SUNY Potsdam

Marianne McKnight
Salt Lake Community College

Keshia Medelin
Los Medanos College

Greg Miller
Hillsborough Community College

James Mills
University of Texas at Brownsville

Walter Miszczenko
College of Western Idaho

Linda Mollno
Cal Poly Pomona/CSULA

Michelle Morris
University of Missouri

Wyatt Moulds
Jones Junior County College

Steven Noll
University of Florids at Gainsville

Jonathon Noyalas
Lord Fairfax Community College

Matthew Osborn
University of Missouri, Kansas City

Chad Pearson
Collin College

Darren J. *Pierson*
Blinn College

Art Pitz
Augustana College

David Price
Santa Fe Community College

Christine Rasmussen
Farleigh Dickinson University

Steven Rauch
Augusta State University

Roger Rawlings
Savannah College of Art and Design

Joel Rhodes
Southeast Missouri State University

Trisha Ring
University of Texas at San Antonio and San Antonio College

Robert Risko
Trinity Valley Community College

Tom Robertson
Community College of Baltimore County

Norman Rodriguez
John Wood Community College

John Sacher
University of Central Florida

Robert Sandow
Lock Haven University

Kyle Scanlan
Mountain Empire Community College

John Schutz
Tennesse Wesleyan College

Todd Shallat
Boise State University

Anthony Stranges
Texas A&M University

Katherine Scott Sturdevant
Rampart Range Campus of Pikes Peak Community College

Scott Seagle
Chattanooga State Community College

Howard Segal
University of Maine

John Shaw
Portland Community College

Edward Shelor
Georgia Military College

Manfred Silva
El Paso Community College

Stuart Smith
Germanna Community College, Fredericksburg

James Smith
Southwest Baptist University

Allen Nathaniel Smith
Ivy Tech Community College

Sherylle Smith
Rowan-Cabarrus Community College

Bruce Smith-Peters
Butte College and California State University, Chico

David Snead
Liberty University Christian College

Melissa Soto-Schwartz
Cuyahoga Community College

Ellen Stone
South Texas College

Dave Tegeder
University of Florida and Santa Fe College

Beverly Tomek
Wharton County Junior College

Christine Trolinger
Butte College

Minoa Uffelman
Austin Peay State

Dianne Walker
Baton Rouge Community College

Steven Wardinski
East Los Angeles College

David Weiland
Collin College

Eddie Weller
San Jacinto College

Christine White
San Jacinto Community College

Benton R. *White*
San Jacinto College South

Scott White
Scottsdale Community College

Linda Wilke Heil
Central Community College, Grand Island

Scott Williams
Weatherford College

Gary Wolgamott
Pittsburg State University

Tim Wood
Southwest Baptist University

Michael Young
Trinity Valley Community College

John Zaborney
University of Maine at Presque Isle

Eloy Zarate
Pasadena City College

Robert Zeidel
University of Wisconsin at Stout

Bill Zeman
Citrus College

A HISTORY FOR THE 21ST CENTURY

1

INSIDE ▶

THE BIG PICTURE

The centuries immediately prior to Columbus's famous voyage to the New World saw major social changes in Western Europe, West Africa, and the diverse native societies of North America. After southern Europeans began exploring and conquering land in Mesoamerica—initiating a complex global exchange of commodities, people, animals, and germs—Europeans and Africans started to arrive in the north as well.

Early American Artifacts. Objects like the water jugs, beads, cat carving, and stone ax pictured here help historians reconstruct some strands of the diverse history of life in North America in the centuries preceding the arrival of Europeans and Africans.

CONVERGENCE OF MANY PEOPLES: AMERICA BEFORE 1600

From some perspectives, U.S. history is a short story. The United States of America was not founded until the last quarter of the eighteenth century, and the ancestors of most of its current citizens arrived in the country far more recently. But the lands that now form the United States have a long history, spanning tens of thousands of years of human habitation, migration, and interaction. As in every other part of the globe, life in the United States today is built atop layers of past events and culture, and U.S. history includes everything we know about that past.

For all but the past few centuries, we find only scattered and obscure clues about the way ordinary people led their lives—whether in America, Africa, Asia, Europe, or anywhere else. Much of what historians know about work, play, and worship in the distant past has been reconstructed from artifacts buried in the earth, changes wrought in the landscape, skeletal remains of people and animals, soil samples, seed deposits, tree rings, glacial ridges, evidence preserved in religious rites, folklore, and language. This is true even of societies where rulers kept written records, such as China eight thousand years ago, Egypt in the era of the pharaohs, and England during the Middle Ages. It is also true of the societies whose writings have been extensively and laboriously preserved by long traditions of religious study, such as India in the Iron Age and the Mediterranean world at the time of Jesus. But in the case of North America, our knowledge of the past is restricted further by the fact that rulers did not maintain written records and religious insights were not passed down on parchment or paper. For this reason, historians have depended on the methods and findings of archaeologists, anthropologists, paleontologists, linguists, and biologists to discover basic facts about politics, religion, and the social order in North America until the seventeenth century.

Scholars have uncovered a fascinating and tumultuous history of diverse societies, cultures, and city-states spread across the North American continent in the thousand years before the arrival of significant numbers of Europeans and Africans in the 1600s. Over the course of that millennium, new North American centers of political power and cultural influence emerged and then dispersed. Meanwhile, religious and political conflicts spurred monarchs in the western part of Europe to sponsor expeditions to the Americas, bringing into contact peoples from the lands that bordered both sides of the Atlantic Ocean. The initial exchanges of people, animals, plants, and germs from three different continents would ultimately trigger profound changes in American life—and in the land itself. In the hundred years after the voyages of Christopher Columbus, the contacts between indigenous (or native) North Americans and the newcomers from across the ocean multiplied and extended. Still, this contact was limited to a few parts of the continent, and its historical significance remained to be seen.

KEY QUESTIONS

- How and over what time frame did human life develop in North America?
- What crucial changes occurred in several North American societies during the warming period?
- What do the rise and fall of Cahokia and the Mississippian culture teach us about North American history before European contact?
- How relevant was religion to European exploration of the Atlantic, and in what specific ways?
- What role did Africa play in the early history of European exploration?
- What was the Columbian Exchange, and how did it influence the New and Old Worlds?

Stone Bird of Prey, Hopewell Culture.

NORTH AMERICA BEFORE CONTACT

The peoples living in North America prior to Columbus's arrival in 1492 were the descendants of migrants from Asia who had arrived approximately fourteen or fifteen thousand years earlier, when those two continents were connected. From the time of these initial migrations, the population of the Americas (a term invented by Europeans) grew to tens of millions as people made their way across and down the landmass. As they migrated, these peoples developed ways of living specific to the climate and landscapes of the regions they settled. They belonged to innumerable tribes, spoke hundreds of quite different languages, and varied widely in subsistence patterns and social arrangements. Yet several centuries before Columbus, major environmental changes and political innovations forged new links among the various societies of North America and created a new world on much of that continent.

EARLY SOCIETIES OF NORTH AMERICA

North America and South America were originally connected to other continents in a supercontinent known as Pangaea, but the Americas separated from the rest millions of years before human life evolved. Only much later in the planet's history did a global cold spell drop the sea level to the point where Siberia and Alaska were rejoined via a land bridge in what is now the Bering Sea (see Map 1.1). Scientists and scholars speak of a region called Beringia, which included the land bridge as well as hundreds of miles of land on both sides. Early humans, who had migrated out of Africa over thousands of years, finally reached North America from Asia at Beringia, where they made their first homes on the continent. Scholars debate the number and timing of these migrations into and across Beringia (and some of the migrants may have traveled along the coast rather than overland), but by the year 10,000 BP (before the present), warmer temperatures submerged the land bridge for the last time. North America became a separate continent again, and the descendants of the Beringia migrants became the indigenous population of a western hemisphere that was now separated from the rest of the human family.

We know very little about these early indigenous Americans, whom archaeologists call Paleo-Indians (ancient Indians), except that they hunted mammoth and bison. Eventually, as larger prey became extinct, they turned to smaller animals and foraged for nuts, berries, and fruit. Paleo-Indians migrated throughout North America, and their descendants adapted to varying local climates and ecologies. Some general patterns linked the whole continent: Major protein sources were hunted and gathered rather than harvested, and unlike in Europe, large domesticated animals like pigs and cows were not available as food sources. Still, different North American peoples lived quite differently from one another. In the Great Basin region between the Rocky Mountains and the Sierra Nevada, native groups subsisted largely on fish, as did those along the coastline of what we now call California. Farther east, they hunted deer and gathered acorns. In all of these regions, the distant descendants of Siberian migrants developed distinct languages, religions, and cultures in the places that now compose the United States.

Paleo-Indians also settled farther south in the hemisphere, forming indigenous tribes and cultures in what we now call Mexico, Central America, and South America. In these warmer climates, the cultivation of maize (Indian corn) supported much larger, denser settlements than in the north. Maize was first grown in Mexico around 5000 BCE (before the Common Era; or B.C., before Christ), and over the next several millennia the crop became the foundation of agricultural societies throughout the region. Complex civilizations flourished in Mesoamerica (see Map 1.1) over a long period that began around 2000 BCE. Cultures like the Olmecs, who were centered around the present-day city of Veracruz on Mexico's Gulf coast; the Mayans, located on the Yucatán Peninsula and in the northern parts of Central America; and the Zapotecs in central Mexico all depended on corn and legumes and sustained the greatest population centers in the hemisphere. By the year 1000 CE (Common Era), the vast majority of people living in the Americas clustered in and around this region.

Farther north, the inhabitants of the lands that became the United States lived in a very different world and had limited direct contact with these populous Mesoamerican societies. Maize cultivation began in the southwestern corner of North America as early as 2000 BCE, but it remained scarce in some parts of the continent. And nowhere north of Mexico, not even in the Southwest, did Americans grow the mix of corn, squashes, and beans that together form a nutritious diet based entirely on plants. Throughout North America, the predominance of hunting, fishing, and gathering meant that populations were smaller and more dispersed than those to the south.

Nonetheless, archaeologists have uncovered evidence of centralized communities in ancient North America. Poverty Point in northeastern Louisiana, site of one of the Americas' first cities, boasted a massive earthwork mound that people from the region used for religious exhibitions and gatherings as early as 1600 BCE. Mounds entailed a great deal of concentrated and organized human labor, and the survival of the Poverty Point mound offers a glimpse of the kinds of cultural and political power that might have developed in ancient North America. The fact that **moundbuilding** appeared first in Louisiana, before any of the Mesoamerican pyramids, makes it the earliest attested example of monumental architecture in the hemisphere.

Corncob Evolution. Corncobs have grown progressively larger over centuries of domestication. The earliest corncobs were small—about the size of a person's thumbnail. Maize cultivation fueled the growth of the earliest-known North American civilizations and continues to sustain life on the continent. Over 125,000 square miles of land in the United States are now devoted to growing corn, which is the dominant ingredient in the modern American diet.

Map 1.1 The Peopling of the Americas. Scholars and scientists continue to uncover new evidence about the migration patterns of the earliest Americans. This map indicates possible routes of those migrations, along with the earliest-known centers of American civilization. Recent research on fossils and genomes suggests that migrants settled the Pacific coast before creating the inland cultures named on this map.

THE AGRICULTURAL REVOLUTION AND THE CITIES OF THE SOUTHWEST

Around the tenth century CE, life in much of North America began to shift dramatically. In widely disparate parts of the continent, Indian groups altered their diets and social arrangements and became more dependent on agriculture. North Americans had planted food sources for centuries, but not until the end of the first millennium did societies in what would become the United States begin to rely on agriculture as a dominant means of subsistence. We have no written records of the wars, political struggles, internal debates, or religious visions that precipitated or accompanied this major change in daily life. But we do know one crucial factor: It got warmer. From about

900 to 1300, in what climatologists call the North Atlantic Warm Period, significantly higher average temperatures increased the number of frost-free days on much of the continent. As growing seasons became longer and more dependable, it was possible to breed new variants of food crops that had grown originally in Mesoamerica. North Americans cultivated a distinctive kind of maize (with eight rows of kernels) that could be harvested sooner than Mexican maize and could therefore thrive in northern climates. Together with locally adapted squashes, gourds, and beans, the maize harvests supported a well-balanced diet that did not require consistent supplements of animal protein. A new agricultural order took hold so firmly that native religions would soon put beans, squashes, and especially maize at the center of their origin stories and religious rituals, which featured corn priests and honored the corn mothers who bestowed the gift of life in the form of corn. Some Indian tribes later paid homage to the trio of beans, squashes, and corn in festivals to the "three sisters."

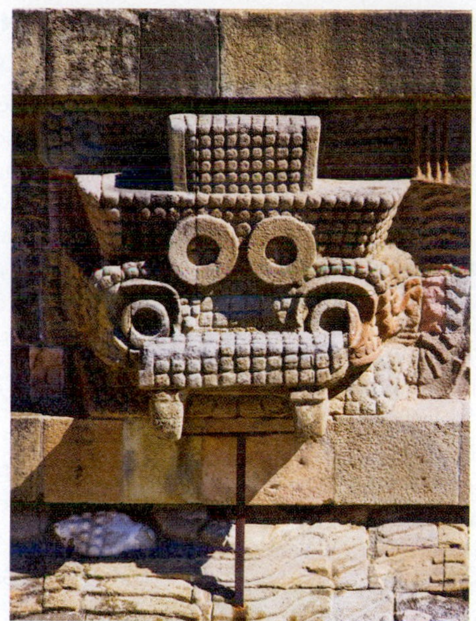

Maya Temple of Quetzalcoatl and Tlaloc, Teotihuacan, Third–Sixth Centuries. The face of the god Tlaloc is represented with a corncob design.

The **agricultural revolution** of the warming era had significant social consequences through much of North America. First, it led to denser living patterns, because raising crops required less territory than hunting and gathering. Indians in the Southwest, for example, developed small farming villages where large groups of relatives shared multiunit dwellings. Because they housed denser, less transient communities, these villages often invested in more substantial building projects than before. The Hohokam people in southern Arizona built canals to irrigate their farmland, as well as subterranean ball courts and storage facilities. In New Mexico, the Mogollon culture designed terraces to help retain soil moisture and experimented with multistory houses made of stone, adobe, and timber.

More dramatically, southwestern Indians formerly known as the Anasazi but now called Ancestral Puebloans built several major cities during this period. In the largest of these, Chaco Canyon in the Four Corners area of northwestern New Mexico, a population of several thousand lived in stone housing blocks, some of them quite elaborate. One of these blocks, built in the eleventh century and later called Pueblo Bonito, contained seven hundred rooms, each of which required cutting and transporting more than forty tons of sandstone. Even more impressive than the physical grandeur of Chaco Canyon was its role as the metropolitan center of a

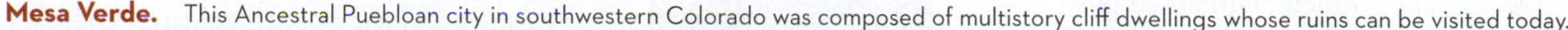

Mesa Verde. This Ancestral Puebloan city in southwestern Colorado was composed of multistory cliff dwellings whose ruins can be visited today.

region where tens of thousands of people made their homes. Over 250 miles of roads flowed in and out of the city, attracting immigrants, produce, political supporters, and religious pilgrims, many of whom came to make astronomical observations and celebrate rites and festivals that marked pivotal moments in the agricultural year.

SOCIAL AND CULTURAL PATTERNS AMONG SOUTHWESTERN PEOPLES

With the transition toward agriculture and urbanization came greater stratification. Some residents of the southwestern cities lived better than others. Those who occupied the largest houses ate more protein, accumulated prestigious goods from distant locations, and were singled out for special honor when they died. And as in other civilizations that left monumental structures for future generations to admire, southwestern construction projects depended on arduous labor, which many archaeologists suspect was coerced from vanquished enemies or from subordinate classes.

For women in the Southwest, the rising importance of agriculture could be empowering, since growing, gathering, and preparing food from the ground was traditionally women's work in most indigenous American cultures. In the arid Four Corners region, unlike in other parts of North America affected by the agricultural revolution of this era, the large-scale irrigation projects necessary for crop cultivation shifted some farming labor into men's hands. The foods they harvested were nonetheless identified with the world of women, as the stories about corn mothers and the three sisters suggest. Perhaps for this reason, households were organized around mothers (and other female relatives), and women maintained possession of the housing units.

The great centers of the Four Corners region began to decline and disperse around the middle of the twelfth century. Sustained droughts undermined the authority of the Chaco Canyon rulers, and large segments of the urban population relocated to smaller communities and more economically and ecologically sustainable living arrangements. Later groups of southwestern Indians retained some aspects of their urban ancestors' culture but favored more participatory religious rites, less dense settlement patterns, and more modest architectural styles. Some scholars have interpreted these cultural patterns among the Pueblo in the late thirteenth and fourteenth centuries as deliberate rejections of the hierarchy and violence of the Chaco Canyon era.

THE RISE AND FALL OF MISSISSIPPIAN CIVILIZATION

As Indians in the Southwest built a new culture around longer growing seasons and crop cultivation, similar transitions were taking place in very different environments on the other side of North America. In the flood plains of the Mississippi River valley, along the Ohio and Arkansas Rivers, and as far away as the Southeast interior, Native Americans were exploiting the climate change to grow the same trio of maize, squashes, and beans (see Map 1.2). Though they spoke different languages and inhabited a vast stretch of land in the eastern half of the continent, many different peoples who made this transition to agriculture were connected to a broad cultural complex that scholars call **Mississippian civilization.**

At the center of this civilization arose a metropolitan center that was bigger than Chaco Canyon and exerted a far greater cultural influence. Later known as Cahokia (its original name has not survived), the city lay just below the confluence of the Mississippi and Missouri Rivers, near present-day East St. Louis, Illinois (see Spaces and Places: Cahokia, Hub City). Cahokia was located in an area that combined rich soil for growing crops with dense nearby woodlands for hunting. More important, perhaps, it enjoyed access to a vast water transportation network that connected it to places through much the continent's interior.

A small settlement had existed at Cahokia since the beginning of the eighth century, but around the year 1050 it started to grow into a large city. Recent archaeological studies generally agree that by the end of the twelfth century, Cahokia (not counting its several suburbs) held between ten and twenty thousand people—a population that would make it the largest city in North America before the eighteenth century. To put that number in a different perspective, more people lived in the city of Cahokia in the year 1200 than inhabited a surrounding region covering 2,500 square miles just two hundred years earlier.

It is impossible to know what drew immigrants from distant places into Cahokia's orbit. Some were probably attracted by rumors of the city's ambitious earthwork mounds.

Chunkey Player Effigy Pipe, 1250–1350, Muskogee County, Oklahoma. The game of chunkey, a powerful symbol of Mississippian culture, remained popular among eastern Indians until lacrosse supplanted it in the nineteenth century.

Map 1.2 The Vast Reach of Mississippian Civilization, ca. 800–1500 CE Mississippian trade routes, cultural connections, and political ties spread through much of the Midwest and Southeast. By 1500, that civilization was thoroughly dispersed, and new nations rose in these territories.

Newcomers might well have glimpsed in those monumental buildings the promise of a richer material life or the embodiment of spiritual wisdom and authority. But why Cahokians embarked on this urban renewal project in the first place remains a bigger mystery. Some scholars have been intrigued by the coincidence of the redevelopment of Cahokia and the appearance of a supernova in the sky beginning July 4, 1054. Perhaps, we might speculate, such an epic cosmic event called forth new attempts to understand or control the universe. Perhaps it bolstered the authority of the Cahokian religion or prepared large numbers of people to accept the proposition that a new era was at hand.

What is clearer from the archaeological evidence is that the capital city of Cahokia had both a powerful pull and a broad reach. From Minnesota down the Mississippi to Louisiana, and from Oklahoma across the Southeast to Florida, artifacts of a single culture appear. Smoking pipes, temple rituals, and sports that originated in the Cahokia area suffused the lives of Indians in the plains and woodlands. Chunkey, a Cahokian version of an older hoop-and-pole game that involved throwing a stone disk across a clay playing field, became an especially prominent feature of Mississippian culture. It served as a ritualized spectator sport, an object of high-stakes gambling, and even an instrument of diplomacy and politics. The ascent of chunkey as the major game of its era both reflected and reinforced the cultural dominance of Cahokian capital, much as particular sports spread British culture in the nineteenth century and U.S. culture in the twentieth.

Powerful city-states anchored Mississippian civilization, and Cahokia was the largest and most influential. Other moundbuilding chiefdoms, including Moundville and Coosa in Alabama, Etowah in Georgia, and Apalachee near Tallahassee, Florida, shared with Cahokia a pattern of striking social inequality. As in many other stratified societies, the differences between chiefs and commoners among the Mississippians were made to seem natural through monumental architecture, the display of prestigious ceremonial goods, and the acquisition and cultivation of esoteric knowledge. All of these factors reinforced the idea that powerful leaders stood somewhere between ordinary human beings and the superhuman forces that controlled the universe. Mississippian chiefdoms also engaged in more organized and sustained warfare, which they relied on to accumulate captives who could serve as a special kind of prestigious good to enhance the status of ruling elites.

Enslaving females was common among the Mississippians, and women were also more likely to die violently than in earlier periods of American history. Skeletal remains in Cahokia provide evidence of elaborate ceremonies involving women's ritual sacrifice. The women selected for sacrifice were disproportionately nonlocal and lower in social status. Indeed, the power of the Mississippian cities rested on rigid social hierarchies and a great deal of violence. Physical anthropologists working with skeletons in Alabama have determined that Indians in the Mississippian era were three times more likely to die violently than their ancestors in the earlier Archaic era and that about one out of three male and one out of four female Mississippians died violent deaths.

In the early 1300s, rather suddenly, this grand civilization began to disintegrate. Cahokia's leadership and prestige were probably weakened by drought, an earthquake, and warfare. The larger economy of the city may also have been damaged by resource depletion, crop failures, and health hazards

SPACES & PLACES

Cahokia, Hub City

Long before Europeans settled the region, a great city stood on a stretch of bottomland on the eastern side of the Mississippi River. For several centuries (longer than the United States has been a nation), the place historians call Cahokia was North America's largest city and the center of an extensive political and cultural empire. A thousand years ago, all roads led to Cahokia. And then it seems to have vanished.

After the urban settlement dispersed around the 1300s, the only traces of this once-mighty civilization were about two hundred pyramids of packed earth, spread out over 3,200 acres. In later centuries, French, Spanish, English, and eventually American travelers encountered these mound-like structures, but they did not see them as evidence of an American Indian city. Nineteenth-century Americans proposed theories of a lost race of pre-Indian moundbuilders, and in the early twentieth century, leading geologists regarded the mounds as natural phenomena. While Americans studied the scrolls, paintings, and hieroglyphs of distant civilizations, they had no idea that a major city had stood on the Illinois side of the Mississippi River.

Cahokia as It May Have Appeared in Its Heyday. The flat-topped pyramid at the center, later called Monks Mound, towered one hundred feet high and spanned sixteen acres at its base.

posed by overcrowding. There may also have been local power struggles, or crises of religious faith, though no traces of such developments have turned up in the soil. What we do know is that the demise of Cahokia was not a local phenomenon. One by one, major Mississippian cities were abandoned during the early fourteenth century, a moment that also marked the beginning of a long cooling period known as the Little Ice Age, which lasted into the nineteenth century. As in the Southwest, changes in the weather appear to have undermined the new cities built by Americans around the rise of three-crop agriculture. The farming practices and diets introduced in the warming period survived, but the great cities did not.

THE DISPERSAL OF THE NORTH AMERICAN POWERS

The end of the Cahokian regime shaped life in a large part of North America as dramatically as the regime itself had. First, as all the migrants who had moved to Cahokia dispersed to other Mississippian cities and to the agricultural settlements created by and for those cities, a major reshuffling of geographical and ethnic boundaries occurred during the fourteenth and fifteenth centuries. The new migrants did not simply return to villages or communities that had existed before the agricultural revolution. Instead they created new decentralized villages, relocated to new regions, forged new political alliances, and built new tribes and nations. Most of the Indian nations that Europeans

The history of that forgotten city lay buried deep in the ground, beneath layers of human activity. Even the mysterious earthen monuments themselves had begun to disappear. By the time of the Civil War many of the great mounds had been leveled. Since the 1960s, however, archaeologists have excavated evidence of a large housing development from the eleventh century. They reconstructed a circle of upright posts that were the basis of a large astronomical observatory. They found burial pits used to honor the city's great chiefs. They identified artifacts, such as distinctive chunkey stones (see p. 9), that established the city's central place in a far-flung culture. And they established a map of the city's earthworks projects, which included a central plaza the size of thirty-five football fields—the biggest planned public space built up to that point in the lands that would become the United States.

Cahokia Today. Monk's Mound, Cahokia Mounds State Historic Site. Monk's Mound, shown here in aerial view, is flanked by two small strands of the vast network of paved roads streaming in and out of St. Louis, Cahokia's modern counterpart.

Prior to Cahokia's rediscovery, French and then American settlers had established a city, St. Louis, in the same area. As the St. Louis metropolitan region grew, many traces of the ancient ruins were destroyed. By the second half of the twentieth century, rental subdivisions in the Illinois suburbs of St. Louis covered the Grand Plaza where Mississippians had once regularly gathered to observe the stars and pay homage to the forces that controlled the universe. Ironically, however, the fact that St. Louis became a bustling U.S. transportation hub may have helped preserve Cahokia's history. In the late 1950s, when the federal government introduced a new interstate highway system, St. Louis was chosen as a gateway city. Once again all roads led to Cahokia, as five different interstate highway routes ribboned through the site that several archaeologists had recently begun to excavate. The possibility that the final remains of the mounds would be leveled to make room for off-ramps galvanized the archaeological community, and the fact that the land now passed into public control prompted a massive study of the site's history. By 1963, as construction began on St. Louis's Gateway Arch monument, scholars pieced together a picture of a forgotten Indian city just across the river.

Think About It

1. Why might Americans in the nineteenth and twentieth centuries have been reluctant to believe that the enormous earthen mounds were once part of an American Indian city?
2. How would you explain the fact that a large city emerged on this location, so close to where St. Louis would be built many centuries later?

later encountered in North America were creations of this post-Mississippian dispersal (see Map 1.2).

Second, relations among the new post-Cahokia villages and tribes were in many cases antagonistic and violent. During their heyday, the Cahokians had introduced new forms of large-scale warfare, but the presence of a regional superpower also enforced a general peace. While Mississippian tribes and villages competed for honor and resources, Cahokian military might tended to discourage all-out wars, and enemies could play out their animosities in games of chunkey. But with the end of the Cahokian regime, new conflicts and rivalries became more lethal. In the late 1970s, researchers digging near Chamberlain, South Dakota, uncovered evidence of a mass killing from the late fourteenth century at Crow Creek near the Missouri River. Nearly five hundred men, women, and children—most or all of an entire village—were murdered, and their bodies mutilated, in an act of bloodshed unmatched in the archaeological records of North America during the Cahokian period. The Crow Creek Massacre offers some indication of what could happen in the American Plains and Midwest in the flux and chaos of the fourteenth century.

From the Missouri River to the Atlantic Ocean, the fourteenth and fifteenth centuries were a time of population movement, shifting trade relations, and political transition. Both the spread of farming during the warming period and the dispersal of the urban chiefdoms after the weather cooled created instability and change. Scholars debate, for example, whether the formation of the powerful Iroquois and Huron confederacies in the Great Lakes region around the beginning of the fifteenth century was the result of the spread, or the fall, of Mississippian civilization. Whatever the case, by the time of Cahokia's decline, events in one part of the continent could affect people far away. Though the extraordinarily diverse array of people whom Europeans would lump together as Indians spoke different languages and belonged to discrete nations, they already lived in a connected world.

CULTURES OF THE PACIFIC COAST

The agricultural revolution of the period bypassed several sparsely populated parts of North America that were too cold (Canada and Alaska) or too arid (Utah and Nevada). Agriculture also made few inroads along the Pacific coast, which nonetheless was by far the most densely populated portion of the country in the era right before Columbus's arrival—about four times as dense as the Northeast or the Southeast. Indigenous Californians were a striking exception to the rule that dense settlement went hand in hand with agriculture.

More than anything else, the abundance of marine life in California and the Pacific Northwest made agriculture unnecessary. Salmon, rather than maize, was the backbone of the economy. But while Indians in the Far West did not farm, they did not live effortlessly off the earth's bounty. Native Californians developed sophisticated techniques for collecting and preparing seeds, roots, and nuts. They also set fires strategically to stimulate the growth of particular plant life, diversify their food sources, facilitate hunting, and adjust to changing climate conditions. Recent research supports the view that native Californians enjoyed more nutritious, varied diets and greater labor efficiency than their agricultural counterparts in the eastern half of the continent.

The diverse ecology of the Pacific coast supported hundreds of different tribes and language communities. West Coast Indians did not develop large chiefdoms. Nonetheless, many California communities underwent some of the same social changes from the eleventh century onward that took place in the urban centers of the Southwest, Midwest, and Southeast. Among the Chumash who lived in the Channel Islands and around the present-day city of Santa Barbara; some of the Pomo groups along the North Central Coast; and the small Shellmound chiefdoms of the San Francisco Bay area, the scale of specialized economic activities (storing salmon and acorns and directing fires) produced elite classes, economic inequality, and the accumulation of private property.

EUROPE AND AFRICA ON THE EVE OF CONTACT

On the other side of the Atlantic, a parallel climatic cycle of a warming period followed by a Little Ice Age affected western European communities as well. A series of economic, political, and intellectual changes put into motion by these trends and others set the stage for explorations that would lead to contact with the Americas. At the same time, kingdoms in West Africa became more deeply enmeshed in Eurasian trade networks. Eventually, the Portuguese set up trading posts there where slaves would be purchased for plantation work. Religious affiliations and rivalries also shaped the course of events in Europe and Africa and provided an important context for subsequent encounters.

CHANGE AND CONFLICT IN NORTHWESTERN EUROPE

Western Europe from the tenth through the thirteenth century (the late Middle Ages or late medieval period) experienced rising temperatures associated with the North Atlantic Warm Period. This climatic change enabled farmers north of the Alps and Pyrenees (especially in what are now France, Germany, Belgium, the Netherlands, and Great Britain; see Map 1.3) to extend the growing season and breed new varieties of food crops, including nutrient-rich legumes. Since Western Europe was already a farming society, the change was less dramatic than the advent of agriculture in North America's Four Corners region or the Mississippi River valley. Nonetheless, the impact was significant. With the rise in productivity and nutrition, the population of northwestern Europe soared.

Then, as in North America, the beginning of the Little Ice Age brought suffering and instability. In Europe, colder temperatures in the early fourteenth century destroyed crops and bred famine, after which devastating diseases swept the continent. Most dramatic was the bubonic plague of 1347–1351, known as the Black Death. Increased warfare had combined with famine and disease to create a demographic catastrophe. By century's end, France had lost approximately 40 percent of its population, and in some areas as much as 90 percent, while almost half of England's people had died. The consequences were far reaching. Previously landless survivors gained new access to property in ravaged areas, and labor shortages triggered population movements and unrest. The traditional social order in which all men and women knew their proper places loosened.

Unlike in North America, instability in England and France during the fourteenth and fifteenth centuries drew people toward big cities rather than away from them. Thus while Indian chiefdoms decentralized, those in Europe began to consolidate into **nation-states** under the control of more powerful monarchs. The kings (and occasionally queens) of Western Europe provided symbols of ethnic and geographical unity within their states and marshaled staggering financial resources. Their aim was to mobilize and equip massive armies for the international wars that consumed the region (especially France, Belgium, and the Netherlands) during this period. European monarchs were also religious figures, occupying a status, like

Indian chiefs, somewhere between the human beings who revered them and the divine forces that authorized their rule. By the end of the fifteenth century, on the eve of the convergence of European, African, and American cultures in what some people began calling the New World, northern Europe was itself a world in transition.

CRUSADES, RECONQUISTA, AND THE BEGINNINGS OF EXPLORATION

As in America over the same period, Europe's northern kingdoms in the Middle Ages had more politically powerful southern neighbors. European monarchs claimed allegiance to **Latin Christendom,** a vast religious community that was centered in

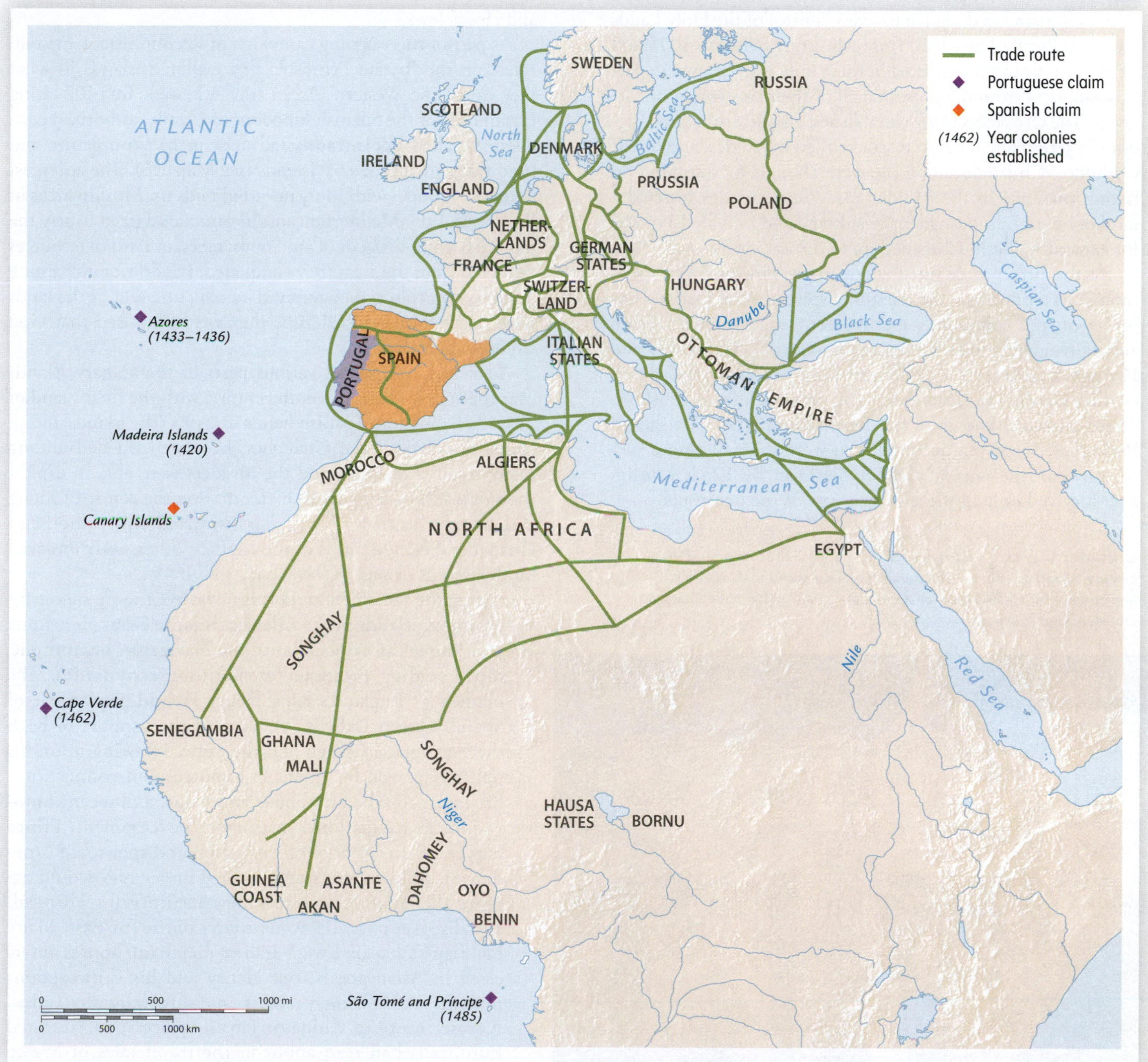

Map 1.3 Western Europe and West Africa on the Eve of Contact, ca. 1400–1500. Networks of long-distance commerce connected Europe and Africa. Along with religious crusades, this web of trade laid the groundwork for future patterns of colonization, conquest, and slave trading. By the last decade of the fifteenth century, before the voyages of Columbus, Spain and Portugal had begun exploring and colonizing islands in the Atlantic Ocean.

the southern part of the continent, in historically influential Mediterranean cities, and unified under the authority of a pope. Latin Christendom saw itself as a universal faith that applied to all countries and lands. Its Catholic Church (the word *catholic* means comprehensive, inclusive, or broad) was able to absorb or subsume older, varied religious traditions throughout the continent.

During the Middle Ages, the unity of Latin Christendom was reinforced by wars against non-Christians, especially in a series of **Crusades** designed to wrest control of the Holy Lands (and specifically Jerusalem) from Muslims. Between 1095 and 1291, European men enlisted in these holy wars, drawn in part by assurances from the pope that all of their sins would be forgiven. The Crusaders briefly established a Latin Christian kingdom in Jerusalem and also massacred Jews, heretics, and Greek Orthodox Christians along the way. Though they secured no lasting presence in the Middle East, the Crusades fostered a kind of broad European identity at home and provided a model for expanding Latin Christendom to distant lands.

By the fifteenth century, increasingly powerful European monarchs tapped into the crusading spirit. In the Iberian Peninsula on the continent's southwestern edge (modern Spain and Portugal), armies from Aragon, Castile, Catalonia, and Portugal had waged a prolonged holy war from the eighth century onward to "reconquer" the peninsula from Muslims. These crusades, known as the Reconquista (the Spanish and Portuguese word for "reconquest"), were generally more successful than the ones in the Middle East. By 1252, Muslim rule survived only in the southern part of the peninsula.

Crusader Culture. Paintings for the medieval era celebrated the military struggles of Latin Christendom against the infidel, as in this depiction of the defense of Constantinople in 1453 against the Ottoman Empire. *Ogier le Danois, 1499 (vellum).*

After stalling during the 1300s, the Reconquista reignited in the fifteenth century. In 1415, Portuguese forces captured the Muslim city of Ceuta on the African side of the Strait of Gibraltar, thereby opening up the Atlantic coast of Africa to Christian ships. In 1469, the marriage of Ferdinand II of Aragon and Isabella of Castile united the Spanish kingdom and reinvigorated the struggle to purify the land of non-Christians. In 1478, Spain initiated both the reconquest of the Canary Islands and an Inquisition to weed out heretics and closet Jews.

As part of this ongoing campaign of Reconquista, Christian rulers on the Iberian Peninsula first explored islands in what they called the Western Ocean (the Atlantic). In 1402, King Enrique III of the Spanish kingdom of Castile authorized conquerors, called **adelantados** (advance men), to organize and fund raids on the Canary Islands (see Map 1.3). The conquest followed a model with roots in earlier raids on Muslim areas in Europe and the Mediterranean: Adelantados agreed to pay the monarch a one-fifth cut of any spoils, taxes, or natural resources extracted from the areas they conquered. In addition to gaining property to exploit, they received a noble title and, if the lands were taken from nonbelievers, they were promised that God would forgive their sins.

Adelantados captured various parts of the Canary Islands over the course of the fifteenth century, with the final island of Tenerife falling into Spanish hands in 1496. The islands' indigenous population, the Guanches, had been divided among many small chiefdoms, and the invaders were able to exploit the animosities among rival chiefdoms over the course of a long and bloody century of war. An estimated thirty thousand Guanches died as a result of the conflict; others were enslaved on the islands or sent as slaves back to Europe.

During the same period, Portugal was even more successful in colonizing islands in the Atlantic. Infante Dom Henrique, also known as Prince Henry the Navigator, became Europe's leading promoter of maritime exploration. The nephew of England's King Henry IV and great-uncle of Spain's Queen Isabella, he enjoyed the support of both the Portuguese Crown and the pope. Drawing upon his political power, his financial resources and connections, his access to scholarly books and maps, and recent innovations in navigational instrument development, Prince Henry set up a school of navigation and sponsored expeditions. Ship captains who trained under him would explore the Atlantic, conquer new territory for Portugal, and discover potential water routes to the Far East. Many of Henry's backers were Italian merchant houses interested in Asian goods, but Henry and his ship captains saw these seafaring projects in more religious terms. A water route to China or Japan—places that educated Europeans had read about in the travel tales of Marco Polo, who had journeyed to Asia in the late thirteenth century—could open up new territories to Latin Christendom and give the Catholic Church a new line of attack in its war against Islam.

In contrast to the Spanish-controlled Canaries, most of the Atlantic islands taken by Portugal were uninhabited. Henry's first target was the Madeira Islands, which he claimed in 1420 on behalf of the Order of Christ, a community of knights to which he belonged. Then, in the 1430s, one of his ship captains found more unpopulated territory farther west, in the Azores. By the middle of the century, Portuguese adventurers had established agricultural colonies in both island chains, relying on the labor of a mix of mostly free settlers and some captives. Henry also sponsored expeditions along the Atlantic coast of Africa. These voyages established trade contacts with the powerful kingdom of Mali, introduced Christianity to West Africa, and, in the 1460s, added the uninhabited islands of Cape Verde to Portugal's growing Atlantic empire.

Closer to the African mainland, the Portuguese claimed a pair of islands in the Gulf of Guinea in 1471, which they colonized in 1485 and named Saö Tome and Principe. Among the original colonists of Saö Tome was a large group of Jewish children who had been taken from their parents in Portugal and brought to the south Atlantic to be brought up as Christians. Quickly, however, the Portuguese began importing African slaves to work on sugar plantations. This colony represented the real beginning of large-scale African slavery in the Atlantic.

After establishing their Atlantic island empire and trading posts along the African coast, the Portuguese-sponsored captains turned their attention to finding the sea route to the East. In 1488, Bartolomeu Dias established the possibility of such a journey when he sailed around the Cape of Good Hope at Africa's southern tip. Ten years later, a Portuguese fleet under the command of Vasco de Gama sailed to India. Portugal would build a vast commercial empire in South Asia, Indonesia, and China over the next centuries, and Catholic missionaries would try to spread Christianity to those lands. But for the history of the Americas, by far the more important consequence of the explorations sponsored by Prince Henry lay in the eastern Atlantic. In the Azores, Madeira, and especially the sugar plantations of Saö Tome, Portugal laid the groundwork for the vast and notorious Atlantic slave system.

WEST AFRICA AND ISLAM

South of the Iberian Peninsula and far closer to the Americas lay another major region that would contribute to the formation of what came to be called the New World. West Africa south of the Sahara Desert, an area framed to the south and west by the Atlantic Ocean (see Map 1.3), covered a large terrain and included many different states and smaller chiefdoms. It was home to a wide range of ethnicities and cultures, hundreds of distinct language communities, and several different religious traditions. Most West Africans were farming people, clustered in small villages and bound by powerful ties to large kin networks, though several important urban centers flourished as well.

A number of states and chiefdoms wielded political power in different parts of the region, but medieval West Africa can be divided into two periods, corresponding with powerful political regimes that dominated much of the region. From the eighth century onward, the kingdom of Ghana controlled a significant empire, centered several hundred miles northwest of the country that bears that name today. Ghana leveraged its extensive gold deposits to establish far-flung trade routes, but attacks from Muslim Berbers in the year 1076 precipitated the decline of its empire during the following century. Ghana's successor, the kingdom of Mali, controlled an even vaster territory and emerged as the imperial superpower and trading center in the thirteenth century.

Mali's rulers adopted Islam, which was spreading south and west from North Africa and the Middle East into the interior of the African continent, during the same period when Christians were expelling Muslims from southern Europe and organizing crusades to Palestine. Via camel caravans, traders introduced Muslim ideas and influences to Mali, along with precious metals, spices, horses, and a range of manufactured goods. The Malian city of Timbuktu became a significant center of Islamic learning, with a university whose faculty was as distinguished and renowned as any in Europe at the time. Islam, a scriptural religion (a faith organized around the reading of sacred texts), flourished along the coasts of the continent and in commercial cities where literacy was more common. In the more rural areas where most West Africans lived, Islam made fewer inroads, though many illiterate peasants learned about the religion through mystic poems composed in vernacular languages (the spoken and written languages of particular regions) rather than in the sacred Arabic.

As trade to the northeast expanded during the late medieval period, the main commodities that West Africans exported were gold and human beings. Slavery thrived in much of the world at this time, and demand for slave labor in Muslim states in North

Malian Emperor Mansa Musa as Depicted in *The Catalan Atlas*, 1375. The artist depicts Mansa Musa holding a gold nugget and a scepter with fleur-de-lys. The emperor made an extravagant and storied pilgrimage to Mecca in 1324 and built splendid mosques in Jenne-Jeno and Gao. For centuries Jenne-Jeno, situated in the floodplain of the Niger River, was the leading urban center in West Africa, but by the year 1200 that city had begun to decline.

African Gold. From the eighth to the sixteenth century, West Africa provided most of Europe's gold.

Africa and the Middle East had soared. In the **African slave trade,** the fact that Islam had spread to Mali without becoming the majority religion of the area probably made a big difference. Muslims preferred to enslave religious outsiders, so non-Muslims from sub-Saharan Africa were valued as laborers, while Muslims from sub-Saharan Africa became trusted trading partners. By around 1500, slaves from Africa replaced those from southeastern Europe (mostly from the Black Sea region) as the primary bound labor force in much of the Muslim heartland. Unlike the men and women sold into slavery in the Americas in subsequent centuries, those who were taken eastward by Muslim traders were mostly employed as domestic servants or concubines, not as agricultural fieldworkers. Two-thirds of the enslaved persons carried from sub-Saharan Africa to the Muslim world were women.

Over the course of the fifteenth century, Malian rule faced rebellions on several fronts. Timbuktu fell to nomadic invaders in 1433, and by 1500 the empire had collapsed as much of its territory came under the control of Songhay, a rival state to the east. During the same period, Portuguese explorers, traders, and missionaries began arriving in West Africa. Mali's authorities resisted the European visitors and forced them to remain on the coast—a ban that protected Europeans from diseases that had spread in the African interior. But even confined to the edge of the continent and reliant upon networks of African merchants to supply the commodities they sought, the Portuguese would have a powerful impact on life in the region.

Farther south along the Gold Coast, in the Kingdom of the Kongo, Portuguese commercial interests established a trading center in 1482 that came to be known as Elmina Castle. The Portuguese used the castle, now the oldest European building in sub-Saharan Africa, to trade for gold, triggering competition for the precious metal within African

Eighteenth-Century Flemish Engraving Depicting the 1491 Portuguese Missions to Africa. King Nzinga, a Nkuwu of the Kingdom of the Kongo, converted to Catholicism and adopted the name King Joao, marking the first foothold of Christianity in West Africa.

St. George's Castle in Modern-Day Ghana, Originally Elmina Castle. In the 1980s Werner Herzog used this location for his film *Cobra Verde*.

societies. A century later, as slaves began to displace gold as West Africa's major export, Elmina Castle would become a major stop on the passage of Africans to the Americas.

CONVERGENCE AND CONTACT

Early Portuguese and Spanish ventures in the eastern Atlantic initiated a larger process of exploration that would ultimately cross the ocean by the end of the fifteenth century. Spain took the lead in this next phase of the age of exploration, turning its attention to the western rim of the Atlantic following the voyage of Columbus to the Caribbean. As in earlier European expeditions to the Azores and Saö Tome, Spain expected lands on the other side of the ocean to yield wealth through the labor of indigenous pagan populations or other enslaved non-Christians. Spanish adelantados quickly established new colonies, both in the Caribbean and in a massive continent just beyond.

COLUMBUS'S FIRST AND SECOND VOYAGES

After its earlier success in the Canary Islands, Spain had not kept up with Portugal's empire-building in the eastern Atlantic, concentrating instead on the wars against Muslim Moors in southern Europe. But once those wars had pushed Islam off the Iberian Peninsula, Spain returned to sponsoring westward exploration. After several unsuccessful overtures to other European monarchs and some failed attempts to secure the sponsorship of Ferdinand and Isabella, an Italian sailor from Genoa named Christopher Columbus was finally appointed as an adelantado for Spain's Queen Isabella in the momentous year of 1492. That January, Spanish forces had captured the stronghold of Granada, ending eight centuries of Islamic rule on the Iberian Peninsula. Later in 1492, Spanish Jews who refused to convert to Christianity were expelled from the country. All three events—Granada's capture, the Jews' expulsion, Columbus's voyage—were closely connected. All were efforts of a rising nation-state to expand its power while spreading the rule of Latin Christendom.

Contrary to popular myth, Christopher Columbus was no visionary geographer. What separated Columbus from the geographical authorities of his day was not his faith that the earth was round (a view they shared) but his erroneous belief that Japan lay close to Europe, just beyond the Canary Islands. Columbus calculated the size of Asia as much larger and that of the earth as much smaller than they actually are, and these errors encouraged him to pursue a westward journey to the Far East that others saw as misguided. Nonetheless, Columbus had on his side a great deal of seafaring experience and an intuitive grasp of the Atlantic's circular wind patterns. Columbus headed south from the Canaries, where he knew that autumn winds blew in an easterly direction. He guessed, correctly, that powerful westerly winds farther north would secure his safe passage home.

Six weeks out from the Canary Islands, Columbus and his three ships dropped anchor at a small island three hundred miles north of Cuba, in part of the present-day Bahamas. Naming the island San Salvador (after the Savior, Jesus Christ), Columbus spent the next three months surveying the other islands in the area and hoping to find a connection to the Grand Khan of China. The Arawak-speaking Tainos, who lived in these islands, fulfilled few of the visitors' expectations of inhabitants of Asia or the East Indies. But Columbus still called them "Indians"—and that name stuck well past the point when it became clear that his ships had not reached the Far East.

Three months after his arrival in the Caribbean, Columbus returned to Europe with evidence of the promising islands he had discovered. At the Spanish court in Barcelona, he displayed parrots and colorful masks that his audience had never seen before. He also produced some gold, which he had found on the large island that he named La Española (Hispaniola, the landmass that now includes Haiti and the Dominican Republic). Finally, he presented seven men, the survivors among the twenty Tainos he had taken aboard his ship for the return voyage. To the Spanish court in 1493, these were men in need of baptism and salvation. To some of the more prescient in attendance, they may also have represented the most valuable resource that Columbus had discovered: an indigenous labor force.

Excited by Columbus's presentation, the Spanish monarchy made him a nobleman and outfitted him for a return trip to Hispaniola. Columbus's second voyage involved seventeen ships carrying over twelve hundred men, including priests, miners, artisans, and soldiers. Importantly, this was a colonization party, not an exploration party. When Columbus arrived in Hispaniola, he discovered that the thirty-nine sailors he had left behind on the first journey had all been killed by the Tainos in response to violence the Europeans had perpetrated against the local population. Undaunted, Columbus and his men began the business of making the new colony profitable. First through diplomatic gift exchanges and then through a heavy tax on the Tainos, the Spanish authorities extracted large quantities of gold from the island. When the local population proved unable to meet the arduous gold tax, the Spanish declared war. By 1496, about one hundred thousand Tainos in Hispaniola (roughly a third of the island's 1492 population) had been killed. By 1499, the surviving inhabitants of Hispaniola were subjected to a regime of forced labor.

SUCCESSOR VOYAGES—AND A NEW CONTINENT DISCOVERED

Using Hispaniola as a base, other Spanish adelantados conquered neighboring islands in the Caribbean, including Puerto Rico (1508), Jamaica (1509), and Cuba (1511). In each case, the invaders proclaimed the sovereignty of the pope and the Spanish monarchy over the island and forced the local population to work for them (see Interpreting the Sources: The Requerimiento). Spain soon boasted an empire in the western Atlantic that rivaled Portugal's imperial domain farther east. Pope Alexander VI had given his blessing to these empires in 1493 and approved the geographical division. Drawing a line on a map of the ocean that southern Europeans were exploring (see Map 1.4), the pope granted all heathen land on one side to Spain and on the other side to Portugal.

Following Columbus's initial voyage, Europeans would learn a great deal about the ocean that he had crossed. On his third trip, in 1498, Columbus ventured south of the Caribbean islands and sailed along rivers in the South American mainland, which he speculated might be attached somehow to China. A different Spanish expedition, a year later, landed in what is now Venezuela. In 1500, Portuguese ships under the command of Pedro Ýlvars Cabral stumbled upon what appeared to be an enormous island, which he dubbed Terra Santa Cruz. A subsequent Portuguese exploration concluded that this territory, which is in northern Brazil, was not an island at all but part of a massive continental landmass.

By the early 1500s, European mapmakers and geographers became increasingly convinced that a large continent, separate from Asia, lay on the western edge of the ocean. A German cartographer named Martin Waldseemüller depicted this continent on a map that he published in 1507. Instead of honoring Columbus, the explorer of the West Indies, Waldseemüller named the continent after Florentine businessman Amerigo Vespucci, who had been sent to Spain as an agent of the Medici banking firm and served as an observer, and then a navigational expert, on the expeditions that reached Venezuela and Brazil. Feminizing Vespucci's first name to suit the imagined gender of a continent, Waldseemüller's map identified the landmass on the other side of the waters as *America*. Support for Waldseemüller's picture of the world came in 1513, when Vasco Núñez de Balboa landed at Panama, crossed the isthmus, and returned to Europe with reports of a large sea on the other side. In 1520, Ferdinand Magellan of Spain sailed around the continent's southern tip (the journey had begun the previous year) and crossed this vast ocean. Magellan himself was killed in the Philippines, but part of his original expedition completed the round trip to Spain, having circumnavigated the globe in three years.

A much clearer view of the other hemisphere now came into focus in Europe. An enormous continent lay between Europe and Asia, and it would be called America. In 1519, the same year that Magellan set out on his round-the-world voyage, a Spanish conquistador would invade Mexico, beginning the establishment of a European colony in the most populous region of this newly named land.

Columbus at the Spanish Court. In this 1870 lithograph, Columbus appears before Queen Isabella and King Ferdinand in 1493. **Question for Analysis:** How does the artist represent the Tainos who were taken from the Caribbean?

Map 1.4 The Spanish Conquest, 1492–1600. In the Treaty of Tordesillas, signed in 1494, Spain and Portugal confirmed the geographical boundary set a year earlier by the pope. The line would have important implications for the settlement of South America, but the pope was not concerned with the geography of the American continents, about which Europeans still knew almost nothing. The line was intended to recognize the colonies that Spain and Portugal had already claimed. **Question for Analysis:** Why might Catholic popes have considered the exploration of the Atlantic Ocean to be part of their domain?

THE SPANISH CONQUEST

From the Caribbean, Spanish conquerors moved to the densely settled regions of Mexico. A military force led by Hernán Cortés invaded the mighty Aztec empire, a well-established civilization with a capital city at Tenochtitlán that was more populous than any metropolis Spaniards had ever encountered. Enlisting the support of other native peoples who resented Aztec rule, Cortés and his allies besieged Tenochtitlán in 1521 and forced its surrender, killing over fifty thousand Aztecs. Cortés ordered the destruction of the city and rebuilt upon its ruins a new capital of Spain's American empire.

Another expedition, led by the conquistador Francisco Pizarro, invaded the western coast of South America. Pizarro sought to

INTERPRETING THE SOURCES

The Requerimiento

As Spanish conquerors arrived in various islands in the western Atlantic during the early sixteenth century, they issued the following proclamation, asserting their rights to rule over the local population. A version of the Requerimiento (requirement) had been used earlier by the Spanish in the Canary Islands, but by 1513 the Spanish were following a standard text composed by a lawyer named Palacios Rubios. Although the text was written (and typically proclaimed) in Castilian Spanish, which presumably no native could understand, the invaders made a point of reading it in the presence of the people to whom it was addressed. When Pedrarias Dávila arrived on the Caribbean island of Dominica in 1513, he had his notary read the Requerimiento and instructed a young native girl (who had been kidnapped, taken to Spain, and then brought back) to help explain its meaning. His audience responded by firing poisoned arrows. On other occasions, the text was read to empty villages or shouted at an island from a ship. Juan de Ayora, one of Pedrarias's commanders, had the Requerimiento read to natives who already had ropes around their necks.

It is impossible to say what this proclamation communicated to the indigenous people of Central America and the Caribbean in the sixteenth century, but the text does offer insight into what the Spanish took to be the justification for their actions.

We ask and require . . . that you consider what we have said to you, and that you take the time that shall be necessary to understand and deliberate upon it, and that you acknowledge the Church as the ruler and superior of the whole world, and the high priest called Pope, and in his name the king and queen . . . our lords, in his place, as superiors and lords and kings of these islands and this mainland. . . .

If you do so [acknowledge the Church as ruler] you will do well, and that which you are obliged to do to their highnesses, and we in their name shall receive you in all love and charity, and shall leave you your wives and your children and your lands free without servitude, that you may do with them and with yourselves freely what you like and think best, and they shall not compel you to turn Christians unless you yourselves, when informed of the truth, should wish to be converted to our holy Catholic faith . . . . as almost all the inhabitants of the rest of the islands have done. And besides this, their highnesses award you many privileges and exemptions and will grant you many benefits.

But if you do not do this or if you maliciously delay in doing it, I certify to you that with the help of God we shall forcefully enter into your country and shall make war against you in all ways and manners that we can, and shall subject you to the yoke and obedience of the Church and their highnesses; we shall take you and your wives and your children and shall make slaves of them, and as such sell and dispose of them as their highnesses may command; and we shall take away your goods and shall do to you all the harm and damage that we can, as to vassals who do not obey and refuse to receive their lord and resist and contradict him; and we protest that the deaths and losses which shall accrue from this are your fault, and not that of their highnesses, or ours, or of these soldiers who come with us. And that we have said this to you and made this Requerimiento we request the notary here present to give us his testimony in writing, and we ask the rest who are present that they should be witnesses of this Requerimiento.

Explore the Source

1. By what authority can the speakers in the text ("we") take the land and lives of the people addressed in the text?
2. According to the Requerimiento, were natives forced to convert to Christianity? What were their options?
3. Why do you think that it was important to the Spanish to have a document like the Requerimiento?

extract wealth from the land of the Incas, who dominated a region of more than nine million inhabitants centered in what is now Peru. In 1532, as the Incans were reeling from civil war and from diseases introduced to the continent by earlier European explorers, Pizarro's small force captured the Incan emperor Atahualpa and held him for a huge ransom in precious metals. The Spanish executed Atahualpa a year later and established the city of Lima. Fighting between Spaniards and Incas continued for years, but another powerful civilization had been subdued.

In Mexico and Peru, as in the Caribbean, Spain established a colonial empire based largely on the exploitation of indigenous labor. Legally speaking, Indians were allowed to remain on their land, but their labor was granted by the Spanish Crown to individual conquerors in a labor regime known as the **encomienda.** Indians did not technically belong to Spanish masters under the encomienda system and could not be passed down as slave property, but they were forced to produce export goods and to labor in mines, sugar mills, and public construction projects. Because Mexico and Peru turned out to hold vast deposits of gold and (especially) silver, the system yielded enormous tangible riches for the Spanish empire. The silver-mining town of Potosí in present-day Bolivia quickly attained a population of 120,000 by 1570 and 160,000 by century's end (surpassing any city on the European continent at the time) and produced forty-five thousand tons of silver over the next two centuries. Within a few generations of Columbus's arrival, Spanish conquests had radically reorganized the political and economic conditions of the most populous parts of the hemisphere.

Potosí Mines, Engraving by Theodor de Bry, 1596. Domingo de Santo Tomás, a Spanish priest who arrived in Peru in 1540, described Potosí as "a mouth of hell, into which a great mass of people enter every year and are sacrificed by the greed of the Spaniards to their 'god.'"

THE COLUMBIAN EXCHANGE

As Spaniards imposed new regimes in the Caribbean and warred against powerful empires in Mexico and South America, they precipitated new flows of people, information, goods, flora, fauna, and microbes between the two sides of the Atlantic Ocean. Scholars refer to this widespread, complex process as the **Columbian exchange.** From one perspective, the most obvious component of the exchange was the new influx of strangers from distant lands to Mesoamerica and the Caribbean. Indeed, approximately three hundred thousand Spaniards immigrated to mainland New Spain during the sixteenth century. The overwhelming majority were male, and most Spanish immigrants married indigenous women and fathered children with them. By the end of the century, towns and cities throughout Mexico and Central America held large numbers of mestizos (Spanish-Indians). More than two hundred thousand enslaved West Africans were brought to Spain's colonies as well in this period, mostly to the West Indies but also to the mainland.

The most striking demographic change, however, was mass death. Spanish conquerors brought guns to the New World and used lethal force to secure the obedience of local populations. But what they could not have known was that they were bearing a far deadlier weapon: disease. Europeans who survived childhood had acquired immunities to smallpox, measles, typhoid fever, and other diseases endemic to their part of the world, but they nonetheless carried those pathogens in their systems. Because indigenous Americans had been isolated from such pathogens for millennia, they lacked immunological defenses against germs introduced by the newcomers beginning with Columbus's first voyage. The total devastation of the Tainos in the Caribbean and the defeat of the Aztec empire were as much the consequence of influenza and smallpox as they were of European military advantages. European disease struck hardest at the old and the young, stripping native societies of both their leadership and their capacity to reproduce. Because population estimates for pre-Columbian America range widely, it is difficult to know with certainty how many native Americans died over the course of the sixteenth century. Even if we accept the most conservative figures, the population of Mexico dropped from eight million to two million during the 1500s. Estimates at the higher end of the scale raise the population loss to twenty-three million. In either case, the destruction of human life was staggering.

Like many other elements of the Columbian exchange, diseases traveled almost exclusively in one direction—toward the Americas. With the exception of syphilis, no deadly American diseases made their way back to Europe. Along with the diseases, humans, animals, and plants moved west rather than east across the ocean. Horses may have been especially startling to indigenous Mesoamericans, since they were instrumental to the conquest, but other animals, including cattle, sheep, and goats multiplied even more rapidly. By the early seventeenth century, there were already nine times as many European animals as American animals in Mexico. Rats and European weeds also made the journey west, allowing what some scholars have described as a wholesale transplanting of European ecosystems.

Other objects flowed mostly in the reverse direction. Some, like gold and silver, involved the extraction of resources from one hemisphere to enrich and ennoble people and nations in the other. But other New World goods, including tobacco and cacao (the plant from which chocolate is derived), built cultural bridges between one part of the Atlantic world and another.

How Much Is That?

Annual Mining Yields from Potosí

By the end of the sixteenth century, Spanish conquerors were overseeing the extraction of about 250 tons of silver every year, valued at approximately 8 million pesos. According to one common historical currency conversion, this would correspond to an annual yield of about 465 million dollars in 2013.

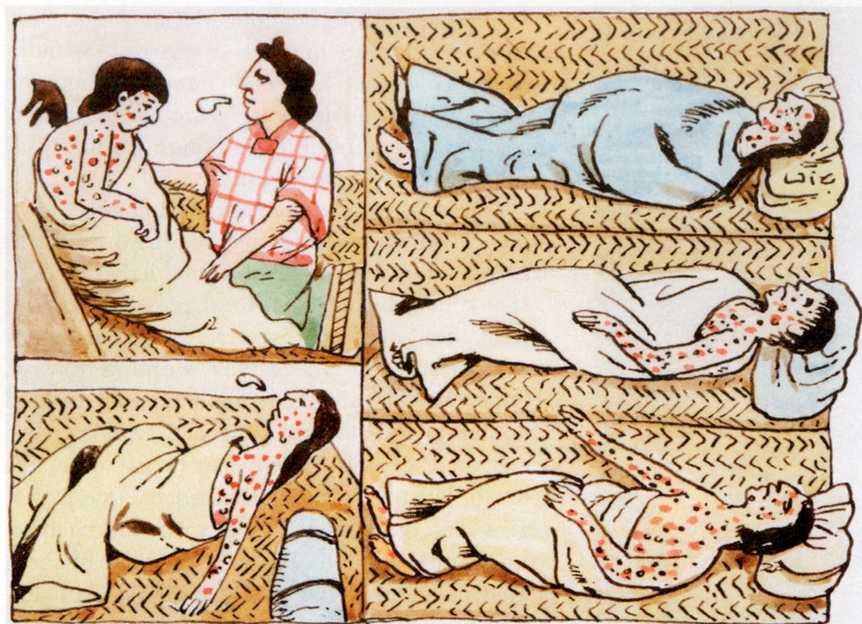

Aztecs Suffering from Smallpox in the Wake of European Contact. This illustration is from *La Historia General de las Cosas de Nueva España*, now known as the *Florentine Codex*, a sixteenth-century ethnography (cultural study) by Spanish Franciscan missionary Bernardino de Sahagún.

Two products cultivated originally in Mesoamerica, tobacco and cacao were special objects of both social exchange and religious ritual among the Aztecs. After they crossed the ocean, tobacco and chocolate came to assume special significance in European culture as well—for their healing properties and their ceremonial role in forging social relationships or marking class distinction. Other American foods would completely transform diets in far-flung parts of the globe. Maize was quickly introduced in West Africa and Europe and from there to the Middle East, India, and China. Potatoes, which had thrived originally in the Andes, came first to Spain in the sixteenth century and later found a home in the cooler and wetter climates of northern Europe. Red tomatoes from the New World entered Italy in the sixteenth century and became a core ingredient in Italian cuisine. The encounter between the Iberian Peninsula and Mesoamerica brought a wide range of new plants—sweet potatoes, pumpkins, pineapples, avocados, peanuts—to the daily tables of men and women who had little other connection to either of those places.

NORTH AMERICA IN THE NEW WORLD

Northern Europe and North America were largely uninvolved in either the fifteenth-century Atlantic explorations or the colonization that followed in Columbus's wake. Indeed, the first chapter of European expansion was dominated by southern Europe (Italian and Iberian seafarers and Iberian monarchs) and focused mostly on the Atlantic islands, the Caribbean, Central America, and the African coast. But northern European countries with access to the Atlantic Ocean, including England and France, were interested in western lands and eager to follow the Spanish and Portuguese examples. Impelled in part by new religious crises and conflicts, northerners joined the world of Atlantic exploration and conquest and brought North America into the orbit of the Columbian exchange.

EARLY NORTHERN EXPLORATION

Northern Europeans had in fact preceded Columbus across the waters by five centuries. The first recorded contacts between Americans and Europeans had taken place around 980, when Norse settlers from Scandinavia colonized the island of Greenland and briefly tried to settle in Newfoundland. By the fifteenth century, however, this encounter was a distant memory in European culture, preserved only in Icelandic sagas. Northern Europeans were not tempted to sea by stories of icy and inhospitable lands.

Northern countries had trouble competing with Spain and Portugal in the business of western exploration and colonization, in part because they lacked comparable financial resources and technical sophistication but also because the areas of the Atlantic world that were closest to them were less inviting. In the wake of Columbus's voyages to the West Indies, King Henry VII of England hired his own Italian navigator, John Cabot (Giovanni Caboto), to sail across the Atlantic from England in 1497. But Cabot did not find in Newfoundland any of the resources that Columbus found in Hispaniola, nor did he discover a northern route to the Far East. Cabot in fact never returned from his second voyage. Other aspiring English conquerors survived to tell their stories but were no more encouraged by what they found along the cold shores of Canada during the Little Ice Age. Though Cabot and his successors had seen vast fisheries in Canada's Grand Banks, these were not enough to interest King Henry or any other European monarch.

France also hired an Italian explorer, Giovanni da Verrazano, who surveyed the North American coast from Maine to North Carolina in 1524, but nothing he saw there intrigued him or his employers. A decade later, Jacques Cartier embarked on the first of another set of French expeditions, this time following the St. Lawrence River through Québec. Cartier returned with stories of large river towns that might be difficult to conquer, but he could report no progress toward a passage to China or Japan. And the cache of diamonds and gold he presented to the French court in 1542 turned out to be quartz crystals and pyrite ("fool's gold").

By the time of these French and English expeditions, Spain had expanded from the Caribbean and Mexico into other parts of North America. By the first half of the sixteenth century, Spain's densely populated colonies in Mexico and South

America were already yielding a huge return in gold and silver. For France and England, much more could be gained by attacking Spanish ships as they returned home than by trying to build a parallel empire farther north, where they found no gold and dim prospects for conscripting a large labor force. Even Spain's initial forays northward, into Florida, the Southwest, and the Great Plains between 1513 and 1546, proved temporary and led only to the conclusion that the land north of Mexico was not worth the trouble. For more than seven decades after Columbus, no significant European colonization projects targeted the areas that became the United States.

PROTESTANT EXPLORERS AND CONQUERORS

While Christians in Spain and Portugal looked to spread their faith to new frontiers in the early sixteenth century, religious life in northern Europe was disrupted by the challenge of the **Protestant Reformation.** In 1517, a monk named Martin Luther in the German town of Wittenberg began calling for reforms in the governance of the Catholic Church, especially an end to the practice of selling indulgences (partial remission for sins). Luther's *Ninety-Five Theses* was a detailed scholarly critique of the authority of the Church to grant pardon and absolution, but because it was reproduced with the new printing techniques that had become available in Europe several decades earlier, it unleashed a more popular controversy. Circulating broadly, Luther's attack quickly touched off larger, wider controversies about papal infallibility and ecclesiastical (church-related) corruption. Parallel critiques of Catholicism soon appeared in other parts of Central Europe. The pope excommunicated Luther, and within a decade of the publication of the *Theses*, a new religious movement was born. Protestants or Lutherans, as the proponents of this movement were called, stressed the view that only God could grant salvation and that human beings could hope to achieve this salvation only through faith. In effect, the Reformation rejected centuries of accumulated religious tradition, ritual, and authority. It also severed the connective tissue that had united Western Europe, at least symbolically, during the Middle Ages.

Sixteenth-Century Print Technology Depicted in a Woodcut Illustration from *The Book of Trades*, 1568. Martin Luther's scholarly disquisition on the sale of indulgences might not have been intended for general consumption, but once translated from Latin to German and set in type, it reached a wide readership. By one count, one out of three books published in German between 1518 and 1525 was authored by Luther.

The Protestant-Catholic split led to bitter and violent internal strife through much of Europe. Because the reformers attracted more followers in the upper part of the continent (in Switzerland and north of the Alps), the Reformation also widened and emphasized the divide between northern and southern countries. In 1534, a major northern power officially broke with Rome when England's King Henry VIII declared himself supreme head of the Church of England and began confiscating and redistributing the lands that had belonged to the Catholic Church. Henry had not been swayed by Luther's ideas; he simply wanted to dissolve his marriage to Catherine of Aragon (who was past childbearing age) in order to produce a male heir with another woman, and he could not receive papal sanction to do so. The English Reformation that Henry initiated preserved many features of Catholic hierarchy, liturgy, and sacrament, but his monarchy was deeply invested in the Protestant rejection of the Roman Church. For if papal authority represented God's will, the king of England was an adulterer and his eventual heir to the throne an illegitimate pretender. Henry's second wife (he would eventually marry six women in succession) did not bear him a male heir, but her daughter, Elizabeth, took the throne in 1558. Elizabeth's claim to legitimacy also depended on a rejection of the pope's authority.

Under Queen Elizabeth I, who ruled until 1603, English naval adventurers known as sea dogs preyed upon Spanish ships at sea and in the Netherlands, both in wartime and in peace. Active from the 1560s until 1605, they defended their piracy as an assault against Catholicism. At this time, England also embarked on its own discovery of the New World. Sea dog Humphrey Gilbert secured a charter from Queen Elizabeth to spread the Christian faith to "remote heathen and barbarous lands" and made two unsuccessful efforts to establish a large colonial estate in Newfoundland. Gilbert died at sea following the second venture in 1583, and the charter was reassigned to his half-brother, Walter Ralegh. Meanwhile, the English Navy's defeat of the vaunted Spanish Armada in 1588 signaled a major shift in the balance of power between Catholic and Protestant powers.

England's Protestant adventurers also took the fight to Ireland. English settlers had been in Ireland since the eleventh century, but in 1565, Queen Elizabeth's government announced a new policy of subjecting all of Ireland to English rule. Because Ireland was Catholic, men like Ralegh and Gilbert financed and directed the conquest of Ireland as part of their wider religious crusade. Englishmen saw their Irish Catholic enemies as quite different from their Spanish ones, however. Gaelic

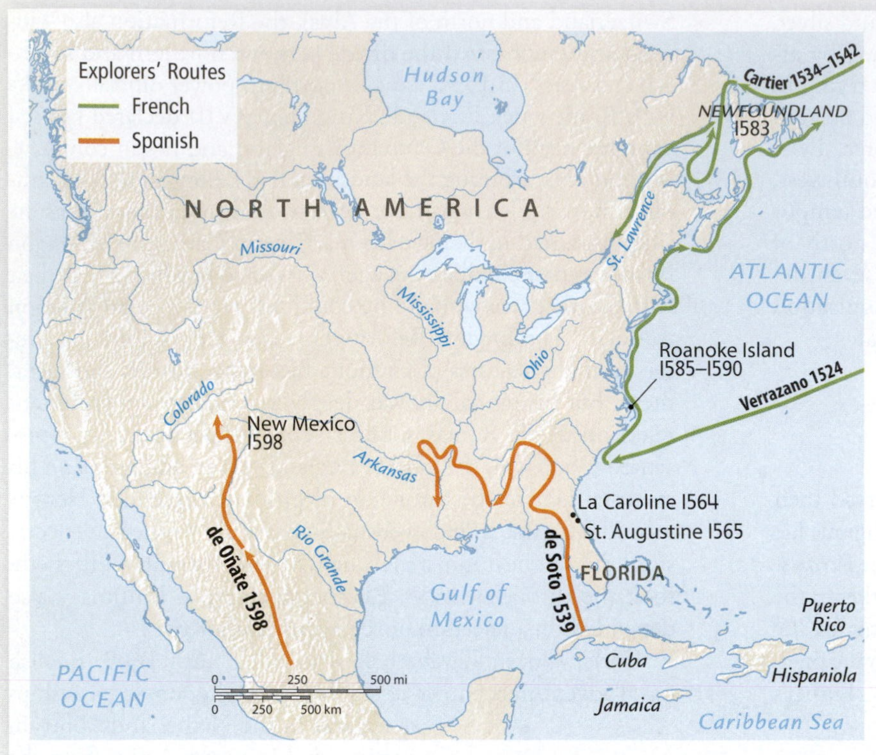

Map 1.5 European Explorations in North America, 1500–1600. Although they established no lasting settlements in North America during the sixteenth century, French and English expeditions explored many parts of the land that became the United States, and contested Spanish efforts at colonizing the mainland.

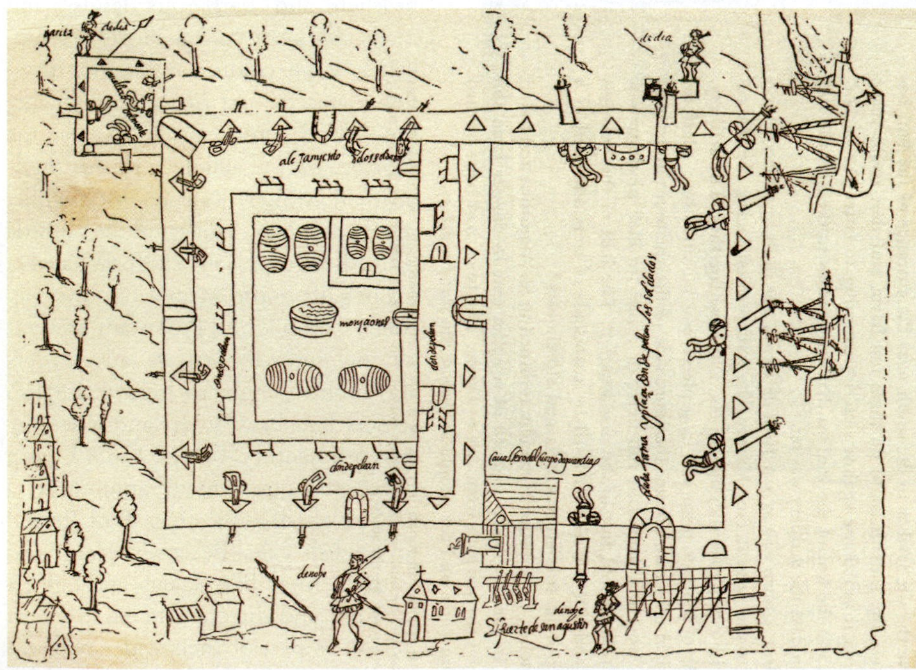

Plan of Fort of St. Augustine, Florida, 1595. The oldest U.S. city began as a Catholic fort designed to ward off Protestant settlement in North America.

Irishmen, living in a world that had not been swept up in Europe's agricultural revolution, appeared to the English as savages, "more uncivill, more uncleanly, more barbarous and more brutish . . . then in any part of the world that is known." Indeed, the English saw Ireland's indigenous population much as Columbus had viewed the natives of Hispaniola. During two long campaigns of brutal suppression, from 1568 to 1583 and from 1594 to 1603, English conquerors followed the model that the Spanish had introduced in the West Atlantic: If Gaelic leaders did not accept English rule and religious authority, they would forfeit their land to men like Ralegh, who would begin the painful process of civilizing the region. Ireland continued to serve as both a parallel theater and a training ground for the Atlantic adventures of the sea dogs and for early English expeditions to the Americas.

The first Protestant crusaders to build colonies in the lands that would later become the United States did not come from England, however (see Map 1.5). Rather, they were Huguenots—Protestants from Catholic France—seeking both a refuge from persecution in Europe and a beachhead in the Americas against the advances of the Catholic armies of King Felipe II of Spain. In 1562, the French pirate and explorer Jean Ribault placed a stone column near the mouth of the St. John's River in the vicinity of present-day Jacksonville, Florida, proclaiming the creation of New France. Two years later, about three hundred French Huguenots settled near Ribault's spot, where they established the colony of La Caroline. The local native population, which had reclaimed Ribault's column for their own purposes (adorning it with magnolias and corn baskets), saw in the French settlement an opportunity for an alliance against a nearby Indian enemy, but this union never materialized. The Spanish, on the other hand, understood the Huguenot settlement for what it was—a Protestant fortress that might later be used to attack Spanish colonies of the Caribbean.

In 1565, Spain dispatched a thousand soldiers under the command of Pedro Menéndez de Avilés to destroy La Caroline. Menéndez captured the fort and executed most of the survivors. According to one report, the Huguenot settlers were hanged under a sign proclaiming "I do this not as to Frenchmen, but as to Lutherans." The major legacy of the short-lived La Caroline settlement was its incitement of the Spanish to colonize Florida in order to keep the Protestants out of the region. In 1565, just days before the attack on La Caroline, Menéndez founded St. Augustine, the oldest city still in existence in the United States.

Following the La Caroline massacre, other Protestant explorers looked elsewhere. Walter Ralegh, observing the failures of Humphrey Gilbert in Newfoundland, selected a far more temperate location much closer to Florida and named it Virginia in honor of Elizabeth I, England's "Virgin Queen." In 1585, Ralegh sent an exploratory party to the region, and they selected for settlement Roanoke Island on the Outer Banks of what is now North Carolina (see Singular Lives: Manteo, Cultural Broker). Five hundred Englishmen (no women) sailed for the new colony in 1585, but mishaps and diversions along the way delayed their arrival and thinned their numbers. After a group returned to Europe for supplies and reinforcements, the remaining Englishmen tried to cajole the local Roanokes into feeding them, and tensions erupted. When Roanoke chief Pemisapan tried to sever all contact with the English, the colonists sensed trouble. Preempting the attack they feared, Roanoke governor Ralph Lane and his men armed themselves, surrounded Pemisapan and his counselors, and initiated an angry exchange. At the prearranged sign of Lane's proclamation "Christ our victory!" the English opened fire, killing the chief and cutting off his head. Soon thereafter, Lane evacuated Roanoke and took most of his party back to England.

A persistent Ralegh sent another expedition to Roanoke in 1587, this time with a party of 110 colonists that included families and now with the goal of eventually settling farther north along the Chesapeake Bay. This venture proved no more successful. Facing a severe drought and mindful of their previous experiences with English settlers, no native groups would help the colonists secure food. Worse, violence erupted again between the newcomers and their hosts. Once more, the colonists dispatched ships to persuade Ralegh to resupply the expedition, but Roanoke was not a priority back in England, which was embroiled in a war with Spain. The ships Ralegh tried to send were detained by a wartime embargo and then diverted to the West Indies to prey on Spanish carriers. When English ships finally reached Roanoke in 1590, the only trace of English settlement was the word *Croatoan*, carved in English letters on a tree. Another Protestant colony had failed.

Algonquian Chief, Watercolor by John White, ca. 1585. The painting recalls artist-colonist White's encounters with Indians in the Outer Banks region. The inscription reads, "The manner of their attire and painting them selves when they goe to their generall huntings, or at theire Solemne feasts." **Question for Analysis:** How does White's 1585 representation of an Indian compare with the 1870 representation on p. 18 of Columbus appearing before the Spanish court?

EARLY CONTACTS IN THE NORTH

Although by 1550 the Columbian exchange had built a bridge across the ocean linking Mesoamerica to West Africa and Western Europe, its impact on North America was slight. In most of the land that would become the United States, native groups experienced little fallout from the conquest in the south or the passage of people, goods, and microbes across the Atlantic Ocean (see Hot Commodities: Cod). But over the second half of the sixteenth century, increasing numbers of North American Indians had some indirect contact with Europe.

Most North American Indians encountered European goods long before they met Europeans. Unfamiliar material objects were introduced to North America by explorers or aspiring colonists who traded European goods with coastal peoples, bestowed them as gifts upon powerful leaders, or simply lost them at sea. The European goods that North Americans valued, such as axe heads, brass kettles, and glass beads, then traveled deep into the interior as they passed from one chief to another along the same routes that had carried other prestigious objects long before European contact. Such unfamiliar goods may have been attached to stories about the peoples who produced or exchanged them, but we do not know what native peoples knew or thought about the world across the ocean.

In a few places, however, live contact between Europeans and Americans was becoming more common. After establishing a permanent mainland outpost in St. Augustine in 1565, Spain also sent an expedition to the upper Rio Grande Valley in 1598 and claimed a new colony, which the party called New Mexico. Catholic missionaries traveled along the Florida peninsula and established missions up the coast as far north as the Chesapeake Bay. Along with Ralegh's various unsuccessful attempts to establish Virginia, the abortive ventures in Newfoundland, and the Huguenot colony at La Caroline, the Spanish outposts contributed to a series of mini-exchanges that had brought select native populations of North America into an Atlantic world. Wherever these exchanges occurred, disease and death followed. An Englishman in Roanoke in 1585 noted that in the Indian

SINGULAR LIVES

Manteo, Cultural Broker

Of the millions of men and women who lived in North America in the sixteenth century, few imprinted their names on the historical record. But the European visitors who explored various parts of the Atlantic coast learned some of these names and recorded valuable details about the lives they represented. When Walter Ralegh's explorers returned in 1584 from their initial voyage to the Carolina coast, they brought two North American men back to London. One of them, Wanchese, was a commoner from Roanoke, where Ralegh hoped to build his colony. The other, Manteo, was a minor chief from a nearby island. When the two men returned to North America the following year, Wanchese bore a dire message to his fellow Algonquian Indians: The English were powerful, ambitious men who should not be trusted or helped. Manteo, on the other hand, embraced his new role as a kind cultural intermediary between the English and the Algonquians, translating one society's words and rituals for the other.

How Manteo felt about the escalating hostilities between the newcomers and the natives is hard to tell from the sources. Although he never changed his name, his trip to England had clearly transformed his identity. Manteo wore English clothing and never returned to the community in which he had grown up, and he advised Sir Richard Grenville (the English commander of the fleet that sailed with Manteo back to Roanoke) on diplomatic matters, earning his trust. Yet he strategically withheld information from the colonists when he needed to and remained an enigmatic figure in the treacherous world of Roanoke politics.

Historians often cite Manteo as a promising example of white-Indian cooperation in the early years of American colonization, but the historical significance of that example is as elusive as the fate of Ralegh's colony. From an English perspective in the 1580s, however, Manteo represented the bright prospects of England's North American crusade. Baptized in 1587 on Roanoke Island, Manteo became the first Indian to convert to Anglicanism.

Think About It

1. Why might the English have brought Manteo and Wanchese to England?
2. How might Manteo have benefited from adapting some of the culture of newcomers whom the Roanoke natives regarded with suspicion?

Susquehannock Tools and Ornaments. These articles were fashioned out of brass stripped from European trade kettles. Before the seventeenth century, natives tended to value the few European goods in circulation mostly for their raw materials or their symbolic associations rather than for their intended uses.

Indian Women Planting Corn. Theodor de Bry's 1590 depiction struck the European newcomers as an odd division of sexual labor. In Europe, fieldwork was considered manly.

HOT COMMODITIES

Cod

Well before Europeans began migrating to North America, they ate American cod. The Atlantic cod fish, *Gadhus morhua*, is an unusually prolific and durable species: omnivorous, resistant to parasites, and highly fecund. From a human perspective, it is also a remarkable food source. Low in fat and high in protein (even by fish standards), cod is well suited to drying and salting and can last a long time. It is also easy to catch. Though Atlantic cod can be found in various regions, the North American banks between Newfoundland and southern New England provide an especially hospitable environment. For centuries, this area has been home to the densest concentration of cod in the world.

Cod Fish European demand for this prolific food source helped stimulate early contact between Western Europe and North America.

Basque fishermen from northern Spain and southwestern France harvested the North Atlantic cod bounty as early as the fourteenth century and began importing vast quantities of dried salt cod to Europe. By the end of the fifteenth century, French, Portuguese, English, and Spanish ships had discovered the secret source of the Basque supply and joined the cod rush. Quickly, cod became a staple of the European diet, accounting for more than half of the fish consumed on the continent by 1550.

European navies and seafaring expeditions valued dried cod because it could sustain a crew over long journeys. But landlocked consumers in Catholic Europe had other reasons to buy fish. Since the fourth century the Catholic Church had condemned eating meat on certain days, and over the subsequent centuries an elaborate calendar of fast days and lean days emerged. Catholics did not eat meat or other "hot" foods on Friday (the day linked to Jesus's crucifixion), during Lent, or on specified holy days. In all, fasts and food taboos (which in some cases forbade dairy, eggs, and wine as well) covered over 100 days per year. In some regions, practically half of the year (182 days) was given over to such fasting. Fish was allowed on fast days, however, and dried cod from the North American banks became a popular, less perishable alternative to local food sources. Western Europeans often ate dried cod with mustard or fatty dairy-based sauces.

Cod became big business in the sixteenth century and contributed to a shipbuilding boom as European merchants competed for the North Atlantic fish trade. The cod trade also habituated European sailors to sailing across the Atlantic. Unlike the gold and silver that Spain extracted from its southern colonies, cod was not a valued currency. And unlike American tobacco, chocolate, or sugar, cod was not really a novel delicacy on the European consumer market. But it was one part of the transatlantic commodity exchange that drew Europe's attention to the northern part of the Americas, encouraging the idea that the region's cold and inhospitable climate might nonetheless hold valuable natural resources.

As fishing crews set up camps to dry their cod haul, they interacted with native populations. Thus through the sixteenth century, fishermen—rather than colonial explorers or priests—initiated the most regular and significant contacts between Europeans and Native Americans.

Think About It

1. Why might cod have been more valuable to Europeans than to North Americans?
2. How might cod have contributed to the eventual colonization of the lands that became the United States and Canada?

villages he visited, "people began to die very fast, and many in short space." Franciscan missionaries claimed to have brought sixteen thousand Florida Indians into the Catholic fold in the early 1600s, but within a few years half of them had died, presumably by contagions borne by the Franciscans. As more European settlements—English, French, Dutch, and Spanish—took hold in the early 1600s, the same diseases that had swept Mexico visited the northern part of the continent.

Though their lives were beginning to intermesh, Indians and Europeans in North America probably formed only vague ideas of each other's societies before the seventeenth century. The newcomers had come to conquer, convert, and extract resources, as the Spanish were doing farther south. But nothing the Europeans saw or heard encouraged optimism on these fronts. Because Indian settlement was scattered (the densest indigenous societies in North America, which were on the Pacific coast, had little contact with Europeans until the eighteenth century), Europeans saw little opportunity to exploit Indian labor. Moreover, gold and silver were elusive. Finally, natives would not provide them food. Some natives appeared receptive to Christianity, but missionaries noticed that those Indians who spent time with them tended to die. As for the natives, who were still living in the migratory and changing world created by the dispersal of the Mississippian powers, they had seen newcomers before. But the hairy men who came by boats brought unfamiliar expectations about how to engage in trade and form alliances. They expected obedience. And while they could not sustain themselves, they seemed to bring death wherever they went.

CONCLUSION

Several decades ago, scholars and writers who were uncomfortable with the conventional notion that Columbus *discovered* the New World began speaking of the European exploration and settlement of the Americas as a *conquest* or an *invasion* rather than a discovery. Such terms apply well to Mexico, Central America, and the Caribbean, where colonization led to the rapid, wholesale destruction of native communities in the sixteenth century. But they are potentially misleading descriptions of what happened north of the Rio Grande before the seventeenth century. The sporadic arrivals of Europeans on the eastern shores of the vast territory that would become the United States did not instantly usher in a new era. Compared to the original Beringian migrations that had populated the continent, the agricultural changes of the warming period that had revolutionized settlement patterns, or the dispersals of peoples that had reshaped national and tribal boundaries in the thirteenth and fourteenth centuries, the events of the 1500s seem less dramatic. After all, much of North America was *already* in flux in 1492.

For the European nations sponsoring these new ventures in North America, the explorations in the Atlantic world were part of a larger process with deep roots in the Middle Ages. Latin Christendom had sent crusaders to distant lands before, without establishing a colonial empire. Northern Europeans had explored cold lands in North America back in the tenth century and had not created a new world. In subsequent centuries, colonization efforts in Newfoundland, La Caroline, and Roanoke came and went. Perhaps the same fate awaited the Spanish colonies of Florida and New Mexico.

In retrospect, however, events in Mesoamerica already showed the possible stakes of European migration to North America. Inspired by their universalistic religion, motivated by international competition, and unknowingly harboring deadly germs, the migrants were capable of turning life in the Americas upside down. Equally ominous, in retrospect, was the emergence of a large trade in West African slaves, who were just beginning to join the great migration.

STUDY TERMS

Beringia (p. 5)
Paleo-Indians (p. 5)
maize (p. 5)
Mesoamerica (p. 5)
Poverty Point (p. 5)
moundbuilding (p. 5)
agricultural revolution (p. 7)
Chaco Canyon (p. 7)
Mississippian civilization (p. 8)
Cahokia (p. 8)
chunkey (p. 9)
Little Ice Age (p. 10)
Crow Creek Massacre (p. 11)
nation-state (p. 12)
Latin Christendom (p. 13)
Crusades (p. 14)
Reconquista (p. 14)
adelantado (p. 14)
Canary Islands (p. 14)
Saö Tome and Principe (p. 15)
Ghana (p. 15)
Mali (p. 15)
African slave trade (p. 16)
Elmina Castle (p. 16)
Tainos (p. 17)
America (p. 18)
encomienda (p. 20)
Potosí (p. 20)
Columbian exchange (p. 21)
mestizo (p. 21)
tobacco (p. 21)
cacao (p. 21)
Greenland (p. 22)
Protestant Reformation (p. 23)
English Reformation (p. 23)
sea dogs (p. 23)
La Caroline (p. 24)
St. Augustine (p. 25)
Roanoke Island (p. 25)

TIMELINE

15,000–14,000 Before Present First migrants cross into North America

5000 BCE Maize cultivation begins in Mexico

1600 BCE Moundbuilding appears in Louisiana

900–1300 CE Warmer temperatures lead to agricultural expansion in North America and northern Europe

900–1150 Ancestral Puebloan (Anasazi) civilization flourishes near Chaco Canyon

1050 Rise of Cahokia

1076 Latin Christendom embarks on Crusades and Reconquista

1300 Little Ice Age begins in North America

1300–1350 Fall of Cahokia

1347 Bubonic plague strikes northern Europe

1433 Fall of Timbuktu

1472 Spain authorizes conquest of the Canary Islands

1482–1485 Portuguese colonize islands, establish trading posts off the African coast

1492 Christopher Columbus arrives in San Salvador

1494 Treaty of Tordesillas divides the New World between Spain and Portugal

1507 Martin Waldseemüller names the American continent

1517 Martin Luther begins Protestant Reformation

1520 Ferdinand Magellan's crew circumnavigates the globe

1521 Hernán Cortés conquers Tenochtitlán

1532 Francisco Pizarro invades Incan empire

1534 Henry VIII breaks from Catholic Church

1564 French settle La Caroline

1565 Spanish found St. Augustine

1585 English establish settlement on Roanoke Island

1588 English Navy defeats Spanish Armada

FURTHER READING

Additional suggested readings are available on the Online Learning Center at www.mhhe.com/becomingamerica1e.

Alfred Crosby, *Ecological Imperialism* (1986), provides a classic account of the damage caused by European pathogens.

Brian Fagan, *Chaco Canyon* (2005), presents current archaeological understandings on the Chaco Canyon site.

Mark Kurlansky, *Cod* (1997), describes the far-reaching historical impact of a transatlantic fish trade that preceded European colonization.

Charles C. Mann, *1491* (2006), opens a wide-angle lens on America before Columbus.

Marcy Norton, *Sacred Gifts, Profane Pleasures* (2008), examines the cultural significance of chocolate and tobacco in the Columbian Exchange.

Michael Oberg, *The Head in Edward Nugent's Hand* (2008), reinterprets the course and significance of the abortive English colony at Roanoke.

Timothy Pauketat, *Cahokia* (2009), relates the remarkable archaeological rediscovery of an ancient city along the Mississippi River.

Daniel K. Richter, *Before the Revolution* (2011), draws powerful parallels between Europe and North America in the periods prior to their contact.

Neal Salisbury, *Manitou and Providence* (1984), considers the significance of early European colonization in North America in terms of the politics and world views of indigenous peoples.

Christina Snyder, *Slavery in Indian Country* (2010), emphasizes the importance of captivity to the history of Indian politics before the arrival of the Europeans.

John Thornton, *Africa and Africans in the Making of the Atlantic World* (1992), highlights the active role of Africans in the Atlantic slave trade and in the larger reshaping of the Americas beginning in the fifteenth century.

Frederick Hadleigh West (ed.), *American Beginnings* (1996), explores the prehistoric world of Beringia.

2

INSIDE

THE BIG PICTURE

Following a few false starts, European colonization took hold along parts of the periphery of North America. Spanish, French, Dutch, and two especially populous and quite different English colonies all reshaped the continent's complex political map, altering the landscape and triggering explosive episodes of native resistance.

Visions of a New World. Martin Pringe, who explored the coast around present-day Massachusetts in 1603 as an agent of English merchants, produced this image of what he called "North Virginia."

1600–1680

EARLY COLONIES

In February 1675, the body of John Sassamon was found under the ice at Assawompset Pond in what is now southeastern Massachusetts. Born a Wampanoag Indian early in the century, Sassamon had been orphaned at a young age and raised by English immigrants as a Christian. Eloquent and literate in both the Massachusett language and English, Sassamon served for several decades as a mediator between Algonquian Indians and the English colonists who lived on the North Atlantic coast. He had worked closely with John Eliot, an English missionary who translated Christian Scriptures into Massachusett, and he studied briefly at Harvard College, a new school founded to train Protestant ministers to preach the gospel in a world the colonists called New England. Sassamon had also advised the powerful Wampanoag leader Metacom, whom the English dubbed King Philip.

Relations between Metacom and the English colony of Plymouth deteriorated in the early 1670s, and in January 1675, Sassamon informed the Plymouth authorities that King Philip was planning to attack them. Josiah Winslow, Plymouth's governor, dismissed the report as the unreliable testimony of an Indian. A week later Sassamon disappeared, and soon thereafter came the discovery of his body. In due course, a witness stepped forward to testify that three of Metacom's advisers were responsible for the killing. After a jury of Englishmen and Christian Indians convicted the men of murder, a Plymouth court ordered their execution.

A protracted and bloody war followed, by some measures the deadliest in American history.

The career of the man at the center of this drama epitomized how intertwined the lives of European settlers and Native Americans had become over the course of the seventeenth century. European colonization on the North American mainland entered a new phase in the early 1600s. By 1614, English, Dutch, French, and Spanish colonizers had secured settlements on North America's Atlantic coast, and in 1638 Sweden established a fur-trading colony in the lower Delaware Valley. These colonies encountered many of the same problems that had plagued the failed ventures of the previous century, but by midcentury their settlements were still standing, and Europeans were enjoying flourishing trade with indigenous peoples. Although the new colonies remained small outposts on the periphery of a region dominated by Indian nations, they had a profound impact on the lands that would become the United States. In addition to the devastating diseases that followed in the colonists' wake, Europeans introduced deadly weapons, ecologically disruptive animals, and unfamiliar ways of using and thinking about land. By the second half of the seventeenth century, European colonization was changing the face of the continent.

In this detail from a larger nineteenth-century painting, George Catlin re-created a meeting in 1682 between the French explorer La Salle and the chief of the Taensa Indians in what today is northeastern Louisiana.

The new colonies varied markedly. French, Dutch, and Swedish settlements were organized around fur trading, whereas English settlements focused on farming. In the Chesapeake Bay region, English colonists grew tobacco on large and relatively isolated plantations, whereas those who lived in New England worked smaller farms and clustered in towns. In Florida and in the Southwest, the Spanish established a mission system to convert Indians and control their labor, whereas English Protestants sought other strategies for spreading the gospel. Religious differences and national rivalries shaped colonial enterprises during this period.

Geographical differences along the Atlantic coast influenced the histories of the new European colonies, but economic and demographic developments mattered as well. Because of social conditions in England, the new English colonies attracted more immigrants than the others. English travelers to the New World included significant numbers of free settlers of both sexes, who sought not to extract precious resources but to build new lives and new communities on American soil. Some English colonists continued to dream of living off the labor of Native Americans, but increasingly they turned to other sources and systems. Eventually, the very different European colonies established in Virginia, New England, New Netherland, New France, and New Mexico during the early seventeenth century would shape settlement patterns for many of the societies that would become the United States.

Despite their differences, all of these colonial experiments shared a tenuous, fragile quality, and by the 1670s, most were facing crises that threatened to extinguish them altogether. The devastating war that erupted in John Sassamon's New England was just one of three major military conflicts in the continent's largest European colonies between 1675 and 1680, ending a long period of tense coexistence that had allowed those colonies to take root.

KEY QUESTIONS

- What different colonial projects did Spain, England, France, and the Netherlands initiate in North America, and why?
- In what crucial ways did the New England and Chesapeake colonies differ?
- Why did tensions arise between colonists and Indians in the various lands Europeans settled in the first half of the seventeenth century?
- How did the three major eruptions of violence in colonial North America between 1676 and 1680 differ from one another?

NEW SPAIN IN NORTH AMERICA

As the seventeenth century opened, Spain was the leading European colonial power in the Americas. Spain's dominion in the New World was located primarily in Central and South America, where colonial authorities exploited the labor of an indigenous population that they supplemented with African slaves. As the Spanish continued their quest for gold, a passage to Asia, and the conversion of the Americas to the Catholic faith, they also sent expeditions northward, where they established smaller colonies in present-day Florida and New Mexico. Their success made Spain the only European power with an established colonial presence in North America.

Multistory Adobe Housing of the Southwestern Pueblos, Taos, New Mexico. From the Spanish word for "town," the term *pueblo* (lowercase) now refers to the adobe-constructed villages. Pueblo (capitalized) Indians are native peoples from the Rio Grande Valley, as well as Zunis and Hopis.

THE ESTABLISHMENT OF NEW MEXICO

By the last quarter of the sixteenth century, Spanish colonization in the Americas had taken a turn. After several decades of destructive conquest (see Chapter 1), the Spanish Crown reconsidered its policies in the New World. Facing severe internal criticism for the brutality of Spanish conduct in Mexico (especially in Bartolomé de Las Casas's *In Defense of the Indians*, which appeared in 1550) and a powerful external challenge from the Protestant Reformation, King Philip II of Spain issued the Ordinances of Discovery in 1573, which renounced and prohibited the wanton massacre of Indians. "Discoveries are not to be called Conquests," the law declared, and should be "carried out peacefully and charitably." On this new model, missionaries would take the lead and direct the pace of all future settlement. Franciscan priests, members of a medieval religious order who had been laboring to convert Mexican Indians since 1524, now sought new territory in which to save souls. Accordingly, in 1581, the Franciscans dispatched an expedition to learn more about the people and the terrain north of the Rio Grande.

On the basis of the Franciscan reports, King Philip authorized a prosperous miner named Juan de Oñate, who had been born in New Spain, to establish the colony of New Mexico. In the spirit of the 1573 Ordinances, the king instructed Oñate that "your main purpose shall be the service of God Our Lord [and] the spreading of His holy Catholic faith," but he added that it would also be necessary to "reduce" and "pacify" the local population. Oñate set out from the Mexican city of Zacatecas in January 1598 with 129 soldiers, seven missionaries, more than 300 other colonists, and lots of sheep, goats, and cattle. He journeyed past long stretches of sparsely inhabited desert into the world of the Pueblos, the name that Spanish colonists coined to designate the diverse Indian peoples they encountered in the Southwest. These Indians descended from the southwestern civilizations that had dispersed after the fall of the major cities in the Four Corners region (see Chapter 1) and from other nomadic groups that had moved to the area around the fourteenth and fifteenth centuries.

Eager to secure the peaceful submission of the Indians he encountered, Oñate staged a series of theatrical ceremonies. His intent was to remind his audiences of the Spanish conquest of Mexico some seventy-five years earlier and to trumpet the benefits of Spanish Catholic rule. Everywhere he went, Oñate marched under a banner bearing the same

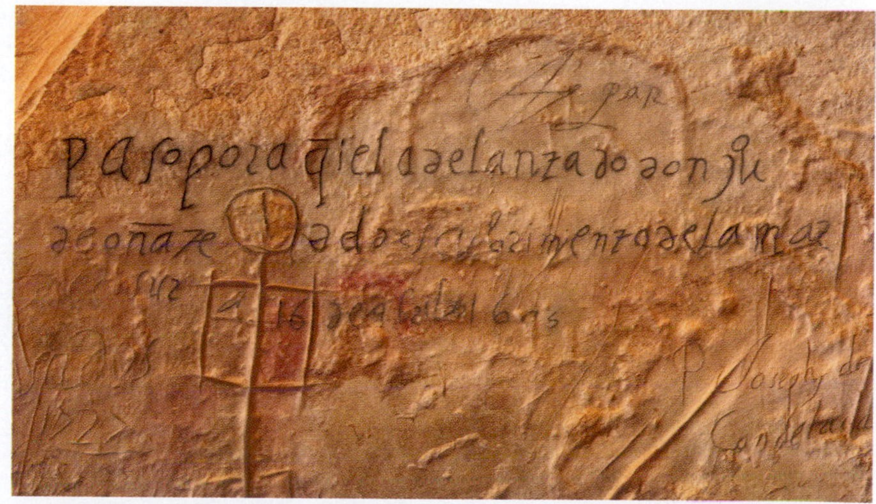

Imperial Graffiti. Juan de Oñate left his mark in the sandstone of what is now known as Inscription Rock, El Morrow National Monument, New Mexico. The translation is, "Passed by here adelantado Juan de Oñate to the discovery of the sea of the south on the 16 April the year 1605." The rock also bears much earlier petroglyphs (carvings on rock) by Pueblo Indians.

religious image that Hernán Cortés had carried upon entering Tenochtitlán in 1519. As part of the ceremony establishing a new colonial capital in a town renamed San Juan de los Caballeros, Oñate gathered the local chiefs for a performance of a medieval play, *The Christians and the Moors*, set during the Spanish Reconquista (see Chapter 1). The play ends with the infidel Moors accepting Christ and submitting to Spanish rule. Oñate expected the Pueblos to get the not-so-subtle message.

Though a number of chiefs pledged fealty to the invaders, tensions between the Spanish and the Indians surfaced quickly. In December 1598, Oñate's nephew Juan de Zaldívar visited the pueblo of Acoma to trade for food. Told that it would take several days to grind the quantity of corn he demanded, Zaldívar withdrew and returned three days later with a heavily armed entourage. Acoma residents killed Zaldívar and some of his party, to which the Spanish responded by launching an all-out attack. Oñate's men razed the Acoma pueblo, killed eight hundred people, and dealt harshly with the survivors. All men and women between the ages of twelve and twenty-five were sentenced to twenty years of servitude. Older men had one foot amputated. Two Indians from other pueblos who had been visiting Acoma were sent back to their communities with their right hands cut off to warn neighboring peoples against resisting the Spanish. Clearly, peaceful missionaries were not calling the shots in New Mexico.

Oñate's violent regime alarmed the Spanish viceroy. His brutality also alienated some of the colonists, who had grown disenchanted with the harsh terrain and were disappointed by the absence of gold. After a lengthy investigation, Spain ordered an end to the exploration of the region, rescinded Oñate's license, and in 1608 threatened to dissolve the colony. But mindful of missionary appeals to the Crown on behalf of the Indians they claimed to have converted already, and concerned about the new English colony of Jamestown established a year earlier in Virginia (which lay much closer to New Mexico on Spanish maps than in reality), Spain elected not to abandon the project altogether, but instead to turn New Mexico into a **royal colony** controlled directly by the Spanish monarchy. By 1610, colonial authorities relocated the Spanish-speaking population to a new capital in Santa Fe, built mainly by Indian laborers. Henceforth New Mexico would be a marginal missionary outpost supported by a small royal subsidy.

THE MISSIONARY REGIME IN THE SOUTHWEST

After 1610, New Mexico became a theocracy run by Franciscan priests who had been instrumental to the missionary effort in central Mexico in the previous century. Moving north from Mexico, Franciscans established mission towns, with large churches in the center, throughout the Rio Grande Valley in what is now north central New Mexico. By 1626, twenty-six missions had been built, and half a century later, more than two thousand colonists occupied these towns. Pueblo Indians visited the missions, often receiving gifts in return for submission to baptism rituals and promises of Christian living.

From this base of operations, the Franciscans launched an attack on traditional Pueblo rites, which revolved around a culture of worship known as the *katsina*. Missionaries outlawed katsina dances and masks and imposed strict penalties for violations of the prohibition. More effectively, they superimposed Christian symbols and rituals onto established patterns of native worship and theology. Pueblo prayer-sticks, for example, became associated with the Christian cross, and landmarks in the Pueblo calendar, such as the winter solstice, acquired links with events in Jesus's life. Although Indians adopted many

Ansel Adams's Photograph of the San Estevan Del Rey Mission Church, Acoma, New Mexico. This Spanish Colonial mission church was founded by Franciscans in 1629.

of these Catholic practices, they resented and resisted Spanish attacks on their religious faith, which they continued to practice in underground structures called *kivas*.

Franciscans also sought to subvert Pueblo gender roles and suppress Pueblo sexual culture. In Pueblo tradition, for example, weaving was men's work, whereas housing construction belonged in the feminine domain. When the missionaries tried to impose a new division of labor, they encountered resistance. "If we compel any man to work on building a house," one missionary noted, "the women laugh at him . . . and he runs away." Spanish missionaries were even more shocked by the sexual practices of the Pueblo, which allegedly included polygamy, extramarital relations, homoeroticism, and the performance of sex acts in sacred rituals. Indeed, native attitudes toward sexuality posed major obstacles to the spread of Catholicism, which held out a model of spiritual life among priests devoid of sexual relations altogether. We have few surviving records of what Pueblo Indians thought of the Franciscans, but the Hopi word for a Spanish priest, *Tota'tsi*, denotes a "tyrant" or a "demanding person."

Detail of the Earliest-Known Map of Santa Fe, New Mexico, from 1767. Spanish missionaries introduced new styles of urban design to North America, based on the 1573 "Royal Ordinances Concerning the Laying Out of Towns," the earliest-known city planning legislation in the lands that became the United States. The original Santa Fe town plan of 1607 featured a central plaza flanked by the parish church (marked "A") on one end and the governor's palace (marked "B") on the other. **Question for Analysis:** How does this plan of parallel and perpendicular streets around a central square differ from the grid plans of modern U.S. cities?

The encounter between Spanish missionaries and Pueblo Indians in seventeenth-century New Mexico bred conflict and animosity. Indians resented the onerous demands for corn and labor upon which the colony depended and chafed against restrictions on their religious worship. Although Spanish policies varied between more and less aggressive enforcement of laws that suppressed Pueblo culture, a general climate of hostility prevailed, punctuated by periodic local rebellions, executions of missionaries by angry Indians, and bloody reprisals by the Spanish. All of these conflicts took place against the larger backdrop of population loss. When Oñate arrived in 1581, more than eighty thousand Pueblo Indians lived in about one hundred villages. Fifty years later, the Indian population had been cut in half. Fifty years after that, only thirty villages survived, holding just seventeen thousand people. As elsewhere in the New World, smallpox and other European diseases accounted for most of the loss of life, but drought, crop failure, and Spanish rule contributed as well. Though many Pueblo had embraced the trappings of Christianity as a strategy for survival, by 1680 the strategy did not seem to be working. That year, Pueblo Indians throughout the Rio Grande Valley rose up in rebellion against Spanish rule, in what was the first successful war of independence against a European colonial power (see States of Emergency: The Pueblo Revolt). The Pueblo Revolt drove the Spanish governor south to El Paso and restored Pueblo autonomy in the Southwest for twelve years.

MISSIONS IN FLORIDA

As in New Mexico, relatively few Spanish settlers lived in the colony of La Florida in the seventeenth century. Because of its strategic importance in battles with pirates and rival European colonies, Florida held many more Spanish soldiers than New Mexico, but the colony's main business was still the spread of Catholicism. Franciscans established forty-four mission towns over a wide swath of land from Savannah all the way west past Tallahassee (see Map 2.1). By many measures their campaign was a great success. Some thirty-five thousand Indians from a range of nations and language groups entered the orbit of these missions, at least nominally embracing the Christian faith. How deeply the new religion entered native cultures and lives is harder to know. A 1612 confession manual, the oldest published text to use an indigenous North American language, instructed priests in how to ask probing questions to Timucuan Indians, designed to regulate their private lives. "Have you had

STATES OF EMERGENCY

The Pueblo Revolt

On August 10, 1680, a Franciscan priest named Juan Pío visited the New Mexican village of Tesuque to perform Mass, as he did every Sunday. But on this day the village was empty. Pío found the townsmen a few miles away, armed and dressed for war. The native men he thought of as his flock promptly killed him. As reports of similar scenes streamed in to Santa Fe from across New Mexico, Spanish authorities understood that a massive rebellion was under way.

Indians had turned the tables on Spaniards in North America. About seventeen thousand men from more than twenty-five independent villages, speaking at least six different languages, managed to coalesce around a single plan of attack. The revolt was directed by a number of leaders, including a medicine man from the San Juan pueblo known as Popé. Five years earlier, when a new governor reinstated a ban on katsina ceremonies, Popé had been among forty-seven medicine men arrested and sentenced to death for violating the law. After the execution of three of the group, a party of Indians stormed the governor's house, holding him hostage until the others were released. This incident might well have convinced Popé and others of the necessity and efficacy of organized violence.

To mobilize the force needed to overthrow the colonial regime, rebel leaders preached a powerful message of religious repentance and revival. If Indians would return to the ways of their ancestors and forsake the false gods of the Spanish, they would enjoy peace and plenty. Supporters of the movement spread their message in secret meetings that took place under the cover of Catholic saints' day celebrations. Once a plan was in place, leaders of different villages communicated through a relay system of knotted cords carried from place to place to signify the number of days until the attack. Seizing a moment of Spanish vulnerability, when supplies were already low, the Pueblos hobbled the colony's defenses by capturing or destroying horses and mules. Then the rebel forces divided the two halves of New Mexico, blocked the roads to Santa Fe, and began dismantling the mission system. In every Spanish outpost, bodies of priests were mutilated, Catholic icons were defaced with excrement, and settlements were razed. Those colonists who managed to escape took refuge in the governor's home in the capital, but rebels besieged Santa Fe for nine days and cut off the city's water supply. A final desperate counterattack by the trapped Spaniards succeeded in forcing the rebels to withdraw, but rather than wait for the next move, the settlers decided to flee the colony. Spain relocated its official base to El Paso, the first permanent Spanish settlement in modern Texas, but did not repossess the New Mexico colony until 1692.

Altar Screen, San Miguel Mission, Santa Fe, New Mexico. In the years 1610–1628, Tlaxcalan Indians under the direction of Franciscan friars constructed this church on the site of an ancient kiva of the Analco Indians. The chapel was damaged by fire during the Pueblo Revolt and rebuilt in 1710.

Think About It

1. Why were the Spanish unprepared for a violent rebellion among an indigenous population that they had subjugated?
2. Why might the rebels have chosen to deface and defile Catholic religious symbols?

intercourse with someone contrary to the ordinary manner?" one such question read. With so few priests administering confessions to so many Indians, however, the system probably had limited reach. Missionaries also tried to stamp out traditional ceremonial sports but ultimately were forced to abandon the effort.

Florida's Indians continued their hunting and farming practices, but the Spanish exacted heavy food and labor taxes to supply the colony's garrisons and missions. These burdens, along with the expansion of Spanish cattle farming, put severe pressures on a population already diminished by European diseases. Indians rebelled against Spanish rule in 1645, 1647, and 1656, but Florida had the military resources to suppress them brutally and decisively. Nothing comparable to the Pueblo Revolt shook Spain's rule in the Southeast.

Map 2.1 Spanish Settlements North of Mexico, ca. 1675. Although they were marginal components of Spain's vast American empire, small Spanish settlements in New Mexico and La Florida stood at the vanguard of a century of European colonization efforts in the lands that became the United States.

NEW FRANCE AND NEW NETHERLAND IN THE IROQUOIS WORLD

Within a short time span, other European powers joined Spain in the competition to colonize North America. French Catholics established their own missions for spreading the faith in the northern part of the continent, primarily around the Great Lakes and in what is now Québec in Canada. But unlike the Spanish colonies, New France in the seventeenth century was organized primarily around trade relationships with Indians. The same was largely true for the new Protestant outposts the Dutch established farther south. Located in areas where Indians were numerous, small settlements of French and Dutch colonists sought initially to collaborate with local powers rather than to subjugate them or exploit native laborers. Nonetheless, these modest trading posts exerted a significant impact. They transformed indigenous communities and cultures throughout a vast region stretching from the Atlantic Ocean to the Great Lakes—in ways Europeans could not have anticipated, let alone intended. For native North Americans as much as for northern European migrants, the seventeenth century saw the making of a new world.

THE IROQUOIS LEAGUE AND EUROPEAN TRADE

In the northeastern part of the continent, Europeans entered a region dominated by a powerful bloc of nations known as the Haudenosaunee, the "People of the Longhouse." This **League of the Iroquois,** as Europeans came to call it, was a political alliance among five native groups located south of Lake Ontario: Mohawks, Senecas, Cayugas, Oneidas, and Onondagas. The league was governed by a council of chiefs appointed by clan matrons in each of the five nations and was designed to accommodate the addition of new members. Native peoples in other parts of North America had been dispersing on the eve of European contact, but the Great Lakes region was an exception. Both the Hurons (who lived on the Canadian side of Lake Ontario) and the Iroquois were consolidating. When northern Europeans arrived in the area, Iroquois Indians described their League as ancient, but most scholars believe it formed in the era immediately preceding European contact as a mechanism for ending a period of constant small-scale warfare. Internal peace also enabled league members to wage much wider and more destructive battles with external enemies.

As the number of French, Dutch, and English colonists arriving in the Great Lakes region grew in the early 1600s, microbes that had been introduced to the coastal areas a century before spread into Iroquois country. Furthermore, because the settlers now included more children, who had acquired fewer immunities than their parents, so-called childhood diseases such as measles and whooping cough wreaked havoc among adults in the nations of the Iroquois League. A deadly smallpox outbreak wiped out more than half of the league's population in the early 1630s. Iroquoian nations responded to such catastrophic losses by raiding other tribes and villages. Scholars refer to these raids as *mourning wars,* since they were intended to bring comfort to the bereaved by striking back in some way at the forces that had slain their loved ones. But the ultimate

HOT COMMODITIES

Beaver

The harsh climate of the northern parts of the continent discouraged early European settlers from trying to grow staple crops or build agricultural colonies, but cold weather presented a particular commercial opportunity. To adapt to their environment, several species of Canadian animals had grown long, luscious pelts. Humans discovered that they could wear these pelts for comfort or prestige. Of all these fur-bearing animals, the most important to the course of North American history was the beaver.

American Beaver This small furry rodent, depicted here in John James Audubon's *The Viviparous Quadrupeds of North America* (mid-19th century), played a powerful role in the ecology of the Northeast. Overhunting in the seventeenth century remade the American landscape.

In the early seventeenth century, broad-brimmed beaver-felt hats became fashionable in Europe. Before 1600, Dutch traders had imported beaver pelts from Russia, but with the growing demand, Russian beavers had been hunted to the point of extinction. In North America, beavers were abundant in 1600, and unlike timber, ice, and other export items in demand in Western Europe and its colonies, pelts were relatively light and easy to transport. Indians had hunted beaver for centuries, but because native people sought pelts strictly for immediate use, animal populations had remained high. Indians expanded their hunting practices only after developing a need for European goods. After all, as one native leader pointed out to a French missionary, the beaver served many purposes well; "it makes kettles, hatchets, swords, knives, bread." And as the Iroquois learned quickly, beavers could also be exchanged for firearms. Whole villages consequently would devote their entire hunting seasons to tracking beaver, neglecting other economic activities and becoming even more dependent on European trade and the political alliances necessary to sustain it.

Because beavers reproduce slowly and lead relatively sedentary lives, they disappeared rapidly from several regions. Areas farther south and closer to the coast were stripped of their beaver populations by the middle of the seventeenth century. The species as a whole proved resilient, but local extinctions altered the landscape in complex ways. Beaver dams played a powerful role in many ecosystems by trapping soil runoff and controlling the water flow. Damming typically had the effect of raising water temperatures and supporting more insects, fish, and waterfowl. The trees that beavers felled, moreover, also supported life forms that nourished larger animals. But once the beavers were removed from the picture, everything changed. Dams disappeared, water flowed freely, soil eroded, and animal protein sources vanished. In their place grew rich fields of tall grass that would become perfect grazing grounds for cattle. Overhunting beaver, in other words, had the remarkable and unintended ecological consequence of creating a landscape that was better suited to cows, pigs, and sheep than to deer, moose, and bears—and thus more hospitable and attractive to European farmers.

Think About It

1. What distinguished European and Indian uses of beaver pelts?
2. Why were Europeans unable to supply their own beaver needs?

goal of Iroquois warfare was to obtain captives, adopt new warriors, and preserve the league's power. During the middle of the seventeenth century, Iroquois nations fought battles with old and new enemies throughout the region. By midcentury, a series of mourning wars with the Huron Confederacy utterly destroyed that nation.

As European germs depopulated Iroquois villages and impelled the survivors to go to war, European trade goods also strengthened the hand of the Iroquois League and ultimately helped its members prevail in those conflicts. Iron blades made traditional Indian weapons far more lethal, and firearms rewrote the rules of native warfare. Iroquois used guns acquired largely from the Dutch to defeat the neighboring Mahicans and corner more of the Dutch market and then exploited that advantage in their mourning wars in the 1640s. Iron tools such as knives, axes, chisels, and awls also changed their daily work habits and artistic practices, and European copper and glass found new practical and aesthetic applications as well. All signaled the power and prestige of the native groups that dominated trade.

Ironically, one of the new trade goods that northern Indians valued most was not imported from Europe at all. **Wampum,** small beads made from the white shells of whelks or the purple shells of quahog clams, was both a local resource and an artifact of European contact. In earlier periods, North Americans had prized the shells and occasionally used them in beaded jewelry. However, it was not until European traders brought the iron tools that made it possible to drill holes in the tiny shells and string them together that Indians could create what counted as true wampum. In the early 1600s, tens of thousands of wampum beads were being produced and traded, in both directions, between colonists and Indians. Wampum became especially important to the public ceremonial life of the Iroquois nations, where an estimated three million wampum beads were in circulation by mid-century. For European settlers, wampum functioned as the dominant currency, at least until significant quantities of silver came in from Europe after 1650. Indians did not typically use wampum as a medium of economic exchange in their own communities, but they prized it for its aesthetic and spiritual value. Iroquoian peoples benefited from the fact that there was a single good that could be traded both to Dutch settlers to the south and to fur-trading Indians in the north, who supplied Iroquois with the thick animal pelts that most interested the European newcomers (see Hot Commodities: Beaver).

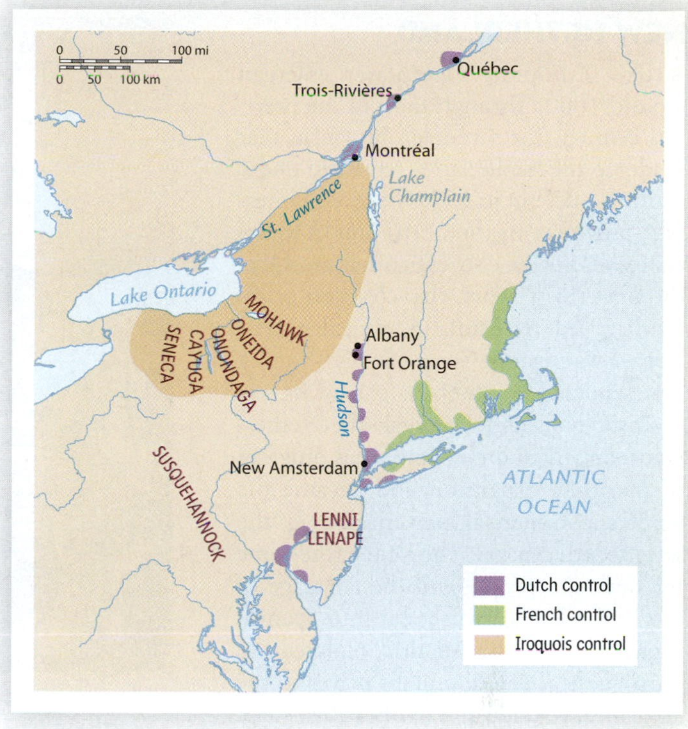

Map 2.2 French and Dutch Settlements in North America, ca. 1660. Though small in population, French and Dutch commercial colonies played crucial economic roles in a region dominated by the Iroquois League.

THE FRENCH IN CANADA

French explorers, traders, and fishing ships had operated along the Atlantic coast of North America during the sixteenth century, and French colonists had tried unsuccessfully to establish footholds along the St. Lawrence River, in Florida, and in Nova Scotia. The first permanent French settlement in the New World began in 1608, when Samuel Champlain led an expedition to find an advantageous spot in the interior of the continent for trading with Indians. Champlain settled on a cliff site along the St. Lawrence River, where the river was narrow enough to be easily defended against European competitors. He called it Québec based on the Algonquian word for a narrow passage. Québec's founding launched the Canadian colony known as New France (see Map 2.2).

Unlike in other European colonies, where trading with Indians supplemented some larger goal of conquest or resource extraction, the French authorities in Canada saw commerce as a goal in itself. Fur trading was a lucrative business, but the Québec colony was vulnerable to English piracy, and the French struggled to protect their main settlement and to set up new towns. France licensed a new investment consortium to run New France in 1628, and these investors reinvigorated the colony by bringing on board Jesuit priests and making missionary activity a fundamental part of French colonization. In the town of Québec, Ursuline nuns offered religious instruction and medical care to local Indian women, while the black-robed Jesuits traveled to Algonquin, Innu, and Wendat camps and villages trying to establish diplomatic inroads into those native communities. As an inducement to conversion, the Jesuits offered lower prices on trade goods to Indians who embraced Christianity. After 1641, converts were also granted the exclusive right to buy guns.

Few settlers came to New France, and hardly any paid their own way. By 1640, more than three decades after the founding of Québec, the French population of North America was less than three hundred. Badly outnumbered by the indigenous population and completely dependent on native peoples for trade, French colonists pursued much more peaceful relations with Indians than did other Europeans. For example, Catholic missionaries in New France tended to be more tolerant than their counterparts in New Spain of traditional native religious practices and beliefs, which they hoped to supplant gradually rather than immediately. Those Frenchmen who were not in the clergy intermarried frequently with native women, a practice endorsed in the 1660s by official French policy. Yet despite New France's more benign colonial practices, the arrival of the French was not a positive development for the region's Huron population. The newcomers spread the same diseases as other European settlers, and competition over the fur trade intensified the military conflicts among Indian nations. New France's Huron allies bore the brunt of these wars.

NEW NETHERLAND

A new European superpower emerged around 1600. Through most of the previous century, the seventeen provinces that made up the Netherlands remained under Spanish rule, but in 1579 the seven Protestant provinces in the north united to declare themselves a sovereign nation. Over the next thirty years, this coalition of republics, led by Holland, waged a protracted war against Spain, finally winning independence in 1609. As part of its war against Spain and Portugal, the Netherlands embarked on an ambitious program of maritime expansion and became the world's commercial powerhouse in the seventeenth century. The Dutch (the name for both the people and the language of the Netherlands) swiftly cut into Spanish trade routes in the Atlantic, replaced the Portuguese as the dominant player in the African slave trade and the Brazilian sugar trade, built a fortress city in what is now Indonesia, captured several small islands in the Caribbean, and eventually contested Portugal's control of Brazil itself. The United Dutch East India Company, a commercial enterprise that oversaw many of these adventures, was less interested in acquiring territory and building colonial plantations than in commanding the seas and dominating global trade.

Advertising America. This Dutch publication from 1671 promoted colonization and celebrated the wonders of a distant world.

As part of this project, the East India Company hired the English ship captain Henry Hudson to explore a northwestern passage to Asia in 1609. Though he did not find such a passage, Hudson sailed into North America along the river that now bears his name. He found willing trade partners near present-day Albany among the Mahicans, who traded furs for axes and beads. Hudson returned to Europe, and his reports encouraged a wave of Dutch commercial expeditions to the region, which the Dutch began calling New Netherland, several years before it became an official colony.

In 1621, when a twelve-year truce between Spain and the Netherlands ended, the Dutch expanded their operations in the Americas and chartered the West India Company. This new corporation focused on pillaging Spanish trading activities in the Atlantic world. To support its war on Spanish commerce, the company also established permanent trading settlements in the area explored by Hudson. The Dutch organized their colony along three major waterways—the North River (later renamed the Hudson), the Fresh (Connecticut) River, and the South (Delaware) River—and recruited migrants to help defend their project against European rivals.

The first permanent Dutch settlers arrived in small groups in 1624 (see Singular Lives: Catalina Trico, Founding Mother), mostly setting up shop at the northern end of the Hudson River in Fort Orange (Albany). Several of the newcomers, however, remained at the harbor on what is now Governor's Island just south of Manhattan. Though they were brought to the New World to staff and protect trading posts, some individuals scoped out the landscape and imagined becoming farmers. As one of them wrote home, "Had we cows, hogs, and other cattle fit for food (which we daily expect in the first ships) we would not wish to return to Holland." Two years later, the West India Company answered those prayers with three ships appropriately named *The Cow*, *The Sheep*, and *The Horse*.

In 1626, the course of Dutch colonization in the Hudson River area took a sharp turn. The Fort Orange settlers allied themselves with the Mahicans, on whose territory they were living. Mohawks from the Iroquois League attacked the Mahicans and killed the commander of the Dutch fort. A new leader named Peter Minuit took over command of the colony and decided to create a new center of operations on the southern tip of Manhattan, which he famously bought from a group of Lenni Lenape Indians for trade goods valued at sixty guilders (see How Much Is That? Manhattan Island). It is hard to know exactly what the Indians thought they were selling Minuit, but it is clear that they remained on the island for years thereafter. Most likely, they were

Depiction of the Conquest of the Silver Fleet. The West India Company's major triumph came in 1628, when Dutch ships captured Spain's treasure fleet as it made its semiannual trip across the Atlantic to fill Spanish coffers with gold and silver from the New World. The enormous haul singlehandedly repaid all of the company's investors and was heralded as a major victory in the Dutch holy war against Catholicism.

SINGULAR LIVES

Catalina Trico, Founding Mother

For more than two centuries, New York has been the leading urban center in the United States, but the city's history is even older than that of the nation. Since the 1620s, a settlement on Manhattan has been drawing immigrants, visitors, and traders from diverse societies and distant continents. Who exactly founded this remarkable polyglot metropolis?

Originally the project of an investment company chartered by the government of the Netherlands, the city that became New York is identified in popular consciousness with a few illustrious individuals. Explorer Henry Hudson became a household name among New Yorkers, but only after the English renamed the river for him in 1664. Peter Minuit, the Dutch West India Company official who ran the New Netherland colony in its early years, gets credit for acquiring land from local Indians. But in many ways the founding New Yorkers were ordinary men and women who chose, for various personal reasons, to make their homes in the New Netherland colony.

Historians have reconstructed some of the calculations and deliberations of a French-speaking Protestant teenager named Catalina Trico, who sailed to the New World from Amsterdam in 1624 as part of the first group of Dutch colonists in Manhattan. Like many newcomers in the Dutch city of Amsterdam, Trico had migrated from Catholic-controlled regions in other parts of the Low Countries, but unlike most of them she decided not to remain in Europe. Four days before embarking on her transatlantic voyage, Trico married Joris Rapalje, a Flemish textile worker. The two of them, along with a small number of adventurous travelers, signed up for six years of labor and service with the Dutch West India Company in return for a promise of land on the other side of the ocean.

One of Trico's distinctions as a pioneering figure in New Amsterdam's early history was the fact that she and Rapalje were among the first to buy land in Manhattan. Not long after arriving, they built two houses on this land, on what is now Pearl Street and was then near the eastern shoreline of the island. Trico and her husband subsequently moved across the river to a new village called Breckelen, where they raised eleven children. Sarah, their oldest daughter, was probably the first child of European descent born in what would become New York City. But Sarah was just the first of Trico's contributions to New York's growing population. Descendants of the Trico-Rapalje union have been estimated at more than one million.

Think About It

1. Catalina's first language was French, not Dutch. Why might she have joined an expedition to create a Dutch-speaking colony in North America?
2. If Catalina Trico was neither the designer of the New Amsterdam settlement nor its governor, in what sense could she be called one of the city's founders?

agreeing to welcome the Dutch onto the island in exchange for the gifts. Minuit set up camp in lower Manhattan, built thirty wooden houses and an earthen fort, and brought the Fort Orange settlers south to the colony's new headquarters. New Amsterdam, as it was called, became a multicultural port town and the center of Dutch colonial government in North America.

Relations between Indians and the New Netherland colonists varied. Like their French counterparts in the north, Dutch participants in the fur trade depended on the cooperation of their commercial partners for a steady supply of beaver pelts. Small communities of Dutch settlers in the upper Hudson cultivated close ties with the Iroquois nations, and Dutch firearms enabled the Mohawks in particular to become a dominant force in the region. Farther south, however, where the beaver population was scarce, colonists depended less on the indigenous population. Dutch settlers in the vicinity of New Amsterdam were more interested in farming. As Dutch farmers' cattle ate Indian corn and as Indians hunted on grounds that the Dutch thought they owned outright because of a sale, conflicts over land spiraled. Frequent skirmishes erupted, and Dutch officials imposed their legal authority over the Indian nations in Manhattan, Long Island, and the lower Hudson Valley with brutal severity. Dutch colonial leaders, unlike those in New France, did not have to worry that such treatment might jeopardize efforts to attract Indians to Christianity. The Dutch did not engage in significant missionary activity, in part because Protestant emphasis on individual Bible reading made it harder to convert nonliterate people.

New Netherland was a small component of a huge far-flung Dutch empire, and the colony attracted few emigrants from the home country. Economic and political conditions in the Netherlands remained favorable, and the West India Company offered scant land incentives to lure people to the New World. Although wealthy stockholders were promised generous "patroonships" (noble landowning positions) along the Hudson River if they could bring their own tenants, only one of these fiefdoms ever materialized.

Of the approximately nine thousand Europeans who lived in the area claimed by the colony, about half came from places other than the Netherlands. Many were Walloons, French-speaking refugees to Holland from what is now Belgium. Others were Sephardi Jews fleeing Brazil and the Caribbean, who were tolerated in New Netherland despite the West India Company's official policy of admitting only adherents of the Dutch Reformed Church. Others were Swedes, who established a colony along the Delaware River under Dutch auspices in 1638. The town of New Amsterdam was especially diverse, as it included Italians, Bavarians, English, and Spaniards as well as Africans who had been brought to the Dutch colony as slaves. By 1664, one-fifth of the town's two thousand residents had been born in Africa.

In 1664, Dutch authority over the colony came to an abrupt formal end when the English invaded and seized control (see Chapter 4). The overall makeup of the colony changed very little during this transition, but the economic and political affairs of the region were now subject to the English Crown. One immediate consequence was official religious toleration. Rather than try to replace the established Dutch church with an official Anglican one, England decided to grant legal recognition to the colony's religious diversity.

How Much Is That?

Manhattan Island

Legend has it that the Dutch bought New York for twenty-four dollars. That was the figure concocted over two hundred years later on the arbitrary basis of the exchange rate for sixty guilders in the mid-nineteenth century. Sixty guilders in the 1620s was more than half the annual salary of a soldier employed by the West India Company and roughly equivalent to other exchanges of goods for land between Dutch traders and natives at the time. Adjusted for inflation, it would have the purchasing power of $888 dollars in 2001, which sounds like a great bargain for Manhattan real estate. But of course neither the buyers nor the sellers believed that they were exchanging a commodity in a real estate market (no such market existed in the 1620s). And while we now gasp at the potential wealth that hung in the balance, even the trifling sum of twenty-four dollars in 1626 represented unimaginable future wealth if invested advantageously. Had the Dutch or the Indians invested that sum at 8 percent interest, it would now be worth more than 100 trillion dollars, far more than the value of Manhattan. At 10 percent interest, the figure would be over 100 quadrillion dollars, enough to buy every piece of real estate in the world.

STUART ENGLAND AND THE SETTLEMENT OF THE CHESAPEAKE

Well before the English conquest of New Netherland, English settlers also built colonies in North America in the early seventeenth century. Although these colonial societies would eventually play dominant roles in the formation of the United States, they did not begin as powerhouses. Having lagged behind other European empires in exploring the New World, the English were seeking to colonize regions that others had considered and rejected. England was still a minor player in the settlement of the Americas when a new colony called Virginia was established in 1607 in what seemed like an inauspicious location. But while French, Dutch, and Spanish colonies continued to attract mostly missionaries and traders, England was the one European country that saw significant emigration to the New World in the seventeenth century. Large numbers of English men and women left their homeland owing to economic crisis, political turmoil, and religious conflict. Many of those emigrants found their way across the Atlantic and some settled in the Chesapeake Bay region, where the first enduring English colony in North America took root.

CRISIS IN ENGLAND

Between 1535 and 1635, the population of England doubled, almost fully recovering from the massive demographic losses of the bubonic plague era (see Chapter 1). England's rapid population growth occurred at a time when colder temperatures yielded smaller harvests and caused severe economic strain. Compounding the crisis was a change in how property owners were using land. In the medieval era, English landowners typically saw themselves as lords with responsibilities to the peasants whose lives they dominated and whose labor they exploited. But as the larger system of feudal obligation loosened after the plague, landowners increasingly saw their land simply as private estates to be managed for profit. During the late sixteenth and early seventeenth centuries, they raised rents, evicted long-standing tenants, converted cultivated fields to pastures for sheep, and built fences around those pastures. Fences, or "enclosures" as they were called, turned land that had been traditionally considered the common possession of a community into a new kind of private property, and the **enclosure movement** became both a cause and a symbol of widespread misery and discontentment among England's rural populace.

These economic developments uprooted people all over the English countryside. As many as 250,000 men, women, and children moved from farms and villages to England's growing cities during this period. Mostly through internal migration, London's population more than doubled between 1550 and 1600 and then roughly doubled again between 1600 and 1650. By 1635, approximately 350,000 people lived there, making London the largest city in Europe—and possibly in the world. But some of those on the move sought to leave the country altogether. Emigration was expensive and in some periods potentially illegal, but the lure of starting over in a new land could be great, especially in times of political turmoil.

The reigns of James I (1603–1625) and his son Charles I (1625–1649), the first two kings of the House of Stuart, stirred up intense conflict over the policies and prerogatives of the monarchy. By 1629, their campaign to expand the power of the Crown reached a new height when Charles decided to rule without Parliament and then enforced a variety of old royal claims in order to collect revenues without relying on Parliament's powers of taxation. When Charles eventually reconvened Parliament in 1640, it refused to authorize his military ventures, and by 1642, Royalists (supporters of the king) and

Parliamentarians were raising competing armies. The political instability of Charles's reign and the violence that ensued during the **English Civil War** of the 1640s fueled emigration further.

But the greatest impetus for leaving England was religious strife, which deeply colored and shaped the period's political divisions. Two overlapping lines of religious conflict emerged in England under Stuart rule. The first was about religious uniformity. In an attempt to centralize religious authority in a time when sects and denominations were proliferating, James I imposed restrictions on Catholics, Presbyterians, and others who did not conform to the Church of England. His most enduring legacy, the famous King James Bible (1611), was part of a campaign to create a distinctively English holy book and to standardize Bible-reading practices. The King James version of Scripture was designed to be read in churches, not in private homes or at informal religious gatherings.

THE
LAMENTABLE
COMPLAINTS
OF
NICK FROTH the Tapſter, and
RVLEROST the Cooke.
Concerning the reſtraint lately ſet forth, againſt drinking, potting, and piping on the Sabbath day, and againſt ſelling meate.

Printed in the yeare, 1641.

Prohibition of Feasting, Merrymaking, and the Opening of Taverns on Sundays. This frontispiece of a comic dialogue was published in response to a law passed in the Puritan British House of Commons.

The fight over centralized worship exposed a larger theological split. On one side stood the Stuart monarchy and leading officials of the Anglican Church, who believed that orderly, communal church services supervised by authorized clergymen were necessary to guide ordinary Christians to accept divine grace and achieve salvation. On the other side stood a growing number of more radical Protestants who stressed the idea that salvation was predestined (in other words, nothing human beings did could bring it about). Further, they objected to the lingering hierarchy, ritualism, and worldliness of England's established church. Known as **Puritans** (though they often referred to themselves simply as the "godly"), these dissenters were strict Calvinist Protestants who charged that the English Reformation had not fully purged itself of Catholic heresy. Puritans clashed bitterly with their opponents over such questions as whether ministers should wear special garments, whether December 25 should be celebrated as a Christian holiday, whether musical instruments belonged in church services, whether it was appropriate to make the sign of the cross during a baptism, and whether it was permissible to dance on the Sabbath. In all cases, the Puritan answer was a resounding no.

Once Charles I assumed the throne, the government took a harder line on these debates and began requiring the practices and rituals to which Puritans objected. By the 1630s, many Puritans felt persecuted and despaired of achieving salvation if they remained in England. Subsequently, when Charles's political opponents gained the upper hand, it was the Anglicans' turn to consider emigration. Throughout the mid-seventeenth century, religious wars helped recruit settlers for England's overseas colonies.

Whether Puritans or Anglicans, Royalists or Parliamentarians, English emigrants looked to the New World for relief from strife and overpopulation at home. They imagined North America as an underinhabited and undercultivated wilderness where they might live without constraint or conflict. America, as one of the early migrants pictured it, contained "vast and unpeopled countries . . . which are fruitful and fit for habitation, being devoid of all civil inhabitants, where there are only savage and brutish men which range up and down, little otherwise than the wild beasts." Some people fantasized that America's fabled natural abundance would release human beings from the biblical curse of having to live by the sweat of one's brow. Others imagined that the widespread availability of land would erase generations of privilege and inherited inequality and create a society of hard-working, independent men living *entirely* by the sweat of their brows. Although the men and women who left England to settle across the ocean in the first half of the seventeenth century hoped for a world that differed from the one they were leaving behind, they also saw themselves as spreading the benefits of their English Protestant civilization. Early English colonists set out to distinguish themselves not only from the Indians they might convert, but also from their Spanish Catholic counterparts, whom they regarded as brutal conquerors.

JAMESTOWN AND POWHATAN

In 1607, seventeen years after the failure of the Roanoke project (see Chapter 1), English colonists made a second attempt at settling the Chesapeake Bay region. Like Walter Ralegh before them, the investors who received a royal charter to establish such a settlement called their project Virginia after the virgin queen, Elizabeth I, who had died in 1603. They also shared many of the aspirations of the adventurers who had tried to build earlier colonies in Newfoundland and Roanoke: They hoped to spread the Protestant faith to the heathen population, thwart the expansion of Catholic Spain, discover gold

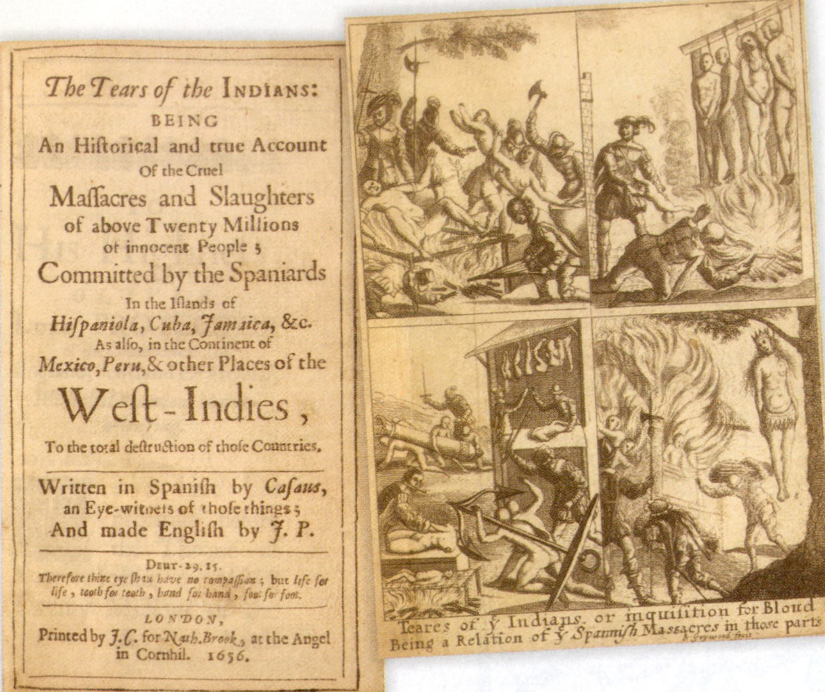
The Tears of the Indians:
BEING
An Hiſtorical and true Account
Of the Cruel
Maſſacres and Slaughters
of above Twenty Millions
of innocent People;
Committed by the Spaniards
In the Iſlands of
Hiſpaniola, Cuba, Jamaica, &c.
As alſo, in the Continent of
Mexico, Peru, & other Places of the
West-Indies,
To the total deſtruction of thoſe Countries.
Written in Spaniſh by *Caſaus,*
an Eye-witneſs of thoſe things;
And made Engliſh by *J. P.*
Deut. 29. 15.
Therefore thine eye ſhall have no compaſſion; but life for life, tooth for tooth, hand for hand, foot for foot.
LONDON,
Printed by *J. C.* for *Nath. Brook,* at the Angel in Cornhil. 1656.

Teares of ỹ Indians, or inquiſition for Bloud:
Being a Relation of ỹ *Spaniſh* Massacres in those parts

Title Page and Frontispiece of 1656 Edition of *The Tears of the Indians.* By 1600, English readers had been exposed to a steady stream of anti-Spanish literature detailing the cruelty of Spain's colonization efforts in the New World. Especially influential were English translations of Bartolomé de Las Casas's *In Defense of the Indians* (1550). Although Las Casas was a Catholic priest, his treatise appeared in English translations under such anti-Catholic titles as *Popery Truly Display'd in its Bloody Colours: Or, a Faithful Narrative of the Horrid and Unexampled Massacres, Butcheries, and all manners of Cruelties that Hell and Malice could invent, committed by the Popish Spanish.*

(or some other valuable good), and find a passage to the Pacific Ocean. To sustain the settlement, Virginia's designers also expected to subdue the local inhabitants, who might then be made to provide the colonists with food. Neither the London investors who financed the scheme nor the original settlers who sailed across the Atlantic knew much about the lands they were set to conquer and claim. The Virginia territory stretched on their maps from present-day North Carolina to New York.

The first ships dropped anchor on April 26, 1607, on swampy marshlands along the James River (named for the new king), close to fifty miles upstream from the Chesapeake Bay. The English settlers selected this particular swampy site, which they called Jamestown, for its utility as a fort to protect against possible attack by the Spanish, who also claimed the Chesapeake region on maps of their domain. Prospects for a thriving colony on the James River were dismal. Jamestown sat in the tidewater region of Tsenacommacah, dominated by a powerful confederacy of thirty Algonquian chiefdoms under the leadership of the paramount chief Powhatan. The European strategy of dividing and conquering small native groups would thus be harder to pursue. In any case, Powhatan's men were wary from their previous encounters with white visitors and initially refused to barter food with the newcomers.

To make matters worse, most of the first English residents of Virginia were either gentlemen or their servants, not farmers accustomed to feeding themselves by raising crops. Compounding this challenge, they arrived during a time of drought. Moreover, the English were highly susceptible to diseases that incubated easily in a warm climate, a malarial swampland, and an unfamiliar ecosystem. Within a few months, half of the original colonists died of illness or starvation. The new settlers who continued to arrive also perished at staggering rates. After the especially brutal winter of 1609–1610, only about sixty English colonists out of five hundred who had made the voyage remained alive in North America, some of them having subsisted on frogs, snakes, or their starved neighbor's corpses. Overall, about four out of five Virginia settlers died within the colony's first decade. And because the early migrants were almost exclusively male, prospects for natural growth among the surviving population were dismal. In its early history, Jamestown was as devastating a failure as Roanoke.

Jamestown enjoyed a few advantages over Roanoke that enabled Virginia to weather these early setbacks and become the first enduring English colony in North America. First, the Virginia Company investors stubbornly refused to pull the plug on the colony, continuing to raise money and recruit migrants even as the project failed to turn a profit. Second, Captain John Smith, a veteran of religious wars against Catholics and Muslims, imposed strict military discipline by which he forced all Jamestown settlers to work the land. Third, Jamestown found a profitable crop. Englishman John Rolfe introduced seeds of the tobacco plant from the West Indies to Virginia soil and in 1612 enjoyed an impressive harvest that was sampled enthusiastically back in England. In 1617, ten years after the first settlers arrived, colonists dispatched the first commercial shipment of tobacco leaves across the Atlantic. The successful cultivation of tobacco boosted the colony's financial prospects, and the Virginia Company began offering land incentives to encourage migration. Over the next five years, Virginia's English population soared from under 400 to 1,240.

Perhaps even more important to the colony's initial survival, however, was the decision by Powhatan's people to trade their corn surplus. Virginians depended for their lives on Indians' grain, and this dependence lay at the foundation of tense and tenuous relations between natives and immigrants during Jamestown's early history. Periodically, Powhatan would impose embargoes on trade with the English, who would then retaliate by attacking Indian villages and raiding the native people's corn stocks. For the first several years of the Jamestown experiment, demanding Englishmen and wary Indians regularly—and violently—skirmished over the corn trade.

From the beginning, Powhatan himself had not been sure what to make of the Virginians. From his perspective, the well-armed immigrants held some attraction as potential allies, and he was pleased to receive gifts from a faraway land. Perhaps to cement an alliance, Powhatan's men captured John Smith in late 1607 and threatened to execute him, only to release him at the last moment. In Smith's retelling of the event, Powhatan stayed the execution because Pocahontas, one of his many daughters, interceded on Smith's behalf. If Smith's story is accurate, Pocahontas was likely participating in a ceremony in which Powhatan ritually adopted Smith and incorporated the English visitors as a subordinate people. The meaning of such a ritual was probably lost on the English, however, who continued to see themselves as conquerors and the Indians as their future subjects.

Powhatan. This image of the Algonquians' paramount chief is a detail from John Smith's 1612 Map of Virginia.

Smith left Virginia soon thereafter as a result of a rebellion against his autocratic leadership, but Pocahontas remained an influential player in the diplomatic relations with the colonists. In 1613, during a period of escalating warfare, the colonists captured Pocahontas and held her as a prisoner in Jamestown. During her year-long incarceration, she converted to Christianity and attracted the attention of John Rolfe. In 1614, Rolfe proposed to Powhatan a marriage with Pocahontas, and the paramount chief accepted eagerly. The marriage between Pocahontas and Rolfe sealed a diplomatic alliance between their peoples and ushered in a brief era of peace for the fledgling Virginia colony. Two years later, Pocahontas sailed across the ocean with her husband and infant son as part of an Indian delegation and was received by King James I of England as a high-profile Protestant convert—evidence of the Virginia colony's success. Pocahontas, who may well have seen the mission as part of her own quest to incorporate the English into her father's kingdom, became fatally ill during the visit and never returned to her home in Tsenacommacah.

Back in Virginia, the peace began to unravel. Powhatan died in 1618, and political power fell to a chief named Opechancanough, who considered the English more trouble than they were worth. In March 1622, Opechancanough launched a series of well-planned assaults on the colonists that killed over three hundred people—more than one-quarter of Virginia's population—in one day. The English settlers responded with a long campaign designed to kill the Indians whom they had once hoped to convert. The governor of Virginia now considered it "infinitely better to have no heathen among us . . . than to be at peace and league with them." After several years of fighting, the English drove their enemies out of their settlement region and dictated peace terms to Opechancanough's men.

Opechancanough's War (sometimes called Opechancanough's Uprising or the Massacre of 1622) marked a turning point—not only in Virginia's relations with Indians, but also in the governing structure of the colony. Alarmed by reports of violence, high death rates, and slow progress on the campaign to spread Christianity, King James I ordered an investigation. Based on the results of the probe, which confirmed suspicions that the colony was badly managed but also encouraged optimism about the value of the tobacco trade, the king revoked the merchant investors' charter in 1624. Henceforth, Virginia would be a royal colony, controlled directly by the English monarch. Under this arrangement, which would prove crucial to the development of Virginia over the next century and a half, the king directly appointed colonial governors and councils. Royal officials could also invalidate any law passed by Virginia's representative assembly, the House of Burgesses, which settlers had established in 1619. Although Virginia, with a population of only 1,200, remained a fragile enterprise in 1624, the English government was now taking a direct interest in the colony's affairs and prospects.

MIGRATION AND GROWTH

Buoyed by thriving tobacco production and better protected against the Indians, the new royal colony grew. By 1624, Virginia was shipping two hundred thousand pounds of tobacco to England. Fourteen years later, that figure had risen to three million. The population climbed steadily as well. By 1619, Virginia landowners were already importing Africans to work their lands (see Chapter 3), but most migrants to the colony at this time were poor young Englishmen who arrived as indentured servants obligated to a master for a specified term. By 1640, eight thousand people lived in the scattered farms and villages of Virginia (see Map 2.3). It was still a small settlement, even compared to other English colonies at the time, such as Barbados and Massachusetts,

Rebecca, the Woman Better Known as Pocahontas. This daughter of Powhatan was originally given the names Amonute and Matoaka. The nickname Pocahontas connoted a playful or mischievous character. Engraved in England in 1616, this is the only portrait of Pocahontas made during her lifetime.

Map 2.3 English Settlements in the Chesapeake, ca. 1607–1660. As in other parts of the American South, the navigable rivers of eastern Virginia enabled farmers to load their crops directly onto ships rather than having to send them by wagon to a market town or port city. The Chesapeake Bay region featured six thousand miles of shoreline; therefore, the English colonists felt little need to develop cities there in the seventeenth century.

but the continued flow of immigrants and the declining mortality rates made Virginia seem viable.

Over the next twenty-five years, however, a much larger society emerged in the Chesapeake region. Massive migrations from England fueled this growth: Between 1645 and 1665, the number of English settlers in Virginia more than tripled. The new Virginians came in two main varieties. Most were indentured servants from the lower ranks of English society. Typically males between the ages of fifteen and twenty-four from the rural southwestern parts of England, these new recruits had decided to take their chances across the ocean, signing up to labor in Virginia in exchange for their transportation costs. In a minority of cases, servants were sent against their will (see Interpreting the Sources: Ballads About Virginia). Descendants of these immigrants would compose a majority of the Virginia colony for the rest of the century.

A second large group of migrants hailed from more prosperous backgrounds. These were elite men and women recruited by the colony's aristocratic governor, Sir William Berkeley, who presided over Virginia from 1642 to 1676. In particular, Berkeley attracted well-to-do migrants from the countryside just south and west of London, especially the younger sons of elite families who did not stand to inherit estates in England. Governor Berkeley offered them large tracts of land in Virginia and vested them with political power. The colony's elite immigrants were almost exclusively adherents of the Anglican Church and supporters of King Charles I during his clashes with Parliament during the English Civil War of the 1640s. After the king was beheaded in 1649 and the Royalists were defeated in battle in 1651, some partisans of the losing side, often referred to as Cavaliers, sought refuge in the New World. The migration of English Cavaliers during the first half of Berkeley's long term in office helped create Virginia's ruling class, and their values and affiliations shaped laws and social hierarchies in the growing colony. The Anglican Church, for example, was the legally established religion of Virginia, and religious minorities, mostly Quakers and Presbyterians, were subject to persecution and expulsion.

The other development contributing to the growth of English settlement in the Chesapeake was the establishment of the neighboring colony of Maryland in 1632. Unlike Virginia, Maryland was a **proprietary colony,** which meant that the king granted land and legal authority over that land to an individual (or a group). In the case of Maryland, the proprietor was Cecilius Calvert, a Catholic whose father was close to King Charles I. Maryland expanded along a similar timeline as its large neighbor to the south, increasing in population from 600 in 1640 to 4,000 twenty years later. Like Virginia, Maryland was a tobacco colony dominated by plantation owners and populated by a steady supply of male indentured servants from southwestern England.

Unlike Virginia, however, Maryland extended religious toleration to all Christians who believed in the Trinity. English Catholics occupied many prominent positions in the early colony's government and built a prosperous minority community that remains thriving and influential in Maryland to this day. Most immigrants to Maryland were not Catholic, however, and the colony's Catholic priests and leaders were careful not to proselytize among Protestant settlers, lest they incur the wrath of the English government. Instead, they encouraged their followers to keep a low public profile. As a result, Maryland contained few churches relative to the population, and religious worship was much less conspicuous there than in other European colonies in seventeenth-century North America.

BACON'S REBELLION

The English Chesapeake was a highly stratified society, divided sharply according to wealth, power, and status. The success of the tobacco economy masked real conflicts over access to land

The Old Brick Church in Smithfield, Virginia. Now known as St. Luke's, the church is the nation's oldest surviving Gothic building. Construction began in 1632 and took about five years to complete. The interior fittings were not fully installed until over two decades later. As the English colony grew and settlers moved farther inland, church construction did not keep pace. Many colonists lived more than five miles away from the nearest house of worship.

and resources. As immigrants streamed in, two of those conflicts hardened. The first was between poorer and wealthier English colonists. By midcentury, a fall in mortality rates meant that more servants were outliving the terms of their indenture and expecting to acquire their own land. Many indenture agreements stipulated that the servant would receive a headright (a legal grant of land) upon completing his term of servitude. But with high land prices propped up by a booming tobacco trade, freed servants were increasingly unable to find suitable farmland. By the 1670s, a majority of the colony was landless, angry, and heavily armed.

The other line of conflict pitted colonists against Indians. An aging Opechancanough mounted a final, deadly, and ultimately unsuccessful attack on Virginians in 1644, and two years later the Indians of the Tsenacommacah region signed a treaty confining their settlement to the north side of the York River. The treaty did little to prevent Virginia's settlers from encroaching on Indian territory, however, especially as English migration increased. Virginia's aspiring landowners coveted Indian lands for tobacco planting, and the colony's growing population of servant animals—cows, pigs, horses, sheep, and goats—routinely grazed beyond the borders of the settlers' farms, destroying Indian cornfields. As a rule, English livestock in Virginia required five to ten acres of woods for every acre their owners devoted to tobacco. Indians often directed their rising anger about English colonization against the encroaching settlers' four-legged vanguard. Pigs appear to have been special targets, and colonists regularly accused Indians of stealing, butchering, or encouraging their dogs to kill English hogs.

Periodic pig-killings and other acts of frontier violence between local Indians and Virginians reinforced a larger development in white-Indian relations in the Chesapeake. As colonists expanded north and west into Tsenacommacah country after the 1646 treaty, they came into more frequent contact with Indian groups beyond the boundaries of the old Powhatan confederation. Through this contact the English learned about far-reaching networks of trade in eastern North America, involving numerous native peoples as well as Spanish and Swedish colonial outposts. At the same time, English settlers also became exposed to raiding Iroquois war parties from the distant north. Not fully understanding this wider geopolitical world into which they had stumbled, anxious colonists associated and conflated the various threats posed by very different groups of Indians.

All of these conflicts converged in 1675 around an Englishman named Nathaniel Bacon, who had arrived in Virginia the previous year. In July, a group of Doeg Indians living on the Maryland side of the Potomac River seized some pigs belonging to a Virginia planter colonist whom they accused of not paying a debt. A series of reprisals followed, involving more

Cecilius Calvert Extends His Map of Maryland to His Grandson, 1669–1670. A court painter of King Charles II produced this portrait. **Question for Analysis:** Why might the youth at the far left have been included in the scene?

INTERPRETING THE SOURCES

Ballads About Virginia

Most of the English migrants to Virginia in the middle of the seventeenth century were unskilled laborers or tenant farmers hoping to escape a life of poverty. Since many of them were illiterate, historians have relatively few sources that document their aspirations, expectations, and disappointments. Several English folk songs composed during the period, however, offer glimpses into the world of these Virginia migrants, often filtered through humor and mockery. One popular ballad, originally published in 1650, tells the story of a weaver who punishes his unfaithful wife by selling her to a ship captain for ten pounds and tricking her into boarding a boat bound for Virginia. The text below is from another seventeenth-century ballad that chronicles the ordeals of women who were duped into sailing to America. Strong evidence supports the view that such practices were not simply the fabrications of balladeers.

Give ear unto a Maid, that lately was betray'd,
And sent into Virginny, O:
In brief I shall declare, what I have suffer'd there,
When that I was weary, weary, weary, weary, O.
[Since] that first I came to the Land of Fame,
Which is called Virginny, O.
The Axe and the Hoe wrought my overthrow.
When that I was weary, weary, weary, weary, O.
Five years served I, under Master Guy,
In the land of Virginny, O;
When she sits at Meat, then I have none to eat,
When that I was weary, weary, weary, weary, O.
. . .
Instead of Beds of Ease, to lye down when I please,
In the Land of Virginny, O;
Upon a bed of straw, I lye down full of woe,
When that I was weary, weary, weary, weary, O.
. . .
Instead of drinking Beer, I drink the water clear,
In the Land of Virginny, O;
Which makes me pale and wan, do all that e'er I can,
When that I was weary, weary, weary, weary, O.
. . .
Then let Maids beware, all by my ill-fare,
In the Land of Virginny, O;
Be sure to stay at home, for if you do here come
You all will be weary, weary, weary, weary, O.

"The Trappan'd Maiden," written in the seventeenth century, reprinted in C. H. Firth, An American Garland: Being a Collection of Ballads Relating to America, 1563-1759 *(Oxford: Blackwell, 1915), pp. 51-53.*

Explore the Source

1. What makes Virginia so unpleasant, according to the song?
2. What had been the speaker's expectations before sailing across the ocean?
3. Who exactly might have "betray'd" the maiden?
4. What does this text suggest about attitudes toward drinking water in seventeenth-century English culture?
5. Why might Virginia have been especially eager to attract female migrants, and why might Englishwomen have been especially reluctant to emigrate there?

parties. When the Susquehannocks, an Iroquoian-speaking people from the north who had moved to Maryland, attacked colonists in the westernmost reaches of Virginia and Maryland settlement, a wave of fear rippled through the colonies.

Bacon, an aristocratic relative of Governor William Berkeley's wife, had become politically estranged from Berkeley and seized the opportunity to lead land-hungry English settlers—mostly current or recent indentured servants—on a series of attacks against what he called "foreign Indians." This campaign drew many followers and supporters in Virginia, but once Bacon sought authorization for a broader war "against all Indians in general," Berkeley balked and declared Bacon a rebel. As landless settlers flouted the governor's orders and refused to abandon their campaign, Virginia descended into political and military chaos. Bacon's supporters elected him to the House of Burgesses, but when he arrived in Jamestown to take his seat, Berkeley had him placed in chains. After a series of blustery maneuvers on both sides, Bacon's men turned their guns on the legislature, extorted a written authorization to lead more raids against Indians, and proceeded to march through the colony. Two armies of Virginians—each comprising English servants, African slaves, and tobacco planters—pillaged the countryside in 1676 and took turns capturing Jamestown, which Bacon ultimately burned to the ground, forcing Berkeley to flee the colony. A few weeks later, however, Bacon contracted dysentery and died, essentially ending the military threat to Berkeley's rule. With the execution of twenty-three of Bacon's followers, order was restored.

Bacon's Rebellion meant different things to different participants. Many Virginians on both sides of this civil war took seriously Bacon's calls for lower taxes and a wider distribution of land and political power in the expanding colony. Others probably saw the battle between Bacon and Berkeley as an internal economic contest pitting those elites who coveted Indian lands against those who valued Indian trade relations. For its part, Virginia's new leadership, which took the reins after Berkeley was recalled to England in 1677, saw one clear lesson in the bloodshed and chaos: A large population of landless settlers posed a grave threat to the political hierarchy. To quell this danger, colonial authorities endorsed Bacon's policy of aggressive expansion into Indian territory in order to open up more land to former indentured servants. They also began encouraging the importation of enslaved Africans, who, because they would be kept in perpetual servitude, would defuse the class struggle within the white population (see Chapter 3.)

From an Indian perspective, Bacon's Rebellion had leveled a devastating blow. Settler attacks scattered the Susquehannocks, forcing them northward to face the violence of their old enemies in the Iroquois League. But Bacon's militia also inflicted heavy casualties upon those Tsenacommacah groups that had been Virginia's allies and trading partners. In 1677, these Indian peoples met with the colony's new governor to sign the Treaty of Middle Plantation, which acknowledged their subjection to English rule and promised them protection from settlers' attacks only if they remained within a three-mile buffer zone of the latter's villages. Effectively, the treaty created the first Indian reservations in the lands that would become the United States.

THE FOUNDING OF NEW ENGLAND

England's other major colonial project during the early seventeenth century—dubbed New England by a royal charter—contrasted sharply with its enterprise in the Chesapeake. Not only were the backgrounds and motives of the New England and Chesapeake colonists quite different, but the physical environments they settled also shaped contrasting societies and radically different ways of life.

New England's settlers arrived as families and included very few enslaved or indentured people. Moreover, unlike the elites who flocked to the Chesapeake, the leading families in these northern colonies were critical of the Anglican Church and supported Parliament, not King Charles I, in the English Civil War of the 1640s. Indeed, the political and religious situation under Charles, along with widespread economic depression and disease, had powerfully influenced their decision to emigrate.

New England was even colder at the time than it is today, and much colder than the Chesapeake. This fact had profound consequences. For one thing, New England's shorter planting season made it less likely to produce a staple crop on a large scale or to enslave a massive workforce to labor on plantations. For another, New England's climate made it a healthier place for English migrants than Virginia, where deadly organisms flourished in the hot summers. Thus, while Virginia needed a constant supply of new migrants simply to maintain its population levels in the first half of the century, New England's original settler group multiplied quickly, doubling every generation throughout the colonial period. Indeed, though founded after the initial settlement of Jamestown, the colonies of Plymouth, Massachusetts Bay, New Haven, Rhode Island, and Connecticut developed earlier than Virginia, experiencing significant growth already in the second quarter of the century. With that growth came the kind of conflicts that flared elsewhere—fierce clashes with Indians and discord within the immigrant community itself.

PILGRIMS AND PURITANS

The earliest English colonists to settle the cold northeastern region of North America were not stirred by visions of a fur-trading empire or a northern route to Asia. They were religious

Jennie Brownscombe's painting *Landing of the Pilgrims*, 1920. This pictorial interpretation highlights the role of women in the original settlement of Plymouth. In fact, the first landing party of the *Mayflower* was entirely male, and this image's central figure, Mary Chilton, was a thirteen-year-old child. **Question for Analysis:** To what extent does this romanticized image of the Pilgrims' landing persist in the imagination of people today?

Seal of the Massachusetts Bay Colony. The words put in the mouth of the Indian figure, "Come Over and Help Us," are drawn from the Bible, from Paul's Epistle to the Philippians.

dissenters. Two groups of English Protestants immigrated to North America starting in the 1620s. Though both were deeply critical of the official religion of England, their emigration experiences differed. The first, called Separatists, had so despaired of the possibility of achieving salvation within what they saw as the insufficiently reformed Church of England that they sought to remove themselves from its corrupting influence. A congregation of Separatists, later known as **Pilgrims,** emigrated illegally for Holland in 1608–1609. But after a few years there, some of the transplants worried about the potential influence of Dutch culture on their children and began casting their sights toward the New World. Rather than settle in Dutch colonies on the Hudson River, the Pilgrim community, who still saw themselves as English, struck a deal with some English investors to help settle Virginia. The first Pilgrim immigrant party set sail for the Chesapeake Bay in 1620 on board the *Mayflower*, but upon stopping in Cape Cod after a storm, they changed their plans. Since they had no legal claim to the land where they were about to disembark, they needed some other basis for forming a colony. Forty-one men aboard the ship signed the famous Mayflower Compact, binding themselves to one another as a single political body and agreeing to build a society on shore based on "just and equal laws."

The *Mayflower* passengers had exhausted most of their food supplies en route and could find no willing trade partners among the native population near their new settlement, which they named Plymouth. Almost half of the original settlers died during the first winter, much like their counterparts in Jamestown. The following year, however, Pokanoket Indians under the leadership of Massasoit decided to open commercial and diplomatic relations with the English in order to strengthen themselves against rivals and enemies. An ambitious and entrepreneurial Pawtuxet Indian named Squanto aided the Plymouth colonists in these negotiations. Squanto had risen to prominence in a region recently turned upside down by diseases introduced to North America by earlier European traders and explorers. One of those explorers had kidnapped Squanto in 1614 and taken him to Europe, where he learned some English. After returning to Massachusetts to discover that he was the sole survivor of a village devastated by an epidemic, Squanto acted as translator and guide for Plymouth and helped broker a treaty between the two peoples. Squanto also helped the Plymouth colony form ties with Indians farther north, linking the Pilgrims to the flourishing beaver pelt trade. Plymouth became an economically viable colony in a short period, though it remained small, containing no more than a couple hundred settlers for much of the 1620s.

A decade after the *Mayflower* docked at Plymouth, a much bigger exodus began arriving on New England's shores. Like the Separatist Pilgrims, these Puritan immigrants were hardline Protestants who had long decried the lingering Catholicism of the Anglican Church, but unlike the Separatists they had hoped to reform the established religion from within. By the late 1620s, however, Puritans had found their place within that religion increasingly untenable and begun sailing toward North America in unprecedented numbers. During the eleven years when King Charles I ruled without Parliament (1629–1640), fifteen to twenty thousand English Puritans moved to New England. More than eight million Americans today can trace their ancestry to this burst of migration. Though many more English emigrants moved to the West Indies and the Chesapeake than to New England during the 1630s, the cultural impact of the New England arrivals exceeded their initial numbers. Because they came in family units, with balanced sex ratios, and because of the healthier climate, the English settlers in Massachusetts multiplied much faster than did their counterparts elsewhere in the New World. By century's end, approximately ninety thousand descendants of this **Great Puritan Migration** lived in New England.

The largest of the New England settlements was called the Massachusetts Bay Colony, founded in 1629 by a consortium of London merchants. Unlike other recipients of royal colonial charters, the Massachusetts Bay Company had been authorized to hold its meetings wherever it pleased. Noting this loophole, the company's Puritan investors decided to immigrate to New England, where the colonists would be able to govern themselves locally, with less interference from London. Although they were a persecuted religious minority in England, Puritan leaders in Massachusetts Bay enjoyed a great deal of power and autonomy. They wished to use that power to do more than convert heathens, engage in lucrative trade, better their economic circumstances, and strike a blow in the ongoing struggle against the Catholic powers. They also aspired to create a new kind of godly society, made up of saintly individuals whose personal piety and commitment to communal living would serve as a model throughout Christendom. In the famous words of John Winthrop, the colony's first governor, "We must consider that we shall be as a city upon a hill" and that "the eyes of all people shall be upon us." They named the actual city they founded in 1630 Boston, and it would remain the major seat of government in colonial New England.

PURITAN SOCIETY, TOWNS, AND RELIGIOUS PRACTICE

Most Puritan immigrants who settled in Massachusetts Bay or its smaller neighbor Plymouth (the two colonies would formally unite as Massachusetts in 1691) arrived in families, and family life remained at the core of colonial society in New England. Colonial leaders spoke and wrote volumes about the importance of families, describing them as "the root whence church and commonwealth cometh." As in other English colonies at the time, each household was organized around the authority of a male patriarch, who commanded the obedience and controlled the labor of his wife, children, servants, and possibly an assortment of others who lived under his roof. Compared to households in the Chesapeake, however, New England households contained fewer servants, more children, and a higher proportion of married couples. Nonetheless, seventeenth-century households differed from modern nuclear families. They more often included multiple generations of kin as well as members who were not related by blood or marriage.

Puritan women had significant opportunities to wield moral authority, especially in church, but family life was not the domain of female influence that it would become in New England culture two centuries later (see Chapter 12). The Puritan family was a male-dominated institution, and Puritan society relied on strict patriarchal discipline to keep all of its members in line and maintain social order. New England laws penalized or prohibited the practice of single adults living alone.

In many ways, however, the most distinctive and fundamental building block of Puritan society in North America was not the family but the town. Unlike settlers in Virginia, who spread out on farms, New Englanders clustered in small tight-knit communities near the coast or along major rivers. When a community grew to a certain size, a group of men would apply to the colonial authorities for permission to found a new town nearby. Towns rather than individuals controlled the distribution of land, which was typically held in common. A town's founding families would assign themselves the lots at the center and allot portions to newcomers. Though individuals claimed the rights to whatever they produced on their assigned lands, their control over that land was subject to the authority and permission of the township.

New England towns were not simply collections of neighbors who settled together. They were religious congregations, bound together by covenants in which town members agreed to build a godly community. Every town included a church, though it might be more accurate to say that every town *was* a church. Not everyone in the town was technically a church member, since membership was available only to those who could convince the community that they had been elected for salvation by divine grace. But everyone was expected (and after 1635, required) to attend services and hear preaching at the local church building, the **meetinghouse.** Church meetings dominated the public life of Puritan towns, and each town's church enjoyed a great deal of autonomy.

Scholars often refer to the brand of Calvinist Protestantism practiced in Puritan New England as Congregationalism since it refused to subordinate local congregations to a central denominational structure or hierarchy. The congregation, in other words, was the only unit of church authority. Congregationalists also sought to maintain a strict division between church and government—not to protect civic life from religious interference but to protect church life from being tainted by profane affairs and considerations. Ministers were not permitted to hold political office, nor were they allowed to perform marriages, which Puritans regarded as strictly civil unions, rather than religious sacraments. The separation between civil and religious authority did not mean religious freedom, however. Violations of religious laws were punishable offenses, and criminal penalties were often based on Scripture. Those who dissented from a town's religious orthodoxy were not free to start their own church.

Town Centers The photograph shows the Old Ship Church Meetinghouse, Hingham, Massachusetts, built in 1681. Church buildings in seventeenth-century New England were small, austere wooden structures. Unpainted and unheated, they were filled with uncomfortable backless benches. Men and women occupied different sections of the meetinghouse and were seated according to age, which was one of the most significant status hierarchies in Puritan culture. Churches also served as town halls where adult men voted, whether or not they were church members.

The shared religious values of New England's Puritans exerted a wide-ranging impact on the Massachusetts Bay and Plymouth colonies. New England towns stripped the traditional English calendar of its saints' days and banned all annual holiday observances, such as Christmas, Easter, and April Fools' Day. As one Massachusetts minister later put it, "New England men came hither to avoid anniversary days." The only holy day on the New England calendar was the Lord's Day, which came once a week and required a complete cessation of work, travel, and amusement.

Musical instruments, pipe smoking, and picking fruit were all forbidden on the Sabbath, as was sexual intercourse. New England colonists often gave their children distinctive biblical names that reflected the high value they placed on reading Scripture. Johns, Sarahs, Marys, and Josephs abounded, but New Englanders also honored more obscure characters like Mehetabel, Abijah, and Mahershalalhashbaz (from the book of Isaiah). Some parents even drew upon ordinary words from the English translation of the Bible, which may account for children named Notwithstanding Griswold and Maybe Barnes.

The Puritan emphasis on reading Scripture also produced a society with broad literacy and a robust culture of reading, writing, and printing. Puritans believed that personal reading of Scripture was a requirement for salvation. Colonial laws therefore obligated parents to teach their children how to read and required towns with fifty families or more to establish a school, though attendance at the school was not mandated. Towns of one hundred families had to provide education in Latin and Greek. In 1636, Massachusetts Bay founded Harvard College in the town of Cambridge to train young men to become ministers. By midcentury, New England colonies were probably the most literate societies in the Americas. In 1660, two out of three men and more than one out of three women were able to sign legal documents, and a great number of those who could not write could still read.

Portrait of Margaret Gibbs, 1670. Contrary to the popular image of Puritans dressed in black, colonial New Englanders tended to wear red, blue, and what they called "sad colors," such as russet. Wearing black was considered flashy and pretentious. Massachusetts sumptuary laws allowed finery such as silk, lace, and single-slit sleeves to be worn only by the families of wealthy and educated men.

New England ministers used the printing press as well as the schoolhouse as a mechanism for spreading literacy. The colony's first press (in fact, the first anywhere in the New World north of Mexico) was shipped from England in December 1638 and established in Cambridge. At first, the colonists used it sparingly, since most of their reading needs were easily supplied from England. But by midcentury, a minister named John Eliot decided to embark on a massive publishing project in order to spread Bible literacy—not to the Puritan settlers in New England towns but to the region's Indians. Eliot learned the Massachusett language and, along with several Christian Indian collaborators, developed a system for rendering Massachusett in the Latin alphabet. Between 1647 and 1689, Eliot published the Indian Library, a series of books of Scripture, catechism, and religious instruction for readers of Massachusett. The paper used to produce two Massachusett versions of the Bible exceeded the entire English-language output of the Cambridge printing press in the decade before Eliot began his project. By 1658, the Indian Library had gotten too vast for a single press, and Eliot ordered another one, along with additional supplies of type, probably to replenish depleted stock of those letters (such as k, m, and w) that appeared more commonly in Massachusett than in English. Eliot flooded the Christian Indian population with Massachusett Scriptures, even though only a small portion of that population was literate. Printing in New England may not have catered to real demands; instead it expressed a religious and cultural ideal.

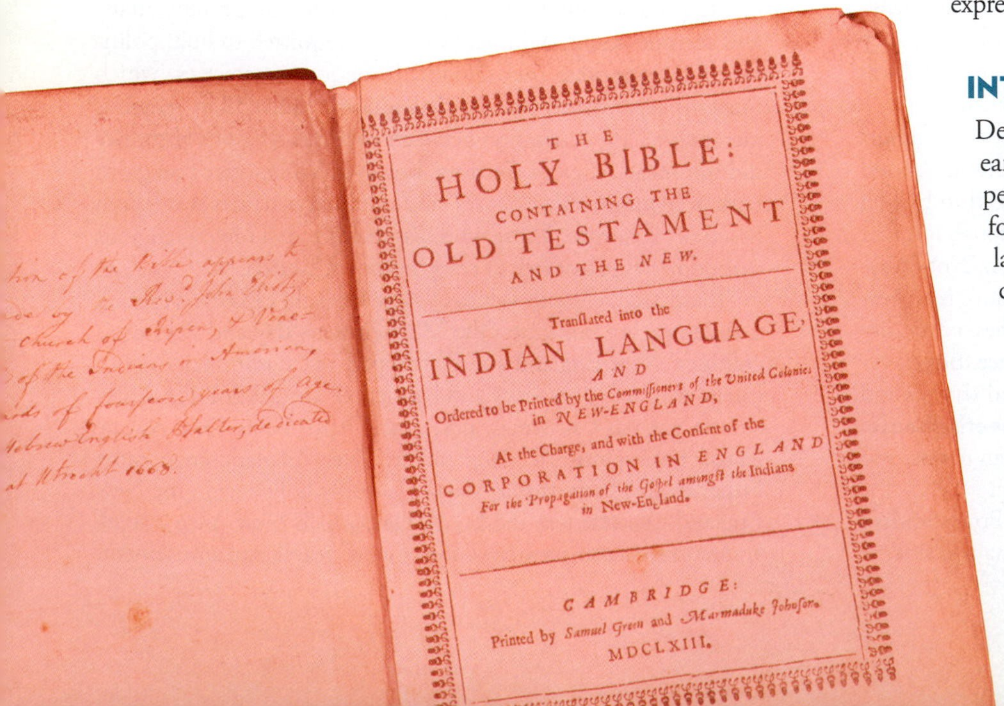

THE
HOLY BIBLE:
CONTAINING THE
OLD TESTAMENT
AND THE NEW.
Translated into the
INDIAN LANGUAGE,
AND
Ordered to be Printed by the Commissioners of the United Colonies in NEW-ENGLAND,
At the Charge, and with the Consent of the
CORPORATION IN ENGLAND
For the Propagation of the Gospel amongst the Indians in New-England.
CAMBRIDGE:
Printed by Samuel Green and Marmaduke Johnson.
MDCLXIII.

Frontispiece and Title Page of the Massachusett Bible, 1663. The earliest printed publications in the lands that became the United States were mostly in the Massachusett language **Question for Analysis:** Why did Puritan missionaries invest so much labor and so many resources in printing religious texts in native languages rather than teaching Indians to read English?

INTERNAL DIVISIONS

Despite their profound sense of shared purpose, early New England colonists did not live in a world of peace and harmony. Small towns in which a few founding patriarchs controlled the distribution of land tended to breed resentments. Moreover, these close-knit communities where everyone was bound together by a religious covenant inevitably presented ample opportunities for neighbors to scrutinize and criticize one another's godliness. Such conflicts contributed to a rising tide of witchcraft accusations that washed over New England during the seventeenth century. Belief in the power of witches was common in England and in other English colonies at the time, but prosecution for witchcraft occurred far more frequently in Massachusetts Bay and Connecticut, especially in the second generation of settlement. Seventy-nine people, mostly but not exclusively women, were accused of being witches in New England between 1647 and 1663, and fifteen were convicted and executed. (Later in the century, the Massachusetts town of Salem would become the site of the most infamous witch trials in the English colonies, but witchcraft accusations had a long history in New England before the events at Salem.) The targets of these prosecutions were often women who had accumulated property and thereby acquired a measure of independence in a society run by men. But the heightened fear that one's neighbors might be using supernatural powers to cause misfortune reflected more general problems that came from interdependent living in small, religious utopias.

Most colonists feared the damages that witches might wreak, but Puritan clergymen also saw witchcraft as a form of heresy, in which the accused stole away from the religious covenant of a community and made a side deal with the devil. New England society was continually haunted by the prospect of broken covenants. Such prospects were woven into the tense fabric of the colonists' religious world view. On the one hand, Puritanism valued individual conscience as the ultimate source of religious authority. But on the other hand, Puritan communities demanded strict conformity to what they regarded as religious truths. Theological dissent constituted grounds for excommunication and exile.

Religious exiles led to the formation of new colonies on the western edges of New England settlement. Roger Williams, a Separatist who arrived in Massachusetts in 1631, took the individualist implications of Puritan theology to a radical extreme. Objecting to mandatory church attendance and to any connection between religious worship and ungodly people, Williams moved toward a larger rejection of state authority. Once he began questioning the rights of the colony to claim land that belonged traditionally to Indians, the Massachusetts General Court ordered him banished. Williams and his followers fled in 1636, first toward Plymouth and then farther south and west to a place he called Providence, on land given to him by the Narragansett Indians. The new settlement, chartered by Parliament in 1644 as Rhode Island, became a colony in its own right. By the law of this new colony, individuals could practice whatever religion they chose, though even there a heretical preacher might be flogged or banished for his views.

Around the same time that Williams fled Massachusetts, a new arrival in Boston named Anne Hutchinson triggered controversy by taking another Protestant principle to its subversive conclusion. Since human beings could be saved only by divine grace and not by their deeds, Hutchinson preached that nothing her New England neighbors did to prepare themselves for salvation—prayer, church attendance, or Sabbath observance—had any effect. Congregationalist ministers who claimed otherwise, she insisted, were peddling falsehoods. Governor Winthrop brought Hutchinson up on charges of "traducing the ministers and their ministry," and his supporters branded Hutchinson's followers as antinomians (those who reject the law). The Massachusetts establishment was especially outraged by Hutchinson's claims to have received direct revelation from God, not through Scripture, and by the fact that she was overstepping the social roles prescribed for women. "You have rather bine a Husband than a Wife and a preacher than a Hearer," one clergyman charged. In 1638, authorities banished Hutchinson from the colony, and she took refuge in Rhode Island.

Another dissenting Puritan minister, Thomas Hooker, left Massachusetts in 1636 to establish a new home in Hartford, in the Connecticut River valley (see Map 2.4). Hundreds of colonists followed Hooker southward, drawn by opportunities to own land, Hooker's considerable talents as a preacher, and his more inclusive approach to religious communal life. Hooker accepted as church members men and women who did not attest to conversion experiences, and allowed those who had not attained church membership to vote in the elections1 of his colony, which he called Connecticut. Two years later, a quite

Map 2.4 English Settlements in New England, ca. 1620–1660. From two small settlements in 1620 and 1630, Puritan colonists spread out into numerous new townships and colonies throughout the region.

different group of New England settlers established New Haven. The New Haven colony set stricter standards for church membership to combat what church authorities saw as increasing laxity in Massachusetts. In 1662, New Haven and Connecticut were joined under a single royal charter, and Hooker's followers dominated the new united colony.

Doctrinal differences and competing visions of church governance separated the various New England colonies during the 1630s and 1640s, but social tensions pulsed throughout the region. As the colonies grew, new commercial opportunities arose. In addition to the fur trade, colonists began clearing forests and exporting timber for use as wine barrels and ship masts. Salted codfish became an even larger export. In smaller towns, most colonists were affected only indirectly by this commercial development and continued to farm for subsistence. But for those living in larger seaport towns such as Boston, Salem, and Plymouth or in newer river settlements such as Springfield and Hartford, political and religious disputes often pitted landowning families trying to defend an older social order against newly wealthy families reaping the benefits of long-distance trade and embracing a more materialistic lifestyle.

Commercial opportunities and material acquisitions may also have contributed to the perception among New England ministers that religious piety and devotion were diminishing. Indeed, after midcentury, rates of church membership began to decline sharply. Part of the problem was a more rigorous application procedure, which required increasingly elaborate demonstrations of personal sanctity. But a bigger factor in the weakening of Puritan zeal in the colonies was the success of the Puritan Revolution in England, which significantly reduced the number of religiously minded migrants. Fewer new settlers arrived in New England after 1650, and those who came more nearly resembled the young men who moved to the Chesapeake during this period. Often farm laborers in the western countryside or servants in the seaport towns, these immigrants joined churches much less commonly than their predecessors had.

After 1650, the founding generation of colonists was in the minority. Facing lower rates of church membership, New England town leaders also worried about losing the offspring of members and argued that this second generation should be generally presumed to be godly even if they had not yet undergone a conversion experience. Most ministers accepted this presumption for the children of church members, but once they too had children, the system ran into trouble. Allowing the third generation to be baptized without evidence of being seized by the Holy Spirit appeared to fly in the face of the Puritan conviction that salvation was bestowed by divine grace, not by birth or upbringing. As a compromise, New England's Congregational Churches introduced the idea of a Half-Way Covenant in 1662, under which the baptized children of full church members occupied a middle status. They could baptize their children, but they could not vote or take communion. Now with multiple grades of membership, some based on pedigree and some based on conversion experiences, and with many more colonists not belonging to the church at all, the older model of a homogeneous religious community had crumbled.

CONFLICTS WITH INDIANS

Ultimately, the most devastating conflicts in seventeenth-century New England occurred between settlers and the region's indigenous residents. Colonists expanded westward and southward from the original colonial outposts into areas that were being quickly depopulated by disease during the first third of the century. The Massachusett people, who had earlier numbered 20,000, were reduced to 750 by 1631. And the worst was yet to come. A smallpox outbreak in 1633 killed as many as 95 percent of the inhabitants in some Indian villages and ravaged parts of the interior that had been spared in earlier epidemics. These calamities facilitated the growth of the New England colonies by allowing settlers to take over abandoned village sites.

At the same time, the depopulation of Indian villages created problems for the colonists. Diseases disrupted power relations among the Algonquian Indians (the language group that linked most native villages in New England) and unsettled political alliances. Some ravaged native villages sought to replenish their military ranks by raiding their neighbors and taking captives. Others could no longer resist the incursions of northern tribes from the Iroquois League, who were seeking to replenish their own thinned ranks. As they expanded in the mid-1630s toward the Connecticut River valley, New England settlers thus entered an increasingly unstable political environment.

They also clashed with the Pequot Indians, the regional power that had dominated the area's wampum trade. Spared the wrath of the earlier wave of diseases that swept through the coastal villages in 1616–1619, the Pequots were hit hard by the 1633 epidemic. From a population of about sixteen thousand at the beginning of the decade, only three thousand remained in 1636. Trying to preserve their position against Dutch, English, and other Indian traders, the Pequots got embroiled in a complicated conflict in 1636–1637. The Puritan colonies turned this conflict, which would become known as the Pequot War, into a test of their own resolve to subjugate natives. After a series of attacks and reprisals between Pequots and colonists, Massachusetts and Connecticut overlooked their theological differences and raised a large joint army. Together with Narragansett and Mohegan Indians, they surrounded the principal Pequot village on the Mystic River in Connecticut and set it ablaze, burning more than three hundred Pequots to death. Survivors were executed, sold into slavery, or delivered by the English as captives to their Indian allies.

Beyond sparking political crises in the region, epidemics also strengthened the hand of Puritan missionaries in their difficult quest to convert Indians. As in other parts of North America, European plagues undermined the authority of native leaders and medicine men, while appearing to demonstrate the power of the invaders' gods. On their deathbeds, many Algonquians accepted Christianity in 1633 and entrusted their children to Puritan families and ministers. The New England colonies were interested primarily in their own godly settlements rather than their heathen neighbors, but a number of Congregationalist ministers devoted themselves to the task of converting Indians. Indian converts were not integrated into New England

English Depiction of the Mystic River Massacre, Engraving by John Underhill, *News from America*, 1638. Pilgrim leader William Bradford described the attack in language reminiscent of the biblical book of Lamentations: "Those that escaped from the fire were slain with the sword; some hewed to pieces, others run threw with their rapiers. . . . It was a fearful sight to see them thus frying in the fier, and the streams of blood quenching the same."

communities but were gathered into so-called **praying towns.** John Eliot founded Natick, the first of these towns, in 1650. Six more were established in Massachusetts Bay over the next few years, and another seven farther inland by 1674. The praying towns were regulated tightly, and Christian Indians were forced to abandon many of their cultural traditions. For residents, these Christian communities appeared to offer a viable refuge from the violence, disease, and instability that were increasingly engulfing the region. Only a small minority of Indians in New England as a whole embraced Christianity or moved to the praying towns, but in eastern Massachusetts and around Plymouth, the figure neared 25 percent.

KING PHILIP'S WAR

Despite the bloody conflict with the Pequots, the New England colonies managed to avoid major violence with the Wampanoag Indians who lived closer to the majority of English settlers along the seaboard in southern Massachusetts and Rhode Island. Wampanoag chief Massasoit had made a peace treaty with the Plymouth colony in 1621, and the arrangement prevailed until Massasoit's death forty years later. Indeed, Massasoit's family and his people had prospered during the period of New England's expansion because the Wampanoags had become crucial trading partners with the English colonists and powerful diplomatic intermediaries between New England and other native groups. But by the time Massasoit died in 1661, the English wanted the Wampanoags' land more than they needed their wampum or political support.

Wamsutta, Massasoit's son and successor as chief, made the colonial authorities nervous, and they forced him to appear in Plymouth for questioning. When Wamsutta died soon after, many Wampanoags suspected the English of having poisoned him. His younger brother Metacom assumed power under the cloud of deteriorating English-Indian relations. Settlers and their cattle had been encroaching on Wampanoag villages and disrupting their subsistence pattern for decades, but by the 1660s the Indian predicament seemed far bleaker. Colonists now outnumbered natives in southern New England by almost three to one, and English courts were regularly asserting their jurisdiction over conflicts between whites and Indians.

Metacom, whom the colonists called Philip, was summoned to Plymouth a decade later over his refusal to obey the colonists' demand that he surrender all of his arms. There he was forced to put his mark (the letter P) on a treaty acknowledging the supremacy of royal authority and Plymouth's colonial government. Metacom began considering his options.

When John Sassamon, Metacom's former trusted aide and translator, informed Plymouth authorities in 1674 that the chief was preparing a revolt, such a plan may only have been in the initial stage. But by the following year, when two of Metacom's advisers were executed for Sassamon's murder (a third was convicted, but his life was spared when the hangman's rope broke and he fell to the ground), the chief had assembled a multinational coalition for an all-out assault on the colonists. Metacom attacked the Plymouth town of Swansea in June 1675. More than fifty New England towns would face such assaults over the next fourteen months, and nearly half of them were destroyed.

Although colonists would call this conflict King Philip's War, it involved many more Algonquian Indians than just Metacom and the Wampanoags. The war was in fact a massive native uprising involving several tribes and many Indian warriors who had previously embraced Christianity. Nipmucs in central Massachusetts joined the attack, as did the Pocumtucks farther west and many Pocasset warriors from the east. The Narragansetts initially sought to remain neutral but were swept into the war once the English colonies attacked their fortified encampment in Rhode Island for harboring the wives and children of warriors who sided with Metacom. Other Indians fought on the colonists' side. Mohegans were a major English ally during the war, while Pequots and Niantics maintained their alliances with the Connecticut colony. Later in the war, Mohawks from the Iroquois League attacked Metacom from the west. Many Christian Indians from the praying towns aided the English war effort, though Massachusetts authorities suspected their loyalties and forcibly transferred Christian Indians in October 1675 to an island in Boston Harbor, where many died of cold or starvation.

Although Indians fought on both sides, to many participants the conflict appeared to be an all-out Indian assault on New England. Puritan minister Increase Mather wrote in his diary that the Indians had "risen almost round the country." And Metacom's men waged their defiant assault in the name of Indians, not just their various tribes or villages. A note tacked to a tree near the burning town of Medfield, Massachusetts, in 1676 warned, "Thou English man hath provoked us to anger & wrat & we care not though we have war with you this 21 years. . . ." While destroying more than twenty-five New England towns, Indians targeted particular symbols of the English way of life, including cattle, fences, and Bibles. According to English reports, Metacom's followers dismembered cows rather than simply killing them and on one occasion buried a Bible inside the stomach of a slain colonist.

Paul Revere's Unflattering Portrait of Metacom, from *The Entertaining History of King Philip's War* (1772). This propaganda tract was a reprint of the *Diary of King Philip's War* (1716) by Benjamin Church, a military captain involved in Metacom's assassination. **Question for Analysis:** What elements of the image reveal the artist's bias?

By the end of 1675, New England society appeared on the brink of collapse. Rhode Island and Connecticut united with the older colonies to create a massive force, but the Indian attacks continued. After a series of assaults in February 1676, the Massachusetts Bay council, anticipating the worst, considered building a wall around Boston. The tide had already begun to turn in the colonists' favor, however. Metacom's supporters began to suffer from food shortages and disease, and the Mohawk attack thwarted their attempt to regroup near Albany, New York. The Indian coalition started to fray, and by summertime, English troops were sweeping through Rhode Island and Connecticut, rounding up rebellious Indians and selling them out of the colonies as slaves. On August 12, a Christian Indian fighting under the English shot Metacom to death.

King Philip's War took more lives in proportion to the population than any subsequent military conflict in American history. Nearly one thousand colonists and more than two thousand Indians died during the attacks. Three thousand other Indians perished of disease or starvation, and another three thousand were exiled or sold into slavery. English settlement was pushed back, at least temporarily, almost to the seaboard, and all four New England colonies were now economically depleted—and thoroughly dependent on England for survival.

CONCLUSION

Despite their crucial differences and bitter rivalries, the European colonies established in North America during the first half of the seventeenth century had much in common. Whether they came to trade, preach, mine, conquer, or farm, European migrants precipitated many of the same devastating changes and bitter conflicts. Strikingly, three large, disparate, and far-flung colonies all suffered violent upheavals in the few years between 1675 and 1680. King Philip's War, Bacon's Rebellion, and the Pueblo Revolt originated in separate circumstances and produced very different political consequences, but all three events were climactic explosions in the tense relations between colonists and natives. These wars culminated decades of accumulated resentment and misunderstanding and reflected powerful processes of economic, ecological, and biological havoc. For natives and newcomers alike, those processes had created a new world, increasingly oriented toward large patterns of global commerce.

Even by 1680, however, Europeans occupied only a small place in North America. Indians controlled most of the continent, and native religions and cultures continued to dominate. In retrospect, the steady growth of England's colonies, which now included the former New Netherland, may appear portentous. As the dust from the conflicts of the 1670s settled, English colonists outnumbered all other Europeans in North America, and their offspring and animals were moving westward and forming new communities on Indian lands. England's colonies did not form a shared world in the seventeenth century, however. The Chesapeake region and New England were in some respects as culturally and economically distinct in 1680 as Catholic New France and Protestant New Netherland had been in 1650. And one of the greatest divisions between those two English colonies was just beginning to emerge.

STUDY TERMS

Ordinances of Discovery (p. 33)
New Mexico (p. 33)
Pueblos (p. 33)
Franciscans (p. 33)
royal colony (p. 34)
Pueblo Revolt (p. 35)
League of the Iroquois (p. 37)
wampum (p. 39)
Québec (p. 39)
the Netherlands (p. 40)
United Dutch East India Company (p. 40)
New Netherland (p. 40)
West India Company (p. 40)
New Amsterdam (p. 41)
enclosure movement (p. 42)
House of Stuart (p. 42)
English Civil War (p. 43)
King James Bible (p. 43)
Puritans (p. 43)
Jamestown (p. 44)
Tsenacommacah (p. 44)
Opechancanough's War (p. 45)
House of Burgesses (p. 45)
proprietary colony (p. 46)
Bacon's Rebellion (p. 48)
Treaty of Middle Plantation (p. 49)
Pilgrims (p. 50)
Mayflower Compact (p. 50)
Plymouth (p. 50)
Great Puritan Migration (p. 50)
Massachusetts Bay Colony (p. 50)
meetinghouse (p. 51)
Congregationalism (p. 51)
Indian Library (p. 52)
witchcraft accusations (p. 53)
Rhode Island (p. 53)
antinomians (p. 53)
Half-Way Covenant (p. 54)
Pequot War (p. 54)
praying towns (p. 55)
King Philip's War (p. 55)

TIMELINE

1598 Juan de Oñate leads expedition to settle New Mexico
1607 Jamestown founded
1608 Samuel Champlain settles Québec
1610 Santa Fe established
1612 Tobacco successfully cultivated in Virginia
1620 *Mayflower* lands in Plymouth
1624 First Dutch settlers arrive in New Netherland

1629 Massachusetts Bay Colony founded
1634 Maryland founded
1636 Roger Williams flees to Providence
1637 Pequot War
1638 New Sweden founded
1642 English Civil War begins
1664 England's first conquest of New Netherland
1675 King Philip's War begins
1676 Metacom killed
1676 Nathaniel Bacon leads rebellion against Virginia
1680 Pueblo Revolt

FURTHER READING

Additional suggested readings are available on the Online Learning Center at www.mhhe.com/becomingamerica1e.

Virginia DeJohn Anderson, *Creatures of Empire* (2004), highlights the role of domestic animals in the colonization of the Chesapeake and New England.

Kathleen Brown, *Good Wives, Nasty Wenches, & Anxious Patriarchs* (1996), puts gender relations at the center of the emergence of Virginia's triracial society.

William Cronon, *Changes in the Land* (1983), explores the environmental impact of European land uses in colonial New England.

David Hackett Fischer, *Albion's Seed* (1989), traces four distinct colonial settlements in English North America to four different regions and cultures in England.

Ramon Gutiérrez, *When Jesus Came, the Corn Mothers Went Away* (1991), shows the centrality of disputes about marriage, gender, and sexuality to the history of Spanish-Indian relations in New Mexico.

David D. Hall, *A Reforming People* (2011), emphasizes the political reforms enacted by New England's colonial leaders.

Carol Karlsen, *The Devil in the Shape of a Woman* (1987), grounds the history of New England witchcraft accusations in the social history of gender relations.

Andrew Knaut, *The Pueblo Revolt of 1680* (1995), covers the dramatic uprising against Spanish authority in New Mexico.

Jill Lepore, *The Name of War* (1998), stresses the role of language and writing in the cultural history of King Philip's War.

Edmund Morgan, *American Slavery, American Freedom* (1975), remains an influential interpretation of early Virginia society and the origins of Bacon's Rebellion.

Daniel Richter, *Facing East from Indian Country* (2001), considers what the establishment of European colonies looked like from the perspective of Native Americans.

Russell Shorto, *The Island at the Center of the World* (2004), presents the early history of New Amsterdam.

3

INSIDE

THE BIG PICTURE

The African slave trade was central to Europe's colonial ventures from their inception, but the institution of chattel slavery took hold slowly and selectively in the lands that would become the United States. By the end of the seventeenth century, however, two distinctive large-scale slave systems emerged in the Chesapeake and the Carolina Lowcountry.

Bound in America. Small numbers of African captives first came to the Chesapeake Bay as enslaved laborers around the beginning of the 1600s. By the nineteenth century, iron shackles such as these represented a vast system of long-established slave societies in the Americas.

1660–1750

SLAVERY & RACE

On May 13, 1643, a man named Francis Payne and a woman named Jane Eltonhead entered into two contracts in Northampton County, Virginia. In the first document, Eltonhead agreed to lease farmland to Payne for the year. Payne would have full control over the planting and would own all of its produce, after paying the rent of 1500 pounds of tobacco and six bushels of corn. The second contract was more momentous. Payne agreed to use the proceeds of the farm to acquire three male servants, aged fifteen to twenty-four, who would serve Eltonhead for at least six years each. In return, Payne would become a free man.

Francis Payne was a slave, Jane Eltonhead's legal property. But by 1649 he had accumulated enough wealth to buy the three servants stipulated in the contract and to secure his own freedom. Seven years later, Payne succeeded in purchasing the freedom of his wife and children, who had remained slaves throughout this period. Enslaved people in Virginia, like Francis Payne and his family, were Africans in origin or descent, and they found themselves in North America as a result of the transatlantic slave trade. The first recorded slave purchase in Virginia dates to 1619, and African slaves had been in the colony even earlier. By the time the English, Spanish, Dutch, and French established permanent colonies on the North American mainland, a massive system of slavery was firmly entrenched elsewhere in the Americas. But on the mainland, in those colonies that would later become the United States, slavery emerged slowly. In English Virginia during the first half of the seventeenth century, a slave like Francis Payne could accumulate wealth, acquire servants, and buy his freedom without alarming the white community. Over the next fifty years, however, the American colonies would build a rigid slave regime, under which stories like Payne's would become increasingly rare.

As slavery became solidly established in England's American colonies, regional variations took shape. Some colonies in the South would become **slave societies,** depending largely on forced African labor for their economic survival. Colonies farther north would become what historians call **societies with slaves,** where enslaved African Americans made up only a small part of the labor force and where family farming predominated. North American slavery would differ fundamentally from larger plantation systems that thrived in the Caribbean and South America. But as in other New World colonies from Canada to Chile, the demand for agricultural labor stimulated a massive forced migration of Africans across the Atlantic that would shape all of colonial America's cultures.

KEY QUESTIONS

- When—and why—did African slavery take hold in the American colonies?
- What was the course of development of the attitudes and laws that allowed slavery to expand?
- What were the experiences of the first generations of African Americans, from enslavement and the Middle Passage to the creation of slave communities with African identities?
- How did slavery differ across the various regions of colonial North America?
- Why was organized slave resistance confined largely to the Carolina Lowcountry?

English tobacco labels, like this one from around 1700, portrayed the system of slave labor taking hold in the Chesapeake colonies.

THE TRANSITION TO SLAVE LABOR

In the first half of the seventeenth century, colonial North America was not a slave society. This did not mean that the men, women, and children who tilled the soil did so voluntarily, cheerfully, or without restraint. Most of them labored under the authority of masters, parents, or husbands. But few of them were defined as someone else's permanent legal property. And before the 1660s, serving a master was not associated with a particular racial or ethnic identity. Enslaved Africans appeared in Spanish Florida as early as the 1560s and in Virginia soon after the founding of Jamestown. But these Africans were few in number and did not initially dominate the agricultural workforce in any North American colony. While thousands of Africans were brought every year in shackles to work on sugar plantations in Brazil and the Caribbean, English colonists on the eastern seaboard relied primarily on European labor. Between 1660 and 1750, however, a crucial transformation took place. Colonists on the American mainland began purchasing more African slaves, exploiting their labor on a grander scale, and creating stark legal distinctions between Europeans and Africans.

BEFORE THE SPREAD OF SLAVERY

The English colonies in North America were agricultural enterprises that depended for their survival and success on a great deal of hard work. Colonists cleared land for farming, worked the fields, grew their own food, cultivated crops or extracted other resources for export, and made much of their own clothing, cleaning products, and household goods. In New England, new immigrants supplied provided much of this labor, arriving in family units and working under the supervision of patriarchs or close-knit religious communities. Colonists in the tobacco-growing Chesapeake depended even more heavily on migrant labor, since Virginians died more quickly than they reproduced during the first half of the century (see Chapter 2). Unlike the New England colonies, however, the Chesapeake could not draw upon a stream of religious dissenters from Europe. Instead, they recruited farm laborers, landless artisans, and restless teenagers from England with promises of wealth and independence in the New World. To pay the high costs of travel, the new recruits, who were overwhelmingly male, contracted to work with employers in Virginia, typically for five to seven years. From the 1620s through the 1670s, approximately 80 percent of all British immigrants to the Chesapeake region paid their passage by signing away their freedom and becoming indentured servants.

Indentured servants were at the mercy of their masters, who could beat them if they did not perform satisfactory labor in the tobacco fields—or sell them to other employers for the duration of the contract. Once the period of indenture was over, servants who survived typically received a small cash payment or a plot of land with which to begin their lives as free people. About half the time, however, indentured servants died before their contracts expired. Despite these odds, indentured servitude continued to lure English migrants to Virginia in significant numbers through the 1650s, supplying the majority of labor in the colony. Working alongside these servants were smaller numbers of involuntary migrants, including petty criminals, political prisoners from Scotland and Ireland, and West Africans sold as slaves to European traders and transported across the Atlantic Ocean.

The West Africans brought to the Chesapeake region between 1620 and 1660 represented a negligible fraction of the enormous slave trade that was supplying the sugar plantations of the Caribbean and Brazil during this period. They also accounted for a very small part of the colony's workforce. Only twenty-three Africans lived in Virginia in 1625, and just three hundred in 1650. As late as 1660, Virginians with African ancestry composed less than 4 percent of the population. In Maryland, people of African birth or descent made up a slightly higher share of the colony, but their numbers were small as well—only about 750 by 1660. This first generation of enslaved Africans in the Chesapeake formed a diverse and cosmopolitan group. Most had come by way of other colonies, such as the English colony of Barbados and the Dutch colony of New Netherland, and were familiar with multiple African and European languages. As an artifact of their time in the Atlantic slave trade, many had Hispanic names.

Africans brought to the Chesapeake before the 1660s came as slaves, not indentured servants. But they performed the same kinds of labor as indentured servants, and they did not always remain enslaved for their entire lives. Though their prospects of achieving freedom were hardly guaranteed, a number of enterprising, industrious, and relatively fortunate men and women managed to purchase their freedom by producing tobacco in excess of what their masters required. In other words, masters were often willing to part with an enslaved laborer as long as they received adequate financial compensation for their investment. Some of these ex-slaves became landowners and even slaveholders. In Northampton County, Virginia, where Francis Payne lived, black landowning was relatively common until the time of Bacon's Rebellion (see Chapter 2). In 1668, about 30 percent of that county's African-descended population was free. The majority remained in bondage, but colonial laws had not yet established the rule that slave status was both permanent and inherited. Slaves might gain their freedom after a period of service, and their children were not necessarily condemned to slavery. The lines between servants and slaves were just beginning to harden in the Chesapeake during the 1660s. White servants and black slaves were different, because the former came to America voluntarily while the latter were brought against their will. Nonetheless, the two groups worked side by side in the tobacco fields, occupied the same quarters, socialized together (occasionally forming romantic relationships), and sometimes collaborated in their attempts to escape. Black and white runaways were often given different punishments, but the fact that they trusted one another enough to engage in risky escape ventures suggests that servants and slaves found common bonds.

In other parts of colonial North America, a similar pattern persisted during the first two-thirds of the seventeenth century. From Puritan Massachusetts to Dutch New Netherland to the Chesapeake, slavery was accepted and legal, but relatively few people were held in bondage. Most of the enslaved were Africans, and most Africans were slaves, but some Africans were free men and women who owned land, testified in courts, and even controlled the labor of others. Native Americans were also taken as slaves, usually as captives of war. Until the last quarter of the seventeenth century, no colony on the continent depended primarily on slave labor.

FROM SERVANTS TO SLAVES IN THE CHESAPEAKE

During the 1660s, Chesapeake landowners began to shift away from indentured servitude and toward race-based **chattel slavery,** a system that treats individuals as personal property that can be bought and sold. Several related developments contributed to this momentous change. In England, a declining birthrate during the civil war of the 1640s and a rise in employment and wages after the restoration of the monarchy reduced some of the pressures that made migrating to the New World attractive. At the same time, English men and women who wanted to emigrate were lured by the promise of a better life in the newer colonies of Pennsylvania, New Jersey, Delaware, and New York (see Chapter 4). All of these factors lessened the supply of white indentured servants to the tobacco colonies at

Slaves Processing Tobacco. Though slavery in the New World had been firmly established by the Spanish and Portuguese since the early sixteenth century, English tobacco growers were the first to import significant numbers of Africans to the North American mainland. Tobacco growing, shown here in a lithograph of a 1790 painting, remained the most common occupation of enslaved laborers in North America throughout the eighteenth century.

a time when the tobacco trade was booming and the demand for field labor was growing.

Meanwhile, African slaves were becoming more available in the Chesapeake. After their victory in the Anglo-Dutch War (see Chapter 4), England began playing a larger role in an Atlantic slave trade that had been dominated up to that point by Holland and Portugal. The Royal African Company was chartered by the English Crown in 1672 to run a slave-buying operation in West Africa, and by the 1680s it was transporting thousands of Africans every year to the New World, mostly to the Caribbean but also to English mainland colonies. Earlier in the century, slaves had been much more expensive and harder to procure than servants, but by the 1680s, the price difference between the two had narrowed considerably (see How Much Is That?). As mortality rates declined, an African laborer who could be kept for life became far more valuable than a European on a six-year contract.

These changes in the international labor market came at a time when Virginia's tobacco planters were growing anxious about the social order of the colony. Bacon's Rebellion alerted large landowners to the dangers of depending on servants, who were now more likely to survive their indentures and demand land. Poor ex-servants allied with slaves and former slaves during the rebellion, and planters began to see how the indenture system could lead to class conflict. If they turned to African slaves instead and assigned them a more clearly inferior status, they could drive a wedge between poor whites and blacks and preempt this conflict. As the demand for African workers rose, slave ships made more frequent trips to the Chesapeake, more slaves became available, and the transition to a slave labor system accelerated. At the time of Bacon's Rebellion, white servants outnumbered black slaves in the Chesapeake by about four to one, but by the early 1690s, the ratio had inverted completely. In the last thirty years of the century, the black population increased fivefold. Unmistakably, the tobacco region was becoming a slave society.

How Much Is That?

Indentured Servants in Chesapeake

By paying approximately 10 pounds to cover the cost of a servant's ocean voyage to the Chesapeake Bay, a tobacco grower in the 1660s could secure four or five years of hard labor. In 2012 values, this purchase price amounts to just over $1800, which is about what a migrant farm worker in the United States earns in two months. But even at the time this labor was a bargain. The typical indentured servant could produce enough tobacco to repay the 10 pounds in two or three months.

CODIFYING BLACK SLAVERY

The transition to slave labor was not simply the result of individual planters' decisions to purchase slaves. Instead, beginning in the 1660s, the Chesapeake colonial governments enacted new laws that recognized and supported slaveholding.

Slaveholding had not been practiced in England for centuries, and nothing in English law provided colonists with clear precedents for holding slaves permanently or for determining the legal status of their children. Drawing on Caribbean models, and especially the sugar island of Barbados, the Virginia legislature in 1662 broke new ground in North America, declaring that slave status was inherited through the mother. This meant that sexual relations between a white man (including a master) and an enslaved woman would produce more slaves for the owner of the woman. This one legal innovation raised the value of enslaved female laborers—and created enormous incentives for rape and forced breeding. Then, five years later, Virginia law reassured slaveholders that slave property would not be undermined if a slave converted to Christianity, affirming that "the conferring of baptisme doth not alter the condition of the person as to his bondage or freedom. . . ." Maryland offered slaveholders the same protection in 1671. Other laws placed bounties on runaways and shielded masters from prosecution for violence against their slaves. All of these laws encouraged tobacco planters to buy African labor as a long-term investment that might supply their labor needs in perpetuity.

Colonial laws from this period made clear that the white society as a whole had an interest in differentiating slaves from servants and regulating relations between Africans and Europeans. Virginia's slave code of 1682, which would be tightened progressively over the following years and copied in Maryland, Delaware, and North Carolina, prohibited slaves from owning weapons, leaving their owners' plantations without permission, or striking any white person, even in self-defense. Both Maryland and Virginia banned marriages between black men and white women—as did Massachusetts (in 1705) and eventually every other colony—thus outlawing a practice that had been tolerated and even recognized earlier in the seventeenth century. Virginia's legislature authorized white citizens to use force to suppress slave rebellions. Finally, in 1691, Virginia made it illegal for masters to free their slaves without paying to have them expelled from the colony. Clearly, colonial lawmakers were not simply seeking to protect a form of property that was becoming more common; they were creating a racially divided slave society where free black people would not be welcome.

Virginia was the most populous English colony in North America in the 1660s, and more African slaves lived in tobacco country than anywhere else on the mainland. But by century's end a larger pattern of slaveholding was emerging in nearby colonies. When New Netherland fell into English hands in 1664, the empire acquired a territory where slavery had been established for several decades. And one year before the establishment of New York, the chartering of South Carolina created the first English colony on the mainland designed from the outset around slavery.

In the South Carolina colony's early years, settlers bought or captured Native American slaves, some of whom they then exported to the West Indies out of fear that local Indians would be more likely to run away and better positioned to organize slave revolts. A third of the colony's enslaved labor force was Indian at the beginning of the century, and until the Yamasee War of 1715 (see Chapter 5) South Carolina slave merchants continued to arm native allies in hopes of encouraging the warfare that supplied the region's Indian slave trade. But South Carolina's founding planters and proprietors had always intended to import African slaves. In an effort to lure planters from Barbados to relocate with their slaves, they instituted **slave codes** that secured the legal status of slavery. South Carolina laws encouraged further growth of the slave system by granting land to any white settler who brought African slaves into the colony. By 1670, half a century before it became the region's major producer of rice, South Carolina already had adopted a plantation system modeled on those of the Caribbean islands. By 1680, South Carolina had a higher proportion of slaves in its total population than any mainland colony, a distinction it would hold throughout the colonial period.

The final major piece of the colonial slavery picture fell into place in 1750. That year, Georgia, founded seventeen years earlier as a refuge colony for debtors and a buffer between South Carolina and Spanish Florida (see Chapter 4), decided to legalize slavery, which a royal decree confirmed in 1751. The legal foundations of slavery throughout British colonies were now firmly established.

ATTITUDES TOWARD RACE

With few exceptions, the men, women, and children who were held as chattel slaves in the colonies that would become the United States were Africans or the descendants of Africans. Many factors contributed to the colonists' decision to enslave Africans rather than Europeans or Indians. Most important was the fact that a thriving traffic in human beings from Africa to the Americas already existed before the mainland English colonies

Manufacturing Molasses in Barbados. By the time Virginia tobacco planters turned to slave labor, a much larger slave system was emerging in the Caribbean, fueled by a rising European demand for sugar.

formed (see Chapter 1). Since a growing global demand for sugar had fueled a steady flow of enslaved African laborers to sugar-producing plantations farther south, mainland planters were participating in an established trade, and captives far from their homelands were deemed easier to control than indigenous slaves. But the flourishing of the transatlantic slave trade was itself a reflection of European beliefs about race, ethnicity, and religion. Europeans saw sub-Saharan Africans as fair game for certain kinds of exploitation that were otherwise taboo.

People throughout the world had practiced slavery, in various forms, for millennia. Often, human beings enslaved people defined as outsiders, such as members of enemy groups as an act or consequence of warfare. The very word *slave*, for example, comes from a Latin word designating a person whose Slavic descent marked him or her as an ethnic outsider. By the twelfth and thirteenth centuries, religious faith played a major role in establishing boundaries. Both Muslim Arabs and Christian Europeans enslaved members of the other group in great numbers. Increasingly, though, they turned their attention to sub-Saharan Africans, most of whom were not protected members of either faith.

Religion would continue to be an important factor in European thinking about slavery in the New World. The Spanish outlawed the enslavement of Native Americans in 1542 (though the practice continued), in part because they saw their mission in the Americas as that of spreading Christianity to the Indians. And when English settlers began importing African slaves to the Chesapeake in the seventeenth century, the question of whether a Christian African could be enslaved worried Virginians and Marylanders. Virginia's 1670 law stipulated that a slave who converted could remain a slave, but not for another twelve years would the colony allow the perpetual enslavement of an African who had been baptized *before* entering the colony.

The transition from servitude to slavery in the Chesapeake involved a shift toward a greater emphasis on race, rather than just religion, as a mark of slave status. The word *racism* would not enter the English language until the 1930s, and the theories of racial difference upon which modern racism rests did not become popular until the nineteenth century. But English colonists inherited a powerful tradition of anti-African prejudice and racial thinking, from both European and Arab sources. By the fifteenth century, the idea that human beings belonged to different families and that some people were condemned by their bloodlines to servitude and persecution (see Interpreting the Sources: The Curse of Ham) was commonplace, especially in the Iberian Peninsula (Spain and Portugal), where Christians developed new theories of blood purity, initially to express

INTERPRETING THE SOURCES

The Curse of Ham

In the history of racial prejudice against sub-Saharan Africans, no text has been as widely discussed and quoted as the so-called curse of Ham from the book of Genesis in the Hebrew Bible. Neither the Hebrew nor the Christian Bible (nor the Qur'an) speaks of racial differences or links slavery with skin color. But as Muslims, Christians, and Jews (a small number of Jewish merchants and planters played a minor role in New World slavery, mostly in the Dutch colonies of Curacao and Suriname) entered the Atlantic slave trade, they found new meaning in an ancient curse that Noah placed upon his son Ham after the great flood.

Before the rise of the African slave trade, the character of Ham had not been identified with the African continent and was rarely associated with blackness. In the eighteenth century, however, the idea that Ham represented sub-Saharan Africa became commonplace. By the nineteenth century, Christian commentators would routinely cite the so-called curse of Ham to justify the enslavement of black people.

The story of the curse appears as Noah's family is about to repopulate the earth. The Biblical passage itself is somewhat enigmatic, and in fact Noah's curse seems to be directed not to Ham but to Ham's son Canaan.

Genesis 8: 18–26:

The sons of Noah, exiting the ark, were Shem, Ham, and Japheth; Ham was the father of Canaan. These three were the sons of Noah, and from them the whole world spread out.

Noah started tilling the soil and planted a vineyard. He drank of the wine and got drunk, and exposed himself inside his tent. Ham, the father of Canaan, saw his father's nakedness and told his two brothers outside. So Shem and Japheth took the garment, placed it on both their shoulders, walked backwards, and covered their father's nakedness; facing backwards, they never saw their father's nakedness. When Noah awakened from his wine, he knew what his youngest son had done. He said: "Cursed be Canaan, a slave of slaves shall he be to his brothers." And he said: "Blessed be the Lord, God of Shem, let Canaan be a slave to him. May God enlarge Japheth, and may he dwell in the tents of Shem, and let Canaan be a slave to him."

Explore the Source

1. In this story, how do some members of the same human family come to be slaves to other members of that family?
2. What is the nature of the crime or sin for which Canaan's slavery is a punishment?
3. Is Noah's pronouncement about Canaan a prediction or a commandment?
4. Why do you suppose American colonists in 1700 might have read this text as a justification of their slave system?

concerns about people suspected of having secret Jewish ancestry. The racial prejudice of Spanish and Portuguese Christians helped justify the African slave trade to the New World.

But if racial prejudice encouraged slavery, slavery also bred racial prejudice. English colonists now viewed Africans less as heathens who might convert and more as black people who were permanently distinct from them. The words *negro* and *slave* became increasingly interchangeable toward the end of the seventeenth century, a shift that marked a major change in colonial life. Before white Virginians began buying large numbers of African slaves, people of African and European descent had much closer social relations, and class was probably more important than ethnicity in determining social status. Free blacks and free whites traded with one another, socialized, and formed friendships, as did enslaved Africans and indentured Europeans. When George Williams, a white seaman, died in 1667, he made his friend Emanuel Driggus, an African and a former slave, the executor of his will. But once tobacco planters shifted from servant to slave labor, and once colonial law defined the boundaries of slavery in racial terms, white and black Virginians now fell on opposite sides of a great divide. Immigrants without African ancestry could exploit new opportunities to own land (wrested from Indians) and achieve economic dependence. And even though class differences remained, poorer free farmers could draw some solace from the idea that their skin color kept them above the degraded status of slaves.

TABLE 3.1 THE ATLANTIC SLAVE TRADE, BY CENTURY

Century	Estimated Number of Enslaved Men, Women, and Children Departing from Africa
Fifteenth	81,000
Sixteenth	338,000
Seventeenth	1,876,000
Eighteenth	6,495,000
Nineteenth	4,027,000

Source: Paul E. Lovejoy, *Transformations in Slavery: A History of Slavery in Africa* (Cambridge: Cambridge University Press, 1983) 19.

AFRICANS IN NORTH AMERICA

The transition to African slavery in England's southern mainland colonies would prove fateful for subsequent American history. But it was a small development in a larger Atlantic slave system that had been in place in South America and the Caribbean for more than a century. The growth of this larger system was in many ways the single dominant event in the development of what Europeans called the New World. From 1500 to 1820, almost four times as many Africans as Europeans left for the Americas. Deported in chains from European trading posts along the shores of West Africa, more than twelve million men, women, and children made the harrowing journey across the Atlantic (Table 3.1). The vast majority hailed from the western portion of the continent most accessible to European traders, but some came from as far east as what is now Mozambique, Tanzania, and the island of Madagascar (see Map 3.1). Only a small fraction—around 5 percent—of the captives disembarked in the North American colonies that became the United States (see Map 3.2). Yet unlike the slaves destined for

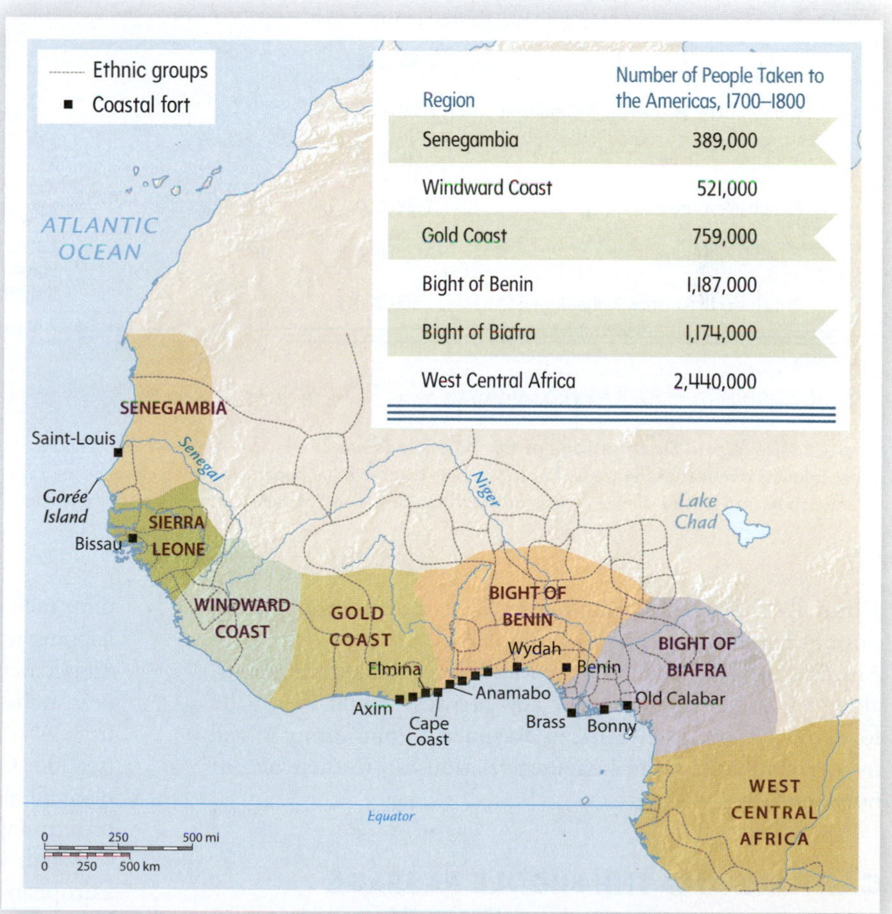

Map 3.1 West African Sources of the Atlantic Slave Trade. Enslaved Africans hailed from very different societies and regions. In the Americas, many maintained distinctive regional identities while also coming to see themselves as Africans.

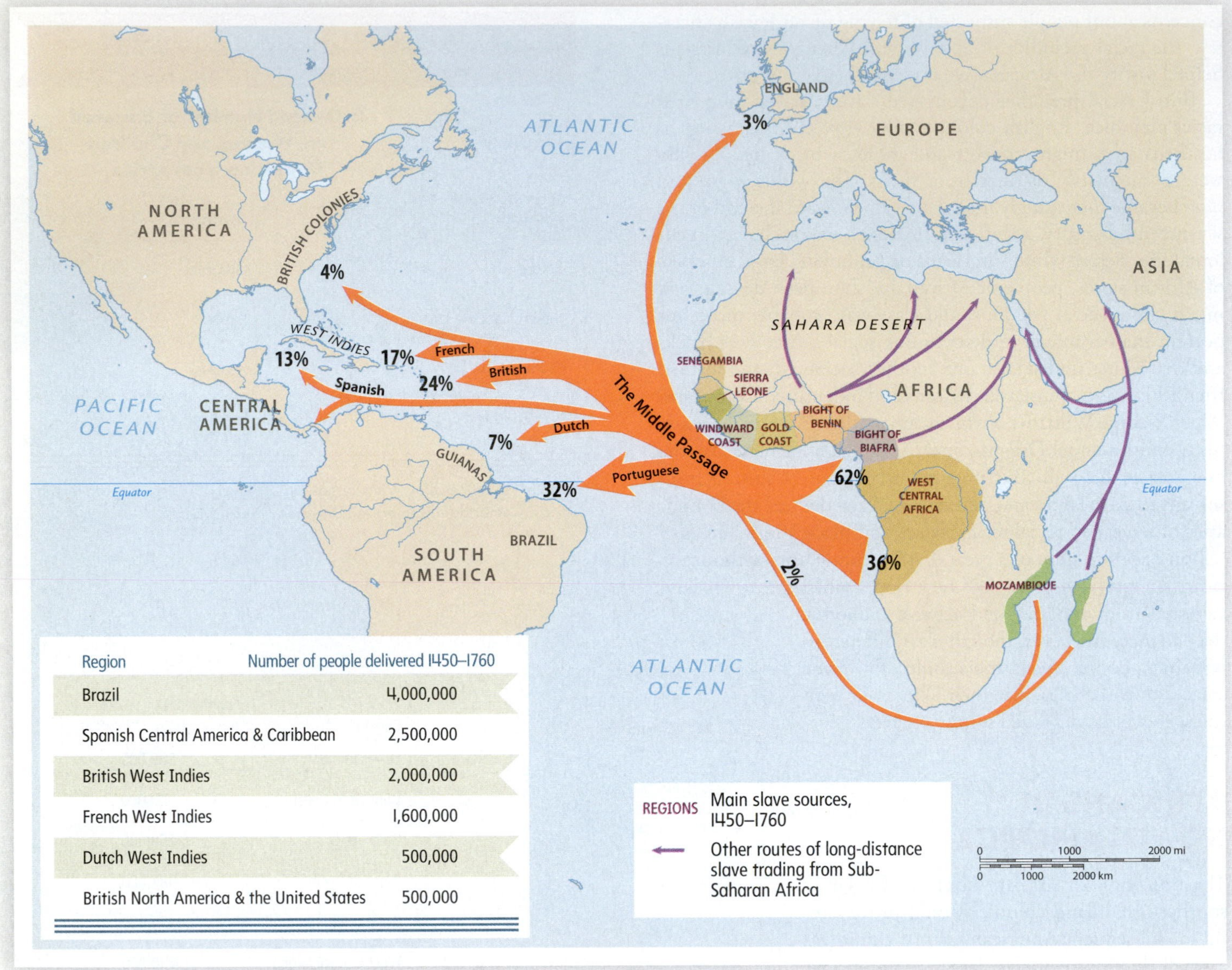

Region	Number of people delivered 1450–1760
Brazil	4,000,000
Spanish Central America & Caribbean	2,500,000
British West Indies	2,000,000
French West Indies	1,600,000
Dutch West Indies	500,000
British North America & the United States	500,000

Map 3.2 New World Destinations of the Atlantic Slave Trade, ca. 1450–1760. Though enslaved Africans arrived in colonies throughout the hemisphere, a few colonies dominated the trade. Recent studies estimate that sugar-producing colonies in Brazil and the Caribbean absorbed approximately 90 percent of the Atlantic slave trade. More slaves were brought to the tiny island of Jamaica than to all the mainland North American colonies combined.

a brutally shortened life toiling in West Indian sugar plantations or South American silver mines, Africans in British North America survived and produced children. Their descendants, along with a steady stream of new arrivals, would eventually form the world's largest African **diaspora,** a community joined by a remembered or an imagined relationship to their distant homeland.

CAPTURE AND THE MIDDLE PASSAGE

European slave traders did not typically seize free people in Africa and ship them across the Atlantic. Rather, they purchased human beings who were already enslaved in Africa. Often captives of war, these men and women were political prisoners or victims of kidnapping raids by predatory African states or enterprising African middlemen seeking to profit from the trade with Europe. European traders purchased slaves with such goods as textiles (often from Asia), metals, weapons, liquor, tobacco, and cowrie shells (see Hot Commodities: Cowrie Shells). These transactions took place all along the western coast of Africa, from as far north as present-day Senegal down to what is now Angola.

Slaves were sold to slave merchants from several different European nations, including Portugal, Holland, England, Denmark, and France, but the slaves themselves represented a far wider array of nations, ethnicities, and languages. Captives came from regions that stretched along 3,500 miles of

Human Cargo This image from Chambon's *Le Commerce de l'Amerique par Marseille* (ca. 1764) depicts "an Englishman licking a Negro's chin to ascertain his age, and to determine from the taste of his sweat if he is sick" and Africans weeping as their loved ones are forced onto a slave ship. **Question for Analysis:** What is the French artist trying to say about the English slave trade that passes through his country?

coastline and extended up to 1,000 miles inland. The men, women, and children shipped to the American colonies did not see themselves as *Africans* but rather as members of villages or language-based ethnic groups. (No large kingdoms or nation-states existed in West Africa during the early years of the slave trade, and the idea that Africans belonged to a single race or culture was a European fiction.) As they gathered in coastal forts where they awaited deportation, captives found themselves massed together with people who spoke unfamiliar languages, hailed from distant lands, or even belonged to enemy states.

The new world to which they were headed was even more unimaginable. No enslaved Africans had returned from the Americas during the seventeenth century with reports of plantation life. Because Europeans were falsely reputed to be cannibals, many of the captives imagined that they were being shipped off to slaughter. What awaited them was in some ways just as horrific. The horrors began with the Atlantic crossing, which Europeans called the **Middle Passage** because the journey formed the second leg of a triangular trade itinerary that brought slave ships from Europe to the African coast, then to the Americas, and then back to Europe. From the perspective of the human cargo, there was nothing triangular or intermediate about this trip. For them, the Middle Passage was an irreversible exile to a life of pain and degradation.

Packed into windowless ship holds and chained together in pairs, the captives lay upon shelves (usually with just two-and-a-half feet between shelves, leaving no room to turn over) for journeys that could last twenty weeks in the early

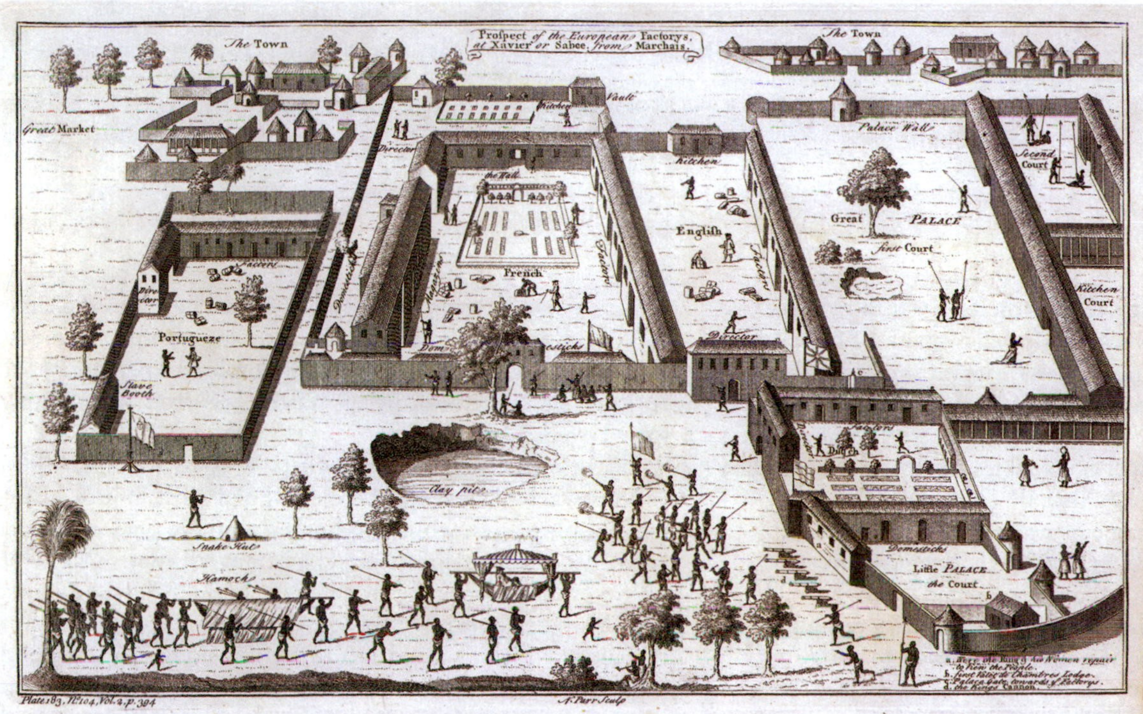

European Slave Camp Portuguese, English, French, and Dutch traders maintained stations in this trading camp, located right next to the king's palace in Savi, the capital of the West African Kingdom of Whydah, ca. 1750.

HOT COMMODITIES

Cowrie Shells

Historians often speak of a triangular trade circuit that connected Western Europe, the American colonies, and West Africa. In the basic model, European nations exported textiles, metals, and manufactured goods to Africa, where they were exchanged for slaves, which were then brought to the colonies, which in turn produced sugar and other raw materials for European consumption. But transatlantic trade in the seventeenth and eighteenth centuries was never a simple triangle. Some ships sailed back and forth directly between Europe and America, while others made several intermediate stops along the way. The triangle model also ignores the important role of Asia in the trade to the New World. Rather than picturing a closed triangle across the Atlantic Ocean, historians are now more likely to describe a complex web of global exchange, involving numerous commodities and disparate economies across the planet.

One crucial player in the new global commerce of goods and labor was the cowrie, a snail-like aquatic creature that lives in the tropical parts of the Indian and Pacific Oceans. Because of their beauty, durability, and distinctiveness, cowrie shells had long been valued, both as prestigious ornaments and as money, in many regions of the world, including Africa. European traders also prized cowrie shells as packing materials that could protect fragile Asian porcelain wares as they traveled in ship holds. But the real value of these early versions of packing peanuts was set by African slave traders along that continent's western coast, where cowrie shells were the leading currency during the seventeenth and early eighteenth centuries. Merchants returning to Europe from China or India would stop in places like the Maldives Islands to purchase the shells and then would export them to Africa in exchange for human beings.

Cowrie Shell Dug out of the Ground near Slave Quarters, Monticello, Virginia. Because of their shape, cowrie shells were often associated with fertility. Their widespread use as money, however, explains the cowrie's Latin name, *Cypraea moneta*.

Modern Cowrie Shells. People today still prize the shells for their beauty.

Because of this global commerce, cowrie shells from the other side of the world have turned up in archaeological excavations in the Chesapeake region. In Yorktown, Virginia, researchers unearthed hundreds of shells in a trash dump from the middle of the eighteenth century, located on property owned by an active slave importer named Phillip Lightfoot II. In Thomas Jefferson's Monticello, archaeologists discovered a cowrie shell in the area where slaves lived. This shell appears to have been worn as jewelry by an African brought to Virginia as a slave, whose name has been lost to us. The Yorktown cowrie testifies to the economic links that bound places like China, the Maldives, France, Benin, Barbados, and Virginia into a single global economy. The Monticello cowrie tells a different story: Men and women, captured and brought to a distant land, wore beautiful shells to retain some connection to a world they would never see again.

Think About It

1. Why did Europeans need cowrie shells in order to buy slave labor?
2. What commodities in European society at the time might be compared to cowrie shells for their beauty, durability, or commercial usefulness?
3. How does the cowrie shell complicate the idea that African slaves were part of a triangular trade?

years of the trade and that even by the eighteenth century rarely took less than five weeks. Ship holds stank of human waste, as the chained passengers would step over one another and relieve themselves in uncovered tubs that were installed for that purpose. Once or twice a day, slaves would be brought up to the deck, still in shackles, to eat, get hosed down, and engage in exercises that their captors mistakenly thought might prevent scurvy. Slaves contracted various illnesses, including dysentery, yellow fever, dehydration, and wound infections from the brands that had been burned onto their bodies. Not surprisingly, death tolls were high, even though ship captains had every incentive to arrive in the Americas with as many living slaves as possible. The Royal African Company's ships lost almost a quarter of their human cargo between 1680 and 1688, and even in the eighteenth century, when faster ships and sanitary improvements lowered mortality rates, it was common for 10 percent of the enslaved passengers to die en route. The dead were simply tossed overboard.

Because African slaves sought to resist their captivity in various ways, slave ships were equipped with mouth openers, thumb screws, whips, and other punitive devices to deal with this rampant problem. Historians estimate that slave mutinies took place on every eight to ten journeys, but most were brutally suppressed by heavily armed ship crews. These rebellions added to the death totals among the captives and offered some clues as to the kind of disciplinary treatment they might expect from their European masters. The crew of

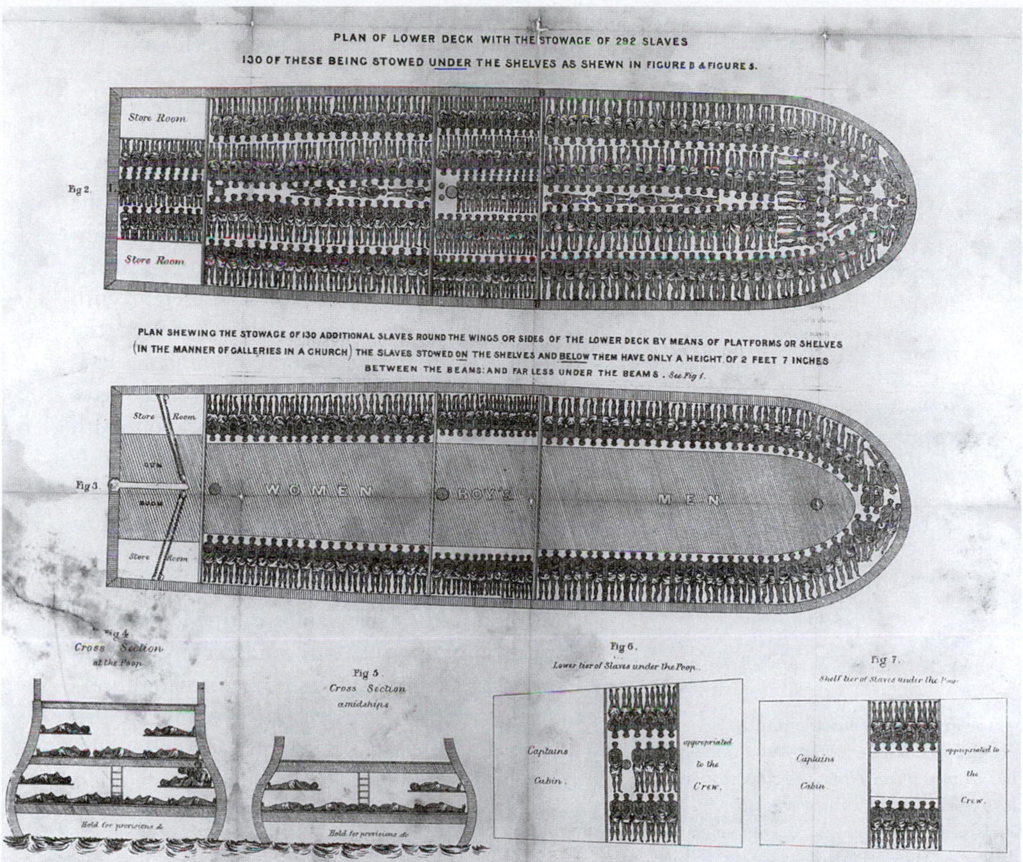

Diagram of the British Slave Ship *Brookes*, ca. 1788. Typically, the ships that carried enslaved Africans across the Atlantic held between 200 and 400 men, women, and children. Though children (most of whom were captured close to the coast) tended to be healthier than adults at the start of the voyage, they were subject to abuse and torture once on board. It was common for girls as young as eight to be sexually assaulted by crew members. This iconic image, engraved by the English abolitionist Thomas Clarkson, was the first visual representation of slave suffering ever produced for a mass audience.

a Danish slave ship in 1709, for example, cut off the right hand of a captive who had led an abortive revolt and exhibited the hand to the rest of the ship. On the following day, his left hand met the same fate. The day after that, the man was decapitated, and his headless torso was displayed for two days. In the face of such brutality, some captives sought to take their own lives by refusing to eat, banging their heads against iron bars, or managing to get to the side of the ship. Thomas Phillips, captain of an English slave ship during the 1690s, described Africans leaping out of boats, "having a more dreadful apprehension of Barbadoes than we have of hell."

The great majority of captives, however, struggled to survive, formed close bonds with their fellow passengers, and tried to prepare themselves for whatever lay at the end of the journey. Upon arrival, slaves were resold, either at fixed prices to eager purchasers who boarded the docked ships or at auctions in the streets, taverns, merchant houses, and public squares of port towns. Most of the new arrivals would then be transported to farms and plantations to perform backbreaking agricultural labor. They had survived one ordeal, but another was just beginning.

BORN INTO SLAVERY

The roughly four hundred thousand Africans brought to North America between 1675 and the American Revolution did not differ fundamentally from the millions transported to sugar-producing colonies in the West Indies or Brazil during the same period. But unlike their kinsmen and compatriots in more tropical climates, North American slaves lived longer on average and had much higher birthrates. This trend exerted a powerful impact on slavery in the mainland colonies.

In most New World slave societies, life expectancy on plantations was very low. Africans lacked immunities to many tropical diseases in the colonies (though epidemiological research suggests that Europeans were even more susceptible), and the debilitating gang labor involved in growing and milling sugar took a devastating toll, especially in Cuba and Brazil but also in the British Caribbean. And because slave owners were constantly replenishing their labor supply by importing African men to replace those who died (slave purchasers consistently preferred male laborers), sex ratios among slave communities were imbalanced and fewer children were born. The high proportion of African-born slaves in most colonies thus produced a vicious cycle of high mortality, low birthrates, and continued importation of African captives. From their formation in the sixteenth and seventeenth centuries until well after the abolition of the slave trade in the early nineteenth century, slave societies throughout Latin America and the West Indies relied on a labor force that was mostly African born.

The one great exception to this rule was mainland North America. Several factors probably contributed to the higher birthrates and lower death rates in Britain's mainland colonies, including climate, diet, work pace, slaveholder practices, and the geographical distribution of slaves. But the crucial point is that the trend was self-perpetuating. Once slave populations began to grow naturally and not simply through importation, sex ratios evened out and birthrates grew even higher. And since more of the population was **creole** (born in the colonies), more slaves had acquired immunities to local disease. American-born mothers' tendency (in accordance with local custom) to wean children at an earlier age than African-born mothers further raised birthrates by reducing the time between pregnancies.

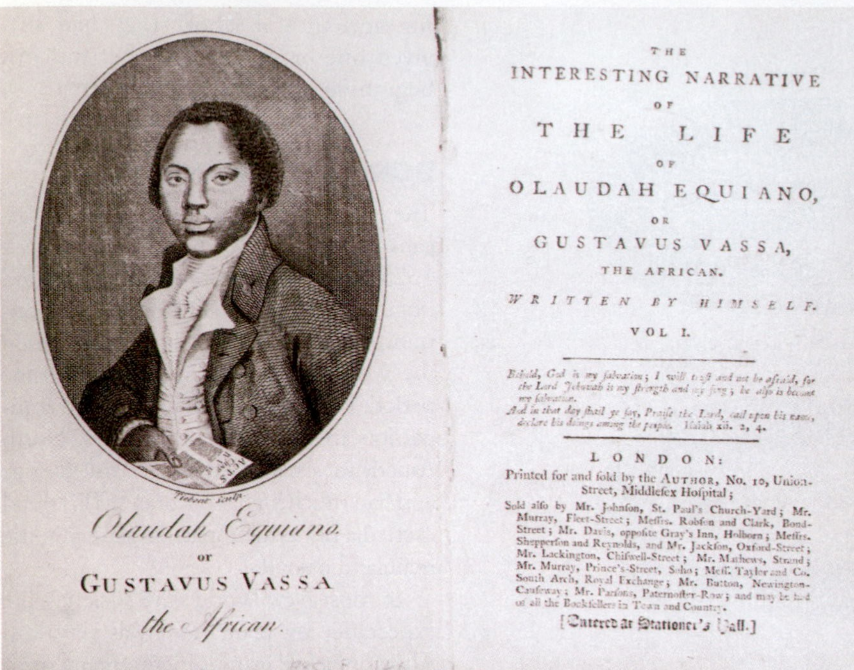

THE
INTERESTING NARRATIVE
OF
THE LIFE
OF
OLAUDAH EQUIANO,
OR
GUSTAVUS VASSA,
THE AFRICAN.
WRITTEN BY HIMSELF.
VOL I.

Behold, God is my ſalvation; I will truſt and not be afraid, for the Lord Jehovah is my ſtrength and my ſong; he alſo is become my ſalvation.
And in that day ſhall ye ſay, Praiſe the Lord, call upon his name, declare his doings among the people. Iſaiah xii. 2, 4.

LONDON:
Printed for and ſold by the AUTHOR, No. 10, Union-Street, Middleſex Hoſpital;
Sold alſo by Mr. Johnſon, St. Paul's Church-Yard; Mr. Murray, Fleet-Street; Meſſrs. Robſon and Clark, Bond-Street; Mr. Davis, oppoſite Gray's Inn, Holborn; Meſſrs. Shepperſon and Reynolds, and Mr. Jackſon, Oxford-Street; Mr. Lackington, Chiſwell-Street; Mr. Mathews, Strand; Mr. Murray, Prince's-Street, Soho; Meſſ. Taylor and Co. South Arch, Royal Exchange; Mr. Button, Newington-Cauſeway; Mr. Parſons, Paternoſter-Row; and may be had of all the Bookſellers in Town and Country.
[Entered at Stationer's Hall.]

Olaudah Equiano. Equiano chronicled the Middle Passage in a famous autobiography, published in 1789. Scholars have questioned the authenticity of parts of his account, but it remains an influential and compelling description of African slavery by a former slave. When the ship carrying Equiano from Africa to the West Indies was boarded by slave traders upon its arrival at port, he and his shipmates still assumed they were destined for a cannibals' feast. "We thought . . . we should be eaten by these ugly men, as they appeared to us," Equiano wrote. "They told us we were not to be eaten, but to work, and were soon to go on land, where we should see many of our country people."

The shift to a mostly creole slave population took place gradually and occurred earlier in the Chesapeake and the North than in South Carolina. Slave populations in Virginia began growing naturally in the 1710s and 1720s. By 1740 only a third of the colony's slaves had been born in Africa. In South Carolina, by contrast, where slaves reproduced more slowly and slaveholders relied more heavily on importation, Africans dominated the slave population until about midcentury. But even in that colony, natural reproduction became the primary contributor to the growth of the slave system. By 1750, the distinctive demographics of North American slavery were clear. The enslaved labor force in the colonies that would become the United States was self-reproducing and mostly born in the New World.

AFRICAN DIASPORA

Creole descendants of Africans in North America undoubtedly experienced slavery differently from African-born slaves much farther south, if for no other reason than they had not been kidnapped from their homes and subjected to the Atlantic crossing. And because they labored on smaller slaveholding units and lived in colonies with larger white populations, North American slaves were in some ways quicker to acculturate to their new surroundings. Nonetheless, African customs, beliefs, memories, and practices survived in the mainland colonies and infused the lives of enslaved Americans.

Even as slave populations became native born, the memory of the old country remained strong during the colonial era. By the time slavery was abolished in the United States after the Civil War, most African Americans would claim several generations of ancestors born on American soil. But in the first half of the eighteenth century, most slaves had either survived the Middle Passage or were the children of survivors. Survivors and their children may have lived in Virginia, Maryland, New York, or South Carolina, but they understood that they came from very different places across the water. As with other immigrants throughout American history, African captives tried to transmit their heritage to their offspring.

Although the slave trade routinely broke up African families, and while no colony granted legal recognition to the marriage or parenthood of enslaved people, Africans in America still managed to select partners and form, maintain, and rebuild family relationships. Slaveholders often encouraged conjugal relations between slaves on the same plantation (or nearby), both to increase their labor force and to prevent slaves from absconding to visit partners elsewhere. Enslaved parents could not protect offspring from the brutal authority of their masters, but they waged a constant struggle to influence their children's development. The naming of slave children presented an early opportunity to remind children of their roots. Slaveholders typically sought to impose English names on newly acquired Africans, but parents generally assumed the right to bestow names on sons and daughters born into bondage. Slaves often observed the West African custom of naming children in accordance with the day of the week on which they were born. A boy born on Friday, for example, might be named Kofi or Cuffee, whereas a girl born on Tuesday would be named some variant of Abena. Other African-language names referred to birth order (the name Sambo, for example, designated a second son) or preserved the memory of relatives still living in the old country.

Outside the bonds of parents and children, African cultures and identities were sustained by growing slave communities. Although slaves did not form a majority in any mainland colony other than South Carolina, they were clustered in particular areas where Africans and their children often predominated. Whether or not they labored on large plantations, slaves conducted most of their social relations with one another during the mid-eighteenth century, and some lived in what essentially was an all-black world. Even in New England, where slaves made up only 3 percent of the population in 1750, Africans and their descendants were sufficiently concentrated in seaports, along rivers, and in particular farm regions that they were able to sustain their own distinctive cuisine, clothing fashions, festivals, and funeral rites, all of which drew upon traditions from Africa.

In areas where slaves predominated, they were also able to preserve their linguistic heritage. Many African-born slaves learned just enough English to recognize some basic work-related commands. In the slave quarters, they spoke in their native tongues or used a patois (mixed language) that integrated African syntax and pronunciation and may have been unintelligible to whites. Slaves in the coastal region of the South Carolina Lowcountry, where blacks vastly outnumbered whites, spoke a patois known as **Gullah,** which became a more formal language of its own by the nineteenth century. Africans who conducted their lives in African languages appear to have been especially likely to try to escape (a large number of advertisements for runaway slaves identify fugitives as speaking little or no English); they were also especially likely to remind other slaves of their common African origins.

14. tf. St. Ann's, July 20, 1779.

RUN AWAY

from the Subſcriber,

About five weeks ago,

A NEGRO BOY, named

JACK,

Of the *Congo* Country,

About 15 or 16 years of age, and has no Brand Mark. —He ſpeaks tolerable good Engliſh, and it is ſuppoſed that he has taken the Clarendon road, being well acquainted in that pariſh.

TWO POUNDS FIFTEEN SHILLINGS Reward will be given for taking him up, and lodging him in any of the Gaols of this Iſland, giving information thereof.

ANDREW BYRNE.

Runaway Slave Advertisement, *Virginia Gazette*, Williamsburg, 1770. Note the reference to the runaway's African birth and lack of proficiency in English.

Although the horrors of the Atlantic crossing may have tested the faith and shaken the world views of many slaves, Africans did not abandon their ancestral religions when they arrived in the American colonies. Before 1750, Africans and their descendants maintained rituals, rites, taboos, and beliefs rooted in a variety of religious traditions. Some were adherents of Islam (see Singular Lives: Ayuba Suleiman Diallo, Redeemed Captive), which had made significant inroads in the Senegambian region from which many slaves came. But most had been raised in religions that were transmitted through oral tradition rather than scripture and that emphasized magic and the conjuring of the spirit world. Many of their beliefs and practices overlapped with those of white Christians at the time, who also sought contact with spirits, consulted sorcerers, and feared the power of witches and wizards. Other African religious traditions, such as marrying more than one woman and burying the dead with food and drink, stood out more conspicuously in colonial America. As the century wore on, more slaveholders and other whites began preaching to the slave population, and

Parrish House, Louisa County, Virginia, and Tobacco Barn, Green Hill Plantation, Campbell County, Virginia. The buildings of both blacks and whites in eighteenth-century Virginia reflected construction patterns imported from West Africa as well as from England. West and Central African homes tended to be small, with few openings other than a doorway. African influence on colonial building also led to the use of thatched roofs. **Questions for Analysis:** What are the most striking common features of the two buildings pictured here? What are some notable differences?

SINGULAR LIVES

Ayuba Suleiman Diallo, Redeemed Captive

Ayuba Suleiman Diallo, who also went by the name Job ben Solomon, was born around 1702 in the West African region of Bondou, between the Senegal and Gambian Rivers. Son of a prosperous Fula merchant, cattle herder, and high priest, Diallo was raised as a Muslim and distinguished himself by memorizing the entire Qur'an as a teenager. One day in 1731, while traveling far from home on business that involved the sale of two slaves owned by his family, Diallo was captured by some Mandingo men and sold to an English slaver, who would bring him in chains to Maryland.

Other men and women aboard the slave ship may have come from equally distinguished backgrounds. Like Diallo, they might have been well off, important personages in their communities who owned slaves themselves. Now they were all thrust together, heads shaven to indicate their status as prisoners, and branded to mark them as property.

Like Diallo, those who survived the Middle Passage were brought ashore in Annapolis, Maryland, where strange men speaking a foreign language put them to work growing tobacco. Each one of them could have told a heart-wrenching story of loneliness and dislocation. Diallo's story entered the historical record as a result of an unusual set of circumstances that would wind up rescuing him, alone among his shipmates, from permanent exile.

Diallo resisted fieldwork, so his master assigned him to cattle herding. This was a trade with which he was familiar and that also allowed him to slip into the woods to fulfill his prayer requirements at prescribed times, though a white boy often followed him, mocking Diallo's devotions and throwing dirt in his face.

Like many newly arrived slaves, Diallo hatched an escape plan, but the odds were stacked against him. Maryland's fugitive slave laws encouraged and empowered anyone (white or Indian) to apprehend black men who might be runaways, and though Diallo made it across the county line, he was soon arrested and jailed in a local tavern. While in custody, he met a man who spoke his native language, and he learned how difficult it would be to escape, so he tried a different approach. Unlike most Africans in North America, Diallo was highly literate, and he wrote a letter in Arabic to his father detailing his predicament and asking to be ransomed. He requested that the letter be delivered to the slave broker in Annapolis who had sold him to his current master, hoping that it might travel back to Senegambia along the other two legs of the triangular trade route that had brought him to North America.

Perhaps because the Arabic letter was a curiosity or perhaps because Diallo's slave translator had intimated to the white Maryland colonists that Diallo's Fula family was rich and powerful, the letter was delivered to Annapolis. From there it was routed to London, where it found its way into the hands of an Arabic professor at Oxford. Translated into English, Diallo's written account of his captivity interested officials of the Royal African Company, who arranged to buy Diallo from his Maryland owner and bring him to England. Diallo learned some English on his way to Europe and negotiated an agreement with the Royal African Company. In return for Diallo's help in securing greater access for British traders to gold, gum, and non-Muslim slaves in the Senegambia, the company would return Diallo to his home and not buy any more Muslim slaves. Late in 1734, Diallo was back in Africa, his horrible ordeal at an end. He soon learned, however, that his father had died, one of his wives had remarried, and wars had ravaged his native land and stripped it of its wealth.

Ayuba Suleiman Diallo. This engraving was published in the English monthly *The Gentleman's Magazine*, 1750.

Think About It

1. How did Diallo's Muslim faith shape his experience of North American slavery?
2. Why might Diallo have imagined that his captors would cooperate in transmitting his letter?
3. How might Diallo have preserved his Muslim identity or his sense of his own elite background had he been forced to remain in the Chesapeake?

by the time of the Revolution a significant portion of the African American population had adapted and adopted some form of Christianity. But before 1750, the religious lives of slaves, whether or not they were exposed to their master's faith, reinforced links with their African heritage.

Africans in America also imported musical instruments, clothing styles, quilting patterns, basket-weaving techniques, medical expertise, tattoos, and other African cultural forms that would connect them to the old country and exert a profound influence on the larger societies in which they lived. African traditions would especially shape speech patterns and foodways now associated with traditional southern culture. Spoonbread, for example, a pudding dish made from cornmeal, evolved from the cooking techniques of slaves seeking to re-create or approximate the traditional African dishes Fufu and Kenkey.

As enslaved people built new communities in the colonies, these African forms would evolve, much as they had back in Africa in the centuries before the slave trade. But the slaves' culture continued to bear the stamp of the worlds from which they had been exiled. Far from losing their African identity in the New World, enslaved men and women actually found that identity. Arriving in America as Igbos, Bambaras, Wolofs, or Yorubas, slaves found common ground as people who had once lived on the African continent and now were part of a diaspora.

Sketch of a Banjo. An African instrument, the banjo was introduced by American slaves in the South. Originally banjos had no frets and were made by stretching a skin over a hollow gourd.

VARIETIES OF COLONIAL SLAVERY

Unlike in later periods, slavery was not confined to a single region of North America during the colonial era. By the eighteenth century, Africans and their descendants were held in legal bondage in English colonies up and down the Atlantic coast and in Spanish and French colonies along the Gulf of Mexico. Most slaves labored in commercial agriculture, producing and processing staple crops for export. Others worked on family farms, in urban workshops, on construction projects, or as domestic servants. Slaves in disparate colonies typically came from different parts of Africa and had varying experiences of the institution of slavery. Under certain conditions, slaves were able to band together to resist their oppression and stage strategic attacks against the regimes under which they labored.

TOBACCO FARMING IN THE CHESAPEAKE

The largest slave system by far in colonial North America emerged in the Chesapeake Bay region. By 1750, three out of five slaves in the thirteen colonies that would become the United States lived in Virginia or Maryland. Most men, women, and children (usually beginning at around age ten or eleven) enslaved in those two colonies cultivated tobacco, which was exported in massive quantities to the British Isles and then sold all over Europe. By 1700, the Chesapeake colonies (including the northeastern corner of North Carolina) were shipping thirty-eight million pounds of tobacco annually, and at various points in the next century, the figure would rise to around sixty million. Later in the colonial period, many Virginia planters began growing wheat alongside or in place of tobacco, but before 1750, the tobacco leaf dominated the local economy.

Tobacco and slavery did not always go hand-in-hand. Tobacco had been the staple crop of the Chesapeake long before Virginia colonists began importing large numbers of Africans, and nonslaveholding family farms continued to grow tobacco during the eighteenth century. But tobacco production and slave labor were certainly compatible. Tobacco growing did not require vast acreage, expensive equipment, or large workforces, so a farmer with only a few slaves could profitably employ them on a tobacco field (though, over time, larger landowners were better able to withstand the impact of soil depletion wrought by tobacco growing). And because soil conducive to tobacco growing abounded in much of the region, this particular staple crop tended to encourage the spread of small slaveholders rather than the amassing of large plantations in just one part of the colony.

Tobacco cultivation exhausted soil quickly, and small farmers and large plantation owners alike often let portions of their land lie fallow for years at a time rather than buying enough slaves to till the entire acreage. While a few wealthy tobacco planters built substantial operations, most slaveholders in the Chesapeake in the middle of the eighteenth century owned five or fewer slaves. The handful of wealthy planters who owned more than a hundred slaves typically divided them among two or three different farms. Still, vast slaveholdings of this size, though common in the West Indies, were rare in Virginia and Maryland.

Compared to other staple crops, tobacco farming required closer supervision because the tobacco leaf was especially fragile, and planters generally observed the rule of assigning an overseer to groups of no more than ten workers. Plantations in the Chesapeake operated on the **gang system,** under which small teams of slaves labored in tandem, straining to match the pace set by a foreman (also a slave), all under the vigilant eye and lash of an overseer. This gang system epitomized not only the demanding nature of tobacco fieldwork but also the high degree of contact between whites and blacks on the plantation. Masters and overseers scrutinized and intervened in the lives of the enslaved to a greater degree in the Chesapeake than in most large New World slave societies during this period.

Needless to say, more frequent contact did not necessarily lead to better treatment. Masters on tobacco plantations may have taken a greater interest in the lives of their slaves, but such interest could lead to whipping, torture, mutilation, or sexual assault. Still, the close bonds that occasionally formed across the color line in eighteenth-century Virginia reflected the distinctive features of the tobacco colonies: Slaves were relatively dispersed, worked in small groups, lived in proximity to their masters, and worked closely with white overseers. These circumstances made it exceedingly difficult for Africans in the Chesapeake to resist their enslavement. Not a single white person was killed in colonial Virginia by an organized slave revolt.

RICE IN THE LOWCOUNTRY

Colonial North America's second largest slave system lay farther south, in the Lowcountry of South Carolina and Georgia. Compared to the Chesapeake system, slavery in the Lowcountry more closely resembled slavery in the Caribbean. Here, absentee masters commonly entrusted large plantations of more than a hundred slaves to the care of managers and overseers. By 1708, less than forty years after its founding, South Carolina had a slave majority and was the only mainland British colony where blacks were not a minority group.

A number of factors shaped the demographics of slavery in South Carolina. First, slavery was established there after indentured servitude had already declined as a viable means of attracting cheap European labor to the colonies. In addition, South Carolina was the southernmost English mainland colony in the late seventeenth century, lying closer to the main routes of the transatlantic slave trade that brought Africans to the Caribbean. And crucially, the colony's first settlers were Barbadians who already owned slaves and were familiar with the trade.

As much as any of those circumstances, however, it was a new crop that sustained the persistent differences between the Lowcountry and the Chesapeake. Rice was still unknown in much of Europe when it was imported to North America from Madagascar in the seventeenth century. West African slaves brought with them experience and expertise in rice cultivation, and South Carolina's planters put them to work clearing swamplands and planting what would become the colony's staple. Slaveholders in the Lowcountry relied particularly on men and women from the Senegambian region, who were familiar with planting, processing, winnowing, and cooking rice. Consequently, the standard South Carolina methods for planting rice—including the use of hoes and coiled baskets and a distinctive sowing technique that involved pressing into the ground with one's heel and covering the seed with one's foot—all closely matched Senegambian practices. African agricultural knowledge and technology made a brutal slave system economically profitable.

Unlike tobacco operations, rice plantations entailed significant start-up costs for draining swamps and building dams, dikes, and ditches. Simply to enter the rice-growing business required a substantial labor force. Those costs also created an economy of scale that encouraged large slaveholding. In addition, rice could be cultivated without close supervision, and the productivity of laborers on rice plantations could be measured more easily than with tobacco, since quantity mattered more than quality. So, instead of the gang system of the Chesapeake, rice planters instituted a **task system** in which slaves were assigned a certain volume and type of work and had to complete it by the end of the day. Typically, an adult slave in mid-eighteenth century South Carolina was required to plant a quarter-acre field in the course of a day. Though an onerous assignment that generally forced bondspeople to supply more of their own food than those in the gang system, the quarter-acre task gave Lowcountry slaves greater control over their time and introduced opportunities to spend their *own* time cultivating private plots for their own consumption.

Pewter Slave Passport. This artifact shows the master's house with slaves' cabins in the background. Tags, badges, and tickets were part of a system of surveillance and control of slaves' movements in Charleston, South Carolina. While metal badges like this one were more common after 1800, tickets identifying a slave's owner and destination were in use in Charleston as early as 1690.

Combined with the size and concentration of the slave population, the task system meant that Africans and their descendants in South Carolina (and later in the coastal areas of Georgia) had less contact with the culture of their masters and were somewhat better positioned to engage in organized resistance. South Carolina was also the only colony before 1733 where slaveholders had to worry that their slaves might flee to the territory of a hostile European power. Spanish Florida, with its capital in nearby St. Augustine, provided an asylum for Africans in South Carolina and inspired slaves to imagine that they might have allies in a showdown with their masters. The Stono Rebellion of 1739 (see States of Emergency: The Stono Rebellion) confirmed the fears of white South Carolinians—and inaugurated an era of extraordinary vigilance about the security of their slave society.

The other major difference between the Chesapeake and the Lowcountry was the presence in South Carolina of an urban center. Because rice was bulkier than tobacco and needed more elaborate processing, the Lowcountry rice economy supported the growth of the region's major port. Charles Town (renamed Charleston after the American Revolution) was the fourth-largest city in British North America by the middle of the eighteenth century. By contrast, in the Chesapeake, tobacco farmers were able to ship their goods to market without the existence of a commercial metropolis. Cities such as Norfolk, Alexandria, and Baltimore grew only once the Chesapeake turned to wheat cultivation after 1750.

Charles Town was not only the principal processing center for the staple crops—rice and, later, indigo, a plant dye exported in large volumes—that were exported to England; it also dominated the colony's import trade in human beings.

STATES OF EMERGENCY

The Stono Rebellion

One Sunday morning in 1739, while many of their masters were attending church services, about twenty slaves assembled near the Stono River twenty miles southwest of Charles Town (the city's original name), South Carolina. Encouraged by reports that a war had erupted been Spain and Britain, the slaves, mostly Angolans, seized arms from a local store, raised a banner, and began beating drums and shouting "Liberty!" in the hope of recruiting more comrades to their cause. They planned to gather an unstoppable force and make their way toward Georgia and then Spanish Florida.

Marching south, the Stono rebels burned homes and killed about twenty white people, including women and children, though they spared a man known to be kind to his slaves. Now a troop of between seventy and ninety, they stopped late that afternoon after traveling ten miles unchecked and set up in an open field. There, they hoped to swell their ranks further and cross the Edisto River the next day. But white colonists had sounded the alarm, perhaps alerted first by the lieutenant governor, who happened to have passed the rebels on the road on his way to a legislative session in Charles Town. Before long, some well-armed planters attacked, and a battle ensued in which many of the rebels were killed. Over the next two days, white colonists, aided by Indians paid to catch slaves, hunted down blacks who had participated in the rebellion, killed them, and placed their heads on poles as a warning to other slaves.

White authorities in South Carolina were not reassured by the successful suppression of the Stono Rebellion. A manhunt for the remaining conspirators continued, and one rebel leader was not captured until 1742. Moreover, slaveholders understood that this was not a one-time threat. The events at Stono came at the end of a decade of rebellions, violent clashes, and foiled conspiracies through much of the Caribbean—in Jamaica, Antigua, Guadalupe, the Bahamas, and in the Danish island of St. John, where a slave revolt controlled the colony for six months in 1733. Compared to those places, where blacks outnumbered whites by as much as ten to one in the eighteenth century, South Carolina's African-descent population (which made up 70 percent of the colony in 1720 and 60 percent in 1750) may have seemed less threatening, but the prospect of mass insurrection was never far from the minds of Lowcountry slaveholders.

In 1740, South Carolina legislators passed the Negro Act, which required every member of a militia to serve in a slave patrol and prohibited masters from manumitting (granting freedom to) their slaves. The following year, the legislature tried to protect whites in the colony by imposing a tariff on slave imports, but the tariff failed to slow the arrival of Africans into the colony. Ultimately, despite their fears of a race war, rice cultivation was too profitable for planters to resist the impulse to buy more slaves.

Think About It

1. What might have discouraged other slaves from joining the Stono Rebellion?
2. Why was the Chesapeake region free of organized violence on the scale of the Stono Rebellion?

Indigo Production Methods in the French West Indies, 1667. Island production practices were similar to those in use in Louisiana and (probably) South Carolina.

Forty percent of all Africans brought to North America before 1808 entered via Charles Town. For that reason, the port is sometimes called the Ellis Island of African America.

SLAVERY IN THE NORTH

Although slavery would later become known as the "peculiar institution" of the South, the colonies north of the Chesapeake Bay also legalized slavery and imported Africans in the seventeenth and eighteenth centuries to labor in a variety of employments. Colonies such as Massachusetts, New York, and Pennsylvania were agricultural, and many of their farms produced and sold surplus crops, but without a major export staple, the scale of commercial agriculture in the North was much smaller and the demand for West African slaves relatively low. By 1750, about 30,000 Africans and their descendants were enslaved in the North, compared to 217,000 in the South.

Still, slavery was an entrenched institution in many parts of the North, not only because English colonists throughout that region profited from slave trading and slave-produced goods, but also because slavery itself was legally sanctioned in the North. The northern colony with the highest enslaved population was New York, where the Dutch had imported Africans as early as 1626. By the time England took over the colony in 1664, black slaves made up a fifth of the population of the city of New Amsterdam, though the line between slaves and other servants under Dutch rule was not as clear as it would become later in the century. The British encouraged the importation of Africans, and during the first four decades of the eighteenth century, the colony's slave population grew faster than the white population. By 1750 there were more than eleven thousand slaves in New York and more than five thousand in neighboring New Jersey, most of whom lived in East Jersey, close to the Hudson River. Slave labor played an important role on commercial wheat farms in the Hudson River Valley and on Long Island. The only northern colony other than New York with at least 10 percent of its population enslaved was Rhode Island, where African laborers were concentrated in seaports and on dairy farms in the Narragansett region.

In the colonial North, Africans and African Americans built roads, herded cattle, and engaged in a variety of skilled artisanal work. Some slaves in New York and New Jersey were field hands or domestic servants, but others worked as carpenters, butchers, weavers, and blacksmiths. One key difference between the slave societies in the South and the societies with slaves in the North was the fact that northern slavery was disproportionately urban. There were not many cities in colonial America, but slavery was prominent in all of them. By 1750, about one-fifth of households in Boston

African Burial Ground National Monument Memorial, New York City. The Negroes Burial Ground was discovered by archaeologists in 1991 and renamed the African Burial Ground two years later.

and one-half of those in New York owned slaves. Slaves themselves formed more than one-third of the population of Kings County (Brooklyn) and close to one-fifth of New York City. Although the overwhelming majority of Africans brought to the New World were put to work on farms, those who wound up living in the North during the eighteenth century were more likely than any other ethnic group (other than Jews) to be living in cities.

Blacks and whites in New York City, Newport (Rhode Island), Philadelphia, and Boston lived and worked alongside one another in the early eighteenth century, though certainly not on terms of equality. Archaeological studies of the remains of black New Yorkers interred in the African Burial Ground suggest that slaves were subjected to far more exploitative labor than white servants, from a very early age.

Living in proximity to white people but not always under the supervision of their masters (who often hired them out to other employers), northern slaves aroused white suspicions of slave revolts. Colonial authorities in the city of New York worried continually about fugitive slaves and revolutionary conspiracies. In 1712, over twenty male and female slaves from the Gold Coast region, joined by some enslaved Indians, staged a violent uprising, setting fire to a building and killing nine white citizens who were trying to extinguish the flames. The militia eventually quashed the rebellion and tortured and executed its ringleaders. The following year, the city council passed a law prohibiting slaves from being in the streets at night without a lantern or a candle. In 1741, an outbreak of fires prompted fears of a more widespread plot, and colonial authorities executed thirty-eight people (thirty-four blacks and four whites), burning some of them alive. Eighty-four other black New Yorkers were deported to the Caribbean.

Execution of Accused Participants in a Plot to Burn New York in 1741. Two of the black men hanged for their alleged role in the slave conspiracy were chained to posts, their corpses left to rot in public view as a warning to other slaves. Others were burned alive.

SLAVERY ON THE GULF COAST

Between 1660 and 1750, the number of African slaves held in North America outside the English-speaking colonies was small. Indians did not enslave Africans during this period, and the French and Spanish slave systems were concentrated in the Caribbean. The Spanish had introduced large numbers of African slaves in Mexico during the 1500s, but this system had declined by the beginning of the following century. In the lands that would become the United States, Spanish and French colonies did not create the kind of commercial agriculture that depended on large numbers of slaves. In 1750, only three hundred Africans were enslaved in Spanish Florida, which continued to provide a refuge for slaves escaping across the border from British colonies. French Louisiana, on the other hand, tried to establish plantation slavery, importing close to six thousand slaves between 1719 and 1743. But slaves lived short, difficult lives in Louisiana, and the colony's enslaved population was less than five thousand in 1750. More slaves lived in New Jersey than in Louisiana.

As a proportion of the colony's population, however, slaves in French Louisiana were far more numerous. Africans and their descendants made up more than half of the colony at midcentury, and slaves from Senegambia (mostly of the Bambara ethnic group) introduced rice cultivation and laid the foundations for the construction of New Orleans by building levees along the Mississippi River and clearing forests. The city was built up in the first half of the eighteenth century by enslaved bricklayers, blacksmiths, wheelwrights, and other laborers imported from Africa. The high proportion of Africans from the same region and ethnicity helped maintain Old World identities among Louisiana's enslaved population. It also raised the danger of rebellion. Two alleged plots were exposed in 1731, one of which was said to involve hundreds of Bambaras from Senegal. Slave insurrections, both real and imagined, impeded the growth of Louisiana under both French and (after 1763) Spanish rule. In the nineteenth century, after it was annexed by the United States, Louisiana would become a leading center of sugar and cotton cultivation and the site of an especially brutal and productive slave system.

***Savages of Several Nations*, by Alexandre de Batz, 1735.** This drawing by a French artist in colonial Louisiana features a person of African descent among indigenous Americans and thus suggests the early fluidity of racial categories in southern Louisiana.

CONCLUSION

By 1750, the British colonial system in North America was closely tied to the Atlantic slave trade. Though Africans in exile had been part of the colonial world as long as Europeans, they had been a small minority for much of the seventeenth century, and their labor had been but a small element in a varied workforce. Over a short time span, however, the colonists' slave-buying spree had made African labor central to the production of staple crops and defined a hard line between slavery and freedom. During that same time period, the slave population shifted. African survivors of the Middle Passage were soon outnumbered by Americans of African descent. And throughout the continent—but especially in the South, where slave populations would continue to grow through the rest of the century—the line between black and white had calcified into a deep and fundamentally violent social divide.

STUDY TERMS

- slave societies (p. 60)
- societies with slaves (p. 60)
- chattel slavery (p. 61)
- Royal African Company (p. 62)
- South Carolina (p. 63)
- slave codes (p. 63)
- diaspora (p. 66)
- Middle Passage (p. 67)
- slave mutinies (p. 68)
- creole (p. 69)
- slave communities (p. 69)
- Gullah (p. 71)
- gang system (p. 73)
- rice (p. 74)
- task system (p. 74)
- Stono Rebellion (p. 74)

TIMELINE

1619 First recorded slave purchase in Virginia

1662 Virginia law makes slave status inheritable through the mother

1663 Carolina founded

1664 England takes over New Netherland, where slavery is well established

1672 Royal African Company formed

1676 Bacon's Rebellion

1712 Slave revolt in New York

1732 Georgia legally established

1739 Stono Rebellion

1741 Alleged slave conspiracy in New York

1751 Slavery legally established in Georgia

FURTHER READING

Additional suggested readings are available on the Online Learning Center at www.mhhe.com/becomingamerica1e.

Ira Berlin, *Many Thousands Gone* (1998), presents an extensive and highly influential account of colonial slavery.

T. H. Breen and Stephen Innes, *"Myne Owne Ground"* (1980), studies the lives and prospects of Africans and their descendants in eastern Virginia, before the entrenchment of chattel slavery in the Chesapeake.

David Brion Davis, *Inhuman Bondage* (2006), synthesizes decades of slavery scholarship, especially on the evolution of Western attitudes about race and freedom.

Michael A. Gomez, *Exchanging Our Country Marks* (1998), emphasizes the retention of particular African religious traditions, languages, and ethnic identities among slaves in North America.

Douglas Grant, *The Fortunate Slave* (1968), reconstructs the life of Ayuba Suleiman Diallo.

Leslie Harris, *In the Shadow of Slavery* (2004), surveys the history of African Americans in colonial New York City.

Winthrop D. Jordan, *White Over Black* (1968), uncovers deep patterns of anti-African prejudice in English thought prior to the entrenchment of North American slavery.

Jill Lepore, *New York Burning* (2006), explores the alleged slave conspiracy that rocked New York in 1741.

Edmund Morgan, *American Slavery, American Freedom* (1975), explains the decline of indentured servitude and the entrenchment of slavery in the Chesapeake after Bacon's Rebellion.

Philip Morgan, *Slave Counterpoint* (1998), compares slavery in the Chesapeake and the Carolina Lowcountry—colonial North America's two largest slave systems.

Stephanie Smallwood, *Saltwater Slavery* (2007), powerfully details the history of the Middle Passage.

Mark Michael Smith (ed.), *Stono* (2005), presents documents and essays on the Stono Rebellion of 1739.

Betty Wood, *Slavery in Colonial America* (2005), summarizes the basic trends and patterns in American slavery prior to the Revolution.

4

INSIDE

THE BIG PICTURE

Following a period of political turmoil, England's royal government consolidated its control over the nation's American colonies. New settlements along the Atlantic seaboard attracted a diverse migration of European Protestants seeking cheap farm plots, but the new dispersed colonial population consumed European goods and forged increasingly strong ties to a growing British Empire.

Middle Colonies. New York, viewed from the southwest in this painting from around 1730, became a bustling port town in the growing British Empire.

1660–1750

BRITISH COLONIES IN AN ATLANTIC ECONOMY

As he recounted over thirty years later, William Moraley had been drinking beer at a London pub when he decided to immigrate to America in 1729. He had fallen on hard times, having been largely cut out of his father's will after he abandoned both a legal education and then a career in the watchmaking trade. A recruiter had spotted him reading advertising posters for foreign lands at the London shipping docks and had brought him to the pub to pitch the idea of signing up to be an indentured servant in the American colonies for five years. The thirty-year-old Moraley set sail, but not for the well-established Chesapeake Bay region, where tobacco planters were completing the momentous shift in labor from European servants to African slaves. Instead his destination was a new port city called Philadelphia in the growing mid-Atlantic colony of Pennsylvania. Upon arrival, his indenture was purchased by a clockmaker in the nearby colony of New Jersey.

The world Moraley entered in 1729 was remarkably different from the early European outposts established on the North American mainland over a century earlier. English colonies now filled in the coastal lands between New England and the Chesapeake and stretched even farther south, all the way to the border with Spanish Florida. A more geographically diverse group of European Protestants was settling the colonies in this period, and most arrived with the goal of acquiring land and living in an agricultural society that was unlike the one emerging on slave plantations in the South. Moraley did not share that ambition. He had no interest in farming or in completing the term of his indenture. Instead he wandered from one village to another, dodging creditors and scouring the growing countryside in vain for a wealthy widow who might support him. After five years in this new land, Moraley gave up his quest and returned penniless to England.

For the majority of European immigrants to the British colonies during the late seventeenth and early eighteenth centuries, however, the move to America was permanent. Most settled in rural areas that probably felt far removed from the worlds they had left behind. But even the most remote farm community during this period was enmeshed in a complex system of commercial and cultural exchange that put people in contact with goods, information, and philosophical and religious ideas from within the colonies and across the world. Part of a growing British Empire, these exchanges were regulated by the British government—but not entirely under its control.

KEY QUESTIONS

- How did the settlement of the various Restoration colonies differ?
- How did the British system of imperial regulation work?
- What characterized the lifestyles of the urban minority and the farming majority in this period?
- What were the Enlightenment and the Great Awakening, and how did they influence life in the colonies?

Protestant immigrants from northern Europe uprooted their lives in response to economic opportunities on the other side of the ocean.

RESTORATION AND EXPANSION

In the 1660s, colonization in North America received a major jolt from political changes in England. Oliver Cromwell, the Puritan leader of the revolutionary movement that had ushered in a decade of Parliamentary rule, died in 1658. Two years later, conservative forces invited Charles II, son of the king whom Cromwell's supporters had executed during the civil war, to take the throne. The **Restoration** of the Stuart Monarchy (1660), as the event was called, led to a new effort on the part of the Crown to expand its overseas empire and coordinate colonial affairs. A series of new colonies appeared in the Restoration era, mostly in the mid-Atlantic area between New England and the Chesapeake, attracting an overseas migration as great as any of the earlier ones. Charles II pursued aggressive policies to wrest trade from the Dutch, and Parliament enacted new laws to wring more profits from North American colonies. England also sought to impose royal authority on the older colonies that had been settled earlier in the century.

CHARLES II AND THE NEW IMPERIAL ORDER

After Charles II returned from exile in 1660 to assume the throne, a host of political and cultural changes swept over England. A new Parliament passed laws to enforce religious conformity, reintroducing the old liturgy, church hierarchy, and holidays that the Puritans had sought to abolish. The king, meanwhile, who had a Catholic mother and eventually converted to Catholicism himself, pulled England back from its role as a crusader for global Protestantism and turned his attention instead to a series of campaigns against the Protestant Netherlands.

Charles II moved quickly to seize Dutch wealth from the seas and from the lucrative Atlantic trade routes that Holland had dominated since early in the century. To compete with the Dutch in the trafficking of human beings, he chartered the Royal African Company (see Chapter 3), which he placed under the directorship of his brother James, the Duke of York. Within months of its official establishment in 1663, the Royal African Company captured Dutch slave-trading posts on Africa's Gold Coast. A year later, the English invaded the Dutch colony of New Netherland. Both the towns of New Amsterdam (renamed New York) and Fort Orange (renamed Albany) promptly surrendered to the invaders, and the Dutch lost their commercial centers in North America. An inconclusive Anglo-Dutch War raged for three years. Though the Dutch recaptured most of their slaving forts in Africa and many of their commercial interests survived the fight, England retained control of New York. One final time, in 1672, Dutch ships managed to retake their lost colony, but in a 1674 treaty the Netherlands renounced its claims on the American continent once and for all.

By virtue of this conquest, the Duke of York became the proprietor of a huge stretch of land that encircled the older New England colonies and ran southwest all the way to the Chesapeake. Other members of King Charles's inner circle also received personal estates within this domain. Beyond enriching his friends and relatives, the king's plan was to enlarge the English empire in America. In the first decade of the Restoration, new colonies were carved out in Carolina, New York, East New Jersey, West New Jersey, and New Hampshire (see Map 4.1). In 1681, another colony was established, in Pennsylvania. Colonial settlement on the North American mainland had been transformed rapidly from a series of independent entities scattered among rival European strongholds to a continuous chain of English colonies between French Canada and Spanish Florida.

While authorizing new settlements, the English government also sought to impose a new order on its American seaboard empire. Rather than allow investor companies or individual proprietors to run independent colonies, both Parliament and the Crown pushed for more centralized control starting in the 1660s. Royal commissioners sailed to America to investigate local affairs, scrutinize colonial charters, and assert royal authority. The main policy thrust behind this move was to make England's American settlements more commercially profitable for the home country.

To support that goal, Parliament passed a series of **Navigation Acts,** which restricted the way commodities produced in English colonies entered international markets and the way commodities produced elsewhere were brought into the colonies. These laws were intended to make sure that English ships and English ports handled the commercial traffic generated by English colonial activity. Such trade restrictions reflected a cluster of ideas (branded **mercantilism** a century later) about how colonization could make a nation rich and powerful by increasing exports, decreasing imports, encouraging shipbuilding and manufacturing, and raising revenues.

The first Navigation Act had been enacted in 1651, under Cromwell's government, to prevent Dutch ships from bringing goods from America, Asia, and Africa into England. But the law had proved difficult to enforce. After the Restoration, a new Parliament expanded this campaign considerably, establishing a new system of commercial regulation that would last until the American Revolution more than a century later. In addition to granting English ships a monopoly on trade out of the colonies, the Navigation Act of 1660 stipulated that certain enumerated articles produced in the colonies—tobacco, cotton, sugar, indigo, dyewoods, and ginger—had to be shipped directly to England (where they would be subject to import taxes) before they could be reexported elsewhere. Three years later, the Staple Act granted England similar privileges for trade *into* the colonies. American colonists could only buy European goods that had passed first through England. Subsequent acts in the 1670s closed loopholes that colonial merchants had exploited to avoid paying customs (import taxes) and established the Lords of Trade to monitor and regulate colonial commerce. Piracy, smuggling, and resistance made it impossible for authorities in London to achieve complete control over American trade, but the Navigation Acts brought significant profits both to English merchants and to the Crown. Trade laws also formed the basis of England's attempts to govern its growing empire.

THE MIDDLE COLONIES

From a North American perspective, the most dramatic change associated with the English Restoration was the growth of England's **Middle Colonies**—New York, New Jersey, Pennsylvania, and Delaware—which were established on land that had been claimed and settled by the Dutch and then granted by Charles II to the Duke of York. The duke entrusted New York to the care of his deputy, Richard Nicolls, who became the colony's governor. In the southwestern part of the territory, the duke also granted land parcels to two other aristocratic supporters of the Stuarts, and these became the colonies of East and West New Jersey.

In 1681, King Charles carved out a 45,000-square-mile colony just west of the Jerseys and the Delaware River as a gift to an aristocrat named William Penn, whose late father (of the same name) had lent money to the king. The younger Penn, recently released from prison for his heretical religious views, had been seeking a refuge for a new religious movement in mid-seventeenth-century England called the Society of Friends, or the Quakers (see below). The king's charter made him the proprietor of a colony called Pennsylvania. A year later, Penn augmented the colony by purchasing additional land on the Atlantic seaboard from the duke. This land, known as the Three Lower Counties, would become the separate colony of Delaware in 1704.

Unlike English settlements in the Chesapeake and New England, the Middle Colonies were built in part on top of an established European colonial project with an ethnically diverse European and African population. New York and New Jersey were superimposed onto New Netherland, which had been settled originally by Walloons (French-speaking refugees from Belgium) and had attracted Germans, Scandinavians, Mennonites, and Jews, among others. The land that became Delaware (added to New Netherland in 1655) had been settled earlier by Swedes and Finns. In the city of New Amsterdam, African slaves and former slaves made up as much as a quarter of the population by the time the English arrived.

This complex history of prior settlement shaped the Middle Colonies. Dutch cultural influences remained especially strong

Map 4.1 British Colonies, ca. 1660–1750. Over the course of a century, the scattered outposts of different European powers in the eastern part of North America (see Map 2.2, for example) were replaced by a continuous chain of seaboard colonies belonging to the same empire.

well after New Netherland's official demise. The Dutch language continued to be spoken in many New York and New Jersey homes and was even more common in church settings. Foods traditionally favored by Dutch farmers, such as beets, endives, spinach, and parsley, figured prominently in local diets. Colonial Christmas observances in this region also bore a heavy Dutch stamp. Although New England Puritans banned celebrating such a holiday, December 25 was a more festive occasion west of the Hudson River, where colonists preserved Dutch practices such as leaving wooden shoes by the door to receive gifts. And although the modern American gift-giving mythology did not emerge until the nineteenth century (see Chapter 12), New York children in the late seventeenth century would have heard of Dutch stories about *Sinter Claes*.

But new communities and different cultural influences also took root in the Middle Colonies beginning in the last quarter

Late-Eighteenth-Century British Painting of a Quaker Meeting. The name *Quakers* began as a disparaging term used by their English detractors, but because it referred to those who "tremble at the word" of God (in the phrase of the Biblical prophet Isaiah), members of the Society of Friends ultimately accepted the designation.

of the seventeenth century. One major source of this change was Quaker migration. Quakerism, a breakaway Christian movement in England, preached the importance of an "inner light" that came from Jesus and lay at the core of every individual. While the Church of England stressed social hierarchy and tradition, and while Puritans regarded salvation as a fate reserved by divine grace for a predestined minority, the Society of Friends attracted followers with a different, encouraging message: Salvation was available to all and required no deference to learned authorities. Quakers also challenged the government by refusing to pay church taxes or swear in court and by advancing ideas of human equality that threatened established divisions based on wealth, social rank, and gender. King Charles's decision to charter William Penn's colony may have reflected his desire to quell domestic dissent by shipping Quakers overseas. Quakers proved eager to escape persecution and join in what Penn called his "Holy Experiment."

English Quakers migrated to various American colonies during the 1650s, but the larger stream began in 1675, when a party of the Society of Friends helped settle West Jersey, the first major American destination for Quaker refugees. Once Pennsylvania was established six years later, the stream became a tide. Close to twenty-three thousand migrants, mostly but not exclusively Quakers, moved to the Delaware Valley between 1675 and 1715. Penn aggressively recruited the majority of these new arrivals from communities of Friends in England, Wales, and Ireland. He also sent promotional tracts and agents to lure Protestants from Holland and the German Rhineland with descriptions of Pennsylvania's fertile farmland and promises of religious freedom. Some new settlers arrived in family groups, whereas others came as individual servants, a social composition that lay somewhere between that of New England and that of the Chesapeake.

Compared to other English colonists, Pennsylvanians enjoyed far more peaceful relations with the continent's native inhabitants. Quaker founder George Fox had visited the Delaware Valley in 1672 and had recommended the region to Penn on the grounds that the Lenni Lenape (whom settlers would later call Delaware Indians) were "very loving." The Delawares, weakened by epidemics earlier in the century and fearful of the growing power of the Iroquois League, eagerly seized the opportunity to form bonds with the newcomers, who came bearing vast quantities of trade goods. Quaker colonists also brought more tolerant views of Indians, and many Quakers were pacifists. Penn was personally committed to preventing the unlawful confiscation of Delaware lands and took pains to make sure that no Indians were dispossessed or evicted without fair negotiation and equitable compensation. Relations between Pennsylvania colonists and the Delaware grew tenser after 1710, when an aging and ailing Penn no longer exerted authority over colonial affairs. Still, a fragile peace would prevail in the colony until the middle of the eighteenth century.

Wampum Belt Depicting Treaty Between William Penn and the Delaware Indians. Historians speak of a "long peace" between natives and Pennsylvania colonists, lasting between the colony's founding and the end of the French and Indian War.

Penn also introduced a political system that was more democratic than any other form of governance in England's American empire. His initial design for the colony, called the Frame of Government, guaranteed individual liberties and religious freedom (though only those who professed faith in Christianity could hold office). It also established a bicameral, or two-chambered, legislature in which a Provincial Council of wealthy landowners initiated laws while a much larger popular Assembly made up of elected representatives reserved the right to approve or reject them. In 1701, Penn revised the Frame of Government in response to political conflict between the two chambers and resistance from the colony's Lower Counties, where most residents were not Quakers. In its place Penn issued a new Charter of Privileges that would serve as Pennsylvania's constitution for the rest of the colonial era. Under the charter, the Lower Colonies could secede and form their own colony. More important, the Provincial Council lost all of its powers, leaving Pennsylvania under the control of a unicameral legislature—the only one of its kind in the American colonies.

THE GLORIOUS REVOLUTION IN NORTH AMERICA

While English settlements grew and proliferated, the Stuart monarchy stepped up its campaign to bring the colonial empire under tighter control. In 1684, England repealed the Massachusetts Bay charter. The following year, King Charles II died, and his brother James (then the Duke of York) assumed the throne as James II of England (and James VII of Scotland). James's elevation had the automatic effect of turning New York, where he had been the proprietor, into a royal colony. The new king set about nullifying the charters of neighboring colonies, redrawing their boundary lines, and reorganizing the English empire north of Maryland into a supercolony called the Dominion of New England. The dominion was to be ruled directly by the king's agent, Edmund Andros, who had previously served as governor of New York. Existing colonial legislatures were to be disbanded, and no new ones could be formed. Andros was instructed to guarantee religious freedom, encourage the importation of African slaves, maintain peaceful relations with Indians, enforce the Navigation Acts, collect taxes on all land sales, and somehow exert absolute authority over the whole region from his headquarters in Boston.

The Andros government met resistance, especially in New England, but soon events in England changed the balance of power altogether. James's ascent in 1685 had been highly controversial because he was a Catholic, but many opponents took comfort in the thought that the new king was elderly and would soon enough be succeeded by one of his Protestant daughters. Then in June 1688, James's second wife, the Catholic Queen Mary of Modena, bore a son who would now be heir to the throne. Fearing a new Catholic dynasty with ties to France, the king's Protestant opponents united behind a plan to replace James with his Anglican daughter Mary and her Dutch husband, William of Orange. William was anxious to forestall an alliance between James and France's King Louis XIV (with whom the Dutch were on the brink of war) and wasted no time in accepting the invitation to rule England, leading an invasion party of forty thousand men across the North Sea. Facing such an overwhelming force, the king's supporters mounted no resistance. James himself escaped the royal palace and threw the Great Seal of England into the Thames River in the belief that William and Mary could not rule without it. Undeterred, supporters of the Dutch invasion maintained that James had vacated the thrones of England, Scotland, and Ireland. In a bloodless regime change known as the Glorious Revolution, King William III and Queen Mary II took over England's growing empire.

When reports of the coup reached Boston, colonists there denounced the Dominion of New England, revived the Massachusetts Bay charter, and put Governor Andros in jail. In Maryland, Protestants took the revolution as a cue to depose the colony's Catholic proprietor. The most dramatic political fallout took place in New York, where a German-born merchant named Jacob Leisler, allied with the old Dutch elite, staged his own revolution in support of the new Protestant monarchy in England. In 1689, Leisler organized a militia, seized the local fort, and established a Committee of Safety to rule the colony. Unlike in Massachusetts and Maryland, Leisler's Rebellion ignited long-simmering political, economic, and ethnic conflicts in New York, and political chaos ensued for two years. When William III sent new a new royal governor named Henry Sloughter to New York in 1691, Leisler challenged his credentials and Sloughter had him tried and brutally executed for treason. The crisis divided the colony and left a legacy of intense partisan strife in New York politics for the next century.

The broader, longer-lasting significance of the Glorious Revolution in North America was a change in colonial policy. Beginning with William and Mary, English monarchs ruled their American possessions with a lighter touch, continuing to insist that the colonies contribute to the commercial growth of the empire but abandoning their predecessors' campaign to make the colonies submit to royal authority. The Protestants who ruled England after 1688 turned their attention to their Catholic rivals and needed colonists' support for a series of wars against the French in North America (see Chapter 5). From 1688 to 1763, a new political order took shape in England's North American colonies, which became "British" when England and Scotland united as Great Britain in 1707. Parliament continued to administer trade policy within the framework of the Navigation Acts, and colonial governors were still appointed by the Crown or by proprietors, but colonial assemblies gained increasing autonomy.

A GROWING WORLD OF MIGRANTS

While events in English politics determined the shape and structure of its colonies, life in those colonies was more visibly and fundamentally changed by the basic fact of massive population growth. In 1650, fewer than 50,000 English settlers occupied the lands that later became the United States. Fifty years later, England's mainland American colonies held more than 250,000 colonists. And fifty years after that, close to a million Europeans and approximately 250,000 Africans lived in British America. Some of this population rise stemmed from high birthrates and increasing life spans, but much of the growth reflected migration from diverse places across the Atlantic. By the eighteenth century, both free and bound newcomers tended to come from lands other than England. As they settled in different regions along the eastern seaboard, they contributed to the development of a range of different colonial societies, some of them ethnically heterogeneous.

NATURAL INCREASE IN NEW ENGLAND

More so than the rest of British North America in 1700, the four New England colonies (Connecticut, Rhode Island, Massachusetts, and New Hampshire; Maine and Vermont were not distinct colonies at this point) consisted primarily of the descendants of English immigrants rather than new arrivals from Europe. After economic conditions improved in England during the Restoration and as persecution of dissenting Protestants eased after the Glorious Revolution, fewer Puritans were motivated to leave the country. In addition, New England was a less attractive destination to those who did want to immigrate because land in that region was scarcer, more expensive, more tightly controlled, and more vulnerable to Indian attack than elsewhere. Some New England colonies even discouraged immigration, passing laws that required ship captains to take responsibility for passengers who were "poor, vicious and infirm" and therefore might become burdens to their new communities.

New England colonies continued to grow after the Restoration in 1660, however, due to natural increase—a surplus of births over deaths. Because so many of the original New England migrants had come over in families, sex ratios were relatively balanced. And although at first they tended to marry later than in some other colonies, New Englanders almost always married. With limited access to contraception, couples produced many offspring, on average about seven or eight infants per woman (see Singular Lives: Sarah Grosvenor, Pregnant Puritan). At the same time, New England's cold climate and well-drained land limited the impact of disease and thus contributed to high average life expectancies relative to other New World societies. In New England's farming villages in the seventeenth century, colonists who reached the age of twenty typically lived to around sixty-five.

High fertility and low mortality enabled a society founded by 20,000 Puritan immigrants in the first half of the seventeenth century to grow into a populous colonial region even after the tide of migration stopped. Natural growth was so great that the region's population continued to double roughly every generation. By 1700, approximately 100,000 people lived in the New England colonies. By 1750, the figure reached 340,000.

As New England families grew, the lands allotted to townships could no longer be subdivided to support all of their founders' descendants. Young men moved to newer towns, migrated westward and northward to unsettled areas, or left New England altogether. From 1670 on, more people moved out of New England than moved in. Connecticut and Massachusetts began

New England Family Values. Large families, of the kind celebrated in this 1804 watercolor family record, helped sustain population growth in the New England colonies long after foreign immigration slackened.

SINGULAR LIVES

Sarah Grosvenor, Pregnant Puritan

Sometime in 1742, a nineteen-year-old woman in the village of Pomfret, Connecticut, discovered that she was pregnant. Sarah Grosvenor and Amasa Sessions, the twenty-seven-year-old presumed father, were not married at the time. But that in itself was no longer remarkable in colonial New England, where premarital intercourse had become much more common. By midcentury, about 25–30 percent of brides in the typical New England town were already pregnant on their wedding night. Grosvenor and Sessions did not get married, however, although the two were members of prominent Pomfret families and would have made a socially suitable match. Nor did they seek another common solution to an unwanted pregnancy and arrange for the offspring to be supported by the community as an illegitimate child. Instead, Sessions hired a man named John Hallowell to prescribe an abortifacient drug. When the drug made Grosvenor ill, Hallowell attempted an abortion procedure, which caused a miscarriage. A month later Grosvenor herself died.

It is hard to know how frequently women or couples in eighteenth-century America sought to terminate pregnancies. Ingesting abortifacients was sufficiently common that Grosvenor could simply refer to it as "taking the trade" when she confided the incident to a friend. Abortion by instrument was probably rarer, though such a procedure, if it took place in the early months of pregnancy before the woman could feel the fetus move, was not in itself a criminal offense in colonial Connecticut. Still, abortions were scandalous (women who assisted in such procedures were vulnerable to witchcraft accusations in the seventeenth century), in large part because they represented brazen attempts to conceal the sin of fornication, or sexual intercourse outside of marriage. Before 1700, New England towns treated such sex as a crime, but by the time of Grosvenor's pregnancy, a new sexual double standard had emerged: Only women were prosecuted for fornication. Sarah Grosvenor might have agreed to "take the trade" to avoid being punished as a fornicator, or to avoid the stigma of bearing a bastard, or for any number of other reasons. But she ultimately seems to have agreed to the abortion procedure under heavy pressure from Sessions and Hallowell, out of fear that an expedited miscarriage was necessary to protect her from mortal danger. In the end, however, it was the abortion itself that took Sarah Grosvenor's life.

The lethal abortion also brought Grosvenor's private relationships to public light. County magistrates began investigating Grosvenor's death in 1745, questioning her former lover, her relatives, and her friends and considering their culpability in her death. Though none of the Pomfret elders appear to have known anything, an inner circle of young people were aware of Grosvenor's predicament, and her sister and cousin had secretly buried the fetus to conceal the abortion. A grand jury indicted only the doctor Hallowell, however, for the "highhanded Misdemeanor" of attempting to harm Grosvenor and her fetus. Hallowell was convicted and sentenced to twenty-nine lashes and two hours of public humiliation, but he broke out of jail and fled the colony. He was never pursued or punished further. Amasa Sessions, who had hired him, remained a prominent and respected citizen in Pomfret.

Last Remains. Apart from this simple Connecticut tombstone, evidence of Sarah Grosvenor's short and tragic life survives in the court testimony of her friends, relatives, and neighbors.

Think About It

1. Why might Connecticut authorities have charged John Hallowell, rather than Amasa Sessions, with a crime?
2. Why was no one charged with murder?

auctioning unsettled land for cash to individual settlers and speculators rather than allocating that land to communities. Although New England life continued to revolve around small, close-knit, religiously homogeneous towns, increasing numbers of New Englanders after 1700 lived either on farms far removed from original settlements or in crowded commercial seaports.

DIVERSE IMMIGRANTS IN THE MIDDLE COLONIES

In the colonies to the south of New England, the population grew much faster as newcomers moved in. Relatively peaceful relations with Indians and prosperity linked to rising international prices for the wheat grown there were among the lures. New York, New Jersey, Delaware, and especially Pennsylvania attracted large numbers of immigrants in the eighteenth century, many from Scotland and northern Ireland. Scots-Irish immigrants to the American colonies (or Scotch-Irish, as they were sometimes called in America) included Scottish Presbyterians whose ancestors had settled in Ireland in the seventeenth century, but the term refers more generally to migrants from all sides of the Irish Sea (see Map 4.2). Driven mainly by poverty and land scarcity, they came from 1717 onward, forming the largest group of European immigrants to British America in the first half of the eighteenth century. Arriving as both free settlers and indentured servants, they made their way to the Shenandoah Valley of Virginia and the Carolina backcountry as well as to the Middle Colonies, drawn by the promise of cheap farmland. By the end of the eighteenth century, more than a third of families listed in the census records of states such as Pennsylvania and North Carolina had Scottish or Irish last names.

Pennsylvania proved even more attractive to migrants from German-speaking lands. Close to thirty-seven thousand German immigrants entered British America between 1700 and 1750, more than twice as many as came from England in that period. German immigration to Pennsylvania had begun with Penn's recruitment campaigns of the previous century, and once Germans established communities there, relatives, neighbors, and coreligionists from Europe were more likely to join them. German colonists did not all emigrate from a single country (Germany was not a unified nation at this time) but came from Westphalia, Alsace, Bavaria, and all parts of the Rhine Valley, including the area that is now in Switzerland (see Map 4.2). What they did share was the German language. English speakers in the colonies came to refer to these people as Pennsylvania Dutch, after the German name for the language, *deutsche*. Many of the migrants had already moved several times back in northern Europe (some of them, ironically, were actually Dutch), but the departure for North America marked a more decisive life change. It also involved significant health risks, both at sea and in the port cities where most migrants disembarked. Germans who sailed from Rotterdam to Philadelphia in 1731 accused their captain of not bringing enough food on board and then charging them exorbitant prices to stay alive. "To keep from starving we had to eat rats and mice. We paid from eight pence to two shillings for a mouse; four pence for a quart of water." German-speaking immigrants to the Middle Colonies were even more likely than those from northern Britain to arrive in family units, and mortality among children was especially high on board these ships. Still, those who survived the dangerous phases of the journey were likely to live as well as or better than the relatives and neighbors they left behind.

Map 4.2 European Migrations to the English/British Colonies, 1700–1750. Protestants from various parts of northwestern Europe and the British Isles were attracted to English-speaking colonies in North America during this period, especially to those established after the Restoration.

By the mid-eighteenth century, European settlement in the Middle Colonies was even more ethnically diverse than it had been at the time of English conquest of New Netherland

Moravians in the American Interior. German-speaking Moravian missionaries baptize Lenape Indians in Bethlehem, Pennsylvania.

(see Interpreting the Sources: Benjamin Franklin on the Population of British America). One thing the overwhelming majority of colonists shared, however, was a Protestant religious affiliation. Many were Presbyterians, while others were Quakers, Lutherans, Anabaptists, Moravians, Mennonites, or Huguenots (French Protestants). But they all worshiped inside the broader Protestant fold. Some significant minority of Irish immigrants may have been Catholic, but if so, most kept that identity concealed. Britain's American empire was not hospitable to Catholic migrants in the first half of the eighteenth century, a point driven home by Parliament in 1740, when it codified the process for becoming colonial citizens. By law, any free white man who resided in a British colony for seven years, swore allegiance to the empire, and had taken Communion in a Protestant church within the previous three months was eligible to own land and participate in elections. Soon after, Parliament revised the rules to make clear that Quakers counted as Protestants and to allow for the possibility of Jewish citizenship, but imperial immigration policy did not welcome Catholics. Jews were a tiny minority in the colonies during this period, concentrated in port towns and subject to some legal restrictions, though Carolina encouraged Jewish immigration. Enslaved Africans were more numerous in the Middle Colonies, and before 1750 only a minority of them identified as Protestants, but they remained largely beyond the bounds of citizenship and they too were concentrated in urban areas (see Chapter 3). The Middle Colonies formed something of a melting pot for Protestants.

CREOLES IN THE CHESAPEAKE

Colonial populations grew steadily in tobacco country as well. High mortality rates and imbalanced sex ratios had checked the natural increase of Virginia and Maryland for much of the seventeenth century, and those colonies had grown entirely through immigration. During the last three decades of the century, when overseas migration to New England slowed, migration to the Chesapeake remained strong; indeed, Virginia and Maryland were the two leading mainland destinations for English immigrants to the New World. Beginning around the same time, birthrates rose, sex ratios evened out, and colonists in the region began living longer on average. With a non-Indian population approaching sixty thousand, Virginia became the most populous colony north of Mexico by 1700. Maryland lagged behind only Virginia and Massachusetts among England's mainland settlements.

After 1680, much of the population growth in the Chesapeake came from the forced migration of Africans. Africans and their descendants made up only 7 percent of the Chesapeake colonies' population in 1680. By 1730, they comprised 27 percent of the population, and by 1750 that figure had risen to 40 percent. By 1710, the enslaved population in Virginia and Maryland already was reproducing itself (see Chapter 3), but planters there continued to purchase laborers at staggering rates. Close to thirty-five thousand Africans of diverse ethnic and geographical backgrounds were brought to the Chesapeake between 1700 and 1740, a number roughly equal to the entire combined populations of New York and Pennsylvania in 1700. Nonetheless, by 1750, 80 percent of enslaved Virginians and Marylanders had never seen Africa. This pattern fit the region's overall demographic change. Between 1680 and 1750, even as the Chesapeake colonies received a more diverse group of newcomers, colonial society was being transformed into a society of creoles—people born in the colonies to parents of European or African ancestry.

The Chesapeake also became the chief destination for a new kind of bound labor. In 1717 and 1718, Parliament revised British criminal codes to encourage new forms of punishment as alternatives to execution. Specifically, the Transportation Act of 1718 authorized judges to exile felons to the American colonies. Over the next half-century, close to fifty thousand transported convicts, mostly young British men convicted of minor crimes, crossed the Atlantic. Overwhelmingly, they were sold as indentured servants in Maryland and Virginia, where many planters, anxious to prevent the formation of a black majority, preferred to purchase white convict labor.

AFRICANS AND EUROPEANS IN THE LOWER SOUTH

In the Lower South, planters' demand for slave labor created a black majority from the early decades of settlement. South Carolina attracted relatively few European immigrants before the 1720s, despite colonial officials' attempts to raise the white population by paying bounties to ship captains who brought white male servants. South Carolina restricted these recruitment efforts to white Protestants and barred the purchase of convicted felons. Authorities worried that convicts might incite slave rebellions and that Catholics might betray the colony to nearby Spanish Florida. More generally, South Carolinians were not optimistic about the ability of Europeans to work in the rice fields. The slave population, by contrast, continued to grow. South Carolina imported as many enslaved Africans between 1700 and 1740 as the two larger Chesapeake colonies combined. Slave imports dropped briefly after the Stono Rebellion (see Chapter 3), and the recruitment of European immigrants picked up slightly around midcentury. Still, whites remained in the minority in South Carolina throughout the colonial era.

The situation in the two British colonies that bordered South Carolina was quite different. North Carolina, which had broken away to form a separate colony in 1712, did not prove as conducive to rice cultivation. Parts of the colony's northeastern section belonged to the Chesapeake region, and farmers there grew tobacco. Coastal areas were given over to pine forests and shipping. Slavery flourished in these regions though in much smaller units than in South Carolina. To the west, however, in the Piedmont and High Country, North Carolina was a land of small farms where slaveholding was uncommon. This region attracted some of the same types of European immigrants who flocked to Pennsylvania. Many of them, in fact, had arrived first in Philadelphia and then migrated south after 1740. Benjamin Franklin later complained that Pennsylvania had lost ten thousand families to North Carolina. Scots-Irish newcomers led this migration, followed by Germans.

INTERPRETING THE SOURCES

Benjamin Franklin on the Population of British America

Born in New England in 1706, Benjamin Franklin ran away to Philadelphia at the age of seventeen and spent much of his adult life there. From his vantage point in the major port of Pennsylvania at midcentury, Franklin offered thoughts about the significance of immigration and population growth in America. In "Observations Concerning the Increase of Mankind, Peopling of Countries, etc." (1755), Franklin noted the relationship between cheap land and expensive labor in America in order to argue that Great Britain should not do "too much to restrain Manufactures in her Colonies" because the colonies would never compete with the mother country in trades that depend on labor. Franklin touted the growing colonial population as a boundless market for British goods and predicted that within a century "the greatest number of Englishmen will be on this Side of the Water."

He worried, however, about the large numbers of non-English settlers that had come to the Middle Colonies. "Why should Pennsylvania, founded by the English, become a Colony of Aliens, who will shortly be so numerous as to Germanize us instead of our Anglifying them, and will never adopt our Language, or Customs, any more than they can acquire our Complexion." Having broached the subject of skin color, Franklin then shared some ideas that might surprise modern American readers.

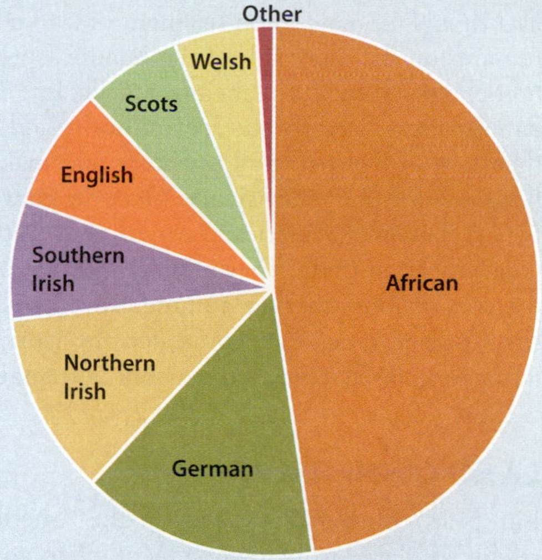

FIGURE 4.1 Immigration to British Mainland North America, 1700–1775. **Question for Analysis:** How might the fact that such a small percentage of immigrants in this period were from England have changed the character of colonial society?
Source: Based on Aaron Fogleman, "Migration to the Thirteen British North American Colonies." *Journal of Interdisciplinary History*, Vol. 22, No. 4. (Spring, 1992), pp. 691–709.

[T]he Number of purely white People in the World is proportionably very small. All *Africa* is black or tawny. *Asia* chiefly tawny. *America* (exclusive of the new Comers) wholly so. And in *Europe*, the *Spaniards, Italians, French, Russians* and *Swedes*, are generally of what we call a swarthy Complexion; as are the Germans also, the *Saxons* only excepted, who with the English make the principal Body of White People on the Face of the Earth. I could wish their Numbers were increased. And while we are, as I may call it, *Scouring* our Planet, by clearing *America* of Woods, and so making this Side of our Globe reflect a brighter Light to the Eyes of Inhabitants in Mars or Venus, why should we in the Sight of Superior Beings, darken its People? why increase the Sons of *Africa*, by Planting them in *America*, where we have so fair an Opportunity, by excluding all Blacks and Tawneys, of increasing the lovely White and Red? But perhaps I am partial to the Complexion of my Country, for such Kind of Partiality is natural to Mankind.

Explore the Source

1. How does Franklin divide humanity by skin color? How many color groupings does he cite? Is skin color a racial classification for Franklin?
2. Why might Franklin have regarded Swedes and Germans as nonwhite?
3. What is Franklin's attitude toward Native Americans, whom he refers to as "Red"?
4. The earlier section of the essay contains other arguments against importing slaves (Franklin would later become a vocal opponent of slavery), but focusing just on this excerpt, what reason does Franklin give for not "planting" the "Sons of Africa" in America?
5. In the last sentence, is Franklin distancing himself from the intolerance of his remarks? Explain.

Farther south, Georgia was created in 1732 as a haven for poor Britons and persecuted European Protestants. Founding leader James Oglethorpe prohibited slavery and limited land ownership and property inheritance in order to preserve the colony as a society of hardworking men who would defend the British Empire against invasion from the south. In its first two decades, Georgia welcomed just over two thousand overseas migrants, including debtors and convicts from England and small farmers from Austria and the Scottish Highlands. But wealthier settlers and migrating slaveholders from South Carolina rebelled against the founders' plans, lobbied Parliament, and forced the colony's trustees to legalize slavery (see Chapter 3) and to cede control of Georgia to the Crown in 1752. Georgia's population at the time was barely over two thousand. Subsequent migration would come mainly from other American colonies and from Africa.

A FARMING SOCIETY IN A COMMERCIAL EMPIRE

Although they hailed from multiple places in Europe and spoke in different languages, dialects, and accents, most immigrants who came voluntarily to North America in the century after the English Restoration shared a common goal. They expected to acquire farmland. By and large, those expectations were fulfilled. Rates of landownership in the colonies were high compared to Europe, though they varied by region and declined over time. Free male colonists, many of whom had been landless peasants on the other side of the Atlantic, spread out with their households from the seaboard and became farmers. Farming families were ruled by paternal authority and sought to sustain themselves by growing all the crops and making all the goods necessary for their subsistence. Over the course of the colonial period, however, American farmers produced more and more goods for local trade. They also became increasingly attuned to patterns of long-distance commerce, centered in a handful of small coastal cities that connected the world of independent farms to a closely regulated network of transatlantic exchange.

LAND OWNERSHIP

European colonists saw land on the American continent as readily available to be owned. More than any other consideration, this is what induced them to uproot their lives and bear the expenses and risks of a transatlantic journey. Land seemed available from a European perspective primarily because the eastern part of North America was much more sparsely inhabited than the northwestern part of Europe, particularly after diseases ravaged America's indigenous population. But land availability was not simply a function of population density. Colonial laws, customs, and practices also made land easier to own than was the case either in Indian country or in Europe.

Traditionally, Native Americans did not regard land as something that could be possessed outright—much as Europeans did not believe that private individuals could buy or sell oceans and rivers. In most native peoples' view, individuals or groups could exchange specific use rights to a piece of land, say for farming, grazing, or hunting, but these ownership claims did not last indefinitely and did not necessarily exclude other users or cover all land uses. From a very different cultural perspective and in very different ways, European societies also traditionally restricted the ability of individuals to own land. In much of Western Europe in the seventeenth century, landowners could not simply sell, give, or bequeath land at will, the way they could with food, animals, houses, and other movable goods. Laws of entail (under which land could be passed on only to children) and primogeniture (under which an entire plot of land had to be passed, undivided, to an eldest son) were designed to keep land within a family's estate. In addition, land in Europe often came with long-standing obligations to feudal lords.

To encourage immigration, Britain's colonial charters stripped away many of these restrictions. Outside New England, colonists had to pay **quitrents,** small perpetual taxes either to the proprietor or directly to the Crown, though these rents proved difficult to collect and often went unpaid. In parts of Maryland and New York, large landowners tried to establish a feudal manor system, under which small farmers and tenants worked on their estates, but because land became so easy to acquire in colonial America as a whole, this system did not thrive. For the most part, American colonists owned land as a **freehold,** which meant that it was viewed as the permanent and exclusive property of an individual (a freeholder) who was free to sell, trade, or give it to others. Consciously departing from older European views of land, and dismissive of the rather different views of Indians, colonists turned land into private property.

By the end of the seventeenth century, land ownership was the norm. Except for those who were legally bound to work as slaves or servants on others' farms, most colonists could afford to acquire their own land. The overwhelming majority of free men owned the land they farmed, either by having purchased a freehold or by simply squatting on (occupying) it. Renting farmland was uncommon between 1660 and 1700, though it existed in pockets of Massachusetts (around Springfield and Salem), Maryland (in Charles County), and New York (in Long Island and the Hudson Valley). These conditions had powerful and paradoxical consequences. Cheap land drew immigrants from Europe while emboldening native-born colonists to marry earlier and thereby produce more children. Both of those trends stimulated population growth, which pushed land prices higher. The higher prices concentrated land in the hands of large landlords and investors rather than freeholders. The ease with which colonists became freeholders in the seventeenth century threatened to undermine that way of life in the eighteenth century.

Older settlements in New England and New York were the first to experience these pressures, but a similar process took place in other colonies as well. During the first half of the eighteenth century, average farm size decreased, while land tenancy became more common. At the same time, though, colonists pushed deeper into Indian country for cheap farmland. Colonial governments encouraged them, offering land grants or tax relief to Protestants who would settle the backcountry and provide a buffer zone between British colonies and their French, Spanish, and Indian neighbors. The westward drift of settlement offset some of the effects of overcrowding and land inflation, and as late as 1750, about two-thirds of free men in all of Britain's mainland colonies owned land. No European society at the time came close to that rate of land ownership. This was the key fact that shaped social and economic life for white settlers in this period.

FARM HOUSEHOLDS: GENDER ROLES AND DAILY LIFE

The crucial building block of colonial society was the farm household, which formed around a male **patriarch.** The typical patriarch inherited or acquired arable land (suitable for growing crops), built a house, and commanded the labor of a wife, his unmarried offspring, and various other dependents, who might include indentured servants, slaves, and wage laborers. In places like the Chesapeake, where people married later and died younger, households often incorporated a complex extended family of children, siblings, and widowed adults from multiple marriages. The core of the household, however, was a relationship between the patriarch and the woman, children, and other laborers who were legally subordinate to him.

Women in the Farm Economy. Colonial women used a spinning wheel, a device introduced many centuries earlier in India, to make yarn for fabric.

Patriarchal relations had long roots in European society, and colonial beliefs about the authority of fathers and husbands drew support from ancient Scripture, but New World conditions gave added force to the patriarchy. Farms in America were larger, more dispersed, and more autonomous than in Europe, and fathers ruled their own landholdings. Unconstrained by rules of entail, the patriarch had greater power to dispose of his property to his sons as he saw fit. Though primogeniture remained common in America in this period, laws in New England and several other colonies allowed fathers to divide up property among several sons if they chose. Colonial patriarchs rarely bestowed real property (land) upon daughters or other female kin, however. Even widows were unlikely to gain control of family resources and might be relegated to back rooms in houses owned by their sons. Land remained under the control of men.

Wives were subordinate to their husbands in the colonies and were expected to obey them, much as servants obeyed masters and children obeyed parents. Whereas men secured their independence through marriage and landowning, women became legally dependent as soon as they wed. A married woman could not make a contract, take someone to court, or possess property in her own right. Husbands were expected to love their wives and treat them kindly, and as one 1726 book put it, the marital relation was "nearest to Equality," as unequal relationships went. Being unable to own land, however, put farm wives in a precarious position.

Still, women played important roles in the farm economy. Both women and men engaged in productive manual labor, though their tasks were generally separated. Men's work typically took place outdoors and focused on such activities as clearing, planting, weeding, harvesting, and herding. While their husbands, sons, servants, and slaves worked in the fields, farm women ran the dairy and egg operations, raised poultry, and tended food gardens. Soap and candle manufacturing were also women's work, as were spinning yarn or thread and sewing garments. Weaving was a male domain in the seventeenth century, and in some places (especially in the Middle Colonies) it remained so through the colonial era, but in New England a decisive shift took place. By 1750, the typical New England farm had a loom operated by a woman.

Women also took charge of food preparation, which by the eighteenth century had become a more complex task on all but the poorest farms. After 1700, farm wives generally used more varied ingredients and cooked a range of different dishes to be eaten with forks and knives, not just spoons (see Hot Commodities: Forks). Farm women also spent large portions of their lives bearing and raising children. Since women in the colonies married young (much younger than in Europe) and did not practice effective contraception, the typical farm wife spent two decades of her life giving birth every 2–2.5 years. Nonetheless, colonial culture did not treat mothering as a separate realm cut off from the rest of farm labor. Childrearing was part and parcel of a woman's contributions to household production.

THE AGRICULTURAL ECONOMY: YEOMAN FARMERS AND THE SPREAD OF COMMERCE

Typical farm households in colonial America in 1700 grew most of the food they ate, sewed most of the clothes they wore, and manufactured the light household goods they used. Colonists aspired to the kind of self-sufficiency that has long been associated with the ideal—and the mythology—of the independent **yeoman farmer** or freeholder. Notwithstanding this ideal, rural Americans also engaged in various forms of trade. Most farmers bartered surplus produce with neighbors for particular goods that they might not own, such as guns and iron farming tools, or for specialized services that they might not be able to provide, such as midwifery and religious instruction. But some farmers also sold their crops for cash, which they accumulated in order to purchase farmland and livestock for their

How Much Is That?

Cattle

Pigs were the leading meat source in colonial America, but cows were even more prized. In addition to their value for beef and dairy products, cattle provided essential labor that fueled the farm economy. Between 1730 and 1750 a yoke of oxen in Connecticut cost between seven and eight British pounds, which is roughly equivalent to $1400-$1500 in today's currency.

HOT COMMODITIES

Forks

John Winthrop, the first governor of the Massachusetts Bay colony, owned a fork. This special utensil, which survives today, distinguished Winthrop from the mass of American colonists in the seventeenth century. A 1630 guide to what prospective colonists needed to bring to New England included a long list of household utensils: "1 iron pot; 1 kettle; 1 frying pan; 1 gridiron; 2 skillets, 1 spit; wooden platters; dishes; spoons trenchers." But no forks.

The fork was introduced by the Venetians around the sixteenth century (though it might have originated earlier, in Byzantium) and spread through the Italian peninsula among people who ate pasta. Forks did not become common in northern Europe until at least the seventeenth century, however, and they were adopted even later in the colonies. Forks do not appear in colonists' estate inventories before 1700, nor do they surface in archaeological digs from the seventeenth century. Well into the eighteenth century, forks were rare luxury goods in North America.

The absence of this simple kitchen implement suggests a very different world of food consumption. Colonists did not typically own any utensil to spear solid food and bring it to their mouths. Some owned knives, but unlike the older English knives that had pointed ends, colonists used newer-style English knives with round blades. Instead, food was eaten with fingers or with spoons. Seventeenth-century cuisine generally suited this arrangement, featuring stews, porridges, and mush that could be consumed out of bowls without cutting or spearing.

During the eighteenth century, colonial eating habits changed. For middling and wealthier farm families, separate dishes of meat, potatoes, and vegetables became more common. They were eaten on plates and tables with forks and knives rather than bowls and laps with spoons and fingers. The proliferation of plates, knives, and forks, mostly imported from Europe, made new food styles possible. But the rising demand for new utensils also reflected new tastes and desires—both for imported food commodities from Asia and the Americas and for the refined habits of bodily control associated with European elites. The fork, the rarest of those utensils in the beginning of the eighteenth century, soon became a required item in the kitchen of respectable farm households.

Think About It

1. Why might the fork have been adopted later than the spoon and the knife in both Europe and the American colonies?
2. Why was the fork a badge of respectability and refinement in the eighteenth century?

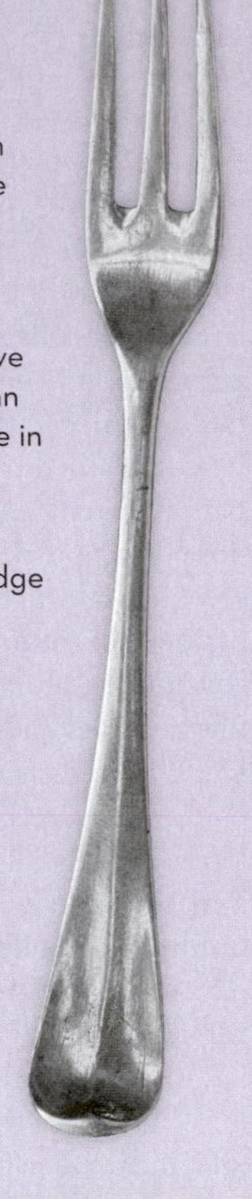

American Silver Fork, ca. 1740s. This simple utensil, which entered colonial America as a luxury item, became the centerpiece of a new relationship to food among most British colonists.

offspring (see How Much Is That?). In addition, colonists increasingly used cash to buy manufactured items that were imported from England under the protection of the Navigation Acts. After 1700, rural Americans began consuming a large volume of foreign-made goods, especially window glass, earthenware, and clothing—most of which they paid for by selling farm produce at local markets. Yet even as they participated in commercial transactions, the majority of American farmers in the colonial period devoted the bulk of their labor and attention to their own families' subsistence before worrying about the demands of distant customers.

Throughout the British colonies, however, market considerations shaped farmers' lives. In the southeastern part of the continent, farmers cultivated tobacco and rice for world markets and were acutely aware of fluctuations in the prices of those commodities. Farming on slave plantations in the South was essentially a commercial enterprise supported by long-distance trade in staple crops and human labor. Farther north and farther inland, farm households grew a more diverse range of crops and sold most of their surplus within their respective colonies. By 1750, many farmers in the Middle Colonies and the northern Chesapeake had begun to grow wheat for markets in Europe and New England. As

Woman's Linen Chemise, ca. 1700. Imported linen clothing became common in America during the first half of the eighteenth century, in part because of rising standards of personal hygiene, which demanded garments that could be washed frequently.

they did so, their livelihoods became more dependent on political and economic developments in far-flung lands, even as they continued to see themselves as independent freeholders.

The other way in which farm households got drawn into the world of market relations was through the land itself. Paradoxically, the fact that land was broadly available for purchase—the very thing that enabled so many immigrant families and their descendants to become economically self-supporting—also turned land into a commodity with fluctuating values. **Land speculation** (buying land to rent it out, resell it, or control its resale value) became common by the eighteenth century. In some colonies, land speculators amassed great estates. New York was an extreme case: Ten or eleven people owned about 75 percent of the land in New York in 1700. But throughout Britain's American colonies, the rising value of land encouraged private individuals to acquire more acreage than a single farm family could till.

RANKS AND "SORTS"

Despite the rise in speculation, cheap land and subsistence farming helped create more egalitarian economic and social conditions for white colonists compared to the places from which they had immigrated. Yet in a society of widespread landholding and no titled nobility, class differences still ran deep. At one extreme stood a small number of aristocrats, such as the proprietary families who governed most of the colonies in the seventeenth century; some fabulously wealthy rice planters in South Carolina; and the lords of manorial estates in New York's Hudson Valley. At the other extreme stood a more substantial number of impoverished men and women who owned little or nothing, including landless tenants, wage laborers, and the growing population of enslaved African Americans. Most colonial farm families, however, lived far from these extremes. In typical settings, actual differences in wealth were less severe, but social hierarchy still prevailed. Colonists drew surprisingly sharp distinctions between **gentry** (people of social refinement and economic privilege) and commoners, even when members of both groups owned sizable farm plots in the same vicinity.

Indeed, European immigrants brought with them longstanding beliefs about class. Those beliefs persisted in North America, despite the mobility and fluidity of colonial society and despite a more even distribution of private property. Colonists perceived differences between farm families of the "better sort" and those of the "meaner sort" (they spoke also of a "middling sort") that were not merely about net worth; people of different ranks, sorts, and degrees inherited a social status that suffused their personality and determined their prospects. Men and women of the highest rank traditionally identified themselves by their distinctive clothing, conduct, and conversation, all of which echoed some of the refinement of European court society. In the crude farming settlements of the early North American colonies, such an identity might have been harder to establish. Even so, around 1700, more rural Americans aspired to genteel status and began investing the profits they made from agricultural surplus and rising land values in a quest to live as gentry.

In the first half of the eighteenth century, several material markers of refinement came to define a growing genteel class in rural America. The gentry wore fine linen shirts and gold belt buckles, served food on porcelain plates, outfitted their homes with maple desks, and drank wine imported from Madeira. By far the most conspicuous signs of class difference in farming communities, however, were mansion houses (see Spaces and Places: Nomini Hall and Carter's Grove). Hundreds of mansions were built in every colony during the eighteenth century, not only in port cities but also on plantations and in villages and small towns. These elegant, two-story brick houses stood in stark contrast to the smaller, simpler homes that wealthier colonists had built a century earlier.

Colonial Mansions. The homes of eighteenth-century colonists differed markedly from the simple residential structures that came before. Homes built in the seventeenth century, even among the elite, were all torn down or modified in later years to accommodate new styles of gentility. But many brick mansions from the eighteenth century, such as the Ridgely house (left) at Eden Hill in Delaware (1749) and the MacPheadris-Warner house (right) in Portsmouth, New Hampshire (1716), survive to this day.

Murals Featuring Mohawk Indians. These scenes grace an interior stairwell of the MacPheadris-Warner house in Portsmouth, New Hampshire.

They stood out even more dramatically against the one-room, unpainted wooden houses of most of the surrounding population.

By later standards, colonial America was ordered rigidly. Even in New England, which had few servants or slaves and no massive estates, churchgoers sat in order of social prominence and entering freshmen at Harvard College were ranked systematically according to their families' position. Throughout the colonies, an entrenched culture of deference (respect) to social superiors helped upper-class families dominate local governments and colonial legislatures. Deference had its limits, though, and colonists of lower rank frequently resisted the social claims of aspiring elites. Especially in the Middle Colonies, ethnic and cultural diversity made it less likely that all the farmers in a region would define social hierarchy the same way or agree on who occupied which position. But the colonies did not dissolve Old World ideas about the social order—and by the eighteenth century, as economic inequality increased, colonial life was becoming more rather than less hierarchical.

URBAN CENTERS AND CITY PEOPLE

Economic stratification was far more pronounced in colonial cities, where prosperous merchants, artisans, wage workers, servants, and slaves lived in proximity to one another. Cities held less than a tenth of the colonial population during this

Philadelphia's Grid Plan. Philadelphia was distinguished by its network of straight streets intersecting at right angles. By 1700, geometrical order became a dominant strategy of colonial town planning south of New England. **Question for Analysis:** How does this town plan compare with that of the Spanish pueblos (see Chapter 2)?

SPACES & PLACES

Nomini Hall and Carter's Grove: Elite Homes in the Chesapeake

Drawing of the Original Georgian-Style, Three-Story Brick Home at Nomini Hall Plantation, Virginia. The original house burned down and was rebuilt in 1850.

Terraced Gardens in Carter's Grove, Virginia. Elegant, manicured outdoor spaces became part of the ideal of genteel refinement for the wealthiest American colonists.

Cheaper land made it possible for a high proportion of colonial households to attain a measure of economic independence. But it also enabled a few very wealthy families to accumulate great wealth and distinguish themselves as local aristocrats in the New World. By around 1725, these wealthy families were asserting their place in American society by building fancy mansions that conformed to the latest fashions in European architecture and landscape design.

Although mansions sprouted up in every colony during the early eighteenth century, many of the grandest colonial homes belonged to southern slaveholders. Robert "King" Carter, whose father had immigrated to Virginia in 1649, owned more land and more slaves than any other English colonist during the second quarter of the eighteenth century. In 1729, the younger Carter built a stately, three-story home in the Georgian style on his Nomini Hall Plantation and began planting elegant gardens. Though the mansion burned down in the nineteenth century, we can still glimpse some of the Carter family's grand aspirations in the restored home and terraced gardens that survive in nearby Carter's Grove, the plantation home of Robert Carter's grandson, Carter Burwell. The main house, built between 1750 and 1755, showcased elegant interiors and fancy brickwork that set the Carters apart from their neighbors and helped support the family's claim to political power in the colony. Even more than books, educational polite conversation, fancy balls, and the other signs of refinement that the Carters cultivated, their mansions in the Virginia countryside stood as monuments to the proposition that British America was a rank-ordered society.

From the perspective of the men and women enslaved by the Carter family, however, the class difference *within* these estates was probably more glaring. Some of them labored on other plantations elsewhere in the colony, rarely visiting the slaveholder's manorial estate. Others lived on site in slave quarters, located in separate buildings on the same property. Archaeologists working in the 1970s discovered the location of the Carter's Grove slave quarters, which were subsequently reconstructed by the Colonial Williamsburg Foundation, and the structures confirm a more general picture of grim living conditions within earshot of the stately Burwell mansion. The luxurious meals served in the main house at Nomini Hall contrasted with the weekly portions of a peck of corn and pound of meat allotted to slaves. And while the Carters hired learned tutors to endow their children with the trappings of gentility, the enslaved were consigned to the cruel treatment of overseers. Architecture reinforced this social hierarchy. Wealthier colonists built houses that segregated private and public spaces and assigned distinctive social functions to specific rooms. But enslaved African Americans (like poorer whites) lived in simple one-room cabins or in partitioned multiroom structures that housed several families in each room. When the slaves at Nomini Hall wished to hold social events, they left their quarters and took over the plantation stables.

Thomas Hudson Portrait of Robert Carter III of Nomini Hall. Commissioned in 1753 during the wealthy, slaveholding Virginian's visit to London, the painting depicts Carter dressed for a masquerade ball.

Think About It

1. Why did Robert "King" Carter invest his tobacco profits in building expensive and conspicuous homes in Virginia rather than living among other elite Englishmen in London?
2. What distinguishes the Nomini Hall home from more modern mansion styles?
3. How might the proliferation of mansion houses have reinforced beliefs about social inequality in a society where landowning was common?

period, but many rural Americans felt their impact. Immigrants, both slave and free, typically landed in bustling ports before settling on farms in the hinterland. Each colony's legislature and governing council met in an urban location. And cities organized the Atlantic trade that shaped life in this farming society. Urban merchants shipped the staple crops grown on rural plantations to foreign markets, and they imported manufactured goods, newspapers, and other scarce commodities. These imports eventually made their way to stores and market stalls in the farm towns and villages where most colonists lived.

Five substantial commercial cities emerged in Britain's mainland colonies before 1750: Boston, Newport (Rhode Island), New York, Philadelphia, and Charleston (South Carolina). They were stretched out along the Atlantic coast, linking their respective hinterlands to a trade centered in and dominated by London. The five principal colonial cities were all small—in 1700 they ranged from about two thousand to about seven thousand in population—and performed many of the same economic functions, but they differed in some important respects. Boston, the oldest of the group (founded in 1630) and the largest town in British North America during this era, most resembled older European port towns. Boston's privately designed streets intersected at irregular angles and in haphazard patterns that gave it the congested appearance and feel of a medieval city. Philadelphia, by contrast, was created in 1682 on a formal grid plan. Newport and New York were closer to Boston, both in the time of their founding and in the layout of their streets, whereas Charleston (Charles Town at the time), with its straight streets, more closely resembled Philadelphia. In other respects, Charleston fit the model of colonial capitals in the British West Indies, busy port cities where enslaved Africans arrived and the staple crops they harvested on local plantations departed. Philadelphia and New York were also entry points for new arrivals, but mostly for voluntary immigrants rather than slaves.

Thousands of colonists made their homes in a number of second-tier cities that grew in the first half of the eighteenth century. Some, such as Williamsburg (Virginia), New Bern (North Carolina), Burlington (New Jersey), and Hartford (Connecticut), were seats of colonial government with large public squares. Others, such as Salem (Massachusetts), Alexandria (Virginia), and Wilmington (North Carolina), were market towns dominated by trade activity. What all of those places had in common was a location on or near the eastern seaboard. Imagined from the inland farming settlements that made up the bulk of the colonies, urban society was a distant reality—a barely visible bridge to the Old World.

ENLIGHTENMENT AND AWAKENING

The colonies' growing and proliferating coastal cities were the conduits not only for trade and immigration but also for the arrival of new ideas and cultural influences from Europe. During the first half of the eighteenth century, urban printers and urban social gatherings helped spread the latest philosophical and theological developments from across the Atlantic. Two quite different but related intellectual movements would exert a powerful influence over colonial culture. One promoted a rational critique of received traditions; the other preached personal reengagement with religion.

TAVERNS, NEWSPAPERS, AND INTELLECTUAL LIFE

Despite their modest size, colonial cities and towns were places of intellectual exchange and ferment. People, goods, and rumors from multiple contents circulated in the streets of these compact port towns. Taverns were especially important sites of information sharing in eighteenth-century urban life. Distinguished from alehouses, which catered to poorer customers and sold beer to go as well as on the premises, the eighteenth-century tavern was a more genteel institution, where middling and elite urbanites might drink wine and engage in polite discussion of commerce and politics. In New York, committees of the legislature even held their meetings in a tavern.

Licensed taverns multiplied and expanded in the middle of the century in the major cities. The fanciest of them were housed in elegant converted mansions located near the busy town docks. Called "public houses" (the origin of the term *pub*), taverns were an urban amenity that made colonial cities feel more like their European counterparts. But in some colonies, they also became centers of political dissent, where the authority of governors and ministers did not necessarily dominate.

Printers also set up shop in cities and began producing the first colonial newspapers. Before 1700, governors and royal officials had prohibited the publication of news in the colonies, out of fear that the circulation of timely political information in print would lead to disorder and undermine the authority of the Crown. But in the years after the Glorious Revolution, Britain grew more confident in the political stability of its colonial system, and the need to promote commerce seemed to justify the small risks that newspapers might foment rebellion. The *Boston News-Letter*, generally considered the first real newspaper in England's colonies, began publication in 1704. Over the next few decades, similar weekly papers were introduced in New York, Philadelphia, Newport, Charleston, Williamsburg, and the Caribbean port cities of Bridgetown (Barbados) and Kingston (Jamaica).

Colonial newspapers did not provide much local news, which was less urgent in cities with only a couple thousand permanent residents, where information traveled quickly by word of mouth. Instead, the papers focused on reports from abroad, especially stories that would be of interest to their merchant readers. Commodity prices, ship arrivals, and developments in European politics and diplomacy dominated the news of the week. Urban newspaper subscribers were eager for reliable information about the British cities with which they traded, especially London, which remained for many colonial merchants the center of their world. Newspapers also included useful advertisements for local commerce, notices of runaway slaves and servants, and entertaining stories reprinted from the English press.

But newspapers also provided printers and their patrons a forum for influencing public opinion on local politics. For this reason, public officials strictly monitored newspapers in the early eighteenth century. In Massachusetts, newspapers were required to secure licenses, and the earliest Boston papers cleared each issue with the governor prior to publication. Benjamin Franklin's older brother James, publisher of the *New England Courant,* tried to operate without a license in the 1720s, but once his paper criticized the colonial authorities, he landed in jail. Banned from the business, Franklin evaded authorities temporarily by listing his younger brother on the masthead as the *Courant*'s publisher. In 1733, a Palatine German immigrant named John Peter Zenger began printing the *New York Weekly Journal,* the first political party newspaper in North America. Zenger printed political essays, mostly written or selected by the leader of a powerful faction hostile to New York's governor. Even some of the advertisements seemed to be satirizing the governor, who had Zenger arrested for the crime of publishing seditious libel.

When the Zenger case came to trial in 1735, his defense lawyer argued both that true statements should not be punished as libelous and that juries were entitled to judge the proper application of a law (rather than simply determining what the facts were in a particular case). Neither position had much support in English law, and the judge explicitly rejected both arguments. Nonetheless the jury acquitted Zenger. Although this famous case was probably not very influential in the history of American libel law, it was celebrated at the time, and continues to be remembered, as a sign of growing popular support for the value of free expression and for the idea that a newspaper could be used to criticize the government.

ENLIGHTENMENT CULTURE

The rising confidence of urban publishers in their right to attack the regime in print was part of a larger set of developments in European thought known as the **Enlightenment.** Over the course of the eighteenth century, French, British, and German philosophers touted scientific experimentation, rational order, and individual reason as the proper way to understand both the natural world and civil society. Enlightenment ideas, which spread to North America during this period, challenged the authority of received tradition and emboldened intellectuals in the colonies to seek new truths through systematic inquiry and public debate. The illustrious career of Benjamin Franklin captured many of the themes and patterns in the American Enlightenment. Franklin was a self-educated urbanite (he moved from Boston to Philadelphia in 1723) who made scientific discoveries, engaged in philosophical speculation, published newspapers, founded libraries and intellectual clubs, ran the post office, and believed fervently in the power of writing and printing to spread the truth.

The Enlightenment directly undermined a number of reigning religious values in colonial life. Influential philosophical texts by early Enlightenment authors such as John Locke, Voltaire, and Jean-Jacques Rousseau encouraged readers, in different ways, to be skeptical of the authority of the clergy, to demand that religion appeal to reason rather than faith, and to look to scientific laws and observations of

N. C. Numb. 1.

The Boſton News-Letter.

Publiſhed by Authority.

From Monday April 17. to Monday April 24. 1704.

London Flying-Poſt from *Decemb.* 2d. to 4th 1703.

LEtters from *Scotland* bring us the Copy of a Sheet lately Printed there, Intituled, *A ſeaſonable Alarm for* Scotland. *In a Letter from a Gentleman in the City, to his Friend in the Country, concerning the preſent Danger of the Kingdom and of the Proteſtant Religion.*

This Letter takes Notice, That Papiſts ſwarm in that Nation, that they traffick more avowedly than formerly, & that of late many Scores of Prieſts and Jeſuites are come thither from *France,* and gone to the North, to the Highlands & other places of the Country. That the Miniſters of the Highlands and North gave in large Liſts of them to the Committee of the General Aſſembly, to be laid before the Privy-Council.

It likewiſe obſerves, that a great Number of other ill-affected perſons are come over from *France,* under pretence of accepting her Majeſty's Gracious Indemnity; but, in reality, to increaſe Diviſions in the Nation, and to entertain a Correſpondence with *France:* That their ill Intentions are evident from their talking big, their owning the Intereſt of the pretended King *James* VIII. their ſecret Cabals, and their buying up of Arms and Ammunition, wherever they can find them.

To this he adds the late Writings and Actings of ſome diſaffected perſons, many of whom are for that Pretender, that ſeveral of them have declar'd they had rather embrace Popery than conform to the preſent Government; that they refuſe to pray for the Queen, but uſe the ambiguous word Soveraign, and ſome of them pray in expreſs Words for the King and Royal Family; and the charitable and generous Prince who has ſhew'd them ſo much Kindneſs. He likewiſe takes notice of Letters not long ago found in Cypher, and directed to a Perſon lately come thither from St. *Germains.*

He ſays that the greateſt Jacobites, who will not qualifie themſelves by taking the Oaths to Her Majeſty, do now with the Papiſts and their Companions from St. *Germains* ſet up for the Liberty of the Subject, contrary to their own Principles, but meerly to keep up a Diviſion in the Nation. He adds, that they aggravate thoſe things which the People complain of, as to *England's* refuſing to allow them a freedom of Trade, *&c.* and do all they can to foment Diviſions betwixt the Nations, and to obſtruct a Redreſs of thoſe things complain'd of.

The Jacobites, he ſays, do all they can to perſwade the Nation that their pretended King is a Proteſtant in his Heart, tho' he dares not declare it while under the Power of *France;* that he is acquainted with the Miſtakes of his Father's Government, will govern us more according to Law, and endear himſelf to his Subjects.

They magnifie the Strength of their own Party, and the Weakneſs and Diviſions of the other, in order to facilitate and haſten their Undertaking; they argue themſelves out of their Fears, and into the higheſt aſſurance of accompliſhing their purpoſe.

From all this he infers, That they have [illegible] Aſſiſtance from *France,* otherwiſe they would never be ſo impudent; and he gives Reaſons for his Apprehenſions that the *French* King may ſend Troops thither this Winter, 1. Becauſe the *Engliſh & Dutch* will not then be at Sea to oppoſe them. 2. He can then beſt ſpare them, the Seaſon of Action beyond Sea being over. 3. The Expectation given him of a conſiderable number to joyn them, may incourage him to the undertaking with fewer Men [illegible] but ſend over a ſufficient number of Of[illegible] with Arms and Ammunition.

He endeavours in the reſt of his Letter to anſwer the fooliſh Pretences of the Pretender [illegible] Proteſtant, and that he will govern us according [illegible] Law. He ſays, that being bred up in the Religion and Politicks of *France,* he is by Education [illegible] ſtated Enemy to our Liberty and Relig[illegible] the Obligations which he and his Fam[illegible] the *French* King, muſt neceſſarily make [illegible] wholly at his Devotion, and to follow hi[illegible] that if he ſit upon the Throne; the thre[illegible] muſt be oblig'd to pay the Debt which h[illegible] *French* King for the Education of himſe[illegible] Entertaining his ſuppoſed Father and [illegible] And ſince the King muſt reſtore him by [illegible] if ever he be reſtored, he will ſee [illegible] his own Debt before thoſe Troops lea[illegible] The Pretender being a good Proficient in [illegible] and *Romiſh* Schools, he will never [illegible] ſufficiently aveng'd, but by the utter Ro[illegible] Proteſtant Subjects, both as Hereticks and [illegible] The late Queen, his pretended Moth[illegible] cold Blood when ſhe was *Queen* of *Britain* [illegible] to turn the Weſt of *Scotland* into a hu[illegible] will be then for doing ſo by the greateſt [illegible] Nation; and, no doubt, is at Pains to ha[illegible] tended Son educated to her own Mini[illegible] he ſays, it were a great Madneſs in th[illegible] take a Prince bred up in the horrid Scho[illegible] titude, Perſecution and Cruelty, and [illegible] Rage and Envy. The *Jacobites,* he ſa[illegible] *Scotland* and at St. *Germains,* are imp[illegible] their preſent Straits, and knowing th[illegible] ſtances cannot be much worſe than [illegible] preſent, are the more inclinable to the [illegible] He adds, That the *French* King knows [illegible] be a more effectual way for himſelf t[illegible] Univerſal Monarchy, and to ruine th[illegible] Intereſt, than by ſetting up the Pretend[illegible] Throne of Great *Britain,* he will in all [illegible] attempt it; and tho' he ſhould be per[illegible] the Deſign would miſcarry in the cloſe, [illegible] not but reap ſome Advantage by im[illegible] three Nations.

From all this the Author concludes [illegible] Intereſt of the Nation, to provide for S[illegible] and ſays, that as many have already [illegible] Alarm, and are furniſhing themſelves [illegible] and Ammunition, he hopes the Gove[illegible] not only allow it, but encourage it [illegible] on ought all to app[illegible]

***Boston News-Letter*, the First Newspaper in British North America.** Its editor, James Campbell, was Boston's postmaster, and his paper originated as a series of handwritten reports to the governors of the New England colonies. In 1704, Campbell began printing it for wider circulation, using both sides of a single sheet. **Questions for Analysis:** What principles guide the layout of the newspaper? What is the lead item or dominant story?

Imagined Interior of the Black Horse Tavern. John Peter Zenger's political patrons gathered in this public space to toast the significance of their victory. Drawing from W. Harrison Baykes, "Old Taverns of New York," ca. 1915.

nature rather than to Scripture for evidence of divine will. Locke, who helped draft the original colonial charter of the Carolina colonies, was an especially influential voice in America. His *Two Treatises on Government* (1689), written in the wake of England's Glorious Revolution, argued that political legitimacy comes from the consent of the governed, not from the biblically ordained powers of patriarchs. But the impact of the Enlightenment's critique of religious traditions affected more than just political thought. Many urban colonists like Franklin, as well as many elite Virginia planters, embraced a deist outlook toward religious matters. **Deists** did not believe in a god who intervenes in the world. Instead, they saw God's powers as built into the natural and moral order of the universe He created.

RELIGIOUS REVIVALS

Although some colonists embraced scientific rationality and what they called "reasonable religion," many more were influenced by European pietist movements that pushed in a different direction. **Pietism,** which promoted rigorous religious observance and stressed intense emotional prayer experiences, spread from German-speaking Europe to the Middle Colonies in the early 1700s. It was part of a broader trend toward popularizing and reinvigorating religious traditions through enthusiastic worship, which was emerging on both sides of the Atlantic and in various religious communities both within and beyond Christianity.

The American experience of pietism and revivalism, which historians call the **Great Awakening,** took place in multiple colonies and in different Protestant denominations from the early 1720s through the mid-1740s. In New Jersey and New York, Presbyterian minister Gilbert Tennent led emotional revivals among Scots-Irish immigrants. Farther north, Congregationalist preacher Jonathan Edwards sought to stem the tide of religious skepticism and indifference in New England. Edwards moved audiences with vivid descriptions of hell and with his admonitions that individuals were utterly and precariously dependent on the creator. In his famous 1741 sermon "Sinners in the Hands of an Angry God," Edwards warned his Massachusetts listeners that "the God who holds you over the pit of hell, much as one holds a spider, or some loathsome insect, over the fire, abhors you, and is dreadfully provoked."

The most popular and effective of the revivalist preachers was George Whitefield (pronounced *Whitfield*), an Englishman affiliated with the new Methodist movement. Whitefield toured North America beginning in 1739 and became something of a celebrity, spellbinding colonists up and down the seaboard with his impassioned, extemporaneous oratorical style. Whitefield attracted crowds in Philadelphia and Boston that were as large as the permanent populations of those cities. Those who could not attend Whitefield's sermons could purchase his tracts, which were sold in mass quantities and promoted through volume discounts and subscription rates.

Tennent, Edwards, Whitefield, and other figures associated with the colonial revivals were not formally connected to a single movement. However, they shared a commitment to personal atonement and individual conversion experiences. Contemporaries dubbed them and their followers New Lights, as opposed to the Old Lights who worried about the excessive enthusiasm of the revivals and their tendency to embolden individuals (including women) to step out of their prescribed social position. In some striking respects, the individualism of the Great Awakening resembled that of the Enlightenment. Although one movement preached rational study and the other valued total faith and emotional expression, both enjoined individuals to defy traditional authority and seek the truth for themselves. In that sense, the cause of John Peter Zenger, who published the sermons of Tennent and Whitefield, was aligned with the evangelical culture of the pietists as well as with the more secular values of Benjamin Franklin. Both forces continued to shape the beliefs of American colonists over the course of the eighteenth century.

Portrait of George Whitefield by John Wollaston, ca. 1742. The popular revivalist preacher had a booming voice that could reportedly be heard at a mile's distance.

CONCLUSION

By 1750, well over a million people lived in Britain's mainland North American colonies, a number roughly equivalent to the population of Scotland at the time. American colonists had spread out across a long coast and well into an expanding backcountry. Though the different colonies continued to vary markedly in population density, ethnic makeup, and religious orientation, and though they grew different crops on different kinds of farms and plantations, they were connected in many ways.

After the Restoration of the monarchy in 1660, England had acquired new territories and asserted royal control over a continuous ring of settlement. Since the Glorious Revolution of 1688, that control had focused on commercial exchange. And especially since the establishment of Great Britain in 1707, a diverse migration from Scotland, Ireland, and the German lands had fueled the colonies' growth and settlement and expanded the reach of an Atlantic commercial empire. From the perspective of someone like Benjamin Franklin, who arrived in Philadelphia just a few years before the indentured servant William Moraley, Britain's American colonies seemed both fundamentally different from and intimately connected with England.

STUDY TERMS

- Restoration (p. 82)
- Anglo-Dutch War (p. 83)
- Navigation Acts (p. 83)
- mercantilism (p. 83)
- enumerated articles (p. 83)
- Staple Act (p. 83)
- Middle Colonies (p. 83)
- Quaker migration (p. 85)
- Charter of Privileges (p. 86)
- Dominion of New England (p. 86)
- Glorious Revolution (p. 86)
- Leisler's Rebellion (p. 86)
- Scots-Irish immigrants (p. 88)
- Pennsylvania Dutch (p. 89)
- transported convicts (p. 90)
- quitrent (p. 92)
- freehold (p. 92)
- patriarch (p. 92)
- yeoman farmer (p. 93)
- land speculation (p. 95)
- gentry (p. 95)
- mansion house (p. 95)
- five substantial commercial cities (p. 98)
- tavern (p. 98)
- colonial newspapers (p. 98)
- Zenger case (p. 99)
- Enlightenment (p. 99)
- Deists (p. 99)
- pietism (p. 100)
- Great Awakening (p. 100)
- New Lights (p. 100)

TIMELINE

1660 Stuart Dynasty restored

Navigation Acts establish new commercial regime in English colonies

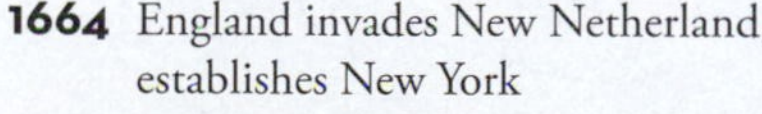

1664 England invades New Netherland, establishes New York

1674 Anglo-Dutch War ends

1675 Quaker migration to North America begins

The Boston News-Letter.

Published by Authority.

1681 Pennsylvania founded

1688 William and Mary assume English throne in Glorious Revolution

1689 Leisler's Rebellion reshapes New York politics

1689 John Locke publishes *Two Treatises on Government*

1704 *Boston News-Letter*, first newspaper in the colonies, begins publication

1707 England and Scotland unite as Great Britain

1717 Scots-Irish migration to North America begins

1732 Georgia established

1735 John Peter Zenger tried for libel

1741 George Whitefield begins preaching tour in North America

FURTHER READING

Additional suggested readings are available on the Online Learning Center at www.mhhe.com/becomingamerica1e.

Bernard Bailyn, *The Peopling of British North America* (1986), sketches broad patterns in eighteenth-century immigration to the American colonies.

Kathleen Brown, *Foul Bodies* (2009), explores changing standards, ideals, and practices of personal hygiene in early America.

Richard Bushman, *The Refinement of America* (1992), follows the spreading cultural ideal of gentility among colonists, expressed in such things as homes, gardens, educational attainments, and personal conduct.

Jon Butler, *Becoming America* (2000), surveys the changes in material, spiritual, and political life that helped form a new American identity in the century before the American Revolution.

David Conroy, *In Public Houses* (1992), illuminates the growing popularity and importance of taverns in the eighteenth century.

James Deetz, *In Small Things Forgotten* (revised ed. 1996), demonstrates how archaeological discoveries illuminate the study of the material life of early America.

Jack Greene, *Pursuits of Happiness* (1988), remains an influential interpretation of the period.

Karen Halttunen, *Murder Most Foul* (1998), studies the changing world views reflected in crime narratives of the colonial era.

David Hancock, *Oceans of Wine* (2009), traces the networks of consumption and culture that formed around the commerce in Madeira wine.

Allan Kulikoff, *From British Peasants to Colonial American Farmers* (2000), emphasizes the importance of land to the expectations and experiences of the British immigrants to North America.

Mark Noll, *The Rise of Evangelicalism* (2003), takes a long view of the role of evangelical preaching in American history.

Mary P. Ryan, *Mysteries of Sex* (2006), includes a survey of changes in gender roles in colonial farm families.

David Shields, *Civil Tongues and Polite Letters in British America* (1997), examines coffeehouses and other urban institutions where ideas and information circulated among colonial elites.

5

INSIDE ▶

THE BIG PICTURE

Britain was one of several imperial players on a continent dominated by Indians during this period. But a major global war reshuffled the American map and created a new frontier between British colonists and Indians of various nations and ethnicities.

Emperor of the Six Nations. This 1710 oil painting by Dutch artist Johannes Verelst depicts Mohawk leader and orator Hendrick Tejonihakarawa (his second name meant "Open the Door"), a major player in diplomatic relations with Great Britain.

1700–1765

EMPIRES, WAR, & THE TRANSFORMATION OF INDIAN COUNTRY

Eliza Pinckney kept in touch with her world by exchanging letters across an ocean. Pinckney, an elite Charleston resident partially responsible for the emergence of indigo as a major export crop in South Carolina, corresponded with friends thousands of miles away in London, which she saw as the center of her universe. Her own location in South Carolina, as she described it in a 1762 letter, was "the Wilds of America" in a "remote Corner of the Globe." By the mid-eighteenth century, many more British colonists, even those less prosperous and privileged than Pinckney, faced east, awaiting news and commodities from the capital of Britain's great empire. From this perspective, the vast and alien interior of the American continent was "the backcountry."

From other vantage points on the continent during the eighteenth century, London was not the hub at all. Although British colonies had expanded significantly since their initial settlement, they were hardly the continent's only powers. Spain and France claimed large swaths of territory and vital political and economic interests in North America, and Spanish and French colonists communicated with different European capitals and approached the North American interior from different directions. Indians controlled most of the continent, and to them London, Paris, and Madrid were remote locales in a land they never expected to see. But over the course of the eighteenth century, the empires commanded from those cities became leading players in the changing politics of North America. Vying with one another and with powerful Indian confederations, they clashed in a series of violent struggles for land, resources, population, and influence.

In contrast to later periods of American history, colonists and Indians did not see themselves as inhabiting two completely separate and antagonistic worlds. The eastern portion of the North American continent was a heterogeneous mosaic of settlements, representing a wide array of ethnic groups, both native and transplanted. Political allegiances in these settlements could be complex, subject to all kinds of local circumstances. But four major powers—Iroquois, French, Spanish, and British—dominated the political geography and organized war and diplomacy during the first half of the eighteenth century.

Of all the societies associated with these powers, Britain's American population was growing the fastest, doubling every twenty-five years during the eighteenth century as it spilled into new settlements. Still, other powers kept the expansion of the British colonies in check, and frequent wars involving alliances of European and native forces preserved a kind of balance among the antagonists. Europe's imperial conflicts provided Indians with a survival map, while imperial growth helped sustain the identities that colonists like Eliza Pinckney used to make sense of their place in the world. Between 1754 and 1763, however, a more decisive war would alter that map forever.

KEY QUESTIONS

- In what significant ways did power and diplomacy in the eastern half of North America shift during this period?
- In what specific ways were British colonists more thoroughly integrated into the British Empire during the eighteenth century?
- How did the French and Indian War fit into the larger, global conflict among European powers?
- Why did 1763 mark a tragic turning point from the perspective of Native Americans east of the Mississippi?

Writing and paper tied European colonists to their growing—and warring—empires.

RIVAL POWERS IN THE EAST

Farmers in Connecticut, artisans in Pennsylvania, and slaveholders in Virginia may have focused primarily on local relationships or on trade patterns that led across the ocean to England, but they were also living in a world shaped by imperial politics. From the perspective of England, Spain, and France, the eastern half of North America was an extension of their empires and another theater in their contest for power. The Iroquois League was the other key player in the political geography of the eastern portion of North America during the first half of the eighteenth century.

THE IROQUOIS LEAGUE AND BRITAIN'S NORTHERN COLONIES

The Haudenosaunee, the five-nation Iroquois League that had used its trading relationships with Dutch and English colonists to achieve military dominance over its enemies during the mid-1600s (see Chapter 2), grew even more powerful as the century wore on. Following the bloody events of 1676–1677, when both New England and the Chesapeake were engulfed with violence, New York governor Edmund Andros initiated diplomatic negotiations with the Iroquoian Mohawks. Andros sought to broker peace between English colonists and Indians, resettle Indian refugees in buffer zones between European colonies, and expand his own political authority in the region. These negotiations established a pattern of councils and treaties between New York and the Iroquois League known as the **Covenant Chain.** Massachusetts, Connecticut, Rhode Island, and Maryland eventually joined in the diplomatic councils, which governed British-Indian relations during the first half of the eighteenth century.

In Covenant Chain negotiations, the Iroquois claimed to speak for all the native groups that conducted trade or interacted with British colonists. The treaties gave the Iroquois security on their eastern front and access to the weapons they needed to attack fur-trading rivals to the west. On the other side, British colonies benefited from more stable partners in the fur trade and relied on the Iroquois nations as buffers and allies in their wars against the French. The Iroquois League grew in size and influence by adopting captives from enemies in the Great Lakes region. The Iroquois also added a sixth nation to the confederacy in the 1720s, following the Tuscarora War of 1711–1713, when an alliance composed of Swiss and German settlers, the colonial militias of North and South Carolina, Yamasee Indians, and other native groups defeated the southern Tuscarora Indians and burned their villages. Between 1,500 and 2,000 surviving Tuscaroras migrated northward from the Carolinas to join the Haudenosaunee.

The Iroquois League proved a powerful ally for Britain's northern colonies over the course of a century of conflict with other empires, but the Iroquois did not always do Britain's bidding. Indeed, when it served their purposes, Iroquois groups made their own peace with the French or with France's Indian allies. In 1701, for example, some Iroquois representatives met the French in Montreal to promise neutrality in exchange for trade and hunting rights in lands north of the Great Lakes. A month earlier, however, other Iroquois had met the English in Albany and acknowledged England's sovereignty over that same land. Iroquois leaders understood the importance of not relying on a single European power and effectively gave both the French and the British empires a reason to maintain good relations with the Six Nations. By around 1720, this strategy had succeeded not only in enhancing Iroquois power but also in securing greater peace between Indians and colonists in North America (see Singular Lives: Sir Willian Johnson, Irish Mohawk).

SPAIN AND FRANCE IN NORTH AMERICA

By the dawn of the eighteenth century, England's Atlantic seaboard settlements were the continent's most populous colonies north of Mexico. Yet poised ominously at the edges of British colonial society were well-armed Spanish and French colonists and their native allies (see Map 5.1).

Spain's North American colonies in 1700 remained minor outposts at the northern edge of a vast empire centered in Mesoamerica, the Caribbean, and the South American mainland. The Pueblo Revolt of 1680 had checked the expansion of Spanish Jesuits into New Mexico, very few Spanish traders had settled in Texas, and the Florida missions had declined. Well into the eighteenth century, fewer than five thousand Spaniards inhabited these three colonies taken together. But Spain was committed to preserving its Florida military bases, primarily to protect its Caribbean empire against the British. Consequently, Spanish Florida sought to extend its political influence over a number of southeastern Indian groups and bestowed gifts and noble titles upon native leaders who had embraced Catholicism. Meanwhile, Indian groups seeking relief from Spain's authority and its labor demands found trading partners and military allies in the British colonies of South Carolina and later Georgia—both of which had been designed to challenge Spanish America.

France's North American empire was far more extensive than Spain's. French traders and missionaries prospered in New France, their scattered settlements stretching westward from Cape Breton Island on Canada's Atlantic coast through the St. Lawrence Valley and the Great Lakes. From there, French colonists extended southward along both banks of the Mississippi River through numerous trading villages in the Illinois territory and down to New Orleans, founded as a French city in 1718. The area from Illinois south was known as Louisiana, and it included a population of several thousand enslaved African Americans in the first half of the century (see Chapter 3). Altogether, about 65,000 people (not counting Indians) lived in French colonies in North America by 1750, at a time when Britain's mainland colonial population approached 1.2 million.

Compared to British America, the French presence, though sparse, was also less divided. French colonies did not have political rivalries and conflicts with one another. For several related reasons, French colonists also enjoyed much closer relations with Native Americans. Because New France's economic basis was animal furs and skins rather than staple agriculture, most French settlers needed Indian trading partners more than they needed Indian land. Moreover, their smaller numbers made the French more obviously dependent on cultivating Indian alliances. Frenchmen, like the Spanish but unlike the English, lived among Indians, intermarried with native women, supplied Indian men with European goods (including weapons), and used these relationships to build a large empire.

Portrait of Catherine Tekakwitha, ca. 1690, by Father Chauchetière. Kateri Tekakwitha (baptized as Catherine) was the daughter of a Mohawk chief and an Algonquin woman who converted to Catholicism under the tutelage of French missionaries near Montreal. Noted during her short life for her piety and her vow of perpetual virginity, Tekakwitha was one of a number of prominent Indian Catholics in French Canada during the late seventeenth century. In 2012 she became the first Native American to be canonized as a saint.

SINGULAR LIVES

Sir William Johnson, Irish Mohawk

William Johnson. In this 1763 portrait, Johnson poses as a British nobleman.

In the North American interior, far from the coastal towns founded in the seventeenth century, British colonists and Native Americans interacted often. William Johnson, an Irish immigrant who settled in New York's Mohawk Valley, at the eastern edge of Iroquois territory, thrived in this environment. Born a Catholic in County Meath in Ireland, Johnson converted to Protestantism and set sail for New York in 1738 to help manage the estate of a wealthy uncle. Johnson became a successful fur trader and merchant and quickly forged connections in New York politics. But he cemented an even more useful political alliance with the Canajoharie Mohawk Indians. During King George's War, Johnson was able to draw upon his influence and friendship with the Mohawk chief Hendrick Theyanoguin to organize bands of Indian men to fight on the British side, notwithstanding the Iroquois League's policy of neutrality.

Johnson's Indian ties were not simply diplomatic. He had learned Mohawk war songs, painted himself as a Mohawk warrior, and received a Mohawk name—Warraghiyagey, meaning "Doer of Great Things" or "Doer of Much Business." Johnson also fathered children with at least two Mohawk women, one of whom, Molly Brant, became his common-law wife.

These cultural bonds enhanced Johnson's standing in the British Empire rather than compromising it. He was appointed New York's agent for negotiations with the Iroquois and later, during the French and Indian War, became British Superintendent of Indian Affairs for the northern colonies, a position he held until his death in 1774. Grateful for his role in the British victory at Lake George in 1755, the Crown conferred upon Johnson the title of baronet, making him one of only two Americans to receive that noble status in the British Empire. Yet despite his elevated social rank, Johnson remained a frontiersman, and he never set foot in the British capital. Instead, he amassed political power and wealth along the Great Lakes, becoming the region's top landowner and a major power broker along the frontier that separated—and connected—Iroquois country and British America. Johnson's career also epitomized the era in white-Indian relations when powerful polities engaged in frequent negotiations to avoid the widespread violence that had torn through the region in the late seventeenth century.

Certifying Diplomacy. In this pictorial detail from a William Johnson certificate, British and Indian officials engage in a peaceful meeting. Johnson would bestow such certificates upon his Indian friends and allies.

Think About It

1. Why was Johnson's willingness to dress like an Indian seen as a political asset within the British Empire rather than a sign of cultural betrayal?
2. Why was it important for his subsequent career that Johnson converted to Protestantism?
3. While many other British colonists formed close bonds with Indians, how did Johnson's Mohawk ties and identity make him a power broker and not simply a link between two cultures?
4. How would you compare Johnson's role as cultural intermediary to that of a seventeenth-century model such as Pocahontas or John Eliot (see Chapter 2)?

IMPERIAL WARS

Conflicts on the other side of the Atlantic shaped relations among the European colonies in North America. After King William III's ascent to the throne in 1689 (see Chapter 4), England renewed its rivalry with Catholic Europe and embarked on the first of a long series of costly wars with France that would re-erupt periodically for more than a century. Between King William's War, which lasted from 1689 to 1697, and the treaty of Ghent in 1815, which ended the War of 1812 (see Chapter 9), England was

Map 5.1 English, Spanish, and French Presence in the Future United States, ca. 1700. While English colonial settlements clumped along the seaboard, French and Spanish outposts were scattered across different parts of the continent. Overwhelmingly, however, North America was populated and controlled by Indians.

embroiled continually in military struggles with France (see Table 5.1). These were not contained, local affairs between the two neighboring countries. In the early wars, England fought as part of large multinational European alliances. More commonly, France would be joined by Spain and by other Catholic allies, while the British might enjoy the support of Protestant forces in northern Europe. In each conflict, hostilities spread beyond Europe to wherever the rivals vied for control.

Beginning with Queen Anne's War in 1702, colonists and Native Americans were drawn into battle in significant numbers. The fight began over the proposed unification of the French and Spanish monarchies and lasted for more than a decade. European armies and navies clashed in far-flung parts of the globe as the two sides raided each other's possessions on the high seas, in the West Indies, Brazil, and North America. English forces from Carolina seized the opportunity to attack St. Augustine and Pensacola in Florida, while the Spanish mounted a counteroffensive against Charleston. France ordered raids into New England, while the English launched an abortive naval expedition to seize Quebec. Relations between different Indian groups proved crucial throughout this war. Creek Indians joined the English attack on Florida for their own reasons, hoping to defeat the Appalachees, who were allied with Spain. Mohawk and Abenaki Indians tied to France carried out attacks against Puritan settlers in Maine and western Massachusetts. Notably, the French did not attack New York, not wanting to antagonize that colony's Iroquois allies, with whom they had recently signed a peace treaty.

TABLE 5.1 IMPERIAL WARS, 1689-1748

Name of War in Europe	Name in British Empire	Main Antagonists	Dates
War of the League of Augsburg (also known as War of the Grand Alliance, Nine Years' War)	King William's War	Austria, Bavaria (and other German states), Britain, France, Holy Roman Empire, Spain, Sweden, United Provinces of the Netherlands	1689–1697
War of Spanish Succession	Queen Anne's War	Bavaria (and other German states), Britain, France, Holy Roman Empire, Prussia, Portugal, Spain, United Provinces of the Netherlands	1702–1713
War of Austrian Succession	King George's War	Austria, Bavaria, Britain, France, Prussia, Saxony, Spain	1744–1748

In the end, Queen Anne's War produced no decisive shift in the balance of power among European empires in North America. As stipulated in the treaty that officially ended the war in 1713, France ceded to Britain some territory in northern and eastern Canada, but Britain, Spain, and France all maintained their major prewar colonies. For Native Americans, on the other hand, the war enhanced the standing of particular confederacies, including the Creeks (who had decimated their enemies) and the Iroquois League (who had maintained their neutrality).

Following a period of relative quiet, Britain exported another long war to North America in 1739. In 1738, a British captain named Robert Jenkins appeared before Parliament holding his pickled left ear, which he claimed had been sliced off several years earlier by a Spanish coast guard official who was enforcing Spain's ban against British trading in the West Indies. The display fanned the flames of British nationalism, anti-Catholic hostility, and commercial ambition, and a year later Parliament declared war against Spain. Once again, fighting broke out on both sides of the ocean. English colonists in America (including George Washington's older brother) signed up for a massive naval expedition to capture Spain's gold trade, but Admiral Edward Vernon's assault on Spanish Cartagena (in present-day Colombia) failed disastrously. Farther north, British ships blockaded Florida, while soldiers from Georgia besieged St. Augustine. South Carolinians stayed out of the fighting, because they did not want to leave their plantations vulnerable in the immediate aftermath of the Stono Rebellion (see Chapter 3). The Spanish broke the siege and counterinvaded Georgia.

The War of Jenkins's Ear, as this inconclusive Anglo-Spanish conflict was dubbed a century later, became part of a wider struggle with France and Spain over control of the Hapsburg monarchy in Austria. The North American theater of this War of the Austrian Succession, known as King George's War, further cemented the bonds between colonists and Britain's transatlantic empire. The only decisive military campaign in America took place in 1745, when 4,300 hundred men, mostly from the New England colonies, captured the strategically significant French fort at Louisbourg on Cape Breton Island, Nova Scotia, giving Britain control over access to the St. Lawrence River. Many New Englanders saw the campaign as part of a Protestant crusade. As one Boston minister exulted, "a great Support of Antichristian Power is taken away, and the visible Kingdom of CHRIST enlarged."

In the complex negotiations ending the war, Britain returned Louisbourg to the French in return for significant concessions in Europe and India. To soften

Siege of Louisbourg. Supported by the British Navy, an attack force of New England colonists captured this pillar of Catholic power in Canada.

the blow to New Englanders, Parliament picked up the tab for the Louisburg campaign, thus underscoring the notion that Americans' local struggles were part of a single imperial operation. The Louisburg campaign had embroiled the Iroquois League, as Indian tribes allied with the French had engaged in retaliatory raids into New York. That colony's governor subsequently pressed the Iroquois to abandon their neutrality pledge, and although the Iroquois resisted this pressure, the Covenant Chain was strained.

FRONTIERS AND BORDERLANDS IN INDIAN COUNTRY

In the eighteenth century, European empires controlled only a small portion of the territory that would eventually become the United States. Most of the continent, on both sides of the Mississippi River, remained Indian country. In eastern North America, Indian country was a large area surrounded by a thinner ring of European settlements that were constantly advancing past their borders (see Map 5.2). There different Indian groups, some of them new to this period, tried to preserve their independence through skillful diplomacy. Farther west, where a small number of French traders and Spanish missionaries operated, Indian nations maintained firmer control.

ALLIANCE AND DIPLOMACY IN THE EAST

Amid the conflicts roiling the rival European empires, most of the eastern half of the continent remained Indian country. South and west of Iroquois territory, much of the American interior had been settled by smaller Indian groups who had migrated to lands depopulated by war and disease. Several new centers of native culture and politics emerged. In the northern reaches of Indian country, refugees from various Algonquian peoples who had been destroyed by the Iroquois in the mid-1600s fled west to the lands bordering Lake Michigan. French traders and missionaries helped mediate conflicts among the refugees, who in turn used French communications networks (trade routes, linked forts, and missionary correspondence) to forge new alliances and create new clusters of villages. Major Indian ethnic groups of the upper Midwest, including the Ottawas, Miamis, Potawatomis, Ojibwas, and Foxes, formed in this way around the beginning of the eighteenth century. These Indians traded with the French, protected New France from the Iroquois League, and even identified with the French Empire, but they also established diplomatic relations with Iroquois groups and sold furs to the English in New York.

Similar patterns appeared throughout Indian country. In the Upper Ohio River valley, Shawnee and Delaware Indians (many of whom had been driven west by land-hungry Pennsylvania settlers and their Iroquois allies) established new villages in the land between the French-allied tribes of the Great Lakes region and England's Middle Colonies. The Ohio Indians, eager to maintain political independence from their powerful British and Iroquois neighbors to the east, cultivated commercial ties with New France as well. Farther southwest, the Choctaw group formed in present-day Mississippi, within the orbit of French Louisiana. Most Choctaw villages allied and traded with the French, but others fought alongside the British. In the southeastern quadrant of the territory, the Creeks and Cherokees emerged in the eighteenth century as new and powerful multiethnic tribes. The Creeks, who had been recruited and armed by South

Map 5.2 Indian Country in an Imperial World, ca. 1720–1750. East of the Mississippi River, native villages and tribes still enjoyed effective sovereignty over most of the land. Rival colonial societies lay on the region's periphery.

Carolina at the end of Queen Anne's War to attack Florida, became the region's leading military power. Different Creek villages allied themselves with French Louisiana and Spanish Florida, conducted trade with both empires, and reduced Creek dependence on Carolina. The Cherokees, who helped Carolina defeat the Creeks in the Yamasee War in 1715 (see Chapter 3), maintained closer ties to British America, but they played one British colony off against another and even pursued alliances with the French. These complex economic and diplomatic relationships were part of a common strategy among eighteenth-century Indians. But they also reflected decentralized leadership in an Indian world—one where communities were on the move, ethnic identities were in flux, and the village remained a fundamental political unit.

Cherokee Chief Austenaco Donning Western Attire During a Visit to London, 1762. Austenaco, a famed orator, and two other Indian leaders met with King George III and sat for portraitist Sir Joshua Reynolds. Over 150 North American Indians made diplomatic journeys to Britain during the seventeenth and eighteenth centuries.

INDIAN POWERS IN THE WEST

Between the Mississippi River and the Pacific Ocean, Indians did not need to exploit any rivalries among European powers. In the West, natives rather than Europeans held sway. Europeans lurked at the edges of this vast territory (see Map 5.3), with French migrants pushing in from the Louisiana colony and Spanish migrants moving up from New Mexico. But French and Spanish colonists had to proceed carefully, eager not to run afoul of the Indian tribes and polities that dominated the region. Yet despite their small numbers and limited settlement, Europeans made a difference.

The different rules governing white-Indian encounters on the other side of the Mississippi were perhaps clearest in southeastern Texas, where small numbers of French and Spanish colonists labored to gain permanent footholds in the early 1700s. France and Spain were not expecting to extract precious metals from the earth or to command plantation labor here. Instead, they were competing to establish relations with the powerful Caddo Indians, who controlled significant territory in what are now eastern Texas and Oklahoma, Louisiana, and Arkansas. French traders held the advantage over Spanish missionaries, since the French did not expect wholesale changes in the religious beliefs, family values, and sexual practices of the Caddos as a condition of doing business. In addition, French traders lived in families and intermarried with Caddos—practices that made them easier to incorporate as allies within a native political system that stressed kin relationships. Spaniards, by contrast, arrived in parties that were suspiciously all-male, though the Caddos were reassured by the ubiquitous images of the Virgin Mary they carried on their banners. From a native perspective, the presence of a woman in a diplomatic ceremony represented a promise of peace, and invoking the Virgin was a way of communicating that promise. Still, the Spanish came to understand that pictures of female saints might not suffice to put the native people at ease. When organizing an expedition to settle the San Antonio River in 1718, the viceroy of New Spain therefore requested only men with families, since "the Indians find it strange that the soldiers do not bring women." Outnumbered and vulnerable, Europeans in Caddo lands relied on diplomacy rather than force or intimidation.

Throughout the West, powerful Indian groups dominated. Beginning in the 1680s, bands of western Sioux Indians swept through the northern plains, gradually controlling land from present-day Minnesota all the way west to the head of the Yellowstone River. Sioux hunting parties followed the buffalo migration during the summer and then moved to woodland areas to trap beaver. In the spring, they traveled east to French trading villages and fairs, where they acquired the guns, ammunition, and horses that secured their military dominance. Western Sioux gradually incorporated European horses (see Hot Commodities: Horses) into their hunting and fighting in the first half of the eighteenth century, but guns and ammunition quickly shifted political relations between western Sioux and their neighbors.

In the southern plains, Comanches, descendants of Shoshone-speaking Indians from the Rocky Mountains, migrated southward to track buffalo and traded hides for horses with Spanish settlers in New Mexico. Spain came to regret its role in the rise in the eighteenth century of the **Comanchería,** an expansive domain of Comanche influence that covered, in present-day terms, western Kansas, eastern Oklahoma, central Texas, and parts of New Mexico. Comanche raids would wreak havoc in Spanish (and later Mexican) settlements for another century. West of the Comanchería, Apaches also benefited from trade with neighboring New Mexico, where Spanish colonial authorities looked for allies against the French-connected Pawnees. New Mexico also shared a tense border with the Navajos, and as the Spanish colony grew slowly over the course of the 1700s, war and diplomacy with the Navajos became a major preoccupation.

At midcentury, European settlement in the western half of the continent remained light. French traders controlled the Mississippi River and were active along the Missouri. French goods circulated extensively through the Plains, Rockies, and Southwest, but no French colonies took hold farther west than eastern Texas. Spanish colonization gained ground but remained confined to the south.

Map 5.3 Indian Powers in the West, ca. 1720–1750. Indian dominance was far more complete west of the Mississippi than in the East. Natives thus felt less need to play rival colonial empires off against one another.

Not until the last third of the century would Spain establish missions and military presidios along the Pacific coast, which remained the most densely settled and least European-influenced portion of western America. Only later, after the imperial map of the continent had shifted dramatically, would Father Junípero Serra found missions in San Diego (1769), Monterey (1770), and San Francisco (1776) and elsewhere along the coast, laying the groundwork for the eventual urbanization of California.

IMPERIAL CONNECTIONS IN BRITISH AMERICA

In some ways, the expansive empires that competed for control over territory in North America were imaginary abstractions. All kinds of cues reminded Americans that they belonged to villages, towns, tribes, churches, colonies, extended families, or historical communities. But what made them feel part of an empire? This was an especially difficult question in the case of what was by far the largest group of European and African colonists on the mainland—those who found themselves living in something called the British Empire. Great Britain was a new entity created by the 1707 Act of Union. Most people who settled in and around Britain's mainland American colonies in the first half of the eighteenth century had never even lived in England or Scotland, let alone in a place called Great Britain. The ties binding British colonists to the empire in 1707 were loose at best. By midcentury, however, new connections among different British colonies linked them both to one another and to the imperial center in London.

CONSUMER CULTURES

As much as any other connection, what made the different colonies seem increasingly British over the course of the 1700s was commerce. Both colonists and Native Americans on the eastern part of the continent purchased similar consumer goods that had been produced overseas and brought to the colonies through British ports on British ships, in compliance with the Navigation Acts. Indians living in territories claimed by Great Britain became major consumers of Old World commodities,

Caddo Man and Woman Dressed in European Trade Goods. French and Spanish colonists vied with each other to establish relations with the powerful Caddos. This early-nineteenth-century watercolor is by Lino Sánchez y Tapia after an original sketch by artist-cartographer José María Sánchez y Tapia.

HOT COMMODITIES

Horses

Romantic images of the Plains Indians feature noble warriors or hunters mounted proudly on their steeds. But where did Indians get horses? Like other indigenous North Americans, the natives of the Great Plains had been nomadic pedestrians who domesticated dogs rather than horses for hunting assistance. In fact, horses had become extinct in the Western Hemisphere during the Pleistocene era. But horses came back to the Indians—from Europe.

Specifically, horses entered the American West through New Mexico, where Spanish colonists introduced them shortly after 1600. Spaniards found the hot, dry Plains grasslands unpromising for colonization. But this terrain proved hospitable to Spanish horses, whose North African breeding helped them withstand high temperatures and survive arid summers.

George Catlin, *Comanche Feats of Horsemanship*, Oil Painting, 1834–1835. The horse, originally a European import, became central to nineteenth-century Americans' romantic images of native life in the West.

Apache and Jumano Indians acquired New Mexican horses early in the seventeenth century through trade and theft, and the animals circulated in sprawling commercial networks that reached as far away as Caddo villages in eastern Texas. More horses entered Indian hands in 1680 when New Mexicans left hundreds behind while fleeing the Pueblo Revolt. Soon after, Comanches shifted to equestrian hunting, and their increased mobility both encouraged and enabled them to conquer their enemies' territory. Comanche power, in turn, helped spread equestrian culture through the Plains.

The equestrian revolution in the Plains had dramatic consequences. Horses were economically efficient since they converted the region's abundant grasses directly into energy. They were politically significant since they allowed warriors to cover, and thereby govern, larger stretches of territory. They lightened the burdens of nomadism, especially for native women, who had carried the materials of camp from place to place during the hunting season. And they created new trade patterns, serving both as a widely valued commodity themselves and as a means for transporting commodities across great distances. Paradoxically, the horse was a European import that wound up helping some Indians achieve prosperity and political autonomy in the face of European incursions. By the second half of the eighteenth century, horses had tipped the balance of political power from Spanish New Mexico to the Comanchería.

The spread of the horse came with serious costs, however. More efficient war-making took a major toll in human life, subjugated many horse-poor Indian groups to a few horse-wealthy ones, and introduced political instability. In addition, equestrianism widened the gap—both in physical distance and in social status—between men's work and women's work, and higher battle fatalities skewed sex ratios in many Indian villages. In the longer term, horses wreaked ecological damage by destroying grasslands, destabilizing bison populations, and disrupting long-standing patterns of economic subsistence.

Think About It

1. How might the introduction of horses have hurt Spain's colonization efforts in North America?
2. Why did southwestern and Plains Indians value horses rather than other domesticated animals imported by the Europeans to the New World?

including weapons, ammunition, iron tools, and woolen textiles. Purchasing such commodities did not necessarily make Indians more like Europeans. European manufacturers designed lighter kettles, axes, and muskets for Indian customers than they did for local markets, whereas textile makers in Belgium and England produced woolen "duffel" or "stroud" cloth specifically for a Native American market. But all of these purchases had an impact on Indian lives and made them dependent on trade relationships that tied Indians to colonists, traversed colonial boundaries, and crossed the ocean.

One of the most devastating commercial relationships between eastern Indians and British colonists involved liquor.

Among all the popular European consumer goods in Indian communities, alcoholic beverages were the ones that were literally consumed. Native villages might hold onto a brass kettle or a woolen blanket for a while, but a barrel of rum was depleted quickly—and tended to stimulate more demand.

The Indian liquor trade developed slowly but steadily in the English colonies during the seventeenth century and became a major force by the mid-eighteenth century. In the 1760s, rum produced in North America from sugar harvested in the French and British West Indies saturated Indian villages deep in the interior of British America. Alcohol presumably brought pleasure, relief, and inspiration to Indian consumers, much as it did to European colonists, and natives incorporated liquor into their festivals and rituals. But both native and colonial observers testified to the horrific damage that came with the liquor trade as domestic violence, illness, addiction, and political instability all followed distilled spirits into Indian country. Benjamin Franklin, a prominent critic of alcohol consumption, observed that if it were "the Design of Providence" to wipe out, gradually, the continent's indigenous population, "it seems not improbable that Rum may be the appointed Means." But despite some attempts to regulate or ban the liquor trade, colonial merchants and officials understood that selling rum to Indian villages was crucial to the larger commercial relationship between Indians and the British Empire. Without the liquor trade, they pointed out, Indians would procure fewer skins and furs for European markets.

Indians were hardly the only Americans to participate in what historians have called Britain's **empire of goods,** a system of commercial exchange that linked a widely dispersed population through the things they bought, consumed, displayed, and coveted. English colonists had long depended on European imports to supply a variety of manufactured commodities that were not produced in North America. By the 1740s, many more of those commodities were available, and colonists demanded and could afford them. Colonial stores filled their shelves with unprecedented volumes and varieties of imported fabric, furniture, and utensils that appealed to colonists' rising aspirations to genteel living (see Chapter 4). Colonial merchants also imported spices, wines, dyes, metals, and other exotic items from places around the globe where British ships traded. Trade to the American colonies skyrocketed during the

MANNER OF INSTRUCTING THE INDIANS.

"Manner of Instructing the Indians." This early-nineteenth-century woodcut shows how white Massachusetts settlers used alcohol to exploit Mashpee Indians. Scholars debate why liquor had such a disastrous impact on Indian communities. Medical researchers find no evidence that Indians have greater physiological susceptibility to alcohol abuse or addiction.

Imported Elegance. Luxurious Georgian-style interiors in colonial America, modeled after English city homes, displayed imported fashions and goods such as hand-painted Chinese wallpaper, British Chippendale furniture, and oriental carpets. The decor here is a recreation by the Metropolitan Museum of Art (New York) of the interior of Philadelphia's Powel House, 1765–1766.

eighteenth century. By midcentury, British exports were rising much faster than the colonial population. From 1720 to 1770, the average colonist's consumption of British exports rose almost 50 percent. In part for that reason, these decades are often described as a period of *Anglicization*—a time of adopting English ways—in American colonial history. But colonists were not simply becoming more English; they were also participating in global exchanges managed by the British Empire.

Consumption connected colonists who hailed from distinct regions in Europe, worshiped in antagonistic religious traditions, and lived in radically different settings. Similar imported ceramic plates, glass mirrors, printed books, and silk gowns appeared in colonial homes from New England to South Carolina, in rural villages as well as port cities. Newspaper advertisements wrapped these consumer goods in an elaborate vocabulary of color, texture, and pattern that kept colonists abreast of the latest trends in British fashion and gave consumers new experiences of choice and control. By the 1760s, the expanding catalogue of British imports shaped the material conditions of most colonists and reminded them how connected they were to a commercial empire.

Had Britain's American colonies manufactured more of their own goods, they might have been more isolated from the empire. British economic policies, however, gave British export merchants special access to American consumers and encouraged colonists to focus on exporting rawer commodities, such as timber, furs, and agricultural surplus. Parliament also explicitly forbade the manufacture of specific goods, such as hats, in the colonies. Yet the bigger obstacle to colonial manufacturing was that because most free colonists wanted to become independent farmers, labor costs were high, and therefore domestic industries could not compete effectively with British products. Even as populations and per-capita income grew, the colonies continued to import everything from paper and ink, to nails and firearms, to wallpaper and handkerchiefs. This shared dependence helped cultivate new connections among residents of the diverse colonies of eastern America.

IMPERIAL COMMUNICATIONS

While administering colonial trade policies designed to bind its American colonies to the larger empire, the British government also took modest steps to build a communications infrastructure in the colonies. In the seventeenth century, letters had been carried by individuals or collected and distributed informally by ship captains. Individual colonies had established limited postal routes, but in 1692 an Englishman named Thomas Neale secured a royal patent to establish post offices in all the major port cities in British America, despite never having set foot in North America. In return for building a network that would convey official communications between London and the colonies, Neale received a potentially lucrative monopoly on mail service in North America. After Neale died, the Crown bought back the royal patent from his widow in 1707 and absorbed colonial mail service into the English post office.

In the Postal Act of 1711, Parliament established the parameters of the colonies' official communications network. As part of the creation of the new entity that was Great Britain, Parliament brought together the mail systems of England, Ireland, Scotland, and North America (both the mainland and the island colonies) into a single bureaucracy that could raise revenue for the empire. In principle, the postal system now connected residents of the different societies in British America, but only insofar as those residents were also part of a bigger network centered in London. Most colonists did not use this service regularly to correspond with England or with other residents of the empire, but the existence of a single channel of communication linking port cities on both sides of the Atlantic gave some force to the claim that the colonies were part of a unified imperial realm.

Brocaded Silk Waistcoat, Spitalfields, England, ca. 1734. The intricate, three-dimensional floral ornamentation is representative of new designs that emerged in the 1730s. Throughout British America, material life acquired a flashier appearance. Clothing, furniture, and wallpaper came in brighter colors by midcentury.

MILITARY ALLIANCE

Britain's empire was a massive commercial operation, involving long-distance exchange and communication, but it was also a military power ready to wage war on land and sea at any opportunity to gain an advantage over its rivals in Catholic Europe. These imperial conflicts thrust together residents of different British North American colonies, because all British settlements became potential targets for the empire's enemies. In periods of imperial war, then, American colonists were likely to feel especially British.

During these wars, militias from the different colonies fought on the same side—often under the command of British officers sent from London—against Indian and French forces.

Further, imperial authorities established forts along frontier areas, which created lines of communication between colonies (see Spaces and Places: Line of Forts, Imperial Outpost). In the 1750s, when conflicts in the Ohio River valley threatened to spread into a larger war with France, Britain's Board of Trade instructed its colonies to coordinate plans for defending the empire's holdings and to strengthen their alliance with the Iroquois League. Accordingly, in the summer of 1754, seven colonies sent delegates to a convention at Albany, which was selected because of its traditional role as a site of Covenant Chain negotiations between New York and the Mohawks. The Albany Convention marked an unprecedented affirmation of the common interests of different societies within Britain's growing empire.

"Join, or Die." Benjamin Franklin's political cartoon, published in the *Pennsylvania Gazette*, May 9, 1754, is most familiar as an icon of unity during the Revolutionary War, but it originally appeared at the time of the Albany Convention. **Questions for Analysis:** Why is the snake divided into eight sections rather than the thirteen that we usually identify as the British colonies?

Delegates in Albany endorsed a Plan of Union, proposed by Benjamin Franklin, to create a single governing authority for defense purposes. According to the plan, a Grand Council of delegates from thirteen mainland colonies would meet annually to consider security measures and to negotiate treaties with Indians that would be binding on all colonies. The council would feature a president appointed by London and would raise indirect taxes for the colonies' common defense. Franklin's proposal was not to create the beginnings of a new autonomous state but to tie the various settlements closer together as parts of a single empire. In any case, the Albany Plan was rejected unanimously by the colonies' assemblies, whose representatives feared that they would lose power. Critics of the proposed union also worried that the plan might entail taxation for common defense and doubted that the colonies could execute a unified policy toward Indians. On the Indian side as well, the Albany gathering bore no obvious fruit. Few non-Mohawk delegates attended, and none of the other Iroquois nations committed themselves to fighting the French. Both the British colonies and their Indian allies were reluctant to commit to Franklin's vision of imperial unity.

THE FRENCH AND INDIAN WAR

Britain and its North American colonies experienced a brief period of relatively peaceful relations with other European powers after the War of the Austrian Succession. Then, in 1754, the empire entered a new imperial war, the first to originate in the colonies themselves (see Map 5.4).

Violence between French and British soldiers in Ohio had escalated quickly in a North American conflict that British colonists would call the French and Indian War, and then spread into a global conflict that struck contemporaries as unprecedented in its scope and magnitude. The global conflict would become known as the Seven Years' War or the Great War for Empire. As a Moravian missionary representing the Pennsylvania colony told an audience of Delaware Indians, "So long as the world has stood there has not been such a War." But not even the missionary could have anticipated or understood the decisive impact that this event would have on North American politics and culture.

WAR ERUPTS IN THE OHIO COUNTRY

Tensions along the borderlands between New France and the British colonies provided the spark that ignited the much wider conflict. Land-seeking British settlers and speculators were pushing west from Pennsylvania and Virginia into the Ohio country, while British merchants were beginning to trade with Indian groups whose allegiances the French could no longer afford to secure with gifts. France began building a series of forts to protect its claims to the region. The largest of these bastions, Fort Duquesne at the meeting of the Ohio, Allegheny, and Monongahela Rivers, was especially threatening to British colonists. French traders used the fort to supply weapons to Delaware and Shawnee Indians who had been driven eastward by the British, and the colonists worried that the well-placed French stronghold would become a base for attacks on British lands.

In May 1754, a small force of Virginia militiamen led by twenty-two-year-old Major George Washington, along with Mingo Indians under the command of the Seneca half-king Tanaghrisson, initiated a surprise attack against French troops in western Pennsylvania and built Fort Necessity just southeast of Fort Duquesne. As British colonial and Iroquois delegates gathered in Albany to plan for the defense of their lands against the French and French-allied Indians, word arrived that Washington had been compelled by enemy forces to surrender the fort.

Clearly, Virginia was now at war, and royal authorities in London sent two regiments of Irish troops under the command of General Edward Braddock to support an invasion of the Ohio River valley. Braddock led a large combined force of British army regulars and colonial militiamen (but no Indian allies) against Fort Duquesne in 1755, only to be routed badly at the Battle of the Monongahela (also known as Braddock's Defeat). A smaller army of French, Ottawas, Ojibwas, and Potawatomis attacked the British, fatally wounding Braddock and thwarting the invasion. Washington managed to form a rear guard, disengage from

SPACES & PLACES

Line of Forts, Imperial Outpost

At the outbreak of King George's War in 1744, Massachusetts leaders worried about the exposure of their western frontier to enemy invasion. Governor William Shirley ordered the construction of a series of military outposts running west of the Connecticut River along the northern border of Massachusetts. The forts were staffed by New England farmers who served in the colonial militia, sometimes accompanied by their families. Each fort was a small log blockhouse, holding about fifty people. In peacetime, this so-called Line of Forts served as trading posts and communications stations for an expanding empire. During the war, however, the forts became a focus of French and Indian attacks on British settlement. Fort Massachusetts, the westernmost of the three major forts on the line, fell to the enemy in 1746, and the men, women, and children living there were taken as prisoners (half of them would die in captivity). But Massachusetts rebuilt the bastion the following year, and the Line of Forts was fully occupied until 1754, the beginning of the next major war.

Many frontier forts from this era of imperial war later became town or city sites (Pittsburgh, Pennsylvania, which was originally the French Fort Duquesne, is the most famous example), but the Line of Forts had all but disappeared from the western New England landscape by 1760. Nonetheless, the fort sites offer historians a rare glimpse of life in midcentury British America. Because the forts were occupied for only a short period, the debris found in the soil can be dated with unusual precision. Unfortunately, Fort Massachusetts now lies beneath a supermarket and parking lot in North Adams, Massachusetts, but the other two forts, Fort Shirley and Fort Pelham, were subjected to thorough archaeological excavations in the 1970s.

Researchers unearthed a remarkable array of metal, glass, and ceramic consumer goods in the soil where the Line of Forts had once stood. Surprisingly few of those artifacts had been made in the New World. The New England farmers who served in the colonial militia and staffed the forts for short stints clearly belonged to the larger consumer culture of the empire of goods. The materials of their daily life were imported from England and closely resembled those of men and women on the other side of the Atlantic. Fort residents smoked pipes, lifted wine glasses, used forks, fired guns, and filled paper sheets that had originated in the Old World and made their way along circuitous but well-worn commercial paths that led to retail stores on the rural frontier. Western Massachusetts marked a vulnerable edge of British settlement, but its settlers also belonged to the heart of the empire.

Line of Forts in Western Massachusetts. This series of short-lived midcentury forts extended the power and presence of the British Empire into Indian Country and toward a Great Lakes region dominated by French colonies and their native allies.

Think About It

1. Why have archaeologists been especially interested in excavating the site of long-abandoned British forts?
2. Taking into account the archaeological findings, how do you imagine that soldiers living in these forts most essentially saw themselves? As Britons? As frontiersmen? As Americans?
3. Though designed for defense, how might these forts have attracted conflict?

the battle, and save a portion of the force from being wiped out, but Braddock's expedition had ended in utter failure. The French also captured the slain general's papers, which revealed the larger British military plan at the time—to capture strategic points along the Great Lakes and in Canada.

For the next three years, the French and their Indian allies racked up a succession of victories. They took control of Lake Ontario in 1756 after capturing Fort Oswego on the lake's New York shore. From there, they drove south into New York and attacked Fort William Henry at the southern end of Lake George with a massive army in 1757. When the fort fell after a six-day siege, the French commander, Marquis de Montcalm, granted the surrendering army the right to leave with their arms and possessions as long as they pledged not to take up arms against France for eighteen months. Such generous terms had ample precedent in European chivalric practices, but the two thousand Indians (about half of whom had traveled hundreds of miles from their homes in the upper Midwest) who had joined the assault felt entitled to their share of captives and war spoils. Acting on those grounds, Indian soldiers attacked the British who were peaceably evacuating the fort. Although the ensuing massacre both frightened and mobilized British colonists, it also

Map 5.4 Global War for Empire, 1754–1763. The Seven Years' War, which actually lasted nine years, counting all of its far-flung theaters, entangled European powers in conflicts as far away as North America, the West Indies, South America, West Africa, South Asia, and the Pacific Ocean.

opened a breach in the French-Indian alliance. Sensing that they played by different rules and had different priorities, the two sides grew reluctant to band together. This change of heart would have great consequences for the war's future course.

Across the Atlantic in Europe, meanwhile, France, Austria, Russia, Saxony, and Sweden banded together in 1756 to block the expansion of Frederick II of Prussia. Great Britain promptly joined the Prussian side, and now the British were fighting a war on two continents. The French took the upper hand in Europe as well, capturing the Mediterranean island of Minorca in the opening naval battle of the Seven Years' War and precipitating a political crisis in London that almost turned out Britain's governing administration. The conflict spread quickly. French and British allies clashed indecisively in both western and central Europe, while French and British trading companies fought in India. From the British standpoint by 1757,

Nineteenth-Century Engraving of the Fort William Henry Massacre. French officials offered to compensate native warriors with two gallons of rum if they would let the British prisoners go, but as one Indian explained to a Frenchman, "I make war for plunder, scalps, and prisoners. You are satisfied with a fort, and you let your enemy and mine live." **Question for Analysis:** What are the sympathies and perspective of this nineteenth-century artist?

however, the most troubling developments were taking place in North America, where France seemed poised to invade New England and conquer the continent.

THE TIDE TURNS

Britain's imperial fortunes improved dramatically in 1758 after two major shifts in policy transformed the war effort. First, colonists turned their attention to improving relations with the native groups in the Ohio country. At the Easton Treaty conference that year, the colony of Pennsylvania committed itself to protecting Delaware Indians' land claims by prohibiting further white settlement north and west of the Alleghenies. Pennsylvania also returned some territory to the Iroquois League that had been ceded four years earlier. With the Ohio Indians no longer at war with Britain, and France's native alliances frayed, the balance of power in the region tilted. Slowly the war in North America became primarily between French and British armies, and France's early advantage disappeared. Feeling vulnerable, the French even blew up Fort Duquesne rather than have it fall into enemy hands.

Britain's other crucial move was to turn to massive deficit spending as Secretary of State William Pitt borrowed heavily to subsidize the North American campaign. Britain thereby offered colonists an inducement to assume a greater share of the fighting. Pitt effectively guaranteed that Parliament would cover the rising costs of the war (for weaponry, provisions, and salaries) if the colonies would provide the manpower. As a result, after 1758, residents of the American colonies accounted for a majority of the enlisted military forces on the British side, putting the French, whose ranks were diminished by the flagging enthusiasm of their Indian allies, at a severe numerical disadvantage. New France's population of men of military age barely reached sixteen thousand at the time of the war, but on the other side, fifty thousand residents of the British North American colonies joined the military effort in 1758 alone.

The new policies had a powerful impact. In July 1759, an army of about 3,500 British soldiers and colonial militiamen, supported by nearly 1,000 Iroquois soldiers, captured Fort Niagara, while British general Jeffrey Amherst led a successful attack on Lake George and forced a French retreat into Canada. Another British force, commanded by James Wolfe, besieged the fortress city of Québec, which was being defended by French commander Marquis de Montcalm. Québec held off the invaders for two months, but in September 1759 the rival armies met on the Plains of Abraham, and Québec fell to the British. The following year, when Montreal fell as well, the surrender of New France was complete. France's close native allies, the Seven Nations of Canada, also made peace with the British. By the close of 1760, Canada was in British hands.

THE END OF WAR

The surrender of New France did not conclude the war in Europe, but there too William Pitt's policies had borne fruit. Britain had increased its financial support to the Prussians and Hanoverians, who exchanged heavy blows with Russia and Austria and tied up French troops on the European continent. Britain won significant victories against thinning French forces in West Africa and the Caribbean in 1759 and off the coast of India in 1760. In an effort to check Britain's imperial expansion and prevent a radical shift in Europe's political balance, Spain entered the war on the side of France in 1762. Havana, the central port of Spain's lucrative

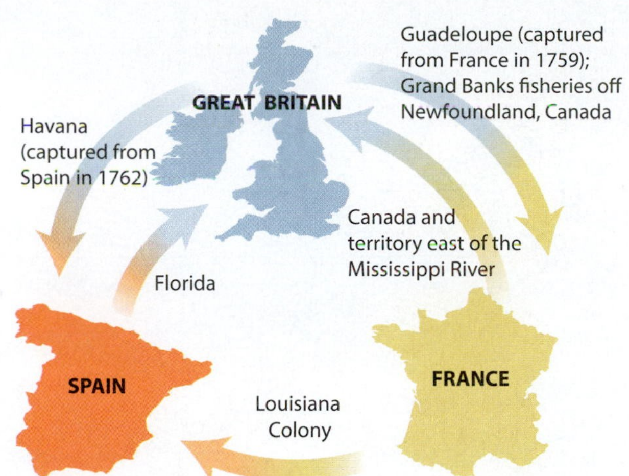

FIGURE 5.1 Key Territorial Exchange in the Treaty of Paris. In sheer land mass, French concessions to Britain were enormous. But France was able to regain control of most of the territories that had been captured in the war, including the Caribbean islands of Guadeloupe, Saint Lucia, and Martinique, the African slave-trading colony of Gorée, and trading posts in India. Spain retained Havana and Manila, which Britain had also taken during the conflict. See Map 5.4

Caribbean empire, then became a British target. Because the British Navy had seized Spain's mail ships, the Spanish in Cuba had no idea that they were at war with Britain and were unprepared for the amphibious attack that came in June 1762. Fifteen thousand British troops, including approximately four thousand volunteers from New York and New England, laid siege to Havana for two months and ultimately captured the strategically valuable city. In October, Spain was forced to surrender the Philippine port of Manila to Britain as well.

Over the course of 1762, Britain's enemies began negotiating an end to the conflict. Whereas treaties concluding earlier imperial wars typically sought to restore some earlier balance of power, the scale of the British victory, especially in the Americas, made such an arrangement unlikely in this case. Pitt hoped to impose a settlement that would permanently hobble France as an imperial rival. Other voices in British politics disagreed, fearing that a one-sided peace would isolate Great Britain from the rest of Europe and lead to future imperial clashes.

The two treaties ending the global conflict, both signed in February 1763, contrasted sharply. The Treaty of Hubertusburg simply restored Austria's and Prussia's prewar borders. The Treaty of Paris, on the other hand, radically altered the geography of France, Spain, and Great Britain's empires (see Figure 5.1). From a territorial standpoint, Britain emerged the big winner from the treaty negotiations. Indeed, in return for some important concessions in Africa, the Caribbean, and India, France transferred Canada and all French territory east of the Mississippi River to Great Britain. British North America now spanned the entire eastern half of the continent, from Hudson Bay down to the Gulf of Mexico.

Britain's territorial acquisitions would yield significant profits from the Great Lakes fur trade and the St. Lawrence fisheries. Had British negotiators been concerned primarily with international commerce, however, they never would have considered trading Havana and Guadeloupe, which exported more sugar than all British possessions combined, for cold stretches of Canadian land. But in 1763, the security of Britain's populous mainland colonies seemed strategically paramount. Removing the French, with their Catholic missions and their diplomatic ties to the continent's indigenous powers, from North America could achieve that goal without destabilizing power relations in Europe. In addition, by eliminating French positions along the Mississippi River and wresting control of Florida and the Gulf Coast from Spain, Britain was now poised to contest Spanish control of the Caribbean (see Map 5.5).

Still, the treaty proved unpopular with many observers in Britain, and Pitt himself denounced the agreement. By letting France keep its maritime possessions in the Caribbean and Newfoundland, he observed, "we have given her the means of recovering her prodigious losses and of becoming once more formidable to us at sea." France would indeed recover from the war soon enough and become a formidable foe for the next half century, but the challenges of the Treaty of Paris to the British Empire would come as much from what the French gave up as what it retained. London now faced the political and financial costs of governing a much vaster colonial society.

A NEW IMPERIAL MAP

The year 1763 would mark the high point in American colonists' sense of belonging to the British Empire. It would also prove to be a turning point. As colonial leaders and British authorities faced the challenges of governing an enlarged domain, North Americans of different ethnicities, religions, and national allegiances struggled to adjust to the decisions made by diplomats on the other side of the Atlantic. Indeed, some inhabitants of the colonies felt compelled to move as a result of the new political map. The most difficult adjustments came in Indian country, where many native groups rejected the Treaty of Paris and fought to preserve their independence. The Indian conflict that followed the British victory in North America would wind up driving a wedge between the interests of colonial settlers and those of the empire.

ASSESSING THE COSTS OF WAR

Britain's stunning and decisive victory in the French and Indian War came at a high price. Immense human sacrifices had been made, both by colonists and by British soldiers and sailors brought from across the ocean. In New England, no military conflict since King Philip's War had killed such a large share of the population. Britain's regular army had suffered at even ghastlier rates. Diseases had ravaged the redcoats, especially in the Caribbean. During the siege of Havana, for example, close to six thousand soldiers and sailors died, mostly from yellow fever, gastric illness, and other diseases.

Map 5.5 North America as Envisioned Under the Treaty of Paris, with Comparison to European Land Claims in 1750. By removing the French from mainland North America, the treaty altered the European map of North America. Note that these maps, like the treaty itself, marked only European land claims, ignoring issues of Indian sovereignty and political power. **Question for Analysis:** How do these pictures of America relate to those in Maps 2.1 and 2.2?

American colonists and British residents weighed the relative significance of these sacrifices differently. Colonists claimed credit for having won the war. Some also wondered why they had put their lives on the line to capture Caribbean islands that would be used as bargaining chips among European powers. British soldiers, on the other hand, saw themselves as protecting the colonists, whom they regarded as ungrateful and often obstructionist. And British officers found colonial soldiers undisciplined—as General James Wolfe put it, "the dirtiest most contemptible cowardly dogs that you can conceive." For their part, some colonial soldiers chafed under British martial law and bitterly resented the arrogance of their commanders from overseas.

The practical question of how to apportion responsibility for the war's astronomical costs proved even more divisive. Britain's victories across the globe and its conquests in New France had been financed by loans from wealthy private investors. When the Seven Years' War started, Britain's national debt stood at 74.6 million pounds. By the time of the treaty, it exceeded 122.6 million pounds despite significant tax hikes during the war years (see How Much Is That?). The annual interest alone on that sum amounted to more than half of the national budget. The British government, now led by Prime Minister George Grenville, sought to pass some of this war debt along to the colonies through new taxes.

What made Grenville's policy especially tricky politically was the fact that colonists were used to paying significantly lower taxes than Britons in the home countries. To British eyes, this consideration only confirmed the equity of asking the colonists to contribute to the costs of administering and defending the empire. But to American colonists, who had come to expect minimal taxation, even a modest assessment felt burdensome. So when Parliament, in the 1764 Sugar Act, sought to shore up a duty, or import tax, on West Indian molasses that the colonists had ignored or circumvented for decades, a firestorm of protest erupted (see Chapter 6). British attempts to trim the massive debt by cutting costs would create other problems, but the policy of raising revenues from American colonists plotted a course of deep political conflict.

How Much Is That?

Britain's Postwar Debt

In 1763, Britain's national debt was £122.6 million. That is equivalent in U.S. dollars to about $18.35 billion in 2013. That figure may not sound staggering in the context of modern policies of deficit spending (the U.S. federal deficit in 2012 stood at $1.089 trillion), but in relation to the size of Britain's national budget and its gross domestic budget, the 1763 debt was much larger.

POPULATIONS ON THE MOVE

The new map created by the 1763 treaty rewrote the boundaries dividing European empires in North America. But the remapping did not automatically and instantaneously alter the character of the societies that had grown on American soil over previous generations. Lands officially labeled as British on the new imperial map did not suddenly become English speaking, Protestant, and loyal to King George III of England. As news of the Treaty of Paris circulated through the continent, colonists and natives had to decide what difference the new boundaries made. Their decisions about whether and where to move shaped postwar North America as well.

Most Indians living in the lands contested during the war rejected and resisted the peace treaty, to which they had not been signatories (see Revolution in Indian Country, below), but several Indian groups in eastern Canada chose to migrate after the war. As British officials and settlers began moving into southern Québec, the Abenakis, who had fought on the French side, headed to the margins of their earlier settlements. The Mi'kmaqs left their homes in Nova Scotia, either for the St. Pierre and Miquelon Islands retained by France in the treaty settlement or for distant parts of Newfoundland where British authority existed only on paper.

Britain's conquest of New France prompted a mass exodus of French soldiers and colonial officials, but most other French Canadians stayed put. Britain hoped to attract Protestant settlers to Québec and to integrate that colony into its empire, but both projects faltered, in part because of the perception that French Canada remained culturally foreign. Indeed, relatively few Britons and British colonists immigrated to Québec in the years after the war, and although Britain set up a Protestant-controlled government that conducted its affairs mostly in English, French-speaking Catholics remained the dominant population in British Quebec. After 1763, French Canadians were living under British sovereignty without adopting British culture.

French colonists in the Great Lakes and Illinois posed a greater problem to the British, since trade, social relations, marriage, and cultural identity had integrated them with Indians. Some British officials favored expelling French colonists from this region. Along the Mississippi River, many of them left voluntarily, crossing west (along with their Indian neighbors) into what was now Spanish Louisiana. Here, though Spain's flag now flew over the forts and cities in this colony, French cultural influence remained strong—and the migration of French speakers across the Mississippi reinforced that influence. The city of St. Louis was established in 1763 on territory that had just been ceded to Spain (though residents did not learn that fact until the following year). But its name, population, architecture, and overall character were distinctly French. Downriver, the older French city of New Orleans also fell to Spanish control, but French influences remained.

The transfer of Louisiana from France to Spain had further, significant consequences: It brought more African slaves to the territory and reshuffled Indian politics in Texas, where Caddo

Colonial Legacies. This 1909 painting of the famous Jackson Square in New Orleans shows the enduring imprint of both French and Spanish rule on the cityscape. The Cabildo (left) was the seat of Spanish colonial government after 1762, while the St. Louis Cathedral (center) reflects the earlier French presence, extending a tradition of Catholic churches on this site dating back to 1718. French architectural influence also appears on the Cabildo's mansard roof, added later.

Indians could no longer exploit the competition between French and Spanish powers. But here too, the removal of French power did not lead to the removal of French people or French culture. In fact, more French people moved to Louisiana under Spanish rule than when it was a French colony.

One remarkable legacy of the postwar French migration is Louisiana's Cajun community. At the war's onset, British authorities in Nova Scotia, suspicious of the loyalties of a large group of French speakers in the settlement of Acadia there, exiled six thousand Acadians to English-speaking colonies farther south. Dispersed through North America in small groups, Acadians faced hostility wherever they landed. Virginia simply refused to admit them. Some sought refuge in France. Meanwhile, New England settlers had moved north to claim the exiled Acadians' farmland. By 1763, a far-flung **Acadian diaspora** of thirteen thousand refugees from Nova Scotia had settled in numerous communities on both sides of the Atlantic Ocean. Only three hundred of them had made their way to French Louisiana, but with the encouragement of Spanish authorities, Acadians began migrating to French-speaking Louisiana and formed a new Cajun culture there. Today, we identify that culture with a complex cuisine that incorporates Louisiana vegetables and various culinary influences from the surrounding Indian and African populations.

In contrast to New France and Louisiana, Spanish Florida evacuated quickly once its territory changed hands. Britain divided the territory into two colonies, West Florida and East Florida, and granted religious toleration to the three thousand Spanish subjects there. But Florida's colonists had shallow attachments to the region and were not eager to stay and test the limits of that religious toleration. With the financial support of the Spanish Empire, which offered them property in Cuba, Florida's colonial population moved south en masse to the center of the Spanish Caribbean.

As Indians, French, and Spanish sought their places within and beyond the expanded borders of British sovereignty, British colonists rushed north to Canada, south to Florida, and especially west into Indian country. Migrating settlers sought lands that now seemed accessible to them—in many cases, lands deep in the interior of the continent that lay well beyond the control of provincial governments. Adding to this flood of colonial settlers was a tidal wave of foreign immigration, which had begun in the prewar years and resumed following the Treaty of Paris. Emigrants came in especially large numbers from Scotland after the war and settled along the periphery of British America—in Georgia, the Carolinas, western Pennsylvania, upper New York, and Canada. Some of these areas were called the backcountry, but from another perspective they now represented the advancing frontier of an aggressive settler society.

REVOLUTION IN INDIAN COUNTRY

The Treaty of Paris outraged the indigenous population of the region where British colonists were finding new homes. Indians had not participated in the treaty negotiations, nor did they consider themselves vanquished. Even those tribes that had fought alongside the French had done so for their own reasons and on their own terms. Moreover, they wondered, by what right could nations from across the ocean dispose of Indian lands to settle their disputes? As a Delaware Indian representative explained to an ambassador from Pennsylvania in 1758, "You white people are the cause of this war; why do not you and the *French* fight in the old country, and on the sea?"

But if Indians objected to the premise of the war, they also understood clearly the ominous implications of its resolution. Throughout the imperial wars of the eighteenth century, Indian groups had fought to preserve their independence by aligning themselves strategically with one or another European power. The ascent of the British and the departure of the French spelled an abrupt end to that political strategy. Now, British forts arose on Indian lands in the trans-Appalachian West, and

Indians could no longer rely on European allies to dislodge the intruders. Indians' resentment of the new local power intensified once they realized that the British were not interested in gift exchanges or diplomacy. General Jeffrey Amherst, the British commander-in-chief, had abandoned such practices, as he did not see "any reason for supplying the Indians with Provisions." Amherst expected Indians to trade furs as dutiful subjects, not as allies—and given the urgent need for fiscal restraint, there was no place in the imperial budget for gifts.

In April 1763, an Ottawa chief named Pontiac convened a war council of Indians from the Great Lakes and the Ohio Valley, urging them to join him in a campaign to purge the land of the British. Pontiac's Rebellion drew on the teachings of Neolin, a Delaware Indian prophet who exhorted Indians of different ethnicities to band together under a common banner, return to their cultural roots, and "live without any Trade or Connection with the White people." Neolin's pan-Indian message lumped together white people, but to Pontiac some white people were much more dangerous than others, and it was the transition from French to British power that alarmed him. "You see as well as I do that we can no longer supply our needs, as we have done, from our brothers the French." For Pontiac, the problem was less that trade with whites had become corrupting than that it had become exploitative: "The English sell us goods twice as dear as the French do, and their goods do not last."

Map 5.6 Pontiac's Rebellion. All across the Great Lakes region, Indians attacked British forts in 1763. At Fort Pitt, one of the only garrisons the British managed to defend, a Delaware chief made the meaning of the rebellion explicit: "You marched your armies into our country, and built forts here, though we told you, again and again, that we wished you to move; this land is ours, and not yours."

Over the next few months, Pontiac and his men seized nine British forts spread over a vast region (see Map 5.6), and they besieged the city of Detroit for half a year. Indians killed five hundred British soldiers and hundreds of white settlers, reclaiming much of the land where the war had begun in 1754. Amherst struggled to amass a force large enough to fight the rebellion. Reinforcements from Havana had been severely diminished by disease, and colonial assemblies, especially in New England, hesitated to commit troops to this second war, which seemed to have little to do with their protection. Through much of the summer of 1763, the British Empire struggled to keep its hold on its western territories.

Committed to using all necessary measures to destroy his Indian enemies, Amherst ordered his officers to take no prisoners. He even contemplated the use of germ warfare, proposing to Colonel Henry Bouquet that the British "Send the Small Pox among those Disaffected Tribes of Indians." Two months earlier, the commander at Fort Pitt appears to have given blankets infected with smallpox to Delaware Indians who had come on a diplomatic mission, but there is no evidence tying that

Mon Frere

La Parole que mon Pere a envoyée
pour faire la Paix je l'accepte, tous mes jeunes Gens
ont enterrés leurs Cassetêtes, je pense que tu oublieras
les mauvaises choses qui sont passées il y a quelque
tems; de meme j'oublirai ce que tu peut m'avoir faire
pour ne penser que de bonne, moi, les Saulteurs, les
Hurons, nous devons t'aller parler quand tu nous
demanderas, fais nous la Reponse, je t'envoye le
Conseil afin que tu le voye, si tu es bien comme
moi tu me feras reponse. Je te souhait le bon Jour.

A Monsieur
Mons.r Gladwin Major
Command.t au Detroit

signé Pondiak

Letter Composed by Pontiac, 1763. The Indian rebel leader's letter, written in French, lifts the siege of Detroit. **Question for Analysis:** What is the significance of Pontiac's use of the French language?

event to Amherst. Historians debate whether British stratagems were in fact responsible for smallpox outbreaks during the spring and summer of Pontiac's Rebellion.

By the fall of 1763, the Indians' war for independence was losing steam. William Johnson used his alliance with the Seven Nations of Canada to put diplomatic pressure on the tribes allied with Pontiac to end the siege of Detroit. The following year, two British armies invaded Ohio and the eastern tribes of Pontiac's coalition made peace. Pontiac himself finally came to terms a year later. Amherst had been recalled to England, and his successors dealt more cautiously with Indians, resuming gift exchanges and relying on diplomatic negotiations.

BRITAIN'S NEW INDIAN POLICIES

Although Pontiac's struggle for independence had failed to remove the British from Indian country, he succeeded in establishing the key point that Indians regarded Ohio and the Great Lakes region as their land. By capturing British forts, besieging British settlements, and killing British colonists, the rebellion persuaded imperial officials that they could not simply incorporate their new territorial acquisitions and rule all of the inhabitants as subjects of the British Crown. In October 1763, with Detroit still under siege, King George III promulgated a royal proclamation (see Interpreting the Sources: The Proclamation of 1763 and the Wampum Belt of 1764) establishing the Appalachian Mountains as the western border of Euro-American settlement. Hereafter, colonists could not settle or purchase land west of the Proclamation Line of 1763 without special royal authorization. Designers of the new policy did not expect the line between white and Indian land to remain fixed, but they did intend to keep firm control over changes to the boundary.

The British had several motivations for creating a partition between Indian land and the colonies. For one thing, the Easton Treaty of 1758, which had helped turn the tide of the

INTERPRETING THE SOURCES

The Proclamation of 1763 and the Wampum Belt of 1764

Britain's royal proclamation of 1763 aimed to solve an immediate political crisis in Indian country, but it would have far-reaching consequences for white-Indian relations, colonial politics, and the legal status of the native peoples of Canada. For decades, this document regulated Indian claims in British North America and established both the legal basis and the legal limitations of those claims. The proclamation even served as a model for an 1840 treaty between the British Empire and the Maori in New Zealand. But the proclamation was a unilateral gesture on the part of the British Crown, not a negotiated treaty. Even so, a year later, two thousand Indians representing twenty-four nations located throughout British North America gathered in Niagara, New York, to ratify the new political order.

At the Niagara convention, William Johnson read the text of the proclamation, and the Indian delegates acknowledged it as the terms of a new peace. To express and codify their agreement, Indians presented a Gus Wen Tah—a two-row belt of purple wampum beads representing the respectful separation of British and Indian nations. Below are excerpts from the proclamation's central provisions regarding Indian lands, accompanied by a picture showing a replica of the wampum belt.

And whereas it is just and reasonable, and essential to our Interest, and the Security of our Colonies, that the several Nations or Tribes of Indians with whom We are connected, and who live under our Protection, should not be molested or disturbed in the Possession of such Parts of Our Dominions and Territories as, not having been ceded to or purchased by Us, are reserved to them or any of them, as their Hunting Grounds.—We do therefore, with the Advice of our Privy Council, declare it to be our Royal Will and Pleasure. that no Governor or Commander in Chief in any of our Colonies of Quebec, East Florida. or West Florida, do presume, upon any Pretence whatever, to grant Warrants of Survey, or pass any Patents for Lands beyond the Bounds of their respective Governments. as described in their Commissions: as also that no Governor or Commander in Chief in any of our other Colonies or Plantations in America do presume for the present, and until our further Pleasure be known, to grant Warrants of Survey, or pass Patents for any Lands beyond the Heads or Sources of any of the Rivers which fall into the Atlantic Ocean from the West and North West, or upon any Lands whatever, which, not having been ceded to or purchased by Us as aforesaid, are reserved to the said Indians, or any of them.

And We do further declare it to be Our Royal Will and Pleasure, for the present as aforesaid, to reserve under our Sovereignty, Protection, and Dominion, for the use of the said Indians, all the Lands and Territories not included within the Limits of Our said Three new Governments, or within the Limits of the Territory granted to the Hudson's Bay Company, as also all the Lands and Territories lying to the Westward of the Sources of the Rivers which fall into the Sea from the West and North West as aforesaid.

And We do hereby strictly forbid, on Pain of our Displeasure, all our loving Subjects from making any Purchases or Settlements whatever, or taking Possession of any of the Lands above reserved without our especial war, committed the empire to protecting the lands of its Indian allies, while the terms of New France's surrender in 1760 obligated Britain to allow those Indians who had sided with the French to "be maintained on the Lands they inhabit." For another thing, as British officials recognized, retarding the westward flow of white settlement would make the colonies easier and cheaper to administer and might redirect Anglo-Protestant migrants toward territories in Canada and Florida where European Catholics had dominated. But the violence ignited by Pontiac made the proclamation's goals appear all the more urgent, because Britain could not afford perpetual war in Indian country. From the standpoint of the empire, restricting settlement was the price of peace in the western part of British America.

The Proclamation of 1763 did not automatically remove white settlers from western lands, nor did it seal off the border to new arrivals from the colonies. The new British policy did discourage settlement, however, especially among land speculators who needed to have their land titles legally recognized in order to secure their investments. Colonists with land claims and large-scale landowning ambitions objected to the proclamation and lobbied imperial officials to grant them land on the western side of the line. George Washington, viewing the proclamation as "a temporary expedient to quiet the Minds of the Indians," advised fellow speculators to scout out good land and stake their claims until the line moved westward or disappeared. Other colonists simply took their chances—and their guns—and moved west. In all of those cases, settlers' demands for access to western lands pitted them against the rule of the empire—and fueled a growing antipathy between Britain and the colonies.

Questions of Indian policy also divided the colonists themselves. On both sides of the new line, backcountry settlers advocated and implemented a harder, more violent approach to clearing Indian land, which sometimes put them at odds with coastal residents. In Pennsylvania, frontier settlers and supporters of westward expansion challenged the political authority of

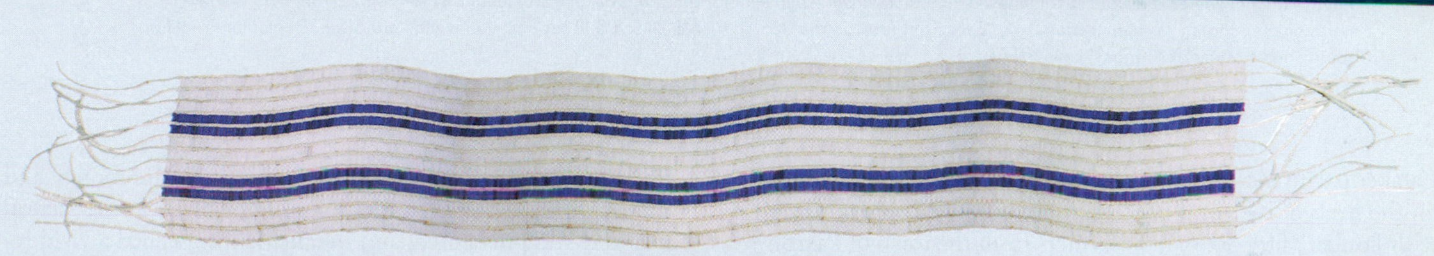

Replica Belt. The original 1764 diplomatic belt would have featured purple wampum arranged in this pattern.

leave and Licence for that Purpose first obtained.

And We do further strictly enjoin and require all Persons whatever who have either wilfully or inadvertently seated themselves upon any Lands within the Countries above described or upon any other Lands which, not having been ceded to or purchased by Us, are still reserved to the said Indians as aforesaid, forthwith to remove themselves from such Settlements.

And whereas great Frauds and Abuses have been committed in purchasing Lands of the Indians, to the great Prejudice of our Interests and to the great Dissatisfaction of the said Indians: In order, therefore, to prevent such Irregularities for the future, and to the end that the Indians may be convinced of our Justice and determined Resolution to remove all reasonable Cause of Discontent, We do with the Advice of our Privy Council strictly enjoin and require, that no private Person do presume to make any purchase from the said Indians of any Lands reserved to the said Indians, within those parts of our Colonies where, We have thought proper to allow Settlement: but that. if at any Time any of the Said Indians should be inclined to dispose of the said Lands, the same shall be Purchased only for Us, in our Name, at some public Meeting or Assembly of the said Indians, to be held for that Purpose by the Governor or Commander in Chief of our Colony respectively within which they shall lie: and in case they shall lie within the limits of any Proprietary Government.

. . .

Given at our Court at St. James's the 7th Day of October 1763. in the Third Year of our Reign.

GOD SAVE THE KING

Explore the Sources

1. Although the Proclamation of 1763 and the wampum belt assert the same terms for white-Indian relations, in what ways do these two kinds of primary sources, the text and the belt, differ?
2. How does the language of the proclamation reveal British attitudes toward Indians? Toward colonists?
3. Why does the proclamation require purchases of Indian land to take place in public meetings?
4. How might various groups of American colonists have responded to the terms and stipulation in the proclamation "that no private Person do presume to make any purchase from the said Indians of any Lands reserved to the said Indians, within those parts of our Colonies where, We have thought proper to allow Settlement?"

Political Cartoon Criticizing the Quakers' Friendly Relations with Indians and Supporting the Paxton Boys, 1764. Quaker merchant Abel James distributes tomahawks to Indians from a barrel belonging to Quaker Party leader Israel Pemberton, who is shown embracing an Indian woman. James says, "Exercise those on the Scotch Irish & Dutch & Ill support you while I am Abel." Benjamin Franklin brandishes a purse of "Pennsylvania Money."

Quaker pacifists centered in Philadelphia. At the end of 1763, on the heels of the royal proclamation and in the midst of war with Pontiac, fifty Scots-Irish farmers from the town of Paxton in Lancaster County went on an Indian-killing spree, murdering Conestogas, a group friendly to the colony, and mutilating their corpses. In January, these farmers, known as the Paxton Boys, led an army of five hundred through the streets of Philadelphia, demanding that the colony allocate money and soldiers to defend the frontier. No one involved in the Paxton massacre was prosecuted, and the incident remained a vivid reminder of how difficult it would be to control violence between whites and Indians. So, despite the assurances of the Proclamation of 1763, British colonists and native Americans continued to live in tense proximity on both sides of the Appalachians.

CONCLUSION

The French and Indian War was a monumentally important event in North American history. Most dramatically, the outcome signaled the end of imperial conflict on the eastern half of the continent that many Indian groups had strategically exploited to maintain their political independence and hold onto their lands. After 1763, for the first time, Indians faced a political map marked by a single eastern frontier, with British colonists advancing westward. The departure of the French also altered the position of the colonists in relation to Great Britain. More than half a century of imperial war and transatlantic commerce had brought the original English colonies closer to one another and more thoroughly identified with the empire and its military power. But now colonists no longer needed imperial protection against France. Instead, they saw a British state preparing to tax them and impeding their access to western lands.

Global conflict had impoverished France, leaving its regime vulnerable to a major revolution before the eighteenth century's end. But the settlement of the French and Indian War would hurt the victor as well. As he surrendered his country's North American colonies, the French foreign minister consoled himself with the prescient prediction that Britain would not be able to maintain control of its growing empire.

STUDY TERMS

- Covenant Chain (p. 104)
- Tuscarora War (p. 105)
- Queen Anne's War (p. 107)
- War of Jenkins's Ear (p. 108)
- King George's War (p. 108)
- Caddo (p. 110)
- Sioux (p. 110)
- Comanchería (p. 110)
- Indian liquor trade (p. 113)
- empire of goods (p. 113)
- Postal Act of 1711 (p. 114)
- Albany Convention (p. 115)
- Plan of Union (p. 115)
- French and Indian War (p. 115)
- Battle of the Monongahela (p. 115)
- Fort William Henry (p. 116)
- Easton Treaty conference (p. 118)
- Plains of Abraham (p. 118)
- Treaty of Paris (p. 119)
- war debt (p. 121)
- Sugar Act (p. 121)
- British Québec (p. 121)
- Spanish Louisiana (p. 121)
- Acadian diaspora (p. 122)
- Pontiac's Rebellion (p. 123)
- Proclamation Line of 1763 (p. 124)
- Paxton Boys (p. 126)

TIMELINE

1689–1697 King William's War (War of the League of Augsburg)

1701 Iroquois settlement at Montreal

1702–1713 Queen Anne's War (War of the Spanish Succession)

1707 Act of Union unites England and Scotland as Great Britain

1711 Postal Act integrates the colonies into
the British mail system

1711 Tuscarora War begins

1715 Yamasee War

1744–1748 King George's War (War of the Austrian Succession)

1754 French and Indian War begins

1754 Albany Congress proposes Plan of Union for intercolonial cooperation

1755 James Braddock's expedition to Fort Duquesne ends in failure

1756 Seven Years' War begins in Europe

1758 Easton Treaty returns Indian lands

1762 Spain enters the war; Britain invades Cuba

1763 Treaty of Paris ends the war

Pontiac's Rebellion begins

King George III issues Proclamation of 1763, recognizing Indian country

Paxton Boys massacre Indians in Lancaster Country, Pennsylvania

FURTHER READING

Additional suggested readings are available on the Online Learning Center at www.mhhe.com/becomingamerica1e.

Fred Anderson, *The War That Made America* (2005), provides a comprehensive account of the war as the major event in the lives of North Americans during the era.

Juliana Barr, *Peace Came in the Form of a Woman* (2007), demonstrates the importance of women to white-Indian diplomacy in the Texas borderlands, a region where natives were politically dominant.

T. H. Breen, *Marketplace of Revolution* (2004), illuminates the growth of Britain's empire of goods in the North American context.

Colin Calloway, *The Scratch of the Pen* (2006), treats 1763 as a pivotal year in the history of North America.

Konstantin Dierks, *In My Power* (2009), probes the development of correspondence and communications infrastructure in the eighteenth century.

Gregory Evans Dowd, *War Under Heaven* (2004), maps the fate and significance of Pontiac's Rebellion.

Pekka Hämäläinen, *The Comanche Empire* (2008), charts the growth of an overlooked political power in the American Plains and Southwest.

James Merrell, *Into the American Woods* (1999), studies the administrators, entrepreneurs, and converts who negotiated the fragile peace between natives and settlers in the Pennsylvania frontier.

Jane Merritt, *At the Crossroads* (2003), connects deteriorating white-Indian relations in the Middle Colonies to new ideas about race.

Daniel Richter, *Facing East from Indian Country* (2001), narrates the European colonization of North America from a native perspective and presents the French and Indian War as a turning point in that story.

Timothy J. Shannon, *Indians and Colonists at the Crossroads of Empire* (2000), places the Albany Plan of Union in the context of imperial politics and disputes some of the received wisdom regarding its provenance.

Peter Silver, *Our Savage Neighbors* (2009), shows how fear of Indian attack united a diverse society of immigrants to the British colonies in the 1750s.

Richard White, *The Middle Ground* (1991), highlights the role of culture in the diplomatic politics of the Great Lakes region in order to rethink the history of white-Indian relations in North America before 1815.

6

INSIDE

Toppling a Regime. Supporters of the colonial rebellion in New York City pull down the statue of King George III in 1776, as depicted by a nineteenth-century artist.

THE BIG PICTURE

After 1765, Britain's attempt to raise revenues in the colonies prompted widespread protests. Dramatic expressions of unrest bubbled up in thirteen of Britain's mainland colonies, both in the seaboard cities and in the backcountry, among men and women with different interests and perspectives. This turmoil reflected varied sources of discontent and ultimately produced a political crisis and a bloody, prolonged war for independence.

1765–1781

CRISIS & WAR

Hauled into court in Salisbury, Connecticut, in 1765 for beating up two men over a business quarrel, Ethan Allen removed his clothing, raised his fist, and branded his accuser a liar. According to court records, Allen, his six-foot, four-inch naked frame towering above everyone else in the room, then announced "with a loud voice . . . that he would spill the blood of any that opposed him." The judge dismissed the charges in return for a promise that Allen would leave town.

Allen continued to run afoul of the local authorities in his next New England community, and in 1769 he bought cheap farmland from New Hampshire and resettled in the Green Mountain region (now in Vermont). Allen and his neighbors soon discovered, however, that their land was claimed by New York. When authorities from New York tried to evict them, men holding New Hampshire deeds formed a militia called the Green Mountain Boys. With Allen as colonel, they terrorized their enemies, often dressing as Indians as they burned the homes or threatened the safety of individuals who claimed New York land titles. For the next five years, Allen led a successful vigilante campaign against those who sought to enforce the authority of the colony of New York.

Ethan Allen and his militia are better remembered today for their role in the massive war that broke out in 1775 and that ultimately severed the links between Great Britain and thirteen of its American colonies. But the Green Mountain Boys did not begin with talk of political independence. Outlaw warriors in the contested interior of northern New England, Allen's men had their own agenda and might easily have stayed out of the war between the rebellious colonies and the British. At least one prominent Green Mountain vigilante even advocated fighting on the British side to help defeat their New York enemies.

The political struggles of the 1770s divided British America in complicated and confusing ways, engulfing and absorbing local conflicts as they unleashed destructive violence up and down the eastern seaboard and beyond. The American Revolution, as these struggles came to be known, drew participants with varied goals and ideas, but over the course of the decade a powerful theme emerged. After the Green Mountain Boys captured the largest fortress in British North America in 1775 and ransacked its liquor supply, they toasted "the liberty and freedom of America." Rebellious colonists often used such language to explain their decision to take up arms against Great Britain. Words like *liberty*, *freedom*, and *independence* meant different things to different people and reflected a range of ideological influences. But amid the carnage and chaos of the revolutionary era, such rhetoric helped cultivate a unified purpose among those colonists who sought to disentangle themselves from the political bonds that had defined their world up to that point.

KEY QUESTIONS

- How did the French and Indian War precipitate a political crisis in the colonies?
- What were the colonists' central grievances, concerns, and beliefs in their growing rebellion against Parliament?
- How does the Revolutionary War fit within a larger history of civil strife, urban unrest, and popular violence in the thirteen colonies?
- What distinctive perspective did African Americans, both free and enslaved, have on the war?
- How did the war unfold and progress, and what were its crucial turning points?

In an era of violent political crisis, colonists waited anxiously for news from distant locales.

THE IMPERIAL CRISIS

During the French and Indian War, the British government and its mainland American colonies had clung tenaciously to one another. But the war left a trail of mutual resentment and staggering debt, and the victory left colonists less dependent on British protection. In an attempt to govern its growing empire, Britain pursued two strategies that alienated colonial leaders and alarmed many segments of the colonial population. First, it stationed more troops in North America. Second, it transferred to American colonists some of the costs of governing the empire. Those two policies became the targets of a new and powerful political opposition in the colonies.

MILITARIZATION OF THE BRITISH COLONIES

British soldiers serving in the French and Indian War had frequently antagonized the colonists they were sent to protect, but Americans nonetheless understood why they were there. Even after the departure of the French in 1763, many colonists appreciated that British troops were suppressing Pontiac's Rebellion and conquering land on the western frontier. By 1765, however, a standing peacetime army of ten thousand British soldiers remained in North America. Colonists were witnessing a striking shift in British imperial policy. After a long period of governing lightly and from afar, Britain was now asserting its power overseas.

In some parts of British America, the presence of red-coated soldiers was reassuring. In Britain's vast Caribbean empire, British warships protected island colonies from their French, Spanish, or Dutch neighbors while army garrisons supported white minorities against the persistent threat of slave rebellions. On most of the mainland, however, British colonies faced neither rival European settlements nor black majorities. In those colonies, Redcoats appeared to be a massive police force.

As he moved troops from Indian country to assume their permanent positions in the eastern settlements, Thomas Gage, commander in chief of Britain's American forces, faced the challenge of housing his men. He requested parliamentary authorization to seize both public and private buildings for this purpose. The British ministry worried about the political fallout from lodging soldiers in private homes, but they passed the Quartering Act of 1765, which gave the army broad access to colonial accommodations. Soldiers could now be placed in inns, livery stables, and houses that sold liquor. If the demand exceeded the capacity of those accommodations, soldiers could also be quartered in "uninhabited houses, outhouses, barns, or other buildings." To some colonists, the new law raised the specter of a military state imposing itself on the rights of private citizens.

TAXATION AND THE QUESTION OF REPRESENTATION

The Quartering Act was not only a military measure; it was a tax, since it required the colonies to pay for housing and feeding soldiers. Colonists had taken on such burdens in the past, but they had done so voluntarily. In mandating that the colonies pay for the empire's military presence, Parliament was bypassing the elected assemblies that had always claimed the right to tax the colonists. Following on the heels of the Sugar Act, which sought to enforce a long-evaded tax on molasses (see Chapter 5), the Quartering Act was part of Britain's prime minister George Grenville's new program of raising revenue and asserting parliamentary supremacy over the colonial legislatures.

Grenville's next move, the Stamp Act (1765), would prove the most controversial. Obligations to accommodate British troops and to pay customs on French molasses had well-established precedents. But with the Stamp Act, Britain broke new ground in the colonies by imposing a direct tax that had nothing to do with the regulation of international commerce. Colonists had to pay a tax on all printed matter and every legal document—newspapers, books, pamphlets, almanacs, liquor licenses, land conveyances, college diplomas, wills, and decks of playing cards. These items were required to bear a special stamp verifying that the tax had been paid. The stamp tax, as it was known, weighed most heavily on colonists in the coastal cities where printing presses were located and paper exchanges were especially common. But because legal documents and papers circulated deep into the interior and throughout British America, the stamp tax touched a broad segment of the population.

Almost immediately, the new tax set off a major political crisis. Although the tax rate was higher in the West Indies than in North America, it was the mainland colonists who responded to the Stamp Act with concerted outrage. Their grievance focused less on the financial burden of the tax than on what they perceived to be an assault on their traditional political rights and privileges as British subjects. Colonial politicians accused the Stamp Act of suppressing their free press by taxing newspapers and violating their rights to jury trials by granting military courts the power to try accused tax evaders. But most of all, they charged, the law infringed on the prerogatives of their elected assemblies and taxed colonists without their consent. Because colonists did not elect members of Parliament, the Stamp Act amounted to taxation without representation.

Opposition to the tax took different forms. Shortly before the new law was to go into effect, representatives from nine

Stamp Act Stamps, 1765. These one-penny stamps were used for newspapers and pamphlets. A similar tax had been in place in Great Britain for a long time, but imposing it in the colonies was a significant innovation in imperial policy.

mainland colonies gathered in New York City, where they composed a petition. Addressing themselves to both Parliament and King George III, members of the 1765 Stamp Act Congress rejected the idea that a distant government could rightfully impose taxes on its American subjects, asserting, "The people of these colonies are not, and from their local circumstances, cannot be represented in the House of Commons." Although the petition was deferential in its tone and philosophical in its approach, by this point angry colonists had already engaged in less polite forms of resistance. In the thirteen oldest British colonies on the mainland (everything south of Canada and north of Florida), resisters formed groups called Sons of Liberty to defy the Stamp Act and mobilized large groups of supporters to take to the streets. In August, a massive crowd in Boston forced the resignation of Andrew Oliver, the colony's designated stamp agent, by hanging him in effigy, destroying his warehouse, and vandalizing his home. In New York, protesters went after the governor himself, parading his effigy, burning his favorite chariot, and intimidating him into surrendering the colony's supply of stamps. By the year's end, tax agents in twelve of the thirteen colonies (all but Georgia) resigned. Royal officials in the colonies quickly concluded that the Stamp Act would be unenforceable.

As reports of petitioning, defiant speeches, and violent protests reached Britain, the government faced added pressure from London merchants who worried about the effects of colonial boycotts on their business. Under the leadership of a new prime minister, Lord Rockingham, Parliament repealed the Stamp Act in 1766 and also lowered the duty on molasses. At the same time, however, Parliament reaffirmed in the Declaratory Act that it had the authority to tax the colonies and that its laws were binding on "the colonies and people of America . . . in all cases whatsoever." Though the controversial tax was now dead, the crisis it had ignited was very much alive. The Stamp Act had unified thirteen of Britain's colonies—remarkably diverse societies with varied economic interests and different histories of settlement—in opposition to the empire and in support of a principle that Parliament had now officially rejected.

IDEALS AND IMAGES OF LIBERTY

A new generation of colonial orators and pamphleteers, including Patrick Henry, Samuel Adams, and James Otis, rose to political prominence during the Stamp Act crisis. They preached about *liberty*, which became the watchword of the colonists' resistance. Liberties, not shillings, the rebellious colonists insisted, were at stake in the dispute over taxation.

Opponents of the stamp tax had various things in mind when they spoke of liberty, including property rights, personal autonomy, and communal prerogatives. And they drew upon different philosophical and historical traditions in arguing that British taxes and the standing army those taxes supported threatened to turn the colonists into slaves. The Patriots, as rebellious colonists began identifying themselves, invoked ancient ideals of the Greek and (especially) Roman republics—a government with no monarch or emperor, a separation of powers, checks and balances among those powers, and great faith in the importance of virtuous, landowning male citizens. They also cited English legal precedents, such as the Magna Carta (1215), which constrained the powers of the king, as well as the long history of political settlements and charters that made up the English constitutional system of government. Many colonists spoke about "natural rights" in the language of the seventeenth-century English philosopher John Locke or that of the moral philosophers of the Scottish Enlightenment. Some critics of imperial policy borrowed concepts of liberty from Protestant theology, while others looked to the humanistic authors of the Italian Renaissance. In short, the ideals of liberty that the Stamp Act threatened had diverse origins and foundations.

Colonists paid special attention to opinions circulating in eighteenth-century England and saw themselves as participants in the ruling country's political discourse. Critics of imperial policy began calling themselves **Whigs,** the name of Britain's more liberal and pro-Parliament political party. They classified their colonial opponents as **Tories** after Britain's royalists, supporters of the king. One powerful strain of political rhetoric among the colonial Whigs echoed English essayists from earlier in the eighteenth century, who opposed the ruling party and nourished a deep suspicion of the corrupting influence of political power and luxury consumer goods. Liberty was always vulnerable, they believed, to the partisan schemes of professional politicians. Liberty was safe when political power lay in the hands of independent landowners whose votes could not be purchased or compromised because they lived virtuous lives free of luxury and debt.

Well-educated critics of imperial policy discussed and disseminated these ideals of liberty in sermons, newspaper articles, and lengthy treatises on politics. Widely read were John Dickinson's influential essays *Letters from a Farmer in Pennsylvania* (1767–1768), which declared that colonists were slaves because they were taxed without consent. But popular participation in the resistance movement depended on a broader cultural celebration of liberty, often involving rituals, ceremonies, symbols, songs, and images rather than learned texts. In New England, for example, colonists imagined liberty in the form of a tree—specifically an elm tree on the property of Deacon Jacob Elliot, who lived on the corner of Essex and Orange streets in Boston. During the Stamp Act crisis, colonists renamed the large elm, originally planted in 1646, the Liberty Tree because it was from its branches that tax agent Andrew Oliver dangled in effigy. The tree quickly became the symbol of the patriotic cause. A month after the big Boston riot, the Sons of Liberty convened under the elm, and all members received silver medals bearing an image of Elliott's tree. In other New England towns and cities, large old-growth elms and oaks

Deacon Jacob Elliot's Liberty Tree, Boston. Elliott's elm tree became a patriotic symbol because of its role in the Stamp Act protest. The tree appeared on a variety of New England banners and flags during the 1770s.

were designated as Liberty Trees and also became sites of public gatherings and protests. One of the first patriotic songs of the revolutionary movement paid homage to the idea of liberty as a tree: "The tree their own hands had to Liberty rear'd," the song ran, "They lived to behold growing strong and revered."

Liberty Trees appeared in other colonies as well, though some used alternative symbols to represent the reigning political ideal. When New Yorkers celebrated the repeal of the Stamp Act in 1766, they erected a ship's mast, dubbed the Liberty Pole, at the center of their festivity. Liberty Poles and Liberty Trees suggested different things about liberty. Elm trees represented liberty as something old, firmly planted, organically connected to the community, and a source of collective protection for those who gathered under its shade. Human-built poles suggested that liberty was something moveable and flexible around which a diverse community might choose to rally. But both trees and poles helped rebellious colonists imagine liberty as something real, not just an abstraction.

THE ESCALATING POLITICAL CONFLICT

Across the Atlantic, a change in the British prime ministry brought William Pitt, the man who had rescued the war effort a decade earlier, back to power. Beset by joint disease, Pitt put Charles Townshend, his chancellor of the exchequer (the national treasury), in charge of colonial policy. Townshend was eager to reduce the home country's military budget and at least as eager to back up the principle expressed in the Declaratory Act—that Parliament had complete legislative authority over the colonies.

The new tax bill Townshend pushed through Parliament in 1767, which became known as the Townshend Duties, introduced new import taxes on glass, lead, paint, paper, and tea. Because these were import duties rather than direct taxes, the law did not provoke as immediate or violent a colonial response as the Stamp Act. But merchants and other Whigs, especially in New England, still objected to the duties, because they recognized the law for what it was: an attempt to raise revenue, not to regulate trade.

Critics of the Townshend Duties were especially galled by the new law's stipulation that some of the revenue would go toward funding the salaries of the colonies' governors and judges. Those officials would thereby become more independent of the elected assemblies and less susceptible to the popular protests that had destroyed the stamp tax. Townshend also established new custom boards and courts to enforce the duties and redeployed more British troops from the west to the seaboard cities. Colonial Whigs saw a conspiracy afoot to deprive them of their liberties.

Taking the lead, Samuel Adams drafted a petition in 1768 on behalf of the Massachusetts House of Representatives, calling upon the lower houses of other British colonies to join in condemning the Townshend Act. Adams's Circular Letter acknowledged parliamentary supremacy, did not threaten any move toward independence, and attracted only mild support from a handful of other colonies. But the British government responded swiftly and forcefully. Lord Hillsborough, now directing colonial policy after Townshend's death, demanded that Massachusetts rescind the letter and ordered the dissolution of any colonial assembly that as much as received the Massachusetts petition. This policy backfired badly. Massachusetts legislators stood defiantly by the Circular Letter, and their counterparts in other colonies rallied to its defense. When the defiant colonial assemblies were dissolved, Whig rhetoric about an imperial design to suppress liberties in America seemed vindicated.

Reorganizing themselves, the Sons of Liberty in Boston began advocating boycotts of British imports as the best way to resist the empire's tax policies. **Nonimportation agreements** caught on only selectively among leading colonial merchants, but by 1770 they had cost Great Britain hundreds of thousands of pounds, and the Townshend Duties had yielded little in the way of revenue. In April of that year, Parliament repealed all of the taxes except for the one on tea. Despite the repeal, however, Britain was now locked in a political showdown with rebellious colonists. The empire's best hope was that divisions among and within the different mainland colonies would make widespread political opposition to British imports and British law and order impossible to sustain.

A DECADE OF POPULAR PROTEST

While Parliament and the colonial assemblies exchanged political maneuvers, a rising tide of angry protest swept through the colonies. Ordinary colonists engaged in daily acts of political expression and resistance. Some actions were directed at the imperial policies that enraged Whig politicians. But popular protest also focused on local grievances and targets, in these cases often dividing colonists rather than bringing them together. Whatever the sources of distress, political passions turned increasingly violent in urban and rural America alike in the years following the Stamp Act controversy.

CONSUMPTION AND NONCONSUMPTION

The political fight between Parliament and the colonial legislatures over taxes and imperial revenue highlighted the importance of colonists' consumer habits. The population of the American colonies had grown so large, and their buying power so great, that Britain was counting on surcharges on the colonists' purchases of imported goods to defray the costs of administering the empire. On the other side, Whig opponents of the new tax policy relied on the threat of a boycott of British imports to provide leverage in their negotiations with the home country.

Urban merchants turned to nonimportation agreements after the Townshend Act of 1767, but at first these agreements were difficult to sustain or enforce. Merchants were reluctant to damage their partnerships overseas and afraid of losing business to local rivals or to other colonial cities. Over the next several years, however, the boycott movement strengthened as rebellious colonists expanded their strategy from nonimportation to nonconsumption. Whereas nonimportation was a deliberate action by large urban buyers, **nonconsumption**—the decision not to buy or use items imported from other countries—entailed a change in the purchasing habits of ordinary men and women throughout the colonies.

The nonconsumption movement, which began in Boston, reinforced nonimportation agreements by calling on colonists to avoid all goods produced in Great Britain. Every purchase became a politically charged act and every article of clothing advertised its wearer's allegiances in the crisis (see Hot Commodities: Homespun Clothing). Consumers became a driving force in the protest of imperial policies, because instead of relying on merchants to cancel orders from British manufacturers, consumers boycotted those merchants who did not do so. In towns and cities in every colony, committees monitored the actions of importers and retailers and punished offenders. Patriots in Lancaster, Pennsylvania, for example, foreswore "any fellowship or correspondence" with merchants who sold imported goods—and even with the consumers who bought them. In New York, nonconsumption activists covered an offending jewelry store with scaffolding. Elsewhere, store owners found their doors and windows smeared with excrement.

The campaign against British goods helped build local communities of activists who joined in shaming their neighbors, but an effective boycott also required long-distance communication and coordination among different colonies. In the same way that their shared consumer habits helped American colonists identify with the British Empire (see Chapter 5), their collective refusal to consume helped them identify with a broad resistance movement. Patriotic boycotts also led to contentious discussions about consumer culture. Nonconsumption advocates, including many Puritan preachers, cited the frivolity of luxuries and preached the virtues of self-sacrifice. Sometimes they cast aspersions on the particular commodities they wished to boycott. Whigs decried the unhealthful effects of tea, for example, and spread the unappetizing and xenophobic rumor that barefoot Cantonese workers stomped the tea leaves into their containers. Poorer colonists also used the nonconsumption campaign to criticize the spending habits of the affluent.

Women played prominent public roles in the colonial boycotts as debates about consumption politicized realms of daily life where women were active as both consumers and producers. Especially in wealthier households, women made significant purchases of imported goods, including clothing, tea, furniture, and utensils. Whig critiques of colonial dependence on British luxury goods often blamed upper-class women for their overconsumption and stigmatized the taste for luxuries as effeminate and dangerous to manly liberty. Such stereotypes made it seem more urgent that female consumers join in the political protests against imperial tax policies. Women's labor moreover assumed even greater significance during the post-1765 crisis than before, because the success of the nonconsumption campaign hinged on the colonists' ability to replace British fabrics and clothing with American-made alternatives. Textile production had become women's work in the eighteenth-century colonial farm household, and women were now called upon to increase their output of homespun cloth.

To publicize women's patriotic contributions to the cause, New England's Whigs organized spinning bees, traditional gatherings where women spun yarn or thread for clothing, often for a local minister. Newspaper editors held up the spinners as symbols of the "industry and frugality of American ladies" and hailed their local contributions to "the political salvation of a whole Continent." Though political publicity stunts, New England spinning bees alluded to the very real fact that countless ordinary women in small towns had to work much harder to support their households' decisions to forgo British imports.

VIOLENCE IN THE COUNTRYSIDE

While consumer boycotts summoned the energies of Patriots in eastern towns and cities and connected their daily activities to public debates about taxation, those in the colonies' rural interior were swept into very different political protests. These conflicts in the countryside had little to do with import duties or the rights of colonial assemblies. Nonetheless, they helped to shape colonial politics after 1765 and contributed to a climate

HOT COMMODITIES

Homespun Clothing

Among the many imported items that tied the American colonies to the British Empire, fabric was by far the most common. Imported clothing dominated American fashion by midcentury, and except for those who were enslaved, most colonists in the 1760s wore British textiles on their bodies every day. The nonimportation movement could not completely change this fact of colonial life, but it exerted powerful pressures to shop—and dress—differently. Opponents of British tax policies boycotted all kinds of popular consumer goods, but clothing was in a category of its own, both because of the importance of textile production to the British economy and because clothing was such a visible and loaded expression of one's identity and solidarity.

Homespun clothing was generally made of coarse linen or wool (or both), but there was no reason why a garment manufactured in the colonies could not appear elegant. Several of the homespun clothes that survive from the late eighteenth century show fashionable cuts and fine tailoring. When George Washington appeared at his inauguration in an American-made suit of fine material and silk stockings, observers mistook his outfit for a foreign import.

For the most part, however, patriotic colonists reveled in homespun's conspicuous simplicity. But only if a homespun garment looked the part could it serve as a badge of support for revolutionary activism. In particular, older and simpler clothing—whether or not it was made from fabric spun in the colonies—best lent support to the cause, because it discouraged the impression that the wearer had violated the boycott. More generally, simple dress embodied a broader poltical ideal celebrated by the rebellious colonists, who associated luxury with aristocracy and effeminacy. In Benjamin Franklin's imagination, the model citizen of a republic appeared "in the plainest Country Garb; his Great Coat was coarse and looked old and thread-bare; his Linnen was homespun; his Beard perhaps of Seven Days Growth, his Shoes thick and heavy, and every Part of his Dress corresponding." As has often been the case in American history, the line between fashion and politics was thin in the era of the Revolution.

Boy's Suit from Virginia, ca. 1780. Though made of coarse homespun cloth, this apparel was cut in the contemporary style.

Think About It

1. How did the homespun movement empower ordinary colonists? How might it have oppressed them?
2. Why were clothes made in America likely to be of inferior quality in the 1760s and 1770s?

of instability. They also readied a cohort of rural American men for armed violence.

Rural violence was often the work of vigilante groups angry at seaboard elites, much like Pennsylvania's Paxton Boys, who massacred Indians and besieged the colonial government in Philadelphia in the aftermath of the French and Indian War (see Chapter 5). Backcountry settlers in South Carolina organized in 1767 to demand government protection against cattle thieves and outlaw gangs. Calling themselves **Regulators,** they policed the frontier and administered extralegal punishments to individuals accused of crimes. Yet though South Carolina Regulators may have been expressing local grievances, they spoke the same political language as Whig merchants protesting the Stamp Act. "We are *Free-men*—British subjects—Not Born Slaves," they insisted, demanding increased representation in colonial government. In neighboring North Carolina, a much larger Regulator movement also protested the underrepresentation of backcountry farmers. North Carolina Regulators expressed particular hostility to wealthy slaveholding elites and protested the legislature's decision to build a lavish governor's mansion in the capital of New Bern. By 1771, most white male residents of the North Carolina backcountry had joined in the violent protest, which withheld tax payment, disrupted court proceedings, and defied the authority of the colonial government.

The two Carolina Regulator movements met different fates. In part because colonial leaders in slave-majority South Carolina worried that violence in the countryside would create the conditions for another slave uprising like the Stono Rebellion of 1739, they sought to mollify the protesters by granting some of their demands. In North Carolina, where the threat of slave revolt seemed more remote and where the social conflict had already widened, colonial authorities violently suppressed the protests, executing leading Regulators and imposing a loyalty oath on Piedmont settlers.

Farther north, tenant farmers and rural squatters in New York's Hudson River valley organized both a rent strike and an armed rebellion in 1766, drawing inspiration from urban protests against the Stamp Act. Angry about high rents and evictions, farmers working plots owned by the Van Cortlandt and Livingston families threatened to murder their manorial landlords. Like the Regulators, rural New Yorkers organized militias and broke open local jails. British troops had to be called in to end their rebellion. The notorious Green Mountain Boys in northern New England (see chapter opening) also began as a band of farmers trying to protect their rights to stay on their land. And like other rural protesters from the period, they defiantly rejected traditional assumptions about deference to social elites or to established law and order. When New York's governor sought to enforce New York land deeds through a proclamation, Ethan Allen responded that the Governor might "stick it in his ars." In the early 1770s, most Whig leaders in coastal towns and cities did not see such rural unrest as part of a larger defense of colonial liberties against British tyranny. Indeed, colonial legislatures were usually the targets rather than the leaders of backcountry rebellions. But armed violence in the continent's interior made the colonies much harder to govern and portended a wider unraveling of Britain's American empire.

URBAN CROWDS AND STREET THEATER

Protesters in large towns and cities were less likely to carry firearms than their rural counterparts, but their dense settlement made violent protest easier to organize and quicker to erupt. Urban rioting was an established tradition in eighteenth-century America, often associated with restoration of law and order rather than its subversion. Urban riots typically involved fifty to a hundred men and targeted property, destroying buildings or goods that were symbolically linked to a common grievance. Rioters claimed to be acting on behalf of the shared norms or values of the entire city, and did not necessarily see themselves as lawbreakers. When rioters were poor, their critics would deride them as dangerous "mobs," a word that came from the Latin term *mobile vulgus*, meaning the fickle or unrooted common people. But one person's mob was another's legitimate crowd action.

The Stamp Act crisis initiated a major escalation in the history of urban rioting. Riots became more frequent, more violent, and involved many more participants, practically obliterating the blurry line between mob action and elite-sanctioned protest. Whig leaders sought to control the 1765 riots, but lower-class urbanites often set the tone, moving beyond attacks on stamps and stamp agents to express anger against the privileges and trappings of wealth. Twelve days after they forced the resignation of the stamp tax collector, rioters in Boston entered the stately home of Thomas Hutchinson, the chief justice of Massachusetts, tore down its brick walls, destroyed his furniture and many of his legal documents, emptied his wine cellar, and stole his cash. Samuel Adams condemned the "truly mobbish nature" of the attack, though many Bostonians on both sides of the conflict recognized it as a central part of the political protest against British authority.

Even after the Stamp Act was repealed, colonial cities became hotbeds of conflict and collective action. One historian has counted 150 different riots in the thirteen colonies in the second half of the 1760s. As with the rural unrest of the period, not every riot was directed against British rule. But they undermined authority, inflamed passions, and habituated colonists to both the threat and the reality of violence.

Riots and demonstrations turned city streets into stages for political performances. Burning effigies, destroying building facades, and loud shouting were common rioting strategies, because they dramatized the power of the crowd and brought shame upon political opponents. Tarring and feathering

Tarring and Feathering. This engraving published in London in 1774 depicts two Bostonian Sons of Liberty torturing a British customs official.

Paul Revere's Engraved Depiction of the Bloody Violence That Patriots Dubbed the Boston Massacre. Neither Revere nor the other engraver from whom he copied this image witnessed the event (which Loyalists and other conservatives referred to as the riot on King Street). The best evidence indicates that British captain Thomas Preston stood in front of his men, in which case it would have been unlikely that he ordered his soldiers to fire. **Question for Analysis:** What can you learn from this image about the identity of the victims?

became a trademark shaming ritual during this period. Tories, haughty colonial officials, or merchants who violated nonimportation agreements might find themselves stripped naked, covered with tar and then feathers, and paraded in the streets. This punishment was not simply a quaint form of humiliation, however. Rioters sometimes upped the stakes by setting the feathers on fire. And when victims eventually sought to remove the tar, their skin would come off in chunks and introduce risks of serious infection.

Urban protests could turn brutal and destructive, but the relative absence of guns among the rioters made fatalities rare. The presence of more British troops on city streets in the late 1760s, however, introduced a more lethal element to the mix. On March 5, 1770, British soldiers guarding a customs house in Boston fired on a crowd of local laborers who were angrily heckling them and pelting them with snowballs and stones. Eleven civilians were struck by gunfire, five of them fatally. After a lengthy trial, the commanding officer and most of the soldiers involved were acquitted, but the Boston Massacre became a rallying cry for rebellious colonists. Broadcast by Paul Revere's famous color engraving of the event, which showed Redcoats shooting civilians at close range, the death of five civilians on the streets of Boston came to stand for the threat to colonial rights and liberties.

THE TEA PARTY AND THE MOVE TO COERCION

Widespread social unrest helped set the stage for a dramatic and fateful urban demonstration in 1773 that fundamentally altered the course of imperial politics. After three years of relative peace between Britain and the colonies over tax policy, Prime Minister Frederick Lord North introduced a law to reinforce the last remaining Townshend duty, the tax on tea. North's principal goal was to bail out the British East India Company, a financially troubled and mismanaged private corporation that sold Chinese tea to British customers. North's Tea Act allowed the company to avoid export taxes, eliminate middlemen, and sell tea directly and inexpensively in America. Because the price would now be lower—even with the import tax—than Dutch tea smuggled into the colonies, North assumed that Americans would happily purchase East India tea and pay the tax. But the Sons of Liberty saw in North's move both an imperious insistence on Parliament's right to tax the unrepresented colonies and a sneaky plot to conceal the tax and induce colonists to pay for the British military presence. Many colonial importers also resented the way the Tea Act bypassed them, selling directly to special agents. Though the tea tax was modest, opponents charged that it threatened a larger political and economic assault on the colonies.

Whig leaders called for tea boycotts, appealing to what was now a familiar strategy of consumer politics and urging colonists to abstain from tea drinking altogether. But Americans were attached to their tea, and total abstinence was an unrealistic goal. And since a great deal of illegally imported Dutch tea was available in colonial stores, it would be impossible to enforce a social taboo against only those tea leaves that came from the British East India Company. Rebellious colonists therefore focused their wrath on the tea shipments, rather than the act of tea drinking, hoping to prevent the new product from landing in the first place. The boats carrying the tea, one Pennsylvania writer warned, were "the true and literal Pandora's box, filled with poverty, oppression, slavery, and every other hated disease." They had to be turned back. As tea shipments headed for the colonies in fall of 1773, activists in the four major mainland port cities threatened the consignment agents who had been specifically authorized to sell the tea. Agents in New York, Philadelphia, and Charleston, mindful of the rising tide of urban violence, decided to resign. Tea shipments to those cities went undelivered or never made it out of local storage.

In Boston, however, the colonial authorities stood firm. Massachusetts governor Thomas Hutchinson, whose two sons had been named

"Man and Child Drinking Tea," ca. 1720. Because tea was associated with elite tastes and social rituals, it had become an especially popular target of lower-class resentment during the consumer protests of the period. **Question for Analysis:** What features of the painting mark tea drinking as an elite activity?

"Americans Throwing Cargoes of the Tea Ships into the River, at Boston," 1789 engraving. The men who boarded the *Dartmouth* and destroyed the tea represented a range of social backgrounds. They dressed as Indians to conceal their identities, intimidate their enemies, and achieve dramatic effects in the theater of urban protests. In addition, they might have wanted to claim a special connection with the American continent, as opposed to Britain (see Chapter 9).

How Much Is That?

The Tea in Boston Harbor

The £10,000 worth of East India tea cast into Boston Harbor in 1773 is equivalent to about $1.45 million in 2013.

as consignment agents, refused to allow the three tea-bearing ships to return to England without unloading their cargo. Hutchinson had been the chief justice during the Stamp Act crisis, and his home had been ransacked. Like his opponents, he now saw the showdown over tea as a crucial test of imperial authority. On December 16, after an anxious stalemate that gripped the city for twenty days of public agitation, a well-organized band of 100 to 150 men, disguised as Indians, climbed aboard the anchored ships, chopped open 342 tea chests with hatchets and axes, and unloaded their contents into Boston Harbor. The Boston Tea Party, as the incident would be named in the 1830s, destroyed about £10,000 worth of property belonging to the East India Company (see How Much is That?) and thwarted the hated tea tax.

The destruction of the tea broke new ground in urban protests to British tax policies, and both King George and Lord North called for a punitive response. Parliament passed four Coercive Acts in the spring of 1774, designed to reassert imperial authority over its rebellious colony and compel Bostonians to compensate the East India Company for the destroyed tea. The new laws closed Boston's harbor and dismantled Massachusetts's self-government by abrogating its colonial charter and suspending all town meetings. Other controversial provisions of the laws protected royal officials from being tried for crimes in the colonies (where popular anger might wield influence) and empowered the colony's royal governor to appoint and fire judges. Parliament also expanded the boundaries of Quebec and granted freedom of religion to Catholics.

The Quebec Act was not part of the Coercive Acts, except in the minds of rebellious colonists. Britain hoped to shore up the political allegiances of its loyal Quebec colony and further isolate Massachusetts and its supporters. But to some colonists, including Virginia land speculators such as George Washington, Thomas Jefferson, and Patrick Henry, the southward expansion of Quebec into the Ohio River valley was a painful reminder that British policy blocked western land settlement. The deeper outrage of the Quebec Act, however, especially in New England, lay in its accommodation to Catholics. To many American Protestants, the conflict with Parliament began to look more like a holy war.

Whig leaders lumped together these five laws—the four Coercive Acts and the Quebec Act—as the "Intolerable Acts," but it was not immediately clear how rebellious colonists would express their intolerance. The British Navy did not need the cooperation of Boston residents to close the port. But the new law amending the Massachusetts charter to make judges, sheriffs, and peace officers directly answerable to the royal governor proved more vulnerable to popular protest. When Crown-appointed officials tried

Protesting the Intolerable Acts. A Virginia merchant signs the Williamsburg Resolutions of 1774, a pledge to observe a moratorium on exporting tobacco. The alternative to bearing the loss of revenue from their most lucrative crop, this scene implies, is public humiliation via the tar and feathers that hang from the courtyard gallows.

to hold court sessions in Massachusetts, outraged farmers and artisans gathered en masse and physically prevented them from doing so. In Worcester County, more than 4,600 men from thirty-seven different towns (about half the county's adult male population) marched to the county seat and blocked access to the courthouse. In other towns throughout the colony, royal officials were threatened and forced to resign. By October 1774, the British Empire no longer controlled the Massachusetts countryside.

MOBILIZING FOR REVOLUTION

Britain's leadership regarded the escalating rebellion in Massachusetts in 1773–1774 as a local crisis that might be isolated. Massachusetts was only one of twenty-six British colonies in the Americas—one of eighteen on the mainland. For Americans enraged by the Intolerable Acts, the challenge lay in cultivating intercolonial ties and coordinating a response to British policies. As they corresponded, convened, and published about the infringements of their liberties, rebellious colonists in thirteen of the mainland colonies built a powerful resistance movement and pushed the imperial conflict to a breaking point.

SPREADING THE WORD

Amid the intensifying crisis, opponents of British policy in North America established procedures and media for circulating news from one colony to another. Virginia took the lead in 1773, establishing a committee to maintain "Correspondence and Communication with our sister colonies," and within a few months almost every other colony followed suit. In Massachusetts, active correspondence committees at the township level had been organizing resistance within the colony since 1772. These Committees of Correspondence played an important practical role in the events leading up to the war and

Opening Prayer at the First Continental Congress. The Continental Congress was an important event simply for mobilizing Patriot leaders and bringing them together on unfamiliar terrain. Many of the delegates had never seen America's largest city, and most had never met one another. John Adams took copious notes on his surroundings, describing every building and street in Philadelphia. As he left Philadelphia, in October 1774, he noted in his diary that "it is not very likely that I shall ever see this part of the world again." In fact it was the first of many stays for the future vice president and second president. This painting shows Anglican reverend Jacob Duché, rector of Christ Church, Philadelphia, leading the opening prayer to Congress.

also provided a model for connecting a dispersed population that had no history of regular contact.

Members of correspondence committees did not hold conventional political positions. Most were not elected, and though all of them came from the circles that dominated local politics, they wielded no formal power and did not pose as replacements for British rule. But any institution of intercolonial communication was a potentially revolutionary threat to the empire, since regulating the flow of goods, persons, and information lay at the core of imperial rule. British authorities and their supporters saw the mere existence of correspondence committees as a political outrage. Massachusetts Tory writer Daniel Leonard called them "the foulest, subtlest and most venomous serpent ever issued from the eggs of sedition." Earlier, colonists had used British communication networks to forge political ties. But the new committees did more than simply forge ties or spread news. By establishing independent channels of political contact, colonists initiated a process of building a nation (see Chapter 7).

Perhaps the most salient achievement of the committees of correspondence was the call for a convention of colonial leaders in Philadelphia in September 1774 to respond to the British crackdown in Boston. Dubbing this gathering a "continental congress," organizers hoped to attract representatives from colonies throughout British North America. Twelve of the invited colonies answered the call (Georgia did not, nor did East and West Florida or any of the three Canadian colonies), sending fifty-six delegates to a meeting that would later become known as the First Continental Congress. Like correspondence committees, congresses were media of communication. Instead of circulating messages, letters, and pamphlets via relay over the wide extent of the colonies, the Continental Congress convened select individuals from their scattered homes to a single location for a face-to-face encounter.

The fifty-six men who gathered in Philadelphia in 1774 were prominent figures in the various colonies, many of whom had acquired renown as orators or pamphleteers in the Whig cause. But they came from disparate places and represented a range of ideological perspectives. Over seven weeks of discussion and deliberation, the delegates expressed and debated different approaches to the crisis. More cautious representatives from the Middle Colonies, such as Joseph Galloway of Pennsylvania, pushed the moderate measure of establishing a special American Parliament in which the colonists would be indirectly represented, but most delegates wanted a more forceful and radical response to the Intolerable Acts. Still, they did not advocate independence from the British Empire. Congress called for peaceful redress of grievances, not armed rebellion, and delegates were careful not to burn all bridges back to where things stood before 1765. They addressed their petitions and resolutions to King George, rather than to Parliament, both as a way of rejecting parliamentary authority and as a way of maintaining a posture of allegiance to the British Crown. Eager not to sever ties with the King, Congress blamed the current crisis and the repressive policies of the past decade on "the devices of wicked Ministers and evil Counsellors."

Exile of the American Company of Comedians to the West Indies. This painting, by Charles Willson Peale, depicts actress Nancy Hallam in 1771 playing cross-dressed as Fidéle in Shakespeare's *Cymbeline*. The Continental Congress expressed its collective disapproval of the theater, banning all plays "and other expensive diversions and entertainments" throughout the colonies and for an indefinite period of time. Proscribing plays was intended both as a boycott of British theatrical culture and as a means of underscoring the solemnity and virtue of the patriotic cause.

Though delegates spoke of liberties and rights, the overriding theme of the First Continental Congress was unity. Defying Parliament's attempt to isolate Boston for that city's seditious behavior, Congress rallied around the Massachusetts resistance, resolving officially "that the town of Boston and province of Massachusetts Bay, are considered by all America as suffering in the common cause." As a concrete demonstration of this unity, Congress agreed to ban all British imports immediately and threatened to block all exports (except rice) to Britain, Ireland, and the British Caribbean the following year if Parliament did not repeal the Coercive Acts. These were timely and momentous measures, but they were intended to weather a storm and restore an older colonial order that had prevailed before the Stamp Act. Only if the British government failed to address their grievances, delegates resolved, would the colonies regroup as a congress the following year.

THE BEGINNINGS OF WAR

Britain did not accede to the demands of the Continental Congress. Though several powerful voices in Parliament urged conciliation and compromise, they were outnumbered. Prime Minister North's government refused to repeal the Coercive Acts, as they had done with the Stamp Act and the Townshend Duties. Instead, North declared Congress an illegal assembly

***Battle of Lexington*, by Amos Doolittle, 1775.** The scene, painted by a young artist sympathetic to the rebellion, shows the British firing on militiamen attempting to flee.

and ordered a naval blockade on the rebellious colonies to prevent them from trading with other nations. And in a move that was bound to lead to bloodshed, North also ordered General Gage to end the rebellion in Massachusetts by arresting its leaders and seizing its munitions supplies.

On April 18, 1775, Gage sent seven hundred soldiers on a night raid from Boston to the town of Concord, where rebel arms were stored. When they arrived the next morning, Gage's soldiers met Patriot militiamen who had been warned by riders from Boston that "the Regulars" were coming. The two forces exchanged fire, first in the nearby town of Lexington and then in Concord itself. The Battle of Lexington and Concord took the lives of seventy-three Redcoats and forty-nine Massachusetts Militiamen. Another 213 men (mostly on the British side) were wounded in the clash. As British soldiers retreated toward Boston without having captured many weapons, more shots were exchanged and the toll rose. From one perspective, this event could have been seen simply as an especially bloody event in the waves of armed violence that had been rippling through the American countryside for a decade. But the involvement of the Royal British Army, which was in the process of deploying twenty thousand additional troops to suppress the colonial rebellion, and the casualties suffered by Gage's army ensured that the battle would have more dramatic implications. In the escalating dispute over Britain's imperial authority, Lexington and Concord struck many participants as an irreparable rupture.

News of the fighting in Lexington and Concord spread quickly, by eighteenth-century standards, thanks to a network of express riders. Word reached Connecticut and Maine by the next day and New York City just three days later. As handwritten reports headed steadily south over the next two weeks by horse, passing from community to community as far as South Carolina (one thousand miles from Boston), colonists gathered at taverns and meetinghouses to react to the event. It was important that these handwritten reports were signed by known members of correspondence committees, because the possibility of false information was all too real. Just six months earlier, mistaken intelligence from Boston had drawn thousands of New England minutemen to defend the Massachusetts capital against a rumored attack that never took place. But when the news of Lexington and Concord came to town, local Patriots respected the authority of the speedy relay network along which it traveled. Men and women living beyond the reaches of this revolutionary network had to wait significantly longer for this news (often until a soldier or traveler happened to pass through their inland communities) and were less likely to feel as though they were witnessing an unfolding imperial drama.

News reports also hastened the spread of the fighting. Less than a month after Lexington and Concord, two distinct groups of New England militiamen (one commanded by Ethan Allen, the other by Benedict Arnold) converged on Fort Ticonderoga in New York and forced a British surrender. Allen then took another fort at nearby Crown Point (see Map 6.1). In capturing the two forts, the rebellious colonists also acquired cannons, mortars, howitzers, and a significant volume of ammunition. By summer, some of those arms had been brought to Boston, where Patriot forces began a siege of the British stronghold in occupied Boston.

Amidst this violent unraveling of the empire, the political leaders of the rebellion reconvened as planned in Philadelphia, this time as thirteen colonies. But despite sharing a name, the Second Continental Congress differed significantly from its predecessor. By May 1775, hopes of peaceful redress had dimmed. The second Congress was not an emergency session with a limited agenda but the beginning of an ongoing conversation among colonial representatives who together formed a makeshift government for the rebellion. Ultimately, this was the government that would cut ties with the empire, but for more than a year Congress refused to do so. They wasted no time, however, in taking command of the war against British rule. Congress created a Continental Army with eighty-eight battalions and appointed George Washington as general. It also authorized the printing of currency in order to pay for the war and sent representatives to negotiate alliances with Indian groups. Congress accounted for these actions in July with the Declaration of the Causes and Necessity for Taking up Arms, but they followed that declaration two days later with an Olive Branch Petition asking George III to intervene and restore peace to the empire. While these mixed messages circulated, Congress also established one institution of civil administration—a continental postal system, which effectively supplanted the British Post Office in the colonies.

Congress was walking a fine line in 1775, acknowledging that a state of war existed, but officially still opening the door to a restoration of the colonies' political status within the empire. In the Olive Branch Petition, the representatives referred to themselves as "your Majesty's faithful subjects" and expressed hope for "a happy and permanent reconciliation." His Majesty was unmoved. On August 23, 1775, King George III declared the thirteen colonies to be in rebellion, marking a political point of no return in the imperial crisis. A year later, Congress would formally declare independence, instruct the colonies to refashion themselves as states, and embark on the project of building a nation (see Chapter 7).

MAKING THE CASE IN PRINT

As members of the Second Continental Congress began coordinating a massive military campaign to beat back British forces, other colonists waged a battle for public opinion. Patriots sought to popularize colonial grievances against Parliament and to drum up support for the war effort. Much of this discussion took place in print. By the time of the Second Congress, thirty-eight different newspapers were circulating in Britain's mainland colonies, and the men who printed those papers were deeply preoccupied with imperial politics. In most cases, printers were early supporters of resistance to parliamentary taxation. The Stamp Act, after all, had been an attack on the printing trade. But whatever their financial interests or their personal politics, printers drew public attention to the dramas of revolution, war, independence, and nation building by flooding American towns with a steady stream of printed essays, sermons, letters, declarations, newspapers, and even almanacs that broadcast the revolutionary changes afoot.

The print medium was especially useful for this purpose because it allowed authors to address their readership without appearing in public gatherings, without claiming any special social standing, and without identifying themselves personally. Sam Adams, for example, contributed frequently to public debates about independence but hardly ever addressed a crowd. And though he became well known during the revolutionary crisis on both sides of the Atlantic, he rarely published under his own name. Instead, Adams adopted more than twenty-five different pseudonyms, which had the intended effect of suggesting that his patriotic views belonged to the general climate of public opinion rather than to the particular perspective of an esteemed individual. Anonymous or pseudonymous publication was a common rhetorical strategy in revolutionary America and had the added benefit of protecting authors from prosecution for treason.

In January 1776, an obscure former corset maker who had recently emigrated from England authored a pamphlet entitled *Common Sense.* Under the cover of anonymity, Thomas Paine ignored the advice of friends and boldly advocated independence, using colorful and provocative language to persuade American readers to abandon hopes of reconciliation and embrace their future as citizens of a democratic republic. While other pamphleteers claimed the rights of British subjects under the Crown, Paine ridiculed the monarchy itself and bid farewell to the "so much boasted constitution of England." The first printing of *Common Sense* sold a thousand copies in a week, and it was reprinted quickly in other towns and cities in seven different colonies, becoming the best-selling pamphlet in the history of colonial America. The remarkable circulation of *Common Sense* emboldened rebellious colonists to believe that they were advocating a popular cause. As one delegate to the Second Congress reported on his way back from North Carolina, the cry throughout the land was "Common sense and Independence." That same year, Paine composed reports on the war for Philadelphia newspapers, as well as a series of thirteen essays, entitled *The American Crisis,* to promote the armed struggle against Britain. Officers in the Continental Army would read passages to inspire and embolden their troops. "These are the times that try men's souls," Paine famously proclaimed at the beginning of the first essay. "Tyranny, like hell, is not easily conquered; yet we have this consolation with us, that the harder the conflict, the more glorious the triumph."

MUSTERING ARMIES

In the war's opening months, colonists volunteered enthusiastically for military duty in the rebel forces. Some joined local militias, serving close to home for short terms—as short as thirty days—while others enlisted in Washington's army. The difference between the two experiences was stark. **Militiamen** generally returned to their farms after the summer, were not forced to surrender entirely to the rigors of military discipline, and often elected their own officers. **Regulars,** as the full-time soldiers were called, typically enlisted for much longer stints, faced more brutal conditions, and suffered much higher casualty rates. Regulars belonged to a professional, hierarchical army whose commissioned officers were appointed by Congress or by provincial governments. Rebel militias fought the opening battles of the Revolutionary War and would prove crucial to the American cause over the coming years, but Patriot leaders understood that without a full-time army under central command, it would be impossible to resist the British for long.

Most American colonists, whatever their political convictions, were reluctant to sign away their freedoms and join the Continental Army. By the end of 1775, once the initial war fervor had subsided, it became more difficult to retain or replace those who had joined. Military recruiters scoured the countryside, visiting local taverns or town squares to make their pitch, but the ranks filled slowly. Washington pushed for longer service terms, cash bounties to attract recruits, or more forceful measures to compel enlistment, but Congress resisted any measure that created a standing army of draftees or hirelings. A year into the war, however, as the British expanded their campaign beyond Massachusetts, Congress was forced to reconsider. By the end of June 1776, Congress was offering ten dollars to men who would enlist for three years. A couple of months later, the bounty was up to twenty dollars, plus a new suit of clothing and one hundred acres of land to anyone who signed on for the entire war. In 1777 Congress also set minimum numbers of men that each state needed to contribute, prompting states to add their own material inducements to meet troop quotas. Maryland offered new recruits an additional forty dollars plus a pair of shoes and stockings. Later in the war, the incentive package for North Carolina recruits included "a prime slave." A Virginia law in 1780, signed by Governor Thomas Jefferson, promised "300 acres of land plus a healthy sound Negro between 20 and 30 years of age or 60 pounds in gold and silver." Such signing bonuses were attractive, especially to poorer colonists, but several states still needed to draft men to fill their quotas. The model of citizen soldiers volunteering to defend their freedom, an ideal cherished by many Patriots, would not suffice in this war.

Still, many Continental soldiers enlisted—out of patriotism, financial need, thirst for adventure, or some combination of motivations. Young boys misrepresented their ages and defied the wishes of parents and masters when army recruiters came to town. Apprentices signed up, even though they could be forced to surrender to their masters whatever bounties they received for their service. And at least one woman, Deborah Sampson of Massachusetts, disguised herself as a man to take up arms against Britain. But for every enthusiastic recruit there were several disgruntled comrades. High rates of desertion and low rates of reenlistment produced a serious problem of troop turnover. Although 230,000 enlisted in the Continental Army over the course of the war, its active duty force rarely exceeded 14,000 at a single time.

Deborah Sampson. Sampson enlisted in the Continental Army under the name Robert Shurtliff. After the war, she went on a lecture tour and became a celebrity. This portrait was published in Massachusetts as the frontispiece of *The Female Review* in 1797.

For most of the war, the ranks of Washington's army were dominated by unmarried teenagers with few opportunities or responsibilities and other colonists without significant property. Several states actively recruited orphaned and impoverished young men or offered pardons to criminals who enlisted. Some army regiments included substantial numbers of recent immigrants, indentured servants, or transported convicts. George Washington officially prohibited the recruitment of slaves or free blacks, but as the conflict wore on that policy was dropped. Approximately five thousand African Americans served in the Continental Army, mostly in northern regiments, and a much smaller number were admitted to state militias.

Commissioned officers, on the other hand, came from genteel social circles and considered themselves a breed apart. Severe differences in pay reflected and reinforced the social divide between officers and enlisted men in the Continental Army. Whereas a colonel received seventy-five dollars per month by 1778, the average private earned just six and two-thirds dollars. Congress awarded the gentlemanly George Washington a monthly salary of five hundred dollars, though he never accepted it. Class tensions within the American army contributed to the high number of mutinies, especially in the final years of the war.

On the other side, the British government could draw on long experience in mobilizing and training a large military force. By the summer of 1776, General William Howe had assembled more than thirty thousand soldiers under his command in New York City, the largest single military force in the eighteenth-century world. But that number fell far short of what Howe had requested. Britain relied even more heavily than the rebellious colonists on financial incentives and heavy-handed recruitment efforts to fill its ranks. Parliament lacked the authority to draft citizens for overseas campaigns, but the army and navy resorted to whatever measures were available, grabbing young men out of jails and poorhouses, impressing the crews of captured ships into British military service, and offering bounties to new recruits in Britain and Ireland. The British government also turned to its traditional German allies, especially the small German state of

Hesse-Cassell, for supplies of professional soldiers. Close to thirty thousand Hessians, as these German-speaking soldiers were called, took up arms during the war, and they made up a major component of the British invasion force on the mainland, though their contracts exempted them from being shipped to the more dangerous Caribbean.

Much more effectively than the American colonists, the British also recruited enslaved African Americans. Before the war, British strategists had argued privately that a colonial rebellion would surely founder because the empire could exploit tensions in a slaveholding society and provoke fears of slave insurrections. In the West Indies, such fears had helped contain anti-imperial protests, and Britain hoped a similar strategy might keep the southern mainland colonies out of any war. In April 1775, as it became clear that Virginia slaveholders were moving toward armed resistance, Governor John Murray, Lord Dunmore, threatened them with an emancipation order. Dunmore had no real intentions of freeing slaves; a slaveholder himself, he did not wish to undermine the institution of slavery in British America. When his own slaves took the bluff seriously and offered to fight against the rebels, a shocked Dunmore threatened to beat them if they raised the subject again. But once war erupted, British officials were less concerned with protecting slavery than with suppressing the rebellion. In November, Governor Dunmore, who had fled the capital of Williamsburg and was now operating aboard a naval ship off the coast, declared martial law and proclaimed liberty for slaves who would bear arms for "His Majesty's Troops."

Lord Dunmore's Proclamation was no general emancipation order, since it officially applied only to able-bodied young male slaves whose masters were disloyal to the Crown, but it had dramatic implications. Already a year earlier, a small number of slaves in Boston had offered their military services to the British in exchange for freedom, but Dunmore's new policy triggered a far more substantial movement toward self-emancipation in the South. On hearing the news, hundreds of enslaved African Americans (including many who were not fit for military service and thus not technically freed by the proclamation) fled plantations in the Norfolk, Virginia area, eluded local slave patrols, and made their ways safely to British lines. Dunmore organized several hundred former slaves into a British Ethiopian Regiment. Tragically, many of the black men, women, and children who took refuge with the British died as the result of a smallpox pandemic, which struck North America during the same years as the Revolutionary War.

As in earlier military conflicts on the American continent, both sides of the Revolutionary War sought to secure military support from Indians. Individual native soliders could be found in one or the other army, but both the British commanders and the Continental Congress relied on diplomatic initiatives to whole Indian villages and communities, rather than trying to recruit individuals. Many Indians fought in the war, mostly on the British side, but they did so as part of their own armed units with their own political agendas (see Indians and the War, below).

By His Excellency the Right Honorable JOHN Earl of DUNMORE, His MAJESTY's Lieutenant and Governor General of the Colony and Dominion of VIRGINIA, and Vice Admiral of the ſame.

A PROCLAMATION.

AS I have ever entertained Hopes, that an Accommodation might have taken Place between GREAT-BRITAIN and this Colony, without being compelled by my Duty to this moſt diſagreeable but now abſolutely neceſſary Step, rendered ſo by a Body of armed Men unlawfully aſſembled, firing on His MAJESTY's Tenders, and the formation of an Army, and that Army now on their March to attack His MAJESTY's Troops and deſtroy the well diſpoſed Subjects of this Colony. To defeat ſuch treaſonable Purpoſes, and that all ſuch Traitors, and their Abettors, may be brought to Juſtice, and that the Peace, and good Order of this Colony may be again reſtored, which the ordinary Courſe of the Civil Law is unable to effect; I have thought fit to iſſue this my Proclamation, hereby declaring, that until the aforeſaid good Purpoſes can be obtained, I do in Virtue of the Power and Authority to ME given, by His MAJESTY, determine to execute Martial Law, and cauſe the ſame to be executed throughout this Colony: and to the end that Peace and good Order may the ſooner be reſtored, I do require every Perſon capable of bearing Arms, to reſort to His MAJESTY's STANDARD, or be looked upon as Traitors to His MAJESTY's Crown and Government, and thereby become liable to the Penalty the Law inflicts upon ſuch Offences; ſuch as forfeiture of Life, confiſcation of Lands, &c. &c. And I do hereby further declare all indented Servants, Negroes, or others, (appertaining to Rebels,) free that are able and willing to bear Arms, they joining His MAJESTY's Troops as ſoon as may be, for the more ſpeedily reducing this Colony to a proper Senſe of their Duty, to His MAJESTY's Crown and Dignity. I do further order, and require, all His MAJESTY's Leige Subjects, to retain their Quitrents, or any other Taxes due or that may become due, in their own Cuſtody, till ſuch Time as Peace may be again reſtored to this at preſent moſt unhappy Country, or demanded of them for their former ſalutary Purpoſes, by Officers properly authoriſed to receive the ſame.

GIVEN under my Hand on board the Ship WILLIAM, off NORFOLK, the 7th Day of NOVEMBER, in the SIXTEENTH Year of His MAJESTY's Reign.

DUNMORE.

(GOD ſave the KING.)

Lord Dunmore's Proclamation. Dunmore's declaration appeared in a printed broadside poster distributed from a ship at the Norfolk harbor. The public display of the proclamation evoked the dreaded specter of a large-scale insurrection. Fomenting slave revolts was quickly added to the list of major colonial grievances against Britain.

MAKING WAR

At the outbreak of the war in 1775, both the British Empire and the rebellious colonists enjoyed distinct military advantages, and each side had some reasons for expecting a swift victory. Britain was the world's naval superpower, and its army was larger and better trained. The British could also exploit political and ethnic divisions within the diverse colonies. The Patriots, on the other hand, drew strength from their familiarity with the terrain and the ardor of local militias to defend their homelands. And although British politicians dismissed the fighting abilities of untrained colonists, the rebels doubted whether Hessian mercenaries would fight valiantly for a cause in which they had no obvious stake. American colonists also benefited from two important circumstances. As an indigenous independence movement, they could prevail simply by a stalemate, whereas the British needed to force a surrender and then reimpose their political will on a hostile population. The thirteen rebellious colonies would be worth little to the home country if they could not be governed. Furthermore, Great Britain had powerful enemies in Europe who might be drawn into the conflict.

In the end, those last strategic considerations would prove crucial, but not before a long and drawn-out war ravaged the eastern part of the continent. British troops won significant battles and occupied major colonial cities for much of the war, but they could neither extinguish the rebellion nor contain the costs and risks of a war that threatened to engulf other parts of the empire.

EARLY CAMPAIGNS

In the months after Lexington and Concord, much of the fighting centered on Massachusetts. Howe's army attacked rebel troops stationed on Breed's Hill across the Charles River from Boston, and eventually drove them away (in a battle named for Bunker Hill, which lay nearby), but only after suffering heavy casualties. Howe remained in occupied Boston, which Washington's army besieged for several months, awaiting further reinforcements and planning another assault on New England. Meanwhile, the Americans took the offensive with an invasion of Quebec in September 1775. The campaign, led by General Richard Montgomery and supported by Colonel Benedict Arnold, moved the conflict outside the rebellious colonies and stirred the passions of New Englanders by giving the struggle for independence the feeling of a religious crusade against Catholics. The day before embarking, soldiers assembled around Newburyport, Massachusetts, and visited the tomb of revivalist preacher George Whitefield (see Chapter 4), whose body had been laid to rest in a nearby church five years earlier. Pious American troops cut pieces of clothing from Whitefield's decomposed skeleton and brought them along as holy relics. One army chaplain looked forward to the invasion of Catholic Quebec as an opportunity to "spread . . . the gospel through this vast extended country, which has been for ages the dwelling of Satan, and reign of Antichrist." Though animated by this religious purpose, many of the Newburyport soldiers fell to hunger and smallpox en route to Quebec. Nor did those who survived the journey fulfill their visions of victory for the Protestant cause. Joined by reinforcements arriving by way of Montreal, Arnold's men attacked the city of Quebec on New Year's Eve but were badly defeated.

The British offensive, meanwhile, focused on New York, where loyalism was stronger. Howe hoped to control the Hudson River, which divided New England from most of New York and from the rest of the colonies, in order to isolate the rebellious New Englanders and put a quick end to the war. Unprecedented numbers of British troops arrived at the southern tip of Manhattan in July 1776, just as the Continental Congress declared independence. Late in August, the British routed the Continentals at the Battle of Long Island, capturing over one thousand prisoners and forcing Washington's retreat to Manhattan. The British attacked Kip's Bay, on Manhattan's East Side, and Washington withdrew again, crossing the Hudson into New Jersey. Understanding the strategic significance of the Hudson River, he ordered his troops to protect fortified positions on its two sides. But in November Howe's pursuing army seized both Fort Washington (in what is now Manhattan's Washington Heights) and Fort Lee (in New Jersey) after a battle that resulted in the capture of more than 2,800 American soldiers, most of whom would later die in captivity. By December, Washington's armies were on the run again, moving westward across the Delaware River and south toward Philadelphia. The fate of the rebellion looked bleak.

As Howe momentarily halted his pursuit with the onset of winter, Washington crossed the Delaware again and attacked Hessian troops stationed in Trenton on December 26, capturing over nine hundred prisoners. Eight days later, after two more trips across the river, Washington's army defeated a British force at Princeton, prompting Howe to withdraw from most of New Jersey. These two victories inflicted only modest damage on British troop levels, but they boosted American morale and stemmed the heavy tide of desertion from the Continental Army. Washington had done nothing to offset the heavy imbalance of manpower and wealth that continued to favor the British, but by eluding disaster in this phase of the invasion and surviving into a new year, the rebellious colonists were raising the costs and lowering the likelihood of Britain's bid to regain the allegiance of the colonies.

SARATOGA AND THE TURNING TIDE

After another year of heavy fighting, during which the British captured the colonists' new national capital of Philadelphia, Britain launched another major offensive to control the Hudson River, targeting the city of Albany, New York. In the summer of 1777, General John Burgoyne led 7,800 British soldiers and a smaller force of Indians on a long southward expedition from Canada into the Hudson Valley. They captured Fort Ticonderoga without a fight and rolled slowly toward Albany. Burgoyne planned to converge with Howe, whose men would move north along the Hudson River from the British stronghold in New York. But Howe sailed south to Philadelphia, home of the Continental Congress. Washington was caught off guard; Congress was forced to flee inland to Lancaster, Pennsylvania; and Philadelphia fell to British hands. But Burgoyne would be as surprised as Washington by Howe's move.

Map 6.1 Key Battles of the Revolutionary War, 1775–1777. The war began in Massachusetts, but after a failed American attack on Canada, a major British invasion of New York shifted the center of the war farther south and west. Burgoyne's surrender at Saratoga in 1777 marked the end of this phase of the war. **Question for Analysis:** What geographical advantages did the British see in deploying troops to New York City?

Other reinforcements for the assault were arriving from the west, as an army of British soldiers, Hessians, Iroquois, and local colonists loyal to Great Britain marched along the Mohawk River toward Albany. But they encountered heavy resistance at Fort Stanwix, a hundred miles west of Albany. A regiment of Continental soldiers held out inside the besieged fort until local militiamen, mostly German speakers whose ancestors had immigrated earlier in the century from the Rhine River region, joined the battle, as did Oneida soldiers who had broken from the Iroquois League to side with the Americans. The bloody fighting in and around Fort Stanwix illustrated the complex ethnic alignments of the Revolution, since Indians, Germans, and New York colonists fought on both sides. The strategic significance of the battle was simpler. By holding the fort, supporters of the rebellion stopped a key part of the Albany invasion in its tracks, foiling the British plan to capture the Hudson and divide the colonies into two noncontiguous parts.

With no help forthcoming from Howe, Burgoyne was now on his own. He encamped at the town of Saratoga, his numbers and supplies depleted by a long journey that had been further slowed by the sabotage efforts of local militiamen. Soon after the Continental Army arrived, Burgoyne attacked on September 19, at Freeman's Farm, winning control of the field, but suffering more casualties than the Americans. A second battle on October 7 proved even costlier for the British, who retreated to Saratoga, but soon found themselves surrounded. Burgoyne surrendered to the Americans on October 17, marking the formal conclusion of the Battle of Saratoga and bringing the invasion of Albany to a disastrous end.

As the news of Saratoga spread through the colonies, Patriots toasted the success of the rebellion and reenacted "General Burgoyne's Surrender" in the form of a dance craze. Such premature celebrations soon subsided, but the reverberations of Saratoga across the ocean would last longer. The defeat exposed Britain's war effort to criticism at home. And in France, where Benjamin Franklin had arrived in December 1776 as an agent of the Continental Congress, reports of the American victory helped persuade King Louis XVI that the colonists' struggle for independence was viable.

Surrender of General Burgoyne, by John Trumbull, 1821. The American colonists' victory at Saratoga would be remembered as the turning point in the war.

FOREIGN INTERVENTIONS

Dreams of American independence, ironically, depended on international opinion and foreign diplomacy. Colonists sought the recognition and support of other nations, but none so badly as that of France, Britain's powerful long-standing enemy. The French had been seeking an opportunity to avenge its defeat in the Seven Years' War, and French officials had in fact been counting on a political crisis in the American colonies to provide such an opportunity. But it was by no means clear in 1775 what role France might play in the Revolutionary War. French support for a doomed rebellion could prove costly. Furthermore, although the colonists' espousal of natural rights and representative government attracted certain French supporters of the Enlightenment, including the Marquis de Lafayette, most of the aristocrats in the court of King Louis viewed the democratic implications of the American Revolution with repugnance or trepidation. The Continental Congress published its Declaration of Independence in part to persuade the French of the legitimacy of the revolution. Still, in the first two years of the war, France provided covert military aid to the colonists but did not officially enter the conflict.

After Saratoga, France did not want to miss its chance to weaken Britain, especially in the Caribbean. Sensitive to the possibility that conciliatory moves from Britain might now lead to peace, France signed a defensive alliance with American representatives in February 1778. Under this agreement, both sides undertook not to make a separate peace with Britain until it formally recognized the colonies' independence. With French intervention seeming imminent, the British government dispatched a commission, led by the Earl of Carlisle, to negotiate an end to the war. Earlier in the year, Lord North had repealed the Tea Act and the Massachusetts Government Act (the abrogation of the colony's charter) but the Carlisle Peace Initiative went further, offering to roll back all post-1763 taxes if the colonists dropped their bid for independence. The alliance with France both emboldened and obligated the Continental Congress to reject those terms, however. Congress ratified the agreement with France and in June the French declared war on Great Britain. Spain joined France in 1779, and a year later the Dutch followed suit.

Although it yielded no immediate results on North American battlefields, the support of Britain's European enemies instantly boosted the Patriots' prospects. French commitments of aid made it less likely that Congress would go bankrupt, and French and Spanish threats to Britain's Caribbean colonies promised to tie up the British Navy and bring some relief to the besieged colonists. A war on the American continent had turned global, again.

THE SOUTHERN CAMPAIGN AND THE BRITISH SURRENDER

While British and American diplomats adjusted to the shifting political landscape, each side pursued new war offensives. The Continental Army and the colonial militias turned their attention to the west, launching attacks in Indian country in 1778 and 1779. Edward Hand routed Shawnee and Delaware Indians near Fort Pitt, while George

Map 6.2 The Southern Front, 1778–1781. Most of the final battles of the American Revolution took place in the South, where brutal fighting between Loyalists and Patriots compounded the devastation wrought by battles between regular armies. British general Cornwallis pursued the forces of Nathanael Greene through the Carolinas, winning several battles at considerable cost, but he eventually decided to abandon the campaign and move his troops to Virginia.

Rogers Clark drove into Illinois, capturing a British fort and seizing Indian villages. As Washington ordered an all-out attack on Britain's Iroquois allies in New York, North Carolina militias destroyed dozens of Cherokee villages in what is now Tennessee.

Britain, meanwhile, embarked on a new strategy for winning the war or at least salvaging a significant part of its mainland empire. Rather than isolate New England, the British now sought to capture the South. A southern campaign, the British hoped, would draw support from Loyalist colonists, ignite fears of slave rebellions, and wrest control of the colonies' most valuable economic resources (see Map 6.2). Landing at the port city of Savannah at the end of 1778, British soldiers propped up a new colonial government in Georgia. A year later, British generals Henry Clinton and Lord Charles Cornwallis sailed south from New York and invaded Charleston, where 5,500 American soldiers surrendered to the British. Continental troops rushed south to thwart the invasion, but were badly defeated in August, 120 miles north of Charleston, in the Battle of Camden.

British successes in Georgia and South Carolina reflected the numerical strength of their forces, as well as valuable intelligence reports sold to them by Benedict Arnold, whose treason was uncovered in the fall of 1780. But Britain was not able to extend its control of the southern coast into the region's interior. The next phase of the campaign was a brutal civil war between Loyalists and Patriots in the Carolinas, where both sides committed vicious acts of torture and mutilation. Guerilla bands and militias on the American side gained the upper hand, winning significant battles at King's Mountain (North Carolina) and Cowpens (South Carolina). Unable to hold the Lower South, British general Cornwallis withdrew northward to Virginia.

Cornwallis captured Williamsburg, moved swiftly through Virginia's Tidewater region, and camped at the small tobacco port of Yorktown on the Chesapeake Bay in the summer of 1781, awaiting additional troops from New York. Learning that the powerful French fleet was sailing north from its main military ventures in the Caribbean, Washington devised a plan to surround Cornwallis. Instructing Marquis de Lafayette to detain the British troops in Yorktown, Washington headed south to Virginia with a French force that had been dispatched to Rhode Island the previous year. Shortly before they arrived, Admiral Francois de Grasse's ships reached the Chesapeake Bay in time to cut off further British reinforcements and prevent Cornwallis from retreating. Surrounded by a larger French-American force, subjected to heavy bombardment, beset by food shortages and smallpox, and denied an escape route, the British surrendered on October 19, yielding approximately 7,500 prisoners to the United States. The stunning American victory at Yorktown destroyed Britain's southern campaign. British forces still controlled New York and Charleston, but threats from France and Spain made Britain's position in North America difficult to sustain. The war, which was now deeply unpopular back in England, shifted to the West Indies (see States of Emergency: The Sack of St. Eustatius) and to the negotiating table.

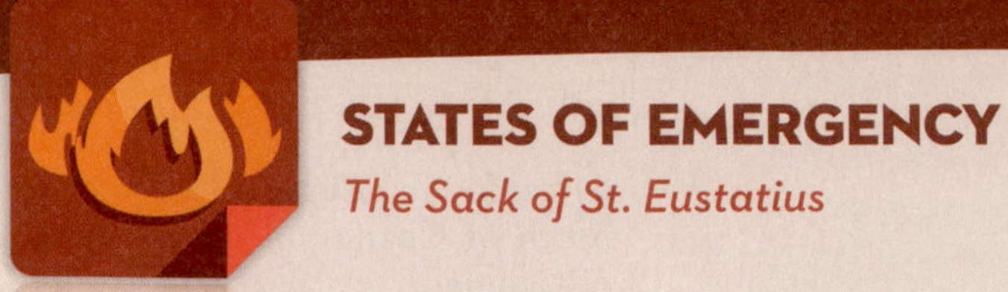

STATES OF EMERGENCY

The Sack of St. Eustatius

On November 16, 1776, a Dutch commander on the small Caribbean island of St. Eustatius fired a cannon, returning the salute of a ship from the new Continental Navy. It was the first foreign salute of the Grand Union Flag (the predecessor to the Stars and Stripes), and thus the first gesture of international recognition in the history of the United States. But over the next few years, this Dutch trading colony, with a land mass of less than seven square miles, played an even more significant role in the course of the Revolution. As a neutral port, the colony was open to American trade, and ships from the United States sailed there frequently during the early years of the war to purchase supplies, including weapons and ammunition, and to retrieve mail from American agents in Europe. Once France entered the war on the side of the United States, both countries used St. Eustatius as a major trading partner. Every night, seven to ten American ships dropped anchor there, bringing indigo and tobacco to exchange for gunpowder, rifles, and naval supplies. British officials blamed this "nest of outlaws" for sustaining the American rebellion, and demanded that the Dutch shut down the trade. When that failed, Great Britain declared war against the Netherlands and ordered an attack on the island.

British forces under the command of Admiral George Rodney arrived in St. Eustatius on February 3, 1781, and the island surrendered almost immediately. Rodney left the Dutch flag flying to ensnare more American and French ships, while his men proceeded to pillage the island of absolutely everything they could find. They confiscated all private property—including kitchen cabinets, the wallets of people walking in the streets, even graves. Rodney did not distinguish between British subjects and others, or between friends and foes of the empire, but he did single out the colony's Jewish community for special abuse. Jewish men were rounded up and stripped of their clothing to expose any concealed money. Some were imprisoned, while others were banished from the island.

Driven by personal greed, anti-Semitism, and a fervent belief that everyone living on St. Eustatius was personally responsible for Britain's military predicament, Rodney flouted international law and codes of military conduct as he turned the island upside down. In the end, however, the chaos and plunder in St. Eustatius may have contributed to the American victory. Preoccupied with despoiling the island, Rodney neglected to pursue other war aims in the Caribbean and failed to block the French fleet as it moved north toward the Chesapeake Bay and the Battle of Yorktown.

Think About It

1. Why did a tiny Caribbean island become a source of major concern to the powerful British Empire?
2. What might the Dutch have hoped to gain from aiding the American rebellion?
3. Why might Rodney have considered it strategically valuable to spend time and energy plundering St. Eustatius while Britain was engaged in a larger war with more powerful enemies?

WHOSE REVOLUTION?

Fighting between France and Great Britain would continue in the Caribbean and on the high seas for another two years, and George Washington feared another attack from British troops still staged in North America, but most Americans understood by the end of 1781 that the rebels had prevailed. Thirteen former British colonies would not be forcibly reintegrated into the empire. What this might ultimately mean for those living in North America remained unclear as diplomats negotiated peace terms and new state and federal governments developed (see Chapter 7). But the war itself shifted power relations among different groups of Americans.

WOMEN IN THE REVOLUTION

American women were formally excluded from military service in the American cause. Whig leaders of the independence movement did not advocate sexual equality or the rights of women to direct political representation. Nonetheless, women had both a role and a stake in the outcome of the revolutionary struggle. The imperial crisis politicized women's activities as consumers, boycotters, manufacturers, and rioters. When war came, women found themselves swept into the chaos and violence of the period even though few of them donned army uniforms. Thousands of women, mostly soldiers' wives, widows, or runaway servants, joined the military community as what were called **camp followers,** serving the Continental Army as nurses, cooks, and laundresses (the British Army retained an even larger community of women in their camps). Those women who remained at home faced difficult decisions about whether and how to support the war effort by concealing men and weapons or by providing food and lodging to soldiers and militiamen. Some women also served as spies for the Patriot cause (see Singular Lives: Patience Wright, Woman under Cover). Finally, they participated by either supporting or discouraging the enlistment of their male relatives.

The war forced women of all classes to declare their political commitments and thereby muddied the neat lines that protected politics as the exclusive concern of elite men. What this portended for women's status in an independent United States

SINGULAR LIVES

Patience Wright, Woman under Cover

In 1772, during a lull in the imperial crisis, a young woman from New Jersey became a cultural sensation in London. Patience Wright was a young widow with five children to support and a remarkable talent for producing uncannily lifelike wax sculptures of people's heads. Hoping to make a living as a portraitist for the rich and famous, she secured a letter of introduction to fellow American Benjamin Franklin, then living in London, who showed her around town and promoted her work. Quickly she amassed a substantial clientele, including lords, ministers, actors, and literary figures. By 1773, even the king and queen, whom Wright (raised as a Quaker not to respect social titles) referred to as "George" and "Charlotte," sat to have their busts sculpted by this American woman.

Beyond her lucrative private commissions, Wright's fame and fortune grew with public exhibitions of her work. Some spectators came to see wax impressions of celebrities, much as they go to wax museums in London or Las Vegas today. But others were curious to see the product of Wright's unusual art. Word spread that Wright sculpted her subjects by studying their faces while holding the clay under her apron, keeping the material warm between her legs and concealing her work as she progressed, until finally lifting the apron to reveal, as if in a moment of birth, the fully formed head.

Over the course of the escalating conflict with the American colonies, Wright became notable in London for reasons other than her art. Forthright about her sympathy for the rebellion, Wright fell from royal favor, and was even suspected of spying for the American cause. She maintained close relationships with a network of American supporters in London and welcomed American prisoners of war into her home. Biographers speculate that Wright may have passed letters and information to her sister in Philadelphia by embedding pieces of paper into her wax sculptures. She never returned to her native land, dying in London in 1786 after a fall.

"The Heads of the Nation in a Right Situation," by John Williams, 1780. This political cartoon features Patience Wright admiring the decapitated heads of three British officials: "This is a sight I have long wish [sic] to see." The cartoon's title plays on the celebrity wax artist's last name.

Think About It

1. In an age before photography, what might have been the special appeal of wax portraiture?
2. Why would the king and queen of England have consented to have their busts sculpted by a widow from New Jersey?
3. What made Patience Wright a potentially valuable asset to the revolutionary cause?

remained unclear. Early in the war, Abigail Adams famously applied the Whig critique of power to the family. She admonished her husband John, as he sat in Philadelphia as a delegate to the Second Continental Congress, not to put "unlimited power in the hands of the Husbands." Observing that "all Men would be tyrants if they could," she warned that "Ladies . . . are determined to foment a Rebelion, and will not hold ourselves bound by any Laws in which we have no voice, or Representation." The Revolution did not, however, produce evidence that a gender conflict was in the offing.

LOYALISTS

Like many anticolonial movements, the armed struggle for American independence was a civil war between two factions of colonists (see Map 6.3). Many **Loyalists,** as they called themselves, continued to see themselves as subjects of the Crown and viewed the rebellion as illegitimate or undesirable. Loyalism was the dominant political stance among white colonists in Canada, Florida, Bermuda, and the British Caribbean, and some opponents of the rebellion in other colonies moved to those parts of the empire early in the crisis. But Loyalists also formed a substantial minority of the population in the thirteen rebellious colonies throughout the war. Some joined the British Army or served in Loyalist militias or guerilla bands. Others lent material support to the British side. Yet others simply expressed their opposition to independence or refused to take loyalty oaths to the rebel governments.

American opponents of the rebellion were not restricted to a particular colony and did not all fit a common profile. Scholars estimate the number of Americans who remained loyal to Great Britain during the war at less than one-fifth of the white population, and Loyalists were a persecuted minority in all thirteen colonies. But loyalism ran high in particular communities, especially in the Southeast and the Middle Colonies. During the war, Loyalists also concentrated in port cities, such as New York, Philadelphia, Charleston, and Savannah, occupied by the British Army. Loyalism was sometimes associated

Map 6.3 A Civil War in Britain's American Colonies. Although the revolutionary upheaval divided families, towns, and colonies, loyalty to the British Empire was much stronger in particular regions.

with conservative political ideologies, but more often it reflected local conflicts and grievances. Many tenant farmers in New York's Hudson Valley opposed the Revolution in part because a single wealthy landlord supported it. An escaped African American slave known as Colonel Tye led Loyalist guerrilla raids against Patriot slaveholders in New Jersey in part to settle old scores with men who had abused him. The brutal and protracted fighting between Loyalists and Whigs in South Carolina was rooted in personal recriminations as much as competing views of parliamentary authority.

One common feature of many white Loyalist communities was their minority status. Men and women who felt vulnerable to the animosities of a hostile majority had greater investment in royal protection and less optimism about a future under popularly elected governments. Immigrant groups who continued to speak Dutch or French rather than English tended to stay loyal, for example, as did some religious minorities. Specific religious minorities opposed the Revolution, or at least refused to participate, as a matter of faith. Approximately eighty thousand Americans belonged to Christian sects that opposed war or the pursuit of political power. Quakers, Mennonites, Moravians, and others objected conscientiously to taking up arms, hiring substitutes, or paying taxes to support the fighting. Quaker meetings disciplined or expelled members for these practices, for taking loyalty oaths, or simply for celebrating Independence Day. Quakers and other pacifists did not, of course, fight on the British side, but neutrality was not a tenable position in the American Revolution. Religious pacifists were seen as Loyalists and subjected to severe punishments, including property confiscation and imprisonment.

During the war, Loyalists of all persuasions suffered from punitive laws and hostile neighbors. After Yorktown, many began to emigrate. Overall, 80,000–100,000 Americans fled or were banished for political reasons during the war era, many in mass emigrations in 1782 and 1783. Some wealthier Loyalists sailed to England, where the British government compensated them for their lost property. More sought new homes in other parts of British America, especially Nova Scotia. These Americans were refugees from a war they had lost, and from a colonial society that had vanished.

SLAVES AND INDEPENDENCE

For the five hundred thousand human beings who were enslaved in the thirteen colonies at the start of the war, the Revolution had special meaning and complex implications. When Patriots claimed to be fighting to preserve their liberty against the threat of slavery, enslaved Americans paid special attention, wondering how their own freedom fit into this political agenda. Some British policymakers assumed that the rebels' ideas about political freedom might undermine colonial slave systems, which is partly why they expected slaveholders to provide powerful conservative voices against the rebellion. Those expectations were partially confirmed in coastal Georgia and South Carolina, and more clearly vindicated in the British West Indies, where white colonists on the islands with the largest slave majorities seemed to show the least enthusiasm for the independence movement. A major slave revolt in Jamaica in 1776 stoked the fears of whites in those colonies. Though the Jamaica revolt was sparked by food shortages resulting from the suspension of American exports, slaveholders there blamed it in part on all the talk circulating that year about the nobility of sacrificing one's life to avoid the fate of being enslaved. Few Whig essayists and orators in the mainland colonies ever made this link explicit, however, and most of the revolutionary leaders accepted the institution of chattel slavery in their midst.

Many black Americans, both free and enslaved, saw great promise in the independence movement. Especially in New England, black preachers and writers embraced the cause of liberty and took white comrades to task for not extending their views on freedom to the plight of American slaves. Identifying with the Patriot cause, free black men took up arms against Britain in disproportionate numbers in the North and played especially significant roles in the early violence in Massachusetts. Earlier in the imperial crisis, enslaved blacks in Massachusetts took their masters to court, relying on liberty-minded juries to affirm their individual emancipation. Jenny Slew initiated one of the first of these **freedom suits** in 1766, persuading a court in Salem that having a white mother made her enslavement illegal. Others made different arguments, tailored to their particular circumstances. After 1773, black New Englanders adopted the strategy of petitioning legislatures for general emancipation, arguing now against the legitimacy of slavery altogether (see Interpreting the Sources: Antislavery Petitions in Massachusetts).

But while some enslaved African Americans in New England turned optimistically to the Revolution, far more slaves, especially in the South, saw prospects for freedom on the British side. For them, it was the war, rather than the independence movement, that inspired dreams of liberation. As a political maneuver designed to frighten slaveholders into loyalty, Lord Dunmore's promise of freedom to African Americans in Virginia backfired. By harboring and arming fugitive slaves, they managed to unite Virginia's slaveholders in opposition to the government and permanently severed their allegiances to the empire. But from the perspective of slaves in Virginia, Dunmore's Proclamation and similar orders by other British commanders were beacons of light. It was a life-changing opportunity for which many had been waiting. As early as 1774, slaves in Boston were reportedly planning to offer their military services to the royal governor in return for their freedom. Throughout the war, whenever British forces occupied port cities in the North, enslaved men, women, and children sought refuge there.

When the heavy fighting shifted to the South after 1778, the scale of this migration exploded. By 1780, when British

Evacuation of Loyalists at the End of the War. In contrast to many other successful revolutions, in the American Revolution, no former Loyalists were tried for treason.

INTERPRETING THE SOURCES

Antislavery Petitions in Massachusetts

Slavery has been around for millennia, and enslaved people have resisted their bondage in countless ways. But petitions of Massachusetts slaves for freedom in the 1770s have no precedent in recorded human history. Slaves had rebelled, escaped, purchased their freedom, or contested the justice of their enslavement, but they had never attacked the justice of the institution of slavery itself. They had never argued, in other words, that slavery is always wrong. The following passages are drawn from petitions to the Massachusetts colonial authorities in 1773 and the Massachusetts State House of Representatives in 1777.

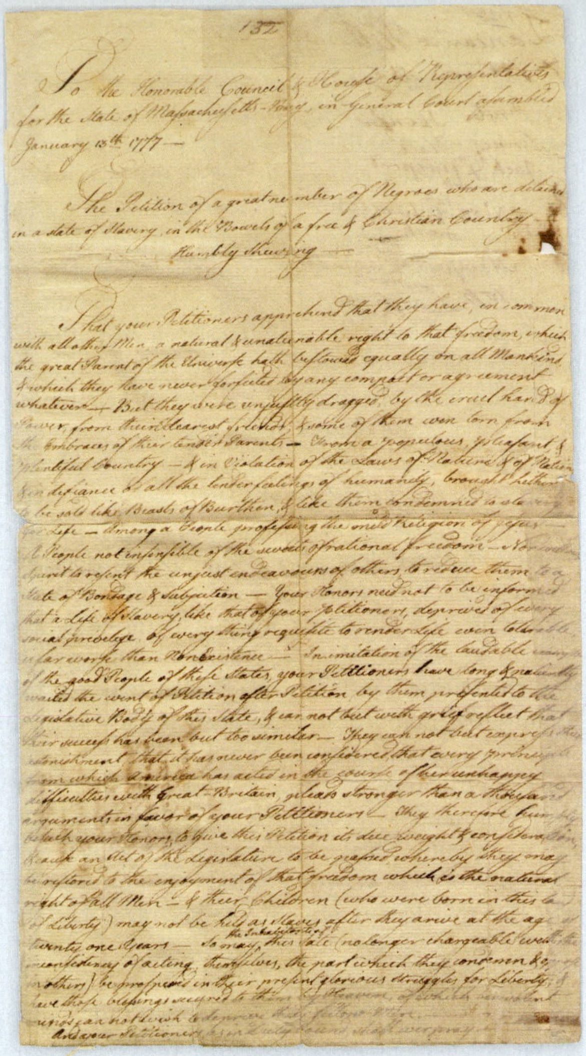

I. Province of the Massachusetts Bay To His Excellency Thomas Hutchinson, Esq; Governor; To The Honorable His Majesty's Council, and To the Honorable House of Representatives in General Court assembled at Boston, the 6th Day of January, 1773. The humble PETITION of many Slaves, living in the Town of Boston, and other Towns in the Province is this, namely That your Excellency and Honors, and the Honorable the Representatives would be pleased to take their unhappy State and Condition under your wise and just Consideration.

We desire to bless God, who loves Mankind, who sent his Son to die for their Salvation, and who is no respecter of Persons; that he hath lately put it into the Hearts of Multitudes on both Sides of the Water, to bear our Burthens, some of whom are Men of great Note and Influence; who have pleaded our Cause with Arguments which we hope will have their weight with this Honorable Court. . . .

We have no Property. We have no Wives. No Children. We have no City. No Country. But we have a Father in Heaven, and we are determined, as far as his Grace shall enable us, and as far as our degraded contemptuous Life will admit, to keep all his Commandments: Especially will we be obedient to our Masters, so long as God in his sovereign Providence shall suffer us to be holden in Bondage.

It would be impudent, if not presumptuous in us, to suggest to your Excellency and Honors any Law or Laws proper to be made, in relation to our unhappy State, which, although our greatest Unhappiness, is not our Fault; and this gives us great Encouragement to pray and hope for such Relief as is consistent with your Wisdom, justice, and Goodness.

We think Ourselves very happy, that we may thus address the Great and General Court of this Province, which great and good Court is to us, the best judge, under God, of what is wise, just and good.

We humbly beg Leave to add but this one Thing more: We pray for such Relief only, which by no Possibility can ever be productive of the least Wrong or Injury to our Masters; but to us will be as Life from the dead.

Signed,
FELIX

II. The petition of A Great Number of Blackes detained in a State of Slavery in the Bowels of a free & christian Country Humbly shuwith [showeth] that your Petitioners Apprehend that Thay [they] have in Common with all other men a Natural and Unaliable [Unalienable] Right to that freedom which the Grat [Great] - Parent of the Unavese [Universe] hath Bestowed equalley on all menkind [mankind] and which they have Never forfuted [forfeited] by Any Compact or Agreement whatever—but thay wher [were] Unjustly Dragged by the hand of cruel Power from their Derest frinds and sum of them Even torn from the Embraces of their tender Parents—from A popolous [populous] Plasant [Pleasant] And plentiful cuntry And in Violation of Laws of Nature and off Nations And in defiance of all the tender feelings of humanity Brough [Brought] hear Either to Be sold Like Beast of Burthen & Like them Condemnd to Slavery for Life—among A People Profesing the Religion of Jesus A people Not Insensible of the Secrets of Rationable Being Nor without spirit to Resent the unjust endeavours of others to Reduce them to A state of Bondage and Subjection your honouer Need not to be informed that A Life of Slavery Like that of your Petioners Deprived of Every social Priviledge of Every thing Requiset [Requisite] to Render Life Tolable [Tolerable] is far [. . .] worse then Nonexistance.

Manuscript Copy of a 1777 Slaves' Petition. Prince Hall and eight other black Bostonians presented this petition to the General Court, stressing that "your petitioners have Long and Patiently waited the Event of petition after petition."

Explore the Sources

1. What are the shared arguments of the two petitions against the legitimacy of slavery?
2. How do the two arguments for freedom differ?
3. How does the later petition appeal to the ideals of the Revolution?
4. Why might the first petitioner have signed his personal name (Felix) if the petition is from "many Slaves"?

ships were traveling along rivers that fed into the Chesapeake Bay, word had circulated through Tidewater plantations and thousands of slaves began plotting their escape. A British naval raid along the Potomac River in 1781, for example, stopped in Mount Vernon, home of George Washington, where fourteen men and three women belonging to the American commander-in-chief climbed aboard. In all, some ten thousand Virginia slaves fled to the British side between 1779 and 1781, constituting what some historians consider the greatest slave rebellion in U.S. history. For most of the participants in this wartime slave rebellion, the decision to run away proved fatal. A majority died of smallpox or various fevers that swept through the British camps. Others lost their lives to starvation or battle wounds during the siege of Yorktown. As the siege tightened, General Cornwallis decided to conserve supplies by sending thousands of black men out of the fortified camp that they had helped build. This gave them a chance to avoid recapture, but exposed them to new perils. Probably no more than one out of six fugitive slaves survived to the end of the war.

Following the Yorktown surrender, it became clear that the slaves who risked their lives for freedom by joining the British had chosen the losing side of the war. For many of the survivors, though, this decision had paid off. When Britain began evacuating, most of the former slaves who had been promised freedom set sail on British ships, mostly for Nova Scotia. Free blacks who had joined the British in New York also left the United States for Canada. Those African Americans who suffered most from the outcome of the Revolutionary War were slaves who belonged to Loyalist masters. Thousands of such men, women, and children, mostly from Georgia and South Carolina, left the United States in bondage, destined for the sugar plantations of the West Indies.

Agrippa Hull. Hull was a free black soldier in the Continental Army. This painting was based on a daguerreotype taken late in his life.

INDIANS AND THE WAR

Even more than the British Empire, which would continue to dominate trade with North America for decades, the biggest losers in the Revolutionary War were the two hundred thousand Native Americans living east of the Mississippi River. Different Indian villages and nations took various positions during the conflict, some switching allegiances at strategic moments in the war. Many sought to remain neutral, but pressures from both armies and encroachments by American settlers often made this difficult. Representatives of the Continental Congress pushed the argument that Indian interests lay in ingratiating themselves with the region's emerging superpower and fighting against the British. In the fall of 1775, a diplomatic mission to western Indians in the Ohio country explained that "the thirteen great Colonies of this Extensive Continent, Comprehending in the whole, at least One Million of Fighting Men, are now so firmly United and Inseparably bound together" that a fight with one colony would incur the wrath of the entire nation. Some Shawnee and Delaware chiefs were persuaded by this threat, but many western warriors were not, and continued violence along the frontier strengthened the hand of those western Indians who advocated fighting to expel the Americans. The ensuing battles in the western theater of the Revolutionary War proved devastating to the region's native population.

In the case of the powerful Iroquois League, the Americans hoped simply to keep them on the sidelines. "This is a family quarrel between us and Old England," one delegate told his Iroquois audience in 1775. Britain lobbied against this course, arguing that "the Americans . . . mean to … take all your Lands from you and destroy your people, for they are all mad, foolish, crazy and full of deceit." The Iroquois maintained their neutrality until the spring of 1777, when the escalating conflict began drawing significant numbers of warriors into the camp of their long-standing British allies. The war strained the League's political unity, however. Most Iroquois, including Mohawks, Onondagas, Cayugas, and Senecas, fought for the British Empire, but many Oneidas and Tuscaroras took up arms for the rebellious colonists. The Revolution ultimately ripped apart the Haudenosaunee, much as it did British America.

Like the majority of Iroquois, most powerful Indian armies wound up siding with Great Britain, typically because their most pressing conflicts were with American settlers who supported the rebellion. Cherokee, Creek, and Choctaw soldiers clashed extensively with American forces in the Southeast. After the war, Cherokee country even provided a haven for white Loyalists. Chickasaws retained their long-standing alliance with the British, though they saw less action during the war. Seminoles in the loyal Florida colonies fought for the Crown as well. All of these nations wound up in a worse position when their allies surrendered.

Regardless of whether they took up arms for Great Britain, the Revolution was a disaster for Indians. The war in Indian country destroyed lives, ravaged the landscape, and sowed political dissension. It also armed American settlers, organized their militias, and gave them war experience, thus decisively tipping the balance of military power between colonists and natives in the eastern half of the continent. Finally, the British had exerted a constraining force on the westward expansion of land-hungry Americans. As much as they had suffered from Britain's expulsion of the French in 1763, they would now mourn the departure of the British.

CONCLUSION

In less than two decades, Britain's North American empire had progressively unraveled. In an attempt to pay back its war debts and finance the administration of its expanded territories, Britain had sent the colonists a tax bill. In response to that bill, colonial leaders articulated political ideas that undermined the authority of the home country and precipitated a standoff. Many British colonies backed away from the standoff because they needed British protection more than they resented its costs. But in thirteen mainland colonies, majorities of the large and growing population of white settlers saw matters differently. Tapping into powerful sources of social conflict, advocates of independence found themselves in a bloody civil war and a protracted revolution.

The American Revolution took an enormous toll on those who lived in and around the thirteen colonies. Over 25,000 soldiers died fighting for independence (approximately 7,000 from battle wounds, 10,000 from disease, and another 8,500 in prison). Thousands more Indians and Loyalists were killed in battle and from disease, and as many as 10,000 enslaved African Americans died pursuing freedom in the chaos of the war. Even larger numbers of Loyalists fled the country. In 1781, even after the Yorktown surrender, civil war persisted in South Carolina, fighting continued in Indian country, and major American cities were under British occupation.

Alongside all of this violence, destruction, and mobility, the rebellious former colonists were building something new. The new republic that would emerge from this political crisis would be shaped by wartime traumas and experiences, but also by the nation-building project that took place in tandem with the Revolution.

STUDY TERMS

Quartering Act of 1765 (p. 131)
Stamp Act (p. 131)
Stamp Act Congress (p. 132)
Sons of Liberty (p. 132)
Declaratory Act (p. 132)
Whigs (p. 132)
Tories (p. 132)
Letters from a Farmer in Pennsylvania (p. 132)
Liberty Tree (p. 132)
Townshend Duties (p. 133)
Circular Letter (p. 133)
nonimportation agreements (p. 133)
nonconsumption (p. 134)
spinning bees (p. 134)
Regulators (p. 135)
Green Mountain Boys (p. 136)
urban rioting (p. 136)
tarring and feathering (p. 136)
Boston Massacre (p. 137)
Tea Act (p. 137)
Boston Tea Party (p. 139)
Coercive Acts (p. 139)
Quebec Act (p. 139)
Committees of Correspondence (p. 140)
First Continental Congress (p. 141)
Battle of Lexington and Concord (p. 142)
Second Continental Congress (p. 142)
Continental Army (p. 143)
Common Sense (p. 143)
militiamen (p. 143)
Regulars (p. 143)
Hessians (p. 145)
Lord Dunmore's Proclamation (p. 145)
invasion of Quebec (p. 146)
Fort Stanwix (p. 147)
Battle of Saratoga (p. 147)
Carlisle Peace Initiative (p. 148)
southern campaign (p. 149)
Yorktown (p. 149)
camp followers (p. 150)
Loyalists (p. 151)
freedom suits (p. 153)
wartime slave rebellion (p. 155)

TIMELINE

1765 Quartering Act passed
Stamp Act passed
Stamp Act protested

1766 Stamp Act repealed
Jenny Slew files one of the colonies' first freedom suits

1767 Townshend Duties passed

1770 All Townshend Duties repealed (except tax on tea)
Boston Massacre

1773 Tea Act passed
Boston Tea Party

1774 Coercive Acts and Quebec Act (also called Intolerable Acts) passed
Committees of Correspondence displace British authority in Massachusetts
First Continental Congress

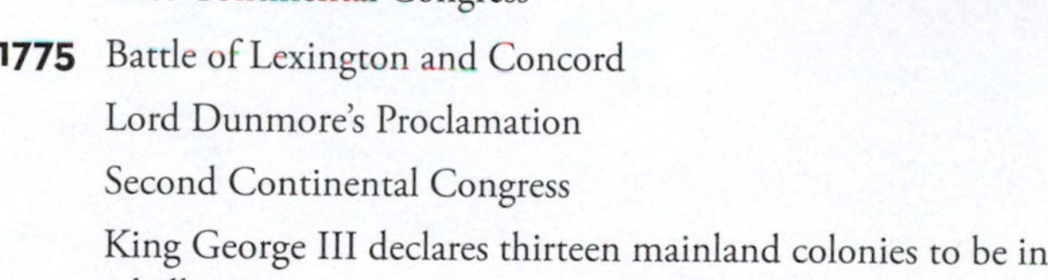

1775 Battle of Lexington and Concord
Lord Dunmore's Proclamation
Second Continental Congress
King George III declares thirteen mainland colonies to be in rebellion

1776 Thomas Paine's *Common Sense* published
Continental Congress declares independence from Great Britain

1777 Iroquois end their neutrality in the Revolutionary War
British general John Burgoyne surrenders at Saratoga

1778 France declares war on Great Britain

1779 Spain declares war on Great Britain

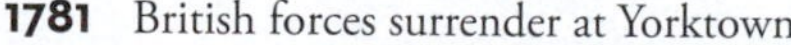

1780 Netherlands declares war on Great Britain
Benedict Arnold's treason uncovered

1781 British forces surrender at Yorktown

FURTHER READING

Additional suggested readings are available on the Online Learning Center at www.mhhe.com/becomingamerica1e.

Colin Calloway, *The American Revolution in Indian Country* (1995), examines the experiences and dilemmas of different Indian communities during the war.

Caroline Cox, *A Proper Sense of Honor* (2007), highlights social conflict within George Washington's army.

Douglas Egerton, *Death or Liberty* (2009), reconstructs the experiences and dilemmas of African Americans during the Revolution.

David Hackett Fischer, *Liberty and Freedom* (2005), shows how two key ideas of the revolutionary cause were represented visually.

Edward Gray and Jane Kamensky (eds.), *Oxford Handbook of the American Revolution* (2013), presents a wide-ranging collection of recent scholarly perspectives on the experience of the war and the meaning of the struggle for independence.

Woody Holton, *Forced Founders* (1999), argues that material interests, and not just abstract ideas, underlay revolutionary sentiment in Virginia.

Holly Mayer, *Belonging to the Army* (1999), reconstructs the world of female "camp followers" in the war.

Robert Middlekauff, *The Glorious Cause* (1982), remains an influential comprehensive narrative of the Revolution.

Gary B. Nash, *The Forgotten Fifth* (2006), rethinks the significance of the war from the perspective of African Americans, including those who joined the British side.

Andrew O'Shaughnessy, *An Empire Divided* (2000), explains why Britain's Caribbean colonies did not join in the revolt against the empire.

Ray Raphael, *A People's History of the American Revolution* (2001), offers a detailed survey of the crisis and the war, emphasizing the experiences of women, the poor, the enslaved, and Indians.

Alfred Young, *Masquerade* (2004), interprets the broader significance of the life and celebrity of Deborah Sampson, the cross-dressing soldier.

7

INSIDE

THE BIG PICTURE

While the rebellious colonists waged war, they also sought to create and utilize new networks of communication in order to define their new nation. The history of the founding documents of the United States unfolded in that context.

A Nation on Paper. Thomas Jefferson's 1784 map of western territories imposed a sense of order over the unknown future of the new republic.

1776–1792

MAKING A NEW NATION

John Adams predicted in 1776 that the anniversary of independence would become a national birthday marked by "pomp and parade, shows, games, sports, guns, bells, bonfires, and illuminations, from one end of the continent to the other from this time forward, forever more." More than two centuries later, the Fourth of July remains the foremost national holiday in the United States, a day for expressing American patriotism and celebrating American independence from Great Britain. Adams's prophecy seems fulfilled in the parades, battle reenactments, backyard barbecues, afternoon baseball games, and shopping sprees of recent decades—except for the odd detail that he expected the celebrations to occur on July 2. Adams had not misplaced or misread his calendar; he simply assumed that Americans would choose to commemorate the date when Congress passed a resolution declaring independence, instead of when it formally approved a written document to that effect two days later.

Adams's mistaken prediction reminds us how difficult it is to pinpoint in retrospect the precise moment when the new nation was born. Why do Americans not celebrate their independence on the April anniversary of the first shots fired at Lexington and Concord in 1775, or the act of Congress the following May that authorized the creation of new governments, or the framing of the first new state constitutions? Why not choose the British surrender at Yorktown in 1781, the Treaty of Paris two years later, or the ratification of the Constitution in 1788?

Among the many decisive turning points in the history of American independence and nation building, the events of July 4, 1776, do not immediately stand out. A signed, written text declaring independence did not suddenly introduce a breach between the colonies and the Crown (which had already happened), nor did it instantly create a new national government (which would come years later). Yet this text and the moment it marked made a difference to the men of the Continental Congress who were charged with organizing the war effort. Even as the British fleet landed in New York and hovered near Charleston, the leadership in Philadelphia carefully considered the best way to express a new political reality. The tactic they chose was an act of communication that helped create a new nation. The military success of the rebellious colonists was only part of the process of making a new nation. July 4th commemorates the larger role of speaking, writing, and publishing in that process.

KEY QUESTIONS

- What were the content, character, and composition history of the documents—the Declaration of Independence, state constitutions, Articles of Confederation, and U.S. Constitution—that established the new American republic?
- How and in what ways was long-distance communication important to nation building?
- What was the significance of slavery in the politics of the early republic?
- Why and how did Americans become interested in plotting the geography of the North American continent?

During the decade and a half following the Declaration, both leaders and ordinary participants in the revolutionary movement tried to make sense of the events of July 1776 and to back up the audacious claim that thirteen long-standing British colonies were now united as free and independent states. New governments had to be designed and implemented, new patterns of communication had to be established, new maps had to be drawn, and a new national identity had to be conceived, represented, and publicized. This period is often identified with two founding documents, the Declaration of Independence and the U.S. Constitution, which stand as powerful—and radically different—symbols of the birth of the nation. But these documents emerged in a larger context of discussion, conflict, and celebration. Nation building was a complex process that unfolded in committee meetings, public parades, newspapers, pamphlets, drinking rituals, popular novels, and the expanding media of communication.

Americans declared their independence in various forms and settings.

DECLARING INDEPENDENCE

The Declaration of Independence has no formal status in American law. One cannot sue a neighbor, challenge a local ordinance, or claim civil rights damages on the basis of the pronouncements in the Declaration. Whatever power or authority it has enjoyed over the course of U.S. history is a function of its status as a sacred text that expresses the nation's founding ideals. But the Declaration did not become national scripture until the nineteenth century. By the twentieth century, the federal government would see fit to exhibit the original parchment text in a national shrine for visitors.

In its day, the Declaration's status was far less clear. Originally a statement by the Continental Congress, the Declaration was at the same time a personal pledge of commitment on the part of the delegates, a public indictment of King George III, and a strategic attempt to persuade the world (and specifically France, whom the Congress sought to recruit as a military ally) that the revolt against British authority was serious and legitimate. Members of the Congress were not entirely certain what it meant to declare independence. Was Congress, as John Adams had suggested early in the process, simply declaring for the record a fact that already existed, or was it somehow bringing a new state of independence into being? This ambiguity persisted as the document circulated in multiple forms and formats across the rebellious colonies.

National Shrine. The physical document identified with American independence had been treated somewhat carelessly by the State Department until 1921, when the Library of Congress took custody of the parchment. During the World War II, the Declaration was removed to Fort Knox under protection of the Secret Service and the U.S. Army. After its safe return to Washington, the Declaration was moved to airtight thermopane containers (with electronic helium detectors) and installed in the National Archives. It remains a tourist attraction by day, but every night the document descends into a fifty-five ton vault of concrete and steel.

DECLARATION BY COMMITTEE

On June 7, 1776, Virginia delegate Richard Henry Lee presented a resolution on the floor of the Continental Congress "that these United Colonies are, and of right ought to be free and independent States." Because several delegations still had instructions from their colonies not to renounce allegiance to Britain, Congress decided to buy time by referring the matter to a smaller committee that would prepare a larger text. The committee consisted of five men: Thomas Jefferson (Virginia), John Adams (Massachusetts), Roger Sherman (Connecticut), Robert Livingston (New York), and Benjamin Franklin (Pennsylvania), though Franklin was stricken with gout and probably did not participate much in the initial deliberations. Jefferson, the junior member of the committee, was chosen as draftsman, charged with producing a case for independence in consultation with other committee members. The text he drafted was presented to Congress on June 28, and the independence resolution passed on July 2 by a vote of twelve to zero (with New York abstaining). But even after that vote, delegates spent the next two days tinkering with the document, making both substantive changes and stylistic edits that Jefferson resisted and resented. A final version was then read aloud, accepted, and approved for publication.

It is hard to determine whether the Declaration was read aloud in Congress solely to secure final approval of its language, or whether the reading itself formed part of the ritual of becoming independent. If the Declaration was simply a legal enactment like a declaration of war, then what mattered was simply that Congress had stated that the former colonies were now free states. But Jefferson himself took seriously the idea that he was drafting a text that would be performed before an audience.

Declarations were a special kind of speech act with a rich history in English politics. Unlike petitions, they did not appeal to the authority of a governing body elsewhere. At the same time, they were more formal than ordinary announcements or pamphlets, which appeared with great frequency in colonial America. This particular declaration served multiple functions. It was supposed to rally popular support in the colonies for the war effort, justify the colonial cause to the "opinions of mankind," announce to other nations that the colonies were available for trade and military alliances, and formally nullify the authority of Great Britain over most of her North American possessions.

THE TEXT OF THE DECLARATION

Written in relatively plain language, Jefferson's draft sought to avoid the stately trappings of royal decrees and express the basic convictions of a broad populace. But for the founding document of a new nation, the Declaration of Independence is also notable for all the things it does not say. The text makes no mention of the history or purpose of English colonization (nothing about the travails of the Jamestown settlers or the lofty visions of the Puritans), omits any reference to the distinctive cultural identity of American colonists, refrains from commenting on the legitimacy of monarchy or aristocracy, and

Early Draft of the Declaration of Independence. Thomas Jefferson was a timid and ineffectual speaker, but he valued the power of oratory and understood his task as draftsman of the Declaration as that of a playwright composing words that would be pronounced dramatically. This early draft included what might appear to be accent marks. Such markings were in fact Jefferson's way of instructing a speaker when to pause between words or phrases.

provides no blueprints for a new republican government—all subjects that could have been both contentious and distracting. Instead, the Declaration confines itself to a fairly specific political argument for revolution.

Though later generations would focus on select phrases from the opening, the bulk and the heart of the text consists of a list of charges against King George III. Like an indictment with dozens of criminal counts, the Declaration lists various "injuries and usurpations," including restricting trade, controlling immigration, imposing taxes, dissolving representative assemblies, maintaining a standing army during peacetime, hiring German mercenaries, and supporting slave revolts. Both in form and in substance, the litany of charges echoed other declarations, resolutions, proclamations, and instructions to delegates that the colonial leadership produced during the crisis. Almost all of the charges referred to events of the past two years, and most were designed to portray the king, in unusually personal terms, as a tyrant. This timeless expression of the first principles of a new nation was in fact a timely political pronouncement.

The more memorable words of the Declaration appear in the opening paragraph. It speaks of the periodic necessity to change governments and appeals to the natural equality of "all men" with their inalienable rights to life, liberty, and the pursuit of happiness. Here, too, the Declaration was breaking little new ground. Jefferson's text drew on the writings of John Locke (the English philosopher who sought to justify the Glorious Revolution of 1688, in which the king was overthrown), on various Scottish Enlightenment thinkers, and most immediately on the model of fellow Virginian George Mason. Mason's draft for a state Declaration of Rights began with the claim that "all men are born equally free and independent, and have certain inherent natural rights, of which they cannot, by any compact, deprive or divest their posterity; among which are the enjoyment of life and liberty . . . and pursuing and obtaining happiness and safety." In elevating "the pursuit of happiness" to the same level as life and liberty, the Declaration of Independence (like the Virginia Declaration) was putting an important spin on the more common English trio of "life, liberty, and property." Both pursuing things and being happy would become central to American identity and ideology over subsequent generations, but even at the time the phrase struck a chord with the colonists. The pursuit of happiness—an idea drawn from Locke and other Enlightenment thinkers—was one of the few phrases in the Declaration's draft to which no delegate appears to have objected. Jefferson and his committee-mates were not coining novel terms or floating alien ideas. They were drafting language they hoped would express the prevailing sentiments of the revolutionary cause.

At the same time, the Declaration was also a personal document. It was not the statement of an abstract populace or a set of colonial governments; it was "A Declaration by the Representatives of the United States of America in General Congress assembled." The delegates themselves speak in this document, "pledg[ing] to each other our lives, our fortunes, and our sacred honor," and sharing the risk of committing treason. Individual signatures reinforced the personal dimension of the Declaration, and over the course of the next several months, delegates who had not affixed their names to earlier versions (including some who had not even been present) took the opportunity to sign.

PUBLICIZING THE DECLARATION

The Declaration was composed for a larger world of public opinion. Although the simple act of writing, signing, or reading aloud this text might have fulfilled the Declaration's claim to "solemnly publish and declare, that these united colonies are and of right ought to be free and independent states," declaring independence would have meant little if it had been confined to the meeting in Philadelphia. John Hancock, president of the Continental Congress, took charge of the elaborate task of informing and persuading his fellow colonists from New England to Georgia that something momentous had taken place on July 4.

Jefferson's Portable Writing Desk. Originally just one member of a drafting committee, Jefferson came to be identified as the Declaration's author.

Spreading the word that independence had been declared involved both writing and speech. According to congressional resolution, the Declaration was to be printed so that copies could be distributed to assemblies, conventions, committees, and militias in every state. But once it arrived at those gatherings, the text would be proclaimed orally. George Washington ordered officers in New York to pick up copies of the text and read it to their soldiers "with an audible voice." Elsewhere colonists gathered in courthouses, churches, and public squares to hear independence pronounced. In Philadelphia, not far from where the Declaration had been carefully composed and contentiously edited, a member of the local Committee of Safety performed the document from the balcony of an astronomical observatory to a chorus of cheers and bells. Colonists responded enthusiastically to these performances. Some communities defaced pictures of George III on tavern signs. New Yorkers destroyed a prominent equestrian statue of the king.

Throughout the war, Americans reenacted the dramatic script of July 4 in everyday acts of celebration. Especially common were festive rituals celebrating the thirteen free and independent states—thirteen gun blasts in a town square or thirteen toasts in a tavern (see Interpreting the Sources: Thirteen Toasts). All of this **street theater** was in turn reported in newspapers and pamphlets, which circulated along with copies of the Declaration itself, helping readers in one part of the continent imagine their celebrations as part of a unified national response. Men and women in the thirteen free and independent states experienced the act of declaration both as a piece of paper and as a shout in the street.

STATE BUILDING

The first independent governments in U.S. history belonged to the individual states. Between 1776 and 1788, these new states united around a common fate and a collective war effort, but they did not form a single coherent political entity. States made their own laws and devised their own political systems, drawing on their different colonial legacies as well as new ideas about legitimate and illegitimate uses of power. Nothing in the Declaration or in any of the other acts of the weak Continental Congress prescribed what exactly a proper republican government would look like. While the Congress, hamstrung by tight restrictions on its power, struggled to keep the states unified during and after the war, it fell to those states to bring a new political order into being.

THE FIRST CONSTITUTIONS

Even before the Continental Congress declared independence from Britain, it instructed the colonies, on May 10, to "adopt such government as shall, in the opinions of the representatives of the people, best conduce to the happiness and safety of their constituents in particular and America in general." Almost immediately, Patriots started amending their colonial charters or drawing up new written constitutions—some permanent, some designed simply to cover the war with Britain. Virginia and New Jersey adopted permanent constitutions within weeks of the congressional call. Over the next two years, eight other states would follow suit, and by the end of the war every rebellious ex-colony had some kind of new constitution in place (Rhode Island and Connecticut simply turned their colonial charters into state constitutions). These documents are often overlooked in retrospect, but at the time they were recognized as the crucial instruments for change in American political life. Jefferson would have preferred to return to Virginia in May 1776 to take part in the design of the new state government, but as the junior member of his delegation he had to remain in Philadelphia to assume the less promising task of declaring national independence. The first state constitutions established the legal frameworks that would secure individual rights and determine who had access to wealth and power in the postcolonial era. They would also provide the bases for constitutional thinking at the national level.

Perhaps the most radical feature of the new state constitutions was the fact that they were written down in the first place. The noun *constitution* had not traditionally denoted a text, and the revered "English constitution" was not a document at all; it referred to the political system itself—to the distribution of power among different political institutions, as worked out in an assemblage of laws, charters, customs, and precedents. Colonists had grown accustomed to written documents (such as royal charters) that defined the terms and conditions of law and government, but those documents were in fact subordinate to a larger system of royal and parliamentary authority that was not written down in any particular place. Written constitutions promised to protect colonists against the abuses of power they had experienced under the English constitution, not only because printed texts could be easily circulated, consulted, and cited, but also because they started from scratch. Written constitutions would stand boldly as the original and supreme law of the land, not depending on any larger or earlier system of authority.

Though they varied significantly from state to state, most of the original constitutions explicitly embraced the idea that legitimate governments drew their power from the consent of the people they governed and were obliged to respect certain **natural rights.** A majority of state constitutions explicitly listed these rights and their derivatives, which typically included civil liberties such as free speech, protection from unjustified searches and seizures, right to trial by jury, and the right to practice one's religious conscience (several states did, however, maintain an established church). In the blueprints for most of the new governments, executive officers (governors) held much less power than their colonial predecessors, and in Georgia and Pennsylvania, the office was abolished altogether. Those two states also eliminated the more aristocratic upper chamber of the legislative branch, but most constitutions provided for **bicameral** (two-chambered) legislatures that wielded

INTERPRETING THE SOURCES

Thirteen Toasts

The era of confederation lasted until 1788, a full five years after the official end of the war. During that period the question of whether the former colonies had become thirteen separate nations or one nation composed of thirteen states remained open. For the most part, the building of new governments and new societies took place at the state level and former colonists likely saw themselves first and foremost as citizens of those states. But a larger national consciousness was spreading at the same time, reinforced by the circulation of printed material and by a postal network that crossed state borders. The practice of offering thirteen patriotic toasts at a tavern, which began as a ritual of wartime solidarity, continued into the 1780s as an expression of this new national consciousness. Although they were spoken to a room of people who knew one another, toasts were printed and reprinted in newspapers and circulated throughout the country.

Toasting rituals drew a wide range of participants into public life, including people who were excluded from voting, serving in the military, or holding office. In Northampton, Massachusetts, a group of women staged their own toasting ceremony to celebrate the conclusion of peace with Great Britain in 1783, after a men's celebration on the previous day paid insufficient attention to female contributions to the cause of independence. As reported in the newspaper, the assembled women drank to:

1. Lady Washington.
2. The Congress.
3. A long continuance to our glorious peace.
4. The Thirteen United States.
5. Success to Independence.
6. May internal disturbances cease.
7. Trade and Commerce throughout the world.
8. Reformation to our husbands.
9. May the gentlemen and the ladies ever unite on joyful occasions.
10. Happiness and prosperity to our families.
11. Reformation to the men in general.
12. May the Protestant religion prevail and flourish through all nations.
13. May reformed husbands ever find obedient wives.

By creating room for the motley mix of social, religious, and political aspirations expressed by these Northampton women, the ritual of thirteen toasts also affirmed the possibility that thirteen very different states could be imagined as one.

Source: Massachusetts Gazette, recorded in David Waldstreicher, *In the Midst of Perpetual Fetes*, Chapel Hill: University of North Carolina Press, 1997 p. 83.

Explore the Source

1. Why do the women toast Lady Washington first?
2. What tensions do you see among the various toasts, especially on issues of gender relations?
3. Whom do you imagine to be the intended audience for these toasts?
4. What do you think is meant by the phrase "reformation to the men in general"?

unprecedented authority and were designed to be especially responsive to electoral pressures.

More significantly, most new state documents broadened participation in public life, by creating more elective offices, mandating more frequent elections, and reducing—but not eliminating—the property requirements for voting or holding office. In many states, close to half the adult white males became eligible to vote. Here, too, Pennsylvania's 1776 constitution was the most radical, granting suffrage to all taxpaying men (including free blacks who qualified as taxpayers). In most states, the fact that only men could vote went without saying, though three states saw fit to make the condition explicit. New Jersey's state constitution, however, opened the door for unmarried women to vote, though that door would be slammed shut early in the next century. Despite such anomalies, the basic character of American politics in the early republic (the early *republics*, really) was established during this era of state constitutionalism.

In the process of building new states on the basis of abstract principles of rights and equality, the framers of these first constitutions faced the problem of slavery. Virginia, the state that held the largest number of enslaved African Americans, was careful not to pitch its influential Declaration of Rights too broadly. George Mason's draft had posited that all men are "born equally free and independent" and could not yield their natural rights, but the delegates at the convention added a phrase to make it clear that those rights were retained only by those who "enter into a state of society," which was understood to exclude slaves. Framers of the Vermont constitution, on the other hand, took the occasion to outlaw slavery explicitly when they drafted their constitution in 1777. Vermont was a small territory (not officially recognized as a state until 1791), and its negligible enslaved population was a drop in the ocean of human bondage that spread over much of the nation. But the enactment was significant. Vermont was the first government to abolish slavery in the New World, and its constitution was the first of the original state-building documents in the United States to extend the rhetoric of equality across racial lines. It was also the only one.

CONFEDERATION

While the states crafted written constitutions that authorized their new governments, no comparable document existed at the national level. For five years after independence was declared, the Continental Congress operated without any formal authority. The purpose of having a single congress governing the thirteen unified states was explicit during wartime. Thirteen states needed a congress to manage the war effort (and to finance it by requisitioning and borrowing funds and by printing paper currency), to conduct international relations, and to run a postal network that crossed state borders. But as the prospect of military success came to appear more likely, it was not clear what kind of government a national congress should or could provide. Back in 1777, shortly after the American victory at Saratoga (see Chapter 6), Congress had passed what it called Articles of Confederation, outlining a structure for a weak central government for what was in many respects not a single nation but a collection of friendly states joined together for common defense. Though the Articles were not ratified by all the member states until 1781, Congress treated the document as a kind of constitution from the time of its initial passage. Since the Articles did not include any executive or judicial branches of government, Congress could act unilaterally to bring the new national government into being. In keeping with the idea that this was a confederation of sovereign states, each state delegation received one vote in Congress, irrespective of its size. When it came to raising funds for the war, states were assessed based on the size of their free populations, but Congress had no power to tax; it could only *ask* the states to contribute money.

A WEAK CENTRAL GOVERNMENT

The relative lack of power granted to the federal Congress under the Articles of Confederation was not an oversight. Recent experiences under British rule left the leaders of the new states suspicious of strong governments and hostile to entrenched bureaucracies exercising authority across large geographical distances. The states certainly needed one another for protection and support, but that did not mean that they wished to submit together to a federal authority located in a capital city. Significantly, the seat of national government migrated among four different cities and towns (Philadelphia, Princeton, Annapolis, and New York) during the 1780s, never coming to rest long enough to create a genuinely national space. As the new federal government began its work, nation builders in Congress and in state politics confronted some of the costs and contradictions of this position.

The new multistate confederation and its weak central government faced the problems of how to repay war debts and how to control lands in the western part of the country. In dealing with the first of those challenges, Congress had no power to impose direct taxes and could only request contributions from the states, much as it had done during the war. States were not especially responsive to these requisitions. Only three of them came up with even half of their assigned quotas between 1781 and 1788 and an especially ill-fated requisition in August 1786 yielded a return of just 2 percent. As an alternative to these inefficient requests, Congress proposed a tariff system, which they called an "impost," that would tax consumers indirectly by collecting 5 percent on the value of imported goods as they entered the country. But the measure needed the approval of all thirteen state legislatures, and first Rhode Island and then New York withheld support.

The confederation's money woes were exacerbated by the general economic chaos of the period. During the war, the Continental Congress and the new state governments had issued close to half a billion dollars' worth of steadily depreciating paper money—notes that were not backed by any promise to redeem them in silver or gold. The value of these Continental dollars had dropped precipitously by war's end, practically to a vanishing point. By the end of 1780, Continental money was trading at a discount of 100 to 1, which represented a 1000% rate of inflation on bills printed between 1775 and 1779. As one farmer put it, wartime paper money was "no Better than oak leaves & fit for nothing But Bum Fodder."

Facing runaway inflation and a postwar depression, caused in part by a trade imbalance once foreign armies left North America and British merchants resumed exporting consumer goods, different groups of Americans in and out of government experimented with new strategies for advantage or survival. A few enterprising merchants from New York and New England began searching for new trading opportunities with distant partners in China and along the Pacific coast of North America. Other investors turned to speculating in the debts racked up by state governments during the war. Gambling that promissory notes from the states might eventually be worth something, speculators purchased these notes at heavy discounts from soldiers (and others who had been paid by the states for supplies) and placed considerable pressure on the new governments to repay them. Debtors, meanwhile, lobbied states to ease the money supply by printing more paper money. So did farmers, a group that included most white American families, who hoped that such a policy might stem a postwar decline in crop prices. Seven states responded by issuing paper money in order to pay off public debts, which pleased both debtors and those who were owed money by the state, but angered other creditors, who would be hurt by inflation. In Rhode Island, the legislature in 1786 authorized an especially large paper issue and declared it legal tender (at face value) for all debts—to the horror of merchants and lenders forced to accept previously worthless currency from customers and borrowers.

In Massachusetts, by contrast, where debtors wielded less influence in the legislature and where a strong tradition of

Continental Bill Designed by Benjamin Franklin. Continental currency helped finance the war effort but was also intended to advertise and promote the cause of independence. This six-dollar note, with its image of a busy beaver, encourages its readers and users to persevere ("Perseverando") in the struggle against Britain. As a symbol of industriousness, the beaver also suggests that hard work and productivity can turn a mere piece of paper into something of real value.

Engraving Depicting Shays' Rebellion, by E. Benjamin Andrews. This 1895 treatment of the regulation movement in western Massachusetts depicts the scene "when the mob attempted to prevent the holding of the Courts of Justice." **Questions for Analysis:** How is the rebellion remembered in this late-nineteenth-century engraving? Does the artist see the disruption of court business as a legitimate act of political resistance?

tax administration had survived from the colonial era, the conflict played out differently. Massachusetts leaned on higher taxes rather than inflationary monetary policies to cover war debts, a preference that favored the interests of eastern merchants over western farmers. The state also imposed new direct taxes that further disadvantaged the rural interior. Several western counties erupted in armed revolt in 1786, conventionally identified with Daniel Shays, a war veteran who was blamed by opponents for leading a rebellion. Shays was not in fact the leader of the angry western farmers (who called their movement a "regulation," rather than a rebellion), though the name Shays' Rebellion survives. The rebels targeted the county courts, disrupting foreclosure proceedings where cashless farmers were losing their land. They were poised to seize a federal arsenal in Springfield when a private army hired by Massachusetts governor James Bowdoin disarmed and imprisoned the rebels. This 1786 uprising put numerous revolutionary leaders (especially Bostonians) in the awkward position of defending the rights of governments to forcibly suppress the resistance of taxpayers. The incident also dramatized the economic and political crisis facing the confederation.

Thomas Jefferson expressed his sympathy for the Massachusetts regulators in letters to several correspondents. "God forbid we should ever be 20 years without such a rebellion," he wrote. Jefferson's response was atypical among the leaders of the Revolution, but it reflected some more widely shared concerns about the dangers of a powerful and distant government. He considered the uprising in western Massachusetts a "rebellion honorably conducted" because it was rooted in the moral consensus of a local agrarian community and fit with that community's understanding of political events, however uninformed he thought they were. The lesson he drew was that state leaders needed to maintain better lines of communication with rural constituents, so that rural communities could remain both virtuous and engaged.

Other national leaders drew quite different lessons from this challenge to state government. To them, violence in western Massachusetts exposed the potential for anarchy latent in the recent rebellion and underscored the need for a strong central government that could collect revenues, set monetary policy, and support the kind of military force that could suppress an insurrection. Although Americans remained divided on these questions, Shays' Rebellion lent urgency to the complaints about the Articles of Confederation and called attention to the difficulties of securing political assent in a geographically dispersed republic.

The westward drift of the American population posed other problems for the weak central government during the confederation period. Congress spent much of its energy during the 1780s trying to settle land disputes between states and impose treaties on the Indians who inhabited and controlled much of that disputed land. In many ways, western lands dominated the politics of the era of confederation. The Articles of Confederation were only ratified in 1781 once Maryland was satisfied by Virginia's renunciation of its claims to land west of Pennsylvania and north of the Ohio River, and further cessions from various states offered the elusive promise of remedying the national government's financial distress. Western lands presented Congress with rare opportunities to play a role in the creation of new states.

A NEW MAP

The new American nation was not simply a set of governments and political institutions. It also corresponded to a body of land. Separation from Britain did not automatically transform the appearance of this terrain, nor did it instantaneously change the way people lived on the land, but the Revolution had profound effects on the way land was imagined and described. In numerous ways, the first generation of independent American governments relied on maps to define the new nation.

IMAGINING A CONTINENT

The leading advocates of revolution did not speak much about the character of American land or the relationship between geography and politics. But from the early days of the imperial crisis, leaders of the resistance to Britain had strategically invoked the idea that American colonies formed a continent as a way to get English-speaking colonists born in the New World to see their interests and identities as united in opposition to those of Parliament. The word *continent* itself connoted a continuous land mass, cutting across various colonial borders, and emphasized the fundamental divide created by the Atlantic Ocean. This way of mapping the colonial world might seem natural in retrospect, but at the time it was something of a bold fiction to imagine all the different nations, societies, tribes, plantations, language groups, and faith communities living in North America as linked simply because they shared a continental setting. Revolutionary leaders, many of whom lived in towns and cities near the seaboard, had more frequent and substantial contact with England than with colonists who dwelled deep in the interior. They also had far more in common with English-speaking Protestants in Great Britain than with the residents of Florida, California, or Apache lands. The very notion that British colonies were part of a single landmass stretching from the Atlantic to the Pacific was relatively novel at the time of the Revolution. For most of the previous two centuries, English mapmakers had typically represented North America either as a series of islands and peninsulas or as a separate region within a larger terrain whose contours were unknown.

The word *continent* gained currency in the 1770s and became crucial to the project of independence. Even though the thirteen colonial societies occupied only a small part of the vast expanse of North America, their leaders created *continental* congresses, mobilized a *continental* army, and attributed their political grievances to the continent itself. As one pamphleteer proclaimed in 1775, "Let English statesmen clamor for power . . . yet the continent of America will contend with equal fervency." In Thomas Paine's *Common Sense*, the Continent (often spelled with a

Earlier Views of North America. The image of the United States as a continent was something of a novelty in the eighteenth century. This 1669 map depicts a series of islands and peninsulas rather than a single land mass.

This sixteenth-century Swiss map puts Mexico at the center of the American land mass and makes Cuba almost as large as the lands that formed the original United States.

capital C) has needs, desires, and even bad habits. But perhaps the best evidence for this new attitude toward the continent lies in the special term that colonists adopted to describe themselves after the Stamp Act crisis. Over and over again, rebellious colonists identified as "Americans," a word that would soon become a national designation but was originally a geographical marker. By calling themselves Americans, as opposed to Virginians or Pennsylvanians, but also as opposed to Englishmen, Europeans, Christians, Baptists, colonists, or gentlemen, the founders of the new republic were identifying with their continent (see Hot Commodities: Maps of the United States).

NATIONAL BOUNDARIES

Neither the Declaration of Independence nor the Articles of Confederation located the new republic geographically. But the third of America's important founding documents did define the new United States as a place on a map. In 1783, representatives of Great Britain and the new U.S. Confederation signed the Treaty of Paris, officially ending the war (see Map 7.1). In recognizing the independence and sovereignty of the United States and "relinquish[ing] all claims to the government, propriety, and territorial rights of the same and every part thereof," the treaty identified the boundaries of the

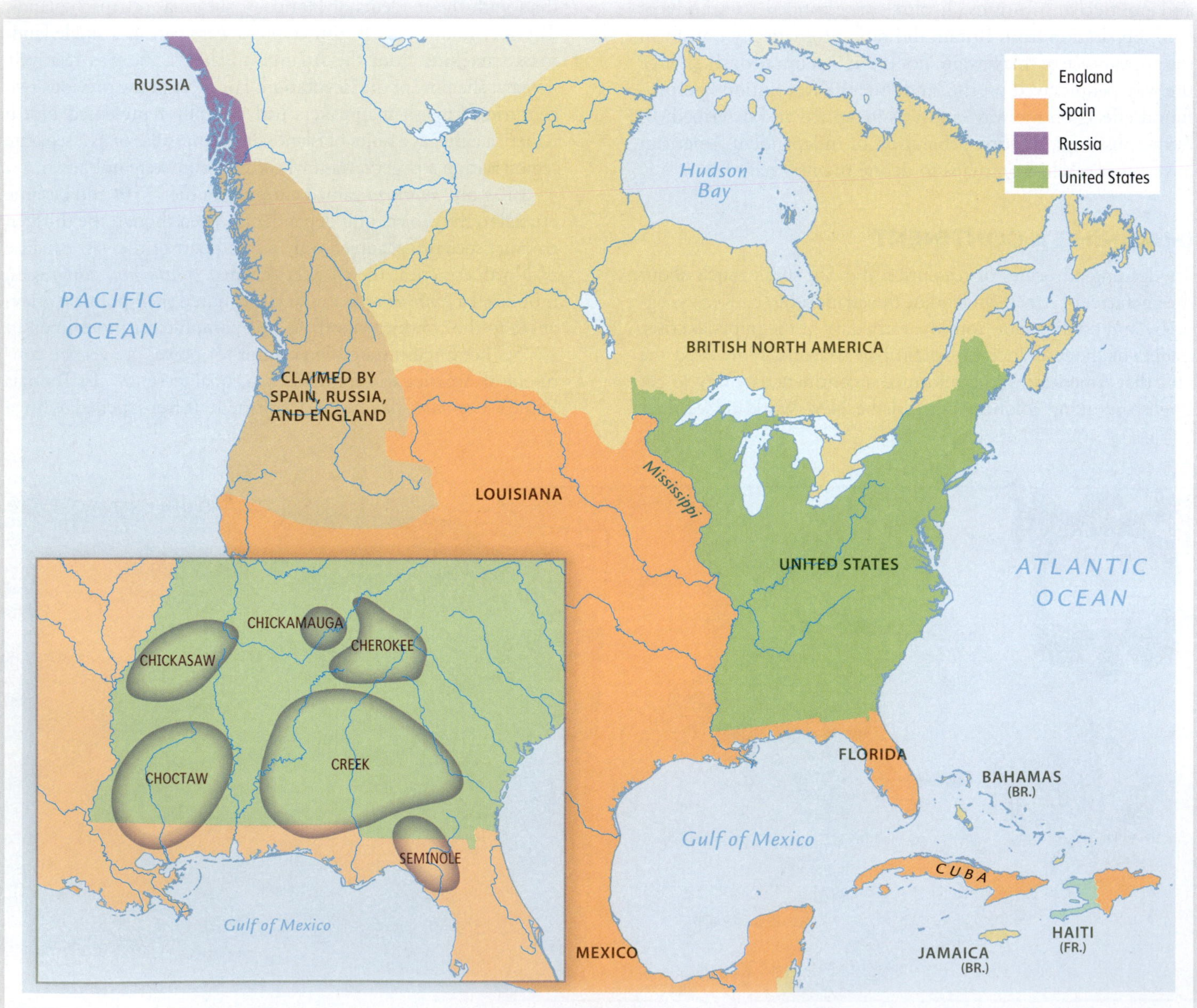

Map 7.1 Treaty of Paris, 1783. Diplomatic negotiations in Europe shifted the map of North America, but the new boundaries ignored the political reality that Indian groups still controlled large portions of the continent. In the Southeast, for example (see inset), nations not recognized in Paris remained dominant political players in the region.

HOT COMMODITIES

Maps of the United States

One of the remarkable innovations of the Revolution was a popular fascination with imagining what the new republic looked like. Often new nations spread images of revolutionary leaders or iconic buildings or battleground sites, but after independence, and especially after the land ordinances, citizens of the United States took particular interest in maps. Jedidiah Morse's textbook *Geography Made Easy* (1784), written shortly after the Treaty of Paris, featured the first published map of the new nation (five years later, another of Morse's geography textbooks would introduce the word *immigrant* into the American vocabulary). Cheap single-sheet national maps became popular consumer items, and large wall maps hung in public offices, coffeehouses, and taverns. Images of the territory of the United States appeared on globes and in pocket atlases, popular almanacs, paintings, card games, and children's puzzles. The proliferation of maps was part of a broader trend toward greater geographical literacy in the late eighteenth century. Land surveying became an important occupation, almanacs began including more geographical data, and geography textbooks like Morse's sold quickly and extensively.

But maps were not simply informative; they were attempts to define the new republic. These nationalistic images stressed the identity between nation and continent, much like the new practice of naming towns, cities, and universities for Christopher Columbus or invoking the figure of Columbia for the United States. Maps of the United States also offered readers a graphic symbol of the United States not based in common language, religion, or history. The outline of the nation as a whole, typically without any stress on the borders separating individual states, became a recognizable icon, a logo for the new republic.

The nationalistic campaign faced an uphill battle, however. During the decades after the Revolution, British printers, mapmakers, and artists continued to dominate the production of geographical images consumed in the new republic. Most maps used in American schools in the 1780s and 1790s continued to depict Europe as the center of the world, with the American continent at the periphery.

Picturing the New Nation. Whereas the Declaration of Independence and the Constitution presented the United States as a political entity, maps and icons, such as the one on this milk jug, depicted the nation graphically as a land mass with a distinctive shape.

Think About It

1. Why might the map of the United States have become an iconic symbol for the new republic?
2. How might the spread of printed maps have contributed to the formation of a centralized federal government?
3. Why might Americans have continued to think of Great Britain as the center of their world, even after 1783?

new nation with great precision (using prose rather than graphics). Article 2 of the treaty cites latitude degrees, distance measurements, and current flow patterns, and refers by name to over a dozen different bodies of water. This was one crucial way to designate a new nation—by marking its international borders.

But mapped boundaries can be deceptive. A nation's borders might be recognized by one neighbor and not another. The United States may have relied on the Treaty of Paris to determine its northern border with British Canada, for example, but the treaty also granted the new nation a southern border with Spanish Florida, and Spain had not been consulted on that part of the treaty. The Spanish did not accept a map that divided Georgia from Florida at the thirty-first parallel, nor did Spain recognize the treaty's authority to grant all U.S. citizens free navigation rights to the Mississippi River. In 1784, Spain barred American ships from the Mississippi and simultaneously cemented alliances with Creek, Choctaw, and Chickasaw Indians in the Southeast. Those native groups were also neighbors of the new United States, and they too had not been consulted on the terms of the Paris treaty.

The Confederation government could not simply take the paper boundaries of the new nation for granted. Shortly after the war came to its official end, Congress moved to establish a boundary with the six Indian nations of the Iroquois League and occupied land in what is now western New York. Geographical and political ambiguity surrounded the negotiations. The Confederation government and the state of New York each claimed rights to make a treaty with the Iroquoian tribes. Meanwhile the Indians and the Americans disagreed as to whether Iroquois land lay between the United States and Canada, or, as the Americans claimed, was surrounded entirely by U.S. territory and effectively conquered. The resulting Treaty of Fort Stanwix (1784) ceded significant Indian land in the Ohio River valley to the United States. The treaty drew unsuccessful challenges from Indians, who were not represented at the negotiations, and was

Map 7.2 Western Land Claims and Cessions, 1784–1802. By persuading the states to drop claims on Indian-dominated territory relinquished by Great Britain in 1783, the confederation government assumed political control of an enormous and potentially valuable stretch of land. **Question for Analysis:** What might have been the fate of this territory, and of the new republic, if the states had not ceded these western lands?

ignored by the state government of New York, which proceeded to appropriate and sell the land. Such treaties made it clear that the new national government possessed the military force to impose international borders on individual Indian tribes but still lacked the administrative capacity to dictate land use to the new states.

In the meantime, the national government needed to resolve boundary disputes between different states, many of which staked ambitious and competing claims to western lands, far in excess of what their colonial population patterns might have suggested (see Map 7.2). Relying on geographical vagueness in their original colonial charters, several states even had claims extending to the Pacific Ocean. Once the Treaty of Paris extinguished British claims to lands east of the Mississippi, states were in a better position to seize some of their western lands, but the national confederation also had its eyes on that prize. In 1781, Congress pressured Virginia, the largest state with the most extensive claims, to accept U.S. sovereignty over territory north of the Ohio River, and over the next five years Massachusetts, Connecticut, New York, and Virginia ceded lands that gave the federal government control over the Northwest Territory. This was a major political victory for the new government and set the stage for the most significant exercise of national will during the confederation period. Significantly, it was an act of mapmaking that plotted the westward future of the nation.

LAND ORDINANCES

After the Treaty of Paris and the state cessions, Congress sought to extend the political and social institutions of the United States of America to new regions subject to its rule. The congressional delegate charged in 1784 with drafting a blueprint for the western lands under federal control was the same man who had been asked eight years earlier to draft a script for independence—Thomas Jefferson. In many ways, his second attempt at creating a nation on paper would be even more ambitious than the first. Jefferson's grand plan for western development was adopted over the next three years in a series of congressional ordinances that organized land in the Northwest Territory and authorized the creation of new states that would join the confederation. Jefferson effectively drew a picture of the land west of the Appalachians as a blank slate of endlessly repeating patterns of identical square sections and subsections. Because Jefferson's plan structured land sales and influenced settlement patterns, this picture remains visible from the air, more than two centuries later, as one flies over the middle of the United States. It also helps explain the preponderance of straight-edged states on the national map.

The first of these land ordinances, passed in 1784, established the basic plan, mapping out ten new self-governing territories that would not be subject to the jurisdiction of any existing states and would eventually become states in their own

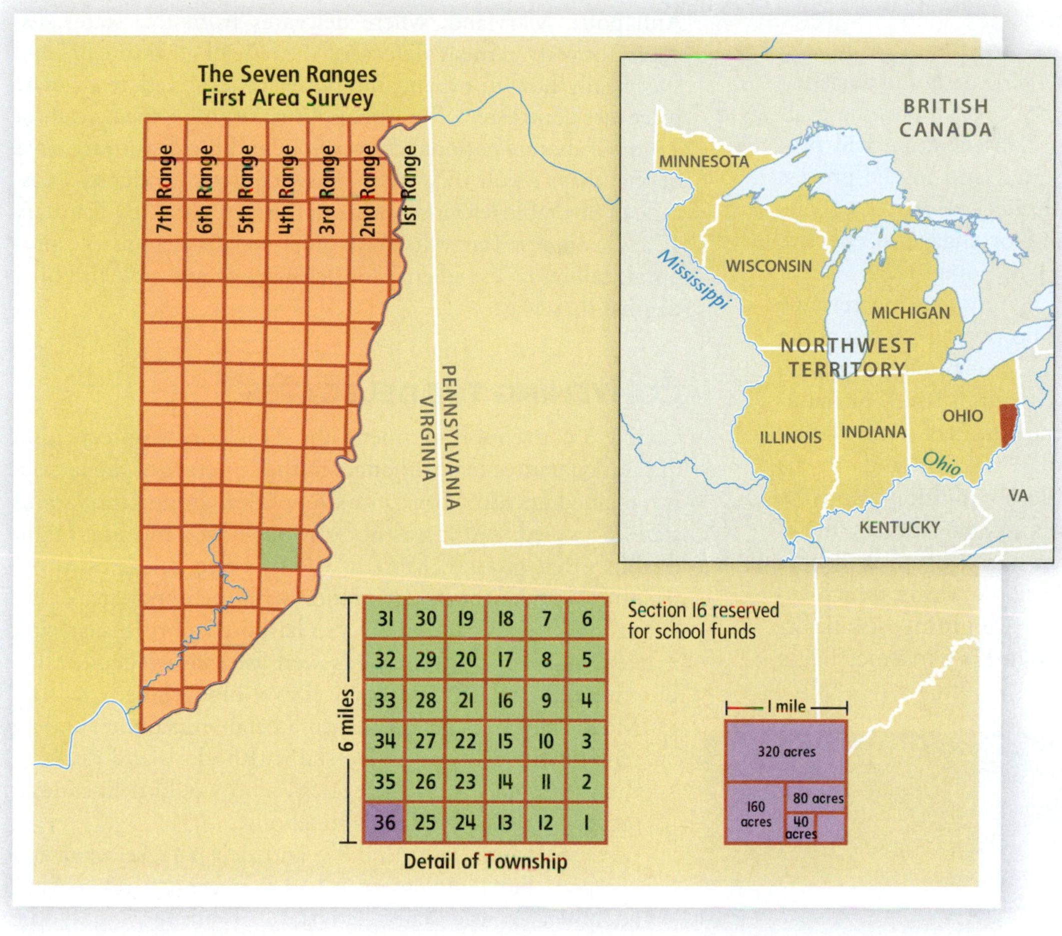

Map 7.3 Plotting the Northwest Territory. The land ordinances imposed a rectilinear grid on the nation's public lands, as shown in this detail from the projected map of southeastern Ohio.

right (see Map 7.3). Their boundaries were composed of straight lines and right angles rather than geographical landmarks (apart from the Ohio and Mississippi Rivers, which framed the entire territory). A year later, the Land Ordinance of 1785 reduced the number of states that would emerge from this territory and introduced a more elaborate division of land: Each of the eventual states would contain townships six miles square, each township contained thirty-six equal sections of one square mile, and each section contained four square farm plots of 160 acres (or sixteen 40-acre farms). Congress stipulated further that at least one section in each township be reserved for education.

The final enactment, the Northwest Ordinance (1787), specified the procedures under which new states would form. Initially a territory would be subject to the authority of an appointed governor, and once it reached a population threshold of five thousand free adult property-owning males its territorial government would qualify for a representative assembly. Once the free population reached sixty thousand, it could call a constitutional convention and apply for statehood. Congress also placed a significant restriction on these territories, which Jefferson had unsuccessfully proposed three years earlier. Slavery would be prohibited in the Northwest, though fugitives escaping across the Ohio River into the territory had to be returned to the South. This prohibition would have significant implications, not only for life and labor in the future states of Ohio, Illinois, Indiana, Michigan, and Wisconsin, but also for North-South relations in the United States and for future debates about the authority of the federal government to restrict slavery. For that reason (along with the fact that it established a model for admitting new states on equal footing with old ones), the Northwest Ordinance would be recognized by later generations as the singular achievement of the confederation. But Jefferson's larger vision of how the nation would expand, which guides all three ordinances, is significant in its own right. The ordinances were not simply ground rules for political growth; they were plans for a new kind of American land that would extend indefinitely.

Jefferson did not invent the idea of a **grid design**—town and city plans in both Europe and the Americas had long expressed a preference for straight lines and right angles. But the Land Ordinance went further by mapping an entire territory (both urban and rural) as a single stretch of graph paper. Such a planning vision treated land as uniform and homogeneous, recognizing no distinctions of topography, demography, history, or proximity to centers of power. This was significant for at least three different reasons. First, it was an appropriate vision for a democratic republic in which the use of land was not constrained by ancient laws, customs, or family claims. Second, it was a blueprint for a national real estate market, in which any plot of land could be easily bought and sold, even by someone who had never seen it. Third, it was a plan for migration, expansion, and conquest, since individuals, families, and communities could simply transplant themselves, relocating ever westward (often into Indian territory) to unknown places that were now likened to the places they left behind. In all of these ways, the congressional plan for the Northwest captured and shaped larger patterns of American national development.

THE CONSTITUTION

Congress's success in mapping western territories and amassing a national domain of land did not solve the most pressing challenges of the 1780s. The Articles of Confederation had protected the sovereignty of the new states, and in the process created a central government with limited power to regulate the economy, maintain a strong army, or engage in effective international diplomacy. Congress might hope to sell western land, but without a stable currency or any existing revenue stream to cover the costs of a military, how was Congress going to enforce treaties with Indians or with Great Britain, negotiate with the Spanish for access to the Mississippi River, or maintain the allegiance and obedience of the hordes of settlers crossing the Appalachians? The value of the western lands to the United States depended on all of those conditions, and the central government lacked the authority to address them. Meanwhile, even the state governments faced severe challenges to their authority from westward population drifts, which fed separatist movements in several states. Mounting dissatisfaction with decentralized government led in 1786 to a meeting in Annapolis, Maryland, where delegates from five states discussed how to "remedy defects of the federal government" and specifically how to expand the power of Congress to regulate interstate commerce. The Annapolis gathering issued a call for a more elaborate national convention, and the disturbing news of the Shays revolt in western Massachusetts produced a cascade of favorable responses from all thirteen states. By February 1787, Congress threw its own puny weight behind the proposal, calling it "expedient" for delegates to assemble in Philadelphia that May.

The Pennsylvania Statehouse Today. The delegates to the Constitutional Convention met at the Pennsylvania statehouse (now known as Independence Hall). On the first day of business, they agreed to a policy of strict secrecy. Doors to the building were closely guarded and the windows remained shut throughout the proceedings, despite oppressive summer weather. The most reliable record historians have of these momentous deliberations comes from James Madison's personal notes, published a half-century later, after his death.

CONVENING THE DELEGATES

Calling a convention to amend the Articles of Confederation did not guarantee major changes in the structure of the nation. It remained unclear what common political ground the various states occupied, and it was not obvious how a meeting might establish that ground. Most of the fifty-five delegates to the meeting shared a general frustration with the impotence of the federal government and many also harbored a broad suspicion that the new state governments were excessively democratic. But this did not translate easily into a blueprint for reform. Much would depend on an unpredictable encounter among representatives from twelve states (Rhode Island declined the invitation to send delegates), who would deliberate in secrecy at the Pennsylvania statehouse.

Once a date had been set and delegates selected and charged, state representatives had to make the trek to Philadelphia. At the scheduled start of business, only the Virginia delegation had managed to muster, and they waited impatiently with their Pennsylvania hosts for several days before enough others arrived to form a quorum. Virginians such as George Washington and James Madison were irritated by the delay, but they seized on the opportunity to set the convention's agenda and propose a model for a new federal government. The Virginia Plan, as it was called, envisioned a complete inversion of the relationship between state and federal government. Under the Articles, Congress represented sovereign states (a bit like the United Nations). Under this new plan, Congress would represent the people living in those states (more like Parliament). Congress would become a bicameral legislature within a three-branch federal government that included an executive officer and a judiciary, and each state's representation within both chambers of Congress would be proportional to its population. Congress would have the power to veto any state law and the authority to use military force against a state that defied a national law.

Though it was ultimately not adopted, the Virginia Plan framed the debate and forced the convention to wrestle immediately with big questions about representation, rather than considering more modest tweaks to the existing framework of national government. Delegates from smaller states (Connecticut, New Jersey, and Delaware), whose constituents would have lost representation under the plan, huddled quickly and devised a counterproposal—known as the New Jersey Plan—that reaffirmed the confederation's principle of giving each state an equal vote in the national government. Battle lines were drawn, and much of the summer would be devoted to working out a compromise, under which states would have equal votes in an aristocratic upper house (called the Senate), where members would sit for long terms and would not have to stand for direct election by the people, while representation in the lower house would be proportional to population. This compromise was necessary to the convention's success, but in many ways it was a predictable outcome once the Virginia Plan had called for two legislative chambers and introduced the concept of proportional representation.

Several members of the first two delegations to show up were instrumental in developing and proposing the Virginia Plan, but one of its major architects was James Madison (from the state that gave the plan its name). Madison had led the original call for the Philadelphia convention, and his theories of national politics would shape the convention's ultimate recommendations. Madison's innovation was to argue that it was possible for a republican government to thrive in a diverse society spread over a large geographical expanse. Rejecting the traditional republican suspicion that central governments were prone to oppress local communities, Madison argued that a national legislature was more likely to act impartially because it would be forced to balance the interests of numerous competing factions and less liable to conspire against the rights of minorities. When delegates from New Jersey and Connecticut complained that Virginia's proposals would benefit the biggest states, Madison responded that populous states like Massachusetts, Pennsylvania, and Virginia were unlikely to have many interests in common or to be able to act in concert.

TALKING ABOUT SLAVERY

The crucial shift toward proportional representation signaled a decisive break from the kind of nation envisioned in the Articles of Confederation. It also forced delegates to confront the explosive issue of how each state's population would be counted. As Madison pointed out in defense of the Virginia Plan, the major political fault line in the United States was not between big states and small ones, but between northern and southern states. The division arose "principally from the effects of their having or not having slaves." The North did in fact have slaves in 1787, but the numbers were small enough to create a clear conflict between the two regions. When it came to apportioning representation in the lower house, Southerners wanted their population counts to include enslaved African Americans, while Northerners, not surprisingly, advocated counting only free persons.

Delegates ultimately settled on the infamous three-fifths clause, which credited states for 60 percent of their slave populations. This formula was not a novel suggestion; it had been introduced four years earlier (by none other than Madison) when the Continental Congress was considering how to assess each state's financial burden. For tax purposes, of course, Northerners wanted the free and the enslaved to count equally, whereas Southerners took the opposite view. Delegates to the Philadelphia convention revived Madison's three-to-five ratio in 1787 as a way of calculating both political representation and tax assessment, but most of them understood that Congress was highly unlikely to engage in any direct taxation. The significance of the three-fifths clause is often misunderstood. It was neither an ingenious solution nor an expression of the mathematics of white racism, but rather a familiar fraction for splitting a crucial political difference. From the perspective of the enslaved, the insult lay less in being counted as only three-fifths of a person than in being counted at all. Disenfranchised slaves had no interest in enhancing the political power of the states in which they were held as property. Ultimately, the Constitution's three-fifths clause would provide a political bonus to slaveholders that would artificially amplify their voice in Congress and in presidential elections right up to the Civil War.

The immediate effect of the three-fifths proposal at the convention was to provoke one of the first national conversations about the legitimacy of human bondage. By 1787, the moral consensus that had supported African slavery in the New World since the early years of European colonization had begun to fray in the North. And while southerners, especially those from South Carolina, had repeatedly warned that any attempt to strip slaveholders of their chattel would instantly dissolve the national confederation, the dynamics of a face-to-face meeting with secret deliberations produced some frank discussion across a growing moral divide. Delegates from the South spoke openly and anxiously about the need for protection against the possibility that Congress would use its powers of taxation to abolish slavery—and threatened on multiple occasions to leave the convention. Several delegates, mostly from the North, took the occasion to denounce slavery, which was, in the words of Pennsylvania delegate Gouverneur Morris, a "nefarious institution" that defied "the most sacred laws of humanity." Regional disagreements over slavery could not be cast simply as North versus South. Delegates from Virginia, where slave populations reproduced themselves naturally and slaveholders were no longer importing human beings from Africa or the West Indies, were willing to join New Englanders in criticizing the international slave trade, and Northerners from small states proved amenable to allying with small slaveholding states on that issue to thwart parts of the Virginia Plan. But these tense and testy discussions supported Madison's observation that slavery mattered more than size as an obstacle to redesigning the national government.

The ultimate resolutions of the slavery debate reflected the discomfort many delegates brought to the subject. Nowhere in the final version of the U.S. Constitution would the words *slave* or *slavery* appear, even though the document contains key provisions intended to protect the interests of slaveholders. The Constitution banned federal interference with the slave trade for twenty years and prohibited state and local governments from impeding the return of fugitive slaves from other states. It also granted slave-rich states extra congressional representation based on their enslaved population—all without ever uttering the crucial word.

WRITING THE CONSTITUTION

By September 8, almost three and a half months after they began their work, delegates had arrived at a set of proposals for a completely new national government, one with enhanced powers and greater insulation from democratic influences. Many important features of the original Virginia Plan, including a bicameral legislature and a three-branch government, survived the long summer of caucusing and negotiation, but the power of the individual states was preserved in some important ways. Both the Senate and the presidency, an executive office chosen by a special gathering of prominent citizens (called an electoral college), recognized the significance of states as fundamental units in the political order. State governments would have some control over their senators and presidential electors, and senators and electors would represent entire states rather than constituencies within those states. Still, the complex system of checks and balances proposed for the new national constitution entailed something much less like a league of states and more like a central government.

The last remaining item on the convention's agenda was to produce a written text that would describe and define the powers of the new government. Five delegates—Madison, Alexander Hamilton (New York), William Samuel Johnson (Connecticut), Rufus King (Massachusetts), and Gouverneur Morris (Pennsylvania)—formed the Committee on Style, which, like the five-man committee that drafted the text of the Declaration of Independence a decade earlier, was charged with choosing the right words to express the intentions of the larger convention. The committee, largely under the leadership of Morris, set about presenting, in crisp and economic language, the various agreements that had been reached over the summer, turning twenty-three different provisions into seven main categories. This work was obviously more than just stylistic and editorial. How the Constitution was organized and the precise language it included would have far-reaching implications. And Morris's preamble, which identified both the authority of the document (the people, not the states) and its goals (forming a more perfect union, securing the blessings of liberty), assigned a specific overriding meaning to the text that a different introduction might not have claimed.

The precise wording of the text made a difference, and Gouverneur Morris could be said to have authored the Constitution in much the same way that Jefferson is credited with the authoring the Declaration (see Singular Lives: Gouverneur Morris, Ghost Writer). But few people (then or now) would identify Morris as the father of the American Constitution, nor is it common to think of the Constitution as having an author at all. (James Madison is widely but misleadingly regarded as the "father" or the architect of the Constitution, because he famously and vigorously defended its plan of government, but not exactly as an author.) This is because the Constitution makes no claim to personal authority, speaking instead on behalf of an abstract "people." Whereas the Declaration was a pledge of personal honor and commitment on the part of specific individuals who were describing current events in urgent language, the Constitution speaks in a more impersonal voice. Though both documents were signed, signatures meant something very different in the case of the Constitution. Thirteen of the original fifty-five delegates had left the convention before the final vote on September 17, and three others opposed the plan, so Benjamin Franklin moved that the Constitution be passed by "unanimous consent of the States present." The men who signed the Constitution were not using personal signatures to authorize the words it contained (as one signs a letter); they were simply attesting to the fact that the state delegations had voted in favor of the document. The words of the Constitution claimed to come directly from "the people"—not from the signers as individual speakers. All of this helps to explain why the Constitution is essentially a printed rather than a written or performed text. Every printed copy of the Constitution has the same significance and authority.

RATIFICATION

The preamble to the Constitution speaks confidently on behalf of "the people of the United States" and their desires, but of course the people had not yet spoken. The blueprint for a new government, which was first presented to the public on September 19, 1787, in a special issue of the *Pennsylvania Packet* newspaper, had been designed by a small and sequestered group of men, less than three-quarters of whom actually voted for final approval. The document did not even bear the official stamp of the existing Congress, which simply passed it along to the states without endorsement. Much work was needed to turn the text hammered out in Philadelphia into the supreme law of the land.

To take effect, the proposed Constitution (according to its own terms) would have to be approved by special ratification conventions in nine states, something supporters recognized would be a challenge. Almost immediately after the Philadelphia meeting adjourned, advocates of ratification, calling themselves Federalists, began organizing conventions in states where success seemed likely. Before the new year, Delaware, New Jersey, and Pennsylvania all ratified. The more interesting and important strategy of the Federalists was to refuse to allow any room in the ratification process for states to give input, propose amendments, express reservations, or vote on particular articles. All the states could do was accept or reject the published Constitution as it was written. This move was designed to prevent the chaos of having to renegotiate new compromises or resubmit amended versions of the text to additional rounds of conventions. It was also consistent with the fiction that the Constitution (which was going to set the rules of government, as opposed to being an act of government) spoke on

SINGULAR LIVES

Gouverneur Morris, Ghost Writer

Lawyers, politicians, and scholars speak of the "framers" of the Constitution, frequently appealing to their ideas and intentions in order to figure out the text's meaning. But who exactly framed the document is open to debate. One place to start is with the man who likely contributed most of the language that became the supreme law of the land in the United States.

Though his face appears on no currency and no state capitals bear his name, Gouverneur Morris (his first name was French but was pronounced *governor* or *gover-NEER* in America) left as powerful an imprint on the new nation as any of the more famous founders. Born into the ruling elites of colonial New York in 1752, Morris joined the revolutionary cause and served briefly as a member of the Continental Congress during the war. But his shining moment came a decade later, after he was elected by the legislature in Pennsylvania (his home since 1778) to represent the state at the Constitutional Convention. Just thirty-five years old, Morris spoke more times at the convention than any other delegate, even though he missed an entire month of the deliberations while attending to private business back home.

Morris was an eloquent and provocative speaker, and many of his contributions shaped the Philadelphia debates. But he was even more effective as a writer and became an obvious choice to serve on the committee that drafted the Constitution. According to other participants, it was Morris who pared the resolutions and compromises produced on the convention floor into the finished product's compact and straightforward articles, which have become the focus of intense scrutiny and debate in American politics ever since. And it was Morris who penned the preamble, which remains the most famous part of the original document.

Morris played no role in the ratification campaign and took no position in the new government. He spent most of the rest of the century in Europe, making money, following the French Revolution as U.S. minister to France, and attending to his busy personal life. Morris would return to the United States in 1798 to make two other great contributions to American history. In 1807, he was appointed by New York State to a commission charged with mapping the future growth of New York City. Three years later the same legislature named him chair of New York's Canal Commission, which recommended building a canal from the Hudson River to the Great Lakes. With less fanfare than the Constitutional Convention, these two commissions would revolutionize market relations in the United States, turn New York into the nation's commercial capital, and utterly transform the city's landscape. One commission designed the grid plan for Manhattan (see Chapter 8); the other created the Erie Canal (see Chapter 10).

Morris died in 1816, before the canal was built and before the gridded streets of New York were graded and settled. But he had reason to be optimistic about these projects. He was less sanguine about his other creation, the Constitution. Late in life, under different political circumstances, Morris came to rue the three-fifths clause and the power it gave to southern states. Privately he advocated a breakup of the union.

Morris's disenchantment with the Constitution he had written is a useful reminder of how hard it is to generalize about the framers. The fifty-five men who haggled in secret over the Constitution were very different from one another. And the man who came up with the words a nation would live by was hardly typical of the gathering. He was far more skeptical than most of his colleagues about the benefits of democracy and did not trust ordinary people to set government policy. He championed a strong presidency in the face of delegates who were more comfortable with legislative authority. He was also far more committed to the rights of minorities. He loved cities and dreaded western expansion. Like Thomas Jefferson (with whom he shared little else), he did not believe in an active god and was not a regular churchgoer. And more than most others at the convention, he bitterly opposed slavery on moral grounds. What Gouverneur Morris meant by "a more perfect union" undoubtedly differed from what Madison would have meant by those same words. But Morris had simply come up with the phrase. Neither he nor any of the other delegates could determine its meaning.

Founding Father Figure. While completing his famous sculpture of George Washington in full military dress, French sculptor Jean-Antoine Houdon used Gouverneur Morris, living in Paris at the time, as a body double. As in the Constitution he drafted, Morris's special role in the creation of this national icon is concealed from public view.

Think About It

1. In what respects was Morris an atypical member of the Constitutional Convention?
2. If Morris composed the text of the Constitution, does that make him its author?
3. What possible similarities does the Constitution share with Morris's two other famous accomplishments?

Mercy Otis Warren (1728–1814), Antifederalist. Warren, a playwright and historian from Massachusetts, worried that the United States covered too vast a territory to be governed by a single legislature. Although women did not ordinarily vote and never held political office, elite women shaped public discourse about government affairs both in print and in polite conversation.

behalf of the people, rather than on behalf of state assemblies or elected representatives. If individual states or politicians proposed amendments, it would be clear that the text did not express the words of "the people." Instead the ratification process presented states with a text written in the name of the people, and it was up to voters to claim the text retroactively or disavow having uttered it.

During the first several months of 1788, ratification battles blazed in several key states. Georgia, which favored a strong National government to protect its border with Spanish Florida, was an easy sell. Connecticut followed soon after, and Maryland and South Carolina also offered hospitable soil for Federalists. But larger states, especially Virginia, Massachusetts, and New York, posed more formidable challenges. **Antifederalists** were strong in those states and raised powerful objections to the proposed Constitution on grounds that it would create an oppressive central government that would trample on the rights for which the Revolution had been fought. A major theme in much Antifederalist rhetoric was long-distance communication. How could a government covering such a vast territory genuinely represent distant constituents and respect local customs and opinions? This concern was especially powerful among backcountry voters, who lived far from the centers of information exchange.

Federalists, on the other hand, were strong in cities and towns nearer the seaboard, and capitalized on their strong support among printers, who were optimistic about a geographically expansive political culture in which citizens took an interest in distant developments and read newspapers. Arguments in favor of ratification dominated the press, most famously in New York City, where Madison, Hamilton, and John Jay collaborated on a series of eighty-five newspaper pieces published between October 1787 and August 1788. The first thirty-six pieces of *The Federalist* appeared together in book form that March, and the rest comprised a second volume published two months later, before eight of the essays had even come out in the newspaper. Though they formed but a small part of the larger print debate over ratification, the essays' three authors eloquently defended the proposed Constitution and, more significantly, offered what future generations would come to regard as the most reliable exposition of its political philosophy. The central theme of this philosophy was the idea that the Constitution represented a system of **checks and balances,** which would protect the new nation against oppression and corruption. Checks and balances referred not only to the division of the government into three branches with separate powers and different domains, but also to the competition of heterogeneous forces, interests, and regions that the Federalist authors believed would prevent any one faction or social group from obtaining excessive power. In this way, its most influential supporters argued, the proposed Constitution would protect the new republic from too much democracy, too much aristocracy, and too much of anything else.

The Preamble to the Constitution: We the People? About 160,000 voters participated in the selection of representatives to the state conventions that debated ratification. Perhaps one hundred thousand of those people voted, however indirectly, to accept this Constitution as the new supreme law of the land. By many measures this was a remarkable democratic achievement, but the number of people who in any sense framed the Constitution falls far shy of the almost three million souls who composed U.S. society at the time. Speaking as the people, those Americans who participated in the creation of this document had to make claims on behalf of a diverse and dispersed population.

We the People of the Un
insure domestic Tranquility, provide for the common defence, prom
and our Posterity, do ordain and establish this Constitution for the
Article I

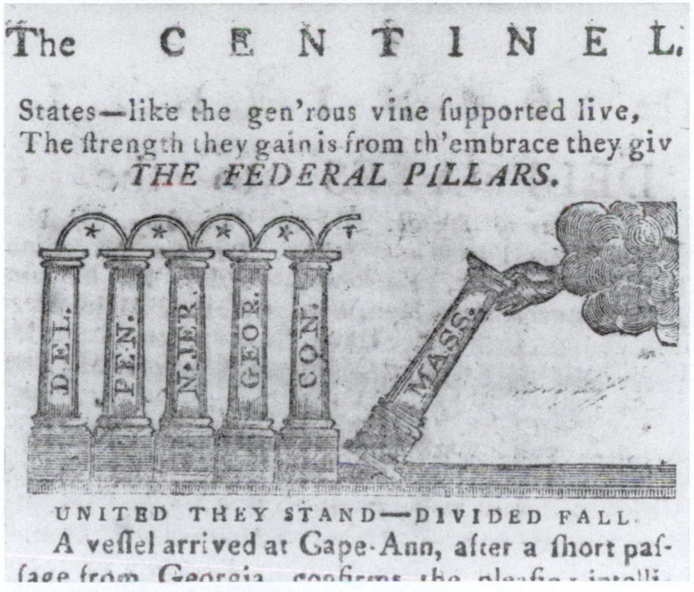

The CENTINEL.

States—like the gen'rous vine ſupported live,
The ſtrength they gain is from th'embrace they giv

THE FEDERAL PILLARS.

DEL. PEN. N.JER. GEOR. CON. MASS.

UNITED THEY STAND—DIVIDED FALL.

A veſſel arrived at Cape-Ann, after a ſhort paſ-

Building the Federal Edifice. Pro-ratification cartoons like this one from the Massachusetts *Centinel* emphasized the structural interdependence of the different states. Propped up by some supernatural hand, Massachusetts adds its pillar to the new government.

Arguments about ratification were not limited to the press. Both proponents and opponents took to public space in rallies, celebrations, bonfires, and other symbolic expressions of support for their positions. In Carlisle, Pennsylvania, for example, Federalists assembled to fire a cannon to salute the Constitution, but they were met by a larger party of Antifederalists, who beat them up, burned an almanac in which the Constitution was printed, and set fire to the cannon itself. Whereas Antifederalists gathered to express the consensus of a local community, Federalists were especially interested in parades and processions that claimed to speak for more abstract collectivities, like the new nation itself. Federalist street theater projected images of unity and wholeness and often used the ritual of the thirteen toasts. Once New Hampshire became the surprise ninth state to ratify, putting the Constitution into effect, Federalists tried to put pressure on Virginia and New York by offering only nine toasts.

Both Virginia (in June) and New York (in July) ratified the Constitution by extraordinarily close margins. In both cases, the promise of subsequent amendments to protect the rights of minorities and individuals helped sway opponents to support ratification. Federalists had refused to amend the text prior to the ratification process (since it would have unraveled the fiction that the Constitution was a founding document that preceded the political actions of the states), but once it was in place, the Constitution's leading advocates in Congress joined critics in supporting a **Bill of Rights,** which contains most of what Americans still regard as the essence of the original Constitution: freedom of speech, assembly, and arms-bearing, as well as freedom from state-established religion, unwarranted searches, self-incrimination, or cruel punishments. The Bill of Rights won congressional approval in September 1789 and by the end of 1791 met the requisite approval of three-fourths of the states. During that two-year period, North Carolina and Rhode Island also ratified the original Constitution, making good on the earlier boast of the delegates in Philadelphia. The Constitution had now been approved by the unanimous consent of the states.

The original U.S. Constitution, despite numerous defects, would wield enormous influence on the development of law and politics both at home and abroad. It did not establish democracy (most Americans remained legally disenfranchised long after ratification), it did not espouse universal human rights (slavery was fully constitutional), and it did not even guarantee basic freedoms of speech, press, assembly, and religion. Even the subsequently adopted Bill of Rights, which prevented Congress from infringing on those rights, allowed states to do as they pleased in this regard. But the Constitution did enshrine fundamental principles of separation of powers and popular sovereignty that remain cornerstones of American government, and its model was adopted wholesale by other republican governments, from Venezuela to the Cherokee Nation, over the next several decades. In the longer term, the constitutionalist idea that national governments ought to be founded upon and bound by a written text remains one of the most significant legacies of American nation building.

THE FIRST PRESIDENT

In keeping with its primary goal of creating a vigorous and energetic national government, the Constitution called for a chief executive who would wield more authority in American political life than any individual since independence was declared. Although no one campaigned for the job, George Washington seemed an obvious candidate by virtue of his broad personal popularity. Washington had participated in the Philadelphia convention as a delegate from Virginia, but had frequently expressed his intention to retire from public life. Still, few doubted that he was the

Fire Bucket Showing George Washington's Face. Washington was celebrated as a strong military leader, likened here to Rome's Julius Caesar.

right man to unite the states and make the new office of president palatable to those who feared executive power. The expectation that Washington would fill the position had largely dissuaded Antifederalists from making the presidency a significant issue in their campaign against the Constitution.

After ratification, Washington maintained a reluctant posture, but the sixty-nine electors, representing eleven states (North Carolina and Rhode Island were not yet on board), did not hesitate to select him unanimously when they gathered in February 1789. The more complicated portion of the process was communicating this decision to the Confederation Congress in New York so that the new president could be inaugurated. Due to frigid weather, it took two months to gather a congressional quorum, and the country was left in a state of limbo without a functioning central government. Finally, on April 6, Congress opened the ballots and announced publicly that Washington had been elected. It would take another week before the president-elect was officially informed, but Washington had already begun to pack his bags for the move from Virginia to New York. The will of the people was clear, he explained in his official response to the election: "I have been accustomed to pay so much respect to the opinion of my fellow citizens that the knowledge of their having given their unanimous suffrages in my favor scarcely leaves me the alternative for an option."

Father for a Republic. George Washington entered office amid lingering concerns that the new constitution might bring back monarchy. The fact that Washington, who appears to have been sterile, sired no natural heirs may have helped allay some of those concerns. "Providence left Washington childless," as the nineteenth-century saying went, "that a nation might call him father."

As he made his slow journey northward, Washington was celebrated in town after town with speeches, toasts, and parades. On the last day of April, the new president was sworn into office in New York's Federal Hall, taking his oath over a Bible brought from a local lodge of the Masonic Order, the secret society to which Washington belonged. After reading the oath prescribed in the Constitution, the officiating chancellor called out to the crowd below the gallery: "Long Live George Washington, President of the United States."

Having inaugurated a new chief executive with much pomp and ceremony, the leaders of the republic faced the challenge of conferring dignity upon the office of the presidency without appearing to have replaced one king with another. Some of the founders, including the new vice president, John Adams, thought that the honor of the nation called for Washington to be addressed with such majestic titles as "His Highness, the President of the United States, and Protector of their Liberties," but advocates of the simpler, republican-sounding "Mr. President" carried the day. The Constitution had clearly delimited the powers of the executive branch, but everyday decisions about protocol, dress, and conduct would also shape the character of the new government.

NATIONAL COMMUNICATION NETWORKS

Documents such as the Declaration of Independence and the Constitution did not simply lay political foundations for a new government; they were also part of a growing communication system. Their power depended on the proposition that citizens of the new republic, however dispersed over the map and however varied in personal circumstances, might imagine themselves as sharing a common identity and participating in a collective conversation. As the new nation emerged, American men and women contributed to this conversation by building a culture around printed texts. A wide range of printed novels, newspapers, and pamphlets circulated among readers in the various states and offered definitions of what people living in the United States had in common, beyond their shared status as subjects of the new national government.

LITERATURE AND THE NEW NATION

The first writer to pose in print the question "What is an American?" was not a delegate to the Continental Congress, a signer of the Declaration, a pamphleteer for independence, or a framer of the Constitution. He was not a native English speaker, nor was he born in North America. Michel Guillaume St. Jean de Crèvecoeur emigrated from France to Canada toward the end of the French and Indian War, subsequently adopted an English name, married a British colonist, and settled on a large plot of land in Orange County, New York. A Loyalist during the revolutionary crisis, Crèvecoeur left the United States in 1781. A year later, a London publisher printed his *Letters from an American Farmer,* a series of literary essays about American life and identity. Presented as the correspondence of a fictional Pennsylvania farmer named James to a genteel and cosmopolitan Londoner, James's letters celebrate an American society in which people of humble origins can willfully remake themselves and achieve social and political equality through owning and cultivating land. James describes a cooperative and responsive natural landscape in North America, devoid of the monumental ruins of Europe, and he contrasts honest rural living with the dehumanizing world of the city. To the question that preoccupies his third letter, "What is an American?", James gives the now-familiar answer that American national identity grows out of economic and political opportunities rather than ethnicity, language, or religion.

Declarations, pamphlets, maps, and constitutions were, among other things, ways of inscribing the new nation on paper and communicating it across distances. But much of what was written, printed, and circulated in the 1770s and 1780s, like Crèvecoeur's original articulation of the American dream, took the form of literature. In published poems, plays, and works of prose fiction, American readers found entertainment, inspiration, and a shared literary culture.

As Crèvecoeur's example highlights, this culture was transatlantic. Texts, books, authors, and fictional characters routinely crossed the ocean in the early years of U.S. literature. In fact, most of the literature consumed by American readers before the nineteenth century was authored in Europe, and especially in England. British authors dominated the American literary marketplace in large part because the absence of copyright laws made it profitable for American publishers to produce cheap pirated editions of foreign works, and English authors were the most accessible and best known. But part of the reason there had never been any copyright legislation in colonial America was that the commercial value of American literature had never been very great. Despite high rates of literacy (among whites), American readers were dispersed widely in a country with poor roads and did not form a major book-buying market for most of the colonial era. After independence, the new states began enacting copyright laws, but they varied in content, were selectively enforced, and did not apply across state lines. In 1790, Congress passed the Federal Copyright Law, and though not many authors or publishers took advantage of it immediately, it signaled the beginnings of literary entertainment as a viable business in the United States. Publishers were still tempted to run the business with foreign authors, however. It would take another forty years until international copyright agreements would protect American authors against unauthorized and uncompensated pirating of their works in foreign countries.

Susanna Rowson (1762–1824). One of the leading novelists in the early United States, Rowson made a living as a professional actress and then as a school headmistress. She was unable to reap much of the profit generated by her best-selling novel *Charlotte Temple*, which was not protected by international copyright agreements.

WOMEN AND THE AMERICAN NOVEL

Novels were the most popular form of literary entertainment in the new nation. English novelists continued to dominate the trade, and no homegrown authors were able to make a living writing fiction for another several decades. Still, several popular and important American novels were published during the end of the eighteenth century. The distinction of being the first American novel is contested, depending on what qualifies a novel as American, but scholars usually bestow that honor on *The Power of Sympathy*, written by the American-born author William Hill Brown. Published in the United States by the influential Worcester publisher Isaiah Thomas in 1789, the year George Washington was inaugurated as the first president, Brown's novel did not achieve much notice during the author's lifetime. Several other novels from the 1790s made a bigger splash. The most successful of these, Susanna Rowson's *Charlotte Temple* (1791), was written in England by an English author who had spent much of her childhood in America. Shortly after her novel appeared, Rowson moved (like her title character) to the United States, where her work became a best seller. *Charlotte Temple* sold an estimated forty to fifty thousand copies in two decades and would be reprinted more than two hundred times, mostly in the nineteenth century.

The plots of many early American novels, including *The Power of Sympathy* and *Charlotte Temple*, feature the motif of seduction, a plot line that both entertained readers and evoked the fragility of the new republic. Would the new nation possess the

***Liberty in the Form of the Goddess of Youth, Giving Support to the Bald Eagle*, by Edward Savage, 1796.** This illustration depicts a popular feminized allegory of the new republic.

necessary virtue to resist the corruption of its political institutions? In each story, a virtuous woman is enticed by a duplicitous lover into a morally compromising and socially damaging sexual relationship. From the start, the national literature of the United States focused attention on questions of women's sexuality and education in the new nation. Brown dedicated his books to "the young ladies, of United Columbia," and claimed that his novel would "expose the fatal consequences, of seduction" Many critics, however, worried that the novels themselves were the seducers; they feared that, as the title of one of many such attacks put it, novel reading was "a Cause of Female Depravity." Like other entertainment media in more recent periods, novels were suspected of thrusting young people into fantasy worlds that prevented them for becoming productive and respectable members of society. But within debates about novels at this moment in American history, cultural critics were particularly concerned with the moral character and influence of women. Whereas the Declaration, the Constitution, and other foundational texts of the nation-building period spoke only of men and rendered women invisible, female perspectives and experiences were central to the novel. Women figured in early U.S literature as authors, readers, and characters, and as symbols of the new republic.

BROADCAST NETWORK

From the standpoint of the nation's founders, writing and print were crucial to sustaining America's republican experiment. To enable the exchange of ideas and information necessary for a national culture or a national politics, a dispersed population had to be connected through some regular system of communication. This was especially important in an overwhelmingly rural nation. Even though most of the founders lived in cities, they imagined the ideal America as a virtuous republic of independent landowners living at comfortable distances from one another and even farther from their seats of government. (Cities, they believed, were threats to the republic, because of the potential for class conflict and mob violence.) How was a dispersed citizenry to become informed and involved in the affairs of government and society?

Five years after the text of the Constitution was printed and sent to the states, Congress enacted a monumental piece of legislation that would address this problem by creating a state-sponsored communication network (see Spaces and Places: The Baltimore Post Office). The Post Office Act of 1792 put Congress in charge of selecting postal routes, protecting the privacy of the mail, and, most important, setting postage rates. More generally, the law laid the foundation for a broadcast network that would circulate political information on a national scale. By taking charge of the designation of routes, Congress could bring postal service to sparsely inhabited areas that might not have generated the mail business to pay for it. By proclaiming the invulnerability of mail to government surveillance, Congress encouraged a freer flow of ideas and information. But the most significant feature of the new, redefined U.S. Post Office was its subsidy for newspapers. In the era of the Articles of Confederation, the Post Office was not required to carry newspapers at all, but under the 1792 law, newspapers could travel up to one hundred miles for one cent and anywhere in the country for 1.5 cents (see How Much Is That?). Furthermore, newspaper publishers could send papers to one another free of charge. This

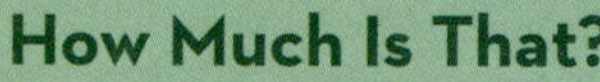

How Much Is That?

News in the Mail

The price of sending a newspaper in 1792, adjusted for inflation, would have been twenty-four cents in 2013, roughly half the cost of mailing a first-class letter and less than one-tenth the cover price of a single copy of the daily *New York Times*.

SPACES AND PLACES

The Baltimore Post Office

Baltimore's First Post Office (Built in 1730). Early post office buildings had not been designed for that purpose and provided little outward sign of their crucial function.

Baltimore Post Office in 1906. This Romanesque Revival building opened in 1889.

Baltimore Main Post Office Today. Opened in 1972, this large structure is located near Interstate 83.

While the war for independence may have been decided on a few key battlefields, the spread of nationalism in the United States took place in countless sites throughout the former thirteen colonies—including streets, courthouses, taverns, schoolrooms, and parlors. Among the most important spaces for the dissemination of ideas and information about the new nation were post offices, where news arrived from other states and from abroad. Post offices were crucial links in the network of printers and publishers that supported the revolution and the nation-building project.

By modern standards, eighteenth-century post offices were inconspicuous and undistinguished, though they served, along with customs houses and military garrisons, as the only visible branch offices of the new federal government. Post offices were small structures built for other purposes and often shared quarters with printing offices, general stores, or personal residences. The first post office in the city of Baltimore was housed in a modest building that had been constructed in 1730 and was notable less for its architecture than for its proprietor. Mary Katherine Goddard was the first postmistress in the United States, a position she occupied between 1775 and 1789. An important figure in early national publishing, she produced the first print version of the Declaration of Independence to include the names of all the signers. But when President Washington took office, his postmaster general replaced Goddard with a man, claiming that he needed someone who could ride a horse. Goddard rallied significant local support but still lost her job.

The bigger change in the Baltimore Post Office after 1789, however, was in the kind of business conducted there. During Goddard's tenure, Baltimore had been one of no more than sixty-nine post offices in the country, and most mail activity was confined to the eastern seaboard. But after the Post Office Act of 1792, the postal system expanded quickly and began broadcasting the activities of the federal government and subsidizing the circulation of political news. The little post office on Front Street would remain a place for locals to pick up newspapers and exchange gossip, but it was now also part of a modern communication network.

Think About It

1. Did Americans consider it legitimate for a woman to run the major federal agency in a leading city in the 1780s?
2. If post offices were the principal conduits of long-distance contact in the United States at this time, why were they so small?
3. What different messages about the power of federal government are projected by the three different post offices in the photographs?

provision basically determined the kind of mail system that would exist in the United States for the next half-century.

By making it cheap to circulate newspapers (and asking letter writers to pay high postage to subsidize that circulation), the federal government made it possible for citizens across the country to have access to political news. And by allowing newspapers to exchange free copies, the law made it likely that the content of that political news would be fairly national and uniform in character—since small-town papers would reprint the articles provided for them by their urban counterparts. The law thus created a relationship between the post and the press in the early republic that made information exchange quite different in two key respects from later periods. First, the mail would carry mostly newspapers rather than letters and would serve as a broadcast medium rather than an interactive one. Second, newspapers would be designed for distant readers as much as for local ones.

The tiny minority of Americans who lived in urban areas by 1790 occupied the front lines of the communication network. They received information faster, were more likely to produce the information consumed elsewhere, and were better integrated into the commercial practices that demanded and rewarded information exchange. But starting in 1792, the U.S. government mitigated some of those differences by turning thousands of towns and villages over an expansive terrain and a diverse society into distribution sites for national news.

CONCLUSION

The revolutionary process of imagining a new nation out of thirteen very different colonies, which had begun two decades earlier with committees of correspondence, was in some important respects now complete. It would be misleading to describe that new nation as having been written into existence, because no piece of paper could by itself create the shifts in allegiance, identity, and authority that nation building entailed. Still, between 1776 and 1792 a series of written and printed documents—declarations, constitutions, pamphlets, maps, novels, and newspapers—circulated in the new republic and made the founding of the United States feasible, conceivable, and meaningful. Several of those documents framed the structure of new state and national governments. With their complex histories now often forgotten, they enjoy sacred status as instruments of historical change and keys to American national identity.

STUDY TERMS

Declaration of Independence (p. 160)
injuries and usurpations (p. 162)
street theater (p. 163)
written constitutions (p. 163)
natural rights (p. 163)
bicameral (p. 163)
Vermont constitution (p. 164)
Articles of Confederation (p. 165)
Continental dollars (p. 165)
Shays' Rebellion (p. 166)
Treaty of Paris (p. 168)
Treaty of Fort Stanwix (p. 169)
Northwest Territory (p. 170)
Land Ordinance of 1785 (p. 171)
Northwest Ordinance (p. 171)
grid design (p. 171)
Virginia Plan (p. 172)
New Jersey Plan (p.173)
three-fifths clause (p. 173)
Committee on Style (p. 174)
ratification conventions (p. 174)
Federalists (p. 174)
Antifederalists (p. 176)
The Federalist (p. 176)
checks and balances (p. 176)
Bill of Rights (p. 177)
Letters from an American Farmer (p. 179)
Federal Copyright Law (p. 179)
Charlotte Temple (p. 179)
Post Office Act of 1792 (p. 180)

TIMELINE

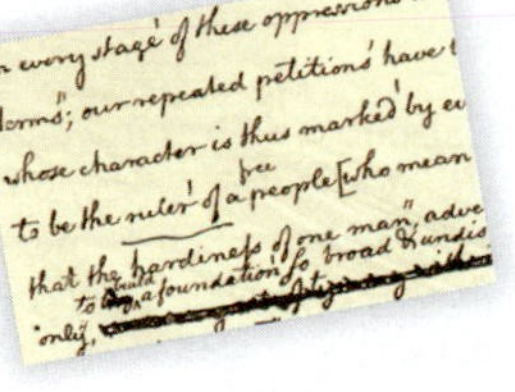
in every stage of these oppressions we
repeated petitions have
whose character is thus marked by
to be the ruler of a free people

1776 Continental Congress declares independence

1776–1778 States create written constitutions

1777 Vermont constitution outlaws slavery

1781 Articles of Confederation ratified

1783 Treaty of Paris signed, officially recognizing the new nation's borders

1785 Land Ordinance divides western territories into gridded squares

1786 Shays' Rebellion erupts in western Massachusetts

1787 Northwest Ordinance prohibits slavery in the Northwest
Constitutional Convention gathers in Philadelphia
Constitution published

1788 *The Federalist*, arguing for ratification, appears in book form
Constitution ratified by nine states

1789 George Washington elected first president

1791 Bill of Rights added to the Constitution
William Hill Brown's *The Power of Sympathy* published

1792 Post Office Act establishes federal control over a national communication network

FURTHER READING

Additional suggested readings are available on the Online Learning Center at www.mhhe.com/becomingamerica1e.

Richard Brookhiser, *Gentleman Revolutionary* (2003), presents a biographical look at the unsung founding father, Gouverneur Morris.

Richard D. Brown, *Knowledge Is Power* (1991), surveys the diffusion of information in early America.

Martin Bruckner, *The Geographic Revolution in Early America* (2006), charts the new ways of writing about space during the colonial and early national periods.

Cathy Davidson, *Revolution and the Word* (1986), examines the importance of novels and novel reading to the founding of the new nation.

Robin Einhorn, *American Taxation, American Slavery* (2006), stresses the interrelation between tax debates and the politics of slavery in the new republic.

Jay Fliegelman, *Declaring Independence* (1993), places Jefferson and the Declaration of Independence within the context of late-eighteenth-century ideas about speech and oral performance.

Pauline Maier, *American Scripture* (1997), demystifies the nation's founding document and details the process by which it acquired its current status as sacred text.

Jack Rakove, *Original Meanings* (1996), provides a thorough study of the constitutional and legal thought of the framers.

Eric Slauter, *The State as a Work of Art*, (2009), explores the broader cultural context for the ratification debates.

Paul Starr, *The Creation of the Media* (2004), emphasizes the role of the Post Office in the creation of a new culture of information exchange and the history of state-sponsored communication.

David Waldstreicher, *In the Midst of Perpetual Fetes* (1997), studies the practices and rituals that created national identity during and after the Revolution.

Kariann Akemi Yokota, *Unbecoming British* (2011), considers the everyday difficulties faced by the Americans in pursuing cultural independence from Britain.

8

INSIDE ▶

THE BIG PICTURE

As population migrated and new societies formed, major divisions emerged over the kind of nation that the United States ought to become.

Finding Their Way. The Lewis and Clark expedition, celebrated in this 1850 painting, reflected a particular vision of how the new nation might develop.

1790–1811

THE EARLY REPUBLIC

In the decades immediately following the American Revolution, respondents to census surveys often lied about their age. This was not in itself remarkable; people had misrepresented how old they were in colonial times as well. What was new was that Americans were now more likely to pretend to be younger rather than older.

New attitudes toward age and aging do not suddenly appear with the publication of a declaration, the ratification of a constitution, or the signing of a treaty. Still, toward the end of the eighteenth century and the beginning of the nineteenth, a change took place throughout American culture—in law, art, and everyday language. Legislatures introduced mandatory retirement laws for public officials. New inheritance laws eroded the long-standing economic advantages of eldest sons. Fewer children were named for their grandparents. Family portraits began positioning parents and children on the same horizontal line. Clothing fashions shifted to emphasize youth and to show younger bodies to advantage. And finally, a new vocabulary emerged for disparaging one's elders. Words like *geezer*, *fogy*, *codger*, and *fuddy-duddy* all entered American speech around this time as contemptuous names for the elderly. Whereas it had once been better to be older (more senior, more venerable), cultural biases now began to favor those whose future lay before them.

Optimism toward youth made sense in the political climate of the early republic, where the founders harbored high hopes for a new democratic nation with its own uncharted future. By the middle of the 1790s, the Constitution was the law of the land, President Washington was beginning his second term in office, a national postal network was in place, and the revolutionary movement to conceive a single nation out of thirteen discrete British colonies was largely complete. But the process of building that nation had only begun. Over the next two decades, the United States would establish new models for political competition and the peaceful transition of power at the highest levels of government. It would create an utterly new seat of national government and confront new dilemmas about slavery, race, and international relations. Most dramatically, the size of its territory would double, and Americans would move beyond the eastern seaboard in greater numbers than ever before, drawn by new towns along a frontier that was constantly shifting farther west. How all of this expansion and movement would change the republic was hard to predict at the end of the eighteenth century. Building a nation required imagining new worlds.

KEY QUESTIONS

- What were the impact and implications of the Haitian Revolution for the young U.S. republic?
- When and how was slavery abolished in the North?
- What two visions of America's national growth underlay the first party system, and how did the two parties differ on national policy?
- Why was Washington, D.C., selected as the new national capital, and how did it develop?
- How did the nation expand westward during the presidency of Thomas Jefferson?

Thomas Jefferson, who was the leading figure in national politics during most of this period and who became the nation's third president, epitomized American optimism about new and imagined worlds. Even as he aged, he sympathized with this cultural trend toward celebrating youth. He once argued that constitutions ought to be reframed every two decades so that no generation would ever be bound by the decisions of its predecessor. Although few of Jefferson's colleagues held that radical position and many of his political opponents detested Jefferson's fondness for innovation, most shared a sense that the new nation was an experiment for which the past offered only limited guidance.

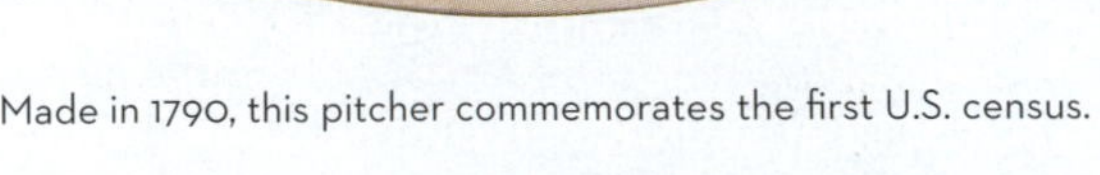

Made in 1790, this pitcher commemorates the first U.S. census.

THE PROBLEM OF SLAVERY

Africans had been enslaved throughout the Americas from the very beginnings of European colonization. For over two centuries, slavery had enjoyed the support of all governments and most religious denominations. In the mid-eighteenth century, however, slaves began to articulate publicly the view that slavery itself was inherently wrong. By the early national period, opponents of slavery were citing the libertarian ideals of the American Revolution and calling for slavery's destruction. At the same time, slaves and free people of color in St. Domingue (renamed Haiti in 1804) were fighting their own war of independence, invoking the same rhetoric of freedom and equality. In the 1790s, it suddenly seemed conceivable that the institution of slavery in the New World was dying.

But any consideration of eliminating slavery in the United States threatened a major source of wealth in the new nation, and any discussion of emancipating African American slaves challenged the unspoken premise that white men should control its politics and economy. Still, the early national era was marked by a serious reassessment of the long-standing system of racial slavery, a hardening of its geographical borders, and the emergence of large free black communities in growing northern cities.

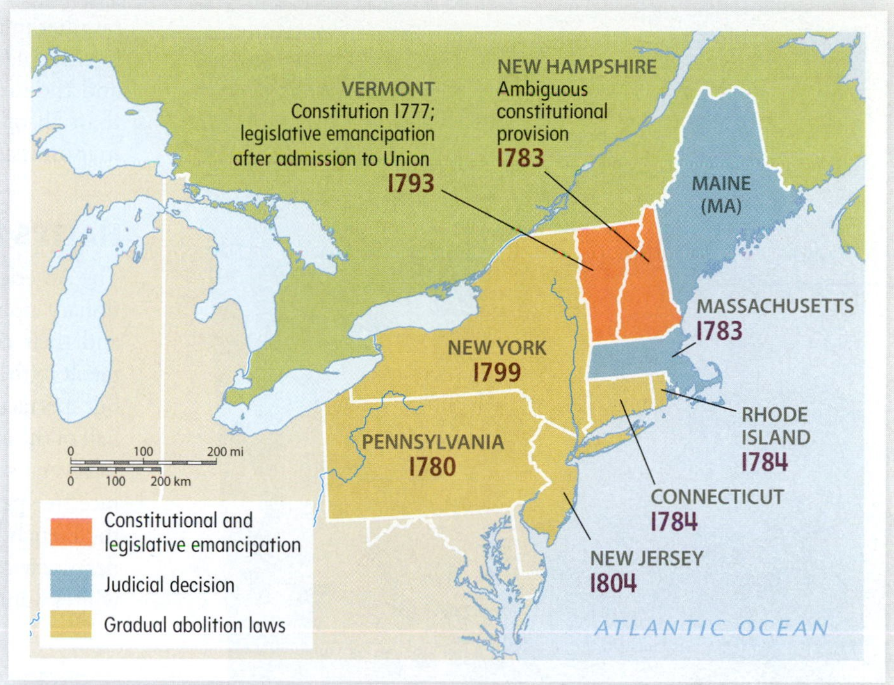

Map 8.1 Gradual Abolition in the North. In the decades following the Revolution, some states abolished slavery by legislative emancipation, others by judicial decision, and others by gradual abolition laws. **Question for Analysis:** What geographical patterns do you notice in the approach of northern states to the legal status of slavery?

SLAVERY SECTIONALIZED

Prompted by petitions from slaves (see Chapter 6) using the language of the new nation's founding documents, and emboldened by assertions of the dignity of labor among white workers, several states began putting slavery on the road to legal extinction during the decades following the Revolution. The institution was most vulnerable in the northern half of the United States, where its scope had been limited. In the North, slavery was not as central to commercial agriculture as it was in the South. Northern slaves were concentrated in towns and cities, where labor was harder to control, free laborers resented the competition, and overall slave populations were relatively small. By the 1770s, only a couple thousand men and women were enslaved in New England (compared to over six hundred thousand in the other nine colonies and millions in the West Indies and Brazil), which lowered both the economic costs and the social implications of abolition. When the aspiring state of Vermont became the first to outlaw slavery in 1777, fewer than two hundred people received their freedom. By 1787, slavery had also become illegal in Massachusetts and New Hampshire, as well as in the Northwest Territory.

In other northern states, a larger enslaved population made legislatures reluctant to free slaves outright, so plans were devised to end slavery more gradually. **Gradual abolition** became the dominant form of legal emancipation in all northern states where significant numbers of men and women were enslaved. Pennsylvania provided the initial model in 1780, with a law that granted eventual freedom to the future offspring of slaves. Any child born to an enslaved woman in Pennsylvania after the law took effect would become legally free upon reaching the age of twenty-eight. A slave born before 1780, on the other hand, would remain enslaved for life. New York and New Jersey adopted similar laws, but significantly later and with much greater impact: more than thirty-two thousand human beings were still enslaved in those two states at the end of the eighteenth century. Gradual abolition was passed in New York in 1799 and five years later in New Jersey, thus completing the legal dismantling of slavery in the North (see Map 8.1).

While a new generation of African Americans achieved their freedom under gradual abolition laws during the early national era, some northern slaveholders responded to the laws by selling their human property (illegally) to states where the institution was still alive and well. In addition, gradual abolition laws did not free any of the men, women, and children who were enslaved when the laws took effect. As a consequence, there were still slaves in Connecticut as late as 1848 and in New Jersey as late as the Civil War. Nonetheless, the acts of northern legislatures had the effect of stopping the growth of slavery in half of the nation, thereby sharpening the divide between a North where slavery would be phased out and a South where it would grow and become entrenched.

For enslaved African Americans living in the South, the decades following the ratification of the Constitution did not lead to mass liberation, though many slaves were granted freedom. Several leading southern plantation owners openly favored some form of gradual abolition, especially in the Upper South (Maryland, Delaware, Virginia, and North Carolina), where a downturn in the tobacco economy made slave labor—which could be costly to maintain and posed a perpetual threat of disorder or

Black Sawyers in Philadelphia. Free people of color outnumbered slaves in the urban North within a decade of the Revolution. New York's free black population was one hundred on the eve of independence but over seven thousand by 1810. In Philadelphia the free black population rose from one thousand in 1783, to six thousand by 1800, and over twelve thousand by 1820.

insurrection—less valuable. State legislatures in the Chesapeake region even debated emancipation bills. None of these laws passed, but new rules made it easier for individual owners to emancipate their slaves. Rates of private **manumission** in Virginia, Maryland, and Delaware increased significantly between 1790 and 1810 (George Washington, upon his death in 1799, freed 124 people he had held as property). By 1810, over three-quarters of Delaware's remaining black population was free, and Baltimore's free black population had increased seventeenfold.

Despite these gains, many more slaves were transported westward over the Appalachian Mountains than were liberated. In those twenty years, Maryland and Virginia sent fifty-six thousand slaves into Kentucky and another twenty-five thousand into Tennessee. Professional slave traders brought some, but most were transported by their owners to work on new farms. In either case, the migration typically broke up a family, because slaveholders often divided up their human property when their sons moved west and because enslaved families in the Chesapeake sometimes lived on multiple neighboring plantations. During this period, coercive migration and the interstate slave trade affected the lives of more slaves than all of the gradual abolition laws and individual acts of manumission combined.

HAITI'S REVOLUTION

The American Revolution was only the first in a series of revolutionary upheavals that would shake the great European powers and their colonies across the Atlantic. The second anticolonial revolt in the Americas took place in St. Domingue, France's small but spectacularly lucrative sugar-producing colony on the western half of the island of Hispaniola. The Haitian Revolution unfolded in several stages and involved several competing groups. Mixed-race free people on the Caribbean island, who were classified in the French Empire as *gens de couleur*, demanded equal rights under a new constitution that had just been written in France. Poor whites wanted a voice in government, and the planter class hoped

Francois-Dominique Toussaint Louverture. Louverture, the son of an African prince, was a leader of the revolution in the French sugar plantation colony of St. Domingue, where slavery was abolished in 1794. France recognized Louverture as the head of the colony in 1800 but two years later sent troops to capture him and reinstate the slave regime. Haitian rebels ultimately won independence from France in 1804.

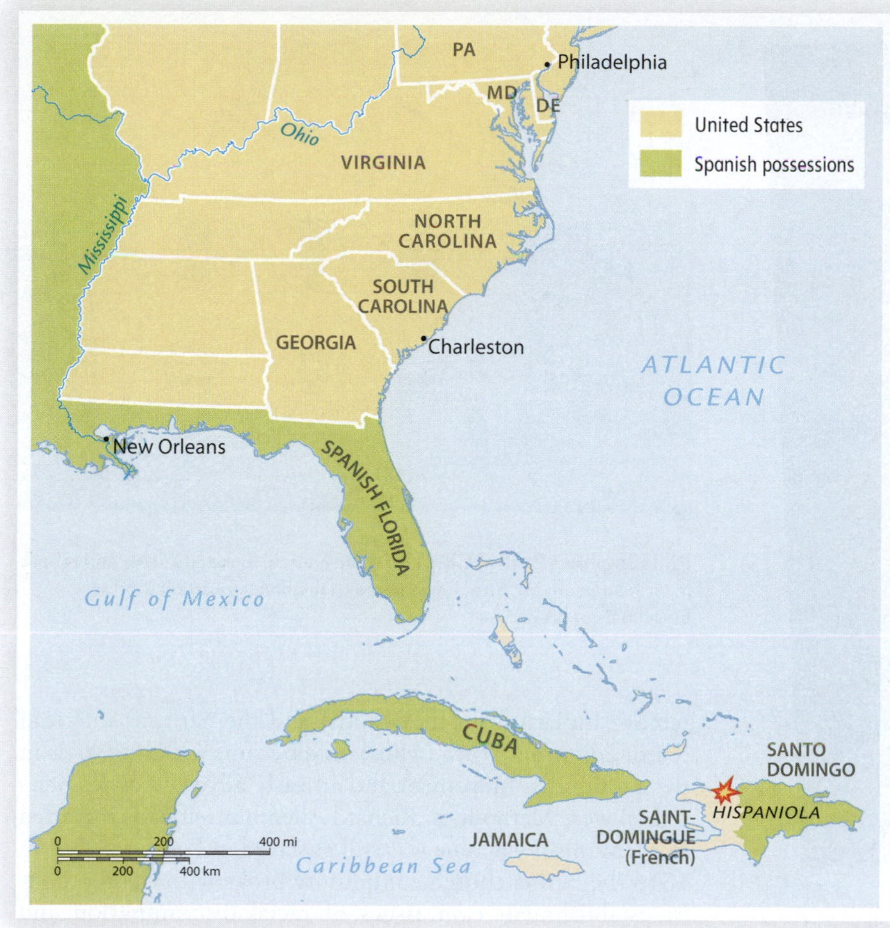

Map 8.2 Slave Revolt in the Caribbean. The small island colony of St. Domingue lay well beyond the borders of the United States but had long occupied a central position in the Atlantic slave trade.

for greater colonial self-rule. In 1791, a fourth group entered the fray, as nearly two thousand of the colony's half-million slaves executed a well-planned attack on sugar plantations.

The combined effect of these eruptions was a complex and protracted civil war, involving multiple groups in the colony and several of France's European rivals, including England. A well-educated former slave named Toussaint Louverture emerged as the leader of a resistance force that would ultimately secure the abolition of slavery in 1794 and create the independent nation of Haiti in 1804. Haiti became the second democratic republic in the New World and the region's first independent black nation (see Map 8.2).

News of the Haitian Revolution traveled quickly to the North American mainland, sparking fears of race war and slave conspiracies. Despite the infrequency of large-scale slave rebellions in their colonies, southern U.S. slaveholders worried intensely about the threat of racial violence that lurked beneath the calm surface of their society, and the revolt in Haiti sounded a powerful alarm. A white witness in Virginia claimed to have overheard two Richmond slaves in 1793 plotting "to kill the white people soon in this place," just as blacks had done "in the French Island." In most southern states, any black who spoke French was treated immediately as a security threat and denied entry at the ports. To enslaved African Americans and a growing number of sympathizers, the end of slavery in St. Domingue signaled that the institution might be destined to crumble elsewhere. To the men who held slaves, the lesson of Haiti was that any end to slavery would be achieved or accompanied by bloodshed.

PHILADELPHIA'S EXPERIMENT

Events in Haiti sent shock waves throughout the United States. They also sent boatloads of white slaveholding refugees northward to American port cities, typically with their human property in tow. In Philadelphia, the nation's capital, about five hundred French-speaking slaves from St. Domingue arrived around 1793, bearing news of violent revolution and eventually joining the city's free black community. Philadelphia was at the time the largest U.S. city, more populous than any community in the Western Hemisphere except for Mexico City. Philadelphia had been an obvious location for the major national gatherings of the revolutionary years and a frequent first stop for foreign visitors to the United States. Many of those foreigners were struck by the significant presence of formerly enslaved African Americans on the streets of the American capital.

The number of ex-slaves living in Philadelphia skyrocketed in the 1790s, as free blacks migrated northward from the Upper South, where legislatures fearing the ripple effects of the Haitian rebellion initiated repressive laws against them. Philadelphia's free black community also included a number of runaway slaves, who took shelter among abolitionists of both races against fugitive slave laws that mandated their return. Networks of free blacks in Philadelphia also helped several visiting African Americans escape their bondage, including a woman named Ona Judge, who had been brought to the capital by her owner, President George Washington. Judge escaped to freedom in 1796, making her way to New Hampshire, where the president's agents sought unsuccessfully to recapture her. Nine months later, Washington's renowned cook, Hercules, absconded as well. Bringing slaves to the nation's capital had become a risky proposition.

Philadelphia's free black community developed during this period a number of new institutions, most significantly a series of seven black churches. These churches included the first black congregations in the United States affiliated with the Episcopalian, Methodist, Presbyterian, and Baptist denominations of Protestant Christianity. Excluded from full

***Pepper-Pot: A Scene in the Philadelphia Market*, by John Lewis Krimmel, 1811.** This painting depicts a free black woman selling spicy Caribbean-style soup. Approximately twenty thousand Haitian exiles arrived in U.S. cities during the 1790s.

Philadelphia's Bethel Church. The church, founded in 1794 and rebuilt in 1805 on South 6th Street, was home to the first African Methodist Episcopal congregation.

citizenship, threatened by fugitive slave laws, and haunted by the specter of a prospering slave system in the South, free blacks relied on their independent churches as a source of social support and an enduring political voice in the struggle against racial inequality.

The largest and most prominent black congregation in Philadelphia, Richard Allen's Bethel church (founded in 1794), reflected in part the rising popularity of Methodism, an English Protestant movement founded in the eighteenth century by John Wesley. The movement's presence was small in the United States at the time of the Revolution, but it grew quickly in the 1790s, spread by itinerant preachers, known as circuit riders, who embarked on evangelical missions throughout rural America. Methodist preachers sought converts across lines of race and class, and their style of worship, which emphasized lay participation and personal enthusiasm rather than the maintenance of social order and hierarchy, struck responsive chords among many disenfranchised Americans, male and female. Several notable leaders of minority communities in the first half of the nineteenth century, including the Pequot William Apess (who would fight U.S. efforts to remove Indians from their lands) and the African American orator Sojourner Truth (who would become a leading voice in the abolitionist movement and an early advocate of women's rights) were Methodists. Richard Allen himself had converted to Methodism when he was still enslaved in Delaware. But in 1816 the Bethel church community broke with the Methodist establishment over issues of racial discrimination and formed the African Methodist Episcopal (A.M.E.) Church, with Allen as its first bishop. Around the same time, the A.M.E. Zion Church in New York began holding services in a converted stable in Lower Manhattan. The A.M.E. Church would serve as the most powerful free black institution in the decades before the Civil War.

The networks of exchange connecting Philadelphia and Haiti carried more than just people and ideas. In July 1793, a deadly fever swept through Philadelphia (see States of Emergency: Yellow Fever in Philadelphia), taking more than four thousand lives and exiling much of the surviving population to the countryside. The capital of the new nation was turned inside out, its municipal government disbanded, and its population literally decimated. We now know that this catastrophic epidemic originated 1,500 miles away in the West Indies.

Philadelphia would not remain the capital of the United States beyond the eighteenth century. But it remained the epicenter of American abolitionism for another two decades after the fever outbreak. Philadelphia would serve as the nation's principal urban laboratory for considering what the United States might look like if slavery were abolished and freed slaves joined whites in building a multiracial society. The violence and discrimination suffered by the Philadelphia black community during the early years of gradual abolition in the North suggested that such a transition might not be smooth or peaceful.

STATES OF EMERGENCY

Yellow Fever in Philadelphia

It began in July 1793 as a handful of gruesome cases of high fever, but within a few weeks the symptoms became familiar to everyone in the nation's largest city: chills, yellow skin and eyes, and black vomit. In August, Philadelphia's most prominent physician, Benjamin Rush, identified the disease as "yellow fever." By September, those with the health and resources to flee the city had done so, abandoning the streets of Philadelphia to the poor, the dying, and the men and women who treated the ill or carted away the fallen.

Yellow Fever Epidemic in Philadelphia. In an era before the rise of germ theories of disease transmission, many physicians blamed the epidemic on environmental factors such as miasma (foul air) in local homes and streets. We now know that the disease spread through insects migrating on ships from distant locales, including the Caribbean.

In the absence of any consensus on what caused the fever (not until 1901 would scientists connect yellow fever to mosquitoes), numerous strategies were adopted to halt transmission. Hoping to ward off the plague with fire, Philadelphians took to setting blazes on street corners, exploding gunpowder, or puffing continuously on cigars. Objects touched by the ill were dipped in vinegar. Rush, one of the signers of the Declaration of Independence and a leading advocate of penal reform and women's education, spent his summer treating fever victims (more than one hundred a day) and used the newspapers to teach readers how to cure themselves. But the papers spread controversy as well as medical information. After Rush counseled readers on the importance of purging and bleeding, rival doctors disagreed vociferously, recommending instead teas and mild barks. Ordinary Philadelphians wrote in to the paper to participate in these debates, to share their own experiences, or to tout various folk remedies.

Philadelphia's African American community became the focus of heated controversy during the epidemic. In the early weeks of the outbreak, the low rates of suffering among blacks fed the popular belief that they were resistant to the fever and could be counted on to care for the ill and tend to the deceased. But black Philadelphians were not immune to the epidemic, nor were their efforts during the crisis appreciated. In his several histories of the yellow fever (the first three of which appeared before year's end), publisher Matthew Carey singled out African American nurses for having profited off the calamity, prompting a powerful response from two emerging leaders of the black community. Former slaves Absalom Jones and Richard Allen, in one of the first published critiques of white prejudice and racial inequality in the United States, took issue with Carey's claims and defended the honor of their race. "We wish not to offend," Jones and Allen wrote, "but when an unprovoked attempt is made, to make us blacker than we are, it becomes less necessary to be over-cautious on that account." Jones and Allen proceeded to narrate the history of the epidemic, offering specific instances of profiteering and misconduct by white Philadelphians and showing how blacks had behaved with courage and honor by comparison.

Though few Philadelphians knew it, the deadly disease had originated in the West Indies (where fever was wiping out French troops trying to suppress the Haitian uprising) and reflected Philadelphia's contacts with the world of Caribbean slavery. But even at the time, it was clear that the fever—like the city itself—was shaped by the politics of race and emancipation.

Think About It

1. Why were cities like Philadelphia particularly vulnerable to epidemic diseases, such as yellow fever?
2. When Jones and Allen wrote that Carey's claims made them "blacker than we are," what did they mean?
3. What did the epidemic reveal about race relations in Philadelphia?

THE BEGINNINGS OF PARTISAN POLITICS

As the home of the new federal government during the 1790s, Philadelphia also became a center of debate among national leaders with competing political visions. Already in President Washington's first term, divisions had emerged within the administration. By his second term, politicians and newspaper editors began organizing themselves into opposing camps with distinct approaches to national policy. Nothing in the Constitution had called for the creation of political parties, and the Constitution's promoters had not expected parties to form in such a large and diverse nation as the United States. Parties had acquired a bad name among the founders, and Thomas Jefferson took pride in 1789 in the fact that he had "never submitted . . . to the creed of any party of men whatever." But a two-party system emerged quickly in the 1790s, and Jefferson stood at the helm of one of the parties. The division reflected serious disagreement over the character of the new nation, how powerful its central government ought to be, and how it should conduct foreign relations.

ALEXANDER HAMILTON'S ECONOMIC AGENDA

Disagreements over the future of the federal government under the new Constitution began with money matters. As the nation's first treasury secretary, Alexander Hamilton sought to use federal power to encourage manufacturing, promote commercial growth, raise revenues for the national treasury, and fortify the political position of the central government. As a crucial first step, he wanted Congress to assume responsibility for debts incurred by the states during the war, a strategy designed to subordinate the states to the federal government and boost the country's credit rating. By presenting the new federal government as a responsible borrower, Hamilton hoped to persuade potential investors that U.S. bonds were safe places to put their money. This, in turn, would give the wealthy a vested interest in the republic's welfare and stability. Public debt, Hamilton argued, would form the "cement of our Union."

This call for **debt assumption** was bold, since the national debt (which included obligations incurred by both state and federal governments to both foreign and domestic lenders) was vast, and could be paid off only by more borrowing. To pull this off, Hamilton proposed selling bonds and paying the interest on those bonds by collecting taxes. Critics objected to the plan on several grounds. Nationalizing the state debts redistributed wealth from those states that had borrowed less (or had paid down their obligations) to those that had borrowed more. Small-debt states like Virginia and Maryland resented having to bear the burden of big-debt states like Massachusetts and Connecticut. Opponents of Hamilton's proposal, led by James Madison, argued further that covering the state debts would simply reward the wealthy speculators who had bought them at discounted rates from soldiers and farmers at the end of the Revolutionary War (see Chapter 7). Moreover, many critics, especially from the South, objected to Hamilton's plan for the same reasons he proposed it: They worried that debt assumption would make the central government powerful at the expense of the sovereignty of the individual states and that it would commit the new republic to a path of commercial growth. But Hamilton's supporters invoked the nation's moral obligation for debts incurred during the struggle for independence. With assumption advocates dominating the Senate and its opponents holding sway in the House, Congress faced a political impasse. Finally, at a 1790 dinner party hosted by Jefferson, a deal was struck whereby southerners would support the assumption bill in return for key northern votes in favor of placing the capital on the Potomac River, between the southern states of Virginia and Maryland (see A Capital on Paper).

To pay down the interest on the bonds that would be used to retire the existing debt, the federal government needed money. Under the new constitution, Congress could have raised funds through direct taxation (on land, property, or persons), but such taxes would have been difficult for a primitive federal bureaucracy to collect from a dispersed population that already paid property taxes to their state governments. Moreover, it would have entailed complex and controversial negotiations over how to apportion the tax burdens of slave states. Alternatively, Congress could impose tariffs on foreign imports or sales taxes on domestic consumption. The 1789 Tariff Act, which set a low tax on imported goods that could be collected at the port and then passed along to consumers, generated sufficient revenue to pay off the federal debt, but more ambitious taxes were needed to finance the bonds that would cover the state debts as well.

Hoping to accomplish two goals simultaneously, Hamilton proposed **protective tariffs** on specific manufactured imports, such as textiles and shoes, which were designed to make American-made goods cheaper than their foreign competition. This would raise revenue while encouraging the growth of the nation's fledgling domestic industries, which were located primarily in New England. Hamilton argued that only by subsidizing the development of American manufacturing could the United States become a truly independent nation. Opponents, especially in the South, argued that such a tariff asked one region to subsidize the economy of another, and that American independence would come with widespread land ownership, not with industrial development. Hamilton's other revenue proposal garnered more support, however. In 1791, and then again in 1794, Congress levied excise taxes on a handful of goods that were deemed luxuries or vices, including snuff, sugar, and distilled spirits (see Hot Commodities: Whiskey).

The final component of Hamilton's economic plan was a Bank of the United States that would help circulate and stabilize paper currency in the new republic. Not a branch of government, but a private, for-profit corporation chartered by the United States and modeled on the Bank of England, the bank would receive deposits from the federal treasury and then issue its own private bank notes that could be used as

HOT COMMODITIES

Whiskey

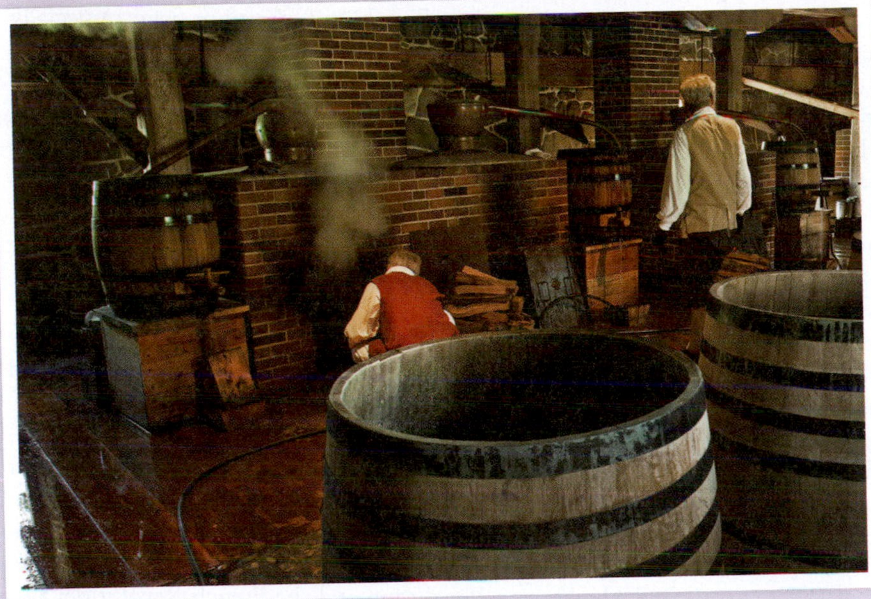

Early National Grain Surplus. George Washington's whiskey distillery, reconstructed at Mount Vernon.

In an effort to raise revenues, Congress acted in 1791 on Hamilton's plan to tax whiskey and other spirits. Unlike tariffs, which could be collected by customs officials at the ports, the whiskey tax applied to a range of distilleries, large and small, across the country. When government officials tried to collect the tax in 1794 from farmers in western Pennsylvania, an area chronically short on currency and generally hostile to taxation, they met stiff resistance. Whiskey rebels intimidated tax collectors, mobilized their militias, and invoked the spirit of the tax protests against Britain that had launched the revolutionary struggle. As many as seven thousand rebels gathered outside Pittsburgh, but took no immediate action. Still, the Whiskey Rebellion was the first major act of resistance to federal authority under the Constitution. Eager to make a show of strength for the new national government, Hamilton and Washington personally rode out with thirteen thousand militiamen, and the rebellion crumbled without a fight.

Behind this famous political crisis lurked a larger development in American life: an explosive growth in the production and consumption of whiskey. Congress might have targeted distilled spirits as luxurious vices, but whiskey drinking was becoming deeply ingrained in the daily habits of Americans across the socioeconomic spectrum. The late-eighteenth and early-nineteenth centuries marked a high point in alcohol consumption generally, and whiskey drinking in particular. The best evidence suggests that during the first third of the nineteenth century the typical American drank more alcohol than at any time before or after. In 1810, American distilleries were producing more than three gallons of distilled liquors—whiskey, rum, gin, and brandy, typically about 90 proof—for every man, woman, and child, and that figure does not include beer, wine, or cider. Overall, Americans consumed about twice as much alcohol per person in 1810 as they do now. Consumption levels would peak in the 1830s and then drop precipitously (see Chapter 12).

Whiskey flowed freely throughout American society during the early decades of the nineteenth century, though certain portions of the population drank more heavily. Women drank less frequently than men and tended to prefer sweetened rum, hard cider, or alcohol-heavy patent medicines. In the South, blacks drank less than whites. Whereas in white homes a julep before breakfast and whiskey at all meals was quite common, slaves (who in some places faced legal obstacles to buying liquor) typically restricted their serious drinking to special occasions and their everyday intake to a shot of whiskey during the cold season. Despite these variations, alcohol was a basic feature of everyday life in this period. Even religious folk drank heartily by later standards. A southern planter who wished to join the Methodist Church had to restrict his intake—within the acceptable daily quota of a quart of peach brandy. Aspiring ministers at the prestigious New England Andover Seminary would regularly and unabashedly down brandy toddies at the local tavern. Drinking was an important social activity, an indispensable form of hospitality and camaraderie. To refuse a drink was to refuse to enter a world of equality and solidarity.

Historians have offered several explanations for the rise of drinking around the turn of the century, but the most important factor was the growth of whiskey production, which made liquor cheap and plentiful. American farmers were producing large surpluses of grain, especially corn, and for those living in the western part of the country, whiskey was an especially efficient way to deliver corn to distant markets. A horse could carry six times the volume of corn in whiskey form, which was easier to store and far less likely to rot. Shipping grain in this form became even more profitable with technological improvements in the distilling process. Between 1802 and 1815, the federal government issued over one hundred patents for new devices to distill whiskey, which encouraged more farmers to become distillers. Once the Republicans repealed Hamilton's whiskey tax in 1802, the price dropped further. The result was a widespread drinking habit that would form a major part of American economy and culture.

Think About It

1. What does the Whiskey Rebellion suggest about federal power under the new Constitution? How did its outcome compare to that of Shays' Rebellion?
2. How did technological innovations affect whiskey consumption?
3. How have attitudes toward alcoholic beverages changed in the United States since the era of the early republic?

legal tender for paying taxes. The government would own 20 percent of the bank's stock and appoint 20 percent of its directors, but the rest would be owned and controlled by private interests. Congress chartered the first Bank of the United States in 1792 (a second bank would be established in 1816; see Chapter 10), though opponents continued to question its legitimacy. Jefferson, Madison, and others argued that the Constitution did not authorize Congress to issue private charters or establish banks. Hamilton defended the bank on the grounds that Congress could adopt any means not prohibited by the Constitution to achieve its constitutional objectives of regulating commerce and maintaining public credit, noting that Article I of the Constitution granted Congress the power to make laws "which shall be necessary and proper" for executing its mandate. Debates over the bank exposed a wide gulf in Washington's cabinet between those who shared Hamilton's **broad construction** of the Constitution and those who favored a **strict construction** that limited the central government to actions enumerated explicitly in the original text.

THE FIRST U.S. PARTY SYSTEM

The polarization of political views within the Washington administration over debt assumption, taxes, and banking split the original federalist supporters of the Constitution into rival factions, with Hamilton leading a group called the **Federalists,** and Jefferson and Madison leading the Democratic-Republicans, also known as **Republicans.** (This is not the modern-day Republican Party, which originated in the 1850s.) The two parties embraced opposing views of the nation's future. Federalists favored a strong national government and envisioned a commercial economy operating out of thriving cities, earning the nation international respect and securing financial confidence in its new government. Their opponents, by contrast, valued an agrarian society of independent landowners and sought to protect those interests against the demands of urban merchants and financiers. Republicans, whose ranks included many who had opposed ratifying the Constitution in the first place, called for a restrained national government with modest expenditures and little need for revenue.

Although the rift between Federalists and Republicans began with debates over specific policies, the nation's first partisan divide reflected broad differences in outlook and ideology. Federalists worried about the threat of too much democracy, whereas Republicans feared a reversion to monarchy. Federalists emphasized the lessons learned under the Articles of Confederation, when a weak central government left the new republic divided and vulnerable. Republicans emphasized the lessons learned in the revolutionary struggle, when local liberties needed to be protected against a powerful and distant British government. Federalists aspired to build a nation that would rival and resemble Great Britain. Republicans were more likely to cite the British government and economy as models to be avoided. By later standards, these two rivals lacked the internal coherence and organizational structure of full-fledged political parties, but the division between Federalists and Republicans was real and the parties appealed to different political constituencies. Republican positions were especially widespread among slaveholders (like Jefferson) in the South, small farmers in the mid-Atlantic states, and the more radically democratic urban artisans in the North. New England provided a stronghold for Federalism. Washington himself tried to stay above the partisan fray, though most of his decisions as president aligned him with the Federalist cause.

FOREIGN REVOLUTIONS

The loudest clashes between the two parties erupted in the arena of foreign relations, where Federalists favored Britain and Republicans sympathized with France. This split reflected different understandings of the legacy of the American Revolution and played out in different responses to two other revolutionary movements that drew immediate inspiration from the United States. More than any other events that took place beyond America's new national borders during this period, the Haitian Revolution and the French Revolution, two separate rebellions that overthrew ruling elites in the name of liberty and equality, tested the limits of the founders' beliefs in democracy and freedom.

The French Revolution was a political crisis that overturned centuries of absolute monarchy and established a period of representative government. The leaders of the new French government abolished feudalism and the traditional privileges of nobles and clergy and issued the Declaration of the Rights of Man and the Citizen, which echoed the American Declaration of Independence in announcing that government derives its power from the consent of the governed. When the uprising began in 1789, many Americans saw a reflection of their own venture in democratic nation-building. But over time, the French cause claimed many more lives than were lost on all the battlefields of the struggle for American independence. Mobs of peasants and urban workers burned aristocratic country homes and rioted in the cities. Becoming more radicalized as a result of pressures from mobilized commoners, the French government ordered the execution of Louis XVI in 1793, and the bloodshed intensified as thousands of suspected political enemies were killed and others died in internal rebellions. Federalists were quick to draw from the French experience negative lessons about the dangers of allowing a non-elite to have power over political affairs. Republicans, by contrast, remained faithful to France's revolutionary cause, despite the violence.

The French revolutionary government faced not only internal rebellions. By 1793, it was also at war with Britain, Spain, Austria, Prussia, and the Dutch Republic. Jefferson, who was Secretary of State, argued that the United States should support France under the 1778 treaty of alliance that had been crucial to the success of the American Revolution, whereas Hamilton argued for suspending the alliance and maintaining relations with Britain, a key trading partner. President Washington, now in his second term, issued a proclamation of U.S. neutrality, but both the French and the British provoked the Americans and fueled the partisan debate. In 1793, the French minister Citizen Edmond-Charles Genêt went over the head of President Washington to enlist Americans to attack British ships and Spanish colonial positions. This meddling in American affairs undermined Washington's neutrality stance, infuriated the Federalists, and embarrassed Jefferson and the Republicans. (A new revolutionary party recalled Genêt as France's ambassador, but fearing the guillotine, Genêt sought and received political asylum in the United States.) Then, in late 1793 and early 1794, British ships began blockading the West Indies and seizing American cargo vessels trading with the French. Britain's Federalist supporters were now on the defensive, and Alexander Hamilton persuaded Washington to send a special envoy to London to settle the dispute.

Supreme Court chief justice John Jay, a pro-British Federalist, returned in 1794 with a treaty that extracted a promise from the British to withdraw their troops from frontier posts in the Northwest Territory, as the Treaty of Paris had specified. The treaty also repaired the new nation's invaluable trading relationship with Britain, which had been broken by the Revolution, but it came at political cost, because it appeared to betray the French. Moreover, southern planters who had lost slaves to the British during the Revolutionary War complained that their compensation claims had not been sufficiently pressed. Republicans vilified Jay's Treaty, but Washington, although disappointed with the terms, supported it as important to avoiding war with Great Britain. The Senate ratified the treaty in June 1795.

Facing strong criticism for his support of the treaty, Washington dared the House of Representatives to impeach him. Many Republicans wanted nothing less. From their perspective, Washington had betrayed both France and the larger cause of revolution in his attempt to placate the British. In an effort to tarnish the president's previously glorious reputation, Republican printers republished a forgotten series of forged letters, allegedly written by Washington to a distant cousin in 1777, expressing doubts about the justice of the colonists' grievance against the British. Washington survived the threat of impeachment. Soon after, he affirmed his intention not to seek a third term, establishing a precedent that would remain until the presidency of Franklin Roosevelt in the twentieth century. The two parties promoted rival candidates, and in the first contested presidential election in U.S. history, Federalist John Adams became the nation's new chief executive. The candidate who ran a close second became his vice president—Republican Thomas Jefferson. Washington's Farewell Address admonished his countrymen to avoid entangling alliances with other nations, but his successor inherited the difficulties that came with neutrality. Outraged by Jay's treaty, France stepped up their attacks on American ships and suspended diplomatic relations with United States. When an American delegation visited France in 1798 to restore the alliance, they were confronted with a series of demands, including a personal bribe to the French foreign minister. In reporting the incident to Congress, President Adams concealed the names of the three French diplomats involved with the letters x, y, and z. News of the incident, dubbed the XYZ Affair, further strained Franco-American relations and plunged the two countries into an undeclared war at sea that lasted until 1800.

Partisan differences over foreign relations also extended to St. Domingue. Federalists were sympathetic to Louverture's revolt against French rule, both because they were hostile to France (and sought to weaken the French position in the Americas) and because fewer Federalists owned slaves and hence they were less concerned about the spread of emancipation or slave insurrection. Republicans, by contrast, sympathized with France and worried about the specter of an independent black republic in the Caribbean that might undermine slavery in the American South. The rebellion in St. Domingue benefited significantly from the outcome of the election of John Adams in 1796. For four years—and for the only time in the first thirty-five years of the U.S. presidency—American foreign policy was directed by a president who did not own slaves and did not come from Virginia. These four years coincided with a critical period in Haiti's independence struggle. Adams and his secretary of state, Thomas Pickering, supported Louverture, recognized his authority, and urged him to declare independence. American ships even bombarded counterrevolutionary forces. Moved largely by a desire to humiliate France and Jefferson's Republican Party, America's only Federalist administration helped establish an independent nation in Latin America that would become a symbol of black pride and revolution throughout the New World. No president after Adams would even recognize (let alone aid) Haiti—not until after the United States had endured its own civil war.

A PARTISAN PRESS

Like other policy clashes between the two parties, the debate over American involvement in foreign affairs flowed through an elaborate network of political newspapers. Philadelphia was the central hub of news production during the 1790s, and would remain so even after the government moved away in 1800, but newspapers sprouted up in every state of the union, in cities and towns of all sizes. In 1795 alone, fifty-three newspapers came into being. Most newspaper publishers sympathized with the Federalist Party, much as printers had supported ratifying the Constitution in 1788, but a handful of opposition papers began to flourish as well. Philadelphia's Benjamin Franklin Bache, the namesake grandson and protégé of America's most famous printer, published the *Aurora General Advertiser*, probably the most important political journal in the early republic. The *Aurora*'s sympathies were explicitly Republican, and Bache did more than any contemporary political figure to tout the virtues of adhering to party principles—contrary to his grandfather's advice.

Another Republican printer, Matthew Lyon of Vermont, stirred even greater controversy. Lyon had emigrated from

"Congressional Pugilists." This cartoon depicts the fight between Federalist Roger Griswold and Republican Matthew Lyon in 1798. Lyon is shown brandishing iron tongs.

Ireland as an indentured servant, and he used his newspaper to launch an unlikely political career that got him elected to Congress. Federalists in Congress ridiculed the plebeian printer as a "beast" and a "fool," to which Lyon responded by spitting in the face of Representative Roger Griswold of Connecticut. When Federalists failed to muster the two-thirds majority necessary to expel Lyon, Griswold resorted to beating his adversary with a hickory stick. Lyon's presence in Congress threatened the establishment, not only because of his background, but also because he represented the potential of newspapers to stir up public opinion and tilt the balance of political power.

As tensions between the United States and France mounted in 1798 in the wake of the XYZ Affair, Federalist leaders began to worry that critics of the administration would undermine the nation's security. Some blamed immigrant radicals, failed revolutionaries in their native lands who had allegedly come to sow disorder in America. But newspapers were especially worrisome to the Federalists. Abigail Adams singled out Bache's *Aurora* as a threat to national unity. "This Bache is cursing & abusing daily," she wrote to her sister. "If that fellow . . . is not suppressed, we shall come to a civil war."

In spring 1798, Congress passed a series of laws designed to protect the nation against that prospect. Several of these laws, dubbed Alien Acts, targeted immigrants by extending the waiting period for obtaining citizenship from five to fourteen years and authorizing the president to detain or expel foreigners during times of war by executive order. Then, Congress addressed the problem of internal enemies by enacting a Sedition Act, which made it a crime to "conspire . . . to oppose any measure . . . of the government of the United States" or to "write, print, utter or publish . . . any false, scandalous and malicious" claims about the government. The Sedition Act criminalized dissent and seemed to violate the First Amendment, but the Federalists who approved the bill in Congress and upheld its constitutionality in the courts argued that it was essential to protect the new nation. "Speech, writing, and printing are the great directors of public opinion, and public opinion is the great director of human action," one judicial supporter explained. There was no such thing as a harmless editorial in the press. Words led directly to action, and newspapers could spread those words to multitudes of actors.

Under the new law, many of the major Republican newspaper editors were arrested, including Matthew Lyon, who was convicted and imprisoned for having charged the Adams administration with caring more about power, pomp, and flattery than the welfare of the people. Sitting in jail, Lyon won reelection to Congress. In the long run, the Sedition Act backfired, because it encouraged the spread of the opposition press it sought to control. Printers, especially Republican printers, were now more likely than before to present themselves as partisan political actors. Between 1798 and the election of 1800, Republican newspapers were cropping up throughout the country.

The Alien and Sedition Acts also aroused a libertarian counterattack from Republicans. In Kentucky and Virginia, state legislatures sought to invalidate the laws, asserting defiantly the rights of states to resist or even nullify congressional laws they deemed unconstitutional. The Kentucky and Virginia Resolutions of 1798, which were secretly authored by James Madison and Vice President Thomas Jefferson, reflected a moment of uncertainty about the power of the central government and became foundational texts in the history of states' rights ideology. But no other states supported the resolutions, and a showdown over federal authority was averted. Still, Jefferson, Madison, and their partisans would soon hold the reins of federal power.

"A BLOODLESS REVOLUTION"

The triumph of Thomas Jefferson over the incumbent John Adams in the election of 1800 was more than just a changing of the guard. For the first time—and after thirteen months of intensive campaigning—control of the presidency shifted from one party to another, bringing to power men who had been branded previously as threats to national security. Jefferson saw his victory as a genuine revolution, on par with that of 1776, which had transformed the "form" but not the "principles of our government." To make the revolution complete, Republicans hoped to scale down the central government and set the new republic on a course that would break from European models of nationhood.

Two factors were critical to the outcome of this close election. One, which was noted repeatedly by both sides, was the power of the recently created Republican newspaper network in influencing voters. The other factor, more striking to northern

Federalists, was the impact of the Constitution's three-fifths clause, which significantly enhanced the voting power of southern states by counting 60 percent of their completely disenfranchised slave population in determining their electoral votes. Without those bonuses, the states won by Adams would have yielded more electoral votes than those won by Jefferson, and the revolution would have been canceled. With the involuntary support of hundreds of thousands of slaves, the slaveholder Jefferson, disparaged by opponents as the "Negro President," took office in the nation's new capital.

The period between the November election and Jefferson's inauguration the following March was marked by grave uncertainty. Though the Republicans had outpolled the Federalists by 73 to 65 electoral votes, the electoral college had failed to produce a clear verdict on the presidency, because Jefferson and his vice-presidential running mate Aaron Burr each received 73 votes. Electors were entitled to vote both for a first and a second choice (the latter would serve as vice president), and parties would instruct their electors to withhold one ballot from the vice-presidential candidate so that he would come in second place. But a New York Republican neglected to play his part, the result was a tie, and Burr refused to concede to Jefferson. The contest then moved to the House of Representatives, where a Federalist majority had to choose between two despised Republican opponents. Only on the thirty-sixth ballot did Jefferson receive the required support of nine state delegations. (By the time of the next presidential election, the Twelfth Amendment would prevent such a recurrence by separating the ballots of presidents and vice presidents.)

After Jefferson was officially elected, Adams devoted the final days of his term to appointing Federalists to positions as judges, diplomats, and military commanders before the Republicans took over. Adams and his newly installed Supreme Court chief justice, John Marshall, spent the month of February preparing and delivering commissions to 217 appointees, working right up to the waning hours of the day before the inauguration. Jefferson and the Republicans decried these tactics and the "midnight judges" that Adams had installed, but they honored all of the appointments that had been fully processed in time.

Aaron Burr (1756–1836). Burr stubbornly refused to concede the presidency to Thomas Jefferson after the election of 1800, forcing the House of Representatives to decide the contest. Four years later, while serving as vice president, Burr killed Alexander Hamilton in a duel in New Jersey and managed to remain in office. Two years after that, he was arrested on charges of raising a private army in the West and conspiring to become emperor of a vast new nation extending from Ohio to Panama.

William Marbury, one of the judges whose commission was not delivered in time, sued the Jefferson administration under the Judiciary Act of 1789 for refusing him the appointment. The Supreme Court (with the same Federalist John Marshall now presiding) ruled that the federal judiciary could not compel a president to process an appointment. More significantly, the Court ruled that the Judiciary Act voted into law by Congress violated the Constitution. *Marbury v. Madison*, decided in 1803, established the important principle of **judicial review,** under which federal courts claim the power to overturn acts of Congress they deem unconstitutional—a power the Constitution did not explicitly grant to the judicial branch. The case had a monumental impact on the future of American law and politics. In the shorter term, the entire ordeal of Marbury's contested commission captured something remarkable about the election of 1800 and the new system of political parties. Change at government's highest level, however bitter and contested, was conducted without violence and according to an understanding of the rule of law shared by both sides.

IMAGINED CITIES

Federalist and Republican visions of the new republic clashed starkly over the future role of American cities. From its founding, the United States was an overwhelmingly rural society, more so than any European nation at the time other than Poland. In 1800, only six places in the young nation had populations over ten thousand, and less than 4 percent of the country's population lived in them. Thomas Jefferson thought little of urban America, and compared cities to "sores on the body politic." But to other founding fathers, many of whom were urbanites themselves, American cities wielded power and importance beyond their number and size because so much traffic (of goods, people, and information) passed through them. Philadelphia was to the United States, the Federalist financier Robert Morris wrote to John Hancock, "what the heart is to the human body in circulating the blood." But whether Americans saw their cities as bodily sores or vital organs, they recognized that urban areas were beginning to grow and proliferate.

Urban growth after the Revolution was not simply the result of migrations or natural increase. American cities were planned, plotted, and imagined. New towns on the frontier were built up in anticipation of future arrivals; older commercial cities on the seaboard were redesigned to accommodate sprawling populations that had not yet appeared; and brand new cities, such as the one that would become the U.S. capital, were projected onto the blank spaces of the national map.

A BRAND NEW CAPITAL

The founders of the new republic expected the federal government to be settled in a city, though which city remained an open question. Compared to European capitals during the same period, the nation's leading metropolis at the time was tiny. By modern standards, Philadelphia after the Revolution hardly seems urban at all. Its population in 1780 (about thirty thousand) would rank below that of Willingboro (New Jersey), Boynton Beach (Florida), Manitowoc (Wisconsin), and many small suburbs two centuries later, and its dense settlement could fit today within the boundaries of several major university campuses. Still, Philadelphia was a bustling, polyglot, cosmopolitan place. It was home to learned societies, a prestigious medical school, a thriving print industry, and the seats of both state and national government. Philadelphians controlled almost a quarter of the country's export trade, and eight Philadelphia newspapers produced much of the news that circulated nationally. If the selection of a national capital had been based on its eminence and influence—or on historical precedent—Philadelphia would have been an obvious choice.

Nonetheless, the national capital moved several times during and after the Revolution. And despite frustration with years of relocating their base of operations from place to place, few of the founders relished the idea of leaving the federal government indefinitely in the clutches of America's most populous and commercially powerful metropolis. In Philadelphia, many worried, the government might be susceptible to the pressures of democratic mobs on the one hand, or commercial cliques on the other. Instead, the founders designed and built a new city, named after George Washington, to house their experiment in decentralized nation-building.

The Constitution had called for the creation of a federal district ("not exceeding ten Miles square") that would not fall under any state's jurisdiction, but the question of where this district would be located was a point of conflict in Congress. Most of the participants in this debate agreed that the new capital ought to be located centrally, but the word *central* was interpreted in multiple ways. Did it refer to longitude, latitude, trade routes, settlement patterns, or national history? In an age when travel was slow and at a moment when the national government's power over the states remained tenuous, Americans in different parts of the country worried about a capital that would be inaccessible to them or beholden to the interests and influences of a rival region. Northerners—especially Pennsylvanians—lobbied for selecting a city at the country's demographic center (counting only white people). Southerners favored a mapmaker's definition of central based on geographical distance, since that would recommend a site farther south than the eight places where national leadership had convened during and after the revolutionary crisis. In the deal that was struck to resolve the impasse over Hamilton's plan for the federal treasury to assume state debts, southerners won a site on the Potomac River, between Virginia and Maryland.

President Washington, who was designated to select the exact site, decided on a spot at the southernmost edge of the 105-mile zone he had been assigned by Congress. Rather than picking any of the existing towns in that district as the capital city, he chose a relatively uninhabited area, where he could create a majestic and thriving metropolis free of corruptions and conflicts of local community interests. The capital plan, designed by the French-born engineer Major Pierre Charles L'Enfant and selected (with several amendments) by the new national government, sought to rival the great urban centers of Europe in scope while embodying principles of rationality and order. (See Interpreting the Sources: Federalist and Republican Plans for a National Capital.)

Promoters of the new capital on the Potomac predicted that it would become the next Rome, attracting and maintaining a population of 160,000 within a few years. Washington and his commissioners were so enthusiastic about the city's prospects that they expected to build the city without any public financing. The plan was to buy an excess of land around the chosen site (ceded by Virginia and Maryland), announce the location, and then sell off the unneeded portion at a profit to pay for the construction of public buildings and urban infrastructure. From the beginning, then, Washington, D.C., was a speculative scheme of the sort that would become familiar in American urban history. For much of their history, cities in the United States have relied on the prospect of rising real estate values (rather than more direct forms of public taxation and expenditure) to cover the costs of urban development. The Rome of the New World would be built by the projected difference between what land was worth today and what it might be worth tomorrow.

Washington's bold scheme to build a new capital through real estate speculation was not necessarily foolish, but he overestimated popular interest in living near the national government. At a special auction in 1791, with Washington, Jefferson, and Madison in attendance, only 35 out of 10,000 lots were sold. The results were no better a year later. Finally, the authorities staged a parade in 1793, and Washington himself stepped up to buy four lots, but few others were sold and the commissioners abandoned the auction strategy altogether. Maryland and Virginia had to provide loans to sustain the project.

D.C.'S HUMBLE BEGINNINGS

When the government moved to the new capital in 1800, only 109 buildings of brick or stone were standing. Few artisans were drawn to the area, and the commissioners had been forced to hire slaves from the neighboring plantations to help with construction. Physically, the town was intensely rustic. Not long after her arrival, First Lady Abigail Adams got lost in the woods for two

INTERPRETING THE SOURCES

Federalist and Republican Plans for a National Capital

Along with the Declaration of Independence, the Constitution, and the Bill of Rights, the design of the capital city ranks among the nation's founding documents. In creating a new capital from scratch, leaders of the early republic were able to imprint their visions of the United States onto paper and potentially onto public space. Republican Thomas Jefferson and Federalist Pierre L'Enfant offered contrasting plans for the city that would both house and represent the new national government.

Jefferson envisioned a small city with a simple grid of streets, with the main government building arrayed in a row across the capital's main street. The dots around the small city indicate the possibility of expanding the city along the same grid pattern, should the need arise. By contrast, L'Enfant's map called for a much larger city. Instead of setting aside space for future growth, L'Enfant boldly anticipated that growth. And instead of adopting the repeating grid plan associated with Philadelphia (see Chapter 4), he drew on models of European imperial capitals, such as Versailles, France, which included diagonals, ovals, and circles. In L'Enfant's plan, different street grids are connected by diagonal avenues that traverse the city in multiple directions. Each avenue would be named for a different state and lined with statues of national heroes. L'Enfant's plan also divided the city into three separate centers of settlement, corresponding with the three branches of government.

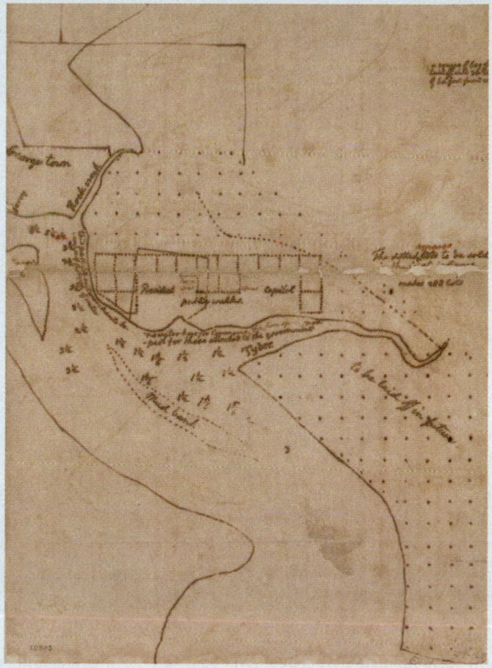

Jefferson's Plan, 1791. Jefferson anticipated a simpler, more functional federal capital, though he left room in his plan for future growth.

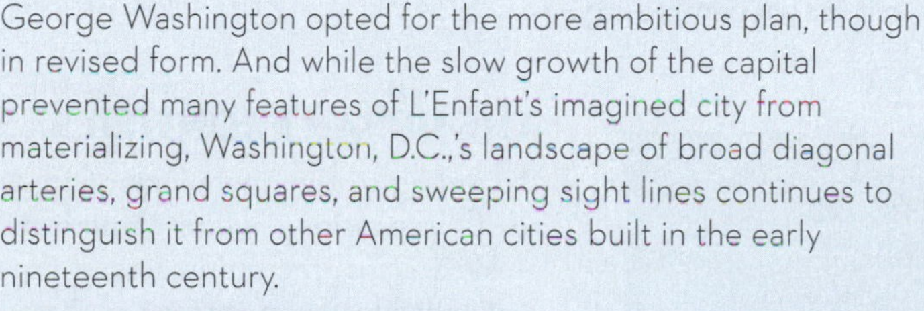

George Washington opted for the more ambitious plan, though in revised form. And while the slow growth of the capital prevented many features of L'Enfant's imagined city from materializing, Washington, D.C.,'s landscape of broad diagonal arteries, grand squares, and sweeping sight lines continues to distinguish it from other American cities built in the early nineteenth century.

Explore the Sources

1. How does Jefferson's plan reflect the ideology of the Republicans?
2. Why might Washington and L'Enfant have favored a city map that was so much bigger than the immediate needs of the national capital?
3. Which features of L'Enfant's plan represent orderliness and practicality? Which features do you think connote urban grandeur?
4. Jefferson complained that L'Enfant's plan "glowed with an iconography of federal supremacy." What does that mean and what features of L'Enfant's plan might have triggered that reaction?

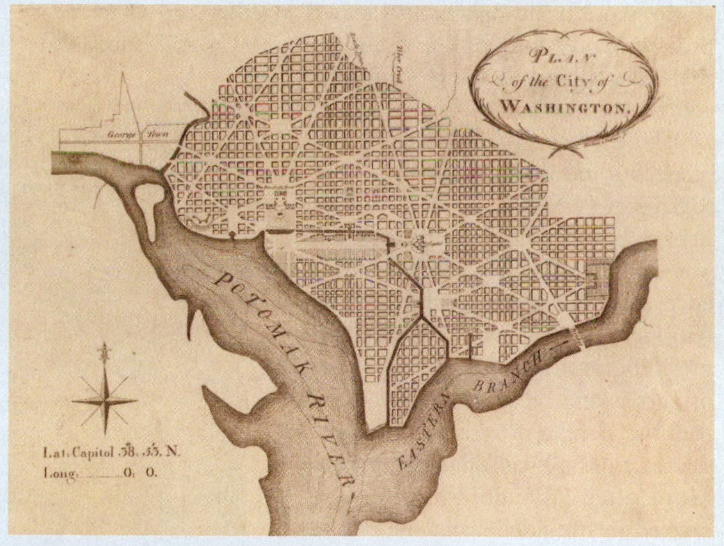

L'Enfant's Plan, 1792. Federalist visions of the new capital emphasized grandeur and aesthetic appeal.

hours and had to hire a vagabond to guide her home. A group of congressmen returning from a dinner party lost their way in the bogs and had to wait until sunrise to return to the capital.

Apart from the postal system, which dispersed the presence of the national government across the country, the federal operation was quite small. When John Adams moved the executive branch of the federal government to the new capital in 1800, the entire records of the Departments of State, War, Navy, Treasury, and Justice occupied seven cases. The Washington community was a small tight-knit group as well. Congressmen and other public

Washington, D.C., around 1803. Hunters and farm animals appear on the streets of the new capital, within sight of the president's house.
Question for Analysis: How does this image square with L'Enfant's city plan?

officials typically stayed in all-male boardinghouses, which were the basic building blocks of early Washington society. Residents of the same boardinghouse socialized together and were even prone to vote along similar lines. Supreme Court justices also shared temporary lodgings while the court was in session.

Women were part of the capital scene, but mostly during the six-week social season. Several wives of prominent public officials who maintained year-round residences exerted influence on Washington culture—and national politics—by cultivating and presiding over an elite parlor culture of parties and receptions where genteel social relations might be conducted and political alliances formed. More often, though, women were pushed to the sidelines of the public sphere of the new capital. Thomas Jefferson, who helped design the city, was especially hostile to the influence of women in politics. When he took over the presidency a year after the government moved there, he famously hosted all-male dinner parties where he enjoyed playing "mother" to his guests.

Washington, D.C., remained for many years a far cry from the New Rome envisioned by its designers. Not until the middle of the nineteenth century would the town begin to fulfill its original promise as a symbol of American grandeur with a full-year residential community.

Dolley Payne Todd Madison (1768–1849). Widowed by the 1793 yellow fever epidemic in Philadelphia, Dolley later married James Madison and became a leading figure in the parlor culture of early Washington, D.C.

THE URBAN FRONTIER

According to the mythology of westward expansion, white Americans trekked across the mountains as rugged individual frontiersmen or hardy family farmers and built primitive societies free of urban influences. In fact the history of American settlement west of the Appalachians began with towns and cities. Before white farmers began tilling soil in the western reaches of the United States, and before settlers swelled the territorial populations in such places as Ohio, Indiana, Kentucky, Illinois, and Missouri, entrepreneurs and government officials were mapping towns, incorporating cities, and projecting urban growth.

Cities were deliberate, forceful impositions on the landscape. Some of these cities began as forts designed to support military conquest. But whether they were military garrisons, fur-trading posts, supply centers, or ambitious commercial villages, cities like St. Louis, Cincinnati, Louisville, Pittsburgh, Lexington, and New Orleans formed an

urban frontier, which was in place before farms were cultivated and before many of their states were admitted to the union. Cities created the possibility of a rural hinterland, and the rural hinterland in turn sustained the growth of cities.

Almost all of the earliest U.S. cities west of the Appalachians were located along major waterways (see Map 8.3). The major exception was Lexington, which was founded in 1775 in the future state of Kentucky and named for the site of the revolutionary battle that had taken place earlier that year in Massachusetts. By 1800, when the state of Kentucky was only eight years old, Lexington held a population of nearly 1,800, making it the most populous community in the western United States.

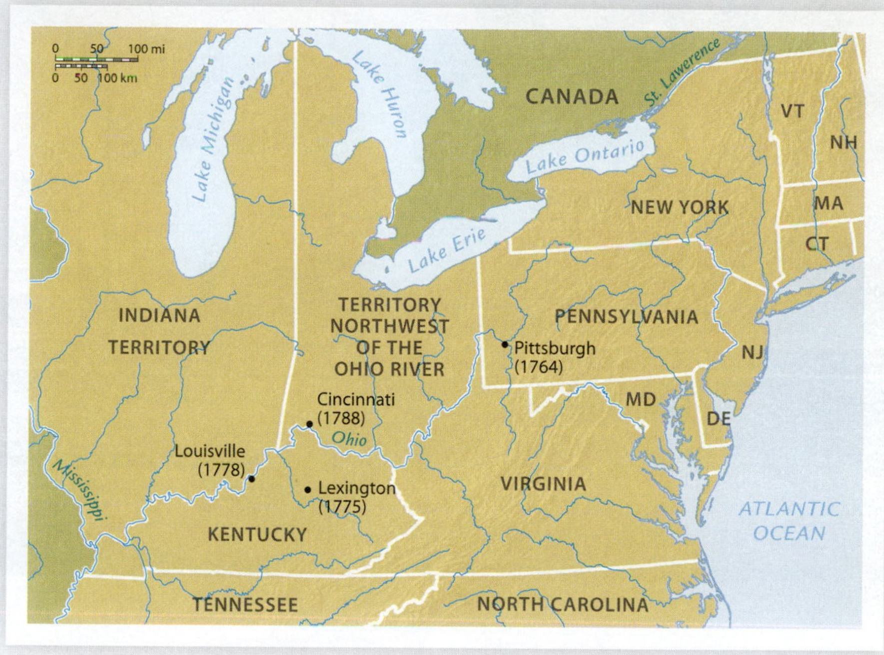

Map 8.3 The Urban Frontier. River cities founded in the eighteenth century helped create the agricultural hinterland and attracted rural migrants to the region.

More typical was Pittsburgh, whose location at the confluence of the Allegheny and Monongahela Rivers, where the Ohio River forms, had made it a contested strategic position in the battles among French, British, and Indian armies during 1750s (see Chapter 5). Laid out as a city in 1764, Pittsburgh grew rapidly during the 1790s with the flow of migrants across the Appalachians. As new arrivals stopped in the city to sell horses and wagons and buy food, furniture, and farm equipment, Pittsburgh became a significant marketplace and catered to a rising demand for manufactured goods. By 1811, iron making was a major local industry and several factories were busily producing nails, household utensils, farm implements, and machine parts. Pittsburgh soon surpassed Lexington in population, and a leading national business publication predicted it would become "the greatest manufacturing city in the world."

Pittsburgh eventually emerged as one of America's industrial centers, but the Ohio River city that would prove more immediately dominant was Cincinnati. Founded in 1788, fifteen years before Ohio entered the union, the "Queen City" became the central market for a vast hinterland, selling merchandise from eastern cities and sugar, cotton, and molasses coming up from New Orleans. Cincinnati's population in 1810 was just over 2,500, but in the ensuing decades it would mushroom into the fifth largest city in the nation.

All of these cities contributed to and depended on the proliferation of riverboats, which carried people and goods along the region's major waterways. During the first decade of the nineteenth century, over 2,500 boats were navigating the Ohio and Mississippi Rivers at any given time, 90 percent of them traveling in the direction of the current. By 1811, the volume of river traffic would increase dramatically due to the introduction of steamboat travel. Robert Fulton initiated the American steamboat era in 1807 by sailing up the Hudson River from New York City to Albany in thirty-two hours. Four years later, Nicholas Roosevelt (whose design ideas Fulton had used) and his wife Lydia Latrobe Roosevelt brought steam travel to the rougher waters of the West. By making a successful voyage from Pittsburgh to New Orleans in 1811–1812, the Roosevelts demonstrated the viability (and profitability) of upriver boat travel in the West.

BOOSTERS, SPECULATORS, AND BANKERS

Inspired by the promising growth of Cincinnati, Pittsburgh, and other early river cities in the West, overland migrants plotted new sites. All along the Ohio River valley and the Great Lakes, ambitious promoters and businessmen laid out towns along grids and touted the glorious economic destinies of their imaginary communities to potential investors and residents. These **boosters,** as historians call them, were not simply investors trying to raise the value of western real estate. They were active shapers of the frontier who thought seriously about urban development. Boosters analyzed climate and natural transportation advantages, developed interesting theories about the gravitational pull that one city exerted on its neighbors, and made predictions about economic and demographic growth. Some of their assessments now seem quite prescient, others less so. For every Cleveland and Indianapolis, there was a Hygeia, a Lystra, and a Franklinville, towns that never made it despite what appeared to be compelling natural advantages and a burst of promotional energy.

What the boosters accurately perceived was the fact that new cities would vie with one another for economic and demographic superiority, even as they contributed to one another's growth. Jefferson's Land Ordinance had mapped the western half of the United States as a blank grid of interchangeable squares (see Chapter 7), but the men who promoted new towns and cities understood that not all locations were the same. Rivers, lakes,

Robert Fulton's *Clermont* on the Hudson, 1813. Steam-powered riverboats would become iconic symbols of the western experience in the mid-nineteenth century. Their introduction in 1811 helped transform the economy and demography of the Mississippi and Ohio river regions.

hills, and valleys shaped the value of individual land holdings, as did politics, entrepreneurial vision, military force, and the flow of capital. Close to two million Americans crossed the Appalachians during the first two decades of the nineteenth century, and most of them farmed. But the value of farmland in Ohio and Kentucky depended on markets for agricultural goods, and cities were crucial in reaching and shaping those markets. As cities got bigger, urban land values skyrocketed, and the boosters who successfully promoted the fortunes of their fledgling communities reaped considerable profits.

City growth along the urban frontier offered another reminder that life in the trans-Appalachian West was far from Jefferson's vision of a nation of simple farming folk. **Land speculators** rather than individual farmers bought up most of the plots sold by the federal government. In 1800, twenty-one speculators claimed one-fourth of Kentucky. Among them was the family of Supreme Court justice John Marshall. Many other founders and leaders of the new nation speculated in western lands as well. Freed from the traditional laws and customs that prevented its transfer from one family or estate to another, land had become another marketable commodity.

The most controversial case of western land speculation took place in the southwestern portion of the country. In 1795 the state of Georgia sold thirty-five million acres of its western reserves to four private companies at suspiciously low prices. The Yazoo lands, as the area became known because of its proximity to the Yazoo tributary of the Mississippi, were then occupied by Cherokees, Creeks, Chickasaws, and Choctaws. Not only Georgia but also the United States, Spain, and Great Britain claimed the land as theirs. Still, the private companies had little trouble unloading tracts of Yazoo land to new investors, including prominent politicians in other parts of the country. Meanwhile, Georgians cried foul over the fact that state legislators who had approved the sale had been bribed with shares of land. The perpetrators were voted out of office, and a new legislature repudiated the Yazoo land deal in 1796. Investors holding worthless shares spent the next decade lobbying the state government for compensation. A commission appointed by President Jefferson (some of whose political allies owned these Yazoo shares) recommended a congressional buyout, precipitating a political split within the Republican ranks. The fate of the Yazoo lands remained tied up in the courts until 1810, when the Supreme Court upheld the original sale. More generally, debates about land deals and land speculation continued to dominate politics throughout the early national era.

Town boosting and land speculation were not the only new entrepreneurial opportunities in the growing urban frontier. By the beginning of the nineteenth century, bankers began to lobby states for charters to establish institutions that would provide

The First U.S. Land Office (1801), Steubenville, Ohio. Land west of the Appalachians was a valuable public asset and provided the principal instrument through which the federal government influenced the demographic and economic development of the country in this period.

SINGULAR LIVES

Andrew Dexter, Rogue Banker in the Wilderness

At the beginning of the nineteenth century, Detroit was not one of the boomtowns of America's urban frontier. A French settlement town founded along the strait off Lake Erie a century earlier, Detroit was captured by the Ottawas and their British allies in 1763 (see Chapter 5) and then given to the United States in 1796 as a provision of Jay's Treaty. In 1805, the federal government designated Detroit as capital of the new Michigan Territory, but white American settlement there was still meager. The total population of Detroit numbered 551, and English speakers were a small minority in the territorial population. When the new territorial governor arrived that year, he was startled to discover that every building in the town had recently burned in a great fire. Five years later, the town remained isolated from other American communities and its population still languished at around 750. To live in Detroit, the governor wrote, was "to remove from the World, and barely exist."

View of Detroit, by George W. Whistler, 1811. The Detroit Bank can be seen in this image.

For a restless Boston schemer named Andrew Dexter, Jr., Detroit's isolation and insignificance made it an ideal place to locate a bank. Born in 1779, Dexter descended from a long line of New Englanders and grew up in Providence, where he attended Rhode Island College (later Brown University). Graduating second in a college class of promising young men, most of whom would become merchants and lawyers, Dexter moved to Boston, embarked on a successful legal practice, and married into a prosperous and influential Boston family. But Dexter aspired to greater wealth and turned to the growing world of finance. Wresting control of a Boston bank in 1806, he acquired or established banks in other places, farther and farther west, including Michigan. Dexter's Detroit bank, the first such institution west of the Alleghenies, printed tens of thousands of dollars' worth of bank notes, sent them back to Boston, and began circulating them with the confidence that few New Englanders (or anyone else for that matter) would ever trek to the Michigan wilderness to present the notes for redemption. As long as no one did so, Dexter and his friends figured, it would make no difference that the Detroit Bank, like most of his financial institutions, held a much smaller supply of gold and silver than its notes promised.

Dexter used this scheme to buy land in Boston and finance the construction of Boston's Exchange Coffee House, which he hoped would become the major commercial center and stock exchange of the region. Upon its completion in 1808, Dexter's lavish Exchange became one of the tallest buildings in the United States. But the notes of the Detroit bank were soon discredited, its charter revoked, and Dexter's paper empire crumpled. Before the building opened for business, a disgraced Dexter fled to Canada, several steps ahead of his creditors, to whom he owed more than a half-million dollars. A decade later, the Coffee House succumbed as well, destroyed by a massive fire in 1818 that firefighting pumps could not reach due to the building's excessive height. Dexter himself ultimately returned to the United States, where he tried his hand at several unsuccessful ventures in the South, and died in 1837 after contracting yellow fever.

Think About It

1. How did Dexter's fraudulent scheme reflect the state of banking in the early nineteenth century?
2. Does Dexter's story emphasize more the connections or the vast distances between Boston and Detroit in the early national period?

white settlers with cash. Banks had to be chartered into existence by special acts of state legislatures because banks actually created money. Before the Civil War, the United States had no uniform government-issued paper currency. Instead, paper money consisted of the various notes of different state-chartered banks, varying in color, size, denomination, and reliability (see Chapter 10). When manufacturers paid their employees or urban customers paid their grocery bills, they were likely using the **bank notes** of some individual bank, which were pieces of paper that the bearer could (in theory) bring to that bank for redemption in silver or gold. Western states were attractive banking centers for investors who saw an advantage in having a remote location that would discourage people from ever presenting their bank notes for redemption (see Singular Lives: Andrew Dexter, Rogue Banker in the Wilderness).

Tontine Coffee House, ca. 1797. Full of printed publications and whispered rumors, coffee houses like the Tontine (left) opened out onto a larger world of goods and ideas, but they were also local hangouts for people who already knew one another. It was at the Tontine, for example, that Alexander Hamilton met with friends in 1804 to discuss his upcoming duel with political rival Aaron Burr, in which Hamilton was killed.

As of 1790, the entire nation had a grand total of four banks. Thirty years later, the number had risen to 328, and many others had come and gone in the interim. Forty new banks were incorporated in Kentucky in 1818 and failed a year later. So long as buyers and sellers maintained faith in the bank's ability to redeem its promissory notes, bank currency would stay in circulation. Banks pumped money into local markets and financed much of the expansion of the American economy.

WALL STREET AND THE NEW YORK GRID

Maps of future cities on the Ohio River and charters for cash-poor banks in remote Michigan villages epitomized the exuberant ambitions of a new generation of merchants and planners. But commercial growth and speculation were not limited to the frontier. Many of the most daring and ambitious planners operated, like Andrew Dexter, in the older cities on the eastern seaboard. There too the impulse to imagine urban growth was taking hold.

By the beginning of the new century, New York (which was then located entirely within the island of Manhattan) had surpassed Philadelphia as the nation's most populous city. The symbolic and practical center of New York's mercantile culture was the Tontine Coffee House on Wall and Water Streets. The Tontine was more than simply a place to drink coffee. It was a clearinghouse of information, both printed and oral, where merchants, lawyers, brokers, and civic leaders went to read newspapers, learn commodity prices, circulate mail, read

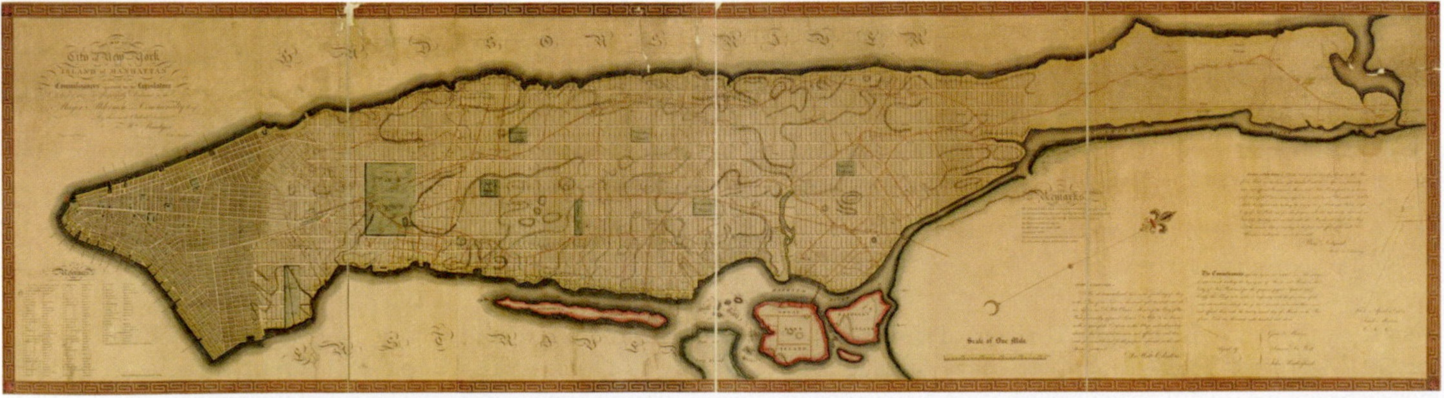

The Commissioners' Map of New York City, 1811. For the first two centuries of its existence, New York was a dense and haphazardly planned collection of winding streets and irregular intersections. In 1811, when fewer than one hundred thousand people lived in Manhattan and settlement barely reached as far north as Houston Street, a commission proposed a grid plan for organizing all future development on the island. Unlike the plan for the nation's capital, the New York plan avoided ovals, circles, or broad diagonal arteries. **Question for Analysis:** How might this map have shaped the settlement patterns of New Yorkers?

incendiary pamphlets, arrange deals, and participate in public life. In 1792, a group of merchants who had been meeting in front of a sycamore tree on Wall Street to devise regulations for public trading of stocks set up shop inside the Tontine building, which opened that year. This was the origin of the New York Stock Exchange.

Anticipating further growth in the city, New York State appointed a commission in 1807 to map streets and direct development on the rest of Manhattan. After debating many plans, the commissioners published a map in 1811 that would leave an enduring imprint on city life. Such a vision of a sprawling city covering the entire island was entirely speculative in 1811, much like the plan for Washington, D.C., or the maps of imaginary metropolises along the Ohio River.

PRESIDENT JEFFERSON AND WESTWARD EXPANSION

Despite its primitive setting in the sparsely settled national capital, the relocated federal government would embark on an ambitious course of national expansion. During the Jefferson administration (1801–1809), the United States took decisive steps in the transition from a set of seaboard settlements to a sprawling continental nation.

REPUBLICANS TAKE POWER

Thomas Jefferson had great expectations for what his revolution of 1800 might bring. In part, he saw his own election as a crushing blow to the monarchical tendencies and aristocratic sympathies of the Federalists, as well as to their program of military spending and high taxes. Once in office, he made a point of avoiding what he took to be the trappings of aristocracy. He abandoned such customs as riding in carriages, maintaining liveried servants, receiving foreign diplomats in special formal attire, or delivering State of the Union messages in person. More generally, he brought enthusiasm about the capacity of the leaders of the republic to remake the world on new foundations. "We can no longer say there is nothing new under the sun," Jefferson wrote to the British scientist and political philosopher Joseph Priestley shortly after the inauguration. "For this whole chapter in the history of man is new."

Many in the revolutionary generation shared Jefferson's suspicion of the dead weight of tradition and his hopeful longing for the possibility of a genuinely new order. To the cohort that was coming of age as Jefferson took office, the allure of the new was even stronger. Jefferson sympathized strongly with this cultural trend. And many of his positions and policies favored the creation of blank slates that bore little imprint of the past. Perhaps nowhere was this clearer than in his long-standing interest in exploring and settling the American West. Jefferson was a cosmopolitan, Francophile intellectual who had spent significant time in Europe, but he looked optimistically westward to an American future on a continent with which he was still largely unfamiliar.

THE LOUISIANA PURCHASE

Ever since the Treaty of Paris, American politicians had been troubled by the Spanish presence at the new republic's southern and western borders. Of particular concern during the 1790s was the fact that Spain, which had claimed the Louisiana Territory from France in 1763, controlled the mouth of the Mississippi River at New Orleans. As American settlers poured into Kentucky and Tennessee, establishing farms near rivers that flowed west, they pressured the federal government to secure free navigation rights on the Mississippi so that they could ship crops down to the Gulf of Mexico and from there to eastern markets. Some radical frontiersmen, including an obscure Tennessee politician named Andrew Jackson who served briefly in Congress during George Washington's second term, threatened to move Kentucky and Tennessee into the Spanish Empire if the United States could not guarantee their access. For a while, Spain granted American farmers the right to ship their goods along the Mississippi through New Orleans and into the Gulf, as part of Pinckney's Treaty of 1795. But Spain revoked these privileges in 1802, and President Jefferson worried about the possibility of war.

As it turned out, Spain had secretly ceded Louisiana back to France two years earlier, though the Spanish were still maintaining a government in New Orleans in an effort to protect their other colonies. Meanwhile, France was having second thoughts about the value of the territory. By 1803, the French cause in St. Domingue was clearly lost (50,000 to 65,000 soldiers had been killed, mostly by disease), and the French emperor Napoleon lacked either the appetite or the resources for further military ventures in his American colonies. Furthermore, the loss of St. Domingue reduced the importance of Louisiana to the French, since Napoleon had valued his mainland colonies largely as a source of food, lumber, and animals for the lucrative sugar plantations in the Caribbean. Anticipating war with Britain, France was motivated to unload Louisiana to another power to avoid having to pay the costs of defending it against the British.

Jefferson had sought to purchase just the city of New Orleans, but Napoleon's representatives responded by offering Jefferson the entire Louisiana Territory, which stretched from the Mississippi to the Rocky

How Much Is That?

The Louisiana Purchase

The $15 million expended on the Louisiana Purchase in 1803 is roughly equivalent to $307 million in 2013 currency, or about 57 cents per acre. The current commercial value of the land itself is difficult to assess since some of it is zoned as parkland and thus not available for private sale, but typical rural land parcels in the state of Louisiana sell for thousands of dollars per acre.

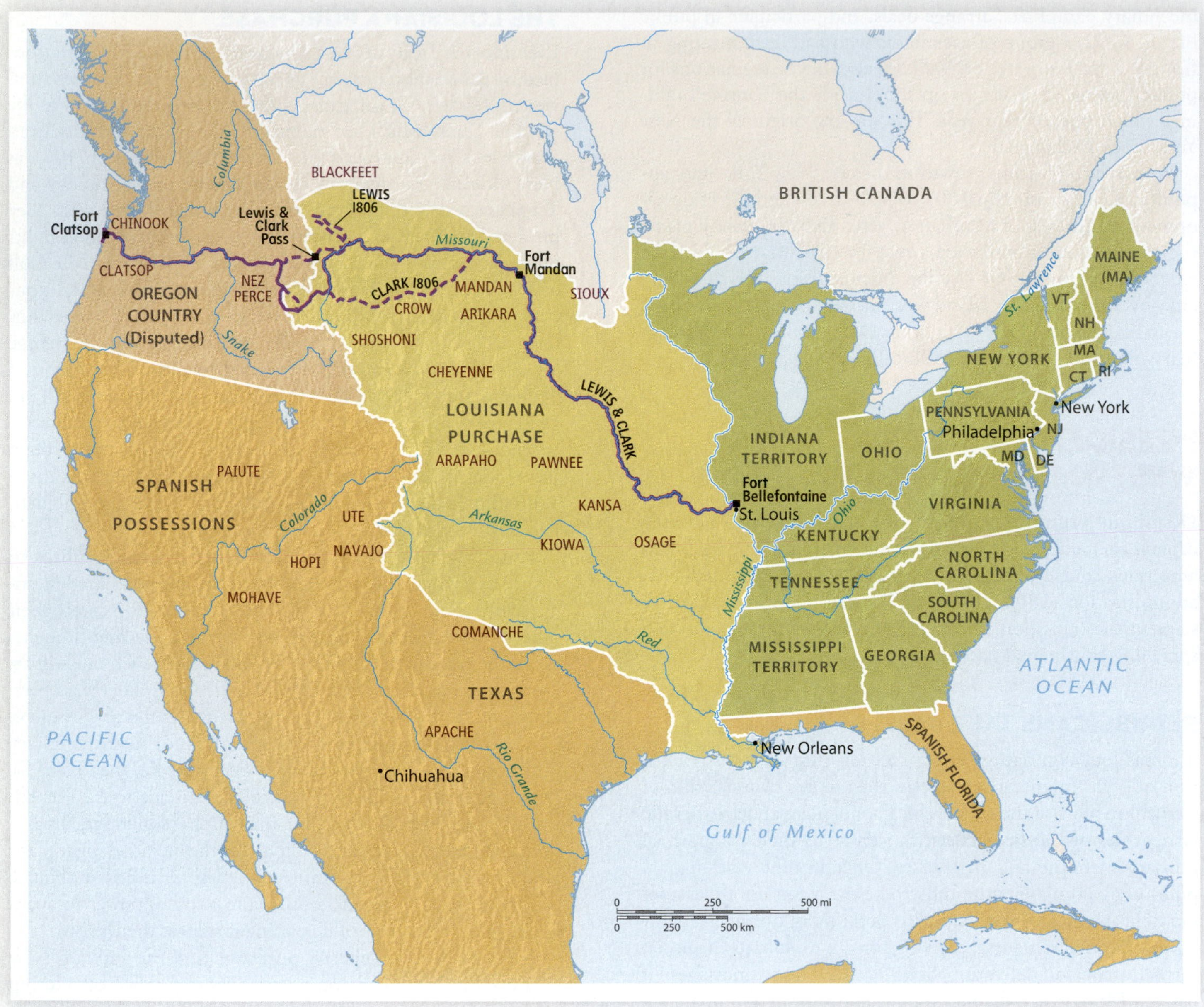

Map 8.4 Doubling the Size of the Nation. Jefferson's Louisiana Purchase was the most significant achievement of his presidency.

Mountains, for the price of $15 million, a figure that included $3.75 million to New England merchants who held claims against the French—and who, Jefferson feared, might otherwise oppose the deal (see How Much Is That?). Jefferson hoped to pay for his new western lands not by tax revenue but by real estate speculation. The government could now trade land west of the Mississippi for Indian land to the east, and sell that land to cotton farmers and speculators at a profit. The Louisiana Purchase treaty, signed in April 1803 and announced to the public on July 4 of that year, instantaneously doubled the size of the United States—at least on paper (see Map 8.4). Ironically, Jefferson's triumph was in large part the consequence of Toussaint Louverture's struggle against French colonial authority in Haiti, a revolt Jefferson feared, opposed, and sought to suppress.

Jefferson seized this unexpected opportunity, despite his own doubts about whether the Constitution authorized the president to buy foreign land and expand the national domain, despite the prospect of opposition from Federalists, and despite the possibility that Spain might not recognize the sale. The last concern was particularly apt. Spain's secret deal with France to return the Louisiana Territory stipulated that the French would not cede the land to another party without offering it back to Spain first.

The allure of western expansion overcame these and other qualms. From Jefferson's perspective, the purchase (which he classified as a treaty, so as to keep within what he regarded as the strict limits of his constitutional authority) addressed a number of concerns in addition to the paramount goal of free access to the Mississippi. The prospect of this massive new terrain for agriculture assuaged Jefferson's fears that the United States would urbanize and turn too quickly to manufacturing. Sudden territorial expansion offered the further benefit of dispersing the population and making it less likely for the new nation to be dominated by a strong central government.

LEWIS AND CLARK: REVEALING THE WEST

Jefferson also looked to the West to help solve what he and many other white Americans perceived to be the nation's Indian problem. He hoped to use the availability of territory on the other side of the Mississippi River to induce Chickasaws, Choctaws, and others to cede lands to cotton planters in the Lower Mississippi Valley. Finally, Louisiana promised to fulfill Jefferson's long-nurtured dream of locating a northwestern route across the continent to the Pacific Ocean.

***Lewis and Clark with Sacagawea*, 1912, by Edgar Samuel Paxson.** Paxson's painting dates to over one hundred years after the Lewis and Clark expedition. Sacagawea, the Shoshoni woman who was a pregnant teenager at the time of the expedition, joined the Corps of Discovery as a translator. She has since appeared on the face of one-dollar U.S. coins.

In January 1803, before the French even broached the subject of Louisiana, Jefferson had sent a confidential message to Congress asking for a modest expenditure to support an expedition of about a dozen men who would travel up the Missouri River, exploring its full length, "even to the Western Ocean." Like the message, the expedition would have to be conducted discreetly, since the men would be traveling through foreign territory. Interestingly, Jefferson explained the need for exploring the Missouri in terms of white-Indian relations. Native tribes, Jefferson observed, were increasingly refusing to cede lands. The only way to accommodate the "rapid increase of our numbers" was to transform the economic basis of native societies so that they would abandon their policy of clinging tenaciously to territory coveted by whites. Jefferson's secret memorandum proposed persuading Indians to adopt agriculture and drawing them into networks of trade in order to "place within their reach those things which will contribute more to the domestic comfort than the possession of extensive but uncultivated wilds." An expedition along the Missouri would serve the goal of establishing cultural contacts and developing commercial connections between the United States and the Indians who lived along the river.

A few months after the secret message to Congress, the Missouri River mission acquired a much a higher profile and far broader significance. Now the expedition would be surveying some of the Louisiana Territory recently added to the United States, territory about which white Americans knew very little. Jefferson entrusted the expedition to his private secretary, Meriwether Lewis, who asked his friend William Clark (a veteran of Indian wars in Ohio) to share the command of the party. Clark recruited a crew of Kentucky woodsmen from around the Ohio River to join a group already assembled by Lewis, and several others were added as the men made their way along the Ohio toward St. Louis, a French trading city that had just been transferred to U.S. control. Once they reached St. Louis, the Corps of Discovery, as the expedition party would be called, set up camp just east of the river, near the site of the present-day town of Hartford, Illinois.

In May 1804, Clark led his crew across the Mississippi and up the Missouri to meet Lewis at the town of St. Charles. By mid-November they had made their way to Fort Mandan, in North Dakota, where they camped for the winter. The multicultural party that formed the Lewis and Clark expedition included southerners, Yankees, immigrants from Ireland and Germany, French Canadians, three men of Indian parentage, and an African American named York, who was enslaved to William Clark and never received any pay for his role in the project. At Fort Mandan they were joined by a French Canadian named Toussaint Charbonneau and his pregnant Shoshoni wife, Sacagawea. Both served the expedition as interpreters, and Sacagawea's presence also helped mark the Corps' mission as peaceful in the eyes of the communities they visited.

A year after leaving their camp at Fort Mandan, the Corps glimpsed the Pacific Ocean. Although they had not found a simple cross-continent waterway, they had identified a route between the Mississippi and the Pacific. Along the way, they had established relations between the United States and numerous Indian nations, while amassing a treasury of geographical, botanical, and zoological knowledge that would fascinate Americans for decades.

CITIES ON THE MISSISSIPPI

When the United States acquired Louisiana from France, it took possession of a number of foreign cities that had been built along the boundaries of the French colonial empire. At the time,

St. Louis was forty years old. Its location atop a limestone bluff just south of the junction of the Mississippi, Missouri, and Illinois Rivers had given the city strategic significance during decades of French-British-Spanish conflict, but the population had grown slowly. St. Louis in 1803 consisted of about two hundred houses and a mostly French population of about a thousand people, two-thirds of whom were cousins. Still, it was the commercial center of the Upper Louisiana Territory and the gateway city to the vast land that Jefferson had acquired unexpectedly.

The real urban prize of the Louisiana Purchase, however, was New Orleans. The French had planned the city on the banks of the river in 1721, laying out a bounded grid of streets, later called the Vieux Carré (old square), about one mile wide and half a mile deep. Later in the century, new suburbs (*faubourgs*) were created beyond the original grid, which remained fortified. The city passed into Spanish hands in 1763, and Americans settled there in large numbers in the 1790s, but the culture remained predominantly French (see Chapter 5). When the United States took over New Orleans, it housed a population (including the *faubourgs*) of just over 8,000, of whom 2,773 were slaves. Another 1,335 were free people of color, *gens de couleur libre* in the local terminology. Over the next six years, a large migration of refugees from Haiti (many of whom arrived in 1809 via Cuba) swelled the city's French-speaking population and changed its racial composition. By 1810, over 63 percent of the residents of New Orleans were descended from Africans.

***A View of New Orleans Taken from the Plantation of Marigny*, by J. L. Bouquet de Woiseri, 1803.** This painting depicts New Orleans at the time it came under U.S. control.

Whereas in the rest of the United States all descendants of Africans were typically classified as black, the law and culture of New Orleans insisted on a more complex set of racial distinctions. Free people of color enjoyed a higher status than those with strictly African ancestry and were granted political rights and social freedoms denied free blacks elsewhere in the South. White visitors were often struck by public romances between white men and women whose partially black racial status would have rendered the relationship taboo or illegal in other states. At **quadroon balls,** as they were called, elite white men paid admission (sometimes quite expensive) to socialize with free women of color. These encounters might lead to arrangements whereby a woman of one-quarter African ancestry would enter into an ongoing sexual relationship with a prosperous man of European descent in return for financial support. Despite the obvious constraints and impositions associated with such a relationship, the women involved would enter the ranks of fashionable New Orleans society.

Public life in New Orleans reflected this complex racial system, as well as the distinctive influences of Catholicism; West Indian dance, music, and clothing; Spanish architecture; and French laws. At the same time, New Orleans's geographical position in the urban frontier would place it at the center of the expanding U.S. economy over the coming decades, a hub city for the flow of goods, information, and slaves.

CAPTIVITY AND THE EMBARGO YEARS

Jefferson's plans to reduce the federal debt, slash military spending, and scale back the activities of the central government were undermined by several developments during his presidency. The first decade of the century saw the new republic fight a war against North African pirates and struggle to avoid military showdowns with both France and Britain. Jefferson decided not to run for reelection in 1808, and his successor James Madison inherited a range of challenging predicaments. Complicated strategies of international diplomacy dominated national politics, framed a divisive debate about the slave trade, and hobbled a growing commercial economy.

WAR IN THE MEDITERRANEAN

Beginning in the late 1600s, the four North African states of Morocco, Algiers, Tunis, and Tripoli controlled the Mediterranean Sea, exacting tribute from countries whose ships wished to participate in the lucrative Mediterranean trade. After independence, the United States made annual payments to secure good relations with these Barbary states, as they were called, and these payoffs consumed a significant portion of the federal budget during the Washington and Adams administrations. Despite the payments, in 1793 Algerian pirates boarded American ships and took 120 hostages in a bid to raise more money. Over the next three years, the fate of the captives became a cause célèbre and accounts of their captivity dominated popular theater and literature. American newspapers reveled in lurid descriptions of Barbary cruelty and portrayed the Muslim world as uncivilized and despotic. After three years, the nation's first hostage crisis ended with a ransom payment of one million dollars.

After Jefferson's election, the Pasha of Tripoli declared war on the United States in the hopes of extorting more money, and the new president responded by sending the navy to the shores of Tripoli. From a military standpoint, the expedition fared poorly for the United States. In 1803, an American battleship ran aground and required a daring rescue effort, led by Stephen Decatur. Another attempt to blow up the Tripoli fleet literally backfired. Finally, an 1804 land attack succeeded in pressuring the Pasha, who decided this war was costing more than it was worth. An 1805 peace treaty ended the first Barbary War (a second war a decade later would finally release the United States from tribute obligations to Muslim states in the Mediterranean), and allowed Jefferson to save face. It also pushed many Republicans to abandon their opposition to maintaining a professional navy.

Decatur's Conflict with the Algerine at Tripoli. In this retrospective portrait from the 1850s, the prominent historical painter Alonzo Chappel dramatizes the heroism of American naval forces and the barbarism of their enemies—represented, for example, by the pirates' clothing, facial hair, and unshod feet.

ENDING THE INTERNATIONAL SLAVE TRADE

American denunciations of hostage taking and white slavery on the Barbary Coast coexisted uneasily with American participation in the capture and enslavement of West Africans. Even many white Americans who were comfortable with owning slaves objected to kidnapping them in the first place. The U.S. Constitution explicitly protected the international slave trade from any congressional interference for two decades after ratification, but by the end of the Barbary Wars that period was drawing to a close. Meanwhile, British opposition to slave trafficking was mounting and the Royal Navy was poised to use its power to abolish the international trade.

Jefferson's annual message to Congress at the end of 1806 called for legislation to ban the importation of slaves into the United States, and after considerable debate about the terms, Congress passed such a law, to take effect in the beginning of 1808 (the earliest allowable date under the Constitution). Many southern slaveholders embraced the ban on slave importation because it raised the value of the slaves they already owned—and because the slave population grew naturally in the American South (unlike every other slave society in the New World, which depended on importation for its growth). But southerners in Congress fought for lighter penalties for slave smuggling and did not want the government to grant freedom to Africans brought illegally to American shores. The final version of the bill allowed smuggled slaves to be handled according to local custom and depended on southern cooperation for its enforcement. Over the next fifty years, many Africans would be brought illegally into the United States. Moreover, this legislation would have no impact on the bustling traffic in human beings that thrived *within* the nation's expanding borders. Still, the black Philadelphia minister Absalom Jones preached a sermon when the new law took effect, proposing January 1 as an annual day of public thanksgiving to commemorate this historic achievement.

NEUTRALITY, IMPRESSMENT, AND EMBARGO

By far the most difficult diplomatic challenge of Jefferson's second term resulted from the Napoleonic Wars, which began in Europe in 1803. Initially, U.S. neutrality in this conflict between France and an alliance of Britain, Russia, and Austria was a source of economic boon. American ships were able to do business with both sides and took over shipping lines between France and its remaining Caribbean colonies that would have been a British target. But as military conflict between France and Britain intensified, both sides began forbidding neutral ships from carrying goods to the other side. Moreover, both worried that America might provide military aid to the enemy.

In 1806 the British began boarding U.S. ships and searching them for suspected arms shipments or for deserters from the Royal Navy. Overall, close to 10,000 sailors on American ships experienced forcible **impressment** into service for Britain between 1793 and 1814. More humiliating for the Americans, in 1807 a British warship sailing off the coast of Virginia opened fire on an American frigate that refused to submit to a search for deserters. Three Americans were killed and sixteen others wounded in this attack on an American ship in U.S. territory. Still Jefferson pursued a course of peace, hoping to avoid a war that would devastate the nation's economy, break the budget of the central government, and demonstrate the military impotence of the new republic.

As an alternative to war, Jefferson and the Republican Congress imposed economic sanctions on the belligerents. The Embargo Act, which passed Congress in December 1807, banned the importation of foreign goods and prohibited American ships from landing in foreign ports without special authorization. Subsequent laws were added to help the federal government enforce this massive and draconian restriction. Jefferson believed that Americans could get by without European manufactured goods for the short time it would take Europeans to appreciate their dependency on American grain, tobacco, and cotton. He miscalculated. The embargo's most severe impact was clearly on the American economy. New England, where the shipping industry was headquartered, suffered most dramatically, but plummeting commodity prices in other parts of the nation spread the pain around. In a single year, U.S. annual exports fell from $108 million to $22 million. Jefferson's embargo proved politically unpopular, and the Federalist Party began to show new signs of life, though the Republican secretary of state James Madison managed to win the election to succeed Jefferson in 1808, in part because the full brunt of the embargo had not yet arrived.

With Madison in office, Congress replaced the embargo with a new Non-Intercourse Act, which opened up American commerce to all nations except France and Britain and promised to resume trade with whichever warring nation would respect U.S. neutrality. Napoleon seized the opportunity and suspended restrictions on American shipping, though French boats continued to intercept American cargo. In 1811, President Madison cut off trade with Britain. At the same time, war between the United States and Britain-supported Indian alliances in the Northwest was putting further strain on Anglo-American relations. The stage was set for more direct conflict between the new republic and its former empire.

CONCLUSION

The period between 1793 and 1811 witnessed a number of remarkable changes and innovations as the new federal government began to operate. Most dramatically, the United States doubled in size, extending across the contested Mississippi River (which it now controlled) all the way to the Rocky Mountains. Slavery was either banned or legally phased out in half of the country, and communities of free blacks were growing in northern cities. A new system of political parties emerged in response to marked differences over policy and ideology, and control of the central government passed peaceably from one party to the other. A new capital city was willed into being on the banks of the Potomac. New networks of political newspapers began exploiting the postal broadcast system that had been set up in 1792, and ambitious speculators pushed the limits of a banking system that barely existed at the start of the period. New cities sprouted up far from the eastern seaboard, and some two million men and women migrated to farmland within market reach of those cities. Some of those migrants went freely; others were brought by force to lands ripe for cultivating cotton. On the international front, the French monarchy had crumbled and France had abandoned its main colonial projects in North America. One war had been declared against the United States by a foreign nation while another, much larger storm was brewing. Though the nation was, by the most generous count, only thirty-five years old in 1811, American society, culture, and landscape had changed in some respects beyond recognition.

STUDY TERMS

gradual abolition (p. 187)
manumission (p. 188)
Haitian Revolution (p. 188)
black churches (p. 189)
Methodism (p. 190)
African Methodist Episcopal (A.M.E.) Church (p. 190)
debt assumption (p. 192)
protective tariffs (p. 192)
Bank of the United States (p. 192)
Whiskey Rebellion (p. 193)
broad construction (p. 194)
strict construction (p. 194)
Federalists (p. 194)
Republicans (p. 194)
French Revolution (p. 194)
Jay's Treaty (p. 195)
XYZ Affair (p. 195)
political newspapers (p. 195)
Alien Acts (p. 196)
Sedition Act (p. 196)
Kentucky and Virginia Resolutions (p. 196)
election of 1800 (p. 196)
midnight judges (p. 197)
judicial review (p. 197)
boardinghouses (p. 200)
urban frontier (p. 201)
steamboat travel (p. 201)
boosters (p. 201)
land speculators (p. 202)
Yazoo land deal (p. 202)
bank notes (p. 203)
Tontine Coffee House (p. 204)
Pinckney's Treaty (p. 205)
Louisiana Purchase (p. 205)
Corps of Discovery (p. 207)
quadroon balls (p. 208)
Barbary War (p. 209)
ban on slave importation (p. 209)
impressment (p. 210)
Embargo Act (p. 210)
Non-Intercourse Act (p. 210)

TIMELINE

1789 George Washington becomes first president
French Revolution begins

1790 Federal government moves to Philadelphia

1791 First Bank of the United States established
Slave rebellion erupts in St. Domingue (Haiti)

1792 Washington reelected

1793 Yellow Fever epidemic hits Philadelphia
Louis XVI of France is guillotined

1794 Bethel church founded by Richard Allen in Philadelphia
Tax on whiskey incites Whiskey Rebellion

1795 Georgia legislatures sells Yazoo lands
Jay's Treaty helps prevent war with Britain but weakens Federalists

1796 John Adams elected president

1798 Alien and Sedition Acts

1799 Gradual abolition enacted in New York

1800 National capital moves to Washington, D.C.
Election of 1800 transfers presidential power to Republicans
Thomas Jefferson and Aaron Burr tie in electoral college

1801 Jefferson takes office

1803 *Marbury v. Madison* establishes power of judicial review
Louisiana Purchase doubles size of U.S. territory

1804 Lewis and Clark expedition
Gradual abolition enacted in New Jersey
Independence declared in St. Domingue (Haiti)

1805 End of First Barbary War

1807 Embargo Act aims at halting European attacks on U.S. ships

1808 James Madison elected president
U.S. ban on importing slaves takes effect

1811 Manhattan grid established

FURTHER READING

Additional suggested readings are available on the Online Learning Center at www.mhhe.com/becomingamerica1e.

Catherine Allgor, *Parlor Politics* (2002), describes the role of elite woman in building an informal public sphere during the early years of Washington, D.C.

Stephen Aron, *How the West Was Lost* (1999), follows the spread of market relations in Kentucky and the transformation of the trans-Appalachian West.

Elizabeth Blackmar, *Manhattan for Rent* (1989), provides some crucial background for understanding the significance of the 1811 New York grid.

Rachel Hope Cleves, *The Reign of Terror* (2009), emphasizes the role of Federalist revulsion to the French Revolution in the development of American humanitarianism.

David B. Davis, *Revolutions: Reflections on American Equality and Foreign Liberations* (1990), probes the relationship between the American revolution and those in France and Haiti.

Stanley Elkins and Eric McKitrick, *The Age of Federalism* (1993), surveys the political history of the new republic.

Simon Finger, *The Contagious City* (2012), provides a medical history of the Philadelphia yellow fever epidemic.

Jane Kamensky, *The Exchange Artist* (2008), presents the dramatic story of Andrew Dexter's Exchange Coffee House in Boston, which brings together the history of city growth, banking, party politics, land speculation, and Jefferson's embargo.

Roger G. Kennedy, *Mr. Jefferson's Lost Cause* (2003), reconsiders the Louisiana Purchase within the context of Jefferson's ideas about land, slavery, and freedom.

Sarah Luria, *Capital Speculations* (2005), interprets the ideas and ideologies behind the planning of Washington, D.C.

Gary B. Nash, *Forging Freedom* (1988), documents the history of Philadelphia's free black community.

Jeffrey Pasley, *The Tyranny of Printers* (2003), offers a detailed guide to the political press in the early republic.

W. J. Rorabaugh, *The Alcoholic Republic: An American Tradition* (1979), covers the boom in whiskey production and consumption during the period.

Jennifer Spear, *Race, Sex, and Social Order in Early New Orleans* (2009), reconstructs the complex racial hierarchies and sexual politics of the French, Spanish, and American city.

Ashli White, *Encountering Revolution* (2010), examines how the Haitian Revolution shaped attitudes toward slavery in the early republic.

9

INSIDE ▶

THE BIG PICTURE

Conflicts between the U.S. government and Indians helped embroil the new nation in a larger war with Great Britain. The war altered the political landscape, paved the way for more westward expansion, and brought about a novel policy of deporting Indians.

Final Salute. British officers bid farewell to their native allies in 1815 in Prairie du Chien (Wisconsin), at the close of a war that would forever alter American Indian history.

WAR, EXPANSION, & INDIAN REMOVAL

On a December night in 1829, a man in full native garb addressed a crowd in New York City. "MY CURSES ON YOU WHITE MEN," he shouted, "MAY THE GREAT SPIRIT CURSE YOU WHEN HE SPEAKS IN HIS WAR VOICE FROM THE CLOUDS! MAY YOUR GRAVES AND THE GRAVES OF YOUR CHILDREN BE IN THE PATH THE RED MEN SHALL TRACE!" At the close of his speech, the large audience responded with a thunderous standing ovation.

The speaker was not an Indian. He was a white Philadelphian named Edwin Forrest, who would become the first person born in the United States to earn an international reputation in the field of acting. And on this night in 1829, Forrest was appearing as the lead character in the premiere performance of a play called *Metamora; or, the Last of the Wampanoags*. The play, which retold the story of King Philip's War in 1675 (see Chapter 2), was a smashing success. Forrest made a hero out of the slain Indian chief and emerged as a major celebrity. Why Forrest was portraying an Indian on a New York stage in 1829, and why white men and women of various classes cheered Metamora's curse on their race, are important questions that require thinking about larger developments in American history over the two decades leading up to the play's production. Although set in the distant past, *Metamora* opened just as the United States was preparing to exile tens of thousands of Indians from their homes in the South to lands west of the Mississippi River. Indian removal, as this government program was called, was the latest turn in a long and violent saga of white-Indian conflict, dating back to King Philip's War and beyond. But it also marked the culmination of a more recent war, one that had ushered in a new chapter in the growth of the young republic.

The War of 1812, as Americans call it, exerted a powerful impact on the nation's economic, cultural, and political development over the next several decades. But it is not often understood how much this event had to do with white-Indian relations. Part of a broad and complex military struggle involving multiple nations and armed forces on two different continents and the high seas, the War of 1812 was in many respects an Indian war. Although the official conflict was with Great Britain, its consequences were felt most clearly, both in the short and the long term, by the native groups who lived between the Appalachian and Allegheny Mountains and the Mississippi River.

The real beginning of the War of 1812 came in 1811, when William Henry Harrison, the governor of the Indiana Territory, led a force of one thousand troops against a predominantly Shawnee Indian community located along the Tippecanoe River. The community, known as Prophetstown, had been a bastion of a resistance among the tribes of the Northwest (and an important ally of Great Britain), and Harrison's victory was celebrated in the United States as a major step in the struggle to clear the territories west of the Appalachians for white settlement. Over the next two decades following Tippecanoe, the new republic would experience a wide range of significant crises and changes, most of which related to the westward drift of the population, both free and slave, and the westward expansion of the market economy. Native Americans suffered grievously from these trends, and the fate of Indians in the eastern half of North America sparked significant debates among white Americans, shaping both national politics and popular entertainment in this period. The theatergoers who flocked to see Forrest's *Metamora* on opening night in 1829 were witnessing the unfolding of that larger dramatic story.

U.S. and Indian forces clash at Tippecanoe.

KEY QUESTIONS

- In what ways were white-Indian conflicts crucial to the War of 1812?
- What were the long-term consequences of the war for Indian life east of the Mississippi?
- How did the first U.S. party system end?
- How did westward expansion relate to developments in the history of slavery, religion, and the American economy?
- In what respects did various parts of the country become more unified or interdependent as a result of developments in slavery, religion, and the economy?
- Why did American art and literature during this period emphasize Indian subject matter?

TECUMSEH AND THE BEGINNINGS OF WAR

Indian tribes had been steadily losing territory to white settlers since the American victory in the war for independence. By 1811, it was clear that the outcome of the American Revolution had been disastrous for Indians living in the new republic. Tribes that had sided with Britain were forced to relinquish their lands after the war. But soon even native groups that had supported independence or remained neutral mourned the departure of the British. The colonists had revolted against, among other things, imperial attempts to create a buffer between Indians and the colonies. Once the war was over, the victorious Americans regarded Indian lands as conquered territory. In response, several native groups had formed an alliance to halt American settlement of the Ohio River valley, but the U.S. troops defeated them at the Battle of Fallen Timbers in 1794 and extracted major land cessions the following year in the Treaty of Greenville. Thereafter, federal agents acquired legal title to vast swathes of Indian land through dubious negotiations with individual Indians who purported to represent tribal interests. Between 1802 and 1805, William Henry Harrison signed seven such treaties, acquiring title over considerable territory in the future states of Indiana, Missouri, Wisconsin, and Illinois at a rate of two cents per acre.

In 1805, a new religious movement began to spread in the region. A Shawnee Indian named Tenskwatawa, who had struggled with alcohol addiction, received a revelation that inspired him to change his life and preach a message of spiritual renewal. Calling for a return to tribal traditions and a rejection of whiskey, imported goods, European foods, intermarriage with whites, and private property, the Shawnee Prophet, as he became known, attracted thousands of followers among the native tribes of the Northwest Territory to his base of operations in a newly established village named Prophetstown (near present-day Lafayette, Indiana). The Prophet's older brother Tecumseh, meanwhile, built a parallel political movement to end the practice of ceding land to the United States. By 1811, Tecumseh's message became a military rallying cry for Indians in different parts of the trans-Appalachian West. Meanwhile, swarms of white settlers were pouring into the region every year. A showdown was imminent.

Tecumseh, Composite Portrait by Artist and Historian Benson J. Lossing. "If it were not for the vicinity of the United States," wrote Tecumseh's adversary William Henry Harrison, "he would perhaps be the founder of an Empire that would rival in glory that of Mexico or Peru." This drawing was based on an 1808 sketch by French trader Pierre Le Dru. Lossing copied and modified the image, replacing Tecumseh's traditional dress with a British military uniform. **Question for Analysis:** Why might the artist have changed Tecumseh's clothing?

In 1809, after several Indian leaders from the Delaware, Miami, and Potawatomi tribes ceded three million acres of Indiana land (including land inhabited by the Shawnees) to Harrison at the Treaty of Fort Wayne, Tecumseh pressed Harrison to rescind the deal. Harrison refused, citing the fact that tribes spoke different languages to argue that a Shawnee Indian had no business commenting on the fairness or legitimacy of land cessions made by Miamis or Potawatomis. His diplomatic efforts rebuffed, Tecumseh devised an ambitious scheme for a confederacy that would unite not only the northwestern tribes but also those in the South. He would draw on the Shawnees' long-standing role as links between northern and southern tribes, and on his own Creek connections, to forge a coordinated military response to American encroachment (see Map 9.1). In 1811, Tecumseh headed south toward Creek country to sell his plan.

Tecumseh arrived among the Creeks at an especially portentous moment. That autumn, a brilliant comet (its tail measuring one hundred million miles long) streaked across the Alabama sky, lending force to Tecumseh's claim that his cause had the blessing of the Great Spirit. By the time Tecumseh returned north, the comet's visibility had dimmed considerably, seeming to follow the charismatic leader home. According to reports circulating among the Creeks, Tecumseh had also threatened to stamp his foot down in Michigan and level the homes of his enemies. When the first of several devastating earthquakes shook the middle of the continent that December (see States of Emergency: The New Madrid Earthquakes), Tecumseh's prophecy was frighteningly fulfilled.

PAN-INDIAN RESISTANCE

Tecumseh made the Prophet's idea of a cultural clash between Indians and whites the basis for an aggressive approach to geopolitics. He claimed that the continent's indigenous tribes shared a common identity and comprised a single political body. In this way, he hoped to avoid the question of which tribal leaders were authorized to negotiate deals with the United States. Local rivalries and intertribal disputes were irrelevant in the larger context of protecting the land. Tribal leaders did not have the authority to negotiate deals with the United States, Tecumseh and Tenskwatawa argued, without the agreement of all Indian tribes. Tecumseh, whose own ancestry was Shawnee, Creek, and white, identified not as member of a particular tribal unit but as an "Indian." "All red men," he insisted, claimed an equal right to the land.

Tenskwatawa and Tecumseh's **pan-Indian** theme was not entirely original; arguments for unity among tribes went back at least half a century (see Chapter 5). But Tecumseh was no ordinary leader. William Henry Harrison described him as "one of those uncommon geniuses, which spring up occasionally to produce revolutions and overturn the established order of things." His message also came at a crucial point in the history of the region, as the white population in the state of Ohio was suddenly more than three times the number of Indians living in the entirety of the original Northwest Territory. With both the British and the French gone from the immediate area, Indian people faced the U.S. threat with more limited options for strategic alliances.

DIVISIONS OVER THE "CIVILIZATION PROGRAM"

Tecumseh's diplomatic journey to the South also coincided with rising internal conflicts among Creeks. Ever since the Washington presidency, the federal government had been pushing a **civilization program,** designed to convert Indians to European ways of living. The program was intended to absorb natives into the new nation as equal citizens, but it also assumed that if Indians began using land differently, they might free territory for white settlement and cultivation. In the words of Benjamin Hawkins, the government official who became the chief Agent for Indian Affairs South of the Ohio in 1796,

STATES OF EMERGENCY

The New Madrid Earthquakes

Legacy of the New Madrid Earthquakes. The current configuration of eighteen-mile-long Reelfoot Lake, in Tennessee and Kentucky, is the result of sinking land and the natural damming of Reelfoot Creek by an earthquake in 1812.

Information traveled slowly in the early nineteenth century, and weeks would elapse before events in the western part of the republic became news in the nation's capital. But when a an earthquake shook the Mississippi River valley shortly after 2 a.m. on December 16, 1811, President Madison sensed the impact almost immediately. Though the epicenter was in southeastern Missouri, where sparse settlement limited the number of deaths, tremors could be felt through most of the United States and in parts of Canada and Mexico. The December catastrophe was the first of three massive earthquakes during a four-month period of seismic activity along the New Madrid (MAD-rid) fault system. The Richter scale was not devised until 1935, but retrospective estimates of the magnitude of the two largest shocks run as high as 8.1, and the area of impact was many times the size of the 1906 earthquake that leveled San Francisco. By most measures, the New Madrid earthquakes of 1811–1812 constitute the largest seismic event in U.S. history.

The immediate impact of the earthquakes was devastating. Those closest to the fault lines described scenes of terror—homes sinking into the earth, trees snapping like twigs, birds screeching deafeningly, and cattle stampeding. One resident of Little Prairie (modern-day Caruthersville, Missouri), which was utterly destroyed by a large aftershock following the first quake, watched the Mississippi River rise up "like a great loaf of bread" and spew water, sand, and black sulfur toward the sky. Ten miles away, a woman walked out to her smokehouse and water well the next morning, only to find them on the other side of the river. On the river itself, sandbars dissolved, uprooted trees accumulated, docked ships found themselves on dry land, and the mighty Mississippi flowed in reverse as powerful waves carried boats upriver. The third quake, on February 7, plunged enough marshland underwater in northwestern Tennessee to create Reelfoot Lake.

Moved by the plight of landowners in the devastated areas, Congress passed the first-ever federal disaster relief legislation in 1815. Residents could exchange their land titles for unclaimed federal land anywhere in the Missouri Territory. But news of the relief offer reached New Madrid slowly. In the meanwhile, land speculators from St. Louis (which was hooked into national communication networks) rushed out to the area to buy up destroyed lots at heavy discounts. Of the 516 exchange certificates issued by the federal government, only 20 went to people who had owned land in the New Madrid region at the time of the quakes.

On a much grander scale, the earthquakes altered the course of white-Indian (and Anglo-American) relations by lending powerful support to Tecumseh's call for Pan-Indian resistance. Traveling through areas close to the epicenter, Tecumseh offered his own compelling interpretation of the natural disaster: "The Great Spirit is angry with our enemies; he speaks, in thunder, and the earth swallows up villages and drinks up the Mississippi." Tecumseh's war against the United States appeared to have divine sanction, and many Native Americans read the events of December, January, and February as ominous rebukes of land cessions, acculturation, and American-style modernization.

White residents of the Mississippi Valley took the same hint, feeling God's anger in the temblors and seeing a call to repentance in the mud, dirt, and debris that littered the landscape. Religious revivals swept the area, and the membership of the Western Methodist Conference rose by 50 percent in a single year. Others found meaning in the fact that a city, founded by visionaries twenty-five years earlier on a promising site, had been wiped off the map. "New Madrid had been designed as the metropolis of the New World," one observer wrote, "but God sees not as man sees."

Think About It

1. How might the earthquakes at New Madrid have been a factor in causing the War of 1812?
2. What differences do you notice between the response to the earthquakes of 1811–1812 and more recent natural disasters? What social or cultural conditions might help explain those differences?

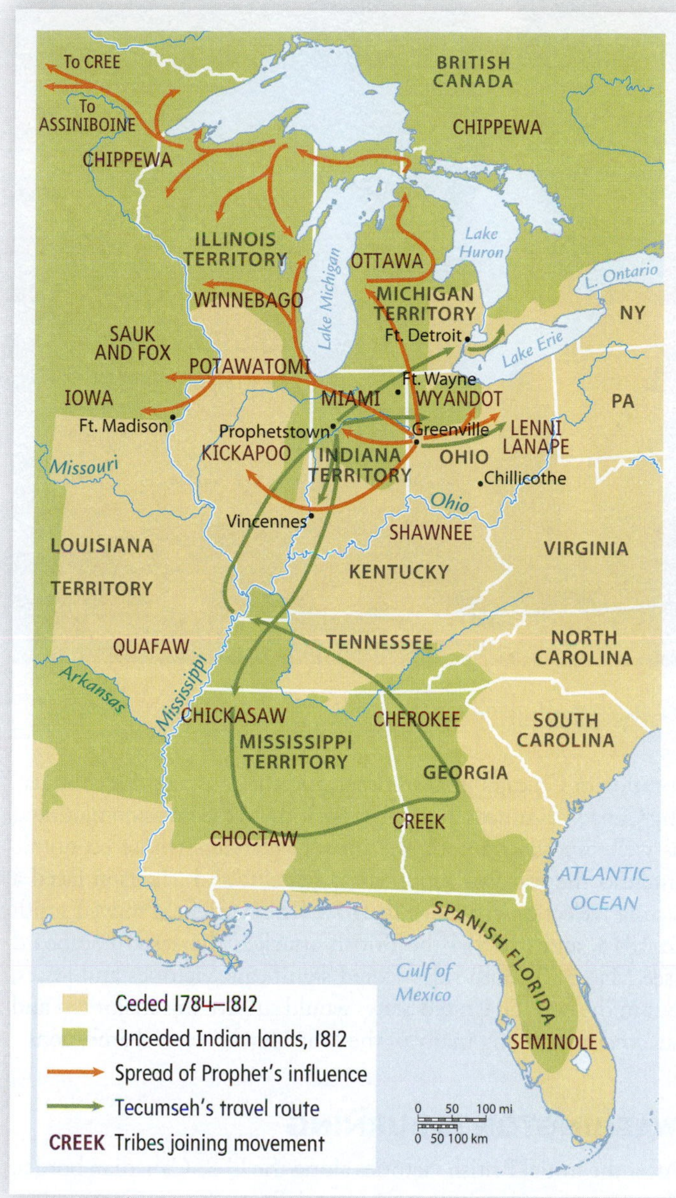

Map 9.1 Tecumseh's Diplomatic Mission. In the summer and fall of 1811, Tecumseh traveled both northwest to British Canada and south to Creek and Chickasaw country in present-day Alabama and Mississippi, traversing three thousand miles in six months.

native tribes needed to be introduced to "a new order of things." A big part of this new order was, quite literally, *things*—private property held and accumulated by individuals. But Hawkins also advocated a larger way of life involving agriculture, fences, reading and writing, European gender roles, and criminal punishments for individuals rather than groups.

As this new order made inroads among the Creeks, a mixed-blood elite prospered, accumulating considerable wealth (including slaves) and power. The disparity between rich and poor Creeks became more apparent after a series of poor harvests during the first decade of the century. Hawkins secured the loyalty of several Creek leaders and warriors through government stipends and debt relief, which further alienated poorer Creeks from Hawkins and the United States. In addition, many Creeks were upset by U.S. plans to build a federal road through their land, increasing the westward traffic of white settlers and enslaved African Americans. By 1811, a civil war was brewing within the Creek nation between supporters and opponents of the U.S. government.

U.S.-INDIAN TENSIONS EXPLODE

Tecumseh and his delegation came to Creek country bearing a pipe symbolizing warfare, but in the presence of Hawkins, Tecumseh appeared to counsel the Creeks not to accept it. A week into the visit, however, Hawkins left and Tecumseh showed his hand. At a large assembly of Creek warriors, the gifted Shawnee orator made a powerful case for Indian unity, resistance, and a return to traditional lifestyles. Many in the audience were swayed, including Hillis Hadjo (also known as Josiah Francis), who would lead the Creek resistance movement. For the most part, however, Tecumseh did not persuade the leaders of the southeastern tribes to join his military alliance.

While Tecumseh was away on his diplomatic mission, Harrison attacked Prophetstown. Tecumseh had instructed his brother to keep the peace during his absence, but the Prophet could not resist the impulse to engage U.S. forces once they encamped outside the town. Harrison's army sustained many casualties, but equipped with superior guns they withstood the raid and proceeded to burn the abandoned Indian settlement to the ground. The Battle of Tippecanoe discredited the Prophet and destroyed his base of operations, but Tecumseh, who would not learn of the fighting for several months, was preparing for a much larger war.

THE WAR HAWKS PREVAIL

Tecumseh's military strategy depended on the revival of alliances with Great Britain, which had vacated the lands east of the Mississippi but still controlled Canada. In the summer of 1812, Tecumseh traveled north to Fort Malden, just across the river from Detroit, to meet with British officials who had promised him supplies in preparation for war. Relations between Britain and the United States had deteriorated rapidly during James Madison's first term, as the Americans sought to preserve their neutrality in the Napoleonic Wars while still engaging in international commerce (see Chapter 8). The impressment of American sailors into the British Navy, which seemed to imply that Americans were still subjects of the British Empire whenever they left U.S. soil, triggered national outrage. But only in 1811, with the looming threat of Britain's support for Tecumseh, did anti-British hostility reach a breaking point. A new generation of congressmen, many of them serving their first terms as Republican representatives of southern and western constituencies, began clamoring for military action. These men, dubbed War Hawks by their opponents, included Kentuckians Henry Clay and Richard Mentor Johnson, South Carolinian John C. Calhoun, and other rising stars in the Republican Party. The War

Civilization Program. This painting shows Benjamin Hawkins instructing Creeks in farming technology.

Hawks presented war as the only honorable response to Britain's humiliating attacks on American ships and American sailors. But to its most ardent supporters, the prospect of war also represented an opportunity to expand northward into British-controlled Canada and southward into Spanish-controlled Florida, where European powers supported Indian attacks against white settlers.

With rising political pressures from within his own party and with the impressment of American sailors still fresh in popular memory, Madison sent Congress a declaration of war on June 1, 1812. A divided vote in Congress, the closest of any formal war declaration in U.S. history, reflected the crucial impetus for the War of 1812. In New England and the mid-Atlantic states, including areas that had suffered especially from Jefferson's embargo on international trade, support for the declaration was lukewarm. But among representatives from the South and the West, who were most concerned about the threat of Tecumseh's confederation, the war resolution passed with little dissent. Despite a recent lull in attacks on American ships, and despite the fact that Britain was about to suspend its blockade on ships doing business with France, the United States decided that the time was right to invade Canada.

THE WAR OF 1812: ESCAPING DISASTER

The War Hawks had predicted a quick and easy victory that would result in the annexation of Canada, but the United States was not prepared militarily for a fight with Britain and its Indian allies. The Americans suffered major defeats near the border in Detroit and at Fort Dearborn (on Lake Michigan near the future location of Chicago) that summer, and the prospects for conquering Canada dimmed. Internal opposition to the invasion mounted as well, especially among the New Englanders whose economic interests the war was supposed to benefit, and Madison faced a strong reelection challenge in 1812. The battlefield moved south in 1813, and in 1814 the British attacked the eastern seaboard (see Map 9.2). Both sides scored significant victories and losses, but in the end the United States would survive this major test and succeed in fulfilling many of the War Hawks' central ambitions.

WASHINGTON IS BURNING

After the initial British victories along the U.S.-Canadian border, American fortunes improved, especially on water. Commodore Oliver H. Perry defeated the British at Put-in-Bay on Lake Erie in September 1813. With control over the lake, U.S. forces were able to cut off the flow of supplies to British forts in Ontario. A month later, Harrison used Lake Erie to launch another invasion of Canada, defeating an Indian and British army along the Thames River. It was during this battle that Tecumseh, who had received a commission as brigadier general in the British army, was fatally shot in the chest. But soon thereafter, the U.S. army failed in an attempt to capture Montreal, while the British successfully took Fort Niagara and burned the frontier city of Buffalo. The northern front of the war had reached a stalemate.

By the middle of 1814, the situation had changed again. British victories over Napoleon in Europe had freed up more troops for a North American surge. From the beginning, antiwar critics had warned that the invasion of Canada might provoke a counterattack against American towns and cities. Those fears now materialized. In August, ten thousand British soldiers

Map 9.2 Major Offensives of the War of 1812. Both the American invasion of Canada and the British counterinvasion of the United States ultimately failed. But decisive U.S. victories against Indians in Alabama and Ohio proved crucial to the long-term consequences of the war.

moved on New York State but were thwarted in a crucial naval battle on Lake Champlain, which probably prevented a successful invasion of the Hudson River valley.

A second British invasion proved more successful. On August 24, 1814, the British sailed into the Chesapeake Bay and five thousand soldiers attacked the nation's capital. First Lady Dolley Madison famously rescued her husband's papers from the invading army, but the presidential residence, the Capitol, a major newspaper office, and a federal arsenal were set ablaze. After sacking Washington, the British proceeded toward Baltimore, the third-largest U.S. city. In a battle memorialized in a poem that would later become the national anthem (see Interpreting the Sources: "The Defence of Fort McHenry"), the Americans succeeded in holding a key fort and the British withdrew, their main mission unaccomplished. The British were joined by more than two thousand enslaved African Americans, who took advantage of the invasion to escape to freedom.

THE HARTFORD CONVENTION

As British forces drove into the heart of the country, antiwar sentiment intensified in the North. Connecticut and Massachusetts protested by withdrawing their militias from federal service, while Federalist leaders throughout New England began organizing a political assault against Madison and the Republicans. At a secret Federalist meeting in December 1814,

***The Taking of the City of Washington in America,* 1814.** Disaster strikes the capital in this contemporary depiction of the British attack on Washington, probably the low point in the American war effort. The burning of the public buildings in the capital was intended in part as retaliation for events in York, Ontario, where U.S. forces had set fire to the provincial Parliament.

known as the Hartford Convention, delegates considered a call for New England to secede from the union, but that motion failed. Instead, they passed resolutions to scrap the three-fifths rule, limit presidents to a single term, bar the election of consecutive presidents from a single state, and require a two-thirds majority in Congress in order to declare war. Such constitutional amendments, Federalists figured, would break the Virginia monopoly on the executive branch, reduce the power of the Republicans, and prevent the South and West from dragging the country into another disastrous expansionist war. While the delegation met in December, they elected not to publicize the platform until January—an unfortunate decision that would prove fatal for the party's prospects.

THE SOUTHERN FRONT

The one region where the Americans clearly prevailed was in the South. The social conflict that had been brewing within the Creek nation intensified after Tecumseh's dramatic visit in 1811. Dissidents known as the Redsticks (after the red clubs they wielded), who had been inspired by Tecumseh's call for resisting white culture and U.S. authority, clashed with the forces of the Creek national council and attacked symbols of the new order—wealth, cattle, cotton, and mixed-race families. They also attacked whites, leading settlers to call for the "dismemberment" and "extermination" of the Creek nation. After a devastating attack by the Redsticks against Fort Mims in 1813, Creeks friendly to Hawkins called for U.S. military intervention. Tennessee general Andrew Jackson rose to national prominence by leading an army of white settlers, Cherokees, and Creeks against the Redsticks, in what is often called the Creek War but was part of the larger War of 1812. Jackson's invasion of Creek country (in present-day Alabama and Georgia) was a major theater of operation in the conflict between the United States and a British-Indian alliance committed to thwarting American expansion.

Jackson suffered numerous personal, political, and military setbacks over ten months of fighting in Creek country. But in one of the bloodiest battles in American-Indian history, he defeated the Redsticks at Horseshoe Bend in March 1814. With the reluctant approval of the federal government, Jackson began dictating peace terms and redistributing Creek land, including that of the Creeks who had sided with him. Jackson forced his Creek allies to cede twenty-three million acres of land, which would become the heart of the Cotton Belt. The Creeks were driven into the northeastern corner of Alabama.

Jackson turned his attention next to Spanish Florida, where British forces had staged the third prong of their invasion (Spain was an ally of Britain in its war against Napoleon). After

INTERPRETING THE SOURCES

"The Defence of Fort McHenry" ("The Star-Spangled Banner")

Shortly after the attack on Washington, Francis Scott Key, a Federalist lawyer from Maryland, was sent to a British ship in the Chesapeake Bay to negotiate the release of a captured American physician. Detained on the ship while the British bombarded Fort McHenry, Key spent the night watching the intense battle. The following morning, when he saw the U.S. flag still flying over the fort, he drafted a poem on the back of a letter. Sold as a celebratory handbill under the title "The Defence of Fort McHenry," Key's poem circulated on the streets of Baltimore and was then set to the tune of a popular British drinking song with a daunting range of one-and-a-half octaves and performed by local actors in taverns. "The Star-Spangled Banner," as it came to be known, was among the handful of most popular patriotic songs in nineteenth-century America, but it did not become the official national anthem of the United States until 1931, well after it had become a fixture at the World Series and other notable baseball games.

A Morning View of the Shelling of Fort McHenry. The thrilling spectacle of this British attack on U.S. soil, with rockets glaring and bombs bursting, has become enshrined by the national anthem as a symbol of American patriotism.

The original poem contained four stanzas, only the first of which is widely performed. In the first stanza, the poet describes the experience of watching the bombardment from the ship and searching the next morning for a sign that the Americans have not surrendered, that the U.S. flag is still waving. The second stanza answers the question—the flag is dimly seen and then comes into clear view—and offers an evocative description of the flying flag as a symbol of the survival of the fort and the resilience of the new nation. The third stanza denigrates the British invaders for polluting American soil and alludes with scorn to the mercenaries ("hirelings") and slaves in their forces. In the final stanza, Key cites the motto "In God is our trust," an early version of the phrase that would become the nation's official motto only in 1956.

Oh, say can you see by the dawn's early light
What so proudly we hailed at the twilight's last gleaming?
Whose broad stripes and bright stars thru the perilous fight,
O'er the ramparts we watched were so gallantly streaming?
And the rocket's red glare, the bombs bursting in air,
Gave proof through the night that our flag was still there.
Oh, say does that star-spangled banner yet wave
O'er the land of the free and the home of the brave?
On the shore, dimly seen through the mists of the deep,
Where the foe's haughty host in dread silence reposes,
What is that which the breeze, o'er the towering steep,
As it fitfully blows, half conceals, half discloses?
Now it catches the gleam of the morning's first beam,
In full glory reflected now shines in the stream:
'Tis the star-spangled banner! Oh long may it wave
O'er the land of the free and the home of the brave!
And where is that band who so vauntingly swore
That the havoc of war and the battle's confusion,
A home and a country should leave us no more!
Their blood has washed out their foul footsteps' pollution.
No refuge could save the hireling and slave
From the terror of flight, or the gloom of the grave:
And the star-spangled banner in triumph doth wave
O'er the land of the free and the home of the brave!
Oh! thus be it ever, when freemen shall stand
Between their loved home and the war's desolation!
Blest with victory and peace, may the heav'n rescued land
Praise the Power that hath made and preserved us a nation.
Then conquer we must, when our cause it is just,
And this be our motto: "In God is our trust."
And the star-spangled banner in triumph shall wave
O'er the land of the free and the home of the brave!

Explore the Source

1. Are there any words in the poem that provide clues to what Key might have believed to be the purpose of this second war with Britain?
2. If the Americans are defending Fort McHenry against British shelling, why does Key say, in the final stanza, "Then conquer we must, when our cause it is just?"
3. Why do you think that the first stanza is the only one that is widely known and sung?

The Hartford Convention in Political Caricature. This cartoon mocks the New England delegates gathering in Hartford as both eager to please the British and afraid to act. In the right corner sits King George III, encouraging the New England secession with promises of "plenty molasses and Codfish; plenty of goods to Smuggle; Honours, titles and Nobility into the bargain."

landing in May 1814, the British joined forces with the Seminole tribe, which had been helping the Spanish repel American forays across the Florida-Georgia border since the beginning of the war. Once again, the conflict between the United States and a neighboring European colonial power merged with a conflict between white American settlers and Indians. In the Spanish colony of East Florida, the clash also pitted slaveholders in Georgia against fugitive slaves living among the Seminoles. As increasing numbers of enslaved African Americans fled across the border, the Seminoles became a mixed-race tribe and their settlements became centers of black-Indian alliance.

Although the British never got very far in their plan to arm and train Seminoles for an invasion of the United States, they built a fort along the Apalachicola River, sixty miles south of the U.S. border. After the war, the Negro Fort, as it came to be known, provided refuge for anxious Seminoles fearing another U.S. invasion, for defeated Redsticks fleeing Creek country, and for runaway slaves from Georgia and Alabama. But in the shorter term, Britain failed to capitalize on its Seminole alliance. In November 1814, Jackson attacked Pensacola, the capital of the separate colony of West Florida, and drove the British from the city.

WAR'S END: THE TREATY OF GHENT AND THE BATTLE OF NEW ORLEANS

By fall 1814, British authorities were looking to make peace. They had managed to repel the U.S. invasion of Canada and humiliated the young republic by burning its new capital. But they had been less successful at defending their Indian allies in the Northwest, and that alliance had proved helpless in resisting the westward incursions of Americans in the South. Eager to bring to an end a long war, Britain entered into talks with the Americans in Ghent, Belgium; no Indian representatives were invited to the negotiations. Britain agreed to return the forts it had seized during the war and to retain the original borders of the United States. In a treaty signed on December 24, both sides effectively abandoned the demands that had brought them into conflict in the first place. Most significant, Britain dropped its insistence on a buffer zone under Indian sovereignty between Canada and the United States, while the United States agreed to recognize all Indian rights and territorial claims from before the war. Had this latter provision been enforced, the Creek land cessions would have been invalidated. Instead, the Treaty of Ghent would mark the end of British interference in U.S.-Indian relations.

Although the war ended officially in Belgium in December, news of the treaty did not reach the U.S. capital until February 13. It would take even longer to reach the Gulf of Mexico, which had become the main stage of the war. After withdrawing from Pensacola, British ships had moved toward New Orleans. There, on New Year's Day, 1815, they shelled the city, but decided to wait a week before launching a ground invasion. Jackson was waiting for them with a motley force that included African Americans, Haitian immigrants, Irish immigrants, Choctaw Indians, French-speaking Louisiana militiamen, volunteers from Jackson's home state of Tennessee, and a band of pirates hostile to the British Royal Navy. The invading army outnumbered Jackson's men by two to one, but due to the superiority of the American guns and some key tactical errors by the British, the attack failed and the British soldiers were massacred. The remaining British forces sailed northeast and on February 11 captured the American fort defending the city of Mobile, but soon thereafter news of the peace treaty arrived.

The Battle of New Orleans did not affect the war's outcome, at least not in the conventional sense of shaping the agreement that formally ended the conflict, which after all had been signed two weeks before the fighting took place. But the battle had important consequences nonetheless. To begin with, the outcome of the war was not determined solely by what was signed at Ghent. Of equal importance was how the British, Indians, and Spanish would approach the military power of the United States in the coming years. From that perspective, the Americans' stunning victory in New Orleans made a statement that Indians in the Southwest were especially likely to notice. Furthermore, because news of Jackson's triumph reached Washington and other eastern cities before anyone in the United States knew about the treaty, the impact of the battle on American perceptions of the war was great. Rather than responding to an inconclusive treaty that cast doubt on why the country had declared war in the first place, Americans reacted first to accounts of Jackson's heroics, and that had important political ramifications. By turning the war into an occasion for patriotic celebration, New Orleans made the Federalist convention at Hartford seem like a gathering of traitors. The Federalists would not survive the blow. At the same time, a new national hero was born in Andrew Jackson.

Negro Fort. For two years, a British-built fort in Spanish Florida stood as a bastion of resistance to southern slavery, U.S. expansion, and the new order being imposed on Native Americans. Andrew Jackson ordered the fort blown up in 1816, killing 270 people. The invaders captured, tortured, and executed leaders of the fort community and sold sixty of the survivors as slaves in the United States. Jackson decided to have the fort rebuilt two years later (when Florida was still part of Spain) and renamed it Fort Gadsden.

Madison was succeeded in 1817 by fellow Virginian James Monroe, who routed his Federalist opponent in the 1816 presidential election by an electoral margin of 183 to 34. The Federalists had been damaged by the successful resolution of a war they had opposed and were then preempted by the Republican embrace of economic policies they had favored. Monroe's landslide victory confirmed the demise of the Federalists as a national party. As the incoming president embarked on a national victory tour, many observers looked toward a period of reconciliation. A Boston newspaper spoke of a new "era of good feelings," a phrase historians have used to denote the period of Monroe's presidency. But the decline of the first two-party system of Federalists and Republicans did not put an end to factional divisions in American politics, nor did it ease tensions between different sections of the country. It simply meant that the most intense political battles at the national level took place within Jefferson's old Republican Party.

The period after the war was defined less by good political feelings than by a series of efforts to expand or shore up the borders of the country and consolidate U.S. control over all of the land east of the Mississippi. With Great Britain no longer supporting Indian resistance, a weakened Spanish empire beginning to fall throughout the Americas, and an aggressive U.S. general riding a wave of national popularity, the Monroe years would mark a pivotal chapter in the history of American expansion.

EXPANSION IN JAMES MONROE'S AMERICA

Having endured a long war and survived a foreign invasion, the Republican leadership exhibited a new spirit of both optimism and urgency about the role of the central government. Though the war had succeeded in clearing major obstacles to westward expansion, it had also exposed the weakness of the U.S. military, the risks of economic dependence on Europe, and the fragility of the nation's communication infrastructure. Republican War Hawks now took the lead in arguing for a nationalist program of expanded government activity, including defense spending, protective tariffs, internal transportation improvements, and a national bank—all measures Republicans had generally opposed before the war.

INVASION OF FLORIDA AND THE EUROPEAN POWERS' WITHDRAWAL

Despite the Treaty of Ghent, the boundaries of the United States remained blurry and contested at the beginning of Monroe's first term. Monroe initiated talks with the British, who were still America's northern neighbors. In the Rush-Bagot Treaty of 1817, both sides committed to disarmament in the Great Lakes. The agreement, which was the first bilateral naval disarmament in the history of international relations, lasted until World War II, when Canada and the United States suspended the treaty to allow naval training. A separate convention the following year set the northern boundary of the Louisiana Purchase at the forty-ninth parallel (which currently divides the United States and Canada from the Minnesota/Manitoba border westward) and established joint British-American occupation of the Oregon Territory. Both of these diplomatic coups were the handiwork of Monroe's secretary of state, John Quincy Adams, who had also led the negotiating team at Ghent.

Facing south, the United States encountered a more difficult situation. The Spanish colonies of East and West Florida bordered the Gulf of Mexico all the way to the Mississippi River, blocking southern American farmers' and merchants' access to Gulf seaports. Equally important, Florida was a refuge for escaped slaves and dispossessed Indians from Georgia and Alabama. Although the destruction of the Negro Fort during the war had landed a severe blow to a stronghold of anti-U.S. militancy, Spanish Florida continued to undermine the security of white settlements and slaveholders' property in the United States.

From the beginning of the nineteenth century, U.S. presidents had sought to acquire Florida, both through diplomacy and by encouraging armed forays and rebellions. But none of these efforts succeeded in wresting Florida from Spain. An exchange of violent attacks between Seminoles and white settlers along the border in 1817 offered the Monroe administration a new opportunity. Andrew Jackson was summoned from Tennessee to lead a force into Florida to attack the Seminoles, but he was ordered not to attack any Spanish forts. Jackson had other ideas. Believing that the colony of East Florida should be ceded to the United States as reparations for the property losses of Americans, Jackson assembled a large army. Crossing into Florida, they killed Indians wherever they found them, including the Creek resistance leader Hillis Hadjo, who was tricked into boarding a U.S. riverboat that was flying the British flag. Then Jackson, either misconstruing or ignoring his orders, moved toward the West Florida capital of Pensacola, alerting its residents that he would "put to death every man found in arms." The Spanish evacuated Pensacola and surrendered in a nearby fort. Jackson announced that he would occupy Florida until the Spanish proved that they could police the border.

Jackson's invasion of Spanish Florida, often called the First Seminole War, became a major international incident and a significant political crisis for Monroe, who needed to assert civilian authority over a popular military hero. Monroe called for the restoration of Spanish authority, but refused to discipline Jackson. Meanwhile, Secretary of State Adams adroitly pressed the Spaniards on the point that they were in no position to defend Florida, much less police its borders. After some negotiations, Spain and the United States signed the Transcontinental Treaty of 1819 (Adams-Onis Treaty), under which Spain not only ceded Florida, but also recognized the Louisiana Purchase and agreed to a boundary between Mexico (a Spanish colony that had been waging rebellion since 1810) and Oregon that would give the United States uncontested access to the Pacific Ocean (see Map 9.4). In return, the United States agreed to pay $5 million in private claims against the Spanish government and conceded that the Louisiana Purchase did not include disputed territory in what is now eastern Texas. Florida was now American territory, and another European power and Indian ally had left the eastern half of the continent.

LATIN AMERICAN INDEPENDENCE AND THE MONROE DOCTRINE

The Florida colonies were not the only ones slipping away from Spain. Independence movements had been gaining momentum in Central and South America since the Napoleonic Wars. Spanish rule had effectively ended in the southern cone of South America by 1818, and colonial authority was teetering both on the northern mainland and in Mexico. In 1822 the United States became the first outside power to establish diplomatic relations with the independent nation of Gran Colombia (comprising Panama, Ecuador, Venezuela, and Colombia). Immediately after, the United States recognized its new neighbor, Mexico. The vast Spanish Empire in the Americas had been reduced to a couple of island colonies.

In 1823, however, Monroe heard rumors that a coalition of conservative European forces led by the Russian tsar was poised to help Spain reconquer its lost American possessions. Facing this unsavory prospect, along with the threat of Russian expansion along the Pacific coast, Adams advised Monroe to introduce a new principle of foreign policy in his annual message to Congress. The Monroe Doctrine held that the United States would not tolerate European interference with the sovereignty of nations in the Americas. The New World was now politically distinct from the Old World, Monroe announced, and "the American continents are henceforth not to be considered as subjects for future colonization by any European powers." In return, America pledged not to intervene in Europe's internal political struggles or in the affairs of existing European colonies (such as Canada, Cuba, and Puerto Rico). The Monroe Doctrine, which would have other important implications for U.S. foreign relations in later periods, was Adams's brainchild (though he did not take public credit for it until the 1840s) and marked the culmination of a ten-year diplomatic campaign to secure the larger objectives of the War of 1812. The doctrine was meant not only to warn the Spanish, French, and Russians against recolonizing Latin America; it was also designed to remove European nations forever as obstacles to America's westward expansion across the continent. Europeans were put on notice not to ally with the Indians who stood in the way.

INTERNAL IMPROVEMENTS, ECONOMIC GROWTH, AND FINANCIAL PANIC

Already in Madison's last years in office (1816–1818), the Republicans had committed themselves to a nationalist program of active government and supported many of the policies previously associated with their political opponents. Even the aging Jefferson (no longer serving in government, but following public life closely from the sidelines) seemed to shed some of his anxiety about commerce, industry, and big government. In 1816 the Republican-dominated Congress enacted a tariff to protect U.S. manufacturers against competition from foreign goods and authorized the creation of a second National Bank. Congress also appropriated $100,000 to extend a national road that would link the eastern seaboard with the Mississippi River (see Map 9.3). The

National Road (also called the Cumberland Road) connected the nation's eastern waterways to those west of the Appalachians and began a period of intense road building and canal construction in the United States (see Chapter 10).

All of these measures reflected Republican optimism about American westward expansion and the party's new vision of the nation as economically interdependent. Farmers and manufacturers, easterners and westerners, lenders and borrowers would all benefit, according to this new platform, from a sound money supply, a diversified economy, and from what were called **internal improvements**—government investments in the improvement of transportation. Kentuckian Henry Clay dubbed this program "the American System" and hitched his personal political fortunes to the promise of economic nationalism, but many of the other original War Hawks shared his perspective. John C. Calhoun, who would later be associated with sectional conflict and the regional interests of the South, was at this time a major proponent of a unified, interdependent nation able to overcome the divisions of distance. "Let us, then, bind the republic together with a perfect system of roads and canals," he proclaimed. "Let us conquer space."

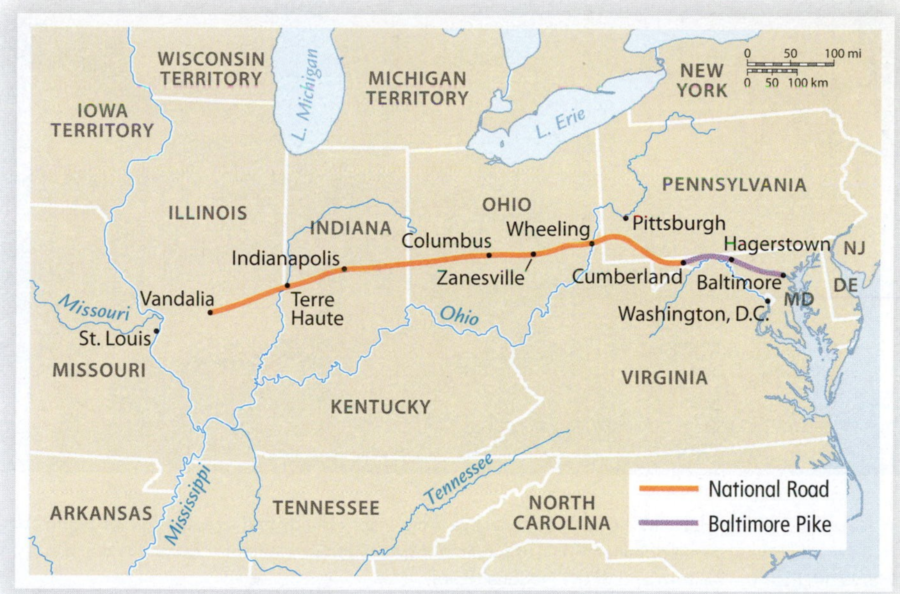

Map 9.3 The National Road. Envisioned by Jefferson after the 1803 Louisiana Purchase as a continuous "line of communication" between the national capital and the city of St. Louis (newly added to the United States), the National Road was surveyed in 1811. By 1818 it had reached Wheeling, Virginia (now West Virginia), on the Ohio River. Because the bulk of the road west of the Ohio River was in the free states of the North, those states drew more migrants, visitors, and trade, though the southern city of Baltimore was also a major beneficiary.

Most of the projects that Clay, Calhoun, and other nationalists envisioned were vetoed by Madison, who harbored doubts as to whether the Constitution authorized building canals and roads. His successor Monroe expressed similar concerns, and the Era of Good Feelings was marked by a conflict between supporters of federal subsidies for transportation and those who worried about either their constitutionality or their costs. But both sides seemed to acknowledge the importance of long-distance transportation to economic growth.

The dangers of economic growth and economic interdependence soon became apparent when a major depression struck the country, the first of several that would recur roughly every two decades over the course of the nineteenth century. Numerous factors contributed to the Panic of 1819, including a rise in foreign imports after the war, rampant land speculation, and a rapid increase in the money supply. Banks and bank notes played an especially dramatic role in the financial chaos of the postwar period. Congress had let the charter of Hamilton's Bank of the United States expire in 1811, ushering in a period of uncontrolled growth in the banking industry. The number of state-chartered banks in the United States more than doubled during the war, and the new banks, mostly in the South and West, printed unprecedented volumes of bank notes without having to worry that a central bank would demand that they be redeemed in specie. After the national capital was captured by Britain in 1814, many of those southern and western banks simply stopped paying specie altogether. In some cases, bank notes from west of the Appalachians had to be discounted by 50 percent for anyone to accept them.

After the war, the Republicans chartered the Second Bank of the United States to stabilize the money supply, but the new central bank was initially reluctant to press other banks to redeem their notes. Instead, the national bank issued large volumes of its own notes, funding loans for land purchases in areas like Alabama that had been conquered by the United States during the war. Steadily, the bank's capital was shifting westward and southward, as branches in the Northeast paid specie to redeem notes printed by the bank's other, more adventurous branches. A new director took the bank's reins in 1819, and exerted much tighter control of the money supply. Meanwhile, the value of American agricultural goods had begun to plummet on foreign markets, as Europe recovered from the Napoleonic Wars and a series of bad harvests. Cotton prices, which had driven the land speculation in Alabama, fell in 1819 to less than half of their 1817 high. When the Bank of the United States started calling in loans and forcing state-chartered banks to do the same, farmers defaulted, land prices dropped, businesses failed, urban artisans lost their jobs, and an epidemic of foreclosure and bankruptcy swept the nation. As one writer in a North Carolina newspaper described it, a "deeper gloom hangs over us than ever was witnessed by the oldest man." Some faulted the bank, others complained of the inadequacy of the tariff protection, others blamed American women and their fondness for luxury goods. Many farmers and artisans grew generally suspicious of the paper economy and the banks that appeared to create and nullify value arbitrarily. Interestingly, no one really blamed the Monroe administration, which was reelected with all but one electoral vote in 1820.

A Republic of Roads. In the early national era, Americans already had a reputation for being constantly on the move. All of this fabled mobility required roads. Road building has been a dominant form of public transportation investment throughout U.S. history. This watercolor depicts the hubbub outside a rural tavern in Maryland, near the eastern end of the National Road.

MISSOURI AND THE NEW GEOGRAPHY OF SLAVERY

As the national economy suffered its first major depression, the political risks of westward expansion became clearer. For two reasons, 1819 marked an important turning point in the political controversy over slavery. First, the land ceded or surrendered by the Creeks, Choctaws, Seminoles, and Spanish during the second decade of the century included millions of acres that were especially suitable for cultivating cotton—and large-scale cotton producers relied on slave labor. With the African slave trade now illegal, the South's slaves became even more valuable as commodities. In the rich soil wrested from Indian control, slaveholders would find new markets for these commodities. Second, with the Indian threat diminished and European powers removed, the Missouri Territory population (which included ten thousand slaves by 1820) grew to the point where it was eligible for statehood. As the Congress of 1817 deliberated over whether to authorize Missourians to draft a constitution and begin the statehood process, slavery was the dominant subject.

Representative James Tallmadge from New York proposed a provision to make Missouri a free state. Specifically, the Tallmadge Amendment prohibited "the introduction of slavery or involuntary servitude . . . except for the punishment of crimes" and stipulated that anyone born a slave in the new state would become free at age twenty-five. With every representative from the South voting against, the amendment still passed the House 78 to 76, but the Senate rejected it and Congress ended its year with the status of Missouri uncertain.

The stalemate over Missouri marked the rekindling of a fight over the balance of power between free and slave states that had flickered during the constitutional convention. Tallmadge offered his amendment to block what he called "the disproportionate power of the slave states." Southerners in turn voted unanimously against the amendment because they too saw this as a showdown over sectional power. If Congress could restrict slavery in Missouri, it could do the same in every new state that would be carved out of the Louisiana Purchase and thereby limit the value of slave property throughout the country. Perhaps more important, a free Missouri might put the entire institution of slavery in political jeopardy. Because each state received two Senate seats no matter the size of its population, maintaining the same number of free and slave states assured the South that Congress would never abolish slavery. Counting Alabama, which was about to enter as a slave state, the union in 1820 consisted of eleven states where slavery was legal and eleven where it had been either outlawed or gradually abolished. Missouri's status would tilt the balance.

When Congress reconvened in 1820, Senator Jesse Thomas, a southern slaveholder now representing the free state of Illinois, suggested a compromise. Missouri would be allowed to enter as a slave state, but would be counterbalanced by the admission of the northeastern (noncontiguous) portion of Massachusetts as the new free state of Maine. More important, Thomas proposed that Missouri be the only part of the Louisiana Purchase north of the 36°30′ latitude where slavery would be permitted (see Map 9.4). The two components of the Missouri Compromise were quite different. The first preserved the balance of power in the Senate through a policy of admitting new states in pairs. But by outlawing slavery in most of the Louisiana Purchase, the second agreement raised the specter of more free states entering the union. This second provision of the compromise made the future status of slavery contingent on geography, rather than political balance in the Senate. By a three-vote margin in the House, this important compromise squeaked through.

In retrospect, the congressional debates over Missouri and the compromise that emerged foretold the growing rift between

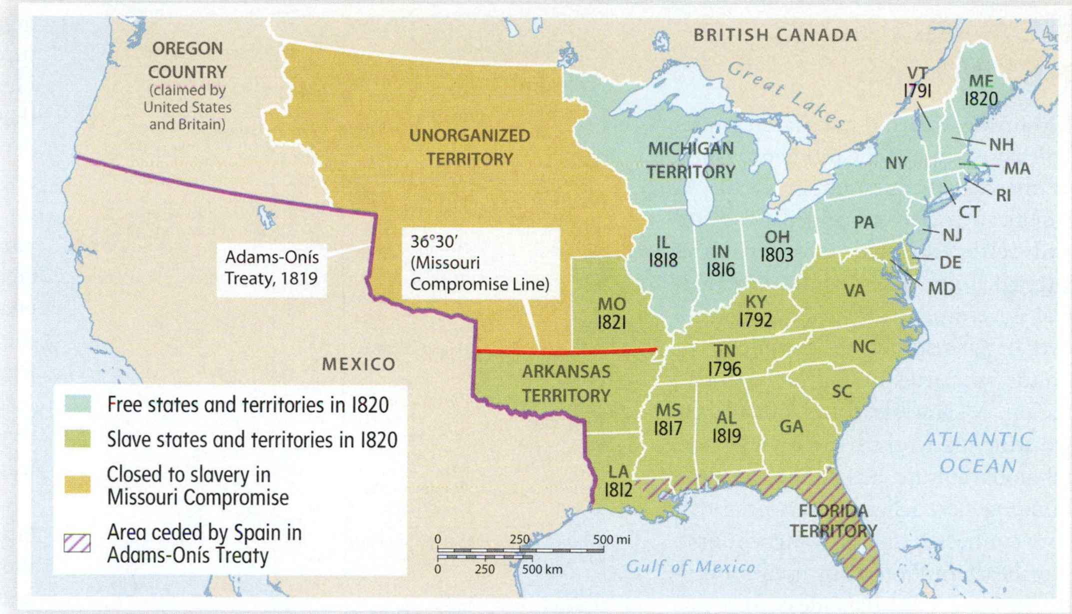

Map 9.4 The Missouri Compromise. The compromise, intended to preserve political balance between slave and free states, presumed that slavery would continue to thrive only below a certain latitude.

North and South. To some observers, those implications seemed clear at the time. Thomas Jefferson likened the debates to "a fire bell in the night" which "awakened and filled me with terror." The geographical boundary recognized by Congress would only harden the moral divide of the slavery question, Jefferson noted, and the union would be doomed. (As Jefferson saw it, the only remaining solution was to deport close to one million slaves.) Secretary of State John Quincy Adams, viewing the debate from the northern side, also saw great portent, and fantasized privately about a violent showdown over the question of slavery.

The Missouri Compromise was an exercise in moral mapmaking, an attempt to preserve a republic, half based on slave labor and half based on free labor, by treating those halves as geographically distinct. Over the next few decades, many forces would threaten that moral map by increasing the flow of goods, persons, and information across this congressionally sanctioned divide between North and South. Even the congressional debate itself seemed to demonstrate how difficult it would be for advocates of the two labor systems to sequester themselves in separate parts of the country.

In the eyes of some southerners, debates over slavery threatened their security by encouraging slave rebellions. Just two years after the Missouri Compromise, those fears were stoked by news of a major plot by slaves and free blacks to set fire to Charleston, South Carolina. The plot was pinned on a man named Denmark Vesey, who had been born a slave in the Caribbean and brought to South Carolina as a boy. Vesey, a skilled carpenter and a self-educated man, managed to purchase his freedom after winning a $1,500 lottery prize in 1800 and rose to a position of influence within Charleston's black community (see How Much Is That?). He had been inspired by events in Haiti and reportedly kept abreast of the congressional deliberations in 1819 and 1820. In 1822, Vesey was arrested along with 130 other black men for planning what would have been the largest peacetime slave rebellion in American history. Using church meetings as a forum for gathering supporters, Vesey had apparently designed the destruction of Charleston, the massacre of its white inhabitants, the pillaging of its arsenal, and a mass exodus of African Americans to Haiti. But the plan was betrayed to the authorities, who convicted Vesey and thirty-four coconspirators in a secret trial and had them hanged. It still stands as the largest number of executions carried out by order of a civilian court in U.S. history.

But in an interesting wrinkle to this remarkable story, historians have now begun to question whether the Denmark Vesey slave conspiracy actually took place. A good deal of evidence supports the theory that the conspiracy was nothing more than a paranoid fantasy on the part of the white authorities, who coerced the confessions that form the basis for the story. We may never know whether Vesey and his codefendants planned an armed rebellion, or whether their conviction says more about the mentality of whites than that of blacks in South Carolina. In either case, the irregular trials and coercive interrogations suggest a moment of panic and hysteria in a slaveholding culture. Even if Vesey and company had been guilty of the alleged plot, the response reflected a heightened security consciousness among southern whites, whose slave system was becoming more economically entrenched and more politically vulnerable (see Chapter 11).

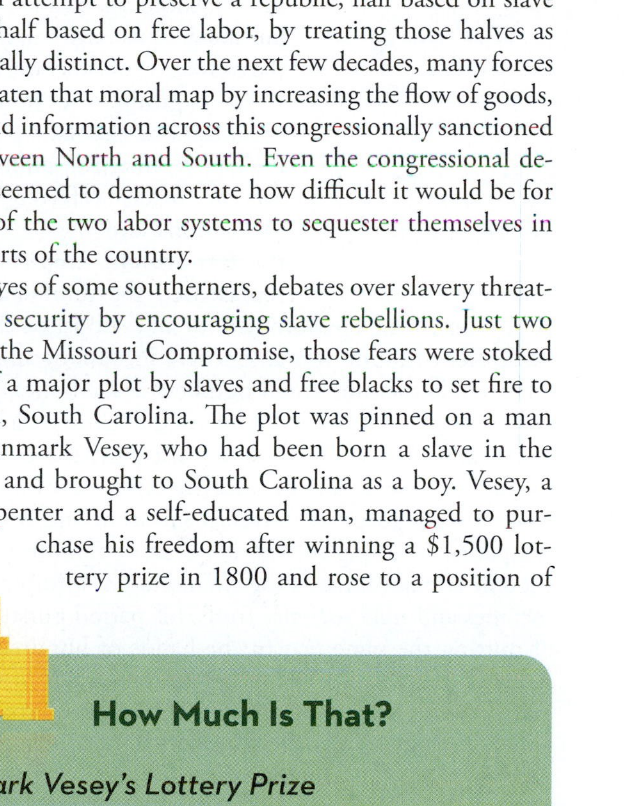

How Much Is That?

Denmark Vesey's Lottery Prize

Adjusted for inflation, the prize would have the buying power of almost $28,000 in 2013—not exactly a jackpot but almost enough to buy a new car or a semester of tuition, room, and board at a private university.

NEW RELIGIOUS NETWORKS

Most Americans did not share Thomas Jefferson's sense of the momentousness of the slavery question in 1820. As American society expanded westward and settlers poured into territories wrested from Indian control, the federal government consolidated control over new territories and designed economic infrastructure for the expanded nation. Meanwhile, forces outside the government worked to create a new religious culture across the country, building new religious networks that also connected the growing country. Northeastern Protestants used print to disseminate Christian ideas to a dispersed populace, while evangelical preachers traversed the countryside, recruiting members to their growing denominations. Church membership doubled across the nation between 1800 and 1820, printed bibles became standard fixtures in American homes, and a new spirit of religious enthusiasm took root in the South and the frontier, especially in areas cleared for white settlement by the war. These developments also presented new opportunities for women to participate in public life at a time when men dominated electoral politics and long-distance commerce.

CLASS No. 1.

Comprises those prisoners who were found guilty and executed.

Prisoners Names.	*Owners' Names.*	*Time of Commit.*	*How Disposed of.*
Peter	James Poyas	June 18	
Ned	Gov. T. Bennett,	do.	Hanged on Tuesday
Rolla	do.	do	the 2d July, 1822,
Batteau	do.	do.	on Blake's lands,
Denmark Vesey	A free black man	22	near Charleston.
Jessy	Thos. Blackwood	23	
John	Elias Horry	July 5	Do. on the Lines near
Gullah Jack	Paul Pritchard	do.	Ch.; Friday July 12.
Mingo	Wm. Harth	June 21	
Lot	Forrester	27	
Joe	P. L. Jore	July 6	
Julius	Thos. Forrest	8	
Tom	Mrs. Russell	10	
Smart	Robt. Anderson	do.	
John	John Robertson	11	
Robert	do.	do.	
Adam	do.	do.	
Polydore	Mrs. Faber	do.	Hanged on the Lines
Bacchus	Benj. Hammet	do.	near Charleston,
Dick	Wm. Sims	13	on Friday, 26th
Pharaoh	— Thompson	do.	July.
Jemmy	Mrs. Clement	18	
Mauidore	Mordecai Cohen	19	
Dean	— Mitchell	do.	
Jack	Mrs. Purcell	12	
Bellisle	Est. of Jos. Yates	18	
Naphur	do.	do.	
Adam	do.	do.	
Jacob	John S. Glen	16	
Charles	John Billings	18	
Jack	N. McNeill	22	
Cæsar	Miss Smith	do.	
Jacob Stagg	Jacob Lankester	23	Do. Tues. July 30.
Tom	Wm. M. Scott	24	
William	Mrs. Garner	Aug. 2	Do. Friday, Aug. 9.

Slave Rebellion Panic. In 1822, Mayor James Hamilton published *Negro Plot: An Account of the Late Intended Insurrection among a Portion of the Blacks of the City of Charleston, South Carolina*. The table documents the thirty-five hangings of sixty-seven convicted. An act of violence that never took place, Vesey's rebellion haunted the imagination of whites in South Carolina and throughout the South. In February 2012, the South Carolina General Assembly passed Senate Resolution S.1214 "to recognize and honor the legacy of Denmark Vesey."

THE BENEVOLENT EMPIRE

By 1815, northeastern elites had lost their political foothold. Many former Federalists, facing the prospects of being shut out of national politics, turned to other strategies for influencing the republic and rescuing it from what they saw as the dangers of revolution. They pinned their hopes on religious institutions. Unlike most European countries at the time, the United States had no official government-sponsored religion. The Bill of Rights had prohibited Congress from establishing a national church, and once Republicans gained power in New England after the War of 1812, the official state churches in that region began to fall as well. By 1818, only one state (Massachusetts) still had an established church. The disestablishment and deregulation of churches created an open market in which a growing range of denominations, sects, and movements competed for souls and membership.

Without a central religious organization supported by public funds, a coterie of charitable societies and nongovernmental organizations emerged in the 1810s to support religion on a national scale. Headquartered in northern cities, these organizations tended to be multidenominational and controlled by laypeople rather than clergy. They focused on goals that were shared widely among Protestant churches, such as increasing biblical literacy, relieving poverty, supporting orphans, spreading the gospel across the globe, and suppressing prostitution. Some of the most important organizations founded during this decade included the American Bible Society (see Hot Commodities: Cheap Printed Bibles), the Sunday and Adult School Union (later the American Missionary Fellowship), and the American Board of Commissioners for Foreign Missions (ABCFM). As its name implied, the ABCFM sponsored missions to distant locations, including the Hawaiian Islands (laying foundations for the eventual American colonization of Hawaii), but much of its early emphasis was on the conversion of American Indians.

As a group, the new religious organizations exerted significant influence in American public life. Observers often referred to these institutions and their leadership as the **Benevolent Empire,** and they represented the unofficial religious establishment in a nation without an established church. The Benevolent Empire was an entirely Protestant affair and did not include the substantial numbers of Catholics, Jews, Unitarians, or freethinkers living in the United States in the 1810s and 1820s. But for the most part, the establishment downplayed sectarian debates in favor of campaigns that spoke the language of universal salvation and humanitarian sympathy. In doing so, the Benevolent Empire managed to become a major force in the circulation of information. Bible societies and tract societies from this period pursued the goal of putting the same text in the hands of hundreds of thousands of people all over the expanding terrain of the United States. While contributing to the spread of Protestant religious ideology, religious publishers also contributed to the development of mass publishing.

THE EVANGELICAL FRONTIER

Alongside the tract societies and missionary organizations that comprised the Benevolent Empire, America's evangelical churches embarked on campaigns to spread their religious

HOT COMMODITIES

Cheap Printed Bibles

Domesticating Scripture. In response to the success of the American Bible Society, rival publishers began offering more elaborate bibles. Itinerant New England folk artist Joseph H. Davis painted small family portraits such as this one from 1836 depicting James and Sarah Tuttle. In many of the images, large family bibles feature prominently amongst other symbols of domestic life.

The ancient Hebrew and Greek texts that most Christians consider Holy Scripture have exerted great cultural influence in America for centuries. When translated into English and bound together in a single volume, this corpus of texts is better known as "the Bible," and it has been the best-selling printed book in U.S. history. But bibles have always come in different forms and formats and the business of making them has had its twists and turns.

Before the Revolution, English bibles were not printed at all in America because the British Crown held a copyright that forbade publishing them in the colonies. When the war for independence broke out, the colonists faced a bible shortage and the Continental Congress considered a desperate plan to import twenty thousand bibles from Holland to address the crisis. After the war, American printers slowly entered the bible business, but the big surge came in 1816, with the founding of the American Bible Society (ABS). Concerned about the spread of heretical religious ideas associated with the Enlightenment and the French Revolution, the ABS's founders sought to save the United States by increasing popular access to the printed translation of the Old and New Testaments. The ABS centralized bible production in New York City, adopted new typesetting technologies (well before any of the major commercial publishing houses), and distributed the bibles through a network of auxiliary branches throughout the country. At a time when print runs of more than two thousand copies of a book were rare, the ABS produced twenty thousand English-language bibles in its first year. Within two decades, the ABS was publishing over three hundred thousand bibles a year.

In 1829 the ABS committed to a goal of putting a bible in every household in the nation over the next two years. The "General Supply," as this program was called, was an unprecedentedly ambitious venture in mass broadcasting. ABS bibles were simple products, presenting the Scriptures in King James translation, but without any additional commentary or homiletic material. The organization's evangelical Protestant supporters had great faith in the power of the book, so long as it made it into the homes of the nation's citizens. Unlike the Gideons International organization, which would begin distributing free bibles in hotel rooms in the beginning of the twentieth century, the ABS rarely gave their goods away, on the theory that owners would value a bible more highly if it had been paid for.

Although they were not free, ABS bibles were very cheap, usually costing much less than a dollar. Other publishers, unable to match ABS prices, were forced to compete in other ways. They devoted themselves instead to producing bibles with extensive commentaries, copious illustrations and maps, lavish bindings, and all kinds of supplemental historical information. The massive effort of northeastern evangelicals to make cheap, simple bibles available to everyone thus had the secondary effect of prompting the spread of a new generation of fancier and more elaborate illuminated bibles that became popular over the course of the nineteenth century.

Think About It

1. How did the proliferation of cheap printed bibles change the attitudes of ordinary Americans toward sacred scripture?
2. Did the American Bible Society's "General Supply" create the equivalent of a national religion?

message orally across the country. They were especially successful in the South and in southern parts of Ohio and Indiana—areas cleared for white settlement by Indian land cessions following the defeat of Tecumseh. The Methodist Church took the lead in this campaign, sending itinerant preachers known as **circuit riders** to small towns and farming communities, much as the American Bible Society disseminated printed books. Circuit riders were typically celibate men who traveled to otherwise isolated rural areas, preaching the gospel, recruiting converts, and organizing small religious communities known as "classes" to reinforce their message while on the road. By 1815, seven thousand classes had been established. By 1830 the number had more than doubled and almost half a million Americans belonged to them. Next to the postal system and the political press, the Methodist network of itinerant preachers and local classes ranks among the major early-nineteenth-century media of information exchange.

Methodists also led the way in sponsoring another form of religious education—the **camp meeting.** These large gatherings attracted converts through powerful emotional appeals. The most famous of the revivals, at Cane Ridge, Kentucky, in 1801, lasted over a week and attracted a crowd estimated at between ten and twenty thousand. Many of those in attendance experienced ecstatic conversion experiences; some fainted, shook violently, or barked like dogs. Camped out in tents on the hillside, the Cane Ridge community was by far the largest settlement in the state of Kentucky during the revival. Over the next forty years, numerous revival meetings of varying sizes appeared throughout the country. Camp meetings like Cane Ridge were early expressions of a later and larger trend toward mass revivals and evangelical fervor (known as the Second Great Awakening), which would take place in the Northeast during the 1830s (see Chapter 10). On the frontier, however, the revivals began earlier, reflecting the power of the Methodist religious network.

Jarena Lee. Born into the free black community of Cape May, New Jersey, in 1783, Lee worked as a domestic servant in the outskirts of Philadelphia until she felt the call to preach at the age of twenty-four. By the 1820s, she was traveling two thousand miles each year as a nonordained itinerant preacher.

The spread of religious enthusiasm in rural America was not confined to a single denomination. Baptist communities, which were less centrally organized than their Methodist counterparts, flourished in many of the same rural areas. Presbyterians also established numerous new evangelical churches during this period. Other evangelicals sought to avoid denomination labels and simply called themselves "Christian." Several important American Protestant groups, including the Disciples of Christ, have their genesis in this antidenominational Christian movement of the 1810s and 1820s. However they were organized or defined, American evangelical communities tended to emphasize broad themes of conversion and rebirth rather than finer points of theological doctrine. The spread of this kind of evangelical Christianity initiated a pattern in American religious life that remains visible today. The part of the country frequently referred to as the Bible Belt is the area that was influenced most powerfully by evangelical campaigns in the first quarter of the nineteenth century. This development was not the result of the cultural isolation of southern communities, but rather the opposite: Evangelicals in the South and the trans-Appalachian West were connected to growing networks of religious preaching and communication.

WOMEN, RELIGION, AND PUBLIC LIFE

In both the North and the South, in frontier churches and in urban religious organizations, evangelical religious networks proved especially attractive to women during the decade after the war. Numerous female preachers, including Jarena Lee of the A.M.E. Church, Harriet Livermore of the nondenominational Christian movement, and the Methodist Phoebe Palmer all achieved renown as public speakers spreading the gospel, though they were not officially ordained as ministers. Ann Hasseltine Judson, who served with her husband as a missionary in Southeast Asia and translated parts of the Bible into Burmese and Thai, became one of the most famous figures in the history of nineteenth-century American missionary activity. Other women founded benevolent associations, organized charities, or served on the governance committees of local congregations.

During a period when women were excluded from politics, civic associations, and the professions, religion offered rare opportunities for public self-expression and communal distinction. Between 1810 and 1830, respectable women largely withdrew from many of the forms of public protest and political speech (such as tavern toasts) that had been common in the revolutionary era. Only in the context of religious life were women able to address male audiences and present themselves publicly without fear of censure. When Fanny Newell, the wife of an itinerant Methodist preacher in Maine, decided to follow her husband's calling, she knew that her audiences would allow her to break a social taboo. "Whatever may be said against a female speaking, or praying in public, I care not," she would tell them, "for when I feel confident that the Lord calls me to speak, I dare not refuse."

Evangelical Protestants would provide models for women's independent participation in public life (see Chapter 12). A few of them, including the writer and reformer Lydia Maria Child, became politically active on behalf of the rights of Indians, a major evangelical concern in the North. Significantly, the first organized petition campaign by women to influence national politics took place in 1830, and its goal was to resist a new initiative to confiscate Indian land.

CIVILIZATION AND REMOVAL

In the history of white-Indian relations in North America, the War of 1812 turned out to be as crucial a turning point as the Seven Years' War of the previous century. During the negotiations following the initial Treaty of Ghent, Britain abandoned all serious resistance to U.S. westward expansion. Although the treaty had called for a return of Indian lands taken during the war, General Jackson ignored the treaty, Presidents Madison and Monroe were eager not to offend the hero of New Orleans, and Britain never pressed the point. Instead, the Creek theater of the war provided a model for a pattern of "treaties"—imposed mostly by Jackson—in which Native Americans ceded lands, white migrants moved in, and tribal territory was brought under the active jurisdiction of the federal government.

By 1820 the United States had consolidated control over all the land east of the Mississippi, but the question of what to do with the 125,000 Native Americans occupying that land remained. Twelve years earlier, President Jefferson had promised western Indians that the "day will soon come when you will unite yourselves with us, join in our great councils, and form a people with us, and we shall all be Americans; you will mix with us by marriage; your blood will run in our veins and will spread with us over this great continent." But American leaders abandoned the assimilationist rhetoric after the war, and a new approach to Indian policy emerged in the 1820s. Instead of pressuring Indians to adapt to a new cultural order, the federal government sought to remove Indians altogether from the eastern half of the continent. Faced with forced exile from their homes, some Native Americans resisted, while others painfully complied with government orders. Responses to the policy were mixed in the white community as well, especially in the Northeast where the new policy struck many observers as cruel or unnecessary. On both sides, the debates about white-Indian coexistence in the United States also reflected new ideas about national identity.

CIVILIZED TRIBES

The process of dispossessing and expelling Indians went most smoothly for the United States in Indiana, Illinois, and other parts of the old Northwest Territory. There officials weakened resistance by bribing tribal leaders and settling debts, inducing many villages and tribes to relocate quietly. The Sac and Fox Indians of the Great Lakes region, however, did take up arms and sought unsuccessfully to stop the American onslaught in the Black Hawk War of 1832. In the South, resistance was more widespread. Five confederations of southern Indians, the so-called **Five Civilized Tribes**—Choctaws, Chickasaws, Creeks, Cherokees, and Seminoles—clung tenaciously to their land and forced the government to demonstrate how far it would go in order to clear land for white settlement.

Significantly, those southern tribes that resisted removal most nearly resembled their white neighbors. They were more settled and agricultural than northern Indians and had developed more sophisticated forms of centralized political authority. Many of their leaders were wealthy planters with mixed ancestry and English-sounding names, and Christianity had made significant inroads within their villages and communities. The native groups that lived within the borders of Georgia, Florida, Tennessee, Mississippi, and Alabama, in other words, had by and large accepted the terms of the civilization program that the United States had proposed earlier in the century as preconditions for equal citizenship and cultural integration.

The Cherokee nation offers the most striking example of this pattern. The Cherokees were an Iroquoian tribe with origins in the Ohio River region that had settled several centuries earlier in the southern portion of the Appalachians. At the beginning of the eighteenth century, they claimed control over an area of roughly 350 by 300 miles, from the Ohio to the Tennessee Rivers and from the Blue Ridge Mountains to the middle of Tennessee. But between 1721 and 1806, the Cherokees, who fought on the losing side of the American Revolution, ceded over 97,000 square miles of land to American colonies or states and had become a small and poor nation centered in northern Georgia. Over the next three decades, the Cherokees rebuilt their society in the shadow of the growing American republic.

Many Cherokees dressed like whites, spoke English, and embraced Christianity. A few were in fact white Loyalists who had fled to Cherokee country after the Revolution, but most were full-blooded Cherokees who had adopted European folkways and practices. The evangelical movement had reached them as well, and they worshiped as Methodists, Baptists, Moravians, Presbyterians, and Congregationalists. By the end of the 1820s, Cherokee society was probably as committed to Christianity as the rest of the Southeast. The Cherokee nation also developed a written constitution in 1827 with a bicameral legislature and a tripartite government modeled explicitly on that of the United States. Finally, in imitation of their white neighbors, Cherokees adopted new ideas about racial hierarchy and instituted slavery. By 1830, about 1,500 African Americans were held as property by Cherokees.

Most strikingly to outside observers, the Cherokees used a written alphabet—an 85-character syllabary devised in 1821 by a man named Sequoyah. (*Syllabary* is the technical term for a writing system, like Korean, where individual characters represent entire syllables.) The Cherokee syllabary proved remarkably effective, and within about a decade most of the Cherokee nation had learned to read, thus eroding one of the most culturally significant differences between whites and Indians in Georgia. Sequoyah's own life was a fascinating example of the complex paths that different Cherokees pursued in response to the shifting politics of U.S.-Indian relations. On the one hand, Sequoyah was a traditionalist who shunned Christianity, did not speak English, and rejected acculturation in general. On the other hand, he fought on the side of Jackson in the Creek War, signed land treaties with the United States, and voluntarily removed to a reservation in Arkansas established by the federal government for Cherokees after the War of 1812.

Sequoyah's Cherokee Syllabary, 1825, and *Cherokee Singing Book*, printed for the American Board of Commissioners for Foreign Missions, Boston, 1846. The new writing system helped introduce mass literacy into Cherokee country.

Sequoyah's syllabary was a source of admiration and fascination to many Americans and made him a celebrity. With little success, white missionaries had sought to teach English-language literacy among the Cherokees (and to translate the Bible into Cherokee words transliterated in English characters), to facilitate the spread of Protestant Christianity. Sequoyah's system, by contrast, seemed to answer the missionaries' prayers. Children who had struggled for years to learn to read English were able to master the syllabary in a matter of days. The new writing system was adopted immediately both by Christian missionaries and by traditional Cherokee medicine men and conjurers. By 1828, Cherokees had produced the first Indian newspaper, the *Cherokee Phoenix and Indian's Advocate*, printed both in English and in Cherokee. In a very short time, the Cherokees had become a prominent advertisement for the willingness and capacity of traditional Indian societies to attain what white Americans regarded as civilization.

ANDREW JACKSON AND INDIAN REMOVAL

Southern Indians were unable to hold on to their land, despite their success in adopting and adapting white culture. The fate of the Cherokees may have been sealed by the discovery of gold on their territory in 1828. But for all the southern Indians, 1828 was an ominous year because of the election of Andrew Jackson as president. Jackson is often remembered more for his connections to the growth of mass democracy and party politics (see Chapter 10), but he had made his name as an Indian fighter and he began his presidency by transforming U.S. policy toward America's native tribes.

Jackson himself did not invent the idea of transporting Indians to territory beyond the Mississippi. Earlier presidents had contemplated schemes to separate Indians and whites or to induce Indians to move west through land exchange. In 1825, President Monroe, just before leaving office, announced a new U.S. program to "remove" Indian tribes "from the lands which they now occupy" to "the country lying westward and northward." But Monroe insisted that the removal must and would take place "on conditions which shall be satisfactory to themselves and honorable to the United States." During the term of John Quincy Adams, Monroe's successor, the federal government negotiated with different tribes in an effort to persuade them to trade their homeland. Both administrations followed U.S. law in treating native tribes as sovereign nations in their own right, and relations with them were established largely by treaty.

For Jackson, on the other hand, Indian removal was not simply a policy objective; it was a national security priority that required immediate attention and forceful action. He viewed the idea of allowing foreign nations to exist within the borders of the United States as a potential danger and an affront to states' rights. Immediately after Jackson's election, Georgia, Alabama, and Mississippi seized the political opportunity and outlawed tribal governments. Supporters of the Cherokees sued the state of Georgia for interfering with the treaty obligations of the United States. In *Worcester v. Georgia* (1832), the Supreme Court under Chief Justice John Marshall ruled that the Georgia laws violated the territorial sovereignty of the Cherokees. But Andrew Jackson refused to enforce the court decision, and the Cherokees realized they could not count on the federal government to intercede in their conflicts with the states.

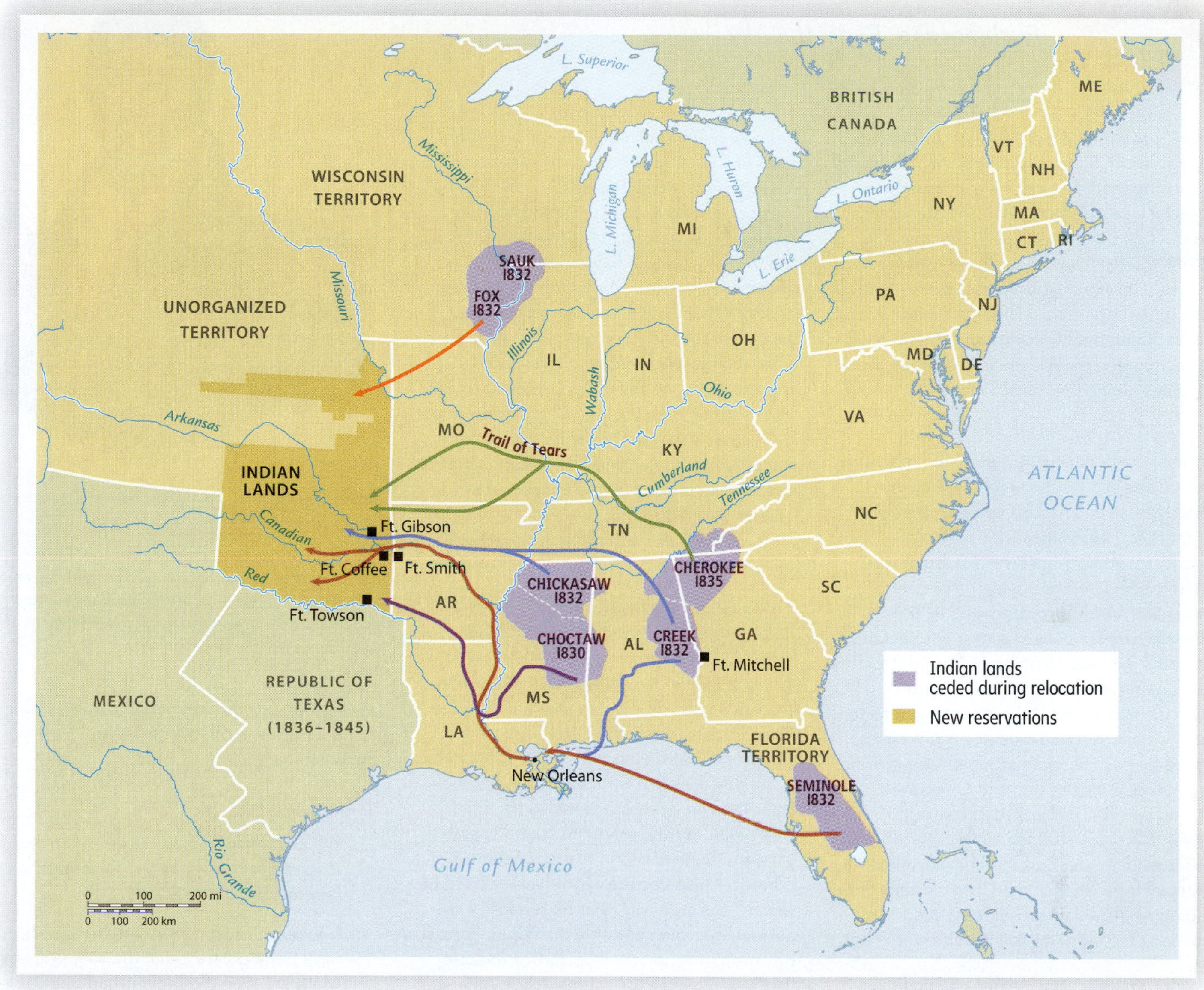

Map 9.5 Indian Removal. Advocates of the proposed removal program claimed that westward migration was in the Indians' own best interests. Andrew Jackson even compared removal to the larger pattern of voluntary mobility for which American society was becoming famous. "Doubtless it will be painful to leave the graves of their fathers," he conceded, "but what do they more than our ancestors did or than our children are now doing?"

The Indian Removal Act became the major political initiative of Jackson's first term in office. In his first annual message to Congress in 1829, he expressed his views on the Indian question. He argued that the earlier federal policy of trying to convert Indians to "the arts of civilization" had always been undermined by the practice of buying Indian lands, which tended to push them further west "into the wilderness." Jackson was clearly giving up on the civilization program. As for the southern Indians who had already acculturated, Jackson advised them to emigrate for their own good, since the federal government had no authority to stop Georgia, Mississippi, and Alabama from seizing their land or expelling them. Jackson repeated this theme in a message to two of the tribes. "Say to my red Choctaw children, and my Chickasaw children," he told an agent, "that their father cannot prevent them from being subject to the laws of the" states. He could only help them if they moved to lands beyond the Mississippi, where their safety would be guaranteed "as long as the grass grows or the water runs." In 1830, Jackson asked Congress to pass an Indian Removal Act authorizing the president to negotiate and oversee the transfer of native tribes remaining east of the Mississippi (see Map 9.5).

Not all white Americans shared Jackson's view that he was benevolently facilitating the next stage of an inevitable historical process. Jeremiah Evarts of the American Board of

SINGULAR LIVES

Pushmataha, Regretful Ally

When Tecumseh visited the Choctaws and Chickasaws in 1811 to rally support for his war against the United States, he encountered a powerful local chief named Pushmataha, who had distinguished himself as a Choctaw warrior and diplomat. Tecumseh's vision would set in motion a dramatic chain of events that transformed white-Indian relations in the United States, but it was Pushmataha's career that epitomized the dilemmas and experiences of Indians during the transformation.

In response to Tecumseh's 1811 appeal, Pushmataha pointed out that Choctaws and Chickasaws had lived peacefully with the United States and had benefited from their contacts and exchanges with white Americans. Furthermore, he argued, it was foolish to declare war against "a people . . . who are far better provided with all the necessary implements of war . . . far beyond that of all our race combined." Yes, whites had committed "outrages" and "unjust encroachments," but the proper response to those violations was diplomacy, not warfare. Moved by Pushmataha's argument (or sharing his political outlook), the joint Choctaw-Chickasaw council rejected Tecumseh's appeal and supported the United States in the impending war. Pushmataha himself led a Choctaw force against the Creek Redsticks, helping Andrew Jackson defeat the Indians who had responded to Tecumseh's war cry.

By 1820, however, Pushmataha had come to see things differently. His former ally Jackson was now pressuring him to trade five million acres of Choctaw territory in Mississippi for western lands, which Pushmataha knew to be both barren and already occupied by white settlers. With Jackson making ominous threats and the Choctaws no longer able to seek alliances with Britain, Spain, or the Creeks, a reluctant Pushmataha was forced to accept the land exchange. Four years later, he led a delegation to Washington in an unsuccessful effort to lobby the federal government to evict white settlers from the new Choctaw holdings in Arkansas. While in the capital, he met with numerous statesmen and foreign dignitaries and sat for a portrait by the famous artist Charles Bird King. Later that year, he contracted a fatal virus and was buried with military honors in the congressional cemetery.

Pushmataha's final legacy to the history of white-Indian relations came through his friendship with the actor Edwin Forrest, whom he met in New Orleans in 1824 when Forrest was on tour with a theatrical troupe. After Forrest took a leave from the troupe, he reported spending time with Pushmataha in the new western Choctaw territory. The actor took an intense interest in the chief. One night, Forrest asked his friend to walk back and forth naked in the moonlight. Whatever else Forrest might have wanted to see, he was studying what he regarded as a perfect specimen of noble manhood. Forrest was preparing, in other words, for the role that would launch his career. When American audiences watched *Metamora*, they were seeing Forrest's impression of a noble Indian, a character he probably based on Pushmataha.

***Pushmataha*, by Charles Bird King.** King's numerous portraits of Indian leaders, which were commissioned by the federal government, became popular attractions in an age when many white observers were interested in catching glimpses of what they saw as a vanishing race.

Think About It

1. Which developments between 1811 and 1820 might have changed Pushmataha's view of the United States?
2. Do you think that Pushmataha would have been portrayed in the same way by white artists if the Indians had been able to thwart Jackson's removal policy?

Commissioners for Foreign Missions led a nationwide campaign against the Indian Removal Act, calling upon Christians all over the country to lobby the federal government against committing what he regarded as a grievous sin. Opposition to the Indian Removal Act was thus one of the first major interventions in American politics by a growing network of Protestant organizations. Congressmen from New England, where evangelical sympathy for the Cherokees ran high and where native tribes had already been dispossessed much earlier, voted overwhelmingly against the bill. Even a few southerners, political opponents of Jackson, opposed the Removal Act. But Jackson's political capital was considerable and overwhelming support for removal in the Southeast proved decisive. In the House, the bill passed by a slim margin of 102 to 97.

Each of the five southern tribes during the 1830s had its own exodus story, but the removal followed a pattern. First the federal government pressured tribal leaders (or putative leaders) to trade their land by pointing out that if they refused the states would take it anyway. Once treaties had been signed, federal troops were called in to enforce the transfer. Indians debated the best course of action, both in traditional tribal meetings and in the newer forums such as the *Cherokee Phoenix*. Some tribes, like the Chickasaws and Choctaws, bargained for the best possible deal and then moved west (see Singular Lives: Pushmataha, Regretful Ally). Others stalled, practiced nonviolent resistance, or, in the exceptional case of the Seminoles, waged a long war. That conflict, often called the Second Seminole War, lasted from 1835 to 1842 and cost

Trail of Tears, 1838. Historical demographers have debated the exact numbers of ethnic Cherokees, other Cherokee citizens, and African American slaves belonging to Cherokee masters who were forcibly marched across the Southeast to Oklahoma as part of the Cherokee removal. Scholars also debate the number who died en route. By all accounts, the episode still stands among the tragic events of the period and as a symbol of the brutal end of white-Indian coexistence in the eastern half of North America.

the government tens of millions of dollars and 1,500 lives. In all, seventy thousand southern Indians were uprooted from their ancestral homes.

The most elaborate and famous of these removals took place in Cherokee country, dragging on past Jackson's eight-year presidency. Jackson's removal policy divided the Cherokees. A Treaty Party, led by wealthy planters Major Ridge and his son John, favored rebuilding the Cherokee nation in the West. The Cherokee National Council, led by John Ross, another wealthy planter and the first principal chief of the Cherokees' new constitutional republic, advocated resistance. Ross had helped to initiate the legal battles for Cherokee rights at the U.S. Supreme Court, and afterward he led a delegation to Washington to negotiate a deal that would allow the nation to remain in its homeland—or at least to delay removal until a time when the political winds in Washington might change. But the Jackson administration negotiated the Treaty of New Echota with the Ridge faction in 1835. Ross petitioned the Senate not to ratify the treaty, but to no avail, and U.S. troops began the process of rounding up Cherokees for deportation. From 1835 to 1840, an estimated sixteen thousand Cherokee citizens and their slaves were forcibly exiled to the Oklahoma territory. Approximately four thousand died as a result of a set of fatal marches in 1838, known as the **Trail of Tears.**

METAMORA, LEATHERSTOCKING, AND THE NEW AMERICAN CULTURE

While the U.S. government was gearing up to remove the five southern tribes, American theatergoers enthusiastically embraced the 1829 drama *Metamora*, which became one of the most widely performed theatrical productions in nineteenth-century America (see page 213). The paradoxical popularity of *Metamora* on the eve of Indian removal was partly a matter of geography. New York spectators in 1829 who applauded Metamora's curse upon white people were far enough removed, both from the seventeenth-century conflicts in their own part of the country and from the frontier clashes that were erupting in their own time, to see Indians as something other than an immediate threat. They could even romanticize Indians. In Georgia, by contrast, the play was less successful. The opening-night audience in Augusta, Georgia, hissed when Metamora chided whites for their treatment of his tribe, and the play was boycotted.

Nonetheless, the theatrical splash of *Metamora* was not primarily a reaction to Indian removal; it was about the culture of white America. *Metamora* was written by John Augustus Stone in response to a prize competition created by the actor Edwin Forrest. The up-and-coming Forrest wanted to promote dramatic arts in the new republic to boost his career and to prove that legitimate theater could be produced in the United States. He invited American playwrights to submit a script that he would perform, stipulating only that "the hero or principal character shall be an aboriginal of this country." Forrest wanted to portray an Indian so that the play would seem distinctively American, and not simply an inferior imitation of European theater. His sympathetic portrayal of an Algonquin warrior was not intended to identify with Indians rather than Puritans, but rather with *Americans* rather than Europeans. Northern audiences responded enthusiastically to this declaration of cultural independence.

Metamora stands in a long tradition in American popular culture, including the Boston Tea Party, of using Indians to claim American-ness. Forrest's drama spawned a rash of Indian plays of varying types on stages all over urban America in the nineteenth century. Biographies of native chiefs became popular at the same time as well, as did Indian characters and themes in American fiction. The author and reformer Lydia Maria Child entered the literary world in 1824 with the anonymous publication of *Hobomok*, a novel about a noble Indian in colonial times who befriended the English and married a white woman. More famously, James Fenimore Cooper's *The Pioneers* appeared in 1823—the first of five historical novels known as the Leatherstocking Tales. Cooper

Edwin Forrest as Metamora: Engraving After Mathew Brady Photograph.
Brady's photograph , ca. 1860, was taken long after Forrest had appeared in this role. Forrest was known for his muscular calves, featured here under his form-fitting pants.

was the first commercially successful American novelist, working at a time when the United States was regarded by Europeans as a cultural wasteland. As late as 1820, a prominent British journal asked the provocative question: "In the four quarters of the globe, who reads an American book?" In the beginning of the decade, Washington Irving's short stories (which included not only "Rip Van Winkle" and "The Legend of Sleepy Hollow" but also "Philip of Pokanoket," another celebration of King Philip) made a strong impression on critics in both Britain and the United States, but Cooper's novels, like Forrest's performances, marked a coming of age for American arts.

Cooper's Leatherstocking novels developed the famous character of Natty Bumppo, a white frontiersman raised among Indians. Bumppo (also called Hawkeye, Leatherstocking, Pathfinder, and Deerslayer) has no trace of Indian descent but clearly has been made stronger and nobler by his relationships with natives. Cooper saw Indians as tragic figures doomed to extinction through violence, but he also saw white American culture as reaping the special benefits of contact with Indian civilization. The double message was that Indians and whites were fundamentally different but also that the history of white-Indian relations had made Americans different from Englishmen.

Novels like *The Pioneers* and plays like *Metamora* were figuring out in the 1820s what gave the United States a distinctive national character. In part, this was a way of persuading other Americans to attend homegrown theater and read their compatriots' literature. But it also reflected a new interest in both American and European thought regarding the idea—often associated with the term *romanticism*—that every nation has a special spirit that its art ought to represent. Indians were crucial to this project of forging a uniquely American culture. Significantly, romantic ideas about Indians in American culture were spreading at a time when whites were giving up on the older project of absorbing Indians into the new republic by spreading the supposedly universal values of farming, literacy, private property, and Christianity.

Lydia Maria Child (1802–1880). Like Washington Irving and James Fenimore Cooper, the novelist and reformer Child turned to the early period of white-Indian contact in the Northeast to tell a distinctively American story. But unlike the *Leatherstocking Tales*, Child's novel took a more hopeful view of the possibility of integrating Indians into American culture.

CONCLUSION

By 1830, it was clear that the second war between the United States and Britain had been more than just a failed American attack on Canada or a valiant attempt to restore American pride. In retrospect, both whites and natives recognized that the War of 1812 had dealt a decisive blow to Indian life in North America. The United States had defeated a major Indian uprising, pushing the Indians' European allies off the continent and consolidating control over half the continent. The territory cleared for white settlement had in turn become a major area of growth for both southern slavery and evangelical Protestantism. The westward spread of slavery also provoked a political crisis over the admission of new states and intensified the pressure to confiscate Indian land. The rise of national organizations to promote evangelical values and practices produced some opposition to that confiscation, but ultimately, a new program of Indian removal prevailed. Uprooted from their homes and exiled to the western territories, Indian society east of the Mississippi had been destroyed. At the same time, Indians began to play an increasingly prominent role in white popular culture, helping whites of European descent to define what was distinctively American about the world they inhabited and the societies they were building.

In 1814, when U.S. diplomats were negotiating a treaty with Great Britain, the War of 1812 might have struck many American observers as misguided or inconclusive. Viewed with the hindsight of two decades, however, the conflict that began in 1811 with an attack on Tecumseh's followers appeared far more momentous. It had affirmed American independence from Great Britain, destroyed the first political party system, reshaped the U.S. map, laid new foundations for American art and entertainment, ended the possibility of peaceful coexistence between whites and natives east of the Mississippi, and brought to a power a new political movement identified with the war's major hero.

STUDY TERMS

- Shawnee Prophet (p. 215)
- pan-Indian (p. 215)
- civilization program (p. 215)
- Battle of Tippecanoe (p. 217)
- War Hawks (p. 217)
- War of 1812 (p. 218)
- Hartford Convention (p. 219)
- Redsticks (p. 220)
- Creek War (p. 220)
- Horseshoe Bend (p. 220)
- Negro Fort (p. 222)
- Battle of New Orleans (p. 223)
- Rush-Bagot Treaty (p. 223)
- First Seminole War (p. 224)
- Transcontinental Treaty of 1819 (Adams-Onis Treaty) (p. 224)
- Gran Colombia (p. 224)
- Monroe Doctrine (p. 224)
- National Road (p. 225)
- internal improvements (p. 225)
- Panic of 1819 (p. 225)
- Second Bank of the United States (p. 225)
- Tallmadge Amendment (p. 226)
- Missouri Compromise (p. 226)
- Denmark Vesey slave conspiracy (p. 227)
- American Board of Commissioners for Foreign Missions (p. 228)
- Benevolent Empire (p. 228)
- circuit riders (p. 229)
- camp meeting (p. 230)
- Cane Ridge (p. 230)
- Five Civilized Tribes (p. 231)
- Cherokee syllabary (p. 231)
- *Worcester v. Georgia* (p. 232)
- Indian Removal Act (p. 233)
- Treaty of New Echota (p. 235)
- Trail of Tears (p. 235)
- *Metamora* (p. 235)
- Leatherstocking Tales (p. 236)

TIMELINE

1811 William Henry Harrison destroys Prophetstown at the Battle of Tippecanoe

Construction begins on National Road

Devastating earthquakes occur along New Madrid fault

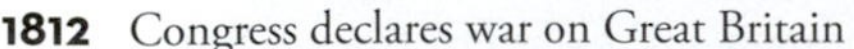

1812 Congress declares war on Great Britain

1813 Tecumseh killed at battle of the Thames

1814 British capture Washington, D.C.

Andrew Jackson defeats the Redsticks at Horseshoe Bend

New England Federalists meet in Hartford

Treaty of Ghent formally ends the war

1815 Americans repel the British at the Battle of New Orleans

1816 American Bible Society formed

Second Bank of the United States chartered

James Monroe elected president

1818 National Road reaches the Ohio River

1819 Jackson invades Florida

U.S. and Spain sign Transcontinental (Adams-Onis) Treaty

Financial panic and widespread bankruptcy strike the nation

1820 Congress enacts Missouri Compromise

1821 Sequoyah devises Cherokee syllabary

1822 U.S. recognizes new independent republics in Latin America

Denmark Vesey and thirty-four others executed on charges of plotting a slave rebellion

1823 Monroe Doctrine propounded

James Fenimore Cooper publishes the first of his Leatherstocking Tales

1828 First issue of *Cherokee Phoenix* appears

Jackson elected president

1829 *Metamora* debuts at New York's Park Theater

Congress passes Indian Removal Act

1832 *Worcester v. Georgia* upholds Cherokees' tribal sovereignty

1835 Second Seminole War begins

Treaty of New Echota transfers Cherokee land to the United States

1838 Cherokees march westward in the Trail of Tears

FURTHER READING

Additional suggested readings are available on the Online Learning Center at www.mhhe.com/becomingamerica1e.

Jay Feldman, *When the Mississippi Ran Backwards* (2005), uses the story of the New Madrid earthquakes to weave together several fascinating events and important developments during the period.

Paul Gutjahr, *An American Bible* (1999), charts the spread and transformation of printed bibles in the United States during the nineteenth century.

Christine Leigh Heyrman, *Southern Cross* (1998), locates the origins of the southern Bible Belt in the activities and accommodations of Baptist, Methodist, and Presbyterian evangelicals during the first third of the nineteenth century.

Daniel Walker Howe, *What Hath God Wrought* (2008), provides a thorough survey of the political history of this period, with an emphasis on religion and communications.

Michael P. Johnson, "Denmark Vesey and his Co-Conspirators," *William and Mary Quarterly*, 58 (October 2001), 915–976, makes the case against the alleged South Carolina slave conspiracy of 1822.

William G. McLoughlin, *Cherokee Renascence in the New Republic* (1992), details the tragic story of Cherokee attempts to hold on to their land by embracing American economic, political, and cultural models.

David Paul Nord, *Faith in Reading* (2004), considers the role of religious publishers as pioneers of American mass media.

Alisse Portnoy, *Their Right to Speak* (2005), describes the rise of women's political activism in the debates over Indian removal.

Karl Raitz and George Thompson (eds.), *The National Road* (1996), sets the first major federal road-building project in the context of larger trends in the celebration of mobility in American culture.

Claudio Saunt, *A New Order of Things* (1999), demonstrates the impact of the new economic order on the Creek Indians before, during, and after the war.

Richard Slotkin, *The Fatal Environment* (1998), offers a compelling reading of Cooper's *Leatherstocking Tales* relevant to the themes of this chapter.

Alan Taylor, *The Civil War of 1812* (2010), proposes an original interpretation of the war as a conflict among English-speaking residents and immigrants in the eastern Great Lakes region over their relationship to the British Empire.

10

INSIDE ▶

THE BIG PICTURE

Expanding circuits of trade and communication fueled the development of big cities, new work patterns, and intense religious movements. Meanwhile, liberal voting laws and a new party system turned democratic politics into a boisterous and inclusive pastime for white men.

First State Election in Detroit, 1837. Electoral politics had become a popular activity for men of different classes by the time of this election.

1825–1844

MARKET SOCIETY & THE BIRTH OF MASS POLITICS

A man walked into a bar in a small Maryland town just after election day in 1834 and made loud, disparaging remarks about the supporters of Senator Henry Clay, the leader of the party that opposed President Andrew Jackson. "Big Bill" Otter, as the man called himself, was a burly plasterer from nearby Emmitsburg who loved causing trouble, and he succeeded that day in provoking one of the Clay partisans in the bar. The offended man called Otter a liar and insisted that "there was as good Clay-men as Jackson-men." When Otter refused to retract his remarks, the Clay man challenged him to a fight. "I told him I could not fight, and never did intend to fight," Otter recalled in his autobiography, "but I can beat any Clay-man belonging to the party in the United States at *butting*." The two men grabbed each other by the ears and butted heads violently. To the great amusement of the other bar patrons, Otter flattened his opponent, sending him "heels over head on the floor." The Clay man asked for a rematch, which produced the same result. By the end of the evening, Otter had head-butted another man (a fellow Jackson supporter who had refused to buy a round of drinks) and then the Clay supporter again. Finally, Otter himself bought drinks for everyone in the bar.

William Otter's postelection brawl was a sign of the new political times. A rural artisan born in England, Otter had minimal formal education and bore little resemblance to the men who had dominated politics in earlier periods

Supporters and spectators throng the 1829 presidential inauguration.

KEY QUESTIONS

- In what ways was the expansion of voting rights around the 1820s significant but limited?
- What was the nature of the pageantry, violence, and partisanship of mass democracy?
- How and why did the Second Party System develop, and how did the Whigs and the Democrats differ from each other?
- How were canal building, urbanization, and the spread of market relations connected?
- What major innovations shaped big-city life?
- What new religious movements and trends emerged in the Erie Canal region?

of American history. And for most of his early adulthood, Otter did not take much interest in affairs of state. But in 1828, twenty-seven years after immigrating to the United States, Otter became a citizen in order to vote for Jackson. Six years later he was defiantly expressing his political views at a tavern. And one year after that, the hard-headed William Otter was elected to public office. Ordinary men like Otter blustered their way into the political world during the second quarter of the nineteenth century, transforming politics from an activity reserved for the wealthy and prominent to an enterprise for the masses.

These years were a period of intense democratization, at least from the perspective of white males like Otter. Participation in elections skyrocketed. New political parties were born, attracting the kinds of passionate loyalty and identification that led men to violence on election days, not only in rural taverns but also in the streets of the nation's largest cities. These developments are sometimes associated with the presidency of Andrew Jackson, who spoke of the common man and appealed to the expanded electorate. But Jackson's opponents also participated in the new, boisterous culture of participatory politics.

The expanding world of politics was connected with the spread of trade networks and the growth of cities. As new transportation links brought much of the country into close commercial contact, rural Americans forged closer ties with the nation's urban centers, and older patterns of work and leisure in those urban centers began to change. During this period, New York emerged as the nation's leading commercial center and a symbol of a distinctive metropolitan way of life. But through much of the Northeast and Midwest, both farmers and city dwellers were participating in activities and institutions, including political parties, labor unions, and religious revivals, that connected them to masses of anonymous strangers.

ANDREW JACKSON AND DEMOCRACY

By modern standards, the United States did not begin as a democracy. In the new American republic, there was no monarchy, nobility, or system of hereditary privilege. And in principle, all citizens were equal before the law. But this did not mean that the mass of people determined the actions of the government or even participated in the political process. The active engagement of large numbers of poor and middle-income Americans in the affairs of state (one of the hallmarks of democracy in the modern world) began in the second quarter of the nineteenth century. Historians sometimes call this development **Jacksonian**

Democracy, but the term is potentially misleading. Jackson's rise to political power was more the consequence of the democratization of American politics than its cause. Still, throughout his presidency, Andrew Jackson symbolized and articulated the growing belief that politics should be driven by the opinions of masses of white men.

UNIVERSAL MANHOOD SUFFRAGE

At the beginning of the nineteenth century, the right to vote or hold public office was linked closely to wealth. In 1800, all but three states required its citizens to own a certain amount of property in order to vote. Outside of New England, few public offices were directly elected; most were either appointed or chosen by representatives. When an office was up for popular vote, the men who stood for election were likely to come from an elite social stratum. Although ordinary Americans could affect the course of political events as soldiers, consumers, rioters, or parents, most did not do so as voters.

During the first quarter of the century, all of this began to change. The six new states that entered the union between 1816 and 1821 (Indiana, Illinois, Alabama, Mississippi, Missouri, and Maine) adopted constitutions with laxer voting requirements than those of the original thirteen. And several older states amended their constitutions to expand the electorate. In some cases, these constitutional changes were fueled by conflicts between Federalists and Republicans or between rival Republican factions seeking to gain electoral advantage by adding new voters to the rolls. But whether it was the result of democratic ideals or political stratagems, the new trend in state constitutions turned voting into a more broadly shared right. The New York State Constitution of 1821, for example, extended the franchise to all adult white male citizens who paid state or local taxes, served in the militia, or worked on the highways. This covered 80 percent of the adult men in a state where, just a year earlier, only one-third of them had been eligible to vote for governor. By 1824, only four states still imposed significant property requirements for voting.

States were also expanding the number of elected government positions. Governorships, which generally had been determined by the legislature, were increasingly subject to popular vote. By the 1840s, it was even common for judges to be elected. States also changed the way presidents were chosen. In 1800, only a third of the states picked presidential electors based directly on a popular vote; by 1824, three-quarters of the states did so. By 1832, when Jackson stood for reelection, every state except for South Carolina conducted a popular vote for the presidency.

The expansion of voting rights and voting opportunities during this period marked the arrival of **universal manhood suffrage.** This nineteenth-century term did not mean that everyone got to vote; it meant that one got to vote by virtue of being a man. Manhood had multiple and varying connotations in nineteenth-century America, but in the context of voting, being a man meant not being a child, a slave, or a woman. The exclusion of children is often taken for granted, but the new suffrage laws of this era typically barred everyone under the age of twenty-one (and in some states, under twenty-five) at a time when life expectancy was much shorter than it is today. Because the median age in the United States in 1824 was seventeen, most people were kept out of the political process for reasons of age alone. The exclusion of women may have seemed natural to many Americans at the time (though some women had voted in New Jersey from 1776 to 1808), but it acquired new significance once men of all classes began voting. Politics became pointedly associated with masculinity in the nineteenth century, which shaped the way it was conducted and understood.

For African Americans, both free and enslaved, the limitations of universal manhood suffrage were far clearer. The same period that brought democratic opportunities to white males closed them down for free men of color. The New York constitution that removed property requirements for whites in 1821 made a point of imposing them on African Americans. New Yorkers of African ancestry had to possess $250 worth of property in order to vote, a restriction that barred all but 298 of the state's 30,000 blacks. Pennsylvania's new constitution in 1838 affirmed that the right to vote, which earlier constitutions had granted to "freemen," explicitly meant white freemen. Black men also lost the legal right to vote in Connecticut, Rhode Island, and North Carolina. And no new state admitted after 1819 (except for Maine, which had been part of an older state) granted voting rights to African Americans. Free black men resisted their exclusion from electoral politics and asserted themselves in the public life of northern cities (see Chapter 13), but most were shut out of the newly expanded political process of the Jacksonian era.

New immigrants from Europe, by contrast, enjoyed significant voting rights under the new state constitutions of this period. In New York, a white immigrant man could vote soon after his arrival in the 1820s. In Illinois, adult white males who had been living in the state for six months could vote, whether or not they had become U.S. citizens. Between 1825 and 1850, massive numbers of Americans entered an unfamiliar world of electoral politics, taking part in what had previously been an elite privilege. No longer a class privilege, voting was now a practice linked to race and gender.

JACKSON'S RISE

In some respects Andrew Jackson was an unlikely champion of these democratizing trends in American politics. Born in the Carolina backcountry in 1767, Jackson became a lawyer and moved west to the frontier city of Nashville in 1788, where he established himself as a successful land speculator, owned a plantation with over one hundred slaves, and married the daughter of the city's founder. He served briefly in Congress in the 1790s, belligerently advocating the interests of western farmers and merchants who sought free access to the Mississippi River. After he returned to private life, the War of 1812 drew him back to public service, and this time he earned nationwide adulation for his role in the Battle of New Orleans. But while his name and story remained the subject of popular legend after the war and into the next decade, Jackson himself stayed out of politics, spending much of the period brooding over perceived insults and mistreatment in connection with his unauthorized ventures into Florida (see Chapter 9). By all appearances, Jackson's glory days were behind him.

An unusual set of political circumstances returned Jackson to the national spotlight. As Monroe's final term in office drew to a close in 1824, no obvious heir was waiting in the wings and a number of candidates emerged. John Quincy Adams, who was Monroe's secretary of state (a traditional steppingstone to the presidency), had distinguished himself in various diplomatic crises and challenges, and might have been the presumptive choice. But after the Panic of 1819, voters and Republican Party leaders were more preoccupied with domestic affairs than with foreign relations, and Adams's perceived hostility to slavery cost him support in the South. A number of slaveholding candidates emerged, including William Crawford (a states' rights advocate who wanted to return to the fiscal conservatism that had dominated the Republican platform before the war), Henry Clay, and John Calhoun (both of whom supported the party's turn toward internal improvements and the national bank). In previous elections, the Republicans had selected their presidential candidates at a **congressional caucus**—a gathering of all the party members in Congress. But with a growing spirit of democracy in the air and the party no longer worried about uniting against a Federalist opposition, the caucus had come to seem more aristocratic and less necessary. Less than a quarter of Congress attended the caucus, and its endorsement of Crawford was of doubtful value. For the first time since its formation in the 1790s, the Republican Party could not coalesce around a single candidate.

In 1822 the crowded presidential field was joined by a surprise contender. In an attempt to block a local rival, a group of Tennessee politicians decided to nominate the hero of New Orleans, and to everyone's surprise Jackson's candidacy caught on in Pennsylvania and North Carolina. The election of 1824 pitted four viable candidates. Jackson, who had been careful not to commit himself on any of the big issues of the day, fared the best (see Table 10.1), but the failure of any candidate to win a majority of the electoral votes meant that, according to the Constitution, the race would be decided by the House of Representatives. Henry Clay was Speaker of the House and wielded considerable influence, but the representatives had to select from the top three electoral vote getters—Jackson, Adams, and Crawford. Clay directed his supporters to back Adams (to whom he was closest ideologically), and by the margin of a single vote in the New York delegation, Adams won. When Clay was subsequently named secretary of state, Jackson and his allies decried the "corrupt bargain" that had determined the outcome and denied Jackson the presidency.

John Quincy Adams, son of the second president, was an accomplished statesman who began public service as secretary

TABLE 10.1 THE PRESIDENTIAL ELECTION OF 1824

Candidate	Percentage of Popular Vote	Electoral Votes
Andrew Jackson	43	99
John Quincy Adams	31	84
William Crawford	13	41
Henry Clay	13	37

Campaign Broadside, 1828. The contest between John Quincy Adams and Andrew Jackson featured smear campaigns in the press. Jackson's supporters labeled Adams an aristocrat for buying billiard tables for the White House and accused the president of having procured young virgins for the czar. Pro-Adams editors in turn called Jackson an adulterer. Both sides evoked the specter of a fragile republic in danger of dissolving. **Question for Analysis:** What does this cartoon suggest about the character and reputation of Jackson (standing)?

of the U.S. legation to St. Petersburg at age fourteen. He was a learned scholar who was fluent in seven languages, and a man with a grand vision for an expanding national government. But the charge of having entered the White House through a back-room deal dogged the Adams presidency, as did the perception that he was an elitist who felt that pubic officials should not be, in Adams's own infamous words, "palsied by the will of our constituents." An outraged Jackson, who had declared himself the champion of those constituents and their will, wasted no time preparing for a rematch in 1828. An army of newspapers friendly to Jackson organized a national public relations campaign, some of it quite vicious. In addition, Adams's slaveholding opponents had learned not to repeat the mistake of dividing their votes among several candidates. In an election that drew three times as many voters as in 1824, Jackson won handily. At the age of sixty-two, the military hero had refashioned himself as a "man of the people" and become the first president from a state west of the Appalachians.

PATRONAGE, PEGGY EATON, AND JACKSON'S FIRST TERM

Jackson's long campaign against President Adams was more than just an attempt to undo the results of an irregular election. Jackson's supporters were building a new national coalition to replace the Jeffersonian party that had splintered by 1824 (see Participatory Politics and the Second Party System, below). Once in office, Jackson's major contribution to the new party system was the practice of using government patronage to reward partisan loyalty. Previous presidents had appointed friends and supporters to vacant positions in the federal government, but Jackson was the first to dismiss large numbers of federal officeholders upon assuming the presidency. He defended the new policy as a reform rooted in the democratic principle that civil servants should rotate rather than forming an entrenched entitled class. "No man has any more intrinsic claim to office than another," he argued. Jackson's critics saw a power grab that threatened to debase civil service. The **spoils system,** as it was called, used the appointive power of the presidency to strengthen party unity and to make party affiliation more important to those who aspired to participate in public life. This system would structure the distribution of federal jobs for the next half-century.

At the top level of the cabinet, Jackson did not simply appoint men who had supported him in the election; he favored those who showed great personal loyalty. Early in Jackson's first term, their loyalty was tested when he named as his new secretary of war a Tennessean named John Henry Eaton, an old friend who had managed Jackson's campaign. Shortly before the inauguration, Eaton had married a much younger woman whose husband had committed suicide a few months earlier. Margaret (or Peggy) Eaton, who cut a scandalous figure in Washington society, was rumored to have been Eaton's mistress while still married to her late husband. Prominent women in the capital, including the wives of cabinet members, ostracized Peggy Eaton for flouting norms of sexual propriety and refused to admit her into polite society. Jackson insisted on Eaton's innocence and likely felt great sympathy for her since his own wife, who died before he was inaugurated, had been wounded by accusations that she had not been legally divorced when she married Jackson. He also resented the fact that the women of Washington were making the rules and defying his orders. Ultimately, he called for the resignation of his entire cabinet (including John Eaton but excluding the postmaster general, whose wife had not participated in the boycott) in order to resolve the conflict. The Peggy Eaton affair underscored the

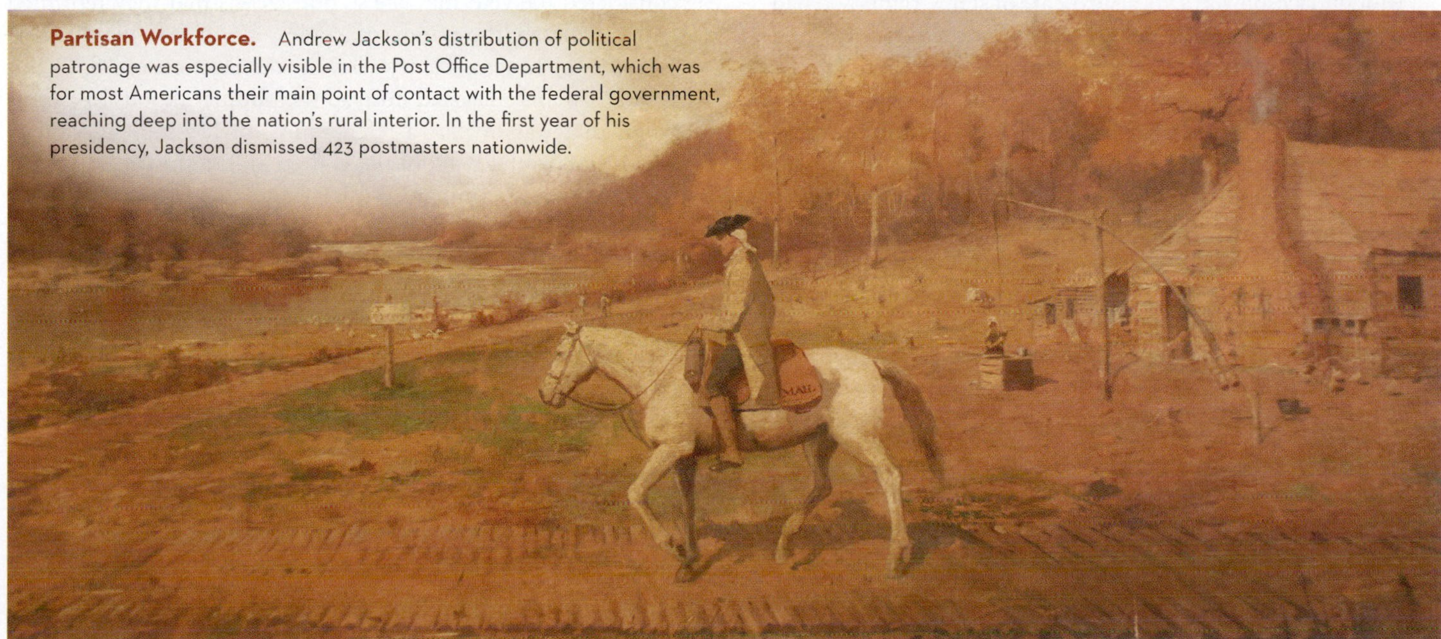

Partisan Workforce. Andrew Jackson's distribution of political patronage was especially visible in the Post Office Department, which was for most Americans their main point of contact with the federal government, reaching deep into the nation's rural interior. In the first year of his presidency, Jackson dismissed 423 postmasters nationwide.

importance of personal relations to the new administration and had significant political consequences both in the short and the long term. In addition to forcing a major turnover in the executive branch, the scandal boosted the political fortunes of Martin Van Buren, a widower who socialized freely and cheerfully with the Eatons, and introduced a breach between Jackson and Vice President John Calhoun, whose wife had spearheaded the boycott. Van Buren, not Calhoun, would inherit Jackson's political mantle and succeed him to the presidency.

While the Eaton scandal simmered, Jackson was devoting himself to the cause of Indian removal. Jackson had achieved renown as an Indian fighter, and his commitment to expelling Indians from the Southeast prompted the major policy initiative of his first term (see Chapter 9). After winning that battle, however, Jackson took on two other causes that would come to define his presidency: one related to federal-state relations and the other to finance. First came the nullification crisis, which reflected and reinforced the growing animosity between Jackson and Calhoun. Calhoun led a revolt by South Carolina against an 1828 increase in the federal tariff on imports that protected northern manufacturers from foreign competition but had no benefit for southern farmers and plantation owners. Indeed, the so-called Tariff of Abominations resulted in higher prices on manufactured goods and indirectly hurt cotton growers by weakening British cotton buyers. Unable to persuade Congress to scrap the tariff, Calhoun anonymously authored a paper that put forward the doctrine that an individual state retained the right to nullify any federal law that it deemed unconstitutional, much like the Kentucky and Virginia Resolutions of 1798 (see Chapter 8). In 1832, when Congress replaced the 1828 tariff with a new one that provided little relief, the South Carolina legislature declared that the tariff law would no longer be operative in the state and no customs would be collected there.

Though Jackson was a vocal advocate of states' rights and had allowed Georgia to ignore the Supreme Court when it came to Indian removal, in this case he insisted on the supreme sovereignty of the federal union and labeled the actions of South Carolina treasonous. He secured congressional authorization for the Force Bill that would allow him to use the military against South Carolina if necessary; he then ordered warships to Charleston harbor. Congressman Henry Clay worked out a compromise tariff bill that persuaded South Carolina to withdraw its nullification, but the point had been made on both sides. South Carolina, which would become the first state to secede from the union three decades later, was on record claiming the right to void an act of Congress. And Andrew Jackson was on record as being willing to wage war against those who defied his authority.

THE BANK WAR AND THE PANIC OF 1837

Jackson's battle against Calhoun and nullification was quickly eclipsed by his political showdown with the Second Bank of the United States. The bank had recovered from the mismanagement of its early years and from the political fallout over the Panic of 1819. The Supreme Court had ruled that its charter did not violate the Constitution, and by 1823 the bank was on solid financial footing under the astute management of Nicholas Biddle, an intellectually accomplished figure with an impressive resumé. When Jackson took office, the bank was regulating the nation's currency supply to the satisfaction of most members of the financial community and the economy was enjoying relative stability. But Jackson came out in opposition to the bank, arguing that it concentrated power in a private corporation.

Fearing that Jackson might cause trouble for the bank when its charter expired in 1836, Biddle and his congressional supporters decided to have the bank apply for early renewal in 1832, so that Jackson would have to approve the new charter or suffer the political consequences in his reelection campaign later that year. Jackson took this as a mortal challenge. When Van Buren visited the president in the White House, he found Jackson lying on a couch. "The bank, Mr. Van Buren," he whispered, "is trying to kill me." He then pressed Van Buren's hand and added: "but I will kill it."

The bank's charter bill passed easily, and Jackson responded by vetoing it. Over the previous forty years, presidents had used this power a total of nine times, and only three times involving important and contested legislation. Jackson vetoed twelve acts of Congress, often citing constitutional grounds. This was perhaps the most significant growth in presidential power associated with Jackson's presidency. More strikingly, the veto message was a venomous and incendiary attack on the central bank, calling it an unfair monopoly that exacerbated the division between rich and poor. "The rich and powerful too often bend government to selfish purposes," Jackson proclaimed, and the bank was just another example of government-supported exploitation of the poor. The bank's supporters considered the veto message so outrageous that they reprinted and circulated thousands of copies, hoping it would help Jackson's opponent, Henry Clay, in the election of 1832. But Biddle and his allies had misread the popular mood. In a campaign that was in part a referendum on Jackson's passionate opposition to the Bank of the United States, the president was reelected overwhelmingly.

Why Jackson hated the bank so passionately and why this particular issue resonated so powerfully among the electorate is the subject of debate. Even within Jackson's own cabinet, there were sharply divided views on what was wrong with Biddle's bank. Some Jacksonians opposed banks in general because banks printed bank notes and created money out of nothing (see Chapter 8). But others objected to the national bank precisely because it regulated other banks and made it *harder* for them to print money. Jackson's veto message probably appealed both to western voters who wanted easier access to credit and to artisans who mistrusted the world of banks and paper.

After the election, three years still remained on the bank's charter, and Biddle was determined to muster sufficient

Bank War. Jackson and Biddle square off in this popular cartoon. Taking a cue from Jackson's political rhetoric, the cartoon depicts the president as the champion of whiskey-drinking frontiersmen, while the Bank of the United States is personified as an aristocratic woman holding a bottle of port.

congressional opposition to overturn the veto. Jackson, meanwhile, sought to undermine Biddle's power and destroy the bank even before its charter lapsed. Over the objections of two secretaries of the treasury, whom he had to fire, Jackson ordered that the federal government withdraw its money from Biddle's bank. Both the rhetoric of the charter veto and Jackson's long-standing discomfort with banks suggested that the president might propose a public alternative for storing government funds and regulating the currency supply. Instead, federal money was simply redeposited in twenty-three state-chartered private banks, many of them owned by associates of well-connected men in Jackson's inner circle of Democratic advisers. Biddle responded to the deposit removal by calling in loans and raising interest rates, thereby limiting the amount of paper money in circulation. This retaliatory act triggered a temporary recession and seemed to confirm Jackson's charge that the bank abused its excessive power for private gain and political influence. The larger problem for Biddle was that without the government deposits, the national bank could exert little control over private banks and the money supply. Private banks printed more money and approved a number of risky loans to investors eager to profit from western lands offered by the federal government (see Interpreting the Sources: Bank Notes). Speculative lending, speculative borrowing, and speculative land purchasing created a major bubble in the economy.

Many of Jackson's supporters had seen his attack on the bank as an indictment of paper money, speculation, and unearned wealth, but the bank war now appeared to have been an act of deregulation, allowing state-chartered private banks to proliferate and to do whatever they wanted. Jackson sought to tame the speculation by requiring payments at federal land offices to be made in gold and silver, but this drained gold and silver out of the banks, exposing them to the risk of not being able to redeem their notes. As Biddle's bank died, Britain's banks tightened the reins on American borrowers, gold and silver stopped flowing in to the United States from abroad, and in 1837 the American economy collapsed for the second time in less than twenty years.

The Panic of 1837 was the result of a complex set of developments in the international economy, but it was seen by many at the time as the result of the Democrats' mismanagement of the economy. Van Buren, who was elected to succeed Jackson in 1836, suffered politically from the economic collapse, but the consequences for the nation as a whole were far more devastating. The ensuing depression lasted for more than six years, the longest and most severe downturn in American history until the Great Depression almost a century later. Business failures began in New Orleans and then spread both through the southwestern part of the country and to New York along the circuits of the cotton trade. Boston merchants gathered in news rooms to learn of the latest bankruptcies in New York, while masses of workers in Philadelphia assembled to denounce banking as "a system of fraud and oppression." Land values declined precipitously (real estate lots in New York worth $480 late in 1836 sold for $50 seven months later), wages plummeted for those workers lucky enough to hold on to their jobs, and despair spread across the country. As the philosopher Ralph Waldo Emerson saw it, "the land stinks with suicide." In many ways the scenes were reminiscent of the smaller collapse in 1819. But by 1837 even fewer Americans were insulated from the instability of the market economy.

DEMOCRACY AND EQUALITY

As Jackson left office in 1837, he continued to rail against banks and paper money. But he took comfort in the fact that in America "the planter, the farmer, the mechanic, and the laborer . . . the bone and sinew of the country . . . [owned] the great mass of our national wealth." Jackson was fond of flattering the common man, but he was not alone in describing the United States in the 1830s as an egalitarian society. European visitors to Jackson's America routinely remarked on the absence of social hierarchy, the blurring of class divisions, and the broad distribution of economic opportunity. Some of these foreign observers liked what they saw, while others found it alarming,

INTERPRETING THE SOURCES

Bank Notes

We are now so accustomed to paper money that we think of the green bills in our wallets simply as cash. But before the Civil War the U.S. government did not print money and there was no such thing as uniform paper currency. The pieces of paper that circulated as money during this era were printed by hundreds of private banks that were chartered by the states in which they were headquartered (see Chapter 8).

Bank notes came in all sizes, colors, and denominations, and no one was required by law to accept them at face value in a transaction. The three-dollar bill pictured here promises that the bearer can exchange the note for three dollars' worth of specie (gold and silver). As long as everyone—storekeepers, landlords, neighbors, and friends—believed that the note *could* be redeemed for specie, it would continue to circulate as three dollars.

As cities grew, commercial exchanges proliferated, banks multiplied, and more men and women labored for cash wages, bank notes such as this became more common features of everyday life. Some of the hostility to the Bank of the United States reflected the frustrations and suspicions of Americans who were newly dependent on this chaotic system.

Three-Dollar Bill, 1850s, Mount Vernon Bank, Providence, Rhode Island. Banknotes from before the Civil War appeared in a bewildering array of denominations, including one cent, nine cents, twelve and a half cents, one dollar seventy-five cents, and three thousand dollars.

Explore the Source

1. What does the image on the bill represent, and why might it have been chosen?
2. If the owner of this bank note wanted to cash it in for gold or silver, what would he or she have had to do?
3. Why was it important for bank notes to bear personal signatures?

but traveler after traveler repeated the same observations: Americans dress in their Sunday best on a daily basis, there are no beggars in the United States, people eat meat three times a day, and any man's son might become the equal of any other man's. Political democracy, it seemed, brought with it social and economic equality. The French aristocrat Alexis de Tocqueville, who visited the United States in 1831 to study its innovative prison system and published a famously perceptive two-volume study of *Democracy in America*, saw "equality of condition" as the most conspicuous feature of American life.

But how equal were conditions in the United States during this period of mass democracy? When making their observations, European visitors tended to ignore or bracket the enslavement of over two million African Americans or the subordinate roles of blacks and women throughout the country. But even among white men, political democracy did not necessarily produce economic equality. Tax records from the period suggest that, contrary to Jackson's claim, a small percentage of the population controlled most of the nation's wealth. By the middle of the century, a majority of Americans owned no taxable property whatsoever. Moreover, most of the wealthy had been born wealthy, while most of those reared in poverty remained poor.

There are several possible explanations for Europeans' exaggerated perceptions of equality in Jackson's America. First, visitors may have seen what they expected to see in a country that had always represented novelty and social fluidity to Europeans. Second, America was being compared to Europe, where fewer individuals owned land and the divide between rich and poor was more extreme. Third, travelers may have associated geographical mobility with social mobility and assumed that, because Americans uprooted and relocated with astonishing frequency, they were ascending the socioeconomic ladder. Finally, even though few Americans were wealthy, many ordinary citizens adopted the refinements that in Europe belonged only to the elite. These signs of privilege included not only clean clothing, protein-heavy diets, and literacy, but also architectural refinements that might have been especially impressive to foreign visitors, such as parlors, open staircases, carpets, and fenced yards with trees and shrubs.

Spreading Gentility. Carpets became increasingly common in middle-class homes during the 1830s and 1840s, as the decorative furnishings of the rich spread to a broader segment of the population.

PARTICIPATORY POLITICS AND THE SECOND PARTY SYSTEM

Jackson's presidency ushered in a new era of mass participation in electoral politics, and expanded voting rights among white men were only part of the explanation. Before the 1830s, even most people who were eligible to vote declined to participate, especially in national elections. But by 1840, close competition between a new system of national parties would lead to turnouts over 70 percent for presidential elections, a trend that would last through much of the century. Even in off years, when the presidency was not at stake, elections drew much higher proportions of eligible voters than presidential contests do today (though the base of eligible voters today is far broader and larger). Elections became popular festivities and party politics drew the kind of boisterous participation and intense loyalty now more commonly associated with sporting events.

A SECOND PARTY SYSTEM

The Age of Jackson was an age of political parties. Having unseated Adams by building a new national coalition over a long campaign, Jackson's supporters sought to turn that coalition into a powerful party. Its lead architect was the New Yorker Martin Van Buren, who had controlled a powerful statewide party organization centered in Albany. The national party created around Jackson's candidacy in 1828 differed from the Republicans and Federalists of the first party system. The Democrats, as Van Buren's party would come to be known, were organized from the grassroots up through a system of nominating conventions on the county and state levels, and regulated by rigid commitments to party unity.

Van Buren reasoned that the country would be better served by competition between two large national parties rather than by a diffuse system of local factions and personal animosities. The clashes between competing national parties would help the masses of American voters identify and express political differences over what constitutes proper government. Van Buren also preferred party rivalries to regional ones. If Jefferson's alliance between artisans and small farmers in New York and slaveholders in Virginia could be revived and extended westward, the nation might avoid a split over slavery.

As the new Jackson alliance solidified, his opponents began reassembling and remodeling the New England–based coalition of nationalist Republicans who had supported Adams. The first rival party to tap into anti-Jackson sentiment was the Antimasons, who organized initially in response to a disappearance in upstate New York. William Morgan, a former member of a Masonic lodge, was rumored to have been abducted and murdered as he was preparing to publish the secrets of that international fraternal order, which had included many of the nation's founders. Antimasons accused Masons of conspiring to undermine the republic by keeping power in the hands of an elite secret society. As their message of transparent government spread west from New York, it attracted voters who suspected Jackson (a Mason) of being a despot. In 1831 the Antimasons introduced the now-standard practice of holding a national convention to set the party's platform and nominate candidates.

Three years later, Jackson's opponents would form a new national party, which they named the Whigs, after the British party that had voiced opposition, especially in the eighteenth century, to excesses of executive power. For the next twenty years, Democrats and Whigs would compete throughout the country in both national and state elections. Despite several significant challenges from third parties, American politics was dominated by these two institutions and their rivalry shaped political debate. For this reason, historians describe the period between the presidency of Jackson and the collapse of the Whigs during the 1850s as the era of the **Second Party System.**

By 1840 the Whigs had adopted many of Van Buren's tactics and had created a successful national party on the Democratic model. That year the Whigs held their first national convention and nominated for the presidency William Henry Harrison, who had led the attack on Tecumseh's followers at Tippecanoe back in 1811. Though Harrison had been born into a wealthy slaveholding family in Virginia and owned a stately home in Ohio, the Whigs celebrated him as a simple frontiersman who drank hard cider and lived in a log cabin. The Whigs, like their rivals, won their first presidential election by nominating an Indian fighter from the War of 1812 and giving him populist credentials.

But Whigs and Democrats were not simply mirror images of each other. They differed on important issues and appealed to different constituencies. Though both parties were committed to national expansion, Whigs tended to support federal interventions in the economy, such as government-sponsored improvements in transportation or tariffs to encourage domestic manufactures. Democrats, by contrast, were more enthusiastic about using federal power for territorial acquisition, as in the case of Jackson's Indian removal policies. Culturally, Whigs tended to embrace the evangelical values of the Benevolent Empire, whereas Democrats courted Catholic immigrants and advocated religious pluralism. Neither party criticized slavery, but Democrats were far more committed to its preservation and placed greater emphasis on an ideology of white supremacy (see Chapter 13).

Part of what made the Second Party System so stable and powerful in this period was the fact that the Whigs and the Democrats were both strong enough to make elections nationally competitive. Between 1834 and 1853, the Democrats won 54 percent of the seats in Congress and a majority of the electoral votes, although Whigs won more popular votes for president, 48.3 percent to 48.1 percent. Unfortunately for the Whigs, both of the men they elected to the presidency, Harrison in 1840 and Zachary Taylor in 1848, died early in their first terms. Harrison in fact died within a month of his inauguration and was succeeded by a vice president, John Tyler, who supported the Democrats on most issues. The Democratic Party may have dominated national policymaking in the 1830s and 1840s, but elections were close enough to maintain the enthusiasm of partisan loyalists on both sides and to discourage the formation of third parties.

CAMPAIGNING IN PRINT

Parties relied heavily on newspapers, pamphlets, and books to broadcast their message to voters. In every state capital in the union, both Whig and Democratic Party organs printed candidates' speeches and rebutted rivals' claims in great detail, drumming up voter interest well in advance of election day. In addition to these standing newspapers, parties produced special periodicals to support particular campaigns. In 1844, before the national conventions, sixty-three papers were published for Henry Clay (Whig) and forty-three for James Polk (Democrat). All of these papers enjoyed cheap postage rates courtesy of the federal government.

By the 1830s, campaign biographies also became a staple of the new political culture. The first books and pamphlets in this genre appeared in 1824, when the leading presidential candidates belonged to the same party and sought to distinguish themselves by touting their personal character and life experience rather than their ideology. But even after the rise of the Second Party System, campaigns used candidates' life stories to appeal to voters. Because overtly campaigning for oneself was frowned upon during this period, candidates did not authorize these biographies and often claimed to have nothing to do with them. Though they shared common themes and strategies, Democratic biographies differed from Whig biographies in subtle but interesting ways. Democrats tended to describe their nominees as ordinary men from humble beginnings who rose to prominence through hard work, whereas Whigs emphasized natural abilities and heroic service to the country. Whig biographies were also far more likely to stress a candidate's moral values, intense religious faith, and abstinence from alcohol. Significantly, campaign biographies from both parties paid little attention to the family relationships of their subjects and assigned women little if any role in the formation of their character. The men described in these books lived in a masculine world, much like the political arena in which they competed (see Hot Commodities: Davy Crockett and His Almanacs).

ROWDY ELECTIONS

In modern democracies, voting is the special ceremony through which the people are entitled and expected to express their will. But for most Americans in the nineteenth century, voting was not the sober, conscientious, private practice we now associate with that ceremony. Voting did not take place in curtained booths; it was performed publicly, often in crowded streets, town squares, county courthouses, or village taverns. In seven states, men exercised their franchise orally, in what was called *viva voce* (live voice) voting. But even paper ballots, which were used in a majority of states by the middle of the nineteenth century, did not shield a voter's preferences from public view. On the contrary, ballots during this period were printed by the political parties themselves, often on distinctively marked or colored paper, and distributed by campaign workers to voters in front of the polling site. Ballots looked and functioned like campaign paraphernalia.

The festivities leading up to election day offered additional opportunities to foster, express, and celebrate party loyalty. Both parties staged rallies and demonstrations in public spaces, featuring banners, floats, and torchlight parades. Except for the crucial fact that they were overwhelmingly male, these rallies resembled religious revival meetings lightly clothed in a common political goal. Speakers made high-pitched emotional appeals about the battle between good and evil, and partisans engaged in lots of singing. Attendance was often enormous. At one 1840 gathering in Dayton, Ohio, William Henry Harrison addressed a crowd of

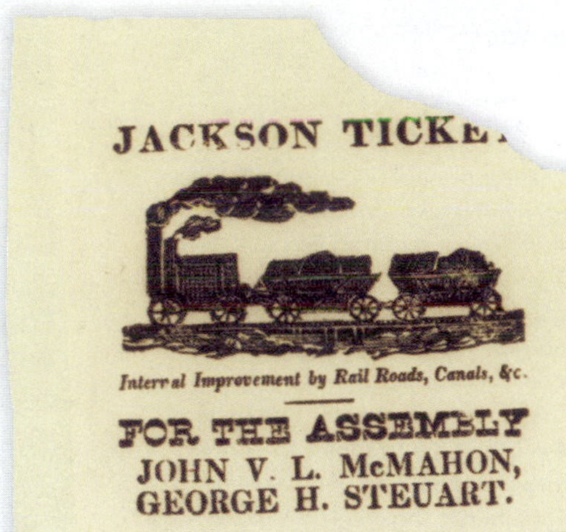

Democratic Election Tickets, 1828. Though they appear to be campaign leaflets, these were actually ballots. Paper ballots in the nineteenth century were slates rather than menus. Instead of selecting from a range of candidates, voters selected a "ticket" and simply dropped it into a box. Parties printed these ballots, which discouraged ticket splitting (voting for candidates from different parties for different races). In these examples from Maryland, a voter would be selecting Jackson for president while simultaneously casting votes for John V. L. McMahon and George H. Steuart, Jacksonians running to represent Baltimore in the state legislature. The depiction of a train was a curious choice for the Democrats since the Whig Party was more identified with transportation improvements during this period. **Question for Analysis:** Compared to modern ballots, do you think these tickets presume more or less knowledge on the part of the average voter about candidates for office?

Whig supporters estimated at one hundred thousand. These outdoor mass meetings relied on pithy slogans and tag lines to define party positions and offered dramatic spectacles that allowed average citizens to feel included in massive contests, where each individual's vote was unlikely to determine the outcome.

Alcohol flowed freely on election days, in urban and rural locales. Local candidates or party officials would treat voters to rounds of drinks as a way of securing partisan loyalty and fostering the solidarity and revelry appropriate to the occasion. Urban elections were especially drunken and violent. During New York's 1834 municipal elections, the first year in which the city elected its mayor, thousands of people engaged in fistfights in the streets, bricks were thrown, gunfire was exchanged, and one side even raided the city arsenal for weapons. When the polls finally closed, city militias had to escort ballot boxes to City Hall.

Drinking, fighting, and gambling reinforced the popular notion that politics was a

Rally for William Henry Harrison. The phrase "keep the ball rolling" has its origins in the 1840 presidential campaign. The line "that swift the ball is rolling on" was used in a Harrison campaign song. Some Whig clubs then built what they called "victory balls," eight- and sometimes twelve-foot balls of canvas, leather, and tin, which they painted with campaign slogans and rolled in rallies and parades. The Tippecanoe Club of Cleveland, Ohio, rolled one such ball across the state.

HOT COMMODITIES

Davy Crockett and His Almanacs

As the Whigs organized in opposition to President Jackson, they searched the political landscape for their own popular western hero. They found David Crockett, a frontiersman from Tennessee who had fought under Jackson against the Creeks and had entered politics in the 1820s.

Long before Davy Crockett became a coonskin-wearing character on a Walt Disney television show in the 1950s, he was a real person from East Tennessee who parlayed his local popularity into a political career and served in Congress for three terms over the period 1827 to 1835. His opposition to Jackson's Indian removal policy led to his election defeat in 1831, but he triumphed again two years later and, with the help of Whig journalists and publishers, presented himself to a wide audience in a series of popular autobiographies designed to boost his prospects for national office. Crockett's autobiographies (some of which were ghostwritten) told of hunting bears and tricking his neighbors, but they also attacked Jackson's military record and referred repeatedly to policy differences between Crockett and Jackson, especially on the national bank. Like Jackson, Crockett portrayed himself as an ordinary man of extraordinary qualities, with virtues and wisdom acquired and demonstrated in frontier life rather than in books, academies, or cosmopolitan social settings. And like Jackson, he depended on a national publishing network to get this message out to voters.

Crockett never fulfilled his political ambitions or those of his Whig promoters. Though he toured the eastern states in 1834 to build support for a possible bid for the presidency, Crockett's political star faded after he lost his seat in Congress in a close election a year later. Tired of Tennessee politics, Crockett left his home and moved farther south. "Since you have chosen to elect a man with a timber toe to succeed me," Crockett was reported to have announced at a hotel bar in Memphis (his Jacksonian opponent had a prosthetic leg), "you may all go to hell and I will go to Texas." Crockett did indeed move to Texas, where he was killed in 1836 at the battle of the Alamo (see Chapter 11).

As a cultural icon, however, Davy Crockett enjoyed great success. The process of turning a Tennessee politician into a mythical figure began in his own lifetime, even before he published his autobiographies. In 1830 a New York writer named James K. Paulding created a play entitled *The Lion of the West,* which featured a new comic character named Colonel Nimrod Wildfire, a powerful hero who was half-man, half-alligator and exposed the pretensions of the snobby and effete. Even before the script had been finished, rumors were identifying Nimrod Wildfire with Congressman Crockett. When the play came to Washington, Crockett rose appreciatively from the audience and exchanged bows with his on-stage counterpart. Already in 1830, Davy Crockett was in part a character in American theatrical entertainment.

By 1835, Crockett's autobiographies were joined by an immensely popular series of

Davy Crockett, Cultural Icon.
The cover of *Davy Crockett's Almanack, 1837,* features the Crockett character in a wildcat skin cap, a year after the real Crockett died in the Alamo. The man featured in the illustration is actually the actor James Hackett, who had played Colonel Nimrod Wildfire on stage.

Congressman David Crockett, 1833.
Crockett's rise to political prominence in the early 1830s epitomized a new age in American politics. As the aristocratic French traveler Alexis de Tocqueville observed with horror in 1831, "The inhabitants of the district in which Memphis is the capital sent to the House of Representatives an individual named David Crockett, who has no education, can read with difficulty, has no property, no fixed residence, but passes his life hunting, selling his game to live, and dwelling continuously in the woods. His competitor, a man of wealth and talent, failed."

Davy Crockett's Almanacks, which continued to be issued for twenty years after his death by urban publishers in the Northeast who had no interest in the politics or the life of the deceased man for whom the almanacs were named. These comic almanacs presented Crockett as a human-animal superhero who kills wild beasts and takes on their qualities. Graphically violent and gory, the Crockett tales often described sadistic behavior toward Indians. Whereas the real David Crockett had stood up to Jackson on the issue of Indian removal, his comic alter-ego would kill an Indian by chewing through his jugular vein and letting him bleed to death. In a later issue of the *Almanack,* the hero brags of killing two Indians: "I smashed number one into injun gravy with my foot, and spread it over number two, and made a dinner for me and my dog. It was superlicious."

Think About It

1. Was David Crockett primarily a politician or a popular entertainer?
2. What does it teach us about American politics and culture during the 1830s that a congressman became the basis for a comic superhero celebrated for sadistic acts of violence?

masculine affair. When Illinois Democratic congressional candidate William May was accused of adultery in 1834, he did not deny the charge. Instead, he responded that his accuser was "some spindle-shanked, toad-eating, man-granny, . . . some *puling* sentimental, *he*-old maid whose cold liver and pulseless heart, never felt a desire which could be tempted." In the age of universal manhood suffrage, rugged masculinity was deemed a political virtue by much of the electorate.

For other Americans, however, all the alcohol, revelry, and violence marked what was undignified and corrupt about politics. This critique often focused more on Democrats than on Whigs, but to many observers, especially native-born Protestants and women, the entire political process seemed tainted. Caroline Kirkland, in an 1839 novel set on the Michigan frontier, mocks the local politician as an ignorant, mercenary man who cares more about getting elected than about any issue. He gets his start in politics by selling hard-boiled eggs to voters on election day as an eight-year-old. "From eggs he advanced to pies, from pies to almanacs, whiskey, powder and shot, foot-balls, playing-cards, and at length," Kirkland informs her readers, "he brought into the field a large turkey, which was tied to a post and stoned to death at twenty-five cents a throw." Men like this epitomized the crude, masculine world of politics that many refined Americans found distasteful. Still, most of those who were eligible to vote did so dutifully, even if it meant holding their noses on the way to the polls.

The Brotherhood of Firemen: Members of the Protector Engine Company, New York, ca. 1850s. Both gangs and fire companies were building blocks of party organizations, especially on the Democratic side.

FIRE COMPANIES, SALOONS, AND BOXERS

In big cities, parties were dominated by brawny and belligerent men who worked the polls and ran for local office. The candidate for mayor might be a prominent businessman or merchant, but the ward bosses who controlled the party's operations at the grassroots level usually rose up from the ranks of gang leading, saloonkeeping, boxing, or firefighting. These men could be counted on to both attract and intimidate voters, and they reinforced the notion that politics was a masculine affair.

In the first half of the nineteenth century, there were no municipal fire departments. Instead, cities depended on volunteer fire companies to extinguish the blazes that erupted regularly in crowded spaces full of wooden buildings. These companies were fraternal organizations that drew men from different classes. They competed to be the first to arrive at the scene of a fire, often fighting one another while buildings burned. Fire companies generated great camaraderie and passion and in some ways were more respectable versions of the street gangs they otherwise resembled.

Saloons played a major role in this urban partisan culture as well, serving as meeting places for politicians and cultivating the solidarity among city dwellers, especially new immigrants. Saloonkeeping, like a leadership position in a fire company, could be a political stepping stone. Boxers also belonged to this world of urban politics. By midcentury, bare-knuckle prize fighting would emerge as a popular modern spectator sport on a national level, but already in the 1830s boxers were local celebrities, identified with particular gangs, saloons, and parties. Political rivals fought in the boxing ring as well as the ballot box, and boxers supplied some of the muscle necessary to win elections.

MARKETS AND CITIES

The rise of mass politics coincided with three other revolutionary developments in American life: the growth of commerce, the quickening pace of transportation and communication, and the emergence of big cities. Commerce was hardly new in the 1820s. For centuries, Americans had been buying and selling land, people, staple crops, and other commodities. But in the early nineteenth century, new patterns of producing, transporting, distributing, and consuming goods changed the daily economic lives of most Americans, especially in the North, bringing them into a national network of regular commercial exchange. Similarly, although cities had existed in North America for many centuries, a handful of places emerged in this period as the nation's first large, impersonal metropolises. Some of these changes were part of the complex process known as **industrialization,** which in its early phases did not primarily involve machines and factories. Industrialization simply meant the reorganization of the production process by employers through the division of labor.

Map 10.1 Canal Network, 1840. Note the geographical distribution of canal projects.

CANALS AND THE TRANSPORTATION REVOLUTION

Artificial waterways powered the growth of the American economy. Because transportation was much cheaper and faster on water than on land, canals sped the circulation of goods across the country and brought more people and places into the world of long-distance trade. Though canals were known in different parts of the world well before the nineteenth century, they had been used sparingly in the United States. After the end of the War of 1812, state governments, merchants, and entrepreneurs embarked on a major canal-building spree. As late as 1820, the total mileage of canals in the United States was lower than one hundred. But over the next three decades, Americans carved out more than three thousand miles of new waterways, mostly with public funding. Much of the construction took place in just a few states (New York, Pennsylvania, and Ohio), but those canals, together with others dug in the Northeast and Midwest, linked most of the country's major rivers and lakes by the middle of the century (see Map 10.1).

In New York, Governor DeWitt Clinton persuaded the state legislature to fund what would become the nation's busiest and most profitable artificial waterway, the Erie Canal. Construction began on the Erie Canal in 1817 and ended in 1825, two years ahead of schedule. "Clinton's Ditch," as it was skeptically dubbed, began in the state capital of Albany on the Hudson River, which flows south to New York City and empties into the Atlantic Ocean. Wending its way north and west from Albany for more than 363 miles, the Canal passed over nineteen stone aqueducts and relied upon eighty-three locks to raise water levels, ultimately reaching its terminus at Buffalo on Lake Erie. The Canal thus allowed for a continuous navigable water passage from the Atlantic Ocean to the Great Lakes. On October 26, 1825, Clinton celebrated this triumph of both civil engineering and public finance with a "Wedding of the Waters" ceremony in New York City. Before the largest public celebration in any U.S. city to that point, Clinton poured a keg of water from Lake Erie into the ocean. In a palpable way, the world was becoming more connected.

The Erie Canal was crucial to the development, during the 1830s and 1840s, of a domestic market within the United States for agricultural produce. No longer would the growth of the American economy depend primarily on foreign trade. Other factors contributed to this development as well, including the proliferation of steamboats, which sped shipping schedules; the westward migration of farmers, which opened new land to cultivation; and the introduction of mechanical reapers, which allowed farmers to harvest larger crops. But canals enabled farmers in the interior of the country to raise crops and livestock for consumers along the eastern seaboard. In turn, canals also opened up new rural markets for manufactured goods from eastern cities. Canals integrated farmland west of the Appalachians into a national water transportation network—and into the market economy.

Though canal construction was costly by the standards of government spending at the time, the investments paid off. Because traffic on the canal was so heavy, New York State brought in five times as much in toll revenues as it owed in interest on debt incurred to finance the project. By 1837, Clinton's Ditch had paid for itself. Even more significant was the canal's impact on the state's economy. A year after the canal's completion, shipping costs from Lake Erie to Manhattan had dropped from $100 a ton to under $9. Within five years, farmers in western New York could sell wheat for a profit in New York City. The new economic equation changed the face of the state. Places that had been wilderness were cleared of trees to make room for farmland and to supply firewood and lumber to the new market towns that were sprouting up along the canal route. Small frontier towns like Buffalo mushroomed into sizable cities, and the brand new city of Rochester quickly emerged as a major processing and manufacturing center. Beyond the borders of the state, the Erie Canal changed the economy and ecology of the Great Lakes region.

Canals were but one component of a national transportation network that carried people and commercial goods. This network, which consisted of paved roads, steam-powered riverboats, and government-contracted mail carriages, also sped the flow of information (see Map 10.2). Apart from smoke signals, carrier pigeons, and a few experiments with optical telegraph relays (which had been introduced on a large scale in the 1790s in France but were used in the United States mostly for ship-to-shore signals), information traveled in this period only as fast as human beings. This meant that improvements in transportation were by definition improvements in communication (see Map 10.3). One measure of the impact of the new transportation network is how quickly people in various parts of the country received national news. When George Washington died in 1799 in Alexandria, Virginia, no one in New York City knew about it for a full week. The news took thirteen days to reach Boston and twenty-four days to reach Cincinnati. Just three decades later, President Jackson's State of the Union address would reach New York in 15.5 hours, Boston in 31 hours, and Cincinnati in just over two days. For those Americans living near these hubs of information exchange, shorter time lags meant new experiences of long-distance connection. It was now possible and meaningful to imagine that two related events could be happening simultaneously in different parts of the country. All of this was before the emergence of a national railroad system and before the introduction of the electromagnetic telegraph. Those advances would happen soon enough. But already in 1840 a revolutionary change had taken place.

URBANIZATION AND CITY GROWTH

Market expansion along the new transportation routes facilitated one of the most important developments in nineteenth-century American history: the transformation of the United States from a rural society to an urban one. When the Erie Canal was completed, the vast majority of Americans lived on

Canal Country. "A new state of things is taking place in consequence of the opening of the New York and Ohio Canals," observed a young man from central Pennsylvania as he passed through Ohio in 1830. "Wheat etc. will now command the land and the country is beginning to assume a new appearance. . . ." In Lockport, New York, the Holland Land Company began selling canal-side parcels to speculators as soon as the state legislature authorized more funding for the Erie Canal Commission in 1816. Between 1820 and 1846, land values along the canal's route grew 91 percent. Like other canals of this era, the Erie Canal was a minimum of four feet deep and allowed boats to be dragged by animals traveling alongside the canal on a towpath. Canal boats traveled at slow speeds, but the reduced friction allowed a single animal to tow fifty-ton barges.

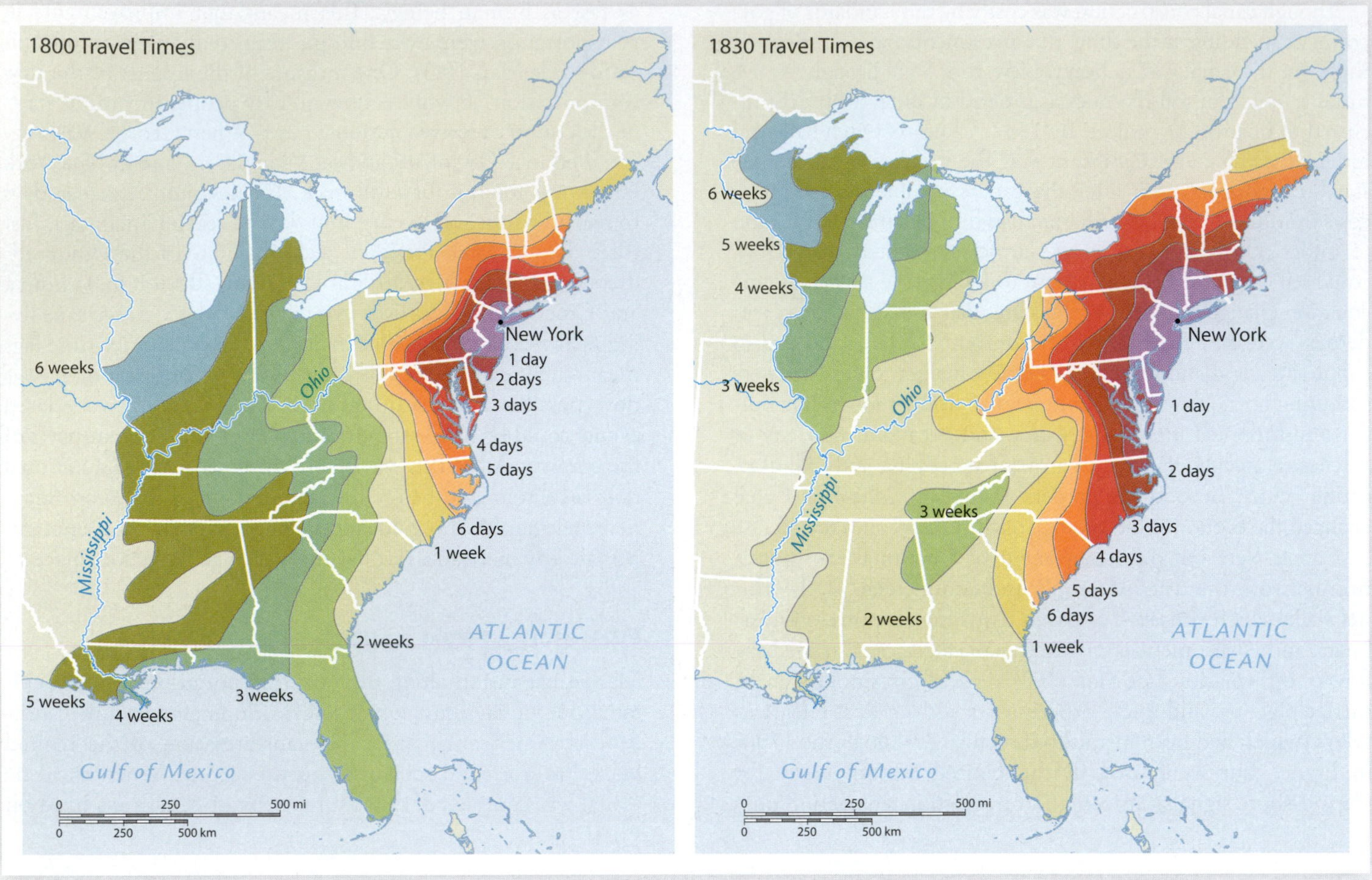

Map 10.2 Travel Times from New York, 1800 and 1830. Persons, goods, and information traveled along the same routes. For Americans living in the rural interior of the country, news arrived in the hands of a less steady stream of travelers, and current events unfolded along a much slower timeline than for those in coastal cities. But the real distances between places were diminishing rapidly, well before the railroad or the telegraph.

farms and in villages. City life remained a minority experience in North America, as it had been for all of recorded history. The 1820 census found that only 7 percent of the population lived in settlements of 2,500 people or more. Over the next hundred years, that proportion would increase steadily, finally reaching a majority by 1920. Many historical factors contributed to this century-long pattern of **urbanization,** but the spread of the market economy was pivotal. The transportation revolution helped convert wilderness into farmland, but it also created new economic opportunities in the cities where agricultural goods were processed, exchanged, and distributed. Before 1830, Cleveland was a tiny village, and Chicago was not even incorporated, but state-funded canals turned them (and countless lesser-known towns across the North and Midwest) into commercial centers by the middle of the century.

At the same time, the United States was becoming urban in another sense as well. What had made the early American republic a society of towns, villages, and farms was not simply the low percentage of people who lived in cities but also the low number of major cities overall and their relatively modest size. In 1800, only six places in the nation had more than ten thousand people and the largest cities claimed barely sixty thousand. By comparison, London's population at the time was 865,000, and Paris had over half a million. Beginning around 1825, several U.S. cities became significant metropolises, and by the middle of the century, big-city life would become a central part of American culture.

The first major modern metropolis in the United States was New York, which became the nation's most populous city at the end of the eighteenth century and has remained so ever since. New York grew quickly in the first quarter of the century, benefiting from transportation links to Britain that gave it competitive advantages over other eastern seaports. But in 1825, New York was still a compact settlement on the southern tip of Manhattan. The opening of the Erie Canal transformed the city, cementing its position as the nation's commercial capital by giving it superior transportation access to the West and making it the major inlet for foreign trade. Over the next thirty-five years, New York's population quintupled to more than eight hundred thousand, swelled by the arrival of rural northeasterners and foreign immigrants seeking better economic opportunities. By 1860 the population of Manhattan (Brooklyn remained a separate city until 1898) exceeded that of twenty of the thirty-three states in the union.

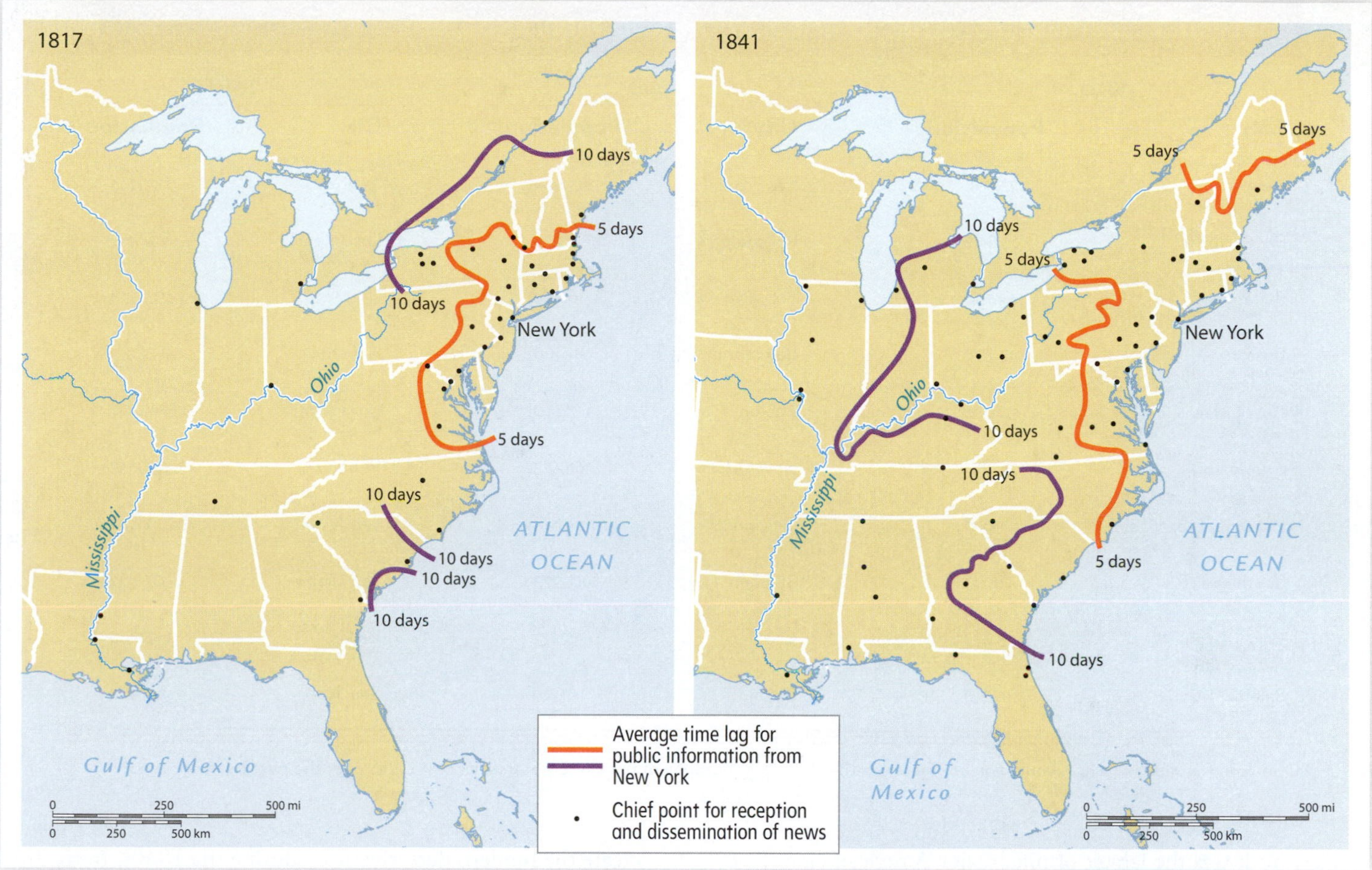

1817

10 days
5 days
10 days
New York
Ohio
5 days
10 days
10 days
10 days
10 days
Mississippi
ATLANTIC OCEAN
Gulf of Mexico

1841

5 days
5 days
10 days
5 days
New York
Ohio
10 days
10 days
Mississippi
5 days
10 days
ATLANTIC OCEAN
Gulf of Mexico

Average time lag for public information from New York

Chief point for reception and dissemination of news

0 250 500 mi
0 250 500 km

Map 10.3 Information Flow from New York. The expanding market society was also a tightening world of information exchange. Whereas Map 10.2 illustrates how long it would take a determined traveler to get from place to place, these maps, by plotting the speed at which public information emanating from New York showed up in 1817 and in 1841, reveal how fast public information tended to move. The maps also indicate the principal points where such information was broadcast and relayed. **Question for Analysis:** How might you account for the change, over these twenty-four years, in which parts of the United States fell within a ten-day news radius of the nation's largest city?

New York at Midcentury. After the opening of the Erie Canal, New York became the largest city in the Western Hemisphere. Although Manhattan would not boast a skyline of tall buildings until well after the Civil War, the crucial period of the city's demographic growth took place between 1825 and 1860. By 1860, Manhattan's population was already closer to what it would be in 2010 than to what it had been in 1820.

TABLE 10. 2 LARGEST U.S. CITIES BY POPULATION: 1820, 1860, AND 2010

1820		1860		2010	
City	**Population**	**City**	**Population**	**City**	**Population**
New York	123,706	New York	813,669	New York	8,175,133
Philadelphia	63,802	Philadelphia	565, 229	Los Angeles	3,792,621
Baltimore	62,738	Brooklyn	266, 661	Chicago	2,695,598
Boston	43,298	Baltimore	212,418	Houston	2,099,451
New Orleans	27,176	Boston	177,840	Philadelphia	1,526,006
Charleston	24,780	New Orleans	168,675	Phoenix	1,445,632
Northern Liberties, PA	19,678	Cincinnati	161,044	San Antonio	1,327,407
Southwark, PA	14,713	St. Louis	160, 773	San Diego	1,307,402
Washington, D.C.	13,247	Chicago	112,172	Dallas	1,197,816
Salem, MA	12,731	Buffalo	81,129	San Jose	945,942

Question for Analysis: How would you characterize the shifting geography of the United States' largest cities over the past two centuries?

New York was the largest of nine major American cities that grew to over one hundred thousand by the 1860 census. Five of these cities were on the Atlantic coast, three (Cincinnati, St. Louis, and New Orleans) were located on major rivers, and another (Chicago) fronted one of the Great Lakes. All were connected through the national network of water transport. Significantly, relatively little of the period's urban growth took place in the South, which benefited much less directly from the new canal projects and, because of the prevalence of slavery, did not attract large numbers of wage laborers. The largest southern cities lay on major waterways at the periphery of the region (Baltimore, St, Louis, and New Orleans). As a whole, the South was a less urban society; its cities were fewer, smaller, and farther between.

CITIES, CROWDS, AND STRANGERS

America's growing cities were not simply bigger in the 1830s than they had been before; they were different social environments. Whereas even the nation's largest urban centers had been compact communities in which people recognized one another (see Chapter 8), cities were now becoming dense worlds of strangers, where newcomers experienced the pleasures, dangers, and alienation of modern anonymous living. It was during this period that residents and visitors in U.S. cities took notice of the new phenomenon of the urban crowd. Edgar Allan Poe, who was a product of this new urban setting, drew upon the mysteriousness of the crowded metropolis to create the modern detective story during the 1840s. In the first of his urban mysteries, "The Man of the Crowd" (1840), Poe's narrator follows an anonymous old man through city streets at night, trying (unsuccessfully) to figure out his story. Cities had become worlds of strangers, and their residents were now members of a crowd.

Several new institutions contributed to the creation of this new urban environment, all of them introduced in a handful of big U.S. cities between 1825 and 1835. The first was fixed-route public transit, which allowed strangers to navigate the city without having to know or communicate with other people. The horse-drawn omnibus (the word was later shortened to *bus*) provided regular service along New York's Broadway beginning in 1829. Within a few years, urban transit companies were operating omnibuses in Boston, Philadelphia, Baltimore, New Orleans, Washington, and Brooklyn. Omnibuses were soon joined by street railway cars, also powered by horses, which became the dominant form of urban transportation by midcentury. Urban transit systems contributed to the sprawling growth of American cities by expanding the distances people could conveniently travel between home and work.

The second major innovation in city life was commercial nightlife, which was marked by the introduction of gaslight. Baltimore was the first city to light its streets with gas lamps in 1817, and New York had adopted the practice by 1825. By later standards, gas lamps provided only partial illumination

***The Boston and Cambridge New Horse Railroad,* Engraving Published in 1856.** Horse-drawn streetcars were the dominant form of urban mass transit in America for most of the nineteenth century, despite the availability of steam power. As in the case of canals, the major innovation of the streetcar lay in the surface on which it ran rather than the structure of the vehicle or the locomotive power on which it relied.

and created none of the spectacle that would be associated with electrified cityscapes at the end of the century. Nonetheless, it signaled an important change in urban living. In earlier periods, city streets were largely empty after nightfall, but the new technologies of outdoor illumination served the needs of a growing market for late-night entertainment. Restaurants, bowling alleys, oyster bars, saloons, cheap theaters, dance halls, and various commercial sex venues catered to this market and changed the look and feel of nighttime in large cities. By mid-century, observers and reformers were describing what went on in cities after dark in lurid and sensational terms. One popular journalist decried "the fearful mysteries of darkness in the metropolis—the festivities of prostitution, . . . the haunts of theft and murder, the scenes of drunkenness and beastly debauch." Put less dramatically, the gas-lit city offered many city dwellers, especially young men, a new world of nighttime activity that we now take for granted.

THE RISE OF THE PENNY PRESS

In addition to streetcars and gas lamps, city people relied on daily newspapers to guide them through unfamiliar urban environments. Newspapers were not new in the second quarter of the nineteenth century, but they were proliferating rapidly and attracting much greater readership. Between 1830 and 1840, the number of daily papers in the United States rose from 65 to 138, and their circulation rose proportionately. This nationwide trend was closely related to the rise of the Second Party System. As in the era of the Federalists and the Republicans, the new national parties relied on networks of loyal newspapers to promote their candidates and broadcast their ideas across the country. With an expanded electorate and intense competition between the two parties, Democrats and Whigs were especially motivated to found newspapers. Many papers, especially outside of big cities, were essentially party organs that brought in little revenue. But if the party emerged victorious at the polls, newspapers' publishers were rewarded with government printing contracts. Other factors contributed to the growth of print journalism on a national scale after 1830, including innovations in transportation, printing, papermaking, and corrective eyewear. But probably no cause was as important as the increased participation of ordinary men in partisan politics.

In big cities, daily news consumption was especially widespread. In New York, one copy of a daily newspaper appeared for every sixteen residents in 1830. Twenty years later, the ratio had dropped to one for every 4.5 residents, and the ratio was one to 2.2 on Sunday. But the bigger change was in the kind of papers that circulated. In 1833, twenty-three-year-old journeyman printer Benjamin Day introduced the first daily to sell for a penny, the *New York Sun,* and within a few months it became the most popular paper in the city. At the time, the leading metropolitan papers of the time cost 6 cents and relied on subscriptions by merchants and lawyers. The *Sun* offered a smaller, cheaper product to a mass readership and employed an army of newsboys to hawk individual copies of the paper in the streets on a daily basis. This model of the penny paper spread quickly to other big cities and changed the news business. The *Boston Daily Times* (1836) took only a few weeks to earn the highest circulation in that city, and the *Baltimore Sun* amassed a circulation three times its nearest competitor before it was nine months old.

The **penny press** initiated new, less affluent readers into the daily habits of reading the news. Some of the early cheap dailies also had ties to working-class politics, but after the Panic of 1837 many of those publications folded. The penny papers that survived the depression attracted readers from different classes and usually disclaimed any formal identification with particular political parties. Newspapers like the *New York Sun*, the *New York Herald*, and their many followers in metropolitan America appealed to a wide local readership by offering popular stories, descriptions of city life, and classified advertising that helped ordinary city dwellers find work, entertainment, services, and consumer products.

The cheap dailies introduced a new brand of journalism to modern urban life. Though they continued older traditions of covering national politics and listing ship arrivals, penny papers pioneered the use of sensational stories to boost circulation. Two years into its existence, the *New York Sun* ran a series of articles, allegedly reprinted from a Scottish scientific journal, describing recent discoveries of life on the moon. The

SINGULAR LIVES

Dorcas Doyen, Tabloid Victim

In the weeks after she was found bludgeoned to death in her bed at a high-end brothel, a woman known as Helen Jewett was probably the most famous person in New York City. Jewett was murdered at the dawn of a new era in the history of American journalism, and the city's cheap newspapers filled their columns with information and misinformation about Jewett and speculation about the crime. Every day, new stories appeared in print, describing a prostitute of unparalleled beauty and charm, who read the novels of Sir Walter Scott and the poetry of Lord Byron and won the hearts of the rich and famous until her tragic demise.

Behind the sensational stories, the woman who adopted the work name "Helen Jewett" led a life that fit some more ordinary patterns in the history of the growing American city. Dorcas Doyen was born in Maine to a poor rural family and worked from a young age as a domestic servant for a prominent judge in Augusta. Forced to leave when it was discovered that she was a sexually active teenager, Doyen moved to larger cities and began working in brothels. She arrived in New York in 1832 at the age of nineteen, part of a tide of young New Englanders migrating to New York in search of social and economic opportunities.

Doyen was just one of many young women who tried to make a living in New York's expanding sex trade, which became more visible and popular during the first half of the nineteenth century. Pushed by low wages to consider alternative or additional work, increasing proportions of women sold sex for money. Though few catered to as elite a clientele as Doyen, a number of women in the sex trade enjoyed considerable autonomy and accumulated significant assets. Between 1830 and 1860, at least twenty-four known New York prostitutes were assessed for $5,000 or more in real property.

Yet sex workers also faced serious risks in nineteenth-century cities. To reduce the dangers of infection and violence, prostitutes sought protection in brothels. But brothels were often attacked in the nineteenth century, and the women who worked there did not enjoy the full protection of the law. Doyen's former lover, Richard Robinson, got away with murder in part because the judge presiding over his trial instructed the jury to disregard the testimony of women in the sex trade. Though Robinson faced a mountain of incriminating evidence, the only witnesses who could place him at the scene of the murder were, of course, prostitutes.

THE REAL ELLEN JEWETT.
From an original Painting taken from Life.

Helen Jewett. The original black-and-white version of this popular image of Jewett in elegant attire was printed shortly after her death. Readers of the story unfolding in the press would recognize the letter in her hand as a hint that she was delivering a message to her lover Richard Robinson, the man charged with her murder.

Think About It

1. How did the timing of Doyen's murder contribute to its status as a sensational event?
2. What larger issues about sex, class, and city life might the murder and the trial have raised for New Yorkers in 1836?

articles' detailed reports of spherical amphibians that rolled instead of walking, blue goats with single horns, two-legged beavers, and short hairy men with bat wings turned out to be fiction, but during the height of the 1835 Moon Hoax controversy, the *Sun*'s circulation soared to almost twenty thousand, making it in all likelihood the best-read daily newspaper in the world.

More often, the leading news stories covered in the penny press were closer to home and rooted in real events. Typically, these stories revolved around sex and violence. Probably the most talked-about news event in urban America during the first decades of the cheap daily press was the 1836 murder of Helen Jewett, a New York sex worker (see Singular Lives: Dorcas Doyen, Tabloid Victim). Accounts of Jewett's life, descriptions of her corpse, and detailed coverage of the trial and acquittal of her accused killer dominated the penny papers, boosted their circulation, and established their new, modern role as an authoritative source of information for events of perceived public interest. In earlier periods, freedom of the press typically meant the right of an editor to criticize the government. By contrast, from the 1830s on, it began to include the right of readers to unimpeded access to information about everything that happened in public life.

WORK, UNIONS, AND CLASS STRUGGLE

Big cities were also transformed during this period by changes in the workplace brought about by industrialization. At this early stage in industrial development (pre–Civil War), only about 10 percent of the labor force was engaged in manufacturing, and most of those workers spent their days in small workshops, making things with their hands, not with automated machinery. In these workshops, industrialization took the form of new strategies for reorganizing craftwork.

Urban employers (master craftsmen and entrepreneurial manufacturers) devised new ways to make the labor process more efficient and profitable, and these new methods changed the customary patterns and rhythms of work and leisure. They eliminated traditional practices such as drinking on the job and Monday absenteeism; they increasingly bought workers' time, rather than their products; and they measured that time with new precision.

Employers also began rationalizing and **deskilling** the production process, dividing it up so as to minimize the amount of skilled labor required. Instead of training apprentices to master various parts of a trade, which they would perform with greater skill and reward over the course of their working lives, masters assigned certain parts of a trade to skilled craftsmen and other parts to workers who would continue to perform just that task. Clothing production, for example, was broken down into cutting, a relatively skilled occupation, and sewing, which could be contracted out to less skilled workers. Shoemaking, similarly, became two distinct tasks. Women were hired to stitch the upper half of shoes for lower rates of pay than men received to construct the outsole, shank, and heel.

The combined effect of deskilling and tighter managerial control was to reduce artisans' expectations for advancement within an occupation and to weaken the association between manual labor and a life calling. This was a dramatic shift in the world view of American craftsmen. Craft traditions that controlled the work experience for centuries began to fade. Elite craftsmen with access to credit and capital withdrew from the workplace and became manufacturing entrepreneurs, while others in the same craft faced a future of wage labor. Many urban workers now identified less with the masters in their own trades and more with those at the same skill level and hierarchical status in other trades.

Beginning in the 1820s, workers in large cities responded to these changes by organizing labor unions. Philadelphia artisans took the lead in this movement, banding together to defend what a group of striking bookbinders called "their inalienable right . . . to affix a price on the only property we have to dispose of: our labor." Tradesmen had asserted their right to set prices on their work before, but only in the second quarter of the nineteenth century did American artisans from different trades coordinate their efforts on the grounds that they were all workers. Labor activists established a General Trades Union in New York in 1833, and over the next few years General Trades Unions sprouted up in more than a dozen U.S. cities. Most workers in New York belonged to such a union in the mid-1830s, as did significant proportions of urban workingmen elsewhere. During a three-year period between 1833 and 1836, American workers went on strike 172 times and were usually successful. Overall, the decade leading up to the 1837 financial collapse marked a high point of union struggles, before hard times, increased foreign immigration, and the use of state force to break strikes diminished the power of organized labor.

Strikes often expressed local grievances, but the central theme of union activity in the 1830s was control over the workplace, and especially the length of the workday. The ten-hour movement was a powerful organizing issue for American labor. Pay standards might vary from craft to craft and from city to city, but capping the workday at ten hours was something all workers could support. Even those who were unemployed stood to gain by limitations on the amount of work employers could demand of an individual laborer, since a shorter day pushed companies to hire more people. By the 1840s, unions and their political supporters (usually from the Democratic Party) had succeeded in establishing a ten-hour norm, beginning a century-long trend toward shorter working days in the United States.

Alarmed by changes in the workplace, urban artisans also turned to electoral politics. Workers' parties formed in Philadelphia and New York in the late 1820s. New York's labor party, led by a radical named Thomas Skidmore who advocated abolishing the private sale or rental of land and granting 160 acres to every man and unmarried woman, attracted considerable support in the 1829 legislative elections. But soon thereafter, labor parties were absorbed or coopted by the Democrats. Urban workingmen tended to support Democratic candidates over Whigs or third-party nominees, and often assumed leadership positions in those local Democratic factions that were more critical than the national party of the emerging industrial order.

Though the new industrial order took hold mostly in small workshop settings, a factory system did appear in a handful of much smaller cities in New England, where innovative technologies were used to convert raw cotton into finished fabrics. The most famous of these textile processing plants were in Waltham, Massachusetts (where the first fully integrated textile factory appeared in 1814) and nearby in the town of Lowell. The **Waltham-Lowell system** employed female employees, mostly single women from New England farm families, and housed them in tightly regulated dormitories. Lowell was widely celebrated as a model of technological progress and worker contentment, and attracted

How Much Is That?

Textile Factory Pay in 1830

Weekly earnings of $3.00 at Lowell in 1830 are equivalent to $75.15 per week in 2013, well below the current minimum wage even for a forty-hour week, let alone for the seventy-three hours put in by female mill workers. Still, young girls and women flocked from New England farms to the mills because they could save up some cash to purchase clothes, amass a dowry, or send money back to their families.

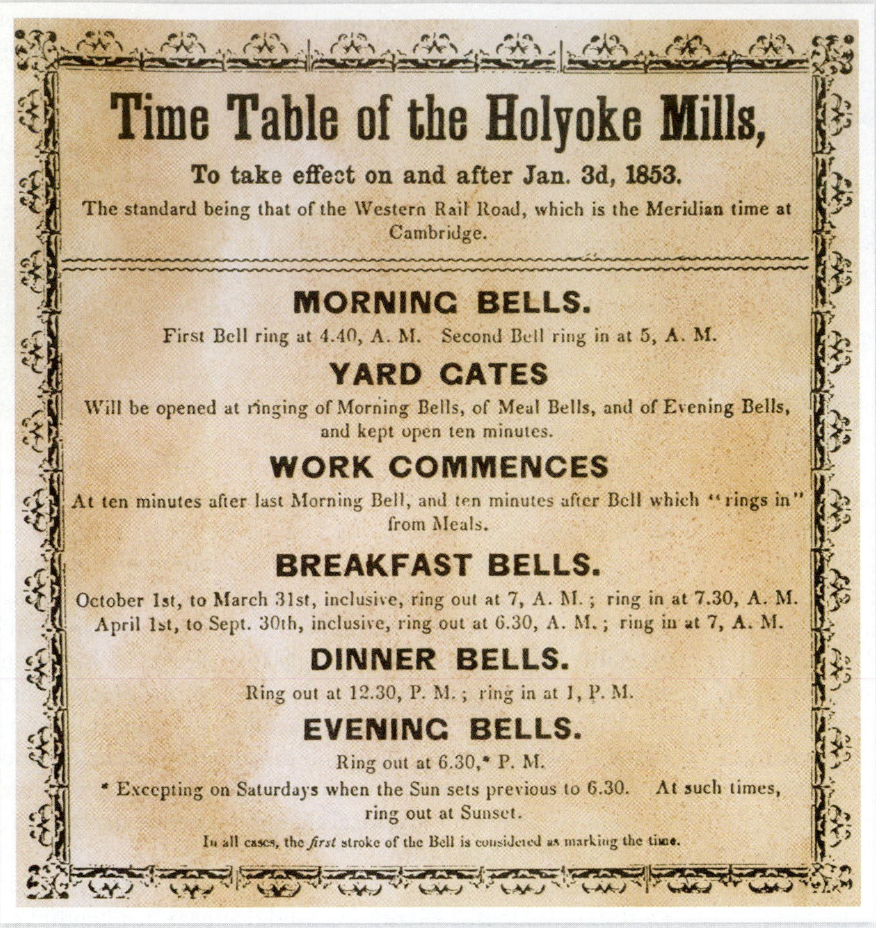
Time Table of the Holyoke Mills,

To take effect on and after Jan. 3d, 1853.

The standard being that of the Western Rail Road, which is the Meridian time at Cambridge.

MORNING BELLS.

First Bell ring at 4.40, A. M. Second Bell ring in at 5, A. M.

YARD GATES

Will be opened at ringing of Morning Bells, of Meal Bells, and of Evening Bells, and kept open ten minutes.

WORK COMMENCES

At ten minutes after last Morning Bell, and ten minutes after Bell which "rings in" from Meals.

BREAKFAST BELLS.

October 1st, to March 31st, inclusive, ring out at 7, A. M.; ring in at 7.30, A. M.
April 1st, to Sept. 30th, inclusive, ring out at 6.30, A. M.; ring in at 7, A. M.

DINNER BELLS.

Ring out at 12.30, P. M.; ring in at 1, P. M.

EVENING BELLS.

Ring out at 6.30,* P. M.

* Excepting on Saturdays when the Sun sets previous to 6.30. At such times, ring out at Sunset.

In all cases, the *first* stroke of the Bell is considered as marking the time.

Time Table of the Holyoke Mills. Though they were unusually large, New England textile mills represented a growing trend toward precise timekeeping at the workplace. Mill operatives worked long hours, six days a week, regulated by an elaborate schedule of bells beginning in this case at 4:40 A.M.

numerous young rural workers for whom a wage of approximately $3 a week represented a significant economic opportunity (see How Much Is That?). By the late 1830s, however, working conditions had deteriorated, and several disenchanted mill employees became labor activists. By the mid-1840s, mill companies began replacing New England farm girls with immigrants, who were less likely to agitate for higher wages and greater control over the workplace. These developments were well publicized at the time, but in the larger scheme of American labor and American urban development, Lowell was anomalous.

MILLENNIALISM AND AWAKENING

The era of canal building and early industrial development also saw the accelerating spread of evangelical Christianity. Church membership doubled between 1800 and 1835 relative to the population, and much of that growth took place in last few years of the period. By the time Tocqueville visited America, it seemed to him that there was no country on earth in which Christianity exercised "a greater influence on the souls of men." At the same time, Americans were also turning to new religious ideas and movements beyond the borders of the major Protestant denominations. Large segments of American society were becoming more intensely religious at the same time that market relations, party politics, wage labor, and urbanization were eroding traditional patterns of living and laying the foundations of a modern culture.

REVIVALS ALONG THE CANAL ROUTE

Religious revivals and mass conversions, which had begun earlier with camp meetings, circuit riders, and tract societies (see Chapter 9), reached a climax after the opening of the Erie Canal. This was the height of what historians call the **Second Great Awakening,** when a charismatic Presbyterian minister named Charles Grandison Finney became the most successful evangelist in the nation. Finney was a lawyer in western New York who knew little about Scripture and had attended church infrequently before he underwent a sudden conversion experience in 1821 and decided to preach. As he informed one of his clients, "I have a retainer from the lord Jesus Christ to plead his cause, and I cannot plead yours."

Finney looked around him at the world being remade by the canal and saw mushrooming towns and cities, Americans uprooting themselves continually in search of new prospects, and new work patterns removing young men from the clutches and scrutiny of their families. He decided the time was right for a massive evangelical campaign. Here, in the part of western New York that came to be known as the **Burned-Over District** because of the religious enthusiasm that blazed through the canal region, Finney staged a series of revivals, culminating in a six-month stint in the booming city of Rochester in 1830 and 1831. He then moved to New York City, where he began preaching to massive audiences in a renovated theater. Over the course of a long career, Finney was credited with bringing about the conversion of half a million souls with his emotional appeals and his message that, contrary to orthodox Calvinist doctrine, human beings were moral free agents who could will their own salvation. He also transformed the conversion experience from a private moment in the individual conscience to a public event—one that competed with the new forms of commercial leisure and entertainment that were emerging in the region's growing cities.

LITH. OF F. PALMER & CO. 88 NASSAU STREET, N.Y. 1850.
THE BROADWAY TABERNACLE.

Charles Grandison Finney Preaching to a New York Audience on Broadway. Using spectacle, advertising, and showmanship, Finney's revivals offered religious excitements that might counteract what he called "the great political and other worldly excitements" of the age.

At first the religious old guard was hostile to Finneyite revivalism and worried about what they saw as a threat to the hierarchies of class and station that secured social order. In 1827, Reverend Lyman Beecher threatened Finney that if the evangelist tried to bring his revivals to Connecticut and Massachusetts he would "call out the artillery-men." But as the market revolution spread, conservative clergymen overcame their scruples about revivalism. Four years after Beecher issued his threat, he was inviting Finney to speak in his own church. Following Finney's spectacular success in Rochester, Beecher declared that his achievements marked "the greatest work of God, and the greatest revival of religion, that the world has ever seen."

The cultural impact of Finney's revivals was considerable, especially among middle-class, native-born Whigs in the North (see Chapter 12). One group for whom the Second Great Awakening proved especially empowering was women. Religious worship provided the principal public occasions in which women rivaled or outnumbered men. In most of the nation's Protestant churches, women formed a majority of those testifying to conversion experiences, signing church covenants, or becoming full members. Women began playing a larger role in determining the religious allegiances of their children. They also were able to assume more prominent positions in public religious life.

AMERICA AS SACRED SOIL: JOSEPH SMITH AND MORDECAI NOAH

While Finney's preaching revitalized and transformed American Protestantism, other religious visions were also taking root in the Burned-Over District. Joseph Smith, Jr., born in 1805, was a farm boy living near Palmyra, New York, when he began receiving revelations warning him to resist the local churches and await further instructions. At the age of seventeen, he announced to his family that an angel had directed him to golden plates buried under ground at the top of a nearby hill. A few years later, after the Smith family lost their farm, young Joseph

SPACES & PLACES

Nauvoo, Illinois

The two biggest cities in the state of Illinois in 1845 had barely existed just fifteen years earlier. In 1830, Chicago was still a Potawatomi village with a population of about two hundred, but within fifteen years it was home to more than twelve thousand people, many of whom were drawn by booster campaigns (see Chapter 8) and the promise of canal projects. The state's other major boomtown, Nauvoo, grew just as quickly, but its appeal was different. Nauvoo emerged when the young Mormon movement chose the site for a religious utopia.

Expelled from their original Zion in Missouri in 1838, five thousand Saints crossed back over the Mississippi and built a new home on a limestone flat in western Illinois, located on a wide bend of the Mississippi River near the border with Iowa. When Joseph Smith chose the site, it was already a town called Commerce, but as Smith recalled later "there was one stone house and three log houses." Renaming it Nauvoo (from the Hebrew word for "beautiful"), Smith transformed it into a thriving city whose population doubled every year from 1839 to 1842 and continued to grow until 1846.

Smith himself became the city's mayor, and in 1844 his followers nominated him for president of the United States. But his rise to power was short lived. Later that year Smith was arrested on charges of treason and jailed in nearby Carthage, the county seat. As he awaited trial, an anti-Mormon mob broke into the jail and shot him dead. The Mormon religion would survive the death of its founder, but the Nauvoo project would not. When Brigham Young led the Saints on their journey to Utah in 1846, the city was largely abandoned.

At the center of this ghost town lay the limestone Nauvoo Temple, a majestic and costly structure sitting atop a bluff, suddenly stripped of its sacred functions. Two years later, arsonists torched the building. Joseph Agnew, an anti-Mormon man from a nearby town who is presumed by most scholars to have been responsible for the fire, later claimed that he had acted out of fear of a Mormon return. Looking back on the fire five years later from Utah, Brigham Young reflected that the temple had "passed into the hands of the enemy, who polluted it to that extent the Lord not only ceased to occupy it, but he loathed to have it called by his name, and permitted the wrath of its possessors to purify it by fire, as a token of what will speedily fall on them and their habitations, unless they repent."

Nauvoo, Illinois, 1846. Though today a small, isolated town of fewer than 1,500 people, Nauvoo was one of the most successful Mississippi River boomtowns in the early 1840s, with a population rivaling that of Chicago. In this 1846 daguerreotype, however, taken shortly after the Mormon exodus, the city was practically uninhabited.

Think About It

1. Despite its special religious mission, in what ways was Nauvoo a typical midwestern boomtown?
2. If Nauvoo continued to attract so many new residents, why did it fail to survive?

received permission from the angel to exhume the plates, along with special stones for translating the texts inscribed on them. Neighbors supported Smith financially during the two years he devoted to producing the text that became the Book of Mormon. Published in 1830 and written in a style similar to the King James translation of the Bible, the Book of Mormon describes the flight of a tribe of ancient Hebrews to the New World, many centuries before Columbus. Jesus had appeared to them after his crucifixion, and their story held the key to restoring the true religion after eighteen centuries of collective error in worldwide Christendom.

Smith's vision and his sacred text helped reunify his disintegrating family during a time of economic upheaval along the canal route. It also formed the basis for a new patriarchal faith and a new Church of Jesus Christ of Latter-day Saints, which he established in 1830. The church appealed to many of his neighbors, and then to a community in Ohio, which Smith soon joined and absorbed. But Ohio was simply a temporary sojourn for Smith, who had announced in 1830 that the Saints (as Smith's followers called themselves) would gather in a new Zion in northwestern Missouri. Beset by dissension and financial troubles after the Panic of 1837, Smith took his flock westward to Missouri, and then in 1839 to Illinois (see Spaces and Places: Nauvoo, Illinois). In each of their homes, the Mormons, as Smith's followers were also called, faced persecution, sometimes for religious heterodoxy, but mostly for being clannish or for seeming to form their own cooperative societies that existed apart from the laws of their neighbors (their doctrines of plural marriage had not yet been publicized and were not a cause of anti-Mormon feeling). Ultimately, in 1844, Smith and his brother were killed by a mob. By then, Mormonism had become a sizable religion outside mainstream Christianity.

Some of the early appeal of the Mormon church can be understood in the context of the social and economic struggles of local farmers hoping to restore a world of patriarchy and community that was threatened by the coming of the Erie Canal. But Mormonism, which is the oldest surviving non-Indian religion born in the United States, was also, at its core, a profoundly American faith. Whereas the New England Puritans had sanctified the New World as a site of religious refuge, a blank slate on which a model community might be transplanted, Mormonism placed the American continent at the center of its sacred geography. According to Smith's teachings, the Garden of Eden had been located in Jackson County, Missouri, and the resurrected Christ had appeared on American soil. For the Mormons, the New World was both a parallel Old World already graced by divine revelation and a new Zion where the Second Coming would be centered.

Around the same time that Smith was visited by his angel, a different utopian vision of America as the center of the world came to Mordecai Manuel Noah. A prominent Jewish playwright, newspaper editor, and politician from New York City, Noah sought to bring all of world Jewry to a colony on Grand Island in the Niagara River near Buffalo. On the day after the Jewish New Year in 1825, Noah appeared at a Buffalo Episcopal church as a "Judge of Israel," dressed in crimson silk robes that he had borrowed from a New York production of Shakespeare's *Richard III*, and proclaimed to a gathering of mostly non-Jewish spectators that a city of refuge for Jews was hereby established. Named Ararat, after the place where the ark of the biblical Noah had come to rest following the flood, Mordecai Noah's colony was intended to attract persecuted Jews from foreign locales to a potentially prosperous settlement along the Erie Canal. Nothing came of the ambitious plan, which was generally ignored or ridiculed in Europe, where most Jews lived. Ironically, however, Noah's dream that the United States would become a haven for European Jews and a center of Jewish life and culture would begin to materialize over the next century.

THE END OF TIME

In different ways, both material progress and religious upheaval inspired many Americans Christians to suspect that they were living in apocalyptic times. **Millennialism,** which is the belief in the imminent arrival of the thousand-year reign of Christ and the angels on earth prior to the Last Judgment, took different forms in American culture in the 1820s and 1830s. Some believed that the millennium was at hand because human beings had brought it about through moral, political, or scientific advances. Others believed that the millennium would begin miraculously and for no reason discernible to humanity. Either way, many Americans believed that the end was near. Joseph Smith had proclaimed in 1835 that "fifty-six years should wind up the scene." Others were even more optimistic or impatient. Various utopian communities, evangelical revivals, and new religions emerged during this period, and they all drew upon the rising millennial expectations of men and women living in the Northeast.

In 1831 a Baptist preacher named William Miller declared that 1843 would be the last "sure year of time" and that Christ would return to earth by April 18, 1844. Miller based his prediction on an interpretation of the Book of Daniel, rather than on any sign in the world around him, but the widespread millennial expectations around him made this prediction seem more plausible. His followers, known as **Millerites,** circulated millions of pages of tracts and preached to half a million listeners (mostly rural and small-town dwellers) in summertime tent meetings between 1842 and 1844. April 18, 1844 came and went without any discernible messianic arrivals, but the Millerites concluded that there had been a miscalculation and that the advent would occur the following Yom Kippur, the Jewish Day of Atonement. With a new target date, Millerites quit their jobs, settled accounts, and rushed to get baptized. But on October 22 (the date of Yom Kippur according to an ancient calendar used by the Karaite sect), Miller's followers were disappointed. Many of them kept the movement alive under new leadership, and became the Seventh-Day Adventists.

Other notable millennialist sects created during this period included the followers of Robert Matthews, a former carpenter in New York, who decided he was a Jewish messiah and called himself the Prophet Matthias. He convinced three wealthy merchants to bankroll his utopian community in the early 1830s, which attracted the ex-slave who would later take the name Sojourner Truth. Matthews was ultimately imprisoned for fraud, one of the first major scandals covered obsessively in New York's penny papers. Equally notorious were John Humphrey Noyes's Perfectionists, who believed that the Second Coming had in fact already taken place. Noyes had been converted by Finney in 1831 and ultimately came to the conclusion that conversion produced complete release from sin. In 1841, he struck out on his own to start a small sect of Perfectionists in Putney, Vermont, where members shared property and practiced what he called "complex marriage" (every man in the community was simultaneously married to every woman), until Noyes was prosecuted for adultery and decided to flee to Oneida, New York.

CONCLUSION

The United States was not yet an industrial power in 1845, and by later standards it was not especially democratic. But market relations and a more participatory political system had begun to erode older patterns of social hierarchy. In the twenty years after the opening of the Erie Canal, enormous changes had taken place across much of the country—at the ballot box, on the farm, in the workshop, at church, and in city streets. A new party system associated with the rise of Andrew Jackson put politics at the center of new mass rituals among white men. Farmers in the continent's interior labored to the uncertain rhythms of distant markets. Artisans and entrepreneurs reorganized the way goods were manufactured. Increasing proportions of Americans crowded into cities and built new kinds of urban communities, including a crowded commercial metropolis in New York. For some men and women, these changes appeared so dramatic as to call for radical adjustments in religious outlook. But even for those who clung to older communities and world views, new political, economic, and social realities were making the country seem both more massive and more interconnected.

STUDY TERMS

- Jacksonian Democracy (p. 242)
- New York State Constitution of 1821 (p. 243)
- universal manhood suffrage (p. 243)
- congressional caucus (p. 244)
- election of 1824 (p. 244)
- "corrupt bargain" (p. 244)
- spoils system (p. 245)
- Peggy Eaton affair (p. 245)
- nullification crisis (p. 246)
- Tariff of Abominations (p. 246)
- Force Bill (p. 246)
- deposit removal (p. 247)
- Panic of 1837 (p. 247)
- equality of condition (p. 248)
- Democrats (p. 249)
- Antimasons (p. 249)
- Whigs (p. 249)
- Second Party System (p. 250)
- paper ballots (p. 250)
- volunteer fire companies (p. 253)
- industrialization (p. 253)
- canals (p. 254)
- Erie Canal (p. 254)
- urbanization (p. 256)
- urban crowd (p. 258)
- omnibus (p. 258)
- gaslight (p. 258)
- *New York Sun* (p. 259)
- penny press (p. 259)
- deskilling (p. 261)
- General Trades Union (p. 261)
- ten-hour movement (p. 261)
- Waltham-Lowell system (p. 261)
- Second Great Awakening (p. 262)
- Burned-Over District (p. 262)
- Book of Mormon (p. 264)
- Church of Jesus Christ of Latter-day Saints (p. 264)
- Ararat (p. 265)
- millennialism (p. 265)
- Millerites (p. 265)
- Prophet Matthias (p. 265)
- Perfectionists (p. 265)

TIMELINE

1821 New York State constitution enfranchises 80 percent of the state's adult men

1824 House of Representatives elects John Quincy Adams president

1825 New York State completes construction of the Erie Canal

Gas lamps appear on the streets of New York

1828 Andrew Jackson defeats Adams in election of 1828

1829 First regular bus service begins in New York City

1830 Congress passes Indian Removal Act

Joseph Smith founds the Church of Jesus Christ of Latter-day Saints

Charles Grandison Finney stages major revival campaign in Rochester, New York

1832 South Carolina nullifies the federal tariff

Jackson vetoes the rechartering of the Second Bank of the United States

1833 *New York Sun* introduced

1834 Whig Party formed

1836 Helen Jewett murdered in New York

David Crockett killed at the Alamo

Martin Van Buren elected president

1837 Economic panic triggers six-year depression

1840 William Henry Harrison's election heralds onset of an era of high voter turnout

1844 Millerites prepare for the imminent return of Jesus Christ

Joseph Smith killed by anti-Mormon mob in Nauvoo, Illinois

FURTHER READING

Additional suggested readings are available on the Online Learning Center at www.mhhe.com/becomingamerica1e.

Peter Baldwin, *In the Watches of the Night* (2012), tracks the growth of nightlife in American cities.

Edward J. Balleisen, *Navigating Failure* (2001), describes the impact of bankruptcy after the Panic of 1837 on larger perceptions of success and failure in American economic life.

Richard Franklin Bensel, *The American Ballot Box in the Mid-Nineteenth Century* (2004), explores the boisterous and often corrupt world of mass voting.

Stuart Blumin and Glenn Altschuler, *The Rude Republic* (2000), offers a corrective to the conventional view that mid-nineteenth-century Americans were all obsessed with politics.

Scott Casper, *Constructing American Lives* (1999), looks at the cultural uses of biography, including biographies of political candidates, during the nineteenth century.

Patricia Cline Cohen, *The Murder of Helen Jewett* (1998), provides a thorough account of the intriguing and tragic life of antebellum New York's most famous murder victim.

Amy Greenberg, *Cause for Alarm* (1998), considers the social composition and cultural function of America's volunteer fire companies.

Bray Hammond, *Banks and Politics in America* (1957), presents a comprehensive explanation of the workings of the Second Bank of the United States and Andrew Jackson's campaign against it.

Bruce Laurie, *Artisans into Workers* (1997), synthesizes a great deal of research on labor history and labor movements during the era of industrialization.

Eric H. Monkkonen, *America Becomes Urban* (1988), puts into historical perspective the remarkable growth of America's urban population in the nineteenth century.

Mary Ryan, *Civic Wars* (1998), describes the vitality of outdoor political life in large U.S. cities in this period.

Michael Schudson, *Discovering the News* (1981), explains the rise of the penny press in this period of political democratization.

Charles Sellers, *The Market Revolution* (1991), explains the political conflicts and religious developments of the period between 1819 and 1846 as responses to the incursion of market relations and market values into everyday life.

Sean Wilentz, *The Rise of American Democracy* (2005), offers an account of American politics that stresses the genuinely democratic impulses reflected in the rise of Andrew Jackson.

11

INSIDE

THE BIG PICTURE

Slavery flourished and grew more entrenched in the American South after 1831, subjugating millions of human beings and igniting a more polarized political debate.

"Old Sarah," Tintype Photograph. The experiences of millions of enslaved African Americans triggered new conflicts in antebellum America.

1831–1844

SLAVERY & THE SOUTH

In February 1831, a solar eclipse darkened the midday sky of Southampton County, Virginia, home to the self-ordained Baptist preacher and slave Nat Turner. Looking skyward, Turner later recalled, he saw "white spirits and black spirits engaged in battle" while "the thunder rolled in the Heavens, and blood flowed in streams." Turner, who claimed direct contact with the Holy Spirit, had waited years for such an omen, ever since a revelation that the day was coming when all the world's hierarchies would crumble. In preparation for the earthly version of the battle he observed in the heavens, Turner recruited several associates. That August, another cosmic spectacle beckoned. A black spot appeared on the sun and crimson flames lit the sky. Judgment Day had come.

Turner's master and his master's family were the first to die in the early morning hours of August 22. Over the next two days, Turner led about sixty slaves as they murdered at least fifty-five white men, women, and children on nearby farms. Virginia militias and white vigilante groups mustered quickly, killing Turner's followers on the spot or after capture. Turner himself, however, escaped. A manhunt ensued, and newspapers speculated wildly about his whereabouts. Various reports placed him across state lines or hidden in a great swamp between Virginia and North Carolina—an area where runaway slaves survived on frogs, terrapins, and snakes. Finally, two months after the insurrection, Turner was discovered hiding in the ground close to home, camouflaged by branches and leaves. In short order, he was convicted and hanged.

Turner's execution sent shock waves through the country. Not a single white person had been killed in a slave revolt in Virginia during the entire colonial era, some 170 years. Slaveholders cited this as proof that slaves lived contentedly within a benevolent institution. At the same time, however, slaveholders worried that the races could never live together in peace and that the potential for extraordinary violence simmered under the surface. The Turner insurrection reinforced this fear.

The year 1831 marked the beginning of a new era in the history of southern slavery. For some whites in the tobacco-growing areas of Virginia and Maryland, Turner's rebellion dramatized the physical dangers of holding large numbers of African Americans in bondage. For most whites in the larger cotton-producing region of the South, however, the lessons were different. As the international demand for cotton soared in the 1830s, so too did the value of slave labor. And to most slaveholders, Turner's revolt pointed not to the dangers of holding slaves but of criticizing slavery. For though he claimed to have seen omens in the skies, it was suspected that Turner, who could read and write, had been inspired by signs of a different kind—those of a growing antislavery movement in the North. Earlier that same year, a white abolitionist in Boston began publishing a weekly newspaper, *The Liberator*, calling for the immediate and uncompensated emancipation of every slave in the United States. Two years before, a free African American had published a powerful critique of slavery and raised the specter of slaves rising up and taking revenge on their masters. Although there is no evidence that Turner had seen either publication, slave owners perceived new dangers in allowing slaves to read, write, and even preach the gospel.

Once a small part of a hemispheric slave system, the American South became one of its main stages in the second quarter of the nineteenth century. From the Caribbean to South America, slave systems were falling. In the American North, slavery was nearing extinction as a result of full or gradual abolition laws passed during the early national era. As slavery became the "peculiar institution" specific to the southern states, southern society grew more distinct and slaveholders less tolerant of anything that might threaten the slave regime. By the 1840s more than two million people were held as property under that regime, many of them living far west of the world turned momentarily upside down by Nat Turner. Under the constraints of an entrenched system of labor discipline and racial subordination, slaves helped build a new culture in the South. At the same time, the entrenchment of southern slavery, in both the economy and national politics, would begin to unsettle the truce between slave and free states that had prevailed since the Missouri Compromise. As the cotton economy boomed, the geographical separation between North and South came to seem more porous, even as attitudes toward slavery hardened and polarized. In a remarkably short period, slavery would become a bitterly divisive issue in American life.

KEY QUESTIONS

- How did the spread of cotton cultivation alter the lives of slaves and slaveholders in the South?
- How did the slave system affect southerners who were neither slaveholders nor enslaved?
- How were plantation discipline and racial hierarchy maintained in slave societies in this period?
- How did family, community, and religious outlook shape men's and women's lives in the South?
- In what ways was the 1830s a pivotal decade in the political status of slavery in the United States?

THE LIBERATOR.

VOL. I.] WILLIAM LLOYD GARRISON AND ISAAC KNAPP, PUBLISHERS. [NO. 2

BOSTON, MASSACHUSETTS.] OUR COUNTRY IS THE WORLD—OUR COUNTRYMEN ARE MANKIND. [SATURDAY, MAY 28, 1831.

THE WORLD OF COTTON

The persistence and expansion of slavery in the United States was driven, above all else, by cotton. When the tobacco market collapsed at the end of the eighteenth century, many prominent southerners began to rethink the region's commitment to human bondage. Some, like Thomas Jefferson, expected slavery to wither away gradually, as planters would diversify their crops and rely less on large-scale gang labor. But cotton changed the script. Beginning in the final decades of the eighteenth century, demand for this raw material grew in the industrial centers of England, where textile production had become mechanized. English manufacturers sold cotton goods to expanding markets throughout the European continent, as well as in Africa, Latin America, and India. As southern planters focused on supplying this growing global trade, slave labor acquired greater value. Slaves were on the move again, uprooted from their homes and treated as chattel within the U.S. slave trade.

COTTON BECOMES KING

Very little cotton had been cultivated on American soil during the colonial period. As late as 1790, annual cotton production in the United States amounted to only three thousand bales. Yet over the next fifty years, cotton would become the dominant staple crop of the South and the nation's leading export. Eli Whitney's invention of the cotton gin (short for *cotton engine*) in 1793 often gets credit for launching the South as cotton supplier to the world, since the gin separated cotton fibers from the seeds more quickly than could human hands alone. It was especially useful in the processing of the short-staple variety of cotton, which grew well in the interior of the country but was difficult to process by hand. The impact of Whitney's machine has been exaggerated, however. Other cotton gins had existed before Whitney's, and short-staple cotton cultivation had already expanded before the invention of the cotton gin, even though the slow purification process created a bottleneck in production. If Whitney had not patented his machine, some other inventor or entrepreneur would have addressed the need soon enough. The machines most responsible for the cotton kingdom were the steam engines that powered textile mills in England. The cotton gin was more the *consequence*, rather than the cause, of growing interest in cotton cultivation.

Neither cotton gins nor steam-powered textile factories instantaneously created a cotton kingdom. Annual cotton production in the United States rose steadily from 3,000 bales in 1790 to 178,000 in 1810 to 300,000 in 1820 and to 700,000 in 1830, as cotton plantations spread westward into land that had been acquired from France and Spain or wrested from Cherokees and Creeks. By 1860, southerners (mostly slaves) were harvesting well over four million bales of cotton each year, which amounted to 68 percent of the world market.

A number of factors put the South in a position to take advantage of the rising global demand for cotton. Though cotton is a sturdy, nonperishable plant that can be shipped across long distances, it only grows in certain climates and requires particular rain patterns and soil conditions that were not found in the North. Southern landowners were also able to command the labor of slaves working in field gangs and thus could grow cotton more efficiently. The turn to cotton cultivation between 1790 and 1830 breathed new life into southern slavery during the same period when northern states were abolishing the institution.

As cotton production took off after 1830, it became the backbone of the regional economy of the U.S. South. Unlike tobacco, rice, and indigo, cotton thrived far from the seaboard, on all kinds of terrain south of the 37° latitude. Whereas sugar and rice cultivation required large investments in expensive machinery, even small-scale slave operations could grow cotton at a profit. Although a small elite group of cotton plantation owners (including twenty-four millionaires, adjusted for inflation, in the town of Natchez, Mississippi, alone) controlled significant proportions of the region's wealth, they represented a tiny fraction of the slaveholding class. The vast majority of slaveholders during the antebellum (pre–Civil War) period owned fewer than twenty slaves, and the cotton trade benefited them too, even if they lived in parts of the South that did not produce cotton (see Map 11.1). Slaveholding tobacco farmers in Virginia, for example, had a stake in the cotton boom because it raised the value of their slaves. By 1840, the economic relationship between cotton and slaveholding was so direct that one could determine the price of a slave by multiplying the price of a pound of cotton by ten thousand (see How Much Is That?).

But while cotton made slavery especially profitable in the South, it also tied the slaveholding states to the larger national economy. Cotton producers shipped their goods to market along the many navigable inland rivers in the South, and cotton traveled along the Mississippi

How Much Is That?

Human Property

Between 1830 and 1850, a twenty-year-old male field slave sold for approximately $900–$950, which is equivalent to an average cost of $25,000 in 2013. Spreading that cost over a thirty-year period of labor, and adding in the yearly cost a slaveholder incurred for maintaining a slave (purchasing and repairing tools, for example), the annual cost of having a slave in 1840 was approximately $51—the equivalent of $1380 in 2013.

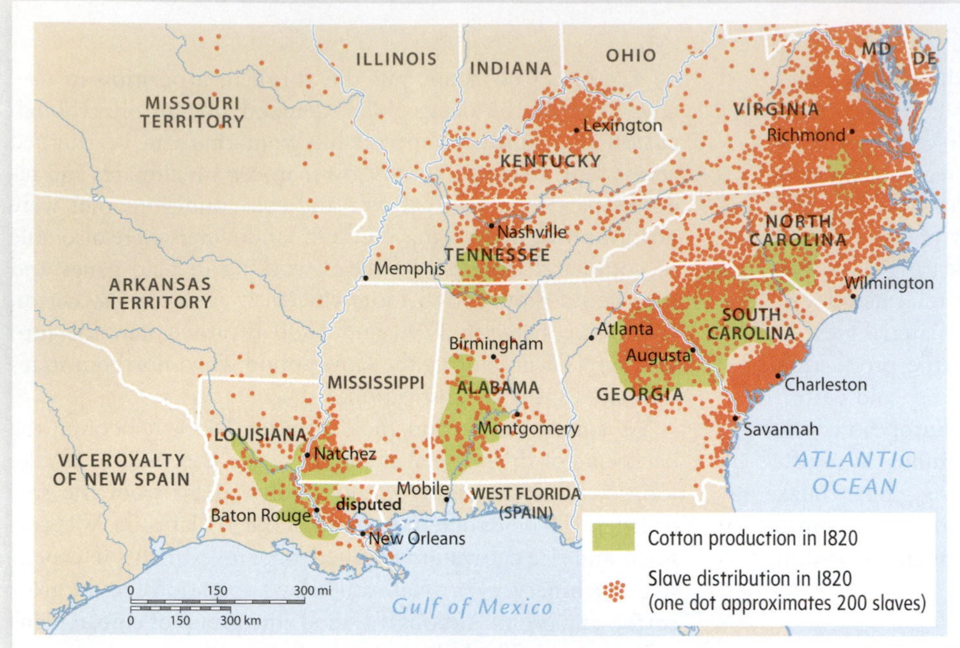

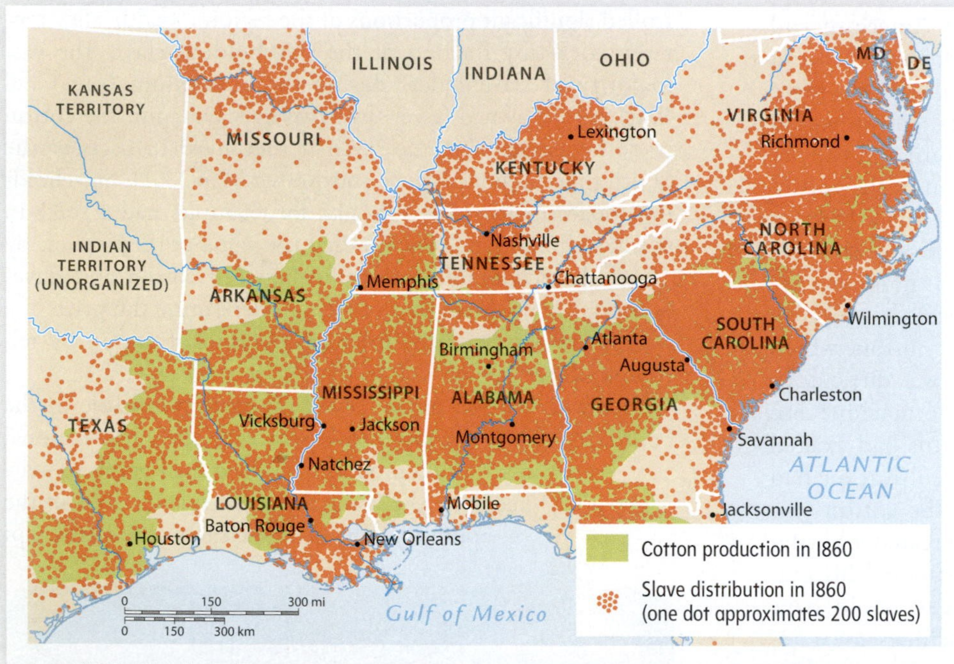

Map 11.1 Cotton and Slavery, 1820–1860. The spread of short-staple cotton cultivation refashioned the map of slavery in the United States in a few decades. South Carolina remained a center of large slaveholdings, but new concentrations of enslaved African Americans emerged in the rich-soil areas of central Alabama and Mississippi. **Question for Analysis:** Where else, other than in cotton country, was slavery growing in this time period?

and throughout the nation's waterway network (see Chapter 10). Because it accounted for more than half of the nation's exports, cotton paid for the nation's imported goods and stimulated industry in the North. New York City was the leading distribution center and outlet for the cotton trade, and its fate as the nation's commercial capital was bound up with cotton—and with slavery. Cotton thus gave the slave South its distinctive economic character, but it also created new forms of national economic interdependence.

THE DOMESTIC SLAVE TRADE

On January 1, 1808, it became illegal to import slaves into the United States (see Chapter 8). Yet while the international slave trade ended, the domestic slave trade intensified. Between 1790 and 1860, slaveholders relocated some one million human beings from Virginia, Maryland, and the Carolinas to states in the interior of the country (see Map 11.2). Some of these men, women, and children traveled with their owners, as entire plantations relocated to cotton country. But two-thirds of the migration took the form of interstate commerce—the slaves were sold to new owners in other states. The number of African Americans sold across state lines in the seven decades between the ratification of the Constitution and the beginning of the Civil War exceeded the number of Africans who had been brought to the thirteen colonies or to the United States during the entire history of the international slave trade.

To slaveholders in the exporting states, the domestic slave trade was a major source of income. For a new class of professional slave traders, the transfer of half a billion dollars in human property was a big and well-organized business. But to the enslaved people involved in this trade, the march westward was a dreadful experience that typically entailed being manacled to one another and confined in pens or ship holds for long periods of time. Being sold also meant being uprooted from home and separated, often permanently, from parents, children, spouses, kin networks, lovers, and friends. About one in four interstate slave sales during this period severed a first marriage, and one in two destroyed a nuclear family of father, mother, and children. Furthermore, laboring conditions in Deep South locales such as Alabama's cotton fields and Louisiana's sugar plantations were often

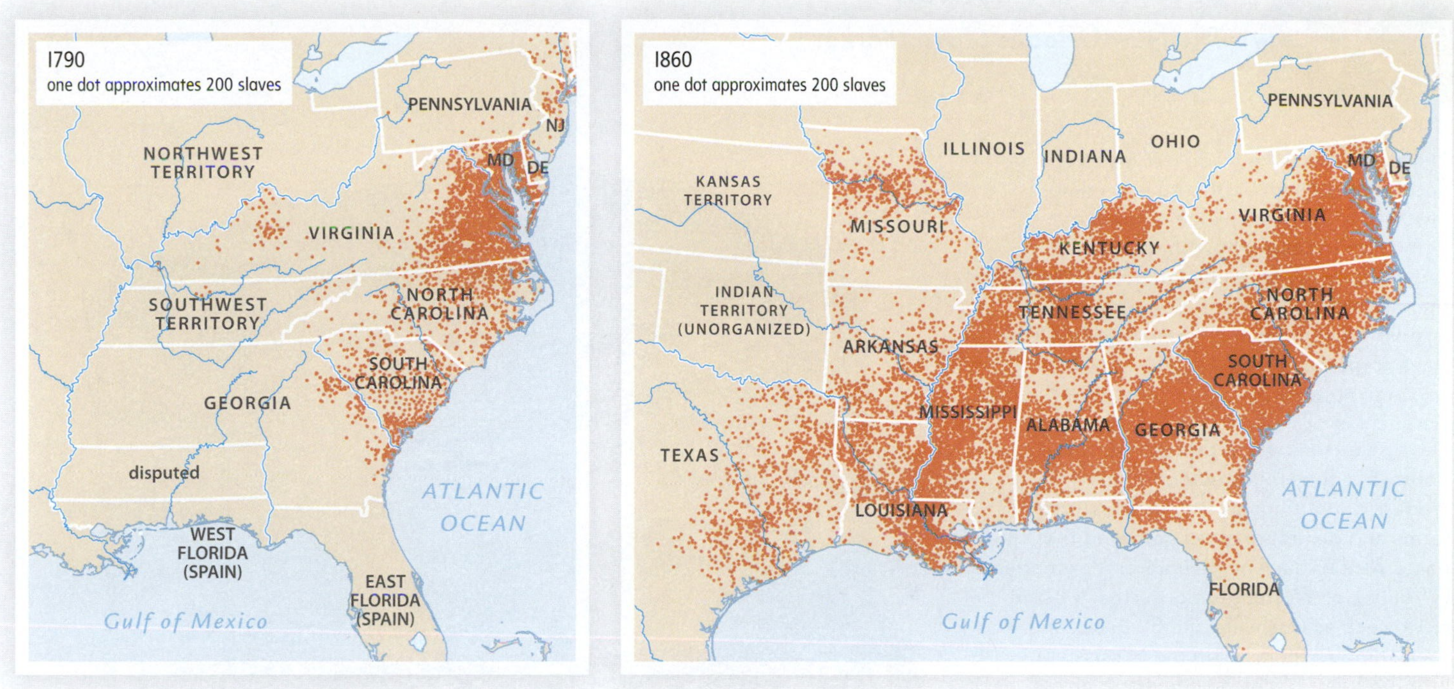

Map 11.2 The Second Middle Passage. This map shows the major patterns of forced migration of enslaved African Americans between 1790 and 1860. The spread of cotton cultivation created a western market for eastern slaves. Approximately one million slaves moved west during this period.

***Hauling the Whole Weeks Picking*, by William Henry Brown, ca. 1842.** This watercolor shows an entire family at work transporting freshly picked cotton.

SPACES & PLACES

The New Orleans Slave Market

The domestic slave trade pervaded the entire antebellum South, quietly (almost invisibly) setting the value of human beings and shaping how they were regarded, treated, and even bred. But in the city of New Orleans, home to the largest slave market in North America, the slave trade appeared in a palpable and concentrated form.

Slave sales took place throughout the South, but they followed certain patterns. Traders bought human beings from rural farms and plantations and gathered them in eastern cities such as Baltimore, Alexandria (Virginia), or Washington or farther west in cities such as Nashville and St. Louis, and then shipped them down the Mississippi into the heart of cotton country. Many of those slaves (thousands each year) wound up in New Orleans, where they were sold, mostly in private arrangements, to buyers from Louisiana, Mississippi, Texas, and Arkansas. Between November and April, the six-month season when 90 percent of the slaves brought to New Orleans were resold, human trafficking was big business in the city.

Sale of Estates, Pictures and Slaves in the Rotunda, New Orleans, 1842. Whereas most slave *labor* took place in rural settings, the slave *trade* cast a spotlight on southern cities.

more brutal than those in the Upper South. For all of these reasons, a master's threats to sell his slaves westward "down the river" if they did not comply with his wishes could be especially traumatizing and effective.

The possibility of sale framed the experience of slavery during the antebellum period. For slaveholders, the slave market determined the value and liquidity of their property. For slaves, it undermined the stability of their most intimate relationships. One slave recalled that he "had a constant dread that Mrs. Moore would be in want of money and sell my dear wife. We constantly dreaded a final separation." Many white southerners considered slave sales distasteful and the professionals who executed those sales disreputable. Georgia even banned the commercial importation of slaves for much of

Slave Coffle. Southern slaves were an intensely mobile population, and their dispersal made it both more difficult to maintain local communities and easier to forge loose bonds of common African American identity. This engraving depicts a coffle (a line of human beings shackled to one another) in Washington, D.C., around 1815 (note the uncompleted Capitol building in the background), though the image probably dates to the 1850s.

The center of this business in the antebellum period was a few blocks from the levee, near the present-day intersection of Chartres Street and Esplanade Avenue. A cluster of trading companies maintained their offices there and also kept slave pens. Though the walls of the pens were as high as twenty feet, trading firms made no secret of what went on behind them. Large signboards marked "Slaves for Sale" hung over their doors, and graphic posters on city walls advertised their trade. Until the practice was outlawed in 1852, slave traders also used the streets in front of their buildings to display and sell their human merchandise. Abraham Lincoln, who visited New Orleans on business in 1829 and 1831, was reportedly disturbed by the spectacle of the city's slave market. One friend claimed that it was here, in the face of the slave pens, that Lincoln's views on slavery were formed.

Think About It

1. Why did New Orleans become a major center of the slave trade?
2. Why were enslaved human beings put on display in a slave market rather than simply bought and sold on paper by people sitting in office buildings?

Urban Slave Trading. Handbills advertising slave sales were a common sight in antebellum New Orleans. This advertisement includes extensive descriptions of human merchandise for sale at auction, boasting of valuable household skills, language fluency, and obedience—except in the case of Frank, who "will occasionally drink, though [is] not a habitual drunkard" and is thus not fully guaranteed by the seller. Note that members of a family—Dandridge, Nancy, and Mary Ann—are being sold separately.

BY

HEWLETT & BRIGHT.

SALE OF

VALUABLE

SLAVES,

(On account of departure)

The Owner of the following named and valuable Slaves, being on the eve of departure for Europe, will cause the same to be offered for sale, at the NEW EXCHANGE, corner of St. Louis and Chartres streets, on *Saturday*, May 16, at Twelve o'Clock, *viz.*

1. SARAH, a mulatress, aged 45 years, a good cook and accustomed to house work in general, is an excellent and faithful nurse for sick persons, and in every respect a first rate character.

2. DENNIS, her son, a mulatto, aged 24 years, a first rate cook and steward for a vessel, having been in that capacity for many years on board one of the Mobile packets; is strictly honest, temperate, and a first rate subject.

3. CHOLE, a mulatress, aged 36 years, she is, without execption, one of the most competent servants in the country, a first rate washer and ironer, does up lace, a good cook, and for a bachelor who wishes a house-keeper she would be invaluable; she is also a good ladies' maid, having travelled to the North in that capacity.

4. FANNY, her daughter, a mulatress, aged 16 years, speaks French and English, is a superior hair-dresser, (pupil of Guilliac,) a good seamstress and ladies' maid, is smart, intelligent, and a first rate character.

5. DANDRIDGE, a mulatoo, aged 26 years, a first rate dining-room servant, a good painter and rough carpenter, and has but few equals for honesty and sobriety.

6. NANCY, his wife, aged about 24 years, a confidential house servant, good seamstress, mantuamaker and tailoress, a good cook, washer and ironer, etc.

7. MARY ANN, her child, a creole, aged 7 years, speaks French and English, is smart, active and intelligent.

8. FANNY or FRANCES, a mulatress, aged 22 years, is a first rate washer and ironer, good cook and house servant, and has an excellent character.

9. EMMA, an orphan, aged 10 or 11 years, speaks French and English, has been in the country 7 years, has been accustomed to waiting on table, sewing etc.; is intelligent and active.

10. FRANK, a mulatto, aged about 32 years speaks French and English, is a first rate hostler and coachman, understands perfectly well the management of horses, and is, in every respect, a first rate character, with the exception that he will occasionally drink, though not an habitual drunkard.

☞ All the above named Slaves are acclimated and excellent subjects; they were purchased by their present vendor many years ago, and will, therefore, be severally warranted against all vices and maladies prescribed by law, save and except FRANK, who is fully guaranteed in every other respect but the one above mentioned.

TERMS:—One-half Cash, and the other half in notes at Six months, drawn and endorsed to the satisfaction of the Vendor, with special mortgage on the Slaves until final payment. The Acts of Sale to be passed before WILLIAM BOSWELL, *Notary Public*, at the expense of the Purchaser.

New-Orleans, May 13, 1835.

this era. But the domestic slave trade lay at the foundation of slavery (see Spaces and Places: The New Orleans Slave Market). As much as corporal punishment, work without wages, inferior legal status for oneself and one's offspring, or lifetime obligation to a master, the prospect and possibility of being sold as property defined what it meant to be a slave in the antebellum South.

POWER AND CONTROL UNDER SLAVERY

Over two million men, women, and children lived as slaves in the United States in 1830, almost all of them in the South. By the time of the Civil War, the slave population would approach four million. There was no single slave experience for all of these people; their situations varied. Many slaves picked cotton in the fields, but others grew hemp, wheat, corn, rice, sugar, or tobacco, while still others performed domestic service, mastered crafts, preached the gospel, managed other slaves, or worked in factories. Some labored in large slave gangs and lived in areas with high black populations, while others belonged to masters with just one or two slaves and lived in towns with large white majorities.

Despite this range of experiences, however, slaves across the South shared the experience of living in a society dominated by free whites. Overall, about one-third of the South was enslaved, though the proportion was somewhat lower in the Upper South and somewhat higher in the Deep South. Even in the Deep South, slaves did not form the kind of black majority found in the Caribbean. Most of the white majority did not own slaves (see Figure 11.1), but they considered slaves to be their inferiors, in need of surveillance and subordination. The lives of slaves were regulated closely, not only by their masters but also by the larger society. Southern slaves thus had to negotiate a brutal system of labor exploitation without the kind of communal support available to enslaved populations in other parts of the world.

PLANTATION LIFE

For about half of southern slaves, life centered on the **plantation,** a large farm where crops were grown primarily for sale in distant markets rather than for local consumption.

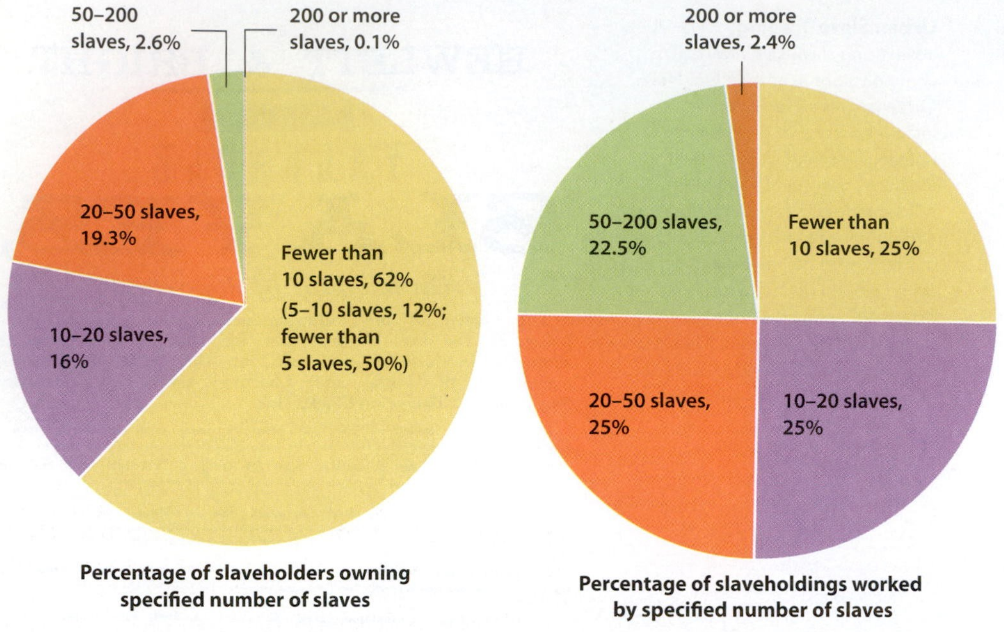

FIGURE 11.1 **Slavery in the American South, 1840.** **Questions for Analysis:** From the perspective of the enslaved, how uncommon was it to live in a household with twenty or more slaves? From the perspective of southern slaveholders, how common were such holdings? How do you explain the difference?

Some slaves, mostly in Louisiana, Mississippi, and South Carolina, toiled on large sugar, cotton, or rice plantations where absentee masters commanded the labor of more than one hundred slaves. But throughout the antebellum era, most slaves lived and worked on smaller plantations and farms, with fewer than thirty slaves, whose owners lived on the property. This meant that masters, mistresses, overseers, white children, and the enslaved lived side by side, and sometimes knew one another intimately, though on grossly unequal terms.

On most plantations, the master's family occupied the big house, while slaves slept in crude one-room log cabins. On larger plantations, the slave quarters formed rows that displayed the wealth of the master but also emphasized the disparity in living conditions of whites and blacks. Slave clothing was also quite primitive, consisting of two to four work suits made from a coarse fabric known as "Negro cloth" that was manufactured in the North and sold to slaveholders.

In areas other than clothing and shelter, slaves tended to benefit more directly from the living standard of their masters. Slaves ate more abundantly and nutritiously than in the colonial period, and received better medical care than most southern whites who did not own slaves. For these reasons, enslaved African Americans grew taller and lived longer than Caribbean slaves, whose masters did not typically reside nearby. More generally, southern slaves enjoyed better basic material conditions than forced laborers in other societies, but had to endure much greater surveillance and interference in their daily lives and were far more vulnerable to sale and forced migration.

About three-quarters of plantation slaves, both male and female, worked as field laborers, toiling six long days (from dawn till dusk) every week, often driven by the lash to produce at an especially intense pace. On Sundays, most fieldworkers had the day off and some used it to cultivate crops for their own use. Many of the slaves who did not work in the fields, including large proportions of children, old men, and women, were house servants, who worked less intensively but with less time off. Smaller numbers

Slave Houses Built on Stilts, Laura Plantation, Vacherie, Louisiana, Early- to Mid-Nineteenth Century. Most slave dwellings for which we have photographic evidence are somewhat unrepresentative, since they were built later and with more durable materials than most. No material traces remain of the housing recalled by Rose Holman, who had been a slave in Mississippi: "We lived in little log houses daubed wid mud an' didn't have no beds—slept on de ground on pallets."

of slaves served as blacksmiths or carpenters, and they were among those most likely to derive satisfaction from their work. Men who labored as slave drivers or foremen enjoyed elevated status on the plantation, and though they risked earning the animosity and contempt of other slaves, drivers more often assumed leadership roles in slave communities. Perhaps the most respected occupations, from the perspective of the enslaved, were preaching and healing, since those skilled services were directed primarily toward other slaves, but these were not full-time responsibilities.

Whatever their occupation or their worksite, slaves were subject to a system of discipline that relied on the threat of violence. Masters, mistresses, and overseers frequently whipped their slaves, and both the lash and the lacerated back became powerful symbols of the evil core of slavery in the rhetoric of abolitionists and the recollections of ex-slaves. Whippings and other forms of corporal punishment were often conducted publicly as a shaming ritual, but the humiliation undoubtedly paled beside the sheer physical torture of some of these tactics. Slaveholders administered punishments such as holding slaves' heads under water, having them mauled by dogs, or castrating them. One North Carolina master was charged in court with beating his pregnant slave "with clubs, iron chains, and other deadly weapons" over a four-month period that ended only with her death.

Most slaveholders condemned the sadistic excesses of such masters, but even those who prided themselves on kindness admitted to regularly beating their slaves. Slaveholders had an interest in limiting the abuse so as not to damage slaves' ability to work (or their resale value), but the fact that states passed laws against the "cruel punishment" of one's slaves suggests that economic interest alone was not sufficient to prevent torture and physical abuse. Escaped slave Henry Bibb described his Kentucky master's ingenious use of a hickory paddle specially designed to beat slaves without inflicting wounds that would be detectable by neighbors or prospective buyers. The paddle was "bored full of quarter-inch auger holes, and every time this is applied to the flesh of a victim, the blood gushes through the holes," or a blister forms. Bibb and his fellow slaves would be tied up and doubled over during the beating, while the paddle struck "those parts of the body which would not be so likely to be seen by those who wanted to buy slaves."

Historians have applied the term **paternalism** to the system of plantation authority in the antebellum South. To describe slaveholders as paternalistic is not to call them benevolent or to label slavery mild. Rather it means that slaveholders knew their slaves intimately, took an active and meddlesome interest in their lives, regarded slaves as childlike inferiors who needed care and protection, and felt entitled to exert absolute patriarchal authority over them. This produced a complex set of constraints and loopholes for slaves to negotiate, and helps to explain some features of slaveholder behavior that at first seem bizarre or inconsistent. The same Louisiana slaveholder who would order mass whippings of all his field laborers simply to instill discipline, for example, also bought them valued Christmas presents from New Orleans. Many slaveholders claimed to love their slaves and would later be shocked to discover, during the Civil War, that these slaves no longer wished to work for them.

FAMILY LIFE AND SEXUAL RELATIONS

Many slaves sought the comforts of family life, but even this institution was subject to interference from white masters. Southern laws did not recognize the marriages of slaves, and the domestic slave trade did not respect their family bonds. Adult males—husbands and fathers—were especially vulnerable to sale, which

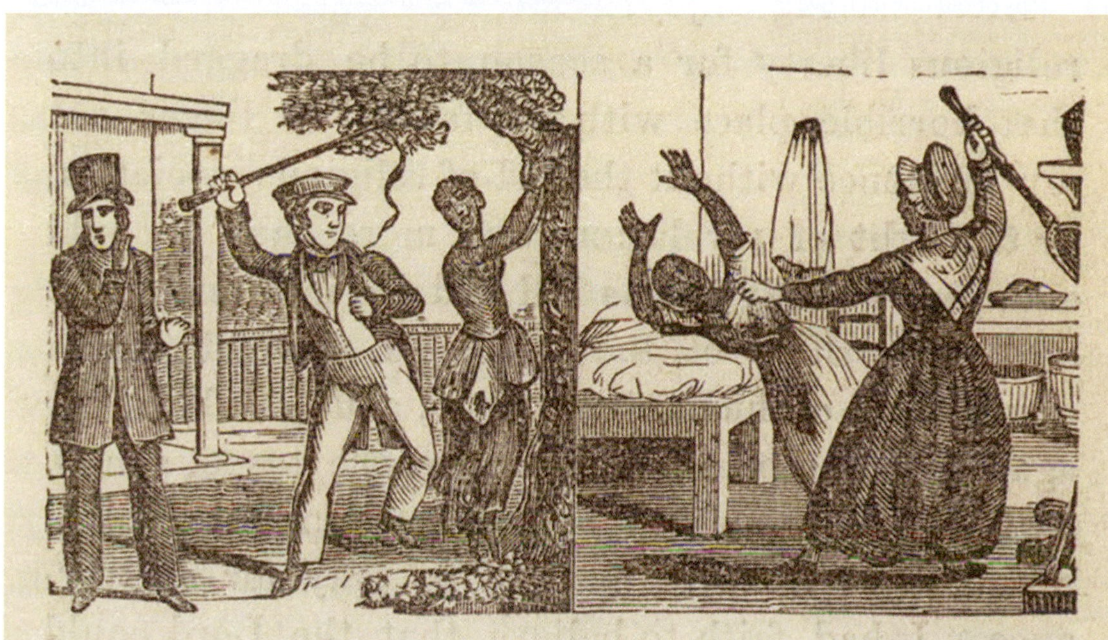

The Lash. In an autobiography that told of his successful escape from slavery, Henry Bibb included a range of engravings and illustrations from abolitionist sources that graphically depicted the violence of southern slaveholding. Here, two scenes of punishment—the whipping of a slave by his master, and the beating of a slave, probably a household servant, by her mistress—suggest the pervasiveness of that cruelty.

may have contributed to the frequency with which slaves named their sons after fathers and grandfathers. As a rule, slave families on larger plantations stood a better chance of remaining intact.

When given the opportunity, slaves managed to form meaningful and lasting family relationships. They cared about patterns of extended kinship and, unlike their white neighbors, avoided marriages with first cousins. The most cherished family ties were those between parents and children. And contrary to a well-entrenched misconception, enslaved children in the antebellum period were mostly raised in two-parent households. Slaveholders had their own reasons for facilitating family formation among slaves. Slaves with family ties on the plantation were less likely to flee or to rebel. Furthermore, both marriage and the prospect of marriage tended to encourage reproduction. In part because they had such a clear interest in the family life of their labor force, masters intervened frequently in slaves' marital lives, by banning marriages off the plantation, for example, or by punishing marital infidelity. Slaves also disapproved of extramarital affairs but did not share the white society's stated discomfort with premarital sexuality.

Living within their masters' households, enslaved people also had to negotiate the sexual demands of whites. Most interracial liaisons in the antebellum South involved white men and enslaved black women, and many were not consensual. Because southern laws did not define the rape of a slave as a crime and because masters had considerable control over the living conditions of their slaves, women on the plantation faced a constant threat of sexual assault. Harriet Jacobs fled her North Carolina home to avoid the unwanted sexual advances of her master and the recriminations of his humiliated wife. Celia, a slave in Missouri, killed her master/rapist and went to the gallows. Far more commonly, sex between white men and black women resulted in an increase in the slave population. In her famous diary, the patrician mistress Mary Boykin Chesnut of South Carolina complained that "like the patriarchs of old our men live in all one house with their wives and concubines, and the mullatoes one sees in every family exactly resemble the white children."

Some masters and slaves formed long-term romantic relationships, and in a few instances enslaved men had such relationships with white women. In general, southerners of both races seem to have been slightly more tolerant of interracial sexuality during this period than they would be after emancipation. But it is important to remember that masters had far more power than slaves and that every sexual encounter took place within an unequal relationship in which slaves had no right of refusal. No slave, male or female, enjoyed any real legal protection against sexual coercion.

SLAVES TO THE STATE

Local communities and state governments shared the slaveholder's interest in maintaining slave discipline, preventing insurrection, and defending the southern slave system against outside criticism. After the Turner rebellion, state legislatures in the South intensified their efforts to regulate the lives of slaves. On the one hand, new laws interfered with the master's control of his plantation, setting minimum standards for food and shelter and making it illegal for masters to murder or mutilate their slaves. At least on the level of formal law, enslaved people enjoyed more protection against inhumane treatment after the 1830s than before, though in practice these laws were rarely enforced. At the same time, the states passed other laws limiting the movements of slaves and prohibiting them from possessing firearms or assembling without white supervision, even for religious services. Most states also made it illegal for whites to teach slaves how to read or write, since legislators feared that a literate slave could forge a pass (see Hot Commodities: Slave Passes), communicate across distances to other slaves, and fall under the influence of antislavery literature.

Restrictions on slave behavior were better enforced than restrictions on slave treatment. All southern states maintained **slave patrols,** whose responsibilities included catching runaways, breaking up large or otherwise suspicious slave gatherings, and monitoring the movements of black people. African Americans traveling through the countryside, free or enslaved, could

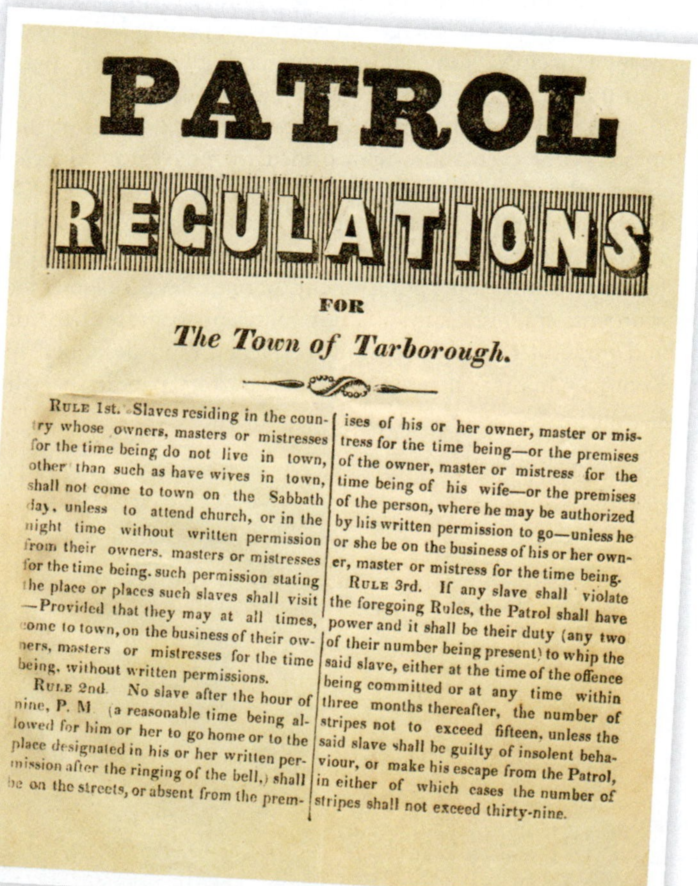

PATROL

REGULATIONS

FOR

The Town of Tarborough.

RULE 1st. Slaves residing in the country whose owners, masters or mistresses for the time being do not live in town, other than such as have wives in town, shall not come to town on the Sabbath day, unless to attend church, or in the night time without written permission from their owners, masters or mistresses for the time being, such permission stating the place or places such slaves shall visit —Provided that they may at all times, come to town, on the business of their owners, masters or mistresses for the time being, without written permissions.

RULE 2nd. No slave after the hour of nine, P. M (a reasonable time being allowed for him or her to go home or to the place designated in his or her written permission after the ringing of the bell,) shall be on the streets, or absent from the premises of his or her owner, master or mistress for the time being—or the premises of the owner, master or mistress for the time being of his wife—or the premises of the person, where he may be authorized by his written permission to go—unless he or she be on the business of his or her owner, master or mistress for the time being.

RULE 3rd. If any slave shall violate the foregoing Rules, the Patrol shall have power and it shall be their duty (any two of their number being present) to whip the said slave, either at the time of the offence being committed or at any time within three months thereafter, the number of stripes not to exceed fifteen, unless the said slave shall be guilty of insolent behaviour, or make his escape from the Patrol, in either of which cases the number of stripes shall not exceed thirty-nine.

Patrol Regulations. After 1830, southern states and local communities passed increasingly restrictive laws governing the free movement of slaves between plantations and in towns. These regulations from Tarboro, North Carolina, include a prohibition on visiting the town on Sundays—the one free day slaves usually had to visit with friends and family—without written permission from their owners.

expect to be apprehended by patrollers ("paddyrollers") asking for their papers. As one ex-slave later recalled, "the paddyrollers they keep close watch on the pore niggers so they have no chance to do anything or go anywhere. They jes' like policemen, only worser." Patrol service was compulsory in several states, and both poor and rich white men staffed these patrols.

Perhaps the most significant initiative in southern slavery after 1830 was a new series of laws making it harder for slaves to achieve their freedom. State legislatures stemmed the tide of private manumissions that had taken place during the decades after the Revolution (see Chapter 8) by limiting the rights of masters to grant or sell freedom to their slaves. States in the Deep South explicitly forbade private acts of emancipation. Whereas the number of private manumissions soared in other societies where slavery remained legal through this period, such as Cuba and Brazil, they declined sharply in the American South. By 1840, free blacks made up only 8 percent of the South's total black population, and a mere 3 percent in the Deep South.

New laws also targeted free blacks, restricting their work options, denying them the right to testify in court against whites, prohibiting their association with slaves, requiring them to carry proof that they themselves were not slaves, and in some cases even forcing them to leave the state or face reenslavement. The southern legal system did not merely protect the property rights of individual slaveholders; it protected a system of racial subordination.

SLAVE RESISTANCE

Working in small slaveholding units, living under the close surveillance of their masters, and surrounded by a powerful and white majority, American slaves were unable to overthrow the regime on the model of Haiti, or even to stage armed revolts with the frequency or magnitude of their counterparts in Jamaica, Cuba, Brazil, or Suriname. Historians have documented at least 250 slave revolts on American soil and another 250 aboard slave ships, but most were limited in scope or impact, peripheral in their location, or relatively early in the history of southern slavery. In fact, after Nat Turner there was no significant slave rebellion inside the South until the Civil War, when slaves took up arms and fought on the side of the Union Army.

But the absence of armed rebellion did not mean that African Americans accepted their fate. In countless ways, slaves sought to resist masters' claims to their labor and their lives. Everyday incidents of work sabotage, malingering, and theft, which whites interpreted as evidence of slaves' innate laziness and mendacity, gave enslaved people a small sense of control over their working conditions. On rare occasions, and when pushed to intolerable limits, a slave would even confront a master or an overseer violently. Paradoxically, a key opportunity for strategic resistance appeared at precisely the moment when slaves seemed utterly powerless: at the point of sale. When slave traders attempted to obtain the highest price for their human merchandise, they depended on the cooperation of the slave, who would be asked by prospective buyers all sorts of questions. In the course of the transaction, slaves had the power to represent their own ages, personal histories, medical conditions, habits, and attitudes. (Some of these statements made their way into court records when white men sued one another over a warranty, which was one of the only instances when slave testimony was introduced in the antebellum court.) In the process of representing himself or herself, a slave might even sabotage or facilitate a proposed sale.

The most straightforward rejection of slavery, of course, was the decision to run away. Exactly how many slaves fled the South each year is hard to determine, but southern newspapers were filled with advertisements for runaways throughout the

Henry "Box" Brown. In perhaps the most unusual and ingenious method of escaping slavery, Henry "Box" Brown had himself mailed, literally, from Richmond to Philadelphia in 1849 in a wooden crate, three feet by two feet, which a white accomplice in Virginia had marked "This side up." Brown rode for 350 miles inside the crate. Emerging after twenty-seven hours, he said "How do you do gentlemen" and promptly passed out. This illustration was sold as an antislavery fundraiser.

period (see Interpreting the Sources: Runaway Slave Advertisements). By 1850, slaveholders were sufficiently concerned with the problem of slaves escaping to the North that they pushed for the enforcement of national fugitive slave laws. Some fugitives, like the famous orator and author Frederick Douglass, used the **Underground Railroad,** a loose network of secret escape routes, sympathetic hosts, and experienced guides, on his way North, though in his autobiography Douglass was careful to conceal the identity of his collaborators.

Successful escapes from the plantation (like prison breaks in later periods) were far less common than their prominence in the popular culture of the time might suggest. Especially after Indian removal, few slaves lived near the borders of states or nations to which they might flee. The thousands who made it safely to the North, to Canada, or to Mexico during this period were, statistically speaking, a drop in the bucket of southern slavery. More frequently, slaves found short-term relief by absconding to a nearby location to avoid or protest mistreatment. The practice of temporary escape was sufficiently common and expected that a South Carolina judge explained in 1839 to a jury charged with deciding whether a particular slave dealer had

HOT COMMODITIES

Slave Passes

In an age before passports, driver's licenses, and Social Security numbers, one class of Americans was nonetheless required to carry identification papers. Already in the seventeenth century, slave societies were using passes to track slaves who were away from their masters. In the antebellum South, this practice was institutionalized to the point that any slave traveling without such a pass was liable to be arrested.

Please to let Benjamin McDaniel pass to Dr. Henkal's in New-Market Shenandoah County Va. and return on Monday or Tuesday night to Montpellier, for Mrs Madison.

June 1st 1843.

Slave Pass. This document grants permission for Benjamin McDaniel to travel to "Dr. Henkal's" in New Market, Virginia, on Thursday June 1, 1843, and return to Montpellier, Virginia, the following Monday or Tuesday. Dr. Solomon Henkel was one of the first doctors on record to practice in New Market.

A slave pass was essentially a letter of introduction from a slaveholder to an unknown white reader, such as a patrolman, authorizing the slave carrying the pass to be out of the master's immediate physical control (which was necessary if masters wished to send their slaves on errands away from the plantation). A typical slave pass was a handwritten note like the following sheet found in the papers of a Missouri slaveholder:

> *Gentilmen let the Boy Barney pass and*
> *repass from the first of june till the 4*
> *To Columbus OM for this date 1852*
> *Samuel Grove*

This surveillance system relied on three important facts about slave life in the South. First, because patrols monitored the movements of slaves in order to protect communities from insurrection, slaves could expect to be routinely inspected. Second, because masters offered substantial rewards for the retrieval of runaways, even white people not serving on patrols might have an incentive to ask a traveling African American for proof of identity. Third, because the free population was mostly literate (the best evidence suggests that approximately 70 percent of the white men in the antebellum South could read) and the enslaved population mostly illiterate (somewhere between 5 and 10 percent of slaves could read during this period), the pass system could function, in theory, as a private communication medium among white people, borne on the bodies of blacks.

But slave passes were imperfect tracking devices. Without other means of corroborating identity, a pass written for one slave could be used by another. Or slaves with legitimate but restricted passes could get a literate friend to alter the date so that it could be used more flexibly. More generally, passes were highly susceptible to forgery. Even a slave with rudimentary writing skills might be able to learn how to copy a handwritten message if it meant being able to visit a relative on another plantation—or if it represented an opportunity to escape to freedom. Buying passes was also an option. A New Orleans newspaper claimed that "any negro can obtain a pass for four bits or a dollar, from miserable wretches who obtain a sold a morally defective slave that "occasional flights of a slave from his master's service for special causes would not constitute any material moral defect."

URBAN SLAVERY

The South as a whole was an overwhelmingly rural region in the antebellum period, and the enslaved were a predominantly rural people. Nonetheless, in 1820, slaves accounted for at least one-fifth of the residents in all major southern cities, and considerably more in some of the largest ones. New Orleans had an African American majority at the beginning of the nineteenth century, and Charleston's population was 58 percent black as late as 1820. But both the slave and the free black populations of southern cities declined over the next several decades, so that by the mid-1840s southern cities were much whiter and slavery was a much less integral part of urban life.

Still, for a significant number of slaves, especially in the first half of the century, city living was a possibility, and by many accounts it was a relatively desirable situation. Slave discipline was much more difficult to maintain in urban settings, where slaves were not engaged in land cultivation and were often

living by such infamous practices." Henry Clay Bruce, who spent the first part of his life as a slave in Virginia and Missouri, recalled that passes could be counterfeited even more cheaply and simply. Since many of the patrolmen he met in Missouri were themselves illiterate, Bruce and his fellow slaves were able to pawn off pages of discarded correspondence as legitimate passes.

Masters worried about slaves forging passes and frequently called attention to this risk in advertisements for runaways who knew how to read and write. In their autobiographies, ex-slaves made the same connection between literacy and freedom and recounted stories of fabricating passes and manumission papers in order to escape. But the obstacles, risks, and deterrents to running away were considerable, even for slaves with access to fake passes, and the number of successful fugitives was far smaller than the number of slaves who could read and write. Literacy was probably less instrumental in slave escapes than either slaveholders or abolitionists claimed. More often, the ability to fake a pass brought moments of relief and freedom within a life of slavery.

Think About It

1. Why was the South's enslaved population primarily illiterate?
2. Why did slaveholders often mention in runaway advertisements whether the fugitive slave could read?
3. How do slave passes compare to bank notes (see Chapter 10)? Which would have been easier to forge?

Pass Inspection. Slave patrols acquired a reputation for viciousness that only grew in the years after 1830, as southern states restricted the movement of both slaves and freedpeople. This image shows an African American surrounded by armed "paddyrollers" and their dog while his pass is scrutinized by lamplight.

INTERPRETING THE SOURCES

Runaway Slave Advertisements

Because most slaves could not write about their lives, historians have relied heavily on the writings of white observers for detailed information about the daily experiences of the enslaved. Slaveholders themselves recorded many observations about their slaves, though of course their impressions and beliefs must be read critically. One especially interesting source of information about how slaves appeared to their masters comes in the form of newspaper advertisements for the retrieval of fugitive slaves.

The following advertisements appeared in the *Baltimore Sun*, the most popular daily newspaper in that city, in the 1840s:

Ranaway from the subscriber, living near Towsontown, on Tuesday, 25th inst., a **NEGRO BOY** by the name of Henry Hilton, about 19 years of age, very dark, and of a sullen look; a small scar on the cheek, occasioned by a burn; had on a dark cassinet pants, blue frock coat, and fine Jefferson boots. The above reward will be paid if returned to me.

DANIEL LEE

December 5, 1845

TWENTY DOLLARS REWARD. Ran away from the subscriber, living in Baltimore county, near the Copper Factory, on the 8th of July, A **NEGRO BOY,** who calls himself Dick Johnson; he is about 5 feet high, and stout built—17 or 18 years of age, with large, heavy eyes, wide mouth, and has lost the toes of his left foot by frost. His clothes were of coarse linen. He was purchased two years ago from Capers Burns who carried on the soap and candle business on Saratoga Street. There is no doubt he is lurking about the city, as he has been seen once or twice lately up town. I will give the above reward to any one who will bring him home to me, or secure him in jail so that I get him again.

LEVI HIPSLEY, near Cub Hill Post Office

August 6, 1844

ONE HUNDRED DOLLARS REWARD. Ran away from the subscriber on or about the 2nd inst, a negro woman named Sophia, though called Sophy. Said runaway negro woman is between thirty eight and forty years of age; bears her age well, is rather above the middle height; of a bright mulatto color; her front teeth are bad, some broken out; speaks very pleasantly; has no marks recollected; and is a very good looking servant.

The above reward will be paid is said runaway is taken without the state of Maryland; a reward of $50 if taken within the state and out of Baltimore City, and $30 is taken within Baltimore City; in each case, said negress to be either returned to her owner or lodged in Baltimore county jail.

TOBIAS E. STANSBURY

Baltimore County, April 26

TWO HUNDRED DOLLARS REWARD. Ran away from the subscriber, living on the north side of Severn, at the Ferry, about sunrise on the morning of the 25th November, a Negro Man, who calls himself HENRY HAMMOND. He was formerly the property of Dr. Rea, from whose estate I purchased him about four years ago. He is about 29 years of age; about 5 feet 6 inches high; very bright color, but not a mulatto; has a scar from the bite of a dog on one of his legs, which was seared with an iron to prevent hydrophobia. The clothing which he took with him, as far as can be ascertained, was a black cloth body coat, and black pantaloons, not very much worn; and plain black Russian hat. His working clothes, which he had on, are, drab pantaloons, which several patches on them, and drab coat, bull woolly; and a pair of new coarse pegged boots. It is probably that he has a pass bearing the name of Samuel Wilson, (a deceased negro) from whose wife he endeavored to obtain said pass during the last summer.

I will give 200 dollars for apprehension of the above described negro, if he is taken out of the state of Maryland; and if taken in the state I will give $100 if safely lodged in jail or delivered to me.

GEORGE B. HAYDEN, Annapolis, Nov. 25

November 26, 1840

Explore the Sources

1. What sorts of signs do these advertisements rely on to help readers identify runaway slaves?
2. What might we conclude about the material conditions of slavery from the information contained in these descriptions?
3. How might the advertisements reflect the distinctive conditions of urban slavery?
4. What do you find most surprising in these advertisements?

contracted out to employers other than their legal owners. The **hiring-out system,** as it was called, meant that slaves worked for bosses whose power over them was restricted. Slaves who were hired out often lived out as well, and chose their own landlords. Some were able to live in small black communities at the periphery of southern cities.

Frederick Douglass, who was enslaved in Baltimore in the 1830s, found urban slavery "a paradise" compared to life on the plantation. From his perspective, the relative freedom enjoyed by the urban slave stemmed from the fact that population density shamed white masters into adhering to higher standards of treatment: "He is a desperate slaveholder, who will shock the humanity of his nonslaveholding neighbors with the cries of his lacerated slave."

For other city slaves, the relative freedom of urban life had to do with the economic conditions of the city. Sally Thomas, a

Virginia-born slave who moved with her master to Nashville, Tennessee, in 1817, hired herself out as a laundress and managed to earn enough to start a laundry business. Renting her own home, signing contracts, possessing property, and negotiating her own social relationships on both sides of the color line (she conceived a child with John Catron, who would later serve on the U.S. Supreme Court), Thomas enjoyed a kind of virtual freedom, even while the state of Tennessee defined her as a slave for all legal purposes. Such cases were far from the norm, but they reflected the greater fluidity of an urban cash economy.

City slaves were also able to live among communities of free people of color. Much like other ethnic minorities in nineteenth-century America, free people of color chose city life over the country and depended on their own churches, fraternal orders, and benevolent societies for social and economic support. But as the number of urban slaves living away from their masters grew after the 1840s southern cities became much more clearly segregated into black and white communities. In the absence of strict master control, white society assumed the role, and both free and enslaved African Americans were subjected to more general forms of social surveillance.

SOUTHERN CULTURES

The antebellum South was organized around the economics of cotton, the demographics of slavery, and the legal regime of white supremacy. But the distinctive texture of southern life was also a matter of culture. Because this culture was destroyed during the Civil War, it is sometimes viewed with nostalgia, as a simpler time of courtly manners and gracious living, at least for those at the top of society. Historians have constructed a more complex and less harmonious view of antebellum life, recognizing that several cultures existed within the South, each with distinct beliefs and rituals that shaped daily life.

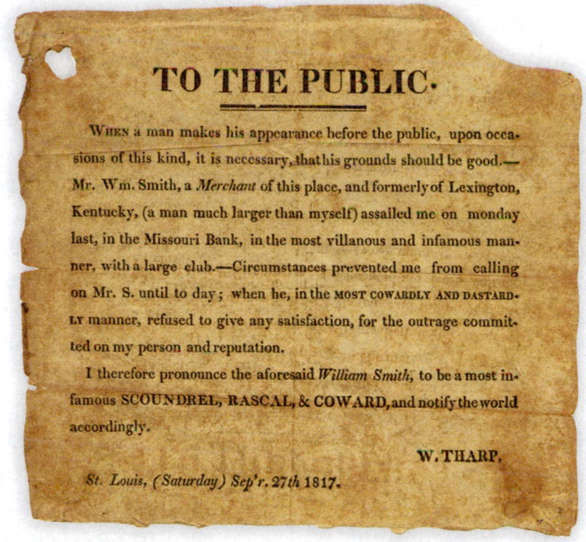

TO THE PUBLIC.

WHEN a man makes his appearance before the public, upon occasions of this kind, it is necessary, that his grounds should be good.— Mr. Wm. Smith, a *Merchant* of this place, and formerly of Lexington, Kentucky, (a man much larger than myself) assailed me on monday last, in the Missouri Bank, in the most villanous and infamous manner, with a large club.—Circumstances prevented me from calling on Mr. S. until to day; when he, in the MOST COWARDLY AND DASTARDLY manner, refused to give any satisfaction, for the outrage committed on my person and reputation.

I therefore pronounce the aforesaid *William Smith*, to be a most infamous SCOUNDREL, RASCAL, & COWARD, and notify the world accordingly.

W. THARP.

St. Louis, (Saturday) Sep'r. 27th 1817.

Dueling Poster. The protocols of honor culture required the issuance of a written public challenge after a long period of negotiation between the representatives of aggrieved parties, such as in this 1817 broadside. William Tharp states that his opponent, William Smith, rebuffed a personal visit to demand the satisfaction of a duel. Smith, a merchant, apparently believed that Tharp, a laborer, lacked the social status necessary to make him an honorable opponent. When he caught Tharp posting notices of challenge on September 28, a fight broke out and Smith was killed. A jury later acquitted Tharp. **Question for Analysis:** Who is the intended audience for Tharp's poster?

CODES OF HONOR AMONG WHITES

As in most other slaveholding societies, the powerful men who ruled in the South put great stock in the concept of **honor.** Their traditional honor culture stressed the importance of personal reputation and relied on public shame, as distinguished from private guilt, to regulate conduct. The honorable gentleman's reputation rested on his ability to demonstrate strength, self-possession, generosity, and honesty in his dealings with others.

On occasion, the code of honor also required displaying a willingness to die in a duel to avenge an insult and maintain one's reputation. Brought to the United States by French naval officers during the Revolution, elaborate codes of conduct for duels (known as "affairs of honor") took hold among both northern and southern elites. After the 1804 killing of Alexander Hamilton by Vice President Aaron Burr, however, popular revulsion toward dueling in the North limited its appeal and use. Dueling was illegal in every state by the 1830s, but in the South what was prohibited by law was sanctioned by custom. As Andrew Jackson's mother had advised him as a young boy, "the law affords no remedy that can satisfy the feelings of a true man." A man of honor, in other words, cannot rely on the law to restore his personal reputation.

Even a physically harmless gesture could be deadly serious to a man of honor. Southern gentlemen stood guard against slights that might bring about dishonor, such as becoming the victim of a humiliating gesture. Once during Andrew Jackson's second term, a disgruntled former naval officer assaulted the president in a ship cabin and attempted to pull his nose. Jackson chased away his attacker with a cane (and refused to have him prosecuted) but was more intent on persuading the public that the nose-pull had failed. Whenever his friend Peggy Eaton teased him about the incident, Jackson would grow quite serious. He would shake his fist, she recalled, and insist that "by the eternal God, madam, no man ever pulled my nose."

White women had honor too, in the sense that they were vulnerable to being dishonored, but their honor consisted almost entirely in sexual chastity and fidelity and did not entitle them to avenge insults or serve in public life. In that sense the culture of honor in the slaveholding South was a white male prerogative. Black women and black men could not participate within this culture of honor because of their status as subordinates.

Indeed the culture of honor is important not only for understanding the world of southern white society, but also for understanding slavery. Southern conceptions of honor were rooted in the domination of other human beings, and even non-gentlemen could claim to be men of honor by owning a couple of slaves or simply by virtue of belonging to a privileged race. At the same time, the treatment of slaves was shaped in part by the dictates of a culture of honor. Plantation punishments—which featured public flogging, enslaved adults beaten by white children, and enslaved women beaten in the presence of their husbands—were not intended solely to secure obedience or heighten productivity. They were also humiliation ceremonies designed to exclude African American slaves from the claims to honor that were treasured by slaveholding men.

Honor culture was not unique to the South, but its prominence in the region's public life found little parallel in the North as the century wore on. The prevalence of honor codes among white southerners may even help to explain certain interesting cultural differences between the two regions, such as the lack of enthusiasm in the antebellum South for forms of entertainment that were popular in the North. White southerners showed less interest in news stories and museum displays that celebrated lies and hoaxes, things that were not laughing matters to men of honor. Perhaps for similar reasons, one historian has argued, the sport of baseball, with its emphasis on such dishonorable habits as stealing and trying to elude capture, did not really catch on in the South until well after the Civil War.

CHRISTIANITY IN BLACK AND WHITE

The southern culture of honor coexisted (not always peacefully) with the influence of evangelical Christianity, which was spreading quickly in the South during the nineteenth century. Especially in the beginning of the century, Baptist and Methodist preachers were the enemies of the culture of honor, in part because they called for the rejection of pastimes and practices that were part of being a gentleman (like gambling, horse racing, and extramarital sex). The evangelical message also encouraged forms of public behavior that were out of place in honor culture, such as ecstatic conversion and enthusiastic surrender before the Holy Spirit. When a gentleman embraced this message, he was unlikely to maintain the proud posture expected of a man of honor, as illustrated in the case of a supporter of nullification who converted during the 1831 revivals (see Chapter 10). As evidence of his conversion, the man claimed that he had been about to challenge a Unionist to a duel, but was now "willing to kiss the dust upon the feet of the Union men if they would only come to Christ."

Evangelical preachers also threatened the dominant culture by putting power in the hands of young, unmarried ministers and pious women, and they frequently blurred the racial divide and the hierarchical division between masters and slaves by emphasizing the need for all human beings to be saved. After 1830, however, as Baptist and Methodist churches in the South began to grow, they became more accommodating of the social order, especially on the subject of slavery. Still, evangelicalism exerted a cultural influence that competed with the code of honor in defining proper masculine conduct for slaveholders.

Christianity made significant inroads among slaves as well. Though their religious practices differed in many respects from those of southern whites, Americans of African descent, by and large, adopted the religion of their masters between 1760 and 1850. By 1860, one in four slaves belonged to a church (as compared to one in three among whites), and many more attended services, heard sermons, or espoused Christian beliefs. Protestant Christianity had become the dominant religion among African Americans.

Although they embraced the religion of the surrounding white society, African Americans in the South were able to infuse Christianity with their own perspectives and circumstances and find within it various resources for dealing with slavery. By choosing particular denominations (mostly Methodist and Baptist), emphasizing particular themes and messages, adopting particular styles of worship, and synthesizing its tenets and practices with those of African religious traditions, slaves carved out a distinctive form of religious expression within what was in some respects a biracial church. Black Christians gravitated toward certain Biblical texts, favoring the exodus narrative, jubilee laws (which called for the emancipation of slaves every fifty years), and the psalms of the Hebrew Scriptures, for example, over the injunctions to obedience in the Pauline epistles of the New Testament, which masters were fond of invoking.

Slaves also brought to the new religion African patterns of call and response (where a preacher or singer alternates lines with a larger chorus or audience), rhythmic singing, and vocal improvisation. Enslaved Christians also developed their own tradition of sacred music, known as **spirituals,** with lyrics that emphasized sorrow, the longing for freedom, and even the possibility of revolution. "He said, and if I had my way," one enduring spiritual intones, "If I had my way, if I had my way,/I'd tear this building down."

Slaveholders were divided about the impact of Christian practice on slaves. Most were driven, both by religious belief and by desire for paternalistic control, to bring slaves into the church. Few saw any inherent conflicts between Christianity and slavery, and most believed that a churchgoing slave would be a more obedient worker. Thomas Affleck, a slaveholder and an agricultural innovator, advised overseers that "an hour devoted every Sabbath morning to [slaves'] moral and religious instruction would prove a great aid to you in bringing about a better state of things amongst the Negroes." Yet at the same time, some slave owners worried that slaves who engaged in ecstatic worship and listened to preachers might resist authority on the plantation. Most troubling, of course, was the specter of the Baptist preacher Nat Turner, whose religious visions led to a bloody slave rebellion. Many masters discouraged slave literacy, even though Protestant faiths stressed the importance of daily Bible reading and study. It is hard to know, of course, to what extent Christian ideas actually shaped slave consciousness, but the best evidence suggests that overall it induced neither feelings of subservience nor impulses to rebel. Slaves probably found within Christianity both reasons to accept their fate in the short term and grounds for expecting freedom in the indefinite future.

SLAVE FOLKWAYS

Christianity provided only some of the resources that African Americans used to build community and find meaning under the brutal conditions of their enslavement. Slaves in southern Louisiana practiced voodoo, a religious tradition that drew upon both African and French Catholic beliefs, and throughout the South, Christianity coexisted with other rituals and world views. Like many southern whites (including many white Christians), slaves cultivated the knowledge of folk medicine, spirit worlds, dream interpretation, and magic. Particular men and women earned special status within the slave community for their skills as conjurers, fortune tellers, or herb doctors, but ordinary slaves also passed on this knowledge (some of which had long African roots) to their children.

Slaves also entertained and instructed their children with a rich body of folktales. Many of these tales featured talking animal characters, such as Fox, Wolf, Rooster, Bear, and the clever Br'er (brother) Rabbit. Animal trickster tales originated in Africa, but as they evolved in the retellings of African American slaves, the animal figures acquired more human characteristics and aspirations. Animal tricksters, unlike the mythic heroes of nineteenth-century white American culture, relied not on superhuman size or strength, but on their wits—and a cunning grasp of their adversaries' habits and weaknesses. Wolf traps the acquisitive Br'er Rabbit with a sticky Tar Baby, but Rabbit dupes Wolf into throwing him into a briar patch, where he can easily escape, by pretending to fear that fate more than any other. Tales in which weaker animals elude or overcome stronger ones had special appeal to subjugated slaves seeking opportunities for resistance and comfort.

In those special moments of respite from the demands of fieldwork, a rich expressive culture of display and festivity developed in and around the slave quarters, especially on larger plantations. Every Sunday, for example, slaves would dress up in their best and most flamboyant clothing. The British actress Fanny Kemble, while living on her husband's Georgia plantation in the 1830s, described the multicolored Sunday attire of her slaves as "the most ludicrous combination of incongruities that you can conceive," but African Americans understood the meaning of these fashion displays as communal events and courtship rituals. Those slaves who were able to cultivate their own small plots of land would often use the proceeds to buy special Sunday outfits. During the week, enslaved women packed their Sunday best in fragrant flowers and herbs. One former slave fondly recalled women who "took their hair down outen the strings" and tucked "honeysuckle and rose petals . . . in dere bosoms." Enslaved African Americans also dressed up for weddings and funerals or on the handful of holidays that enlivened the slave calendar. In the festival of Jonkonnu (or John Canoe), which was observed around Christmas time in parts of North Carolina and southern Virginia during the antebellum period, bands of black men wearing elaborate costumes and playing musical instruments marched through the countryside, entering plantation homes and asking white landowners for money or drinks. And throughout the South, slave communities enjoyed log-rolling or corn-shucking festivals at critical junctures in the work cycle.

"Red Set Girls, and Jack-in-the-Green," 1837. African traditions were preserved more easily in slave communities in the Caribbean, where African-born slaves formed a much larger share of the population. But Caribbean celebrations of festivals such as Jonkonnu, depicted in this lithograph by the Jamaican Jewish artist Issac Mendes Belisario, had modest counterparts in many parts of the U.S. South.

SINGULAR LIVES

Frances Webb Bumpass, Evangelical Editor

White women in the antebellum South played a variety of social roles, not all of which fit easily into the familiar stereotypes of plantation mistresses and farm wives. Frances Webb was raised in Virginia and North Carolina, where she was given a substantial education that included private tutelage in Greek. In 1839, at the age of twenty, she met an itinerant Methodist minister named Sidney Bumpass, and she married him in 1842. After a number of posts in different rural congregations, the Bumpasses opened a school in Greensboro, North Carolina, and in 1851 Sidney, who had acquired a printing press, began publishing a weekly Methodist newspaper. In December of that year, however, Sidney died from typhoid fever and Frances, suddenly a thirty-two-year-old widow, assumed the reins. Despite early opposition from the Methodist Conference, which considered a woman's stewardship of a religious newspaper unseemly, Frances Bumpass ran the *Weekly Message* for twenty years, focusing much of the paper's attention on subjects related to female education. From the perspective of women's literary history in the South, Frances Bumpass was something of a pioneer.

On the contentious questions of slavery and race, Frances Bumpass was in some respects more conventional. Though she and her husband sought to spread Methodism to African Americans and opposed a white lynch mob that attacked free blacks, they did not express fundamental objections to the racial order of the American South. Like most white southerners, the Bumpasses did not own slaves, and like many white evangelical leaders in the region, Frances focused her daily life on spiritual matters that had little to do with politics or labor arrangements. In her private writings, however, she expressed ambivalence toward the slave system. She wrote in an 1844 diary entry about "the evils of slavery" and spoke of the possibility of moving to a free state. But Bumpass did not necessarily mean that slaveholding was sinful or wrong; she simply saw slaves as difficult to manage. Slaves are "a continual source of trouble" to their owners, she elaborated, "vexing them, and causing much sin."

Most of all, Bumpass worried about the possibility of a slave revolt. Rumors of such a revolt in North Carolina in 1844 prompted her to confess to her diary of a tendency to "dwell too much on . . . imaginary scenes of murder." These images kept her up at night and, once she did fall asleep, they would awaken her with sudden dread. Bumpass would turn to her faith on such occasions, which helped her manage the fear of latent violence built into southern race relations. Still, her frightened perspective offers clues as to how white southerners, even those with no obvious material investment in slavery, might have regarded the prospect of African American emancipation.

Frances Webb Bumpass. Like most nonslaveholding whites, this evangelical newspaper publisher had no wish to subvert the South's racial hierarchy.

Think About It

1. Looking back at other examples from Chapters 8–10, how do you think Bumpass's career as a newspaper editor reflected the limitations and possibilities of women's participation in nineteenth-century public life?
2. What do you think Bumpass might have had in mind when she wrote in her diary that slaves vexed their owners and "caused much sin?"
3. If armed slave rebellions were so uncommon in the South, why did the fear of them keep Bumpass awake at night?

THE CULTURE OF COMMON WHITE FOLK

Most white southerners did not own slaves and did not belong to slave-owning families. As a group, they represented a lower class, since this majority owned less than 10 percent of the region's wealth by the end of the antebellum period. But not all of them were impoverished. Some were subsistence farmers tilling poor soil in the hilly backcountry, far from the large plantations. Others lived in cities, including a growing population of foreign immigrants by the 1850s. But large numbers were more substantial landowners, often called **yeoman farmers,** who grew crops for market as well as for subsistence. Yeomen lived on small family farms where men, women, and children worked together as a household, much like modest landowners in the Midwest, where slavery was illegal (see Singular Lives: Frances Webb Bumpass, Evangelical Editor).

Unlike the wealthy planters, and more so than independent farmers in the North, the common folk of the southern hill country still inhabited a world that was relatively cut off from the communication networks that were beginning to reshape the country in the 1830s and 1840s (see Chapter 10). By national standards, they had low literacy rates and were unlikely to engage in regular contact with people beyond their communities and families. Like enslaved African Americans, poorer white farming families in the South maintained a rich folk culture that bore the traces of traditions from across the Atlantic. In many parts of the South, the music of nonslaveholding whites, for example, with its five-tone scales and distinctive singing style, resembled that of the Scottish lowlands or southeastern England, where many of their ancestors had lived. The common folk of the South also tended to preserve traditional beliefs in ghosts, witches, conjurers, and weather omens.

Despite the great cultural differences separating planters from yeoman farmers and common white folk, whites in the South shared some basic convictions. Although nonslaveholding white men formed a majority of the southern electorate, they never posed a serious threat to the institution of slavery. Some aspired to acquire slaves in the future and supported slavery for many of the same reasons that people who do not own real estate today nonetheless support the rights and privileges of homeowners. Other yeoman farmers, who may not have aspired to enter the ranks of slaveholders, nonetheless defended slavery because they shared with the planters a world view that valued hierarchy, submission, and obedience. These farmers commanded the labor of white women and children in their own families, rather than enslaved African Americans, and saw themselves as masters with an interest in maintaining social order. But whatever their views on slavery, most white Southerners regarded the prospect of emancipating African Americans as frightening. Accounts of violence in Haiti and the bloody example of Nat Turner reinforced the widespread notion that the end of slavery would lead to racial conflict. As one poor white man told a northern traveler, "I reckon the majority would be right glad if we could get rid of the niggers. But it wouldn't never do to free 'em and leave 'em here. I don't know anybody, hardly, in favor of that." Poorer whites in the South benefited, at least psychologically, from the privileges of racial superiority in a mixed-race society. But probably many would have been happy to live like family farmers in northern states such as Illinois, where black people were not tolerated at all, either free or enslaved. What they did not want was to live with emancipated slaves.

TABLE 11.1 THE ABOLITION OF SLAVERY IN THE AMERICAS, 1777-1833

State or Region	Date Slavery Outlawed	Means
Vermont	1777	Constitutional mandate
Pennsylvania	1780	Gradual abolition
Massachusetts, New Hampshire	1783	Judicial ruling
Connecticut, Rhode Island	1784	Gradual abolition
Northwest Territory	1787	Continental Congress
Upper Canada	1793	Colonial law
New York	1799	Gradual abolition
Lower Canada (Quebec)	1803	Judicial ruling
New Jersey	1804	Gradual abolition
Haiti	1804	Armed revolution
Argentina	1813	Gradual abolition
Gran Colombia	1821	Gradual abolition
Chile	1823	Legal prohibition
Mexico	1829	Legal prohibition
Bolivia	1831	Legal prohibition
British West Indies	1833	Act of Parliament

SLAVERY, POLITICS, AND SECTIONAL CONFLICT

At various points in late eighteenth and early nineteenth centuries, the practice of slaveholding had fallen under political attack. In the 1830s, however, new factors heated up the slavery issue. When Great Britain banned slavery in its West Indian colonies and slavery was dismantled in the new independent republics of South America (see Table 11.1), the South became the largest slaveholding society in the hemisphere. Together with the Russian Empire, with its millions of serfs, the American South was now heavily identified with a form of labor discipline and class division that was being rejected by much of the modern world. Southern slaveholders and their political allies came increasingly under attack, both from northern abolitionists who spoke out against the injustice to slaves and from northern politicians enraged by the political power of slaveholders on the national stage. In this polarized climate, all three branches of the federal government became embroiled in new outbreaks of the slavery debate.

ANTISLAVERY RUMBLINGS AND ATTEMPTS AT CENSORSHIP

The Missouri Compromise in 1820 (see Chapter 9) had succeeded in keeping the issue of slavery off the congressional agenda for fifteen years. But in 1835, a Maine representative introduced a petition signed by 172 women in his district calling for the abolition of slavery in Washington, D.C., the only part of the country over which Congress had uncontested jurisdiction. In prior years, such a petition would have been referred to a committee and quietly disposed of without serious consideration, but the new spotlight on southern slavery prompted the House of Representatives to avoid the petition altogether. Voting to table the motion, they simply set it aside without any official action. This prompted a series of maneuvers between northern Whigs and proslavery Democrats (from both regions) over the question of whether Congress would even acknowledge the criticism of slavery in its chambers.

First, a representative from Vermont made a motion to print the petition, noting that the signers were respectable citizens and not members of some radical abolitionist society. In response, a New York Democrat allied with Martin Van Buren moved to table the motion to print. Two days later, another New Englander presented another antislavery petition, and James Henry Hammond of South Carolina moved that the petition "not be received." This was unprecedented. Petitions from citizens went routinely unheeded but had never been refused altogether. House Democrats, seeking to avoid a damaging sectional split within Van Buren's coalition on the eve of the 1836 election, then passed a gag rule on all slavery petitions, requiring that they be tabled immediately after being presented by title. The gag rule, which remained in effect in the House of Representatives from 1836 to 1844, prevented the antislavery views of northern citizens from being aired in Congress.

This crisis over antislavery petitions reflected southern panic over the sudden rise of a radical abolitionist movement in the North. Northern reformers had criticized slavery before, but most of their efforts had focused on ending the slave trade and their proposals to emancipate slaves involved gradual schemes that worked within existing systems of authority and enlisted the support and cooperation of slaveholders. The leading antislavery organization in the United States before

ABOLITION FROWNED DOWN.

Stifling Debate. This political cartoon published in New York in 1839 satirizes the gag rule that prohibited discussions of abolition in the House of Representatives. Two slaves cower behind a bale of cotton and witness the collapse of John Quincy Adams atop a pile of petitions, *The Emancipator* newspaper, and a resolution calling for the recognition of Haiti. Waddy Thompson, Jr., a proslavery Whig congressman from South Carolina, glowers at Adams.

the 1830s was the American Colonization Society (founded in 1816), which briefly united opponents of slavery and anxious slaveholders around a plan to relocate slaves to Africa. Opponents of slavery turned to colonization as the best chance for achieving emancipation in the South, whereas slaveholders saw in it a way to deport free blacks who might otherwise encourage slave rebellions. Advocates in both regions also defended colonization as a way of bringing Christianity to Africa. The American Colonization Society succeeded in 1822 in establishing the colony of Liberia on Africa's west coast (its national capital still bears the name Monrovia, in honor of the American president at the time of its creation), and colonization briefly enjoyed widespread support among a range of prominent political leaders in both regions. But by 1825, this alliance began to splinter. Slaveholders now saw colonization as part of a larger plan of emancipation, which they objected to on economic as well as ideological grounds. And for a new generation of abolitionists, colonization came to seem both racist and unlikely to end slavery.

Between 1825 and 1835, gradual approaches to ending slavery gave way to a new radicalism among both black and white abolitionists. In 1829, the *Ethiopian Manifesto* of Robert Alexander Young, a free black from New York, prophesied the imminent arrival of a black messiah who would lead slaves to freedom and execute divine judgment against slaveholders. Seven months later, a free black from Boston named David Walker published his *Appeal . . . to the Coloured Citizens of the World*, which explicitly rejected the idea of colonization. In 1831, a white New Englander named William Lloyd Garrison began publishing his antislavery newspaper, *The Liberator*, advocating the immediate and uncompensated emancipation of all slaves. In 1833, the American Anti-Slavery Society was formed, providing an institutional base for a new abolitionist movement.

The new antislavery movement was based in the North, but white southerners had reason to worry about the circulation of these ideas within their communities. Walker sent his pamphlets southward by stitching them into the jackets he sold to black sailors. Garrison and the American Anti-Slavery Society relied on a more conventional medium: the U.S. mail. Taking advantage of the low postage rate charged to newspapers, they inundated the South with their publications. During the summer of 1835, abolitionists sent over 175,000 pieces of mail into the South, an amount equal to the entire output of the southern periodical press. In certain rural districts, these abolitionist papers would comprise the

Charleston Post Office. Southerners accused abolitionists of "pour[ing] their poisons into the national chalice" and being accessories to the murderous rampage of Nat Turner. In this abolitionist depiction of the 1835 Charleston post office raid, a poster offering a "$20000 reward for Tappan" refers to a bounty set by the city of New Orleans on American Anti-Slavery Society founder Arthur Tappan.

overwhelming majority of the printed information arriving each day by mail.

Southerners tried various means to dam the southward flow of abolitionist tracts and to prevent them from reaching African Americans. In 1831, Georgetown (in the District of Columbia) passed a law prohibiting free blacks from taking copies of *The Liberator* out of the post office. If caught, they faced a $25 fine and thirty days in jail. If they could not pay the fine, they could be sold into slavery for four months. In 1835, a group of Charleston citizens calling themselves lynch men raided the post office at night, confiscated an unsolicited mass mailing from the American Anti-Slavery Society, and burned the offending publications in the streets of the city, along with effigies of leading abolitionists, before a crowd of two thousand. Significantly, the South found an ally in the White House. President Jackson considered abolitionists "monsters" who fomented slave uprisings and deserved "to atone for this wicked attempt with their lives," and he instructed his postmaster general not to deliver antislavery publications unless a subscriber demanded them. In the event that someone did, his or her name would be published. With the federal government's blessing, local postmasters thus quietly censored the mail.

The mass circulation of new antislavery ideas formed the backdrop for the fight in Congress about how to deal with abolitionist petitions. The postal system was making it difficult to maintain a clear geographical barrier between the North and South, thwarting the South's attempt to control how slavery was discussed within its borders. So Jackson and his party tried to impede the flow of antislavery mail and suppress the discussion of petitions to Congress, whose records circulated in the national press. But the petition gag proved in some ways counterproductive. Former president John Quincy Adams, now serving in the House of Representatives, waged a strenuous campaign to affirm the constitutional right of petitioning, drawing more public attention to the debate over discussing slavery than it would otherwise have attracted. Abolitionist petition drives, now protesting the gag rule in addition to the earlier cause, garnered even more signatures. The tabled petitions filled a 600-square-foot room in the Capitol building, from the floor to its 14-foot ceiling.

PROSLAVERY DEFIANCE

The southern defense of slavery assumed a new form by the 1830s. Whereas earlier many white southerners had conceded that slavery was problematic or even undesirable, such views quickly became taboo. Fearing slave insurrections like Nat Turner's, responding to attacks from the North, and feeling isolated in the face of a growing international rejection of slavery, Southerners began to assert that their labor system was a blessing, not a curse. No longer a "necessary evil" or an "irremediable evil," slavery was now, in the words of James Henry Hammond, "the greatest of all blessings which a kind Providence has bestowed upon our glorious region."

Slavery's defenders often began with the observation that abolition was impossible. For one thing, slave property was too valuable. The British government had ended slavery in the West Indies by compensating slave owners. But how would the federal government come up with $900 million to emancipated southern slaves, when all federal revenues amounted to only about $25 million a year? Furthermore, they argued, it would be impracticable to send two million slaves back to Africa and dangerous to leave them on American soil where they would cause disorder and initiate racial warfare. But the **proslavery ideology** that flourished in the South after 1830 also relied on a large arsenal of arguments for why slavery was in fact desirable.

Some of the proslavery arguments had been around for a while, introduced in the North during the eighteenth century when slaveholding fell under moral attack there. Southern Christians cited the Biblical laws and precedents permitting slaveholding and invoked the "curse of Ham" from Genesis (see Chapter 3) to explain the enslavement of Africans. They also presented black slavery as part of a divine plan to Christianize the heathens of Africa. But proslavery advocates also advanced newer arguments during the antebellum period. Increasingly, slavery was justified with reference to the innate racial inferiority of black people, which southerners supported with the latest scientific theories and vocabulary developed at leading northern universities. In addition, southern politicians and writers contrasted slavery with the wage labor system that was spreading in the North and in Britain, claiming that plantation slaves were better treated than factory workers. These arguments would grow more elaborate and intense as sectional tensions escalated in the 1850s (see Chapter 14).

THE SLAVE POWER AND CONSPIRACY THEORIES

Proslavery arguments may have bolstered white southerners' commitment to their labor system, but it was the U.S. Constitution and the two-party system that provided the ultimate defense of slavery during this period. By counting 60 percent of the growing slave population, the Constitution's three-fifths clause inflated the South's representation both in Congress and in the electoral college that determined the presidency, which helped offset the population growth in other regions. Had slaves been excluded from the count, southern voices in Congress would have been fewer and the nation would have elected a very different set of presidents. Slaveholders held the office of the presidency for fifty of the office's first sixty-two years.

In a subtler manner, the party system protected slavery by allowing a solid faction within the Democratic Party to control national elections. In a closely competitive two-party system, a majority within the majority party (which can in theory consist of just over 25 percent of the total electorate) can prevail, so long as everyone else maintains party unity. Because southerners held sway among Democrats, and because other Democrats remained more committed to the primacy of the party than to any other cause, southern Democrats could set policies and nominate candidates. Northerners who rose to prominence within the party had to be acceptable to the South. Southerners wielded less power among the Whigs, but they too needed to remain competitive in the South to have a chance at winning national elections.

These circumstances lent credibility to a new rhetorical device that entered the American political vocabulary in the 1830s. Northerners began to speak of a **Slave Power,** an insidious force in American history through which a small circle of wealthy slaveholders manipulated the political system for their own benefit. The charge was first developed by abolitionists, but it spread quickly to mainstream northern politicians who claimed no particular sympathy for the enslaved. What was evil about the Slave Power, from this perspective, was more the conspiratorial scheming and the acquisitive appetites of the slaveholding class and less the injustice of treating another human being as property. In this view, the primary victim of slavery was thus not the slave, but the free institutions of the American republic. Such arguments would help spread hostility toward slaveholders among nonabolitionists and would eventually create problems for Democrats in the North.

The Slave Power thesis was part of a larger trend in antebellum political rhetoric toward conspiracy theories. Perhaps because the nation was still relatively young and itself the result of revolution, Americans were quick to suspect secret plots to subvert the republic. Charges of conspiracy had a long history in Anglo-American politics, dating back to English fears of Catholic designs on the throne, and such rhetoric had played an important role in the American Revolution. But in the 1830s and 1840s, subversion charges were leveled much more broadly and promiscuously—at Catholics, Mormons, Masons, or the directors of the national bank. The escalating slavery conflict was especially ripe for such heated accusations. On the southern side, conspiracy theories focused on the abolitionists, whom proslavery politicians accused of stealing slaves and plotting slave rebellions. Southerners evoked the specter of secret midnight meetings, "where the bubbling cauldron of abolition was fulfilled with its pestilential materials, and the fire beneath kindled by the breath of the fanatics." Most provocatively, both sides alleged that conspirators of the other region were motivated by a desire to have sex with enslaved women.

One key difference between the competing conspiracy theories in the slavery debates of the 1830s, however, was the fact that abolitionists were a fringe minority in the North whose views were considered beyond the pale of congressional deliberation and unfit for the U.S. mail. By contrast, leading slaveholders held major political positions throughout the South.

SEMINOLES, TEXANS, AND THE SLAVERY CONFLICT

The federal government sought to massage or avoid a number of potential conflicts over slavery during this period but generally acted in support of slaveholders' interests. Jackson's Indian removal policies had cleared the way for the expansion of the cotton kingdom, and his successors continued those policies at considerable cost. When Seminole Indians in Florida resisted removal, the U.S. Army pursued them over the course of a seven-year guerilla war. Seminole resistance was by some definitions a slave rebellion, since hundreds of escaped African Americans and many descendants of former slaves were part of the Seminole nation. The federal government's extraordinary commitment to removing this single native group reflected the threat that a Florida haven for runaways posed to nearby slaveholders. The Second Seminole War, as historians often label the conflict, lasted from 1835 to 1842, and ultimately succeeded in forcing the removal of three thousand Seminoles to Oklahoma. But it cost the federal government $20 million, and 1,500 American soldiers died in the course of the battle.

On the western frontier of the cotton kingdom, the federal government set its sights on Texas, a province at the outer reaches of the new nation of Mexico. Mexico had achieved independence of Spain in 1821, but Texas lay far from the Mexican capital and much of its territory was populated and controlled by Comanche, Apache, or Kiowa Indians. The Mexican government welcomed Anglo settlers to Texas, with the proviso that they obey Mexican laws, learn Spanish, and attend Catholic mass. Ignoring those conditions, many white southerners (mostly slaveholders) answered the call. Mexico abolished slavery in 1829 but declined to enforce the ban in Texas. By 1830, the coastal region of eastern Texas had twenty thousand white American settlers and one thousand slaves brought in to grow cotton. Mexico grew alarmed and banned further migration, but Americans continued to immigrate illegally into Texas, and by 1835 they outnumbered Mexicans there ten to one.

Sensing their numerical power and fearing Mexican attempts to reassert control over the province, American settlers in Texas organized a rebellion. English-speaking whites objected to being taxed and complained of lack of military protection against Indians. But most of all, they sought to preempt enforcement of national laws, including the ban on slavery. In 1836, joined by several leading Mexicans in the region, they declared independence.

Mexican president Antonio López de Santa Anna led a military attack against the rebellion and captured the makeshift rebel garrison in San Antonio at the Battle of the Alamo. Mexican troops killed all 187 defenders of the fort, including the

Santa Anna's Surrender. This 1836 cartoon imagines Santa Anna and his brother groveling as they turn themselves over to Sam Houston. "I consent to remain your prisoner, most excellent sir!!" the Mexican leader tells Houston—a depiction that undoubtedly pleased Texans and Americans who had taken "Remember the Alamo" as a battle cry. **Question for Analysis:** How does the cartoonist's representation of the Mexican surrender square with the Mexican Senate's insistence that Santa Anna was coerced into recognizing Texan independence?

former Whig congressman David Crockett. The Texans, regrouped under the command of Sam Houston, ambushed Santa Anna's army near the San Jacinto River and took the president prisoner. Threatened with his life, Santa Anna signed treaties recognizing Texan independence and agreeing to keep his troops south of the Rio Grande. The Mexican Congress refused to ratify this coerced treaty, and Mexico continued to claim Texas as its own territory.

Houston and the Texans expected the United States to annex the new independent nation, but the politics of slavery dictated a different response. President Jackson recognized that adding a new slaveholding territory would jeopardize northern support for his party's presidential candidate, Martin van Buren, on the eve of election. Jackson waited for his last day in office to recognize the new Texas Republic, with a southern border at the Rio Grande, based on Santa Anna's controversial treaty. But neither he nor Van Buren proposed annexation. Texas remained an independent slave state, called the Lone Star Republic, for the next decade, enjoying friendly relations with the United States and attracting 100,000 American immigrants with generous land grants. The ultimate status of this disputed territory awaited resolution.

THE *AMISTAD* CASE

The Van Buren administration was not able to control the debate over slavery as smoothly when fifty-three African slaves, sold to Portuguese merchants and brought illegally to the Spanish colony of Cuba, made their way through the U.S. justice system. On July 1, 1839, a twenty-five-year-old man from Sierra Leone known as Joseph Cinqué (his

1841.] ANTI-SLAVERY ALMANAC. 23

counsel to defend them. S. S. Jocelyn, Joshua Leavitt, and Lewis Tappan, are the committee, and the donations can be sent to Lewis Tappan, Treasurer, No. 122 Pearl street, New-York.

DESCRIPTION OF CINQUEZ, GRAB-EAU, AND JAMES COVEY THE INTERPRETER.

SING-GBE, [Cingue,] (generally spelt *Cinquez*) was born in Ma-ni, in Dzho-poa, *i. e.*, in *the open land*, in the Mendi country. His mother is dead, and he lived with his father. He has a wife and three children, one son and two daughters. His king, Ka-lum-bo, lived at Kaw-men-di, a large town in the Men-di country. He is a planter of rice, and never owned or sold slaves. He was seized by four men, when traveling in the road, his right hand tied to his neck. Ma-ya-gi-la-lo sold him to Ba-ma-dzha, son of Shaka, king of Gen-du-ma, in the Vai country. Ba-ma-dzha carried him to Lomboko and sold him to a Spaniard. At Lomboko he was transferred to a slave-ship, and taken to Havana.

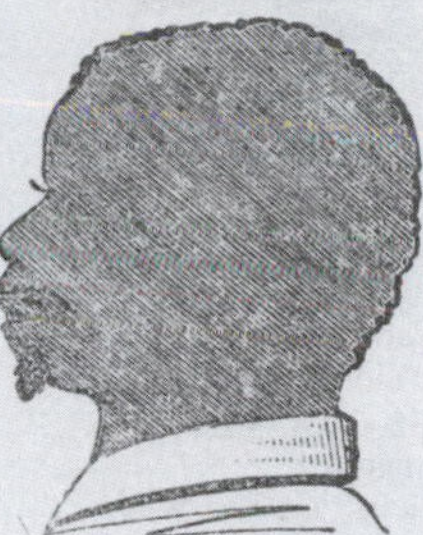

GI-LA-BA-RU, [Grab-eau,] (*have mercy on me,*) was born at Fu-lu, in the Men-di country, two moons' journey into the interior. He was the next after Cingue in command of the Amistad. His parents are dead, one brother and one sister living. He is married, but no children; he is a planter of rice. He was caught on the road when going to Taurang, in the Bandi country, to buy clothes. His uncle had bought two slaves in Bandi, and gave them in payment for a debt; one of them ran away, and he (Grab-ean) was taken for him. He was then sold to a Vai-man, who sold him to Laigo, a Spaniard, at Lomboko.

JAMES COVEY, the interpreter for the Africans, is apparently about twenty years of age; was born at Benderi in the Men-di country. Covey was taken by three men, in the evening, from his parents' house, he was carried to the Bullom country, and sold as a slave to the king of the Bulloms. He was afterwards sold to a Portuguese, living near Mani. After staying in this place about one month, Covey was put on board a Portuguese slave-ship, which was captured by a British armed vessel, and carried into Sierra Leone. Covey thus obtained his freedom, and remained in this place five or six years, and was taught to read and write in the English language, in the schools of the Church Missionary Society. Covey's original name was *Kaw-we-li*, which signifies, in Mendi, *war-road*, i. e., a road dangerous to pass, for fear of being taken captive. In Nov. 1838, he enlisted as a sailor on board the British brig of war Buzzard, commanded by Captain Fitzgerald. It was on board this vessel, when at New-York, in Oct. 1839, that James was found, and by the kindness of Capt. Fitzgerald his services as an interpreter were procured.

***Amistad* Captives.** For eighteen months, the thirty-six African men and four children who had survived the ordeal of enslavement and mutiny were imprisoned in Connecticut. Thousands of visitors paid twelve and a half cents each to see the men, who were exhibited as "African Savages." John Warner Barber's illustrations of the captives showed each only in profile, though he also provided capsule biographies stressing their lives and families in Africa.

original Mendean name was Sengbeh Pieh) led a mutiny aboard the Spanish ship *Amistad* as it was transporting them from Havana to another Cuban port. Using a nail to pick the locks on his collar, Cinqué similarly freed the other captives, and the group armed themselves with sugar cane knives and killed the captain. They ordered a Spanish slave merchant to sail the ship back to Africa, but he steered a northward course and the ship was ultimately intercepted by a U.S. ship off the coast of Long Island. The American captain towed the ship to New London, Connecticut, and a federal judge ordered that the African captives be jailed in New Haven pending a determination of their legal status. Were they Spanish property? Were they pirates who had illegally seized control of a Spanish vessel? Or were they free human beings who had themselves been illegally seized by pirates?

President Van Buren and his secretary of state, John Forsyth, supported the Spanish government's insistence that the Africans were Cuban-born slaves who ought to be forcibly returned to their Cuban masters. Because the Spanish had signed a treaty with Great Britain honoring the British ban on the international slave trade, they could not admit that the slaves were taken from Africa. (Cuba imported more than 180,000 African slaves during the 1830s, despite the ban.) But Van Buren was unable to keep the case out of the U.S. judicial system, where a federal court tried to determine whether the Africans were legally enslaved. Crucial to the captives' case was the argument that they neither spoke nor understood Spanish. To help make this argument, a distinguished linguist on the Yale faculty found an African sailor in New York who spoke the Mende language and served as a court interpreter for the captives' testimony. The judge ruled that the captives had in fact been taken from Africa and that their enslavement was therefore not recognized by any law—American, Spanish, or international.

The Van Buren administration appealed the decision to the Supreme Court, where John Quincy Adams argued the Africans' case, invoking the Declaration of Independence and the natural right to rebel against slavery. In 1841, the Supreme Court upheld the decision in favor of the West Africans, setting free all of the *Amistad* captives except for a man named Antonio who had been raised in Cuba as a slave (abolitionists succeeded in smuggling Antonio off to Montreal after the ruling). The Court made clear, however, that wherever slavery was legal, which of course included the American South, no right of rebellion existed. Had the men aboard the slave ship been legally enslaved in Cuba, or in Alabama, they would have been returned to their owners.

The *Amistad* case dramatized the plight of slaves for northern audiences. It also underscored how difficult it was to draw rigid lines between legal slavery and illegal kidnapping and posed troubling questions about the conflict between the property rights of slaveholders and the natural right of self-defense invoked by rebellious slaves. And as an event in international diplomacy, the *Amistad* crisis raised the possibility that changes in *international* slavery politics might affect the federal government's ability to manage the conflict between North and South. The Supreme Court's ruling thwarted the will of the president and alarmed slaveholders, but it also averted a possible war with the British, who might have imposed a blockade of Cuba, in defiance of the Monroe Doctrine.

"Joseph Cinquez [Cinqué] Addressing His Compatriots on Board the Spanish Schooner *Amistad*." This 1839 lithograph by John Childs depicts the leader of the *Amistad* rebellion as a prophetic orator enthralling his audience on board the slave ship.

CONCLUSION

During the fifteen years after Nat Turner's insurrection, the slave system in the South became more firmly entrenched. While enslaved African Americans struggled to carve out places of autonomy and comfort, their prospects for emancipation dimmed considerably. Despite a dip in the late 1830s, the cotton economy boomed and the market for slave labor made every slave vulnerable to sale and forced migration. Paradoxically, the growth of cotton intensified some of the social and cultural differences between the North and the South, even as it made the two regions more economically interdependent.

Meanwhile, a polarized and vitriolic debate over what do about slavery left slaveholders feeling increasingly insecure, despite the extraordinary power they wielded in the political system. A tense and fragile peace held between the slave states and the rest of the country, but events like Texan independence and the *Amistad* rebellion showed how hard this peace would be to maintain. If the United States were to expand southward or westward, peace would certainly have to be renegotiated.

STUDY TERMS

cotton gin (p. 271)
plantation (p. 271)
field laborers (p. 276)
house servants (p. 276)
corporal punishment (p. 277)
paternalism (p. 277)
slave patrols (p. 278)
Underground Railroad (p. 280)
hiring-out system (p. 282)
honor (p. 283)
spirituals (p. 284)
animal trickster tales (p. 285)
yeoman farmers (p. 285)
gag rule (p. 288)
American Colonization Society (p. 289)
Liberia (p. 289)
lynch men (p. 290)
proslavery ideology (p. 290)
Slave Power (p. 291)
conspiracy theories (p. 291)
Second Seminole War (p. 291)
Battle of the Alamo (p. 291)
Lone Star Republic (p. 292)
Amistad case (p. 293)

TIMELINE

1829 David Walker publishes *Appeal . . . to the Coloured Citizens of the World*

1831 William Lloyd Garrison begins publishing *The Liberator*

Nat Turner leads a slave rebellion in Virginia

1833 American Anti-Slavery Society formed

British Parliament abolishes slavery in Britain's colonies

1835 Antislavery petitions spark controversy in Congress

Charleston "lynch men" raid the post office to destroy antislavery publications

Second Seminole War begins

1836 Houses passes the gag rule, preventing the discussion of slavery

Antonio López de Santa Anna defeats Texan rebels in the Battle of the Alamo

Texas declares independence from Mexico

1839 Joseph Cinqué leads a mutiny of kidnapped Africans aboard the *Amistad*

1841 Supreme Court rules in favor of the *Amistad* captives

FURTHER READING

Additional suggested readings are available on the Online Learning Center at www.mhhe.com/becomingamerica1e.

David Brion Davis, *Inhuman Bondage* (2006), places the history of slavery in the antebellum South in the larger context of the end of slavery in the New World and includes a concise account of the *Amistad* crisis.

Thavolia Glymph, *Out of the House of Bondage* (2008), stresses the extent of women's power and violence on southern plantations.

Kenneth Greenberg, *Honor and Slavery* (1996), reinterprets the southern culture of honor, and presents a case for why slaveholders showed little interest in baseball.

Ariela Gross, *Double Character* (2000), shows how slaves' dual status as property and moral agent complicated everyday legal disputes in the courtrooms of the Deep South.

Martha Hodes, *White Women, Black Men* (1999), examines the history of illicit sexual relations between white women and black men in the antebellum South.

Walter Johnson, *Soul by Soul* (1999), uncovers the world of the domestic slave trade and demonstrates how the prospect of sale shaped the meaning of slavery in this period.

Peter Kolchin, *American Slavery* (1993), offers a succinct synthesis of several decades of historical scholarship on slavery in the United States.

Lawrence W. Levine, *Black Culture and Black Consciousness* (1977), recovers and analyzes the meaning of slaves' folktales, music, and expressive culture.

Stephanie McCurry, *Masters of Small Worlds* (1995), studies yeoman farm families in South Carolina and considers their ideological relationship to slavery.

Dylan Penningroth, *The Claims of Kinfolk* (2003), uncovers the role of property ownership among the enslaved.

Leonard Richards, *The Slave Power* (2000), shows how the southern defense of slavery shaped national politics through the workings of the Second Party System.

Brenda E. Stevenson, *Life in Black and White* (1997), updates the long-standing and contentious scholarly inquiry into the nature and persistence of slaves' family structures.

John Michael Vlach, *Back of the Big House* (1993), reconstructs the architecture and material culture of the plantation.

12

INSIDE ▶

THE BIG PICTURE

A variety of reform movements spread among the growing ranks of middle-class northerners, reflecting evangelical zeal about social change and promulgating new ideals of masculinity and femininity. Reformers found themselves at odds with major sectors of U.S. society, including Catholic immigrants, the slaveholding South, and supporters of the Democratic Party.

Making a New Man. A father fulfills his family duties by signing the temperance pledge.

1831–1848

ERA OF MIDDLE-CLASS REFORM

One night in 1842, a widow in Utica, a growing New York town along the Erie Canal route, waited up anxiously for the return of her son. When he failed to come home, she made her way to a local brothel and called to him through the locked door of one of the bedrooms. The brothelkeeper tossed the mother down a flight of stairs, but when she arrived at her home, her son was waiting for her, ashamed and repentant.

The story of the bold widow appeared in the reports of Utica's Female Moral Reform Society and presented a parable for an important new development in northern culture during this period. The fatherless son in this parable, like many young men who moved to the region's growing cities, lives free of paternal authority and enjoys the pleasures of the marketplace. His mother hopes to influence him at home but is forced by his absence to seek him out, bringing her maternal authority to the sinful world of the brothel. Risking exposure to the vices of the city, entering spaces ordinarily barred to respectable women, and suffering physical abuse in the process, the mother persuades her wayward son to mend his ways. In publicizing this victory in the battle against promiscuity and prostitution, Utica's female reformers were also narrating their own efforts to go out into the world, shout outside of locked doors, and wield their motherly influence over a wayward generation.

By the 1830s, the North was full of men and women who called themselves *reformers*. Not all of them followed the intrepid example of the Utica widow, but most shared the humanistic optimism of the eminent philosopher Ralph Waldo Emerson, who made a name for himself lecturing to packed houses. "What is man born for," Emerson asked rhetorically, "but to be a Reformer, a Re-maker of what man has made?" The culture of reform in the North covered a wide terrain. Some of the causes that the reformers embraced appear in retrospect humane and progressive, such as women's rights, public education, and prison reform. Others might seem more utopian, such as pacifism and cooperative farming. Still others strike modern Americans as repressive or bigoted, such as Sabbatarianism and anti-Catholicism. The most popular and prestigious reform movement was the temperance campaign, which sought to persuade people to abstain from drinking alcohol. The most socially and politically disruptive was abolitionism.

KEY QUESTIONS

- What prominent middle-class reform causes emerged in the North during the 1830s and 1840s?
- How did these reform causes relate to the social and economic circumstances of northern middle-class life?
- What ideological themes connected the temperance movement to abolitionism and to other reform causes?
- How did new ideals of domesticity help give birth to a feminist movement?
- How did Irish immigration shape the culture of middle-class reform?

These different movements and projects shared some basic themes and appealed to a particular population. Antebellum reform causes attracted mostly native-born northern Protestants in the 1830s and 1840s and reflected a larger outlook associated with the growing middle class. Middle-class northerners were not simply those whose income levels fell in the middle of the economic spectrum. They distinguished themselves through their occupations, homes, family arrangements, gender roles, sober habits, and world view. Reform movements would help to identify middle-class Americans and to define their culture.

During this same period, however, another powerful culture emerged in the northern states. Catholic immigrants, many of them from Ireland, moved to the United States in unprecedented numbers, bringing different attitudes from those of the reformers and challenging their authority. The reformers' ideals became the subject of culture wars between natives and newcomers, which contributed both to the friction between Democrats (who were popular among the newcomers) and Whigs (who fared better among reformers) and to the brewing conflict between the North and the South.

This 1846 lithograph depicts the nine stages of "The Drunkard's Progress," from respectability to ruin.

On the whole, southerners steered clear of the movements and campaigns that spread quickly in other parts of the nation during this period. A North Carolina editor bragged that the southern press rejected "the isms which infest Europe and the Eastern and Western states of this country." Self-improvement schemes, reform associations, and utopian social visions were viewed warily south of the Mason-Dixon Line, both because those movements included antislavery voices in the North and because southern slaveholders tended to be social conservatives. Reform remained controversial in the North as well, but a host of powerful campaigns to change individuals, communities, and government policy gained critical momentum and transformed American life.

THE CULTURE OF REFORM IN THE NORTH

Reform movements took root among a growing body of northerners who formed what we would now recognize as a modern middle class. Members of this class lived in towns and cities and worked in a variety of occupations and earned a range of incomes. Their swelling ranks included shopkeepers, small-scale merchants, factory managers, lawyers, doctors, teachers, clerks, and many others, along with their families. For the most part, they all regarded themselves as people who worked with their heads, rather than their hands. As much as income level, the hardening separation between manual and nonmanual labor during the early phases of American industrialization (see Chapter 10) marked the divide between the working class and the middle class by the middle of the nineteenth century. Nonmanual workers were more likely to receive salaries rather than hourly wages; they enjoyed greater prospects for advancement; and their work was more likely to require and reward entrepreneurialism.

Reform movements appealed especially to this class. Middle-class Americans did not own large farms and were not masters of inheritable trades. Instead, they aspired to transmit to their children those values, habits, and appearances that might secure their position in a new economy. They also worried about how the spread of commerce and cities might undermine their children's character. And they increasingly worried about threats to the social order posed by growing numbers of manual workers who did not attend their churches, live in their neighborhoods, or share their spheres of social influence. Reformist impulses reflected many of these concerns.

The middle-class men and women who called themselves reformers did not form a political party or build a single organization. They did not always agree on the merits of every reform cause nor did they unite around a single strategy for pursuing reformist goals. What they shared was a confidence that righteous individuals should take moral responsibility for making themselves and their neighbors better people. Armed with this confidence and with an evangelical fervor, reinforced during the Second Great Awakening, about what was right and wrong, reformers set out to reform themselves, their communities, and the society at large.

SELF-IMPROVEMENT

One of the cornerstones of reform ideology was the ideal of individual self-improvement. Young adults, especially men, were encouraged to discipline their habits, develop their characters, and expand their horizons. Many influential thinkers espoused this ideal, but none so powerfully as Ralph Waldo Emerson, a Unitarian minister from Boston who resigned his pulpit in 1832, rejected organized religion and other traditional institutions, and celebrated individual intuition as the source of true knowledge. Emerson encouraged Americans to trust that intuition and rely on themselves. Along with Henry David Thoreau, Margaret Fuller, and other New England philosophers and critics known as transcendentalists, Emerson believed in human perfectibility and preached that God was present in man and in nature.

Emerson spread his ideas about self-reliance as a touring lecturer, part of a network of speakers and adult education offerings known as the lyceum movement. Beginning in the 1820s, lyceum societies sponsored public lectures on science, literature, history, philosophy, archaeology, and other subjects through much of the North, and were especially popular in New England and the Midwest. By the mid-1830s, attending lectures had become one of the most common and respected leisure activities among middle-class adults. Through these lectures, a corps of speakers on the lyceum circuit exerted a powerful influence over a dispersed population. Emerson himself was a tireless public speaker, addressing audiences in hundreds of towns spread across twenty different states.

At a time when literacy was widespread but opportunities for formal education remained quite limited, most northern cities and towns supported lyceums and debating societies. Larger cities also sponsored lending libraries and schools for workingmen. Young adults participated in these institutions not only for education and entertainment, but also as a way of demonstrating their commitment to a project that many lyceum lectures stressed: making oneself better.

ASSOCIATIONS AND UTOPIAS

Even as lecturers preached individual self-reliance and self-improvement, members of the middle class assumed that young people stood a better chance of improving themselves in groups. Sponsors of lectures and debates were just a few examples of the **voluntary associations** that Americans formed in unprecedented numbers during the 1830s and 1840s. The small city of Utica, for example, with fewer than ten thousand inhabitants, listed forty-one of these associations in its city directory for 1832. Voluntary associations included an array of charities, benevolent societies, fraternal orders, self-improvement associations, and religious groups, but whatever their purpose they encouraged sociability and strengthened peer cultures.

Voluntary associations often called themselves reform societies and devoted themselves to reform causes. These were the building blocks of the new reform

Ralph Waldo Emerson. Emerson's lectures resonated with a rising number of middle-class men and women who sought to escape the shackles of traditional institutions and remake the world.

culture and tended to be local institutions, though sometimes they were affiliated with larger national networks. In certain ways, reform associations resembled political parties. The crucial difference was that the former attracted and included women as well as men. Many associations espoused religious ideals and attracted evangelical Christians, but they stood outside the formal structure of churches and denominations.

Associations in the antebellum North appealed to a mobile population seeking community, and the men and women who were drawn to the project of reform in this period wanted to build better communities and not just better individuals. In some cases, the impulse to improve communities led reformers to withdraw from the larger society. Millennial religious sects, such as the Mormons or the Perfectionists (see Chapter 10), were famous examples of movements to fashion new social communities from scratch, but a host of more secular communes and experiments in cooperative living arose during this period as well. Robert Owen, a Scottish industrialist worried about the social effects of the factory system, built a model industrial community in New Harmony, Indiana in 1825. Rejecting private property, religion, and marriage, Owen attracted nine hundred colonists to his community. One of Owen's followers, his fellow Scottish socialist Frances Wright, bought land in western Tennessee and formed the community of Nashoba, on which she settled slaves whom she had purchased. The slaves would earn their freedom in five years and would be encouraged to intermarry with whites. Wright's community fell apart after a few years, and she became a symbol of sexual license and heretical religious views.

The most famous of the **utopian communities** of this period appeared in West Roxbury, Massachusetts, in 1841, where Emerson, Fuller, and other transcendentalists established Brook Farm, a cooperative agricultural community committed to high thinking and plain living. Brook Farm lasted only a few years, as did the substantial number of American communities organized around the cooperative ideals of the influential French thinker Charles Fourier. Still, experiments in noncompetitive communal living continued to attract reformers who were disturbed by the spread of capitalism, at least in certain parts of the country. Only 2 of the 130 cooperative utopias founded in the United States between 1800 and 1860 were located in the South.

REFORMING THE STATE

Self-improvement programs and utopian communities were often associated with free-thinkers (atheists and other critics of religion) but the most popular and successful movements to change society at large grew out of religious forces and impulses. The first organized campaign to bring the nation's conduct in line with religious dictates was **Sabbatarianism,** the movement to enforce Sabbath observance. American Sabbatarians sought, first in 1810 and then more forcefully between 1826 and 1831, to bar the transmission of mail on Sunday. The particular target was significant. Travel for any worldly purpose violated many American Protestants' convictions about proper Sabbath observance, and the postal service represented the secular realms of commerce and politics more generally. Moreover, since collecting, delivering, and distributing mail was the federal government's main activity as far as most Americans could see, evangelical Christians selected the Post Office Department as the best place to launch a campaign to reform the government.

Sabbatarians mounted national petition drives, but they faced opposition from a number of groups. Merchants insisted that the disruption of mail service would make business difficult and retard economic growth. Free thinkers, non-Protestants, and Protestant evangelicals from the newer denominations (especially Baptists) argued that legislating Sabbath observance amounted to state-sponsored religion and impinged on freedom of conscience. Many of President Andrew Jackson's political supporters were suspicious of the evangelical leaders who spearheaded the Sabbatarian campaign, several of whom also opposed Indian removal and questioned slavery. The Sabbath mails movement failed to achieve its goal (Sunday delivery would not be suspended until 1912), but it helped to organize evangelical reformers and spread the powerful idea that because Americans were connected economically they belonged to the same moral universe and therefore were responsible for one another's sins.

Several of the other campaigns to reform society through government action focused on the issue of punishment. Opponents of the death penalty organized an antigallows movement in the 1830s and 1840s, drawing support from numerous ministers, politicians, and journalists and stirring up an evangelical fervor associated with other reform causes in the North. In the mid-1830s, Pennsylvania and New York abolished public executions, and Maine passed a law stipulating that criminals convicted of capital offenses be confined in a state prison for a year and that they be executed only upon the issuance of a written warrant at the discretion of the governor. By midcentury, the antigallows movement succeeded in persuading three state legislatures—Michigan, Rhode Island, and Wisconsin—to ban the death penalty altogether, making them the first governments in modern times to abolish capital punishment on a permanent basis.

More generally, reformers questioned the use of violence as a means of correction. Traditional practices of corporal punishment came under attack in the North, where reformers believed that criminals would be corrected more effectively by moral influence, guilty conscience, and surveillance than by physical beating or public humiliation. Congress even considered abolishing the time-honored practice of flogging in the U.S. Navy, but the measure faced unanimous opposition among representatives from the South, where the lash remained a respected symbol of patriarchal authority and social order. As alternatives to floggings and beheadings, northern states built innovative prisons, which were now intended not simply to

Prison Reform. The Auburn Prison was built in 1816, and twelve prisons of this type were in operation in the United States by 1840.

keep offenders in custody while they awaited a more decisive punishment (or until their debts were paid) but to remake them as law-abiding citizens. Philadelphia's Eastern State Penitentiary placed convicted criminals under solitary confinement and enforced silence, in the hopes that they would be moved to repent their misdeeds. The Philadelphia model drew much interest in various parts of the world, but most states built a different—and cheaper—kind of prison, modeled on the one in Auburn, New York. In Auburn-style prisons, inmates performed hard group labor that was sold cheaply to private contractors to pay the costs of their incarceration.

TEMPERANCE AND SELF-CONTROL

The most popular and broad based of all the antebellum reform movements targeted entrenched traditions of drinking. By 1830, Americans were consuming more hard liquor per capita than at any time before or since—nearly triple today's rate. But over the next two decades, a temperance movement curbed national alcohol consumption and turned the refusal to drink into a badge of middle-class respectability. In dramatizing the evils of liquor, temperance advocates also emphasized key ideological themes that would tie together many of the disparate reform movements in the antebellum North. This evangelical campaign to stamp out drinking provided both common ground and formative training for activists and leaders in those other causes.

TAKING THE PLEDGE

As evidence mounted of the dire consequences of alcohol addiction for family life, workplace productivity, and individual health, reformers took aim at American drinking habits. In 1826, a group of New England ministers founded the American Society for the Promotion of Temperance and launched a national campaign to refashion the public image of alcoholic beverages. Drinks that had commonly been considered healthy were now stigmatized as "demon rum," a poison that led to poverty, crime, and violence. Though these reformers used the word *temperance,* they were not advocating moderation. Members of the new organization were asked to indicate their pledge of commitment to the cause by marking a "T" for total abstinence next to their signature, hence the word ***teetotaler.*** Within seven years of its founding, the American Temperance Society (as it came to be known) claimed a million members.

Early temperance advocates pushed for legislation to limit the sale of alcohol, and over the next two decades they were able boast of some modest successes, mostly in the Northeast. By 1855, thirteen states had enacted some form of alcohol restriction, though most of those laws were challenged successfully in courts. For the growing temperance movement, however, these legislative efforts were not the main battleground. The thrust of the movement, especially after 1840, lay not in the passage of restrictive laws but in the promotion and celebration of a sober lifestyle. Temperance groups like the Washingtonians (founded in 1840) and the Sons of Temperance (1842) were not lobbying organizations seeking the attention

HOT COMMODITIES

Cold Water

Water covers most of the earth's surface, but its availability for human use can never be taken for granted. Even in our society, where access to drinkable water is considered a basic necessity, private water-bottling is big business. Only in the past century and a half have local governments in the United States assumed the burden of supplying water to their citizens. Before the middle of the nineteenth century, residents of big cities relied on communal wells, maintained their own cisterns, collected roof runoff, or purchased water from private companies. As populations grew, however, these methods proved inadequate to the changing demands of firefighting, public health, and personal hygiene. Between 1837 and 1848, Philadelphia, New York, and Boston all invested public funds in reservoirs and aqueducts. In a short time, water supply became a public utility.

Cold Water Soldiers on Parade, 1848. Temperance reformers join in the celebration of the completion of Boston's first municipal water system.

Like other debates about municipal finance and regulation during this period, the question of whether government ought to intervene in the water business pitted poorer residents, who believed that the necessities of life should be shared by everyone, against wealthier residents, who advocated private competition. In this case, however, the supporters of public ownership found a powerful ally in middle-class reformers, who saw moral benefits in water. Starting in the 1830s, northern reformers advanced new medical theories about the links between dirt and disease and touted the special advantages of soft water (as opposed to the hard water that collected in wells) for washing food, clothing, and bodies. But the greatest advantage of clean water, reformers argued, was as an alternative beverage to alcohol. In the eighteenth century, distilled spirits had been considered a healthful complement to water—a mixer (or even a chaser!) that made water palatable and innocuous. By the 1830s, the conventional wisdom was shifting. By providing a clean water supply, governments would be removing one of the motivations for drinking liquor.

Temperance reformers supported public water projects as part of a larger campaign to turn clean, cold water into America's drink of choice. "Cold water" became a standard euphemism for events and organizations that shunned alcohol. Temperance societies called themselves "cold water armies," staged "cold water celebrations" on July 4th, and sang "cold water melodies" that praised the virtues and pleasures of this alternative beverage. In an 1842 Washingtonian song, set to the tune of "Yankee Doodle," the final verse proclaims:

> *I'll not touch the poisonous stuff,*
> *Since all the brooks are free, sir;*
> *Give me cold water, 'tis enough,*
> *That cannot injure me, sir.*

Think About It

1. Why did middle-class reformers not rely on private competition to provide water to urban residents?
2. What might have been some of the arguments against this reform?
3. How did antebellum reformers spread their theory that drinking water was good for one's health?

of politicians; they were fraternal associations designed to recruit members to sign abstinence pledges. In the first six years of its existence, the Sons of Temperance grew to six thousand units and two hundred thousand paying members, all of whom had taken such a pledge.

The temperance organizations of the 1840s stressed moral suasion rather than coercion and believed that even confirmed drunkards could be rescued from a life of ruin. To support their members' attempts to resist liquor, they created alcohol-free forms of entertainment and sociability, featuring picnics, parades, concerts, and dances (see Hot Commodities: Cold Water). This alternative popular culture competed with the three main venues of male-dominated social life during the period—the theater, the tavern, and the political party—in which drinking played a central role. Washingtonians and Sons of Temperance mostly targeted men and promoted new ideals of masculinity, but they were joined in these efforts by auxiliary female groups: the Martha Washington Societies and the Daughters of Temperance.

Already by 1840, the national consumption of alcohol had declined by more than two-thirds. A profound transformation in everyday life was under way. Yet the impact of temperance reform across the country was uneven. Most of the pledges came from New England, western New York, New Jersey, and Pennsylvania. In the South and the West, and in urban neighborhoods dominated by artisans, laborers, and immigrants, temperance reform enjoyed less prestige and older patterns of drinking persisted. Alcohol continued to wreak havoc in Indian communities as well, though some native groups began to resist the liquor trade around this time. The Pawnee Indians of the Great Plains regulated the supply of liquor, for example, and by the 1850s alcohol was totally banned from Pawnee villages. This was the result of powerful local leadership, however, rather than the influence of a national reform movement.

"An Address Delivered by Abraham Lincoln Before the Springfield Washington Temperance Society." There was some unintended irony in naming a temperance organization after George Washington, who had been a whiskey distiller, but the name reflected a desire to link alcohol reform to patriotism. Addressing a Washingtonian Society in Illinois in 1842, a young politician named Abraham Lincoln compared the "temperance revolution" to the revolution against Britain in 1776. In temperance, Lincoln proclaimed, "we find a stronger bondage broken, a viler slavery manumitted, and a greater tyrant deposed."

SENSATIONALISM AND THE PERILS OF DRINK

Temperance reformers hoped that a culture of sober camaraderie would support young men in their resolve to abstain from drinking, but they also turned to more sensational methods for sounding the alarm against alcohol. Reams of fictional temperance tales filled the pages of popular magazines during the 1840s, warning readers of the horrifying effects of alcohol on personal prospects and family tranquility. Temperance novels and plays enjoyed a heyday as well. Walt Whitman, before becoming a famous poet, began his literary career at the age of twenty-three with a novel entitled *Franklin Evans, or, The Inebriate* (1842). It sold more copies during the author's lifetime than any of his other publications. The novel, which he later disclaimed as a piece of "damned rot" written over the course of three days with the help of a bottle of port, concerned the travails of a young alcoholic from the North who visits a friend on a Virginia plantation, falls for an enslaved woman, and in a drunken state decides to marry and manumit her. Upon gaining sobriety, he regrets these actions, and he subsequently falls for a white woman from the North. His wife becomes jealous, murders her rival, and then kills herself. Such contrived, sensational plots were staples of temperance fiction in the 1840s. The most successful temperance author of the era was Timothy Shay Arthur, whose *Ten Nights in a Bar-Room* (1854) became one of the best-selling American novels of the nineteenth century.

Temperance fiction frightened (and perhaps entertained) readers with stories of fortunes squandered, marriages sundered, and lives lost. Reformers also circulated images of crazed drunkards and the cowering victims of their violent outbursts. Finally, temperance lecturers sought to convert the masses by offering personal testimonies of the horrors of drinking. John B. Gough was a former bookbinder and actor who moved audiences all across the country with accounts of his drunken past and dramatic performances of the *delirium tremens,* a physiological condition caused by alcohol abuse. Gough gained special notoriety in 1845, when he disappeared for a week in New York and was discovered seven days later, intoxicated, in a house of ill repute. Gough claimed that enemies had slipped a drug into his glass of cherry soda and dragged him to the brothel to discredit him. Much of the public appears to have accepted this explanation for his fall off the wagon, and Gough's career as a spokesman for the temperance cause continued to flourish. Gough's spectacular lapse reinforced the temperance message that alcohol was a dangerous foe that could never be vanquished permanently.

SEX AND THE SECRET VICE

Though the term *temperance* referred specifically to drinking, and temperance lecturers regarded alcohol as the singular cause of all human misfortune, the campaign against liquor also stressed a broader ethic of **bodily self-control.** The impulse to consume alcohol was one of several appetites and instincts that needed to be suppressed. Reformers during this period worried especially about the sexual appetites of men. The middle-class male was expected to control his sexual instincts as well as his drinking habits.

Women reformers took the lead in an evangelical campaign against sexual vice. The American Female Moral Reform Society, which grew to more than one hundred chapters within

"The Drunkard's Home." This illustration, accompanying a temperance tale, dramatizes the threat that intoxicated men posed to their families. Temperance fiction often featured villainous husbands who beat their wives while under the influence and initiated their sons into the dangerous world of the tavern.

ten years of its founding in 1834, targeted male depravity and challenged the traditional double standard that condemned prostitution and female promiscuity while condoning the sexual activity of men. In New York, the moral reformers organized a petition drive to persuade the state legislature to outlaw seduction. More generally, the moral reform movement sought to instill in men a new, chaste attitude toward their own sexuality.

While the moral reform movement targeted men who patronized sex workers or seduced young women, others worried more about what men (and women too) did when they were alone. Beginning in the 1830s, an antimasturbation movement took hold in the United States, as doctors, lecturers, and childrearing manuals initiated a major public discussion of the dangers of what they called the solitary vice or the secret vice. Reformist tracts described the horrors of this widespread practice and linked it with numerous physical ailments and with insanity. Temperance lecturer Sylvester Graham led the crusade, and other evangelical physiologists echoed his message, describing masturbation as the definitive problem of the age (see Singular Lives: Sylvester Graham, Diet Crusader). Reformers worried especially about very young boys initiating one another into the dark world of self-abuse, though Graham's disciple Mary Gove insisted that it was a common problem among girls as well. Much of the anxiety focused on boys living away from their parents, or young men in cities who worked in the new economy. As one reformer put it, the dangers of masturbation loomed larger for "students, merchant's clerks, printers and shoemakers [than for] young men who labor at agricultural employments or active mechanical trades." Masturbation, like drinking, was considered to be a dangerous habit that launched a young man down a steady path to ruin.

The masturbation scare of the 1830s should not be misunderstood as traditional superstition or Victorian prudery. Reformers who argued that masturbation caused debility, insanity, and death were not recycling old folk beliefs. They were espousing newfangled medical theories and citing the latest scientific studies in an optimistic attempt to change the world. Their emphasis on self-control linked their campaign

"The Total S'iety, A Comic Song," 1840. Temperance lectures persuaded countless audience members to sign pledges in the 1840s. Note how the drawing on this sheet music cover mocks the speaker as a drunken hypocrite, with a red nose and a bottle in his pocket. **Question for Analysis:** How do the posters on the wall behind the audience fit with the speaker's message?

SINGULAR LIVES

Sylvester Graham, Diet Crusader

Among the many men and women who took the temperance podium in the 1830s, only one remains a household name. Sylvester Graham was a Connecticut-born physician and Presbyterian minister who began preaching against alcohol but broadened his message to attack masturbation and all habits that he believed led to drink, lust, and a general sapping of the body's vitality. For Graham, the real problem was stimulation, and he urged his growing band of followers to abstain from coffee, tobacco, and frequent sexual intercourse—which meant more than a few times in one's life. (Graham himself was the seventeenth child of parents who clearly did not practice such restraint.) Graham also shunned meat, spices, snacking between meals, restrictive clothing, and soft bedding.

Graham's greatest notoriety came in the field of dietary reform. Reaching wide audiences through his popular lectures and books, he preached that the key to human happiness lay in the stomach. If people would adhere to a strict regimen of small portions of unstimulating food consumed at regular hours, they would be able to live long, chaste lives. Among the obstacles to such a life, Graham believed, was the refined white bread that was popular in urban settings. Graham invented his own bread recipe in 1829, using coarse whole-wheat flour and avoiding all chemical additives. The original "Graham cracker," which was a good deal blander than its modern descendants, consisted of this special flour.

Though he was an idiosyncratic and controversial thinker, drawing the wrath of butchers and bakers and the ridicule of many of his contemporaries, Graham was in many ways the quintessential antebellum reformer. He preached temperance, bodily control, and chastity. He instructed young men on how to conduct more respectable lives and resist the temptations of the marketplace. And he believed that new medical notions could create happier human beings. In retrospect, many of his ideas seem more mainstream. Vegetarianism is no longer a novelty, and grocery stores in many parts of the country cater to those who prefer whole grains or unprocessed food. Even more Americans share Graham's faith that proper diet holds the key to health and happiness. Perhaps Graham's most enduring legacy appears on the American breakfast table. He had been a major proponent of early morning meals consisting of whole grains. One of his most influential followers, Dr. John Harvey Kellogg, experimented with flakes of different grains in an effort to find the perfect meal to lower the sex drives of the patients at his sanitarium. In 1906, Kellogg's brother Will began marketing the result under the brand name Corn Flakes.

Sylvester Graham. Ralph Waldo Emerson dubbed Graham "the poet of bran and pumpkins."

Think About It

1. How does the graham cracker reflect the ideals of the temperance movement?
2. Do you see Graham as more of a medical reformer or a moralist? Why?

to many of the other reform movements of their day. Reformers were not prudish men and women who were uncomfortable discussing sex. On the contrary, crusaders against the secret vice argued that masturbation needed to be discussed openly, not only between parents and children, but in public life as well.

ABOLITIONISTS

A subset of the men and women who joined the temperance crusade also believed that slaveholding was sinful. **Abolitionists,** as they were called, remained a small group in the North throughout the 1830s and 1840s, but they hailed from the same evangelical circles as other, more popular, reformers and stressed many of the same reform themes. Almost all abolitionists, both white and black, advocated temperance, for example. But their radical views on slavery threatened the political compromises on which the federal union rested and challenged racial hierarchy in the North as well as the South.

IMMEDIATISM

What distinguished the new generation of abolitionist reformers that rose to prominence around 1830 (see Chapter 11) was their commitment to immediate rather than gradual solutions to the problem of slavery. From the 1790s to the 1820s, antislavery campaigns in both Britain and the United States had focused on stopping the slave trade or developing complex

"Am I Not a Man and a Brother?" This image was an icon of the American Anti-Slavery Society, the leading organization of immediatist abolition. Based on a design by British abolitionists in the 1780s, it originally appeared as a mass-produced miniature sculpture suitable for setting in jewelry. **Questions for Analysis:** Why is the slave on his knees? Why might abolitionists have chosen to display this image rather than one of a slave picking cotton, suffering corporal punishment, or rising up in rebellion?

projects, such as African colonization, that worked within existing systems of authority and enlisted the cooperation of slaveholders. By 1830, gradualist compromises had been discredited, attacked by black abolitionists as racist and by slaveholders as too dangerous. In their place arose a powerful approach known by historians as **immediatism.** It was not the dominant view in the North, not even among those who found slavery repugnant. Though many northerners objected to slave *trading* and viewed the political power of slaveholders with suspicion, the men and women who wanted to *abolish* slavery wherever it existed in the United States formed a tiny minority. Still, this new and radical ideology would frame the national slavery debate.

By the 1830s, abolitionists were calling for the immediate emancipation of all slaves, without compensation to slave owners. This was a radical position by the standards of antislavery thought at the time. Britain's Emancipation Act of 1833, which ended slavery in the West Indies, offered twenty million pounds in compensation, to be supplemented for six years by the unpaid labor of black "apprentices." Northern abolitionists, many of whom were evangelical Christians, wanted none of that. They were not interested in economic ramifications or political timetables. Slavery was inherently sinful and emancipation had to be instantaneous and unmediated. Like a religious convert at a mass revival or a drunkard freeing himself from whiskey, slaveholders and slaves needed to break the chains of human bondage.

Abolitionism was not only a radical stance toward the slavery question; it was also a fundamental critique of the social order. Although most white northerners, whatever they thought about slavery, held conservative attitudes toward American race relations, the abolitionists did not. Both blacks like James Forten and Sojourner Truth and whites like William Lloyd Garrison and Angelina Grimké advocated racial equality. Garrison drew special notoriety for his views. When critics charged, as they often did, that abolitionists were driven by a desire for interracial sex, Garrison took the occasion to make it clear that he did in fact foresee and favor marriage between whites and blacks.

Garrison and his most radical allies were countercultural critics. Although many of them had social and economic affiliations with an elite merchant class, and the evangelical religion they espoused and many of the other reforms they advocated had cultural prestige, their opposition to slavery put them at the margins of mainstream politics. For the Garrisonians, the sin of slavery turned the nation's sacred symbols into objects of scorn. On July 4th, which abolitionists viewed as the darkest day on the calendar, Garrison publicly burned a copy of the Constitution. Governments, churches, and even the Bible, whatever texts or institutions condoned slavery, became targets of the Garrisonians' wrath.

SLAVE TESTIMONY

Some of the most ardent and influential abolitionists were men and women who had been born into bondage. Ex-slaves were able to help the abolitionist cause by offering first-hand testimony about the brutal treatment they received while enslaved and by demonstrating their own humanity and their own capacity for citizenship. The most famous of these former slaves was Frederick Douglass, who escaped from his Maryland owner in 1838, settled in Massachusetts, and joined the American Anti-Slavery Society. Douglass was a major sensation on the abolitionist lecture circuit, helping raise funds with his vivid accounts of plantation life. Audience members were sometimes drawn to his talks by curiosity or skepticism that an African American raised in bondage could be so eloquent.

In part to dispel the suspicions they encountered on the lecture tour, former slaves like Douglass also published autobiographies. **Slave narratives,** as historians and literary critics call them, are invaluable sources of information about the experience of slavery, but they were also commercial publications designed to attract readers and yield revenue, often for the author. Moreover, they were abolitionist tracts designed to persuade readers of the evil of slavery in the American South by using particular rhetorical techniques. One of the most important strategies of the slave narrative was to prove its authenticity by naming actual slaveholders or by including letters from respected members of the white community asserting that the ex-slave in question actually wrote the book. Proslavery apologists were quick to challenge the truthfulness—and the authorship—of published slave narratives. On one occasion, the American Anti-Slavery Society even recalled the autobiography of fugitive slave James Williams because they could not corroborate the details of his story. Questions surrounding the authenticity of abolitionist slave narratives continue to haunt scholars today. The now-canonical slave narrative of Harriet Jacobs, who wrote under the name Linda Brent, was widely believed to be have been composed by white abolitionist Lydia Maria Child until it was proved in the early 1980s to be Jacobs's own work.

Frederick Douglass, ca. 1850. Perhaps the most prominent American abolitionist, ex-slave Douglass attacked the institution of slavery in lectures, newspapers, and a widely circulated memoir.

MOB VIOLENCE

Unlike the advocates of other reforms, abolitionists were targets of major violence and repression throughout much of the North, especially in the years 1834–1838, when abolitionism was a new and disruptive force in national politics (see Chapter 11). Anti-abolitionist riots, often led by prominent members of the community, disrupted antislavery meetings and destroyed the homes and offices of the movement's leaders. Mobs also turned their wrath on churches where abolitionists preached and blacks and whites prayed together. Occasionally, abolitionists suffered serious injuries during these riots, and one antislavery editor was killed defending his printing press (see States of Emergency: The Murder of Elijah Lovejoy).

Mob leaders were often Democratic politicians eager to maintain their coalition with southerners, and their posters criticized abolitionists for sowing sectional discord. But anti-abolitionists were also trying to control race relations in northern cities. Rioters attacked free blacks, whether or not they were outspoken on the slavery question. They targeted places where whites and blacks socialized, and they decried abolitionists as **amalgamationists**—people who supported or desired interracial sexual unions. Participants in these riots may also have identified abolitionism with elitism, with England, or with the larger agenda of middle-class reform. A mob in Wilkes-Barre, Pennsylvania, for example, dragged an abolitionist named William Gildersleeve to the local tavern in 1839 and forced him to have a drink.

"Practical Amalgamation," 1839. Abolitionists were ridiculed in the popular press by writers and cartoonists who accused them of having sexual motivations and warned that the emancipation of slaves would lead to disorder in northern race relations.

STATES OF EMERGENCY

The Murder of Elijah Lovejoy

The anti-abolitionist mobs that formed in the North during the 1830s were violent and destructive, but only once did they murder a white abolitionist. Elijah P. Lovejoy grew up in Maine, moved west in his mid-twenties, and settled in St. Louis, where he worked as a schoolmaster and then as the editor of an anti-Jackson newspaper. By 1833, Lovejoy (now an ordained Presbyterian minister) was publisher of the *Observer*, which regularly condemned slavery and Catholicism. Both positions earned him bitter enemies in St. Louis, a city with a significant Catholic population and many slave owners. Some of these enemies destroyed his printing press and forced him out of town.

Stopping the Presses. Anti-abolitionists set fire to Elijah Lovejoy's warehouse in Alton, Illinois. Lovejoy was killed in the attack.

Hoping to find a safer environment in a free state, Lovejoy moved his operation across the Mississippi River to the city of Alton, Illinois. Alton's citizens took less offense at anti-Catholic writings, but they were deeply intolerant of Lovejoy's abolitionism, which had grown more immediatist and increasingly militant. Twice more, Lovejoy lost his printing press to angry mobs. When a fourth printing press was due to arrive from Cincinnati in 1837, Lovejoy and his supporters armed themselves with pistols in anticipation of another attack. After it was delivered, local citizens surrounded the warehouse where the new press was being stored, and tried to set fire to the roof. Raising his gun to ward off one of the assailants, Lovejoy was shot dead.

John Quincy Adams described the killing of Lovejoy as "a shock as of an earthquake throughout this continent, which will be felt in the most distant regions of the earth." To most northerners, Lovejoy became a martyr who had died defending the freedom of the press. To leading anti-abolitionists in the North who had supported riots in their own cities, the incident in Alton served as a chastening reminder of the risks of rallying mobs to police the slavery debate. To abolitionists, on the other hand, Lovejoy's murder confirmed the brutality that underlay the slave regime. Some of the Garrisonians also found support for their radical commitment to nonviolence, since Lovejoy was killed while bearing arms. Several abolitionists, especially Quakers, criticized Lovejoy for brandishing a "carnal weapon," even in self-defense. Angelina Grimké proclaimed that "there is no such thing as trusting in God and *pistols* at the same time."

Think About It

1. Why did Lovejoy's printing press become the focus of so much passionate interest on all sides?
2. Why might the residents of a state like Illinois, which did not allow slavery, have bitterly opposed Lovejoy's *Observer*?

Farther south, abolitionists were even less popular, but southerners were able to use the law, rather than mob violence, to suppress abolitionist activity. Local ordinances targeted antislavery publications and their authors. The Georgia legislature placed a bounty on Garrison, offering $5,000 to anyone who would bring him to Georgia to face criminal charges (see How Much Is That?). Abolitionists steered clear of the South during the 1830s.

How Much Is That?

Garrison's Bounty

The $5000 offered by Georgia for the apprehension of the abolitionist William Lloyd Garrison is equivalent to about $134,000 in 2013 dollars. By comparison, the FBI currently offers rewards of just $100,000 for help apprehending the criminals on its Ten Most Wanted Fugitives list.

INTERNAL DIVISIONS

As the abolitionist movement grew in the 1830s, members began to question two controversial parts of the new ideology. Garrison had advocated a policy of **nonresistance,** which meant that abolitionists, like other reformers, would rely on moral suasion rather than physical force to bring about social change. But for Garrison, it also meant not relying on state power or political elections. Abolitionists wrote petitions to Congress in the 1830s, but many of their leaders refused to support candidates for office and even opposed voting, since it implied cooperation with a slaveholding political system. This posture put the Garrisonians at loggerheads with **political abolitionists** like James Birney and Gerrit Smith, who saw in the political process an opportunity to exert significant influence over national policy. Because competition between Whigs and Democrats was close in most states, these abolitionists reasoned, even a modest number of voters committed to a single issue could hold the balance of power.

Abolitionists also divided over the role of women in the movement. As in other antebellum reform campaigns, women participated actively in abolitionist efforts. Angelina Grimké, author of *Appeal to the Christian Women of the South* (1836), grew up in a slaveholding family in South Carolina and moved north, where she and her sister Sarah became fixtures on the antislavery lecture circuit. According to witnesses, Angelina Grimké could command the undivided attention of immense audiences for two hours at a time. Other women, including Lucretia Mott, Lydia Maria Child, Maria Weston Chapman, and Abby Kelley, also assumed leadership positions in the American Anti-Slavery Society. But by the end of the decade, many supporters of the growing movement were objecting to the role that women were playing, criticizing both the practice of female abolitionists addressing mixed-sex audiences and their embrace of women's rights. When Kelley was appointed to a key committee of the American Anti-Slavery Society at its 1840 convention, a substantial minority of delegates bolted the room and formed their own organization. The 1840 schism within the abolitionist ranks divided the Garrisonians, who were committed to sexual equality and opposed to political action, from those abolitionists who wanted to focus exclusively on slavery. One dissenter explained his resignation from the Board of Managers of the Massachusetts chapter of the American Anti-Slavery Society as follows: "The Society is no longer an *Anti-Slavery* Society *simply*, but . . . has become a *women's rights, no-government-Anti-Slavery Society*." That same year, political abolitionists launched the Liberty Party, a national political party defined entirely by its opposition to slavery. James Birney was the party's presidential nominee.

ABOLITIONISTS

BEWARE.

THE Citizens of Cincinnati, embracing every class, interested in the prosperity of the City, sat- [illegible]ed that the business of the place is receiving [illegible] stab from the wicked and misguided operations of the abolitionists, are resolved to arrest their course. The destruction of their Press on the night of the 12th Instant, may be taken as a warning. As there are some worthy citizens engaged in the unholy cause of annoying our southern neighbors, they are appealed to, to pause before they bring things to a crisis. If an attempt is made to re-establish their press, it will be viewed as an act of defiance to an already outraged community, and on their heads be the res[illegible] which will follow.

Every kind of expostulation and remonstrance has been resorted to in vain---longer patience would be criminal. The plan is matured to eradicate an evil which every citizen feels is undermining his business and property.

Anti-Abolitionist Handbill, Cincinnati, 1836. Shortly after James Birney began publishing an abolitionist newspaper, angry citizens broke into his office and tried to destroy his printing press. This poster blasts the "unholy cause of annoying our southern neighbors" and warns that any resumption of publication "will be viewed as an act of defiance to an already outraged community." Birney defied the warning, and on July 30, hundreds of whites in Cincinnati rioted against the paper and attacked the city's free black community.

The two major issues over which abolitionists divided—the role of women and the legitimacy of political action—were closely related because politics was a masculine arena in the antebellum period. Abolitionists who favored political action were urging reformers to focus on a world in which women had no legal voice and men were the crucial audience. From this perspective, women who played an active role in the movement were entering a male preserve and behaving like men. For the Garrisonians, on the other hand, abolitionism was about moral suasion and not politics, so it was perfectly appropriate for women to be active in the movement. At the same time, the Garrisonians' rejection of political action was also a rejection of the kind of violent, drunken masculinity that dominated mass politics. Like many others in the larger world of reform to which abolitionism belonged, key figures in the antislavery movement saw themselves as trying to create a different kind of man, more sober and self-controlled. Some

Hutchinson Family Singers. Like the temperance movement, abolitionism spawned its own theatrical culture. The Hutchinson family of New Hampshire (including the ten brothers pictured here) formed a popular singing group in 1840 and sang about slavery. They often performed at antislavery rallies and more generally identified with the reform causes of the era. "Yes we're friends of emancipation," the lyrics of their most famous song announced, "we are all teetotalers/ And have sign'd the Temp'rance pledge." **Question for Analysis:** What kind of masculinity do the Hutchinson brothers project in this posed photograph?

of them also began to wonder whether the nation might be better served by a political process in which both men and women participated.

DOMESTICITY AND GENDER

The reform impulses that drove movements like temperance and abolition reinforced a growing interest among native-born middle-class Protestants in the question of how to exert moral influence over other people. This was a particularly pressing issue when it came to their own children. Especially in towns and cities, middle-class fathers had little of the power enjoyed by traditional household patriarchs (see Chapter 4) who commanded family labor and controlled the inheritance of farmland. In a more mobile, market-oriented society, parents and community leaders sought new ways to shape character and cultivate marketable skills in the next generation. Around the 1830s, reformers began addressing those concerns by touting the home as a space of intimacy and tranquility presided over by a nurturing mother. Those who celebrated this ideal of domestic life promoted new roles for men and women and new beliefs about the significance of sexual difference that would have a powerful impact on modern American culture. The **cult of domesticity,** as historians call this ideology, spread through fashion magazines, holiday observances, and an expanding consumer culture. It also contributed, paradoxically, to the birth of the country's first feminist movement.

MEN'S AND WOMEN'S SEPARATE SPHERES

In earlier periods of American history, men and women had of course led different lives, enjoyed different rights, assumed different responsibilities, and faced different challenges. But only in the nineteenth century did Americans come to believe that the sexes ought to occupy **separate spheres** of activity and influence. "Domestic life is a woman's sphere," an advice book from 1832 explained to its readers, "and it is here that she is most usefully as well as most appropriately employed." Men, on the other hand, belonged in the workplace, absorbed in the pursuit of financial gain. This was not a time-honored cliché, but rather an outlook that was catching on, a reform idea of sorts.

Traditionally, the home had been a site of production where both men and women worked under the control of a male head-of-household. But by the 1830s, changes in the nature of work were making it possible to think of workplaces and domestic spaces as distinct. Especially in the more urban parts of the North, fewer workers lived with their employers or labored under the roof of a master. Those who worked for cash wages and produced for distant markets were less likely to perform that work where they slept and less likely to share that work with their blood relatives. At the same time, middle-class Americans were marrying later, having fewer children, and living in more tightly defined kin groups, often consisting of just a nuclear family. All of these conditions encouraged middle-class men and women to imagine the home as something opposed to work.

The home, according to the new apostles of domesticity, should be a female-dominated private zone insulated from the rough-and-tumble public worlds of the marketplace, the street, and the ballot box. Increasingly in the nineteenth century, middle-class homes were subdivided architecturally into a semipublic downstairs consisting of common areas and parlors and an upstairs consisting of private bedrooms and nurseries. Redefined in this way, the home now appeared as a feminine domain, linked to women not just by convention but also by nature. In countless magazine articles, domestic manuals, advice books, and medical journals, authors of both sexes introduced the idea that women were naturally suited to private life. Catharine Beecher, perhaps the best-known author of housekeeping guides during this period, called domestic life "a woman's sphere" and discouraged her readers from venturing beyond its bounds. "There is . . . something unfeminine in independence. It is contrary to nature, and therefore it offends. . . ." Earlier images of women as cruel, manipulative, and domineering receded from mainstream culture—or were directed largely toward lower-class women and the sexually deviant women who filled the pages of sensationalist literature. In their place came images of women as vulnerable and infantilized. These were new beliefs, bolstered by the prestige of modern science. A medical professor explained to his exclusively male gynecology class in 1847 that the female head is "almost too small for intellect but just big enough for love."

What suited women to the task of running the home, according to the domestic reformers, was precisely this capacity for love. Loving mothers could build character in their children (and their husbands) because the objects of that love would be receptive to maternal influence and would wind up internalizing the proper values of sobriety, thrift, honesty, and self-control. Throughout the reform culture, men and women paid tribute to the shrine of what they called true motherhood. As one Methodist tract put it, "Her love can only be excelled by the love of God."

Those who celebrated domesticity spoke of it as an oasis of personal relations unsullied by the conflicts of a materialistic world. But working-class Americans could not afford to live up to this middle-class ideal. Only a small minority of male urban artisans could support their families on a single income, and most poorer women left the home to work in factories, sweatshops, or, more often, as domestic servants in middle-class homes. While the work of housewives was defined outside the wage labor model, household work was often wage labor when performed by an outsider. For home and work to become distinct in middle-class America, there had to be a pool of women available for low-paid work outside of their own homes. And for middle-class children to stay home longer, there had to be a pool of young girls entering the market at an early age to help service the domestic hearth. Domesticity thus reinforced class divisions—divisions that often overlapped with those of race and ethnicity. In the 1840s in Philadelphia, for example, one in five adult blacks lived as a servant in a white household.

WHITE-COLLAR MEN

As the home became a feminine domain identified with middle-class women, middle-class men spent more time in places where they dominated. To the horror of reformers, some sought pleasure and camaraderie among men of different classes in the urban world of saloons, brothels, and theaters. Others enjoyed more respectable associations with members of their own class, such as debating societies and baseball clubs. Men could also carve out within the middle-class home some rooms of their own, such as a study or a library. But the most respectable masculine space within the new world of separate spheres was the office.

The office became the distinctive work environment for non-manual workers during this era, especially for legions of young men employed as clerks in such businesses as dry-goods stores, mercantile firms, or banks. Though an entry-level clerkship

Early Baseball Players. Baseball, modeled on an English children's game called rounders, was played by adults in American cities earlier in the nineteenth century, but its history as an organized sport began in the 1840s. The first baseball teams were middle-class fraternal clubs, such as the New York Knickerbocker Club, whose members appear above. (Alexander Cartwright, in the middle of the back row, is often credited with having devised the original rules of the sport.) Clubs like the Knickerbockers provided avenues for young men to enjoy respectable pleasures that did not involve gambling or violence.

might not pay much more than the wages of a young cabinetmaker or a tailor, clerks were apprentices in an expanding world of commercial opportunity, part of a new breed of middle-class employees whose identity came not from the craft they performed but from the social status associated with commerce and capitalism. A clerk's tasks might be monotonous, and he might spend the entire day copying letters, but it was respectable work. In the clerical office, the young man demonstrated the kind of character and self-control that middle-class homes were supposed to instill.

Reformers emphasized and enforced the link between respectable habits and the market economy through a new institution that produced and disseminated credit ratings. In 1841, an evangelical New York merchant named Lewis Tappan, who was prominent in the antislavery movement, opened the Mercantile Agency, the nation's first credit bureau. Starting out with his abolitionist friends, Tappan developed a vast network of informants scattered throughout the country, who supplied his office with financial reports and character references for tens of thousands of men engaged in commerce. Merchants eager to determine whether a firm or an individual buyer in a distant locale was a good credit risk could purchase this information from the agency. Tappan's files, inscribed in large red books held in New York, contained information about how much a man was worth and how reliably he paid his bills, but it also assessed his drinking habits, his personal life, and his moral reputation. The Mercantile Agency's success spawned numerous competitors, and Tappan's company eventually became Dun and Bradstreet, America's leading broker of credit information.

MAGAZINES, HOLIDAYS, AND CONSUMPTION

New ideals of femininity, masculinity, homemaking, and family life lay at the center of an expanding middle-class culture. This culture was spread not only in schoolrooms, lecture halls, and dining room tables, but also in mass publications, such as advice books and periodicals. National magazines directed at female readers were especially important in disseminating ideas about domesticity and respectability. The first highly successful women's magazine, *Godey's Lady's Book* (founded in 1830), featured articles, stories, and poems by famous authors alongside fashion advice, architectural plans, and moral instruction. *Godey's*, with a circulation of 150,000 by 1860, exerted an enormous influence on women's clothing styles and the magazine became one of the principal arbiters of middle-class taste.

Magazines like *Godey's* instructed middle-class readers in the proper ways to dress, shop, socialize, mourn the dead, give gifts, or celebrate holidays. In fact, such magazines were at the center of new efforts to reform the calendar by promoting holidays that took place in the home and centered around the family. Sarah Josepha Hale, the editor of *Godey's*, waged a lifelong campaign to create a national holiday based on the religious thanksgiving fasts and feasts of New England Puritans. In 1863, Hale's campaign bore fruit, and Thanksgiving, which was already a popular middle-class custom in the Northeast, became an official observance identified with a domestic meal.

The modern American Christmas also emerged in this period as a family-centered holiday. Before the antebellum period, Christmas was a time of feasting, public drunkenness, and outdoor revelry. Several of the American colonies had discouraged (or even prohibited) the observance of December 25, in part because it was originally a pagan holiday that the Catholic Church had linked to December 25 without Scriptural basis, but also because it was a time of social disorder. Between the 1820s and 1850s, Christmas was transformed into a family festivity celebrated largely indoors, focused on the exchange of gifts, and identified with the jolly figure of Santa Claus, who enters the home and rewards good children. By the 1830s, observers were already complaining that "All the children are expecting presents," and stores began bombarding potential customers with advertisements for Christmas gifts. Manufacturers, merchants, newspaper editors, and advertisers promoted the idea of Christmas as a time when material longings might be legitimately indulged and luxury items might be purchased and given as tokens of affection—especially the kind of parental affection that was becoming the hallmark of the new middle-class nuclear family.

Santa Claus Comes to Town. Though nominally connected to a bishop canonized as St. Nicholas, the modern Santa Claus is an American figure, popularized in the 1822 poem "A Visit from St. Nicholas." By the 1840s, he had become a common commercial icon. In this 1850s illustration, which retains some of the revelry of earlier Christmas traditions, Santa visits "his young friends in the United States."

Modeling Domesticity. *Godey's* dress illustrations, which appeared in elaborate color plates by the time of the Civil War, heralded the arrival of the modern fashion magazine, but they were part of a larger reform campaign to spread the cult of domesticity to middle-class readers.

Elizabeth Cady Stanton, One of the Signers of the 1848 Declaration of Sentiments. At her own marriage ceremony, Stanton famously refused to utter the conventional vow to obey her husband.

THE RISE OF FEMINISM

Though all the cultural emphasis on home and family imposed significant burdens and restrictions on American women, it also provided the basis for some new arguments on behalf of women's rights. Celebrations of domesticity and motherhood assigned special significance to mothers in shaping the country's values and made women the guardians of social order. And all the talk about how men and women were fundamentally different sorts of creatures made it more plausible to argue that female purity suited them for moral leadership and not simply for subservience.

Northerners who were actively involved in the reform movements of the period were most likely to sympathize with such arguments. If maternal affection and moral suasion were the way to change the hearts and minds of drunkards, slaveholders, criminals, or wayward children, then women had a special moral authority to address social problems. But women active in causes such as temperance and abolition found the taboo against female participation in public life to be powerful. They also began to see more clearly the forms of second-class citizenship to which women were subjected. As Angelina Grimké wrote to Catharine Beecher, "the investigation of the rights of the slave has led me to a better understanding of my own."

By around 1840, a new feminist reform movement was emerging out of abolitionism. Early advocates of **women's rights** adopted many of the forms of social analysis that critics of slavery had developed, invoking similar ideals of social inclusion, equality, and human rights. Early feminists also shared with the abolitionists a foundation in the evangelical churches, where women had been playing active roles since the beginning of the century. Abolitionism thrust women onto the stage of local and national politics and gave them valuable training in political organizing, fundraising, lecturing, and pamphleteering.

The campaign for women's rights gathered momentum in a series of conventions during the 1840s, the most famous of which took place in 1848 in Seneca Falls, New York. Organized by Lucretia Mott and Elizabeth Cady Stanton, the Seneca Falls Convention issued a Declaration of Sentiments, modeled explicitly on the Declaration of Independence, proclaiming the self-evident truth "that all men and women are created equal." Seneca Falls launched a feminist movement designed to secure equal status for women under the law. Feminist reformers focused on a few basic rights: women ought to have the same legal control over their wages and

Anti-Suffrage Cartoon, 1869. More than two decades after the Seneca Falls Convention, women were no closer to being able to vote. Popular lithographs continued to mock the prospect of female participation in political life as a threat to established gender norms and social order. **Questions for Analysis:** According to the artist, what is the problem with female suffrage? What allegedly unfeminine behaviors are imagined in this cartoon? Which feminine behaviors does the cartoonist imagine as a threat to the political system?

property, the same rights to form contracts and inherit, and the same rights to custody and guardianship over children. Finally, women ought to have the same right to suffrage—voting in popular elections.

Women's suffrage became the most important goal of the antebellum feminist movement, the one demand that symbolized and could potentially secure all of the others. It was also the most controversial. A resolution demanding the vote for women barely passed the Seneca Falls Convention. Although other planks in the feminist platform met with some success in the state legislatures, suffrage did not. Even after the Civil War, when amendments to the Constitution enshrined and extended the principle of equal protection and expanded voting rights to include African Americans, women were still excluded from the electoral process.

The new feminist movement was most successful in securing women's economic rights. According to the prevailing legal doctrine of **coverture,** a wife was legally subsumed to the identity of her husband, bound to obey his orders and incapable of owning property, contracting her own debts, or appearing in court as her own legal person except under unusual circumstances. By the middle of the century, coverture was beginning to decline, especially in matters of property ownership. Mississippi passed a married women's property act in 1839, and by 1860, fourteen states had enacted similar laws allowing wives to control the property they brought to the marriage or to acquire property while married that would not automatically belong to their husbands. Such reforms ran counter to the ideology of separate spheres, which stipulated that certain aspects of economic life belonged in the male domain. Other improvements in women's legal status seemed more consistent with that ideology. Most states began awarding custody for children to mothers rather than fathers during the antebellum era, but not on the grounds that men and women deserved equal rights. This new legal practice reflected beliefs that childrearing was crucial to social order and that mothers were naturally better suited to that task.

RELIGIOUS CONFLICT

Even in the North, not everyone embraced the culture of reform. Radical movements, such abolitionism and women's suffrage, certainly rankled the mainstream, but even the basic beliefs about self-control, character, conscience, and faith that dominated middle-class culture at the time were potentially controversial. Some of the biggest culture wars in the antebellum North pitted Protestants against Catholics. Reformers were overwhelmingly Protestant, and many of them saw Catholicism as an obstacle to reform. This view became more widespread during the 1830s and 1840s, just as Catholic immigrants were changing the demographic character of the country and challenging the authority of Protestant reformers.

ANTI-CATHOLICISM

Though most Americans would now regard hostility to Catholics and the Catholic Church as a form of bigotry, anti-Catholicism in the antebellum period was pursued by many native-born Protestants as a major reform cause. Leaders of temperance, antislavery, and other reform crusades often portrayed Catholicism as a threat to the free institutions of the American republic, as a form of religious superstition that blocked the path to salvation, or as a conservative social force that prevented individuals from taking control of their own lives. These were not uncommon views in the United States at the time. New Englanders claimed a long tradition of anti-Catholicism going back to the Puritan founding of their colonies, but even in other parts of the country, a general fear of conspiracies (see Chapter 11) and foreign influences exposed American Catholics to the suspicion that they were taking orders from the Pope.

In the 1830s, anti-Catholicism began to intensify in the North. A number of factors contributed to this trend, including Catholic immigration to the United States, a major international revival in Catholic piety and theology, and the general influence of evangelical Protestantism in American public life. Anti-Catholicism flourished at the same time as movements such as temperance and antislavery. In 1834, an anti-Catholic mob burned an Ursuline convent in Charlestown, Massachusetts, in response to a rumor that a nun was being held there against her wishes. Later that same year, Samuel F. B. Morse, the man who would develop the electromagnetic telegraph and help introduce photography to the United States, published a series of letters claiming that European monarchs had enlisted the Catholic Church in a scheme to undermine democracy in the United Sates by encouraging Catholic immigration to the American West. The following year, the eminent minister Lyman Beecher (father of Catharine Beecher and the famous antislavery novelist Harriet Beecher Stowe), whose anti-Catholic sermons had helped inspire the convent attack, warned that Catholic schools in the United States were trying to indoctrinate American children for nefarious purposes. Then, in 1836, Maria Monk's alleged exposé of her experiences at a Montreal nunnery (see Interpreting the Sources: The Awful Disclosures of Maria Monk), published with the support of powerful New England elites, became a phenomenal best-seller.

Anti-Catholic conspiracy theories found a receptive audience among reform-minded Protestants, and especially among abolitionists. Though the most radical antislavery voices criticized clergy and established religious authority more generally, abolitionists singled out the Catholic Church as an enemy of freedom comparable to the Slave Power. Abolitionists resented

Nativist Rioters Gather Outside the Girard Bank in Philadelphia. This 1844 daguerreotype may be the oldest photographic record of an urban riot and stands as a landmark in the history of photojournalism. **Question for Analysis:** How does the appearance of the crowd in this image challenge modern assumptions about rioting?

INTERPRETING THE SOURCES

The Awful Disclosures of Maria Monk

Of all the anti-Catholic writings produced in the United States, none was read more widely than a book entitled *Awful Disclosures, by Maria Monk, of the Hotel Dieu Nunnery of Montreal,* which Monk herself published in 1836. Monk recounted her life in the Montreal convent, telling lurid stories of sex and murder while confirming her readers' suspicions that Catholicism was a religion that despised the Bible, kept its adherents ignorant, and thrived on secrecy and privilege. Like many other popular captivity stories of the time, including those of fugitive slaves, Monk's book ends with a description of her escape from the convent.

Though *Awful Disclosures* was presented as nonfiction, many readers doubted its truthfulness. Ultimately, Monk's tale would be exposed as a fabrication. Still, it sold three hundred thousand copies over the next twenty-five years, becoming one of the best-selling books by an American author before the Civil War, second only to *Uncle Tom's Cabin* (see Chapter 14).

Early editions of the book included a foldout map showing the interior and exterior layouts of the convent. Following are excerpts from the sixth chapter.

The [Mother] Superior now informed me . . . that one of my great duties was, to obey the priests in all things; and this I soon learnt, to my utter astonishment and horror, was to live in the practice of criminal intercourse with them. . . . Doubts, she declared, were among our greatest enemies. They would lead us to question every point of duty, and induce us to waver at every step. They arose only from remaining imperfection, and were always evidence of sin. . . . Priests, she insisted, could not sin. It was a thing impossible. Every thing they did, and wished, was of course right. . . . She gave me another piece of information which excited other feelings in me, scarcely less dreadful. Infants were sometimes born in the convent: but they were always baptized and immediately strangled! This secured their everlasting happiness; for the baptism purified them for all sinfulness, and being sent out of the world before they had time to do anything wrong, they were at once admitted into heaven. How happy, she exclaimed, are those who secure immortal happiness to such little beings! Their little souls would thank those who kill their bodies, if they had in their power!

Explore the Sources

1. What connections does the narrator make between Catholic religious ideas and the sex and infanticide that go on in the convent?
2. How might this text have been designed specifically to outrage readers who valued antebellum ideals of domesticity and motherhood?
3. Why do you think the author begins the book with detailed illustrations of the convent? How might the illustrations contribute to the book's message?

the fact that the Catholic Church accepted slavery, but like many reformers they also hated Catholicism on its own terms. "In this country, popery finds its appropriate ally in the institution of slavery," wrote an Ohio abolitionist. "They are both kindred systems. One enslaves the mind, the other both mind and body." Because Catholicism insisted on the infallibility of its own leaders, Protestant reformers charged, the Church is the natural enemy of democracy and human progress. "The Catholic Church opposes everything which favors democracy and the natural rights of man," wrote the abolitionist and transcendentalist Theodore Parker. On the other side of the divide, Catholic priests and intellectuals mistrusted the reform movements and their belief in the infallibility of individual conscience. Catholics, both in the United States and abroad, criticized Protestant reformers for a naïve faith in human freedom, for elevating individuals over communities, and for favoring social changes that would lead to chaos, bloodshed, and true despotism.

Conflicts between Protestants and Catholics increased in the 1840s, as the Catholic population of the United States grew. On the outskirts of Philadelphia, two bloody riots broke out during the summer of 1844 between Irish-born Catholics and native-born Protestants. Two Catholic churches and many homes were destroyed, and rioters on both sides were killed. Because the conflict pitted immigrant newcomers against **nativists** (advocates of the interests of native-born citizens and opponents of immigration), the riots are often categorized as nativist violence. But the core grievances on both sides of the Philadelphia riots had more to do with religion than with turf battles between recent arrivals and more established communities. Although nativism would become a powerful force in American politics in the 1850s (see Chapter 14), anti-Catholicism was even more widespread. And whereas virtually all nativists in the antebellum North were anti-Catholic, not all anti-Catholics were nativist. Especially after the Revolutions of 1848, when the Catholic Church played an important role in thwarting liberal nationalist uprisings in France, Italy, Austria, Hungary, and elsewhere in Europe, anti-Catholicism flourished among many Americans (including German immigrants, socialists, and land reformers) who had no sympathy whatsoever for nativism.

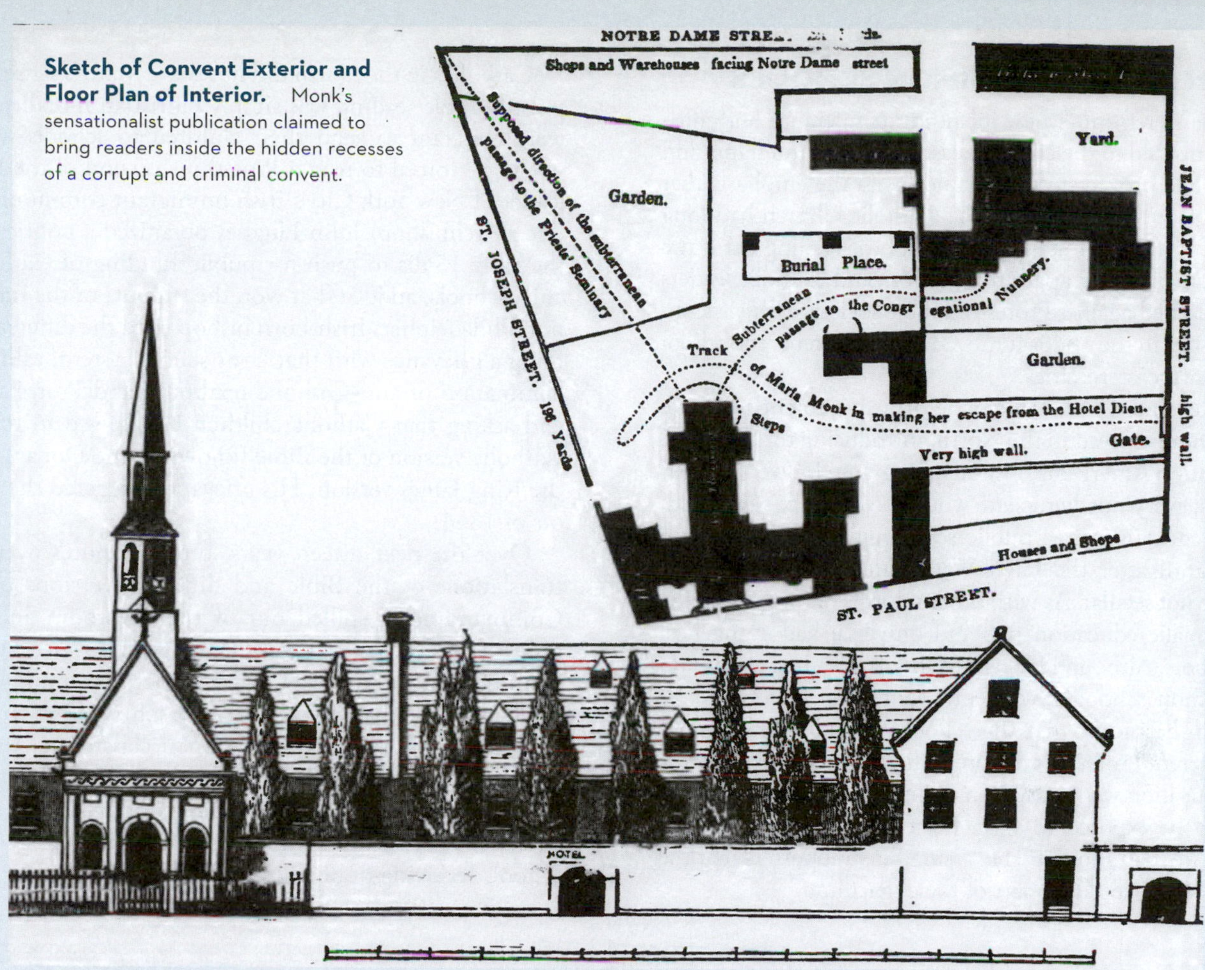

Sketch of Convent Exterior and Floor Plan of Interior. Monk's sensationalist publication claimed to bring readers inside the hidden recesses of a corrupt and criminal convent.

IRISH IMMIGRATION AND THE POTATO FAMINE

Although anti-Catholic prejudice originated in global religious conflicts rather than ethnic hostilities in the United States, one American ethnic group bore the brunt of that prejudice. The experiences and perspectives of Irish Americans shaped the politics of evangelical reform in the antebellum era. The high point of Irish immigration to the United States would take place in the decade after 1845, but already by the 1830s the flow of immigrants from Ireland struck most observers at the time as a dramatic change. Driven by land scarcity and overpopulation and drawn by cheaper overseas transportation, Irish men, women, and children moved to the northeastern part of the United States in large numbers in the 1830s, coming mostly from Catholic areas in southern and western Ireland. For the first time in U.S. history, a majority of Irish immigrants were now Catholic.

Irish Catholics in the United States identified strongly with their religion and not simply with their land of origin. The new immigrants built newspapers, like the *Catholic Herald* in Philadelphia, the *Catholic Telegraph* in Cincinnati, and the *Pilot* in Boston, that addressed their readers as a specifically Catholic community. The leaders of the new immigrant communities were typically priests and bishops. By 1840, American Catholicism was already linked in the popular imagination with Irish immigrants living in the fast-growing cities of the North.

In 1845, a natural disaster in Ireland prompted an exodus that would swell the Irish Catholic population in the United States to unimagined proportions. A fungus struck the Irish potato crop, which was the main food source of poor farmers who cultivated small plots of rented land controlled by English and Anglo-Irish landlords. The fungus charred the leaves of the potato plant and made them disintegrate. It wiped out 30–40 percent of the country's potato crop in 1845, and the following year it devastated the crop entirely. Ireland's potato harvests would not recover until the middle of the 1850s. By that point, the Irish potato famine had killed between 1 and 1.5 million people, out of a prefamine population of 8 million. Another 1.5 million came to America, between 1845 and 1854, part of the greatest wave of immigration, as a proportion of the U.S. population, in the nation's history (see Chapter 14). In the process, Catholicism became the largest single religious denomination in America.

RELIGION AND THE COMMON SCHOOLS

Although many reform issues, including temperance and antislavery, contributed to the cultural clash between Protestants and Catholics, none proved quite so explosive as the emphasis that Protestants placed on the Bible. The Catholic Church had long been critical of the Protestant prescription of reading Scripture without commentary as a path to salvation, and Catholic leaders had long preached against Protestant bible societies. This was an old conflict, but in the 1840s it moved to a new arena: the school systems of northeastern cities.

Starting around 1840, a major reform movement to create **common schools** spread in the North, introducing the system of public education Americans now take for granted. Over the next twenty years, every northern state would provide tax-supported, tuition-free education (free public schooling did not appear in the South until after the Civil War). But the earliest public schools were not secular. As with other reforms of the period, the impulse to make education free and universal had evangelical Protestant roots. Although Horace Mann, the leading champion of the common school movement, wanted the schools to be nonsectarian, he meant that the schools should not take sides between different Protestant denominations. Mann believed in a universal education where children of different backgrounds and faiths would be exposed to what he took to be the common ground of Christian morality. He assured his supporters that the King James Bible would be part of the curriculum.

Catholics in the North did not share Mann's sense that compulsory Bible reading was simply Christian morality, and they were reluctant to send their children to schools where they would be forced to read a Protestant version of the Bible. The leader of New York City's Irish immigrant community, Bishop (later Archbishop) John Hughes organized a political party in the early 1840s to push for public funding of Catholic parochial schools, an idea that won the support of the state's governor. Philadelphia's Irish-born bishop tried the different tactic of filing a grievance with that city's school system, calling for the elimination of anti-Catholic textbooks and Protestant hymns and asking that Catholic children be allowed to read from a Catholic version of the Bible (known as the Douay) instead of the King James version. His grievance triggered the bloody riots of 1844.

Over the next fifteen years, bitter disputes over different translations of the Bible and different versions of the Ten Commandments spilled out of the classroom and into the political arena. Reformers did not want to give up on their commitment to expose all children, perhaps immigrants most of all, to what they saw as the core Christian faith. But they did not want Catholic Bibles in their classroom. And they especially did not want to use taxpayer money to support Catholic schools. To avoid giving such support, states ultimately decided to exclude religious instruction altogether from schools receiving public funding.

CONCLUSION

By midcentury, movements promoting temperance, abolitionism, women's rights, universal education, and anti-Catholicism had become familiar features of public life in the North, as had a varied menu of self-improvement programs, cooperative communities, and social taboos. These were the product of a middle-class culture of reform that emerged during the same period when slavery was driving a wider and more permanent wedge between the two sections of the country. The culture of reform did not go uncontested; it created new lines of social conflict and hardened old ones. But the broader assumptions about individual responsibility, social change, and family life that the reformers shared and reinforced were gaining power and influence. By mid-century, these ideas were reshaping everyday life in the North.

STUDY TERMS

- transcendentalists (p. 299)
- lyceum movement (p. 299)
- voluntary associations (p. 299)
- New Harmony (p. 300)
- utopian communities (p. 300)
- Brook Farm (p. 300)
- Sabbatarianism (p. 300)
- antigallows movement (p. 300)
- corporal punishment (p. 300)
- prisons (p. 300)
- teetotaler (p. 301)
- American Temperance Society (p. 301)
- Washingtonians (p. 301)
- Sons of Temperance (p. 301)
- temperance novels (p. 303)
- bodily self-control (p. 303)
- the secret vice (p. 304)
- abolitionists (p. 305)
- immediatism (p. 306)
- racial equality (p. 306)
- slave narratives (p. 306)
- anti-abolitionist riots (p. 307)

TIMELINE

1826 American Temperance Society forms in Boston

1830 *Godey's Lady's Book* introduced

1831 William Lloyd Garrison begins publishing *The Liberator*

1832 Ralph Waldo Emerson resigns pulpit and embarks on new philosophical path

1833 American Anti-Slavery Society formed1834 Anti-abolitionist riots break out in the North

American Female Moral Reform Society formed

1836 Maria Monk's *Awful Disclosures* published

1837 Elijah Lovejoy killed in Alton, Illinois

1840 Abolitionists split over issues of political action and the role of women

1844 Catholic-Protestant riots erupt around Philadelphia

1845 Frederick Douglass publishes his autobiography

Potato famine begins in Ireland

Temperance advocate John Gough discovered drunk in a New York brothel

1848 Seneca Falls Convention enacts Declaration of Sentiments

Revolutionary movements in Europe reinforce anti-Catholicism in the United States

FURTHER READING

Additional suggested readings are available on the Online Learning Center at www.mhhe.com/becomingamerica1e.

Thomas Augst, *The Clerk's Tale* (2003), looks at the struggles of young middle-class men to establish their character and answer the moral demands associated with white-collar work.

Stuart Blumin, *The Emergence of the Middle Class* (1989), traces the development of a self-conscious American middle class in antebellum cities.

Nancy Cott, *Bonds of Womanhood* (1977), illuminates the relationship between the cult of domesticity and the emergence of feminism.

Bruce Dorsey, *Reforming Men and Women* (2002), emphasizes the importance of new ideas about gender to reform movements in Philadelphia.

Karen Halttunen, *Confidence Men and Painted Women* (1982), studies the role of etiquette guides in spreading new standards of middle-class behavior.

Helen Lefkowitz Horowitz, *Attitudes Toward Sex in Antebellum America* (2006), surveys some very different views toward human sexuality during this era.

Nancy Isenberg, *Sex and Citizenship in Antebellum America* (1998), explicates the ideas of the women's rights movement.

Henry Mayer, *All on Fire* (1998), details the life of William Lloyd Garrison.

John T. McGreevy, *Catholicism and American Freedom* (2003), treats the conflicts between Catholics and Protestants in antebellum America as a clash between competing ideas of freedom.

Stephen Nissenbaum, *The Battle for Christmas* (1997), offers an interpretation of the rise of the modern American Christmas and the birth of Santa Claus in the nineteenth century.

Elaine Frantz Parsons, *Manhood Lost* (2003), connects the temperance movement to changing ideas about gender and increased women's participation in public life.

Mary P. Ryan, *Cradle of the Middle Class* (1983), documents how transformations in family life in the Erie Canal region laid the foundation for middle-class values.

13

California News. War, conquest, and long-distance communications stoked the fires of westward expansion.

INSIDE

THE BIG PICTURE

Following the momentous 1844 election, the United States embarked on a course of aggressive territorial expansion that led to a costly and controversial war with Mexico and expanded the nation's border to the Pacific. Nationalistic themes also reverberated in popular entertainment, literature, and new patterns of travel and communication.

1844–1854

EXPANSION, NATIONALISM, & AMERICAN POPULAR CULTURE

Writing in a New York literary magazine in 1845, James Kennard, Jr., of New Hampshire posed a question of some importance to the magazine's elite readership. "Who are our National Poets?" asked Kennard provocatively. Ever since 1776, Americans had been trying to declare their cultural independence. This required proving not only that artists in the new republic could create plays, novels, paintings, and poems of comparable merit to the best European works, but also that American art expressed the special circumstances of American life and the particular genius of the American people. Beginning in the 1820s, white Americans often produced works of art and literature that featured Indian subject matter in order to distinguish American culture from that of England or the European continent (see Chapter 9). But Kennard wanted more than just distinctively American subject matter. He wanted distinctively American artists, uncorrupted by the influences of other national traditions. Surveying the cultural landscape in 1845, Kennard argued that the real national artists were slaves. "The negro poets . . . in the swamps of Carolinas," he imagined, produced original poems that were then recorded by whites, reproduced on the minstrel stage by white actors in blackface, and spread all over the globe. And this, according to Kennard, was American culture.

Kennard's essay was both playful and perverse, but his ideas reflected two important developments in American life by 1845. One was a rising nationalism among many sectors of the population, energized by mounting confidence in the unique character of the United States and new expectations that the nation would continue to grow. The same year Kennard's essay appeared, a new Democratic president entered office with a powerful commitment to national expansion. James Knox Polk believed that it was the destiny of the United States to stretch across the continent to the Pacific. By the time he left office four years later, his vision had been realized and the nation had doubled in size. Territorial growth was fueled in part by mass migrations of American settlers seeking cheaper land, but it was mostly the product of a major military invasion of neighboring Mexico. The U.S.-Mexican War would dominate Polk's presidency, unsettling the political rivalries between slave and free states and between Democrats and Whigs. The 1848 discovery of gold in the foothills of the newly acquired American territory of California, a find that Polk corroborated in his farewell address, accelerated both westward expansion and the political conflicts it triggered.

KEY QUESTIONS

- How did ideas about the United States' national destiny influence the decision to extend U.S. sovereignty over new territory?
- What were the causes of the U.S.-Mexican War?
- What major westward migrations occurred in the United States in this period, and how did they differ from one another?
- What were the leading popular entertainments in the United States in these years, and how did they help shape national identity?
- How did communication and publishing contribute to American nationalism?

Kennard's essay also indicated the importance of popular culture to the new American nationalism. Actors, athletes, singers, and dancers enjoyed mass celebrity during the 1840s and 1850s, and their performances became occasions for expressing national pride and building national identity. The particular performances that Kennard cited, which purported to represent plantation slavery, became especially popular and politically significant. Minstrel shows depicted the bodies, voices, and experiences of African Americans, but they also spread new ideas about whiteness and helped to define America's national identity as specifically white, just as war supporters were Americans describing the Mexican enemy as a different race. Minstrel skits and songs also provided important venues and vehicles for spreading the expansionist ideology of Polk and the Democrats. Even more genteel artists, such as the novelists and poets who participated in the era's literary renaissance, would take an interest in the territorial growth of the United States and the spread of its political institutions.

Blackface minstrelsy became popular nationalist entertainment.

Not all Americans supported the war against Mexico or clamored for westward expansion. For many northern Whigs, for example, nationalism meant tightening the bonds of commerce and communication across the country rather than adding new territories. They pushed for cheaper postage rates and celebrated the spread of telegraph wires and railroad tracks. But Americans in both parties and regions developed grander and more ambitious visions of the republic's historical destiny and global reach.

MANIFEST DESTINY AND THE ROAD TO WAR

Nationalist movements in the United States looked to the west in the 1840s, imagining a country that spanned the continent. Access to the Pacific Ocean had been an explicit goal of the United States since before the days of the Lewis and Clark expedition (see Chapter 8). What was new was the argument that westward expansion was more than simply good trade policy or military strategy; it was now more often described as the fulfillment of the nation's destiny. Several powerful obstacles stood in the way of this destiny, however (see Map 13.1). The British still claimed the Oregon Territory, which had been ruled since 1818 under a "joint occupation" agreement with the United States. Further south, various native groups, especially the Apache, Comanche, Navajo, and Kiowas, imposed their considerable military power over large regions. Even more of the Southwest lay within the political borders of Mexico, which had been an independent republic since 1821 and held a population of around seven million in the 1840s. During the space of a few years, the United States committed itself to the project of wresting enough land from these other powers to realize the dream of a transcontinental nation.

TEXAS AND THE POLITICS OF EXPANSION

By the 1840s, debates about territorial expansion focused on the borderland with Mexico. Texas had declared independence from Mexico in 1836 (see Chapter 11), but the Mexican government refused to recognize either its independence or the Lone Star Republic's claim to extend all the way to the

Map 13.1 North America in 1844. Between the two independent republics of Mexico and the United States lay a disputed region that included the Lone Star Republic of Texas, whose borders and status Mexico did not recognize. In addition, powerful Indian polities such as the Apache, Comanche, and Kiowa held sway in much of northern Mexico and the U.S. West.

Rio Grande (see disputed area on Map 13.1). Violence flared frequently between Texas and Mexico in the decade following independence, which intensified tensions between Mexico and the United States. Ironically, Mexico had encouraged the emigration of white, American settlers to Texas in the 1820s in an ill-fated attempt to create a buffer that would impede U.S. expansion into northern Mexico and protect Mexicans from Comanche attacks. But now Texas was independent, dominated by English speakers with allegiance to the United States and desires to join the union. No longer a buffer, Texas was a prime target for foreign annexation and attack.

Though the prospect of annexing Texas appealed to many Americans, opponents (mostly northern Whigs) argued that annexation was tantamount to declaring war against Mexico. Some also worried that taking Texas would embroil the United States in a struggle with the Comanche Indians, who remained the major military power in that region. But the greatest opposition to annexation came from northerners concerned about the spread of slavery and the balance of power between slave states and free states in the Senate. By 1840, the question of Texas had become the primary touchstone for sectional conflict over slavery.

During the Texas controversy, the White House was occupied by John Tyler, who succeeded to office in 1841 upon the death of William Henry Harrison, just thirty-one days into his term (see Chapter 10). A slaveholding Virginia Democrat who had alienated the Jacksonian establishment in the 1830s by supporting states' rights, Tyler was tapped by the Whigs for vice president in 1840 in an effort to attract southern support. He shared few of his new party's views, however, and they disowned him soon after he became president. Planning to run for reelection as an independent candidate, Tyler advocated adding Texas and instructed Secretary of State John C. Calhoun to prepare an annexation treaty with Texas in 1844. But Calhoun fanned the flames of the slavery controversy by arguing that annexation was necessary to foil British plans to encourage abolition in the Lone Star Republic. Calhoun also took the occasion, in a letter to the British minister, to tout the benefits of slavery. With the approach of the 1844 presidential election, a divided Senate rejected the annexation treaty.

THE ELECTION OF 1844

As both major parties headed toward their nominating conventions, it seemed possible that the burning question of Texas might not be a major campaign issue. The Whigs rallied behind Henry Clay, who was known to oppose annexation but sought to avoid the controversy. On the Democratic side, former president Martin Van Buren was the presumed nominee, and he too intended to avoid the annexation question and run largely on the economic issues (such as bank regulation, tariffs, and internal improvements) that had dominated the campaigns of the previous decade. But Van Buren faced opposition within his party, especially among annexation advocates. After successfully pushing a rule requiring the nominee to get a two-thirds majority of the delegates, the rebels threw their support to Lewis Cass of Michigan (an annexationist) and the convention was deadlocked. Finally, on the ninth ballot, a surprise candidate emerged. James Knox Polk, a Tennessee slaveholder who had been Speaker of the House and a protégé of Andrew Jackson, won the Democratic nomination and became the standard-bearer of a party suddenly committed to annexing Texas.

To shore up their support in the North, the Democrats called for the "re-occupation" of Oregon from Britain as well as the "re-annexation of Texas" (which Democrats claimed had been included in the 1803 Louisiana Purchase from France). Slavery was unlikely to flourish in the Oregon Territory, which was being settled by families planning to work the land themselves, and the eventual admission of a free state from the Northwest could appease northerners by balancing out Texas. Polk's campaign trumpeted the Oregon cause more loudly than Texas, making northern rather than southern territory the symbol of the party's expansionist ideology. But everyone understood that a vote for Polk was a vote for taking Texas. This turn of events undercut President Tyler's hopes to win reelection as an independent on an expansionist platform. Rather than split the southern vote, Tyler endorsed Polk and withdrew from the race.

Faced with an expansionist opponent, Clay could no longer dodge the Texas question. Trying to hedge his bets, he claimed to be willing to consider annexation if it could be achieved "without dishonor, without war, with the common consent of the Union, and upon just and fair terms." This position reassured none of the expansionists, but it alarmed slavery opponents in the North. In an extremely close election, voters opposed to slavery and annexation made a difference. Although abolitionist candidate James Birney, running on the Liberty Party ticket, polled only 2.3 percent of the total, he drew enough support away from Clay in Michigan and New York to secure victory for Polk (see Map 13.2). In one of the most consequential elections in American history, the Democrats recaptured the presidency and claimed a popular mandate for aggressive expansionist policies.

Before leaving office, President Tyler invoked this mandate and asked Congress to admit Texas to the union. Congressional Democrats were able to win approval for Texas annexation by treating it as an application for statehood, which required only a majority in both houses, rather than a treaty with a foreign nation, which required a two-thirds majority that the Democrats did not have. John Quincy Adams, one of the bill's bitterest opponents, remarked that this maneuver had violated the Constitution, reducing it to "a menstruous rag." Over such objections, Texas entered the union, its status and borders still angrily contested by Mexico.

YOUNG AMERICA, RACE, AND MANIFEST DESTINY

As they contemplated and justified annexing and conquering western lands, Americans spoke explicitly about what they saw as the character of their nation. It was in this

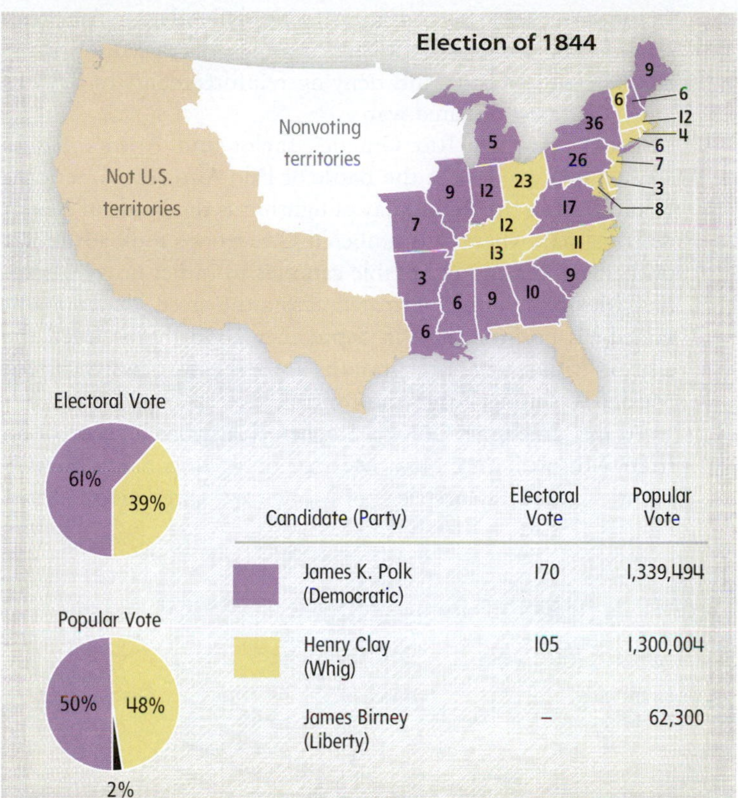

Map 13.2 Election of 1844.

context that the famous words **manifest destiny** entered the political vocabulary. The phrase was introduced in the pages of John L. O'Sullivan's journal, *The United States Magazine and Democratic Review*, in 1839, though the term was probably coined by one of his writers, Jane McManus Storm, who published under the name C. Montgomery. In 1845, Storm used the term in widely circulated articles to argue for acquiring more territory. Annexing Texas, she wrote, would fulfill "our manifest destiny to overspread the continent allotted by Providence for our yearly multiplying millions." The American claim to greater Oregon was said to rest on the exact same foundation—"our manifest destiny to overspread and to possess the whole of the continent which Providence has given for the development of the great experiment of liberty."

As both a political slogan and a political argument, "manifest destiny" meant a few things. First, expansionists were claiming that the westward spread of the United States was not simply a matter of policy or expedience; it was preordained by divine will. Second, the divine plan for the United States to expand was revealed not in sacred texts or prophecies, but in the working of history itself. The growth of the American population and its steady westward migration was what made this destiny clear, or *manifest*. Third, America was destined to expand in order to model and spread its free and democratic political institutions. "A higher than earthly power still guards and directs our destiny," wrote Polk's secretary of the treasury, "and has selected our great and happy country as a . . . centre of attraction for all the nations of the world." *Manifest destiny* expressed a utopian vision of the United States, propelled by the hand of God in history, introducing new political ideals to a changing planet.

Older countries might stake their claims to territory in the past—treaties, traditions, generations of occupancy—but the new ideologues of American expansion emphasized the future and touted the youth of the republic as a reason why older nations ought to give way to U.S. interests. American expansionists in the late 1840s rallied under the banner of **Young America,** a name introduced earlier in the decade by the philosopher and lecturer Ralph Waldo Emerson. Significantly, the Young America moniker was adopted both by politicians advocating American expansion and by writers like Herman Melville, Walt Whitman, and Nathaniel Hawthorne, who advocated a distinctive American literature (see National Literature, below).

But manifest destiny was a racial ideology as well. If America's youthfulness became an argument for why Great Britain ought to concede Oregon, what about Mexico, which was a new republic as well? Expansionists made many arguments against Mexican claims to greater Texas, including the point that Mexico had failed to colonize its northern states successfully because it had not wrested control of that territory from Indians. Ultimately, however, what seemed to justify taking Mexican lands was the fact that Mexico was a racially mixed society that therefore did not share the national destiny of the United States. When John O'Sullivan and others celebrated the movement of settlers westward, they called it an "irresistible army of Anglo-Saxon emigration." In the words of a Maryland congressman, "We must march from Texas straight to the Pacific ocean, and be bounded only by its roaring wave. . . . It is the destiny of the white race, it is the destiny of the Anglo-Saxon race." Manifest destiny meant white destiny.

WAR AND CONQUEST

Polk entered office with Texas already annexed and his eye on the Pacific Ocean. He hoped to acquire both the Oregon Territory and Mexican California in order to bring the harbors of San Diego, San Francisco, and the Puget Sound under U.S. control. Polk wished to avoid military conflict with Great Britain and acquire as much of Oregon as possible through negotiations while he prepared to invade Mexico. He expected war with Mexico to be relatively brief, since Mexico would not be able to defend its northern states while simultaneously waging war against raiding Indian armies. Despite repeated battlefield victories, the U.S.-Mexican War dragged on for seventeen months, taking many lives and provoking serious political debates about the future of the union.

THE INVASION OF MEXICO

Mexico did not recognize the U.S. annexation of Texas. Moreover, Mexico disputed the boundaries that the United States had claimed for Texas, citing the traditional boundary of the Nueces River, not the Rio Grande as Texans had asserted. (The Rio Grande border also included the commercial centers of Santa Fe, Albuquerque, and Taos; see Map 13.3.) For the United States to press its claim to the region between the two rivers, it would need to send troops into land that Mexico viewed as its own. Polk did so quickly, ordering General Zachary Taylor to take up a position along the Rio Grande. Predictably, Mexico's general Mariano Arista responded by launching an attack against Taylor's men in late April 1846. When news of the attack reached Washington, Polk (who had been preparing a war message anyway) announced to Congress that "the cup of forbearance has been exhausted." Mexico had "invaded our territory, and shed American blood upon American soil." Facing a choice between accepting Polk's account of the conflict with Mexico and denying reinforcements to Taylor's army, Congress declared war.

Back along the Rio Grande, Taylor and Arista's armies clashed for two days in the Battle of Palo Alto (the Americans would refer to the second day of fighting as the Battle of Resaca de la Palma), where outnumbered U.S. troops took advantage of their lighter, more portable cannons to inflict heavy casualties. Mexican soldiers retreated across the river, Taylor maintained his position, and in September 1846, he besieged the city of Monterrey. Five months into the war, northeastern Mexico was under American control.

At the same time, Colonel Stephen Kearny led an expedition from Missouri into New Mexico, occupying Santa Fe two months before Taylor's siege of Monterrey. Three months later,

Map 13.3 Major Battles of the U.S.-Mexican War. After sending troops into the disputed territory west of the Nueces River, the United States launched a multi-front invasion of its neighboring republic.

Kearny marched into San Diego, California, entering a Mexican state where, farther north, the explorer John Frémont had initiated a revolt of American settlers against Mexican rule earlier in the year. Though the fighting was fierce, the two-pronged invasion of northern Mexico by Taylor and Kearny seemed to be working. In a final burst of resistance, General Santa Anna (whom the Americans had naively brought back to Mexico from Cuban exile in the hopes that he would help negotiate a peace) mustered a massive army to expel the invaders from Monterrey. But in the Battle of Buena Vista (February 1847), where both sides suffered heavy loss of life, Taylor's troops fought to a standstill, and Santa Anna decided to withdraw southward. The Mexicans had missed their best chance to resist the invasion.

Despite the succession of victories, American war aims remained elusive. Had the United States simply wanted to annex and defend greater Texas, the conflict might have ended. But all along Polk had wanted the invasion to force Mexico to negotiate a settlement that would cede New Mexico and California as well. In 1845, before the war began, he sent minister John Slidell to Mexico to offer cash for all of these territories (including $25 million for California), but the Mexicans had rebuffed him, and a slew of U.S. military victories in the north had not changed their minds. The United States decided that the only way to force Mexico to negotiate would be to bring the war south to the capital.

For the second phase of the war, Polk called upon General Winfield Scott, rather than Taylor, to land a large force on the Gulf coast city of Veracruz and march from there to Mexico City. Following lengthy preparations, Scott arrived in Veracruz in March 1847, occupied the city after an eighteen-day siege, and headed west. After defeating a force led by Santa Anna at Cerro Gordo on April 17 and 18, Scott's army moved slowly toward the capital. On September 14, Mexico City's authorities surrendered, and the U.S. flag was hoisted above the Mexican National Palace.

FOLLOWING THE WAR AT HOME

More than any prior war in American history, the conflict with Mexico unfolded in full view of the populace. Though it took place on foreign soil, the war engaged all Americans because they had unprecedented access to its progress. This was the first war to be covered by the new mass medium of the cheap daily press (see Chapter 10). Newspapers all over the country actively relayed news from the front. In New Orleans, which was the principal staging point for troops, supplies, and information, nine daily newspapers competed for the most up-to-the-minute accounts of the war.

The U.S.-Mexican War was also the first American military conflict to take place after the introduction of the electromagnetic telegraph in 1844 (see National Communication, below).

***War News from Mexico*, by Richard Caton Woodville, 1848.** Americans gathered at post offices, telegraph offices, and newspaper offices to receive and discuss the war's progress. Most of these spaces were dominated by men, but note here the presence of a woman leaning out the window of the hotel to listen to the discussion. **Questions for Analysis:** What seems to be the perspective of the African American man and child in the foreground? Why might the artist have included them?

Within weeks of the war's outbreak, messages could be exchanged instantaneously between New York and Washington. By the war's end, New York was connected via telegraph wire to Charleston, South Carolina. News could now travel from New Orleans to the national capital within three days. Whereas just three decades earlier, no one in Washington knew of the Battle of New Orleans until weeks after it had taken place, residents of one city now formed something closer to a real-time audience for events in the other. Slow communication between President Polk and his officers on the Mexican battlefields continued to plague the chain of command and affect the conduct of the war, but many Americans, especially those living in cities, could experience the course of the conflict as a series of current events.

A majority of Americans greeted the war news enthusiastically. The Declaration of War and the early successes at Palo Alto and Resaca de La Palma fanned the flames of patriotism throughout the country. Books, pamphlets, plays, and songs about the war proliferated, especially in the urban North. In New York theaters, actors and actresses interrupted their scenes to deliver passionate addresses in support of the war effort. Stores advertised special consumer goods, including Palo Alto hats and Palo Alto root beer.

War fever also helped swell the ranks of the army, which at the time war was declared consisted of barely seven thousand personnel. Young men rushed to enlist, quickly filling the fifty thousand spots called for by Congress. Volunteers were encouraged not only by the promise of generous land bounties in any territory that might be conquered, but also by a variety of well-publicized patriotic gestures of local governments and businesses. Volunteers in Indiana were promised an extension on their taxes. State quotas filled quickly, prompting men to cross state lines to volunteer for the war.

Soldiers came from all walks of life, including men who were not yet U.S. citizens and even a few Indians. About half of the enlisted men were foreign immigrants, many of them Catholics from Ireland. The Mexican army sought to lure Catholic immigrant soldiers away from the U.S. military with pamphlets and posters, asking why they participated in the invasion of a Catholic country alongside "those who put fire to your temples in Boston and Philadelphia." Some Irish immigrants switched sides, and close to three hundred of them were organized into the San Patricio battalion, which fought for Mexico in the battle of Buena Vista. The San Patricios were in the minority, however. Thousands of Irish immigrants fought for the United States (forming over a quarter of the soldiers under Zachary Taylor's command). The war gave them an opportunity to demonstrate their fitness for American citizenship—an opportunity denied to African Americans. By taking up arms against a Catholic country on behalf of their new country, Irish immigrants made a powerful claim to the destiny of white America.

WAR AND SLAVERY

From the start, the war had its critics in the United States. Many northeastern Whigs vocally opposed Polk's claim that Mexico had started the war, and they denounced the invasion

***The Hanging of the San Patricio Battalion Deserters at the Battle of Chapultepec, September 1847*, by Sam Chamberlain.** The immigrants who joined this battalion represented a small fraction of the 9,207 U.S. soldiers (all volunteers) who deserted during the U.S.-Mexican War as the war dragged on beyond most volunteers' expectations. This was the highest rate of desertion in any American war. Chamberlain fought in Mexico at the Battle of Buena Vista and also deserted in 1849. He later became colonel of the all-black Fifth Massachusetts Volunteer Cavalry Regiment during the Civil War.

at every stage. As a young Whig congressman, Abraham Lincoln branded it a "war in conquest fought to catch votes" and repeatedly challenged the Democrats to identify the precise spot where U.S. soil had been attacked. The Massachusetts legislature branded the invasion "wanton, unjust and unconstitutional" and a "war against humanity." Nonetheless, Whigs continued to vote for war appropriations, claiming that they did not wish to deny the soldiers the support they needed.

The war's most outspoken opponents attacked it as a war for slavery. The abolitionist ex-slave Frederick Douglass railed against the "disgraceful, cruel, and iniquitous war with our sister republic." Henry David Thoreau refused to pay taxes to support the war, and the night he spent in jail for this defiance became the basis for his famous 1849 essay, *Resistance to Civil Government*. Radical abolitionist William Lloyd Garrison went so far as to root for the success of the Mexicans. "We only hope that, if blood has had to flow," he wrote, "that it has been that of the Americans."

Though most northerners did not adopt the views of Douglass, Thoreau, or Garrison, they were still attuned to the connection between the war and slavery. Some northern expansionists who had supported Polk's aggressive stance on both Oregon and Texas began to wonder about Polk's priorities once they saw how differently the two frontiers were handled. Whereas the United States mounted a costly invasion of Mexico, Polk settled the Oregon question through diplomacy. After the British proposed a settlement at the forty-ninth parallel (far short of the Democrats' campaign promise to push for all of Oregon), Polk submitted the Oregon settlement treaty to the Senate, where it was ratified in June 1846 with minor revisions (see Map 13.4). After the Oregon compromise, more northern and western Democrats began expressing doubts about the wisdom of war policy in Mexico. Manifest destiny held broad national appeal, but the U.S.-Mexican War was more popular in the South than in the North.

The sectional divide over the war came to a head in August 1846, when Pennsylvania representative David Wilmot proposed a rider to a war appropriations bill, prohibiting slavery in any of the Mexican territories that might be acquired in the war. Wilmot, a Democrat, was not an abolitionist and made clear that his intention was to preserve the West as a place where white men could till the soil "without the disgrace which association with Negro slavery brings upon free labor." Polk expressed shock that anyone would see a connection between "slavery and making peace with Mexico," but Wilmot's northern Democratic colleagues were eager to sever any possible connection between their support of the war and the westward extension of slavery. The Wilmot Proviso passed in the House, but the larger appropriations bill stalled in the Senate. After the 1846 elections, when Whigs won control of the House, the Proviso passed there again, but Texas provided the necessary two-vote margin to defeat it in the Senate. Although the proviso never became law, ten state legislatures endorsed it, and it became a rallying cry for northern Democrats uncomfortable with their party's slavery stance. The popularity of Wilmot's Proviso cast a political pall over the war effort, hinting that the addition of new territory might bring new troubles to Washington. It also augured deep fissures within the Democratic Party.

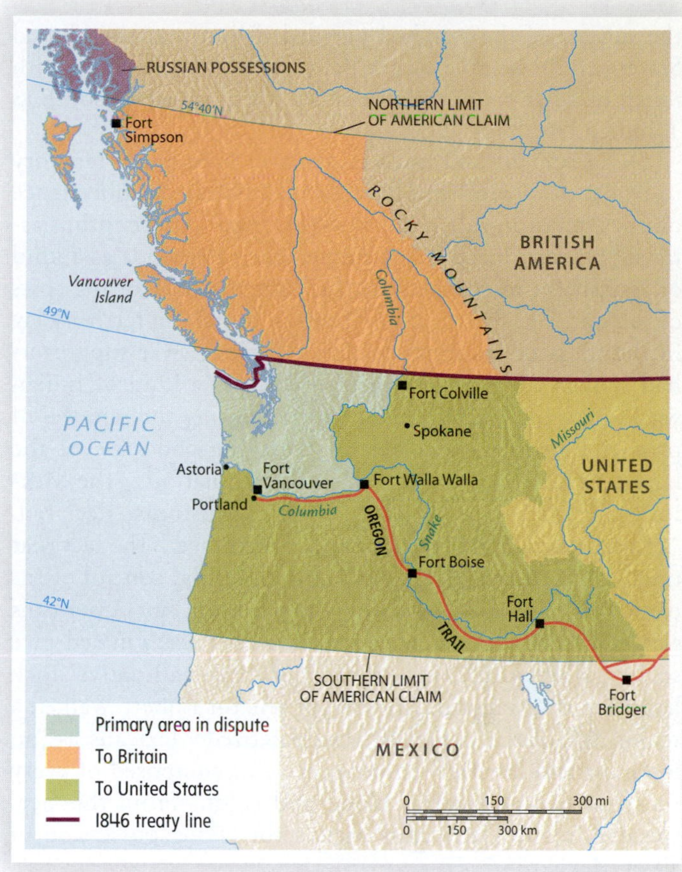

Map 13.4 Settlement of the Oregon Question. An 1846 treaty between Britain and the United States set the boundary at the forty-ninth parallel with the exception of Vancouver Island, which remained under British control.

SURRENDER AND THE MEXICAN CESSION

Even after the fall of its national capital, the Mexican government (temporarily relocated to Querétaro, 125 miles away) refused to make land concessions that were satisfactory to the United States. Part of the problem was that, by the end of 1847, the U.S. position was unclear, because American political opinion was deeply divided over what to ask for. Whigs now controlled the House of Representatives and many Whigs opposed acquiring any new territory. Polk's long-standing war aim had been to wrest all of New Mexico and Alta California from the Mexicans and gain recognition of the Rio Grande as the border of Texas. But the success of the war had persuaded him that the United States should be able to get Baja California too along with much of what is now northeastern Mexico—as far south as Tampico (see Map 13.3).

Disagreement and uncertainty over how much territory to demand was not simply tactical; it reflected ambivalence on the American side, even among the war's most enthusiastic supporters. Hard-liners framed their demands as a kind of assessment to compensate the United States for the costs of the war. But their real justification for taking territory lay in the ideas of manifest destiny. All along, war supporters had spoken of the invasion of Mexico as a kind of Indian war, where the United States was expediting the removal of primitive peoples who were not making good use of the land—rather than vanquishing a foreign nation. "The Mexicans are *Aboriginal Indians*," one expansionist declared, "and they must share the destiny of their race." The fact that much of northern Mexico was still under the control of Indian nations seemed to support this notion, but Americans also emphasized the fact that Mexico itself was a mixed-race society, where the lines between European and native stock had been transgressed. Mississippi senator Robert Walker, a major ally of the president, characterized Mexicans as "an ignorant and fanatical colored race . . . composed of every poisonous compound of blood and color." From this perspective, many Democrats argued for taking possession of all of Mexico.

But the analogy between invading Mexico and removing Indians proved deeply misleading. U.S. soldiers encountered established cities, many of them older and larger than anything they had seen before. If the United States were to annex all of Mexico, what would they do with its seven million inhabitants? Would they simply absorb the country and extend citizenship to people they considered racially inferior? Would they subjugate Mexico as a colonial dependency? Would they enslave the population or incorporate Mexico's system of peonage into the southern slave economy? Or would they, as one senator recommended, dispossess Mexicans and place them on reservations? All of these options were unpalatable to most Americans, and Polk pushed instead for taking only those portions of Mexico that would not force the federal government to choose between its commitment to white supremacy and its commitment to republican equality.

Polk had entrusted the task of securing a peace treaty with Mexico to Nicholas Trist, a former protégé of Thomas Jefferson and aide to Andrew Jackson. Unbeknownst to the president, Trist harbored deep objections to the U.S. invasion of Mexico and was far more eager than Polk to make peace. But Trist found negotiations with Mexico difficult, and in October 1847 Polk decided to recall him, partly as a tactical maneuver to make the United States seem less eager to make peace. The recall message (which was too sensitive to be conveyed via telegraph) took a month to reach Trist, who decided to ignore it, on the grounds that political developments in Mexico had created a timely opportunity to negotiate a deal. Two and a half months after being recalled, Trist reached an agreement with a new Mexican government. Under the Treaty of Guadalupe Hidalgo, signed in Mexico on February 2, 1848, the United States acquired five hundred thousand square miles of Mexican territory (not counting Texas), an area that covered the future states of California, New Mexico, Arizona, Utah, and Nevada and included the coveted Pacific harbors of San Francisco, San Diego, and Monterey. In return, the United States assumed $3.25 million in private claims against Mexico and paid the Mexican government $15 million (see How Much Is That?). The United States also agreed to grant citizenship to all Mexicans residing in the ceded territories, to assume responsibility for preventing all Indian raids into Mexican territory, and to prohibit the enslavement of Mexicans captured by Indians on either side of the new border.

Polk was furious with Trist for disobeying his orders and disappointed that the agreement did not wrest even more territory from Mexico. But with congressional opposition to the war mounting and guerrilla attacks against the U.S. invasion force taking a toll, the president submitted the treaty to the Senate, where it was ratified in March. After seventeen months, a long and costly war had come to an end. Not counting the treaty payments, the United States spent $98 million on the war effort, far more than anyone had expected. More tragically, 12,518 U.S. soldiers were killed, most of them as a result of disease. This would be the last great burst of American territorial acquisition on the North American continent. With the exception of a small slice of the southern parts of present-day New Mexico and Arizona acquired in the 1853 Gadsden Purchase to facilitate a railroad route, the United States had achieved its current contiguous borders (see Map 13.5).

How Much Is That?

The Mexican Cession

By the standards of the time, the $15 million Mexico received for the lands ceded to the United States was trifling. It is dwarfed by the amount Mexico spent waging the war (nearly $100 million, not counting pensions) and the amount the United States offered Spain ($50-100 million) later that same year in an unsuccessful bid to purchase Cuba. In 2013 dollars, the sum represents approximately $440 million, or $1.31 per acre.

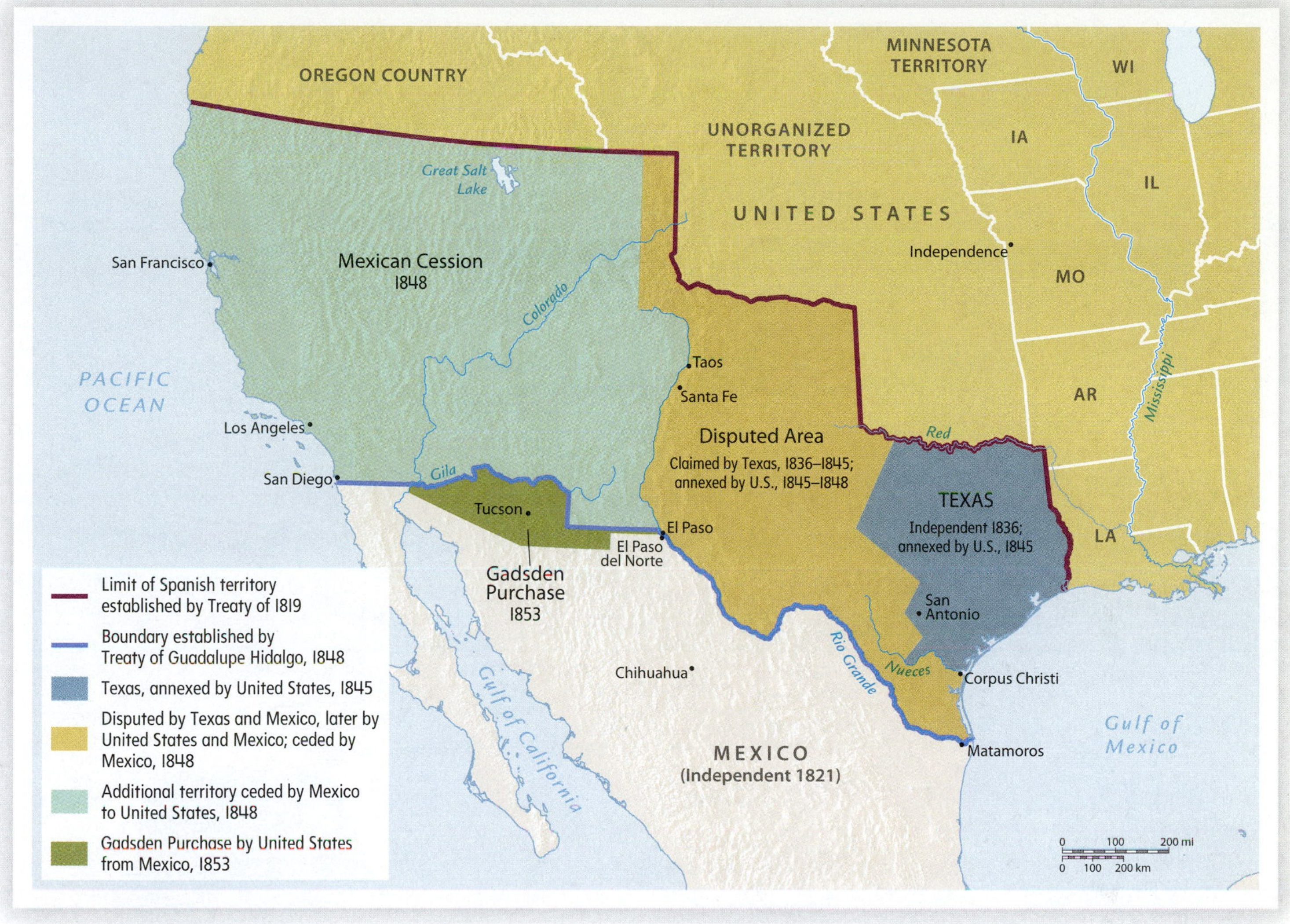

Map 13.5 The United States in 1854. After a decade of annexation, border settlement, war, and land purchase, the nation had extended its sovereignty over the continent and claimed its current continental borders.

EXPANDING WEST

America's westward expansion during the middle of the nineteenth century followed two paths. The United States used diplomacy and military force to extend its sovereignty over the western third of the continent, pursuing what politicians, journalists, and artists described as the nation's historical destiny. At the same time, westward expansion was the result of countless individual and group decisions by Americans and foreign immigrants to pick up stakes and pursue opportunities in those lands that the United States was in the process of conquering.

OVERLAND MIGRATION

During the first third of the nineteenth century, the few Americans who traversed the South Pass of the Rocky Mountains had been fur traders. But in the early 1840s, two well-publicized expeditions established the feasibility of a two-thousand-mile wagon voyage from the Missouri River to the Pacific Ocean in about six months. By 1850, the number of annual migrants on the **Overland Trail** reached over fifty-five thousand.

Typical overland travel parties in the 1840s formed wagon trains each spring in what were called jumping-off cities along the Missouri River, namely Independence and St. Joseph, in Missouri, and Council Bluffs, Iowa (see Map 13.6). Most of the men and women who embarked on the Overland Trail were midwestern white family farmers who lived in Missouri, Illinois, Iowa, and Indiana. They were transient people who had moved at least once before, often several times, in search of cheap, arable land farther west. Crossing the Rockies entailed a bigger commitment, however, since the supplies necessary for the journey cost about $600. But the lure of a homestead in Oregon was great, even before the United States took possession in 1846.

The decision to travel west was usually made by a man on behalf of his wife and children. Women often resented the move,

Map 13.6 The Overland Trail. Between 1846 and 1860, over two hundred thousand travelers trekked from the Missouri River across the Rockies to the west coast, typically in canvas-covered wagons, each weighing between 2,000 and 2,500 pounds and pulled by teams of oxen and mules.

especially the dissolution of their social networks, but they had no social or legal foundation for contesting their husbands' decisions. Wagon trains brought different families together, however, creating mini-societies with their own organization and social world.

Overland migrants passed through Indian lands, including areas controlled by the relatively nomadic tribes of the southern plains whose raids on northern Mexico had made it difficult for the Mexicans to resist the U.S. invasion. But Indian attacks on American travel parties were rare, especially before 1854. The route was not without peril, however. Diseases such as cholera took the lives of thousands of migrants. Overland travelers also needed to time their movements carefully. In 1846, for example, the Donner party started too late and took an ill-advised shortcut across the Utah desert, where many of their animals died, forcing them to cut loose wagons and supplies. They made their way to Truckee Lake (later renamed Donner Lake), the last serious mountain barrier, but became trapped by heavy snowfalls for four months. The ghastly and well-publicized tale of their ordeal, including starvation and cannibalism, dramatized the perils of the Overland Trail.

GOLD DISCOVERED IN CALIFORNIA

Before 1848, Oregon was the primary Pacific destination of westward migrants. But in January of that year, while Nicholas Trist was in Mexico City negotiating an end to the war, James Marshall discovered gold in the middle of the Mexican state of Alta California, which Trist was at that very moment demanding from Mexico as the price of peace. The world did not immediately pay attention to Marshall's discovery at Sutter's Mill. But by June word had spread to the San Francisco Bay region, where men left their homes, their military posts, and their ships in droves to pan

The Overland Trail, ca. 1871. Luminist painter Albert Bierstadt, famous for his large canvases of dramatically lit mountain landscapes, made several expeditions to the American West starting in 1859. In painting the wagon train at dusk, Bierstadt prioritized romantic setting over fact. The travelers would have had to make camp before nightfall.

Donner Lake in California's Sierra Nevada. One of the most famous tales of western migration took place near here. Trapped by snow in this treacherous terrain, seventeen members of the Donner party tried to make it out of the mountains on foot but could not get beyond the snow on the western slope. Only seven of the seventeen survived, subsisting on the corpses of those who did not make it. Back in the main camps, thirteen migrants would starve to death and become food for the others before the rescue parties arrived.

for gold in the foothills of the Sierra Nevada. Later that summer, the news had reached Hawaii and the west coast of Mexico. By the end of the year, newspapers all over the Atlantic seaboard were fanning the flames of gold fever. In less than twelve months, about eighty thousand people descended on California, now part of the United States. A year later, in 1850, California would draft a state constitution and enter the union as part of a national compromise over slavery (see Chapter 14). By 1854, Marshall's discovery had attracted more than three hundred thousand people to California.

The California gold rush differed from other migrations to the American West. Only a portion of the newcomers took the Overland Trail. Most arrived by ship, even those from the eastern half of North America. Some sailed around Cape Horn at the tip of South America, while others traveled by steamship to Panama or Nicaragua, crossed the isthmus by foot, mule, and canoe (there was no canal in Panama), and boarded another ship on the Pacific side. Gold rush migrants were also far more heterogeneous in origin. In contrast to the white midwestern farmers who packed the wagon trains of the more steady overland migration, those who followed the scent of gold hailed from many different places, especially Chile, Mexico, China, Australia, France, and the United States. The people who rushed to California between 1848 and 1854 thus had a very different relationship to the larger project of U.S. territorial

French Guidebook to California, 1850. In Paris, which was reeling from social unrest and failed revolution, news of the gold rush struck fast and hard. Within a year of the discovery of gold in California, advertisements were flooding the papers and sprouting up on walls all over the city. Between 1849 and 1850, eighty-three French companies were formed to sponsor digging expeditions. In all, over twenty thousand French-speaking people joined the gold rush.

expansion than homesteaders heading to Oregon. For some of the new arrivals, the journey to the Sierra was northward or eastward, rather than westward. For many of them, it was their first encounter with the United States.

Immigrants arrived in large numbers from the Cantonese-speaking parts of southern China, especially from the Pearl River delta, where the First Opium War had left a legacy of economic hardship. Most were young single men bent on bringing wealth back home. A minority were women, brought over to work as prostitutes in gold rush cities or in the mines. African Americans came as well, mostly as slaves brought by their owners to a territory in which the legal status of chattel slavery remained uncertain at first. The largest and most influential group of **forty-niners,** as the migrants became known, were white, English-speaking Americans, mainly from New England and the mid-Atlantic states. Mostly middle-class men, these gold seekers came as temporary migrants hoping to return to the communities from which they hailed with greater wealth and enhanced status. Few struck it rich, but gold brought people from all over the world and built new polyglot worlds on the California coast.

"California Gold Diggers: Mining Operations on the Western Shore of the Sacramento River," ca. 1849–1852. This lithograph depicts the range of ethnicities and nationalities of the men who mined gold.

"View of San Francisco, Formerly Yerba Buena, in 1846-7 Before the Discovery of Gold." Prior to the gold rush, Yerba Buena was a compact trading village at the northeastern corner of present-day San Francisco.

San Francisco Harbor, ca. 1850. Almost overnight, San Francisco became a dense urban settlement.

The other distinguishing characteristic of the gold rush migration was its gender imbalance. Forty-niners were overwhelmingly male, and men outnumbered women by as much as ten to one in the mining areas. Migrants complained of the absence of women and the domesticating influence they were supposed to provide. Prostitution flourished in the mines and especially in the growing cities on the San Francisco Bay and along the rivers, often involving women from France and China. But this only confirmed the sense of transplanted northeasterners that they were living in a masculine world cut off from female society. Gold rush culture was rugged and male dominated; the major events of interest and the chief topics of discussion were, as one newcomer reported, "gambling, Duelling, Murdering, Lectioneering and Digging." There were also other, less violent, expressions of this all-male culture. Out in the mining camps, men joined together for festive merriment and dancing, partnering up with one another. On one occasion in the town of Angel's Camp, half the assembled, marked by colorful patches on their pants, would be ladies for the evening. But for most Anglo men, the absence of white, middle-class women was an excuse to construct a social world that featured the rough, same-sex pleasures of the bachelor culture that thrived in eastern cities at the time.

NATIVES AND CALIFORNIOS

For the people who had been living in California long before the 1840s, the gold rush brought about even more momentous changes than the U.S.-Mexican War. At the beginning of the decade, over 150,000 Native Americans lived in California. This represented about half the size of the indigenous population just seventy years earlier, when Spanish settlement began introducing new diseases to the region. But relatively few Hispanic colonists immigrated to California. Indians made up over 90 percent of the population in 1848, even after a malaria epidemic had almost wiped out native life in the Central Valley and after the U.S. invasion. The discovery of gold completely changed the demographic situation. Within a few years, whites outnumbered natives by about two to one.

Because Mexico had granted citizenship to the native population in 1824, California's Indians were eligible, in theory, to become U.S. citizens under the 1848 treaty. Instead, Indians were banished, relegated to second-class citizenship, or simply killed by private militias financed by the State of California. Their livelihoods disrupted by the tide of migrants, surviving Indians developed new economic activities and resources, including stealing and selling horses but also performing their Indian identities in the immigrant towns. Within a few years of the gold rush, small groups of natives would dance in ceremonial regalia for spectators and then pass around the hat.

California's much smaller Mexican population, the **Californios,** already outnumbered by Americans even before California was ceded to the United States, also struggled to survive the onslaught of new arrivals (see Singular Lives: John Rollin Ridge, Cherokee Novelist). Although the new state constitution of 1850 granted rights only to "free white persons," this category included Mexicans of Spanish descent. Wealthy Californio rancheros, who had received substantial land grants from the Mexican government, were represented in the framing of a new state constitution and sought to define themselves as white in the eyes of the law. They held significant political power in southern California, where the gold rush had not diluted their strength. But after California joined the union, Anglos began challenging the rancheros' land titles in court and pressuring them to sell.

SINGULAR LIVES

John Rollin Ridge, Cherokee Novelist

When Andrew Jackson removed Indian tribes from the Southeast, he promised them security in western lands. But southeastern Indians did not simply relocate and disappear. Facing internal divisions, conflicts with the native population of their new homelands, and the westward march of white American settlement and U.S. territorial sovereignty, groups like the Cherokees enjoyed none of the peace promised by removal advocates.

The remarkable career of John Rollin Ridge, also called Yellow Bird, dramatized the dilemmas and fate of the Cherokee diaspora in the era of U.S. expansion. Ridge came from a distinguished and politically powerful Cherokee family. His grandfather had fought alongside Jackson in the Creek War, his father (who attended a missionary boarding school in Connecticut) became a prosperous landowner and slaveholder, and his cousin Elias Boudinot founded the Cherokee *Phoenix*. All three signed the controversial Treaty of New Echota that transferred Cherokee land to the United States and moved voluntarily to Oklahoma in 1836, using their cash settlement with the United States to establish stores that would serve the new arrivals. But when those Cherokees who had opposed the treaty arrived two years later along the Trail of Tears, the Ridge family became the targets of bitter animosity. In 1839, when John Rollin Ridge was twelve years old, treaty opponents executed his father in front of his eyes.

Young Ridge's white mother moved him to Arkansas and then sent him to be educated in Massachusetts. He returned to Arkansas at age twenty, took up the law, and, like his father before him, married a white woman. But the feud between the two Cherokee groups followed Ridge to Arkansas, and when he killed a man over a conflict about a horse, he decided to flee rather than face Cherokee justice. Ridge traveled first to Missouri in 1849, and a year later joined the exodus to California. After a brief and unhappy stint in the mines, Ridge turned to writing and in 1854 produced the first novel published by a Native American author.

Ridge's novel, *The Life and Adventures of Joaquin Murieta*, was based loosely on the life of a Mexican bandit who had become a legend in the American mining camps. In Ridge's version, Joaquin is a noble and honest Mexican miner who turns to crime to avenge the rape of his wife by white Americans. The novel condemns white racism and criticizes whites for failing to live up to the individualist values that Ridge admired in American culture. Ridge's attitude toward Mexicans seemed more ambivalent. Joaquin is a superhero, but the book's preface makes a point of distinguishing him from other, lesser Mexicans. On the surface, the novel raised questions about what it meant to be an American in this new land, but it also reflected its biracial author's own conflicted relationship to the United States. Though he shared his family's interest in acculturation and adaptation, John Rollin Ridge had spent his life fleeing violence, racism, and family vengeance, and his novel transported those themes to the nation's westernmost setting. Despite Ridge's embrace of white civilization, he criticized the U.S. government's Indian policies, clung to his Cherokee identity, aspired to launch a Cherokee newspaper, and longed to return to the Cherokee Nation, which he hoped would enter the union as its own state. Thwarted in that effort, Ridge remained a Californian. He died in 1867.

John Rollin Ridge and His Daughter, Alice Bird. Author of one of the earliest novels in California, Ridge remains an important figure in the region's literary history.

Think About It

1. How did John Rollin Ridge fit into the larger pattern of California migration during the gold rush?
2. Why might a Cherokee author have identified with a Mexican bandit in gold rush California?

Farther north and inland, Anglo Americans used their superior numbers to muscle Mexicans (and other groups) out of the gold mines. In April 1850, the newly formed state legislature passed the first of two Foreign Miners Taxes, which imposed a prohibitive fee of twenty dollars a month on all non-American miners. It was ultimately reduced and then repealed, in part because of the organized opposition of European and South American gold seekers. A more modest imposition of the tax was reintroduced a year later, aimed largely at Chinese miners.

SAN FRANCISCO: INSTANT CITY

To get to the mines, most gold seekers passed through harbor towns on the San Francisco Bay, creating in the process a bustling urban society. The largest of these towns had been founded in 1835 by William Richardson, an independent entrepreneur of British birth who secured a private land grant from the Mexican government in the hopes of trading with small Mexican communities around the bay. Originally called Yerba Buena, the town was renamed San Francisco in January 1847, which may have contributed to the city's growth by identifying the new settlement with the more famous bay. When the gold rush hit, news, goods, and packages destined for the mines via the San Francisco Bay were addressed to San Francisco rather than to the rival town of Francesca, later named Benicia, which stood at the gateway to the interior. At the time gold was discovered, about a thousand people lived in San Francisco; just eight years later, it was home to fifty thousand.

For many migrants, the booming economy of San Francisco was enough of a lure to detain or divert them from the mines. Wages in many sectors of the local economy skyrocketed. Washing clothes became so expensive, for example, that some residents sent their laundry to Hawaii, while others simply bought new clothes when their favored garments got too soiled. One enterprising new arrival from New York brought with him 1,500 outdated copies of the daily *Tribune*, a two-cent paper, and sold them quickly and easily for a dollar each.

"Lola Has Come." In a city with few women, Lola Montez became a major superstar in 1853, personifying San Francisco's culture of male-oriented sensational entertainment, where she assumed the mantle of the nation's leading sex symbol. Born Eliza Gilbert in Ireland in 1818, Montez moved to Spain as a young woman, adopted a Spanish name, and entertained European audiences with her "spider dance," in which she writhed provocatively and removed clothing while appearing to shake a spider off her body. In this cartoon, Montez performs before a theatrical manager and two other men. **Question for Analysis:** Why does the man reading a book cover his eyes?

Land values in the city soared, so that urban real estate became as much of a bonanza as mining claims. Some of these economic pressures and opportunities were the result of the sudden influx of gold. But many of them came from the compression of older patterns of urban growth into such a short time. "It's an odd place," a new arrival said of San Francisco in 1849. "[I]t is not created in the ordinary way but hatched like chickens by artificial heat."

Not all of the residents of San Francisco approved of the rough masculine culture that characterized the instant city as well as the mines. Opponents of this culture, mostly middle-class, American-born Protestants, saw disorder both in the violent streets and in the corruption of the city's nascent political institutions. In 1851, they formed a Committee of Vigilance to execute "prompt and summary punishment" of public offenders. Over the next two years, they took ninety-one prisoners, exiling about a third of them from the city, whipping one, and hanging four others. Five years later, a more ambitious Committee of Vigilance arose. They captured a shipment of federal arms intended for the state militia and arrested the chief justice of the state's supreme court. For ninety-nine days, the committee ruled the city, jailing and executing men associated with gambling, commercial sex, political corruption, and the Democratic Party.

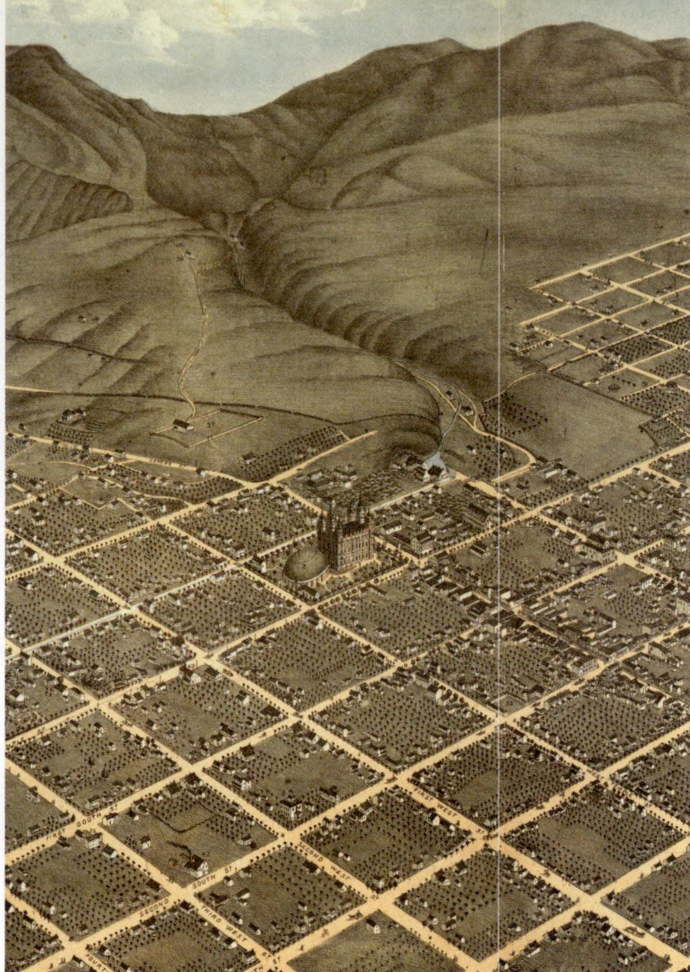

Bird's-Eye View of Salt Lake City, 1870. The temple city of the Church of Latter-Day Saints grew almost instantaneously, holding 4,200 people within a year of it creation. But unlike San Francisco, Salt Lake City was a carefully planned and controlled urban space, where wide streets were laid out on a flat grid, land was divided by lottery, and real estate speculation was prohibited.

MORMON EXODUS

Oregon-bound families and gold seekers in California pursued new economic opportunities in the American West, but the large migration of Mormons from Illinois to the Utah desert had different motivations. After the murder of their prophet Joseph Smith in Nauvoo (see Chapter 10), Brigham Young took over the church, made provisional peace with the community's enemies, and led a Mormon exodus to a promised land in the West in 1846. In contrast to other overland travelers, Young chose a location where he figured the prospects for agriculture or mineral extraction were so poor that no one would bother them. Whereas other westward migrants were following or anticipating the progress of U.S. territorial expansion, the Mormons were seeking a distant refuge from the United States. From their perspective, the American continent was sacred, but the American nation was a place of persecution. The promised land near the Great Salt Lake was technically Mexican territory when Young arrived with the vanguard of his followers in 1847, but Young envisioned a society where the church held all political power and no other sovereign nation had real jurisdiction.

Young declared the existence of a state called Deseret (derived from a word meaning "honeybee" in the Book of Mormon) and renounced any intention "to have any trade or commerce with the gentile world." The self-sufficient economy of Deseret depended on a complex system of irrigation works and a cooperative ethos that contrasted sharply with the competitive individualism of the California gold rush. By 1852, twenty thousand Mormon converts had settled in the Utah Territory, which was by that point part of the United States but largely ignored by the federal government. That year, Young first proclaimed publicly that the church sanctioned plural marriage (for men only), more widely known as polygamy. Outcry over this aspect of Mormon doctrine prompted the federal government to send troops to Utah in 1857 to assert U.S. sovereignty over the territory. More than a year later, after a prolonged standoff with federal forces and a massacre of non-Mormon overland migrants by a Mormon militia, the Mormon government negotiated a peace deal, agreeing to accept the sovereignty of the United States in return for a withdrawal of the troops and promises of freedom of religion in Utah.

NATIONALISM AND POPULAR THEATER

Most Americans living in the age of nationalist expansion did not enlist in Taylor's army, trek across the Rockies, or sail to California in search of gold. Many of them experienced

STATES OF EMERGENCY

The Astor Place Riot

Prior to the Civil War, the bloodiest riot in an American city began over a performance of *Macbeth*. In May 1849, two rival actors with a history of deep personal animosity were starring simultaneously in competing New York productions of the Shakespeare play. One was the English actor William Macready; the other was the American Edward Forrest of *Metamora* fame (see Chapter 9). Forrest's partisans managed to disrupt Macready's performance at the recently opened Astor Place Opera House at the intersection of Broadway and the Bowery, drowning out his lines with catcalls and hisses, pelting him with potatoes, pieces of wood, and stink bombs, and driving him offstage. Set to return to his homeland, the mortified English actor was persuaded to stay by a letter signed by forty-seven prominent citizens (among them the writers Washington Irving and Herman Melville) and promising the restoration of order at Macready's next performance.

This time precautions were taken. Only respectable gentlemen known to be friendly to Macready could purchase tickets. Policemen moved about the audience, and the Seventh Regiment state militia stood close by. Though a big crowd gathered outside the opera house, the play began smoothly. But soon after, the performance was disrupted, some arrests were made inside the theater, and the men on the street grew angrier. Members of the crowd tore up iron railings, broke into a marble yard, and started chucking rocks at the theater. Militiamen appeared on the scene. They first fired into the air and then turned their firearms on the crowd, killing twenty-two people and injuring over fifty others.

How could Shakespearean drama stir up such bitter and violent passions? The Astor Place Riot of 1849 was not simply a theater review turned nasty. The issues raised and the animosities vented extended to fundamental questions of politics, class relations, and national identity. To the crowd assembled outside the theater, Macready and the opera house represented, among other things, aristocratic privileges and foreign influence on American popular culture. But the conflict also pitted competing visions of how one ought to behave at the theater. The signatories of the letter imploring Macready to stay saw theater as an art form to be appreciated respectfully by a city's leading citizens. The hundreds who stormed the opera house saw things differently. In the words of the lawyer defending the riot's organizers, "The right to hiss an actor off the stage is an undisputed right of anyone who goes into a theatre." The Astor Place Riot marked a turning point in this debate. The courts did not buy the rioters' free speech argument and ruled that purchasing a ticket entitled spectators to nothing other than the right to a seat. What they did in that seat would be subject to the dictates of the theater manager.

WORKING MEN
SHALL
AMERICANS
OR
ENGLISH RULE!
IN THIS CITY!
The crew of the British Steamer, have threatened all Americans who shall dare to express their opinions this night at the
ENGLISH ARISTOCRATIC!
OPERA HOUSE!
We advocate no violence but a free expression of opinion to all public men.
WORKINGMEN! FREEMEN!!
STAND BY YOUR
LAWFUL RIGHTS!
AMERICAN COMMITTEE.

Astor Place Riot Broadside. Organizers of the riot, who included the nationalist author Ned Buntline, creator of the Buffalo Bill character, summoned Forrest's supporters to the scene with posters like this, which skillfully appealed to patriotic sentiments.

Think About It

1. Why might Forrest's supporters have objected to an English actor?
2. How might Irish immigrants and native-born American workers have read the poster differently but still found common cause in the riot?
3. Why did the rioters think that the theater was an important and appropriate place to express one's views and opinions?
4. What does the event suggest about the status of Shakespeare's plays in American culture in 1849?

nationalism and expansion primarily as ideas, sources of inspiration or humor, and subjects of conversation and debate. This period of war, annexation, and westward migration was also a time of major growth and consolidation in American popular culture. Americans of different classes flocked especially to the theater in the mid-nineteenth century, and stage performances became major venues for spreading—and testing—ideas about politics and nationality.

BOISTEROUS AUDIENCES

Theatergoing in U.S. cities during the first half of the nineteenth century was strikingly different from the quiet, decorous experience we now associate with dramatic entertainment. Instead of sitting in silent, rapt attention, audience members shouted, wandered around, got drunk, and engaged in all kinds of informal behavior—including spitting, throwing nutshells, and breastfeeding. When spectators disapproved of a performance,

Barnum's American Museum, New York City. Between 1841, when P. T. Barnum purchased the museum, and 1865, when it burned to the ground, the American Museum was the grand cathedral of middle-class entertainment. A massive building by contemporary standards, it contained six floors of exhibition space by 1865 and formed one of the most imposing and recognizable landmarks on the New York cityscape.

they might groan, hiss, shower the offending actor with fruits and vegetables, or wreak more serious havoc (see States of Emergency: The Astor Place Riot). When they approved, they might press an actor to repeat a line (or an entire scene). On other occasions, audience members might caution a stage character to beware of some imminent danger, or they might suddenly disrupt a performance of Shakespeare with a rendition of "Yankee Doodle." Lights were left on, so that spectators could see and be seen. The audience was part of the show.

Significantly, these theater audiences tended to be heavily male. Before the 1850s, respectable women saw plays only in the company of a male escort and tended to avoid the theater altogether. In most cities, prostitutes were admitted free of charge to a designated tier of the gallery, where they might negotiate and even consummate their business. But theaters, like saloons and polling places, were sites of public life where men dominated. This not only licensed drunkenness and rough behavior; it also marked theaters as appropriate places to air political views and allegiances.

P. T. BARNUM AND MUSEUM THEATER

Now remembered mostly for his later association with the American circus, Phineas Taylor Barnum was famous in his time as a curator of curious exhibitions, an impresario of popular entertainments, and a master of deceptions. Barnum was a founding father in the world of mass culture. He shaped and marketed commercial entertainment for multiple generations of Americans in the nineteenth century. Raised in Connecticut in 1810, Barnum moved to New York City in his early twenties in search of opportunities to make money by catering, as he later put it, to "that insatiate want of human nature—the love of amusement." Barnum's opportunity came knocking in 1835 in the form of a slave named Joice Heth, who was reputed to be 161 years old and have nursed a young George Washington. Barnum purchased her for $1,000 and peddled her and her bogus story throughout the Northeast. Thus began the career of America's greatest showman. Seven years later, Barnum had another major hit on his hands in the form of the Fejee Mermaid, which was actually made from the body of a fish and the head and hands of a monkey and exhibited to a skeptical but fascinated paying public as a major scientific discovery.

Such popular hoaxes, or "humbugs," as they were called, made Barnum a household name and drew customers to his American Museum on New York's Broadway. The museum would become the best attended entertainment venue in the United States by the late 1840s. For twenty-five cents admission, New Yorkers and the growing body of out-of-town visitors would tour a collection featuring exotic animals and fish, skeletons, ethnological artifacts, recent inventions, wax portraits, and various curiosities. Or they might observe a baby contest or enjoy the performance of the talented or freakish. Barnum's museum combined the zoo, the aquarium, the natural history museum, the circus, the lecture hall, and the art gallery.

In 1850, Barnum's Museum also became an important theater. But instead of offering the typical stage entertainment of the era, Barnum dedicated the museum's lecture room to what he called "moral drama," a form of theater introduced in Boston a few years earlier by Moses Kimball. **Moral drama,** or "museum theater," as it was sometimes called, promised its patrons stage entertainment without any of the profanity or lewdness with which theater had long been associated. The plays themselves were typically melodramas that reinforced the popular middle-class reform causes of the era (see Chapter 12). Titles such as W. H. Smith's *The Drunkard,* Charles Saunders's *The Gambler,* and F. S. Hill's *Six Degrees of Crime; or Wine, Women, Gambling, Theft, and the Scaffold* reassured spectators that any depiction of vice would be framed by a morally instructive lesson. Museum theater managers also exerted tight control over their lecture halls, guaranteeing that the boisterous behavior of the traditional theater audience would not be tolerated.

These innovations were designed to make theatergoing a legitimate activity for women and families. Museum theater helped expand the American theater audience, repackaging the drama as a site of moral education, and redefining theater as a mixed-gender activity. By the end of the century, women would outnumber men in American theater audiences. More immediately, Barnum's lecture hall would provide the stage for numerous plays about slavery and race that would shape national debates in the antebellum era.

BLACKFACE MINSTRELSY

The new moral melodramas competed with Shakespearean tragedies and plays about the war in Mexico for the attention and disposable income of America's growing theater audiences, but no form of staged entertainment proved quite so popular in this period as **blackface minstrelsy.** Blackface entertainment took many forms in nineteenth-century America and proved adaptable to many different dramatic genres (including Shakespeare and moral melodrama), but its defining feature was the appearance on a public stage of a performer, typically but not necessarily a white man, with burnt cork or black paint on his face. Introduced in large northern cities around 1830, it achieved the height of its popularity in the late 1840s, and remained the dominant form of homegrown theater throughout the antebellum period and for some time thereafter. Blackface shows were immensely popular, but they also bore the stamp of elite approval. Minstrel troupes performed for several presidents, including Abraham Lincoln. It was the music of the blackface show that critics celebrated as America's national art.

Different blackface performers followed the same basic format, employed the same stock characters, and showcased many of the same songs and dances. American audiences through much of the North, Midwest, and far West were consuming essentially the same entertainment product (blackface was somewhat less popular in the South, in part because it was a primarily urban form of entertainment). The standard minstrel troupe featured four or five blackface performers wearing oversized, ragged costumes, and armed with banjos, fiddles, bone castanets, and tambourines. The show typically consisted of three parts: a selection of songs; a medley of novelty acts such as farcical dialogues, stump speeches riddled with malapropisms, and drag performances; and a narrative skit, usually set in the South, with dancing, music, and burlesque.

In these performances, the use of blackface was linked with representations of African Americans. The two stock characters who reappeared most frequently on the blackface stage popularized two stereotypes of black America. **Jim Crow** (which was the name of both a character and a dance) was a happy-go-lucky, contented plantation slave. Zip Coon, his northern counterpart, was an urban dandy, prone to mispronouncing or misusing big words, possessed of an inflated sense of social importance, and given to excesses of predatory sexual desire.

Much blackface performance rested on a foundation of racial contempt and animosity. White people dressed up as black people and ridiculed their bodies, their speech patterns, their

Virginia Serenaders, Sheet Music, 1844. By the 1840s, blackface minstrel troupes were appearing in most big cities in the North, filling five huge theaters in New York, for example, where large auditoriums seated several thousand spectators. **Question for Analysis:** Why does the title page show the Serenaders both in and out of their blackface costume?

INTERPRETING THE SOURCES

"Oh! Susanna"

It is difficult for modern readers to appreciate just how mainstream blackface entertainment was in the nineteenth century and how enduring its impact on American popular culture has been. Though its overt and crass racism might make it seem like a distant episode in the American past, much of what is now fondly remembered as classic American music had its origins on the blackface stage. The works of Stephen Foster are a good example. Foster's best-known songs, including "Camptown Races" (1850), "Old Folks at Home" (1851), "Jeannie with the Light Brown Hair" (1854), and "Old Black Joe" (1860), were written for the minstrel stage and designed to be sung with black inflections and performed in blackface. The original lyrics of one of Foster's best-known compositions, "Oh! Susanna" (1848), show this connection explicitly:

I came from Alabama, Wid a banjo on my knee,
I'm gwyne to Louisiana, My true love for to see.
It rain'd all night the day I left, The weather it was dry,
The sun so hot I froze to death; Susanna, don't you cry.
Chorus:
Oh! Susanna, Oh don't you cry for me,
cos' I've come from Alabama, Wid my banjo on my knee
I jumped aboard the telegraph, And trabbled down the riber,
De lectric fluid magnified, And killed five hundred nigger.
De bullgine bust, de horse run off, I really thought I'd die;
I shut my eyes to hold my breath, Susanna don't you cry.
CHO: Oh Susanna...
I had a dream the odder night, When ebery thing was still
I thought I saw Susanna A Coming down de hill;
The buck-wheat cake was in her mouth, The tear was in her eye;
Says I, "I'm coing from de south, Susanna, don't you cry."
CHO: Oh Susanna &c.
I soon will be in New Orleans, And den I'll look all round,
And When I find Susanna, I will fall upon de ground.
And If I do not find her, Dis Darkie'l surely die,
And when I'm dead and buried, Susanna, don't you cry.
CHO: Oh Susanna &c

OH, SUSANNA.

Written by S. C. Foster. Sung by Wood's Minstrels, 414 Broadway.

I've come from Alabama with the banjo on my knee,
I'm gwine to Louisiana my true lub for to see.
It rained all night the day I left, the wedder it was dry,
De sun so hot I froze to deff, Susanna don't you cry.

CHORUS AND REPART.

Oh, Susanna, don't you cry for me,
I've come from Alabama,
With the banjo on my knee.

Sheet Music for Stephen Foster's "Oh! Susanna!" Born near Pittsburgh in 1826, Foster moved to New York as a young man to become a songwriter. He stayed there until his alcohol-accelerated demise in 1864, but in his short career he became the first American to earn a living by writing music. While tens of thousands of urban Americans heard Foster's songs at blackface performances, many more encountered them in more intimate and informal settings, performed by amateurs who bought the sheet music.

Explore the Source

1. Who is the speaker, and why might he and Susanna be living apart?
2. Does the song present the speaker in a sympathetic light?
3. How would you explain why this song became the anthem of white gold-seekers bound for California in 1849?

social aspirations, and their claims to human dignity—all before an appreciative white audience. Enjoying a blackface performance was a way of claiming one's whiteness, which is part of the reason the shows proved particularly popular among new immigrants from Ireland, who hoped to gain equality with their nativist detractors under the white banner.

But the appeal of blackface to urban audiences went beyond racism. Many of the skits and songs did not touch on explicitly racist themes but used blackface to mark the performance as popular rather than elitist. Jim Crow and Zip Coon were American types who exposed the pretensions of the well-born and often had the last laugh. As such, blackface performances helped white Americans declare cultural independence from Europe. In addition, under the protective cover of blackface comedy, bawdy burlesque humor could be indulged, and transgressive sexual pleasures, such as cross-dressing and homoeroticism, could be both expressed and disclaimed. Blackface also created a sense of common culture among a transient urban population. Many of the most popular songs from the blackface stage, such as "The Old Folks at Home," "My Old Kentucky Home," and "Oh! Susanna" drew on themes of displacement and longing for home (see Interpreting the Sources: "Oh! Susanna"). Finally, skits and songs about carefree characters leading undisciplined work lives may have appealed with special force to an urban working class facing the early stages of industrialization.

Blackface promoters claimed that minstrel songs and dances were rooted in the slave experience and that blackface shows were what James Kennard called "operas of negro life." But blackface, like all popular American theater, was an urban phenomenon.

Minstrel composers grew up mostly in frontier cities like Pittsburgh and Cincinnati, and their intial audiences were in places like New York and Philadelphia. There is no evidence that blackface entertainment was the product of slaves or a reflection of slave life. Instead, it reflected white perceptions and fantasies of African American life in the North. Blackface emerged in places of racial intermingling and was a product of the encounter between white performers and the free people of color who sang, danced, dressed expressively, paraded, and socialized in the public spaces of northern and midwestern cities. Famous African American performers, such as William Henry Lane would appear on the blackface stage, and minstrel song lyrics referred to events and personages in the black dance world. Less flatteringly, blackface publicized the forms of ridicule by which whites attacked the aspirations of emancipated urban blacks to assert their freedom in public space.

Although blackface was a mass entertainment form that drew fans from across the social and political spectrum, it enjoyed a special relationship with the ideology and culture of the Democratic Party. Most of the major minstrel performers and composers were identified with the Democrats. Henry Wood, New York's leading minstrel promoter, was the brother of Benjamin and Fernando Wood, two of the leading Democratic politicians of the 1850s. Stephen Foster, blackface's preeminent composer, was related by marriage to Democratic president James Buchanan and wrote Democratic campaign songs. Blackface performances tended to embrace what the party stood for in the North—westward expansion, aggressive nationalism, anti-abolitionism, inclusive definitions of whiteness that accommodated recent immigrants, deep suspicion of reformers and evangelical pieties, and the championing of urban working-class entertainment tastes in defiance of elitist prejudices.

William Henry Lane. Better known as Master Juba, Lane achieved a transatlantic reputation as an acrobatic dancer and is sometimes credited as the inventor of tap dancing.

NATIONAL COMMUNICATION

Much as the original creation of the United States had required new processes of communication (see Chapter 7), the territorial expansion of the American republic posed new communication challenges. The expanded nation required new infrastructure and new symbols of shared identity to bind together a diverse citizenry spreading to unfamiliar parts of the continent. Already in the 1840s, a network of railroad tracks was beginning to form in the Northeast. By the middle of the next decade, the railroad would thoroughly displace the canal system as the nation's most powerful force and most conspicuous symbol of economic consolidation and long-distance connection (see Chapter 14). But long-distance communication in this period was not simply about building roads, canals, or rail lines. Various important innovations in the way Americans communicated with one another facilitated the mobility of people and ideas in the era of national expansion.

THE TELEGRAPH

During the early decades of the nineteenth century, the time it took for information to pass between one part of the country and another had been radically reduced—by improved roads, artificial waterways, entrepreneurial news providers, and more frequent and dense patterns of travel and commerce. But generally speaking, information moved only as fast as the human beings or animals that conveyed it. The exceptions to this rule were various optical signal systems, which had been introduced in France in the 1790s. These signal systems, which involved a series of visual displays relayed from one hill or tower to another, were known as *telegraphs*. Already in 1820, forty-five American newspapers used that word in their names to express the ideal of rapid communication over distances. Optical telegraphy was expensive to set up and limited in its reach, but in 1837 Samuel Morse (a painter by training) and Joseph Henry (a physicist) demonstrated the possibility of transmitting electromagnetic signals over wires. Morse, who secured a federal patent for the electromagnetic telegraph in 1840, synthesized and applied the discoveries and inventions of numerous scientists, promoted the new device with great vigor, and also developed a code that would become the international language of telegraphy.

Hyer versus Sullivan. In this 1849 bare-knuckle fight, one of the first American sports events to be followed by a national audience, American-born Bowery butcher Tom Hyer (the taller boxer) knocked out Irish immigrant Yankee Sullivan in less than twenty minutes.

In 1843, Morse persuaded Congress to appropriate $30,000 for the construction of a telegraph line between Washington and Baltimore. Though he squandered $23,000 of the grant trying to bury the wires below ground, Morse succeeded in building the line, and on May 22, 1844, he successfully transmitted the Biblical phrase "What hath god wrought" across forty miles. Morse fully expected the federal government to purchase his patent and regulate the use of the telegraph through the Post Office. He offered the patent for $100,000 and tried to drum up support by staging exhibitions and chess games over the wires. But Congress refused, and Morse turned to private investors, who funded the rapid construction of telegraph lines. By 1850, twelve thousand miles of telegraph wire stretched across the eastern half of the continent; by 1853, the total reached twenty-three thousand miles.

Because sending a message across these wires was extremely expensive—as much as $1 per word in the early years—the telegraph did not transform the way Americans communicated with one another. Telegraphy was used mostly by merchants, bankers, and others who needed to check someone's credit, relay commodity prices, or lock in the terms of a commercial transaction. But the impact of Morse's device on popular culture was nonetheless considerable, because the telegraph affected the way news was reported. In 1846, six major New York dailies agreed to share the costs of transmitting news from the Mexican War. This arrangement did not simply make it possible for New Yorkers to follow the war as it unfolded; it created the first wire service, called the Associated Press. Wire services created a new standard for speedy news flow and helped turn newspaper offices in large urban centers into major gathering spots for the reception of official information.

Although initially intended to harness the power of the telegraph for relaying war news, wire services could be used as well to turn other items of popular interest into mass media events. When boxers Tom Hyer and Yankee Sullivan squared off in a $10,000, winner-take-all prize fight in 1849, the bout attracted considerable interest. Partisans of Hyer (a native-born Whig) and Sullivan (an Irish-born Democrat who would later die in a San Francisco jail, facing trial at the hand of the Committee of Vigilance) identified passionately with their respective champions and wagered an estimated $300,000 on the outcome. Because prize-fighting was illegal, the Hyer versus Sullivan match was held in a secret location in Kent County, Maryland, in front of only a few hundred spectators. But all over urban America, fans crowded around newspaper offices to hear the results relayed round-by-round. In this way, the telegraph helped create the modern sports event as a contest followed in real time by a national audience.

Mail Call. Post office lines in San Francisco and Sacramento were notoriously long, and numerous reports told of men refusing offers of five, ten, even twenty dollars for their spot on line. Forty-niners were eager for news from home—and eager to show those they had left behind that their letters were more precious than money. Images of post office crowds were often designed as stationery in California and used for mailing letters home.

CHEAP POSTAGE

Although the federal government got out of the telegraph business, it continued to provide the infrastructure for national communication through the U.S. Post Office. During this period, postal service underwent a major transformation, however. In its early decades, the Post Office had been used primarily by merchants to conduct business and by publishers to circulate newspapers. Up until the 1840s, the mail was important for ordinary Americans primarily as a source of news. Sending a letter to friends or relatives was a significant event reserved for special occasions, except for those wealthy enough to afford very high rates of postage. Letter writers (or, more typically, letter recipients) were charged per sheet of paper and according to distance. Postage on a two-page letter traveling four hundred miles, say from Albany to Pittsburgh, would be fifty cents—more than half the average daily wage of the time. By the early 1840s, it cost eighteen and a half cents to mail a one-page letter from New York City up the Hudson River to Troy, New York, but just twelve cents to ship a barrel of flour over the same distance.

Beginning in 1845, a major change took place in the history of postal correspondence. Around the same time that private telegraph companies began assuming some of the role in news broadcasting and commercial exchange that had been the domain of the Post Office, Congress decided to enact postage reform, helping to turn the nation's postal system into a popular interactive medium. According to a new law in 1845, letters would now be assessed primarily on the basis of weight rather than distance, and rates were lowered radically to five cents per half-ounce for close distances and ten cents per half-ounce for greater distances. The Postal Act of 1851 extended this reform by setting the basic letter rate at five cents for a half-ounce letter addressed virtually anywhere in the country. If the sender prepaid the postage (for which purpose postage stamps had been introduced in 1847), it would cost only three cents. Citing a model introduced a few years earlier in Great Britain, postal reformers argued that the lower rates would be offset by the much higher volume of correspondence, because more Americans would develop new letter-writing habits. Lower postage was especially popular among Whigs, who placed a high premium on literacy and saw improvements in long-distance communication as essential to national expansion. But the fact that congressmen from both parties supported the reforms reflected their general optimism that enough Americans would want to send letters across the expanding nation to justify the new strategy. The era of postal reform marked the emergence of the mail as a popular medium for maintaining personal relationships at a distance.

Postal reductions and westward expansion went hand in hand. Westward migrants were especially likely to want to correspond with the communities they left behind. And events like the war with Mexico and the California gold rush dramatized before a national audience the utility of a postal network for connecting temporarily separated family members. Forty-niners left for California with promises to send news (and wealth) back to their wives and children, and upon arrival they

HOT COMMODITIES

Daguerreotype Portraits

When photography was introduced in France and Britain in 1839, its inventors and promoters imagined it would be primarily suitable for still-life depictions and landscapes. There was little reason to expect the camera to be used for personal portraiture. The daguerreotyping procedure, named for the French inventor Louis-Jacques-Mandé Daguerre, could produce remarkably faithful images, but it required lengthy exposure times—five minutes to an hour in its early years. Even once exposure times were reduced to twenty seconds, the composure necessary to sit for a portrait could be excruciating. Daguerreotype artists would position their subjects against iron head rests, and many early portraits show men and women in apparent discomfort.

Nonetheless, portraiture quickly became the dominant use of the daguerreotype in the United States. By midcentury, 90 percent of daguerreotypes taken nationwide were posed portraits of individuals or (less commonly) families. Daguerreotype portrait studios became big business, especially in cities. Within a decade of Daguerre's invention there were a hundred such studios in New York alone. And in the instant city of San Francisco, dozens of daguerreotype studios and salons appeared within a few years of the discovery of gold.

Daguerreotypes allowed middle-class families the opportunity to emulate the traditionally genteel, even aristocratic practice of displaying the portraits of relatives and ancestors. They also allowed Americans on the move to maintain visual contact with friends and family living at a distance. After the postage reductions of 1845 and 1851, daguerreotype portraits also became mobile. Before 1845, enclosing a picture in the mail would have doubled the cost of sending a one-page letter, but once the Post Office began charging by weight rather than by the sheet, photographs could be included at no extra charge.

Think About It

1. Why would photographic portraits have been especially popular in American cities and in California?
2. How might the circulation of photographic portraits have changed social relationships in the United States?

I Sell the Shadow to Support the Substance.
SOJOURNER TRUTH.

Sojourner Truth's Carte de Visite. After the introduction of photography, Americans could exchange calling cards that featured their own likenesses. By 1851, wet-plate collodion processes allowed for the mechanical reproduction of unlimited (and cheap) copies of a single image, and politicians, authors, and actors began using these cartes de visite as a form of publicity. The abolitionist orator Sojourner Truth used cartes de visite to support herself and raise funds for her cause.

wrote frequently of their desire for letters from home (see Hot Commodities: Daguerreotype Portraits). On "steamer days," when mail from the eastern states would be unloaded, the post offices in Sacramento and San Francisco became mob scenes.

NATIONAL LITERATURE

The decade after President Polk's election was also a time of explosive growth in American literature. An expanding publishing industry, headquartered in northeastern cities, circulated unprecedented volumes of fiction. Americans read much of this fiction in serial installments in newspapers and magazines, or in cheap soft-covered pamphlets sent in the mail. Because there were no international copyright laws (Congress was more interested in promoting the spread of reading than in protecting the property rights of authors), publishers could reprint foreign works without having to pay royalties. But several American authors produced best-selling books as well. Female novelists such as Maria Cummins, Susan Warner, and Fanny Fern reached tens of thousands of readers in the middle of the nineteenth century with fiction that explored and celebrated the private feelings and sympathies of their characters and focused on family relationships. This body of novels, often classified by critics as **sentimental literature,** included Harriet Beecher Stowe's antislavery novel *Uncle Tom's Cabin* (see Chapter 14), which would become the best-selling American novel of the century.

Stowe's novel also had elements of another popular fiction genre, often designated **sensational literature** and typically authored by men. Best-selling sensational fiction included the adventure stories and melodramas of the nativist author Ned Buntline, reform tracts such as T. S. Arthur's *Ten Nights in a Bar-Room* (see Chapter 12), the soft-core pornographic novels of George Thompson, and George Lippard's *The Quaker City*. Lippard's 1845 novel, which was based on a Philadelphia murder that had dominated the local news, promised to expose the "Secret Life of Philadelphia" and entertained readers with stories of seduction, rape, murder, and the corruption of city life. Lippard himself was a prominent advocate of westward expansion and donated much of the money he earned from his literary career to a campaign for distributing western land to the nation's urban working class. More generally, popular sensationalist fiction after 1845 celebrated the expanding American frontier as a place where adventurous men from different classes, parties, and regions could overcome their differences and unite under the banner of American manhood.

It was in this same short period that the poets, novelists, and essayists now considered the giants of nineteenth-century literature produced their classic works. Herman Melville, Walt Whitman, Edgar Allan Poe, Emily Dickinson, Ralph Waldo Emerson, Henry David Thoreau, and Nathaniel Hawthorne were not nearly as well read in their day as Warner, Lippard, or Stowe, but by the middle of the twentieth century, they became part of the American cultural canon and their work came to represent what critics call the **American Renaissance.** Their most enduring writing (including *Moby Dick*, *The Scarlet Letter*, *Walden*, and *Leaves of Grass*) first appeared in print in the years 1850–1855, at a time when Americans were grappling with the implications of their expanded nation.

Several of the leading figures in the American Renaissance, including Melville, Whitman, and Hawthorne, were part of a New York–based literary circle that revolved around the nation's most famous expansionist journal, the *Democratic Review*. The journal's literary editor, Evert Duyckinck, became a spokesman for the Young America movement in American literature. Authors in this circle cared deeply about politics and attributed enormous political significance to literature. They were optimistic about the United States and eager to enhance its reputation, spread its influence, and expand its territorial sovereignty. They also supported nationalist republican movements in Europe (see The Revolutions of 1848), were obsessed with youth, were friendly to the labor movement, and favored extending suffrage across class lines. But they were far cooler to middle-class reform causes such as temperance, women's suffrage, and abolitionism; and like the blackface performers and promoters, they were strongly identified with the Democratic Party.

THE AMERICAN NATION IN THE WORLD

Because the Mexican cession and the Oregon settlement added territories that extended the United States to the Pacific and established what are more or less the nation's current continental borders, it is tempting to think that the project of expansionism was complete and America's manifest destiny fulfilled. But nationalists in 1848 did not see it that way. Many American politicians, writers, and adventurers gazed with interest at other parts of the globe and saw new opportunities for American influence and new frontiers for U.S. expansion.

THE REVOLUTIONS OF 1848

On February 21, 1848, with new the Treaty of Guadalupe Hidalgo freshly arrived at the U.S. capital, Americans learned of the Paris uprising that signaled the beginning of a new revolution against the French monarchy. This was the first of the revolutions of 1848, which erupted through much of the European continent. Over the course of the year, liberal nationalist movements sought to establish new republican governments within the sprawling, multiethnic Hapsburg Empire centered in Austria. Uprisings in Hungary, Bohemia, German-speaking lands, the Balkan region, and the Italian peninsula declared independence from the Hapsburgs and envisioned a new era of liberal nation-states in central Europe. By 1849, however, some of the coalitions that had supported these uprisings had fallen apart and conservative forces were able to restore Hapsburg rule.

American nationalists greeted the revolutions of 1848 enthusiastically. Many relished the prospect of the toppling of old European regimes. Some celebrated the idea that republican revolutions were extending an American empire of liberty eastward. When the exiled Hungarian nationalist leader Lajos Kossuth toured the United States in 1851, following the defeat of his revolution by Russian forces, he received a hero's welcome throughout the country. Tens of thousands of spectators met his ship upon arrival in New York, a congressional banquet was held in his honor, and Kossuth paraphernalia appeared in stores across the nation. Supporters of the Young America movement were among Kossuth's loudest fans and portrayed him as the representative of American freedom in an Old World ruled by despots.

Kossuth hoped to parlay his American popularity into foreign aid that would enable him to launch a second revolution, but here he failed. Though private individuals donated to the Hungarian cause, the U.S. government was loath to antagonize the Hapsburgs and become enmeshed in European wars. And over the course of his visit, the Kossuth mania subsided. Irish Americans, many of whom saw Kossuth as an enemy of the Catholic Church, grew critical. Southerners worried that his speeches on behalf of freedom would embolden the critics of slavery. Kossuth was careful to avoid that topic, but this only alienated abolitionists, who accused him of pandering or hypocrisy. Unable to navigate the tensions of U.S. sectional politics, he headed back to Europe in 1852 without having achieved his real goal, but the American nationalism that had turned Kossuth into a star did not diminish.

FILIBUSTERS

The Treaty of Guadalupe Hidalgo did not satisfy many Americans' desires for territorial expansion. Democrats in particular clamored for further acquisitions and made expansionism a consistent plank in their party platform even after the war. In 1848, they ran Lewis Cass for president against the Whigs' war hero, Zachary Taylor. Cass had advocated taking all of Mexico during the war and supported annexing Cuba as well. Cass was defeated by Taylor (who died in 1850 and was succeeded by Millard Fillmore), but Democrats continued to push for expansion into Mexico, Central America, the Caribbean, and the

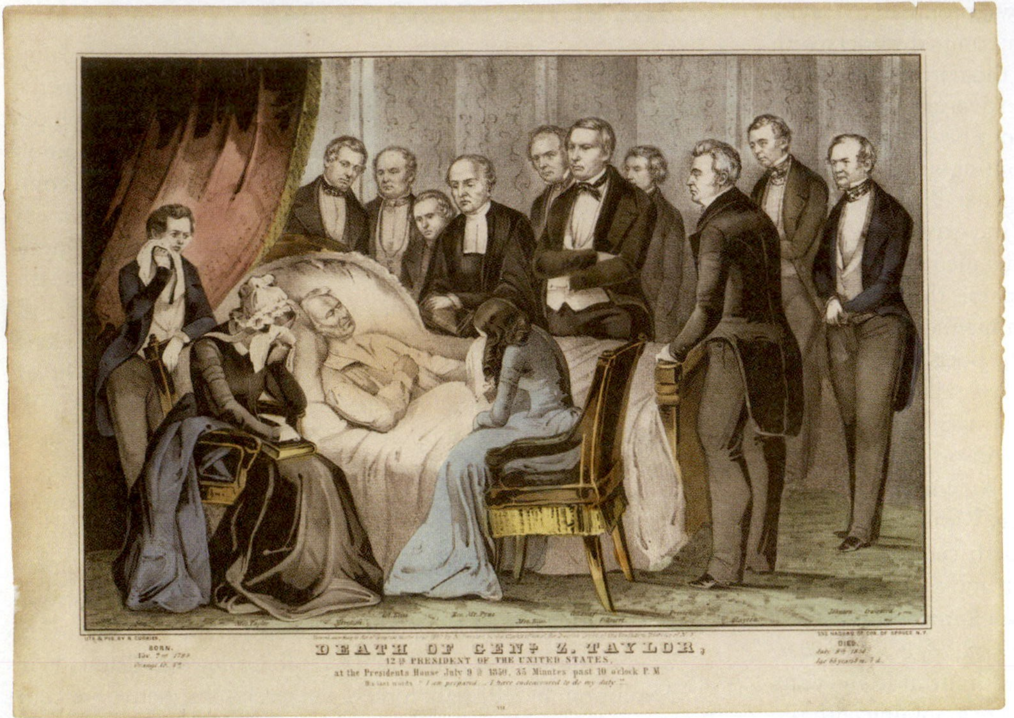

President Taylor's Death. Like William Henry Harrison (the only other Whig elected to the presidency), Zachary Taylor served a short term in office. Conspiracy theorists would later accuse the Slave Power of orchestrating the deaths of these two presidents out of fear that they would thwart the expansion of slavery. Forensic evidence supports the hypothesis that Taylor died from acute gastroenteritis.

Pacific. When Democrats retook the presidency in 1852 with the election of Franklin Pierce, the United States pressed Mexico to cede more land, resulting in the Gadsden Purchase, and tried hard to wrest Cuba from the Spanish.

Where the U.S. government failed or refused to go, individual American citizens took matters into their own hands. The Mexican War triggered a rash of filibuster campaigns in which private armies used American territory and American expansionist ideals as a launching pad for invading foreign countries. Derived from a Spanish word meaning freebooter (pirate), American **filibusters** (the word denotes both the invader and the invasion) entered British Canada, Mexico, Ecuador, Honduras, Cuba, and Nicaragua—and contemplated invasions of the Hawaiian Islands. These campaigns violated international law, which the United States had reaffirmed in the 1818 Neutrality Act, and the federal government officially disavowed them. But filibusters enjoyed significant popularity during the postwar years, in both the North and the South, especially among Democrats.

Filibusters were motivated by various desires for private gain, adventure, and masculine honor, but most of the men who led these expeditions also imagined that they would ultimately be extending U.S. sovereignty over new land. This was not an entirely unreasonable expectation. After all, Texas provided a model for how a revolution by Americans acting without the sanction of their government could ultimately bring about annexation. The filibusters who invaded Sonora, Cuba, or Nicaragua anticipated a similar process as they sought to fulfill the nation's manifest destiny.

Though thousands of Americans participated in the filibusters, they did not succeed. Joseph Morehead's foray into the Mexican state of Sonora was rebuffed in Baja California in 1851. California state senator Henry Crabb met his death while leading a similar expedition in 1857. Venezuela-born Narciso López founded the Junta Cubana in New York in 1848, attracting significant American support for his attempt at revolution in Cuba, but he was executed on the island in 1851. Tennessean William Walker seized power in Nicaragua from 1855 to 1857 (he reintroduced slavery there, hoping to attract southern support for annexation), but he was ousted and eventually shot to death in Honduras in 1860.

In retrospect, these ventures may seem foolhardy, but filibusters saw themselves as the vanguard of American imperial expansion, fighting on the side of history. They had no reason to believe that the pace of U.S. territorial acquisition would slacken. In 1853, the *Democratic Review* (a prominent supporter of the López filibuster) imagined the nation's borders creeping progressively southward into Mexico and spreading "a penumbra over the West Indies." Several years later the magazine asserted that "no well-informed person entertains the shadow of a doubt" that Cuba and Mexico would become states in the growing union.

NEW COMMERCIAL FRONTIERS

Whigs were less eager to add new territory to a nation already beset by sectional controversy over the extension of slavery. Instead they sought to expand the nation's power and influence by opening up new trade networks and building a commercial empire in the Pacific. Whig president Fillmore instructed naval commander Matthew Perry to sail to Japan with heavily armed ships, to pressure the Japanese to open up their ports to American traders. The first Perry expedition reached Edo (now called Tokyo) in 1853 and conveyed a letter from President Fillmore. A year later, a second expedition resulted in the signing of the Treaty of Kanagawa, under which Japan agreed to limited diplomatic and commercial relations with the United States. The United States would now be able to compete in the growing world of Pacific trade.

CONCLUSION

A decade after Congress voted to annex Texas, the United States was a sprawling transcontinental nation with new links to the Pacific world. Many of its citizens expected further extension of the nation's borders and harbored ambitions for an expansive American empire. But even the way things stood in 1854, the United States had become a very different place in a very short time. Territorial expansion attracted new streams of foreign migration and accelerated the dispersal of the native-born population. Various forces, including railroads, telegraph wires, cheap postage, print culture, and commercial entertainment, helped forge links among a mobile populace. But the era of nationalist expansion would pose new threats to the political unity of the country. By 1854, the compromises and coalitions that had contained sectional conflict over slavery were already straining and struggling to survive.

STUDY TERMS

Texas annexation (p. 324)
manifest destiny (p. 325)
Young America (p. 325)
electromagnetic telegraph (p. 327)
San Patricio battalion (p. 328)
Resistance to Civil Government (p. 329)
Oregon settlement (p. 329)
Wilmot Proviso (p. 329)
Treaty of Guadalupe Hidalgo (p. 330)
Gadsden Purchase (p. 330)
Overland Trail (p. 331)
Donner party (p. 332)
California gold rush (p. 333)
forty-niners (p. 334)
Californios (p. 335)
Foreign Miners Taxes (p. 336)
Committee of Vigilance (p. 338)
Mormon exodus (p. 338)
Deseret (p. 338)
Astor Place Riot (p. 339)
American Museum (p. 340)
moral drama (p. 341)
blackface minstrelsy (p. 341)
Jim Crow (p. 341)
Associated Press (p. 344)
Hyer versus Sullivan (p. 344)
postage reform (p. 345)
sentimental literature (p. 346)
sensational literature (p. 346)
American Renaissance (p. 347)
revolutions of 1848 (p. 347)
filibusters (p. 348)

TIMELINE

1844 Samuel Morse successfully demonstrates electromagnetic telegraph

James Knox Polk elected president on an expansionist platform

1845 Texas annexed

First postage reduction passed by Congress

1846 Congress declares war on Mexico

Britain and United States settle Oregon boundary

Associated Press created in New York

Brigham Young leads Mormon exodus to Utah

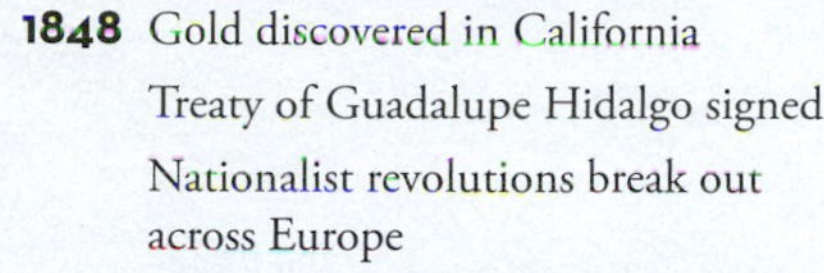

1848 Gold discovered in California

Treaty of Guadalupe Hidalgo signed

Nationalist revolutions break out across Europe

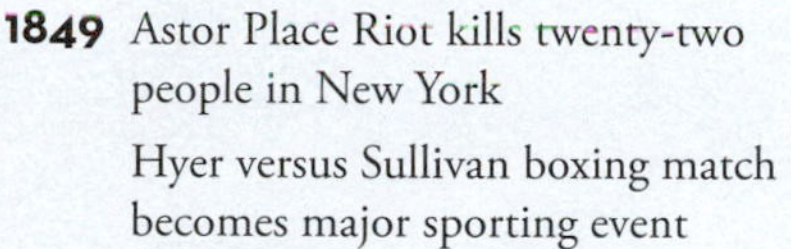

1849 Astor Place Riot kills twenty-two people in New York

Hyer versus Sullivan boxing match becomes major sporting event

WORKING MEN
SHALL
AMERICANS
OR
ENGLISH RULE!
IN THIS CITY!
ENGLISH ARISTOCRATIC!
OPERA HOUSE!
WORKINGMEN! FREEMEN!!
STAND BY YOUR
LAWFUL RIGHTS!
AMERICAN COMMITTEE.

1853 Matthew Perry's expedition arrives in Japan

United States acquires additional land from Mexico in the Gadsden Purchase

1854 Treaty of Kanagawa initiates new era of Pacific trade relations

1855 William Walker assumes power in Nicaragua

1856 For the second time, a Committee of Vigilance takes over San Francisco

FURTHER READING

Additional suggested readings are available on the Online Learning Center at www.mhhe.com/becomingamerica1e.

James Cook, *The Arts of Deception* (2001), treats P. T. Barnum as the central figure in a popular culture obsessed with fraudulent or misleading appearances.

Brian DeLay, *War of a Thousand Deserts* (2008), explains the importance of Indian raids to the course of Mexican history and the success of the U.S. invasion of Mexico.

John Mack Faragher, *Women and Men on the Overland Trail* (1979), explores the experiences and world views of rural white midwesterners who trekked across the Rockies at midcentury.

Amy Greenberg, *Manifest Manhood and the Antebellum American Empire* (2005), shows the importance of competing ideas of masculinity in the controversies over filibuster expeditions and nationalist expansion.

Amy Greenberg, *A Wicked War* (2012), chronicles the political dramas and bitter controversies surrounding the U.S. invasion of Mexico.

Daniel Walker Howe, *What Hath God Wrought* (2007), includes an especially strong account of the politics of the U.S.-Mexican War and the role of information exchange in that event.

Albert Hurtado, *Indian Survival on the California Frontier* (1990), details the impact of Mexican and American settlements on native life in California.

Susan Lee Johnson, *Roaring Camp* (2000), studies gender roles in the southern mining camps of the California gold rush.

Alexander Saxton, *The Rise and Fall of the White Republic* (1991), illuminates the connections between American popular culture and Democratic Party politics.

Shelley Streeby, *American Sensations* (2002), analyzes the images of Mexico, race, and imperial expansion that suffused popular literature during this period.

Graham White and Shane White, *Stylin'* (1998), describes the expressive culture of free blacks in the North, which became the subject of racist ridicule on the blackface stage.

14

INSIDE

THE BIG PICTURE

Newly acquired territory and expanding networks of transportation pushed the United States to determine the status of slavery in the western half of the continent. Compromises and stratagems designed to preserve the political balance between the North and the South wound up intensifying the conflict between increasingly incompatible positions on slavery and crippling both major political parties. In the new geography of the 1850s, the western states of Illinois and Missouri now appeared central to the future of the union.

Dismal Swamp. Runaway slaves often negotiated treacherous terrain, and their flight sparked political instability. (Thomas Moran, *Slave Hunt, Dismal Swamp, Virginia*. © 2014 Philbrook Museum of Art, Inc., Tulsa, Oklahoma.)

1848–1860

A UNION UNRAVELING

On June 2, 1854, life in the city of Boston ground to a halt as its inhabitants gathered to watch a single African American man walk down the middle of State Street on a Friday afternoon. A military force of nearly one thousand men cleared the streets and guarded the man's procession with orders to fire on the crowd if necessary. Anthony Burns, the man of the hour, was an enslaved Virginian who had run away to Boston and become an active member of that city's free black community. But a month earlier, his putative owner, Charles Francis Suttle, had secured an arrest warrant for Burns under the controversial Fugitive Slave Act that had been passed four years earlier. Having been certified as the man named in the warrant, Burns was now in military custody, bound for the South.

From the moment Suttle's warrant was issued, the city of Boston had been awash in agitation over the case. Boston's abolitionists pursued a wide range of legal and extralegal strategies to secure Burns's release. Hours of prestigious legal counsel, reams of inflammatory handbills, and dozens of impassioned exhortations from Protestant pulpits were mustered in his defense. There was even an attempt at armed rescue, in which genteel clergymen, Harvard law students, black dockworkers, and prominent white attorneys wielded axes and pistols and mounted battering rams. This assault on his jail cell failed to free Burns and resulted in the death of James Batchelder, an Irish-born truckman who was part of the marshal's guard. Finally, several of Burns's supporters, both white and black, tried unsuccessfully to purchase him from Suttle.

On the other side of this battle stood not only Suttle, the Virginia slaveholder, but also the federal government, which spent $14,000 to secure Burns's return to Virginia and demonstrate its commitment to the recapture of fugitive slaves. Some of the Bostonians lining State Street on June 2 were on the government's side. A few were conservative elites and merchants in the cotton business who feared the shocking turn to civil disobedience in their city and sought to preserve good relations with the South. But more were Irish immigrants hostile to abolitionism and to the nativist Protestants who rallied to Burns's defense. Many of these immigrants staffed the marshal's guard and the militia. At the end of Burns's procession, gleeful militiamen taunted the fugitive with a chorus of the popular blackface minstrel strong, "Carry Me Back to Old Virginny." And with that, Anthony Burns boarded a ship and returned to slavery.

KEY QUESTIONS

- How did the Compromise of 1850 unsettle the political conflict over slavery?
- Which events escalated and dramatized the antagonism between proponents and opponents of the westward expansion of slavery?
- How did changes in transportation infrastructure encourage new experiences of time and space and forge stronger connections between particular regions?
- How did ideas about work, race, and religion, shape the escalating sectional conflict?
- What factors contributed to the breakdown of the two-party system?

Anthony Burns was by no means the first fugitive slave to be recovered in the North (or even in Boston) after 1850, but this particular trial pricked white consciences and fired the imaginations of previously inert supporters of free labor. His forced return to Virginia (where he sat in a Richmond jail cell until his friends managed to purchase his freedom) stoked the flames of political conflict in places like Boston but also underscored a bigger threat to national unity. Fugitive slave cases unsettled the moral boundaries of slavery. The United States was a nation half slave and half free, but those two halves were increasingly entangled and interconnected. Laws requiring the citizens of Massachusetts to enforce the claims of Virginia slaveholders helped burst the illusion that free and slave states could peacefully coexist as separate cultural and political worlds.

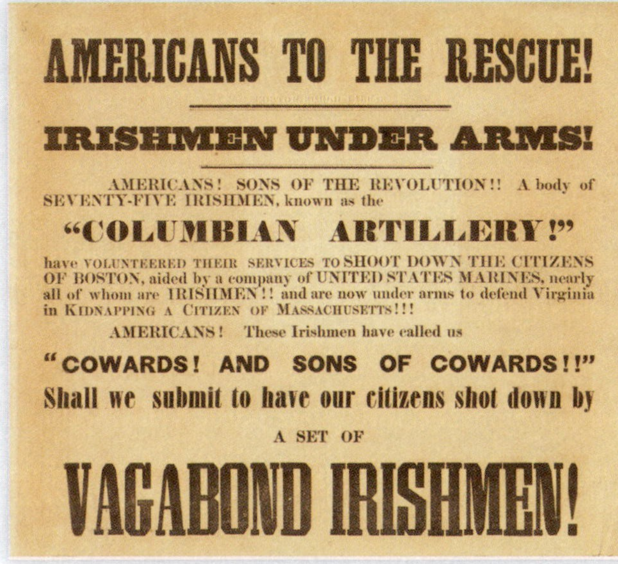

Antislavery (and anti-Irish) posters rallied Bostonians to the defense of a fugitive.

One of the central paradoxes of the 1850s was that southerners and northerners gravitated toward irreconcilably opposed positions on the slavery question, even as the nation as a whole became, in other ways, more unified. Economic ties, expanded communication, population movement, and, most dramatically, an emerging railroad system all reshuffled the national map, making distant places seem more connected. The emerging lines of long-distance connection tended to run along an east-west axis, however, speeding the east-west flow of people, commodities, and information and forging new coalitions between northerners and midwesterners. Newly acquired western territories, over a thousand miles away from the nation's capital, became the subjects of intense debate on the Atlantic seaboard and strained the relationship between North and South.

The political system that had produced compromise in 1820 began to buckle under the weight of the Mexican Cession of 1848, and sectional tensions escalated on a number of connected fronts: in the western territories, on the streets of Boston, in the halls of Congress, at the Supreme Court, and at the geographical borders that purportedly divided North from South. National political parties that had once appealed to voters on both sides of this sectional partition could no longer do so, and by the end of the 1850s a stark choice between two hostile political positions would rip the nation apart.

COMPROMISES AND BOUNDARIES

The Mexican cession of 1848 extended U.S. sovereignty over foreign lands and populations and fulfilled expansionists' dreams of a transcontinental nation. But the new map of the United States raised novel questions about the character of that nation (see Map 13.5). As the federal government sought to organize its newly acquired territories and admit states into the union, the thirty-year political truce brokered by the Missouri Compromise broke down. Instead of extending the horizontal divide between slavery and free labor westward at the 36°30′ latitude, Congress relied on a complex set of new compromises to maintain the political balance between North and South.

THE ELECTION OF 1848

Although David Wilmot's 1846 proposal to ban slavery in any territory acquired as a result of the war against Mexico failed to become law (see Chapter 13), it provided the rallying cry for a new political movement in the North. Few supporters of the Wilmot Proviso advocated abolishing slavery where it existed or freeing any of the three million African Americans held in bondage at the time. But they insisted that Congress had the right to regulate slavery in territories that had not yet become states, and most of them wished to preserve the nation's western lands as "free soil" for white settlers. As the 1848 election approached and the two major parties refused to embrace free soil principles, many northerners bolted the Whigs and the Democrats to form a Free Soil Party, nominating a ticket of Democratic ex-president Martin Van Buren and Boston's Whig leader Charles Francis Adams (son of John Quincy Adams).

The Free Soil coalition drew many Wilmot Proviso supporters from both major parties in the most populous northern states, as well as more hard-core antislavery voters who had cast their ballots for the Liberty Party four years earlier. But they failed to win any states and captured only 10 percent of the popular vote. Competing closely in both slave and free states were the two major-party contenders, war hero Zachary Taylor, a Louisiana slaveholder running on the Whig ticket, and Lewis Cass, a Michigan Democrat who favored aggressive westward expansion and did not seem to care whether slavery entered the new territories. Taylor narrowly won the contest, helped in part by the defections of Democrats in New York to Van Buren. The election of 1848 seemed to demonstrate that the major parties could maintain their national coalitions even in the face of the slavery controversy. But the ominous appearance of Van Buren, the architect of the Second Party System (see Chapter 10), at the head of an army of rebellious northern Democrats, foretold troubles for the political order.

THE COMPROMISE OF 1850

Upon taking office in 1849, President Taylor surprised his southern supporters by charting a course that seemed likely to help the North. Hoping to preempt controversy over the status of slavery in the new territories, Taylor began pushing for immediate statehood for California and New Mexico, where American settlers had already drafted and adopted free-labor constitutions. Southerners in both parties protested this plan, however, and a major debate over the westward expansion of slavery ensued.

Some Democrats proposed using the Missouri Compromise line and simply dividing the new territories between the North and the South (see Map 14.1). Missouri senator Thomas Benton, who had helped broker the original 1820 compromise, continued to pin his hopes on the geographical line and to tout the special role of St. Louis as a central city that could lead the nation down a middle path on the slavery question. But congressional opinion was now more polarized than it had been thirty years earlier. The idea of cutting the national map in half and splitting the difference had become unacceptable to increasing numbers of Americans on both sides. Antislavery senators like Salmon P. Chase and William H. Seward spoke for a growing body of northern politicians who would not countenance the introduction of slavery into any part of the country where it was not already legal. Proslavery spokesman John C. Calhoun, on the other hand, now took the view that the federal government had no constitutional right to restrict slavery at all. During the 1850s, this view became the party line among southerners known as **fire-eaters,** who felt that any concession on slavery would lead to abolition. A third position, which Cass had embraced during the presidential campaign, favored letting the status of slavery in the West be determined by **popular sovereignty**—a vote of a territory's local settlers. Illinois Democrat Stephen A. Douglas touted popular sovereignty as a viable political compromise, but it marked a major departure from the principles of earlier compromises, because it ceded a crucial element of federal control over the territories and did nothing to secure the balance of power in the Senate.

After months of debate and the sudden death of President Taylor, Congress passed a series of laws, which together became known as the Compromise of 1850. Authored by an aging Henry Clay and refined by Stephen Douglas, the compromise was not a single piece of legislation (which could not pass) but rather a cluster of different measures that Congress enacted separately. Taken together, the compromise appeared to give something to each side of the debate (see Table 14.1). It admitted

TABLE 14.1 MAJOR PROVISIONS OF THE COMPROMISE OF 1850

Advantages to the South: Stricter fugitive slave law; status of slavery in New Mexico and Utah territories to be determined by popular sovereignty (despite Utah's location north of the Missouri Compromise line); Texas receives debt relief; slavery not abolished in D.C.
Advantages to the North: California admitted as a free state; Texas relinquishes western land claims; slave trade abolished in D.C.

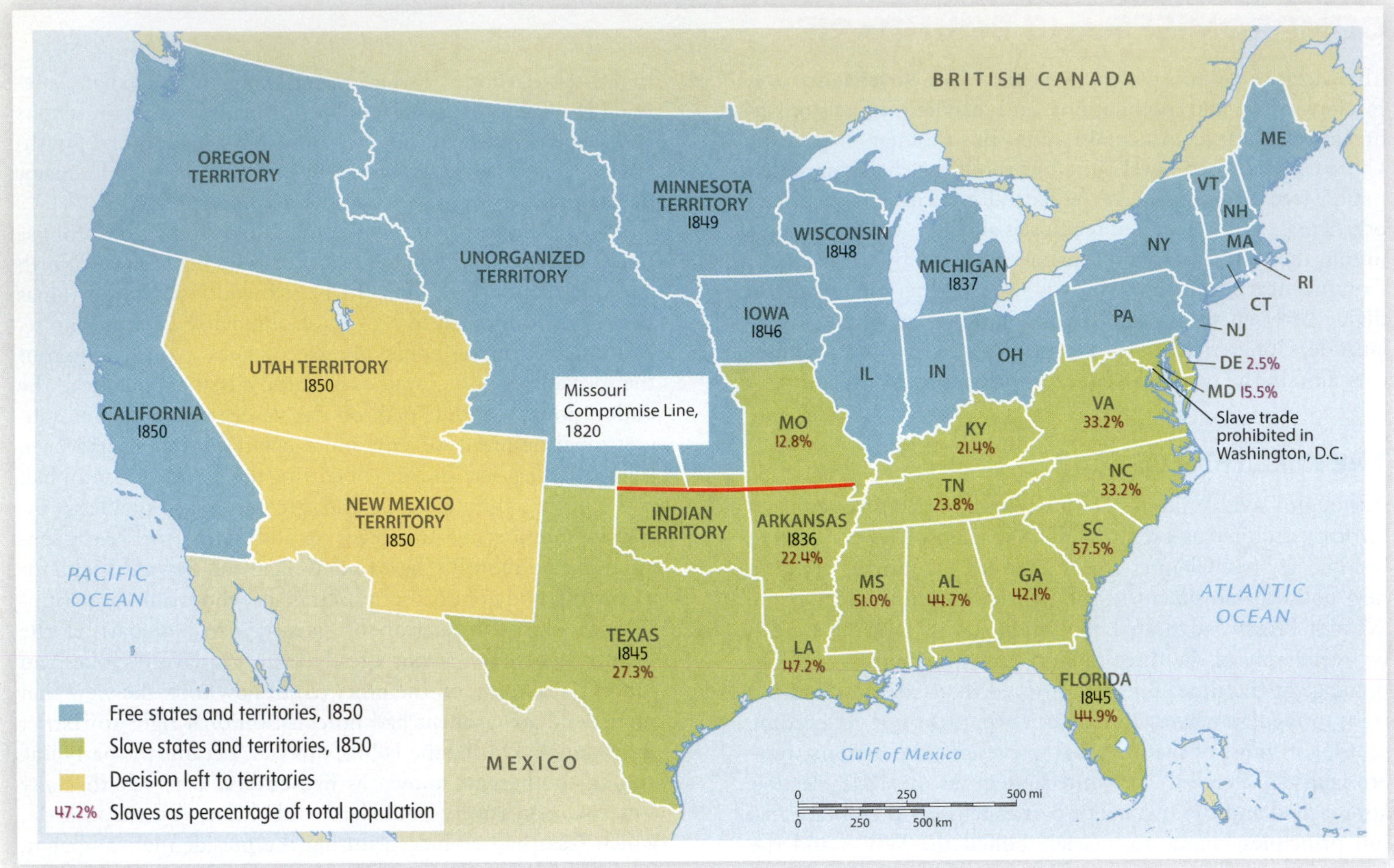

Map 14.1 The Compromise of 1850 (with the Missouri Compromise line shown). The compromise preserved the balance between slave and free states but introduced new principles for determining the status of slavery in the western half of the continent. Note that extending the Missouri Compromise line westward would have split California into two states with a border just north of Los Angeles.

California as a free state but determined that the status of slavery in the new territories of New Mexico and Utah would be decided by popular sovereignty at a later point, when those territories were ready for statehood. New Mexico also received a generous eastern boundary that had previously been contested by Texas. At the same time, Congress abolished the slave trade, but not slavery itself, in the nation's capital. As the linchpin of the deal, a stricter fugitive slave law went into effect, making it easier for slaveholders to recover their human property in other parts of the country.

Because the Compromise of 1850 contained so many different provisions, observers could (and did) disagree about which section's interests or which approach to the slavery question had prevailed. With the addition of California, free states now outnumbered slaves states by sixteen to fifteen, giving them two more votes in the Senate. But slave states could hope to restore the balance in the future, now that Congress had opened the door for popular sovereignty in the other western territories. The South could also take comfort from the fact that Congress had still refused to abolish slavery anywhere, even in Washington, D.C., where it had sole jurisdiction. The clear losers in the debate were those who had favored updating and extending the Missouri Compromise. That model of managing the slavery conflict was now obsolete.

FUGITIVE SLAVES

By far the most controversial plank of the Compromise of 1850 was the Fugitive Slave Act. There was nothing new about the legal requirement that people legally enslaved in one state had to be returned to their owners, even if they escaped to another part of the country where slavery was illegal. Such a provision appeared explicitly in the U.S. Constitution and was reinforced by congressional legislation in 1793. But the 1850 Fugitive Slave Act tilted the legal scales decisively against accused runaways and dramatically increased the obligation of citizens in free states to cooperate with slave catchers. According to the new law, someone charged with being a runaway slave was not entitled to a jury trial and could not use most customary forms of legal defense. An alleged fugitive could not contest the legality of slavery, nor could he or she even contest the claim that he or she was legally enslaved; the only permissible

Debating the Fugitive Slave Act in Congress. In this 1855 engraving depicting debate over the Compromise of 1850, Senator Henry Clay speaks to his colleagues. The fugitive slave issue stirred passionate rhetoric like that of George Julian, a Free Soil representative from Indiana: If "I believed the people I represent were base enough to become the miserable flunkies of a God-forsaken southern slave hunter by joining him or his constable in the blood-hound chase of a panting slave, I would scorn to hold a seat on this floor by their suffrages, and I would denounce them as fit subjects themselves for the lash of the slave-driver."

defense was that he or she was not the person listed on the warrant. The trial of an accused runaway would be a summary proceeding before a federal magistrate, enforced immediately and without possibility of appeal. The act also offered financial incentives for magistrates to certify a suspect as a fugitive slave and empowered federal marshals to require citizens' help in enforcing the law.

The Fugitive Slave Act brought the slavery conflict from the halls of Congress to the towns and cities of the North and West. Slaveholders and their agents pursued runaways in border states, deep into New England, and as far away as California. In short order, New York, Philadelphia, Harrisburg, Syracuse, and Detroit became battlegrounds, as ex-slaves, free blacks, and white abolitionists resisted the new law. In Christiana, Pennsylvania, armed African Americans killed two white men from Maryland who were trying to recover a fugitive. In Boston, which had been a magnet for escaped slaves, as many as one-fifth of the city's black residents were subject to being reclaimed as property under the Fugitive Slave Act, and many others worried about being mistakenly apprehended or falsely accused. A substantial portion of the community fled to Canada during the immediate aftermath of the Compromise of 1850. But most stayed, and Boston became the main stage for the fight over enforcing the new law. In 1851, black Bostonians successfully rescued Frederick "Shadrach" Minkins from federal marshals and sent him off to Canada. Two months later, the marshals prevailed in the recapture of another Boston fugitive, Thomas Sims. And in 1854, the Anthony Burns case (see opening vignette) proved a galling and humiliating defeat for Boston's antislavery community.

In the six years following passage of the Fugitive Slave Act, three runaways were forcibly rescued from their captors, whereas almost two hundred people were returned to bondage. Both numbers are negligible in the context of more than three million slaves and over a thousand runaways a year. But the impact on white opinion in the North was far greater. By bringing the drama of slave capture to northern soil, the Fugitive Slave Act blurred the lines between North and South and gave credence to the

"Police Conveying Sims to Vessel," 1851. The recapture of Thomas Sims became an initial test case for the constitutionality of the Fugitive Slave Act. Lemuel Shaw, chief justice of the Massachusetts Supreme Court, ruled in favor of the act. Shaw was Herman Melville's father-in-law, and Melville's famous story *Billy Budd,* which explores the conflict between law and moral conscience, has been read as an allegorical meditation on the Fugitive Slave Act.

abolitionist argument that slavery was not simply a southern institution. Garrison and his followers had insisted since the 1830s that every citizen of the United States bore moral responsibility for slavery. After 1850, the logic of that position was especially compelling. Federal magistrates and marshals made it clear that slavery had legal legitimacy in Boston and Detroit, and not just in Charleston and New Orleans. Individual states sought to nullify or thwart the Fugitive Slave Act, but it was a crucial part of the political compromise over slavery in the territories, and the federal government was committed to its enforcement.

UNCLE TOM'S CABIN

Against the backdrop of the new moral and political map created by the Fugitive Slave Act, Harriet Beecher Stowe was persuaded by her friends to write *Uncle Tom's Cabin.* Stowe grew up the daughter of Lyman Beecher, New England's leading Congregationalist minister. From age twenty-one to age thirty-nine, Stowe lived in Cincinnati, the largest city on the Ohio River, which was one of the major borders between free states and slave states. Stowe's novel would reinforce the Ohio River's place in the popular imagination as the symbolic divide between southern slavery and northern freedom. In one of the book's most haunting scenes, the heroine (an enslaved woman named Eliza) flees across the frozen river clutching her son Harry, with a slave trader and his dogs in hot pursuit. But much of the novel describes the horrors of plantation life for those held in bondage on the other side of the water.

Stowe painted a picture of the South that emphasized the domestic slave trade and its tendency to break up slave families, but it also contained sensational descriptions of cruel and sadistic masters. The book also dealt with themes that were standard fare in the sentimental literature of the day (see Chapter 13), such as the nurturing home and courageous patience in the face of suffering. *Uncle Tom's Cabin* was serialized in the antislavery paper *The National Era* in 1851–1852 and then published as a book in May 1852. The novel was phenomenally successful. By 1857, half a million copies had been sold in the United States and over a million in England. It was translated into French, Italian, German, Russian, Finnish, Javanese, Hindi, Armenian, and many other languages. No book other than the Bible was as widely purchased in nineteenth-century America.

Like the Fugitive Slave Act itself, *Uncle Tom's Cabin* brought vivid images of slavery to northern audiences and raised the volume of sectional conflict. Southern readers paid attention to Stowe's novel as well, and they attacked it bitterly. Southern reviewers criticized her for describing slavery without ever having visited a plantation, and several charged that she must have been a depraved woman indeed to make up such scenes of sensational cruelty from her own imagination. Others responded with novels of their own. Books like *Uncle Robin in his Cabin in Virginia and Tom without One in Boston* (1855) and *New England's Chattels* (1858) made the familiar proslavery argument that southern slaves were better off than workers in the North. Other responses to Stowe's novel were less literary. In 1853, she received in the mail, presumably from the South, a package containing a black human ear.

Uncle Tom's Cabin was a media sensation, but its popularity did not necessarily mean that Stowe had persuaded her mass audience that slavery was cruel and immoral. Much of the American

Southerners Respond to Stowe. Mary Henderson Eastman's 1852 novel *Aunt Phillis's Cabin* is among the better-known literary responses to Harriet Beecher Stowe's novel. Eastman's book sold between 20,000 and 30,000 copies the year it was released.

public knew Stowe's story and her characters through the theater, where Stowe had little or no control over the content. Under copyright laws of the time, playwrights were free to adapt any popular story to the stage without much concern for the original. Within a year of the novel's publication, there were four versions on the New York stage, and another eleven in England. By end of the century, five hundred Uncle Tom companies would be touring the United States. It is estimated that fifty people eventually saw the play for every one person who read the novel. Uncle Tom plays varied widely in their politics, and several of them changed the plot to downplay the novel's abolitionism. Henry J. Conway's highly successful stage adaptation began appearing on American stages by 1853, and P. T. Barnum assured audiences that this version of the play did "not foolishly and unjustly elevate the Negro above the white man." Several playwrights and theater promoters used *Uncle Tom's Cabin* as a vehicle for blackface minstrelsy (see Chapter 13), and many northern theatergoers encountered Stowe's characters first as comic caricatures. An 1854 minstrel version of *Uncle Tom's Cabin* in St. Louis turned Stowe herself into such a caricature, dubbed Harriet Screecher Blow.

Years later, Abraham Lincoln was reputed to have greeted Stowe with the observation that she was "the little woman who wrote the book that made this great war," because she mobilized humanitarian sympathy for the plight of the enslaved. But Stowe could no more control the meaning of her novel than she could direct the course of political events around her. *Uncle Tom's Cabin* became a major part of the culture of the 1850s, a touchstone in the polarizing debate over slavery. It did not, however, turn the North into a region of abolitionists.

RAILROAD NATION

The controversies over fugitive slaves and slavery in the territories divided a nation that was in some respects more connected than ever before. America in the 1850s was linked by canals, telegraph wires, postal service, mass publishing, and ever-intensifying commercial contacts. But the most visible source and symbol of national connection was the railroad network. Rail transportation, which lay at the center of a broad change in American attitudes toward time, distance, and geography, would also reshape the debate over slavery. Fugitive slaves and other abolitionists used the metaphor of an Underground Railroad to designate a far-flung web of safe houses and accomplices through which tens of thousands of runaways from southern bondage made their way to northern states, Canada, Mexico, or the Bahamas. The above-ground system that inspired its name was also breaking down the walls that enclosed the southern slave system. Railroad development affected perceptions of proximity; introduced new patterns of work, trade, and travel; mobilized the nation's labor force; stimulated heavy industry; and transformed the landscape of the country. Crucially, it forged special ties between free-labor states in the East and those in the West. In all of these ways, the economic and social changes wrought by new transportation patterns during the 1850s further altered the map of slavery politics.

THE RAIL NETWORK

Railroads had been part of American life since the 1820s, when horses pulled cars along the tracks of the Baltimore and Ohio railroad line. Those tracks soon accommodated steam locomotives and governments began subsidizing the construction of new lines. By the end of the 1830s, the United States had more than twice as many miles of railroad track as all of Europe combined. Track construction slowed in the years following the 1837 depression, but then rebounded on a much larger scale.

Horse-Drawn Passenger Car on the Baltimore and Ohio Line, 1830. Although railroads soon became associated with steam locomotion, they began with more traditional power sources. Crucial investment decisions to designate routes and lay track preceded the introduction of faster and longer vehicles.

Between 1848 and 1860, the United States became a nation of railroad lines. Track mileage soared during that period, from five thousand to thirty thousand miles, and a rail network centered in the Midwest surpassed the canal network as a conduit of long-distance travel and trade.

Railroad construction was not simply the result of new technologies. An extraordinary amount of private and public investment was necessary to finance the high initial costs of building the new train network. Railroad companies borrowed money from European banks, sold stock to farmers who lived along their routes, and benefited from extraordinary government munificence. State governments contributed 45 percent of the capital that financed the early construction of railroads. Starting in 1850, the federal government got in on the act as well, providing a land grant of several million acres to the Illinois Central railroad—the first of forty land grants to railroad corporations in the 1850s. By the end of the decade, the combined public and private investment in U.S. railroads had exceeded $1.1 billion (see How Much Is That?).

The rapid growth of the rail network in the 1850s transformed American life in innumerable ways. By lowering the cost of transporting farm produce, the railroad brought new areas of the country into the orbit of long-distance trade. Canals had exerted a similar impact a generation earlier (see Chapter 10), but the railroad reached places that lay far from navigable waterways. Train transportation was also better protected than water travel against adverse weather conditions and afforded farmers more consistent access to urban markets. As rail lines spread, American farmers settled vast swaths of grassland west of the Great Lakes, planted wheat and corn, and created the prairie landscape that now characterizes much of the central and north-central region of the United States. Railroad companies actively encouraged this process, using posters, pamphlets, and handbills to attract settlers to the prairies adjacent to their lines.

By radically reducing the duration of journeys between different parts of the country, especially in the North, railroads also changed popular travel habits, enabling new forms of vacationing and sightseeing and increasing the ease with which middle-class and elite Americans maintained relationships with distant friends and family. In the thirty years after the first railroad tracks were laid, trips that took weeks were reduced to a matter of a couple of days. By 1857, virtually the entire Northeast lay within a day's travel radius of New York City (see Map 14.2).

In contrast to Europe, where the railroad met significant opposition and resistance, Americans by and large celebrated the arrival of tracks and trains. In Europe, rail lines were superimposed on existing roads and highways and were often experienced as disruptions in the rhythm of prior ways of living, working, and moving. In the United States, by contrast, much of the rail network staked out new roads altogether and thus symbolized growth and expansion into new terrain. Urbanites and municipalities, worrying about steam explosions, restricted the use of railroad cars on city streets. At least in the period before the Civil War, however, most Americans tended to regard the new machines with considerable optimism. Whereas, in Europe, mechanical innovations were commonly associated with the breakdown of craft traditions and the displacement of workers, mechanization in the United States appeared first and most conspicuously in the domains of transportation and agriculture, rather than in industrial production. American journalists, critics, artists, and politicians commonly described new technologies as sublime works of art, and perhaps no new technology impressed them more than the steam locomotive. An 1851 issue of the magazine *Scientific American* called the

How Much Is That?

Railroad Investment

The capital invested in railroad construction during the 1850s reached the equivalent of $23.6 billion in 2011 dollars. This represented an unprecedented venture in transportation financing but would not stand out today, in an age of more complex infrastructural improvements. New York's ambitious Second Avenue Subway line, which began construction in 2007, is projected to cost $17 billion.

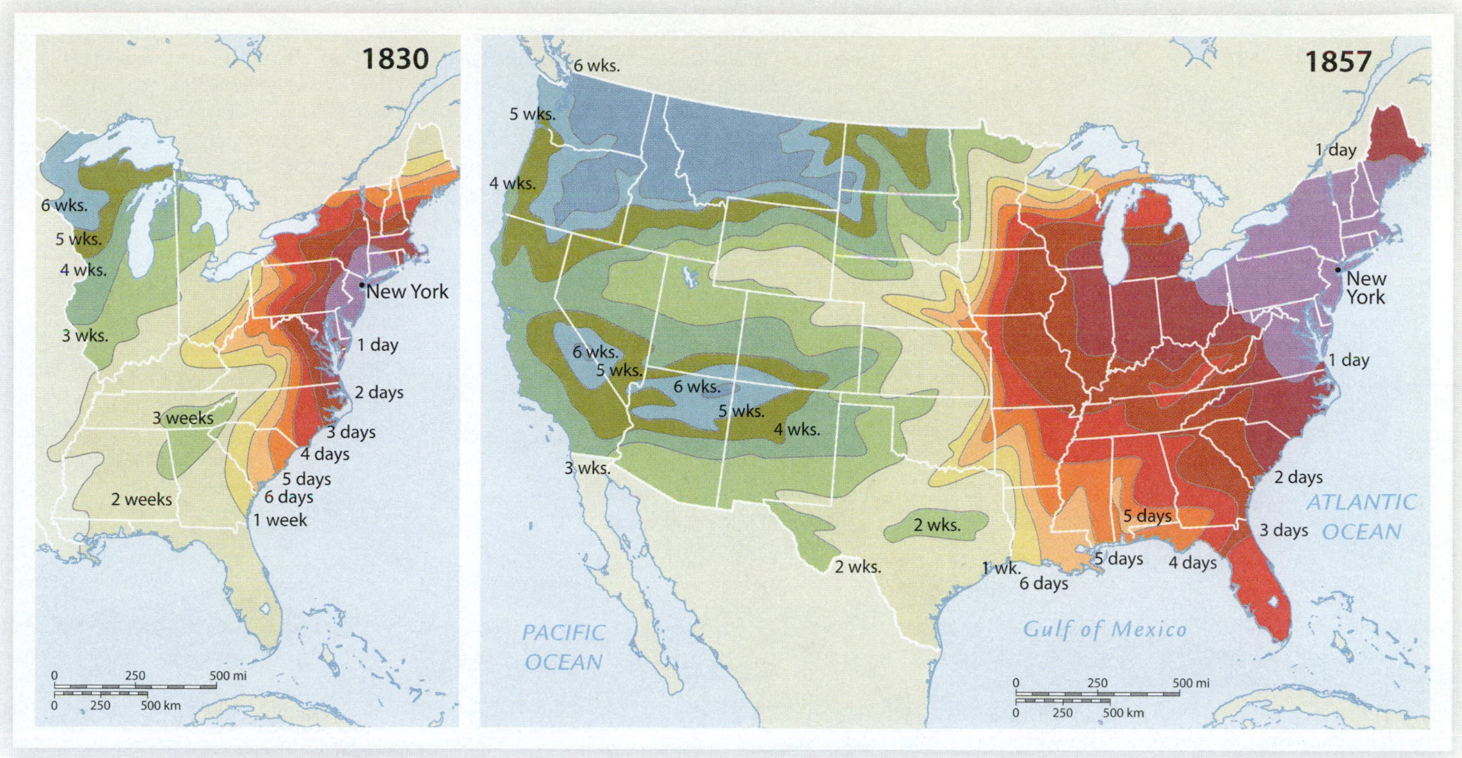

Map 14.2 Travel Times from New York City, 1830 and 1857. Before the railroad network was in place, a trip from Indiana or Illinois to New York City took two to three weeks, but by the early 1850s, it could be accomplished in less than two days.

Railroad Passenger Car. American rail passengers sat in large cars modeled on ship cabins rather than in small compartments like those offered by European trains from the same period. And unlike in Europe, rail travel in the United States was not segmented into multiple classes. A heterogeneous mix of passengers shared the same accommodations, though some trains reserved separate sections (and, in exceptional cases, special carriages) for women.

The Bucolic American Locomotive, 1855. George Inness was commissioned by the Delaware, Lackawanna and Western Railroad to produce a work of art that could be used in the company's advertisements. Pictorial representations of the railroad typically showed rural scenes rather than urban settings and tended to integrate trains and tracks into a bucolic natural landscape. Because land was cheaper and labor more expensive in the United States than in Europe, American railroad lines often followed curved paths around natural obstacles, and this feature further linked the American railroad to rural rather than urban aesthetics.

"sublime and terrific" spectacle of a large train, hurtling along at the profoundly unfamiliar speed of thirty miles an hour, "one of the grandest sights in the world."

By the 1850s, these large trains were speeding through every state in the union except for Arkansas (see Map 14.3), but the network was far denser in some regions than others. Eastern states like Maryland, Pennsylvania, and New York had been centers of early railroad development, but by midcentury the focus of new construction had moved westward, with Ohio, Indiana, and Illinois leading the way. The other significant trend was that rail traffic tended to flow in an east-west direction rather than north-south. Rail cars transported commodities, tourists, and migrants along east-west routes and forged tighter credit relationships between communities along the Atlantic seaboard and those at similar latitudes in the Great Lakes, or along the Ohio, Mississippi, and Missouri Rivers. By the 1850s, one of the chief effects of the national rail network was to integrate the North with the West. And in both of those regions, a handful of large cities became the central destinations for the people and goods that rode the rails.

THE RISE OF CHICAGO

"Railroads in Europe are built to connect centers of population," the prominent New York newspaper editor Horace Greeley observed. But in the American West, "the railroad itself builds cities." Nowhere was this phenomenon more apparent than in Chicago, Illinois. In 1830, Chicago (whose name means "place of the wild garlic") was a fur-trading village with a population of about two hundred Potawatomi, French, and Anglo inhabitants. After the U.S. Army vanquished the Sac and Fox Indians in 1832, American settlers began entering the area in larger numbers and boosters began imagining a city. The town's prospects brightened considerably with the help of private investment capital from New York as well as a harbor project that turned Chicago into a port on Lake Michigan and the Illinois legislature's decision to build a canal with a Chicago terminus. Just over twelve thousand people lived in Chicago in 1845, and in 1848, the year the canal opened, the population reached twenty thousand. But between 1848 and 1860, the city grew more than fivefold. By 1860, Chicago had a population of 112,000 and was the industrial and commercial center of a vast and productive agricultural region.

The railroad was crucial to the spectacular emergence of Chicago as the big city of the American West. In 1848, construction began on the Galena and Chicago Union Railroad line, which was intended to connect Chicago to Galena, a lead-mining town in the northwestern corner of Illinois. Though it never reached Galena, the line quickly made Chicago the major destination for wheat grown north and west of the city. Soon eleven other rail lines would follow, linking Chicago to farms, towns, and cities in all four directions. Midwestern wheat farmers dispatched their goods and directed their energy toward Chicago, and through Chicago they were connected to regions and markets farther east.

Significantly, no railroad line ran *through* Chicago. Because it was either the eastern terminus or the western terminus of those eleven lines, Chicago provided the bridge between the two halves of the nation's rail network. And because it was also the major

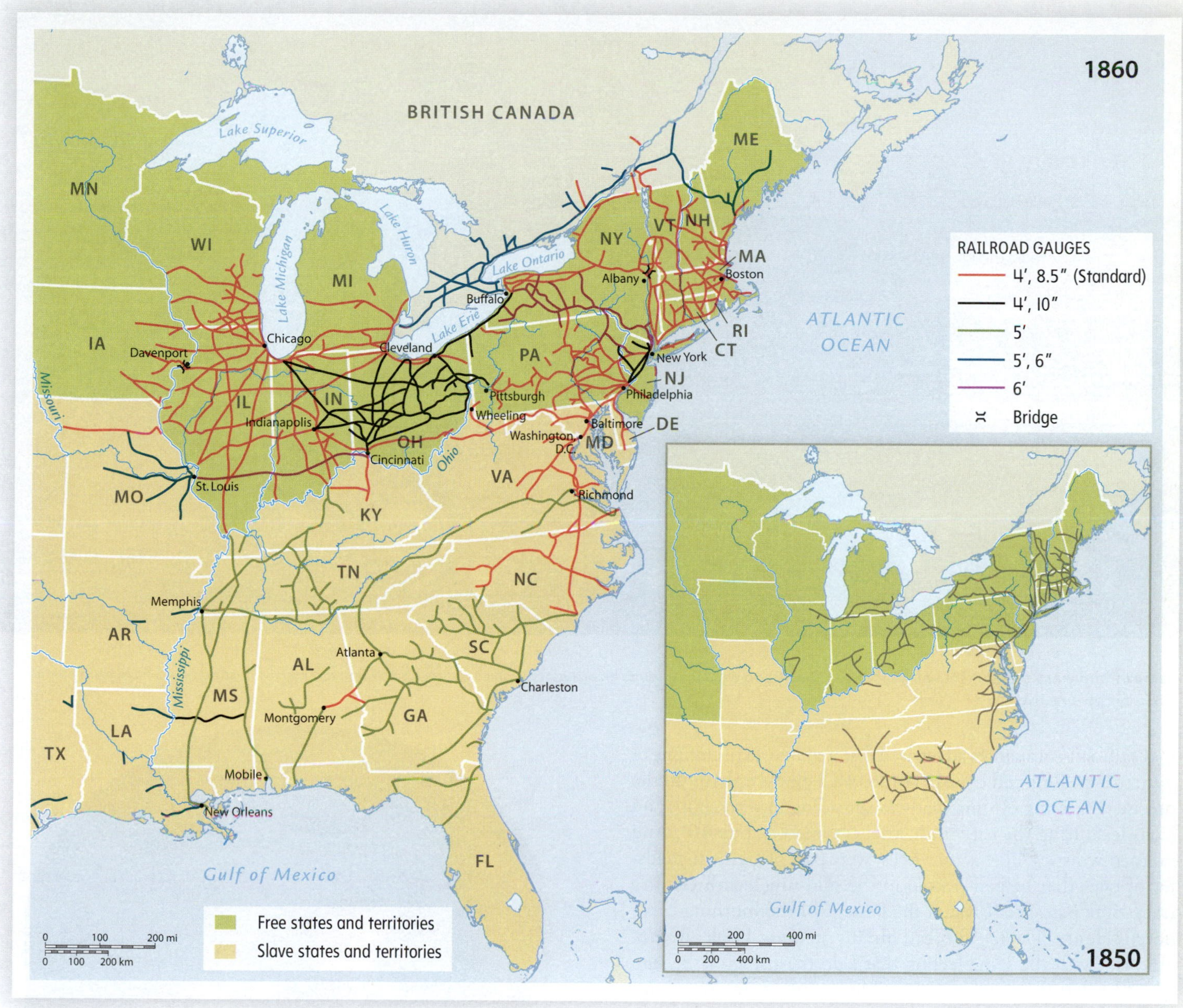

Map 14.3 Growth of the Rail Network, 1850–1860. Over the course of a single decade, railroads helped remap economic and social relations in the United States. **Questions for Analysis:** How did the development of railroad lines bring certain sections of the country closer? How did the lack of track gauge alignment between different lines contribute to the growth of Chicago?

port on Lake Michigan, Chicago offered a transfer point between rail travel and water travel. These considerations put Chicago at the center of the nation's commercial map. Farm products were loaded onto trains throughout Illinois, Iowa, Wisconsin, and Missouri and assembled in Chicago for redistribution or resale eastward. In the other direction, manufactured goods shipped from eastern cities, and especially New York, would be disassembled in Chicago and redistributed or resold westward.

Evidence of Chicago's central place on the rail map sprouted up all over the city. In 1847, Cyrus McCormick's mechanical reaper factory relocated to Chicago, producing the powerful new devices (invented in 1831) that dramatically increased farm productivity in the city's hinterland. A year later, the Chicago Board of Trade opened. Grain elevators (see Hot Commodities: Grain), lumberyards, and animal pens dotted the cityscape. By the end of the 1850s, one of the great industrial cities of the nineteenth century had come into being.

RAILROADS AND TIME

As railroad service proliferated, Americans acquired new reasons to care about exactly what time it was. The faster speed of train travel encouraged passengers to think in smaller increments of time, and the precise departure and arrival times

James Palmatary's 1857 View of Chicago. Barely two decades after its incorporation, Chicago was a sprawling metropolis best depicted from an imaginary bird's-eye perspective.

that railroad companies advertised fostered new expectations of punctuality. Railroad culture reinforced a new emphasis on the precise reckoning of time that was spreading in workshops and factories during the early industrial era (see Chapter 10). And railroad whistles, like factory bells, were part of a growing cluster of cues that helped people in the mid-nineteenth century track time passage. "I watch the passage of the morning cars," noted Henry David Thoreau in his famous book *Walden* (1854), "with the same feeling that I do the rising of the sun, which is hardly more regular." More and more Americans could also consult clocks in their homes and watches in their pockets. The industrial production of clocks had taken off in the United States during the 1830s, and the first watch factory opened in 1850. The North dominated timepiece production, but clocks and watches became common amenities throughout the country by the 1850s. Americans in all regions paid more attention to these devices and grew more likely to think of time as something that needed to be tracked mechanically, rather than simply by astronomical observation or by attending to the natural rhythms of the day.

In the age of telegraphs and railroads, however, it quickly became a problem that clocks and watches in one place were out of sync with those in another town or state. Noon in Hartford, Connecticut, for example, preceded noon in Albany, New York,

***Listening to Father's Watch* (1857).** Clocks and watches symbolized the growing attention to precise timekeeping in this era.

HOT COMMODITIES

Grain

The railroad empire centered in Chicago was built on grain. Farmers settling along the railroad routes cultivated unprecedented volumes of corn and wheat with the hopes of sending it eastward via Chicago. By 1856, with skyrocketing European demand for wheat as a result of the Crimean War, twenty-one million bushels of grain passed through the city in a single year. Chicago was more than just a convenient stopover for agricultural products en route to customers on the Atlantic seaboard and in Europe. The city's grain business helped turned prairie crops into abstract commodities.

Along with the railroad itself, the invention that allowed Chicagoans to organize—and dominate—the grain trade was the steam-powered grain elevator, which was first used in Buffalo in 1842 and introduced in Chicago in 1848. The new elevators were enormous warehouses that used machines to load, weigh, and unload the vast quantities of grain stored there. Usually owned by railroad companies, grain elevators employed chutes to empty the contents of rail cars directly into their storage facilities. This radically reduced the costs of transferring the grain and gave Chicago a big competitive advantage over cities like St. Louis, which relied mostly on water transportation. Within a few years, Chicago's ten massive grain elevators were housing four million bushels of wheat at a time.

Grain elevators also mixed the grain of different farmers into one undifferentiated mass that could be sold by weight. As long as buyers and sellers could agree that the grain in a particular elevator was of similar quality, one bushel was interchangeable for another and it was unnecessary to track the grain belonging to particular farmers. To facilitate this, a new private organization called the Chicago Board of Trade (founded in 1848) distinguished grades of grain quality and established standards for each grade. Grain sellers would receive a receipt from an elevator for depositing a certain amount of grain (measured in sixty-pound bushels) of a particular grade, and they could then redeem their receipt for an equal quantity of similar-grade grain at any other elevator. Under this system, grain became a kind of money, and grain receipts a form of paper currency that could be exchanged by people who had no interest in actually owning grain, much as bank notes could circulate among people who had no intention to redeem them for silver or gold. Elevator receipts also made it easier for speculators to bet on the price of grain. Buying a grain receipt was essentially an investment in grain, which the buyer could resell for profit or loss at a later date. And with the arrival in Chicago of the telegraph (in the same year as the elevator and the Board of Trade), Chicago grain receipts could be traded in places like New York. In the space of a decade, the same railroad network that caused wheat and corn to sprout all over the midwestern prairie and turned Chicago into a city flowing with grain also created a second market in grain, far removed from the world of farmers and crops.

Think About It

1. How did storing grain in elevators rather than in farmers' sacks change the way merchants thought about individual shipments of grain?
2. Why was it necessary or useful to create a grading system for grain quality?
3. How might the efficiency of this grain elevator system have contributed to the perception on the East Coast that Chicago was the commercial center of the West?

because the sun appears at its apex at different points, varying with longitude. If a passenger set his watch to noon in St. Louis, it would be ten minutes behind the clocks in Chicago by the time his train arrived. And if that passenger was also the train's engineer, the difference could make it hard to maintain schedules and avoid traffic jams or train collisions. Telegraphs exposed these time disparities as well. A merchant house in Philadelphia and a bank in New York might both close at 5 p.m., but if they tried to do business together over the wires they might discover to their frustration that they actually closed at different times.

Telegraphs also offered a possible solution, however. Using telegraphy, railroad companies in New England began coordinating their schedules in 1849, agreeing to use a time two minutes after the true astronomical time of Boston, as determined by a particular Boston clockmaker named William Bond. British railroads had done something similar two years earlier, and it quickly set standard British time. Railroads had the effect of standardizing timekeeping in the United States as well, though it was not until 1883 that the railroads mapped out time zones for the nation and not until 1918 that the United States recognized that map and turned railroad time into official time. In the shorter term, however, railroad time coordinated the activities of those Americans along the northern corridor who were integrated more intensively into the rail network.

INDUSTRY AND WAGES

The rail network also shaped the slavery conflict by accelerating the process of industrialization in the North. Track building spurred iron processing, fuel consumption led to coal mining, and the growth of commerce stimulated all kinds of manufacturing. Faster travel opportunities and new travel routes encouraged laborers, including massive numbers of new immigrants, to move to U.S. cities for work opportunities. Outside of the South, the railroads reinforced the steady rise in the proportion of Americans who worked for wages. In 1800, only about 10 percent of the U.S. workforce was employed on a wage basis; by 1860, the figure would be 40 percent, mostly in the North. By 1850, for the first time, the number of wage earners in the United States exceeded the number of slaves. Wage earners belonged to a new working class comprised of men and women who were not bound to their employers but had no independent means of support. On average, they were paid less than most experts at the time thought was necessary to support oneself (let alone a family), and their wages declined, relative to inflation, over the course of the 1850s. Wage workers did not own their tools, could not set the value of their labor, had little or nothing in common with the men who employed them, and depended on their employers in new and unsettling ways.

Wage labor itself, rather than factory conditions, long hours, or mechanization, was the most controversial feature of the new world of industrial work. Wage laborers had long been stigmatized as dependent and vulnerable, and by midcentury they were becoming the norm in most states where slavery was illegal. Both proslavery ideologues in the South and labor leaders in the North spoke of **wage slavery** and compared the plight of immigrant workers in northern cities to that of plantation slaves (see Interpreting the Sources: George Fitzhugh on Industrial Labor). Arguments about wage slavery often created alliances between

INTERPRETING THE SOURCES

George Fitzhugh on Industrial Labor

When defenders of southern slavery cited the impoverished conditions of laborers in the North or in England, their point was usually to liken "wage slaves" to "chattel slaves." Abolitionists were hypocrites, they charged, for condemning slaveholders while condoning the mistreatment of workers in their own backyards. Every society had a lower class that performed menial tasks, ran the proslavery refrain, so it was unfair and unwise to single out plantation slavery for censure. But as the political conflict over slavery intensified, southerners began to insist that their own form of labor discipline was morally and politically *superior* to the industrial labor system emerging in the North.

For many critics of "wage slavery" or (as they sometimes called it) "white slavery," the southern system was better because it confined slavery to a stigmatized race of people who did not deserve the benefits of freedom. But Virginian George Fitzhugh, perhaps the most radical proslavery ideologue of the 1850s, pursued the defense of slavery to its logical conclusion: Since slavery was really a benign system, then white workers would also be better off under its regime. In the process of defending the social and economic order of the South, Fitzhugh offered a powerful critique of free labor and of competitive capitalist society.

From *Sociology for the South, or the Failure of Free Society* (1854)

More than half of the white citizens of the North are common laborers, either in the field, or as body or house servants. They perform the same services that our slaves do. They serve their employers for hire; they have quite as little option whether they shall so serve, or not, as our slaves, for it is wholly insufficient for their comfortable maintenance, whilst we always keep our slaves in comfort, in return for their past, present, or expected labor. The socialists say wages is slavery. It is a gross libel on slavery. Wages are given in time of vigorous health and strength, and denied when most needed, when sickness or old age has overtaken us. The slave is never without a master to maintain him. The free laborer, though willing to work, cannot always find an employer. He is then without a home and without wages!

From *Cannibals All! or, Slaves Without Masters* (1857)

It is impossible to place labor and capital in harmonious or friendly relations, except by the means of slavery, which identifies their interests. Would [a northerner] lay his capital out in land and negroes, he might be sure, in whatever hands it came, that it would be employed to protect laborers, not to oppress them; for when slaves are worth near a thousand dollars a head, they will be carefully and well provided for. In any other investment he may make of it, it will be used as an engine to squeeze the largest amount of labor from the poor, for the least amount of allowance. We say allowance, not wages; for neither slaves nor free laborers get wages, in the popular sense of the term: that is, the employer or capitalist pays them from nothing of his own, but allows them a part, generally a very small part, of the proceeds of their own labor. Free laborers pay one another, for labor creates all values, and capital, after taking the lion's share by its taxing power, but pays the so-called wages of one laborer from the proceeds of the labor of another.

Do not the past history and present condition of Free Society in Western Europe (where alone the experiment has been fully tried,) prove that it is attended with greater evils, moral and physical, than Slave Society? . . .

But our Southern slavery has become a benign and protective institution, and our negroes are confessedly better off than any free laboring population in the world. How can we contend that white slavery is wrong, whilst all the great body of free laborers are starving; and slaves, white or black, throughout the world, are enjoying comfort?

Explore the Sources

1. In what respects, according to Fitzhugh, do slaves and wage workers share the same status?
2. By what standard does Fitzhugh consider slaves to be better off than wage workers?
3. How does slavery, from Fitzhugh's perspective, prevent class conflict?
4. How might a critic of slavery respond to Fitzhugh's argument?

radicals who sought to improve the lot of white workers and wealthy slaveholders who sought to protect their property. Mike Walsh, an Irish-born labor radical in New York who was elected to Congress in 1852, was both a vociferous critic of capitalism and a staunch defender of slavery and the South.

In the South, the national rail network also had a significant impact on economic and social life but did not alter the labor system. International demand for cotton kept prices high during the 1850s, and the southern economy boomed. Slavery was compatible with railroads, mechanization, and even mass production. Enslaved people worked in mills and mines as well as cotton fields. Thousands of Virginia slaves worked in factories in the 1850s, for example, producing flavored plugs of chewing tobacco. But the economic success of slavery inhibited the spread of wage labor. As wage labor spread in the North, the difference between North and South became increasingly framed in those terms. By the 1850s, northern critics of slavery began using the model of wage labor to define what was wrong with slavery: enslaved workers were not paid cash wages, did not sign contracts, and did not move freely from job to job in search of higher pay.

POLITICAL REALIGNMENT

From its inception, the Second Party System of competition between Democrats and Whigs had been designed to build national coalitions and forestall political conflicts between North and South. The election of 1848 had exposed strains in that system, and the sectional truce that had been declared in the Compromise of 1850 was fragile from the start. By not extending the Missouri Compromise, Congress had signaled that the status of slavery in the western territories would have to be settled by some new principle. Sooner or later, the political parties would need to stake out positions on what those principles would be. Significantly, it was the spread of the rail network that brought such conflicts to the fore sooner rather than later. Territories on the western side of the Mississippi now became major battlegrounds in an increasingly polarized and suddenly violent struggle over slavery. In the face of this challenge, Democrats and Whigs lost their grips on their coalitions and the nation inched closer to disunion.

KANSAS AND NEBRASKA

In the 1852 presidential election, the Democrats and their standard-bearer Franklin Pierce stood by the Compromise of 1850 and won a decisive victory with landslide margins in the Deep South. But the Compromise of 1850 had been vague on the crucial question of the day, which was whether and under what terms slavery would be introduced into the western half of the continent. Significantly, the admission of California, which straddled the 36°30′ line, implied that the geographical divide laid out in the Missouri Compromise to divide slave and free states would not be in effect, at least in the lands taken from Mexico. California was a free state because the gold rush had drawn settlers who supported a free-state constitution, not because of the Missouri line. Because the Missouri Compromise held little sway in the Mexican Cession, southerners may have imagined that it would ultimately become obsolete in the Louisiana Purchase as well, but this was far less clear.

The vast stretch of Louisiana Purchase land that had not yet been organized into territories (see Map 14.4) was still sparsely settled in the early 1850s. Congress would have had no incentive to prepare these lands for statehood had it not been for the spread of the railroad network. Prospects of a rail line spanning the continent drew considerable interest after 1848. The Pierce administration pushed for the 1853 Gadsden Purchase with precisely this goal in mind (see Chapter 13): The additional land acquired from Mexico would enable the construction of a line between New Orleans and San Diego and connect the South to the nation's western territories. But politicians and investors in the Midwest envisioned a more northerly route to the Pacific Ocean. St. Louisans such as Thomas Hart Benton touted the advantages of their city as the gateway to the Pacific, and the state of Missouri invested massively in railroad construction throughout the decade in the hopes of boosting that prospect. But Chicago had already emerged as the leading western terminus of rail traffic from New York and the hub of an expanding regional rail network between the Ohio and Mississippi Rivers. Illinois politicians were in a strong position to nominate their leading city as a terminus for the western half of a transcontinental rail line. To facilitate this development, Stephen Douglas (in his capacity as chairman of the Senate committee on territories) crafted a bill covering the entire unorganized portion of the Louisiana Purchase (from the western borders of Missouri, Iowa, and Minnesota to the Rocky Mountains, as far north as the Canadian border), which he called the Nebraska Territory.

Seeking southern support for his railroad vision and eager to spread his program of popular sovereignty as a model for dealing with slavery in the West, Douglas included language in his Nebraska bill stipulating that "all questions pertaining to slavery in the Territories, and in the new states to be formed therefrom are to be left to the people residing therein." Worried that the bill would still wind up adding free states to the union, the South pressed Douglas for two key amendments. First, the law would repeal the provision of the Missouri Compromise that banned slavery north of 36°30′, so that slaveholders could move into the proposed Nebraska territory. Second, the area under consideration would be split into two territories, Nebraska and Kansas, the latter adjacent to the slave state of Missouri and potentially attractive to slaveholders. With the strong backing of President Pierce, near-unanimous support from the South, and enough votes from northern Democrats, the Kansas-Nebraska Act passed by margins of 113 to 100 in the House and 37 to 14 in the Senate.

The Kansas-Nebraska Act outraged northern congressmen, who denounced the compromise as a violation of the sacred compact of the Missouri Compromise. Texan Sam Houston, one of the lone dissenters from the South, pointed out that Congress was also reneging on the promises made during Indian removal to reserve land west of the Mississippi for the

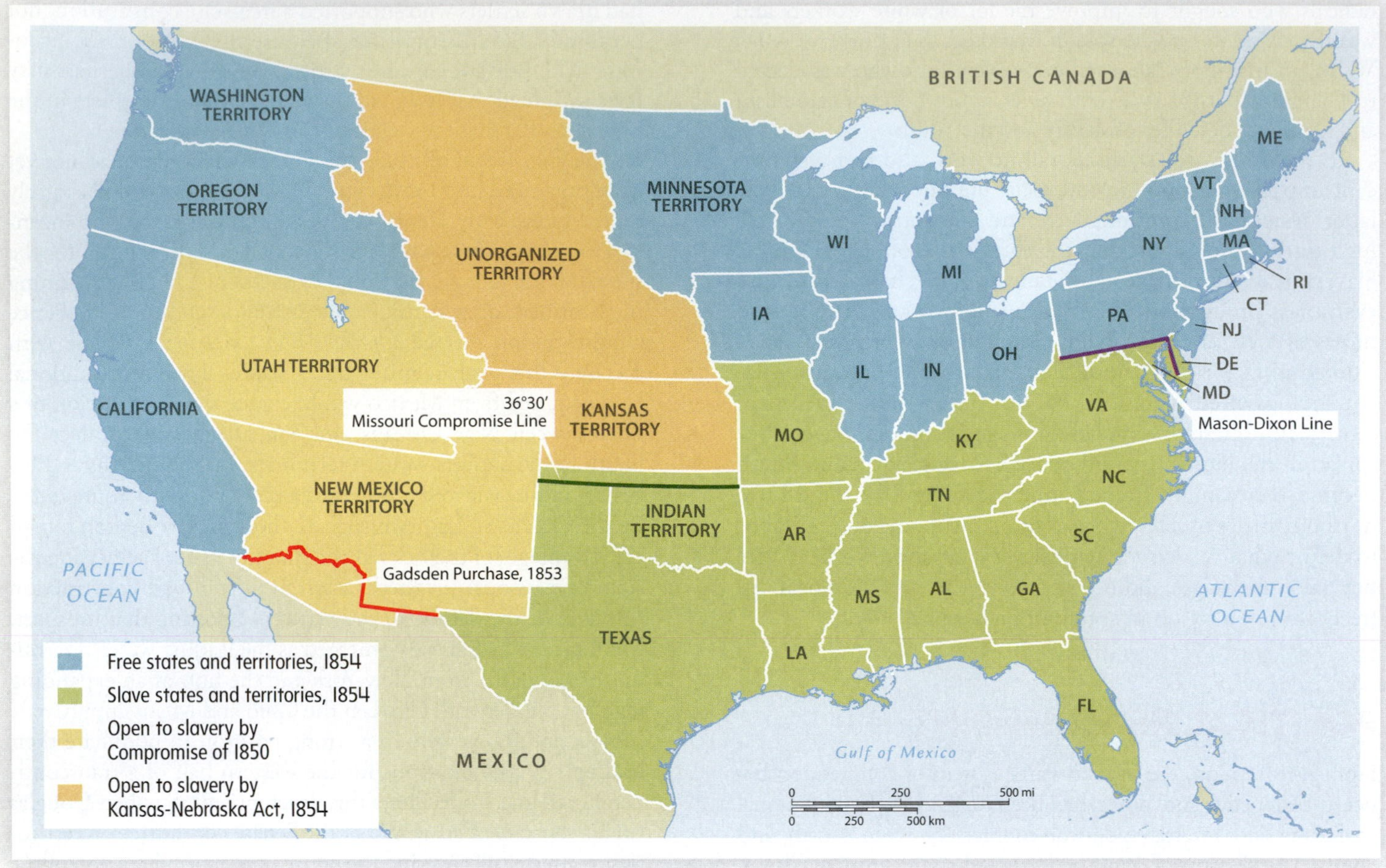

Map 14.4 The Kansas-Nebraska Act. By remapping new territories to facilitate the construction of new rail lines to the West, Congress set up a political showdown over slavery in the lands just west of Missouri.

permanent occupation of native groups exiled from their lands in the 1830s. As Houston observed ruefully, Kansas-Nebraska marked the official abandonment of the idea of a serious boundary between the United States and Indian country. Indian Territory, as it was still called, was confined to a much smaller area (see Map 14.4), and earlier assurances that Native Americans could live on this land "as long as the grass shall grow and water run" were quickly forgotten.

But few Americans focused on the implications of Kansas-Nebraska for Shawnee, Delaware, or Chickasaw Indians. The real outrage of Douglas's bill lay in its implications for the slavery controversy. On the same day that Anthony Burns was arraigned in Boston, Massachusetts senator Charles Sumner introduced a two-hundred-foot-long petition signed by over three thousand ministers and written by celebrity author Harriet Beecher Stowe, calling the new law "a great moral wrong . . . a breach of faith . . . exposing [the nation] to the righteous judgments of the Almighty. . . ." As Sumner saw it, the one positive consequence of the bill was that, by scrapping the Missouri Compromise (which abolitionists like Sumner saw as having been immoral in the first place), it made all future deals impossible: "Thus it puts Freedom and Slavery face to face, and bids them grapple. Who can doubt the result?"

The more immediate result, however, was a fatal blow to the Second Party System, dividing the country politically along sectional lines. The Whig Party had maintained ranks in 1850, but when northern Whigs refused to support the Kansas-Nebraska Act, their southern colleagues deserted the party, leading to its collapse. Enough Democrats had stood by Douglas's bill to make it law, but the 1854 congressional elections showed that Douglas and Pierce had miscalculated. Kansas-Nebraska alienated so many northerners that the Democrats lost more than two-thirds of their House seats in the North to opponents from a host of free soil parties and "anti-Nebraska" coalitions.

THE KNOW-NOTHINGS

In the immediate wake of the collapse of the Whigs, the American Party, also known as the Know-Nothing Party, appeared to be poised for national prominence. The Know-Nothings originated in a cluster of nativist secret societies, which coalesced in 1850 as the Order of the Star-Spangled Banner. Members of the order were committed to protecting the United States and the vision of its founders from what they saw as the menace of Catholic immigration. By 1850, Irish comprised 43 percent of the growing foreign-born population of the United States. By decade's end, Catholics (including many German immigrants) would form the nation's largest religious denomination. Tensions between native-born Protestants and Catholic immigrants, especially those from Ireland, ran high in the 1850s, often flaring into violence.

Hostility to Irish Catholic immigrants reflected a number of forces and prejudices. Anglo Americans had inherited a long tradition of regarding Irish people as savage and inferior (see Chapter 1), and such views acquired more authority and prestige from new scientific theories about racial difference. For other nativists, the problem with Irish immigrants was more religious than racial. In the antebellum era, the Catholic Church became the focus of intense suspicion and hostility among temperance advocates, abolitionists, evangelical preachers, and other middle-class reformers (see Chapter 12), and nativists found common cause with those reformers who objected to Catholicism even if they welcomed immigration. Finally, nativists could point to the growing political power of Irish and German Democratic voters in large U.S. cities, where immigrants and their children typically made up more than half the population.

THE DEAD SERGEANT IN TWENTY-SECOND STREET.

Anti-Irish Caricatures in the Mainstream Press. This illustration from a slightly later book about the New York Draft Riots (see Chapter 15) draws on middle-class descriptions of Irishmen as having "Celtic physiognomy," black skin, and "brutish" or "simian" features. Here they are also depicted as inhumane, abusing the body of a militiaman killed in the rioting.

In 1851, the Order of the Star-Spangled Banner created the American Party and shrouded its workings with secret rituals. "I know nothing," was a standard early response to queries about the party's membership and goals, which gave birth to the popular nickname. But by 1854, the Know-Nothing Party was operating in full view of the electorate and poised to capitalize on the Kansas-Nebraska crisis. In July 1854, American Party delegates from thirteen states promulgated a platform calling for restrictions on naturalization (the process of becoming a U.S. citizen) and the exclusion of Catholics from holding public office. Despite their focus on what seemed like a narrow political agenda, the Know-Nothings had significant appeal to party-less Whigs and disaffected northern Democrats. Forty Know-Nothing candidates were elected to Congress, along with many more state legislators. The party swept through much of New England, replaced the Whigs as the major opposition party in most border states, and attracted significant chunks of the electorate in New York, Pennsylvania, and California. Know-Nothings even drew support in the South, where voters anxious to preserve the union looked to the American Party for a way out of sectional conflict.

In the Northeast, where anti-Catholicism and antislavery often went hand-in-hand, the Know-Nothings ran against the Kansas-Nebraska Act and became the party of middle-class reform. Know-Nothings captured the Massachusetts legislature and governorship in 1854, for example, and proceeded to implement antislavery and reformist goals. They enacted personal liberty laws designed to thwart the Fugitive Slave Act, along with a law that allowed juries to rule on the justice of a law as well as the facts of a case. They abolished imprisonment for debt, passed child labor legislation, instituted a married women's property act, came close to abolishing the death penalty, and, in April 1855, officially desegregated the Boston schools. In a mix of reform agendas that might seem stranger now than it did in 1854, the Massachusetts Know-Nothings also sought to deport Irish paupers and to require immigrants to have twenty-one years of residency prior to voting. Outside of the Northeast, however, Know-Nothings did not run as an antislavery party. And in many parts of the country, the perceived threat of immigrants or Catholics was not powerful enough to organize an enduring political party. Within a couple of years, the Know-Nothings receded as a force in national politics.

BLEEDING KANSAS, BLEEDING SUMNER

By 1855, all eyes turned to Kansas, which had been designed by Congress as a territory where slavery might take legal root through popular sovereignty. Nothing in the congressional legislation specified how exactly the people of the territory would express their will. Who was eligible to vote in the elections establishing a new government in Kansas, and when would such elections take place? Partisans in the slavery conflict mobilized for a showdown with few clear rules.

With railroad lines connecting the Atlantic seaboard to Illinois and Missouri, traveling to the western territories from the Northeast was an easier proposition. Already a year earlier, twelve hundred settlers had been dispatched to Kansas by the Emigrant Aid Society, an antislavery organization based in Massachusetts. Thousands more settlers moved to Kansas under their own auspices from the Midwest, and most of them were committed to the goal of keeping slaves (and all African Americans) out of Kansas. These migrants were preceded, however, by western Missourians who crossed the border to vote for proslavery members of the new territorial legislature. David Atchison, a former Missouri senator, led the charge westward, urging his neighbors to "kill every God-damned abolitionist in the Territory" and protect the region against the free soil onslaught. As Atchison saw it, the fate of slavery hung in the balance. "If we win we carry slavery to the Pacific Ocean, if we fail we lose Missouri, Arkansas, and Texas and all the territories."

Although fewer than three thousand white settlers lived in Kansas at the time of the March election, more than 6,300 votes were cast and the proslavery forces prevailed. Free-state voters immediately charged fraud on the part of Atchison's "border ruffians," declared the new legislature "bogus," and established a rival government. Kansas now had two territorial legislatures, enacting different laws and proposing competing state constitutions. The proslavery legislature, headquartered in the town of Lecompton, quickly passed laws making it a crime to speak against slavery and a capital offense to aid a runaway

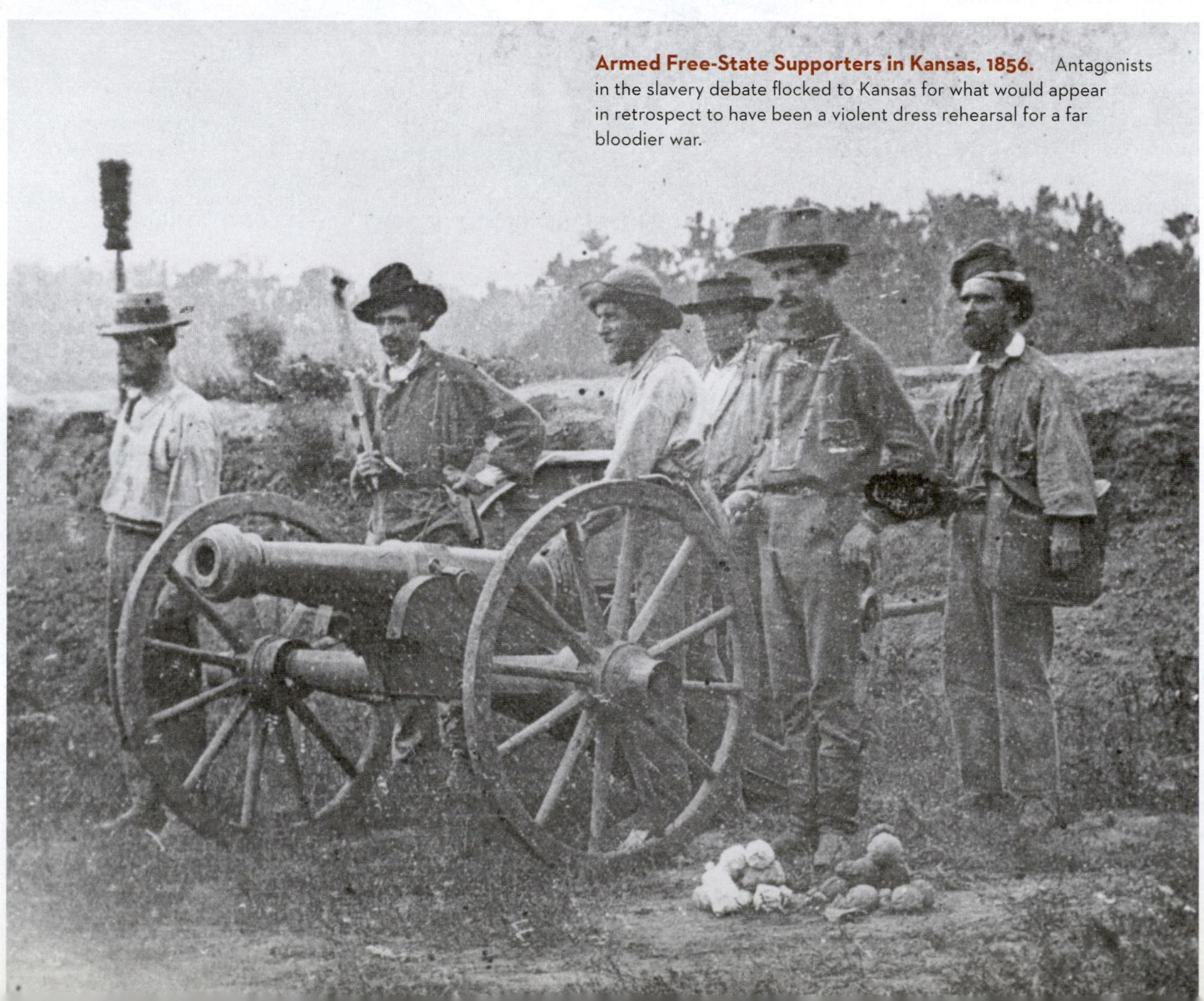

Armed Free-State Supporters in Kansas, 1856. Antagonists in the slavery debate flocked to Kansas for what would appear in retrospect to have been a violent dress rehearsal for a far bloodier war.

slave. Its rival, centered in the town of Lawrence, banned both slavery and free blacks from the territory. Over the objections of the territorial governor, President Pierce recognized the Lecompton government, as did the U.S. Senate, whereas the House recognized the one in Lawrence.

Disputed elections often turned violent in antebellum America, but the scale and stakes of the Kansas conflict broke new ground. Armed proslavery Missourians, who had crossed the border before the election in order to vote, now did so to enforce the election's results. They were joined by other southern settlers and supported by agents of the federal government. Free soil settlers, for their part, requested help from supporters in Ohio, New York, and New England. Antislavery organizations sent Sharpe's rifles to Kansas, sometimes in crates marked "Bibles." The stage was set for a civil war.

After a series of smaller skirmishes, Lecompton men raided Lawrence in May 1856 and destroyed numerous buildings, including newspaper offices and the governor's house. In retaliation, an abolitionist named John Brown led a small party (including his sons) on an attack against proslavery settlers at Pottawatomie Creek, killing five people and mutilating their corpses. In the guerilla war that ensued over the next few months, close to two hundred people were killed and $2 million worth of property was destroyed.

The fighting in what newspapers began calling "Bleeding Kansas" failed to resolve the legal status of slavery. Its principal effect on the larger debate was to replace abstract fears about geographical principles and popular sovereignty with concrete and frightening images of real enemies. Northern newspapers described boorish Missourians wielding bowie knives, while the South read about self-righteous zealots brandishing rifles.

During the height of the Kansas violence, Senator Charles Sumner of Massachusetts issued a venomous two-day attack from the Senate floor on "The Crime Against Kansas." In Sumner's words, the Missourians who had gone into Kansas to fight for slavery were "hirelings picked from the drunken spew and vomit of an uneasy civilization." Invoking familiar antislavery rhetoric about slaveholder lust, Sumner decried "the rape of virgin territory," and the South's "depraved longing for a new slave State." He singled out a particular southern senator, Andrew P. Butler of South Carolina, as a liar whose fondness for slavery resembled a man chasing after a harlot.

From the perspective of southern notions of honor, this was not simply political rhetoric; Sumner's words belonged to the class of insulting speech acts that could only be avenged by personal acts of violence. Sumner's goal had not been to antagonize anyone in the Senate chamber, much less to sway any of his colleagues' views on slavery. The real intended audience for this speech, which he had prepared carefully beforehand, was the antislavery public who would read it in print. But three days after the speech, Butler's nephew, a young South Carolina congressman named Preston Brooks, approached Sumner as he sat at his Senate desk preparing copies of the inflammatory text for mailing. After announcing that he had carefully read the contents of the speech, Brooks began beating Sumner over the head with a cane. The Massachusetts senator was trapped behind his bolted desk as Brooks continued to pummel him. By the time Sumner managed to pull the desk out from its moorings, his head had split open. Several senators tried to intercede, but two southerners prevented anyone from getting to Brooks before Sumner had been beaten unconscious.

The shocking incident played out differently on the two sides of the sectional divide. Southerners saw Brooks as a hero, whereas northerners turned Sumner into a martyr. A northern majority in Congress censured Brooks, while a united South prevented his expulsion. Both men were enthusiastically reelected by their constituents, though in Sumner's case this meant leaving his seat unoccupied for three years while he recovered from his head injury. Brooks's admirers sent him souvenir canes in the mail.

A new political party in the North, founded in 1854 during the Kansas-Nebraska controversy, seized upon the two events of May 1856 to launch their first presidential campaign. Calling themselves Republicans, the latest entrants to national politics invoked the specter of Bleeding Kansas and "Bleeding Sumner" to mount a sectional campaign that renounced all hopes of winning votes in the Deep South. To lead their ticket, the Republicans nominated John C. Frémont, who had helped wrest California from Mexican control. The Democrats replaced Pierce with James Buchanan, and the Know-Nothings nominated the former Whig president Millard Fillmore. Buchanan won the election, but Frémont's showing was quite remarkable (see Table 14.2). As a first-time contender, the Republicans took a third of the popular vote without appealing to southern voters. The results confirmed that

TABLE 14.2 ELECTION OF 1856

Candidate	Party	Electoral Vote	Popular Vote	Percent of Popular Vote
James Buchanan	Democratic	174	1,836,072	45.3
John C. Fremont	Republican	114	1,342,345	33.1
Millard Fillmore	American	8	871,731	21.6

Republicans had absorbed the remnants of the Liberty Party and supplanted the Know-Nothings among antislavery voters in the North. More ominously for the Democrats, Buchanan drew only 45 percent of the vote and lost most of the free states. Had the Democrats' northern opponents rallied behind one candidate, a president could have been elected without a single electoral vote from the South.

DRED SCOTT AND THE END OF COMPROMISE

In his inaugural address, President Buchanan expressed the view that the status of slavery in the territories was really a judicial question that would be "speedily and finally settled" by the U.S. Supreme Court. What Buchanan had in mind was a legal battle over the fate of two Missourians, Dred and Harriet Scott. The case had been moving through the court system for eleven years and would finally be decided two days after Buchanan's 1857 inauguration.

Dred Scott was born into slavery around 1800 in Virginia, and was taken westward by his owner, first to Alabama and then to St. Louis. After his owner's death, Scott was sold to an army surgeon named John Emerson, who brought Scott with him to Fort Armstrong in Illinois and then to Fort Snelling in the Wisconsin Territory, where Scott met and married another slave named Harriet Robinson. After a brief trip to Louisiana and another stint at Fort Snelling, Emerson decided to leave Dred and Harriet Scott in St. Louis, renting their labor out to others. After Emerson's death in 1843, his widow Irene Emerson inherited the estate and continued to rent out the Scotts. Dred Scott's many moves were not unusual among enslaved African Americans, and his status as a hired-out urban slave was common in a city like St. Louis (see Singular Lives: Elizabeth Keckley, Free Seamstress). But in 1846, Dred Scott took the uncommon step of suing for his freedom and that of Harriet and their two daughters, claiming that having lived in a free state (Illinois) and a free territory (Wisconsin) a decade earlier meant that he and Harriet were no longer slaves.

Scott lost his first case on technical grounds in 1847, but three years later a St. Louis jury ruled in his favor. Irene Emerson's lawyers appealed, however, and the Missouri Supreme Court reversed the decision in 1852. Scott then initiated a new suit in federal court, this time targeting Irene Emerson's brother John Sanford, a New York merchant who had been acting on his sister's behalf. (A Supreme Court official later misspelled Sanford's name on court documents, and the case would forever be known as *Dred Scott v. Sandford.*) The federal judge instructed the jury that the state of Missouri could determine the Scotts' legal status, and the jury upheld the state court decision. Scott appealed the case to the Supreme Court in 1854. All the while, he and his family remained wards of the St. Louis County sheriff, who rented them out and held the proceeds in escrow pending a final resolution of the question of whether they were slaves (in which case Irene Emerson was owed rent)

FRANK LESLIE'S ILLUSTRATED NEWSPAPER

No. 82.—VOL. IV.] NEW YORK, SATURDAY, JUNE 27, 1857. [PRICE 6 CENTS.

TO TOURISTS AND TRAVELLERS.

VISIT TO DRED SCOTT—HIS FAMILY—INCIDENTS OF HIS LIFE—DECISION OF THE SUPREME COURT.

Dred and Harriet Scott. Shortly after the 1857 Supreme Court decision, the sons of Dred Scott's original owner purchased him and his family and manumitted them. Less than a year later, Dred died of tuberculosis. Harriet lived for another eighteen years. One of their daughters lived to be ninety-nine and died in the 1950s.

or free (in which case they were owed wages). Ten years after the Scotts' original claim for freedom, their case was heard by the Supreme Court.

Arguments in the case of *Dred Scott v. Sandford* began in 1856. In May, the court decided to call a recess until after the presidential election and scheduled new arguments for December. At issue now was not only the freedom of the Scotts, but also the more momentous questions of whether free blacks had a right to sue in federal courts and whether Congress had been authorized to prohibit slavery in the territories. On March 6, 1857, Chief Justice Roger B. Taney, a former slaveholder who years earlier had served as Andrew Jackson's secretary of the treasury during the bank war, read the opinion of the court for a full two hours. Dred Scott was not entitled to sue, Taney ruled, because Dred Scott was black. Black people were a degraded

SINGULAR LIVES

Elizabeth Keckley, Free Seamstress

In October 1860, one month before the fateful presidential election that would bring Lincoln to office and spark southern secession, the nation's capital turned its attention to a visit from the Prince of Wales, the nineteen-year-old who would later become King Edward VII of England. In preparation for a formal dinner honoring the prince, Elizabeth Keckley went shopping for elegant dress materials. A seamstress and fashion consultant for several elite Washington clients, Keckley was selecting lace trimming for Mary Anne Randolph Custis Lee, the great granddaughter of Martha Washington and the wife of Colonel Robert E. Lee, who had just led the force that quashed John Brown's rebellion.

Keckley had recently moved from St. Louis but would soon become a well-known figure in Washington society. The following March, she met Mary Todd Lincoln at the new president's inauguration and was hired as the first lady's personal "modiste" (a fashionable dressmaker) and confidante. During the Lincoln presidency, Keckley designed Lincoln's event wardrobe and became one of her closest friends.

What makes the story of Elizabeth Keckley (her name was sometimes spelled Keckly) striking is the fact that just five years before Lincoln's election she had been a slave. Born into bondage in 1818 near Peterson, Virginia, Keckley endured an especially brutal youth that featured savage beatings and repeated sexual assault (some of which she later described in her 1868 autobiography). In 1847, her master moved her to St. Louis, where he rented out her labor to local white families. Keckley developed her talents as a seamstress and cultivated a clientele and a network of supporters whom she would ultimately draw upon in her bid for freedom. Living in St. Louis also put Keckley in contact with the city's sizable free black community, which by 1850 was more numerous than the enslaved population.

Keckley's life in St. Louis overlapped with that of the city's two most famous black residents of the antebellum period, Dred and Harriet Scott. Keckley's main connection to the Scott case was through her owner, Hugh Garland, the lawyer who successfully represented Scott's owners in the Missouri courts. Garland was a steadfast supporter of the rights of slaveholders, and he was not eager to grant Keckley her freedom when she asked him to manumit her in 1850. But Garland needed cash badly, and after much resistance, he agreed in 1852 to free Keckley in return for $1,200. Over the next three years, Keckley worked to raise the large sum. Keckley remained in St. Louis for several years while she repaid those who had helped her purchase her freedom. In 1860, she moved to Baltimore and then to Washington, D.C., where the former slave became active in black philanthropic causes and a minor celebrity in the capital's social circles.

Elizabeth Keckley. Born a slave in Virginia, Keckley found freedom in St. Louis and later became a successful businesswoman in the nation's capital.

Think About It

1. How was an enslaved African American able to use domestic service to escape bondage in St. Louis?
2. Why would Keckley's rise to celebrity have been less likely had she remained in a rural location in Virginia and not moved to Missouri?

race, "so far inferior, that they had no rights which the white man was bound to respect." The founders had not intended the descendants of slaves to become citizens, and free blacks could not attain U.S. citizenship, even if they were citizens of individual states.

This sweeping claim ought to have ended the matter, but the chief justice (like President Buchanan) was eager to resolve the question that was on the minds of the white electorate. Even though it should have made no difference to Scott's case, Taney proceeded to rule the Missouri Compromise unconstitutional and to deny that Congress could prohibit slavery in the territories. The clause in the Constitution authorizing Congress to regulate the territories applied only to those territories possessed or contemplated in 1787, according to Taney. Furthermore, he argued, slaves were property, and as such were protected against government seizure by the Fifth Amendment. This last claim meant that even leaving the slavery question to popular sovereignty was unconstitutional, since Congress could not grant a territorial government any authority that it did not possess. The Court as a whole supported Taney's decision by a seven-to-two vote, though the six concurring justices each wrote individual opinions, and they did not all affirm the entirety of Taney's rationale. But Taney was the chief justice and his majority opinion appeared to be the new of the land.

SPACES & PLACES

Mount Vernon

Mount Vernon. As in Abraham Lincoln's famous "House-Divided" speech, Ann Cunningham and the Mount Vernon Ladies' Association offered a house as a symbol of national unity.

Amid the widening sectional rift over slavery, a group of women decided to turn the plantation where George Washington was buried into a symbol of national unity. Mount Vernon, located near Alexandria, Virginia, had been the founding father's home until his death in 1799, and had been passed down to a series of heirs over the next half a century. In 1850, Washington's great grand-nephew, John Augustine Washington III, signed a contract with a steamboat company to bring visitors to the plantation, and Mount Vernon quickly became a tourist attraction. As the traffic increased, deteriorating conditions on the property began to alarm those who saw Washington's burial site as a sacred place. More worrisome to them were the rumors that Washington's heirs might sell Mount Vernon to entrepreneurs who would turn the plantation into a theme park or another Barnum's Museum.

Ann Pamela Cunningham, the daughter of a wealthy South

FEAR AND CRISIS

Buchanan's confidence that the *Scott* decision had settled the slavery controversy once and for all was deeply misplaced. Instead, Taney's opinion became the centerpiece of sectional conflict. Republicans renewed charges of a Slave Power conspiracy that now controlled both the presidency and the Supreme Court. Northern Democrats found themselves on the defensive and rifts within the party widened. As the next presidential election loomed, an eruption of abolitionist violence in Virginia augured unimaginable bloodshed.

THE LINCOLN-DOUGLAS DEBATES

Senator Stephen Douglas's political career was instantly jeopardized by the *Dred Scott* decision. Having staked his fortunes on the ideal of popular sovereignty as a solution to the slavery problem, he now faced a Supreme Court decision that appeared to undermine it by completely deregulating slavery. A practical test of the status of popular sovereignty came in 1858, when Buchanan sought statehood for Kansas under the proslavery Lecompton Constitution, which had not been submitted to popular ratification. The president, invoking *Dred Scott,* believed that slavery was now legal in the territories "by virtue of the Constitution." But Douglas continued to champion popular sovereignty and joined Republicans in blocking the statehood bill. Douglas stuck to his principle, but in the new political landscape created by Taney's decision, this now cost him southern support.

Having stood up to the administration on the Kansas question, Douglas returned triumphantly to Illinois to campaign for reelection. His opponent was a former Whig legislator and congressman named Abraham Lincoln who had emerged as the leader of the new Republican party in the

Carolina slaveholder, spearheaded a campaign to purchase Mount Vernon from John Augustine Washington in order to preserve it against the ravages of time and commercialization. Appealing initially to "Ladies of the South," Cunningham warned that Washington's home was in danger of being engulfed by the "blackening smoke and deafening machinery" of northern industry. But she soon broadened her pitch to include women throughout the nation. Patriotic women, Cunningham argued, would band together to save Mount Vernon, even as men resorted to blows and arms over the extension of slavery. The Mount Vernon Ladies' Association (MVLA) was incorporated in 1856, the same year that violence erupted in Kansas and on the floor of the U.S. Senate.

The founders of the MVLA designed an elaborate fundraising structure, with Cunningham as the national regent and vice regents in each state overseeing local committees. Both prominent and ordinary women from all parts of the country joined the campaign, and their efforts were supported by public lectures, magazine articles, and pictorial exhibitions stressing the virtues of Washington and the worthiness of the cause. Even with the national economy plunging into a deep depression, the MVLA raised John Augustine Washington's $200,000 asking price (see How Much Is That?).

The MVLA envisioned Mount Vernon as a kind of shrine, but instead of building a monument or a mausoleum, it presented the Washington plantation as first and foremost a home. This resonated with the popular idea that the nation's first president was a model of civic virtue because he retired to his private, farming life after serving his two terms in office. It also fit the emerging gender ideals of the period. Cunningham and the other Mount Vernon Ladies were trying to rescue a domestic setting and suggesting that a private home could provide a haven from the political conflicts that were wracking the nation.

Keeping the issue of slavery out of the Mount Vernon campaign was especially challenging, because Mount Vernon was not simply a home; it was also a plantation with slaves. In his will, George Washington had emancipated all 123 people who were his sole legal property, but most of the slaves living on the Mount Vernon plantation at the time of his death belonged, strictly speaking, to Martha, and they remained in bondage. Mount Vernon heirs continued to own, purchase, and rent out slaves. Some abolitionists supported the MVLA campaign in order to redeem George Washington's legacy from slavery (the plantation operation was to be shut down and the slaves moved out), but many refused to do business with slaveholders. In 1858, the MVLA made a hefty down payment on the property and took title to the new national shrine. With the money he received, John Augustine Washington bought another plantation and eight additional slaves.

How Much Is That?

Mount Vernon

The $200,000 raised by the MVLA to buy Mount Vernon represents the buying power of $5.6 million in 2013, or about 3-4 times the assessed value of President Obama's home in Chicago.

Think About It

1. Why might a movement to turn Mount Vernon into a national shrine have emerged specifically in the 1850s?
2. How might white people in the North and the South have interpreted the legacy of Washington and his home differently?

state. Raised in a yeoman farming family that had moved west from Kentucky, to Indiana, and then to Illinois in search of cheaper land opportunities, Lincoln had become a store clerk and then a lawyer, entering a middle-class culture of respectability marked by temperance, self-control, and self-education. On the subject of slavery, Lincoln had been a supporter of the Wilmot Proviso and marched in step with moderate antislavery opinion in Illinois. He bitterly opposed opening new territories to slavery, favored gradual emancipation where slavery existed, and spoke of a time when free blacks might be colonized to West Africa, where they might enjoy their rights unfettered by racial prejudice.

Ordinarily, Douglas would have been a heavy favorite in this race. But widespread disenchantment with the Democrats in the wake of a major economic depression in 1857 made every Democratic senator vulnerable. Lincoln shrewdly challenged the incumbent to a series of seven debates, where he pushed Douglas to square his doctrine of popular sovereignty with Taney's decision in *Dred Scott.* Lincoln hoped to link Douglas to Taney and persuade Illinois voters that their free soil was not safe on his watch. Taking a text from the Gospels, "A house divided against itself cannot stand," Lincoln argued that the extension of slavery westward would ultimately bring slavery to free states as well. "I believe this government cannot endure, permanently, half slave and half free. I do not expect the Union to be dissolved—I do not expect the house to fall—but I do expect it will cease to be divided. It will become all one thing or all the other. Either the opponents of slavery will arrest the further spread of it, and place it where the public mind shall rest in the belief that it is in the course of ultimate extinction; or its advocates will push it forward, till it shall become alike lawful in all the States, old as well as new—North as well as South" (see Spaces and Places: Mount Vernon).

Lincoln-Douglas Debates, 1858. On the campaign trail, Lincoln tried to defend himself against charges of being an abolitionist and an amalgamationist. "Now I protest against that counterfeit logic which concludes that, because I do not want a black woman for a slave I must necessarily want her for a wife. I need not have her for either, I can just leave her alone."

Douglas rejected Lincoln's dire predictions and resisted Lincoln's attempts to get him to admit that new states could no longer decide the fate of slavery on an individual basis. In their Freeport, Illinois, debate, Douglas insisted that although the Supreme Court barred settlers from outlawing slavery in the territories, settlers could still make slavery unworkable by refusing to enact laws necessary to protect it. The Freeport Doctrine was probably plausible and palatable enough to persuade his Democratic constituents that Douglas was not beholden to the Slave Power. Free of that grip, Douglas counterattacked with the devastating charge that Lincoln was an abolitionist who favored racial equality, two things Lincoln vigorously denied.

Since senators were not directly elected before the twentieth century, the 1858 Lincoln-Douglas race was determined by the elections for state legislators. Republicans drew more votes and Lincoln's supporters gained more legislative seats, but because the Democrats held more of the seats that were not up for election that year, Douglas won narrowly. It had been a costly victory, however. Roger Taney and Abraham Lincoln had made Douglas choose between his short-term and long-term political future. The Freeport Doctrine shored up his credentials in Illinois, but it thoroughly discredited him in the South.

JOHN BROWN'S RAID

On October 16, 1859, John Brown, the religious zealot who had massacred proslavery settlers in Kansas three years earlier, crossed the Potomac River from Maryland to Virginia with nineteen men, five of them African Americans. His immediate objective was to seize a federal arsenal in Harpers Ferry, Virginia (now West Virginia), and secure arms for a slave insurrection. Ultimately, Brown sought, in his words, "to purge this land with blood." In its first goal, John Brown's raid was a failure. Local militiamen surrounded the arsenal, a force of U.S. Marines led by Robert E. Lee arrived, half of Brown's party was killed, Brown himself was wounded, and all the survivors were captured. Slaves on nearby plantations did not take the raid as a cue to revolt, and the immediate threat was thwarted. Virginia convicted Brown quickly of treason and conspiracy, and hanged him on December 2.

Although most northerners, including most Republican officials, repudiated Brown's raid, several abolitionists, both white and black, had supported Brown's plan in advance and many others celebrated his effort after it failed. Expressions of abolitionist support for Brown alarmed white southerners. Both Lydia Maria Child and Ralph Waldo Emerson compared his martyrdom to that of Jesus and predicted that hanging him would turn the gallows and the scaffold into sacred symbols. William Lloyd Garrison, who had always preached nonviolence, wished "success to every Slave insurrection at the South and in every country." On the day of the hanging, bells tolled in many New England towns.

If Nat Turner had initiated a period of proslavery defiance, John Brown brought it to a hysterical climax. One Atlanta newspaper announced that "we regard every man in our midst an enemy . . . who does not boldly declare that he believes African slavery to be a social, moral, and political blessing." Statements about slavery had become a matter of life and death.

***The Last Moments of John Brown*, by Thomas Hovenden, 1884.** Hailed and mourned by abolitionists in the Northeast and upper Midwest, Brown appeared to southerners as a harbinger of mortal danger for whites living in a biracial slave society.

THE ELECTION OF 1860

At the time of Brown's hanging, a presidential campaign was already under way. Predictably, the Democratic convention in Charleston, South Carolina, featured a showdown between northern delegates who supported Douglas's program of popular sovereignty and southerners who advocated federal laws protecting slavery in the territories. Douglas corralled the simple majority of votes to install a popular sovereignty plank in the party platform but lacked the two-thirds majority necessary to nominate him. Once the popular sovereignty plank passed, delegates from the Deep South bolted the convention. Douglas's supporters reconvened in Baltimore to nominate him, but southern Democrats staged their own convention and nominated Buchanan's vice president, John C. Breckinridge of Kentucky, on a proslavery platform. More moderate southerners, including many former Whigs, turned to John Bell of Tennessee, who ran on the Constitutional Union ticket, which affirmed the union and law and order over sectional concerns.

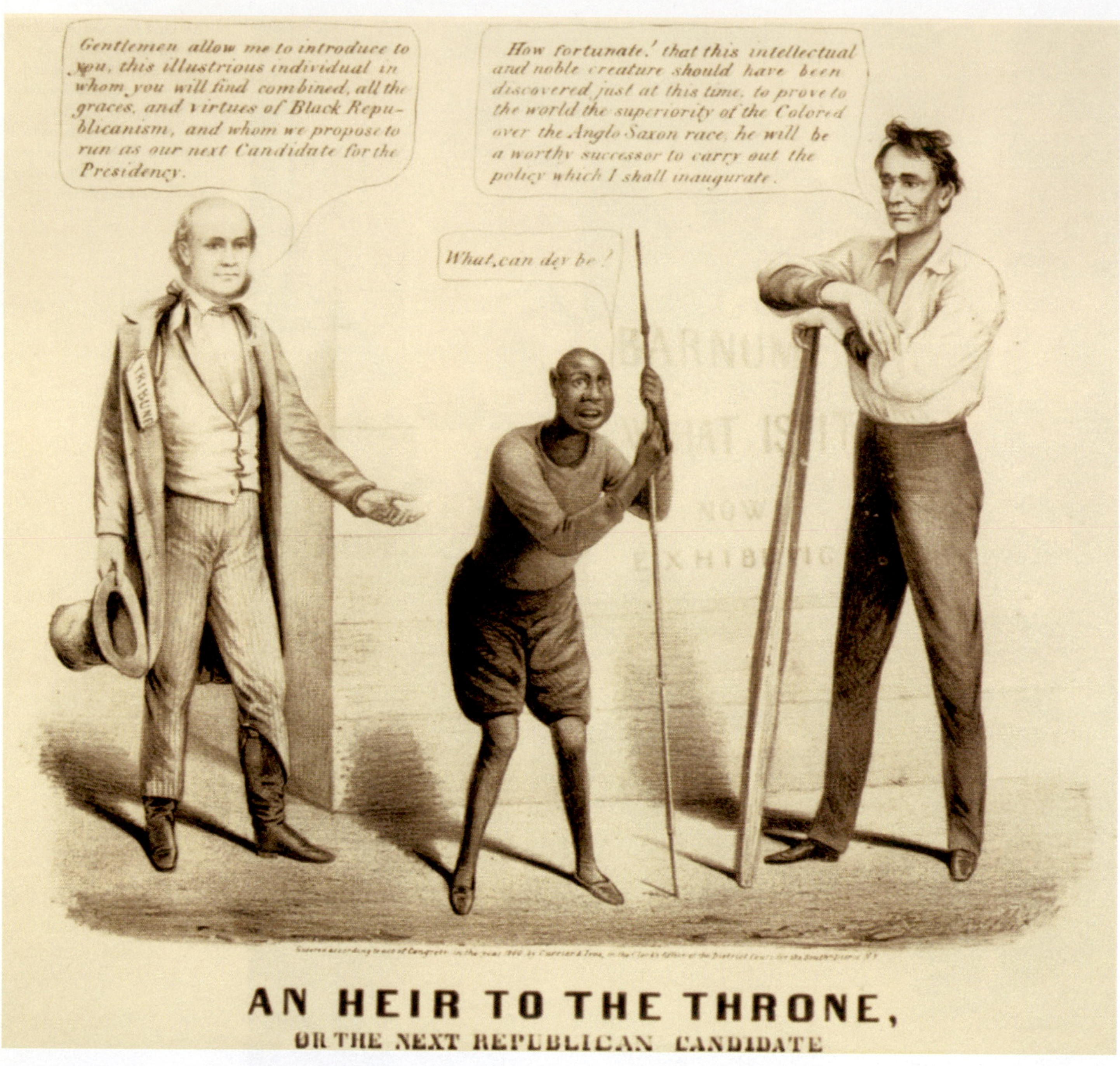

Currier and Ives Cartoon—Election of 1860. In an attempt to taint Lincoln with the brush of abolitionism, the Democrats invoked a popular "What Is It?" exhibit from Barnum's Museum. For the exhibit, Barnum hired an African American man named William Henry Johnson, who was developmentally disabled and microcephalic, dressed him in a fur suit, and asked viewers to decide "whether it is human or animal." Lincoln's actual running mate, Hannibal Hamlin, was dark skinned, and Democratic newspapers fanned speculations about his racial identity. The *Charleston Mercury* claimed that Hamlin "had negro blood in his veins and . . . one of his children had kinky hair." **Question for Analysis:** What was this cartoon trying to suggest about Lincoln's views on racial equality?

The decisive split in the old Democratic coalition left the South vulnerable to an antislavery takeover of the presidency. But to take advantage of this opportunity, the Republicans needed to sweep the North. Even more so than in 1856, the Republicans could expect no votes in the South. In most slave states, no Republican ballots would even be printed. Republicans understood that they would not be running against Breckinridge. Their real opponent was Douglas, whom they needed to defeat in nearly every free state. Rather than risk it all on a more prominent antislavery politician,

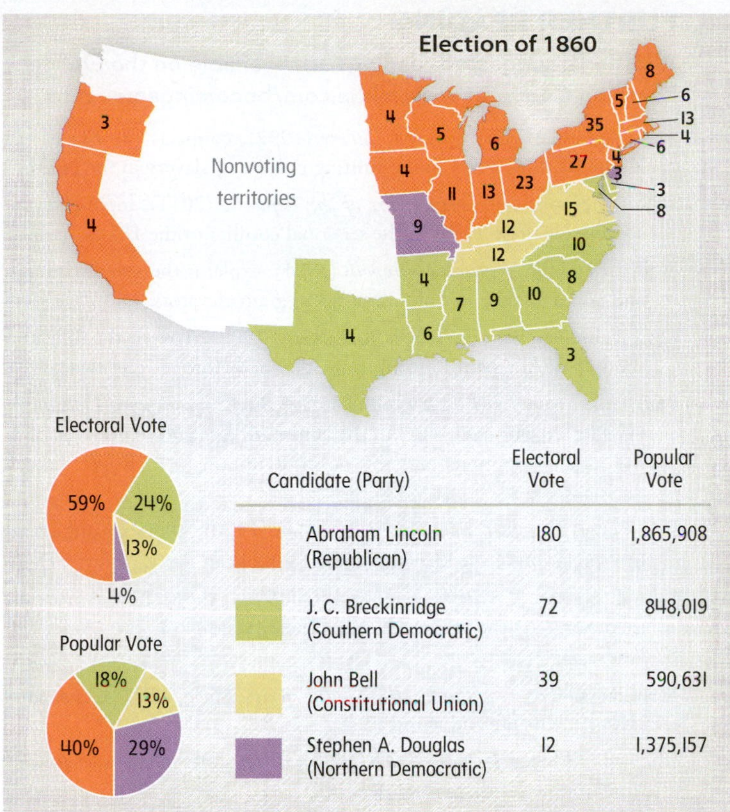

Candidate (Party)	Electoral Vote	Popular Vote
Abraham Lincoln (Republican)	180	1,865,908
J. C. Breckinridge (Southern Democratic)	72	848,019
John Bell (Constitutional Union)	39	590,631
Stephen A. Douglas (Northern Democratic)	12	1,375,157

Map 14.5 Election of 1860.

like William Seward of New York or Salmon Chase of Ohio, they nominated Abraham Lincoln, whose moderate views on slavery and lack of association with nativism made him a safer choice. Lincoln was also from Illinois, a state that had become more prominent in the railroad era, whose eleven electoral votes might prove crucial to securing a Republican majority. Lincoln ran on a free-labor platform that offered northern voters additional incentives to vote Republican that had little to do with slavery, including protective tariffs, homesteads, and internal improvements. The Republicans, not facing any nativist opposition and hoping to cut into the Democratic base, also affirmed the political rights of immigrants.

In a tense election that drew the largest turnout in U.S. history to that point, Lincoln captured the electoral majority (see Map 14.5). He won every state where slavery was illegal except for New Jersey (which he split with Douglas), and that was more than enough to win the election. Though his overall share of the popular vote was just 40 percent, Lincoln won majorities in the most populous states. Although Douglas ran competitively in much of the North, he won no free states outright. Douglas finished second in the popular vote but dead last in the vote that mattered. Divided between North and South, the Democratic Party was no longer a national force. Without its protection, slavery now seemed vulnerable to assault from the federal government.

CONCLUSION

Lincoln's election in 1860 was no ordinary shift in political power. For the first time in U.S. history, a president had been elected on a platform that was explicitly critical of slavery. The Republicans had also seized the presidency without a single electoral vote from a southern state, a sure sign that the South had lost its veto power over national policy. Equally ominous, from the perspective of the South, was the fact that the Democratic Party had splintered. During the three decades of sustained public debate about the legitimacy of slavery, both northern and southern Democrats had provided crucial political protection for southern slaveholding. Without that protection, slavery now rested on shakier ground.

The collapse of the Democratic coalition was the result of many forces and circumstances. The Mexican cession, westward migration, and the California gold rush forced Congress to make new decisions about slavery in the territories. New political compromises stirred up conflicts that had been held in check by older political compromises. Meanwhile, foreign immigration had greatly increased the population (and the political power) of the free states, while new patterns of transportation and communication had made it harder to insulate one part of the country from another. The older model of compromise, which relied on geographical distance, was systematically dismantled over the course of the decade, first in the Compromise of 1850, then in the Kansas-Nebraska Act, and finally in *Dred Scott*.

By 1860, the map no longer provided a viable means of splitting political differences. Instead, American voters faced two radically different options. A Democratic Supreme Court proposed a bold solution that deregulated slavery in the name of the sanctity of private property. The new Republican opposition offered an alternative model of regulating slavery and celebrating freely contracting laborers. In the new cultural and political landscape created during the 1850s, the Republicans won.

STUDY TERMS

Free Soil Party (p. 353)
fire-eaters (p. 353)
popular sovereignty (p. 353)
Compromise of 1850 (p. 353)
Fugitive Slave Act (p. 354)
Uncle Tom's Cabin (p. 356)
Chicago (p. 360)
grain elevator (p. 361)
wage slavery (p. 364)
Kansas-Nebraska Act (p. 365)
Know-Nothing Party (p. 366)
Bleeding Kansas (p. 369)
Republicans (p. 369)
Dred Scott v. Sandford (p. 370)
Lecompton Constitution (p. 372)
Freeport Doctrine (p. 374)
John Brown's raid (p. 374)

TIMELINE

1848 United States acquires Mexican cession in the Treaty of Guadalupe Hidalgo

Galena and Illinois Railroad begins service

Chicago Board of Trade founded

Zachary Taylor elected president

1850 California admitted as a free state as part of congressional compromise

1852 *Uncle Tom's Cabin* published in book form

1853 Gadsden Purchase obtained from Mexico in anticipation of railroad route

1854 Congress passes Kansas-Nebraska Act

Anthony Burns captured in Boston and returned to bondage in Virginia

Know-Nothing Party scores major electoral victories

1856 Violence erupts in Kansas between supporters of rival territorial governments

Preston Brooks bludgeons Charles Sumner on the Senate floor

Republican Party emerges as a political force in the North and West

1857 Roger B. Taney announces *Dred Scott v. Sandford* decision

1858 Congress rejects Kansas's Lecompton Constitution

Abraham Lincoln and Stephen Douglas debate in Illinois

1859 John Brown leads raid on federal arsenal in Harpers Ferry, Virginia

John Brown is hanged

1860 Lincoln wins four-way presidential race

FURTHER READING

Additional suggested readings are available on the Online Learning Center at www.mhhe.com/becomingamerica1e.

Tyler Anbinder, *Nativism and Slavery* (1992), connects the rise of the Know-Nothing Party to the shifting politics of slavery in the North.

Adam Arenson, *The Great Heart of the Republic* (2011), highlights the special role of St. Louis in the sectional conflict of the 1850s.

William Cronon, *Nature's Metropolis* (1991), explains the rise of Chicago and highlights the role of railroads and grain elevators.

Don Fehrenbacher, *Prelude to Greatness* (1962), covers the life and thought of Abraham Lincoln in the decade before his presidency.

Paul Finkelman, *Dred Scott v. Sandford: A Brief History with Documents* (1997), lays out the history of the landmark case and reproduces both the judicial opinions and the political responses to Roger Taney's decision.

Eric Foner, *Free Soil, Free Labor, Free Men* (1970), offers an influential interpretation of the ideology of the Republican Party.

John F. Kasson, *Civilizing the Machine* (1976), shows how Americans incorporated the railroad into their vision of the American landscape.

Stephen Oates, *To Purge This Land with Blood* (1984), presents John Brown's life and world view.

Michael O'Malley, *Keeping Watch* (1990), traces shifts in attitudes toward time in nineteenth-century America.

Mark M. Smith, *Mastered by the Clock* (1997), challenges the myth that the antebellum South was a society not yet permeated by modern time-consciousness.

Albert J. von Frank, *The Trials of Anthony Burns* (1998), demonstrates how a single fugitive slave case precipitated a cultural crisis in New England.

Gavin Wright, *The Political Economy of the Cotton South* (1978), provides a quantitative analysis of the role of slaves and slavery in the southern economy.

15

INSIDE ▶

THE BIG PICTURE

The Civil War plunged the nation into an unexpectedly long period of carnage, chaos, and dislocation. Uniformed soldiers massacred one another on open battlefields, and civilians endured and engaged in guerrilla raids, urban riots, and plantation escapes. Meanwhile, new media brought images of the war's toll into homes far removed from the fighting.

Mourning Daguerreotype. A brutal war brought death and destruction to families across the country.

1861–1865

DISUNION & WAR

On a Sunday in February 1862, much of the population of Nashville, Tennessee, was sitting dutifully in church when news arrived that the city was about to be attacked. Ministers released their congregations, but Nashville residents were unsure how to prepare for what lay ahead. Louisa Pearl described her neighbors "hurrying to & fro like crazy people not knowing what to do." By the end of the day, the post office had closed, newspaper presses stood idle, and state government officials were escaping the city on trains. Soldiers charged with protecting the city prepared to leave as well, but first they seized horses, mules, and carriages, destroyed bridges and other resources that might be of use to the enemy, and looted private property. Banks shut, stores were emptied, and utter chaos reigned. Pearl began to hope that the invaders would finally arrive.

The army advancing on Nashville in 1862 marched under the banner of the United States. To most of the city's white population, however, the troops represented a foreign enemy. The political split between slave and free states in the 1850s had turned quickly into a brutal civil war between foes who saw each other as belonging to alien cultures, distant homelands, and distinct nations. The reality, of course, was that the soldiers attacking Nashville and those fleeing the city had a great deal in common. Most men on both the Union and the Confederate sides spoke English, shared a similar European ancestry and Christian religious identity, venerated the same founding fathers, and claimed the legacy of the same American Revolution.

Civil War events and themes came to dominate popular art, music, and literature.

KEY QUESTIONS

- What course of events led from Abraham Lincoln's election to military conflict between North and South?
- Why were white southerners threatened by Lincoln's election?
- In what stages did Union war policy toward slavery and emancipation unfold?
- What were the major battles, campaigns, and turning points of the Civil War?
- What were the experiences and significance of black soldiers in the Union Army?
- How did the war bring disorder and violence to Americans living far from major battlefields?
- Through what media, new and old, did Americans on the home front experience the war?

Those fighting for the Union in the Civil War years of 1861 to 1865 saw themselves as continuing the revolutionary struggle to build a viable democratic republic based on majority rule, whereas their counterparts on the Confederate side saw themselves as reasserting the revolutionary right to dissolve existing governments in order to protect local freedoms. Despite that stark ideological division, allegiances could shift and blur. In border states like Tennessee, which had seceded from the union a year earlier, men from the same towns fought on opposite sides of the conflict. In many parts of the country, people switched, suppressed, or misrepresented their loyalties over the course of the fighting, adding to the climate of chaos and confusion. The war divided neighborhoods and families, and not just the nation.

But it was the division of the United States into two large military apparatuses with massive armies that took the greatest and most unimaginable toll. Scholars now estimate that as many as 750,000 U.S. soldiers perished in the Civil War, more than the number who died in all other American wars combined between 1775 and 1945. Another fifty thousand civilians lost their lives as a result of diseases, food shortages, guerrilla warfare, and urban riots that accompanied the war. The death total was only the most tragic of the war's terrible consequences. Limbs were shattered, homes destroyed, fortunes squandered, communities divided, families torn apart. The Civil War brought the United States unprecedented carnage, devastation, and chaos.

For many Americans, the war was also a time of possibilities. Southern whites in the eleven states that seceded from the United States built a new nation. At the same time, a federal Union now firmly controlled by northern Republicans expanded the role of the central government in new areas and directions. More dramatically, enslaved African Americans found opportunities amid the carnage and chaos to renegotiate their relationships with their masters, escape their bondage, take up arms against the slave regime, and turn the Union war effort, slowly, into a crusade against slavery.

SECESSION

With remarkable speed and efficiency, the states in the Lower South responded to the 1860 presidential election by severing their ties to the United States. They left the union as individual states, claiming either the right to secede or the right of revolution, but they had no intention of remaining independent entities. By the time Abraham Lincoln took office, the rebellious states had coalesced to form their own rival government and were preparing for the possibility of war. Unionists throughout the country devised plans to woo back the seceded states, or at least to prevent other slave states from joining them, but the incoming administration proved unable to reassure the South that slavery would be safe under a Republican regime. Within a month of his inauguration, President Lincoln had to decide whether to enforce federal authority in a rebellious South Carolina. When he did, shots were fired, more states seceded, and war began.

THE CONFEDERATION OF THE COTTON STATES

To most southern whites, Lincoln's victory at the polls meant that the federal government was now in the clutches of a radical party that secretly supported John Brown and openly sought to destroy the South's way of life. Even though Democrats still controlled Congress and the Supreme Court, and even though Lincoln had insisted during the campaign that he had no desire to restrict slavery where it was already legal, leaders in the states most committed to slavery did not want to wait to see what the new government might do. Immediately after receiving news of the election, South Carolina's state legislature called a convention to consider the question of secession. By a vote of 169 to 0, the convention passed an ordinance on December 20, 1860, declaring that "the union now subsisting between South Carolina and other States, under the name of the 'United States of America,' is hereby dissolved." Though acting alone, South Carolinians saw themselves as the vanguard of a larger revolution to build a new nation. "The tea has been thrown overboard," a Charleston newspaper announced, "the revolution of 1860 has been initiated."

While South Carolina was voting to secede, other states in the cotton kingdom were working toward the same goals. Alabama and Mississippi dispatched representatives to the other slave states to drum up support for a southern confederation. **Secession commissioners,** as these representatives were called, also came from South Carolina, Georgia, and Louisiana, lobbying more states to secede. Wherever they traveled in the South, the commissioners sounded the same basic themes. The "Black Republicans," as southerners generally labeled Lincoln's party, intended to abolish slavery and elevate blacks to positions of social and political equality. Commissioners also warned audiences that abolitionism would lead either to a race war or to the "amalgamation" of the two races. In the southernmost states, the commissioners were often preaching to the choir. Newspapers, ministers, and secessionist delegates in the Lower South were expressing and stoking the same fears. "Submission to Black Republicanism," one Alabama secessionist predicted, meant forcing "our wives and daughters [to] choose between death and gratifying the hellish lust of the negro." If the South wanted to avoid this dire scenario, delegates to these secession conventions argued, they needed to act preemptively. One by one, six more state conventions voted to secede. By February 1, Mississippi, Florida, Alabama, Georgia, Louisiana, and Texas had followed in South Carolina's footsteps. Three days later, delegates from the seceding states met in Montgomery, Alabama, and established the Confederate States of America, with a new constitution and Jefferson Davis of Mississippi as its president (see Map 15.1).

Though the seven rebellious states made it explicit that they were leaving the union over the issue of slavery, they defended their right do so in terms of state sovereignty. Because states had ratified the U.S. Constitution, they argued, states could withdraw from it as well. Some secession leaders claimed that even if states did not have the constitutional right to secede, they nonetheless had a natural "right of revolution," much like the revolutionaries of 1776. In his inaugural address, President Jefferson Davis (who took office two weeks before Lincoln), emphasized the rights of states and individuals to resist oppressive government. But if the *justification* for secession lay in abstract principles of **states' rights,** the real *cause* for which the Lower South was willing to risk the consequences of secession was slavery and racial supremacy. One month after the Confederacy was established, its vice president, Alexander Stephens, announced that the core principle of the new government was "the great truth that the negro is not equal to the white man; that slavery, subordination to the superior race, is his natural and moral condition."

THE UPPER SOUTH IN THE BALANCE

The seven states that formed the Confederacy in February 1861 represented only about half of the slave South. In the eight other slave states (North Carolina, Virginia, Maryland, Delaware, Kentucky, Tennessee, Missouri, and Arkansas), arguments for secession fell short. Slaveholders made up smaller percentages of the white population in those states and consequently wielded less political power. In the larger cities in the Upper South, especially Baltimore, St. Louis, and Richmond, growing numbers of white artisans and European immigrants were unenthusiastic about slavery and indifferent to calls for a preemptive strike against a possible Republican antislavery agenda. Many slaveholders in the Upper South also supported staying in the union, because they worried that their property would be less safe if the nation split in two. Slaveholders in states bordering the North were especially dependent on federal fugitive slave laws; if their states seceded, the North would have no political incentive to maintain or enforce those laws. And throughout the Upper South, unionists touted the close economic ties that bound them to their northern neighbors. In Missouri, for example, opponents of secession argued effectively that leaving

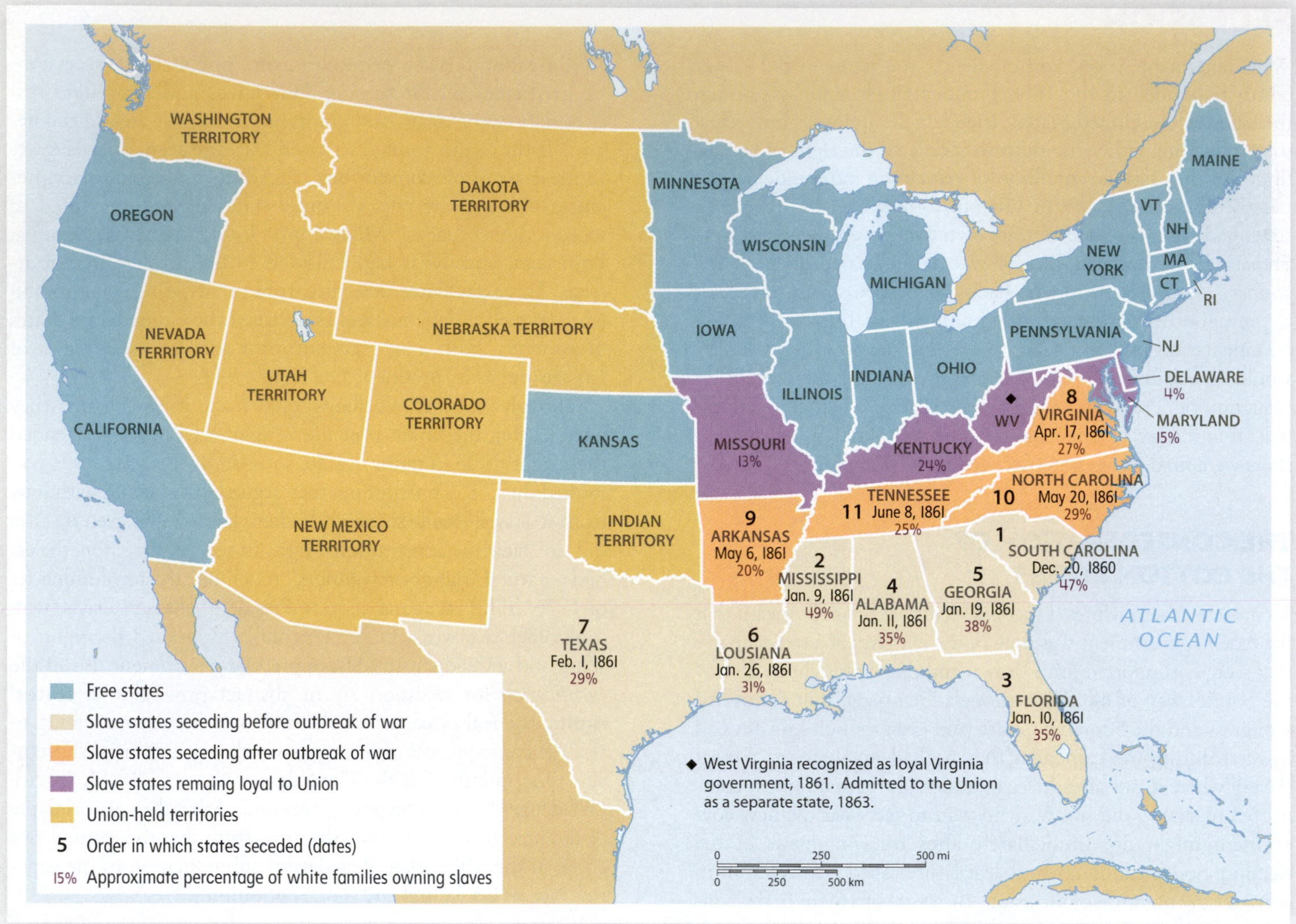

Map 15.1. Secession in Two Stages. Seven states in the Lower South seceded between Lincoln's election in November 1860 and his inauguration four months later. Those in the Upper South did not secede until after the firing on Fort Sumter. Four other slave states remained in the union. **Question for Analysis:** How did the decision to secede correlate to the extent of slave ownership?

the union would end the building of the transcontinental railroad and thwart the state's economic development.

Secessionists tried to persuade nonslaveholding whites throughout the South that they too had a stake in the perpetuation of the region's labor system. Slavery exempted poorer whites from belonging to the menial class, slaveholders argued. In the words of the governor of Georgia, "the poor white laborer . . . belongs to the only true aristocracy" in the South, "the race of *white men*." Upcountry farmers in the Lower South may have warmed to appeals to racial supremacy, but those in the Upper South were less moved. Perhaps because several of those states had relatively small black populations, the prospect of interracial unions, slave insurrections, and race war may have seemed less real.

Both the new Confederacy and Lincoln's government-in-waiting understood that the Upper South held the key to the fate of the secession movement. By themselves, the seven seceded states faced grim prospects for resisting the United States. The eight northernmost slave states held more than half of the South's population and about two-thirds of the white population that would be called on to defend the region in the event of war. And though the Lower South was rich with cotton and slaves, the Upper South accounted for most of the South's livestock and food supply and the vast majority of its industrial capacity. During the months between the establishment of the Confederacy and Lincoln's inauguration, both sides sought, above all, to avoid alienating the Upper South.

COMPROMISE PLANS

As states began seceding, proponents of national reconciliation urged various compromises that would reassure the South that slavery was safe. Outgoing President Buchanan, who denied that states had any right to secede but also denied the federal government the authority to compel them back into the union, called on the North to help return fugitive slaves, support plans to add Cuba as a slave state, and pass a constitutional amendment protecting slavery in all territories. Most northerners refused to take this proposal seriously, deriding it as essentially the political platform of the Slave Power. Special committees in Congress, composed of men from both regions and both parties, gathered to consider other strategies for compromise. John J. Crittenden, a Whig from Kentucky, crafted a proposal in the Senate to assuage southern fears by passing a series of irrevocable constitutional amendments. The first plank of the Crittenden Compromise would have prevented the federal government from ever interfering with slavery in the states where it was legal in 1861. The second plank would have barred Congress from outlawing slavery in the national capital—unless the voters there requested it and the neighboring states of Virginia and Maryland had already abolished slavery. The final piece of the plan extended the geographical line of the Missouri Compromise to divide slave soil from free soil in all territories "now held, or hereafter acquired."

Many prominent Republicans appeared willing to sign on to this compromise, but the president-elect instructed them not to. Writing from his home in Illinois, Lincoln told his supporters in Congress not to budge on the question of extending slavery into the territories. Other issues, such as fugitive slave enforcement and protections for slavery where it was legal, were open to negotiation, but not this one. The Senate rejected Crittenden's plan. Congress took other measures to stem the tide of secession, including the approval of a proposed constitutional amendment forever prohibiting the federal government from abolishing slavery in the states. Such gestures probably helped keep the Upper South in the union a little longer, but by the time Lincoln took office on March 4, 1861, neither the secessionists nor the Republicans were eager to compromise.

In his inaugural address, Lincoln insisted that secession was unacceptable and vowed to use "all powers at my disposal" to maintain federal property in the rebellious states. At the same time, he extended a hand to the Upper South, repeating his campaign pledge not "to interfere with the institution of slavery where it exists." Above all, he appealed to patriotism and to the "bonds of affection" uniting all Americans, to the "mystic chords of memory, stretching from every battle-field, and patriot grave, to every living heart and hearthstone, all over this broad land." Confederate leaders seized upon Lincoln's implied threat to use force against the South and labeled it a "Declaration of War." But the crucial audiences for the speech—the Democrats in the North whose support Lincoln would need in order to back up his threats and the unionists in the Upper South whose hand Lincoln needed to strengthen—seemed willing to give the new president a chance.

FORT SUMTER

Lincoln's impossible quest to appear both firm and conciliatory faced a severe test the day after his inauguration, when he received word from the commanding officer at a federal garrison in South Carolina that supplies were running out. Fort Sumter lay four miles from the heart of the port city of Charleston, in the first state to have seceded from the union. Resupplying the fort would be read as an act of military aggression and might nudge the Upper South into the Confederate fold. But evacuating the fort would appear to recognize the Confederacy and might also embolden the Upper South to secede. Caught in this bind, but facing mounting pressure from northerners to act against the rebellion, Lincoln announced his intention to dispatch unarmed ships carrying only food supplies. The ball was now in the Confederacy's court.

Jefferson Davis understood that a federal invasion of the South would unite the region. Lincoln's gambit had dared Davis to fire the first shot, but so long as federal troops retaliated, the effect would be the same. As the Virginia-born secessionist Edmund Ruffin wrote in his diary in Charleston, "the shedding of blood will serve to change many voters in the hesitating states," making them "zealous for immediate secession." Not wanting to fire on the unarmed supply boats, Davis ordered General P. G. T. Beauregard to take the fort before the boats arrived. On April 12, Beauregard's troops fired on Fort Sumter, and after thirty-three hours of bombardment, the undermanned federal garrison surrendered to the Confederacy.

In the North, the attack on Fort Sumter provoked an immediate outpouring of righteous indignation and patriotic fervor. The outcry among Republicans was predictable, but even in Democratic strongholds, the image of the U.S. flag coming down under fire in South Carolina was too much to bear. In New York City, whose mayor had recently floated the idea that the city should secede and form an independent political jurisdiction with ties to both the North and the South, 250,000 people turned out for a pro-union rally. In Chicago, Democrat Stephen Douglas captured the new mood: "Every man must be for the United States or against it. There can be no neutrals in this war, *only patriots—or traitors*." Lincoln's immediate call for seventy-five thousand militiamen to put down the rebellion was answered quickly and enthusiastically throughout the region.

In the Upper South, by contrast, the militia summons had the opposite effect. Leaders in those states denounced Lincoln for authorizing an invasion of the South and made it clear that they would play no part in a crusade of "northern aggression." Two days after Lincoln called for troops, the crucial state of Virginia (the most populous in the South) voted to secede. Arkansas followed soon thereafter, as did Tennessee and North Carolina. Kentucky, Maryland, and Missouri ultimately remained in the union, but only after protracted political battles and—in the case of Maryland and especially Missouri—armed clashes between the two sides. Arguments for secession in those states described the Lower South states as "sisters" and appealed to a widespread view of the South as a single and distinct culture threatened by strangers. Secessionists invoked this regional identity and spoke the language of loyalty and honor (see Chapter 11). But even after Fort Sumter, slavery remained the crucial factor in determining attitudes toward secession. Delegates who owned significant numbers of slaves and represented counties with higher slave populations voted overwhelmingly to secede. Delaware, with a tiny enslaved population, was the only slave state without a significant secession movement.

As the dust settled from the Fort Sumter bombardment, a new national map emerged. The Confederacy, with its capital now relocated to Richmond, Virginia, contained eleven southern states, which held just under 30 percent of the nation's population; more than a third of the people living in the Confederacy were enslaved. In the three border states of Kentucky, Maryland, and Missouri, the U.S. flag still flew, but the

Multilingual Union Recruitment Poster, New York. Neither side anticipated the unprecedented manpower that the war would entail. Lincoln's request for troops in April 1861 sought seventy-five thousand militiamen (almost five times the size of the federal army at the time) for a period of ninety days. The Confederacy had begun earlier and more ambitiously, authorizing an armed force of one hundred thousand men to serve for twelve months. By the end of the war, more than 2.2 million had served on the Union side, and close to 900,000 (three-quarters of the white men of military age in the South) had fought for the Confederacy.

population remained more divided. The vast majority of Americans lived farther north, in the other sixteen states. They clung to a vision of a single unified nation.

THE CONFEDERACY UNDER SIEGE, 1861–1862

Badly overmatched in population, infrastructure, and resources (see Table 15.1), the Confederacy could count on one crucial advantage. Like the American colonists in their struggle for independence against Great Britain, the South did not have to conquer or occupy enemy territory; they simply needed to survive the Union onslaught and force a stalemate. The Civil War would be fought largely on southern soil, and Confederate soldiers would be defending their homeland. But this tactical and psychological edge also meant that southern towns, cities, and farms would bear the brunt of the military conflict. Union forces invaded from a number of directions, leaving trails of death and destruction in Virginia and Tennessee, and occupying territory along coasts and rivers in many parts of the South. In the first year and a half of the war, Confederate forces resisted the invasion effectively in the eastern theater, whereas Union armies advanced with greater ease on the western front. As casualties and costs mounted, both sides were disabused of their initial hopes that the Civil War would be a quick affair.

TABLE 15.1 COMPARISON OF CONFEDERATE AND UNION RESOURCES

Resource	Confederacy	Union
Population	39%	61%
Railroad mileage	34%	66%
Farms	33%	67%
Wealth produced	25%	75%
Factories	19%	81%

PREPARING FOR WAR

Both the United States and the Confederacy were unprepared, in multiple ways, for the vast project of war making that lay ahead of them. The South needed to create a new national government and new national institutions (an army, a navy, a treasury, a post office) from scratch. But even in the North, where such institutions were already in place, the military was small, dispersed, and disorganized, and officer ranks had been thinned by southern defections. Because federal bureaucracies were modest in size and not yet capable of coordinating a massive war effort, northern states recruited and outfitted their own soldiers at the outset of the war. Different states negotiated separately with European arms dealers and domestic clothing suppliers, which proved costly and inefficient. Over the next few years, both the Confederacy and (especially) the United States would expand and centralize their government operations in order to deal with the unprecedented and unanticipated scale of the war.

Both Union and Confederate leaders expected the war to be brief, their confidence reflecting a mixture of political calculation and cultural prejudice. Southerners knew how difficult it would be for the Union to invade and occupy a territory of 750,000 square miles. They doubted that Yankees, whom they saw as cowardly and pragmatic, had the stomach for the kind of fighting that would be required. Southern strategists and propagandists also argued that England's dependence on cotton would lead the British government to recognize the Confederacy and intervene in the war. Northerners, for their part, regarded the South as lazy and economically backward, incapable of sustaining a rebellion once the federal government committed to suppressing it. Republicans in the North also saw secession as serving the agenda of the Slave Power, an elite cabal of fire-eating plantation owners. If federal troops made a show of force, many Union politicians figured, nonslaveholders in the South would refuse to fight and more moderate voices in the rebellious states would prevail.

In keeping with their diplomatic objectives and their expectations of a short and limited war, both sides downplayed the issue of slavery. Lincoln crafted the early war effort with an eye toward boosting union strength in the border states. His goal was to quickly suppress a rebellion, not to precipitate a broad revolution in labor or race relations. If unionist leaders in Kentucky, Missouri, or Maryland interpreted the federal war effort as an attack on slavery, Lincoln warned, they might well switch sides. In addition, talking about slavery in the North ran the risk of turning the war into a Republican project, and Lincoln needed bipartisan support for his mobilization efforts. Jefferson Davis also had an interest in avoiding the subject of slavery. Great Britain was far less likely to recognize the Confederacy or intervene in the war if the southern cause were identified with an institution that the British government had abolished in the West Indies and loudly opposed elsewhere. And once the Union armies invaded, it was easy enough to mobilize an army of nonslaveholding white men by asking them to defend their homelands, without having to stress the benefits of white supremacy or the dangers of race war. As two central governments prepared for a military showdown and two armies mustered near the Maryland-Virginia border, a strange silence surrounded the main political controversy that had provoked the crisis.

Civil War Uniforms. (*Top*) Uniform shell jacket of the 71st Pennsylvania Infantry; (*bottom*) Confederate uniform jacket made of homespun cloth. The different uniforms that various state regiments (both North and South) used during the early months of the war caused terrible consequences. In the 1861 Battle of Wilson Creek (Missouri), Union soldiers mistook a group of gray-clad Arkansas soldiers for Iowa volunteers, who also dressed in gray. After the Union men were massacred, Union commanders mandated the wearing of blue uniforms.

A THWARTED INVASION

Feeling pressure from newspapers and politicians in the North to invade Virginia, Lincoln directed General Irvin McDowell to devise an attack in July 1861. McDowell had thirty-five thousand men under his command, mostly untrained recruits nearing the end of their ninety-day commitments. His plan was to move against the twenty thousand Confederate soldiers defending the Manassas railroad junction in northern Virginia, about thirty miles from Washington. A victory there would disrupt the Confederate supply lines, demoralize the South, and pave the way for a march on the new capital at Richmond. But McDowell's troops moved too slowly, a spy ring in Washington led by Rose O'Neal Greenhow alerted General Beauregard to the impending attack, and Union forces in the Shenandoah Valley failed to tie up Confederate general Joseph E. Johnston's reinforcement army of eleven thousand men. By the time the invading army reached Manassas on July 21, the two sides were roughly equal in size. At first McDowell's forces seemed to prevail, but by midafternoon the tide turned, and exhausted Union soldiers began retreating. The orderly retreat of companies turned quickly into the frenetic flight of individual men. A congressman, who had joined the crowds that came down from Washington to watch the battle, looked on with horror at the fleeing, frightened soldiers. "We called to them," he reported, "called them to stop, implored them to stand . . . ; no mortal ever saw such a mass of ghastly wretches."

The First Battle of Bull Run, named for the branch of the Potomac River where much of the fighting took place (the South called it the Battle of Manassas), was a decisive victory for the Confederacy and a major event in the war. Compared to later Civil War battles, the number of casualties was modest, but the 800 soldiers from both sides killed on that day (not counting another 450 mortally wounded) exceeded anything

Americans had seen before. And the political and psychological impact of the chaotic retreat from Virginia ran even deeper. Southerners, finding confirmation of their view of a cowardly North incapable of manly combat, began celebrating their independence. One Richmond newspaper exulted: "The breakdown of the Yankee race, their unfitness for empire, forces dominion on the South. . . .We must adapt ourselves to our new destiny." The North was deeply humiliated, and Lincoln and his generals dug in their heels for what they now accepted would be a much longer struggle.

In the immediate aftermath of Bull Run, Lincoln authorized the recruitment of a million soldiers to serve three-year terms and appointed George B. McClellan the commander of a newly formed Army of the Potomac. A skilled administrator, McClellan built a vast and well-disciplined force, though he was notoriously reluctant to bring it into battle, perhaps mindful of McDowell's failed offensive. McClellan, a Democrat, also clashed with the Republican leadership, including Lincoln, whom he held in low regard and aspired to replace as president. To the great frustration of the Republicans, McClellan held back from attacking the South for months, apart from a single disastrous foray in October 1861, which resulted in the massacre of Union troops at Ball's Bluff.

More than a year after Fort Sumter, and ten months after the Bull Run debacle, McClellan finally ordered a march on Richmond, moving 130,000 soldiers to Norfolk, at the mouth of the James River, and marching inland from there (see Map 15.2). Confederate forces, led by Johnston and then by Robert E. Lee, blocked their onslaught in what was called the Seven Days Battle (June 25–July 1, 1862). The smaller southern army suffered many more casualties, but McClellan withdrew his men back to Washington. Two months later, another Union assault on Manassas met with defeat. Lee then seized the offensive, hoping to take the war into Union territory and compel the North to surrender. On September 17, 1862, the bloodiest day in U.S. history to that point, the Union was able to claim victory in the Battle of Antietam, in Maryland, its first such success on the eastern war front. But three months later, Lee's army successfully defended its position near Fredericksburg, Virginia, killing or wounding thirteen thousand Union troops. As 1862 drew to a close, the Confederates had succeeded in protecting their capital and keeping the invading army out of Virginia.

THE WESTERN FRONT AND THE NAVAL BLOCKADE

Although the U.S. Army of the Potomac faltered, northerners found more cheering news from other theaters of the war. Under the command of General Ulysses S. Grant, an undistinguished graduate of West Point who had been working as a store clerk in western Illinois when the war began, Union forces moved into Tennessee in February 1862 and captured key river positions in successful battles at Fort Henry and Fort Donelson (see Map 15.2). Two months later, Grant prevailed again in the Battle of Shiloh, but at a cost in human life that seemed astonishing at the time. Each side suffered about ten thousand dead and wounded. William Tecumseh Sherman, Grant's right-hand man, wrote home about the spectacle of "piles of dead soldiers' mangled bodies . . . without hands and legs." The Union was winning in Tennessee, but the scale of the carnage persuaded many of the victorious northern soldiers that the war would drag on far longer than expected. To Grant, the lesson of Shiloh was that the Union could not be preserved "except by complete conquest."

The Union war effort also succeeded at sea. From the beginning, General-in-Chief Winfield Scott had advocated a strategy of isolating the South by blockading the sea and controlling the Mississippi River. Sealing off 3,550 miles of Confederate coastline was a tall order for a U.S. Navy with few ships and no beachheads for supplying those ships. But northern boats quickly captured key harbors in the south Atlantic and put the naval blockade into effect. In April 1862, the U.S. Navy took New Orleans, the South's largest port city. As a result of naval success and Grant's victories, large sections of the South were under Union control by the spring of 1862.

The Confederates sought to break the blockade by developing a new weapon: the ironclad warship. A redesigned wooden ship called the *Virginia*, outfitted with an armor plate, destroyed two wooden U.S. ships before being confronted by the Union's own ironclad, the *Monitor*. An inconclusive battle between the two ships on March 9, 1862, dampened southern hopes of reopening their maritime trade. The South also hoped that foreign intervention might end the blockade. Newspapers and political leaders throughout the South urged planters to stop growing and shipping cotton, hoping this might induce textile manufacturers in Great Britain and France to pressure their governments to recognize the Confederacy. But this unofficial cotton embargo had the unintended effect of making the northern blockade seem more effective, which in turn obligated Britain and France to respect it under international law. And as the war dragged on, the embargo wound up impoverishing the South and denying the Confederacy valuable resources. Meanwhile, European textile manufacturers survived without cotton from the South, both because they had stockpiled southern exports during the years before the war and because cotton from Egypt and India filled the void. France and Britain did not extend recognition and the blockade remained in place. Individual ships continued to make it through in both directions, but the Union's command of the seas had an increasingly devastating effect on the Confederate economy.

WEST OF THE MISSISSIPPI: NATIVE AMERICANS JOIN THE FRAY

Although most of the storied battles of the Civil War occurred in the eastern half of the country, fighting spilled into territories on the western side of the Mississippi River as well. Here, as in Tennessee, Union armies gained the upper hand. Confederate forces scored an early bloody victory in the Battle of Wilson's Creek, near Springfield, Missouri, after which pro-Confederate

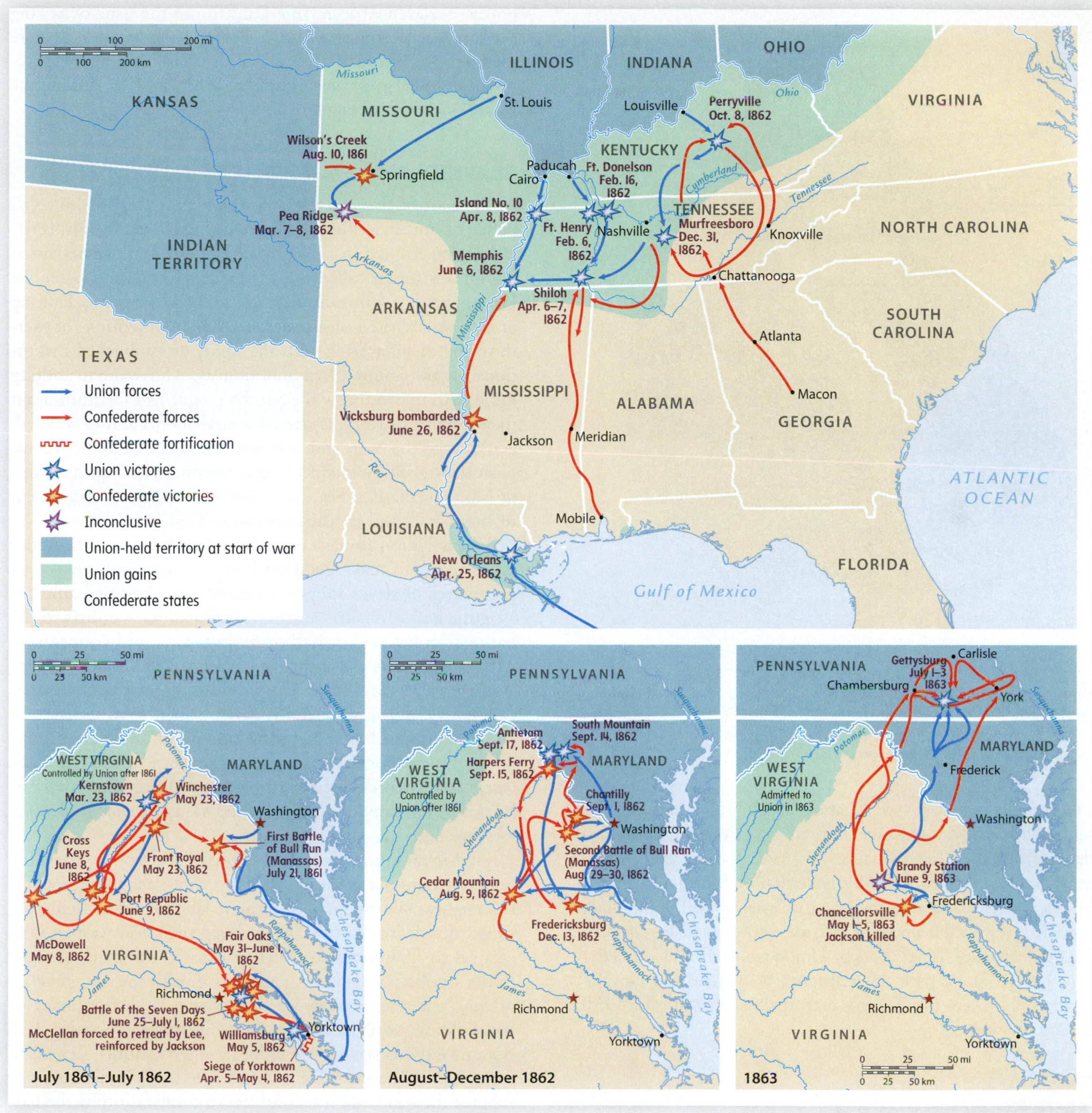

Map 15.2 Western and Eastern Theaters of the Civil War, 1861–1863. Confederate forces vigorously rebuffed the Union incursion into Virginia, the major eastern front of the first part of the war. By contrast, Union armies enjoyed great success in the West, where victories in Louisiana and Tennessee gave the North control of the Mississippi River.

Missouri militiamen were able to capture the southwestern part of that state. But federal forces soon drove them out, and Missouri remained in the union. Three other states west of the Mississippi (Texas, Louisiana, and Arkansas) were part of the Confederacy, and by spring 1862, Union troops occupied parts of both Louisiana and Arkansas. Confederate general Earl Van Dorn tried to launch a northward attack from Arkansas into Missouri. He commanded a force of sixteen thousand, which included regiments of Cherokees and other Indians who had been exiled from Georgia and Alabama in the 1830s by

Cherokee Leader Stand Watie. After supporting John Ridge's Treaty Party and voluntarily moving west in the 1830s, Stand Watie organized an Indian regiment for the Confederacy when the Civil War broke out. He became principal chief of the Confederate Cherokees in 1862.

southern slaveholders (see Chapter 9) but now allied themselves with the Confederacy as their best hope for independence from the United States. In March 1862, Van Dorn's army was scattered by a much smaller Union force in the battle of Pea Ridge. That same month, Confederate forces that had marched westward from Texas into the territory of New Mexico were defeated at Glorieta Pass by Union troops from Colorado. This failure, along with the resistance of Apache and Navajo Indians, blocked the South's attempt to expand westward during the war.

THE SLAVERY WAR

During the first two years of the war, Lincoln repeatedly insisted that the North was fighting to preserve the national union, not to abolish slavery. This position proved difficult to sustain, for several reasons. First, not everyone in the Union chain of command shared or respected Lincoln's commitment to keeping the question of slavery out of the war. Second, the large-scale invasion of the South inevitably shook up relations between masters and slaves, irrespective of official federal policy. Enslaved African Americans forced the issue by seizing their own opportunities to participate in the war and liberate themselves. Finally, by the end of 1862, Lincoln and the Republican leadership came around to the view that winning the war might require emancipation.

SLAVERY AND WAR POLICY

At the start of the war, most northerners supported Lincoln's policy of not undermining slavery in the South. In July 1861, as fighting erupted in Bull Run, the House and Senate passed resolutions (often called the Crittenden Resolution, after the House version) affirming that the United States was fighting only to defend the Constitution and had no intention "of overthrowing or interfering with the rights or established institutions" of the South. Even abolitionists, who wanted nothing more than to overthrow the South's established institution, bit their tongues in 1861, understanding that only a unified North could wage this war, and that war was most likely to accomplish their goals. William Lloyd Garrison, invoking the words of Moses at the Red Sea, counseled the antislavery movement to "stand still, and see the salvation of God."

When Union forces entered the South, they were under strict orders to make good on Lincoln's reassurances. As the first waves of slaves sought refuge in Union army camps in Virginia and Missouri, northern commanders confirmed the national policy of not harboring runaways and cooperating with slaveholders' attempts to recover their human property. But from the start, many Union military personnel violated this policy. Some were motivated by their own antislavery convictions and by the growing clamor among Republicans in Washington against the use of northern soldiers as slave catchers. Others decided to employ or protect runaway slaves because they provided or promised valuable pieces of military intelligence.

Higher-ranking Union officers began questioning Lincoln's policy of noninterference, once it became clear that the Confederate war effort depended on slave labor. General Benjamin Butler decided to classify the enslaved men and women who escaped to Union camps in Virginia as "contraband of war." Butler's policy, which was endorsed quickly by the general-in-chief and the secretary of war, accepted the legitimacy of slaveholding, while striking a blow against the South's slave system. Virginia slaves were indeed property, Butler seemed to concede, but like any other property used by disloyal citizens to support the rebellion, it was subject to confiscation by the federal government. With this justification, Butler began sheltering and employing runaway slaves. The men, women, and children who came to Butler's camps were not legally free, but because they were **contrabands,** their masters could no longer compel their labor or control their lives. In August 1861, Congress reinforced the contraband policy by passing the first Confiscation Act, which authorized the capture of any property enlisted in the rebellion, including all slaves "employed in or upon any fort, navy yard, dock, armory, ship, entrenchment,

Contrabands in Union Army Camp. Enslaved African Americans seized the opportunity represented by the war to flee to Union lines, hoping to secure freedom.

or in any military or naval service." Then, in March 1862, Congress prohibited army officers from returning escaped slaves—a complete reversal of the original Union policy. For many enslaved men and women in the Confederate States, the invading armies now represented a real alternative to slavery.

Still, the Lincoln administration steered clear of larger plans to emancipate slaves during the first year of the war. When General John C. Frémont, the former Republican candidate for president, declared martial law in Missouri in August 1861, he announced that all slaves belonging to rebellious masters were hereby free. But Lincoln asked, and ultimately ordered, Frémont to rescind the order. Secretary of War Simon Cameron raised the idea of arming slaves to help suppress the rebellion, but Lincoln rejected the recommendation and reassigned Cameron (who was regarded as incompetent) to an ambassadorship in Russia. As the fighting dragged on, however Lincoln's approach to the slavery question shifted. Losing confidence that there was any point in cultivating unionist supporters in the states that had seceded, and slightly less worried about risking the support of the loyal border states, he moved gingerly (and always a step behind Congress) toward the position that preserving slavery might not be compatible with the war to preserve the union. He approached the subject cautiously, endorsing gradual, compensated emancipation in the slave states that had not seceded and sending freed blacks out of the country to colonies in Africa.

EMANCIPATION

In April 1862, Congress voted to abolish slavery in the District of Columbia. Slaveholders were to be compensated for their losses and Congress backed Lincoln's goal of promoting the colonization of former slaves, yet the law was still a momentous development. A century after the rumblings of abolitionism had first appeared in American politics and culture, and a year after the Civil War erupted, the federal government freed slaves through legislation for the first time. Washington's three thousand slaves were a small beginning. Over the next year, military realities would embolden the federal government to contemplate larger assaults on slavery. Two main developments propelled this process. First, as U.S. forces pushed deeper into the Confederacy, more enslaved people appeared in Union camps or fell into Union hands as contrabands of war. Second, over the course of 1862, northern politicians and military officials lost their earlier faith in the existence of unionist sentiment in the South. The Union army grew more dependent on black labor and assistance and less committed to cooperating with slaveholders.

Back in Washington, Republicans ratified and reinforced the changes that were taking place on the ground in the South. In June 1862, Congress prohibited slavery in the territories and began preparing for the readmission of the northwestern portion of Virginia as the new free-labor state of West Virginia. A month later, Lincoln warned congressmen from the border states that slavery was likely to be destroyed in their states "by the mere incidents of the war." Congress then passed a Second Confiscation Act, which went much further than the first in authorizing the Union Army to harbor runaway slaves. Whereas the 1861 law had permitted the seizure of any slave being used in the Confederate war effort, the new act applied to the slaves of any masters who supported the rebellion. Congress also passed a Militia Act, authorizing the army to employ "persons of African descent" in suppressing the rebellion and emancipate any slave who accepted such employment. Lincoln then acted on this authorization, ordering his generals to seize slaves in the Confederacy, employ them "for military and naval purposes," and pay them wages.

By the end of July, Lincoln had decided that the only way to defeat the Confederacy was to strip it entirely of its labor force and enlist black support for the Union war cause. Rather than lure the seceding states back into the Union by promising not to interfere with slavery, the North would threaten them with the slave rebellion that the Confederacy had most feared all along. Not wanting his new policy to appear as an act of desperation, Lincoln waited patiently for a Union military triumph. When Lee's invasion of the North was blocked at Antietam that September, Lincoln saw his chance. On September 22, 1862, Lincoln's Emancipation Proclamation declared that as of the new year, all slaves in rebellious states would be "then, thenceforward, and forever free." The South was put on notice that the invading army was now formally allied with the slaves.

On January 1, 1863, Lincoln's signed the Emancipation Proclamation. Since it applied only to those states that had seceded and to the parts of those states that were not currently occupied by Union forces, the Proclamation did not abolish slavery in the United States. Still, its consequences were profound. In the North, Lincoln's order aroused the Democratic opposition, leaving Republicans politically vulnerable to the charge that they were waging a war for social revolution, not for the Constitution. In Europe, the same signals were greeted more enthusiastically

Proclaiming Liberty. A Union officer addresses a crowd of formerly enslaved African Americans in Louisiana in the wake of the Emancipation Proclamation. The original caption of this drawing characterizes the speech as an explanation of "the duties of freedom."

and probably doomed any possibility that Britain or Russia (which had recently emancipated its serf population) would recognize the Confederacy. In the South, both whites and blacks took Lincoln's order quite seriously as a call to slave insurrection. General Beauregard threatened to retaliate by executing Union prisoners of war. Jefferson Davis called the Proclamation "the most execrable measure in the history of guilty man." Enslaved African Americans throughout the South, even in areas not covered by the proclamation or far from the advance of Union troops, rejoiced at the news, which passed quickly through word of mouth along what contemporaries called a "grapevine telegraph" that linked slaves across plantations. Several slaveholders reported first hearing about the Proclamation from their slaves. In northern cities and in occupied areas of the Confederacy, black men and women ushered in January 1 as the dawn of a Jubilee, the biblical year of freedom for all slaves.

BLACKS IN THE UNION ARMY

Even before the Emancipation Proclamation, enslaved African Americans had been flocking to contraband camps, seeking both their own freedom and the opportunity to fight against the Confederacy. Abolitionists, black and white, had argued for enlisting African Americans, hoping that by participating in the Union war effort, black men might stake their claims to full and equal citizenship. Free blacks had been excluded from militia service in the antebellum North, and northern states refused to mobilize them during the first part of the war. But by 1863, the North's demand for men exceeded the supply of white volunteers. Brutal battles had depleted the Union ranks, and every successful incursion into Confederate terrain required a larger and larger occupation force. Once the Emancipation Proclamation had turned a war to save the union into a war against slaveholding, more whites in the North warmed to the idea of letting free blacks in the North and contrabands in the occupied South put their own lives at risk for that war effort.

The recruitment of regiments of what the Army called Colored Troops began slowly, first in parts of occupied Louisiana and South Carolina, and then in the New England states of Massachusetts, Rhode Island, and Connecticut, where the political resistance to arming African Americans was likely to be lightest. A few months later, the Lincoln War Department authorized other northern states to follow suit. Free blacks in the North quickly filled the new regiments that were established for them, but most of the black military contribution would come from other parts of the country. Only forty-six thousand African American males of military age lived in the free states. More than twice that number were held in bondage in the loyal slave states, but these areas were specifically exempted from the Emancipation Proclamation. Mobilizing black soldiers in the border states was a politically sensitive process, since it involved arming men who were legally enslaved, but Union recruiters fanned out to plantations in Maryland, Missouri, and Tennessee in 1863, and slaves enlisted in droves. Slaveholders tried unsuccessfully to slow the exodus, sometimes by threatening to punish the wives and children of men who enlisted, but the recruitment of slaves continued, and it severely undermined the slave regime. Overall, 180,000 men, mostly escaped or confiscated slaves recruited from the border states and the Confederacy, fought in the Army, and another 10,000 in the Navy.

Black soldiers encountered significant discrimination in the Union military. The War Department refused to commission black officers and insisted on paying lower wages to African American recruits. While white soldiers earned a minimum of $13 per month, their black counterparts received only $10 (regardless of rank). In late 1863, a South Carolina infantry regiment, led by Sergeant William Walker, protested the injustice of this arrangement by refusing to perform their duties. Walker was court-martialed and executed.

African American soldiers also faced special risks on the battlefields. The South refused to treat blacks in the Union Army according to the conventional rules of combat, and Confederate soldiers frequently shot at black soldiers rather than taking them prisoner. As the *Arkansas Gazette* explained this policy, "we cannot treat negroes . . . as prisoners of war without a destruction of the social system for which we contend." In the infamous Fort Pillow Massacre (1864), Confederate troops in Tennessee slaughtered almost two hundred black soldiers after they had surrendered. Officers (white or black) who commanded the Colored Troops were also singled out for mistreatment. When Colonel Robert Gould Shaw, the white commander of the famous all-black Fifty-Fourth Massachusetts Volunteer Infantry Regiment, was killed in South Carolina in 1863, the victorious southern army refused to surrender his body for burial. When Captain Andre Cailloux, a free black from New Orleans, fell while attacking a Confederate fort in Louisiana that same year, southern snipers prevented Union personnel from retrieving his body during a truce. Cailloux's corpse lay unburied for forty-seven days.

WHITE SOLDIERS' ATTITUDES TOWARD SLAVERY

The shift in Union war aims affected and reflected the attitudes of white soldiers as well as black ones. Most men who fought in the Civil War, on both sides, were neither slaves nor slaveholders. But they too cared about slavery

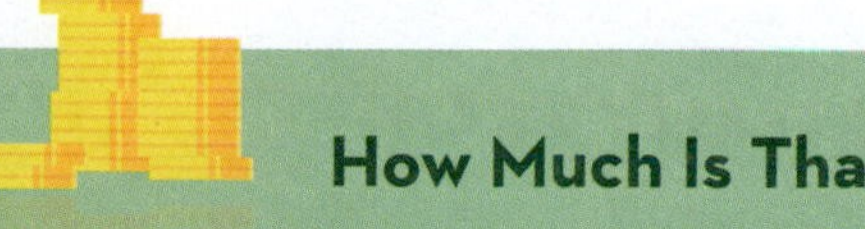

How Much Is That?

Union Army Wages

The ten dollars paid to black soldiers a month represented a buying power equivalent to about $185 in 2013. The higher pay rate for white soliders works out to a minimum wage of just over $240 per month.

and its relationship to the causes they were defending. From the time they joined the Confederate Army, southern men saw themselves as protecting their homeland against invasion, and the presence or prospect of free black men with guns was a big part of what was threatening about the invasion. Already by 1862, a Confederate soldiers' newspaper insisted that "any man who pretends to believe that this is not a war for the emancipation of the blacks, and . . . a stirring up of servile insurrections, is either a fool or a liar."

Union soldiers entered the war with a wider range of attitudes toward slaves. Most of the northern men who signed up for battle hated slavery and blamed a slaveholding oligarchy for undermining the republic and starting the war, and many of them saw free labor as a big part of what was at stake in a war to preserve the United States (much as Americans would talk about fighting for free enterprise a century later). But only a minority saw the fate of four million southern slaves as a cause worth dying for. Lincoln's new war policies tested the allegiance of most Union soldiers, who did not want to fight for emancipation. The months after the Emancipation Proclamation was announced marked a low period in troop morale on the Union side. Desertion became more frequent and grumbling grew louder.

Over the course of 1863, however, many rank-and-file soldiers began to see things differently. Because antiwar Democrats, dubbed **Copperheads** by their opponents, attacked Lincoln for turning the Civil War into a crusade against slavery, those who criticized the Emancipation Proclamation risked being linked with the war's critics. Furthermore, the service of black men in the Union military and their contributions to the war effort altered many northern whites' perspectives on race relations in the South. When Sam Evans of Ohio volunteered to serve with the U.S. Colored Troops in May 1863, for example, his father was aghast, writing that he "would rather clean out S__thouses at ten cents pr day" than assume such a "degraded" status. Sam explained that this was an easier way for him to become an officer, and reminded his father that the new policy would save white lives. By the end of the war, however, both father and son supported black enlistment as a matter of principle and advocated granting black men the right to vote. Northerners who had despised abolitionism in 1862 came to endorse the goal of ending slavery in the South.

THE WAR'S MANY FRONTS

Though the Civil War is typically imagined as having taken place on specific battle sites in rural America, the violence spilled over beyond the borders of the battlefields, blurring the lines between soldiers and civilians and touching the lives of men, women, and children across the country. Those who lived in the many paths traced by the clashing armies fell victim to stray bullets, errant cannon fire, or shells left behind. Especially in the South, civilians suffered at the hands of occupation forces. In the border states or in large cities, neighbors of different convictions and allegiances were swept up in guerrilla attacks, civil unrest, or violence between slaves and masters. The mass movements of troops and refugees and the accumulation of carcasses and wounded bodies also accelerated the spread of disease. For Americans spared these ravages, the war's destructiveness was brought home by the loss of loved ones, the constant reports of death, and new graphic depictions of the mounting carnage.

OCCUPIED TERRITORY

The Civil War was a brutal struggle for territory. For four years, Union and Confederate armies fought to control towns, cities, and large swaths of contested land, which meant that many parts of the country were subjected to military occupation. In portions of seceded states, such as eastern Tennessee and southwestern Virginia, Confederate forces controlled regions where the local population supported the Union. On a few occasions, when Robert E. Lee invaded Maryland, and then Pennsylvania, northerners endured an enemy invasion. But most of the war was fought in and over the South. To win, the Union needed to assert federal authority and take forcible possession of the seceding states. For most of the war, Union soldiers occupied much of Virginia (in the northern, eastern, and southeastern parts of the state), the Carolina coastline, southeastern Louisiana, middle and western Tennessee, and portions of Arkansas, northern Mississippi, and northern Alabama. These occupied areas included many of the South's major cities, such as New Orleans, Memphis, Nashville, Norfolk, and Alexandria. Later in the war, Charleston, Savannah, and Wilmington would also fall to federal forces. Overall, more than a hundred towns and cities in the South became Union army garrisons for at least part of the Civil War (see Map 15.3).

Federal military officials may have described their job as liberating the South from the clutches of secessionist oligarchs, but the South's white population regarded them as invading armies. No one knew for certain what life would be like under Yankee occupation, but popular stereotypes about the North may have predisposed white southerners to believe rumors that the invaders were there to steal slaves, pillage property, and rape women. One woman in Winchester, Virginia, recorded her own horror at seeing these alien soldiers arrive. Never before had she beheld "so many faces where evil predominated—a kind of sinister expression—horrible to look at." Hundreds of thousands of southerners lived under this army's occupation or fled their homes to escape such a fate. Slaveholders often sent their slaves into the interior of the region to avoid losing valuable human property. For those who remained, the reality of military occupation rarely lived up to their worst fears. During the early months of the occupation, Union soldiers actively enforced slave codes and even whipped slaves who disobeyed their masters. Overall, however, the effects of the invasion were devastatingly disruptive to southern life. In cities and towns,

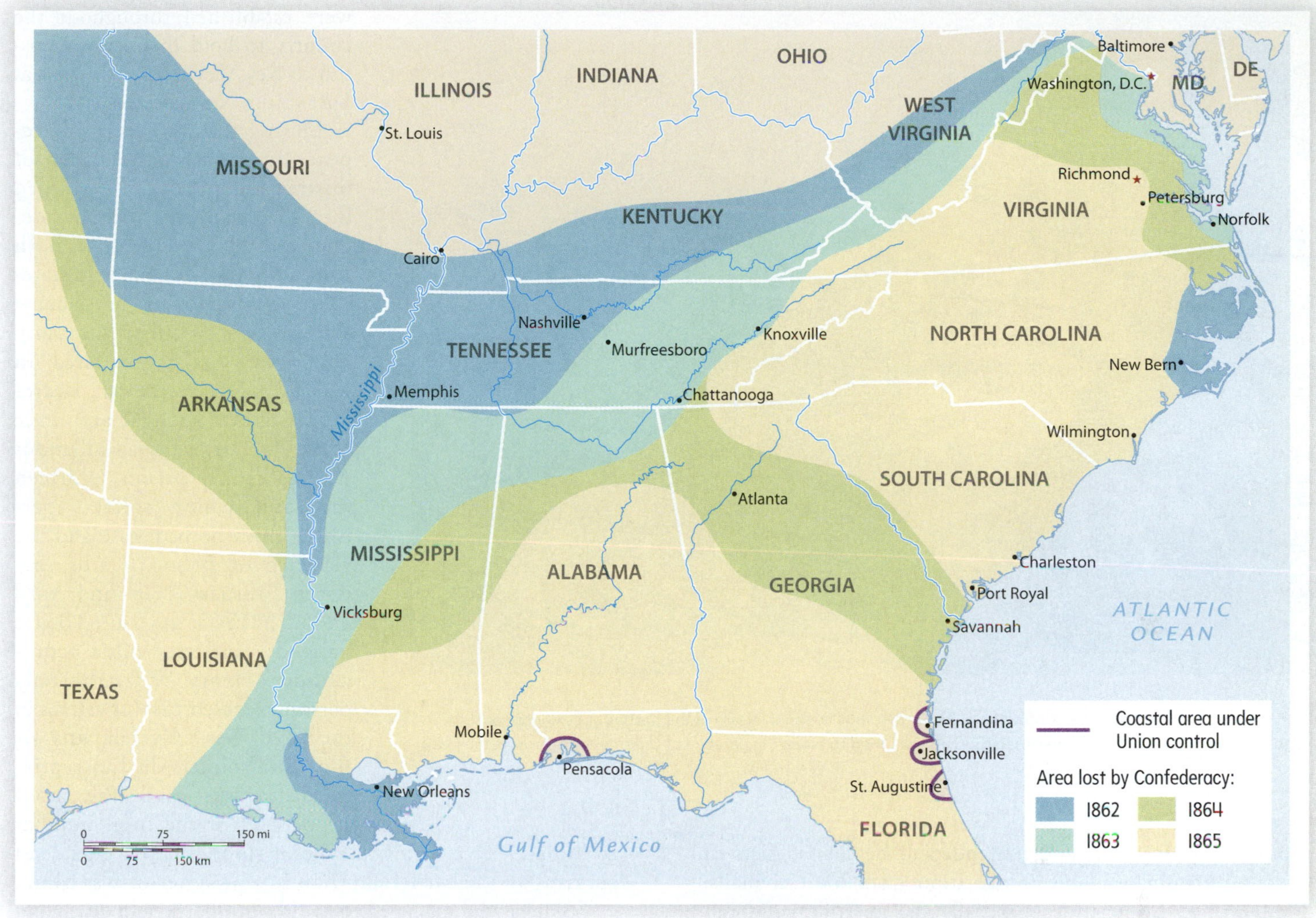

Map 15.3 The Union-Occupied South. In large sections of the South, the war brought military occupation rather than Confederate rule.

trade was disrupted, employment opportunities disappeared, and food and fuel supplies were quickly depleted. In rural areas near the federal garrisons, farms and villages were raided periodically for supplies. And in the zones that fell between the occupied territory and the Confederate-controlled interior, deprivation and anarchy prevailed.

GUERRILLA WARFARE

Even in loyal states, Union soldiers were sometimes treated like occupying armies. When the Sixth Massachusetts Volunteer Infantry Regiment passed through the streets of Baltimore shortly after the attack on Fort Sumter, local whites rioted in the streets and killed four members of the regiment. In Missouri, which federal troops had kept in the Union fold in 1861, the Union imposed martial law throughout the war and tried more civilians under its authority than in all of the occupied states combined. Meanwhile, the state's Confederate sympathizers waged ongoing guerrilla campaigns against federal troops and their supporters.

Guerrilla warfare in Missouri was in some ways a continuation of the battles over slavery that had erupted along and across the border with Kansas in the 1850s (see Chapter 14). Pro-Confederate guerrillas, known as **Bushwhackers,** terrorized the Missouri countryside throughout the war period. Mostly very young men from rural backgrounds, the Bushwhackers were loosely organized and had no formal connection to the Confederacy. But they targeted Union supporters and saw their own acts of looting, arson, torture, and murder as part of a broader revolutionary struggle to defend their homelands against Lincoln's invasion. They were pursued both by Union troops enforcing martial law in Missouri and by Kansas regiments stationed along Missouri's western border. These cross-border raiders were known as **Jayhawkers.** To be "jayhawked" meant to be the victim of looting attacks by Union troops, whereas to be "bushwhacked" meant to suffer the same fate at the hands of the guerrillas.

Both in the border states and in the occupied South, soldiers and guerrillas added to the confusion by concealing their identities. In Mississippi, for example, Union scouts dressed in

Attack on the Massachusetts Sixth. On April 19, 1861, the anniversary of the battles of Lexington and Concord, supporters of the Confederacy in Baltimore tried to block the passage of Union troops through their city.

Confederate uniforms and pretended to be sick soldiers in order to acquire valuable information from local civilians. Many armed combatants (especially the guerrillas) did not wear uniforms at all, and left it to their victims to figure out how thefts, beatings, rapes, or executions fit into the larger meaning of the war.

PRISONS, HOSPITALS, AND BURIAL GROUNDS

Most of the war's major battles lasted no more than a few days, but for many of the young men involved, the end of a battle signaled the beginning of a new ordeal. Approximately 674,000 soldiers were captured during the Civil War, and 410,000 were held in some form of military custody. Early in the war, the two armies sometimes released prisoners immediately, agreeing to parole equal numbers of men of corresponding rank. For a one-year period in the middle of the war, large-scale prisoner exchanges were conducted at two specified locations in Virginia and Mississippi. But by the middle of 1863, these arrangements broke down, in part because of the Confederacy's refusal to accord black soldiers the status of war prisoners, but also because the Union authorities concluded that the South, with its much smaller population of eligible soldiers, needed the exchange more than the North did. By 1864, the number of war prisoners on both sides soared. Over 150 compounds were established throughout the country to hold them, from Boston to Key West and as far west as Fort Craig, New Mexico.

During the war, each side repeatedly accused the other of mistreating prisoners. Crowded into small barracks without adequate food or clothing, both southern and northern inmates suffered miserably. One Alabama artilleryman described the camp where he was incarcerated in Elmira, New York, as "nearer Hades than I thought any place could be." In Georgia's infamous Andersonville prison, thirteen thousand Union soldiers perished, from both disease and the violence of prison guards, between February 1864 and April 1865. (In 1865, the United States hanged Andersonville's commander, Henry Wirz, the only person executed for war crimes in the Civil War.) Overall, fifty-six thousand soldiers died in captivity during the Civil War, about 13 percent of the total number of inmates. Statistically, a soldier stood a better chance of survival on the battlefield than in a prisoner-of-war camp.

Soldiers who managed to avoid both battlefield death and imprisonment often wound up in military hospitals, which were established in towns and cities throughout the major war theaters. Richmond alone had thirty-four hospitals, the largest of which (Chimborazo) held eight thousand patients at a time and treated seventy-six thousand wounded and sick Confederate soldiers over the course of the conflict. Union casualties filled an even larger number of hospital beds in the U.S. capital.

The Civil War took place at a point in American history when techniques of killing had advanced more quickly than techniques of healing. Soldiers bore muzzle-loading rifles with three times the firing range of the arms that had been used in the war against Mexico just over a decade earlier. New, more powerful portable cannons, which had been developed in France, mowed down soldiers in unprecedented numbers. Meanwhile, medical practices remained primitive by the standards of just a few decades later. Doctors understood very little about germs and antisepsis and spread numerous diseases through unclean instruments and hospital conditions. The availability of anesthetics encouraged doctors to amputate wounded and infected limbs, which probably saved many lives, but unsanitary surgical practices may have nullified some of the benefits. The scalpel used to stop

Union Military Prison, Camp Morton, Indianapolis. Originally a training facility before it was converted to a prison for Confederate soldiers, Camp Morton occupied a thirty-six-acre site covering an area now bounded by Talbott Street, Central Avenue, Twenty-Second Street, and Nineteenth Street in Indiana's capital city. Despite the Lincoln administration's insistence that secession was illegal and its supporters were criminals rather than foreign enemies, the Union treated captured Confederate soldiers as enemy combatants instead of as traitors or terrorists.

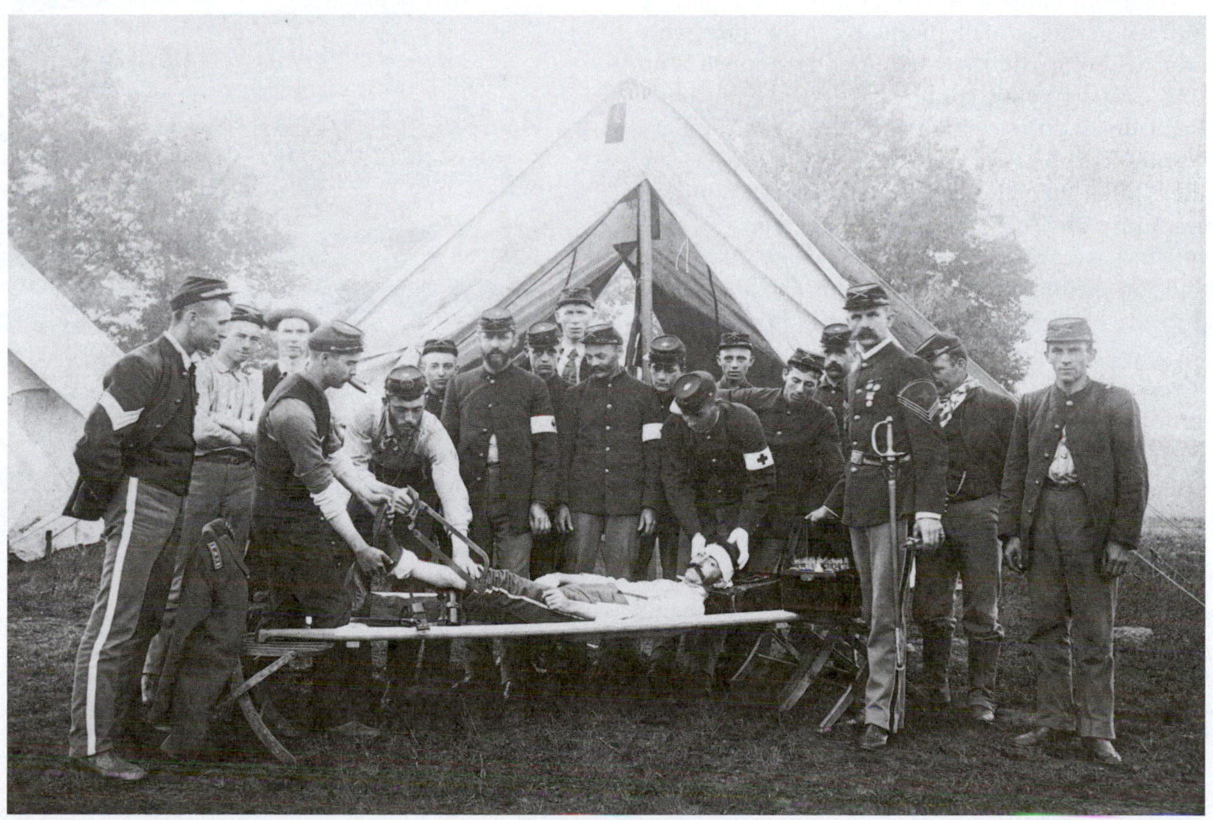

Amputation Procedure, Gettysburg, 1863. Surgeries were often performed outdoors for better lighting conditions. Doctors amputated fifty thousand limbs over the course of the war, and about 75 percent of the patients survived. Between 1861 and 1873, the United States awarded eighty-five new patents for prosthetic legs.

an injured leg from infecting one body would spread the infection to another. Military hospitals treated more than just bullet wounds. Soldiers, many of whom hailed from isolated rural areas where they had been exposed to fewer diseases, were devastated by epidemics of measles, mumps, and smallpox, as well as recurrent outbreaks of malaria, typhoid, and dysentery. Twice as many soldiers died from disease as from battle injuries.

Disease swept quickly through the war-torn areas, paying no respect to the distinction between soldiers and civilians. Military camps, hospitals, and prisons became breeding grounds for contagion and produced staggering mortality rates. At one contraband camp near Nashville, 25 percent of the ex-slaves assembled there died in a three-month stretch. But disease could hardly be contained in these places. In crowded cities with transient populations, epidemics spread just as quickly. President Lincoln's eleven-year-old son Willie died of typhoid fever during the war, probably the result of water contamination in Washington, D.C.

Dealing with the dead was at least as difficult as dealing with the injured and ill. Civil War battles yielded grotesque harvests of dead bodies, which needed to be disposed of, both out of respect for the deceased and out of concern for the living. Officials on both sides worried that leaving corpses to decompose on the battlefields would not only hurt troop morale but also imperil hygiene because corpses might emit dangerous effluvia. Burying the dead was part of the burden of soldiering, usually borne by the victors, who controlled the field of battle after the shooting stopped. But the escalating casualty totals could easily overwhelm both the surviving army and the civilian population. At the Battle of Gettysburg in 1863 (see The War's End), three days of fighting killed 7,000 men and left 22,000 others wounded. A local community of 2,400 had to bear the impact of this carnage, which was compounded by the death of 3,000 horses (in all, an estimated 1.5 million horses and mules were killed in the Civil War). About six million pounds of carcasses lay upon the fields of this one Pennsylvania town. For several months, nearby residents would walk around with peppermint oil or pennyroyal to combat the powerful stench of death.

Broadly shared beliefs about the afterlife and theories about the spread of disease demanded that fallen soldiers be buried in the earth, as had been the long-standing practice in Western warfare. But the Civil War introduced new standards for naming, honoring, and commemorating the dead. And for many soldiers and their loved ones, the prospect of mass, anonymous burial on the battlefield was disturbing. Grieving families wanted corpses brought home, so that they could positively identify their loved ones and lay them to rest in a family setting.

The heavy traffic in bodies created a market for new kinds of coffins. Because wooden boxes were more liable to break in transit and did not seal in odors, delivery companies required that bodies be conveyed in metal caskets. Entrepreneurs designed coffins that were lined with zinc and sealed for long journeys. Other companies offered coffins filled with ice or embalming services, which became widespread during the Civil War and set new protocols for the handling of dead bodies in peacetime as well. By the middle of the war, the Union Army also began building large-scale cemeteries next to major battlegrounds, both to speed up the burial process and to memorialize the sacrifices of the men who died in battle. The Confederacy lacked the resources to engage in similar cemetery-building projects.

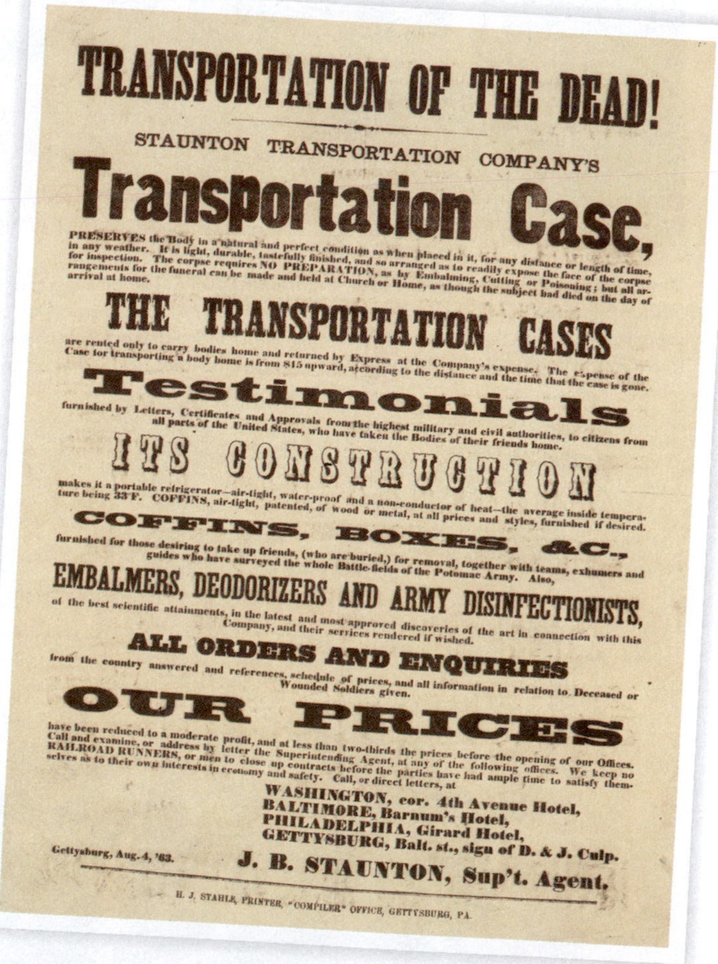

"Transportation of the Dead." The demand for transporting dead soldiers created a major business opportunity for coffin manufacturers, embalmers, and private delivery companies. After the Battle of Gettysburg in 1863, J. B. Staunton advertised a special refrigerated coffin for transporting corpses from the battlefield to the families of the deceased. The Staunton Transportation Company touted its coffins as "light, durable, tastefully finished, and so arranged as to readily expose the face of the corpse for inspection." **Question for Analysis:** What anxieties or fears might manufacturers have been trying to assuage when they assured customers that new coffins allowed for the easy inspection of dead bodies?

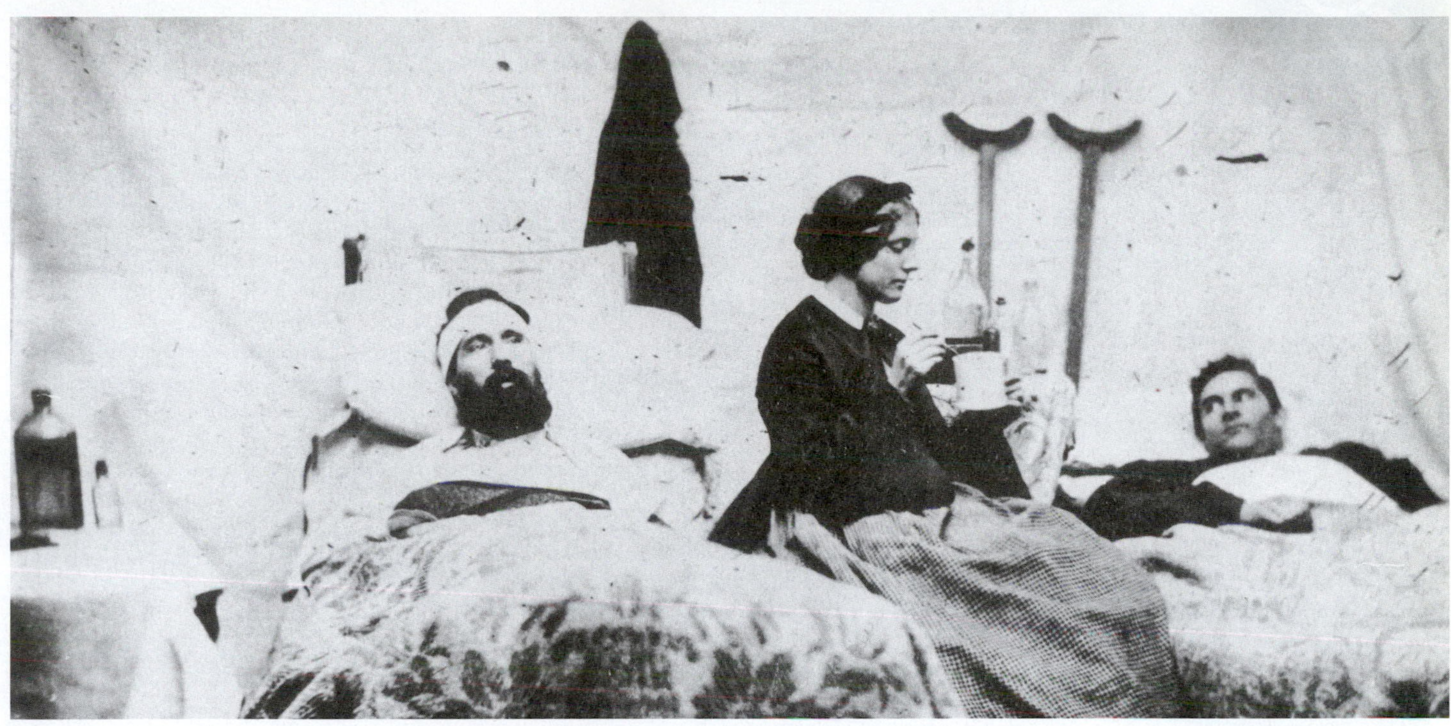

Feeding the Wounded, Carlisle Barracks, Pennsylvania. Hospital service brought large numbers of women to the war front. Drawings and photographs of hospital scenes often highlighted the heroism of nurses and placed them in the foreground of military coverage.

To address the enormous administrative and humanitarian challenges posed by all the death and suffering produced by war, an unusual private organization emerged on the Union side. Founded in New York at the start of the war, the Women's Central Association of Relief for the Sick and Wounded of the Army was an elite philanthropic organization in the larger tradition of antebellum reform (see Chapter 12), but in a time of expanding federal power and growing government bureaucracy, the organization's leaders sought official recognition from Washington and widened its goals beyond simply providing relief. Renamed the United States Sanitary Commission and authorized to act as a federal agency, it collected millions of dollars in private donations, but it turned its main attention to compiling vital statistics and hospital records, studying military hygiene, recruiting and training nurses, and supporting the Union war campaign by improving the health and expediting the convalescence of northern soldiers. In its official reports, the commission stressed rationality, discipline, and efficiency, rather than humanitarian sympathy. Distinguished men from prosperous backgrounds dominated the organization's leadership structure, but the Sanitary Commission also provided many opportunities for women to play significant roles in the northern war effort. Prominent commission nurses, such as Mary Livermore, Eliza Howland, Georgeanna Woolsey, Louisa May Alcott, and Katherine Prescott Wormeley, were only a few of the approximately twenty thousand Union and Confederate women who served in the war as medical caregivers, but they helped turn the position of Civil War nurse into a platform for various women's reform causes.

HOME FRONTS

Far from the cemeteries, military hospitals, garrison towns, and killing fields, Americans tracked the events of the war closely, like no prior event in the nation's history. As in the U.S.-Mexican war, newspapers and telegraph transmissions relayed current military news, but the passage of fifteen years had increased the reach of the telegraph system and the circulation of the press. Moreover, compared to the Mexican case, Civil War developments took place much closer to American news and telegraph networks. And finally, the massive mobilization of young men gave most readers, North and South, special reasons to attend to the news. Newspapers regularly printed casualty lists, which friends and relatives of soldiers scoured nervously. In larger cities, newspaper offices posted the latest headlines as they came in via telegraph onto large bulletin boards that attracted large public gatherings during major battles.

Civilians also followed the war through three new cultural practices that had become widespread during the antebellum period: postal service, pictorial magazines, and photography. First, the battlefields were connected to the home front through the mail. Civil War armies were the most literate mass fighting forces in history to that point (more than 85 percent

INTERPRETING THE SOURCES

Walt Whitman's Condolence Letters

In December 1862, after the Brooklyn poet and journalist Walt Whitman received the distressing news that his brother George was among the wounded in Fredericksburg, he headed south to the front to search for him. George Whitman was not badly wounded, it turned out, and had returned to active duty but. Walt Whitman remained on the Virginia battlefield for eight days and then took a part-time job in Washington so that he could devote himself to visiting military hospitals. By his own count, Whitman made six hundred hospital visits to somewhere between 80,000 and 100,000 dying or wounded soldiers over the next three years. Among the services and comforts he offered these men, Whitman wrote numerous condolence letters to the families of soldiers who did not survive. Below are some excerpts from an 1863 letter to the family of a soldier from Breesport, New York, who had been a musician in the Union Army:

Much of the time his breathing was hard, his throat worked—they tried to keep him up by giving him stimulants, milk-punch, wine &c—these perhaps affected him, for often his mind wandered somewhat—I would say, Erastus, don't you remember me, dear son?—can't you call me by name? . . .

I was very anxious he should be saved, & so were they all—he was well used by the attendants—poor boy, I can see him as I write—he was tanned & had a fine head of hair, & looked good in the face when he first came, & was in pretty good flesh too—(had his hair cut close about ten or twelve days before he died)—He never complained—but it looked pitiful to see him lying there, with such a look out of his eyes. He had large clear eyes, they seemed to talk better than words—I assure you I was attracted to him much—Many nights I sat in the hospital by his bedside till far in the night—The lights would be put out—Yet I would sit there silently, hours, late, perhaps fanning him—he always liked to have me sit there, but never cared to talk—I shall never forget those nights, it was a curious & solemn scene, the sick & wounded lying around in their cots, just visible in the darkness, & this dear young man close at hand lying on what proved to be his death bed I do not know his past life, but what I do know, & what I saw of him, he was a noble boy—I felt he was one I should get very much attached to. I think you have reason to be proud of such a son, & all his relatives have cause to treasure his memory. . . .

I write to you this letter, because I would do something at least in his memory—his fate was a hard one, to die so—He is one of the thousands of our unknown American young men in the ranks about whom there is no record or fame, no fuss made about their dying so unknown, but I find in them the real precious & royal ones of this land, giving themselves up, aye even their young and precious lives, in their country's cause—Poor dear son, though you were not my son, I felt to love you as a son, what short time I saw you sick & dying here—it is as well as it is, perhaps better-for who knows whether he is not better off, that patient & sweet young soul, to go, than we are to stay? So farewell, dear boy—it was my opportunity to be with you in your last rapid days of death—no chance as I have said to do any thing particular, for nothing [could be done—only you did not lay] here & die among strangers without having one at hand who loved you dearly, & to whom you have your dying kiss. . . .

Walt Whitman to the parents of Erastus Haskell (Mr. & Mrs. SB Haskell), August 10, 1863

Explore the Source

1. What consolation does Whitman offer the dead soldier's parents about the conditions of his death?
2. What does Whitman report about the young man's physical condition in the hospital?
3. Given the fact that hundreds of thousands of ordinary Americans died during the war and the sight of wounded patients became exceedingly common (Whitman himself visited close to one hundred thousand of them), what might be Whitman's point in calling men like Erastus Haskell "royal" and "precious"?

of the soldiers involved in the war could both read and write), and the men who enlisted in this war had grown up during the period when lower postage rates had transformed the mail into a popular tool for maintaining contact with distant friends and family. According to one estimate, soldiers in the Civil War sent or received an average of 180,000 letters every single day. Soldiers' correspondence, which was rarely censored by the authorities (though sometimes intercepted by the enemy,) provided readers back home with detailed information about army life and made the war seem much closer. Letters from the front also brought dreaded reports of injury or death (see Interpreting the Sources: Walt Whitman's Condolence Letters). In the South, mail service was much less comprehensive and reliable, both because its new mail service had to compete with the War Department for limited resources, personnel, and transportation infrastructure and because the Confederate Post Office was firmly committed to not running a deficit. Nonetheless, Confederate soldiers also spent much of their time writing letters and southern families anxiously awaited their arrival.

Second, Americans saw the war through a series of mass-circulation **pictorial magazines** that shaped the popular imagination of battles, armies, and the enemy, especially for northern readers (see Hot Commodities: Civil War Board Games). These weekly publications, founded mostly in the 1850s, sold hundreds of thousands of copies of a single issue

HOT COMMODITIES

Civil War Board Games

The Civil War mobilized millions of soldiers, health care workers, merchants, couriers, refugees, and runaway slaves, sending them great distances all over the continent. But a majority of the country remained at home during the war. Americans on the home front imagined the conflict through a steady supply of media coverage and consumer goods—including pictures, songs, and mail envelopes with patriotic emblems—bringing the war into the parlors, studies, and living rooms of middle-class families, especially in the North.

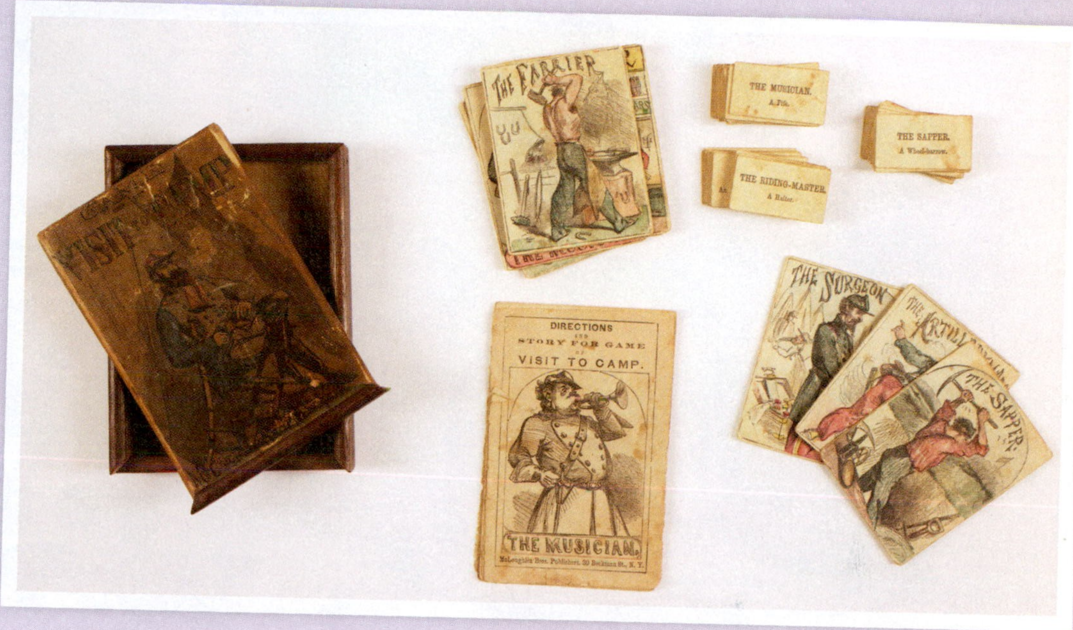

"Visit to Camp" Board Game. This game familiarized northern consumers with important figures in Civil War military life, such as "The Surgeon," "The Sutler" (supplier of nonmilitary supplies to the troops), and "The Musician."

Entrepreneurial publishers in northern cities even produced and peddled Civil War games. Board games, many of them imported and adapted from India via Great Britain, had been growing in popularity in the United States during the nineteenth century, but the Civil War marked a major takeoff in the game industry. In 1860, Milton Bradley, a young New England inventor and entrepreneur, introduced a board game called the Checkered Game of Life, in which players advance strategically across a sixty-four-square checkerboard, following a journey from infancy to old age, navigating the ups and downs of fortune and competing with other players in a search for individual prosperity. Bradley sold forty thousand copies of the game in its first year and parlayed that success into a company that became America's leading producer of board games. Much of that early success came from Union soldiers who brought Bradley's portable box of backgammon, chess, checkers, and the Checkered Game of Life to distract and entertain them on the front.

For those who stayed behind, games featured the war itself. Decks of playing cards depicted the rigors of camp life or featured pictures of fifty-two Union officers. The Game of Secession, a version of the ancient snakes-and-letters game genre and similiar to the modern Chutes and Ladders board game, followed the events of the political conflict. Another game, entitled The Game of the Rebellion, promoted itself by promising "Ladies, Gentlemen and Children a chance to 'fight the rebels by their own firesides.'"

Think About It

1. If the war brought death and destruction to so many American families, why were war games popular?
2. Why might Civil War games have been more popular in the North than in the South?

and featured lithographed engravings and drawings of current events. Prominent papers included *Harper's Weekly*, the *New York Illustrated News*, and the spectacularly successful *Frank Leslie's Illustrated Newspaper*, which was selling as many as 347,000 copies of a single issue by 1860. When the war broke out, *Frank Leslie's* (like most mass newspapers based in the North) decided to forsake its southern readers and assume a pro-Union stance. The decision paid off handsomely, and *Leslie's* became the magazine of record in many northern households. Together, the three leading pictorial magazines of the era supplied a northern audience with a steady stream of military portraits, battle panoramas, and illustrations of parades, fairs, recruitment centers, and hospitals. Even Union troops, with first-hand access to the events of the war, were avid consumers of the pictorial press. Southern readers, by contrast, had to make do with the much scantier offerings of the *Southern Illustrated News* (which had trouble hiring good engravers and filled its columns mostly

Winslow Homer, "News of the War," from *Harper's Weekly*, July 14, 1862. Homer, a successful painter, was among a number of regular contributors of war drawings to the pictorial newspapers. To this day, history books rely heavily on these illustrations to imagine and represent the Civil War. **Question for Analysis:** How is this montage of scenes a commentary on the role of writing and print in the popular experience of the war?

***A Sharpshooter's Last Sleep*, by Alexander Gardner.** Gardner, a Scottish immigrant, produced many of the most haunting and enduring photographs of the war. Mathew Brady, who exhibited Gardner's battle images without attribution, is often credited as the official photographer of the Civil War.

***A Burial Party on the Battle-Field of Cold Harbor*, by John Reekie and Alexander Gardner.** Because equipment was heavy and exposure times were long, photographs of the war depicted still scenes before or after a battle rather than action shots from the fighting. **Question for Analysis:** What might the photographer be trying to convey by arranging this posed scene of African American men gathering long-decomposed body parts?

Mathew Brady's Lincoln. Brady's many photographs of Lincoln helped turn him into a broadly recognizable political celebrity unlike any previous president.

with text) and two other pictorial papers that operated only briefly. White southerners could not stomach the northern options, however. "The pictures in 'Harper's Weekly' and 'Frank Leslie's' tell more lies than Satan himself," wrote one Georgia woman in her diary. "I get in such a rage when I look at them that I sometimes take off my slipper and beat the senseless paper with it."

Third, whereas pictorial magazines offered artists' perspectives on the events of the war, the new medium of photography offered the promise of more direct access to the front. Though a few rare daguerreotypes had been taken during the war against Mexico, and some Americans had seen photographic images taken in the Crimean War in southeastern Europe (1853–1856), the Civil War was the first U.S. military conflict to be viewed through the camera lens. Because of the heavy equipment and lengthy exposure times entailed, Civil War photographs were not action shots on the battlefield. Instead, they typically featured still scenes of camp life. Often they emphasized death. Most of the photographs of the war front were exhibited and published by Mathew Brady, whose photo galleries in New York and Washington introduced many Americans to the shocking spectacle of corpses piled on the fields of Antietam. Brady was the most famous photographer of his era, and it was to Brady that President Lincoln had turned, both in the presidential campaign and during his time in office, to help fashion his image. But Brady did not take the classic war photographs that bore his name. Most were the work of Timothy O'Sullivan or Alexander Gardner, artists in Brady's employ. In all, Brady oversaw and underwrote the production of some ten thousand photographic plates during the Civil War.

THE WAR'S END, 1863-1865

For most Americans, at home or in uniform, the second half of this unimaginably long war brought only more deprivation, destruction, and sadness. In hindsight, however, the Union war effort clearly had turned a corner during the summer of 1863. Crucial battles that summer depleted the southern ranks and set up further Union incursions into Confederate territory. Lincoln regained the support of northern voters, elevated a different general to supreme command of Union forces, and presided over the slow, bloody end of the conflict. All the while, his party had been building a much more powerful federal government, authorized not only to wage war but also to remake the nation.

KEY UNION VICTORIES

Though the North had occupied New Orleans and won decisive victories in Tennessee, General Grant still did not have control of the Mississippi River. After an unsuccessful attempt to capture the strategically crucial Confederate stronghold of Vicksburg, Grant decided in May 1863 to besiege the city and try to force its surrender. For six weeks, Confederate soldiers and Vicksburg residents suffered from hunger and disease, trying to survive on whatever food sources they could obtain, which reportedly included mules, dogs, snakes, and boiled shoe leather. On July 4, Confederate General John Pemberton surrendered to Grant. The city of Vicksburg would not hold Fourth of July celebrations until after World War II.

Meanwhile to the east (see Map 15.4), General Lee's Confederate troops had won a major battle in Chancellorsville, Virginia, shortly before Grant began the siege of Vicksburg. Seeking to take quick advantage of the victory, Lee marched an army of seventy-five thousand men northward through Maryland and into Pennsylvania, hoping to inflict a heavy blow on the North, threaten Philadelphia and Baltimore, and force Lincoln to negotiate a peace settlement. On June 28, 1863, Union troops led by George Meade interrupted Lee's march near the town of Gettysburg, which was at the hub of several roads in the area. On July 1, the two armies began exchanging fire in what was to become the most famous battle of the Civil War (see inset in Map 15.4). On the first day, the Confederate forces broke the Union lines and seemed headed to another victory, but the next morning brought Union reinforcements and the northerners defended their elevated positions. Undaunted, Lee ordered an ill-advised frontal attack on Cemetery Ridge, the center of the enemy lines, on July 3. The charge was led by General George Pickett, whose men stretched across an open field, forming a mile-wide target for Union cannons and guns. The killing on this last day of the Battle of Gettysburg brought Lee's casualties to twenty-eight thousand men, forcing him to withdraw to Virginia. Almost as many northern soldiers were killed or wounded, but these were losses the larger Union Army could more easily survive. Just one day before the fall of Vicksburg, Lee's invasion of the North ended in failure.

LINCOLN'S WAR

By many measures, the first half of Abraham Lincoln's term in office was a colossal failure. The union fell apart on his watch and the country was plunged into a devastating war. He seriously overestimated the extent of support for the union that could be rallied in the Upper South, and his attempts to placate slaveholders backfired. Then, two years into his term, his shift of course toward emancipation won him new enemies in the North. State legislatures in Indiana and his home state of Illinois passed resolutions calling for peace, and Copperhead leader Clement Vallandigham of Ohio condemned the war on the floor of Congress. As support for the war ebbed, Lincoln responded by suppressing civic liberties, using his military authority to order the arrest of anyone engaging in "disloyal" activities. He had Vallandigham arrested, for example, and expelled across enemy lines to Tennessee. (Vallandigham escaped to Canada and later won the 1863 Democratic nomination for Ohio governorship in absentia.) After the war, the Supreme Court would rule against one of Lincoln's tactics, the subjection of U.S. citizens to military tribunals in circumstances where civilian courts are in operation. On the second anniversary of Lincoln's inauguration, the South was still out of the Union, more than a hundred thousand soldiers had perished, the nation's economy was in crisis, and Democrats were accusing him of having abandoned the Constitution.

A year before facing reelection, Lincoln seized the occasion of a ceremony dedicating a new national cemetery in Gettysburg to redefine the war effort. The main speaker at this event, held on November 19, 1863, was not the president, but Edward Everett, a distinguished Massachusetts statesman who addressed a crowd of fifteen thousand for two hours. Lincoln followed with what was listed in the program as "Dedicatory Remarks" and consisted of ten short sentences. These remarks, which came to be known as the Gettysburg Address, paid homage to the men "who here gave their lives" at the nearby battlefield so that the "nation might live." But in giving meaning to their sacrifice, Lincoln made it clear what he thought the war was about. He did not mention the word *union.* Nor did he speak of the Constitution, which his political opponents invoked repeatedly in their attack on the war. Instead, the president harked back to a moment before the Constitution. "Four score and seven years ago," Lincoln began, "our fathers brought forth on this continent a new nation, conceived in liberty, and dedicated to the proposition that all men are created equal." The nation was created on July 4, 1776, he reminded his listeners, with the Declaration of Independence. The founding ideals of that nation, which existed before individual states were formed and before those states cobbled together a constitution, were freedom and equality. The Civil War, Lincoln insisted, would determine whether a nation founded on those ideals could survive.

Lincoln's Democratic critics ridiculed the "dishwatery utterances" of the Gettysburg Address and intensified their campaign to unseat him. Lincoln himself seemed convinced that

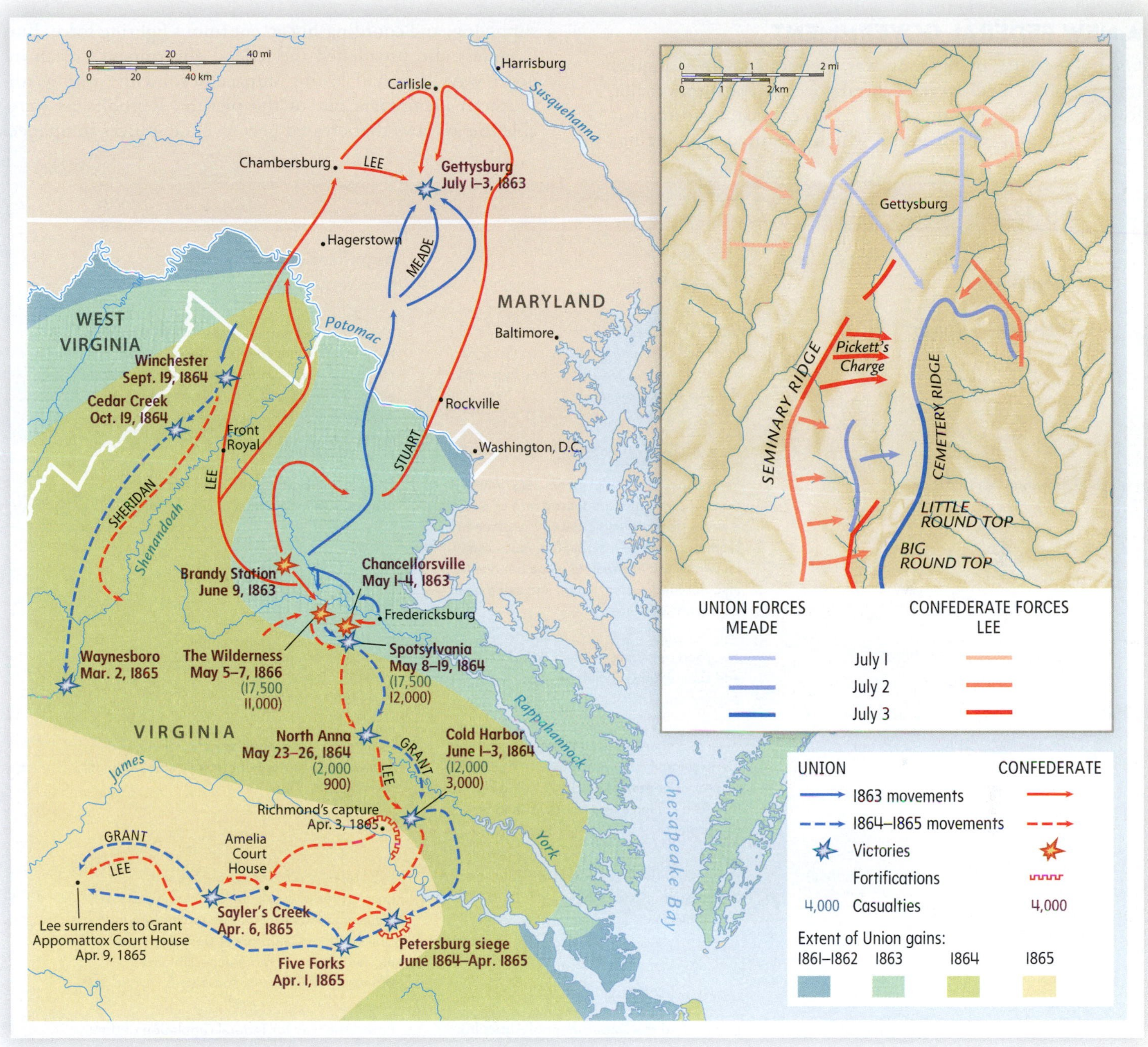

Map 15.4 The War in the East, 1863–1865. The tide of the war shifted decisively after 1863, with key Union victories in both Virginia and the Southeast.

the war's slow progress would doom his reelection chances. Democrats ran on a slogan advocating "the Union as it was, the Constitution as it is," reminding voters that Lincoln's transformed war aims violated the Constitution (which protected slavery) and pursued a broader social agenda. The Democrats' problem, though, was that their slogan barely masked a split between those who favored a return to the pre-1861 union by suing for peace, and those who advocated pressing on with the war but renouncing emancipation. They nominated General McClellan, who supported continuing the war, but they also produced a peace platform. Republicans battered the Democrats with the charge of favoring surrender, and the Union war fortunes improved enough by the election of 1864 to produce a wide margin of victory for Lincoln (who won every state except Kentucky, Delaware, and McClellan's home state of New Jersey) and increased Republican majorities in Congress. Lincoln's party was granted a new mandate to continue the war and pursue its national vision.

A NEW FEDERAL GOVERNMENT

Over the course of the long war, Republicans in Congress transformed a small, weak central government into a major force in the nation's economic life. Part of the transformation lay in the war effort itself, which required mobilizing, supplying, and coordinating an enormous fighting force. But Congress also broadened the federal government's reach in other ways that had lasting impact beyond the war. With southern Democrats out of the picture, Republicans were able to pass laws that created new revenue sources to finance

TABLE 15.2 MAJOR FEDERAL LEGISLATION, 1862-1864

Legislation	What It Did	Significance or Postwar Consequences
Homestead Act (1862)	Entitled settlers (including immigrants who intended to become citizens) to 160 free acres of western land after they had worked the plot for five years.	Made it easier and cheaper for small farmers to get land. Over the next seventy years, more than four hundred thousand families acquired farms under the Homestead Act. Also encouraged westward settlement and precipitated conflicts with Indians.
Revenue Act (1862)	Established a national income tax, which taxed income at a graduated rate of between 3 and 5 percent, and created the office of Commissioner of Internal Revenue—today known as the Internal Revenue Service (IRS); also outlined excise, liquor, and sales taxes on dozens of items.	Established both the IRS and the first progressive income tax in U.S. history.
General Pension Act (1862)	Awarded pensions to disabled soldiers and their widows, children, and dependent sisters.	Created a model for a social security system.
Pacific Railroad Act (1862)	Awarded charters to the Union Pacific and Central Pacific Railroads to construct a transcontinental railroad, providing one hundred million acres of public land for the project.	Facilitated the growth of national markets and western settlement (after completion of the railroad in 1869).
Morrill Land-Grant College Act (1862)	Provided federal support and public land to the states for establishing agricultural and mechanical arts (engineering) colleges.	Facilitated the founding of research universities in every state (including Cornell, Massachusetts Institute of Technology, and University of California at Berkeley), making higher education more accessible to a broader proportion of Americans.
Act to Establish a Department of Agriculture (1862)	Established the Department of Agriculture, which was responsible for distributing information and seeds to farmers and collecting statistics on American agriculture.	Paved the way for federal regulation of the crops that Americans grow and consume.
Legal Tender Act (1862) and National Banking Act (1863)	Established a national currency and supported the market for federal government bonds.	Created the United States' first national currency.
Conscription Act (1863)	Instituted a federal draft for the first time in U.S. history.	Formed the basis for drafts in future U.S. wars. Resistance to the draft exploded into the New York Draft Riots in July 1863.
Act to Amend the Laws Relating to the Post-Office Department (1863)	Made several changes to the postal service, including the introduction of free home delivery for forty-nine cities.	Initiated the process of turning mail service into a standard feature of American home life.

the war, established welfare programs for veterans and their families, and stimulated economic growth through policies that favored business and encouraged western expansion (see Table 15.2).

Although many wartime laws would have far-reaching consequences for the postwar nation, the most dramatic and controversial at the time was the Conscription Act (1863), which instituted a federal draft. Bypassing state governments, the law declared all unmarried white men between the ages of twenty and forty-five (and all married ones between twenty and thirty-five) eligible for forced military service. Federal agents would go from door to door collecting names, which would then be entered into a draft lottery. Congress passed the law in March 1863, at a low moment in the war, when the Union faced both a shortage of manpower and a crisis of morale. The Confederacy (despite its earlier espousal of states' rights) had instituted a national draft a year earlier, but in the North the Conscription Act was an unprecedented exercise of federal power and it triggered loud protests. Prominent newspapers denounced the United States as "one grand military dictatorship," and one Democratic daily explained the draft as an attempt to "kill off Democrats and stuff ballot-boxes with bogus soldier votes." The most galling part of the law was a provision that allowed men to avoid military service by paying a $300 bounty or securing a substitute. This exemption had been intended to prevent a black market for substitutes (which would not benefit the government and could put the cost out of reach for most Americans), but it had the effect of suggesting that the draft was for poor men, not rich ones. The draft met resistance throughout the North, from Massachusetts to Minnesota, but the most deadly explosion of antidraft protest erupted in New York City, which for four hot days in July 1863 became engulfed in violence (see States of Emergency: The New York Draft Riots). But draft quotas were ultimately met. The federal government succeeded in administering a massive forced mobilization of men, providing a large enough army to win the war.

GRANT'S COMMAND

By the end of 1863, the Union had won another important victory in Tennessee, defeating Confederate forces at Chattanooga (see Map 15.5). Impressed with Grant's record,

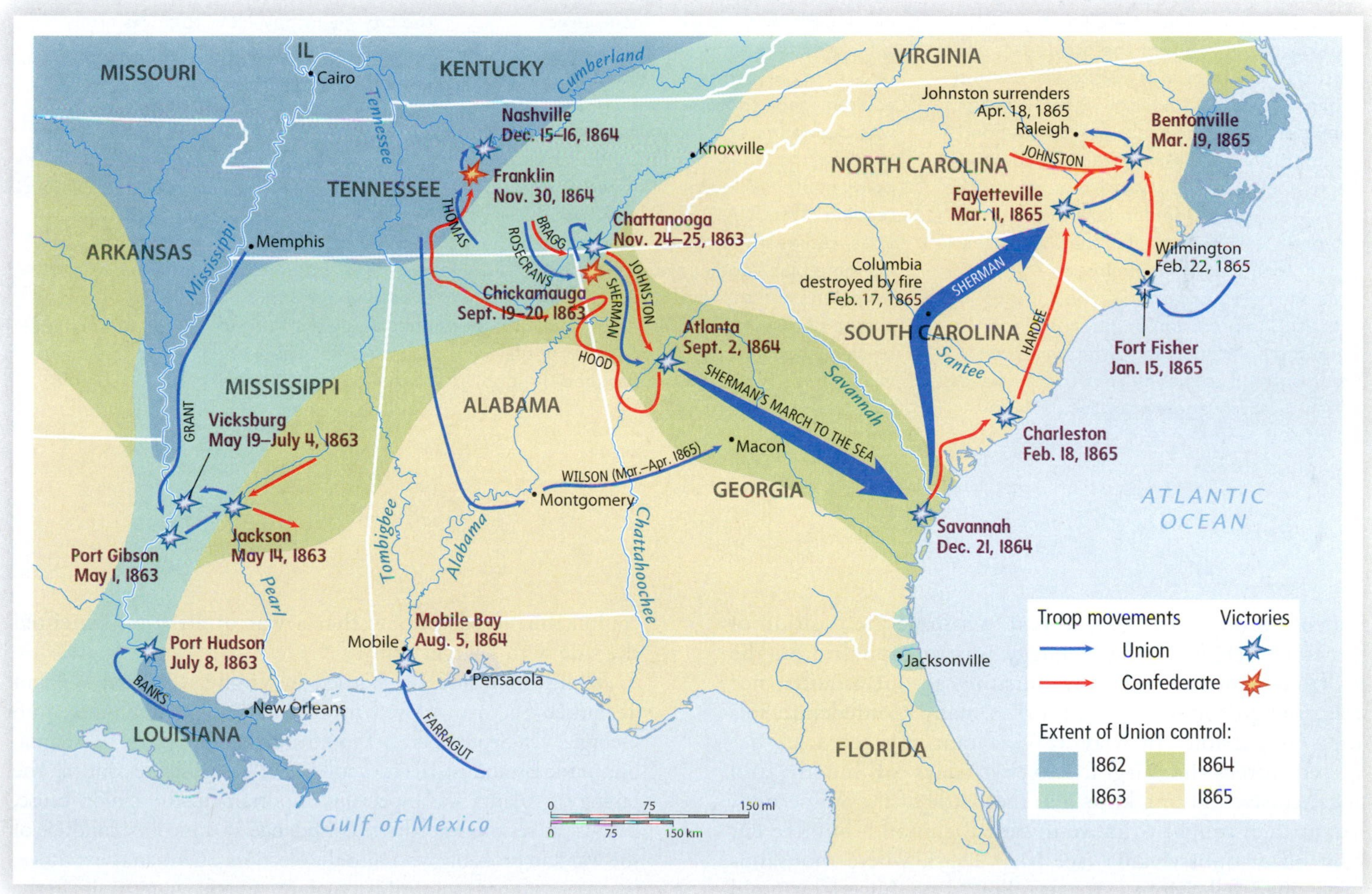

Map 15.5 The War in the West and Southeast, 1863–1865. Crucial northern victories in Chattanooga and Atlanta set up Sherman's ground invasion of the Southeast. While massive armies wore each other down in Virginia, Union forces prevailed decisively elsewhere, conquering major southern cities.

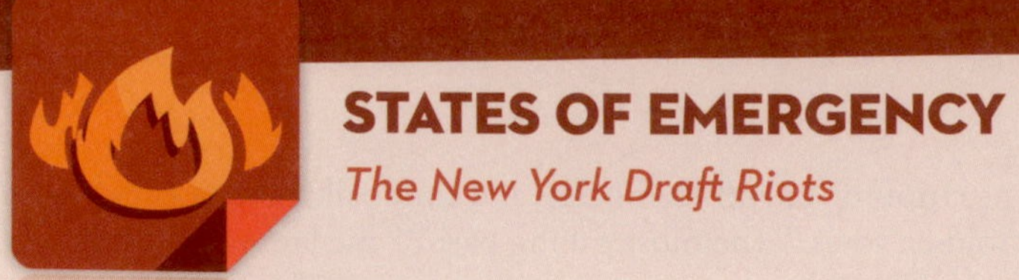

STATES OF EMERGENCY

The New York Draft Riots

Just days after the Battle of Gettysburg, as the army of Robert E. Lee headed back to the South, the largest city in the Union fell under violent attack. From the perspective of some New Yorkers, especially African Americans and Republicans, the attack came from *within*, in the form a massive riot by opponents of the federal draft, mostly immigrants and the children of immigrants. From the perspective of other New Yorkers, who probably formed the majority, the attack came from without, when the Union army invaded New York to help police control the city and reassert federal authority to impose the hated draft. From our later vantage point, the New York Draft Riots constituted a mini Civil War deep in Union territory.

The initial riot took place on Monday, July 13, 1863, on the second day of the lottery's operation. Lottery numbers had been drawn without incident the previous Saturday, but after a day off to discuss and organize, workers, most of whom were Irish immigrants, left their jobs and surrounded the draft office on Manhattan's Third Avenue. Like a majority of New Yorkers, the protesters were Democrats, and their sympathy for the war effort had diminished significantly once Lincoln began proclaiming emancipation. The $300 substitution provision underscored for them the point that poor white men were being sent off to die in order to free slaves. When the draft agents began to run the lottery that morning, the protesters beat the policemen who were guarding the building and then burned it down. From there, the opposition to the draft turned toward a violent purge of all symbols and instruments of Republican Party rule, including police officials, abolitionists, the offices of the New York *Tribune* and the New York *Times*, wealthy homes, various philanthropic institutions, and, most of all, African Americans.

That afternoon, rioters ransacked and torched the Colored Orphan Asylum, which housed over two hundred black children (the children escaped and took refuge in an almshouse on Blackwell's Island). Over the next two days, the crowds grew even more violent, and some of the original supporters of the uprising switched sides and began defending homes and property against looting. Blacks (who were themselves subject to the draft) remained principal targets of the rioters' wrath, and any who could manage to leave town did so. Those who did not escape, including women, children, the elderly, and the infirm, risked being beaten, killed, or mutilated. A sign reading "$100 REWARD FOR A NEGRO" appeared near the docks. A handful of mangled black bodies swung from lampposts. On the third day of the riots the corpse of a twenty-two-year-old disabled black coachman, cut down by order of the military, was rehanged and dragged through the streets by the genitals.

For three days, chaos reigned in the city. Omnibuses and streetcars were idle, businesses were closed, stores were looted, and houses were burned. Companies tried desperately to protect their offices, sometimes by bribing riot leaders, sometimes by stationing workers on rooftops with pots of boiling oil. Smoke filled the streets, billowing above the city. Police clashed violently with crowds. Policemen were mercilessly beaten to death—in one case the beating lasted six hours. On the other side, rioters were bludgeoned with clubs, shot in the head, or tossed out of upper-story windows.

Finally, on Wednesday night, Union soldiers began arriving by the thousands from Gettysburg. By the next day, the troops had subdued the rioters, broken through the barricades, and commenced occupying the city. By Friday, New York was firmly under the control of the army. The local government managed to quiet the draft resistance by paying substitution fees, and the federal draft was not seriously disrupted. Over one hundred people were killed in the riot (the vast majority of whom were on the side of the draft protesters), a small figure by the standards of the larger war but still the single bloodiest event in New York's history. Hundreds of buildings were burned, $5 million worth of property vanished, and New York's African American population was scattered by a vicious pogrom.

Lincoln brought the general east to assume the position of general-in-chief. Grant's strategy was to capitalize on the North's manpower edge by pursuing all-out assaults, not releasing prisoners, and killing as many Confederate soldiers as possible. In May 1864, Grant engaged Lee's depleted forces in Virginia in two days of bloody and inconclusive fighting known as the Battle of the Wilderness. Grant then sought to move toward Richmond, but Lee cut him off at Spotsylvania (see Map 15.4), where thousands more men fell. More carnage followed on June 1, at Cold Harbor. Grant was no closer to capturing the Confederate capital, but he also knew that a war of attrition benefited the side with a larger army.

While Grant and Lee battled in Virginia, General William Tecumseh Sherman moved from Chattanooga, Tennessee, into Georgia. On September 2, 1864, he captured the city of Atlanta, one of the last industrial cities still under Confederate control. The taking of Atlanta was especially important to the Union cause, because it restored northern confidence in Lincoln's conduct of the war and probably won him the election. Sherman's next move, however, was not against the remaining Confederate armies in the Southeast but against the Southeast itself (see Map 15.5). He

Fanning the Flames. In this anti-Irish and pro-Republican drawing, Governor Horatio Seymour (a Democrat) is depicted as a rabble rouser making common cause with Irish rioters, whom the artist ridicules as apelike. Not all Irish supported the riots, and many of the police and soldiers were also Irish immigrants. But a majority of the rioters were Irish, a fact that their opponents stressed repeatedly. Because Irish immigrants were associated with the two powerful institutions that embraced their entry into this country—the Democratic Party and the Catholic Church—many people blamed both Seymour and Archbishop John Hughes for failing to stop the riots. Democratic and Catholic identity was, in fact, a rallying point for rioters.

Think About It

1. Why did rioters attack free blacks in the North if their stated goal was to stop or protest the draft?
2. The Confederacy, which had implemented an earlier conscription law, offered exemptions to one white man from every plantation that had twenty or more slaves, seemingly favoring the wealthiest households. Why do you think no comparable draft riots erupted in the South in response to that draft?

moved his troops three hundred miles east toward Savannah, destroying bridges, factories, railroad lines, and everything valuable that lay in his path. The goal of Sherman's March to the Sea, as he put it, was to make the South "so sick of war that generations would pass away before they would again appeal to it."

SURRENDER AND ASSASSINATION

By the end of 1864, the Union troops had won another large battle in Nashville and Sherman's men had captured Savannah. Sherman then decided to bring the war back to South Carolina, where it had started almost four years earlier. As Columbia, the state capital, went up in a blaze, Confederate forces began evacuating South Carolina, hoping to unite with other armies in North Carolina to stop Sherman. Meanwhile, Lee had decided to move south from Petersburg, Virginia, leaving the Confederate capital of Richmond exposed. Grant's armies took Richmond and attacked Lee's outnumbered and exhausted forces as they retreated. On April 9, Lee surrendered to Grant at the Appomattox Court House in Virginia, under generous terms that allowed Lee's men to keep their horses and effectively granted them immunity from treason charges. Over the next

SINGULAR LIVES

Jesse James, Confederate Guerrilla

Few men rival Jesse James in the pantheon of American folk heroes. A Robin Hood figure who reputedly robbed banks to help the poor, the mythical Jesse James was a Wild West celebrity. The historical person behind the legend, however, came to his career of violence as a guerrilla fighting for slavery and the Confederacy in war-torn Missouri. Even by the standards of the Civil War, this was an especially dangerous and chaotic place to be. Rent by bitter internal divisions and subject to martial law, Missouri lost a third of its population to death, exile, and displacement during the war. And for a teenaged guerrilla operating beyond the conflict's formal borders, the Civil War lasted beyond Robert E. Lee's surrender in 1865.

Jesse James was born in 1847 in Clay County in northwestern Missouri to Robert and Zerelda James, hemp farmers who owned a small number of slaves. When war erupted, Jesse was barely a teenager, but his older brother Frank, aged eighteen, joined a local secessionist unit and fought against federal troops. After his unit was defeated in 1862, Frank James surrendered and returned home to Clay County, where he and his family lived resentfully under martial law and supported guerrilla attacks against their local adversaries. Frank spent much of the war in pro-Confederate bushwhacker gangs, and in 1864, his sixteen-year-old brother Jesse joined him. Their activities consisted mostly of killing farmers who supported the Union and fighting the Missouri State Militiamen who sought to enforce martial law. Their mother fully supported her sons' actions, and when Frank and Jesse entered the ranks of "Bloody Bill" Anderson's guerrilla band, Zerelda's family farm served as Anderson's home base. While serving under Bloody Bill, the James brothers looted the town of Centralia, Missouri, shot unarmed Union soldiers in cold blood, and mutilated their corpses. After Anderson met his demise, Jesse James escaped to Texas with another bushwhacking gang.

Jesse James, Guerrilla Field Commander. James is remembered in American culture as a populist bank robber, but his depredations began as part of the Confederate guerrilla effort.

In May 1865, a year after the war officially ended, James and his gang plundered its way back into Missouri, still fighting for the surrendered Confederate cause. James participated in an attempt to capture the city of Lexington, which had been the site of two battles earlier in the war, and was shot in the chest by a Wisconsin cavalryman. He survived the wound and rejoined his fellow bushwhackers in their ongoing campaign of resistance and revenge against Unionists. The campaign now included bank robbery. Archie Clement, the gang leader whom James had followed to Texas, became the prime suspect in an 1866 armed attack on a bank owned by Republicans in Clay County, the first daytime bank robbery in U.S. history. James turned to robbing banks as well, targeting institutions owned by his political enemies and striking symbolic blows in an ongoing local guerrilla war over slavery and secession. For James, that war had begun a decade earlier in Kansas, when he was just a boy, and the accumulated grievances and vendettas assured that it would continue for some time.

Think About It

1. How did Jesse James's role in the Civil War reflect the particular situation of Missouri in the conflict?
2. Do you see James as a soldier, a political terrorist, or a gang member?
3. How might James's identity as a pro-Confederate guerrilla have helped turn him into a celebrated outlaw?

"Jeff in Petticoats: A Song for the Times." One month after Lee's surrender, Union soldiers in rural Georgia finally captured Jefferson Davis, who had fled Richmond with his cabinet and remained a fugitive in the South. Because Davis reportedly disguised himself by wearing his wife's overcoat, northerners ridiculed him as a cross-dresser.

two weeks, other Confederate armies would abandon the cause as well. The Civil War was over (see Singular Lives: Jesse James, Confederate Guerrilla).

For African Americans in the South, the Confederacy's surrender confirmed what had been happening throughout the war. The institution of slavery had been undermined steadily, first by the arrival of the Union forces, then by the actions of the enslaved, and eventually by the policies of the federal government. On every plantation in the South, this process played out differently, depending on location and varying with the circumstances of each master-slave relationship. Many enslaved people left their homes, while others stayed, concealing their plans as they awaited the resolution of the conflict. Some took the opportunity to renegotiate the terms of their service to their masters, while others sought to even old scores. In one dramatic scene in Virginia in 1864, three former slaves (under the protection of Union general Edward Wild) took turns whipping a slaveholder who had abused them. In different ways and to different degrees, most of the four million men, women, and children who had been held as property at the start of the war now enjoyed some measure of freedom or relief. Legally, slaves in the loyal border states had not been emancipated, but after the election of 1864, the enhanced Republican majority in Congress was able to pass a constitutional amendment to free them as well. On January 31, 1865, the Thirteenth Amendment, which banned slavery except as punishment for crime, was submitted to the states for ratification (see Chapter 16).

With the Confederate surrender and the abolition of slavery imminent, Lincoln now faced the challenges of reintegrating the rebellious states into what had become a very different nation. Without conceding the Republican position that secession was illegal and treasonous, he needed to devise a plan for granting amnesty to the millions who had supported the rebellion and the hundreds of thousands who had taken up arms against the United States. On April 14, Good Friday, Lincoln took time away from this project to attend a play, *Our American Cousin*, which was being performed at Washington's Ford's Theatre. During the play, an actor named John Wilkes Booth sneaked into Lincoln's box and shot him in the head. By the next morning, the president of the United States was dead.

Lincoln, long a controversial figure in American politics, became an instant martyr throughout the North. His death seemed to stand in some way for all the suffering the nation had undergone, and perhaps to atone for all the violence it had perpetrated. In words that recalled Lincoln's own speech at Gettysburg but also compared his death to that of Christ, a Providence, Rhode Island, minister captured a common theme in northern eulogies: "One man has died for the people, in order that the whole nation might not perish."

CONCLUSION

Four years earlier, back in the winter that stretched between Lincoln's election and his inauguration, the leading citizens of South Carolina had tried to reassure one another that leaving the United States would not lead to war. James Chesnut, Jr., who had resigned from the U.S. Senate four days after Lincoln's election, promised to drink any blood that would be spilled over disunion. Newspaper editor Robert Barnwell Rhett reputedly offered to eat all the bodies that might be killed. Chesnut and Rhett were bluffing, of course, trying to convince other slaveholders and slave states to join their cause—precisely to avoid the prospect of bloodshed that they dismissed. Chesnut's wife, Mary, understood the urgency of this political stance. "We have risked all, and must play our best," she noted in her diary, "for the stake is life and death." But whatever they might have feared, no one in South Carolina (or anywhere else) could have imagined just how much death was at stake—how much blood would flow across the country over the next four years.

By 1865, approximately 2.5 percent of the nation's population had been killed in the war (an equivalent loss today would exceed seven million lives). In the South, where about one in five white men of military age perished, whole cities had been leveled. Communities in both the North and the South were awash in prosthetic limbs and covered in mourning crepe. The amount of money expended by the North alone in waging this war would have been enough to purchase every slave in the South in 1861, set up each emancipated family with forty acres and a mule, and compensate them for years of back wages. But of course slaveholders in 1861 had not been interested in selling slaves their freedom, and few white Americans, North or South, were willing to share the continent (let alone their own land) with four million free people of color. Few white Americans were interested in emancipation at all in 1861. But four years later, everything had changed. What this change meant for national politics, the economy, and the lives of four million freed people remained profoundly uncertain.

STUDY TERMS

secession commissioners (p. 383)

Confederate States of America (p. 383)

states' rights (p. 383)

Crittenden Compromise (p. 385)

Fort Sumter (p. 385)

First Battle of Bull Run (Manassas) (p. 387)

Army of the Potomac (p. 388)

Battle of Antietam (p. 388)

Battle of Shiloh (p. 388)

naval blockade (p. 388)

Crittenden Resolution (p. 390)

contrabands (p. 390)

Confiscation Act (p. 390)

Second Confiscation Act (p. 391)

Emancipation Proclamation (p. 392)

Colored Troops (p. 393)

Fort Pillow Massacre (p. 393)

Copperheads (p. 394)

military occupation (p. 394)

guerrilla warfare (p. 395)

Bushwhackers (p. 395)

Jayhawkers (p. 395)

Andersonville prison (p. 396)

United States Sanitary Commission (p. 399)

casualty lists (p. 399)

pictorial magazines (p. 400)

Civil War photographs (p. 403)

siege of Vicksburg (p. 404)

Battle of Gettysburg (p. 404)

Gettysburg Address (p. 404)

election of 1864 (p. 405)

Conscription Act (p. 407)

New York Draft Riots (p. 408)

Battle of the Wilderness (p. 408)

March to the Sea (p. 409)

Thirteenth Amendment (p. 411)

TIMELINE

1860 Abraham Lincoln elected president

South Carolina votes to secede from the United States

1861 Confederate States of America established

Confederate troops attack Fort Sumter

Congress passes Crittenden Resolution

First Battle of Bull Run (Battle of Manassas)

Congress passes Confiscation Act

1862 Battle of Shiloh

U.S. Navy captures New Orleans

Congress abolishes slavery in the District of Columbia

Congress passes Second Confiscation Act

Battle of Antietam

Lincoln delivers the Emancipation Proclamation

1863 U.S. begins forming Colored Troops

Congress passes Conscription Act, instituting a federal draft

U.S. troops begin the siege of Vicksburg

Battle of Gettysburg

New York Draft Riots

Lincoln's Gettysburg Address

1864 African American soldiers massacred at Fort Pillow

Battle of the Wilderness

Union general William Tecumseh Sherman's March to the Sea begins

Lincoln reelected

1865 Confederate general Robert E. Lee surrenders to Union forces

Lincoln assassinated

FURTHER READING

Additional suggested readings are available on the Online Learning Center at www.mhhe.com/becomingamerica1e.

Stephen Ash, *When the Yankees Came* (1995), covers the experiences and horrors of life in the occupied South during the war.

Ira Berlin, Barbara Fields, et al., *Slaves No More* (1992), draws on a massive documentary study of emancipation to offer an account of the end of slavery, told in part from the perspective of the enslaved.

Alice Fahs, *Imagined Civil War* (2003), focuses on the war as reflected in the popular culture of the period, especially in fiction.

Drew Gilpin Faust, *This Republic of Suffering* (2008), treats the Civil War as a major event in the history of American attitudes toward death.

James McPherson, *Battle Cry of Freedom* (1988), remains the most influential and comprehensive narrative of the causes, course, and consequences of the war.

Chandra Manning, *What This Cruel War Was Over* (2007), examines soldiers' correspondence to explore their views toward slavery, secession, and the meaning of the conflict.

Heather Cox Richardson, *The Greatest Nation of the Earth* (1997), traces the role of the wartime Congress in transforming the role of the federal government and shaping the postwar nation.

Barnet Schechter, *The Devil's Own Work* (2007), narrates the 1863 draft riots in New York.

Yael Sternhell, *Routes of War* (2012), places the dramatic movements of soldiers, deserters, refugees, and escaped slaves at the center of the South's wartime experience.

T. J. Stiles, *Jesse James: Last Rebel of the Civil War* (2002), presents the life of the famous Missouri bandit in the context of local guerrilla fighting and the Confederate cause.

Alan Trachtenberg, *Reading American Photographs* (1989), interprets the classic photographs published and exhibited by Mathew Brady.

Garry Wills, *Lincoln at Gettysburg* (1992), treats Lincoln's speech as a foundational moment in the remaking of the United States.

16

A New South. Institutions like Richmond's First African Church helped build communities of freedpeople and encouraged optimism about the possibilities of a free and inclusive southern society.

INSIDE

THE BIG PICTURE

After the war, "reconstructing" the South and reintegrating the seceded states into the union was a complex and contested process. Spurred by the demands, aspirations, and new political power of ex-slaves, Republicans in Congress laid the groundwork for major changes in southern politics and culture, only to see those changes reversed.

1862–1883

SOUTHERN RECONSTRUCTION

In May 1865, just a month after Confederate forces surrendered at Appomattox, rumors about the future of the defeated South spread quickly along the Cotton Belt. Beginning on the Carolina coast, recently freed slaves whispered of a coming "Christmas Jubilee" in which the federal government would confiscate the slaveholders' great plantations, divide them into small farms, and "give the land to the colored people." The rumor traveled quickly inland, and from cities to farms, along the oral "grapevine telegraph" that had served as an informal communication network among slaves. By the end of summer, millions of rural freedpeople believed that it was only a matter of time before the federal government took action. Meanwhile, a different rumor spread among the South's white communities. Many white southerners predicted that, around Christmas time, armed mobs of freedpeople would seize the old slave plantations. By December 1865, talk of a "Jubilee Insurrection" and a second civil war, this time between black and white southerners, echoed across the wartorn region.

As it turned out, neither "jubilee" came to pass. Although the federal government distributed some land to freedpeople, it did not embark on a large-scale confiscation of the plantations. Nor did the freedpeople rise up and take white people's property by force. But the rumors were significant all the same. They were the opening shots in a long struggle to determine how and by whom the South's devastated economy, culture, and political system would be reconstructed.

For the freedpeople, the Civil War had been a war against slavery. If their hard-won freedom was to be meaningful, the federal government would have to give them access to the land of their former masters. This would be a practical guarantee of their economic independence as well as a symbolic acknowledgment of their freedom. With their own small farms, freedpeople could reunite and sustain their families, lead independent lives, and build strong, prosperous communities. Freedpeople also knew that breaking up the plantations would weaken the white elite; deprived of their plantations, former masters would never again wield the enormous economic and political power they had enjoyed before the Civil War. Ex-slaveholders sensed that their position was precarious. Rumors of a Christmas insurrection fueled their distrust of free blacks and promoted a racist solidarity against black efforts to gain equality.

KEY QUESTIONS

- What role did newly emancipated slaves play in setting the terms for political change in the South?
- How did Presidential and Congressional Reconstruction plans differ, and why did Congressional Reconstruction triumph in a political sense?
- In what ways did the new state governments in the South both fulfill and disappoint freedpeople's political aspirations?
- Why had Republicans failed to maintain control of state governments in the South by the mid-1870s?
- What were the terms of the political and cultural compromise that ended the North's commitment to enforcing emancipation and equality in the South?

Freedpeople's efforts to define and claim their freedom, and their former masters' opposition to these efforts, lie at the heart of the era of Reconstruction (1862–1883). The term *Reconstruction* refers both to federal policies to reintegrate the states that had seceded from the union and to the remarkable political, cultural, and economic revolution that took place in the South during these years. Reconstruction unfolded in three distinct phases. In the first, Wartime Reconstruction, President Lincoln and Congress began debating how to bring the South back into the union—well before the northern victory had been declared. With the war won, Reconstruction entered its second phase, Presidential Reconstruction, in which President Andrew Johnson suspended land distribution and former slave masters tried to subordinate African Americans and return them to plantation labor. The third and most dramatic phase, Congressional Reconstruction, began in 1866, when Republicans in Congress rejected Johnson's approach and set the South on the path to building the Western world's first racially inclusive democracy. Vibrant black communities emerged, built on the twin pillars of independent churches and schools. And for the first time, black men participated actively in state, local, and federal government and served on juries, in the judiciary, and as police.

Five generations of a black family pose for a white photographer on a South Carolina plantation in 1862.

The South's new democracy soon came under relentless attack. Every Reconstruction government fell by 1877, and by 1883 the Supreme Court had limited the scope of key civil rights legislation. The nation's remarkable democratic experiment all but collapsed. Yet African Americans' aspiration to landownership, autonomy, and full citizenship endured. And the churches, schools, and cultural institutions that had been founded during Reconstruction continued to inspire, protect, and energize black communities for many decades to come.

WARTIME RECONSTRUCTION

Already in 1862, just a year into the Civil War, President Lincoln and congressional leaders had spoken of the need for a postwar plan of what they called "national reconstruction." Initially, Reconstruction simply referred to the legal terms and conditions under which the Confederate states would be readmitted to the union once they had surrendered. But as slaves fled their masters and streamed across Union lines, they forced lawmakers and the president to confront the issue of slavery (see Chapter 15) and gradually turned the freedom of four million African Americans into a core issue of the war. Over the two and a half years following Lincoln's Emancipation Proclamation in January 1863, the president and Congress debated the South's future. Each side held different views about how to deal with the old southern ruling class and ensure the freedom of ex-slaves. As the war escalated and damage to the South grew, the challenges of postwar recovery multiplied.

LINCOLN'S TEN PERCENT PLAN

The Union's scorched-earth warfare pounded southern cities and towns into rubble and tore up miles of railroads and highways. Farmland lay charred and infertile, while forests were stripped by both sides for fuel and materiel. After the war turned decisively in the Union's favor late in 1863, the need to formulate a more thorough plan of southern Reconstruction became urgent.

Lincoln and congressional lawmakers found no clear guidance in the federal Constitution for how to reclaim or readmit seceding states following a civil war. The Constitution was silent on the question of whether the Confederate states should be punished for their actions. Likewise, it was unclear how active a role, if any, the federal government should play in reconstructing the economies, political institutions, and social fabric of the rebel states. It also gave no indication of whether the authority to reconstruct the union and the South lay primarily with Congress or with the president.

As Union lawmakers and leaders grappled with these thorny constitutional questions, they slowly formulated two quite different conceptions of Reconstruction.

Masters of Their Destiny. Slaves fled their masters and poured across Union lines in 1862, compelling the federal government to abandon its policy of return. Accepting the end of slavery became the supreme condition for the Confederate states' readmission to the union.

Advancing the case for what came to be called the Ten Percent Plan (officially titled the "Proclamation of Amnesty and Reconstruction"), Lincoln argued that the authority to reintegrate the South into the union lay with the president and that harsh punishment was neither justified nor legal. The Confederate states might claim they had legally seceded from the union, Lincoln asserted, but in the eyes of the law they had not. Consequently, southern state governments were essentially legitimate. Though he would later toughen his position, in 1863 Lincoln believed that taking a heavy hand against the South would prove counterproductive. "We shall sooner have the fowl by hatching the egg than by smashing it," he argued. The best way to help the South recover and to reunite the nation was to punish only the small minority of men who had led the Confederacy, and quickly usher southern lawmakers back into Congress.

Lincoln presented his Ten Percent Plan in December 1863. Under this proposal, the rebel states would have to accept the end of slavery, but as long as at least ten percent of the number of voters in 1860 took a loyalty oath to the union, that state could hold elections and rejoin the United States. Leaders of the Confederacy would not be allowed to hold office, but most other white southern men would be given full amnesty and regain their political rights.

EARLY CONGRESSIONAL INITIATIVES

To implement his plan, Lincoln needed the consent of Congress, which had sole constitutional authority to seat (or refuse to seat) members of the House of Representatives and

Senate. Northern Democrats and some conservative Republicans supported Lincoln's initiative. But it failed to impress moderate Republicans, and it bitterly disappointed a vocal minority known as the **Radical Republicans.** This congressional faction, made up largely of abolitionists, believed that the new rights of freedpeople might not be properly protected if the process were hurried and that southern elites might try to reintroduce slavery. Leading Radical Thaddeus Stevens also claimed that, contrary to Lincoln's view that secession never occurred, the Confederates *had* left the union and had done so illegally. They could rejoin the union only by being readmitted as new states, Stevens concluded, and Reconstruction thus fell entirely under congressional authority, because only Congress had the power to admit new states to the union. And Congress should therefore make much stiffer demands on the Confederate states before readmitting them.

With the support of a number of moderates, Radical Republicans presented the Wade-Davis Bill of 1864 in an effort to slow down the process of readmission and assert congressional control over Reconstruction. It provided that once the majority of a southern state's voters pledged allegiance to the union, the president would appoint a governor and direct him to call an election for a state constitutional convention. Convention delegates would write a fresh state constitution, prohibit slavery, and disenfranchise Confederate leaders. The bill also provided that only those men who swore an oath that they had not taken up arms against the federal government would be eligible to participate in the convention. Because so many white men had served in the Confederate military, this would have disqualified much of the prewar southern electorate.

Lincoln considered the Wade-Davis bill a direct challenge to his authority and his own Reconstruction plan. He refused to sign the bill. Enraged, Radical Republicans and a growing cadre of moderates in turn enacted several bold new laws aimed at ensuring the emancipation of the slaves and laying out the goals of Reconstruction. In January 1865, Congress passed the Thirteenth Amendment to the U.S. Constitution, which prohibited slavery and involuntary servitude in all forms except as punishment for crime. (This exemption allowed northern states to continue their long-standing practice of putting prisoners to forced labor.) The Emancipation Proclamation had abolished slavery only in the rebellious states (not in Missouri, Kentucky, West Virginia, Maryland, or Delaware) and as a wartime measure.

Mourning and Mobilization. As Lincoln's funeral train wended its way to Illinois, tens of thousands of mourners lined city streets and railroad tracks. In the process, northerners became more receptive to Radical Republicans' call for lasting change in the South.

The amendment, which Lincoln supported vigorously, would bring an end to legalized slavery in the United States.

Two months later, Congress established the Bureau of Refugees, Freedmen, and Abandoned Lands (or the Freedmen's Bureau), a special agency of the War Department, and charged it with overseeing southern Reconstruction. Under the directorship of General Oliver O. Howard of the U.S. Army, the Bureau set about feeding the millions of former slaves and poor white southerners who faced starvation in the winter of 1865 due to the destruction of crops, livestock, and granaries. These initiatives were reinforced on the ground in the South when General Sherman issued Special Field Order No. 15, ordering the distribution of forty-acre sections of land to ex-slaves in the Union-occupied Sea Islands and Carolina Lowcountry. Under this plan, some forty thousand freedpeople settled on some four hundred thousand acres of land. Observing the mounting support in Congress for a more thorough Reconstruction of the South, Lincoln pragmatically endorsed certain demands of the Radicals—including giving propertied black men the vote.

LINCOLN'S ASSASSINATION AND NORTHERN SENTIMENT

By April 9, 1865, the day that General Robert E. Lee surrendered the Northern Department of the Confederate Army at Appomattox, Lincoln and Congress agreed that the supreme precondition for the South's readmission into the union would be acceptance of emancipation. The South would be reconstructed and readmitted as a free society, and only as a free society. Beyond that certainty, however, a great deal of doubt remained about what course Reconstruction and reunion might take.

John Wilkes Booth's shooting of Lincoln, less than a week after Lee's surrender (see Chapter 15), altered the political equation. When Lincoln died the following morning, waves of grief and fear swept across northern cities and towns. Although Booth and his associates had acted alone, rumors spread that they had been part of a Confederate-backed conspiracy to overthrow the federal government, halt the South's surrender, and reignite the war. Booth was indeed a Confederate sympathizer, but speculation about a Confederate plot had no basis in fact. Still, the rumors strengthened northern antipathy toward the southern leadership.

As public anxiety intensified, Lincoln's body was placed in a coffin and hoisted onto a funeral train. The locomotive embarked on a solemn, 1,700-mile railroad procession from the capital through Philadelphia, New York, Buffalo, and Chicago before carrying Lincoln to his final resting place in Springfield, Illinois. Seven million mourners lined the route, and millions more saw photographs of the procession in the press. As the train wound its way west, public opinion swung swiftly and decisively behind the Radical Republicans and their call for a thorough and exacting reconstruction of the South. The Radicals stepped up their campaign.

CLAIMING THE FUTURE

Northerners were hardly the only Americans to face tremendous uncertainty in the spring of 1865. In the South, the war and emancipation had destroyed the legal right to buy, sell, and own human beings. But there was no consensus as to what freedom would mean in practice, or what kind of society the South should become. In the first few years after the war, freedpeople, white farmers, planters, and the Freedmen's Bureau all explored the meaning of emancipation. They did so not only in political speeches and in the press but also in their everyday actions, parades, songs, and dress, and in the stories they told about "slavery days" and the war that had led to slavery's destruction.

FREEDPEOPLE CLAIM THEIR FREEDOM

Though it ended slavery, the Civil War wreaked havoc in the lives of four million ex-slaves in the South. Approximately half a million of them had escaped to freedom during the course of the conflict, and they were especially vulnerable to diseases that came with the mass mobilization of soldiers and refugees. Tens of thousands of ex-slaves died in a smallpox epidemic that erupted in Washington, D.C., in 1862 and spread to the Upper South over the next two years. Those who remained on plantations during the war suffered as well. Facing poverty, physical hardship, and a major medical crisis that historians are just beginning to uncover, freedpeople assumed the historic task of claiming their newfound freedom, performing hundreds of small acts that had been forbidden to them as slaves. Freedpeople laid down tools, walked off plantations, and crisscrossed the countryside looking for loved ones who had been sold and scattered under slavery. They gathered in abandoned halls, railroad cars, barns, cabins, and makeshift structures. It was during these early days of freedom that the rumors of land distribution circulated among blacks in the rural South.

In cities, black southerners joyously celebrated their freedom with an important American ritual from which they had been previously barred—the street procession (see Hot Commodities: Dressing for Freedom). In Charleston, black clergy and the Colored Men's Twenty-First Regiment led off a parade of ten thousand black men, women, and children, lifting banners that proclaimed freedom and asserted the rights of black men to vote. Just as free white men had done for decades, the men marched by trade or occupation. A flotilla carrying tableaux of the Old South, complete with auction block and actors playing the role of slaves and auctioneer, confronted white onlookers with the horror of their supposedly benign institution. The prominent position of uniformed black soldiers in these parades linked their military service to their claim to full citizenship—and signaled to white southerners that black communities were prepared to protect themselves by force if necessary.

Through the remainder of 1865, blacks in the South exercised their new freedoms and began building their future as independent citizens. Ex-slaves overcame hunger, bombed-out

HOT COMMODITIES

Dressing for Freedom: Silks and Satins

On a spring day in 1865, a joyous crowd of black people, clad in what one observer described as brilliant "silks and satins of all the colors of the rainbow," gathered on a main thoroughfare in Charleston, South Carolina. Just hours before, the revelers had been informed of their emancipation from slavery. They shed their work clothes, helped themselves to their former masters' and mistresses' fine suits and dresses, and headed into town to celebrate their freedom. Millions of other former slaves across the South marked emancipation in much the same way that year.

Going out publicly in colorful, fancy clothing was one particularly vivid means by which freedpeople registered their freedom and staked a claim to full membership in American society. Under slavery, most had been compelled to wear relatively plain, white or undyed cotton garments that were suited to hard labor in the fields; their simple clothes also signaled to everybody that the wearer was a slave (rather than a free black person). Once free, former slaves dressed up brightly and promenaded in town squares to exhibit their liberty—including the freedom to wear whatever style of clothing they pleased.

Dress remained an important form of self-expression and marker of identity during and after Reconstruction. Dressing stylishly also signaled a desire to participate as equals in consumer culture. Once stores reopened and trade with the North resumed, southern black women purchased fine textiles, buttons, and lace to sew into stylish dresses, bonnets, and blouses. Urban black women sometimes modeled their clothing on the latest New York fashions, which they had seen in the new mass-circulation national magazines of the era. But many others incorporated fine materials into their own distinctive designs, blending expensive fabrics with more affordable ones (including textiles and trim salvaged from upholstery and other household sources). Both poor and middling black women dressed in "ladylike" ways that emphasized their femininity and respectability and asserted equality with whites. Parasols and crepe veils of the sort that adorned fashionable whites became popular accessories. Regardless of their trade or occupation, black men wore topcoats and hats in public, particularly to church on Sundays. And men and women alike dressed to attend the theater and other public entertainments alongside whites—much to the annoyance of the latter.

Such stylish dressing frequently offended whites, who generally thought of African Americans as social inferiors whose dress should reflect their supposedly humble station in life. Some white men went so far as to violently cut new clothes off the backs of former slaves on the grounds that they were being "uppity"—aspiring to a social status above that of laborer. Other whites, who failed to see the historical significance of the colorful clothing, were appalled by the bright new fashions. As Belle Kearney, the daughter of a former slaveholder put it, black women had "bought brilliant-hued stuffs and had them made with the most bizarre effects." And some could not understand why even the poorest African Americans spent their precious wages on fashion. Why must black people have "parasols when they ha'n't got no shoes?" chastised a Charleston proprietor. "Because, although we are poor, we are free," might have come the answer.

Free Expression. Black Americans celebrated their freedom not only in formal speeches about slavery and the war, but in music, dress, and their use of public space. This young man, dressed in fashionable morning coat, top hat, and leather shoes, exudes the self-assurance and pride that many African Americans expressed during Reconstruction—and many white people found threatening.

Think About It

1. Why might recently emancipated African Americans have valued clothing over other kinds of consumer goods, such as carpets, dishes, and pianos?
2. Why were many whites offended by the flashy outfits of freedpeople?

roads, and a chronic shortage of money and credit to reconstitute their families, establish rudimentary schools, and found their own churches. Uncertain whether federal Reconstruction policy would protect them and concerned about white southerners' refusal to disarm the militias, freedmen organized their own militias and drilled with the discipline many had learned in the Union Army.

Above all, freedpeople made it clear that they no longer wanted to grow cotton for their old masters, not even for wages. Instead they took steps to acquire their own small farms on which they could raise a few head of livestock and grow a variety of produce. Ex-slaves who had escaped to the North during the war returned home with the hope of claiming the land they and their forebears had worked for generations. "Our wives, our children, our husbands has been sold over and over again to purchase the lands we now locates upon," declared one freedman. "[F]or that reason we have a divine right to the land."

Many stayed on the plantations and some pressed their former masters for the tools, stock, seed, and capital needed to fence and transform the war-ravaged land into working farms. Some claimed back pay, although it is unlikely that they expected to receive it. As Jourdon Anderson, an ex-slave who had moved to Ohio, taunted his former master: "I served you faithfully for thirty-two years, and Mandy twenty years. At $25 a month for me, and $2 a week for Mandy, our earnings would amount to $11,680. . . . Please send the money by Adams Express."

Lost Limbs. Injury and amputation disabled many soldiers and prevented them from being productive family farmers or factory workers. Injured and disabled men filled American towns and cities in the postwar decades. These paired photos show Confederate veterans Henry J. and Levi Jasper Walker before and after the war. Beginning with San Francisco in 1867, several U.S. municipalities passed "unsightly beggar ordinances," prohibiting the exhibition of maimed or unsightly bodies in public space.

For many ex-slaves, freedom meant that families could now live together without fear of being separated by a master, and black males could assume their place at the head of the household. Like white fathers and husbands, the male head of house would assume a range of rights (such as the right to discipline his children and wife, and the right to make contracts on the family's behalf) and claim responsibility for the household as breadwinner and decision maker. This arrangement provided for the welfare of wives and children, but it also withheld certain rights, such as the right to own property, from married women.

In 1865, a small but growing number of freedpeople began to argue that black heads of household (and African American men in general) should have the right to vote and hold public office. "Slavery is not abolished until the black man has the ballot," argued Frederick Douglass. For Douglass and many black southerners, the ballot was both the supreme symbol of freedom and the practical means by which African Americans would be able to protect their newfound rights.

RURAL WORLDS LOST: WHITE FARMERS

The war had been a calamity for the South's white yeomen farmers and their way of life. Many yeomen, especially in the Appalachian region, had opposed secession. But the Confederate government had conscripted vast numbers of them, and they had performed most of the fighting and borne the brunt of the fatalities. As the war escalated and the Confederacy requisitioned their mules, crops, and supplies, many farming families were left all but destitute. "We are in this county as poor as people ever gets to be to live," lamented one Alabama farmer. For many yeomen families who had lost limbs to the cause of secession, a return to prewar farm life was all but impossible.

Many southern farmers returned home in the summer of 1865 embittered with the planter class that had led them to war. Much like the freedpeople, they resisted having to go to work for planters as subordinated wage laborers producing food and raw materials for distant markets. Instead their goal was to rebuild their own small farms, growing crops and raising livestock for themselves and the local marketplace. Growing numbers of yeomen now joined the local Union Leagues, the southern chapters of the northern Republican clubs that had been founded during the war in support of Lincoln's war policies. In Alabama, over three thousand men had officially joined the leagues by December 1865, and many thousands more were affiliated informally. These leagues worked hard to limit the immense political and social power of the planter "aristocracy."

Some also joined the freedpeople in calling for a general distribution of the slaveholders' plantations. "We should tuk the land," wrote one white farmer, "[and] split it, and gin part to the [freedpeople] and part to me and t'other Union fellers."

PLANTERS AND POWER

Planters, the wealthy slaveholding class that had dominated southern politics and society before the war, sought full restoration of their power, status, and way of life in the aftermath of the conflict. Planters had convinced themselves that slavery was a benevolent and Christian institution and that their slaves had been quite content with it. Many were therefore shocked by their slaves' great joy in being freed. Even more perplexing was their former slaves' refusal to continue working for them, even for wages. On one plantation in South Carolina, where freedpeople had divided the plantation into small farms for themselves, the former master was outraged by what he called the freedpeople's "recklessness and ingratitude." Many former masters and mistresses misread ex-slaves' desire to work for themselves as laziness. "Their idea of work, unaided by the stern law of necessity, is very vague," wrote Fan Butler, the daughter of a wealthy ex-slaveholding family in Georgia. "I don't think one does a really honest full day's work. . . . They are affectionate and often trustworthy and honest, but so hopelessly lazy as to be almost worthless as laborers." Planters' most immediate desire was to force their former slaves back to work on their great cotton, sugar, rice, and tobacco plantations. They also wanted to ensure that, whatever form Reconstruction took, it did not destroy their political and economic power.

THE FREEDMEN'S BUREAU

As the freedpeople, yeomanry, and planters hashed out their visions of a new South in 1865, the Freedmen's Bureau extended the federal presence on the frontlines of southern Reconstruction. The Bureau's tasks were overwhelmingly complex and often contradictory. In a world turned upside down, the Bureau had to get food to millions of freedpeople and poor white southerners, help refugees relocate their families, and secure civil peace. The Bureau also needed a way to identify and track the population it was assisting. This in itself was an enormous task partly because, under slavery, many African Americans had not used a surname. The Bureau had first to persuade several million ex-slaves to adopt—and keep—a permanent family name, and then register as many of the names as possible. In its first year, the Bureau was expected to do all this on an initial shoestring budget of just $27,000 and with a staff of only a few hundred people (see How Much Is That?).

Above all, the Bureau's mandate was to prepare ex-slaves for a peaceful transition to freedom. Initially, official Bureau policy was entirely unclear about what form this freedom would take. Many Bureau agents drew on the abolitionist belief that a free society was one in which people voluntarily entered into contracts that imposed certain duties and obligations in return for certain benefits. Labor and marriage contracts were the focus of their efforts. Bureau officials shared the freedpeople's belief that freedom was connected with land ownership, however. By November 1865, the Bureau had confiscated 850,000 acres of land and was ready to rent it out (and eventually sell it) to the freedpeople in 40-acre lots. The Bureau awaited orders from the federal government.

How Much Is That?

Relief for Ex-Slaves

In today's dollars, the value of the Freedmen's Bureau's budget of $27,000 would be just over $399,000—a drop in the bucket compared with the magnitude of the South's devastation.

PATHS TOWARD RECONSTRUCTION

Divisions between congressional and presidential visions for bringing the South back into the union widened in the wake of Lincoln's assassination. Vice President Andrew Johnson, who was inaugurated as president shortly after Lincoln was pronounced dead, was a yeoman farmer and unionist from the former slave state of Tennessee. A self-made man who loathed aristocracy, his political priority had been the permanent disempowerment of the southern planter elite. "Damn the Negroes," he had declared during the war. "I am fighting those traitrous aristocrats, their masters." But as it became clear that black southerners wanted full legal equality, Johnson reversed course and began working for the restoration of the planters as the South's political leaders. This provoked outrage in Congress, and lawmakers eventually wrested control of Reconstruction from Johnson and set the South on the road to becoming the Western world's first truly racially inclusive democracy.

ANDREW JOHNSON AND PRESIDENTIAL RECONSTRUCTION

Early on in his administration, Johnson supported the abolition of slavery by requiring southern states to ratify the Thirteenth Amendment as a condition for reentry into the union. (Indeed, Georgia's vote provided the three-fourths majority that allowed the amendment to be adopted in December 1865.) He did so not because he deemed slavery an unjust institution but because it gave the planter class enormous power in southern society and in the republic as a whole. On the question of whether black people should have full political and civil rights, Johnson was blunt: "White men alone," he declared, "must manage the South."

Because Congress remained in recess for much of 1865, from April until December, Johnson moved forward with

Reconstruction without congressional oversight. He appointed provisional governors in each of the southern states and directed them to call constitutional conventions. In a series of executive orders, he mandated that white men could regain their property rights and vote for delegates to their states' conventions by taking an oath of loyalty to the United States. However, he disqualified Confederate leaders and those who owned property worth more than $20,000. He also instructed state conventions to repudiate the debts of the Confederacy, a move that hurt planters who had invested their fortunes in war bonds. Although not as sweeping as the Radical Republicans' plan, Johnson's early initiatives seemed an important step toward dislodging the planter class from power.

Once it became evident by midsummer that the planters would not surrender their land and power without a fight, Johnson abandoned his initial plan. Rather than mobilizing a coalition of freedpeople, yeomen, and Republicans to take on the planters, he chose to incorporate the powerful ex-slaveholders into Reconstruction. He issued thousands of pardons to the wealthy men disqualified under his original plan. He also authorized provisional governors to raise militias, thereby allowing planters to revive the old slave patrols and rearm ex-soldiers. Most critically, Johnson blocked the confiscation and division of plantations. He ordered that all confiscated land be returned to the planters (including the forty thousand acres that Sherman had distributed in the Sea Islands).

As Christmas approached and rumors of a massive transfer of land to the freedpeople circulated along the Cotton Belt, Johnson ordered the Freedmen's Bureau to inform the freedpeople that no large-scale redistribution would be forthcoming. The Bureau now uniformly urged freedpeople to sign labor contracts with the planters and return to plantation labor. "You must labor for what you get like other people," the officials warned. Those who helped themselves to planters' property could expect to be "punished with utmost severity." This reversal in federal policy resulted in massive displacements of African Americans. Some twenty thousand lost land in southeastern Virginia alone.

As a final concession, Johnson agreed to the planters' request that Union troops be gradually withdrawn from the South. Proof that Presidential Reconstruction had allowed the old slaveholding class to return to power came in the congressional elections of 1865. Every southern state refused African Americans the right to vote. White southerners elected twenty-four ex-Confederate lawmakers, state officers, and military commanders (including four Confederate generals). Georgia voted the former vice president of the Confederacy, Alexander Stephens, into the U.S. Senate.

BLACK CODES

Under Presidential Reconstruction policies, many ex-slaveholders and Confederate leaders were also elected to state legislatures. With the exception of North Carolina, all the southern states enacted a harsh set of laws known as the **Black Codes.** These laws gave black southerners the right to make contracts and use the courts, but they also attempted to turn the freedpeople into a compliant labor force for the planters. The codes denied freedpeople their own farms, prohibited them from hunting and fishing for food, and refused them access to money and credit (see Interpreting the Sources: Mississippi's Black Code, 1865). Some laws went so far as to require all black southerners to sign year-long labor contracts. One state's code banned freedpeople from performing any kind of labor besides plantation labor or domestic service. Black workers who quit their positions and looked for better wages and conditions faced forfeiture of all wages earned and could be forced to return to their original employer. Most codes limited the legal ability of African Americans to work as independent artisans, mechanics, and shopkeepers by requiring all aspiring black businesspeople to apply for costly licenses. Like slaves, freedpeople were prohibited from hunting, bearing arms, and raising militias; and taking part in games, begging, or other diversions from supervised labor were grounds for arrest as a vagrant. The codes also established a new category of racial crime: Discourtesy and other allegedly offensive behavior against whites by anyone classified as a negro were punishable by the old slavery method of whipping.

Black southerners did their best to resist the codes. Many refused to be forced into exploitative labor contracts. Rumors that Congress would soon distribute land helped many African Americans hold out against signing contracts. "I ain't going to bind myself," one freedman in South Carolina informed a planter in late 1865, "not till I can see better." But when President Johnson made it clear that there would be no large-scale distribution of land, freedpeople reluctantly signed agreements. Prohibited from making an independent living, many ex-slaves had no choice but to return to work for their old masters. In Congress, however, the Black Codes backfired on their southern authors. Both the codes and freedpeople's protests confirmed many Republicans' suspicions that the planters were reintroducing slavery through a back door.

CONGRESS TAKES CONTROL

Moderate and Radical Republicans in Congress had differed for some time on the goals of Reconstruction. Moderates wanted to establish basic legal rights for the freedpeople, such as the right to make contracts and the right to protection from racial discrimination. They believed that once freedpeople had acquired such rights, they would be able to defend their interests in court. At least initially, moderates were not committed to extending to freedmen the right to vote or hold political office. Most also opposed land redistribution. But because Johnson's Reconstruction failed to purge the South of slavery and allowed ex-Confederates to retake power, moderates joined Radical Republicans in calling for a more aggressive plan of **Congressional Reconstruction.** Like moderates, Radical Republicans supported legal reform. But they believed that without universal male suffrage, black southerners' freedom was in perpetual jeopardy. People could only protect their rights,

INTERPRETING THE SOURCES

Mississippi's Black Code, 1865

Though they varied from state to state, planter-dominated governments throughout most of the South passed restrictive laws, called Black Codes, designed to reestablish their authority in the aftermath of the legal emancipation of slaves. Below is an example from Mississippi.

This Indenture, made this 19th day of August, in the year eighteen hundred & sixty five between Lieut A. S. Dial A. A. Supt. F.B. 7th Dist Va of the one part, and John F. Hawkins of the County of Bedford of the other part, **Witnesseth**, That the said Lieut A. S. Dial &c. &c. by virtue of the authority in him vested as Military (~~Commandant~~ agent) aforesaid, hath put and bound, and doth by **These Presents**, put and bind Susan a free Girl of color, of the said County, and being of the age of Five years, to be **Apprenticed** to the said John F. Hawkins to learn the Business of a house servant, and with him to dwell and remain and serve until she, the said Susan, shall obtain the age of Eighteen years; during all which time, she, the said Susan, faithfully shall serve and obey, all secrets keep, and all lawful commands willingly do and perform; and shall not absent herself from the service of her Master day or night, without his leave; but shall, in all things, as a faithful Apprentice, behave herself towards her master, and all his family, during the said term: and the said John F. Hawkins doth hereby covenant, promise and agree to, and with the said Lieut A. S. Dial &c and his successors in office, that he the said John F. Hawkins will instruct said Apprentice in the business of a house servant (~~which now~~ area useth) shall and will teach and instruct, or cause to be taught and instructed in the best manner that he can, and shall and will provide and allow unto the said Apprentice, during all the said term, competent and sufficient meat, drink, washing lodging, apparel, and all other things necessary for the said Apprentice to have, and that he will well and truly pay to the said Susan at the end of her term of apprenticeship aforesaid, the sum of Twenty dollars, lawful money of Virginia; and that during the term aforesaid he will instruct, or cause to be instructed, the said Susan, in reading, writing and arithmetic, as far as the Rule of Three.

Witness, the following signatures and seals of the parties.

M. B. Chase
Chf. Clk.

A. S. Dial [SEAL]
1st Lt. & A. A. Supt. F.B. 7th Dist. Va.
John F. Hawkins [SEAL]

"Free to Work." Under the Black Codes, planter-dominated legislatures tried to force freedpeople, including children, to enter into year-long labor contracts for work they once performed as slaves.

1. Civil Rights of Freedmen In Mississippi

Sec.1. *Be it enacted* . . . That all freedmen, free negroes, and mulattoes may sue and be sued, implead and be impleaded, in all the courts of law and equity of this State, and may acquire personal property, and choses in action, by descent or purchase, and may dispose of the same in the same manner and to the same extent that white persons may: *Provided*, That the provisions of this section shall not be so construed as to allow any freedman, free negro, or mulatto to rent or lease any lands or tenements except in incorporated cities or towns, in which places the corporate authorities shall control the same. . . .

2. Mississippi Vagrant Law

Sec. 1. *Be it enacted, etc.* . . . That all rogues and vagabonds, idle and dissipated persons, beggars, jugglers, or persons practicing unlawful games or plays, runaways, common drunkards, common night-walkers, pilferers, lewd, wanton, or lascivious persons, in speech or behavior, common railers and brawlers, persons who neglect their calling or employment, misspend what they earn, or do not provide for the support of themselves or their families, or dependents, and all other idle and disorderly persons, including all who neglect all lawful business, habitually misspend their time by frequenting houses of ill-fame, gaming-houses, or tippling shops, shall be deemed and considered vagrants . . . and upon conviction thereof shall be fined not exceeding one hundred dollars, with all accruing costs, and be imprisoned at the discretion of the court, not exceeding ten days.

Sec. 2. . . . All freedmen, free negroes and mulattoes in this State, over the age of eighteen years, found on the second Monday in January, 1866, or thereafter, with no lawful employment or business, or found unlawfully assembling themselves together, either in the day or night time, and all white persons so assembling themselves with freedmen, free negroes or mulattoes, or usually associating with freedmen, free negroes or mulattoes, on terms of equality, or living in adultery or fornication with a freed woman, free negro or mulatto, shall be deemed vagrants, and on conviction thereof shall be fined in a sum not exceeding, in the case of a freedman, free negro or mulatto, fifty dollars, and a white man two hundred dollars, and imprisoned at the discretion of the court, the free negro not exceeding ten days, and the white man not exceeding six months. . . .

3. Penal Laws of Mississippi

Sec. 1. *Be it enacted* . . . That no freedman, free negro or mulatto, not in the military service of the United States government, and not licensed so to do by the board of police of his or her county, shall keep or carry fire-arms of any kind, or any ammunition, dirk or bowie knife, and on conviction thereof in the county court shall be punished by fine, not exceeding ten dollars, and pay the costs of such proceedings, and all such arms or ammunition shall be forfeited to the informer; and it shall be the duty of every civil and military officer to arrest any freedman, free negro, or mulatto found with any such arms or ammunition, and cause him or her to be committed to trial in default of bail.

Source: Mississippi Slave Code, 1848, Hutchinson, Code of Mississippi, 512-17; 16.8; 16.9: §1, Vagrancy Act of Mississippi, 1865; Kermit L. Hall, Paul Finkelman, and James W. Ely, Jr., *American Legal History: Cases and Materials* (Oxford: Oxford University Press, 2010), 351-353.

Explore the Source

1. Why might white lawmakers have seized upon vagrancy as the focus of a Black Code?
2. What role do the authors of this code envision for people of color in the post-slavery South?
3. Why might lawmakers have banned marriage between black people and white people?

Radicals argued, when they were able to participate fully in elections and government. Unlike moderates, Radical Republicans were also passionately committed to land redistribution and insisted that the federal government had the authority to break up the great plantations. In the view of Thaddeus Stevens, the government should seize all 394 million acres of the "70,000 proud, bloated and defiant rebels" and redistribute them to the freedpeople. By the end of 1865, a new coalition of moderates and Radicals in Congress stood opposed to Presidential Reconstruction.

When Congress reconvened in December, the new coalition exercised Congress's constitutional right to refuse to seat the southern Congressmen elected under Johnson's watch. Lawmakers then established the powerful Joint House and Senate Committee on Reconstruction. In early 1866, the Committee held public hearings about the Black Codes and mistreatment of freedpeople under the new southern governments. On the basis of this evidence, the committee sponsored a series of groundbreaking laws. These included a new Freedmen's Bureau Bill, which renewed the Bureau for another year and widened its powers. The Bureau was granted the authority to cancel the repressive labor contracts that many black southerners had been compelled to sign. In direct opposition to Johnson's policy, the bill also provided for the distribution of land to the freedpeople and the establishment of military courts to enforce their legal rights.

The Face of Radical Reconstruction. Congressman Thaddeus Stevens of Pennsylvania poses hand-on-heart above a law book placed on a floral tablecloth. Radical Republicans like Stevens claimed that law and morality required the redistribution of former slaveholders' plantations to the freedpeople. **Questions for Analysis:** What is the meaning of Stevens's pose? Why does he include a law book?

The Committee also sponsored the nation's first civil rights bill, which recognized all people born in the United States (except Native Americans) as national citizens and conferred upon them equal rights before the law. The bill empowered the federal government to prosecute states that deprived citizens of their citizenship or denied them their equal legal rights. President Johnson vetoed both bills, on the grounds that they were an unwarranted extension of federal power over the states, but Republicans eventually had enough votes in Congress to override him and enact these landmark bills into law.

THE FOURTEENTH AMENDMENT, VIOLENT BACKLASH, AND IMPEACHMENT

In 1866, shortly after the enactment of the Civil Rights Act, Congress passed the Fourteenth Amendment to the Constitution and sent it to the states for ratification. This was the first comprehensive civil rights amendment since the 1780s and marked a significant departure from previous citizenship law. The amendment provided that birth on U.S. soil established American citizenship, making citizens of most freedpeople (again, Native Americans were excluded). Consistent with the moderate Republican agenda, the amendment guaranteed to all citizens the full "privileges and immunities" of citizenship and to equal protection of the laws at both state and federal levels. States were prohibited from depriving citizens of life, liberty, or property without first allowing them to defend those rights in a court of law.

The Fourteenth Amendment also made an important contribution to the electoral system. It changed federal voting law by counting all persons (except Native Americans) in each state into the electoral base. Any state that barred male adult citizens from voting in state or federal elections would be penalized by a reduction in its number of representatives and presidential electors. This sent a clear message to the South that the disenfranchisement of adult men on explicit racial grounds would reduce the region's political power at the federal level. Despite the lobbying efforts of women's suffrage advocates, however, the amendment did not penalize states that withheld the franchise from women.

Congress sent the Fourteenth Amendment to the states, where a three-fourths majority was needed for adoption. To secure the necessary approval of a number of southern states, Congress stipulated that any state that ratified the amendment would be readmitted to the union. Johnson, meanwhile, opposed the amendment and urged his supporters to reject it. Ironically, Johnson's home state of Tennessee was the only one of the eleven former Confederate states to vote in its favor. It was readmitted to the union in 1866.

The Fourteenth Amendment and the Civil Rights Act provoked a backlash of anti-black violence across the South in the summer of 1866, with race riots breaking out in Memphis, New Orleans, and several other southern cities. Thousands of smaller incidents of beatings and murder were reported. In New Orleans, a mob of white men, led by police, attacked Republican delegates on their way to a constitutional convention. The assaults soon spiraled into a spree of violence that left fifty people (mostly black bystanders and constitutional delegates) dead and dozens more injured. Although mob violence was carried out by a wide cross-section of white society, it was often instigated by planters and merchants who sought to subordinate black people to their employers and exclude them and white Republicans from the halls of political power.

Opposing Reconstruction. Planters and their allies railed against the Fourteenth Amendment and Congress's renewal of the Freedmen's Bureau. This crude cartoon illustrates the view of many planters that northerners and the federal government were catering to the natural indolence of freedpeople by mistakenly granting them the rights of aspiring farmers and citizens.

The waves of riots and murders were intended to put Republicans on notice that white southerners would take up arms against black enfranchisement and any federal intervention in the region's affairs. Mob action also announced that to be a true southerner one had to be white. As many whites saw it, the war might have been lost and slavery abolished, but southern white men alone would govern the South.

Violent white opposition only strengthened the hand of Radical Republicans in Congress. The riots convinced remaining moderates that legal reform was not enough, and the federal government's slow response to widespread violence also persuaded them that Andrew Johnson was abnegating his presidential duties. In December 1866, Congress finally took complete control of Reconstruction. Lawmakers began by establishing universal male suffrage in the western federal territories and Washington, D.C. The following year, Radicals enacted the sweeping legislation they believed was crucial to the success of Reconstruction. The Reconstruction Act of 1867 declared that, with the exception of Tennessee, none of the governments established in the former Confederate states under President Johnson's Reconstruction policy were legal. The act divided the South into five military districts, to be administered directly by federal military officers who would register all eligible adult men and do whatever was necessary to protect citizens' property and lives. Southern states were to call conventions, rewrite their constitutions to include universal male suffrage, and hold elections to elect new, racially inclusive governments. Finally, Congress mandated that southern states could reenter the union only once they had disenfranchised ex-Confederate leaders and granted the vote to freedmen.

Radicals were reasonably confident that the U.S. Army would cooperate and enforce the act. Secretary of War Edwin Stanton was broadly sympathetic to their agenda, but Stanton answered directly to the president. Congress therefore enacted the Tenure of Office Act (1867), which prohibited the president from sacking cabinet members whose appointment had required Senate approval. This precipitated a final confrontation between the beleaguered president and an ever-more confident Congress. Ignoring the law, Johnson attempted to hand Stanton his notice. Stanton refused and barricaded himself in his office for three days while House Republicans voted to impeach Johnson. In the Senate, the vote fell just one short of the number needed for a conviction, and Johnson was acquitted. But impeachment effectively neutralized him. Free of Johnson's oversight, Stanton halted the withdrawal of federal troops from the South.

Johnson left office the following year, when the country went to the polls to elect a new president. Former Union war hero and Radical sympathizer General Ulysses S. Grant defeated Democrat Horatio Seymour by a large majority in the electoral college. But Grant won a slimmer majority of the popular vote (309,684 out of a total of 5,716,082 votes). Black voters had played an important role in Grant's election, rewarding the party that had been responsible for abolishing slavery and establishing civil rights. Consequently, Republicans became even more firmly committed to protecting black suffrage, while the Democratic Party determined to limit it severely.

With the president now firmly behind Radical Reconstruction, Congress pushed the third and final Reconstruction amendment. The Fifteenth Amendment, passed in 1869 and ratified in 1870, provided that a citizen's right to vote could not be denied or altered by either state or federal government "on account of race, color, or previous condition of servitude." Like the Fourteenth Amendment, the Fifteenth was aimed

Memphis Riots, 1866. Whites who opposed black rights torched a freedpeople's schoolhouse in this outbreak of anti-black violence.

primarily at the South, but its provisions applied to the entire country. Because southern states could not be relied on to protect freedmen's right to vote, Congress gave itself the authority to enforce the amendment. The amendment became law in early 1870, once two-thirds of the states had ratified it.

TOWARD A RACIALLY INCLUSIVE DEMOCRACY

Freedpeople were overjoyed by the Reconstruction Act of 1867, which promised them true freedom and equality. In southern cities, many defied the unfair contracts they had been forced to sign. They desegregated the streetcars, refusing to sit in the back of the bus, and insisted on paying the same price as white people for the same goods and services. All over the South, African Americans convened spontaneous, mass meetings to mark the dawn of a new era. Itinerant lecturers and preachers, mostly black but some white, carried the news to the countryside. Planters looked on as black laborers walked off plantations, attended political rallies, and signed up en masse to join Republican Union Leagues, just as white farmers had done after the war.

Convening in churches, schools, the woods, and the fields, Union Leagues initiated hundreds of thousands of black Americans into political life for the first time. Organizers typically placed a Bible, a copy of the Declaration of Independence, and a farming implement on a table and then solemnly administered oaths of allegiance to the league and the Republican Party. League orators then educated members about the electoral process and the system of government and held "colored men's conventions" that, despite their name, drew masses of women and children as well as men. Rural blacks, meanwhile, turned the conventions and leagues into vehicles for putting education, labor, and, especially, land reform on the Republicans' political agenda. As one orator reminded a crowd of freedpeople at an Alabama convention, "Didn't you clear the white folks land?" "Yes," the crowd roared, "and we have a right to it!" Rural freedpeople were once again hopeful that land and democracy were on their way.

As black southerners mobilized politically, the U.S. Army set about registering adult black men and other eligible voters in the region. Sending a small crew of registrars all over the South on horseback, the Army worked closely with the Union Leagues to execute the biggest government-led voter registration drive in American history. Freedmen once again laid down tools and flocked to towns, inspired by the hope that registration would finally lend them a political voice and lead to land redistribution.

Elections for delegates to the constitutional conventions in the South got under way in late 1867 and continued through 1869. Under military protection, between 70 percent and 90 percent of southern black men went to the polls, voting overwhelmingly for the party that had enfranchised them. About 75 percent of southern white men participated, with the

Faces of a New Government. Voters in Louisiana and elsewhere in the South elected delegates to rewrite their state constitutions. Twenty-nine black men served at the constitutional convention in Louisiana in 1868.

rest either boycotting the elections or disqualified by their role in the Confederacy. Republicans won a majority of delegates in every state. Just over half these Republican delegates were white southerners, most of whom were upcountry yeomen, small merchants, and artisans. One in every four Republican delegates was black and 15 percent of the delegates were transplanted northerners. With the prodding of the federal government, the South became the first region in the nation to implement universal male suffrage and to hold racially inclusive elections.

When the first conventions finally met in the state capitals, in the fall of 1867, the scene was nothing short of astonishing. Just three years earlier, slavery had ruled the South. Now, as one sympathetic British observer commented, "black men and white men sit side by side," to rewrite the state constitutions. These remarkable conventions framed constitutions that were more democratic and egalitarian than anything Americans, North or South, had known before. Every new constitution guaranteed southern men their civil and political rights regardless of race. All also repealed the Black Codes. They reduced the number of capital crimes and abolished the punishment most symbolic of slavery—whipping—and the penalty of imprisonment for debt. Many constitutions contained provisions for establishing public school systems and poverty relief programs, and some established basic legal rights for women. At several conventions, freedmen voiced support for giving women the vote, on the grounds that it was an "inherent right," but the measures failed to pass.

Although the conventions established legal equality, they did not mandate a systematic redistribution of land. With rural black delegates a minority in many conventions, and many white Republicans anxious that confiscation of planters' land would provoke violence, redistribution proposals did not carry the day.

RECONSTRUCTION GOVERNMENTS

In the months following the constitutional conventions, southerners mobilized to take part in their first racially inclusive elections for federal, state, and local governments. Whereas the smaller Democratic and Whig Parties attracted white planters and merchants, Republicans drew a large coalition of blacks and whites. Black churches played a critical role as bases for Republican mobilization, as did the Union Leagues. Leaders soon emerged to express and press black political demands. "We claim exactly the same rights, privileges and immunities as are enjoyed by white men," delegates to an Alabama political convention declared. "[W]e ask for nothing more and will be content with nothing less."

Black candidates for office were drawn from diverse backgrounds. Some had been free and living in the South for generations. Others were northerners, including fugitive slaves who returned to the South after the war to participate in Reconstruction. Some worked for the Freedmen's Bureau, and others were educators, ministers, shopkeepers, or artisans. Notably, however, few candidates were drawn from the single largest population of black southerners—the impoverished freedpeople who had once slaved for the planters. Rural freedpeople often favored black representatives who were literate or owned property in the belief that they would more effectively advance the interests and aspirations of former slaves.

A broad group of white Republicans formed the most powerful faction of the Republican Party, supplying just over half its elected officials and occupying many of the most powerful positions in state government. Southern Democrats derided this powerful white minority by calling them **scalawags,** slang for runty, useless farm animals. The white Republican coalition was comprised largely of upcountry yeomen who had been quietly building their own Union Leagues since 1865. A small number of planters and former Democratic leaders signed up as well. Some elite southerners pragmatically cast their lot with the Republicans, convinced that the Democrats' days in the South appeared numbered because of black enfranchisement. Others genuinely embraced the Republican ideology of legal equality and free labor. Aware that northern Republicans were aggressively pursuing large-scale investment and development in the American West, some ex-planters also considered the party more likely to attract northern investment capital to the South.

"Electioneering at the South." Black candidates campaigned for office in the 1867 and 1868 elections, often at small gatherings such as the one illustrated here. Notice that women are in attendance but seated separately from enfranchised men.

and retain their earnings independent of their husbands.

Reconstruction governments undertook the most ambitious health, education, and welfare programs the country had even seen. They established the South's first public schools, on the principle that a decent education is a right of freedom and the basis of democratic citizenship. Legislatures also directed the construction of hospitals, asylums, and penitentiaries and looked for ways to adapt these northern institutions to the values of the new, democratic South. In North Carolina, for example, lawmakers rejected the practice of putting convicts to forced labor for private manufacturers, and introduced a variety of educational, vocational, and religious programs designed to rehabilitate offenders. Some states, including Texas, integrated their police forces. For the first time in American history, black people wore law enforcement badges and exercised the protective and peacekeeping powers of the state. All these reforms were undertaken without federal funding.

Whites from the North made up the remainder of the South's Republican base. Southern Democrats referred to them as **carpetbaggers,** deriding them as impoverished and ill-educated scoundrels who had packed up all their worldly belongings in travel bags made of carpet and headed south to "fatten on our misfortunes." The great majority of former northerners, however, were neither poor nor illiterate, and the majority had no interest in gaining political office. Many were lawyers, teachers, and doctors with families and high hopes for the project of emancipation and a free South. A great number were Union veterans and some were aspiring farmers and artisans. Just like migrants to the West during this period, many families moved south in search of land, small business opportunities, and an agrarian way of life that industrialization and the rise of wage labor in the northeastern states were threatening to destroy.

Throughout the South, voters elected Republican-dominated legislatures in 1867 (see Map 16.1). These **Reconstruction governments,** which ruled from a few months to nine years, acted on the egalitarian principles laid down in the new state constitutions. Many eliminated property requirements for voting and established universal male suffrage. Georgia, North Carolina, and South Carolina led the way on the nationwide struggle to give women the right to hold property

Legislative changes also helped produce a new racially inclusive legal culture in the South. For the first time, African Americans served on juries in large numbers and some served as judges. They made wide use of the court system to enforce their newfound rights, crowding courts that had once been off-limits. For black women, who had legal though not political rights, the courts and the legal system became a vehicle to gain some measure of protection from intimidation and harm. Like most Americans, black women assumed that women were naturally subordinate to men, but they insisted that domestic violence be treated as criminal conduct rather than as a right belonging to a male employer or head of household.

In the economic sphere, the new Republican state governments generally aimed to lessen the South's dependence on cotton, which had lost value when India, Egypt, West Africa, and Brazil entered the market during the Civil War. In 1868, lawmakers responded by looking for ways to encourage

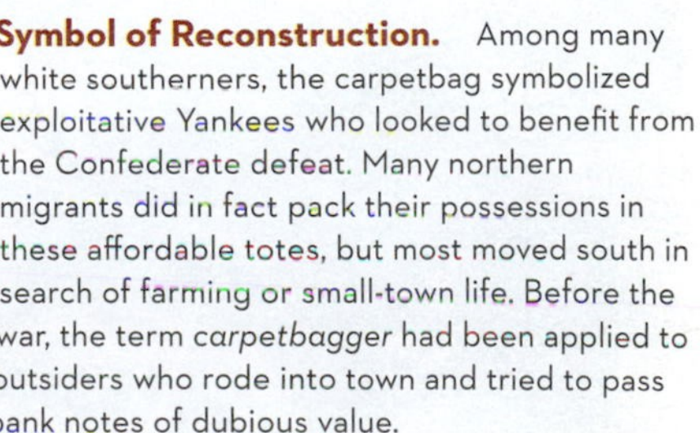

Symbol of Reconstruction. Among many white southerners, the carpetbag symbolized exploitative Yankees who looked to benefit from the Confederate defeat. Many northern migrants did in fact pack their possessions in these affordable totes, but most moved south in search of farming or small-town life. Before the war, the term *carpetbagger* had been applied to outsiders who rode into town and tried to pass bank notes of dubious value.

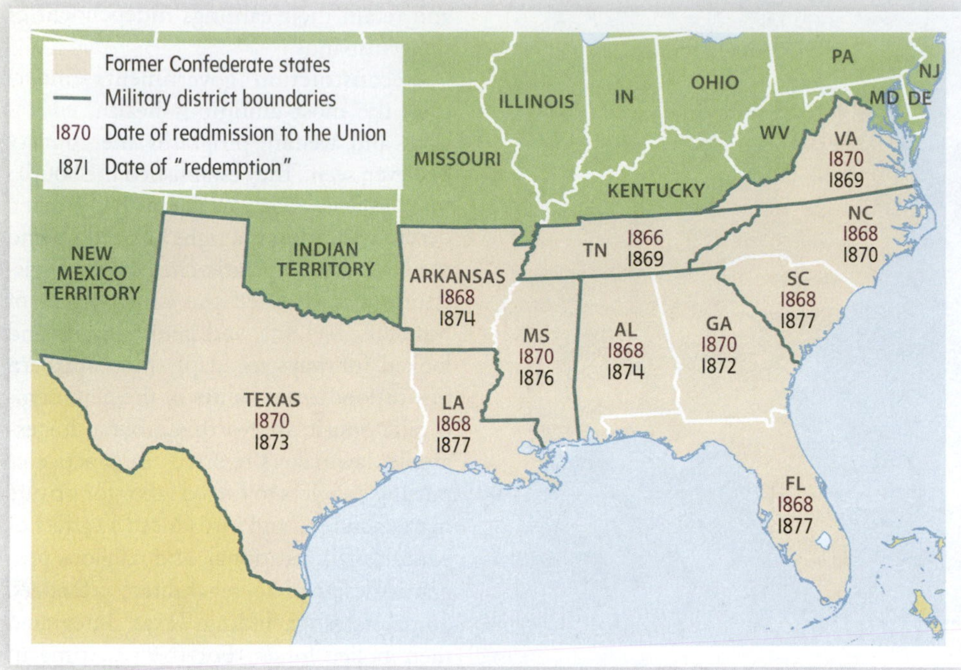

Map 16.1 Southern State Governments During Reconstruction. Every former Confederate state elected a Reconstruction government in 1867, and African Americans served in the legislature of every Reconstruction government in the South—in stark contrast to the situation in the North at the time. Reconstruction governments qualified southern states for readmission to the union but were dismantled ("redeemed") in the 1870s.

farmers and planters to plant different, more lucrative crops. They also invested in expanding the school system in the hope that this would lead to diversification of the economy as a whole. And like northern legislatures, they fostered the construction of railroads that would integrate their states into the national and global economy and attract investors.

These economic policies sidestepped freedpeople's early demands for land redistribution. In the end, the states made little effort to resettle freedmen and poor whites on their own small farms. South Carolina made farms available at an affordable price to fourteen thousand African Americans, but this was the major exception. Some legislators worried that it would alienate white voters. Others argued that depriving planters of their property was illegal and immoral. Instead, most lawmakers preferred to assist rural freedpeople with legislation that protected them from undue exploitation at the hands of planters.

Khangaon Cotton Market, India, 1870. While the South was fighting the Civil War, the British Empire looked for an alternative supply of cotton in India, Egypt, and elsewhere. After the war, southern cotton growers found themselves in competition with these new suppliers.

Although the states did not deliver on rural freedpeople's most pressing request, freedpeople nonetheless supported their new system of democratic government. The fact that black men participated in governing their states and the nation was itself highly significant. All told, over six hundred black men served in southern legislatures during Reconstruction, and sixteen in Congress. In 1870, Hiram Revels, a minister and educator who had helped raise black regiments during the war, became the first African American elected to the U.S. Senate. Twenty black men served as governors and high-ranking cabinet ministers. Black officeholding in the United States was groundbreaking, but white critics of Reconstruction overstated its magnitude. Although only 20 percent of all Republican officeholders during Reconstruction were black, critics routinely referred to southern governments as "Negro rule."

RECONSTRUCTING SOUTHERN SOCIETY

By 1871, all of the former Confederate states had met the requirements laid down by the Reconstruction Act and rejoined the union. The United States was whole and the key political aims of Reconstruction had been fulfilled. But southern Reconstruction was more than a political project. The workplaces, churches, schools, and many of the other institutions that black southerners founded in the early years of peace set in motion lasting social and cultural change among freedpeople. African Americans carved out new identities, drew emotional and spiritual sustenance, and forged new forms of artistic and moral expression. Likewise, white communities also underwent broad social and cultural changes in these years. Many white farmers lost family farms and were drawn into the sharecropping system.

PATTERNS OF WORK

In the rural South, farm labor and daily life settled into new patterns, as landless blacks and whites struggled to maintain some measure of independence from landholders. Labor patterns varied by region. The rice-growing areas of South Carolina and Georgia typically adopted the task system, under which agricultural workers were paid a set amount for each task they performed, rather than an hourly wage. On the sugar plantations of Louisiana, meanwhile, freedpeople worked under the contract system for hourly or weekly wages under close supervision. In the cotton and tobacco belts, where the majority of black southerners lived, sharecropping emerged as the dominant mode of farming among both whites and blacks. The sharecropper and his family rented part of a large plantation, where they lived and grew the tobacco or cotton crop. At harvest, the family divided the crop between themselves and the landowner (as payment for rent). Sometimes they gave a portion to local merchants and planters in payment for seed and equipment.

Although sharecropping was not the system of freehold farming for which the freedpeople had hoped, it enabled them to live as families and to work without overseers. It also held out the promise of eventual ownership of land. In theory a sharecropper could save enough money from the sale of his surplus crops to purchase his own farm. In practice, however, it was very difficult. Just 20 percent of black southerners owned land by 1877. Freedwomen's aspiration to withdraw from field and domestic service in order to work as wives and mothers in their own homes was partially realized in the late 1860s. But by the 1880s, over half of all southern black women were working for wages.

Sharecropping, along with the states' efforts to lay railroads and reintegrate the South into the global economy, brought about significant changes in the southern landscape. As the great plantations of the cotton-growing region were divided up and rented out as farms, some eight thousand stores sprang up across the Cotton Belt to meet sharecroppers' growing demand for food, farming supplies, and housewares. Country villages proliferated, typically following newly laid railroads along which cotton, farming supplies, consumer goods, and mail flowed.

As the global price of cotton recovered in the late 1860s, yeomen farmers and sharecroppers increasingly committed all their land to raising the "white gold." Despite states' encouragement of diversification, southern farming became increasingly monocultural—that is, devoted to a single crop. Integration into the global marketplace meant farmers and sharecroppers benefited from the rising prices of cotton. But they also became vulnerable to slumps. When the global price of cotton plummeted in the depression of 1873–1878, tens of thousands lost all their land and income. With fields committed solely to cotton, crop failure could be financially devastating. Many growers abandoned the traditional practice of crop rotation (which allowed the soil to recover) in order to maximize production. This change depleted the soil of nutrients, and cotton crops grew less robustly and lost much of their resistance to pests, rot, and disease. Monoculture had important social consequences, too. Sharecroppers' reliance on cotton made them more dependent on the merchants and planters who gave them credit and access to the global marketplace.

THE HEART OF THE COMMUNITY: THE CHURCH

Other areas of black southern life thrived under Reconstruction. The churches that blacks had created in the early days of freedom remained the only black institutions not connected in some way to planters and to white authority. Indeed, churches continued to be the principal spaces within which freedpeople experienced and expressed their political and spiritual independence. Black ministers from the North spearheaded a large-scale missionary drive into the South, as did northern branches of the Episcopal, Presbyterian, and Congregational churches. These missions resulted in the construction of hundreds of independent black church buildings. Their commitment to teaching

SINGULAR LIVES

Ella Sheppard, Spiritual Singer

As well as participating fully in the world's first racially inclusive democracy, African Americans energized their communities and transformed American culture through a great surge of creativity in the musical, literary, and performing arts. Although they remembered slavery as the brutal and unjust institution it had always been, black musicians also recovered and celebrated the unique musical form that slaves had created—the slave spiritual, which mixed African vocal styles with the language and imagery of English hymns. In the 1870s, Ella Sheppard and fellow musicians of the all-African American Jubilee Singers transcribed and performed dozens of these spirituals, introducing the nation and the world to America's first homegrown musical tradition.

Singing Freedom. The Jubilee Singers, with Ella Sheppard (standing, center), pose for the photograph that would be their carte-de-visite.

Sheppard was born a slave in Tennessee in 1851, and her experience of slavery inspired what went on to be the most famous of the slave spirituals—"Swing Low, Sweet Chariot." One day, her mother discovered that their mistress had been bribing young Ella (with buttered biscuits and sweet cakes) to spy on her. Reacting in "agony of soul and despair," Ella's mother tried to drown herself and her daughter. But an elder intervened, with the words that would later become the chorus of the well-known spiritual. Soon after, Ella's father, a former slave who had saved enough to buy his freedom, paid the $350 needed to free Ella. When creditors threatened to re-enslave Ella's stepmother to satisfy her father's debts, the family fled Tennessee for Cincinnati. Here, Ella took piano and singing lessons, becoming an accomplished enough musician that she was able to support her family after her father died in 1866.

Like many African Americans who escaped the slave states, seventeen-year-old Ella returned in 1868 to help build the South's new democracy. She taught piano in Nashville and used the proceeds to enroll at Fisk University (which had been founded by the American Missionary Association two years earlier for the purpose of educating freedpeople). As the pianist for the Fisk choir, Ella went on fundraising tours for the school in 1871, performing standard popular and classical songs—and the occasional spiritual. The choir's mostly white evangelical audiences applauded respectfully for the standard tunes, but cheered wildly for the spirituals. The director promptly changed the choir's name to the Jubilee Singers (in honor of emancipation) and Ella assumed responsibility for collecting and producing the popular slave songs. The choir returned home with $20,000—enough money to build a new campus.

Fisk became a distinguished liberal arts college and the Jubilee Singers went on to tour the North, Britain, and western Europe to great acclaim. Commenting on the state of American music in the 1890s, the distinguished European composer Antonin Dvořák wrote of the choir's spirituals, "These beautiful and varied themes are the product of the soil. They are American . . . and [they have] all that is needed for a great and noble school of music." In the 1910s, the choir recorded many of the spirituals that Ella Sheppard had remembered and preserved. Long after Reconstruction was defeated, these same slave songs served as an important source for America's other distinctive contributions to music—jazz, the blues, rock 'n' roll, and rap.

Think About It

1. What aspects of the history of slavery did the music of the Jubilee Singers seek to preserve? Why?
2. Why do you think white audiences in America and Europe valued spiritual songs?

freedpeople to read and write also played a crucial role in lifting black southerners' reading literacy (but not writing literacy) rate from just 5 percent in 1870 to 70 percent by 1890.

The new churches were also vital political centers. Urban ministers exhorted their congregations to participate fully in political life. Clergy accounted for 40 percent of all black office-holders. Many, including African Methodist Episcopal minister Charles H. Pearce, considered religion and politics inseparable: "A man in this State cannot do his duty," Pearce instructed, "except he looks out for the political interests of his people."

In the countryside, visiting itinerant and circuit preachers tied sharecropping families together in networks that sometimes stretched over several counties. Traveling preachers fostered the sharing of information and forged a larger sense of community among rural black people. In both city and country, women came to occupy important positions of spiritual and institutional authority. Although barred from ordination as ministers, they organized missionary societies, literacy programs, and exercised considerable influence over church activities in general.

Black churches developed their own distinctive theology. Free of the oversight of white ministers, rural congregants drew on the old folk religion that they had secretly forged as slaves in the secluded "hush arbors" and "praying grounds" of the plantations. Black ministers built upon the slave preachers' emphasis on faith as the crucial source of resistance to oppression, and freedpeople carried forward the slave tradition of exuberant, expressive worship. Congregations clapped and danced and sang old slave songs about freedom as well as new gospel songs celebrating emancipation as the work of God (see Singular Lives: Ella Sheppard, Spiritual Singer). Firm in the belief that their faith, above all else, had carried them through to freedom, congregants sang of the coming of a New Jerusalem: "See what wonder Jesus done/ O no man can hinder me!"

SCHOOLS AND AID SOCIETIES

Much like churches, schools became a symbol of freedom and a central institution in the everyday life of both rural and urban black southerners. Many freedpeople prized literacy, which had been forbidden under slavery, as the key both to economic and cultural progress and to spiritual salvation. As one man put it, "ole missus used to read the good book to us on Sunday evenin's, but she mostly read dem places where it says, 'Servants obey your masters.' . . . Now we is free, there's heaps of tings in that old book we is just suffering to learn."

Black people founded and staffed many schools, but northern religious and reform organizations also played an important role, employing some 1,400 white teachers and missionaries for black schools and donating thousands of schoolbooks to the cause. By 1870, there were four thousand freedpeople's schools and over one in every ten freed youth attended them. Six years later, over half of all freed youth were in school. Some states tried to establish integrated schools, but white parents generally rejected them and the initiative was abandoned.

Throughout Reconstruction, learning to read and write remained a dangerous activity. Fiercely protective of what they saw as an exclusive privilege, whites in many parts of the South stole or destroyed black children's precious books and assaulted black students on their way to and from school. Black children responded by changing their routes or concealing their books. In some rural communities, parents sent their children away to school in towns where there was safety in numbers. On more than one occasion, schoolteachers confronted and dispersed white mobs intent on closing their schools.

Alongside churches and schools, freedpeople established a wide range of mutual aid societies, including organizations to help the sick and the elderly, savings banks, firefighting

Freedmen's Bureau School, South Carolina. Freedpeople's schools were both symbols of and training grounds for freedom, but attending them could be life threatening. "When we sent our children to school in the morning," reflected Colonel Douglass Wilson, a former slave and veteran of the Union Army whose son was beaten by whites for attending school, "we had no idea that we should see them return home alive in the evening."

companies, tenants' clubs (to defend sharecroppers' rights), and labor associations. In the cities, where the black urban population was doubling, freedpeople set up debating clubs, drama groups, and trade associations to promote black culture and industry. These organizations formed a vital network among black southerners and served as an important foundation on which they built strong, independent communities.

CHALLENGES TO RECONSTRUCTION

By 1870, Reconstruction had transformed culture, politics, and the economy in the South. Nine of the eleven ex-Confederate states had Republican legislatures. For the first time in the nation's history, a small but significant minority of black men exercised authority as lawmakers, judges, sheriffs, and militia officers. Most freedpeople (like many white farmers) still believed that if they worked hard enough, landownership and full independence were possible. But in the early 1870s, the tide turned against the South's revolution. Harsh economic conditions bred resentment against the new governments, just as the federal government's resolve to ensure their success weakened. Across much of the South, the ideology of white supremacy tightened its hold, in large part through the rise of Ku Klux Klan.

THE AILING SOUTHERN ECONOMY

Republican-led state governments continued their efforts to rebuild the South and complete its transition from a slave society to a free labor democracy, but they could not do it alone. The northern investment that was necessary to southern Reconstruction never materialized, going instead to lucrative mining and railroad opportunities in the West (see Chapter 17). Northern businessmen distrusted the South's radically democratic governments and the white yeomen and black southerners who often served in them. White violence against blacks also undermined northern business confidence in the South, persuading investors that it remained an unstable, risky place. The South was "the last region on earth," despaired prominent Republican George Templeton Strong, in which "a Northern or European capitalist [would] invest a dollar."

The federal government did not help the southern rebuilding effort either. Like northern investors, the government preferred to work with private corporations in the West. Southern states racked up massive debts as they opened schools and rebuilt towns, with some states' deficits quadrupling in just a few years. Legislators responded by raising taxes and attempting to broaden the tax base. But most southerners were poor and possessed little in the way of taxable assets or income. State governments therefore turned to the elite planters who owned significant amounts of real estate and other assets. Higher taxes, in turn, hardened the opposition to Reconstruction among planters, who also resented the tendency of Reconstruction governments to award building and other lucrative contracts to unionists.

Planters soon found new allies among the growing number of poorer white farmers who had owned land before the Civil War but who had lost their farms due to debts acquired in the South's harsh economic climate. Although their predicament was the result of the cash-starved economy, crop failures, and the volatile global cotton market, white farmers tended to focus their frustration on closer and more concrete targets—Republican lawmakers and the freedpeople. Many blamed Reconstruction for depriving them of their land, freedom, and autonomy.

THE MAKING OF WHITE SUPREMACY

In these desperate economic times, the ideology of white supremacy gained momentum. Sometimes white supremacy spread slowly and in subtle forms. At other times it exploded in spectacular acts of violence. Racial segregation of the sort that had been common in the private hotels, trains, and steamboats of the antebellum North quietly took root in many southern states. Prominent and well-to-do black Americans were often refused admission to first-class railroad cars and steamship berths. Oscar J. Dunn, the lieutenant governor of Louisiana, for example, was barred from traveling in a first-class railcar in his own state. Likewise, the eminent Frederick Douglass paid full fare for first-class tickets while traveling in the South, only to be consigned to the crowded, filthy, and smoke-filled second-class car. Planters and white storekeepers often refused to do business with black Republicans, and white state and county officials neglected to carry out the directives of higher-ranking black officials.

The ex-Confederate militias that President Johnson had allowed to rearm in 1865 morphed into secret societies and paramilitary organizations such as the White Leagues and Red Shirts. These groups frequently threatened, terrified, and beat African Americans who tried to vote or otherwise assert their independence. The Ku Klux Klan, led by ex-Confederate general Nathan Bedford Forrest, was the largest and most infamous of these secret leagues. Masking themselves in white sheets or colorful costumes, Klansmen galloped across the countryside at night, looking for black men they considered a threat to white political and economic interests. Upon arriving at a victim's home, the Klan performed elaborate rituals of violence and humiliation that were designed to put black men in their subordinate place. These performances drew on popular southern theater, blackface minstrelsy, and folk music to stage terrifying dramatizations of white men's supposed superiority. Northern newspapers and leaflets reported these events in lavish detail, creating a national audience for the Klan's acts of terrorism.

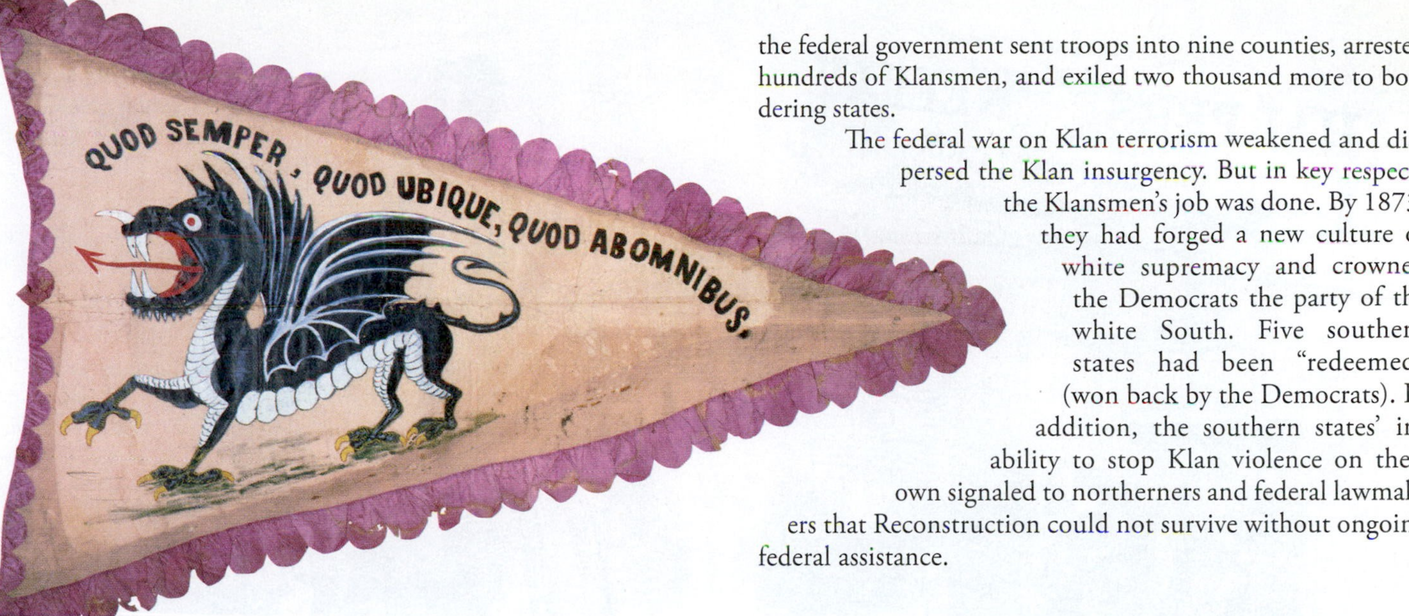

Klan Culture. As in this flag, ca. 1865–1866, featuring a ferocious dragon, costumed Klansmen appealed to established theatrical, minstrel, and folk traditions in their effort to drum up support for white supremacy.

With its popular cultural references and its skillful appeals to white racism and anxieties about Reconstruction, the Klan won instant support among white southerners. Among those who joined were Democratic politicians, planters, members of smaller secret societies and paramilitary organizations, common criminals, and struggling white farmers, shopkeepers, and workers who feared competition from black people. Musicians, circus performers, and actors also belonged, playing central roles in the Klan's highly theatrical performances.

While sending a chilling message to black communities, the Klan's violent spectacles simultaneously informed white southerners that the defenders of white supremacy were on the march once more. Many quietly heralded the Klan as a patriotic liberation army and gave them aid and comfort. They heeded the Klan's call to join the Democratic Party and rebuild its political power. And they began to feel bound together by race, despite the regional and economic differences that had divided them in the past.

Republican state governments were generally unable or unwilling to confront the Klan, fearing that such confrontation might spark an all-out race war. But Congress tried to assist by enacting the Enforcement Act of 1870, which prohibited the use of force or threat of force against anyone trying to vote or attempting to register to vote, and the Ku Klux Klan Act (1871), which gave the federal government broad powers to arrest and prosecute individuals who conspired to deprive citizens of their right to vote, hold office, and serve on juries. Under the act, federal officers rounded up and prosecuted hundreds of Klansmen in North Carolina and Mississippi. Dozens were convicted and sent to prison. In South Carolina in 1872, the federal government sent troops into nine counties, arrested hundreds of Klansmen, and exiled two thousand more to bordering states.

The federal war on Klan terrorism weakened and dispersed the Klan insurgency. But in key respects the Klansmen's job was done. By 1873, they had forged a new culture of white supremacy and crowned the Democrats the party of the white South. Five southern states had been "redeemed" (won back by the Democrats). In addition, the southern states' inability to stop Klan violence on their own signaled to northerners and federal lawmakers that Reconstruction could not survive without ongoing federal assistance.

REPUBLICANS DIVIDED

As the Klan battled the federal government in the South, some prominent members of the northern Republican Party broke away to form the Liberal Republican Party. Although they supported the new constitutional amendments, Liberal Republicans were highly critical of the Klan enforcement acts on the grounds that the laws vested excessive police power in the hands of federal government at the expense of the states. Government ought to be small, they held, and it should be run by the most skilled and respectable members of society. Representing the growing middle class of the urban North, these Republicans also claimed that the South's racially inclusive democracy gave the "ignorant" laboring poor too much power. Liberals sought the reenfranchisement of ex-Confederates, arguing that their exclusion from political life deprived the South of some of its "best men."

Republican governments in the South were weakened further by internal divisions. New ideological differences emerged in these years between black and white Republicans and even among black Republicans. Most agreed on the necessity of equal civil and political rights, but they diverged on political and economic issues. Black Republicans tended to favor governmental funding of schools, infrastructure, and other public goods and supported higher taxes as a way of providing these things. White Republicans were more likely to object to tax increases and, although they supported black voting rights, many objected to African Americans assuming positions of leadership in the party.

As the Klan and the Democratic Party surged in white popularity, white Republicans increasingly asked their black brethren to forgo leadership positions for the sake of retaining white voters. Black Republicans in many states fought against their marginalization. In some states, they forced out white leaders who blocked the black majority's will and replaced them with black leaders. But many white southern Republicans responded by abandoning the party.

Caricaturing Reconstruction. By 1874, many northerners who had strongly supported Reconstruction were critical of the South's new governments. One such critic, *Harper's Weekly* cartoonist Thomas Nast, crudely depicted black lawmakers as apelike and unfit for public office. Such racism did not go unanswered, however. The *New York Daily Graphic* responded with an unflattering illustration of Nast and the headline, "I Wonder How Harper's Artist Likes To Be Offensively Caricatured Himself?"

THE DEATH OF RECONSTRUCTION

After 1873, the ailing Republican congressional coalition that had been the driving force of southern Reconstruction finally fell apart. "Radicalism is dissolving—going to pieces," one southern Democrat exulted quite accurately. Vigilante violence, legal setbacks, economic depression, and the hardening of northern sentiment all combined to allow the Democratic opposition, known as Redeemers, to take control of the last remaining Reconstruction governments.

SOUTHERN MILITIAS MOBILIZE

The campaign of violence against southern blacks accelerated in 1873, despite the Klan's defeat. The single deadliest attack occurred on Easter Sunday, 1873, at the Colfax courthouse in Grant Parish, Louisiana, where armed members of the White League paramilitary attempted to unseat the newly elected Republican judge and registrar. Although a black regiment of the state militia defended the building, it was overwhelmed when the league unleashed a cannon and set the courthouse on fire. By the end of the siege, more than 280 black men lay dead, including 50 who had surrendered (just three white men lost their lives). The following year the league armed fourteen-thousand-odd men and marched on the Louisiana capitol, where they battled the state militia, overthrew the Republican government, and installed a white Democrat at its head. Federal troops put down the rebellion, but the spectacle of thousands of armed white men besieging a state government further persuaded many white northerners that the challenge of Reconstruction was too great.

In the wake of the Colfax violence, recruitment to the White Leagues grew steadily. The devastating effects of the massacre were reinforced in 1876, when the Supreme Court heard the appeals of three white men involved in the crime. The men had been prosecuted under the Enforcement Act of 1870 for depriving the victims of their civil rights. In *U.S. v. Cruikshank* (1876), the Court overturned their convictions on the technical grounds that the original charge had not identified race as the motivation for the massacre. The justices also ruled that the Fourteenth and Fifteenth Amendments did not authorize the federal government to prosecute and punish private organizations such as the White Leagues. Like news of the massacre itself, this decision emboldened white supremacists and reassured white southerners that the federal government would no longer intervene on black southerners' behalf.

REMEMBERING THE WAR, FORGETTING SLAVERY

Northerners' support for Reconstruction depended in part on their belief that the Civil War had been a struggle against slavery and that victory would not be complete until the freedmen achieved full legal and political equality. Immediately after the war, northern Memorial Day parades, speeches, war monuments, and graveyard services celebrated emancipation as the chief goal and sweetest fruit of victory. But after 1873, commemorations increasingly avoided mentioning slavery. Instead, they underlined the necessity of forgiving the South. Unionists and Confederates had fought with equal valor, white northerners emphasized, and now it was time to reunify as Americans. As one veteran Union officer put it, "over the grave of buried bygones, rejoice that . . . as soldiers and citizens, we know no North, no South, no East, no West—only one country and one flag." Memorial Day celebrations now enacted a collective forgetting of the Civil War as a war against slavery. Although some northerners, including Frederick Douglass, objected, by 1876 few remembered that emancipation had been the war's central achievement.

A complementary change also took place within the South. Under Reconstruction governments, black and unionist militias had played prominent roles in the South's annual Decoration Day festivities, which had celebrated the war for its destruction of slavery. But in the growing number of Democratic states, Decoration Day became a celebration of Confederate veterans and their heroism. Black citizens could march only at the back of the procession. In 1874, for the first time, white northerners and southerners participated in the same Memorial Day celebrations. Northerners now decorated the graves of Confederate and not just Union soldiers. Memorial Day became a tribute to a reconciled white nation. Increasing numbers of white Americans tacitly acknowledged that full national reunion would be possible only if the federal government abandoned its support of Southern democracy.

This new approach to Memorial Day paralleled new political alliances between North and South. Liberal Republicans began to work with southern Democratic Redeemers for the restoration of peace and commerce in the South. They agreed that

Honoring the Confederate Cause. Richmond, Virginia, held its first annual Confederate veterans' parade in 1875. The parades continued through the 1910s.

mob violence would stop only when the federal government ceased to play an active role in the South and black men no longer governed. As New York Liberal Republican E. L. Godkin put it, once the federal government departed, "the negro will disappear from the field of national politics. Henceforth the nation, as a nation, will have nothing more to do with him."

RECONSTRUCTION'S DAY IN COURT

In 1875, in one last bid in Congress to save Reconstruction, Radical Republican Charles Sumner sponsored legislation that outlawed racial discrimination in every state of the union. The Civil Rights Act of 1875 declared that it was government's duty to treat people equally and justly, irrespective of their race, color, religion, nativity, or political belief, and that all people were entitled to the full and equal enjoyment of any public inn, theater, transportation system, or place of amusement. The law broke important new ground for protecting the rights of African Americans as consumers of goods and services.

But as Congress enacted Reconstruction laws, other parts of the government, especially the courts, blunted their impact. Federal circuit courts heard dozens of cases under the Civil Rights Act of 1875, but the federal government made little effort to enforce the law. It was left up to victims of racial discrimination to bring a lawsuit, and the expense of doing so discouraged legal action. In those cases that made it to court, judges did not interpret the act as a mandate to integrate public amenities. Instead, they took it to mean that public amusements and transportation systems were to ensure that separate, first-class accommodation and other services were also available for people of color.

The Supreme Court further undermined Reconstruction, first by striking down state and federal loyalty laws, thereby opening the way for ex-Confederates to return to southern politics. Subsequently, in the *Slaughterhouse Cases* of 1873, the Court ruled that the Fourteenth Amendment only protected the rights of federal citizenship and that the states were free to limit other rights (such as the right to education and welfare) on the basis of race (See Spaces and Places: The Crescent City Slaughterhouse). Three years later, in *U.S. v. Cruikshank*, the Court overturned the convictions of the perpetrators of the Colfax massacre, ruling that the Fourteenth Amendment protected an individual's rights from violation by a state government, but not by private individuals and mobs. These cases made it clear that neither the federal government nor the federal courts were likely to intervene on behalf of black southerners or the ideal of racially inclusive democracy. Southern Democrats would have a free hand.

THE ELECTION OF 1876

Sensing that Reconstruction's end was within reach, southern Democrats in 1875 announced the Mississippi Plan. They openly called upon their partisans to carry that state's upcoming election "peaceably, but by force if necessary." In a departure from earlier Klan tactics, heavily armed white militias deployed openly and without disguise, preventing some sixty thousand black and white Republicans from voting and thereby securing a Democratic victory. In the wake of this success, Democrats in the remaining Republican states organized white electoral militias as well.

President Grant also sensed the shifting political winds. Mindful of the 1876 election, he slowly withdrew federal support from the ailing southern Republicans. He withheld troops when they were needed to defend black voters from murderous mobs and all but dropped enforcement of the Ku Klux Klan Act. Grant also quietly extended patronage and aid to moderate southern Democrats in an effort to build a new alliance.

Grant's effort failed. In 1876, a series of financial scandals involving some of his cabinet members permanently tainted his administration and, ironically, associated him

"The negroes of the South are free—free as air," says the parliamentary Watterson. This is what the *State*, a well-known Democratic organ of Tennessee, says, in huge capitals, on the subject: "Let it be known before the election that the farmers have agreed to spot every leading Radical negro in the county, and treat him as an enemy for all time to come. The rotten ring must and shall be broken at any and all costs. The Democrats have determined to withdraw all employment from their enemies. Let this fact be known."

Force Unmasked. Violence against black voters and white Republicans became direct and well organized beginning in 1873. This cartoon satirizes the idea that elections in the South were "free."

SPACES & PLACES

The Crescent City Slaughterhouse: Battlefield of Reconstruction

Crescent City Landing and Slaughter-House. Shown in this 1875 drawing, the plant held a licensed monopoly on slaughtering business in the New Orleans area.

In 1869, Louisiana became one of the first states in the union to regulate the meat supply in the service of public health and economic efficiency. Like other Reconstruction legislators, Louisiana lawmakers envisioned a far more active role for state government than under slavery. Most believed it was the state's duty to provide all citizens with basic health care, free education, and protection from racial discrimination. Before the Civil War, hundreds of butchers had hand-slaughtered livestock in the backrooms of their shops, disposing of the blood, offal, and other waste products in residential streets and the Mississippi River (some even used the putrid matter as building material and as filler for potholes). As in many cities, conditions were unsanitary, often resulting in the sale of spoiled and disease-ridden meat and deadly outbreaks of cholera and yellow fever. The Slaughterhouse Act of 1869 aimed to end the sale of rotten meat and turn the meat business into a clean, efficient, large-scale industry. Lawmakers also wanted to ensure that consumers were charged a fair price for their beef, mutton, and pork, regardless of race, and that the traditionally white-dominated craft of butchering was opened to black men.

The act established a public corporation to oversee the entire process of butchery for the city of New Orleans. All commercial swine, cattle, and sheep were transported live to one large, central state-supervised meatpacking plant—the Crescent City Landing and Slaughter-House. Meat inspectors determined whether arriving livestock were disease free and fit for processing. Licensed butchers then slaughtered, dressed, and packed the meat under the supervision of public officers, who inspected it a second time to ensure it was fit for consumption. Under the direction of the state health board, physicians regularly conducted sanitary inspections of the slaughterhouse. Its location on the Mississippi River, some miles downstream from the city, ensured that waste products no longer rotted in city streets but floated down the river and into the sea instead.

Both the efficiency of Louisiana's meat industry and city sanitation improved dramatically as a result of the new law. But it effectively relocated the environmental hazard from people to marine life, resulting in the depletion of many species of fish and plant life in the Mississippi basin. The Crescent City slaughterhouse also soon became a highly controversial symbol of southern Reconstruction. Many of the city's white butchers objected to the centralization of their trade, the tough new sanitary laws, and the inclusion of black butchers. They secured a prominent attorney, John A. Campbell, and challenged the law's constitutionality. Campbell, a former Supreme Court justice and the Confederacy's assistant secretary of war, argued that the slaughterhouse law imposed a form of "involuntary servitude" on the white butchers and was therefore unconstitutional under the Thirteenth Amendment, which prohibited slavery. He also maintained that the law interfered with the butchers' right to make a living and thereby contravened the Fourteenth Amendment's guarantee of citizens' economic rights.

The Supreme Court rejected the white butchers' claim in 1873, and the Crescent City slaughterhouse continued to operate. But the Court used the occasion to further limit the scope of Reconstruction's rights revolution, ruling that federal courts could only protect the rights of citizens in relation to federal laws and that the states were free to define and limit other rights—including the supposed right of local butchers to slaughter hogs as and where they saw fit. This important ruling signaled to southern Democrats that the federal courts would not actively oppose their efforts to retake state government, dismantle Reconstruction, and strip back the rights of black southerners.

Think About It

1. How were issues of civil rights and public health entangled in the Slaughterhouse Act of 1869?
2. Why did it take a Reconstruction government to pass laws regulating meat safety?
3. How did Campbell, a former Confederate leader, use the ideals of Reconstruction to argue against Reconstruction policies?

with the southern Republicans from whom he had tried to distance himself. Congressional Republicans took stock of Grant's plummeting popularity and looked for a new candidate. They settled on a mild-mannered conservative from Ohio, Rutherford B. Hayes, in the hope that his reputation for honesty would reunite the party and restore its tarnished name. The Democrats nominated Samuel B. Tilden, whose platform differed little from that of Hayes, but who had earned a national reputation as the reformer who brought down New York City's corrupt Tweed administration (see Chapter 18).

Tilden carried all of the South's Democratic states and won the national popular vote by a margin of 250,000 (see Map 16.2). But in the electoral college, he fell one vote shy of the 185 needed to win the election. Both sides claimed victory in the three remaining southern Republican states (South Carolina, Florida, and Louisiana). If all three were counted for Hayes, the Republicans would retain the White House. But if even one were counted for Tilden, the Democrats would win. Neither party would concede defeat. Democrats warned gravely of raising militias and ominously declared "Tilden or Fight!" Congress appointed an electoral commission to count the votes and resolve the standoff. The commission voted eight to seven, along party lines, to declare Hayes the victor. Democrats resisted. But in March 1877, following a long, secret meeting between leading southern Democrats and five Republicans close to Hayes, the Democrats capitulated and consented to a Hayes presidency.

The price the Republicans paid was something many Liberal Republicans had wanted for some time. In exchange for the presidency, the Republicans quietly consented to a "new southern policy" that would leave white southerners to run their own political affairs. Known as the Compromise of 1877 (or, in Radical Republican circles, the "Corrupt Bargain of 1877"), that agreement left freedpeople and the South's remarkable democratic experiment to the mercy of southern Democrats and their militias. President Hayes ordered the last few U.S. troops in the South to stand down and Democrats ousted the three remaining Republican governments. The South had been "redeemed"; Reconstruction was dead.

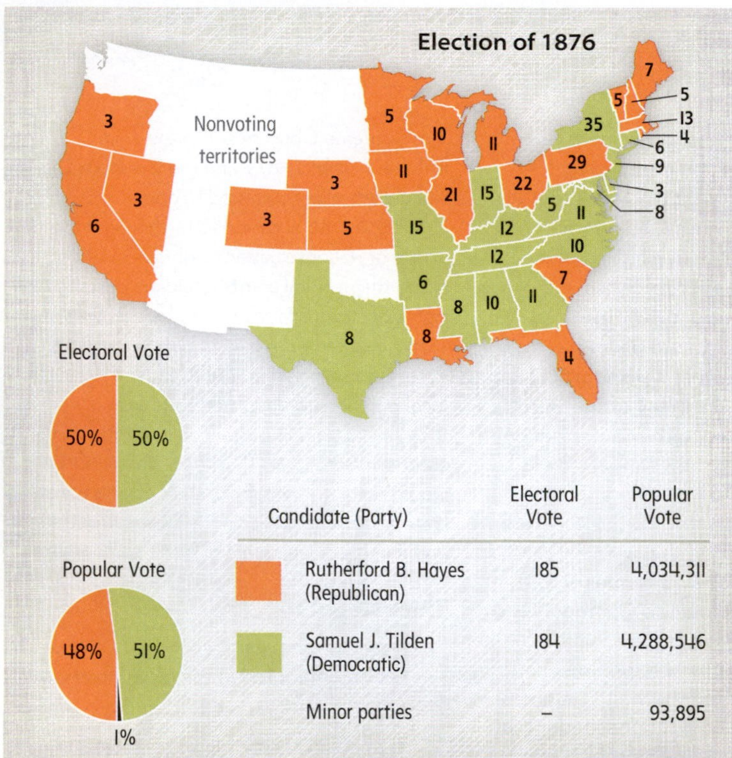

Map 16.2 Election of 1876. For the first time since 1824, the candidate with the most votes failed to win the presidency. But Hayes's victory was not simply the result of the peculiarities of the electoral college system; it was the fruit of a political deal that ended the nation's project of reconstructing the South.

BURYING RECONSTRUCTION

In 1878, Congress passed the Posse Comitatus Act, which prohibited the federal government from using the army to enforce the law—including laws that protected voters from violence and intimidation in the South. Five years later, Reconstruction received a lethal blow when the Supreme Court heard the 1883 *Civil Rights Cases.* These cases arose from lawsuits brought by black citizens in California, Kansas, Missouri, New York, and Tennessee who had been refused access to public theaters, hotels, and railroad cars on account of their race. The Court ruled that the Fourteenth Amendment did not bar racial discrimination by a private business such as a theater. It added that most of the Civil Rights Act of 1875 was unconstitutional because the authority to protect citizens from discrimination lay not with the federal government but with the states. The black press condemned the Court's decision as an ultimate betrayal of the Civil War and Reconstruction. Few white people commented. The editors of the Liberal Republican journal *The Nation* noted approvingly "how completely the extravagant expectations as well as the fierce passions of the war have died out." The Court had buried Reconstruction's final remains.

By 1883, freedpeople's hopes and dreams for a thoroughgoing reconstruction of the South's society, economy, and politics were all but dashed. Nevertheless, Reconstruction remained one of the most important periods of the nation's history. Although African Americans suffered a great defeat, they were not the passive victims of circumstance. Throughout the era, they played a crucial and active role in trying to shape their destiny and that of the South and the nation. Many of the institutions that freedpeople established during Reconstruction, such as churches and mutual aid associations, outlived the demise of democratic government in the South and continued to be vital sources of African American autonomy and cultural life.

Election Stalemate. Congressmen and members of the public, including women, packed the U.S. Supreme Court in 1877 to witness the proceedings of the electoral commission. Democrats refused to accept the commission's ruling that Rutherford B. Hayes had won the presidential election of 1876, and the outcome was instead decided in a secret meeting between southern Democrats and Hayes's Republican allies.

CONCLUSION

First as slaves, and then as freedpeople, black southerners played a central role in each of the three stages of Reconstruction. During the war, it was slaves who forced the issue of emancipation onto the federal war agenda through their exodus across Union lines. President Lincoln subsequently resolved to expand Wartime Reconstruction to include the abolition of slavery, the confiscation and redistribution of some former slave plantations, and stricter criteria for the readmission of former Confederate states. Talk of a great redistribution of land put further moral pressure on Lincoln and the federal government to finish off the work of the war against slavery. Lincoln subsequently drafted a program for the construction of a more racially inclusive South.

President Johnson put Lincoln's plan of Reconstruction on hold. Making it clear that his opposition to black enfranchisement was greater than his hatred of the planter class, he set about restoring former slaveholders to power. But freedpeople's refusal to comply with the repressive laws enacted on Johnson's watch emboldened Republicans in Congress to reject the restoration of the old ruling class and to help freedpeople build the world's first racially inclusive democracy. Congress enacted key civil rights reforms and empowered the U.S. Army to enforce the law. As a result, men who had been slaves just a few years before served in the South's new government and on juries, the judiciary, and police forces.

Aware that Reconstruction would deprive them of their power, planters waged a bitter campaign against the South's Reconstruction governments and Congress. A growing cross-section of white southerners waged small-scale warfare against black voters, white Republicans, and anyone who supported black rights. Violence against black southerners wore down northern voters' commitment to Reconstruction and the Supreme Court further undermined Reconstruction by limiting the reach of key civil rights legislation. Facing economic hardships, many white southerners who had not opposed Reconstruction blamed the region's misfortunes on Republican rule. And, as memories of the war against slavery faded, more and more northerners came to think of the Civil War as a tragic conflict among brothers, rather than a heroic fight against slavery. They called for reconciliation with the white South and ceased to support the South's Republican governments.

As a result of all these factors—vigilante violence, legal defeat, economic depression, the hardening of northern sentiment, and white people's amnesia about slavery—every Reconstruction government fell by 1877. The Civil Rights Cases of 1883 confirmed the end of an era. But black Americans' aspirations to landownership, freedom, and full citizenship endured, as did the cultural institutions they established during Reconstruction. Although the scope of the Thirteenth, Fourteenth, and Fifteenth Amendments was severely limited, Congress did not repeal them. In the 1950s and 1960s, almost a century after their enactment, they would become indispensable tools of liberation in a new and powerful civil rights movement.

STUDY TERMS

- Reconstruction (p. 417)
- Ten Percent Plan (p. 417)
- Radical Republicans (p. 418)
- Wade-Davis Bill (p. 418)
- Thirteenth Amendment (p. 418)
- Freedmen's Bureau (p. 419)
- Union Leagues (p. 421)
- Black Codes (p. 423)
- Congressional Reconstruction (p. 423)
- Fourteenth Amendment (p. 425)
- Reconstruction Act of 1867 (p. 426)
- Tenure of Office Act (p. 426)
- Fifteenth Amendment (p. 426)
- scalawags (p. 428)
- carpetbaggers (p. 429)
- Reconstruction governments (p. 429)
- Jubilee Singers (p. 432)
- Ku Klux Klan (p. 434)
- Liberal Republican Party (p. 435)
- Redeemers (p. 436)
- Civil Rights Act of 1875 (p. 438)
- *Slaughterhouse Cases* (p. 438)
- Mississippi Plan (p. 438)
- Compromise of 1877 (p. 440)
- Posse Comitatus Act (p. 440)
- *Civil Rights Cases* (p. 440)

TIMELINE

1862 Wartime Reconstruction begins

1863 President Abraham Lincoln issues Emancipation Proclamation and Ten Percent Plan

1864 Lincoln vetoes Wade-Davis Bill

1865 Congress sends Thirteenth Amendment to the states for ratification

Freedpeople celebrate emancipation in jubilee parades and gatherings

Congress establishes Freedmen's Bureau

Lincoln is assassinated and Andrew Johnson becomes president

Presidential Reconstruction begins

Southern states enact Black Codes (1865–1866)

1866 Congress passes Civil Rights Act

Congress sends Fourteenth Amendment to the states for ratification

1867 Congressional Reconstruction begins

Congress passes Reconstruction Act

U.S. Army undertakes largest voter registration drive in American history

Southerners elect racially inclusive governments, sheriffs, and judiciaries

1868 House of Representatives impeaches Johnson

Ulysses S. Grant elected president

Ku Klux Klan begins night raids

1870 Enforcement Act authorizes federal government to prosecute Klansmen

1871 Jubilee Singers revive slave spirituals to great acclaim

1872 The Liberal Republican Party opposes President Grant and Radical Reconstruction

Grant reelected

Official Memorial Day celebrations cease to mention slavery

1873 Supreme Court limits reach of the Fourteenth Amendment in *Slaughterhouse Cases*

African Americans massacred at Colfax County Courthouse, Louisiana

Ex-Confederate and Union soldiers commemorate the war together

1874 White militias mobilize against white Republicans and black voters

1875 Congress passes Civil Rights Act

1876 Presidential election between Rutherford B. Hayes and Samuel Tilden leads to a deadlock

1877 Political bargain results in Hayes's presidency

U.S. Army stands down in the South

Last three southern Republican governments fall

1878 Congress passes Posse Comitatus Act, prohibiting the army from law enforcement

1883 The Supreme Court declares Civil Rights Act of 1875 unconstitutional

FURTHER READING

Additional suggested readings are available on the Online Learning Center at www.mhhe.com/becomingamerica1e.

David Blight, *Race and Reunion* (2001), illuminates the process by which white Americans came to accept white southerners' view of the conflict.

Thomas J. Brown, ed., *Reconstructions: New Perspectives on the Postbellum United States* (2006), explores recent themes in the study of Reconstruction.

Jim Downs, *Sick from Freedom* (2012), documents the devastating impact of war and emancipation on the health of freed slaves.

Laura F. Edwards, *Gendered Strife and Confusion* (1997), examines the impact of Reconstruction on private life and gender roles in a North Carolina county.

Barbara J. Fields, *Slavery and Freedom on the Middle Ground* (1985), charts the passage from slavery to emancipation in the important border state of Maryland.

Eric Foner, *Reconstruction: America's Unfinished Revolution* (1988), remains the most systematic and detailed treatment of southern Reconstruction.

Steven Hahn, *A Nation Under Our Feet* (2003), provides a wide-ranging study of rural blacks' fight for political and economic power.

Leon Litwack, *Been in the Storm So Long* (1979), considers the early phase of Reconstruction and the responses of freedpeople and ex-slaveholders to emancipation.

Elaine Franz Parsons, "Midnight Rangers: Costume and Performance in the Reconstruction-Era Ku Klux Klan," *Journal of American History* (2005), highlights the Klan's use of popular cultural forms to communicate the goals of white supremacy.

Elizabeth Regosin, *Freedom's Promise* (2002), traces freedpeople's efforts to re-create family relationships and establish legal families and households.

Heather Cox Richardson, *West from Appomattox* (2007), argues that southern Reconstruction was part of a larger project of national reconstruction that unfolded in the North and West as well.

Amy Dru Stanley, *From Bondage to Freedom* (1998), explores the centrality of contracts to debates over freedom and slavery in nineteenth-century America.

Shane White and Graham White, *Stylin': African American Expressive Culture from Its Beginnings to the Zoot Suit* (1998), shows how African American traditions of style and self-presentation became a resource for surviving slavery and defining freedom.

17

INSIDE ▶

THE BIG PICTURE

Mythologized as the gunslinging Wild West, the lands west of the Mississippi River in fact encompassed many peoples, cultures, environments, and frontiers. After the Civil War, as government and the railroads conquered Indian lands and opened them to settlement, western resources powered American industrialization and gave rise to new fantasies of freedom, opportunity, and adventure. Colossal fortunes were made, but for many, life "out West" was marred by hardship and dispossession.

***Design for The Western Frontier, First Phase*, by Tom Lea, 1935.** As Lea's mural suggests, the post–Civil War West was a place of immense cultural and environmental diversity.

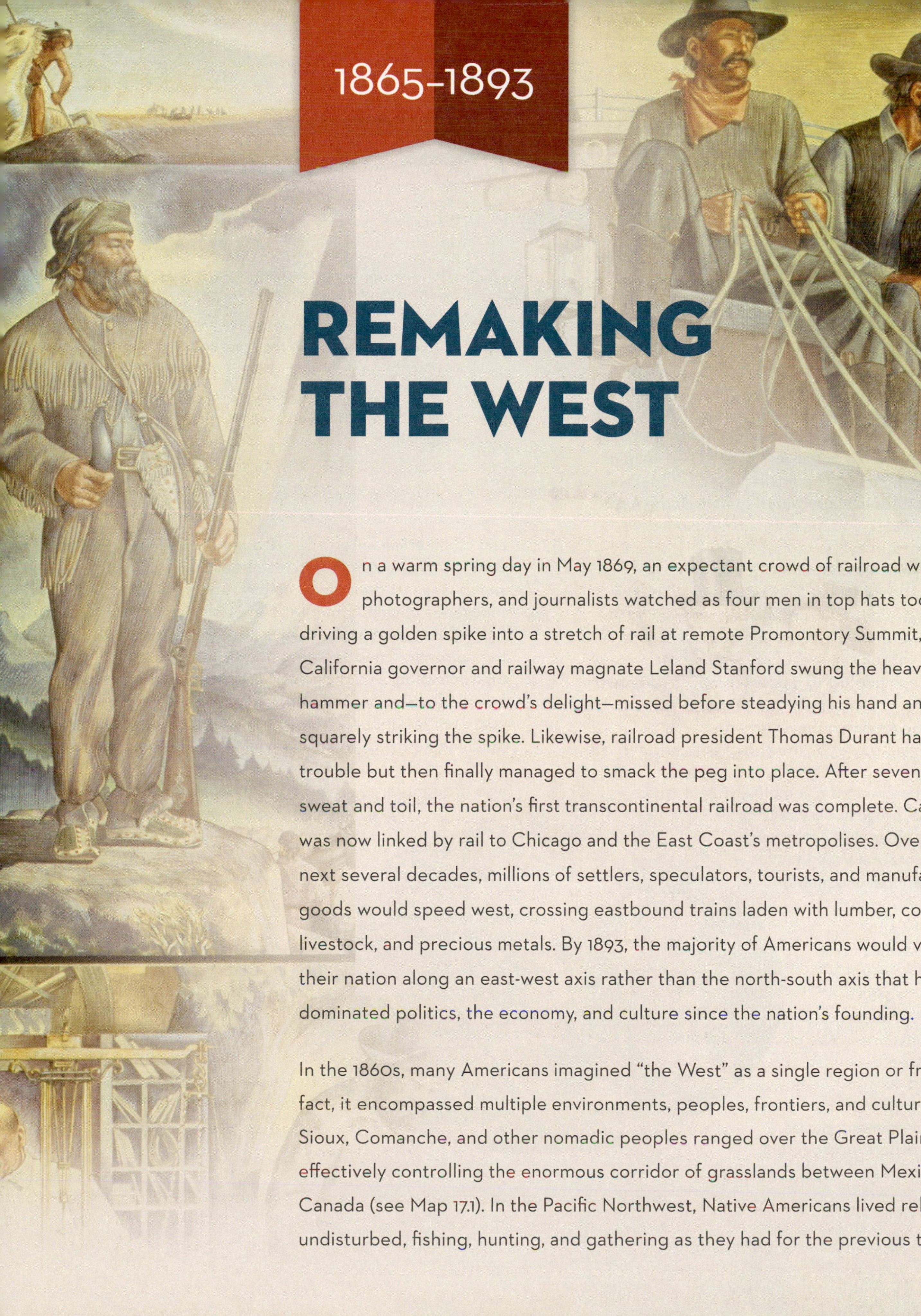

1865–1893

REMAKING THE WEST

On a warm spring day in May 1869, an expectant crowd of railroad workers, photographers, and journalists watched as four men in top hats took turns driving a golden spike into a stretch of rail at remote Promontory Summit, Utah. California governor and railway magnate Leland Stanford swung the heavy hammer and—to the crowd's delight—missed before steadying his hand and squarely striking the spike. Likewise, railroad president Thomas Durant had trouble but then finally managed to smack the peg into place. After seven years of sweat and toil, the nation's first transcontinental railroad was complete. California was now linked by rail to Chicago and the East Coast's metropolises. Over the next several decades, millions of settlers, speculators, tourists, and manufactured goods would speed west, crossing eastbound trains laden with lumber, coal, grain, livestock, and precious metals. By 1893, the majority of Americans would visualize their nation along an east-west axis rather than the north-south axis that had dominated politics, the economy, and culture since the nation's founding.

In the 1860s, many Americans imagined "the West" as a single region or frontier. In fact, it encompassed multiple environments, peoples, frontiers, and cultures. Sioux, Comanche, and other nomadic peoples ranged over the Great Plains, effectively controlling the enormous corridor of grasslands between Mexico and Canada (see Map 17.1). In the Pacific Northwest, Native Americans lived relatively undisturbed, fishing, hunting, and gathering as they had for the previous ten thousand years. Miners, lumberjacks, and fur traders of European, Russian, Euro-American, and Chinese origin added to the mix. In the Southwest, Hispanos and Tejanos (Spanish-speaking residents of New Mexico and Texas, respectively), Native Americans, and Anglo-Americans lived and worked in small farming communities. California, which had achieved statehood in 1850, was home to an even more diverse mix of foreign and American-born peoples, the majority of whom lived in San Francisco, a global nexus of trade, information, and culture.

As railroad tycoon Leland Stanford and his fellow entrepreneurs and investors had hoped, the transcontinental railroad forever changed the West's subregions—though not always as they had imagined. Railroads helped knit the smaller regions together as a single "West" and incorporated them into the nation. Often in concert with the railroad companies, government surveyors mapped unknown terrain, identified valuable natural resources, and sold or gave away millions of acres of land to settlers. With the protection of the U.S. Army, the railroads paved the way for government, investors, speculators, and farmers to exploit the West's rich natural resources. This development fueled a burst of industrial growth "back East" (a term popularized in the 1870s) that turned the nation into the world's greatest manufacturing power by the end of the century.

Incorporation proved a complex, violent, and paradoxical process. Journalists, novelists, artists, and performers helped incorporate the West into the national imagination as a land of freedom, opportunity, and adventure—and a place that could heal and reunite the post-Civil War nation. Western development drove the United States' economic growth and contributed to the expansion of the federal government. But as waves of settlers, prospectors, and commercial enterprises flooded the region, conflicts over territory and resources erupted. Native Americans lost their lands, culture, and, in hundreds of thousands of cases, their lives—though not without a fight. Chinese immigrants, indispensable in building the railroads, faced seething hostility and discrimination, as did Hispanic and African Americans. Eventually, tensions mounted among competing communities of Euro-Americans, with large-scale ranching, farming, and mining interests edging out small producers, sometimes violently. Incorporation also brought far-reaching environmental change. "Out West," as Americans now described the region, new cities rose in the desert, enormous stretches of virgin forest were felled, and the Plains peoples, wildlife, and **open range** gave way to wheat, cattle, and miles of barbed wire.

California governor Leland Stanford drives a golden spike into the last stretch of North America's first transcontinental railroad at Promontory Summit, Utah.

KEY QUESTIONS

- How, by whom, and to what effect were the West's many subregions incorporated into the rest of the nation?
- What role did the federal government play in "opening" and developing the West?
- Which Native American peoples were living in the West and how did they respond to the newcomers? What other conflicts occurred in the West at this time?
- How and why did the West captivate the public imagination?

Map 17.1 The West's Many Biomes. Biomes are large geographical areas with similar or unique soils, plants, animals, and climate. Although many mid-nineteenth-century Americans thought of the West as a single region or frontier, the biomes of the American West were diverse—far more so than those of the Northeast and South—and presented particular challenges to conquest and settlement. Great conifer forests covered much of the Pacific Northwest, giving way to high alpine terrain to the east and, to the south, in present-day California, a combination of deciduous forest, beach and marshland, farmland, and desert. Deserts were the norm in most of the Southwest and much of present-day Utah, Nevada, and Nebraska. Two of the world's largest mountain ranges, the Rockies and the Sierra, ran the length of the West, as did the semiarid grasslands of the Great Plains.

CONQUEST AND INCORPORATION

During and after the Civil War, the federal government offered fresh incentives to businesses to increase their western investments, particularly in railroads. Federal surveyors and geologists fanned out over the West's subregions, sending a steady flow of information and images back East, and settlers applied to the government for parcels of farmland. Aggressively promoting settlement, the railroad companies sold millions of acres of land to prospective farmers, sight unseen.

Meanwhile, the U.S. Army endeavored to make the region safe for development, using a combination of force and negotiation to relocate Native Americans wherever they occupied desirable territory. Native peoples resisted in some instances and pragmatically yielded in others. But even once they agreed to relocate to new homelands—which the government guaranteed them in perpetuity—prospectors, settlers, and commercial interests encroached once more, triggering another round of conflict. Indian peoples sometimes prevailed. By 1893, however, the railroads, the U.S. Army, and resettlement had conquered and incorporated the many Wests into the United States.

MAPPING THE LAND

Contrary to the myth that cowboys won the West, the federal government was the single most important force in the region's conquest, settlement, and ultimate incorporation into the United States. Since the 1790s, people had debated how best to settle and develop America's many Wests—and what role, if any, slavery should play. The Mexican-American War of 1846–1848 had popularized the idea that the nation had a God-given "manifest destiny" to expand across the North American continent (see Chapter 13), and this conviction had strengthened as Americans poured into California's goldfields after 1848. During the Civil War, as a precaution against Confederate expansion in the West, the Republican Congress moved quickly to designate remaining western lands as federal territories. The government also began the difficult and costly work of surveying the West's subregions—the crucial first step to conquering, railroading, mining, dividing, and selling the land.

Surveying accelerated after the war. In 1867 alone, surveyors from the General Land Office and the U.S. Army Corps of Engineers undertook studies of vast expanses of California, Colorado, Utah, Nevada, Nebraska, and Wyoming. Engineers were also dispatched to Alaska, which the United States had recently purchased from Russia for the modest sum of $7.2 million (the equivalent of $110 million today—a bargain). For the first time, Congress specified that the geology of the territories, including information about waterways and the presence of useful minerals such as gold and coal, was to be the principal objective of the expeditions. Clarence King, a Yale-trained geologist and mountaineer, led one such survey along the fortieth parallel, the future route of the transcontinental railroad, and published a popular illustrated account of the expedition in the *Atlantic Monthly* in 1872.

By shaving years of precious time off the planning process, these federal surveys directly stimulated the development of private mining in the West. The government surveys also fostered a new way of seeing and thinking about the West. Before the war, most Americans pictured the West as sublime nature or a divine "Eden," very much as the artist Albert Bierstadt had depicted it in his famous paintings. Once the surveys got under way in 1867, however, a deluge of photographs, paintings, and

The Army and the West. The U.S. Army played a crucial role in western expansion, not only as a conquering force but also through the collection and dissemination of information on climate, geology, and topography.

Shifting Views of the West. Popular images of "the West" began to change in the 1860s, from the sublime emphasis of Alfred Bierstadt (top) to the utilitarianism of the photographers and painters who pictured the region as a land of exploitable natural resources (bottom).

press reports from the expeditions depicted western mountains, rivers, and giant redwood forests as promising "natural resources" ripe for exploitation. Consequently, for many Americans "the West" denoted a single, enormous reservoir of raw materials just waiting to be extracted and fed into the furnaces of the country's industries.

RAILROADI[illegible]

T[illegible] crucial role in the laying o[illegible] which in turn sped conque[illegible]opment (see Map 17.2). Und[illegible] and 1864, railroad companie[illegible]ion acres of unclaimed western land and huge sums of capital in the form of government bonds. The new laws authorized the companies to issue their own bonds in order to generate additional funds for the project. The initial motivation—depriving the Confederacy of an opportunity for expansion—was military rather than economic in nature. But as news filtered back about the West's epic natural resources, the federal government reconceived railroad building as vital to the nation's economic development.

State and local governments joined in the railroad fever, buying masses of railroad company bonds and making land cheaply or freely available for railroad construction. Small settlements, eager to recruit farmers and connect with mass markets back East, lobbied strenuously to get on a railroad route. For many such communities, being connected determined their economic viability.

Major railroads in 1870
Major railroads added 1870–1890
First transcontinental railroad

Map 17.2 Connecting the West. After the first transcontinental railroad was completed in 1869, railroad companies rushed to build dozens of major lines and hundreds of smaller ones across the Great Plains. This dense network sped conquest and settlement. By enabling the large-scale extraction and transportation of the West's metals, coal, livestock, and lumber, it also fueled industrialization.

The Chinese and the Railroads. Of the 13,500 men who built the eastward leg of the first transcontinental railroad, over 12,000 were Chinese immigrants. Toiling twelve hours a day, six days a week, for the equivalent (in today's dollars) of less than $520 a month, they excavated tunnels through solid granite, constructed bridges over deep mountain valleys, and laid hundreds of miles of track—all by hand, using picks, shovels, and baskets (to remove the debris).

Building bridges over deep ravines, blasting tunnels through mountain ranges, grading the earth's uneven surface, and laying mile after mile of rail line were expensive and dangerous tasks. Believing they could not lose on the government-backed schemes, northeastern bankers scrambled to buy into the rail enterprise. Crucially, government took much of the risk out of the enterprise, providing land and effectively promising to bail out companies that encountered financial difficulties. The U.S. Army provided security, especially on the plains, where Native American peoples were far from pleased about the arrival of the "iron horse."

The federal government also ensured that the railroad and other developers secured large, cheap labor forces. For example, when the Central Pacific Railroad decided to replace most of its higher-wage, strike-prone Irish railroad workers with lower-wage Chinese laborers, the United States negotiated the Treaty of Burlingame (1868) with the Chinese government, promising Chinese citizens the right of immigration to the United States, as well as access to schooling and protection from discrimination. (In return, American missionaries and businessmen were allowed to travel and work freely in China.) The Central Pacific and other railroad companies recruited thousands of peasants from Guangdong and other rural Chinese provinces. By 1870, one in four waged laborers in California was Chinese.

THE CONTESTED PLAINS

The corridor of grasslands running the length of North America was home to over a dozen Indian peoples, including the Lakota (the westernmost tribes of the large Sioux nation), Cheyenne, and Comanche (see Map 17.3). Most were nomadic hunters who followed migratory antelopes and **Plains bison,** more commonly known as buffalo. A few centuries before Europeans had arrived in North America, a long-term drought had forced most Indians off the parched grasslands and into the surrounding valleys, where they established farming communities. When Europeans arrived with horses, the newcomers unintentionally provided the means by which many Indians were able to return to the plains after 1700. European horses revolutionized plains life by allowing Indians to travel greater distances and move their campsites more easily than before, as well as improve their hunting yields. (The American horse had died out in the Americas over six thousand years earlier.)

The U.S. government had forcibly removed thousands of southern Indians onto the plains during the Indian removal campaigns of the 1820s and 1830s. Competition heated up for territory that often extended up to seven hundred miles, and inter-Indian wars broke out. By the 1850s, Plains Indians numbered more than two hundred thousand. Treaties designated the region "Indian country," and the United States promised to protect the inhabitants and their homelands "for as long as the grass shall grow" in exchange for the right to lay roads, establish posts, and secure safe passage for Americans headed west.

Until the Civil War, the government and white American settlers showed little interest in the plains. Although a small numbers of settlers had been making their way west for some years, the native peoples still controlled much of the region. But when the Civil War pushed up the price of wheat, hundreds of thousands of white settlers (some with slaves) poured

The Buffalo. The more than sixty million buffalo that roamed the plains before the Civil War were the material and spiritual foundation of Plains Indian life. Painter and traveler George Catlin was one of the few whites to live among the northern Plains peoples prior to the war. His paintings are among the few surviving depictions of Indian life, including the vital activity of buffalo hunting.

Map 17.3 Conquest and Incorporation, 1850–1890. This map tracks the United States' conquest of the West's many Indian peoples in the years 1850–1890 and the major battles in which Indians attempted to turn back the conquest. The reservations to which most were confined by 1890 occupied a fraction of the land to which their parents and grandparents had access just forty years earlier.

into western Missouri with the intention of planting the lucrative crop. Once peace returned, the Homestead Act of 1862 spurred further expansion. This remarkably egalitarian law made 160-acre lots of "public land" (typically, Indian hunting grounds) available to anyone age twenty-one or older who was an American citizen or who intended to become a citizen, regardless of race, sex, or other status. The government charged just $1.25 an acre and gave the land to the claimant free of charge once he or she had "…ed" it for five straight years (see How Much Is That?).

sustain the Indians' way of life, however, and the annuities were far less than the government had promised. Desperate for relief, in 1862 the Santee Sioux requested food and other aid from the region's federal agent. Rebuffed, they raided surrounding farms and posts, killing five hundred Anglo men, women, and children in what became known as the Santee Rebellion. In reprisal, the U.S. Army hanged thirty-eight Sioux raiders, imprisoned hundreds more, and deported the rest to the Black Hills in far-flung Dakota Territory. The army also extended its operations deep into the plains for the first time, battling with Lakota

Sand Creek Massacre. Cheyenne warrior Howling Wolf personally witnessed the massacre, which he recollected in this drawing made eleven years later while he was a prisoner of war in Fort Marion, Florida. Other incarcerated warriors created similar "ledger art"—pictures drawn on blank account ledgers, the only material available to them. Taking inspiration from the older art form of buffalo hide drawings, most ledger art depicted battles with settlers and the U.S. Army.

had been raiding Hispanic and Pueblo farming settlements since 1700) stole horses and supplies from the Anglo-American newcomers. Wherever Indians attacked Americans, the settlers responded with a scorched-earth policy.

Plains Indians still dominated the region, but the constant fighting was taking its toll. Significantly, the warfare divided Indians on the question of whether to negotiate with the newcomers or stand and fight. Certain factions of the Cheyenne and the Arapaho requested peace in 1864. Among them, conciliatory Cheyenne chief Black Kettle led seven hundred men, women, and children to a campsite in Sand Hills, Colorado, declaring his wish for peace. By then, however, the settlers' militia was intent on violence. On November 29, 1864, militia colonel John M. Chivington led his men on a bloody rampage through the Indian camp, ordering the killing and scalping of every person, "big and small." Desperate to avert a massacre, Black Kettle waved both a U.S. flag and the white flag of surrender, but the militia advanced anyway and slew hundreds of his people. (Black Kettle survived, only to be killed four years later in a U.S. Army attack on his camp in Washita, in present-day Oklahoma.) Settlers cheered Chivington's Sand Creek Massacre, but back East, most newspapers and Congress condemned his butchery.

How Much Is That?

The Homestead Act's 160 Acres

To attract settlers to the West, the Homestead Act offered 160 acres of public land at $1.25 an acre, for a total of $200. Adjusting for inflation, that would be about $28 per acre and $4,534 respectively, today. But was $1.25 an acre affordable for the average American in 1862? In the 1860s, a farm laborer's average wage was $13.70 a month, about the same pay that white Union soldiers made during the Civil War. At that rate, a farmhand or soldier would have to save almost 15 months' earnings to purchase 160 acres. That might sound like a lot, but remember that a homesteader could get the land *for free* if he or she made improvements to it and resided on it continuously for five years. All the homesteader would need to pay was a total of $18 in fees—$408 in 2012 dollars—or less than two months' wages. Despite these seemingly low costs, however, only 40 percent of homesteaders were able to successfully file their claims and own their 160 acres of land. Some could not afford seed, supplies, and livestock. Others sold out to big agricultural interests. And for many, farming the arid lands of the new western territories was simply too difficult.

WAR, RELOCATION, AND RESISTANCE

The Sand Creek atrocities united the Plains Indians in the belief that neither the settlers nor the U.S. government could be trusted and that negotiating with them was futile. Plains violence subsequently spread. The Sioux, Cheyenne, and Arapaho retaliated for the Sand Creek episode by burning all the stage stations and ranges of the South Platte and killing dozens of Americans. The army brought in sixty thousand U.S. reinforcements, including two African American battalions, in 1866. Unused to the grassy, flat expanse of the plains, the troops moved slowly and inefficiently, repeatedly losing the enemy's trail. They became disoriented, lost, and hungry—and one entire column of eighty-two men was fatally ambushed. Even help from the Sioux's longtime enemy, the Pawnees, was not enough to secure a U.S. victory in the Great Sioux War of 1866–1868.

The cost of the war mounted, with no end in sight. Under pressure from Congress, General William Tecumseh Sherman, who had famously commanded Union troops in the southern theater during the Civil War, reluctantly negotiated the Sioux Treaty of 1868, which permanently reserved the northern Black Hills in Dakota Territory and the adjoining land in Wyoming, Montana, and Nebraska for the Sioux peoples. In exchange for the cessation of hostilities, the United States also relinquished the Bozeman trail, which crossed Sioux hunting grounds in northeastern Wyoming—a great though temporary victory for the Sioux (see Map 17.3). On the southern plains, eighty-six thousand Indians agreed to move to a reservation in Oklahoma, and by 1868, the Kiowa, Comanche, Cheyenne, and Arapaho had also signed treaties agreeing to relocate. Most southwestern peoples, including the Apache and Navaho, followed suit.

The ink on the treaties of 1867–1868 had barely dried before the Comanche in north Texas recommenced their raids on American settlers who once more were encroaching on guaranteed lands. On the central plains, the Cheyenne resumed attacks on both Pawnee enemies and American settlers. In the north, some leaders, among them Sitting Bull, the new chief of the Hunkpapa branch of the Lakota Sioux, refused to recognize the Sioux Treaty of 1868 and raided forts, settlers, and railway surveyors. The U.S. Army spent the winter of 1868–1869 preparing for fresh campaigns and designated the southern plains a "free fire zone" in which soldiers were authorized to shoot any and all Indians on sight. Over the next ten years, the army proceeded to clear the length and breadth of the plains, relocating the entire population of Indians to far-flung reservations.

This was not the first time in modern history that armies had driven out unwanted populations to make way for economic development. The English, for instance, had cleared tens of thousands of farmers off the Scottish Highlands in the eighteenth and early nineteenth centuries, establishing large sheep stations capable of employing England's masses and forcibly relocating the Highlanders to coastal fishing villages. Before the Civil War, America's own Indian removal policies effectively cleared Cherokee and other native peoples off coveted farmland in Georgia and elsewhere. But the plains clearances were far more ferocious than either of these removals, ultimately approaching genocide—the systematic eradication of an entire people—in both scale and intent.

Treaty of Fort Laramie. General William Tecumseh Sherman and Sioux chiefs signed the treaty at Sioux Wigwam, 1868.

FIGHTING BACK

In the Great Sioux Reservation of Dakota, which the treaty of 1868 had reserved for the exclusive use of the Sioux, hostilities erupted in 1875 following the discovery of gold in the reservation's Black Hills area and the ensuing arrival of thousands of American prospectors. The hills were the most sacred of the Lakota Sioux's lands, and the native people defended their holy sites accordingly, killing trespassers and raiding the mining camps. When the Lakota rejected a government

Bison Dance. As U.S. Army officials well knew, the bison was a key source of nourishment, shelter, and tools for Plains peoples and a valuable commodity that could be exchanged for horses, weapons, and other goods. It also served as the foundation of spirituality, identity, and way of life. In Sioux culture, the bison's spirit controlled matters of love and family and nurtured all living things. The rhythms of life, intertribal relations, and important ceremonies were all structured around the bison's migratory seasons. **Questions for Analysis:** Why might the bison have acquired such enormous cultural importance in Plains societies? Why might the army have decided to exterminate them? What effects might their practical extinction have had on Plains peoples?

offer to buy the gold-rich hills, General Philip Sheridan persuaded President Ulysses S. Grant that the Indians should be forced off the land altogether. Within a year, the United States was waging the Great Sioux War of 1876–1877.

Led by Lakota chiefs Crazy Horse, Sitting Bull, and Rain-in-the-Face, the Sioux claimed an early victory over the U.S. Army when well-known Indian fighter General George Armstrong Custer unwittingly marched his troops straight into the Sioux's war base in June 1876. Incorrectly assuming that he had come across a small encampment, Custer had divided his troops in two, personally leading a charge into what turned out to be 2,500 massed, well-armed Sioux warriors. The colonel and all 265 of his men were killed. Newspapers around the nation spread word of "Custer's Last Stand" at the Battle of Little Big Horn just as the nation was celebrating the wonders of American technology at the Centennial in Philadelphia (see Chapter 18). With white Americans appalled by the slaughter and shocked that Indians were capable of defeating the mighty U.S. Army, public opinion back East swung against the Sioux—and all Plains Indians. The settlers' long-held view that the army should use any means necessary to wipe the Indians off the plains became majority opinion and official U.S. policy.

Thousands of U.S. troops now deployed to the Black Hills. Within a few months, most of the Sioux warriors had surrendered or been killed, with the notable exception of Sitting Bull, who fled to Canada (see Singular Lives: Sitting Bull: Warrior, Chief, and Symbol of Resistance). Aware of the Plains bison's essential place in Sioux life, General Sheridan directed troops to eradicate the beasts. The herds were already in decline due to commercialized hunting and disease, but the order to obliterate them resulted in their near-extinction, with just twenty-three animals from the original herd surviving undetected in a remote valley in Yellowstone Park. These were the ancestors of the three thousand wild Plains bison alive in the United States today.

Large-scale armed resistance on the plains ended with the Sioux defeat in 1877, but a number of smaller rebellions broke out elsewhere. In the Southwest, Apaches rode well beyond the bounds of their government-enforced reservation, raiding settlers as late as the 1880s, when the last few surrendered. In Oregon and Idaho, the Nez Percé Indians fought settlers who encroached on their lands. When U.S. forces attempted to relocate the Nez Percé to a reservation, they fled with their leader, Chief Joseph, in the hope of escaping to Canada. Known in the press as "the Red Napoleon," Chief Joseph led his people 1,700 miles over some of the roughest terrain in North America. The army eventually caught up, and Chief Joseph, believing that his people would be allowed to return home, surrendered without a struggle. In fact, the U.S. government relocated them, first to eastern Kansas, then to Oklahoma, and eventually to Washington Territory.

The Plains Indians won several battles in the course of which they inflicted heavy losses on U.S. forces, but they did not win the war. Outgunned and outnumbered, they eventually lost

SINGULAR LIVES

Sitting Bull: Warrior, Chief, and Symbol of Resistance

Sitting Bull, as Himself, in William "Buffalo Bill" Cody's Wild West Show. Some historians argue that Cody, a former army scout and buffalo hunter, was exploiting the Lakota chief for his own ends. Others point out that Sitting Bull and other Lakota held Cody in highest regard as a fellow warrior and as one of the few white men who respected—and was prepared to educate the world about—Plains culture and history.

No Indian chief defied American power more vehemently than Hunkpapa Lakota chief Sitting Bull. Born around 1831 in present-day South Dakota, Sitting Bull learned the arts of war and buffalo hunting at an early age, earning his first warrior's red feather and victory feast at age fourteen after daringly felling an enemy Crow with a single blow of the tomahawk. His first encounter with U.S. soldiers came in 1863 as troops attacked the Plains Lakota in retaliation for the Santee Rebellion (in which the Lakota had played no role). By 1865, Sitting Bull was leading raids and was known among whites and Indians alike as a fearless and brilliant warrior—one who, like the male buffalo, planted his hind legs firmly on the ground, reared up, and refused to submit.

Seemingly immune to enemy bullets and uncannily calm under fire (he once packed and smoked his tobacco pipe midbattle), Sitting Bull was also revered as a man of immense spiritual powers—including the power of prophecy. The future was very much on Lakota minds after the Civil War, as Americans encroached ever deeper into Lakota hunting grounds and the prized buffalo grew scarce. When a wave of gold prospectors penetrated the sacred Black Hills in 1876, Sitting Bull had a dream in which men fell like grasshoppers out of the sky. Mustering his allies, Sitting Bull and 2,500 warriors dug in at Little Big Horn, preparing to defend their homeland. General Custer's Seventh Cavalry blundered into the encampment and fell—like grasshoppers—to a hail of Lakota fire.

Aware that the full fury of the U.S. Army would soon be unleashed, Sitting Bull led five hundred Lakota to safety in Canada. Four years later, finding it impossible to care for his exiled people in the absence of the buffalo, the chief reached an agreement with the American authorities to return with his people to Standing Rock Reservation near his birthplace. Worrying that the chief would stir up fresh resistance, federal Indian agent James McLaughlin arranged for him and his warriors to be held as prisoners of war at Fort Randall over three hundred miles away.

In 1883, Sitting Bull returned to Standing Rock, where the federal program to turn Indians into farmers was in full swing. Determined to break the chief's will and diminish his stature, agent McLaughlin forced him to perform farm labor. But Sitting Bull

people in secret and, when the opportunity presented itself, joining Buffalo Bill's Wild West show (see p. 467)—in which he played himself, in full war costume, reenacting "Custer's Last Stand." Contrary to McLaughlin's expectations, the show only increased the chief's prestige. Sitting Bull and other Lakota warriors traveled extensively, performing the Lakota's proud way of life for millions of awe-inspired Americans. As befits chiefs, the Lakota performers met the president and European royalty. Having observed American culture and politics firsthand, Sitting Bull returned home with fresh insights on how the Lakota could survive in their harsh new world. He insisted, for instance, that his children learn to read and write so that they might work with the Americans.

The chief remained a thorn in the side of the Bureau of Indian Affairs to his dying day—an occasion that the bureau directly hastened. In 1890, as a new spiritual movement known as the Ghost Dance unnerved whites from New Mexico to the Dakotas, federal authorities worried that Sitting Bull was preparing to lead a rebellion. Under orders from McLaughlin, Lakota police stormed the chief's cabin and arrested him. A fierce gunfight ensued that ended in the death of Sitting Bull. Fearing that the powerful chief might yet inspire resistance from the grave, McLaughlin had him buried at Fort Yates sixty miles away. The chief's descendants reinterred his remains on the Standing Rock Reservation in 1953 and, sixty years later, gave the University of Copenhagen permission to sequence his DNA using a lock of hair retrieved by a U.S. Army surgeon shortly after his death. Sitting Bull will be the first

sequenced. The procedure will cast light on the complicated process by which humans first crossed into America from Russia at the end of the last Ice Age to become the diverse "first peoples" of the Americas. He has also been immortalized in dozens of plays, films, novels, computer games, songs, U.S. postage stamps, and, most recently, in President Barack Obama's children's book of great Americans, *Of Thee I Sing: A Letter to My Daughters* (2010).

Think About It

1. Why do you think Sitting Bull was so acclaimed among the Lakota, even before 1876?
2. Who or what was Sitting Bull's enemy—and did he ever fully surrender?
3. Did Sitting Bull "sell out" by joining Buffalo Bill's Wild West show?
4. What accounts for late nineteenth-century Americans' ambivalence about Sitting Bull? Why might many Americans today consider Sitti[illegible] Bull a hero?

"Civilizing" Native Peoples. As part of the government's detribalization program, thousands of Indian children were taken from their families and sent to one of over 475 federal and private boarding schools. The Plains Indian children shown here attended the Carlisle School in Pennsylvania, whose motto was "To civilize the Indian, get him into civilization. To keep him civilized, let him stay." "Civilizing" the native children involved cutting their hair (a traumatic event, particularly for boys, because long hair was associated with manhood), dressing them in Euro-American clothing, subjecting them to military-style discipline, giving them Anglo names, and prohibiting the use of their native language. **Questions for Analysis:** Why might missionaries and the Bureau of Indian Affairs have been so committed to "civilizing" Indians in the 1870s and 1880s? Why do you think the schools banned Indian languages and hairstyles?

most of their lands. Legal redress was not an option, as Indians were not citizens and therefore were deprived of the Fourteenth Amendment's guaranteed access to the courts. By 1890, the majority of Indians were contained on reservations far from home (see Map 17.3). The few peoples allowed to stay in their homelands were those who had allied with the United States, as the Crow and Shoshoni had done during the Sioux Wars. Regardless of the location of their reservations, all Indians were expected to stay there—or face being hunted down and possibly killed.

HUNTERS INTO FARMERS

Turning Indians into farmers was the principal goal of federal reservation policy in the 1870s and 1880s. Together with white missionaries, teachers, and philanthropists, federal officials also attempted to substitute Christianity and the nuclear family (composed of two married, heterosexual parents and their children) for the Indians' tribal way of life. Farming and the Bible, according to the Bureau of Indian Affairs, would "civilize" the Indians and turn their nomadic tribes into settled, self-sustaining communities. Missionaries fanned out across the reservations and went to work stamping out traditional beliefs and rituals and replacing them with Christian practice. Agents at the Bureau of Indian Affairs targeted children, arguing that separating them from their parents was the most effective way to "civilize" the culture. Bureau boarding schools gave the children new names, dressed them in American clothes, taught them Anglo etiquette, and educated them in reading, writing, and arithmetic.

For the most part, missionaries and agents were well-meaning people. They believed that they were playing a key role in saving the Indians both from annihilation by the army and from "heathen" ways that supposedly doomed their chances of survival in the modern world. Often the children or grandchildren of abolitionists, the missionaries implicitly rejected the older view that Native Americans were savages who were biologically incapable of "civilization." At the same time, though, most missionaries dismissed Indians' existing cultures as inferior and blindly assumed that Indian society should and could be reconstructed in a matter of a few years.

Not surprisingly, the effort to turn Indians into Christian farmers failed. Indians persisted in trying to hunt and, when game grew sparse, became dependent on the government's Indian agents for food. The agents, employees of the Bureau of Indian Affairs, were either contemptuous of the Indians' supposed inability to farm or grew frustrated with their own government for not doing more to help with the transition. Even if the Indians had wanted or known how to farm, the reservations to which they were banished were mostly arid and all but unworkable. And although the reservations were guaranteed by treaty, the swelling tide of developers, prospectors, and railroad builders continued to press in on the reserves.

By the 1880s, lawmakers and philanthropists were rethinking the reservation policy. White activists of the Indian Rights Association argued that the reservations were poverty traps that reduced inhabitants to an unhealthy dependency on the federal government. The publication of Helen Hunt Jackson's book *A Century of Dishonor* (1882) persuaded many Americans that Indians were being so badly treated that whole peoples were perishing. Congress debated possible solutions and eventually agreed to implement a system of private property, reasoning that if Indians were able to own their own farms, they would acquire an interest in the land and be motivated to farm it. In 1887, the Dawes Severalty Act divided the reservations into small parcels. Each household was entitled to a 160-acre parcel that would become the private property of the head of household, and single adults would receive 80 acres each. The law's sponsor, Massachusetts senator Henry L. Dawes, theorized that private land ownership would turn Indians into self-sustaining farmers and assimilate them into American society. As an added incentive, Indians who accepted the offer of land would be eligible for U.S. citizenship.

Indian chiefs opposed the Dawes act on the grounds that it attacked the tribal foundation of their societies, in which the tribe as a whole owned the land. Many were also suspicious of a clause in the law providing that after distribution of the lots, any surplus reservation land would become U.S. government property. But there was little the chiefs could do to stop the law's implementation. Over the next few years, millions of acres were transformed into private lots, the title passing to individual Indian "land owners." The government sold to white settlers the enormous surplus of land that resulted from there being far more land than was needed under the allotment scheme.

From Oklahoma to the West Coast, posters advertising "Indian land for sale" triggered land rushes. Sometimes tens of thousands of reservation acres were sold off in a single day. By the 1930s, the amount of land possessed by Indian tribes and individuals had dropped from 138 million to just 47 million acres. As the chiefs had feared, the communal character of Indian culture was all but broken. But privatization did not result in either the large-scale Americanization of Indians, as Dawes had promised, or the eradication of poverty. By 1900, only 54,000 of 250,000 Indians had opted for U.S. citizenship.

THE GHOST DANCE AND WOUNDED KNEE

Like many of the world's dispossessed peoples, western Indians responded to the gradual breakup of their lands and culture with a surge of religious prophecy and ritual. In 1889, two years after the passage of the Dawes Severalty Act, a new religious movement emerged among the Paiute people in Nevada. Paiute shaman and medicine man Wovoka claimed to have had a prophetic vision that the Native American dead would one day return and that whites, their guns, and whiskey would disappear from North America. In the meantime, Wovoka preached, Native Americans should live in peace, sobriety, and prayerfulness, enacting an ancient round dance at frequent intervals. The Paiute thereupon began extended revivals in which they performed what came to be known as the Ghost Dance. By 1890, other suffering peoples had adapted it to their own particular belief systems. Throughout the West, the Ghost Dance served as a form of mourning, an act of prophecy, and a source of resistance to cultural decimation.

Although Wovoka's message was pacifist, it was not long before the Ghost Dance was adapted to more confrontational ends. Older chiefs and warriors among the Sioux and Lakota led Ghost Dances that lasted days at a time, during which the tribe's men, women, and children entered a trancelike state, hailing the imminent arrival of a whole new world. Federal agents reacted with terror. "Indians are dancing in the snow and are wild and crazy," telegraphed one in 1890—*"we need protection and we need it now."* The government dispatched the U.S. cavalry, but before they could get there, several chiefs and Ghost Dancers took refuge in the Badlands section of the Pine Ridge Reservation.

A few days after Christmas 1890, the cavalry finally caught up with a large group of Ghost Dancers at their Wounded Knee campsite. The soldiers surrounded the camp and dug in for the night. Early next morning the sounds of rifle and machine gun fire echoed across the reservation. The soldiers had been disarming a handful of warriors when a gun accidentally went off, triggering a hail of fire from the cavalry. Within ten minutes, at least 153 Sioux men, women, and children were killed, many shot in the back as they ran from the soldiers. Twenty-five soldiers also lost their lives—almost all to friendly fire amid the chaos. A few hours later, a blizzard blanketed the scene, freezing the bodies where they lay. Lakota medicine man and eyewitness Black Elk reflected that not only innocent people but "something else died there in the bloody mud, and was buried in the blizzard. A people's dream died there. It was a beautiful dream . . . the nation's hoop is broken and scattered. There is no center any longer, and the sacred tree is dead."

As news of the Wounded Knee massacre spread, a vocal minority of the public expressed outrage, mostly in the Northeast. General Nelson Miles condemned the attack and relieved the cavalry's commanding officer, Colonel James Forsyth, of his authority. But no court-martial was held, and a military commission of inquiry found that Forsyth was not responsible for the massacre. Majority public opinion was favorable toward both the cavalry's actions and the slowly unfolding genocide of western Indians. As L. Frank Baum, future author of *The Wonderful Wizard of Oz* (1900), wrote approvingly in a newspaper column a few days later, "Our only safety depends upon the total extirmination [sic] of the Indians. Having wronged them for centuries we had better, in order to protect our civilization, follow it up by one more wrong and wipe these untamed and untamable creatures from the face of the earth." In 1891, twenty soldiers were awarded the highest military decoration—the Medal of Honor—for their role at Wounded Knee.

BONANZAS, FEVERS, AND BUSTS

More than any other region of the United States, the post–Civil War West was a land of unprecedented booms and devastating busts. Mineral strikes, land rushes, and cattle surpluses drew hundreds of thousands of people to the region, all looking to get rich or achieve the life they had dreamed of but most failing to do so. The bonanzas helped create new American mining, farming, and ranching frontiers as newcomers spilled into areas often previously occupied or claimed by Indians. These frontiers advanced at different speeds and in various directions, and only farming conformed in any way to the myth of westward expansion. But all these enterprises tended to take the same broad pattern: Individual settlers with a modest claim would move in, followed by large-scale operators who would force most small operators out of the business and into waged labor. Both farmers and ranchers literally lost more and more ground to powerful interests.

MEN, WOMEN, AND MINING

Contrary to the popular myth of westward expansion, American miners and mining companies typically moved in an eastward direction after the 1850s, from San Francisco and the

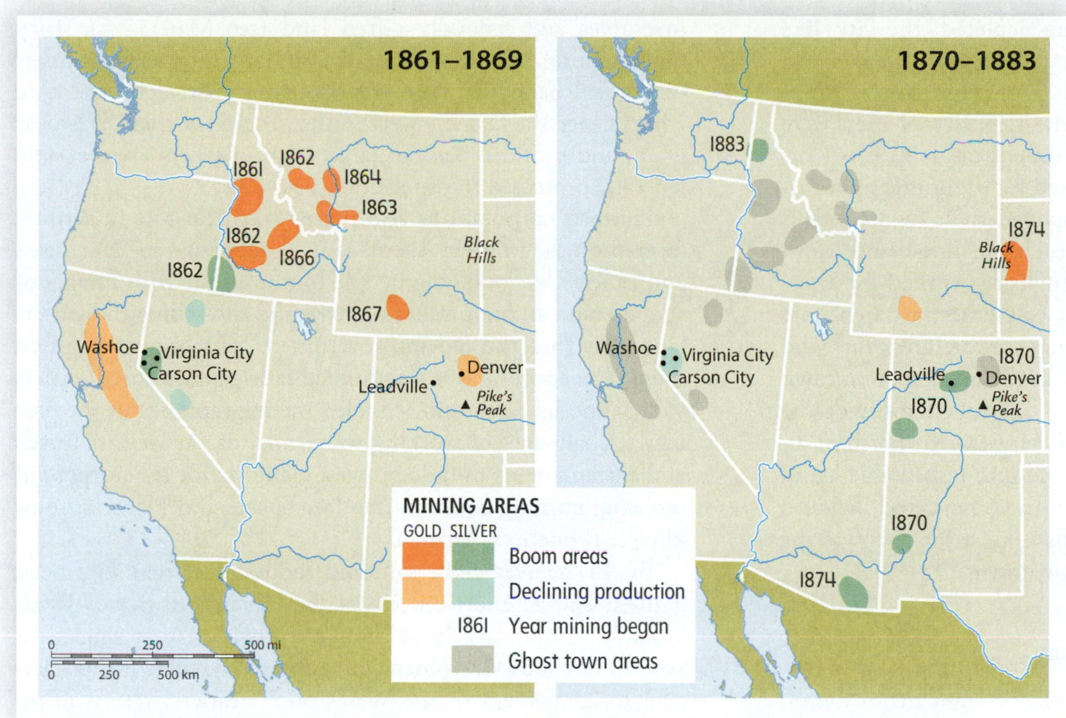

Map 17.4 From Boomtown to Ghost Town, 1861–1883. Unlike farming and ranching, which moved westward and northward, respectively, the **mining frontier** swept eastward from California. Once a valuable mineral such as gold or silver was "struck," prospectors poured in and towns sprang up, seemingly in a matter of weeks. As supplies of the precious metal dwindled, the miners moved on, leaving a succession of "ghost towns" behind them.

Sierras into Nevada, Utah, Idaho, and Dakota Territory (see Map 17.4). In the Washoe Basin in 1859, prospector Henry Comstock struck one of the richest veins of silver in North America. But mining the Comstock Lode required heavy, expensive equipment. Many entrepreneurs raised money for genuine mining operations by selling stock on the San Francisco securities exchange. Some, however, swindled investors by selling shares in nonexistent mines, unworkable sites, or imaginary companies. Thousands of speculators lost their life savings. Those who were lucky—or clever—enough to invest in trustworthy companies grew rich on the $300 million worth of silver—the equivalent of more than $7 billion today—extracted from the vein.

Once the transcontinental railroad was completed and tributaries added, prospectors flowed in ever-larger numbers east from California. News of a strike, including the reports of the 1875 gold strike in the Black Hills of the Lakota Sioux Indians, would set off a frantic rush. Most strikes followed a boom-and-bust model similar to California's experience of the gold rush after 1848. Upon reports of the discovery of a precious metal, thousands of prospectors would descend on the site, stake their claims, and extract what they could, using picks, shovels, threshers, and pans in a process called **placer mining.** If the miners trespassed on Indian hunting grounds, local Indians would terrorize, kill, or otherwise try to run them off the land, and the U.S. Army would respond with a violent campaign to clear the tribe in question. In general, placer miners were a diverse lot, made up of Chinese, Peruvians, Irish, Poles, Germans, Mexicans, white Americans, and Hispanos. Smaller numbers of prospectors from Japan, Turkey, Samoa, and Native American lands also appeared.

For a short time—up to a year or two—the placer miners had relative success. Boomtowns sprang up, catering to miners' needs and making small fortunes for local storekeepers and saloon and brothel operators. But the miners soon depleted the easily extracted minerals, leaving only deposits buried deep in the ground and embedded in solid quartz. As at Comstock, retrieving these minerals required heavy equipment, large workforces of paid laborers, and a lot of capital. **Commercial mining enterprises** set up business, and independent miners soon found themselves either moving on or accepting a waged position in the local company. Through a variety of extractive techniques, the company would pull millions of dollars' worth of minerals from the ground. The environment surrounding the mine became a great pile of rubble, stripped of its forests due to the need for timber supports and other mine-related construction. By 1875, over a thousand stamping mills pressed ore, and the industry directly employed more than four thousand men.

Comstock's skilled laborers were well remunerated by the standards of the day, but the work was dangerous. Descending as deep as three thousand feet into the earth, company miners encountered stifling heat, unsteady shafts, and toxic air. Once extraction was complete or the market collapsed, the boom became a bust. The cycle of prospecting, conflict with Indians, commercialization, and environmental destruction began again elsewhere.

Many of the mining towns that sprouted alongside major strikes bore little resemblance to the lawless outposts imagined in Wild West fiction and Hollywood movies. Virginia City, which bordered the Comstock Lode, had an abundance of churches, schools, theaters, and family homes. While still outnumbered by men two to one in 1880, women had a significant presence, keeping house, providing lodging, teaching school, or cooking for miners. A small percentage of the city's women worked as prostitutes. By the mid-1870s, Virginia City was an industrial hub of over twenty-five thousand people, one of the largest cities in the West after San Francisco and Los

Angeles. When the silver veins were depleted, the city, like other mining boomtowns, became a ghost town.

Prostitution and gambling were far more common in camps and smaller mining towns, where the majority of men were single. Thousands of women, both Americans as well as Chinese and European immigrants, looked for economic opportunity in such communities. Some opened their own brothels and made a fortune. Others—particularly Chinese and Mongolian women who did not speak English—worked for a pittance or nothing. Untold thousands of Chinese women were sold by impoverished parents to Chinese or foreign agents who in turn sold them to brothel keepers. In the mining boomtown of Helena, Montana, white women controlled most of the brothels and reported high levels of property ownership, although they were rarely if ever accepted into respectable Montana society. Chinese sex workers, on the other hand, held no property and plied their trade, usually against their will, in the male-controlled brothels of local Chinatowns.

FARMERS AND LAND FEVER

Like miners, American farming settlers brought major demographic, cultural, and environmental change to the West. In some respects, the **farming frontier** conformed more closely to the one imagined by northeasterners. It generally moved westward along the railroad and the overland trails. However, far from being independent of government aid, as popular mythology held, farming frontiers were driven by federal incentives and federally gifted land (see Map 17.5). They moved along the new, federally funded transportation networks and benefited from the security provided by the U.S. Army. Once the farmers were settled, they sent their livestock, grain, and produce back to large urban markets via the same federally protected transportation networks.

Railroad corporations also played a critical role in settling farmers on the frontier. Agents fanned out across the Northeast and Europe, encouraging people to move west with images of verdant land and boundless opportunity and selling the settlers land that that the federal government had originally gifted them. The corporations also funded mortgages, carried settlers west at special rates, and schooled the migrants about the particular challenges of working western lands. As well, railroads and entrepreneurs founded towns, expressly for the purpose of servicing farming communities [see Spaces and Places: Pumpkinville (Phoenix), Arizona].

By 1873, over eight hundred thousand settlers had been granted 160-acre sections under the Homestead Act of 1862. Notably, thanks largely to the law's provision that single, divorced, or widowed women could apply, anywhere from 5 percent to 22 percent of the West's homesteaders were women, depending on the county. Not all were unmarried, however, as an unknown number had concealed their marital status in order to double the size of their husband's holdings. Years after Wyoming's Eleanor Pruitt Stuart published a popular memoir about the rewards of homesteading for the single woman, for instance, it was revealed that she had been married all along. Still, never before had such a high percentage of the nation's women owned land. The experience of working one's own farm, although tough, often proved exhilarating. Idealized stories of the fiercely independent female homesteader became a literary genre and a common feature of popular magazines. The woman homesteader who was prepared to put in the hard work, wrote Stuart, "will have independence, plenty to eat all the time, and a home of her own in the end."

Regardless of their sex, homesteaders met with mixed success. As early as the 1870s, it was clear that the 160-acre sections were usually too small given the West's aridity and the large-scale nature of grain production. Congress subsequently offered farmers twice that amount under the Timber Culture Act of 1873, with the proviso that each homesteader plant forty acres of trees on the parcel. This condition reflected the popular misconception that trees would attract rain to arid regions while also underscoring the federal government's commitment to pushing settlement into less desirable, drier regions of the plains. Much the same logic was behind the Desert Land Act of 1877, which made land cheaply available on the condition that the owner would irrigate part of the land.

Opened to homesteaders under federal Homestead Acts, 1862-1916

Opened to homesteaders under Texas Homestead Act, 1839

Map 17.5 Homesteaders and the Settlement of the West. Together with railroad grants, the Homestead Act of 1862 was the federal government's most effective tool for settling and incorporating the West. Under the act, settlers established farms on over 270 million acres of territory.

The following year, the Timber and Stone Act offered nonarable land for sale for just $2.25 (the equivalent of about $50 today) per acre.

All told, the nation's homesteaders planted over forty million acres of corn and twenty million of hay and wheat, and they added millions of acres of cotton and oats to the nation's supplies. Yet only about half the new migrants were able to continue farming. Often, the lush land depicted in railroad brochures turned out to be too arid, infertile, or insect-plagued for farming. Settlers frequently found themselves in competition with large-scale landowners who had found legal and illegal ways to manipulate government land grants and acquire thousands of acres of the best and most arable land.

Much as the mining companies edged out individual prospectors, agricultural operations displaced family farmers. Large-scale grain growers on the plains had the money to build silos, put heavy machinery such as the improved McCormick reaper and the new steam tractor to work on the land, and drill deep-water wells. In the early 1870s, as these expensive new farming technologies raised output both in the West and throughout the world, prices of wheat and other cereals plummeted, driving thousands of small farmers out of the market. Many of those prairie farmers who did hold onto their homesteads lived in tiny cottages made out of sod—a mix of earth and roots—and eked out a meager existence on the land. Locust plagues made life even harder on the central plains, striking repeatedly in the 1870s. As in the cotton belt South, Protestantism flourished across the prairie in these years, and itinerant and circuit preachers traveled from town to town, knitting isolated farming families into a community and sustaining them in the face of tremendous natural and social adversity. Small farmers also organized local and, eventually, national organizations to support and promote their interests and way of life.

In Texas, a new organization, the Farmers' Alliance, provided cooperative storage facilities, which freed farmers from their dependence on expensive third parties (see Chapter 19). Farther north, membership in the National Grange of the Patrons of Husbandry swelled to almost a million by 1875. Particularly in the wheat-growing areas of Nebraska and the northern plains, **Grangers,** as members of the organization were called, held meetings and picnics and lobbied state legislatures to regulate the prices of the railroad transport and grain storage facilities on which they depended for getting their grain to market. Railroads and wholesalers objected, but in the groundbreaking case of *Munn v. Illinois* (1876), the Supreme Court declared that the states could regulate commerce wherever there was a public interest in doing so.

Farther west, California rapidly became a land of sweeping estates rather than family farms. Entrepreneurial landholders found creative ways around restrictions in the Homestead and Timber Culture Acts and quickly amassed great tracts of the most productive rural land. Crops were tended and harvested by migrant Chinese and Mexican laborers, who like many white farmers had difficulty acquiring and retaining their own land.

Grain Elevators. Storage facilities known as grain elevators were among the earliest commercial entities to be subjected to commercial regulation in the name of the public interest.

CATTLEMEN AND COWBOYS

The American **ranching frontier** originated in Texas and west Louisiana in the 1840s, when Euro-Americans began replacing the Mexican rancheros who had run goats, sheep, and the mighty Texas Longhorn cattle since the late seventeenth century. Before the Civil War, cattlemen had mustered their relatively small herds and driven them on the hoof or railroaded them to New Orleans, the meat-slaughtering capital of the South. In the early 1850s, some cattle were also driven west via El Paso to California, where the gold rush created a lucrative market for beef.

The loss of the Louisiana railroad during the war led a handful of enterprising cattlemen to drive their steers north into Kansas, New Mexico, and Colorado, where rail links connected them to Chicago, the North's main meatpacking center. Wartime demand was so high that the cattlemen began rounding up free-ranging herds on Indian land and branding

SPACES & PLACES

Pumpkinville (Phoenix), Arizona

Most migrants to the West, whatever their ethnic background, aspired to become landowning farmers. But a significant minority saw an opportunity in providing the goods and services that the farming and mining communities would need. Hundreds of towns sprang up—some seemingly overnight. A few, such as the Union Colony in Colorado (founded in 1868 and subsequently renamed Greeley, after New York publisher Horace Greeley, its principal sponsor) were privately organized utopian settlements in which only people of "good moral standing"—and white skin—qualified for residency. Others were built by the U.S. Army for the express purpose of facilitating American expansion. More typically, as in the case of Pumpkinville, Arizona, an entrepreneur or group of investors chose a promising site—close to mines, fertile land, or a railway hub—and set about developing a town.

Pumpkinville, like many of the West's "new" towns, was built atop the ruins of an earlier Native American settlement. Indian settlements had typically been close to the West's most precious natural resource, water, which was crucial for both survival and agriculture. In Pumpkinville's case, the Hohokam people had diverted water from the Salt River, in Arizona's upper Sonoran Desert, via a 150-mile system of canals and irrigation ditches that rivaled the complexity of the famous canals of ancient Egypt and China. The American waterways, built between 700 and 1450 AD, had enabled the Hohokam to farm cotton, tobacco, maize, beans, and pumpkin and to build a greater metropolitan area composed of several villages and towns, complete with public plazas, multistory stone or adobe buildings, ball courts, and common ovens for cooking bread and meat. In the fifteenth century, a long-term drought forced the Indians to abandon their towns, and the canals fell into disrepair. But as entrepreneur and Confederate veteran Jack Swilling immediately grasped on a tour of the valley in 1867, the ruins, together with the area's rich soil, were a clue that the site might be an excellent location for a farming settlement. Apache raiders might pose a threat, but the U.S. Army had recently built nearby Fort McDowell and established good relations with the Pima and Maricopa Indians, who offered to protect Americans.

Swilling rebuilt the ancient canal system and, as his predecessors had done, began growing acres of pumpkins. Naming the area Pumpkinville, he soon branched out into wheat, corn, and barley culture and planted a vineyard and orchards. Within a year, other farmers purchased land. Swilling opened a flour mill, and the federal government established a post office. In 1869, the farmers agreed that Pumpkinville's name should be changed to something more dynamic. Swilling favored Stonewall, after Confederate general Stonewall Jackson. But his associate Phillip Darrel Duppa suggested the name Phoenix, after the great bird of mythology that had crashed and burned in the Arabian Desert, only to rise from the ashes and begin its life anew.

Jack Swilling. The entrepreneur raised money from friends to establish the Swilling Irrigating and Canal Company, which renovated and extended the ancient Hohokam canal system and enabled the growth of Pumpkinville/Phoenix. A swashbuckling southerner who farmed, developed real estate, opened Arizona's first winery, and owned several saloons, Swilling died an early death in jail after he was mistakenly arrested in central Arizona on suspicion of a stage coach robbery.

them as their own private property. The wartime reorientation of ranching proved permanent. In 1865, Texas cattle fetched ten times as much money in Chicago as in the South, largely because most northern consumers—unlike war-ravaged southerners—could afford to make meat a daily staple. The Indian clearances turned much of the plains into a safe, open, and free range for cattle. The U.S. government in turn proved a reliably hungry customer. Cattlemen supplied the two hundred thousand troops stationed in the West and, as the army enforced the Indian reservation system, the federal government purchased additional meat for the increasingly dependent Indians.

In 1874, after several years of growth, Phoenix was granted a land patent by President Ulysses S. Grant, authorizing the sale of downtown lots three miles west of Swilling's estate. Hispanics—some of whose forebears had farmed and ranched the Southwest since the eighteenth century—played an important role in the city's "rebirth" and expansion. Almost half the city's residents were Hispanic in the 1870s, and they literally built much of the city, sun-drying bricks for construction, building homes and businesses, and laying roads and railways. Relations between Hispanics and "Anglos" (as white people, regardless of linguistic or national affiliation, came to be known) were relatively harmonious through the 1880s. With a population of around 1,700 in 1880, folks often knew one another and had business or other ties. The groups intermarried, sent their children to the same schools, and frequently were bilingual. When the city as a whole celebrated Mexican Independence Day in 1885, the daily Anglo-owned newspaper published both Spanish and English reports on the festivities.

Aerial Map of Phoenix, 1885. This view highlights the redeveloped canals that made the city possible. Like the brilliantly hued bird of mythology, the desert city of Phoenix rose from the "ashes" of the Hohokam civilization that preceded it—though this map's emphasis on the city's modern features erases all signs of that history. A few years later, the city council completed the erasure, replacing the Indian-named streets with numbered streets and avenues. Today, greater Phoenix is home to 4.2 million people and is the nation's twelfth most populous metropolitan area.

The town rapidly acquired a public school, stores, banks, and a telegraph office—and sixteen saloons. In the late 1880s, a rail spur connected the town to the transcontinental Southern Pacific Railroad, and the federal government named Phoenix the capital of Arizona Territory. The railway boosted trade and population growth. Anglo migrants flooded the area, soon outnumbering Hispanics by more than eight to one and dominating farming, commerce, and banking. Relations between the two groups deteriorated after 1890, fueled by an Anglo-led campaign against teaching Spanish in the schools. After 1900, Phoenix, like many southwestern cities, segregated its public schools, and intermarriage between Hispanics and Anglos became rare.

From its earliest days—and like many western towns—Phoenix was strongly Democratic. The city defined itself against both the Republican-dominated government in Washington, D.C., and the Wall Street bankers who helped bankroll western development. From the Phoenicians' perspective, both East Coast institutions were distant, out-of-touch, and unduly powerful. Although the region would not have prospered without federal support for land grants, irrigation projects, and protection from hostile Indians, the themes of regional independence and untrustworthy federal government continue to dominate political debate in many parts of the West today.

Think About It

1. Why might Pumpkinville settlers have preferred the name "Phoenix" over "Stonewall"?
2. What might the story of Phoenix's founding tell us about Americans' complex relationship to Indians, both living and dead? What might it say about the newcomers' attitude toward the desert environment?
3. What could explain the relatively harmonious relations between Hispanics and Anglos in the 1870s and 1880s?

Enormous cattle drives of more than ten thousand beasts became a common sight and sound on the plains as thousands of wage-labor cowboys drove millions of thundering steers northward each year (see Map 17.6). The number of cattle grew from fifteen million in 1870 to thirty-five million by 1900, by which time Chicago controlled over 90 percent of the nation's cattle market. The drives turned a handful of cattlemen into millionaire "cattle barons" and ranching into a multimillion-dollar business that attracted investors from New York, Boston, and Europe.

By the mid-1870s, the ranching frontier was controlled predominantly by white cattle barons and their East Coast and European investors. However the range itself was racially and ethnically

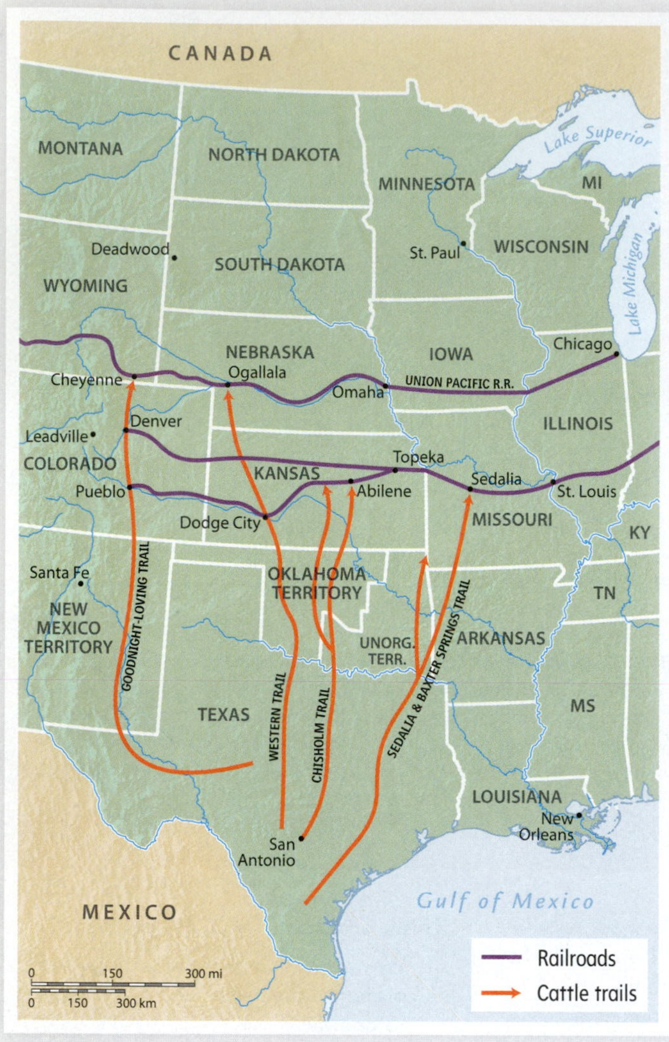

Map 17.6 Driving Cattle North. Dust flew as small armies of cowboys drove hundreds of thousands of cattle northward across the Texas plains in the 1870s. Each trail connected with a railway line, and from there the livestock were freighted to urban slaughterhouses in Chicago, Baltimore, and other major American cities.

Nat Love. More than one in three cowboys was nonwhite, and a significant minority were ex-slaves. Born a slave in Tennessee in 1854, Nat Love went west in the 1870s looking for work as a cowboy. In 1907, he recounted his adventures in a popular autobiography that, like most Wild West writing, played up the romantic, gunslinging image of ranchers that readers had come to expect.

diverse. Contrary to the image presented in twentieth-century cowboy movies, a full third of the West's thirty-five thousand cowboys were Mexican, Indian, or African American—many were former slaves who had left the South and its plantations for the dream of opportunity, freedom, and adventure. Cowboys mixed freely and intimately with one another, generating their own distinct culture, complete with songs, stories, and lingo.

Popular magazines and cheap paperbacks depicted cowboys' lives as romantic, glamorous, and adventure filled. By 1900, this idealized cowboy was a national icon and a figure that embodied the mythology of America as a land of romantic and ruggedly masculine individuals. The reality of work on the range was another matter. Most cowboys rode for long hours in extreme environmental conditions and were poorly compensated. "Oh the cowboy's life is a dreary, dreary life," one campfire song went. "All out in the midnight rain; I'm almost froze with the water on my clothes." During the heyday of the long cattle drives (1865–1885), it took gangs of ten to fifteen herders and over one hundred horses to drive thousands of steers north. A cook accompanied the cowboys, serving unpalatable dried or canned food from a chuck wagon. Most cowboys were young, and few lasted in the business more than a couple of drives. In the dry season, the dust was suffocating, coating the cowboy's face, clothes, and lungs. When the weather was not scorching, it was freezing—and bothered or spooked steers could easily stampede, at great risk to cowboys' life and limb.

THE CATTLE WARS

The era of long cattle drives on the open range drew to a close in the late 1880s. By then, the cattle barons were running so many cattle that the grasslands could no longer sustain them. The rapid

HOT COMMODITIES

Barbed Wire

Because the Indians dominated the prairie until the 1870s, there was little farming and, therefore, fencing in the region. Typically made out of stone, wood, hedge, or brick, fences were expensive and difficult to build—particularly on prairies, where raw materials for building them were scarce. As the Indians were cleared from the land, cattlemen turned the plains into an enormous "open range" along which they drove their stock to market, accessing watering holes along the way.

All that began to change in the late 1870s, as thousands of farmers bought lots on the prairie and as patented, cheap, and easy-to-install fences flooded the market. Made of twisted strands of wire with threaded protrusions, these various forms of "barbed wire" were "bull strong and hog tight," as one manufacturer boasted. In conjunction with the Indian clearances and western land sales, the new approach to fencing sped the enclosure and division of the plains into private property.

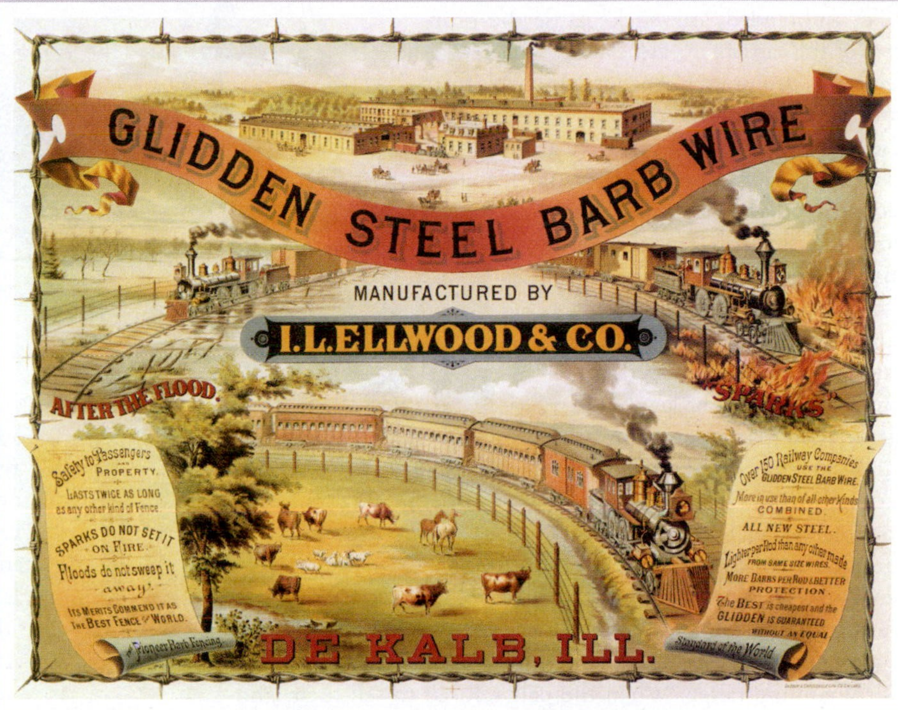

Advertisement for Glidden Steel Barb Wire. One of a thousand designs that came on the market in the 1870s, Joseph Glidden's patented "barb wire" is the type most commonly seen today. Its popularity derived partly from its superior design and partly from the fact that Glidden successfully sued his competitors for patent infringement.

By 1880, settlers were buying eighty million pounds of barbed wire each year, and over a thousand designs were available, many with colorful names such as Split Diamond, Necktie, and Arrow Plate. Farmers enclosed millions of acres of land in just a few years, often blocking access to the watering holes on which cattle drivers depended (and on which Plains Indians had relied before them). Cattlemen objected fiercely, and vigilante fence-cutters swooped down to remove the barriers. Fence cutting became a felony in Texas and other states, and the cattlemen eventually lost the battle against enclosure. But the wealthiest cattlemen adapted to the times, buying up small ranches and farms in the 1890s and accumulating vast holdings.

Railroads were also major consumers of barbed wire, lining the tracks so that livestock would not stray onto the rails. The U.S. government became another top customer as agents laced "the devil's rope," as Indians called it, around forts and reservations, both to keep settlers out and to hold the Indians in. The use of barbed wire as a weapon of war grew internationally in the nineteenth and twentieth centuries, as governments built detention camps and defensive structures and militarized borders. Originally used as a cheap and efficient farm fence, barbed wire had become a universal symbol of war and repression by the mid-twentieth century.

Think About It

1. Why might plains farmers have been so keen to put up fences?
2. What impact did barbed wire have on the plains and their inhabitants?
3. What does the widespread use of barbed wire tell us about farmers' attitudes toward the plains environment?

growth of the herds also forced down the price of beef, crimping profits. After a few years of unusually mild winters and cool summers, the intense climate returned with a vengeance in 1886. Millions of cattle died on the plains that winter. Some ranchers lost 90 percent of their herds, and northeastern and European investors pulled their money from the cattle business.

Efforts by small-scale ranchers to obtain, feed, and protect their own herds also posed a threat to cattle barons in the 1880s. Acquiring 160-acre parcels under the Homestead Act, many ranchers planted hay feed and, for the first time, strung barbed wire fences across the plains—sometimes around water sources (see Hot Commodities: Barbed Wire). With enclosure, old-style cattle drives became far more difficult, much to the cattle barons' consternation. The cattlemen prevailed upon the Wyoming Territory legislature to pass a Maverick Law (1884), which made all wild, unbranded "maverick" cattle the property of the cattlemen's association. This law effectively prohibited smaller ranchers from rounding up mavericks and branding them as their own. "If you stole a few cattle," small ranchers bitterly objected, "you were a rustler," but if you had stolen a few thousand mavericks back in the 1860s, when the range was still Indian land, "you were a cattleman." A number of small ranchers were prosecuted under the law, but juries refused to convict them.

When the courts offered the barons no relief, they resorted to violence. In 1889, cattlemen targeted two homesteaders, Ellen ("Ella") Liddy Watson ("Cattle Kate") and James Averell, each the owner of homestead ranches on the Wyoming range. When the pair refused to sell their land to the cattlemen, vigilantes lynched them. This brazen act of violence galvanized small ranchers, who banded together in Johnson County, northern Wyoming, to protect their property. Events came to a head in the Johnson County War of 1892. Desperate to maintain their monopoly, the barons hired fifty Texas gunmen and sent them to northern Wyoming, where they shot and killed four men associated with the small ranchers. Horrified locals formed their own vigilante force. A blood bath was averted only when President Benjamin Harrison, acting on a desperate telegram from the cattlemen, sent the U.S. Army to restore order, with no further loss of life on either side.

Neither the cattle barons nor their hired guns were prosecuted for the murders. But their efforts to avert the closing of the range came to nothing. Enclosure made sense in light of overgrazing and the return of harsh winters. As fencing accelerated, cattlemen simply joined the rush. Ironically, enclosure, which had originated as a way for small ranchers to maintain their independence, inaugurated a new kind of baron—the ranch baron. A handful of cattlemen bought up vast swaths of the range and soon dominated the cattle business once again.

Ellen Liddy Watson, Riding Tall. Women in the West often enjoyed much greater personal freedom than their counterparts back East, but that freedom occasionally came at a terrible cost. Having divorced an abusive husband, moved west, and acquired her own farm under the Homestead Act, Ellen Liddy Watson was not about to back down when a cattleman demanded she sell him her land. Standing six feet tall and unafraid of asserting her rights, Watson was a formidable opponent and an unconventional woman by the standards of the time. Cattlemen defamed her as "Cattle Kate," accusing her of acquiring cattle by selling sexual favors to cowboys. When she again refused to sell her land, they lynched her.

REINVENTING THE WEST

Migrants' expectations of the West frequently clashed with reality. The economic hardships, climatic extremes, and practical challenges of settler life came as an unwelcome surprise to many. White settlers—who accounted for about 70 percent of the total population by the 1880s—tended to blame other ethnic groups (and increasingly the federal government) for their misfortunes. Prejudice against Chinese, Hispanics, Native Americans, and other "alien" groups hardened into violence, dispossession, and segregation. The vision of the West as a "white man's country"—and as a place where nonwhites were strictly subordinate—was realized through law. The idea of the Wild West was popularized in dime novels, pulp magazines, newspapers, and traveling vaudeville shows that depicted the conquest of the West as heroic, divinely ordained, and a victory for the nation and humankind. Americans continued to think of the West as a place where a white man could get rich quick, but mass culture also began portraying California as an Arcadian paradise of peace, harmony, and natural abundance.

EXCLUDING THE CHINESE

Westerners of all backgrounds closely followed the post-Civil War reconstruction of the South, correctly recognizing that it had important consequences for their own region. The Fifteenth Amendment to the U.S. Constitution, which prohibited racial disenfranchisement, provoked heated controversy, particularly in California and Oregon. The few thousand African Americans who lived in these states in the late 1860s were not the principal concern. Rather, many West Coast whites worried that Reconstruction would inevitably lead to the enfranchisement of the region's tens of thousands of Chinese, Hispanic, and American Indian residents. "How long would we have prosperity," asked one Oregon newspaper, "when four races, separate, distinct and antagonistic should be at the polls and contend for control of government?"

Anti-Chinese sentiment in particular had been building throughout the 1860s, as the Chinese population of California grew. Chinese settlements dotted the California countryside, home to the thousands of farmworkers who annually brought in the harvest and fruit crops. The workers concentrated in the citrus belt, where they developed a packing system in which each piece of fruit was meticulously wrapped in tissue paper before being packed in wooden crates to be displayed at city groceries all over the country. By 1870, over half of California's farmworkers were Chinese.

California Democrats used the issue of minority rights to scare white farmers and workers to the polls in 1868 and 1870. Republicans, they claimed, were committed to land monopoly, railroad corporations, and black and Chinese rights at the expense of white farmers, workers, small businessmen, and widows. Both Oregon and California voted against ratification of the Fifteenth Amendment (which became law nonetheless). To the question posed in Democratic Party leaflet, "Shall Negroes and Chinamen Vote in California?" they answered a resounding "NO!" Black suffrage and Chinese competition for jobs were two sides of the same coin of white disempowerment, Democrats argued, and both threatened the interests and honor of white men. Appealing to whites' racial and economic anxieties, the Democrats warned of an "Asiatic" push for power and of a despotic alliance of "the Mongolian and Indian and African." They eventually prevailed upon Western state legislatures to pass **anti-miscegenation laws,** which prohibited white people from marrying a Native American or person of Chinese, Japanese, Filipino, or other Asian descent. In an effort to assuage these anxieties (and attract votes), the Republican-dominated Congress enacted a Naturalization Act in 1870 that effectively barred Chinese from voting by denying them the privilege of becoming American citizens.

When a global economic recession known as the Long Depression struck in 1873, causing unemployment to spiral, anti-Chinese rhetoric escalated into forcible action and spread to other states. White farmworkers rallied in San Francisco to demand the dismissal of Chinese workers, and vigilantes rode across the Sacramento Valley burning Chinese settlements along the way. White employers who refused to lay off their Chinese workers suffered arson attacks. By 1875, anti-Chinese sentiment was so widespread that Congress enacted the Page Act, the first of two laws limiting Chinese immigration. The new law provided that all Chinese women seeking entry into the United States could be interrogated and excluded if suspected of being prostitutes. Enforcement effectively halted the flow of women, further challenging the viability of Chinese communities.

Seven years later, the Chinese Exclusion Act barred Chinese laborers from entering the country and prohibited people born in China from naturalizing as U.S. citizens. Acts of arson and beatings flared repeatedly in the subsequent years. Chinese Americans retreated to the cities, where they found work in laundries, restaurants, and other service industries. Deprived of their cheap labor force, agricultural employers turned to Japan, which supplied thirty thousand workers after 1890. It was not long before the intense anti-Chinese racism was redirected to the Japanese, a development that led California lawmakers to prohibit the ownership or long-term leasing of land by Asian "aliens" in 1913.

WILDING THE WEST

Before movies and television, vaudeville theater was the most popular form of mass culture—and it helped generate some of the most enduring myths about the West and its peoples. Beginning in the 1870s and gaining widespread popularity in the 1880s, a new kind of vaudeville show reinforced and expanded the idea of white supremacy in the West. Performances presented the region as a wilderness within which white American men realized their fullest potential as individuals. Among the shows, Chicago's *The Scouts of the Prairie* blended history, patriotism, and action-adventure to create an image of the West as the triumphant culmination of American nation building.

The most famous of these performances was Buffalo Bill's Wild West show. In 1874, New Yorker William "Buffalo Bill" Cody, a former hunter and scout for the U.S. Army's plains division, had teamed up with James Butler "Wild Bill" Hickok to take a prairie-themed show on the road. The performances, which typically depicted heroic battles with Indians and exciting bison hunts, proved outrageously popular across the United States, especially in the East. Building on his success, Cody put together Buffalo Bill's Wild West show in 1883. A mix of circus, theater, and documentary, the show included guests whom the press had already made famous as archetypal western figures. Sharpshooter Annie Oakley played herself in embellished reconstructions of gunfights, and Sitting Bull appeared in full battle dress along with twenty Sioux warriors (see Singular Lives: Sitting Bull). Typically staged in sprawling fairgrounds, the show boasted live bison hunts and cattle roundups and simulated well-known battles, including "Custer's Last Stand."

In Cody's West, gunfights, stagecoach robberies, and epic battles were everyday events that offered excitement and opportunities for heroism. Breaking with the usual depiction, Cody's West was big enough for women and Native Americans, too. Years before cinema, television, and the Internet, the action taught Americans—and Europeans, when Cody took the show across the Atlantic—the popular myth of an "untamed" and romantic western frontier. The dust flew, gunfire crackled, and horses thundered, forever imprinting the sights, sounds, and smells of Cody's West on the spectator's memory.

As Buffalo Bill's show traveled the world in the 1880s, the railroads' emerging tourism industry reinforced certain parts of his vision. Railroad promotions no longer portrayed the West as a collection of immense natural resources, ripe for exploitation, as they had initially done immediately after the Civil War. Instead, tourist pamphlets and advertising promoted the majestic wilderness, noble "savages," and various Wild West curiosities. Fitting out trains with larger windows, more comfortable seats, and sleeping and buffet cars, operators promised tourists a thrilling adventure from the safety and comfort of a train.

A flood of dime novels, newspapers, and magazines, replete with images of gunfighters and bandits, sublime landscapes, exotic (but unthreatening) Indians, and bountiful nature, completed the West's transformation—at least in the eyes of a majority of Americans—into the Wild West. Even scholars reinforced the romantic idea of the untamed West. "The existence of an area of free land," wrote historian Frederick Jackson Turner in 1893, "its continuous recession, and the advance of American settlement westward explain American development." The western frontier was the crucible of the American democratic spirit, Turner's influential **frontier thesis** insisted, and it produced a new kind of citizen: rugged, fierce, entrepreneurial, and uniquely American.

Turner ignored the West's northern ranching frontier, the eastward-moving mining frontier, and the complex history of the region's multiple peoples and cultures. But his frontier thesis nevertheless became the lens through which most Americans saw western history. Decades later, Hollywood and television would repeat the theme, and President John F. Kennedy would celebrate space exploration as America's "new frontier" (see Chapter 28). Historians also remained

INTERPRETING THE SOURCES

Advertising the Dream: Palmdale, California

Advertisers played a critical role in shaping Americans' perceptions of California, particularly once the second and third transcontinental railroads boosted travel to the West coast. This 1888 promotional map of Palmdale, a real estate development in the southern Californian desert, typified boosters' efforts to sell land to aspiring migrants back East. Before video, air travel, and color photography, advertisers worked hard to persuade easterners to invest sight unseen in the California dream. Although Palmdale was initially successful, the extreme desert climate soon overwhelmed the townspeople. A flood in 1893 followed by an eleven-year drought drove away most residents, and the town slowly disappeared back into the desert.

Explore the Source

1. What kind of life would a resident of Palmdale lead, according to its promoters? In the 1870s and 1880s, who might have desired that kind of life?
2. Why might the developers have called their town Palmdale?
3. How do the promoters deal with the fact that Palmdale is in a desert—an environment that many people at the time considered uninhabitable?
4. Why might Palmdale's street plan have followed this particular design? What do you think the street names were designed to convey to prospective buyers?

Illustrated Map of Palmdale, San Diego County, 1888. Advertising aimed at prospective homebuyers featured Palmdale's "lucky horseshoe" town plan and supposedly lush environment.

enthralled by the idea of the Wild West until the 1960s, when the civil rights movement led them to question its assumptions and accuracy.

CALIFORNIA DREAMING

California held a special place in the larger mythology of the American West. It had been the subject of individual and collective aspirations long before the 1870s. Whether it was the "Gold Mountain" of which immigrants from Guangdong dreamed or the resource-rich region that, in the words of Karl Marx, promised to turn the Asia-Pacific region into the world's mightiest economy, the "Golden State" captured imaginations around the globe. But in the 1870s, a diverse range of writers, artists, scholars, naturalists, and business interests began depicting California as promising much more than economic wealth. In the eyes of many, it was the place where America's promise—which they interpreted as personal freedom, unspoiled nature, modern technology, and instant wealth—was most likely to be realized (see Interpreting the Sources: Advertising the Dream: Palmdale, California).

California's popular historian Hurbert Howe Bancroft painted the state as a place in which ordinary American men could do extraordinary things. Unlike the citizens of great East coast and European cities, Californians were not weighed down by the past or encumbered by arcane rules, attitudes, and institutions. They had never practiced chattel slavery, and the state had emerged from the Civil War relatively unscathed. Nowhere in the United States or the world, argued Bancroft, was a man freer to pursue his ambitions, whatever they might be. Americans had turned California from a "wilderness into a garden of latter-day civilization."

The free Californians that Bancroft and others had in mind were the minority of inhabitants who were white and male. They were not the women, Chinese, Native Americans, Hispanics, and African Americans who together accounted for over 70 percent of California's population. Bancroft's works were also full of factual errors, especially when it came to the state's violent beginnings and ugly history of racism and genocide (which he largely ignored). But the books nevertheless proved influential, generating a powerful "California fable" that mythologized the state's past and celebrated its supposed future.

A torrent of newspaper and magazine articles further fed Americans' imagination of California as a land of untouched possibility. In his column in the *Los Angeles Times*, journalist Charles Lummis described entering California following a months-long trek from industrial Ohio. "God's country . . . was carpeted with myriad wild flowers, birds filled the air with song, and clouds of butterflies fluttered past me," Lummis wrote. "I waded clear, icy trout brooks, startled innumerable flocks of quail, and ate fruit from the gold-laden trees of the first orange orchards I have ever seen."

The fact that the countryside was blanketed by enormous commercial crops rather than a patchwork of family farms seemed not to register in most Americans' minds. But Californians knew better. Henry George, who had gone west from Pennsylvania in the 1850s and worked his way up from typesetting apprentice to editor in the San Francisco newspaper industry, was the keenest observer of what seemed to be the creeping economic inequality of post–Civil War California. Ascribing rural and urban poverty to the rise of the land barons and the railroads (which monopolized enormous amounts of land), George declared the foundation of California rotten.

Later, in his best seller *Progress and Poverty* (1879), George charged that land policy, corruption, and rampant speculation had deprived the overwhelming majority of Californians of small farms, agrarian communities, and the California dream. "The promised land," he lamented, "flies before us like a mirage." Far from conceding defeat, however, George called upon Californians—and eventually the nation—to work together for land reform and to turn the mirage into reality. Like most Americans, even George still believed that new beginnings and equality of opportunity were possible on earth and that they were most likely to be realized not in Europe or Asia or Latin America but in the United States—most likely, in California.

CONCLUSION

More than any other region of the United States, "the West" of the post-Civil War period was a place of extremes. Between 1865 and 1893, railroads and federally underwritten settlement supplemented the region's climatic and topological extremes with colossal booms and ruinous busts, great hopes and tragic genocides. Whole cities, cultures, and ecosystems were created, destroyed, and reinvented in just a few years. Americans had witnessed breathtaking change before, but never had it come so fast and furiously or with such dramatic effect. By the 1890s, in less than thirty years, disparate and partly unconquered lands had become, in the minds of westerners and other Americans alike, a single, distinctive region. And that region had been quite thoroughly incorporated into the nation's economy, political system, and culture.

Western conquest and settlement in turn remade the nation. The region's minerals, timber, meat, and wheat fed the juggernaut of eastern industrial development and helped create a class of bankers and industrialists of unprecedented wealth. With the help of railroad promotions, mass-circulation magazines, and vaudeville shows, the region fed imaginations, too. The mythological West was partly the product of distinctly eastern fantasies, whether of the "get rich quick," agrarian republican, or civilizing kind. But the West itself—its peoples, topography, climate, and ecosystems—fired those fantasies and, at times, challenged and even bitterly disappointed them. When it became clear that greater economic and environmental forces were thwarting most settlers' aspirations, the West remained, in the eyes of most observers, the place where a freer, more prosperous, and happier life might still be possible.

STUDY TERMS

open range (p. 446)
Pacific Railway Acts (p. 449)
Treaty of Burlingame (p. 451)
Plains bison (p. 451)
Homestead Act (p. 452)
Santee Rebellion (p. 452)
Sand Creek Massacre (p. 453)
Great Sioux War of 1866–1868 (p. 454)
Sioux Treaty of 1868 (p. 454)
Great Sioux War of 1876–1877 (p. 455)
Battle of Little Big Horn (p. 455)
Dawes Severalty Act (p. 457)
Wounded Knee massacre (p. 458)
Comstock Lode (p. 459)
mining frontier (p. 459)
placer mining (p. 459)
commercial mining enterprises (p. 459)
farming frontier (p. 460)
Grangers (p. 461)
ranching frontier (p. 461)
free range (p. 462)
Maverick Law (p. 466)
Johnson County War (p. 466)
anti-miscegenation laws (p. 467)
Naturalization Act (p. 467)
Chinese Exclusion Act (p. 467)
Buffalo Bill's Wild West show (p. 467)
frontier thesis (p. 468)

TIMELINE

1859 Comstock Lode discovered in Nevada

1862 Pacific Railway Act enables building of a transcontinental railroad
Homestead Act passed

1864 Pacific Railway Act enlarges land grants from ten to twenty square miles
Sand Creek Massacre

1865 First Sioux War begins after U.S. attempts to remove Montana Sioux from the plains

1868 Treaty of Burlingame negotiated with China, encouraging Chinese immigration
Sioux Treaty promises Dakota Black Hills territory to all six Sioux tribes

1869 Transcontinental railroad completed

1870 Naturalization Act allows only whites and persons of African descent to become naturalized citizens

1873 Virginia City silver and gold lode discovered in Nevada
Timber Culture Act encourages timber cultivation in the plains

1875 Gold struck in Black Hills
Membership in the National Grange of the Patrons of Husbandry at one million

1876 *Munn v. Illinois* establishes states' right to regulate commerce
Second Sioux War begins, triggered by discovery of gold in the Black Hills
Battle of Little Big Horn

1877 Desert Land Act encourages the irrigation of dry lands in the West and further development
Farmers' Alliance formed in Texas

1878 Timber and Stone Act offers sale of nonarable land for mining and logging

1882 Helen Hunt Jackson publishes *A Century of Dishonor*
Chinese Exclusion Act bans Chinese immigration

1883 William F. Cody debuts *Buffalo Bill's Wild West Show* in Omaha, Nebraska

1884 Maverick Law in Wyoming passed

1887 Dawes Severalty Act breaks reservation lands into 160-acre lots

1889 Ghost Dance movement begins under Wovoka's leadership

1890 More than 150 Sioux Indians massacred at Wounded Knee

1892 Conflict between small ranchers and large cattlemen erupts into the Johnson County War in Wyoming

1893 Frederick Jackson Turner asserts that the frontier created America's distinctive democratic culture

FURTHER READING

Additional suggested readings are available on the Online Learning Center at www.mhhe.com/becomingamerica1e.

Sucheng Chan, *This Bittersweet Soil: The Chinese in California Agriculture, 1860–1910* (1987), traces Chinese immigrants' role in the development of California agriculture.

Emily Greenwald, *Reconfiguring the Reservation: The Nez Perces, Jicarilla Apaches, and the Dawes Act* (2002), looks at how Native Americans responded to land allotment under the Dawes Act.

Julie Roy Jeffrey, *Frontier Women: The Trans-Mississippi West, 1840–1880* (1998), describes women's frontier experiences and their efforts to bring domesticity and "civilization" to the West.

Joy S. Kasson, *Buffalo Bill's Wild West: Celebrity, Memory, and Popular History* (2001), explores the role of memory and celebrity in constructing popular representations of the West.

Kerwin Lee Klein, *Frontiers of Historical Imagination: Narrating the European Conquest of Native America, 1890–1990,* tracks American intellectuals' changing understanding of the European conquest of Native America.

Patricia Nelson Limerick, *A Legacy of Conquest* (1987), considers conquest as the predominant feature that ties the West's various territories and inhabitants together.

Jeffrey Ostler, *The Lakotas and the Black Hills: The Struggle for Sacred Ground* (2010), examines the Lakotas' and the U.S. government's competing claims over the Black Hills.

Alexander Saxton, *The Indispensable Enemy: Labor and the Anti-Chinese Movement in California* (1971), examines the origins of anti-Chinese sentiment in California and the role that labor organizations played in Chinese exclusion.

Kevin Starr, *Americans and the California Dream, 1850–1915* (1986), shows how ideas, perceptions, and myths shaped California.

Elliot West, *The Contested Plains: Indians, Goldseekers, and the Rush to Colorado* (1998), examines the Colorado gold rush's impact on the Plains Indians and highlights the role of environment in the ensuing conflicts.

Richard White, *Railroaded: The Transcontinentals and the Making of Modern America* (2011), traces the rise of transcontinental railroads and the transformative effect they had on the political, economic, social, and physical landscapes.

Donald Worster, *Rivers of Empire: Water, Aridity, and the Growth of the American West* (1985), examines the role water rights played in California's social, political, and economic development.

18

INSIDE ▶

Pleasures of Consumption. A well-dressed crowd takes in the brightly lit Christmas scene at R. H. Macy's department store in 1884.

THE BIG PICTURE

As railroads and factories boomed after the Civil War, the colossal forces of industrialization forever changed the experience of time, work, nature, recreation, and city life. Whole new classes emerged and a modern consumer culture was born. But industrial society also proved unstable, subject not only to great booms but devastating busts, industrial violence, and environmental despoliation.

1865–1885

INDUSTRIALIZING AMERICA

Like millions of Americans in the summer of 1876, sixteen-year-old James Sanders traveled a great distance from home to attend the nation's lavish birthday celebration, the Centennial Exhibition in Philadelphia. A horse-drawn coach carried him and his father from remote Montana Territory to Idaho, where they boarded a train bound for the transcontinental railroad network. Speeding eastward, James wrote excitedly in his diary about the 2,880-foot-long rail bridge that spanned the Missouri River and other feats of engineering that made their journey possible. Once in Philadelphia, James was enthralled by the displays in Machinery Hall, where the world's largest steam engine powered dozens of innovative machines—including the first soda fountain and a contraption that automatically sealed the tops of tin cans. He marveled at Alexander Graham Bell's newfangled telephone and the first incandescent (electric) lightbulb, and tasted strange new consumer foods, such as popcorn, canned beans, and an unfamiliar fruit—the banana (imported from Brazil). Overwhelmed, James opened his diary and painstakingly listed the dimensions and features of each of the hundreds of new machines, buildings, and products on display.

The America that the young westerner encountered was in the throes of one of the most dramatic social revolutions the world has ever seen. In just twenty years (1865 to 1885), the United States was transformed from a modest-sized manufacturing nation to an industrial goliath without economic rival on the world stage. A tremendous burst of technological innovation enabled the production of masses of goods and foodstuffs and the construction of some of the world's largest bridges, buildings, and factories. As young James observed, the transcontinental rail network made it possible to move vast quantities of raw materials, people, and manufactured goods over great distances quickly and relatively cheaply. The railroads, and the telegraphs that typically ran alongside them, also constituted the world's densest communication network, helping to create a single national market that stretched from California to New York and from Canada to the Mexican border.

KEY QUESTIONS

- How did the new industrial network transform American life and the economy?
- What new tensions arose as society industrialized?
- Where did commercialized recreation and mass consumption come from, and how did they change urban culture?
- In what ways did industrialization alter the environment?

Visitors to the Centennial Exhibition climb what eventually became the Statue of Liberty's arm and torch.

While turning the United States into a leading manufacturing power, the industrial and communication revolution also transformed Americans' way of life, identities, and aspirations. Experiences of leisure, the city, foodways, love, childhood, the built and natural environments—and even time itself—all underwent profound change. Bankers and industrialists accumulated wealth more rapidly and on a much greater scale than before, often as a result of speculation in railroad construction. Many of the "new rich" used their wealth to finance the building of whole new cities, such as Chicago, and to transform New York into a global metropolitan center. Across the nation, cities acquired palatial department stores, museums, opera houses, luxury hotels, and—in a monument to the railroads that helped create such enormous wealth—cathedral-like railway stations.

It was partly for this newly wealthy elite that the era came to be known as the **Gilded Age.** Mark Twain and Charles Dudley Warner coined the term as the title for their 1872 novel, in which they satirized the new rich for their extravagant displays of wealth. Not everyone shared in the good times. In many parts of the country, family farms were unable to compete with large-scale commercial agriculture, and the environment was irreparably damaged in the process of obtaining the coal, lumber, and oil that drove industrial growth. In the cities, a grinding poverty took hold in the poorest immigrant neighborhoods, and deadly fires and violent riots broke out with surprising frequency. The dynamic new economy also proved unstable, frequently swinging from boom to bust. By the time of the Exhibition in 1876, it was clear that the forces of industrialization could be as destructive as they were creative.

THE INDUSTRIAL NETWORKING OF AMERICA

The United States' transformation into the world's most productive economy was made possible by new networks of mass communication and transportation. With the completion of the transcontinental railroad in 1869 (see Chapter 17), raw materials, workers, and goods crossed the country with unprecedented speed and at a lower cost than ever before. Trainloads of lumber, coal, iron, cereals, livestock, precious metals, and cotton roared out of the West and South and into the northern industrial states. Manufactured goods, mail, and magazines thundered back along the same rails. Farm hands, miners, and factory workers deployed by train to regions hungry for their labor, and quickly moved again when needed elsewhere. Whole new towns and farming districts sprang up alongside the railroads, and by 1890 Chicago—the hub of the transcontinental network—would become the nation's second-largest city, after New York (see Map 18.1). Although industry grew faster than ever before, large areas of the country, including much of the Deep South, remained unindustrialized and fell even further behind the national average in income, education, and health.

RAILROADS AND THE BIRTH OF BIG BUSINESS

Railroad companies laid some 128,000 miles of track across the United States between 1865 and 1890, connecting much of the nation. Many of the companies were owned by the same entrepreneurial industrialists and bankers who had helped finance the Union's war effort. Investors such as California's Leland Stanford and Pennsylvania's Jay Cooke understood that a national network would enable the freighting of huge volumes of raw materials from the West to factories in the Northeast and Midwest while also creating an expansive national market for goods and information.

Both railroad construction and the finished network radically increased the pace of American industrialization. Laying tracks required heavy machinery and millions of steel rails and rail equipment. American steel output soared from ten thousand tons a year in the 1860s to almost six million tons by 1895. By 1900, the United States was producing more steel than any other nation in the world. Railroad companies built hundreds of railway stations and purchased thousands of freight, stock, and passenger cars, making the railcar and rail equipment business one of the nation's largest and most profitable industries. Keeping the steam engines stoked required millions of tons of coal each year. In response, the railroads' fuel suppliers stepped up production and employed masses of new workers. In all of these growing industries, workers had to be outfitted and fed, which further boosted textile and agricultural production.

Trains became important for transporting workers as well as goods. Thousands of young, unskilled migrant laborers "hopped" trains—riding without a ticket—looking for gainful employment in seasonal businesses such as fruit picking or fluctuating businesses such as copper mining. **Tramping,** as it was called, was quite commonplace after the Civil War, and railroad companies turned a blind eye to it. Many Americans

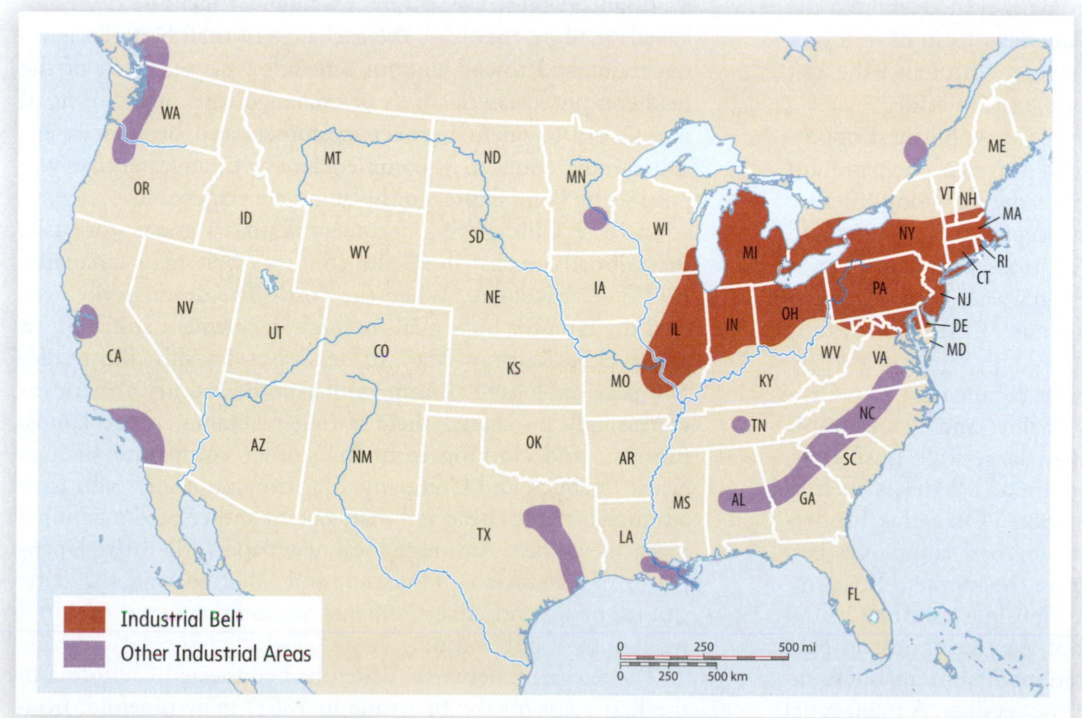

Map 18.1 The Industrial Belt
After the Civil War, manufacturers constructed thousands of factories along the railroad corridors running from Illinois to the East coast. New interregional railroads connected this "Industrial Belt" to the mines, forests, ranches, farms, and wheat and cotton fields of the West and South. Industry also took root in other regions, including the tobacco- and cotton-growing areas of the South, but on a far smaller scale than in the Industrial Belt.

Riding in Style. The luxuriousness of the new Pullman railroad cars—complete with tobacco spittoons—helped make railroad tourism popular and profitable.

considered tramping a normal phase in a young male worker's life, and some, including Walt Whitman, even celebrated the mobility it afforded as a distinctly American form of freedom. "I inhale great draughts of space," wrote Whitman, "the east and west are mine and north and the south are mine."

Paying passengers brought with them new business opportunities. George Pullman anticipated travelers' demand for more comfortable accommodations on the new long-distance hauls. He designed the first luxury sleeping car in 1865 and built an enormous factory for their mass production, near Chicago, two years later. His Pullman Palace Car Company assembled and contracted out thousands of their plush, fully staffed cars to the railroad companies.

As the railroad boomed, the largest companies—the Central Pacific, Union Pacific, Kansas Pacific, and Pennsylvania Railroads—became the country's first large-scale businesses, the precursor to the modern corporation. Magnates such as Jason "Jay" Gould and the "Commodore" Cornelius Vanderbilt aggressively bought out smaller railroad companies and competed with one other to dominate the market. The companies were complex, labor-intensive businesses. The Central Pacific, for example, needed a staff of over ten thousand people to issue tickets, manage the stations, maintain lines and engines, serve passengers, and advertise services. A managerial class of technicians, accountants, and clerical workers was born, and this in turn stimulated the invention of a host of technologies and office equipment (such as the typewriter, which, after 1880, allowed a trained typist to type 50–120 words per minute, as compared with the 25–30 words per minute that a skilled scribe could manage).

The construction of monumental, multiacre terminals in Chicago, Boston, Philadelphia, and New York forcefully reminded city dwellers of the centrality of the railroad to urban prosperity and the new industrial economy. Soon, no aspiring city was complete without one. The soaring, cathedral-like stations also embodied their sponsors' unflappable confidence in themselves and the future.

COMPLETING THE INFORMATION NETWORK

The railroads helped extend the mail and telegraph networks that were completed in the late 1860s and 1870s—creating a national information network that greatly sped the flow of news and marketing materials around the country. The U.S. Railway Mail Service, established in 1869, the same year in which the transcontinental railroad was completed, carried and sorted mail overnight in special mail cars. Eventually, trackside cranes allowed "mail on-the-fly"—the exchange of mail between moving trains and towns without scheduled stops. Much of the mail comprised checks, bills of exchange, and other forms of promissory payment between customers and businesses, enabling transactions to be completed many times faster than was possible by Pony Express or horse-drawn stagecoach.

In 1872, Chicago's Montgomery Ward dry goods store used the railroads to distribute the country's first mass-circulated mail order catalogue. When the post office dramatically lowered the rates for bulk mail in 1885, department stores began using U.S. Railway Mail to send out lavishly illustrated, 500-page catalogs to customers all over the country. Americans increasingly purchased their sewing machines, home lamps, firearms, and clothing from mail order companies such as Sears, Roebuck and Company. Magazine publishers also took advantage of the cheap rail mail system and created a national magazine market. Although local newspapers still thrived, people in San Francisco, Houston, and Chicago read the same stories, news, and advertisements as easterners, and within a week or so of publication.

The telegraph network (which had connected California to the East coast for the first time in 1861) grew ninefold, from

Sears, Roebuck and Co. Catalog, 1895. The company's mail order catalog was typical of those that department stores sent out along the rails.

32,000 miles of wire in 1862, to 291,000 miles by 1880. Even remote areas of the country, such as Wyoming and Oregon, were connected, and in 1866 the *Great Eastern* steam ship laid the first reliable telegraph cable between North America and Europe. Higher quality cable increased communication speeds fifty times over the pre–Civil War rate, to eight words a minute. Other innovations, such as Thomas Edison's quadruplex lines (which allowed the transmission of two messages simultaneously in both directions), led to the circulation of much greater volumes of information.

Much like today's Internet, the telegraph network proved extremely popular with Americans. By 1880, more than thirty-two million messages buzzed along the wires each year. Telegraphed information became a valuable commodity. Investors and newspaper editors paid significant sums for news and information. Stock exchanges installed the new, high-speed Universal Printing Telegraph, which printed stock symbols, their prices, and the number of stocks bought and sold on a paper ribbon (which permitted brokers and reporters to follow price fluctuations). The leading telegraph company, Western Union, introduced the first money transfer service in 1871, enabling money to be "wired" across the country in a matter of minutes. The first systematic weather forecast started in 1869, when the Cincinnati Astronomical Observatory requested that observers from all around the country use the telegraph to report their local weather. The observatory used the data to track storms, and to map and forecast the weather—and then sent out the information along the wires. In the 1870s, the U.S. Army Signals Corps used the same system to establish the weather agency that would eventually become the National Weather Service.

The telegraph network also changed the way Americans experienced national and international events. Local newspapers reported remote disasters and other events within hours of their occurrence, often underscoring their dramatic content. Readers clamored for information about wars, fires, European and American exploration of Asia and Africa, and scientific and technological discoveries. In 1869, the *New York Herald* commissioned writer Henry Morton Stanley to "find" the Scottish missionary and explorer, Dr. David Livingstone, who was allegedly lost in Zanzibar, Africa. Although Dr. Livingstone did not consider himself lost, American newspaper readers thrilled to stories of Stanley's adventure in Africa and his eventual "rescue" of the doctor.

THE CONSTRUCTION BOOM

The Gilded Age was also an era of rapid urban expansion, particularly in the Northeast and Midwest. Older cities more than quadrupled their population in the three decades following the war, and new cities sprang up along the rail lines. Chicago, a vital nexus in east-west commerce, became the fastest growing city in the world and America's second largest city after New York. Tens of thousands of new European and American migrants arrived each year to find work in the city's booming meat, railroad, and construction industries. Whereas older cities used expensive, durable materials such as marble and stone in their construction projects, developers in newer cities such as Chicago and San Francisco worked with lumber milled from the surrounding countryside. In Chicago, whole neighborhoods made of wood were erected in just a few weeks.

Many northeastern cities undertook massive public works projects between 1865 and 1871. City governments paid for the projects by selling bonds to wealthy industrialists, bankers, and merchants in both the United States and Europe. These private-public partnerships sparked one of the biggest construction booms in American history, providing tens of thousands of workers with employment and generating unprecedented profits for developers. They also gave the cities their present-day form and character.

In New York, Democratic Party leader William "Boss" Tweed (see Chapter 19) undertook a massive construction and public

Opening of the Brooklyn Bridge, 1883. Tens of thousands gathered to witness the event. The crowd was so huge that twelve people were stampeded to death. **Questions for Analysis:** What do the artists try to emphasize in this picture of the Brooklyn Bridge? Why was bridging the river between Brooklyn and Manhattan an occasion for mass celebration?

works program in 1870. He commissioned the building of thousands of sewers and water and gas pipe lines and authorized the construction of New York's 1811 grid plan, which called for wide modern avenues bisected at regular intervals by numbered cross streets in upper Manhattan. The laying of infrastructure stimulated a swarm of private housing construction projects along the new routes, most of it of far higher quality than the older tenements of lower Manhattan. A few blocks west, New York's booming financial industry bankrolled a great wave of demolition and reconstruction. Dozens of new banks, insurance companies, and commodities exchanges established their headquarters on or near Wall Street. Buildings began to move skyward, topping a record seven and a half floors in 1870.

Another record was broken that year when construction got under way on the largest project ever before built on American soil—the Brooklyn Bridge. Connecting the largest and third-largest cities in America (New York City and Brooklyn, which had not yet merged), the bridge became a celebrated icon of progress, industry, and urban growth.

MASS PRODUCTION COMES OF AGE

Before the Civil War, industrialization had been confined mostly to the textile industry and a handful of other businesses such as clock making. The United States had imported the majority of its manufactures from Britain. After the war, the rapid growth of cities and the railroads' ability to move masses of raw materials, goods, people, and information fueled the industrialization of the economy as a whole. Manufacturers, mining companies, food growers, and service providers all looked for ways of producing the greatest volume of goods and services in the shortest time, and with the aid of machinery wherever possible. They also began experimenting with new ways of efficiently organizing their businesses and advertising the unprecedented volume of goods they were producing. The result was a revolution not only in the workplace but also in American culture at large.

In heavy industry and manufacturing, employers transformed "the American System" of manufacturing (which had been used in some factories since the 1810s) into a system of mass production. They divided the production process into many different phases, none of which required a great deal of skilled labor, and most of which could be performed in sequence in one large factory. In the manufacture of lightbulbs, for example, one worker would spend her day repeatedly inserting filaments into thousands of bulbs. Another closed the bulbs and tested them on an electrified plate. Some wrapped the bulbs in protective paper, and others simply fastened labels to finished packages. By the 1880s, mass production principles were being applied in other areas, including commercial

The Great Union Stockyards of Chicago, 1878. The railroad network helped make Chicago the center of the emerging meat industry. This aerial view of the Union Stockyards shows the rails on which livestock rolled in from the West and the 375-acre stockyards in which they were held, slaughtered, and processed.

Southern California Citrus Fair, Chicago, 1886. Purpose-built refrigerated fruit cars, small armies of low-wage migrant workers, and an extensive national railroad network made it possible for California orange growers to harvest and ship millions of navel oranges to midwestern and East coast cities every year. Growers used the new color advertising and city fairs to entice consumers to brighten their tables with the fruit during dark winter days.

laundries, which replaced hand ironing with heavy steamrollers and substituted strong chemical cleansers for soap to speed up the washing process.

The production, processing, and distribution of food were also industrialized in these years. Railroads made it possible to distribute mass amounts of grains, meat, fish, dairy, and fruit and vegetables. Rail lines connected the fisheries and orange groves of California and the wheat-growing and cattle-ranching plains of Minnesota and Texas to the grocery stores, dining tables, and food carts of the big northeastern cities. Whereas before the 1870s, city people bought locally produced food, by 1900 most ate food that had been rail freighted from thousands of miles away.

Meat was the first food to become a large-scale industry. Rail lines made it relatively easy to transport livestock from the West to slaughterhouses in Chicago, and the advent of efficient ice and refrigerated cars meant that the meat could be processed, packaged, and freighted over many miles to big East coast cities and Europe. In 1864, a consortium of nine railroad companies opened the world's largest stockyards outside of Chicago. Hogs were slaughtered and processed at the unprecedented rate of over a million a year by the 1870s—or approximately twenty thousand a week. Most of the meat was packed onto nearby railcars and sent east to New York and other big cities.

Northeasterners were initially suspicious of nonlocal meat and sausage—a sentiment encouraged by local slaughterers and butchers whose jobs were threatened by Chicago's meatpacking industry and who hung window signs reading "No Chicago-dressed meats sold here!" When meat came prepackaged or already ground into sausage, it was difficult to tell whether it was fresh and disease free. But the steady supply and lower price of mass-processed meat soon overcame consumers' resistance (see How Much Is That?). Unable to compete, local slaughterhouses and beef farming declined and city dwellers stopped keeping hogs. By 1900, most urban consumers ceased to know where the livestock they were eating were from, or how they had been raised and processed. (New York, where local kosher slaughterhouses continued to supply

How Much Is That?

A Pound of Bacon

By 1881, the price of bacon—one of the most affordable meats and an important component of the working-class diet—had fallen to just 14 cents per pound, or about $3.28 in today's dollars. Thanks to refrigerated railcars and Chicago's "disassembly line," which sped up the slaughtering, dressing, and packaging of meat, bringing home the bacon had never been cheaper.

Jewish consumers, and San Francisco, where citizens insisted on keeping meat local, were the only major exceptions.)

By 1885, food production was a major industry, and food was becoming a mass produced commodity. Across all social classes, Americans' consumption of fresh and locally produced foods and raw ingredients such as flour and baking soda gradually declined, while sales of processed, refrigerated, and manufactured foods climbed steadily. By 1900, manufactured food accounted for one-third of the value of all commodities produced in the United States.

THE ENERGY REVOLUTION

Keeping the new industrial economy running required large amounts of power. For the first time, fossil fuels such as coal and petroleum—drilled from deposits deep within the earth's crust—became essential. Demand for coal skyrocketed. Coal fired the steam engines that drove the trains and much of the heavy industrial machinery. Gas derived from coal lit the streetlamps that many cities installed in the 1880s, and lump coal eventually fueled the first electricity stations (which enabled the construction of the first urban electric tramways, beginning with the Richmond, Virginia, system in 1888). By then, fossil-fuel-based electricity had become a common power source in a variety of businesses.

Demand for petroleum products boomed, and the nation began its long-term dependency on fossil oil. Before the Civil War, people had fueled their lamps and heaters with a wide range of whale, wood, and animal-based oils. In 1862, after the federal government levied a tax on the alcohol used in the most popular lamp oil, petroleum-derived kerosene (which did not contain alcohol) became the dominant fuel source for home lighting. Although petroleum would not be widely used as engine fuel until the early twentieth century, petroleum byproducts were used as lubricants for the increasing number of machine gears and other moving parts. As the need for these products expanded, dozens of oil fields sprang up in Pennsylvania, Ohio, and West Virginia. As in the railroad industry, large-scale businesses such as John D. Rockefeller's Standard Oil company soon emerged to dominate the market.

Surprisingly, industrialization also increased the country's dependence on a much older source of power—the horse. Although coal-fired steam engines powered the nation's trains, horses were the principal source of motor power elsewhere. Horses hauled street trams, carried firefighters and their engines to emergencies, and transported food and goods off boats and docks. In the farming sector, horses were needed to draw the heavy, mechanized threshers that sorted grain and the wagons that carried produce to the canneries and railway depots. Even the "iron horse" railroad engines depended on horses to deliver the coal that fired their boilers. For the first time, in the 1870s, the equine population of major cities such as Boston exceeded the number of human residents. Breeders also successfully doubled the weight—and hauling power—of the average city horse from 900 to 1,800 pounds.

CORPORATE MONOPOLIES

It was in the energy and railway sectors that the **modern corporation** first emerged. Before the Civil War, state or local government had issued certain groups of individuals a charter, granting them the right to incorporate their business, usually for the purposes of constructing a utility of public value (such as a dam or railroad). Incorporation allowed the business to hire, fire, and make contracts, much like a "natural person." Most important, it also took much of the risk out of business ventures by protecting the owners from personal liability for the corporation's debts (should the company go bust, for instance). After the war, railroads and other big businesses sought to extend the scope of incorporation to include all manner of activities, not just those of obvious public benefit.

Railroad lawyers also began to push the courts to grant corporations the same rights of due process guaranteed persons under the Fourteenth Amendment. The Supreme Court eventually complied, in 1882, by which time most legislatures had dropped the traditional public service requirement. The modern corporation also had a distinctive organizational structure, with a large class of managers (including accountants, clerks, and lawyers) responsible for overseeing everyday operations.

A few Gilded Age corporations became trusts or **monopolies.** Building on the business model of the great railroad companies, John D. Rockefeller, owner of the

Get Your Standard Oil Kerosene Here! By integrating all phases of production and distribution, setting prices lower than his competitors, and opening retail outlets that stocked general provisions and just one brand of kerosene—his own—John D. Rockefeller was able to dominate the home lamp fuel market.

Standard Oil Company, moved aggressively to corner the petroleum market. His company took control of the entire process, from drilling through piping and refining, barreling, distributing, wholesaling, and retailing. Rockefeller systematically cut his prices so low that smaller producers could not compete. General stores had to stock the cheaper Standard Oil kerosene or lose customers.

Tactics such as these gave Rockefeller a near-monopoly in oil, and by 1879 he controlled 90 percent of the nation's oil production. Carnegie Steel, Western Union telegraph and, eventually, the electric companies established similar monopolies using the same approach. Likewise, in food production, Henry Heinz, National Biscuit, Quaker Oats, Campbell, and the Swift and Armour meat corporations consolidated and came to dominate the canned goods, cookie, cereals, soups, and meat markets, respectively. A handful of businesses even dominated the state prison systems, putting some thirty thousand convicts to work in manufacturing, mining, railroad construction, and commercialized agriculture by 1886. Although the modern corporation made industry more productive than ever before, most Americans were ambivalent about it—and, as business leaders eventually learned, they were outright hostile toward the monopolistic kind (see Chapter 20).

SPEED AND TIME IN INDUSTRIAL CULTURE

America's industrial network changed the experience of speed, time, and distance. The transcontinental railroad made it possible to reach the opposite coast in seven days rather than many weeks. The ability to move rapidly across vast distances made the traditional practice of local timekeeping seem impractical. Before 1883, most towns estimated time locally by synchronizing clocks and watches according to the position of the sun. Noon in Los Angeles might be 12:18 p.m. in San Francisco and 12:16 p.m. in Seattle. This created considerable difficulty for railroads that needed precise schedules. One solution was to telegraph time from astronomical observatories (which charged a fee for the service) to the stations. Conductors set their pocket watches according to each station clock as they stopped along the line. Rail stations mounted several clocks, showing passengers the time in a number of different cities.

But this complex system proved deeply confusing for travelers. Consequently, in 1883 the railroad corporations adopted four standardized regional time zones—Eastern, Central, Mountain, and Pacific. Americans generally accepted the change, and at noon, on November 18, they set their watches and clocks accordingly. The following year, the United States, Britain, and Europe agreed on international time zones.

Americans also came to experience and celebrate speed on a scale and with an intensity unknown before the Civil War. In cities, speed competitions of various kinds became popular amusements, and the word *record* took on its current meaning as the highest rate ever attained. Thoroughbred horse racing, which was organized and commercialized for the first time in the late 1860s, became a popular attraction for middle-class and upper-middle-class people. Illegal betting pools formed in the cities, and bookies used the telegraph system to send near-instantaneous reports of the races and winners.

Telegraph operators, typeface setters, steel drivers, and dozens of other tradesmen took considerable pride in their ability to do skilled work at great speed. In a world in which the skilled trades were increasingly endangered by mechanization, audiences thrilled to the virtuosity of the racing telegraphers and typesetters in speed competitions. Especially as more women entered the trades, male "swifts" used the races to maintain their domination of the field. New experiences of speed were often thrilling—but they could also be troubling. Some commentators even argued that time pressures were affecting Americans' health and well-being (see Interpreting the Sources: George M. Beard, *American Nervousness*).

Typesetters Rule. Despite the mechanization of other phases of the printing process, setting the metal typeface on printing plates remained a time-consuming and highly skilled task requiring the typesetter to position each individual letter by hand. Here students at the historically black Claflin University in Orangeburg, South Carolina, set type and run the school's printing press.

INTERPRETING THE SOURCES

George M. Beard, American Nervousness

Gilded Age Americans were thrilled and fascinated by speed in all its forms. But in the 1880s, a growing number of social observers warned that America's competitive, speed-oriented culture was endangering people's physical and mental health. One such critic, Dr. George M. Beard, cautioned that a new and distinctively American disease—"neurasthenia" (literally, weakness of the nerves)—was on the rise. Beard's book, *American Nervousness: Its Causes and Consequences* (1881), proved especially influential among physicians and affluent and elite Americans, many of whom were already worried about the physical and spiritual side effects of the nation's transition from an agrarian to an advanced industrial society. By the 1890s, tens of thousands of wealthy urbanites had been diagnosed with neurasthenia and were undergoing calming and revitalizing therapies in serene mountain sanitariums and health spas. For those unable to afford such facilities, a slew of cheap commercial elixirs and tonics (including Coca-Cola) promised to counter the supposedly enervating side effects of modern life.

A new crop of diseases has sprung up in America, of which Great Britain until lately knew nothing, or but little. A class of functional diseases of the nervous system . . . seem to have taken root under the American sky, where their seed is being distributed . . . . No [other] form of civilization . . . possessed such maladies. Among the signs of American nervousness are . . . susceptibility to stimulants and narcotics; . . . nervous exhaustion; hay fever; neuralgia; . . . early and rapid decay of teeth; premature baldness; . . . [and] sensitiveness to cold and heat. . . .

The perfection of clocks and the invention of watches have something to do with modern nervousness, since they compel us to be on time, and excite the habit of looking to see the precise moment, so as not to be late for trains or appointments. . . . Punctuality is a greater thief of nervous force than is procrastination. . . . We are under constant strain, mostly unconscious, oftentimes in sleeping as well as in waking hours, to get somewhere or do something at some definite moment. . . . The telegraph is a cause of nervousness the potency of which is little understood. Before the days of Morse and his rivals, merchants were far less worried than now and less business was transacted in a given time; prices fluctuated far less rapidly, and the fluctuations which now are transmitted instantaneously over the world were only known then by the slow communication of sailing vessels or steamships. . . . [Now], every cut in prices in the wholesale lines in the smallest of the Western cities becomes known in less than an hour all over the Union; thus competition is diffused and intensified.

Explore the Source

1. In Beard's view, what is the relationship between the relatively new technologies of the Gilded Age and Americans' health?
2. Why, according to Beard, might Americans be more prone to nervous diseases than other peoples?
3. Why do you think Beard's work made good sense to some Gilded Age Americans? For whom might it have been irrelevant?

YEARS OF UNREST

The sense that industrialization could be a disruptive as well as a creative force intensified during the boom years of the late 1860s and early 1870s. Industrialization generated unprecedented inequalities and new kinds of social crisis, suffering, and tension. Also, the economy proved prone to wild swings between prosperous booms and devastating busts. In 1873, the country was thrown into the longest, most severe recession it had ever seen. Four years later, with no signs of relief on the horizon, workers undertook the country's first nationwide railroad strike. Business was paralyzed, the federal government stepped in, and the U.S. Army was deployed against civilians in the North.

NEW CLASSES, NEW ASPIRATIONS

The rapid growth of American industry attracted an average of three hundred thousand laborers per year to the United States between 1865 and 1871—many more than in the prewar years (although an even larger wave of immigration was to follow). European workers and peasants accounted for most of the mass migration, but significant numbers of immigrants also arrived from Southeast China and Mexico. The great majority of European immigrants settled in and around industrial cities such as Detroit, New York, and Chicago, whereas Chinese and Mexican immigrants were concentrated in the West (see Chapter 17). Immigrants typically found themselves in the lower classes of American society, offered employment in the least skilled, worst paid, and most dangerous jobs, such as deep shaft mining and sweatshop clothing manufacture. White native-born workers were more likely to perform skilled labor, whether in smaller-scale workshops (such as shoe, cigar, and printing works) or large-scale industries such as the steel industry. Protestants tended to achieve higher paid positions faster than Catholics. And men were paid a significantly higher wage than women.

Immediately after the Civil War, skilled white workers were generally optimistic that the tremendous economic growth of the time was good for them and good for the republic. Like the

***The Bulls and Bears in the Market*, by William Holbrook, 1879.** Holbrook's painting imagines the Wall Street metaphor of bull and bear markets—upward and downward market trends—coming to life in a melee of disorder and violence. Like Holbrook, many Americans worried that the new industrial economy was highly volatile and that its creative potential was accompanied by an awesome capacity for destruction.

skilled workers of the pre–Civil War period, they thought of wage earning as a temporary phase of life. Many aspired to accumulate enough savings to one day open their own workshops. Believing upward mobility was imminent, they pressed employers and legislators to reduce work hours from ten or twelve hours to eight hours per day, so as to leave eight hours for "self-improvement" in the form of education, recreation, and community work (and eight hours for sleep). But skilled workers became less optimistic in the early 1870s, as machinery and technological innovation rendered their skills obsolete. Meanwhile, unskilled, underpaid industrial jobs grew. Few workers accumulated enough savings to start their own businesses, and many felt trapped in industrial labor.

Industrialization also brought about important changes within the North's wealthiest classes. The great convergence of immigrant labor, massive investment, and technological innovation brought the owners of the railroad, steel, oil, and food companies unprecedented wealth. Although merchants—the most prominent prewar elite—remained dominant among New York's wealthy, industrialists and bankers were clearly on the rise. Industrialists and bankers grew wealthier than established merchants and exercised more power in the new industrial economy.

Clerical workers, accountants, lawyers, and other white-collar workers also began to see themselves differently as their number grew and they played an increasingly important role in American life. Before 1865, few thought of these various professions as making up a single middle class. But during the 1870s, white-collar workers came to forge a new, middle-class identity and way of life. Whereas before the Civil War they had celebrated skilled work and farming as the sources of republican virtue, in the 1870s they increasingly viewed intellectual work and the higher technical arts as the most honorable forms of labor. Most middle-class occupations established associations and imposed standards on practitioners in an effort to promote professionalism and distinguish themselves from the "lower" trades and industries (such as carpentry and manufacturing). New York City lawyers, for example, established the Association of the Bar in 1870, declaring that law was a "noble profession" and not a "trade with the rest."

RIOT, FIRE, AND FLU

Both the pace of change and the development of a large working class concerned many middle- and upper-class Americans. In the cities, in particular, the visible presence of poverty provoked widespread anxiety. Bankers, industrialists, and an increasing number of middle-class commentators argued that cities were disorderly, dangerous places. Many also feared that a potentially violent revolutionary movement was taking root amongst workers and the poor.

A series of dramatic and well-publicized events in the United States and Europe in the early 1870s fueled this anxiety. In March 1871, the transatlantic telegraph broke news of a large-scale workers' uprising in Paris, France. Workers took over their city government in response to the French president's unpopular effort to disarm the citizens' militia. The Paris Commune, as the workers' government was known, implemented many of the social reforms that workers in America and Europe had been demanding since the end of the Civil War, including a shorter workday. The Communards barricaded the streets to defend against the French army and took a number of prominent and wealthy Parisians hostage. Although the army defeated the Communards in a matter of weeks, the fierce battles and consequent fires claimed the lives of over twenty-five thousand Parisians (including many of the hostages).

News and images of the workers' uprising sparked panic among the middle and propertied classes of Britain, Europe, and the United States. In America, elites and the middle class worried that the Commune would be the first in a worldwide spate of workers' insurrections against property interests. "The reign of the Commune," declared *The Nation*'s editor, "strikingly illustrates the truth of observation that the barbarians . . . live not in the forests, but in the heart of our large cities." Calvinist minister and social reformer Charles Loring Brace cautioned that "there are just the same explosive social elements beneath the surface of New York as of Paris." Brace and others labeled the urban poor "the dangerous classes."

A few months after the Commune, a large-scale riot in New York escalated fears. Tensions between Irish Protestants and Irish Catholics had been mounting since the New York City Draft Riots of 1863. In July 1871, the New York City government denied Irish Protestants' request for a parade permit, on the grounds that the previous year's parade had sparked a deadly riot. But pressure from the city's Protestant elite led to a reversal of this decision. The parade went ahead as planned with a route that would take the Protestants (also known as Orangemen) through the city's Irish Catholic neighborhoods. The governor of New York took the precaution of calling out the National Guard to line the parade route. As the parade got under way, the streets erupted in riot. The police charged the Catholic crowds and the National Guard opened fire. By the end of the day, at least 63 people had been killed and over 140 seriously injured. Almost all the fatalities were Irish Catholics, and not a single Orangeman died. The middle-class press blamed the disorder on Irish Catholics, warning that they posed as much of a threat as Parisian Communards, and condemned Boss Tweed's government for tolerating their alleged conduct.

Anxieties about urban disorder and working-class rebellion continued to grow after the Great Chicago Fire of October 1871. The fire raced along Chicago's wooden sidewalks and swallowed up thousands of its wooden buildings in a great cauldron of flames. By the time the fire burnt itself out three days later, it had killed three hundred people, razed eighteen thousand commercial buildings and homes, and thrown tens of thousands of Chicagoans into the streets (see States of Emergency: The Great Chicago Fire). Anxious that the disaster would launch the city into full-scale panic, the mayor declared martial law and requested U.S. Army general Philip Sheridan to maintain order. Like the Paris Commune and the New York riots, the fire became the object of anxious discussion about "the dangerous classes" and a symbol of the potentially catastrophic effects of rapid industrial growth.

It was amid this general feeling of unease and social tension that the country entered its first full-scale energy crisis. The Great Epizootic of 1872 was probably the worst pandemic of horse influenza the world has ever seen and, because horses were essential to industrial society, it paralyzed key sectors of the economy and brought whole cities to a standstill. The epidemic probably started near Toronto, Canada, in September 1872. Infected horses coughed, developed high fevers, and slumped to the floor of their stalls, helpless, for days at a time. The virus spread quickly southward to Boston, New York, Philadelphia, Washington, D.C., and Charleston. These cities' filthy, cramped, multilevel stables proved a perfect incubator for the contagion. The virus soon swept westward, striking down Chicago's horses along the way, and south to Florida and Cuba as well. By December, almost the entire horse population of North America was afflicted.

Most of the horses eventually recovered. But the epidemic temporarily wrought havoc on cities, factories, and countryside. Everywhere, men formed teams to draw carts, wagons, and reapers in an effort to restart the economy. Mass transit systems ground to a halt. City fires raged out of control, as horse-drawn fire engines were hauled to the scene by hand. In one such emergency, the Great Fire of Boston, fourteen people died and over 776 buildings were lost. Goods and rotting food piled up on docks that horse-drawn wagons typically serviced. Coal mines and other industries all but ceased operations, as did the trains. Food production was also disrupted, because farmers' horses could no longer draw the heavy, mechanized threshers and ploughs or take the usual wagonloads of produce to market. Even national security was affected. In the Southwest, for example, the U.S. Cavalry (and their Apache combatants) were compelled to dismount their ailing horses and wage war on foot.

THE DEPRESSION YEARS

By 1873, after more than a decade of meteoric growth, the national economy was dangerously overextended. The United States' capacity to grow, refine, manufacture, and freight massive volumes of food, raw materials, and goods far exceeded the nation's (and the world's) capacity to absorb them. Goods piled up, prices fell, and industry's profits shrank. Meanwhile, entrepreneurs' feverish drive to raise the capital necessary to lay railroads and build great cities had led many banks to issue too much stock and grant massive loans to risky borrowers. President Ulysses S. Grant had gradually tightened the money supply, with the result that money and credit were increasingly scarce.

Under these conditions, the failure of the venerable Jay Cooke and Company bank (which had financed the Union

STATES OF EMERGENCY

The Great Chicago Fire

The careless flicking of a cigarette butt into a barn was probably what ignited the most devastating urban fire of the nineteenth century on October 8, 1871. Powerful winds propelled the blaze, creating new fire centers, devouring whole neighborhoods, and creating a heat so intense that mortar dissolved, iron melted, and trees exploded from the heat of their own resin. Marble mansions and flimsy immigrant tenements alike fell to the flames. Even sturdy downtown railroad stations, post offices, theaters, and municipal buildings crumbled. By the time the fire burned itself out, three hundred people had died, and the flames had consumed 50 million feet of milled timber, 1.5 million bushels of wheat and corn, and 80,000 tons of coal.

***Chicago in Flames: Scene at Randolph Street Bridge*, Currier and Ives Lithograph, ca. 1872–1874.** In their colorful depictions of the Great Chicago Fire, printmakers Currier and Ives captured many Americans' growing anxiety that rapid industrialization was unleashing destructive societal forces. In this popular print, unrealistic sky-high flames tower over a helpless city.

Three other large-scale fires broke out that day, all around the shores of Lake Michigan. By far the worst was in rural Peshtigo, Wisconsin, where 2,500 people died (more than eight times the number in Chicago). But it was the idea of a great American commercial city in flames that gripped the nation's imagination. The new, high-volume telegraph system and the trans-Atlantic cable transmitted news of the Great Chicago Fire around the country and the world, making it the nation's first instantaneously reported catastrophe. People in New York, London, and San Francisco read in awe of the speed with which the city was being destroyed and of the fire's warlike horrors. The financial markets spun into turmoil as the city melted into air. National magazines sent photographers to Illinois to document the ruins and for weeks afterward flooded readers with images of the gutted city.

Although fires were common occurrences in Chicago, many commentators interpreted the inferno as a sign of growing urban disorder. The *New York Times* published the alleged confession of an exiled Paris Communard who, the newspaper claimed, had ignited the fire "to humble the men who had waxed rich at the expense of the poor." More typically, the press blamed the fire on Irish immigrant Catherine O'Leary, whose cow was reported to have kicked over a lantern she had negligently left in her barn. (In fact, two young men had probably started the fire by accident.) For many middle-class Americans, O'Leary and Chicago's working poor symbolized the threat that Irish and other ethnic immigrants supposedly posed to America's dominant white, Protestant culture. The press reported on the "awful democracy" the fire unleashed, and its displacement onto the streets of a great mass of people drawn from all classes and ethnicities. Poorer Chicagoans did not attack or rob the well-to-do, but many middle-class and wealthy Americans insisted that they were poised to do so. The U.S. Army's "prompt, bold and patriotic action," wrote one editor, had saved the city from almost certainly being "destroyed by the cutthroats and vagabonds."

Think About It

1. Why did the Great Chicago Fire captivate the public imagination more than the other fires that happened that day?
2. What role did mass media play in shaping people's perception of the fire?
3. Why were middle-class Americans quick to blame immigrants, the working class, and the urban poor for the fire?
4. Why did some newspapers consider the displacement of peoples from all classes and ethnicities an "awful democracy"?

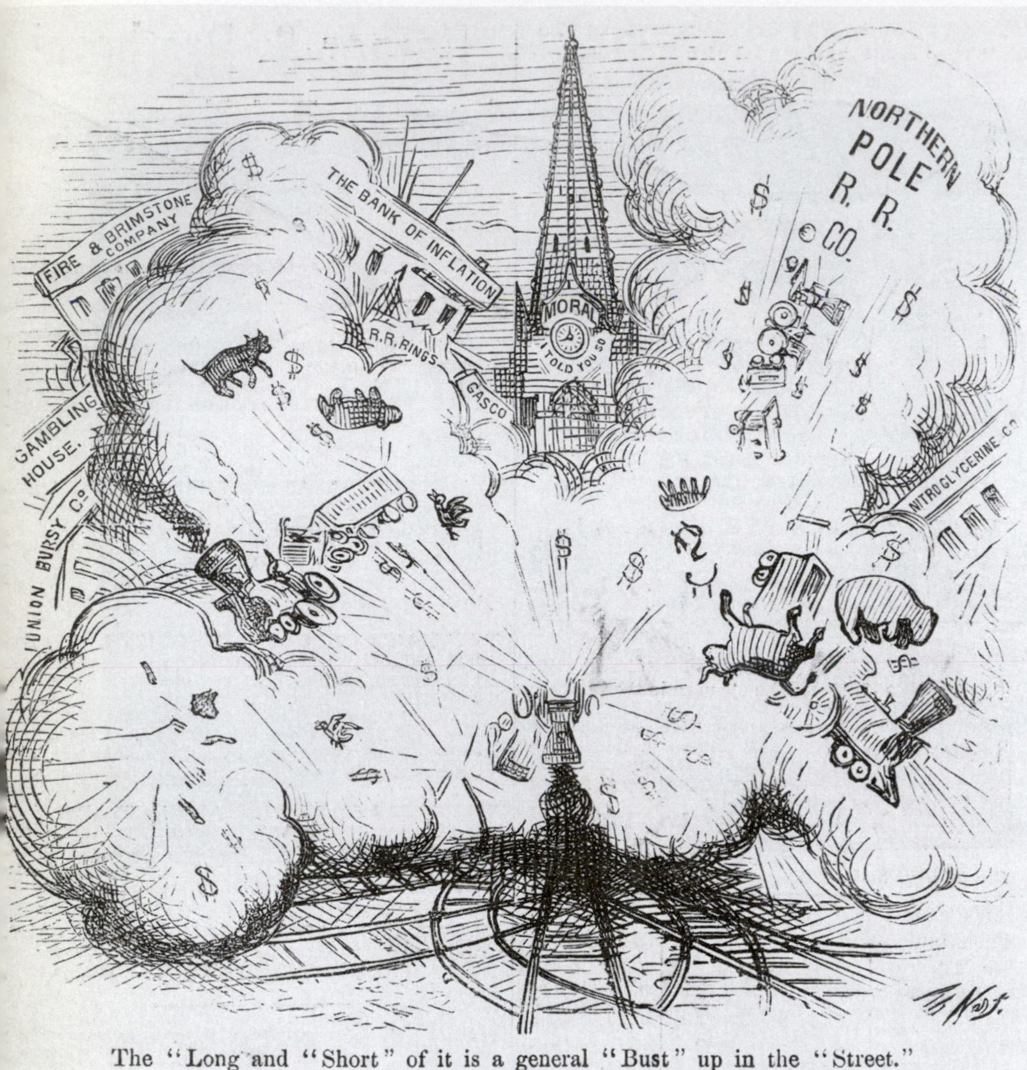

The "Long" and "Short" of it is a general "Bust" up in the "Street."

Wall Street Goes Bust. This Thomas Nast cartoon, which shows railroad companies, banks, and bulls exploding in the air above Wall Street, satirizes the self-destructive tendency of financial speculation. By presenting Trinity Church and its "morality" sign as unscathed by the explosion, Nast suggests that Wall Street is the victim of its own speculative immorality.

war effort and the second transcontinental railroad) triggered a general financial panic. Customers raced to withdraw their savings, but the banks, which had loaned their customers' money to other enterprises, could not meet the demand. Stockholders panicked and placed massive sell orders. Overwhelmed, the New York Stock Exchange closed its doors for ten days, prompting a series of other business failures and tipping the national economy into a deep recession known as the Long Depression. Lasting until early 1879, the recession was the most severe the country had ever experienced.

The Long Depression intensified both the destructive and the creative forces of industrialization. Over eighteen thousand business failed in two years, and more than half the country's railroad companies and banks went bankrupt. But this enabled large-scale corporations such as Rockefeller's Standard Oil to aggressively buy out failing enterprises for a fraction of their worth. In each of the steel, oil, coal, banking, wheat, processed food, meat, and rail sectors, the pre-depression tendency toward efficient, large-scale corporations was greatly accelerated.

The depression threw four million people out of work. Those who remained employed suffered wage cuts of up to 50 percent. Northern cities suspended city-funded construction projects, putting thousands out of work. As the international price of cotton fell by almost 50 percent, cotton growers experienced a devastating drop in their income. Many small artisans and businesses in the South entered bankruptcy and even some of the region's largest industries (including the Tredegar Iron Works, in Richmond) collapsed. The Freedmen's Savings Bank failed, taking with it the life savings of tens of thousands of black sharecroppers and laborers. In the West, the price of food crops such as wheat and corn also declined dramatically, with ruinous consequences for farmers. Thousands of family-owned farms failed, and many families were forced to leave the land.

Tensions between workers and employers escalated around the country. In spring 1874, tens of thousands of hungry, unemployed laborers staged mass demonstrations in the nation's cities, demanding "Work or Bread!" and the resumption of publicly funded works projects. Railroad workers, miners, and textile hands struck as well. But as the search for work and relief became more desperate, employers found it easier to find men willing to break strikes. Police and state militias violently dispersed strikers in New York, Chicago, and San Francisco. The union movement lost all but 50,000 of its 300,000 members, and the number of national unions fell from thirty-three to just nine.

Many workers hit the rails in search of employment. But employment was hard to find, and wages were often so low as to barely cover the cost of daily bread. As a result, tens of thousands of migrant laborers had little choice but to keep tramping and seek food and shelter from state and private charities.

Urban middle-class commentators interpreted the desperate poverty of migrant workers as a refusal to work and a grave threat to the social order. They no longer thought of tramping as something socially useful and instead coined the pejorative word *tramp* to describe the migrant unemployed. "An army of tramps" was ranging over the countryside, many newspaper editors warned, living off of public assistance, refusing to do an honest day's work, and helping themselves to whatever they wanted from local citizens and their homes. Although the unemployment was caused by a lack of jobs, critics argued that migrant workers' poverty stemmed from the fact they were not subject to the disciplinary institutions of home, workplace, and church. Further, state and city government should prevail on them to accept all work offered, regardless of the wage rate, and public and private charity should be ended. Lawmakers enacted anti-tramp and **vagrancy laws** that resembled the southern black codes of 1865 (see Chapter 16) and that compelled poor adults to carry proof of employment and/or a fixed abode. Tens of thousands of unemployed people—including novelist Jack London—were arrested and sentenced to hard labor in the county penitentiary or on farms.

Workers, farmers, and small ranchers all faced similar pressures during the recession. But racial divisions among them often widened as they competed for jobs and income. Hispanic farmers and sheep herders in New Mexico and Arizona fared poorly during the recession, as white ranchers and developers used intimidation and force to sweep thousands off of their farms and take possession of their land. As competition for jobs tightened during the recession, white workers stereotyped Chinese as slave-like laborers and scapegoated them as the cause of white unemployment, particularly in the West. Protests culminated in the passage of the Chinese Exclusion Act in 1883 (see Chapter 17).

THE GREAT RAILROAD STRIKE OF 1877

Four years into the Long Depression, workers undertook the nation's first countrywide strike in protest of low wages, unemployment, and the general condition of the economy. Significantly, the strike began in a company of the type that had driven the economic revolution—a railroad company. It spread westward along the very same lines that had facilitated the industrial boom.

The strike began in June 1877, when the Baltimore and Ohio Railroad Company announced that employees' wages were to be cut by 10 percent. It was the second time that year that such a cut was made. Employees in Martinsburg, West Virginia, spontaneously expressed their dismay at the news by refusing to let trains pass until their wages were restored. The governor sent in the militia to disperse the crowd and get the trains running again. But the militiamen, who were drawn from the general citizenry and were suffering from the depression as well, sympathized with the strikers and refused to use force against them. The president of the railroad company requested federal troops, who succeeded in freeing up one rail line. But townspeople and local boatmen and coal miners joined the strike, derailed the train, and overwhelmed the troops.

From there, the strike quickly spread up the railway lines, through Maryland and Pennsylvania and then west to Chicago and on to California (see Map 18.2). Eventually, two-thirds of the country's railroad lines were closed down. Workers in other industries struck in sympathy. Some, such as the workers of St. Louis, Missouri, even took control of city government. The national economy all but ground to a halt for almost two weeks. Across the United States, big business raised private militias to break the strikes. Laborers responded by burning down railway facilities and pulling up lines. The strike ended only when President Rutherford B. Hayes ordered federal troops to get the trains running again. Soldiers and private militias dashed from city to city, freeing up stretches of railroad and putting railroads and industry back to work.

The depression and strike of 1877 marked a watershed in American history. Despite their defeat, labor leaders across the country were encouraged by the strength of feeling and organizational capacity of local unions. Workers had demonstrated that the same rail and telegraph networks that drove American industry enabled labor to mobilize on a national scale. The unions resolved to build a national labor movement and went on to found the Federation of Organized Trades and Labor Unions in 1881 (which became the American Federation of Labor in 1886).

Eager to avert future strikes, the federal and state legislatures enacted conspiracy statutes aimed specifically at unions and strikes. State governments authorized the building of National Guard armories in the cities and strengthened the state militias. Industrialists and railway owners hired Pinkerton detectives (from Allan Pinkerton's rapidly growing detective agency) to spy on workers and break up unions. Employers and workers now considered their interests and world views as irreconcilably opposed. Their bitter struggle would be a key issue in American politics for the next three decades (see Chapter 19).

The depression and strike also taught industrialists and bankers that although the economy was spectacularly dynamic, it was highly unstable. They looked for ways to end price wars and the intensive competition that had characterized the pre-depression era. They also began looking overseas for markets that would raise demand for American goods, theorizing that exports would help keep prices high, which would keep workers in steady employment and avert calamitous events such as the railroad strike. As economist David A. Wells put it, America must export its surplus goods "or we are certain to be smothered in our own grease." East Asia took on new significance as a potentially massive market. The governor of the cotton-growing state of Georgia expressed the hopes of many industrialists when he declared, "It is my dream to see in every village [in Georgia] . . . a cotton factory to convert the raw material of the neighborhood into fabrics which shall warm the limbs of Japanese and Chinese."

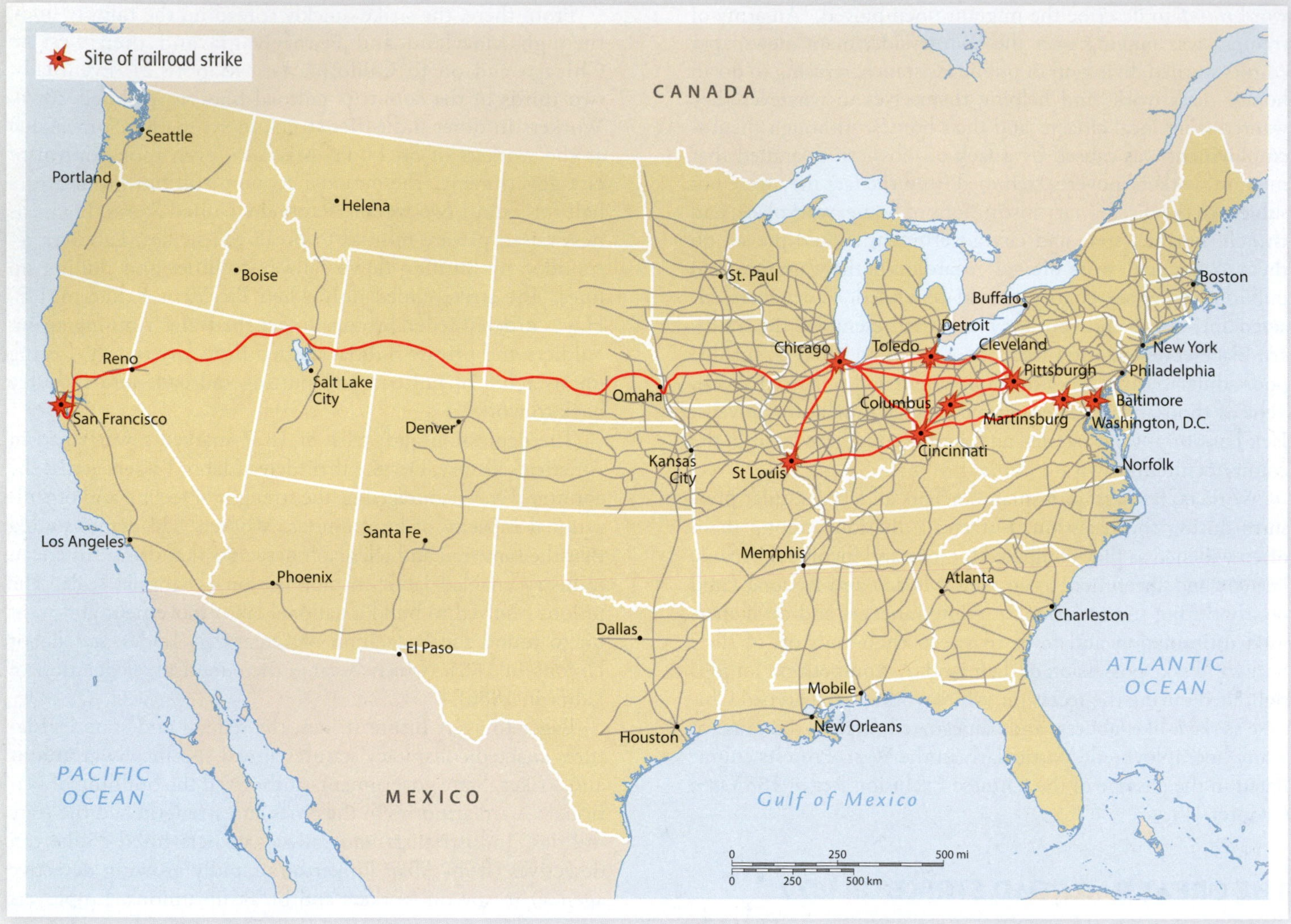

Map 18.2 The Great Railroad Strike Paralyzes the Economy. Although railroads were the arteries of industrialization, pumping millions of tons of raw materials into Industrial Belt factories each month, they also made manufacturing susceptible to stoppages. Blocking just one main trunk line could bring whole industries to a halt. In 1877, strike action spread along the railroad lines from tiny Martinsburg, West Virginia, through the Industrial Belt and on to San Francisco. The nation's industrial economy literally ground to a standstill.

SOCIETY AND CULTURE IN THE GILDED AGE CITY

As the creative and destructive forces of industrialization exerted themselves in the 1870s and 1880s, urban society and culture were dramatically transformed. First and foremost, a culture of **mass consumption** took root as middle-class Americans began to associate happiness and well-being with the purchase of goods and services in the new institution of the department store. Recreation also became something people could purchase, and even immigrant and working-class people could afford the new amusement parks that were built in this period. Meanwhile, the industrialists, railroad magnates, financiers, and entrepreneurial merchants who profited so handsomely from industrialization found new ways to represent their wealth and exercise their power. Attitudes about the institution of marriage and sexual morality also began to shift during this period, and conservatives organized to fight perceived threats to the established social order.

CATHEDRALS OF CONSUMPTION: THE RISE OF THE DEPARTMENT STORE

Industrial America's move toward a culture of mass consumption was most evident in the spectacular new city department stores that opened in the 1860s and 1870s. Before the Civil War, merchants had generally adhered to the republican ethos of masking wealth and stocking few luxury items. In New York in the 1860s, Alexander T. Stewart was the first of several merchants to abandon the antebellum suspicion of luxury. His great Iron Palace dry goods store encouraged an ethos of consumption for pleasure among the small section of New York society that could afford expensive and exotic goods. He loaded his "palace" with sumptuous items from Europe, China, Japan, Russia, and Central Asia. Whereas stores of the pre–Civil War period were housed in relatively modest buildings, Stewart's covered an entire city block and was adorned by a magisterial marble façade. Towering windows displayed gorgeous silk gowns, fine camelhair shawls, hand-knotted Persian rugs, exquisite furs, and other luxury items rarely seen in earlier years.

Other merchants built on Stewart's example, introducing middle-class consumers to the culture of consumption. In Philadelphia, John Wanamaker opened a palatial store in the Grand Depot railway station in 1876 (see Singular Lives: John Wanamaker, Department Store Magnate). In Chicago, the department store that became Marshall Field's occupied a six-story building adorned with a marble façade and towering Corinthian columns. The spectacular scale and lavish use of marble, glass, and soaring columns evoked the cathedrals and stately architecture of earlier societies—brightly celebrating the pleasures of consumption. Color posters and large billboards (and, after 1892, signs made with electric lightbulbs) also advertised department stores and their wares. Window displays, which functioned as street-level advertisements, became a highly profitable art form.

Department stores changed the way people used and related to the city's commercial district. The district became a destination not just for workers and businessmen but for shoppers—and window shoppers, too. Most significantly, they brought middle- and upper-class women into streets that had previously been the exclusive sphere of men (and, by night, prostitutes). The *New York Herald*, for example, commended Stewart's Iron Palace as "a beautiful spot" in which women could "wile away [their] leisure hours." The stores helped set women on the road to replacing their husbands as the principal shoppers for household goods. Through the exercise of their newfound purchasing power, women also became part of the city's public and commercial life for the first time. Many would eventually argue that women's new and important role as household economists merited giving them full civil and voting rights (see Chapter 19).

Department stores changed not only those who could afford to shop in them but the broader culture of the cities as well. Displays anticipated and promoted what would be called the **American dream**—the idea that with hard work, every American could achieve prosperity, happiness, and upward mobility. "In a dazzlingly beautiful place called a 'department store,'" recalled Mary Antin, a Russian-Jewish immigrant, she and her sister "exchanged our hateful home-made European costumes . . . for real American machine-made garments, and issued forth glorified in each other's eyes." Immigrants and other laboring people would often sew their own clothes based on designs they had seen in store windows. Guidebooks and a new kind of publication—the fashion magazine—also taught consumers in the cities and beyond how to dress and how to decorate their homes. For the first time, to be an American meant having the money and freedom to consume.

Selling Consumption. Advertising and display were critical tactics in department store sales strategies. Long a part of the newspaper business, advertising became its own industry in 1870s when the first independent agencies were founded. The Louis Prang agency used the new color lithography to produce bright, pocket-sized advertisement cards, such as this Valentine, for stores and manufacturers.

INHABITING THE CITY

As department stores changed the look and feel of the cities' commercial districts, urban communities began to change the way they inhabited and imagined the city. Palatial homes, sumptuous fashions, and lavish balls announced the newfound economic power of industrialists and bankers to older members of the establishment, whose wealth had come from preindustrial sources such as the fur trade and land speculation. The new rich—industrialists, railroad owners, financiers, and entrepreneurial store owners—broke with the pre–Civil War practice of dressing modestly and living in relatively plain homes. Disavowing the traditional ideal of social equality, they began displaying their wealth far more conspicuously. In New York, Alexander T. Stewart built the first great palatial residence on Fifth Avenue in the style of **Second Empire** architecture beloved of wealthy Parisians. Through the 1870s and 1880s, East coast elites constructed dozens of residences modeled on Stewart's. In San Francisco, the West's largest city, newly enriched railroad and silver magnates built enormous Italianate and Victorian homes on Nob Hill. In both cities, the new wealthy promenaded down city streets in splashy carriages modeled on that of the French empress Eugénie, wore clothes modeled directly on Parisian high fashion, and moored luxury European-made yachts at city yacht clubs. New magazines, such as *Decorator* and *Furnisher* reported on the latest interior designs, while *Harper's Bazaar* covered debutante balls and other glamorous exploits of the wealthy.

SINGULAR LIVES

John Wanamaker, Department Store Magnate

John Wanamaker's Grand Depot. The huge store opened to the crowds of the Centennial Exhibition in 1876, only to reopen a year later as a remarkable new kind of store. The store's design was modeled on open-air European markets like Les Halles in Paris. Almost anything that could be bought in the United States could be found at Wanamaker's, and in 1878 the store became the first department store with electric lighting.

The modern concept of "shopping" as a pleasurable, uplifting, and even magical experience was popularized by John Wanamaker, the proprietor of Philadelphia's first department store. Wanamaker, the son of a rural brick maker, combined his retailing skills (acquired while working as a clerk in a local dry goods store) with his devout Presbyterian conviction that all people should be treated equally. In the 1860s, his "Oak Hall" men and boys' clothing store applied the still-novel practice of charging the same price for the same good (the "fixed price system"), rather than forcing customers to haggle.

But it was at his palatial Philadelphia department store, the Grand Depot, that he most enduringly shaped the emerging consumer culture. The enterprising Wanamaker opened his massive men's clothing store in late 1875, hoping to snag the millions of visitors scheduled to tour the Centennial Exhibition the following summer. Touring the exhibition himself, he was so impressed by the architecture and variety and opulence of goods on display that he temporarily closed the Grand Depot and renovated it, top to bottom. The new, improved store had three acres of shopping on a single floor containing 129 counters. The sumptuous displays and stunning architecture were aimed less at men (who had traditionally done the shopping) than at women. And, unlike A. T. Stewart's famously expensive Iron Palace in New York, the Grand Depot was aimed squarely at the emerging middle class. Products were luxurious but affordable, appealing both to middle-class pocketbooks and middle-class desires to emulate the wealthy.

Beneath the store's magical aura lay a very rational set of accounting, marketing, and sales techniques. Wanamaker believed that providing service to the customer was essential, and that making customers feel special would further spark their imaginations . . . and open their pocketbooks. Soon his store offered child care for shopping mothers, live music, and the novel "money-back" guarantee. In-store fashion shows educated and excited shoppers about the new season (and showed them how perilously "out of date" last year's clothes and furnishings had become). The stores' layouts were designed for browsing, a new marketing technique that encouraged shoppers to circulate and see, touch, and dream about as many products as possible. Wanamaker not only insisted that the "customer is king"—he coined the well-known phrase. All this made him the third wealthiest man in America and one of the nation's most popular magnates, especially among the consumerist middle class.

Think About It

1. Why might Wanamaker have wanted to transform shopping into a pleasurable pastime aimed especially at women?
2. How might this new approach have transformed women's relationship to money, the city, and their families?

Displaying Wealth: The Mansion of Alexander T. Stewart. Stewart was the first of many entrepreneurs to build and live in a mansion modeled on the grand style of Second Empire French architecture. In this 1876 engraving, his Fifth Avenue home, built in 1869–1870, dwarfs the far plainer brownstone housing that New York's wealthy had traditionally favored (on the left). The embellished style and use of expensive building materials such as marble and copper embodied the consumerist ethos on which Stewart had made his fortune.

The new wealthy also nurtured a reputation for public generosity, particularly in the arts. In New York, Alexander T. Stewart, J. P. Morgan, and others spearheaded campaigns to build the Metropolitan Museum of Art and the Natural History Museum—the country's first large, public museums. Much as railroad owners had harnessed the backing of the federal government in their ventures, they sought and pursued massive public assistance from city government. After being rejected for membership in the old elite's opera house, many of the same wealthy subscribers founded the rival Metropolitan Opera. Panoramic city maps, which had been invented in the 1830s, grew especially popular as the new monumental architecture became a common sight. Merchants, industrialists, and city officials commissioned maps that emphasized the scale and grandeur of such buildings and conveyed their limitless confidence in industrial America.

Middle-class urban dwellers established their own distinctive neighborhoods. In New York, a new architectural style emerged—the French Flat apartment building. These buildings emulated the style of Stewart's Second Empire mansion, distinguishing them from laborers' plain tenement buildings, but on a smaller scale. Typically, they contained several apartments rather than a single family home. Hundreds were built in the 1860s and 1870s (before giving way to much larger middle-class apartment buildings). In San Francisco, middle-class housing also expanded dramatically, with 1,600 new homes built in 1876 alone—many resembling the palatial Victorian homes of the city's most affluent citizens.

Most city dwellers lived neither in a mansion nor in French Flats or a Victorian home but in a working-class building known as a **tenement.** In mid-nineteenth-century New York, tenements were four stories tall and stood on standard lots that were 25 feet wide and 100 feet deep. Each floor contained four two-roomed apartments, most of which were dark, poorly ventilated, overcrowded, and breeding grounds for disease. The annual death rate in tenement neighborhoods approached 10 percent—significantly higher than in other parts of the city. In the 1860s and 1870s, concerned lawmakers ordered the city to spray tenement districts with disinfectant. They also required landlords to construct fire escapes and install sewer pipes and flushable toilets. Every inhabitable room was to have a window to the outside. Subsequently, hundreds of new tenements were constructed in "dumbbell" style, each with a large front room, a narrower middle room, and a larger back room—all with a window, which often opened onto an airshaft. In the older buildings, landlords were compelled to carve 46,000 windows into the walls. With the invention of steel frame construction in the early 1880s, developers constructed tenement buildings up to seven floors high. Immigrant neighborhoods such as New York's Lower East Side became even more crowded, with upwards of 1,500 dwellers per square city block.

Safety laws and new design improved the tenements in some respects but made life much more unhealthy in others. Landlords squeezed several families into the new three-room apartments, instead of the single family for which they were intended. In overcrowded conditions, the new fire escapes became useful storage spaces for all kinds of things, including "quilts and clothes," as one tenant reported, and "chairs, tin boxes, ice boxes, dogs, birds, cats, rabbits, jars . . . big parrots screeching at each other, canaries singing, and children playing." Tenants often threw garbage down the airshafts, creating an unhealthy stench,

Tenement Squalor, 1889. Even after states passed laws in the 1860s and 1870s aimed at improving living conditions, Gilded Age tenements remained overcrowded, filthy, poorly ventilated, and without running water. Jacob Riis's photograph "Five Cents Lodging, Bayard Street, 1889" starkly immortalizes a family living in a tenement on New York's Lower East Side. The photograph comes from the Danish immigrant Riis's pathbreaking work of photojournalism, *How the Other Half Lives* (1890).

and the airshafts amplified ordinary household sounds to an unbearable level. Many landlords ignored the sewage regulations, with the result that tenants were compelled to use nonflushing privies out back. Few tenements had running water.

CHEAP AMUSEMENTS

Commercialized recreation, which traced its roots to the pre–Civil War city, expanded and changed dramatically in the Gilded Age. For the first time, large numbers of city dwellers had both disposable income—more money than they needed for food, shelter, and other basic necessities—and significant leisure time. In addition, recreational entrepreneurs invented profitable new pastimes and found ways of making older, noncommercial forms pay. Increasingly, city dwellers of all classes sought recreational pleasure and self-fulfillment through the purchase of "cheap amusements."

Working-class urbanites spent more time at new resorts such as Coney Island, nine miles from New York City. Every Sunday, tens of thousands of working-class men, women, and children experienced the island's attractions. They climbed aboard the world's first roller coaster and took the elevator up the three-hundred-foot Iron Tower for a bird's-eye view of the city. Immigrant shopkeepers offered simpler amusements such as shooting clay ducks and fortune telling. A ten-block area known as the "Gut" housed dance halls, brothels, dog-fighting arenas, and saloons—and a street named after the city's bawdy Bowery district. Families and amorous couples found relief from the dark, crowded tenements on the island's expansive golden beaches. City trolley companies opened similar amusement parks at Cedar Point in Ohio, Riverview in Chicago, and Mountain Park in Massachusetts in the 1880s and 1890s.

Through these leisure activities, a more inclusive, working-class culture took shape. The boundaries separating ethnic immigrant groups (who worked in different industries and in separate parts of the city during the week) began to dissolve as the diverse crowds enjoyed amusements together. Boundaries between the sexes also softened as men and women took rides together and broke the old convention of sex-segregated swimming. Poor and working-class women exercised new freedoms and asserted their independence at the parks (and in city dance halls). One boundary that cheap amusements did not dissolve, however, was that between black people and white people. Pools, beaches, skating rinks, and bowling allies remained racially segregated.

Middle-class recreation involved strolling in city parks, singing around pianos in parlors, and attending outdoor band concerts. Middle-class people attended baseball games, whose structure, rules, civility, and entrance fee made it far more appealing than prize fighting, blood sports, and other workers' amusements. Parks modeled on New York's Central Park were built in other major cities. But by the 1890s, middle-class youth began following the example of the working class, patronizing Coney Island, Chicago's Riverview, and other amusement parks.

For men of all classes, a large and highly organized sex industry provided another form of cheap amusement—if a disreputable one. A feature of city life since the eighteenth century, prostitution became a large and specialized industry during the Gilded Age. Thousands of female "camp followers" who had plied their

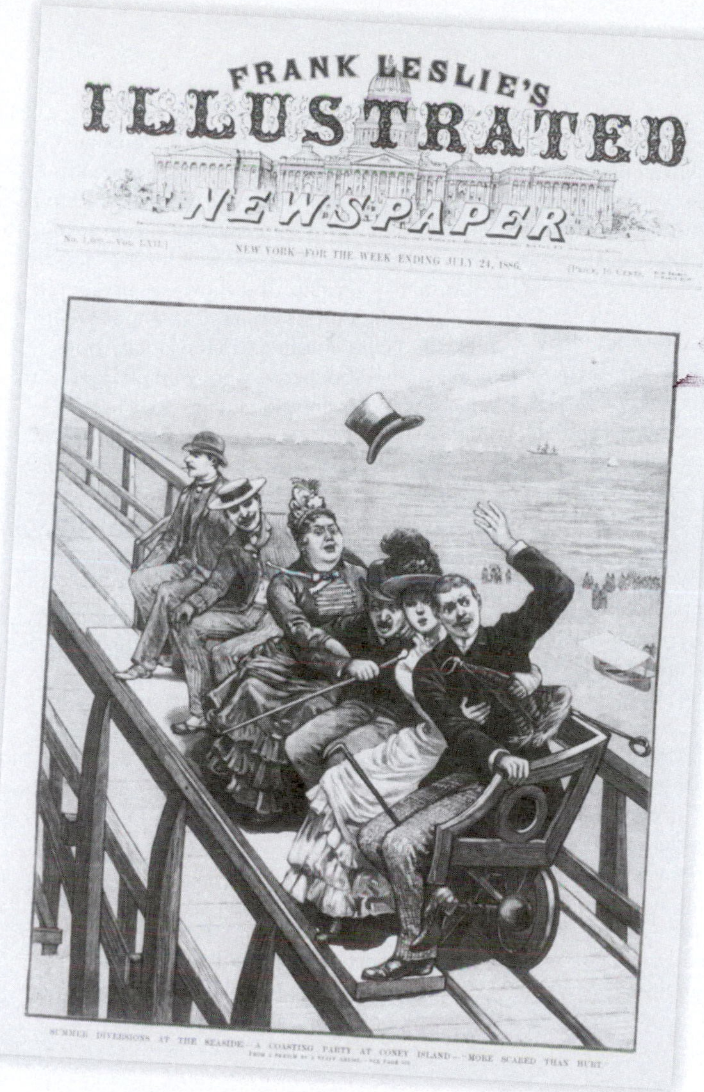

FRANK LESLIE'S ILLUSTRATED NEWSPAPER

NEW YORK—FOR THE WEEK ENDING JULY 24, 1886.

SUMMER DIVERSIONS AT THE SEASIDE—A COASTING PARTY AT CONEY ISLAND—"MORE SCARED THAN HURT."

"A Coasting Party at Coney Island," 1886. At Coney Island, young men and women were able to mingle in ways that were not permitted at home.

trade with troops during the Civil War settled in New York and other urban centers. In many cities, the police, politicians, and the sex trade were interconnected. Saloon- and brothelkeepers paid police for protection (from the law and others). The police retained a portion of the fee for their station house and passed along the rest to local politicians. By 1876, the payoffs had been standardized, with set fees for police protection and other services (see Hot Commodities: The Concert-Saloon).

WOMEN, GENDER, AND THE CULTURE WARS

Women's place in northern society changed dramatically following the Civil War. The deaths of 364,000 Union soldiers widowed tens of thousands of them and deprived many families of their breadwinners. For the first time, large numbers of women entered the workforce as missionaries, teachers, and nurses. Many women also became more active in social reform. The high incidence of alcoholism among veterans helped generate support for the founding of the Women's Christian Temperance Union (WCTU) in 1873. The WCTU went on to become the principal vehicle by which middle-class women (who still could not vote) participated in politics, spearheading reform projects such as the establishment of lunchrooms, libraries, and kindergartens for the poor. Members also advocated for prison reform, the eight-hour workday, and a public health system.

Some of the same women who unsuccessfully advocated for federal voting rights between 1865 and 1873 redirected their campaign for women's suffrage to the state level (see Chapter 19). Others tried to change conventional gender roles and marital and sexual relations. Suffragist Elizabeth Cady Stanton spoke out in favor of birth control and more liberal divorce laws. Victoria W. Woodhull, a newspaper publisher and the first woman to found a Wall Street brokerage, rejected the conventional monogamous marriage. In her newspaper, Woodhull (or "Mrs. Satan," as her critics called her) advocated "free love"—the idea that adults should be free to love whom they wanted, when they wanted.

Middle-class conservatives such as the leading Protestant preacher of the age, the Reverend Henry Ward Beecher of Brooklyn, were quick to condemn free love as unchristian and unnatural. But in 1872 Woodhull struck back, publicizing Beecher's secret adulterous affair with the wife of a parishioner and sarcastically declaring him a secret supporter of free love. Beecher remained silent on the matter. However, Anthony Comstock, a parishioner who had been pressuring city police to close down erotica stores, succeeded in getting Woodhull arrested and jailed. Woodhull was charged with circulating obscene literature (the stories about Beecher). Although the court eventually dismissed the case, the national press exploded in heated debate about sexual freedom, the right to privacy, women's rights, and the institution of marriage.

The Woodhull-Beecher scandal galvanized elite and middle-class opposition to women's rights and sexual and marital reform. A new force appeared in American cultural politics in 1873. The New York Society for the Suppression of Vice was the first of several conservative lobby groups to champion traditional marriage and to crusade against anything that seemed to threaten marriage and procreative marital sex. Under the leadership of Anthony Comstock, the Society persuaded many middle-class and wealthy urbanites that Woodhull's free love idea, the growth of a freer sexual culture (in places like Coney Island), and the thriving prostitution business undermined the social order. The Society secured generous funding from J. P. Morgan and others of the cities' wealthiest citizens and began a two-decades long campaign against birth control, women's independence, erotic art and literature, and prostitution.

Comstock mobilized congressional support for the enactment of the nation's first sweeping federal censorship law. The Comstock Act of 1873 law banned the mailing of material deemed "obscene, indecent, or immoral" through the U.S. Post Office. "Obscene" was defined very broadly to include condoms,

HOT COMMODITIES

The Concert-Saloon

Depending on whom you spoke to in the Gilded Age, concert-saloons were the zenith of personal freedom, places to make a buck, or dens of vice and iniquity. All three characterizations contained a germ of truth. The distinctive new entertainment venues, which sprouted in dozens of cities after the Civil War, combined the theater, brothel, and bar, with a stage downstairs and rooms for rent upstairs. Reflecting the cosmopolitan nature of America's bigger cities, the stage shows borrowed from French vaudeville, Italian opera, German beer gardens, and London music halls. Male patrons sang along as they were served food and wine by "waiter girls" looking for additional business.

Like industrial society at large, the concern-saloons' offerings were increasingly specialized. Some catered to uptown patricians, whereas others attracted working-class "roughed necks" (such as the sixty-thousand-odd sailors that docked in New York each year). In the 1880s, establishments also tended to be grouped together according to the kinds of services provided. Male performers known as "Nancys" and "fairies" performed in elaborate women's clothes at male-only venues such as New York's The Slide and the Columbia Club. Those managing the prostitution side of the trade kept their workers to a strict timetable. In one working-class establishment, women worked on average seventy to one hundred encounters per week, with each appointment lasting ten to fifteen minutes.

Condemned by morals crusaders yet protected by the police (whom the owners paid off), the concert-saloons were a fact of urban life. But as department stores and female shoppers began changing the character of the city, some concert-saloon owners cleaned up their acts. In New York, Antonio Pastor, a former clown and entrepreneurial concert-saloon proprietor, recognized that the respectable women whom department stores were drawing to the commercial districts might be persuaded to spend their money on the concert-saloon—provided the venues were made clean, safe, and respectable. In 1881, he announced the opening of the "New Fourteenth Street Theater" in New York's Union Square shopping district, and the arrival of "the first specialty and vaudeville theater of America, catering to polite tastes." His series of short acts included ethnic songs and dances, blackface comedy, and puppetry, and it drew women and men from across the social spectrum.

Building on Pastor's approach, Benjamin Franklin Keith opened a similar venue in Boston in 1883. Audiences were treated to a series of skits lasting anywhere from seven to twenty minutes, all of which were suitable for family viewing. The show was presented in elegant, purpose-built theaters that were staffed by uniformed ushers, ladies' room maids, and bouncers, who were charged with ejecting unruly male patrons. Keith and Pastor had created a new, respectable form of vaudeville and it quickly became the most popular—and profitable—form of entertainment in the country. The newly polite concert-saloon would go on, in the early twentieth century, to serve as the model for the first big cinemas. Most of the older-style concert-saloons fared less well once middle-class reformers pressured lawmakers to reorganize urban police departments and enforce antiprostitution laws in the 1890s and 1900s.

Think About It

1. Why were brothel concert-saloons such thriving businesses in the Gilded Age?
2. What does the advent of the "polite" concert-saloon and its vaudeville variety say about popular attitudes toward the city, entertainment, and women?

information about birth control, and depictions of the human body. Comstock was appointed special agent of the Post Office, and U.S. marshals were instructed to seize and destroy offending materials. Violators of the postal clauses could be imprisoned and put to hard labor for up to five years and fined up to $2,000. Comstock and the Society proceeded to comb New York—and dozens of other cities—looking for obscene material. By 1915, Comstock had arrested 3,700 people and ordered the destruction of over fifty tons of obscene books, four million obscene pictures, and almost seventeen thousand photographic plates.Much of the material was erotic in nature, but some of it, such as Dr. E. B. Foote's best-selling *Medical Common Sense*, included frank discussions of marriage and sexual morality. By censoring the mails, Comstock succeeded in stanching not only the circulation of pornography but also the free flow of ideas, texts, images, and medical studies concerning sexuality and the human body.

The conservative impulse among many middle- and upper-class Americans also emerged in a slew of new guidebooks aimed at teaching women of modest means how to become good wives and homemakers. In 1869, Henry Ward Beecher's sisters, Harriet (author of *Uncle Tom's Cabin*) and Catherine, published a best-selling guide, entitled *The American Woman's Home, or Principles of Domestic Science; Being a Guide to the Formation and Maintenance of Economical, Healthful, Beautiful and Christian Homes*. Advocating "modes of economizing labor, time, and expenses, so as to secure health, thrift, and domestic happiness to persons of limited means, in a measure rarely attained even by those who possess wealth," the authors envisioned wives and mothers as effective domestic managers. The book offered numerous hints for efficient kitchen design and the art of home decoration. Above all, the Beechers instructed women on the importance of being cheerful, so as to create cheerful environments for their husbands and children. Careful decoration with

Homemaking Explained. Guides such as the Beecher sisters' *American Woman's Home* instructed women of modest means that their role in life was to be a cheerful household manager. The homemaker's duties included the emotional labor of making the home a place for the rejuvenation of a hardworking husband—with a smile.

colorful prints, wallpapers, and tablecloths would "renovate degraded man and clothe all clime with beauty." Another guidebook, by Louisa May Alcott (author of *Little Women*), reiterated the point in a chapter devoted to cheerfulness, writing that the homemaker's duty was to create a relaxed and comfortable environment for male breadwinners—and to always wear a smile.

THE INDUSTRIALIZED ENVIRONMENT

The same processes of industrialization that transformed cities also brought sweeping changes in the environment. The ways in which Americans used, experienced, and thought about land, air, water, plants, animals, food, noise, and even human and horse excrement changed dramatically after 1865. Industrialization and development brought to an end older, customary uses of the land. Hunting, open range grazing, gleaning and gathering, fishing, and the collection of firewood were strictly regulated for the first time. Direct access to free or common sources of food, fuel, and shelter became a rarity. Customary practices that had helped feed and shelter poorer rural people (including, in many parts of the West, Native Americans) became criminal offenses. The meaning of nature changed, as people made weary by city life sought spiritual rejuvenation in sublime landscapes or withdrew to a new kind of rural space they called **"the country."**

LAND, WATERWAYS, AND FORESTS

The two decades following the Civil War saw widespread deforestation in every region of the country. Forests were felled both for lumber (which was used as fuel, building materials, railroad sleepers, and fencing) and to clear land for farming. In Vermont, which had been heavily forested before the Civil War, almost 70 percent of the state's spruce, fir, hemlock and other trees were felled by 1880. The midwestern ecosystem was permanently transformed as lumberjacks felled whole forests on the periphery of Chicago and Lake Michigan, sending the wood to Chicago for use in building and railroad construction. Likewise, parts of Northern California and the Pacific Northwest were cleared for redwood, oak, and other timbers used in the construction of boomtowns such as San Francisco.

In some sections of society, attitudes toward wildlife underwent a significant shift in the 1870s. Before the Civil War, when large parts of the country were yet to be conquered and incorporated, wildlife had seemed inexhaustible. After the war, it became clear that development, industrialization, and commercialized agriculture threatened whole species with extinction. The loss of forests was also a loss of animal habitat. Moose, elk, bears, wolves, mountain lions, and diverse species

Coos Bay Lumber Company Steam Donkeys, Oregon. After 1881, the use of "steam donkeys"—steam-driven winches that dragged felled trees out of the forest and into mills or onto logging trains—and advances in milling technology sped deforestation in California and the Pacific Northwest.

of birds all went into decline. The well-documented fate of the Plains bison, which was hunted to near extinction, gravely underscored the point (see Chapter 17).

Perhaps surprisingly, elite sportsmen took the lead in wildlife conservation. Contrasting the poorer "game butchers," "fish pirates," and "pothunters" to "gentleman sportsmen" such as themselves, they decried those who hunted for food on the grounds that they were lazy, ignorant folk who "chose not to work for a living." Wealthy hunters lobbied state legislatures for game laws and a licensing system that would exclude everyone but sports hunters. In the name of conservation, many states passed restrictive laws that made it very difficult for poorer people to meet their meat needs through hunting.

The federal government also became involved in conservation, becoming the first in the world to develop a coordinated policy. The policy developed along two different axes. One involved the regulation of certain commercially valuable resources that threatened to run dry or become extinct. Following reports from worried fishermen that catches were rapidly declining, Congress issued a joint resolution in 1871 establishing the Commission of Fish and Fisheries (which surveyed fish stocks). However, the official view tended to confirm the long-standing (and erroneous) idea that the sea's fish populations were inexhaustible. As Spencer Baird, the first U.S. commissioner of Fish and Fisheries, declared in 1873, "The principle may safely be considered as established that line-fishing, no matter how extensively prosecuted, will never materially affect the supply of fish in the sea."

The federal government's second line of approach involved the preservation of public lands—and their animal and birdlife—as national parks. The Yellowstone Act of 1871 provided that two million acres in northwestern Wyoming were to be protected as a public "pleasuring-ground" for the "preservation . . . of all timber, mineral deposits, natural curiosities or wonders . . . and their retention in their natural condition." In 1891, Congress authorized the president to create federal forests as a way of protecting topsoil and watersheds.

URBAN ECOLOGY

The ecology of cities and the ecological impact of cities on the countryside also changed dramatically in these years. Just as the advent of refrigerated railcars separated city people from the environment in which their food was raised and processed, the installation of city sewers further cut city people's sense of connection with the larger environment. Before the installation of sewer lines in the 1870s and 1880s, human excrement had been considered a useful byproduct. Cities had employed small armies of tub men to collect and carry "night soil" out into the surrounding farmland, where it was returned to the soil as a nutrient-rich fertilizer (though also a potentially dangerous one, as it often carried disease-causing pathogens and worm eggs). This practice helped bind city people with the countryside and gave them an understanding of their place in the food chain. By 1880, however, city dwellers were flushing much of their human waste into sewers. Tub men were becoming a thing of the past. People became less aware of their everyday impact on the environment, adopting a "flush it and forget it" mentality in which excrement was no longer understood as a useful fertilizer but as "waste."

Piping sewage out of the cities improved them by reducing disease rates and lessening the stench. But it also had a radical effect on the ecology of the surrounding countryside. City sewers emptied raw, untreated excrement into rivers, lakes, and oceans. This caused algae blooms in the waterways, which in turn deprived fish of oxygen and drastically reduced their numbers and the diversity of species. The dumping of industrial waste and refinery runoffs added to the effect. By 1886, the fisheries had been severely depleted, and toxicity levels had made much of the fish dangerous to eat.

One kind of waste that the cities produced in prodigious amounts—horse manure—did make it back into the soil. The great mass of manure that tramway and other horses daily deposited into the streets was not flushed but rather collected and rail freighted to rural areas, where it was sold as fertilizer to farmers. Cities required the tram companies to perform the work as a condition of operation. Whereas farmers had previously found manure locally, they now came to rely on the cheap by-product of city life. Chicago's slaughter yards also sold millions of tons of waste blood and bones as fertilizer, and, beginning in 1868, phosphate mines in South Carolina supplemented the nation's fertilizer supply with a powerful new, phosphate-based product. The multibillion-dollar American fertilizer industry grew directly out of these practices.

REMAKING NATURE AND INVENTING "THE COUNTRY"

As industrialization and urbanization proceeded apace, many middle-class and upper-class Americans developed what they experienced as a deeply spiritual connection with the land, waterways, and forests. The word *nature* came to represent sublime landscapes supposedly untouched by human hands, and a place to which those worn down by life in industrial society could retreat for spiritual solace. Scottish-born explorer and botanist John Muir most famously expressed this new relationship with the environment in the magazine articles he authored in the 1870s. Muir trekked from Kentucky to Florida, recording his observation of blossoms, plants, and wildlife in his journal and eventually spent some years exploring Yosemite in California. Muir wrote eloquently of the conversion-like experience he had when he first pondered the beauty of a wild orchid. "I never before saw a plant so full of life; so perfectly spiritual," wrote Muir. "[I]t seemed pure enough for the throne of its Creator."

The new way of seeing the land as untouched tended to erase the memory of Native Americans and early European and Mexican settlers who had lived on and often changed the land (through use of fire and husbandry, for example). Physically getting to nature also depended upon the very tools of industry—such as railroads—from which nature worshippers sought a reprieve. But the new, spiritual conception of nature gave rise to conservation organizations and nature clubs that actively sought to protect species. Northeasterners founded the Appalachian Mountain Club in 1876 and began conducting guided tours of the Adirondacks and White Mountains. In 1892, Muir cofounded the Sierra Club, which went on to become the leading champion of conservation in the twentieth century.

Prosperous urban Americans created another environmental space in the 1870s and 1880s. As farming in the Northeast declined and railroads connected rural areas with the cities,

John Muir, Disciple of Nature. Carrying copies of John Milton's *Paradise Lost*, Scottish poet Robert Burns's works, and the New Testament on his travels, John Muir filed numerous stories in which he marveled at the Edenic qualities of the plants, valleys, streams, and mountain peaks he encountered. In 1903, he persuaded President Theodore Roosevelt, left, to turn the Yosemite valley—pictured here behind Roosevelt and Muir—into a national park.

farmhouses and cottages became picturesque retreats for weary city folk. Such areas became known as "the country" and served as an intermediate space between sublime nature and the consumerist city. After farming became unviable in Poland Spring, Maine, in the 1860s, the owners of one large farm turned their old farmhouse into a spa. With the rise of advertising and rail tourism in the early 1870s, they opened a large hotel—the Poland Spring House—in 1876. Visitors came from all over the country, and the family also began bottling and selling the fresh spring water. Similar health resorts opened in Vermont, Massachusetts, and upstate New York.

When middle-class urbanites went to the country, they sought out picturesque scenery and romanticized what they imagined to be the virtuous, rural life. Many sought a return to America's agrarian roots. In fact, the modern railroad and the telegraph system had helped create "the country" by boosting large-scale western agriculture (at the expense of northeastern farms). And the "traditional" farming life, even in New England, had been hardworking and even stressful. But visitors from the city could only see the country as "authentic," "quaint," and delightfully "old-fashioned."

Wealthy urbanites also developed a relationship with the new, intermediate space of the country. Beginning in 1882, they built expansive "country clubs" on the edges of cities, and poured money into landscaped grounds, lavish clubrooms, tennis courts, and (beginning in the late 1880s) golf and polo courses. Many clubs offered gentleman sportsmen and lady sportswomen the opportunity to practice their hunting skills on clay pigeon shooting ranges. Whole families went to the clubs together, seeking a retreat from the hurly-burly of city life. Membership was strictly regulated along religious, racial, and class lines. Clubs such as the Country Club of Brookline, Massachusetts, became important social institutions to which the rich and aspiring sought to belong.

CONCLUSION

In the twenty years following the end of the Civil War, America ceased to be a nation of farmers, artisans, and small businessmen and became one of the world's wealthiest industrial societies. Although the majority of Americans still lived and worked in rural areas, by 1885 over half of all American workers were wage earners rather than owning their own farm or business. A great network of telegraphs and rails knitted together disparate regions of the country, shrinking the physical and cultural distances between them. Significant events in one part of the country—such as the Great Chicago Fire—were keenly felt and followed in other parts of the country. And, for the first time, much of the nation was also linked into a global communication network along which news, ideas, money, and information flowed at near-instantaneous speeds. By the 1890s, many Americans thought of themselves as members of communities and classes that cut across national borders.

A new consumer culture formed in the cities, transforming the look, rhythm, and experience of urban life. By the 1880s, that culture was radiating out across America via railroads and wires, magazines, mail order catalogs, and cheap prints and books. It would eventually saturate much of the nation. New York, with its new opera house, museums, department stores, and skyscrapers, confirmed its position as the nation's industrial and financial capital, and entered the ranks of cosmopolitan, international cities. Amid the rapid and profound changes, nature came to have a deeply spiritual significance and the country offered prosperous urbanites a respite from industrial life.

The colossal forces of industrialization proved to be immensely creative, and tragically destructive. Poverty took hold of a significant minority of urban immigrants. Periods of prosperity and rising wages were bookended by devastating recessions. By 1877, deep distrust marked relations between workers and industrialists and bankers. Workers responded by organizing a new trade-union movement. Industrialists moved to expand and consolidate their holdings and stabilize the market.

Following the Long Depression (1873–1879), popular perceptions of leading industrialists such as Carnegie, Rockefeller, Vanderbilt, Cooke, and Heinz began to change. Across the social spectrum, Americans began questioning the lack of government regulation of the often disastrously volatile economy. Kansas farmers complained that the railroads on which they depended to get their produce to market were run by "robber barons" who monopolized the service and fixed the freight prices ruinously high. Middle-class urbanites worried that the immense economic power of industrialists, who were neither democratically elected nor accountable to public oversight, was a threat to democracy. As Henry George put it in his best-selling book *Progress and Poverty* (1879), "This association of poverty with progress is the great enigma of our times. So long as the increased wealth which modern progress brings goes but to build up great fortunes, to increase luxury and make sharper the contrast between the House of Have and House of Have Want, progress is not real and is not permanent." In the 1880s and 1890s, Americans' unease with the industrial world they had wrought would be expressed and confronted in the political arena.

STUDY TERMS

Centennial Exhibition (p. 473)
Gilded Age (p. 474)
tramping (p. 475)
Pullman Palace Car Company (p. 476)
Sears, Roebuck and Company (p. 476)
Brooklyn Bridge (p. 478)
Standard Oil (p. 480)
modern corporation (p. 480)
monopoly (p. 480)
standardized regional time zones (p. 481)
Paris Commune (p. 484)
Great Chicago Fire (p. 484)
Great Epizootic of 1872 (p. 484)
Long Depression (p. 486)
vagrancy laws (p. 487)
mass consumption (p. 488)
Iron Palace (p. 488)
American dream (p. 489)
Second Empire (p. 489)
French Flat (p. 491)
tenement (p. 491)
Coney Island (p. 492)
New York Society for the Suppression of Vice (p. 493)
Comstock Act (p. 493)
"the country" (p. 495)

TIMELINE

1865 Civil War ends

1866 Transatlantic telegraph connects North America and Europe

1869 Transcontinental railroad completed
U.S. Railway Mail Service begins operating.
Luxury Pullman railcars popularize long-distance travel
The Beecher sisters publish *American Woman's Home*

1871 Victoria Woodhull sparks national debate about free love
French workers declare the Paris Commune
Orangemen riots erupt in New York
Fire destroys Peshtigo, Wisconsin, and the city of Chicago

1872 Yellowstone National Park established
Montgomery Ward issues first mail order catalog
Economy slows after Great Epizootic sickens nation's horses

1873 Long Depression starts

1875 Newspaper and telegraph companies construct world's tallest office buildings

1876 Centennial Exhibition begins
John Wanamaker opens Grand Depot department store
Philadelphia Appalachian Mountain Club founded
Poland Spring House, a country spa, opens in Maine

1877 Wage cuts trigger Great Railroad Strike

1879 Long Depression ends
Henry George writes *Progress and Poverty*

1880 Golden Gate Park completed in San Francisco

1881 George M. Beard publishes *American Nervousness*

1882 Congress excludes all Chinese immigration
The first country club opens in Brookline, Massachusetts

1883 Brooklyn Bridge opens
Standardized regional time zones established
Metropolitan Opera performs its first opera
Benjamin Franklin Keith creates respectable vaudeville

1884 World's first roller coaster opens at Coney Island

1885 Department stores distribute lavish mail order catalogs

FURTHER READING

Additional suggested readings are available on the Online Learning Center at www.mhhe.com/becomingamerica1e.

Tim Cresswell, *The Tramp in America* (2001), describes the changing fortunes and social status of migrant laborers and the poor.

William Cronon, *Nature's Metropolis: Chicago and the Great West* (1991), explores the ecological and economic relationship between Chicago and the hinterland.

Rebecca Edwards, *New Spirits: Americans in the Gilded Age* (2005), offers a thorough treatment of Gilded Age economics, culture, and politics.

Richard J. Hooker, *Food and Drink in America: A History* (1981), traces Americans' changing foodways.

Roger Horowitz, *Putting Meat on the American Table* (1981), examines the rise of the meat industry.

William Leach, *Land of Desire: Merchants, Power, and the Rise of a New American Culture* (1994), traces the rise of the department store and birth of consumer culture.

Michael O'Malley, *Keeping Watch: A History of American Time* (1990), tracks American timekeeping practices and attitudes toward time.

Kathy Peiss, *Cheap Amusements: Working Women and Leisure in Turn-of-the-Century New York* (1986), explores working-class leisure in late-nineteenth-century New York.

Andrea L. Smalley, "'Our Lady Sportsmen': Gender, Class, and Conservation in Sport Hunting Magazines, 1873–1920," *Journal of Gilded Age and Progressive Era* (October 2005), surveys wealthy hunters' exclusion of subsistence hunters and elite women's entry to the sport.

Carl Smith, *Urban Disorder and the Shape of Belief: The Great Chicago Fire, the Haymarket Bomb, and the Model Town of Pullman* (1995), probes the meanings of the Chicago fire and Americans' anxieties about their rapidly changing world.

Mark David Spence, *Dispossessing the Wilderness* (2000), discusses the complex origins of the national parks and late-nineteenth-century attitudes toward wilderness.

Alan Trachtenberg, *The Incorporation of America: Culture and Society in the Gilded Age* (1982), offers an interdisciplinary study of how the idea and institution of the corporation have influenced American culture.

19

INSIDE ▶

THE BIG PICTURE

Saloons, parades, and a partisan press fueled a lifelong passion for party politics among most Gilded Age men, and women became involved through various reform movements. Lobbyists targeted the federal government, transforming the way lawmakers did business. For their part, increasingly disillusioned workers, farmers, and the unemployed eventually took matters into their own hands.

Street Politics. Gilded Age Americans of all ages and backgrounds took part in boisterous political parades in election years.

1878–1896

POLITICS & DISCONTENT IN THE GILDED AGE

Under the glare of gaslights and the glow of hundreds of Chinese lanterns, the uniformed men of the "York Escort" marched into the town square in New Haven, Connecticut. As fireworks exploded overhead and a brass band belted out "The Star-Spangled Banner," three other columns of marchers, each named after a leading city Democrat and bearing bright-burning torches, arrived. Well-heeled women watched the procession from the windows of surrounding homes, and throngs jostled for a better view on the street. It was July 1876, and New Haven was preparing for a presidential election.

Far from being a singular event, such parades occurred nightly throughout the nation in the lead-up to presidential elections during the Gilded Age. They were essential to a political system that was built on fierce loyalty to party and high voter turnout. The men who marched or who cheered on the marchers believed that the political system belonged to them as voters. Although most women could not vote and could only express support from the sidelines, many felt included in the democratic process. Others pursued an expanded role in politics and government.

This culture of mass politics was remarkably stable in the years 1876–1892. Voter turnouts were higher than at any other time in American history. Despite ongoing harassment, African American men continued to vote in the South in large numbers until the mid-1890s, and although women could not vote in most parts

A torchlight parade marching up Pennsylvania Avenue toward the White House celebrates Rutherford B. Hayes's 1877 inauguration.

KEY QUESTIONS

- Why were the vast majority of men so passionately involved in electoral politics during the Gilded Age?
- What changes did women seek in American culture and politics, and how did they make their voices heard?
- How did lobbyists become powerful in Washington, and what impact did they have on the federal government?
- Why did so many people eventually become disillusioned with government and the two-party system—and what did they do about it?
- How and why did the Jim Crow system of racial segregation and political disenfranchisement take root in the South?

of the country, they worked within the political system as advocates, lobbyists, and authorities on health, welfare, and education. It surprised political party leaders when, in 1892, the robust world of Gilded Age politics quite suddenly threatened to collapse. A viable third political party emerged to challenge the major parties and the political system that supported them. Southern states moved to disenfranchise African American men. By 1896, politics as usual was no longer possible.

AGE OF MASS POLITICS

Unlike most people today, Gilded Age Americans had a passionate and lifelong loyalty to either the Republican or the Democratic Party. Membership in one or the other was a critical element of most men's identity—on a par with religious affiliation and ethnicity—and men publicly affirmed that identity throughout their lives. The cardinal rule of Gilded Age politics was unwavering support of one's party on election day, regardless of the candidate's experience, policies, or character. But being a Republican or a Democrat meant much more than voting loyally. It also meant seeing the world through a particular lens and feeling a sense of belonging in a community of like-minded people. The all-male world of the saloon played a key role in this political world, as did the partisan press and colorful, boisterous parades. These factors helped raise voting rates to the highest they have ever been in American history.

POLITICAL MACHINES AND THEIR CRITICS

A distinctive kind of organization—the **political machine**—played a central role in city life and politics in the Gilded Age. At a time when cities expanded far faster than government, the political machines performed many of the economic and welfare tasks that government plays today. The machine consisted of a loose-knit network of political party members (known as "ward bosses" and lieutenants) who dispensed jobs, legal assistance, food, and other resources to the urban poor. European peasants and workers arriving in cities from San Francisco to New York eagerly turned to the machines for help as they grappled with the many challenges of urban life. In return, the immigrants gave the party their votes on election day. Ward bosses also helped millions of immigrants naturalize as American citizens, paying the fees and doing the paperwork.

Most urban machines were Democratic and run by Irish Americans and Irish immigrants who spoke English and often had a history of political organizing against the English colonizers back in Ireland. But the machines also absorbed a large portion of immigrants from elsewhere in Europe, and it was commonplace for an Irish boss to attend Italian baptisms and Jewish bar mitzvahs. Ward bosses reported informally to a citywide boss, who was often a charismatic and shrewd politician. Whenever the machine won control of city government (which happened frequently), the boss and his lieutenants appointed sympathetic party members to positions of power, including the judiciary, sanitation department, and police force. The chief prerequisite for appointment was not experience or skills but loyalty to the party machine.

Political machines were also moneymakers for the boss and his lieutenants, who often made significant fortunes through their political connections. Bosses knew in advance that property values in a certain neighborhood would rise because a new tramline or street was being planned for construction, and they would buy low before plans were announced. Bosses received kickbacks from contractors as a "thank you" for city construction projects and shook down saloonkeepers and others for money in return for protection. Critics condemned such profits as "graft," a dishonorable way of making money at the expense of others. But machine defenders claimed that there was a difference between honest and dishonest graft, and that the former was simply about capitalizing on opportunities that came their way, the same as anybody else would. "I seen my opportunities and I took 'em," declared George Washington Plunkitt, the boss of New York's Democratic machine, Tammany Hall. Founded in 1789, Tammany was among the most powerful of the urban machines, having harnessed the support of New York's growing immigrant population in the 1830s and 1840s.

The machines were subject to growing criticism before the Civil War, particularly among native-born, middle-class Americans who resented the machines' capture of the immigrant vote and considered the reciprocal arrangement of votes-for-jobs corrupt. Such objections intensified in the 1870s and 1880s. Some critics disdained the Irish and other immigrants as unfit to vote and condemned the machines for exploiting them for their own purposes. But others opposed the machines on the grounds that they routinely stole from the public treasury and bought elections. In New York City in 1886, for instance, Henry George organized an unlikely coalition of socialists, anti-monopolists, trade-union activists, single-taxers, and middle-class reformers against Tammany and other machines and called for an end to "the extortion and speculation by which a standing army of professional politicians corrupt the public whom they plunder."

SALOONS AND POLITICS

Awash in grog, ale, and male conviviality, city saloons were the most important sites of working-class male recreation in the last third of the nineteenth century. But they were also indispensable economic and political institutions. Most functioned as "reciprocity machines" in which patrons, saloonkeepers, and politicians traded jobs, votes, favors, and drinks and forged crucial political networks. In some cities, one in every two saloonkeepers was a ward boss for the Democratic Party. In many urban places, more saloonkeepers than any other occupation group served in city government. Almost half of New York City's twenty-four aldermen were bar owners in 1890, and Tammany Hall's boss, George Washington Plunkett,

Tammany on the Prowl. Originally a benevolent society founded in 1789, New York's Tammany Hall became one of the most powerful and successful of the urban political machines—and the target of attacks by native-born Republicans such as cartoonist Thomas Nast, who considered machine rule a threat to democracy. Nast was the first of several cartoonists to depict Tammany as a voracious tiger that lived off graft and clawed and mauled the people and the city that its leaders claimed to champion.

HOT COMMODITIES

Votes for Sale!

In contrast to the system today, parties, rather than the government, printed, distributed, and counted the ballots in the Gilded Age, and voters could fill out the ballot anywhere before depositing it in a ballot box. Voting did not take place in secret, and party officials frequently supervised—and influenced—a voter's choice. One flagrant form of influence was a cash payment for the right vote. Although probably no more than 20 percent of votes were bought in any one election, the practice was open and routine. "Votes will be bought if you just shake the cash at them," one aide explained to his congressman. Particularly in northern swing states such as Ohio and New York, where presidential elections were generally close, vote buying could determine the outcome of the election.

Vote buying was well organized and well funded. Both parties paid and shipped in voters from other districts or states to pack the vote, and both paid local "floaters" and "lost nerves" (men who showed signs of breaking with their party and voting for the opposition) to remain loyal. Many loyal voters were also paid as a way of compensating them for losing a few hours' wages due to taking time off to vote. The going rate for a vote in the 1880s was generally between $1 and $2 (about $23 and $47 in today's dollars) and, much as the price of sugar, kerosene, and other commodities went up when demand was high and supply was low, the price of votes could fluctuate. Votes were more valuable in particularly close races than in clear-cut elections, and floaters often raised the price for the party that was lagging and desperate for support. In New York in 1880, for example, an observer reported that 20 percent of one district's votes had been purchased for the relatively high price of between $2 and $5.

Party bosses systematically coordinated the purchase of votes, spreading "soap" (as vote-buying funds were known) across the state and instructing district and ward bosses to dispense it appropriately. In Indiana, in the bitterly contested presidential election of 1888, a high-ranking Republican popularly known as Two Dollar Dudley (for the amount he paid for a vote) openly wrote his county chairmen with strict instructions for getting out and paying for the vote. Wherever third parties such as the Anti-Monopoly Party looked likely to win, Republicans and Democrats concentrated their vote-buying efforts in those districts. In many cities on election day, party workers mustered floaters and lost nerves at saloons, paid them a cash fee, helped them fill out a ballot, and then promptly marched them down the street to the polling booth.

Political leaders and many citizens considered vote buying a necessary part of politics. But in the mid-1880s, a growing chorus of voices objected to the principle of vote buying and to the party patronage system generally. Third-party supporters soon blamed their defeats on vote buying and vowed to abolish the practice. The growing number of urban middle-class critics who believed that uneducated immigrants should not vote, because they were allegedly ignorant and easily manipulated by party bosses, also condemned vote buying. In the mainstream press, buying votes came to symbolize everything that middle-class people considered corrupt about the political machines and the patronage system. Mounting criticism led almost every state to mandate the "Australian" or secret ballot system, under which government printed the ballots (which listed all candidates) and voting was conducted in secret in voting booths. The new system made vote buying more difficult, though the practice persisted into the early twentieth century.

worked closely with saloonkeepers. One Chicago saloon was known as the "Democratic Headquarters of the Eighteenth Ward." Machine politicians worked closely with saloonkeepers to organize voters at elections. This could be expensive, as one of the ways politicians worked for votes was by "treating" or buying rounds of drinks for the patrons (see Hot Commodities: Votes for Sale!).

ELECTION CAMPAIGNS AND THE PAGEANTRY OF MASS POLITICS

From June until November in national election years, campaigning spilled beyond the saloons and into the streets. As one surprised Scottish observer, James Bryce, recalled in 1888, for months before election day, "usually with brass bands, flags, and badges, crowds of cheering spectators are the order of the day and night, from end to end of the country." Americans' tradition of taking politics into the streets stretched back to the mid-eighteenth century. But it was in the Gilded Age, when most men could vote regardless of race or class, that the spirited parades, impassioned oratory, and ongoing festivities became a form of mass entertainment that initiated huge numbers of people into the political process. Parties competed with each other to make the events as large and spectacular as possible, partly to reinforce party loyalty and partly because they believed a massive showing could demoralize the other party and reduce its turnout on election day.

Party members carefully orchestrated election festivities through two different kinds of clubs: marching clubs and political clubs. **Marching clubs** loudly paraded through towns and cities after dark several times a week for at least two or three months before the election. In an effort to draw northern support, Republican "Boys in Blue" evoked the memory of the Civil War and reminded voters of the Democrats' close association with the Confederacy. Southern Democrats did the opposite, linking Republicans with the "northern war of aggression." Northern Democrats either avoided the topic of the Civil War and named clubs after their hero, President

Think About It

1. The vote-buying system was well entrenched by the 1880s and efficient by some accounts. Explain the concerns of those who opposed the practice of spreading "soap" in order to sway voters.
2. In what ways did the voters themselves encourage vote buying?
3. Why do you think proponents of the Australian ballot thought their system would put an end to vote buying?

Tammany Vote for Sale. This 1884 cartoon associates the conventional practice of vote buying with what a growing number of Americans believed was the corruption of politics in general. The powerful political machine Tammany Hall is depicted as auctioning off Irish votes to the highest bidder in return for patronage.

Andrew Jackson, or they called their clubs the "White Boys in Blue"—an attempt to draw white voters by appealing to racial prejudice and reminding them that black voters were overwhelmingly Republican.

Political clubs sprouted in both rural and urban areas in the months before the presidential elections. Such clubs were particularly active in the six "swing" states that tended to decide elections in this period: New York, New Jersey, Connecticut, Ohio, Indiana, and Illinois. Typically named after the party's candidate, the city clubs generally organized by social or ethnic group (such as Irish Catholics in San Francisco, Germans in New York, and so forth) or, occasionally, by factory or business. Veterans, who had their own associations and regiments, established clubs, as did other communities of people (including New York's deaf mutes, in the 1880 election).

Political clubs were themselves models of democracy. Founders elected an executive board and wrote a constitution and rules of order (which new members swore to abide by). They rented campaign rooms for the duration of the election, setting up presses for printing campaign literature and coordinating parades, rallies, and stump speeches for their ward or county. These localized arrangements were a highly effective way of reaching voters, and they were also relatively inexpensive because participants freely volunteered their labor, materials, and organizing energy.

Congressional, state, and local politicians typically joined in the festivities and gave stump speeches, sometimes with oratory brilliant enough to hold listeners' attention for two or three hours. Rather than traveling to meet voters, however, presidential nominees traditionally stayed at home and had surrogates hit the campaign trail for them. In a new twist, the Republican Party transported thousands of young voters, businessmen, and recently naturalized immigrants to Ohio to hear their candidate, James A. Garfield, give inspirational "front porch speeches" in the campaign of 1880. Significantly, the parties often brought women to hear their candidates because, although women could not vote, they were likely to influence male relatives who could.

Campaigning by Porch. Beginning with James A. Garfield in 1880, several presidential candidates (including William McKinley, pictured here) ran their electoral campaigns from their own front porch.

THE PARTISAN PRESS

The press also played a key role in election campaigning (and in everyday politics) by being a mouthpiece for the parties. As had been the case since the 1850s, over 95 percent of American newspapers were openly aligned with either the Democratic or the Republican Party.

The daily press and the parties advanced each other's interests. Newspapers publicized the party's platform and saved candidates the expense of printing their own campaign literature. In return, politicians commonly made donations to local newspapers, and the parties often employed newspaper companies to print the ballots. If the editor's party won office, lucrative government printing and advertising contracts usually followed. Editors were also rewarded with government posts, including the well-paying job of U.S. postmaster.

To boost circulation and sell ads, editors catered to the partisan passions of their readers, referring to the opposition as "enemies" and openly accusing them of engaging in all manner of corruption and villainy. It was not unusual for partisan newspapers to report the same event in wildly divergent ways, with Republican papers emphasizing that a Republican-led legislative session was a rousing success for the citizenry, and the Democratic newspapers reporting the opposite. Because readers looked to the newspaper primarily for affirmation of their political outlook, few were concerned about or aware of the discrepancy.

Most daily newspapers covered only state and local politics, but in the 1880s, Joseph Pulitzer's *New York World* became the first to systematically cover national politics, with an emphasis on scandals and corruption. The *World* told stories from the perspective of ordinary working people, using sensationalist headlines and graphics. Readers were enthralled, and the *World*'s readership more than tripled (from 30,000 to 100,000) in just a few months.

New engraving and printing technology made possible lavishly illustrated weeklies such as *Harper's Weekly* and *Frank Leslie's Illustrated Newspaper* that complemented the daily press. Although they sometimes covered breaking news, the weeklies specialized in giving readers a visual experience of key national events. Weeklies also featured political cartoons that poked fun—often viciously—at the opposition. Cartoonists became famous and well-paid shapers of public opinion with real power to effect change. The most famous cartoonist of the 1870s, Republican Thomas Nast, played a key role in bringing down Tammany boss, William Tweed, who was prosecuted and imprisoned for embezzlement of public funds.

Although the press remained male dominated, a growing number of women began working in newsrooms in the 1880s. For the first time, a few moved from the women's pages (which dealt exclusively with homemaking and other domestic activities) to general news sections. Most explored

VERYTHING OBNOXIOUS TO US, SHALL BE ABOLISHED.
AUGHTER OF PEACEFUL W-ABIDING IRISH CITIZENS MASSACRED BY RIOTOUS MILITIA.
SEE THE IRISH PAPERS.
FENIAN COUNCILS
HANG THE DUTCH GOVERNOR
ENGLISH GOLD
RUM
"IT IS DOUBTFUL IF THE AMERICAN REPUBLIC CAN STAND
THE TABLET
OUR LIBERTY HAS BEEN TAKEN AWAY.
KILLING ORANGEMEN
DOWN WITH THE BASE HIRELING POLICE.
PEACEFUL CITIZENS MUST AVENGE THE MASSACRE OF THE 12TH INSTANT.
THE WRETCH THE BUTCHER OF DUTCH DESCENT.
MASS MEETING
WE MUST RULE.
GUN POWDER
UNCLE SAM'S
SPIRIT OF 76
Th. Nast
THE USUAL IRISH WAY OF DOING THINGS.

Cartoonists as Opinion Shapers. The influential cartoonist Thomas Nast transformed the cruder cartoons of earlier eras by dropping the speech balloons that flowed from characters' mouths and instead crafting detailed, highly expressive figures that conveyed the point with as few words as possible. Nast's harsh attacks helped to decide elections and, in the latter part of his career especially, to popularize racist and xenophobic images of Irish immigrants, African Americans, and Chinese people.

issues of poverty and exploitation in a newsworthy, sensationalist way that would attract readers (see Singular Lives: Nellie Bly, Investigative Journalist).

ELECTORAL MAPMAKING

Voters' strong loyalty to party meant that party membership in any given electoral ward or district was the single most important predictor of election results. But Americans were highly mobile, which meant that the party affiliation of many districts often changed dramatically between elections (as members of one party moved out of the district and partisans of another moved in). As a consequence, the party in power in the state legislature constantly redrew the electoral map—sometimes with dizzying speed—to maximize the party's number of legislators (see Figure 19.1). In Ohio between 1876 and 1886, for instance, lawmakers redrew the electoral districts six times, with the unsettling result that some voters could claim that they had lived in several different districts without ever having moved.

This partisan redrawing of district lines—a practice known as **gerrymandering**—usually proceeded by concentrating members of the opposing party in just a handful of districts. Such redistricting gave the minority power massive majorities in a few districts but preserved the incumbents' hold over the majority of districts. As one Illinois Republican explained his party's strategy in the 1882 redistricting: "Put as large a Democratic majority as possible into the Democratic districts, and spread the Republican majorities over as many districts as possible to make them Republican."

Gerrymandering became a hotly debated issue in the late 1880s, when citizens in many northern states became frustrated with the constantly moving political map. They organized massive anti-gerrymandering rallies at which angry voters displayed maps that revealed the partisan motivation behind redistricting. Although Democrats were as guilty of gerrymandering as Republicans, the rallies persuaded the Democratic leadership that the party might pick up votes if it promised to end the practice. But when Democrats were elected, they reneged on their promise and redrew district lines in their own favor. The Republicans went to court, winning injunctions against redistricting in New Jersey, Wisconsin, and Michigan. Nevertheless, gerrymandering continued into the mid-1890s, and wherever Republicans regained power, they substituted their old gerrymandered districts for the Democrats'.

THE SOUTH AND BIRACIAL POLITICS

Despite the defeat of Reconstruction, the place of black southerners in politics was still an open question in the 1880s. African American men did not automatically lose the vote when "Redeemer" Democrats took power, and, despite the violence against them, they remained active in defense of their rights and political interests through the 1880s. As in the North, newspapers played

SINGULAR LIVES

Nellie Bly, Investigative Journalist

Female reporters were among the growing number of women who ventured into public affairs for the first time during the Gilded Age. Elizabeth Cochran, who later assumed the pen name Nellie Bly, was born into an affluent family, but her father died in 1870 when she was just six years old, leaving her mother to care for their unusually large family of fifteen children. Judge Cochran left no will and, in an era when "respectable" women did not enter paid employment, the family eventually lost everything, including its stately mansion. Nine hard years passed before Elizabeth—who was already known as the most rebellious and headstrong of the Cochran clan—took matters into her own hands and enrolled at Indiana Normal School's teacher-training program (one of the few professional programs, besides nursing, open to women at the time). After just one semester, however, the ambitious young student had to drop out, as she could not afford the school fees. Cochran moved to Philadelphia, where she found low-wage work at a boarding house. She struggled to support herself and her mother—and continued to dream of becoming a teacher and writer.

Then as now, making a living through writing was extremely difficult. Most writers were independently wealthy. Those without means usually supported themselves through teaching or completing a journalism apprenticeship and working at a newspaper. Barred from journalism apprenticeships, aspiring female journalists looked for unconventional ways to catch the attention of editors and publishers. Cochran saw her opportunity in 1886 when a Philadelphia columnist criticized women who worked, writing that women's place was in the home. Outraged, Cochran penned a letter to the editor that was so well written and so passionately argued that the newspaper hired her on the spot. Journalism was considered a rough-and-tumble man's world, and it was conventional that women writers publish under an assumed name, preserving their "privacy." Cochran adopted the pen name Nellie Bly and started work on the "woman's page"—which offered recipes and articles on home decorating, fashion, and gardening. She eventually persuaded the editor to send her to Mexico, where she reported on everyday life. But she soon found herself back on the woman's page. Frustrated, Cochran wrote the editor, "I'm off for New York. Look out for me. Bly."

Cochran contacted *New York World* publisher Joseph Pulitzer, who commissioned her to investigate the infamous city insane asylum on New York's Blackwell's Island. The twenty-three-year-old feigned insanity and arranged to be committed to the asylum, subsequently writing a series of sensationalist articles about her experiences as a patient (published under the eye-catching headline "Behind Asylum Bars" and including an episode on forced labor entitled, "The Girl Who Makes Boxes: Nellie Bly Tells How It Feels to Be a White Slave"). The series was a hit with readers. Cochran went on to write other exposés of injustice and abuse, in which she featured as participant and heroine. Every major newspaper in the nation subsequently hired a "girl stunt reporter" who, like Cochrane, went undercover and wrote about the experiences of immigrants, prisoners, child laborers, and other struggling Americans.

NELLIE PRACTICES INSANITY AT HOME.

Playing the Part. Women reporters ventured into public affairs in the 1880s through both suffrage newspapers and a new genre of investigative reporting. An illustration for Nellie Bly's exposé of New York's insane asylum, this drawing depicts the author preparing to enter under cover.

Such reporting helped educate middle-class readers about the plight of the poor and generated public support for social reform. It also reinforced the relatively new idea that women were expert authorities on social suffering and enlightened welfare policy. Along the way, the talented and resourceful "Nellie Bly" became a household name.

Think About It

1. Why might girl stunt reporters have been such a hit with readers during the Gilded Age?
2. What made Cochran a gender rebel by Gilded Age standards?
3. Explain how journalism such as Cochran's might have helped or harmed society's most downtrodden people.

an important role. By the 1880s, between 20 percent and 30 percent of African Americans over the age of ten could read and write, and those who could not read for themselves attended newspaper readings in churches and schools and at public gatherings. African Americans edited more than fifty southern newspapers and published handbills, circulars, and pamphlets for mass distribution. These publications knitted African American communities together in a communication network that facilitated political mobilization.

The Republican Party remained dominant among black southerners, who continued to work with white Republicans for better schools, roads, and other improvements. But some

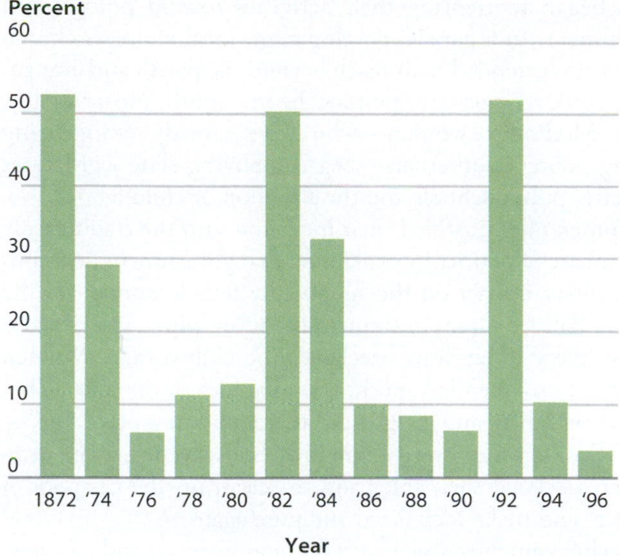

FIGURE 19.1 Percentage of House Districts Redrawn, 1872–1896. Members of the winning party frequently redrew the electoral map to split or isolate the opposing party's voters and to create new districts that were likely to support their own party in the next election.

Exoduster Family, Nicodemus, Kansas. Minister W. H. Smith cofounded Nicodemus with five other Exodusters in 1877. The town eventually grew to a population of seven hundred and supported two newspapers and three churches.

internal divisions arose within African American communities, especially over the question of whether they should remain in the South. Established leaders urged southern blacks to stay and work toward a better South, but independent African American candidates and third parties based in the cotton-growing regions of Alabama, Mississippi, and elsewhere argued for mass migration. The **Exodusters** relocated to Kansas, in response to the defeat of Reconstruction and the growing threat of a white supremacist social order. Emigrants to Liberia (in Africa) wished to leave America altogether in the hope of founding their own people and nation. Most black southerners did not migrate, however. And those who stayed remained politically active, usually in the Republican Party, through the 1880s.

WOMEN IN POLITICS

In almost every state of the union during the Gilded Age, electoral politics remained an exclusively male domain. Before and immediately after the Civil War, advocates of voting rights for women had waged a series of spirited and well-publicized campaigns for women's enfranchisement. Almost all of these failed, however. Other than in the Utah and Wyoming Territories, women could not vote, join the major parties, or hold electoral office. Through the 1880s and 1890s, suffragists struggled on with their campaigns for women's enfranchisement. For the first time in American history, millions of middle-class women found alternative ways to participate in politics and government. Building on their experience as homemakers and mothers, middle-class women carved out a place for themselves as authorities on health, welfare, sanitation, and related public policy issues.

CAMPAIGNING FOR SUFFRAGE

Campaigns for women's voting rights were spearheaded by two rival women's rights organizations. The National Woman Suffrage Association, which had been founded by Susan B. Anthony and Elizabeth Cady Stanton in 1869, pressed for a federal constitutional amendment to enfranchise women and a host of other reforms, such as the right of married women to own property. The rival American Woman Suffrage Association lobbied chiefly for the women's vote at the state level.

Both associations held hundreds of rallies, published dozens of suffrage newspapers, organized speaking tours and door-to-door campaigns, and lobbied Congress for relief.

But men voted down eleven state referenda to enfranchise women. Congress even took a step backward by depriving Utah women of their voting rights in 1887, as punishment for that territory's refusal to prohibit polygamy (a practice endorsed by the Church of Jesus Christ of Latter-day Saints until 1890). Only in the 1890s did suffragists make significant headway, winning votes for women in four states, beginning with Wyoming. All-male electorates in the states of Colorado, Utah, and Idaho gave women the vote by 1896 (see Map 19.3). But it would be over twenty years before women won the right to vote in federal elections (see Chapter 20).

TEMPERANCE CRUSADERS AND CLUBWOMEN

In the face of ongoing exclusion from politics, millions of middle-class women found other, less direct ways to participate. Changes in family size and the home helped make this possible. The average number of children per family dropped for middle-class women from seven or eight in the early nineteenth century to only three or four by 1890, expanding women's free time. (Immigrant and working-class women still tended to have larger families.) The advent of labor-saving technologies—such as wringer washing machines and canned food—also freed many middle-class women from long hours of homemaking.

The single largest organization for women's political involvement was the Woman's Christian Temperance Union (WCTU), which was founded as a prohibitionist organization in 1873. Under the leadership of Frances Willard, it expanded its activities after 1879 to welfare and health issues and began lobbying state and federal government for reform. The women of the WCTU set up lunchrooms and soup kitchens for the needy, opened kindergartens and libraries for immigrants and other poor workers, and installed thousands of water fountains in town squares and parks. In Chicago, the WCTU ran a homeless shelter, a lodging house, a free medical dispensary, an industrial school, and two nurseries.

The organization also weighed in on health care, prison reform, and public health debates. It vigorously supported women's suffrage campaigns in the belief that enfranchised women would cast their vote in favor of prohibition. (Unsurprisingly, saloonkeepers and bar patrons were overwhelmingly opposed to the enfranchisement of women for the same reason, and drinkers chased prominent suffragist Susan B. Anthony out of town on more than one occasion.) In their local WCTU chapters, women received a political education, learning the traditionally male art of oratory and debate, identifying issues of public concern, and acquiring lobbying and publicity skills. Such activities helped draw more than a million women to the organization by the late 1880s—making it one of the largest grassroots movements in the nation, and a training ground for women's involvement in politics.

Across the nation, college-educated and middle-class women also organized thousands of voluntary women's clubs and associations that sought to influence legislation. Existing women's clubs began reorienting their activities toward politics and government. In a parallel development, local women's church groups also extended their reach beyond the parish and evangelizing work to legislative politics. In the South, most notably, white Methodist women—who were already evangelizing among poorer southerners—began lobbying state legislatures for better public schools and the abolition of child labor.

Women often justified their incursion into the traditionally male sphere of politics by explaining that government decisions had a direct impact on the supposedly female domain of the home. "Politics comes in through the water pipes, gas jets, and almost every other way," declared one clubwoman. Women reformers also upended another popular idea of the time—that politics was dirty and rough, and therefore not a place for "ladies." Evoking the image of the tidy housekeeper, women reformers declared their intention to "clean up the cesspool of politics" and make it civilized and pure again.

As clubwomen engaged with the working poor and educated themselves about politics, they became far more aware of the magnitude of problems such as poverty and disease, and of the limits of small voluntary groups' ability to alleviate suffering. The answer, many clubwomen came to believe, lay with state and city governments. As one Southern Methodist woman put it, "the state is God's ministry of organization, through which he must work." In the cities, leaders of the big, nondenominational clubs did not invoke God's ministry, but they agreed that the state ought to play a far more active role in caring for its citizens. In Chicago and elsewhere, women's clubs prevailed upon lawmakers to establish protective agencies for children and to prohibit domestic violence. They lobbied for cleaner water, better public schools, and sanitized streets. And they won the right to vote in school board and other local elections. By the early 1890s, many groups moved beyond the city and state levels to form national associations along the lines of the WCTU.

THE SETTLEMENT MOVEMENT AND MUNICIPAL POLITICS

Middle-class women also entered politics in the Gilded Age through the settlement movement, a welfare experiment begun at the Toynbee Settlement Hall in London, England, in 1884. At Toynbee, college students and graduates were invited to "settle" in working-class districts and to learn about poor communities and help improve them. Inspired by her 1888 visit to the hall, American college-graduate Jane Addams used money she had inherited from her father to purchase a dilapidated mansion in a slum district of Chicago and turn it into a community center. Across the nation, other middle-class women soon opened similar houses.

Initially, Addams's Hull House sought to "uplift" the neighborhood's poor by offering music, history, fine art, literature, and other cultural programs. These programs often reflected the particular values of Addams and other middle-class reformers, but many immigrants found the settlement houses to be excellent resources for stabilizing their lives and strengthening

Hull House Women's Basketball Team, Chicago, 1896. Settlement houses provided important services for immigrants, but they almost always did so with a reformist agenda intended to create better-assimilated and more productive workers. Founder Jane Addams believed that team sports such as basketball could help future factory workers reorient their ideas about success and cooperation to fit better into a work environment of specialized skills, where individual contributions were not always clearly related to the final product.

community ties. In Chicago, for instance, one Greek immigrant, who complained that he had yet to meet a Chicagoan who was interested in classical Athens, was thrilled to find a picture of the Acropolis at Hull House—and an audience of American women who valued his heritage. As immigrants flocked to the houses, Addams and her fellow volunteers discovered that the urban poor were also educating the reformers on the harsh realities of slum life and industrial toil. Consequently, in the early 1890s, the settlement houses expanded their scope beyond cultural uplift to tackling urban poverty directly.

The reformers lobbied city government for better sanitation, housing codes, and factory safety inspections and set up clinics and playgrounds for immigrant children. Soon, settlement leaders were serving on state charities boards and official commissions of inquiry into working and living conditions. In Chicago, Hull House women were instrumental in the establishment of the nation's first juvenile justice system (which, in theory, took into account children's special needs and developed special remedial programs that kept them off the streets and out of prison). Like clubwomen, settlement workers built on their experience and status in the domestic sphere to pressure the state to play a more active role in regard to children, immigrants, and the poor.

NATIONAL POLITICS

The federal government was not as visible in most Americans' lives during the Gilded Age as it is today or as it was in the South during Reconstruction. Party machines, the courts, and state and city government performed many of the welfare, penal, taxation, and economic roles that we now associate with federal government. Congress enacted only a handful of major laws in the two decades between 1877 and 1896, and the president's most challenging assignment was to appoint party supporters to federal offices.

Despite its relatively low profile, however, the federal government was an essential force in American life. Far from taking a hands-off approach to the economy, Congress and most of the presidents worked closely with big business to build Americans' dynamic new industrial world, protecting industrialists from overseas competition and the demands of striking workers. The government also continued to support western development through land grants and other incentives (see Chapter 17). Professional lobbyists became an essential part of Washington life and exerted tremendous influence over the lawmaking process. Most voters remained more or less content with the system. But a growing minority objected that the government seemed unresponsive to their needs. By the 1890s, millions of Americans were demanding an end to "politics as usual."

REPUBLIC OF LOBBYISTS

A visitor to the House of Representatives in the Gilded Age would likely have encountered a scene resembling a raucous city saloon. The din of multiple conversations, the stench of tobacco smoke, and constant, restless motion pervaded the chamber. Lawmakers rarely paid attention to whomever was speaking. They ignored calls to order, yelled at each other across the chamber, and spat long streams of tobacco juice at spittoons fitted to every desk. Members wandered in and out at random intervals, sometimes to take a bath in one of nine oversized tubs recently installed beneath the chamber, and other times to take a nap.

This disorderly scene reflected a fundamental shift in the way Congress performed its duty to legislate. In the 1870s, the chamber ceased to be a place in which representatives routinely debated bills, listened to one another, and decided how to vote. Instead, they (and most senators) generally determined their votes ahead of time in hallways, meeting rooms, parlors, and dining rooms. Almost always, they returned to vote on legislation only after meeting with lobbyists employed by corporations, individuals, or (occasionally) foreign governments.

Lobbying was not a new phenomenon in American political life, but it became a much larger, more professionalized, and better funded enterprise in the Gilded Age. Whenever Congress was in session, professional lobbyists jammed the hallways, offering legislators cash bribes, cheap loans, and special favors in return for favorable laws, tax breaks, and subsidies that promoted their interests. (At a time when senators were appointed by state legislatures rather than direct vote, lobbyists also bribed state lawmakers to make sympathetic appointments.) Businesses hired former congressmen who were willing to use their government connections, and they also turned to female lobbyists in the belief that congressmen were unlikely to break gender etiquette by ignoring or slighting a woman. Clients sponsored "pleasant parlors" for congressmen, where women hosted lavish suppers and served fine wines—a welcome relief from Washington's usual boardinghouse fare.

Lobbyists also transformed capital city life, generating demand for better restaurants, hotels, and other amenities. Complaining that in Washington "the rent is high, the food is bad, the dust is disgusting and the mud is deep," some disgruntled lobbyists and congressmen proposed moving the capital to prosperous St. Louis, Missouri. In response, Washington officials began a massive renovation: streets were paved, old sewers and rank-smelling canals were filled in, and low-lying sections of the city were raised out of the marshes. The government installed a state-of-the-art public tram system, and dozens of restaurants and hotels opened to facilitate the wining and dining of lawmakers.

Professional lobbying was so entrenched by 1880 that both politicians and businessmen felt compelled to engage in it. Not accepting such hospitality, bribes, and "gifts" was often politically costly for lawmakers. At the next election, frustrated lobbyists and their clients simply redirected their money toward other, more sympathetic candidates. At the same time, however, some businessmen began to resent that they had to spend significant sums of money hiring lobbyists and paying for lavish hotels, meals, and bribes. One railroad owner, Collis Huntington of the Central Pacific corporation, complained he had to hire over two hundred lobbyists, including the Associated Press's Washington correspondent, for just one session of Congress.

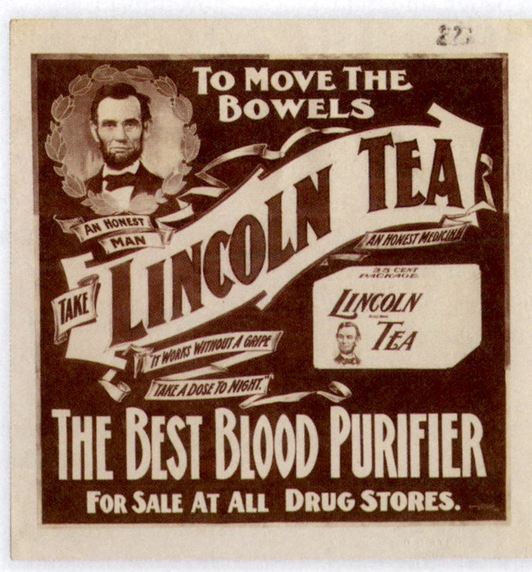

Selling the Presidency. Trade cards such as this example used images of popular presidents to promote products. This card associates "honest Abe" with a purportedly honest remedy: blood-purifying tea.

VETERANS AND THE FOUNDATIONS OF THE WELFARE STATE

Lobbying reinforced the legislature's tendency to concern itself almost solely with matters of commerce, as did the failure of either party to control Congress long enough to enact reforms. Congress passed only a handful of major laws between 1877 and 1896. However, lawmakers did establish a number of new agencies (including the Bureaus of Labor, Education, Statistics, and Fish and Fisheries and the U.S. Geological Survey), and they doubled the size of the federal bureaucracy. Most notably, Congress expanded the Civil War veterans' pension system—America's first federal welfare system. Union veterans lobbied successfully for pensions, both for themselves and their dependents. The system was paid for by the money that flowed into the U.S. treasury from the tariff (tax) on imported goods and, as tariff revenue grew in the late 1880s, coverage was gradually extended. By the end of the century, a majority of northern men and thousands of soldiers' widows and dependents collected a pension, and the system was the second costliest item on the federal budget (after government borrowing).

THE PRESIDENCY AND THE SPOILS SYSTEM

The office of the president had tremendous symbolic value in the Gilded Age. Former presidents such as Abraham Lincoln and John Adams signified reliability, optimism, and strength—so much so that advertisers often used their images on colorful trade cards promoting everything from hand soaps to blood-purifying teas. But in terms of policymaking, the office was weak by the standards of Civil War and post-1930s America. Andrew Johnson's impeachment in 1866 and Congress's limitation of executive power after the war (see Chapter 16) had left the office of the president with just one major task: the distribution of the federal government's 100,000-odd positions. "The President may be compared to the senior or managing clerk in a large business establishment," wrote an uninspired James Bryce, and his "chief function is to select his subordinates."

Presidents entered the White House indebted to the patronage networks of party members who had campaigned for them, and they paid off their political debts by appointing supporters to salaried government positions and distributing other "spoils" (resources) of office. Under this **spoils system,** the positions went to party supporters, who then kicked back a portion of their government salary to the party treasury. The spoils system dated back to the era of Andrew Jackson, and most Americans had long accepted it. But as industrialization and the development of the West transformed American life, many citizens became concerned with the scale of the spoils and government's increasingly cozy relationship with big business. The unprecedented wealth generated by industrialization and western development added tremendous value to political office. Politicians, from the president on down to the town alderman, now had the power to authorize and fund multimillion-dollar construction, railroad, and industrial projects. Consequently, transcontinental railroads and other interests began paying lawmakers far more handsomely for favorable legislation (including land grants, tax breaks, bonds, and cheap loans).

CIVIL SERVICE REFORM AND THE GARFIELD ASSASSINATION

Development projects frequently generated spectacular profits for business owners, but they also often came at the expense of aspiring farmers, ranchers, workers, small businesspeople, and the public interest. The series of financial scandals that rocked the Grant administration in the 1870s (see Chapter 16) produced a small but vocal movement within the Republican Party to limit patronage and loosen the ties between big business and government. Republicans split into two factions during Rutherford B. Hayes's administration (1876–1880). Stalwarts supported patronage, whereas reformists, derisively named Half-Breeds (on the grounds that they were not fully Republican), argued that one way to limit big business's influence on government was to dismantle party patronage networks and establish a federal civil service. The qualifications for becoming a postmaster or U.S. marshal, insisted the Half-Breeds, should not be party loyalty but skills and demonstrated experience.

A fierce struggle broke out among Republicans when Stalwart Ulysses S. Grant and Half-Breed candidate Senator James G. Blaine of Maine squared off against each other at the party's national convention in Chicago in 1880. Half-Breeds refused to give Grant the nomination on grounds of corruption and excessive patronage. But the real issue at stake—the independence of government—was overshadowed quickly as each side became focused solely on winning the nomination. The factions deadlocked and the delegates voted an unprecedented thirty-three times without a clear victor emerging. On the thirty-fourth vote, a little-known compromise candidate, former Union general and U.S. congressman James Garfield of Ohio, emerged as an uncontroversial contender and went on to win the candidacy. In a gesture of conciliation, he chose a Stalwart, Chester Arthur, as his running mate.

Like the Republicans, the Democrats chose a former Union general, Winfield S. Hancock, to run for the presidency in 1880. The Greenback-Labor Party, a small third party established in 1876 that supported monetary reform, the eight-hour workday, and a federal income tax, also nominated an ex-Union general, James B. Weaver. As the campaign wore on, the parties lapsed into personal attacks. Hancock, who had never held elective office and so had no record of political corruption, promoted himself as clean and incorruptible and spent much of the campaign trying to discredit Garfield for his involvement with the scandal-ridden Grant administration. But Hancock's detractors ridiculed him for his lack of political experience and claimed he was the puppet of powerful southern planters. The Republicans printed a pamphlet on Hancock's political achievements, consisting of a title page and seven blank pages. The election was typical of the age: Voter turnout was high (around 80 percent of all voters), and the two major parties' electoral platforms were almost indistinguishable. On election day, Garfield easily won the electoral college, but the popular vote was much closer, with Garfield winning by a margin of only eight thousand votes. Weaver received a disappointing three hundred thousand votes.

Once in office, President Garfield faced the usual tens of thousands of office seekers requesting patronage. But he proved himself an ally of reform, refusing to quickly distribute the posts, and supporting the Half-Breeds' call for a federal civil service. He also confronted a leading Stalwart, Senator Roscoe Conkling, by refusing to appoint the senator's preferred candidate to the important position of tariff collector at the New York Customs House (where the federal treasury collected millions of dollars in tariff fees on imported goods). The senator, who had long controlled the lucrative customs house, fought a bitter battle against Garfield and what he called the "snivel service" initiative. But the Stalwarts made little headway, and an enraged Conkling quit Congress in protest, returning to work as a highly paid railroad attorney.

Some weeks later, a deranged lawyer and Stalwart by the name of Charles Guiteau shot the president as he waited for a train at a Washington, D.C., railroad station. Guiteau, who had unsuccessfully petitioned Garfield for the position of consul general to Paris, reportedly yelled, "I am a Stalwart and Arthur is president now!" as he pulled the trigger. Garfield was confined to bed and lingered for three months before passing. The unhinged assassin, who chose to defend himself in a circus-like proceeding described by the press as the "trial of the century," was convicted and hanged.

Garfield's assassination drew public sympathy to the cause of civil service reform and further discredited the Stalwarts, giving Congress the majority needed to pass the Civil Service Act in 1883. One of the few significant federal laws enacted during the Gilded Age, the act made some 10 percent of all federal positions subject to civil service rules, under which candidates had to take a competitive examination and federal offices had to appoint the top performers. Sensing that the tide was changing, President Arthur disappointed his Stalwart allies by signing the act. Stalwartism was weakened, and by 1900 almost one hundred thousand federal employees (40 percent of the total) had been appointed through the civil service system.

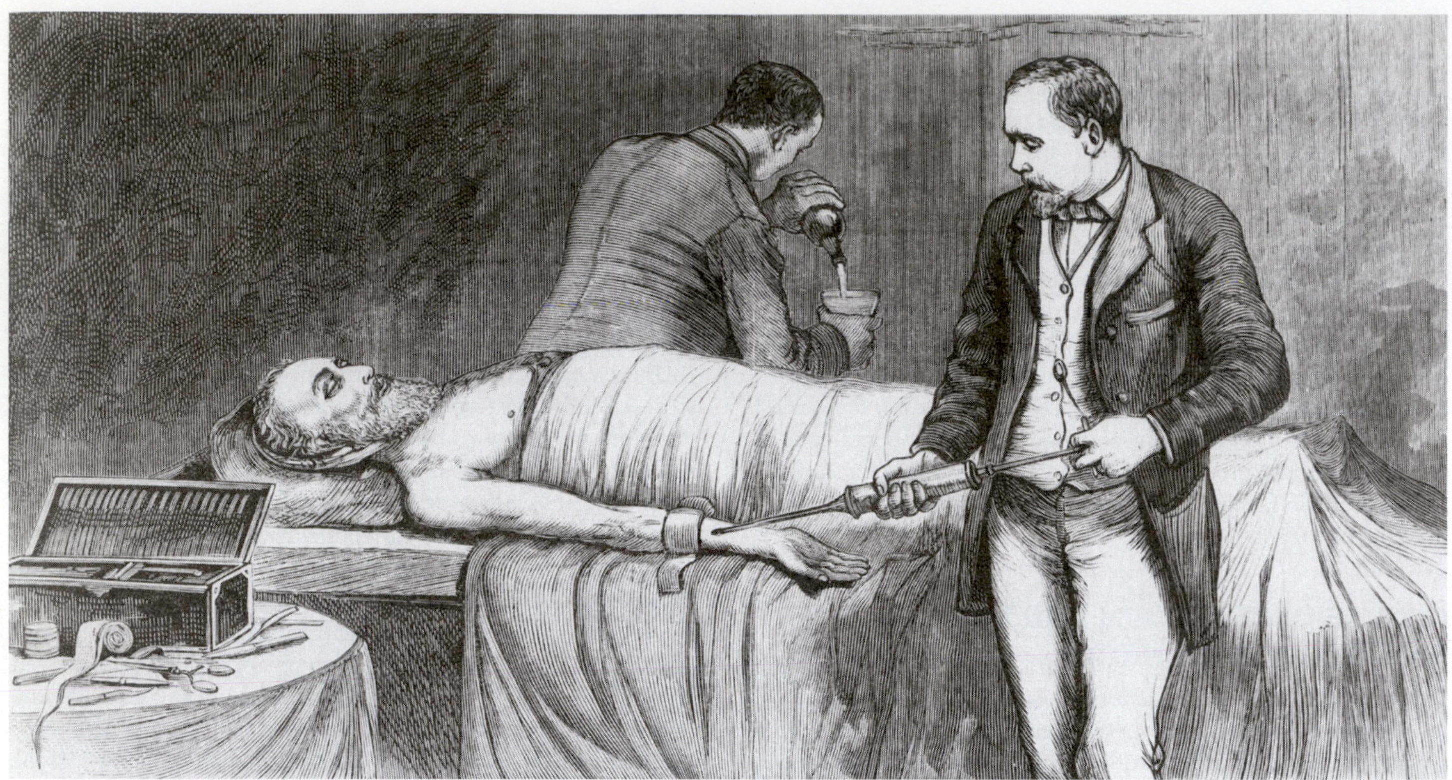

Embalming a President. After Charles Guiteau shot President Garfield in 1881, the weekly press closely followed the fallen president's last few, painful, bedridden months and dramatized the treatment of his body in death. In this macabre illustration, a mortician pumps embalming fluid (probably arsenic) into the deceased man's veins.

DEBATING THE TARIFF

In most federal elections between 1880 and 1896, the two major parties' electoral platforms were remarkably similar. The great majority of voters cast their ballots on the basis of party loyalty rather than policy questions, and so the parties spent little time framing and debating substantive issues (such as foreign policy or western development). But the parties differed on two key issues about which Americans from all walks of life cared passionately: the tariff on foreign-made products and the money supply.

For most of the nineteenth century, the U.S. government had protected American industry from overseas competition by forcing up the prices of foreign goods. Importers and overseas manufacturers paid the Treasury a tariff on the goods' value at the port of entry, and they passed this cost to consumers by raising the goods' price. Before the Civil War, the tariff had protected America's small and struggling manufacturing sector. But by the 1870s, American industries were highly profitable and globally competitive and large numbers of voters believed that protection was no longer necessary.

The increasingly heated debate over the tariff reflected two competing visions of American government. Democrats envisioned America as a free-market society in which federal government played only a minimal role. National government ought to concern itself only with overseas trade, international relations, and war making—not the regulation of Americans' lives, morals, and the economy (unless the issue was the impact of large, interstate corporations on citizens as consumers). Conversely, Republicans advocated an expansive, protectionist government that promoted economic development and the moral welfare of the nation. Republican administrations typically imposed a tariff of upwards of 50 percent, which made imported goods so expensive that most consumers had little choice but to buy American. High tariffs were bad for consumers, argued Democrats, and damaged the republic by creating an extremely wealthy class of American industrialists at the expense of everyone else. Republicans countered that protective tariffs would help maintain high employment levels in industry and enrich the federal treasury.

THE MONEY QUESTION

The other most passionately debated political issue of the age was money. Today's monetary system (which consists of one currency: the **greenback** dollar) did not exist in the Gilded Age. Instead, several kinds of money were in circulation. People could take silver and gold to any U.S. mint and pass it through a window for conversion into coins. The value of this kind of money was pegged to the price of silver and gold on the open market. Just as they are today, greenbacks were a kind of "token money" that was not guaranteed by precious metals in the Treasury but by government bonds. The value of these bonds fluctuated significantly, depending on investors' confidence in the government, which made the greenbacks' value unstable. Even more confusing, privately owned banks, rather than the federal government, printed money (bank notes). Depending on what form the money took, a dollar could be worth a lot more in silver or gold than in greenback or bank note form.

Gilded Age Americans agreed that the nation's monetary system was in need of drastic reform. But there was no consensus on how to reform it. The great "money question" became an urgent political issue when an acute shortage of currency struck in the early 1870s. Homeowners with mortgages and farmers who borrowed to pay for land and supplies favored a system of cheaper greenbacks that would get more money into circulation and thus lower interest rates and make loans easier to obtain. However, bankers and creditors, who preferred debts to be repaid in the more valuable bimetallic money, demanded the currency's withdrawal. The Republican government, which was generally friendly toward bankers and industry, agreed and gradually withdrew about one-fifth of circulating greenbacks by 1875.

The money question was complicated further by Congress's response to changes in the supply of silver. Since 1834, the price of silver for the purpose of minting had been set by law at one-sixteenth that of gold, a ratio that corresponded roughly to the prices of silver and gold on the open market at that time. By the 1860s, silver was worth a lot more than one-sixteenth the value of gold, and people preferred to sell their silver to jewelers and other craftsmen for the higher price. As the coinage of silver all but ceased, Congress voted in 1873 to discontinue it altogether and permit only the minting of gold. Few people objected. But once newly discovered veins of silver in the West flooded the market, the price of silver dropped precipitously and demand for silver coinage revived. Mining interests lobbied hard for the reintroduction of silver-backed currency, because the federal government would have to purchase thousands of tons of silver from them. And farmers—increasingly indebted and desperate for more and cheaper money—concurred.

The money shortage was aggravated again in 1876 when Congress ordered that, beginning in 1879, the currency would move to a single **gold standard,** with all greenbacks redeemable in gold coin. Outraged farmers in the Midwest formed the Greenback Party, which called for more greenbacks and an end to the gold standard (see Interpreting the Sources: Thomas Nast, "Milk Tickets for Babies"). If government could choose to issue money backed by a metal such as gold, argued the Greenbackers, it could also issue money backed by bonds—or any kind of wealth.

Congress responded with two compromise solutions, neither of which stabilized the monetary system or fully satisfied anybody. The first, in 1876, required the Treasury to purchase between $2 million and $4 million worth of silver each year, and to mint $1 silver coins. In practice, however, the law did not satisfy indebted farmers and mining interests, because Treasury officials—who favored the gold standard—always bought only the minimum ($2 million) of silver required by law. By the late 1880s, frustrated farmers and mining interests were labeling the original suspension of silver coinage in 1873 the "Crime of '73" and demanding **free silver**—the unlimited coinage of silver. Congress enacted the Sherman Silver Purchase Act of 1890, which required the government to purchase an extra 4.5 million ounces of silver bullion for coinage and issue bank notes that could be redeemed in silver or gold. From the Silverites' perspective, this injected some, though not enough, fresh silver into the market. Meanwhile, bankers argued that it further destabilized the monetary system—and possibly put America in danger of losing foreign investors.

DEMOCRATS RETURN: THE FIRST ONE-TERM PRESIDENCY OF GROVER CLEVELAND

The Democrats' close association with southern secession and the Confederacy—which Republicans reinforced every election by waving the bloody shirt (see Chapter 16)—ensured that the Republican Party dominated the presidency and Congress for almost two decades after the Civil War. This began to change after the defeat of Reconstruction, as Democrats used all means at their disposal to build a solid southern base. Realizing that they could not win the presidency on southern votes alone, in the run-up to the election of 1884 they looked for ways to rebuild in the North. They nominated New York governor Grover Cleveland for president in the hope that he would help make the national party acceptable to a majority of northern voters.

At a time when a growing number of Americans were suspicious of big business, Cleveland astutely promoted himself as a champion of the people against special interests (especially the railroad companies), and spoke out against the Republican policies of high tariffs and government subsidization of corporations. Pulitzer's *World* supported him, as did a small but influential group of independent Republicans. Labeled Mugwumps (a term derived from an Algonquian word for chieftain or independent leader) by the disapproving Republican press, these dissenters were mostly Anglo-Saxon professionals who were critical of both machine politics and the increasingly powerful generation of financial and industrial magnates who held sway in federal government. Mugwumps condemned lobbying, the spoils system, and high-level corruption and called for a return to policies that benefited the public as a whole rather than special interests.

James G. Blaine, Cleveland's Republican opponent and formerly a member of the Grant administration, calculated that if he pressed for a moderate tariff and government subsidy of business, northern workers would support him because they believed these policies generated jobs. Blaine also actively courted Irish American voters, who had traditionally voted Democratic but who, he reasoned, could be won over to a high-tariff policy.

INTERPRETING THE SOURCES

Thomas Nast, "Milk Tickets for Babies"

The money question reached a fever pitch in 1876 when farmers deluged Congress with petitions objecting to the imposition of a single gold standard on greenbacks and formed the Greenback Party. Money was simply a token of value, they insisted, and the government could create money in any form it chose, whether paper, metal, or stone. "Gold is not money until coined and made money by the law," declared one advocate, "[and] paper is equally money, when conditioned and issued according to the law." The Greenbackers' concept of money eventually became the foundation of our own monetary system, but in the Gilded Age, most Americans considered it a lunatic proposition. This 1876 cartoon, "Milk Tickets for Babies," by influential Republican artist Thomas Nast, lambastes the Greenbackers' idea.

MILK-TICKETS FOR BABIES, IN PLACE OF MILK.

7

Thomas Nast, "Milk Tickets For Babies," in David A. Wells, *Robinson Crusoe's Money*, 1876.

Explore the Source

1. What is absurd about the Greenback Party's concept of money, according to Nast's cartoon?
2. Why, in the 1870s and 1880s, might Nast and most Republicans have supported a single gold standard for greenbacks?
3. Why do you think Nast chose the images of babies, milk, and cows to make his point?

The race was among the closest and bitterest of the Gilded Age. The Republican press charged that Cleveland had fathered an illegitimate child, while Cleveland's campaign lambasted Blaine for allegedly accepting bribes from railroads and other interests while a member of Congress. (Evidence suggests that both claims were true.) Ultimately, Blaine could not shake the taint of corruption. In the last week of the election, the Republican campaign made a costly blunder when a pro-Blaine Protestant preacher denounced the Democrats as the party of "rum, Romanism, and rebellion." When it was reported in the press, Blaine refused to distance himself from this blatantly anti-Irish slur. Cleveland secured both the Irish American and the Mugwump vote and was victorious on election day. Democrats held the White House for the first time since before the Civil War. In the wake of the Republicans' defeat, the word *Mugwump* became an enduring term of abuse for those who broke the cardinal rule of Gilded Age politics—unwavering loyalty to party on election day.

As president, Cleveland helped make the Democratic national party respectable again among many northern voters—including Mugwump exiles from the Republican Party. He played an instrumental role in the enactment of one of the most important laws of the period—the Interstate Commerce Act of 1887. Passed in response to a Supreme Court ruling in 1886 that the states could not regulate interstate railroads and their prices, the act laid the groundwork for federal regulations that would ensure fair prices and conditions for all customers. In the same spirit of opposition to special interests, Cleveland arranged for the return to the federal government of some western lands that private companies and individuals had acquired fraudulently.

Cleveland also strengthened the office of the president relative to an all-powerful Congress. Much as Andrew Jackson had done in the 1830s (see Chapter 10), he consistently defined the president's role as that of protector of the people against congressional lawmakers beholden to special interests. He asserted his will over federal lawmakers by vetoing 414 bills between 1884 and 1888—more than twice the number vetoed by all previous presidents combined, and more than any subsequent

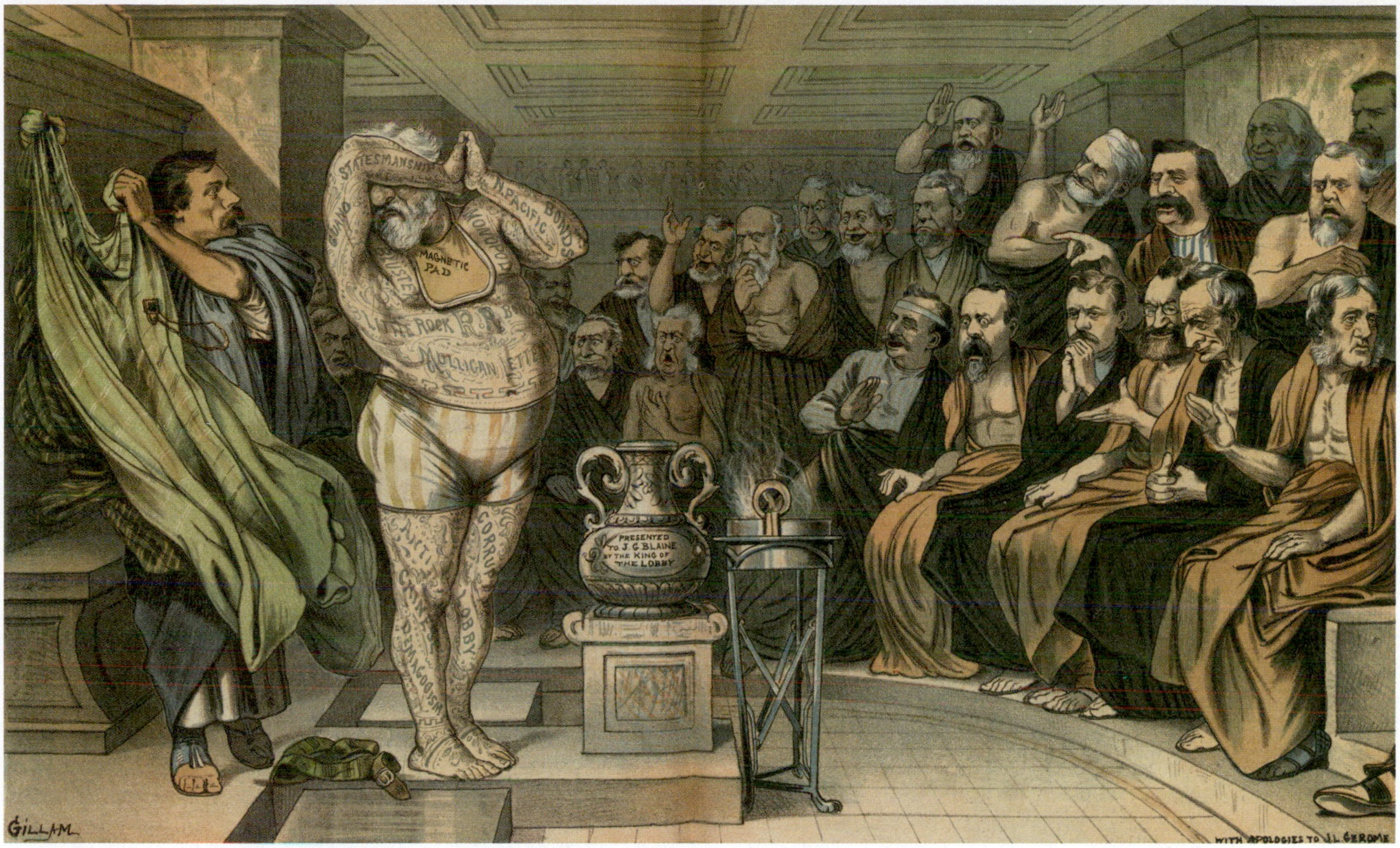

"James Blaine: Tattooed Man." In the 1884 election, Democrats accused Republican presidential nominee James G. Blaine of corruption. Here he is depicted as a tattooed person of uncertain gender, with the marks of corruption printed indelibly on his skin.

president in a single term. Although Cleveland was the most assertive president of the Gilded Age, his actions did not always work in his or his party's favor. The intended recipients of federal aid in the vetoed bills were usually businesses, but sometimes they were communities struck by natural and other disasters, and some of these communities voted Democratic. Following a severe drought in Texas, for instance, Congress wanted to give struggling farmers $10,000 worth of free seed. But Cleveland, who favored small government, killed the Texas Seed Bill, declaring that such aid only made Americans unhealthily dependent on government and weakened the "sturdiness of our national character" (see How Much Is That?).

This Texas seed controversy rankled with western Democrats and was a warning sign that although many

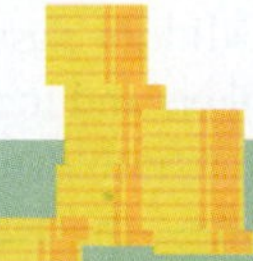

How Much Is That?

President Cleveland's Seed Bill Veto

It may seem absurd that Grover Cleveland's presidency ran into trouble over the president's veto of a $10,000 appropriation for wheat grain for drought-stricken Texas farmers. Even taking inflation into account, the $10,000 would be worth only $252,000 today—a drop in the bucket for a Congress that spends over $3 trillion annually. Because wheat grain was much more expensive in 1888, $10,000 would have bought only 139 bushels back then, whereas the equivalent today would buy an astounding 33,000 bushels! To understand the controversy, we need additional information. When we examine Congress's usual expenditures for the time, for instance, it becomes clear that $10,000 was a relatively large amount in the Gilded Age, accounting for 10 percent of the government's total free seed fund. More importantly, philosophical differences about the role and methods of government made the seed bill controversial. The bill's supporters viewed government as an active participant in the economy, but Cleveland believed that the economy functioned best when the government left farmers and business owners alone. Emergency bailouts, he argued, only encouraged unhealthy dependency—and stuck taxpayers with the bill.

Americans were critical of massive federal aid to big business, they expected government to aid specific communities in times of need. Cleveland also vetoed dozens of private congressional bills that allocated pension money to particular individuals and groups. These vetoes pleased critics of patronage but alienated Democrats whose bills were vetoed—and it angered voters, including well-organized veterans, who had hoped for more aid.

Criticism within the party mounted as Cleveland made tariff reduction the key plank in his reelection campaign for 1888. With the tariff generating ever-larger surpluses for the federal government (over $114 million in 1888—or $2.9 billion today), Cleveland announced to Congress that the tariff ought to be permanently lowered. The western and southern sections of the party enthusiastically greeted Cleveland's decision enthusiastically, but most northeastern Democrats, including the powerful Tammany Hall machine in Cleveland's home state, withdrew their support. Detecting the Democrats' division over the issue, Benjamin Harrison, the Republican candidate and a former Civil War general, made a high tariff the central plank in his election platform.

The presidential election of 1888 was even more bitterly fought than the previous one. Whereas Cleveland followed tradition and left campaigning to his running mate, Harrison used his front porch speeches to repeatedly argue that a high tariff was good for workers and the nation. The first nominee to tightly control press coverage of his speeches and meetings, Harrison was careful to avoid a repeat of Blaine's "rum, Romanism, and rebellion" blunder. Businessmen contributed an unprecedented $3 million (over $75 million today) to his campaign and prominent New York Republican Thomas Platt spent $150,000 purchasing votes for Harrison in Cleveland's home state. Both parties paid the poll taxes of some one hundred thousand poor people and covered immigrants' naturalization fees in many cities and towns so that they could vote.

On election day, voter fraud and ballot tampering were rife. In West Virginia, twelve thousand more people voted than were eligible to do so. In Arkansas, campaign printing presses were smashed, newspaper reporters were driven out of town, and the content of ten precincts' ballot boxes was destroyed. At the end of the day, when all surviving ballots were counted, Cleveland won the popular vote but lost the electoral college. For the first time since 1872, Republicans swept both houses and the presidency.

TIDES OF POLITICAL DISCONTENT

Although elections were passionately contested and the great majority of male citizens voted in the 1880s, relatively little changed in American politics and government in that decade. Third parties never captured more than a small percentage of the vote, and partisanship remained vital and strong. But dramatic and important changes were taking place elsewhere in American life, and these eventually had an impact on politics. In a time of rapid industrial and cultural change, farmers, workers, small business owners, bankers, and corporate leaders all formulated new and often conflicting visions of government and society. Many also created vast, locally rooted networks of alliances and unions that tried to adapt to the industrializing world by identifying common concerns and offering members mutual aid, education, and economic advancement. These cooperative networks transformed lives and aspirations—and they also sowed seeds of political discontent.

THE ANTI-MONOPOLY MOVEMENT

In the early 1880s, as corporations strengthened and acquired new legal rights (see Chapter 18), many Americans grew concerned about the power of big business. Large corporations' ability to set prices for essential goods and services, and consumers' relative lack of power to do anything but pay those prices, became a focal point of growing anti-monopoly protest. Numerous critics argued that railroad magnates such as Jay Gould behaved like the barons of feudal Germany, whose control of road, canal, and river tolls enriched them at the expense of ordinary people. The idea that the railroad owners were indirectly stealing from consumers (by setting freight rates too high) struck a chord with many struggling farmers, who also faced escalating prices for grain storage and higher interest rates on loans. Many industrial workers agreed. In California, the Workingman's Party called for the end of the "land monopoly" held by the five largest railroad companies. On the Fourth of July, diverse gatherings of farmers, laborers, and union leaders read aloud a modified Declaration of Independence in which they called for relief from monopolies and an end to economic injustice.

Middle-class Americans also worried that the power of the bankers and industrialists, who were neither elected nor accountable to public oversight, was a threat to democracy. In 1882, Carl Schurz, the Republican editor of the *New York Evening Post*, criticized the unprecedented economic power of the "robber barons" in a speech at Harvard University, and the pro-business *New York Times* lamented that magnates were routinely buying political favors in state legislatures. Concerned clergy, such as former antislavery campaigner Parker Pillsbury, warned that the growth of large-scale monopolies would only result in more "strikes, tramps, paupers, idiots, lunatics and criminals."

Across the country, those opposed to monopolies met to strategize about how to weaken the robber barons and advance social justice. In 1884, a nationwide Anti-Monopoly Party was founded in Chicago that included in its platform higher taxes for the wealthy, the direct election of senators, and legislation that would break up the trusts. Activists and anti-monopoly clubs secured the passage of laws regulating monopolies in several states. One constitutional amendment declared, "Monopolies shall never be allowed in [Washington] state."

In practice, the states were limited in what they could do to regulate corporations that spanned the continent. And although the Anti-Monopoly Party fielded a presidential candidate in the 1884 election (former U.S. Army general Benjamin

Butler), he polled only 176,000 votes out of ten million and the party soon dissolved. Still, the major parties took note of the popular outcry, and in the next presidential election (1888) both included antitrust planks in their electoral platforms. In 1890, Congress passed the Sherman Antitrust Act, which made it an offense to "monopolize" or conspire to monopolize "any part of the trade or commerce among the several states." The act broke ground for the federal government by empowering it to prosecute interstate organizations, such as corporations. But the law provided no means of enforcement and, ironically, the federal courts tended to enforce it not against corporations, but against the trade unions, ruling that unions conspired to build their own kind of monopoly—a monopoly over workers.

WORKERS AND THE PRODUCERS' REPUBLIC

The Knights of Labor, which was founded as a secret society of tailors in Philadelphia in 1869, emerged in the 1880s as the largest national workers' organization, with over seven hundred thousand members nationwide. Under the leadership of Terence Powderly, the Knights dropped their secrecy and openly spearheaded campaigns for the eight-hour day, an end to child and convict labor, and various political reforms such as women's rights and a graduated income tax. The Knights aimed to create what they called "one great solidarity" among people employed in productive labor, regardless of gender, ethnic, religious, and other differences. Like skilled workers in the antebellum era, the Knights were critical of the wage labor system and rejected the idea that it was a permanent feature of American life. They hoped that waged workers would have the opportunity to one day become small business owners or farmers. Reforming the wage system so as to make that aspiration a reality was one of their chief goals.

Black Knights. Although African Americans joined the Knights of Labor in large numbers, the Knights' southern chapters remained segregated. When Frank J. Ferrell, an African American Knight from New York City's Assembly 49, gave a short speech at the organization's 1886 convention in Richmond, Virginia, there were threats of mob violence.

Only those whom the Knights did not consider **producers** were barred from joining. Bankers, lawyers, liquor store owners, and gamblers—all of whom were said to unjustly profit from the labor of others—were excluded. People of Chinese descent were refused on the grounds that they provided a cheap form of labor that damaged the interests of other workers. (In fact, Chinese workers attempted to unionize and demand higher wages wherever they could.) The Knights' leadership opposed the use of strikes, preferring boycotts of the offending company's products and political lobbying. But the membership often took matters into their own hands. In 1884, for instance, members successfully struck against the Southwestern Railroad, which was owned by prominent magnate Jay Gould. Rather than stopping all trains, as workers had done in 1877, the strikers made the strategic decision to stop only freight trains. Pleased they were not being delayed, passengers were far more sympathetic to the strikers, and the state governors refused to dispatch the militias against striking workers. Eventually, Gould was compelled to honor a union contract, which implicitly recognized the union's right to exist. News of this victory had an immediate impact on Knights' membership, which grew from under 150,000 to 700,000 in two years.

Many workers were drawn to the Knights, but a small but vociferous minority argued for far more radical social change. Self-proclaimed **anarchists** in New York and elsewhere claimed that it was a myth that workers in America enjoyed the natural right to life and liberty and that America was instead an oppressive "grand temple of Usury, Gambling, and Cut-Throatism." The nation's fastest-growing city (Chicago) emerged as the leading anarchist city, particularly once Germany's autocratic government sent thousands of radical workers into exile in the early 1880s. As much a cultural as a political movement, Chicago's anarchist community organized some two dozen social clubs, ran dances and beer festivals, and published several newspapers (with a combined circulation of thirty thousand). At parades and rallies, leaders condemned the prevailing system of private property as a form of organized theft that protected the rich few at the expense of the exploited many. Society, these anarchists argued, ought to be reorganized into a series of self-governing cooperatives.

Employers and many middle-class Americans responded with derision, alarm, and incomprehension. Anarchists "parade at night with their black and red flags in the very shadow of the

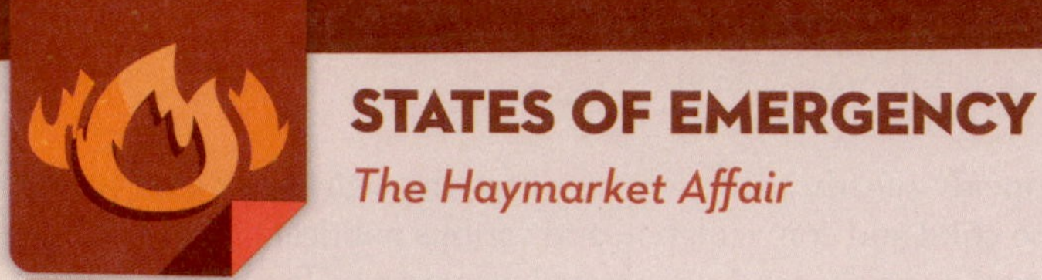

STATES OF EMERGENCY

The Haymarket Affair

In May 1886, Chicago's anarchist leaders responded to the deaths of four strikers at the McCormick Harvester Company by calling a rally in Haymarket Square, where 1,300 workers assembled the following evening. The gathering was orderly, but as the crowd was dispersing under police supervision, an unknown person threw a dynamite bomb, instantly killing a policeman and wounding many others. Police shot into the crowd, and some workers returned fire. Five minutes later, seven police and four civilians lay dead. In the ensuing hours, police rounded up eight anarchists (six of whom were German speaking) and charged them with murder. The bomb thrower was never identified. Despite a complete lack of evidence, the men were swiftly convicted, and four were executed. In 1893, Governor Peter Altgeld pardoned the three surviving men.

The Haymarket Affair had far-reaching consequences for politics and culture. At a time when anxieties about debt, economic depression, and the changing demographics of American society ran high, it associated immigrants with radicalism in the minds of many native-born Americans. The ensuing hysteria and crackdown set the pattern for the "red scares" of 1919 and the early 1950s (see Chapters 22 and 26). Foreignness was considered a sign of radicalism, and radicalism was seen as "un-American." Although the vast majority of protestors at Haymarket had been orderly, and although many were native born, newspapers railed at this "invasion of . . . long-haired, wild eyed, bad-smelling, atheistic, reckless foreign wretches." Law-and-order leagues and secret fraternal societies, such as the Patriotic Order Sons of America, launched anti-immigrant campaigns. City and state governments redoubled their efforts to build imposing fortress-like armories near immigrant neighborhoods. Well into the twentieth century, the specter of a dynamite-throwing immigrant haunted public debate about immigration policy, and many native-born Americans perceived immigrants as lawless, potentially violent, and a threat to the nation.

Haymarket also proved a near-fatal blow for the Knights of Labor. Although the Knights had no involvement with the bombing and denounced it, the mass press closely identified the organization with radicalism. Membership fell dramatically. The Knights survived a few years longer in the South, going on to organize a general strike among ten thousand black sugarcane workers in Louisiana in 1887. (That strike was violently repressed by state militia, at the loss of fifty black workers' lives, and the Southern Knights collapsed in its wake.) In the industrial states, some trade unions—which had competed with the Knights for leadership on labor issues—lumped the Knights' producerism with anarchism and communism and inaccurately dismissed them all as foreign agitation. The unions established the American Federation of Labor and proceeded to reorganize the labor movement as something almost exclusively for white, male, skilled workers. Only the typographers and cigar makers' unions admitted women. Insisting that workers needed to focus exclusively on the goal of higher wages, and not systematic social and economic reform, the future leader of the Federation, Samuel Gompers, declared: "The way out of the wage system is through higher wages."

Think About It

1. Labor organizer John Swinton declared that the Haymarket bomb was "a godsend to the enemies of the labor movement." What did he mean, and did his assessment prove accurate?
2. Explain why labor unions limited their membership and their focus in the aftermath of the Haymarket Affair.

buildings which have furnished them full employment," wrote the editor of the *Chicago Tribune*, "and threaten the destruction of the buildings . . . which they were paid to construct! What do the leaders of this unreasoning, ignorant, inconsistent association mean?"

INDUSTRIAL CONFLICT AND THE NEW NATIVISM

Almost ten thousand industrial and agricultural strikes broke out across the United States in the 1880s, and strike activity continued through the 1890s in many counties (see Map 19.1). Some strikes were carefully planned in advance; others were a spontaneous response to an employer's sudden change in work rules or an unfair dismissal of a coworker. Both kinds were a forceful way of expressing workers' grievances and demands, such as for an eight-hour day and higher wages. But refusing to work as normal and asserting their freedom from employers was also exhilarating and empowering. Longer strikes were often community-building events in which workers and family members performed songs, staged parades and pageants, and engaged in lengthy oratory, much as at election time. Workers also called sympathy strikes in which they showed their support for striking laborers in other industries and in other parts of the country.

Strike activity peaked in 1885–1886, during a particularly turbulent period that culminated in a mass strike known as the Great Upheaval. The country had recently entered a depression, and hundreds of thousands of people had lost their jobs

The Haymarket Bomb. The Haymarket Affair affirmed the perception of many native-born Americans that European radicals were fomenting revolution in the United States and that they should be jailed or deported.

or suffered severe pay cuts. Workers called another strike on Gould's Southwestern railroad in spring 1886, after the company fired a union spokesman for attending a meeting on company time. The Great Southwestern Strike spread rapidly along the rail lines of Texas, Missouri, Kansas, and Arkansas, eventually paralyzing the entire southwestern railroad system. When militiamen, strikebreakers, and Pinkertons (agents of the Pinkerton Detective Agency, a private security company) attempted to get the engines rolling again, armed strikers sabotaged the trains, soaped the rails, and tampered with the switches. Deputies and militiamen clashed repeatedly with strikers, resulting in thousands of arrests and injuries and an unknown number of deaths. In East St. Louis, the Knights held massive funeral processions for the deceased.

In the Northeast and Midwest, workers and unions campaigning for the eight-hour day called a general, nationwide strike for May 1, 1886. A much smaller number than expected (about three hundred thousand versus upward of a million) struck in Chicago, New York, Detroit, and elsewhere. At first the protests were peaceful, but on May 4, police shot and killed four strikers at the McCormick Harvester Company in Chicago after a crowd surged toward the strikebreakers. The next evening, a rally held in Chicago's Haymarket Square to protest the previous day's deaths also turned violent. Following the Haymarket Affair (see States of Emergency: The Haymarket Affair), hundreds of labor leaders and suspected radicals were detained across the country, and the Great Southwestern Strike and the eight-hour movement collapsed. Convinced that the

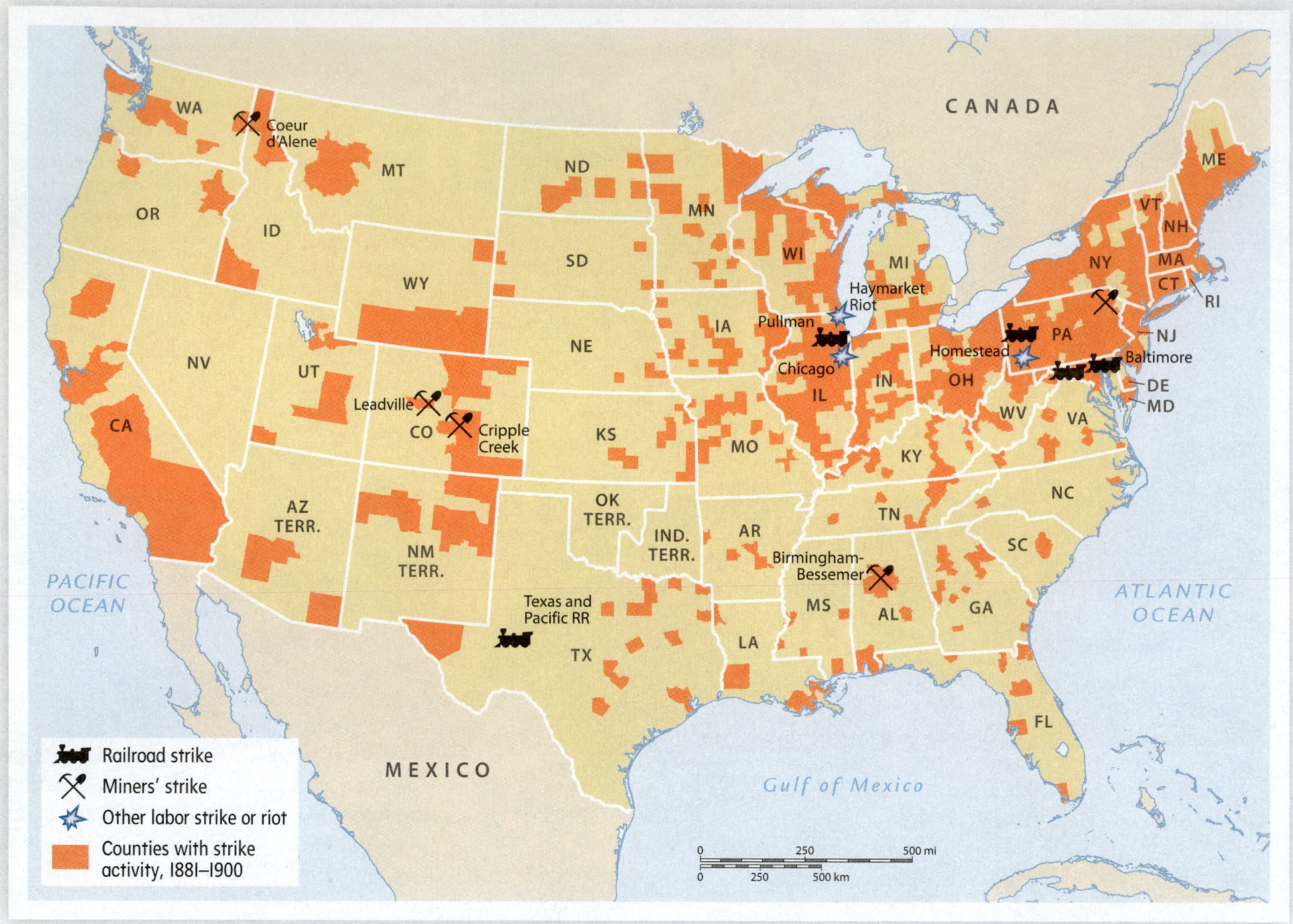

Map 19.1 Labor Strikes, 1881–1900. Crushing recessions, accompanied by deep wage cuts and mass joblessness, motivated millions of workers to lay down their tools and demand better wages, an eight-hour workday, and the right to organize a union.

violence was connected to foreign agitators, a new nativist movement to restrict immigration swept through northeastern and midwestern cities.

"BRAINS, PUSH, AND ENTERPRISE": FARMERS AND RURAL MODERNIZATION

Like many industrial workers, large numbers of farmers in the South, West, and Midwest banded together in the 1880s. Black, Hispanic, and white farmers all founded farming associations dedicated to cooperative action. The largest of these were the all-white Southern Farmers' Alliance, established in Texas in 1879 and counting over a million members by 1890, and the one-million-strong Colored Farmers' Alliance, established in 1886. The Northern Alliance and related organizations, such as the Agricultural Wheel, also attracted hundreds of thousands of farmers and other rural people. Like the Knights, the Alliances welcomed producers (including women) and barred "nonproducers" such as lawyers, bankers, and saloonkeepers. In the South, white and black women joined the Alliances in far greater numbers than any other southern organization. Many former members of the Greenback Party also joined.

These Farmers' Alliances brought farmers hope that they could survive the financial and physical hardships of rural life, and they did so by demonstrating the power of cooperation to put farming on a "modern, business basis," in the words of Southern Alliance leader Charles W. Macune. Putting farming on a business basis meant connecting farms to the telegraph and railroad networks (enabling farmers to get stock and produce to market) and making those services affordable. It also required introducing the latest agricultural science and labor-saving machinery to farming, and securing cheap credit and affordable storage facilities. The Alliances also established a series of cooperatives, such as the Texas Exchange, which

Fantastical Farmers' Alliance. This cartoon from the January 1891 cover of the urban satirical magazine *Judge* lampoons the demands of the Farmers' Alliance as reflective of a backward "hayseed" organization. In fact, Alliance members pushed to modernize farming.

eliminated the middleman and gave farmers direct access to the cotton and other agricultural markets. In California, fruit growers established similar exchanges, connecting small citrus and other growers with the national and global markets.

Education also played a key role. Leaders argued that broad education and the exchange of ideas would help farmers modernize their farms. It would also close the steadily widening income gap between rural and urban America. The Southern Alliance aimed to become the "most powerful and complete educator of modern times," organizing lecture circuits and adult education, and opening libraries throughout the West and South. Women used the Alliance as a venue for organizing for prohibition, lobbying for the vote, and gaining access to labor-saving technology (such as sewing and washing machines) for the home. Alliance leaders argued that by helping farming women to become better mothers and educators, the health and prosperity of the next generation of farmers would dramatically improve.

The Alliances called upon legislators and political candidates to be more responsive to farmer-constituents and even set up a lobbying office in Washington. Their demands congealed into a single program for reform in 1890, when the largest Farmers' Alliances called a national conference in Ocala, Florida. The Ocala Demands condemned the Sherman Silver Purchase Act as inadequate and called for the free coinage of silver, an increase in the money supply, abolition of national (private) banks, and an end to the high tariff. They also demanded the establishment of state subtreasuries where farmers could store grain and other crops in government-owned warehouses, releasing more onto the market when the price was high, and less when it was low. Alliance leaders argued that the nation's great communication network of roads, telegraphs, and railroads served the same purpose as public roads and therefore should be put under "state and federal control and supervision." Finally, the farmers called for a radical overhaul of the electoral system that they believed had stifled their voice in federal government: They demanded a direct vote for the U.S. Senate.

Republicans and Democrats included some of the Ocala demands in their electoral platforms, but once elected, they rarely carried through. A handful of western states enacted reforms advanced by the Alliances, but many of the problems farmers faced required federal action. And in Washington, big business remained more influential than ever before.

THE COLLAPSE OF GILDED AGE POLITICS

The Gilded Age system of mass politics proved remarkably resilient in the face of the challenges of the 1880s. But in the early 1890s, it began to collapse. The Farmers' Alliances and an agricultural recession that escalated into the worst depression of the nineteenth century proved a catalyst to change. The farmers' Populist Party gained momentum, turning the traditional two-party system into a three-way race. Realizing they could no longer afford to ignore farmers or rely on automatic party loyalty, Republicans and Democrats hastily reorganized themselves and rewrote their electoral platforms. In the South, Democrats worked to strengthen their base by attracting white Populists and depriving black men (most of whom voted Republican) of the vote.

As pressure mounted on the existing political system, new racial and religious hierarchies began to harden. Southern states compounded the removal of black voters from the polity by enacting racial segregation laws that further deprived African Americans of full citizenship. The full impact of these events would become evident in 1896—a pivotal year that would seal the fate of the Gilded Age system of mass politics and give birth to a new political order.

THE POPULIST CHALLENGE AND THE ELECTION OF 1892

By 1892, farmers' patience with the major parties had run dry. At camps and rallies across the nation, Alliance members sang songs about the failure of Republicans and Democrats to take farmers' concerns seriously and their intention to quit the party: "I was a party man one time," went one popular song, but "The party would not mind me/So now I'm working for myself/The party's left behind me/A true and independent man/You ever more shall find me." Farmers did not quit politics altogether, however. Rather, they determined to establish their own, independent political party.

Early in 1892, a presidential election year, the Farmers' Alliance called a convention in St. Louis, Missouri. Thousands of southerners and westerners, including farmers, supporters of the Prohibition Party, western middle-class reformers, trade unionists, and the remnants of the Knights of Labor, met to establish the People's Party **(Populists).** "The time has arrived," declared L. L. Polk in his welcoming remarks, "for the great West, the great South, and the great Northwest, to link their hands and hearts together and march to the ballot box, take possession of government, restore it to the principles of our fathers, and run it in the interest of the people." Their platform, based on the Ocala Demands, also reached out to urban northerners and industrial workers by including the eight-hour workday, further restrictions on immigration, and a ban on employers' use of private armies (especially the Pinkertons) to break strikes. Rural women, who had been active in the Alliances, flocked to the party, and many went on to be some of its most exciting orators.

At the Populist Party convention in Omaha, Nebraska, Ignatius Donnelly directly linked the plight of workers and farmers and accused the dominant parties of purposely ignoring the real issues facing most Americans. In an electrifying speech (that was subsequently printed and circulated among millions of voters), Donnelly thundered that "the controlling influences dominating the old political parties have allowed the existing dreadful conditions to develop. (T)hey propose to drown the cries of a plundered people with the uproar of a sham battle over the tariff, so that corporations, national banks, rings, trusts, 'watered stocks,' the demonetization of silver, and the oppressions of usurers, may all be lost sight of." The true America, argued Donnelly, was a country of producers—farmers, small businesspeople, and workers—and producers were being swallowed up by greedy corporations and a government dominated by business interests.

The true purpose of government, the delegates declared, was to ensure that "oppression, injustice, and poverty shall eventually cease in the land." In an effort to appeal to both northern

Populist Party Orator and Suffragette Mary Elizabeth Lease, ca. 1890. A hardscrabble Kansas farmer and mother of four, Lease lectured for the party and challenged farmers everywhere to "raise less corn and more hell."

and southern voters, they nominated former Union Army general James B. Weaver for the presidency and former Confederate general James G. Field as his running mate. Some southern Populists also courted black voters. "You are kept apart," Tom Watson informed mixed audiences in Georgia, "that you may be separately fleeced of your earnings."

Democrats nominated former president Grover Cleveland and waged a campaign that picked up on some of the same issues that Populists were pressing. On election day, Populists won three western governorships, some 1,500 state legislative posts, and fifteen congressional seats. In the presidential race, Weaver and Field garnered a million popular votes and twenty-two electoral votes. But, for the first time since before the Civil War, the Democrats swept Congress and the White House (see Map 19.2). In the South, where Democratic leaders warned of "Negro supremacy" and intimidated voters at the polls, white voters were solidly Democratic. Populists won little of the support they had hoped for in the Northeast, and black voters everywhere tended to support Republicans. As the Populists had hoped, thousands of Republican voters changed their affiliation—but they switched to the Democrats rather than the People's Party.

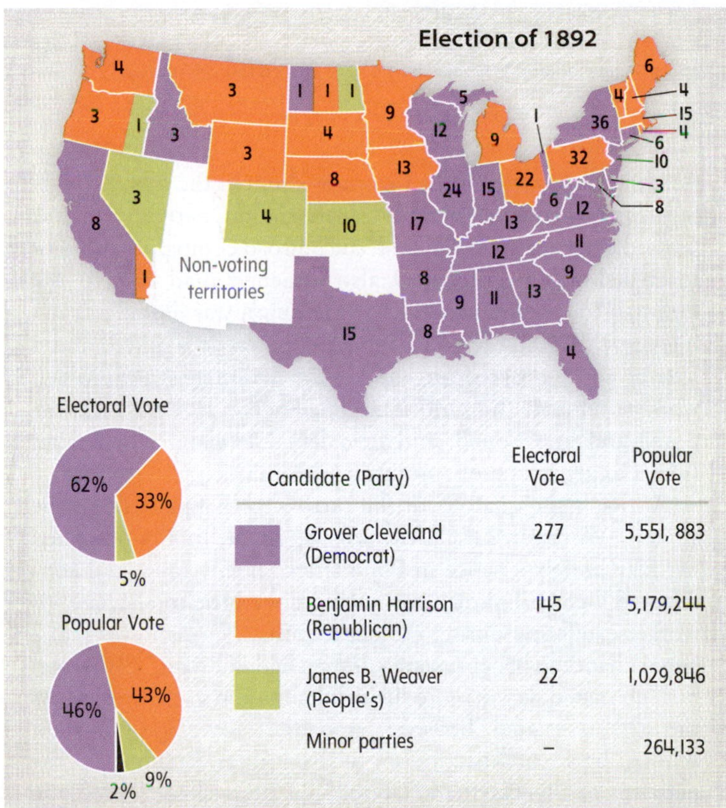

Candidate (Party)	Electoral Vote	Popular Vote
Grover Cleveland (Democrat)	277	5,551, 883
Benjamin Harrison (Republican)	145	5,179,244
James B. Weaver (People's)	22	1,029,846
Minor parties	–	264,133

Map 19.2 Election of 1892. The results of the presidential election underscored the appeal of the People's Party among westerners. The Populists' 9 percent of the popular vote was a blunt reminder to both major parties that the era of voters' unquestioning loyalty to party might be drawing to an end.

DEMOCRATS AND DEPRESSION

Shortly after Grover Cleveland's second inauguration, and as the agricultural recession spread to other sectors of the economy, Americans confronted the worst depression of the nineteenth century. Beginning in early 1893, fifteen thousand businesses failed and five hundred banks closed their doors. Unemployment rose to between 20 percent and 28 percent, and economic activity shrank by 25 percent. Farmers were hit particularly hard, as prices for crops, vegetables, and meat sank lower than the costs of production. Wages were cut by up to 40 percent in some industries. When one of the country's largest, and supposedly most stable, corporations—the National Cordage Company—declared bankruptcy in May 1893, investors panicked, selling their stocks and bonds. The Panic of 1893 triggered a run on the banks, many of which collapsed, and investors began hording their cash.

The roots of the depression were complex, but northeastern bankers and other opponents of silver-backed money insisted that the Sherman Silver Purchase Act of 1890 was largely to blame. Critics argued that by putting silver on a par with gold, the act had sparked inflation and injected uncertainty into the currency. As they had predicted, investors were moving money out of the United States to economies that used the more stable gold standard. This and the decline of tariff revenue (from depressed imports) were draining the Treasury of its gold. Equally alarmingly, a growing number of foreign governments were now refusing to accept American dollars.

In August 1893, under increasing pressure to act, President Cleveland called the first emergency session of Congress since Abraham Lincoln had sought a declaration of war in 1861. Despite vigorous opposition from the rural southern and western wings of his party, Cleveland pinned the cause of the depression on the "truce" of 1890 (the Sherman Act). "The people of the United States are entitled to a sound and stable currency and to money recognized as such on every exchange and in every market of the world," he declared. "Their Government has no right to injure them by financial experiments opposed to the policy and practice of other civilized states With that he requested—and received—congressional repeal of the act.

The discontinuation of silver-backed money stabilized the monetary system, but it did not end the depression. Unemployment, starvation, and homelessness worsened both in cities and in the countryside in late 1893. Middle-class people also began to lose their homes as they lost income and interest rates on their mortgages rose. In rural America, no amount of hard work seemed enough to survive, and states reported that suicide and insanity rates were climbing.

Workers, farmers, and Populist leaders called upon the federal government to alleviate poverty, restore employment, and save foreclosed farms. But Cleveland, who remained a free-market Democrat and proponent of small government, insisted that only the revival of investment would generate jobs and return the country to prosperity. The only action he was

Pullman: A Model Company Town? Taken just a year before the violent Pullman strike in 1894, this photograph depicts a factory shift change at the Pullman Car Works and suggests the image of the town and company that its founder hoped to project: orderly, docile, efficient workers whose relations with management were harmonious.

U.S. Cavalry Breaks the Pullman Strike. This newspaper illustration typified the mainstream press's coverage of the strikers, the federal government, and railroad companies. **Questions for Analysis:** How are the strikers and cavalry portrayed? What might this cartoon tell us about the artist's perception of the role of government and its relationship to business and striking workers? Who else might have shared this perception?

prepared to take was to attract private confidence and investment in the American economy. In a bid to restore the government's gold reserves, the president worked with leading financier John Piermont Morgan to sell Treasury bonds overseas. The program succeeded financially, but politically it further damaged Cleveland's standing in the eyes of many ordinary Americans by associating him with one of the best-known banker "robber barons" of the day.

STRIKERS AND MARCHERS

Industrial workers and the unemployed organized large-scale protests in early 1894—just as they had done during the Long Depression of 1873–1879 and the depression of 1885–1886. In Pennsylvania, 125,000 coal miners struck for the restoration of wages in Pennsylvania. As in the 1870s and 1880s, railway workers exercised their unique power to paralyze an economy that depended on rail networks. Workers at the Pullman Palace Car factory in Chicago struck following a series of five pay cuts (totaling between 25 percent and 40 percent of wages) and the firing of one-third of the employees in 1894. The price of Pullman shares was holding up on the stock market, workers exclaimed, but George Pullman's company town was cutting wages while holding rents and food prices steady.

When Pullman refused to negotiate with the American Railway Union, which combined engineers, switchmen, and brakemen, the union called for a boycott of all Pullman cars. Across the country, railroad workers shunted the cars into sidings, and the nation's vital transportation network all but ground to a halt. As in the past, the railroad companies brought in strikebreakers. But they also attached mail cars to the Pullman trains, and argued that the union was illegally delaying the U.S. Railway Mail Service. The tactic worked, and a federal court ordered an end to the Pullman strike. When workers refused, the union's leader, Eugene V. Debs, was arrested and imprisoned, and President Cleveland sent federal troops to get the trains running again.

At first some quarters of the press were sympathetic to the strikers. Writing for the *New York World*, Nellie Bly described her firsthand experience in Pullman's company town and condemned George Pullman for having done little to alleviate his workers' suffering during the depression. "No man ever had a better chance to benefit mankind than had Pullman," Bly wrote, but "no man deserves more the condemnation of the world." As the strike escalated, however, empathetic coverage was soon eclipsed by strenuous criticism of the strikers. Building on the nativism of the Haymarket years, the press characterized the Pullman strike as an anarchistic, immigrant-driven assault on American laws and institutions—even though Debs and many railroad workers were native-born Americans and subscribed to a cooperative, workingmen's republicanism similar to that of the Knights of Labor. (Debs later embraced socialism, after his experience at Pullman and his time in prison.) As the boycott spread along the railroad lines, and violence escalated, most newspapers framed the struggle as a battle for the nation's soul, in which strikers were attacking America itself. Using imagery of Uncle Sam and the Stars and Stripes, many newspapers declared that the "Strike Is Now War" and that "the nation was in the grips of a rebellion." Once the army had crushed the strike, the *Chicago Tribune* equated the strikers with the defeated (and treasonous) Confederacy: "Debs has reached his Appomattox."

Living Petition: The First March on Washington. Coxey's Army was the first, but several other unemployed "armies" had converged on Washington from California and elsewhere by the end of 1894.

A new form of public protest emerged amid the conflicts of the 1890s. Frustrated with the conventional methods of communicating with Congress (via written petition and the ballot box), Populist Jacob Coxey organized the first march on Washington, in 1894. Calling it a "living petition" and bearing nothing but white flags, Coxey's Army of some five hundred unemployed people walked from Ohio to the capital to demand government relief from unemployment. Coxey was arrested when he attempted to address marchers from the steps of the capitol, and the U.S. Army dispersed the crowd. But Coxey and his fellow marchers had already succeeded in raising public awareness of the extreme plight of the unemployed and had popularized the novel idea that the federal government should do more to address it.

Support for the Populists surged around the nation, and the party won 40 percent more votes in the midterm elections of 1894 than in 1892. Cleveland's Democratic Party suffered heavy losses. Even in the party's traditional stronghold of the West, many Democrats voted Republican and others voted Populist. In the Northeast, large numbers of workers who typically voted Democratic cast their ballots for the Republicans. Although the Populists did poorly (again) in the Northeast and Midwest, in many western and southern states they became one of the two largest parties. The election established that American politics was now a three-way race, and that Republicans and Democrats could no longer rely on voters' passionate party loyalty. Elections would have to be fought on the issues.

JIM CROW AND THE NEW RACIAL ORDER

The Democrats sacrificed the rights of African Americans in their efforts to win over white Populists. In the South, Democratic lawmakers legalized segregation in public places, passing city ordinances that restricted where blacks could sit on street cars and trains and forbade them from using certain water fountains (which the civic-minded southern women's clubs had installed in the 1880s). Southern states also mandated racial segregation of the schools, barring people of African American descent from attending "white" schools and colleges. These laws together became known, after 1904, as the **Jim Crow laws,** a reference to the white stereotype of an African American man—named Jim Crow—made famous by the blackface minstrelsy shows of the antebellum period (see Chapter 13).

As part of Jim Crow, lawmakers also disenfranchised black voters, bringing to an end the historic period of black participation in politics that had begun with Radical Reconstruction. Beginning with Florida in 1889, the southern states amended their constitutions to exclude black men from voting (see Map 19.3). Mindful that federal laws prohibited disenfranchisement on the basis of race, the conventions avoided explicitly racial language. Most instead required all voters to pass a literacy test, in the belief that this would automatically disqualify the 50 percent or more of black men who were illiterate. Tests were administered by local white officials who used the slightest pretext (such as a stumble, or reading too slowly) to bar literate black men as well. Several also required voters to pay a poll tax. (Many poor, semiliterate white voters who were likely to support the Republicans or Populists also lost the vote under these laws.) The federal government did nothing. In Congress, House Republicans passed a voters' rights bill, aimed at enforcing the Fifteenth Amendment and protecting black voters in the South. But a coalition of Democrats and western Republicans defeated the bill in the Senate.

African Americans' subordinate place in southern society was violently reinforced. In Wilmington, North Carolina, and other

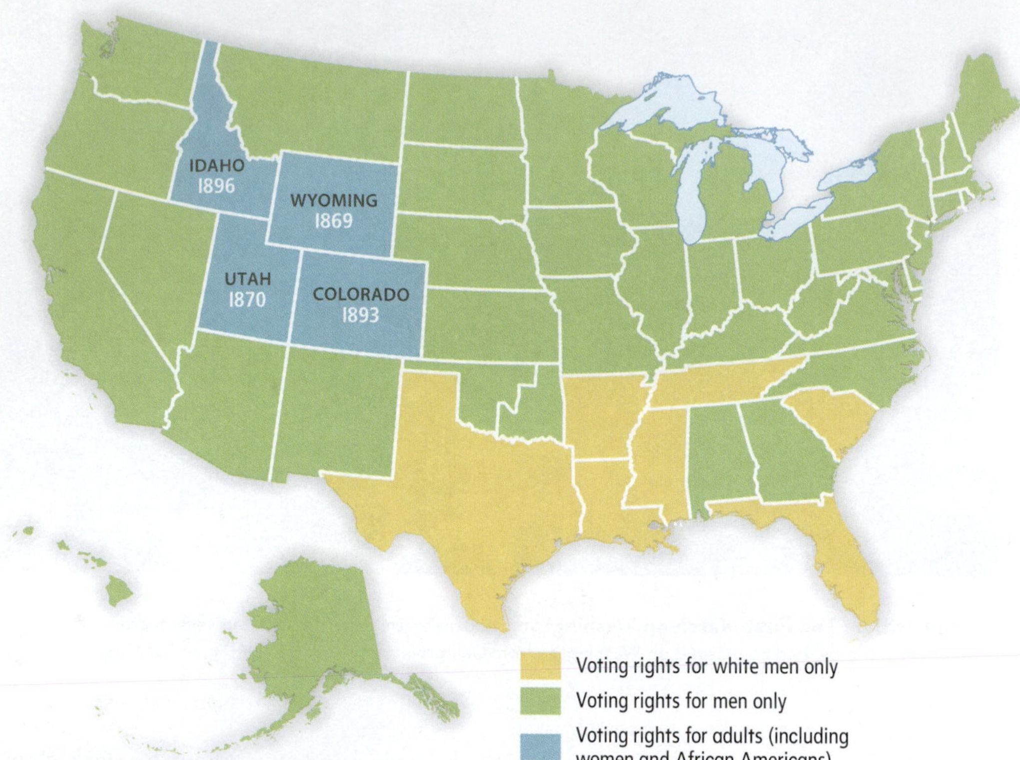

Map 19.3 Democracy in America, 1900. As late as 1900, less than 50 percent of the adult population was eligible to vote in state or federal elections. As this map indicates, there were only four states in which both white women and African Americans could vote for state or federal legislators. Most white women would not gain the vote until a majority of the states ratified the Nineteenth Amendment in 1920. In the South, poll taxes, literacy tests, and other devices disenfranchised hundreds of thousands of African American men.

towns where African Americans were prospering or still had the vote, race riots broke out over the election of African Americans to local government. A wave of **lynching** also got under way. Over 4,743 people (90 percent of whom were black) were lynched between 1882 and 1965. At the peak of lynching, in the late 1890s, almost three black people a week were murdered by white mobs. In the Cotton Belt, the victims were often black laborers. In towns, a significant number were doctors, teachers, and other aspiring middle-class African Americans who were the target of white resentment. The states of the Deep South—Mississippi, Georgia, Alabama, Louisiana, and South Carolina—had the highest incidence. Nearly 40 percent of all southern lynchings took place publicly in town squares, in full view of photographers and reporters. Railroads began running excursions, school was let out, and officers of the law turned a blind eye (and sometimes participated). Whites of both genders and from across the social spectrum participated.

Lynchings were repeated again and again across the South, as whites aimed to teach African Americans an unforgettable lesson about their place in southern society. "I was not yet five years old," wrote Benjamin Mays, recollecting the day a white mob rode up to his father in 1898 and forced him to remove his hat and bow, "but I have never forgotten them. . . . That mob is my earliest memory." It also strengthened the culture of segregation and white racial identity throughout the region, and persuaded a growing number of black southerners that full freedom would not be possible in the South. Ida B. Wells, a black teacher and newspaper owner and editor, fled the South for New York and Chicago after covering the lynching of Thomas Moss, an upwardly mobile grocery store owner. She built an antilynching movement and lectured prolifically on the subject in the North and Europe. Thanks to her efforts, antilynching bills were introduced to Congress in the 1910s and 1930s. But they were voted down repeatedly.

Ida B. Wells, Crusader for Justice. The daughter of former slaves, Wells attended a freedmen's school and went on to study at Fisk University in Nashville, Tennessee. Like many black southerners in the 1880s, she resisted local efforts to segregate trains and public spaces, suing a railroad company that had ejected her from one of its "whites only" cars in 1883.

Outside the South, too, segregation took hold in the 1890s. More laws forbidding interracial marriages were passed in western states than southern ones in these years. Anglos were prohibited from marrying Chinese, Indians, and black Americans. Across the country, for the first time, Jews were systematically excluded from elite colleges, country clubs, and resorts. Even the New York Union League, which Jews had helped establish during the Civil War, closed their doors to Jewish Americans. The YMCA initially resisted calls for the racially segregated clubs but capitulated in 1900. Professional baseball, which had some mixed leagues and teams in the 1880s, adopted segregation as well.

In 1896, in *Plessy v. Ferguson,* the U.S. Supreme Court ruled that cities and states had a legal right to segregate public amenities. Jim Crow laws were constitutional, the Court held, provided that African American amenities were of equal quality to those of whites. Although the *Plessy* case concerned streetcars in Louisiana and was relevant chiefly to southern states, the Court's new "separate but equal" doctrine applied across the union—and also carried great symbolic force. In the wake of the decision, southern states and cities passed hundreds of laws and ordinances requiring strict segregation of schools, hospitals, and all public amenities. Even in death the races were to be kept separate by law, in segregated cemeteries. In theory, the so-called colored amenities such as schools and railroad cars were of equal quality, but in practice, they were markedly inferior.

REMAKING THE AMERICAN POLITICAL SYSTEM

The forces of racial segregation and disenfranchisement, Populism, economic depression, and industrial conflict converged directly on the election of 1896. The election completed the demise of the party system that had dominated American politics for the previous forty years. As the election of 1894 had shown, voter loyalty to party could no longer be counted on, and the election would have to be run on the issues. Each of the three parties strategized over which issues would draw the most voters away from the other two. Taking note of their weakness in the Northeast and Midwest, as well as criticism from the middle-class press, Populists pragmatically dropped most of their more radical planks. Free silver became their central issue in the hope that Democrats who felt betrayed by President Cleveland's endorsement of the gold standard would flock to them. In fact, Democrats dropped Cleveland from their ticket, and shrewdly incorporated silver into their own platform. They also nominated a close ally of the Populists, William Jennings Bryan of Nebraska, for the presidency. Western Populists proposed that the two parties align and won out over southern opposition. Bryan became the Populists' candidate as well.

Bryan, a striking and charismatic orator with evangelizing flair, roared around the country making impassioned stump speeches in the name of struggling workers, farmers, and the West's central place in American life. "Burn down your cities and leave our farms," he warned voters, "and your cities will spring up again as if by magic; but destroy our farms and the grass will grow in the streets of every city in the country." Above all, Bryan returned repeatedly to the harm that Cleveland's abolition of silver money had inflicted on rural folk. Rallying voters with a lofty rhetoric of good and evil, he exclaimed, "We will answer their demand for a gold standard by saying to them: You shall not press down upon the brow of labor this crown of thorns, you shall not crucify mankind upon a cross of gold."

The Republicans stood firm with northeastern industrial and banking interests, nominating William McKinley and committing themselves to the gold standard. But they also reached out to two other northeastern constituencies—industrial workers, many of whom had voted Republican for the first time in the previous election, and urban middle-class voters who fundamentally distrusted rural western Populists and southern Democrats. Republicans received a significant boost when labor leader Samuel Gompers and the American Federation of Labor withdrew support from Bryan.

With the help of campaign manager Mark Hanna, McKinley lobbied the public directly for its support. In the words of Theodore Roosevelt, Hanna marketed McKinley "as if he were a patent medicine." In the wake of the Pullman strike, Hanna easily whipped up middle-class anxieties about mobs taking over the country and used this image to raise more money from big business than had any other Gilded Age candidate. Women's greatly increased presence in politics (through clubs, temperance, and settlement work) did not escape Hanna's attention, either. Women's rights, equal opportunity and equal pay, and "protection to the home" all became planks in McKinley's platform.

On election day, the Republicans tightened their hold on the Northeast and Midwest and were able to dominate national politics for the next eighteen years (see Map 19.4).

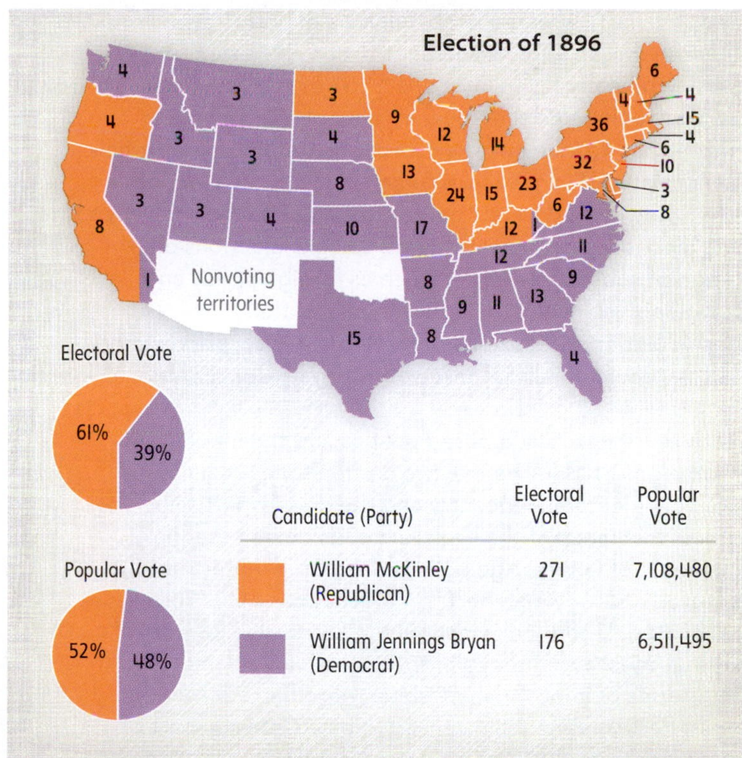

Map 19.4 Election of 1896. The rural-urban divide played a far more prominent role in the election of 1896 than in other Gilded Age elections. Although McKinley defeated Bryan by ninety-five electoral votes, his support came almost entirely from the urbanized Industrial Belt (plus California and Oregon). Conversely, rural southern and western states voted overwhelmingly for Bryan.

Subsequently, they took much of the West as well. In the South, the party lost heavily. As the southern states completed the work of disfranchising the Republicans' base—black and poor white voters—that party finally collapsed as a viable force in southern politics. (The southern wing of the party would not begin to recover until the late 1960s; see Chapter 28.)

Ironically, the party that had been the catalyst for political change, the Populists, collapsed. Alarmed that anti-corporate forces were poised to take the reins of government, big business lavishly funded the dominant parties and paid journalists to attack Populist ideas. The Populists' small budget made it hard to respond effectively. Mass circulation newspapers were aligned with the dominant parties, depriving Populists of a direct pathway to a mass audience, and the major parties argued that the best way for voters to bring about change was through the established parties—not via a young, inexperienced third party. Some mainstream candidates also adopted Populist planks, effectively depriving the Populist candidates of some of their support. Especially in the South, Democrats drew many white Populists back into the party fold.

Above all, the growing cultural divide between city dwellers and rural people made the Populists' task an extremely difficult one. Urban people knew little about America's rural cultures and farmers' struggles, and farmers had little understanding of city life. Some (though not all) Populist leaders were virulently anti-Semitic and anti-urban, and many claimed that there was a vast conspiracy of bankers against farmers and workers. Such rhetoric led the urban press to relentlessly ridicule the Populists as unsophisticated hayseeds and wide-eyed fanatics, dismissing not only their extreme ideas but their more moderate ones as well." Although the Populists ran in 1896 on the least radical of the platform's planks, they could not shake the aura of fanaticism.

CONCLUSION

Populism played a key role in bringing about an end to the culture of patronage and party loyalty that had characterized the political system for much of the nineteenth century. The People's Party wrested large numbers of voters away from the Republican and Democratic Parties. Even though the party ultimately failed in its quest to destroy the major parties, it changed the way they did politics. The major parties had to innovate their election strategies and rethink their relationship to voters. Beginning with the election of 1896, they ceased to rely on voters' loyalty as the sole way to win elections and instead started to fight elections on a range of substantive issues (such as foreign policy and taxation). The major parties also realized that gerrymandering was not a fail-safe tool for securing victory, as they could no longer take voters' loyalty for granted.

With the shift to issue-based politics and the media-savvy campaigns of Mark Hanna, two cornerstones of mass politics—electoral pageantry and the deeply partisan press—lost much of their relevance. As these essential elements of Gilded Age politics dissipated, voter turnout entered a steady decline, from which it has never fully recovered. Disfranchisement in the South also lowered voting rates, as hundreds of thousands of black men and thousands of impoverished whites were barred from the polls. Party membership ceased to be an integral part of most men's identity. The age of mass politics was at an end.

STUDY TERMS

political machine (p. 502)
Tammany Hall (p. 503)
marching clubs (p. 504)
political clubs (p. 505)
New York World (p. 506)
gerrymandering (p. 507)
Exodusters (p. 509)
Liberia (p. 509)
National Woman Suffrage Association (p. 509)
American Woman Suffrage Association (p. 509)
Hull House (p. 510)
lobbyists (p. 511)
Civil War veterans' pension system (p. 512)
spoils system (p. 513)
Stalwarts (p. 513)
Half-Breeds (p. 513)
Civil Service Act (p. 513)
greenback (p. 514)
gold standard (p. 515)
free silver (p. 515)
election of 1884 (p. 515)
rum, Romanism, and rebellion (p. 516)
Interstate Commerce Act of 1887 (p. 516)
election of 1888 (p. 518)
anti-monopoly (p. 518)
Sherman Antitrust Act (p. 519)
Knights of Labor (p. 519)
producers (p. 519)
anarchists (p. 519)
Great Upheaval (p. 520)
Haymarket Affair (p. 520)
Farmers' Alliances (p. 522)
Ocala Demands (p. 523)
Populists (p. 524)
Panic of 1893 (p. 525)
Pullman strike (p. 526)
Coxey's Army (p. 527)
Jim Crow laws (p. 527)
lynching (p. 528)
Plessy v. Ferguson (p. 529)
election of 1896 (p. 529)
cross of gold (p. 529)

TIMELINE

1879 Woman's Christian Temperance Union expands into welfare, health, and political lobbying

Currency moves to gold standard

Southern Farmers' Alliance formed

1880 Mugwumps condemn patronage system

Republican James Garfield elected president

1881 Charles Guiteau assassinates President Garfield

1882 Lynching rates begin to climb

1883 African Americans join the Knights of Labor

1884 Anti-Monopoly Party founded

Knights of Labor win strike against Southwestern Railroad

Democrat Grover Cleveland elected president

1885 Depression begins (ends in 1886)

1886 Anti-immigrant American Party forms following Haymarket Affair

Colored Farmers' Alliance established

1887 Interstate Commerce Act authorizes federal government to regulate interstate railroads

1888 Republican Benjamin Harrison elected president

1889 Hull House opens in Chicago

Florida is the first of ten southern states to indirectly disenfranchise black voters

1890 Sherman Silver Purchase Act injects silver into money supply

Sherman Antitrust Act authorizes federal government to dismantle trusts

Farmers' Ocala Demands call for free coinage of silver, subtreasuries, abolition of national banks, and direct elections for the Senate

1892 The People's Party founded

Democrats sweep White House and Congress

1893 Financial panic sparks economic depression

President Cleveland calls emergency session of Congress

1894 Coxey's army marches on Washington, D.C.

Pullman and other labor strikes briefly paralyze economy

Populists do well in midterm elections

1896 Supreme Court rules racial segregation is constitutional (in *Plessy v. Ferguson*)

William McKinley elected president.

People's Party collapses

FURTHER READING

Additional suggested readings are available on the Online Learning Center at www.mhhe.com/becomingamerica1e.

Lucy G. Barber, *Marching on Washington, The Forging of an American Political Tradition* (2002), narrates the history of marching on the capital as a form of political protest.

Charles W. Calhoun, *Minority Victory: Gilded Age Politics and the Front Porch Campaign of 1888* (2008), contextualizes the rise of modern campaigning in the late nineteenth century.

Rebecca Edwards, *New Spirits: Americans in the Gilded Age* (2007), argues that the Gilded Age was a threshold to modernity in part because of the period's eruptive conflicts over increasing racial, ethnic, intellectual, and political diversity.

Lawrence Goodwyn, *The Populist Moment: A Short History of the Agrarian Revolt in America* (1978), claims that the movement's elite leadership failed to foster the democratic organization and administration that could have built a "movement culture."

Morton Keller, *Affairs of State: Public Life in Late Nineteenth Century America* (1977), traces the era's complex relationship to centralization, reform, and active national government.

Michael McGerr, *Decline of Popular Politics: The American North, 1865–1928* (1988), examines the rise and fall of nineteenth-century partisan campaign culture.

Charles Postel, *The Populist Vision* (2007), illuminates the Farmers' Alliance's drive for rural modernization and the fruition of Populism.

Madelon Powers, *Faces Along the Bar: Lore and Order in the Workingman's Saloon, 1870–1920* (1998), analyzes the centrality of the barroom to politics and workingmen's culture.

Joel Silbey, *American Political Nation 1838–1893* (1994), explores the raucous partisan culture of the Second Party System.

Carl Smith, *Urban Disorder and the Shape of Belief: The Great Chicago Fire, the Haymarket Bomb, and the Model Town of Pullman* (1995), examines the meanings of the Haymarket Affair and Americans' anxieties about their rapidly changing world.

Mark Wahlgren Summers, *Party Games: Getting, Keeping, and Using Power in Gilded Age Politics* (2004), traces vote buying and other electoral tactics of the Gilded Age.

Robert E. Weir, *Beyond Labor's Veil: The Culture of the Knights of Labor* (1996), describes the cultural, religious, musical, literary, and artistic history of the Knights of Labor.

20

INSIDE ▶

THE BIG PICTURE

An influx of non-Anglo immigrants and rural Americans energized and remade urban culture. Fresh ideas and new approaches emerged as city dwellers grappled with the promise and problems of modern industrial life. Optimistic that progress was possible, millions of middle-class Americans banded together, publicized social problems, suggested solutions, and ran for political office.

Atlantic Crossings. Over 12 million immigrants, mostly non-English speakers from Europe, entered the United States via the Ellis Island inspection station in New York harbor.

1896–1914

THE PROGRESSIVE ERA

In fall 1913, an ordinary laborer by the name of Tom Brown was committed to New York's Auburn state prison. Upon arriving, Brown exchanged his civilian clothes and personal belongings for the standard-issue convict's uniform. A clerk examined him, noting six tattoos on his left bicep, and the prison barber trimmed his hair to regulation short back and sides. A guard then marched him to his new home—a cold stone cell measuring just four feet by seven feet. With the turn of a heavy iron key, Tom Brown became a prisoner of the Empire State.

Though Brown's incarceration appeared typical, newspaper headlines revealed that it had been anything but routine. The *New York Journal* put it dramatically: "Millionaire Head of Penitentiary Commission Takes His Place in Auburn, as Thomas Brown, and Works at Sorting Straw—Has Receiver of Stolen Goods for His Mate at Table—Eats Plain Fare and Seems to Like It—Shut Off From World." Tom Brown was in fact Thomas Mott Osborne, and Osborne was neither a laborer nor a convicted felon but a wealthy New York manufacturer and state prison official. He had volunteered to be temporarily incarcerated in order to study prisons from the convict's perspective. Following his "release" a week later, Osborne dedicated his life to reforming a justice system that, in his view, only perpetuated a vicious cycle of social dysfunction, violence, and repeat offending.

Osborne's voluntary incarceration was highly unusual, but he was not alone in his pursuit of fundamental social change in the early decades of the twentieth century. Millions of Americans were organizing to reform dysfunctional prisons, outdated school systems, dangerously unregulated food and water supplies, and antiquated welfare agencies. As in the South during Reconstruction, this remarkable burst of reform activity accompanied and responded to the colossal upheavals associated with industrialization, urbanization, and mass immigration. Reformers fervently believed that voluntary community work, active local government, and the application of scientific and technical principles would solve the nation's problems. Their abiding faith in the nation's capacity for progress led them to identify themselves as "progressives." Later, in the far more conservative 1920s and early 1930s, liberal commentators would wistfully characterize the years between 1896 and 1914 as the Progressive Era, a period when Americans had worked together for the good of the whole.

Historians now think of the Progressive Era not only as an age of big ideas and ambitious reforms, but also as a deeply complex period, fraught with contradictions. Industrialization and urbanization finally displaced agriculture as the driving forces of the American economy. High wages and decent working conditions emerged in some industries, whereas in others, workers barely made subsistence wages and faced constant danger of injury or death. The nation grew more religiously and culturally diverse, yet racial segregation became the norm in all regions. Industrialization, urbanization, and mass migration evoked nostalgia for a supposedly simpler, more virtuous past yet also inspired boundless confidence in the powers of technology, community, and media to solve the nation's social problems.

Prison reformer Thomas Mott Osborne underwent a week's voluntary incarceration to study prison conditions firsthand. Osborne, right, poses here outside one of the Auburn prison cells in which he was held.

KEY QUESTIONS

- In what ways did the powerful new technologies of mass production and mass entertainment change everyday life?
- Why did more Americans than ever before quit rural life and move to the city?
- What caused the color line to harden, and how did African Americans respond to it?
- How did new immigrants from southern and eastern Europe transform American culture and society, and how did living in the United States change them?
- What was progressivism, what were its religious and intellectual roots, and why were so many people drawn to it?

INDUSTRY TRIUMPHANT

By 1896, the colossal forces of industrialization, unleashed by the Civil War and fueled by westward expansion, had permanently changed American culture, politics, and society. Industrialization continued to bring wondrous technological innovations, higher industrial output, and floods of new consumer goods. More Americans than ever worked for large corporations and spent their growing disposable income on a dazzling array of goods and services. Tired of the bitter labor conflicts of the Gilded Age, some industrialists began paying their workers far higher wages than ever before. But not everyone was better off. Sweatshops, life-endangering work, and grinding poverty were still commonplace, and devastating recessions continued to throw the economy, small businesses, and workers into crisis. Unions remained all but illegal, and workers' discontent over inequality was high. Monopolization—the concentration of power in one or two enormous corporations—continued unabated. Yet signs of change were afoot. Labor leaders, middle-class reformers, and a small but growing number of politicians searched for ways to stabilize the economy, check the power of monopolies, improve working conditions, abolish child labor, and avert industrial conflict.

GROWTH AND CONSOLIDATION

The economy grew steadily in a number of sectors, both old and new. The biggest economic boost came from manufacturing, which added $8 billion to the U.S. gross national product by 1909, almost twice its contribution just nine years earlier. Steel production soared during the same time, as did the extraction of coal, petroleum, precious metals, and several other nonfood commodities. By the second decade of the twentieth century, Americans were also producing record volumes of consumer goods, including cars, small-scale refrigerators, safety razors, phonographs, and bottled soft drinks, that had not been widely available in the previous century. Already an industrial giant in the Gilded Age, by the Progressive Era the United States exceeded the combined industrial output of Britain, France, and Germany.

As it grew, American industry consolidated under the control of a small number of powerful corporations. The depression of the 1890s had handed Gilded Age robber barons an opportunity to buy out competing firms and control prices, and the end of the depression in 1897 triggered a six-year period of widespread **merger and integration** involving $7.5 billion of capital and absorbing 40 percent of the country's industrial production. In fifty different industries, a single company now controlled at least 60 percent of production.

Most dramatically, the six years of consolidation produced near-monopolies in several of the nation's largest industries. The U.S. Steel Corporation, formed in 1901 through a merger of Carnegie Steel and two other companies, controlled about 80 percent of the country's steel production and became the world's first-ever billion-dollar corporation. Tobacco, railroads, oil, life insurance, and several other industries also came to be dominated by one or two large companies. In theory, monopolies, because of their enormous scale, limited waste and optimized productive efficiency. In practice, however, they often raised prices (because of lack of competition) and cut their workers' wages. Many Americans also worried that such vast concentrations of wealth and industrial power, if left unchecked, would enrich a small minority at the expense of the great majority and corrupt the political process.

MAKING WORK SCIENTIFIC

Newly enlarged corporations did not need to worry as much about price competition, but they faced the challenges of coordinating increasingly complex and geographically dispersed businesses. In many industries, companies instituted new practices of systematic management featuring detailed record-keeping and new techniques of cost-benefit analysis. The objective was to reduce a company's dependence on the habits, talents, knowledge, or personal connections of individual employees, whether they were foremen, line workers, or branch managers, and to rely instead on standard written procedures.

Frederick W. Taylor, a management consultant in the steel industry, took the idea of systematic management to a new level. Taylor argued that American businesses could reduce their labor costs by making sure their workers were not expending any wasted energy. There was one ideal way to perform any industrial task, Taylor believed, and he conducted numerous "time and motion studies" during the first decade of the century to break down the labor process into smaller, measurable components and to set guidelines for every worker. He then relied on wage incentives to get workers to meet new standards of productivity. Taylor's program of **scientific management** had some appeal among employers, though many were not convinced that it actually increased productivity. Not surprisingly, workers deeply resented this new assault on their autonomy and often sabotaged Taylor's time and motion studies. Even industries that shunned Taylor's methods shared his interest in maximizing efficiency by breaking down the production process into more focused and monotonous tasks. Industrialization in the nineteenth century had consistently involved such a subdivision of labor into less skilled components. By the end of the century, the meatpacking trade had instituted a

Gospel of Efficiency. Frederick W. Taylor's book *The Principles of Scientific Management* (1911) became the classic study in the emerging field of management science. However, many workers and some industrialists criticized Taylor's "science" as inhumane and even absurd, as this cartoon suggests.

"disassembly line" that quadrupled production rates by subdividing the skilled labor of meat production into the separate but sequential tasks of killing, pumping, splitting, carving, and packing.

Michigan mechanic Henry Ford, who founded the Ford Motor Company in 1903, was one of several manufacturers who adapted the meatpacking system to the mass production of consumer goods. By 1914, his **assembly line** boosted production of the company's Model T cars from a few thousand to hundreds of thousands a year. It also allowed Ford to replace skilled craftsmen with cheaper operatives and to rely on the mechanized conveyor belt—rather than overseers—to set and accelerate the pace of work. The company wanted to hire inexperienced workers, one of its engineers said, "who have nothing to unlearn, . . . and will simply do what they are told, over and over again, from bell-time to bell-time." To attract operatives to perform such monotonous work under strict managerial control, Ford offered the unusually high wage of $5 a day for eight hours of work (the equivalent of $114 a day today). Ford theorized that this generous wage would also stimulate the economy by enabling workers to buy more expensive consumer goods—including his cars.

Because workers burned out quickly in the new system, companies that adopted the assembly line faced high employee turnover. Nonetheless, the technology became standard in the auto and other industries. By speeding the production process, the moving assembly line helped turn the car into an affordable mass consumer good (see Hot Commodities: The Automobile). By paying his workers well and making cars affordable (see How Much Is That?), Ford became known as the man who both democratized driving and invented the high-wage, high-consumption economy. In the 1930s, "Fordism" became shorthand for an entire economic system—one that allowed for mass employment, high wages, mass production, and mass consumption.

How Much Is That?

The 1908 and 1914 Fords

If we adjust for inflation, the $850 price tag of a 1908 Ford car, produced before the introduction of the moving auto assembly line, would be $21,394 today. At that price, which was significantly more than the average worker's annual wages, Ford sold just 10,607 cars. By 1914, however, Ford's introduction of the moving assembly line had driven down the price to $360—the equivalent of just $8,131 today! The lower price point helped push up sales seventyfold, to 730,041.

LABOR DISCONTENT

Whereas the economic crises of the 1890s had fueled bitter confrontations between capital and labor, the recovery produced more muted forms of class conflict. In urban America, organized labor made some headway during the Progressive Era. The depression of the 1890s had destroyed the last remnants of the Knights of Labor and decimated the American Federation of Labor (AFL). Indeed, by 1897, AFL membership had dropped well below half a million, or less than 5 percent of the wage labor force. Then, over the next seven years, American workers unionized in droves, raising union membership above two million. The AFL sought to use the consolidation of American business to workers' advantage by negotiating contracts across entire industries, and consequently unions in a number of trades were able to secure higher wages and shorter workdays. But in focusing mostly on skilled craftwork, the AFL largely ignored women, African Americans, new immigrants, and the rising number of unskilled laborers working in the nation's factories.

Although organized labor did relatively well in some sectors, unions had to contend with "open shop" campaigns sponsored by the National Association of Manufacturers and designed to keep unions out of the workplace. In arenas where employers were smaller and less organized, such as in New York's garment trade, grassroots labor activists were more successful (see States of Emergency box later in this chapter). In 1909, twenty thousand female garment workers staged a general walkout, forced three hundred businesses to accede to their demands, and helped revive unionization efforts in the trade.

While the AFL and its affiliated unions pursued better pay and conditions in particular trades and industries, other movements tapped into larger discontent with the division of wealth and power in the United States at this time. Founded in 1905, an industrial union called the Industrial Workers of the World (IWW) explicitly appealed to immigrants, African Americans, women, and other laborers whom the AFL had ignored or excluded. Unlike the AFL, the "Wobblies," as IWW members were known—and whose motto was "An injury to one is an injury to all"—aimed to build one big union and to wage an international revolution. Their goal was nothing less than to wrest control of the means of production from capitalists. Particularly in the West, IWW leaders such as Elizabeth Gurley Flynn pioneered street demonstrations to bring attention to the plight of the nation's most impoverished workers. Employers and authorities responded by dispatching brass bands to drown them out or by dispersing them by force. Subsequently, the IWW led some of the first campaigns for free speech rights. By 1912, the Wobblies counted fifty thousand members and enjoyed the support of hundreds of thousands more.

Less radical in rhetoric was the U.S. Socialist Party, founded in 1900. The Socialists opted to work within the established political system, preaching economic cooperation and democratic opportunity and calling for the nationalization of

HOT COMMODITIES

The Automobile

Car Club. Although cars quickly became icons of masculinity, women (including avid motorists such as etiquette guru Emily Post and writers Edith Wharton and Gertrude Stein) did drive cars in the early years of the twentieth century, and studies showed a lower accident rate among female drivers. Men nevertheless ridiculed women who took the wheel and excluded them from New York's Automobile Club of America.

No consumer good so starkly divides the nineteenth from the twentieth century as the automobile. Prior to 1900, cars were virtually unknown in most of the United States. Maryland had granted a patent for a steam auto as early as 1787, a motor vehicle had been successfully test-driven in 1805, and the first internal combustion engine was built in 1860. But cars had simply never caught on in the nineteenth century.

The main obstacle to getting cars on the roads was the roads themselves. As late as the 1890s, half of the streets in major U.S. cities were unpaved, and smooth road surfaces were virtually nonexistent outside cities. Without paved roads, cars remained exotic luxury items, about as practical as trains would have been without rail tracks. The Good Roads Movement spread through the country around the turn of the twentieth century, advocating that the nation's idle convicts be put to work on road improvement. Local and state governments took on the task, reasoning that it was healthier for prisoners to do strenuous outdoor work than to sit idle in prison cells. The smooth roads that were the product of this effort literally paved the way for the automobile.

Not surprisingly, cars appeared first in cities, which had the densest concentration of drivable surfaces. More surprisingly, the automobile appealed to many urbanites and progressive reformers as a solution to the problem of urban pollution. The advent of cars not only would reduce the number of horses fouling up the streets with their waste, but also would help clean up the miasma of mud and dust that so many streets had become. Furthermore, cars could traverse the same distance at greater speeds, thus reducing the volume of street traffic at any given point. However, as cars proliferated, city leaders worried about the increase in vehicle speed. Consequently, traffic codes appeared beginning in 1897, and several states laws required cars to be preceded by a man on foot carrying a red flag.

The expansion of roads made car travel possible, yet few Americans could afford to own them until Henry Ford's Model T put the automobile in reach of the masses. Still, a great deal of cultural groundwork was necessary to ignite the American romance with the car. By 1910, car companies were buying one-eighth of the advertisements in mass-circulation magazines. Seven years later, the proportion had risen to one-fourth. Popular music contributed as well, helping to construct the car as a symbol of sexual freedom. Composer Rudolph Anderson's 1899 song spoke of "Love in an Automobile" at a time when only two thousand Americans owned cars. A 1905 hit made the point more explicitly: "You can go as far as you like with me, Lucille, in my merry Oldsmobile." The car was quickly becoming a unique consumer good. Whereas in 1895, only four automobiles were registered in the United States, by 1910 almost half a million were. By 1915, the National Highway Association (a champion of the Good Roads Movement) was calling on the nation's one million drivers to "see America" on the new and improved highway system. Association president Charles Henry Davis declared auto tourism to be "almost a duty of all patriotic citizens"!

Think About It

1. What kinds of arguments were likely to persuade politicians to allocate public funds for paving roads?
2. Why do you think car manufacturers promoted their product as an icon of sexual freedom? Why did most people think of the car as a specifically masculine commodity?

Poster for IWW Pageant. Aided by middle-class radicals and wealthy donors, the IWW organized an elaborate pageant in New York City's Madison Square Garden in 1913, hoping to raise funds and foster public support for striking silk workers in Paterson, New Jersey. A cast of one thousand workers enacted the dramatic story of the IWW-led battle between the working class and employers. But the Wobblies raised only $150 for the strikers, and the workers' absence from the picket lines caused the strike to collapse.

railroads and utilities. Eugene V. Debs, the former railway union leader who had played a key role in the Pullman Strike (see Chapter 19), led the Socialist Party during the Progressive Era, running for president five times between 1900 and 1920. In the Socialists' first serious presidential campaign, in 1904, Debs won over 400,000 votes, and eight years later he polled more than 900,000. Although even the latter showing amounted to only 6 percent of the electorate, it cut into Democratic support in the Northeast and Midwest and represented a striking success for a third party. Clearly, even in times of economic growth, various groups of Americans were raising serious concerns about capitalism. These objections would frame a larger discussion in this era about the relationship between government and private enterprise.

THE URBAN AGE

Other than industrialization, no development at the dawn of the twentieth century was more transformative of the nation as a whole than mass urbanization. City populations, already growing steadily in the Gilded Age, exploded during the Progressive Era. Millions from rural America flocked to the cities—or dreamed of doing so—in search of employment, new experiences, and the ready abundance of consumer goods. At the same time, continuous streams of immigrants disembarked at the nation's ports and built their own thriving urban communities. The flood of people into the cities more than quintupled the nation's urban population between 1896 and 1917, to over fifty-four million (see Map 20.1). Immigrants from southern and eastern Europe eclipsed those from northern Europe, and American cities became far more diverse than ever before. As new forms of recreation and entertainment proliferated, so did slums and sweatshops. The color line hemmed in racial minorities, and white and commercial areas of the city gained electric streetlights and mass transit systems. Middle-class women, who had first ventured into commercial districts as shoppers during the Gilded Age, now entered the workplace in significant numbers, too. And, for the first time in the country's history, urban life and the city dweller replaced family farm life and the yeoman farmer as the embodiment of what it meant to be American.

LEAVING THE LAND

As in earlier periods of U.S. history, an influx of new residents was the main driver of urban growth. Indeed, millions of people made their way to America's cities in the Progressive Era—and a significant minority came from within the United States. Although the agricultural economy was flourishing and 120 million acres of new farmland had come into use, much of this growth was due to large-scale commercial farming. Yeomen farmers continued to struggle with the same pressures of rising debt, falling income, and a declining standard of living that had sparked farmers' protests in the late nineteenth century.

In light of these conditions, a steady stream of young people left the land in these years in search of fresh opportunity and excitement in the city. Magazine images of city dancehalls, amusement parks, department stores, street life, crowded baseball stadiums, and skyscrapers made rural life seem dull and stifling by comparison. As Cicely Rand, a character in a popular play, put it in 1909, "Who wants to smell new-mown hay, if he can breathe in gasoline on Fifth Ave instead! Think of the theaters! The crowds! Think of being able to go out on the street and see someone you don't know by sight."

African Americans were among the millions of Americans who migrated to cities in large numbers in these years. At first, many moved to southern cities, hoping to escape the crushing poverty of tenant farming and racial oppression that kept them "in their place." They found instead that southern cities offered no refuge from Jim Crow segregation and discrimination. Further,

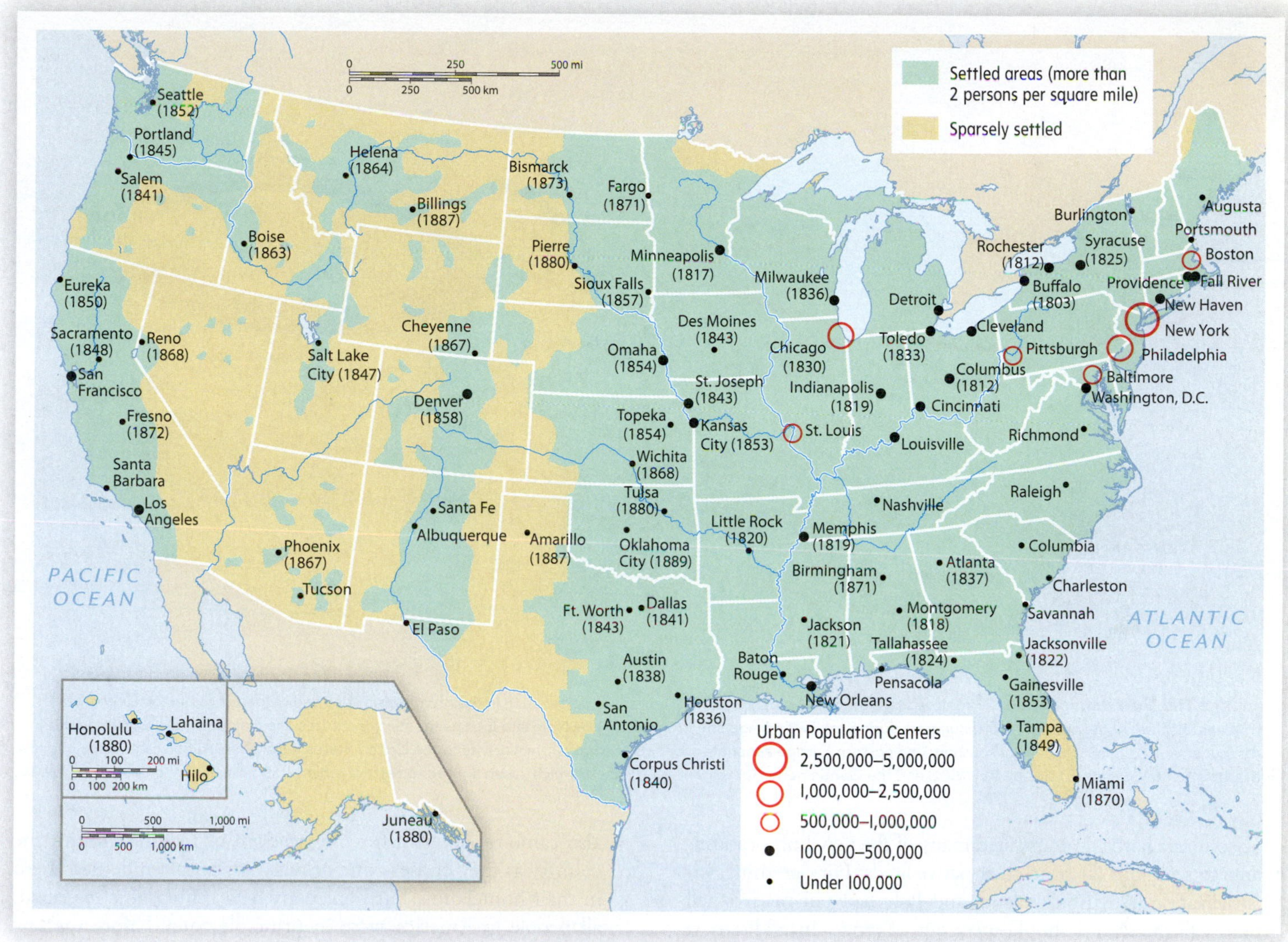

Map 20.1 Urbanizing America. By 1900, the United States was well on its way to becoming an urban nation. Two in five inhabitants lived in cities (defined as settlements of 2,500 or more people), more than double the rate in 1860. New York was the second-largest metropolis in the world (after London), with a population of 3.5 million, while Philadelphia and Chicago each counted over a million inhabitants. Urbanization continued apace through the Progressive Era, and by 1920 just over half the population was urban.

when black communities grew and prospered, whites in neighboring communities became resentful and even more hostile. Tensions boiled over in Atlanta in 1906 when 10,000–15,000 whites went on a violent rampage that left four black men dead and hundreds of black professionals and college students jailed. As racial segregation hardened and lynch mobs went unchecked, thousands of African Americans resolved to quit the South and head to northern cities in search of jobs, decent schools, and civil rights. This exodus would accelerate to become the Great Migration during World War I (see Chapter 22).

THE NEW IMMIGRATION

The fifteen million immigrants who came to the United States between 1890 and 1914 played an even larger role in urban growth than did the newcomers from rural America. Almost nine million immigrants arrived in the first decade of the twentieth century alone, forming the largest wave of immigration the country has ever seen (see Map 20.2). Although the new arrivals left their homelands under many of the same circumstances that had motivated earlier immigrants, observers called them the "new immigrants" because their nationalities and ethnicities were new to the immigrant mix. Indeed, after 1893, more than two-thirds came from eastern and southern Europe—the Italian peninsula, the Austro-Hungarian Empire, Russia, Greece, and Romania—rather than from the traditional sources of immigration, namely Britain, Ireland, Holland, Germany, Sweden, Norway, and Switzerland. This new wave also included large numbers of Mexicans and Japanese who settled in the West. Over two-thirds of all the new immigrants arrived through New York, and although most eventually moved on, the vast majority made cities their home.

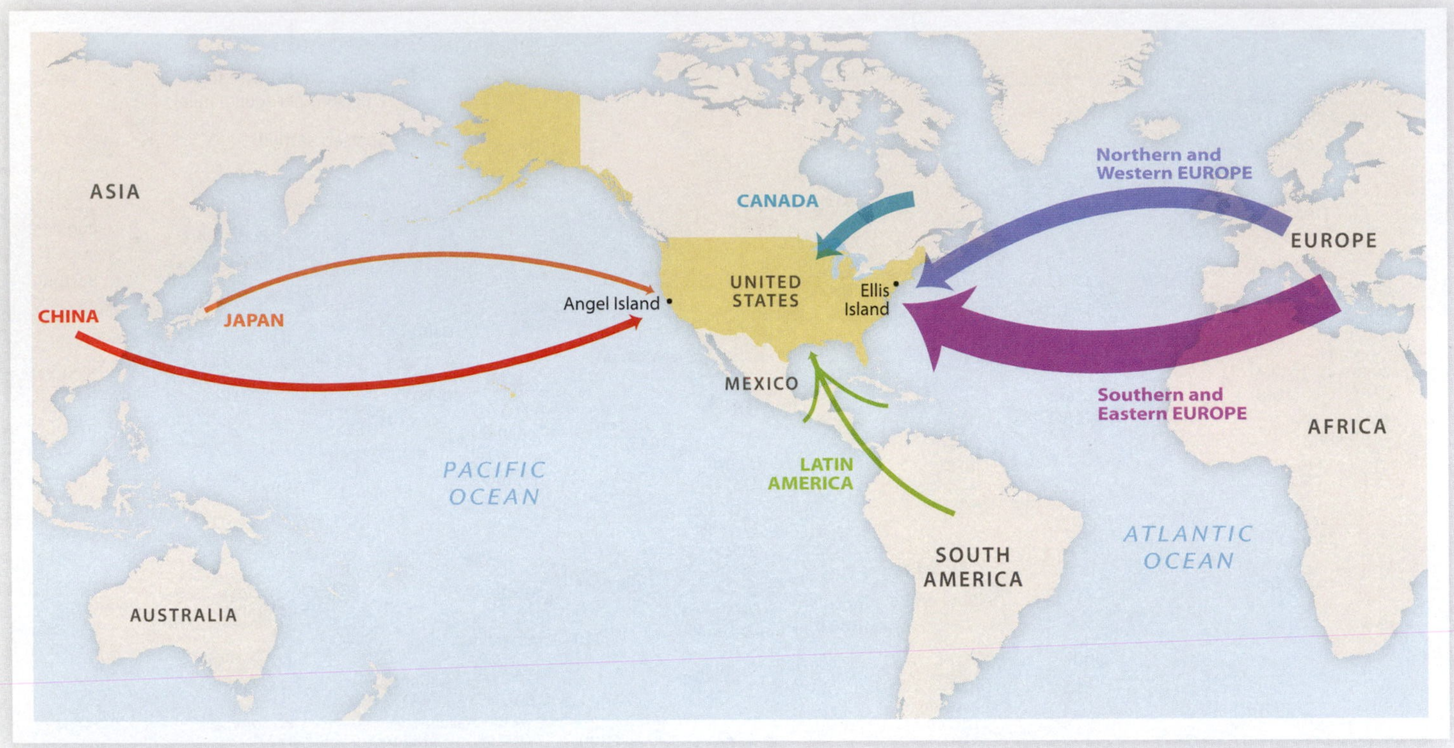

Map 20.2 The New Immigration. Prompted by economic hardship, political crisis, and persecution in their home countries and by better pay in the United States, Europeans left their homelands in record numbers during the Gilded Age and Progressive Era. Northern Europeans still constituted the majority in the 1880s and early 1890s, but after 1893 immigrants from southern and eastern Europe accounted for two-thirds of all immigrants to the United States. Asian immigration rates remained low, due largely to the Chinese Exclusion Act (1882) and the Gentlemen's Agreement (1907), under which Japan agreed to restrict emigration from Japan to the United States.

Economic hardship motivated many of the new European migrants to seek jobs far from their native lands. For one thing, industrialization in Russia, Poland, and Italy had put many small artisans, farmers, and shopkeepers out of work. In addition, a population boom in southern and eastern Europe in the 1880s and 1890s had made work scarcer, food more expensive, and wages considerably lower than before. Meanwhile, many foreign governments had also forcibly redistributed farmland, displacing hundreds of thousands of families. U.S. companies saw opportunity in all this hardship. Hoping to lower their labor costs by hiring more workers—and finding those willing to work for less especially appealing—employers advertised for workers in hard-hit areas and sent agents to recruit them. Consequently, many young men left for the United States with the intention of working hard, making money with which to pay off debts at home, and returning to the old country. Indeed, more than half of Italian immigrants and a significant number of Croatian, Polish, Serbian, and Greek workers returned to Europe between 1897 and 1906.

Other immigrants chose the United States as their final destination, attracted by its promise of religious freedom and social equality. In the Russian Empire, where Jews had faced legal restrictions and persecution for centuries, a false rumor that a Jew had assassinated Czar Alexander II sparked a violent pogrom (an officially sanctioned, organized attack) in 1881. After mobs stormed, burned, and pillaged Jewish villages, more than two million Jews fled Russia. Eastern and southern Europeans also came to America for the freedom of moving around the country as they chose—one of many rights often denied them in their homelands. Further, many new immigrants reasoned, all people in America were in principle equal before the law regardless of their occupation, religion, or nationality—as long as they could be counted as white.

Among all the new immigrant groups, the decision to stay in the United States could set off a chain migration. Once a few families or individuals from a village had decided to settle, other members of that village soon followed. Typically, the first wave of immigrants paid the passage for almost three out of every five subsequent immigrants.

THE IMMIGRANT METROPOLIS

A variety of resources helped immigrants make sense of and cope with the large, impersonal cities in which they found themselves (see Map 20.3). The first such resource was the family unit. Indeed, immigrants often found work through their family and its village connections. Although immigrants typically moved several times in a ten-year period in search of better housing and jobs, they almost always moved as a family. For a while, Italians were the one major exception to the rule, since most Italian immigrants were individual men intending to return. By the 1910s, however, Italians were emigrating as families and following much the same pattern as other immigrant groups.

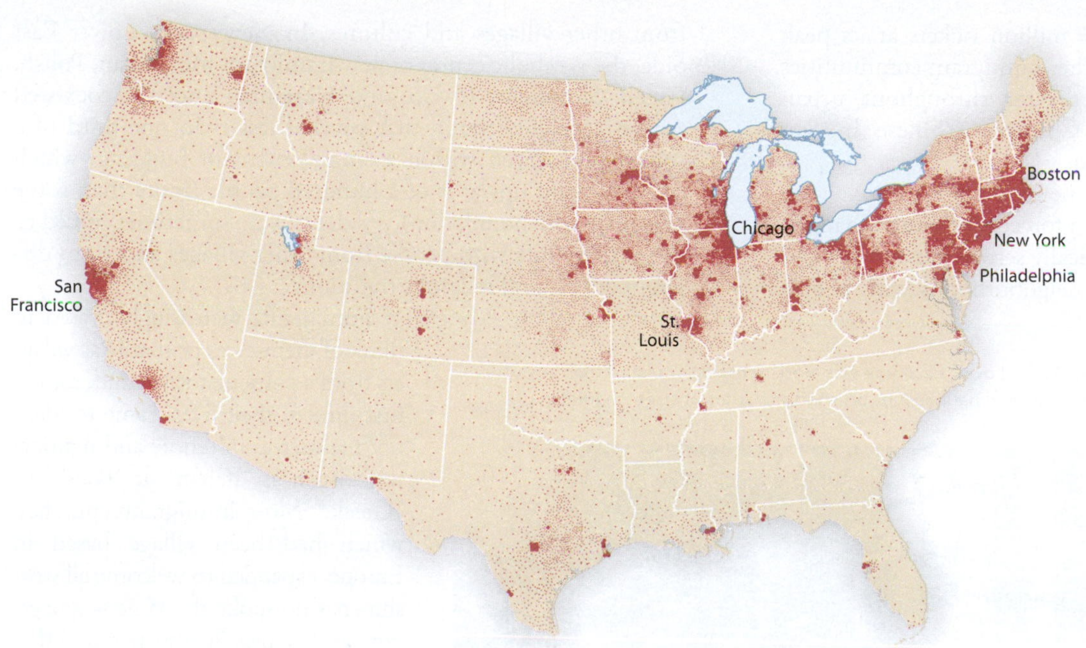

Map 20.3 Immigrant Cities. The vast majority of European immigrants to the United States settled in cities and other industrial regions.

Because kinship networks helped newcomers find work, particular immigrant groups eventually became concentrated in specific trades. In this way, for example, Italians gained control of construction and barbershop jobs in Philadelphia, Pittsburgh, and Buffalo. Similarly, Serbs and Croats cornered freight handling in New York, while Poles waited on most of the tables in Chicago's thriving restaurants. Although ethnic labor networks guaranteed the immigrant a job, it was often the only job he or she could get.

The first generation of new immigrants strove to preserve much of the old culture. Many newcomers lived among people from their village or shtetl and set up the same kinds of societies and institutions they had had at home. Southern Italians reestablished the *padrone* system, under which a well-connected member of the village helped find jobs for fellow villagers and negotiated with employers on workers' behalf. American insurance agencies refused to insure the new immigrants, so many communities set up their own health, welfare, and death benefit societies. Similarly, banks would not extend credit to immigrant borrowers (partly because of prejudice and partly because of the risk that the immigrant would return home and default on the loan), so immigrants established their own mutual aid societies and community banks.

Immigrants also banded together through churches, synagogues, and religious rites. Most new immigrants were Catholic or Jewish, but rather than joining the churches and synagogues already established by Irish Catholics, German Catholics, or German Jews, they built new institutions. In their own places of worship, the newcomers practiced rituals and celebrated beliefs that more established immigrants ridiculed as superstitious and unsophisticated. Irish Catholics, for example, commonly thought of Italians as pagans and criticized their devotion to pilgrimages, shrines, and saints' cards. German Jews, who attended Reform synagogues and conducted prayers partially in English, mocked eastern Europeans who spoke Yiddish, dressed traditionally or covered their hair, and rigorously observed the details of Jewish law.

Other, more secular institutions reinforced ties to the old country. By the time the United States entered the First World War in 1917, some 1,323 foreign-language newspapers were in operation in America. Over half of them served groups (such as Germans, Swedes, Norwegians, and Bohemians) that had established themselves in the previous century, but there were also 77 newspapers in Polish and 103 in Italian. Abraham D. Cahan's *Jewish Daily Forward*, which had the highest circulation of any non-English daily in the country, was just one of five Yiddish papers that appeared every day on the streets of New York during this period.

Bank of Italy Resources
OVER 847 MILLIONS
The resources of *California's largest bank* represent close to a *billion* dollars ... *a vast amount of wealth*

Advertisement for the Bank of Italy, ca. 1920. By 1920, the Bank of Italy was California's largest bank. Founded by Amadeo Giannini, the son of immigrants from northern Italy, the bank attracted the business of hundreds of thousands of immigrants whom other lenders shunned. In 1928, it assumed the new name Bank of America and, in the twenty-first century, went on to become the world's largest commercial bank.

New York's Jews also supported the Yiddish theater, which had originated in eastern Europe in the 1870s but had grown significantly in the United States. Presenting romantic musicals, adaptations of Shakespeare, and dramatic renditions of the dilemmas, predicaments, and pathos of the Jewish immigrant experience, the Yiddish stage supported over one thousand shows a year and sold about two million tickets at its peak around the turn of the century. Other immigrant communities also attended foreign-language theater throughout urban America, including Swedes in Chicago, Chinese in San Francisco, and Mexicans in El Paso.

Despite these continuities with newcomers' traditional cultures, life in the immigrant city also forced significant changes. Although the new immigrants typically settled close to kin and other villagers, they shared their neighborhoods with people from other villages and cultures. In New York's Lower East Side, the symbolic center of new immigrant life, Italian, Polish, Greek, Slovakian, Jewish, and Ukrainian enclaves coexisted within a neighborhood that covered less than one-third of a square mile. Even within a single tenement building, which could contain upwards of a hundred people (more than some villages' entire population), residents were sometimes forced to live side by side with people from other villages and from different ethnic and religious traditions.

Hester Street Market, ca. 1900. New York's Lower East Side was more densely populated than any other part of the country. Immigrants of many religions and nationalities brushed shoulders at street markets.

Immigrants increasingly ceased to think of themselves primarily as villagers from a particular town and, for the first time in their lives, came to identify themselves in ethnic and national terms such as "Italian" or "Polish" or "Greek." Most immigrant churches, which had been village based in Europe, expanded to welcome all worshipers who spoke the same language. Foreign-language newspapers and theaters reinforced this trend because of their need to build an audience that was larger than a few dozen people from a particular village.

Many second- and third-generation immigrants eventually assumed a hybrid or "hyphenated" national identity in an effort to emphasize the fact they had been born in America. Growing numbers of Italians and Poles, for example, began to think of themselves as "Italian-American" or "Polish-American." The public schools, which prohibited the use of any language but English, played a key role in the creation of this hybrid identity. New cultures emerged that were neither traditionally American nor European but a blend of both. Ethnic clothing styles incorporated American fabrics and buttons, and immigrant musicians introduced American musical instruments (such as trumpets and saxophones) into traditional folk music.

For those newcomers seeking to adapt to their new homes, American consumer culture offered gateways to the world of the city. Mary Antin, a Jewish immigrant in New York, recalled in her 1912 memoir walking up Broadway on Saturday nights with her friends, staring at the lavish display windows. More conspicuous advertising, fancier display windows, and new electrified signage beckoned immigrants with the promise that they could live modern, up-to-date American lives simply by buying things. The children of new immigrants were especially eager consumers, hoping that by participating in the consumer culture, they would both show that they fit into American society and distance themselves from the old-fashioned ways of their parents.

MASS ENTERTAINMENT AND THE RISE OF CINEMA

The new immigration coincided with the explosion of mass commercial entertainment in urban America, and immigrants in turn helped boost demand for cheap entertainment. Theaters, bars, cheap museums, circuses, spectator sports, and concert halls had thrived in U.S. cities since the 1830s, but now the audiences for these venues were bigger and more socioeconomically diverse than ever before. Immigrants flocked to theaters and concert halls, but many of the seats were also filled by clerical employees, members of a growing white-collar workforce (1.7 million by 1910) with more leisure time and disposable income to spend on cheap entertainment. The adoption of the shorter, eight-hour day in skilled industries such as building, printing, and automaking also swelled audiences by adding to the pool of people with time and money on their hands.

In a significant departure from the past, women joined men in these venues, as did growing numbers of middle-class youth. Large numbers of young, unmarried female clerical workers as well as adolescent working-class girls living away from their families in boardinghouses or rented apartments (known as "furnished rooms") looked for entertainment outside the home and in the company of boys and men. Older members of the native-born middle and upper classes often looked askance at these mixed-sex activities and openly worried about their impact on public morality—and their daughters' reputations.

Japanese Garden at the St. Louis World's Fair, 1904. The fair invited visitors to experience—and stare at—cultures that most white Americans considered exotic and mysterious.

Couples on dates, as well as singles in groups, rubbed elbows with families at amusement parks, which were popularized by a series of six world's fairs that attracted tens of millions of visitors between 1893 (Chicago) and 1904 (St. Louis). Once beyond the turnstiles, fair visitors entered an exotic playground featuring Egyptian belly dancers, simulated space travel, and miniature models of the city of Jerusalem. The spirit of the fairs was preserved year-round in places like Revere Beach (Boston), Euclid Beach (outside Cleveland), Meramec Falls (near St. Louis), The Chutes (San Francisco), and the grandest and most famous of all, New York's Coney Island. These resorts on the outskirts of town offered city dwellers cheap and easy escape from their working lives.

By far the most popular form of commercial entertainment during the Progressive Era was the theater. By 1900, New York boasted more theaters than any city in the world; in 1910, the total seating capacity, including movie houses, was close to two million. Like many American cities, San Francisco chalked up an estimated weekly theater attendance that substantially surpassed its total population. Many different kinds of dramatic performance appeared on American stages at the turn of the century, but none was as popular as the new form of vaudeville that had emerged in the 1880s (see Chapter 18). The cleaned-up version of vaudeville's traditionally bawdy entertainment drew record numbers of new immigrants, women, and, increasingly, middle-class families. For the first time, Jewish immigrants and their children figured prominently on the vaudeville stage, among them Sophie Tucker, Eddie Cantor, and Groucho Marx [see Singular Lives: Ehrich Weiss (Harry Houdini), Escape Artist].

Second to theater in popularity was baseball, a sport that spectators in northern cities had watched for decades. Although the National and American Leagues had been founded in the 1876 and 1901, respectively, it was not until the Progressive Era that they became a single entertainment franchise with consistent mass popularity. The leagues signed a joint operating agreement in 1903, and the World Series began that year. Attendance doubled in the five years between 1903 and 1908 as fans filled new purpose-built stadiums that could accommodate more than sixty thousand spectators. Though the performers were all male, women joined men in the bleachers, a fact reflected in the

SINGULAR LIVES

Ehrich Weiss (Harry Houdini), Escape Artist

For talented new immigrants, the vaudeville stage provided a rare opportunity to gain security and prosperity in their new home. For Ehrich Weiss, born a Hungarian Jew in Budapest in 1874, it was the launch pad for a career as Harry Houdini, the most famous escape artist of all time.

Harry Houdini Wows a Crowd. A handcuffed and chained Houdini prepares to plunge into the river below—and miraculously escape his bonds.

Weiss's family immigrated to the United States in 1876, first living in Wisconsin, where Ehrich Weiss (as Houdini) would later claim to have been born. In 1887, when Ehrich was thirteen, his father, a rabbi, moved the family to New York and became a garment worker. At seventeen, Ehrich began doing magic shows at Coney Island, and a couple of years later, he and his younger brother, Theo, performed at the 1893 World Exposition in Chicago. The duo achieved some renown as part of a magic act dubbed "the Brothers Houdini," a name that evoked the great French illusionist Jean-Eugène Robert-Houdin. From there, "Harry Houdini," as Erich now called himself, started appearing in cheap New York theaters and then in more respectable vaudeville houses, perfecting an act that featured needle-swallowing tricks, handcuff escapes, and other remarkable displays of strength, ingenuity, or deception that captivated audiences. Houdini toured the country, generating publicity for his act by announcing in each new town that he could escape from any handcuffs provided by the local police. Then, at the beginning of the new century, Harry Houdini and his stage partner (and wife) Bess took their show abroad. America's great escape artist quickly became an international celebrity.

Houdini's act had several appeals. For some spectators, his ability to free himself from handcuffs or a straitjacket was truly supernatural, suggesting some link with mysterious powers and unseen worlds. (Houdini went on, in the 1920s, to debunk psychics and spiritualism, but much of his audience continued to believe that he himself had supernatural power.) Others may have been drawn by the challenge of uncovering his secrets, which often involved tools or keys hidden on his person, the athleticism of his acrobatic maneuvers, or the sheer spectacle of his mostly naked body. For Weiss, the role of Houdini the escape artist fit the experience of an immigrant who had left his home, discarded the religious tradition of his father, and made his own way in a new land, without having to endure the constraints of factory labor or office work.

Think About It

1. What traditional values did Houdini's act flaunt? What did his performances celebrate?
2. How would you explain the name Harry Houdini? Why would a Jew from Hungary have taken a stage name that sounded neither Jewish nor Hungarian?

famous song "Take Me Out to the Ball Game" (1908), a tune popularized on the vaudeville stage. In the song's chorus—the only part ever chanted at baseball stadiums nowadays—a "baseball-mad" young woman pleads with her beau not to take her to the theater next Saturday but instead to bring her to the ballpark for their date.

Vaudeville shows, amusements parks, and baseball games, however, would all face competition from new entertainment technology that had the advantage of being much less expensive to produce and put on than live performances. The phonograph, which had been invented as a dictation device for businesses, caught on instead among music lovers. In 1890, a San Francisco saloon installed nickel slot machines that bar patrons enthusiastically fed in order to hear low-quality music recordings. A few years later, new machines were offering moving pictures. Thomas Edison's Kinetoscope was a small viewing device that ran a strip of film (a French invention) across a lighted background. Edison sold his Kinetoscope to entertainment parlors, which in turn charged customers a nickel to peer into the machine and watch a twenty-second film of a dancer doing a pirouette or an acrobat flying across a room. By 1900, nickel machines were featuring such titillating silent movies as *Serpentine Dancers*, *How Girls Go to Bed*, and *How Girls Undress*.

Edison also acquired the rights to produce the machine that would change the way Americans experienced the movies. His Vitascope projected images from film far enough and brightly enough that viewers could watch the movie together in a theater rather than individually in front of a single machine. By 1899, hundreds of small cinemas had opened across the United States, many in storefronts. Larger vaudeville theaters soon installed projectors, squeezing out small operations. Soon after, a Pittsburgh vaudeville impresario opened the Nickelodeon, a venue devoted entirely to showing moving pictures. Already by 1908, some eight thousand theaters on this model had opened in American cities. The five-cent admission fee ($1.26 in today's dollar) was considerably cheaper than tickets to the theater, and by 1910 an estimated twenty-six million Americans were going to the movies every week.

Cinema for Everybody. Viewers were amazed and even shocked by their first experience of moving pictures. When the image of an approaching train or a runaway horse was first projected in theaters, spectators often leaped out of their seats with fright. **Questions for Analysis:** Why might silent films have drawn such diverse audiences? Why did so many of the earliest films feature a moving object or animal?

Cinema often built on familiar themes and experiences and drew from existing commercial entertainments and news sources, such as variety shows, amusement parks, daily newspapers, weeklies and magazines, and cheap fiction. Short silent movies known as "topicals" informed viewers about current events, including the Spanish-American War of 1898 (see Chapter 21) and the San Francisco earthquake and fire of 1906, which filmmakers depicted using scale models.

THE COLOR LINE

Although the world of commercial entertainment welcomed and integrated new immigrants, it did little to mend the United States' racial divide. African Americans remained second-class citizens in these years, even in the North. Southern states continued to enact and enforce segregation laws, and de facto (nonlegislated) segregation became entrenched elsewhere. In first-class theaters in New York and Chicago, managers refused to seat African Americans anywhere but in the gallery. Many other commercial leisure establishments denied admittance outright to African Americans, a phenomenon that appears to have been on the rise. Indeed, a journalist writing in 1907 described the practice of excluding African Americans from hotels, restaurants, and confectionery stores in Boston. Only a few years earlier, he claimed, none of these establishments had black patrons. African Americans contested discriminatory policies in court and occasionally won, as in the case of G. O. Cochran, who sued a Los Angeles theater for not letting him sit on the first floor and won a judgment of fifty dollars (worth about $1,260 today). These incidents did little to stem the larger trend, however, which was a steady hardening of the color line.

Johnson Versus Jeffries. Jack Johnson's defeat of Jim Jeffries in Reno, Nevada, on July 4, 1910, precipitated nationwide race riots in which at least twenty-five people, mostly blacks, were killed.

In response to discrimination, African Americans opened their own theaters and performance spaces and patronized clubs in black bohemian neighborhoods such as New York's Tenderloin and Chicago's South Side, where they enjoyed African American musical forms such as Ragtime. In mainstream entertainment culture, however, African Americans were often objects of amusement, ridicule, or derision. Whether belittled in coon songs on the vaudeville stage or depicted as savages in world's fair exhibitions, mascots at baseball games, buffoons in amusement park concessions, and dim-witted children or predatory rapists in silent films, African Americans were routinely denigrated.

One black American did manage to become a celebrity in mainstream entertainment culture during the Progressive Era, however—the prizefighter Jack Johnson. Victorious against numerous white opponents, Johnson reigned as heavyweight champion of the world from 1908 to 1915. He had defended his title against a succession of so-called great white hopes, most famously the champion Jim Jeffries, who came out of retirement in 1910 "to prove that a white man is better than a Negro." Jeffries lost. Because of his success in the ring and his relationships with white women, however, Johnson was feared by whites and subjected to police harassment—and ultimately to criminal prosecution.

Discrimination extended well beyond the entertainment world. In northern cities, the residential segregation of Hispanics and people of Chinese or African descent was not mandated by law. But native-born white Americans and European immigrants distinguished themselves as racially "white," left neighborhoods that housed people of color, and signed agreements known as **real estate covenants** pledging that they would not sell or rent their homes to a person of color. When a white homeowner sold to a person of color, the homeowners' association took the case to court—and won (on the grounds that the vendor had broken the covenant). In a few places, such as Springfield, Illinois, in 1908, white mobs torched black homes and businesses and physically drove African Americans out of town.

Europeans immigrants who had not identified as white before coming to the United States quickly learned that, in America, the color line was the principal marker of status and that they would enjoy full rights and freedoms only if they were considered white. The same ethnic labor networks that extended employment opportunities to newcomers and their children also squeezed black workers out of trades they had once dominated. In Philadelphia, for instance, black men were gradually excluded from the traditionally black business of barbershops. Once locked out, their children no longer had access to that labor network. The AFL's exclusion of black workers further limited opportunities. For the first time, a small but growing stratum of urban blacks faced chronic unemployment over two or more generations.

NEW BUILT ENVIRONMENTS

As racial lines hardened and racial minorities became concentrated in urban "ghettos," white neighborhoods and white commercial zones changed dramatically. Here electric streetcars largely supplanted horse-drawn streetcars, effectively doubling the distance one could travel to work or to shop in a given block of time. The faster streetcars, which averaged twelve miles per hour, encouraged both urban sprawl and suburbanization. They also increased everyday mobility within the city. By the end of the

Monument to Shopping. With the help of investment banks, Woolworth had expanded quickly from eighteen to six hundred branches and become the nation's preeminent chain store. At a construction cost of $13.5 million (the equivalent of over $309 million today), New York's Woolworth Building stood as a monument to consumer capitalism. For the building's opening ceremony, President Woodrow Wilson pressed a button in Washington, D.C., that illuminated eighty thousand lightbulbs in the building. Reportedly, the flash could be seen at a distance of one hundred miles.

nineteenth century, the average person living in a city of ten thousand or more rode public transportation 252 times in the course of a year. As both Boston and New York opened subway systems (in 1897 and 1904, respectively), electric streetcars were moved below ground, where they had an uncontested right-of-way.

While rapid transit lines fanned out across the city, skyscrapers pierced—and utterly transformed—the urban skyline. Nineteenth-century U.S. cities were dense and bustling, but they had few tall buildings. Even as late as the 1880s, the tallest built object in the United States' largest city was New York's Trinity Church, whose spire rose a modest 284 feet. By the turn of the century, much taller buildings, supported by steel cages, would tower above Chicago (known as the birthplace of the skyscraper) and New York City. By 1913, Manhattan was home to almost one thousand buildings with eleven to twenty stories and another fifty-one edifices with twenty-one to sixty stories. That year saw the opening of the world's tallest building to date, the Woolworth Building on Broadway, standing 792 feet tall, or close to three times the height of Trinity Church.

Electrification was the other major change in the American city's physical appearance during the Progressive Era. Some of the earliest customers for Thomas Edison's lighting plants were urban entertainment centers: Harry Hill's Concert Saloon in New York, Chicago's Academy of Music, and the St. Charles Hotel in New Orleans. The real impact of electricity on city life, however, was felt outdoors as urban America's main streets became "Great White Ways" that were brightly illuminated by dense concentrations of electric lights. In New York City, the brightest lights of all dazzled on advertising signs. On Broadway, the signs flashed automatically, switching letters to alternate messages or to simulate movement, and by 1910 the street boasted more than twenty blocks of electrical advertisements. Some signs, such as the Roman Chariot Race, a seventy-two-foot-tall advertisement complete with the optical illusion of movement, became major tourist attractions.

Be Prepared! The Boy Scouts of America, founded in 1910, blended military and wilderness training with lessons in "patriotism, courage, self-reliance, and kindred values." Two years later, Juliette Gordon Low founded the Girl Scouts of America, which introduced girls to wilderness training and housekeeping while also encouraging them to consider careers in business, the arts, science, and social work.

THE URBAN MIDDLE CLASS

The urban middle class, which had grown steadily since the Civil War, experienced considerable change in the Progressive Era. In particular, attitudes toward gender roles and family life shifted. On the one hand, the older idea that women were naturally suited to nurturing nuclear families and to overseeing domestic life remained deeply entrenched. On the other hand, more women were finding their prescribed roles unfulfilling. Many middle-class women developed new career and recreational aspirations as educational opportunities increased, especially at demanding all-women's colleges founded in the last third of the nineteenth century, and as birth rates fell. The proliferation of new, time-saving household appliances, commercial bakeries, packaged foods, and ready-made clothing lightened women's household labor load. Moreover, the widespread belief that women were morally superior to men may have dampened the romantic allure of marriage itself. Women who came of age toward the end of the nineteenth century were less likely to marry than at any time in American history before or since.

Middle-class men, for their part, had grown increasingly estranged from the feminized family life they claimed to esteem. They also worried that their urban, white-collar jobs were emasculating them. And because children entered college or the workforce later than in earlier generations, men feared that their sons would be spoiled and weakened by the female-dominated home. Many men, both elites and members of the middle class, began extolling highly masculine activities such as hunting and boxing and spending more time in same-sex clubs and settings. Boys' clubs that placed particular emphasis on creating independent, physically competent men also became popular. Scouting groups, such as the Society of the Sons of Daniel Boone, organized boys into forts, took them out of the cities, and taught wilderness skills.

THE BIRTH OF PROGRESSIVISM

The pace of economic, political, and cultural change in the late nineteenth and early twentieth centuries was relentless. "Never in the history of the world was society in so terrific flux as it is right now," wrote novelist Jack London in 1907. "An unseen and fearful revolution is taking place in the fiber and structure of society." By 1900, the small, agrarian, and relatively homogeneous republic in which most Americans over the age of thirty had grown up had been replaced by a massive, diverse, industrial, and urban society. Industrialization had made the nation wealthier than ever before, but it had also brought high levels of poverty, toxic and unsafe food, destruction of the wilderness, violent industrial conflict, and countless slums and sweatshops.

Although middle-class and wealthy Americans were among the beneficiaries of the new economy, by 1896 a growing number were unsettled by its negative side effects. Many also worried that the nation was losing its moral compass. Around the country and especially in cities, progressive activists mobilized for reform. Far from building a single, coherent movement or political party, progressives tended to focus on a particular social or political problem or cluster of problems at one time, such as the dilapidated prison system or the lack of city sanitation services. Most of the reformers were college-educated men and women who believed in the power of education, rationality, science, and technology to solve the United States' most pressing problems. Many also drew upon older American traditions of moral order and evangelical reform, and some enthusiastically adopted new ideas from across the Atlantic. They skillfully used the press, cinema, and advertising to publicize their causes and generate popular support for their reforms.

PROGRESSIVISM'S EVANGELICAL ROOTS

Urban, evangelical Protestant churches were key sources of progressive activism and ideology. In the wake of the crushing depression of the 1890s, the clergy and congregations of some city churches rethought the older Protestant view that poor people brought hunger, unemployment, and disease upon themselves. Looking back over the Gilded Age, many urban clergy observed that a cycle of economic boom and bust had thrown up to 40 percent of Americans into severe distress in every decade since the Civil War. Some preached a Social Gospel, arguing that poverty's causes could be traced to society's most basic institutional arrangements rather than to the victims' laziness, avarice, or other moral failing. God-fearing Protestants could not hope for salvation if they ignored the vast poverty of their fellow man, they proclaimed. Salvation required that Christians join the struggle for what many called social justice on earth.

Although the Social Gospel never completely eclipsed the older strain of American Protestantism that blamed the poor for their own predicament, it heavily influenced a generation of middle-class churchgoers, as well as prominent business and political leaders (including Thomas Mott Osborne, the millionaire prison reformer profiled in the chapter introduction). The movement gained momentum as it was embraced by Protestant Americans who published influential magazines, dominated higher education, and ran major charities.

The urban churches associated with the Social Gospel movement took a multipronged approach to "lifting up" the poor. New recreation programs gave immigrants an alternative to vice. The churches also worked with secular associations to produce social surveys of whole neighborhoods, mapping the ethnicities of poor areas, building by building, and locating churches, synagogues, saloons, schools, and brothels. Reformers used the maps to decide where to start recreational, educational, and welfare programs. And they identified areas considered ripe for the recruitment of newcomers to Protestantism. In 1910–1911 alone, social surveys were the basis of evangelical revival drives in some eighty-eight cities.

Many evangelical reformers saw conversion to Protestantism as the only way to turn immigrants into Americans—and to end prejudice against them. As one manual, entitled *Aliens or Americans?*, instructed readers, Americans ought to take "responsibility for the salvation of these commonly despised foreigners" and "evangelize" (recruit) them. "The trouble is that the alien and the American do not know each other. Did it ever occur to you that you could do something directly for the evangelization of the Greek or Italian fruit vender or bootblack or laborer?" The evangelical impulse thus inspired reformers to sympathize with the immigrant poor but to criticize their cultural and religious traditions.

ATLANTIC CROSSINGS

Progressivism was also shaped by the larger web of trade, ideas, and industry that tied together the United States and Europe. Whereas Americans had once associated poverty, crime, and social discord with the Old World, the traumatic depressions of the Gilded Age made clear that their country was not immune to these problems and that cities such as New York, Atlanta, and Portland faced many of the same challenges as Paris, Manchester, and Munich. Like Jane Addams, an early pioneer of social work, thousands of concerned middle-class Americans made their way to European cities and universities in the 1890s and 1900s to study their approach to social reform.

In Britain, the investigators found social policies that together served as a safety net for society's most vulnerable and unlucky members. Elderly people who could no longer work were supported by a national old-age pension system. When workers fell ill, they received medical care through a compulsory system of national health care. In mining and other highly dangerous industries, government boards had the authority to set wages at a minimum, livable level. If workers lost their jobs, state-run employment agencies helped them find employment and, in some cases, tided them over with state-sponsored unemployment insurance.

Reformers discovered similar practices in Germany, Australia, France, and New Zealand. The French government, they found, aimed to avert strikes and protect workers (who typically wielded less power than employers in negotiations over wages and conditions) by providing public mediation for industrial conflicts. All four countries funded these systems, at least in part, through progressive taxation, under which poorer people with little money to spare paid a low tax while the wealthy paid progressively higher taxes, depending on their income and assets. American reformers took many of these ideas home, publicized them, and called upon Republicans and Democrats to endorse them.

These reformers' findings were reinforced by the growing number of highly educated experts with doctoral degrees in economics, law, and government. Around this time, a new generation of American economists had been trained in graduate programs in Germany, home to the world's leading economics departments (American colleges still lacked graduate programs in most disciplines). At the University of Berlin and elsewhere, students developed a rigorous critique of the laissez-faire model of free-market economics that had guided American political economy since before the Civil War. The free market was a fiction, they insisted, and institutional forces, such as labor unions and laws mandating minimum wages and workplace safety, could keep the workforce healthy and productive while stabilizing industrial relations. Returning home, the young economists educated an entire generation of American college students about the need for regulation and served on government commissions charged with improving relations between workers and employers.

W. E. B. Du Bois. Initially, Du Bois was the only African American in a leadership position at the NAACP. He edited the organization's journal, *The Crisis: A Record of the Darker Races*, the stated purpose of which was to "set forth those facts and arguments which show the danger of race prejudice, particularly as manifested today toward colored people."

A MIDDLE-CLASS MOVEMENT

Progressive ideals and methods were especially appealing to the new urban middle class. Typically, college-educated, salaried employees embraced the latest scientific discoveries and put great value on professional training and expertise. They believed that European models offered a rational analysis of the roots of disorder and a set of practical tools and solutions. Social problems were to be addressed by trained, credentialed experts applying scientific methods of investigation and analysis. In this vein, progressive-minded accountants, lawyers, doctors, and engineers all worked through their professional associations to reserve their respective fields for credentialed practitioners. The American Medical Association, for example, successfully lobbied state legislatures for laws prohibiting midwives, osteopaths (who rejected pharmaceutical approaches to health, in favor of physical manipulation), and anyone without a medical degree from prescribing medication, performing certain procedures, or calling themselves doctors.

Progressive reformers also pushed for the professionalization of **social work,** the culmination of a trend toward a more scientific approach to providing relief to the poor. By the 1910s, reformers were creating training programs for social work practitioners and bringing the study of poverty, juvenile delinquency, and housing into the orbit of the university. Women were encouraged to enter the social work profession, which seemed to be an extension of their role in the earlier poverty-relief movements, and it was partly for this reason that social work paid less handsomely than medicine or engineering. Middle-class progressives were especially concerned with child welfare and argued that society ought to protect younger people from premature adulthood. Progressive women successfully lobbied city government and private philanthropists to build the first public playgrounds for children, pressing for the need to structure children's time and take them off the streets. For the first time, child development itself became the object of sustained research, as did a brand new category of young people—adolescents.

The suggestion that social suffering and disorder originated in the upper and working classes was naturally appealing to the middle class. Connecting the economists' critique with Social Gospel's emphasis on moral purpose, many people believed that the free-market ideology of the Gilded Age had produced a nation of selfish individuals who put their own narrow self-interest ahead of the good of the whole. Consequently, they condemned elite bankers and industrialists for throwing lavish banquets while the poor could barely find enough bread to eat. At the same time, however, they denounced workers for striking and disrupting the social peace with callous disregard for others.

For the most part, white progressives were little concerned with the plight of African Americans in either the South or the northern cities. They were equally uninterested in the discrimination suffered by Hispanics, Chinese, and Japanese in the western states. Among the exceptions was Jane Addams, who condemned segregation as an obstacle to improving African American living and working conditions and raised money for the Frederick Douglass Center, a multiracial settlement house that provided services and relief to the poor.

However, even Addams did not prioritize racial discrimination as a pressing social problem. That task fell to a new generation of African American intellectuals and activists who strenuously criticized both white progressives' acquiescence to racism and the accommodationism of many older black leaders. African Americans would make no progress, argued W. E. B. Du Bois in *The Souls of Black Folk* (1903), until they had full political and social rights. Du Bois, who had studied at Fisk, Harvard, and the University of Berlin, thus rejected Booker T. Washington's view that African Americans should concentrate on developing trade skills and fitting into a segregated society. Answering Du Bois's call, a handful of supporters gathered on the Canadian side of Niagara Falls in 1905, declaring that "we do not hesitate to complain, and to complain loudly and insistently." Five years later, Du Bois's Niagara Movement, along with several white progressives and benefactors, helped found the National Association for the Advancement of Colored People (NAACP).

The NAACP struggled to reverse the tide of discrimination through its anti-segregationist journal and a series of lawsuits. But the organization was small and lacked grassroots support among black communities. African Americans would join in much larger numbers in the 1920s and 1930s, however, carrying the organization to significant legal victories (see Chapters 23 and 24).

FEMINIST PROGRESSIVES

Progressives often, though not always, supported woman suffrage and an expanded social role for women. Without necessarily questioning beliefs about stark gender differences that they inherited from the previous century, progressive reformers looked for ways to widen women's role in the public sphere, to bridge the gap between male and female experiences of the family, and to make family life more attractive and fulfilling. Though they varied in their emphasis and strategy, progressives of different stripes supported giving women more control over sexual relations, reproduction, and family size and eliminating the sexual double standard that forced men and women of the same class to live by different sexual codes. Progressive activists also pushed for greater opportunities for women outside the home.

In the spirit of these reformist times, suffragists renewed their push for women's voting rights. Activists claimed that by denying women the vote, the nation was depriving itself of the full benefits of women's acknowledged expertise in matters of welfare, family, health, and educational policy. In 1900, despite local suffragist agitation, women could vote in only four lightly populated states in the West—Wyoming, Colorado, Idaho, and Utah. In 1909, the National American Woman Suffrage Association (NAWSA), in an effort to draw national attention to their cause, coordinated the first of a series of street rallies. Marchers reported overcoming deep feelings of trepidation as they broke class and gender norms and took to Main Street.

Suffragists also called on the department stores they frequented to support the cause. Soon, retail shops were incorporating pro-suffrage colors and symbols in their window displays.

Women Take to the Streets A year before the NAWSA held street rallies, the California Equal Suffrage Association staged a street demonstration for women's voting rights. Such protests were an exhilarating expression of women's growing public role and their newfound willingness to forcefully demand their rights.

Macy's department store in New York City advertised special parade marching outfits for suffragists, and the movement's supporters named Macy's their "headquarters for suffrage supplies." By 1914, suffragists had won voting rights for women in California, Arizona, Kansas, and Oregon. However, some women remained frustrated with the snail's pace of reform. One disgruntled faction broke away from the NAWSA in 1913 to form the Congressional Union, which pressed for a woman suffrage amendment to the federal constitution. Three years later, the members of this splinter group would celebrate their success (see Chapter 22).

Other women reformers made women's labor reform their primary goal, sometimes acting in concert with female labor unions. The National Consumers League (NCL), a women's organization founded in 1889, led the charge. The League operated on the premise that middle-class women exercised significant power in the emerging consumer society as household shoppers. "To live means to buy," League leader Florence Kelley reminded female consumers, and "to buy means to have power, to have power means to have responsibility" (see Interpreting the Sources: Florence Kelley on Consumer Power). Consumers, in other words, could reward manufacturers and store owners by buying from them and could punish others by shopping elsewhere. The NCL urged consumers to boycott any store that failed to pay female sales clerks a minimum wage of $6 per week (about $152 in today's dollars) or forced them to work more than twelve hours per day or six days per week. A well-publicized "white list" informed shoppers of which vendors met NCL standards. Further, together with the International Ladies' Garment Workers' Union, the NCL distributed white labels that approved manufacturers could affix to their products.

Although most progressive women were dedicated to political causes such as woman suffrage and the improvement of women's working conditions, some considered themselves "bohemian" and pursued literary and sexual experimentation. In New York's Greenwich Village, a small but influential group of twenty-five highly educated women founded the Heterodoxy Club, an association that promoted members' self-development and critiqued the conventional model of gender relations in which women were economically and psychologically dependent on men. "We intend simply to be ourselves," one member declared, "not just our little female selves, but our whole big human selves."

In a related vein, immigrant and anarchist Emma Goldman toured the country as a fiery champion of free speech, free love, modern dance and theater, and labor rights. Goldman, whose speeches drew workers as well as middle-class people, spoke openly and frankly about women's sexuality and their need for both economic independence and control over reproduction (through access to birth control, which was still illegal). Such ideas were still too radical for most American women. But they proved appealing to the growing number of younger middle-class women who had moved into clerical, sales, and publishing work after 1900.

***Mr. and Mrs. Isaac Newton Phelps Stokes*, by John Singer Sargent.** In an era when physical and economic activities were opening to women for the first time, Sargent's portrait of this newlywed couple evoked the energy and self-confidence of the middle-class "New Woman." **Questions for Analysis:** What does Sargent's depiction of Mrs. Stokes's clothing, demeanor, and name suggest about her life? How does Sargent represent the marital bond between Mr. and Mrs. Stokes?

INTERPRETING THE SOURCES

Florence Kelley on Consumer Power

National Consumers League leader Florence Kelley wrote the following article, published in a leading sociological journal, in the hopes of persuading fellow progressives to support the League's campaign to abolish child labor, improve working conditions for women, and end "sweated" and "drudge" labor (in which workers toiled so relentlessly that they became sick or even died). Here Kelley argues that consumers are not powerless to change the conditions under which so many workers suffered. If consumers could learn more about the source of the goods they buy, their composition, and the conditions under which they are made, they would reject the products of unethical manufacturers. Both workplace safety laws and the contents labels of today's packaged foods and beverages can be credited to the success of consumer awareness drives such as the League's.

The underlying principles of the Consumers' League are few and simple. They are partly economic and partly moral. . . . In a civilized community every person is a consumer. From the cradle (which may be of wood or of metal, with rockers or without them) to the grave (to which an urn may be preferred), throughout our lives we are choosing, or choice is made for us, as to the disposal of money . . . we help to decide, however unconsciously, how our fellowmen shall spend their time in making what we buy. A man is largely what his work makes him— an artist, an artisan, a handicraftsman, a drudge, a sweaters' victim, or, scarcely less to be pitied, a sweater.

While . . . the whole body of consumers determine . . . what shall be produced, the individual consumer has, at the present time, for want of organization and technical knowledge, no adequate means of making his wishes felt, of making his demand an effective demand. . . . A painful type of the ineffectual consumer may be found in the colony of Italian immigrants in any one of our great cities. These support at least one store for the sale of imported maccaroni [sic], vermicelli, sausage (Bologna and other sorts), olive oil, Chianti wine, and Italian cheese and chestnuts. These articles are all excessively costly . . . but the immigrants are accustomed to using them, and they prefer a less quantity of these kinds of foods rather than a greater abundance of the cheaper and more accessible supplies by which they are surrounded. The pitiful result is that the importer buys the least quantity of the real Italian product requisite for the purpose of admixture with American adulterants. The most flagrant example of this is, perhaps, . . . Italian olive oil, of which virtually none, really pure, is placed upon the market, for sale at retail.

What the Italian immigrants really get is the familiar Italian label, the well-known package with contents tasting more or less as they used to taste at home in Italy. What the actual ingredients may be they know as little as we know when we place our so-called maple syrup, or our so-called butter, or honey, on our hot cakes at a hotel in the city. The demand of the Italians in America for Italian products, although large, persistent, and maintained at a heavy sacrifice on the part of the purchasers, is not an effective demand, because the immigrants have neither the knowledge nor the organization wherewith to enforce it.

Source: Florence Kelley, "Aims and Principles of the Consumer's League." *American Journal of Sociology,* 5, no. 3 (November 1899).

White Labels. League campaigns argued persuasively that sweatshops and garment factories bred diseases that were spread not only to workers but to consumers as well. White labels were designed to help consumers make informed choices about products and to shop in the confidence that they were purchasing goods that had been produced under humane working conditions.

Explore the Source

1. In Kelley's view, what makes the consumer's decision to purchase any given product both an economic and a moral issue?
2. What is Kelley's attitude toward Italian immigrants? What are "ineffectual consumers"?

SPECTACLES OF REFORM

Regardless of their chosen cause, progressives were savvy communicators who pursued their reform agenda by using mass media to publicize the evils they saw in American society. They conducted investigations, often operating under cover (as in the case of Thomas Mott Osborne), employed press agents, and published their results before a mass audience. Progressives were familiar with new advertising techniques as well as with the principle, drawn from consumer culture, that people's desires and aspirations could be stimulated and directed. Fervently believing in the power of facts to ignite reform, they adapted some of these powerful techniques and became adept publicists for their causes.

The most successful progressive publicists were journalists and photojournalists, known as **muckrakers,** who exposed corruption in government, the horrors of poverty, outrageous working conditions, and the sinister influence of big business on American life. Their work appeared in new affordable magazines with wide national circulation, such as *The New Republic*, *Everybody's*, *Cosmopolitan*, *Collier's*, and most notably *McClure's*, whose star writer Lincoln Steffens penned some of the era's most influential investigative journalism.

In 1901 and 1902, Steffens exposed graft in the municipal governments of St. Louis, Minneapolis, Chicago, Pittsburgh, Philadelphia, and New York in a series of articles entitled "The Shame of the Cities," which then became a best-selling book. Steffens documented dozens of cases in which elite, respectable businessmen had illegally bought favors from city government and influenced elections. The "shame" was that corruption and greed had produced slums and squalor, rather than the other way around (as many earlier critics had argued). *McClure's* also published Ida Tarbell's series "The History of the Standard Oil Company" (1902–1903), which portrayed John Rockefeller as a ruthless and arrogant businessman whose public generosity was designed to conceal his cutthroat takeover of the oil industry.

Perhaps the most sensational muckraker was Upton Sinclair, who went undercover into Chicago's meat processing plants. His best-selling novel, *The Jungle* (1906), depicted the exploitation and abuse of immigrant meatpackers through the story of a Lithuanian family whose dream of making it in America is destroyed by deceitful bosses and merciless foremen. But the novel's most palpable effect was to disgust middle-class consumers with vivid descriptions of the rat dung, spoiled meat, and fecal matter that manufacturers routinely ground into sausage meat. Hitting consumers in the stomach was politically effective: Congress quickly enacted laws calling for meat inspection. The trials of slum life, however, remained much the same.

Cinema proved to be another powerful medium for swaying hearts and minds, although many progressives initially condemned movies and nickelodeons as corruptive, time-wasting amusements. But eventually, progressives recruited filmmakers to shoot a new genre—the documentary—that supported reform efforts. The New York–based Joint Committee on Prison Reform, for instance, retained twenty-two-year-old Katherine Russell Bleecker to make documentaries on prison reform and to dramatize Thomas Mott Osborne's voluntary incarceration. Such films proved popular among the reform-minded middle class, and premieres frequently sold out. A number of leading filmmakers were themselves progressives, and the superior craftsmanship they brought to the art form made their movies popular with mass audiences. Particularly after 1907, when clear story lines became a central feature of movies and when large-scale theaters began replacing the tiny nickelodeons, directors adapted plays with progressive themes to the screen.

Muckraking journalists and filmmakers made a heart-wrenching spectacle of working-class life that they consciously molded to stimulate demands for reform. Other spectacles occurred spontaneously, to both tragic and galvanizing effect. Among these, the deadly fire at the Triangle Shirtwaist Company, which killed over one hundred female garment workers in New York in 1911, gruesomely brought to the nation's attention the plight of several hundred thousand sweatshop workers (see States of Emergency: The Triangle Shirtwaist Fire). Armed with the horrifying facts of the disaster, reformers in many states were able to secure passage of the nation's first tough work-safety regulations and to close down multiple sweatshops.

CLEANING UP THE CITY

Of all the progressive causes, the city and its problems were the most pressing. Most progressive reformers were city people themselves, but they distrusted the apparent chaos and disorder of city life. Among the many evils they targeted, machine politics and political corruption, unsanitary and overcrowded tenements, and urban poverty loomed large. When reformers promised to "clean up the city," they simultaneously referred to the establishment of honest government, the provision of decent sanitation and waste disposal services, and the imposition of Protestant norms of social conduct.

THE SANITIZED CITY

Nineteenth-century cities were dirty, smelly places by modern standards, and reformers saw the foul streets in poor neighborhoods in particular as incubators of disease and moral decay. By 1900, breakthroughs in germ science had firmly established the bacteriological origins of common and frequently fatal diseases such as tuberculosis. *How the Other Half Lives,* Jacob Riis's influential exposé of tenement life in New York, had also linked dirt and mud with urban poverty. Progressives pressed for modern sanitation services that would make the disposal of garbage and human waste a basic amenity of city life. George E. Waring, the father of modern municipal sanitation, led the charge in the mid-1890s as New York's sanitation commissioner. Waring, an engineer who had designed drainage systems for Central Park and sewer systems for Memphis, Tennessee, organized a well-disciplined army of street cleaners, known as the White Wings, who swept slum streets and emptied the ash barrels that dropped filth on the sidewalks.

Sanitation reformers saw their mission as both practical and moral. Waring's broom not only removed disease-causing waste, exclaimed one advocate, "it swept the cobwebs out of our civic brain and conscience, and set up a standard of a citizen's duty." Waring also initiated a recycling program and became a national advocate for sewer construction. In 1880, U.S. cities provided only 598 miles of waterworks, but by 1909, 24,972 miles of sewer system were in operation in urban America.

STATES OF EMERGENCY

The Triangle Shirtwaist Fire

Fires were common occurrences in American cities before 1930, destroying buildings and taking lives with almost numbing frequency. Whole sections of New York City, Chicago, Boston, and San Francisco had been devastated at one time or another. But the fire that blazed through the top floors of the ten-story Asch building in New York's Greenwich Village on March 25, 1911, shocked the nation and rallied popular opinion around a range of reforms.

From street level, witnesses could see a fire rip through the top of the building, while firefighters vainly tried to extinguish the blaze with ladders that reached only six flights high (just a few decades earlier, virtually no building in the city was taller than six stories). What they saw next was far more horrifying. Trapped inside their burning workplaces, dozens of young women jumped out of windows in desperation, forty-six of them plunging to their deaths. When the smoke cleared, another hundred lay dead inside the building. While the majority were women, thirty of the victims were men.

The top three floors of the building had been rented out to the Triangle Waist Company (also known as the Triangle Shirtwaist Company), which ran a sweatshop employing five hundred young women, mostly immigrants from southern Italy and eastern Europe. One Jewish immigrant from Lithuania, who had worked at the factory not long before the fire, recalled that her "starting wage was just one dollar and a half [worth $34 today] a week—a long week—consisting more often than not, of seven days." Long hours and low wages were by no means unique in New York's garment trade, which had already become the focus of tense labor conflicts as immigrant women sought to unionize. But Triangle had so far managed to keep the union out, and the company set working conditions unilaterally.

Low wages and long hours did not cause the fire, of course, but investigations after the fire revealed that the factory had violated existing building codes. Several workers also charged that managers were in the habit of locking the shop floors, a practice that certainly would have contributed to the massive loss of life. More generally, the sensational fire ripped the roof off of the sweatshop industry, calling attention to the vulnerability (and, as many saw it, the degradation) of young women in the garment trade. Unions made the fire a rallying cry for collective bargaining and workers' control. Progressive reformers, who had been long stressing the connection between unventilated, unsafe buildings and the perpetuation of poverty, seized the moment to build support for their campaigns of social welfare and workplace safety. And for decades to come, labor leaders, immigrants, and liberal politicians would invoke the tragic fire as an argument for government regulation. "We banded ourselves together . . . moved by a sense of stricken guilt," wrote Frances Perkins, an eyewitness to the carnage and a future U.S. secretary of labor, "to prevent this kind of disaster from ever happening again."

Think About It

1. Triangle company owners Isaac Harris and Max Blanck were acquitted of manslaughter charges in the fire. What advantages do you think the sweatshop owners had over the workers when the case was brought to court?
2. What difference might it have made to progressive reformers if the victims had been older, male, Protestant, or native born?

Sweatshop Inferno. The fire's victims could have been saved if the employer had unlocked the fire escapes. The disaster galvanized New York City and state legislators to enact workplace safety laws. Other states soon followed.

WAR ON VICE

To many progressives, what made cities and slums dirty was not simply mud, horse deposits, and stagnant water but the allegedly immoral habits of their residents. Alcohol was an especially important target because it lay at the center of both the commercial nightlife that progressives judged to be immoral and the machine politics that they considered corrupt. Though reformers did not succeed in outlawing the sale or consumption of liquor until after World War I, **Prohibition,** as the movement was called starting in 1900, was a major progressive goal going into the twentieth century. Organizations such as the Woman's Christian Temperance Union and the Anti-Saloon League gained strength during the Progressive Era, drawing mostly Protestant middle-class men and women who identified with other reform crusades. Because saloons, beer gardens, and wine shops were important communal institutions for Germans, Italians, and many other immigrant groups, progressive campaigns touched off bitter culture clashes. From the perspective of many immigrants, the progressives' prohibition crusades constituted an attack not only on alcohol consumption but also on a whole way of life.

Working in parallel to the Prohibition movement, anti-prostitution organizations, such as the Social Purity Alliance and the American Society of Sanitary and Moral Prophylaxis, spent a great deal of time and money on exposing commercial sex rings and publicly shaming prostitutes' clients. New York City's Committee of Fifteen, formed in 1900, investigated the extent of prostitution in that city and published its shocking findings in a book entitled *The Social Evil* (1902). Another New York organization, the Committee of Fourteen, comprising settlement house workers and Prohibition activists, sent undercover agents to dancehalls and entertainment venues to identify sex workers and lobbied for stricter enforcement of anti-prostitution laws.

The progressive assault on the sex trade served the larger purpose of policing urban sexuality—and especially urban newcomers. The annual reports of the Committee of Fourteen routinely called attention to the high proportions of immigrants in the sex trade. In 1910, Congress passed a law authorizing the deportation of immigrants who worked in any "music or dance hall or other place of amusement or resort habitually frequented by prostitutes." That same year, the notorious Mann Act (1910), officially called the White Slave Traffic

Prohibition Crusade. The Woman's Christian Temperance Union began a national campaign for the federal prohibition of alcohol in 1909. Like many prohibitionists, these Birmingham, Alabama, women claimed to have God's support for their cause.

Act, made it a federal crime for anyone to transport a woman across state lines for "prostitution or debauchery, or for any other immoral purpose." The vagueness of that last phrase empowered federal agents to prosecute all kinds of sexual behavior, including nonmarital, teenage, and interracial intercourse. Two years later, African American boxing champion Jack Johnson was arrested under this law for traveling with a white woman, his future wife Lucille Cameron, from Pittsburgh to Chicago. When the charges were dropped, a different white woman accused him of having transported her across state lines for "immoral purposes" in 1909–1910. Rather than face the new charges (and an all-white jury), Johnson fled the country.

PURIFYING POLITICS

When it came to city government, progressives emphatically wanted to place administration in the hands of experts and professionals rather than machine politicians and their friends. Progressives offered compelling practical reasons for this preference, arguing that machine politics at the city level led to poor public services, rising taxes, and the manipulation of naive and uninformed voters (especially immigrants). After 1901, reformers embarked on a nationwide movement to put city government on a business basis and under the control of either citizen commissions or city managers. Hundreds of cities followed the example of Dayton, Ohio, which elected city commissioners and hired professional managers to administer city services.

But much more was at stake in urban political reform than economic efficiency. Advocates of the business model considered their reforms a crucial part of the larger war for the soul of the city. From the perspective of William T. Stead, author of the popular text *If Christ Came to Chicago* (1894), and Charles Parkhurst, a New England minister who moved to a Presbyterian pulpit in New York in 1880, the city's salvation lay in the purification of not only its vice but its politics as well. Moral reform and political reform went hand in hand because, in Parkhurst's words, drinking, gambling, and sex formed in the "slimy, oozy soil of Tammany Hall." Tammany and the other political machines that ignored and even supported taverns and commercialized sex would have to go.

THE CITY BEAUTIFUL

Many of the same people who sponsored anti-vice raids, urban sanitization, and the purification of city politics also championed the City Beautiful Movement. Launched for the 1893 Chicago Exposition, and flourishing first in Chicago, Detroit, and Washington, D.C., the movement focused less on vice and political corruption than on urban aesthetics. But it aimed for much the same result: Its advocates argued that beautified public spaces would inspire moral and civic virtue among the city's inhabitants. For the first time, municipal leaders enlisted artists and architects in the project of producing civic loyalty by adorning cities with statues, fountains, landscaped boulevards, and stately city halls. According to the motto of New York's Municipal Art Society, "To make us love our city, we must make our city lovely." By 1905, over 2,400 "improvement societies" had cropped up in U.S. cities.

At the same time, several cities also began to develop integrated approaches to city growth—and many U.S. cities today demonstrate the enduring legacy of this Progressive Era movement. The 1901 new master plan for Washington, D.C., realigned the Mall and sited the Jefferson and Lincoln Memorials. Civic center districts, with their clusters of municipal buildings, libraries, museums, and opera houses, also began appearing at this time, as did many of the United States' grand railroad stations, including Washington's Union Station and New York City's Grand Central Terminal, which remain architectural jewels of urban America.

THE NATIONAL PROGRESSIVE MOVEMENT

As progressive initiatives proceeded on the city level, a diverse set of reformers set out to bring the nation as a whole in line with their distinctive vision of fairness, moral order, and efficiency. Some reformers sought to change public opinion, others ran for office, and still others built new organizations and institutions. Though they did not coordinate their activities in any formal way and did not always agree on every issue, together they formed an unofficial movement for social and political change that spanned the country and fulfilled many of their goals in a short period of time. Successful presidential candidates such as Theodore Roosevelt were canny observers of the surging progressive impulse among voters and harnessed it to ride into power. Once in the White House, they attempted to balance the call for reform with the more conservative forces of big business. This delicate balancing act resulted in the enactment of many progressive programs—but it also limited their scope and efficacy.

ELECTORAL REFORM

Weakening the power of political parties in state and federal politics was a major objective of many progressives, who believed that skilled, educated experts would be more likely to emerge and win office if the parties did not control the nomination process. Consequently, progressives supported primary elections that would allow voters to influence party nominations (and in the process would weaken party cohesion). **Ballot initiatives** and **referenda,** by which voters propose or enact legislation, as well as **recalls,** which allow voters to remove an officeholder, were other innovations of the period. So was the short ballot, which meant having fewer offices elected at the same time and which enabled voters to cast their ballots for individual candidates rather than entire party slates. Progressives also pushed to let voters rather than state legislatures elect U.S. senators.

Progressives were confident that educated voters acting without the mediation of political parties would make better decisions. They also believed that government worked most efficiently and fairly when headed by civic-minded reformers who were nonpartisan and thus not tainted by politics. The progressives' antipathy to partisanship and to politics, which remains extraordinarily influential in American public life today, broke from the powerful tradition that held that political parties allowed voters to make clear choices between competing ideologies.

Barring individuals whom they considered unsuitable for full citizenship from voting was another progressive initiative. By 1910, nine northern states indirectly restricted voting among many naturalized immigrants by requiring them to read English. Seven southern states imposed literacy tests aimed primarily at African Americans and impoverished whites. By these means, hundreds of thousands of voters were deprived of the right to vote. In addition, voter turnout in national elections began what would turn out to be a long-term decline, from a peak of over 80 percent in 1890 to about 48 percent in 1996.

PROGRESSIVE POLITICS AND GOVERNMENT REGULATION

While muckrakers and organizers mobilized public opinion on behalf of various progressive causes, reformers simultaneously seized crucial positions of political power. Progressive factions, coalitions, or parties, for example, took over several state governments in these years. In Wisconsin, Robert M. La Follette, elected governor in 1900, instituted the most far-reaching reforms, including new taxes on railroad profits and inheritances. Other new governors embraced various parts of the progressive agenda, including Hiram Johnson (California), Charles Evans Hughes (New York), James K. Vardaman (Mississippi), and Woodrow Wilson (New Jersey).

More significantly, Vice President Theodore Roosevelt succeeded to the presidency in 1901 after an anarchist assassinated President William McKinley. Roosevelt, the youngest president in U.S. history (at age forty-two when he first took the oath of office) and the only one born in the nation's largest city, took office with strong progressive credentials. The product of a privileged family and an elite education, Roosevelt had entered city politics and served as New York City's police commissioner under the reform administration of William Strong, devoting himself to anti-vice campaigns. In the brewing late-nineteenth-century conflict between capital and labor, Roosevelt appeared to stake out what was becoming the progressive middle ground. Though suspicious of unions and hostile to working-class radicalism, he was also critical of big business. "I know the banker, the merchant and the railroad king well too," Roosevelt told a friend, "and *they* also need education and sound chastisement." During his first term, Roosevelt repeatedly used his presidency, which he called a "bully pulpit," to preach against both class division and materialism. (*Bully* is slang for "wonderful" or "superb.")

The popular Roosevelt nudged the Republican Party toward accepting a major expansion of the federal government's role in regulating the economy. At first he focused on monopolies, authorizing the Justice Department to prosecute companies that violated the Sherman Antitrust Act, starting with J. P. Morgan's railroad conglomerate, the Northern Securities Company. Some progressives and most radicals called for the abolition of monopolies, but Roosevelt advocated merely for their regulation on the grounds that the tremendous efficiencies such organizations made possible could be harnessed for the public good. The Supreme Court ruled in the government's favor in 1904, prompting Roosevelt's administration to bring an unprecedented forty-four antitrust lawsuits over the next five years. Shrewdly, Roosevelt made much of his reputation as a trust buster. But he was careful only to take on cases involving unpopular corporations or those that had offended him, and he did not seek a rigorous system of checks against the concentration of economic power.

Elected in his own right to a second term in 1904, Roosevelt's antitrust rhetoric intensified, and he called for government regulation that would rein in the worst excesses of the wealthiest corporations—and thus undercut some of the more radical attacks on industry then being waged on the left. Now buffeted by the support of progressive reformers and by the readers of muckraking exposés, Roosevelt called for an expansion of the role of the Interstate Commerce Commission, which had been created two decades earlier but given a very narrow charge. The Hepburn Act of 1906 fulfilled this goal by granting the commission the authority to set railroad rates and supervise railroad company bookkeeping practices.

Later that year, in the wake of Upton Sinclair's startling exposé of conditions in the Chicago meatpacking industry, Congress passed the Meat Inspection Act (1906), which authorized the Agriculture Department to investigate stockyards and attest to the quality of commercial meat. The Pure Food and Drug Act (1906) further extended the reach of government as a consumer protection agency by creating the Food and Drug Administration. Roosevelt enthusiastically backed these measures, which were helped by fears that Europeans might ban the importation of processed foods from the United States. The progressive critique of unrestrained wealth and the free market was now enshrined in federal law.

ROOSEVELT AND CONSERVATION

Roosevelt's other major domestic policy achievement lay in the area of conservation. An outdoorsman with keen interest in the natural world, Roosevelt was the first president to treat the despoliation of the American landscape as a political problem and a policy priority. Already in his first message to Congress, Roosevelt had called for laws to protect western lands held by the federal government. A year later he supported legislation to fund irrigation and reclamation projects, in so doing opening his first rift with conservatives from his party. In his second term (which began in 1905), Roosevelt helped create a major bureaucracy called the U.S. Forest Service, with his friend Gifford Pinchot as chief forester. Pinchot and Roosevelt oversaw the establishment of vast new national parks in the Rockies and wildlife preserves all over the country (see Map 20.4).

The conservation movement had begun earlier (see Chapter 18), and conservation was not a major preoccupation of the progressives, most of whom were urbanites focused on city problems. Still, the idea that certain lands ought to be withdrawn from the marketplace and treated as public rather than private resources suited progressive sensibilities—and won middle-class support.

PROGRESSIVE LEGISLATION IN THE TAFT YEARS

During Roosevelt's presidency, progressive voices within the Republican Party had been powerful enough to enact the program of government regulation that Roosevelt advocated. But under his handpicked successor, William Howard Taft (president from 1909 to 1913), the party drifted back toward its earlier pro-business conservatism. For example, Taft raised tariffs, a move that benefited big business and alienated many progressives. Divided between progressives and conservatives, the Republicans lost control of the House of Representatives in 1910. But progressive Republicans formed an alliance with pro-labor Democrats, passing a series of reforms that benefited

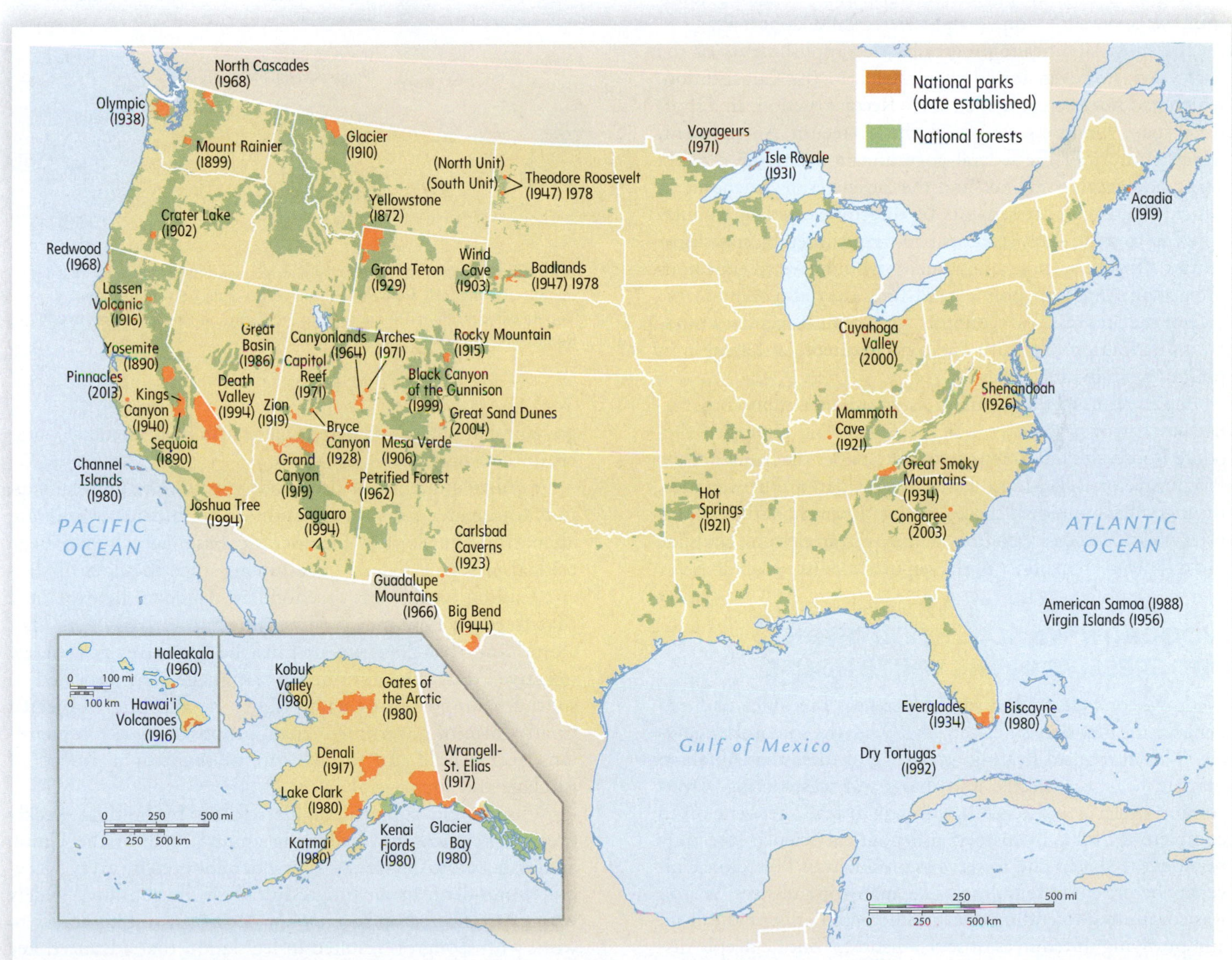

Map 20.4 Growth of National Parks. The conservation cause received a boost from Theodore Roosevelt and other progressives, whose efforts tripled the number of national parks from just three (Yellowstone, Yosemite, and Sequoia) in 1896 to nine by 1914. Since then, the system has grown to include fifty-nine parks.

workers, including new regulations for mine and railroad safety and an **eight-hour day** for federal employees. In another telling example of the overlapping interests between labor and the progressives, this same Congress also ended Sunday mail delivery, fulfilling a century-old evangelical reform goal while also giving postal clerks their Sundays off.

Meanwhile at the state level, progressive lawmakers responded to the protests of the National Consumers League by limiting women's work hours to ten. The controversial laws met with opposition from employers, as well as from some women workers who objected that they were not children and did not need the protection of either concerned middle-class consumers or a paternalist state. The Supreme Court decided in *Muller v. Oregon* (1908) that states could protect women and children from excessive exploitation in factories and laundries by limiting work hours to ten per day. A number of states subsequently enacted protective legislation, including minimum wage laws for women and stricter child labor laws.

The most significant progressive accomplishments of the Taft years, however, found their way into the Constitution, which had not been amended since Reconstruction. In a short time span, Congress proposed the Sixteenth Amendment, which authorized the federal government to impose a direct and graduated income tax, and the Seventeenth Amendment, which mandated that senators be directly elected by popular vote (up to that point, senators had been chosen by state legislatures). Together, these amendments would have an enormous impact on American politics and life. They also went to the core of the progressives' economic and political agenda: a modest redistribution of wealth and a more direct participation in politics by individual voters.

As Taft returned the Republicans toward their more conservative base, many progressives bolted the party and supported Theodore Roosevelt's bid to return to office under the banner of the Progressive or Bull Moose Party in 1912. In a four-way race, the incumbent president chalked up just 1 percent of the electoral vote, while Democrat Woodrow Wilson won an electoral landslide but did not get a majority of the popular vote (see Map 20.5).

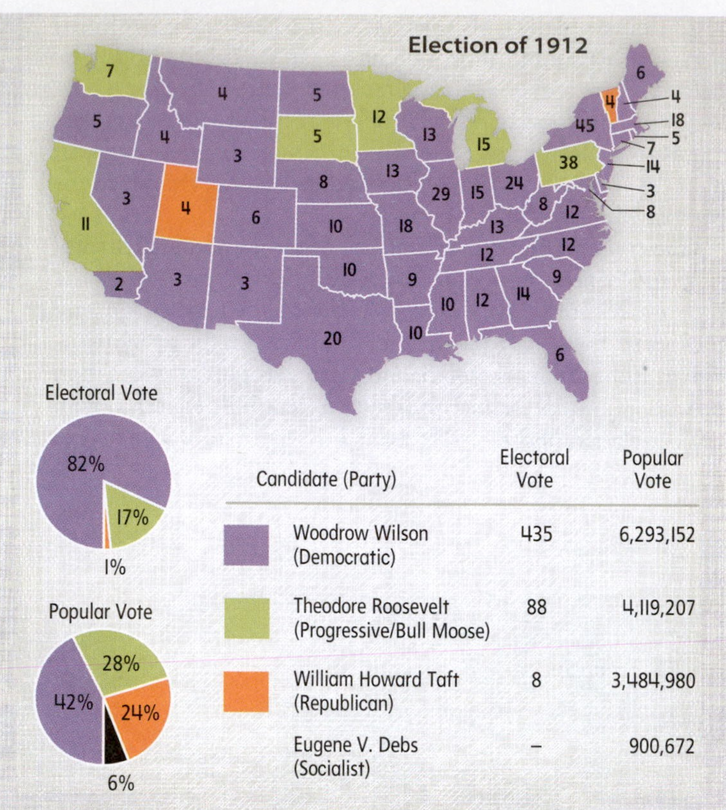

Map 20.5 Election of 1912. Democratic candidate Woodrow Wilson benefited immensely from Republican voters' split between former Republican president Theodore Roosevelt and the more conservative Republican president, William Howard Taft.

WOODROW WILSON: A SOUTHERN PROGRESSIVE IN THE WHITE HOUSE

With Wilson's election, a southerner held the office of president for the first time since the Civil War. The son of slaveholders, Wilson recalled hearing at the age of three that Abraham Lincoln had been elected and that a war was coming. Overcoming dyslexia and teaching himself to read, he went on to complete a Ph.D. in history and political science (the only president to do so) and to serve as president of Princeton University before entering politics. Like many progressives, Wilson was committed to ending class conflict, containing radicalism, and purifying the sources of social disorder. But he deeply disappointed African Americans—and the handful of white progressives who supported civil rights—by segregating government offices and demoting or firing black federal workers in the South.

A skilled strategist, Wilson rode the wave of popular support for greater federal regulation of big business while not alienating the South's Democratic base, which had been critical of strong federal government since the days of slavery. Calling for a "New Freedom" in America, he explained that freedom now meant something more than being "left alone" and that government must be "positive, not merely negative." But, he cautioned in language that appealed to southern supporters of states' rights, he absolutely objected to any form of government that "proposed to set up guardians over people and to take care of them by a process of tutelage and supervision."

Wilson built support for his reforms by holding weekly press conferences and delivering annual State of the Union addresses before Congress—a practice adopted by every subsequent president. In the progressive spirit, he consulted widely with experts before making policy decisions, and his ability to work with Congress resulted in legislation that advanced key parts of the progressive agenda. Wilson also lowered Taft's unpopular tariffs and backed the Clayton Antitrust Act (1914),

President Woodrow Wilson at the Old Ball Game. Although he was not the first president to throw the first ball of the season at a Washington Senators game (Taft had that distinction), Wilson embraced mass culture and adeptly used it to augment his popularity.

which punished businesses that combined to restrain or monopolize trade and limited the courts' ability to issue injunctions against striking unions. Wilson, however, was not as anti-business as many progressives would have liked. For example, he wound down the Justice Department's prosecution of trusts, diverting cases to the new Federal Trade Commission, a nonjudicial body that heard complaints against large corporations but had no enforcement powers.

Perhaps the most enduring of Wilson's policies was his overhaul of the nation's volatile banking system. Like a number of his reforms, the Federal Reserve Act (1913) satisfied many competing interests, including the southern and western farmers who had demanded greater federal control of the money supply since the days of Greenback Party, and bankers who wanted a centralized banking system. By insuring that banks could issue more money in times of falling prices and less money during inflationary periods, the new Federal Reserve Board established a way for the government to stabilize the economy. The system succeeded in stabilizing the currency and freeing up credit for small businesses and eventually farmers. Whether it would put an end to the harsh recessions that Americans had endured every decade since the Civil War was as yet untested.

CONCLUSION

At the beginning of the Progressive Era, it was clear that urbanization and a new wave of mass immigration were permanently transforming the nation. Whereas most of the population had worked in agriculture just a generation earlier, the majority of Americans were now employed in factories, small businesses, and large corporations. One in three people lived in a city, and new immigrants from southern and eastern Europe were turning America's relatively homogeneous cities into lively centers of religious, linguistic, and cultural diversity.

Native-born Americans approved of some of these changes and criticized others. Middle-class urbanites mostly welcomed the growth of large industrial corporations, but they worried as slums and sweatshops, previously associated only with Europe, proliferated. Some enjoyed the new dancehalls, cinemas, and amusement parks that served urban immigrants, but many more feared that such places corroded "traditional American" values. The majority agreed that industrialization, urbanization, and the new immigration had made many existing institutions and laws woefully obsolete and that new ideas and approaches to education, immigration, health, and a variety of other public goods were sorely needed. Across the nation, concerned citizens organized petitions, ran publicity campaigns, conducted expert studies, and ran for local office. Their campaigns were many and diverse. Whatever their particular cause, however, most progressives sought to build a society in which monopolies were regulated in the public's interest and in which voluntary associations worked with government to protect children, immigrants, and other vulnerable members of society from poverty, disease, and exploitation.

By 1914, progressive reformers could claim a number of major victories in their battles for regulating big business, weakening the political party system, protecting workers, and cleaning up big cities. They also had reason to be optimistic about their campaign for woman suffrage and their evangelical crusades against alcohol, commercial sex, and non-Protestant cultures. It would have been hard to predict which progressive reforms would appear, a century later, as forward strides in a longer story of national progress—and which would look like wrong turns or bigotry-driven missteps.

STUDY TERMS

merger and integration (p. 535)
U.S. Steel Corporation (p. 535)
systematic management (p. 535)
time and motion studies (p. 535)
scientific management (p. 535)
assembly line (p. 536)
Model T (p. 536)
Industrial Workers of the World (p. 536)
Socialist Party (p. 536)
foreign-language newspapers (p. 541)
Yiddish theater (p. 541)
"Take Me Out to the Ball Game" (p. 545)
Nickelodeon (p. 545)
real estate covenants (p. 547)
skyscrapers (p. 548)
Social Gospel (p. 549)
social work (p. 550)
National Association for the Advancement of Colored People (p. 551)
National American Woman Suffrage Association (p. 551)
National Consumers League (p. 552)
muckrakers (p. 554)
McClure's (p. 554)
The Jungle (p. 554)
Prohibition (p. 556)
Woman's Christian Temperance Union (p. 556)
Anti-Saloon League (p. 556)
Mann Act (p. 556)
City Beautiful Movement (p. 557)
ballot initiatives (p. 557)
referenda (p. 557)
recalls (p. 557)
Hepburn Act (p. 558)
Meat Inspection Act (p. 558)
Pure Food and Drug Act (p. 558)
eight-hour day (p. 560)
Sixteenth Amendment (p. 560)
Seventeenth Amendment (p. 560)
New Freedom (p. 560)
Federal Trade Commission (p. 561)
Federal Reserve Act (p. 561)

TIMELINE

1896 William McKinley elected president

1897 Depressions ends
First U.S. subway line opens, in Boston

1900 U.S. Socialist Party founded
McKinley reelected president
Robert La Follette elected governor of Wisconsin
Committee of Fifteen formed in New York to investigate sex trade

1901 Theodore Roosevelt takes office after McKinley's assassination
U.S. Steel Corporation formed
Lincoln Steffens begins exposé of municipal corruption

1903 Major League Baseball consolidated

1904 Roosevelt elected for second term
Supreme Court breaks up the Northern Securities trust

1905 Industrial Workers of the World (IWW) founded
African American newspaper *Chicago Defender* founded, promotes *Great Migration*
Nickelodeon movie theaters introduced

1906 Earthquake and fire destroy large sections of San Francisco
Hepburn Act facilitates railroad regulation
Upton Sinclair's *The Jungle* published

1909 General walkout by twenty thousand New York female garment workers
Organization that becomes NAACP founded

1910 Jack Johnson defends heavyweight title against Jim Jeffries
Boy Scouts of America founded
Congress passes the Mann Act

1911 Fire at Triangle Shirtwaist Factory kills 146 garment workers

1912 Woodrow Wilson elected president

1913 Sixteenth Amendment (income tax) ratified

IWW produces Paterson Pageant

Seventeenth Amendment (direct election of senators) ratified

Woolworth Building opens in New York

Federal Reserve Board regulates the money market

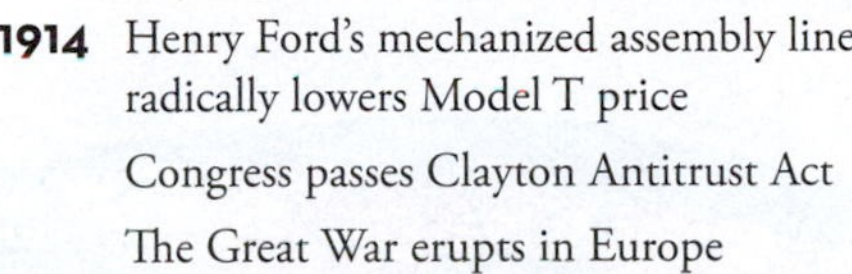

1914 Henry Ford's mechanized assembly line radically lowers Model T price

Congress passes Clayton Antitrust Act

The Great War erupts in Europe

FURTHER READING

Additional suggested readings are available on the Online Learning Center at www.mhhe.com/becomingamerica1e.

Paul Boyer, *Urban Masses and Moral Order in America, 1820 –1920* (1978), places Progressive Era urban reform in the context of long-term struggles to impose order in the city.

Grace Elizabeth Hale, *Making Whiteness: The Culture of Segregation in the South, 1880–1940* (1998), explains how people of European descent came to imagine themselves as white and how people of color were marginalized in the process.

Samuel P. Hays, *Conservation and the Gospel of Efficiency: The Progressive Conservation Movement* (1999), describes the origins and inherent tensions of conservationism.

Andrew Heinze, *Adapting to Abundance* (1992), shows how Jewish immigrants assimilated into American culture through a fusion of consumption with social and religious traditions.

Robert D. Johnston, *The Radical Middle Class: Populist Democracy and the Question of Capitalism in Progressive Era Portland, Oregon* (2003), argues that Portland's small-business people and skilled workers drove the city's progressive movement.

Jackson Lears, *Rebirth of a Nation: The Making of Modern America, 1877–1920* (2009), shows how a fervent desire for moral regeneration animated progressivism.

David Levering Lewis, *W. E. B. Du Bois, 1868–1919: Biography of a Race* (1994), analyzes the history of the African American experience of Jim Crow through the life and work of Du Bois.

Michael McGerr, *A Fierce Discontent: The Rise and Fall of the Progressive Movement in America, 1870–1920* (2003), emphasizes the diverse sensibilities and commitments that characterized the progressives.

Clay McShane, *Down the Asphalt Path: The Automobile and the American City* (1995), argues that attitudes toward public spaces, especially streets, had to change before the automobile could become popular.

Daniel Rodgers, *Atlantic Crossings* (2000), tracks the trans-Atlantic networks of experts and reformers and the European influences on American progressives.

Christine Stansell, *American Moderns: Bohemian New York and the Creation of a New Century* (Princeton, 2000), examines the flourishing experimentalism of Greenwich Village writers, libertines, and activists and their impact on American culture.

Robert Wiebe, *The Search for Order, 1877–1920* (1966), argues that progressive reform was a direct response to the disorienting impact of modernization.

21

INSIDE ▶

THE BIG PICTURE

Missionaries and traders led the way into China, Africa, and Latin America, forging networks, publicizing foreign cultures, and stoking expansionist ambitions at home. Following a short, victorious war with Spain, the United States controversially acquired an empire of its own and was drawn into a bitter war of insurgency.

Evangelizing China: Cartoon from *Puck* Magazine. Missionaries carried America's evangelical frontier—and in some cases, U.S. military and commercial interests—into East Asia. This cartoon's original caption pungently observed, "According to the ideas of our missionary maniacs, the Chinaman must be converted, even if it takes the whole military and naval forces of the two greatest nations of the world to do it."

1880–1914

BIRTH OF A GREAT POWER: THE UNITED STATES & THE WORLD

Marching through the stifling heat of Yangcun, China, in the summer of 1900, a regiment of American troops stumbled into a deadly ambush. Several U.S. soldiers were mortally wounded, but many returned fire, felling some assailants and scattering the rest. The troops resumed their march to Peking (Beijing), where Chinese rebels known as the Boxers were threatening to massacre nine hundred European and American missionaries, businessmen, and military personnel. Joining forces with British troops, the Americans stormed the city's wall, overcoming heavy fire from Gatling machine guns. Scaling a second wall, the American troops beat the British to the terrified westerners and freed them, killing dozens of Chinese fighters along the way.

As dramatic as these events were, they occurred not in China but in packed arenas around the United States, enacted by a cast of over five hundred actors from Buffalo Bill's Wild West show. Although inspired by real events, the carefully scripted spectacle played fast and loose with the facts in an effort to portray the Boxer Rebellion as an epic "Wild West" battle between civilized Americans and merciless savages. There had been, in fact, no ambush at Yangcun—only an incident involving friendly fire from the United States' Russian allies. The British, not the Americans, had reached the foreign legation first. And the Boxers were not "savages" but nationalist peasants (or "patriots," as writer Mark Twain called them) who sought Chinese unity and independence from foreign powers. Yet the idea that the U.S. experience in China was a continuation of the glorious history of America's western frontier was in certain respects apt.

KEY QUESTIONS

- What new transnational networks of communication, trade, investment, and moral reform emerged in this era, and how did they help the United States become a great power?
- Who took the nation to war with Spain, and what was the war's impact on U.S. culture, politics, and world standing?
- How did the peoples of the Philippines, Mexico, and elsewhere respond to American efforts to liberate them from oppressive regimes?
- In what ways did popular ideas about race and gender shape U.S. foreign policy and vice versa?
- Why did the United States insist on free trade in China and throughout the world?

Toward the end of the nineteenth century, many American missionaries, entrepreneurs, traders, and manufacturers saw the non-Western world as the next frontier. Spreading out along the religious, trade, and information networks that European powers had built over the previous few decades, these Americans drew their nation and government into much closer contact with non-Western peoples. Missionaries and reformers used their networks to raise churchgoers' awareness of famines, epidemics, and mass murder—and funds for relief programs. To protect American life and property abroad, the United States began rebuilding its navy. And a small but growing chorus of business, political, and religious leaders prevailed on the government to play a more active role in the world. When the Spanish Empire violently repressed Cuban nationalists who were demanding independence from Spain, Americans were outraged. Within three years, the United States went to war, aiming to liberate Cuba from the Spanish Empire. A spectacular success, the Spanish-American War established the United States as a world-class power—and, ironically, gave the country an empire of island colonies.

The mass press, moving pictures, popular songs, and spectacles like Buffalo Bill's Wild West show all reinforced the view that the United States was destined to spread its ideals and way of life around the world, as it had done across the North American continent. But certain realities disrupted this vision. Unlike in the West, ordinary Americans generally did not want to settle in the tropics. All over the world, moreover, colonized peoples were beginning to demand their right to national self-determination. Many Americans opposed colonization, particularly once Filipino nationalists took up arms against the new U.S. administration that had been established in their country. By 1908, the U.S. government had abandoned the policy of ruling the colonies directly, in favor of extending financial aid, incentives, and loans. Although the colonial idea was dead, this new approach still led to frequent armed intervention and the suppression of nationalist movements in Mexico, Central America, and the Caribbean.

Audiences were so moved by the Buffalo Bill show's depiction of the Boxer Rebellion that they cried and jumped out of their seats as the actors playing European and American soldiers fell in the "Rescue of Peking."

NETWORKING THE WORLD

In the 1880s and 1890s, as the U.S. Army put down the last few Native American resistance movements and the West was fully incorporated into the nation, many Americans looked overseas for new spiritual and commercial frontiers. Missionaries' gaze fell mostly on Asia and the Pacific, where Europe's great empires (and, after 1895, the empire of Japan) had widely colonized the native peoples. American clergy expanded their activities faster and farther than ever before thanks to the transportation and communication networks put in place by the colonial powers. Flooding American church publications, magazines, and newspapers with reports and vivid images of foreign lands, the missionaries stimulated considerable popular interest and sympathy for foreign victims of famine and genocide. Meanwhile, business was also eager to exploit the new networks. However, as American missions and business aspirations grew in the 1890s, so did European and Japanese efforts to exclude the United States from their colonies.

SPEEDING THE GOSPEL

Although some Protestant American missionaries had ventured overseas in the nineteenth century, most others had focused on converting the peoples of the American West. By the Progressive Era, the spiritual frontier had moved to the Asia-Pacific region, which attracted the attention of an unprecedented number of evangelical clergy and moral reformers. This upsurge was enabled partly by the European empires' conquest and colonization of much of Asia and Africa in the 1880s and 1890s and the telegraph, road, and rail networks that those empires often forced colonized populations to build. Missionaries were quick to realize that these networks, together with the addition of dozens of new steamship routes, allowed them to travel quickly and relatively safely into vast and often densely populated non-Christian areas. Converting and integrating non-Christian peoples into a global "Christian Kingdom" now seemed possible. As one missionary excitedly reported in the 1890s, "[S]tudents of Christendom are awaking, with steam and electricity to carry us to the ends of the earth in a month, with a typewriter and telegraph for our epistles [letters], and bicycle and railway to speed the gospel."

These new technologies and networks were also powerful tools for publicizing missionaries' efforts, raising funds, and recruiting. New England missionaries Margaret and Mary Leitch were the first Americans to systematically telegraph and write letters home with news of their evangelical, educational, and health work in British India. In the late 1880s and early 1890s, they returned home briefly to present dramatic photographic slide shows designed to incite clergy and laity to support their cause. These and similar efforts in the 1890s raised significant sums of money and helped draw thousands of American clergy, doctors, and teachers into overseas mission work. Indian and Chinese converts also petitioned American churches for aid, often with the help of missionaries like the Leitch sisters.

Around the same time, and partly as a result of missionary publicity campaigns, Protestant clergy organized revival meetings that inspired young adults to dedicate themselves to the conversion of non-Christian peoples. The first such meeting, convened in 1886 in the woods of Northfield, Massachusetts, attracted 251 students from all over the nation, 100 of whom pledged to become overseas missionaries. Over the next two summers, 2,200 students followed suit, and the newly organized Student Volunteer Movement for Foreign Missions (SVM) announced members' ambitious goal of the "evangelization of the world in this generation." Fundraising and recruitment accelerated through the turn of the century with the help of the 660,000-strong Young People's Society of Christian Endeavor. In addition, the Young Men's and Young Women's Christian Associations (YMCA and YWCA) and the Woman's Christian Temperance Movement (WCTU) provided support by setting up offices, raising funds, and establishing Christian colleges in Asia. New magazines and journals such as *Christian Endeavor* and *National Geographic* documented the cultures and lands in which the missionaries worked, kindling American readers' interest in China, India, and other non-Christian parts of the world. The flood of information also drew explorers, tourists, and consumers, thus sparking new opportunities for tour operators and retailers. Although most missionaries were white, upwards of a hundred African American missionaries also set sail in these years, primarily to Africa, which was in the throes of European colonization (see Singular Lives: William Henry Sheppard, Missionary and Human Rights Advocate).

By 1905, tens of thousands of missionaries and reformers, financially supported by millions of American churchgoers and philanthropists, were at work in the Asia-Pacific region and elsewhere. Although missions varied in their methods and priorities, the experience of overseas work changed both the missionaries and American churches. When clergy first entered the field in large numbers in the early 1890s, their principal aim was to replace non-Christian belief systems, values, and rituals with Protestant ones. Their chief method was preaching the gospel. Once on the ground, however, they typically found that the purely spiritual tenets of Protestant Christianity held little attraction for Hindus, Muslims, Buddhists, and Russian Orthodox Christians. Conversely, food, shelter, and other material resources were immensely attractive, particularly in lands wracked by famine. As the clergy's missions grew, they placed greater emphasis on education, nutrition, health care, and recreational activities—much as progressive reformers were doing in the immigrant and poor neighborhoods of the United States' big cities.

To some extent, locals initiated the shift to social uplift by teaching missionaries about their particular needs. The missionaries were eager to help, but most also saw locals' appeals as an opportunity to Americanize them—whether through housing designs that reflected modern American ideas or by classes

SINGULAR LIVES

William Henry Sheppard, Missionary and Human Rights Advocate

By 1892, all but one African empire had fallen to the European powers' "scramble" to colonize Africa. Deep in central Africa, in what is today the Democratic Republic of Congo, the Kingdom of Kuba (also known as Boshongo and Bakuba) still thrived (see Map 21.1). Founded in the seventeenth century, multiethnic Kuba grew wealthy on New World crops such as cassava, maize, beans, and tobacco (acquired through coastal neighbors). The capital, Mushenge, was a thriving center of trade and culture, with a population of ten thousand and buildings, marketplaces, and streets that followed much the same grid pattern found in modern American cities. A succession of kings had foiled the efforts of Westerners to penetrate the Kuba territory by threatening to behead any subject who harbored or guided foreigners. Even the precise location of Mushenge remained unknown to outsiders—until 1892, when Kuba officials arrested an American explorer and missionary and sent him to Mushenge to face the king.

The man they arrested, the Reverend William Henry Sheppard, was a long way from home. Born in 1865 in Waynesboro, Virginia, Sheppard had dreamed of the adventure and spiritual challenge of missionary work in Africa. The son of an African American father (probably a former slave) and a white mother, he worked as a stable boy and waiter, putting himself through high school and college. He was subsequently ordained a minister of the Southern Presbyterian Church and transferred to a parish in Atlanta. In 1888, Sheppard requested that the church establish a mission to Central Africa. The church was initially reluctant. European colonizers had recently expelled African American missionaries from the continent, and in the United States missionary work was fast becoming the exclusive prerogative of white men. But Sheppard persisted, and in 1890 the Presbyterian leadership relented, with the proviso that a white minister accompany every African American missionary into the field. At the age of twenty-four, Sheppard set sail for Africa.

Map 21.1 Colonization and the Congo. Although European powers had colonized of much of Africa by the mid-1890s, the Kingdom of Kuba and the Zappo Zap people remained independent. With the support of King Leopold of Belgium, however, the Zappo Zap destroyed Kuba in 1898. Belgium subsequently colonized both peoples.

Like other American missionaries, Sheppard initially followed in the tracks of Europe's expansionist empires. Arriving in western Congo, he and his white counterpart, the Reverend Samuel Lapsley, used ports, roads, maps, and postal and telegraphic services provided by Belgium's king Leopold II, who controlled much of the territory adjoining Kuba and personally agreed to support Sheppard's mission. Leopold had little interest in the spiritual side of Sheppard's work, but he was eager to make inroads into Kuba and to gather intelligence on rubber trees and other potentially lucrative resources. Sheppard learned Bantu, the language of Kuba, which helped save his life following his arrest for trespassing on Kuba land. At Mushenge, the

in American-style government and business. These conflicting goals often caused considerable tension between the colonial populations and the missionaries.

The emphasis on uplift was also hastened by the entry of large numbers of men into missionary work. Women had long played an important role in churches and were an increasingly powerful presence in social reform (see Chapters 19 and 20). The one-million-strong WCTU was a growing power in overseas reform work, taking its social agenda of prohibition, women's suffrage, fair pay for women workers, and anti-prostitution to the colonial world. Concerned, however, that women played too active a role and that Asian peoples might perceive Christianity as weak and feminine, organizations such as the all-male SVM and the YMCA promoted what they called "muscular Christianity." Combining spiritual and athletic training and emphasizing the cultivation of "manly virtues," these well-funded programs recruited young Asian men for education in business, government, and morals. Male missionary recruitment skyrocketed in the 1890s and had almost tripled by the decade's end. Whereas wealthy donors such as John D. Rockefeller bankrolled initiatives and sports and cultural facilities abroad, women's missionary organizations were forced to scrape together whatever funding they could.

Defending Kuba. Sheppard (far right), whom the peoples of Congo called the "black white man," provided one of the few surviving accounts of a precolonial African state (the Kingdom of Kuba) and became a leading critic of European colonialism. His and other reports of Belgian atrocities inspired Mark Twain's satire *King Leopold's Soliloquy: A Defense of His Congo Rule* (1905) and Joseph Conrad's *Heart of Darkness* (1899, 1902).

king of Kuba pronounced him the resurrected spirit of an earlier king and authorized him to build a church. In the United States, Sheppard was hailed as the "Black Livingstone" (in a reference to the famous white missionary-explorer Dr. David Livingstone).

Sheppard's experiences profoundly altered his view of the peoples of Congo, European colonization, and the nature of his mission. He arrived in Africa expecting to convert and civilize "heathen savages" but soon realized, especially after his sojourn in Mushenge, that he had in fact "entered a land of civilization." Like many missionaries, he became a proponent of human rights—and a vociferous critic of European colonization. Contrary to outward appearances, King Leopold's profitable colony was built on slave labor and systematic violence, leading to the deaths of up to 50 percent of the region's population. Bearing witness to the atrocities, Sheppard cofounded the Congo Reform Association in 1904, one of the first international human rights organizations, and published a detailed account of the abuses under Leopold. Subsequently, a Belgian corporation based in Congo sued Sheppard for defamation. The case, which was tried in the colony's Belgian-run court system, drew international attention and helped speed reform of the brutal labor system, though not an end to colonialism. Sheppard was acquitted, largely because the court feared that the United States, whose people and government were outraged by the atrocities, would demand that Belgium relinquish its African colonies. Despite Sheppard's best efforts, Kuba was invaded by Belgian allies, the Nsapo (or Zappo Zap), in 1899 and subsequently colonized by the Belgians.

Think About It

1. Why might Sheppard have been surprised by the civilization he found in Kuba?
2. What does Sheppard's experience in Africa tell us about missionaries' role in the European colonization of Africa?
3. Why do you think Sheppard became an outspoken critic of colonialism?

THE BIRTH OF FOREIGN AID

Neither the concept of a **humanitarian crisis** (such as the 2010 earthquake in Haiti, which resulted in three hundred thousand deaths) nor the idea that powerful nations should intervene in crises beyond their borders was a familiar idea in the nineteenth century. But the rapid growth of American missionary networks in the early Progressive Era fostered much greater awareness of mass suffering and a fervent desire, especially among middle-class and upper-middle-class Protestants, to provide large-scale relief to the afflicted.

The first crisis that missionaries systematically documented and publicized came in 1891–1892, when twenty million Russians faced starvation following the failure of that nation's wheat harvest (see Map 21.2). Although Russia was itself an empire, Protestant missionaries had been actively seeking to convert millions of its Orthodox Christians since the 1880s. When the crops failed, the missionaries reported on the resulting famine and raised much-needed funds from concerned American churchgoers. Five years later, when an even worse famine afflicted British India, they again led the charge to raise funds and sent millions of tons of midwestern wheat and corn to the victims. U.S. farmers were eager to oblige, in part out of their new sense of Christian duty toward foreign peoples but also because mechanized farming had produced a grain glut, which

Making a New Colonial Man. By 1904, the YMCA boasted eight offices in China, six in Japan, and ten in India. Twelve years later, the organization operated in fifty-five countries. Aimed at producing the "new colonial man," these establishments trained young men in reading, writing, arithmetic, business, bible study, and athletics.

depressed prices and highlighted the need for overseas markets. This time, the missionaries and their allies also persuaded Congress to deploy the navy to deliver the aid.

Mass slaughter of one people by another people or government (which would come to be known as genocide in the 1940s) also fell under heightened scrutiny. Genocide was not a new phenomenon or concern. Like Europe's governments, the United States had sometimes expressed concern about mass killings, particularly where Christians were the victims. But neither the government nor the churches had sought to intervene systematically on the side of the victims. Things changed dramatically in 1894–1896. The once-powerful Ottoman Empire was facing the breakup of its Asian and African colonies and a surge of independence movements in its European provinces. The empire authorized local government to purge sections of the Gregorian Armenian population, a Christian minority calling for revolution against their Muslim Ottoman overlords. Missionaries working in the area reported mass killings of Armenian men and women, widespread torture and rape, and the orphaning of upwards of 500,000 children. Assessments of fatalities varied wildly, from 13,432 according to Ottoman officials, to up to 300,000 as reported by Armenian historians.

Back in America, missionaries and the press reported hundreds of thousands of deaths, the pillaging of Christian churches and businesses, and forced conversions to Islam. The WCTU acted swiftly, proclaiming the mass orphaning of Armenians a humanitarian crisis and calling upon Congress and "our home-loving republic [to exert] moral and material influence" to end the atrocities. At a time when international law was weak and poorly defined, the distinguished economist Charlotte Perkins Gilman implored the United States to develop international law to "restrain, prohibit, punish . . . best of all to prevent" genocide. Concerned citizens also formed the National Armenian Relief Committee—which John D. Rockefeller generously funded—and for the first time the American Red Cross launched a relief program outside the United States, to aid the Armenian refugees. Congress formally condemned the sultan of the Ottoman Empire for the massacre of one hundred thousand Armenians.

Within just a few years, missionaries had persuaded many lawmakers and private citizens that the United States owed a moral duty to intervene in cases of mass starvation and genocide beyond its borders. That conviction deepened through the late 1890s and into the twentieth century. Aid and other forms of support were also increasingly extended to non-Christian peoples, including the Jewish victims of a series of pogroms

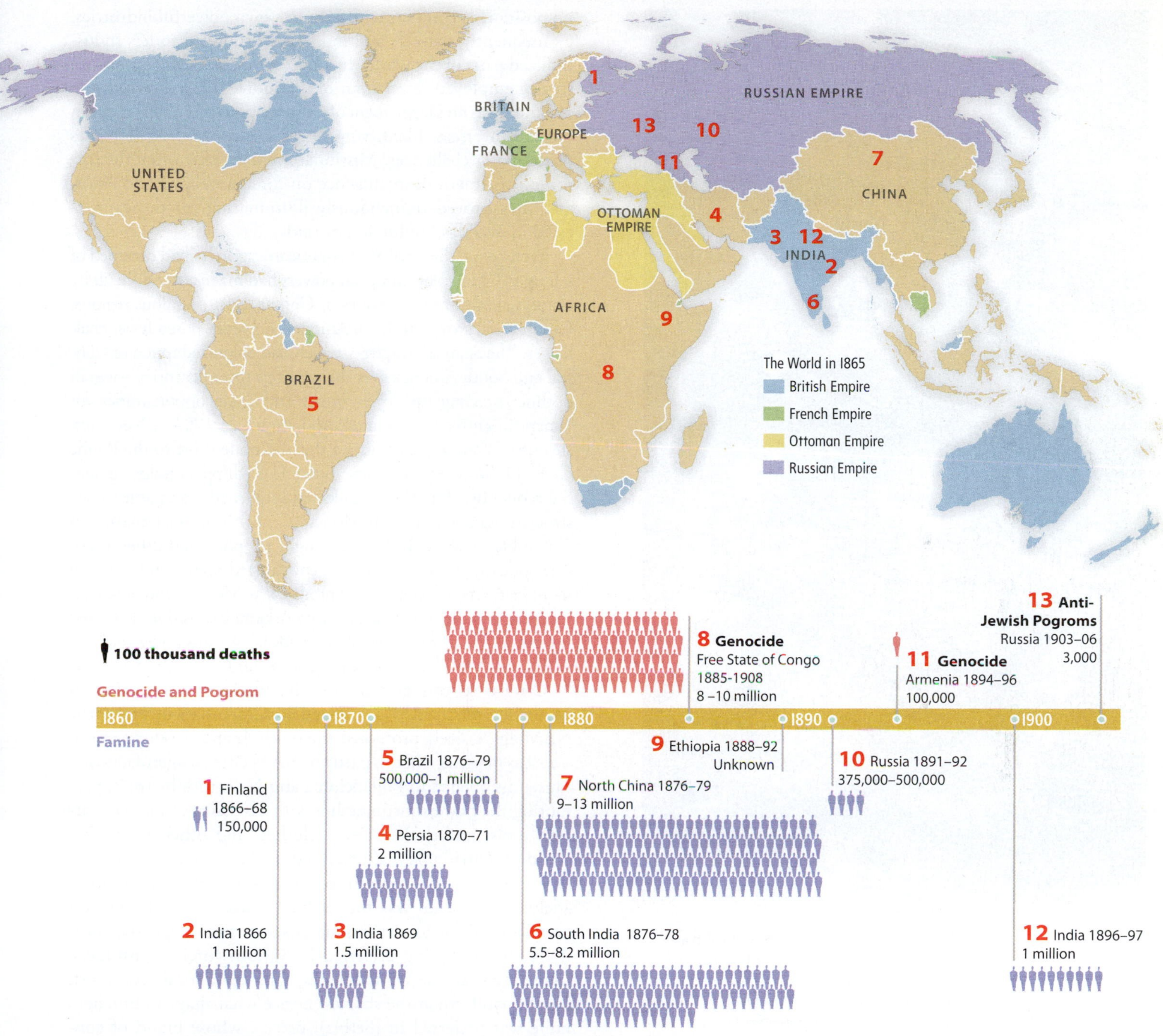

Map 21.2 Humanitarian Crises, 1865–1906. This map of the world, which shows the four most powerful empires and their colonies, tracks some of the major famines and other crises that broke out between 1865 and 1906. Although several such catastrophes struck Ireland, India, China, and other places in these years, large-scale voluntary and governmental aid programs did not get under way in the United States until American missionaries and the press began vividly documenting the disasters in the 1890s.

that erupted in Russia between 1903 and 1906. Under mounting pressure from Jewish American leaders, President Theodore Roosevelt condemned the czarist government for its implicit promotion of the anti-Semitic riots. Congress issued a joint resolution stating that "the people of the United States are horrified by the reports of the massacre of Hebrews in Russia, on account of their race and religion."

THE SEARCH FOR NEW MARKETS

U.S. exports—80 percent of which were wheat and other agricultural products—had grown slowly but steadily in the two decades since 1875. After the devastating depression of 1893, industries began systematically to seek overseas markets for their growing mountains of excess goods. As unsold stoves, carriages, and other goods piled up in warehouses, many observers argued that America's

The Missionary's Many Roles. Missionaries sometimes acted as middlemen for American business and spokespersons for the U.S. government. Presbyterian missionary Horace Allen used his close connections with Korea's King Kojong (shown) to secure lucrative railway construction and gold mining contracts for U.S. companies.

productive capacity far outstretched the nation's ability to consume. The solution, in industrialists' minds, was to build overseas markets that could consume the excess production and, in theory, keep American factories humming and profits growing. Aware that economic depressions also brought strikes, radicalism, and the People's Party (see Chapter 19), a growing number of bankers and manufacturers also believed that overseas markets were key to the survival of the United States' largely unregulated market economy.

The obvious market for American goods was Europe. Except for a handful of large corporations (such as Singer Sewing Machine and Standard Oil), however, manufacturers were in no position to compete with Europe's own powerful industries. Consequently, bankers and industrialists looked to less industrialized parts of the world. In an age when the U.S. diplomatic service employed fewer than one hundred officers worldwide and there was no Department of Commerce to promote American business overseas, identifying likely markets and trade routes posed major challenges. Missionary reports were often the sole source of American intelligence on foreign peoples and lands, and they proved tremendously illuminating for those interested in overseas production or trade.

Even before the Civil War, American exporters had dreamed of selling to China, but European powers had made entry difficult by claiming exclusive trade zones in China's most populous regions. Commercial growth in Latin America, however, posed fewer challenges. The Spanish Empire—which had colonized much of Central and South America over the previous three centuries—was in decline, opening up development and trade opportunities for American entrepreneurs and corporations. In 1894, a New York steamship company established the first trade route to the Pacific Coast of South America, and other U.S. shippers followed suit. Subsequently, American banks and railroad companies constructed major railways in Mexico, Costa Rica, Guatemala, and Colombia in 1895–1896 and bought up ports and other assets. The southern trade paper *Dixie* encouraged textile and clothing manufacturers to exhibit their products at Mexico's industrial exhibition, and organizers of the 1895 Atlanta Exposition dedicated the entire fair to the "foreign trade idea." Within a few months, U.S. exports to Latin America began to climb.

Critical to this growth was the National Association of Manufacturers (NAM). Founded in Cincinnati in 1895, the NAM aggressively promoted the research and development of overseas markets. Thanks partly to NAM efforts, manufacturing museums opened in Philadelphia and New York in 1897, promoting the new exporting ethos with extensive displays of foreign tools, household objects, clothes, and other goods that could potentially be manufactured in the United States. Long before the State Department provided such information, Philadelphia's museum was the leading source of intelligence on everything from local shipping costs to the design specifications and packaging preferred by various foreign customers. "Where else in the United States," boasted a local economist, "could you learn at the shortest notice what shape of butcher's knife was preferred in [Serbia], or . . . whose brand of condensed milk was in favor in Colombo? . . .What would be the freight on forty brass bedsteads ordered from Rangoon? How would you write 'Handle with care' in Russian?"

Manufacturers' drive for overseas markets soon bore fruit. As a share of exports, consumer and industrial products more than doubled in value, from about 15 percent of all exports in the 1880s to almost 34 percent by 1900. For the first time in the nation's history, the total value of U.S. exports exceeded the value of imports—a positive balance of trade that would last until the late 1960s (see Figure 21.1). As a result of NAM's lobbying, Congress established the Department of Commerce in 1903. American industries also set up shop on location.

Foreign Intelligence. The Philadelphia Commercial Museum operated a Bureau of Information dedicated to helping American companies develop overseas markets. The bureau became the leading source of intelligence on foreign markets, peoples, and governments.

SEA POWER

The navy had all but scuttled its fleet after the Civil War, when the federal government turned its attention to conquering the West and reconstructing the South. But as American missionary and trade networks spread across the Pacific and Caribbean in the 1880s, businesses with overseas interests prevailed on Congress to provide protection for American trade routes and ships. Consequently, the United States acquired thirty-three light ("brown-water") cruisers and gunboats and, in 1887, built a coaling and repair station at Pearl Harbor, Hawaii. Hawaii was not yet a U.S. territory, but American sugar planters had used their considerable economic power to convinced Hawaii's King Kalakaua to authorize the new station. Two years later, the United States established a joint protectorate of Samoa with Germany and Britain, extending the reach of its navy farther into the South Pacific.

The rapid growth of American missionary and business activity in the 1890s intensified the demand for a much larger fleet—one that could protect American property and trade interests and the thousands of U.S. citizens evangelizing or doing business abroad. Pressure also mounted as the European empires accelerated their scramble to colonize large swaths of Asia and Africa. Building dozens of heavy, oceangoing ("blue-water") warships, the European powers' new fleets were designed specifically to do large-scale battle with one another and to enhance each empire's prestige and colonial aspirations. U.S. ships were all but useless against these floating fortresses.

Earlier in the decade, the growing gap between the navies of Europe and the United States had caught the attention of Captain Alfred T. Mahan, a self-taught naval historian at the U.S. Naval College. In *The Influence of Sea Power Upon History, 1660–1783* (1890), Mahan argued that the key to imperial power had always been control of the seas. Drawing on the social Darwinist belief that only the fittest individuals and races will survive, he also hypothesized that all nations aggressively struggle for survival and that they do so by constantly expanding the markets for their goods and by maintaining powerful navies that can protect those markets. In light of the empires' naval arms race, the United States' lightweight fleet, argued Mahan, was woefully inadequate to the task. Mahan's treatise attracted considerable attention in Europe—affirming the empires' decisions to expand their navies. After languishing in the United States for a few years, Mahan's book became essential reading for the growing number of politicians, businessmen, and naval officers who favored a more aggressive foreign policy and a sustained program of expansionism.

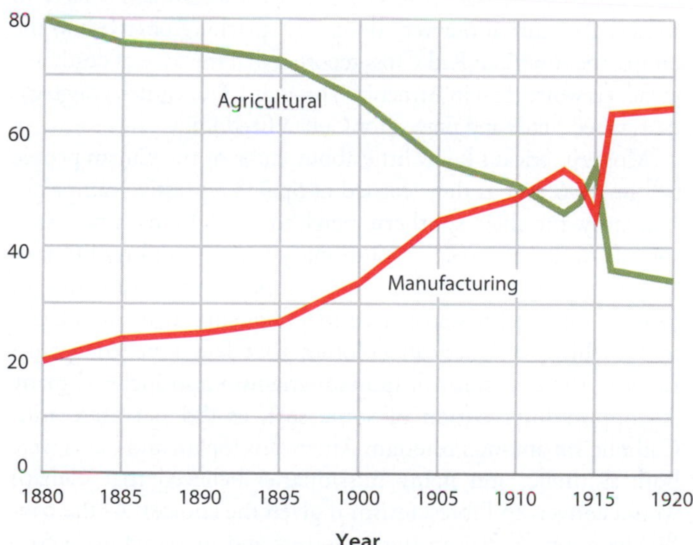

FIGURE 21.1 Exports, 1880–1920: Manufacturing Takes the Lead. American manufacturing grew increasingly vital to the U.S. economy and international trade in the 1890s, more than doubling its share of total exports between 1890 and 1913. Although agricultural exports continued to grow in value, their importance to overall trade fell significantly due to lower prices and the manufacturing boom. The outbreak of World War I in 1914, which threatened to starve over ten million people in northern Europe, temporarily boosted U.S. agricultural exports in 1914–1915. But exports of meat, dairy, grain, and other food products soon resumed their general downward trajectory (to around 10 percent of total exports today).

VISIONS OF GLOBAL EXPANSION

The new global networks of the 1890s and the religious, cultural, and commercial exchanges they enabled propelled more Americans into the world than ever before. Through them, the United States also came into much more direct contact—and potential conflict—with the world's great empires and the peoples and politics of Asia-Pacific and Latin America. The official policy of isolationism, which since the 1860s had kept the United States out of most international affairs, seemed to many observers to be out of step with reality.

Among other critics of isolationism, Republicans Theodore Roosevelt and Henry Cabot Lodge tirelessly lobbied for a far more ambitious navy-building program. Citing Mahan, they argued that the United States must become a first-rate maritime power and follow the great empires' lead in acquiring overseas colonies (something that Mahan had never advocated, although he did support the acquisition of overseas naval bases). They and other proponents of empire building came to be known as **expansionists**—a term they embraced, in large part because, in a nation that was avowedly republican, the word *imperialists* conjured corrupt European monarchies.

Many expansionists worried as well that Americans were growing overly civilized and effeminate due to the closure of the western frontier and, for middle- and upper-class men, the increasing ease of urban life. Women's rapid ascent in certain areas of government and progressive reform also concerned them (see Chapters 19 and 20). To counter these trends, in Roosevelt's view, men should seek psychological, physical, and spiritual renewal in encounters with untamed nature and the "savages" of the world. American manliness—and therefore the nation's well-being—required that men constantly conquer the wilderness. And given that America's West was no longer "wild," men would have to seek adventure in the "savage" world beyond the boundaries of Europe and the United States—ideally in a war of colonization.

Democratic president Grover Cleveland, who served from 1885 to 1889 and again from 1893 to 1897, firmly opposed the acquisition of colonies. Cleveland agreed, however, that existing trade routes needed greater protection, and he vigorously pressed Congress to commission the construction of five new blue-water battleships, bringing the total to nine. Similarly, Secretary of State Richard Olney declared that American economic health, and especially the maintenance of "free access to all markets," depended on its naval power. In 1896, the navy quietly drew up war plans, including a strategy for wresting the Philippines from its Spanish occupiers, should Americans and their interests be threatened in Asia.

FROM DIPLOMACY TO WAR

Although expansionists envisioned the acquisition of colonies and the United States' admission to the ranks of the great powers Britain, France, Germany, Austria-Hungary, and Russia, they had no master blueprint for empire building. But the small-scale efforts that had been under way in the missionary, commercial, and naval arenas laid some of the groundwork for expansion by drawing an increasing number of citizens and U.S. interests overseas and by priming Americans and their federal government to intervene in humanitarian crises. Consequently, when the Spanish Empire ruthlessly repressed the Cuban independence movement in 1895, the United States brought diplomatic and moral pressure to bear on behalf of the victims. Seeing opportunity in the widespread outrage raining down on Spain, expansionists pushed for an armed response. For a time, the majority of Americans opposed war, but Spain's stonewalling of U.S. diplomacy, along with a barrage of horrific images and stories in the press, soon persuaded many Americans that armed force was necessary.

CRISIS IN CUBA

Americans learned of the humanitarian crisis unfolding in the Spanish colony of Cuba in 1895. Military governor Valeriano Weyler, responding to a large-scale revolt by Cubans seeking independence from Spain, had ordered the torching of crops and homes and was detaining tens of thousands of displaced peasants in filthy, disease-ridden "reconcentration camps." Over 12 percent of Cuba's population perished in the first three months alone.

American missionary and reform organizations sounded the alarm, documenting the Cubans' suffering, and rallying aid in the form of donations, food, and children's clothing. The proximity of Cuba to the United States convinced many church leaders that the country had an even greater duty to aid the suffering peasants. "We must not consent," editorialized the evangelical *Christian Union*, "to another Armenia at our very doors." Dispatching observers to the camps, the American Red Cross reported that the scale of death was in fact far worse than in Armenia. Through 1896, church congregations raised funds and prayed for Cuban freedom.

Most Americans knew little about Cuba or the Cuban people before 1896, but as they learned of Spain's repressive campaign, sympathy for their southern neighbor's plight became widespread. Americans' own revolutionary heritage and tradition of anti-imperialism primed them to support the overthrow of Spanish rule, and newspaper editors frequently compared Cuba to the thirteen American colonies that had rebelled against Britain. The new spirit of humanitarianism also inclined many to support intervention of some sort, as did pervasive anti-Catholicism among Protestant Americans (Spain and Cuba were both Catholic, and many missionaries believed that Cubans would convert to Protestantism if given the choice). As the conflict wore on, American sugar growers and investors, who controlled over 50 percent of Cuba's sugar plantations, also entreated the federal government to act. Across the United States, thousands of concerned citizens marched in protest of Weyler's policies. Popular antipathy toward the Spanish was so great that both the Republican and the Democratic parties added Cuban independence planks to their 1896 election platforms.

Exactly how the United States should intervene was a matter for debate. The majority of newspapers argued that the United States should supply aid and moral support and use diplomatic channels to bring about Cuba's liberation. Yet from early on, a vocal minority of **jingoes**—ultra-patriots who favored the threat or use of armed force—called on the United States to take a much tougher stance. Seeking to boost newspaper sales, Joseph Pulitzer's *New York World* and William Randolph Hearst's *New York Journal* advocated armed intervention, splashing ever more sensationalist headlines of Spanish depravity and Cuban heroism across their front pages. Such **yellow journalism** mixed fact and fiction to argue that the U.S. government should come to the rescue of the Cuban people, much as any chivalric knight would have rescued a maiden in distress. One typical *Journal* story told of eighteen-year-old Evangelina Cisneros, an elite Cuban who was accused of aiding the rebellion and jailed under allegedly horrific conditions because she resisted the sexual advances of Spanish soldiers. When a petition for her release failed, a Hearst correspondent bribed the jailers to free Cisneros and smuggled her to New York, where she received a rapturous welcome. The following day, the *Journal* boasted (untruthfully) that its manly correspondent had bravely scaled the jail and broken Cisneros out himself, thereby achieving "at a single stroke what . . . red tape diplomacy had failed to bring about in many months."

Much the same strain of jingoism could be heard across small-town America. As early as 1895, local militias organized expressly for the purpose of fighting Spain on behalf of Cuba. Several members of Congress drew on long-standing stereotypes of Catholic and Spanish brutality to make the case for armed intervention. Spanish soldiers, exaggerated Nebraska senator William V. Allen, were "gathering up little girls . . . and selling them into a species of slavery . . . and a life of shame." They were also snatching Cuban babies from their mother's breasts and dashing their brains out, according to Indiana representative Alexander Hardy. Such lurid stories were almost always untrue, although it was the case that tens of thousands of peasants were dying of starvation and disease in the camps. By the end of 1897, many Americans were persuaded that diplomacy was inadequate and that force or the threat of force should be used to expel Spain from Cuba.

WAR WITH SPAIN

Cleveland's successor in the White House, the Republican William McKinley, considered war an expensive and uncertain venture, and he worried that a rush to arms—as the jingoes demanded—could result in defeat and damage his reelection chances in 1900. On the other hand, appearing weak or cowardly was also a liability. Further, like many Republicans, McKinley was committed to expanding U.S. commercial and military interests overseas. Consequently, he played a delicate balancing act, openly applying diplomatic pressure on Spain to

Men of the USS *Maine*. The USS *Maine*'s baseball team won the popular navy series in 1897 with the help of star pitcher William Lambert (back right). As newspapers reported, however, all but one player lost their lives six months later in the *Maine* disaster. News of their deaths added to Americans' outrage—and swung baseball's National League behind the call for war.

quit Cuba while at the same time secretly planning for war. In September 1897, the president once again informed Spain that the war in Cuba had to end and that the United States would take unspecified measures if it did not.

The implied threat appeared to work. Weyler was relieved of his duties, and the Spanish government entered negotiations with the rebels. In January 1898, however, a small pro-Spanish portion of the Cuban population rioted in protest. Amid the chaos, McKinley sent the battle cruiser USS *Maine* into Havana harbor, hoping that its presence would deter attacks on Americans and their property and pressure Spain to continue to pursue peace. Soon afterward, a leaked letter from the Spanish ambassador in Washington revealed that Spain intended to continue fighting the rebels and that the ambassador considered McKinley a weak "would-be politician." "Worst Insult to the United States in History," declared the headline of the *New York Journal* (which had also received a copy of the leaked communication), further fueling McKinley's anger and frustration with the Spanish.

Defending Hawaiian Sovereignty. Queen Lili'uokalani inherited the Hawaiian throne from her father, Kalakaua, in 1891. She also inherited a thorny set of political problems. Most Hawaiians resented the "Bayonet Constitution" of 1887, which had been forced on her father by expatriot American sugar planters and which stripped the monarchy of its power. When Lili'uokalani proposed a new constitution in 1893—one that enfranchised Hawaii's Asian and Polynesian populations and restored the crown's right of veto over legislation—the planters and overseas business interests overthrew her. U.S. Marines, deployed to keep the peace, effectively prevented the monarch's forces from defending the government and enabled coup leaders to declare a republic.

As tensions neared the breaking point, the *Maine* exploded and sank in Havana harbor, taking 267 U.S. seamen with it. Although a Spanish-led investigation found no evidence of foul play, suspicion immediately fell on Spain. Within days, the front page of the *New York Journal* illustrated the method that Spanish agents had allegedly used to bomb the ship. McKinley, who doubted that Spain was responsible, ordered a court of inquiry. But many members of Congress, already convinced of Spain's guilt, unanimously passed a $50 million defense appropriation bill in expectation of war. The court of inquiry reported a month later that the explosion was caused by an unknown external source. Although the investigators did not explicitly blame Spain, their finding confirmed lawmakers' suspicions, and many Republicans and Democrats now demanded war. (The exact cause of the *Maine* blast remains a mystery, despite several subsequent investigations.)

Unaware that McKinley was already strategizing for war, a diverse chorus of Americans strongly criticized the president's diplomacy, questioned his resolve, and warned that Britain or Germany might soon exploit the Cuban chaos to stage a land grab if the United States did not act. The critics' motivations were varied. Shippers and American sugar interests claimed that the instability was damaging U.S. economic interests, having collapsed trade worth $100 million a year. Democratic lawmakers who had favored a negotiated peace demanded retribution for the alleged insult to U.S. honor. "I am no jingo," Representative William Sulzer explained, presuming the *Maine* explosion to have been Spanish in origin, "but there are things more horrible than war. I would rather be dead upon the battlefield than live under the white flag of national disgrace, . . . cowardice, . . . decay, and . . . disintegration." African American associations and the labor unions—both of which saw Spanish rule as a form of slavery—joined mainstream newspapers and leading literary figures to demand war "for the sake of humanity." Even most missionaries now pressed for war.

Finally, in April 1898, with the support of most of the press and the nation, McKinley asked Congress to authorize the use of force to bring peace to Cuba "in the name of humanity and in the name of civilization." Significantly, he dodged the question of Cuban independence, leaving open the possibility of U.S. occupation or even annexation. Worried lawmakers consequently passed the Teller Amendment, which stated that the United States would not formally annex Cuba, and demanded that Spain quit the island immediately or face war. When McKinley delivered the ultimatum, Spain responded by cutting diplomatic ties and preemptively declaring war. The U.S. navy blockaded Cuba, and on April 24, 1898, Congress declared war on Spain.

Although all eyes were on Cuba, the first and most decisive battle of the Spanish-American War occurred over nine thousand miles away in the Spanish colony of the Philippines (using the navy's war plan from 1896). On May 1, with the aid of intelligence supplied by Filipino nationalists, Commodore George Dewey's Asiatic fleet staged a surprise dawn attack in Manila Bay, sinking Spain's entire Western Pacific fleet at the cost of just one American life. The scope of the war quickly widened, as the navy requested additional forces and soldiers to assist in the capture of the city of Manila and as the forces of Filipino nationalist leader Emilio Aguinaldo joined the war against Spain (see Map 21.3).

Back home, two hundred thousand men rushed to volunteer for service in the nation's twenty-eight-thousand-strong army, now recalled from service in the western states. By mid-May, voluntary and regular troops had landed in Manila, becoming the first U.S. battalions ever to enter ground combat outside North America. Maneuvers began in Cuba in July and were over by mid-August, thanks largely to Cuban fighters who had already cleared the countryside of most of the Spanish forces. The few remaining Spanish soldiers, poorly trained and equipped, fell easily to the well-armed Americans—especially regiments that had prior experience fighting Native Americans in the West. The United States also took the Spanish colony of Puerto Rico in just three days and occupied Guam. And in June 1898, with the help of American sugar planters who had orchestrated a coup against Hawaii's recently ascended Queen Lili'uokalani five years earlier, the United States annexed the Hawaiian Islands.

Within four months, the United States had won its first overseas war and acquired an empire of islands. With just 379 American soldiers killed in action, the press pronounced it a terrific success. In fact, over ten times as many soldiers had died from tropical diseases, such as malaria and yellow fever, contracted in the course of duty. Although this shocking mortality rate received little mention in the press, it prompted the U.S. Army to study tropical diseases, leading to the important discovery in 1900 that malaria and yellow fever are carried by waterborne mosquitoes.

WAR STORIES

The Spanish-American War captured the national imagination. Volunteers flocked to join the military, and thousands of reform societies mobilized to provide troops with supplies, money, and medical care. The early victory at Manila

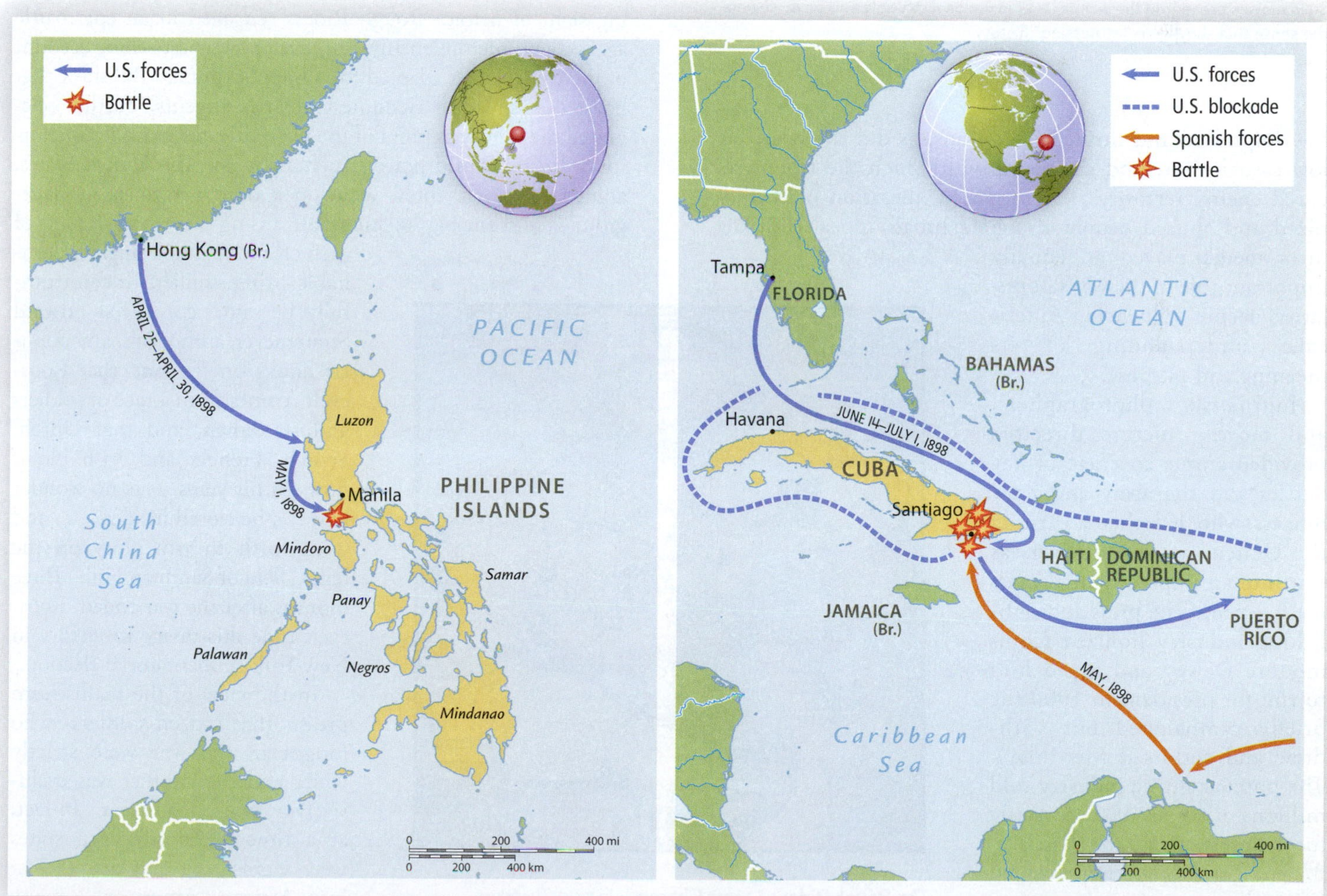

Map 21.3 The Spanish-American War, 1898. In Cuba, the battlefield action in Theodore Roosevelt's "splendid little war" lasted little more than a week, largely because Cuban rebels and the U.S. naval blockades had substantially worn down the enemy in advance of the American deployment. Halfway across the world, in the Philippines, American forces shocked and impressed the great powers of Europe by sinking Spain's entire Pacific fleet and defeating its ground troops in just three months.

War Movies. The Spanish-American War was the first to be filmed, and these "moving pictures" contributed significantly to the war's popularity. Although the film was of poor quality by today's standards, audiences thrilled to Thomas Edison's footage of events such as Commodore Dewey's landing in Manila Bay and his simulation (sometimes with toy boats) of battle scenes. Such movies presented the war as an epic national struggle and gave viewers the sense that they were "witnessing" history.

Bay impressed and thrilled Americans, as did the relatively low casualty rate and the speed with which the troops secured enemy territory. The supposed liberation of a colonized and abused people also held broad appeal. But the mass media played an equally important role in the war's popularity, deeply influencing Americans' understanding of its meaning and purpose.

Journalists, photographers, and moving picture directors provided ample coverage of key battles and the army and navy officers who led them, turning the United States' first overseas war into an unprecedented mass media event. The press and publishing industry lionized Commodore Dewey and urged him to run for president in 1900 (he briefly campaigned but withdrew and endorsed McKinley). The popular music industry sold millions of copies of sheet music for titles such as *The Battle of Manila*, and advertisers cashed in on the war, promoting everything from American flags to "Dewey's favorite armchair"—"large, roomy, massive, handsome and comfortable."

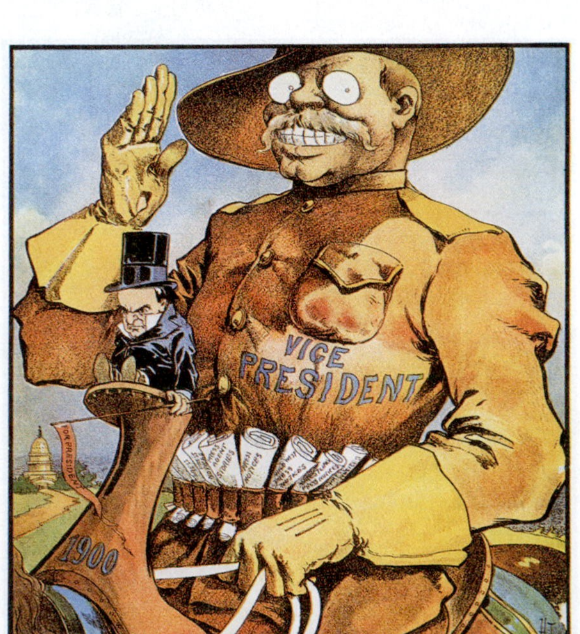

The Rough Rider's Latest Charge. In 1900, Theodore Roosevelt again assumed his Rough Rider persona to run for, and win, the vice presidency of the United States. Many observers believed that Vice President Roosevelt called the shots in the McKinley administration and that the president (pictured on the horn of Roosevelt's saddle) had little choice but to "go along for the ride."

More than anyone else, Theodore Roosevelt detected political opportunity in the new relationship between war and the mass media. Immediately resigning his position as assistant secretary of the navy, Roosevelt enlisted to lead a force of 450 volunteers—among them, a number of popular baseball players and several journalists—into battle in Cuba. He bravely, and at times recklessly, led his volunteers up heavily fortified San Juan Hill alongside four battalions of experienced African American regulars. By the battle's end, one in five men lay dead. Many more would later succumb to injury or illness. But Colonel Roosevelt emerged unscathed (save for a bullet graze on his wrist)—and a hero.

Roosevelt's heroic status had as much to do with his publicity efforts as his leadership skills. Even before Cuba, Roosevelt insisted that the war effort was the triumphant extension of what many believed to be the manly, frontier spirit that had supposedly conquered and civilized the American West. In an iconic image drawn directly from the immensely popular Wild West shows of Buffalo Bill, Roosevelt and his soldiers stormed into battle on horseback. Roosevelt's cavalry charge provided the journalists and illustrators embedded in his unit with the thrilling sight of heroic "Rough Riders" engaged in an epic battle against a murderous enemy. Roosevelt's own best-selling account of the charge, later adapted for a popular Buffalo Bill show that boasted a "squad of Genuine Cuban Insurgents," further celebrated the victory as proof of the United States' martial superiority over Old World powers such as Spain. The United States, argued Roosevelt, threw white men drawn from many backgrounds into one big "melting pot," fusing the strongest traits of each ethnicity into a single indomitable citizen-soldier. "It can truthfully be said," concurred Edward Stratemeyer, author of many popular books on the war, that Roosevelt "comes from a race of soldiers and statesmen, and that Dutch, Scotch, French, and Irish blood flows in his veins. It is no wonder that . . . he closed his desk . . . and went forth to win glory on the battle-field of San Juan Hill." Three months after the war ended, Roosevelt rode this image to victory in New York's gubernatorial election.

In the view of the mainstream press, the citizen-soldiers who fought in the war were strictly white and the conflict was exclusively a "white man's war." In fact, at a time when southern states were segregating and disfranchising African Americans, many black men were particularly keen to serve because they saw the war as an opportunity to demonstrate their loyalty and fitness for full

Common Ground. The white press and political leaders claimed that victory in the Spanish-American War—and especially the liberation of Cuba from Spain—had reconciled North and South. President McKinley reinforced this message on a victory tour of the South, proclaiming the war's "magic healing, which has closed ancient wounds and effaced their scars." **Questions for Analysis:** What role is assigned to the girl labeled "Cuba" in this scene? What does the picture's composition tell us about the photographer's perceptions of the U.S. role in Cuba—and of Cuba's role in the United States?

citizenship. If the rights and benefits of citizenship were forged through military service—as most Americans had believed since the War of Independence—then African American military service posed a challenge to the new Jim Crow culture. Roosevelt refused to allow black soldiers to serve under his command (a policy that effectively limited press coverage of their service) and blocked their admission to officer ranks. The press and moving pictures drew an implicit color line between white and African American soldiers, all but ignoring the contributions of the latter. Where African Americans did appear, they did so only as cowards who abandoned their posts. In fact, the African American regiments served with valor in Cuba, saving Roosevelt's Rough Riders from defeat and obeying orders more consistently than white soldiers.

With the help of the mass media, the nation's first large-scale conflict since the Civil War also became a galvanizing force for sectional reconciliation. Newspapers, parades, cartoons, popular stories, and moving pictures all emphasized that northern and southern whites had reconciled to fight alongside each other in the common patriotic cause of Cuban liberation. "It was roses, roses, all the way," exclaimed Henry Cabot Lodge on the occasion of the Massachusetts soldiers' departure from the port of Baltimore, Maryland. "[T]ears were in my eyes. . . . The war of 1861 was over at last." Members of Congress likewise reached across the old sectional divide to declare the "late unpleasantness" between South and North a thing of the past. A year later, the Confederate war dead were reinterred in Arlington National Cemetery alongside their Union "brothers." Such sentiment came largely at the cost of returning African American soldiers, who were excluded from the main victory parades, refused service throughout the South despite wearing the uniform, and beaten for insisting on equal treatment.

EMPIRE OF ISLANDS

The fact that thousands of Americans died as a result of the war did not dampen the public's enthusiasm for what became known as "the splendid little war." Victory had delivered five foreign territories and made the United States a great power—one of just a handful of nations to command an overseas empire. "What passes before our eyes," marveled the semiofficial newspaper of the French government, "is the appearance of a new power of the first order." The London *Times* concurred: "In the future America will play a part in the general affairs of the world such as she had never played before." Americans passionately debated how the United States should handle Spain's former colonies and whether they should be immediately given their independence. Congress eventually authorized the president to establish jurisdiction over them—and, for the first time, the United States became a colonial power beyond the North American continent (see Map 21.4). In the Philippines, however, the burdens of colonial empire weighed heavily, and the "splendid little war" soon morphed into the

Map 21.4 America's Tropical Empire, 1900. The United States had already annexed several islands in the Pacific by the time the Spanish-American War broke out in 1898. Victory resulted in the acquisition of several ex-Spanish possessions, all of which lay on or close to the Tropic of Cancer.

nation's first—and seemingly endless—overseas war of occupation. The brutality of the guerrilla warfare reprised some of the bloodiest battles of the Indian wars in the U.S. West, and news of massacres soon soured Americans' support for what ironically had become a colonialist war for empire.

THE NEW COLONIAL POWER

Even before the guns fell silent, the McKinley administration considered the question of the future of the four island territories it would soon wrest from Spain. As reports filtered back from Cuba and the Philippines, the president determined that neither population was "ready" for independence. Cubans turned out to be far from the light-skinned brothers-in-arms that Americans had imagined them to be. Roosevelt contemptuously reported that they were "squealing, water-melon eating imbeciles and infants," while McKinley worried that they lacked the cultural and material resources to sustain independent government. Worse still, in McKinley's mind, was the prospect that Cuba and the Philippines might be capable of independence but oppose American interests in the regions.

McKinley consequently sought both to free the islands from Spanish tutelage and to take control of them. Under the Treaty of Paris (1898), the United States proposed to occupy Cuba and take legal possession of Puerto Rico and Guam. (The United States could not legally annex Cuba due to the Teller Amendment, but occupation still gave the United States control.) As well, in a clause that shocked and dismayed the Filipino nationalists who had fought alongside American troops, the United States agreed to buy the Philippines from Spain for $20 million (see How Much Is That?).

Overwhelmingly united in support of the war, Americans were divided over the treaty. The chief conflict was whether the United States should take Spain's island colonies for itself or immediately grant them independence. In the Senate, which has to consent to treaties by a two-thirds vote before they become law, McKinley's supporters insisted that because the Philippine islands had 175 different languages and lacked a common language and cohesive culture, national unity and independent government were impossible. The resulting instability would be an invitation for Britain, Germany, or another empire to step in and annex the Philippines—potentially

How Much Is That?

The Philippines

The purchase price of the Philippines—$20 million, or $543 million in today's dollars—may seem like a steal for the United States. But the Philippines remains the most expensive territorial acquisition in the nation's history. The United States paid the Russians just $7.2 million ($181 million today) for Alaska in 1867, and the enormous Louisiana Territory cost only $15 million in 1803 ($226 million today). The truly controversial aspect of the Philippines purchase was not the price but the fact that the United States, like the empires of Europe and Japan, was acquiring overseas colonies.

threatening U.S. interests throughout Asia. Others argued that simply by defeating the Spanish, the United States had acquired a legal right of possession and that to give up the islands would be a betrayal of the soldiers who had sacrificed their lives for the nation. Senator Albert Beveridge of Indiana, an outspoken proponent of colonization, added that God had been preparing English-speaking people for a thousand years to be "master organizers of the world [and] to establish system where chaos reigns." It was the nation's duty—or the **white man's burden**—to "uplift," "civilize," and "modernize" the "backward" peoples of the world. Many missionaries, though less outspoken than Beveridge, concurred and were eager to begin missions in the island colonies.

A vociferous minority dissented, worrying that annexation and direct rule posed certain political, biological, and economic threats to the republic. Traditionally, U.S. territorial expansion—exclusively transcontinental and westward moving—had turned conquered or purchased land into federal territories that eventually applied for statehood and admission to the union. All inhabitants of the states were citizens or could naturalize unless they were Chinese or Native American (see Chapter 17). Overseas annexation therefore raised the possibility that new populations, mostly people of color, could become American citizens—something that a majority of white Americans opposed on racial, religious, and economic grounds. Some native-born Protestants, who already worried about declining birthrates among Anglo Americans and the influx of Mexicans and southern and eastern Europeans, also feared that Asians and Latinos would further "corrupt" America's Anglo gene pool by intermarrying and becoming the majority population. And although labor leaders had been staunch supporters of the war, they worried that annexation would flood the United States with cheap Asian and Caribbean labor.

Others argued that annexation would betray America's proud republican and anti-imperial traditions. Mark Twain and Jane Addams, outspoken critics of imperialism, added that annexation would also betray those Filipino nationalists who had fought and died alongside American troops believing that they were fighting for independence. (Although Commodore Dewey had not promised independence, he had treated Aguinaldo's forces as informal allies, leading them to believe that the United States supported their cause.) The United States should intervene on behalf of subjugated peoples, but only to liberate them—not to colonize them anew. Above all, Filipinos should have a say in their own destiny.

Although divided, large numbers of Americans—and the majority of the press—appeared to be in favor of annexation and direct rule. Expansionists scoffed at anti-imperialism, insisting that colonization without consultation was a legitimate continuation of U.S. territorial expansion. After all, Florida's Seminole Indians, declared Roosevelt, "had not been consulted in the sale [of Florida to the United States]." Many Senate Democrats who had initially opposed the treaty were now persuaded that temporary annexation would make it possible for the Philippines to become independent. With their support, the Senate ratified the treaty in late 1899, officially transferring Spain's empire of tropical islands to the United States. In the same session, Democrats sponsored a resolution supporting eventual Philippine independence, only to be defeated by a single vote. McKinley immediately issued a decree establishing military governments in the former colonies.

BLOWBACK: THE FILIPINO INSURGENCY

The treaty proved far less popular in the tropics. As the Senate debated, Aguinaldo formed an independent government in the Philippines in the hope of preempting U.S. annexation. News of McKinley's decree sparked an instant nationalist rebellion and led to three years of bloody guerrilla warfare.

In Manila—the old imperial capital and stronghold of the nationalist leadership—the United States fought Aguinaldo's men street by street, killing or arresting rebels and suspected rebels on sight. Establishing no fewer than eight security agencies and laying down a state-of-the-art telephone network and street lamp grid, the Americans turned Manila into the most heavily surveilled city in the world. As the nationalist movement was crushed, Aguinaldo retreated to the countryside. By 1902, the military had intelligence files for 200,000 of the city's 300,000 residents, and strict censorship laws that made it a crime to advocate independence had effectively silenced all remaining dissent. Back home in the United States, military personnel who had served in the Philippines would help adapt these surveillance techniques for domestic use against radicals during World War I. They also helped found the United States' new Bureau of Intelligence in 1907—which became the Federal Bureau of Investigation, or FBI, in the 1920s.

In the Philippine countryside, however, the United States encountered a far more intractable form of warfare. At a disadvantage due to the unfamiliar jungle terrain, the tropical climate, and the absence of maps, roads, and communication networks, the military had first to send scores of cartographers and surveyors into potentially hostile provinces. Meanwhile, upwards of one hundred thousand peasants joined Aguinaldo's forces, and though generally poorly armed, they knew the lay of the land and enjoyed the support of most locals.

As allies became enemies, Americans' initial openness to and curiosity about Filipinos quickly gave way to contempt and fear. Officers and soldiers—many of whom had served at Wounded Knee and other Indian campaigns—typically saw service in the Philippines as "frontier duty" and the Filipinos as inferior natives or "negroes" unprotected by the laws of war (which prohibited the torture and massacre of civilized but not "savage" peoples). Frustrated by the rebels' tendency to blend in with the civilian population, U.S. forces began detaining civilians, burning villages, and torturing suspects. In diaries and letters home, servicemen recorded using the same brutal tactics deployed against Native Americans on the western prairies. The "[rebels] have caused so much trouble & murdered so many of our boys," explained Corporal Chriss A. Bell, "that [U.S. soldiers] recognize them no longer but shoot on sight all natives. Natives will not or cannot understand kind & civilized treatment. If you treat them as equals they will think you are afraid of them & murder you."

Filipino insurgents responded by committing their own atrocities. In 1901, at Samar, they ambushed and killed U.S. soldiers and then stuffed molasses into disemboweled bodies as a way of attracting ants. Outraged at this desecration, an American provincial governor, General Jacob H. Smith, retaliated with an order to kill all local men and boys over the age of ten and to burn whole villages. Unknown numbers of civilians died in the campaign, and almost three hundred thousand survivors were rounded up and moved to disease-ridden "protection zones." "Civilize 'em with a Krag" (gun) became a popular song among the troops.

McKinley Campaigns on Prosperity and Prestige. The Republican campaign drew a vivid line between Democratic and Republican rule by pointing to the return of prosperity, industrial peace, the gold standard, wartime victory, and an expanded role for the United States in the world.

THE HOME FRONT

Initially, most of the press and moving pictures depicted the United States' involvement in the Philippines war positively. Magazines, journals, and newspapers fired readers' interest with maps of America's new possessions, key battles, and vivid descriptions of the newly colonized peoples. But newspapers' maps typically simplified the often-challenging terrain, leaving readers with the false impression that conquest would be easy and fast. Cheap paperbacks known as dime novels celebrated the war as a regenerative force in American life. Much as in the West, "civilized people," wrote Roosevelt in one popular book, were pushing into "wastes" where "barbarians" lurked, and improving the world as they went. In 1900, once the military's information bureau flooded the press with stories of atrocities committed against U.S. troops, newspapers affirmed that "we are not dealing with a civilized people" and that the United States should respond accordingly.

With press support for the war, and with the popular Theodore Roosevelt as his running mate, McKinley entered the election of 1900 confident. The Spanish-American War had stimulated a recovery from the depression of 1893–1898 and was wildly popular among voters. Republican campaign literature moreover directly appealed to middle-class voters, many of whom believed that it was the nation's dutiful mission to uplift less advanced peoples and spread American values. On election day, McKinley easily beat the Democratic candidate, William Jennings Bryan, an outspoken critic of direct rule. Bryan's defeat came as a blow to Filipino nationalists. Recognizing that McKinley's reelection meant that the United States would continue the war, many moderates in the Philippines now pressed for peace.

Peace, however, came neither fast nor easily. Although Aguinaldo was captured in 1901 and the United States had pacified many of the Philippine islands, the military was committed to the eradication of resistance rather than a negotiated peace. It might be necessary, argued General William Shafter, "to kill half of the Filipinos in order that the remaining half . . . may be advanced to a higher plane of life than their semi-barbarous state affords." As the war ground on into the new century, Americans grew pessimistic that it would ever end. A force of 175,000 Americans, at a cost of $160 million, had not been enough to wipe out the nationalists. Over four thousand American soldiers—almost ten times the number who died in combat during the Spanish-American War—and between 200,000 and 700,000 Filipinos had perished. News of massacred women and children leaked out, partly through the effort of British investigative journalists and the failure of censors to vet each and every soldier's letter. And in an alarming parallel to Cuban reconcentration camps, thousands of civilians were reported to have perished in the protection zones. "About 8,000 have been completely civilized and sent to heaven," quipped an outraged Andrew Carnegie. "I hope you like it."

Senate hearings in 1902 made official what many Americans privately knew to be true—that U.S. officers were ordering soldiers to kill women and children, often in retaliation against Filipino fighters. Once the champion of national liberation and humanitarian intervention, the United States now appeared no different from the European empires it had once condemned. In the wake of the hearings, William James, the nation's leading philosopher, charged that the Philippine-American War was "a damning indictment of that whole bloated ideal term, 'civilization'." Echoing Carnegie, William Jennings Bryan declared that neither missionaries nor armies could "beat blessings" into Filipinos. Even William Graham Sumner, a once-staunch supporter of colonization, fumed that instead of "civilizing the lower races . . . we have exterminated them."

NATION BUILDING IN THE COLONIES

It fell to Theodore Roosevelt—an outspoken champion of colonial imperialism—to resolve the conflict and reframe U.S. policy in the colonies. Becoming president in 1901 following the assassination of McKinley, the pragmatic Roosevelt recognized that much of the press and many American voters no longer supported direct colonization. He resolved to prepare Cuba and the Philippines for independence—and as quickly as possible. In 1901, the Platt Amendment authorized Cubans to establish a fully independent government but with the proviso that the United States could intervene by force if Cuban independence or individuals' lives, liberty, or property were threatened. Cuba signed a treaty based on the amendment in 1903, consenting to lease land at Guantánamo Bay to the United States in perpetuity for the purpose of building a navy base.

Working closely with Secretary of War Elihu Root and Philippines civil governor William Howard Taft, Roosevelt accelerated the development of educational, civic, and other programs with the aim of building an American-style democracy in the Philippines. The decision to transform the island colonies rapidly into independent nation-states drew on and reinforced many progressive ideas and reform efforts under way in the United States (see Chapter 20). The Philippines became an intensive laboratory of progressive nation-building—and the first of many foreign countries in the twentieth century to undergo a process of direct Americanization.

In true progressive style, nation building blended privately funded initiatives and volunteerism with federal programs. An army of almost three thousand American teachers volunteered to teach English, arithmetic, and civics in the Philippines. Drawn from nearly every state, these men and women viewed their work as a noble effort to liberate Filipinos from their supposed state of ignorance. Empowering them with a common language (English), they believed, was the essential first step toward nationhood and a vital part of the civilizing process. The new schools were aimed especially at Filipino elites and key minorities, and as Governor Taft started elections, he extended voting rights first of all to these educated men.

Protestant missionaries also arrived in force as both teachers and evangelizers. Committed to spreading certain Protestant values, and realizing that soldiers and other Americans in the colonies might not share these values, they became as concerned about the U.S. soldiers' moral conduct as they were about Filipino souls. They were shocked, for instance, to find that many bordellos draped the U.S. flag across their entryway—to attract soldiers—and that troops were getting drunk with Filipinos. Missionaries and the WCTU pressed the secretary of war to prohibit drinking among the troops and objected to the army's practice of inspecting prostitutes and licensing those deemed "clean" (free of sexually transmitted infections). The flag, argued the WCTU's Katherine Stevenson, should "stand in the Far East as the symbol of righteousness"—not licensed vice. Men, she added, should be held equally responsible for the spread of sexual diseases. As a result, the army issued new regulations subjecting the troops to sexual examination and abolishing the licensing system. Officers were instructed to lead by example as abstinent and sober gentlemen. The unlicensed bordellos, however, endured.

Meanwhile, civil governor Taft set about establishing an American-style legal system, complete with a Supreme Court and new legal code. Taft substituted private property rights for various forms of communal and feudal property, thus freeing up land to be divided and bought and sold, just as in the United States. In areas that had been pacified, he also replaced Spanish courts and tribunals with American legal institutions. Taft's motivation was partly to provide U.S. investors with a predictable and familiar legal environment. "The army has brought the Philippines to the point where they offer a ready and attractive field for investment and enterprise," he wrote in 1902, "but to make this possible there must be mining laws, homestead and land laws, general transportation laws, banking and currency laws." In the same vein, the army prioritized road and bridge construction, and the Signal Corps built national telephone and telegraph networks. But such programs were also intended to foster a democratic system of government, claimed Taft, by giving Filipinos a sense of collective responsibility and commitment to their new government.

A similar logic prevailed in architecture and city planning. Many of Spain's imperial buildings in the Philippines, erected in the seventeenth and eighteenth centuries, were crumbling—the relics of a despised and outmoded form of colonialism. Taft's government proposed to replace them (and local indigenous housing) with buildings that in theory promoted American culture, values, and good government. In 1904, Daniel Burnham planned the redevelopment of Manila as a national capital and the construction of a new, summer capital in temperate Baguio (for those months in which Americans found Manila too hot and humid). Burnham, who designed the layout of the World's Columbian Exposition in Chicago in 1893 and was a major proponent of the City Beautiful movement, envisioned an ideal progressive city for the tropics, complete with "hotels, official buildings [and] residences, court houses, schools, sanitariums, playgrounds, railroad terminals, business section, markets, . . . [a] country club"—and churches. Criticizing old Manila as "ill-suited for the abode of white men," Burnham redeveloped the city, opening its extensive waterways as canals and laying rail lines to transport people and goods. Due to Congress's changing budget priorities after 1906, Burnham's long-term Manila plans were only partially implemented, but work in temperate Baguio proceeded. New government offices were built using the relatively modern material of reinforced concrete, which was strong, easy to clean, and appropriate to the buildings' "dignity and permanency."

By the 1910s, nation building in the Philippines had produced an educated, English-speaking elite, a viable U.S.-style legal system, and a strong, centralized security force. Filipinos were now participating in local government in many regions. However,

The Moro Massacre in the Philippines. General Leonard Wood led eight hundred heavily armed U.S. soldiers in an attack on Moro men, women, and children who had fled U.S. jurisdiction for the Bud Dajo volcano in 1906. Misleadingly dubbed the "Battle of the Crater" by the press, the campaign was in fact a massacre of almost a thousand civilians—as this disturbing photo, which surfaced some years later, suggested. Unlike previous slaughters, however, it did not result in any courts martial or Senate investigations, perhaps because the army's information bureau succeeded in portraying the Moros as religious fanatics who deserved their fate.

INTERPRETING THE SOURCES

Imperial Eyes: Inspecting the Filipino Village, Louisiana Purchase Exposition

Colonial researchers and U.S. authorities installed the first "living exhibit" of Filipino tribal life at the Pan-American Exposition in Buffalo, New York, in 1901. Three years later, on the centennial of another pivotal event in U.S. expansion—the Louisiana Purchase—the world's fair in St. Louis featured a forty-seven-acre living exhibit built and inhabited by more than 1,200 Filipinos drawn from twenty tribes. Former Philippines governor William Howard Taft, now the secretary of war, helped engineer the installation, which consisted of six villages and staged the varied clothing, shelters, hunting and gathering techniques, and wedding rituals of the tribes. The exhibit, pictured here, proved the most popular at the fair. Visitors learned that both the "red man of America and the brown man of Oceania" were the "ward of Uncle Sam" but that the Filipinos, unlike the Native Americans, were well on their way to "development" thanks to American schools, law, clothing, architecture, and tools.

Simulation of Filipino Village, Louisiana Purchase Exposition, St. Louis, 1904.

Explore the Source

1. How might the construction of paths and viewing platforms have shaped visitors' responses to the simulated village and its inhabitants?
2. In what ways might this "exhibit" have confirmed the view of many white Americans that they belonged to a superior race? How might it have challenged them?

the policy backfired in other areas. In Muslim-dominated Moroland, for example, the chief sultan had signed a treaty accepting U.S. sovereignty in exchange for American recognition of Islam and the local laws and government. But when nation building got under way in earnest, the new Moroland governor, U.S. general Leonard Wood, revoked the treaty, thereby sparking a bloody rebellion that lasted through 1913. As the death toll among the Moro people climbed into the thousands, an exasperated Roosevelt declared that the Philippines was the United States' "heel of Achilles" and should be made independent as soon as possible. Three years later, the Jones Act (1916) established a Filipino legislature and committed the United States to Philippines independence, which did not become official until 1946.

RACE AND EMPIRE

U.S. scientific and other research also flourished in the islands during these years, transforming the fields of ethnography, tropical medicine, and the natural sciences and making possible many important discoveries, such as tropical vaccines. Teams of doctors and scientists succeeded in stamping out leprosy and other vicious diseases. Yet some research was poorly conceived and based on invalid—and often racist—assumptions. Doctors, naturalists, and anthropologists, for example, used invalid sampling techniques to examine and measure hundreds of people and then presented their work as scientific proof that Filipinos were racially inferior to peoples of European origin. In one of many such studies, Robert Bennett Bean, a physician working in a health clinic in the Philippine municipality of Taytay, charted and contrasted the "average Taytayan" with the "average European" and used photographs of his subjects to argue that Filipinos were less evolved. Bean also claimed, erroneously, that he had occasionally spotted Neanderthal men among the population.

Although lacking scientific validity, such work affirmed the misconception that human beings belonged to distinct biological races, the most evolved of which was the Anglo American. The pseudo-scientific ideology of race grew in popularity in the United States (see Interpreting the Sources: Imperial Eyes) and in turn helped justify the exclusion of people of color from the full rights of citizenship.

Racial ideology also influenced American attitudes toward the legal status of people born in the colonies. Between 1901 and 1904, the Supreme Court ruled in fourteen *Insular Cases* on the legality of the United States' acquisition of overseas possessions and the eligibility of colonized populations for U.S. citizenship and constitutional rights. The cases were initially brought by importers insisting that goods from Puerto Rico and the Philippines should not be subject to tariffs or seized as illegal imports because the islands were legally part of the United States. But the Supreme Court recognized that the question of the legal status of imported goods would also have implications for the legal status of foreign peoples subject to U.S. control. In a contradictory finding, the justices ruled that that Puerto Rico, the Philippines, Hawaii, and other new acquisitions were American soil but that the Constitution did not automatically extend to them.

Under this new doctrine of territorial incorporation, the Court gave Congress the authority to rule the possessions as it wished and provided that Filipinos, Hawaiians, and Puerto Ricans would enjoy the full rights of U.S. citizens only if and when Congress admitted their islands as states of the union. The Court elaborated in a case brought on behalf of twenty-one-year-old Puerto Rican immigrant, Isabel Gonzales, ruling that although subject to U.S. jurisdiction, Gonzales (and all persons born in U.S. possessions) were U.S. "nationals"—not U.S. citizens.

INFORMAL EMPIRE

As the United States retreated from European-style colonialism, it embraced economic forms of expansionism while continuing to build the navy and deepen its presence in the Pacific. The federal government began working far more closely with banks and private financial institutions to exercise influence through the extension of loans, bonds, and other financial instruments. Beginning with Theodore Roosevelt, the executive arm of government increasingly bypassed Congress in its dealings with other nations, instead entering into informal agreements in "memoranda" and "notes" rather than formal treaties (for which Senate approval was needed). Roosevelt also asserted the right of the United States to get involved in Latin American affairs when American property rights or unpaid debts were at stake, a position further embroiling the country in its neighbors' affairs. Roosevelt's successor, William Henry Taft, struggled to avoid military interventions in the region, but when nationalists struggled to overthrow pro-American governments, the United States responded by sending in marines. With Woodrow Wilson at the helm after 1912, the earlier impulse to intervene aggressively was revived.

OPENING THE DOOR TO CHINA

The Philippines provided the United States, for the first time, a territorial foothold in East Asia—and, promisingly, a stepping-stone to China and its potentially massive commercial market. However, the German, Russian, French, Japanese, and British empires had gotten to China first, leasing and in some cases conquering territory and claiming exclusive spheres of influence (trade and development monopolies from which other nations were excluded). The ongoing disintegration of the ruling Qing Dynasty (1644–1911) threatened to fragment China further and to trigger an all-out land grab among the empires. American missionaries and commercial interests raised the alarm, calling on the United States to step up its role in maintaining their access to the troubled nation.

Although emboldened by the success of the war with Spain, the United States had neither the will nor the military capability to join the imperial scramble. Nonetheless, in 1899, Secretary of State John Hay sent the first of two **Open Door** notes to the governments of Europe and Japan, insisting that all nations had a right to trade with China. Wishing to avert conflict (because they were afraid that the newly confident United States might ally with an enemy), the imperial governments evaded the matter—whereupon Hay promptly proclaimed victory and announced that every empire had accepted the Open Door principle.

A year later, in 1900, the United States sent 2,500 troops stationed in the Philippines to China to help put down the Boxer Rebellion, an uprising in which thousands of Chinese protested the foreign presence on Chinese soil. Hay now penned a second Open Door note, this time asserting a right to protect American lives and property and to trade freely and equally in the region. He furthermore declared that China must remain united (rather than being divided among the European and Japanese empires) and that it owed the United States $333 million in damages resulting from the rebellion. Again, the European and Japanese empires neither accepted nor rejected the note—and the Russians ignored it, stationing 175,000 troops in Manchuria. But the empires quietly decided not to carve up the rest of China, primarily because they feared that doing so would ignite an all-out war among themselves. From the U.S. perspective, the imperial powers' decision confirmed the United States' newfound respect as a world power.

Despite the Open Door policy, trade with China leveled off during Roosevelt's presidency, partly because Congress renewed the ban on Chinese immigration in 1904 and thereby prompted a mass boycott of U.S.-made goods in China. Roosevelt himself undermined the Open Door policy by cooperating with the British in China in the belief that an alliance with the world's largest empire would best protect U.S. interests. Although only an informal alliance, this Anglo-American cooperation ended over a century of animosity between Britain and its former American colony and became a cornerstone of U.S. foreign policy into the twenty-first century. Britain's newest ally, the aggressively resurgent Japanese Empire, also became a friend to the United States. Japan had long sought influence over its Korean neighbor, and in 1904 Roosevelt determined that the best way of protecting U.S. rail, mining, and other interests was to informally recognize Japan's close—and domineering—relationship with the Korean peninsula. A year later, the United States and Japan agreed in a memorandum that the United States would not interfere with Japanese designs on Korea as long as Japan left the Philippines to the United States.

RIVALS FOR THE PACIFIC

The Russian Empire's decision to ignore the second Open Door note and to occupy Manchuria infuriated the Japanese, whom the European powers had pressured to withdraw from Manchuria several years earlier. Much as the United States had done in 1898 at Manila Bay, Japan shocked the world with a devastating attack on the Russian fleet at Port Arthur, Manchuria, in 1904—the first engagement in what would be the Russo-Japanese War. The destruction of Russia's Pacific fleet upset the delicate balance among the empires and threatened to close the United States' door to China. It also gave notice that Japan was an aspiring power in the Pacific. Roosevelt immediately invited the combatants to a meeting at Portsmouth, New Hampshire, calculating that the best way to protect American interests was to broker peace. After tense negotiations, Roosevelt offered a compromise solution that redistributed disputed territory and rail lines, removed Russian troops, and satisfied both sides. The Treaty of Portsmouth (1905) earned Roosevelt the Nobel Peace Prize. The Japanese rewarded the United States by reopening southern Manchuria to American trade, but Japan drew the line at American investment.

Although Roosevelt sought to advance U.S. interests in East Asia, he did so by making informal agreements with an occupying power (Japan) that, in effect, fostered Japan's expansion and sacrificed the principle of China's territorial integrity. U.S. bankers and leading American diplomats were unconvinced that this was the correct approach—particularly because it permitted Japan's embargo on foreign investment in Japanese-controlled areas. Disapproval spread in the United States in 1906 as Japanese nationalists pressured their government to further restrict U.S. access to Manchuria and rioted against the Treaty of Portsmouth.

That same year, relations deteriorated further when the San Francisco school board decided to segregate all Japanese American and Japanese immigrant schoolchildren in a new Asian-only public school. In Japan, the press and public objected strenuously. In the United States, Roosevelt blasted the decision as a "wicked absurdity." Transporting the entire school board to Washington, D.C., the president pressed members to reverse segregation in exchange for a commitment from the Japanese government to restrict the immigration of Japanese laborers to the United States. The Japanese consented to this so-called Gentlemen's Agreement in 1907.

Sensing Americans' growing uneasiness over the Japanese Empire's rapid expansion, Roosevelt also took the opportunity to prevail on Congress to expand the navy again and to build more bases. He announced that a "Great White Fleet" of U.S.

Pageant of Sea Power. The United States' Great White Fleet steams into Sydney harbor, Australia.

battleships would circumnavigate the globe, making calls in Australia, the Middle East, and Europe—as well as Japan. The tour powerfully impressed upon Japan (and other empires) that the United States was a formidable naval power. Shortly after the fleet left Tokyo, Japan recognized the Pacific as an open trade route and promised the United States equal access to China. The world's empires had entered a new naval arms race—one that, by 1914, would bring Europe to the brink of a catastrophic war.

REVIVING THE MONROE DOCTRINE

While gradually relinquishing direct control over Cuba and the Philippines, President Roosevelt nevertheless asserted the right to intervene in the affairs of Latin American and Caribbean countries (see Map 21.5). In his first annual message to Congress in 1901, Roosevelt announced that the United States guaranteed the "commercial independence of the Americas." But he added that the United States would not prevent European nations from taking punitive action against a Latin American or Caribbean nation in the event that the latter defaulted on debts or staged a revolution that endangered European interests.

Roosevelt had in mind Venezuelan dictator Cipriano Castro's refusal to repay millions of dollars' worth of debts and bonds held by German and British investors. With tacit U.S. support, Germany and Great Britain proceeded to bombard Venezuelan forts and seized the country's ports in 1902. But a year later, when Germany repeated the bombardment, Roosevelt changed his position, declaring such action unacceptable and dispatching Admiral Dewey's fleet to underscore his point. The Germans withdrew.

Map 21.5 U.S. Intervention in Latin America, 1895–1940. Although the United States opted for an "informal" and largely nonterritorial form of empire in Latin America, it nonetheless repeatedly deployed money and troops to the region whenever strategic or American business interests were deemed to be at risk.

Events in the small Caribbean nation of the Dominican Republic further persuaded Roosevelt that a statement of U.S. policy in the Western Hemisphere was overdue. A nationalist revolution there threatened German as well as certain American interests. In 1904, Roosevelt clarified that the United States was now an "international police power" that would ensure its neighbors paid their debts and honored property rights—and would deploy force against them if necessary. This Roosevelt Corollary turned the Monroe Doctrine's prohibition of European intervention into an assertion of U.S. police power over the entire Western Hemisphere. Roosevelt prevailed on the Dominican Republic's government to allow the United States to take over the nation's customs house (through which all imports arrived and were taxed), reserving 45 percent of the takings for the Dominicans and placing most of the rest in an American trust fund out of which the country's creditors would be paid.

In Cuba, under the pro-U.S. president Tomás Estrada Palma, American investment flourished in the cattle, tobacco, and other industries, quadrupling by 1913. Almost half of all Cuban sugar mills were U.S. owned by 1920. Whenever nationalists objected too loudly or threatened rebellion, the United States dispatched troops. In 1906, for example, Roosevelt sent a navy cruiser and secretary of war William Howard Taft to Cuba to restore order. Taft, former governor of the Philippines and future president, established a civilian government, placing five thousand U.S. troops at its disposal. But in contrast to the situation in the Philippines, there was no real effort to build a U.S.-style democracy. Instead, the objective, as in the Dominican Republic, was to make Cuba an orderly, stable environment amenable to American business. Having achieved that goal by 1908, the troops withdrew.

The United States also extended its influence in the Caribbean and Central America through the construction of a canal connecting the Pacific and Atlantic oceans. "No single great material work which remains to be undertaken on this continent," Roosevelt declared, "is as of such consequence to the American people." When the Colombian government proved reluctant to cede control of Panama, President Roosevelt and Panamanian business interests organized a coup, created an independent nation (Panama), and installed a pro-American government. Work began on the canal in 1904 and, after early setbacks, was completed in 1914 (see Spaces and Places: The Panama Canal).

DOLLAR DIPLOMACY

William Howard Taft continued to use the Roosevelt Corollary as a compass for Latin American policy when he became president in 1909. But Taft knew from experience that armed intervention was both costly and risky. Even if successful, it could damage the United States' image abroad, fuel anti-U.S. sentiment, and provoke criticism at home. Consequently he initially placed far more emphasis on using American financial power to sway governments to conduct business in ways that were friendly to U.S. interests. The federal government had cooperated with U.S. banks and industry to influence developments overseas before, but the relationship grew far closer under Taft. Adopting a strategy that would be dubbed **dollar diplomacy,** the State Department worked with U.S. banks to buy up Latin American debts and offer new loans for development as a way of gaining political influence in these "client" states.

Despite Taft's effort to "substitute dollars for bullets," the United States turned repeatedly to the use of military force in the Progressive Era. Latin American states still defaulted on loans—only now they were loans made by U.S. banks and guaranteed by the U.S. government. In the Dominican Republic, the local economy recovered through the new arrangement, but nationalist dissent was fueled by the perception that the United States was running the nation's economy. When that country's pro-American president was assassinated in 1911, U.S. marines arrived to enforce order—and ended up occupying the republic, where they would remain until 1922. In a now depressingly familiar pattern, the United States sent marines to Cuba again in 1912 and 1917. The region became caught in a cycle of financial dependency, nationalist rebellion, and armed U.S. intervention (see Hot Commodities: Bananas).

WAR IN MEXICO

By the time Democrat Woodrow Wilson was elected president in 1912, the sight of U.S. Marines landing on the shores of Caribbean and Latin American nations was not unusual. However, nothing in the administrations of Roosevelt and Taft approached the scale or frequency of the intervention that occurred under President Woodrow Wilson. Indeed, Wilson dispatched more U.S. battleships to Caribbean harbors than did Taft and Roosevelt combined. But he added to Taft's pro-business foreign policy a strong moral commitment to improve and uplift the world—and a willingness to send in ground troops to do it.

U.S. investments had grown exponentially throughout Latin America during the Roosevelt and Taft years but nowhere faster than in Mexico. Doubling their investment after 1900, American coal, railroad, and oil companies owned almost half of all Mexican land and over 75 percent of its silver, lead, and copper mines by 1910. However, Mexico was ruled by an increasingly unpredictable tyrant, Porfirio Díaz, whose brutality toward his own people and disregard for law were infamous. Many Americans applauded when, in 1911, an uprising by Mexican rebels ousted the longtime dictator and replaced his lawless government with a constitutional republic and an American-style democracy. The new president, Francisco I. Madero, and the tiny middle class that aspired to govern were soon assailed by an enormous and long-suffering peasantry demanding "Mexico for Mexicans." Much like nationalists in China and elsewhere, they called for the repatriation of all U.S.- and foreign-owned mines and land. In the absence of a popular government, Mexico descended into a bloody civil

SPACES & PLACES

The Panama Canal

Traders, investors, and seafarers had long dreamed of carving a canal through the crooked finger of land that separates the Pacific and Atlantic oceans (see Map 21.5). For centuries, European ships bound for the Pacific had had to navigate down the coast of South America and cross to the other ocean via the treacherous waters of Cape Horn. The sea voyage between New York and San Francisco was thirteen thousand miles long and took several arduous months to complete. Alternatively, ships could drop their cargo and passengers on the Central American isthmus, where rail tracks crossed a fifty-mile span to the opposite coast—but few did, as that method was expensive and slow. Farther north, the transcontinental railroad made it easier to transport goods, people, and raw materials between coasts, but it could not keep pace with the booming demand for freight space.

Linking the Oceans. Much of the U.S. press viewed progress on the canal as a patriotic extension of American power abroad. Although enormous steam-operated bulldozers did most of the heavy lifting, this cartoon depicts the workers as an army of brave, pick-and-shovel soldiers led by Roosevelt—much like the Rough Riders of San Juan Hill.

war. By 1912, rival armies of peasants roamed the countryside, raiding silver mines, haciendas (estates) of local gentry, and, occasionally, small U.S. border towns. Hundreds of Mexicans and sixty-three Americans lost their lives in the violence.

These events were closely followed by President Wilson, the southwestern states, and the many U.S. corporations with investments across the border. When Madero was killed in a coup in early 1913, Wilson took the unusual step of refusing to recognize the government of rebel leader Victoriano Huerta. Insisting that Huerta step down, Wilson dispatched ten thousand troops and a fleet of warships to the border but stopped short of invading. He instead pursued a strategy of indirect intervention, providing military support such as technical expertise and munitions to popular peasant leader General Francisco "Pancho" Villa. Villa, whose equestrian skills and rough charisma made him popular with the U.S. press, accepted the aid happily and with the belief that the United States would support a united and independent Mexico.

By 1914, Villa's forces were still making little headway. Wilson resolved to send U.S. troops to topple Huerta's regime directly. But Villa did not support an invasion, and Huerta had carefully abstained from any actions that might have been legitimate grounds for a U.S. attack, such as confiscating American property. The provocation for war soon came, however, when local Mexican police arrested a small boatload of U.S. sailors who had illegally entered the government-controlled town of Tampico. Eager to avert armed conflict, Huerta immediately apologized and released the sailors. But with the backing of Wilson, Rear Admiral Henry T. Mayo forced a showdown, demanding that Huerta give the United

In the 1870s, European and American business interests identified tropical Panama—a lush jungle territory belonging to Colombia—as the most logical site for a canal. President Ulysses S. Grant sent investigators to the area, but a French company beat the United States to the draw, leasing Panama from Colombia and securing construction rights. In the early 1880s, thousands of laborers, mostly locals of African or Native American descent, cut a narrow passage through the jungle and began digging a channel. Using the latest steam-driven ditch-diggers, workers made steady progress. Back in Europe, company directors celebrated, confident that modern technology was conquering the rugged terrain, uniting the world's mightiest oceans, and enriching investors.

When the rainy season arrived, however, work literally bogged down. The French workers overseeing the local laborers were unfamiliar with tropical seasons, terrain, and diseases. Despite locals' advice to suspend operations until the return of the dry season, the company pressed on. Snakes, spiders, swamps, disease-carrying mosquitoes, and driving rain made the work dangerous and at times impossible. Over four hundred workers succumbed to heat stroke, malaria, yellow fever, or smallpox. The Chagres River repeatedly burst its banks (as it did every season), sweeping away personnel and equipment and turning the construction site to mud. This pattern was repeated annually for the next six years. By 1888, only eleven miles of canal had been dug—at the cost of over twenty thousand lives.

Progress on the canal ground to a halt until 1902, when the United States agreed to purchase development rights from the French and to negotiate a treaty with the Colombian government guaranteeing U.S. control of the canal. When Colombia proved reluctant, President Roosevelt dispatched the USS *Nashville* to Colombian waters and worked with Panamanian business interests to overthrow the Colombian government. The coup took only a few hours and was relatively bloodless, as Colombian troops were paid off. Roosevelt later defended his legally questionable actions, bragging that it was only because he "took Panama and let Congress debate" that the United States was able to proceed with the canal. With Colombia neutralized, the United States bought the French company's lease (for $10 million) and devised an American-style constitution for the new, "independent" nation of Panama. Work on the canal resumed in 1904.

Like the French, the American workers at first ignored local advice, with equally fatal consequences. Within a year, the Roosevelt administration changed tack, largely at the instigation of chief engineer John Stevens, who had built railroads through the challenging terrain of the Pacific Northwest. Stevens began by ordering a massive sanitization operation, on the rationale that an effective workforce was a healthy one. With the help of the U.S. Army's sanitation office, he implemented mosquito abatement programs, such as draining swamps and constructing sewers, and built hospitals, schools, housing, churches, and hotels—all equipped with mosquito screens. Malaria and yellow fever were all but eliminated, though over five thousand people died before the programs took effect. When Stevens recommenced work on the canal, he abandoned the French plans for digging a sea-level channel, instead devising a series of locks and dams that lifted ships to an enormous artificial lake in the middle of Panama and then lowered them down the other side. America retained control of the Canal Zone, which officially opened in 1914, until the end of the twentieth century, when Panama agreed to take full control in exchange for guaranteeing the canal's neutrality.

Think About It

1. What was so attractive, from the perspective of the U.S. government and business, about the possibility of linking the Atlantic and Pacific Oceans?
2. Why might the Colombian government have been reluctant to relinquish control over its Panamanian territory?
3. Why do you think Stevens insisted on building schools, churches, and housing for the workers?

States a twenty-one-gun salute—a highly symbolic act of domination to which the Mexicans were unlikely to submit. Now desperate to avoid conflict, Huerta consented, but with the proviso that the United States offer a reciprocal salute to Mexico. Wilson refused, suspended negotiations, and asked Congress to use armed force "to obtain from General Huerta . . . the fullest recognition of the rights and dignity of the United States."

Congress consented, and in May 1914, six thousand troops of the same American Expeditionary Force (AEF) that had fought in the Philippines poured over the border and headed south to the important port city of Veracruz. Under General John Pershing and with the support of U.S. battleships and destroyers, the AEF quickly took control of Veracruz, where it proceeded to set up a model progressive municipality. President Wilson did not, however, send troops to secure U.S. property, much to the frustration of American mine owners and their Republican supporters. Huerta was overthrown, and Venustiano Carranza established a new government. But by the end of 1914, the U.S. invasion had backfired badly by unifying Mexico's warring factions, who agreed on little besides the idea that the nation's future should be solely in Mexican hands. Pancho Villa now condemned the United States. Pershing pursued him and in so doing effectively turned Villa into a nationalist war hero—and the mass of Mexicans into passionate critics of the United States.

In the United States, the invasion proved divisive, reigniting older debates about colonial empire and whether the country should acquire and hold colonies. In theory, progressives supported republican revolutions and the establishment

HOT COMMODITIES

Bananas

The cheapest and most popular fruit in the United States today, the banana was once an exotic luxury found only on the tables of the nation's wealthiest few. Its fruit rich in calories and nutrients, the tropical banana "tree" (technically an herb) originated in South and Southeast Asia and was among the first edible plants to be cultivated, over seven thousand years ago. By 1000 AD, several of the plant's two hundred varieties had migrated to Africa, the Middle East, and Polynesia. But it was not until the sixteenth century that European slaveholders introduced the plant to Latin America and the Caribbean, principally as a cheap source of calories for slaves. As late as 1890, most North Americans had never seen a banana, let alone tasted one. A single fruit of the sweet and brightly jacketed Gros Michel variety cost the equivalent of two dollars—approximately ten times what it costs today. And because genteel consumers considered the fruit's natural appearance lewd, bananas came pre-peeled, chopped, and politely wrapped in tin foil.

The United States' "informal empire" rapidly turned the once-exotic banana into an everyday staple—and an American icon. As investors shifted their attention south of the United States in the 1880s, Boston seafarer Lorenzo Dow Baker joined forces with businessman Andrew Preston to start the world's first commercial banana plantation, in Jamaica. With the help of refrigerated "banana boats" and rail cars, their Boston Fruit Company exported millions of Gros Michels to the Northeast each year. The trade proved a boon to tourism, too, as boats relieved of their fruit cargo in Boston returned with Americans eager to see the tropics. Meanwhile, in Costa Rica, American investor Minor C. Keith secured eight hundred thousand acres of land and rights to the port of Limón in exchange for building a fifty-mile railroad. When construction proved slow and unprofitable, Keith planted out his acreage with Gros Michels, eventually gaining a monopoly over the southeastern United States.

Keith's banana empire merged with the Boston Fruit Company in 1899 to form the mighty United Fruit Company (UFC, now Chiquita). UFC turned millions of acres into banana plantations throughout Latin America and the Caribbean. Cheap labor

Pancho Villa, from Hero to Villain. The charismatic leader of northern Mexican rebels and a U.S. ally, Villa was introduced to Americans by the Biograph movie studio, which sent a camera crew along to follow his expeditions in 1912 and portrayed him as a noble, virile white man—much as the media had celebrated the Rough Rider Theodore Roosevelt. After Villa later resisted the U.S. invasion, however, he was portrayed as a murderous bandit of racially "mixed"—not white—heritage.

of U.S.-style democracies around the world. But they also passionately debated the role that the United States should play in other people's revolutions. Some observers joined the call of muckraker Lincoln Steffens and Wisconsin senator Robert La Follette to immediately withdraw the troops from Mexico, accusing the Wilson administration of putting private profits ahead of the national interest. Others, such as William Jennings Bryan, argued that now that the United States was involved, it owed a duty to tutor Mexicans in the art and science of democratic government. Mexicans were as yet incapable of governing themselves, argued Bryan, invoking the same racial and paternalistic logic of the "white man's burden" with which many progressives had justified U.S. intervention in Cuba and the Philippines. Many Republicans took a much harder line in favor of full-scale intervention, citing the urgency of protecting property (most expressly, American-owned mines) and making Mexico financially stable. The situation became stalemated and would not be resolved for another two years.

allowed the company to drop the price of bananas to half that of apples, the cheapest U.S.-grown fruit. The company mass-marketed bananas year-round, selling them in their skin and in bunches, boasting that the fruit's protective layer afforded sanitary advantages and eye-catching appeal. UFC produced cookbooks with banana recipes, school atlases identified Latin America as home to the banana, and banana peel jokes and comedy sketches proliferated (although few people ever accidentally slipped on a banana peel). Before long, racy lyrics played on the banana's supposedly suggestive shape, with Bo Carter singing, "I Wanna Put My Banana in Your Fruit Basket" and Memphis Minnie lamenting her "Banana Man Blues." Much as the industry had hoped, Americans had fallen in love with the banana.

Together, the industry and Americans' love of bananas helped consolidate U.S. power in Latin America and the Caribbean. UFC protected its million-dollar banana business there by persuading governments to grant the company huge tracts of land, thereby excluding local farmers and peasants from joining the industry. The company controlled major railways, the Great White shipping line (the world's largest privately own fleet), and, after 1913, radio and telegraph services. During the nationalist uprisings that periodically swept these regions after 1900, UFC supported right-wing governments in Cuba, Guatemala, the Dominican Republic, Colombia, Haiti, and Mexico and helped topple nationalist and socialist regimes. In return, government security forces repressed labor strikes, most violently in Magdalena, Colombia, in 1928, when troops massacred peaceful demonstrators.

The company's immense political power inspired writer O. Henry to describe Central American and Caribbean nations as "banana republics" whose governments were mere puppets of the banana industry. By the 1950s, UFC's holdings in Guatemala were so substantial that, at the company's urging, the administration of U.S. president Dwight D. Eisenhower orchestrated a coup against the democratically elected government after it proposed to redistribute land to the nation's struggling peasantry (see Chapter 27).

Think About It

1. How did the interests of the U.S. government in the Caribbean and Latin America compare with those of the United Fruit Company?
2. How did UFC become so powerful in these regions?
3. Why do you think UFC did not want American consumers to hear about working conditions and the repression of unions and strikes on the banana plantations?

CONCLUSION

The United States' transformation into a great power in 1898 appeared sudden but was in fact the product of complex processes of religious, commercial, political, and military growth over the previous years. By the mid-1890s, U.S. missionaries and their reform networks had persuaded most Americans and their leaders that the United States owed a moral duty to intervene in humanitarian crises beyond its borders. That conviction and U.S. aspirations in East Asia and Latin America propelled the United States into Cuba and the Spanish-American War—and helped keep the United States in the Philippines and Cuba years after the Spanish colonizers had been expelled. Arriving as liberators in the Philippines, U.S. troops quickly became subjugators, at the cost of high human and monetary losses on both sides.

U.S. voters soon rejected colonization and European-style formal empire. Consequently, after 1901, the government experimented with other ways to protect Americans, promote their interests, and advance the nation's strategic position. For the first time overseas, the federal government worked closely with banks and industry to cultivate access to foreign markets and resources and to head off the world's other great powers. Parts of Latin America and the Caribbean became tightly entwined with U.S. interests, and both regions became caught in a cycle of nationalist revolution and U.S.-backed repression. In Mexico, Woodrow Wilson extended this model of foreign policy to include progressive programs of uplift and republican state-building that in many ways resembled the earlier Philippines projects, with equally mixed results.

The emergence of the United States as a great power between 1893 and 1914 occurred in the context of a game-changing scramble for territory, resources, and prestige among the world's established empires. Under way since the 1880s, this competition intensified again after 1907, the year Roosevelt's Great White Fleet set sail, as each empire raced to build the largest navy and most advanced weaponry the world had ever seen. Germany, Austria-Hungary, and Italy would promise one another military support in the event of an attack, and Britain would soon ally with France and Russia. Both alliances would rush to ink military treaties with Europe's smaller, independent nations. Where escalating tensions would lead—and where the United States would fit in this precarious balance of power—was far from obvious. In the summer of 1914, the answer to the first question would become shockingly clear.

STUDY TERMS

Student Volunteer Movement for Foreign Missions (p. 567)
humanitarian crisis (p. 569)
expansionist (p. 574)
jingoes (p. 575)
yellow journalism (p. 575)
Teller Amendment (p. 576)
Spanish-American War (p. 576)
Rough Riders (p. 578)
Treaty of Paris (p. 580)
white man's burden (p. 581)
Platt Amendment (p. 583)
Jones Act (p. 585)
Insular Cases (p. 586)
spheres of influence (p. 586)
Open Door (p. 586)
Anglo-American cooperation (p. 586)
Treaty of Portsmouth (p. 587)
Gentlemen's Agreement (p. 587)
Roosevelt Corollary (p. 589)
dollar diplomacy (p. 589)
American Expeditionary Force (p. 591)

TIMELINE

1884 European empires accelerate conquest and colonization of Africa

1886 Student Volunteer Movement for Foreign Missions founded

1887 United States builds naval coaling station at Pearl Harbor, Hawaii

1890 Alfred T. Mahan publishes *The Influence of Sea Power Upon History*

1891–1892 Americans send wheat following the Russian harvest failure

1895 National Association of Manufacturers founded

1895–1896 Congress condemns Ottoman Empire for allowing Armenian massacres

1898 USS *Maine* explodes in Havana harbor

Filipino, Cuban, and U.S. forces defeat Spain in Spanish-American War

Hawaii is annexed

United States buys Philippines from Spain for $20 million

U.S. occupation of Philippines encounters opposition at home and in the Philippines

American anti-colonialists decry U.S. foreign policy

1899 United States insists on Open Door for trade and investment in China

Reverend William Henry Sheppard publicizes atrocities in the Congo

1900 Chinese nationalists rebel against foreign presence (Boxer Rebellion)

1900 President William McKinley reelected on victory against Spain

1901 Philippine-American War escalates, leading Theodore Roosevelt to prepare Philippines for independence

Revived Monroe Doctrine authorizes military action in Latin America and the Caribbean

1901–1904 Supreme Court rules in the *Insular Cases* that the Constitution does not automatically extend to U.S. possessions

1904 United States begins work on Panama Canal

1905 Japan wins Russo-Japanese War

Roosevelt brokers Treaty of Portsmouth (between Russia and Japan)

U.S. railroad companies gain access to Manchuria

Mark Twain blasts imperialism in his biting satire *King Leopold's Soliloquy*

1907 Japan consents to halt Japanese workers' immigration into United States under "Gentlemen's Agreement"

1903–1906 Roosevelt and Congress criticize anti-Semitic pogroms in Russia

1909 President William H. Taft pursues dollar diplomacy

1910 Americans own 50 percent of Mexican land

1911 U.S. Marines occupy the Dominican Republic

Mexican nationalists call for repatriation of land and resources

1912 U.S. Marines occupy Cuba

Mexican civil war breaks out

1914 American Expeditionary Force invades Mexico

Panama Canal opens

FURTHER READING

Additional suggested readings are available on the Online Learning Center at www.mhhe.com/becomingamerica1e.

Howard K. Beale, *Theodore Roosevelt and the Rise of America to World Power* (1956), explores Roosevelt's revival of the Monroe Doctrine and his promotion of U.S. power elsewhere in the world.

Gail Bederman, *Manliness and Civilization: A Cultural History of Gender and Race in the United States, 1880–1917* (1995), shows how and why elite Americans of the late nineteenth and early twentieth centuries paradoxically admired "primitive" men of color while proclaiming the superiority of "civilized" white men.

Vincent J. Cirillo, *Bullets and Bacilli: The Spanish-American War and Military Medicine* (2004), explains how the war ultimately advanced tropical medicine, surgery, and sanitation.

Warren I. Cohen, *America's Response to China: A History of Sino-American Relations* (2000), argues that China and the United States developed a mutually beneficial relationship in the late nineteenth and early twentieth centuries.

Kristin L. Hoganson, *Fighting for American Manhood: How Gender Politics Provoked the Spanish-American and Philippine-American Wars* (1998), assesses late-nineteenth-century conceptions of gender and their impact on the decision to go to war.

Edward S. Kaplan, *U.S. Imperialism in Latin America* (1997), traces William Jennings Bryan's attitudes toward Latin America before, during, and after his tenure as secretary of state.

Paul A. Kramer, *The Blood of Government: Race, Empire, the United States, and the Philippines* (2006), analyzes the emergence of new racial ideologies during the Philippine-American War and explains how empire building subsequently transformed ideas of race and nation.

Walter LaFeber, *The New Empire: An Interpretation of American Expansion, 1860–1898* (1998), explores the economic, ideological, and geopolitical motivations behind U.S. foreign policy.

Resil B. Mojares, *The War Against the Americans: Resistance and Collaboration in Cebu, 1899–1906* (1999), describes the Philippine-American War from the perspective of the Philippines' Cebu people.

Emily Rosenberg, *Financial Missionaries to the World* (1999), argues that the United States used dollar diplomacy—private bank loans and financial advice—to win influence over foreign governments.

Ian Tyrrell, *Reforming the World: The Creation of America's Moral Empire* (2010), traces the growth of American reform and missionary networks during the late nineteenth century and reformers' subsequent impact on U.S. foreign policy.

Richard P. Tucker, *Insatiable Appetite: The United States and the Ecological Degradation of the Tropical World* (2000), explores the ecological impact of U.S. expansion in the tropics and the ways in which investors and landowners sought to legitimate their actions.

22

INSIDE ▶

THE BIG PICTURE

Mobilization for World War I transformed everything from the food Americans ate and the movies they watched to race relations, women's rights, and the relationship between government and business. Although the United States emerged as the world's leading economic and military power, President Woodrow Wilson was unable to turn progressives' dream of American global leadership into a reality.

COLORED MAN IS NO SLACKER

Hellfighters. Four hundred thousand African American men served in World War I—and, following victory, the survivors returned home to claim the full rights of citizenship.

WAR & PEACE

For ten months in 1915, San Francisco was the site of a celebration of American and global progress. Some nineteen million visitors to the city's Panama-Pacific International Exposition wandered up the "Avenue of Progress," where exhibits traced humankind's evolution from lower primates in their jungle habitat to worker-citizens in a dynamic industrial world. Familiar Progressive Era themes about the dangers of cheap amusements and the promise of science, technology, and international cooperation suffused the exhibition palaces. A colorful pageant of nations reenacted the world's advance from the old "Spirit of War" to the "Spirit of Peace."

Yet something was amiss. Official exhibitors from the British, German, and Russian empires, which had become embroiled in armed conflict the year before, failed to show. Spectators were both thrilled and perplexed by the exposition's incongruous finale, in which a full-scale battleship anchored in San Francisco Bay was blown up in honor of the new "Age of Peace." The disconnect between the official optimism of the exhibition and the grisly reality of the war raging abroad was reinforced daily by newspaper headlines describing the carnage on Europe's numerous battlegrounds.

The outbreak of the war in 1914 horrified most Americans. The vast majority of citizens, including President Woodrow Wilson, initially wanted nothing to do with it. But as the hostilities escalated, a small but vocal coalition of conservatives and internationally aware progressives made the case for entering the "Great War." The president eventually agreed, calculating that U.S. involvement would generate an unprecedented opportunity to end European colonialism and reshape the global order along cooperative, progressive lines. In 1917, for the first time since the Civil War, the federal government mobilized the great mass of citizens, creating a raft of agencies to coordinate the economy, publicize the war effort, control communication networks, and raise an army of almost five million troops. As U.S. soldiers deployed to France, the balance of military power tipped in the Allies' favor.

KEY QUESTIONS

- What were the causes of World War I, and how did Americans respond to the outbreak of hostilities?
- Why did the United States enter the war?
- What impact did U.S. participation have on the nation's world standing?
- What role did cinema, the press, and other culture industries play in the mobilization effort?
- How did U.S. servicemen and women, including African Americans and other minorities, experience the war and its aftermath?
- Why did progressive reform collapse once peace returned?

While the war went relatively well for the United States and President Wilson, the transition to peace fared miserably. Wilson's plans for a new global order met with stiff opposition both at home and abroad. As U.S. war industries ground to a halt and millions of returning servicemen competed for a shrinking pool of jobs, the nation entered a violent period of racial and industrial unrest. The Wilson administration appeared to be losing control on both the international and the domestic fronts. In 1920, the Department of Justice erroneously concluded that the U.S. government was in imminent danger of being overthrown, and undertook the single biggest mass arrest of critics, radicals, and other dissenters in American history. These tumultuous events brought the Progressive Era to an abrupt and unexpected end.

Planned at a time of widespread optimism about humanity's capacity for peace and progress, the opening of the Panama-Pacific International Exposition in 1915 in fact coincided with the deadliest war the world had ever seen.

CLASH OF EMPIRES

The European empires' scramble for territory, resources, and prestige, under way since the 1880s (see Chapter 21), intensified after 1900 as each one raced to build large navies and advanced weaponry. The imperial powers formed two competing alliances whose members promised one another military support in the event of an attack. Both alliances also rushed to sign military treaties with Europe's smaller, independent nations—and grew increasingly anxious that the loss of even one such country to the other side would weaken them. Tensions eventually focused on the Balkans, where the Austro-Hungarian and Russian empires vied for dominance. When nationalist Serbs, who were allied with Russia, assassinated the heir to the Austro-Hungarian monarch in the Balkan city of Sarajevo in June 1914, a chain reaction in just a few weeks drew all of Europe's great empires into what would later be known as World War I. Americans were appalled that modern civilizations would turn their weapons against one another.

ARMS, ALLIANCES, AND ANXIETY

By the 1900s, Europe's imperial rivals (now joined by a rapidly expanding Japan) were engaged in a full-blown arms race. France and Germany almost doubled the size of their standing armies, and all the contenders stockpiled the lethal new weapons that the industrial revolution had made possible. These machine guns, howitzers (light mortars that could fire high enough to surmount rivers, buildings, and other obstacles in the line of fire), and powerful big-gun battleships known as dreadnoughts were capable of unleashing death on an unprecedented scale and at record-breaking speed.

Intense military, economic, and territorial rivalry put pressure on the empires to form alliances that they hoped would stabilize Europe by acting as a deterrent to war. By 1914, the British had secretly aligned with France and Russia (the Triple Entente), promising military support in the event of an attack. Germany and Austria-Hungary, which had joined forces in the 1870s, added Italy to their bloc, now called the Triple Alliance. Because individual members of the Triple Alliance and the Triple Entente had also pledged to protect most of Europe's smaller, independent nations, almost the entire continent was absorbed into this system—and an attack on one small nation would likely draw all the empires into conflict.

For a time, the alliance and the entente were equally strong, and this **balance of power** appeared to make war unlikely. Then, in the 1910s, as the arms buildup intensified and the ever-expanding network of alliances absorbed the remaining smaller nations, the great powers began to worry that the collapse or defection of just one smaller nation would weaken the entire bloc and render it vulnerable to attack. Consequently, in early 1914, military leaders secretly began drawing up battle plans while their governments accelerated arms-building programs. This activity further raised tensions between the blocs' leaders, who became increasingly anxious that their rivals might soon attack.

Although relations between the two sides were growing more volatile, the suggestion that Europe's empires would ever deploy their deadly weapons against each other seemed absurd to most Americans and Europeans in early 1914. Why would "white civilization," as President Woodrow Wilson put it, turn against itself? The fact that Europe had seen war as recently as 1870 (when Prussia invaded France) and that millions of people had experienced the Civil War firsthand did not shake most Americans' faith that the modern world had transcended mass violence and ascended to a more enlightened order. The hardening of segregationist culture, which had made race the key dividing line in U.S. society by the 1910s, also blinded most Americans to the possibility that people of the "same race" might make war on each other. However, the depth of the European rivalries did not escape the attention of Wilson's envoy to Europe, who warned in early 1914 that "militarism has run stark mad" and "there is some day to be an awful cataclysm."

BETWEEN EMPIRES: CRISIS IN THE BALKANS

The most unstable region of Europe in these years was the Balkans. The Balkan peninsula was home to Romanians, Serbs, Bulgarians, and other peoples who had long been subjects of either the Austro-Hungarian Empire or the centuries-old power known as the Ottoman Empire, based in what is now Turkey (see Map 22.1). Known to Americans and western Europeans alike as the "sick man of Europe," the Ottoman Empire had steadily weakened and contracted during the nineteenth and early twentieth centuries, unable to compete with the industrial and military might of the other great powers. As the Ottomans gradually lost control of their Balkan territories, the Russian and Austro-Hungarian empires vied for influence, eager to absorb the region.

The Balkan peoples had different aspirations. As in Mexico, China, and other parts of the world subject to the interventionism of larger powers (see Chapter 21), a number of popular nationalist movements had emerged in the region. Romanian, Serbian, and other nationalist movements demanded unification of their respective ethnic groups and national independence, or **self-determination.** Balkan nationalists were particularly threatening to Austria-Hungary, whose leaders feared that the cry for self-determination would spread to their own empire and possibly spark nationalist rebellion among Poles, Czechs, and other Austro-Hungarian subjects. Eager to capitalize on the Ottomans' crumbling empire and nip Balkan nationalism in the bud, Austria-Hungary expanded into the Balkans in 1909 by annexing Bosnia, a small province with a sizable Serbian population.

Annexation only further inflamed the nationalist passions of independent Serbia, whose leaders demanded that Bosnia be liberated and allowed to unite with all southern Slavs to form an independent Serbian state. The Serbians' call fell on deaf ears, however. Their frustrations boiling over, members of a radical Serbian militia named Unity or Death took matters into their own hands on June 1914 and gunned down Austria's heir to the throne, Archduke Franz Ferdinand, and his wife on the streets of Sarajevo, Bosnia.

BATTLE FOR EUROPE

Austria-Hungary immediately demanded that the Serbian government crack down on radical nationalists and issued a stringent ten-point ultimatum in late July. The Serbs, realizing that failure to meet these demands could mean war, hastily complied with all except one of them. But Austria-Hungary had in fact already resolved to invade Serbia—despite warnings by Russia's foreign minister that such an action would "[set] fire to Europe."

On the pretext of Serbia's noncompliance with the ultimatum, Austria-Hungary declared war on Serbia on July 28. In response, Russia mobilized troops, and Germany followed four days later, preemptively declaring war on Russia and Russia's ally, France. The chain reaction accelerated when Germany invaded Belgium a few days later, in preparation for

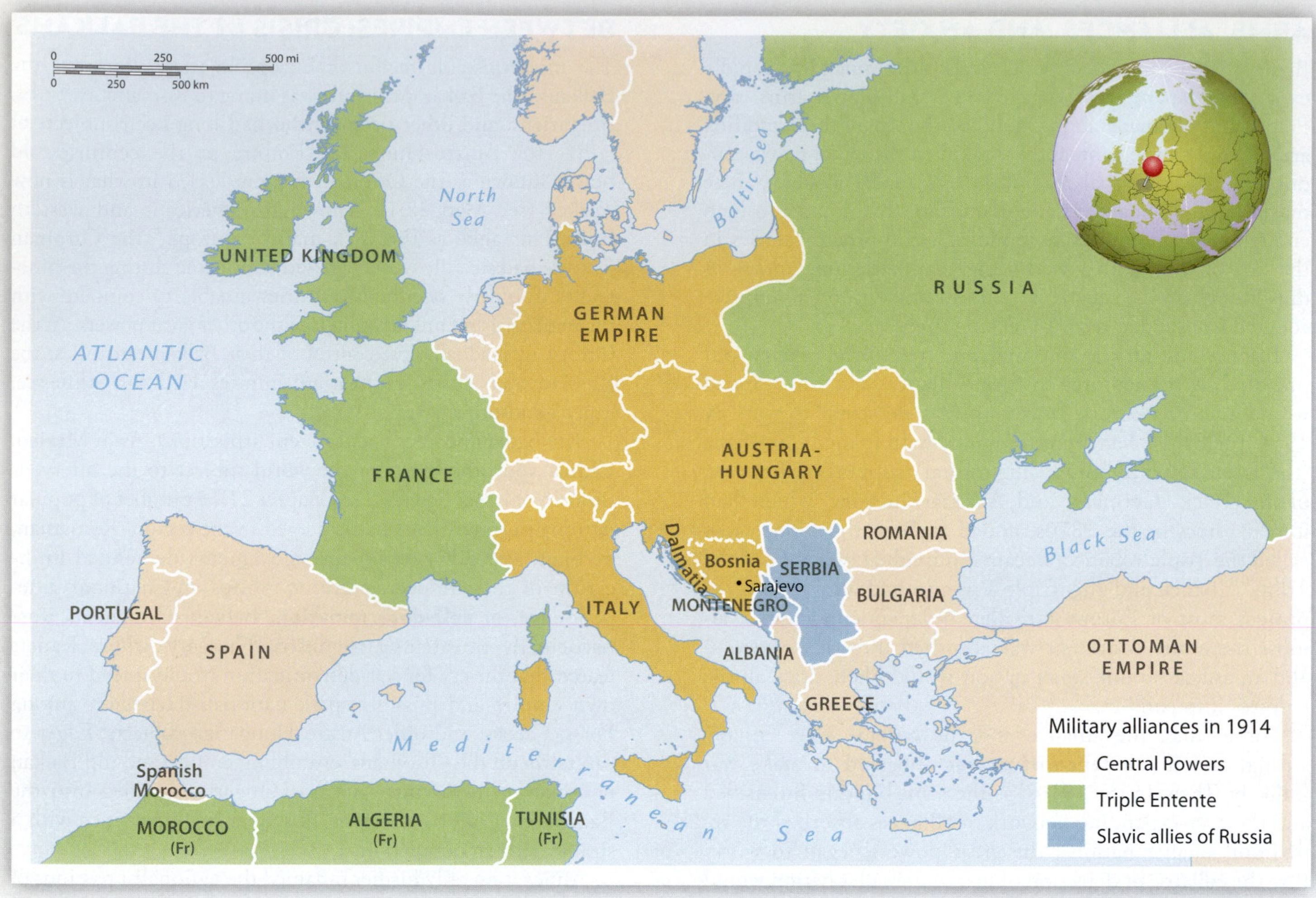

Map 22.1 The Road to World War I. In the context of Europe's system of military alliances, localized conflict over the small territory of Bosnia triggered a clash of empires.

an assault on France, leading Great Britain to declare war on the invaders. In seven short days, Europe's empires had been sucked into war by the very alliance system that was supposed to avert violence.

Throughout Europe, people poured into streets and town squares in joyous celebration. Relieved that the mounting tension between the blocs had broken, and anticipating that the hostilities would be short and relatively bloodless, the vast majority welcomed war. Many also believed that the war would reunite their peoples behind a common purpose after several years of wrenching industrial strikes and political divisions. Young men eagerly enlisted, suffragists called for women to support the war, and socialists, progressives, and conservatives forgot their differences. "This war is war to protect justice and civilization," declared one Russian socialist, echoing the thoughts of millions of Europeans. "It is a *war against war*," he insisted, and it would bring "disarmament and universal peace."

The Germans' battle plan was to take France before the Russians had a chance to attack from the east. The Germans moved quickly and effectively through Belgium in August, reaching the outskirts of Paris in just four weeks. But after Belgium's initial collapse, a resistance movement sprang to life, sabotaging German supply lines and generally slowing the advance on Paris. The first few detachments of British troops reinforced the French army, which used every available vehicle—from Parisian taxicabs to bicycles—to deliver soldiers to the Western Front. As the Belgian resistance and French and British armies slowed Germany's advance, Russian troops attacked Germany from the east, forcing the Germans to transfer over one hundred thousand troops from the Western to the Eastern Front. Weakened in the west, Germany lost fifty miles or more of French territory by December. In the east, however, Germany and Austria-Hungary hammered the Russians, at the cost of hundreds of thousands of lives, and drove deep into Russia. Meanwhile in the Pacific, Japan joined forces with Britain and forcibly took possession of German Samoa and parts of German-held China.

By early 1915, the war that people thought would be over by Christmas 1914 showed no signs of abating. In fact, the war was showing every sign that it would be the bloodiest military conflict the world had ever seen. Both the Central Powers (as Germany, Austria-Hungary, the Ottoman Empire, and Bulgaria became known) and the Allied Powers (Britain, France, Russia, Japan, and Italy—which had pragmatically switched sides) had dug in for the winter, constructing a long line of parallel trenches that acted as shelters along the fronts. Generals sent men out of the trenches in continuous waves of attack aimed at pushing the enemy back just a few hundred feet at a time. Both sides mixed the firepower of modern weaponry with old-fashioned arms and strategy to particularly lethal effect. Men armed with old technology such as bayonets, sabers, and single-shot rifles ran directly at the enemy's machine guns and rapid-fire artillery.

About 1.5 million men died in the first three months of this **trench warfare** on the Western Front alone—more than twice the number that had perished in the entire American Civil War. Millions more would die the following year as Europe's empires unleashed tanks and aerial and chemical warfare on the enemy for the first time in history. "Every foot of ground contested," one German soldier reported of the nightmarish scene he encountered every time his regiment advanced on the Western Front, "everywhere bodies—rows of them! All the trees shot to pieces; the whole ground churned up a yard deep by the heaviest shells; dead animals; houses and churches utterly destroyed . . . [a] gigantic burial ground and the reek of corpses." Life in the trenches was hardly easier, particularly as the winter brought driving snow and rain. The shelters filled up with mud, disease was rife, and men often suffered a mental breakdown over the carnage they had witnessed. Some literally shot themselves in the foot so as to be sent to the hospital and avoid being ordered back into battle.

As staggering as they were, battlefield mortality rates were not as high as they might have been. Against orders, many battalions on both sides observed an unspoken rule that battle was to be avoided if possible. "Don't fire at us," as one experienced soldier explained the arrangement to a newly enlisted man, "and we'll not fire at you." Soldiers on both sides tacitly agreed to hold fire while the enemy was eating meals, and occasionally combatants would even play soccer together, between trenches. The two sides frequently buried their dead in one common grave.

THE VIEW FROM AMERICA

Americans were mostly united in their shock and disgust at the turn of events in Europe. They were also relieved that a large body of water lay between themselves and the battlefields. "I thank Heaven for many things," wrote the U.S. ambassador to Britain, "first, the Atlantic Ocean." Addressing Americans on August 4, 1914, President Wilson called on the nation to remain neutral and "impartial in thought as well as action."

Drawn as they were from multiple ethnic, religious, and political backgrounds, Americans were divided in their sympathies for the antagonists. Most native-born Protestants were overwhelmingly sympathetic to Britain and its allies France and Russia. Many Americans, regardless of ethnicity, also considered Britain the "mother" of liberty and democracy and a natural U.S. ally. The tens of thousands of Serbs, Croats, and Slovaks who had settled in midwestern cities such as Milwaukee and Chicago opposed Austria-Hungary, whereas Russian Jews and exiled socialists hoped that the war might finally topple the tsarist regime in Russia that had long persecuted them. Unsurprisingly, German Americans (who numbered about 8.25 million, or 11 percent of the U.S. population) mostly sympathized with Germany and Austria-Hungary, and they mobilized to keep the United States out of a war that it would likely fight on the side of Britain. The nation's 4.5 million Irish Americans were also strongly critical of Ireland's British overlords. Regardless of Americans' sympathies, however, the great majority of people in the United States viewed the war as Europe's problem and supported U.S. neutrality.

Chemical Weapons. Exposure to the most commonly used chemical agent during the war—mustard gas—blinded the victim and caused the skin to bubble and blister painfully, often through clothes and usually twenty-four hours after exposure. Inhaled in concentrated form, frequently when soldiers were sleeping, it burned the troops' lungs, leading to long periods of convalescence and high cancer rates. Graphic images were strictly censored, but photographs occasionally filtered through.

BIRTH OF THE PEACE MOVEMENT

Progressives watched in dismay as their European networks of reformers, progressive universities, and philanthropic societies abandoned international cooperation in favor of narrow national self-interest. In 1914–1915, American progressives generally agreed that the war was a limited, regional conflict confined to Europe and that neither U.S. interests nor progressive principles of social justice would be well served by getting involved. They also worried that American involvement would derail important reform initiatives at home, such as national child labor reform.

Progressive women were particularly vocal in their opposition, and some even attempted to stop the war. New York's suffragists staged a silent parade for peace in August 1914, drawing a diverse array of conservative, progressive, radical, African American, white, Chinese, immigrant, and native-born women. Women had a special stake in the largely male domain of war, the suffragists argued, due to their essential role as mothers and homemakers. "I Didn't Raise My Boy to Be a Soldier" went the first antiwar song to be commercially recorded. "I brought him up to be my pride and joy."

Eager to build a peace movement, suffragist leaders called on respected reformer Jane Addams to help organize a peace convention, which was held in Washington, D.C., in January 1915 and attended by over three thousand women. Elected leader of the newly formed Women's Peace Party, Addams assembled a delegation to attend an international women's conference in The Hague and to demand peace, multilateral disarmament, and the right of all nations to self-determination. Although the initiative did not alter the war's course, it laid the foundation of the first American peace movement, for which Addams would become the first woman to receive the Nobel Peace Prize, in 1931.

THE CASE FOR PREPAREDNESS

Swimming against the American mainstream in 1916, Theodore Roosevelt and many other Republicans continued to be hawkish champions of a U.S. military buildup. They made the case for national **preparedness**—the position that the United States should build its armed forces in preparation for joining the fight on the side of Britain. The view of many Americans that war was a barbaric relic of premodern times was nothing but "flabby pacifism," Roosevelt argued, and the progressive idea that nations should act multilaterally, in cooperation with one another, was dangerously unrealistic. Although once the self-anointed champion of progressivism, Roosevelt had long since lost that title to Woodrow Wilson (in the 1912 election). He now railed against Wilson, gathering around himself a cohort of self-identified conservatives whose defining belief was that all nations pursued—and *should* pursue—their own national interest or else risk decline into feeble unmanliness and domination by another power. In the present case, Roosevelt argued, American self-interest dictated preparation for—and eventual entry into—the war.

Roosevelt's **conservative nationalism** appealed to military leaders, the financial sector (which had bankrolled and profited from the Spanish-American War), and Republicans of the older generation. The majority of Americans, however, preferred neutrality. Consequently, Roosevelt and other conservatives took the case for preparedness directly to consumers, publicizing it through songs, the press, and movies. Filmmakers evoked the specter of marauding German troops (pejoratively called "the Hun") terrorizing the United States and its women and exposed the folly of an unprepared military. One film, *The Battle Cry of Peace* (1915), depicted the imaginary destruction of New York City and its people by an unnamed navy and an army of fanatical invaders whose spiked helmets suggested German origin. In *The Fall of a Nation* (1916), a character who looks suspiciously like the pacifist secretary of state, William Jennings Bryan, persuades Americans that reason and generosity are all that are needed to defeat imperial aggression—only to be proven drastically wrong. Pacifist filmmakers responded with antiwar movies such as *Civilization* (1916), in which a submarine commander intent on torpedoing a civilian ocean liner meets Jesus and devotes his life to peacemaking instead. Ironically, this and other antiwar films identified the war and its brutality with "the Hun," thereby inadvertently reinforcing anti-German sentiment.

Roosevelt's conservative nationalism soon attracted more adherents, largely among the growing and diverse communities of men and women who saw themselves as defenders of what they believed were "true" American values. Conservative women's organizations such as the United Daughters of the Confederacy (a patriotic hereditary society) abandoned their previous opposition to the war and now argued that preparedness was the best way to protect American homes. The Daughters of the American Revolution joined other conservative patriotic societies such as the American Defense Society to call upon the United States to begin arming. Most mass circulation newspapers entered on the side of conservatives, carrying lurid stories of German atrocities and remaining conspicuously silent on the carnage inflicted by Britain and its allies. One important exception was the William Randolph Hearst news corporation, whose owner's vehement disapproval of the British Empire led him to throw his weight behind Wilson and those calling for neutrality.

THE ROAD TO WAR

Despite the growing conservative movement and widespread anti-German feeling, most Americans still supported neutrality in 1916 and believed that the war was of little consequence to them. In fact, however, the war significantly affected the U.S. economy, national security, and the country's standing in the world. Wilson began rethinking his policy of neutrality in 1916, and progressives—who retained considerable political power—grew divided on the question. Many dropped their former opposition to the war after they observed the tremendous expansion of government power that had occurred throughout Europe as a result of war mobilization. Wilson and other progressives also now saw the war as a prime vehicle for a crusade to bring American-style democracy to a troubled world.

THE COMPLEXITIES OF NEUTRALITY

As 1916 dawned, progressives were largely united and in a relatively strong position in national politics. Congress enacted a series of laws that fulfilled key progressive aims, including the Revenue Act (1916), which raised the income tax rate for most people to 2 percent and imposed a 15-percent inheritance tax on the very wealthy (those who earned over $2 million, or $40 million today). The Adamson Act (1916) guaranteed railroad workers an eight-hour day—something for which workers in many industries had been striving since the 1870s. The Keating-Owen Act (1916) abolished child labor (at least until 1918, when the Supreme Court declared the law an unconstitutional interference with states' right to regulate their own internal commerce). Wilson also repeatedly affirmed the neutrality that most progressives and a distinct majority of Americans favored.

As the war escalated, however, the United States' strong cultural, economic, and diplomatic ties to Britain undercut Wilson's official policy of neutrality. Within months of the outbreak of hostilities, the war lifted the flagging U.S. economy out of severe industrial recession and drove unemployment down to historic lows. The vast majority of American arms, food, and consumer goods found their way to Britain and France, thanks in large part to the British navy's blockade of the Atlantic. Exports to the Allies quadrupled between 1914 and 1916, while exports to an increasingly hungry German populace dropped from $354 million a year to barely $2 million. Headed by Herbert Hoover, a major food relief operation also got under way in late 1914 for Britain's starving ally, Belgium, in the wake of Germany's devastating attack. Wilson approved massive loans (a total of $2.3 billion, or $48 billion today) for the Allies, but the Germans received just over a tenth of that amount. From the German perspective, it appeared that the United States had implicitly aligned with the Allies from the start.

Join the Navy! Proponents of preparedness urged American men to enlist in the armed forces in the wake of the *Lusitania* tragedy. This poster was sponsored by a chapter of the pro-militarization Navy League and a bank.

Britain's and Germany's naval strategies also affected the United States. Almost immediately after war broke out, Britain's Royal Navy blockaded Germany in an effort to cut off its trade networks and starve it of imported food, war materiel, and consumer goods. Desperate to break the embargo but lacking the firepower of the British dreadnoughts, the German navy launched *unterseeboot* (U-boat, or submarine) attacks on British commercial ships and naval boats. Over two hundred American oceangoing passengers died between 1914 and 1917, the victims of unannounced German U-boat attacks. Among them were 128 Americans who lost their lives when a U-boat opened fire on the British passenger liner *Lusitania* in May 1915, killing 1,198 passengers. Theodore Roosevelt and fellow conservative nationalists immediately called for war, but Wilson and most Americans remained committed to neutrality.

Wilson sharply rebuked the German government and demanded (and received) an apology, but he made no threat of action. At the same time, however, he ignored the advice of Secretary of State Bryan to reassure the Germans privately that he expected a peaceful resolution of the incident. Meanwhile, Wilson began to support preparedness. He announced a navy-building plan, designed to put the United States on par with the world's largest fleet, Britain's Royal Navy, by 1920, and called for the expansion of the army. When Bryan resigned in protest, Wilson replaced him with State Department attorney Robert Lansing, who believed that U.S. entry into the war on Britain's side was only a matter of time.

After more Americans died or were seriously injured in U-boat attacks, Wilson threatened to break off diplomatic ties with Berlin—a response the Germans mistakenly interpreted as an indirect threat to go to war. Although the Germans estimated that U.S. involvement would pose only a minor setback (because they believed it would take the United States a long time to raise and mobilize forces), they were eager to avoid even minor naval skirmishes. Consequently, the German High Command ordered U-boats to cease surprise attacks on ocean liners and other merchant vessels.

Despite his strides toward preparedness in 1916, Wilson remained unconvinced that the United States should enter the war. He was certain, however, that

Promising Peace. Woodrow Wilson successfully ran in the 1916 presidential election on the slogan "He kept us out of war." Although it referred originally to the Mexican War, many Americans misremembered it as a pledge to keep the United States out of the Great War.

he could not win the election of 1916 on a preparedness platform. Instead, he walked a line between the pacifism of most voters and the increasing popularity of preparedness. "There is such a thing as a man being too proud to fight," Wilson reassured Americans in an effort to appear both strong and resolutely opposed to war. "There is such a thing as a nation being so right that it does not need to convince others by force that it is right." The election was one of the closest in presidential history, with Wilson defeating Republican Charles Evan Hughes by only twenty-three electoral votes and under six hundred thousand popular votes (see Map 22.2). Women voters, who were especially likely to be pacifist, cast the decisive ballots, with ten out of the twelve states that had granted women voting rights supporting Wilson.

PROGRESSIVE CRUSADERS

After two years, the conflict abroad had turned deadlier than any war the world had ever seen. As its effects radiated well beyond Europe, to both the United States and the great powers' colonies, people began referring to it as the Great War (it earned the title "World War I" only after World War II). To the extent that the United States had commercial and other interests in Asia and Africa, the war's expansion had important consequences for American foreign policy. Conservatives and progressives alike agreed that the United States should have a say in any postwar settlement over the fate of those regions and the empires that had started the war.

A growing faction of progressives began viewing the war as an opportunity to turn the federal government into a powerful engine for national reform. They saw that Germany, Britain, France, and Austria-Hungary had rapidly built good-quality workers' housing, enacted public health care, coordinated the wartime economy, and mediated labor disputes in the effort to strengthen their populations' capacity for war. U.S. entry into the war, many argued, presented an unprecedented opportunity to advance progressive causes. Above all, war mobilization would put the public's well-being ahead of the interests of private individuals and classes.

The suggestion that progressives could both improve on European wartime reforms and demonstrate the superiority of the American democratic model was also deeply appealing. The missionary zeal that had suffused progressivism since the 1890s disposed many observers to believe that the United States had a special redemptive role in the war. President Wilson, who referred to himself as a "missionary diplomat," was among these **progressive idealists** who envisioned a heroic United States bringing sanity to Europe, ending the slaughter, and redeeming the world. In early 1917, he attempted to mediate between the combatants, to whom he presented a plan for a new, postwar system of international relations based on cooperation. Calling for a "peace without victory," Wilson proposed that all nations were equal and should respect the others' right to exist. The missionary diplomat met only with derision and silence, however. "Peace without victory," writer Anatole France sneered, "is bread without yeast, love without quarrels, a camel without hump." Neither side would budge, and in February the Germans resumed unrestricted submarine warfare against American as well as British vessels.

The failure of U.S. mediation fractured the progressive consensus at home, convincing Wilson and his fellow idealists that neutrality had failed. Wilson now agreed with conservative nationalists and a growing number of progressives that the Germans were a threat to American trade with Europe and possibly posed a danger in the Western Hemisphere as well. Wilson's turn away from neutrality led the prominent pacifist Emma Goldman to quip that she saw no difference between Roosevelt, "the born bully who carries a club," and Wilson, "the history professor who uses the smooth polished mask."

The United States withdrew its diplomats from Germany in early February 1917 in protest of the U-boat warfare, and goods bound for the Allies piled up on American wharves as crossing the Atlantic became too risky. Two weeks later, the British showed U.S. officials a telegram they had intercepted from German foreign minister Arthur Zimmermann and decoded. The Zimmermann Telegram proposed that Mexico and Germany join forces if the United States entered the war, and, in return Germany would help restore to Mexico all territory lost in the Mexican-American War of 1848 (including Texas,

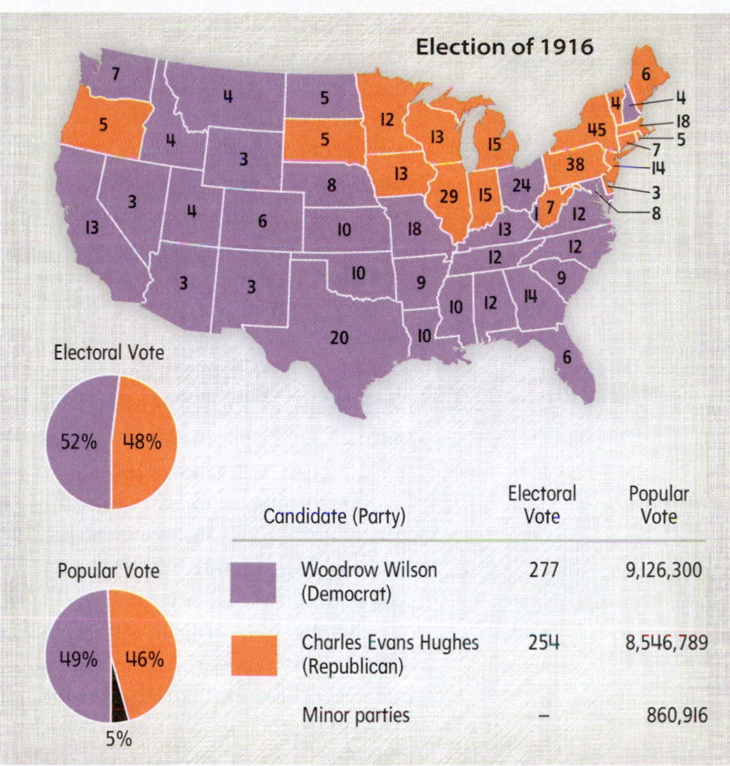

Election of 1916
Electoral Vote
52%
48%
Popular Vote
49%
46%
5%
Candidate (Party)
Electoral Vote
Popular Vote
Woodrow Wilson (Democrat) 277 9,126,300
Charles Evans Hughes (Republican) 254 8,546,789
Minor parties – 860,916

Map 22.2 Election of 1916.

Arizona, New Mexico, and California). Mexico never responded, but Wilson was enraged by the leaked communiqué. He asked Congress for permission to arm U.S. merchant ships so that they could defend themselves, and released the telegram to the press in an effort to firm up popular support for the measure. Although antiwar senators Robert La Follette and George Norris filibustered the request, Wilson ordered the ships armed.

Wilson's release of the telegram inflamed popular opinion in favor of war against Germany. Subsequent events sealed the nation's fate. The Germans sank over ten U.S. ships in the following weeks, destroying three in one seventy-two-hour period alone. On April 2, Wilson addressed Congress and requested a declaration of war against Germany. Congress complied, although fifty representatives, including Jeanette Rankin—the first woman ever elected to Congress—voted against going to war. "I felt the first time the first woman had a chance to say no to war," Rankin later recalled, "she should say it."

In his speech, Wilson framed the country's entry as an imperative crusade—a "sacred democratic mission"—to halt imperialism and militarism and bring freedom and security to the world. The American people, he exclaimed, must wage a fight for "a universal dominion of right, by such a concert of free peoples as shall bring peace and safety to all nations and at last make the world itself free." Wilson probably genuinely believed that it was the United States' holy mission "not to serve ourselves," as he once put it, "but to serve mankind" and make the world "safe for democracy." At the same time, he was keenly aware that despite the Zimmermann outrage and the attacks on commercial ships, many millions of Americans still did not support war. Persuading them of the righteousness of that decision would become one of the defining characteristics of Wilson's administration—and of the entire war effort.

WARTIME GOVERNMENT

By the summer of 1917, American soldiers were sorely needed in France, where the war had bogged down in the mud-filled trenches and desolate battlefields. The war had become an endurance race in which the victor was certain to be the nation (or bloc) that could sustain production of the vast quantities of food and materiel that were needed on the battlefronts and in Europe's towns and cities. The U.S. role would be both military and economic, therefore, and would require the government to mobilize the nation's resources fully. President Wilson convened a series of powerful committees, answerable directly to his cabinet. Thousands of progressive experts went to work for new and existing federal agencies, raising and training an army, coordinating industry and agriculture, cranking out war propaganda, and mobilizing women as factory workers and household budgeters.

THE COLLECTIVIST STATE

The U.S. government adapted Britain's policy of **war collectivism** by which the government had taken direct control of the economy for the purpose of optimizing the war effort. Because the British government's policies of rationing and speeding up production had undermined popular support for the war and pitted employers against workers, the Wilson administration avoided outright rationing and invited union leaders and captains of industry to work together to help direct the economy. Government boards, made up of labor leaders, industrialists, and various experts, coordinated every aspect of the economy, from fuel consumption, industrial output, food production, and railroads to garbage disposal, household management, and oversight of prisons (whose inmates voluntarily donated millions of gallons of blood for Allied soldiers injured in battle). Even time was regulated, with the adoption in 1918 of daylight saving, which extended the hours of natural light and conserved the energy that would have otherwise been used to light the workplace. Standard time zones also became federal law, although most states had adopted the system in the 1870s.

Progressive experts and advocates entered government service in droves to head new agencies and serve as foot soldiers in the emerging bureaucracies. The War Industries Board (WIB, established in July 1917) played the central role in coordinating the war economy and fulfilling the needs of the Allies and U.S. military. Directed by progressive Democrat and financier Bernard Baruch, the WIB established War Service Committees

Sow the seeds of Victory!
plant & raise your own vegetables
WRITE TO THE NATIONAL WAR GARDEN COMMISSION ~ WASHINGTON, D.C. for free books on gardening, canning & drying.
JAMES MONTGOMERY FLAGG
"Every Garden a Munition Plant"
Charles Lathrop Pack, President

Reorganizing the Food System. The Food Administration implored housewives to "sow the seeds of victory" by planting their own vegetable patches and conserving the nation's food supply. Millions complied, with the unexpected result that American consumption of fresh fruit and vegetables rose during the war years.

beginning in 1918 to make supply agreements with each of five hundred industries, from munitions to face cream. The Price Fixing Committee persuaded companies to sell their wares at an agreed-on price so that there would be no price wars or gouging (overcharging). The government paid the companies on a favorable cost-plus basis, which meant that contractors pocketed a significant profit. Although the WIB had no formal authority to punish uncooperative companies, its directors extracted cooperation by threatening to expose noncompliant industries as unpatriotic and withholding lucrative government contracts.

For the first time in American history, the government helped set wages for industrial workers. The National War Labor Board (NWLB, 1918) got workers and business leaders to negotiate mutually agreeable conditions and wages. The board mediated over 1,200 disputes and encouraged equal wages for women; it also made strikes illegal in return for allowing workers to unionize. Minimum wages and working conditions for labor in every important war industry were set, and the eight-hour day became standard, as did overtime pay (at a rate of time-and-a-half). Thanks to the board's insistence that business work with organized labor, the unions added 1.5 million members in just two years.

Herbert Hoover returned from his highly successful campaign (to feed Belgium) to lead Wilson's Food Administration (FA). Hoover proceeded to set the prices of household foods such as wheat, sugar, and coffee and to procure basic foodstuffs for the Allies and U.S. armed forces. In establishing high prices for wheat and other commodities, the FA encouraged an increase in production that in turn provided much-needed economic relief to farmers and enormous profits to agribusiness. Federal agents fanned out across the rural hinterland, offering expert help to farmers and distributing fuel, equipment, and fertilizer to regions deemed wartime priorities. Scout troops, prisoners, and housewives planted vegetable gardens to boost production, and some twenty thousand urban college women joined the federal Women's Land Army as "farmerettes" who performed essential farm work in place of men who had been drafted.

At the other end of the food chain, Hoover stopped short of the unpopular British model of rationing and instead urged housewives to be patriotic and reduce household consumption voluntarily through "Wheatless Mondays" and "Meatless Tuesdays." "Food Will Win the War—Don't Waste It!" one poster declared. Curbing one's appetite would help avert "strikes, riots and disorders which would destroy our economic and financial efficiency," claimed another. Restaurants complied with the call to conserve certain foods, substituting whale (which could still be legally hunted), rabbit, and horsemeat for the beef, chicken, and pork that were needed in Europe. Over five hundred thousand volunteers went door-to-door across the United States to ask adults and children to sign pledges that they would not waste food or let mothers and wives cook uneconomically.

FINANCING THE WAR

Wars have always been expensive, and World War I was no exception. The War Finance Corporation (WFC) drew vast sums of money from the new Federal Reserve System for loans to essential industries. The United States also loaned $11 billion to the Allies, but because they spent most of that money on American goods, the loan amounted to an infusion of wealth into the U.S. economy. By 1918, the United States was the world's biggest lender—a position it retained until the twenty-first century, when China took the lead. All told, the government loans to American industries and the Allies, combined with the cost of the extensive military and civil programs, amounted to over $30 billion (see How Much Is That?). This huge sum was partly paid for by the War Revenue Act of 1917, which hiked the tax rate from 15 percent to 67 percent for the small percentage of top earners who made over $2 million a year and which taxed most Americans at rates of just 4–10 percent of their income.

How Much Is That?

Paying for the Great War

In monetary terms, World War I was the most expensive war the United States had yet fought. The country's nineteen-month intervention cost $30 billion, or, adjusting for inflation, the equivalent of nearly $500 billion today. By comparison, the Civil War cost $83 billion in today's dollars. As compared with the war in Iraq (2003–2011), which cost about $31 billion per month, the Great War cost $26 billion per month. A notable difference between these wars, however, was that the government mobilized the entire nation for World War I, unlike the war in Iraq, with the result that Americans enjoyed rising wages and almost full employment. In the short run, the Great War was great for the U.S. economy.

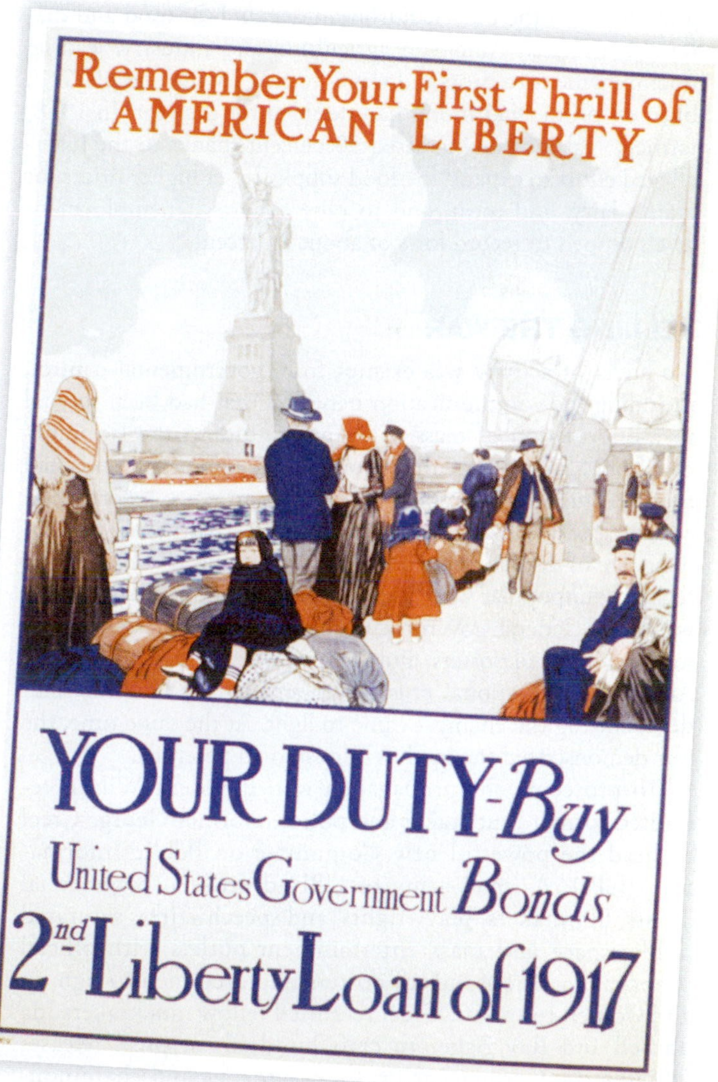

Immigrants and the War. The government informed immigrants that there was no better way to prove their patriotism than by buying liberty bonds and conserving food. Millions of immigrants bought liberty bonds, but as immigrants' low wages rose during the war, many spent their extra income on previously unaffordable foods. **Questions for Analysis:** Why should immigrants contribute to the war effort, according to this WFC poster? How is the United States depicted? What assumption does the poster's designer make about its target audience?

The government also raised capital through the sale of liberty bonds to the public. Citizens could purchase bonds at an interest rate of around 4 percent a year and cash them in thirty years later. When the first round of bonds failed to sell out, the government hired actors, advertisers, artists, and journalists to wage a massive publicity campaign. Millions of posters, buttons, and window stickers exhorted consumers to support the fight against German autocracy. Organizations from across the political spectrum, from the Girl Scouts of America and immigrant welfare leagues to the nativist Ku Klux Klan, devoted themselves to selling the bonds. All told, bond sales raised an astounding $23 billion for the war effort.

Although the war was costly, it also spurred economic growth. From the outset, European demand for food and materiel stimulated American agriculture and industry, leading unemployment to drop and wages to rise. By the end of 1917, business profits had more than doubled for the year. In 1918, farmers' real income increased 30 percent thanks to the federally led effort to expand the food supply, to set higher prices for grain, dairy, and meat, and to raise exports. Unemployment levels dipped to record lows of about 2 percent.

SELLING THE WAR

No arena of activity was exempt from governmental control, including the communication networks that had been so vital to the formation of mass consumer culture in the late nineteenth and early twentieth centuries. Although propaganda had been an important weapon of government since before 1848 and the Mexican-American War, it became particularly crucial in an age of diverse visual and print media and at the start of a relatively unpopular war. For the first time, the strategic uses to which the federal government could put the press, cinema, mass-reproduced posters, and telephone networks—promoting America's international crusade, energizing the citizenry, and demoralizing the enemy—came to light. At the same time, the war demonstrated the media's oppositional potential.

To prosecute the propaganda war, President Wilson recruited former muckraker and police reformer George Creel to head the powerful new Committee on Public Information (CPI). A small army of CPI advertisers, commercial artists, filmmakers, playwrights, and speechwriters saturated public space and mass entertainment outlets with official propaganda. Thousands of posters implored men to sign up and women to ration. Creel recruited fellow muckrakers Ida Tarbell and Ray Baker to craft hundreds of press releases vilifying the Germans as Prussian autocrats and championing the U.S. effort to liberate the world. Some seventy-five thousand "Four-Minute Men" delivered patriotic speeches to cinema audiences during the four-minute breaks between movie reels. The CPI also commissioned the first official daily government newspaper and the first government-made films. *America's Answer to the Hun* (1918), which was distributed to over six thousand cinemas, carefully documented the troops' journey to France; the distribution of food, locomotives, and other supplies; and the U.S. infantry's triumphant charge into combat at Cantigny. Filmmakers not in the employ of the CPI soon began making anti-German movies starring well-known actresses, including "America's Sweetheart," Mary Pickford (see Singular Lives: Mary Pickford: Actor, Producer, Entrepreneur).

Tapping into the growing use of sex and gender in mass advertising, CPI artists crafted commercial images of women that were designed to "sell" the war effort. Under the artistic direction of Charles Dana Gibson, whose pen-and-ink drawings of the robust, liberated "Gibson Girl" had redefined American ideals of feminine beauty in the 1890s, the CPI distributed images of women as both sexually desirable and assertive. Millions of recruitment posters and magazine advertisements featured shapely and attractive women who looked the viewer directly in the eye and challenged him to "join up!" Other, less racy depictions of women as pure and devoted housewives and mothers projected an image of the home as an equally important front in the war for global progress. Still other posters and pamphlets luridly portrayed the Germans as bloodthirsty monsters intent on raping "civilization" and crushing "liberty"—which were usually portrayed as women or the Statue of Liberty.

Much of this propaganda demonized the enemy, even though the vast majority of German soldiers were no more and no less morally debased than Allied soldiers. Nonetheless, CPI publicists theorized that by portraying Germany as an antidemocratic "autocracy" and idealizing the U.S. war effort as a righteous war for democracy, Americans would be far more motivated to win. Their propaganda reinforced this idea by portraying German emperor Kaiser Wilhelm II as a tyrannical autocrat who would stop at nothing to halt the spread of democracy. All things German fell under suspicion, including German language terms, which the CPI ordered removed from the vocabulary. Consumers, for example, were called upon to eat "liberty cabbage" rather than the German-named sauerkraut. Energetic allies advanced the CPI's propaganda campaign. Evangelical Christian ministers exhorted their congregations to support the American mission to save the world and claimed the war effort had the approval of God. "It is Bill (Kaiser William of Germany) against Woodrow," the Reverend Billy Sunday thundered, "Germany against America, Hell against Heaven."

THE SURVEILLANCE STATE

The flip side of the federal propaganda machine was increased surveillance and censorship of people and ideas that the government deemed unpatriotic. Postal workers opened mail addressed to or from people with German-sounding names, and public schools stopped teaching German. Local and state government cleared German authors off library shelves and banned performances of Beethoven, Wagner, and other leading German composers. Nativists such as Madison Grant, whose best-seller *The Passing of the Great Race* (1916) argued that only northern

SINGULAR LIVES

Mary Pickford: Actor, Producer, Entrepreneur

The first and biggest female silent movie "star," Mary Pickford defined new standards of American femininity during the Great War and was one of several celebrities whom the federal government recruited to promote the war effort. Born in Toronto, Canada, in 1892 as Gladys Louise Smith, she moved from the New York stage to the new medium of silent narrative film when director D. W. Griffith auditioned her at his Biograph Company in Brooklyn in 1909. Pickford played hundreds of Biograph roles before the company relocated to Los Angeles, where studio space was cheap and natural light plentiful. In the time before actors were identified in movie credit roles, few film actors gained recognition. However, when audiences soon began recognizing and demanding Pickford, the company launched its first publicity campaign around "the Girl with the Golden Curls."

As war broke out in Europe, Pickford starred in the box office smash *Hearts Adrift* (1914), in which she and a stranger fall in love while marooned on a desert island, and she was one of the first actors to have her name boldly displayed on publicity posters. Whether playing a woman or a girl, Pickford turned on the same youthful charm, finding a giant fan base as the pure and wholesome "America's Sweetheart." With the European film industry severely disrupted by the war, American movies and actors such as Pickford became market leaders. By 1916, Pickford was earning significantly more (at $500/week) than almost all other actors and had become the nation's most famous and critically acclaimed screen actor.

"America's Sweetheart." Mary Pickford is surrounded by menacing German soldiers in *The Little American*. After the war, Pickford became the most powerful woman in Hollywood, co-founding the major film studio United Artists as well as the Academy of Motion Picture Arts and Sciences.

Once the United States entered the war, Pickford further cultivated her all-American persona when she joined actors Charles Chaplin and Douglas Fairbanks on the payroll of the Committee on Public Information (CPI) to promote sales of liberty bonds. Drawing audiences of over fifty thousand people, she helped sell millions of dollars' worth of bonds, wrapping herself in the American flag and even auctioning off one of her famous curls. She also starred in Cecil B. De Mille's *The Little American* (1917), the poignant story of an American woman (Pickford) who bravely crosses the Atlantic in search of her German American beloved, who has been inexplicably drafted into the German army. Enduring both a U-boat attack and capture by Germans intent on raping her, Pickford escapes and helps French soldiers kill all the Germans with the exception of her beloved—whom she escorts back to the United States, where he will be humanely treated as a prisoner-of-war. *The Little American* was unusual in showing a feisty young woman outwitting the German war machine.

Think About It

1. What did Mary Pickford contribute to the CPI's war effort?
2. How might Pickford have benefited from her work for the CPI?
3. In what ways did Pickford conform to conventional gender roles of the Progressive Era, and in what ways did she challenge them?

INTERPRETING THE SOURCES

Satirizing the War Effort

The Wobblies (members of the IWW) were highly critical of the war and the American role in it. The lyrics of "Christians at War" were written by U.S. Army captain and IWW sympathizer John Kendrick in 1915 and later published in the *Little Red Song Book* (1917). Set to the well-known tune of "Onward, Christian Soldiers"—a rousing Civil War–era hymn usually played to stir soldiers' martial spirit—it criticizes the alleged hypocrisy of a war waged by Christians against other Christians. The parody enraged the proponents of preparedness, who later used it to whip up popular support for new sedition laws. Prosecutors also presented the lyrics as evidence of the Wobblies' alleged atheism and disloyalty and as grounds for their deportation.

"Onward, Christian Soldiers"
Lyrics by Sabine Baring Gould, 1865

Onward, Christian soldiers, marching as to war,
With the cross of Jesus going on before.
Christ, the royal Master, leads against the foe;
Forward into battle see his banners go!
Onward, Christian soldiers, marching as to war,
With the cross of Jesus going on before.
. . .
Like a mighty army moves the church of God;
brothers, we are treading where the saints have trod.
We are not divided, all one body we,
one in hope and doctrine, one in charity.
Onward, Christian soldiers, marching as to war,
With the cross of Jesus going on before.

"Christians at War"
Lyrics by John F. Kendrick, 1917
(Tune: "Onward, Christian Soldiers")

Onward, Christian soldiers! Duty's way is plain:
Slay your Christian neighbors, or by them be slain.
Pulpiteers are spouting effervescent swill,
God above is calling you to rob and rape and kill,
All your acts are sanctified by the lamb on high;
If you love the Holy Ghost, go murder, pray and die.
. . .
Onward, Christian soldiers! Blighting all you meet,
Trampling human freedom under pious feet.
Praise the Lord whose dollar sign dupes his favored race!
Make the foreign trash respect your bullion brand of grace.
Trust in mock salvation, serve as pirates' tools;
History will say of you: "That pack of G-- d--- fools."

Explore the Source

1. Why might Kendrick have set this lyric to the tune "Onward, Christian Soldiers"?
2. Who or what is Kendrick criticizing?
3. According to the author, what role does money play in the war?
4. From Kendrick's vantage point, why will future generations have a low opinion of those who fought in the Great War?

European peoples were capable of assimilation as Americans, fed popular suspicion of Italians, Poles, Russians, and Germans (even though Germans were technically northern European). Although the war had slowed European immigration to a trickle, Congress passed the Literacy Act of 1917, which effectively barred entry to poorer immigrants by requiring them to pass a literacy test in their native language.

While local government and civic associations put much of the German population under surveillance, the federal government specifically targeted war critics and radical labor organizations that argued that the conflict was nothing but a "rich man's war" over ill-begotten resources such as Europe's income-generating colonies. Such critics presented a triple threat in the government's eyes. For one thing, their radicalism might deter corporate leaders from joining with workers and more moderate unions to build a progressive nation. For another, these war critics might also radicalize moderate workers and undermine their willingness to cooperate with the government and corporations. Worst of all from the administration's perspective, these dissidents could use the mass media to erode Americans' support for the war effort.

At Wilson's prompting, Congress enacted a suite of surveillance laws. The Espionage Act (1917) prohibited spying, interfering with the draft, and "false statements" that might impede military success. The Alien Act (1918) authorized the commissioner of immigration to deport immigrants suspected of hostile actions and beliefs, and the Sedition Act (1918) criminalized making, speaking, or printing statements that intended to cast "contempt, scorn, or disrepute" on the American "form of government" or to advocate interference with the war effort. All three laws gave the government broad latitude for the suppression of anything that could be construed as criticism of the government or its policies. The postmaster general was granted wide-ranging powers to ban from the U.S. Postal Service any material he determined to be treasonous. Anyone convicted of antiwar activities could be imprisoned for up to twenty years. The laws reverberated far beyond radical circles, prompting publishing houses and movie studios voluntarily to withdraw material that authorities might construe as unpatriotic.

The government's principal targets, however, were the speeches, publications, and organizational activities of the Industrial Workers of the World (IWW), Socialist Party, and

United Mine Workers (see Interpreting the Sources: Satirizing the War Effort). At first, in 1917, the U.S. Postal Service suppressed issues of radical newspapers such as the IWW's *The Masses* and the socialist *Appeal to Reason* and deprived other newsletters of the cheap second-class postage that made their circulation possible. Soon, the postmaster general ruled that no publication could question the government's motives for entering the war or say that the government was a "tool of Wall Street."

The Justice Department quickly widened the campaign by issuing tin-star badges to vigilante groups, such as the 250,000-strong American Protective League, and instructing members to report on the activities of their neighbors. Federal attorneys prosecuted over 2,200 socialists and radicals, including Rose Pastor Stokes, who received a ten-year prison sentence for writing a letter to a Kansas City newspaper stating, "No government that is for the profiteers can also be for the people, and I am for the people and the government is for the profiteers." The following year, socialist leader Eugene Debs was sentenced to ten years' imprisonment for uttering the words "The master classes declare war while the subject classes fight them." Stokes and Debs were joined in prison by all 113 IWW leaders, whose imprisonment effectively crushed that organization.

The federal campaign against free speech was the most extensive the United States had ever seen. Few progressives spoke out, in part because they supported Wilson's overall program for the collectivist state and in part because the civil liberties of individuals and minorities had never been their major priority. In New York, however, a young progressive and conscientious objector named Roger Baldwin gathered together an emergency committee of attorneys to provide legal defense for dissenters. Free speech was an inalienable right of all Americans, Baldwin argued, and the American Civil Liberties Union, as the group came to be known, would "get a lot of good flags, talk a good deal about the Constitution and what our forefathers wanted to make of this country, and . . . show that we are the folks that really stand for the spirit of our institutions."

AMERICANS AT WAR

By the beginning of 1918, the CPI's propaganda machine, the government's war collectivism, and the campaign to silence critics had helped turn an unpopular war into a wildly popular one. The peace movement had all but withered away, and even outspoken pacifists such as Jane Addams lost heart and ceased to oppose the war actively. Contrary to Germany's predictions, American forces organized quickly and efficiently, deploying to France in a matter of months. Mobilization transformed the identity and aspirations of the four million men who served, in both positive and negative ways. Although U.S. soldiers saw relatively little action at first, their mere presence in France—and their eventual entry into combat—turned a stalemated war into an Allied victory. Back home, meanwhile, the collectivized state and mass mobilization altered almost every aspect of American life and opened up new opportunities for women and minorities.

FIT TO FIGHT

When it came to building the American Expeditionary Force (AEF), the United States benefited from observing the British, whose mistakes had hampered the rapid deployment and effectiveness of their forces. Instead of relying solely on a voluntary army (as the British originally had), the United States, on June 6, 1917, began conscripting all fit and healthy men aged eighteen to thirty under the Selective Service Act (1917). An amendment in 1918 would raise the eligible age to forty-five. Some 2.8 million men were eventually drafted, and another

Pershing Arrives in Paris. When the AEF arrived in France, the commanding general, John Pershing, rode to the tomb of the Marquis de Lafayette, who had commanded the French forces that fought on the American side during the War of Independence. "Lafayette," Pershing's French-speaking aide declared, "nous sommes ici [we are here]!"

2 million volunteered. To the dismay of the Germans, who had gambled that the United States would need months to deploy, the first of the two million soldiers who ultimately saw combat in France, sailed from New York on June 14, 1917, along with several thousand nurses. The troops departed to the rousing hymn "Onward Christian Soldiers," while impassioned orators exhorted them to "win the world" for freedom. Arriving in Paris on July 4, the AEF was greeted as heroes who would help the French vanquish the conquering Germans and end the war.

Most recruits had received their training at a camp in their home state before deploying to Europe. Training conscripts to shoot straight and follow orders was only a small part of the trainees' crash course in soldiering. Thousands of experts in hygiene, human relations, morale, and welfare worked with the army to help build the world's strongest—and most virtuous—fighting force. The War Department's Commission on Training Camp Activities (CTCA) banned alcohol in the training camps, much to the approval of temperance advocates, in the name of making recruits both morally and physically fit to fight. The sexual practices of the soldiers (many of whom were single men) also occupied the thoughts of the CTCA and its various experts. Some worried about the potential for sexually transmitted infections—and about 10 percent of the recruits did contract an infection (probably from local prostitutes). The vast majority of CTCA authorities, however, were concerned chiefly with the men's morals and the distinct possibility that the United States' "crusaders for democracy" would be corrupted by the time they reached Europe.

Progressive voluntary organizations also worked with the army and navy to boost morale and promote personal morality, chiefly by structuring the soldiers' leisure time and making camp life in both France and the United States as close to wholesome home life as possible. The YMCA organized Bible classes, and the Jewish Welfare Board sent song leaders. Major league baseball teams played exhibition games, and popular actors and musicians performed at the camps. "Onward Christian Soldiers" rang through the training centers, as did a modified version of the "Battle Hymn of the Republic," proclaiming the United States' "sacred mission" to "fight for world-wide freedom." The army also did its own outreach to U.S. citizens, producing lavish military reviews such as Private Irving Berlin's popular "Yip! Yip! Yaphank!" which promoted and poked fun at military life.

Consistent with previous practice, the AEF's four hundred thousand African American servicemen were barred from certain amenities at the training camps and directed to back rows of assembly halls by the same "Whites Only" signs that were by now planted everywhere in the South. Likewise, other minorities, including the 18,000 Puerto Ricans who served in the armed forces and the 5,700 Filipinos who served in the navy, were subjected to segregation and mostly confined to menial labor. Tensions mounted, particularly in the South, as thousands of black and white conscripts mustered in training camps in the summer of 1917. Tensions erupted, most lethally in Houston, Texas, where African American troops from the North refused to obey Jim Crow rules. Whites tormented black soldiers to the point that they rioted and opened fire, and seventeen white men and two African Americans perished in the fray. In response, the army hanged nineteen black soldiers and President Wilson temporarily suspended black recruitment.

Unlike the army, viruses did not discriminate, as the troops discovered the following year when the deadly "Spanish flu" tore through the training camps, felling thousands of soldiers. Over a thousand men died at Camp Sherman, Ohio, for instance, in three weeks. Infected soldiers then carried the virus to Europe, where it was transmitted and carried around the world by troop transports and hospital ships to fatal effect. By 1919, more than twenty-one million people around the world had died, and another thirty to eighty million would perish by 1921. All told, sixty-two thousand American soldiers died from influenza and other diseases—eleven thousand more than were killed in battle.

HELLFIGHTERS AND DOUGHBOYS

Although the American troops began deploying to France in June 1917, it was not until the summer of 1918—four years into the war—that U.S. units entered combat. AEF commander John Pershing was adamant that the United States would remain an independent "associated" power with full control over its own troops (with the notable exception of the 369th African American regiment; see below). For reasons of national pride and because the Allied generals' strategy had resulted in millions of deaths, Pershing did not entrust American troops to French and British command during the German advance of early 1918. Until then, Americans mostly played a support role, even as the Germans advanced to within sixty miles of Paris.

Military Life. Millions of enlisted men awoke to the early-morning blast of a camp bugle, one of several aspects of camp life that became a familiar symbol of wartime thanks to composer Irving Berlin, an army private at Camp Upton, New York. In the song "Oh, How I Hate to Get Up in the Morning," Berlin jested, "Someday I'm going to murder the bugler—Someday they're going to find him dead."

Americans in Paris. American "doughboys" (soldiers) proceed through the boulevards of Paris in November 1918. Although the origins of the term *doughboy* are still debated, U.S. soldiers were known to spend their "dough" liberally on French businesses and in so doing became a hit among many locals.

While they waited to deploy, the soldiers got to experience a culture that in many ways was profoundly different from their own. Paris, in particular, was an exciting and eye-opening adventure. Paid at a much higher rate than their British and French counterparts, and free of the tightly controlled training camps, American soldiers spent liberally on local wines, women, and entertainment. Unlike in America, prostitution was considered a natural if unrespectable part of urban life. Much to the consternation of U.S. officials, the troops flocked to red light districts. Army administrators pleaded with French officials to close the brothels and, when they refused, warned the soldiers that local women suffered from sexually transmitted infections. "A German Bullet Is Cleaner Than a Whore," advised one Army poster. Ultimately, it was a losing battle, however, and AEF officers began handing out condoms.

For many troops, Paris was the first large city they had ever experienced. Men with rural roots later recalled how the freedoms possible in a large, cosmopolitan city forever changed their lives. The thought of returning to farm life after the war became unthinkable. "How ya going to keep 'em down on the farm," one popular song went, "after they've seen Paree?" The experience led hundreds of thousands of rural and small-town men to resettle in cities after the war, and this trend further accelerated the depopulation of the American countryside.

For African Americans soldiers, deployment to France proved an especially revelatory experience. Unlike back home, white people did not automatically segregate and exclude them, and they received tremendous gratitude for their support work. Black army bands found an appreciative audience for jazz and ragtime, which most French people had never heard before and which sparked a tremendous following for what many Europeans considered the United States' only truly original art form. Feeling deep pride, African American servicemen grew determined to challenge their second-class citizenship at home.

On the U.S. military bases, however, the vast majority of African Americans soldiers continued to suffer discrimination. They found themselves barred from combat and serving strictly in labor units, hauling trash, unloading supplies, or digging trenches. When the NAACP protested, the War Department allowed some black servicemen to fight, but most African Americans still wielded many more brooms and shovels than rifles. One exception to the no-combat rule was the "Harlem Hellfighters" 369th infantry regiment from New York, which had trained as a National Guard unit before the war and was clearly ready for the front lines. After white southern officers warned General John Pershing that whites would not stand for African Americans in combat, the regiment was seconded to the French Army and went on to distinguished service on the Western Front.

Harlem Hellfighters Cross the Rhine. This poster reminds viewers that the 369th African American regiment was the first Allied unit to cross the Rhine River into Germany. The artist incorrectly portrayed the Americans in full U.S. uniform. In fact, they fought under French command, in U.S. uniforms but wearing the French "Adrian" helmet. **Questions for Analysis:** What connections did the artist draw between the Civil War and the Great War? Why are those connections significant? Why might the artist have chosen to show the 369th wearing U.S. helmets, even though they entered battle in French headgear?

EQUAL PARTNERS: WOMEN, MINORITIES, AND UNIONS WAGE WAR

The government's mass mobilization program, which aimed at recruiting every American into the war effort, enabled labor unions, civilian workers, minorities, and women to contribute directly to the wartime economy. With millions of men conscripted and immigration suspended, employers recruited these groups in the tens of thousands. In the West and Southwest, thousands of Mexican Americans quit their low-paying, hard-toiling farm jobs and joined the industrial workforce. Many of these workers were American citizens, but many others were refugees from the Mexican Revolution (1910–1917).

Seeking to boost production without provoking labor unrest, employers offered many labor incentives for the first time, including employee disability insurance, child-care services, athletic programs, savings programs, and other attractive benefits. Personnel departments, which only 5 percent of corporations had established before the war, became an indispensable part of most companies. A number of corporations also introduced worker representation plans, under which employees nominated delegates to meet with employers regularly in the name of what many called industrial democracy.

Workers were happy with many of the new benefits. However, they strongly preferred their own labor unions to the worker representation system, which employers often used for surveillance purposes. Thanks largely to the government's treatment of the American Federation of Labor (AFL) as a wartime partner, unions grew dramatically, taking AFL membership from two million in 1916 to three million in 1919. Almost five million Americans belonged to a labor union in 1919—double the number before the war—and some industries (notably train service workers) were 90 percent unionized (see Figure 22.1). Organized labor enjoyed newfound respectability as government and business attempted to work cooperatively with them. Although employers preferred their own version of industrial democracy, for the first time in American history they had firsthand experience of the advantages of cooperating with the unions.

African American, Asian American, and Hispanic American civilians enthusiastically joined the war effort. Most dramatically, the humming wartime economy gave the **Great Migration** of African Americans out of the South a tremendous boost. Between 1916 and 1919, over five hundred thousand left permanently, mostly following railroad lines northward from North and South Carolina to New York and Philadelphia or from Mississippi, Alabama, Arkansas, and Louisiana to Detroit,

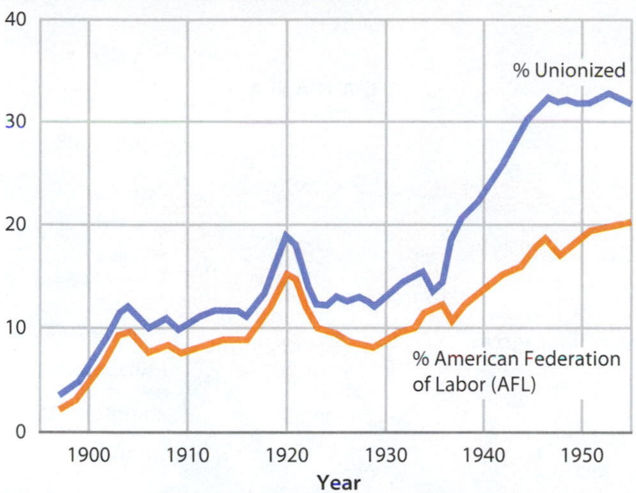

FIGURE 22.1 Percentage of Unionized Workers in Nonagricultural Work, 1900–1955. A growing proportion of workers joined labor unions in the Progressive Era. Union membership rates peaked during and immediately after World War I, when the federal government actively worked with unions and employers to maximize wartime production, and again during the New Deal and World War II. Membership rates dropped significantly after the crackdown on striking workers and radicals in 1919–1920 and remained relatively flat until the New Deal (see Chapter 24).

Cleveland, and Chicago (see Map 22.3). The black population of Detroit increased sixfold; in Cleveland it tripled. In sheer size, however, the largest migrations were to New York and Chicago, both of which attracted more than sixty thousand black southerners during these years. They came for the wartime North's rising wages and in the hope of finding a freer, better life—and because they sought release from the South's unyielding culture of segregation and lynching. Men secured work in the steel, meatpacking, and automobile industries, whereas women mostly took domestic jobs as maids and cooks. When women could find industrial work, they preferred its shorter hours (about forty-eight, compared to upwards of ninety-four in domestic service) and higher wages, and the autonomy it afforded.

Much as the drain of white men out of the workforce and into the military attracted African American and other minority men, it also drew white women. Indeed, white women moved into waged work of all kinds, from clerical jobs to auto assembly. Over one million mostly single women who had never worked outside the home became wage earners, and millions more left low-paying domestic labor to take jobs as streetcar conductors, secretaries, telephone operators, and munitions makers, among others. The shortage of men in the professions also led many professional schools, such as medical programs, to admit women for the first time. In addition, thousands of "women-at-arms" bucked gender conventions by joining militias in their home states, asserting a right to take up arms in the defense of themselves and the nation. "Whether we vote or not," Lurana Sheldon Ferris of the Maine Women's Defense Club insisted, "we are going to shoot." Gun manufacturers supported the clubs, but the image of women serving as soldiers—conventionally, a man's role—proved far more threatening to most people than the idea that women were joining the war effort in factories and on farms.

Thirty-four thousand women did sign up for service in the armed forces and the navy, mostly as nurses, and they also served in the marines as clerical workers. Women eagerly applied to be "Hello Girls" (telephone receptionists) for the army near the front lines in France (450 got the job, and 10 received congressional citations for bravery under enemy fire). Some twenty thousand Navy "Yeomanettes" and army nurses worked in France, many on "moving hospitals"—trains equipped with medical supplies that could transport up to four hundred injured soldiers back from the front lines. Encountering discriminatory exclusion from official rank, nurses campaigned unsuccessfully for full inclusion in the rights and privileges of the military world.

American women also helped through private organizations such as the YWCA. Mary Borden, a wealthy college-educated

Women Who Shoot. Although these Yeomanettes drilled with rifles at the naval training base in San Francisco, they were not permitted to serve in a combat role and were confined largely to nursing and clerical duty.

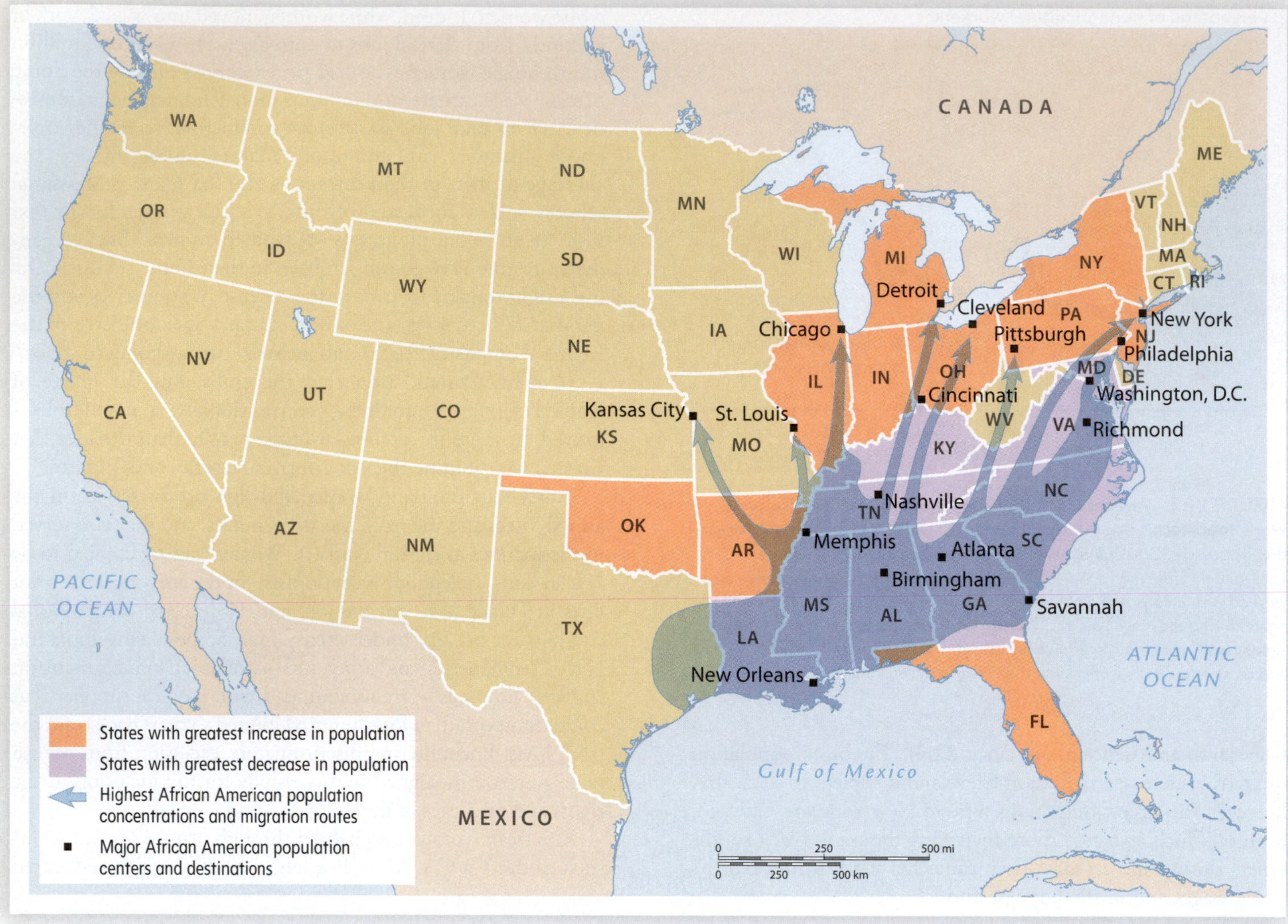

Map 22.3 The Great Migration, 1916–1930. As the Great Migration gathered speed during the war, African Americans went from being an overwhelmingly rural ethnic group to a predominantly urban one.

nurse who established her own hospital near the front lines, was one of many who witnessed the relentless cycle of injury, healing, and reinjury that countless soldiers endured. "Just as you send your clothes to the laundry and mend them when they come back," wrote a disheartened Borden, "so we send our men to the trenches and mend them when they come back again. You send your socks . . . again and again just as many times as they will stand it . . . we send our men to the war again and again . . . just until they are dead."

Back home, temperance organizations, long a magnet for women reformers, got a welcome boost from the army's decision to ban alcohol in the camps. They now renewed their campaign to enforce temperance in American society at large. Eighteen strongly Protestant states had already prohibited the sale of alcohol (see Chapter 20), but heavily urbanized states with larger immigrant populations that were often more tolerant of alcohol consumption had not. Prohibitionists capitalized on the perception that beer drinking was German, unpatriotic, and wasteful, and persuaded federal lawmakers to pass the Eighteenth Amendment, which banned the manufacture and sale of alcoholic beverages. The law went into effect in 1920.

The war also led suffragists to renew their campaign for women's voting rights. Despite their public service, in 1917 women could vote in only twelve states, mostly western, and there was but one woman serving in Congress (Jeannette Rankin of Montana). Even though Woodrow Wilson owed his narrow reelection the year before to women voters in those states, he openly opposed women's suffrage. In the winter of 1917, as Wilson toured Europe to promote his vision of freedom and peace, suffragist Alice Paul and the newly established National Woman's Party set up a continuous vigil outside the White House. Bearing placards that called upon the president to recognize women's contribution to the war effort and to practice at home the democracy that he preached abroad, the protestors won extensive press coverage when

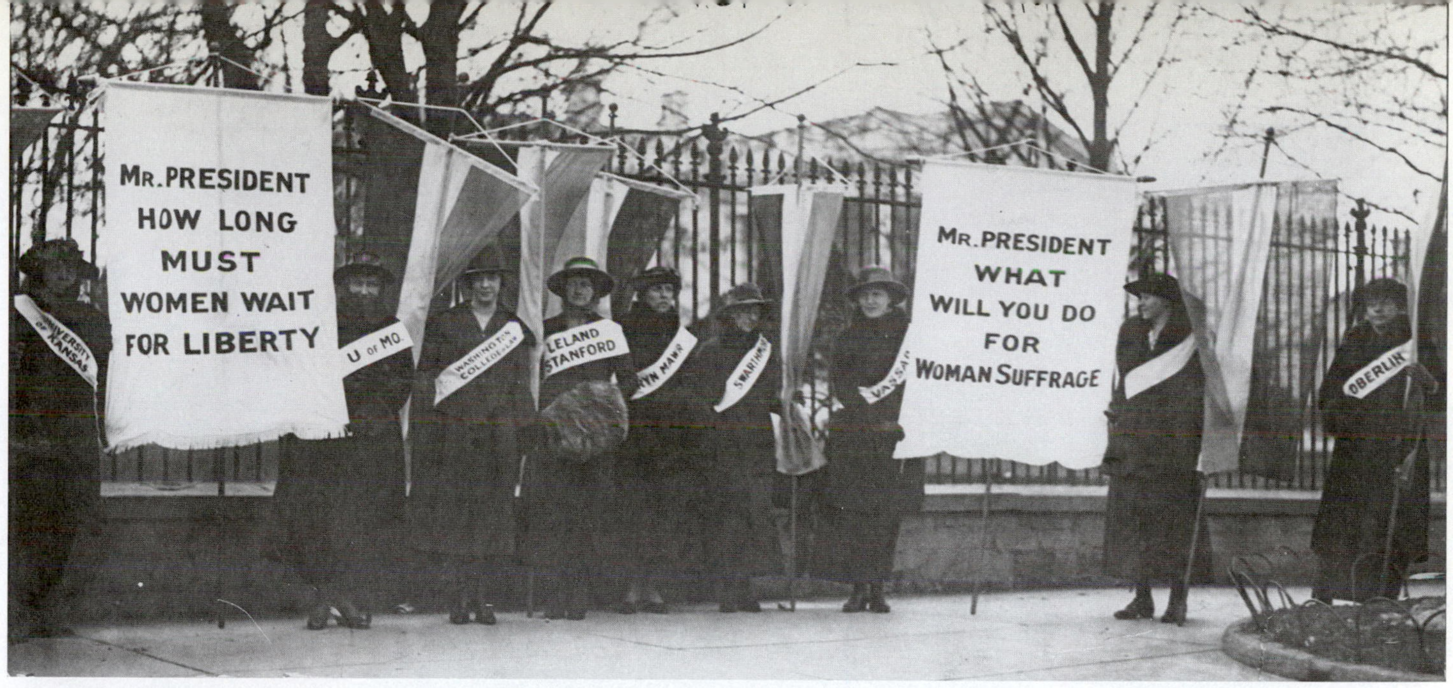

Demanding Democracy at Home. As Alice Paul and sister suffragists had hoped, press photographs that showed placards questioning Wilson's commitment to democracy humiliated the president and pressured him to support voting rights for women.

they were arrested and beaten for allegedly blocking traffic outside the executive mansion. Convicted and imprisoned, Paul began a well-documented hunger strike that, along with her subsequent force-feeding, became a source of mounting embarrassment for Wilson.

Women's lack of voting rights at a time when the government demanded women's full participation, coupled with police brutality against the suffragists, starkly contradicted Wilson's claim that the United States was bringing democracy to the world. Although some suffragists remained critical of the war, Carrie Chapman Catt, the leader of the National American Woman Suffrage Association, pragmatically endorsed Wilson's stand on the war while calling on him to recognize women's vital contributions. Finally, in the summer of 1918, the president dropped his opposition and announced that women's suffrage was "vital to winning the war." In the ensuing midterm elections, suffragists lobbied against the few remaining holdouts in the Senate; most of the opposing legislators subsequently lost their seats. When Congress reconvened in May 1919, both houses voted to support the Nineteenth Amendment giving women the vote. By election day 1920, three-quarters of the states had ratified the amendment. Seventy-two years after women had demanded the vote in Seneca Falls, the first women to vote legally in a presidential election cast their ballots.

AMERICANS ON THE BATTLEFIELD

Around the same time that President Wilson changed his mind about women's suffrage, U.S. soldiers finally entered combat in large numbers. In June 1918, several hundred thousand Americans joined the Allies and marched to the battle zone—and into the mud and misery of trench living. Deploying from the trenches in torrential rain, the troops slept, ate, and fought in damp and rotting uniforms and boots, constantly battling colds, pneumonia, skin infections, and flu. When they climbed to the surface, it was to advance through woods and fields—passing by thousands of broken and dying soldiers—while under fire from artillery shells, clouds of poison gas, and a thick hail of bullets. Mortality rates were staggering. In the campaign to retake Belleau Wood, for example, five thousand of eight thousand U.S. marines fell (see Hot Commodities: Blood).

The first major independent American campaign took place outside Paris, where 550,000 U.S. troops helped the French retake Château-Thierry (see Map 22.4). Gaining momentum, Pershing's million-strong force punched through German lines, pushing them over one hundred miles back toward Germany. By the end of August, American forces had successfully repelled the enemy at Rheims, in northeastern France. Pelted by rain, the AEF and Allies launched a third major campaign the following month, the Meuse-Argonne offensive, which finally pushed the Germans out of France and cut them off from their supply lines.

Reeling from the thrust and convinced they could no longer win, German generals unexpectedly called for an armistice in late October. On November 11, 1918, just six months after the first significant deployment of U.S. troops, the war that had ground on for four long years and claimed nineteen million lives lurched to an end. The American death toll stood at 117,465, making World War I the third most lethal conflict in the nation's history after the Civil War and World War II. Almost all the fighting, suffering, and dying had fallen on the peoples of Europe. But American combat troops, coming at a time when the war was stalemated and both sides were nearing economic and physical collapse, gave Britain and its allies the extra push they needed to tip the scales in their favor.

Map 22.4 The United States in Combat: Major Battles. The Germans gained significant territory in the spring of 1918, but when the Americans began a counteroffensive in the late summer, Germany was left no choice but to call for an armistice.

WINNING THE PEACE

When hostilities ceased in late 1918, the struggle to determine the terms of the peace began in earnest. The United States was widely credited for having financed, supported, and enabled the Allies' victory, and President Wilson stepped confidently forward to offer his vision of a world order without empires or cataclysmic conflict. The United States was not the only country that aspired to global leadership, however. The new government of Bolshevik Russia also had plans for the world.

HOT COMMODITIES

Blood

Demand for blood leaped during the Great War as new technologies of warfare filled ambulances and hospitals with critically wounded soldiers in desperate need of blood transfusions. Hematology (blood science), however, significantly lagged behind the weapons industry. There was still no tried-and-tested way of preserving blood, a highly perishable substance, and doctors were only dimly aware of the importance of matching the patient's blood type with the donor's. Blood could be transfused only directly, via a short rubber tube connecting donor and recipient arm-to-arm. Difficult and unhygienic, a transfusion could endanger or even kill the patient.

All this changed when Oswald Hope Robertson, a British-born physician and researcher at the Rockefeller Institute, New York, volunteered for the U.S. Army and shipped out to the Western Front. Robertson had recently discovered a way of preserving blood for up to twenty-six days, by mixing it with sodium citrate. The new process made the blood storable until needed. The battlefield provided a perfect laboratory for refining and developing Robertson's indirect transfusion method, which turned blood into a commodity that could be pumped, bottled, transported, and potentially sold (as soldiers with minor injuries learned when they traded a pint of blood for two weeks' leave). Dozens of Western Front "blood depots," hospitals, makeshift first aid camps, and ambulances used Robertson's transfuser, and the device saved tens of thousands of lives.

Stories of heroic donors sacrificing a pint of their blood for a fellow soldier filled U.S. newspapers and magazines and captured the public's imagination. Several movies lionized donors, but others explored anxieties about the possible effects of the transfusion of men's blood into women, Jews' blood into Christians, and animals' blood into humans. The possibility of transfusions from African Americans to whites drew the most attention, particularly in southern states that had legislated the "one drop (of blood)" rule in the 1910s, decreeing that only persons who had no African-descended ancestors qualified as white. (Despite a mountain of scientific evidence that African American blood was exactly the same substance that flowed in white people's veins, most U.S. hospitals segregated their blood supplies well into the 1960s.)

After the war, hospitals and research institutions lost access to the army's enormous pool of donors. So-called "canned blood" temporarily fell out of use, and improved methods of arm-to-arm transfusion became the norm as doctors argued that fresh blood was of higher quality. (Direct transfusion also made it possible to know who—and what race—the donor was.) Hospitals and private agencies advertised for civilian donors; some donors were volunteers, but many were paid. In large cities, a highly competitive market emerged, with blood sometimes fetching as much as $100/pint ($1,061 in today's dollars). A lucrative source of cash, frequent blood donation proved particularly attractive to poorer people, especially during the Great Depression of the 1930s. The first "blood bank"—modeled on Robertson's original blood depot—opened at Cook County Hospital, Chicago, in 1937.

Think About It

1. How did the field of hematology benefit from the Great War?
2. What threat might blood transfusions have posed to southern segregation?
3. Why might health boards have considered the unregulated market in blood to be exploitative?

COMPETING VISIONS: PROGRESSIVES AND BOLSHEVIKS

In March 1917, a month before the United States entered the war, a revolution had swept across Russia. As a democratic parliament replaced centuries-old tsarist rule, American progressives cheered the change in regime as another sign that the forces of global democracy were destined to overcome autocracy. In November, however, Russian communists known as Bolsheviks led a revolution against their nation's fragile young democracy. Viewing Europe's war as costly and corrupt, the Bolsheviks immediately called for an armistice with Germany and withdrew from the Allied Powers. Abolishing the parliament, they constructed what their leader, Vladimir Illich Lenin, described as a "dictatorship of the proletariat," in which the workers' unions (or soviets) that made up the Communist Party would rule in the alleged best interests of all workers.

Americans learned of the **Bolshevik Revolution** largely through the reporting of progressive journalist John Reed. In his bracing account *Ten Days That Shook the World* (1919), Reed grasped that the Bolshevik Revolution was a working-class uprising of historic and global magnitude and that it would likely have ramifications far beyond Russia's borders. He also reported on the Bolsheviks' discovery of archival documents showing that the tsar and other imperial allies had secretly agreed to divide up the world among themselves after the war. This revelation was a stark reminder that Europe's empires had no intention of making the world "safe for democracy," as President Wilson had insisted, but that they aspired to smash Germany and the other Central Powers and tighten their hold over the globe.

Like American progressives and conservative nationalists, the Bolsheviks were inspired by a particular world view that they believed was applicable to the world at large. In certain respects, their vision of the world and methods of recruitment were indistinguishable from those of progressives. Progressives and Bolsheviks opposed European-style imperialism and supported self-determination—the right of all nations to be free. Both tried to skirt official channels and communicate directly with other empires' subjects and citizens. Both opposed monarchies and supported popular rule (although they disagreed about what "popular rule" was), and both had a crusading spirit, a determination to bring about global change. Key aspects of their respective visions of modernity were in conflict, however—chiefly, their economic visions. Bolsheviks were committed to the socialization (government ownership) of factories, land, and other means of production, whereas progressives opposed socialization and advocated a responsible capitalism in which the state played a mediating role between employers and workers. By the beginning of 1918, Wilson and the Bolshevik leader Lenin were locked in competition for the ideological leadership of the world.

Lenin Addresses the World. Following the Bolshevik Revolution, leader Vladimir Illich Lenin emerged as Wilson's chief rival on the global stage.

WILSON'S NEW WORLD ORDER

Wilson presented his ideas before Congress in January 1918. The first five of his Fourteen Points called for an "open" world in which all peoples enjoyed freedom of the seas, equal trade opportunities, arms reduction, and the end of colonialism. The right of Europe's many minorities to self-determination was the subject of points six through thirteen. (Much to the disappointment of Indian and other subject peoples of the European empires, the right of non-European peoples to self-determination was ignored.) The fourteenth point called for a "general association of nations" that would ensure the independence and security of all the world's states.

Two months later, the Russian government established the Third Communist International (Comintern), a global movement with an open commitment to struggle "by all available means, including armed force, for the overthrow of the international bourgeoisie and for the creation of an international Soviet republic as a transition stage to the complete abolition of the State." Bolshevism seemed to be gathering support in Germany following the armistice, as well as elsewhere in Europe. In Mexico, the government had enacted a radical constitution that declared all mineral wealth the property of the nation. In the United States, a small group of American socialists broke away from Eugene Debs's American Socialist Party and established the Communist Labor Party. Conservatives and progressives alike worried that the world was on the verge of communist revolution.

Wilson hastily publicized his peace plan as a just alternative both to Allied plans for continued empire and to the Bolshevik call for a workers' revolution. Disinclined to liberate their colonies or consent to American global leadership, the Allied Powers initially rejected Wilson's peace plan. However, once U.S. troops forced an armistice with Germany in November 1918 and Wilson threatened to suspend exports of American goods to the Allies, they grudgingly consented to use the Fourteen Points as a basis for peace negotiations. In December, Wilson arrived in Europe and was mobbed by deliriously happy crowds—some carrying banners with the words "Redeemer of Humanity"—at every stop. Appalled by the carnage and desperate to avert another global catastrophe, many ordinary Europeans hailed Wilson as the man who would ensure that the Great War was "the war that will end war" (in the words of English novelist H. G. Wells). Colonized peoples from Africa and the Middle East to China and Southeast Asia also saluted Wilson, hoping that he would force the Allies to recognize their right of self-determination.

The negotiations began in Paris in January 1919 and extended to April, with the United States, Britain, France, and Italy present. Wilson entered the Paris Peace Conference buoyed by the outpouring of popular support. The Allied leaders, however, accustomed to making decisions with little regard for public opinion, worked tirelessly to preserve the old international system of colonies, secrecy, and spheres of interest. The negotiations occurred in secret, and neither Bolshevik Russia nor Germany was admitted to the table. In the end, the Allies opposed all but two principles in Wilson's plan. They looked to the heavily industrialized German economy as a source of reparations for the devastating costs of the war and also insisted that Germany be punished through enormous reparations of over $33 billion ($433 billion in today's dollars). Wilson got nowhere with the free seas and free trade points of his plan for a new world order.

The principle of self-determination in Europe was largely honored, in part because it suited the Allies to break up the Austro-Hungarian Empire and parts of what had been the tsar's empire. Austria, Czechoslovakia, Romania, Finland, Poland, and five Balkan states were given independence. Self-determination for Germany's colonies, however, fell by the wayside, with large parts of the Middle East (including Syria, Jordan, and Palestine) becoming mandates—a type of colony—of Britain and France. Chinese students launched an anti-imperialist movement as a result of the Japanese acquisition of a formerly German province, and French Vietnamese were bitterly disappointed by Wilson's lack of response to their call for self-determination.

THE DREAM OF COLLECTIVE SECURITY

The other provision that survived the Paris Peace Conference was Wilson's fourteenth point. Wilson drafted the covenant for a **League of Nations,** which provided for a permanent council of the five biggest world powers and the election of representatives for the smaller nations. Consistent with progressive principles, a general assembly of all nations was to meet regularly to discuss issues of global importance, and in Article 10 the members pledged to protect all members from aggression or threat—by force if necessary.

Germany and the Allies all signed the resulting Treaty of Versailles in June 1919. For Germany, the treaty was humiliating. Not only did it deprive the country of over 10 percent of its population and colonial territory, but it also subjected the Germans to massive reparations that would cast the nation into abject depression for fifteen years. Wilson returned to the United States to seek the Senate's approval of the treaty, satisfied that at the very least he had provided the world with a means to maintain peace through the League. But conservative nationalists and Republican senators greeted the president with hostility. They worried that League membership would compromise America's sovereign right to act in its own best interests—and possibly even authorize the use of force against the United States. Some progressive senators, while applauding the League, opposed ratification because the treaty kept the Allies' empires intact.

Wilson was convinced that signing the treaty was both right and righteous, a part of the divine plan for America and the world. "The stage is set," he informed the Senate, "the destiny disclosed. It has come about by no plan of our conceiving, but by the hand of God, who led us into this way." Increasingly isolated from his more flexible supporters and enraged by his conservative critics, the uncompromising Wilson intensively lobbied senators for their unqualified support. Suffering a minor stroke, he refused to convalesce as per doctors' orders, instead embarking on a ten-thousand-mile train trip around the United States and delivering over forty impassioned and often delirious speeches in support of the treaty. Collapsing in Colorado, he returned to Washington, where he suffered a devastating stroke that left him partly paralyzed.

Ailing President. Some months following President Wilson's stroke, and just before the 1920 Democratic Party convention, this photo was staged as part of the administration's effort to show that the president remained in command of himself and the country. Wilson, whose right side was unaffected by the stroke, is pictured in right profile with his wife, Edith Bolling Galt Wilson, at his paralyzed left side.

With the help of his wife Edith, his personal assistant, and his doctors, the bedridden Wilson continued to serve. He remained adamant that no compromise was acceptable, and issued scathing attacks on all opponents. He ultimately lost the battle, however, when the Senate, in 1920, failed to muster the two-thirds majority needed to ratify the treaty. That vote proved the final, fatal blow to Wilson and his progressive vision of a peaceful, multilateral world.

THE GREAT UNREST

Like the international transition to peace, the road to peace domestically was far from smooth. The Wilson administration was unprepared for the complex task of demobilization. On the day of the armistice, in November 1918, the various government boards and agencies scrambled to cancel all their contracts for food and supplies and lifted price controls. War industries wound down and wheat silos overflowed. The economic boom of the war

Writing History with Lightning. D. W. Griffith's 1915 film brilliantly innovated the techniques of motion picture production. At the same time, its inaccurate and racist retelling of Reconstruction sparked riots and the founding of the second Ku Klux Klan.

gains permanent, they met with considerable resistance—and a government that appeared to have lost its way.

RACIST BACKLASH

White hostility toward African Americans had been hardening since the 1890s and had escalated in 1915 with the release of the racist motion picture *The Clansman.* Based on a novel by writer Thomas Dixon, the film portrayed the original Ku Klux Klan of the Reconstruction era as the heroic saviors of white womanhood and the nation. Lavishly produced, this first cinematic dramatization of American history was a box-office smash and the first movie to be shown at the White House. President Wilson was dazzled, according to Dixon, exclaiming that "it is like writing history with lightning . . . [M]y only regret is that it is all so terribly true."

Shocked by the film's blatant racism and the president's positive response, Jane Addams and other progressives prevailed upon director D. W. Griffith to cut some of the film's most offensive scenes and retitle it *The Birth of a Nation.* At a time of increased black migration to northern cities, however, even the edited version galvanized many white people into "defending" their exclusively white neighborhoods, jobs, and schools. Whites in Boston and elsewhere rioted at the film's premiere. Within weeks of its debut, Southern Methodist minister William J. Simmons announced the formation of the second Ku Klux Klan (KKK), pledging to advance the causes of white supremacy and patriotism everywhere.

As the nation entered World War I, white mobs hauled African American migrants off trains headed to Chicago, and all-white draft boards disproportionately drafted African Americans (40 percent more often than whites). Lynching rates almost doubled between 1917 and 1919, and at least ten black victims were murdered in army uniform. Bloody race riots broke out in at least six cities during 1917, including East St. Louis, where black neighborhoods were burned to the ground and thirty-nine African Americans and nine whites were killed. In an NAACP-

years continued for a short time, but in 1919 inflation set in at an annual rate of 15 percent. Wages dropped, the market for consumer goods collapsed, and recession loomed. As African Americans, white workers, and women strove to make their wartime sponsored "silent parade" down Manhattan's Fifth Avenue in July 1917, some marchers carried placards that asked, "Mr. President, why not make America safe for democracy?" Wilson was silent.

It was to this hostile environment that African American and other minority soldiers returned after the war. Minorities returned with great hopes for a more inclusive and equal society. For instance, Chinese American veterans, who had been barred from citizenship under the Chinese Exclusion Act (1882), were hopeful that, having served their country in wartime, they might at last become citizens. But these aspirations were thwarted. (Not until 1935, when Congress passed the Nye-Lae Bill, was citizenship granted to all noncitizen veterans of World War I.)

African American and Mexican American veterans were already citizens. But segregation and other forms of discrimination had deprived them of the full benefits of citizenship since the nineteenth century. Having received a generally warm welcome in France and having risked their lives for their country, black veterans were determined to reassert their rights at home. The uniform was a powerful symbol of their service and, once back home, many African American veterans would "polish everything up fine, and *strut* in the uniform of the United States Army," as Mamie Garvin Fields, an African American living in South Carolina, recalled. At first, white people stood back. But within weeks, bands of resentful whites started assaulting the young veterans, throwing them off trains, and beating or intimidating them. These encounters always involved desecrating the veteran's uniform, pulling off its buttons, and tearing it to shreds—a stark reminder to African Americans that they were not full citizens. Violence against African American civilians also escalated as discharged soldiers attempted to reenter the workforce. Competition for jobs stirred further white working-class animosity toward increasingly confident African American men.

U.S. cities were seething by the summer of 1919, when no less than twenty-five urban race riots broke out. In many urban locales, black Americans fought back against the white mobs. Chicago's deadly race riot, in July 1919, exemplified what was becoming a familiar story of American race relations. When an African American boy swimming in Lake Michigan started to drift toward a white beach, white people threw stones at him, causing him to lose consciousness and drown. Enraged black Chicagoans marched into the white neighborhoods in protest. White crowds then stormed into black neighborhoods and began shooting, beating, and stabbing black people and burning their homes and businesses. Over a five-day period, twenty-three African Americans and fifteen white Americans were killed.

That African Americans had actively struck back further enraged many white people and swelled the ranks of the KKK, not only in the South but also in the West and Midwest. Some whites even perceived such defiance as evidence of the presence of bolshevism on American soil, imagining

African Americans March Against Violence. Carrying reminders of African Americans' long-standing sacrifice for their country, ten thousand men, women, and children marched in silent protest of the recent violence in East St. Louis.

African Americans' "uppityness" as part of a global communist revolution, even though African Americans had no connection with Russia and needed no prompting to defend themselves and their homes.

WORKERS PRESS THEIR CLAIMS

Workers in general also attempted to parlay their wartime advances, such as the recognition of unions and the forty-hour workweek, into permanent progress on the grounds that these represented the "democratization of industry." Employers, however, rushed to roll back workers' gains and to eject the government from its mediating role. Women largely quit industrial work under pressure from both the government and the unions.

Industrial workers battled back against declining wages and the shrinking role of unions. Adopting the Wilsonian rhetoric of the democratic fight against autocracy, workers denounced as "Prussian" and "autocratic" employers' effort to return to the prewar status quo, in which employers typically set wages and work hours without consultation or government oversight. The unions demanded a continuation of the wartime model of cooperation between employers and unions; the 40- to 48-hour week; and union recognition as their reward for having bought liberty bonds, toiled long hours, or shipped out to Europe to risk limb and life for democracy. "For why we buy Liberty Bonds? For the Mills? No, for freedom and America—for everybody," declared one Polish mill worker. "No more work like a horse and wagon. For 8-hour day."

In the biggest labor action since the Great Railroad Strike of 1877, the unions organized a series of strikes involving over four million workers. In Boston, even the police department refused to work, plunging the city into chaos and leading Massachusetts governor Calvin Coolidge to call out the state militia. The most paralyzing strike, that of the steelworkers, was centered in Chicago but spread across the Northeast and Midwest in September. Some 350,000 steelworkers demanded an eight-hour day and union recognition. Employers responded violently, bringing in private armies to break up the picket lines and deliver strikebreakers to the factories. Eighteen strikers were killed in one of several riots that erupted. Eventually, the steel strike was broken, as the workers failed to shut down the steelworks and middle-class Americans signaled that they were unsympathetic to the cause.

THE RED SUMMER OF 1919

In April 1919, as industrial strife and racial tension mounted, twelve parcel bombs were sent anonymously through the U.S. mail to prominent political leaders, judges, and industrialists. Some of the bombs exploded, and the U.S. Post Office intercepted others. No one died, although one person was seriously injured. Two months later, eight bombs in eight cities, from San Francisco to Washington, D.C., exploded within a few minutes of one another, including one at the home of Attorney General A. Mitchell Palmer. The perpetrators of these campaigns were never identified. The labor unions denied having had a role and condemned the attacks. The bombers' anonymity heightened elite and middle-class fears that revolutionary bolshevism was spreading from Russia to the United States.

As more race riots and strikes broke out in the summer of 1919, the press blamed "armed revolutionaries" and a creeping international bolshevism. Although America's Communist Labor Party was very small by European standards, its existence and the possibility of an organized connection between the Bolsheviks and American radicals concerned both conservatives and a growing number of progressives. Suspicion also fell on striking workers. The *Philadelphia Inquirer* exemplified this perspective when its editor stated that the steel strike was "penetrated with the Bolshevik idea . . . steeped in the doctrines of class struggle and social overthrow." The press and middle America seemed to forget that AFL head Samuel Gompers and many other U.S. union leaders were strongly anti-communist, not to mention antiradical and often anti-immigrant.

As the press whipped up fears of bolshevism, hysteria gripped the country. Known as the **Red Scare,** this alarm over a supposed Bolshevist plot was heightened by a number of civic organizations affiliated with and funded by big business. The National Civic Federation, the National Association of Manufacturers, and the American Defense Society (which was funded by John D. Rockefeller and J. P. Morgan) all decried organized labor as

Police on Strike. The Massachusetts militia—helped by Harvard University students and faculty—guarded smashed storefronts in Boston during a two-day police strike in 1919. The strike helped to fuel middle-class fears that the nation was teetering on the edge of revolution.

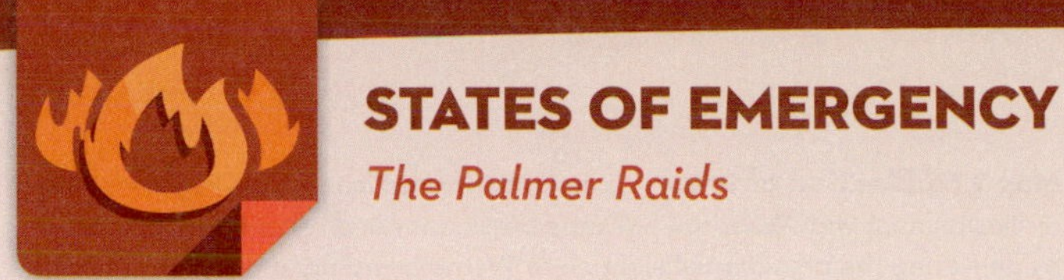

STATES OF EMERGENCY

The Palmer Raids

New Year's Day, 1920, promised to be a great day in the promising career of A. Mitchell Palmer. The "Fighting Quaker" had served as Woodrow Wilson's attorney general since early 1919. A former member of Congress from Pennsylvania, known for his passionate progressivism and his defense of the idea that the government's "power of self-preservation has no limits other than the extent of [an] emergency," Palmer had announced another raid on communists and other subversives. These dangerous revolutionaries, he explained, held large caches of explosives and arms and planned to unleash them on the government.

On the appointed day, federal agents swept thirty-three cities in twenty-three states, arresting thousands of revolutionaries and seizing their weapons cache, which turned out to consist of just three handguns. Police found no explosives, no machine guns, and no bolt-action, single-shot rifles of the sort issued to millions of soldiers during the war—none of the weapons one might suppose revolutionaries would make it their business to possess. Of the four thousand to six thousand people arrested, several hundred radicals had very probably planned or undertaken sabotage or other violent action against government officials and employers. However, many of the targeted individuals simply held radical beliefs or had spoken critically about the government. The majority had not broken any law or declaimed the government but were "guilty" only of being of eastern European or Russian extraction. Authorities deported five hundred of the detainees, many to Russia—a country most had never set foot in or had resided in only as a child. Few received trials, and those who were not deported were eventually released because of the lack of evidence against them.

Palmer, a man with presidential ambitions, was undaunted by the raids' failure to uncover evidence of a revolutionary plot. He and his assistant, J. Edgar Hoover (who would go on to direct the FBI), responded with a huge propaganda campaign against domestic radicalism in general and bolshevism in particular. On May Day (May 1, International Workers Day), they warned, radicals would attempt a coup against the U.S. government. Tensions mounted as May approached, and the National Guard went on alert. But May Day came and went without incident. Palmer's political career and the legitimacy of his policing campaigns were in shreds. Nonetheless, the raids, undertaken in the name of emergency, had effectively strangled American radicalism and chilled free speech.

Think About It

1. What did Palmer mean when he said that the government's "power of self-preservation has no limits other than the extent of [an] emergency"?
2. Why might Palmer have continued to insist on the existence of a communist plot to overthrow the government even though earlier raids uncovered no weapon caches?
3. Why were so many innocent immigrants caught up in Palmer's dragnet?

communistic and warned that dangerous revolutionaries were threatening American democracy. Other organizations, most notably the Ku Klux Klan (which was not backed by big business), took matters into their own hands. Vigilantes across the country sacked the offices of various socialist organizations—as well as antisocialist labor unions. Members of the IWW, which was already quite weak following the wartime crackdown, were beaten and lynched.

Suspicion spread to colleges and major research universities. Allegedly radical faculty members were fired, and radical literature was swept off library and bookstore shelves. Thirty-odd states enacted peacetime sedition laws mandating severe prison sentences for anyone convicted of fomenting revolution. By the end of the summer, over three hundred people had been imprisoned under these laws, some for simply voicing criticism of the government.

Finally, the federal government swung into action. In November 1919, Attorney General Palmer ordered federal police to conduct the first of several extensive and well-publicized dragnets of any organizations deemed radical. Most socialist, anarchist, and other leftist organizations and presses were squashed; the remainder got a powerful message that to engage in radical criticism of the government or of capitalism was to court state repression. The Palmer raids also sent an implicit warning to the labor movement, leading the AFL to harden its anti-Bolshevik stance and to distance itself further from potential socialist allies (see States of Emergency: The Palmer Raids). Radical ideas, organizations, and advocates would be largely absent from the public sphere until the 1930s.

END OF THE PROGRESSIVE ERA

Although Palmer and other Wilson cabinet members had been well-known progressives, progressivism fared badly in the waves of unrest and repression that followed the war. Reformers from Jane Addams to John Dewey found themselves under sustained attack from conservatives and business leaders keen to roll back many of progressives' wartime gains. Although they tended to be fierce critics of bolshevism, progressives were now tarred with the brush of anti-communist fear-mongering, and consequently many withdrew from public life. An ironic verse captured the fate of many progressives: "So when I disagree with you I'll call you Bol-she-vik! veek! veek! It's a scream and it's a shriek. It's a rapid-fire response to any heresy you speak."

Many progressives were enraged by Wilson's dismantling of the wartime state and Palmer's crackdown. "I hated the new state, its brutalities, its ignorance, its unpatriotic patriotism," lamented Frederic Howe, Wilson's disenchanted commissioner of immigration. "I wanted to protest against the destruction of my government, my democracy, my America." Jane Addams

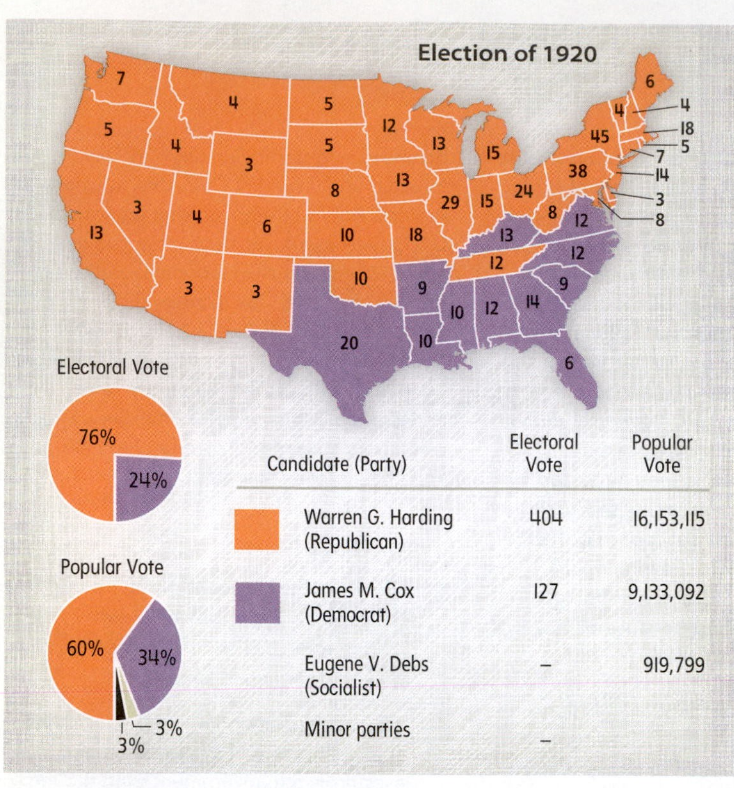

Candidate (Party)	Electoral Vote	Popular Vote
Warren G. Harding (Republican)	404	16,153,115
James M. Cox (Democrat)	127	9,133,092
Eugene V. Debs (Socialist)	–	919,799
Minor parties	–	

Map 22.5 Election of 1920. A majority of American voters registered their disillusionment with Woodrow Wilson's presidency and recent public disorder by delivering the presidential election to Warren Harding and the Republicans. Harding took 37 of 48 states and won 60 percent of the popular vote.

lost her once "unlimited faith in the president," ruefully noting the disparity between Wilson's fight for freedom abroad and his government's suppression of speech at home.

A recession hit with full force in 1920, knocking 10 percent off the gross national product, bankrupting 100,000 businesses, forcing 453,000 farmers off the land, and throwing almost five million Americans out of a job. The presidential elections of 1920 served as a referendum on the fate of progressivism and the direction of the nation. The Democrats offered a continuation of Wilsonian progressivism, including the unpopular stance on the League of Nations. In place of the ailing Wilson, progressive Ohio governor James Cox won the presidential nomination, with Franklin D. Roosevelt running as his vice president. The Republicans fielded another Ohioan, little-known senator Warren G. Harding, who promised to return the country to "normalcy." Governor Calvin Coolidge, who had won the support of business and northern conservatives for his handling of the Boston police strike, completed the Republican ticket as Harding's running mate. The Republicans won in a landslide victory (see Map 22.5).

CONCLUSION

The years 1914 to 1919 proved to be some of the most tumultuous of the twentieth century, and they shaped American politics—and global affairs—for several decades to come. Within a few years, most Americans would look back on the war not as a crusade for democracy but as a bleak and senseless tragedy. Writers such as Mary Borden and John Dos Passos, who had themselves survived the killing fields of Europe, bemoaned the fate of their "lost generation" and condemned the war as a meaningless slaughter. "You died," a disenchanted character in Ernest Hemingway's *A Farewell to Arms* put it bluntly, refusing to distinguish between his commanding officers and the enemy: "They threw you in and told you the rules and the first time they caught you off base they killed you." Above all, the bloodbath in Europe shattered the common progressive belief that civilized peoples no longer used violence to settle their differences.

Equally, by 1920 the progressive vision of collective security and collectivized government were lost causes. The United States never joined the League of Nations, and Woodrow Wilson died in 1924, a broken man. As a final sign of the failure of his diplomacy, Germany, which Wilson had tried to shield from the vindictive instincts of the Allies, failed to issue the usual condolences or lower its embassy flag upon the president's passing. With the election of Warren Harding in 1920, progressivism seemed in full retreat. Yet significant strains of progressive thought and a handful of progressive-minded politicians persisted into the 1920s. When the Great Depression devastated the nation and scrambled conservative politics in the early 1930s, the progressives' wartime state would prove a rich reservoir of ideas, personnel, and practical solutions.

STUDY TERMS

balance of power (p. 599)
self-determination (p. 599)
Western Front (p. 600)
Eastern Front (p. 600)
Central Powers (p. 601)
Allied Powers (p. 601)
trench warfare (p. 601)
Women's Peace Party (p. 602)
preparedness (p. 602)
conservative nationalism (p. 602)
Revenue Act (p. 603)
Lusitania (p. 603)
progressive idealists (p. 604)
Zimmermann Telegram (p. 604)
war collectivism (p. 605)
War Industries Board (p. 605)
National War Labor Board (p. 606)
Food Administration (p. 606)
liberty bonds (p. 608)
Committee on Public Information (p. 608)
Espionage Act (p. 610)
Alien Act (p. 610)
Sedition Act (p. 610)
American Civil Liberties Union (p. 611)
Selective Service Act (p. 611)
Great Migration (p. 614)
Eighteenth Amendment (p. 616)
National Woman's Party (p. 616)
Nineteenth Amendment (p. 617)
Meuse-Argonne offensive (p. 617)

- Bolshevik Revolution (p. 619)
- Fourteen Points (p. 620)
- Third Communist International (p. 620)
- Paris Peace Conference (p. 620)
- League of Nations (p. 621)
- Treaty of Versailles (p. 621)
- *The Birth of a Nation* (p. 622)
- Ku Klux Klan (p. 622)
- Red Scare (p. 624)
- Palmer raids (p. 625)

TIMELINE

1914 Austria-Hungary invades Bosnia

President Woodrow Wilson calls for neutrality after war breaks out in Europe.

British naval blockade cuts trade with Germany

Trench warfare claims 1.5 million lives

1915 Panama-Pacific International Exposition opens

Women's Peace Party demands peace and national self-determination at the Hague

Second Ku Klux Klan is founded following premiere of *The Clansman/The Birth of A Nation*

Wilsons reaffirms neutrality but undertakes military buildup after German submarine sinks *Lusitania*

1916 Wilson is narrowly reelected

Progressives divide over the question of entering the war

1917 Britain intercepts the Zimmermann Telegram

United States declares war and commences mass conscription under the Selective Services Act

Bolsheviks seize power in Russia and sign armistice with Germany

Committee on Public Information, War Industries Board, and Food Administration mobilize the nation for war

The National Women's Party pickets the White House

Race riots kill dozens in East St. Louis

Congress enacts the Espionage Act

1918 Wilson presents the Fourteen Points

Congress passes the Eighteenth Amendment (instituting Prohibition; comes into force, 1920)

U.S. troops enter combat

The "Spanish flu" claims the first of 50–100 million lives globally

U.S. forces overwhelm Germans at Château-Thierry

Germany calls for armistice

1919 Wilson attends Paris Peace Conference while war industries and economy collapse at home

Great powers sign Treaty of Versailles

Race riots and labor strikes break out in dozens of American cities

Attorney General A. Mitchell Palmer orders raids on suspected subversives

U.S. Senate refuses to ratify Treaty of Versailles

Congress enacts Nineteenth Amendment (women's suffrage)

1920 Women vote for the first time in a presidential election

Republican Warren Harding is elected president

FURTHER READING

Additional suggested readings are available on the Online Learning Center at www.mhhe.com/becomingamerica1e.

Christopher Capozzola, *Uncle Sam Wants You: World War I and the Making of the Modern American Citizen* (2008), traces the role of local authorities—from librarians to postmasters—in the drive to suppress dissent and activate citizens as volunteers in surveillance efforts.

John Milton Cooper, *Woodrow Wilson: A Biography* (2009), comprehensively treats Wilson's life, political career, progressive vision, and segregationist politics.

Alan Dawley, *Changing the World: American Progressives in War and Revolution* (2005), explores progressives' messianic mission to bring peace and security to the world and the differences among them.

Ellis Hawley, *The Great War and the Search for Modern Order* (revised edition, 1997), analyzes progressives' use and understanding of the war.

Kimberly Jensen, *Mobilizing Minerva: American Women in the First World War* (2008), recounts how women joined the fight on and off the battlefield with a view to claiming the full rights of citizenship.

Jennifer Keene, *Doughboys, the Great War, and the Remaking of America* (2001), traces the draftees' experience of war, from conscription through deployment and combat to demobilization and the campaign for veterans' benefits.

Margaret MacMillan, *Paris 1919: Six Months That Changed the World* (2003), recounts the negotiations and backroom horse-trading behind the Treaty of Versailles that ultimately thwarted most of Woodrow Wilson's Fourteen Points.

Malcolm D. Magee, *What the World Should Be: Woodrow Wilson and the Crafting of a Faith-Based Foreign Policy* (2008), explores Wilson's religious convictions in relation to his crusade for peace and democracy.

Erez Manela, *The Wilsonian Moment: Self-Determination and the International Origins of Anticolonial Nationalism* (2008), examines the colonized world's enthusiastic response to Wilson's call for self-determination and subsequent disappointment.

David S. Patterson, *The Search for Negotiated Peace: Women's Activism and Citizen Diplomacy in World War I* (2009), traces the founding of the modern American peace movement and the critical role that suffragists played.

Stephen Ponder, *Managing the Press: Origins of the Media Presidency, 1897–1933*, argues that, like Presidents William McKinley and Theodore Roosevelt, Woodrow Wilson grasped the political importance of shaping public opinion, but that his administration also went one step further, attempting to control all news regarding government.

Robert H. Zieger, *America's Great War: World War I and the American Experience* (2000), offers a comprehensive account of the experiences of women, progressives, and African Americans during the war.

23

INSIDE ▶

THE BIG PICTURE

Jazz, radio, and youth culture burst onto the scene, dismantling old conventions and forging new ones. Business thrived and industrial workers enjoyed their highest standard of living yet. But modern life also brought with it new social divisions, and unchecked financial speculation triggered a devastating economic crash.

Heavenly Airwaves. Aimee Semple McPherson was the most popular of several evangelical pastors to build a mass congregation using leading-edge technology and publicity techniques.

AMERICA IN THE JAZZ AGE

On the evening of Friday, January 16, 1920, millions of Americans gathered in homes, bars, and churches to mark the death of "John Barleycorn," the personification of beer and whiskey. At the stroke of midnight, the Volstead Act would go into effect, criminalizing the production, sale, and transportation of alcoholic beverages. In the nation's capital, Secretary of the Navy Franklin D. Roosevelt sipped champagne with college classmates. Across the Potomac, the Reverend Billy Sunday bellowed over a twenty-foot coffin in a mock funeral before a congregation of fifteen thousand people: "John Barleycorn, we bury you because . . . you disfigured our bodies; you ruined our nervous system; you dethroned our reason; you caused idiocy and insanity; . . . you destroyed both soul and body; you darkened our homes; you broke our hearts. . . . Farewell, you good-for-nothing, God-forsaken, iniquitous, blear-eyed [sic], bloated-faced, old imp of perdition!" Three hours later, as the clock struck twelve in Los Angeles, saloons emptied out for the last time. Patrons glumly followed jazz bands and cabaret dancers down Main Street to the Eagle café, where "mourners" somberly gathered around yet another Barleycorn coffin to pay their final respects.

The following day, the officially "dry" nation entered a thirteen-year period of widespread lawlessness, as bootleggers, smugglers, and gangsters filled demand for spirits, wine, and beer across the nation. Especially in cities, organized crime burst forth on an unprecedented scale, turning a massive profit by quenching

Americans' thirst for alcohol—and their desire for live jazz, "hot" dancing, and glamorous venues. Young adults in particular reveled in what appeared to be a freer, more expressive culture, celebrating the flamboyant "anything goes" attitude of the day. It was the era of the flapper, the slummer, and the celebrity—the "Jazz Age," as coined by novelist F. Scott Fitzgerald. And, for the first time in the country's history, African American writers and musicians won considerable recognition among white audiences and a foothold in the culture industry.

KEY QUESTIONS

- What caused the consumer economy to boom in the 1920s and then crash?
- In what ways did advertising, radio, and mass spectacle change everyday life?
- What were the consequences of Prohibition?
- Why and among which groups of Americans were fundamentalist and evangelical strains of Christianity increasingly popular?
- Why did the Great Migration accelerate, and how did African Americans experience the opportunities and barriers they encountered in northern cities?

The period was also one in which skilled American workers commanded the highest standard of living of any workers in the Western world. Republican administrations supported pro-business tax and trade policies, and banks and business made borrowing available on a wider scale than ever before. An emerging advertising industry used the new medium of radio to flood homes throughout the country with the promise of better living through amazing appliances and foods. Nationally syndicated radio shows, movies, and magazine advertisements all reinforced the idea that the "good life" and personal fulfillment could be attained through the purchase of goods. Parades sponsored by department stores heightened the excitement of buying in the holiday season. Mass consumer culture, long in development, was coming of age.

Yet the nation was far from united in embracing these changes. As homeowners, drivers, and vacationers, Americans happily participated in consumer culture, but many also lamented the loss of what they claimed were traditional American values. Catholic bishops threatening mass boycotts managed to "clean up" the movies, while parents and Christian clergy launched less successful campaigns to ban jazz. Fundamentalist Christians clashed with liberal Christians over modern science, sweeping the country into a passionate debate about evolution. At the extreme end of the culture wars, the second Ku Klux Klan attracted hundreds of thousands of Americans with its agenda of "purifying" communities by driving out bootleggers, immigrants, Catholics, Jews, and African Americans.

Tombstones marking the "death" of John Barleycorn popped up in churchyards, town squares, and private yards all over the United States on January 17, 1920, the day that Prohibition took effect.

Although the economy expanded, large sections of the population could not afford to participate fully in the new consumer culture. Farmers and low-skilled workers saw their incomes decline over the decade, and by 1928 more than half of Americans were living on or under the poverty line (the bare minimum of food needed to survive). Adding to the structural weakness of the consumer economy were the startling growth in personal and commercial debt and the overvaluation of stocks and real estate. The decade was to close as dramatically as it opened, with the Wall Street crash, which exposed these underlying weaknesses and sent the entire nation reeling.

THE TRIUMPH OF CONSUMER CAPITALISM

By 1922, the nation had recovered from the severe industrial recession that had followed World War I. Unemployment dropped to record lows and real wages rose in most sectors, securing for many industrial workers the highest standard of living in the world. For the first time, consumer goods—especially automobiles and home appliances, but also radios, movies, household chemicals, and electricity—played a crucial role in the growing economy. Production expanded at the lightning rate of about 5 percent per year through 1929, by which time factories were pumping out 64 percent more consumer goods than in 1920. The chief engines of this boom were the federal government's pro-business policies, the advent of easier credit, new attitudes toward money, changes in advertising and media networks, and the spread of Henry Ford's model of a high-wage, high-consumption economy. Get-rich-quick schemes abounded, and for the first time, large numbers of workers invested. Many profited, but several spectacular busts caused hundreds of thousands of people to lose some or all of their life savings.

THE REPUBLICANS RETURN

Although mainly remembered for the corruption scandals that tarnished the last year of his presidency, Republican Warren G. Harding (elected in 1920) was a relatively popular president, associated neither with World War I nor with the painful period of "readjustment" that had followed. Most Americans instead identified him with industrial growth, rising wages, and a cascade of affordable consumer goods.

Although elected on an anti-progressive platform, Harding's cabinet was a mix of conservatives, businessmen, and some independents with progressive credentials (including Herbert Hoover). Harding's declaration, at his inauguration in 1921, that he would return the country to "normalcy" was in practice a blend of conservative and progressive principles. He immediately asked Congress to cut the income taxes that had soured so many middle- and upper-income Americans on progressivism. Lawmakers obliged, cutting wartime luxury taxes in 1921 and reducing the highest income tax rate to 33 percent. But they refused to trim the excess profits tax or abolish the estate tax. Two years later, however, the administration persuaded Congress to lower corporate taxes and cut the upper-income tax rate again, to just 25 percent. The Federal Trade Commission ceased to enforce the antitrust laws that progressives had championed.

These policies explicitly aimed to create an environment that was favorable to business. They generated an infusion of cash into the economy, which in turn stimulated investment. But Harding's administration did not pursue a pure laissez-faire policy of small government and nonintervention in the economy, as is popularly believed. Some parts of government grew rather than shrank in the 1920s. In particular, the Department of Commerce expanded dramatically under the leadership of Herbert Hoover. A believer in free markets, Hoover nonetheless insisted that businessmen should engage in "voluntary cooperation" with government and workers, on the grounds that cooperation made American business more efficient and therefore more profitable and internationally competitive. The Commerce Department worked closely with the corporate sector to establish voluntary trade associations, which set industrywide standards for goods and services, and to set voluntary wage and price controls. In a holdover from the Progressive Era, Commerce and other federal agencies also generated and distributed all kinds of information that was useful for business, including production statistics and trade forecasts.

Internationally, the Harding administration rejected Wilsonian diplomacy and refused to join the League of Nations. The United States quietly moved away from the military interventionism that had characterized policy in Central America during the Progressive Era. America did not retreat into

Warren G. Harding. Poet E. E. Cummings may have lampooned President Harding as "the only man, woman or child who wrote a simple declarative sentence with seven grammatical errors," but Americans mostly welcomed Harding's apparent vigor, reassuring demeanor, and frankness. Harding appears here with his beloved dog, Laddie Boy.

isolationism, however, as many progressives had forecasted. In a move that delighted most struggling progressives, the United States, Britain, France, and Germany signed the Kellogg-Briand Pact (1928), which prohibited war among the signatories. Harding recognized Mexico's government (in exchange for compensation for American property losses during the revolution) and Secretary of State Charles Evan Hughes negotiated the Washington Naval Treaties (1921–1922), under which Japan, Britain, France, and Italy pledged to suspend the renewed naval arms race and to honor America's Open Door policy (see Chapter 21).

Most significantly, Harding eased the way for U.S. trade and investment overseas by dispatching trade attachés, expanding overseas embassies, and facilitating the flow of information between host countries and American business. Corporations such as Ford Motors, weapons giant Du Pont de Nemours, and Hollywood's MGM Studios opened dozens of production facilities in Europe, Latin America, and Australia. American engineering and production methods became highly influential, even in communist Russia, where leader Vladimir Illich Lenin proclaimed Ford's assembly line the key to modernization.

ENGINES OF PROSPERITY

The automobile industry became a major driver of the national economy in the 1920s as it directly employed 7 percent of all industrial workers and generated jobs in countless related industries, including road building, petroleum, insurance, steel, glass, rubber, and tourism. Once dominated by Henry Ford, whose no-frills Model T accounted for 54 percent of all new car sales in the early 1920s, the auto industry after 1924 followed the General Motors (GM) emphasis on comfort, style, and power—as well as new features such as automatic windshield wipers. Rather than presenting its product as uniform and unchanging, GM applied marketing principles that the fashion industry had perfected in the Progressive Era. The company regularly updated and innovated its automobiles, ran lavish advertising campaigns announcing the release of the latest model, and built the first capacious, floodlit "showrooms." The emphasis now was all about consumer choice. Compelled to follow GM's lead, Ford introduced the Model A, a more luxurious car that, in line with the new ethos of consumer choice, was available in a variety of colors and body styles.

Although the Model T was obsolete by 1927, Ford's management model of high wages and assembly line manufacture became a pillar of the consumer economy. More skilled industries and businesses followed his example of paying workers at historically high rates that enabled them to buy consumer goods, in turn stimulating demand and increasing consumption. Employers also theorized that workers' emerging identity as consumers made them more content with their employers and less open to unionization or radicalization. With the widespread adoption of **Fordism,** workers' wages rose steadily after 1922 and assembly lines helped drive prices to historic lows. Employees' purchasing power increased dramatically and, by 1929, America's high-skill workers could afford more and higher quality consumer goods than any other labor force in the world.

Higher wages, however, came at a price. As before World War I, manufacturers vehemently opposed unionization, only their tactics were now largely indirect and nonviolent. Many offered various services that unions would have otherwise provided—such as workers' insurance, pensions, and disability support. They also instituted raises to reward long-term service and gave workers paid vacations. Workers did not benefit equally, however. Like many employers, the Chicago meat and steel industries reached a tacit agreement with skilled white workers that they would keep immigrant and black labor separate from native Protestant workers, and lavished more benefits on the latter. Employers generally concentrated African Americans in the least skilled positions, such as cleaning and hauling and gave European immigrants and first-generation Americans semiskilled work. The best-paid, skilled positions and benefits were reserved for native-born white Protestant men. Much as employers had hoped, union membership continued to decline through the decade.

Many industrialists and the State Department also promoted Fordism overseas as the key to political stability and economic vitality. With the approval of European labor leaders, Ford paid workers in his European factories the same real wages as his employees in Detroit received—a policy that unnerved government leaders, who worried that other workers would strike for the same high wages. European labor organizations and U.S. industry also boasted of American workers' unrivaled purchasing power, touting their "standard of living" as the highest in the world. To demonstrate their point visually, Ford and Boston department store magnate Edward Filene sent a series of display trunks to Europe, each containing what they claimed were the clothes of an "average" American family of four, photographs of their housing, and detailed household budgets. Spectators were amazed to learn that every year the typical American husband purchased five shirts, two cotton suits, two ties, two pairs of leather shoes, and nine pairs of work gloves and that his wife and children were likewise clad in new, fine-quality, store-bought clothing. Exhibits such as these inevitably exaggerated what the average family could afford and ignored the fact that European governments and unions provided social services. But skilled American workers indisputably had considerably more money and goods than Europe's—and they were the envy of workers and labor leaders everywhere.

ADVERTISING THE GOOD LIFE

Advertisers played a central role both in boosting sales of consumer goods and, more profoundly, in changing people's attitudes toward money, consumption, and the meaning of happiness. Aware that mass advertising was critical to consumption, business spent on average $3.2 billion ($41 billion in today's dollars) on advertising each year—about 50 percent more than the nation spent annually on K–12 education. The volume of magazine, billboard, and newspaper advertising more than quadrupled between 1917 and 1929, aiming to stimulate among Americans the conscious desire to consume.

Advertising used a host of new strategies to convince Americans that purchasing the latest clothes, gadgets, cars, foods, and other consumer goods would lead to health, happiness, and prosperity. Adopting the tie-in technique that the federal government had used to great effect during World War I advertisers recruited famous figures from the mass media, such as well-known baseball players and movie stars, linking the celebrity's material success and happiness with their product. Signaling a shift away from nineteenth-century values, advertising now emphasized the celebrity's consumption habits and way of life rather than the hard work, solid character, or frugality that earlier advertising had highlighted. The new approach both encouraged ordinary people to fantasize about the good life and persuaded them that they, too, could attain the same lifestyle as the rich and famous.

Celebrity Sells. Celebrities and mass advertising emerged hand-in-hand in the 1920s, as this candy wrapper, bearing Babe Ruth's image and endorsement, testifies.

More than anyone else, baseball player George Herman "Babe" Ruth embodied the emerging celebrity culture. His fame was in large part made by—and in turn helped to make—the advertising business. Traded to the New York Yankees from the Boston Red Sox in 1920, Ruth hit a record-smashing sixty home runs during a single season, a feat that made him the undisputed king of baseball until 1961, when Roger Maris broke Ruth's record. Earning about $100,000 a year (the equivalent of $1.2 million today), Ruth was the first ballplayer to outearn many top executives, including the president of the United States (see How Much Is That?). Born and raised in a working-class Baltimore neighborhood, Ruth reveled in his triumphs on the diamond and embraced his newfound consumer power. He spent liberally on luxury goods—in full view of the mass media. Advertisers paid "the Bambino" handsomely for his endorsements, and both Hollywood and Ruth cashed in on his celebrity status. Advertising turned dozens of actors and athletes into stars in this way—and helped spread the consumer ethos in the process.

How Much Is That?

Babe Ruth's Paycheck

Americans were awed by the earnings of Babe Ruth, who made an unprecedented $100,000 per year from his baseball contract alone. Adjusted for inflation, the Bambino's salary would be worth $1.2 million today—considerably less than the $29 million annual paycheck of top earner Alex Rodriguez.

The transformation of actors, singers, and sports heroes into mass celebrities quickly spread through the culture at large via magazine and newspaper articles and profiles in newsreels—short films about current events that theaters screened before the feature movie. For the first time, newspapers and magazines became deeply dependent on revenues from commercial advertising. *Time*, *The New Yorker*, and *Better Homes and Gardens* were just a few of the dozens of new magazines stuffed full of advertisements—which themselves were far more visually compelling than before. "A magazine," observed one advertising executive, "is simply a device to induce people to read advertising." In an effort to make products memorable, advertisers also designed logos and catchy brand names that manufacturers then turned into trademarked property by registering them at the U.S. Patent Office. This government service, which enabled manufacturers to legally own product names, logos, and advertising images (and prevent rivals from using them), was an essential part of branding.

Advertisers also attempted to elevate their trade to a respectable occupation, pressing business schools to offer classes in marketing and advertising and publishing a plethora of manuals on the so-called science of selling. When studies revealed that four out of every five purchasers of consumer goods were women, many commentators correctly argued that the traditional working family, headed by a male breadwinner who made most budgetary decisions, was obsolete. "The typical American man," observed Christine Frederick in her leading manual, *Mrs. Consumer*, "seems to enjoy himself most at earning, while content to leave the pleasure of spending to his women. . . . Such a condition puts buying power into women's hands on a tremendously broad scale." Targeting white women became the new standard in advertising, and the psychology of women came to be the principal object of study. Most white advertisers reinforced the color line by largely ignoring African Americans or by drawing on stereotypical images (see Interpreting the Sources: Advertisement for Aunt Jemima Self-Raising Pancake Mix).

According to advertising manuals, women could be persuaded most effectively by appeals to their supposed insecurities and implicit warnings about the embarrassment caused by the failure to use certain products. Marriage, children, friends, and a comfortable life would bypass the woman who forgot (or never knew) that she was supposed to use a particular deodorant, toothpaste, or laundry detergent. A new generation of etiquette books reinforced this notion, and many women came to see products that were once luxuries as necessities.

Advertisers' emphasis on fitting in soon spread, especially among another demographic they deemed impressionable—youth. In advertising and cinema, the rail-thin flapper replaced the hourglass Gibson Girl, and dieting and "reducing" programs, books, and aids became popular for the first time. A lucrative beauty industry responded to—and shaped—young women's changing mode of self-presentation. Beauty shops increased eightfold during the decade and millions of young women adopted one or another fad diet, such as the Hollywood 18-Day Diet (which allowed only 585 calories a day—about a quarter of the 2,000 calories that the U.S. Drug and Food Administration recommends for women today). Many entrepreneurial women, including Elizabeth Arden and Madame C. J. Walker, founded cosmetic companies, and thousands of other white and African American women built careers in the industry. By the late 1920s, the beauty industry had successfully enticed the mothers and aunts of young women to pursue the "youthful" spirit, too.

Making Makeup Respectable. Some of the entrepreneurs who reaped vast fortunes in the beauty industry had turned household products into commercially viable cosmetics that were aimed at overcoming middle-class women's association of makeup with prostitution. The first successful mascara, for instance, was a mix of coal dust and Vaseline that Chicago entrepreneur T. L. Williams had seen his sister Mabel applying to her lashes and that he later branded as Maybelline. In this photograph, flapper actress Colleen Moore explains how to apply Winx, a rival eyelash darkener: "Curl back the lashes with the mascara brush, first brushing them clean of any face powder." **Questions for Analysis:** What is new about the standard of femininity portrayed here? In what ways does the photograph's underlying message aim to overcome makeup's traditional association with prostitution?

The branding principle also influenced the retail industry, chiefly through the development of **chain stores.** Seeking to drive "mom-and-pop" gasoline outlets—which usually consisted of a lone pump and a nondescript shack—out of business, the Socony-Vacuum Oil Company built a series of gas stations resembling colonial homes, while Wadham's gas chain erected distinctive Chinese pagodas. Chain grocery stores also came to dominate much of the food market, with A&P's 15,400 stores leading the charge. Such chains could purchase in large quantities from suppliers at a reduced price and undersell independent grocers (causing many to go bankrupt). Most groceries adopted the self-service model of Tennessee's Piggly Wiggly, which allowed shoppers to browse and select their own items, much as they were used to doing in department stores. This in turn led food manufacturers to invest heavily in eye-catching packaging and advertising.

The use of architecture to establish brand recognition was not confined to chains. With the automobile boom, a new kind of building—large-scale models of consumer products—proliferated, typically on roadsides. Enormous coffeepots, windmills, and pigs, along with gigantic milk cans and hats, caught the eye of passersby and advertised the business inside. Neon signs and oversize advertising billboards also made their first appearance in the mid-1920s.

NETWORKING THE AIRWAVES: THE BIRTH OF BROADCASTING

The world's first broadcasting system—radio—also sped the spread of consumer culture. Although commercial shippers, the military, and hobbyists had used radio since the 1910s, it was not until 1922 that manufacturers and advertisers recognized its potential as a medium for instantaneous mass communication. Radio offered unprecedented access to a mass market of consumers—and unlike mail, railroads, the telegraph, and telephones, it did not require enormous amounts of land, labor, money, and time to build. (It did, however, require electric power.)

Once the business world reconceptualized radio as a mass advertising network, hundreds and then thousands of companies began operating stations. Western Electric and General Electric manufactured receivers that were more appealing to consumers, substituting loudspeakers for the old headphones and redesigning the sets to resemble elegant furniture. The same companies made homes radio-ready by connecting millions of homes to the electricity grid, doubling the proportion of homes with electricity, from 35 percent in 1920 to almost 70 percent by 1930.

Advertising and radio grew hand in glove, with the former generating much-needed revenue for radio and the latter extending advertisers' reach to audiences of tens of millions of people. Local businesses and national corporations frequently sponsored radio shows (such as the *The Gold Dust Twins,* named for a household scouring product), and many also recorded advertisements for their products. By 1925, 2.75 million radio receivers were in operation and approximately 10 percent of all homes had a radio. Five years later, one in three families owned a radio and the majority of Americans got their news that way rather than from newspapers (see Map 23.1). Although music constituted 70 percent of

Birth of the Chain Restaurant. The White Castle hamburger chain modeled its restaurants on Chicago's famous Water Tower, blending modern cinderblock construction with a medieval castle appearance. Founded in Wichita, Kansas, the company grew to include 113 "castles" by 1931. In light of earlier scandals in the sausage and ground meat industries, White Castle's open floor plan allowed customers to see how—and with what ingredients—their hamburgers were made.

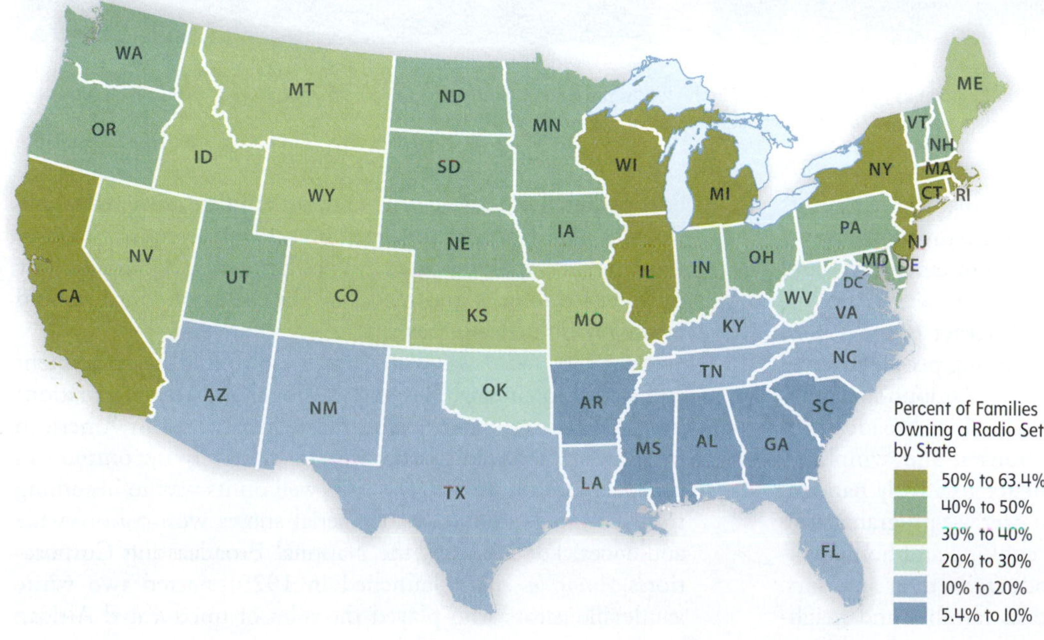

Map 23.1 Radio Set Ownership, 1930. Few people owned electric radio sets before 1920, but they had become commonplace across much of the nation by 1930. States in which few homes had electricity, such as Mississippi and Alabama, missed out on the radio sets and the new mass culture they broadcast.

Domesticating Radio. Westinghouse and other companies redesigned radios in the 1920s, promoting them as pleasing parlor furniture around which the family could gather comfortably rather than as complicated technical devices best housed in a garage or workshop.

broadcast content in the early 1920s, radio also turned events such as trials, parades, and baseball games into broadcast events that a mass of listeners could experience simultaneously—and far more intimately—than ever before.

Like television in the 1950s and the Internet in the 1990s, radio quickly transformed everyday life. Young people in small towns everywhere heard the latest jazz from cosmopolitan cities and gathered together to dance to the radio. Live broadcasts of performances from dancehalls, opera houses, and symphony halls were popular, expanding the audience to a truly national one. By the mid-1920s, talk shows and exercise programs were also popular. Housewives tuned in for cooking and homemaking shows, many built around the products of their sponsors. New patterns of socializing developed as families and neighbors gathered at radio parties and, on Sundays, listened to nationally renowned evangelical preachers. Even in prisons, wardens such as Sing Sing's Lewis E. Lawes piped radio (strictly censored) into cells and mess halls in the hope that it would positively influence inmates.

By 1930, radio was also a major source of entertainment and a rival to cinema. Although regional and ethnic variations persisted (including in California, where Mexican American radio flourished), and radio was still relatively uncommon in the Deep South, the medium was well on its way to becoming truly national. A slew of new serial shows won countrywide audiences. For instance, the National Broadcasting Corporation's *Amos 'n' Andy,* launched in 1929, starred two white vaudeville actors who played the roles of uneducated African

INTERPRETING THE SOURCES

Advertisement for Aunt Jemima Self-Raising Pancake Mix

The figure of "Aunt Jemima" was a stock character from blackface minstrel shows of the nineteenth century, in which white men applied blackened cork to their faces and lampooned African American women as "happy slaves" and "mammies." The character made her first appearance on cans of R. T. Davis Milling Company's self-raising pancake mix in 1889. Four years later, the company hired a former Tennessee slave, Nancy Green, to play the role of Aunt Jemima at a pancake demonstration stand at the World's Columbian Exposition in Chicago. The mill subsequently sent Green around the nation promoting the mix as Aunt Jemima, altering the image to resemble Green. In the 1920s, mass marketing and colorful cardboard packaging made "Aunt Jemima" the most familiar advertising icon in the United States. Consumers believed she was a real person rather than the creation of the Davis mill's advertising department. Nancy Green died in 1923, and the company subsequently hired dozens of African American women to play the role locally.

Stereotypes in Advertising. In the 1920s, artist N. C. Wyeth was hired to produce a series of advertisements that placed the fictional figure of Aunt Jemima in significant historical moments in order to legitimate the invented personality. This oil painting, which appeared in an advertisement for the Aunt Jemima pancake mix, placed the famous character at the 1893 World's Columbian Exposition in Chicago, where, the ad copy said, excitement for "her" pancakes created such a disturbance that the "Columbian Guards had to come and keep the crowd moving."

Explore the Source

1. On what stereotypes does the image of Aunt Jemima draw?
2. Why do you think advertisers of the 1920s tried to sell pancake mix this way?
3. What desires might advertisers have aimed to stir in potential consumers?
4. How do you think this image may have reinforced the ideology of racial segregation?

American migrants from the South. Much in the same vein as advertising, the show played to popular white stereotypes of black southerners as comic bumblers who constantly fell prey to get-rich-quick schemes. An instant hit, the program raised sales of radio receivers 25 percent in 1929 alone and launched a raft of new expressions (including "Holy mackerel!" and "Ain't dat sumpin'?"). Despite criticism from the National Association for the Advancement of Colored People (NAACP), by 1931 over forty million Americans (almost two-thirds of all listeners) tuned in to *Amos 'n' Andy* every night.

THE CULTURE OF CREDIT

Along with advertising and radio, greater access to credit and changing attitudes toward debt sped the transition to a consumer-oriented economy. Consumer credit, which was not available to most Americans before 1920, expanded dramatically when GM offered a monthly installment purchase plan, which enabled people to put down a deposit and drive home with a new car. This form of credit boosted car sales threefold, accounting for 75 percent of new car sales by 1924.

Some manufacturers, including Henry Ford, still demanded cash payment in full, arguing that the installment plan subverted individuals' desire to work hard and save up for the things they wanted. But consumers and most other manufacturers rapidly embraced the system. By 1929, installment purchases accounted for 60 percent to 90 percent of all "big ticket" goods, including vacuum cleaners, radios, refrigerators, automobiles, and furniture. At the same time, rules governing housing mortgages were relaxed in some areas, and home buyers had to pay only 10 percent—instead of the formidable 50 percent—as a down payment.

Installment purchasing put expensive goods within reach of many upper-working-class and middle-class people and reinforced the consumerist attitude that the good life meant acquiring the latest appliances and other goods. It also taught consumers how to budget in order to meet their monthly payments, because missing payments could result in repossession. Older ideals of frugality, thrift, and living debt-free now seemed obsolete and potentially a drag on the economy. For the first time, going into debt for the sake of consumption was respectable.

SPECULATORS AND SWINDLERS

Another kind of debt, brokers' loans, also became respectable and commonplace. Whereas banks and wealthy investors had traditionally paid cash for stocks and bonds, the middlemen who placed orders began advancing them loans with which to pay for investments. Soon, steel, automobile, and other manufacturing companies began to deal in brokers' loans, and by 1928 around $9 billion ($119 billion in today's dollars) in loans were being offered annually. Together with federal tax cuts, the loans generated millions of dollars for investment on the stock market, fueling one of the strongest bull markets in American history. At its height, the *New York Times* industrial index (a measure of the aggregate price of stocks) increased 85 percent in just twenty months, as compared to an average of 16 percent. Easier credit, however, also vastly increased the debt levels of banks and industry and encouraged investors to invest in far riskier enterprises.

For the first time, skilled workers, small businesspeople, and salaried employees infused the markets with an enormous amount of cash. "If a man saves $15 a week and invests in common stocks," GM executive John J. Raskob informed magazine readers, "at the end of 20 years, he will have at least $80,000 . . . not only can [he] be rich . . . but [he] *ought* to be rich." An unprecedented number of Americans (four million) bought shares on the stock market, and millions more invested directly in oil, real estate, mining, and other ventures. Some investments were sound, but a speculative fever—fueled by media and advertising—swept the nation and drew unsuspecting investors into dubious and even criminal get-rich-quick schemes (see Hot Commodities: Miami Beach).

The fresh source of investment dollars also proved a boon for swindlers who peddled fake companies and capitalized on new investors' enthusiasm (which often far outstripped their financial expertise). Although swindlers were nothing new, their frauds were more numerous and on a much larger scale than before. Deploying the same advertising tactics used by manufacturers and department stores, they posted glossy advertisement on billboards and used the new copying technologies of addressographs and multigraphs to mass-mail professional-looking advertisements promising instant riches. The advent of more sophisticated monetary instruments, such as coupons, also created new opportunities for fraud.

One such opportunist, Charles Ponzi, realized that due to changes in the exchange rate of the U.S. dollar, he could buy postal coupons in Spain or Italy and then sell them for a 100-percent profit in the United States. Setting up shop in Boston, Ponzi doubled initial investors' money within ninety days, news of which attracted thirty thousand new subscribers. Soon, the press lauded him as a "wizard of finance" and "America's most talked-about man." Within a few months, however, orders for coupon purchases outnumbered actual coupons, forcing Ponzi to pay off early investors using money from more recent subscribers. All went well until investors grew suspicious and, in a panic, tried to cash-out their shares. Redemptions vastly outstripped Ponzi's cash reserves, and the company collapsed, bringing down thousands of small investors (and several banks) with it. Ponzi was later convicted on mail fraud charges and served several years in federal prison, but millions of people continued to be seduced by other "Ponzi schemes."

Scandal also struck the Harding administration when it surfaced that some cabinet members had illegally awarded contracts to corporations by dodging bidding procedures. The most infamous was the Teapot Dome scandal (1922–1923), in which the federal government had illegally leased out governmental oil reserves at Teapot Dome, Wyoming, and Elk Hills, California. Albert Fall, Harding's secretary of the interior, was later convicted of accepting bribes and sentenced to prison. Harding himself died of a heart attack just as the scandals began to break. Vice President Calvin Coolidge assumed office and proceeded to clean up much of the corruption that had marred the previous four years.

AGE OF MASS SPECTACLE

By 1920, for the first time ever, a majority of Americans (52 percent) lived in cities—and nineteen million more urbanized in the course of the decade. Most dwelled in big metropolitan centers such as St. Louis, San Francisco, and New York, but almost as many Americans (seventeen million) inhabited mid-size towns of between ten thousand and one hundred thousand people. Urbanization fed the growth of a culture industry that provided entertainment on a massive scale and drove out thousands of smaller, independent companies. Baseball team owners built giant new stadiums to attract millions of working-class and middle-class spectators and, with the help of radio and newsreels, turned the "national pastime" into a mass spectacle. Motion pictures became a respectable form of entertainment for middle-class people in sumptuous new "movie palaces." Everywhere, department stores sponsored enormous parades promoting the consumerist potential of Christmas.

MAKING A SPECTACLE OF SPORTS

Major league baseball began the decade under a cloud of distrust and sagging ticket sales when eight Chicago White Sox players were indicted for accepting bribes. (High-stakes gamblers had allegedly paid them to lose the 1919 World Series to the Cincinnati Reds—and they obliged.) Viewing the Black Sox scandal as a publicity disaster for the sport, team owners decided to establish a baseball commission, charged with restoring public confidence and ticket sales. The chief commissioner fired the White Sox eight and mandated the use of a harder, faster ball, which sped up play by making it easier for batsmen (most famously, Babe Ruth) to slug home runs. Pitchers were banned from spitting tobacco juice

HOT COMMODITIES

Miami Beach

In 1910, the swampy, mosquito-ridden islands of Biscayne Bay, Florida, hardly seemed habitable, let alone desirable as a vacation destination. But Indiana entrepreneur, auto racer, and highway developer Carl Fisher saw tremendous potential in what was to become the resort city of Miami Beach. Fisher soon bought land, erected a bridge and two hotels, and launched two great highway-building projects—the Lincoln Highway, connecting the Pacific and Atlantic coasts, and the Dixie Highway, running from Canada to the foot of his Miami bridge. By 1920, the highways and rail connections were complete and Fisher had dredged the bay, built several residential islands, and created a harbor into which larger vessels could sail. He was ready to sell land, sand, and sun in his manufactured paradise.

Tourists, retirees, and other potential buyers, however, had little interest in a region long considered a rural backwater. Consequently, Fisher hired publicist Steve Hannigan to target major urban centers, especially in the Northeast and Midwest, filling newspapers and magazines with enticing images of golden sand and "bathing beauties." A giant Times Square billboard on display during New York's chilly winter boasted, "It's June in Florida"—and showed middle-class motorists driving down the sleek Dixie Highway to paradise. It was one of the most successful publicity campaigns in history.

Publicity Stunt. Golf professional John Brophy teed off on Rosie the elephant's back in one of many publicity shots for Miami Beach. Another photograph showed President Harding using Rosie as a golf caddy.

Sales rocketed, helping to launch Miami Beach and the entire "Sunshine State" into prominence. The permanent population of Fisher's island city more than quintupled to 5,000 by 1924, and mainland Miami ballooned from 5,500 to 150,000 residents (25,000 of whom were real estate agents). Other developers saturated magazines and the mail with colorful advertisements, and thousands of parcels of land—once swampland or orange groves—were bought, subdivided, and sold each year. Traffic crawled bumper to bumper on the Dixie Highway, the trains were overflowing, and the *Miami Herald* included five hundred pages of real estate advertising. Land values shot up so rapidly—a parcel bought for $2,500 in 1923, for example, was sold for $35,000 two years later—that purchasers began to treat property as an investment rather than as a place for prospective homes, hoping to resell at enormous profits a few months later.

Vast fortunes were made, Fisher's foremost among them. But Florida's modern-day "land fever" drove prices so high that they far outstripped value. In 1925, the Internal Revenue Service threatened to tax speculators who made massive profits by "flipping" properties. Newspapers reported that swindlers were selling lots on unbuildable land or near towns that did not exist. Sensing that the market might soon lose steam, major developers withdrew. The following year, a hurricane devastated Miami Beach and much of South Florida, killing four hundred people, destroying thousands of homes, and returning several developments to the swamps. Newsreels and photographs of the destruction replaced the enticing images of reclining beauties. Real estate prices crashed—and took down thousands of investors, including Fisher, and the state's economy with them. Satirizing Florida's boom and bust a few years later, comedian Groucho Marx cracked in the film *The Cocoanuts* (1929), "Now folks, everybody this way for the grand swindle! Buy a lot, you can have any kind of house you want, you can get wood or brick or stucco—oh boy, can you get stucco!"

Think About It

1. What developments outside Florida made Miami Beach a viable commercial venture?
2. What could have been done to control the overvaluation of properties?
3. Who or what burst Florida's real estate bubble?
4. What does the popularity of Miami Beach say about American values, beliefs, and practices during the 1920s?

Sport for the Masses. Erected in 1922, Yankee Stadium featured three tiers that seated fifty-eight thousand fans. It was the world's largest sporting venue at the time. Ballparks became the mass staging ground for an elaborate celebration of the game, fans, and star players.

or other sticky substances on the ball (which made its trajectory more uneven and less hittable), and the ball was replaced whenever it became so muddy that the hitter couldn't see it. By 1922, the game was faster moving and higher scoring, and fans flocked to the bleachers in massive new stadiums.

In baseball's off-season, boxing matches and football games drew equally large crowds. Previously a disreputable (and, in all but two states, illegal) sport, boxing followed baseball's lead in establishing commissions designed to put prizefighting on a credible, legal, and money-making basis. Promoters and advertisers helped turn prizefighters into major celebrities capable of drawing upwards of a million dollars in box office sales for a single match. College football also boomed for the first time, along with rising college enrollments and the growth of alumni fundraising. Dozens of colleges built enormous venues, many of which rivaled even Yankee Stadium in seating capacity and ticket revenues. As in baseball, football promoters cooperated to reinvent the game as a faster, more exciting, crowd-pleasing sport.

These sports made extensive use of radio and movies to extend their mass fan base. Previously, the World Series telegraphed play-by-play action to scoreboards in town squares and meeting halls all over the United States. But for the first time, in 1922, the series (between New York's Giants and Yankees) was also broadcast over the radio. Listeners were amazed to hear not only the commentator but also the crowd, the umpire, and even, according to one newspaper, "the voice of the boy selling ice cream cones." Broadcasting the series was an experiment and, for a time, New York's teams resisted making it a permanent feature (anxious that radio's realistic quality would keep fans at home). But western teams such as Cleveland and Detroit eagerly adopted the technology, and, by 1930, popular demand for broadcasts had spread back East.

A new type of celebrity entered U.S. culture—the radio commentator. Commentators strove to make the experience even more real to listeners by using vivid and imaginative language and a rhythm and tone of voice that conveyed the excitement of a home run, knockout, or touchdown. "You must make each of your listeners, though miles from the spot, feel that he or she, too, is there," instructed one producer of baseball radio, "watching the movements of the games, the color, the flags, the pop-bottles thrown in the air; the straw hats demolished, Gloria Swanson arriving in her new ermine coat; and [the coach] in his dugout. . . ." Capturing listeners' imaginations, broadcasters helped turn sports into spectacular entertainments experienced simultaneously by millions of people. As fans tuned in to "live" sports at home, the town squares to which crowds had once flocked for telegraphed coverage fell silent.

THE BIG SCREEN

Like baseball, movie studios had a rough time early in the decade, when they were dogged by a series of sexual and criminal scandals that threatened to damage their reputation and box office sales. Much as baseball's owners had done, Hollywood studios countered with a lengthy and wildly successful campaign to save their reputation and autonomy, setting standards of decency for the industry and recruiting former postmaster general William Hays to enforce standards.

The strategy worked. Millions of middle-class people now flocked to films—traditionally a working-class entertainment. Weekly movie attendance doubled from forty million to over eighty million by 1928, and for the first time, cinema was the beneficiary of large-scale investment from Wall Street banks (such as Goldman Sachs, which poured $850 million into the industry

The Spectacle of Flight. Spectacles often reverberated in fashion. After Fox Studios filmed Charles Lindbergh's completion of his trans-Atlantic flight, for instance, hundreds of thousands of men began wearing the famed aviator's style of leather flight jacket. Both radio and film recorded Lindbergh's return to Washington, D.C., from France in 1927 and the subsequent parade welcoming him to New York.

annually by the end of the decade). Picture palaces grew in size and majesty, seating upwards of six thousand viewers. Cinemas redesigned movie going as an all-encompassing experience that in theory transported audiences into a world of opulence, pleasure, and fantasy. In some theaters, uniformed ushers (an innovation of newly respectable vaudeville theaters in the 1890s) greeted patrons under elegant, sparkling chandeliers and enormous domes of the sort found in European palaces and cathedrals. Others, such as Houston's air-conditioned Majestic, used an "atmospheric" design that simulated an open-air theater, complete with a black-blue "night sky," twinkling stars, and mobile clouds. Full orchestras accompanied the silent movies that still dominated most theaters in the 1920s.

The content and staging of movies changed in similar ways. By mid-decade, studios were using elaborate sets, often for historically themed movies such as *Ben Hur* (in which ancient Rome's Circus Maximus was reproduced in startling detail) and war films. Sumptuous sets continued the theme of cinema as an experience of fantasy and altered reality. New genres—many still popular today—also emerged, including feature-length westerns, horror films, animation, and slapstick comedies. After 1927, the new and highly topical genre of the gangster movie swept through cinemas. Warner Brothers added sound to *The Jazz Singer* in 1927, but "talking pictures" became standard only after 1930.

PARADING COMMERCE

Other activities also became large-scale commercial spectacles. Retail stores and business districts drew on Americans' long and distinguished history of political and commemorative parades to stage lively, entertaining spectacles of consumerism. Many of the parades that welcomed home soldiers in 1919 were sponsored by department stores. Unlike the somber parades of earlier years, however, these sensational entertainments featured streams of colorful light and bejeweled "triumph" arches. Subsequently, many cities appointed parade committees to welcome visitors officially and to mark sporting victories and civic milestones. When downtown Chicago, for instance, replaced gas streetlights with electric lights, chain stores, cinemas, and other businesses joined in throwing consumers a three-night street parade, complete with brilliantly colored searchlights, jazz bands, and outlandish decorations.

Such grand parades soon became regular events, nudging earlier, more community-oriented parades (such as the "ragamuffin" processions of costumed immigrant children) off the

Putting Santa to Work. Cartoonist Thomas Nast had popularized the jolly, red-suited version of Santa Claus in the 1860s. But it was not until the 1920s that department stores and advertisers turned Santa into an advocate for the consumerist version of Christmas with which we are familiar today.

streets. Pre-Christmas parades were the most lavish, aiming to transform the holiday season into an occasion for mass consumption, particularly of toys. Macy's, home to the world's largest toy department, launched the first of its famous parades on Thanksgiving Day, 1924. Employees marched in costumes as sheiks, acrobats, and princesses; caged wild animals and floats were driven along the route; and the entire procession climaxed in the arrival of Santa Claus at the store's massive Christmas grotto. By the late 1920s, Santa Claus was a fixture of department store parades everywhere. Fittingly, the decade closed with the single largest commercial celebration of Christmas to date, in Los Angeles, where the movie industry joined hands with department stores to mark the opening of the cities' holiday season with a joyful parade of enormous fairy-tale figures.

NEW CULTURES

City life, with its bright lights, commercialized recreations, and promise of personal and economic opportunity, had eclipsed farm life as the American ideal in the Progressive Era. Together with the culture industry, it now completed the shift away from the nineteenth-century Victorian values of thrift, modesty, and restraint to a more "modern" emphasis on personal expression through consumption. Movies, advertising, and the tabloids presented the underground culture of nightclubs and bars as glamorous, and the popular perception that individuals were free to consume as they saw fit encouraged people to flout Prohibition. In the cities, people in their twenties identified for the first time as a distinctive new generation in opposition to their parents and grandparents. Emulating big-screen stars, young women broke with decades of tradition by bobbing their hair, cutting their hems short, and entering nightclubs and restaurants unaccompanied by men. Although African Americans encountered new barriers in the cities of the North, they also forged groundbreaking forms of musical, literary, and visual art.

EXPERIENCING PROHIBITION

Prohibition both suppressed national alcohol consumption by an estimated 60 percent and stimulated the growth of the country's first large-scale criminal syndicates. The federal government's first chief of enforcement for Prohibition swore

St. Valentine's Day Massacre. Turf wars between competing gangs in Chicago climaxed in the infamous St. Valentine's Day Massacre of 1929. Posing as police officers, unknown men—probably from Al Capone's gang—disarmed members of the rival gang of George "Bugs" Moran and massacred them. Here, Chicago authorities reenact the likely scene.

that "this law will be obeyed in the cities . . . we shall see that the [liquor] is not manufactured, sold, nor given, nor hauled in anything on the surface of the earth nor under the earth nor in the air." Within days of John Barleycorn's funeral, an army of bootleggers began to manufacture or smuggle liquor. A common ploy of the bootleggers—adding water, flavoring, and pure alcohol to gin and whiskey to enlarge its volume—led city barmen to invent flavored "cocktails" to improve the taste. Even more commonly, suppliers diverted alcohol that had been intended for commercial or industrial use and redistilled it as a drinkable substance. Farmers and workers who could not afford such black-market drink brewed their own beer and moonshine. Those who were especially hard-up imbibed beverages made from household products containing alcohol, such as aftershave lotion and hair tonic; thousands of people were sickened and died as a result.

Profiting from Prohibition. Milk and Coca-Cola were marketed aggressively as alternatives to alcoholic beverages—and their consumption soared during Prohibition.

In the big cities, urban gangs transformed themselves into sophisticated business enterprises that smuggled, distilled, or redistilled beverages. Mixing violence with conventional business techniques, these crime syndicates provided not only the alcohol but also the venues for drinking it. New types of drinking establishments—the **speakeasy** and the nightclub—offered urbanites a glamorous setting, the latest band music, and inviting dance floors. They were also a place for people to mingle, often across racial and class lines.

Although gangsters did not hesitate to use violence, in other ways they brought much the same approach to their customers as did other large-scale enterprises in the era. Crucially, they aimed to maintain stable, lucrative commercial relationships with consumers who happened to want an illegal substance. Unlike thieves, who stole from their victims, gangsters delivered to customers—and tried to keep them happy. Running the organization smoothly required the adoption of modern business techniques, including financial planning, advertising, the maintenance of communication networks, double-entry bookkeeping, and regular payrolls. Rival gangs often waged price wars before resorting to machine guns.

Thanks to the gangs, liquor became a $2-billion-per-year illegal industry. Federal law enforcement, with its far smaller $2 million budget, stood impotent to stop its flow. The country's most notorious gangster, Chicago's Al Capone, was never charged with any crimes other than tax evasion, for which he was sent to federal prison in 1932. Like other mob bosses, Capone paid off local politicians and police and enjoyed a degree of protection. More important, by the mid-1920s, legitimate business, legal, and political leaders socialized in speakeasies and nightclubs that were either owned or protected by the crime syndicates. Chicago's mayor proclaimed openly that he was "as wet as the middle of the Atlantic Ocean."

Well into the 1920s, movies and magazines celebrated speakeasies and nightclubs, and tabloids featured photographs of revelers, feeding the aura of excitement and imbuing the scofflaws' actions with a degree of legitimacy. A whole new vocabulary for being in a state of drunkenness (*fried*, *potted*, and *shellacked*, among them) entered the English language, and popular songs such as "If I Meet the Guy Who Made This County Dry" parodied well-known tunes. Although built on illegality, speakeasies and nightclubs had become an integral part of urban life, and many of the old immigrant saloons continued to function despite the ban. Looking back on the 1920s, the majority of Americans would consider Prohibition an abject failure that bred contempt for the law and spawned illegal enterprises. In 1933, Congress agreed, repealing the Eighteenth Amendment (see Chapter 24).

AFRICAN AMERICANS CONFRONT CITY LIFE

Over seven hundred thousand African Americans poured into northern cities between 1920 and 1930, continuing their Great Migration from the South in search of waged work and a better, freer life. Once settled, the majority of newcomers rented apartments in mostly African American neighborhoods, such as Chicago's South Side and Detroit's Black Bottom (named for its rich marsh soils). As African American men went to work in unskilled and semiskilled industrial work, black women typically found employment as domestic servants for white families.

At the beginning of the decade, African Americans and whites shared workplaces, public schools, and city parks and recreational sites. When white people began leaving the city for new suburban developments, however, the public schools grew less diverse. Moreover, when municipalities made swimming pools and other amenities coed for the first time, they also segregated them racially, out of the prejudiced belief that African American men could not be trusted around white women. Yet the entrenched white prejudice that kept African Americans living in their own neighborhoods and swimming separately from whites also made those neighborhoods relatively independent of white oversight. One Chicago migrant, gospel singer Mahalia Jackson, later recalled that, returning from labor for a white business or family at the end of the day, the black worker could "lay down his burden of being a colored person in the white man's world and lead his own life."

A small but growing minority of the migrants were lawyers, doctors, and other professionals, many of whom were self-employed and could afford to purchase a home. But these African Americans bumped up hard against the informal segregation that had first taken root in northern cities earlier in the century. Although the North was free of segregationist legislation, many key business institutions adopted racially exclusive rules—with enormous consequences for African Americans. Suburban developers, for example, agreed to refrain from selling lots and houses to black people, and restrictive covenants that prevented white homeowners from selling to African Americans (see Chapter 20) became widespread. Real estate agencies adopted similarly racist rules and regulations that prevented them from showing homes in predominantly white neighborhoods to black buyers. Many bankers tacitly agreed not to extend mortgages to African Americans, and most refused mortgages for properties in white neighborhoods. Banks also systematically charged higher interest rates on loans for African American clients, on the questionable grounds that these clients were more of a risk, and insurance agents tacitly agreed to withhold home insurance. From Berkeley, California, to Long Island, New York, institutional discrimination was the norm by 1930.

The NAACP fought a number of cases, both high profile and more ordinary, against these practices—with mixed results. The most famous of these involved Ossian Sweet, an African American physician who had saved enough money from his medical practice to purchase a home in a white working-class suburb of Detroit in 1925. On moving day, Sweet and his wife were met by an angry mob of white neighbors intent on running the couple out of their home. Defiant, Sweet resolved to defend his property by force, as he was legally entitled to do. In the anger-fueled violence that ensued, one neighbor lay dead, and Sweet was charged with murder. Retaining one of the most renowned criminal defenders of the age, Clarence Darrow, the NAACP skillfully used the case to put racism on trial. Sweet was eventually acquitted—but the restrictive practices that he confronted persisted well into the 1960s.

The NAACP was not the only major organization supporting African Americans during this period of intense discrimination. Hundreds of thousands of urban African Americans also joined the Universal Negro Improvement Association (UNIA), an organization founded by Jamaican-born Marcus Garvey, who espoused racial separatism and the development of black businesses and institutions. A superb communicator and energetic entrepreneur, Garvey published a popular newspaper called *The Negro World* and broadcast radio messages of black pride to well over a million UNIA members. Consistent with the booster spirit of the era, he also established a grocery chain and the Negro Factories Corporation—which ambitiously aimed to manufacture every kind of consumer good available to Americans. As well, Garvey's Black Star shipping line transported interested African Americans to Africa in a Back to Africa movement for the purpose of building Liberia, the first independent, all-African nation-state. The program collapsed in 1922 amid charges of fraud and mismanagement (although Liberia survived), and in 1927 Garvey was convicted of mail fraud and deported to Jamaica. Nonetheless, his larger movement had nurtured a sense of racial pride that long outlasted his departure.

THE HARLEM RENAISSANCE AND THE JAZZ AGE

Of all the predominantly black neighborhoods, Harlem, in Manhattan, proved an especially strong magnet for black southerners (and African Caribbeans). Migrants made up roughly 30 percent of Harlem's population in 1920 and over 76 percent by the end of the decade. Here flourished a remarkable community of talented young black writers, artists, and intellectuals—most of whom were part of the small but growing black middle class. Commentators called this intense percolation of art and ideas the "New Negro Renaissance" and the "New Negro Movement," in reference to the Harlem writer Alain Locke. Historians have since renamed the movement the **Harlem Renaissance** in recognition of the special role that New York City played in this rich cultural ferment.

Central to Harlem's renaissance was the renewed sense of pride many African Americans felt in the wake of World War I (see Chapter 22). Alain Locke rejected the idea, common among whites, that black people lacked culture, and instead defined the "New Negro" as a person who took pride in being both of African descent and American. Poet Langston Hughes gave voice to this spirit when he declared "I am a Negro—and beautiful." Asserting this attitude publicly—or even thinking it privately—was a truly radical act in a society that was increasingly segregated and intolerant of African American claims to full citizenship.

In the arena of the big screen, independent movie directors such as Oscar Micheaux, who relocated from Chicago to Harlem in 1919, countered Hollywood's negative portrayal of black people. Casting African Americans (rather than white actors in blackface) in starring roles, Micheaux portrayed his characters as overcoming racial discrimination and thriving in the city. Shot on shoestring budgets and lacking access to major distribution networks, most "race movies" nevertheless drew huge audiences of African Americans. Writers and artists reached back to African roots to explore and extol the richness of black American culture. Importantly, they also firmly rejected the commonplace view that

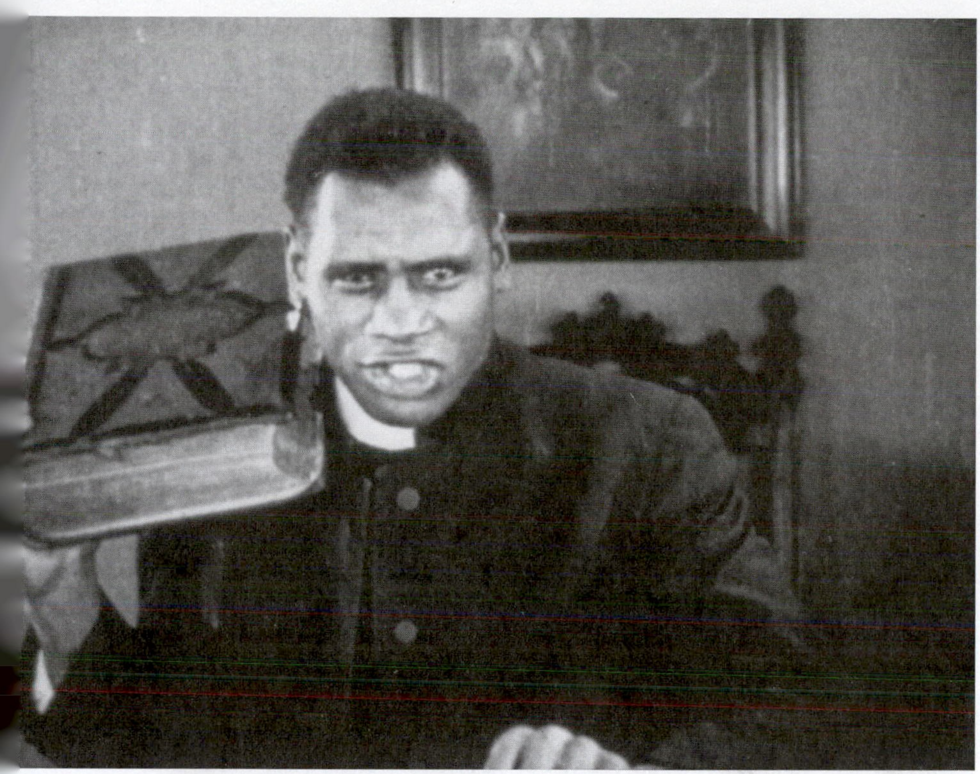

Still from *Body and Soul*. White-owned studios neglected African American actors, but the popular performer Paul Robeson found a starring role in Oscar Micheaux's *Body and Soul*—a biting social critique of the role of clergy in African American society, in which Robeson plays both a corrupt preacher and the preacher's honest brother.

African Americans were the source of the so-called Negro problem—the decades-old perspective, held by almost all whites, that it was difficult if not impossible for black people to integrate fully into U.S. society.

Many Harlem intellectuals and artists sought to express and make sense of the experience of the Great Migration and the excitements and challenges of life in northern cities. A few, such as African Caribbean Claude McKay, fused their writing with organized, black liberation politics. More than most, McKay drew out the radical political implications of the New Negro movement. "If we must die," he wrote in reference to the race riots that roiled U.S. cities in 1919, "let it not be like hogs/ Hunted and penned in an inglorious spot/ . . . Like men we'll face the murderous, cowardly pack/Pressed to the wall, dying, but fighting back!" For the most part, however, the Harlem Renaissance was not overtly political. Art, literature, film, music, and theater, in Alain Locke's view, were far more promising vehicles for raising African Americans' pride in themselves—and, ultimately, their socioeconomic status. By the mid-1920s, well-known white critics and publishers were convinced both of the literary and commercial value of the works of Zora Neale Hurston, Locke, and Hughes and published these and other writers to widespread acclaim among educated whites.

As Harlem's renaissance unfolded in the early 1920s, Chicago emerged as the capital of jazz. With its roots in minstrelsy, New Orleans' ragtime music, and the tunes of brass bands, this unique African American art form had no written score. Instead, jazz musicians improvised, playing with the melody and accenting, disrupting, and embellishing as they went along. Initially performing only in African American communities, jazz bands were enthusiastically received in Paris during the Great War (see Chapter 22) and later debuted in American nightclubs. In the 1920s, the gangsters who often owned the speakeasies and nightclubs were among the first to put all–African American jazz bands on their payrolls and pay them a decent wage. Famous jazzman Louis Armstrong, for example, got his first "gig" working for the club of New Orleans mobster Henry Matranga.

Spurred by "hot jazz," whose blazingly fast tempo appealed to dance lovers, the record business by 1923 was issuing thousands of jazz recordings a year. In a sign of the times, many of these tunes were recorded by white bands that had learned from African American performers, because the record companies felt white consumers would find white musicians more palatable. Radio stations initially barred African Americans from playing at all. But Louis Armstrong and His Hot Five and other African American bands still found an enormous audience, and they eventually conquered the radio market as well.

CULTIVATING YOUTH

By the mid-1920s, Harlem's Cotton Club and Apollo Theater were attracting young white urban sophisticates, many of them the sons and daughters of upper-middle-class professionals. Since the 1910s, these "slummers," as they were often called, had been gradually casting off the Victorian morality they associated with older generations. Whereas their parents worried about the corrupting influence of cities, slummers experienced urban modernity—with its cinemas, theaters, speakeasies, and relative degree of anonymity—as liberating. They eagerly sought the kinds of intellectual, social, political, and sexual stimulation that the city made available, and they thrilled to the sights and sounds of immigrant and bohemian neighborhoods such as San Francisco's Polk Street district and Chicago's South Side. In their eyes, African American music, art, and other cultural forms were more "real," vital, and lively than their parents' Progressive Era culture. Well-heeled, many also enjoyed the feeling of entering a neighborhood that their parents would not dream of setting foot in, and breaking white society's double taboo against socializing with African Americans and poor people.

Many slummers considered themselves champions of African American culture, and several went on to fund black artists and their projects generously. Most, however, also

TABLE 23.1 YOUTH, SLANG, AND POPULAR CULTURE

Word	Meaning	Source
applesauce	nonsense or flattery	T. A. Dorgan comic strip, 1919
baloney	nonsense	from *bologna* (Italian sausage)
bee's knees	terrific (usually in reference to new dance move or song)	Unknown
clam	a dollar	Unknown
fire extinguisher	a chaperone	Unknown
flipper	male companion of the flapper	Unknown
gin mill	speakeasy/bar	Unknown
goofy	in love	Unknown
hair of the dog	a shot of alcohol	Unknown
heebie-jeebies	shaking or feeling of discomfort	Billy DeBeck comic strip, 1923
knock up	to make pregnant	Unknown
Let's blouse.	Let's leave.	Unknown
on the lam	fleeing the police	Unknown
Rhatz!	How disappointing!	Unknown
sap	an idiot or a fool	Unknown
sheik	rebellious young man who dressed like heartthrob Rudolph Valentino	Rudolph Valentino movie, *The Sheik*, 1921
upchuck	vomit	Unknown
wet blanket	someone who doesn't like whoopee (see below)	Unknown
whoopee	raucous fun	G. Kahn song, "Making Whoopee," 1928
zozzled	drunk	Unknown

brought a subtle racism to bear in their praise of black jazz, blues, literature, and art, which they typically celebrated as "primitive" and exotic. The first generation to come of age in a predominately consumerist society, many also treated African American music and literature solely as commodities to be consumed for their enjoyment rather than as explorations of the complex realities of urban migration, Jim Crow, and the memory of slavery.

Other, middle-class young people also chose to rebel against the culture of their parents. For the first time, particularly in big cities but increasingly in mid-size towns, an entire cohort of young white Americans thought of themselves as a unique generation, complete with distinct attitudes, fashion sense, and rules of conduct. This new "youth" generation was the first to embrace dating, jazz and jazz dancing, and cinema—previously associated with immigrant working-class people and African Americans.

The music industry also played a major role in the formation of the new youth culture. Before the Great War, most Americans purchased popular music in the form of sheet music, which they performed at home, usually at the piano. Sheet music sales remained strong through the 1920s, but increasingly radio broadcasts, technical improvements in phonographs, talking pictures, and the proliferation of speakeasies changed the way Americans experienced music. Youth in particular abandoned the conventional activity of playing piano and embraced listening (and dancing). As the new media brought musical genres such as Tin Pan Alley, hot jazz, commercial jazz, blues, and hillbilly music to a national audience for the first time, a fiercely competitive recording industry took root.

NEW FREEDOMS AND LIMITS FOR WOMEN

Urban youth defined themselves in a variety of ways, but the most vivid—and, for some, threatening—emblem of their new culture was the **flapper.** The young women known as flappers embodied a new, more assertive femininity in the way they dressed, spoke, and interacted with men. "Breezy, slangy, and informal in manner," wrote Preston W. Slosson in 1929, the flapper was "slim and boyish in form; covered in silk and fur that clung to her as close as onion skin; with carmined [reddened] lips, plucked eyebrows and close-fitting helmet of hair—gay, plucky and confident." These young women self-consciously transgressed gender conventions by smoking cigarettes and drinking gin cocktails, venturing into speakeasies unaccompanied by men, and dancing in ways that involved far more physical contact and flirtation with the opposite sex than Victorian conventions permitted. The short, androgynously "bobbed" haircut they favored boldly rejected their mothers' standards of femininity.

Flappers also toppled class norms that held that rouge and mascara, tight-fitting clothes, drinking, and "wild" dancing were strictly for prostitutes and working-class women. Many flappers claimed new sexual freedoms, challenging the long-standing prohibition on premarital sex. Although birth control remained illegal unless prescribed by a physician for medical reasons, its use became more commonplace. In 1921, long-time birth control advocate Margaret Sanger established the American Birth Control League, a research and educational organization promoting the principle that "every woman must possess the power and freedom to prevent conception." Two years later, the nation's first legal contraception clinic, run by physicians in consultation with Sanger, opened in New York. The clinic served only married women who wanted to limit the size of their families, but it helped make contraception more respectable, though only in big cities and mostly among Protestant women.

Young women's newfound independence was made possible partly by the disposable income that came with their employment as telephone operators, clerical workers, and department store assistants. Yet the great majority still aspired to marry and have children, and most stepped out of nightclubs and offices for good and into the familiar role of homemaker by the age of twenty-five. Meanwhile, those members of their mother's generation who had struggled long and hard to win women's voting rights extended their fight for equality. African American feminists called on white suffragists to help restore voting rights in the South, where virtually all African American adults were deprived of the vote (see Chapter 19). White feminists, however, were more concerned with the economic and legal status of white northern women, and, by the early 1920s, were divided in a bitter internal debate over the true meaning of women's liberation.

For Alice Paul and the National Woman's Party (NWP), the next logical step for women was absolute equality in access to employment, education, the courts, and all the rights and privileges of U.S. citizenship. Despite recent gains, women were still paid up to 75 percent less than men in the same line of work, barred from many colleges and universities, and unable to take out a mortgage or apply for an installment purchase plan in their own name. Following intensive lobbying by the NWP, Congress debated an Equal Rights Amendment (ERA) to the Constitution, which proposed eliminating all legal distinctions "on account of sex." But other women's organizations opposed the ERA. Leading the charge, Carrie Chapman Catt and the influential League of Women Voters argued that the constitutional amendment would disastrously outlaw existing legislation that singled out women for special protection—such as laws guaranteeing mothers' pensions and limiting women's work hours. The ERA was defeated, and despite winning congressional approval several decades later, in 1972, it would fail to muster the requisite two-thirds support at the state level.

NEW DIVIDES

Not everyone welcomed the momentous cultural changes of the 1920s. Many white Americans believed that bootleggers, flappers, movie stars, Catholic and Jewish immigrants, and African Americans threatened the United States' traditional values and the morality of its youth. The decade began with the rapid growth of the second Ku Klux Klan, which called for an end to mass immigration, the enforcement of Prohibition, racial "purity," antiradicalism, and the patriarchal family. Later, Hollywood became the target of a campaign by the Roman Catholic Church against glamorous depictions of gangsters and "loose" women and negative portrayals of members of the clergy and law enforcers. Particularly in the West, South, and Midwest, fundamentalist Protestant clergy broke away from established churches to rally rural and newly urbanized people around a form of Christianity they described as "old-time religion." Although these conservative movements condemned big-city culture and called for a return to tradition, they were as much shaped by modern society as were the urban cultural forms they criticized. Most conservative activists used modern methods of mass communication, publicity, fundraising, and advertising, and all promoted a vision of society that their parents and grandparents would have found alien.

THE WOMEN AND MEN OF THE KU KLUX KLAN

Founded by William Simmons in Georgia in 1915 (see Chapter 22), the second Ku Klux Klan counted more than four million members by 1924—comprising more Americans than belonged to all labor unions combined and approximately 15 percent of the U.S. population. Although the Klan remained strong in the South, it drew its largest membership from the small and mid-size cities of the West and Midwest (see Map 23.2). Its single biggest membership was in Indiana, and Chicago and Detroit counted over fifty thousand and thirty-five thousand members, respectively. Virtually all members were white Protestants.

The Klan's rapid growth stemmed in part from its aggressive advocacy of immigration restriction, which tapped into deep strains of nativism and antiradicalism that had intensified in many white Protestant communities during World War I (see Chapter 22). Taking a leaf out of advertising manuals, in 1921 the Klan's leadership appointed a "publicity relations" director who proceeded to target those western and midwestern cities to which large numbers of African Americans and Catholic and Jewish immigrants were migrating. The Klan's appeal was particularly strong among shopkeepers, office workers, small business operators, factory foremen, skilled tradesmen, and schoolteachers. Having more disposable income than their parents, these lower-middle-class Americans typically owned an automobile and a modest home, worked a relatively short forty-five-hour week, and had enough disposable income to go on vacation, buy household appliances, and support a wife as a full-time homemaker. But many believed that immigrants and African American migrants posed a threat to their rising standard of living. Store owners, for instance, feared losing customers to immigrant shopkeepers who might be willing to work longer hours and set lower prices (in fact, chain stores such as Woolworth turned out to be a greater threat). Skilled autoworkers in Detroit and elsewhere shared this concern, and white homeowners everywhere worried that property values would decline if African Americans, Jews, or Catholics moved into the neighborhood.

As the Klan recruited, many communities also organized lodge halls (made up of skilled tradesmen and foremen) and storekeepers' associations for the purpose of excluding black and immigrant newcomers. Neighborhood protective associations, which promoted racially exclusive home deeds that

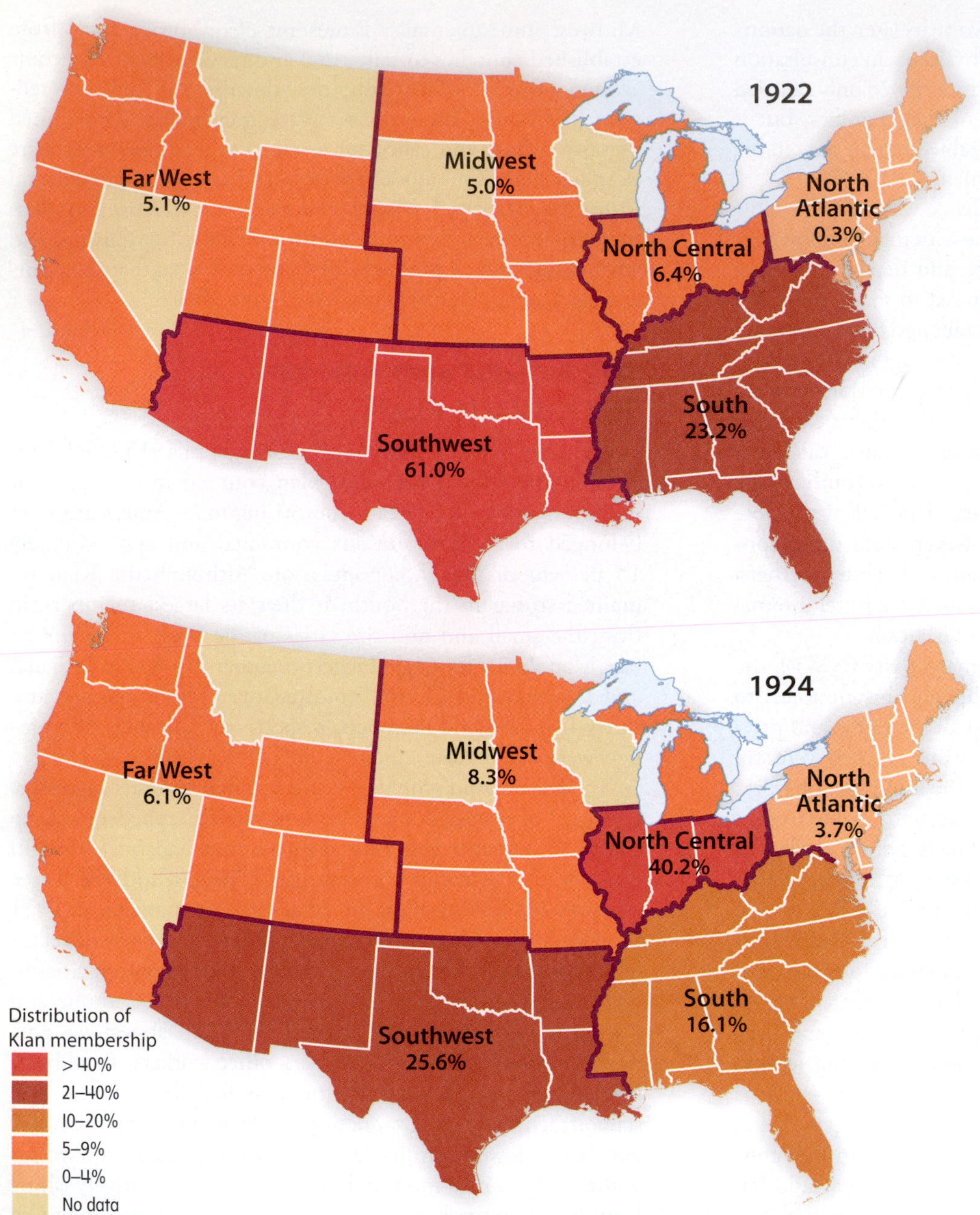

Map 23.2 Membership of the Ku Klux Klan by Region. The Klan's membership rolls swelled after 1921 as recruiters targeted new regions such as the Midwest and the North Central states. These maps, which show the distribution of Klan membership, illustrate the effectiveness of the conservative organization's campaigns in these areas.

prohibited sales and rentals to African Americans and other groups, were also common. The Klan both drew their membership from these exclusionary associations and helped spread them. Operating as one enormous fraternal society, it provided members with business connections, a vast network of brothers, and services of various kinds.

The Klan's appeal was also cultural. Many believed that black and non-Protestant newcomers were diluting, destroying, and perverting what they took to be true American virtues—sobriety, Protestantism, patriotism, and so-called racial purity. Klan pronouncements against the nation's growing religious and cultural diversity—or what Klansmen called "the mongrelization of America"—attracted hundreds of thousands, as did state-level campaigns to close all parochial (Roman Catholic) schools. The Klan's version of family values, which held that fathers were the rightful head of household and that women were subordinate to men, also appealed to those who worried that youth culture and women's expanding roles were weakening the moral fabric of society. Klan leaders decried premarital sex and working mothers and called for compulsory Bible reading in the schools and tougher divorce laws. While there was some variation among the priorities of local Klaverns (as Klan chapters were known), they were united in their commitment to enforcing "law and order"—particularly the laws against the production and sale of alcohol. (Many temperance crusaders and members of the Anti-Saloon League joined the Klan.)

The Klan often harassed and terrorized people they considered alien and un-American, including African Americans, Jews, Catholics, and radicals. Klaverns mounted consumer boycotts against immigrant and black-owned businesses, hogtied bootleggers, and shut down nightclubs. Often operating outside the law, they committed arson, tarred and feathered some of their victims, and publicly whipped (and even lynched) others. Accused adulterers and suspected communists were subject to beatings. But the Klan also pursued its vision through the ballot box and via lobbyists. As hundreds of Klan members ran for elective office, millions of voters supported them. The Klan even established a national office, which proceeded to stage lavish annual parades in Washington, D.C. By 1921, the organization was spearheading a mass movement to pressure Congress to drastically restrict immigration.

The Klan Marches. Waving the stars and stripes, tens of thousands of men and women marched proudly through the nation's capital in white robes, silk sashes, and conical hats in the annual KKK parade. **Questions for Analysis:** Why might the Klan have wanted to march in the nation's capital? Why might Klan members have been comfortable marching without the masks worn by the first Ku Klux Klan during Reconstruction? Women rarely marched in American street parades before the twentieth century. What might this parade's inclusion of women tell us about the Klan's attitudes toward them?

POLICING THE BORDERS

The call for immigration restriction received a boost from the American Federation of Labor, whose leaders argued that immigrant workers drove down wages. Big business also joined the chorus, believing that immigrants were more likely to be Bolshevik labor organizers. By 1920, immigration from southern and eastern Europe had resumed, whereas Mexican immigration, which had accelerated during World War I due to the wartime labor shortage in the United States and the failure of the Mexican Revolution to alleviate rural poverty, continued to climb. In California and the Southwest, Mexican migrants performed much of the low-wage seasonal agricultural and ranching labor on which large commercial food producers depended.

Calls to close the borders reached a fevered pitch in 1921, when Italian immigrants and anarchists Nicola Sacco and Bartolomeo Vanzetti were found guilty of double murder in Massachusetts and sentenced to death. Convicted on highly questionable evidence, Sacco and Vanzetti were in all likelihood the innocent victims of the virulent nativism that gripped the nation at that time. But the majority of native-born Americans saw the verdict as a mandate to restrict immigration. Not since the early 1880s and the exclusion of Chinese immigrants had Congress been pressured so strongly to close the borders. With hundreds of Klansmen poised to run for office in the midterm elections of 1922, lawmakers hastily enacted the Immigration Act (1921), which more than halved the number of immigrants entering legally in 1922.

However, the nativist coalition would not rest until the United States' "golden door" was securely closed, especially to Mexicans and eastern and southern Europeans (see Figure 23.1). Subsequently, the National Origins Act (1924) stipulated that only 150,000 immigrants could enter the country annually, and it fixed immigration numbers by country of origin in favor of British, Scandinavian, and German nationals. The law set quotas for each country at 2 percent of the number of its emigrants living in the United States in 1890, before the majority of southern and eastern European immigrants had arrived. In deference to Californian and southwestern nativists,

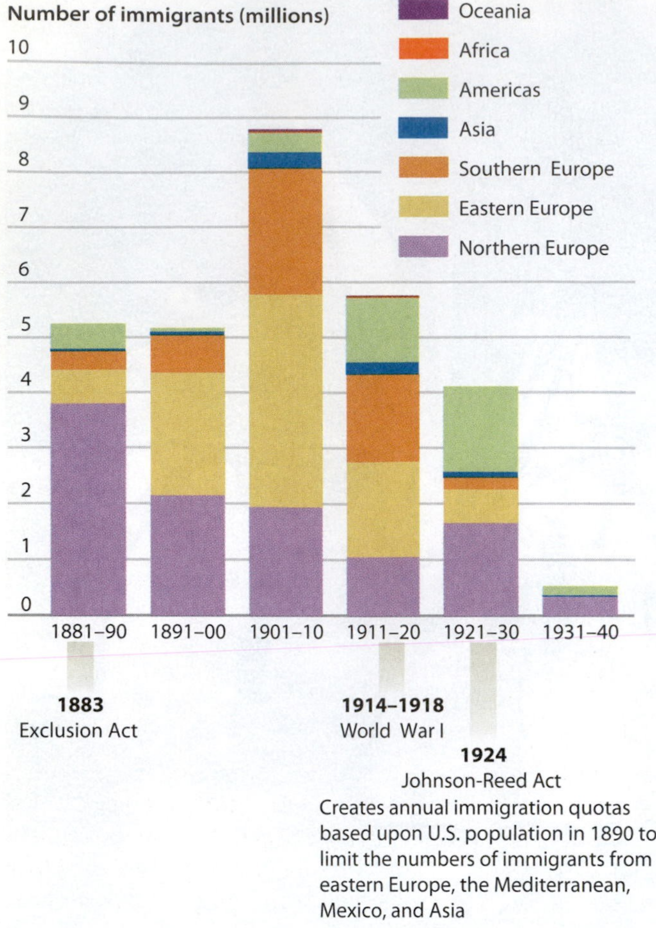

FIGURE 23.1 The "New Immigration" Ends. The disruptions of World War I had already suspended most legal and illegal immigration to the United States by 1915. Immigration picked up again after the war, but the Immigration Act of 1924 slammed the door on the great majority of "new immigrants" who were from eastern and southern Europe. Immigration from these nations plummeted 98 percent, while immigration from northern Europe fell on average just 27 percent. The act also extended Chinese exclusion to all of Asia, with the exception of the Philippines (a U.S. territory). Most Mexican immigration, which accounted for the majority of immigrants from the Americas, also became illegal in 1924. However, as illustrated here, Mexican immigration actually increased in the second half of the 1920s because of demand for cheap agricultural labor.

the law also established the Border Patrol and headquartered it in El Paso, Texas. With the stroke of a pen, most of the tens of thousands of Mexican migrants who entered the United States each year acquired a new status—**illegal alien.** Despite the law, Mexican immigration continued to increase as demand for cheap agricultural labor soared. By 1927, over 1.2 million Mexican immigrants lived in the United States—ten times the number in 1900—and the U.S.-Mexico border was the nation's major port of entry.

With the passage of immigration restrictions, the Klan achieved its most popular goal, and its membership declined. It all but collapsed following reports in 1925 that its leader, Grand Dragon David Stephenson, had been arrested for rape and kidnap. Nonetheless, many of the Klan's exclusionary practices and racist attitudes endured in real estate, banking, advertising, and popular culture.

CENSORSHIP WARS

Most Americans did not belong to the Ku Klux Klan. Yet many did share the Klan's belief in the Victorian values of feminine modesty, temperance, and thrift and were increasingly anxious about the direction in which the culture seemed to be headed. Attracted to many of the benefits of consumer society, they nonetheless resented and feared some of its other aspects. They worried that the same youth who had previously looked to parents, teachers, and church ministers for moral guidance now were consulting their peers and the culture industry for cues. They condemned movies, tabloids, and radio for their glamorized depictions of gangsters, jazz, and speakeasies and objected to uncritical portrayals of sex, adultery, and homosexuality.

As weekly attendance numbers at the movies grew to one hundred million by 1927, making movies the premier form of entertainment, the pressure to censor content mounted once more. The would-be censors whom the Hays Office (see p. 640) had appeased in the mid-1920s remobilized late in the decade, at the same time that gangster movies were appearing. For the first time, Catholic clergy and organizations took the lead, demanding that industry censorship move beyond the removal of mere obscenity (nudity and cursing) to what they called the enforcement of community and moral standards. Films must never lower the audience's moral standards, they insisted, and should always promote the "correct standards of life." The law ought never to be lampooned or criticized, and movies could depict evil only as long as they clearly condemned it.

Eager to consolidate his power over the studios, William Hays enthusiastically drafted a motion picture code that was based on these principles and that detailed the kinds of scenes that would be banned. The studios initially rejected the resulting Hays Code. However, once Catholic bishops threatened mass boycotts and a major Hollywood investor, A. H. Giannini of the Bank of America, joined the campaign, they caved in. From 1933 until the 1950s, movies had no depictions of sexual passion, homosexuality, adultery, interracial relationships, or sympathetic gangsters. Police always got their man, and even married couples slept in separate beds.

Significantly, publishers successfully defeated legal efforts to censor literature—which received less scrutiny than films did from the clergy, largely because the latter believed that cinema was a powerful, mass medium and that literature's impact was limited. But concerned parents and Protestant and Catholic clergy waged campaigns against dances like the fox trot and the Charleston and above all the "devil's music"—jazz. Pointing to the possibility that the word *jazz* was derived from the southern vernacular term *jass*, meaning sexual intercourse, they proclaimed the musical genre a "moral disaster." "Does Jazz Put the Sin in Syncopation?" worried the president of the General Federation of Women's Clubs. Henry Ford

Beach Censors. Many states and private beach clubs responded to the advent of "bathing beauty" contests and more revealing swimwear by hiring "beach censors" to eject women whose suits were "indecently brief." Some even prescribed the maximum amount of flesh that could be exposed between a woman's hem and knee.

answered in the affirmative, condemning jazz as "moron music . . . suggestive of cave love." Older white citizens imagined young white women being seduced by African American trumpet and saxophone players into immoral and even criminal behavior and went so far as to blame youth's newfound rebelliousness on the music. These critics failed to dampen the appeal of either jazz or dancing—and may even have enhanced their allure. Eager to avert censorship, the recording and broadcasting industries, however, gradually sanitized the commercial image of jazz and its performers.

PROTESTANTS DIVIDED

The vast majority of Americans belonged to a Christian church in the 1920s (see Map 23.3). On average there was one place of worship per thousand inhabitants—about the same ratio as today. Due partly to the arrival of new immigrants over the previous three decades, however, religious diversity *within* Christianity was at an all-time high. More people belonged to the Roman Catholic Church than any other religion (a fact that explains in part why Hollywood took the threat of the bishops' consumer boycott so seriously). But the overwhelming majority of Christians—two-thirds—were Protestant.

Although church membership was high, it was dropping compared to earlier times, with fewer Americans attending church on a weekly basis or supporting the churches financially. People who

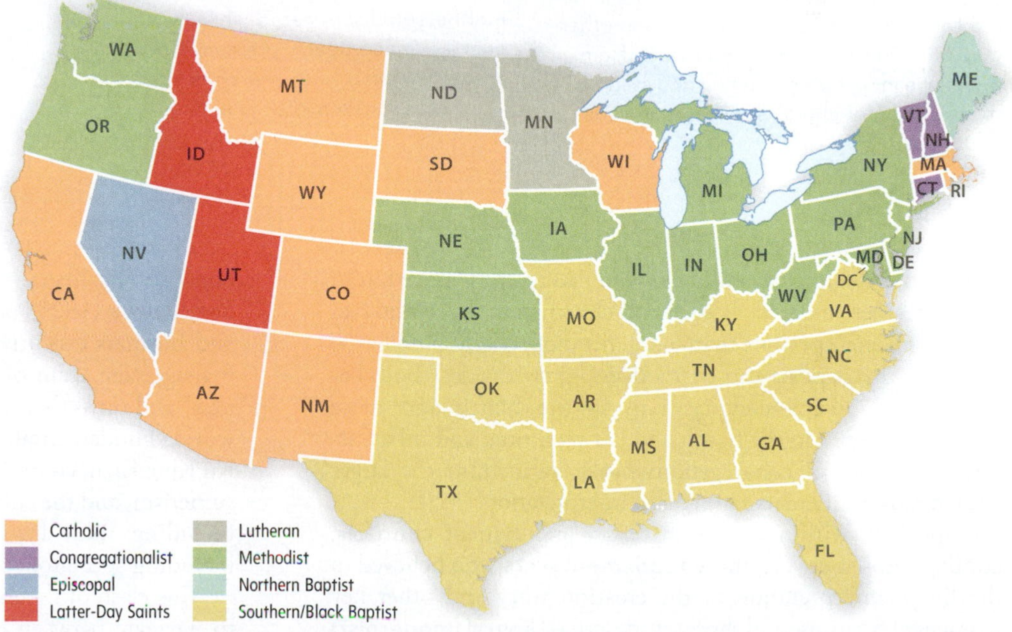

Map 23.3 The Geography of Religion, 1929. This map illustrates the strength of Baptists in the South; Lutherans in the upper Midwest; Mormons in Idaho and Utah; and Catholics and Methodists across a wide range of states. Jews made up only a small portion (4 percent) of the U.S. population.

SINGULAR LIVES

Aimee Semple McPherson, Modern Evangelist

Born and raised in rural Ontario, Canada, Aimee Semple McPherson (see chapter opening) became a sensation—one of the most successful revivalists of 1920s America. The secret of her success? A novel mix of Pentecostal theology, which emphasizes a direct, emotionally intense experience of God, plus state-of-the-art mass communication techniques. It was in San Diego, California, whose pleasant climate had long been a magnet for thousands of sick and convalescing people, that McPherson first gained fame as an evangelical faith healer. Among the suffering, McPherson was said to have performed countless "miracle healings" of invalids, blind people, and the terminally ill.

Gaining a devoted following along with steady revenue, McPherson moved to Los Angeles in 1922, where her enormous Angelus Temple seated five thousand worshippers under its sparkling cinema-like dome. Millions more followed her services on the church's radio station, KFSG, the most powerful transmitter in Los Angeles. McPherson's Church of the Foursquare Gospel offered a softer alternative to Billy Sunday's bare-knuckle preaching, promising boundless love to those who dedicated themselves to God. McPherson condemned the corrosive impact of Hollywood and other popular culture but borrowed heavily from the movie industry's marketing and staging techniques. Her church services featured mock battles between God and Satan, complete with smoking artillery, bolts of lightning, hot air balloons, and a scoreboard.

McPherson showed millions of worshipers and fans—many of whom were rural migrants to the city—how to reconcile life in a fast-paced consumer society with fundamentalist interpretations of Scripture. Although she wore the flowing robes of a preacher while in church, she was also unafraid of flapper accessories like lipstick and mascara and presented herself as a modern, sexually attractive woman—who sometimes motorcycled up the center aisle of the church. A successful entrepreneur, she also raised millions of dollars and added a college, overseas missions, and a publishing house to her empire. She was seemingly afraid of no one, including Commerce Secretary Herbert Hoover, who ordered her radio station to use a less powerful transmitter (because it was disrupting other stations). "Please order your minions of Satan to leave my station alone," McPherson retorted on air. "You cannot expect the Almighty to abide by your wavelength nonsense . . . . I must fit into His wavelength reception."

Followers were grief stricken when McPherson disappeared while swimming at nearby Venice Beach, presumed drowned, in 1926. An enormous search ensued, without result. A month later the evangelist reappeared near the Mexican border, claiming that she had been abducted and tortured before making her escape across the desert. When the tabloids fueled rumors that she had actually eloped, gotten an abortion, or had cosmetic surgery in Mexico, McPherson was hauled before the courts on charges of obstructing justice. The district attorney eventually dropped the charges, and McPherson returned to her ministry. But her shiny appeal had been tarnished. Rival fundamentalist ministers—all men—openly criticized her as a sinner and an unnatural usurper of male authority. Shortly after, *Elmer Gantry* (1927), a best-selling novel by Sinclair Lewis, implicitly lampooned McPherson and permanently discredited her in the eyes of most followers.

Think About It

1. How do you think McPherson reconciled her modern flair for publicity and spectacle with her fundamentalist reading of Scripture?
2. In what ways did McPherson break the gender stereotypes of the 1920s, and in what ways did she affirm them?
3. What commonplace anxieties and aspirations did McPherson tap in her message and methods?

lived in the countryside and those who had recently moved from rural areas were more likely to attend church than those who had dwelled in cities for more than one generation. Many churches—especially the Baptists and Methodists—grew divided, both between more liberal congregations in the North and more conservative ones in the South and between rural and urban areas. A number of congregations broke away from the larger churches over differences in biblical interpretation.

Especially within the Presbyterian and Baptist churches, conflicts arose between those **fundamentalists** who believed in the literal interpretation of the creation story and other key passages of Scripture and those self-described **liberal (modernist) Christians** who embraced science—including the theory of evolution—and welcomed women's increased autonomy and many (but not all) aspects of mass consumer society. A best-selling book among liberal Christians, Bruce Barton's *The Man Nobody Knows* (1925) portrayed Jesus as a charismatic salesman and business executive (like Barton himself) who creates his management team of twelve "from the bottom ranks of business" and turns their enterprise into the greatest business in the world. Fundamentalists, many of whom also belonged to the Ku Klux Klan, countered that secularism, certain strains of consumerism, and the culture industries were destroying old values, including "blue laws" that banned commercial activities—including spectator sports—on Sunday.

This clash of theologies reflected the larger problem of how to navigate between older and newer value systems in an increasingly consumption-oriented society. Fundamentalist preachers did not fully reject consumer society, and liberal Christians did not uncritically embrace every part of it. Both accepted some aspects of the new and blended them with the old. And both sides worried that movies and other mass entertainments were pulling parishioners away from the church or, as one minister complained, leaving them in a "dazed, comatose state" during sermons.

The effort to reconcile faith and modern culture also found expression in religious revivals that, ironically, took the form of mass spectacles. At large-scale services (some of which were broadcast), charismatic evangelists called upon Christians to repent and recommit themselves to God. The Reverend Billy Sunday was the first fundamentalist evangelical to run his church as a modern business, complete with advertising and publicity sections. A one-time star of the Chicago White Stockings baseball team, Sunday renounced the high life and his baseball contract to become the nation's most famous traveling evangelist in the 1910s and 1920s. Declaring that liquor was "God's worst enemy and Hell's best friend" and that David "soaked Goliath right between the lamps and he went down for the count," his sermons were blunt, rich with masculine imagery, and deeply reassuring to millions of mostly rural and recently urbanized Protestants. In 1922, Aimee Semple McPherson, a charismatic Pentecostal minister, innovated Sunday's model to include publicity stunts borrowed directly from Hollywood (see Singular Lives: Aimee Semple McPherson, Modern Evangelist).

As the revivals proceeded, a less flamboyant form of fundamentalism spread through many of America's small towns and rural areas. Legislatures were soon debating bills sponsored by fundamentalists—and, particularly in the South and parts of the Midwest, were making them law. In Tennessee, one such statute prohibited the teaching of the Darwinian theory of evolution in public schools and fined offenders up to $500.

In 1925, liberal clergy and the American Civil Liberties Union resolved to fight the Tennessee law. They recruited local teacher John Thomas Scopes to teach evolution in his high school classroom. Following Scopes's arrest and indictment, the Monkey Trial, as radio and the press dubbed it, became an epic courtroom battle and a media event. In the trial, Scopes's attorney, Clarence Darrow, crossed rhetorical swords with the old populist crusader—and recent convert to fundamentalism—William Jennings Bryan (see Chapter 19). Calling Bryan to the stand as an expert in Scripture, Darrow fooled the aging fundamentalist into admitting that he doubted biblical stories such as Jonah's transformative sojourn in the belly of a whale. Despite his humiliation of Bryan in the mass media, Darrow lost the case. Scopes was convicted. The line hardened between fundamentalists and liberals—and in some states today, teaching Darwin's theory is still controversial.

END OF AN ERA

In 1927, sociologists Robert and Helen Lynd reported in an exhaustive study that the townspeople of Muncie, Indiana (which they called Middletown), cared more about their leisure time and purchasing power than politics. Although the Lynds may have exaggerated, voting rates had continued their post-1896 decline, and the mass media were transforming elections. Political leaders now hired their own publicity agents and addressed the public directly in radio broadcasts rather than through the press. In 1928, presidential nominees Herbert Hoover and Al Smith were the first to make talking pictures for their campaigns. Regardless of party affiliation, most electoral candidates positioned themselves as the champions of Americans' consumer-driven standard of living. Cultural factors played more of a role in elections, and social conservatives, such as Herbert Hoover, tended to win.

When Hoover entered the White House in January 1929, the economy seemed robust and the stock market was bullish. But certain structural weaknesses, including Americans' debt and poverty levels, had worsened during the 1920s. At no point in the nation's history had the income gap been wider. Later in the year, following a period of particularly wild speculation on Wall Street, a handful of major investors quietly pulled their capital out of the stock market in the belief that the markets were overvalued. One fateful morning in October, as thousands of smaller investors rushed to follow suit, the New York Stock Exchange went into free fall.

THE RISE OF HERBERT HOOVER

In 1927, while on a fishing trip, Calvin Coolidge stunned the nation by announcing that he would not be running for reelection. Coolidge had never relished the office, considering it more of a noble duty of guardianship than a valuable opportunity to bring about change. With the economy relatively buoyant and no major political crises in sight, he was content to retire from politics.

Herbert Hoover was the clear choice to lead the Republican ticket in the 1928 election. He had a distinguished track record as one the most promising and capable members of all three previous administrations. An engineer by training, Hoover benefited from a resumé that uncannily placed him in the center of almost every significant national event of the previous twenty-five years. Beginning with his role as fundraiser for the Panama-Pacific International Exposition of 1915, he had gone on to direct the campaign to feed a starving Belgium in 1916, to great acclaim. He became a household name as coordinator of the United States' food industry during World War I, and he had served as secretary of commerce in an era in which business and employment boomed. Moreover, just a few months prior to Coolidge's announcement, Hoover had become a national hero as the director of the federal relief effort in one of the greatest peacetime disasters in American history—the Great Mississippi Flood of 1927 (see States of Emergency: Politics of Disaster).

Like a growing number of politicians, Hoover retained a publicity agent in 1926 who worked to ensure that his client's service to the nation was well publicized. Hoover won the Republican nomination for the election of 1928 easily and, in his acceptance speech, declared that the United States was nearing

STATES OF EMERGENCY

Politics of Disaster: The Great Mississippi Flood of 1927

Rooftop Rescue. National Guard aircraft rescue Arkansas victims off their roofs during the Great Mississippi Flood of 1927.

In the spring of 1927, following weeks of rain and an unusually heavy thaw in the Great Lakes region, the Mississippi River burst its banks across seven states, displacing hundreds of thousands of people, mostly farmers, and submerging millions of acres of farmland. Spring flooding was nothing new. Native Americans had called the river Mississippi—"father of waters"—for good reason, and it had flooded every few years for centuries, changing its course and the surrounding landscape. In the eighteenth century, French settlers found some of the richest soil in the world, thanks to layers of alluvium that the swollen river had repeatedly deposited. Carving up the delta for farms and plantations, settlers built levees to keep the river from swamping their crops. In flood, however, the river always found a route to the ocean through undammed areas or over the weakest levees. As Mark Twain put it, no one "could tame the lawless stream . . . say to it, Go here, Go there."

Eventually, in 1879, Congress began work with the U.S. Army Corps of Engineers to reinforce and complete the patchwork of levees. By the 1920s, state and federal government had lined the full length of the river's thousand miles. The levees, announced the chief of engineers in 1926, were "now in condition to prevent the destructive effects of floods." In fact, a devastating flood was far more likely than before, as the natural spillways that had released the enormous pressure of the swollen river had been eliminated and logging and development had cleared much of the remaining forest—vital for absorbing excess water. The mighty Mississippi had no place to go but over the levees and into the surrounding countryside the following spring.

Over a million people were affected, and the flood wreaked an estimated $400 million worth of damage ($5.2 billion in today's dollars). In the first-ever federal relief effort, President Coolidge dispatched Herbert Hoover to oversee rescue and reconstruction. A master of both publicity and large-scale coordination, Hoover deployed the press, newsreels men, the army, private and federal airplanes, and radio broadcasters to survey the damage and relay critical information. He housed 350,000 displaced persons in tent cities within several days and, with help from the Red Cross, coordinated thirty-one thousand volunteers, the army and navy, and a national fundraising drive (which generated $17 million). He ordered towns that had been spared to take in thousands of refugees. The national media recorded everything.

Remarkably, given the magnitude of the disaster, only 246 people died—1,590 fewer than in Hurricane Katrina in 2005, which ravaged a smaller area. On the waterlogged ground, however, some victims fared better than others. Despite Hoover's orders that the hundreds of thousands of affected African American sharecroppers should receive equal aid, many were forcibly pressed into labor on the levees or denied shelter. When the NAACP presented Hoover with evidence that white soldiers were sexually assaulting African American women, he refused to take action. Within weeks, African American blues artists had recorded the first of thirty songs lamenting the flood and the government's subsequent reconstruction effort. News of conditions—and Hoover's reluctance to wield the power of federal government on African Americans' behalf—spread through Chicago, Detroit, and New York, provoking African Americans' historic drift out of the Republican Party and into the Democratic fold. African American disaffection would not cost Hoover the presidency in 1928, but the drift to the Democrats gathered momentum and would be instrumental to his defeat in 1932.

Think About It

1. Was the flood of 1927 a natural, manmade, or other kind of disaster?
2. What made Hoover a particularly good candidate to direct the relief effort?
3. Why do you think Hoover's relief operation made him a hero among many white people?

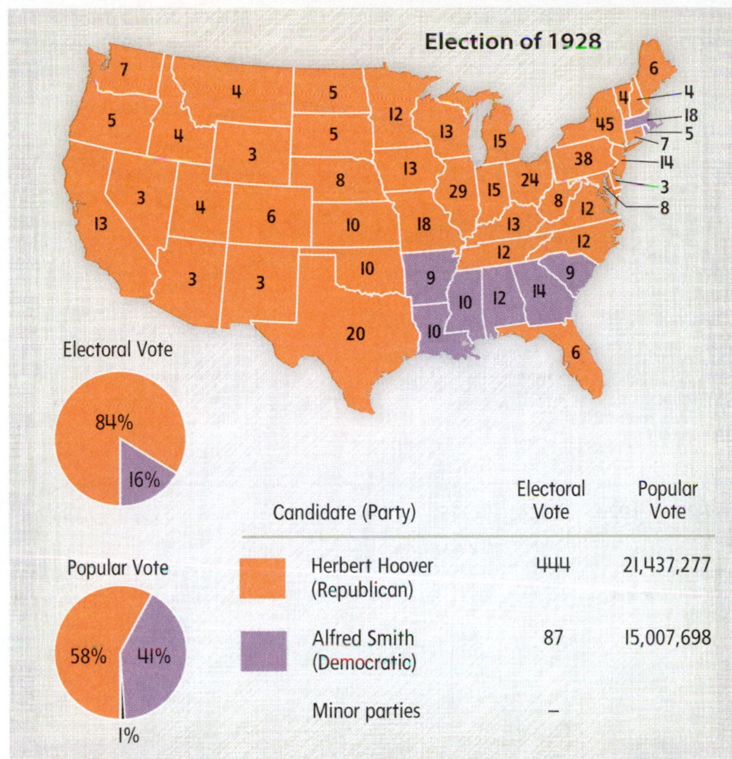

Candidate (Party)	Electoral Vote	Popular Vote
Herbert Hoover (Republican)	444	21,437,277
Alfred Smith (Democratic)	87	15,007,698
Minor parties	–	

Map 23.4 Election of 1928. Although voters were divided on cultural issues such as Prohibition, most associated the Republican Party with the economic boom on the 1920s and consequently returned a Republican, Herbert Hoover, to the White House.

its "final triumph over poverty"—even though almost 50 percent of Americans, mostly in rural, Democratic areas, were on the poverty line. Going into the election, the Republicans made a single, bold consumerist promise: "a chicken in every pot and a car in every garage." The Democrats meanwhile fielded New York governor Alfred E. Smith, who was popular in the party's urban wing but who did not appeal to the Democrats' white rural base. On many economic issues, Hoover and Smith were surprisingly close. "Hoover says the tariff will be kept up," joked celebrity Will Rogers. "Smith says the tariff will not be lowered. Hoover is in favor of prosperity. Smith says he highly endorses prosperity."

Despite the parties' similar economic platforms, voters interpreted the election as a choice between two clearly opposing cultures. The Iowa-born Hoover represented traditional values to his fellow white Protestant voters. Smith, born and raised in New York City, was the child of Catholic immigrants and the first Catholic to run for president. As the presidential contest unfolded, traditionalists disapproved of Smith's (unsuccessful) campaign to end Prohibition, and he failed to rally many Democrats behind the usual class and economic issues. Fundamentalist ministers everywhere launched an all-out campaign against Smith, whom one evangelical called "that nominee of the worst forces of Hell" who would soon make the United States "100% Catholic, Drunk, and Illiterate."

The Ku Klux Klan also mobilized, greeting Smith in Oklahoma City with a burning cross planted near a local Baptist church whose minister had warned that a vote for Al Smith was a vote against Christ. Smith's supporters countered that anyone who did not vote for him was a "bumpkin," a "moron," and "hopelessly uneducable," thereby reinforcing small-town perceptions of the New Yorker as a condescending elitist. (Smith's New York accent was also a liability, especially in his radio addresses.) While Smith carried the nation's twelve largest cities and benefited from most white southerners' refusal to vote Republican, the election of 1928 was a landslide victory for Hoover (see Map 23.4).

PERILS OF PROSPERITY

Although the stock market was surging forward when Herbert Hoover took office in 1929, key sectors in the economy had ceased to perform well (see Figure 23.2). Spending in automobiles and construction—two of the boom industries of the 1920s—had been in decline for two years. In other sectors, consumers were not buying as many goods as the factories were producing. The reasons for the slowdown were numerous and complex. Many skilled workers had enjoyed wage increases, but elsewhere (particularly in agriculture, steel, coal, and other heavy industries) wages had stagnated, leaving workers with little disposable income. By 1928, companies also had far more plant space—factories, warehouses, and equipment—and employees than they needed. Corporations downsized in response to this problem, thereby expanding the pool of Americans who could not afford consumer goods. In addition, the wealthy had benefited from the boom disproportionately, with 2 percent of Americans commanding 28 percent of national income while a majority—60 percent—received just under one-quarter of it. This high concentration of wealth among a small minority deprived the economy of money that might otherwise have gone to employees through higher wages. Ultimately it deprived the consumer economy of demand.

All told, more than 50 percent of Americans were living on or under the poverty line and had little or no disposable income for consumer goods. Farmers struggled especially hard as they endured an agricultural depression that lasted the entire decade. Depressed prices for meat and produce and the steep price of farm machinery led farmers who owned their property to mortgage it as a way of boosting income, while sharecroppers and renters sought other kinds of loans. By 1928, with no sign of improvement, many farmers were unable to service their loans, defaulted on their payments, and lost their farms to foreclosure. The ripple effect of this wave of foreclosures hit small rural banks hard, causing many to fail.

The dramatic growth of consumer and commercial debt in the 1920s freed up money for consumption and investment.

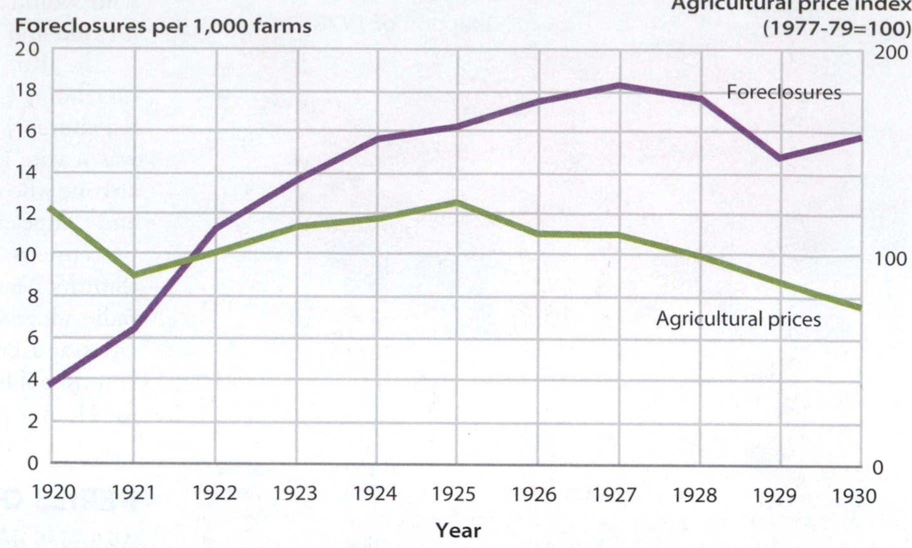

FIGURE 23.2 Uneven Prosperity. Although industrial and agricultural output shot up in the 1920s and skilled workers' wages rose, large segments of the population did not share in the prosperity. Farmers in particular suffered from low prices for their produce, and many were forced to mortgage their land. As prices continued to drop, foreclosure rates more than quadrupled. This graph compares the agricultural price index—the average price that producers received for their product each year—with the rate of farm foreclosures.

Motorized Farming. Farmers' use of motorized equipment such as this McCormick Deering Farmall tractor and reaper often came at the cost of mortgaging the farm and further depressing the price their harvest could fetch (because such equipment raised output).

But it also made the economy appear much stronger than it really was. People were spending money they had not yet earned or accumulated—a fine practice as long as the economy expanded fast enough for them to reap the profits, but dangerous if growth slowed. The lightning-fast extension of credit domestically was paralleled in international finance, with the European allies together owing the U.S. Treasury upwards of $9 billion ($118 billion in today's dollars) at the end of the Great War. Looking for a way to repay these loans, at Versailles Britain and France had insisted on hefty reparations from Germany and Austria (see Chapter 22). But the defeated nations' economies were even more precarious. A vicious cycle of credit and debt emerged in which U.S. banks loaned money to European nations that in turn used these loans to pay off their U.S. government loans. By the late 1920s, Europe was caught in a sinkhole of debt, and American banks were dependent on debtors that lacked the means to repay them. The banks began to respond to the international situation in 1928 by raising interest rates and sometimes refusing to lend to Europe. Consequently, by the end of the year, European governments were on the verge of defaulting on their loans altogether.

Desperate Acts. Having lost an unknown amount of money in the Wall Street crash, this investor was willing to sell his car for as little as $100, about 5 percent of its value.

THE GREAT CRASH

Despite these structural vulnerabilities in the domestic and international economies, investment on U.S. stock markets boomed well into 1929. By September, stock prices had been driven up over 50 percent since January 1. Much as in the Florida land rush, major investors now began worrying that the market could be tremendously overvalued. News that building construction and new car sales had sagged further fueled anxiety, as did rumors that major investors were withdrawing in the expectation of a correction (that is, a decline). On Thursday, October 24, after weeks of uncertainty and volatility, investors rushed to sell their securities on the United States' main market, the New York Stock Exchange. But they could find no buyers, and the price of stocks plummeted. After other investors panicked, by lunchtime the market had suffered a staggering $9 billion loss ($118 billion in today's dollars). Despite the efforts of the J. P. Morgan bank to buy up masses of unwanted securities, a move that briefly stabilized the market, on the following Tuesday, October 29, investors dumped as many shares as they could. The result was the single largest one-day loss in history.

Finance company Goldman Sachs lost nearly half its value, and even the most stable corporations, such as General Electric, Standard Oil, and AT&T, lost up to 40 percent of their value. Fistfights broke out on the trading floor as brokers jostled to sell as quickly as possible. By the time the Wall Street crash was over, the panic had spread to other financial districts, and brokers were desperately demanding the repayment of investors' loans. Although reports of suicide were greatly exaggerated, a number of prominent investors took their lives that day—including the president of the Union Cigar Company (which had lost half its value in a matter of minutes), who jumped to his death from the ledge of a Manhattan hotel.

The market stabilized over the next few weeks, but it commenced a slow downward trajectory. Although hundreds of thousands of Americans had lost their fortunes, neither bankers nor ordinary citizens thought the panic was different in nature from the devastating busts of past decades. A few weeks later, financier Bernard Baruch reflected, "Financial storm definitely past," and President Hoover concurred that "the fundamental business of the country is sound." But the basic structural problems in the domestic and international economy remained—and were aggravated by the sudden loss of investment capital, the radical decline of consumer spending power, and industries' need to lay off workers due to the contraction of demand. Although Americans barely realized it in 1929, the single worst economic catastrophe in the nation's history was just beginning.

CONCLUSION

Reflecting on the 1920s two years after the Wall Street crash, novelist F. Scott Fitzgerald pronounced the Jazz Age dead. It "had a wild youth and a heady middle age," Fitzgerald's obituary for the era recollected, "but it was not to be. Somebody had blundered and the most expensive orgy in history was over." Fitzgerald was correct that Americans, wealthy and poor, had sustained enormous financial losses in 1929 and that the unbounded optimism of so many was fading. But many of the 1920s' new cultural forms and networks survived the economic cataclysm. The basic formulae of advertising, filmmaking, and radio broadcasting remained in place and were adapted to new needs and challenges. Youth culture endured, and mass spectacle became even more ubiquitous in subsequent years. Politics grew closer to the art and science of mass publicity.

The cultural forms that did not fare so well tended to be the ones with which white rural and small-town Protestant Americans most identified. Already struggling, many rural communities disintegrated altogether after the crash, and with them went their civil and church networks. By late 1929, the United States stood on the threshold of a radically different world.

STUDY TERMS

Washington Naval Treaties (p. 632)
Fordism (p. 632)
chain stores (p. 634)
Amos 'n' Andy (p. 636)
Teapot Dome (p. 639)
Black Sox scandal (p. 639)
speakeasy (p. 643)
Back to Africa movement (p. 644)
Harlem Renaissance (p. 644)
flapper (p. 646)
Equal Rights Amendment (p. 647)
second Ku Klux Klan (p. 647)
Sacco and Vanzetti (p. 649)
National Origins Act (p. 649)
illegal alien (p. 650)
Hays Code (p. 650)
fundamentalists (p. 652)
liberal (modernist) Christians (p. 652)
Monkey Trial (p. 653)
Great Mississippi Flood (p. 653)
Wall Street crash (p. 657)

TIMELINE

1920 Volstead Act launches Prohibition
Majority of Americans live in cities for first time
Warren Harding elected president
General Motors promotes installment plans
Movie *The Flapper* popularizes bobbed hair and higher hemlines for young women

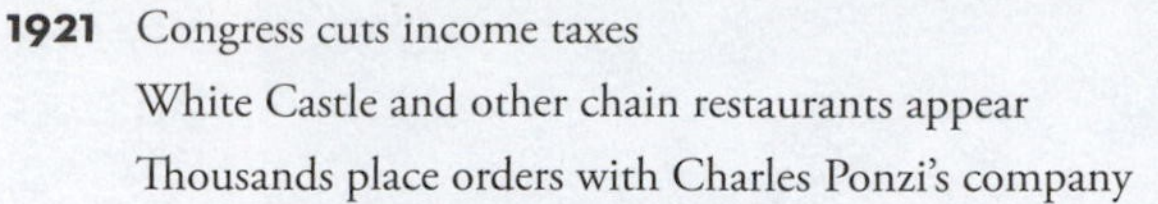

1921 Congress cuts income taxes
White Castle and other chain restaurants appear
Thousands place orders with Charles Ponzi's company

1922 The great powers sign Washington Naval Treaties, restricting naval arms
Radio begins commercial broadcasts
Recession ends except in agricultural sector
Hollywood studios establish Hays Office in wake of scandals
Aimee Semple McPherson broadcasts first sermon from Angelus Temple

1923 Corporate taxes lowered
Calvin Coolidge becomes president following Harding's death

1924 Congress restricts immigration
The Teapot Dome scandal breaks
Ku Klux Klan counts over four million members

1925 Dr. Ossian Sweet tried for murder after defending his home
Alain Locke publishes his essay "The New Negro"
John Scopes is convicted of breaking Tennessee's anti-evolution law

1926 Florida real estate bubble bursts
Herbert Hoover hires a publicity agent
Ford shifts production from Model T to Model A

1927 Movie *The Jazz Singer* features a partial soundtrack
Catholic clergy demand tougher censorship system for Hollywood
One million people are displaced by the flooding Mississippi River

1928 Herbert Hoover wins presidency in a landslide election
Construction and new automobile sales slow
Farmers default on loans at record high rates

1929 Advertising revenues reach $3.4 billion
NBC broadcasts *Amos 'n' Andy*
Bloody St. Valentine's Day Massacre in Chicago gangster wars
European workers marvel at Ford's traveling trunk show
New York Stock Exchange crashes

FURTHER READING

Additional suggested readings are available on the Online Learning Center at www.mhhe.com/becomingamerica1e.

Kathleen M. Blee, *Women of the Klan: Racism and Gender in the 1920s* (1992), analyzes women's contradictory role in the Klan.

Pete Daniel, *Deep'n as It Come: The 1927 Mississippi River Flood* (1996), examines the flood's social, cultural, and political effects.

Nicholas R. Grossman, *The Promised Land: The Great Black Migration and How It Changed America* (1991), portrays African Americans' varied experiences of resettling in Chicago and their challenges and triumphs in making a new life.

Nathan Irving Huggins, *Harlem Renaissance* (1971), explores the work of leading figures and its impact on American culture.

Kenneth Jackson, *The Ku Klux Klan in the City, 1915–1930* (1992), shows that the Klan grew most dramatically in the newer cities of the Midwest and West.

David E. Kyvig, *Daily Life in the United States, 1920–1940* (2002), explores the way people adopted and adapted automobiles, radio, and other new phenomena in everyday life.

William Leuchtenberg, *Perils of Prosperity* (2nd ed., 1993), shows how the United States' transition from an agrarian to a modern consumer society concentrated enormous power in the hands of big business and created a culture in which money was a dominant value.

David Levering Lewis, *When Harlem Was in Vogue* (1981), shows how a complex convergence of people, ideas, politics, and art made Harlem the site of the United States' most vital interwar cultural movement.

Roland Marchand, *Advertising the American Dream: Making Way for Modernity, 1920–1940* (1985), probes how advertisers drew on mass media and photography and other art forms to shape and promote the consumption ethic.

Mae M. Ngai, *Impossible Subjects: Illegal Aliens and the Making of Modern America,* traces the emergence of the category "illegal alien."

Kathy Peiss, *Hope in a Jar: The Making of America's Beauty Culture* (1999), tracks the careers of the women who built the beauty industry and shows how female consumers' own aspirations contributed to its success.

Jules Tygiel, *Baseball as History* (1996), includes an essay looking at the sport's relation to the advent of radio and its impact on the ways Americans experienced the world.

24

INSIDE ▶

THE BIG PICTURE

As the Great Depression ground on and unemployment escalated, Americans looked to churches, voluntary associations, and ultimately to the federal government to get the nation on its feet. Government programs provided unprecedented material and psychological relief on a mass scale. Consumer culture became more homogeneous, while the arts proved to be vital resources for a population struggling to cope with the nation's worst-ever depression.

Hard Times. Margaret Bourke-White's disturbing photograph, first published in *Life* magazine in 1937, became an iconic image of the Great Depression.

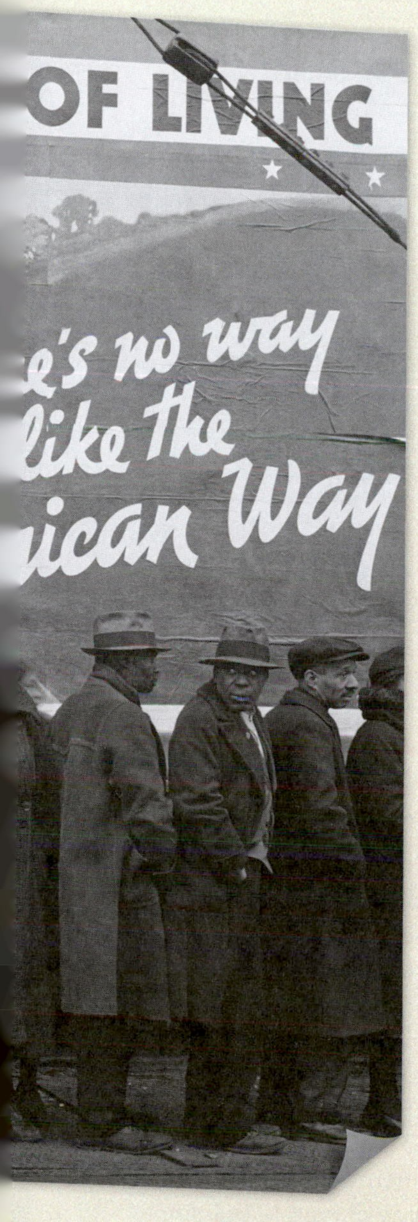

AMERICA REMADE: THE GREAT DEPRESSION & THE NEW DEAL

Driving across the parched plains of the Texas panhandle one Sunday afternoon in 1935, the Phillips family was surprised to see a strange, billowing mass reaching thousands of feet into the blue sky and heading straight toward them. Within minutes, the air turned thick as the cloud of grit and sand pelted the family's Ford Model A. Desperate to escape, the Phillipses abandoned their car and scrambled blindly toward an old hut, where they took shelter with ten others huddling in the dark. Four hours later, the frightened inhabitants emerged to a nearly unrecognizable, dust-encrusted landscape.

Similar episodes were repeated across the southern plains over the next several years. Extreme weather was nothing new to plains folk. For four years they had endured record drought and dozens of long, slow dust storms that ruined crops, buried homes, and coated everything inside and out with a dense film. But the swirling dark towers of sand were something new and lethal. They literally whipped the earth out from under one's feet, destroying millions of acres of crops, suffocating thousands of livestock, and killing dozens of people.

Beyond the plains, the great majority of Americans also felt as though the ground was disappearing under their feet in the 1930s. After the Wall Street crash of 1929, the prosperity and optimism of 1920s urban America evaporated. Contrary

In his 1933 work *Dust Bowl*, Texan painter Alexandre Hogue illustrated the ravages of the "black blizzards" on the grasslands of his boyhood.

KEY QUESTIONS

- What were the causes of the Great Depression?
- How did the Depression affect American culture, politics, and daily life?
- In what ways were the First and the Second New Deals different?
- How did ordinary people's experience of the Depression vary depending on their race, ethnicity, sex, and geographical location?
- What role did the arts, advertising, and the culture industries play during the Depression?
- How did conservatives, liberals, leftists, and other commentators respond to the dramatic increase in federal government authority brought by the New Deal?

to the popular view that the economy would bounce back, it did not. And as the economy unraveled, over one in five Americans lost their jobs; another three million lost their land. Most Americans learned to "live lean" in these years, improvising novel ways of surviving and coping with life's stresses and uncertainties. A growing number also demanded federal government action. Committed to the idea that big business would revive employment of its own accord, President Herbert Hoover resisted such calls until well into 1931. When he finally took action, it was too little, too late, and the electorate voted him out of office in a landslide.

Hoover's successor was elected on a vague platform that included a "new deal" for Americans and an acknowledgment that the unbridled forces of free-market capitalism had brought the Great Depression—by then, the worst economic downturn in U.S. and global history. Franklin D. Roosevelt and his cabinet commenced a thorough retooling of the American economy. Lacking a grand plan, Roosevelt's experimental New Deal nevertheless gradually changed government and society and produced a novel political ideology, New Deal liberalism. Government regulation of business stabilized the economy and stimulated consumption, while social security, farm subsidies, and housing assistance integrated one in three Americans into a vast new network of entitlements (federal services and payments). Although in theory all Americans benefited from the New Deal, in practice some benefited far more than others.

Besides reform, other forces remade American life in the 1930s. Consumer culture expanded its reach and influence, taking advantage of new national communication networks and Americans' desire for at least temporary release from the stresses and strains of the Depression. A distinctive American diet emerged, as did a consumer rights movement that demanded better labeling and more control over product contents. Thanks largely to massive government funding, the arts flourished and became a vital source of morale building in these hardest of times.

HERBERT HOOVER AND HARD TIMES

Immediately following the Wall Street crash of 1929, President Herbert Hoover cut taxes on the theory that this measure would give consumers more disposable income and stimulate investment. The Republican president reassured the nation that the economy was "fundamentally sound" and had suffered only a temporary setback. Hard work, private and state relief organizations, and business leadership would reverse the slump. Having directed the nation's two greatest humanitarian relief efforts—the Belgian food drive of 1915 and the Mississippi flood of 1927—to wide acclaim, Hoover enjoyed the support of most Americans. But over the next few years, as millions lost their jobs and homes or were thrown off their land, voters grew disillusioned with Hoover's approach.

THE UNRAVELING ECONOMY

The stock market recovered temporarily but then continued its descent through 1931. Companies once thought to be invincible, such as U.S. Steel, lost 90 percent of their stock value and were forced to close many plants. By 1930, twenty-six thousand businesses had gone bust. As the surviving industries operated at less than a fifth of their previous capacity, newspapers grimly reported massive layoffs. Meanwhile, the American depression spread to the global financial system as troubled U.S. banks recalled loans from Germany and Austria. A chain reaction began when Germany defaulted on reparations to France and Britain, causing those nations to default on their U.S. loans. After American depositors, fearing that international defaults threatened their own savings, rushed to withdraw their funds, more U.S. banks failed. In an effort to discourage borrowing, the Federal Reserve tightened credit sharply, causing interest rates to spike and putting pressure on banks, especially rural and ethnic ones. Upwards of five thousand banks failed by 1932—and took the savings of nine million Americans with them.

By 1931, the depression had become a global crisis, but its effects were especially crippling in the United States. The U.S. economy was less regulated than Europe's and therefore more prone to extreme booms and busts. Only Germany, with its crushing war debt and 30 percent unemployment rate, fared worse. U.S. workers and farmers were hit hard. Some industrial cities, such as Detroit and Flint, Michigan—both hubs of the auto industry—were devastated. In Chicago and Cleveland in 1932, unemployment rates jumped to 50 percent, while the Ohio cities of Akron and Toledo counted even higher rates of people out of work (see Table 24.1). Nationwide, one in four Americans were thrown out of work by 1932. Those who remained employed often worked shorter hours for lower wages, as full-time work became a rarity. Unlike many European nations, the United States lacked a safety net of federal unemployment insurance, health care, and social security that might have saved millions of people from abject poverty. With far less income—or none at all—trickling in, over half a million people lost their homes to foreclosure and millions more were evicted from rental properties.

The depression affected all workers, but it hurt some more than others. Working women were the first to lose their jobs in the popular belief that men needed the work more (for both psychological and economic reasons) and that jobs for women were a luxury that society could no longer afford. Local governments and employers' associations campaigned against women's employment, and all but 25 percent of school districts banned female teachers. As the depression wore on, however, more women were compelled to work, often because their husband's incomes had been cut so severely. Now barred from many skilled and professional occupations, most could find only domestic or part-time jobs.

TABLE 24.1 UNEMPLOYMENT RATES IN SELECT CITIES, 1932

City	Rate (percent)
Chicago, Illinois	50
Cleveland, Ohio	50
Akron, Ohio	60
Toledo, Ohio	80

Employers also enforced existing racial hierarchies that excluded African Americans, Latinos, and Asians from certain skilled positions and professions. Companies routinely fired people of color first to free up jobs for whites. By 1932, African American men were twice as likely as white men to be unemployed. Black working women suffered triple the unemployment rate of white women, largely because employers replaced them with the flood of white women entering domestic and service occupations. As joblessness spread, once-vibrant African American neighborhoods such as Chicago's South Side and New York's Harlem suffered disproportionate levels of poverty and despair.

The crash of 1929 accelerated the ongoing mass migration of small farmers off the land. By then, prices for meat, dairy, and produce had already dropped to ruinous levels, and debt and foreclosure rates were rising. Falling prices and the rapid expansion of large-scale agribusiness in the 1920s further pressured small farmers and sharecroppers, forcing six million to quit the land by 1929. After the crash, millions more left—some sped by the prolonged drought that struck the plains in the early 1930s (see Leaving the Dust Bowl, below). Over the next three years, almost one-third of all farming families lost their land when they could not make mortgage payments. In the hardest-stung rural regions, parents had little choice but to cut children's meals from three to two per day. Across the country, hospitals observed record numbers of illnesses and deaths from malnutrition.

Many middle-class Americans experienced a sudden fall in their fortunes. Doctors, attorneys, teachers, and other college-educated people all suffered salary cuts. Many also lost their life savings, disposable income, and credit. Even the wealthiest Americans were affected. Although most generally maintained their high standard of living, they lost between 50 percent and 90 percent of their investments—and some were ruined. As sales of homes, cars, and other big-ticket consumer goods plummeted, more plant closures and layoffs followed.

THE LIMITS OF VOLUNTARISM

Much as he had done throughout his distinguished career in government, President Hoover hewed to a policy of **voluntarism**—the idea that the federal government, rather than legislating solutions, should work collaboratively with big business, the states, and voluntary relief organizations to resolve the crisis. Shortly after the crash, Hoover persuaded business leaders to pledge to maintain wage and employment levels. He also convened the Emergency Committee for Employment, which worked with charities to coordinate unemployment relief. As Hoover had hoped, city government, charities, and churches and synagogues rallied, setting up soup kitchens and providing shelter and other essentials, and eight states gave the unemployed direct financial assistance.

Despite business's pledge, however, the layoffs and foreclosures continued, approaching record levels in 1931. Relief organizations were quickly overwhelmed. With the business sector unable to find its own way out of the downward spiral, President Hoover's faith in voluntarism wavered. Calling upon state and local governments to invest in public projects such as road construction, the president conceded that government might need to take a more direct role in what he was the first to call the United States' "Great Depression."

The president's first step was to help burdened farmers. In an effort to protect American growers from overseas competition, Hoover signed the Hawley-Smoot Tariff (1930), which imposed heavy taxes on food imports. He also reluctantly authorized the single largest peacetime increase in federal spending for large-scale public projects ($700 million, or $9.8 billion in today's dollars), in the hope that government could put millions of people back to work. The president moreover directed the Reconstruction Finance Corporation, a federal agency established in early 1932, to provide $300 million in stimulus loans to banks, insurers, and railroads and other corporations. In the same year, congressional Democrats prevailed on a hesitant Hoover to sign the Federal Home Loan Bank Act, by which thousands of homeowners refinanced their mortgages and avoided foreclosure, and the Emergency Relief Act, which authorized the Reconstruction Finance Corporation to extend loans to the struggling states.

Hoover's initiatives, however, did not stem the powerful tide of the Depression. Although the scale of the federal programs was unprecedented, it was dwarfed by the enormous costs of the Depression. Workers, farmers, and the middle class continued to struggle, and the Hawley-Smoot Tariff triggered a disastrous trade war in which foreign governments boycotted American goods. U.S. exports consequently fell by over 50 percent in the following year, and the unemployment rate tripled, to almost 25 percent, by 1932.

LIVING LEAN

Left largely to their own devices under Hoover's voluntarist policies, Americans coped as best they could by learning to "live lean." Millions hit road and rail in search of work, and thousands of homeless families set up shantytowns on the periphery of cities, typically alongside rail lines and near city dumps. They called these settlements **Hoovervilles** in ironic reference to a president who appeared unmoved by their plight.

Two million urban people traversed the country looking for work in 1930—among them, 250,000 teenage boys and "sisters of the road" (homeless women). As in previous recessions, several thousand urban families headed for the countryside, hoping to farm their own food. But starting a farm from scratch, with little experience and even less capital, proved a grueling and often impossible task. For the first time in the nation's history, more people (especially Italians and Mexican immigrants) left the United States than entered it. Many departed of their own accord, in search of work, but for most Mexicans, emigration was forcible. As unemployment climbed and Americans grew hungry for any work they could find, a wave of anti-Mexican feeling among white workers, unions, and local government broke over Southern California and the Southwest. Courting voters ahead of the 1932 election, Hoover announced a **repatriation** policy to send Mexican nationals back to Mexico. By 1940, city, federal, and county governments had forcibly "repatriated" upwards of 450,000 mostly rural Mexicans—along with over 35,000 American citizens mistaken for Mexican nationals.

The most desperate people scrimped on meals, trawling through trash to find food if necessary, and cut all nonessential spending. Middle-class women, who in the 1920s had opted to dress their children in store-bought clothing rather than sewing from scratch, learned anew how to darn socks, knit, and sew clothes. Aunts, uncles, grandparents, and other relatives moved in with nuclear families, and children found themselves sharing their bedrooms—and even their beds—with cousins and siblings. As couples delayed marriage, children, and the expense of having a family, the national birthrate fell almost a quarter, to just over seven babies per hundred women (a historic low).

The emotional effects of the economic crisis were no less severe. By 1932, popular optimism that business was "sound and prosperous" (Hoover's words) had given way to fear and despondency. Psychological distress took many forms. In a culture in which urban men's identity rested on their role as family breadwinner, widespread job loss among men set off a full-scale crisis of masculinity. "The moral fiber of the American man," lamented popular novelist Sherwood Anderson, "through being without a job, losing a sense of being some part of the moving world of activity, so essential to an American man's sense of his manhood—the loss of this essential something in the jobless can never be measured in dollars."

Many unemployed men, particularly in industries that prized physical strength, felt humiliated by their loss of status. Fathers who had once put ample food on the table and fed their family's consumerist desires now considered themselves failures. Publications with titles such as "The Decline of the Male," "The Lure of the Helpless Male," and "Fallen Fathers" reinforced their sense of defeat. Demoralized and deeply

Moving to Hooverville. By 1931, Herbert Hoover's name became synonymous with the Depression and government inaction. The millions who lost their homes and livelihoods coped as well as they could, many of them constructing makeshift shacks in city parks and urban peripheries. They turned newspapers—the multiple layers of which provided insulation in cold weather—into "Hoover blankets" and referred to empty pockets as "Hoover flags."

ashamed, most men suffered in silence. Some left home, however, and others took their own lives, pushing the nation's suicide rate to an all-time high.

MOBILIZING FOR CHANGE

Although most Americans concentrated on day-to-day survival, some also began to organize for change. In 1932, farmers banded together to prevent the banks and sheriffs from seizing their properties and evicting their families. Midwestern farmers set up the Farmers' Holiday Association, which coordinated an effort to prevent foreclosure auctions and, in some states, dumped large quantities of milk and vegetables in protest of low prices. Kentucky coal miners struck over a 10 percent wage cut in 1931, and the following year, Ford Motor Company workers walked off the job. Both strikes were violently broken, but employers' use of armed force against the workers enraged many people around the nation and fueled a revival of the labor movement.

In dozens of cities, unemployed people rioted over unaffordable rent and food. In some thirty-seven states, they joined associations known as unemployed councils. Although some were founded by the American Communist Party (which counted just twelve thousand members in 1930), the majority of the councils' three hundred thousand members were neither communist nor politically motivated. Rather, in the early years of the Depression, most councils were committed primarily to what they called "self-help"—finding ways to feed, shelter, and otherwise protect their members.

Self-help flourished everywhere. In Seattle, unemployed councils fed the jobless by borrowing fishermen's boats and securing local farmers' permission for workers to pick over lower quality produce. In Pennsylvania, twenty thousand unemployed coal miners dug small mines on company land and sold the "bootlegged" coal. In Chicago, whenever a sheriff evicted a family and put their belongings out on the street, the local council immediately dispatched a band of neighbors to reopen the home, return the property, and occupy the city's poor relief office until officials agreed to pay the family's rent. Such actions were sometimes illegal, but Americans were generally sympathetic, and officials seldom prosecuted. Chicago's city government eventually suspended the evictions.

Schemes such as these softened the blows of unemployment, but they did not address the root cause. Gradually, Americans began to demand more systematic relief, protesting the federal government's relative lack of action. Hoover refused a plea for increased federal aid to the unemployed and to low-wage workers. Millions of jobless people interpreted this refusal as callous disregard for their plight. By

Dispersing the Veterans. Caught on newsreel and in the press, the images of soldiers using guns, tanks, and fire to disperse the Bonus Marchers shocked and repelled many Americans. **Questions for Analysis:** What message do you think such displays of force were intended to convey to the veterans and to Americans generally? Why were such photographs so damaging to the Hoover administration?

the end of 1931, the once-popular Hoover was well on his way to becoming the most reviled president in the nation's history.

The largest and most effective protest came in June 1932 as twenty thousand unemployed World War I veterans and their families marched from all corners of the country to the nation's capital. Once there, this Bonus Army demanded early payment of veterans' bonuses that were due in 1945. Rebuffed by President Hoover, the veterans set up camp and refused to leave, hoisting banners with messages such as "We were heroes in 1917, but we're bums now." Most of the campers dispersed when the Senate voted down a House bill for the immediate payment of their bonuses, but two thousand dug in. Increasingly embarrassed, the president ultimately ordered the U.S. Army to disperse the remaining protestors. A fleet of six tanks and two regiments of the Third Cavalry razed the campsite, injuring over a hundred veterans (and killing one baby) in the process.

THE ELECTION OF 1932

Following the routing of the Bonus Army, public opinion swung even more strongly against Hoover. Nonetheless, going into the election of 1932, Republicans retained the embattled Hoover as their candidate. Franklin D. Roosevelt (FDR), a wealthy New York politician and distant cousin of former president Theodore Roosevelt, won the Democratic nomination. Permanently paralyzed from the waist down by polio, which he had contracted at the age of thirty-nine, Roosevelt brought to the Democratic ticket boundless optimism and the fighting spirit that had carried him through his health crisis. As governor of New York since 1928, FDR had actively promoted state relief programs. His track record led party members to agree that he, more than any other Democrat, had the right experience to guide the nation out of the Depression.

Drawing strength from the popular disaffection with Hoover, Roosevelt lambasted the president for his evident lack of leadership, proclaiming that his opponent's insides were "made of jelly." FDR promised a "new deal for the American people" based on fresh ideas and the willingness to experiment. Other than ending voluntarism, it was unclear—both to FDR and to voters—exactly what the **New Deal** would involve. But the Democrat's resolve to end the Depression and to lead boldly struck a chord with voters, who carried him into the White House with a significant majority (see Map 24.1). By also electing a Democratic House and Senate, voters effectively empowered FDR to carry out his agenda.

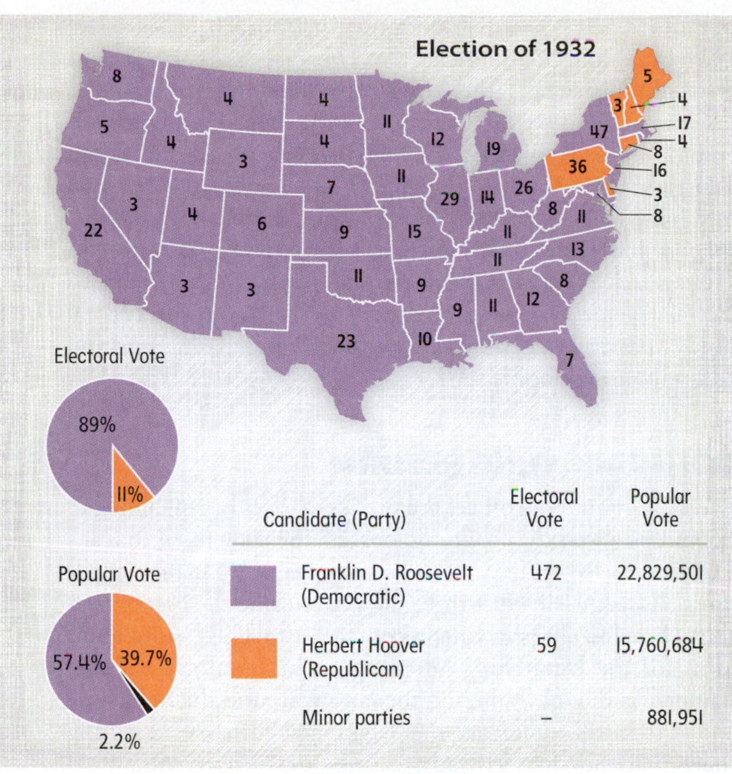

Candidate (Party)	Electoral Vote	Popular Vote
Franklin D. Roosevelt (Democratic)	472	22,829,501
Herbert Hoover (Republican)	59	15,760,684
Minor parties	–	881,951

Map 24.1 Election of 1932. FDR won 57.4 percent of the popular vote and 472 electoral votes to Hoover's 59.

FRANKLIN D. ROOSEVELT AND THE FIRST NEW DEAL

The U.S. economy was at its lowest ebb when FDR was inaugurated in March 1933. One in every three adults was unemployed, and almost half the nation was at or below the poverty line. A deep, collective anxiety gripped all but the wealthiest Americans. The new president was convinced that the free-market system could survive only if it were thoroughly reformed. He also believed that he needed to act swiftly and decisively—and, unlike his predecessor, he understood that success would depend partly on the government's ability to communicate directly and persuasively with citizens. The First New Deal was as much a sustained campaign against popular fear and lack of confidence as it was a set of structural economic reforms. FDR set out to rebuild Americans' confidence in government, the free-market system, and themselves. Within days of his inauguration, he took the first of several emergency actions and recruited a team of leading economists, sociologists, and planners to draft long-term reforms. Lacking a master plan, the First New Deal was a trial-by-error process of experimentation and innovation.

EMERGENCY REFORM

FDR wasted no time in launching what historians call the First New Deal (1933–1934). Within three days of entering office, he took the unprecedented step of closing the nation's banks, effectively ending the run on banks, which had escalated between the election and Roosevelt's inauguration. The president also sent Congress an emergency bill that protected the larger institutions from the cascading bankruptcies of smaller ones. The resulting Emergency Banking Act (1933) directed the Treasury to inspect all banks and to reopen only those that could afford to operate. Federal assistance was extended to many of the more stable banks, while dozens of weaker ones were subject to mandatory reorganization.

Twenty-four hours later, FDR successfully pressed Congress to cut government salaries and veterans' pensions by almost 15 percent, a move that instantly trimmed $1 billion from the federal budget—and that boldly signaled to business that FDR was prepared to cut government spending. By the end of the week, FDR had backed a third major bill—a modification of the Volstead Act that would allow the production and sale of beer. Roosevelt thereby sought to free the federal government from the expense of enforcing an unpopular law and to empower the states to tax the popular beverage. He also supported the full repeal of the rest of Prohibition, which Congress carried out later in 1933.

RECONSTRUCTING THE ECONOMY

Having taken swift emergency action, the administration embarked on the hard work of framing legislation aimed at reorganizing and stabilizing every major sector of the economy. All New Dealers shared the goal of reviving the economy, but disagreement existed over how to do so. The New Dealers tended to fall within one of two camps. One group believed that private interests—farmers, business leaders, workers—should dominate the planning process. The other camp argued that the government should be the principal planning agent in the new economy. Both approaches influenced the extraordinarily comprehensive set of reforms that the Roosevelt administration shepherded through Congress in what has come to be called the **first hundred days** (March 9–June 17, 1933).

Tackling the decimated farming sector first, the Agricultural Adjustment Act (1933) buoyed the prices of basic agricultural products such as wheat and corn and thus provided some immediate relief for beleaguered farmers. Reforming the financial sector—whose reckless practices had helped run up stock and property values in the late 1920s—was next. Under the Truth in Securities Act (1933), all corporations issuing new shares had to provide the public with complete and accurate information about their securities, including financial accounts that theoretically enabled investors to assess a company's viability. Congress also established the Federal Deposit Insurance Corporation (FDIC), which insured deposits in banks so that customers would not rush to withdraw their funds in mass panic, plunging the banks into crisis. The following year, FDR also established the Security and Exchange Commission, which he charged with policing the stock market. The new Federal Housing Administration made fair, affordable mortgages available by insuring bank loans extended for the purpose of home purchase or construction.

Relieving unemployment was also a priority in FDR's first hundred days. Rather than giving cash handouts to America's fifteen million jobless, however, the administration endeavored to put men back to work in the belief that paid employment would restore self-respect and affirm their identity as productive breadwinners and citizens. Under the new Federal Emergency Relief Administration (FERA), the government established a series of massive new public employment schemes, many aimed at improving roads, bridges, and other infrastructure. Over four million people worked on road, school, and park construction under the direction of FERA's Civil Works Association between 1934 and 1936. By 1937, the Civilian Conservation Corps was providing work and training for six hundred thousand young men through energetic, highly disciplined work in the nation's parks and wilderness areas. Other massive public works were undertaken in the First New Deal by the Tennessee Valley Authority, including the world's largest hydroelectric project (see Networking Rural America, below).

The most significant and ambitious reform of the First New Deal was the National Industrial Recovery Act, a sweeping law that fundamentally altered U.S. industrial relations and dramatically extended public work schemes. This act was a compromise between the United States Chamber of Commerce—a powerful business lobby that wanted the right to stabilize prices across entire industries—and the Democratic Party's commitment to organized labor. The law authorized businesses to set prices for any given industry and guaranteed workers the right to join a union and to collectively bargain with their employers. It also authorized the creation of the National Recovery Administration (NRA), which worked with business to establish production codes that specified work hours, wage rates, and the quality and quantity of products for over seven hundred industries. As well, the NRA brought government, business, and labor together to negotiate and agree on fair wages and prices.

Eagle of Recovery. Stores and other business eagerly posted the NRA eagle, and seventy-five million people saw it each week in Hollywood movie credits. The eagle holds a cog to represent industry and a lightning bolt to symbolize power.

By the end of 1933, the government had invested $6 billion in over 13,000 federal projects and 2,500 local projects that together employed over five million Americans. The sweep of these agricultural, financial, unemployment, and environmental reforms—all undertaken in just over three months—radically altered both the function and the extent of federal government. Never before, in times of peace, had the government taken such an aggressive and visible role in American life. Even in the long-dormant arena of Indian affairs, the government took dramatic action to ease poverty and reempower the nation's most disenfranchised communities. Known as the Indian New Deal, the Indian Reorganization Act (1934) ended the half-century-old system of allotment (which broke up communal lands and allotted them to individual Indian owners; see Chapter 17). It also authorized tribes to write their own constitutions and returned the management of communal lands to tribal councils. Federal funds were made available to the tribes for purchasing land and educational development.

COMMUNICATING REFORM

Even before entering office, the president-elect began talking to the public about the economic crisis. "The only thing to fear," FDR counseled millions of radio listeners in his inaugural address, "is fear itself." Just three days later came the first of over thirty **fireside chats** in which Roosevelt explained and sold his ideas for the New Deal. Adopting an informal and fatherly manner, as though gathering the family around the hearth, he aimed to instill confidence in a frightened citizenry, reassuring them that they had a steady, caring, and utterly committed president who took their suffering seriously. "I never saw him," reflected one listener, "but I knew him. Can you have forgotten how, with his voice, he came into our house, the President of these United States, calling us friends. . . ."

Radio broadcasts were not the only way FDR's government informed, persuaded, and reassured the American public about the First New Deal. Drawing on the latest advertising techniques, the government also used print, visual media (such as billboards), documentary movies, and even the relatively new strategy of product branding. General Hugh S. Johnson, director of the National Recovery Administration, ordered the design of a Blue Eagle icon and authorized all businesses that complied with NRA code standards to display the eagle. "When every American housewife understands that the Blue Eagle on everything that she permits into her home is a symbol of its restoration to security," proclaimed Johnson, pointing to women's important role as household shopper, "may

God have mercy on the man or group of men who attempt to trifle with this bird." Business rushed to display the banner, and by 1934 the eagle had become a ubiquitous symbol of economic recovery.

POPULAR RESPONSES

By mid-1934, the First New Deal had achieved two of its three key objectives. The panic and fear that had gripped the nation under Hoover had been expelled. In their place arose a cautious optimism that the Depression might soon end and that FDR would be the one to end it. The reforms had also averted the complete collapse of the nation's financial system and stimulated production. However, they had not ended the Depression or even significantly ameliorated some of its worst effects. In 1935, ten million Americans were still without work, and millions more could not make ends meet.

The sluggish economy invited a barrage of criticism. Breaking with FDR in 1933, charismatic senator Huey P. Long of Louisiana went on national radio to advocate a far more radical redistribution of wealth. His Share-Our-Wealth Plan called for high taxes for the wealthy, government-guaranteed subsidies of $5,000 for families, and an annual minimum wage of $2,500. Though highly controversial, Long's plan proved popular enough that he considered running against FDR for the Democratic Party's nomination for president in the next election. An assassin's bullet, however, would deprive Long of that opportunity—and his life—in 1935.

Workers and labor unions also grew impatient. With the enactment of the National Industrial Recovery Act, union membership ballooned—especially in big industries, such as automobiles—from a few hundred thousand to 3.6 million by 1935 (about 14 percent of the industrial workforce) and to 10 million by 1941. Their confidence renewed, the unions insisted that government could do much more to help workers and the unemployed. Many protested that the National Recovery Administration was not procuring true cooperation between business and labor. In particular, many of the largest corporations shaped production codes to their own needs, at workers' expense. Employers also continued to slash wages.

In 1934, over 1.5 million workers expressed their dissatisfaction by staging more than two thousand strikes. Most of the work stoppages were in protest of repeated wage cuts, and many were spontaneous. When employers recruited strikebreakers from among the unemployed, violence erupted. In one such episode, one thousand workers responded to the use of strikebreakers in the Electric Auto-Lite factory in Toledo, Ohio, by surrounding the plant. When another nine thousand supporters joined the picket line, the police and the National Guard attempted to disperse them, and a bloody battle ensued.

Of all the protests, the San Francisco waterfront strike became the most vivid—and most publicized—demonstration of workers' surging strength. As in other industries, dockworkers' union membership rates had soared to 95 percent following passage of the National Industrial Recovery Act. In the summer of 1934, a small but determined faction led by communist Harry Bridges walked out in protest of the "shape-up" system by which dockworkers mustered at 6 a.m. every day in the hope that the company foreman would employ them. When shippers attempted to replace the strikers, workers in dozens of other San Francisco industries stopped work, paralyzing the city. As gas stations ran dry and San Franciscans began hoarding food, National Recovery Administration director General Hugh S. Johnson publicly

Battle of the Radio Waves. FDR's radio voice was reassuring for countless listeners facing a world of uncertainty and suffering. Others were swayed by Father Charles Coughlin, who grimly warned that things were only getting worse—and that FDR was part of the problem. Coughlin's increasingly extreme rhetoric led the Columbia Broadcasting System (CBS) to cancel his contract in mid-1933. The media-savvy priest, however, soon founded his own network, funded by more than $5 million in listener contributions.

condemned the San Francisco general strike as a "civil war." After a few days, the American Federation of Labor agreed, distancing themselves from the dockworkers and calling for an end to the strike. The dockworkers eventually won their original demand, but not before they fought deadly pitched battles with National Guard, police, and private security forces.

Other critics condemned New Deal initiatives as too timid—though not because they had failed to empower unions and workers. From Detroit, Catholic "Radio Priest" Charles Coughlin raged against the president for refusing to take direct control of the nation's banks and to increase the money supply, a move that Coughlin thought would enable homeowners to pay their mortgages. Father Coughlin's weekly sermons reached forty million listeners—an astounding 60 percent of the national radio audience. While FDR counseled against "fear itself," Coughlin fear-mongered on a massive scale, warning that an international conspiracy of bankers, Jews, communists, and Wall Street brokers was running America. Millions joined his National Union for Social Justice, which demanded nationalization—that is, government takeover—of all banks, some industries, and the railroads.

BUSINESS AGAINST REFORM

Many business leaders were equally perturbed by the First New Deal, though on radically different grounds from both Coughlin and workers. Leading financiers and industrialists initially rejected FDR's argument that capitalism's future lay in its reform. Establishing the Liberty League in 1934, they condemned the New Deal as anti-capitalist and un-American and lobbied hard for its defeat. They were joined by the National Association of Manufacturers, which launched a full-scale media campaign against the reforms, claiming that they were "socialistic" and a radical departure from established principles. Pointing to the shutdown in San Francisco, the pro-business *Los Angeles Times* insisted that the protesters' action had not been a general strike but "an insurrection—a Communist-inspired and led revolt against organized government."

A majority of justices on the U.S. Supreme Court agreed. Dominated by an older generation that was committed to the principle of liberty of contract (which held that unions and collective bargaining impinged on the freedom to negotiate one's own job contract), the Court struck down key reforms. The first case involved New York's Schechter Poultry Company, which had been convicted in a state court of selling diseased chickens to consumers in violation of the National Recovery Administration's poultry code. In 1935, Schechter appealed the case all the way to the U.S. Supreme Court, which reversed the conviction on the grounds that the executive branch of the federal government lacked the constitutional authority to regulate commerce in New York or any other state. The government was forced to disband the codes system, and the use of the Blue Eagle was prohibited. Shortly afterward, the Court rejected the Agriculture Adjustment Act, a coal conservation measure, and New York State's minimum wage law. In light of these restrictive judicial rulings, the future of the New Deal appeared bleak.

THE SECOND NEW DEAL

By 1935, the First New Deal was under attack from business, a conservative Supreme Court, masses of disaffected workers, and an increasingly frustrated middle class. Faced with a choice between reversing or extending reform, FDR chose the latter. He abandoned his conciliatory approach to big business and began publicly deriding the "money classes," boasting that "we have earned the hatred of entrenched greed." Such rhetoric drew implicitly on the United States' populist tradition of suspicion toward large corporations and banks (see Chapters 19 and 20). It also implicitly acknowledged that millions of voters were persuaded by Father Coughlin and more moderate critics that the banks were an obstacle to prosperity. With an election year looming, decrying big business promised to earn back the support of millions of disillusioned voters. The president was also genuinely convinced that greater economic stimulation and the redistribution of a larger portion of the nation's wealth to the American people were vital to rebuilding the economy.

EXTENDING REFORM

In a nod to the labor unions' growing power, the first major reform of the Second New Deal was the Wagner Act (1935), which provided that all nonagricultural workers could join unions and prohibited employers from firing or otherwise coercing workers who chose to do so. The law also established a nonpartisan board that would supervise union elections and enforce collective bargaining rather than merely allow it—union goals since the Gilded Age. The Social Security Act (1935) provided that employers and employees would pay a tax into a general fund that would pay retired workers a pension. The same law also established the first direct federal assistance to the unemployed, imposing a tax on employers that funded compensation for anyone recently thrown out of work.

FDR also fortified existing employment programs, including the Works Progress Administration (WPA), which now became the principal federal relief agency. Over the next eight years, 8.5 million Americans would work for the WPA. The federal government would invest $10.5 billion in WPA projects, which included construction, art, and architecture (and even a program to build swimming pools; see Spaces and Places: Swope Park Swimming Pool, Kansas City, Missouri). On the income side, the Revenue Act of 1935 raised taxes on estates, personal income, and corporations. Although the law brought in only $250 million in tax revenues each year, it symbolized the government's tougher stance toward large corporations and the superwealthy—and reassured middle- and working-class voters of FDR's commitment to a more equitable distribution of wealth. Finally, racial injustice drew the attention of some members of the Roosevelt administration. Mary McLeod Bethune, a college president and a member of Roosevelt's "Black Cabinet" (a group that advised the president on African American

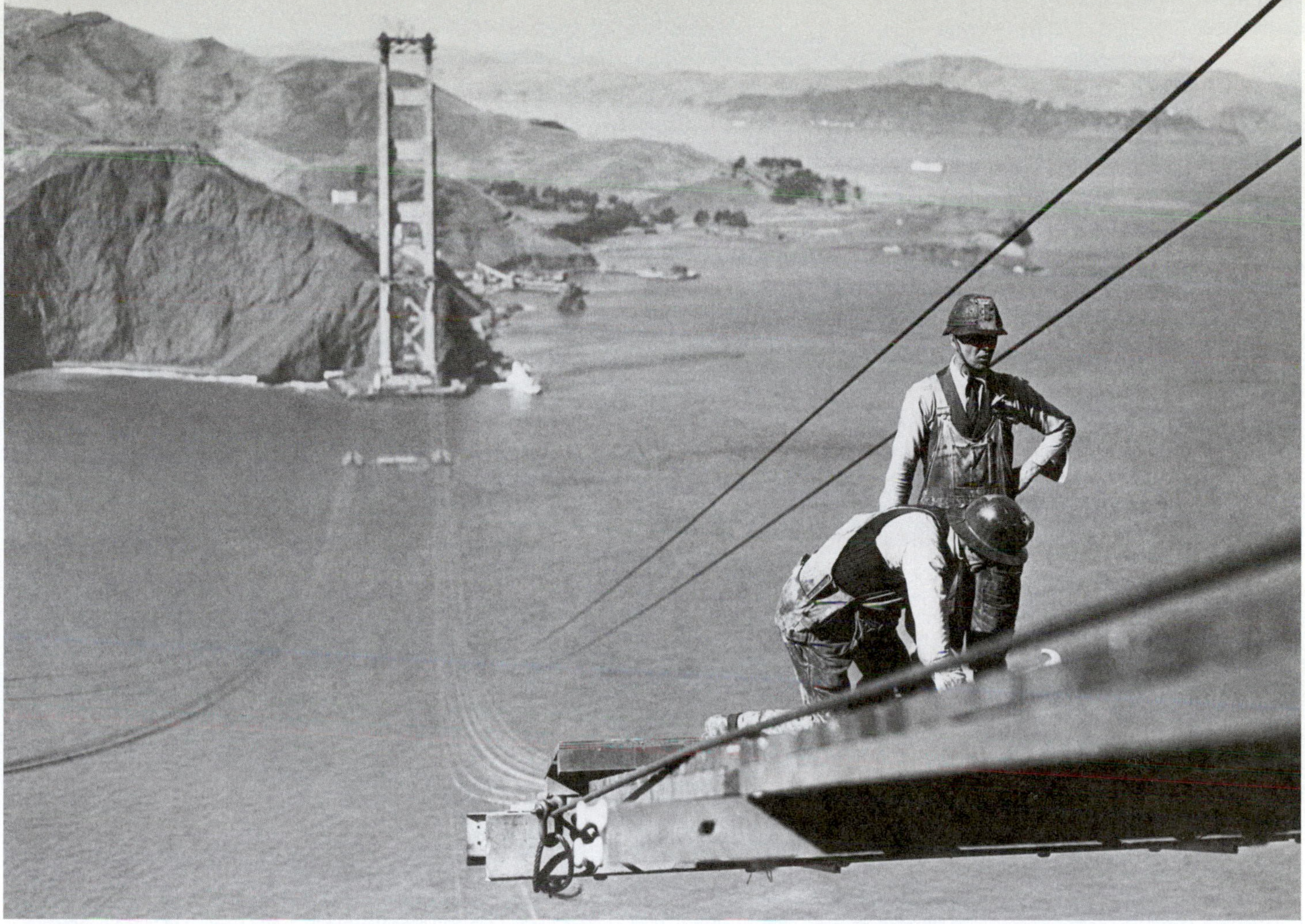

Bridging Unemployment. Although the state of California was responsible for commissioning the building of a new bridge over the Golden Gate to San Francisco Bay in 1926, the WPA played a vital role once construction began in 1933. WPA workers laid the bridge's approach ramps and roads. Large public projects put people back to work and revived their sense of dignity.

affairs), pressed FDR to recognize the Depression's disproportionate toll on African Americans. Bethune also worked with the new National Youth Administration to ensure that more than two hundred thousand African American youth received the same training opportunities available to young white people.

THE ELECTION OF 1936

Powered by diverse popular support for his initiatives, FDR competed in the election of 1936 with a much broader, and even more solid, base of support than in 1932. The majority of voters appeared convinced by his argument that "to preserve [capitalism] we had to reform." White workers, unions, African Americans in the North (those in the South had limited voting rights), ethnic and religious minorities, middle-class professionals, pensioners, and even progressive Republicans reelected FDR in the biggest landslide victory in the nation's history (see Map 24.2). Father Coughlin's National Union for Social Justice, which had fielded a number

Candidate (Party)	Electoral Vote	Popular Vote
Franklin D. Roosevelt (Democratic)	523	27,757,333
Alfred M. Landon (Republican)	8	16,684,231
William Lemke (Union)	–	882,479

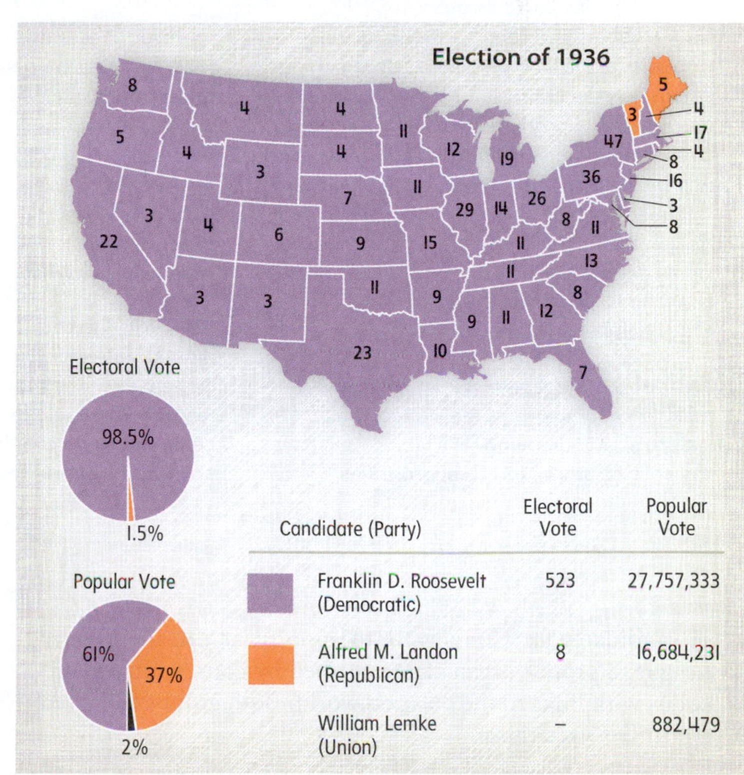

Map 24.2 Election of 1936. Roosevelt won every state except Maine and Vermont—more states than any other candidate in history.

SPACES & PLACES

Swope Park Swimming Pool, Kansas City, Missouri

Swimming in the Depression. Completed in 1940, the Swope Park swimming pool was one of fourteen pools constructed in the drought-stricken state of Missouri during the New Deal. Swope Park was popular with the public, but municipal authorities refused to admit African Americans until 1955. Many Depression-era pools have fallen into disrepair in recent years, but the WPA brass plaques that record the government's effort to democratize swimming can still be glimpsed near many pool entrances.

One of the most beloved initiatives of the New Deal, especially among children and youth, was the national swimming pools project. Through the WPA, the federal government built over eight hundred pools across the nation, mostly in small towns and rural areas, and restored hundreds more. Many new pools, including Swope Park in Kansas City, were larger than a football field, and lifeguards used small rowboats to patrol them. Hundreds included diving and wading pools.

Pool construction provided employment for thousands of laborers, landscape designers, architects, concrete manufacturers, and engineers left jobless by the Depression. It also provided work for unemployed sculptors and painters, whose art still adorns many facilities today. But beyond job creation, the pools project—like other WPA initiatives—aimed to improve the nation's health and morale at a time of rampant distress. For a dime or two, families could forget their troubles and spend a whole day poolside, picnicking on grassy banks or playing on the pool's sandy "beach." Such facilities also contributed to national fitness by making swimming affordable for everyone and by introducing a generation of children to aquatic sports. Young swimmers who had gotten their start in government-sponsored pools began breaking world records, and by the 1950s, the United States dominated Olympic swimming events.

The pools project went a long way toward making swimming—and staying cool in an era before air conditioning—available to all. As in the case of other New Deal programs, however, access was unequal. Although federal dollars funded the pools, local government retained control over the rules and regulations under which they operated. Consequently, in the South most pools were reserved exclusively for white patrons (as was Swope Park). In some instances, separate facilities were built for African Americans and Hispanics.

Although northern and western states did not legislate racial segregation, white communities there prevailed on pool managers to exclude or segregate people of color. White parents insisted that their children swim separately from African Americans, on the grounds that "mixing" the two groups of scantily clad swimmers would lead to interracial romance—or more.

Think About It

1. Why were so many public amenities, including pools, built during the Depression?
2. Why do you think the pools and learning to swim were so popular in the Depression years?
3. What impact, if any, do you think these popular amenities had on people's attitudes toward government?

of candidates for Congress, fared poorly, as did the Liberty League, a protest organization formed by conservative Democrats with links to the business world. Both groups collapsed after FDR's reelection.

The president interpreted his landslide victory as a mandate to extend the Second New Deal (see Table 24.2). To that end, he consolidated his authority as president, insulating many federal agencies from congressional oversight and

TABLE 24.2 MAJOR ACTS AND AGENCIES OF THE FIRST AND SECOND NEW DEALS

Year	Acts and Agencies	Status
First New Deal		
1933	Repeal of Prohibition	Remains in force
	Agricultural Adjustment Act (AAA)	Supreme Court voided, 1936
	National Industrial Recovery Act (NIRA)	Supreme Court voided, 1935
	Public Works Administration (PWA)	Functions transferred to FWA, 1943
	Federal Emergency Relief Administration (FERA)	Superseded by WPA, 1935
	Civil Works Administration (CWA)	Roosevelt suspended, 1934
	Glass-Steagall Act	Key provisions repealed, 1999
	Federal Deposit Insurance Corporation (FDIC)	Still operating
	Civilian Conservation Corps (CCC)	Dissolved, 1942
	Tennessee Valley Authority (TVA)	Roosevelt suspended, 1934
		Still operating
1934	Indian Reorganization Act (IRA)	Remains in force
	Federal Communications Commission (FCC)	Still operating
	Federal Housing Administration (FHA)	Still operating
	Securities and Exchange Commission (SEC)	Still operating
Second New Deal		
1935	National Labor Relations Board (NLRB)	Still operating
	National Youth Administration (NYA)	Dissolved, 1943
	Rural Electrification Administration (REA)	Absorbed by Rural Utilities Service, 1949
	Social Security Act	Remains in force
	Works Progress Administration (WPA)	Dissolved, 1943
1937	Farm Security Administration (FSA)	Replaced by Farmers Home Administration, 1946
1939	Federal Works Agency (FWA)	Dissolved, 1949

creating six new assistant positions in the cabinet, each directly answerable to the White House. Roosevelt's only remaining opponent was the Supreme Court. Because the justices were lifelong appointees, the Court's opposition posed a real and ongoing threat. Taking the offense, FDR asked Congress for legislation that would radically alter the structure of the Court by ultimately expanding the number of justices from nine to fifteen. This **court-packing** scheme would allow him to nominate enough sympathetic justices to outweigh the conservatives. In the end, however, Congress rejected the scheme. Still, FDR's well-publicized threat appeared to serve his purpose, as the justices subsequently affirmed the constitutionality of New Deal legislation.

A NEW DEAL FOR THE ARTS

The Great Depression brought a surge of activity in the arts, largely because President Roosevelt believed that professional artists, like other workers, needed employment and that the creative arts were crucial to raising the nation's morale. At no other time has government funded the arts as generously as it did between 1935 and 1943, allocating around $100 million, equivalent to $1.7 billion today. And neither before nor since have artists so emphatically shaped local and national culture.

Most government funding for the arts was channeled via the WPA, which created four federal "projects" (agencies) representing the visual arts, theater, music, and writing. The forty thousand artists employed by the WPA fanned out into every state, often working in remote areas that had never before seen art exhibitions or professional performances—or been the subject of films, books, and other artwork. The Federal Music Project alone put to work over fifteen thousand unemployed musicians to perform for public and radio audiences. By 1940, the project had also provided music lessons for eighteen million eager American students.

Painters and sculptors of the Federal Art Project transformed tens of thousands of public spaces—including parks, schools, and post offices—with vibrant murals, sculptures, and paintings. Much of this work portrayed scenes from early

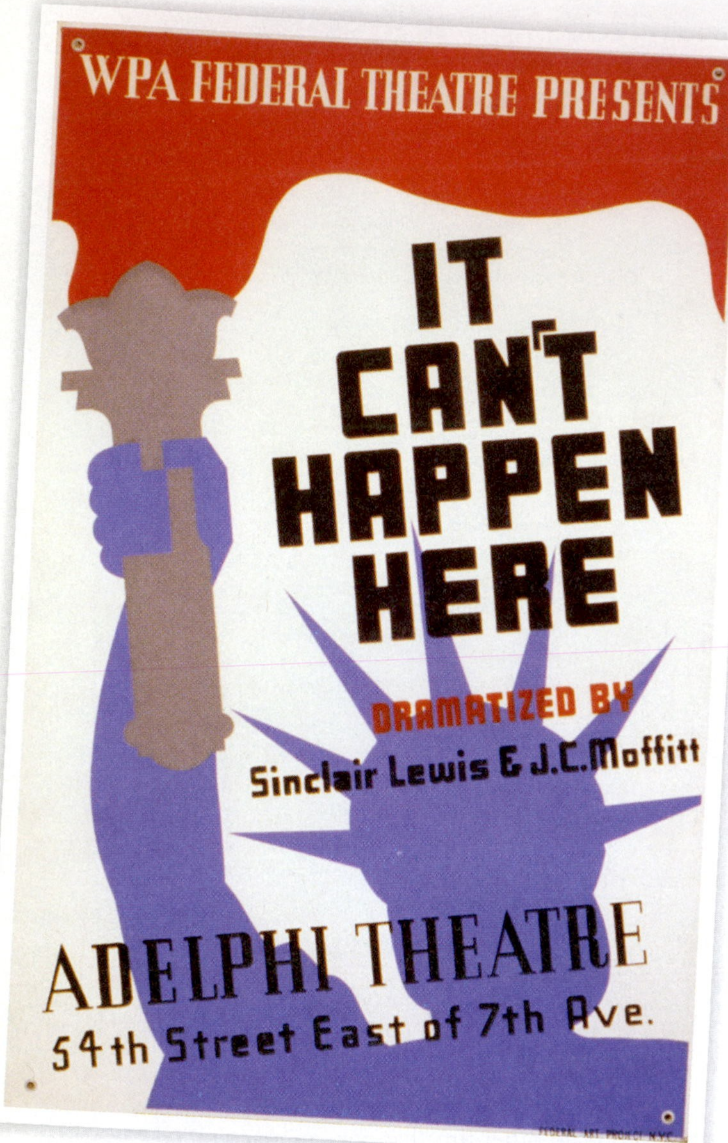

A New Deal for Actors. The Federal Theatre Project hired thousands of unemployed playwrights, actors, and stagehands; reopened shuttered theaters; and built dozens of new venues around the nation. Federally sponsored productions such as *It Can't Happen Here* opened in multiple states and theaters.

How Much Is That?

Funding the New Deal

Although it was the biggest bill that the U.S. government had ever racked up, the price tag for the New Deal's efforts to revive the American economy was comparatively low by today's standards. All told, New Deal construction, art, agricultural, industrial, housing, and welfare programs cost around $32 billion—the equivalent of $500 billion today. In contrast, the federal bailouts of banks, the auto industry, and other key sectors during the Great Recession of 2007-2009 totaled over $4.6 trillion—more than nine times as much. Cost wasn't the only difference between the two sets of legislation, however. Unlike the Bush-Obama stimulus programs, which aimed at encouraging job growth, Roosevelt's policies directly created jobs and influenced business to do so. The WPA alone directly generated over eight million jobs between 1935 and 1943, mostly in construction. The Great Recession bailouts, although costlier, created about half that many jobs.

America, which many artists depicted nostalgically as a happy and prosperous place unlike their own world. There followed an outpouring of books, magazines, and movies on the American past, and the theme also influenced home design and decoration. Some artists, however, chose contemporary, and often quite controversial, subject matter, such as labor strikes. The Federal Theatre Project sponsored even bolder work, starting with Sinclair Lewis's *It Can't Happen Here* (1935), a satire about a populist presidential candidate who promises to return the United States to prosperity but instead puts the nation on the path to fascism.

Edgier still was The Living Newspaper series, in which playwrights took a controversial issue from newspaper headlines and worked with unemployed journalists to develop a script on that theme. *Injunction Granted* (1936), for example, lampooned business tycoons such as H. J. Heinz and encouraged workers to join a radical union. Warned by WPA administrators that such explicitly political material might lead to a loss of federal funding, directors toned down subsequent plays. Nonetheless, they continued to champion the concerns of ordinary workers and consumers and to provide much needed employment to actors and other theater workers.

Many of the journalists, novelists, and other writers employed by the Federal Writers Project went to work on a series of WPA guidebooks to every state in the nation. These lengthy volumes offered the most exhaustive historical and cultural guide to America ever produced. Each contained essays on the state's history and culture, major cities, and tourist attractions, and many also collected oral histories from remote or little-understood communities of sharecroppers, former slaves, and migrant workers. Some state governments, particularly in the South, objected to the writers' liberalism and decided to publish no more than a few hundred copies of their work. But the guides' focus on the lives of ordinary people influenced American literature for years to come—and launched the careers of Richard Wright, Studs Terkel, and dozens of other influential writers of the post-Depression era.

Honoring the Past. FDR was deeply committed to educating the nation about its history, folklore, and heritage. He also believed that historic preservation—like labor relations and education—was too important a task to leave to private organizations. The federal government preserved historic sites, recorded the histories of cities and states, and collected oral histories. One project, the Slave Narratives, recorded the memories of former slaves, including one-hundred-year-old Josh Tarbutton, pictured here. These oral histories remain an essential resource for our understanding of the Old South.

ADAPTING CONSUMER CULTURE

Consumer culture suffered a heavy economic blow in the Depression's early stages. But as advertisers responded to hard times with new messages aimed at thrifty homemakers, American consumption patterns grew far more homogenized than before. At the same time, the large-scale purveyors of commercial entertainment found a larger audience among the unemployed and those simply looking for a cheap escape from their woes. By the late 1930s, tens of millions ate the new "American diet," watched the same upbeat Hollywood films, whistled the same catchy advertising jingles, and buried themselves in the same best-selling novels. Optimistic and nostalgic themes prevailed, and consumers took comfort in participating in a truly national culture. But consumer tastes also fragmented in new ways, as the Depression and New Deal stimulated the formation of novel identities—and potential markets—such as that of the "teenager." Not everyone was content with the expansion of advertising and consumer industries. A new consumer rights movement insisted that ordinary people should have more say over the quality and content of products and the truthfulness of advertising—and by the mid-1930s, concerned citizens called on Congress to enact a New Deal for consumers.

ENTERTAINING THE NATION

Forced unemployment and underemployment gave millions of Americans up to fifty extra hours of spare time each week. The New Deal also expanded many workers' spare time by cutting the waged workweek to just forty hours (a historic low) and capping it with the two-day rest known as "the week-end." (Until the 1930s, only organized workers in building and construction, the clothing and needle trades, and printing and publishing had won that concession from employers.) Americans explored new ways of meaningfully filling their increased free time. Knitting, reading, and other solitary pastimes became popular. Millions joined hobby, bowling, or athletic clubs. A miniature golf craze—spurred by competitions featuring large cash prizes—swept the nation. And a softball tournament at the Chicago World's Fair of 1933 turned baseball's younger sibling into a popular pastime.

Although the Depression initially had an adverse effect on Hollywood and other culture industries, companies saw tremendous long-term potential in the sudden expansion of spare time and people's creative efforts to fill it. Consumers wanted to escape the harsh realities of contemporary life—and upbeat and pleasurable movies, books, and other media were ideally suited to that purpose. Firms adopting this strategy grew dramatically, producing dozens of "hits" (a new term in the 1930s), whereas realistic and critical treatments of Depression-era themes mostly failed.

Record sales—which had lagged behind sheet music sales in the 1920s—boomed, thanks partly to the industry's decision to halve the price of discs and to introduce cheap record players. Eager to integrate consumers into a single national market, Columbia and Decca led the way by softening the sound of jazz and blues and homogenizing the equally diverse traditions of country music. The introduction of jukeboxes to restaurants, soda fountains, and other venues after 1933 further sped the emergence of a national record market. By the end of 1935, millions of Americans eagerly tuned in to the National Broadcast Corporation (NBC) *Your Lucky Strike Hit Parade* radio show, which counted down the ten best-selling hits of the week. (The show was named after the sponsor's cigarette brand; also see Hot Commodities: Cigarettes.) The same year, a derivative of jazz—an energetic, rhythmic form of dance music known as swing—swept the nation, accounting for almost one-third of all record sales for the remainder of the decade.

HOT COMMODITIES

Cigarettes

More than any other consumer product, the cigarette enjoyed a remarkable trajectory from obscurity in the early twentieth century to icon of modern American life by 1941. Its mass appeal testifies to the tremendous power of advertising and the resilience of consumer culture in the Depression era. Although they were cheap and mass produced, cigarettes before 1930 were the least popular way of consuming tobacco, trailing pipes, chewing tobacco, and cigars. Smoking, mostly a private activity undertaken in one's parlor or study, was widely seen as a self-indulgent vice. Cigarettes grew popular among soldiers during World War I, but it was not until the late 1920s that cigarette manufacturers successfully marketed their products to a broad cross-section of U.S. society. Hollywood was key to their success.

The American Tobacco Company (ATC) was the first of several firms to seize on the new technology of the "talking pictures" as a vehicle for changing attitudes toward cigarettes. Launching the Precious Voice campaign in 1927, ATC recruited Al Jolson, star of the first talking picture, *The Jazz Singer* (1927), to endorse Lucky Strikes. By the early 1930s, dozens of other stars had signed up to appear in magazine ads describing cigarettes as both enlivening and good for the vocal chords. Because famous film star Carole Lombard "acts 12 hours a day," one ad read, "her singing teacher urged her to choose a light smoke—Luckies. . . ." Suddenly cigarettes seemed glamorous, healthful, slimming, and pleasurable. Manufacturers also sponsored radio shows and prevailed on Hollywood studios to have their stars smoke on the big screen.

Despite the Depression, cigarette sales climbed steeply, proving that the campaigns were working. The old criticism that smoking was a vice only made cigarettes more alluring, turning the slender white tubes into a symbol of the pleasures of consumption. By 1935, more advertising dollars were spent promoting cigarettes than any other industry besides automobiles, and tobacco had become the United States' fourth-largest cash crop after cotton, wheat, and corn.

As the New Deal got under way, advertisers claimed that cigarette smoking was also good for the nation. Advertisements frequently linked cigarettes to the federal government's agricultural policies, especially New Deal programs aimed at improving tobacco yields and quality. When the first of a string of medical studies suggested a link between smoking and disease, the industry amplified its claim that cigarettes were "good for you." Professional athletes touted the enlivening effects of smoking, and the industry aggressively courted doctors, hoping to convince them that smoking was fine, particularly if patients switched to their latest filtered brand. Advertisements appeared in medical journals, and R. J. Reynolds launched its long-running "More Doctors Smoke Camels" campaign. Although it is unclear whether more doctors did in fact choose Camels, by 1941 the majority of doctors smoked cigarettes, as did most American men and women.

Where smoking had once been confined to the home, public places such as restaurants, bars, trains, offices, theaters, and even elevators now thronged with smokers—and filled with smoke. In 1964, the federal government acknowledged that smoking was the leading cause of lung cancer among Americans and launched the first of several public health campaigns against the habit.

Smoke and Mirrors. To combat medical reports in the early 1930s that smoking might cause disease, cigarette manufacturers waged aggressive advertising campaigns that promoted their product as not only glamorous but also healthful.

Think About It

1. Why did smoking, an added expense, become so popular at a time when most people were short of cash?
2. Why did cigarette manufacturers turn to actors, athletes, and doctors to promote their product?
3. According to advertising campaigns, how would smoking cigarettes improve consumers' lives?

As in the music industry, Depression-era publishers were most successful with titles that distracted readers from the harsh realities of life. For instance, detective novels, which accounted for more than half of all book sales, involved readers in intricate mysteries, often transporting them to exotic or luxurious locales. The authors of the second most popular literary genre, historical fiction, took readers back to a happier time in the nation's past, much as most painters, architects, and interior design experts were doing. Book clubs, such as the Literary Guild and Book-of-the-Month Club, selected a fresh title each month for tens of thousands of avid subscribers, often turning little-known books into instant best sellers. New genres such as pulp magazines and comic books became wildly popular, and Superman became a mass phenomenon in 1938, fighting for social causes of the sort that the New Deal promoted—and tirelessly rescuing young women from certain doom.

Lady Sings the Blues. Many music executives believed that African American singers and musicians would not sell on the predominantly white market and so cultivated white "crooners" such as Bing Crosby. A minority of industry leaders, however, promoted soulful African American singers, including Billie Holiday, whose blues broke new musical ground, challenged the color line, and portrayed black women's lives and sexuality in a positive light.

Of all the mass media, cinema most tightly integrated consumers into a single national audience, although radio came in a close second. Movie attendance had initially fallen off after the Wall Street crash, to about $75 million in box office sales per week, and this decline forced almost a third of all cinemas to close. By 1934, attendance was springing back, and within a few years Americans were watching more "talking pictures" than ever before. The cinema chains of the 1920s grew bigger, absorbing many of the smaller operations that had been forced to close. As cinema empires mushroomed, moviegoers in New York and Chicago increasingly watched the same movies, newsreels, shorts, and advertisements as audiences in Houston and Seattle—and their children attended the same Saturday matinees.

With just a few exceptions, most Hollywood movies avoided direct mention of the Depression. Convinced that Americans wanted to escape grim reality for a few hours each week, the studios cranked out dozens of light, entertaining movies. President Roosevelt commended Hollywood for making it possible for every American to "pay 15 cents, go to a movie . . . and forget his troubles." Among the diverting genres, musicals proved particularly popular, following Warner Brothers' release in 1933 of *42nd Street*, which told the story of a plucky young chorus girl struggling to become a Broadway star. The movie's toe-tapping melodies, cheering message, and elegant "streamlined" set

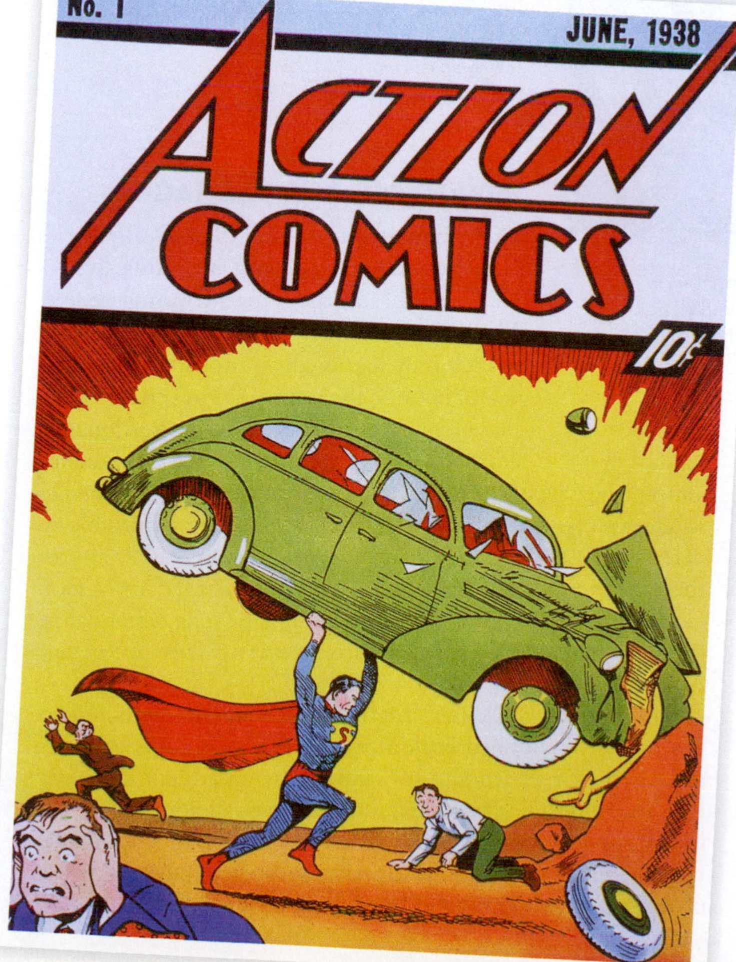

Superheroes for Troubled Times. At a time of crisis for American masculinity, Superman's appeal lay partly in his dual character as Clark Kent, the mild-mannered newspaper reporter who, as Superman, possessed secret powers and the ability to become the strongest, most virile man in the world. **Questions for Analysis:** Why might Clark Kent's possession of hidden powers have been particularly appealing during the Great Depression? Why might the idea of a "superhero" have been equally attractive?

Get Happy. Like advertisers and politicians, Hollywood tried to instill a spirit of optimism in consumers that prosperity would soon return. The first child star, Shirley Temple, embodied positive spirit with her precocious self-confidence, shiny blonde locks, and popular songs such as "You've Gotta S-M-I-L-E to Be H-A-P-P-Y."

Hollywood Goes Epic. Critics disparaged Margaret Mitchell's novel *Gone with the Wind* (1936) as bad history and tawdry melodrama. Some condemned its racism. But Depression-era readers made it an all-time best seller, and Hollywood's Warner Brothers turned it into one of most popular movies of all time in 1939. In this scene, hero Rhett Butler's use of profanity ("Frankly, my dear, I don't give a damn") thrilled audiences and made the moment one of the most memorable in movie history.

made it the first of many musicals to enthrall audiences—and to break box office records.

Other genres indirectly engaged audiences' Depression-era fears and desires and sought to reassure viewers. New "screwball comedies" typically poked fun at a rich eccentric who became romantically attached to a working- or middle-class protagonist. Offering the latter a chance at upward mobility and sudden success, such stories resonated powerfully at a time of widespread joblessness and anxieties about gender roles. Horror films portrayed—and slayed—a raft of terrifying monsters, including Dracula and Frankenstein. And by 1933, gangster movies were glamorizing Federal Bureau of Investigation agents who killed gangsters and brought law and order to the city.

INVENTING THE TEENAGER

High unemployment and New Deal policies also effected lasting change in youths' lives—and in adults' attitudes toward young people. Most conspicuously, attending high school (which only half of all youth had done before 1930) became the norm. The towering unemployment rates of the era disproportionately affected young Americans, who accounted for almost a quarter of the fifteen million thrown out of work. As in subsequent recessions, enrolling in school made it possible to delay entry into a difficult job market, and by 1940, almost three-quarters of all high-school-age youth stayed in school. College attendance grew by half, although, by today's standards, the rate remained low, with just three in every twenty college-age Americans enrolled.

Throughout the cities, high school students gathered in basements, abandoned buildings, and the backrooms of stores to form their own "congresses" and "cellar" or athletic clubs. By the late 1930s, almost a third of all American adolescents belonged to a club. The clubs provided members with dance nights, freedom from adult supervision, status, the recognition of their peers, and sometimes even the possibility of employment.

Like the city neighborhoods in which they arose, clubs were often organized along racial and ethnic lines. Significantly, they fostered a new social identity—that of the teenager, who was neither a child nor an adult but an adolescent who spent most of his or her time in the company of peers. A distinct teen culture emerged with its own unique slang, including *going steady* to refer to a teenage couple's agreement to date only each other, and *parking*, which meant cuddling and kissing in an automobile, usually after dark.

Before long, federal youth agencies and sociologists grew concerned that teenage clubs were encouraging truancy and petty crime (some did, but many did not) and that teens' newfound independence made them vulnerable to subversion. Many parents moreover worried that teens' peers had more influence over their children than did traditional authority figures. WPA youth agencies tried working with teens to redirect them "back into the fold of the school," offering after-school vocational and recreational programs. But as one agency worker despaired, these efforts generally failed because youth preferred "paying 25 cents admission every Friday night to a [club] dance . . . to the accompaniment of a Victrola [record player]" over free, supervised events at the local school gymnasium. Teenagers—and adults' perceptions that they were a vulnerable and potentially disruptive force in society—were here to stay.

Ever watchful for social trends that might entail new commercial possibilities, the powerful forces of advertising targeted teenagers for the first time. Record companies and jazz musicians promoted music specifically aimed at them, sparking the swing dance craze and a run on the short white "bobby socks" that teenage girls wore while jitterbugging. Even products that seemingly had nothing to do with teens, such as baker's yeast and peanuts, now promised to clear teens' acne or energize them and make them the most popular boys or girls in school. Magazines such as *American Girl* and *Boy's Life* encouraged teens to acquire the skills and personality traits that would make them responsible adults and consumers. The content of these publications reinforced conventional gender roles, informing girls that marriage and children were the highest achievement in life and downplaying the possibility of a career or anything else that might put them in competition with boys and men.

Marijuana: Evil Weed. Although urban teenagers mostly wanted greater autonomy in the late 1930s, parents, Congress, and federal agencies worried that demagogues and criminals might subvert them. Nazis' and fascists' recent radicalization of disillusioned youth in Europe fueled anxieties and justified the expansion of federal youth programs such as the Federal Bureau of Narcotics' anti-marijuana campaign.

REFINING THE AMERICAN DIET

Like other industrialists, food manufacturers for several decades had hired armies of advertisers and branding experts to pitch their products. But it was only during the Depression—and with help from radio advertising—that the food industry was able to turn regional markets into a single national market. A distinctive American diet, consisting of the same range of everyday foodstuffs and recipes, displaced most immigrant-ethnic cuisines (with the exception of simple Italian foods, such as spaghetti and meatballs). Regional cuisines—among them Louisiana's Cajun, midwestern German and Scandinavian, and southwestern Mexican—were sidelined to county fairs and local festivals.

Americans began eating many of the brands and foodstuffs we recognize today. Instead of a cooked breakfast or unprocessed dry cereal, for instance, consumers filled their bowls with Wheaties, Cheerioats (later renamed Cheerios), or Grape-Nuts, all of which they first heard about on the radio or saw in national magazines. Highly processed white bread replaced brown and whole grain loaves, and margarine—a butter substitute that the dairy industry had attempted to block since the nineteenth century—won a small but growing segment of the market.

You've Got Spam. Introduced by Hormel in 1937, the mix of pork products marketed as Spam fit the typical profile of a 1930s foodstuff: cheap, processed, nonperishable, and convenient.

Although the new national diet consisted of many of the same meats, grains, vegetables, and fruits as before, manufacturers now commonly blended the food with new chemical preservatives, colorings, coagulants, and other agents. New laboratory-produced preservatives made possible the production of "pre-prepared" foods containing highly perishable ingredients such as raw egg and dairy products. Coagulants and other agents stopped manufactured foodstuffs from separating or acquiring an unappetizing texture or appearance, and chemical coloring enhanced the look of freshness and goodness. Instead of spending time making mayonnaise from scratch or having to throw stale crackers into the trash, a 1930s housewife could reach for the Miracle Whip or open a package of Ritz crackers that would stay fresh for weeks.

Some nutritionists questioned the health value of pre-prepared foods, and consumer rights advocates warned of possible adverse health effects. Food processors, however, correctly calculated that middle-class housewives, who typically lost their domestic servants when the Depression hit and now had to do the cooking themselves, wanted to spend less time in the kitchen. Cheap pre-prepared foods would allow them to do so.

ADVERTISING WARS

Manufacturers' success during this period of economic hardship largely came courtesy of advertisers, who adapted their techniques to the times. Conscious of the public's rejection of the fantasy-driven messages of the 1920s, they now emphasized the product—its quality, affordability, and immediate gratifications to be had by buying it. As in the culture industries, the vast majority avoided direct mention of the Depression (which, they feared, might lead consumers to close their wallets) but implicitly acknowledged the crisis by hinting or even declaring that "prosperity is just around the corner." Most printed advertisements provided hard information about products and prices, replacing the lavish, colorful illustrations of the previous decade with bold, black and white print and photographs, which were also less expensive to produce. Coupons also became a common way of attracting customers.

Meanwhile, for the first time, American homes filled with the sound of lively advertising jingles from the commercial sponsors of popular radio shows. Through their sponsorship of new, nationally syndicated programs such as *The Jack Benny Show*, advertisers turned obscure brands such as Pepsodent, Jell-O, Lucky Strike, and Pabst Blue Ribbon into household names—sometimes overnight.

Even as consumers were being bombarded with national advertising, they were also becoming more aware of its powers of manipulation. The consumer movement of the Progressive Era, which had collapsed after World War I, had already begun to revive in the late 1920s with the publication of Stuart Chase and Frederick J. Schlink's best-seller *Your Money's Worth* (1927). Most advertising, argued Chase and Schlink, deliberately deceived consumers and lacked social value. But it was only with the Depression and consumers' shock at the financial collapse that consumer awareness became a mass phenomenon. By the early 1930s, dozens of books, magazines, and pamphlets were declaring deceptive advertising a major social problem.

The publication of Schlink and Alfred Kallet's *100,000,000 Guinea Pigs: Dangers in Everyday Foods, Drugs, and Cosmetics* (1933) also brought the quality of consumer goods under scrutiny. Of special concern were products that contained life-threatening chemicals and other agents. Hundreds of thousands of concerned citizens flocked to new organizations such as Consumer Research Incorporated, which assessed the composition and quality of home appliances, foods, and other goods and exposed fraudulent advertising. Other, more radical **consumer rights** groups such as the Consumers Union argued that business was pounding the nation with so many commercial messages that civic and religious values were collapsing.

Both wings of the consumer rights movement lobbied Congress and state legislatures for "truth-in-advertising" laws and stricter quality controls on foods, pharmaceuticals, and other goods. Seeking to put objective information in consumers' hands, they also called upon the federal government to rate all goods for their safety and quality. Advertisers and manufacturers meanwhile launched a counteroffensive, insisting that advertising was a form of free speech and thus protected from government censorship under the Constitution. They offered instead to regulate themselves as an industry (like Hollywood) and to establish their own truth-in-advertising codes. Though sympathetic to consumers, President Roosevelt did not weigh in on the problem. Poorly funded and vastly outmaneuvered, consumer rights advocates settled for the watered-down Food, Drug, and Cosmetics Act of 1938, which required drug makers to prove the safety of their products before selling them to the public.

RURAL WORLDS TRANSFORMED

Although cities were the hub of American life, politics, and consumer culture in the 1930s, the nation was far from fully urbanized. Almost two in five people lived in rural areas, and in 1935 a record thirty-three million people made their homes on farms. Still, farming had been under siege since the agricultural recession of the early 1920s, and hundreds of thousands of farmers had left the land in the 1920s. The Great Depression, which caused thousands of rural banks to fail, accelerated the rural exodus. To make matters worse, a severe drought struck in 1931, causing crop failures in every state but Maine and Vermont and turning the southern plains into a giant dust bowl. President Roosevelt extended expert assistance, research, and funding to farming. But millions of farmers were displaced. Hundreds of thousands from the dust-stricken plains subsequently headed to California and the Pacific Northwest in search of bountiful orchards, green valleys, and a fresh start.

DEMISE OF SHARECROPPING AND TENANT FARMING

The Agricultural Adjustment Act of 1933 was the first of many federal efforts to relieve farmers and reconstruct the farming sector. It sought to raise prices and farmers' incomes by paying farmers to plant one-third fewer acres and raise one-third fewer animals. All farmers qualified for this program, which was funded by a consumer tax on processed food. Farmers killed six million pigs and destroyed tens of millions of acres of grain and cotton crops in the first year to meet the law's requirements. Opponents of government intervention in agriculture meanwhile raged at the "slaughter of the little pigs." The scheme appeared to work, however, forcing up prices and saving many farmers—at least for another year or two.

Unfortunately, the Agricultural Adjustment Act had unintended consequences. Paying farmers to destroy crops left many growers—particularly tenant farmers and sharecroppers—without a lasting source of income or the means to pay their landlords. Landlords often took the subsidies for themselves and used the money to replace sharecroppers and tenant farmers with the latest mechanical plows, harvesters, and tractors. Within a few years, hundreds of thousands were thrown off the land, and sharecropping and tenant farming became all but extinct. Although the government attempted to resettle the displaced farmers, fewer than five thousand consented; others preferred to migrate under their own steam.

After the Supreme Court, in 1936, ruled the Agricultural Adjustment Act's food tax unconstitutional, the new Farm Security Administration (FSA) helped tenant farmers purchase their own farms. But the program was underfunded and did little to stem farmers' migration. All told, more than 3.5 million Americans left their farms by 1940, returning almost ten million acres of farmland to nature. Most moved locally, but over a million headed to the agricultural "Golden State" of California, where they boosted that state's population by more than 20 percent in just a few years.

Who's Afraid of the Big New Deal? Released in 1933, Walt Disney's *The Three Little Pigs* drew on the controversy surrounding the government-led hog slaughter of that year. Critics interpreted the Big Bad Wolf as the federal government, but others saw the Great Depression as the real "wolf at the door" and the New Deal as the third little pig's solid brick house. The image was also put to work by critics of Prohibition, who portrayed lawmakers opposed to the repeal of the Volstead Act as killjoys or worse.

LEAVING THE DUST BOWL

The exodus of farmers was particularly pronounced on the plains of Kansas, eastern Colorado, and the panhandles of Texas and Oklahoma (see Map 24.3). Farming had always been tough in the region, with its extreme weather, wind-whipped prairie fires, and periodic droughts. By the 1930s, years of intensive wheat cultivation had stripped the terrain of grasses and other vegetation that stabilized the soil. Drought struck in 1931, causing massive dust storms known as "dusters." Three years later, the worst storms in memory buried whole farms in thick black sand, stripping the earth of three hundred million tons of soil and carrying some of it—along with the taste and smell of the plains—all the way to New York City. Less dramatic but no less destructive were sand blows, which formed high drifts and coated everything and everybody with thick dust. Dusters and black blizzards continued to wreak havoc across the **Dust Bowl** through 1939.

Initially most farmers had responded stoically on the belief that the rains would return the following year. Many had approached the situation with dark humor. "Great bargains in real estate," one shop window sign read, in reference to fifty-foot soil drifts; "bring your own container." Local chambers of commerce insisted that the region was just fine and angrily criticized the few newspapers that declared the storms a catastrophe. But the drought continued—and when the first black blizzards struck, many farmers' faith in the future crumbled. Calling upon President Roosevelt to act, they insisted that the drought, not social factors such as grass clearance and soil exhaustion, was the root cause of their troubles. Water was needed, they declared, and the federal government ought to dam and divert rivers to give it to them.

As plains dust fell like snow on the National Mall, the Roosevelt administration resolved to act. Over the following several years, the government spent more money on the Dust Bowl than on any other region in the nation. Despite farmers' insistence that water was the issue, the FSA soon realized that the problem was far graver and more complicated and that ecological, economic, and cultural factors—including the popular attitude that land was primarily there to be exploited—would have to change. In 1935, federal dollars poured into disease prevention, literacy, soil conservation, and a host of other programs.

The aid enabled many farmers to stay on the land—and they rewarded FDR by voting for him in the election of 1936. But the poorest sharecroppers continued to leave. Thousands of "Okies"—poor white rural folk from Oklahoma and other plains states—joined the swelling migration to California. Processions of their dust-encrusted cars rumbled over the state line. However, many of the newcomers found California inhospitable. Police, coping with their own poor and destitute, sometimes turned back the migrants. Everywhere, the downtrodden Okies faced something they had never experienced before—explicit discrimination. Signs such as "Negroes and

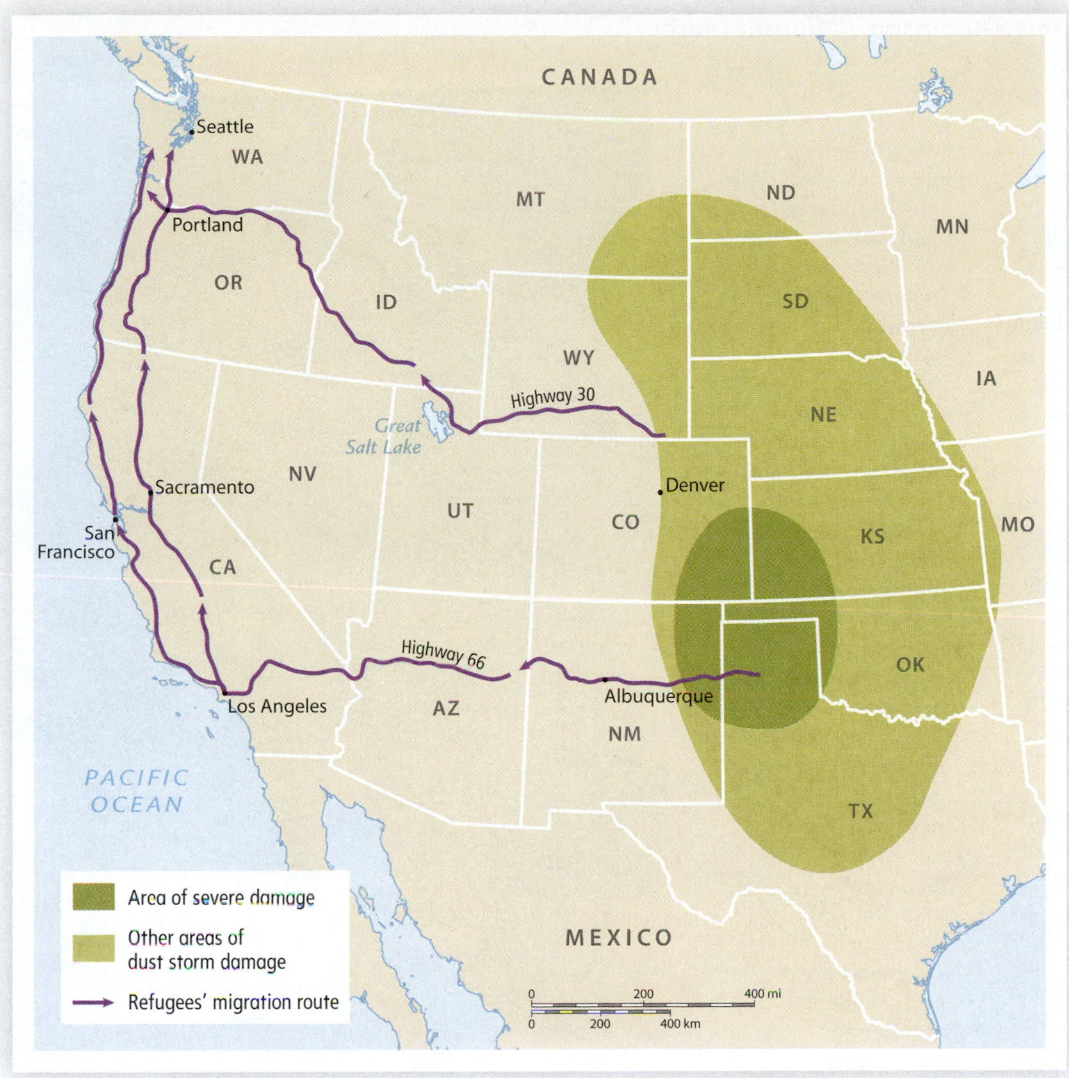

Map 24.3 Dust Bowl Migrants. Beginning in 1931, blinding dust storms destroyed millions of acres of crops, killed livestock, and left much of the land barren and open to more dusters. The storms accelerated the exodus of farmers to California.

Okies Upstairs" directed the newcomers to segregated seating or excluded them altogether.

Barred from many towns, thousands squatted in camps they called "Little Oklahomas." About 175,000 found seasonal waged work on "factory farms," where they replaced Mexican workers who were being repatriated. The rest moved northward from camp to camp and seasonal job to seasonal job in search of a way to survive.

ENVISIONING THE DEPRESSION

Not all Californians treated the impoverished migrants hostilely. A small group of photographers, writers, and social critics who had been documenting the Depression's impact on Californians soon became interested in the Dust Bowl migrants' experiences and origins. Several, including journalist John Steinbeck and photographer Dorothea Lange, made the reverse trek to the plains. They discovered that the same forces of large-scale agribusiness that were at work in California had contributed significantly to the ecological and social ravages of the Dust Bowl.

Subsequently, the FSA sponsored Lange and other professional photographers and filmmakers to document the everyday life of sharecroppers, coal miners, food processors, migrant laborers, and displaced families across the United States (see Singular Lives: Florence Owens Thompson, "Migrant Mother"). The FSA published many of more than a million images in newspapers and magazines. Impressed by the stills—and the public's fascination with them—independent publishers founded new photo-magazines such as *Life*, sending dozens of photographers out to do similar shoots. Among the most famous works of Depression-era photojournalism was *Let Us Now Praise Famous Men* (1941), a joint effort by writer James Agee and photographer Walker Evans that meticulously detailed the plight of the Dust Bowl's besieged farmers.

This extensive body of photographic work informed city dwellers about the diverse and difficult experiences that many of their fellow Americans were enduring. (It also sparked a boom in the sale of portable cameras—particularly Kodak's new, easy-to-use Brownie.) More than the printed word or drawings, photographs of malnourished, dispirited, and prematurely aged men and women struck a deep emotional chord and built sympathy for farmers' plights—and wide support for the rural New Deal. FSA photographers also laid the path for John Steinbeck's 1939 novel *The Grapes of Wrath*, probably the most important literary work of the Great Depression. Among the few best-selling novels to earn the widespread praise of literary critics (and a Nobel Prize), Steinbeck's story traced the Joad family's harrowing experience of the Dust Bowl. Director John Ford's film adaptation of the novel—for

SINGULAR LIVES

Florence Owens Thompson, "Migrant Mother"

Born to Cherokee parents in the impoverished Indian Territory (Oklahoma) in 1903, Florence Owens Thompson, now a young adult, moved to the California with her husband, Cleo, in 1926 in search of a better life. The Thompsons settled in California's Central Valley, where Cleo found steady work at a sawmill. But when the Great Depression hit, the mill folded. Cleo died shortly afterward, leaving Florence alone with five hungry mouths to feed. She did what hundreds of thousands of penniless Americans did in the 1930s: she hit the road—family in tow—as a migrant farmworker.

At first, Thompson picked cotton, receiving fifty cents for every hundred pounds and clearing no more than $2.00 a day (about $28 in today's dollars). After sunset, she worked as a washer at local restaurants for a penny per dish plus leftovers. As soon as the children were physically able, they joined their mother in the fields. Getting an education was all but impossible, and even when the children attended school, the migratory nature of farmwork meant that they were soon uprooted. Like other Depression-era migrants, Thompson and her children lived in their automobile and roadside canvas tent. On one occasion, in 1936, the car broke down on U.S. Highway 101. Thompson pulled into a pea pickers' camp and dispatched two sons to the nearest town to fetch the necessary car part. When she began cooking dinner on a portable stove, hungry children from the camp pleaded to be fed, explaining that the pea harvest was poor that year and they were subsisting on nothing but birds and raw vegetables. Her sons returned an hour or two later, and after feeding the camp's kids, the family hit the road again.

It was at the pea pickers' camp that FSA photographer Dorothea Lange encountered Thompson and her children. According to Thompson's daughter, Lange asked to take their picture, explaining that the photographs would help document the migrants' plight. She did not ask their names and promised that the photos would never be published. In fact, one appeared in newspapers across the country over the next few days. The anonymous "Migrant Mother" soon became the most iconic image of the Great Depression.

For many Americans, then and now, Lange's photograph captures Thompson's internal strength—and humanity's irreducible nobility under even the direst of circumstances. But Thompson felt betrayed, humiliated, and misrepresented. She and her children also claimed later that her frown was uncharacteristic and that she was a far more joyful and lively person than the photograph suggested. It did not help that Lange implied that the Thompsons were pea pickers and declared (incorrectly) that they had just sold their tires for food. Yet Lange's poignant photograph undeniably drew much-needed attention to farmworkers' poverty. The portrait generated considerable empathy among middle-class and wealthy Americans, who had little understanding of rural poverty, and helped persuade many to support the New Deal. The government also swiftly dispatched twenty thousand pounds of food to the pea pickers' camp, though the Thompsons were long gone by then.

Florence Owens Thompson. Dorothea Lange's photo of Thompson, aged thirty-three, became the most widely recognized documentary photograph of the Great Depression. Lange took the portrait during a ten-minute rest stop while en route to her next assignment.

The family continued toiling as farmworkers, until 1942, when Thompson found full-time employment as a hospital worker in the employment boom that resulted from America's entry into World War II. She died of cancer at the age of eighty in 1983, shortly after a local newspaper traced Thompson and brought her story to light. The striking image of American's most famous "Migrant Mother" once again inspired an outpouring of sympathy—this time in the form of donations that helped cover Thompson's hospital costs.

Think About It

1. Why did the 1931 closure of the mill where Florence Thompson's husband worked have such a drastic impact on on her and her children?
2. Why were migrant farmworkers so poorly paid?
3. Why might Thompson have resented the publication of Lange's "Migrant Mother"? Was it exploitative?
4. What was it about the photograph that made it the Depression's most enduring image?

which he drew on the stark and haunting FSA photographs—sealed the Okies' place in history as the face of the Great Depression.

NETWORKING RURAL AMERICA

At the beginning of the 1930s, only 10 percent of American farms had electricity. The vast majority of farmers relied on coal, wood, and candles for light and heat. Farmers' dependency on these premodern sources of power both compromised their standard of living and symbolized the gap between urban and supposedly "backward" rural life. One of the largest projects of the New Deal, the Tennessee Valley Authority (TVA, founded 1933) networked millions of impoverished southerners into a regional electricity grid for the first time—effectively extending the New Deal to some of the nation's most isolated and destitute communities.

The TVA grew out of a long-standing controversy in American politics over the use and protection of the nation's water supply. Reformers had long urged the government to harness the energy of the country's rivers for hydroelectricity In May 1933, the Roosevelt administration decided to take over work under way on a dam at Muscle Shoals on the Tennessee River. Over the next few years, the TVA improved water transportation, built five dams, and upgraded twenty others. These projects all but eliminated flooding and brought electric power to poor communities in eight southern states.

By 1937, the TVA was one of the United States' largest and cheapest suppliers of power. By setting electricity prices low, the TVA also helped bring prices down in the rest of the nation. The government worked with power companies and community groups to wire other rural areas, and by 1940 over a third of all farms had electricity (see Map 24.4). Electrification changed the practical side of farm life by enabling the use of

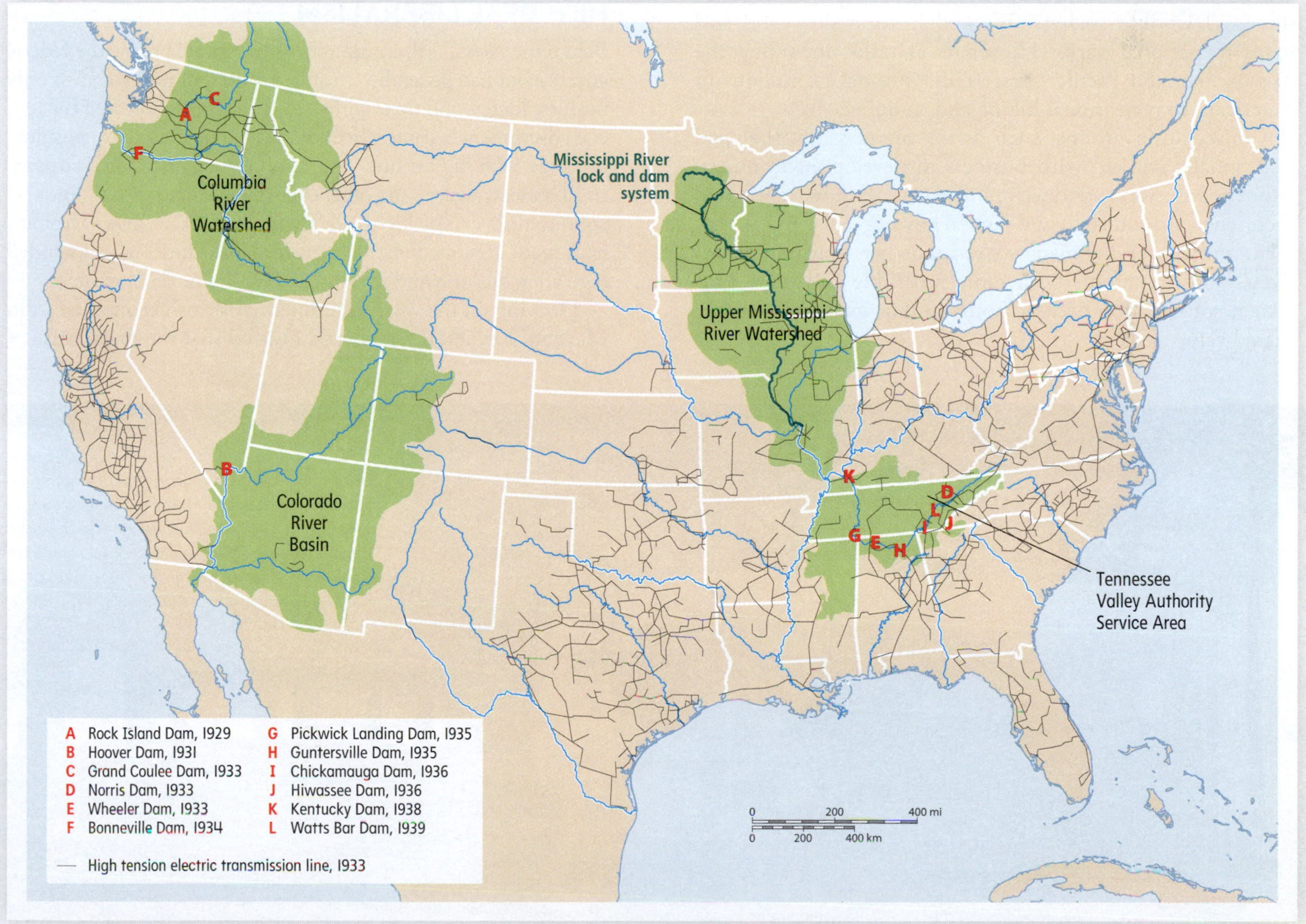

Map 24.4 Networking Rural America. Farm productivity climbed as a result of the TVA initiatives, and their success inspired similar projects on the Colorado, Missouri, and Columbia Rivers. In the 1960s, TVA projects would also serve as a model for U.S.-backed development in Southeast Asia.

labor-saving tools and appliances, and it integrated farming families into national consumer culture via the radio. Working with local communities, the TVA introduced fertilizer, built flood control gates, reforested the land, and conserved the soil. Many farmers subsequently felt less isolated, less ignored by the government, and more included in modern life.

A NEW DEAL FOR THE ENVIRONMENT

As well as expanding the federal role in agriculture, the New Deal transformed wastelands and other unfarmed parts of the American landscape and changed popular attitudes toward forests, wetlands, and native species. Federal agencies conserved millions of acres of soil and planted hundreds of millions of trees, including 220 million along the ninety-ninth meridian running from Texas to Canada. In addition, young men in the Civilian Conservation Corps planted some two billion trees on private and public wastelands that within a few years had reforested more than half of all the land that has ever been reforested in the United States. Other government projects restocked rivers and lakes with a billion fish, built thirty thousand wildlife shelters, restored historic sites, and laid roads to national parks. Hundreds of trails, including the Appalachian and Pacific Crest Trails, introduced millions of Americans to recreational hiking and camping.

Conservation groups, such as the Sierra Club, that had traditionally worked with business to develop environmentally friendly ways of developing resources now reoriented themselves around state and federal governments. As government and conservationists worked together to make forests, rivers, and mountains both more accessible and more protected, conservation became both a public goal and a widely shared value.

LIBERALISM AND ITS DISCONTENTS

The New Deal took shape via experimentation and innovation rather than according to a master plan. But by the late 1930s, the experiment had generated a new concept of government, society, and culture. This New Deal liberalism sought to use federal government to mitigate the worst excesses of the free-market system, and it enduringly transformed the nation. Widely popular, New Deal liberalism nevertheless struck some Americans as still too limited in scope. A loose coalition of leftists offered an alternative vision of the United States as a diverse country in which all people were free and equal and where government guaranteed everyone a free education, health care, and the basic necessities of life. For others—particularly Republicans, the southern wing of the Democratic Party, and sections of the labor movement—the New Deal was a dangerous power-grab by government. As the nation entered a new recession in 1937, Roosevelt lost both political support for some programs and his will to forge others.

NEW DEAL LIBERALISM

Before the New Deal, in matters of economic policy, the federal government had generally consulted with and responded to only business leaders and their lobbyists. After 1932, however, the federal government became a **broker state** as officials now consulted not only with big business but also with labor unions, farmers, small business owners, and other constituencies and tried to "broker" compromises acceptable to all. By the late 1930s, New Deal liberals were arguing that the government's duties also included regulating business and investing in economic development.

Drawing on the work of influential British economist John Maynard Keynes, these liberals insisted that the main cause of

Past Tents. Cheaper automobiles and new roads drew millions of Americans to car camping. For many middle-class families, camping meant an annual vacation in a state park or national park, and camping became an important summer ritual—one that in turn fostered conservationism. For poor migrants, however, roadside camping was a necessity, not a choice.

recession was poor consumer demand rather than declining production, as economists had believed. The practical upshot of **Keynesianism,** as the theory became known, was that government should actively stimulate consumer demand by lowering interest rates (making money cheaper and more available) and investing directly in the housing sector, agriculture, industry, interstate transportation, and science and technology. Such an approach, liberals asserted, promoted growth and smoothed capitalism's destructive boom-and-bust cycles, which had produced a severe recession—and two long depressions—every decade since the Civil War. Government should also invest in its citizens and help them move into the middle class by providing subsidized mortgages, free education, and a safety net for those who were unable to support themselves, whether due to age, illness, or misfortune. These ambitious goals required higher taxation.

By 1940, one in three Americans was receiving some kind of direct federal aid. Seniors collected Social Security, and many homeowners had mortgage guarantees. Loans and subsidies were available for farm or industrial development. By British, Japanese, and European standards, the New Deal state was still relatively weak, and it relied on states and municipalities to oversee a number of its programs. But by American standards, it was a radical departure from previous practice. Washington, D.C., became a symbol of politics and political power as never before.

New Deal liberalism also reshaped the Democratic Party, which successfully cemented a coalition among various constituencies that were not necessarily sympathetic to one another. Unionized labor, women of all classes, white ethnic immigrants, black northerners, and white southerners were the basis of the party's power through the 1960s. For the first time, Jews and Catholics served in high-ranking government positions.

The New Deal coalition was often an uneasy one, however, particularly in matters of gender and race. Women were officially discouraged from working in paid employment through official propaganda and the lower wages they received, despite the fact that almost all working-class women—and a significant number of their middle-class counterparts—worked out of necessity. At the same time, women played a vastly expanded role in the New Deal government. First lady Eleanor Roosevelt by turns shocked and impressed Americans as the first president's wife to play an active and public role in government. An experienced educator, labor advocate, and Democratic campaigner, she held press conferences, toured the country giving speeches on her husband's behalf, and openly advocated for equal rights for women and minorities. FDR's cabinet included Frances Perkins, secretary of labor and the first woman to serve in any cabinet, and over a dozen women served in executive-level positions in the Treasury, State Department, and other government agencies.

African Americans had a more mixed experience of the New Deal. Although Roosevelt appointed over forty African Americans to executive positions in the federal government, the president and many liberal lawmakers were less than eager to confront the fact that minorities were disproportionately bearing the brunt of the Depression. Nor was FDR, whose New Deal initiatives required the support of southern segregationists in Congress, willing to fight the injustices of racial segregation, disenfranchisement, and racial violence. Privately critical of lynching, the president nevertheless refused to support an anti-lynching bill (which consequently was defeated in Congress).

In theory, New Deal programs were race-blind. In practice, they either failed to benefit most African Americans or imposed southern-style segregation (the Civilian Conservation Corps camps, for instance, were segregated, as was federal theater). The New Deal's reliance on local authorities to implement and manage most programs meant that they were subject to local prejudice. Across the country, local governments almost always segregated federally funded housing, and the Federal Housing Administration approved the same restrictive real estate covenants that had excluded African Americans from white neighborhoods in the 1920s. Low-income African American housing was targeted for demolition, and although the slums were often dilapidated, they were also home to tens of thousands of people and the foundation of the community (see Interpreting the Sources: Lester Melrose and Casey Bill Weldon, "W.P.A. Blues"). A majority of African Americans, moreover, did not qualify for Social Security because most were agricultural or domestic workers, and those categories of labor were excluded. For the most part, liberals would not actively embrace civil rights as a matter of federal action until the 1960s—and when they did, many southern Democrats quit the party.

RISE OF THE LEFT

Liberalism was not the only new political movement to congeal amid the extraordinary conditions of the Great Depression. Communist, socialist, and related left-wing organizations all underwent significant growth. Although New Deal liberals shared some of the Left's goals, the latter pushed for even greater government involvement in the economy, including government ownership of utilities, and unlike liberals openly demanded full racial equality.

Frustrated with both the government and the American Federation of Labor's disapproval of many strikes, a small cadre of unionists formed the Congress of Industrial Organizations (CIO) in 1938. The CIO, which had begun as a subcommittee of the American Federation of Labor (AFL) three years earlier, unionized Mexican Americans, African Americans, and other populations that the AFL had traditionally spurned. For the first time, a major labor organization made racial justice a central objective. The CIO also welcomed over eight hundred thousand women to its ranks and, unlike the AFL, accepted members of America's small communist party. (A number of CIO leaders, though not a lot of its rank-and-file members, belonged to the party.) The CIO argued that the New Deal had not gone far enough toward protecting workers from exploitation. In particular, the union called upon Congress to explicitly

INTERPRETING THE SOURCES

Lester Melrose and Casey Bill Weldon, "W.P.A. Blues"

Blues, gospel, jazz, and work songs of the 1930s often expressed African Americans' complex relationship with FDR and the New Deal. Many blacks were angered by FDR's failure to support anti-lynching legislation and his acquiescence to discriminatory practices within New Deal agencies. Others lamented life in the Depression and the hardships of being poor, black, and voiceless. Yet the overwhelming majority supported him in each of three elections, hoping that the New Deal might deliver not only jobs but equality and justice. Lester Melrose and Casey Bill Weldon's blues song "W.P.A. Blues," in which the WPA brings employment to a struggling town but also demolishes a home, encapsulates African Americans' ambivalence. The witty lyrics of "W.P.A. Blues" (recorded in 1936) and dozens of other songs provide the best record we have of African American experiences and perceptions of the New Deal.

Everybody's working in this town and it's worrying me night and day
Everybody's working in this town and it's worrying me night and day
If that mean working too, have to work for the W.P.A.
Well well the landlord come this morning and he knocked on my door
He asked me if I was going to pay my rent no more
He said you have to move if you can't pay
And then he turned and he walked slowly away
So I have to try find me some other place to stay
That housewrecking crew's coming from the W.P.A.
Well well went to the relief station and I didn't have a cent
If that's the only way you stand you don't have to pay no rent
So when I got back home, they was tacking a notice on the door
This house is condemned and you can't live there no more
So a notion struck me, I better be on my way
They're going to tear my house down, that crew from the W.P.A.
Well well I went out next morning I put a lock on my door
I thought I would move but I have no place to go
The real estate people they all done got so
They don't rent to no relief clients no more
So I know, have to walk the streets night and day
Because that wrecking crew's coming from that W.P.A.
Well well a notion struck me, I'll try to stay a day or two
But I soon found out that that wouldn't do
Early next morning while I was laying in my bed
I heard a mighty rumbling and the bricks come tumbling down on my head
So I had to start ducking and dodging and be on my way
They was tearing my house down on me, that crew from that W.P.A.

Explore the Source

1. What is the protagonist's predicament?
2. How do the lyrics present the WPA?
3. Who are the "real estate people," and why might they have stopped renting to "relief people" (welfare recipients)?
4. Why might this song have been popular among African Americans?

recognize workers' rights to unionize and to bargain collectively with employers for industrywide contracts.

The American Communist Party (CPUSA)—a legal and relatively open organization in the 1930s—grew from just a few thousand to over 100,000 card-carrying members. Even larger numbers of Americans were sympathetic "fellow travelers" or cycled through the party at some point. For the first time in American history, the CPUSA enjoyed a degree of respectability among the working class and the middle class, and even in the mass media.

At a time when liberals shied away from demanding full racial equality and acquiesced to the inequitable implementation of the New Deal, racial justice also found a champion in the CPUSA. Even the National Association for the Advancement of Colored People was hesitant to tackle the unduly high levels of poverty, disease, and miscarriages of justice that African Americans endured, fearing that taking on such a cause might jeopardize the organization's respectable, middle-class reputation and goals. Only the CPUSA was prepared to defend poor African American sharecroppers and laborers wrongly accused of crimes—as the nine Scottsboro Boys were in 1931.

The Scottsboro Boys, nine black teenagers, had been convicted and sentenced to death for the alleged rape of two transient white women in Alabama. The CPUSA paid top New York attorney Samuel Leibowitz to lead the youths' appeal. Despite glaring contradictions in the young women's testimony, and national media coverage notwithstanding, the Alabama Supreme Court affirmed the convictions. In 1932, the U.S. Supreme Court overturned the Alabama decision in the groundbreaking case of *Powell v. Alabama*, ruling that the young men's right of due process had been denied. (A long series of retrials ensued, during which five of the young men were reconvicted and four were freed.) At a time when most white people accepted racial inequality, the CPUSA argued tirelessly that African Americans and other minorities were entitled to nothing less than full civil, political, and social equality.

Communists and the CIO also joined the **Popular Front**—a loose international coalition of leftists that was formed in 1935 with the goal of stopping the advance of fascism in Spain, Germany, and elsewhere in Europe (see Chapter 25). In the United States, the CPUSA abandoned its previous commitment to overthrowing the capitalist system and, together with other front members, threw its weight behind the New Deal. As well as running soup kitchens, adult education classes, and housing programs, the Popular Front helped drive the tremendous upsurge in artistic production that the New Deal had set in motion. A new conception of the United States emerged—as a racially, ethnically diverse nation that celebrated differences and valued the active participation of all people in civic and cultural life.

CONSERVATIVE REBIRTH

Although they were in the minority, conservative lawmakers and others who opposed an expanded role for government were equally active. In some instances, as in the advertising industry, business lobbies brought pressure to bear on Congress to water down legislation. The American Medical Association, for instance, spent considerable funds defeating a proposal for a system of national health insurance. Although southern Democrats often supported key New Deal reforms—and lapped up federal dollars as eagerly as the North—they were uniformly opposed to any initiative that might deprive the southern states of local control over federal resources. FDR's attempt to restructure the Supreme Court and to strengthen the executive also alienated many southerners, who criticized his actions as a federal power-grab at the expense of the South. Above all, southern Democrats feared that leftists might soon persuade Roosevelt (whose wife, Eleanor Roosevelt, openly supported civil rights) to attack racial segregation and disfranchisement.

Conservative congressmen in both parties went on the offense in 1937. The House Un-American Activities Committee (HUAC) investigated allegedly subversive and disloyal activities among federal and private employees. The committee chair, Texas Democrat Martin Dies, subpoenaed hundreds of people, many because of ties to the Communist Party. Dies's real intention, however, was to discredit some of the most outspoken northern New Dealers, especially those working for the WPA, and to warn Roosevelt off exerting greater federal control of the New Deal. The committee turned up relatively little evidence, but the hearings helped turn the relatively small anti-communist movement into a larger, far more mainstream conservative network. Leaders of the AFL, which now faced competition from the more radical CIO, became more audibly anti-communist. Worried that communists were spreading atheist values, Catholic leaders also spoke out, and Catholic workers began building anti-communist blocs within the unions.

Opposition to leftist causes of various kinds also grew within the federal government itself, particularly in the Federal Bureau of Investigation (FBI). Although Roosevelt had authorized the FBI to engage in limited political surveillance in 1934—specifically, of German Americans suspected of producing Nazi propaganda—FBI director J. Edgar Hoover radically expanded this mandate to include leftists, liberals, students, free speech advocates, and even liberal congressmen and Supreme Court justices. Through wiretaps, break-ins, and burglaries, the staunchly conservative Hoover built extensive (and secret) information files on thousands of Americans. He then selectively leaked information to conservative lawmakers and organizations such as the American Legion, who used it to discredit the New Deal by arguing that Russian-led communists had infiltrated government. This relationship laid much of the institutional and cultural groundwork for the anti-communist crusade of Wisconsin senator Joseph McCarthy (see Chapter 26).

THE ROOSEVELT RECESSION

Although unemployment and poverty levels remained high in 1937, the nation's gross domestic product had risen an average of 10 percent per year since 1933. On the strength of these gains, FDR cut federal spending on employment and other programs. The cuts unexpectedly triggered an immediate uptick in unemployment of about 1.5 million Americans. Fearing a recession, the new Federal Reserve swiftly lowered interest rates, which precipitated a run on the stock market. The country's economic growth consequently slowed, and unemployment jumped again, from 14 percent to 19 percent. Approximately ten million workers lost their jobs, and industrial output and real income declined to 1933 levels. The nation had entered what many would call the Roosevelt recession.

Aware that conservatives would not support more taxes, the president opted for a new practice that would become known as pump priming, in which the government injected money into new employment programs. Conservative Democrats balked but Roosevelt fought back, campaigning against several of his own southern party members in the 1938 midterm elections. His strategy backfired, however, and the intraparty split widened. The rift pushed voters toward the Republicans, who picked up dozens of seats in the House, eight seats in the Senate, and thirteen governorships. These results signaled that the popular mandate FDR had won in 1936 had fractured and was diminishing. With Roosevelt pursuing no major legislation after 1938, the New Deal appeared to have stalled.

CONCLUSION

The New Deal did not end the Depression. Significantly, however, it relieved the suffering of tens of millions of people and enduringly changed American politics, life, and culture. Before 1933, the federal government had been relatively weak and inactive in peacetime. Its principal arenas of action had been interstate commerce and foreign policy, and it therefore lacked the administrative and financial capacity to respond effectively to the unemployment, poverty, and distress that overwhelmed so many Americans after 1929. Although some Progressive Era reformers had envisioned a far more hands-on role for federal government, it took the Great Depression and President Franklin D. Roosevelt's experimental relief programs to kindle popular support for active government. It was only then that a new vision of government—New Deal liberalism—emerged and found broad support. Mass culture, with its powerful new radio and cinema networks, played a key role in galvanizing public opinion in favor of reform. Many Americans were critical of the rapid expansion of advertising, but the industry aggressively fended off most efforts at regulation.

By the mid-1930s, the federal government was more present, responsible, and visible in every sphere of American life. Thanks to Social Security and other entitlement programs, the United States had a rudimentary welfare system for the first time. At both the state and the federal levels, government grew substantially, as did Americans' reliance on it. By 1940, more than a million Americans worked permanently for the civil service, about eight hundred thousand more than in 1930. The New Deal also transformed industrial relations—which had long been rocky and sometimes violent. Unions became legitimate organizations in the eyes of most Americans, and employers no longer called upon militias, the U.S. Army, or private security forces to disperse strikes. For the most part, workers confined their actions to coordinated, peaceable picketing and filed grievances with the National Labor Relations Board. The New Deal's reinvention of government had brought relief and hope to a nation on its knees.

In 1939, however, it was by no means obvious that the New Deal would have a lasting legacy. Opposition within the Democratic and Republican Parties and among southern voters had effectively paralyzed reform. What seemed clear, in the wake of Germany's invasion of Czechoslovakia and Poland in 1939, was that the forces of fascism and Nazism were on the march and that the world was facing another catastrophic global conflict.

STUDY TERMS

voluntarism (p. 664)
Hawley-Smoot Tariff (p. 664)
Reconstruction Finance Corporation (p. 664)
Hoovervilles (p. 664)
repatriation (p. 664)
unemployed councils (p. 665)
Bonus Army (p. 666)
New Deal (p. 666)
First New Deal (p. 667)
first hundred days (p. 667)
Agricultural Adjustment Act (p. 667)
Civilian Conservation Corps (p. 668)
National Industrial Recovery Act (p. 668)
National Recovery Administration (p. 668)
Indian New Deal (p. 668)
fireside chats (p. 668)
Blue Eagle (p. 668)
Share-Our-Wealth Plan (p. 669)
San Francisco general strike (p. 670)
National Union for Social Justice (p. 670)
Liberty League (p. 670)
Schechter Poultry Company (p. 670)
Wagner Act (p. 670)
Social Security Act (p. 670)
Works Progress Administration (p. 670)
court-packing (p. 673)
The Living Newspaper (p. 674)
WPA guidebooks (p. 674)
teenager (p. 675)
American diet (p. 675)
consumer rights (p. 681)
Farm Security Administration (p. 681)
Dust Bowl (p. 682)
Tennessee Valley Authority (p. 685)
broker state (p. 686)
Keynesianism (p. 687)
Congress of Industrial Organizations (p. 687)
Scottsboro Boys (p. 688)
Popular Front (p. 689)
House Un-American Activities Committee (p. 689)
Roosevelt recession (p. 689)

TIMELINE

1929 Wall Street crash

Repatriation program begins mass expulsion of 450,000 Mexicans

1930 Hoovervilles proliferate

Severe drought hits most states, accelerating rural migration

Advertisers reinvent cigarettes, sparking a twenty-five-year smoking craze

1931 President Herbert Hoover initiates first bailout for business (Reconstruction Finance Corporation)

Scottsboro Boys are sentenced to the electric chair

1932 50-percent to 80-percent unemployment rates cripple the Industrial Belt

U.S. Army forcibly disperses Bonus Army in Washington, D.C.

Franklin D. Roosevelt wins election and Democrats sweep Congress

1933 First New Deal under way in Roosevelt's First Hundred Days

Roosevelt's first "fireside chat" is broadcast

Agricultural Adjustment Act buoys food prices

Congress regulates banking sector and the stock market

Federal Housing Administration offers fair, affordable mortgages

Federal Emergency Relief Administration establishes massive public employment schemes

National Industrial Recovery Act brings unions, government, and business together to establish fair wages and prices.

Tennessee Valley Authority begins massive development project in the South

Schlink and Kallet call for stricter regulation of food, drugs, and cosmetics

1934 A general strike paralyzes San Francisco, and 2,000 strikes erupt nationally

Father Charles Coughlin claims Jews, Communists, and bankers are conspiring to rule the United States

Escapist music, movies, and fiction are best sellers

1935 Supreme Court finds key New Deal acts unconstitutional

Second New Deal protects union members, establishes Social Security, and establishes Works Progress Administration

Revenue Act raises taxes to pay for relief programs

First of many "black blizzards" hits the Dust Bowl

American communists join the Popular Front and openly support the New Deal

"Swing" dance craze sweeps the nation

1936 Roosevelt is reelected

Federally funded arts thrive

Florence Owen Thompson, "Migrant Mother," becomes the face of poverty

1937 Roosevelt threatens to increase Supreme Court bench to fifteen

House Un-American Activities Committee fails to discredit the New Deal as a communist plot

Roosevelt cuts federal spending, triggering a recession

1938 Leftist workers form the Congress of Industrial Organizations, welcoming women and minorities

Republicans pick up multiple seats in Congress

The New Deal stalls

FURTHER READING

Additional suggested readings are available on the Online Learning Center at www.mhhe.com/becomingamerica1e.

Anthony Badger, *The First Hundred Days* (2008), examines the vital early days of Franklin D. Roosevelt's presidency.

Francisco Balderrama, *Decade of Betrayal: Mexican Repatriation in the 1930s* (2006), traces the rise of nativism and Mexican repatriation.

Alan Brinkley, *Voices of Protest: Huey Long, Father Coughlin, and the Great Depression* (1982), assesses conservative challenges to the New Deal.

Lizabeth Cohen, *Making a New Deal: Industrial Workers in Chicago, 1919–1939*, analyzes workers' influence on the New Deal.

Blanch Wiesen Cooke, *Eleanor Roosevelt; Volume 2: The Defining Years, 1933–1938* (2001), maps the first lady's influence on housing, racial, and women's issues.

Morris Dickstein, *Dancing in the Dark: A Cultural History of the Great Depression* (2010), shows how the arts and culture industries boosted morale in one of the most trying eras of the nation's history.

David Kennedy, *Freedom from Fear: The American People in Depression and War, 1929–45* (1999), narrates the story of the Great Depression and the New Deal.

Bruce Lenthal, *Radio's America: The Great Depression and the Rise of Modern Mass Culture* (2007), charts the immense impact radio had on the lives on Americans and mass culture.

William E. Leuchtenberg, *Franklin D. Roosevelt and the New Deal* (1963), offers a classic political history of the era.

Neil M. Maher, *Nature's New Deal: The Civilian Conservation Corps and the Roots of the American Environmental Movement* (2007), tracks the government's response to a variety of environmental disasters.

Patricia L. Sullivan, *Days of Hope: Race and Democracy in the New Deal Era* (1996), examines the response of southern liberals, black activists, labor organizers, and Communist Party workers to the Depression and New Deal.

Donald Worster, *Dust Bowl: The Southern Plains in the 1930s* (2004), chronicles the region's ecological, political, and cultural history.

25

INSIDE ▶

Promoting Unity. Allies' cannons simultaneously blast into the sky—and against the fascist war machine—in this official U.S. poster from 1943.

THE BIG PICTURE

The United States eventually entered World War II, throwing its full military, economic, and cultural might into the fight against fascism. Wartime mobilization ended the Great Depression, spurred suburbanization, and turned the United States into the leading superpower. A new vision of America as an ethnically and racially inclusive consumer society emerged, although minorities' everyday experiences still diverged significantly from that ideal.

1939–1945

AMERICA GOES TO WAR

Far from the popular dancehalls of New York City and Chicago, the unmistakable blasts of live American swing jazz pierced England's quiet country air. The setting seems incongruous, but for thousands of U.S. servicemen gathered in paddocks, airplane hangars, and barns in the summer of 1944, the catchy rhythms of Glenn Miller's Army Air Force Band brought them "home" to happier times, loving sweethearts, and the freedoms of civilian life. Already the king of swing before the war, Miller had volunteered for the army in 1942, determined to entertain the millions of troops stationed at home and abroad. Turning traditional military band music on its head, Captain Miller assembled the biggest and best swing band the world had ever heard, taking his musicians on a grueling eight-hundred-gig tour of England. By the end of the war, swing was a proven morale builder and a global symbol of American freedom.

Like World War I, World War II was a war of production in which each combatant rapidly converted its entire economy to the manufacture of war materiel and strove to outproduce the others. But the duration and massive scale of the United States' wartime conversion had a much more transformative effect than previously. It forever changed cities and industrialized whole regions. The rate of urbanization tripled and suburbs proliferated. Conversion also turned the United States into the world's most powerful military and economic nation, a development that President Franklin D. Roosevelt anticipated as early as 1939.

Winning was not just a military and an economic challenge; it was also a cultural and an ideological struggle. The fascist regimes that had risen to power in Europe and Japan in the 1930s espoused deeply racist world views according to which their own peoples were genetically and culturally superior to others. Nazi Germany in particular carried out systematic campaigns to "purify" its citizenry, stripping German Jews and other "undesirables" of their rights and herding them into labor camps (and, eventually, death camps). Democracy, according to fascists, was a decadent American idea that pretended that all people were equal and that dangerously mixed multiple ethnicities and races into one "bastard" nation. Fascist states tried to stamp out American music, movies, dress styles, and ideas—even banning swing in the 1930s.

KEY QUESTIONS

- How did World War II influence the U.S. economy, mass culture, and the cities?
- What role did the culture industries play in the Allies' victory over fascism?
- How did women and minorities experience mobilization, and how did the war change gender and race relations?
- What were the long-term consequences of U.S. involvement in the war?
- What were the war's human and other costs?

Military top brass at first grumbled that Glenn Miller's swing music—with its jazz roots and sensual physicality—was not fit for the troops. The soldiers' overwhelmingly positive response soon convinced them otherwise.

At first, the U.S. government did not realize that these same culture industries could be important weapons of war. Roosevelt even briefly considered closing the advertising business as "non-essential." But the culture industries flooded American radio, movies, and magazines with patriotic material persuading the government otherwise. A new, inclusive concept of what it meant to be an American came to the fore. Although this picture of an ethnically and racially inclusive democracy did not square with many minorities' experience, it gradually gained official recognition and became a rallying point for the nation's epic fight against fascism.

A WORLD AGAIN AT WAR

The Great Depression wrought drastic changes worldwide. It destabilized governments everywhere and plunged millions into distress. Americans responded mostly by strengthening their democratic institutions, but racist and authoritarian regimes rose to power in Japan, Spain, Italy, and Germany. These governments subscribed to the ideology of fascism—the idea that a struggling nation could be revived only by a charismatic dictator who exerted complete control over the nation's legal institutions, education system, culture industries, and economy. Wherever they seized power, fascist states imposed ultraconservative values, oppressed minorities, and propagated a cult-like devotion to the leader. Believing that war was a rejuvenating force, they also built large armies—and eventually deployed them against neighboring nations. Great Britain and France tried to negotiate with German dictator Adolf Hitler, but their efforts failed, and by late 1939 Europe was at war. Although a vocal minority of American writers, publishers, and other artists argued that the United States needed to confront global fascism directly, the great majority of Americans opposed U.S. entry into the conflict. Prosperity was "just around the corner," many believed, and involvement in yet another European war would surely derail the long-awaited recovery.

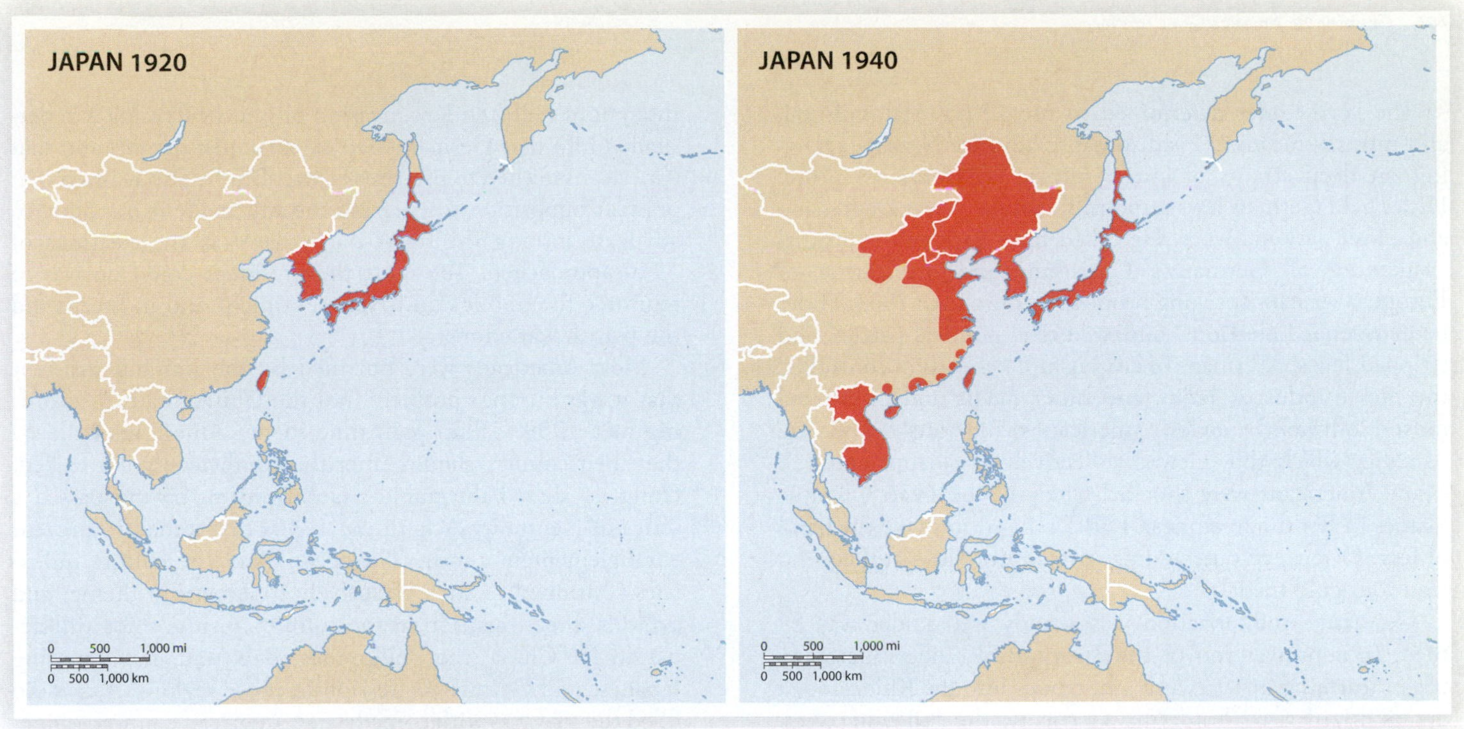

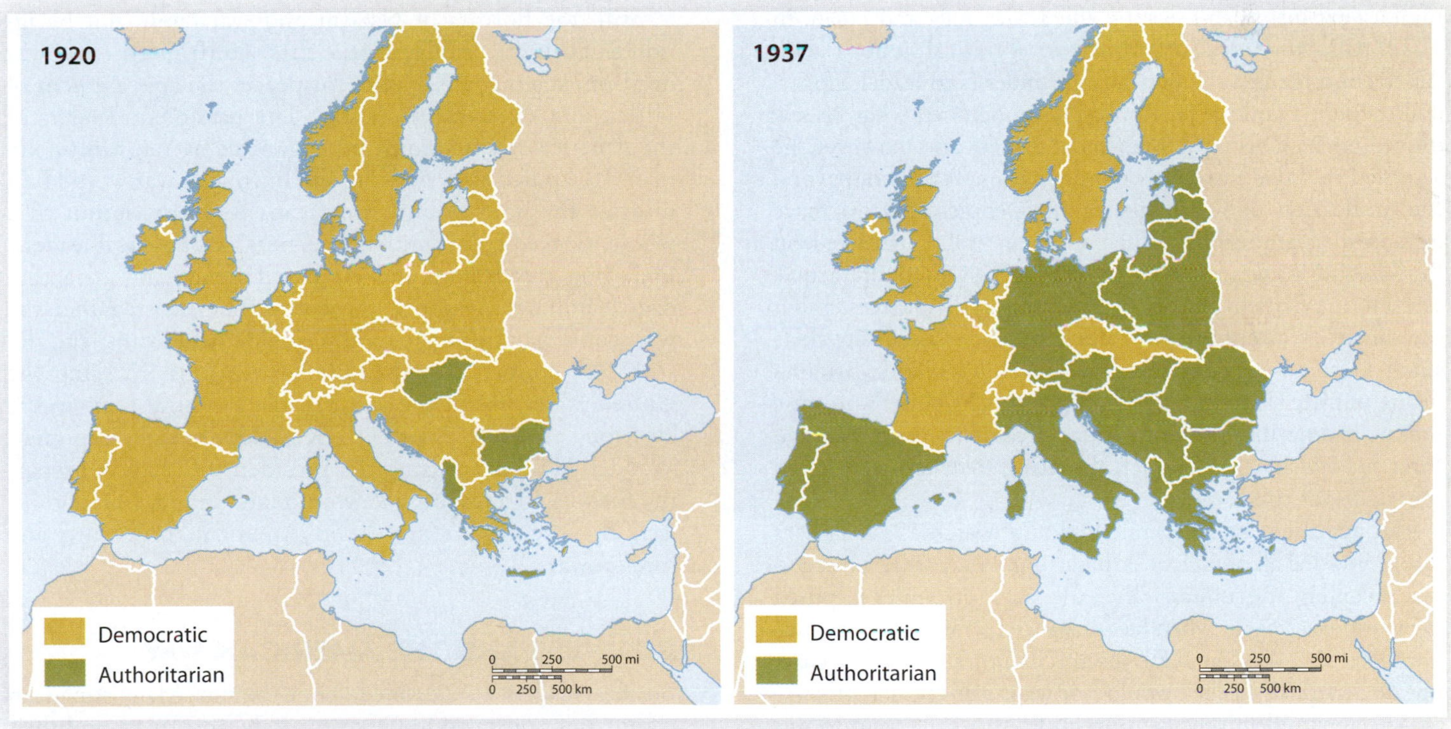

Map 25.1 Fascism on the March. Fascist and other authoritarian regimes came to power in East Asia and Europe in the 1920s and 1930s. By 1937, the fascist governments of Germany, Italy, and Japan had embarked on a period of aggressive, unchecked expansion.

THE MARCH OF FASCISM

When its troops swarmed into Manchuria in northeast Asia in 1931, Japan became the first fascist nation to expand aggressively (see Map 25.1). Hungry for iron, oil, and other natural resources, the Japanese launched a full-scale invasion of the rest of China six years later. In the meantime, fascist Italian dictator Benito Mussolini invaded Ethiopia in 1935. Although the League of Nations condemned the aggressors, it lacked the will and ability to take action. The League's timidity in turn emboldened German chancellor Adolf Hitler, whose fascist National Socialist Party (Nazis) had risen to power in 1932, to escalate German expansion.

The Nazi leader determined to use all political, cultural, and military means at his disposal to advance Nazism. Drawing on deep strains of anti-Semitism in German culture, Hitler held German Jews responsible for the Great Depression and other national woes. He called for a nationalist spiritual awakening of Germany's Christians and unification of Europe's German- speaking peoples. By the end of 1933, Hitler had suspended elections, outlawed rival political parties, and stripped Jewish Germans of citizenship. Nazis soon controlled the movie industry, radio, and other media and prohibited most Hollywood movies, American swing music, and jazz dancing (which they viewed collectively as corrupt culture). Many Americans were shocked when, at the 1936 Olympic Games in Berlin, an enraged Hitler refused to shake the hand of Jesse Owens, an outstanding African American athlete who won four gold medals.

Germany's militarization was already well under way by then. In contravention of the Treaty of Versailles, Germany began rearming in 1935 and sent troops into the Rhineland, a demilitarized zone bordering Germany, the following year. When the League of Nations again stalled, Hitler accelerated military expansion and secretly allied with Italy and Japan. In 1938, Germany declared *Anschluss* (political union) with Austria and merged the two nations under Nazi leadership.

President Franklin D. Roosevelt condemned what he saw unfolding in Germany. Like most Americans, however, he assumed that the Nazis were simply nationalists who, beyond the unification of German-speaking peoples, did not have expansionist ambitions. When German troops gathered on the Czechoslovakian border in 1938, FDR therefore acquiesced to the British strategy of appeasing Hitler, agreeing that the dictator's intention was to occupy only Czechoslovakia's small German-speaking region, the Sudetenland. Britain's prime minister Neville Chamberlin accepted Hitler's promise that he had no intention of a broader campaign and returned from negotiations in Munich declaring that he had secured "peace in our time."

But appeasement failed miserably. In March 1939, Hitler's troops invaded all of Czechoslovakia—and they stood poised to take Poland by the summer. Then the mercurial Hitler surprised the world once again when he announced a mutual nonaggression pact with the Nazis' foe Joseph Stalin, the Soviet dictator. The leaders pledged they would not wage war on each other—an agreement effectively assuring Hitler that if he went to war against the West, he would have to fight on only one front (against Britain and France in western Europe) and not two. Germany's state-of-the-art tanks and artillery took Poland with lightning speed on September 1. On September 3, Britain and France declared war on Germany. World War II had begun.

ISOLATIONIST AMERICA

Two days after Britain and France declared war on Germany, FDR affirmed U.S. neutrality while also acknowledging that he could not "ask that every American remain neutral in thought as well." Hitler's invasion of Czechoslovakia had persuaded him that Germany had expansionist dreams and that Americans needed to prepare for war. But he also realized that popular opposition to entering the war made it impolitic to advocate joining the fray—particularly as the elections of 1940 approached. The most the president could do was to reinforce the public's anti-Nazi sentiment and indirectly aid the British war effort.

Most Americans were horrified by the war but insistent that it was Europe's problem, not the United States'. According to a 1939 Gallup poll, nine in ten Americans believed that their country should enter the conflict only if attacked. Congress shared the public's **isolationism,** having passed a series of Neutrality Acts in the 1930s that aimed to prevent entanglement in another European war. The culture industries continued to stick exclusively to American themes and avoided direct mention of the conflict. Cruise ships still departed for China, the Philippines, Bali, and Java, ignoring Japanese and German aggression in those regions. And radio filled the airwaves with comedy and American country, swing, and light popular music.

Still, the horrors of Nazism and war could not be ignored entirely. College students confronted the war head-on, staging mass rallies for peace, the appeasement of Hitler, and American isolation. The passionate leaders of the America First Committee, organized at Yale University in 1940, argued that entering the European war would be a disaster for both young Americans and the nation as a whole. Backed by prominent business and political leaders, including Henry Ford and Herbert Hoover, and attracting over a million members, the committee insisted that the war would bankrupt the nation, divide Americans, and destroy the country's democratic institutions. Keeping the United States out of the war became a central issue in the election of 1940, with FDR's Republican opponent Wendell Willkie accusing the president of secretly preparing for war. In a response he would later regret, FDR promised that he would not "send American boys into any foreign wars."

BUSINESS AND THE AMERICAN WAY

Business leaders were divided about the war. Many American corporations operated in Germany, Italy, and Japan, and their chief executives therefore vociferously supported U.S. neutrality. Others remained quiet, calculating that FDR would eventually take the nation to war and demand their full support. Either way, the war was above all a complicating factor in an already troubled political environment. From corporate leaders' perspective, the Great Depression, the consumer rights movement, New Deal regulation, and public disillusionment with big business posed much more immediate threats. For some months before the war, many leading American corporations had already been planning a publicity blitz to counter these challenges.

A Promising Future. Originally intended to mark the 150th anniversary of George Washington's swearing-in as the first president, the 1939 World's Fair became a publicity campaign for corporate America. An enormous diorama of a prosperous, futuristic "Democracity" redefined democracy as the "right to choose" from among a rich and varied supply of consumer goods. Other exhibits included fully automated kitchens, new food products such as Wonder Bread, and television broadcasting, which had been invented a few years earlier but would not become popular until after the war.

The public relations campaign kicked off at the 1939 World's Fair in Flushing Meadows, New York. A dazzling celebration of the "world of tomorrow," the fair's exhibits included an enormous scale model of "America in 1960," complete with futuristic suburban housing, sleek skyscrapers, hydroelectric dams, and scientifically advanced farms, all connected via the first multilane highways. Product-themed architecture, audio tours, and oversized company logos promoted what corporate sponsors referred to as the **American way**—a blend of consumerism, technological innovation, responsible corporate leadership, and antiunionism.

The overarching message was that democracy meant individual freedom of choice—the choice of where to live, whom to work for, what to eat, and what car to drive. According to this vision of America, responsible corporations rather than government were the true guardians of freedom. Furthermore, wherever government regulation occurred, whether in Nazi Germany or New Deal America, it was un-American and an inherent threat to freedom. The fair's enormous scale, sleek design, and optimistic vision caught the imagination of a generation of Americans and provided business with a public relations model that would endure into the early twenty-first century.

CONFRONTING FASCISM

Most Americans responded enthusiastically to the advertisers' optimistic images of future prosperity and mass consumption. A small but outspoken minority of self-identified **internationalists,** however, worked tirelessly to disrupt what they viewed as Americans' false sense of security and misplaced optimism about the future. Internationalist journalists, artists, publishers, and scholars highlighted the United States' long-standing ties to Europe, now under full-scale attack by the Nazis. Well-known critic Lewis Mumford argued in *Faith for Living* (1940) that the United States owed a moral duty, not only to its citizens but to all humanity, to halt the Nazi war machine. Nazism, Mumford wrote, was an assault on civilization itself, and isolationists were "passive barbarians" who inadvertently fueled the fascist war effort.

Scholars such as Mumford reached only a limited, highly educated readership. But through the media of radio, film, and magazines, international artists and reporters documented the destructive force of the Nazis for masses of Americans. Their work slowly changed Americans' minds about the war. As the Battle of Britain got under way in 1940, radio broadcaster Edward R. Murrow filed harrowing—and frighteningly real—reports from London, where German aerial bombers were reducing sections of the city to rubble. Taking cover in bomb shelters and clambering over smoking ruins, Murrow vividly described everything he saw and memorably interviewed locals about "the blitz." Like no other medium, Murrow's radio broadcasts personalized the war, empathically connecting tens of millions of Americans with Londoners and their struggles and triumphs.

Many Americans learned more about the Nazis' global ambitions from Charlie Chaplin's popular movie *The Great Dictator* (1940). Years before the mainstream press reported on Hitler's war against Jews, Chaplin's dark comedy publicized the widespread use of concentration camps and Nazi visions of world domination. Pushing the case for U.S. intervention further, Timely Comics introduced millions of readers to the heroic Captain America, and the Captain's "Sentinels of Liberty" fan club pushed sales of the popular comic series higher than best-selling *Time* magazine. Many other internationalist artists also decried isolationism—among them newspaper cartoonist Theodor Geisel, known to later generations of American children as Dr. Seuss.

Gradually, internationalist art and journalism changed many Americans' minds about neutrality. Before long, themes of death, destruction, and evil surfaced even in mainstream movies that supposedly had nothing to do with fascism or war, and this trend suggested that the violence occurring in Europe and Asia was neither as remote nor as irrelevant as the public had assumed. In 1941, most Americans still opposed U.S. entry, but almost one in five favored war with Germany and Italy (double

Images of War. Much as Edward R. Murrow made the Battle of Britain real for radio's mass audience, the vivid photojournalism of *Look* and *Life* magazines presented millions of Americans with haunting images of a devastated Europe and awesome displays of Nazi might. Here, St. Paul's Cathedral towers above bombed-out remains of London's Ludgate Hill district.

Raising the Alarm. Accompanied by his likable teenage sidekick Bucky, Captain America was the first major superhero to fight the Nazis and the Japanese. The Captain was the crusading alter ego of a quiet and unassuming civilian, the frail, pasty Steve Rogers. This postal stamp from 2007 commemorates the character's immense popularity during World War II. **Questions for Analysis:** Why might the comic's creators have portrayed Steve Rogers (who miraculously morphed into Captain America) as a weakling? Why do you think the comic featured a teenage buddy? How might the Captain America series have prepared Americans for war?

the number in 1939). Almost half supported indirect forms of military intervention, such as loaning U.S. battleships to Britain's Royal Navy.

UNDECLARED WAR

Although FDR was legally bound to keep the United States out of the war, he did all he could to aid the British against Hitler and to prepare Americans for war. The president had been waging an indirect, undeclared war on Germany for almost two years by the time the Japanese executed a surprise attack on the Pacific fleet at Pearl Harbor, Hawaii, in December 1941. As Americans reacted with shock to the magnitude and audacity of the attack, isolationism rapidly turned to a thirst for revenge. Roosevelt now had a popular mandate and full congressional support for war.

AIDING THE ALLIES

FDR skillfully juggled the contending demands of president and commander in chief, diverting as much aid as possible to the British while repeatedly reassuring the American people that helping the Allies was the only way to preserve U.S. neutrality. All the while, he slowly prepared the nation for war. The war he had in mind was Europe's. Before Pearl Harbor, Japanese aggression rarely figured in his calculations or public addresses. He considered Nazism the overriding threat to American interests and assumed that an attack on the United States would come from Germany. Roosevelt preferred to keep U.S.-Japan relations as peaceable as possible, though he did boost aid to Chinese forces fighting the Japanese invaders. Trade with Japan was still worth over $227 million in 1940 ($3.7 billion today), and although the federal government forbade the export of metals to Japan because it was used in weaponry, American oil flowed into Japan through much of 1941, literally fueling its war machine.

By the end of 1939, FDR had persuaded Congress to authorize the United States to sell arms to European democracies provided they paid cash and collected the arms themselves. Soon after implementing this cash-and-carry arrangement, the United States gave Britain a fleet of fifty outmoded destroyers in exchange for the right to establish naval bases in Canada and the West Indies. As a precaution against potential acts of espionage, the United States interned the first of nineteen thousand German and Italian nationals. Some of them happened to be sailors on shore leave when war broke out in Europe, but most were deported (as suspected agents) from Latin American countries at the insistence of the U.S. State Department.

PREPARING FOR WAR

Through most of 1940, an election year, the Roosevelt administration quietly promoted awareness and preparedness by publishing articles in popular magazines such as *Look* and encouraging editors to dispatch news reporters to the war zones. Such efforts even extended to radio and the movies. When United Artists threatened to cease production of Charlie Chaplin's *The Great Dictator* on the grounds that it was anti-German, Roosevelt's top adviser flew to Hollywood to encourage Chaplin personally to see the film through. At FDR's instigation, Congress authorized the first peacetime draft in the nation's history. Under the Selective Service Act (1940), nine hundred thousand draftees were to be drawn each year from the nation's population of men aged twenty to thirty-six and subjected to military training. The government also commissioned the construction of fifty thousand warplanes—the single largest arms buildup in U.S. peacetime history.

As FDR prepared the country for war in the run-up to the election of 1940, he remained silent on whether he would run for an unprecedented third consecutive term in the White House. Neither seeking the Democratic nomination nor withdrawing from the race, he effectively ensured that potential rivals gained no traction within the Democratic Party (which formally renominated him in the summer of 1940). The Republicans tapped Wendell Willkie, a charismatic industrialist who charged that the New Deal was stifling business and that FDR was secretly plotting for war. With the majority of voters favoring isolationism, both candidates pledged to keep the nation out of the conflict. Willkie ran an unusually energetic campaign, with his free-market policies attracting strong support in the Northeast and Midwest. But many Americans still blamed big business, with which Willkie was closely associated, for the Great Depression. On election day, FDR won 449 electoral college votes to Willkie's 82; he captured 55 percent of the popular vote.

Once reelected, Roosevelt built the case for war more openly and directly. In his **Four Freedoms** speech to Congress, broadcast live in January 1941, he declared that "[i]n the future days, we look forward to a world founded upon four freedoms"—the freedoms of speech and worship and the freedom from fear and economic want. However, the president continued, unless Congress swiftly authorized increased production and sale of war supplies, violent dictatorships would trample those freedoms. Roosevelt's moving words would be broadcast, quoted, and invoked around the world for the remainder of the war.

Following the speech, Congress passed the Lend-Lease Act (1941), giving the government wide latitude to supply defense materiel to "any country whose defense the president deems vital to the defense of the United States." Although voters' continuing isolationism made Roosevelt hesitant to boost British supplies immediately, he nevertheless extended U.S. Navy patrols halfway across the Atlantic and deployed over four thousand troops to Greenland and British-occupied Iceland.

Events took a dramatic turn a few months later, when Germany attacked the Soviet Union (communist Russia) on the unfounded assumption that the Soviets were about to invade Germany. One of the greatest strategic bungles in military history, the attack opened the bloodiest, costliest front in the war—and became the catalyst for open U.S. support of the Allies. Roosevelt dispatched the first of $11 billion worth of materiel to Russia and arranged to meet personally for the first time with British prime minister Winston Churchill. Strong willed and opinionated, Churchill nevertheless bonded with FDR. Churchill's respect for the American leader deepened, and Roosevelt's commitment to helping Britain was sealed.

The president, believing that the United States was not yet ready to engage, was careful not to promise armed intervention. He did agree to deploy the U.S. Navy to protect British merchant ships between North America and Iceland. He also promised that when the United States went to war, America would prioritize the fight against Germany rather than Japan. In an implicit acknowledgment that the United States would soon join the war, the two leaders signed the Atlantic Charter (1941), a blueprint for the postwar global order. Recognizing the principles of collective security, free trade, and national self-determination, the charter subsequently drew the Soviets' support and set in motion the founding of the United Nations in 1945.

ATTACK ON PEARL HARBOR

By the fall of 1941, Roosevelt believed that war with Germany was imminent but that it would take a "shock" to persuade Congress to declare it. In the meantime, as he informed Prime Minister Churchill, he would "become more and more provocative. If the Germans [do] not like it, they [can] attack American forces." The anticipated incident came in October,

Never Again. Although the dawn raid at Pearl Harbor was a tactical victory for Japan, in the long run it was a strategic disaster. Enraged Americans vowed to bring the full force of the United States' military down on Japan. The U.S. government and corporations such as Bethlehem Steel reinforced the popular resolve with colorful posters imploring Americans to "avenge Pearl Harbor!"

when a German U-boat attacked the USS *Kearny* near Iceland, killing eleven servicemen. Shortly afterward, the Germans torpedoed another U.S. destroyer, at the cost of one hundred American lives. At Roosevelt's request, Congress repealed key sections of the Neutrality Act of 1939, allowing U.S. merchant ships once again to transport munitions directly to the Allies. Legislators' and voters' support for all-out war meanwhile remained uncertain.

By this time, the United States had suspended oil exports to Japan, largely under pressure from the British. But Roosevelt still sought a peaceful way forward in the Pacific, not wishing to imperil the pending war with Germany. The United States assured Japan that trade would be restored if the latter agreed to four principles of conduct—freedom of the seas, free trade, respect of other nations' sovereignty, and nonintervention in other countries' affairs. Fearing that such an agreement would strip them of their Chinese acquisitions, the Japanese rejected these principles and expedited preparations to seize Dutch and British oil fields in Southeast Asia. In early December 1941, U.S. military code-breakers informed Roosevelt that Japan appeared to be mobilizing for a campaign and that a large fleet of Japanese ships was headed south, most probably to Southeast Asia's oil fields.

Military intercepts gave no indication of an even larger movement of aircraft carriers and other vessels eastward across the Pacific toward Hawaii. As it happens, the fleet had avoided detection by suspending all radio contact. At dawn on December 7, 1941, 350 Japanese carrier planes departed for the U.S. Naval Base at Pearl Harbor, where they carried out a deadly surprise attack that killed 2,403 Americans and damaged or destroyed twenty-one ships. Americans were appalled at the loss of life and the fact that the attack came on a Sunday, with no explicit warning. Even the most ardent isolationists now pressed for war.

Roosevelt immediately asked Congress to declare war on Japan. All but one lawmaker (Representative Jeanette Rankin, who had also voted against U.S. entry into World War I) voted in favor. Three days later, the Germans—in a blunder that would return to haunt them—declared war on the United States, believing they could easily rout its much smaller and supposedly less disciplined military. Congress reciprocated and, for the second time in twenty-five years, the United States was officially at war with Germany.

HOME FRONTS

In five short days, the United States had gone from Allies' friend to active partner in a global war. Declaring war put sudden and immense pressure on the government and the American people. Millions of men and women volunteered to serve in the armed forces or help out on the home front, while the federal government moved swiftly to increase the military draft and convert the economy to wartime production. Conversion accelerated migration, particularly among African Americans, as twenty-seven million people (one in four Americans) left home in search of war-related employment. The war gave millions their first well-paid, full-time jobs, changing the demographics of many cities and populating the Sunbelt, the generally warm region that stretches from southern California through the southwestern and southern states to Florida. For 110,000 people of Japanese descent, however, wartime migration was the result of government-ordered internment—and an unmitigated disaster.

DEMOCRACY'S ARMY

Galvanized by Pearl Harbor, millions of Americans volunteered for armed service. The hundreds of local draft boards established under the Selective Service Act of 1940 called up millions more. All told, over sixteen million men and women

No More Business as Usual. As the nation mobilized in 1942, families, neighborhood associations, businesses, and civic clubs hoisted millions of American flags and posted thousands of patriotic signs along highways. Patriotic graffiti appeared in the restrooms of restaurants and bars, on advertising billboards, and on private homes. Small business owners hung "gone to war" signs in their windows, and propaganda posters such as the one above reminded consumers that they would have to sacrifice, even at Christmas.

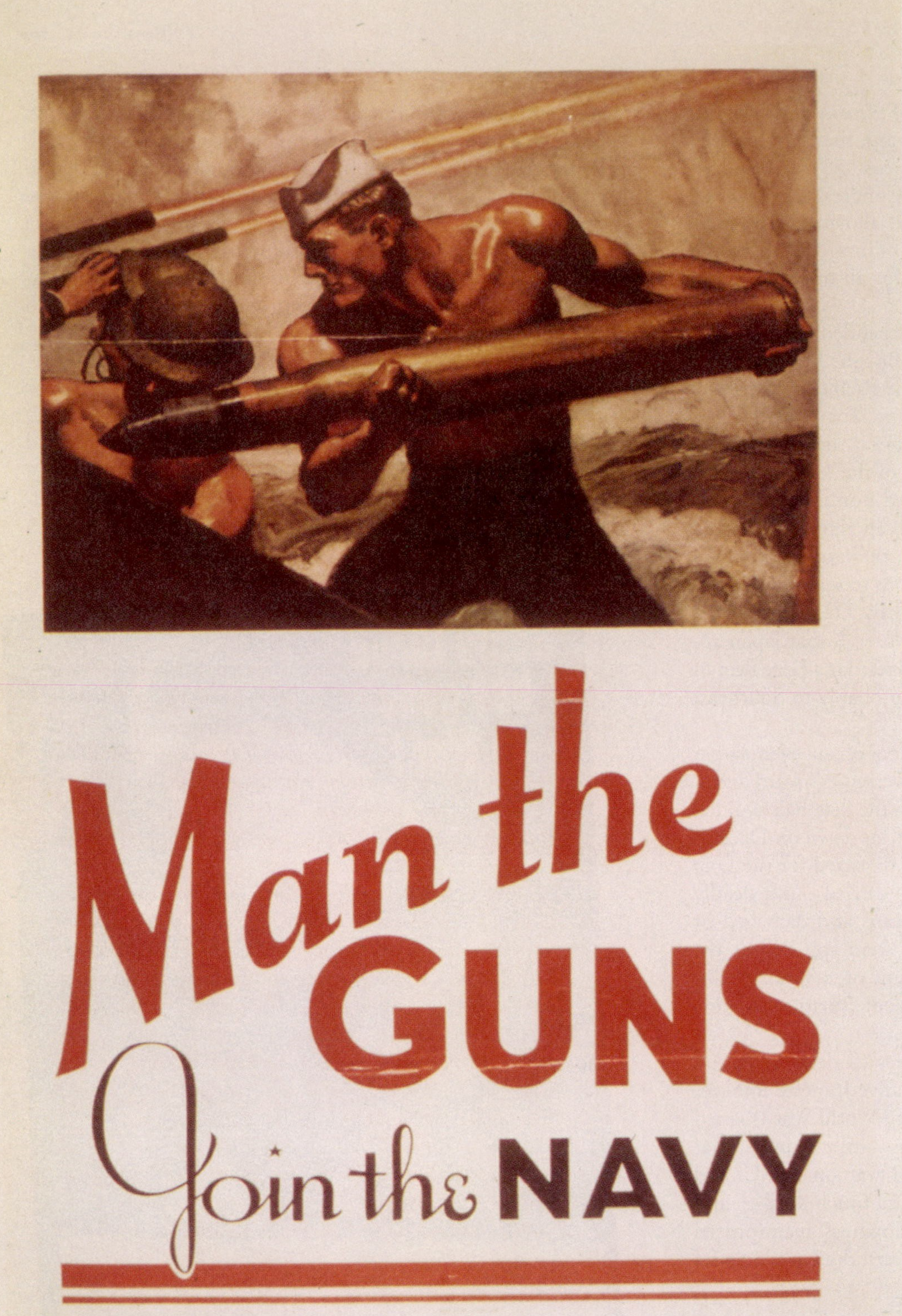
Man the
GUNS
Join the NAVY

America Calling. Drawing on popular imagery from cartoons and comics, government recruitment posters emphasized the muscular, manly qualities of servicemen, often in sexually suggestive ways.

would serve in uniform over the next four years, a full ten million in the army alone. By 1943, most families had one or more members in the military and the nation had the largest citizen-soldier army the world had ever seen.

America's armed forces—and the army in particular—were the most diverse in modern times. Large numbers of people of African, Mexican, Native American, and Chinese descent served, as did masses of Italian, Irish, German, and other Euro-Americans (see Table 25.1). More than four hundred Navajo Indians encoded vital messages and orders in their native language for the Marines' signal corps. Over thirty thousand Japanese Americans also volunteered for service (see Singular Lives: Ben Kuroki, U.S. Airman), including six thousand who performed vital translation and code-breaking work for the Military Intelligence Service. Volunteers and draftees were migrant farm hands, factory workers, lawyers, doctors, and Hollywood celebrities—people drawn from across the nation and every occupation.

Most servicemen drilled, fought, and socialized together. But African Americans were segregated and barred from combat, despite the Selective Service Act's prohibition of "discrimination on account of color." Although many blacks were eager to join the navy or marines, they were often denied entry and redirected to the army. Increasingly frustrated, the National Association for the Advancement of Colored People demanded that African Americans be allowed to serve to the fullest capacity. To this end, A. Philip Randolph (president of the Brotherhood of Sleeping Car Porters, the nation's largest black union), and other civil rights leaders commenced a Double V campaign in 1942, calling upon the government to commit to victory both in the war overseas and over racism at home. The navy and marines began accepting African Americans, and the army increased recruitment. But not until 1944, when the United States needed more combat soldiers in the final advance across Europe, were African American units permitted to fight—and the call to desegregate the armed forces went nowhere until 1948.

America's 350,000 servicewomen served mostly in the Women's Army Corps (WACs) or the navy's women's corps, typically as nurses or clerical workers. Although barred from

TABLE 25.1 U.S. ARMED FORCES BY RACE AND ETHNICITY

	Number Who Served	Percentage of All Who Served	Percentage of Their Race/ Ethnicity
African Americans	1 million	6.3	12
Euro-Americans	14 million	90	11
Chinese Americans	13,000	0.1	5
Japanese Americans	30,000	0.2	12
Mexican Americans	500,000	3.2	26
Native Americans	25,000	0.2	7

Although the vast majority of those in the armed forces were white, a greater proportion of the African American, Japanese American, and Mexican American populations served in the war.

combat, many women worked on the front lines, where they tended to the sick and wounded and carried out vital and often dangerous communication work. The thousand-strong Women's Air Service Pilots (WASPs) personally delivered every new U.S. Army Air Force plane from the factory to its U.S. base, disproving the popular perception that women were unsuited to piloting. Although many military women called on the armed forces to grant them full military status, they were denied this status, along with the veteran's benefits that came with it.

A WAR OF PRODUCTION

Waging war on a global scale did more to end the Great Depression than all New Deal programs combined. Demand for ships, airplanes, guns, and other war materiel lifted heavy industry out of the economic doldrums, taking with it many of the extractive industries, such as coal, copper, and rubber. Farmers grew 30 percent more crops in order to feed the armed forces and the Allies. By the end of the war, almost all industrial production was war related and business profits skyrocketed to double what they had been in 1941. Most importantly, unemployment fell to almost nothing. No other four-year period, before or since, has witnessed such a striking recovery (see How Much Is That?).

The engine of this spectacular growth was government spending. By raising corporate and individual taxes and borrowing money, the federal government pumped an unprecedented $100 billion annually ($1.5 billion today) into war-related production as well as clothing, feeding, arming, and transporting the armed forces. Wartime spending in turn created full employment for farmers and workers—and robust profits for business.

As soon as the United States entered the war, Roosevelt invited business leaders to Washington, D.C., appointing several to run key government agencies. Of these, the powerful War Production Board awarded war contracts worth billions of dollars to various industries and offered auto manufacturers and other businesses subsidies and tax breaks as incentives for converting to war production. To sweeten the deal, the Department of Justice suspended most of its antitrust lawsuits (initiated against a number of corporations during the New Deal) and offered to build new plants for the manufacturers, free of charge.

Big business benefited from this partnership more than small enterprise, winning over the great majority of war contracts and growing even larger as a result. Government preferred big business because, as Roosevelt put it, victory required an "overwhelming [and] crushing superiority of equipment," which only the nation's manufacturing giants could deliver. Federal-corporate cooperation engendered a close and lasting relationship between the two, fostering a new economic sector (the defense industry) that still provides employment for millions of Americans today. By 1945, new and converted factories had turned out 196,000 airplanes, 86,000 tanks, 6,500 ships, and over 15 million rifles—outproducing the enemy Axis powers by a ratio of four to one.

How Much Is That?

Mobilizing for War

Mobilization for the war lifted the American economy out of the Great Depression, but it also cost the U.S. government an unprecedented $280 billion—or the equivalent of a whopping $3.5 trillion today.

AMERICANS ON THE MOVE

The proliferation and expansion of war industries accelerated urban migration. That trend only intensified as the war wore on. The departure of millions of men for military service created a labor shortage, especially in urban industries, just as demand began to climb. Rural migrants stepped into the jobs. California's shipyards and airplane industry attracted over two million people, while many poor white southerners flocked to the enormous shipyards of Virginia and the factories of the Midwest. By mid-1942, the highways were packed, bumper-to-bumper, as migrant families made their way to Los Angeles, Oakland, Atlanta, Detroit, and

SINGULAR LIVES

Ben Kuroki, U.S. Airman

In the days following the bombing of Pearl Harbor, hundreds of thousands of young Americans volunteered for the armed forces. Among these patriots, Ben Kuroki and his brother Fred drove 150 miles to a recruiting station in their home state of Nebraska. Initially rejected as "unfit for service" due to their Japanese American heritage, the brothers made their way to another station and were instantly accepted by a recruiting agent whose more pressing concern was the $2 commission he received for each recruit. Ben Kuroki became a tail-gunner in a B-24, one of the few Japanese Americans permitted to fly bombing missions for the U.S. Army Air Force. By the end of the war, he was among the most decorated airmen in the service.

Born in small-town Nebraska during World War I, Kuroki was one of ten children of Japanese immigrant parents. Kuroki enjoyed the same childhood as most other Nebraskan children, experiencing virtually none of the discrimination and enmity that the *Nisei* (children of Japanese immigrants) suffered on the Pacific coast. But in training camp, Kuroki was bewildered to discover that many of his fellow airmen considered him racially inferior. He learned that the best way to survive was to do his job well while attracting minimal attention. When Kuroki's squadron received orders to ship out to the Pacific, he was grounded because the Army forbade Japanese Americans from entering combat. Bitterly disappointed, he pleaded to be posted to Europe. Noting the airman's exemplary record, the commanding officer consented.

Despite the grueling bombing missions, Europe proved a welcome respite from discrimination. Like Kuroki's childhood friends in Nebraska, Europeans accepted him first and foremost as the American he had always been. Gradually, his white crew came to respect and admire him, nicknaming him "Honorable Son." They flew a punishing thirty missions over German targets, stopping only when they were shot down over fascist Spanish territory. Kuroki and the crew were held captive for three months until the State Department negotiated their release. The young tail-gunner returned to the United States, where he was awarded the first of three Distinguished Flying Crosses.

In 1944, as the army grew desperate for more recruits, the government turned to untapped populations, such as the 110,000 interned Japanese Americans. The army now championed the exceptional young airman as an example of its supposedly enlightened policies—and as someone who could persuade internees to enlist. Sought out by the press and radio, Kuroki received rousing applause at public appearances in New York and San Francisco. But he still suffered discrimination. "I don't know for sure if it's safe to walk the streets of my own country," he reflected sadly, having been refused hotel, taxicab, and restaurant service. He was appalled to learn that the vast majority of Japanese soldiers—like African Americans—served in their own segregated regiments. Returning to battle in the Pacific, he was nearly killed by a knife-wielding GI who screamed "Damn the Japs!"

After the war, Kuroki campaigned against racism and became the first Japanese American to own and edit an English-language newspaper. "Not only did I go to war to fight the fascist ideas of Germany and Japan," he explained on a nationwide speaking tour, "but also to fight against a few Americans who fail to understand the principles of freedom and equality upon which this country was founded." He had flown a record fifty-eight missions during the war, but, he declared, "I've got one more mission to go . . . the fight against prejudice and race hatred. I call it my 59th mission, and I have a hunch I won't be fighting alone."

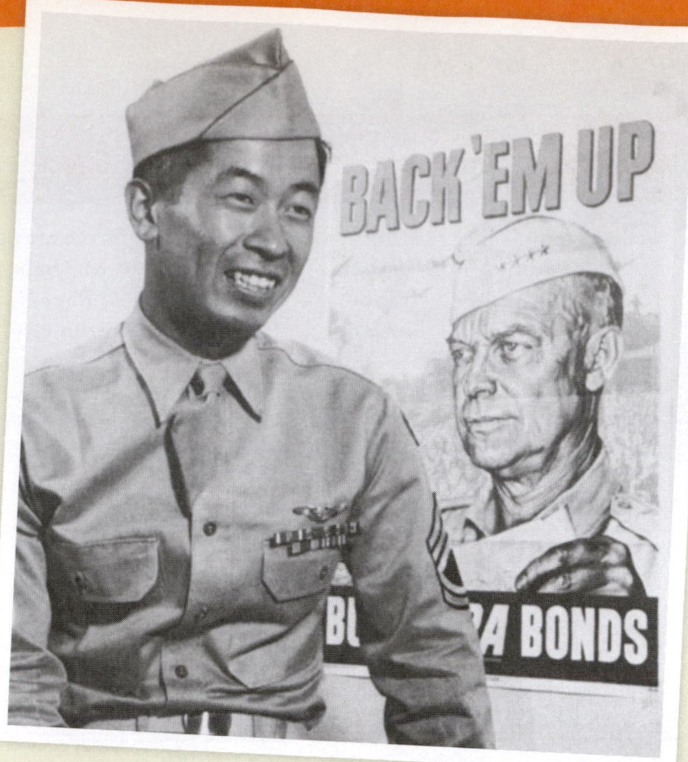

Fighting Injustice at Home and Abroad. Decorated airman Ben Kuroki helped the government recruit interned Japanese Americans to the war effort. After the war, he campaigned for full civil rights for minorities.

Think About It

1. Although a Japanese American, Ben Kuroki did not experience discrimination until he tried to enlist in the military. What might this say about regional variations in race relations?
2. How might Kuroki's military experience have changed him? How might his service have changed the attitudes of his crew and superior officers?

other "arsenals of democracy" (see Map 25.2). "It made me think of *The Grapes of Wrath*," one California migrant reflected, "minus the poverty and hopelessness."

Many white women were especially eager to step into factory jobs, from which most had been previously barred. The War Production Board and other federal agencies worked with business to recruit housewives, while millions of other women quit their low-wage jobs for the war industries. Whereas women had made up just one-quarter of the national labor force before the war, by 1945 they accounted for one-third of

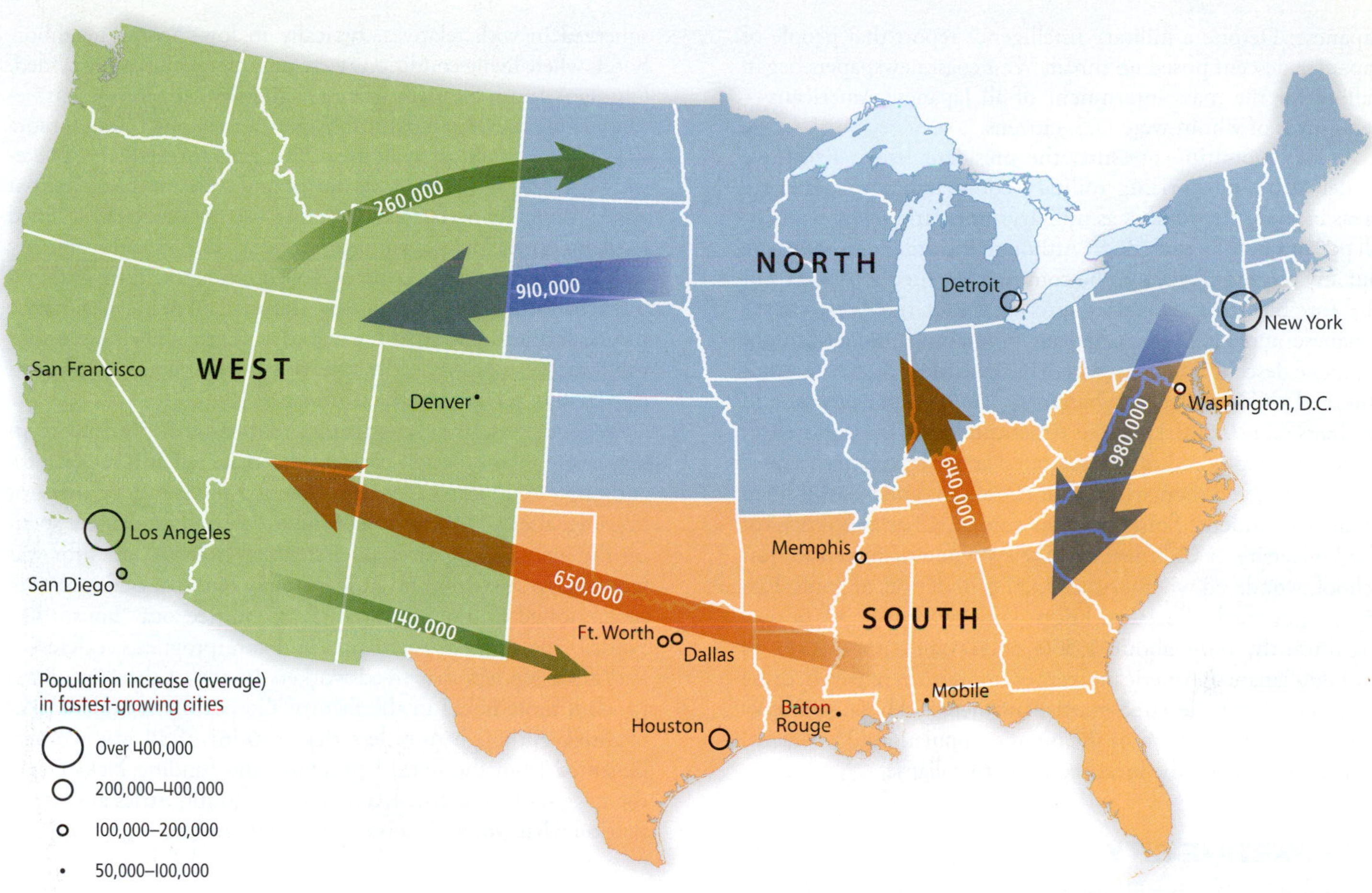

Map 25.2 Mobile America, 1940–1950. The war accelerated U.S. urbanization and drew hundreds of thousands of migrants to shipyards and to factories churning out armaments and other essential war manufactures.

all workers. For the first time, women became postal deliverers, bus drivers, welders, riveters, and mechanics.

Demand for food climbed sharply during the war, with the result that the U.S. government reversed its Depression-era policy of expelling Mexican nationals. In 1942, hundreds of thousands of ***braceros*** (literally, "helping arms") entered the United States legally as a massive agricultural labor force. Meanwhile, tens of thousands of Mexican Americans sought better-paying employment in California's war industries. Although initially shut out by employers and white-dominated unions, tens of thousands found well-paying positions in shipyards and factories as demand for skilled labor skyrocketed.

Joining the war workforce also appealed to African Americans, many of whom had long endured poverty and segregation in the South or been excluded from skilled labor in northern industry. Tens of thousands moved to California seeking work in the humming shipyards and airplane assembly lines, establishing a large presence in San Francisco and Oakland and more than doubling Los Angeles' black community. But most looked for industrial work in Detroit, Chicago, and the other more familiar cities of the Midwest and Northeast.

Although they found employment, minorities still encountered racial discrimination as employers consistently passed over them for jobs and promotions. In 1941, A. Philip Randolph planned a massive protest march on Washington, D.C. President Roosevelt, concerned that the march would divide Americans and provide grist for the Nazi propaganda mill, immediately issued an executive order banning racial discrimination by any employer with a government contract. The Fair Employment Practices Commission was appointed to enforce the order, and Randolph called off the march. Although many employers initially resisted the order, the rising demand for workers eventually led them to hire large numbers of African Americans. Black workers were denied most managerial positions, but by 1943, the number in skilled positions more than doubled.

For many Japanese Americans, however, wartime mobility was neither hopeful nor just. Although the United States was at war with Germany, Italy, and Japan, the government singled out Japanese Americans alone as high security risks. In California especially, years of racial prejudice toward people of Japanese descent and other Asian Americans bubbled over into outright hatred following Pearl Harbor. Several attacks occurred, sometimes against Chinese Americans mistaken for

Japanese. Despite a military intelligence report that people of Japanese descent posed no threat, West coast newspapers began calling for the mass internment of all Japanese Americans—two-thirds of whom were U.S. citizens.

Under mounting pressure, the president issued Executive Order 9066, authorizing military commanders to designate areas in the United States as military zones "from which any or all persons may be excluded." Although the order did not single out any one ethnic group, the commanders used it to carry out the forcible relocation and internment of the West coast's Japanese and Japanese American population. (Americans of Japanese descent living elsewhere in the United States were not interned.) Compelled to abandon their homes, schools, and businesses, 110,000 Japanese Americans were incarcerated in remote barbed-wired camps scattered across the western states. Most considered themselves loyal Americans and were stunned at their treatment. Some, such as student Charles Kikucki of the University of California, Berkeley, who was forced to quit school, wondered whether the "U.S. is in danger of going Fascist too, or maybe Socialist. I don't know what to think or do." Significantly, only about 1,500 of Hawaii's population of 220,000 Japanese Americans were ever interned, in part because FDR had already declared martial law there and because interning such a large portion of the islands' population (35 percent) would have caused the local economy to collapse.

THE WARTIME CITY

The rise of fascism abroad and the sweeping mobilization for war permanently changed the size and character of American cities (see Spaces and Places: Washington, D.C., Global Capital). With events in Europe came an exodus of painters, writers, filmmakers, and other artists—many, though not all, Jewish—from Germany and elsewhere. As the Nazis stormed through Europe, a mass of artists and intellectuals relocated to New York City, where they discovered a vibrant population of American thinkers and artists. Together, these communities turned New York into the capital of the art world and a global center of intellectual life.

Other Europeans fled to Los Angeles, turning parts of that city into "Berlin in exile." European Jews had long been an important presence in Los Angeles, having played a leading role in the creation of the movie industry—a relatively new enterprise that, unlike publishing and many older industries, was open to Jews. As émigré writers and artists took up residence in Westwood and nearby areas, a city that had revolved around private home life acquired a dynamic public culture of cafés, restaurants, and nightlife—more like the cosmopolitan cities of Europe. Many émigrés also brought with them a greater openness about sexuality and sexual expression. The movie industry reflected these changes, with émigré actresses such as Greta Garbo and Marlene Dietrich bringing the European-style *femme fatale* to American audiences.

Meanwhile, the mass migration of rural folk to the city brought with it an acute housing shortage and consequent overcrowding. In the industrial cities, African Americans mostly squeezed in with relatives, typically in low-income neighborhoods where living conditions were unsanitary and overcrowded. Chicago's South Side, for instance, grew by 50 percent as it became home to 300,000 African Americans, about 100,000 more than the area could safely house. Other migrants settled in makeshift shantytowns outside city limits and near war factories that had sprouted up on farmland. Both settlement patterns strained local fire departments, garbage services, schools, and policing well beyond capacity. As parents went to work, their children often wandered the streets or were dropped off at the local movie theater for the duration of the workday. Racial and class tensions mounted, leading to deadly race riots in Harlem, Detroit, and dozens of other cities in the summer of 1943.

Federal agencies subsequently spent some $350 million on services for the besieged cities under the Lanham Act (1940). Although legislators had never intended the law to be used for housing, after 1943 almost half the authorized funds were spent on the manufacture of easily assembled housing units for war workers. To save time and money, many of the new homes were prefabricated in assembly lines that churned out "houses like Fords." The rest was spent on child-care programs, cafeterias, and other services that freed workers (many of them mothers) to work more hours in the factory. Corporations built similar facilities. Although only less than a third of all war workers benefited from the federal program, the funding kick-started the flagging U.S. construction and design industries and set in motion what would be a postwar suburban housing boom.

CONSUMER CULTURE IN WARTIME

World War II was not just a war of production; it was also a war of consumption. Wartime conversion generated huge demand for a wide range of materials found in common consumer goods. Consequently, the government called on consumers to curtail their use of everything from silk stockings (reserving the silk for use in parachutes) to automobiles (which depended on valuable rubber, steel, and gasoline). Household recycling was mandated on a scale that was unprecedented and that has not been seen since. Paper became scarce, and the government even considered suspending the advertising industry for the war's duration. Advertising agencies hastily made themselves relevant by promoting patriotism, federal wartime programs, and collective sacrifice. In Hollywood, a new conception of the nation emerged—an America that celebrated diversity and pulled together in the fight against fascism.

CONSUMERS, RATIONING, AND SACRIFICE

Beginning in early 1942, the federal war machine introduced rationing, which both limited the availability of many consumer products and evenly distributed them across the population to make it harder for the wealthy and profiteers to stockpile scarce goods. The government also issued guidelines for the recycling of metals, fats, and other household waste. Many

SPACES & PLACES

Washington, D.C., Global Capital

Perhaps no U.S. city was as transformed by the war as Washington, D.C. An influx of thousands of diplomats and Allied military officers turned the city from an almost sleepy town into the symbolic and practical capital of the free world. Over 130,000 Americans moved to the District of Columbia to staff the wartime federal agencies, almost doubling the city's population—and triggering a housing crisis. Most of the newcomers were female clerical workers, but many became uniformed members of the Women's Auxiliary Army Corps (WAAC, which later became the WAC). With so many local men shipping out to war, the city's gender ratio became heavily skewed toward women. Both white and African American women found new opportunities for employment, and the WAAC struck an unusual blow for racial justice by enlisting proportionately equal numbers of both.

Washington, D.C., War Capital. Wartime conversion even extended to the capital's Mall, where dozens of cheap, hastily constructed buildings accommodated new federal agencies.

The physical appearance and feeling of the city also changed dramatically. For the first time since the Civil War, Washington was fortified. Antiaircraft guns were installed on the city's periphery, and air-raid sirens were mounted on buildings. Complete blackouts of the city occurred on a regular basis. Even the taxicabs were retrofitted to serve as ambulances in the event of an air raid. The White House got its first permanent security guards, and bayonet-wielding marines guarded important sites such as the Capitol building. Dozens of prefabricated buildings were put up to accommodate federal agencies. These were disassembled after the war, but other buildings, such as the Pentagon, were permanent—a continuing reminder of the nation's new role in the world and the growing importance of the military in government and American life.

Think About It

1. In what ways were the changes in the nation's capital similar to changes under way in other cities during the war? What was different?
2. What was so unusual, in 1942, about the WAAC's decision to enlist proportionately equal numbers of African American and white women? Why might this policy have been especially significant in a city like Washington, D.C.?

consumers voluntarily boosted the flow of essential materials into war production by rummaging through their attics and cellars for items like old copper alarm clocks, rubber water bottles, and brass bedsteads. Neighborhood businesses encouraged such resourcefulness and served as collection points for salvageable junk, while government-employed songwriters filled the airwaves with catchy jingles like "Junk Ain't Junk No More ('Cause It Will Win the War)" and "Cash Your Trash."

All adult citizens were issued ration books containing stamps and coupons with which they paid for goods. Rubber was withdrawn from the market altogether (leading to a shortage of tires), the paper that books and magazines were printed on was rationed, and toys contained so many essential materials that the industry almost collapsed. Authorities forbade motorists to drive faster than 35 miles per hour and allotted just two gallons of gas each week per household. Long-distance vacations consequently became difficult for most people and became illegal in 1943, when auto travel for pleasure was banned. By then, coffee, fats, meats, sugar, and canned vegetables were all rationed. Most of these foodstuffs were redirected to servicemen and servicewomen, who, when not in combat, consumed a remarkable five thousand calories a day, making them the best-fed military in the world.

Rationing fundamentally altered everyday life and made private decisions about household consumption an important public matter. Consumerism and "the American way" seemed remote from wartime realities. But the great majority of Americans cooperated with the new system and looked for creative ways to fill the gap. Many recycled their existing wardrobes, refashioning old wool suits to make more fashionable items. Homemade clothing became so commonplace that the sewing pattern business boomed. (Some people resisted the conservative trend, however; see Hot Commodities: The Zoot Suit.) With guidance from the Department of Agriculture, citizens planted over twenty million "victory gardens" and were eating so many vegetables by the war's end that vitamin intake rose by over 10 percent (a boom in supplements also helped). Consumers substituted fish and eggs for meat and ate meals at the factory cafeteria or at new drive-in "car-hop" restaurants—neither of which was subject to meat rationing and both of which offered what would soon be known as "fast food."

A black market also thrived, and the majority of people used it some of the time. The rationing system of coupons, ration books, and blackout dates was complex and difficult to follow, even for the patriotic majority. Although designed to keep the flow of goods relatively steady, rationing sometimes resulted in rushes and long shortages, particularly of food. Millions of Americans went without meat, for example, in the harsh winter of 1942–1943 because of widespread hording in advance of stricter rationing.

Consequently, "Mr. Black," as the illegal market in rationed goods was known, stepped up. Criminal syndicates (many of which had provided liquor during Prohibition) printed counterfeit coupons or stole legitimate ones for gas and tires and sold them at a substantial markup. One in five legitimate businesses also looked for ways to dodge rationing laws, particularly in the meat industry. Although the government charged almost 15 percent of the nation's merchants with breaches of the ration laws, the courts mostly treated them leniently. The practice of supplementing rations was commonplace, and the courts were reluctant to undermine patriotism at such a crucial time.

SELLING THE "GOOD WAR"

The war first threatened and then saved the advertising business. Initially deemed a wasteful "nonessential industry" by the federal government, advertising enterprises faced the possibility of heavy taxation or even closure for the duration of the war. But advertisers fought back, seeking to persuade the government that advertising was in fact essential. By promoting military recruitment, women's work, wartime rationing, and other government initiatives, advertisers strove to win government approval. They understood that appealing to Americans' intense wartime patriotism was the best way to strengthen consumers' faith in business, explain why certain goods and services were in short supply, and build consumer loyalty for the time when peace and mass consumption would return.

Advertisers worked through the War Advertising Council, a nonprofit organization that consulted with the government and encouraged "A War Message in Every Ad." The letter V (for victory) became ubiquitous in magazine advertisements,

"Tonight
I leaned across
10,000 miles and
kissed you!"
COPYRIGHT 1943 THE GRUEN WATCH COMPANY — PRINTED IN U. S. A.

Staying Relevant. As metals, cloth, and other materials were diverted to the war effort and mass consumption fell drastically, manufacturers and department stores kept their brands in circulation with the help of patriotic war-themed advertisements like this 1943 ad for Gruen watches.

HOT COMMODITIES

The Zoot Suit

The fashion industry prospered during the war despite textile rationing. Clothing styles changed dramatically in these years. The rationing of wool, silk, nylon, and other textiles inspired shorter, boxier designs that used less fabric. And with government publicity encouraging consumers to economize, lavish self-presentation—even by movie stars—became socially unacceptable. Bucking the strict new conventions, however, many young men sported suits with unusually long, wide-shouldered jackets and pleated trousers "pegged" at the ankle.

Originally worn by a handful of Harlem jazz musicians in the late 1930s, these "zoot suits" caught on among youth, particularly urban African Americans and Mexican Americans. Brightly colored and typically worn in conjunction with a duck-tailed hairstyle and wide-brimmed sombrero, the zoot suit was the pride of many young Mexican Americans' wardrobe. Adding to the garments' expense was the fact that the "drapes" were usually tailor made (because clothing manufacturers were subject to rationing laws) and a large quantity of fabric was required to make them. Young men saved up all their wages to buy just one suit, and friends exchanged drapes. Ideal for dancing due to its pegged trouser cuff, the zoot suit was a bold expression of status and personal freedom.

The Zoot Suit. By the war's end, fashion-conscious white youth were sporting the controversial look popularized by young Mexican Americans and African Americans, and many ex-soldiers soon joined them.

In the eyes of many white Americans, the zoot suit was an unpatriotic waste of essential war material and an insult to the principle of personal sacrifice. Syndicated comic strip artist Al Capp singled out the zoot suit as a symbol of subversion and treachery, ending one cartoon strip with a mob rampaging through clothing stores, destroying the offending suits. The fact that most "zoot suiters" were minorities further encouraged critics to view the wearers as un-American draft dodgers and delinquents. Los Angeles' growing Mexican American community fell under special scrutiny. Although the proportion of the Mexican American population that served in the military was higher than any other group's (see Table 25.1), white Californians worried that these men were unpatriotic and were taking valuable jobs and housing (and possibly white women, too). Soon Los Angeles police were routinely beating and arresting young zoot suiters.

Tensions boiled over in 1943, when a group of white sailors on shore leave reported that several "Mexicans" had attacked them. (The incident was a typical barroom brawl that had begun when two Anglo sailors tried to pick up two Mexican American women.) Over two hundred sailors swarmed into the Mexican American barrio, singling out every zoot suiter they encountered and ordering them to strip their pants or face a beating. The police joined the melee, arresting and beating the victims. The **zoot suit sailor riots** lasted for five nights, during which thousands of soldiers, marines, police officers, and sailors "pantsed" hundreds of zoot suiters, shredding their jackets and dishing out beatings to "offenders" who resisted. Many zoot suiters were forcibly given a military haircut, too. Miraculously, no zoot suiter died; the sailors' chief target was actually the suit itself. Indeed, the men in uniform wanted most to destroy the symbol of two precious things they had been compelled to sacrifice: freedom of choice and their individuality.

Think About It

1. Why do you think young Mexican American men favored the expensive and stylish zoot suit over other forms of dress during the war?
2. Why did the rioters target the zoot suit and forcibly trim the young men's hair?
3. What might the duration of the riots and the fact that the police joined the rioters tell us about what it was like being young, Mexican American, and male in wartime Los Angeles?

on billboards, and even on clothing and in women's hairstyles. Corporate film departments cranked out dozens of movies that celebrated their company's contribution to wartime production. Some advertisers barely mentioned the products they were advertising and focused mostly on the patriotic message. Many popularized the idea that Americans were fighting for "the American way"—or what corporations were now calling the **Fifth Freedom** (after FDR's Four Freedom's speech). Picking up where the New York World's Fair left off, they pushed the idea that, after the war, business should be free of regulation.

At a time when women were streaming into industrial labor, advertising forged new images of ideal womanhood that promoted the recruitment of women into factory work. "These jobs will have to be glorified," the federal government advised, "as a patriotic war service if American women are to be persuaded to take them and stick to them." The standard Depression-era image of the highly feminine, stay-at-home mom gave way to images of physically capable welders and victory gardeners and of heroic nurses and ambulance drivers—all proudly and happily doing their part. The widespread image of "Rosie the Riveter" became symbolic of women's war effort (see Interpreting the Sources: Imagining Rosie the Riveter).

Advertisers' war promotions paid off handsomely, with revenues growing about 70 percent between 1941 and 1945. Advertisers also worked for the government, which hired thousands of artists, photographers, writers, and filmmakers for its chief propaganda organ, the Office of War Information (OWI, established 1942). The OWI pumped out millions of colorful posters urging citizens to buy war bonds, recycle essential materials, plant victory gardens, and resist the temptation to discuss the location of their loved ones serving abroad. "Loose Lips Sink Ships!" advised one poster, and

INTERPRETING THE SOURCES

Imagining Rosie the Riveter

Millions of married and single American women entered the industrial workforce for the first time during World War II, spurred on by recruitment campaigns and the imaginary wartime heroine "Rosie the Riveter." Rosie first appeared in a hit song as a champion riveter on a warplane assembly line who was "making history [and] working for victory." Images of various Rosies subsequently surfaced in popular magazines and in-house publications, as well as on recruitment posters, and the name became shorthand for women war workers. Norman Rockwell's famous interpretation, in which Rosie strikes the same saintly pose as Isaiah in Michelangelo's Sistine Chapel fresco, appeared on the cover of *The Saturday Evening Post* in 1943. Like other artists and advertisers, Rockwell tried to strike a balance between new ideals of female toughness and older ideals of a soft, unthreatening femininity. Rosie disappeared from advertising after the war, when business, the government, and returning servicemen called on women to return to the home.

Explore the Source

1. In what ways does Rockwell's Rosie depart from the feminine norms of the 1930s?
2. Why do you think Rockwell chose a biblical figure as a model for Rosie?
3. Why might Rosie have been such an appealing image during the war?

PRODUCTION
Stop this monster that stops at nothing... PRODUCE to the limit!
This is YOUR war!

The Face of the Enemy. Visual portrayals of the enemy were crucial in the OWI's campaign to promote the "good war," and the government collaborated with artists, museums, and advertisers to communicate the apparent evilness of the enemy. Germans were often portrayed as heartless autocrats and murderers, whereas the Japanese were almost always shown as vicious, subhuman "monkeymen."

"Keep It Under Your Stetson!" warned another. Such rousing appeals gave Americans concrete advice on how to contribute to the war effort. Appearing in restaurants, town squares, school canteens, and highways, visual propaganda also impressed upon Americans that regardless of their differences, they were in the fight together. (The race riots of 1943, however, demonstrated the limits of this feeling of camaraderie.)

Depicting combat proved more difficult. Government propaganda oscillated between sanitized depictions of heroic soldiers marching into combat in crisp, neatly pressed uniforms and bloody images of mangled servicemen supposedly killed because someone "blabbed." As one frustrated newspaper editor complained, OWI officials were "alternately [dosing] the public with stimulants and depressants in accordance with the mood they desire to create." But Americans remained committed to the war.

PATRIOTIC HOLLYWOOD

Like the advertising industry, Hollywood eagerly pitched in on the war effort. Despite its self-policing efforts in the 1930s, the movie industry retained an aura of moral corruption and remained a favorite target of evangelical Protestants, the Catholic Church, and anticommunist investigators. The Department of Justice was also investigating the big studios for breach of antitrust laws. The war presented Hollywood with a perfect opportunity to prove that it was an upstanding institution, worthy of respect and official approval.

Thousands of technicians, directors, and actors volunteered for military or civilian service. Clark Gable and Jimmy Stewart were among those who enlisted—in so doing, contributing to a shortage of leading men. Bette Davis, Rita Hayworth, and other glamorous stars led rallies for war bonds, appeared at military recruitment drives, and dressed down (so as to publicly observe the spirit

Rise of the Pinup. One of Hollywood's first and most popular "pinup girls," Rita Hayworth presented a picture of wholesome American femininity and a fantasy of sexual encounter. Aimed at lonely troops far from home, such images appeared in countless U.S. military lockers, tents, tanks, bomber planes, and barracks around the world. Although far less explicit than most fashion magazines are today, pinups pushed the boundaries of conventional 1940s decency—and, after the war, stirred demand for more explicit sexual imagery among millions of returning troops.

of clothing rations). Many helped out as dishwashers and servers in soldiers' canteens, which became makeshift theaters where soldiers saw performances and got to meet the stars. All told, the Hollywood Victory Committee sent almost seven thousand actors, actresses, comedians, and musicians overseas to entertain the troops and raise morale.

Dozens of directors made movies with war themes. Distinguished director Frank Capra became an army officer and filmed a series of *Why We Fight* documentaries that millions of soldiers watched. On the home front, the big studios enthusiastically cooperated with federal agencies such as the OWI's Bureau of Motion Pictures (BMP), which encouraged the studios to produce prowar films for civilians (and censored any that cast the war effort or the United States in a negative light). "At every opportunity," BMP guidelines implored, "show people bringing their own sugar when invited out to dinner, carrying their own parcels when shopping . . . uncomplainingly giving up their seats for servicemen . . . accepting dim-out restrictions, tire and gas rationing cheerfully." Even westerns, musicals, and other genres that were not explicitly about the war were subject to censorship and promoted wartime goals.

Authorities decreed that the United States' allies were also to be treated sympathetically following protests in U.S.-occupied Iceland about a Hollywood movie that portrayed local men as moronic peasants who lost their girlfriends to suave American GIs. The BMP made it clear that presenting the Soviet Union positively was especially important now that it was an ally. Both Hollywood and the magazine industry obliged, and Roosevelt made a point of sending a film favorable to the Soviets, *Mission to Moscow*, directly to Joseph Stalin in 1943 with a note assuring him that the United States "has no axes to grind."

Directors relished the opportunity to break from the escapist fare of the Depression and early war period and to instead make films about something as consequential and noble as the war. Observed one industry reporter, "No longer is it necessary to cloak the more serious thoughts . . . behind a melodramatic yarn or sugarcoat the message." With the encouragement of the federal government, many filmmakers defined their own "American way"—a vision of the United States as a diverse but unified society. Popular Depression-era films in which the super-rich were ignored, vilified, or ridiculed gave way to movies that showed big business in a positive light, working harmoniously with government and labor in a common cause. On the silver screen, workers did not strike and consumers willingly sacrificed for the good of the nation. Most significantly, the United States was an ethnically, and occasionally racially, inclusive society, in stark contrast to fascist Germany and Japan. The nation's strength, according to Hollywood's **pluralist nationalist** vision, derived from the unification of all Americans as a single people.

Groundbreaking scenes showed ethnically diverse and racially integrated battalions that included African Americans, even though in reality the armed forces were still segregated. Irish, Italian, Latino, Jewish, and African American men battled heroically, side by side. In Alfred Hitchcock's popular film *Lifeboat* (1944), an African American serviceman helps disarm a Nazi in a scene that buoyed hopes that the armed forces might soon integrate. Japanese Americans, however, were conspicuously absent from the films because of widespread prejudice and the fact that the actors had been interned. Chinese American actors were usually assigned the role of the despised Japanese enemy since directors believed that most Americans could not tell Asians apart.

Such films proved popular, although servicemen considered the depictions of combat absurd and preferred escapist movies. Cinemas sold U.S. war bonds (accounting for more than 20 percent of sales). The federal government dropped its antitrust investigations, and box office sales and studio profits soared to record highs. Hollywood had at last attained the official acceptance it craved. But the industry had changed along the way. Movies on controversial topics such as poverty and racial and class conflict were no longer acceptable. "We'll

War Films for Women. Two popular new genres, both designed to stoke morale, entered Hollywood's repertoire in the war years: the combat movie and the "weepy," or women's, film. Some combat films featured a male shirker who subsequently had a life-altering experience (such as falling in love) that inspired him to join the war effort. The popular weepy *Since You Went Away* told the story of a mother and her two daughters patriotically coping with food shortages, planting victory gardens, enduring erratic train service, and building bombs. **Questions for Analysis:** Why did Hollywood create films primarily for female audiences? How might weepies have helped women get through the war?

have no more *Grapes of Wrath*," one industry leader warned the Screen Writers Guild in 1945, "no more films that deal with the seamy side of American life . . . [or] that treat the banker as a villain." This conservative impulse would strengthen as the war ended.

YANKS ABOUT TOWN

In the course of the war, millions of American servicemen and servicewomen were stationed in or near dozens of overseas cities, including Sydney, Australia; Paris, France; and Cairo, Egypt. As they spread their consumerist values, Coca-Cola, nylon stockings, and Camel cigarettes gained global circulation for the first time, both as consumer goods and as emblems of American democracy. Although swing had already won an international following, the U.S. military helped turn it into a global symbol of anti-fascism and a morale builder for the troops. The Armed Forces Network (AFN), which broadcast to troops at home and around the world, played more swing than any other genre, as did the OWI's radio station, the Voice of America, which aired from over forty stations worldwide by the war's end.

AFN shows included the romantic, big-band music of Glenn Miller, aimed primarily at white audiences, and "Jubilee," which featured African American bands. Miller and hundreds of other jazz musicians enlisted and were deployed all over the world. By 1943, swing was so popular that both the Nazis and the Japanese broadcast their own versions in the vain hope that Allied troops would switch sides.

Other performers toured under the auspices of the United Service Organization (USO), a voluntary group that located halls, barns, and spacious outdoor venues for the purpose of staging almost three hundred thousand musical, comedic, and other shows for the troops. Whether bored and waiting for deployment or exhausted and shell shocked, troops were hungry for the sweet sights and sounds of home.

The performances brought back "something of those days when we were all happy and free," one serviceman explained. The shows also bolstered Hollywood's claims that the entertainment industries were patriotic, essential contributors to the fight.

WAGING WAR

The overseas war effort presented immense military, diplomatic, and personal challenges—many, unforeseen. Although President Roosevelt had originally planned for U.S. troops to join the British in a joint invasion of German-occupied Europe, the United States struck first and hardest against Japan in the Pacific. U.S. troops soon became embroiled in extremely bloody warfare in which neither side took prisoners and both treated the enemy as subhuman. Meanwhile, the Soviet Union's gains against the Germans in eastern Europe led the president to rethink his approach to the postwar peace. Roosevelt pragmatically recognized the reality of Soviet and British spheres of interest and insisted that the Allies recognize those of the United States. Instead of calling for one big postwar conference, as Woodrow Wilson had done at Versailles, the United States convened many smaller meetings with the British and Soviets during the war. Roosevelt gradually hammered out a plan for the United Nations, which he saw as essential to postwar peace, security, and U.S. interests.

Coca-Cola: Refreshing the World. Corporal William Jones washes down a doughnut with a Coke after his liberation from a German POW camp in 1945. Already one of the nation's most popular beverages, the nonalcoholic and distinctively bottled "soft drink" Coca-Cola was distributed in vast quantities to servicemen and servicewomen in place of "hard" alcoholic beverages. Military personnel loved the sweet, caffeinated product and the price—a nickel a bottle, half the usual cost. By war's end, Coke was a leading symbol of the United States and the world's best-selling consumer product.

THE BIG THREE

Immediately following the U.S. declaration of war in 1941, Roosevelt commended the new "Grand Alliance" among the United States, the Soviet Union, and Great Britain (the "Big Three") and reiterated his pledge of putting Europe first, ahead of the Pacific war. The besieged Allies heaved a sigh of relief. But U.S. entry did not immediately reverse fascism's onslaught in either Europe or the Pacific. German troops thrust deep into Soviet territory in 1942, in search of oil, wheat, and a compliant labor force. Millions of Soviet civilians and soldiers perished in the defense of their homeland—more than the U.S., British, and French fatalities combined. At the same time, Germany invaded North Africa, threatening vital trade routes, and stepped up its U-boat attacks in the Atlantic.

Desperate for help, the Soviets urgently pressed their allies to launch a massive invasion of western Europe across the English Channel to divert German troops from the Soviet Union. U.S. war strategy called for such an invasion—dubbed Operation Overlord—but with the American war industries just beginning to meet production goals, the United States was in no position in 1942 to carry it out. Such an attack became possible the following year, but British strategy complicated matters. Although Churchill assured the Soviets that Operation Overlord would proceed in the spring of 1943, he in fact waged many small-scale attacks on the war's periphery, near Britain's valuable colonies. A brilliant and ruthless strategist, Churchill was in no hurry to relieve the Soviets' suffering, probably calculating that a weaker Soviet Union would be less threatening to British interests in the long run.

Roosevelt reluctantly deferred to Churchill, sending U.S. troops to North Africa in 1942 on the British insistence that Nazi-controlled Europe should be retaken initially from the

Map 25.3 The Allied Advance in Africa and Europe. By the end of summer 1943, the Allies had opened two fronts in the European war. With British prime minister Winston Churchill refusing to open a Western Front until relatively late in the war, Soviet soldiers and civilians fought more battles and lost more lives (fourteen to seventeen million civilians and soldiers) than any other ally—a fact that later bolstered Soviet claims over eastern Europe. As this map illustrates, the Soviets had severely weakened Axis forces by the time British and U.S. forces launched an assault on Nazi-occupied France.

south. In November, British and U.S. troops carried out Operation TORCH, invading French North Africa (then under the control of Vichy France, the portion of France that had allied with Nazi Germany in an effort to avert full occupation). American GIs expected an easy campaign. In fact, the inexperienced, undertrained troops met with fierce resistance from Vichy forces before finally securing Morocco, Oran, and Algiers. Troop training intensified, and in early 1943 the United States and Britain pushed German forces out of Tunisia by using a two-army "pincer movement" to flank the enemy. By May 1943, the Germans had surrendered Africa and all 275,000 troops stationed there. Germany's Mediterranean forces, sent to reinforce Tunisia, had all but collapsed, leaving the Allies in full control of North Africa and with a clear shot across the Mediterranean to southern Europe (see Map 25.3).

The Allied drive into southern Europe came via the Italian island of Sicily in the summer of 1943. The meticulously planned Operation Husky began with a campaign of deception that led the German high command to expect the Allied assault would come not in Italy but in Greece. As Hitler deployed troops to Greek beaches, the Allies unleashed a massive aerial bombing of Sicily's Axis airbases. The largest amphibious (waterborne) operation of the war followed a month later, winning the island for the Allies. Despite careful planning, however, Operation Husky was only moderately successful. The Allies' seizure of Sicily triggered the overthrow of Italian dictator Benito Mussolini and made much of the Mediterranean safe again for Allied shipping. But through poor coordination of their forces, Allied commanders let thousands of German soldiers withdraw and regroup, rendering the Allies' subsequent invasion of Italy far more costly than it might otherwise have been.

As the African and Mediterranean campaigns proceeded, tensions mounted within the Grand Alliance. By early 1943, it was evident to the Soviets that Operation Overlord had stalled. Left to bear the brunt of Nazi aggression, the Soviets grew bitter, particularly with Britain. Roosevelt sent more bomber planes to the Soviet Union and worked hard to restore Soviet confidence in the Alliance. Hitler's fortunes were reversed by the harsh Soviet winter and massive native resistance (which had been fortified with the help of the new U.S. bombers). The Soviets' repulsion of the Germans at Stalingrad in the fall and winter of 1942 cost two million Russian lives and killed or wounded over five hundred thousand Axis soldiers. The battle proved the most decisive of the European war and by mid-1943 the Soviets had pushed Hitler's army back as far as the Baltic states (see Map 25.3). With a new front opening in southern Europe, the Germans were overcommitted, underresourced, and, with the deployment of U.S. forces in North Africa and the Mediterranean, outgunned. It was only a matter of time before the Allies launched a final attack on Germany itself.

RECLAIMING THE PACIFIC

The situation in the Pacific was also bleak for the United States in 1942. While the navy scrambled to recover from the Pearl Harbor raid, Japan was blasting through Filipino and U.S. forces in an effort to take the Philippines, a strategically important country that was a stone's throw away from mineral-rich Australia. (The million barrels of oil that the United States stored just outside Manila were also attractive to the Japanese.) Thousands of U.S. and Filipino troops perished before commanding officer Douglas MacArthur was finally forced to relinquish the Bataan peninsula and flee to Australia. Japanese planes dropped English-language messages on the remaining U.S. and Filipino troops, urging them to surrender and reassuring them of humane treatment, in accordance with international law. Over seventy-five thousand U.S. and Filipino soldiers did surrender. But despite reassurances, around four hundred Filipino officers and soldiers were summarily executed and the rest sent on a grueling sixty-mile march to an abandoned U.S. base. Deprived of food and water and driven at a relentless pace, ten thousand prisoners of war died on the infamous Bataan Death March.

By the summer of 1942, Japan held vital territory in the South Pacific, Southeast Asia, and even the Indian subcontinent (see Map 25.4). The U.S. response—implemented in tandem with Australia and New Zealand—was originally two pronged. General MacArthur would coordinate the retaking of Japanese-occupied islands in the western Pacific while Admiral Chester Nimitz concentrated on attacking Japan and its central Pacific possessions. Ultimately, according to the plan, Allied forces would conduct a massive ground invasion of Japan. Under Nimitz, the U.S. Navy won a strategic victory at the Battle of the Coral Sea in May 1942, using aircraft carrier planes to dive-bomb the Japanese fleet and halt its advance on Australia. The Japanese sank more Allied ships, but the Allies sank some of Japan's best aircraft carriers—and for the first time in the war, Japan had to retreat. A month later, at the Battle of Midway, U.S. dive bombers notched up a second victory, turning back a Japanese bid for islands that could have served as a base from which to bomb the United States. Japan consequently lost its naval superiority, and the door now opened to an American advance. Emboldened, MacArthur's ground troops embarked on the first of several island-hopping campaigns, beginning in the Solomon Islands in 1942 and slowly working their way back to the Philippines in 1944.

Many servicemen in the Pacific and elsewhere spent a lot of time waiting—sometimes for months on end—for deployment to battle. The great majority, having only ever seen combat in movies, were exuberant about the prospect of getting their "hands on the Japs" or taking "a crack" at Germany. "I came here to see action and I hope this is the biggest battle of all time," one seaman wrote home. The possibility of defeat or death rarely entered the troops' minds at that point. "You hear . . . see . . . and read of casualties," explained a serviceman in North Africa, "but you believe it will never happen to you." Once they entered battle, however, such bravado turned to a feeling of absolute powerlessness in the face of the world's most technologically advanced weaponry. After seeing combat, upwards of one in twenty soldiers (313,000) likely suffered from what psychiatrists today call posttraumatic stress disorder (PTSD). "[I was] very emotionally unhinged, maybe for five years after the war," recalled decorated infantryman Paul Fussell, "and at parties I would break into tears."

The savagery of Bataan set the tone for subsequent Pacific battles, all of which were far bloodier and more vicious—on both sides—than anything Americans suffered or inflicted in Europe or North Africa. In the earliest encounters, U.S. soldiers were shocked to find that the Japanese frequently took no prisoners and often bound, tortured, and disemboweled survivors. Weak or injured Japanese soldiers were abandoned to die on their own, whereas Americans tried hard to save their wounded—which, as the enemy understood, left

Map 25.4 The Pacific War. Allied forces pressed slowly but surely northwestward beginning from the Coral Sea and Guadalcanal to the Philippines and eventually on to Iwo Jima and Okinawa. The idea behind this "island-hopping" strategy was to bypass or leapfrog the most heavily fortified Japanese positions and to capture lightly defended islands that could serve as bases from which to attack Japan itself.

them vulnerable to attack. In Japanese warrior culture, surrender was a shameful betrayal of family, nation, and the military. Getting wounded or falling into enemy hands was a disgrace deserving of death. Consequently, Japanese troops did all they could, including suicide bombing, to avoid capture. As grim reality dawned on American GIs, they too began fighting to the bitter end, taking few prisoners and often brutally violating the laws of war. As one officer put it, having witnessed the Japanese style of warfare firsthand, "the old rules of war [underwent] a swift change in me."

The 2000-Yard Stare. The incessant pounding of mechanized artillery and the eerie whistle of incoming shells appearing seemingly out of nowhere shattered the nerves of even the toughest of men. This iconic painting by war correspondent Tom Lea captured the numbing effect that millions of servicemen experienced.

PLANNING THE PEACE

Although victory seemed distant in 1942, Roosevelt had already begun planning the postwar peace. During this early phase, FDR's vision of collective security (first articulated by Churchill and Roosevelt at the Atlantic Conference, which secretly took place on the USS *Augusta* off the coast of Newfoundland in 1941) owed much to former president Woodrow Wilson's idealist internationalism. Wilson's reputation, which had suffered ridicule and scorn through the 1930s, had revived as the costs of not implementing his original vision of international relations became apparent. Popular magazines, movies, plays, and books celebrated the former president's life and legacy—particularly his concept of the League of Nations (which was never fully enacted). At its 1944 national convention, the Democratic Party paid tribute to Wilson for the first time since World War I.

FDR's admiration of his predecessor, however, waned during the war. Studying Wilson's approach at the Versailles treaty negotiations of 1919, FDR was struck by his costly failure to bring about a just peace and a viable system of collective security. Wilson, in FDR's opinion, had overestimated his influence and underestimated the enduring strength of Europe's old balance-of-power system, to ultimately catastrophic effect. Determined not to repeat Wilson's mistakes, FDR abandoned the Wilsonian principle that defeated powers should have a say in the terms of their surrender, and determined that the United States would directly oversee the reconstruction of their governments, economies, and cultures.

Unlike Wilson, Roosevelt embraced power politics and accepted that the British would not disband their empire any more than the Soviets would budge on their wish for a pro-Soviet Eastern Europe. The Soviet Union's stunning repulsion of German forces made it conceivable that Hitler would be beaten sooner rather than later and gave the Soviets new bargaining power. Conversely, Britain's increasing dependency on American armed forces put it in a weaker position. At the Tehran Conference in Iran in late 1943, the United States conceded that, as compensation for their terrible losses, the Soviets could keep most of the Baltic states and large parts of Poland to create a security buffer between Germany and the USSR. The Big Three also agreed to establish an international security organization and to manage the new world order themselves. The Soviets pledged to fight Japan once Hitler had been defeated, and Roosevelt compelled Churchill to expedite Operation Overlord. From that moment on, Great Britain was the junior partner to the American superpower.

By 1944, U.S. foreign policy had adapted to the reality of Soviet and British power while at the same time strengthening its claims to Latin America as an exclusive zone of U.S. interest. Rather than viewing the heavily armed powers as a threat to global security, the president now saw them as the only forces capable of guaranteeing international peace. Work was under way on three international organizations that would stabilize global markets, deter economic depression, and provide collective security. In July 1944, representatives from forty-four nations convened in Bretton Woods, New Hampshire, to establish the World Bank and the International Monetary Fund, which extended loans for postwar reconstruction and development and stabilized global finances. Later that year, the Big Three met with China in Washington, D.C., to draft the Charter of the United Nations. The founding document provided for a strong executive board (the Security Council) composed of Britain, the Soviet Union, France, China, and the United States, and a weaker assembly of member-nations. The following year, the fifty member-nations of the United Nations convened for the first time in San Francisco, California, and unanimously approved the charter.

MARCHING TO BERLIN

Once the United States had asserted its leadership role, Operation Overlord kicked into high gear (see Map 25.3). More than 1.5 million Allied troops departed England in early June 1944 in the world's largest flotilla of vessels. Much as in Sicily, a massive airborne assault softened German defenses before 160,000 troops landed in German-occupied Normandy, France, on D-Day (June 6, 1944). Wave after wave of foot soldiers stormed up the heavily fortified beaches as U.S. paratroopers of the 101st Airborne Division landed behind the beach to destroy enemy gun batteries. German fire felled upwards of 4,200 men, but the Allied infantrymen won a beachhead, allowing reinforcements to go ashore safely.

Three thousand miles away, Soviet forces pinned down German regiments in eastern Europe, making it impossible for Hitler to send reinforcements to France. Attacked on both flanks, the Germans lost Paris and most of Belgium by August. Germany desperately rallied its retreating forces in December in the Battle of the Bulge, causing the Allied advance to bog down. The fatigued German forces were ultimately no match, however, for the combined strength of the Allies.

As Allied forces advanced steadily on Berlin in the fall of 1944, Roosevelt campaigned for his fourth and, as it turned out, final presidential election. New York governor Thomas Dewey won the Republican nomination, and his party once again ran against the New Deal. The president looked tired. Rumors of health trouble circulated in the press. Southern Democrats prevailed on FDR to drop his left-leaning vice president, Henry Wallace, who had spoken out against racism on several occasions, in favor of moderate Missouri senator Harry S Truman. Polls suggested that the Republicans stood a good chance of winning. But U.S. victories on the battlefield and in international diplomacy buoyed the president, as did an open-car tour of several states that scotched rumors of his failing health. FDR won 53 percent of the popular vote and all but ninety-nine electoral votes.

His presidency secured, and an Allied victory all but certain, Roosevelt met secretly with Churchill and Stalin for a third time, on this occasion in Soviet Crimea in February 1945. Each leader entered the Yalta Conference with clear goals for the postwar global order—and each had to make significant compromises. The Soviets were in a strong bargaining position, having made deep incursions into German-held Poland, Hungary, and Czechoslovakia. At Yalta, they made it clear that they were not about to give up those countries. Roosevelt secured an agreement to proceed with a first meeting of the United Nations, the recognition of China as a great power, and a Soviet pledge to join the fight against Japan in the Pacific. But he and the British had to give way on free and fair elections for Poland, and the most they could get from Stalin was a pledge to allow Eastern Europeans to vote on whether they wanted to be independent. Churchill managed to keep Britain's colonies intact but was blocked by the Soviets from giving France a large part of Germany.

The exhausted president returned to the United States confident that American interests had been advanced. Within days, the United States and Britain unleashed a fierce aerial "carpet-bombing" over Dresden, Berlin, and other German cities, killing or seriously wounding over a million civilians and soldiers. Following an address to Congress, Roosevelt retreated to the peace and quiet of Warm Springs, Georgia, for a few days' rest. On April 12, 1945, he suffered a fatal stroke. Americans, Britons, and Soviets alike were rocked by the news of FDR's death. Many U.S. soldiers wept openly, as did Churchill. Republican Senate leader Robert A. Taft called Roosevelt "the greatest figure of our time" and commended him as a man whose "words and actions were more important than those of any other man." To many Americans, Roosevelt was the man who had led the nation out of the worst depression in history and safely through the world's most destructive war. They worried whether they would ever again have a president of his caliber and integrity.

It would fall to Vice President Truman—a man with little diplomatic experience—to end the war and guide the nation to peace. By late April 1945, Soviet troops had arrived on the periphery of Berlin, and the British and Americans were not far off. Having hidden in an underground bunker with his staff, Hitler committed suicide on April 30. Two days later, the Soviets swept through the city, and by the end of the week, Germany had surrendered unconditionally. The European war was over. It had cost the lives of 9,385,000 Allied soldiers—including 9 million Soviet soldiers and 135,576 American servicemen and servicewomen. Upwards of forty-four million civilians, including over twenty-three million in the Soviet Union, had perished.

FACING THE HOLOCAUST

As the Allied soldiers advanced through Germany and Poland, they found grisly evidence of Hitler's **final solution** to "the Jewish problem"—the slaughter of six million Jews and six million communists, Poles, Slavs, Roma (gypsies), gays, Jehovah's Witnesses, and other minorities that the Nazis deemed "un-desirable." In Auschwitz, Buchenwald, and several other locations, soldiers found huge death camps—some containing emaciated survivors—in which the victims had been systematically starved and gassed, or shot as the Nazis retreated.

Documenting the Holocaust. Like most governments, the United States turned a blind eye to the plight of Europe's Jews under Hitler. The State Department withheld entry visas from the majority of Jewish refugees in the 1930s—and turned back a ship containing over nine hundred Jewish exiles from Hamburg, Germany, in 1939. As the mass killings began in 1942, officials decreased the number of visas granted to Jewish exiles. Not until the late 1940s, with the publication of graphic photographs of Nazi death camps in *Life* and other popular newsmagazines, did Americans recognize that the Holocaust had taken place.

Although most Americans knew of the Nazi persecution of the Jews during the 1930s, few were aware that genocide had gotten under way in 1942. Hitler's regime denied the fact (even to the German people) and went to considerable lengths to keep the program secret. Firsthand accounts began leaking out in late 1942. But the Roosevelt administration found it hard to believe that anyone—even the Nazis—would undertake such a horrific campaign. Long-standing anti-Semitism also blinded most American officials to the fragmentary evidence and made them unwilling to take action even once the genocide was indisputable. But in 1944, as the evidence mounted and the World Jewish Council implored the United States to intervene, Roosevelt briefly considered sending the U.S. Army Air Force to bomb the death camps. The War Department was opposed on the grounds that the attacks would be a "diversion" from the war effort. The president ultimately decided he could not justify killing innocent Jewish civilians—even though the Nazis were systematically gassing them.

Roosevelt had also worried that taking action would alienate Congress and voters (particularly in 1944, an election year). Instead of a direct response, he established an independent War Refugee Board (WRB), which used public and private funds to set up refugee camps for Jews in Allied Europe and Palestine. The WRB saved two hundred thousand Jews. But the United States and its Allies left the vast majority of European Jews (along with other minorities) to face the Nazis alone. By the time Allied troops stumbled on the gas chambers, two-thirds of Europe's entire population of Jews had perished. After the war, the United States would prosecute the first-ever international war crimes at the Nuremberg trials, sentencing top Nazi leaders to death for their role in the Holocaust. The United States also tried Japanese war criminals at the Tokyo Trials of 1946–1948.

DAWN OF THE NUCLEAR AGE

Victory in the Pacific seemed assured by mid-1945. Japan had lost most of its fleet in the epic battle for the Philippines, while U.S. bombing missions over Tokyo and elsewhere had killed over three hundred thousand civilians and decimated the Japanese war industries. MacArthur and Nimitz were advancing toward mainland Japan, and the United States was hopeful the enemy would surrender. But Japan continued fighting. In the battles of Iwo Jima and Okinawa (1945), Japanese pilots flew their bombers directly into U.S. ships, while thousands of soldiers sacrificed their lives defending mere inches of territory. Most American soldiers killed in the Pacific war died in the grinding battles of 1944–1945. The War Department estimated that another 250,000 would perish in the planned invasion of Japan.

When the United States secretly tested the world's first atomic bomb, at Alamogordo, New Mexico, in the summer of 1945, it was immediately clear that the country possessed a weapon of catastrophic and unprecedented force—and that it could end the Pacific war sooner rather than later. Six years earlier, European physicists led by Albert Einstein had secretly informed Roosevelt that the Nazis were probably developing nuclear weapons and that Hitler would not hesitate to use them. The president promptly recruited Einstein and dozens of other physicists—many of whom were German Jewish refugees—to develop the atomic bomb as part of the top-secret Manhattan Project (1942–1945). When the bomb was finally tested at Alamogordo, its force shot debris eight miles into the sky and knocked project personnel, located several miles away, off their feet. "No matter what else might happen," one awestruck witness, General Thomas Farrell, reported to Supreme Allied Commander General Dwight Eisenhower, "we now have the means to insure [the war's] speedy conclusion and save thousands of American lives."

Exactly how the bomb should be used was a matter for debate. The Manhattan Project's scientific director, J. Robert Oppenheimer, and a number of other officials had profound moral reservations about dropping the bomb on civilians. "Now," a tearful Oppenheimer quoted Hindu scripture after the Alamogordo test, "I am become Death, the destroyer of worlds." Having witnessed its colossal destructive power, a delegation urged President Truman to invite the Japanese to view a test demonstration that, in theory, would persuade them to immediately surrender. But Truman and the War Department rejected their plea on the grounds that the United States possessed only three of the new devices and that a misfire (which could easily happen) would be embarrassing and a waste of precious materiel.

Truman saw many advantages and few drawbacks to dropping the bomb. Whereas earlier in the war, the Allies had been loath to bomb civilians, the aerial bombings of 1945 and the race to end the war as quickly as possible had desensitized most policymakers to massive civilian losses. For their part, Secretary of War Henry Stimson and his top military advisers had always assumed that Japan would be bombed into submission. They informed the president that a land invasion would cost anything from half a million to a million American lives, an exaggeration of the military's analysis of 250,000. Inheriting the presidency so late in the war, Truman was disinclined to interfere with the military's plans and even less prepared to endanger American lives. He was aware that public support was virtually assured given most Americans' desire to avenge Pearl Harbor and their intense animosity toward the Japanese.

Relations with the Soviets also figured in Truman's calculations. The president had received news of the test while in negotiations with Stalin and Churchill—and he immediately realized that dropping the bomb on Japan would establish American military supremacy. It would also negate the need for the Soviets to enter the Pacific war and consequently limit their claims over Japan and Japanese-occupied China. Truman decided to proceed.

In late July, the president demanded Japan's "unconditional surrender" and threatened "prompt and utter destruction" if none was forthcoming. Japan remained silent. Eleven days later, on August 6, 1945, the *Enola Gay* released an atomic bomb over the city of Hiroshima. Two observation planes recorded a blinding flash followed by a towering, roiling mushroom cloud of debris, dust, and smoke that rose thousands of feet. On the ground, a wave of blistering heat engulfed the city and its inhabitants, ripping foliage off trees, blowing buildings apart, and stripping the skin off of human flesh. The bomb killed 130,000 civilians (over one-third of the city's population), severely injured and sickened 100,000, and leveled four in every five buildings.

The United States fully expected Japan to surrender unconditionally—but it did not. The OWI dropped millions of pamphlets over Japanese cities, describing the suffering of the people of Hiroshima and warning that other attacks would swiftly follow if Japan did not give up. On August 9 the United States dropped a second bomb, this time on Nagasaki—to almost as devastating an effect. Galvanized at last by the fascist regime's sacrifice of so many civilians, moderates took control of the Japanese government. Japan informally surrendered on August 14 and again, in an official ceremony aboard the USS *Missouri*, on September 2, 1945. Americans celebrated; World War II was over. In the words of Winston Churchill, the United States now stood at "the summit of the world."

CONCLUSION

The legacies of World War II were profound and many, both for the United States and the world. Over 60 million people, including 418,500 Americans, had perished. Millions more had been dislocated, their homes destroyed. Throughout Europe and Asia, dozens of cities lay in rubble, and communication, transportation, and industrial networks were ruined. Nationalist anticolonial movements had been galvanized by the war, and the French and Dutch each soon entered new wars in Vietnam and Indonesia, respectively. Economically broken, the British reluctantly prepared to exit from India, the jewel in the crown of their once-great empire.

The United States roared out of the war as the world's wealthiest, most productive, best armed, and most confident nation—a superpower. The war had turned the Great Depression on its head, more than doubling the size of the economy between 1939 and 1945 and producing full employment. After 1945, most factories reverted to peacetime production, but many continued to manufacture war-related technology and became the basis of the nation's first permanent defense industry. Universities built on their new stature as a vital source of research and development in arms and other industries. Business confidence returned—as had citizens' confidence in big business. For the first time, the United States had majority influence over international institutions such as the United Nations. For all these reasons, the United States would play a leading role—financially, technologically, and culturally—in the reconstruction of Europe and Japan.

Although the war had taken its deadliest toll on the Soviet Union, that country's remarkable push into central Europe secured it a place at the table as the other superpower. The Soviets were keenly aware that their ally, the United States, was in sole possession of atomic weaponry. And in the wake of their massive losses and the bitter memory of Winston Churchill's refusal to come to the USSR's aid in a timely manner, the Soviets determined to break that monopoly.

STUDY TERMS

- isolationism (p. 696)
- America First Committee (p. 696)
- American way (p. 697)
- internationalists (p. 697)
- Captain America (p. 698)
- cash-and-carry (p. 699)
- Selective Service Act (p. 699)
- Four Freedoms (p. 700)
- Lend-Lease Act (p. 700)
- Atlantic Charter (p. 700)
- United Nations (p. 700)
- Double V campaign (p. 702)
- War Production Board (p. 703)
- *braceros* (p. 705)
- Fair Employment Practices Commission (p. 705)
- Executive Order 9066 (p. 706)
- Zoot Suit Sailor Riots (p. 709)
- Fifth Freedom (p. 710)
- Office of War Information (p. 710)
- Bureau of Motion Pictures (p. 712)
- pluralist nationalist (p. 712)
- Voice of America (p. 713)
- United Services Organization (p. 713)
- Operation Overlord (p. 714)
- Bataan Death March (p. 716)
- Tehran Conference (p. 719)
- World Bank (p. 719)
- International Monetary Fund (p. 719)
- D-Day (p. 719)
- Yalta Conference (p. 719)
- final solution (p. 720)
- Nuremberg trials (p. 721)
- Manhattan Project (p. 721)

TIMELINE

1931–1938 Fascist regimes in Japan, Italy, and Germany begin military expansion

1938 Hitler forces *Anschluss* (unification) with Austria

British prime minister Neville Chamberlain appeases Hitler in Munich

1939 Forty-four million Americans attend World's Fair in Flushing Meadows, New York

Britain and France declare war on Germany after Hitler invades Poland

President Franklin Roosevelt reaffirms U.S. neutrality but indirectly aids British war effort

1940 Voters return FDR to White House

Edward R. Murrow vividly reports on the Germans' aerial bombing of London

First 900,000 Americans drafted into military under Selective Service Act

1941 FDR proclaims "Four Freedoms"

Captain America makes his debut, fighting Nazis

U.S. economy booms on strength of Allies' wartime needs

Germany unexpectedly attacks the Soviets, opening a second front in the European war

FDR and British prime minister Winston Churchill sign the Atlantic Charter

United States declares war on Japan following Japanese attack at Pearl Harbor, and Germany and Italy declare war on the United States

1942 Hitler orders the extermination of European Jews and other minorities

A. Philip Randolph calls for a "Double V" victory over racism at home and fascism abroad

Japanese Americans living on West Coast are interned under Executive Order 9066

U.S. forces enter combat in the Pacific, Southeast Asia, and North Africa

The top-secret Manhattan Project gets under way

1943 Suburbanization accelerates

Race riots break out in many U.S. cities

The United Service Organization takes American popular culture to the troops

Allies secure Africa; Soviet Union repels German forces

Planning for the postwar new world order gets under way at the Tehran Conference

1944 Allied troops storm Normandy beaches on D-Day

United States and its allies establish the World Bank and International Monetary Fund

Big Three and China draft Charter of the United Nations

FDR is reelected for a fourth term

1945 Big Three agree to a new world order in which the Soviets exercise influence over Eastern Europe

Harry S Truman becomes president after FDR suffers a fatal stroke

Hitler commits suicide in a Berlin bunker; Germany surrenders

United States drops atomic bombs on Hiroshima and Nagasaki; Japan surrenders

1946 Allies try German and Japanese leaders as war criminals

FURTHER READING

Additional suggested readings are available on the Online Learning Center at www.mhhe.com/becomingamerica1e.

Luis Alvarez, *The Power of the Zoot* (2009), explores Mexican American youths' use of popular culture to challenge conformity during World War II.

Steven Casey, *Cautious Crusade: Franklin D. Roosevelt, American Public Opinion, and the War Against Nazi Germany* (2004), tracks FDR's efforts to persuade Americans of the Nazi threat and the constraints that public opinion imposed on him.

Thomas Doherty, *Projections of War: Hollywood, American Culture, and World War II* (1999), depicts Hollywood's role in promoting patriotism and support for the war.

John Dower, *War Without Mercy* (1986), reveals the influence of intensely racist sentiments on American and Japanese war tactics and relations.

Paul Fussell, *Wartime: Understanding and Behavior in the Second World War* (1990), examines soldiers' experience and understanding of the war.

Maureen Honey, *Bitter Fruit: African American Women in World War II* (1999), relates black women's diverse experiences of wartime mobilization.

John Keegan, *The Second World War* (2005), provides a comprehensive military history of the war on all fronts, including U.S. involvement.

Daniel Kryder, *Divided Arsenal* (2000), explores the effects of the federal government's wartime labor and military policies on African American workers and soldiers.

Gerald Linderman, *The World Within War* (1997), investigates the transformative power of combat, arguing that soldiers experienced the war in vastly different ways than did other Americans.

Margaret Regis, *When Our Mothers Went to War* (2008), broadly surveys the many ways women were involved with and experienced World War II.

Ronald Takaki, *Double Victory* (2000), highlights the contradictions inherent in the United States' fight for democracy abroad within the context of racial discrimination at home.

Thomas W. Zeiler, *Unconditional Defeat: Japan, America, and the End of World War II* (2004), assesses the last two years of war between the United States and Japan, with a focus on combat.

26

INSIDE ▶

THE BIG PICTURE

Americans faced fresh challenges immediately after World War II. Millions of ex-servicemen competed for jobs, racist violence surged, relations with the Soviet Union soured, and citizens worried that the Great Depression would return. The consumer economy soon roared back to life, however, thanks partly to massive government investment in veterans and infrastructure. Suburbanization and television transformed American culture and politics, as did the so-called Cold War with the Soviets, which fueled anxieties about communism and spurred the creation of the nation's first peacetime defense industry.

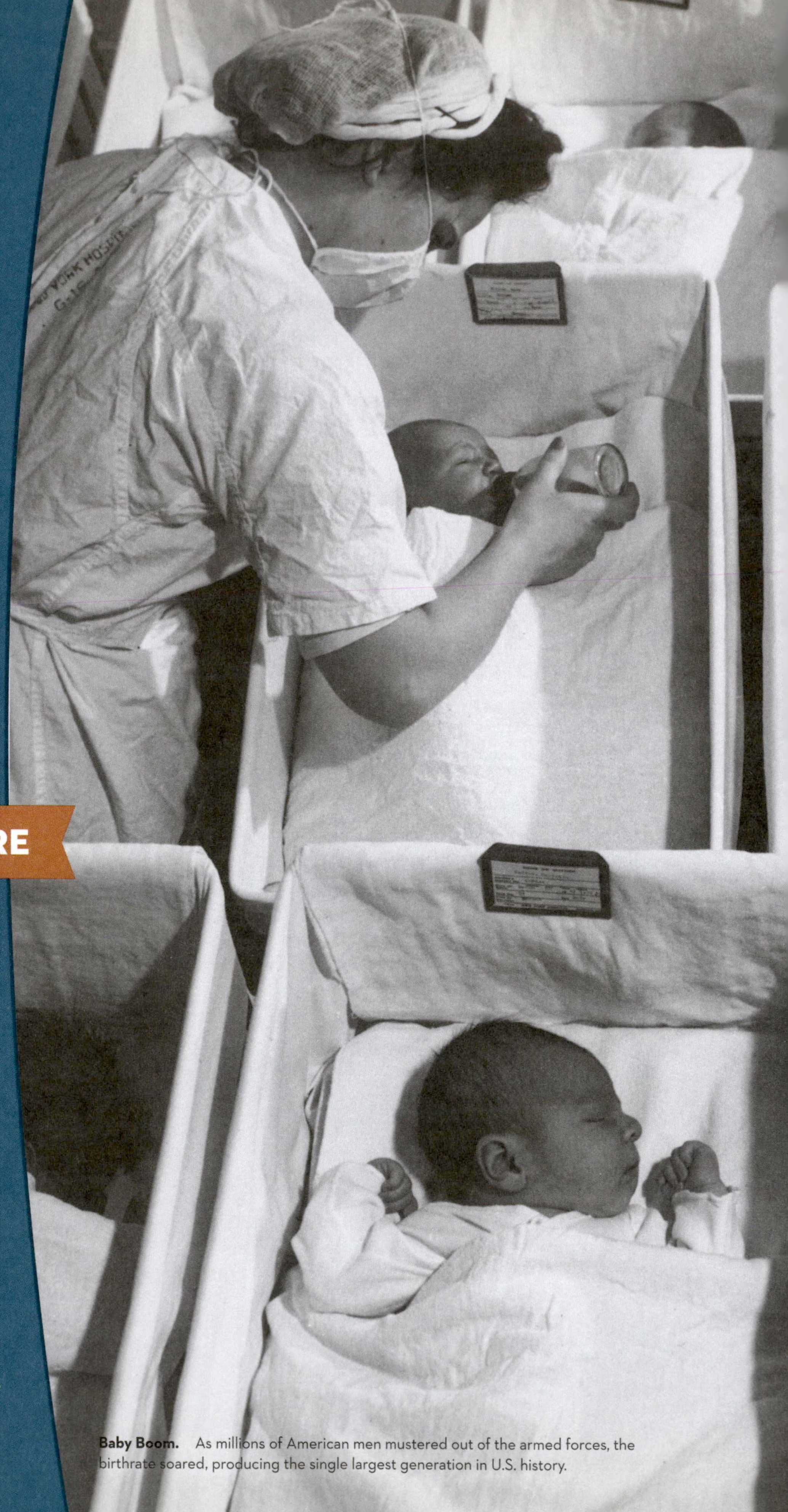

Baby Boom. As millions of American men mustered out of the armed forces, the birthrate soared, producing the single largest generation in U.S. history.

1945–1953

POSTWAR AMERICA

The audiences that flocked to opening night of *High Noon* in 1952 had high expectations for Hollywood's latest Western. Billboard advertisements for the movie, which starred Gary Cooper and Grace Kelly, showed the lone town marshal—a man "too proud to run"—poised to do battle against hardened outlaws. In fact, the movie disappointed most viewers, who complained about the lack of action. An apparent sleeper, *High Noon* continued to play around the country, however, and gradually attracted fans—and a different kind of criticism. Viewers with liberal politics celebrated the film, interpreting the townspeople's abandonment of the brave marshal as the moral failure of Hollywood to stand by fellow actors and writers accused of being communist. From the opposite perspective, many anti-communists condemned *High Noon* as an "un-American" defense of communists.

The film's content and controversial reception expressed the deep political and cultural divisions of the postwar years. The era's rancor and anxiety contrasted sharply with the sense of oneness and jubilation that swept the nation after Japan's surrender in 1945. Although the horrors of battle traumatized countless individuals, veterans' hopes for their own and the nation's future ran high.

GARY COOPER
when the hands point straight up... the excitement starts at
"HIGH NOON"

High Noon lacked most elements of classic Hollywood Westerns—including ruggedly beautiful scenery—and many liberals interpreted it as a critique of anti-communism in the movie industry.

KEY QUESTIONS

- What foreign and domestic challenges did the United States face immediately following World War II?
- How did the Cold War affect American politics and culture?
- Why did the American middle class thrive in the postwar era, and what role did the government play in sustaining its newfound affluence?
- What controversial new ideas and movements flourished after World War II?
- What accounts for the rise and fall of McCarthyism?

President Harry S Truman plotted a peaceful "reconversion" to a civilian society and agreed to a plan of peace and reconstruction with the United States' ally and chief rival, the Soviet Union. The last thing on American minds in early 1946 was the possibility of a major conflict with the Soviets.

The transition from war to peace proved difficult on all fronts, however. Finding jobs, housing, and colleges for the millions of returning veterans was a colossal challenge. Congress stonewalled many of Truman's initiatives, and state and local government, which administered many of the federal postwar programs, frequently withheld the new entitlements from African Americans and other minorities. Meanwhile, as Soviet and U.S. diplomats wrangled over the peace terms, high-ranking American officials grew convinced that the Soviets were seeking influence well beyond their neighboring states. By late 1946, the United States sought to block Soviet ambitions in Eastern Europe. Relatively cooperative competitors during the war, by 1948 the two countries saw each other as the crucible of evil.

Truman prepared Americans for what came to be known as the Cold War, chiefly by pouring resources into programs designed to strengthen the nation's military, economy, and morale. The economy boomed—but so did anti-communist fervor. Many leftists and critics of Cold War policy were dismissed from their jobs, and even New Deal liberals faced public censure for allegedly tolerating communists. Yet new forms of dissent bubbled up in the arts, academia, and mass culture. And, unexpectedly, the Cold War energized the civil rights movement.

A MEANINGFUL VICTORY

As peace returned in August 1945, most Americans were optimistic that reconversion would set the nation on the road to prosperity. African Americans and other minorities were also hopeful that they would finally win full legal equality. But change proved slow and difficult. The military discharged thirty-five thousand servicemen and servicewomen each day, overwhelming the job, food, and housing markets, and it took months for factories to retool for civilian production. Many Americans worried that without a mighty war effort to keep the fires of production burning, the recent economic depression would return. A majority of whites opposed civil rights reform, some violently. As wartime unity dissipated, anxiety and moral ambiguity became major themes in the arts and mass culture.

CHALLENGES OF RECONVERSION

The advent of peace abruptly changed almost every aspect of American life and politics. For the previous four years, the entire nation—its economy, people, and culture industries—had been devoted to the war effort. Before the war, a depression had mired the nation's business and progress. Now, at war's end, military contracts for weapons and other materiel were canceled, and industry ground to a halt. Wages fell, jobs dried up, and three million American workers, from the automobile to the coffin-making industry, participated in hundreds of strikes. Protest marches erupted in many cities, and a cloud of worry over a renewed depression hung over the nation.

However, the combination of high wages and wartime rationing meant that a majority of Americans had accumulated substantial savings. With the return of peace, they were eager to spend on all kinds of goods and services, and they flooded the market with money. Industry's reconversion to consumer production was slow, however, and inflation spiraled until 1948, when factories again began churning out goods.

In the meantime, men returned to their traditional roles as wage earners and heads of household, and government and business encouraged wage-earning women to return to the home. Most of the nineteen million women who had earned a wage during the war viewed their employment as temporary and looked forward to resuming domestic life. Others, though, were reluctant to lose their jobs and the independence, sense of fulfillment, and purchasing power that came with wages.

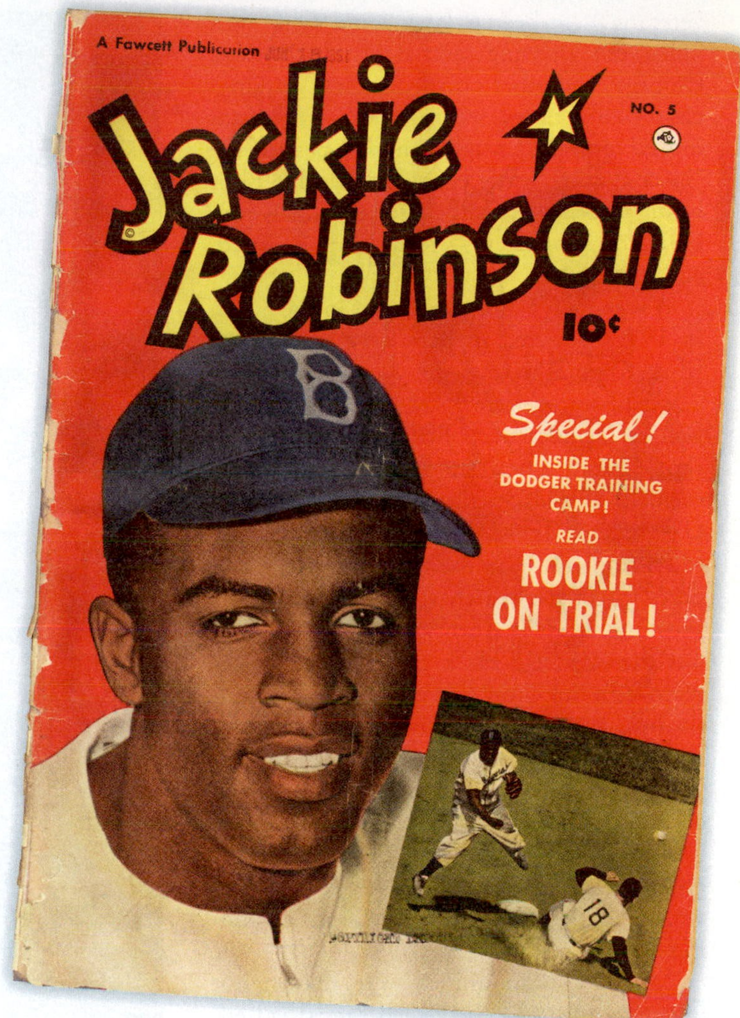

Desegregating Baseball. Brooklyn Dodger Jackie Robinson became an inspiring symbol of the struggle for civil rights, but he endured taunts even from Dodgers fans. Years would pass before Major League Baseball drafted significant numbers of minority athletes.

FIGHTING RACISM AT HOME

Having risked life and limb for the nation, many African Americans and other minorities sought to translate the defeat of racist Nazi Germany into victory over racism and poverty at home. Their military service emboldened them to claim the right to have the same high-wage jobs and housing opportunities, to attend the same schools, and to swim in the same public pools as whites. Although disenfranchisement and segregation were still in force in the South, tens of thousands of black southern veterans attempted to register to vote and refused to ride in the back of the bus. The number of African American newspapers grew and circulated widely through black neighborhoods.

The culture industries tentatively embraced racial equality. Record companies noted that a growing number of white people were buying African American "race music" (blues). Recognizing the potential for a mass audience, they renamed and repackaged the music as "rhythm and blues." In sports, ex-army lieutenant Jackie Robinson in 1947 became the first African American to play in Major League Baseball since the 1890s.

Yet the barriers to full inclusion remained, even outside the Jim Crow South. In the Southwest, whites still excluded most Mexican Americans and Native Americans from their neighborhoods and schools and barred them from voting. Minority veterans were beaten (and some were even killed) for asserting their rights. In Detroit, Chicago, and other northern cities, working-class whites rioted when African Americans moved into white neighborhoods, beating the "interlopers." Nearly everywhere Jackie Robinson appeared, white baseball fans—even Dodgers supporters—threatened, taunted, and spat on him.

A wave of lynching broke out in the South in 1946, powered in part by a revived Ku Klux Klan. Abetting the Klansmen's campaign of terror were local law enforcers, as well as Democratic politicians eager to prevent African Americans from voting against them. If any black tries to organize to vote, U.S. senator Theodore Bilbo exhorted white Mississippians, "Use the tar and feathers and don't forget the matches." In one especially shocking incident, a white conductor gouged out the eyes of a black ex-marine who had removed a Jim Crow sign on an Alabama trolley bus, and the sheriff shot the former serviceman dead. In another episode, a group of white men ambushed two African American couples as they drove across Monroe, Georgia, killing all four. "This time it has gone too far," an African American veteran wrote President Truman. "[The Klan] are killing our women."

Minority communities were shaken but undeterred. Life in the armed forces had encouraged many not only to stand up for their rights but also to appreciate the importance of disciplined cooperation among allies. Departing from its usual refusal to work with more radical organizations, the National Association for the Advancement of Colored People (NAACP) cooperated with the communist Civil Rights Organization and the National Negro Congress to demand a federal investigation of the Monroe Ford lynching. In response, Truman established the President's Committee on Civil Rights (1946) and introduced anti-lynching legislation (the passage of which southern congressmen successfully blocked, just as before the war).

Uneasy Homecoming. In *Key Largo* (1948), jobless veteran Major Frank McCloud (Humphrey Bogart) travels to the Florida Keys to pay respects to his fallen buddy's father. As a hurricane bears down, McCloud and other hotel guests are held captive by an old-time gangster who dreams of a return to the "good old days" of Prohibition. The morally disillusioned McCloud must decide whether he will take the easy way out (submit to the bullying gangster) or assume a moral stand (fight the gangster and his retrograde vision of America). McCloud chooses to fight. The message in this and other postwar films was that in the United States, individuals had both the freedom and the responsibility to reinvent themselves.

NEW ANXIETIES

Advertisers and the other culture industries widely celebrated the return of peace and painted America as a nation bonded in victory and unscarred by the most destructive war in global history. One of the sweetest fruits of victory, advertisers suggested in 1946, was the freedom to consume again. However, a more nuanced, ambivalent perspective also emerged. Visual artists (including many veterans) translated the image of a nuclear explosion—and the suffering of its victims—into jarring works of art that questioned the morality of nuclear technology. As more gruesome evidence of the scale and depravity of the Nazis' Holocaust emerged, intellectuals and artists in the United States and elsewhere probed into whether humanity as a whole was hurtling toward self-destruction.

Other works in the immediate postwar years explored the trauma of veterans' homecoming and frequently portrayed an alienating shift from the barracks and battlefield to the family's front parlor. In films such as *The Best Years of Our Lives* (1946), husbands return to find their wives involved with other men, their parents dead, and their old jobs filled by juniors. Veterans struggled with physically disability and traumatic memories of war, sometimes turning to alcohol and crime and losing their faith in humanity. Another unnerving picture of postwar America emerged in a new genre called film noir ("black film"). Noir movies depicted ordinary men, often veterans, engaging in paranoid self-destructive behavior, frequently over a femme fatale who causes them to spiral into crime and ultimately death. As in many of the returning veteran films, the postwar world appeared claustrophobic and morally ambiguous. Usually shot in black and white and featuring looming shadows, film noir challenged the image of the bright, wholesome life that advertisers and many of the culture industries were propagating.

CONSOLIDATING THE NEW DEAL

Planning a smooth transition to peace had been a priority for Presidents Roosevelt and Truman. The latter was especially eager to avoid the violence that had attended the reconversion of the economy after World War I (see Chapter 22). Truman believed that a revival of the New Deal, which had stalled in Congress after 1938, would be the surest way to restore prosperity. If the government invested heavily in education, health, and job training and ensured full or near-full employment, argued Truman, mass consumption would grow the economy and spread prosperity. Furthermore, extending popular social and labor reforms and regulating big business would seal middle-class support for Truman's Democratic Party.

As part of this strategy, Truman sought to strengthen his standing among African Americans, expressing outrage at the South's "organized terror." He endorsed voting rights, fair wages, and decent housing for all Americans regardless of race; and he desegregated the armed forces in 1948. But Truman's cabinet, like Roosevelt's, contained several conservative southern Democrats, and any legislation he proposed also required the consent of southern lawmakers. When directed by Truman to investigate the South's lynching outbreak, the attorney general, a white Texas Democrat, conducted a feeble inquiry. Stubbornly opposed to federal intervention in the South's segregation of the races, southerners blocked many federal employment and welfare initiatives that might have ensured equal treatment for African Americans. Although Truman's moral outrage over inequities was genuine, his commitment to reform rarely produced results.

Like FDR and many other Democrats of the era, Truman was influenced by British economist John Maynard Keynes. A well-paid, fully employed workforce, according to Keynes, would drive the economy by buying consumer goods, boost tax revenue, and stoke the government with funds to spend on urgent social and educational initiatives. Such programs, Keynes believed, would in turn produce a skilled workforce and thereby propel technical innovation. The government's job, in this view, was to ensure full employment and mass consumption. The 1920s provided the model for how *not* to organize the economy, according to Keynes. In that decade, wages and salaries had not kept pace with the economic boom, with the deleterious consequences that too few people could become mass consumers and that a minority of Americans held a concentration of the wealth. As Keynes saw it, the uneven distribution of wealth and purchasing power had produced the Great Depression.

Tailoring Keynesian theory to the U.S. economy, scholar Chester Bowles singled out two crucial economic sectors for government investment—housing and agriculture. Moreover, to raise consumers' income, Bowles recommended increasing Social Security benefits, hiking up the minimum wage, and reducing the tax burden on most taxpayers. Truman wasted no time pursuing reform. Within days of the Japanese surrender, he proposed an increase in the minimum wage from forty to sixty-five cents an hour, the expansion of Social Security, and a new Fair Employment Practices Act. He also called for the construction of dams and other large-scale projects in the rapidly growing West, and housing for hundreds of thousands of returning veterans. Finding markets for farmers' surplus production and ensuring that all children were adequately nourished would be other presidential priorities. "No nation," Truman remarked, "is any healthier than its children or more prosperous than its farmers."

The School Lunch law, enacted in 1946, authorized the U.S. Department of Agriculture to purchase surplus meat, dairy, and grain and redistribute it free of charge to the nation's neediest children. School lunches became one of the most popular government programs in U.S. history. The capstone of the proposed reforms was universal health care, which most other industrial democracies had provided to their citizens since the early twentieth century. The idea of national health care enjoyed widespread postwar support, particularly among workers. Most Republican and southern Democratic lawmakers opposed it, however, as did the powerful American Medical Association, which argued that state-funded health care would diminish quality (and potentially physicians' income). FDR, an adept politician, had tried but failed to pass health care reform in the 1930s. Ultimately, Truman—who lacked both political experience and the skills to marshal public support—also failed.

REPUBLICAN RESURGENCE

As the 1946 midterm elections approached and strikes, race riots, and lynching spiked, Republican campaign posters asked, "Had enough?" A majority of voters, including many African Americans frustrated by the Truman administration's failure to stop lynching, answered in the affirmative. With Republicans taking control of both houses, the death of reform and rollback of the New Deal were almost certain. As expected, Republican lawmakers slashed government spending and reduced business regulations, including the wartime price controls that had prevented inflation. Inflation soon rocketed to 35 percent—over ten times what it is today. Citizens appealed to Truman for relief but met with apparent resignation, while leading Senate Republican Robert Taft advised Americans to simply "eat less" and "tighten their belts."

Conservatives and some business owners also decried the New Deal as a form of communism. Taft led the charge against the Wagner Act (1935), a cornerstone of the New Deal, which had legalized the practice of hiring all-union workforces (see Chapter 24). The resulting Taft-Hartley Act (1947) prohibited workers' solidarity and "wildcat" strikes and permitted the states to pass "right-to-work" laws that limited the unions' ability to recruit workers. Taft-Hartley also outlawed union donations to federal political campaigns, a measure that weakened the unions' political clout and cut off a principal source of Democratic campaign financing. Although organized labor lobbied against the bill and Truman condemned it as "dangerous intrusion on free speech," Congress overrode the president's veto. Corporations welcomed the legislation, as did many southern state lawmakers, who promptly passed right-to-work laws to attract industry to their region.

SUPERPOWER AMERICA

The Republicans' effort to roll back the New Deal came at a time of deteriorating U.S. relations with the Soviet Union. During the war's latter years, the two allies had devised the institutional framework of the postwar global order, tacitly agreeing to respect each other's interests in Europe and East Asia. In 1946, the "big two" continued to be allies and friendly rivals. A few State Department officials, however, suspected that the Soviet effort to cultivate close ties with Eastern Europe was part of a master plan for global domination. Similarly, members of Stalin's government viewed American efforts to open markets in Eastern European countries (traditional Soviet trading partners) as a bid for economic dominance. As relations soured, Truman came to believe that the Soviet Union posed an enormous threat to the United States and world peace. In 1947, facing low voter support and fresh accusations that communists had infiltrated his administration, the president resolved to use all means available short of direct military engagement to thwart Soviet expansion.

THE BIG TWO

At a series of Allied conferences in 1945–1947, American and Soviet leaders pursued what they took to be their nation's interests. The United States pressed for free trade and American-style elections throughout Europe and Asia, believing that these goals would rebuild and stabilize the world while also providing American manufacturers and agribusiness with vital markets. U.S. negotiators realized that America's monopoly of atomic technology and its industrial and financial supremacy made it the sole "superpower" at the table. While few of these negotiators trusted Stalin, they knew that cooperation with him was a route to expanding U.S. interests.

U.S.-Soviet Cooperation. In 1945, the Truman administration sought a cooperative relationship with the Soviets, the president noting in his diary that the Russians have "always been our friends . . . I can't see any reason why they shouldn't always be." Truman would reverse his opinion of Soviet leader Stalin the following year.

In 1946, the Soviet army's occupation of Eastern Europe gave the Soviets significant control over that region, which the British and Americans had accepted grudgingly. Having lost twenty-seven million people to the Nazi war machine, the Soviets sought to ensure that Poland, Hungary, and other Eastern states never again fell into hostile hands or became corridors for another German invasion. Stalin knew that the Nazis had risen to power in Germany through free elections. He therefore reneged on his promise to hold free elections throughout Eastern Europe and did so only where communists or leftist parties were popular. Stalin also opposed free trade, recognizing that open commerce with American corporations would increase U.S. political and cultural influence in the region. At the same time, however, the weaker Soviets, to avoid antagonizing the American superpower, rarely engaged directly in influencing elections.

As the Soviet occupation of Eastern Europe continued, however, the Truman administration split over the best approach, and American foreign policy shifted. Increasingly, Truman's plainspoken and sometimes quick-tempered manner set the tone. Secretary of State James Byrnes began pressing for free trade and free elections and for reminding the Soviets of the United States' awesome atomic capability. Secretary of War Henry Stimson and Secretary of Commerce Henry Wallace opposed this "atomic diplomacy" on the grounds that threats could lead the Soviets to distrust the United States—and even accelerate the development of their own atomic program. In their view, the Soviets merely wanted to secure their western borders by ensuring that Eastern Europe remained friendly or neutral. But the State Department and Truman were increasingly convinced that Soviet interests in Eastern Europe were far more sinister.

Former British prime minister Winston Churchill reinforced this suspicion in an electrifying speech he gave in the president's home state of Missouri in 1946. Exaggerating the Soviet role in Eastern Europe, Churchill cautioned that "an **iron curtain** has descended across the continent." Over half of Europe, he continued, was subject "not only to Soviet influence but to a very high and in some cases increasing measure of control from Moscow," and local leftists were working in "absolute obedience to the directions they receive from the Communist center." In fact, most Eastern European communists and other leftists were proudly independent of the Soviets—even openly critical. Nonetheless, Churchill's brilliant oratory sent a chill down the spine of many Americans. Churchill even inferred that Soviet ambitions, if left unchecked, could force the United States into war, just as German aspirations had forced Britain and France into World War II.

FROM RIVALRY TO COLD WAR

Numerous State Department officials and several cabinet members were receptive to Churchill's call to confront the Soviets. Just a month earlier, U.S. diplomat George F. Kennan wired an influential message from Moscow, where Allied talks were taking place, in which he warned that the Soviets perceived the United States as an enemy and that they aimed to control Eastern Europe directly. Kennan's alarming long telegram convinced many State Department officials that Soviet leaders were intent on spreading Soviet-style communism. By mid-1946, Secretary of the Navy James V. Forrestal concluded that the USSR was aggressively expansionist. Stalin could not be trusted, he insisted: "We tried that once with Hitler."

The analogy between Britain's disastrous appeasement of Nazi Germany at Munich in the 1930s and American policy toward the Soviets was popular among State Department officials. In the wake of the bloodiest war in history, the Truman administration was anxious not to repeat Britain's mistakes in dealing with Nazi Germany. But the analogy was flawed. The war had left Soviet society shattered, and unlike the Nazis, the Soviets had neither the desire nor the might to be a power player outside Eastern Europe. Their overarching aim was to ensure that nonhostile governments ruled their immediate neighbors. Yet Soviet communism, like Nazism, was totalitarian (rule by dictatorship), and most Americans saw little difference between the two ideologies.

More and more, U.S. foreign policymakers viewed each step the Soviets took toward securing their borders as further evidence of Nazi-like expansionism. And wherever local communists or socialists gained political power, Truman blamed Soviet-directed subversion. Increasingly, the State Department adopted confrontation over diplomacy and negotiation. At Truman's behest, the United States in late 1946 began wielding foreign aid as a weapon, withholding reconstruction loans from both the Soviets and leftist Eastern European governments. The unintended consequence was to drive cash-starved governments closer to the Soviets.

In early 1947, eager to support U.S.-friendly governments in the Mediterranean, where the Soviets aimed to protect their southern borders, Truman sought money and military advisers to prop up the regimes of Greece and Turkey. The president argued that leftist nationalists were threatening the Greek people's "freedom" with Soviet help. If Congress did not vote to send the Greeks and Turks $400 million in military and economic aid, Truman warned, U.S. interests and peace would be imperiled. The president's Truman Doctrine encouraged the United States to "support free peoples who are resisting attempted subjugation by armed minorities or by outside pressures." However, the Greek government was a dictatorship, and the leftist nationalists (whom the Soviet Union had in fact refused to help) wanted democratic reform.

Although the president felt genuine concern about Soviet ambitions in Europe, he and his State Department advisers exaggerated the threat to persuade lawmakers to act. The scare tactic worked—Congress funded military and economic aid to Greece—and became a hallmark of Truman's relationship with Congress in foreign policy matters. As well as winning congressional support, this approach silenced Republican critics who had claimed that Democrats were soft on communism. A few months later, Truman publicly condemned the Soviets as a threat to the American way of life. All federal employees were ordered to take a loyalty oath and submit to background screening. Over the next four years, more than 2,700 civil servants were dismissed for allegedly holding radical views or being a member of the Communist Party (which, however, remained legal until 1954).

Truman made clear that the United States was at war. The chief objectives would be to contain the growth of Soviet influence around the world. But unlike a conventional "hot" war, which involved direct military engagement with the enemy, this **Cold War** would be fought with economic, cultural, psychological, and political weapons.

THE STRATEGY OF CONTAINMENT

The case for waging the Cold War won further support in Congress and the State and Defense departments with the publication in 1947 of an anonymously authored article in the well-respected journal *Foreign Affairs*. Writing under the pseudonym of "X," the author insisted that "the main element of any United States policy toward the Soviet Union must be a long-term, patient but firm and vigilant **containment** of Russian expansive tendencies." Although expansionist, X continued, the Soviet government had been severely weakened by World War II and was likely to collapse soon. The United States could speed that collapse with "counterforce"—the strategy of containment—applied whenever the Soviets flexed their muscles around the globe.

X's article sparked vigorous debate about the extent of the Soviet threat and the question of whether the United States should apply diplomatic, military, cultural, economic, or a combination of various forms of counterforce to the Soviets. Journalist Walter Lippmann accused the State Department of abandoning diplomacy and committing the United States to funding an array of anti-communist "satellites, clients, dependents and puppets" that included oppressive dictatorships (like the Greek government). This approach would stretch American resources to the limit, threaten the United States' reputation abroad, and endanger prosperity at home (because taxpayers would have to foot the enormous cost of mounting such a fierce campaign).

Key cabinet members and many War Department staffers also dismissed containment and criticized the Truman Doctrine as unnecessarily confrontational. But the president had been gradually squelching dissent in his cabinet, having fired one of the doctrine's biggest critics, Secretary of Commerce Wallace, and replaced Secretary of War Stimson. Disagreement evaporated further once it was revealed that X was George Kennan, the respected U.S. diplomat to the Soviet Union. Kennan's stature and knowledge of the Soviets clinched congressional, military, and State Department support. Containment became the foundation of U.S. foreign policy for the next forty years.

Just two years earlier, U.S. officials had viewed the world as a complex array of cultures, governments, and alliances. Once containment became official policy in 1947, successive U.S. administrations increasingly saw Europe and other world regions in black and white: either pro-American and anti-Soviet or pro-Soviet and anti-American. Viewed through the lens of containment, politically unstable countries appeared threatening to U.S. interests and global peace. Consequently, American foreign policy aimed at restoring stability—even if it meant aiding corrupt and tyrannical regimes.

This rigid mentality led Truman and his successors to treat anticolonial and pro-democracy movements from the Dutch East Indies (Indonesia) and French Indochina (Vietnam) to South Africa and Iran as threats rather than opportunities to promote democracy and capitalism. Although freedom fighters in these nations typically sought independence from all outside influence (including the Soviet Union's), the State Department frequently believed they were directed from Moscow. "Like medieval theologians," Democratic senator William Fulbright sadly reflected years later, "we had a philosophy that explained everything to us in advance, and everything that did not fit could be readily identified as a fraud or as an illusion." By 1949, the Soviet Union had embraced a similar world view.

COLD WAR IN EUROPE

Truman spared no expense to implement containment by bolstering American influence in any part of the world deemed ripe for Soviet subversion. In a reversal of policy, the United States offered aid to Eastern Europe, calculating that injections of capital would free the region from the Soviets' grip. Stalin, however, refused the aid and angrily declared that the world was now irreversibly divided between capitalist and communist forces. Believing that communism was likely to take root during hard economic times, the Truman administration now tried to shore up Western Europe's sagging economies.

Truman's Marshall Plan (1948) provided massive funding for the recovery of the Western European nations. A centerpiece of the containment strategy in Europe, it pumped a total of $12.4 billion into France, Germany, and other Western European economies between 1948 and 1951. Each Western European government consulted with an official American adviser about how best to use the money. At first, most aid was spent on U.S. food and consumer goods, thus supporting U.S. manufacturing and hastening the reconversion to peacetime production. Eventually, however, Marshall Plan dollars were used to modernize European industry to aid European economic revival.

Like Truman, the Pentagon hyped the Soviet threat in Europe and built support in Congress and among voters for the Cold War. Military leaders pressed for weapons development, overseas bases, and formal military alliances with other democratic nations. Although the Soviets were still reeling from their wartime losses, Pentagon analysts reported in 1947 that the USSR would be able to overrun Britain and Western Europe in six months and inflict serious damage on Alaska and the Pacific Northwest. Armed with this alarming report, Truman asked Congress to pass the comprehensive National Security Act (1947), which provided for the militarization of the Cold War. This law replaced the War Department with the Department of Defense and the National Security Council, a presidential advisory board. A third organization created under the act—the Central Intelligence Agency (CIA)—began recruiting agents for subversive actions in Eastern Europe.

By 1950, the Marshall Plan was also a factor in the militarization of the Cold War. Beginning in the late 1940s, Marshall money helped fund Western Europe's militaries, integrating them into a modernized anti-Soviet bloc. By 1951, over 80 percent of all Marshall funds were invested in Western Europe's militaries. Congress justified this shift in U.S. aid in the name of "national security," releasing reports from the Pentagon and State Department that warned of various Soviet threats.

Stalin viewed these developments as a betrayal of the two powers' tacit agreement to honor each other's respective spheres of interest. The Soviet Union was not intervening in Canada, Mexico, or even Western Europe, the Soviet premier protested, so why would the United States intrude in Russia's backyard (Eastern Europe)? Increasingly, the Soviets believed that the true goal of U.S. foreign policy, like that of Nazi Germany, was global domination. So, in 1948, fearing a threat to their security, the Soviets pursued absolute control over Eastern Europe and secretly began a nuclear arms program. That same year, Stalin asserted his control of the region by sealing off rail, land, and water access to Germany's capital, Berlin, which lay inside the Soviet-occupied zone of Europe but was administered by all four Allies (the United States, Britain, France, and the USSR).

Now cut off from urgently needed provisions, Berliners faced dwindling food supplies. Truman responded decisively, seizing on a 1945 agreement that guaranteed airborne access to Berlin and sending upwards of 1,500 cargo planes, laden with flour, wheat, meat, and other foods, into the city each day. The Soviets dared not risk a direct confrontation by shooting down the cargo planes, and the Berlin Airlift continued feeding the city's residents for ten months. Humiliated, the Soviets called off the blockade in May 1949.

The British, Canadian, and French air forces had all participated in the airlift, a cooperative effort that further advanced the emergence of a Western European military bloc. In April 1949, nine months into the airlift, the United States signed a treaty with Canada and ten European nations that specified that an "armed attack against one or more" would be considered an attack against them all. The agreement created the North Atlantic Treaty Organization (NATO). Some congressmen argued that NATO's existence could draw the United States into another European war. But most lawmakers believed that the nation had to defend itself and its allies from Soviet aggression and that the treaty served notice that such aggression would not be tolerated. Once Congress approved NATO, lawmakers voted to send an extra $1 billion worth of military aid to the United States' partners. The Soviets registered their displeasure by publicly testing their first atom bomb in August 1949—an act that shocked Americans—and establishing a Soviet military alliance with Eastern Europe, the Warsaw Pact. Truman responded by authorizing the construction of three hundred atomic bombs.

The militarization of the Cold War had far-reaching consequences. For the first time in American history, the weapons industry flourished in peacetime. Instead of all but dismantling the armed forces, the Truman administration maintained a sizable military and channeled billions of dollars into weapons research (see Figure 26.1). As Congress funded war-related scientific research,

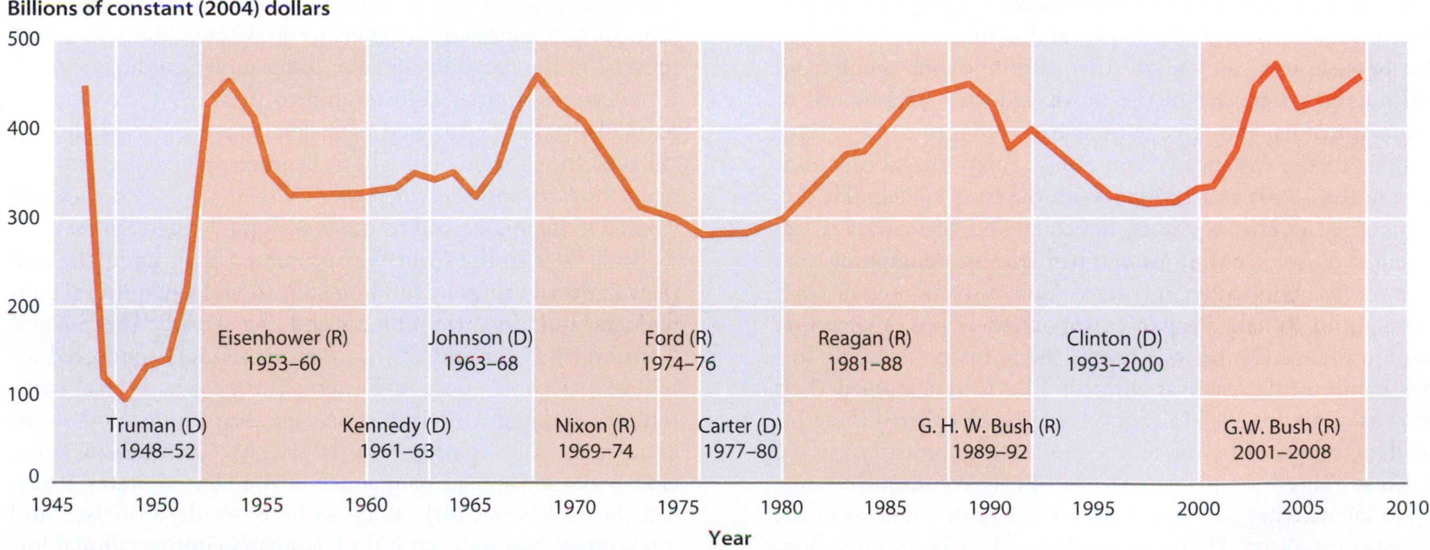

FIGURE 26.1 The Defense Boom, 1946-2008. U.S. defense spending fell dramatically after World War II but spiraled upward as the Cold War got under way in earnest in 1948. A president's party affiliation did not determine the level of spending. The defense budget rose significantly under Presidents Truman, Johnson, and Carter (all Democrats) as well as Reagan and George W. Bush (Republicans). It declined under Democrats Kennedy and Clinton and Republicans Eisenhower, Nixon, Ford, and George H. W. Bush.

government, universities, and weapons manufacturers joined forces in a giant **military-industrial complex.** All told, the Cold War, which lasted until 1991, cost the equivalent of over $19 trillion (in today's dollars). By 1950, more than one in seven jobs nationally was defense related. Weapons research and development kindled innovation in other parts of the economy, including the pharmaceutical, airplane, and communication industries, and prompted the expansion of universities.

COLD WAR POLITICS

The transformation of the Soviets from ally to enemy had major implications for the American political system and, especially, the Democratic Party. In 1947, Republican lawmakers reconvened the House Un-American Activities Committee (HUAC) in hopes of exposing communists in Truman's administration, discrediting the New Deal, and achieving a Republican victory in the 1948 presidential election. HUAC uncovered little that could damage the Truman administration—until the committee heard evidence from a conservative *Time* magazine editor that a prominent liberal diplomat, Alger Hiss, had passed confidential information to the Soviets in 1937–1938. Subpoenaed by the committee, Hiss vehemently denied the charge. Although Hiss was never tried for the alleged crime, Representative Richard Nixon of California pursued him relentlessly, and a federal court finally convicted Hiss of perjury in 1950, sentencing him to prison. The investigation, although inconclusive, cast suspicion on liberals, particularly Democrats in the State Department. The anxieties about subversion that the committee whipped up led most Democrats to distance themselves from both communists and left-leaning liberals.

Hollywood, which had enjoyed close ties with Roosevelt's wartime government, was HUAC's next target. Walt Disney, Jack Warner, and other Hollywood studio heads gladly cooperated, partly because of their own anti-communist beliefs but also because they wanted to drive striking labor unions and leftist scriptwriters out of the movie industry. (Thousands of actors, directors, and screenwriters had belonged or been sympathetic to the American Communist Party, a legal organization, in the 1930s and 1940s.) With the studios' help, HUAC subpoenaed dozens of actors, directors, and screenwriters, accusing them of communist sympathies and demanding that they testify about other suspected "subversives." Actors Gary Cooper and Ronald Reagan corroborated HUAC's view that communist subversion was rife in the industry. As some former communists, such as director Elia Kazan, named their peers as communists, Hollywood studios blacklisted these individuals and thereby forced them out of the industry.

Most Hollywood personnel resisted HUAC's inquiry, refusing to say whether they "were or ever had been members of the Communist Party." High-profile stars such as Humphrey Bogart and Lauren Bacall helped launch a counterattack on HUAC by asserting that Hollywood personnel, like other Americans, were entitled to their First Amendment rights of freedom of speech and assembly. The discrediting of HUAC stanched the investigations in late 1947. By then, however, the studios had already begun blacklisting, effectively ending the careers of hundreds of writers, actors, and directors. The following year, the members of a group known as the Hollywood Ten were convicted of contempt of Congress for refusing to testify and were sentenced to prison. In 1951, HUAC reconvened and expanded its hunt for communists.

THE CULTURAL COLD WAR

As in the two world wars, mass culture and propaganda were indispensable to the Cold War and shaped Americans' perceptions of the Soviet Union as an enemy and foreigners' perceptions of the United States as a friend. In the wake of HUAC's Hollywood hearings, the major studios released a wave of anti-Soviet films. Some exposed the bleak conditions of life in the Soviet Union and Eastern Europe and cautioned that American communists were on Moscow's payroll. *Iron Curtain* tells the story of a real-life Soviet code-breaker who flees political oppression to be free in the United States, only to find American communists committing espionage for the Soviets. Movies about World War II claimed that the Soviets, although nominally U.S. allies, were potentially an even greater threat to world peace than the Nazis. Once the arch-enemy, Germany was reborn as a vital new ally.

Beyond Hollywood, the government directly sponsored art, music, education, and literature to counter both homegrown and foreign criticism of U.S. foreign policy. Government officials were selective about the kinds of culture they would sponsor to represent the United States. For instance, Secretary of State George C. Marshall canceled an international tour of Modernist American art following protests that it was overly abstract, incomprehensible, and un-American. The Truman administration also established the Fulbright Program (1948), which sent American college faculty and students overseas for a year or two and brought well-educated foreigners to the United States to attend university. The program aimed to foster understanding between Americans and other cultures and to promote U.S. values—particularly those associated with democracy and capitalism—abroad. Once foreign Fulbright students completed their studies, many rose to positions of power in their own countries and worked to maintain good relations with the United States.

Both sides in the Cold War promoted their countries and their national values by funding educational and cultural conferences and organizations around the world. The Soviets' Cominform (Communist Information Service) sponsored international conferences in Eastern Europe where local communists declared American-style capitalism the enemy of art, democracy, and freedom. In 1949, the Cominform audaciously cosponsored a conference in the United States' financial heart—New York City—where resident artists and intellectuals had been critical of Truman's confrontational foreign policy. The New York conference underscored the need for a more systematic approach to the promotion of American culture abroad. To this end, the CIA secretly funded the Congress for Cultural Freedom, which attracted thinkers from across the political spectrum. Further, to counter negative portrayals of the United States, the State Department took over the radio broadcasts of Voice of America, which had broadcast American music and propaganda during World War II, and began transmitting directly to the Soviets.

INFRASTRUCTURES OF CONSUMPTION

As the Truman administration launched the Cold War, it also began to invest heavily in infrastructure at home through policies that strengthened the United States' consumer economy and society. Under Truman the federal government invested in education, the defense industry, agriculture, and highway construction. Federal stimulation of the economy increased, promoting home ownership, suburbanization, a baby boom, and consumer demand for everything from baby formula to lawn mowers. Infrastructural investment generated an educated workforce capable of remarkable innovation. Business would have preferred to deal with nonunionized labor and continued to fight regulation and corporate taxes, but most employers grudgingly adapted to new realities.

AMERICANIZING GLOBAL MARKETS

By 1947, the new international monetary system established at Bretton Woods, New Hampshire, was propelling American economic growth (see Chapter 25). The low interest rates set for the massive loans that U.S. banks made available to foreign countries through the Bretton Woods system made these loans appealing to both cash-starved Europe and the developing world. They came with strict conditions, though—notably the right to sell large quantities of U.S. goods to the borrowing nation.

The Bretton Woods system put the United States in a strong position relative to the economically decimated Soviet Union, which could not offer Europe and other regions the same level of financial aid and therefore lost out on potential trade opportunities. The American position was strengthened in 1947 when the United States, Britain, France, China, and many smaller nations signed the General Agreement on Tariffs and Trade (GATT), which obliged the signatories to enter trade talks aimed at reducing tariffs on foreign imports. Because the war had doubled U.S. productive capacity while wrecking that of Europe and the Soviet Union, GATT primarily benefited American manufacturers by opening markets for a variety of consumer goods as well as industrial equipment. European demand stimulated the reconversion of U.S. industry to peacetime production, providing millions of jobs for Americans.

TRUMAN'S FAIR DEAL AND THE ELECTION OF 1948

Despite encouraging signs that the economy was turning around in 1947, Truman's prospects—and the New Deal legacy—looked bleak going into the presidential election of 1948. Voter support plummeted as fast as Truman's initiatives failed in Congress. The tenuous alliance that FDR had built between conservative and liberal Democrats finally fell apart. Former cabinet member Henry Wallace recruited members for his new Progressive Party, while white southerners defected to the independent Dixiecrats, who opposed civil rights. To make matters worse, Truman's Republican opponent, Thomas E. Dewey, enjoyed a national reputation as governor of New York and tough-talking, crime-busting prosecutor.

Truman recognized, however, that the majority of Americans still wanted job security, high-wage jobs, low inflation, decent housing and schools, and access to consumer goods. He understood that most minorities desired these same things—as well as the civil rights that would secure entry to

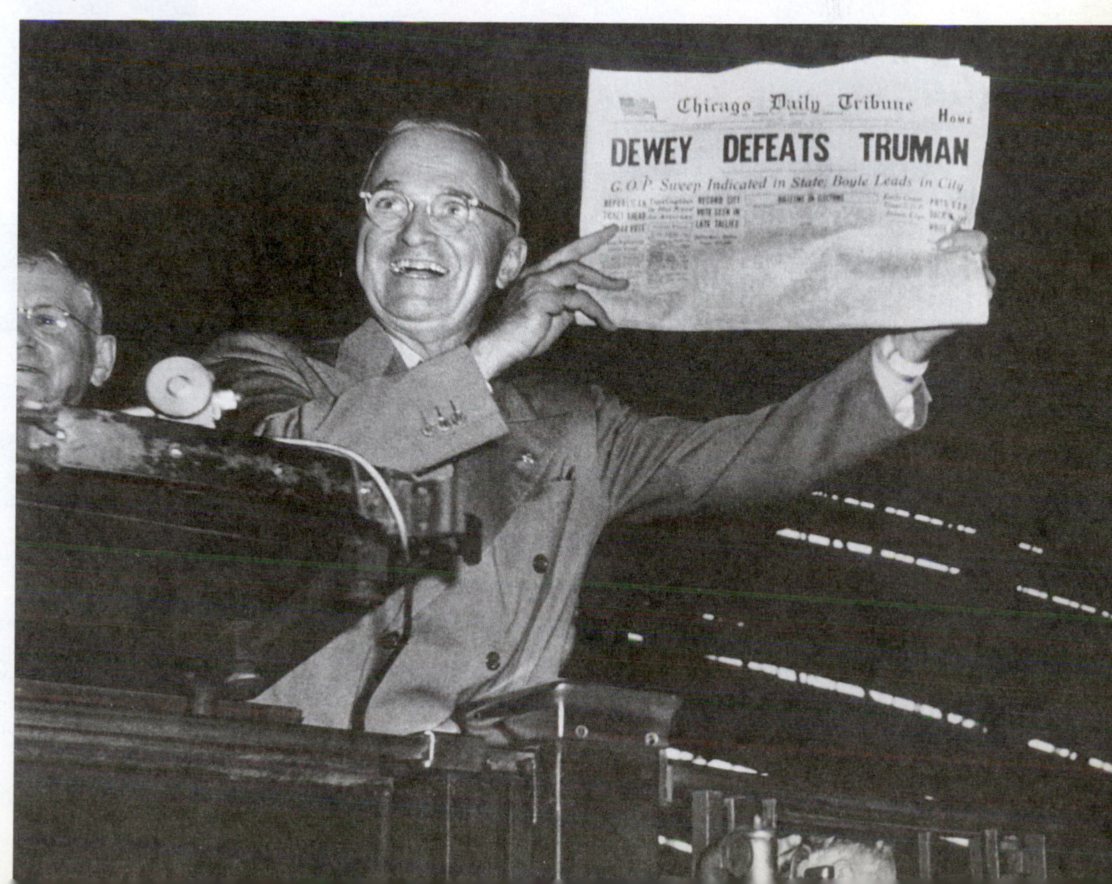

Rush to Judgment. On election day, 1948, midwestern and eastern newspapers rushed to print the next morning's headlines, prematurely declaring victory for Republican Thomas E. Dewey. A triumphant President Truman holds aloft one such newspaper.

the middle class. In consultation with his advisers, Truman resolved to shake off his inept image, reasserting his vision for what he later would call his **Fair Deal** for America. Embarking on a grueling tour of 356 U.S. towns and cities in the summer of 1948, Truman hammered the Republican Party as arrogantly out-of-touch with ordinary Americans and pressed for the repeal of the unpopular Taft-Hartley Act that limited labor's ability to strike. He also included a strong civil rights platform, becoming the first president to campaign in the historically influential African American neighborhood of Harlem, New York, and ordering the desegregation of the armed forces. The fact that his short, frank, and forceful speeches were often broadcast live allowed Truman to bypass the press—which mostly favored Dewey—and to speak to millions of citizens directly.

Truman's confidence was buoyed as Marshall money began stimulating American industry. Unemployment dropped, new car sales surged, and images of an array of new consumer goods saturated the mass media. Yet pollsters remained adamant that Truman would lose the presidency. On election day, Dewey took an early lead and appeared to have won as the sun set in his home state of New York. But later that night, voting returns in the western states chipped away at his lead, eventually delivering the election to Truman. In the end, Dewey lost and the Democrats retook both houses of Congress (see Map 26.1).

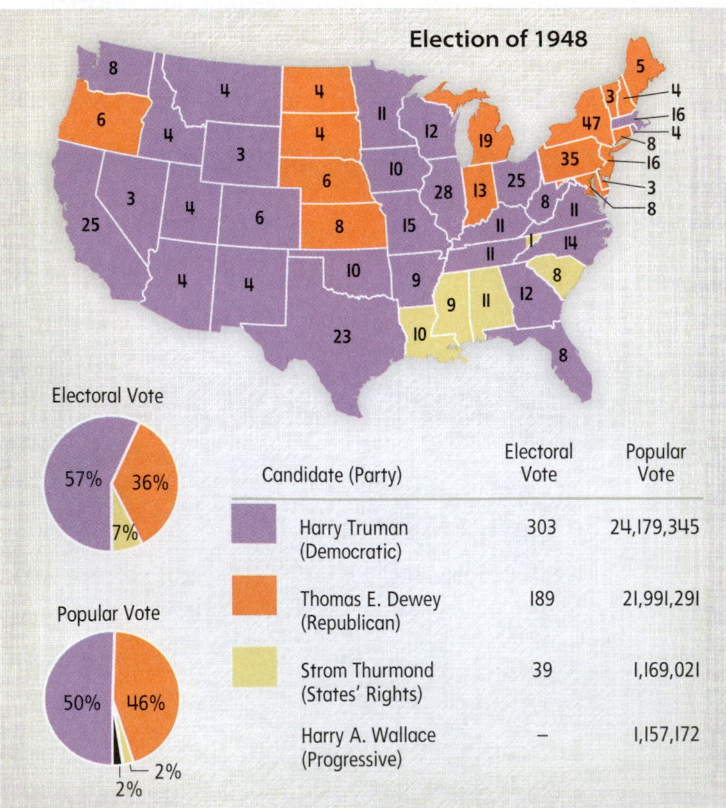

	Candidate (Party)	Electoral Vote	Popular Vote
	Harry Truman (Democratic)	303	24,179,345
	Thomas E. Dewey (Republican)	189	21,991,291
	Strom Thurmond (States' Rights)	39	1,169,021
	Harry A. Wallace (Progressive)	–	1,157,172

Map 26.1 Election of 1948.

Unionized workers, the urban middle class, and a majority of white southerners had voted Democratic. Pleased that Truman had finally desegregated the armed forces, African Americans in northern cities tipped the election in his favor.

INVESTING IN VETERANS

Victory in hand, Truman pushed forward with government investment on a large scale, targeting farming and food, college education, and housing. To raise workers' standard of living and make them mass consumers, the new Democratic Congress raised the minimum wage almost 88 percent, to 75 cents per hour. Under the Servicemen's Readjustment Act of 1944 (the G.I. Bill), the government paid college tuition and fees for hundreds of the 2.2 million eligible veterans. By making possible veterans' education, including job placement services and vocational training programs, the bill catalyzed rapid growth in universities and put the nation on the path to having the world's best-educated workforce.

Free Education for Veterans. The G.I. Bill's original sponsors were determined to avoid the confusion and political conflict over veterans' pensions that had followed World War I. The Restaurant Institute of Connecticut, which later became the world-famous Culinary Institute of America, was one of many vocational schools founded on G.I. Bill money.

After 1947, the G.I. Bill's low-interest home loans, requiring no down payment, turned the housing shortage into a construction boom. By 1950, for the first time in the country's history, the majority of families owned their own home. The Housing Act (1949) further funded research on the mass production of housing and authorized the construction of almost a million homes and rental subsidies for low-income Americans. By the early 1950s, the government was directly subsidizing the home construction industry and making Federal Housing Administration loans for first-time buyers affordable for most Americans. The federal government spent over $14 billion on World War II veterans.

Although most veterans benefited directly from the G.I. Bill, several minorities did not. Indeed, a Veteran Affairs ruling in 1945 disqualified the thousands of servicemen and servicewomen who had been dismissed from the military on grounds of homosexual conduct. Larger demographic minorities also fared badly. Locally, the schools, businesses, and developers that benefited from the federal stimulus prioritized white veterans at the expense of people of color. Most southern colleges continued to exclude African Americans, while northern colleges imposed racial quotas. The G.I. Bill also had the effect of reversing women's upward trend in college enrollments. Although "G.I. Janes" gained access, they accounted for just 2 percent of all eligible veterans. These limitations hampered them from joining the affluent society.

SELLING THE SUBURBAN DREAM

Increasingly, first-time homebuyers purchased a relatively new kind of home—a mass-produced house—in a novel type of settlement: a suburb. Although architects and planners had experimented with suburban design for years, it was not until the passage of the G.I. Bill that the construction of these planned communities boomed and that suburban homes became affordable for working and middle-class Americans. Federal and state governments stimulated suburbanization by subsidizing developers, making home loans affordable, and laying miles and miles of highways and waterlines that made the countryside more habitable (see Spaces and Places: Lakewood Park Suburban Development, Los Angeles). A tenfold increase in new car sales by 1955 and relatively cheap gas also fueled suburban development. Significantly, mass production perfected in the war industries' housing projects allowed a developer to erect upwards of twenty thousand such tract houses in fewer than two years. By 1950, just over half of all Americans lived in "suburbia."

Former U.S. Navy builder William Levitt pioneered the large-scale construction of tract housing. Cutting production costs and adapting Ford's assembly-line principles, Levitt assigned a separate work crew to each of twenty-six stages of construction. Standardized, often prefabricated, materials were assembled atop a concrete slab foundation. Originally intended as rental housing, Levittown homes could be bought for little more than a year's rent once federal housing loans became available. With a price tag of just over $7,000, homes in Levittown came within the reach of most skilled factory workers—unless they were African American, Asian American,

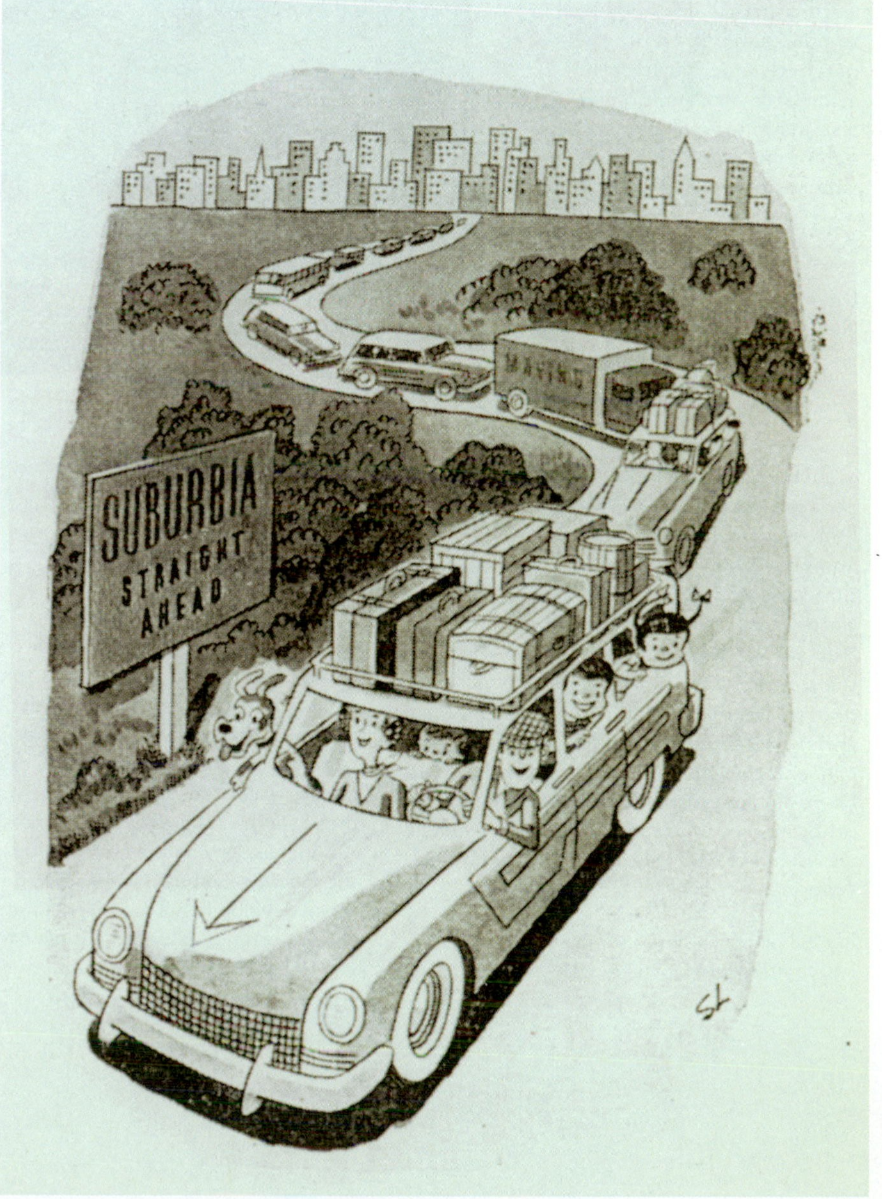

Leaving the City. Thanks to modern construction and financing methods, builders like Levitt and Sons made suburban homeownership affordable to millions. **Questions for Analysis:** To whom and what might the cartoonist be appealing? What lifestyle might await the new suburban home buyers?

SPACES & PLACES

Lakewood Park Suburban Development, Los Angeles

Suburban developments shot up across the United States after 1947 but nowhere faster than in the Sunbelt, the warm region spanning southern California through Arizona and Texas to Louisiana and Florida. The growing defense industry and number of civilian employers fleeing the Industrial Belt for the South's right-to-work states (legalized by the Taft-Hartley law) accelerated suburbanization in the region. In southern California and other desert environments, state and federal water projects made it possible to build suburbs on otherwise parched land. The advent of affordable air conditioning also made these regions habitable. Many Sunbelt suburbs grew so fast that they were soon able to incorporate as independent cities.

Mass-Produced Housing. William Garnett's famous photographs emphasized the uniform pattern and mass production of the Lakewood development—and what readers of the 1950s saw as the miracle of modern development.

Developed in the southern California desert in 1949, the misleadingly named suburb of Lakewood Park was close to military bases and the burgeoning defense industry from which it attracted likely first-time homebuyers. The suburb comprised almost seventeen thousand homes, three million feet of waterlines, and one of the nation's first "full-service" shopping centers. In 1950, the developer commissioned photographer William Garnett to take an aerial shot of Lakewood for use in a glossy presentation book aimed at potential homebuyers. *Business Week* and several other magazines soon published the image and commended Lakewood as a symbol of American progress.

In 1954, when the expanding city of Long Beach attempted to take over Lakewood Park, residents incorporated their own city and thus paved the way for local control. Other fledgling western towns soon followed, becoming "contract cities" that hired out for trash collection and other municipal services rather than providing these services themselves. For many Americans, leaving the cramped quarters of the big city and buying a home in one of these developments promised a better life, the opportunity to become mass consumers, and entry into the middle class.

Think About It

1. What aspects of suburban development does Garnett's photograph emphasize?
2. What made Lakewood Park possible in the 1940s?
3. Why might developers and consumers have celebrated Lakewood when this image first appeared?
4. What aspects of the development might later generations have critiqued?

or another minority (see How Much Is That?). Indeed, a racial covenant restricted the sale and resale of Levittown homes to "Caucasians" only.

News media proclaimed Levitt a national hero and made his Levittowns (and their racially restrictive covenant) the national model of suburban development. As the Cold War escalated, developers linked housing to the **nuclear family** (two married, heterosexual parents and an average of three children; extended family not included), consumer culture, and the defense of democracy. According to advertisers, these institutions lay at the heart of "the American way of life."

Most suburbs contained no or only a few parks and other public amenities, which were expensive to maintain. Consistent with the new emphasis on consumption, however, many suburbs boasted sprawling shopping centers. New homes, after all, required a host of appliances and services. Furniture sales shot up 240 percent between 1945 and 1950; lawn mower sales, by nearly 1,000 percent in roughly the same period. The number of televisions in U.S. homes catapulted from around forty thousand in 1947 to over forty million a decade later. At first, television was dominated by serious dramas broadcast live from the television studio. As with radio, however, advertisers pressed television programmers to adopt more exciting and glamorous programs, including game shows.

The baby boom and the emergence of the nuclear family further stimulated demand for suburban homes and lifestyles. Returning soldiers, eager to marry, pushed matrimony rates up by more than 25 percent and spurred a baby boom that would last until 1964. The **baby boomers,** as the generation born between 1946 and 1964 came to be known, was the largest generational group in American history—and the first fully suburbanized one. In combination with their parents' rising wages and access to cheap mortgages, baby boomers served as a growing market for disposable diapers, children's books, and baby food (see Hot Commodities: Baby Food).

How Much Is That?

A Home in Levittown

Earning an average yearly wage of around $3,000 and qualifying for cheap government-backed mortgages, white workers could easily afford a $7,000 home in Levittown, New York, in 1947. Adjusted for inflation, the cost was the equivalent of just $70,000, with a down payment of only $2,000. Today, the average Levittown home sells for around $329,000 and with a minimum down payment of $60,000—a sticker price that puts these homes well out of reach of the average American.

Backyard Paradise. The gas-powered lawn mower industry thrived after the war as wives prevailed on their husbands to maintain the family's new suburban lawn—and husbands looked for a way to cut the time and effort spent on the chore. Of all home appliances, the power lawn mower became the single most recognizable symbol of postwar suburbia.

UNIONS AND BENEFITS

As white workers moved to new suburbs or bought city homes, many continued to belong to labor unions. For the most part, unions retained the legitimacy and official recognition they had won during the New Deal and World War II. Over a third of all nonagricultural workers belonged to a union by the 1950s, down slightly from the 40 percent peak of the war years. Unions helped American workers secure the highest wages in the industrialized world. High wages in turn fed the consumer economy. By 1950, most Americans spent over a third of their income on consumer goods, such as home freezers and televisions, and on services that were once considered luxuries. More remarkable yet, they deposited an average of 8 percent of their income into a savings account—far more than at any previous time in American history. (The historically high saving rate increased until the 1980s, when it declined steeply, to around zero in 2004.)

HOT COMMODITIES

Baby Food

Boomer Bonanza. Baby foods such as Gerber's had been around since the late 1920s, but only after World War II and an industry-wide advertising campaign did a majority of American moms substitute them for breast milk.

Seventy years ago, the idea of baby food—solid foods, such as meats and vegetables, that are mashed, strained, and bottled or canned for infant consumption—would have struck most Americans as absurd. For centuries, the sole nutrition source for most babies was breast milk, produced either by the mother or, among the wealthy, by a "wet nurse" who breast-fed the mother's infant. In early twentieth century, a small but growing number of mothers supplemented breast milk with evaporated milk. Then, when scientists in the 1920s discovered that fruit and vegetables contained vitamins and minerals, the first-ever commercial baby food that was not milk-based, Gerber's mashed peas, appeared. Still, not until 1948 did a majority of mothers embrace baby food and infant formula. Demand tripled between 1949 and 1951, and five years later, only 18 percent of American babies were breast-fed. Outselling all other processed foods, baby food had become a billion-dollar-a-year business in just eight years.

Coinciding with the baby food craze, the baby boom drove up sales. Prepackaged and supposedly nutritious, baby food appealed to American women for its convenience and purported health benefits. But deeper influences, including changing ideas about parenting and infant psychology, also turned baby food into a hot commodity. Especially as prosperity returned after the war, older parenting manuals that advised putting babies on a strict feeding schedule and ignoring their cries for breast milk seemed out of step with a culture that celebrated personal fulfillment through consumption. Millions of parents were excited, then, when pediatrician Dr. Benjamin Spock published a manual detailing a relaxed approach to parenting. In his best-selling *Common Sense Book of Baby and Child Care* (1946), Spock released mothers from the guilt of withholding food and comfort, advising them to "follow your instincts. . . . Let your child tell you when he's hungry, not the clock." Spock also recommended switching from breast milk to infant formula at the early age of three to seven months and introducing solids before age one.

Food manufacturers were quick to cite Spock's recommendations, claiming in advertisements and baby-care manuals that baby food was essential for the baby's psychological and nutritional health. Beech-Nut mailed out millions of coupons for free jars of baby food, at one point sending every new mother a congratulatory letter. Gerber's, Heinz, and other manufacturers hired dieticians to inform mothers, doctors, and maternity ward staff about the benefits of eating as many solid foods as early on as possible, sometimes at four weeks. Doctors sent free samples home with nursing mothers.

The Cold War era's faith in science and technology—widely believed to be the United States' most powerful weapons against the Soviets—also sped the adoption of baby food. Produced in dozens of flavors, recommended by doctors, and nutrient dense, baby food was science and technology in a jar. It quickly came to symbolize the advanced nature not just of U.S. science and technology but of American civilization generally. Women could feed their babies without baring their breasts, as supposedly "backward" and "savage" people did. And unlike "savages," an entire generation of advanced American babies learned to wield that powerful symbol of civilization: the spoon.

Think About It

1. Why might the novel product of baby food have especially appealed to mothers in the postwar period?
2. Why did parenting styles change so dramatically after the war?
3. How do postwar attitudes toward infants compare with attitudes today?

Many workers also received health care and other benefits for the first time, owing principally to a union drive to get employers to add benefits to labor contracts. Detroit's skilled autoworkers, led by Walter Reuther of the United Auto Workers (UAW), signed such an agreement with employers in 1950. Known as the Treaty of Detroit, the contract guaranteed, for an unprecedented five-year period, high wages, paid holidays, and generous health care and pensions. These benefits, combined with steady wage increases, gave American autoworkers the highest standard of living of any industrial labor force in the world. In return, the UAW tacitly agreed to drop its insistence on overseeing management and to remain loyal to employers.

Benefits soon became a standard condition of employment in about a third of all industries. They proved a mixed blessing for workers as a whole, however. Wherever unions were strong, members could secure health care coverage. But the contracts generally covered only employees who belonged to powerful unions such as the UAW—most of whom were skilled, white, and male. Typically, neither unskilled workers (often African American) nor agricultural laborers (often Latino or African American) qualified, and smaller businesses rarely offered benefits. Tensions mounted between workers with benefits and those without, often along racial lines. Content with the new arrangement, the powerful unions ceased to lobby for Truman's proposed national health care system, depriving that initiative of its wealthiest, best-organized champions.

CROSSCURRENTS

By 1950, the United States was well on its way to what would be a spectacular, twenty-five-year period of strong economic growth and low unemployment. This economic boom was fueled partly by the Cold War and ongoing government investment in infrastructure. For the first time in U.S. history, the majority of American men worked a single well-paid job, possessed a college or high school diploma, and owned their own home. White male minorities—Jews, Catholics, and European immigrants—entered college or vocational school for the first time, bought suburban homes, and joined the middle class in unprecedented numbers.

Most African Americans, Latinos, and other minorities, however, did not get ahead in the postwar years, no matter how hard they worked. These communities and their white allies pointed out the embarrassing gap between reality and the United States' Cold War image as the global champion of freedom and prosperity. Furthermore, approval of the consumer society and the U.S. government's policy of Cold War was hardly unanimous. Some critics condemned suburban life as antidemocratic and soul destroying. Others, in search of personal or aesthetic experience, shunned politics and the consumerist world to forge daring and controversial new art forms.

UNEVEN AFFLUENCE

Despite the march of affluence in the postwar years, about one in three Americans remained poor or grew poorer. Cultural, political, and legal barriers prevented most African Americans and Latinos, for example, from sharing in the prosperity. Reform bumped up against the brick wall of southern Democrats' segregationism and refusal to grant federal agencies greater authority over local affairs for fear that the federal government would treat all races equally. Rather than entrusting resources to federal agencies, lawmakers put the administration of school lunches, college loans, and housing aid in the hands of local and state authorities. The majority of white southerners no longer tolerated lynching by the late 1940s, but their representatives blocked the passage of a federal anti-lynching law in 1949. Truman's initiatives to protect voting rights in the South and establish a commission on racial discrimination in the workplace suffered the same fate. When Congress did enact Fair Deal initiatives that might have helped minorities and poor whites, it often underfunded the programs.

Across the nation, local agencies reviewed people's eligibility for federal entitlements. However, particularly in the South, these agencies disqualified minorities. Mississippi, for instance, guaranteed over three thousand federal home mortgage loans for veterans in 1947 but gave just two of those loans to African Americans. In New York, African Americans were the recipients of just one in a thousand veteran loans and 2 percent of all conventional mortgages. Colleges exercised similar exclusionary practices. Three decades before affirmative action programs would help underrepresented minorities gain employment or entry to college, the Fair Deal was implicitly operating as a form of affirmative action targeted at whites.

THE DEINDUSTRIALIZING CITY

While the suburbs boomed in the late 1940s and early 1950s, many American cities—especially in the Northeast—slowly lost jobs, industry, and their broad tax base. Typically, the cities' loss was the suburbs' gain. This shift meant that minorities, who had little choice but to remain in the city, lost ground while whites, more likely to suburbanize, advanced. Federal investment enabled city-based defense industries to relocate to the suburban Sunbelt, where they built on cheap land close to military bases. Oakland, California, for example, lost thousands of defense-related jobs when the war industries wound down. But even the throbbing capital of auto production, Detroit, experienced creeping job loss, particularly among semiskilled and unskilled workers, who were disproportionately African American.

Even as corporate profits soared, city-based manufacturers looked for ways to expand production, cut costs, and limit their dealings with assertive labor unions. The Ford Motor Company established an Automation Department in 1947, targeting the company's River Rouge, Michigan, plant and other city plants with strong UAW chapters for the installation of automated equipment. Soon automation was heralded as

Shuttered Factories. Abandoned workshops such as this textile plant in Massachusetts became a common sight in the 1950s as manufacturers left cities where labor unions were strong and relocated to southern states with right-to-work laws and weak unions.

the next phase of industrialization and the key to raising the U.S. standard of living. Although automation led to job losses, the UAW accepted it as long as employers agreed to retrain or find other work for the union's chief constituency: skilled workers. Management and the union's national leadership agreed that unskilled, semiskilled, and recent hires would be let go first. Because these workers were more likely to be African American or Latino, unemployment rates among these minorities rose faster than among whites.

To trim costs, raise profits, and disentangle themselves from unions, industrial employers also scaled back urban operations or even quit the city altogether. Most opened plants in the suburban and rural areas of the Midwest or the "right-to-work" states of the South, where labor was less unionized and local government offered substantial tax breaks. General Motors spent $3.4 billion on new plants, while smaller manufacturers followed GM and Ford to the suburbs, a move further eroding the cities' tax base. By 1960, thousands of urban factories had closed, throwing tens of thousands of people out of work and leaving behind buildings that, just a few years earlier, were buzzing with activity.

RACE AND SUBURBANIZATION

Creeping unemployment hit urban minorities particularly hard, but it was not the only challenge people of color faced. Across the nation, federal housing policy, the suburban boom, and racial segregation interacted to promote the breakdown of low-income neighborhoods and reinforce racial discrimination.

Federal loan policy aggravated the situation by awarding mortgages on the basis of neighborhood rather than the individual applicant's credit-worthiness. Beginning in 1947, the government and private lenders divided cities into four zones, ranking them from most likely to hold or increase their value to least likely to do so. The latter neighborhoods were usually shaded red on residential security maps, and their residents were **redlined**—automatically denied a mortgage—regardless of income. Long-standing patterns of discrimination and segregation dovetailed with the practice of redlining. Since the turn of the century, real estate covenants and other forms of segregation had forced most African Americans and Latinos to live in red zone neighborhoods, often poorly serviced by government and neglected by slumlords. Denied an ownership stake in their neighborhood, red zone minorities saw their property values and quality of life decline further.

Many urban whites took advantage of federal mortgages and packed up for the suburbs. During this "white flight," African American and Latino communities spilled out of their crowded, segregated neighborhoods into white working-class areas with higher-quality housing. Those whites who had not yet joined the flight to the suburbs feared that the arrival of minorities would lead to the redlining of their neighborhoods and cause property values to plunge. White parents also shuddered at the thought of racially diverse schools and their daughters dating—or

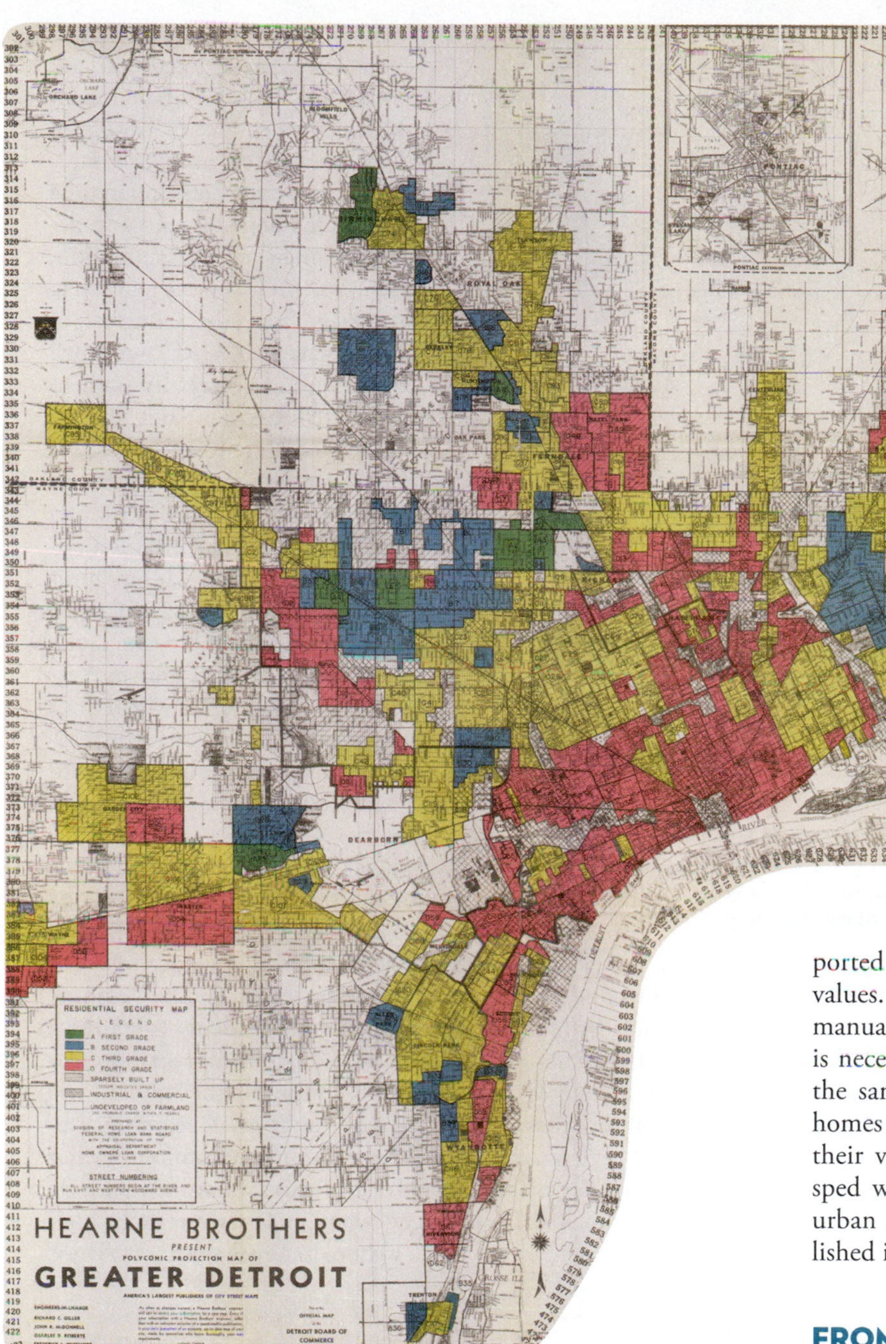

Mapping Race, Institutionalizing Inequality. Residential security maps, created by the Roosevelt administration as a tool for targeting lower-income neighborhoods in need of housing assistance, were used after the war by banks and federal loan officers to identify African American neighborhoods and areas where the number of minorities was increasing. Such neighborhoods ran the risk of being redlined—disqualified from eligibility for a mortgage.

marrying—an African American or Latino. Urban whites living in transitioning neighborhoods consequently joined the rush to the suburbs or organized to "defend" their turf. In New York City and elsewhere, the youth clubs of the 1930s morphed into neighborhood gangs that patrolled "their" territory and kept outsiders from using local pools and parks.

In Atlanta, neo-fascist youth gangs mobilized to stop the flow of African Americans into all-white areas. "There are two ways to fight this thing," one young neo-fascist explained to white residents of a transitioning neighborhood. "With ballots and bullets. We are going to try ballots first!" The youths' embrace of Nazism was too extreme for most white southerners, particularly once these young fascists were convicted of crimes, including the murder of a young African American man who wandered into a white Atlanta neighborhood. But the Ku Klux Klan, with which more whites were comfortable, picked up the slack. Organizing "neighborhood defense" groups, the Klan became a force in local politics by 1950.

When it came to real estate, federal agencies rarely challenged local racism and even supported it in the name of maintaining social peace and property values. "If a neighborhood is to retain stability," the official manual of the Federal Housing Authority (FHA) directed, "it is necessary that properties shall continue to be occupied by the same social and racial classes." According to the FHA, homes owned by African Americans were unlikely to maintain their value. In effect, federal policies bolstered segregation, sped white flight to the suburbs, and further impoverished urban African Americans and Latinos. The patterns established in the postwar years would intensify in future years.

FROM SOCIAL JUSTICE TO CIVIL RIGHTS

After the war, certain social observers connected the plight of many African Americans with that of colonized peoples, especially those in Africa and Asia. Among these champions of freedom, an aging W. E. B. Du Bois called on the United States to make good on its claim to leadership of the "free world." As the Cold War escalated, however, the government became increasingly embarrassed by Du Bois and other critics who, to Soviet propagandists' delight, publicized the hypocrisy of the United States' claim to leadership despite widespread injustice. The government confiscated Du Bois's passport. The culture industries soon joined in, censuring critics and striking the name of social-justice advocate, popular singer, and retired football star Paul Robeson from the list of football's All-Americans.

In northern cities, many African Americans, Latinos, and left-leaning whites reacted with distress to what they saw unfolding in their neighborhoods and workplaces. Workers at Ford's River Rouge plant and militant chapters of the union movement raised the alarm. But middle-class African Americans and civil rights organizations focused on the South, where over 60 percent of all African Americans lived and where segregation and disfranchisement were legally mandated. In 1944, the NAACP had won a victory when the Supreme Court outlawed white-only primaries, preparing a path for African American political participation in the South. This victory encouraged the NAACP to pursue a strategy that focused on courtroom battles for civil rights rather than the social-justice issues of poverty, joblessness, and urban decay. Especially once the United States entered the Cold War, the NAACP distanced itself from both the left's broad social-justice agenda and the anticolonial movements of Africa and Asia. The organization declared its commitment to anti-communism and cultivated its reputation for middle-class respectability.

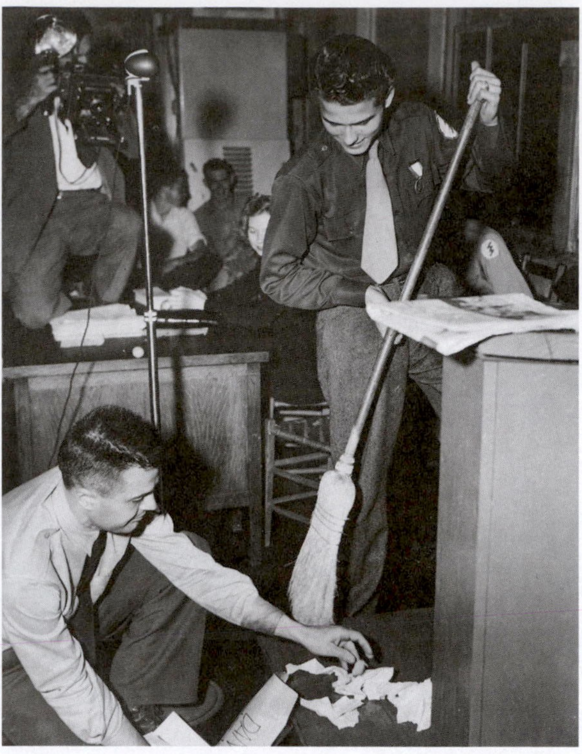

Enforcing Segregation. A self-proclaimed neo-fascist gang, the Columbians, Inc., used the threatening lightning bolt imagery of the elite Nazi *Schutzstaffel* (or Protection Squadron, which carried out the Holocaust) to warn African Americans and real estate agents that Atlanta's Ashby Street neighborhood was "off limits."

Civil rights advocates notched up another victory in 1946, after African American Irene Morgan was convicted of a misdemeanor in Virginia for refusing to move to the back of a bus that was en route to another state. Morgan appealed her case to the Supreme Court. In *Morgan v. Virginia,* a majority of the justices found in her favor, outlawing segregation in interstate transportation (see Map 26.2). In 1948, the Supreme Court prohibited racist housing covenants and forbade graduate schools that received federal funds from barring applicants on account of race. State courts also acted against legalized racism. The same year, California's Supreme Court overturned California's fifty-year-old ban on interracial marriage. New organizations, such as the League of United Latin American Citizens, also began challenging racist laws and institutions in court.

Although important, the courtroom victories were largely symbolic. The states were often slow to comply, and local jurisdictions sometimes refused outright, knowing that the federal government was unlikely to enforce the law. Even in California, voters overwhelmingly retained racial covenants. In response to the South's ongoing refusal to desegregate interstate transportation, sixteen African American and white northerners from the Congress of Racial Equality (CORE)—a small Christian pacifist organization in Chicago—embarked in April 1947 on a "Journey of Reconciliation" to challenge the segregation of interstate bus services directly. Boarding two buses in Washington, D.C., African American CORE members sat up front while white members sat in back. Touring fifteen southern cities, the riders encountered little resistance except in North Carolina, where three were arrested. CORE's action emboldened local African Americans to refuse to sit in the back of the bus on interstate routes.

Black southerners devised additional strategies to counter inequality. In several cases, young African Americans who refused to accept second-class status led protests. In Farmville, Virginia, Barbara Rose Johnson, a sixteen-year-old student, organized a strike at her all–African American high school in 1951 to protest the state's chronic underfunding of the school. The NAACP soon began working with Johnson, developing a legal challenge against school segregation and conjoining her case with that of another African American student, Linda Brown, who had been denied entry to her white-only high school in Topeka, Kansas. These

The Price of the AFRO Is 7 Cents In D.C.—Pay No More

WASHINGTON AFRO AMERICAN

COMING! COMING! Two new comics that you'll enjoy — Starting June 22.

54th Year, No. 43

WASHINGTON, D.C., JUNE 8, 1946

28 PAGES

JC Bus Travel Outlawed

Supreme Court Votes 6-1 in Morgan Case

Jurists Rule State Laws Place Undue Burden on Interstate Travel

Jim crow on Southern busses is dead.

Reversing the opinion of the Supreme Court of Appeals of Virginia in the Irene Morgan case, the United States Supreme Court on Monday, by a 6 to 1 vote, ruled that State jim-crow laws are not applicable to interstate bus transportation.

The majority opinion, which was read by Justice Stanley

Chronology of Morgan Case

Uphill Fight Took Two Years

1. Arrested July 16, 1944.
2. Fined $10 by Trial Judge, Oct. 18, 1944.
3. Conviction Upheld by Virginia Court, June 6, 1945.
4. Petition for Rehearing Denied September 4, 1945.
5. Appealed to Supreme Court, March 2, 1946.
6. Decision Reversed, June 3, 1946.

held that State segregation laws imposed "an undue burden on interstate commerce."

Interstate passengers coming from the North were not being segregated Wednesday, on either the Greyhound or Trailways bus lines running into Richmond. Those coming from the South were still seated from the rear, it was learned.

Managers of the Richmond terminals told the AFRO they were awaiting advice from their home offices before instructing drivers not to enforce the outlawed Virginia Statute.

The law calling for the segregation of passengers on buses in Virginia was enacted in 1930, while the statute applying to trains was put on the books in 1902.

Fined $10 for Refusing to Move

The validity of the Virginia statute was challenged by Mrs. Irene Morgan of Baltimore, who appealed from a Virginia Supreme Court decision upholding the imposition of a $10 fine on her by a Middlesex County circuit court judge for refusing to move to the rear of the bus.

Mrs. Morgan had been arrested on a warrant on July 15, 1944, after she refused to move to the rear of the bus

Her Fight Ends Bus Jim Crow

MRS. IRENE MORGAN of Baltimore and New York, who was plaintiff in the NAACP suit against the State of Virginia, which resulted in the Supreme Court ruling Monday ending segregation of races on all buses traveling between the States regardless of local laws.

Cases of Bus Jim Crow Show Barbarity of Policy

Pickets March in Protest; Choir Sings

U. S. Sues Klan for Unpaid Taxes

Georgia's Governor Also Cracking Down on Order

FBI PROBE ASKED

Organization Big Factor in Gubernatorial Drive

By CARDELL W. M'VICKERS

(See Campbell Cartoon on Editorial Page)

ATLANTA—The United States Government Thursday entered the arena in the growing battle to squelch the revival of the Ku Klux Klan when suit was filed against the hooded order seeking recovery of $685,305 in back income taxes.

the week

'Metamorphosis' of the Colonel

By VINCENT TUBBS

The Old Days

Hundreds Ignore Line to Hear Tuskegee Concert

Dr. Patterson Refused to Cancel Date at DAR Constitution Hall

Refuses Proceeds

Endorsing Groups

Court-Ordered Desegregation. The African American press informed readers of the Supreme Court's order to desegregate interstate transportation.

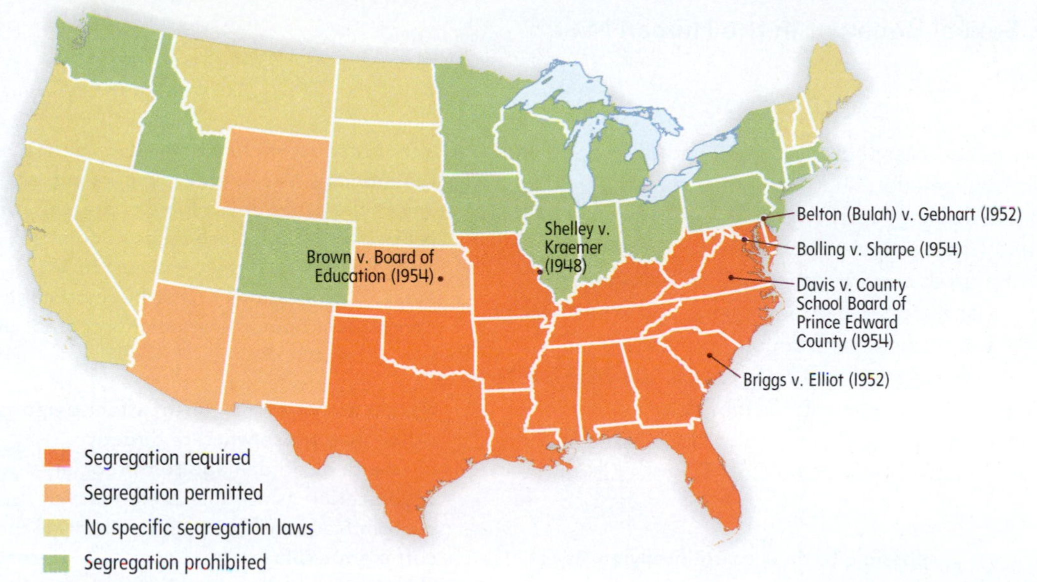

Map 26.2 Segregated America, 1950. Civil rights organizations won a number of important cases between 1944 and 1950. Yet as this map indicates, states were slow to implement federal court orders. It would be another five years before a systematic campaign of civil disobedience began to desegregate buses, lunch bars, and schools throughout the South.

students' experiences became the basis of the historic case *Brown v. Board of Education* (1954), in which the Supreme Court declared segregated schools unconstitutional (see Chapter 27).

CHALLENGING CONVENTION

By 1950, mass culture, from television to magazines and music, presented suburban family life as the sweet fruit of citizenship in the world's richest, most democratic nation. But many writers, filmmakers, and other artists opted instead to explore the anxieties and limitations of modern American life. The HUAC investigations had chilled political dissent, however, and few artists and social commentators were prepared to criticize suburban culture or Cold War policy explicitly.

The few Americans who did directly criticize the consumer society were mostly scholars supported by prestigious universities. In *The Lonely Crowd* (1950), Harvard sociologist David Riesman and fellow authors argued that consumerism had caused middle-class Americans to lose their inner compass and instead to focus outward, seeking the social approval of others. "The other-directed person," the authors later clarified, "wants to be loved rather than esteemed." The cost of becoming other-directed, they believed, was a loss of individuality, oversensitivity to others' expectations, and the death of creativity.

The suggestion that the postwar consumer society was warping Americans' sense of identity recurred in C. Wright Mills's *White Collar* (1951). Sociologist Mills lamented the spread of what he called the "sales mentality" in American society. White-collar Americans (office rather than factory or field workers), he argued, emphasized having a cheerful, well-rounded personality that helped "make the sale." The salesman personality had become so pervasive, said Mills, that people related to one another as salesmen even when they were not selling anything. "Men are estranged from one another," Mills wrote, "as each secretly tries to make an instrument of the other."

Harvard-educated biologist Alfred Kinsey challenged a very different aspect of American culture—attitudes toward sex and sexuality. In *Sexual Behavior in the Human Male* (1948), he criticized the conventional view that men's sexual experiences and predilections were mostly fixed and heterosexual. Instead, Kinsey's interviews with some four thousand American men suggested that most men had a range of sexual experiences in the course of their lifetimes. Kinsey's report earned its author extensive media coverage. The book shocked some Americans, who looked for evidence of communist subversion. But in a Cold War culture that celebrated science, Dr. Kinsey's use of scientific language and his affiliation with the respectable Rockefeller Foundation conferred immense authority on his work, and the report became a best seller (see Interpreting the Sources: Alfred Kinsey, *Sexual Behavior in the Human Male*).

A small group of artists also radically challenged convention after the war. Leading American painters such as Jackson Pollock and Mark Rothko produced **abstract expressionist** works in which they rejected the realist images of New Deal–era art—popular portraits of everyday life and people—in favor of abstract work that was neither easily understood nor obviously political. The artists also found advertising and other commercial images manipulative and banal. Art, many of the rebel painters argued, was the expression of the artist's own personal experience and feelings, which were often in turmoil and almost always restless. Such artwork tended to be rough, explosive, and large scale, requiring tremendous athleticism by the artist.

White women such as Lee Krasner and African American artists such as Hale Woodruff and Hughie Lee-Smith also produced critically acclaimed signature works in these years. But almost all the leading Abstract Expressionists were white men who dismissed others' work as insufficiently abstract. Despite their self-promoting chauvinism, however, the aggressive young artists created an important, distinctly American art form that transformed the meaning and purpose of art.

INTERPRETING THE SOURCES

Alfred Kinsey, Sexual Behavior in the Human Male

In the postwar years, Alfred Kinsey made sex a respectable topic of study and, among college-educated communities, public conversation. Although well-educated Americans were already familiar with the works of early-twentieth-century psychoanalyst Sigmund Freud (who had written extensively on sexuality), Kinsey was the first to study the sexual behavior of a great mass of Americans. A biologist by training, Kinsey presented his findings in language designed to persuade the reader of the scientific rigor and legitimacy of his sex studies. Far from putting readers off, Kinsey's dry and even quite tedious prose functioned as a Trojan horse, allowing him to smuggle a taboo topic into public discourse. Together with *Sexual Behavior in the Human Female* (1953), his report on male sexuality sold almost a million copies and was referenced widely in the press, Hollywood movies, and even Cole Porter's hit song "Too Darned Hot."

For some time now there has been an increasing awareness among many people of the desirability of obtaining data about sex which would represent an accumulation of scientific fact completely divorced from questions of moral value and social custom. Practicing physicians find thousands of their patients in need of such objective data. Psychiatrists . . . find that . . . patients need help in resolving the sexual conflicts that have arisen in their lives. An increasing number of persons would like to bring an educated intelligence into the consideration of such matters as sexual adjustments in marriage, the sexual guidance of children, the pre-marital sexual adjustments of youth, sex education, sexual activities which are in conflict with the mores [moral conventions]. . . . Before it is possible to think scientifically on any of these matters, more needs to be known about the actual behavior of people. . . .

[H]uman sexual behavior represents one of the least explored segments of biology, psychology, and sociology. . . . [M]ore has been known about the sexual behavior of . . . farm and laboratory animals. In our Western European-American culture, sexual responses, more than any other physiologic activities, have been subject to religious evaluation, social taboo, and formal legislation. . . . Sexual responses . . . involve emotional changes which are more intense than those associated with any other sort of physiologic activity. For that reason, it is difficult to comprehend how any society could become as concerned about respiratory functioning, . . . digestive functioning, . . . excretory functioning, or any of the other physiologic processes. It is probable that the close association of sex, religious values, rituals, and custom in most . . . civilizations . . . has been primarily consequent upon the emotional content of sexual behavior.

Sexual activities may [also] affect persons other than those who are directly involved, or do damage to the social organization as a whole. Defenders of . . . custom frequently contend that this is the sufficient explanation of society's interest in the individual's sexual behavior; but this is probably a . . . rationalization that fails to take into account the historic data on the origin of the custom. It is ordinarily said that criminal law is designed to protect property and persons, and if society's only interest in controlling sex behavior were to protect persons, then the criminal codes concerned with assault and battery should provide adequate protection. The fact that there is a body of sex laws . . . apart from the laws protecting persons is evidence . . . that [sex laws protect] custom. [This is why] sex customs and sex law . . . are defended with more emotion than the laws that concern property or person. The failure of the scientist to go further than he has in

THE COLD WAR HEATS UP

Cold War tensions mounted in 1949 following the installment of communist governments in East Asia and the Soviets' first successful nuclear test. Although the communist governments of China and North Korea were independent of the Soviets, American leaders viewed them as puppets of Stalin and therefore a threat to be contained. Criticized widely for "losing" China, President Truman set the nation on course for a huge military buildup that would further escalate U.S.-Soviet tensions. Despite Truman's get-tough approach, however, conservative and moderate Republicans amplified their criticism, preparing the way for Senator Joseph McCarthy to conduct modern-day witch hunts for suspected communists within the U.S. government. When communist North Korea invaded South Korea soon afterward, Truman believed he had little choice but to take the nation into the first armed conflict of the Cold War.

THE COLD WAR IN ASIA

Although containment originated in American efforts to block Soviet influence in Europe, it soon became the guiding star of U.S. policy globally. With the militarization of the Cold War, Japan, which lies just a few hundred miles off the coast of the eastern Soviet Union, acquired new strategic importance, principally as a site for U.S. naval and air bases. In 1948, Truman abandoned efforts to establish an open democracy and a New Deal government in Japan, clamping down on the nation's unions and suspending reparations to the Soviets. The State studies of sex is undoubtedly a reflection of society's attitude in this field. . . .

The present study, then, represents an attempt to accumulate an objectively determined body of fact about sex which strictly avoids social or moral interpretations of the fact. Each person who reads this report will want to make interpretations in accordance with his understanding of moral values and significances; but that is not part of the scientific method and, indeed, scientists have no special capacities for making such evaluations.

Source: Kinsey, A. C., Pomeroy, W. B., & Martin, C. E. (1948). *Sexual behavior in the human male.* Indiana University Press, pp. 3–5; originally published by W. B. Saunders Company, 1948. Reprinted by permission of The Kinsey Institute for Research in Sex, Gender, and Reproduction, Inc.

Explore the Source

1. Why, according to Kinsey, is sex worth studying?
2. Who or what might Kinsey have been arguing against in the late 1940s?
3. Why might Kinsey have insisted on separating scientific study from moral interpretation? Is Kinsey being purely objective in this excerpt, as he infers? Explain.

The Science of Sex. Alfred Kinsey both jolted and titillated readers with his frank discussions of sex and the diversity of Americans' sexual experience.

Department also deregulated Japan's economy and reinstated a number of wartime leaders. Events in neighboring China further persuaded Truman that a pro-U.S. Japan was more important than a democratic one. The communist forces of Mao Zedong were poised to overthrow the unpopular nationalist government of Jiang Jieshi. In early 1949, despite $3 billion of U.S. military and economic aid, the nationalists all but collapsed, fleeing to Formosa (Taiwan). A triumphant Mao proclaimed the People's Republic of China in October 1949. By that time, another neighbor, North Korea, had also established a communist government.

Coming on the heels of the Soviets' first successful test of an atomic bomb, the news that China had fallen to communism rattled many Americans. Viewing the world through the Cold War lens, most assumed that Stalin was behind the Chinese Revolution and that Mao was a Soviet puppet. In fact, Mao was resolutely independent, and Stalin had supported the nationalists after the war, counseling a disillusioned Mao to do the same (probably because Stalin calculated that the U.S.-backed nationalists would provide a stronger check against the possible resurgence of Japanese militarism). The Soviet leader also withheld large-scale aid from the Chinese communists and privately derided Mao as a "cave-dweller-like Marxist." Despite weak Soviet support, however, Mao went on to lead China for almost thirty years, until his death in 1976.

In need of allies and concerned about the possible military revival of Japan, Mao pursued a treaty of friendship with the Soviet Union. Stalin was unenthusiastic but eventually obliged, and the two nations promised to come to each other's aid in the event of armed attack. Truman interpreted the treaty as further evidence that the Soviets were calling the shots in China and refused to officially recognize the new government. Non-recognition put China out-of-bounds for American trade for almost thirty years, hardened Mao's antipathy toward the United States, and spurred Chinese militarism.

The "loss of China" to communism led Truman to order a sweeping study of U.S. military and foreign policy. Coauthored by George Kennan, Dean Acheson, and other high-ranking officials, National Security Council Report 68 (NSC-68) cast the Soviets as an apocalyptic global threat. The report urged the president to meet that threat through a policy of containment and a massive military buildup. Truman at first rejected the recommendations on the grounds that the military strategy would cost billions more than his federal budget allowed. When communist North Korea invaded South Korea in June 1950, however, he accepted the report. NSC-68 was the foundation of U.S. foreign policy for the next twenty years.

EVANGELIZING THE COLD WAR

Despite Truman's anti-Soviet policies, Republican critics condemned the president and the Democratic Party for allegedly losing China. Truman countered in 1950 with an exhaustive State Department report that explained that the United States could not have saved China's failing nationalist government. But critics trumpeted the study as evidence of the president's failure to contain communism. When Alger Hiss was convicted in federal court in the same month, the anti-Truman chorus grew even louder. Powerful conservatives stoked popular fears that communists were infiltrating American society and politics, sparking the second **Red Scare** in the nation's history. (The first had followed World War I and the Bolshevik Revolution; see Chapter 22.)

As part of this movement, *Time* magazine publisher Henry Luce joined forces with media magnate William Randolph Hearst to finance and publicize the religious revivals of a little-known Protestant evangelist, Billy Graham (see Singular Lives: Henry Luce, Opinion Maker). The Reverend Graham's fiery anti-communist speeches, delivered over the radio and at a tent revival in Los Angeles, attracted a mass audience. Graham described the Cold War confrontation as an apocalyptic battle between Christ and Antichrist: "The only way that we're going to win that battle," he declared, "is for America to turn back to God and back to Christ and back to the Bible at this hour!" By 1950, millions of Americans had signed on to Graham's Cold War religious revival.

Compounding the president's troubles, in early 1950 a little-known Republican senator from Wisconsin, Joseph McCarthy, shot to national prominence after he announced that 205 alleged Communist Party members were employed by the State Department. The charges were baseless, and McCarthy kept changing the number on his list. To investigate the matter, Senate Democrats established the Tydings Committee, whose final report dismissed the demagogic McCarthy's accusations as a "fraud and a hoax" designed to confuse Americans. Nonetheless, Republican senators, conservative Democrats, and conservative publishers sided with McCarthy. That same year, Congress passed the McCarran Internal Security Bill (1950), which required communist groups to register with the government and authorized the detention of suspected subversives during times of war or "internal security emergencies." Truman vetoed the bill, denouncing it as "the greatest danger to freedom of speech, press, and assembly since the Alien and Sedition Laws of 1798." But Congress overrode his veto and the bill became law.

THE KOREAN WAR

Truman's popularity—already in decline—slumped to an all-time low in the early months of 1950. But the tide turned in June, when communist North Korea invaded South Korea. Five years earlier, after Allied forces had liberated Korea from Japan, the United States and the Soviets had partitioned Korea along the thirty-eighth parallel, an arrangement formalized in 1948. Soviet troops had remained in North Korea until 1949 and installed a pro-communist government. Likewise, U.S. forces had handed off power to a sympathetic government and withdrew. North Korean leader Kim Il-sung, eager to reunite the nation under his communist government, took the withdrawal of U.S. forces as a sign that Truman no longer had an interest in Korean affairs and invaded in 1950.

The unexpected invasion shocked Truman and his critics alike. Many U.S. officials feared that World War III had begun. Convinced that the Soviets were calling the shots, Truman viewed the invasion as the first of a series of Soviet-directed aggressions against Asia—and ultimately the world. "If we let Korea down," he cautioned, "the Soviet(s) will keep right on going. . . ." The U.S. prevailed on the UN Security Council to charge North Korea with a "breach of the peace" and to authorize UN troops to intervene. Truman then dispatched aircraft and warships to Asian territories. Bypassing his critics in Congress, Truman exercised the "police power" of the president to send American ground troops. The Cold War had become hot; Truman's popularity instantly rebounded.

Strains had been building between the two Koreas and within South Korea for years. Although the North's leader, Kim Il-sung, was a communist, and the South's president, Syngman Rhee, an ultraconservative, both were ardent nationalists who resented Soviet and American domination of the peninsula. But each resented his Korean rival more and was strongly committed to reuniting the entire nation under his own regime. In 1949, Kim Il-sung had secured Stalin's permission to "liberate the Fatherland" and unite Korea. Contrary to U.S. assumptions, however, the Soviet leader had refused to get directly involved. Fearing war with the United States, Stalin instead advised the North Koreans to seek support from China's Mao. The Chinese leader, preoccupied with planning the invasions of Taiwan and Tibet, was equally unenthusiastic, until American

SINGULAR LIVES

Henry Luce, Opinion Maker

Born in China during the Spanish-American War (1898), and dying seventy-odd years later as hundreds of thousands of American soldiers shipped out to Vietnam, Henry Luce lived a life that spanned the era in which the United States burst onto the international scene and became a superpower. As the publisher of *Time*, the United States' top-circulation newsmagazine, Luce helped shape ordinary Americans' perceptions of the nation's newfound power after World War II. He outspokenly rejected the Cold War strategy of containment as being "too soft" on the Soviets, favoring direct military confrontation, including the use of short-range nuclear weapons, wherever the Soviets extended their influence. Although his hawkish ideas had little direct impact on U.S. foreign policy, Luce fueled American apprehensions about the Soviets and helped legitimize the military buildup of the 1950s.

The shy son of devout American missionaries, Luce spent most of his childhood in boarding school in China before coming to the United States at age fifteen. Intellectually insatiable and deeply ambitious, he and an associate founded *Time* magazine in 1923. Under Luce's direction, *Time* broke journalistic boundaries by replacing dry, factual accounts with richly detailed stories that emphasized the "newsmakers" and personalities behind the news. Articles crammed with "knowing details"—such as whether this or that congressman sweated profusely or had hands resembling meat hooks—appealed in a culture fascinated with celebrity. Luce followed *Time* with *Life* (the first and most influential photographic magazine), *Fortune* (the popular business weekly), and *Sports Illustrated*, again applying the winning formula of putting people and personality at the center of the story. Radio tie-ins soon followed. By World War II, the man whom associates typically described as awkward, friendless, and lonely was connecting with tens of millions of devoted readers each week.

Luce openly used his magazines to try to influence Americans' understanding of global and national affairs—most famously in the 1941 *Life* editorial "The American Century." Americans were "the inheritors of all the great principles of Western Civilization," he averred, and it was now "time to be the powerhouse from which [American] ideals spread throughout the world." That mission became ever more urgent, at least in Luce's mind, after World War II. Restless by nature, Luce revamped his publications in an effort to focus Americans' attention on what he saw as the looming Soviet threat and the need to promote U.S. business and democracy overseas. *Fortune* was to "assist in the development of American Business Enterprise at home and abroad," chiefly by carrying exciting stories of American business successes and dropping its usual diversity of opinion in favor of an unabashedly pro-corporate ideology. *Time* relentlessly harangued President Truman for seeking peace in Korea and allegedly "losing China," angrily describing Truman's diplomacy as the "greatest betrayal" of the century. The magazine also became a virtual Republican mouthpiece in 1952, when Luce helped persuade Dwight D. Eisenhower to run for the presidency and dispatched his two best writers to help out Eisenhower's campaign.

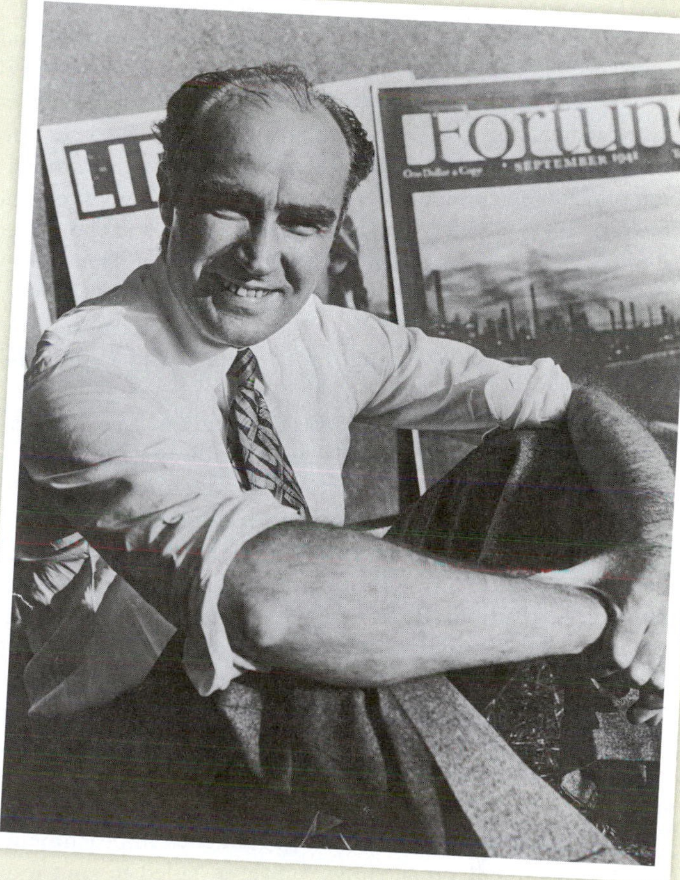

Henry Luce. The publisher strikes a casual pose in front of two of his influential magazines.

Critics complained that Luce's magazines "disguised opinion as fact." But readers could not get enough, purchasing upwards of twenty million copies a week by 1953 and turning Luce's corporation, Time Inc., into the world's most profitable media empire. Time Inc. subsequently acquired television stations and merged with Warner Communications, forming the multinational media corporation Time Warner Inc. in 1989.

Think About It

1. What accounts for Americans' receptiveness to the personality-driven style of newsmagazines like *Time* in the postwar era?
2. Why might critics have objected to the magazines' blending of fact and opinion?

troops and battleships began amassing in the region. Persuaded that China's security was imperiled, Mao dispatched 250,000 soldiers to the war zone in October 1950. The Soviets began to supply secret air cover as well as training and equipment for the North Koreans and Chinese.

The United States initially suffered heavy troop losses and costly delays. Conditions worsened as Chinese strategists exploited the Americans' low expectations of China's peasant army, which pretended to retreat only to draw U.S. forces into a deadly trap. This effective tactic enraged the U.S. commanding officer, General Douglas MacArthur, who then vowed not only to defeat North Korea but to crush China and the Soviet Union, too. President Truman and Secretary of State Dean Acheson, however, favored a more restrained **limited war** that focused on defeating North Korea with conventional (nonnuclear) weapons and avoiding direct conflict with China and the USSR.

The concept of limited war was unpopular with the American people, particularly once Truman indicated that he was interested in negotiating an armistice and reinstating the old border. Republicans and many in the military criticized him as a weak-kneed "appeaser" of communism. The fanatical Senator McCarthy accused the president of being a "sinister monster of many heads and many tentacles, a monster conceived in the Kremlin. . . ." In Korea, General MacArthur publicly taunted his commander in chief for being "soft" on communism—a charge that prompted Truman to relieve the insubordinate MacArthur of all duties and to replace him with General Matthew Ridgeway. Truman's dismissal of the nation's most famous war hero was hugely unpopular, and Republican leaders called for the president's impeachment. The impeachment proceedings, however, failed to gain momentum in Congress.

Meanwhile, the war became stalemated, and Stalin now mocked the United States for being incapable of subduing a weak nation of peasants. By 1953, over 2.5 million North Koreans and more than 1 million South Koreans had been killed. Over 33,000 Americans and 150,000 Chinese soldiers had also lost their lives in what was rapidly becoming one of the deadliest wars of the twentieth century.

MCCARTHY'S REIGN

As the Korean War bogged down, Senator McCarthy widened his witch hunt. Although his specific charges of State Department disloyalty had been shown to be baseless, he began accusing more fellow Americans of being agents of Soviet communism. The senator worked with conservatives in the media to publicize his attacks, using his chairmanship of a minor Senate subcommittee to conduct hearings and confront supposed subversives. Although the federal government sorely needed East Asia experts as the war in Korea escalated, McCarthy prevailed on the State Department to dismiss them on the dubious grounds that they were responsible for communist victory in China.

McCarthy's place in the national limelight steadily grew. He campaigned for dozens of fellow Republicans in the 1950 and 1952 elections, issuing dire warnings about Soviet plans for world domination and accusing Democratic incumbents of sheltering communists and traitors. Every Republican candidate for whom McCarthy campaigned in 1950 won, boosting his power in the Senate and making him the party's chief strategist. Although his anti-communist tirades played particularly well among conservative Republicans, McCarthy, who was Catholic, also gained support in Democratic strongholds, especially in Catholic and Eastern European communities. Although traditionally Democratic, many Catholics admired the senator for wielding influence in the overwhelmingly Protestant arena of national politics. In the wake of the Soviet crackdown in Poland and elsewhere, many Americans of Eastern European descent praised his uncompromising anti-communism.

McCarthyism, the practice of accusing people of communism without any evidence, received a boost from the states, many of which established their own investigatory committees and fired employees suspected of subversion. Seeking to benefit from the upswing in anti-communism, Democrats reconvened HUAC in 1951 and expanded their blacklisting. A number of conservative organizations, including the American Legion, also joined the effort. Soon, local anti-communist groups were prevailing on libraries and schools throughout the country to remove "communistic" novels and nonfiction. Even books about Robin Hood (who, as legend has it, stole from the rich and gave to the poor) were censored as subversive. The Supreme Court denied free speech rights in *Dennis v. United States* (1951), upholding the incarceration of Communist Party leaders on the basis of their beliefs rather than their actions.

Bucked up by the groundswell of support and the absence of criticism, McCarthyites accused the growing civil rights movement of being a Soviet-backed effort to subvert American society. Under J. Edgar Hoover, the Federal Bureau of Investigation (FBI) stepped up its monitoring of civil rights organizations, even though few had any connection to communism. The Justice Department prosecuted a number of alleged spies, including Julius and Ethel Rosenberg, a Jewish working-class couple from New York who belonged to the American Communist Party. In a sensational trial in 1951, the jury convicted both of having passed "the secret of the atomic bomb" to the Soviets during World War II. Subsequent evidence established that Julius Rosenberg had indeed passed on information, including crude diagrams of an implosion device, but that it was so vague as to be almost worthless to Soviet scientists. Although there was virtually no evidence against his wife, both Rosenbergs were sentenced to the electric chair and executed in 1953.

The Rosenberg case confirmed for McCarthy and his supporters that subversion was widespread. In his boldest move to date, McCarthy set his sights on the Defense Department and its secretary, George C. Marshall. The distinguished former general had overseen U.S. military operations during

Surviving McCarthyism. Hollywood and television star Judy Holliday was called before HUAC in 1952 after the anti-communist publication *Red Channels* identified her as a communist sympathizer. Although Holliday had an extraordinarily high IQ, she was frequently cast in movies as a "dumb blonde"—a role she put to good use when questioned by HUAC members, who were unable to get a straight answer from the apparently "befuddled" star. Holliday was temporarily dropped from television, but her movie career thrived. **Questions for Analysis:** Why do you think Holliday's "dumb blonde" act was so effective in the HUAC hearings? What might her experience reveal about gender stereotypes of the postwar period?

World War II and drafted the plans for European reconstruction. In a widely publicized speech before the Senate in 1951, McCarthy accused Marshall, who had helped shape U.S.-China policy, of losing China to communism and being part of a vast "conspiracy . . . to diminish the United States in world affairs, to weaken us militarily, to confuse our spirit with talk of surrender in the Far East and to impair our will to resist evil." Appalled by the vicious attack, the secretary resigned. For McCarthy and his supporters, Marshall's resignation was proof that subversives had infiltrated the U.S. government. Two years later, Marshall was awarded the Nobel Peace Prize for the Marshall Plan.

As McCarthyism spread, the new medium of television became an important battleground. American Business Consultants, Inc. (ABC), founded by businessmen and former FBI agents in 1947, claimed that the Cominform and the American Communist Party were using radio and television dramas and news programs to subvert families. According to the ABC's publication, 151 journalists, writers, broadcasters, actors, and musicians were communists or communist sympathizers. The Columbia Broadcasting Corporation (CBS) responded by issuing a loyalty oath to be signed by all employees, under threat of dismissal.

Although small numbers of Soviet spies were at work in the United States and thousands of Americans belonged to the American Communist Party, the overwhelming majority of people caught up in McCarthyism's net had broken no law. Some held communist beliefs, belonged to the party, or defended communists' rights to their beliefs. Most were patriots, and dozens, like George C. Marshall, had a record of distinguished service to the nation. But even where proof of subversion was lacking, thousands found themselves blacklisted and unemployed. Fear of blacklisting spread like wildfire after 1950, tamping down political debate and artistic expression for the rest of the decade. Many innocent victims would not work again until 1962, when the courts finally banned blacklisting.

THE ELECTION OF 1952: EISENHOWER VICTORIOUS

Allegations of subversion in the federal government became a hot topic in the presidential election of 1952, as did Truman's limited but seemingly endless war in Korea. Taking stock of his dismal voter approval ratings, the president declined to run for

Ike Versus Egghead. Unlike Democrat Adlai Stevenson, who stuck to established media such as radio and print, General Dwight Eisenhower exploited television to get out his message, instantly identifying himself with suburban consumers and their love of new technology. Alongside the optimistic, dynamic, and battle-proven Ike, Stevenson seemed old-fashioned, overly intellectual (an "egghead"), and—as a well-publicized photograph of a hole in one of his shoes suggested—homespun.

reelection. Adlai Stevenson, the governor of Illinois and former State Department attorney, headed the Democratic ticket. The erudite Stevenson tried desperately to turn voters' attention to the Democrats' domestic achievements of the past twenty years and warned that Republican rule might plunge the nation into another depression. But his opponent, former general Dwight D. "Ike" Eisenhower, kept the focus on Korea, pledging to end the war. He also vowed to rein in government spending but, much to the disappointment of party conservatives, stopped short of promising to abolish existing programs.

The first presidential candidate to run television campaign ads, Eisenhower entered millions of suburban living rooms across the nation. His choice of the popular medium affirmed his party's commitment to technology and consumption. But his strategy also called on less forward-looking forces. Indeed, although Eisenhower privately despised Joseph McCarthy's mudslinging tactics, he publicly agreed with the influential senator's goals and sought his support. The tactic worked. On election day, Ike won 55 percent of the popular vote and all but nine states. Stevenson attracted support from the urban middle class but lost critical votes among the conservative southern Democrats, Catholics, and Americans of Eastern European descent whom McCarthy had mobilized. The Republicans had broken the Democrats' twenty-year hold on the White House.

When the reviled Soviet leader Joseph Stalin died a few months into Eisenhower's presidency, relations with the Soviet Union seemed more hopeful. Stalin's successor, Nikita Khrushchev, denounced the deceased leader's iron-fisted rule and declared him guilty of causing millions of deaths through political violence and misguided agricultural policies (which had resulted in famine twenty years earlier). In April 1953, Eisenhower lamented the U.S. military buildup, publicly declaring that "(e)very gun that is made, every warship launched, every rocket fired signifies, in the final sense, a theft from those who hunger and are not fed, those who are cold and are not clothed." Equally critical of the vast expense borne by American taxpayers, he questioned the priorities of military over social spending. A few months later, Eisenhower negotiated an end to the stalled Korean War. North Korea and South Korea agreed on a new border, which more or less followed the old one, and established a demilitarized zone between the two countries. An end to the Cold War with the Soviets seemed possible.

Eisenhower and other leading Republicans gradually distanced themselves from McCarthy and his virulent anti-communism. McCarthy responded by criticizing the new president for failing to purge all suspected subversives from government and condemning him—on national television—for abandoning the effort to locate U.S. pilots missing in action since the Korean War. Eisenhower, however, refused to be drawn into open conflict with the senator, betting that McCarthy's inflammatory antics would soon cost the senator his popular support. McCarthy renewed his pursuit of

Television Rules. By 1953, television was eclipsing radio and newspapers as the single most important medium in politics. Candidates who performed well on television were more likely to win elections and garner popular support for their initiatives. Even Senator Joseph McCarthy turned to television to reach a mass audience. However, the alcoholic, bullying, and untelegenic McCarthy was unsuited to the medium—a reality that hastened his demise.

communists, investigating the U.S. Army in 1953. The televised spectacle of McCarthy verbally bullying uniformed officers—one a well-known war hero—and making wild accusations against the nation's military leaders offended many Americans. McCarthy's allies increasingly saw the senator as a liability to the cause of anti-communism.

In a blistering televised indictment of McCarthy, television broadcaster Edward R. Murrow declared that "we must not confuse dissent with disloyalty. We must remember always that accusation is not proof and that conviction depends upon evidence and due process of law. We will not walk in fear, one of another." Coming from Murrow—whose radio broadcasts from London during the German blitz had earned him nationwide admiration—these words carried great moral weight. McCarthy's popular support, already at low ebb, collapsed. Soon afterward the Senate censured McCarthy (on an unrelated charge) and effectively destroyed his political career.

CONCLUSION

The postwar era began as a time of both uncertainty and hope. Americans struggled to make sense of the global war they had just fought and their nation's emergence as a superpower. The United States, along with the Soviet Union, was now one of just two world powers capable of exerting influence over other nations and peoples. Leaders on both sides believed that a cooperative relationship was desirable, and both were initially prepared to respect the other's security needs and geographical spheres of interest. But as the superpowers began securing their respective interests, a growing faction of the Truman administration determined that the Soviets aspired to spread their influence and ideology beyond their obvious sphere of interest. That perspective became official policy, leading the United States to act to frustrate Soviet ambitions. The Soviets in turn interpreted the American stance as a hostile bid to dominate the globe. By 1948, the self-perpetuating cycle of mutual threats, suspicion, and propaganda—the Cold War—had set in.

The United States' ascent to superpower and the advent of the Cold War profoundly influenced the nation's economy, politics, and culture. The federal government invested in society on levels previously seen only in wartime. The spending, however, occurred almost exclusively in arenas such as national defense and college education. The financial stimulus sped economic growth and suburbanization and helped lift large numbers of working-class Americans into the middle class. Meanwhile, social programs, such as health care and poverty relief, mostly failed to gain congressional support. African Americans pointed to the discrepancy between the official view of the United States as land of freedom and democracy on the one hand, and the disproportionate levels of poverty, unemployment, and lack of opportunity in their communities on the other hand. By the 1950s, the anti-communist climate and ongoing white resistance to racial equality forced the freedom movement to narrow its focus and concentrate on courtroom battles for legal equality.

Culturally, the Cold War had contradictory effects, creating a repressive atmosphere in which novel explorations of the self nevertheless occurred. Politically, it spawned new tactics in the struggles between and within the parties. Although the Truman administration genuinely believed that the Soviets were a threat, officials knowingly used scare tactics to jolt Congress and the American people into supporting the Cold War. Ironically, Truman's critics adopted his harsh rhetoric and turned it against him—and all liberal Democrats. As a result, neither a leftist critique nor liberal or moderate dissent about the conflict with the Soviet Union became permissible.

From the vantage point of today, the Cold War may seem to have been inevitable, but it was not. The conflict was born of a series of calculations, some genuine and morally guided, others cynical and political. In 1953, following the death of Joseph Stalin and the election of Dwight D. Eisenhower, the wisdom of waging the Cold War once again became open to debate.

STUDY TERMS

President's Committee on Civil Rights (p. 728)
Taft-Hartley Act (p. 730)
iron curtain (p. 731)
long telegram (p. 731)
Truman Doctrine (p. 731)
Cold War (p. 732)
containment (p. 732)
Marshall Plan (p. 732)
National Security Act (p. 732)
Berlin Airlift (p. 733)
North Atlantic Treaty Organization (p. 733)
Warsaw Pact (p. 733)
military-industrial complex (p. 734)
House Un-American Activities Committee (p. 734)
Congress for Cultural Freedom (p. 734)
Fair Deal (p. 736)
Servicemen's Readjustment Act (p. 736)
Levittown (p. 737)
nuclear family (p. 739)
baby boomers (p. 739)
Treaty of Detroit (p. 741)
redlined (p. 742)
Congress of Racial Equality (p. 744)
abstract expressionist (p. 745)
National Security Council Report 68 (NSC-68) (p. 748)
second Red Scare (p. 748)
limited war (p. 750)
McCarthyism (p. 750)

TIMELINE

1945 Japan surrenders; World War II ends

1946 Baby boom begins
Revival of Ku Klux Klan results in lynchings across South
Winston Churchill's "iron curtain" speech
Benjamin Spock publishes *The Common Sense Book of Baby and Child Care*

1947 President Harry S Truman declares a Cold War against the Soviet Union
Congress passes Taft-Hartley Act
Levittown homes for sale
House Un-American Activities Committee (HUAC) reconvenes
Jackie Robinson makes his Major League Baseball debut
National Security Act is passed
Suburbia booms
Federal and private lenders "redline" mortgage loans

1948 Truman is reelected president
Hollywood Ten are convicted of contempt of Congress and imprisoned
U.S. Army is desegregated
Alfred Kinsey publishes *Sexual Behavior in the Human Male*
Soviet Union secretly begins nuclear arms program
Marshall Plan is established
Berlin Airlift begins

1949 North Atlantic Treaty Organization (NATO) is founded
Warsaw Pact is signed
Soviet Union tests first atomic bomb
Congress passes Housing Act
Mao Zedong declares a communist People's Republic of China

1950 North Korea invades South Korea, sparking the Korean War
McCarran Internal Security Bill is passed
Majority of American families own their own home

1950–1953 McCarthyism reigns

1952 Dwight D. Eisenhower is elected president

1953 Julius and Ethel Rosenberg are executed
Joseph Stalin dies

FURTHER READING

Additional suggested readings are available on the Online Learning Center at www.mhhe.com/becomingamerica1e.

Glenn C. Altschuler and Stuart Blumin, *The G.I. Bill: The New Deal for Veterans* (2009), explores the origins of the G.I. Bill and its transformative effect on universities, cities, suburbs, employment, and family life.

Carol Anderson, *Eyes Off the Prize: The United States and the African American Struggle for Human Rights, 1944–1955* (2003), explains why the NAACP abandoned its wartime emphasis on social justice and human rights in favor of a narrower civil rights agenda.

Rosalyn Baxandall and Elizabeth Ewen, *Picture Windows: How the Suburbs Happened* (2001), analyzes suburbanization from the perspective of the first wave of suburban residents.

Alan Brinkley, *The Publisher: Henry Luce and His American Century* (2010), offers a detailed account of Luce's life, career, and legacy.

Lizabeth Cohen, *A Consumers' Republic: The Politics of Mass Consumption in Postwar America* (2003), shows how mass consumption empowered many consumers but also deepened racial and class inequalities.

Bruce Cumings, *The Origins of the Korean War* (1980), explores the origins of the first armed conflict of the Cold War.

John Lewis Gaddis, *The Cold War: A New History* (2006), argues that nuclear arms programs profoundly influenced the course of the Cold War.

Jonathan P. Herzog, *The Spiritual-Industrial Complex: America's Religious Battle Against Communism in the Early Cold War* (2011), examines the religious lens through which American leaders viewed the Soviet Union and the religious institutions they conscripted in the war effort.

Ira Katznelson, *When Affirmative Action Was White: An Untold History of Racial Inequality in Twentieth-Century America* (2006), argues that entitlement programs associated with the Fair Deal were a form of affirmative action for white Americans.

David Oshinsky, *A Conspiracy So Immense: The World of Joseph McCarthy* (1983), takes an in-depth look at McCarthy's world view and political ambitions.

Robert O. Self, *American Babylon: Race and the Struggle for Postwar Oakland* (2003), traces the rise of suburbia, the decline of the city, and the impact of federal programs on African Americans.

Jules Tygiel, *Baseball's Great Experiment: Jackie Robinson and His Legacy* (1997), explores the lives of African American ballplayers and the desegregation of Major League Baseball.

27

INSIDE

Sounds of Freedom. Champions of the defense industry claimed that the suburban way of life to which most Americans aspired in the 1950s depended on the nation's commitment to waging and winning the Cold War.

THE BIG PICTURE

Suburbanization, unparalleled levels of affluence, and an ideology of religious unity created a pervasive image of the United States as a thriving and cohesive society. Contrary to appearances, however, widespread poverty and racial discrimination persisted. As the Cold War became an arms race, many Americans lived in fear of nuclear annihilation. The illusion of consensus was challenged head-on by a resurgent civil rights movement and diverse cultural rebellions.

1953–1960

AGE OF AFFLUENCE

Reciting the Pledge of Allegiance was a familiar American ritual by the 1950s. Authored in 1892 by Christian socialist Francis Bellamy, the pledge was originally conceived as a way of affirming the nation's duty toward its poorer, less advantaged citizens and of assimilating immigrants into the United States' English-speaking culture. The pledge underwent minor revisions in the 1920s, and by 1945, over thirty states required public school children to recite it each morning in front of the flag. The pledge contained no reference to God until 1954 when, at the suggestion of President Dwight D. Eisenhower and with Congress's consent, "under God" was added. Reciting the amended version on the steps of the Capitol on Flag Day, Eisenhower called upon all Americans to "honor our colors," dedicate themselves to "the Almighty," and give "prayerful consideration" to the duties and privileges of citizenship. "We are all soldiers now," he continued, and the most powerful weapon in the fight against Soviet communism was Americans' spiritual faith.

Previous presidents, including Abraham Lincoln, had invoked God and flag at times of epic national struggle. Never before, however, had a president or Congress attempted to systematically imbue the signs, symbols, and official discourse of government with sacred meaning. The bipartisan effort began in 1953 during President Eisenhower's first year in office when the U.S. Post Office embossed the words "In God We Trust" on the eight-cent stamp. The following year, Eisenhower asked the world—and ordered all federal employees—to join Americans in a "Prayer for Peace." In 1955, Congress opened a prayer room featuring a stained glass portrait of George Washington kneeling below the inscription, "Preserve me, O God, for in thee do I put my trust." A few months later, Congress voted to replace the nation's unofficial motto, "E Pluribus Unum" (Latin for "one out of many," a slogan favored by the founding fathers) with "In God We Trust."

KEY QUESTIONS

- What were the signs of growing U.S. affluence, and who shared in the new prosperity?
- How did the Cold War affect American culture and vice versa?
- How did changing forms of cultural expression reinforce and/or threaten consumerism and social conformity?
- What were the milestone events in the civil rights movement of the 1950s?
- What new ideologies of conservatism emerged in the 1950s, and from where?

The explosion of spiritual symbolism in the 1950s was not the result of a sudden surge of popular belief in God, which already hovered around 96 percent at the start of the decade. Instead, it was a product of the Eisenhower administration's drive to reunite Americans on the heels of Joseph McCarthy's divisive anti-communist campaigns, while also validating the United States' Cold War struggle against the "godless" Soviet Union. Such symbolism and rhetoric, which invoked belief in God but referenced no particular religion, was broadly appealing to Americans of all faiths in the 1950s. Since World War II, the idea that America was a unique "tri-faith" nation of Protestants, Catholics, and Jews had been gaining popularity. And at a time of unprecedented affluence, representations of the nation as a diverse community of believers also reminded Americans and the world, in the words of influential Presbyterian minister George Docherty, that their country was more than "the material total of baseball games, hot dogs, Coca-Cola, television, deep freezers, and other gadgets."

Seeking to unite Americans of all faiths behind the nation's Cold War effort, Congress voted in 1955 to print the motto "In God We Trust" on all U.S. currency. Bills like this one—with the now-familiar phrase—were first issued in 1957.

Together, the Cold War, consumerism, and the spread of tri-faith ideology generated mass consensus about the country's purpose and character. Regardless of religion or ethnicity, most Americans believed, if a person played by the rules, the rewards would be entry into the middle class, access to the world's largest consumer economy, and enduring happiness. This belief proved so pervasive that, even today, Hollywood and most other culture industries present the 1950s as a decade of blissful suburban conformity, ideal family life, and universal affluence. The reality was far more complex. By decade's end, one in four Americans still lived in poverty. Although the vigorous political debates of previous eras petered out, other forms of dissent and experimentation proliferated. Radical new forms of thought, expression, and experience were percolating in youth culture, poetry and literature, and the performing arts. And African Americans continued building the freedom movement that would one day transform the nation.

AFFLUENT AMERICA

By the time Dwight D. Eisenhower entered the White House, in 1953, the nation was well on its way to one of the most remarkable periods of economic growth in its history. The "great expansion," which began in 1948 and lasted until the mid-1970s, was made possible by unprecedented levels of government investment in education, scientific research, defense, and infrastructure. Although the economy had expanded at comparable rates before, only a minority of the American people had been lifted into the middle class. Now, in the 1950s, a majority shared in the nation's prosperity. President Eisenhower charted a moderate course, continuing and increasing government investment in infrastructure while holding welfare spending constant. Industry boomed, new communication and transportation networks multiplied, and wages rose steadily. Corporations invested heavily in research and development, unions won higher wages and better benefits for workers, and the middle class spent its money freely on consumer goods. By 1955, the average American had almost five times as much disposable income as fifteen years earlier, and a growing number had access to revolutionary new forms of credit. Against the backdrop of the Cold War, manufacturers and the culture industries expertly tapped into consumers' desires for security and comfort. Thousands of new products, many using plastics and chemicals developed by the defense industry, flooded the market, while the mass media celebrated the suburban home as a haven of family togetherness.

MODERN REPUBLICANISM

Most of the political and cultural groundwork for prosperity had been laid during the New Deal, the war, and the transition to peacetime under Democratic presidents Franklin D. Roosevelt and Harry S Truman. With the election of Republican Dwight D. "Ike" Eisenhower to the presidency in 1952, it was unclear whether the government would continue funding the programs that had been so essential to the growth and financial well-being of the middle class. Having vowed to curtail government spending and work more closely with big business, Eisenhower appointed prominent corporate leaders and one labor leader to his cabinet, instructing them to recommend budget cuts. Former president of General Motors Charles Erwin Wilson went to work as secretary of defense, declaring that "what's good for GM is good for America." Liberals worried, as journalist Richard Strout put it, that "the next four years may see the biggest lobby drive since [President] Grant's day to loot the public domain, reverse history, and crown big business. Ike has picked a cabinet of eight millionaires and one plumber."

But the president surprised many Americans when he refused to defund the New Deal and concentrated instead on trimming military spending. The former U.S. Army general warned the conservative wing of his party against abolishing Social Security, unemployment insurance, or labor laws and farm programs. As Eisenhower recognized, the overwhelming majority of voters liked these programs, and any politician who tried to dismantle them would be committing electoral suicide. He also believed that a strong middle class was the basis of peace and prosperity. Ike therefore pursued a conciliatory middle path in which federal government actively promoted the interests both of corporations and middle-class Americans.

Much as before, America continued to have a mixed economy in which government was active in regulating and guiding key sectors of the nation's economic life. Branding his domestic agenda **modern Republicanism,** Eisenhower extended popular programs such as education grants for veterans and affordable government-backed mortgages, both of which elevated millions more Americans into the middle class after 1953. The government also began constructing the federal interstate highway system, in turn accelerating the process of suburbanization that had been under way since the war.

Salaries and the wages of skilled workers rose steadily during the decade. Medium family income almost doubled, and real wages (which took inflation into account) grew over 30 percent between 1950 and 1960, leaving more money for nonessential goods and services. Although whites experienced greater upward mobility than other Americans, minorities partook in the nation's affluence in far larger numbers than ever before. By 1960, an African American middle class—comprising skilled workers, teachers, doctors, lawyers, and other professionals—had emerged. Almost 2.5 million African Americans owned homes in the suburbs. Although confined to predominantly black suburbs, most considered their circumstances vastly superior to earlier times.

THE CREDIT REVOLUTION

In the corporate and industrial sectors, many employees enjoyed four full weeks of paid vacation each year. This benefit was largely the fruit of labor unions' campaigns, but by the mid-1950s, employers had come to believe that vacations rejuvenated workers and improved productivity. With paid vacation time, Americans traveled for pleasure more than ever before, typically by car to national parks and other tourist attractions, but also on the world's first commercial jet liners. A large-scale **service economy**—restaurant, hotel, travel, and related services—developed. More generally, white-collar "desk" jobs grew more numerous as corporations expanded. By 1956, half of all U.S. nonagricultural jobs were white collar.

Higher wages and increased leisure time also stimulated the emergence of more flexible forms of credit. Although consumers had purchased cars, homes, and home appliances on credit since the 1920s, it wasn't until 1950 that the first general-purpose charge card appeared. Designed specifically with the traveler and diner in mind, the Diner's Club card could be used at a variety of restaurants (initially in New York, but by the 1960s internationally). The leading travel agency, American Express, soon followed suit. Although the new charge cards were popular, the account still had to be paid in full each month and the cards could be used only for dining or travel.

Recognizing the potentially huge market for credit cards, the Bank of America experimented with the first general-purpose revolving credit card, mailing unsolicited cards to hundreds of thousands of Californians in 1958. The forerunner of Visa, the BankAmericard allowed the holder to carry a balance while servicing his or her debt, and to charge a variety of goods and services. Unaccustomed to this novel form of credit, over one in every five users defaulted in the first year alone. And in an era before credit rating agencies and picture identification, fraud was rampant. Still, the bank persisted, improving systems for vetting customers' creditworthiness and mounting a massive public relations campaign.

TELEVISING SUBURBIA

The advent of credit cards boosted consumerism by making it possible to "buy now, pay later." But it was the relatively new media of television that most powerfully stimulated consumers' tastes and aspirations—and shaped their purchasing patterns. Although regular programming had been under way since 1946 and broadcasts of major political and sports events had aired since the 1920s, it was not until the 1950s that television stations realized the medium's full potential and that the great majority of Americans owned a TV set. Before then, broadcasters had treated television as an extension of radio, using it to beam live theater and traditional variety shows as radio did, usually to a local or regional audience. This programming reflected the fact that many stations, including the "big three" networks—National Broadcasting Company (NBC), American Broadcasting Company (ABC), and Columbia Broadcasting System (CBS)—were originally radio broadcasters.

In the early 1950s, the big three recognized that television was a dynamic visual medium—less like radio and more like the movies—that could potentially reach a national audience. Each of the three companies integrated their local stations into a national network on which they broadcast the same programs. To improve viewers' visual experience, the larger stations rushed to develop mobile cameras, new videorecording technology, and elaborate studio sets. Television acting became highly physical, with actors expressing themselves through energetic antics and exaggerated facial gestures, much as in the movies. By 1955, television had mostly lost its serious and reflective qualities and had become a visually powerful medium that primarily appealed to viewers' emotions, particularly their sense of humor.

Love in the 'Burbs. As in a number of well-established sitcoms, the family in *I Love Lucy* "moved" from their New York City apartment to a spacious house in suburbia (and, in reality, from New York to a stage set in Los Angeles, California).

The new shows targeted the rising white suburban middle class. But programmers estimated that idealized depictions of suburban life would appeal to viewers of all backgrounds, as well as to GM marketers and other corporate sponsors who pitched their advertising to suburban consumers. Situation comedies with domestic settings and familiar family themes dominated viewer ratings. Shows that featured urban working-class families either folded or attempted to suburbanize. Sitcom characters strove to create a peaceful haven at home, complete with the latest fashions, foods, and appliances, including the ubiquitous TV set. As in advertising, the emphasis was on the family's domestic togetherness and on joyfully eating, playing, and watching television together. Such shows offered a comforting and entertaining vision of viewers' own suburban lives and whetted city dwellers' appetite for the suburbs. The folding TV tray, designed to facilitate eating dinner while one watched television, became ubiquitous in suburban households.

The new TV programs generally downplayed regional, ethnic, religious, and class differences, emphasizing a relatively homogeneous American identity. Although more than one in three women went out to work in the 1950s, television's women were stay-at-home moms and wives. African American actors and people of Asian or Mexican descent rarely appeared, and scripts avoided direct mention of the burgeoning civil rights movement, the nuclear arms buildup, and other controversial topics. Yet television's obsessive focus on white, suburban family life indirectly acknowledged that disturbing events were unfolding in the real world. And the characters' comic efforts to perform the role of perfect suburban housewife or calm, competent dad unintentionally questioned gender norms. For the most part, however, audiences and producers alike thought of the shows as affirmations of the pleasures and basic goodness of suburban life.

Suburban life was also affirmed in TV quiz shows, a precursor of "reality television" that was especially popular in the mid-1950s. Led by *The $64,000 Question*, which edged out *I Love Lucy* for most popular series in 1956, these shows attracted major corporate sponsorship. Contestants competed for large amounts of cash, household appliances, and automobiles, and the winners returned to the show the following week. But as it became clear in 1958, the producers of one popular show, *Twenty-One*, had been prepping contestants, giving them answers in advance, and teaching them to feign surprise for the cameras. Subsequently, a congressional investigation revealed that the shows commonly eliminated some contestants while aiding others in an effort to elevate ratings.

The discoveries temporarily shook audiences' faith in television. But by then, television had become a fixture in most families' everyday lives. Much as the networks had hoped, by 1960 over 90 percent of American homes owned a TV set. Along the way, soaring TV production costs had forced most local providers out of the market. Meanwhile, corporate sponsors all but abandoned radio, permanently diminishing the former's influence and funding and reducing radio programming to popular music and news shows. (One important exception to the general decline was African American radio, which expanded dramatically after the war.) At the same time, Hollywood box-office sales plunged, pushed along by middle-class Americans' flight to the suburbs—and away from the cinemas, most of which were urban. The movie industry tried to lure viewers back by producing spectacular epics, such as *Ben-Hur*, that were shot in "Technicolor" and ill suited to small black-and-white TV screens. Although many of these films—which were often biblically themed—were smash hits, the days had passed when the average American went to the movies once a week.

Fixing the Quiz. Although quiz shows insisted that the competition was fair, one disillusioned player, a Jewish working-class man by the name of Herbert Stempel, publicly claimed that *Twenty One*'s producer had ordered him to "lose" against a popular returning contestant (and erudite Columbia University instructor), Charles Van Doren (pictured here on the right). Reflecting television's visual nature, sponsors often insisted that "attractive" players—typically white, well-groomed men—be "helped" to win. A New York grand jury found Stempel's claim to be true, whereupon quiz show ratings collapsed. Congress outlawed quiz show fixing in 1960. **Questions for Analysis:** Why might producers have wanted attractive players to win? What may have made Van Doren attractive in their eyes? What do you think made such shows extremely popular in the 1950s?

Hollywood Strikes Back. Hollywood experimented with gimmicks to draw viewers back to the silver screen, including shaking theater seats, a crude version of 3D (pictured here), and the "Smell-a-tron"—a contraption that simulated the movie's "smell track."

VEHICLES OF DESIRE

More than any other industry, U.S. carmakers powerfully influenced the national economy, culture, and everyday life in the 1950s. Although they had promoted the automobile as an expression of freedom and social mobility since the late 1920s, it was only after 1950 that the automobile became the single most important symbol of American prosperity. For the first time, designers prioritized form over function, adding features that made little difference to the cars' technical performance but radically transformed its appearance. Instead of every few years, car styles were now altered each September, when new models were unveiled. Previous models became obsolete, even though they generally had the same engines and chassis. This system of "planned obsolescence" soon became standard for other consumer goods as well.

Aimed at suburban families, cars became larger and more comfortable than ever before (or since). Marketers reasoned that consumers wanted the feel of luxury and were prepared to pay for it. Embellished tail fins (which were intended to reduce drag but quickly became a purely decorative feature), chrome-encrusted grilles, and bulbous fender accessories replaced the sleek, modernist lines of the 1930s car. In an era in which Americans commonly considered science and technology the engines of progress, stylists turned car tails into rocket-like appendages, stoking consumers' fantasies of speed and space exploration. Meanwhile, the front end became far more feminine through the use of curves, oversized bumpers, and bulging headlamps. By 1955, automobiles had become, as some observers put it, "wildly imaginative metallic sculpture" designed to tap into consumers' desires and pocketbooks.

Auto manufacturers spent more money than almost any other industry on advertising, allotting hundreds of millions of dollars each year for TV sponsorship and magazine ads. Flashy auto shows, complete with dancing girls, popular singers, and masters of ceremony, turned the technically oriented trade exhibits of the 1930s into mass spectacles. They also began encouraging families to buy a second car and spent considerable sums marketing cars to women by adding features such as power steering, power brakes, vanity mirrors, and attractive carpets. By 1955, Americans were spending almost

Putting on a Show. GM, the largest of the "big three" carmakers (the others were Ford and Chrysler), helped forge a new automobile culture with its annual "Motorama" show. Popular bands and glittering showgirls performed for rapt audiences as cars such as this Oldsmobile Delta revolved on spotlighted turntables.

20 percent of gross national product on new automobile purchases. Although the competitive feeling of having to "keep up with the Joneses" was as old as consumer culture itself, the social pressure to do so increased dramatically and helped drive mass consumption of automobiles and other consumer goods to an all-time high.

To further promote car sales, the auto industry lobbied hard for the construction of an interstate highway system. President Eisenhower had been impressed by the German military's rapid deployment along the broad, multiple lanes of Hitler's *autobahn* during World War II and saw the proposed system as a critical part of the nation's defense strategy. Presented to Congress as such, the bill that would become the National Interstate and Defense Highways Act (1956) authorized the largest public works project to date, at the cost of an astounding $25 billion—footed mostly by taxpayers via a gas tax. Much as the auto industry had projected, the interstates helped transform the bordering farmland into strings of suburbs and, along the way, clinched the automobile's place at the heart of American life and culture (see Map 27.1).

The threefold increase in cars on the road in the 1950s drove up oil consumption, a trend that had challenging and far-reaching effects on U.S foreign policy, domestic politics, and, more noticeably, the environment. Now the mere act of getting to work generated significant pollution. Indeed, highway commuting vastly increased the amount of gasoline burned, making exhaust fumes the top air pollutant. In 1955, reporters popularized the term *smog* to refer to the thick mixture of exhaust and damp sea air that blanketed Los Angeles every summer. On bad days, visibility was limited to three blocks, and Los Angelinos suffered respiratory failure, nausea, and vomiting. As the problem worsened, Congress enacted the Air Pollution Control Act (1955), the first federal law authorizing the states and local government to regulate air pollution.

Demand for oil skyrocketed. U.S. oil interests acquired substantial holdings in the Middle East for the first time. In 1953, Congress authorized the states to make forty billion acres of the nation's ocean bed available to oil companies for the purpose of offshore drilling.

CULTURE OF CONVENIENCE

Another ubiquitous symbol of America in the 1950s was the glamorous housewife in her technologically advanced kitchen—women's natural domain and the nerve center of family life, according to period sitcoms and their sponsors. Indeed, popular culture almost always pictured women in immaculate kitchens,

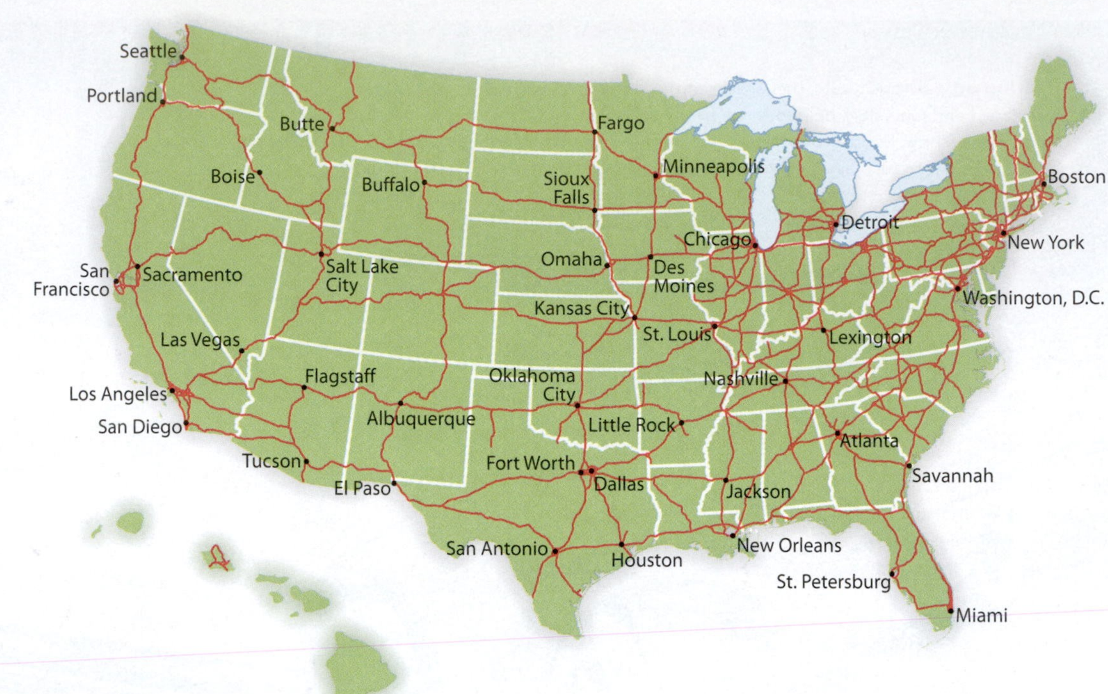

Map 27.1 The Dwight D. Eisenhower System of Interstate and Defense Highways. The publicly funded interstate network, constructed between 1956 and the 1970s, made an already-mobile nation even more mobile. It also proved a boon to business, which used the free network and large-capacity trucks to move goods quickly and relatively cheaply to cities and suburbs. By the early 1970s, the interstate and the eighteen-wheel "Big Mack" diesel truck, introduced in 1962, had effectively replaced the railroad as both engine and symbol of the modern U.S. economy.

surrounded by the latest appliances and wearing up-to-the-moment fashions under impractically frilly aprons. The only image of working women that appeared with any frequency was that of the glamorous "air hostess" serving food and beverages to airplane passengers. Although these images were highly idealized, the production, preparation, and consumption of food underwent an enormous shift in the 1950s—with profound consequences for women's lives, the rhythm of everyday life, and (eventually) Americans' health.

By the mid-fifties, households spent on average almost a third more of their income on food than they had spent before World War II (26 percent as opposed to 20 percent). Consumption of meat, especially steak, which Americans had long associated with prosperity, rose dramatically. Shoppers also expended a growing portion of the food budget on convenience foods—processed, prepackaged fare that could be prepared fast and with minimal effort. Wartime innovations in growing, processing, preservation, and packaging made these new products possible. The supermarkets that sprang up near suburbs aided distribution, stocking their aisles with hundreds of brightly packaged, flash-frozen, freeze-dried, refrigerated, and chemically preserved foods. Sweetened and colored cereals, whipped cream in a can, processed cheese products, and instant everything all made their debut. Even fruits and vegetables were likely to come wrapped in cellophane, another wartime innovation that extended shelf life by restricting exposure to air.

Heat, Then Serve. Before there was food television, there was television food. A perfect marriage between the culture of convenience and television, the TV dinner hit supermarkets in 1954. Consumed in front of the screen, the meal came in a package resembling a television. Related products, including TV trays and snack food, also became popular—even in the White House.

Many women were at first reluctant to use the strange new products. But like auto manufacturers, processed food marketers tapped into the era's love of science, boasting that their products were the very latest in meal technology. Marketers promised a more fulfilling life with more "quality" family time, courtesy of the attractive labor-saving devices such as cake mixers and dishwashers that featured prominently in advertisements. A profusion of commercial cookbooks, such as General Mills's best-selling *Betty Crocker's Illustrated*

Cookbook, taught women how to prepare dishes using the new processed foods. By 1960, over 70 percent of the nation's food was sold through supermarkets, the majority of it processed. Food preparation had never been as quick or easy. At the same time, though, convenience foods made the traditional, feminine skills of home cooking and grocery selection obsolete, fueling feelings of despair and uselessness among millions of housewives (see Chapter 28).

GLOBALIZING THE COLD WAR

Suburban life was inherently attractive to most Americans at the start of the 1950s—and, thanks to television and advertising, it became more so. But as the decade progressed, troubling world events also drove many people toward the suburban comforts of home, family togetherness, and material consumption. Foremost among these was the resurgence of the Cold War in 1954. Although Soviet-U.S. tensions had shown signs of thawing, both nations now embarked on a nuclear arms race, building ballistic missiles capable of razing entire nations. Containing communism continued to be the overarching principle of American foreign policy. In Europe, containment mostly meant using cultural forms, such as jazz, to persuade the citizenry that they ought to ally with the United States and adopt an American-style free market. U.S. propaganda meanwhile emphasized America's technological superiority, whether in outer space or in the inner sanctum of the suburban kitchen. In Africa, Asia, and Latin America, however, containment took the form of stifling any nationalist movement deemed threatening to U.S. military or commercial interests. As both the Soviets and the United States tried to conscript the emerging nations, the Cold War widened to a global scale.

NUCLEAR STRATEGIES

Cold War tensions appeared to be easing in 1953. The fiery Soviet premier Joseph Stalin had died, the Korean War was over, and President Eisenhower had announced to the world that the USSR and the United States now had greater "chances for peace." But instead of dissipating, the Cold War assumed new and potentially more lethal forms. The Soviets, under the leadership of Premier Nikita Khrushchev, remained skeptical of Eisenhower's professed desire for friendlier relations and continued their country's nuclear buildup. Although Eisenhower trimmed defense spending in 1953, he accelerated America's nuclear program. Completing a review of the Soviets' military capacity in 1954, the president's new secretary of state, John Foster Dulles, advocated "massive retaliation" through the early use of nuclear weapons in the event that the Soviets threatened the United States.

Massive retaliation became the foundation of Eisenhower's New Look foreign policy, which called for a smaller conventional military force during peacetime but a larger nuclear arms stockpile (see Figure 27.1). The military soon acquired

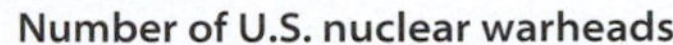

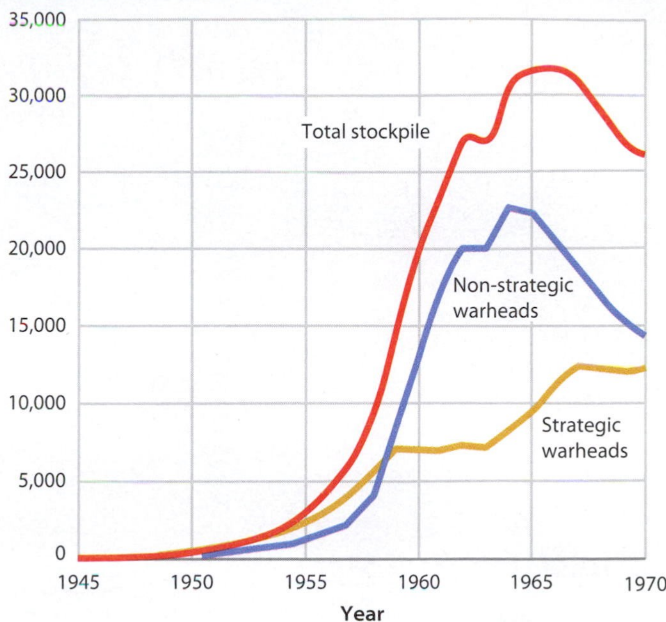

FIGURE 27.1 U.S. Nuclear Armory, 1945–1970. Eisenhower justified his decision to expand the nation's nuclear stockpile as a move that would ultimately save money. Although a single nuclear bomb cost upwards of $1 million, it could annihilate a major city such as Moscow at a much lower cost than conventional weaponry—a grim reality leading to the phrase "more bang for the buck."

dozens of thermonuclear weapons that could unleash five hundred times more force than the fission bombs used on the relatively small cities of Hiroshima and Nagasaki during World War II.

The Soviets did not lag far behind in the arms race, and the French, British, and Chinese also acquired thermonuclear weapons. Briefly, in 1955, the Soviet Union and the United States sought to deescalate the buildup, entering negotiations to prohibit the use and manufacture of nuclear weapons. Although the United States nearly signed the treaty, officials backed off at the last moment, convinced that the Soviets would cheat. Hopes rose anew the following year when Khrushchev publicly denounced his predecessor, Joseph Stalin, for engaging in the mass murder of millions of his opponents and called for "peaceful coexistence" with the United States. A few months later, however, Soviet troops brutally put down an uprising among Hungarian anti-communists, making reconciliation with the United States all but impossible. The two superpowers could agree only to halt nuclear testing—which by 1958 had been shown to pose a health threat to the millions of people exposed to the fallout. But the test ban lasted only three years. The size of the U.S. nuclear arsenal grew from a thousand warheads in 1953 to eighteen thousand just seven years later.

As both sides assembled their arsenals, the United States developed a negotiating style known as **nuclear brinksmanship**—refusing to back down in a crisis even if that position meant

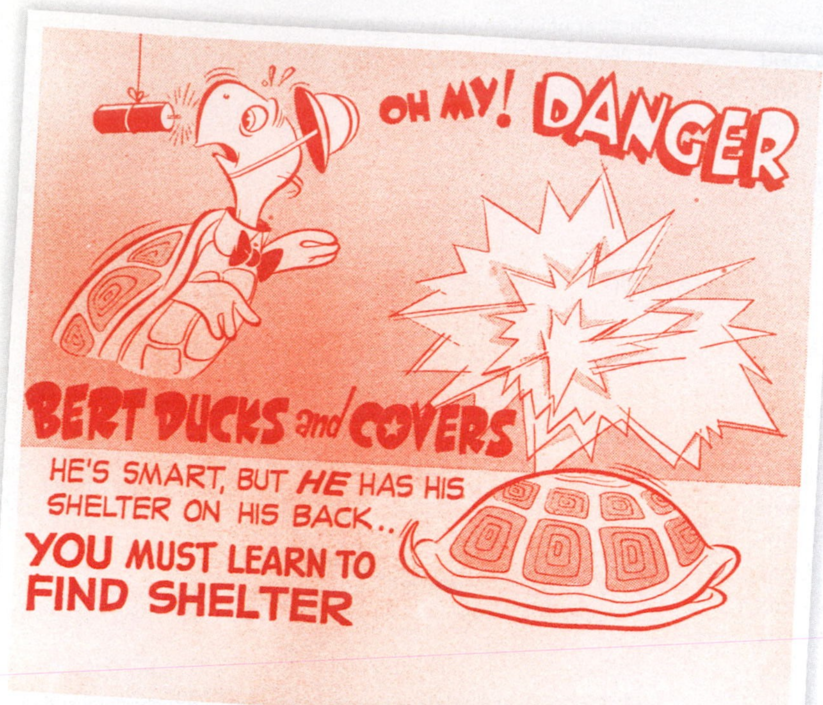

Duck and Cover. Animated character Bert the Turtle taught millions of American schoolchildren to "duck and cover"—drop into the fetal position under their desks and cover their heads with their hands—in the event of a nuclear attack. In theory, the maneuver would prevent them from running to the window after a nuclear flash (which, seconds later, would shatter the windows and potentially injure them) and would shelter them from falling debris. **Questions for Analysis:** In what ways might Bert the Turtle have reassured American schoolchildren? In what ways might the "duck and cover" cartoon have made them more anxious? Did educational films like these promote—or undermine—popular support for the Cold War?

taking the nation to the brink of nuclear war. This approach was applied to communist China when Chinese forces bombarded Taiwanese possessions in 1954–1955 and President Eisenhower announced that he would not hesitate to use nuclear weapons "just exactly as you would use a bullet."

Paradoxically, the threat of nuclear war probably decreased the chances of armed conflict between the two superpowers because neither side wanted to initiate a war that would almost certainly result in mutual destruction. But the American people's sense of vulnerability mounted steadily. Nuclear air-raid drills in schools, along with sobering government films about how to survive a nuclear attack, only fed anxieties. The manufacturers of underground fallout shelters sold millions of units to suburbanites, and the federal government installed large shelters in all the cities—a constant and visible reminder of the nuclear threat. When the Soviets reported in August 1957 that they had successfully tested the world's first intercontinental ballistic missile (ICBM), Americans were stunned. The Atlantic and Pacific Oceans—the vast natural barriers between Eurasia and North America that had made Americans feel safe for so long—were instantly rendered irrelevant.

THE GREAT TECHNOLOGY RACE

The nuclear arms competition was part of the much broader science and technology race between the two nations. Americans were still reeling from the news that Soviet missiles could reach U.S. soil when the Soviets launched the world's first satellite, in October 1957. Signals from *Sputnik* were picked up by a receiving station on Long Island and eventually broadcast around the world. Orbiting directly over American territory, the craft convinced many people that the United States was inadequately defended—and left them wondering why Americans, with their allegedly superior technology, hadn't beaten the Soviets to space.

Sputnik marked a symbolic victory for the Soviets. Since the early 1950s, both sides in the Cold War had pointed to their technological and scientific innovations as positive proof of the superiority of their respective political and economic systems. Shortly after *Sputnik*'s launch, the President's Science Advisory Committee issued the Gaither Report (1957), which confirmed what many Americans feared: that the Soviets were more militarily advanced than the United States and that their economy was growing faster. Not only did the Gaither Report provide fuel for the arms buildup, but it also prompted Eisenhower to prevail on Congress to expand funding for research and development significantly. A new aeronautics agency—the National Aeronautics and Space Administration (NASA)—was charged with beating the Soviets in the "space race," and the National Defense Education Act (1958) provided for hundreds of millions of dollars of federal aid for new university programs in science, mathematics, technology, and foreign languages (the latter would be needed in the drive to win the allegiance and oversee the modernization of developing nations). Research universities, especially the University of California at Berkeley and the Massachusetts Institute of Technology, became indispensable to the Cold War effort, and federal money became crucial to their teaching and research programs.

As the technology race intensified, the U.S. government worked with business leaders on a spate of new advertisements, films, and television programs that extolled the superiority of American science and technology. According to this publicity material, the whole world—not just Americans—benefited from U.S. ingenuity. Whereas the emphasis at the beginning of the decade was mostly on military weapons and miracle medicines (such as the polio vaccine), after 1956 it widened to embrace domestic technologies, particularly those associated with kitchens, families, and suburban homes. This dimension of Cold War rivalry climaxed with the Kitchen Debate between Soviet premier Nikita Khrushchev and U.S.

vice president Richard Nixon in Moscow in 1959. Nixon argued that American technology had achieved something that no other nation had achieved: freeing women from the drudgery of household labor (see Spaces and Places: The Cold War Kitchen).

Both opponents in the Cold War also expanded their efforts to persuade foreign peoples of the superiority of their side's approach to economics, politics, and culture. To this end, Eisenhower in 1953 founded the United States Information Agency (USIA), the single largest government information agency in the world. The USIA spent $2 billion annually on radio, television, library and museum exhibitions, movies, magazines, and live performances. "People's Capitalism," the first of several ambitious campaigns, promoted American consumer capitalism abroad and also aimed at "re-educating the American people to our way of life." Official material claimed that, unlike their counterparts in Europe and the Soviet Union, ordinary workers invested in the stock market and were therefore "business owners" who exercised far more freedom and enjoyed much greater equality than Europeans and Soviet citizens. The government canceled the campaign only a year later, however, after universities and popular magazines such as *Time* disputed the claim that workers truly "owned" American business.

Other, less explicitly political campaigns were more enduring. Among them, the People to People program distributed donated magazines and books to overseas youth and families. The Camp Fire Girls made photo albums of their homes for foreign girls, and eventually the USIA organized a student exchange program. The Jazz Ambassadors program sent Dizzy Gillespie, Benny Goodman, Sarah Vaughan, and dozens of other jazz giants ("jambassadors") through southern Europe and the Middle East. These tours, many of which featured African American musicians, showcased the United States' contribution to global culture and refuted the common European and Soviet criticism that Americans were gross materialists. Eisenhower hoped that the jazz tours would also counter the popular perception overseas that African Americans could never succeed in America. In addition, the U.S. government systematically exported Hollywood cowboy movies in the belief that the freedom and rugged individualism of the stock cowboy character (which dated back to Buffalo Bill's Wild West Shows) had universal appeal.

COMPETING FOR THE THIRD WORLD

Racial segregation and disfranchisement in the South had long undermined U.S. claims to global moral leadership. As the Cold War progressed, Jim Crow became even more of a liability. While the Soviet Union and United States had been vying for power in the Northern Hemisphere, dozens of anticolonial movements in Africa, South and Southeast Asia, and the Middle East had mobilized to demand national independence from European colonial powers. Between 1945 and 1960, thirty-six nations, including Ghana, India, and Pakistan, won their independence. Most emerging nations were in the Southern Hemisphere, and all were agricultural societies populated by people of color. **Decolonization,** the process by which colonies demanded and gained independence, was in full swing—and Americans and Soviets alike sought to sway the new nations to their side. State Department officials, who continued to see the world through the lens of containment, interpreted Third World independence struggles as signs that the Soviet enemy was expanding its territorial, economic, and ideological reach. Both sides viewed the decolonizing nations with a mix of hope and fear and as potential sites for demonstrating the superiority of their own model of development. Each superpower thus formulated plans for massive "modernizing" infrastructural projects, such as hydroelectric dams and power grids, and sought military alliances and material opportunities, such as freer access to the Middle East's oil. And both pressured the newly independent nations to choose sides in the Cold War.

In theory, the United States' own revolutionary past and its Cold War identity as the "leader of the free world" made it a natural ally for the world's independence movements. Initially, many nationalists—including Vietnamese revolutionary Ho Chi Minh—courted American support, drawing from the Declaration of Independence to frame arguments for their liberation from colonial powers. But by the mid-1950s, nationalists grew suspicious of both the United States and the Soviet Union. The persistence of Jim Crow in the American South cast doubt on the United States' commitment to the full independence of peoples of color and became a worry that no amount of jazz diplomacy could assuage. Also, while proclaiming its commitment to the independence of all colonized peoples, the United States quietly backed France, Portugal, and other Cold War allies in their intentions to retain their colonies, by force if necessary. By 1954, the United States had abandoned the postwar policy of offering foreign aid strictly to democratically elected governments and instead extended support to any government, whether democratic or despotic, that the State Department deemed an ally.

Both superpowers forcefully demonstrated their intolerance for governments that opposed their interests. In particular, the United States rejected one of the common ambitions of many decolonized nations—to return to the people those resources and vital industries that the colonial power had owned and developed. According to Secretary of State John Foster Dulles, this process of **nationalization** not only deprived U.S. corporations of existing or potential opportunities but also was a dangerous form of communism. Consequently, the Central Intelligence Agency staged successful coups against "unfriendly" democratically elected governments in Iran and Guatemala in 1953–1954 after they tried to confiscate oilfields and unused farmland, respectively, from Western corporations. The Soviets were equally prepared to intervene in other nations' affairs. When Hungary's new government tried to exit the Warsaw Pact (the Soviet military alliance), for instance, Khrushchev sent tanks to crush it. For both superpowers, direct intervention

SPACES & PLACES

The Cold War Kitchen

In 1959, the U.S. government sponsored the American National Exhibition in Moscow. The display focused on automobiles, home appliances, fashions, and other consumer goods, and nearly three million people flocked to see it. The central exhibit was a ranch-style suburban home, complete with model kitchen. On opening day, after sipping a cocktail of Pepsi-Cola and vodka—supposedly symbolic of the two nations' mutual "friendship"—Vice President Richard Nixon showed Premier Nikita Khrushchev around the model home.

Capitalism Versus Communism. In the Kitchen Debate, Nixon and Khrushchev argued over the respective virtues of their nations' economic and political systems. The American free enterprise system, Nixon stressed, made homes affordable and produced innovative technologies, such as dishwashers, that liberated housewives from domestic drudgery. Khrushchev countered that the Soviets' system guaranteed all citizens a home by virtue of being born in the Soviet Union, whereas "[i]n America, if you don't have a dollar, you have a right to choose between sleeping in a house or on the pavement."

A heated, impromptu debate broke out in the kitchen over the significance of the United States' having more and better household appliances. Nixon argued that such technology was vital to the progress of nation as a whole. Freedom, in his view, meant the ability to choose among consumer goods as well as the right to speak and think as one wished. It also meant that women were relieved from the backbreaking aspects of household work. Rather than heaving coal and cooking on coal stoves, American women simply turned on gas or electric ovens. With electric refrigerators, there was no more mopping up after leaky iceboxes that needed constant refreshing. All this freed women, according to Nixon, to fulfill their "natural" roles as supportive wives, loving mothers, and capable homemakers. Khrushchev countered that in the Soviet Union, people did not have "the capitalist attitude toward women" and that citizens were concerned less with gadgetry and more "on the things that really matter," such as providing housing and health care for all and eliminating poverty.

Americans greeted the Kitchen Debate, which was televised, as a triumph for the nation. The episode also boosted Nixon's reputation as a possible successor to President Eisenhower. Meanwhile, Eisenhower sought to capitalize on the moment and further to ease tensions between the superpowers by inviting Khrushchev to the United States. To the media's delight, in September 1959 the premier and his family embarked on a tour of the great icons of 1950s' American culture: a supermarket, a technologically advanced farm, the bustling metropolis of New York, and a Hollywood movie set. At each stop, the feisty and telegenic Khrushchev sparred openly with his hosts over the advantages and disadvantages of American-style capitalism. At the end of the visit, Eisenhower and Khrushchev jointly pledged to work toward general disarmament and to settle "all outstanding international questions . . . not by the application of force, but by peaceful means through negotiations."

Think About It

1. Why might Americans of the 1950s have thought that Nixon won the Kitchen Debate?
2. Why might Nixon have chosen the kitchen as a good place to debate Khrushchev?
3. What, if anything, might the Kitchen Debate tell us about attitudes toward women in the 1950s?
4. Why do you think the Soviet and U.S. leaders chose to stage their public debates in a mock kitchen, in a supermarket, on a technologically advanced farm, and in Hollywood and not in a more formal setting, such as a town hall?

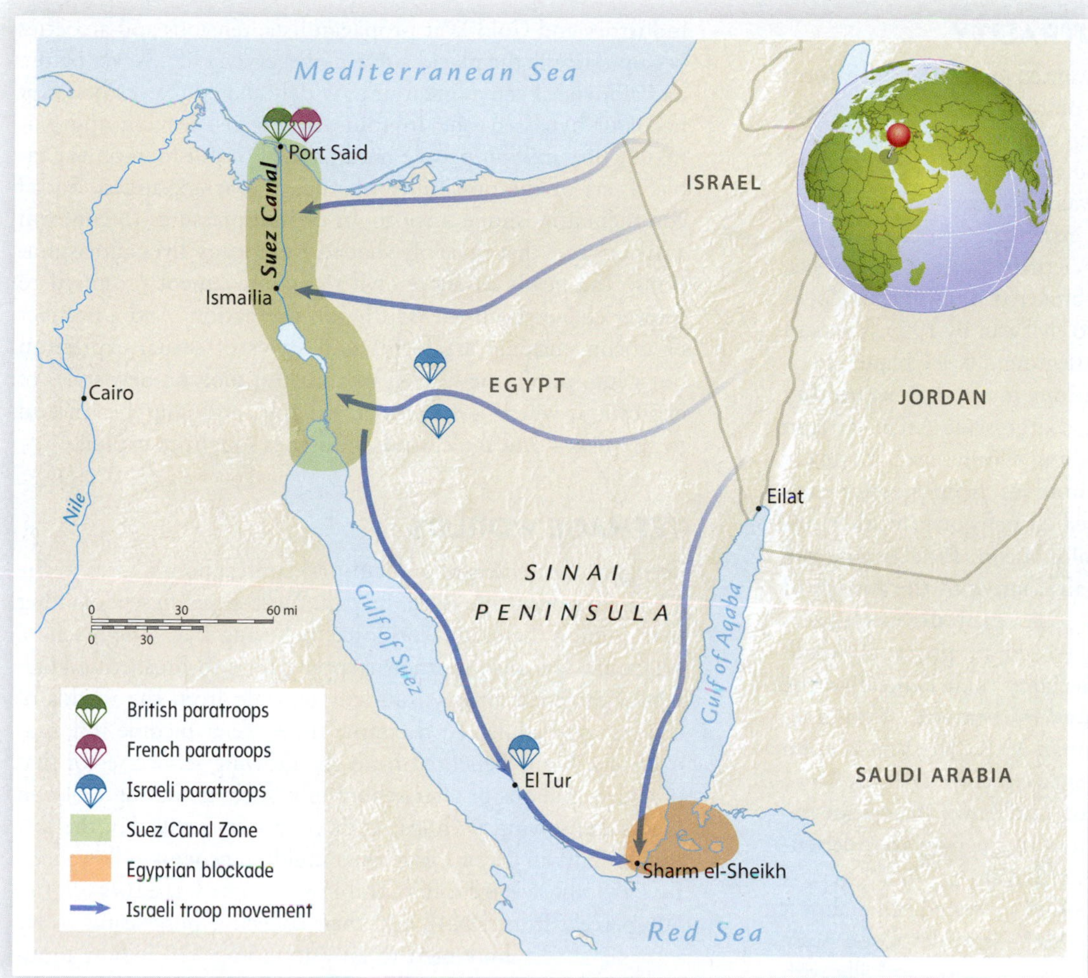

Map 27.2 The Suez Crisis and Gaza Invasion, 1955. Rising Arab nationalism, Israel's search for security in a hostile region, and the West's escalating demand for oil made the Middle East a Cold War hot spot. These forces collided in 1955 when the French, British, Egyptian, and Israeli governments mobilized troops in the strategic areas of the Suez Canal and Gaza Strip.

created new allies. But, in the U.S. case, it also led whole populations to question the sincerity of America's commitment to democracy and fanned the flames of militant anti-Americanism.

Nowhere was this truer than in the Middle East, where the United States had developed significant economic and strategic interests during and immediately after World War II. By the 1950s, American companies were producing almost half of all Middle Eastern oil, and the region supplied about 90 percent of Europe's petroleum needs. U.S. and European leaders grew concerned when nationalist Egyptian leader Gamal Abdel Nasser promised to nationalize the Suez Canal, a British-controlled gateway to the oilfields in 1952 (see Map 27.2). Eager to maintain good relations in the region, the British agreed to a gradual withdrawal over several years. Armed conflict appeared to have been averted. But when Israel invaded the Egyptian-controlled Gaza Strip in 1955 in retaliation for a Palestinian raid on an Israeli army patrol, a chain reaction began.

Convinced that Israeli forces now posed a threat to Egypt, Nasser signed an arms deal with communist Czechoslovakia, in so doing fueling American fears that Egypt might align with the Soviets. Secretary Dulles at first took a conciliatory approach, offering to finance a massive public works project in Egypt, the Aswan Dam. But Nasser refused to repudiate the arms deal and subsequently entered an anti-Israel alliance with Egypt's Arab neighbors. Dulles retaliated by publicly canceling the dam financing. Humiliated, Nasser ordered Egyptian troops to storm the Suez Canal. Events threatened to spiral out of control when, unbeknownst to U.S. officials, British, French, and Israeli troops invaded Egypt and attempted to retake the canal. Enraged at his allies' lack of consultation, President Eisenhower demanded their immediate withdrawal. Only after the president suspended economic aid and threatened to impose sanctions on Britain, France, and Israel did they leave. United Nations peacekeeping forces then took control of the canal, effectively depriving Egypt of a strategic artery and hardening anti-American sentiment in the Arab nations. Eager to firm up American power in an unstable region, Eisenhower patched up relations with Israel, and in 1958 the United States made the first of dozens of arms sale to the young state.

THE CHALLENGE OF NEUTRALITY

Few leaders of decolonized nations wanted to develop a new form of dependency—**neocolonialism**—on rich nations or to transfer access to their resources to American corporations or the Soviet government. Even fewer were willing to become pawns in yet another, potentially catastrophic, rivalry between foreign powers. Many were aware of the disastrous experience of decolonization that was unfolding in Indochina (Vietnam), where the Soviets, the United States, and China had brokered transition independence, only to plunge the nation into civil war. By 1955, Vietnam had become a bloody Cold War battleground (see Chapter 28).

Leaders of the decolonized nations made their neutrality explicit in 1955 at the world's first large-scale Asian-African meeting. Convening at the Bandung Conference in newly independent Indonesia, representatives from twenty-nine Asian and African nations pledged to help one another oppose both colonialism and neocolonialism. Proclaiming the birth of the "Third World"—an alternative to the worlds of Soviet communism and American capitalism—leaders condemned the Cold War and vowed to promote world peace and cooperation. Having declared their neutrality, the new nations joined the **nonaligned movement,** simultaneously conceived by Indian statesman V. K. Krishna Menon and communist Yugoslavian leader Josep Broz Tito. By 1961 Yugoslavia and 120 Asian, African, and Latin American nations had pledged their commitment to steering an independent "middle path" through the Cold War.

Dismayed, the United States boldly increased aid—almost quadrupling it between 1952 and 1960—in order to persuade Third World governments to resist nationalization and ally with the United States. The State Department dropped its earlier emphasis on the importance of democracy building and began funding any regime that appeared likely to protect and advance American interests. The new U.S. Agency for International Development worked with private organizations such as the Rockefeller, Ford, and Carnegie Foundations to train Third World leaders in fighting communism and building industrial economies.

These tactics were generally ineffective and sometimes worked against U.S. interests. Many Third World governments simply grew expert at playing one Cold War power against the other, extracting large sums of economic and military aid from both but all the while remaining officially neutral. The United States also lost popular support and stirred up anti-Americanism wherever it aided repressive regimes. Vice President Richard Nixon learned firsthand about the mood change in 1958, when he was mobbed and almost killed on an official visit to Caracas, Venezuela. "Go away, Nixon!" yelled the infuriated crowd, "We won't forget [the CIA-backed coup in] Guatemala!"

CULTURE REBELS

While the United States struggled to recruit the independent-minded Third World, various challenges were brewing at home. Contrary to the upbeat image projected by the culture industries and Cold War propagandists, tensions and anxieties began to ripple the placid surface of everyday life. Never before had affluence been as great or as widely shared. Nevertheless, it had still bypassed one in four Americans, leaving approximately fifty million people hard pressed to put food on the table. Fears of the possibility of nuclear war abounded. Social commentators shone a spotlight on the pressures to conform and consume that invisibly shaped Americans' lives and aspirations. The newly assertive civil rights movement promised to forever change both the South and the nation. And a number of unconventional art forms and styles of sexual expression burst into public view. Teen culture also took on new styles of expression, which government, schools, and churches moved to suppress—and the culture industries sought to exploit.

TEENAGE WORLDS

Teenagers first emerged as a cultural and economic force in the 1950s. In a departure from the past, most stayed in school rather than joining the adult workforce, believing that a high school education was an important steppingstone to prosperity. High school provided an environment separate from the worlds of children and adults. At the same time, teens' income rose dramatically. Many benefited from the growing service sector that provided millions of after-school jobs such as waiting tables in diners and serving as "hops" at drive-in restaurants. For the first time, suburban parents gave their children generous allowances. By 1959, the average teen's combined income was $10/week (up 500 percent from 1944), and their collective purchasing power amounted to an astounding $10 billion annually (see How Much Is That?).

How Much Is That?

Teen Income and Purchasing Power

Life for 1950s teenagers was markedly different from that of previous generations. Generally, teens stayed in school longer, had less pressure to contribute to the family income, and enjoyed more leisure time. Allowances from their affluent parents, combined with an abundance of part-time jobs in the service sector, afforded the average teenager a $10/week income in 1959—that's about $78 today. This income went a long way toward buying 15-cent McDonald's cheeseburgers and 5-cent Coca-Colas and Hershey's chocolate bars. It also left plenty of money for 51-cent tickets to popular movies such as *North by Northwest*, *Some Like It Hot*, and Disney's *Sleeping Beauty*, as well as for $1 records. Teens' purchasing power made them highly sought-after consumers. And if teens wanted to be popular—and in the 1950s, they did—they prolifically spent their discretionary income.

Unlike their counterparts in previous eras, teens got to keep their earnings—and spend it on consumer goods and services of their choice. Manufacturers and the culture industries were acutely aware of the profits to be made by shaping and tapping into teens' tastes. Eugene Gilbert, a young entrepreneur who established Gilbert Teen Age Enterprises while still a high school student in the late 1940s, was among the first to survey his peers about their likes and dislikes with a view to selling the results to interested companies. By the mid-1950s, Gilbert's clients included major candy, soft drink, and clothing manufacturers, and he was writing the nationally syndicated newspaper column, "What Young People Are Thinking."

Movies, clothes, and radio programs designed especially with the teenager in mind flooded the market. In 1955, *Teen* was the first of over a dozen new magazines to target youth. All stressed the importance of physical appearance and popularity, both of which could supposedly be attained by purchasing the right clothing, personal products, and records. Television was much slower to appeal to teens, emphasizing family fare above all else—though music shows such as *American Bandstand* grew more teen oriented. Teens were the new "big-time consumer in the U.S. economy," announced *Life* magazine in 1959, and they would spend $1 billion more than GM made from car sales that year.

In some respects, teens' aspirations differed little from their parents'. The desire to consume was hardly rebellious, but teens used consumer goods and services to push the boundaries of convention. Teenage boys often customized their cars, chopping down the bodies and rebuilding and personalizing them as racing cars or "hot rods." Both illegal and thrilling, drag racing became popular and a source of considerable status. **Cruising** was even more central to suburban teenage life. Escaping parents and younger siblings for a few hours, teens cruised around together (often in the family car) with no single destination in mind. New drive-in diners and movies catered to them by allowing "parking" in relative privacy. Heavy petting became commonplace, and a significant minority of teens had sexual intercourse. The average age at marriage dropped to just twenty-two by the end of the decade, and the proportion of white brides who were pregnant on their wedding day more than doubled.

Parents, teachers, police, and other adults widely disapproved of these activities—and were generally anxious about teens' increased autonomy (see Interpreting the Sources: The Going-Steady Controversy). Youth's insistence on having separate activities challenged the dominant 1950s ideal of family togetherness. Parents considered cruising aimless and lazy and worried that teens were engaging in sexual and even criminal activities. Although many teens were sexually active, parents' fears were fueled by an outpouring of alarmist books and Hollywood movies portraying teens as morally lost, sexually precocious, and prone to violence. Marlon Brando's performance in *The Wild One* (1954) as an antisocial, jeans-wearing biker whose gang terrorizes an innocent town horrified parents and thrilled teenage audiences everywhere. But no one captured teen angst as well as James Dean in *Rebel Without a Cause* (1955). The film's sullen and restless seventeen-year-old Jim Stark (Dean) bridled against his parents, who led a dull suburban life punctuated by marital fights that his mother always seemed to win.

Such portrayals of teen culture helped convince many adults that an epidemic of juvenile delinquency was sweeping the nation. Many states tightened abortion and contraception laws in an attempt to discourage teens from having

Weak Fathers, Rebellious Sons. A bleak portrait of disaffected suburban youth, *Rebel Without a Cause* blamed young men's supposed alienation on weak fathers who had been feminized by suburban life. Here, Mr. Stark, wearing his wife's frilly apron, appears feminine and powerless.

INTERPRETING THE SOURCES

The Going-Steady Controversy

Teenage dating patterns changed dramatically in the 1950s. Much to the dismay of parents, teachers, religious authorities, and even some teenagers, teens started dating at a much earlier age—typically between the ages of 12 and 14. Instead of dating dozens of peers, as teens had before World War II, they also confined themselves to "going steady" with just one person. Going steady was not a new concept, but its meaning and function changed from an informal engagement that led directly to marriage to an intimate relationship that carried no expectation of marriage. By 1957, two in three high school students were going steady. The *Life* magazine article from which these excerpts were taken featured interviews with teens and parents about the new custom and included a summary of the Catholic Church's position.

Interview with parents

Mrs. Hunsberger: My concern is that [teens who are going steady] don't have any fun. At a dance you have to be with your date all evening. And they don't have many friends. I said to my son, "Why don't you stop by so-and-so's house? He said, "Oh I couldn't . . . she goes steady." He couldn't stop in to see a girl he has known since second grade.

Mr. Barber: Have any of you noticed . . . whether children's steady dating has tended to lead any toward promiscuity? *Dr. Scambler*: Young people today have a far better sense of morals than we think. *Mr. Doney*: But back of our minds, when we talk about steady dating, isn't that what we are suspicious of? *Mrs. Doney*: I think so. *Mrs. Sculley*: More stress should be put on sports and athletic activity rather than this emotional part.

Interview with teenagers

Bob: When I first became a high school freshman last fall, I found it an awful difference from eighth grade (*Laughs*). There were an awful lot of new things to get used to and I feel that particularly in the beginning of your teens it is this striving for security that makes going steady seem the ideal arrangement, because it does offer security for both of the kids. . . . *Sue*: In high school you really go steady just to go out.

Judy: If you go steady in high school you haven't got time to think about getting married. You're so busy with sports and dates and what other people are doing. Look, I've got eight or nine years before I'm really ready to raise my own family, and stuff like that. There are so many things I want to do. I want to travel and oh, I want to write, I guess. Parents who think that their kids when they go steady are automatically engaged to be engaged are taking it much too seriously. . . .

Chris: If two people have gone steady for a while, they're much more likely to do things and try things they shouldn't (*Protests of "No"*). I would, I know (*Cries of "Oh"*). *Sue*: Going steady means that two people are not just best friends but a little more than friends.

Summary of Catholic Church's position

Boys and girls who go steady "start making bad confessions, then no confessions, followed by no sacraments, no Mass, finally no faith" (quote from *Information*, Catholic magazine).

Source: "Debate About Going Steady: Parents, Teen-Agers Differ on a Spreading U.S. Custom," *Life*, September 9, 1957.

Explore the Source

1. What made parents of the 1950s so worried that their teenage children were going steady?
2. Why do you think most teens in that era chose to date one person exclusively?
3. Why might *Life* magazine have interviewed teens about their attitudes toward dating—and what does this tell us about the changing place of teens and teen culture in American society?

sexual relations. In 1954–1955, Senator Estes Kefauver of Tennessee convened a subcommittee on sex and violence in popular culture and its effects on teens. Although unable to prove any direct connection, the Kefauver Committee condemned the movies, comics, and television for glamorizing delinquency and criticized the federal government for failing to "protect the Nation's children." Congress took no action, but the culture industries, worried about the prospect of federal censorship, pulled their more salacious material. Publishers established an industry-wide censorship body and replaced horror, crime, and sensationalist comics, which accounted for over half of all comic books, with more "wholesome" titles such as *The Flash* and other superhero stories. Anxious to avoid being closed down, drive-in theater operators hired security guards to shine flashlights through car windows so as to put a stop to heavy petting. Manufacturers began pitching their products as "good," "respectable," and "wholesome" (see Hot Commodities: Blue Jeans).

RACE, SEX, AND ROCK 'N' ROLL

In the midst of intensifying concerns about teen delinquency, a raucous new musical form burst into national prominence. Rock 'n' roll was a hard-driving combination of amplified guitar riffs, fast dance beats, and raw, suggestive lyrics. Its closest relative, rhythm and blues (R&B), was performed almost exclusively in African American communities and had been unknown to most white youth until 1954, when Bill Haley and His Comets, an all-white band with a country music background, recorded a version of Big Joe Turner's R&B song "Shake, Rattle, and Roll." Few white teens had ever heard anything so raucous and sexually frank. It was an instant hit. Haley followed with other singles, including "Rock Around the Clock" in 1955, which eventually sold a record-breaking 25 million copies.

The growing popularity of rock 'n' roll was partly due to the fact that white teens were already pushing the boundaries of acceptable sexuality and looking for new ways to express and define themselves. The music's intrinsic physicality and frank suggestiveness were perfectly matched to their quest. In live performances, the new technology of electric guitar and bass enabled four and five-person bands to create heart-thumping walls of sound, previously possible only with orchestras of 30 or 40 musicians and for ten times the cost. The arrival of new, affordable record players and the cheap three-minute "45s" (7" gramophone records) suited both rock 'n' roll songs and teen budgets. For some white teenagers, rock 'n' roll's African American roots also gave it an appealing rebellious quality.

Above all, it was white disc jockeys, producers, and managers who made rock 'n' roll popular by bringing it to white teens' attention. Alan Freed, a white disc jockey based in Cleveland in the early 1950s, was among the first to play African American R&B on his radio show and to host racially integrated concerts and dances. Winning fans and notoriety, Freed moved to New York in 1954, where he popularized the term *rock 'n' roll* and played both African American and white artists for a largely teen audience. By 1955, three black musicians, Little Richard, Bo Diddley, and Chuck Berry, were dominating the national charts—a distinction that was unimaginable just a few years earlier.

In the early 1950s, R&B had also caught the ear of white record producer and entrepreneur Sam Phillips. Phillips had been recording African American blues musicians at his independent studio, Sun Records, in Memphis, Tennessee, since 1952. Although the records sold well, Phillips was convinced that racial prejudice would prevent African American artists from ever winning mass appeal. Consequently, he began recording white musicians who blended country music with rhythm and blues to produce a new genre, rockabilly. The formula was a success, and soon millions of Americans were listening to the music of Johnny Cash, Roy Orbison, and Carl Perkins.

Soon the bigger record labels became interested in Sun Record's most successful artist—a working-class 20-year-old from Mississippi named Elvis Presley. Presley's sound, looks, and famously physical performance style, all of which drew directly on African American performance, made him a smash hit among teen audiences. Not everyone liked Elvis Presley, however. The working-class Presley was little more than a "male burlesque dancer . . . [with an] unnecessary bump and grind routine," wrote one disapproving reporter in 1956, and his acts were "vulgar and animalistic." Catholic Cardinal Francis Spellman, the archbishop of New York, voiced even graver concerns, claiming that Presley's 1955 performance on *The Ed Sullivan Show* was proof that teenagers were in thrall of a new

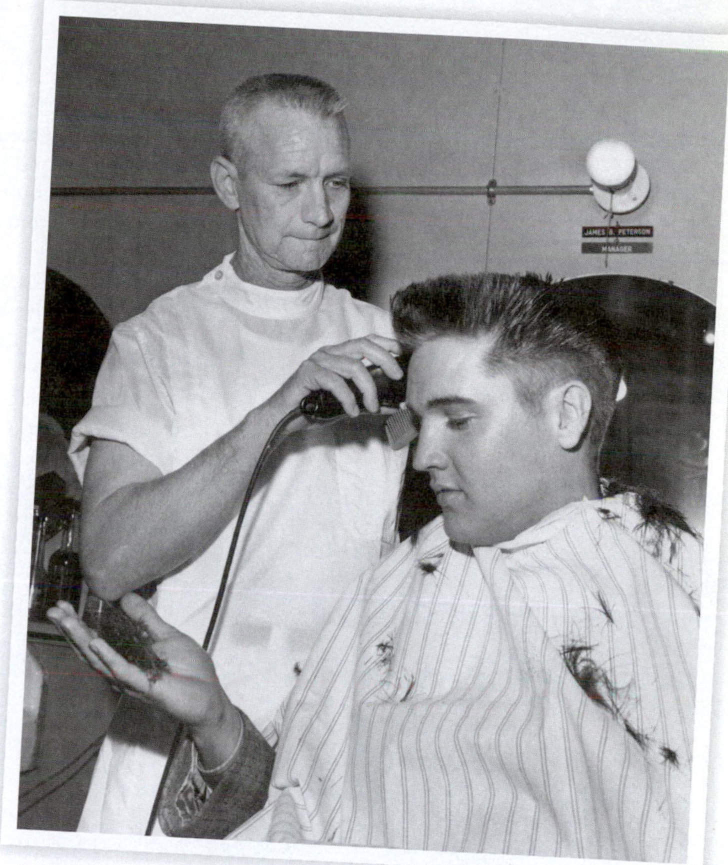

Elvis Presley, Patriot. With the help of publicists and his manager, Elvis went from threatening long-haired rock 'n' roller in 1957 to a dreamy, crew-cut Cold Warrior in 1958.

"creed of dishonesty, violence, lust, and degradation." Rock 'n' roll "plunges men's minds into degrading and immoral depths," pronounced a young Baptist minister by the name of Martin Luther King, Jr. in *Ebony* magazine. Of the thousands of articles published in the 1950s, only one (in *Harper's* magazine) recognized Presley's prodigious talents. Almost all the rest saw the Elvis phenomenon as corruptive of youth.

Pressure mounted on the federal government to investigate the new musical form, leading senators John F. Kennedy and Barry Goldwater to press for legislation against the way record companies paid disc jockeys to promote the latest songs on the airwaves. This practice, known as payola, had been common for years, and efforts to stop it masked a larger impulse to censor rock 'n' roll. Houston, Boston, Baltimore, Atlanta and a dozen other cities prohibited live concerts, and in 1959 a House subcommittee declared its intention to "save" America from rock 'n' roll.

Eager to avoid government censorship, TV and some of the larger record companies tried to make rock 'n' roll more respectable and "family-friendly." Most celebrity rebels were quite easily tamed—and often amenable to toning down, especially where lucrative contracts were at stake. Elvis Presley's publicists emphasized the performer's churchgoing

HOT COMMODITIES

Blue Jeans

"Blue jeans, the most durable and once the most wholesome kind of American clothes, are getting a bad name," lamented the *New York Times* in 1959. Young hoodlums and "motorcycle boys" were wearing them "in anything but a neat manner," and schools, theaters, and restaurants everywhere were banning them.

Denim jeans had come a long way since western miners and farmers had first pulled on Levi Strauss's button-flied, hardwearing, copper-riveted work pants in the mid-nineteenth century. Building on Buffalo Bill's vision of a romantic and heroic West, the first cowboy movies had popularized jeans among male consumers back East—especially once the Lee Company introduced the more convenient "Amazing Hookless Fastener" (the zipper) line in 1927. Blue jeans became respectable middle-class wear during the Great Depression, even for women, who bought millions of the new, side-zippered "Lady Levi" in 1935. Affordable, durable, and unmistakably western, jeans seemed to symbolize Americans' common struggle at a time of great hardship—and the belief that this, too, would pass.

As prosperity returned after World War II, middle-class adults shed their jeans in favor of dressier, more expensive pants (for men) or skirts and dresses (for women). Jeans also became the subject of heated debate—and widespread censure. When Levi's ran an advertising campaign in 1949 with the slogan "Denim: Right for [High] School," many parents complained that jeans were far too informal for the classroom. Flush with allowances, teens responded by buying more jeans. Some, particularly young men in gangs, turned the pants into a statement of their toughness and supposed nonconformity, wearing them a little loose, rolling up the cuffs, and strapping big black leather belts around their hips. Worried that the popular new look was offending their European hosts, U.S. military bases in Germany banned blue jeans and other "teenage attire" for off-duty soldiers in 1953.

Right for School? Marlon Brando's cuffed-jeans-and-leather-jacket look, borrowed from street gangs, sparked a national craze among teens when his film *The Wild One* (1953) was released.

Anguished suburban mothers complained to advice columnists about daughters in jeans, while etiquette experts counseled that jeans were okay for the backyard but should never be worn shopping or on city streets. "Dressing like a hoyden [a tomboy or boisterous girl]," warned one expert, "invariably seems to heighten the temptation to behave like one."

By the time rebellious Hollywood idols James Dean and Marlon Brando swaggered across the big screen in cuffed jeans, t-shirts, and leather motorcycle jackets in 1953-1955, the association of blue jeans with juvenile delinquency had been cemented. Newspaper headlines told of "blue jeans gangs" (some, all-girl), robbing grocery stores and creating mayhem. The jeans industry, which had never promoted its products as "rebel wear," panicked, especially when schools, restaurants, and theaters began banning jeans and as sales of more "respectable" chinos, twills, cords, and "buckled-in-back" pants soared. France, Norway, Indonesia, and Soviet bloc nations joined the ban. Concerned manufacturers established Denim Councils aimed at reestablishing the respectability of jeans and introduced "Ivy League" jeans—"a natty new look for clean cut American boys." Neatly buttoned up the back and cut slim (but not tight), the jeans were a flop. By the 1960s, jeans makers had accepted that it was rebel symbolism that drove sales—and adjusted their ad campaigns accordingly.

Think About It

1. What might account for teenagers' passion for blue jeans in the 1950s?
2. What do you think the history of blue jeans indicates about teenagers' attitudes toward consumer culture and about manufacturers' approach to teens?
3. How rebellious was a teenager being when she or he pulled on a pair of blue jeans? Against what was the teen rebelling?

childhood and strong family ties. At a time when all young men had to serve in the armed forces, Presley was subsequently drafted into the U.S. Army—after which he abandoned his rockabilly quiff (which combined a pompadour and flat-top hairstyle), sensual snarl, and provocative performance style.

Despite pressures to become respectable, neither rock 'n' roll nor its rebellious spirit died. In 1959, African American rhythm and blues musician Ray Charles once more shocked parents and thrilled teens with his raunchy 1959 hit "What'd I Say?" Emerging and "breakthrough" artists such as Charles constantly innovated the raucous new musical form, pushing the boundaries still farther, while the record industry strove to sidestep censorship and churn out hits. Teens' idolization of rebellious, sexually expressive stars, and their eagerness to spend freely on records and other products that symbolized rebellion (blue jeans, t-shirts, gum, cigarettes, hair cream, make-up), made huge profits for the record and related industries.

What'd He Say? Borrowing from gospel, Ray Charles seemingly thumbed his nose at disapproving church ministers with his sexually raw interpretation of the African American church ritual of call and response. Banned from both white and African American radio stations in 1959, "What'd I Say?" won Charles a rabid teen following—once a "cleaner" version was released.

THE BEATS AND THE AVANT-GARDE

Rock 'n' roll may have challenged standards of middle-class respectability, but it also generally accepted and reinforced consumer culture's emphasis on self-expression, conformity (among peers), and fulfillment through shopping. A far more radical critique was posed by a growing number of young artists who rejected consumerism. Among them, a community of novelists and poets known as the Beats wrote caustically of what they saw as the overbearing conformism and emptiness of mass culture. Some also derided the banality of American politics, and all rejected conventional literary genres.

In the first reading of *Howl* in San Francisco in 1955, Beat poet Allen Ginsberg protested the "Robot apartments! Invincible suburbs! Skeleton treasures! Blind capitals! Demonic industries!" of modern life. Reciting long lines that jammed words together, defying the rules of punctuation and leaving the reader breathless, Ginsberg denounced the destructive forces of commercialism and intolerance. "My generation," exclaimed the poet, had had the "absolute heart of the poem of life butchered out of their own bodies," their creative energies destroyed by "the nightmare of Moloch [commercialism]." In a similar vein, Ginsberg's friend Jack Kerouac penned spontaneous, free-form fantasies of freedom from responsibility and the strictures of a culture he found deadening. Kerouac's *On the Road* (1956), completed following a cross-country car trip from New York to San Francisco, celebrated personal experience, perpetual motion, and boundless life force.

Kerouac and other Beats condemned the strict conformism of the suburban ideal of married heterosexual life. Ginsberg's work went farthest, invoking the pleasures of anal sex—at a time when sodomy was a crime in every state—and casual sex with strangers. Many Beats also experimented freely with mind-altering drugs, including alcohol, marijuana, and peyote, in the pursuit of pleasure and intellectual insight. The publication of *Howl* in 1956 resulted in obscenity charges, mass confiscations of the poem, and a widely publicized trial in San Francisco. Backed by the American Civil Liberties Union, the publisher's attorney persuaded the judge that the poem "does have some redeeming social importance." The trial helped push sales of *Howl* to over 10,000 and eventually gained its author the grudging respect of mainstream media, including *Time* and *Life* magazines. *Howl* is now considered a classic of American poetry.

Important critiques of consumerism and conventional values also developed among a young generation of experimental or **avant-garde** (literally, "advance guard") visual and performing artists. These individuals questioned popular assumptions about the meaning of reality and advocated a radical new consciousness of being. They rejected the idea, advanced by painter Jackson Pollock and other leading postwar artists in the 1940s (see Chapter 26),

On the Beat. With its poetry readings, "cool jazz" performances, and printing press, City Lights Bookstore was ground zero for the Beat movement. Here, Beats Bob Donlin, Neal Cassady, Allen Ginsberg, Robert LaVigne, and Lawrence Ferlinghetti pose outside the store.

that art was the expression of the artist's inner emotional truth. Instead, art's mission was to lead audiences to experience sounds, sights, language, human movement, and their own bodies in ways they had never thought possible. The avant-garde carried out its reformist cause by breaking down the conventions of individual art forms, the boundaries between the arts, and the usual distinction between performers and audience.

The live performance of *4'33"* by composer John Cage exemplified avant-garde art. In this 1952 piece, Cage placed a world-renowned pianist alone on the stage with a piano, instructing him to sit silently and without moving (apart from opening and closing the piano lid three times). The only sounds heard in the four-minute, thirty-three-second performance were the unintentional noises of the audience. By leading listeners to become conscious of these sounds, Cage overturned expectations about what music and performance were—and conferred value on the accidental "sounds of silence." In a related vein, choreographer Merce Cunningham shocked the ballet world in 1953 with a performance in which parts of the solo dancer's body moved separately—and often jarringly—in no particular order and with no discernible rhythm or unifying theme. By refusing to tell a story, Cunningham's work broke with the conventions of both classical ballet and the expressive, modern dance that Martha Graham had pioneered in the 1930s and 1940s.

Cage and Cunningham also collaborated—often with visual artists—on some of the world's first multimedia projects. At one such experimental performance, held at Black Mountain College in rural North Carolina, where many avant-garde artists were in residence, performers created dance in real time, as they went along, according to a dance score that was not revealed to them until the event. Enormous, painted white panels by artist Robert Rauschenberg hung overhead, and musicians and dancers performed not on a stage but in the middle of an enormous dining hall. Refusing the convention of following the music, the dancers performed as though there were no music. Films and slides were projected on the walls, and Cage "played" the radio while other musicians played unconventional instruments (including buckets of water).

The works' emphasis on accident and coincidence was intended to engage the audience in actively making sense of their experience. This approach directly rejected the manipulative marketing campaigns of the era's consumer industries, which strove to control both the meaning of products and the supposedly passive consumers who obediently bought them. Many Beats and avant-garde artists drew on non-Western traditions, especially Zen Buddhism, to create anti-consumerist experiences that were anarchic and playful. Older, more established American artists and art critics found their work meaningless—and, in the 1950s, the culture industries rejected them as unprofitable. In the 1960s, however, when defying authority and criticizing consumerism became popular, the groundbreaking ideas of the Beats, Cage, and Cunningham found fresh relevance.

CRITIQUING MASS SOCIETY

Writers working within existing genres also offered stark critiques of a suburban culture in which large corporations were both mass employers and providers of consumer products and services. In Sloan Wilson's best-selling novel *The Man in the Gray Flannel Suit* (1955), the main character is a white-collar worker and World War II veteran who feels like a soulless and powerless automaton. Going to work day in and day out, he returns home each night to his stay-at-home wife and television-addicted children. Having survived the trauma of war, the character wonders about the meaning and value of his existence and ultimately turns down a high-powered job for the sake of spending more time with his family. The theme of the disempowering effects of white-collar work surfaced again in the best-selling nonfiction study *The Organization Man* (1956) by William Whyte. Corporate employees, argued Whyte, were more concerned with getting along and working as a team in the interests of their employer than with being autonomous, creative, and self-reliant contributors. The results were a disturbing mass conformity and a loss of masculinity.

Advertising also came under attack. In *The Hidden Persuaders* (1957), journalist Vance Packard showed how advertisers were using psychology to subtly manipulate the desires and behavior of Americans consumers. Although Packard overstated his claim that advertisers were brainwashing consumers, his analysis of advertising's aims and methods was broadly correct. Advertisers were openly tapping into people's desire to conform, to feel secure, and to love and be loved. Philosopher Theodor Adorno, a German-Jewish exile, advanced a withering attack on advertising, Hollywood, and consumer society more generally, charging that mass culture was destroying "people's last possibility of experiencing themselves." In a related vein, Sociologist C. Wright Mills argued in *The Power Elite* (1956) that the elites who ran corporations and government bureaucracies exercised enormous power through mostly invisible channels—and that this power was largely unaccountable to voters.

THE FREEDOM MOVEMENT

In 1954, despite social critics' bleak assessment of contemporary culture, many African Americans were cautiously optimistic that revolutionary social change was near at hand. That year, the Supreme Court ruled that racial segregation in schools was unconstitutional. As the United States tried to recruit support for the Cold War in the Third World, the federal government began advising federal courts that legalized segregation was damaging the country's reputation overseas. Pointing to the contradiction between the image of America as the leader of the free world and the reality of racial segregation, African Americans mobilized to force integration nonviolently. Their efforts were the cornerstone of the first mass freedom movement since Reconstruction (1865–1877). This time, unlike the last, the movement would forever change the nation.

LITIGATING SEGREGATION

Despite the promising political and legal headway made in the immediate postwar years, the civil rights movement's prospects appeared dim at the dawn of the 1950s. President Truman's earlier efforts to roll back Jim Crow had collapsed, and mass actions against segregation had tailed off. President Eisenhower, who had all but ignored racial inequality in his electoral campaign, went so far as to criticize going to court to attain justice for African Americans. It was impossible, Eisenhower declared, to "change the hearts and minds of men with laws or decisions." Southern segregation was still mandated by law. Most northern cities, including Boston, New York, and Chicago, did not explicitly legislate racial separation, but restrictive real estate covenants, discriminatory lending, and other racist practices enforced a system of **de facto segregation** (see Chapter 26).

Lacking both popular momentum and a sympathetic White House, civil rights organizations resolved to step up their legal campaign against southern segregation. Leading a team of attorneys for the National Association for the Advancement of Colored People (NAACP), Thurgood Marshall decided to combine five lawsuits that parents had already initiated against local school boards into a single suit, *Brown v. Board of Education of Topeka, Kansas* (1954). In the case that gave the suit its name, Oliver Brown, an African American veteran and welder from Kansas, sued the Topeka school board for barring his eight-year-old daughter from attending the local whites-only elementary school. Another case grew out of the actions of high school student Barbara Johns and 450 fellow African American students, who had walked out of their segregated Virginia high school in protest of its dilapidated state.

Challenging the principle of "separate but equal" head on—rather than fighting for equal funding for segregated schools, which implied an acceptance of the principle of racial separation—Marshall argued that racial segregation violated the Fourteenth Amendment's guarantee of equal protection. Overturning the decision in *Plessy v. Ferguson* (1896), the Supreme Court agreed: Segregation of the schools was unconstitutional. African Americans and their civil rights allies celebrated the historic decision. But it was unclear whether the federal government would enforce the law and desegregate the schools. President Eisenhower, in whose hands the responsibility rested, remained aloof, even when African American teenager Emmett Till was brutally murdered in Mississippi in 1955 for allegedly whistling at a white woman. Federal inaction spurred southern segregationists to flout federal law. It also affirmed segregationists' belief that they would defeat integration—and gave them time to mobilize white support for segregation.

THE MONTGOMERY BUS BOYCOTT

Between 1954 and 1957, it fell to African Americans to enforce the law and desegregate the South. In this cause, they literally used their own bodies. In December 1955, Rosa Parks, a longtime member of the NAACP and resident of Montgomery, Alabama, refused to give up her seat to a white rider on a city bus, as a local ordinance had required African Americans to do since the late nineteenth century. Parks was immediately arrested and jailed, whereupon the African American community mounted a boycott of the bus service. Rather than patronize the segregated service, members of the community walked miles to work or formed car pools. Led by twenty-six-year-old Baptist pastor Martin Luther King, Jr., the boycott caused the bus company to fail and the town's white-owned business district to suffer. Nonetheless, the white townspeople stood firm—until the U.S. Supreme Court struck down segregation on all forms of public transportation (in *Browder v. Gayle*, 1956).

Nonviolent Protest. Rosa Parks was arrested, fingerprinted, and jailed for refusing to give up her seat in the "whites only" section of the bus. She and other civil rights workers consciously courted arrest and prosecution in an effort to publicize the injustice and hypocrisy of a democracy in which citizens would be jailed or beaten if they sat in the wrong place or drank from the wrong fountain.

The Montgomery boycott created a model of nonviolent protest and propelled Martin Luther King, Jr., to national prominence. It also gave birth to the Southern Christian Leadership Conference (SCLC, founded in January 1957). Led by King and the Reverend Ralph Abernathy, SCLC drew together dozens of black churchwomen with years of organizing experience and trained African Americans in the use of nonviolent protest against segregation. Blending Indian nationalist leader Mahatma Gandhi's practice of civil disobedience with a Christian conception of brotherly love, King wrote that he "had come to see early that [nonviolence] was one of the most potent weapons available to the Negro in his struggle for freedom." Other southern towns began mounting boycotts modeled on Montgomery.

Many white southerners were enraged by the Montgomery boycott, the *Brown* decision, and subsequent efforts to integrate the South. Virginia senator Harry F. Byrd called for—and got—"massive resistance" to integration. In Congress, 101 lawmakers signed the Southern Manifesto, denouncing the Supreme Court ruling as a "clear abuse of judicial power" and pressing whites to defy court-ordered integration. Over five thousand southerners joined White Citizens' Councils that had been established after the war, and even the Ku Klux Klan revived, its membership swelling to 1920s levels. Over five hundred acts of Klan-sponsored violence and thousands of other assaults ensued. Recognizing the new, integrationist sensibility of much of the growing teen culture, the Klan and the Citizens' Councils also physically attacked integrated venues. Popular African American performers, including Alabama-born singer Nat King Cole, were knocked off the stage, and Klansmen threatened to run rock 'n' rollers out of town.

BIRTH OF A MASS MOVEMENT

Despite the assaults and civil unrest, the federal government still refused to enforce the law. Tensions in the South came to a head in the fall of 1957 when a group of African American students (dubbed the "Little Rock Nine") were denied access to the whites-only Central High School in Little Rock under orders from Arkansas governor Orval Faubus. One student was turned away from the school's main entrance by Arkansas national guardsmen and then surrounded by a mob of white students and adults who hurled obscenities and threatened to lynch her (see Singular Lives: Elizabeth Eckford, "Little Rock Nine" Student). Such intimidation was nothing new, but photographs of the incident reached the national press, provoking outrage both overseas and in the United States. Governor Faubus's flagrant violation of federal law put tremendous pressure on President Eisenhower to intervene, something he was previously reluctant to do. The outrage was so palpable, and the spectacle so embarrassing internationally, that a few days later the president ordered eleven thousand troops to deploy to Little Rock to enforce the law. It was the first time since Reconstruction that federal troops had helped African Americans secure their rights. Eckford and the rest of the Little Rock Nine successfully enrolled at Central High—and made history.

Little Rock proved a turning point for the civil rights movement. Thanks largely to the television networks, the spectacle showed Americans and the world the extremes to which white segregationists were prepared to go to save Jim Crow. With popular support for integration building, civil rights activists now had reason to hope that the federal government would throw its weight behind them. As donations poured into the SCLC, the organization was able to train thousands more African Americans in civil disobedience.

CHALLENGING INEQUALITY IN THE WEST

African Americans were not the only minority to insist on their civil rights in the 1950s. People of Mexican ethnicity pursued a similar goal for themselves. Mexican and Mexican American communities had continued to grow in the states after World War II, partly because the U.S. government continued the *bracero* ("helping hands") program that allowed Mexican laborers temporary legal entrance to the United States and partly because agribusiness offered them ample low-wage work. Each

Mass Deportation. In 1954, the federal government swept through the fields of California and the Southwest looking for "wetbacks" to deport. *Wetback* was a common derogatory term for a Mexican who had illegally crossed into the United States by swimming across the Rio Grande. Here, Los Angeles police detain ten men who had allegedly entered the United States as stowaways on a train.

year, about one hundred thousand Mexicans crossed the border to labor in the orchards and fields of Texas and California. Many returned home after the harvest, but others stayed on, some legally and others illegally.

Although employers welcomed and depended on these workers, they generally opposed Mexicans' permanent settlement in the United States, fearing that Americanization would raise the price of their labor. Like the majority of white Americans, they also believed that people of Mexican descent were good for farm work but unfit for full American citizenship. Consequently, Mexican nationals and Mexican American citizens faced systematic discrimination that was very similar (and in some cases identical) to Jim Crow laws. Although they were citizens of the United States, Mexican Americans were routinely denied the right to serve on juries, assemble freely, and vote.

Pressured by state and local governments, the federal government deported over a million Mexican farmworkers in 1954. Most of those rounded up under Operation Wetback were "undocumented" and had not been recruited through the *bracero* program. While the federal Border Patrol clamped down on the undocumented, the federal government responded to agribusiness's growing demand for cheap farm labor by almost tripling the number of documented *braceros* allowed to enter the United States (to around four hundred thousand) in 1955. As a result, Mexican communities actually grew in the United States through the 1950s, and the *braceros* remained a cheap source of labor, far cheaper than Mexican American labor.

After the mass deportation, Mexican American citizens, thousands of whom had been living in the United States for several generations, were often misidentified as "wetbacks." Many felt increasingly unwelcome in their own country. But a growing number fought back. Older civil rights organizations, such as the League of United Latin American Citizens (see Chapter 26), were joined by newer groups, including the American G.I. Forum (AGIF), a Latino veterans' group. Just as African Americans were doing, these organizations appealed to the courts to overturn segregation and other forms of discrimination. Proclaiming that "Education Is Our Freedom and Freedom Should Be Everybody's Business," AGIF led a series of successful lawsuits against the segregation of schools—and, in one case, graveyards—in Texas and California.

In 1954, the same year in which the U.S. Supreme Court decided *Brown v. Board of Education*, the Court addressed the issue of the exclusion of Hispanics from juries. Having been convicted of murder by an all-white jury in Jackson, Texas, farmworker Pete Hernandez appealed on the grounds that the jury could be impartial only if people of all races were allowed to serve. In *Hernandez v. Texas* (1954), the Supreme Court agreed, ruling that all racial groups in the United States were entitled to equal protection under the Fourteenth Amendment.

REIMAGINING GOVERNMENT

As the freedom movement mobilized, conservatives began the long-term project of updating their ideology and building movements of their own. They started several important "think tanks" (organizations that undertake research and engage in political advocacy), including two that championed a new concept of free enterprise. Libertarians such as Ayn Rand grew immensely popular, as did a number of new conservative religious organizations. Some were merely anti-communist. But others were also committed to overturning Eisenhower's modern Republicanism and rolling back the New Deal, on the grounds that government regulation of business—especially government protection of unions—impinged on human freedom. By 1960, **neoconservatism** was a small but growing force in American politics.

GOSPELS OF FREE ENTERPRISE

A number of conservative think tanks drew together business leaders and intellectuals (typically journalists and economists) for the purpose of formulating and promoting an updated version of

SINGULAR LIVES

Elizabeth Eckford, "Little Rock Nine" Student

By the 1950s, a majority of Americans considered high school a teenage rite of passage and an essential step toward achieving upward mobility and a secure place in the middle class. In the age of affluence, public schools often boasted a new gym, up-to-date classrooms, and well-trained teachers. In the South, however, the best schools were strictly for "whites only," and African Americans were consigned to "colored" schools that were grossly underfunded, understaffed, and dilapidated. Even after the Supreme Court ordered school desegregation in 1954, a number of states stubbornly refused. Three years later, many white southerners still insisted that nothing had changed—and that nothing would change.

But for fifteen-year-old Elizabeth Eckford, the Supreme Court's ruling had changed everything. The studious daughter of a dining car maintenance worker and a teacher, Eckford was determined to claim her right to the same education and opportunities that white teens enjoyed. In the fall of 1957, with the encouragement and support of local civil rights activist and newspaper publisher Daisy Bates, Eckford and eight other African American teenagers made a plan to enroll at Central High School in Little Rock, Arkansas. The school board allowed them to register, but Arkansas governor Orval Faubus overrode its decision, dispatching the National Guard to prevent the African American students from attending classes.

On the first day of school, Eckford arrived alone at the front entrance, unaware that the other African American students were convening in the rear. The guardsmen barred her way, forcing her to retreat through an angry mob of whites. Eventually, Grace Lorch, a white civil rights activist and labor unionist, escorted Eckford home. Local newspaper photographer Will Counts captured the disturbing events. When the national press then published one of his photos, Elizabeth Eckford became the face of African Americans' collective courage and dignity as freedom fighters.

Counts's photograph revealed the ugliness of segregation, frozen in time in the contorted facial expression of white student Hazel Bryan as she hurled obscenities at Eckford. Public outrage finally persuaded President Eisenhower to send the 101st Airborne to enforce the law. A few weeks later, under the protection of federal troops, Eckford and the rest of the Little Rock Nine were finally able to enter Central High. Many whites, including Hazel Bryan, subsequently transferred to a different school in protest. Although the federal troops stayed on in Little Rock for a year, Eckford and the other African American students suffered physical and verbal abuse from white students.

In a final push to resist integration, Governor Faubus ordered all Little Rock high schools to close their doors in 1958 (they reopened the following year). Determined to earn her high school diploma, Eckford completed her studies via correspondence classes. After attending a predominantly white college in Illinois, she eventually received her bachelor's degree in history at Central State University, an African American university in Ohio. In 1982, Eckford accepted Hazel Bryan Massery's apology for her abusive behavior on that fateful day in 1957. Arkansas-born president Bill Clinton presented Eckford and the rest of the Little Rock Nine with the country's highest civilian award, the Congressional Gold Medal, in 1999.

Think About It

1. Why did Eckford encounter so much hostility when she tried to exercise her constitutional right, guaranteed by the Supreme Court in *Brown v. Board of Education* (1954), to attend her local high school?
2. What role did media, both television and print, play in the outcome of the desegregation efforts at Central High?
3. Why might Counts's photograph have been so shocking to white northerners, given that de facto segregation was the norm in most northern cities?

the nineteenth-century ideology of laissez-faire economics. The Mont Pelerin Society, an international organization cofounded by Austrian economist Friedrich Hayek, promoted the concept of what Hayek called **free enterprise**—the controversial idea that business should be free of almost all legal constraints. In Hayek's view, the absence of government restraint on business was the basis not only of all economic life but of freedom itself.

Funded in the United States by former DuPont executive Jasper Crane, the Mont Pelerin Society aggressively advanced the free enterprise idea. Within a year, the society counted among its ranks several corporate leaders, conservative magazine editors, and President Eisenhower's chief economic adviser. Although it failed to change the Keynesian orientation of most university economics departments, it gave corporate leaders the simple yet powerful concept of free enterprise. The ideology spread through corporate executives' offices in the 1960s, and, a decade later, through the universities, too. By 1980, it would be official Republican economic policy (see Chapter 30).

Novelist and essayist Ayn Rand popularized a related but different strain of free enterprise thought in the same years. Rand, one of the few female intellectuals on either the left or the right to win a mass audience in the 1950s, had emigrated from communist Russia twenty-five years earlier. Having initially struggled as a Hollywood screenwriter, Rand in 1943 published a best-selling novel, *The Fountainhead*, the story of an independent-minded architect who chooses to remain true to his own artistic vision rather than to give in to either fashion or tradition. Rand subsequently supported a variety of anti-communist

Documenting Hate. Will Counts's photographs of events at Central High, such as this one showing Elizabeth Eckford after she was denied entrance to the school, brought moral pressure to bear on President Eisenhower to enforce southern desegregation.

causes and, in 1957, published her most famous work, *Atlas Shrugged*. This thousand-page novel explained that the human being is a "heroic being" whose principal purpose is to selfishly seek happiness through creative production and the exercise of reason. Avowedly anti-mystical as well as radically individualistic, Rand condemned not only communism and New Deal liberalism but all forms of Christianity as fatally "irrational."

Rand's books sold in the millions and introduced a new generation of Americans to her particular brand of **libertarianism,** the view that all individuals have exclusive ownership rights over themselves and that they are therefore morally entitled to acquire property rights in other things. Rand's libertarianism proved particularly popular among businessmen, who found in it a moral justification for the self-interested pursuit of profit. But a number of other conservatives rejected its atheistic aspects. Among these, a right-wing Los Angeles group called Spiritual Mobilization helped popularize a theological justification for free-market economics. "The blessings of capitalism," the movement's leader and founder, the Reverend James Fifield proselytized, "come from God." The organization produced a magazine, a radio program, and held regular conferences for clergy—all of which promoted the idea that every Christian's duty was to minimize the role of government in American life and to seek personal profit. The movement faltered by 1960, however, thanks in large part to its leadership's pursuit of inner spiritual exploration (which in some cases involved experimentation with psychoactive drugs).

Other conservative Christian organizations became major forces in politics. Founded in 1958 by Robert Welch, Jr., a retired

Boston candy manufacturer, the anti-communist John Birch Society was named for a Baptist missionary killed by Chinese communist forces in 1945. With generous support from Koch Industries, one of the largest privately owned businesses in the United States and still a generous donor to conservative causes, the society argued that bankers and socialists were conspiring to take over the U.S. government with the goal of handing it over to "a one-world international socialist order." By 1960, the society had recruited one hundred thousand members and was mobilizing them for grassroots activism. Birchers ran for school boards, lobbied politicians, and pressured corporate sponsors to boycott "liberal" TV programming.

Although popular, both the John Birch Society and Ayn Rand were too extreme for William F. Buckley, Jr., and a number of other leading Christian conservatives. All objected to Rand's atheism, and most distanced themselves from Welch after he accused President Eisenhower of being a "communist tool." Buckley, a wealthy Catholic from Connecticut, set out to define the boundaries and "true" meaning of a new American conservatism. His journal, the *National Review*, founded in 1955, fused libertarianism with conservative morality to become the leading conservative publication of the era. As well as excluding "fringe" conservatisms such as the Birchers', Buckley's circle broke with older conservatives who advocated American isolationism, and instead embraced the Cold War, the nuclear arms race, and aggressive foreign intervention. Buckley also repeatedly disavowed older conservatives' anti-Semitism, arguing that Western civilization had been built on a single Judeo-Christian morality.

Despite their important differences, the conservatives of the 1950s were united in their rejection of civil rights for African Americans and other minorities. Whites were entitled to enforce racial segregation because, according to Buckley, "for the time being, [whites are] the advanced race." The Birchers held that the Constitution could in no way be interpreted to support the equality of African Americans and that the Reverend Dr. Martin Luther King, Jr. and the civil rights movement were parts of a "communist plot." Such vehement opposition appealed to many white Americans and helped launch a political movement that would eventually, in the 1980s, turn back the tide of New Deal liberalism and the freedom movement (see Chapter 30).

NEW CORPORATE AGENDAS

Conservatives updated their ideology in an effort to respond to national and global events they found troubling, including the uptick in Soviet propaganda, American cultural rebellions, and the rise of the civil rights movement. They were especially disturbed by an emerging pattern of industrial relations in which corporate power was checked in part by labor unions and government. Under the general rubric of the so-called Treaty of Detroit, most unions abandoned their decades-long demand to participate in corporate management, while management recognized the unions' right to strike under certain circumstances (see Chapter 26). Government subjected both sides to rules and regulations concerning working conditions and other aspects of production. Both sides generally accepted the arrangement.

Union delegates and management periodically negotiated wages and benefits, and if all went smoothly, the delegates announced the terms of the new contract to workers. When wages were rising, as they were until 1957, unions' popularity and membership surged. Because skilled labor was in high demand, unionized workers who were employed by large automakers and other industries were able to extend benefits such as health care. When negotiations broke down, strike actions proliferated, with an average of 350 legal actions each year and hundreds more unauthorized ones. But these rarely proliferated into general strikes, and neither the government nor most corporations considered them a threat to the rule of law.

A minority of corporations, however, were eager to dismantle this system of industrial relations and, especially, to avoid having to deal with labor unions. General Electric (GE) spearheaded these efforts with an ambitious public relations campaign to undermine the unions and to promote the relatively new concept of free enterprise.

As part of a strategy to sap union strength and repeal labor regulations, GE vice president Lemuel Ricketts Boulware changed the corporate culture, making seminars, readings, and book groups on the concept of free enterprise an essential part of company life. An older generation of administrators, most of whom had risen through the ranks from the shop floor, was replaced by college-educated professionals who had little practical background in the industry but an abiding commitment to free enterprise. Labor relations at GE changed dramatically. Instead of hashing out a compromise with the unions, the new managers listened respectfully and quietly to union leaders' demands but refused to negotiate. Some days later the company would announce the terms of the new contract, which sometimes included raises and benefits. Workers could accept or reject the terms, but the unions could not claim the usual victory. Managers explained that if workers rejected the contract and struck for more, GE would have no choice but to relocate to the South, which was mostly nonunionized. Some factories did move. By the late 1950s, the mere hint of shuttering a plant persuaded workers to accept each new contract.

Persuading consumers and the business press that the free enterprise model was the best thing for America also became part of GE's strategy. In 1953, the company hired Hollywood actor Ronald Reagan as its official spokesperson. Reagan communicated with millions of Americans as the host of television's popular *GE Theater*—and the friendly face of GE. He also toured company plants, chatting informally with workers (who were generally thrilled to meet him) and giving speeches about the virtues of free enterprise. Reagan's good looks, reassuring voice, and sunny disposition made him the perfect company spokesman.

The business press lauded Boulwarism, as GE's new approach to labor negotiations came to be called, for its tough antiunion policies and active promotion of free enterprise ideology. But through most of the fifties, few industries were able or willing to emulate the GE model because so many depended on northern cities' highly skilled and thoroughly unionized labor. Most large manufacturers were also still reconciled to the existence of unions. However, the balance of power began to shift in 1957 when the worst recession since the 1930s struck. As production slowed and profits dipped, many companies singled out pensions, high wages, and paid vacation as untenable costs. A growing number, moreover, attempted to block union membership drives. A new kind of contractor appeared on many company payrolls—the labor relations consultant—whose job was to persuade workers that unions were disruptive, potentially violent, and opposed to the individual employee's best interests. Corporate donations to conservative think tanks surged after 1957, tightening the bond with conservative activists and disseminating the gospel of free enterprise across corporate culture.

The recession of 1957–1958 also had a galvanizing effect on business's involvement in electoral politics and its relations with the public at large. Several of the largest corporations began organizing workshops for managers on how to run for—and win—office in the 1958 midterm elections. Company newsletters reported on the record of national and local politicians, assessing their loyalty to free enterprise and their impact on the company's interests. GE and others vigorously campaigned to spread the South's antiunion "right-to-work" laws to California and other western states. "The American corporation has rediscovered politics," announced *Fortune* business magazine in 1958. The campaigns for antiunion legislation in the western states failed, due both to the unions' well-organized opposition and to most voters' reluctance to give more power to corporations. Still, the effort forged a new network among like-minded politicians, corporate executives, and conservative organizations, setting in motion a resurgence of conservatism in the Republican Party in the 1960s (see Chapter 28).

THE ELECTION OF 1960

Neoconservatism was one among many new forces with which the Democratic and Republican Parties had to grapple in the run-up to the 1960 presidential election—and it was by no means the most challenging factor. In 1960, voters' confidence that the nation was headed in the right direction gave way to widespread jitters about the faltering economy, the South's expanding freedom movement, and the Cold War. Although Khrushchev's American tour had helped thaw relations, tensions mounted once again as talks about Berlin's fate got under way. The former German capital, located deep in Soviet-dominated East Germany, had been divided and governed by France, Britain, the United States, and the Soviet Union since the end of World War II. But the Soviets had always viewed the other nations' military presence in the city as a security threat and had periodically demanded that they withdraw.

Western and Soviet leaders met in Paris in the spring of 1960 to confront once again the thorny issue of Berlin. A few days into meeting, however, Premier Khrushchev shocked the world with the news that a U.S. spy plane had been shot down over Soviet territory. President Eisenhower initially denied most of the report, claiming that the downed aircraft was a weather plane that had accidentally strayed into Soviet airspace. But a few days later, Khrushchev presented both the wreckage of the "U-2" spy plane and the captured U.S. pilot, Francis Gary Powers. A standoff ensued, and an enraged Khrushchev stormed out of the Berlin talks. The more personal approach to diplomacy that Eisenhower had championed the previous year seemed not to be working. Once again, Americans grew anxious that the Cold War was escalating.

With Eisenhower serving his second term (and thus ineligible to run again, according to the restrictions of the Twenty-second Amendment, ratified in 1951), the Republicans nominated Vice President Richard Nixon of California. Nixon, who enjoyed tremendous popularity as the "winner" of the Kitchen Debate, campaigned on a Cold War platform, pledging to bring his considerable experience to bear on U.S. dealings with the Soviet Union. The Democratic nominee, John F. Kennedy, focused on both foreign policy and domestic issues, especially the recession and job losses, for which he blamed the Republican incumbents. Although Kennedy knew that the United States was winning the arms race, he lambasted the Republicans for the alleged "missile gap" and promised to close it. The forty-seven-year-old Nixon insisted that the forty-three-year-old Kennedy was far too young and inexperienced to guide the United States through the complexities of the Cold War. Kennedy responded that the new decade demanded fresh, new ideas, not the stale old policies of the aging Eisenhower—Nixon administration.

Although from a wealthy, politically connected family, Kennedy was a Roman Catholic and had to overcome considerable prejudice among Protestant voters, even in his own party. Americans had never elected a Catholic president before, largely because many Protestant voters believed that the church might try to influence him. But the idea that Catholics and Jews were as American as Protestants had grown more popular since the war. Rather than dodge the issue, Kennedy addressed it directly, proclaiming his belief in the separation of church and state and affirming that the United States was a tri-faith nation. "I believe in an America that is officially neither Catholic, Protestant, or Jewish," the candidate declared before a gathering of Houston's white Protestant ministers, "I do not speak for my church on public matters, and the church does not speak for me." Partly to overcome Protestant resistance (which was dominant in the South), Kennedy chose a Protestant, Texas senator Lyndon B. Johnson, as his running mate. Johnson campaigned hard, winning Kennedy substantial support among white southerners.

Most preelection polls placed Nixon ahead of Kennedy with the slightest of margins. The turning point came in the fall of 1960, when the candidates agreed to take part in the first-ever televised presidential debate. Over seventy million viewers tuned in, and several million others listened via radio. A relaxed and confident Kennedy answered journalists' questions with ease and self-assurance. Nixon, recently hospitalized for an infected knee, appeared pale, underweight, and stressed. Polls later showed that a majority of TV viewers believed that Kennedy had won the debate but that radio listeners believed he had lost. In the new age of television, candidates' looks, body language, and style made all the difference. The Democratic campaign also publicized Kennedy's acts of courage and heroism during World War II, including saving his crewmates from probable death when a Japanese destroyer rammed his torpedo boat. The well-publicized stylishness of his wife, Jacqueline, reinforced Kennedy's image as a robust and youthful candidate.

Voters were energized by the new forms of electioneering and the choices before them. Almost two-thirds of all voters cast a ballot on election day—a greater proportion than in any election since 1908. The race was one of the tightest in history, with Kennedy winning by just 118,500 of 68.8 million popular votes. (The electoral vote margin was wider, with Kennedy taking 56 percent.) In the South, Kennedy and Johnson succeeded in assuaging many Protestants' fears of a Catholic president. In the North, they drew more Catholics into the electorate. Significantly, Kennedy also won the support of African Americans after he telephoned Coretta Scott King, the wife of Martin Luther King, Jr., who had been arrested in Georgia during a civil rights march. As Kennedy worked to free King, Nixon remained silent, virtually reversing the goodwill that President Eisenhower had earned among African Americans for sending federal troops to Little Rock in 1957.

Television Transforms Politics. Fatigued but refusing to wear stage makeup for the cameras, Republican candidate Richard Nixon looked pasty and unshaven in his first televised debate. Tan, clean-cut, relaxed, and intellectually nimble, his Democratic opponent, John F. Kennedy, came across on television as the debate's clear winner.

CONCLUSION

Many people today fondly remember the 1950s as a period of consensus, stability, and widely shared affluence—a golden era in which Americans "got along," families were strong, and the nation waged an unambiguously just war for freedom. Others consider the decade a period of stifling conformity and cultural conservatism. Both characterizations contain a germ of truth, but neither adequately captures the complexities of this rich and paradoxical era.

By any monetary measure, the middle class had never had it so good. They earned significantly more, lived in bigger houses, drove larger cars, had more college education, took longer vacations, enjoyed better benefits, and spent their disposable income on a greater range of consumer products than any other middle class in world history. For most suburbanites, economic growth and technological possibilities seemed as boundless as their optimism. But one in four Americans did not share in the affluence, and a significant minority were still subject to second-class citizenship and legal discrimination.

Even in the affluent suburbs, many struggled with new anxieties, most associated with the very same technologies they celebrated. Convenience foods and appliances freed up time but incubated feelings of futility and worthlessness among homemakers. Although it ostensibly protected Americans, the buildup of the nation's nuclear armory fueled fears of nuclear annihilation and drove defense spending to new heights. Reflecting on the rapid growth of the U.S. military and defense contracting over the previous decade, President Eisenhower warned in his farewell speech of the immense cost and the potential dangers of the new defense industry. "We recognize the imperative need for this development," he explained, "but . . . in the councils of government, we must guard against the acquisition of unwarranted influence, whether sought or unsought, by the military-industrial complex. The potential for the disastrous rise of misplaced power exists, and will persist."

The fate of the individual in America's mass consumer society was also very much on people's minds. The world's first generation of self-identified teenagers eagerly participated in the consumer culture that adults had created, but they frequently used it to challenge convention about everything from sex to self-expression and the meaning of freedom. The freedom movement forced the issue of African Americans' individual rights into the consciousness—and conscience—of the nation. Avant-garde artists and radical social critics exposed and critiqued what they saw as the moral dangers of mass consumption, cookie-cutter suburbs, and an advertising-soaked society that seemed to have little time for reflection, dissent, or art. And a new generation of conservative thinkers and corporate leaders argued that unions and other forms of collectivism were eroding individual freedoms. As John F. Kennedy assumed the presidential reins in 1961, the nation's cultural and political ferment began to bubble over.

STUDY TERMS

modern Republicanism (p. 759)
service economy (p. 759)
National Interstate and Defense Highways Act (p. 763)
Air Pollution Control Act (p. 763)
convenience foods (p. 764)
New Look foreign policy (p. 765)
nuclear brinksmanship (p. 765)
Sputnik (p. 766)
Gaither Report (p. 766)
National Aeronautics and Space Administration (p. 766)
National Defense Education Act (p. 766)
Kitchen Debate (p. 766)
United States Information Agency (p. 767)
Jazz Ambassadors (p. 767)
decolonization (p. 767)
nationalization (p. 767)
neocolonialism (p. 770)
nonaligned movement (p. 770)
cruising (p. 771)
Kefauver Committee (p. 772)
rock 'n' roll (p. 772)
rhythm and blues (p. 772)
payola (p. 773)
Beats (p. 775)
avant-garde (p. 775)
de facto segregation (p. 777)
Brown v. Board of Education of Topeka, Kansas (p. 777)
Southern Christian Leadership Conference (p. 778)
Southern Manifesto (p. 778)
Operation Wetback (p. 779)
American G.I. Forum (p. 779)
Hernandez v. Texas (p. 779)
neoconservatism (p. 779)
free enterprise (p. 780)
libertarianism (p. 781)
John Birch Society (p. 782)
Boulwarism (p. 782)

TIMELINE

1953 Soviet leader Joseph Stalin dies
President Eisenhower unexpectedly protects New Deal and trims military spending
Schools, U.S. military, and several foreign countries ban blue jeans

1954 Congress inserts phrase "under God" in Pledge of Allegiance
Chinese invasion of Taiwan tests U.S. brinksmanship policy
Supreme Court rules "separate but equal" not valid in education
Operation Wetback deports over a million Mexicans

1955 Air Pollution Control Act attempts to stem air pollution
First issues of influential *National Review* published
Walt Disney opens Disneyland
James Dean confronts suburban culture in *Rebel Without a Cause*
Montgomery bus boycott challenges segregation on public transportation

1956 Alan Ginsberg's *Howl* decries conformity
National Interstate and Defense Highway Act establishes interstate highway system
Elvis Presley releases "Heartbreak Hotel"

1957 Soviets successfully test world's first ICBM
Little Rock Nine challenge segregation at Central High School

1958 GE sponsors conservative electoral candidates
Pan American Airways flies first intercontinental flight

1959 Kitchen Debate brings the home into the Cold War struggle

1960 ABC, CBS, and NBC broadcast Kennedy-Nixon debates
John F. Kennedy is first Catholic to be elected president

FURTHER READING

Additional suggested readings are available on the Online Learning Center at www.mhhe.com/becomingamerica1e.

Thomas Borstelmann, *The Cold War and the Color Line: American Race Relations in the Global Arena* (2001), examines U.S. race relations within the broader context of post–World War II global decolonization.

Stephanie Coontz, *The Way We Never Were: American Families and the Nostalgia Trap* (1992), questions myths and uncovers the reality of family life in America.

James Gilbert, *A Cycle of Outrage: America's Reaction to the Juvenile Delinquent in the 1950s* (1986), focuses on how changing social mores and concerns over national security redefined delinquency and contributed to an urgent sense that delinquency was a threat to national security.

Jonathan P. Herzog, *The Spiritual-Industrial Complex: America's Religious Battle Against Communism in the Early Cold War* (2011), reveals the interconnectedness of religion and politics in the early Cold War era.

Michael Klarman, *From Jim Crow to Civil Rights: The Supreme Court and the Struggle for Racial Equality* (2004), sets the 1954 *Brown v. Board of Education* case within the broader context of race-based Supreme Court cases.

Karal Ann Marling, *As Seen on TV: The Visual Culture of Everyday Life in the 1950s* (1994), highlights the significance of television to the expanding American consumer culture.

Elaine Tyler May, *Homeward Bound: American Families in the Cold War Era* (1988), explains that the Cold War influenced even Americans' private lives.

Grace Palladino, *Teenagers: An American History* (1997), traces the post–World War II transformation of adolescence as a distinct life stage and analyzes the significant role teenagers have played as consumers.

Kim Phillips-Fein, *Invisible Hands: The Making of the Conservative Movement from the New Deal to Reagan* (2009), examines the cultural, economic, and political factors that contributed to the formation of the modern conservative movement.

Kevin M. Schultz, *Tri-Faith America: How Catholics and Jews Held Postwar America to Its Protestant Promise* (2011), traces the popularization of the idea that the United States is a tri-faith nation and explores the debates over religious pluralism.

Jason Sokol, *There Goes My Everything: White Southerners in the Age of Civil Rights* (2006), considers the civil rights era from the perspective of white southerners who navigated change and confusion as the world in which they grew up was transformed.

Penny von Eschen, *Satchmo Blows Up the World: Jazz Ambassadors Play the Cold War* (2004), investigates the Cold War practice of sending jazz musicians to other countries as cultural emissaries.

Odd Arne Westad, *The Global Cold War: Third World Interventions and the Making of Our Times* (2007), probes how the U.S. and Soviet ideological struggle engulfed parts of Asia, Africa, and Latin America, exacerbating tensions within those countries.

28

INSIDE ▶

THE BIG PICTURE

Youth came to the fore in the 1960s as never before, energizing the freedom movement and forging new forms of artistic and political expression. Congress enacted milestone civil rights and anti-poverty legislation, but for many Americans it was too little, too late. As urban neighborhoods rebelled, the government enlarged its involvement in the Vietnam War. By 1968, the antiwar movement and a multitude of disaffected communities were demanding radical change, and civil and political violence was spiraling out of control.

Stop! In the Name of Love. Detroit's Supremes burst onto the music scene in the early 1960s with catchy, bittersweet love songs that captured the seemingly boundless optimism and openness of baby boomer youth culture.

ERA OF DREAMS & DISCONTENT

Every Friday night between 1966 and 1969, the USS *Enterprise*, the spaceship at the center of NBC's popular *Star Trek* television series, ventured into outer space—"the final frontier . . . where no man has gone before"—and into Americans' living rooms. *Star Trek* projected the older genre of the Western adventure story into the twenty-third century and outer space, using the setting to explore urgent moral questions of the day. Futuristic technology, including laser guns known as "phasers" and "teleporters" that "beamed" crew members between the spaceship and alien planets, reinforced Cold War ideas about the link between technology and human progress. *Enterprise* captain James Kirk and his crew repeatedly brokered peace agreements between warring "races" that looked suspiciously like Russians and Americans. On one occasion, barefoot, colorfully dressed youths strongly resembling hippies searched for Eden and staged a "sit-in" on the *Enterprise*—before hijacking it. Over and over, the *Enterprise*'s multiracial crew was seduced by strange utopian societies, only to find themselves trapped in a totalitarian nightmare.

Star Trek offered a vision of the United States as a technologically advanced and enlightened multicultural society that would triumph over war and despair. The 1960s began on a similarly hopeful note with the election of the youthful, dynamic John F. Kennedy to the presidency. An outpouring of art, music, and fashion that drew inspiration from the avant-garde culture of the 1950s put an end to the prior decade's celebration of conformity and primed baby boomers to question authority and challenge convention. In these same years, the leadership of the southern freedom movement shifted to a younger, more ambitious generation whose nonviolent sit-ins and calls for a "second Reconstruction" attracted the support of millions of Americans. Congress enacted sweeping civil rights reform and the most ambitious social and environmental initiatives since the New Deal.

KEY QUESTIONS

- Why did so many Americans have such high hopes for the Kennedy administration?
- What were U.S. foreign policy goals under Kennedy and Johnson, and how did the Cuban missile crisis affect Cold War policy?
- How did the African American civil rights movement's strategy, aims, and personnel change between 1960 and 1965?
- What were the origins and impacts of the social movements of the late 1960s?
- What were the chief cultural, political, and economic divisions in American society at the end of the 1960s?

Spock, *Star Trek*'s chief science officer, gains an understanding of the "hippie" phenomenon in which youth rejected social convention and embraced free love, nature, drugs, communal life, and utopia.

Even as progress was made, however, political conflict of an intensity unseen since 1919 rocked the nation. Violence roiled the South in the early part of the decade, as diehard segregationists harassed, beat, and even murdered young civil rights workers. The brutality continued with a string of assassinations, starting with President Kennedy's in Dallas, Texas, in 1963. In the latter half of the decade, urban riots razed whole neighborhoods. Frustrated with the slow pace of change, minority youth leaders forged new, far more militant organizations that rejected the freedom movement's earlier, nonviolent tactics. Internationally, the United States stepped up its Cold War operations, including assassinations and military campaigns, in the developing world. By the end of the decade, hundreds of thousands of troops had entered combat in Vietnam. The war further divided Americans along generational, racial, and class lines, with no end in sight.

THE KENNEDY YEARS

At age forty-three, John Fitzgerald Kennedy (JFK) was the youngest man ever elected U.S. president. Consistent with his electoral campaign, the incoming president offered a vision of the nation as energetic, youthful, optimistic, and adventuresome. The United States would conquer both the New Frontier of space, promised Kennedy, and the old enemies of disease, poverty, tyranny, and war. Although JFK's legislative record lagged behind his rhetoric, his words resonated in a culture that had grown restless. By 1960, many middle-class Americans were questioning their suburban, consumerist values and becoming receptive to artistic innovation and unconventional ideas. Along with a reinvigorated civil rights movement, this cultural shift set the stage for an anti-authoritarian rebellion.

NEW VISION, NEW FRONTIERS

JFK advanced his vision of the United States' future in his inaugural address in January 1961. "[W]e stand today on the edge of a New Frontier," he proclaimed, "—the frontier of the 1960s, the frontier of unknown opportunities and perils, the frontier of unfilled hopes and unfilled threats." The "torch [has been] passed to a new generation," he continued, and as president he would lead Americans through the exciting and uncharted territory of the new decade. Science, social reform, education, and economics would unlock the doors to national greatness. With this vision in mind, Kennedy rejected the military-style hierarchy that his predecessor Dwight D. Eisenhower had imposed on the cabinet in favor of a consultative model designed to unleash creative thinking. He appointed only the "best and brightest" to his cabinet—most with graduate degrees from top-flight schools.

Among the most urgent problems Kennedy confronted was the persistence of Jim Crow in the South. However, his small margin of victory (only 118,500 votes) and the dominance of conservative southern Democrats in Congress initially made him reluctant to press for comprehensive civil rights legislation. Instead, JFK extended existing New Deal programs. The reforms were modest by the standards of previous Democratic administrations but substantial by comparison with the Eisenhower years. At JFK's initiative, Congress increased Social Security benefits by 20 percent and raised the minimum wage by 25 percent over two years, to $1.25/hour (see How Much Is That?).

Health services were added for disabled children, retirees, and pregnant women, and food stamps were reintroduced. Ambitious new legislation also sought to revitalize the cities, which had been especially hard-hit by the outflow of jobs and taxpayers to the suburbs. The Housing Bill of 1961 authorized the federal government to build one hundred thousand urban units, develop mass transit, and provide affordable housing for low- and middle-income urbanites. When Kennedy's Presidential Commission on the Status of Women, headed by Eleanor Roosevelt, reported that women were typically paid far less than men, the Equal Pay Act of 1963 prohibited wage inequality based on sex. The wage gap, by which employers paid women on average less than half what they paid men, diminished slowly until 1980.

CELEBRITY PRESIDENT

Kennedy's presidency made an enormous impact on U.S. culture—and vice versa. Although other presidents had skillfully used mass media to boost their popularity, Kennedy was the first to harness the public's adoration of celebrities. His magnetism and grasp of public relations quickly made him a major media personality and the subject of countless artworks, books, films, and TV shows. His emphasis on fresh ideas appealed widely in a culture that celebrated youth and innovation. Kennedy also constantly emphasized vigor, vitality, and courage in his addresses and self-presentation, which was unprecedentedly casual. Masking the pain he endured from an endocrine disorder called Addison's disease, JFK took well-publicized daily swims and played touch football games on the White House lawn, inspiring a national fitness craze.

Under the direction of the president's fashionable wife, Jacqueline, the White House became synonymous with glamour and sophistication. Distinguished writers, musicians,

How Much Is That?

The Federal Minimum Wage

Although it doesn't sound like much, the federal minimum wage (FMW) of $1.25/hour bought a lot more in 1963 than it does today. Back then, $1.25 could buy what $9.37 buys now. The current FMW ($7.25/hour) has therefore *decreased* in real terms by almost 30 percent.

JFK: Celebrity Politician. President John F. Kennedy's frequent appearances in published photographs and on TV shows emphasized his fitness, informality, and magnetism. Television especially made Kennedy appear far more approachable than previous presidents, and his virile sexuality made him seem like a Hollywood star. Despite being married, he had liaisons with many women, including box office icon Marilyn Monroe, while in office.

artists, scholars, and Hollywood actors visited frequently, leading commentators to liken the Kennedy White House to Camelot, the legendary King Arthur's magical court (an idea originally promoted by Jacqueline Kennedy). Above all, the Kennedy White House gave the new sensibility of openness, experimentation, and youthfulness its official seal.

END OF CONSENSUS

Just ten years earlier, Kennedy's elegant parties, informality, and embrace of celebrity would have scandalized most Americans. By the early 1960s, thanks largely to the boundary-busting effects of rock 'n' roll, avant-garde art, and the freedom movement, a growing proportion of middle-class Americans were bending, and even breaking, many contemporary social conventions. Above all, they began questioning the authority of **the establishment,** a term that generally served as shorthand for long-standing social conventions, entrenched elites, and political and cultural institutions. Questioning authority—whether in the arts, politics, the family, church, or school—came into vogue in the Kennedy years, particularly among young urbanites.

In the arts, the rebellious Pop Art movement challenged conventional perceptions of American society, drawing on the familiar imagery and objects of consumer culture, including comics, advertising, and packaging, to challenge the idea that art was only for the elite. Practitioners such as Andy Warhol used mass production techniques to undermine the idea that a work of art could not be a copy and had to be abstract or inaccessible. Collaborative street events known as "happenings," which brought together many kinds of art, technology, and everyday experience, popped up in unexpected places. Building on ideas first explored by the 1950s avant-garde, happenings such as Jim Dine's *Car Crash*, which simulated the sensory experience of a car collision, turned audiences into participants, implicitly challenging the idea that the artists were the sole creators of "art." "Minimalist" artists also rebelled against convention, specifically the 1950s love of decoration and detail. Clean lines, cool tones, and simplicity replaced the busy embellishment of older design.

African American artists had challenged various aspects of Jim Crow since the 1890s and questioned other social conventions as well. Jazz and R&B had won large followings, but it was not until the 1960s that black artists in other fields attracted racially diverse mass audiences. In New York, Alvin Ailey and his American Dance Theater performed *Revelations* (1960), an emotionally intense story of the black experience from slavery to the present day. This critically acclaimed work incorporated blues, gospel music, and historical narrative and critiqued the commonplace perception that the black historical experience was simply one of victimization and degradation. In music, too, black musicians and lesser-known record labels such as Detroit's Motown Record Corporation attracted an integrated, mass audience for a new kind of music known as "soul," which combined gospel and R&B. In 1961, The Marvelettes' "Please Mr. Postman" was the first of 110 Motown soul tunes to win a racially mixed audience and hit number one on the American Billboard chart.

Like rock 'n' roll and blue jeans in the 1950s, much of the antiestablishment ethos of the early 1960s was absorbed and adopted by Hollywood and the other culture industries. Fully aware of youths' purchasing power, advertisers increasingly pitched to what they called the "Now Generation." White youths' newfound desire to be "cool" and "hip" (terms borrowed from African American culture) was fed and spread as advertisers skillfully turned youths' dissent into a selling point. Still, the commercialization of dissent helped bury the conformist ethos of the 1950s and affirmed the social value of challenging convention. And, after 1964, questioning authority became the hallmark of the powerful new social movements that burst onto the American political scene (see A Nation at War, below).

Boots Made for Walking. By 1963, the clothing industry had fashioned boots and miniskirts into a national craze. The items' popularity also reflected young women's newfound desire to assert their sexuality and equality with men. As Nancy Sinatra sang to her lying, cheating man in 1966: "These boots are made for walking, and that's just what they'll do. One of these days these boots are gonna walk all over you."

THE OTHER AMERICANS

Not everyone bucked convention or participated in the newly hip consumer culture. Although most Americans had long enjoyed a higher standard of living than their European counterparts, poverty remained a constant reality for many, even during economic booms. Poverty rates, although steadily declining, stood at 22 percent when Kennedy took office.

In one sense, poverty had changed dramatically in the postwar years, from a predominantly rural to a mostly urban phenomenon. As upwardly mobile whites moved to the suburbs, poorer urbanites had little choice but to stay put. They were joined by an influx of impoverished rural folk who could no longer survive in the increasingly mechanized business of farming but who possessed few urban skills. In another sense, however, poverty had changed depressingly little. It still afflicted African Americans disproportionately, at over twice the rate for whites. Latinos also suffered disproportionately, while Native Americans endured the highest poverty rate of all. Although non-Latino whites still made up the majority of the impoverished masses nationwide, African Americans and Latinos composed the great majority of the new urban poor.

Politicians, scholars, and affluent Americans had mostly ignored the scourge of poverty in the 1950s. It was a rural and distant problem for most, and the popular misconception that all Americans were prospering blinded them to the facts. In the early 1960s, however, the scale of urban poverty and a series of studies punctured popular illusions. Jane Jacobs's *The Death and Life of Great American Cities* showed that federal money made available to city government under the Housing Acts of 1949 and 1954 had in fact aggravated urban poverty. Mayors, bankers, and real estate developers had bulldozed the slums to make way for expressways, skyscrapers, civic centers, and middle-class apartment blocks. These **urban renewal** programs not only exiled the poor (typically, African Americans) to the city's fringes, but also broke up neighborhood and kinship networks that had helped poor families cope with their challenges. As developers emptied the inner city of its residents and replaced homes with vast "dead zones" of concrete plazas and elevated highways, cities became less safe. Crime rose steadily.

Poverty further forced its way onto Americans' radar in 1962 with the publication of social critic Michael Harrington's *The Other America*. That America, wrote Harrington, "is populated by failures, by those driven from the land and bewildered by the city, by old people suddenly confronted with the torments of loneliness and poverty, and by minorities facing a wall of prejudice." Many Americans were shocked by Harrington's findings, and the president won support in Congress for programs aimed at the urban poor. Legislators earmarked $2 billion for encouraging businesses to relocate to economically depressed areas and to set up training programs for the unemployed. Given the extent of the problem, however, Kennedy's program struck many concerned citizens (including those in impoverished communities) as inadequate.

KENNEDY'S COLD WAR POLICY

True to his electoral platform, President Kennedy strove to close the "missile gap", strengthen the military, and lay to rest the impression that, as a liberal Democrat, he was "soft on communism." The misconception that liberals, who typically supported protections for labor, a federal welfare system, and government-sponsored health care, were communist sympathizers had dogged northern Democrats since the Second Red Scare of the postwar era (see Chapter 26). The fact that there was no missile gap and that the last Democratic president, Harry S Truman, had started the Cold War did not stop Republicans or the conservative press from questioning Kennedy's commitment to waging the Cold War.

Like Truman before him, JFK was tough on the Soviets and eager to show it. He immediately increased the defense budget by 15 percent and expedited the construction of overseas military bases (see Map 28.1). The U.S. nuclear capability grew sevenfold between 1961 and 1963, and over a quarter-million U.S. personnel were stationed overseas. The Soviet Union's launch of the world's first manned spaceship in early 1961 further persuaded JFK that putting an American on the moon was a top priority. Soon afterward, NASA announced the Apollo space program (which culminated in the first moonwalk in 1969), and astronaut John Glenn, in 1962, became the first American to orbit the earth.

The developing world remained a crucial arena of the Cold War. Containing communism and stabilizing governments in Latin America, especially in light of recent anti-American protests (see Chapter 27), assumed new urgency. The Kennedy administration's strategy, much like Eisenhower's, was to stabilize U.S.-friendly governments regardless of whether they were democratic or had committed human rights abuses. As well as boosting foreign aid by $20 billion, the government established the Peace Corps, which sent idealistic students to Latin America and elsewhere to provide educational, health, and technical services. Kennedy explained the logic behind this initiative as an effort to extend foreign policy beyond formal agreements and pledges of support. "Peace does not rest in the charters and covenants alone," he told the United Nations in 1963. "It lies in the hearts and minds of all people."

The combination of monetary and expert aid was intended to relieve the material and psychological conditions of poverty under which communism and anti-Americanism were thought to thrive. As insurance, however, the government also opened special military camps in which U.S. officers trained Latin American police and paramilitaries in guerrilla warfare. American Special Forces (commandos known as Green Berets) trained in jungle warfare in the expectation that they might someday be needed in the global war on communism.

Kennedy's first foreign policy challenge was a botched invasion of Cuba undertaken by a force of Cuban ex-patriots in 1961. Two years earlier, socialist revolutionary Fidel Castro had led a popular uprising against the military dictatorship of Fulgencio Batista. Castro's victory had abruptly ended a twenty-five-year period of repressive right-wing rule and was putting

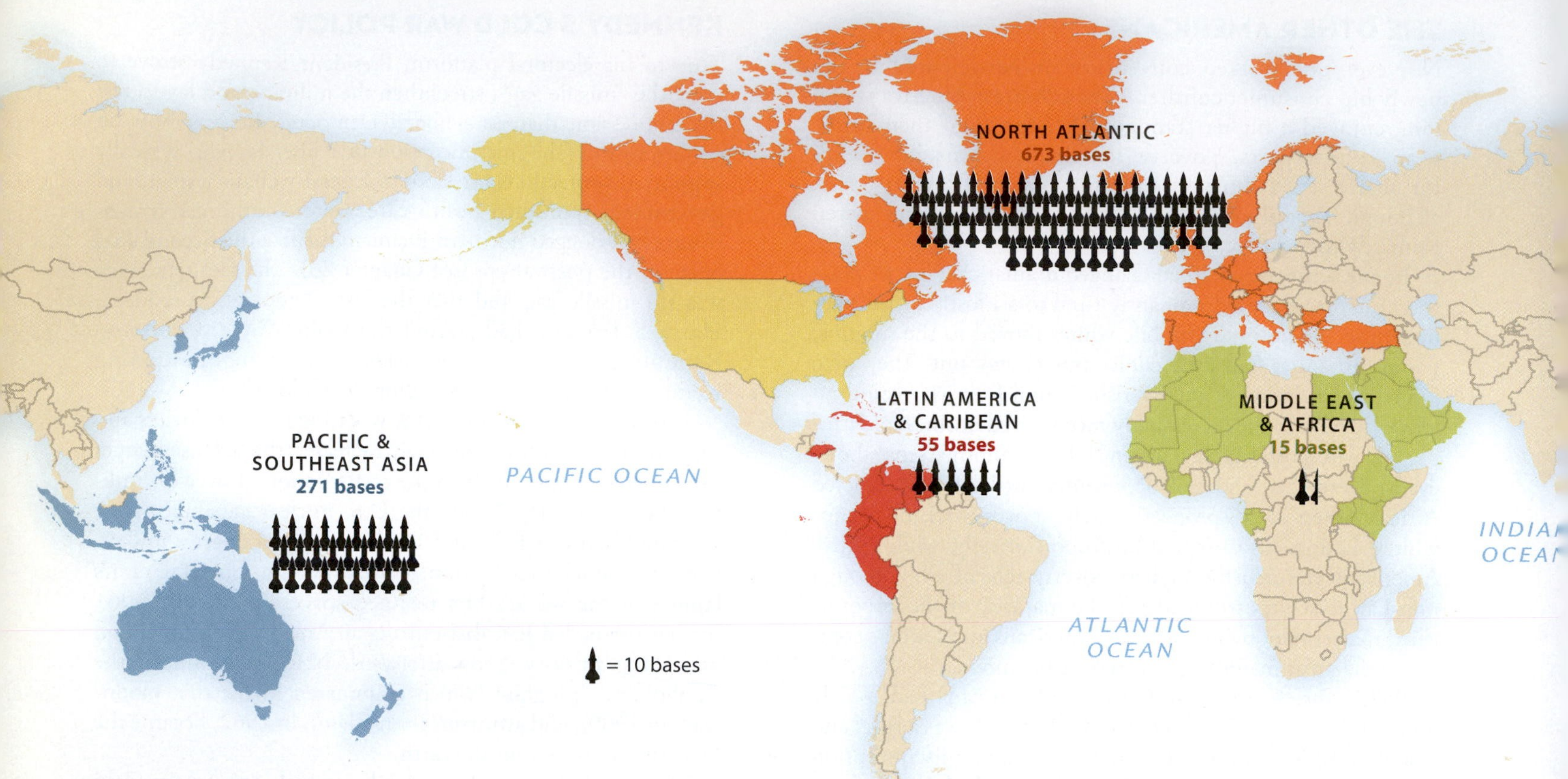

Map 28.1 The U.S. Security Network, 1967. Under President Kennedy, the U.S. security network expanded to include over 30 nations, 275 military bases, and 400 intercontinental ballistic missiles. By 1967, it included 1,014 foreign bases—more than at any time since World War II (and any time since).

American business interests in Cuba at risk. Although Castro had not immediately implemented socialist reforms, the U.S. government feared he soon would, and worried that the popular young leader was inspiring other revolutionaries in the Caribbean and Central America.

Under President Eisenhower, the Central Intelligence Agency (CIA) had trained a force of Cuban exiles intent on mounting an invasion and overthrowing Castro. Although he worried that the operation might backfire, Kennedy allowed it to proceed. In April 1961, U.S. bombers attacked Cuban airfields, and a few days later, 1,400 émigré troops stormed Cuba's Bay of Pigs. Much to Kennedy's embarrassment, the Cuban military quickly captured most of the rebels and paraded them on live television. Castro eventually returned all but eleven to the United States in exchange for food and medicine. The humiliating episode led Kennedy and Secretary of Defense Robert McNamara to look for a new, more effective strategy. The CIA consequently made several unsuccessful assassination attempts on Castro. The government also began planning operations in which U.S. soldiers would not only coordinate but also expertly execute covert actions in the region.

CONFRONTING KHRUSHCHEV

U.S.-Soviet relations meanwhile grew increasingly tense. The president's well-publicized commitment to nuclear buildup and his decision in 1961 to place Soviet-targeted intercontinental ballistic missiles (ICBMs) in Turkey and Italy, within striking distance of Moscow, had heated up the nuclear arms race. The Soviet leader again demanded that American, British, and French troops withdraw from Berlin on the grounds that their presence so close to the Soviet Union and deep inside East Germany threatened Soviet security. Adding to Soviet concerns, upwards of thirty thousand East Berliners were fleeing to the West every month. JFK acknowledged the Soviets' security concerns but refused to withdraw. Raising the stakes, the president went on national television to ask Congress for the authority to call up military reservists and to fund a massive civil defense program, complete with fallout shelters, for West Berlin. Berlin had become the Cold War's ground zero.

Tensions came to a head in the fall of 1961 when communist-allied East Germany, with Soviet consent, constructed a massive, fortified wall that split Berlin in two. The Berlin Wall staunched the flow of refugees out of East Germany and isolated West Berlin. Although Kennedy objected and mobilized U.S. forces, he was ultimately unprepared to take the United States to war over the development. In Berlin, however, an American general took matters into his own hands, arming ten U.S. tanks with bulldozer attachments for the purpose of flattening the wall. As American tanks squared off against Soviet tanks, the two superpowers edged to the verge of hostilities. On learning of the standoff, Kennedy opened secret, high-level talks with Khrushchev. After sixteen hours of tense negotiation, both sides stood down.

The subsequent period of relative calm was short lived. In 1962, the Soviets and Cuba secretly agreed to install nuclear warheads on Cuban territory. Cuban intelligence sources had revealed the existence of U.S.-backed assassination plots and large-scale military exercises in the Caribbean that appeared preparatory for an invasion of Cuba. Castro reasoned that aligning with the Soviets—and accepting much needed economic and military aid—was essential to the Cuban Revolution's survival. The Soviets welcomed the opportunity, seeing it as a way of balancing out America's recent installation of nuclear warheads in Turkey. In October 1962, an American U-2 spy plane confirmed that the Soviets had established missile sites in Cuba.

News of the installations—which put ninety-two million Americans in the direct line of nuclear fire—sent the Kennedy cabinet into full crisis mode. A hastily-convened emergency committee put four options for resolving the Cuban Missile Crisis on the table: "Shoot them out," "squeeze them out," "talk them out," and "buy them out." Although some diplomats suggested a negotiated solution, the committee focused only on military options, including a full-scale invasion and aerial bombing. Members finally settled on a naval blockade that would halt all shipments into and out of Cuba.

With the blockade in place, President Kennedy went on national television to demand that the Soviets immediately end "this clandestine, reckless, and provocative threat to world peace" or face the full force of U.S. military might. But tensions only escalated when Soviet warships approached U.S. forces. Nerve-wracked commanders on both sides nearly fired on each other, and the U.S. Strategic Air Command went on nuclear alert. On October 27, a Soviet missile took down an American U-2 spy plane over Cuba. The superpowers were on the precipice of war. Across the United States—and much of the world—citizens were terrified that nuclear war was imminent. Thousands fled major cities on the eastern seaboard, and millions more stocked their bomb shelters.

Faced with the stark reality that military pressure was not working and that it might spark a catastrophic nuclear war, Kennedy negotiated. He accepted Khrushchev's offer to remove the missiles in exchange for an assurance that the United States would not invade Cuba and that he would withdraw U.S. nuclear missiles from Turkey and Italy. The Soviets pulled out, and U.S. forces stood down. The crisis had passed.

In the wake of the crisis, the United States and the Soviets tempered their rhetoric, eager to avoid another nuclear standoff. Kennedy called for arms control and the two leaders established a "hot line" (emergency telephone line) between Moscow and Washington. A treaty banned underwater and aerial nuclear testing. Yet Kennedy's cabinet still believed, despite evidence to the contrary, that the United States' superior military force and the country's hard-nosed willingness to "get tough" with the enemy had worked.

THE ROAD TO VIETNAM

While the eyes of the world were on Berlin and Cuba, the United States had quietly increased its involvement in Southeast Asia. In 1961, shortly after the Bay of Pigs fiasco, President Kennedy had sent five hundred Green Berets and military advisers to South Vietnam, where the unpopular, U.S.-backed government of Ngo Dinh Diem was teetering near collapse. Just twenty years earlier, South Vietnam had been part of French Indochina, a colony of France. Japan occupied Indochina for much of World War II, and when the Allies defeated Japan in 1945, Vietnamese nationalists known as the Viet Minh demanded independence for their country. France, however, sent troops to reassert French rule. Led by socialist Ho Chi Minh, the educated son of a well-known Confucian scholar, the Viet Minh began a nine-year guerilla war against the French.

As a young man, Ho had lived and worked in the United States, Britain, France, and communist Russia. He was hopeful that the United States would support Vietnamese independence and based the Viet Minh's founding principles directly on the Declaration of Independence. President Truman, however, backed France and, after 1947, reiterated the U.S. policy of containing communism in all its forms —including Ho's plans to break up the great colonial plantations and redistribute land to the peasantry. The Soviets and communist China (after 1949) filled the vacuum, sending supplies and equipment to the struggling guerrilla army.

Outgunned and outspent, the Viet Minh appeared to be losing the war when, in an extraordinary operation that took the world by surprise, the guerrillas stormed the French stronghold at Dien Bien Phu. The besieged French called for a ceasefire and ultimately agreed to dissolve Indochina. Under the Geneva Accords of 1954, the former colony was divided along the seventeenth parallel between the Viet Minh's Democratic Republic of Vietnam in the north, and the loyalists' State of Vietnam to the south (see Map 28.2). The separation was intended to be temporary and the Accords also provided that a national unification election would be held in 1956. Before then, however, Ngo Dinh Diem, a member of the loyalist landholding elite, grabbed power after rigging a referendum and declared the founding of a rival Republic of Vietnam. The unpopular Diem delayed the unification election indefinitely.

Map 28.2 The Road to Vietnam. President Kennedy never intended for U.S. troops to fight a war in Southeast Asia. Because he subscribed to the domino theory of Soviet expansion, however, he was committed to funding and training the anticommunist government of Ngo Dinh Diem in South Vietnam. When Diem's forces failed to quell the Viet Cong, Kennedy dispatched sixteen thousand U.S. personnel, many of whom entered combat. U.S. involvement would escalate in subsequent years.

By 1961, a broad cross-section of the southern Vietnamese people was rebelling against Diem and his fellow landholders in protest of unjust land laws and religious persecution. (Diem and the elite were Catholic, whereas the vast majority of Vietnamese were Buddhist.) A small cadre of educated communists, known as the National Liberation Front (NLF, or Viet Cong), joined the southern insurgency. Soon, the Soviet-friendly government of North Vietnam offered the NLF support. Few Vietnamese on either side considered their struggle a Cold War conflict. But Kennedy and McNamara, viewing these developments through the lens of containment, determined that Vietnam was a crucial front of the Cold War.

By 1963, over sixteen thousand American soldiers were assisting Diem and even entering combat on his behalf. Victory over the NLF became a formal objective of U.S. foreign policy. Although aware of Diem's corruption and human rights abuses, the United States viewed him as a crucial ally. But after Diem ordered a series of brutal attacks on peaceful Buddhist protesters, the State Department realized that the leader was a liability and a recruiting tool for the enemy. In November 1963, with the backing of the CIA, Diem's generals ousted him and established a military regime. Stability proved elusive, however, and the new regime was soon overthrown by another elite faction. The civil war raged on.

YOUTH AND THE FREEDOM MOVEMENT

Back on the domestic front, as President Kennedy stalled on civil rights reform, a younger generation of activists gained momentum in the South. These impassioned youths pushed the freedom movement toward a bolder, more confrontational strategy by physically integrating lunch counters, bus terminals, and other public spaces around the South. Segregationists met their efforts with an epidemic of violence, which in turned publicized African Americans' plight. Tens of thousands of white Northerners joined the freedom movement, and President Kennedy finally called for new civil rights legislation to stop the violence.

STUDENTS EMPOWER THE MOVEMENT

Prosperous Greensboro, North Carolina, home to excellent public schools and two leading black colleges, seemed like the last place where the African American freedom movement would confront Jim Crow. Greensboro's white leaders prided themselves on their relatively progressive politics and the civility with which townspeople treated one another, even across the color line. African Americans voted and ran for office, and when the Supreme Court ordered schools to desegregate in 1954, the city complied. Despite appearances, though, segregation still held sway. Only a few African Americans had been admitted to white schools by 1960, and blacks remained subject to segregation in restaurants, employment, and public amenities.

In the spring of 1960, four African American freshmen from North Carolina Agricultural and Technical College courageously demonstrated that Jim Crow was alive and well in Greensboro. Respectably dressed in suit and tie, the students entered a Woolworth's store and, after buying a few items, sat at the segregated lunch counter. Refused service, the four remained at the counter for almost an hour before leaving. The following day, they returned with twenty-three other students—and they repeated their action every day through the end of the week, by which time some white students from a local women's college had also joined the protest. Reporters began covering the **sit-in,** and within weeks, similar protests had spread to fifty-four southern cities. Several thousand young African Americans were arrested, and many more assaulted by enraged whites. Nonetheless, the protests continued. In the North, too, thousands of whites and African American students sat in at Woolworth's counters to protest the chain's enforcement of southern segregation.

The sit-ins marked a change of strategy, aims, and personnel for the freedom movement. Unlike the carefully planned actions of the 1950s, the new protests began as spontaneous acts of defiance, uncoordinated by the National Association for the Advancement of Colored People (NAACP) or other established civil rights groups and led by young people, mostly college students. The protesters bravely used their bodies to integrate lunch counters and, eventually, all kinds of segregated spaces. Perfectly suited for the television age, such tactics gave news teams plenty of vivid footage—and won the protesters plenty of publicity. The new approach provoked white segregationists into spectacular acts of violence that appalled many northerners, mobilizing popular support for change. Such actions empowered individual protesters by letting their voices be heard and changing the national conversation.

As the sit-ins spread, their message also became far more ambitious: not only must the South end segregation, but the entire nation, including the federal government, must do whatever was necessary to reverse centuries of discrimination and inequality. A new organization, the Student Nonviolent Coordinating Committee (SNCC, pronounced "Snick"), was founded in Raleigh, North Carolina, a few months after the Greensboro sit-ins. The first student-led civil rights organization, SNCC became the driving force of the freedom movement. Idealistic and brimming with confidence, SNCC founders understood that they were making history and believed that their courage and moral rectitude would triumph over injustice.

Thousands of young African Americans joined SNCC. In the North, many white students who were previously uninterested in politics also signed up. The remarkable sight of African American youths quietly exposing the brutality of Jim Crow shook many people out of their complacency and showed them that positive change was possible. SNCC also appealed at a time when many white students sensed that their suburban, consumerist lives lacked meaning. SNCC activists "lived on a fuller level of feeling than any people I'd ever seen," commented Tom Hayden, a University of Michigan senior who later cofounded the radical Students for a Democratic Society.

GOVERNMENT INDECISION

SNCC's strategy influenced other civil rights organizations. In the spring of 1961, the Congress of Racial Equality (CORE, founded in 1941) organized the first of several freedom rides in which

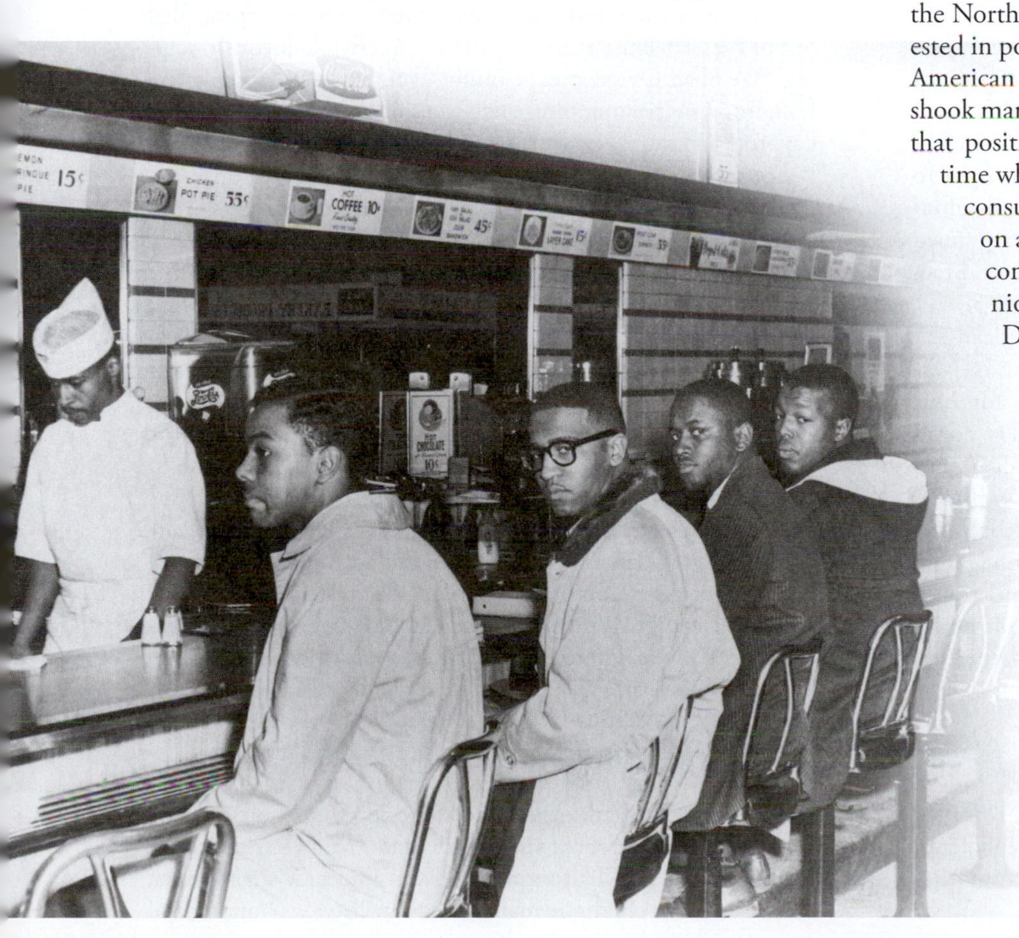

Students Integrate Greensboro. When a group of working-class whites heckled the "Greensboro Four" and their fellow protesters, the local college football team protected them. Stunned, the angry whites demanded, "Who do you think you are?"—to which the athletes replied, "We the Union Army." **Questions for Analysis:** Why were whites so surprised that African Americans sat down at a Greensboro lunch counter? What made the protest effective? Why might the football players have identified themselves as the Union Army?

interracial groups traveled by public buses across the South to test the enforcement of federal court orders to desegregate buses and terminals. CORE's founder, James Farmer, knew that the riders were likely to provoke violence among whites. He understood, however, that such a reaction, while endangering lives, presented a prime opportunity to further galvanize public (and potentially federal) support for enforcing federal law. True to expectations, white segregationists viciously beat the activists at almost every stop, even firebombing the buses. Local police rarely intervened and on more than one occasion gave Ku Klux Klansmen time to beat riders before stepping in to "protect" them.

The Kennedy administration remained reluctant to act, largely because the president feared losing the support of powerful southern Democrats in Congress. But the televised spectacle of white mob violence was undermining the United States' image abroad at an especially tense stage of the Cold War. Caught between conflicting imperatives, the administration tried to persuade white southern leaders and civil rights organizations to avoid violence. Attorney General Robert Kennedy, brother of JFK, requested that Alabama's governor ensure that activists proceeded without harassment through his state. Despite assurances, however, local police stood by as white segregationists beat riders senseless.

The Kennedys also urged SNCC members to focus on registering black voters instead of staging sit-ins. SNCC eventually agreed, sending hundreds of young African American and white activists out across the South in 1962. Mississippi, a Deep South state with a brutal record on race relations, became the testing ground. With the help of the NAACP and Harlem-born activist Robert Moses, students worked with locals there, opening "freedom schools" that taught reading, math, and history as well as strategies for passing the **literacy test** that had been used to deny African Americans the vote since 1890. Thousands of laborers and farmers passed the test, but state registrars failed them anyway. Organizers were beaten and even killed, and registration rates remained low.

Later that year, James Meredith, an African American Air Force veteran who attempted to register at the all-white University of Mississippi in Oxford, compelled the Kennedy administration to intervene further. After the governor refused to admit Meredith and whites rioted, the president ordered in five hundred federal marshals to enforce the law. Incensed whites battled the marshals with guns, bats, pipes, and firebombs, prompting JFK to send in the army. Privately, the president determined that Congress would probably have to enact civil rights legislation if African Americans were to be fully free. But in 1962, he remained fearful of southern lawmakers—and hopeful that the crisis would resolve itself.

TURNING THE TIDE

Neither the freedom movement nor southern whites backed down. Indeed, 1963 saw more mass protests and more violence against nonviolent African American citizens than any other year in the movement's history.

In the first half of the year, Martin Luther King, Jr., and other leaders in the Southern Christian Leadership Conference (SCLC), a black civil rights organization (see Chapter 27), had identified Birmingham as the ideal place in which to intensify the freedom struggle. Thoroughly segregated, the city had a history of violence against African Americans. Police chief Eugene "Bull" Connor and his force were allied to the local Klan and enjoyed the support of the most outspoken segregationist in the South, Alabama governor George C. Wallace. Confronting segregation in Birmingham would provoke Connor into a savage crackdown—and thrust the freedom movement back into the national spotlight.

The Birmingham protests began in April 1963 with a boycott of local department stores and a street march by hundreds of worshippers from the Sixteenth Street Baptist Church, SCLC's organizing base. On this occasion, Bull Connor's men acted cautiously, depriving the protesters of a newsworthy event. After Martin Luther King, Jr., defied a local court order to cease demonstrations, he was arrested and jailed for nine days. From his cell, King penned his "Letter from Birmingham Jail," a response to local white clergy who had acknowledged the injustices of segregation but urged African Americans to be patient. King reminded the clergy of the humiliation and inequities to which African Americans were subjected daily, and called upon them to commit fully to ending racial prejudice.

After King's release, the SCLC redoubled its determination to provoke Connor. Leaders organized a children's march in which over a thousand youngsters, aged six to eighteen, filed out of the Sixteenth Street Baptist Church while joyously singing "We Shall Overcome." Connor again ordered police to refrain from intervening. But when the children marched the next day, too, Connor's men unleashed the full force of their fury. Police attack dogs dragged some youngsters to the ground, while firemen used high-pressure hoses to disperse others. Television images of uniformed men attacking nonviolent children triggered mass outrage. President Kennedy declared that the "shameful events" had been "so much more eloquently reported by the news camera than by any number of explanatory words." The images disgraced Birmingham, and the name Bull Connor became synonymous with segregationist hate.

The children's march turned the tide. Embarrassed by the international spectacle of brutality—and worried that it might damage trade deals with the city's steel industry—Birmingham's business elite prevailed on stores and restaurants to desegregate and to hire African Americans at all ranks. Now emboldened, hundreds of thousands of previously hesitant African Americans across the nation joined the movement. Protests against inequality in housing, education, and employment erupted in 186 cities, including Birmingham, Alabama. And for the first time, President Kennedy endorsed the goals of desegregation and equal rights, ordering his advisers to draft the most comprehensive civil rights legislation in history.

Southern segregationists were the one group unmoved by Birmingham. Their most violent advocates registered their fury in the murder of Mississippi's NAACP leader, Medgar Evers, shortly after the children's march. Then in 1964, as hundreds of

Brutality Unleashed. President Kennedy was shocked when he saw this photograph on the front page of *The New York Times* (May 4, 1963). The stunning image starkly captures a 17-year-old civil rights demonstrator being attacked by a police dog in Birmingham, Alabama. Such photographs and reports of ongoing violence against demonstrators persuaded Kennedy of the urgent need for new civil rights legislation.

northern students fanned out across the South during the Freedom Summer to register African American voters, Klansmen murdered three young activists, including two white volunteers. These acts broadcast the message that some segregationists were prepared to use any means necessary—including terrorism—to stop the country's "second Reconstruction."

MARCHING FOR FREEDOM AND JOBS

The well-publicized events in Birmingham and Mississippi reverberated just as loudly in African American communities outside the South. Building on the president's newfound commitment and on the momentum of a massive Great March to Freedom in Detroit in June 1963, movement organizations, trade unions, and churches cooperated on an ambitious plan for a new display of their solidarity. On August 28, 1963, a quarter of a million people gathered at the Lincoln Memorial in Washington, D.C. The largest public demonstration in U.S. history to that time, the March on Washington for Jobs and Freedom was broadcast live, reaching a national audience of tens of millions and millions more overseas. Cameras strung from atop the Washington Monument captured the length and breadth of the protest beneath. The images of a sprawling, racially integrated crowd assembled peacefully on the Mall were unprecedented. The occasion remains an iconic and, for many people, a sacred moment in American history.

That day, Martin Luther King delivered a more powerful version of a speech he had given during the Great March in Detroit. "I have a dream," the leader proclaimed, "[that] my four children will one day live in a nation where they will not be judged by the color of their skin but the content of their character." Young SNCC chairman John Lewis had planned to demand "Justice Now!" for African Americans and to criticize President Kennedy's civil rights promise as "too little, too late." At the last minute, however, King and fellow SCLC leaders persuaded Lewis to temper his anger. African American vocalists Mahalia Jackson and Marian Anderson sang civil rights standards, and young white folk singers, including Bob Dylan and Joan Baez, performed African American freedom songs.

The March on Washington brought African Americans and whites together as never before. King's conciliatory vision of the American dream galvanized individuals of all backgrounds. Nevertheless, according to Gallup polls, over a third of the nation's population still held an unfavorable view of the civil rights leader, and even more disapproved of the freedom movement. Moreover, the disagreement between SNCC and older-generation activists over John Lewis's intended speech foreshadowed a deeper split in the freedom movement. Younger activists were losing patience with nonviolence, particularly as more and more SNCC organizers suffered beatings, harassment, and killings. They also doubted that voter registration drives and efforts to integrate schools and restaurants were enough to address the plight of most African Americans, and believed that ambitious economic, educational, welfare, and health reforms were also urgently needed. Two years of hard, life-endangering work among Mississippi's rural poor had enlarged voter rolls by a paltry four thousand new registrants. And just a month after the March on Washington, segregationists bombed Birmingham's Sixteenth Street Baptist Church, killing four young girls.

Appealing for Freedom. Although Fannie Lou Hamer, Ella Baker, Rosa Parks, and thousands of African American churchwomen had played crucial roles in building the movement for blacks' civil rights, no woman was permitted to speak at the March on Washington. Still, female performers, among them Mahalia Jackson, had a powerful effect, inspiring the freedom movement and its supporters with spiritual songs of resilience and hope.

ASSASSINATION OF JFK

The recharged civil rights movement and the uptick in segregationist violence in 1963 finally persuaded JFK to order the Department of Justice to draft comprehensive civil rights legislation. Later that year, the president also ordered his advisers to devise a systematic antipoverty program. Departing from New Deal principles, they recommended cutting corporate taxes, which in theory would allow business to invest more in production and job creation; advisers also argued that stimulating business in this way would make the U.S. economy far stronger than the Soviets'. Congress eventually enacted a massive tax cut and authorized a series of new aid programs.

However, President Kennedy did not live to see Congress pass his reforms. On November 22, 1963, as he was campaigning for reelection, the president was gunned down while traveling in a motorcade in Dallas, Texas. TV networks aired news of the assassination to a stunned national audience minutes later. JFK's violent death shook the nation more deeply than any event since World War II. Televised and photographic images of the open limousine, the bullet's impact, and Jackie Kennedy's bloodstained pink suit were seared into the nation's memory.

The prime suspect, Lee Harvey Oswald, was soon arrested. Events took an even more unimaginable turn when a local nightclub owner, Jack Ruby, shot and killed Oswald—on live television—while the latter was in police custody. As it happens, both men had ties to organized crime, a link prompting suspicion of a conspiracy. Kennedy's successor, Lyndon B. Johnson, announced that a commission headed by Chief Justice Earl Warren would investigate. The Warren Commission determined that Oswald and Ruby had acted alone, but many Americans did not accept this conclusion, and conspiracy theories proliferated. Despite the lack of any solid evidence that Oswald had been part of a larger plot, a sense of uncertainty shrouded the assassination. What was certain was that many Americans had lost, in the words of *New York Times* columnist James Reston, "not only the president but the promise."

Johnson Becomes President. After President Kennedy's death, Vice President Lyndon B. Johnson, pictured here on Air Force One beside his wife Lady Bird and Jacqueline Kennedy, was hastily sworn in as president while the plane was still on the ground in Dallas. Because no Bible was available, Johnson became the first president to take the oath of office on a missal (liturgical book).

Vain, loud, aggressive, and—by the standards of East coast elites—unforgivably coarse, the Texan marked an abrupt departure from JFK's smooth style and approach. He shunned celebrity, preferring to work behind the scenes, where his ability to browbeat and entice lawmakers into supporting his initiatives was unmatched. More so than Kennedy, the new president wholeheartedly supported the New Deal and was strongly committed to wielding federal power to effect social change. As a lawmaker from a segregated state, Johnson had previously remained aloof from civil rights controversies, but by the late 1950s, he supported equal rights for African Americans. Above all, he was extremely ambitious. As president, he was determined to leave a legacy even greater than that of FDR, with whom he frequently compared himself.

Eager to harness Kennedy's popularity for his own ends, in December 1963 Johnson called upon Congress to carry out the deceased president's legislative agenda. The first bill LBJ pushed through Congress was Kennedy's tax cut, which he knew Republicans would support. Their good will secured, Johnson then had enough votes to neutralize the southern Democrats and drive JFK's civil rights bill through Congress. A major victory for the freedom movement, the Civil Rights Act of 1964 prohibited discrimination in employment and public facilities, effectively rendering southern segregation a federal crime. The law also made it illegal to discriminate on the basis of sex.

Next prioritizing JFK's proposed antipoverty legislation, Johnson called for a systematic "War on Poverty." The centerpiece of this "war"—the Economic Opportunity Act of 1964—was the most sweeping welfare reform since the New Deal. However, where the New Deal had created jobs through large-scale public works, Johnson's War on Poverty aimed to equip the poor with the skills and education with which to improve their standard of living. Under the law, the new Office of Economic Opportunity (OEO) involved local communities in framing and carrying out education, job training, and other programs. Over the next year, the OEO spent $1 billion on new programs such as Job Corps, a vocational program for inner-city youths, and Head Start, which enrolled impoverished children in preschool. Upward Bound prepared high school students for college, and other programs helped rural families to improve their land and small businesses to expand.

TOWARD THE GREAT SOCIETY

The United States was unsettled as 1963 drew to a close. Segregationist violence raged, and young activists grew impatient. With President Kennedy's assassination, many Americans wondered if the nation was beginning a violent new chapter in its history. President Lyndon B. Johnson optimistically argued that government action could end social conflict and spread prosperity to even the most impoverished Americans. In 1964, the vast majority of voters enthusiastically supported Johnson's liberal vision, returning him to the White House and giving Democrats control of Congress. Meanwhile, feminists, environmentalists, and other social critics joined the call for reform.

LBJ'S LEGISLATIVE AGENDA

Raised amid grinding poverty in hardscrabble Texas hill country, Lyndon B. Johnson (LBJ) had taught school before moving to Washington, D.C., to join FDR's New Deal campaign to rebuild the depressed American economy. Johnson skillfully carved out a political career, serving first as secretary for a Democratic congressman in the 1930s and subsequently as a U.S. representative for Texas and Senate majority leader. LBJ's biggest break came in 1960 when Kennedy, to firm up southern support, had asked him to run for vice president.

The quite modest funding for these measures amounted to just one-tenth of that spent on the Works Progress Administration during the New Deal. Kennedy's space initiative cost twice as much. Nonetheless, Johnson and his advisers believed that his programs, in concert with the tax cut, would be far more effective than the New Deal. According to the theory of **growth liberalism,** after a few years most of the poor would be equipped with job skills that would allow them to find decent employment and ultimately to enter the working class. The tax cut would stimulate business to create jobs and raise wages, putting more money in consumers' pockets. In turn, consumers would buy more, and this newfound purchasing power would further stimulate production and job growth (provided that consumers bought U.S.-made goods). By costing less and delivering more, Johnson believed, such a program would appeal to almost everyone.

In practice, growth liberalism was more complicated, and the policy had unintended consequences. Just as advocates for the tax cut predicted, the economy grew at a remarkable rate of 7–9 percent annually for the next three years, faster than at any other time in the twentieth century. Unemployment dropped to under 5 percent, and poverty levels also fell dramatically (see Figure 28.1). The Economic Opportunity Act helped millions of Americans out of poverty by enabling youths to stay in school and indigent children to learn to read and write. In many urban communities, however, the "opportunity" promised by the OEO was too little, too late. It fostered protest, both among the minorities it was intended to help and among working-class whites who resented what they saw as unfair "handouts" to minority communities.

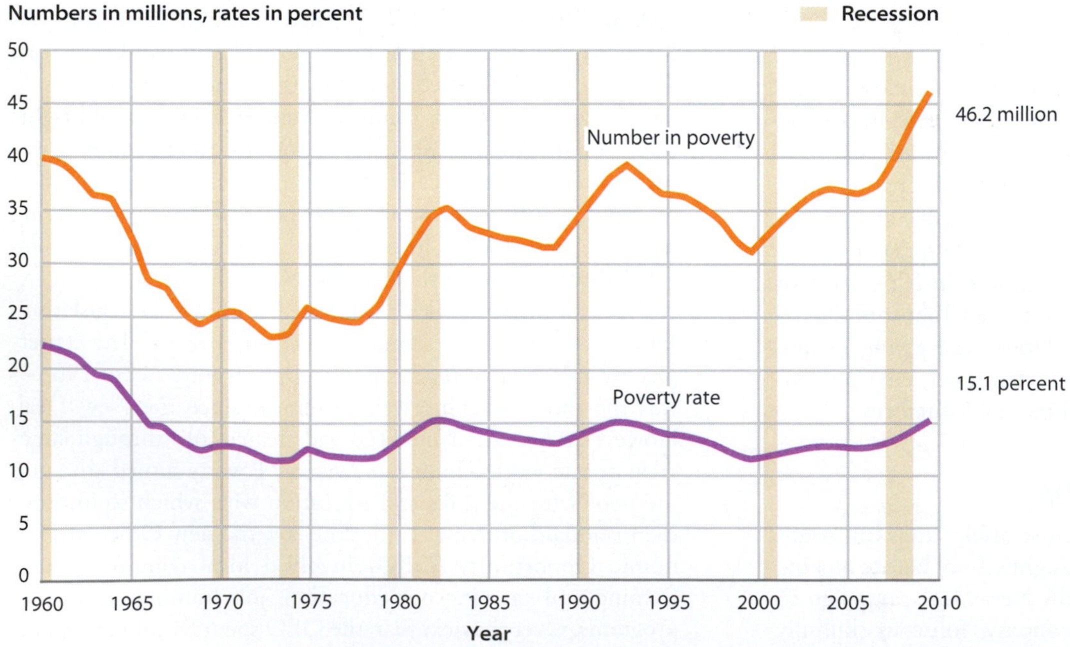

THE ELECTION OF 1964

With major legislative victories in hand, Johnson confidently campaigned for reelection. The country was on the road to building a Great Society, he announced, and government would end poverty and racial injustice, and enable all children to develop their talents. Leisure time would be used for personal reflection and improvement, and "the city of man [would serve] not only the needs of the body and the demands of commerce but the desire for beauty and hunger for community." Students roared their approval when Johnson asked whether they would join "the battle to build the Great Society."

Adoring crowds greeted LBJ on the campaign trail, and he enjoyed consistently high support in opinion polls. Yet at the Democratic National Convention that summer, he faced attacks from both the conservative and the younger, more radical wings of his party. The racially integrated Mississippi Freedom Democratic Party (MFDP) demanded to be seated as the legitimate representatives of Mississippi, while the official (all-white) southern delegations threatened a walkout if the convention obliged. MFDP delegate Fannie Lou Hamer testified on national television about the beatings she had received when trying to register to vote in Mississippi. When Johnson attempted to broker a deal, promising the MFDP just two unofficial seats, SNCC and other young African Americans felt betrayed. "We didn't come all this way for no two seats," Hamer reprimanded Johnson. The 1964 convention proved a turning point in the party's relationship with the freedom movement, as young African American activists began to question Johnson's as well as white liberals' commitment to racial justice.

At the Republican National Convention, delegates chose Barry Goldwater to run against Johnson. The federal government, argued the conservative Goldwater, should not support welfare or education. But government should, he stressed, fund an enormous military-industrial complex to fight communism and even use nuclear arms, if necessary, to defeat communism in Vietnam. Above all, the federal government should not interfere with state affairs, including the "right" of southern states to segregate.

Goldwater, although popular among conservatives, seemed radically out-of-step with the majority of voters. Although southern Democrats ran their own candidate for president (segregationist Alabama governor George C. Wallace), Johnson soared to

FIGURE 28.1 Poverty Rate and Number of People in Poverty, 1960–2010. Although protests exploded in the cities after 1964, poverty rates declined steadily from 19 percent to a near-record low of 12 percent in 1979. Poverty has generally hovered in the 10- to 15-percent range ever since, with the exceptions of 1983 (following a recession), 1993 (after large welfare cuts), and 2010 (during the Great Recession).

victory on election day, winning 90 percent of the electoral college and an all-time record of 61 percent of the popular vote. The Democrats gained over two-thirds of the seats in both houses of Congress, winning a free hand in the legislative process. Americans had given the president a mandate for change. At the same time, however, Goldwater picked up five Deep South states, the first Republican since Reconstruction to do so, and the segregationist Wallace won primaries in two midwestern states. Beneath the tide of popular liberalism, an undertow of conservative dissent and opposition to civil rights gathered strength.

HIGH TIDE OF LIBERALISM

Johnson's landslide victory put the Great Society within reach. The administration submitted almost ninety bills in 1965, ranging from revisions to health and welfare policies to environmental and immigration reform (see Table 28.1). In what the news media called a "political miracle," Congress enacted almost every single bill. Eradicating poverty remained a priority, as lawmakers doubled the OEO's funding to $2 billion annually. The president pushed through the Voting Rights Act of 1965, under which the federal government installed new registrars in any state that refused to register African Americans. Consequently, black voting rates shot up, with Mississippi witnessing a ninefold increase in two years, from just 7 percent in 1964 to 60 percent in 1966.

The Immigration and Nationality Act of 1965 also struck a blow against discrimination by abolishing the national origins quota that had barred Asians, Africans, and Latin Americans from immigrating to the United States. Although the number of immigrants from any one nation was still capped, the law gave priority to individuals with desirable work skills and those with family in the United States.

The most enduring—and popular—reforms were in health care. Although the majority of Americans had supported a government-funded health care system since the 1930s, the powerful American Medical Association had blocked such initiatives in Congress. Johnson decided against taking on the medical establishment and instead pushed through Congress government-funded health care for society's two most vulnerable groups. After 1965, Medicare paid for the medical needs of senior citizens, and under Medicaid the federal government and the states covered the medical expenses of poor Americans of all ages.

TABLE 28.1 CONGRESS ENACTS THE GREAT SOCIETY

1964	Civil Rights Act prohibits racial and gender discrimination in workplaces and public services.
1965	Congress funds schools in impoverished districts. College funding is expanded. Medicare and Medicaid are established. Voting Rights Act protects minority voters. Immigration and Nationality Act abolishes national quotas. Federal funding for the arts and the humanities is reestablished.
1966	Model Cities Act targets slums for improvement and involves urban communities in planning and development.
1967	Food stamps program is expanded for those unable to work.
1968	Congress prohibits discrimination in housing.

WOMEN CHALLENGE CONVENTION

Like most people of color, white middle-class women in 1960s America were barred from many of the economic and cultural opportunities available to most white men. Although, unlike most minorities, they enjoyed the material benefits of suburban life, few women held political office, and those who pursued careers were mostly confined to low-paid sales or clerical work. Universities limited female admissions. The rigid ideology of suburban housewifery—with its emphasis on homemaking, the culture of convenience, and caregiving—also severely limited women's ability to flourish. Confused and unhappy, a significant minority began taking sedatives and tranquilizers, almost quadrupling the nation's consumption between 1950 and 1965, from 30 million to 123 million prescriptions per year.

Other American women wrestled with the confining aspects of suburban life more constructively. Some became active in church groups or local school boards. Others, inspired by the publication of Julia Child's *Mastering the Art of French Cooking* in 1961 (and by Child's subsequent television show), rejected the deskilling effects of suburban life and taught themselves the pleasures and artistry of fine cooking. When Betty Friedan, a former labor organizer turned suburban homemaker, wrote of the frustration and despair many suburban women felt, hundreds of thousands of housewives recognized themselves instantly. Much as Friedan suggested, many resolved to radically break the suburban mold by going (or returning) to college and embarking on meaningful careers (see Interpreting the Sources: Betty Friedan, *The Feminine Mystique*).

Friedan sparked a revival of feminism among middle-class women and helped convince Congress to protect women's basic rights. The Equal Pay Act of 1963 provided that women be paid the same amount of money for the same job, and the Civil Rights Act of 1964 explicitly protected the rights of women. Under President Johnson, the Equal Employment Opportunity Commission forced hundreds of employers to comply with the laws, and women's wages climbed gradually. Friedan and other liberal feminists went on to cofound a new feminist group, the National Organization for Women (NOW), in 1966. Broadly modeled on the freedom movement, NOW not only demanded women's equal access to jobs, education, housing loans, and other resources, but also launched media campaigns against sexist stereotyping in mass culture.

ENVIRONMENTAL AWAKENING

Environmental reform was also on Johnson's agenda. The dense patchwork of suburbs, shopping malls, and highways that now covered millions of acres of former farmland and

INTERPRETING THE SOURCES

Betty Friedan, The Feminine Mystique

A wide-ranging critique of American gender relations, Betty Friedan's *The Feminine Mystique* (1953) condemned advertisers, the mass media, the legal and medical establishments, and social scientists for leading women to believe that happiness came only through motherhood and homemaking. Women, Friedan wrote, were trapped in a "mystique of feminine fulfillment," and when they inevitably became frustrated and unhappy, they blamed themselves rather than sexist ideology. Women were far from the monodimensional housewives portrayed a few years earlier by Vice President Richard Nixon in the "Kitchen Debates." In fact, women possessed an innate desire and capacity to become multidimensional human beings, argued Friedan. In this excerpt, she explains the origins of the "feminine mystique" and its effect on women's aspirations.

The problem lay buried, unspoken, for many years in the minds of American women. It was a strange stirring, a sense of dissatisfaction, a yearning that women suffered in the middle of the twentieth century in the United States. Each suburban wife struggled with it alone. As she made the beds, shopped for groceries, matched slipcover material, ate peanut butter sandwiches with her children, chauffeured Cub Scouts and Brownies, lay beside her husband at night—she was afraid to ask even of herself the silent question—"Is this all?"

For over fifteen years there was no word of this yearning in the millions of words written about women, for women, in all the columns, books and articles by experts telling women their role was to seek fulfillment as wives and mothers. Over and over women heard in voices of tradition and of Freudian sophistication that they could desire no greater destiny than to glory in their own femininity. Experts told them how to catch a man and keep him, how to breastfeed children and handle their toilet training, how to cope with sibling rivalry and adolescent rebellion; how to buy a dishwasher, bake bread, cook gourmet snails, and build a swimming pool with their own hands; how to dress, look, and act more feminine and make marriage more exciting; how to keep their husbands from dying young and their sons from growing into delinquents. . . .

In the fifteen years after World War II, this mystique of feminine fulfillment became the cherished and self-perpetuating core of contemporary American culture. Millions of women lived their lives in the image of those pretty pictures of the American suburban housewife, kissing their husbands goodbye in front of the picture window, depositing their stationwagonsful of children at school, and smiling as they ran the new electric waxer over the spotless kitchen floor. They baked their own bread, sewed their own and their children's clothes, kept their new washing machines and dryers running all day. They changed the sheets on the beds twice a week instead of once, took the rug-hooking class in adult education, and pitied their poor frustrated mothers, who had dreamed of having a career. Their only dream was to be perfect wives and mothers; their highest ambition to have five children and a beautiful house, their only fight to get and keep their husbands. They had no thought for the unfeminine problems of the world outside the home; they wanted the men to make the major decisions. They gloried in their role as women, and wrote proudly on the census blank: "Occupation: housewife."

Explore the Source

1. According to Friedan, what were so many women yearning for in the fifteen years following World War II?
2. What is the "mystique of feminine fulfillment," and what makes it "self-perpetuating"?
3. How, in Friedan's view, did experts and mass culture shape women's experiences and expectations?

desert had drastically altered the natural environment. Everyday acts of consumption had become significant sources of pollution. A boom in refrigeration and air conditioning released large quantities of ozone-damaging chlorofluorocarbons into the air, and highway commuting made smog a fact of life. Millions of gallons of harmful chemical agents such as the insecticide DDT had been sprayed in an effort to eradicate malaria, a disease carried by mosquitoes. By 1963, large amounts of radiation had also been released into the atmosphere by over 400 atomic bomb tests, 259 of which occurred over U.S. territory.

The nation's soil and groundwater had also deteriorated. Fifty percent of suburbs were not connected to sewer lines. Suburbanites typically flushed kitchen, laundry, and bathroom wastewater into large septic tanks buried in their backyards, which in turn dispersed the runoff into the ground. This technology worked well for farmers, whose extensive pastures could soak up and neutralize the sludge. But small suburban yards could not absorb it, and it seeped into drinking wells and streams, where it occasionally caused infectious outbreaks.

Feeding the surging population and tailoring food to suburban tastes were also transforming farming and rural ecosystems. In the Midwest, enormous monocultural "cities" of wheat, corn, and potatoes owned by giant agribusinesses swallowed up more diverse family farms. Major producers adapted the "factory farm," which egg growers had pioneered in the 1920s, to livestock. Several large-scale hog, dairy, and beef growers permanently transferred their livestock from grassy open fields and plains to covered or uncovered pens where grain and vitamins would nourish them for the duration of their lives. These methods revolutionized agricultural production by overcoming natural constraints such as seasons, nightfall, and the need for grassy pasture. Production tripled, and food became cheaper than at any other point in American history.

The new methods also bred new problems, however. Family farmers could not compete with agribusiness, with the result that fourteen million farmers (almost two-thirds of the national total) left the land between 1945 and 1970. On the monocultural factory farms that replaced them, crops and animals were vulnerable to infection. The use of antibiotics and chemical fertilizers, pesticides, and insecticides accelerated, and a vicious cycle began in which pests and bacteria grew immune to chemical agents.

Greening the Highways. Lady Bird Johnson, as First Lady, championed many environmental causes, among them a campaign to beautify the nation's highways. Here, she and a young citizen plant a tree on Arbor Day, 1968.

In 1961, when it became clear that thalidomide, a new morning sickness medication, caused grotesque birth deformities, many Americans began questioning the nation's embrace of "wonder drugs" and other chemically based "miracles of science." Around the same time, Rachel Carson, a biologist and accomplished nature writer, was noticing subtle changes in the environment, such as a striking decrease since the 1940s of birds and birdsong in the springtime. In *Silent Spring* (1962), Carson laid out a mass of evidence that many pesticides, including DDT, were "biocides" that destroyed not just insects but birds, fish, and entire ecosystems. Carson's study won a mass audience and launched a new environmental movement. Advocates emphasized the need to sustain the health, beauty, and permanence of the environment and all its inhabitants and publicized the impact of pollution, toxins, and certain kinds of mining and development on ecosystems and the quality of life.

Lawmakers were receptive to the environmentalists' concerns. In 1964, Johnson signed the Wilderness Act, putting nine million acres of federal land off-limits for commercial development. The law reflected the new ethos in defining wilderness as a place where "man and his own works [do not] dominate the landscape" but "where the earth and community of life are untrammeled by man, where man himself is a visitor who does not remain." Then in 1965, the president pledged to preserve a "green legacy" for future Americans. The Clean Water Act required states to issue quality standards for interstate waters, and the new Clean Air Act directed the government to set and enforce auto emission standards. DDT was finally outlawed for agricultural use in 1972. Environmentalism had made great strides. The new laws and consumer concern, however, also prompted chemical companies and agribusinesses to invest millions of dollars to block future regulation.

A NATION AT WAR

As liberalism crested in American society, the U.S.-backed government in South Vietnam teetered once more. Johnson had inherited the "Vietnam problem" from Kennedy, who had inherited it from Eisenhower. Like both former presidents, LBJ regarded Vietnam as the epicenter of the nation's confrontation with communism. He agonized over sending young Americans to fight half a world away. In his mind, though, to disengage would be worse—and potentially damaging to his presidency. As he sent hundreds of thousands of young G.I.s to Vietnam, unrest grew at home. Urban African American youths vented their rage and frustration over police harassment, lack of economic opportunity, and the slow pace of reform. On campuses, meanwhile, white middle-class students called for radical change and an end to the war. By 1968, federal troops and National Guardsmen were not only fighting a war in Vietnam but containing one at home.

AMERICANIZING THE VIETNAM WAR

In the summer of 1964, LBJ determined to repel both South Vietnam's NLF (Viet Cong) rebels and North Vietnam's communist government. He began looking for ways to persuade Congress to authorize and fund a wider war. The opportunity presented itself in August 1964, when reports filtered back to Washington, D.C., that North Vietnamese torpedo boats had fired on a U.S. destroyer stationed in the Gulf of Tonkin off the North's eastern shore (see Map 28.2). Although it later came to light that the "attack" had consisted of a single bullet to the ship's hull, Johnson immediately pressed Congress to allow him to "take all necessary measures to repel any armed attack against the forces of the United States and to prevent further aggression." All but two senators consented. The Gulf of Tonkin Resolution gave the president a blank check and free rein in Vietnam.

Concerned that escalation might be divisive in an election year, Johnson waited until 1965 before authorizing the first of hundreds of air raids on North Vietnam and the mass deployment of U.S. troops in the South. By 1968, over a half-million American troops had shipped out under Operation Rolling Thunder, and over three million tons of explosives had been dropped on Vietnam. Initially, the two strategic objectives were to avoid drawing neighboring China into the conflict and to force North Vietnam to abandon the goal of reuniting the nation under communist control. Less than half the size of Texas and populated largely by peasants, Vietnam seemed to Johnson and his military advisers relatively easy to subdue, and they hoped that it would provide a model example of what the United States was capable of in the developing world. In fact, the arrival of U.S. troops drove many neutral Vietnamese into the arms of Viet Minh leader Ho Chi Minh.

A TEENAGE ARMY

In previous wars, American soldiers had typically ranged in age from eighteen to forty and had come from all classes and backgrounds. In contrast, the Vietnam War was fought mostly by blue-collar and impoverished youths. More than two-thirds of the soldiers who served had volunteered, eager to pursue the economic opportunities promised by U.S. military life. The average age of U.S. soldiers in Vietnam was nineteen, compared with twenty-six during World War II, and a large minority were seventeen or younger. Over 30 percent were African American. All told, 3.5 million servicemen—the majority of them teenagers—and a nursing force of 11,000 women served in Vietnam between 1965 and 1972.

Soldiering in southern Vietnam, the site of most of the ground war, was especially challenging, and little in the young G.I.s' experience prepared them for it. They were fighting a people they did not understand, in alien terrain and for reasons that made little sense to them (see Singular Lives: Tim O'Brien, G.I.). The jungle environment was oppressively humid, hot, and hazardous. The enemy knew the home terrain far better and continually caught the Americans in booby traps and lethal ambushes. With minimal training in warfare, G.I.s often moved loudly through the jungle, even talking and singing. Morale was low through most of the war. Because tours of duty lasted just a year, troops who did develop jungle skills were soon replaced with fresh, inexperienced recruits. As spirits sagged, the incidence of "fragging"—killing one's commanding officer, typically by throwing a fragmentation grenade—climbed.

Many soldiers could not or would not distinguish fighters from civilians. Although some G.I.s befriended locals, widespread anti-Asian racism led to the assumption that all Vietnamese were actively hostile and aiding the guerrillas. U.S. forces consequently killed thousands of Vietnamese civilians. In reprisal, the Viet Cong and North Vietnamese systematically mistreated and even tortured U.S. prisoners of war. Brutality reigned on both sides. In one of the worst instances, 105 G.I.s from Charlie Company, which had recently lost several men in Viet Cong raids, executed over 400 women, children, and elderly people in a single village in 1968. The My Lai Massacre remained a secret for over a year, until a soldier wrote the president and Congress about the crime. A commanding officer, Lieutenant William Calley, was subsequently found guilty of murder and served four years under house arrest.

Despite the United States' vastly superior military and economic power, the war bogged down. As frustrations mounted, the Pentagon doubled down on its strategy of combining a mass of ground troops with the latest in aerial technology. Beginning in late 1965, the United States dropped millions of bombs filled with napalm, an acidic gel that ignited in flames, instantly clearing the jungle and searing the skin of anyone caught in its path. By 1968, nearly one in three Vietnamese had lost their homes to such tactics, and fifty-two thousand civilians were dead. In addition, millions of gallons of toxic herbicides and defoliants, including Agent Orange, were sprayed over farmland and paddies. Although principally intended to deprive enemy forces of their food supply, the attacks wiped out civilian farms and resulted in the birth of a half-million deformed babies. The destruction of farmland forcibly urbanized a society that had been overwhelmingly rural just a year earlier.

URBAN REBELLIONS

Like the young G.I.s in Vietnam, many urban African Americans saw little to celebrate in the long, hot summer of 1965. The freedom movement had integrated much of the South and forced civil and voting rights legislation through Congress. These developments, however, had little impact on the miseries of the urban poor in the North and West. Nor did Johnson's War on Poverty seem to be making a difference. Schools were grossly inadequate, children often went hungry, crime rates were high, and unemployment frequently ran into the third generation. Routinely, city police forces (overwhelmingly white) dealt brutally with the community, particularly youth. After 1964, many young men confronted a grim choice: they could stay or they could escape—but only by enlisting and risking life and limb in Vietnam.

Impoverished urbanites around the nation made it clear that their aspirations were different from the ones envisioned for them by the southern freedom movement, Johnson's War on Poverty, and most white liberals. The pride that many white Americans took in the Civil Rights Act and their view that the nation had now reversed its long history of racism angered minorities. Local communities began using the OEO programs to mobilize against city corruption and to take control of school boards, police departments, and housing authorities. The urban poor were an important political force in the 1964 elections, participating as never before in local democracy. Disgruntled mayors, developers, and police chiefs accused President Johnson of fomenting "class warfare." Putting politics ahead of principle and facing escalating costs in Vietnam, the president subsequently let funding for many antipoverty programs lapse.

SINGULAR LIVES

Tim O'Brien, G.I.

"The Bouncing Betty is feared most," G.I. Tim O'Brien wrote of wading through rice paddies riddled with enemy mines. "It leaps out of its nest in the earth and when it hits its apex, it explodes, reliable and deadly. . . . More destructive . . . are the booby-trapped mortar and artillery rounds. They hang from trees. They nestle in shrubbery. They lie under the sand. . . . They haunted us."

Like hundreds of thousands of young American men in 1969, the twenty-two-year-old O'Brien found himself trapped in a war that seemed unpredictable, futile, and meaningless. Drafted the summer he graduated from college, he briefly considered dodging the draft and escaping to Canada—particularly once the Draft Board classified him as infantry, the most perilous category of service. O'Brien had attended peace rallies while a political science major at Macalester College. But the fear of shaming himself and his family, and of living in exile (possibly for the rest of his life), trumped his impulse to flee. While most of his college friends got deferments or doctor's notes, O'Brien gritted his teeth and entered basic training in the fall of 1968.

The son of an insurance salesman and an elementary school teacher, O'Brien had grown up in Worthington, Minnesota, population 9,921. Both of his parents had served in World War II. Like most boys his age, he and his pals had played war games, dressing up in old army surplus gear and "fighting" the Japanese (as his father had served at Okinawa and Iwo Jima) or reenacting famous battles with the Plains Indians. Worthington was much less "fun" for teens, however, especially in the early 1960s, when big-city culture, with its convention-busting fashions, music, and lifestyles, was making small-town America seem sleepy and old-fashioned by comparison. Ironically, O'Brien escaped "dullsville" with the help of one of its long-standing institutions—the local library. Plato, Aristotle, and other great thinkers opened his mind and kindled his imagination. When he later considered fleeing the draft, he recalled that Socrates, when given the opportunity to escape Athens and the death penalty, chose to stay because Athens was where he had made his life.

After completing basic training at Fort Lewis, Washington, in 1969, O'Brien shipped out to join the "American Division" (5th Battalion, 46th Infantry) in Quang Ngai province. Although none of the new recruits knew it, a year earlier members of the division had carried out an attack that would later become infamous as the My Lai Massacre. O'Brien and his platoon noticed only that locals seemed quietly hostile and not a little afraid of their "liberators." Frightened and alienated, O'Brien started jotting down his thoughts and experiences for local Minnesota newspapers. Soon he was filing stories for the *Washington Post* and *Playboy* magazine. In excruciating detail he related the terrors of mine-strewn landscapes, bullets flying out of nowhere, and long hours in foxholes and paddy fields. Even Plato and Aristotle seemed to lose meaning in this "wrong war," as O'Brien called it, and the only glimmer of hope was the heroic conduct of one of his infantry captains. After O'Brien completed his year-long tour, he entered a Ph.D. program in political science at Harvard, eventually becoming a full-time writer. O'Brien's *If I Die in a Combat Zone: Box Me Up and Ship Me Home* (1973) was the first and best-received memoir by an infantryman, and his later *The Things They Carried* (1990) blended fiction and autobiography to startling and memorable effect.

Think About It

1. Why might so many of the young men who opposed the war have complied with the draft, as O'Brien did?
2. Why might the war have produced feelings of alienation and meaningless?

But African American leaders were determined to compel the government to honor the pledge to eradicate poverty. Starting in 1964, activists demanded not just their civil rights (freedom from discrimination), but also their social rights. As citizens of the richest nation on earth, they insisted, African Americans were entitled to decent jobs, good schools, a police force that served and protected them, and—where families were unable to make ends meet—financial assistance from the government. In a sign that the freedom movement was at last taking note of their plight, Martin Luther King, Jr., called for a Bill of Rights for the Disadvantaged. Like the G.I. Bill of 1944, his draft legislation would make college education, low-interest housing loans, job training, and other vital programs available to those who had been deprived of opportunity. As well as abolishing poverty, argued King, the government should prioritize African Americans as a disadvantaged group that had been oppressed, exploited, and abandoned for over three centuries. The connection King drew between targeted federal programs and the history of slavery and Jim Crow was one of the earliest calls for **affirmative action.**

Emotions boiled over in the summer of 1965 when a white California Highway Patrolman took a young African American who had allegedly resisted arrest into custody in the Watts district of Los Angeles. For five days, young men looted stores and burned the neighborhood, throwing bottles and stones at police and overturning cars. "If I've got to die, I ain't dying in Vietnam," one youth declared, "I'm dying right here." It took a force of sixteen thousand police and National Guardsmen to restore order, at the cost of thirty-four lives, four thousand arrests, and the destruction of $45 million worth of property. Dozens of other major rebellions, typically triggered by an arrest or other police action, broke out in northern and western cities over the next three years (see States of Emergency: The Detroit Rebellion, 1967).

STATES OF EMERGENCY

The Detroit Rebellion, 1967

On a hot summer's night in Detroit, July 1967, friends and family gathered at a bar to welcome two young African American soldiers home after a year's tour of duty in Vietnam. Although the two men's identities are unknown, the events that unfolded in the ensuing hours catapulted Detroit and its impoverished African American community into the headlines and, ultimately, the history books. The celebration was taking place in a "blind pig"—an unlicensed bar of the kind that Americans had patronized during Prohibition and which were still common in the inner city. Predominantly white police forces routinely raided such establishments, arresting and, in Detroit's case, even beating patrons. On this occasion, police arrested all eighty-two revelers, including the young servicemen, brutalizing several in the process.

Usually, such raids went smoothly for the police. On this night, however, a crowd gathered outside the bar and demanded the patrons' immediate release. Soon, someone in the crowd threw a bottle, smashing a police car window. Somebody else heaved a trash basket through a store window, and within minutes more bottles, trash cans, and bricks went flying. The protest quickly spread into other African American neighborhoods. Young men looted stores and set them on fire throughout the night. By morning, Detroit was in the grip of the deadliest riot since the New York City Draft Riots of 1863. By the time the U.S. Army and the Michigan National Guard restored order three days later, forty-three people had been killed (almost all were African American residents, and most had been shot by police and the National Guard), and three square miles of the city were destroyed. Detroit looked less like the once-proud capital of the U.S. auto industry than the smoldering ruins of a bombed-out European city in World War II.

Although the catalyst for the uprising was police brutality, the root causes ran far deeper. African American frustration and anger had been building for years. The black community, which made up 30 percent of Detroit's population, was especially hard hit by most auto manufacturers' departure from the city after 1945. The unemployment rate hovered at double that of whites, and racially restrictive housing practices still enforced an informal segregation. African Americans put up with poorer schools, health services, and recreational facilities. Police officers, business owners, and landlords were almost all white and commonly dealt with African Americans disrespectfully. Inner-city residents routinely paid up to 20 percent more for groceries and other goods, partly because the cheap new supermarkets were located in far-off white suburbs and partly because of overt discrimination. White residents had recently voted down a ballot measure raising taxes for the improvement of city schools.

Urban Uprising. The Detroit rebellion was just one of 167 urban uprisings in the summer of 1967, but it was by far the worst. Ironically, the biggest victim, after those who lost their lives, was the city itself. The rebellion sped the exodus of businesses and middle-class residents, more than tripling the annual rate of white flight in the following year and further depriving the city of much-needed employment and tax revenue.

Detroit's African American youths were particularly disillusioned with their increasingly bleak prospects. Like other minority youths in the 1960s, many were drawn to a more militant approach and to demanding faster, more systematic change. Even though Detroit had received more federal aid from President Johnson's War on Poverty than any other city besides New York, it was too little, too late. Subsequently, when police closed down the veterans' homecoming celebration on that hot July night in 1967, Detroit burned.

Think About It

1. Given the multitude of problems plaguing American inner cities in the 1960s, why was police brutality typically the trigger for urban rebellions?
2. Why might Detroit youths have protested by rioting rather than engaging in other, more peaceful forms of collective action?
3. Why might youths have experienced their actions as "empowering?" Was destroying property actually empowering? Explain.

BLACK POWER

Out of the smoke and ashes, new social movements arose and existing ones grew more militant. The urban uprisings had animated many young African American civil rights activists, including members of SNCC. Unlike the rioters, most had middle-class backgrounds and were college educated. But many saw in what they called "ghetto rebellions" a new and energetic force that could turn the freedom movement, with its limited civil rights agenda, into a social revolution. In 1966, SNCC's Stokely Carmichael urged African Americans to embrace what he called Black Power— "black people coming together to form a political force and either electing representatives or forcing their representatives to speak their needs." Black Power quickly became the clarion call of a young generation of African American college students. SNCC and CORE leaders expelled white members, arguing that whites should concentrate on fighting racism in their own communities.

Malcolm X Speaks. The charismatic activist gained an international audience when he argued the affirmative in a debate held at Oxford University, England, on the topic of "Extremism in the defense of liberty is no vice; moderation in the pursuit of justice is no virtue."

The concept of African American solidarity was also echoed in the teachings of the Nation of Islam, a Muslim organization founded in Detroit in the 1930s that challenged African Americans to take pride in their heritage and their skin color. The Black Muslims, as members were known, called upon African Americans to open their eyes to the history of violent racism. "Blacks" were a superior race from the Black Muslim perspective, and whites were devils whose ultimate fate was annihilation. The Nation of Islam's most brilliant rhetorician, Harlem minister Malcolm X, pressed African Americans to take control of their own lives. While respecting the law and remaining courteous and peaceful, the minister nonetheless instructed his followers to send anyone who "puts a hand on you . . . to the cemetery."

By the early 1960s, Malcolm X had grown openly critical of the freedom movement and its integrationist goals. Nonviolence, in Malcolm X's view, was both poor strategy and morally suspect in the context of African Americans' historical experience of white racism. Then in 1964, Malcolm X broke from the Nation of Islam to build his own movement and declared his willingness to work with the civil rights movement. Following a life-changing pilgrimage to Mecca, he rejected the narrow ideology of racial separatism and embraced a broader world view in which the revolutionary struggle for justice, rather than the race of the revolutionary, was what mattered. "We've got to be more flexible," he pronounced in late 1964, "I don't care what a person looks like or where they come from. My mind is wide open to anybody who will help get the ape [oppressors] off our backs."

Widely admired by activists and drawing considerable media attention, Malcolm X became a hated man among the leadership of the Nation of Islam. An assassin's bullet ended his life in February 1965, but his call to self-defense echoed in the urban rebellions of the next three summers and in the growing Black Power movement.

Black power was also championed by the Black Panther Party for Self-Defense, founded in Oakland, California, in 1965, a few months after the Watts rebellion. The "Panthers" established a wide range of programs for the hard-up community, including children's breakfasts, point duty at dangerous intersections, and health clinics. Condemning the government's failure to provide basic services for African Americans, the party even set up its own shadow cabinet and assumed the responsibilities of an independent state. "Minister of Defense" Huey Newton organized an armed security force that vowed to protect and serve the community and to "police the police." The Panthers paired these programs with confrontational rhetoric such as "Off the pigs!" (kill the police) and "Power to the people!" Packing weapons and sporting stylish leather jackets, berets, and natural hairstyles, the youthful Panthers powerfully countered the image of African Americans as helpless victims. The mass media thrilled to the spectacle, and within a year, Detroit, New York, and dozens of other cities had Panther branches.

Although legal, the Panthers' activism, guns, and rhetoric threatened authorities and many white people. Calling the Panthers "the greatest threat to the internal security of the country," FBI director J. Edgar Hoover worked with federal agents and local police to infiltrate the radicals' ranks and provoke them into illegal acts. Some Panthers lost their lives in the confrontations; for example, Chicago's up-and-coming Panther leader, Fred Hampton, was shot and killed in a joint FBI-police operation while sleeping in his bed in 1969. Power struggles erupted within the party, and by 1972, much of the leadership was dead, exiled, imprisoned, or in hiding.

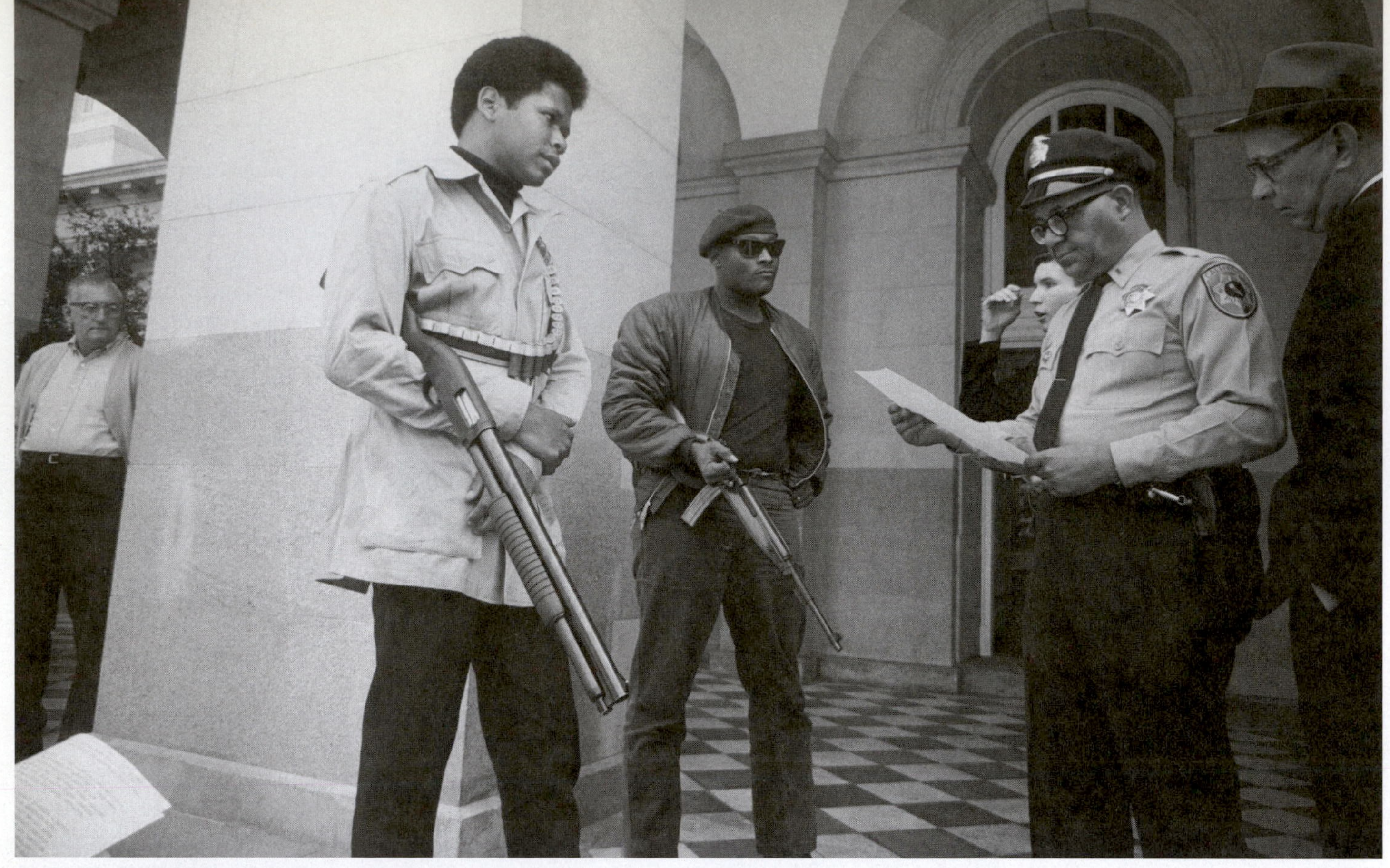

Power to the People! The Black Panthers gained a mass following when they protested a ban on unconcealed weapons by parading through the state capitol in Sacramento, California, carrying loaded guns.

YOUTH RENEW THE LEFT

The Vietnam War and urban rebellions had also radicalized white middle-class college students, and by the mid-1960s, many identified with the New Left. This social movement's roots reached back to 1956, when thousands of disillusioned leftists in Europe and the United States quit the communist party in protest of the Soviets' ruthless suppression of Hungary's democracy movement. In Britain and France, ex-communists condemned Soviet-style government and rejected the idea that organizing the working class into labor unions was the only way to achieve social justice. Instead, they argued, activists and intellectuals should pursue change on many fronts, including within popular culture, political institutions, and interpersonal relations.

American college students were introduced to these ideas by sociologist C. Wright Mills, one of the few Americans to have written critically about U.S. society in the 1950s (see Chapter 27). In his 1960 "Open Letter to the New Left," Mills argued that "students, . . . young professionals, . . . writers [and] the young intelligentsia" had supplanted industrial workers as history makers. Youth were changing the world, he argued, chiefly by challenging cultural and political institutions head-on. Against the backdrop of the youthful SNCC sit-ins of 1960–1962 and middle-class students' growing conviction that something was broken in their suburbanized society, Mills's claims had tremendous appeal.

On northern and western campuses, small groups met to discuss the state of U.S. democracy. Among them, Students for a Democratic Society (SDS), founded in 1960 as an offshoot of an older socialist organization, rapidly emerged as the leading New Left group. Outlining members' objectives in 1962 in the Port Huron Statement, SDS leader Tom Hayden wrote that many students had grown up in relative comfort but had been shaken from their apathy, as young adults, by the virulent racism that thrived in their own country and by the threat of nuclear annihilation.

The cause of these troubles, according to Hayden, was that "the American political system is not the democratic model of which its glorifiers speak." Far from involving the citizenry in governing, a complex of corporate, military, and political power separated the people "from power, from relevant knowledge, from pinnacles of decision making." SDS's solution was "participatory democracy": much like the freedom movement (which many SDS members also joined), students needed to mobilize for civil rights, nuclear disarmament, and urban relief. They should democratize all powerful institutions—from corporations to trade unions, schools, and the military—by making them accountable to ordinary people. Further, on campuses everywhere, students "must make debate and controversy . . . the common style for educational life."

SDS and its ideal of participatory democracy grew steadily more popular. The organization received a boost in the fall of 1964 when University of California at Berkeley students challenged a campus rule prohibiting the advocacy of political causes on campus. Conservative, liberal, and radical students all agreed that the rule violated free speech rights, and rallied peacefully to demand that the university rescind its policy. When the administration refused, the protests continued for weeks, climaxing in a mass nonviolent protest. The university's Board of Regents finally honored the students' free speech rights in 1965, and numerous other campuses followed suit. Thousands of U.S. students went on to demand their free speech rights and an overhaul of higher education, from curricula to the structures of decision making.

Reclaiming Free Speech. The arrest of a student for distributing civil rights literature at the University of California at Berkeley launched the free speech movement on campuses around the nation. Climbing atop a police cruiser, free speech advocate Mario Savio declared, "There comes a time when the operation of the machine becomes so odious, makes you so sick at heart, that you can't take part. . . . And you've got to put your bodies upon the gears and upon the wheels, upon the levers, upon all the apparatus, and you've got to make it stop."

THE ANTIWAR MOVEMENT

Student movements also demanded an end to the Vietnam War. In 1965, SDS organized the first of many large-scale antiwar demonstrations, with twenty-five thousand students marching on Washington, D.C. Students went on strike nationwide, calling on universities to cut ties with corporations and government agencies associated with the war. Protests escalated when the Johnson administration made graduate students eligible for the draft in 1967. Students and sympathetic faculty held "teach-ins" about U.S. foreign policy, the effects of Agent Orange and napalm, and the need for participatory democracy at home.

Antiwar sentiment spread beyond campuses to other arenas. In early 1967, two thousand women from the group Women Strike for Peace demonstrated outside the Pentagon, waving signs that read "Not Our Sons, Not Your Sons, Not Their Sons." As troop fatalities rose and the nightly TV news beamed horrifying images of the war into American living rooms, much of the mainstream media came to oppose the war. A number of professional organizations and thousands of clergy, from all denominations, called for an end to hostilities. Some opponents objected to the war on moral grounds, but the majority argued from the practical perspective that it was unwinnable and socially divisive.

The young men whom the war affected most acutely responded in a variety of ways. All men over the age of 18 were eligible to be drafted, but in practice many middle-class and affluent men legally deferred service by enrolling in college or graduate school or using family connections to serve out the war at home in the National Guard. To illegally "dodge" the draft, some 60,000 fled to Canada or Mexico, and over 170,000 declared that they were conscientious objectors—a status that allowed them to serve in a nonmilitary capacity. Others feigned insanity, got a doctor's note, or admitted to homosexuality. Hundreds of thousands more opposed the war but went to Vietnam anyway, some out of patriotic duty and others because military service seemed the only way out of poverty. For their part, many troops felt personally attacked by the antiwar movement and were keenly aware of the class difference between themselves and the protesters. For the next three decades, presidential electoral campaigns would make the candidates' Vietnam service record—or evasion of service—a key election issue.

President Johnson derided war critics as "nervous Nellies." Despite mounting evidence that the Vietnamese were winning, he insisted that the United States stay the course. Half of all Americans still supported his policy in 1966, but their enthusiasm was flagging. Although the war's cost had spiraled skyward, the president delayed asking Congress for an unpopular tax increase so as to give the public the impression that the United States was prevailing. When he finally requested the tax hike, Congress obliged only on the condition that funding for many Great Society programs be cut. Appalled, Martin Luther King, Jr., condemned the government for unleashing violence overseas and abandoning the war on injustice at home.

By late 1967, a broad antiwar coalition had formed among radicals, pacifists, and liberals. The era's first mass antiwar demonstration drew four hundred thousand protesters to New York City. According to a Gallup poll, less than half the population now supported the war. For the first time, protests turned violent as activists in Oakland, California, tried to close down an army recruiting station and police responded with tear gas and batons. In the nation's capital, a mass of demonstrators gathered at the Lincoln Memorial and then marched to the Pentagon. Over thirty thousand protesters converged on the building, and hundreds broke through police and military lines. The antiwar movement was now actively resisting the government. When a distant trumpet sounded at the Washington, D.C., protest, writer and antiwar advocate Norman Mailer was reminded of the Civil War. "The ghosts of old battles were wheeling like clouds over Washington," Mailer wrote. The Vietnam War had come home.

DEFYING AUTHORITY, MAKING COMMUNITY

The African American freedom movement pioneered two models for social change: the nonviolent civil rights model of the early 1960s and the group solidarity model of the Black Power movement. As Native Americans, Hispanics, disillusioned white youths, women, and gays and lesbians also confronted discrimination and other problems, activists from these communities borrowed from the freedom movement, adapting its strategies and tactics to their needs. When they encountered governmental indifference, repression, or dishonesty, the young activists visibly occupied public spaces, forged new identities, and openly challenged convention. By 1967, defying authority, whether of the government, parents, or mainstream ideology, had become a reflex for a diverse mass of young Americans.

NATIVE AMERICANS DECOLONIZE

A new sense of cultural cohesion within and among Native American tribes emerged in the 1950s, which in turn stimulated fresh demands for reform. A younger generation of leaders formed the National Indian Youth Council (NIYC), announcing their intention to resist assimilation into white American society and demanding federal relief from poverty and other social ills. Although President Johnson eventually pledged federal funds, for many tribes this help was too little, too late.

Young Indian activists, many of whom were college educated, mirrored the analysis of power advanced by Black Power militants. "We are not free," explained NIYC leader Clyde Warrior, "[as] we are not allowed to make those basic human choices about our personal life and the destiny of our communities." Native Americans had been reduced to the same condition to which the colonized peoples of the developing world had been reduced, Warrior argued, and, like colonial subjects the world over, they were now asserting their right to self-determination.

Whereas NIYC forcefully articulated the principle of autonomy and organized nonviolent protests such as "fish-ins" to enforce treaty rights, the American Indian Movement (AIM) became the vehicle for more militant activism. Founded in Minneapolis in 1968, this grassroots organization acted on behalf of the United States' three hundred thousand urban Indians who suffered disproportionately from poverty, unemployment, ill health, and police abuse. Security patrols, health clinics, schools, legal clinics, and food programs were established. Before long, AIM activists were also working in rural areas, where they attracted a mass following. The movement's "Red Power" message sparked the growth of other militant native groups, including Indians of all Nations, which went on to occupy Alcatraz Island in 1969 in protest of illegal seizures of Indian land.

BROWN POWER

Meanwhile, Americans of Mexican and Puerto Rican descent confronted ongoing inequities with greater organization and determination than ever before. In California and the Southwest, where hundreds of thousands of Mexican Americans and Mexican migrants toiled in low-wage agricultural labor, Cesar Chavez and Dolores Huerta established the United Farm Workers of America union. Chavez, an Arizona-born farmworker, employed nonviolent tactics and worked with the media to spotlight the workers' plight. His devout Roman Catholicism and insistence on nonviolence won the farmworkers' movement widespread support. In 1965, he and Huerta launched a massive consumer boycott of table grapes that eventually forced the largest growers to recognize the union, pay higher wages, and improve working conditions.

In the cities, younger Mexican Americans (many of whom were third-generation citizens) jumpstarted older campaigns against persistent inequality in education, housing, and employment. Many Mexican American youth declared their identity and political consciousness as Chicanos—Americans of Mexican descent—and insisted that their community take great pride in its unique culture, language, and history. Chapters of Young Citizens for Community Action, a grassroots organization founded in Los Angeles in 1966, spread quickly to dozens of other cities, introducing Latino youth to nonviolent civil rights activism. In 1968, they renamed their group the Brown Berets, dressed in military fatigues, and asserted that they, like the Black Panthers, would protect the *barrio* (neighborhood) from violence.

On the East coast, Puerto Rican Americans founded community action groups and, like other young activists, grew militant after 1967. As the Vietnam War wore on and activists clashed with police, the Young Lords promoted cultural pride, leftist politics, and withdrawal from Vietnam. Chicano and Puerto Rican students also joined with their Asian American

Viva Mi Raza!/Long Live My People! Both a political and a cultural movement, Chicano activism inspired a flowering of politically conscious visual, literary, and performance art. This mural, located in Chicano Park in San Diego, California, draws on Mexican, Aztec, Polynesian, U.S., and Japanese motifs to highlight the diverse roots of Chicano culture and experience.

and African American counterparts to push for curriculum reform on university campuses. After a long strike by minority students in 1968, San Francisco State University became the first U.S. college to establish an ethnic studies program.

THE COUNTERCULTURE

As antiwar demonstrators, grassroots radicals, and minority activists clashed with authorities, white youths began congregating in urban enclaves and experimenting with a way of life and a set of values that diverged sharply from those of their parents. Many were college students from suburban homes; the great majority opposed the war. But unlike the leaders of other movements, their critique of American society was chiefly cultural and spiritual. Like the Beats of the 1950s, they believed that something was deeply wrong with American culture, and that it was time to overthrow it. Contemporary observers referred to adherents as "hippies," a term that referenced the older word *hipster*, which was probably of African American origin and described those who were up-to-date and culturally aware.

Hippie **counterculture** took many forms, whether communal farming, living in a youthful enclave in cities like Atlanta and San Francisco, or simply "hanging out" and listening to rock music. The movement was nevertheless united in its search for new identities, new experiences, and true community. Most hippies embarked on this odyssey with the aid of mind-altering drugs. Initially, the drug of choice was marijuana, which had added appeal as a substance long associated with African American and Mexican minorities and, more recently, white rock musicians. Getting "stoned" reportedly enabled many hippies to experience music, sex, and everyday life in new and interesting ways. Far less potent than today's varieties, marijuana produced a gentle high that facilitated users' desire to escape their violent and divided society. Passing a hand-rolled "joint" around a circle of strangers and friends also gave them an enhanced sense of community.

After 1966, a far more potent substance became popular. The hallucinogen lysergic acid diethylamide (LSD, or "acid") promised to jolt users out of their present reality and send them on a spiritual path of self-discovery. Introduced to the United States as a psychiatric medication in the 1950s, it gained prominence in 1963 when former Harvard psychology professor Timothy Leary promoted its alleged transformative effects. Leary's advice to "turn on, tune in, drop out" found an eager audience in San Francisco, especially in the countercultural district of Haight-Ashbury. LSD use multiplied and transformed the counterculture. Frequent users—or "freaks"—publicly dramatized their disavowal of conventional society by wearing brightly colored clothes, beads, and bells. They also discarded "oppressive" undergarments and took new names that symbolized their rejection of modern ways (such as Wildflower and Berry). Condemning science and Western philosophy as instruments of social control, hippies and freaks drew on Eastern mysticism, formed chant circles, and made wild, psychedelic street art.

Piece of My Heart. Janis Joplin transfixed crowds with her gritty blues vocals and her enraptured performances. Joplin's raw and sexually assertive stage presence, which drew directly on the work of black artists such as Big Mama Thornton, earned her a place in the "boys' club" of rock 'n' roll greats. For a woman ahead of her times, that club proved both an exciting and a desperately lonely place.

Freaks viewed sex as the ultimate act of liberation and an experience to be had as often and with as many people as possible. The growing availability of the contraceptive pill, which freed women to have sex with little risk of pregnancy, also fueled what many claimed was a **sexual revolution.** Hippie newspapers championed free sex, while rock music smashed other taboos. Singing frankly about tripping, sex, and liberation, performers such as Janis Joplin, Jefferson Airplane, The Doors, and Jimi Hendrix gave voice to the new culture of rebellion.Youth responded enthusiastically and, much to the dismay of parents and local authorities, converged in their thousands on the nation's first-ever rock festival, held in Monterey, California.

Although centered largely on youth, the counterculture permanently transformed American culture. After writer Tom Wolfe documented the San Francisco scene in *The Electric Kool-Aid Acid Test* (1968), it seemed that hippie youth everywhere began "tripping." By 1969, the counterculture's music, sexual attitudes, and look had spread to universities and even to high schools and suburbs (see Hot Commodities: Hair). To many observers, the acid-inflected youth culture signaled a welcome and dramatic break from the past, but to others it was hardly radical or even novel. Experience-enhancing drugs such as nicotine, alcohol, and antianxiety medication had been around for some years. Furthermore, the idea that a drug—or a soft drink or convenience food or an automobile—could transform one's life was a familiar refrain of consumer culture. Indeed, astute advertising agencies quickly capitalized on the counterculture, packaging goods as "hip" and recruiting rock stars to promote products.

Even the sexual revolution was less radical than its progenitors claimed. Premarital sex among women had been steadily increasing since World War II, and mainstream culture had celebrated the work of sexologists such as Sigmund Freud and Alfred Kinsey since the early twentieth century. The advent of the birth control pill did not, in and of itself, change the power dynamics between men and women and in some ways merely reinforced the sexist convention that women's purpose was to serve men (in this instance, sexually).

WOMEN'S LIBERATION

Many young women soon discovered that when it came to matters of sex and gender, most supposedly radical men were just as blind as "the establishment." After 1965, a younger generation of feminists began advocating an all-out gender revolution. Most were white college students who had been politicized by the Vietnam War, Black Power, and the New Left. They had become disenchanted with their relegation to support roles, such as cooking and secretarial work, as well as their exclusion from leadership and decision making.

The young feminists broadened NOW's legal reform agenda to demand the complete cultural and political liberation of women. Many of the constraints on women's lives arose in the home and especially in their personal relations with men, argued the activists. Cooking, housekeeping, parenting, and child care were not mandated by law but enforced by popular attitudes and assumptions that women were better suited to (and naturally enjoyed) such work. No law explicitly provided that women's bodies were intended to serve men, sexually or otherwise, but most men and the culture at large treated women's bodies as though these were their primary functions. Men's attitudes and behavior toward women and their bodies would have to change, leaders of the **women's liberation** movement insisted.

HOT COMMODITIES

Hair

With its airy bouffants, cheeky moptops, elegant pageboys, natural Afros, and stringy hippie dos, the 1960s has long been associated with hair. It may therefore be surprising that the hair industry ended the "great American hair decade" in a droopy slump. What happened—and what might the history of hair tell us about the sixties?

Hair has been a key medium of artistic and political expression for centuries, and barbers, stylists, and hair product manufacturers have catered to and shaped tastes since at least 3000 BCE. In ancient Egypt, for instance, grooming and styling were so important among the affluent that hairdressing was a revered trade. With the rise of the modern beauty industry, hair became big business, as stylists and manufacturers catered not only to wealthy customers but also to mass consumers. Advertisers, stylists, and the makers of hair products wielded far more influence than before, using radio, color magazines, and, in the 1950s, television to powerfully mold mass taste.

The American Tribal Love-Rock Musical. Overflowing with profanity, explicit sexuality, open nudity, positive depictions of drug use, and a crowd of long- and Afro-haired actors, the rock musical *Hair* flouted convention as no musical before it. Within a year of opening in 1967, it was Broadway's biggest hit—and a target of conservative Christians.

It was not until the early 1960s, however, that hair became the leading sector of the beauty industry. Women's hair went big, as swept-up beehives and puffed-up bouffants (popularized by first lady Jackie Kennedy) turned hairspray into the nation's top-selling beauty product. Manufacturers promoted new chemical aids, especially easy-to-use blonding agents for women. Because dyed hair was associated with "loose women," advertisers substituted ordinary, though attractive, suburban homemakers for the glamorous actresses who had once endorsed their products. "If I've only one life, let me live it as a blonde," said one housewife in an advertisement for Lady Clairol cream bleach. By 1962, one in two American women was lightening her hair, up from just 7 percent in the late 1950s. Most African American women did not bleach, but many straightened their hair, as they had since at least the 1920s, in conformity with industry-set standards of beauty.

The cultural and political eruptions of the mid-1960s changed people's conception of hair and, for a time, turned the beauty industry on its head. As Black Power and the slogan "Black is beautiful" caught on, African American youths of both sexes embraced a "natural" or "Afro" look (which a small number of black avant-garde artists and writers had been wearing since the 1950s). For many youths, the new style signaled liberation, ethnic pride, and their rejection of white norms and the older generation's "go slow" tactics in the struggle for civil rights. The fashion soon spread to whites with curly or kinky hair, particularly young Jews who wanted to affirm their ethnic identity. Hippies of both sexes grew their hair long, typically parting it in the middle, and threading flowers or wrapping a bandana around it. By 1969, millions of college students, antiwar activists, and teens were sporting long or Afro-style hair.

These diverse "natural" hairstyles all signaled the wearer's rejection of consumer culture, segregation and other forms of oppression, the Vietnam War, and the presumed authority of parents and other elders. Unsurprisingly, neither "the establishment" nor the hair industry approved, the latter losing billions of dollars because of lower demand for its products and services. Thousands of barbershops and hair salons went bust. The industry rebounded in the early 1970s, but only once the anticonsumerist movements of the late 1960s had expired and young people were open, once again, to products and services. The Afro survived, but mostly as a fashion statement and largely stripped of its radical liberationist roots.

Think About It

1. Why did Americans care so much about how they—and other people—wore their hair in the 1960s?
2. Who or what was threatened by "natural" hairstyles?

The principal organizing tool of women's liberation was "consciousness raising" (CR). In New York, San Francisco, and other major cities in 1967–1968, feminists convened thousands of CR workshops in which a dozen or so women discussed their personal experiences, frustrations, and desires. In theory, the process validated participants by revealing that they shared certain experiences. It also led them to realize that regardless of their personal backgrounds, men exercised inordinate power over them in the family, the workplace, popular culture, and even in radical organizations. Branding this power as "patriarchy," the young feminists resolved to resist and overthrow it, both in daily life and in the mass media and other institutions.

OUT OF THE CLOSET

Gay, lesbian, and transgender Americans remained the least visible, least cohesive, and least understood minorities in these years. Sodomy laws, which theoretically applied to everyone but in practice targeted gay men, were still on the books in every state. Gays, lesbians, and transgender people were frequently arrested at bars and fired from their jobs if word of their sexuality got out. Admitting to being gay or lesbian was grounds for losing custody of one's children. Further, the federal government had routinely continued to purge suspected homosexuals from government agencies, a practice begun in the McCarthy era. Whether blue collar, affluent, white, or minority, the vast majority of gays and lesbians had little choice but to lead outwardly straight lives and express their sexuality, if at all, "in the closet"—that is, in secret.

As sexual outlaws, gays and lesbians found it hard to organize and to lobby publicly for legal reform. Sustained advocacy become possible only once gays began to live more openly in their own urban enclaves, as many did by the mid-1960s. Taking a leaf out of the freedom movement's book, gay and lesbian societies began sitting in and picketing against discrimination at local restaurants and businesses. As a rising number of gays and lesbians identified themselves publicly at these protests, others grew emboldened to "come out" and live more openly. While most remained closeted at work, large numbers came out to their families. Many parents and siblings disapproved, but others were supportive.

Like African American leaders of the pre-militant era, gay and lesbian protesters initially emphasized their respectability and patriotism, referring to themselves as "homophile" rather than "homosexual" (a strategy that deemphasized sex) and wearing business attire to sit-ins and pickets. These tactics changed once grassroots organizing accelerated, particularly in New York City and San Francisco, where the largest gay, lesbian, and transgender populations lived. Founded in 1964, the San Franciscan Society for Individual Rights (SIR) concentrated on building community by sponsoring dinners, softball games, field trips, drag shows, and other events. By 1968, thousands of gays, lesbians, and transgender people had joined SIR and similar organizations.

Although SIR helped develop a sense of community, poor and working-class gays led the way in collectively defending themselves and their way of life. In 1966, transgender prostitutes in San Francisco's red light district rioted against police harassment at a local all-night restaurant. Homophile advocates kept their distance, but many other gays felt empowered by the unexpected display of defiance. Dozens of young gays rebelled in Los Angeles the following year, after police beat up revelers for kissing at a bar on New Year's Eve. The most spectacular rebellion came in New York's Greenwich Village in 1969, when impoverished gay and transgender youths fought police for five nights after a routine raid at a bar called the Stonewall Inn. Although the Stonewall Riots did not end police harassment, they were a catalyst for community building, bringing gays from all walks of life together for the first time in common purpose and spurring the growth of the gay rights movement.

CHALLENGING LAW AND ORDER

The explosion of oppositional ideas and movements radically challenged both social convention and the structures of political power. By 1968, the Johnson administration was facing escalating social revolution at home and a resurgent enemy abroad. Opposition to the war spread, and small bands of student demonstrators started fighting back against riot police and National Guardsmen. Outside the Democratic National Convention in Chicago, events spiraled into violence as the authorities ordered thousands of police and soldiers to use any means necessary to disperse protesters. The televised spectacle of disorder only hardened radicals' resolve. Unexpectedly, however, media coverage also helped hand the 1968 presidential election to Republican candidate Richard M. Nixon.

DAYS OF RAGE

Politically, the year 1968 was among the most pivotal of the twentieth century, matched only by 1919 in the intensity of its violence and the depth of its divisiveness. The year began with a joint Viet Cong–North Vietnamese attack on every U.S. base and major city in southern Vietnam. Although U.S. troops repelled the assaults, the massive Tet Offensive (named for *Tet*, the Vietnamese New Year) took Americans and their government by surprise. Just a few weeks before, President Johnson's military advisers had announced that the North was in disarray and that the United States could now see "some light at the end of the tunnel." After Tet, respected TV newscaster Walter Cronkite echoed the shock of many Americans when he asked, "What the Hell is going on? I thought we were winning the war."

President Johnson's approval ratings sank to 26 percent. The president confronted the harsh reality that the Viet Cong and North Vietnamese seemed even less likely to surrender than ever before. On live television on March 31, 1968, LBJ announced that the United States would limit its bombing campaign and open peace talks. He further stunned the nation when he stated that he would not seek reelection. Both decisions were major victories for the antiwar movement. But by declaring his intentions, Johnson had rendered himself a "lame duck"—a politician who lacks the ability to initiate and carry out major decisions. In effect, Johnson left the nation adrift and rudderless.

In the meantime, Martin Luther King, Jr., had been organizing a Poor People's Campaign and mass march on Washington to demand a federal jobs program and other assistance. When African American sanitation workers struck for higher wages in Memphis, Tennessee, King seized on their case as an illustration of the plight of all low-wage and unemployed Americans. Tensions escalated in Memphis when young Black Power militants rioted while King—who continued to advocate nonviolence—and the sanitation workers marched peacefully. On April 4, 1968, a white assassin shot and killed King as he stood on the balcony of a Memphis motel. That night, African Americans in over 120 cities expressed their grief and rage in an outburst of rioting.

Antiwar protests broke out on over two hundred college campuses later that spring. In an angry chant aimed at Johnson, students yelled, "Hey, Hey, LBJ; how many kids have you killed today?" The nightly news showed riot police and National Guardsmen deploying to multiple cities and campuses. At Columbia University, students occupied buildings and demanded an end to their school's involvement in the war and the proposed construction of a university gymnasium in a Harlem park. After city police evicted and beat the occupiers, the students followed up with the longest campus strike in American history, effectively closing the university. The media, countercultural youth, and leaders of the SDS and Black Panthers converged on the campus and turned Columbia into a center for radical protest.

By the summer of 1968, many Americans feared that the nation was on the verge of a civil war. Some believed that U.S. radicalism might even be a front for a global revolution. Stoking the latter speculation were developments in Europe, Japan, Latin America, and the British Commonwealth, where students clashed violently with police. In May 1968, students in France united with workers in a nationwide strike that nearly toppled the government. Peace talks with North Vietnam had broken down in May, and students—along with the majority of Americans—were dismayed when President Johnson sent another two hundred thousand troops off to war. In June, violence flared again back home when a Palestinian émigré assassinated Robert F. Kennedy in retaliation for the latter's promise that, if elected president, he would deliver fifty fighter jets to Israel. (Kennedy had been seeking the Democratic Party's presidential nomination.)

Justice on Trial. Eight men, including Jerry Rubin, Abbie Hoffman, and Rennie Davis (pictured here), were tried for conspiring to incite violence at the 1968 Democratic National Convention in Chicago. Many Americans reacted in shock when judge Julius Hoffman ordered one of the eight—Black Panther Bobby Seale, who defended himself in court—bound and gagged. Five of the defendants were found guilty, but an appeals court overturned the convictions due to the trial judge's obvious bias.

By midsummer 1968, a small but growing minority of student protesters had abandoned nonviolence and were waging pitched battles with police in Berkeley and elsewhere. Many students developed a fascination with violence and claimed to feel newly empowered—much as minority youth, with whom they identified despite being middle class, had felt in the urban rebellions. Tensions mounted as the Democratic Party prepared for its national convention in Chicago in August. Over ten thousand students and other young people descended on the city, camping out in downtown parks to protest the government's Vietnam policy. A splinter group of SDS, the Youth International Party (the "Yippies"), enacted its opposition through street theater, flag burning, and nominating a live pig for president. For the first time in American history, the president stayed away from his own party's convention.

Chicago mayor Richard Daley (a Democrat) dispatched thousands of police, who unleashed tear gas and their nightsticks on protesters, the press, and bystanders alike. Although most protesters retreated and some counseled nonviolence, many fought back. Peace was eventually restored. Whether it had been a "police riot" (as a federal commission later described it) or violent rebellion, most people agreed that the Chicago conflagration had damaged the Democratic Party.

ELECTION OF 1968

Senator Eugene McCarthy, a liberal who supported an immediate end to the Vietnam War, had won more primary votes than any other Democratic candidate in the 1968 presidential campaign. Yet the national convention in Chicago nominated Johnson's loyal friend and vice president, Hubert Humphrey. Delegates also voted for a contradictory platform that promised more troop deployments while promoting a diplomatic solution in Vietnam. Humphrey's nomination not only split the party but also alienated millions of younger voters, liberals, and leftists.

Moderate and conservative Democrats were also alienated. Many had looked on in horror as TV coverage showed protesters and police clashing outside the convention. These events—which followed years of urban uprisings, student protests, and countercultural rebellion—convinced many blue-collar workers that the party had forgotten them. The Democrats, in their view, had become "bleeding heart" elitists who seemed to care only for the well-being of the country's most oppressed minorities. White workers also felt that they, more than any other group, had dutifully shouldered the burden of Vietnam and that the government was wrong in allowing middle-class kids to engage in disrespectful acts such as flag burning. And most white southerners (and a significant minority of white northerners) had still not forgiven the Democrats for pushing through civil rights reform.

Just as in 1964, Alabama governor George C. Wallace tried to mold such discontent into political support for an independent run for president. The politician who benefited most, however, was Republican Richard M. Nixon, who had been forced out of politics several years earlier, having lost both the California gubernatorial election of 1962 and the presidential election of 1960. Nixon waged a brilliant electoral campaign aimed at bringing both white working-class northerners and segregationist southern Democrats into the Republican fold. Under this **southern strategy,** Nixon courted powerful segregationist politicians, secretly promising to relax enforcement of federal civil rights laws. At the same time, he attracted northern workers' support by pledging to represent the "great majority of Americans, the forgotten Americans, the nonshouters, the nondemonstrators." Neoconservative Republicans in California and elsewhere had been running a grassroots campaign of their own since the late 1950s, aimed specifically at whites who resented the freedom movement. In a thinly disguised appeal to white racism, Nixon vowed to return the nation to "law and order."

On election day, Nixon beat Humphrey by 500,000 popular votes and 110 electoral votes (see Map 28.3). The white South voted widely for Nixon or Wallace (who won ten million popular and forty-six electoral votes), effectively running the Democrats out of office. Democrats also lost important gubernatorial races, including in California, where Republican candidate and former General Electric spokesman Ronald Reagan had promised to "clean up the mess at Berkeley."

As president, Nixon would carry out a two-pronged strategy of governance. Proclaiming his intention to secure "peace with honor" in Vietnam, he pursued a policy of Vietnamization by which he steadily decreased U.S. troop levels and thereby put

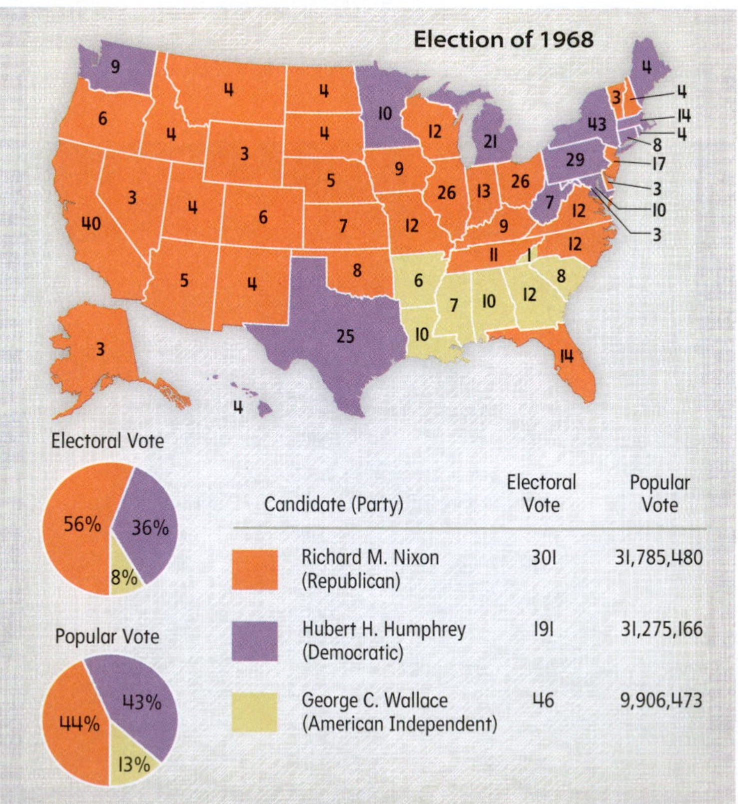

Election of 1968
Electoral Vote
56%
36%
8%
Popular Vote
44%
43%
13%
Candidate (Party) | Electoral Vote | Popular Vote
Richard M. Nixon (Republican) | 301 | 31,785,480
Hubert H. Humphrey (Democratic) | 191 | 31,275,166
George C. Wallace (American Independent) | 46 | 9,906,473

Map 28.3 Election of 1968.

After Woodstock. Attracting over half a million fans in the summer of 1969, Woodstock was the largest, most famous multi-day music festival of the decade. Long after the guitars and drums fell silent, Woodstock remained a popular but controversial symbol of the times. For many baby boomers, it marked the apex of American culture and a crowning achievement of their generation. Conservatives saw the event as a symbol of everything that was wrong with the counterculture, and leftist radicals of all ages generally dismissed it as a distraction. Whatever one's perspective, what would come after Woodstock and the heady, turbulent years of the 1960s remained unknown.

responsibility for fighting the war in South Vietnamese hands. Domestically, he built on his southern strategy, promoting himself as the champion of "ordinary Americans" (especially white blue-collar workers and southerners) and branding protesters, hippies, and the radical left as unpatriotic. Nixon linked his policies with patriotism and identified dissent as an unpatriotic threat to American freedom. He would never allow the government, he promised in 1969, "to be dictated by the minority . . . who try to impose [their opinion] on the Nation by mounting demonstrations in the street."

CONCLUSION

Interviewed in 1969 in a San Francisco jail cell by a sympathetic Swedish journalist, Angela Davis was asked about the "revolutionary" tactics of the Black Power movement. Davis, a radical intellectual and activist associated with the Black Panthers, answered that grassroots organizing of the sort the Panthers championed was a revolutionary way to empower communities. The reporter repeated the question, as though Davis had failed to answer. "Oh, so you're really asking me about *violence*?" Davis asked, taken aback. "I grew up in Birmingham, Alabama," she continued slowly, "and I lived across the street from the Sixteenth Street Baptist Church." It was the same church where children peacefully marching for freedom had been beaten by police and where four little girls had been killed in a bombing in 1963. Parents had to patrol the neighborhood for days afterward, Davis recounted. Why were white reporters, in light of the wave of segregationist violence that had broken over the South earlier that decade, making violence an issue now that African Americans were talking about their right to defend themselves? Why weren't reporters asking die-hard segregationists about violence? Davis promptly ended the interview, lamenting that the journalist obviously understood "nothing at all."

The exchange captured much of the optimism, anger, and confusion of the 1960s. Most Americans, especially African Americans, began the decade rejecting violence, whether as a tool of protest or as a weapon of government. The freedom movement practiced mass nonviolence. When

President Lyndon Johnson Americanized the Vietnam War, clergy members, mothers, professional associations, and a new generation of students forged a peace movement that dissented nonviolently. And hundreds of thousands of white middle-class youths rejected violence and embraced a counterculture focused on nature, sex, community, and spiritual exploration.

But segregationists and southern police forces had resorted to violence in their endeavor to halt desegregation. Impoverished urban minorities eventually lost patience with the slow pace of change, communicating their frustration through rioting and armed self-defense. Local, state, and federal government responded with force. By the late 1960s, as police cracked down on college students and antiwar protesters, many young whites also ran out of patience. Even the counterculture fell victim to the increasing social violence. By late 1969, violence was breaking out at the hallowed rock festivals that had symbolized peace and love just a few months before. Demand for illegal substances spawned drug gangs whose members in turn waged deadly turf warfare. As the decade closed, the dreams and disillusionment of the era collided—with lasting consequences for American culture and politics.

STUDY TERMS

Equal Pay Act of 1963 (p. 789)
Camelot (p. 790)
the establishment (p. 790)
urban renewal (p. 791)
Apollo space program (p. 791)
Bay of Pigs (p. 792)
Berlin Wall (p. 792)
Cuban missile crisis (p. 793)
Viet Minh (p. 793)
Geneva Accords of 1954 (p. 793)
National Liberation Front (p. 794)
sit-in (p. 795)
Student Nonviolent Coordinating Committee (p. 795)
freedom rides (p. 795)
literacy test (p. 796)
Freedom Summer (p. 797)
March on Washington for Jobs and Freedom (p. 797)
Warren Commission (p. 798)
Civil Rights Act of 1964 (p. 799)
Economic Opportunity Act of 1964 (p. 799)
growth liberalism (p. 800)
Great Society (p. 800)
Voting Rights Act of 1965 (p. 801)
Immigration and Nationality Act of 1965 (p. 801)
Medicare (p. 801)
Medicaid (p. 801)
National Organization for Women (p. 801)
Wilderness Act (p. 803)
Gulf of Tonkin Resolution (p. 803)
My Lai Massacre (p. 804)
Bill of Rights for the Disadvantaged (p. 805)
affirmative action (p. 805)
Black Power (p. 807)
Nation of Islam (p. 807)
Black Panther Party for Self-Defense (p. 807)
New Left (p. 808)
Port Huron Statement (p. 808)
American Indian Movement (p. 810)
United Farm Workers of America (p. 810)
counterculture (p. 811)
sexual revolution (p. 812)
women's liberation (p. 812)
Stonewall Riots (p. 814)
Tet Offensive (p. 814)
southern strategy (p. 816)

TIMELINE

1960 Greensboro Four "sit in" at a Woolworth's lunch counter in North Carolina
Student Nonviolent Coordinating Committee (SNCC) founded
John F. Kennedy elected president

1961 Kennedy establishes Peace Corp by signing Executive Order 10924
Bay of Pigs invasion of Cuba fails
Congress of Racial Equality (CORE) organizes first Freedom Rides
Construction begins on Berlin Wall

1962 Andy Warhol exhibits Campbell's Soup can paintings in Los Angeles
Michael Harrington's *The Other America* exposes U.S. poverty
Students for a Democratic Society (SDS) issues Port Huron Statement
Cuban missile crisis brings United States and USSR to the brink of nuclear war
Rachel Carson's *Silent Spring* exposes pesticides' detrimental side effects

1963 Equal Pay Act prohibits gender-based pay inequity
250,000 people attend March on Washington for Freedom and Jobs
Betty Friedan's *The Feminine Mystique* reawakens feminism
Police violently repress Children's Crusade in Alabama
LSD use rises after Timothy Leary advises youth to "turn on, tune in, drop out"
Lyndon B. Johnson assumes presidency after John F. Kennedy is assassinated

1964 U.C. Berkeley students spark the free speech movement on American campuses
Johnson begins War on Poverty
Johnson signs Civil Rights Act
Tonkin Gulf Resolution escalates Vietnam War

1965 Medicaid and Medicare provide health care for the poor and the elderly
United Farm Workers of America leads boycott against table grapes
Malcolm X is assassinated

1966 SNCC and CORE expel white members
National Organization for Women seeks gender equality
Black Panther Party is established in Oakland, California

1967 Federal troops deploy to Detroit
FBI infiltrates Black Panther Party

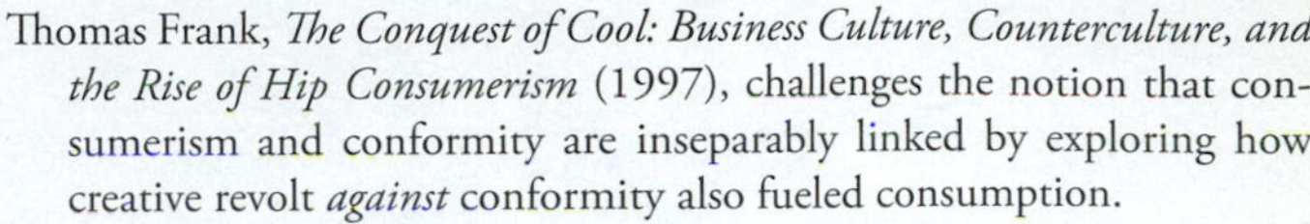

1968 American Indian Movement established

Brown Berets organize for Chicano rights

Women's liberationists protest Miss America Pageant

Martin Luther King, Jr., and Robert F. Kennedy are assassinated

Police violently disperse protesters at Democratic National Convention in Chicago

Richard M. Nixon is elected president

1969 Neil Armstrong walks on moon

500,000 attend countercultural rock concert at Woodstock

Stonewall Riots call public attention to police harassment of gays

Members of Indians of All Nations occupy Alcatraz Island

FURTHER READING

Additional suggested readings are available on the Online Learning Center at www.mhhe.com/becomingamerica1e.

Joshua Bloom and Waldo E. Martin, Jr., *Black Against Empire: The History and Politics of the Black Panther Party* (2013), gives a comprehensive history of the Panthers' ideas, personnel, and programs.

Aniko Bodroghkozy, *Groove Tube: Sixties Television and the Youth Rebellion* (2001), demonstrates the infusion of counterculture into mainstream entertainment through the medium of television.

Alice Echols, *Scars of Sweet Paradise: The Life and Times of Janis Joplin* (2000), is an incisive cultural history of Joplin's career and of the tumultuous era that made and unmade her.

David Farber, *The Age of Great Dreams: America in the 1960s* (1994), provides an overview of changes and events in the 1960s, explaining that many significant trends and notions were grounded in earlier decades.

Thomas Frank, *The Conquest of Cool: Business Culture, Counterculture, and the Rise of Hip Consumerism* (1997), challenges the notion that consumerism and conformity are inseparably linked by exploring how creative revolt *against* conformity also fueled consumption.

Todd Gitlin, *The Sixties: Years of Hope, Days of Rage* (1993), evaluates the rise and fall of the student New Left through the lens of the author's experience with Students for a Democratic Society.

Michael Herr, *Dispatches* (1977), relates a first-hand account of the horrors and hardships of the Vietnam War from the perspective of a frontline journalist.

George Herring, *America's Longest War: The United States and Vietnam, 1950–1975* (2001), integrates the economic, military, and political history of the Vietnam War.

Maurice Isserman and Michael Kazin, *America Divided: The Civil War of the 1960s* (2008), explores tensions inherent in oppositional political, cultural, and social movements of the 1960s.

Felicia Kornbluh, *The Battle for Welfare Rights: Politics and Poverty in Modern America* (2007), posits that welfare rights activism went beyond seeking economic equality in an effort to more fully extend the benefits and entitlements of American citizenship.

Lisa Law, *Flashing on the Sixties* (2000), visually chronicles the art, music, and fashion of the sixties.

Peter B. Levy, ed., *America in the Sixties—Right, Left, and Center: A Documentary History* (1998), represents the 1960s through the perspectives of both liberals and conservatives, as well as New Left and Right student groups.

Charles Payne, *I've Got the Light of Freedom: The Organizing Tradition and the Mississippi Freedom Struggle* (2007), challenges the standard narrative that places men and the church at the center of the civil rights movement through a focus on oral histories from Greenwood, Mississippi.

29

INSIDE ▶

THE BIG PICTURE

In the aftermath of the 1960s, various groups of Americans seized upon some of the goals and rhetoric of the civil rights struggle and the counterculture to build new social and cultural movements, both liberal and conservative. As an ambitious Republican president sought to turn the shifting cultural climate to his party's advantage, international political crises and a global economic downturn further divided the country.

Roller Disco. New styles of urban expression became enduring symbols of a contentious and transformative decade.

1970–1979

REACTION, RECESSION, & GLOBALIZATION

On November 27, 1978, Dan White, carrying a loaded handgun, entered San Francisco's City Hall through a first floor window. Having resigned earlier in the month from his membership on San Francisco's Board of Supervisors, White was now asking to be reinstated. Frustrated by Mayor George Moscone's refusal to reappoint him, White confronted the mayor, drew his weapon, and shot him dead. He then found Supervisor Harvey Milk and killed him as well.

White's double murder was another in a long series of violent acts that punctuated American political life in the years between the assassination of President John F. Kennedy in 1963 and the nonfatal shooting of President Ronald Reagan in 1981. After Malcolm X, Martin Luther King, Jr., and Robert Kennedy were gunned down in the 1960s, a would-be assassin took aim at presidential candidate George C. Wallace in 1972, and two women separately attempted to kill President Gerald Ford in 1975. The following year, Martin Scorsese's movie *Taxi Driver* haunted audiences with the homicidal fantasies of a deranged New York cabbie who plots to assassinate a presidential candidate. The story had roots in the diaries of the man who shot Wallace, and the movie in turn inspired a real-life attempt against Reagan five years later. In a period of rising political antagonisms, proliferating gun ownership, and expanding media coverage, assassinations had become preoccupying events in American culture.

The gunshots that rang out in San Francisco's City Hall echoed another deadly episode with local connections. Just nine days earlier, California congressman Leo Ryan had been killed in Guyana, in South America, where he was investigating abuse charges against an agricultural commune, the Peoples Temple, run by a charismatic former San Franciscan named Jim Jones. When disaffected members of the commune attempted to leave Guyana with the congressman and his entourage, Temple security forces opened fire on the group. The following day, Jones ordered his followers to drink poisoned Flavor-Aid, precipitating a mass suicide/infanticide that catapulted the Jonestown death toll to 918, including 276 children.

KEY QUESTIONS

- How did the civil rights and Black Power movements influence the political consciousness of other ethnicities and interest groups?
- What were the central elements of Richard Nixon's cultural strategy for appealing to specific constituencies who had traditionally voted for Democrats?
- How did the end of the Vietnam War fit into larger changes in U.S. foreign policy under Nixon?
- What were the course and impact of the Watergate scandal?
- How did the economic crisis of the 1970s reflect global developments and shape popular perceptions of the American city?
- How did the spread of evangelical Christianity influence American politics?

Media coverage of Jonestown and the Moscone-Milk murders spotlighted disturbing problems in American culture, including the malignant magnetism of religious cults, deep political and racial divisions, and the numbing frequency of violent crime. Jim Jones had espoused radical left-wing views, and though he was white, many of his followers were African American. Dan White was a former policeman and firefighter, a culturally conservative Catholic who positioned himself as tough on crime and a defender of traditional values against a local counterculture. In contrast, George Moscone was a popular liberal, and Harvey Milk the first self-identified gay person elected to public office in California history. When a jury of white, straight, mostly Catholic San Franciscans convicted White of the lesser charge of voluntary manslaughter, the city's gay community erupted in angry protest. Local police officers, many of whom had expressed support for White, then raided a gay bar in the Castro neighborhood and beat patrons.

Like many divisive events in the 1970s, the violence that gripped San Francisco in November 1978 bore the stamp of the social movements of the preceding decade. Struggles for freedom and liberation in the 1960s had divided the country along lines of race, ethnicity, gender, sexuality, and religion, and these divisions were broadcast in news reports, popular films, and new television programming. As political leaders sought to build fresh alliances within this fragmented culture, a revived Republican Party gained ground in the new political landscape—until a political scandal forced the once-powerful President Richard Nixon to resign from office in disgrace.

Before Nixon's resignation, his government struggled to cope with an economic crisis that would define the 1970s in the eyes of many Americans. Inflation, unemployment, and the decline of industrial manufacturing in the North and Midwest brought crime waves and poverty to the nation's cities and contributed to the sharpest rise in the cost of living since the Civil War. The economic downturn eroded long-standing assumptions about growth and progress, while new developments in international politics, commerce, and finance persuaded more Americans, both in and out of government, that they were living on a smaller, more interdependent planet.

Taxi Driver cabbie Travis Bickle (played by Robert De Niro) stoked fears of urban danger and political assassination.

PROTEST AND LIBERATION IN A DIVIDED NATION

The civil rights reforms of the Great Society and the oppositional social movements of the 1960s left a complex legacy. Federal government policies designed to promote racial integration ignited conflicts, especially in the North. There, various groups of white Americans began to see civil rights as a zero-sum game in which black advances came at their expense. At the same time, the tactics and language of the civil rights and Black Power movements inspired other Americans to celebrate their ethnic identities and organize political protest. Feminists, frustrated by their second-class status within the civil rights struggle, sought to apply the lessons of that movement to women in general. For these new assertions of political power, black America provided a model of group solidarity and personal liberation. The United States in the 1970s incubated an array of new solidarities and liberation programs, for groups and individuals alike (see Singular Lives: Curt Flood, Activist Athlete.)

DESEGREGATION BATTLES

By 1970, U.S. courts had grown impatient with the failure of the nation's public schools to achieve racial integration with the "deliberate speed" mandated in the 1954 *Brown v. Board of Education* decision (see Chapter 27). In a case involving North Carolina schools, the Supreme Court ruled in 1971 that transporting schoolchildren from one area to another was an acceptable method of ending segregation. Federal courts subsequently began ordering school districts with established patterns of racial segregation to apply this remedy of **busing.** White parents and politicians in Massachusetts, Michigan, Ohio, California, Kentucky, Virginia, Maryland, and elsewhere staged angry protests against the policy of "forced busing." Anti-busing protests sometimes turned ugly. In 1975 close to ten thousand white protesters confronted police in Jefferson County, Kentucky, calling them "pigs" and throwing rocks and bottles at them.

Some of the most notorious protests took place in the predominantly Irish area of South Boston, Massachusetts, whose schools were being merged with those of the mostly black neighborhood of Roxbury. In 1974, white parents organized as ROAR (Restore Our Alienated Rights) and refused to cooperate with the court order. White students threw rocks at buses carrying blacks and chanted racist slogans. Black parents were also wary of sending their children into hostile territory, and black students retaliated with violence of their own. Despite the intense opposition, the courts continued to oversee the desegregation of Boston's public schools for the next fifteen years.

Among both white and black parents, busing children out of their neighborhoods proved an unpopular strategy for achieving integration, although it was primarily whites who resisted the law. When resistance failed to roll back mandatory integration, opponents of busing sought ways around the law. In a momentous decision, *Milliken v. Bradley* (1974), the Supreme Court confined desegregation remedies to areas within a single metropolitan district. This ruling meant that schools in a suburban community did not have to integrate with schools in a neighboring city. In places like Detroit, where the *Milliken* case originated, white middle-class families could now avoid busing by moving to the suburbs. Such white flight contributed to the declining population and tax base of northern cities during the

White Protest. Suburban mothers picket in opposition to busing in St. Louis, Missouri, September 1971.

SINGULAR LIVES

Curt Flood, Activist Athlete

On January, 3, 1970, an African American man named Curt Flood appeared on national television, defiantly describing himself as "a well-paid slave." His interviewer, sportscaster Howard Cosell, was familiar with the well-paid part, as was much of the viewing audience. Flood, a star centerfielder for the St. Louis Cardinals during the 1960s, had helped the team to three World Series appearances and secured a reputation as one of baseball's premier defensive players. In 1969, he had earned $90,000—about ten times the median annual U.S. income at the time. Flood was not complaining about money, however. What irked the proud man from Oakland, California, who had grown up in a ghetto and endured hardships and humiliation on his way up the ranks of the game, was that he had been traded, against his will, from the Cardinals to the Philadelphia Phillies. As he sat in the interview chair, Flood was in the midst of a protracted legal battle against Major League Baseball that had gone all the way to the Supreme Court. And he was calling himself a slave.

Flood was challenging the "reserve clause" in Major League Baseball contracts, which granted teams exclusive rights to a player's services, even after the contract expired. Teams routinely traded their exclusive rights, in which case the player was bound to move. Flood did not especially wish to relocate to Philadelphia and play for the Phillies, in part because he perceived their owner to be racist. What outraged him more, though, was the trade's implication that he was "a piece of property to be bought and sold irrespective of my wishes." With the financial support of the baseball players' union, Flood sacrificed his career to challenge the reserve clause in federal court in 1970.

His prospects were dim. Although the clause granted baseball franchises unusual monopolies, the Supreme Court had ruled in 1922 that baseball was not interstate commerce (because individual games were played within state borders) and therefore not subject to federal antitrust legislation. With that precedent in place for almost five decades, federal district courts and appeals courts ruled against Flood. Undeterred, Flood appealed to the Supreme Court. Throughout the process, Flood's suit received scant support from former baseball players or from baseball fans, most of whom considered the reserve clause necessary to the game. The only retired stars who testified on Flood's behalf were outsiders themselves—Jackie Robinson, who had broken baseball's color line (see Chapter 26), and Hank Greenberg, who had endured anti-Semitic taunts and opposition during his long and successful career.

The final blow to Flood's campaign came in 1972 when a five-to-three majority of the Supreme Court upheld the lower courts' decisions. Specifically, the Court ruled that although baseball really *was* interstate commerce, it had been granted a special exemption from antitrust laws, and therefore the reserve clause needed to be negotiated through collective bargaining, not in the courts. Flood, who had missed the 1970 season and then played only thirteen games for the Washington Senators (to whom he consented to be traded) in 1971, decided to retire. However, for the baseball union that had supported his lawsuit, the next chapter was far brighter. Pressured to negotiate the reserve clause at the bargaining table, baseball owners agreed to submit disputes to independent arbitrators. In landmark decisions in 1974 and 1975, arbitrators declared three players (all white pitchers) free agents, setting off a bidding war and demonstrating to players and fans the market value of their services. The reserve clause was abolished, free agency was introduced, and Curt Flood's cause prevailed, though too late for him to benefit.

Think About It

1. How did Curt Flood's suit enhance the bargaining position of the players' union?
2. How was Flood's challenge to Major League Baseball an outgrowth of the civil rights struggles of the 1960s?
3. What aspects of U.S. slavery did Flood have in mind when he called himself "a well-paid slave?"

Free Agent. Curt Flood, the man who challenged baseball's reserve clause at the cost of his career, poses with his portrait of Martin Luther King, Jr. Though Flood was largely remembered as a martyr to the cause of players' rights, his challenge also had political overtones. Indeed, Flood had long been sensitized to issues of injustice, especially racial injustice.

1970s and deprived urban schools of funding. In the South, where segregated white and black schools often existed in the same communities, white families chose a different strategy for resisting integration. In the 1960s, they had already begun withdrawing their children from public schools and enrolling them in private academies. The proliferation of all-white private schools, many with religious affiliations, throughout the South during the 1970s contributed to the spread of evangelical Christianity there.

Reclaiming Heritage. Actor Levar Burton starred as the enslaved Kunta Kinte in the immensely popular *Roots* television series. The series finale still ranks as the third most-watched television program in U.S. history.

POLITICS OF PRIDE

The white backlash against civil rights initiatives was matched by an increasing interest among white Americans in emulating parts of the black liberation struggle. Black Power rhetoric had spread to Chicano, Latino, American Indian, and Asian American activists by the late 1960s (see Chapter 28), and soon other marginalized groups not defined by ethnicity or descent—among them women, gays and lesbians, senior citizens, and people with disabilities—began appropriating the language of power, pride, and separatism to help secure equal rights and promote self-esteem.

A similar upsurge in the politics of group pride took place among white people, especially the descendants of southern and eastern Europeans who had immigrated to the United States between the 1880s and 1920s. After decades of identifying as white Americans and seeking entry into the cultural mainstream of America's melting pot, a new generation began celebrating their distinctive identity as Italians, Jews, Poles, Greeks, Slovaks, Ukrainians, or other ethnic Europeans. Inspired by the political mobilization of African Americans, participants in this **ethnic revival** also saw new appeal in identifying as something other than white. As Slovak American theologian and political philosopher Michael Novak argued, his people bore no special responsibility for racial inequality in the United States. "Our ancestors owned no slaves," Novak wrote in his best-selling book *The Rise of the Unmeltable Ethnics* (1972). "Most of us ceased being serfs only in the last two hundred years."

The white ethnic revival of the 1970s took highly visible forms, from popular T-shirts proclaiming ethnic pride ("Kiss Me, I'm Irish"), to television shows with unapologetically ethnic characters (Italians like Arthur Fonzarelli on *Happy Days* and Laverne DeFazio on *Laverne and Shirley*, or Jews like Rhoda Morgenstern on *Rhoda* and Gabe Kotter on *Welcome Back, Kotter*) to the establishment of government-sponsored ethnic heritage programs. New local museums chronicled the experiences of Hungarian, Czech, German, and other immigrant groups in the United States, while best-selling books sought to preserve artifacts and peddle memories of the Old Country. Census Bureau surveys from early in the 1970s found many more people identifying themselves as Polish Americans or Ukrainian Americans, for example, than had done so in the previous decade.

More generally, Americans became intensely interested in recovering their roots in the 1970s, spawning an unprecedented spike in genealogical research and heritage journeys to ancestral lands. Here, too, black Americans provided a powerful model. The television mini-series *Roots* (1977), based on a historical novel by Alex Haley, followed seven generations of an African American family in slavery and freedom. Some 85 percent of American television households tuned in to at least part of the eight-episode series, with a majority of episodes averaging over eighty million viewers. Most of them saw *Roots* not as a distinctive story about the legacy of slavery but as a broader story about the links between foreign ancestors and American descendants. Following Haley's example, Americans flocked to libraries and historical societies in search of their own ethnic pasts.

Identifying with one's ethnic group could entail political activism as well. Organizations such as the Irish Northern Aid Committee (founded in 1970) and the American Committee for Democracy and Freedom in Greece (1967) mobilized ethnic pride for nationalistic political causes, often focused abroad. The early 1970s saw a new activism among young Jews, many of whom were inspired and emboldened by the stunning military victory of Israel against Egyptian, Syrian, and Jordanian forces in the 1967 Six Day War. Meir Kahane's Jewish Defense League (JDL), founded the following year in New York as a nationalist vigilante group to resist anti-Semitism, modeled itself in many respects on the Black Power movement. League members adopted a clenched-fist logo, organized armed community patrols, and even called themselves "Jewish Panthers." The JDL attracted a small right-wing minority with its call for violent confrontations with local enemies, but it also stood at the radical vanguard of a growing political movement to protest the treatment of Jews in the Soviet Union.

The politics of ethnic pride was sometimes divisive in the 1970s, but many Americans came together in a new celebration

Family Values. Francis Ford Coppola's *Godfather* films celebrated the Italian immigrant experience and endorsed their characters' family allegiances and ethnic traditionalism as noble American traits.

of the American immigrant experience, not as a story of assimilation but as a process in which families preserved and transmitted their rich cultural heritages. Ellis Island, New York's bustling immigrant depot between 1892 and 1924, became the symbolic center of this celebration. The federal government began restoring the forgotten island in the 1960s, and by the nation's bicentennial year of 1976, the National Park Service was offering tours of the facility, which would eventually house a major immigration museum. Ellis Island National Monument pays tribute to immigrants to the United States from different places and in various periods, including those who arrived in other harbors, on other coasts, and across other borders. However, the ethnic revival that fueled the restoration project focused mostly on those groups that had settled in and around New York during the island's heyday. As new streams of nonwhite foreign immigrants from places other than Europe began entering the United States after 1965, Poles, Jews, Slavs, and especially Italians came to appear in the popular imagination as classic, prototypical Americans.

FEMINISM, FAMILY LIFE, AND THE SEXUAL REVOLUTION

Like other 1960s struggles for equal rights, the women's movement had taken a radical turn by the end of that decade. Feminist activists increasingly described sexism and male supremacy as the fundamental evil in society and called for a major reordering of gender roles. Much like advocates of Black Power and ethnic pride, some radical feminist organizers embraced separatism. They encouraged women to invest their political energies in female-led causes that made the liberation of women (rather than civil rights, socialism, disarmament, the end of the Vietnam War, or the decolonization of the developing world) the primary objective.

Radical feminism, as this movement was called by the end of the 1960s, pushed public discussion of gender issues beyond the goals of equality and fulfillment that had dominated the early consciousness-raising movement (see Chapter 28). The new agenda posed troubling questions about sexuality, reproduction, and childrearing. Radical feminists advocated public investments in child care and pushed for the freedom to terminate an unwanted pregnancy—a goal that received a significant boost in 1973 when the Supreme Court legalized abortion (see Evangelical Counterculture, below). More provocatively, they also pointed to the dangers of maintaining heterosexual relationships with men.

As its critique of sexism intensified, the feminist movement struggled to deal with internal rifts over issues of class, race, and especially sexual orientation. Partly in an effort to unify the movement by highlighting what all women shared, many feminists in the 1970s embraced a new posture, sometimes called cultural feminism, that emphasized the essential differences between men and women. In the words of Jane Alpert, "Biology is . . . the source and not the enemy of feminist revolution." Alpert, disavowing her radical past as a leftist activist, now downplayed the importance of class and race relations and rejected the politics of the New Left. Alpert, Robin Morgan, and other cultural feminists contrasted nurturing female values with the controlling, violent tendencies of men and advocated the creation of alternative female communities. They were less interested in debates about equal pay and public access, leaving those struggles to more mainstream liberal feminists. Instead, cultural feminists politicized personal life, social arrangements, and sexuality.

Feminism called close public attention to revolutionary shifts in sexual attitudes and experiences that were taking place in the 1970s. Cultural constraints and personal inhibitions that had long regulated the behavior of youths, middle-class adults, and women of all ages began to melt away. Men and women expressed greater interest in their own sexual pleasure, in sexual relationships outside the bounds of a lifelong monogamous commitment, and in sexual acts other than heterosexual intercourse. Some feminists saw these developments as encouraging signs of women's liberation from what author Germaine Greer called "doglike devotion" to husbands and boyfriends. Others, including many cultural feminists, suspected that the sexual revolution was simply unleashing aggressive male sexuality and objectifying women.

There was no mistaking the revolution, however, because much of what changed in the early 1970s was the ease and enthusiasm with which sex was publicly discussed and depicted (see Hot Commodities: Pornographic Feature Films). Americans eagerly sought out information about sex, turning memoirs like Xaviera Hollander's *The Happy Hooker* (1971) and manuals like David Reuben's *Everything You Always Wanted to Know About Sex (But Were Afraid to Ask)* (1969) and Alex Comfort's *The Joy of Sex* (1972) into runaway best sellers. In 1971, Reuben's guidebook outsold the New English Bible in the United States. Comfort, whose manual featured illustrations of sexual acts and positions, captured the permissive sexual ethos of the new decade and envisioned a time "when we may regard chastity as no more a virtue than malnutrition."

The movement of gays and lesbians to stop concealing their sexual orientations reflected and reinforced this new culture of sexual candor. After the Stonewall Riots in 1969 (see Chapter 28), gay and lesbian activists emphasized the need for homosexual men and women to "come out" and become visible. Gay pride parades, marking the anniversary of the riots, spread through urban America by 1971 and contributed to the public presence of sexuality in American life. The ideals of gay *pride* and gay *liberation* (two words that reflected the influence of Black Power), however, required more than parades. Gays and lesbians came out to family members and friends, asking for an acknowledgement of their private selves and often demanding a greater degree of honesty and transparency in talking about sex more generally.

Not all of the public discussion of sex during the early 1970s was celebratory. Social conservatives and religious groups decried the loosening of sexual mores and joined with the feminist organization Women Against Pornography in calling special attention to the degrading effects of pornographic films and magazines. Congress funded the President's Commission on Obscenity and Pornography in 1969, and when its report turned up no evidence of the negative social impact of pornography, President Richard Nixon and the U.S. Senate rejected the findings. Mainstream media also sounded alarms about the new sexual culture. A 1972 *Time* magazine cover story on teenage sexuality in the United States described an epidemic of sexually transmitted infections, abortion, and out-of-wedlock births among teens and suggested that teens themselves felt uneasy about the "almost unlimited new sexual license" in American high schools and colleges.

Critics worried especially about the impact of the sexual revolution on family life. The twelve-episode PBS television documentary *An American Family* (1973) focused some of this criticism. The series, which attracted an unexpectedly robust weekly audience of ten million viewers, followed the daily life of the Louds, a family in suburban California with five children. Over the course of the documentary's filming in 1971, the life of this ostensibly typical family had taken surprising turns. Pat Loud kicked her husband Bill out of the house, citing sexual infidelity and absenteeism, while their oldest son, Lance, came out as gay. Viewers followed the United States' first reality show with great interest, but cultural commentators seized on the breakdown of order and authority in the Loud family and turned the Louds into symbols of fractured marriage (divorce rates would climb by 67 percent nationwide over the course of the decade) and permissive parenting. Cosmopolitan observers wondered what this documentary said about their own culture, and some longed for the orderly, patriarchal families that they associated with an earlier generation of white immigrants. Reflecting on *An American Family* in the *New York Times*, the feminist journalist Anne Roiphe questioned the benefits of American assimilation. Referring to the fictional Italian mafia family glamorized in the *Godfather* novel and movie, she wrote: "Maybe it's better to be a Corleone than a Loud, better to be tribal and ethnocentric than urbane and adrift."

THERAPEUTIC CULTURE

Beyond the realm of sex, the 1970s witnessed a general rise in individual quests for personal fulfillment and meaning. A rash of popular self-improvement regimes catered to these yearnings. Former used-car salesman Werner Erhard founded Erhard Seminars Training (est) in San Francisco in 1971. Est attracted hundreds of thousands of people to seminars in which individuals learned to "take responsibility" for their life circumstances. Meditation and yoga also took off in the 1970s, as did new strategies of psychotherapy, dieting, and bodybuilding. Cultural critics saw these developments as evidence of a narcissistic culture in which men and women who had been committed to changing the world a few years earlier suddenly were turning inward to explore and rediscover themselves.

The popular journalist and author Tom Wolfe labeled the 1970s the Me Decade in 1976. However, not all the efforts at self-transformation were entirely individualistic. Massive religious cults and movements, such as the Reverend Sun Myung Moon's Unification Church and the International Society for Krishna Consciousness (Hare Krishna), submerged the individual identities of their adherents, as did smaller utopian communities such as Jim Jones's Peoples Temple.

HOT COMMODITIES

Pornographic Feature Films

For most of the twentieth century, sexually explicit movies were shown in private settings or marginal venues beyond the bounds of social respectability. Known as "stag films" or "blue movies," they typically ran for fifteen minutes without sound or story line, featured performers with their faces concealed, and were produced illegally. Then, in the 1970s, hard-core pornographic film entered the mainstream with high-production, feature-length narratives that played in large public movie houses.

The mainstreaming of pornography was part of a broader sexual revolution. By the 1970s, Americans were consuming unprecedented volumes of sexually explicit books, magazines, and songs, which were protected by a series of Supreme Court decisions in the mid-1960s that blunted most state obscenity laws. More than the law had changed, however; the sexual revolution was a sea change in popular attitudes. Movies with sexual themes and nudity received restrictive ratings from the motion picture industry, but for many respectable middle-class adults, an X rating was not a deal breaker. John Schlesinger's *Midnight Cowboy* (1969) won the Academy Award for Best Picture despite being rated X, but X-rated films such as *Behind the Green Door* (1972), *Deep Throat* (1972), and *The Devil in Miss Jones* (1973) broke new cinematic ground. They did not simply use explicit language and depict sex acts; in these hard-core films, sex acts consumed a majority of the screen time. They presented such spectacles as group sex, masturbation, sadomasochism, and sexual coercion. They also focused on the sexual desires of their female protagonists.

The films were fantastically successful. Jim and Artie Mitchell's *Behind the Green Door*, produced for $60,000, reaped $1 million in ticket sales from its first nationwide release and eventually grossed over $25 million. Gerard Damiano's *Deep Throat*, which ran for close to four hundred straight weeks in some U.S. theaters, was both cheaper to make and more lucrative, with estimates of *Deep Throat*'s gross sales ranging as high as $600 million. *Deep Throat* even became the chic movie choice among the rich and famous. Republican vice president Spiro Agnew saw videotapes of the film at the home of singer Frank Sinatra. Soon middle-class married couples began attending pornographic features together and *Deep Throat* became a date movie.

The unexpected commercial success of *Deep Throat* and other hard-core films sparked a powerful backlash among government authorities and concerned citizens. FBI investigators arrested Damiano and targeted his movie throughout the country. Local officials sought to block screenings, and states banned the film and brought charges against those involved in its production and distribution. Actor Harry Reems, *Deep Throat*'s male lead, was convicted on federal obscenity charges in Tennessee, a state that prosecutors had chosen for its presumed hostility to the permissive sexual culture in which the film had premiered. Reems was held to a new obscenity standard—which granted works of entertainment First Amendment protections only if they possessed "serious literary, artistic, political, or scientific merit"—introduced by a more conservative Supreme Court in 1973. Because the new standard appeared after *Deep Throat* was filmed, the conviction was overturned on appeal, the charges were subsequently dropped, and Reems avoided jail time. Still, the film remained controversial, and not only among social conservatives. Many radical feminists criticized the new X-rated blockbusters as degrading, hostile, and dangerous to women, and in 1978, activists in New York founded Women Against Pornography, which favored banning hard-core films. Other feminists defended the new pornography, either in the name of free speech or out of faith in the larger benefits of frank discussions of female sexual pleasure.

Think About It

1. Why might government officials have been concerned about the popularity of hard-core feature films in the early 1970s?
2. How might we distinguish the cultural impact of films like *Deep Throat*, which played in movie theaters, from the impact of more recent pornography, which is consumed largely at home on DVDs or via the Internet?

Personal quests also brought new recruits to older religious traditions. Evangelical Christianity experienced enormous growth during the 1970s (see Evangelical Counterculture, below), especially outside the established evangelical denominations. A loosely defined Jesus movement swept through Texas, California, and elsewhere and helped lay the groundwork for the growth of evangelical megachurches with independent ministries. Around the same time, Chabad Hasidism launched outreach programs to unaffiliated American Jews, attracting adherents through a similar blend of less formal worship and charismatic leadership. Religious revivals competed effectively with self-help programs for the commitments and resources of a rising number of young men and women seeking new spiritual and psychological anchors.

RICHARD NIXON'S AGENDA

Richard Nixon was an astute observer of these trends in politics and culture. After winning narrow election in 1968 in a three-way race, he worked to build majority support for his vision of America. Central to both the vision and the political strategy was his faith that a "silent majority" of Americans was rejecting the cultural politics of the 1960s and seeking a restoration of order at home and honor abroad. Cultural changes sweeping the country in the early 1970s, Nixon and his advisers believed, could clarify the differences between him and his political opponents. Facing a war that was going terribly, a stagnating economy, and a new set of international crises and challenges, Nixon

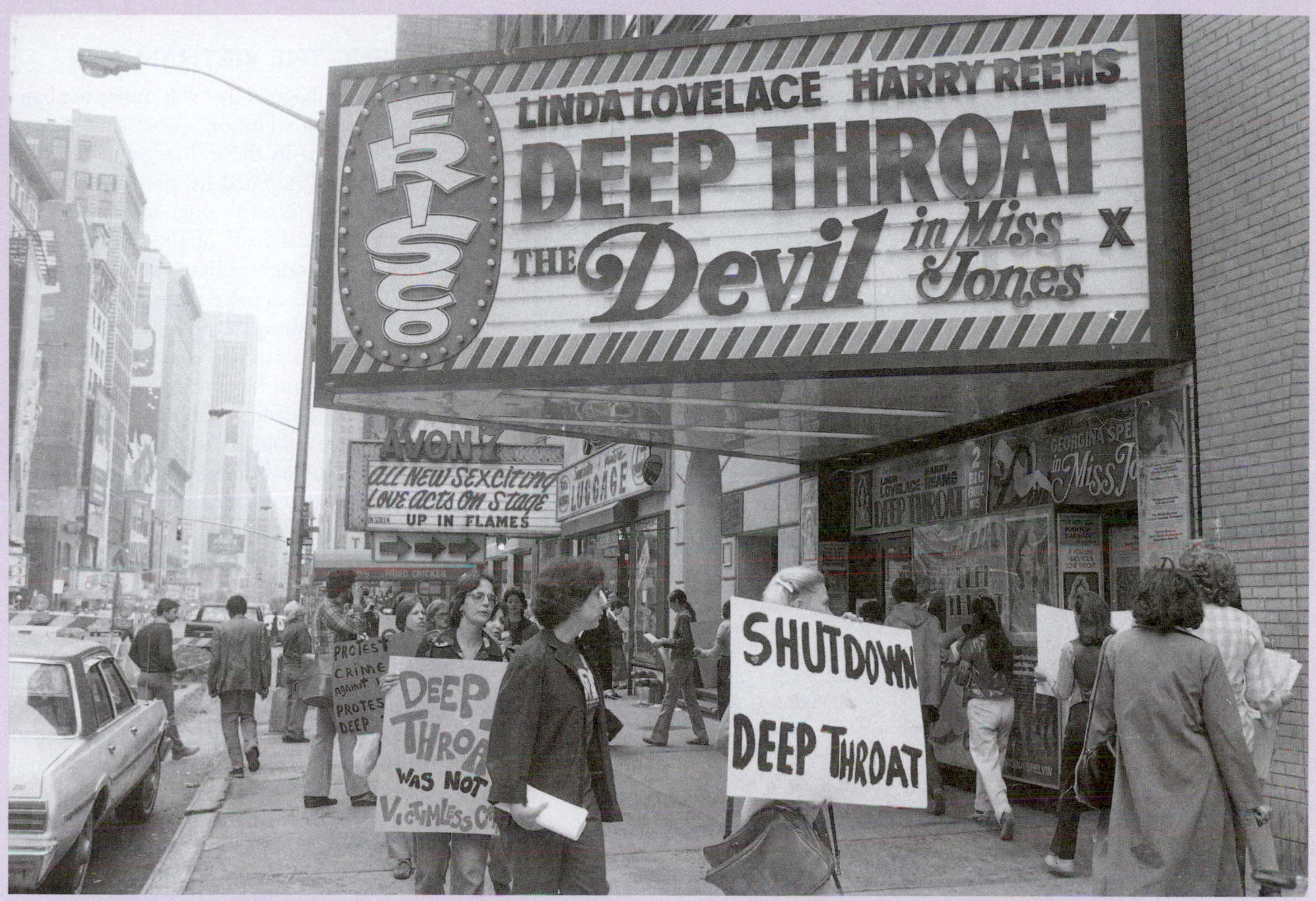

Pornography Wars. In 1980, protesters picketed the New York theater that was screening *Deep Throat* and *The Devil in Miss Jones*. *Deep Throat* became a special target of feminist ire, in part because its star actress, Linda Lovelace, claimed that an abusive boyfriend had forced her to participate.

nonetheless kept to his political strategy, exerted presidential power in both foreign and domestic affairs, expanded the federal government's reach, and implemented a political program designed to cement his new majority.

A NEW POLITICAL COALITION

As Nixon understood, the nation's civil rights struggles and the wrenching internal conflict over Vietnam had opened a crack in the Democrats' New Deal coalition. George C. Wallace's independent presidential candidacy had exposed the growing fracture in 1968, and Nixon and his advisers saw an opportunity to rebuild the Republican Party by attracting Wallace's white base in the South and his working-class supporters in the North. Southern whites could take comfort in Nixon's lack of interest in mandating racial integration. At least initially, Nixon discouraged the IRS from denying tax breaks to the private academies that had been created to maintain segregation. "Whites in Mississippi can't send their kids to schools that are 90 percent black," he told an aide, "they've got to set up private schools." Nixon eventually retreated from that stance, but throughout his presidency he criticized "forced busing" and even supported a constitutional amendment that would end the practice. School desegregation was in fact taking place in the South on Nixon's watch, but rather than claiming credit for the achievement, the president underscored his sympathy for the anti-busing movement.

Country Values. In 1969, the country hit "Okie from Muskogee" by Merle Haggard and the Strangers declared: "We don't smoke marijuana in Muskogee/ We don't take our trips on LSD/ We don't burn our draft cards down on Main Street/ Cuz we like livin' right and bein' free." President Nixon, seeking to ally his party with nonelite Americans who were alienated from the drug culture and the antiwar movement, invited the band to play at the White House.

Opposition to busing also boosted Nixon's standing among white northerners. However, his hopes to lure northern blue-collar union voters from their traditional home in the Democratic Party also rested on the conviction that white ethnics shared his core cultural values. Nixon believed that patriotism, support for the Vietnam War, traditional sexual morality and gender norms, and antipathy toward the counterculture could unite people with different economic interests. Partway through his first term, he envisioned a "new coalition based on silent majority, blue-collar Catholics, Poles, Italians, [and] Irish." Not all ethnic groups would join this coalition, Nixon warned his advisers: "No promise with Jews and Negroes." Still, his **blue-collar strategy** could succeed by finding common cultural ground with enough of the participants in the ethnic revival of the times.

Among Nixon's inner circle, Special Counsel Charles Colson pushed the Republican Party to abandon or downplay its long-standing hostility to organized labor. Colson hoped that in future elections, the religious, moral, and foreign policy outlooks of union members might trump their bread-and-butter economic concerns and their traditional party allegiances. As a counterpart to Nixon's pitch to white Catholics in the urban North, the president also stressed the links between the values of Republicans and those of country music. In earlier periods of the party's history, both of these appeals would have been most unlikely.

WIDENING THE VIETNAM WAR

Nixon had campaigned in 1968 under the banner of "Peace with Honor," promising to end U.S. involvement in the military and political debacle that had doomed his predecessor Lyndon B. Johnson. Nixon's dual strategy was to reduce the political costs of the Vietnam War while keeping enough military pressure on the North Vietnamese to force them to the negotiating table. Pursuing a policy that became known as Vietnamization, Nixon announced in 1969 that he would be shifting the burden of ground combat to South Vietnam. By training South Vietnamese soldiers and supporting them with arms and aerial bombardment, the United States could lower its troop levels, a change Nixon figured would make the war more popular. The Nixon administration also altered the military draft so that fewer American men would be subject to conscription, and began the move toward a volunteer army. Between 1969 and 1972, the number of U.S. servicemen in Indochina dropped steeply from more than half a million to approximately sixty thousand.

While radically reducing its troop commitments, the United States nonetheless broadened the scope of the war. Nixon and Henry Kissinger, the former Harvard professor who served as Nixon's main adviser for military affairs and foreign policy, decided to attack military bases in neutral Cambodia that the administration believed were sustaining the North Vietnamese. Without telling Congress, Nixon ordered a secret invasion into Cambodian territory that led to the overthrow of the country's government. Once a pro-American regime assumed power, Nixon decided to publicize plans for the attack that was already taking place, not anticipating the reaction it would trigger. Congress protested the invasion by rescinding the Gulf of Tonkin resolution that had granted earlier authorization for the war effort. In 1973, memories of this secret invasion of Cambodia would help secure passage, over Nixon's veto, of the War Powers Resolution limiting the authority of a president to wage war without congressional consent.

Masses of Americans reacted to the Cambodia announcement with immediate outrage. In May 1970, a revived antiwar movement staged huge rallies across the country. Four college students on the mostly working-class campus of Kent State (Ohio) University were killed by National Guardsmen, while two others were gunned down by police at Jackson State, a historically black college in Mississippi. The killings at Kent State and Jackson State prompted more demonstrations and further tarnished the image of the war. Not everyone sympathized with the slain college students or their cause, however. Construction workers in New York City rioted in the streets, beat antiwar demonstrators, and raised a U.S. flag that had been lowered to honor the Kent State victims. On May 20, the Building and Construction Trades Council of Greater New York, led by Peter Brennan, organized a hard hat rally that drew one hundred thousand blue-collar workers to a patriotic demonstration of support for Nixon and the war.

Nixon took comfort in the support of blue-collar workers but grew obsessed with the mounting antiwar criticism. In 1969, Americans learned the details of a 1968 incident in which U.S. soldiers under the command of Lieutenant William Calley had killed 350 civilians in the South Vietnamese village of My Lai. Calley's trial and conviction in 1971 confirmed the grisly details of the massacre and cast the war in an especially unfavorable light. That same year, the *New York Times* began publishing the Pentagon Papers, a leaked set of documents produced by the Defense Department under President Johnson. The papers proved that the Johnson administration had lied about the goals and progress of the Vietnam War. Nixon sought a court injunction to prevent their publication, and when that tactic failed he authorized a campaign to discredit Daniel Ellsberg, the antiwar former military analyst who had given the documents to the *Times*. Using a team of "plumbers" that had been established to prevent leaks of politically sensitive information, White House officials orchestrated a burglary at the office of Ellsberg's psychiatrist, in an unsuccessful attempt to find embarrassing information with which to silence Ellsberg.

DOMESTIC POLITICS AND THE EXPANDING WELFARE STATE

Nixon's domestic agenda proved less divisive. Both his instincts and his blue-collar strategy pushed him to seek a middle ground on economic issues. Making no effort to roll back Great Society programs, Nixon's administration continued the federal war on poverty. On his watch and with his approval, Congress raised food stamp support and indexed

Blue-Collar Protest. Donning hard hats, construction workers express their support for President Nixon and call for the impeachment New York's "red mayor" John Lindsay (a liberal Republican). Nixon and Charles Colson wooed rally leader Peter Brennan as a political ally, and ultimately Nixon appointed him secretary of labor.

Social Security to the rising cost of living. The president also proposed the Family Assistance Plan, which would have replaced welfare payments with a federally guaranteed income of $1,600 for a family of four (see How Much Is That?). In this case, Nixon's middle ground proved less popular. Conservatives balked at the idea of government handouts, and liberals objected to the notion that a family could survive on such an income. The plan died in the Senate. Still, Nixon could claim credit for having tried to reform welfare, and his defeated proposal could do no political harm.

How Much Is That?

Nixon's Family Assistance Plan

President Nixon's proposed Family Assistance Plan would have guaranteed a monthly income of $1,600 for a family of four in 1969. That amount would have had a purchasing power of $9,510 per month ($114,120 per year) in 2010. By contrast, the average family of four on welfare in 2010 received a cash payment of just $412 per month ($4,944 per year) from the federal government via Temporary Assistance for Needy Families.

Civil rights issues proved trickier, as Nixon sought to pursue racial equality while still shoring up his position among southern whites and blue-collar white workers. Rather than championing integration, Nixon offered economic encouragements to African Americans by supporting minority-owned businesses and employment initiatives. His administration expanded a Johnson-era program to push companies that contracted with the federal government to employ black and Hispanic workers. Nixon's Revised Philadelphia Plan, which set goals for minority hiring by federal building contractors in Philadelphia in 1969, marked an early milestone in the history of affirmative action. However, when the white ethnic workers he was trying to woo began protesting the Philadelphia Plan, Nixon was quick to compromise and make the hiring guidelines voluntary.

The administration's most liberal policy decisions related to the environment. Mindful of rising public concern over public health hazards and long-term ecological deterioration, Nixon signed the National Environmental Policy Act (1969), the Clean Air Act Extension (1970), and the Environmental Protection Act (1970). Together these landmark laws mandated environmental impact statements for public projects, set new pollution standards, authorized citizen suits against polluters, and created a major federal agency for environmental issues. To protect against smaller-scale environmental dangers, Nixon also signed the Occupational Safety and Health Act (1970), which he called "one of the most important

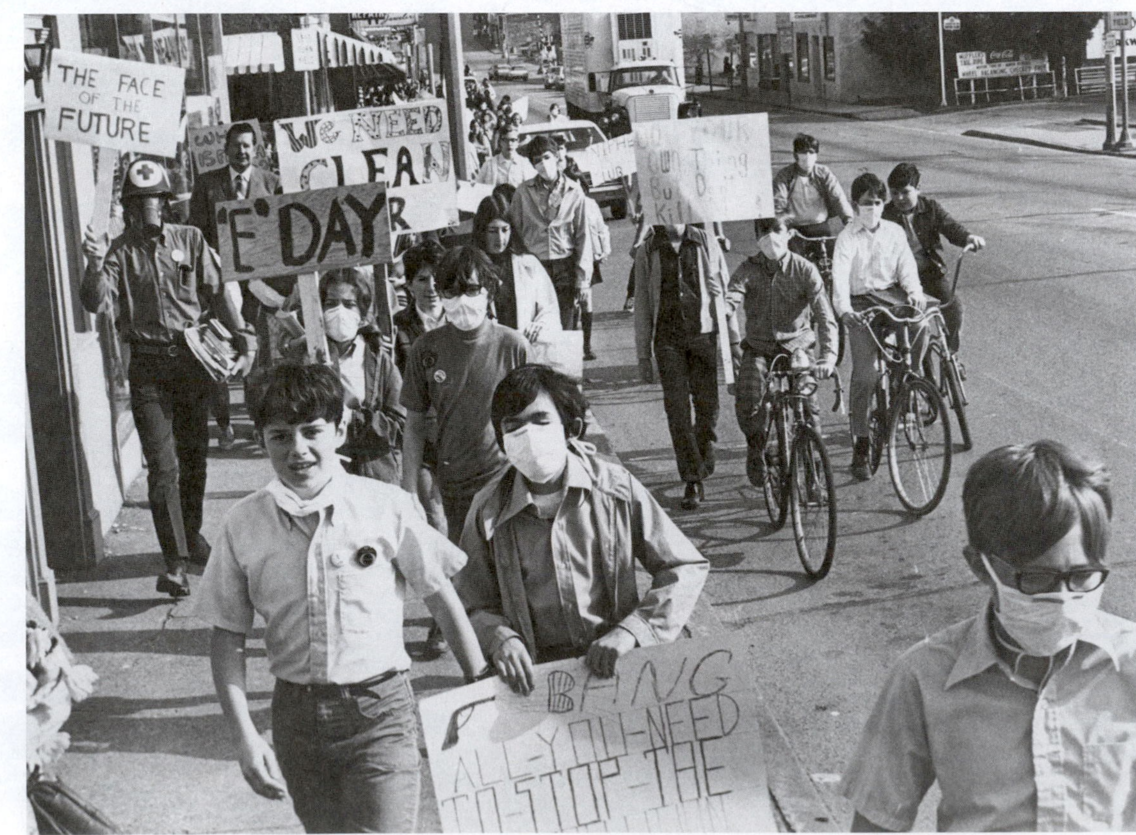

The First Earth Day. Junior high school students march through a suburban business district outside St. Louis on April 22, 1970. Earth Day celebrations drew some twenty million participants across the country that year in a collective demonstration of concern for the planet's fragility. Democrats, liberals, and environmental activists dominated the public events of the day, and President Nixon declined to attend. Nonetheless, he announced through an aide that he would be following the festivities, and he pledged his support to an antipollution campaign.

pieces of legislation . . . ever passed by the Congress." Though some Republicans resented federal regulation of workplace conditions and the bureaucracy it created, occupational safety was a popular issue among workers—a crucial segment of Nixon's new political coalition.

By far the biggest challenge Nixon faced as head of a growing federal government came from the nation's economic woes. Nixon entered office during a period of increased industrial competition from Japan and Western Europe and rising international prices for raw materials, especially oil (see Energy Shocks and the Global Economy, below). He also inherited a federal deficit that had escalated along with the costly war in Vietnam. Both factors contributed to a spike in inflation, which approached 6 percent by 1970 and hurt the Republicans in the midterm elections that year. Americans also worried about the declining demand for their manufactured goods. For the first year since 1893, the United States imported more than it exported in 1971.

That year, Nixon made two major economic moves. First, he attacked inflation by ordering a ninety-day freeze on wages and prices, after which he set up wage and price guidelines that would be administered by a federal price board. **Wage and price controls** were generally popular, but they poisoned Nixon's relations with the labor movement. Further, though they curbed inflation temporarily, prices skyrocketed again soon after. Nixon's other initiative was to take the United States off the gold standard, decoupling the dollar from the value of gold and thereby dismantling the Bretton Woods system that had regulated the currencies of industrial nations since the end of World War II (see Chapter 25). This strategy lowered the value of the dollar, which Nixon hoped would reverse the trade deficit, but it also created a volatile international currency market. Throughout his presidency, Nixon struggled to tame the economy, wavering between spending and cutting and toggling between lowering interest rates to spur growth and cutting them to check inflation.

HENRY KISSINGER, REALISM, AND DÉTENTE

The nation's economic troubles pointed increasingly toward global developments and international relations, areas where Nixon's ambitions and interests lay. Kissinger, who served in Nixon's first term as national security adviser, guided Nixon away from hard-line Cold War positions. Eager to avoid further disastrous entanglements like Vietnam and to reduce the costs and dangers of a nuclear arms race, Kissinger promoted a new foreign-policy approach. Kissinger's realism, as it was sometimes called, deemphasized ideological saber-rattling in favor of quiet negotiations and manipulations designed to preserve a balance of international power in an increasingly multipower world and to promote the United States' practical political interests around the globe.

Most significantly, the new approach featured a softer stance toward the USSR. Kissinger believed that by easing tensions with its traditional enemy—a policy known as **détente,** from the French word for relaxation—Americans could achieve more of their political goals without war and the Soviets could be induced to push the North Vietnamese to the bargaining table. The Soviet Union had its own motivations for pursuing such a course, but Nixon added pressure by making overtures to communist China, a country the United States had refused to recognize. After dispatching Kissinger on a secret mission to make arrangements, Nixon traveled to Beijing in February 1972, becoming the first sitting U.S. president to visit the Chinese mainland. Protected by his long-standing anticommunist credentials from political attacks at home, Nixon initiated diplomatic exchanges with the People's Republic of China and paved the way for Mao Zedong's government to join the United Nations.

By 1972, China, the United States, and the Soviet Union were each worried about the prospects of closer ties between the other two. Soviet premier Leonid Brezhnev responded to Nixon's China trip by inviting the president to Moscow, where the two leaders signed an arms limitation treaty, SALT I, that had been under negotiation since the start of Nixon's presidency. Both sides agreed not to deploy any nuclear missiles exceeding existing levels and pledged further arms reduction talks. Nixon failed, however, to leverage this new relationship to end the Vietnam War.

Once tensions with the Soviet Union and China eased, Nixon's foreign policy entailed avoiding direct military conflicts elsewhere and choosing allies based on practical rather than ideological considerations. Criticized both by conservatives for abandoning the fight against communism and by liberals for supporting autocratic regimes, Kissinger continued to support quiet interventions and covert operations to prop up any government that seemed friendly to an immediate American interest. The United States relied on regional allies like Iran, Israel, Zaire, South Africa, and Japan to help stop the spread of communism but did not interfere in the domestic affairs of friendly nations. When a socialist government came to power in Chile in 1970, however, Nixon's new posture was tested. Fearing communism's spread to the rest of Latin America, Nixon authorized the CIA to help undermine the democratically elected regime of Salvador Allende and had Kissinger funnel arms to Allende's opponents. Three years later, Augusto Pinochet seized power in Chile in a military coup. Pinochet's brutal dictatorship would last for two decades, far longer than the U.S. administration that had helped bring it about.

REPUBLICAN TRIUMPH, REPUBLICAN DISGRACE

Nixon stood for reelection in 1972 as a powerful incumbent with a promising strategy for expanding his political base. But he was not one to leave things to chance, and his unscrupulous actions during the campaign precipitated a complex chain of events that would stun the nation, lead to his downfall, and remake American politics.

THE LANDSLIDE ELECTION OF 1972

Despite the troubled economy and his failure to end the Vietnam War, Nixon enjoyed strong support. He seemed to be taking steps to deal with the nation's problems. Even if some of those steps (such as invading Cambodia and freezing wages) outraged or antagonized large constituencies, he maintained confidence that his basic strategy—running against the values of the 1960s counterculture and social movements while not dismantling any of the political programs of the Great Society—would solidify his new majority. His biggest concern was the prospect of facing another third-party candidacy of George C. Wallace, who was running for president again in the Democratic primaries. That threat was eliminated on May 15, 1972, however. Arthur Bremer, who had originally planned to assassinate Nixon as a way of demonstrating his manhood to the world, settled instead for shooting Wallace at a Maryland shopping center. The next day, Wallace won the Maryland and Michigan primaries, but he was paralyzed from the waist down and unable to continue his campaign.

The Democrats had grounds for optimism as well, especially when the Twenty-sixth Amendment lowered the voting age from twenty-one to eighteen in 1970. Nixon tried to appeal to these new voters by narrowing and then ending the draft, but Democrats hoped that an influx of young men and women into the political process would favor a liberal and more idealistic alternative to the president. Young, idealistic voters did in fact play a significant role in the campaign, but mostly in helping to pick the Democratic nominee, a development that wound up playing into the incumbent's hands.

From Nixon's perspective, the more liberal an opponent, the better, since a left-leaning Democratic nominee would enable him both to claim the center and sharpen his message about cultural values. Nixon's campaign organization, the Committee to Re-elect the President (CREEP), sought to undermine the candidacies of more centrist Democratic hopefuls, especially the presumed frontrunner, Maine senator Edmund Muskie. In the New Hampshire primary, Nixon operatives phoned voters at uncivilized hours, pretending to be Muskie campaign volunteers from Harlem. CREEP also forged a letter to a New Hampshire newspaper reporting that a Muskie staffer had used the term *Canuck* to disparage Americans of French-Canadian descent. When Muskie's margin of victory in New Hampshire fell far short of expectations, many Democrats began looking elsewhere for a candidate. Liberal South Dakota senator George McGovern was well positioned to benefit from Muskie's problems, more democratic nomination rules, and the Twenty-sixth Amendment. With Wallace drawing conservative votes away from centrist candidates earlier in the campaign, McGovern was able to secure the nomination.

McGovern was the liberal opponent of Nixon's dreams. The South Dakotan's support for racial integration and amnesty for draft evaders would not go down well with white voters in the South. Further, although McGovern had the

Conservative Working-Class Hero. Archie Bunker, played by the very liberal actor Carroll O'Connor, became a cultural icon on the hit television series *All in the Family*, which ranked number one in the Nielsen viewership ratings from 1971 to 1976. Bunker was designed by the show's writers to expose the clueless prejudices of an older generation, but he came to symbolize blue-collar support for President Nixon.

most pro-labor voting record of any major-party candidate in U.S. history, blue-collar voters did not identify with him or his followers. At the contentious Democratic convention in Miami that summer, one labor leader complained of seeing "too much hair and not enough cigars." During the roll-call vote, a few conservative delegates protested by casting their ballots for Archie Bunker, the bigoted white protagonist of the television sitcom *All in the Family* (1971–1979), who had become a spokesman for blue-collar values in the culture wars of the 1970s. Republicans saw their opportunity. At Nixon's instigation, their party platform abandoned its traditional hostility to labor unions, instead praising them for "advancing the well-being not only of their members but also of our entire free-enterprise system." The AFL-CIO decided to sit out the election.

The remaining challenge for Nixon's reelection bid was the ongoing war in Vietnam. In the hopes of ending the conflict in time for the vote, Nixon changed his position that North Vietnamese troops would have to leave the south as a condition of any peace agreement. Armed with this major concession, Kissinger met secretly with North Vietnamese foreign secretary Le Duc Tho in Paris to negotiate a cease-fire. On October 26, less than two weeks before election day, they reached a tentative accord. Nixon could now tell the American public that "peace is at hand." (Shortly after the election, the Kissinger-Tho agreement fell apart and the war continued.)

Nixon's margin in the electoral college was greater than that of any president in U.S. history. He beat McGovern in forty-nine of fifty states, losing only in Massachusetts and the heavily African American District of Columbia. No Republican had ever swept the South, and this election marked the culmination of a major realignment among white southern voters. Many in Nixon's inner circle also interpreted the results as a vindication of the Republicans' strategy of appealing to working-class white ethnics. As Patrick Buchanan, the aide who had coined the phrase "silent majority," argued, the election was a decisive battle in a cultural civil war, and it signaled "a victory of 'Middle America' over the celebrants of Woodstock Nation."

SCANDAL AND RESIGNATION

Nixon had not run his campaign like an incumbent cruising toward a landslide reelection. CREEP had aggressively raised millions of dollars in campaign gifts, including illegal contributions from major corporations. It had also unleashed an array of stealthy maneuvers designed to eliminate any possibility of an upset. One of those maneuvers backfired on an unimaginable scale. In June 1972, five men were caught breaking in to the Democratic National Committee headquarters in the Watergate apartment complex in Washington. Administration officials categorically denied any involvement in what they dismissed as a "third-rate burglary attempt." Nonetheless, the men arrested turned out to have connections to CREEP, and an FBI investigation began ferreting out evidence suggesting that high-ranking figures in the Nixon campaign had ordered the break-in. Reporters for the *Washington Post*, relying on an anonymous informant nicknamed Deep Throat after the popular pornographic movie, uncovered some of these links after the election—and thereby stoked the flames of a major political scandal.

The following year, when the Watergate burglars were brought to trial, things took a bad turn for Nixon. Just prior to sentencing, defendant James McCord decided to cooperate with the prosecution and wrote a letter to the judge implicating Nixon administration officials in both the break-in and the cover-up. One of the officials fingered by McCord, White House counsel John Dean, broke ranks as well, and a chain of accusations now led all the way up the administration's ladder.

From May to August 1973, mounting public interest in the scandal focused on the U.S. Senate, where a Select Committee on Presidential Campaign Activities was investigating the Watergate incident. The Senate was controlled by Democrats, who had every motivation to expose the Nixon administration, but even Republicans were shocked by the committee's disclosures. Two disturbing pictures emerged over the summer. First, the Watergate break-in fit into a larger pattern of brazen and illegal campaign activities. Second, Nixon aides had engaged in an elaborate and concerted attempt to obstruct justice and impede the Watergate investigation. In a decade when Americans spent unprecedented amounts of time in front of their televisions (see Table 29.1), the three major television networks devoted an average of five hours of broadcast time to the hearings during their first five days, while PBS aired complete video recordings of the daily proceedings every evening. A third-rate burglary attempt had become a national obsession.

As the revelations multiplied and more members of his administration were implicated, Nixon maintained his personal innocence. Denying prior knowledge of the break-in or any connection to the cover-up, he famously repeated that he was "not a crook," even as the ground beneath him was crumbling. Testimony before the Senate revealed that White House conversations were meticulously recorded, and investigators now demanded the tapes. Nixon refused, and when the special independent prosecutor he had appointed to deal with Watergate subpoenaed the tapes in October 1973, the president ordered Attorney General Elliot Richardson to fire the prosecutor. Richardson resigned in protest, as did his deputy. Solicitor General Robert Bork, as third in command, agreed to do Nixon's bidding.

These chaotic events, dubbed the Saturday Night Massacre, inflicted heavy political damage. A new special prosecutor picked up where his predecessor had left off. In early August 1974, after a unanimous Supreme Court rejected Nixon's argument that "executive privilege" entitled him to withhold the tapes, the recorded conversations revealed conclusively that Nixon had been fully involved in the cover-up from the beginning.

Even before the final release of the unedited tapes, the House Judiciary Committee had initiated impeachment proceedings against the president. Earlier in the process, many Democrats in Congress would have been reluctant to push for Nixon's resignation, out of fear that the succession of Vice President Spiro Agnew, the administration's conservative attack dog, would be

TABLE 29.1 TELEVISION VIEWERSHIP

Americans spent progressively more time in front of the television set between 1950 and 1985. The figures for the 1970s are especially significant because, prior to the proliferation of cable broadcasting, with its more diverse programming, television broadcasting was still controlled by three major national networks. In the 1970s, televised news, series, and specials dominated the collective culture of the United States.

Year	Average Viewing Time per Day
1950	4 hr. 35 min.
1955	4 hr. 51 min.
1960	5 hr. 6 min.
1965	5 hr. 29 min.
1970	5 hr. 56 min.
1975	6 hr. 7 min.
1980	6 hr. 36 min.
1985	7 hr. 10 min.
1990	6 hr. 53 min.

far worse than leaving a politically hobbled Nixon in office. In October 1973, however, Agnew himself resigned after pleading no contest to tax-evasion charges as part of a plea bargain to avoid conviction on more serious counts of accepting bribes. Nixon appointed the less controversial and more politically moderate Gerald Ford to replace Agnew, a move that effectively cleared a path for Nixon's own departure.

Facing certain impeachment and likely removal from office, Nixon announced his resignation on August 8, becoming the only American president to leave office alive before the end of his term. He had left a powerful stamp on U.S. foreign policy and a host of new domestic initiatives. His more immediate legacy, however, was broad cynicism about crooked politicians and deep disapproval of the Republican Party. In the November 1974 elections, Democrats added significantly to their majorities in both houses of Congress.

GERALD FORD: UNELECTED PRESIDENT

Seven other sitting vice presidents had succeeded to the presidency before Gerald Ford, but Ford was the first to become chief executive without having been elected as vice president. He inherited both an economy under stress and the tarnished reputation of the Nixon administration (see Interpreting the Sources: Chevy Chase as Gerald Ford on *Saturday Night Live.*)

Whatever hopes Ford might have had to divest himself of the Watergate legacy were extinguished when he issued a presidential pardon to former president Nixon for crimes committed in office. Ford hoped to steer the nation past the scandal and avoid the divisive spectacle of a protracted court trial, but most Americans wondered whether Nixon and Ford had struck a deal. Seven high-ranking Nixon aides served prison time for their role in Watergate, including former attorney general John Mitchell, White House chief of staff H. R. Haldeman, and Charles Colson, the leading architect of the Republicans' blue-collar strategy. Nixon himself, however, was now immune from prosecution.

Ford directed most of his energies to tackling the troubled economy (see Recession and Urban Crisis, below). He also had to deal with the war in Indochina, which had not ended in 1972 despite Nixon and Kissinger's preelection assurances. The South Vietnamese had scuttled the cease-fire in December 1972 by insisting on the withdrawal of North Vietnamese troops, and the United States responded by stepping up its aerial assault. A peace treaty was finally signed in Paris in January 1973, ending the American invasion of the region. However, with North Vietnamese forces remaining in the South, the war was far from over.

After more than a year of devastating battles between the two sides, North Vietnam launched a major invasion in March 1975, and Congress refused South Vietnamese appeals for support. American embassy officials in Saigon evacuated the country just before communist forces reached the capital. The fall of Saigon in April 1975 marked the end of the Vietnam War and the larger Indochina conflict, with all of Vietnam now firmly under communist control. A month later came another blow in the region, as forces from the Cambodian Khmer Rouge (the communist party that had assumed power earlier in the year) boarded the U.S. ship *Mayaguez* and took its crew hostage. Henry Kissinger, who had remained in Ford's White House as secretary of state, thought the situation required a demonstration of power rather than diplomatic finesse, and consequently the president ordered both a rescue operation and renewed bombing of Cambodia. The *Mayaguez* rescue succeeded in freeing the ship and its crew but lost more lives than it saved.

Ford also faced some intense personal scares while in office. In two separate incidents in 1975, just three weeks apart, someone tried to kill him. On September 5 in Sacramento, Lynette "Squeaky" Fromme pointed a loaded pistol at the president. Fromme was a member of the Manson Family cult, a criminal group implicated in several California murders. Although there was no bullet in the firing chamber when a Secret Service agent wrested the gun from her hands, Fromme was sentenced to life imprisonment for attempted assassination. Seventeen days later in San Francisco, Sara Jane Moore (who had no connection to Fromme or the Manson group) managed to fire a shot at Ford, but a bystander intervened and the bullet struck a wall, ricocheted off the curb, and hit a taxi driver in the groin. The two unsuccessful assassination

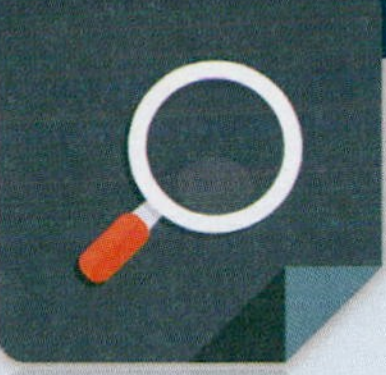

INTERPRETING THE SOURCES

Chevy Chase as Gerald Ford on Saturday Night Live

Entering the White House under the cloud of Watergate and amid an economic downturn, Gerald Ford also had the misfortune of being targeted for parody by a new sketch comedy show that premiered in 1975. Airing on Saturdays at 11:30 p.m., *NBC's Saturday Night* (renamed *Saturday Night Live* a year later) would establish a tradition of impersonating and caricaturing politicians, from Ford to Bill Clinton to Sarah Palin and beyond. On November 8, in the show's fourth episode, comedian Chevy Chase introduced his slapstick impression of the president tripping over the stage. The routine, which Chase repeated regularly over the next year, alluded to an oft-broadcast incident from May 1975 when Ford slipped in Austria while exiting Air Force One. Chase reinforced a popular perception of Ford—an athletic man who had been a star football player—as physically clumsy.

Below is a photograph of Chase as Ford, along with an excerpt from one of his sketches.

"Operation Stumblebum"

FORD: [looks around the Oval Office] I just don't see what's so awful about this room, personally.

WHITE HOUSE PRESS SECRETARY: No, Sir, *Oval*. It's the *Oval* Office, sir.

FORD: Ah!

PRESS SECRETARY: Not awful, Oval—round.

REPORTER: Mr. President: Peter Aaron, *Washington Gazette*.

FORD: Yes, Mr. Aaron.

REPORTER: Mr. President, what is your reaction to the recent allegations of CIA activities in Italy?

FORD: [gets his sleeve caught in the microphones]

PRESS SECRETARY: I think what the president is trying to say is— [Chase leans forward and hits his head on the podium]

FORD: No problem! No problem! I'd be happy— [slips and falls on the ground]

Explore the Sources

1. What is the connection between physical and mental clumsiness in "Operation Stumblebum"?
2. How might impressions of politicians on popular comedy shows compete with these figures' appearances in news broadcasts, press conferences, and presidential debates in shaping public opinion?
3. Like other vice presidents who succeeded to office, Ford had been called an "accidental president." How did jokes about his clumsiness alter the meaning of that phrase—or reinforce its implications?

attempts appeared unrelated to Ford's low popularity, but they dramatized the rising violence and chaos that accompanied his tenure.

THE ELECTION OF 1976

President Ford faced the election of 1976 with all the disadvantages of incumbency and few of the benefits. He was held responsible for the nation's hard times and, on account of the Nixon pardon, was tarred with the brush of Watergate. Further, unlike most presidential bids for a second term, his candidacy put Ford on the national ballot for the first time.

Ford fended off a surprisingly serious challenge from the party's right wing in the person of former California governor (and movie actor) Ronald Reagan and limped toward renomination. Democratic officials and voters, eyeing an opportunity and eager not to repeat the mistakes of 1972, rallied around a relatively unknown governor, James (Jimmy) Carter of Georgia. Carter's lack of Washington experience and connections played as an advantage in the wake of Watergate. As a devout, born-again Christian, white southerner, Carter moreover was far less vulnerable to the Republican political strategy that Nixon had introduced.

Still, as November approached, polls showed the two candidates locked in a close battle. Ford appeared to hurt himself in televised debates late in the campaign, especially when he tried to insist that the Soviet Union did not exert political domination over Eastern Europe. On election day, Carter edged out Ford 50–48 percent in the popular vote and prevailed in the electoral college by a margin of 297–240, mostly by capturing all but one of the former Confederate states that Nixon had won in the two previous presidential contests. Ford's brief and unexpected stay in the White House had come to an end.

RECESSION AND URBAN CRISIS

A disturbing set of economic developments preoccupied the presidencies of all three men who occupied the White House during the 1970s. International financial pressures, ballooning inflation, the loss of union jobs, and shrinkage in American productivity led to the most severe economic crisis since the Great Depression. As Americans suffered a drop in their standard of living, the once-proud cities of the Northeast, especially New York, became symbols of the crime, grime, and corruption that accompanied—and highlighted—the nation's economic decline.

ENERGY SHOCKS AND THE GLOBAL ECONOMY

By the 1970s, Americans had come to depend on ever-increasing quantities of oil. Although the United States remained the world's largest oil producer in 1970, foreign production had risen dramatically in recent years, especially in the Middle East. The increased oil supply kept prices low and encouraged consumer appetites and habits in Europe, Japan, and the United States. Meanwhile, in 1960, oil-rich nations in the developing world, led by Saudi Arabia and Venezuela, had formed the Organization of the Petroleum Exporting Countries (OPEC) in an effort to exert controls on prices.

After Nixon abandoned the gold standard in 1971, OPEC nations started pegging the price of petroleum to the value of gold rather than to the depreciating U.S. dollar. This shift effectively raised costs for American consumers. Around the same time, U.S. oil demand rose sharply, more than doubling between 1965 and 1973, and domestic production (now diminished by environmental reforms that limited coal as an alternative energy resource) failed to keep pace, leaving the nation dependent on foreign imports and vulnerable to OPEC. By the fall of 1973, the price of oil was climbing steeply.

Then, in October 1973, war broke out in the Middle East when Egyptian and Syrian forces launched a surprise attack against Israel on the Jewish holy day of Yom Kippur. The war threatened to become another dangerous proxy conflict between the Soviet Union, which was resupplying Egypt and Syria, and the United States, which was supporting Israel. For the first time since the Cuban missile crisis, U.S. forces were put on a worldwide nuclear alert. A nuclear showdown was averted, but Arab oil exporters brought the Yom Kippur War to American shores in a new way. By imposing an embargo on sales to the United States, oil producers radically diminished the supply to American markets. As the price of a barrel of crude oil consequently—and suddenly—quadrupled, the United States faced its first national **energy crisis.**

The war lasted less than three weeks, as Israel survived an invasion from Egypt and launched counteroffensives into both

Ground to a Halt. Cars in Portland, Oregon, line up for gas during the energy crisis. Gas rationing programs permitted drivers to purchase fuel only on alternate days. On even dates, only cars with license plates ending in even digits could buy gas, and the opposite was true on odd dates.

Syria and Egypt. However, the embargo, which remained in place until March 17, 1974, had proven effective. Mindful of its impact, Nixon and Kissinger pressured Israel to accept a cease-fire rather than press its advantage. The crisis had demonstrated the vulnerability of the United States to political pressures from the global energy economy.

Back home, the fallout from the energy crisis continued to rain down for the embargo's duration. Fifteen states and the District of Columbia instituted gas rationing, and in some places, service stations simply stopped selling gasoline. To encourage conservation, Congress introduced a national speed limit of fifty-five miles per hour on interstate highways and imposed daylight saving time for all of 1974. That same year, NASCAR decided to reduce the distances of all auto races by 10 percent. Responding to powerful pressures from an agitated populace, Congress took more aggressive measures, passing a mandatory fuel allocation bill to press large U.S. oil companies to lower their prices and to force them to sell to independent refiners and distributors. Although it was not the only symptom of a global economic downturn, the energy crisis introduced those Americans who had known only growth and prosperity to the concept of a shortage. It also threatened, according to a leading pollster who had surveyed American attitudes on the subject, to produce "social instability of the magnitude of the depression."

STAGFLATION AND DEINDUSTRIALIZATION

The uptick in energy prices quickly undid any check on inflation from wage and price controls or other government actions. The annual inflation rate hit 6.2 percent in 1973 (almost twice the previous year's level), and in 1974 it rose to an astonishing 11 percent, the highest figure in decades. Ordinarily, inflation accompanied economic growth and full or high employment, but the skyrocketing inflation of the 1970s coincided with a sluggish economy and high jobless figures in both the United States and Western Europe. U.S. unemployment rates jumped from 3.5 percent in 1969 to an annual high of 8.5 percent in 1975. Further, after decades of growth, the value of the gross domestic product began to drop around mid-decade. To describe this unusual combination of higher consumer prices and economic stagnation, economists coined the term **stagflation.**

National rates of economic misery masked the fact that certain regions and populations were hit much harder than others. Job losses were heaviest in the manufacturing sectors of the Northeast and Midwest, the same places that suffered most from mushrooming energy prices. These regions—economic powerhouses in earlier periods—bore the brunt of the United States' decline as an industrial manufacturer in the face of foreign competition. The impact of deindustrialization on older U.S. cities during this era was staggering. Between 1967 and 1987, manufacturing jobs in Philadelphia dropped by 64 percent, in Chicago by 60 percent, and in New York by 58 percent. Many jobs simply disappeared as factories shut down or relocated to other parts of the world. At the same time, employment was migrating to other sectors of the economy, such as service work. Jobs were also drawn to warmer parts of the country, especially southern and western states where right-to-work laws lowered labor costs by prohibiting collective bargaining contracts that required a company to hire union members.

U.S. industrial decline thinned the ranks of unions and weakened the labor movement, which was in turn less able to deliver concrete benefits to members. Organized labor made significant gains in the public sector, however, where unions negotiated not with private employers but with the government. From 1955 to 1975, union membership in the public sector leaped by 1,000 percent, and the American Federation of State, County, and Municipal Employees (AFSCME) became the fastest-growing union under the AFL-CIO umbrella. States began rescinding laws that barred public employees from going on strike. President Nixon, who had taken a conciliatory stance toward striking postal workers and air traffic controllers in 1970, also signed a 1974 law that protected the hours and wages of government employees at the state and local levels.

By 1975, when a new, Democrat-dominated Congress convened, the prospects looked good for passage of a sweeping law that would extend to government workers the union rights guaranteed to those in the private sector under the Wagner Act (see Chapter 24). As the economic crisis stripped states and municipalities of their tax bases, however, public unions lost ground. In the political arena, labor leaders focused on legislation designed to achieve full employment, but as long as American businesses and consumers were preoccupied with inflation, labor drew minimal support for its program.

Despite the sluggish national economy, certain areas experienced growth during the period. Migration to the Sunbelt fueled building there, and cities like Phoenix, San Jose, and Las Vegas emerged as major metropolitan areas. In addition, the 1970s was a time of innovation in American business and technology. Bar codes, in vitro fertilization, home computers, e-mail, VHS recorders, CAT scans, MRIs, and ultrasound all made their first appearances during this decade. Most Americans experienced the 1970s nonetheless as a time of depleted resources, declining personal wealth, and diminishing economic expectations.

URBAN DECLINE, URBAN DYSTOPIA

Amid the general economic misery, northeastern and midwestern cities became notorious sites of poverty, crime, racial conflict, population loss, and fiscal crisis. The decline of traditional urban centers reflected several global and local factors, including the international narcotics trade and white flight, but mostly it underscored the nation's larger economic changes and challenges. Film, television, and news media paid unprecedented attention to urban America, and specifically to New York, the largest U.S. city, to represent the nation's troubles in the 1970s.

Crime was an especially disturbing symptom and symbol of the nation's economic distress, and industrial cities became particularly dangerous places. Responding to a Justice Department survey, thirty-seven million Americans (representing one-quarter of the nation's households) reported having been victims of rape, robbery, assault, burglary, larceny, or car theft in 1973. By mid-decade, residents of U.S. cities ranked crime as a much bigger concern than either inflation or unemployment. Fear of crime prompted many Americans to arm themselves. Between 1964 and 1981, membership in the National Rifle Association climbed more than 300 percent.

Much of the growth in gun ownership took place outside city bounds, but media images of urban America in the 1970s reinforced the idea that one needed weapons to survive in the big city. Michael Winner's film *Death Wish* (1974) starred Charles Bronson as a New York architect whose wife is killed and whose daughter is raped by local thugs. Bronson's character visits Arizona on business, where he is taken to a shooting range and given a handgun. Returning home, he becomes an urban vigilante, bringing frontier justice to the New York subways. Without universally endorsing the vigilantism of *Death Wish*, many other popular films set in New York during the period, including *Shaft* (1971), *Taxi Driver* (1976), and *Marathon Man* (1976), depicted a city where armed men needed to take the law into their own hands. As these and other contemporary movies—such as *The French Connection* (1971), *Serpico* (1973), and *Dog Day Afternoon* (1975)—suggested, part of the problem was that law enforcement agencies had lost or ceded control of American cities, a phenomenon publicized in New York by shocking disclosures of police corruption in the Knapp Commission hearings of 1971.

Popular fascination with New York as a dystopia, a symbol of everything negative in American society, extended beyond film. Television sitcoms showed renewed interest in urban life at the moment when cities appeared to be dysfunctional and in decline. At the start of the decade, networks canceled four of the most popular shows of the 1960s, all with rural settings: *Green Acres*, *Mayberry RFD*, *The Beverly Hillbillies*, and *Petticoat Junction*. In their place arose new comedies about the modern city. Norman Lear and Bud Yorkin produced comedies (*All in the Family*, *Sanford and Son*, *Maude*, *Good Times*, *The Jeffersons*) that portrayed urban families and focused on contemporary issues of race relations, class identity, and gender politics. Around the same time, MTM Enterprises introduced a new brand of urban workplace comedy—beginning with *The Mary Tyler Moore Show* and *The Bob Newhart Show* and moving to *Barney Miller* and *Taxi*—that

Brand-New Twins. The World Trade Center towers, which opened in 1972 and 1973, symbolized New York City's aspirations for renewed grandeur in an age of global finance. At first, the towers seemed to be a failure, sustaining high vacancy rates and quickly being eclipsed in height by Chicago's Sears Tower. By 2001, when the twin towers were destroyed by terrorists and mourned by the American populace, the buildings' status both as icons of New York prosperity and as symbolic links between the city and the nation had been cemented.

Disco Demolition Night at Chicago's Comiskey Park, July 12, 1979. Responding to a local radio station's promotion, approximately 90,000 people showed up at Comiskey, a 52,000-seat baseball stadium. They had been lured by the promise that their disco records would be exploded on field between games of a doubleheader. Participants stormed the field, lit fires, rioted, and tore up the playing area, forcing the White Sox to forfeit the second game. The broader antidisco backlash that inspired the event mocked the music as formulaic and commercialized, but distaste for disco often represented a rejection of an effeminate musical genre associated with gay culture and urban life.

featured characters who did not live in nuclear family units. Urban sitcoms of the economic crisis era, especially those set in New York, emphasized crime, dirt, and social conflict rather than cosmopolitan glamour.

New York promoted itself as a stage for entertainment, in part as a way of boosting business during a time of fiscal crisis. Mayor John Lindsay, who presided over the city from 1966 through 1973, created the Mayor's Office of Film, Theater, and Broadcasting at the start of his first term, and his efforts helped set off a boom in television and film production in New York. As the city lost thousands of manufacturing jobs annually, its entertainment industry thrived, though not enough to balance the budget. By 1975, New York City stood at the brink of municipal bankruptcy and looked to Washington for aid. When President Ford initially vowed to veto any congressional bailout of the nation's largest city, the tabloid New York *Daily News* fabricated a quotation for an infamous headline: "Ford to New York: Drop Dead." The headline might have hurt Ford's electoral prospects in New York (Jimmy Carter would win the state in the election a year later), but the federal government's reluctance to come to the city's aid reflected a troubled relationship between American society and its urban problems.

In the end, however, Ford and the nation did not let New York drop dead. Indeed, federal—and state—aid helped the city bail out of its budget crisis. As a condition of the financial relief, New York's municipal priorities were set by bankers who were removed from the electoral process. Thereafter, an Emergency Financial Control Board would review all city contracts and impose austerity measures on city services. In the second half of the decade, a new, rebranded city had embarked on its road to economic recovery. A 1977 "I Love New York" campaign launched a process of restoring the city's wounded pride, closing its commercial sex districts, adding police, and cultivating international tourism and financial investment.

NEW URBAN MUSIC

Various new musical forms emerged from American cities during this period of industrial decline and economic frustration. In abandoned factories and warehouses in the Northeast, discotheques attracted patrons with funk and soul-influenced dance music. Disco, as the music was called, stressed personal liberation and flashy clothing statements rather than social protest, thereby providing more ammunition for those who criticized 1970s culture as narcissistic. But disco music also brought pleasure to a diverse urban populace. Originating in black and gay music venues in the early 1970s, disco became an integrating force in American urban nightlife by the decade's end. Like many hit films of the times, the disco celebration *Saturday Night Fever* (1977) features an Italian working-class hero, but dancing in that movie connects men and women of different classes and races, a hallmark of the disco era.

Around the same time, block parties among African American and Latino New Yorkers introduced hip hop music, in which DJs isolated and replayed portions of popular funk, soul, and disco songs on turntables and MCs rapped over the music. Some music historians argue that stereo equipment looted during the 1977 New York blackout helped spread hip hop techniques and parties (see States of Emergency: The New York City Blackout of 1977). In 1979, The Sugar Hill Gang's "Rapper's Delight," a song lasting close to fifteen minutes, popularized the genre for listeners across the country.

STATES OF EMERGENCY

The New York City Blackout of 1977

Through much of the twentieth century, New York City's bright electric lights distinguished nighttime in the United States' largest city, enhancing the city's claims to metropolitan grandeur and captivating the national imagination. On the evening of July 13, 1977, however, the city went suddenly and frighteningly dark. This was not the first time the lights went out in New York. Twelve years earlier, a regional blackout had shut down power through much of the Northeast. But the 1977 blackout was limited to New York City, and it struck during an economic downturn, at the end of a scorching summer day, when New Yorkers were reeling from the unsolved and ongoing crimes of a notorious serial killer. Unlike the 1965 blackout, whose occurrence at dusk gave residents some daylight time to prepare for the night ahead, the 1977 outage had an immediate visual impact.

Dark Skyline. Against this backdrop, a prolonged riot of looting and arson engulfed much of the city, unlike anything that New York had experienced since the draft riots of the Civil War—which coincidentally had begun on the exact same date 114 years earlier.

The blackout was triggered by lightning strikes that tripped breakers and downed transmission lines at the plants of Con Edison, New York's power provider. Defective equipment and inadequate responses by the power company exacerbated the situation, and by 9:37 p.m. almost the entire city was without electricity, which was not restored until late the next day. What caused the crime spree that ensued is harder to determine. Looting erupted in thirty-one different neighborhoods throughout the city, but Brooklyn, New York's most populous borough, felt the heaviest impact. In Brooklyn's Bushwick neighborhood, fires consumed whole blocks. Bushwick had been a middle-class area in the 1950s, but white flight, the decline of the Brooklyn Navy Yard, and the razing of single-family housing to make room for new housing projects had turned it into one of the city's poorest districts. By 1977, 80 percent of Bushwick residents were unemployed and the neighborhood had the highest infant mortality rate in the city. With the power down and police and firefighting services strained, desperate and angry residents found both an opportunity to steal and an outlet for their rage.

When the lights finally came back on, New Yorkers tallied up the heavy toll: stores destroyed, buildings burned to the ground, 4,500 individuals arrested (most of them in a single mass sweep), and more than $300 million in damage. City officials blamed Con Edison officials, who in turn called the outage an act of God and blamed the city for the poverty that lay at the root of the rioting. New York voters rejected incumbent mayor Abe Beame four months later, electing tough-on-crime candidate Ed Koch. To the rest of the country, viewing darkened skylines and burning houses on the evening news, the events of July 13–14, 1977, seemed to confirm what so many headlines, television shows, and movies had suggested: The great metropolis had declined.

Think About It

1. Why might a power outage have encouraged angry residents to riot and loot?
2. How did the fact that the 1977 blackout affected New York alone, rather than the larger region, contribute to the meaning of the event?

American punk rock also originated during the urban crisis years of the 1970s, but it appealed primarily to young white listeners. Bands like the Ramones, who hailed from Queens, New York, stripped 1970s rock music of its heavy production and instrumental virtuosity, presenting short, energetic songs with simple messages of despair, alienation, or defiance. Other pioneering punk bands, including the Patti Smith Group, Blondie, and Richard Hell and the Voidoids, also originated in New York City. Though influenced by contemporary developments in British music and culture, punk rock in the United States was heavily identified with New York and reflected the city's status as a symbol of despair.

JIMMY CARTER AND THE POLITICS OF MALAISE

Although many of the worst moments in the economic downturn took place on Nixon's or Ford's watch, Jimmy Carter's presidency coincided with the era's deepest pessimism. By the late 1970s, discussions of economic shortages and shortfalls had begun to treat those phenomena as metaphors for perhaps larger problems. Carter was a religious, introspective man who eagerly took up these themes, often to his political detriment. Whereas Nixon had exploited cultural anxieties, Carter preferred to diagnose them.

In July 1979, as inflation soared and another OPEC price increase plunged the United States into a second energy crisis, Carter retreated to Camp David to reflect on the nation's problems. Rather than consulting with economists or geologists to devise a new energy policy, the president invited some 130 clergy, community leaders, academics, businesspeople, and others to help him reflect on the psychological and spiritual dimensions of the economic crisis. Speaking on national television after this retreat, Carter outlined a series of energy initiatives. More memorably, however, he insisted that the United States was facing a "crisis of confidence," a threat that "strikes at the very heart and soul and spirit of our national will." As Carter saw it, Americans no longer believed they could contribute positively to their own government and no longer looked optimistically to the future. They had also become distracted by materialistic desires. "Owning *things* and consuming *things*," he proclaimed, sounding like a preacher, "does not satisfy our longing for meaning."

The unusual address became known as the malaise speech, though Carter never actually uttered that word, and it proved politically damaging. Critics accused the president of blaming Americans for the economic crisis and belittling their material concerns. Notably, the idea of a national malaise caught on, however. Even many of Carter's opponents and detractors seemed to agree that inflation rates and energy crises had psychological implications and correlations. Still, they wanted a president who would rise above the popular despair and project energetic confidence in the face of all the evidence of economic decline.

CULTURE WARS AND CONSERVATIVE BACKLASH

During the Ford and Carter years of the mid-1970s, fallout from the Watergate scandal, combined with the severe economic downturn, appeared to have undone Nixon's strategy for building a new Republican majority. Indeed, by 1977, Democrats controlled both houses of Congress and the White House, and the cultural values of the silent majority no longer dominated the national political dialogue. All along, though, a more lasting rightward turn in culture and politics was taking place. Nixon had expected his majority to express its disapproval of the social and political upheaval associated with the 1960s by acting patriotically, voting for Republicans, and supporting the status quo. What actually happened was more remarkable: Conservative Americans, and especially evangelical Protestants, built a counterculture of their own and mobilized their constituencies for a new set of battles over gender roles, race relations, cultural values, and the role of government.

EVANGELICAL COUNTERCULTURE

Evangelical Protestantism enjoyed a rebirth in the 1970s, comparable in some ways to the great religious revivals and awakenings of the eighteenth and nineteenth centuries. Evangelical denominations like the Southern Baptist Convention grew quickly over the decade, while more liberal mainstream churches declined in membership. Some of the most spectacular growth took place among Pentecostals, both white and black, and other evangelical churches not affiliated with larger ecclesiastical bodies. By 1976—"the year of the evangelical," according to *Newsweek* magazine—more than one in three Americans identified themselves to pollsters as "born again" or "evangelical" Christians. That same year, the United States elected Jimmy Carter, its first born-again president.

Personal evangelical faith often fit into a larger conservative world view, nurtured in an older network of institutions that included churches, Bible colleges, Christian booksellers, and campus groups. Evangelicalism in the 1970s also spread through new avenues, however. Among them were FM radio stations that catered specifically to born-again listeners and new cable television channels and satellite technology through which evangelical preachers reached ever-wider audiences. Reverend Pat Robertson's Christian Broadcasting Network, founded in 1961, launched its own cable network in 1977, which eventually became the Family Channel. Robertson had many colleagues and competitors. By the end of the decade, Jerry Falwell's *Old Time Gospel Hour* was drawing more than 1.4 million viewers nationwide. Evangelical consumer goods also flourished, including contemporary Christian music and a booming publishing industry that sold over a billion dollars a year in Christian self-help books, fiction, theology, greeting cards, and other printed goods. Men and women uncomfortable with the secular values and sexual content of mainstream popular entertainment and literature flocked to a burgeoning alternative culture.

In the preceding decades, conservative evangelicals had mostly avoided politics. While liberal ministers, rabbis, and priests advocated social reforms in the 1960s and led their parishioners on campaigns for civil rights and peace, figures like Falwell had preferred to focus on questions of salvation. "Preachers are not called to be politicians," Falwell insisted in 1965. Over the course of the 1970s, however, the wall separating spiritual and political affairs began to crumble within the growing evangelical culture.

Among other factors, two specific controversies drew evangelicals into politics. First, in 1973, the Supreme Court ruled in *Roe v. Wade* that laws prohibiting abortion violated a women's constitutional right to privacy. The decision had powerful and immediate implications for gender relations, women's health, and family life (forty-six states had some statutory limitation on abortion in 1973). To evangelicals, who deplored many of those implications, *Roe* made the federal government an active agent in the spread of sinful behavior. The ensuing abortion controversy also forged an important alliance between evangelical Protestants and Roman Catholics, two traditional foes in American culture and politics. As the decade wore on, political controversy about race also pulled evangelicals into the political fray. Specifically, more evangelical Christians were mobilized in opposition to IRS policies that threatened the tax-exempt status of private religious schools over questions of racial integration.

Born Again. One intriguing bridge between the new religious right and Nixon's earlier cultural strategy was Charles Colson (in glasses), shown here watching the actor who would portray him in the 1978 biopic *Born Again*. Incarcerated for his role in Watergate, Colson emerged from prison a born-again Christian. He founded an evangelical prison ministry and became a major voice in conservative politics, reframing older attacks on the sexual revolution in the name of his newfound faith.

By the decade's end, evangelicals had emerged as an identifiable mass constituency. Falwell, who had changed his mind on the value of political action, founded an organization called the Moral Majority in 1979 to harness the power of that constituency. Evangelicals began taking over local school boards, running for state office, and getting elected to Congress. They created political action committees, lobbied legislators, and turned out voters. Ironically, the politicization of the evangelical counterculture in the late 1970s put it at loggerheads with the nation's born-again president, whose views on many issues, but especially foreign policy, evangelicals did not share. Embracing the Republicans, the Moral Majority harked back to the rhetoric of Nixon's silent majority a decade earlier.

RISE AND FALL OF THE ERA

A touchstone issue for evangelical Christians and cultural conservatives in the 1970s was the battle over women's rights. Prompted by the women's movement, Congress in 1972 approved a constitutional amendment ensuring that "equality of rights under the law shall not be denied or abridged by the United States or by any State on account of sex." Such an amendment had been considered and rejected fifty years earlier, but in 1972 it sparked little opposition. The Equal Rights Amendment (ERA) met overwhelming, bipartisan approval in both chambers of Congress (354–23 in the House and 84–8 in the Senate) and moved to the states for what most observers expected would be speedy ratification. Within the year, thirty of the required thirty-eight state legislatures had ratified.

By 1974, however, the momentum had stalled. Despite the official support of both major parties, a number of state legislatures balked. Leading the public opposition was Phyllis Schlafly, who had organized a campaign called STOP ERA in October 1972 after the amendment already had passed in twenty-two states. Schlafly painted the ERA as an assault on the rights of housewives. By nullifying the legal differences between husbands and wives, Schlafly and her supporters argued, the amendment would leave married women dependent and unprotected. The ratification process slowed to a crawl in mid-decade, and by 1979, when the seven-year limit established by Congress was set to expire, only thirty-five states had ratified. Though those states represented over three-quarters of the nation's population, their approval was insufficient. Congress voted to extend the deadline by three years, but nothing changed. The ERA was dead.

Religious opposition had been crucial to the outcome of the ERA debate. Schlafly's STOP ERA and Beverly LaHaye's Concerned Women for America (founded in 1979) had attracted significant support from evangelical women, as well as from conservative Catholics and especially Mormons. The states that blocked the amendment included most of the South, where the evangelical movement was strongest, and three western states (Utah, Nevada, and Arizona) where Mormons enjoyed considerable voting power. These various religious conservatives saw the ERA as a broad cultural threat that went beyond the danger to housewives. Schlafly in 1972 had also founded the Eagle Forum, a political organization that linked ERA opposition to antiabortion activism and a host of other causes associated with the defense of traditional gender roles and the idea of family values.

By the second half of the decade, this political defense of the American family focused on homosexuality. Conservative recording artist Anita Bryant led a "Save Our Children"

Blocking the ERA. Phyllis Schlafly rallies ERA opponents in the Illinois capitol.

campaign in 1977 that successfully repealed a Dade County (Florida) civil rights ordinance prohibiting discrimination against gays and lesbians. Bryant conducted similar campaigns elsewhere and offered support to the 1978 Briggs Initiative, a statewide ballot proposition in California that would have authorized the firing of any public school employee who engaged in "public homosexual conduct," which included making statements implicitly defending the rights of gays. In November the bill went down in defeat, having been opposed by several prominent politicians from both parties and countered by a massive door-to-door campaign organized by the state's gay rights activists, including Harvey Milk just before his assassination later that month (see the chapter introduction).

AFFIRMATIVE ACTION

Sexual politics mobilized many conservative Americans, but others turned rightward over issues of race. White voters, including those who now identified more closely with their distinctive ethnic heritage, increasingly resented the special attention paid by federal and state governments to African Americans. Many Italian, Polish, and Jewish Americans in particular became outspoken critics of affirmative action programs in hiring and school admissions, which they dubbed "reverse discrimination" against whites.

In *Bakke v. Regents of the University of California* (1978), the Supreme Court weighed in on this contentious issue. The justices reviewed the case of a white medical school applicant who believed he had been denied admission to the University of California, Davis, in favor of less deserving minority students. In a complex five-to-four decision, the Court ruled that the university's policy of setting aside a certain number of medical school slots on the basis of race was constitutionally prohibited, though the university was entitled to consider race in its admissions process. Affirmative action was fine, in other words, but numerical quotas were not. The following year, however, the Court ruled differently in a case involving affirmative action in the blue-collar workplace. Brian Weber, a white Louisiana steel worker, challenged a company-union agreement that admitted equal numbers of black and white unskilled employees into a training program until the proportion of black skilled workers in the plant corresponded to the overall numbers on the factory floor. *United Steelworkers of America v. Weber,* which differed from *Bakke* in several respects (the steel company was private and the affirmative action remedy was transitional), upheld affirmative action in American industrial hiring just at the moment when the United States was deindustrializing.

TAX REVOLT

The conservative coalition of the 1970s mobilized new constituencies angered by the social movements of the previous decade, but it also tapped into traditional opposition to taxation and government regulation. A strand of libertarianism (seemingly in tension with religious conservatives' emphasis on duty and constraint) was especially popular in the West, where conservatives objected to federal rules on land development, water use, grazing, hunting, and deforestation.

Westerners also took the lead in resisting taxes. In 1978, voters in California, by a two-to-one margin, approved Howard Jarvis's Proposition 13, which capped state property taxes at 1 percent and limited future tax assessments as long as property was not sold. Support for the measure was driven in part by concerns over inflation, which raised homeowners' tax liability without improving their standard of living. California voters had discovered that property taxes were one bill they could cut. Proposition 13 also reflected—and fed—a growing pessimism about government and what it could do. The pessimism proved self-fulfilling. In one stroke, California lost $7 billion in revenues, and the state's services (especially education) deteriorated quickly. The political allure of the tax revolt was great, however. Caps on taxes succeeded in trimming budgets without targeting particular social programs and transferred to legislatures the politically costly business of deciding where to make the cuts. Other states began following suit. Strict taboos against property tax increases became the cornerstone of conservative politics.

COLD WAR AND HUMAN RIGHTS

In both politics and culture, the 1970s saw a rising awareness of international interdependence. As the global circulation of currency, natural resources, consumer goods, information, ideas, germs, pollutants, and people accelerated, Americans struggled to make sense of their shifting place in a shrinking world. Like Nixon and Kissinger earlier in the decade, Jimmy Carter sought to move away from Cold War views of a worldwide contest against communism. Carter groped for new foundations for American foreign policy and began to invoke the language of a growing human rights movement. By the decade's end, however, he found himself reasserting U.S. interests in the face of severe challenges to its authority in the world.

HELSINKI AND THE INTERNATIONAL HUMAN RIGHTS MOVEMENT

Under détente, Henry Kissinger's enduring achievement during the Nixon and Ford administrations, both sides in the Cold War accepted parity and stability as the goals of U.S.-Soviet diplomacy. Such acceptance had been built in to arms limitation negotiations, and in the summer of 1975 the United States joined thirty-four other nations in Helsinki, Finland, for the Conference on Security and Co-operation in Europe. The Helsinki Accords signed at that momentous gathering recognized the boundaries of Europe that had been established after World War II but contested during the Cold War. This recognition of communist governments in the Eastern bloc, although a significant achievement for the Soviets, left President Ford and other Western leaders vulnerable to the charge that they had surrendered the Cold War. Nonetheless, the agreement was consistent with the goals of détente.

Contrary to American and Soviet expectations, however, Article VII of the Helsinki Accords, which affirmed human rights and basic freedoms, wound up signifying a new direction in international relations. Political dissidents in the Soviet Union and Eastern Europe drew inspiration from the agreement in their campaigns for political change in their societies, while a growing chorus of their supporters in the West invoked Helsinki as a new basis for activism. American politicians took particular interest in the rights of Soviet subjects. In 1974, Senator Henry Jackson and Representative Charles Vanik introduced a law withholding trade privileges from nations that denied their citizens the right of emigration. Designed primarily to protest Soviet restrictions on the USSR's Jewish population, the Jackson-Vanik Amendment (which passed unanimously in both houses of Congress) appealed to broadly shared American beliefs about freedom and mobility. At the same time, it united critics of détente from both sides of the political aisle. Conservatives who felt that Kissinger was accommodating the spread of communism joined liberals who felt that he was turning a blind eye to abuses of individual rights. The specific right of Soviet Jews to emigrate became a rallying cry and a launching pad for a number of different political developments that emerged and diverged in the 1970s: renewed anticommunism, revived American Jewish ethnic identity, and a new global movement to hold national governments accountable to universal standards of human rights.

Although the idea was an old one, human rights became a political buzzword in the United States in the 1970s. Don Fraser, a Democratic congressman from Minnesota, began pressing the Nixon administration in 1973 to monitor the human rights records of nations that received U.S. aid, a position that Congress increasingly favored during the Nixon and Ford years. Meanwhile, liberals in government and academia who had prioritized disarmament in previous years turned their attention to human rights. Finally, a new set of nongovernmental organizations (NGOs) assumed leadership of an **international human rights movement.** The London-based organization Amnesty International, with growing support in the United States, received the 1977 Nobel Peace Prize for its campaign to end torture. The American NGO Helsinki Watch was founded in 1978 to monitor Soviet compliance with the Helsinki Accords, but the organization soon expanded its oversight to Central America and other parts of the world, shaming governments that violated human rights standards.

INTERNATIONALISM AND JIMMY CARTER'S AMERICA

Human rights organizations were often international in composition as well as in focus. At the United Nations, which had enshrined human rights at the center of its mission in 1948 and sponsored the first international conference on the subject in 1968, nations began speaking more frequently and confidently about human rights goals and violations. Such rhetoric competed with new forms of nationalism in the developing world and older expressions of the importance of national sovereignty. But they also reflected a growing global consciousness. In the United States, this consciousness was reinforced in a number of arenas. Earth Day celebrations and the environmental movement called attention to the fact that Americans belonged to a fragile planet, not simply a nation. The *Voyager* launches in 1977, which sent unmanned satellites into space, took advantage of a rare planetary alignment but also underscored the common position of the earth's inhabitants. Two years later, the World Health Organization, a UN agency, announced the eradication of smallpox, which had killed an estimated three hundred million people in the twentieth century to that point. In a project that highlighted both the global circulation of pathogens and the international cooperation necessary to contain them, smallpox became the first infectious disease to be wiped off the face of the earth.

Small World. The northern hemisphere as captured in a 1971 NASA photograph. Space travel and new satellite technologies introduced Americans to images of the earth as unified, interdependent, and vulnerable.

Global sensibilities also shaped American foreign policy during the Carter years. Far more than his immediate predecessors, Carter emphasized the role of universal human rights standards, the importance of adhering to international law, and the value of the goodwill of other nations. Under Carter, the United States signed two major international human rights agreements, the International Covenant on Civil and Political Rights and the International Covenant on Economic, Social, and Cultural Rights, though in neither case did he press the Senate to ratify those agreements (the United States has never ratified the covenant on economic, social, and cultural rights). Carter also lent his support to a congressional campaign to improve the lives of women worldwide. Under Nixon, women's rights activists had pushed the passage of the Percy Amendment, which directed U.S. foreign aid toward the goal of women's economic integration in the developing world. Carter created a special division within the USAID agency to further this goal.

Ideological commitments to internationalism and human rights prompted Carter to cut off aid to Argentina's military dictatorship in 1978 and to advocate a treaty ceding the Panama Canal to local control. In 1979, he used the rising moral authority of the United States to broker the historic Camp David peace treaty between Israel and Egypt. When left-wing rebels in Nicaragua rose up in 1977 against a dictatorship that had been friendly to the United States, Carter insisted that aid to the government be tied to human rights. As the revolution escalated, Carter stayed out of the conflict in order to avoid a repetition of the Vietnam War, though his neutrality drew criticism from those more fully committed to human rights in Central America.

IRAN, AFGHANISTAN, AND THE UNRAVELING OF CARTER'S FOREIGN POLICY

Despite the new direction of Carter's foreign policy, the United States retained certain strategic allies irrespective of their commitment to human rights. Among these allies was the oil-rich nation of Iran. U.S. support for Shah Mohammad Reza Pahlavi, Iran's long-reigning monarch with a long record of human rights violations, went back decades. In 1979, however, when an Islamic revolution overthrew the Shah's government, that support became costly. Carter allowed the Shah into the United States to seek medical treatment, effectively providing asylum from the punishment intended for him in Iran. In response, followers of the Ayatollah Khomeini—the Shia Islamic cleric who had led the revolt against the Shah and succeeded him as Iran's political leader—stormed the U.S. embassy in Teheran on November 4 and took fifty-three Americans hostage in an effort to force the United States to extradite the Shah. The Iran hostage crisis dragged on more than a year, through the rest of Carter's term.

Before the end of 1979, Carter's problems were compounded when the USSR invaded Afghanistan. Though the Soviet Union insisted that it was simply maintaining its power in the region, Carter worried that the Soviets were advancing toward Iran in an attempt to control the world's oil supplies. The United States suddenly found itself back in the Cold War, but with neither the diplomatic leverage to influence Soviet behavior nor the willingness to risk a showdown. Carter responded by announcing a boycott of the 1980 Moscow Olympics, suspending arms limitation talks, raising military spending, and funding Islamic revolutionary forces in Afghanistan.

Though some critics read the events in Iran and Afghanistan as indictments of policies put in place by Kissinger, most Americans saw them as exposing the nation's impotence. As oil shortages and higher energy prices loomed, Carter switched from idealism to tough talk. In his January 1980 State of the Union address, the president announced a new policy, the Carter Doctrine. "Let our position be absolutely clear," he warned. "An attempt by any outside force to gain control of the Persian Gulf region will be regarded as an assault on the vital interests of the United States of America, and such an assault will be repelled by any means necessary, including military force." Internationalism and human rights were receding in the face of a political crisis—and the Carter presidency was on the ropes.

CONCLUSION

Television's fictional Archie Bunker was both a symbol and a critic of the 1970s. The politically liberal producers and writers of *All in the Family* presented Archie as a man who had been bypassed by historical changes—racial integration, women's liberation, the sexual revolution, international cooperation—that he neither appreciated nor entirely understood. But he also articulated a backlash that was gaining political momentum. As he groused over Jimmy Carter's election in a 1976 episode, Archie warned his liberal son-in-law that four years later, things would come around. In a laugh line, he predicted that the United States would get Ronald Reagan in 1980.

STUDY TERMS

busing (p. 823)
ethnic revival (p. 825)
Roots (p. 825)
radical feminism (p. 826)
gay pride parades (p. 827)
Me Decade (p. 827)
blue-collar strategy (p. 830)
Vietnamization (p. 830)
War Powers Resolution (p. 830)
My Lai (p. 831)
Pentagon Papers (p. 831)
Revised Philadelphia Plan (p. 832)
Environmental Protection Act (p. 832)
Occupational Safety and Health Act (p. 832)
wage and price controls (p. 833)
détente (p. 833)
SALT I (p. 833)
Twenty-sixth Amendment (p. 834)
Committee to Re-elect the President (p. 834)
Watergate (p. 835)
Saturday Night Massacre (p. 835)
fall of Saigon (p. 836)
Organization of the Petroleum Exporting Countries (p. 838)
Yom Kippur War (p. 838)
energy crisis (p. 838)
stagflation (p. 839)
disco (p. 841)
malaise speech (p. 843)
Roe v. Wade (p. 844)
Moral Majority (p. 844)
Equal Rights Amendment (p. 844)
Briggs Initiative (p. 845)
Bakke v. Regents of the University of California (p. 845)
United Steelworkers of America v. Weber (p. 845)
Proposition 13 (p. 846)
Helsinki Accords (p. 846)
Jackson-Vanik Amendment (p. 846)
international human rights movement (p. 846)
Camp David peace treaty (p. 847)
Carter Doctrine (p. 848)

TIMELINE

1970 Secret invasion of Cambodia announced
Student protesters killed at Kent State and Jackson State
Nixon signs Environmental Protection Act and Occupational Safety and Health Act
First Earth Day celebrated

1971 *All in the Family* premieres
Nixon takes United States off gold standard

1972 Nixon visits China
George C. Wallace paralyzed in assassination attempt
Behind the Green Door and *Deep Throat* inaugurate new age of pornography
Equal Rights Amendment approved by Congress and sent to states for ratification
United States and Soviet Union sign SALT I agreement
Burglars arrested at Watergate apartment complex
Nixon reelected president in a landslide

1973 Supreme Court protects abortion rights in *Roe v. Wade*

Senate committee conducts hearings on Watergate cover-up

Yom Kippur War and Arab oil embargo precipitate prolonged energy crisis

1974 White parents in South Boston organize opposition to forced busing

Nixon resigns

President Gerald Ford pardons Nixon for crimes committed in office

Annual inflation rate hits 11 percent

1975 Saigon falls, ending Vietnam War

Helsinki Accords ratified

New York faces municipal bankruptcy

1976 Jimmy Carter defeats Ford in presidential election

1977 *Roots* mini-series spawns renewed interest in family histories

New York City blackout sparks mass looting and riots

Amnesty International wins Nobel Peace Prize

1978 Supreme Court rejects affirmative action quotas in *Bakke* case

California voters pass Proposition 13

1979 Jerry Falwell founds Moral Majority

Deadline for ERA ratification passes

Carter brokers Camp David peace treaty between Egypt and Israel

Carter gives malaise speech

Iranian students take American hostages in Teheran

USSR invades Afghanistan

FURTHER READING

Additional suggested readings are available on the Online Learning Center at www.mhhe.com/becomingamerica1e.

Daniel Carter, *The Politics of Rage* (1995), explores the broader significance and impact of George C. Wallace's campaigns for the presidency.

Stanley Corkin, *Starring New York* (2011), studies the representation of New York in popular films of the 1970s.

Jefferson Cowie, *Stayin' Alive* (2010), documents the emergence of Nixon's blue-collar strategy and puts labor and class relations at the center of 1970s political history.

Alice Echols, *Daring to Be Bad* (1989), charts the rise and splintering of radical feminism.

Alice Echols, *Hot Stuff* (2010), celebrates the role of disco music in integrating American nightlife and transforming gay culture.

Niall Ferguson et al. (eds.), *The Shock of the Global* (2010), puts the American experience of the 1970s in international context.

Matthew Frye Jacobson, *Roots Too* (2006), examines the white ethnic revival of the 1970s.

Bethany Moreton, *To Serve God and Wal-Mart* (2009), illuminates the connections between consumer culture and conservative ideology in the 1970s through a study of the world's largest private company.

Samuel Moyn, *The Last Utopia* (2010), locates the intellectual origins of the modern human rights movement in the 1970s.

Heather Murray, *Not in This Family* (2010), treats the coming-out dramas of gay and lesbian Americans and their straight families as part of a new ethic of sexual revelation in this period.

Daniel Sargent, *A Superpower Transformed* (2014), recasts the history of American foreign policy in the 1970s against the backdrop of global changes in energy politics, finance, and human rights ideology.

Bruce Schulman and Julian Zelizer (eds.), *Rightward Bound* (2008), collects recent scholarship on the conservative revival of the 1970s.

30

INSIDE

THE BIG PICTURE

Deindustrialization accelerated as President Ronald Reagan, elected on the promise of restoring prosperity and downsizing government, slashed taxes and welfare spending and revived the Cold War. The consumer economy boomed and innovative new technologies, art forms, and protest strategies proliferated. Yet certain chronic problems—homelessness, poverty, a sky-high federal budget deficit—and the frightening specter of the AIDS epidemic cast a dark shadow.

Cultural Ferment. Unfashionable since the late 1960s, conspicuous consumption roared back to life in the 1980s, accompanied by edgy new expressive forms such as rap music, graffiti art, and satirical billboards like mass media artist Barbara Kruger's critique of commercialism, pictured here.

1980–1992

DEINDUSTRIALIZING AMERICA

High wages, generous job benefits, and decent public schools had been the norm in thriving Flint, Michigan, in the mid-twentieth century. The site of the nation's first sit-down strike and the birthplace of the United Auto Workers (1936–1937), Flint had helped inaugurate the era of high-paying, secure employment for skilled American workers. But no sooner had the "Auto City" earned its prosperous reputation than its white middle class began moving to larger, greener suburbs. As tax revenues drained out of the city, public amenities decayed. Flint's troubles only intensified when auto sales collapsed during the oil crisis of 1973 and the industry lost market share to more fuel-efficient Japanese and European cars. General Motors (GM), Flint's top employer, laid off tens of thousands and relocated factories to Mexico. All these developments—and their pernicious effect on Flint citizens—were chronicled by little-known filmmaker and Flint native Michael Moore. *Roger and Me* (1989) became the decade's blockbuster documentary film, turning the once-proud Auto City into the symbol of the worst excesses of urban deindustrialization.

Industrial Belt cities had been slowly losing factories and jobs (typically to southern states) since the 1930s, but it was only in the 1980s that tens of millions of jobs were relocated overseas. Flint's collapse reflected powerful national and global forces that together turned the traditional industrial zone of the United

Manufacturers shuttered factories in record numbers in the 1980s, turning Detroit and the rest of the United States' once-booming Industrial Belt into a "Rust Belt" of abandoned plants, mass unemployment, and crumbling infrastructure.

KEY QUESTIONS

- How did deindustrialization influence U.S. politics, society, and culture?
- Why was President Ronald Reagan so popular, and what were his administration's legacies?
- Why did the consumer economy and the middle class thrive during the 1980s, while economic inequality spiraled upward?
- What were the origins, outcome, and significance of the culture wars?
- How did the Soviet Union's collapse affect the United States and the world?

States into the "Rust Belt" and the fruit orchards of California's Santa Clara Valley into Silicon Valley. President Ronald Reagan's economic conservatism greatly accelerated deindustrialization and the associated problems of white flight and urban decay. Reagan strove to reverse New Deal and Great Society policies—to free businesses from financial, health, safety, and labor regulations and to make deep cuts in welfare programs. Cutting taxes became the war cry of conservatives. At the same time, Reagan's administration renewed the Cold War and strengthened the military. With the leap in defense spending, the economy boomed, mass culture reveled in the new affluence, and conservatives rejoiced in their growing political influence.

Despite the decade's reputation as one of the most conservative in the country's history, however, dissent and new forms of radicalism flourished in equal measure. Opposition to Reaganism was not confined to the metropolitan coasts but took root in the southern and midwestern heartland as well. Progressives successfully defended many of the hard-earned victories of the New Deal and the civil rights era, forcing Reagan's rollback to a halt. The president's critics also constrained most of his more hawkish foreign policy ambitions. New cultural and political ground was broken through rap music, experimental writing, documentary filmmaking, and more. Many youths, often led by progressive musicians, developed an awareness of global issues, such as South African apartheid, and felt their generation's electoral clout. In schools and, to an extent, the workplace, multiculturalism also advanced. And, following the discovery and spread of a fatal new virus, gay men and lesbians took their campaign for visibility and rights to the streets and Congress.

NATION AT THE CROSSROADS

In 1980, an unusually large number of Americans were disillusioned with the direction of their lives and the nation. The economy had yet to recover from the oil shocks of the 1970s, prices were rising, and unemployment hovered at a post-1950 high. President Jimmy Carter seemed defeated by the economy and global events. Millions of people living in the developing world, however, felt differently about the United States and its future. In the wake of the 1965 Immigration and Nationality Act, which had opened the gates to non-European immigrants, hundreds of thousands of Asians and Latin Americans immigrated to the United States, seeking prosperity and freedom from persecution. Although many native-born citizens celebrated the renewal of multiculturalism, others worried that immigrants were taking citizens' jobs, collecting welfare, and threatening American cultural values.

THE FALTERING ECONOMY

Most Americans began the new decade with a mix of anxiety, frustration, and fear. The spectacular period of economic growth and low unemployment ushered in by World War II had ended in 1973 and, seven years later, was yet to return.

The steel, automotive, and other industries were shrinking and losing valuable markets to more efficient European and Japanese manufacturers. In the summer of 1980, inflation mounted to almost 14 percent (over four times what it is today), and productivity sank to its lowest rate since 1940. European and Japanese industry was booming, having taken almost a quarter of the world market away from U.S. industrial producers. The stock market had fallen, and unemployment had risen to around 7.5 percent.

Several years after Watergate and the communist victory in Vietnam, confidence in the government remained low. More recently, the Soviets had ignored U.S. calls to halt their invasion of Afghanistan, and the United States had bungled efforts to free the American hostages in Iran. Polls showed that faith in business, the press, the legal profession, the military, and the medical establishment had also hit an all-time low. Less than a third of Americans, according to Gallup polls, had full confidence in public schools (down sharply from the mid-1960s), and only 12 percent thought that "things are going well in the United States"—a historic low. For the first time since World War II, a majority of Americans believed that their quality of life and future prospects had dimmed over the previous five years.

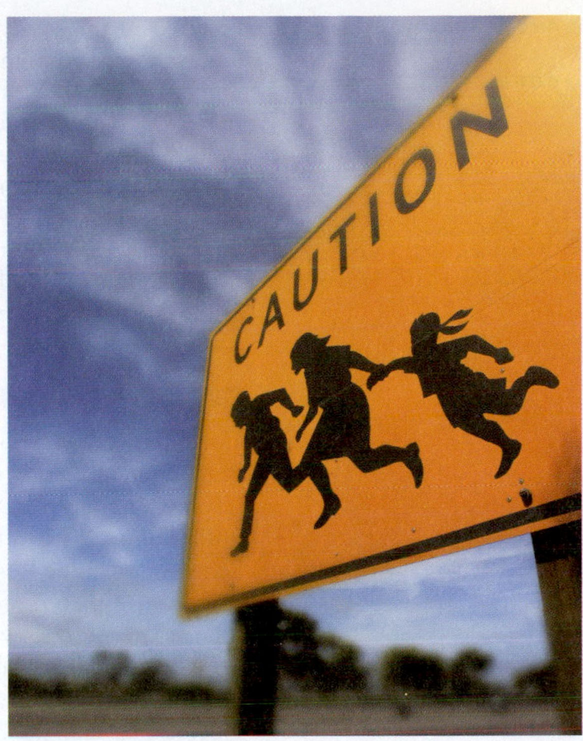

Immigrants Crossing. This haunting road sign, which first cropped up on the border zone sections of California's I-5 in 1990, warned motorists to watch for families of illegal immigrants crossing traffic lanes. By then, over a hundred illegal immigrants, most let off on I-5 by human traffickers, had been killed by passing vehicles.

THIRD WORLD IMMIGRANTS

Not everyone was disillusioned. Between 1965 and 1980, over eight million people had immigrated legally to the United States—and the flow of both legal and illegal immigrants accelerated in the new decade. For the first time, the great majority of immigrants were not from Europe. One in two came from Latin America, and most of the rest were from Asia (generally China, the Philippines, and South Korea). Much as immigrants before them, they came to escape economic pressures or political and religious persecution. Besides their excellent work ethic and will to succeed, few brought any assets with them. Most found employment in the service industries, manufacturing, or agriculture—low-pay sectors in which American citizens were reluctant to work.

Immigration from Mexico surged after that nation experienced a series of economic shocks in the 1970s and near bankruptcy in the 1980s. Hundreds of thousands of Mexicans, mostly impoverished farmers, hopped the border in search of agricultural work. A half-million others went to work for General Motors and other U.S. manufacturers that had set up dozens of *maquilas* (assembly plants) in northern Mexico, a region that the Mexican government had designated a **free trade zone** in 1965. The zone, which offered American corporations tax breaks, cheap labor, and other incentives, boomed in the 1980s. (It would eventually serve as the model for turning all of North America into a free trade zone; see Chapter 31.) Ironically, however, the *maquilas* made no difference to Mexico's unemployment rate and even spurred immigration to the United States. The reason was that the *maquilas'* managers, fearing that male workers would be more likely to demand higher wages and unionize, widely employed young rural women who were entering the workforce for the first time. Thus the mass migration of Mexican men to the United States grew steadily.

Mexican and other newcomers were changing the United States' demographic and cultural makeup (see Figure 30.1), especially in the Southwest, where the number of Mexican Americans tripled between 1970 and 1990, and in the West, where the Asian American population increased sixfold. Not since the Progressive Era and the influx of Southern and Eastern Europeans was the country as linguistically and culturally diverse. The influence of the new Chinese and Mexican immigrants on American culture was apparent, particularly in cuisine, where Szechuan, Oaxacan, and other unfamiliar regional styles, together with Tex-Mex and other fusion foods, became widely popular. Spanish-language television, which had grown from a single station in San Antonio, Texas, in 1955 to a regional network by 1980, became a truly national phenomenon in 1986 when greeting cards giant Hallmark Cards bought and expanded the network, renaming it Univision.

Many Americans welcomed the nation's new diversity. Children's television shows such as *Sesame Street* actively promoted the United States' increasingly multicultural reality, and *Condo*, the first English-language sitcom to feature an upwardly mobile Hispanic family, aired on ABC in 1983. Many school boards developed curricula to help immigrants from Mexico, China, and elsewhere settle in. Other Americans, however,

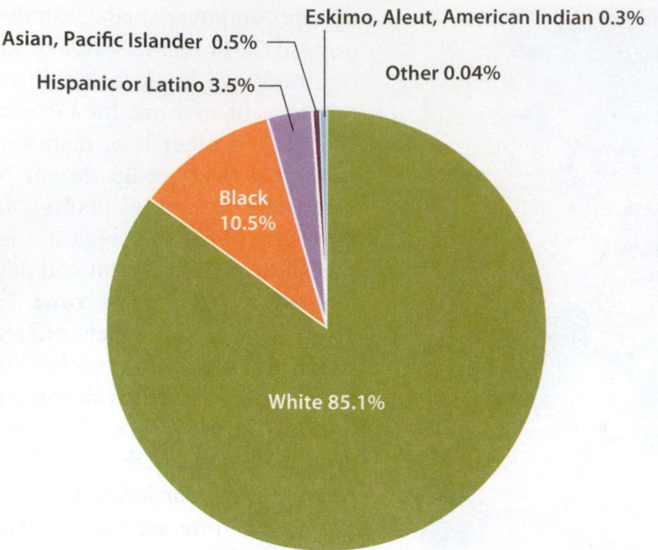

U.S. Ethnicity by Percentage, 1960

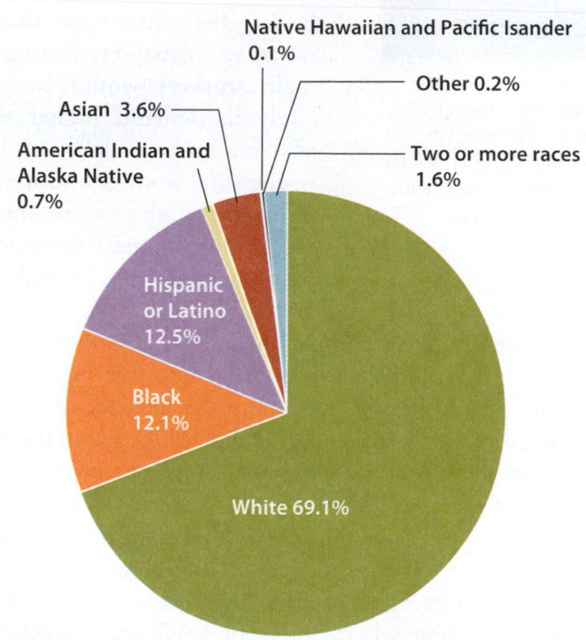

U.S. Ethnicity by Percentage, 2000

FIGURE 30.1 We, the New Americans. The nation's demographics, which had already changed in the wake of the Immigration and Nationality Act, shifted even more dramatically in the 1980s with an uptick in illegal immigration and a high birthrate among the new immigrants. By 2000, the Hispanic and Latino populations combined, both immigrant and citizen, had more than tripled since 1960, and the Asian population had grown over sevenfold.

objected to the steady growth of the "nonwhite" population and wondered what impact it might have on their way of life. Some also feared that the influx of a relatively poor population in need of schools, housing, and medical services would bleed state and federal budgets, even though immigrants overall generated billions in tax revenue. In many parts of the country, including the Southwest, Hispanics faced ongoing discrimination and hostility. Immigration—both legal and illegal—was fast becoming one of the most controversial political questions of the late twentieth century.

CONSERVATIVE REVIVAL

Conservative leaders benefited immensely from popular fears of Mexican and other new immigrants groups, and some conservatives actively played on such fears. Widespread middle-class disillusionment with the stagnating economy and the United States' humiliating loss in Vietnam also provided grist for the conservative mill. A growing number of Americans proved responsive to conservative calls to cut taxes and, in foreign policy, to "make America great again."

A variety of conservative organizations began attracting mass membership and significant cash donations. Building on the electronic ministries of the late 1970s, the reverend Pat Robertson and fundamentalist preacher Jerry Falwell drew millions more viewers and mounted passionate attacks on welfare programs, abortion, and homosexuality. Conservative Catholics found themselves agreeing that gays, feminists, and liberals were unraveling the nation's moral fiber. Together, they promoted conservative Christian candidates for office, the adoption of "Christian values" in public institutions, and conservative Christian control of the Republican Party. By 1990, Pat Robertson's Christian Coalition, founded the previous year, counted 1.6 million members and dominated the party in more than a dozen states.

As the economy and Carter's presidency continued to stall in 1980, subscriptions to the conservative *National Review* rocketed. Think tanks such as the American Enterprise Institute advanced the theory of **supply-side economics.** Supply-siders insisted that tax revenues were maximized not by higher tax rates (which allegedly discouraged workers and businesses from working harder and producing more) but, paradoxically, by lower tax rates. Lowering tax rates, advocates argued, would motivate workers to produce or "supply" more, thereby creating jobs and more tax revenue, and boost the supply of money for fresh investments.

Supply-side economics reversed the previous forty years of Keynesian economics, which held that government should stimulate demand for goods and services and that this policy would in turn lift production. The supply-side approach gained little traction among economists, most of whom viewed it, in the words of economist Paul Krugman, as "crank doctrine." Nevertheless, it appealed to neoconservative editors and publicists, as well as to voters who had supported the tax revolt in California and elsewhere in 1978 (see Chapter 29).

ELECTION OF 1980

By mid-1980, every indicator suggested that the U.S. economy was the worst it had been since the Great Depression. Heading into the election, both the struggling economy and President Carter's pessimistic message about America's dimmed prospects proved to be a gift to Republicans. Former Hollywood actor and General Electric spokesperson Ronald Reagan appeared to be the perfect choice for the Republican nominee. Indeed, his optimistic and reassuring persona would prove a tremendous asset for the party. Reagan evoked an allegedly simpler, more prosperous period of the nation's history: the 1950s. At the same time, his campaign successfully connected the Democrats with the tumultuous 1960s—an association that would damage them again in the 1984 and 1988 elections. In an age when television had eclipsed newspapers as the most influential medium in politics, Reagan's communication skills, acting experience, and star quality inspired sorely needed confidence. He easily won the Republican nomination.

Campaigning for president, Reagan tapped into Richard Nixon's "silent majority" of Americans who were frustrated by the sputtering economy and Carter's apparent paralysis. Reagan picked up on three intense dislikes of many white middle-class and working-class voters—the civil rights movement, antiwar protesters, and the liberalism of the Supreme Court under Chief Justice Earl Warren—and drew directly on popular anti-tax sentiment. The solution to the nation's problems was relatively simply, according to Reagan. Government had become unwieldy and too expensive, and a thicket of regulations was ensnarling free enterprise. Such controls ought to be abolished so that business might grow and prosper. Consistent with the theory of supply-side economics, Reagan argued that **deregulation** in turn would have a "trickle-down effect" that would bring more jobs, higher pay, and better goods and services. In addition, the problems of poverty and crime would be solved if the poor took responsibility for themselves rather than depended on government "handouts." The message was appealing to over 50 percent of voters, and Reagan swept to power over Carter with 489 electoral votes (91 percent of the total; see Map 30.1). Reagan's embrace of Nixon's southern

Patriotic Appeal. Seeking to ignite voters' optimism while acknowledging the economic and political woes of the 1970s, Reagan and his running mate George H. W. Bush vowed to restore the nation to greatness. **Questions for Analysis:** Why might making "America great again" have been such an appealing idea in 1980? What did it mean?

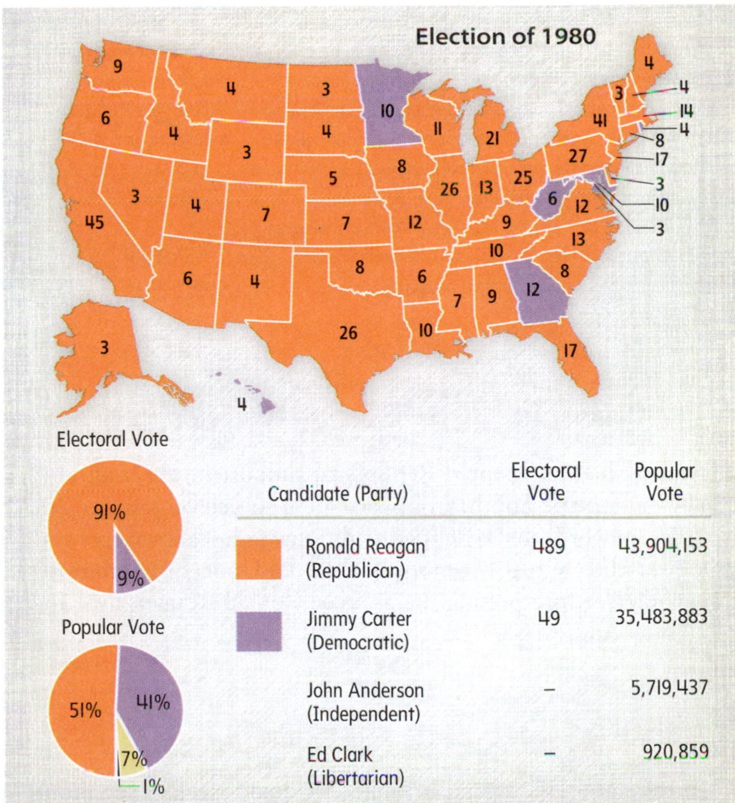

Candidate (Party)	Electoral Vote	Popular Vote
Ronald Reagan (Republican)	489	43,904,153
Jimmy Carter (Democratic)	49	35,483,883
John Anderson (Independent)	–	5,719,437
Ed Clark (Libertarian)	–	920,859

Map 30.1 Election of 1980.

INTERPRETING THE SOURCES

Ronald Reagan, First Inaugural Address, January 1981

Dubbed the "Great Communicator," Ronald Reagan plied an oratorical style that permanently transformed the way Americans thought about and debated politics and government. Many middle-class citizens, disillusioned with politicians and fearful of national economic decline, found his speeches simple, direct, sincere, and above all optimistic. Others dismissed his words as simplistic or wrongheaded. In fact, Reagan's speeches were far more complex than either his supporters or his opponents realized. Like Franklin D. Roosevelt, Reagan took familiar words and political concepts such as "equal opportunity" and "special interests" and redefined them in ways that made millions of citizens feel that he understood their hopes and fears. Duly acknowledged, many Americans were eager to throw their support behind the new president and his small-government, pro-business agenda. Reagan's first inaugural address, excerpted here, stands as a prime example of his complex rhetoric.

The economic ills we suffer have come upon us over several decades. They will not go away in days, weeks, or months, but they will go away. They will go away because we, as Americans, have the capacity now, as we have had in the past, to do whatever needs to be done to preserve this last and greatest bastion of freedom.

In this present crisis, government is not the solution to our problem. . . .

We hear much of special interest groups. Our concern must be for a special interest group that has been too long neglected. It knows no sectional boundaries or ethnic and racial divisions, and it crosses political party lines. It is made up of men and women who raise our food, patrol our streets, man our mines and our factories, teach our children, keep our homes, and heal us when we are sick—professionals, industrialists, shopkeepers, clerks, cabbies, and truckdrivers. They are, in short, "We the people," this breed called Americans.

Well, this administration's objective will be a healthy, vigorous, growing economy that provides equal opportunity for all Americans, with no barriers born of bigotry or discrimination. Putting America back to work means putting all Americans back to work. . . .

We are a nation that has a government—not the other way around. And this makes us special among the nations of the Earth. Our Government has no power except that granted it by the people. It is time to check and reverse the growth of government which shows signs of having grown beyond the consent of the governed.

It is my intention to curb the size and influence of the Federal establishment and to demand recognition of the distinction between the powers granted to the Federal Government and those reserved to the States or to the people. . . .

Now, so there will be no misunderstanding, it is not my intention to do away with government. It is, rather, to make it work—work with us, not over us; to stand by our side, not ride on our back. . . .

We are not, as some would have us believe, doomed to an inevitable decline. I do not believe in a fate that will fall on us no matter what we do. I do believe in a fate that will fall on us if we do nothing. So, with all the creative energy at our command, let us begin an era of national renewal. Let us renew our determination, our courage, and our strength. And let us renew our faith and our hope. . . .

Explore the Source

1. Why might Reagan have referred to ordinary working people as a "special interest group that has been too long neglected"?
2. What do you think members of the civil rights and women's liberation movements might have said about Reagan's definition of "equal opportunity"?
3. What is the relationship, according to Reagan, between the federal government and the economic crisis?

strategy had augmented Republican support in the traditionally democratic South. In his inaugural speech on January 20, 1981, in words that redefined traditional political concepts and views, the "Great Communicator" laid out his ambitious agenda (see Interpreting the Sources: Ronald Reagan, First Inaugural Address).

REVERSING THE NEW DEAL

In the name of "less government," Ronald Reagan set about cutting taxes and abolishing many of the costly regulations to which business was subject. Although he slashed antipoverty welfare programs, he was unable or unwilling to cut the expensive programs from which his middle-class base benefited. Meanwhile, federal spending grew during these years, as the president followed through on his promise to rebuild and expand the military. With lawmakers unable to balance the budget, the United States borrowed heavily and consequently became a debtor nation for the first time since World War I. Deregulation fiercely eroded labor union power—a primary goal of conservatives. But scandals and popular discontent with environmental deregulation impeded the administration from taking deregulation as far as Reagan wanted, and many key New Deal programs, such as Social Security, also survived.

REAGANOMICS: REINING IN BIG GOVERNMENT

Reagan's economic electoral plank—dubbed **Reaganomics**—emphasized lower taxes, less federal spending, and fewer regulations for business. Within weeks of entering office, the president assembled a team of advisers who favored supply-side economics. The president asked lawmakers to lower federal income taxes by 25 percent over the next three years. Congress consented, passing the Economic Recovery Tax Act of 1981, which cut all tax levels and dropped the wealthiest Americans' annual rate from 70 to 50 percent. (In 1985, Congress halved the latter to just 28 percent for top earners—a historic low.) At the president's insistence, tax rates on corporate profit, inherited wealth, and other forms of income were also slashed.

Shrinking government and trimming spending proved far more challenging, mostly because they fell victim to another election promise—to grow national defense. The president secured massive spending increases for nuclear and conventional weaponry and salary hikes for most military personnel. Beginning in 1983, the government also spent billions on the president's controversial new Strategic Defense Initiative (SDI, or "Star Wars"), a missile defense system that would allegedly use satellite weaponry to intercept incoming Soviet missiles. All told, military spending swelled by $2 trillion during Reagan's presidency (see The Cold War Renewed, below).

The administration paid the growing defense bill in part by diverting $25 billion from Great Society welfare programs such as food stamps, school lunches, and low-income housing. Most Americans still believed that welfare programs were a necessary part of the social safety net. Consequently, the administration had to work hard to win voter support for the cuts. Seizing on the stereotype of single, urban, African American mothers as **welfare queens,** Reagan officials painted the poor as parasites who lived lazily at the expense of hardworking taxpayers. In fact, the vast majority of the neediest beneficiaries barely made ends meet, and middle-class entitlements such as Medicare, Social Security, and housing loans cost taxpayers far more than antipoverty programs. The administration feared, however, that cutting these would alienate middle-class voters.

As tax revenues dropped and government spending soared, the federal government's budget deficit ballooned from $100 billion in 1980 to $150 billion in 1981. Unable to rebalance the budget, the administration was forced to borrow. Beginning in 1981 and continuing for the next nine years, the government racked up a record $3 trillion in debt, borrowed from a mix of foreign and domestic lenders (see How Much Is That?). A few years before, the United States had been the world's largest creditor nation, but by the end of the 1980s it was the top debtor. Despite the huge loans and the cuts to welfare, moreover, annual budget deficits quintupled between 1981 and 1990 from $59 billion to over $300 billion.

How Much Is That?

The U.S. Debt

The United States has carried government debt—the money owed to banks and other investors, foreign governments, or federal trust funds such as Social Security—since 1792. But it was only in the 1980s that the debt began to spiral, more than tripling during that decade and quintupling again by 2012. In the 1980s, the combination of higher spending, especially in defense, and lower tax revenue led the government to borrow an unprecedented $3 trillion, or $5.47 trillion today. That amount could buy twenty-four million homes (with an average cost back then of $125,000) or a brand-new midsize car for every man, woman, and child in the United States. Paradoxically, the rocketing debt was an indicator of investors' confidence that the economy was growing. Eager to profit from the interest on the loans, and certain that the government could easily repay them, investors gladly extended credit.

EMPOWERING CORPORATIONS

Freeing corporations from the tangle of regulations to which they had been subject since the New Deal was another Reagan priority. In the late 1970s, President Jimmy Carter had begun opening up key industries to competition from new, more efficient businesses. Reagan, however, radically accelerated deregulation, targeting environmental, safety, consumer, and labor standards in particular. After appointing sympathetic officials to each of the federal regulatory agencies, the president ordered cost-benefit analyses of all new regulatory initiatives. Only those regulations whose benefits outweighed their costs were to be enforced. The administration also pruned agencies' funding by an average of 12 percent, laying off about 15 percent of their staffs by 1984.

Deregulation freed corporations from the expense of implementing costly health and other regulations. Detroit automakers, having long lobbied for relief from safety and emissions regulations, persuaded Reagan to delay the implementation of tougher standards, including new rules that required better tire safety, lower carbon dioxide emissions, and passenger-side air bags. The government also delayed implementation of regulations in the natural gas and electricity sectors.

Of all sectors, finance and banking were the most aggressively deregulated. Reagan weakened the ability of the Securities and Exchange Commission to effectively oversee the stock market, on the grounds that the agency was stifling the creative forces of investment. Relaxation of rules governing consumer credit led to a boom in credit card use and rapid growth of consumer debt (see Figure 30.2). Small savings and loan associations, which were originally intended to offer

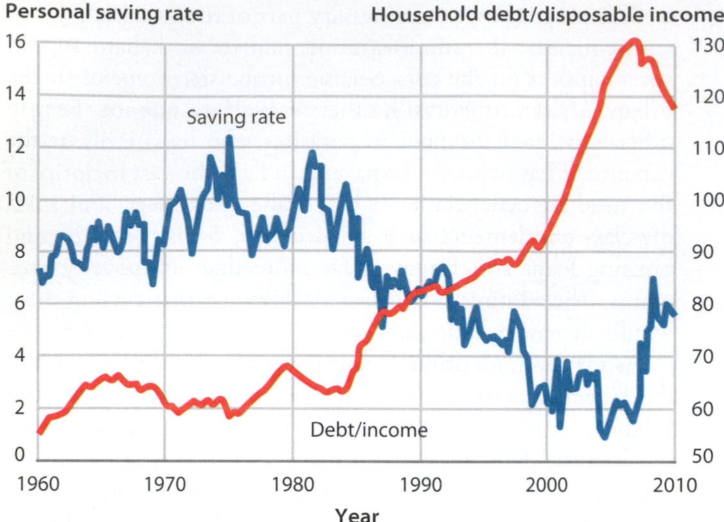

FIGURE 30.2 A Nation of Debtors. Banking deregulation, which boosted the availability of mortgages and credit cards, encouraged lower saving rates and record household debt, including consumer and mortgage debt. By 2007, the average household debt was an unprecedented 130 percent of household income. Meanwhile, the saving rate plunged from over 11 percent in the early 1980s to an all-time low of 1.7 percent in 2006.

middle-class families affordable mortgages, were authorized to act more like banks and to offer a range of services. This new flexibility encouraged many savings and loan associations to abandon their traditional mission and to pursue large profits. It also led them to take on higher and more complex levels of risk, such as in the real estate market. Ultimately, thousands of the associations, along with over 1,600 banks that were also overleveraged, failed. Because the Federal Deposit Insurance Corporation insured many of the institutions, taxpayers and the federal government were left with a $164 billion bill ($299 billion in today's dollars). Although some institutions repaid the bailout in the 1990s, taxpayers footed over two-thirds of the final bill.

In communications, the government dropped its longstanding insistence that the airwaves belonged to the people and that commercial broadcasters must serve the public. Under the leadership of Reagan appointee Mark Fowler, the Federal Communication Commission gave broadcasters a free hand to determine the quality and quantity of programming. Companies could now also own up to twelve stations and run any amount of advertising they saw fit. Most important, cable television secured the authority to compete fully with broadcast television and was no longer required to provide public, educational, and government access. With the start-up of new "genre stations"—Music Television (MTV), CNN, The Discovery Channel, QVC, and many more—a new age of televised mass culture dawned. The big three broadcast networks, NBC, CBS, and ABC, began losing audiences to the new cable channel. It was a blow from which they never fully recovered.

Music Television. Parental and Christian groups condemned cable newcomer MTV's frequent depictions of sex, drug use, and violence, and the music industry worried that the channel prized slick production over musical talent. However, MTV soon appeased most critics by banning explicit material, and Michael Jackson, with his 1983 hit "Thriller," proved that great music could be presented in well-produced videos—and could sell millions of records.

WEAKENING ORGANIZED LABOR

Meanwhile, the 1980s was turning out to be the most disastrous decade for organized labor since the 1920s. After fifty years of growth or relative stability, labor unions lost millions of members and much of their status and power. This decline was due partly to deindustrialization and the shift to a service economy, both of which accelerated in the 1980s in the United States and Europe. But organized labor's decline was both faster and more devastating in the United States than elsewhere, largely because the federal government, unlike most other governments, successfully implemented antiunion policies that encouraged employers to disregard unions and the principles laid down in Walter Reuther's Treaty of Detroit in 1950 (see Chapter 26.)

The president made it clear that he neither respected the unions nor felt compelled to negotiate with them. When

13,000 air traffic controllers struck in 1981 over stagnating salaries, Reagan fired them, broke their union, and temporarily put the military in charge of air traffic. Big business applauded, but the government's actions sent shockwaves through organized labor. Many employers treated Reagan's audacious move, and his appointment of antiunionists to the National Labor Relations Board (NLRB) and the Department of Labor, as a permission note to ignore key labor laws. Workers who tried to unionize were illegally fired, and employers replaced hundreds of thousands of unionized employees with temporary laborers who were nonunionized and not entitled to costly benefits.

The unions filed grievances, but the NLRB often stood back, halving its prounion rulings. In a significant number of cases in 1984, the board effectively authorized employers to bypass negotiations with the unions. Such decisions encouraged the new phenomenon of **downsizing,** by which large corporations hired consultants and attorneys who helped them dodge labor laws and lay off employees, especially unionized workers. Downsizing led to the loss of over forty-five million jobs between 1979 and 1995. Most of the laid-off employees found new employment, though it was unlikely to be unionized work and typically did not include benefits such as health insurance. The days of the comfortable, one-income family, already in decline, had passed. By 1990, maintaining a middle-class lifestyle required both parents to work, and almost 60 percent of married mothers were employed outside the home, compared to fewer than one in two in 1980 and one in three in 1960.

Reagan's antiunion policy was wildly successful. Union membership, already declining, plummeted. Whereas almost one in four employees in the private sector had belonged to a union in 1979, fewer than one in six belonged by 1984. By the end of Reagan's second term, barely one in every ten employees was unionized. State and federal workers, who were generally well protected by law, continued to join unions at the same or a greater rate during these years and would not be targeted for deregulation until the twenty-first century.

THE ENVIRONMENT AND THE LIMITS OF DEREGULATION

Another radical policy reversal came in the area of the environment. As California governor in 1967–1975, Reagan had sided with environmentalists over issues such as the construction of a massive dam on the Eel River. By 1981, however, he believed that environmental regulation, like other government controls, was stifling business. Reagan played to antienvironmentalists with off-the-cuff comments such as "trees cause more pollution than automobiles do." Such talk impressed the western rangers, mining companies, and large property holders who had waged the 1970s "Sagebrush Rebellion" to demand that state and local authorities take possession of valuable federal land and make it available for development. They now had a champion at government's highest level.

The president rewarded antienvironmentalists' support by naming them to key positions in the government's environmental agencies. Before his appointment as secretary of the interior, attorney James Watt of Wyoming had specialized in finding legal ways to bypass environmental regulations so as to allow mining companies and other commercial interests access to protected land. Watt had claimed at his Senate confirmation that the imminent return of Jesus Christ obviated the need for federal land management. Once in charge of national parks and wildlife refuges, Watt made no secret of his contempt for environmentalism or his intention to open all unused federal land to mining and oil drilling interests by 2000.

Over the next two years, Watt quintupled the amount of land leased to mining companies and significantly expanded offshore drilling. His brash style and unrealistic goals alienated even many conservative Republicans, however, and he resigned two years into the job. Other, less outspoken deregulators made greater inroads. Colorado corporate attorney Anne Gorsuch headed the Environmental Protection Agency, which proceeded to drop lawsuits against polluters and relax antipesticide and clean air regulations. Forest Service chief John Crowell and Land Management Bureau head Robert Burford together facilitated the path of miners, drillers, and foresters onto previously protected land. Meanwhile, the sale of land-use rights at bargain-basement prices deprived the deficit-plagued federal treasury of their full market value.

This swift reversal of policy enraged environmentalists and stunned the public. Americans of all backgrounds enjoyed recreational activities in the national parks and forests. Almost everyone wanted clean, toxin-free air and drinking water. Increased drilling, mining, and timber felling threatened not only the natural world but also the billion-dollar wilderness recreation business and millions of jobs. A series of environmental disasters further impressed upon the public the need for tougher safety, labor, and other regulations. In 1984, a gas leak from the Union Carbide pesticide plant in Bhopal, India, killed over three thousand people. Two years later, the Chernobyl nuclear reactor in the Soviet Union melted down, spewing radioactive fallout across Belarus and Ukraine. And in 1989, the oil tanker *Exxon Valdez* ran aground off Alaska, releasing up to 750,000 barrels of crude oil onto the pristine coastline. An investigation by the National Transportation Safety Board found that the Exxon shipping company had failed to provide an adequately rested crew and to maintain its anticollision radar system, which would have warned of the impending danger.

Although two of these disasters occurred overseas, in all three cases lax or nonexistent labor and safety regulations were a major contributing factor—and were headline news in the United States and around the world. Concerned Americans joined the Sierra Club and other environmental groups in droves and loudly protested environmental and other forms of deregulation. Not wishing to alienate large numbers of voters, the Reagan administration began ratcheting back its deregulation policy in the election year of 1984. In his second term,

Limiting Deregulation. Shocking photographs and video of the *Exxon Valdez* spill, which killed more than 100,000 seabirds, over 2,800 sea otters, and other wildlife, persuaded many Americans that potential polluters, such as the oil shipping industry, should be regulated more rigorously.

Reagan would settle for ensuring that Congress passed no new environmental regulations. In 1990, Congress passed a new Pollution Act, which, among other things, banned dangerous, single-hull oil tankers such as the *Exxon Valdez*.

THE COLD WAR RENEWED

In foreign policy, expanding the military and reasserting U.S. power became Reagan's primary objectives. Critics complained that the president's grasp of the basic facts of global history and international affairs was tenuous at best. Nonetheless, his foreign policy proved popular at home and relatively effective abroad. Reagan drew on his remarkable ability to tap into voters' fears and aspirations and framed a simple, broadly appealing approach. The United States must use its military might and diplomatic power to confront Soviet communism, he asserted, while actively improving the world for all. Blending his characteristic idealism with hard-nosed pragmatism, Reagan justified massive increases in military spending both in stark terms, painting the Soviet Union as an evil empire, and in lofty rhetoric that appealed to Americans' sense of their nation as the historic champion of freedom. "We have it in our power," declared the president optimistically in 1981, "to begin the world over again."

Beginning the world over again had particular resonance in the wake of the disastrous Vietnam War, the oil shocks, the humiliation in Iran, and the Soviet invasion of Afghanistan. Reagan's military buildup and blunt anti-Soviet rhetoric rekindled the Cold War, reversing more than a decade of U.S. foreign policy that had emphasized the need for peaceful coexistence with the United States' superpower rival. The new approach also went beyond the older doctrine of containment, which had sought to block the spread of communism to Europe and the impoverished nations of the developing world in the 1950s and 1960s. Under Reagan, the objective was no less than the total defeat of Soviet communism. Military buildup, reasoned the president and his advisers, would force an arms race that would bankrupt the Soviet economy and spark an anticommunist revolution.

With the overthrow of the Soviet system in mind, in 1981 the president slapped trade sanctions on the USSR after Poland's pro-Soviet government suppressed an independent workers' organization named Solidarity. Two years later, after a Russian pilot shot down a Korean airliner that had wandered off-course and deep into Soviet airspace, the administration restricted commercial flights to the USSR.

Fighting the Soviets' Third World allies once again became an important part of U.S. foreign policy. Indeed, Reagan renewed U.S. financial and covert military operations against communist and other leftist movements, siding with extreme right-wing governments, dictatorships, and rebels much as the administrations of Eisenhower, Kennedy, and Johnson had. Announcing the Reagan Doctrine, the president declared before the world that the United States would actively support "freedom fighters" in the global struggle against communism. Subsequently, the United States accelerated financial and military aid for the anticommunist *mujahidin* who were battling Soviet occupiers in a very uneven match in Afghanistan. Using portable American-made Stinger missiles capable of taking down the Soviets' helicopters and jets, Afghan soldiers leveled the playing field and forced a stalemate—and, in 1988, Soviet withdrawal.

The administration most forcefully applied the Reagan Doctrine in Latin America and the Caribbean. In Nicaragua, leftist nationalists known as the Sandinistas had overthrown the pro-U.S. dictatorship of Anastasio Somoza García two years before Reagan took office. When the Nicaraguan nationalists, in 1981, extended their revolution to neighboring El Salvador, where a right-wing military dictatorship held power, Reagan authorized the CIA to covertly fund, arm, and train thousands of anti-Sandinista counterrevolutionaries known as Contras. El Salvador descended into a bloody civil war in which right-wing death squads eventually killed over forty thousand civilians and rebels. A similar scenario unfolded in

Guatemala. Two years later, the president sent U.S. troops to the island nation of Grenada (a former British colony) to overthrow its socialist government, which had recently staged a violent coup that potentially endangered one thousand American citizens living on the island.

The UN General Assembly condemned the invasion of Grenada by a vote of 108 to 9 (with 27 abstentions), and documentary evidence of the death squads' horrifying killings in El Salvador and Guatemala soon leaked out. The State Department denied involvement, going so far as to claim that one massacre of innocent civilians, at El Mozote in El Salvador, had never happened. As the evidence mounted, however, protests broke out on American college campuses and around the world. In 1984, Congress prohibited the government from directing military aid to the anti-Sandinista Contras.

Even as the Cold War seemed to be escalating once more, a different, less familiar threat emerged. In 1982, Israel, a U.S. ally, had invaded Lebanon, which was in the throes of a bloody civil war and had become a base from which guerrilla fighters from the Palestinian Liberation Organization (PLO) were launching attacks on Israel. Along with other nations, the United States sent a peacekeeping force to Lebanon to oversee the evacuation of PLO guerrillas and to stabilize the country. Resentment of the peacekeepers mounted among Lebanon's Muslim and Druze communities, particularly after U.S. forces bombed Druze civilians thought to be waging war on the Lebanese government. A few months later, two truck bombs exploded at the U.S. and French barracks, killing 241 American servicemen and 58 French paratroopers. The Islamic Jihad organization (later known as Hezbollah, a militant Shi'a Islamic group funded by Iran) claimed responsibility for the Beirut barracks bombing, and President Reagan quickly recalled U.S. troops. The president vowed to punish such terrorism. This new kind of enemy, however, would prove far more elusive than nation states such as the Soviet Union—and its number and grievances would multiply through the turn of twentieth century.

MORNING IN AMERICA

Reagan faced significant challenges as he headed into his reelection campaign in 1984. Although the administration had succeeded in weakening the unions and deregulating finance, manufacturing, and other industries, such policies had encountered strong headwinds. Scandals, moreover, had engulfed some of Reagan's top deregulators, and many Americans opposed the nuclear arms buildup and renewal of the Cold War.

The Democrats nominated Walter Mondale, vice president under Jimmy Carter, and (for the first time in history) chose a woman, Geraldine Ferraro, for vice president. Mondale railed at Reagan for starting a nuclear arms race, pursuing economic policies that favored the rich, and racking up a crushing federal debt. Taxes would have to be raised, warned the Democrat, and the budget would have to be balanced.

Reagan stayed positive, rejecting what his campaign managers called Mondale's "typical tax-and-spend, gloom-and-doom" assessment of the state of the nation and commending Americans for the "thousand dreams inside [their] hearts." The economy had recovered from the recession of 1981–1982 and was growing faster than at any other point since the 1950s. The nation's future was bright, Reagan proclaimed while campaigning in New Jersey—and it rested on "the message of hope in the songs of a man so many young Americans admire, New Jersey's Bruce Springsteen." The rocker's "Born in the USA" for a time became the campaign's anthem, even though Springsteen was a Democrat and the song criticized the nation's ill treatment of an unemployed Vietnam veteran.

The Republicans also flooded television with advertisements that celebrated the return of economic growth. One especially effective ad opened with scenes of Americans going off to work while a calm, confident narrator declares, "It's morning again in America." More men and women were employed than ever before, the narrator continued, mortgage rates and inflation were down, marriage rates were up, and "under the leadership of President Reagan, our country is prouder and stronger and better." Why would Americans "ever want to return to where we were less than four short years ago?" Voters agreed, delivering forty-nine of the fifty states and 59 percent of the popular vote to Reagan in a landslide election.

LAW-AND-ORDER PRESIDENCY

Abandoning his deregulation drive, the president now focused on passing immigration reform, waging the first large-scale **war on drugs,** and building a more conservative Supreme Court. The Immigration Reform and Control Act of 1986 made it an offense to knowingly hire immigrants who had entered the country illegally, and granted amnesty to three million illegal immigrants. The same year, the president signed a powerful law enforcement bill that significantly toughened the penalties for drug offenses and poured $2 billion into policing. First Lady Nancy Reagan meanwhile led an antidrug campaign urging youth to "Just Say No" to drugs. Both initiatives proved deeply controversial, particularly once it became clear that the penalties for possessing crack cocaine, a cheap and especially addictive street drug that was inundating the inner city, were much harsher than for regular cocaine, the drug of choice among more affluent users.

When three out of the nine presiding justices on the Supreme Court, including Chief Justice Warren Burger, retired in the 1980s, Reagan seized the opportunity to appoint conservatives to the bench. In his first term, the president had nominated Sandra Day O'Connor, an Arizona judge and former Republican politician. The first woman to serve on the Court, O'Connor hewed to the conservative judicial philosophy known as **New Federalism,** which held that the courts should force the federal government to devolve as much regulatory power as possible to the states. In his second term, Reagan's conservative nominees shared O'Connor's New Federalist perspective but also advocated a far stronger executive with far-reaching police powers and relative immunity from congressional oversight. Nominees argued for an "originalist" reading of the Constitution, according to which its true meaning could be found only in the intentions of the framers. The Constitution's authors, according to originalists, could not have intended to license the great civil rights, health, labor, and welfare reforms of the mid-twentieth century.

Antonin Scalia, a brilliant rhetorician, New Federalist, and originalist, was easily confirmed. However, the Senate drew the line at Robert Bork, a harsh critic of civil rights, women's rights, and the right to privacy. Following vehement opposition from Democratic senator Edward Kennedy, the NAACP, and women's rights groups, the Senate refused to confirm Bork. Reagan then nominated Anthony Kennedy, who had worked with the president when the latter was California governor. A conservative who was less ideological than other Reagan nominees, Kennedy won a relatively smooth confirmation in 1987.

The court's New Federalist turn was all but assured with the confirmation of justice William Rehnquist as Chief Justice in 1986 despite acrimonious debate in the Senate. Over the next nineteen years, Rehnquist would steer the Court in an aggressively conservative direction, overseeing an end to court-ordered busing, limiting the scope of federal laws, loosening protections for prisoners, and declaring capital punishment constitutional. President George H. W. Bush's successful nomination of David Souter in 1990 should theoretically have clinched a conservative majority in the Court. But in the meantime, Sandra Day O'Connor and Anthony Kennedy had unexpectedly become "swing votes," sometimes voting with the conservatives and other times against them.

Justice Sandra Day O'Connor. Although nominated by President Reagan, Justice O'Connor sometimes surprised Americans by opposing her conservative colleagues in key decisions. In 1989, for instance, she blocked Antonin Scalia's effort to overturn *Roe v. Wade*, thereby preserving abortion rights. Despite the occasional defeat, however, the majority of justices increasingly voted conservative—especially when it came to labor rights and the rights of prisoners and defendants.

COLD WAR THAW

Although Reagan made law and order the key focus of his second term, it came to light in late 1986 that high-ranking administration officials had been secretly selling antitank and antiaircraft missiles to Iran in exchange for Iran's help freeing seven American hostages held by Hezbollah in Lebanon. The proceeds from these arms sales were deposited in a Swiss bank account and then wired to the anti-Sandinista Contra rebels in Nicaragua, in contravention of Congress's explicit ban.

Top advisers oversaw the arrangement, and President Reagan probably knew of it. When Congress investigated, however, a mid-rank officer, Marine lieutenant colonel Oliver North, denied that the president had any knowledge, took the fall on national television, and defended his actions as just and patriotic. North and eleven Reagan staff members were indicted and convicted in 1988 (North's conviction was reversed a year later on technical grounds). Reagan himself escaped the Iran-Contra scandal unscathed, proving that he was the "Teflon president" to whom "dirt" never stuck.

Iran-Contra was soon eclipsed in the news by an unexpected thaw in U.S.-Soviet relations. The death of hard-line Soviet leader Leonid Brezhnev in 1982 had ushered in a period of rethinking and reform within the Kremlin. In 1985, a young Mikhail Gorbachev took power. Gorbachev pledged to implement a policy of *perestroika*—the restructuring of the depressed Soviet economy along market-oriented lines. He also promised a new era of *glasnost*, or political openness. To carry out these reforms, however, the Soviet leader needed to suspend the USSR's costly nuclear arms program, much as Reagan and his advisers had calculated.

Reaching out to Reagan, Gorbachev requested a meeting to discuss arms reduction. Reagan convened with the Soviet leader in Reykjavik, Iceland, in 1986. Under the Intermediate-Range Nuclear Forces Treaty that came out of the Reykjavik Summit, the two superpowers agreed to destroy all mid-range missiles in Europe. Reagan ceased to refer to the Soviet Union as the "evil empire" and advocated cooperation instead. The end of the Cold War was imminent.

THE NEW GILDED AGE

Reaganomics and deregulation had mixed but lasting results. Much as in the Gilded Age, consumer culture expanded dramatically, breaking into new territory such as the classroom and medicine. Consumers enjoyed far greater choice and lower prices for everything from air travel to long-distance telephone service. However, Wall Street and Main Street experienced this shift very differently. As in the Gilded Age, business leaders benefited far more than middle-income Americans. The poorest Americans grew poorer. The infusion of income at the highest ranks stimulated consumption—and prompted the culture industries to promote and extol affluence in the population at large. The movies and other culture industries nostalgically portrayed the 1950s as the ideal era of American prosperity and peace. The causes and impact of the US failure in Vietnam, also proved a recurring and controversial issue in culture and politics alike.

THE ECONOMY'S "GREAT EXPANSION"

Although the first three years of Reaganomics had resulted in a towering national debt and rising budget deficits, by 1983 Reagan fiscal policies had jumpstarted the economy and vanquished the spiraling inflation of the previous decade. For the next twenty-four years, the economy underwent what economists call the Great Expansion. As measured by continuous increases in gross domestic product, the economy grew by an average of about 6 percent a year for the next eight years—the longest peacetime expansion on record. Interrupted only by two eight-month recessions, it continued to boom until 2007 (see Chapter 31).

Although some of the new growth came from traditional sectors such as automobiles, oil, chemicals, and steel, most was generated by service industries. Banking and finance, the trades (such as electrical and plumbing services), information services, restaurants, entertainment, and tourism together led the boom. Many corporations, including fast food, retail, and manufacturing giants, underwent **vertical integration**, taking control of every step of the business, from production to finishing and distribution. The decade was also marked by large-scale consolidation of the media, with just fifty conglomerates owning almost all movie companies, magazines, newspapers, publishing enterprises, and broadcasting outlets by 1990. The majority of Americans now owned a TV that was hooked up to cable and a video recorder. Almost 50 percent had video game systems—a technology virtually unknown before the 1980s.

Introducing Macintosh. Like many computer companies, Apple was based in California's Santa Clara Valley (dubbed Silicon Valley). The company began life in the home garage of a future CEO, Steve Jobs (pictured here in 1984), in Los Altos before moving to Cupertino, eight miles away, in 1977. Close to the renowned computer science departments of Stanford University and the University of California at Berkeley, Cupertino offered cheap land, a stream of talented computer scientists, and space for expansion.

Heavy industry and manufacturing, the twin engines of U.S. prosperity since the Gilded Age, lost more ground to foreign producers. In 1984, for the first time since 1915, the United States imported more goods and money than it exported. Much of the trade deficit arose from Japan's phenomenal rise as an economic superpower and one of the world's leading producers of cars and electronics. U.S. automakers found it increasingly difficult to compete with Japan's cheaper, more fuel-efficient cars. American factories closed, and once-prosperous towns such as Flint, Michigan, went into steep decline. By 1990, journalists had renamed the nation's Industrial Belt, which stretched from the steel and coal works of Pennsylvania through the factories and auto-assembly lines of Ohio and Michigan, the "Rust Belt."

The single manufacturing industry that experienced steady growth in the 1980s was a relatively new one. The makers of personal computers (PCs) had shrunk the room-size computer processors that the military had developed during World War II down to the size of a relatively affordable microchip. In 1984, the PC enjoyed its first major commercial success with the release of Apple's Macintosh. Meanwhile, software designers Bill Gates and Paul Allen had developed a powerful new operating system, MS-DOS, which they sold to Apple competitors. The precursor to Windows, the system went on to be used on the vast majority of the world's PCs.

CELEBRATING AFFLUENCE

Much like their Gilded Age counterparts, many of the wealthiest Americans engaged in "conspicuous consumption" as they purchased expensive European cars, constructed lavish mansions, and threw posh parties. Tirelessly tracking the spending frenzy, the media glorified the new live-for-today attitude. Books, movies, advertisements, TV shows, and clothing styles exalted affluence, stimulating the desire among less well-off Americans to emulate the look and feel of the "good life." TV shows such as *Lifestyles of the Rich and Famous* paid homage to excess as a value worthy of pursuit and imitation.

Americans also thrilled to the stories of successful corporate titans. Among them was Lee Iacocca, Chrysler's CEO, who had saved the foundering automaker (with the help of a $1.5 billion loan from the U.S. government) and made it profitable again. Donald Trump, a real estate developer, energetically promoted himself and his taste for excess, feeding the media stories of his high-rolling lifestyle and building the extravagant Trump Towers in New York City.

Whereas fashion had emphasized individuality, creativity, and even resourcefulness in the 1960s and 1970s, excess now became the aim. White women lopped off their long, natural locks and opted instead for voluminous blow-dried and "permed" hairstyles. Male rock bands such as Def Leppard followed suit. Women's clothing, embellished with shoulder pads, ruffles, and rhinestones, emphasized glamour. For men, formal black-tie dinner suits made a comeback. When high-end clothing designers, such as Giorgio Armani, Ralph Lauren, and Calvin Klein, produced "designer jeans" and underwear, eager consumers paid unprecedentedly high prices.

REVISING HISTORY

As part of the shift in attitudes toward the glorification of wealth, a nostalgic vision of the 1950s also predominated in mass culture, as did reinterpretations of the turbulent sixties. President Reagan made explicit appeals to Americans to restore what he thought of as the affluent, decent 1950s. Reinforcing Reagan's perspective, a wave of Hollywood movies created an artificial memory of the fifties as a harmonious, universally prosperous, and morally uncomplicated time. *Diner* (1982), *The Right Stuff* (1983), *Back to the Future* (1985), *Peggy Sue Got Married* (1986), and *La Bamba* (1987) portrayed the period in glowing terms—conveniently writing McCarthyism, racial segregation, the decaying inner city, suburban sprawl, and women's subordination out of the script.

Other mass culture dealt with the legacy of the 1960s and Vietnam. Although a minority of radicals from the 1960s continued on in politics, by 1980 most hippies and radicals had abandoned the counterculture or protest politics, embarked on careers, bought their first home, and become "yuppies" (young upwardly mobile urban professionals). Many now looked for a way to square their past with the present—and to come to terms with their newfound affluence. One popular movie, *The Big Chill* (1983), tells the story of a group of old friends from the 1960s who have a reunion in 1982 following the suicide of a college buddy. While the friends lament the loss of the camaraderie, idealism, and exhilaration of the sixties, most of the characters find a way of justifying their new lives and pursuit of wealth. TV shows echoed this theme: "If we can't have the revolution," an ex-hippie remarked on the yuppie-centered drama *thirtysomething*, "we might as well have a great breakfast room."

American Bling. Later dubbed "McMansions," ostentatious homes became fashionable in the 1980s, as mass culture rejected the last remnants of the 1960s' anti-commercialism and once again embraced conspicuous consumption. **Question for Analysis:** What does this McMansion's attention to detail, usually found on much larger homes, suggest about the owner's aspirations?

The renewal of the Cold War inspired a series of blockbuster action adventure movies, many of which addressed the United States' failure in Vietnam. In *Top Gun* (1986), the decade's most popular movie, an airman whose father went missing-in-action during the Vietnam

Rewriting Vietnam. After reporters overheard President Reagan at a press conference saying, "Boy, after seeing *Rambo* last night, I know what to do next time this happens," the photomontage satirist Alfred Gescheidt produced this image. The montage captured what many Americans loved—or hated—about Reagan's foreign policy and tough talk.

War confronts his inner demons by becoming an ace fighter pilot, using the latest technology to shoot down enemy planes. *Rambo: First Blood Part II* (1985) also attempted to cure the "Vietnam syndrome"—Americans' loss of confidence in the nation's ability to win a war. In this high-action film, muscleman Sylvester Stallone played a soldier who is sent back to Vietnam to find long-lost American POWs—a goal he accomplishes by singlehandedly massacring their Vietnamese captors. In case the point was lost on audiences, Stallone's character asks his superior officer, "Sir, do we get to win this time?" Other films, such as Oliver Stone's *Platoon* (1986), refused to let audiences forget the war's moral and political complexities. Showing combat in graphically realistic detail, Stone's movie portrayed the divisions within a platoon, U.S. violence against civilians, and young soldiers' terrifying experiences of jungle warfare.

NEW FRONTIERS OF CONSUMERISM

Advertisers and merchandisers had long ago saturated urban spaces with commercial messages and imagery. They had entered private homes via radio, television, the movies, magazines, mass mailings, and product packaging. But they had not yet infiltrated classrooms or children's playtime and meals. In the 1980s, deregulation encouraged many industries to break past the remaining boundaries and also to transform the meaning of shopping itself.

Advertisers and merchandisers created a separate fantasy world for kids. Indeed, deregulation of TV advertising meant that advertisers could aim program-length commercials at children. Typically starring a licensed movie or TV action figure such as Darth Vader or a Smurf, these ads were intended to spur product sales. The plan worked. Whereas only one in ten toys sold in the United States was based on a licensed character in 1980, almost two-thirds were by 1990. Even public television followed suit, selling licensed *Sesame Street* characters to close funding gaps.

Toy companies and fast food interests broke new ground by collaborating on a large scale, as eateries such as McDonald's and Burger King offered children "free" gifts such as plastic cups and plates featuring favorite TV and movie characters. In 1984, a new cable TV station, Nickelodeon, aimed its shows and advertisements specifically at children. And corporations entered the classroom for the first time, distributing free products and services in exchange for adding the company name and products to the curriculum. Thousands of schoolchildren, for example, learned about volcanoes—and a delicious new candy—with the help of General Mills' Fruit Gushers (which exploded like a volcano). By the mid-1990s, 350 corporations were running similar educational programs.

As the child's world became ever more commercialized, tag, dodge ball, and other social games that required little equipment declined in popularity. Parents' lawsuits against schools that allowed rough-and-tumble games (which could result in injury to children) led some schools to ban these traditional pastimes. The relatively new medium of video games also sped the decline. Beginning in the early 1980s, children and teens fed billions of quarters to oversized video machines in game arcades or played on first-generation home consoles (see Hot Commodities: *Pac-Man* and the Popularization of Virtual Reality).

Later on, smaller, more sophisticated Nintendo games for the home replaced the arcades. By the end of the decade, children were playing more at home and less in public playgrounds—a trend that would accelerate as video games continued to grow in popularity. Like their parents, millions of children now thought of playtime as the consumption of commercial goods and services.

Even the activity of shopping changed during the 1980s. Shopping ceased to be merely a means to an end (consuming goods) and became a popular form of recreation. Large-scale malls and gallerias were the most common shopping destination, displacing "Main Street" stores. Movie theaters opened, and a new species of "themed" chain stores and restaurants (including Hooters and Hard Rock Cafe) turned the malls into multiuse spaces where entertainment, browsing, dating, hanging out, and spending time with the family blended with and enhanced the shopping experience.

HOT COMMODITIES

Pac-Man and the Popularization of Virtual Reality

Although the first video games appeared in arcades in the 1970s, the majority of Americans, as late as 1980, had never played one. Then came *Pac-Man*—the arcade video game that revolutionized gaming, created a mass market, and, over a decade before the spread of the Internet, introduced millions of Americans to virtual reality. After inserting a quarter in the machine, the player, represented as a yellow disc named "Pac-Man," ate as many moving dots as possible while being chased by four "evil" ghosts and making his or her way through a series of labyrinths. As the player gobbled dots, the *Pac-Man* icon issued a cute "wocka-wocka" swallowing sound. The game seems simple by today's standards. Back then, though, players (who were accustomed to simple shooting and racing games) had never seen or heard anything like it.

Contrary to industry expectations, the game was an instant hit, generating a *Pac-Man* fever that turned it into the best-selling arcade game of all time. Various versions became available for the first generation of home computers, including the best-selling Atari 2600 and Commodore 64. The icon soon starred in a Hanna-Barbera cartoon series and appeared on everything from stickers and lunchboxes to pajamas and belt buckles. Pac-Man even became an "old-fashioned" wind-up toy and a character in board games. By 1982, the game was so popular that hundreds of towns prohibited arcades outright, condemning them as "sirens" that lured children (and their lunch money) away from school.

Ms. Pac-Man. In 1982 alone, Americans fed thirty-two *billion* quarters into *Pac-Man* machines. Although successfully completing all 256 stages of the game was theoretically possible, it was not until 1999—nineteen years into the game's life—that a player, thirty-three-year-old Billy Mitchell, actually "won"!

Pac-Man's mass appeal lay partly in its reinvention of the player's role from noninteractive to active participant in a virtual world. Unlike in earlier video games, the player was a character, the *Pac-Man* icon, and this player-character participated virtually in the action. He or she could advance the plot by gobbling more dots and staying alive. The action itself was structured differently than before, with the player generally trying to elude rather than confront enemies. "Power-ups" rewarded players by briefly empowering them to "eat" enemy ghosts and by breaking the tension with comical interludes. Far from the dark and overtly violent graphics of earlier shooting games, *Pac-Man*'s icons were light, colorful, and "cute."

All these features made *Pac-Man* a perfect match for a culture that emphasized instant gratification. And in turning "gobbling" into lighthearted play, *Pac-Man* literally mirrored the era's unambiguous celebration of consumption. It proved irresistible not only to existing video gamers—the vast majority of whom were boys—but also to new participants, including girls. In 1981, the game's U.S. distributor sought to capitalize on girls' interest by releasing *Ms. Pac-Man*.

Pac-Man's virtual technology made it an important precursor of many of today's interactive video games and helped create a culture that was receptive to more complex forms of virtual reality. Although today's Lara Croft and the Assassins of the *Assassin's Creed* series look nothing like *Pac-Man*, in technological and cultural terms, they—and the worlds they allow us to inhabit—are his descendants and heirs.

Think About It

1. Given the state of American politics and culture in 1980, why might millions of people have flocked to play a virtual reality game like *Pac-Man*? Why do you think the game was so addictive?
2. In what ways, if any, did *Pac-Man* transform the meaning of play?

Consumers mostly went along with the new meaning of shopping and with commerce's expansion into previously protected spheres. They committed much more of their income to consumption and significantly less to their savings—which fell by two-thirds, from an average 9 percent of income to just 2.8 percent by 1986. Like the federal government, Americans also went deeper into debt to maintain their spending levels, expending an average of 20 percent more of their income on installment debt plans than they had in the 1970s.

Good Time, Great Toys. Fast food chains worked with Hollywood to produce tie-ins that simultaneously attracted younger customers and families to their restaurants and made money for film companies. Darth Vader, the villain in *Star Wars*, was one especially popular action figure given away by Burger King. George Lucas Films celebrated the first fast food–toy tie-in when customers received free *Star Wars* paraphernalia with their burgers and fries. The campaign's success led to an explosion of such collaboration.

NEW AND OLD INEQUALITIES

Although the economy surged and the average American's paycheck fattened during the 1980s, the majority nonetheless fell behind relative to overall growth of income. For the first time since the 1920s, the lion's share of the new prosperity went to the wealthiest 1 percent of citizens. The average American's pretax income increased 7 percent during the decade, while the top 1 percent's income shot up by an astounding 107 percent. Other statistics confirmed that the tide was not lifting all boats equally. Large-scale investors, bankers, and celebrities had always outearned most other Americans, but in the 1980s their remuneration grew exponentially faster. Whereas in the 1970s, top basketball or football stars earned on average eight times what an average American earned, by the end of the 1980s they were making fifty times the average wage. The **affluence gap** between the wealthiest and the majority had been greater only in the Gilded Age.

If middle-income Americans prospered only partially from the boom, it bypassed the poor altogether. Overall poverty rates rose between 1980 and 1988, from 11.7 to 13.5 percent, the highest level since the 1950s. African Americans and female-headed households (some of which were also African American) were especially hard hit. Children's poverty rate rose from about 18 percent to almost 20 percent, or 50 percent in the case of African Americans. Minorities also bore the brunt of unemployment, with African American men experiencing almost twice the level of joblessness as other men. Retired Americans (who, before the New Deal, had traditionally endured high levels of poverty) were saved, however, largely because Social Security and Medicare were still intact.

At no time since the Great Depression was homelessness such a large and visible phenomenon. The number of homeless Americans more than tripled between 1980 and 1988 from 125,000 to 402,000. Cuts to welfare programs and institutions such as hospitals and psychiatric institutions turned tens of thousands of vulnerable citizens onto the streets. The majority were single, unemployed people who had spent time in prison or a mental institution. In many cities, over a third were Vietnam veterans, and a majority battled alcoholism or drug addiction.

Homeless advocates pressed for low-cost federal housing and drug rehabilitation programs but made little headway. Shelters could not keep pace, and many homeless people bedded down in cardboard boxes or abandoned buildings. Unknown just a few years earlier, the homeless "squeegee guy" (who, in hopes of earning a quarter or two, cleaned drivers' windshields as they waited at red lights) became ubiquitous—an ever-present reminder that the new, deindustrializing order was creating not only unparalleled wealth and opportunity, but also poverty and social dysfunction.

REINVENTING DISSENT

Most liberal and leftist baby boomers considered the 1980s an unmitigated triumph for conservative politics and culture. Convinced that consumerism had reduced the population to selfish, mindless automatons who cared little about oppression or inequality, many checked out of politics altogether. Other baby boomers "sold out," treating the culture of affluence as the logical extension of the sixties' emphasis on self-exploration and personal fulfillment. The new poverty and social dysfunction did not go entirely unchallenged, however, and neither Reaganism nor conservative culture was as successful or as far reaching as critics assumed. A small but vocal minority of leftist and liberal baby boomers adapted old strategies to new challenges. Novel oppositional networks and fresh forms of cultural and political expression emerged. As well, progressive members of the younger, more diverse Generation X (born between 1964 and 1979) began formulating their own radically democratic visions.

THE NEW ACTIVISM

President Reagan and his conservative supporters attempted to return the United States to an idealized 1950s, but their agenda in fact had the effect of provoking new forms of dissent and forging new, "progressive" networks comprising liberals and leftists. On college campuses especially, young Americans mobilized to pressure the government, business, and other major institutions to change course on an array of domestic and international issues. Although radicals from the 1960s were involved in the new movements, both their personnel and many of their methods differed from those of two decades earlier. They and **Generation X** distanced themselves from the antiestablishment politics of the 1960s, which had ended in violence, repression, and questionable gains. Many engaged in direct action of the sort pioneered by the freedom movement, the Black Panthers, and the Yippies, but they hoped to change particular policies rather than overthrow "the system." Some also tried to reform the establishment from within—a strategy that 1960s radicals would have rejected as selling-out. Protest in the 1980s was typically more tactical and less idealistic, though no less determined. Activists generally had narrower goals and used the mass media to build rather than to alienate "mainstream" support.

Former 1960s activists and Generation X progressives first came together over the staggering nuclear buildup. Inspired by mass antinuclear demonstrations in Europe in 1981, a grassroots movement took shape. Veteran activists, in a widely circulated pamphlet, "A Call to Halt the Nuclear Arms Race," proposed a freeze on nuclear arms manufacture and urged the United States and the Soviet Union to shrink nuclear arsenals. The document's clear, sensible language was highly influential among antinuclear activists and palatable to the mass media. Local organizers across the United States rallied popular support for a freeze, attracting celebrity backing from Bruce Springsteen and others. Distancing themselves from the "peacenik" rhetoric and look of the 1960s, organizers emphasized that the arms race jeopardized families—and that voters were footing the enormous cost of nuclear warheads.

By 1982, hundreds of towns, including almost 90 percent of those in Vermont, had passed freeze resolutions. The same year, in the largest protest march in the nation's history, 750,000 men, women, and children rallied peacefully in Central Park and demanded that the Soviets and the United States freeze the testing, production, and deployment of nuclear arms. The crowd was not only orderly but also far more diverse

Nuclear Nightmares. Convinced that Americans would be traumatized by the made-for-TV movie *The Day After*, thousands of school administrators—along with ABC officials—set up counseling facilities and discussion groups for viewers. Ronald Reagan recorded in his diary that the film was "very effective and made me depressed."

than prior mass protests. "It's not just hippies and crazies anymore," one demonstrator told the press. Then in 1982, tens of thousands of people attended a fundraising concert at Pasadena's Rose Bowl for a televised mass "aid" concert aimed at raising cash and publicizing the antinuclear movement. These tactics proved quite successful, with Michigan, New Jersey, Oregon, and five other states supporting nuclear-freeze ballot initiatives in the 1982 elections. The following year, a record one hundred million viewers tuned into ABC television's *The Day After* (1983), a movie about the possible impact of a nuclear attack on Kansas and Missouri. Although the Reagan administration criticized the freeze movement at first, the president quietly began exploring arms reduction.

GOING GLOBAL

The antinuclear movement introduced a new generation of Americans to progressive politics and raised their awareness of their country's role as a wealthy superpower in a globalizing world. Primed by the antinuclear cause, many began following U.S. foreign policy in Central America in the early 1980s. Thousands of college students joined the voluntary organization Witness for Peace. Small groups of "witnesses" went to Guatemala, El Salvador, and Nicaragua in the hope that their presence—and their cameras and notebooks—would deter the Contra death squads. The witnesses forged tight bonds and a sense of solidarity with both the suffering civilian population and the leftist Sandinista leadership.

In the United States, over three hundred sympathetic churches and synagogues started the sanctuary movement in 1982. These institutions established a new "underground railroad" for Salvadoran and Guatemalan civilians fleeing the Contra death squads. The network was much like the one that had once aided fugitive slaves on their journey north. Refugees recounted their horrific experiences of Contra and other right-wing violence (see Singular Lives: Adriana Rodriguez, Political Refugee). Their stories, together with a cascade of artistic and literary work by fellow survivors, revealed the nefarious uses to which U.S. taxpayers' money was being put. Secular activists also publicized the atrocities, criticizing U.S. foreign policy as the latest instance of American "imperialism." As well as organizing street demonstrations, activists lobbied Congress to investigate the death squads and stop U.S. funding. By 1986, when the Iran-Contra scandal broke, most Americans opposed further U.S. intervention in Central America.

Activists' other major cause in these years was South Africa's anti-apartheid movement. For many decades, South Africa's white minority had deprived all nonwhites of the vote, imposed racial segregation, and forced much of the black population to live on hardscrabble *Bantustans* (all-black reservations). Anti-apartheid protest in the United States reached back to the 1960s and earlier, but it was only in the mid-1980s that a popular movement flourished. The protesters focused on one very specific issue—large-scale U.S. investment in South Africa. Such investment, activists argued, not only benefited from apartheid but perpetuated it.

In the late 1970s, anti-apartheid activists had first targeted a handful of universities (whose large pension funds often held South African investments) and major corporations. The effort sprang back to life in 1985, after American television broadcast images of the South African military brutally suppressing black protesters in Soweto, an urban area near Johannesburg, South Africa's largest city. Students across the nation staged sit-ins in campus buildings. Others constructed and inhabited mock shantytowns in the middle of their college campuses—a symbol of South Africa's poor black townships and *Bantustans*. The shanties proved a headache for college administrators, who wanted to protect free speech rights but worried about the shanties' safety and appearance. But the installations were a catalyst for campus-wide debate. Even at more conservative colleges, such as Dartmouth, more than 40 percent of students supported divestment. The cause got a further boost in late 1985 when a diverse group of well-known musicians, including Run DMC, Bono, and Bonnie Raitt,

Musicians Against Apartheid Progressive students and musicians used the mass media (including MTV) to build popular support for divestment in South Africa. By 1989, more than 80 percent of all U.S. colleges and universities had divested from the country, Congress had banned new investment, and state and local government pension funds had withdrawn almost $20 billion.

SINGULAR LIVES

Adriana Rodriguez, Political Refugee

Aged twenty-three, Adriana Rodriguez in 1981 was an energetic nursing student, committed to serving some of the most vulnerable citizens of her native El Salvador. Between classes in San Salvador, the nation's capital, she volunteered at a nearby clinic that served elderly people, women, and children who had fled the brewing civil war between El Salvador's brutal military regime and pro-democracy forces. Rodriguez, like many Salvadorans, was still hopeful that the citizenry would prevail, much as in neighboring Nicaragua, where the pro-democracy movement had triumphed.

Over the next two years, however, El Salvador's infamous right-wing death squads openly killed sixteen thousand Salvadorans, "disappeared" and tortured thousands more, and turned the nation into a magnet for leftist revolutionaries. By 1983, most Salvadorans no longer believed that democratic change was possible—especially once it became clear that the United States, which had tentatively supported the new Nicaraguan government in 1979, was aiding both the right-wing Contras and El Salvador's military regime (under the Reagan Doctrine). As the war escalated, even those who merely helped the refugees were fired, expelled from school, and harassed by the military. The persecution grew steadily more violent. In 1982, one of Rodriguez's coworkers was abducted from the refugee clinic by heavily armed men and never seen again. Rodriguez struggled on with her work, ignoring threats and harassment. Later that year, however, after her fiancé and father were brutally murdered, she joined the mass exodus out of El Salvador.

Rodriguez eventually sought sanctuary in the United States as a political refugee, traveling through war-wracked Guatemala and Mexico before crossing into the United States in late 1982. The U.S. government classified her and other Central American refugees as "economic migrants" who, fleeing poverty rather than persecution, did not qualify for political asylum. Rodriguez, like her compatriots, was classified as an illegal alien. Undeterred, and with help from the Sanctuary movement, she stayed on in the United States and eventually found work in New York—once again for a refugee organization.

Why did the United States refuse to grant asylum to most Salvadoran victims of political violence? In the 1970s, Congress had prohibited the United States from aiding governments that tortured or perpetrated other human rights abuses. Acknowledging the migrants' status as political refugees would have implicitly recognized the fact that the Salvadoran regime was abusing human rights.

Think About It

1. How might the implementation of the Reagan Doctrine have indirectly affected Rodriguez's life and the people of El Salvador?
2. Why do you think Rodriguez sought political asylum in the United States rather than somewhere else, even though it was common knowledge that the Reagan administration supported El Salvador's regime?
3. How might granting Rodriquez political refugee status have endangered the implementation of the Reagan Doctrine?

produced a music video in which they condemned apartheid and pledged never to perform in the South African resort of Sun City.

President Reagan, while conceding that apartheid was wrong, insisted that the United States and American corporations ought to pursue "constructive engagement" with the regime. However, progressives' efforts brought considerable pressure to bear on Reagan and Congress. In 1986, a year after the protests, lawmakers passed the Comprehensive Anti-Apartheid Act over Reagan's veto. The law banned new investment in South Africa, the sale of military and policing equipment, and the importation of South African goods. In combination with other nations' divestment campaigns, these prohibitions drained capital out of South Africa. The proapartheid regime began to contemplate reform, releasing African National Congress leader Nelson Mandela from prison in 1989. The following year, the embattled government set about dismantling apartheid and preparing the nation for its first democratic election.

ELECTING AFRICAN AMERICANS

Although the African American–owned Black Entertainment Television (BET) acquired its own cable channel in 1983, much of the U.S. media was still overwhelmingly run by whites. Together with most conservative politicians, the media portrayed African Americans either as an underclass that had tragically failed to capitalize on civil rights reform or as criminal "welfare queens" and "crackheads." Fighting such stereotyping—as well as the devastating effects of deindustrialization, the dismantling of welfare programs, and the crack cocaine epidemic—became major priorities for African American activists in the 1980s. They continued building grassroots organizations and, for the first time since Reconstruction, moved into electoral politics in large numbers.

New groups such as POWER (People Organized for Welfare and Employment Rights) took on the Reagan administration's attack on Great Society programs by organizing voter registration drives. A significant upturn in voting rates helped to push the number of African American mayors from only a few in 1965 to 316 by 1990. Chicago, Washington, D.C., New York City, and Los Angeles all elected African American mayors. Drawing support from African Americans, whites, Latinos, and Asian Americans, over twenty black candidates also won seats in Congress.

Most African American politicians had come up through the freedom movement. Jesse Jackson, a former aide to Martin Luther King, Jr., vividly described U.S. voters as a "rainbow coalition" of all races, religions, occupations, and ethnicities. Excited and hopeful, several million African Americans registered and cast their first vote in the Democratic primary of 1984, in which the most prominent progressive to run for the nomination was Jackson himself. The candidate's multiracial Rainbow Coalition delivered him a number of states and forced Democratic Party leaders to take him seriously.

On the Campaign Stump. Jesse Jackson delivers a speech in Chicago during his 1984 presidential bid.

Promoting economic justice for all, Jackson boldly argued that poverty was not just an African American issue and that "most poor are White women, infants, children, and old people." But his candidacy collapsed unexpectedly when, in an aside to a journalist, he used anti-Semitic slurs. Jackson redoubled his electoral efforts in 1988, reaching out to Hispanics, rural whites, and the working class. While his progressive platform garnered widespread support, the Democratic Party ultimately chose Michael Dukakis, a centrist white candidate, instead. Still, Jackson's candidacy had made history, and it would help lay the path for Barack Obama's successful bid for the presidential nomination twenty years later.

African Americans had more success in Congress and in city government. Democrat Harold Washington, elected to Congress in 1980, vociferously opposed Reaganomics, the nuclear buildup, and Central American policy. Later elected mayor of Chicago, Washington dismantled that city's entrenched patronage system, which had traditionally excluded African Americans and minorities. He also passed a Tenants' Bill of Rights before dying suddenly a few months into his tenure. In Washington, D.C., Mayor Marion Barry, a former member of the Student Nonviolent Coordinating Committee, improved city services, founded a summer jobs program for youth, restored ten thousand decrepit housing units, and instigated a transparent financial accounting system. Commending New York City as a "gorgeous mosaic" of diversity, that city's black mayor, David Dinkins, focused on reducing crime. After his first year in office (1990), crime rates dropped for thirty-six straight months.

Many of the most egregious forms of racism had diminished by the 1980s, but prejudice still abounded, particularly against African American lawmakers and mayors. Chicago's Mayor Washington, like other African American mayors, had to deal with some white constituents' suspicions that he would serve only the black community. Although New York crime rates dropped under Mayor Dinkins, white New Yorkers believed they were rising, and the misperception helped Republican Rudolph Giuliani to win the mayoral election of 1993 on a promise to "restore" law and order. And despite his achievements as three-term mayor of the nation's capital, Marion Barry was embroiled in a drug scandal that ended his tenure and affirmed ugly stereotypes about African Americans. (After serving jail time, the popular Barry won reelection to a fourth term, in 1994.)

ACTING UP

Gays, lesbians, and transgender people also mobilized to elect sympathetic legislators and continue the reform drive of past decades. The outbreak of a lethal new disease had a galvanizing effect. A mysterious illness swept through the gay male communities of San Francisco and New York in 1980, sickening and eventually killing almost all those who contracted it. For months, no one understood the disease or why it struck gay men disproportionately. In 1982, American physicians finally named it AIDS, or acquired immune deficiency syndrome. The following year, a French physician discovered the causative virus—HIV, the human immunodeficiency virus. Unprotected sex and the reuse of dirty injection-drug needles were the principal transmission routes.

Almost one hundred thousand Americans died of AIDS in the 1980s—almost twice the number killed in World War I—and the disease would fell twenty million people worldwide by 2000. With gay men the first-known AIDS victims, the Reagan administration was reluctant to declare a national health emergency. Money that could have been spent on researching the virus was withheld as some Reagan advisers speculated that AIDS was God's punishment for gays. Not until 1987, after tens of thousands of deaths, did the Reagan administration acknowledge that there was an AIDS epidemic and that anyone, regardless of sexual orientation, could contract it. Yet the government still resisted declaring a national health emergency and refused to educate the public about condom use (which greatly reduces HIV transmission).

Enraged by official indifference, gay men and their supporters founded the AIDS Coalition to Unleash Power (ACT UP) in 1987. The group put antidiscrimination laws on city and state ballots, staged media stunts such as "die-ins" at busy city intersections, distributed millions of condoms, and marched to demand that the government take AIDS seriously. ACT UP also stormed medical conventions of virologists and pharmaceutical companies, insisting that they invest more in the study of HIV. Fusing visual art and politics, the coalition produced striking posters, stickers, and other art forms that criticized the government's slow response to AIDS. Such campaigns educated

Memorializing the Victims of AIDS. Gay rights activist Cleve Jones turned to art as a vehicle for honoring the thousands of Americans who had died of AIDS and for challenging the Reagan administration's failure to fund AIDS research. Conceived of by Jones, the Memorial Quilt, pictured here on the Mall in Washington, D.C., in 1987, originally consisted of 1,920 panels, each naming an AIDS victim and sewn by a friend or loved one. Activists then carried the quilt across the United States on a twenty-city tour, collecting panels along the way. The quilt today consists of 48,000 panels memorializing more than 94,000 people.

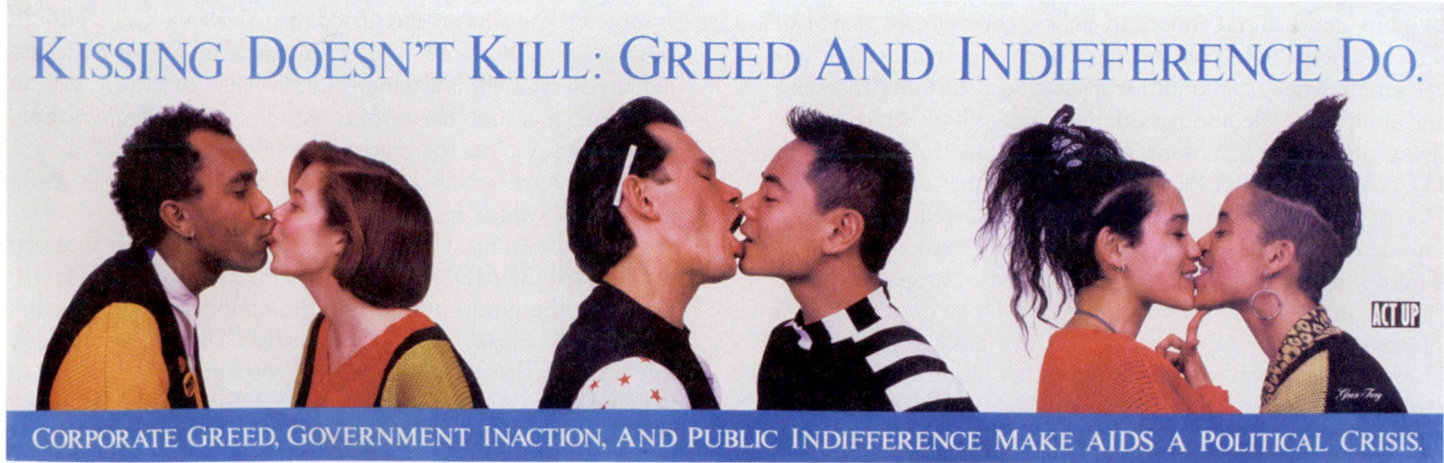

KISSING DOESN'T KILL: GREED AND INDIFFERENCE DO.
ACT UP
CORPORATE GREED, GOVERNMENT INACTION, AND PUBLIC INDIFFERENCE MAKE AIDS A POLITICAL CRISIS.

AIDS Education. Independent artist collectives used guerrilla marketing to spread ACT UP's messages. In New York City, San Francisco, and elsewhere, gay-positive and AIDS education posters appeared in subway cars and taxi cabs and on lampposts, billboards, and bus panels. This New York City bus panel from 1989 informed viewers that "Kissing Doesn't Kill: Greed and Indifference Do." **Questions for Analysis:** What is this image's message? What made it so attention-grabbing in 1989?

gays and straights alike about safer sex and encouraged the former to take pride in themselves and their sexuality.

ACT UP members made a point of being open, honest, and unapologetic about their sexual orientation, thus emboldening millions of younger Americans to "come out" (of the closet) and declare their gay, lesbian, or "queer" sexual orientation. Other groups soon formed, including Lesbian Nation, whose founders had been active in ACT UP, and Queer Nation, an all-inclusive coalition that mounted street demonstrations against discrimination and homophobia (hatred of gays), chanting "We're here! We're queer! Get used to it!"

ART OF DISSENT

The AIDS crisis was a strong catalyst for radical artists in New York, San Francisco, and other major cities. But it was just one among many new forces to which artists responded in the 1980s. Indeed, the decade witnessed the birth of novel genres of music, visual art, philosophy, writing, and documentary-film making. Together these laid the foundation for much of today's art and popular culture.

Gangstas with Attitude. Many white Americans and older-generation African Americans objected to rap's focus on sex and drugs and joined feminists who condemned the apparent misogyny of the lyrics. Calls for censorship heightened in 1988 when gangsta rappers N.W.A, pictured here, released a song containing an expletive aimed at the police.

Rock music continued to innovate and to serve as a vital channel for social criticism and artistic experimentation. Various subgenres of heavy metal—a fast, loud, distorted rock style—thrived among young white working-class audiences. Although metal was generally apolitical, it challenged the cultural norms of the 1980s, attracting criticism in particular from conservative Christians who objected to some songs' violent, sexual, and potentially blasphemous content. Another new musical genre fused punk and rock to produce "alternative rock." Bands such as R.E.M. and Sonic Youth experimented with feedback and other forms of white noise, pairing sound with poetic lyrics, and recording strictly on independent labels. Women artists, such as Pat Benatar, Joan Jett, and Chrissie Hynde burst onto the male-dominated rock scene with a raw assertiveness not seen since Patti Smith's punk rock debut in the 1970s. Less experimental but far more political and popular, Bruce Springsteen recorded songs of biting social criticism.

Some of the hardest-hitting, most innovative cultural production came from African American communities. A cohort of women writers, including Toni Morrison and Alice Walker, explored controversial themes such as slavery and racism and equally challenging issues like incest, sexual discovery, and spirituality. Their work implicitly confronted the "welfare queen" and "crackhead" mythologies circulating in some sections of the white media and found a mass audience as well as critical acclaim. On the big screen, independent filmmakers Spike Lee and John Singleton probed contemporary black life in movies such as *Do the Right Thing* (1989) and *Boyz n the Hood* (1991). Lee and Singleton neither shied away from themes of drug dealing, gangs, and street crime nor condoned the mainstream media's negative characterization of African Americans.

Perhaps the most radical and enduring art form to develop in the 1980s, rap music interwove social criticism with rhyme and poetry, performance art, and music. In 1990, New York's Public Enemy rapped about whites' fears of interracial relationships on their album *Fear of a Black Planet* and condemned the usual slowness of emergency response units to come to the aid of African Americans in "911 Is a Joke." Ice-T and other creators of "gangsta rap" (which emerged first in Los Angeles) used edgier rhymes but a slower beat and frequently documented gang life, drug dealing, sex, and making money. Although rap was largely male dominated and often misogynist, female rappers such as Roxanne Shanté, Salt-N-Pepa, and Queen Latifah won significant followings and rapped about empowered women.

Rap's critical edge also came through in stories about police harassment, poverty, and poor schools, all of which continued to be an ever-present reality in African American neighborhoods in U.S. cities through the turn of the decade. In 1991, television viewers were shocked by a widely disseminated video that showed Los Angeles police brutally beating an African American motorist, Rodney King. The following year, when a jury acquitted four of the five white police officers who had participated in the beating, LA's African American neighborhoods erupted in a riot that left fifty-three people dead and two thousand injured.

As in previous decades, radical musicians and other artists tended to define themselves against mass culture. Yet, as in the past, they enduringly changed mass culture—and in some cases even joined it (but not before "cleaning up their act"). At first wary of heavy metal, for instance, MTV worked with some of the bands to produce a tamer and telegenic version of it, and, by the late 1980s, *Headbangers' Ball* was the network's most popular show. Guerrilla artists' positive images of gays and lesbians influenced the imagery used in Calvin Klein advertisements and other promotions. And rap became the foundation of a multibillion-dollar music industry that would win broad appeal among American youth as a whole in the 1990s.

TOWARD A NEW WORLD ORDER

By 1988, the United States and much of the Western world were in the throes of a powerful cultural, political, and economic shift. In a sign of things to come, certain cultural phenomena, such as the inclusion of minority and women authors in college curricula, gay visibility, and rap music, became hotly contested. In televised congressional sessions, debate focused increasingly on cultural issues and personal character rather than on substantive matters. The new style of discourse animated electoral politics and gave the presidential campaign of Republican George H. W. Bush an edge over his Democratic opponent in the 1988 election. President Bush faced new challenges, especially in foreign policy, where the Cold War's end generated fresh crises and novel opportunities.

THE NEW CULTURAL POLITICS

Not everyone appreciated the radical new forms of artistic and personal expression. Mass culture's ready embrace of leading-edge art set off alarm bells in conservative circles. Critics of various persuasions railed against rap music, positive depictions of gays and lesbians, and multiculturalism, and in so doing found new common ground among themselves. Allan Bloom, a classics scholar, attracted considerable publicity with his claims that multiculturalism and former-sixties radicals were sabotaging the education system. Soon, abortion, women's rights, contraception, homosexuality, hip-hop, and sexually explicit art were in conservatives' crosshairs (see States of Emergency: The Culture Wars).

The era's **culture wars** found a welcoming home—and eager flag bearers—in Congress. Although lawmakers' rhetorical styles had shifted over the years, in the mid-1980s both the tone and the target of debate changed in striking new ways. For the first time, House proceedings were televised live (on the new cable station C-Span), inviting a potentially enormous audience. Lawmakers realized that they could use the new medium to build their base and profile. Playing to the camera rather than engaging in genuine debate, several abandoned the nitty-gritty detail of most House business for pronouncements on controversial cultural issues and fiery displays of oratory. In fact, few people watched C-Span, but the news networks, which drew large audiences, rebroadcast the lively footage. Gradually, debate focused less on substantive issues and more on the opposition's supposed character flaws. Rhetoric sharpened and grew more divisive, and bipartisan cooperation became difficult.

In particular, a freshman lawmaker from Georgia, Republican Newt Gingrich, perfected the art of colorful and inflammatory oratory. Gingrich determined to make a name for himself as a fearless foe of Democrats, progressives, and liberal culture. He frequently waited for the close of House business and, with the cameras still rolling but the chamber empty, lambasted the absent Democratic lawmakers and challenged them to defend themselves—condemning their failure to do so. (From the TV viewer's perspective, it appeared that the Democrats were unresponsive when in fact they had all gone home.) In 1987, Gingrich honed his rhetoric and claimed that Democrats and Republicans were in a "civil war." "This war has to be fought," he elaborated in a speech to the Enterprise Institute, "with a scale and a duration and a savagery that is only true of civil wars."

In a nation in which six hundred thousand souls had fought and died in a civil war, such language marked a brash departure from the norms of congressional debate. It also helped set the tone for the divisive politics and congressional "gridlock" of the 1990s and 2000s. For its authors, though, it proved an extremely useful tool. Gingrich's mastery of the new form helped push him to the forefront of the Republican Party.

THE ELECTION OF 1988

Although Ronald Reagan had succeeded only partially in reversing the New Deal, his antitax rhetoric and cultural conservatism had proved popular not only among conservatives, but also with middle-class and wealthy Americans generally. A substantial minority of Democratic voters had switched their allegiance to Reagan in 1980, and more did so in 1984. By 1988, these "Reagan Democrats" were the swing voters whose ballots decided elections. Consequently, both parties put the Reagan Democrats' concerns and values at the center of their campaigns. Democratic Party leaders began distancing themselves from the New Deal and the idea that wealthy Americans should carry a greater tax burden than other citizens. In economic matters, the terms of debate had trended significantly to the right—and would stay there until the Great Recession of 2007–2009.

Reagan's successor, George H. W. Bush, had little in common with the president and was disliked by conservatives. Bush hailed from a wealthy, well-connected New England

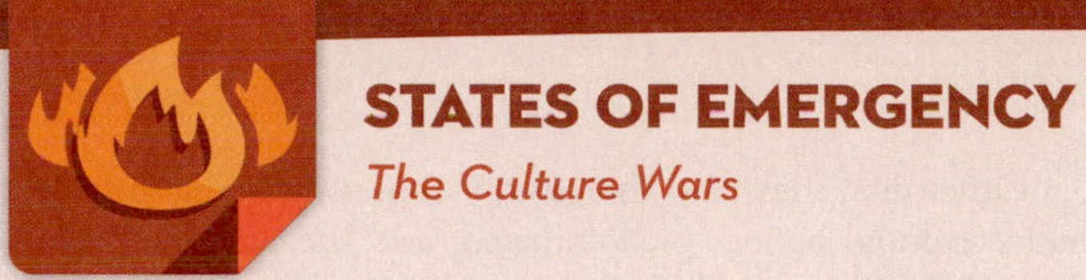

STATES OF EMERGENCY

The Culture Wars

Most people today would define *emergency* as a natural or manmade crisis, such as a flood, fire, or military attack, that endangers (or threatens to endanger) life and limb on a grand scale. But at various times in the past, including the period 1986–1992, a significant portion of the American population believed that their nation was in the grip of a moral and cultural emergency. In the late eighties, many people, most of whom identified as conservative, feared that a pernicious relativism was replacing "traditional" standards and beliefs in everything from art and mass culture to college curricula and sexual mores. In particular, critics claimed, the relativist idea that there are no universal standards (values that hold true regardless of place and time) was sabotaging Americans' ability to discern between "true" art and worthless junk, great literature and mere entertainment, and, most worryingly, right and wrong.

University of Chicago professor Allan Bloom was among the first to advance such claims. New cultural forms and technologies like MTV and the popular Sony Walkman (one of the first portable music players), Bloom asserted in 1987, were inundating youth with meaningless "lowbrow" entertainment that fueled a lust for sex, violence, and money. In his best-selling book *The Closing of the American Mind* (1987), he objected further that college students were being forced to read "lesser" authors such as Kate Chopin and W. E. B. Du Bois at the expense of Shakespeare, Plato, and other canonical writers. The reason for this development, Bloom argued, was that liberal and leftist baby boomers had infiltrated college faculties to promote an inferior, multicultural curriculum. "Tenured radicals" (and the "culture elite," as conservatives described liberal filmmakers and TV programmers) were forcing their biased, "politically correct" ideas down the throats of the younger generation.

Although many schools had added women and minority authors to syllabi, few had expelled the canons of Western literature and philosophy. Nonetheless, the curriculum controversy opened up a broader set of debates about the nature of American institutions and the place of Christianity in them. With renewed energy, conservatives pursued prayer in public schools, the return of capital punishment (which had declined dramatically in the United States in the 1960s and 1970s), the abolition of abortion, and broader gun rights.

Conservatives were not the only ones proclaiming a state of emergency in the eighties. Feminists were having their own culture war over the flourishing pornography industry, with some arguing that pornographic images were degrading and inherently violent toward women, and other, "pro-sex" feminists countering that women often found the material sexually liberating. Conservatives sided with the anti-pornography lobby and, in 1989, introduced a bill forbidding the National Endowment for the Arts (NEA) to fund any "obscene" or "indecent" work. The NEA complied, pulling arts funding from dozens of artists whose work conservatives might deem offensive. Many of the affected artists worked with gay/lesbian and feminist themes, prompting the criticism that the NEA's decisions were based on politics rather than artistic merit. When radical performance artists Holly Hughes, Karen Finley, John Fleck, and Tim Miller lost their funding, they sued the NEA and won an out-of-court settlement.

Federal support of the arts never fully recovered, and conservatives in Congress proceeded to shear the NEA budget by almost 50 percent in 1996. But such victories did little to halt the spread of the cultural phenomena to which conservatives objected. Hip-hop boomed, college students read more women and minority writers, the Supreme Court upheld abortion rights, and, although still rare, positive portrayals of same-sex relations appeared in the mass media (beginning with the baby boomer TV drama *thirtysomething* in 1989 and continuing with *L.A. Law*, the first TV show to air a same-sex kiss, in 1991). By then, pornographic video—most of which depicted heterosexual relations—was a $1.6 billion-per-year business. For the time being, the nation's strong free speech tradition, combined with the tremendous force of mass culture, appeared to have won the "war." Conservatives would renew their struggle in the 2000s, largely in response to the advent of same-sex marital rights (see Chapter 31).

Think About It

1. Why might conservatives of the 1980s have cared so much about college reading lists?
2. What gave mass culture so much force that it overcame the strenuous, well-organized opposition of conservatives and anti-pornography feminists?

family, and he had amassed millions in the Texas oil business before entering politics in 1964. Neither a native westerner nor a religious conservative, Bush was part of the older, East coast establishment that espoused economic conservatism but took more moderate positions on social issues. Despite his lack of conservative credentials, Bush had garnered considerable good will as Reagan's vice president and outspent his rivals in the primaries. He easily won the Republican nomination. In his acceptance speech, Bush embraced the conservative social agenda, opposing abortion rights and supporting prayer in public schools, capital punishment, and gun rights. His choice of a religious conservative, Senator Dan Quayle, as his running mate further reassured conservatives. Bush also promised to balance the budget without raising taxes, exhorting voters to "Read my lips: No new taxes."

The run-up to the election reflected the uncivil turn that congressional politics had taken. Both parties waged intensely personal attacks on the candidates. A relatively new phenomenon,

attack ads (political advertisements emphasizing the opponent's alleged character flaws rather than substantive issues) saturated the media. Democrats derided Republican vice-presidential candidate Quayle for his grammatical errors and poor grasp of current events. Republicans assailed the Democratic nominee, Michael Dukakis, as a Harvard-educated elitist and a "card-carrying liberal." Such ads were aimed at firming up the Republicans' base of southern, working-class midwestern, and suburban whites.

Dukakis tried to rescue his candidacy—and American liberalism—by claiming that he was proud to be a liberal. Trying to shuck the Democrats' reputation for weak foreign policy, he asserted that he would be strong in dealing with the world. In response, Republicans lampooned his weak campaign and released a law-and-order ad attacking Dukakis's record as Massachusetts governor. The ad told how convicted murderer and rapist Willy Horton, an African American, skipped the state while out of prison on a weekend pass and subsequently brutally assaulted a young couple. Although the basic story was accurate, the ad's imagery, text, and voice-over fanned white stereotypes of African American men. (In 1991, Bush's chief campaign strategist would apologize for the ad.) The tactic worked; Bush won the election with 54 percent of the popular vote and 426 electoral college votes to Dukakis's 111. However, the Democrats gained control of Congress.

DOMESTIC GRIDLOCK

Promising a continuation of Reagan-era policies, President Bush vetoed dozens of bills that would have imposed new regulations on employers and campaign financing. But the administration was forced to confront the gaping budget deficit of the Reagan years. Despite his "no new taxes" pledge, Bush, in an effort to balance the budget, recommended a small tax hike for high-income earners, as well as steeper taxes on cigarettes, gas, alcohol, and luxury items. The Democratic Congress consented. The new tax revenues, however, barely made a dent in the deficit. And under Bush, spending continued to spiral, particularly in middle-class entitlement programs such as Medicare and Social Security.

Lawmakers enacted some significant legislation between 1988 and 1992. The Americans with Disabilities Act of 1990 was the widest-ranging civil rights law to be established since the 1960s. Based on the idea that people with mental or physical disabilities have a right to participate fully in society, the law prohibited employers from discriminating against such individuals and directed businesses, restaurants, and schools to provide suitable access. Although conservatives on the Supreme Court subsequently narrowed the law's scope, its passage represented a signal victory for civil rights advocates. Congress and the president also reauthorized the Clean Air Act (1990) and the new Immigration Act (1990), the latter increasing the number of immigrants legally admitted to the country and dropping the ban on homosexual immigrants.

Other than these laws, however, Congress achieved little. Divisive cultural politics predominated, and the president vetoed many bills. Bipartisanship, already endangered, gave way to what the news media called "gridlock." Unable to advance their broader agenda, conservative Republicans targeted avant-garde art, rap music, and other radical cultural forms for criticism and censorship.

Bush's first Supreme Court nominee, David Souter, was relatively uncontroversial, although feminists opposed him for his antiabortion stance. But when President Bush nominated conservative judge Clarence Thomas, an African American, to replace retiring liberal justice Thurgood Marshall, controversy erupted. The American Bar Association ranked Thomas's skills as a judge lower than those of any justice in thirty years. Even more damaging, Anita Hill, a professor of law from the University of Oklahoma, testified in Congress that Thomas had sexually harassed her while they were working together at the Equal Employment Opportunity Commission in the 1980s. On national television, the all-white and all-male Senate panel seemed to side with Thomas and against Hill, who was also African American. When Thomas accused Hill and his Democratic critics of a "high-tech lynching," many critics backed off, and Thomas was confirmed.

NEW ALLIES, NEW ENEMIES

The U.S.-Soviet thaw quickened during Bush's first year in office, bringing about the most momentous change in European history since World War II. Eastern Europeans rose up against their Soviet-backed governments to demand an end to state corruption, official repression, and their comparatively low standard of living. In refraining from sending in Russian troops, Soviet president Mikhail Gorbachev implicitly consented to the breakup of the vast Soviet empire. Beginning with Poland in June 1989, the Soviet bloc regimes toppled one after the other, most replaced by freely elected governments. In a highly symbolic and emotionally charged act, East and West Germans used picks, shovels, and bare hands to tear down the Berlin Wall in November. With the support of President Bush, the two Germanys reunified in 1990. Former Soviet bloc nations applied to join the NATO security pact, and Western Europe created a common economic market. A united Europe was on its way to becoming a powerful new global force.

The popular uprisings in Eastern Europe reverberated around the world. In 1989, tens of thousands of college students in Beijing demonstrated against China's communist government and demanded democratization and economic reforms. The world watched, on video smuggled out of Beijing, as the demonstrators faced down tanks and heavily armed soldiers in Tiananmen Square. Unlike the Soviets, however, the Chinese regime cracked down, killing hundreds of students and arresting over ten thousand more. Meanwhile, twelve out of fifteen Soviet republics peacefully seceded from the Soviet Union and formed a new confederation, the Commonwealth of Independent States. While Gorbachev's policies had been popular at first, the abrupt shift to a market economy had resulted in poverty for many and immense wealth for some. Bridling at the new inequality and loss of Soviet power, hard-line communists in Moscow staged a brief coup. The revolt was put down, but Gorbachev had lost much of his power, and he resigned on December 25, 1991. The next day, the Soviet Union was officially dissolved.

For forty-four years, the Soviet Union had been the enemy against which the United States had defined all its foreign policy. The Soviets' demise not only destroyed the Cold War's bipolar system of international relations but also created a vacuum of ideas in the highest U.S. diplomatic circles. With the Soviets gone, a whole new raft of challenges materialized. For better or for worse, the Soviets had played a stabilizing influence in Eastern Europe, Central Asia, and other regions. Repressive new regimes took the place of the old communist regimes, and in Yugoslavia, a bloody civil war broke out, culminating in the genocide of Bosnia's Muslims. Although the nuclear arms race was over, it had spawned the spread of atomic technology to other nations, including North Korea, Israel, India, and Pakistan. Further, with the demise of the Soviet military, the security of hundreds of nuclear warheads now became uncertain.

Among the other important legacies of the Cold War was the survival of repressive regimes that had once been supported by military and financial aid from the Soviet Union or the United States or both. In Central America, one such regime, that of right-wing Panamanian dictator Manuel Noriega, had been a valuable and well-compensated ally in the U.S.-sponsored war against Sandinista leftism in the mid-1980s. More recently, however, Noriega had used his U.S.-funded military to join the multibillion-dollar business of drug trafficking. Indicted by a Florida jury on trafficking charges, Noriega became an embarrassment for the Bush administration. To make matters worse, Noriega also began staging anti-*yanqui* (anti-American) rallies. In December 1989, President Bush took Americans and much of the wider world by surprise when he sent twenty-five thousand U.S. troops to Panama to depose Noriega. Hundreds of civilians and Panamanian soldiers perished in Operation Just Cause, and the dictator was eventually sent to Florida to stand trial for drug crimes.

THE PERSIAN GULF WAR

Another U.S.-supported strongman, Saddam Hussein, proved both a problem and an opportunity for the Bush administration. For some years, the United States had sent financial and military aid to Hussein's regime in its war with Iran, hoping to prevent wealthy Iran from gaining control of Persian Gulf oil. But in August 1990, Iraqi troops marched into oil-rich Kuwait (see Map 30.2), claiming it as a province

Map 30.2 The Persian Gulf War. Swift and effective, Operation Desert Storm laid to rest many Americans' lingering concerns over the power of U.S. military forces in the wake of Vietnam. This map demonstrates the speed and scale of the campaign.

The Bloodless War. The Persian Gulf War was the most televised of all wars to that time. Due to restrictions on news reporters, however, audiences saw only a sanitized version of the war—without the blood, gore, and body bags that had undermined popular support for the Vietnam War. Several American photojournalists documented the violence of the Persian Gulf War, including the so-called Highway of Death (pictured here) along which U.S. forces bombarded Iraqi soldiers as they retreated across northern Kuwait. But news corporations, eager to maintain good relations with the U.S. government, successfully withheld such images from the American public.

of Iraq. President Bush and European leaders condemned the action, which placed Iraq in a strategic position to gain control of a large portion of the world's oil supply, and demanded an immediate withdrawal. The president deployed two hundred thousand troops to Saudi Arabia to convey the seriousness of his request. The United Nations backed his ultimatum that Iraq quit Kuwait by January 15, 1991, or face the consequences.

The proposed Kuwait operation, by far the biggest since the 1960s, was both an opportunity to vindicate the U.S. military for the fiasco in Vietnam and a potential disaster. Secretary of Defense Dick Cheney and Bush's advisers argued that U.S. failure in Vietnam was due largely to two controllable factors: the absence of military control over the mass media, which meant that American civilians witnessed the gruesome nature of the war and consequently opposed it, and the failure to amass forces before engaging the enemy. Determined not to repeat history, Bush ordered another 250,000 troops to Saudi Arabia and strategized an aerial bombing campaign that would destroy Iraqi military bases and infrastructure before U.S. troops were deployed. He also directed that the military tightly control the media's access to the theater of war.

Hussein ignored the deadline for withdrawal, and on January 17, 1991, Operation Desert Storm began. Putting the principle of overwhelming force into action, the U.S. military began pounding strategic sites in Baghdad remotely via a fleet of cruise missiles. After five weeks of intense bombing, 450,000 U.S. and Allied troops swept across the Saudi-Kuwait border, driving the Iraqis out of Kuwait in less than four days. U.S. forces stopped at the Iraqi border, largely because the international coalition that backed Kuwait's liberation would not consent to a full-scale invasion of Iraq. As Hussein conceded defeat, the president rejoiced, "By God, we've kicked the Vietnam syndrome once and for all."

Although upwards of 20,000 Iraqi and 114 U.S. troops had died in combat, television viewers had seen none of the blood and gore of the battlefield. Instead, TV coverage was confined mainly to tracking the computer-guided "smart bombs" that were fired on Baghdad, mostly at night. The footage, resembling video game graphics, presented the U.S.-led campaign as a high-tech, minimally violent, and "surgically precise" operation. Censors pulled the occasional video or photograph that suggested otherwise from circulation in the United States.

CONCLUSION

The United States began the 1980s at a crossroads and ended the decade on a wide-open road of global domination and economic growth. Deindustrialization and a conservative resurgence—dual forces that had been gathering strength for three decades—had effected a seismic shift in the nation's political and cultural landscape. In 1980, Republicans thundered into the White House on a promise to "return" the country to the optimistic, self-confident, and harmonious society it had supposedly been in the 1950s. Though inaccurate, Ronald Reagan's idealized vision of the fifties resonated broadly at a time when Americans were disillusioned with the faltering economy, perceived drifts in moral standards, and seemingly weak political leadership.

Although Reagan was one of the twentieth century's most popular presidents, his legacy is among the most complex. In the name of freeing the economy from government's heavy hand, his administration commenced a sweeping program of deregulation that did little for small business owners but a great deal for corporations. And even though the president pledged that he would bridle government spending, the federal deficit almost tripled in size under his watch, due mainly to increased military spending. By the decade's end, New Deal liberalism, the reigning paradigm of government since the mid-1930s, had been all but discredited. The economy was booming. Yet economic inequality was greater than at any time since the 1920s, and the deregulation of banking had resulted in the financial failure of the savings and loan associations. Even the Cold War victory was tempered by the sobering news that potentially catastrophic threats such as terrorism and genocide were multiplying.

Equally profound cultural shifts accompanied the political, economic, and national security changes. Mass culture celebrated affluence and turned shopping into a leisure activity. At the same time, a younger generation of artists, writers, musicians, and activists invented new forms of expression and challenged basic assumptions about biological and social realities. Young artists who explored alternative sexualities or brought to life the everyday lives of minority and poor Americans found receptive audiences. By the decade's end, alternative images, sounds, and ideas were filtering into mass culture. Despite official condemnation by most Republicans, many churches, and traditional Democrats, mainstream culture was embracing diversity as never before. Whether the potent cultural shifts and the policy failures of the Reagan-Bush years would register at the political level would be tested in the 1992 presidential election.

STUDY TERMS

free trade zone (p. 853)
Christian Coalition (p. 854)
supply-side economics (p. 854)
deregulation (p. 855)
Reaganomics (p. 857)
welfare queens (p. 857)
savings and loan associations (p. 857)
downsizing (p. 859)
evil empire (p. 860)
Reagan Doctrine (p. 860)
Sandinistas (p. 860)
Beirut barracks bombing (p. 861)
war on drugs (p. 861)
New Federalism (p. 861)
Iran-Contra scandal (p. 862)
Reykjavik Summit (p. 862)
vertical integration (p. 863)
personal computers (p. 863)
yuppies (p. 864)
affluence gap (p. 867)
homelessness (p. 867)
Generation X (p. 868)
sanctuary movement (p. 869)
Comprehensive Anti-Apartheid Act (p. 870)
Rainbow Coalition (p. 871)
AIDS Coalition to Unleash Power (p. 871)
culture wars (p. 874)
Reagan Democrats (p. 874)
attack ads (p. 876)
Americans with Disabilities Act (p. 876)
Operation Desert Storm (p. 878)

TIMELINE

1980 Ronald Reagan wins presidency in landslide election

Pac-Man released

1981 Congress begins deregulation and slashes taxes on income, capital gains, and inheritance

Reagan accelerates Carter's nuclear arms buildup, increases defense spending, and implements Reagan Doctrine

Sandra Day O'Connor is first woman appointed to Supreme Court

1982 750,000 Americans march in New York against nuclear arms buildup

First AIDS cases are observed.

1983 Terrorists attack U.S. and French barracks in Beirut, Lebanon, killing 299

Economy commences twenty-four-year-long "Great Expansion"

First "McMansions" built in California

Congress cuts $25 billion from welfare programs

Michael Jackson's song "Thriller" is released

1984 Reagan slows deregulation and is reelected in landslide

Apple transforms personal computing with Macintosh release

Jesse Jackson becomes first African American to run for nomination as the Democratic Party's candidate for president

1985 Soviet premier Mikhail Gorbachev undertakes reform of Soviet economy and political system

Rambo "wins" fight against United States' Vietnamese enemies

Anti-apartheid movement reinvigorated after scenes of brutality in Soweto are broadcast on American TV

1986 Iran-Contra scandal breaks

War on drugs begins

Reagan and Gorbachev agree to nuclear arms reduction at Reykjavik Summit

1987 Allan Bloom publishes *The Closing of the American Mind*

ACT UP publicizes AIDS crisis and government inaction

Toni Morrison explores slavery's psychological impact in *Beloved*

1988 Homeless Americans number 402,000, up almost 300,000 since 1980

Los Angeles–based N.W.A popularizes gangsta rap

George H. W. Bush elected president

1989 Supreme Court preserves abortion rights

United States invades Panama

1990 Half of all U.S. households own video game system

Congress bans discrimination against Americans with disabilities

Budget deficit reaches $300 billion: Bush reneges on promise not to raise new taxes

1991 Operation Desert Storm pushes Iraq out of Kuwait

1992 Fifty-three people killed in Los Angeles riots

FURTHER READING

Additional suggested readings are available on the Online Learning Center at www.mhhe.com/becomingamerica1e.

William C. Berman, *America's Right Turn: From Nixon to Bush* (1994), explains how social conservatives became allied with economic conservatives, to devastating effect for liberal U.S. politics.

Michael A. Bernstein and David E. Adler, *Understanding American Economic Decline* (1994), explores various aspects of the changing American economy.

Jeff Chang, *Can't Stop Won't Stop: A History of the Hip-Hop Generation* (2005), traces hip-hop from its Jamaican roots and Bronx birthplace to the U.S. mainstream.

Robert M. Collins, *Transforming America: Politics and Culture During the Reagan Years* (2009), shows how Reagan's combination of conservative ideology and political pragmatism enabled him to implement his policies.

Thomas Byrne Edsall, *The New Politics of Inequality* (1989), tracks the impact of lower taxes and social spending cuts.

E. Anne Kaplan, *Rocking Around the Clock: Music Television, Postmodernism, and Consumer Culture* (1987), explains MTV's tremendous appeal in the 1980s and its relation to global youth culture.

Michael Katz, *The Undeserving Poor: From the War on Poverty to the War on Welfare* (1992), charts the origins and impact of Reagan-era welfare policy.

Bradford Martin, *The Other Eighties: A Secret History of America in the Age of Reagan* (2011), explores the dissent and oppositional movements that flourished in the eighties.

Lisa McGirr, *Suburban Warriors: The Origins of the New American Right* (2002), examines the social roots and fruition of the conservative populism that helped elect Reagan and transformed American politics.

John Prado, *How the Cold War Ended: Debating and Doing History* (2010), incorporates Soviet and European sources to argue that internal transformations within the Soviet Union contributed significantly to U.S. victory in the Cold War.

Michael Shaller, *Reckoning with Reagan: America and Its President in the 1980s* (1994), comprehensively analyzes both Reagan's immense popularity and his impact on foreign, social, and economic policy.

Randy Shilts, *And the Band Played On: Politics, People, and the AIDS Epidemic* (1987), discusses the early impact of AIDS.

David Sirota, *Back to Our Future* (2011), offers an entertaining yet insightful exploration of the eighties' popular culture and its long-term effects on American politics and society.

31

New Year, New Millennium. Revelers ring in a new year and a new millennium in Times Square, New York City, January 1, 2000.

INSIDE ▶

THE BIG PICTURE

Barriers to international trade, investment, and communication were lowered, with mixed results at home and abroad. Disruptive new technologies sped economic globalization but also amplified opposition and dissent. Americans had just begun debating the pros and cons of their globalizing world when terrorists struck and the nation again went to war.

GLOBALIZING AMERICA, 1992 TO THE PRESENT

In 1998, the international science journal *Nature* confirmed that DNA testing had proved that President Thomas Jefferson had almost certainly fathered a son with his slave Sally Hemings. The online article grabbed headlines around the world and prompted biographers and historians to rewrite history. Although the president of the all-white Monticello Association invited Jefferson's African American descendants to the annual family reunion, other association members rejected the validity of the genetic study and barred the Jefferson-Hemings descendants from officially joining the family. Undeterred, the Jefferson-Hemings formed an association of their own and opened it to all descendants of Thomas Jefferson and his household.

The Jefferson family controversy offers an illuminating snapshot of American culture at the turn of the millennium. New technologies, particularly in genetic science, computing, and mass communication, were changing people's conception and experience of reality. The policy of economic globalization—under which the United States and other nations dismantled certain trade and investment barriers—facilitated the flood of cheaper and faster computers and the distribution of information. It also stimulated international collaboration among scientists and other scholars, which resulted in major discoveries (including the genetic makeup of the Jefferson family tree). The related policy of deregulation, which abolished various labor, financial, and trade regulations, also fueled economic

The Hemings-Jefferson family gathers at Monticello, Thomas Jefferson's plantation, for their reunion in 1999.

KEY QUESTIONS

- In what ways did Bill Clinton and the New Democrats transform their party and reshape the federal government?
- How did different communities of Americans experience and respond to economic globalization?
- What were the catalysts for and effects of the Digital Revolution?
- How did George W. Bush's administration respond to the 9/11 terrorist attacks?
- What caused the Great Recession of 2007–2009?
- What changes did the Tea Party and Occupy Wall Street seek, and what impact did they have?

growth and innovation, as did the privatization of certain public services and resources. Economic globalization, deregulation, and privatization together underwrote the Digital Revolution—the mass digitization of information and widespread adoption of the Internet and cellular phones. That revolution in turn sped globalization.

The confluence of these globalizing forces profoundly transformed life, culture, politics, and even the environment in the United States and throughout the world. Much like the industrial revolution of the nineteenth century, economic globalization proved awesomely creative yet also colossally destructive. As formerly rural countries such as India, Vietnam, and China became the world's manufacturing powerhouses, American manufacturers left the United States in droves, taking jobs and tax revenue with them. The boom in financial, information, and other services revitalized many American cities in the 1990s but also launched rents and prices skyward, compelling poorer people to relocate to cheaper, decaying suburbs. The rapid expansion of the Internet promoted the free exchange of information and cut business costs, but it also led to mass piracy of music and other intellectual property and rendered the usual way of doing business obsolete. A speculative bubble formed in the high-tech sector and then burst in 2000, leaving the entire economy in recession.

Americans were only just beginning to grapple with the complexities of their globalizing world when terrorists struck on September 11, 2001. The foreign wars that followed became the most talked-about issues of the day. It was not until 2008, when the worst recession since the Great Depression threw millions of Americans out of home and work, that the nation directly confronted the thorny legacies of globalization, deregulation, and privatization.

BILL CLINTON AND THE NEW DEMOCRATS

In 1991, most Americans associated prosperity and the flourishing economy with the Republicans. Even some Democrats believed that the party's New Deal liberalism—high taxes, regulations on business, and comprehensive social services—were outmoded, unrealistic, and unlikely to win votes. A younger generation of "New Democrats" emerged and successfully campaigned to elect William Jefferson "Bill" Clinton to the presidency. At first, the Clinton administration promoted globalization, reshaped welfare, deregulated business, raised taxes, and appointed dozens of women and minorities to offices traditionally held by white men. The president and the nation faced multiple challenges domestically and internationally, however. Gridlock set in when the Republicans won Congress in 1994. Homegrown antigovernment terrorist groups proliferated, and the United States became a target of radical Islamist terrorists.

REINVENTING THE DEMOCRATIC PARTY: THE ELECTION OF 1992

Democratic prospects in the 1992 presidential election seemed dim at the beginning of the decade. As President Bush's approval rating soared to an unprecedented 90 percent, Democratic leaders in Washington, D.C., were convinced that a fourth Republican presidential victory was inevitable. Although the economy was in recession and middle-class income had not kept pace with national economic growth, the majority of voters believed that the Republicans would restore prosperity. Many Americans credited Republican leadership with the collapse of the Soviet Union, and the victory in the Persian Gulf War seemed to indicate that the Bush administration had put the "Vietnam Syndrome" to rest.

Not all Democrats were pessimistic. Bill Clinton sensed an opportunity in the spiraling federal deficit and trillion-dollar federal debt of the Republican administrations. Voters were sick of Washington gridlock, he theorized, and the slow pace of economic recovery. As Arkansas governor, Clinton had steadily promoted a new approach to government. A leading member of a group of younger politicians known as New Democrats, Clinton advocated centrist policies that rejected the expansive (and expensive) government that Franklin D. Roosevelt and Lyndon B. Johnson had championed. Specifically, the New Democrats combined liberal cultural policies, such as women's and gay rights, with certain conservative economic policies, including reducing the federal deficit and streamlining government bureaucracy. New Democrats also took a generally conservative approach to criminal justice, supporting the death penalty and mandatory minimum sentences for drug, property, and violent crimes.

Clinton announced his candidacy for the Democratic nomination in October 1991, proclaiming himself a Washington outsider who would break partisan gridlock, grow the economy, and move the country beyond divisive cultural politics. Clinton also insisted that the welfare system should promote self-responsibility by making benefits contingent on working or actively looking for work. This stance appealed both to the mass of swing voters who had voted for Ronald Reagan in the 1980s and to baby boomer Democrats who had grown prosperous and considered the "old Democratic Party" outmoded.

Clinton out-organized his rivals and consolidated support among southern and midwestern voters by pointing to his record as a tough-on-crime governor. On the eve of the New Hampshire primary, Governor Clinton flew home to ensure that the state of Arkansas dutifully carried out the execution of Ricky Ray Lector, a murderer with an intellectual disability. His choice of U.S. senator Albert ("Al") Gore, a New Democrat and U.S. Army veteran, as running mate pleased party members and further distanced Clinton from "old Democrats." Clinton easily won the nomination.

The Republicans once again cast their lot with George H. W. Bush, even though conservatives widely criticized his decision to raise taxes and to sign civil rights legislation into law. Many Republicans were drawn to newcomer H. Ross Perot, a Texas billionaire who entered the race as an independent, tapping into voters' exasperation with the mess in Washington, the federal deficit, and sluggish job growth. In an effort to mobilize the support of conservatives and Reagan Democrats, Bush tarred the Democratic nominee as a liberal, draft-dodging antiwar hippie who had smoked marijuana.

A charismatic speaker who made many middle-class Americans feel as though he was on their side, Clinton skillfully deflected the attacks, at one point declaring that he had not "inhaled" marijuana smoke. He also concentrated on building his support base. Although Bush enjoyed stronger business backing

Candidate Clinton, Sax Man. Fresh-faced, saxophone-playing Bill Clinton hit a high note with baby boomers and young people alike when he appeared on Arsenio Hall's popular late night talk show in the summer of 1992.

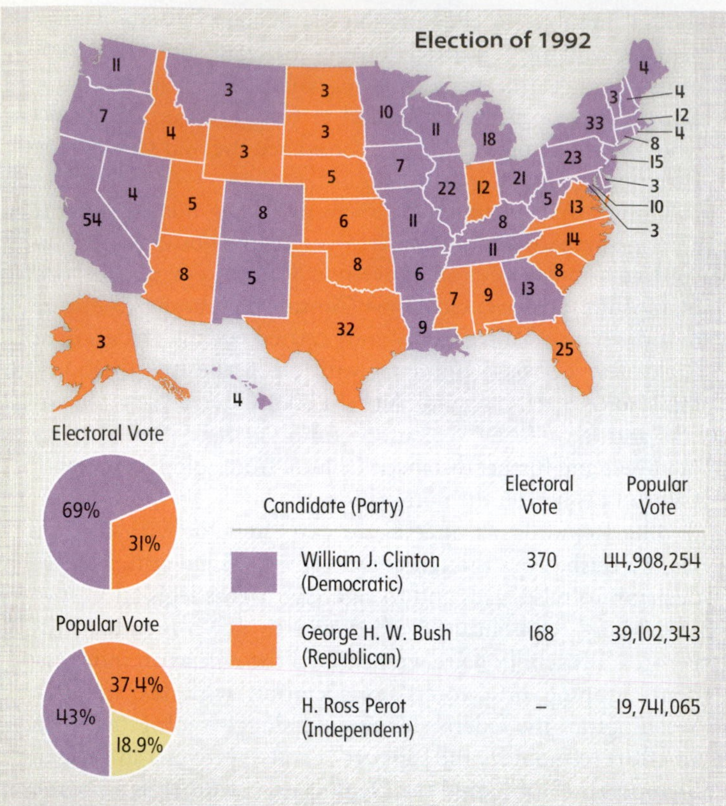

Candidate (Party)	Electoral Vote	Popular Vote
William J. Clinton (Democratic)	370	44,908,254
George H. W. Bush (Republican)	168	39,102,343
H. Ross Perot (Independent)	–	19,741,065

Map 31.1 Election of 1992.

overall, Clinton secured important allies—particularly among New York's investment banks and Silicon Valley's computing companies. Above all, Clinton's speeches stayed on-point, relentlessly returning to the economic issues about which the majority of voters cared most. "It's the economy, stupid," became the campaign's slogan and most popular bumper sticker. Clinton carried the election and, for the first time since the 1960s, the Democrats won Louisiana, Arkansas, and Georgia (see Map 31.1).

NEW DEMOCRATS IN GOVERNMENT

Clinton entered office determined to change both government and the Democratic Party. He made strong strides toward the latter goal, ensuring that New Democrats and their philosophy guided policymaking. His record in government was more mixed, with some important early achievements followed by a legislative logjam after 1994. Delivering on his promise to make government "look like America," Clinton appointed more women and minorities to cabinet positions than any previous president. Madeleine K. Albright, an international relations advisor and professor of Eastern European studies, served as the nation's first female secretary of state, and Janet Reno became the first female attorney general. Clinton also appointed to the cabinet three African Americans and the first Asian American (Secretary of Commerce Norman Y. Mineta). Well over half of Clinton's first 129 appointments to the federal courts—where judges were overwhelmingly white and male—were women or minorities.

In Congress, the president pushed through an increase in the Earned Income Tax Credit for low-wage earners, which effectively reduced their taxes and carried their income over the poverty line. Clinton also scored a victory when Congress approved the North American Free Trade Agreement (NAFTA) in 1993. That agreement abolished tariffs (importation taxes) between Mexico, the United States, and Canada, creating a common market in which goods could flow freely across borders. Although many labor unions objected that U.S. jobs, especially in the auto industry, would be lost to Mexico, the New Democrats argued that NAFTA would promote prosperity by opening Canada and Mexico to U.S.-made goods (see Globalization and Its Critics, below).

Clinton's other top priority was eliminating the $4.4 trillion budget deficit that he inherited from Republican administrations. In his first four years in office, the president pushed through $241 billion in new taxes while approving $255 billion in spending cuts, reducing the deficit by almost $500 billion. As the economy sprang back from the recession of 1991–1992, tax revenues poured into the Treasury. By the time Clinton left office in 2000, he had turned the national deficit into a surplus.

The administration racked up other significant victories. In the arena of women's rights, the Family and Medical Leave Act (1993) authorized unpaid leave for childbirth, adoption, and family medical issues, while the Violence Against Women Act (1994) funded rape crisis centers and resources for battered women. Clinton's Violent Crime Control and Law Enforcement Act (1994) significantly enlarged the scope of capital punishment by imposing the death penalty for crimes such as large-scale drug running. In addition, federal prison construction expanded dramatically, and the law prescribed stiffer sentences for violent offenders (see How Much Is That? and Figure 31.1). However, health

How Much Is That?

Funding Crime Control and Law Enforcement

As the federal government pared welfare spending in the 1990s, it spent lavishly on prisons, law enforcement, and crime prevention. The Violent Crime Control and Law Enforcement Act (1994) may have been the "the toughest and smartest crime bill in our history," as President Clinton claimed, but it was certainly the most expensive. Over $9.6 billion—the equivalent of over $14 billion today—flowed into new prison construction. Another $8.8 billion (over $13 billion today) was spent on hiring one hundred thousand new police officers. All told, the law authorized the government to spend an unprecedented $30 billion (more than $45 billion today) on criminal justice.

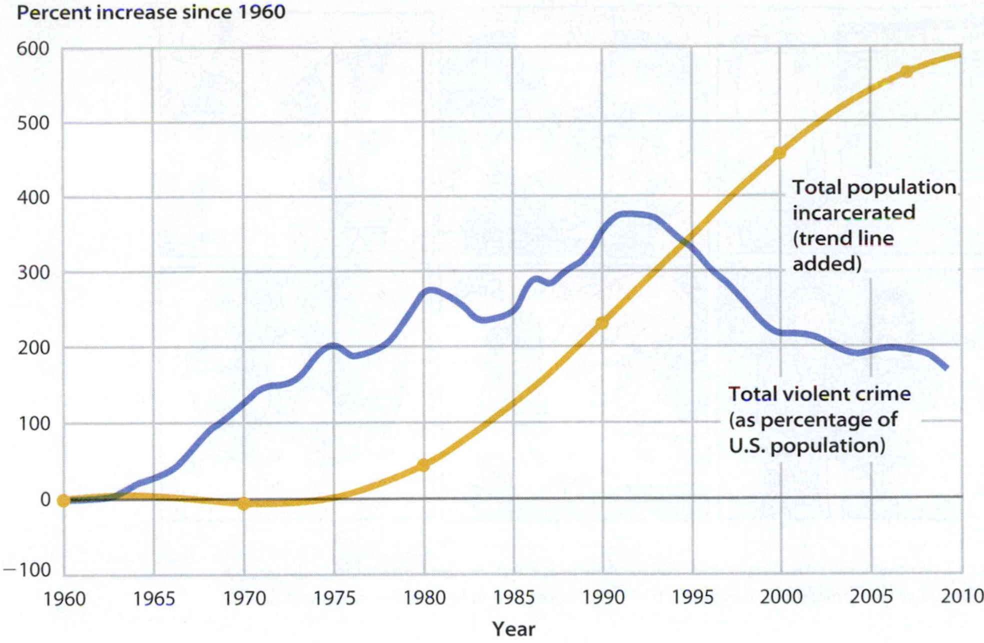

FIGURE 31.1 The Prison Boom. After remaining relatively flat through the 1950s and 1960s, the incarceration rate began to climb in the mid-1970s, as policing and sentencing practices shifted to a more conservative model of criminal justice. Despite a drop in violent crime after 1993, the incarceration rate continued its upward trajectory until 2010, by which time the proportion of Americans behind bars was six times what it had been in 1975.

care reform, a major goal of the administration, failed miserably. First lady Hillary Clinton headed a campaign to make health care available to all working Americans under a plan that would have required employers to provide insurance for every employee. Republicans and health insurers argued that the plan deprived consumers of a choice of health insurers, and the initiative failed.

CONGRESSIONAL BATTLE LINES

In November 1994, Republicans won a majority in both houses of Congress for the first time in forty years. Led by House Speaker Newt Gingrich, the party issued its Contract with America. Although the New Democrats had achieved major spending cuts and beefed up law enforcement, the Republican proposals called for cuts to Social Security and Medicare, further expansion of prison and policing programs, tax cuts, and decreases in business regulation. Republicans also fought back against tighter gun control laws and demanded Social Security reform.

As well, affirmative action became a target on the grounds that it discriminated against white people—especially white men. The centerpiece of the "contract" was a constitutional amendment that would have required Congress and the president to balance the federal budget, which had been in deficit since the beginning of the Reagan era.

The constitutional amendment failed, but the Republicans passed other bills. When President Clinton vetoed the proposed budget, House Republicans withheld emergency funding, a move necessitating a shutdown of nonessential government departments. Although lawmakers blamed Clinton for the closures, the majority of voters held Congress responsible. Consequently, the Republican leadership dropped its insistence on cuts to Medicare and Social Security. President Clinton also softened his position as he conceded in January 1996 that the "era of big government is over." A few months later he signed the revised budget.

Defending middle-class entitlements such as Medicare became the president's chief concern. In the face of relentless Republican pressure to shear welfare programs further, Clinton signed into law the most sweeping welfare reform since the 1960s. The Personal Responsibility and Work Opportunity Act (1996) ended monetary aid to dependent children, required unemployed adults to find work within two years, and limited cash aid to vulnerable families to five years. Critically, the law also shifted to state government the power to make decisions concerning the distribution of many welfare benefits. The reforms saved the federal government less than 1 percent of its annual budget, but their impact on the poor was immediate, with monetary aid to the nation's neediest families dwindling to one-third of its pre-reform level.

CLINTON'S SECOND TERM: GRIDLOCK AND SCANDAL

Buoyed by the rebounding economy and the electorate's anger over the shutdown of the federal government, Clinton easily won reelection in 1996. The Republicans nevertheless held on to majorities in the House and the Senate. The next four years would be characterized by political deadlock and a White House scandal.

In 1994, Congress had appointed a special prosecutor, Kenneth Starr, to investigate Bill and Hillary Clinton's involvement in an Arkansas property development known as Whitewater. Starr relentlessly pursued evidence against the Clintons. In 1998, unable to uncover any substantive evidence of wrongdoing, Starr and his grand jury resolved to follow up on rumors that the president was romantically involved with

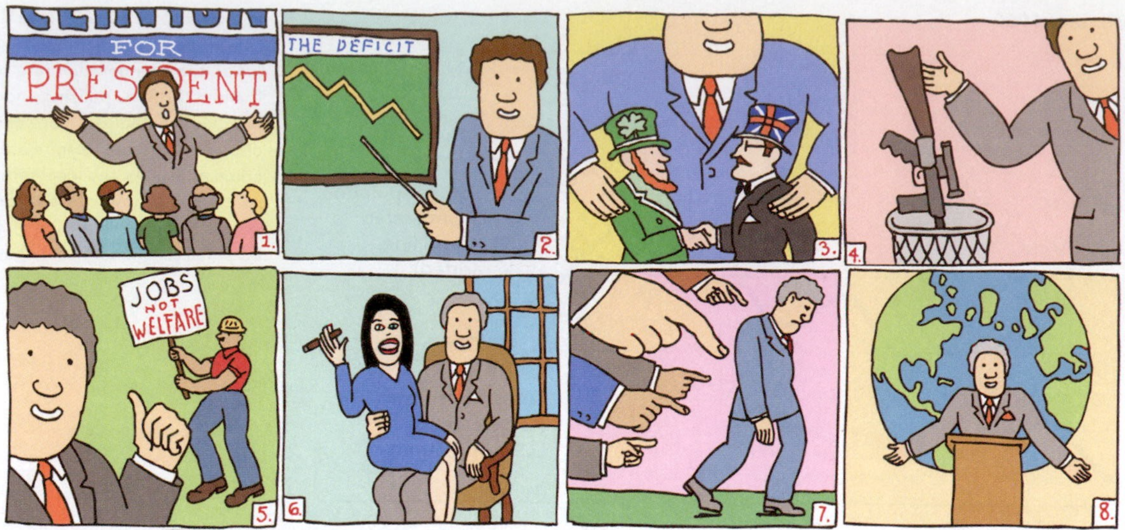

Clinton Impeached. Cartoonist Seymour Chwast satirized the House of Representatives for impeaching Clinton by suggesting that the president's dalliance with Monica Lewinsky was a trivial transgression in light of his major political achievements. © 2005 by Seymour Chwast. Reprinted with permission.

young White House intern Monica Lewinsky. After initially declaring that he "did not have sexual relations with that woman," the president eventually admitted that he had had "inappropriate intimate contact" with Lewinsky. Starr wrote a report to Congress, summarizing events and recommending impeachment charges against the president. Several prominent Democrats condemned Clinton's behavior.

Starr's report seemed certain to ensure Clinton's impeachment and removal from office. But many Americans were more shocked by the report than by the presidential philandering. When Hillary Clinton appeared on television beside her husband, most people decided that her husband's affair was a private matter. Regardless, House Republicans voted to impeach Clinton on four counts. Starr's efforts to remove Clinton from office ultimately stalled in the Senate, but the taint of sexual infidelity lingered for the remainder of his presidency.

THE NEW EXTREMISM

Although Clinton was relatively popular and far more conservative than his Democratic—and some of his Republican—predecessors, antigovernment extremism mushroomed during his tenure. Indeed, whereas violent crime decreased in the 1990s, domestic terrorism increased. A minority of discontented citizens, most of whom were white, male, and working class, joined armed militias, founded white supremacist organizations, and declared themselves the only true Christians. Convinced that the United Nations would take over the country and that the federal government was plotting to destroy liberty, many began stockpiling weapons and running training camps in remote areas. To these militias, the passage in 1993 of the Brady Handgun Violence Prevention Act, which imposed a five-day waiting period and background check for all handgun purchases, was positive proof of the coming crackdown. Some took the words of Thomas Jefferson out of context, arguing that "the tree of liberty must be refreshed from time to time with the blood of patriots and tyrants."

Local, state, and federal police openly worried that such extreme rhetoric might soon morph into violence. When agents from the Federal Bureau of Alcohol, Tobacco, and Firearms (ATF) learned that an armed religious cult in Waco, Texas, the Branch Davidians, had been stockpiling weapons in 1993, they secured a warrant to search the group's premises. Although the weapons were acquired legally, informants suggested that the Davidians were modifying them to be machine guns (the possession of which was a crime). ATF agents swooped in on the Waco compound one morning in February 1993, sparking a gunfight that lasted several hours and left four ATF agents and five Davidians dead. After a tense seven-week standoff followed, the attorney general finally ordered federal agents to clear the compound using tear gas. A fast-moving fire erupted, claiming the lives of fifty adults and twenty-five children.

A federal probe later determined that one or more Davidians had ignited the conflagration by pouring fuel on the ground. But extremist militias grew even more distrusting of the federal government. On the two-year anniversary of the Waco siege, militia members used a massive fertilizer bomb to blow up a federal building in Oklahoma City, killing 168 people and wounding almost 700. The worst terrorist attack in American history up to that point, the Oklahoma City bombing had been plotted and carried out by Timothy McVeigh, a Gulf War veteran and antigovernment radical, and Terry Nichols, also a veteran and a sometime gun dealer. Both men had argued that the government was too big and taxes too high. In 1997, McVeigh was tried and found guilty of a capital crime. He died by lethal injection in 2001. Nichols is serving 161 life terms in federal prison.

Nongovernmental entities were also subject to politically motivated violence in these years. Abortion clinics and their

Tragedy at Waco. Americans followed the astonishing events unfolding at Waco on live television. They watched as FBI agents tried in vain to get leader David Koresh and his Branch Davidians to surrender, and were horrified when the compound burst into what would be deadly flames.

personnel, for example, became the targets of extreme antiabortionists in a wave of attacks. Although the leading antiabortion organization, Operation Rescue, did not advocate violence, members did engage in confrontational tactics such as blocking clinic access and taunting patients and employees. Tensions heightened, and by 2000, eight employees had been shot and killed, and several clinics bombed.

Mass shootings escalated despite the tough new gun control and crime prevention laws. The 1990s saw twenty-three armed rampages—almost three times as many as in the previous decade. The shootings typically involved a lone gunman, disaffected by his business or employment experience. In a disturbing new development, however, high school students or recently graduated students were among the perpetrators. In the most lethal attack involving young people, two heavily armed teens shot and killed twelve schoolmates and a teacher in a rampage at Columbine (Colorado) High School in 1999. The boys were alienated bullying victims who had written admiringly of the Oklahoma bombing. A new round of gun control advocacy followed, but the National Rifle Association and gun manufacturers thwarted reform efforts, and the Assault Weapons Ban expired in 2004.

GLOBALIZATION AND ITS CRITICS

Relatively few Americans were familiar with the term **globalization** at the beginning of President Clinton's first term. By 2000, however, the majority understood the concept to mean free-flowing trade and investment among nations, without traditional barriers such as tariffs and taxes. By then, most people had also formed a strong opinion about whether economic globalization was good or bad. Regardless, globalization accelerated dramatically in the 1990s. In the United States, NAFTA sped the process on a regional level, as did the rapid growth of the European Economic Community, which admitted former Soviet bloc nations after 1992 and became the European Union (EU) in 1993. Both George H. W. Bush and Bill Clinton promoted globalization and supported NAFTA.

The most powerful champion of economic globalization was not a single nation or government but the World Trade Organization (WTO), which the United States and other advanced industrial nations jointly founded in 1995. The WTO replaced the General Agreement on Tariffs and Trade (GATT), which had regulated international commerce since 1948. The new organization successfully negotiated the opening of formerly protected economies (most notably those of the developing world and the former Soviet bloc) to large-scale investment and trade. The WTO's vision of the post–Cold War world was essentially the same neoliberal vision that Friedrich Hayek and other conservative economists had been promoting since the 1940s (see Chapter 27). The goal was a single global market, freed from costly constraints such as environmental regulations, minimum-wage laws, taxes, and tariffs. WTO leaders worked closely with the International Monetary Fund, the World Bank, and corporate leaders to develop Structural Adjustment Programs (SAPs) that attached strict conditions to financial aid for developing economies. Such governments would be eligible for aid only if they agreed to slash social spending, taxation, and tariffs.

American Icon. Thanks to economic globalization, the golden arches of McDonald's sprouted in such unlikely places as Red Square in Moscow, Mecca in Saudi Arabia, and Shenzen, China (pictured here).

The dissolution of trade and investment barriers proved a boon to U.S.—and, to some extent, European—corporations. McDonald's multiplied its franchises worldwide, turning the "golden arches" into a ubiquitous symbol of globalization. The Walt Disney Company opened Euro Disney in Paris in 1992, and iconic American brands such as Nike, Levi's, and Gap flooded Europe, Asia, Africa, and Latin America (though in many places the items were cheap, pirated copies). Thanks to the relaxation of trade barriers, Microsoft became the dominant force in computing software during the 1990s. Apple, a respected but small player in the personal computer market, catapulted to a major global brand with the release of its iPod line in 2001. Even trash became a globally traded commodity (see Hot Commodities: Garbage). National economies, such as those of India and Vietnam, flourished, and a small but prosperous white-collar class emerged. As manufacturing shifted to the developing world, the price of consumer electronics, computers, clothing, furniture, and automobiles dropped substantially in the United States. More consumer goods became available to more people for much less than ever before.

Yet economic globalization also compounded the inequality between the wealthiest elites and the world's poorest farmers and industrial workers. In many regions, particularly Africa and Central America, it helped deliver precious natural resources, such as metals, minerals, waterways, and forests, into the hands of U.S. and European megacorporations. Local elites often benefited from such deals, but because the corporations were generally exempt from taxation or minimum-wage laws, ordinary people gained little. At the same time, the vast majority of people were subject to much stiffer immigration laws that made it difficult or impossible to seek higher-paying jobs in Europe or the United States. In the latter, the auto industry and numerous clothing, appliance, and machine manufacturers moved their plants to other countries, such as Mexico and Vietnam, where labor was far cheaper and nonunionized. Well-paid manufacturing jobs with benefits became a rarity in the United States. Struggling industrial hubs such as Detroit and Cleveland lost more jobs and gained notoriety for crime, high unemployment, and crumbling infrastructure.

Globalization's side effects became subject to mounting criticism in the mid-1990s. Some critics opposed economic globalization outright. French farmer José Bovée famously declared, "The world is not for sale!" and coordinated mass dumpings of manure on McDonald's restaurants in France. In Chiapas, Mexico, peasants formed the Zapatista Army of National Liberation, declaring war against NAFTA and the Mexican government for suspending crop subsidies. In 1996, using the new technology of the Internet, the Zapatistas convened an international meeting and cofounded an international forum—Peoples' Global Action. The forum coordinated dozens of street protests, acts of civil disobedience, and direct actions around the world. It also spawned the first of several massive antiglobalization street demonstrations in 1999.

In the United States, most critics called not for an end to globalization but for a different kind of globalization. Billionaire investor and philanthropist George Soros condemned what he called the reigning "market fundamentalism" that claimed to spread prosperity but in fact concentrated wealth in the hands of a shrinking elite. Nobel Prize–winning economist Joseph Stiglitz added that current policies gave big business a free hand to put profit making above all other considerations, including human rights, social justice, and the environment. Both men called for regulation and a more democratic, transparent system of decision making within global agencies and corporations.

Upwards of forty thousand Americans reinforced such criticisms when they converged on the Seattle meeting of the WTO in November 1999. The majority marched peacefully to the WTO convention center, jamming the streets and making it impossible for WTO delegates to proceed to the meeting. Smaller, more radical groups vandalized symbols of global corporate capitalism, including the Bank of America, the Gap, McDonald's, and Starbucks. Overwhelmed by the crowd's size and attacks on property, police panicked and began teargasing

HOT COMMODITIES

Garbage

Trash Nation. Before recycling became mandatory in many cities, barges like the Mobro 4000 were a familiar sight.

Garbage has long been a valuable commodity. Traveling peddlers once paid householders for their used rags, tin, and rubber, selling their haul to industry. Until the introduction of sewers and toilets in the late nineteenth century, cities' "night soil" (human waste) was sold to farmers by the cartload for use as fertilizer. Over ten thousand hauling companies picked up city and suburban trash in the mid-twentieth century and transformed it into valuable (if toxic and sometimes unstable) landfill.

Environmentalism, the privatization of city sanitation services, and deregulation changed all that—and transformed trash into a billion-dollar-a-year industry. In 1987, the widely reported story of the Mobro 4000 trash barge sailing up and down the eastern seaboard, looking in vain for an open landfill, rudely awakened Americans to the fact that their society was producing far more trash than it could absorb. Within months, the Environmental Protection Agency (EPA) listed waste prevention and recycling as top priorities. Three-quarters of the states and the District of Columbia passed recycling laws, and the pressure of public opinion led corporations such as McDonald's and Coca-Cola to substitute recycled and recyclable materials for Styrofoam, which is neither recyclable nor biodegradable.

The EPA's enforcement of tough new standards for landfills resulted in the closure of hundreds of small landfill businesses that could not afford to update equipment. Likewise, new EPA standards for garbage trucks squeezed smaller operators out of business. By 2000, just four, enormous garbage corporations controlled the national market. Citizens became garbage literate as they learned to interpret recycling codes (numbered 1–7) on the bottom of plastics and separated paper from plastic, glass, and cans. Greater interaction with trash reinforced the idea that consumption has environmental consequences—and that recycling for the sake of the planet was a moral imperative. Eleven states and dozens of cities mandated recycling, and some, such as New York, even fined citizens who did not separate their rubbish. In 1993, President Clinton's executive order 12873 required federal agencies to use recycled and environmentally safe products.

All these developments drove up the monetary value of garbage. Recycling programs generated a constant supply of bottles, tins, paper, and plastic. It wasn't long before the Chicago Board of Trade, which handles the market in agricultural futures, opened the first Recyclables Exchange, a national marketplace in which millions of dollars of garbage are bought and sold daily.

As globalization removed trade barriers, a thriving export trade also emerged, and by 2010, "scrap and trash" (including metals from old appliances) had become the nation's top export.

Think About It

1. Why did the value of trash increase exponentially in the 1990s?
2. In what ways does the recent history of trash illustrate the globalization process that characterized the post-1992 era?

and beating the protesters indiscriminately. The "Battle of Seattle" delayed the start of the WTO sessions. More importantly, the antiglobalization movement and its ideas became the subject of extended debate in the mainstream media for the first time. The swell of popular feeling led President Clinton to press the WTO to mandate basic labor rights in all member nations, but delegates concluded that enforcement of such rights would be impossible.

THE UNITED STATES IN A GLOBALIZING WORLD

Other than in the spheres of international trade and investment, the U.S. role in the post–Cold War world remained uncertain at the beginning of Bill Clinton's presidency. Like Jimmy Carter, Clinton envisioned the United States as a protector of human rights and a powerful conciliator between warring nations. Balancing these aspirations against U.S. economic and military interests, however, proved deeply challenging. In 1992, President George H. W. Bush had dispatched U.S. Marines to the starving, war-torn nation of Somalia in eastern Africa for the purpose of restoring peace and distributing humanitarian aid. Objecting to the presence of foreign troops on Somali soil, tribal warlord Mohammed Farah Aidid killed fifty UN peacekeepers in 1993. President Clinton immediately deployed Marines against Aidid. Hundreds of Somalian civilians lost their lives in the ensuing campaign, but Aidid and his forces eluded the Marines, ambushing and killing eighteen U.S. soldiers in Mogadishu. Americans watched the TV news in revulsion as Aidid's men triumphantly dragged one Marine's body through the streets. The United States withdrew from Somalia soon after.

Within months, another human rights crisis erupted just 1,200 miles away from Somalia, in war-ravaged and ethnically divided Rwanda. In 1994, the majority Hutu population rose up against the nation's Tutsi minority. In twelve weeks, Hutu forces and local militias slaughtered over eight hundred thousand of their fellow citizens. Although the United Nations had a peacekeeping force in Rwanda, the United States and other Security Council members were reluctant to become directly involved. The largest force on the ground, Belgian peacekeepers, withdrew midway through the attacks. Chastened by the Somalian experience, President Clinton decided not to commit U.S. forces, asserting that the conflict was not genocidal. When the extent of the violence became undeniable, however, he and the United Nations conceded that genocide had indeed occurred.

Revelations of the Rwandan genocide persuaded Clinton to intervene in another ethic conflict, this time in Eastern Europe. After the Soviet Union's dissolution, the Balkan country of Yugoslavia had splintered into several ethnically defined nations. In ethnically diverse Bosnia, the Orthodox Christian Serb population relentlessly attacked Muslim citizens. The violence continued for four years, but Clinton was reluctant to intervene. Then, in 1995, concerned that genocide might be under way, the president authorized air strikes against the Serbs. A cease-fire and a temporary end to the war followed within two weeks. A few years later, however, Serbian president Slobodan Milošević embarked on another campaign of "ethnic cleansing," deploying troops and militias against hundreds of thousands of Albanian Muslims living in southern Serbia. Clinton again ordered U.S.-NATO airstrikes against the Serbs. Milošević's popularity plummeted, and he lost the 2000 election. He died before the international war crimes tribunal could try him for crimes against humanity.

Peacemaking was also on Clinton's foreign policy agenda. The president traveled to Ireland several times in an effort to broker a settlement between Great Britain and the British colony of Northern Ireland. Although it took some years, the sides reached agreement. Progress was also made in the Middle East in 1993, when Clinton orchestrated a historic meeting between Israeli prime minister Yitzhak Rabin and Palestinian leader Yasser Arafat. However, extremists on both sides sabotaged the peace effort. A right-wing Israeli assassinated the liberal Rabin, and subsequent elections propelled hard-liner Benjamin Netanyahu into power. Both he and Arafat subsequently abandoned the peace process, and negotiations did not resume until 1999. Although agreement seemed imminent in 2000, zealots on both sides once again derailed the talks, and violence escalated.

Meanwhile, Americans became targets of international terrorism. During the 1980s, new strains of extremism had emerged in Afghanistan, where Muslim fighters, led by the radical Islamist Taliban movement, had fought a decade-long war to repel the Soviet invasion (see Chapter 30). Young Muslim men from the Middle East and South Asia had flocked to Afghanistan to join the fight, which was bankrolled almost

Genocide in Rwanda. Hutu nationalists, such as the young men pictured here, slaughtered 800,000 of Rwanda's Tutsi and any Hutu who supported peaceful coexistence with the Tutsi. In 1999, President Clinton expressed profound regret about U.S. inaction, asserting that 5,000 Marines could have saved 500,000 Rwandan lives.

entirely by the United States and Saudi Arabia. Once the Soviets withdrew in 1989 and the Taliban formed a government, many Saudi Arabian fighters, including Osama bin Laden, returned home. When Iraq invaded Kuwait in 1990, Bin Laden offered the Saudi government the use of his fighters—known by then as **al-Qaeda** (literally, "the base")—to protect the nation's oilfields. The Saudi government rejected the offer and instead provided facilities for the U.S. forces that would eventually drive Saddam Hussein's army out of Kuwait. Enraged that the Saudis had invited non-Muslim forces onto their soil (which many Muslims consider sacred), al-Qaeda plotted revenge against the United States.

Al-Qaeda's network expanded in the 1990s to include radical Islamist operatives, fundraisers, and sympathizers around the world. A small number of operatives who had trained in al-Qaeda's Afghanistan camps lived and worked in the United States. Many condemned what they saw as unjustified U.S. support of Israel, and some began plotting terrorist attacks in the early 1990s. In 1993, several such extremists bombed the World Trade Center in New York City, parking an explosives-packed truck in the basement of one of the towers. A thousand people were injured, and six lost their lives.

Overseas, terrorists targeted U.S. military and diplomatic personnel. A truck bomb killed several U.S. airmen in Saudi Arabia in 1996, and massive bombs ripped through U.S. embassies in eastern Africa two years later, killing several hundred people. The most daring attack to that point came in 2000 in Yemen, when a small bomb-carrying boat pulled alongside the USS *Cole* and exploded. Seventeen U.S. servicemen died in the blast. The bombers were later identified as Islamist radicals with al-Qaeda ties.

The few Americans who had heard of al-Qaeda in 2000 had tended to think of the organization as nothing more than a motley crew of religious fanatics. In fact, the United States was facing a nontraditional enemy with global reach and military and economic might. Far from being old-fashioned or antimodern, moreover, al-Qaeda was using global networks—commercial air routes, international banking, and the emerging technology of the Internet—to recruit followers and wage war.

BRAVE NEW CULTURE

The Internet spread like wildfire across the nation and the world in the 1990s. By mid-decade, tens of millions were going online each day to conduct business, socialize, play, shop, do research, or follow the news. The Internet sped the emergence of a postindustrial economy in which the main products were information and related services. At the same time, breakthroughs in medical and biological science remade the conventional understanding of life and provided tools to extend and manipulate it. Immigration, meanwhile, was altering the country's national, religious, and ethnic makeup. All these changes were controversial, and their long-term consequences unknown.

THE DIGITAL REVOLUTION

Digitization—the transformation of objects, images, sounds, and signals into binary code (1's and 0's)—was not a new technology. Computers, all of which use digital technology, dated back to the 1950s and had become commonplace on college campuses in the 1980s. But it was only in the 1990s that computing and electronic manufacturers, the culture industries, universities, and consumers began to realize the full potential of digitization. The world-altering **Digital Revolution** was under way, and it was ushering in a new era: the Information Age.

Seeking faster, more efficient communication, whether locally or globally, two new kinds of digital networks emerged—the Internet and, especially after 2001, cellular phone networks. The Internet, a global system of millions of local and national networks, had its roots in a digital communications system developed by the U.S. military in the late 1960s and adapted for campus use in the 1980s. In 1991, Timothy Berners-Lee, a Massachusetts Institute of Technology computer scientist, found a seamless way to link documents and other content to the Internet. His World Wide Web sparked the development of user-friendly web browsers and helped turn the Internet into a mass medium (see Spaces and Places: The World Wide Web).

Much like radio in the 1920s, the Internet of the 1990s was neither coordinated by government nor dominated by a single corporation. Anyone could set up a website, and millions of Americans did. The Internet's radically decentralized nature allowed artists, writers, small-business operators, and entertainers to communicate cheaply and directly with a world of users. Internet entrepreneurs also recognized the potential, developing profitable sites such as AuctionWeb (later renamed eBay) and search engines such as Netscape Navigator and Yahoo. In 1995, Netscape was the first of dozens of Internet companies to go public, raising $12 billion in the most successful stock market flotation to date. Netscape's financial home run incited hundreds of other Internet businesses to issue public offerings. Between 1995 and 2000, investors rushed to support these startups and "dot-coms" (named for their commercial web addresses). Business's use of the Internet grew fiftyfold, from just 1 percent of all telecommunicated business information in 1993 to 50 percent by 2000. Ten years later, 97 percent of all telecommunicated business information was transmitted via the Internet.

Online communities formed as users connected with friends and like-minded strangers around the world. These "virtual" communities, most of them noncommercial, stimulated the formation of the first for-profit social networks in the late 1990s. As the Internet took off, digital innovations made it far easier to create, copy, and share or sell music, images, personal correspondence, and business documents. Consumers approved, especially as the price of digital cameras and other electronics fell thanks to economic globalization, which enabled manufacturers to use cheap developing world labor. Whereas only 15 percent of American households owned a computer in 1990, by 2000 that proportion had risen to 51 percent, and the real price of a standard personal computer had been halved.

THE NEW ECONOMY

The Internet played a key role in the development of what many commentators called the **New Economy.** This economy was based not on capitalism's traditional sectors of industry and agriculture but on the kinds of technology and information services in which the Internet specialized. In 1994, Vice President Al Gore declared that Americans were building a "global information infrastructure" that would enable the world's peoples to derive "robust and sustainable economic progress, strong democracies, . . . improved healthcare, and—ultimately—a greater sense of shared stewardship of our small planet." Microsoft CEO Bill Gates wrote in his book *The Road Ahead* (1995) that the Internet would positively change everything from the classroom and the home to entertainment and the workplace. Networked stock exchanges and other financial markets would no longer need expensive brokers as intermediaries and would become transparent and accessible to all.

SPACES & PLACES

The World Wide Web

In the 1990s, Americans used the revolutionary World Wide Web technology to build a radically new online or virtual space. This space existed in no one physical place but in a network of fiber-optic cables, satellites, personal digital devices, network browsers, computer mainframes, and (eventually) wireless signals. Originally intended, in its inventors' words, "to give universal access to a large universe of documents," the web quickly became the basis of an enormous virtual space complete with multiple market, recreational, educational, business, and social meeting "places."

Some observers claimed that the early web had created a "digital commons"—an open space to which all people had access as free and equal individuals. Others conceptualized it as the new Wild West—a virtual utopia free of the oppressive constraints of law, powerful corporations, and government. The Electronic Frontier Foundation, founded in 1990 by computer technicians, lobbied hard to keep the Internet free of restrictions on speech and expression. The group also saw the web as a space in which individuals could carry on private conversations without the risk of eavesdropping by the government or others.

By 1996, big business was claiming parts of the web's virtual space. As web "real estate" (addresses or URLs: uniform resource locators) increased in value, the equivalent of a land rush ensued. Enterprising individuals registered thousands of addresses as they calculated—correctly—that McDonald's, Coca-Cola, and other corporate giants would buy up all Internet addresses containing their names or slogans. Although commercialization made the digital commons idea less workable, it greatly expanded the number and kind of virtual meeting places. The makeoutclub.com, one of the first for-profit social spaces, gathered music and underground fashion news for "indierockers, hardcore kids, record collectors, artists, bloggers, and hopeless romantics."

Such niche marketing soon went mainstream with the emergence of Friendster, MySpace, and LinkedIn. Advertisers flocked to the sites in an effort to reach a mass audience. Dating services such as match.com, founded in 1993, provided a space in which singles could "meet" and get to know one another, even across vast distances. Demand for social media in turn sparked the creation, after 2002, of new programs aimed at facilitating much higher, more user-friendly levels of interaction and collaboration in what is often referred to as Web 2.0. One pioneer, Facebook, went on to build the world's largest, most profitable social networking site.

With the web came new anxieties. Many critics worried that the web—and the Digital Revolution generally—was substituting a virtual world for "real" places, people, and experiences. Psychologists warned that exposing children to virtual reality could interfere with their cognitive development. (This possibility struck a chord with Silicon Valley executives, many of whom began sending their own children to computer-free kindergartens and elementary schools.) Others warned against the nation's growing reliance on an Internet that might spread corrupting software "bugs" and pernicious "viruses." Citizens, businesses, and government agencies worried that computers and data storage facilities might fail on January 1, 2000, because their clocks used two instead of four digits to denote the year. (Potentially, this could have resulted in massive data loss.)

Besides the ongoing problem of piracy, most worries proved misplaced. In 1999, government and business methodically upgraded their systems, and as the world rang in the year 2000, hardly any systems faltered. The web's virtual space actually boosted physical interaction among people in real time and space. Most users of online dating services, for example, wanted to connect with someone who lived within a twenty-five-mile radius and to meet their "date" in person as soon as possible. Also, as wireless Internet connections brought people into cafés, libraries, and other "real" social spaces, demand for such venues grew. Further, social networks and online advertising helped everything from restaurants, nightclubs, and opera houses to local flower shows, churches, and temples to draw mass audiences.

Think About It

1. Why do you think the Internet grew so quickly in the 1990s?
2. What were some unexpected effects of the rise of new social media, such as online chat rooms and dating services?
3. In what ways, if any, was the Internet a force for globalization?

Online America. Artists used powerful new image and mapping programs to generate startling representations of the world's newfound Internet "connectivity." Such "infographics" blurred the line between art and information and registered the geographical unevenness of Internet access, but they did not highlight the digital divide by which the majority of African Americans and other minorities were unable to gain such access. By 2010, however, over 80 percent of all U.S. Hispanics and whites and 71 percent of African Americans had achieved access.

Many Americans agreed that the Internet was a democratizing force, but others worried that it was exacerbating inequality. By 2000, over half of all whites had Internet access but only one in three African Americans was connected. Hispanics fared only slightly better. Social commentators worried that the Digital Revolution might be leaving minorities behind and limiting their employment and educational opportunities. In 2000, President Clinton addressed this **digital divide** in his State of the Union speech, underscoring the need to open up the Internet and the New Economy to everyone.

Minority online connectivity improved steadily during the 2000s, but the gap between the real income of nonmanagerial workers and that of the wealthiest Americans continued its post-1977 march to levels unseen since the Great Depression. The digital divide was closing, but the economic divide was even wider than it had been in the 1980s.

Part of the reason was that, unlike the Ford Motor Company and other industrial giants, computing companies were not large-scale employers. Although they paid their U.S.-based staff exceptionally well, high-tech powerhouses such as Microsoft and Netscape employed a relatively small proportion of the workforce. Computer manufacturers had moved most of their factories to China by 2000. Another problem was that investors overestimated the value of technology stocks, thereby driving their price artificially high. With stock prices rising, many dot-coms took on debt in the belief that their growing stock value and rapidly expanding customer base would cover the difference. When the overpriced stocks crashed in March 2000, most dot-coms (or "dot bombs," as some derided them) were ruined. Only the largest companies, including Amazon, Google, and eBay, survived the dot-com crash and rode out the recession that followed.

Other victims of the Digital Revolution were newspaper and book publishers, television networks, and music studios whose "old media" found it difficult to compete with the Internet. With its easily copied electronic texts, the Internet brought the price of information and entertainment down so dramatically—sometimes to zero—that consumers were increasingly unwilling to pay the usual price for their news, books, movies, and music. Some newspaper publishers, such as the *New York Times*, added subscription-based online editions, but many others ceased publication. The music industry, which had traditionally relied on the analog technology of the long-playing record (which was difficult to reproduce), all but collapsed as Internet users began uploading and sharing their music libraries, making free use of new online services such as Napster.

Some Internet entrepreneurs sought to profit, and a new kind of crime—**Internet piracy,** the large-scale copying of copyrighted music, text, and film—became a billion-dollar-a-year industry. Apple's iTunes, introduced in 2001, aimed to bring order to this arena of the Internet (as well as to turn a profit). However, piracy remains one of the New Economy's biggest problems.

RECONCEIVING THE MEANING OF LIFE

The Digital Revolution also gave rise to a new field of knowledge—**biotechnology** (or "biotech")—that both transformed medical science and challenged conventional morality.

Hello, Dolly. The first mammal to be cloned successfully from an adult mammal's cell was a female domestic sheep named Dolly. The fact that she had three mothers—one provided the egg, another supplied the DNA, and a third carried the fetus—made Dolly the world's most famous and most controversial sheep. Her well-publicized birth in Scotland in 1996 sparked passionate debate over the moral and psychological ramifications of cloning. **Question for Analysis:** Why do you think the popular press, including leading magazines like *Time*, considered Dolly newsworthy?

Between 1995 and 2001, international teams of geneticists used unprecedentedly powerful computer processors to sequence and map the genome—an organism's entire genetic information—of humans, viruses, and other life forms. Through this work, scientists discovered human genetic abnormalities correlated with cancer, autism, and other illnesses and conditions. It became clear that genes may change or express themselves differently over a person's lifetime. In a related vein, new research on stem cells—cells that reproduce a variety of other cells—became the basis of radical new therapies for treating bone marrow disorders. For the first time, healthy stem cells were transferred into the patient's marrow, where they produced healthy rather than diseased cells.

The revelations afforded by biotech inspired tremendous hope among medical professionals and the public that genetic therapies would one day cure cancer, heart disease, brain damage, and other life-threatening conditions. The advances also kindled controversy and opposition. Some stem cell research involved the use of human embryos, which were destroyed in the process of extracting the stem cells. Antiabortionists condemned the procedure outright, arguing that human life is sacred even in embryo form. Consequently, in 2001 President George W. Bush ordered that federal funding for stem cell research should apply only to existing stem cells. His order effectively halted the use of embryos until President Barack Obama overturned the restriction in 2009.

Biotech also began to transform the conditions under which life was created—as well as long-standing social conventions about sexuality and parenting. Although the United States' first "test-tube baby" was born in 1978, it was not until the 1990s that the use of assisted reproductive technology (ART), including sperm donation and in vitro fertilization, became commonplace among wealthy and middle-class Americans. Sperm banks, which collected and stored cryogenically frozen sperm, multiplied in major cities in the late 1990s and advertised on the Internet. The technology became particularly popular among Generation X women (born between 1964 and 1979) who had focused on career building in their twenties and delayed pregnancy until later.

The Promise and Challenge of Biotech. The TV series *Battlestar Galactica* (2004–2009) was one of many productions to register Americans' deep ambivalence toward the revolutionary technologies of the late twentieth century. Created by humans, the Cylon robots develop the biotechnological means to appear, feel, and act human. In their bid to destroy their makers, the Cylons use their masters' computer networks to turn humans' own weapons systems against themselves. Yet injections of Cylon "blood," a genetically enhanced version of human blood, are discovered to cure cancer—a fantasy echoing popular hopes about biotechnology.

ART was originally aimed at helping married heterosexual couples suffering from infertility to conceive a child from their own genetic material. But the technology had far broader implications. Where a male partner's sperm was immotile or otherwise damaged, heterosexual couples were able to use donated sperm to produce a child genetically unrelated to his or her father (unless the donor was related to the father). ART also made it much easier for single women and women in same-sex relationships to conceive a child—with the consequence that the number of children born to lesbian couples increased exponentially. Many conservatives charged that donor sperm resulted in illegitimate children, even within heterosexual marriage, and that same-sex parenting was a sin. Moderate critics worried that children would not develop healthily if raised outside the institution of heterosexual marriage. Despite these objections, ART had accounted for over forty-one thousand births in the United States by 2006, or slightly over 1 percent of total births that year.

Biotech revolutionized the U.S. food chain as well. In the 1990s, geneticists and biologists discovered ways of directly manipulating the genetic matter of plants to maximize growth and render them resistant to disease and pests. Led by former

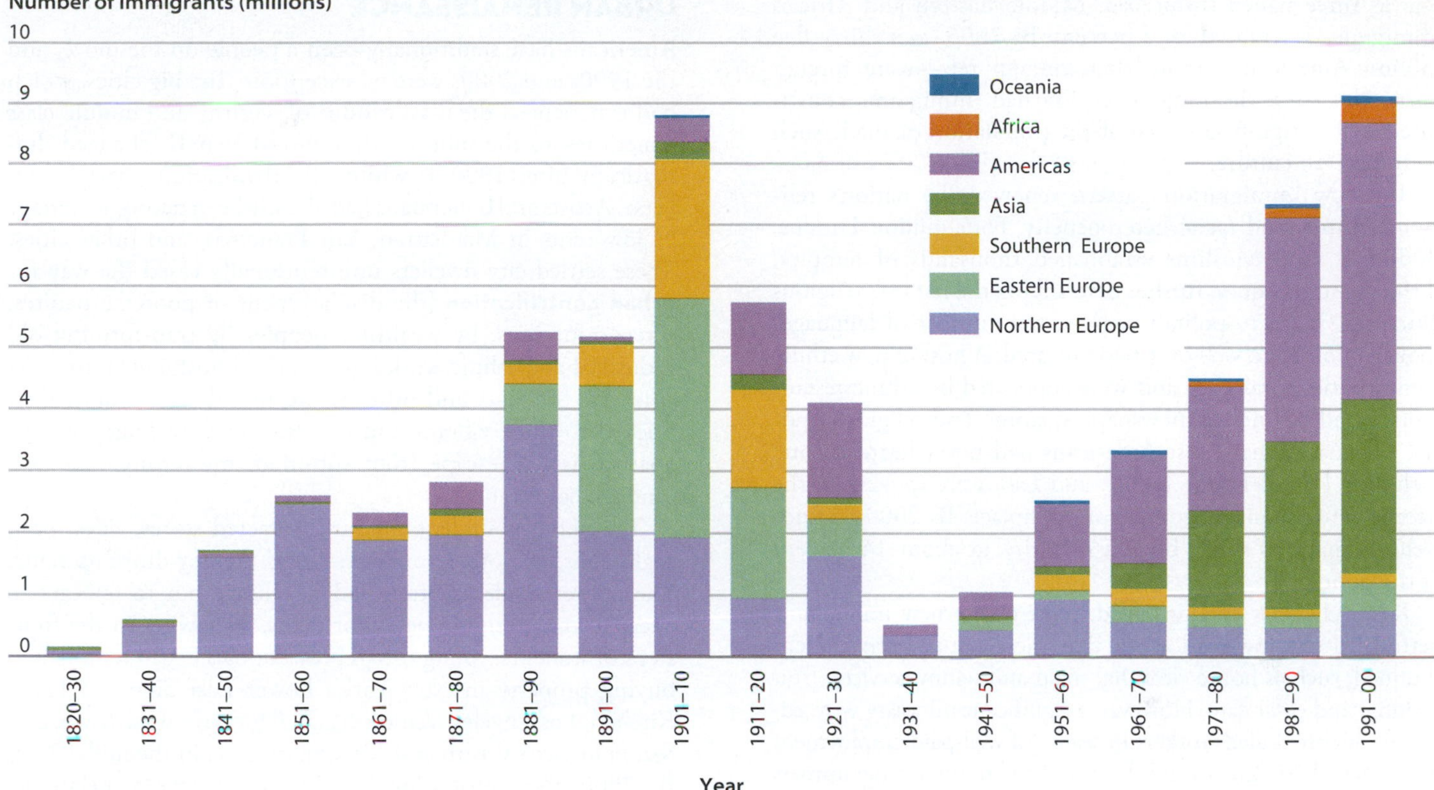

FIGURE 31.2 **Globalizing Immigration, 1820–2000.** The principal source of immigration shifted from Europe to Asia, Africa, and Latin America after 1965.

chemical producer Monsanto, agribusiness developed genetically modified seeds for sale to farmers worldwide. By 2000, over a million U.S. acres were planted with genetically modified soybeans, cotton, maize, and canola. It also became possible for the first time to patent and legally own genes—the raw material of life itself. By 2010, upwards of 60 percent of all packaged foods in the United States contained genetically modified plant matter.

RENEWING DIVERSITY

As technological innovation accelerated, the meaning of "American" was changing rapidly. Legal and illegal immigration to the United States increased dramatically in the 1990s, and for the first time in the nation's history, the great majority of migrants did not come from Europe (see Figure 31.2). Almost half were from Latin America and the Caribbean, and

Pledging Allegiance. The rate at which eligible immigrants naturalized (became U.S. citizens) increased dramatically from about 47 percent in 1996 to 59 percent by 2006. Hispanic naturalization almost doubled. These military personnel pictured at a naturalization ceremony were just a few of the one million or so foreign-born permanent residents who became citizens each year.

one in three hailed from Asia. Middle Eastern and African immigrants accounted for 5 percent. By 2006, over thirty-five million Americans—more than one in ten—were foreign born. Not since the Progressive Era had immigrants constituted such a significant slice of the population or made such an impact on culture.

The new immigration pattern renewed the nation's religious, ethnic, and racial heterogeneity. Four million Hindus, Buddhists, and Muslims established thousands of temples, shrines, and mosques, further diversifying the nation's religious pluralism. In metropolitan centers, the number of languages spoken climbed to well over two hundred. A host of new ethnic communities sprang up and were supported by ethnic restaurants, small businesses, newspapers, stores, and religious leaders. Languages that most Americans had never heard before, including Hindi, Urdu, Arabic, and Lao, were spoken on the streets, while Spanish became commonplace. By 2000, Latinos were the nation's single biggest majority, at about 14 percent of the population.

Relatively poor and unskilled, most of the new immigrants performed the low-paid work that most native-born citizens shunned, such as house cleaning, maid and nanny services, fruit picking, and elder care. However, a significant minority were educated, highly skilled workers in search of well-paid employment in the New Economy. A full third of the computer programmers working in Silicon Valley were foreign born. University-educated immigrants also entered the arts and the film industry, where they produced a new genre of globally conscious work. Taiwan-born Ang Lee, director of *The Wedding Banquet* (1993), made several critically acclaimed films about cultural differences between and among immigrants and a series of blockbuster movies, including *Brokeback Mountain* (2005), many of which framed American subject matter in ways that were designed to appeal to a global audience.

The newcomers received a mixed welcome in their adoptive home. Many Americans and much of the mainstream media celebrated the renewal of diversity and the birth of what they hoped would be a truly multicultural society. Employers were generally welcoming, though unless the workers were highly skilled engineers or computer programmers, the wage scale did not reflect their enthusiasm, and employers frequently suppressed immigrants' efforts to unionize.

In California, where native-born whites were fast ceasing to be in the majority, voters supported propositions aimed at limiting public services and education for Latinos. In 1996, Californians also passed the highly controversial Proposition 209, which prohibited universities from taking the race, sex, or ethnicity of college applicants into account as a way of achieving diversity. Voters, especially in the Southwest, put pressure on the federal government to halt illegal immigration, particularly from Mexico. The Immigration and Naturalization Service (INS) beefed up border patrols and opened dozens of prisons for over-stayers and undocumented "aliens." By 2000, more than sixty thousand immigrants were incarcerated.

URBAN RENAISSANCE

Americans have traditionally been a people on the move, and the 1990s and 2000s were no exception. The big cities, which had experienced the mass exodus of wealthy and middle-class Americans to the suburbs after World War II, changed dramatically after 1990 as white suburbanization began to reverse. Artists and bohemians had already been taking advantage of low rents in Manhattan, San Francisco, and other cities. These settled city dwellers unintentionally eased the way for **urban gentrification** (the displacement of poorer urbanites, often minorities, by wealthier people) by transforming old industrial and ethnic working-class neighborhoods into artist colonies. Students and other white middle-class youth then flocked to these vibrant and diverse zones, seeking low-rent apartments, an escape from suburban monotony, and new kinds of community.

The flood of students in turn attracted stores, cafés, bars, nightclubs, and other amenities—and thereby drove up rents. The poorer residents often had no choice but to relocate to cheaper, more remote neighborhoods. Following in the footsteps of students, young urban professionals began renting and buying property in New York's Lower East Side and Hell's Kitchen, Los Angeles' Venice Beach, Chicago's West Town, and San Francisco's Castro and Mission districts in the mid-1990s. By 2000, these professionals gentrified dozens of neighborhoods that suburbanites once considered too dangerous or dirty for residence.

Television sitcoms also returned from suburb to city in the 1990s, led by *Seinfeld* and then *Friends* and *Sex in the City*. All three shows were set in New York and featured a circle of friends rather than the suburban family of earlier sitcoms. Gentrification resumed after the dot-com crash of 2000, as baby boomers—often the parents of urbanizing young professionals—migrated to the cities in large numbers.

Economic globalization and the Digital Revolution sped gentrification, chiefly because professionals who had once worked in the industrial sector (which had fueled suburbanization) now worked for financial and related informational services, most of which were city based. Urban mayors and police departments also worked hard to attract business and affluent residents, adopting "zero-tolerance" policies aimed at petty crime, drug use, panhandling, and conspicuous homelessness. Urbanizing professionals were motivated, too, by the promise of diversity (even though their own migration actually homogenized cities) and freedom from highway commuting. The perceived possibility of personal growth—most significantly, the ability to live in an internationally diverse area or the freedom to lead an openly gay life—was also a major motivating factor.

Many urban communities fought gentrification. Some opponents, including New York's Lower East Side Collective, worked to save the many community gardens and playgrounds that longtime residents had planted on abandoned sites and which developers eyed for condominium construction.

Tenants' unions took landlords to court to fight illegal or unfair evictions, which spiked in the 1990s as landlords attempted to raise rents. Although homeless people found it especially difficult to organize, small groups, such as Picture the Homeless, popped up in major cities in the late 1990s. Notably, many used the Internet to organize protests and publicize their plight. Nonetheless, gentrification appeared unstoppable—until the worst recession since the Great Depression struck the global economy in 2007 (see The Great Recession, below).

GEORGE W. BUSH AND THE WAR ON TERROR

Having presided over one of the most impressive economic booms in the nation's history, the Democrats were stunned when their candidate lost to a Republican in the 2000 presidential elections. President George W. Bush proceeded to implement his program of "compassionate conservatism," a mixture of social reform and massive tax cuts. The recession was far from over on September 11, 2001, when al-Qaeda terrorists hijacked four commercial flights in U.S. airspace, turning the planes into weapons and killing thousands of American civilians. The Bush administration declared a "war on terror" and initiated military actions in Afghanistan and, later, Iraq. Although al-Qaeda leaders escaped from Afghanistan, the military campaigns overthrew the Afghan and Iraqi regimes. Peace proved hard to maintain, however, as the United States became bogged down in seemingly endless wars of insurgency. At home, Hurricane Katrina claimed thousands of lives and all but destroyed New Orleans. Disillusioned voters gave both houses of Congress to the Democrats in 2006.

THE ELECTION OF 2000

The Republicans faced an uphill battle going into the election of 2000. Bill Clinton was still among the most popular presidents in the nation's history. Many middle-class and wealthy Americans now associated him and his New Democrat policies—rather than the Republican Party—with boom times. Although the boom had turned to bust in the dot-com meltdown of March 2000, the majority of voters still gave Clinton high marks for his overall handling of the economy. Seeking to emphasize continuity and to build on the administration's relative popularity, the Democrats nominated Vice President Al Gore, a former Tennessee senator with over eighteen years' experience in national politics.

Republicans gave the nod to George W. Bush, Texas governor and the son of former president George H. W. Bush. Although Gore and Bush both came from wealthy, politically connected families, the two men had little in common. Unlike Gore, Bush lacked a track record in national and global politics, and unlike Bush, Gore had little business experience. The cerebral Democrat understood and promoted "big ideas" like the global information superhighway and international cooperation on global warming, whereas the down-home Republican professed relative ignorance on these matters and took more interest in the lives and aspirations of ordinary Americans. The two men's personal styles moreover could hardly have been more at odds. Bush was most at ease in informal situations and had a remarkable ability to connect on a personal level, even with political opponents. Informality made Gore uncomfortable—he was most at home behind a podium or in front of a full session of the Senate. Except for contrasting views on the environment, their policies were not that different. Both supported deregulation, economic globalization, and the New Economy. Consequently, both campaigns relentlessly picked on the perceived weaknesses in the other candidate's personal style—and the mass media piled on.

The Gore campaign assumed that a Democratic victory was assured. Bush's strategists worked hard to separate their candidate from the extreme conservative wing of the Republican Party, promoting him as a "compassionate conservative" who cared about education and society's neediest as well as balancing the federal budget. Promising tax cuts, Bush campaigners also succeeded in painting Gore as an elitist policy wonk who had little in common with the average American. One well-publicized poll in October 2000 showed that more people "would rather sit down to drink a beer" with Bush than with Gore. By then, the candidates were in a statistical dead heat. In such a close race, the fact that well-known consumer advocate Ralph Nader was polling a few percent as the Green Party's nominee became a serious threat, particularly to the Democrats, the party most likely to lose votes to Nader. Founded in 1991, the Green Party ran on an environmentalist and socially conscious platform and attracted left-leaning voters disillusioned with the Democrats' embrace of economic globalization and free-market policies.

On election day, Gore won the popular vote by more than five hundred thousand ballots. Millions of Americans went to sleep that night assuming a Democratic victory. The next morning, they learned that Bush had carried Florida and its twenty-five electoral votes, in so doing winning the electoral college and the presidency (see Map 31.2). Although an automatic electronic recount of the Florida vote was under way by then, the Democrats immediately called for a hand count of the Florida ballots, on the grounds that the automatic recount would likely be riddled with errors. Evidence had surfaced that, in some precincts, officials had barred African American voters from casting their ballots (which most likely would have been for Gore) on dubious grounds such as a typo in the registration information or misidentification as a disenfranchised felon.

The Republicans asked the Supreme Court to stop the hand count. The justices divided sharply over the case, voting five to four along party lines to deny the Democrats their request. Al Gore conceded the presidency on December 13, 2000.

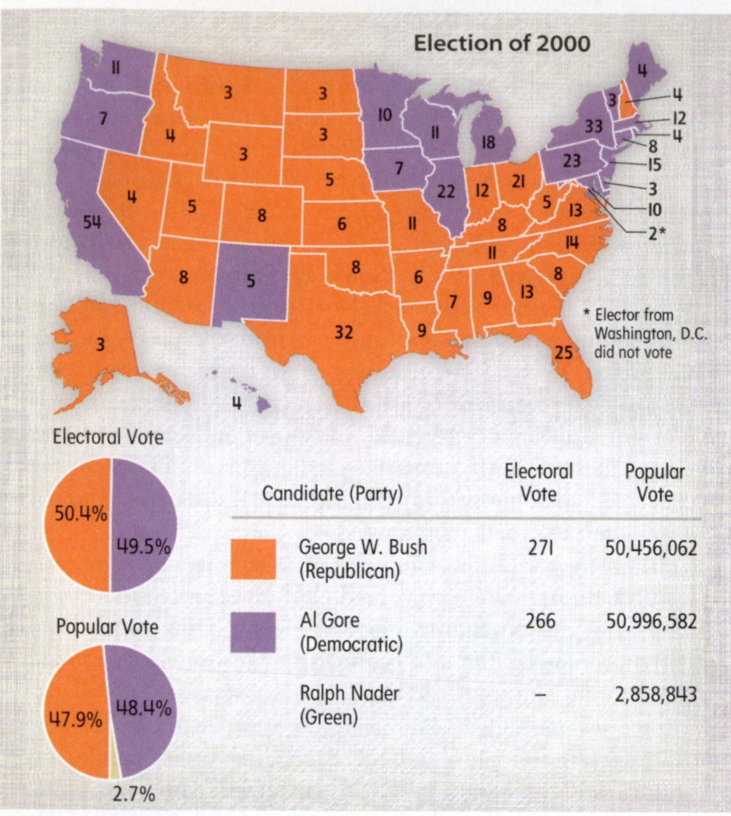

Candidate (Party)	Electoral Vote	Popular Vote
George W. Bush (Republican)	271	50,456,062
Al Gore (Democratic)	266	50,996,582
Ralph Nader (Green)	–	2,858,843

Map 31.2 Election of 2000.

COMPASSIONATE CONSERVATISM IN ACTION

George W. Bush delivered swiftly and decisively on many of his basic campaign pledges. Drawing heavily on his father's circle of moderate Republicans to fill key cabinet positions, the younger Bush also pleased his party's religious wing by appointing several conservatives. General Colin Powell, a moderate and former commander of the U.S. Armed Forces, became the first African American secretary of state, while the ultraconservative John Ashcroft was eventually appointed attorney general.

Religious conservatives were also pleased when the president established the White House Office of Faith-Based and Community Initiatives, which increased the ability of churches and other religious organizations to draw on federal funding for social programs aimed at vulnerable populations such as prisoners and the unemployed. Some critics argued that the office contravened the constitutional separation of church and state. Federal courts subsequently ruled that federal funding could not be used for programs that promoted prayer or other devotional practices. The office and many other programs survived, however, their budget growing to over $2 billion annually by 2005.

Reducing taxes was also a high priority. In 2001, Congress passed Bush's tax bill, which retroactively refunded taxpayers $300 to $600 each. For most Americans, the refund was equivalent to an extra can of soda every day for less than a year, but it was tremendously popular. In the same legislation, Bush approved a tax reduction plan that cut taxes for the next ten years, to the tune of over $1.3 trillion. Two years later, Congress trimmed another $320 billion in tax revenue. Though widely welcomed by taxpayers, the cuts helped put the government budget back into deficit for the first time since the mid-1990s. Further, the great bulk of the cuts went to the wealthiest minority of Americans.

The tax cuts were purportedly designed to kick-start the economy, which had stalled in the wake of the dot-com crash of 2000. But the economy continued to slip into recession in the summer of 2001, fueled by an energy crisis. Gas prices rose to their highest point in history, to over $1.90 a gallon. In California, severe power cuts—imposed by major suppliers—afflicted millions of consumers. The president responded by proposing the construction of more power plants, mines, and oil rigs, some on protected federal lands such as the Alaskan and Arctic wildernesses. The Senate blocked the Arctic plans, but Bush forged ahead elsewhere. The United States also withdrew from the Kyoto Protocol on the basis that—despite a global scientific consensus—the theory of global warming was "bad science." And whereas the Clinton administration had taken early steps to lessen U.S. dependency on fossil fuel, Bush signed the Energy Policy Act of 2005, which injected almost $14 billion into the coal, oil, and nuclear industries.

Social policy changed more in emphasis than in orientation under President Bush. The No Child Left Behind Act (2002) greatly expanded the federal government's role in education. All schools were to meet state testing standards or face a loss of federal funding. The act, which gained bipartisan support, also increased federal aid for education by $4 billion. In addition, a new health care law advanced federal funds to private insurers to encourage them to compete with the government's Medicare system. The same law also gave prescription drug benefits to the elderly for the first time.

Bush's initiatives had mixed results. Schools struggled to comply with No Child Left Behind and were hampered by ongoing state budget crises. The great majority of elders were pleased with subsidized prescription drugs, but at a cost of over $500 billion a year, it strained the federal budget. Moreover, Bush-era health reform did nothing to help the forty-six million or so Americans who were uninsured and who consequently had little or no access to health care.

AL-QAEDA ATTACKS

Nothing defined George W. Bush's administration more acutely than its response to the terrorist attacks of September 11, 2001. That morning, nineteen al-Qaeda operatives boarded commercial jets in Boston, Newark, and the nation's capital, hijacked them, and flew them toward the foremost symbols of American power. Two slammed into New York City's World Trade Center (the Twin Towers), ultimately causing them to collapse and killing over 2,700 civilians, police, and emergency workers. A

Rekindling the Culture Wars. Attorney general nominee John Ashcroft's controversial views on homosexuality, abortion, the place of religion in public life, and art made for a contentious confirmation process in the Senate. Once confirmed, Ashcroft famously ordered the Department of Justice's twelve-foot-high seminude statues, including the Spirit of Justice, pictured here, covered in blue drapes.

third jetliner hit the Pentagon and killed 125 personnel and all the passengers. A fourth plane crashed in a field near Shanksville, Pennsylvania, after passengers wrestled with the hijackers; everyone on board perished. All told, the terrorists claimed the lives of 2,977 people.

Shockwaves rolled over the world. President Bush's popularity soared, and across the nation, Americans flew the flag at half-mast in honor of the dead. Memorials and shrines were laid out in capitals and small towns across every continent. Dozens of foreign governments expressed their profound grief and affirmed their willingness to work with the United States to ensure that such attacks never happened again. The events that the media now simply referred to as 9/11 brought the nation together for the first time in decades. For a brief few weeks, the culture wars, ideological differences, and partisan fighting were forgotten. As the Bush administration formulated a response, however, both national unity and global sympathy for the United States fractured.

On September 20, 2001, in an address to Congress and the American people, the president announced a **war on terror.** He asserted that the true target of terrorists—al-Qaeda and others—was American freedom. "Our war on terror," Bush continued, "begins with al-Qaeda, but it does not end there. It will not end until every terrorist group of global reach has been found, stopped, and defeated." The brainchild of Defense Secretary Donald Rumsfeld, Vice President Dick Cheney, and national security adviser Paul Wolfowitz, the war on terror envisioned an ongoing military, ideological, diplomatic, and economic campaign against terrorist organizations (including al-Qaeda and other Islamist groups) and, if necessary, the nations that harbored them.

Potentially global in scope, the campaign had no end date and no clear strategic objectives. Then, in what came to be known as the Bush Doctrine, the United States asserted the right to preemptively strike any nation harboring terrorists even though that nation's government had not itself attacked the United States. This open-ended approach gave the president maximal flexibility to determine the campaign's duration, objectives, and location—and paved the path for the rapid expansion of presidential power. Bush also pushed the USA PATRIOT Act through Congress six weeks after the attacks. This controversial law (whose name is an acronym for Uniting and Strengthening America by Providing Appropriate Tools Required to Intercept and Obstruct Terrorism) forcefully enhanced presidential power. It reduced restrictions on law enforcement's ability to conduct surveillance within the United States and gave authorities more discretion to detain and deport immigrants suspected of terrorism. It also expanded the definition of terrorism to include domestic terrorism, thereby potentially subjecting U.S. citizens to much greater surveillance than was previously legal.

THE WAR ON TERROR

Shortly after announcing the war on terror, President Bush requested international support for military operations against the terrorist network and its Taliban hosts in Afghanistan. The Taliban refused to hand over Osama bin Laden and in October the United States and Britain began the aerial bombing of Afghanistan. On the ground, anti-Taliban rebels known as the United Islamic Front (UIF, or the Northern Alliance) invaded Taliban territory, working with U.S. forces to overthrow the government. By December 2001, this joint effort had destroyed both the Taliban government and al-Qaeda's mountain headquarters in Tora Bora (see Map 31.3). Under United Nations auspices, UIF and other anti-Taliban leaders convened a few weeks later to establish an interim government. The new regime repealed Taliban religious laws and drafted a U.S.-style constitution. A special UN force, headed by American general David Petraeus, was charged with maintaining security in and around the Afghan capital, Kabul.

Entailing the loss of fewer than one hundred American lives and bringing a regime change to Afghanistan, this short period of fighting boosted the Bush administration's popularity at home. Afghanistan was relatively peaceful for the following few years. However, hundreds of al-Qaeda operatives, including leader Osama bin Laden, had slipped out of Afghanistan during the bombing campaign. Many regrouped in the so-called tribal lands on the Afghan-Pakistani border, over which no national government had effective control (see Map 31.3). The Taliban were also reorganizing in southern Afghanistan.

In the international sphere, the United States encountered criticism for not having worked with the UN Security Council to win authorization for the war. The Bush administration argued that it had been an "act of collective self-defense" requiring no Security Council resolution. Nonetheless, the administration's willingness to go to war unilaterally, without UN involvement, proved highly controversial overseas and at home.

Critics' concern turned to shock when, in January 2002, President Bush announced that Iraq, Iran, and North Korea were an "axis of evil" whose activities might soon warrant U.S. intervention. Although the three nations had little in common—and

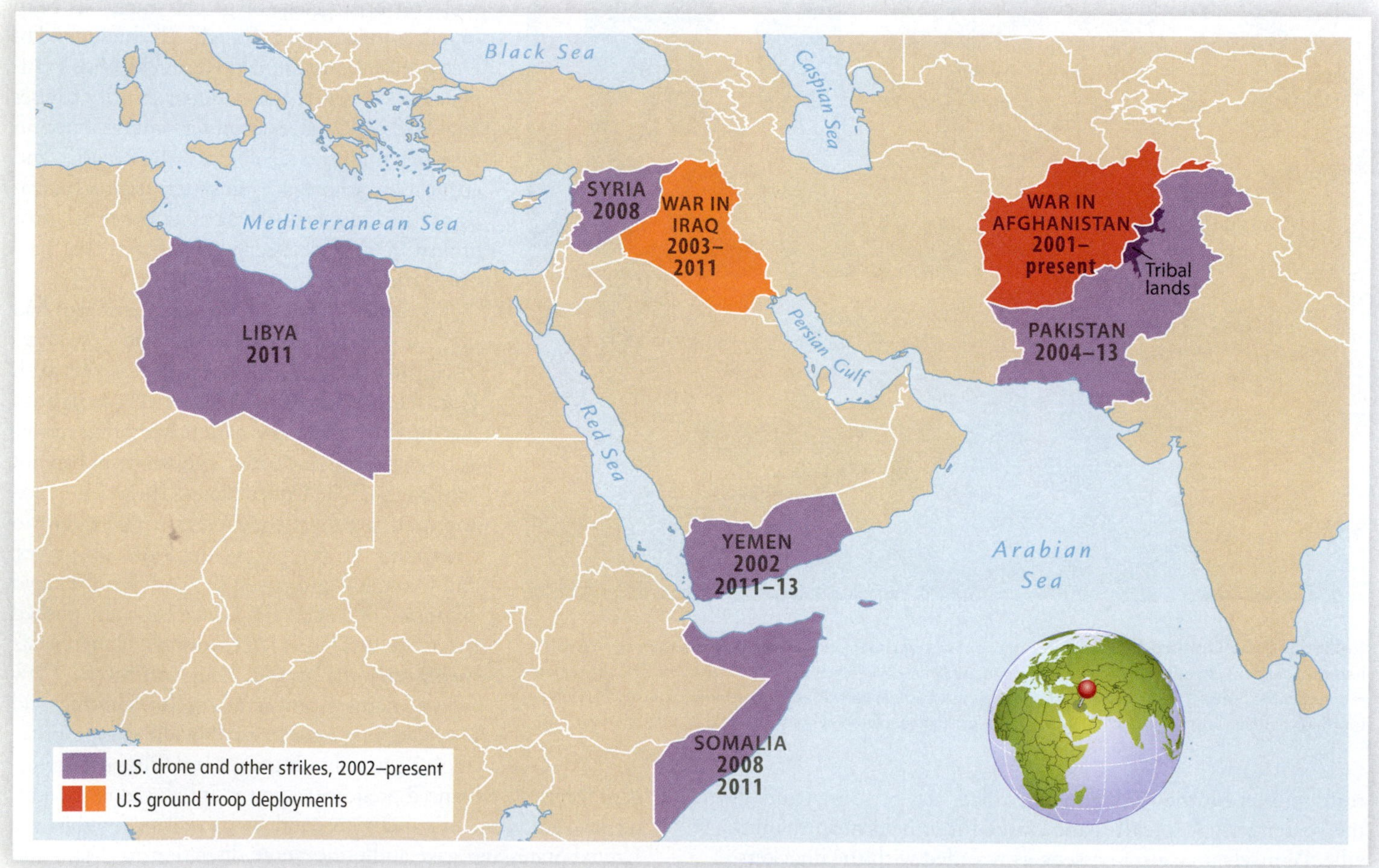

Map 31.3 U.S. Military Intervention, 2001–2013. In the course of the war on terror, British and U.S. forces began a massive aerial bombing of Afghanistan on October 7, 2001, about one month after the al-Qaeda attacks on the United States. Two years later, U.S. and allied forces went to war with Iraq. The United States also controversially conducted a series of drone strikes and other attacks on suspected terrorist targets in Libya, Yemen, Pakistan, Somalia, and Syria.

Iran and Iraq were bitter enemies—Bush linked them with al-Qaeda and proclaimed them the single biggest threat to the United States. The administration expanded on this idea in the National Security Strategy of 2002 (NSS-2002)—the most important statement of U.S. foreign policy since NSC-68 outlined the principle of containment (see Chapter 26). NSS-2002 enshrined the Bush Doctrine and proclaimed that the United States would directly aid foreign nations that were attempting to develop U.S.-style democratic and economic institutions.

Critics charged that the United States was embarking on an aggressive new foreign policy in defiance of international law. Their fears were confirmed a few months later when President Bush announced that Iraq had developed weapons of mass destruction (WMD) and that, as a consequence, Iraqi leader Saddam Hussein would have to be removed, by force if necessary. Among the "hawks" (proponents of war) in Bush's cabinet, Secretary Rumsfeld was particularly influential. The elder President Bush, he argued, had squandered the opportunity, in the Persian Gulf War, to invade Iraq, depose Hussein, and construct an American-style democracy. Democratizing Iraq, he insisted, would spur similar movements throughout the Middle East, potentially opening up the region to U.S. investment and oil interests. In the hawks' opinion, September 11 provided an opportunity to remake the entire region.

THE IRAQ WAR

Much of the world opposed precipitous action against Iraq, especially without hard evidence. Bush therefore reluctantly agreed to let UN weapons inspectors search for proof that Iraq possessed WMD. Although the inspections unearthed nothing, in early 2003 Secretary of State Colin Powell presented the case for an invasion to the United Nations. U.S. intelligence, Powell claimed, had established that WMD were hidden away in Hussein's palaces, underground bunkers, and mobile facilities. (The claims later proved false.) Soon afterward, Bush announced that the United States was going to war with Iraq. Congress authorized him to use force, but with the exceptions of Britain and Australia, all traditional U.S. allies refused to support the war. Still hoping for a modicum of international support, Bush turned to former Eastern bloc nations, to which he offered U.S. aid and preferred immigration status if they agreed to join a "coalition of the willing."

Crushing aerial bombing campaigns began in March 2003. Within three weeks, U.S. ground troops overthrew the Iraqi government and occupied the capital, Baghdad. Saddam Hussein eluded U.S. forces, but by May 1, the United States had gained control of much of the nation. President Bush proclaimed victory.

From the administration's perspective, the invasion could hardly have been more successful. No one, however, had

Proclaiming Victory. In a carefully choreographed media spectacle, a navy jet carrying President George W. Bush landed on the USS *Lincoln* aircraft carrier, anchored off California. Standing beneath a "Mission Accomplished" banner and surrounded by cheering sailors, the president proclaimed that major combat operations had ended in Iraq. **Questions for Analysis:** Why might President Bush and his advisors have chosen the USS *Lincoln* as the backdrop to the announcement that the United States had accomplished its goals in Iraq? What does this event tell us about Bush's domestic challenges during the war on terror?

planned for the peace. In the absence of police authority, Iraqis ransacked factories, power plants, museums, stores, military arsenals, and palaces. U.S. troops stood by as food, water, gasoline, and electricity ran short. Out of the chaos and dysfunction, an anti-American insurgency emerged. Led at first by members of the Sunni (the Muslim minority to which Hussein had belonged), the insurgents incessantly attacked coalition forces. Majority Shi'a Muslims faced off against the Sunni, threatening to plunge the nation into a civil war. Soon, al-Qaeda, which had not had a presence in Iraq, infiltrated the country and recruited thousands of new members and allies. Far from being accomplished, the U.S. mission was just beginning.

THE ELECTION OF 2004

The war on terror and the Iraq War initially raised President Bush's popularity, with two in every three voters rating him favorably in 2003. But when the insurgencies escalated in early 2004, an election year, his ratings fell. They slipped further when photographs surfaced of U.S. troops torturing and sexually humiliating suspected insurgents in Abu Ghraib prison in Baghdad. Al-Qaeda and other radical Islamists seized on the images as proof of Americans' hatred of Islam and of the falsity of U.S. claims to democratizing Iraq. America's Muslim allies wondered how the U.S. military could have permitted such conduct, and Americans of all political persuasions expressed their disgust. Shortly afterward, the public also learned of harsh treatment at Guantánamo Bay, the Cuban site of a U.S. detention camp that held Afghan and Iraqi prisoners.

As the insurgency ground on and revelations of abuse spiraled, Bush's ratings collapsed. Whether the use of stress positions and waterboarding (simulated drowning) constituted torture became major election issues. Republican strategist Karl Rove recommended that Bush's best shot at reelection was to appeal to Americans' patriotism while disentangling the nation from Iraq and escalating the culture wars (which would bring out conservative voters). Accordingly, Bush apologized for the Abu Ghraib incidents, and expedited plans to transfer power to a new Iraqi government. In June 2004, the United States handed over sovereignty, leaving behind 130,000 U.S. troops to protect the new government and train Iraqi security forces.

Abu Ghraib. Leaked to the media in early 2004, this image of a detainee at Abu Ghraib, hooded and apparently wired for electrocution, stunned and enraged people around the world. A Defense Department inquiry subsequently confirmed that physical, psychological, and sexual abuse was widespread at the prison, further eroding Americans' support of the war.

Domestically, the cultural issue most likely to mobilize conservatives was gay marriage, which Massachusetts had legalized earlier in 2004. Conservatives were already dismayed by *Lawrence v. Texas* (2003), in which the Supreme Court ruled that sexual relations between consenting adults of the same sex were constitutionally protected. Led by Vermont, several states had also legislated civil unions for same-sex couples. Adopting Rove's strategy, Bush declared his opposition to same-sex marriage, and Republican activists put antigay initiatives on the ballot in over two dozen states in the hope that the initiatives would bring conservative voters to the polls.

Several Democrats vied for their party's presidential nomination. The progressive Howard Dean, governor of Vermont, campaigned directly against the Iraq War. U.S. representative Dennis Kucinich, who had always opposed the war, asked why so many Democratic lawmakers had supported the president's unilateral intervention. Retired general Wesley Clark also joined the race, vowing to get the country out of Iraq. Ultimately, though, U.S. senator John Kerry, a decorated Vietnam veteran with strong support among the party elite, won the nomination.

Kerry avoided the inflammatory issue of gay marriage and concentrated on channeling patriotism toward what he saw as a more responsible approach to the war on terror. His war hero status was his strongest suit against a president who had sat out the Vietnam War from the safety of the Texas National Guard. However, Republicans turned Kerry's war record into a liability in campaign advertisements that alleged falsely that the candidate had lied to earn his war medals. His opponents also produced evidence that Kerry was a "flip-flopper" with no consistent point of view. (In fact, Kerry had voted more consistently in the Senate than most long-term senators.) On election day, a higher proportion of voters turned out than in any election besides the bitter contest of 1968. Exit polls confirmed that Rove's strategy of energizing conservative voters had worked.

CRISES AT HOME AND ABROAD

The challenges of governing multiplied during Bush's second term. In August 2005, Hurricane Katrina lashed the Caribbean and the coasts of Florida, Mississippi, Louisiana, Alabama, and Texas, where it left a

Hurricane Katrina. Stories of heroism and of communities pulling together emerged following Katrina. Locals, college students, and philanthropic groups mobilized to begin the long, hard work of rebuilding New Orleans. Nothing, however, could soften the hard reality that thousands of citizens had been left to fend for themselves in their greatest hour of need.

long trail of devastation. On August 29, most of New Orleans's old flood levees failed, plunging 80 percent of the city under water. On some parts of the coast, the ocean flooded up to twelve miles inland. The storm's destructive effects were compounded by human missteps, including the failure of federal, state, and local governments to strengthen levees needing repair. Evacuation orders had come without the human resources to aid citizens who did not own a car or had nowhere to go.

In New Orleans, once the levees broke, the rescue effort took days to mount and hundreds perished while waiting for help. By the time relief arrived, over 1,800 people had died and $81 billion worth of damage had been done. Televised footage of the devastation—and the absence of a coordinated rescue effort in the first crucial days—shocked people the world over. Many condemned Bush and the Federal Emergency Management Administration (FEMA) for having abandoned the poor and failing the first duty of government to protect its citizens. The fact that most of the stranded were African American raised the question of whether the government would have handled the disaster differently had the victims been white. A collective feeling of shame spread over the nation, and President Bush's popularity sank to new lows.

The tragedy in New Orleans coincided with an eruption of insurgent violence in Iraq. By the end of 2005, more U.S. troops had died during the "peace" than during the initial war. Unknown tens of thousands of Iraqis had also perished, and the war had grown deeply unpopular at home. The majority of Americans now believed that the war was a mistake. Voters reinforced this message in the midterm elections of 2006, delivering both houses to the Democrats. Defense Secretary Rumsfeld resigned and was replaced by Robert Gates, former Central Intelligence Agency director under the elder Bush. When asked at his Senate confirmation hearings about the war in Iraq, Gates said the United States was neither winning nor losing. The new secretary's solution was a troop surge—an infusion of twenty thousand extra troops to train the Iraqi military to take control of the insurgency. The surge appeared to work, as violence decreased in major cities. As soon as the president was able to claim credit in Iraq, however, the worst recession since the Great Depression struck at home.

THE GREAT RECESSION

Although the economy appeared healthy in 2006–2007, the housing and banking sectors were stumbling. In October 2007, the stock market commenced a contraction that lasted for two years. With banks unable or unwilling to offer regular business loans, companies laid off millions of workers. Thousands of businesses failed. Deprived of tax revenue and under strain from people in need, the states slashed their budgets. The recession was the last straw for the majority of voters already disillusioned with the Bush administration.

THE HOUSING BUBBLE

Trouble had been brewing for some years in the U.S. economy. With house prices rising rapidly in the mid-2000s, the construction sector had built suburban houses, urban high-rises, and retirement villages at record speed. Supply began outstripping demand in 2006, causing home values in many regions to fall. Meanwhile, the deregulation of the banking and mortgage industries (begun in the Clinton years) had enabled many lenders to offer homebuyers a flexible new kind of loan. Adjustable rate mortgages (ARMs) began with a low interest rate that then reset to a higher rate after a few years. Lenders also relaxed standards, encouraging even risky lenders to take on "jumbo" mortgages (over $417,000) that they could not afford. As the first ARMs began resetting in 2006–2007, tens of thousands of homeowners were unable to make their higher mortgage payments. Foreclosures mounted; hundreds of thousands lost their homes.

The nation's largest banks had heavily invested in securities that were backed by these risky "subprime" mortgages. Just ten years earlier, such securities, which made the financial markets vulnerable to problems in the housing market, had been illegal. However, beginning with the repeal of the Glass-Steagall Act in 1999, the government had gradually removed the firewall between the two kinds of financial instruments. Regulations were loosened again in 2004, when the U.S. comptroller of the currency ordered the states' attorneys general, who had traditionally regulated the banks, to end their watchdog role. Banks and a new kind of investment fund for billionaire investors—hedge funds—rushed to buy up the mortgage-backed securities. In 2008, once the banks realized that many securities were next to worthless, they stopped offering regular loans to business, causing widespread panic and triggering the biggest stock market crash since 1929.

Investors lost over $7 trillion in just weeks, and the respected investment bank Lehman Brothers failed. Other big banks teetered on the edge of failure, as did the U.S. auto industry. As the securities and housing markets shed trillions, American consumers drastically curtailed their spending, which caused the consumer economy to contract rapidly. Thousands of small and medium-size businesses folded and millions of Americans defaulted on their mortgages. The economy cast off 8.7 million jobs between 2007 and 2010, with minorities bearing the brunt of the damage. Middle-class Americans were also afflicted by rising unemployment, which passed the 10 percent mark in 2008, as well as by the sudden depletion of their retirement funds (invested largely in stocks). Reeling from the loss of tax revenue, the states drastically cut health, welfare, and education spending. The nation had entered what would become the longest recession since the Great Depression.

The Foreclosure Crisis. Abandoned and foreclosed homes became a common sight across the United States in 2008. As well as causing financial ruin and heartache for millions of families, foreclosures had unexpected environmental consequences. In California, for instance, abandoned swimming pools caused an uptick in the mosquito population and consequent outbreaks of mosquito-borne West Nile virus.

SAVING THE NEW ECONOMY

The economic crisis spread quickly to other world regions. It was sped by the same transnational channels of trade and investment forged by economic globalization and deregulation. Only countries that had not deregulated their banking systems—such as Canada—were spared financial chaos (but still suffered from the contraction in global trade). Iceland, Ireland, Greece, Italy, and Spain essentially went bankrupt. The booming Chinese economy slowed as a result of the drastic drop in American spending on consumer goods. Demand for oil dropped, pitching even wealthy oil-producing nations into recession.

Many governments, including those of the United States, China, Great Britain, and Germany, determined that huge bailouts were necessary to save their national economies. American car manufacturers requested a $50 billion loan from the U.S. government in September 2008. Congress loaned half that amount, and in

December, President Bush agreed to an additional bailout of $17 billion. Bush also asked Congress to pass the Troubled Asset Relief Program (TARP), which provided the stricken banks with $700 billion in loans under the Emergency Economic Stabilization Act of 2008. Although this was an enormous sum, trillions more would be needed if the financial auto, housing, and manufacturing sectors were to recover. But 2008 was an election year, and political campaigning eclipsed further action on the economy.

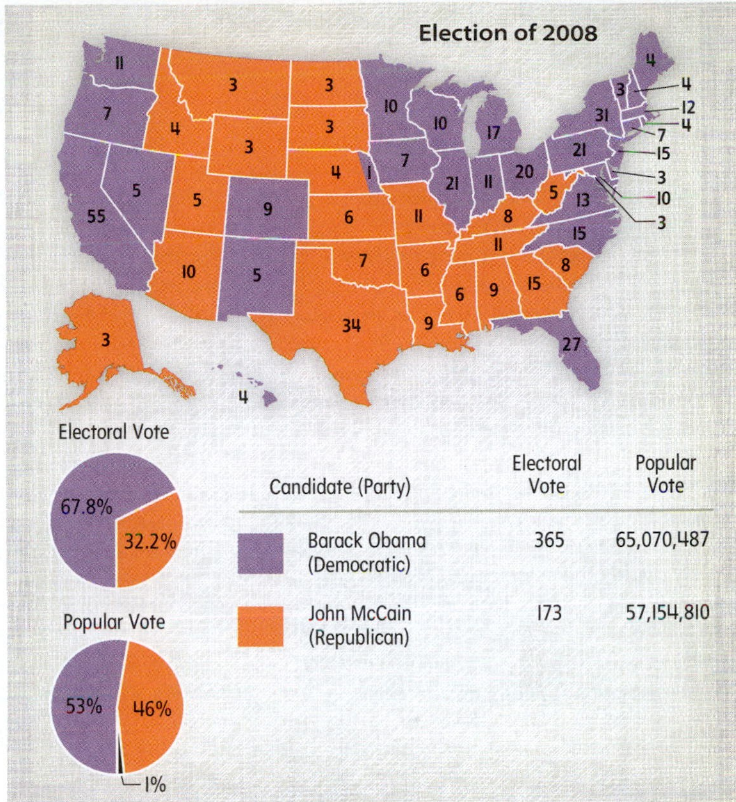

Map 31.4 Election of 2008.

THE ELECTION OF 2008

The United States stood at a crossroads. Americans took stock of the devastated housing market, spiraling unemployment, and bank bailouts. Many wondered whether the New Economy—the deregulation of business, historically low taxes, and curtailed welfare spending—was sustainable in the long term. The war in Iraq, which had claimed over three thousand American lives by 2008, was improving in some respects but was unfinished and widely unpopular. Painful images of New Orleans's suffering citizens were still fresh in the public's mind, and the question of whether the mass of displaced persons could return home remained unanswered. Forty-five million Americans—over 15 percent of the population—had no health insurance, with no relief in sight. Amid these uncertainties, an unusual set of contenders for the presidency and vice presidency emerged. For the first time in American history, an African American and a woman, both Democrats, were serious rivals for the highest office in the land.

New York senator (and former first lady) Hillary Rodham Clinton campaigned on the theme of change. A younger politician, Illinois senator Barack Obama, did not have the benefit of Clinton's extensive fundraising network, but his campaign made groundbreaking use of the Internet to reach millions of Americans, raising small donations from a sea of supporters and inspiring youth to get involved. Like Clinton, Obama and his running mate, Senator Joseph Biden, ran on a message of change—"change we can believe in." Obama was a moderate Democrat who favored deliberation and mediation over the divisive confrontationalism that had characterized American politics since the 1980s. Committed to freedom and equality, he was also pragmatic about the constraints and challenges he would encounter if elected (see Interpreting the Sources: Barack Obama, "A More Perfect Union"). The Democratic primary was close, but by late summer Obama had sewn up the nomination.

The Republicans fielded John McCain, a seventy-two-year-old decorated navy veteran and seasoned senator from Arizona. McCain distanced himself from the Bush administration by claiming that he was a "maverick" Republican who stood up for what was right, regardless of party. He presented himself as an elder statesman who would bring a steady hand and a lifetime of political experience to the presidency. Americans were surprised when he chose little-known Alaska governor Sarah Palin as his running mate. Palin—young, charismatic, and ultraconservative—was a hit among the party's evangelical base. In speeches and debates, however, she showed little grasp of global affairs or the stricken economy. Many Republicans questioned McCain's choice.

The recession, the protracted war, McCain's risky nod to Palin, and the Democrats' youth-centered campaign joined forces to deliver the election to Obama. Winning both the popular vote and the electoral college, the Democrat swept the Northeast, the Midwest, and the West Coast and picked up three Republican states in the South (see Map 31.4). Obama failed to win a majority of the vote only among people older than sixty-five and white voters (43 percent of whom cast their ballots for him). Almost all African Americans supported the new president, as did a majority of Hispanics.

RENEWING THE DREAM

Perhaps no president-elect since John F. Kennedy inspired so much hope among so many Americans as Barack Obama. Millions saw in him the promise of an end to war and the abuse of enemy detainees, a rapid return to prosperity, and equality and freedom for all. Many were convinced that the nation was embarking on a new and better era. With the election of a president born in 1961, the nation appeared to have moved on from the divisive politics of the previous forty years.

INTERPRETING THE SOURCES

Barack Obama, "A More Perfect Union," Speech Given in Philadelphia, March 2008

Two hundred and twenty one years ago, in a hall that still stands across the street, a group of men gathered and, with these simple words, launched America's improbable experiment in democracy. Farmers and scholars; statesmen and patriots who had traveled across an ocean to escape tyranny and persecution finally made real their declaration of independence at a Philadelphia convention that lasted through the spring of 1787.

The document they produced was eventually signed but ultimately unfinished. It was stained by this nation's original sin of slavery, a question that divided the colonies and brought the convention to a stalemate until the founders chose to allow the slave trade to continue for at least twenty more years, and to leave any final resolution to future generations.

Of course, the answer to the slavery question was already embedded within our Constitution—a Constitution that had at its very core the ideal of equal citizenship under the law; a Constitution that promised its people liberty, and justice, and a union that could be and should be perfected over time.

And yet words on a parchment would not be enough to deliver slaves from bondage, or provide men and women of every color and creed their full rights and obligations as citizens of the United States. What would be needed were Americans in successive generations who were willing to do their part—through protests and struggle, on the streets and in the courts, through a civil war and civil disobedience and always at great risk—to narrow that gap between the promise of our ideals and the reality of their time.

This was one of the tasks we set forth at the beginning of this campaign—to continue the long march of those who came before us, a march for a more just, more equal, more free, more caring and more prosperous America. I chose to run for the presidency at this moment in history because I believe deeply that we cannot solve the challenges of our time unless we solve them together—unless we perfect our union by understanding that we may have different stories, but we hold common hopes; that we may not look the same and we may not have come from the same place, but we all want to move in the same direction—towards a better future for our children and our grandchildren.

This belief comes from my unyielding faith in the decency and generosity of the American people. But it also comes from my own American story.

I am the son of a black man from Kenya and a white woman from Kansas. I was raised with the help of a white grandfather who survived a Depression to serve in Patton's Army during World War II and a white grandmother who worked on a bomber assembly line at Fort Leavenworth while he was overseas. I've gone to some of the best schools in America and lived in one of the world's poorest nations. I am married to a black American who carries within her the blood of slaves and slaveowners—an inheritance we pass on to our two precious daughters. I have brothers, sisters, nieces, nephews, uncles and cousins, of every race and every hue, scattered across three continents, and for as long as I live, I will never forget that in no other country on Earth is my story even possible.

It's a story that hasn't made me the most conventional candidate. But it is a story that has seared into my genetic makeup the idea that this nation is more than the sum of its parts—that out of many, we are truly one. . . .

[R]ace is an issue that I believe this nation cannot afford to ignore right now. . . .

The fact is that the comments that have been made and the issues that have surfaced over the last few weeks reflect the complexities of race in this country that we've never really worked through—a part of our union that we have yet to perfect. And if we walk away now, if we simply retreat into our respective corners, we will never be able to come together and solve challenges like health care, or education, or the need to find good jobs for every American.

Understanding this reality requires a reminder of how we arrived at this point. As William Faulkner once wrote, "The past isn't dead and buried. In fact, it isn't even past." We do not need to recite here the history of racial injustice in this country. But we do need to remind ourselves that so many of the disparities that exist in the African-American community today can be directly traced to inequalities passed on from an earlier generation that suffered under the brutal legacy of slavery and Jim Crow.

Explore the Source

1. In what ways, according to Obama, does the history of slavery still influence the United States? Why is the past not "past," in William Faulkner's words?
2. How does Obama position his candidacy in relation to American history?
3. Despite the history of slavery and segregation, what makes the United States one nation, in Obama's opinion?

In his inaugural address on a frigid January 20, 2009, the new president outlined his aspirations before a crowd of millions. He would take "bold and swift" action to create jobs and lay the foundation of a new, more solid economy. Infrastructure (including the Internet) would be rebuilt and extended so that all Americans would benefit. The government, Obama hinted, would not let market forces plunge the nation into such a crisis again but would keep a "watchful eye" over them. The United States would "responsibly leave Iraq" and "seek a new way forward" with the Muslim world, based on mutual interest and respect. The president added that government was only part of the solution. "What is required of us now," he said, summoning up the memory of

End of an Era. Millions of Americans who had tuned into the televised inauguration of Barack Obama watched as Bush vice president Dick Cheney, temporarily confined to a wheelchair, left Washington, D.C., by helicopter. For many progressives, Cheney's departure from the nation's capital symbolized the end of a terrible chapter in the country's history. For conservatives, whose voter base was significantly older than Obama's, the inauguration reinforced anxieties that conservatives' cultural and political influence over the nation was coming to an end.

JFK, "is a new era of responsibility—a recognition, on the part of every American, that we have duties to ourselves, our nation and the world, duties that we . . . seize gladly, firm in the knowledge that there is nothing so satisfying to the spirit, so defining of our character than giving our all to a difficult task." Such heightened expectations, however, were inevitably disappointed.

CHALLENGES OF LEADERSHIP

As Obama had also noted in his inaugural, "gathering clouds and raging storms" were all around. Dispersing them would be a task of mammoth proportions. In his first few months, the president announced the closure of Guantánamo Bay prison, prohibited torture, lifted Bush's ban on embryonic stem cell research, and began looking for ways to improve relations with the Muslim world. The president also nominated the first Hispanic Supreme Court justice, Sonia Sotomayor (confirmed in 2009), and successfully steered a new budget through Congress, authorizing $800 billion for the limping construction industry, the states, and an extension of unemployment benefits. This "stimulus" was designed to jumpstart the sluggish economy. However, economists agreed that more than three or four times that amount was needed if the stimulus was to be more than a Band-Aid. Obama's financial advisers warned against expanding the stimulus, and the president followed their advice.

The nation's expensive and inequitable health care system had long been a Democratic reform priority. With the exception of Lyndon B. Johnson, who had established Medicare, no president had succeeded in systematically reforming health care. Obama was well aware of Hillary Clinton's failed attempt to introduce a universal health care system in the mid-1990s and of the ongoing influence of the health insurance industry in Congress. In characteristically pragmatic fashion, he worked with insurers and other interested parties to hash out a plan that gave all Americans access to health care. Modeled on Massachusetts' new system, the Patient Protection and Affordable Care Act (2010) struck a compromise among interests. While eliminating the most problematic aspects of the existing system (including denial of coverage for preexisting conditions and lifetime limits), the act pacified insurers by mandating that all Americans carry insurance. Employers were required to provide insurance, and poorer citizens would be subsidized so that they, too, could afford insurance.

Although some observers considered "Obamacare" a remarkable achievement given the political constraints, many others were bitterly critical. The progressive wing of the Democratic Party accused the president of "selling out" to private health care interests. Conservatives railed against "health care rationing" and a "government takeover." Not a single Republican voted for the bill in the House.

The Tea Party—a loose coalition of conservative, evangelical, and libertarian Republicans—mobilized against the reform both before and after the act was passed. Although the Tea Party had little direct impact on the law itself, members deployed the Internet to tremendous effect, using health care reform as a lightning rod for the conservative agenda. Wealthy backers flushed the Tea Party with cash, and the conservative arm of the media eagerly publicized its rallies and protests. By 2010, the Tea Party movement was bringing heavy pressure to bear on the Republican Party. Over 130 Tea Party–endorsed Republicans were elected to Congress in the midterm elections, with the result that congressional Republicans moved farther to the right than at any other point in the nation's history.

President Obama continued to try to work with Congress on key initiatives, including tax reform. The influential Tea Party legislators refused bipartisanship, however, and threatened to close down government if federal spending were not curtailed drastically. Obama also faced a potentially enormous challenge from the conservative-dominated Supreme Court. In *Citizens United v. Federal Election Commission* (2010), the Court ruled that government could not restrict political expenditures by corporations and unions—a decision widely believed to favor Republicans because wealthy corporate donors tended to give to that party. Obama's single most important achievement, health care reform, was also in danger of being overturned by the conservative Court.

On the left, Obama faced a different populist mobilization, as protesters began camping out near Wall Street, the United States' financial hub, in downtown Manhattan. The thousands of youth who flocked to Zuccotti Park and endorsed its Occupy Wall Street message had a range of grievances, most arising out of the Great Recession. The majority gathered peacefully to protest corporate influence in Congress, the government's failure to prosecute the financiers who had played a role in the global economic crisis, and rising economic inequality. By remaining in the park, the protesters believed they were symbolically "taking back" American democracy from powerful private interests.

Using social media, the Occupy protest movement caught fire in the fall of 2011, sparking similar actions in cities and on college campuses across the United States. In many states, students protested skyrocketing college fees, which had doubled since 2007 and left individuals unable to complete their degrees or mired in debt. Protesters fastened on the title of an article by economist Joseph Stiglitz, "Of the 1%, by the 1%, for the 1%," in which he claimed that the wealthiest 1 percent of Americans owned over 40 percent of U.S. wealth—and were essentially running the government. "We are the 99 percent!" crowds chanted. Although eventually dispersed, the protesters had changed the terms of public debate about the Great Recession and the New Economy. Not since the 1960s had the mainstream media—and Democratic members of Congress—openly discussed the problems of economic inequality and of corporate influence on American democracy.

THE ELECTION OF 2012

These complex issues came to a head in the 2012 election. In the first election since the *Citizens United* case removed most limits from campaign financing, donors spent more money than in any previous presidential contest. Corporations, wealthy individuals, and Super PACS (political action committees that paid for independent messages on various issues) raised over $4 billion, much of it from anonymous sources.

Barack Obama and Joseph Biden again headed the Democratic ticket, with little controversy. The Republican primaries, on the other hand, were bitterly and broadly contested. The unusually large field of candidates included experienced politicians such as libertarian and former congressman Ron Paul, ex-Speaker of the House Newt Gingrich, and former Pennsylvania senator Rick Santorum. Five governors and ex-governors also vied for the nomination, as did Tea Party–favorite representative Michele Bachmann and the moderate Republican and former ambassador to China Jon Huntsman. Businessmen Herman Cain and Donald Trump entered the fray. The field drew candidates from every geographical region and divided along ideological lines among evangelical, libertarian, and moderate Republicans. Voters and much of the media registered their collective lack of confidence in the field by repeatedly elevating one candidate to frontrunner position and then replacing him or her with another.

As primary voting dragged on, former businessman and Massachusetts governor Mitt Romney slowly notched up victories. Originally a moderate Republican, Romney changed his position on key issues, such as health care and abortion, to match what appeared to be the deepening conservatism of his party. These shifts troubled both moderate and conservative Republicans and allowed his opponents in the primaries to relentlessly portray him as a flip-flopper. Although Romney clinched the nomination in early June, no faction of his party was wholly enthusiastic about his candidacy.

The issues of jobs, the federal budget deficit, taxation and spending, the future of middle-class entitlement programs, health care reform, and immigration dominated the election. Unemployment was still unacceptably high and the economic recovery slower than expected. But Obama was able to point to major achievements in foreign policy, including withdrawing most troops from Iraq, as he had promised he would in the 2008 election, and killing al-Qaeda leader Osama bin Laden in a daring raid in Pakistan in May 2011. The president chalked up a major victory the following year, when the Supreme Court unexpectedly upheld the constitutionality of the signal achievement of his domestic policy—health care reform—in *National Federation of Independent Business v. Sebelius* (2012).

Romney performed exceedingly well in the first presidential debate. But he made a series of missteps during his campaign. On one damaging occasion captured in a video leaked to the media, Romney announced to a donor group that 47 percent of Americans considered themselves "victims" and were "dependent on government" By August, betting agencies and statistical analysts considered Obama the probable winner. Yet as late as November 5, most of the news media and the parties painted the election as too close to call. When voters cast their ballots the following day, Obama won 51 percent of the popular vote to Romney's 47 percent and 332 electoral votes to Romney's 206, securing a second term.

In his second inaugural, Obama outlined what some commentators called a "New Liberal" agenda. He spoke positively and at length about the need for a social safety net, a robust middle class, and tougher regulation of big business. He also, for the first time in inaugural history, directly referred to gay people and affirmed what he claimed was their right to equality under the law. Turning to economic matters, the president went on to pronounce, "We the people understand that our country cannot succeed when a shrinking few do very well and a growing many barely make it. We believe that America's prosperity must rest upon the broad shoulders of a rising middle class." As rhetoric, Obama's speech marked a distinct departure from the free-market ideology of both the Republicans and the Clinton-Gore New Democrats. Whether it would launch a new kind of politics and a new era remained to be seen.

CONCLUSION

The years after 1992 witnessed often breathtaking economic, cultural, and political changes. Together, economic globalization and the Digital Revolution created a whole new world for peoples around the globe. Work, the economy, the divide between public and private life, consumption and recreation patterns, and even the meaning of friendship changed profoundly and lastingly. The Internet and cellular technology brought people together cheaply (or even for free) across vast divides of space and culture. Information of all kinds, from scholarly studies and popular magazines to stock prices and government reports, became available to anyone with an Internet connection. Overseas, globalization's deregulation of banking enabled the development of microcredit schemes, funded by Americans and aimed at liberating poor and oppressed communities from the bonds of debt and dependency.

But globalization and associated developments brought with them colossal powers of destruction. Older ways of life and patterns of thought were swept aside. By the early 2000s, well-paid manufacturing jobs with benefits and a forty-hour workweek were relics of the past. In a development that some people celebrated, digital technologies rendered music, literature, film, and even top-secret defense documents defenseless against piracy. The middle class lost ground relative to the wealthiest Americans, while economic inequality reached its highest peak since 1928. And as banks and the housing industry were freed from most regulatory oversight, many made risky investments and became dangerously over-leveraged, with the result that the nation was tipped into the single worst recession since the Great Depression.

The American people had not stood at such a vital crossroads since the 1930s. Never before had the way forward seemed so unclear. Coming to terms with the digital, globalized economy and its awesome powers of creation and destruction promised to be among the greatest challenges of the twenty-first century.

STUDY TERMS

North American Free Trade Agreement (p. 886)
Contract with America (p. 887)
Personal Responsibility and Work Opportunity Act (p. 887)
globalization (p. 889)
World Trade Organization (p. 889)
Peoples' Global Action (p. 890)
Rwandan genocide (p. 892)
al-Qaeda (p. 893)
Digital Revolution (p. 893)
Internet (p. 893)
World Wide Web (p. 893)
New Economy (p. 894)
digital divide (p. 895)
dot-com crash (p. 895)
Internet piracy (p. 895)
biotechnology (p. 895)
genome (p. 896)
stem cells (p. 896)
urban gentrification (p. 898)
war on terror (p. 901)
Bush Doctrine (p. 901)
USA PATRIOT Act (p. 901)
National Security Strategy of 2002 (p. 903)
weapons of mass destruction (p. 903)
gay marriage (p. 904)
Hurricane Katrina (p. 904)
troop surge (p. 905)
adjustable rate mortgages (p. 906)
Troubled Asset Relief Program (p. 907)
Patient Protection and Affordable Care Act (p. 909)
Tea Party (p. 909)
Occupy Wall Street (p. 910)

TIMELINE

1992 William Jefferson "Bill" Clinton elected president

1993 The Mosaic web browser popularizes the World Wide Web.

United States, Canada, and Mexico sign NAFTA

Waco standoff ends violently

Al-Qaeda affiliates detonate truck bomb under World Trade Center

1994 Violent Crime Control and Law Enforcement Act bans assault weapons and speeds new prison construction

1995 Antigovernment militiamen bomb federal building in Oklahoma City

World Trade Organization founded, prompting U.S. manufacturers to accelerate relocation overseas

Republicans in Congress shut down government in protest of President Clinton's veto of budget.

1996 Cloned sheep Dolly is born.

Personal Responsibility and Work Opportunity Act cuts welfare benefits and compels beneficiaries to find work

1998 Geneticists confirm Thomas Jefferson fathered a child with slave Sally Hemings

Federal budget runs surplus for the first time since 1970

1999 Police clash with antiglobalization protesters in Seattle

Joint U.S.-NATO force strikes Serbian military

2000 Dot-com crash causes tech stocks to lose almost 80 percent of their value by 2002

Islamist radicals bomb USS *Cole* off Yemen coast

George W. Bush elected president

2001 Federal budget reenters deficit

Al-Qaeda operatives attack World Trade Center and Pentagon

UN forces bomb al-Qaeda stronghold in Afghanistan

2003 United States and allies invade Iraq and topple Saddam Hussein

2004 Photographs of torture and simulated torture at Abu Ghraib go viral

Facebook goes online

Gay couple legally weds in Massachusetts, first state to legalize same-sex marriage

2005 Hurricane Katrina ravages Gulf Coast locales

2007 Great Recession begins as housing and stock markets crash

2008 President Bush secures $700 billion federal bailout for stricken banks

Barack Obama elected president

2010 Congress overhauls health care system, mandating insurance

Tea Party asserts control of the Republican Party

Corporations spend record amounts on election campaigns

2011 Occupy Wall Street sparks anti-corporate protests

Last U.S. troops leave Iraq

2012 Supreme Court finds health care reform constitutional

United States and NATO announce two-year drawdown of foreign troops in Afghanistan

2013 Supreme Court rules Voting Rights Act of 1965 unconstitutional

Supreme Court directs federal government to recognize gay marriage

Republican House of Representatives shuts down government in dispute over funding for Obamacare

FURTHER READING

Additional suggested readings are available on the Online Learning Center at www.mhhe.com/becomingamerica1e.

William C. Berman, *From the Center to the Edge: The Politics and Policies of the Clinton Presidency* (2001), explains how and why Bill Clinton's policies came to consolidate Ronald Reagan's.

Jason Burke, *The 9/11 Wars* (2011), explores the diverse wars that followed in the wake of al-Qaeda's attacks on the World Trade Center and the Pentagon.

James W. Cortada, *The Digital Flood: The Diffusion of Information Technology Across the U.S., Europe, and Asia* (2012), traces the spread of computing and information across much of the world.

Colin Harrison, *American Culture in the 1990s* (2010), analyses key cultural and political events of the 1990s and their legacies.

James T. Kloppenberg, *Reading Obama: Dreams, Hope, and the American Political Tradition* (2011), explores Barack Obama's commitment to freedom, equality, and deliberative politics.

Jaron Lanier, *You Are Not a Gadget: A Manifesto* (2010), argues that programming decisions at the beginning of the Digital Revolution have fundamentally transformed our culture, and not necessarily for the better.

Jeffrey Melnick, *9/11 Culture* (2009), analyzes cultural responses to the terrorist attacks of September 11, 2001.

Williamson Murray and Robert H. Scales, *The Iraq War: A Military History* (2003), analyzes the aims, strategy, tactics, and battlefield experiences of both sides in the war.

Steven E. Schier, ed., *The Postmodern Presidency: Bill Clinton's Legacy in U.S. Politics* (2000), traces Clinton's courtship of public opinion and explains the significance of his celebrity status.

Rebecca Solnit, *A Paradise Built in Hell: The Extraordinary Communities That Arise in Disaster* (2009), recounts how new communities and ideals emerged out of natural and human-made disasters such as Hurricane Katrina.

Julian E. Zelizer, ed., *The Presidency of George W. Bush: A First Historical Assessment* (2010), collects historians' contextualization of various aspects of Bush's administration, from corporate bailouts to compassionate conservatism and the war on terror.

APPENDIX

THE DECLARATION OF INDEPENDENCE

IN CONGRESS, JULY 4, 1776,

THE UNANIMOUS DECLARATION OF THE THIRTEEN UNITED STATES OF AMERICA

When, in the course of human events, it becomes necessary for one people to dissolve the political bands which have connected them with another, and to assume, among the powers of the earth, the separate and equal station to which the laws of nature and of nature's God entitle them, a decent respect to the opinions of mankind requires that they should declare the causes which impel them to the separation.

We hold these truths to be self-evident, that all men are created equal; that they are endowed by their Creator with certain unalienable rights; that among these, are life, liberty, and the pursuit of happiness. That, to secure these rights, governments are instituted among men, deriving their just powers from the consent of the governed; that, whenever any form of government becomes destructive of these ends, it is the right of the people to alter or to abolish it, and to institute a new government, laying its foundation on such principles, and organizing its powers in such form, as to them shall seem most likely to effect their safety and happiness. Prudence, indeed, will dictate that governments long established, should not be changed for light and transient causes; and, accordingly, all experience hath shown, that mankind are more disposed to suffer, while evils are sufferable, than to right themselves by abolishing the forms to which they are accustomed. But, when a long train of abuses and usurpations, pursuing invariably the same object, evinces a design to reduce them under absolute despotism, it is their right, it is their duty, to throw off such government and to provide new guards for their future security. Such has been the patient sufferance of these colonies, and such is now the necessity which constrains them to alter their former systems of government. The history of the present King of Great Britain is a history of repeated injuries and usurpations, all having, in direct object, the establishment of an absolute tyranny over these States. To prove this, let facts be submitted to a candid world:

He has refused his assent to laws the most wholesome and necessary for the public good.

He has forbidden his governors to pass laws of immediate and pressing importance, unless suspended in their operation till his assent should be obtained; and, when so suspended, he has utterly neglected to attend to them.

He has refused to pass other laws for the accommodation of large districts of people, unless those people would relinquish the right of representation in the legislature; a right inestimable to them, and formidable to tyrants only.

He has called together legislative bodies at places unusual, uncomfortable, and distant from the depository of their public records, for the sole purpose of fatiguing them into compliance with his measures.

He has dissolved representative houses repeatedly for opposing, with manly firmness, his invasions on the rights of the people.

He has refused, for a long time after such dissolutions, to cause others to be elected; whereby the legislative powers, incapable of annihilation, have returned to the people at large for their exercise; the state remaining, in the meantime, exposed to all the danger of invasion from without, and convulsions within.

He has endeavored to prevent the population of these States; for that purpose, obstructing the laws for naturalization of foreigners, refusing to pass others to encourage their migration hither, and raising the conditions of new appropriations of lands.

He has obstructed the administration of justice, by refusing his assent to laws for establishing judiciary powers.

He has made judges dependent on his will alone, for the tenure of their offices, and the amount and payment of their salaries.

He has erected a multitude of new offices, and sent hither swarms of officers to harass our people, and eat out their substance.

He has kept among us, in time of peace, standing armies, without the consent of our legislatures.

He has affected to render the military independent of, and superior to, the civil power.

He has combined, with others, to subject us to a jurisdiction foreign to our Constitution, and unacknowledged by our laws; giving his assent to their acts of pretended legislation:

For quartering large bodies of armed troops among us:

For protecting them by a mock trial, from punishment, for any murders which they should commit on the inhabitants of these States:

For cutting off our trade with all parts of the world:

For imposing taxes on us without our consent:

For depriving us, in many cases, of the benefit of trial by jury:

For transporting us beyond seas to be tried for pretended offences:

For abolishing the free system of English laws in a neighboring province, establishing therein an arbitrary government, and enlarging its boundaries, so as to render it at once an example and fit instrument for introducing the same absolute rule into these colonies:

For taking away our charters, abolishing our most valuable laws, and altering, fundamentally, the powers of our governments:

For suspending our own legislatures, and declaring themselves invested with power to legislate for us in all cases whatsoever.

He has abdicated government here, by declaring us out of his protection, and waging war against us.

He has plundered our seas, ravaged our coasts, burnt our towns, and destroyed the lives of our people.

He is, at this time, transporting large armies of foreign mercenaries to complete the works of death, desolation, and tyranny, already begun, with circumstances of cruelty and perfidy scarcely paralleled in the most barbarous ages, and totally unworthy the head of a civilized nation.

He has constrained our fellow citizens, taken captive on the high seas, to bear arms against their country, to become the executioners of their friends, and brethren, or to fall themselves by their hands.

He has excited domestic insurrections amongst us, and has endeavored to bring on the inhabitants of our frontiers, the merciless Indian savages, whose known rule of warfare is an undistinguished destruction of all ages, sexes, and conditions.

In every stage of these oppressions, we have petitioned for redress, in the most humble terms; our repeated petitions have been answered only by repeated injury. A prince, whose character is thus marked by every act which may define a tyrant, is unfit to be the ruler of a free people.

Nor have we been wanting in attention to our British brethren. We have warned them, from time to time, of attempts made by their legislature to extend an unwarrantable jurisdiction over us. We have reminded them of the circumstances of our emigration and settlement here. We have appealed to their native justice and magnanimity, and we have conjured them, by the ties of our common kindred, to disavow these usurpations, which would inevitably interrupt our connections and correspondence. They, too, have been deaf to the voice of justice and consanguinity. We must, therefore, acquiesce in the necessity which denounces our separation, and hold them as we hold the rest of mankind, enemies in war, in peace, friends.

We, therefore, the representatives of the United States of America, in general Congress assembled, appealing to the Supreme Judge of the world for the rectitude of our intentions, do, in the name, and by the authority of the good people of these colonies, solemnly publish and declare, that these united colonies are, and of right ought to be, free and independent states: that they are absolved from all allegiance to the British Crown, and that all political connection between them and the state of Great Britain is, and ought to be, totally dissolved; and that, as free and independent states, they have full power to levy war, conclude peace, contract alliances, establish commerce, and to do all other acts and things which independent states may of right do. And, for the support of this declaration, with a firm reliance on the protection of Divine Providence, we mutually pledge to each other our lives, our fortunes, and our sacred honor.

The foregoing Declaration was, by order of Congress, engrossed, and signed by the following members:

JOHN HANCOCK

NEW HAMPSHIRE
Josiah Bartlett
William Whipple
Matthew Thornton

MASSACHUSETTS BAY
Samuel Adams
John Adams
Robert Treat Paine
Elbridge Gerry

RHODE ISLAND
Stephen Hopkins
William Ellery

CONNECTICUT
Roger Sherman
Samuel Huntington
William Williams
Oliver Wolcott

NEW YORK
William Floyd
Philip Livingston
Francis Lewis
Lewis Morris

NEW JERSEY
Richard Stockton
John Witherspoon
Francis Hopkinson
John Hart
Abraham Clark

PENNSYLVANIA
Robert Morris
Benjamin Rush
Benjamin Franklin
John Morton
George Clymer
James Smith
George Taylor
James Wilson
George Ross

DELAWARE
Caesar Rodney
George Read
Thomas M'Kean

MARYLAND
Samuel Chase
William Paca
Thomas Stone
Charles Carroll, of Carrollton

VIRGINIA
George Wythe
Richard Henry Lee
Thomas Jefferson
Benjamin Harrison
Thomas Nelson, Jr.
Francis Lightfoot Lee
Carter Braxton

NORTH CAROLINA
William Hooper
Joseph Hewes
John Penn

SOUTH CAROLINA
Edward Rutledge
Thomas Heyward, Jr.
Thomas Lynch, Jr.
Arthur Middleton

GEORGIA
Button Gwinnett
Lyman Hall
George Walton

Resolved, That copies of the Declaration be sent to the several assemblies, conventions, and committees, or councils of safety, and to the several commanding officers of the continental troops; that it be proclaimed in each of the United States, at the head of the army.

THE CONSTITUTION OF THE UNITED STATES OF AMERICA[1]

We the People of the United States, in Order to form a more perfect Union, establish Justice, insure domestic Tranquility, provide for the common defence, promote the general Welfare, and secure the Blessings of Liberty to ourselves and our Posterity, do ordain and establish this CONSTITUTION for the United States of America.

ARTICLE I

Section 1

All legislative Powers herein granted shall be vested in a Congress of the United States, which shall consist of a Senate and House of Representatives.

Section 2

The House of Representatives shall be composed of Members chosen every second Year by the People of the several States, and the Electors in each State shall have the Qualifications requisite for Electors of the most numerous Branch of the State Legislature.

No Person shall be a Representative who shall not have attained to the Age of twenty-five Years, and been seven Years a Citizen of the United States, and who shall not, when elected, be an Inhabitant of that State in which he shall be chosen.

[Representatives and direct Taxes[2] shall be apportioned among the several States which may be included within this Union, according to their respective Numbers, which shall be determined by adding to the whole Number of free Persons, including those bound to Service for a Term of Years, and excluding Indians not taxed, three fifths of all other Persons.][3] The actual Enumeration shall be made within three Years after the first Meeting of the Congress of the United States, and within every subsequent Term of ten Years, in such Manner as they shall by Law direct. The Number of Representatives shall not exceed one for every thirty Thousand, but each State shall have at Least one Representative; and until such enumeration shall be made, the State of New Hampshire shall be entitled to chuse three, Massachusetts eight, Rhode-Island and Providence Plantations one, Connecticut five, New York six, New Jersey four, Pennsylvania eight, Delaware one, Maryland six, Virginia ten, North Carolina five, South Carolina five, and Georgia three.

When vacancies happen in the Representation from any State, the Executive Authority thereof shall issue Writs of Election to fill such Vacancies.

The House of Representatives shall chuse their Speaker and other Officers; and shall have the sole Power of Impeachment.

Section 3

The Senate of the United States shall be composed of two Senators from each State, chosen by the Legislature thereof, for six Years; and each Senator shall have one Vote.

Immediately after they shall be assembled in Consequence of the first Election, they shall be divided as equally as may be into three Classes. The Seats of the Senators of the first Class shall be vacated at the Expiration of the second Year, of the second Class at the Expiration of the fourth Year, and of the third Class at the Expiration of the sixth Year, so that one-third may be chosen every second Year; and if Vacancies happen by Resignation, or otherwise, during the Recess of the Legislature of any State, the Executive thereof may make temporary Appointments until the next Meeting of the Legislature, which shall then fill such Vacancies.

No Person shall be a Senator who shall not have attained to the Age of thirty Years, and been nine Years a Citizen of the United States, and who shall not, when elected, be an Inhabitant of that State for which he shall be chosen.

The Vice President of the United States shall be President of the Senate, but shall have no vote, unless they be equally divided.

The Senate shall chuse their other Officers, and also a President pro tempore, in the absence of the Vice President, or when he shall exercise the Office of President of the United States.

The Senate shall have the sole Power to try all Impeachments. When sitting for that purpose they shall be on Oath or Affirmation. When the President of the United States is tried, the Chief Justice shall preside: And no person shall be convicted without the Concurrence of two thirds of the Members present.

Judgment in Cases of Impeachment shall not extend further than to removal from Office, and disqualification to hold and enjoy any Office of honor, Trust, or Profit under the United States: but the Party convicted shall nevertheless be liable and subject to Indictment, Trial, Judgment, and Punishment, according to Law.

Section 4

The Times, Places and Manner of holding Elections for Senators and Representatives, shall be prescribed in each State by the Legislature thereof; but the Congress may at any time by Law make or alter such Regulations, except as to the Places of Chusing Senators.

[1]This version follows the original Constitution in capitalization and spelling. It is adapted from the text published by the United States Department of the Interior, Office of Education.
[2]Altered by the Sixteenth Amendment.
[3]Negated by the Fourteenth Amendment.

The Congress shall assemble at least once in every Year, and such Meeting shall be on the first Monday in December, unless they shall by Law appoint a different Day.

Section 5

Each House shall be the Judge of the Elections, Returns and Qualifications of its own Members, and a Majority of each shall constitute a Quorum to do Business; but a smaller number may adjourn from day to day, and may be authorized to compel the Attendance of absent Members, in such Manner, and under such Penalties, as each House may provide.

Each House may determine the Rules of its Proceedings, punish its Members for disorderly Behaviour, and, with the Concurrence of two thirds, expel a Member.

Each House shall keep a Journal of its Proceedings, and from time to time publish the same, excepting such Parts as may in their Judgment require Secrecy; and the Yeas and Nays of the Members of either House on any question shall, at the Desire of one fifth of those Present, be entered on the Journal.

Neither House, during the Session of Congress, shall, without the Consent of the other, adjourn for more than three days, nor to any other Place than that in which the two Houses shall be sitting.

Section 6

The Senators and Representatives shall receive a Compensation for their Services, to be ascertained by Law, and paid out of the Treasury of the United States. They shall in all Cases, except Treason, Felony, and Breach of the Peace, be privileged from Arrest during their Attendance at the Session of their respective Houses, and in going to and returning from the same; and for any Speech or Debate in either House, they shall not be questioned in any other Place.

No Senator or Representative shall, during the Time for which he was elected, be appointed to any civil Office under the Authority of the United States, which shall have been created, or the Emoluments whereof shall have been increased, during such time; and no Person holding any Office under the United States shall be a Member of either House during his continuance in Office.

Section 7

All Bills for raising Revenue shall originate in the House of Representatives; but the Senate may propose or concur with Amendments as on other bills.

Every Bill which shall have passed the House of Representatives and the Senate, shall, before it become a Law, be presented to the President of the United States; If he approve he shall sign it, but if not he shall return it, with his Objections, to that House in which it shall have originated, who shall enter the Objections at large on their Journal, and proceed to reconsider it. If after such Reconsideration two thirds of that House shall agree to pass the bill, it shall be sent, together with the objections, to the other House, by which it shall likewise be reconsidered, and if approved by two thirds of that House, it shall become a Law. But in all such Cases the Votes of both Houses shall be determined by Yeas and Nays, and the Names of the Persons voting for and against the Bill shall be entered on the Journal of each House respectively. If any Bill shall not be returned by the President within ten Days (Sundays excepted) after it shall have been presented to him, the Same shall be a Law, in like Manner as if he had signed it, unless the Congress by their Adjournment prevent its Return, in which Case it shall not be a Law.

Every Order, Resolution, or Vote to which the Concurrence of the Senate and House of Representatives may be necessary (except on a question of Adjournment) shall be presented to the President of the United States; and before the Same shall take Effect, shall be approved by him, or being disapproved by him, shall be repassed by two thirds of the Senate and House of Representatives, according to the Rules and Limitations prescribed in the Case of a Bill.

Section 8

The Congress shall have Power To lay and collect Taxes, Duties, Imposts and Excises, to pay the Debts and provide for the common Defence and general Welfare of the United States; but all Duties, Imposts and Excises shall be uniform throughout the United States;

To borrow money on the credit of the United States;

To regulate Commerce with foreign Nations, and among the several States, and with the Indian Tribes;

To establish an uniform rule of Naturalization, and uniform Laws on the subject of Bankruptcies throughout the United States;

To coin Money, regulate the Value thereof, and of foreign Coin, and fix the Standard of Weights and Measures;

To provide for the Punishment of counterfeiting the Securities and current Coin of the United States;

To establish Post Offices and post Roads;

To promote the Progress of Science and useful Arts, by securing for limited Times to Authors and Inventors the exclusive Right to their respective Writings and Discoveries;

To constitute Tribunals inferior to the Supreme Court;

To define and punish Piracies and Felonies committed on the high Seas, and Offenses against the Law of Nations;

To declare War, grant Letters of Marque and Reprisal, and make Rules concerning Captures on Land and Water;

To raise and support Armies, but no Appropriation of Money to that Use shall be for a longer Term than two Years;

To provide and maintain a Navy;

To make Rules for the Government and Regulation of the land and naval forces;

To provide for calling forth the Militia to execute the Laws of the Union, suppress Insurrections and repel Invasions;

To provide for organizing, arming, and disciplining the Militia, and for government such Part of them as may be employed in the Service of the United States, reserving to the States respectively, the Appointment of the Officers, and the Authority of training the Militia according to the discipline prescribed by Congress;

To exercise exclusive Legislation in all Cases whatsoever, over such District (not exceeding ten Miles square) as may, by Cession of particular States, and the acceptance of Congress, become the Seat of the Government of the United States, and to exercise like Authority over all Places purchased by the Consent of the Legislature of the State in which the Same shall be, for the Erection of Forts, Magazines, Arsenals, Dock-yards, and other needful Buildings;—And

To make all Laws which shall be necessary and proper for carrying into Execution the foregoing Powers, and all other Powers vested by this Constitution in the Government of the United States, or in any Department or Officer thereof.

Section 9

The Migration or Importation of such Persons as any of the States now existing shall think proper to admit, shall not be prohibited by the Congress prior to the Year one thousand eight hundred and eight, but a tax or duty may be imposed on such Importation, not exceeding ten dollars for each Person.

The privilege of the Writ of Habeas Corpus shall not be suspended, unless when in Cases of Rebellion or Invasion the public Safety may require it.

No bill of Attainder or ex post facto Law shall be passed.

No capitation, or other direct, Tax shall be laid unless in Proportion to the Census or Enumeration herein before directed to be taken.

No Tax or Duty shall be laid on Articles exported from any State.

No Preference shall be given by any Regulation of Commerce or Revenue to the Ports of one State over those of another: nor shall Vessels bound to, or from, one State, be obliged to enter, clear, or pay Duties in another.

No Money shall be drawn from the Treasury, but in Consequence of Appropriations made by Law; and a regular Statement and Account of the Receipts and Expenditures of all public Money shall be published from time to time.

No Title of Nobility shall be granted by the United States: And no Person holding any Office of Profit or Trust under them, shall, without the Consent of the Congress, accept of any present, Emolument, Office, or Title, of any kind whatever, from any King, Prince, or foreign State.

Section 10

No State shall enter into any Treaty, Alliance, or Confederation; grant Letters of Marque and Reprisal; coin Money; emit Bills of Credit; make any Thing but gold and silver Coin a Tender in Payment of Debts; pass any Bill of Attainder, ex post facto Law, or Law impairing the Obligation of Contracts, or grant any Title of Nobility.

No State shall, without the Consent of the Congress, lay any Imposts or Duties on Imports or Exports, except what may be absolutely necessary for executing its inspection Laws; and the net Produce of all Duties and Imposts, laid by any State on Imports or Exports, shall be for the use of the Treasury of the United States; and all such Laws shall be subject to the Revision and Control of the Congress.

No state shall, without the Consent of Congress, lay any duty of Tonnage, keep Troops, or Ships of War in time of Peace, enter into any Agreement or Compact with another State, or with a foreign Power, or engage in War, unless actually invaded, or in such imminent Danger as will not admit of delay.

ARTICLE II

Section 1

The executive Power shall be vested in a President of the United States of America. He shall hold his Office during the Term of four years, and, together with the Vice President, chosen for the same Term, be elected, as follows:

Each State shall appoint, in such Manner as the Legislature thereof may direct, a Number of Electors, equal to the whole Number of Senators and Representatives to which the State may be entitled in the Congress: but no Senator or Representative, or Person holding an Office of Trust or Profit under the United States, shall be appointed an Elector.

[The Electors shall meet in their respective States, and vote by Ballot for two persons, of whom one at least shall not be an Inhabitant of the same State with themselves. And they shall make a List of all the Persons voted for, and of the Number of Votes for each; which List they shall sign and certify, and transmit sealed to the Seat of the Government of the United States, directed to the President of the Senate. The President of the Senate shall, in the Presence of the Senate and House of Representatives, open all the Certificates, and the Votes shall then be counted. The Person having the greatest Number of Votes shall be the President, if such Number be a Majority of the whole Number of Electors appointed; and if there be more than one who have such Majority, and have an equal Number of Votes, then the House of Representatives shall immediately chuse by Ballot one of them for President; and if no Person have a Majority, then from the five highest on the List the said House shall in like Manner chuse the President. But in chusing the President, the Votes shall be taken by States, the Representation from each State having one Vote; a quorum for this Purpose shall consist of a Member or Members from two-thirds of the States, and a Majority of all the States shall be necessary to a Choice. In every Case, after the Choice of the President, the Person having the greatest Number of Votes of the Electors shall be the Vice President. But if there should remain two or more who have equal votes, the Senate shall chuse from them by Ballot the Vice President.][4]

[4]Revised by the Twelfth Amendment.

The Congress may determine the Time of chusing the Electors, and the Day on which they shall give their Votes; which Day shall be the same throughout the United States.

No person except a natural-born Citizen, or a Citizen of the United States, at the time of the Adoption of this Constitution, shall be eligible to the Office of President; neither shall any Person be eligible to that Office who shall not have attained to the Age of thirty-five years, and been fourteen Years a Resident within the United States.

In Case of the Removal of the President from Office, or of his Death, Resignation, or Inability to discharge the Powers and Duties of the said Office, the same shall devolve on the Vice President, and the Congress may by Law provide for the Case of Removal, Death, Resignation, or Inability, both of the President and Vice President, declaring what Officer shall then act as President, and such Officer shall act accordingly, until the disability be removed, or a President shall be elected.

The President shall, at stated Times, receive for his Services a Compensation, which shall neither be increased nor diminished during the Period for which he shall have been elected, and he shall not receive within that Period any other Emolument from the United States, or any of them.

Before he enter on the execution of his Office, he shall take the following Oath or Affirmation:—"I do solemnly swear (or affirm) that I will faithfully execute the Office of President of the United States, and will, to the best of my Ability, preserve, protect, and defend the Constitution of the United States."

Section 2

The President shall be Commander in Chief of the Army and Navy of the United States, and of the Militia of the several States, when called into the actual Service of the United States; he may require the Opinion, in writing, of the principal Officer in each of the executive Departments, upon any subject relating to the Duties of their respective Offices, and he shall have Power to Grant Reprieves and Pardons for Offenses against the United States, except in Cases of Impeachment.

He shall have Power, by and with the Advice and Consent of the Senate, to make Treaties, provided two-thirds of the Senators present concur; and he shall nominate, and by and with the Advice and Consent of the Senate, shall appoint Ambassadors, other public Ministers and Consuls, Judges of the supreme Court, and all other Officers of the United States, whose Appointments are not herein otherwise provided for, and which shall be established by Law: but the Congress may by Law vest the Appointment of such inferior Officers, as they think proper, in the President alone, in the Courts of Law, or in the Heads of Departments.

The President shall have Power to fill up all Vacancies that may happen during the Recess of the Senate, by granting Commissions which shall expire at the End of their next Session.

Section 3

He shall from time to time give to the Congress Information of the State of the Union, and recommend to their Consideration such Measures as he shall judge necessary and expedient; he may, on extraordinary occasions, convene both Houses, or either of them, and in Case of Disagreement between them, with respect to the Time of Adjournment, he may adjourn them to such Time as he shall think proper; he shall receive Ambassadors and other public Ministers; he shall take care that the Laws be faithfully executed, and shall Commission all the Officers of the United States.

Section 4

The President, Vice President and all civil Officers of the United States, shall be removed from Office on Impeachment for, and Conviction of, Treason, Bribery, or other high Crimes and Misdemeanors.

ARTICLE III

Section 1

The judicial Power of the United States, shall be vested in one supreme Court, and in such inferior Courts as the Congress may from time to time ordain and establish. The Judges, both of the supreme and inferior Courts, shall hold their Offices during good Behaviour, and shall, at stated Times, receive for their Services, a Compensation, which shall not be diminished during their Continuance in Office.

Section 2

The judicial Power shall extend to all Cases, in Law and Equity, arising under this Constitution, the Laws of the United States, and Treaties made, or which shall be made, under their Authority;—to all Cases affecting ambassadors, other public ministers and consuls;—to all cases of admiralty and maritime Jurisdiction;—to Controversies to which the United States shall be a Party;—to Controversies between two or more States;—between a State and Citizens of another State;[5]—between Citizens of different States—between Citizens of the same State claiming Lands under Grants of different States, and between a State, or the Citizens thereof, and foreign States, Citizens, or Subjects.

In all Cases affecting Ambassadors, other public Ministers and Consuls, and those in which a State shall be Party, the supreme Court shall have original Jurisdiction. In all the other Cases before mentioned, the supreme Court shall have appellate Jurisdiction, both as to Law and Fact, with such Exceptions, and under such Regulations as the Congress shall make.

The trial of all Crimes, except in Cases of Impeachment, shall be by Jury; and such Trial shall be held in the State where the said Crimes shall have been committed; but when not committed within any State, the Trial shall be at such Place or Places as the Congress may by Law have directed.

[5]Qualified by the Eleventh Amendment.

Section 3

Treason against the United States, shall consist only in levying War against them, or in adhering to their Enemies, giving them Aid and Comfort. No Person shall be convicted of Treason unless on the Testimony of two Witnesses to the same overt Act, or on Confession in open Court.

The Congress shall have power to declare the Punishment of Treason, but no Attainder of Treason shall work Corruption of Blood, or Forfeiture except during the Life of the Person attainted.

ARTICLE IV

Section 1

Full Faith and Credit shall be given in each State to the public Acts, Records, and judicial Proceedings of every other State. And the Congress may by general Laws prescribe the Manner in which such Acts, Records and Proceedings shall be proved, and the Effect thereof.

Section 2

The Citizens of each State shall be entitled to all Privileges and Immunities of Citizens in the several States.

A Person charged in any State with Treason, Felony, or other Crime, who shall flee from Justice, and be found in another State, shall on demand of the executive Authority of the State from which he fled, be delivered up, to be removed to the State having Jurisdiction of the crime.

No Person held to Service or Labour in one State, under the Laws thereof, escaping into another, shall, in Consequence of any Law or Regulation therein, be discharged from such Service or Labour, but shall be delivered up on Claim of the Party to whom such Service or Labour may be due.

Section 3

New States may be admitted by the Congress into this Union; but no new State shall be formed or erected within the Jurisdiction of any other State; nor any State be formed by the Junction of two or more States, or parts of States, without the Consent of the Legislatures of the States concerned as well as of the Congress.

The Congress shall have Power to dispose of and make all needful Rules and Regulations respecting the Territory or other Property belonging to the United States; and nothing in this Constitution shall be so construed as to Prejudice any Claims of the United States, or of any particular State.

Section 4

The United States shall guarantee to every State in this Union a Republican Form of Government, and shall protect each of them against Invasion; and on Application of the Legislature, or of the Executive (when the Legislature cannot be convened) against domestic Violence.

ARTICLE V

The Congress, whenever two-thirds of both Houses shall deem it necessary, shall propose Amendments to this Constitution, or, on the Application of the Legislatures of two-thirds of the several States, shall call a Convention for proposing Amendments, which, in either Case, shall be valid to all Intents and Purposes, as part of this Constitution, when ratified by the Legislatures of three-fourths of the several States, or by Conventions in three-fourths thereof, as the one or the other Mode of Ratification may be proposed by the Congress; Provided that no Amendment which may be made prior to the Year One thousand eight hundred and eight shall in any Manner affect the first and fourth Clauses in the Ninth Section of the first Article; and that no State, without its Consent, shall be deprived of its equal Suffrage in the Senate.

ARTICLE VI

All Debts contracted and Engagements entered into, before the Adoption of this Constitution, shall be as valid against the United States under this Constitution, as under the Confederation.

This Constitution, and the Laws of the United States which shall be made in Pursuance thereof; and all Treaties made, or which shall be made, under the Authority of the United States, shall be the supreme Law of the Land; and the Judges in every State shall be bound thereby, any Thing in the Constitution or Laws of any State to the Contrary notwithstanding.

The Senators and Representatives before mentioned, and the Members of the several State Legislatures, and all executive and judicial Officers, both of the United States and of the several States, shall be bound by Oath or Affirmation to support this Constitution; but no religious Tests shall ever be required as a qualification to any Office or public Trust under the United States.

ARTICLE VII

The Ratification of the Conventions of nine States shall be sufficient for the Establishment of this Constitution between the States so ratifying the same.

Done in Convention by the Unanimous Consent of the States present the Seventeenth Day of September in the Year of our Lord one thousand seven hundred and Eighty seven, and of the Independence of the United States of America the Twelfth. In Witness whereof We have hereunto subscribed our Names.[6]

[6]These are the full names of the signers, which in some cases are not the signatures on the document.

GEORGE WASHINGTON
PRESIDENT AND DEPUTY FROM VIRGINIA

NEW HAMPSHIRE
John Langdon
Nicholas Gilman

MASSACHUSETTS
Nathaniel Gorham
Rufus King

CONNECTICUT
William Samuel Johnson
Roger Sherman

NEW YORK
Alexander Hamilton

NEW JERSEY
William Livingston
David Brearley
William Paterson
Jonathan Dayton

PENNSYLVANIA
Benjamin Franklin
Thomas Mifflin
Robert Morris
George Clymer
Thomas FitzSimons
Jared Ingersoll
James Wilson
Gouverneur Morris

DELAWARE
George Read
Gunning Bedford, Jr.
John Dickinson
Richard Bassett
Jacob Broom

MARYLAND
James McHenry
Daniel of St. Thomas Jenifer
Daniel Carroll

VIRGINIA
John Blair
James Madison, Jr.

NORTH CAROLINA
William Blount
Richard Dobbs Spaight
Hugh Williamson

SOUTH CAROLINA
John Rutledge
Charles Cotesworth Pinckney
Charles Pinckney
Pierce Butler

GEORGIA
William Few
Abraham Baldwin

Articles in Addition to, and Amendment of, the Constitution of the United States of America, Proposed by Congress, and Ratified by the Legislatures of the Several States, Pursuant to the Fifth Article of the Original Constitution[7]

[AMENDMENT I]

Congress shall make no law respecting an establishment of religion, or prohibiting the free exercise thereof; or abridging the freedom of speech, or of the press; or the right of the people peaceably to assemble, and to petition the Government for a redress of grievances.

[AMENDMENT II]

A well regulated Militia, being necessary to the security of a free State, the right of the people to keep and bear Arms shall not be infringed.

[AMENDMENT III]

No Soldier shall, in time of peace, be quartered in any house, without the consent of the Owner, nor in time of war, but in a manner to be prescribed by law.

[AMENDMENT IV]

The right of the people to be secure in their persons, houses, papers, and effects, against unreasonable searches and seizures, shall not be violated, and no Warrants shall issue, but upon probable cause, supported by Oath or affirmation, and particularly describing the place to be searched, and the persons or things to be seized.

[7]This heading appears only in the joint resolution submitting the first ten amendments, known as the Bill of Rights.

[AMENDMENT V]

No person shall be held to answer for a capital or otherwise infamous crime, unless on a presentment or indictment of a Grand Jury, except in cases arising in the land or naval forces, or in the Militia, when in actual service in time of War or public danger; nor shall any person be subject for the same offence to be twice put in jeopardy of life or limb; nor shall be compelled in any criminal case to be a witness against himself, nor be deprived of life, liberty, or property, without due process of law; nor shall private property be taken for public use, without just compensation.

[AMENDMENT VI]

In all criminal prosecutions, the accused shall enjoy the right to a speedy and public trial, by an impartial jury of the State and district wherein the crime shall have been committed, which district shall have been previously ascertained by law, and to be informed of the nature and cause of the accusation; to be confronted with the witnesses against him; to have compulsory process for obtaining witnesses in his favour, and to have the Assistance of Counsel for his defence.

[AMENDMENT VII]

In suits at common law, where the value in controversy shall exceed twenty dollars, the right of trial by jury shall be preserved, and no fact tried by a jury, shall be otherwise reexamined in any Court of the United States, than according to the rules of the common law.

[AMENDMENT VIII]

Excessive bail shall not be required, nor excessive fines imposed, nor cruel and unusual punishments inflicted.

[AMENDMENT IX]

The enumeration of the Constitution, of certain rights, shall not be construed to deny or disparage others retained by the people.

[AMENDMENT X]

The powers not delegated to the United States by the Constitution, nor prohibited by it to the States, are reserved to the States respectively, or to the people.
[Amendments I–X, in force 1791.]

[AMENDMENT XI][8]

The Judicial power of the United States shall not be construed to extend to any suit in law or equity, commenced or prosecuted against one of the United States by Citizens of another State, or by Citizens or Subjects of any Foreign State.

[AMENDMENT XII][9]

The Electors shall meet in their respective States and vote by ballot for President and Vice-President, one of whom, at least, shall not be an inhabitant of the same State with themselves; they shall name in their ballots the person voted for as President, and in distinct ballots the person voted for as Vice-President, and they shall make distinct lists of all persons voted for as President, and of all persons voted for as Vice-President, and of the number of votes for each, which lists they shall sign and certify, and transmit sealed to the seat of the government of the United States, directed to the President of the Senate;—The President of the Senate shall, in the presence of the Senate and House of Representatives, open all the certificates and the votes shall then be counted;—The person having the greatest number of votes for President, shall be the President, if such number be a majority of the whole number of Electors appointed; and if no person have such majority, then from the persons having the highest numbers not exceeding three on the list of those voted for as President, the House of Representatives shall choose immediately, by ballot, the President. But in choosing the President, the votes shall be taken by states, the representation from each state having one vote; a quorum for this purpose shall consist of a member or members from two-thirds of the states, and a majority of all the states shall be necessary to a choice. And if the House of Representatives shall not choose a President whenever the right of choice shall devolve upon them, before the fourth day of March next following, then the Vice-President shall act as President, as in the case of the death or other constitutional disability of the President.—The person having the greatest number of votes as Vice-President, shall be the Vice-President, if such number be a majority of the whole number of Electors appointed, and if no person have a majority, then from the two highest numbers on the list, the Senate shall choose the Vice-President; a quorum for the purpose shall consist of two-thirds of the whole number of Senators, and a majority of the whole number shall be necessary to a choice. But no person constitutionally ineligible to the office of President shall be eligible to that of Vice-President of the United States.

[AMENDMENT XIII][10]

Section 1

Neither slavery nor involuntary servitude, except as a punishment for crime whereof the party shall have been duly convicted, shall exist within the United States, or any place subject to their jurisdiction.

Section 2

Congress shall have power to enforce this article by appropriate legislation.

[AMENDMENT XIV][11]

Section 1

All persons born or naturalized in the United States, and subject to the jurisdiction thereof, are citizens of the United States and of the State wherein they reside. No State shall abridge the privileges or immunities of citizens of the United States; nor shall any State deprive any person of life, liberty, or property, without due process of law; nor deny to any person within its jurisdiction the equal protection of the laws.

Section 2

Representatives shall be apportioned among the several States according to their respective numbers, counting the whole number of persons in each State, excluding Indians not taxed. But when the right to vote at any election for the choice of electors for President and Vice-President of the United States, Representatives in Congress, the Executive and Judicial officers

[8]Adopted in 1798.
[9]Adopted in 1804.
[10]Adopted in 1865.
[11]Adopted in 1868.

of a State, or the members of the Legislature thereof, is denied to any of the male inhabitants of such State, being twenty-one years of age, and citizens of the United States, or in any way abridged, except for participation in rebellion, or other crime, the basis of representation therein shall be reduced in the proportion which the number of such male citizens shall bear to the whole number of male citizens twenty-one years of age in such State.

Section 3

No person shall be a Senator or Representative in Congress, or elector of President and Vice-President, or hold any office, civil or military, under the United States, or under any State, who, having previously taken an oath, as a member of Congress, or as an officer of the United States, or as a member of any State legislature, or as an executive or judicial officer of any State, to support the Constitution of the United States, shall have engaged in insurrection or rebellion against the same, or given aid or comfort to the enemies thereof. But Congress may by a vote of two-thirds of each House, remove such disability.

Section 4

The validity of the public debt of the United States, authorized by law, including debts incurred for payment of pensions and bounties for services in suppressing insurrection or rebellion, shall not be questioned. But neither the United States nor any State shall assume or pay any debts or obligation incurred in aid of insurrection or rebellion against the United States, or any claim for the loss or emancipation of any slave; but all such debts, obligations, and claims shall be held illegal and void.

Section 5

The Congress shall have the power to enforce, by appropriate legislation, the provisions of this article.

[AMENDMENT XV][12]

Section 1

The right of citizens of the United States to vote shall not be denied or abridged by the United States or by any State on account of race, color, or previous condition of servitude—

Section 2

The Congress shall have power to enforce this article by appropriate legislation.

[12]Adopted in 1870.

[AMENDMENT XVI][13]

The Congress shall have power to lay and collect taxes on incomes, from whatever source derived, without apportionment among the several States, and without regard to any census or enumeration.

[AMENDMENT XVII][14]

The Senate of the United States shall be composed of two Senators from each State, elected by the people thereof, for six years; and each Senator shall have one vote. The electors in each State shall have the qualifications requisite for electors of the most numerous branch of the State legislatures.

When vacancies happen in the representation of any State in the Senate, the executive authority of such State shall issue writs of election to fill such vacancies: Provided, That the legislature of any State may empower the executive thereof to make temporary appointments until the people fill the vacancies by election as the legislature may direct.

This amendment shall not be so construed as to affect the election or term of any Senator chosen before it becomes valid as part of the Constitution.

[AMENDMENT XVIII][15]

Section 1

After one year from the ratification of this article the manufacture, sale, or transportation of intoxicating liquors within, the importation thereof into, or the exportation thereof from the United States and all territory subject to the jurisdiction thereof for beverage purposes is hereby prohibited.

Section 2

The Congress and the several States shall have concurrent power to enforce this article by appropriate legislation.

Section 3

This article shall be inoperative unless it shall have been ratified as an amendment to the Constitution by the legislatures of the several States, as provided in the Constitution, within seven years from the date of the submission hereof to the States by the Congress.

[AMENDMENT XIX][16]

The right of citizens of the United States to vote shall not be denied or abridged by the United States or by any State on account of sex.

[13]Adopted in 1913.
[14]Adopted in 1913.
[15]Adopted in 1918.
[16]Adopted in 1920.

Congress shall have power to enforce this article by appropriate legislation.

[AMENDMENT XX][17]

Section 1

The terms of the President and Vice-President shall end at noon on the 20th day of January, and the terms of Senators and Representatives at noon on the 3d day of January, of the years in which such terms would have ended if this article had not been ratified; and the terms of their successors shall then begin.

Section 2

The Congress shall assemble at least once in every year, and such meeting shall begin at noon on the 3d day of January, unless they shall by law appoint a different day.

Section 3

If, at the time fixed for the beginning of the term of the President, the President elect shall have died, the Vice-President elect shall become President. If a President shall not have been chosen before the time fixed for the beginning of his term or if the President elect shall have failed to qualify, then the Vice-President elect shall act as President until a President shall have qualified; and the Congress may by law provide for the case wherein neither a President elect nor a Vice-President elect shall have qualified, declaring who shall then act as President, or the manner in which one who is to act shall be selected, and such person shall act accordingly until a President or Vice-President shall have qualified.

Section 4

The Congress may by law provide for the case of the death of any of the persons from whom the House of Representatives may choose a President whenever the right of choice shall have devolved upon them, and for the case of the death of any of the persons from whom the Senate may choose a Vice-President whenever the right of choice shall have devolved upon them.

Section 5

Sections 1 and 2 shall take effect on the 15th day of October following the ratification of this article.

Section 6

This article shall be inoperative unless it shall have been ratified as an amendment to the Constitution by the legislatures of three-fourths of the several States within seven years from the date of its submission.

[17]Adopted in 1933.

[AMENDMENT XXI][18]

Section 1

The eighteenth article of amendment to the Constitution of the United States is hereby repealed.

Section 2

The transportation or importation into any State, Territory, or possession of the United States for delivery or use therein of intoxicating liquors, in violation of the laws thereof, is hereby prohibited.

Section 3

This article shall be inoperative unless it shall have been ratified as an amendment to the Constitution by conventions in the several States, as provided in the Constitution, within seven years from the date of the submission hereof to the States by the Congress.

[AMENDMENT XXII][19]

No person shall be elected to the office of the President more than twice, and no person who has held the office of President, or acted as President, for more than two years of a term to which some other person was elected President shall be elected to the office of the President more than once.

But this Article shall not apply to any person holding the office of President when this Article was proposed by the Congress, and shall not prevent any person who may be holding the office of President, or acting as President, during the term within which this Article becomes operative from holding the office of President or acting as President during the remainder of such term.

This article shall be inoperative unless it shall have been ratified as an amendment to the Constitution by the legislatures of three-fourths of the several states within seven years from the date of its submission to the states by the Congress.

[AMENDMENT XXIII][20]

Section 1

The District constituting the seat of Government of the United States shall appoint in such manner as the Congress may direct:

[18]Adopted in 1933.
[19]Adopted in 1951.
[20]Adopted in 1961.

A number of electors of President and Vice-President equal to the whole number of Senators and Representatives in Congress to which the District would be entitled if it were a State, but in no event more than the least populous State; they shall be in addition to those appointed by the States, but they shall be considered, for the purpose of the election of President and Vice-President, to be electors appointed by a State; and they shall meet in the District and perform such duties as provided by the twelfth article of amendment.

Section 2

The Congress shall have power to enforce this article by appropriate legislation.

[AMENDMENT XXIV][21]

Section 1

The right of citizens of the United States to vote in any primary or other election for President or Vice-President, for electors for President or Vice-President, or for Senator or Representative in Congress, shall not be denied or abridged by the United States or any state by reason of failure to pay any poll tax or other tax.

Section 2

The Congress shall have the power to enforce this article by appropriate legislation.

[AMENDMENT XXV][22]

Section 1

In case of the removal of the President from office or of his death or resignation, the Vice-President shall become President.

Section 2

Whenever there is a vacancy in the office of the Vice President, the President shall nominate a Vice President who shall take office upon confirmation by a majority vote of both Houses of Congress.

Section 3

Whenever the President transmits to the President Pro Tempore of the Senate and the Speaker of the House of Representatives his written declaration that he is unable to discharge the powers and duties of his office, and until he transmits to them a written declaration to the contrary, such powers and duties shall be discharged by the Vice-President as Acting President.

Section 4

Whenever the Vice-President and a majority of either the principal officers of the executive departments or of such other body as Congress may by law provide, transmit to the President Pro Tempore of the Senate and the Speaker of the House of Representatives their written declaration that the President is unable to discharge the powers and duties of his office, the Vice President shall immediately assume the powers and duties of the office as Acting President.

Thereafter, when the President transmits to the President Pro Tempore of the Senate and the Speaker of the House of Representatives his written declaration that no inability exists, he shall resume the powers and duties of his office unless the Vice President and a majority of either the principal officers of the executive departments or of such other body as Congress may by law provide, transmit within four days to the President Pro Tempore of the Senate and the Speaker of the House of Representatives their written declaration that the President is unable to discharge the powers and duties of his office. Thereupon Congress shall decide the issue, assembling within forty-eight hours for that purpose if not in session. If the Congress, within twenty-one days after receipt of the latter written declaration, or, if Congress is not in session, within twenty-one days after Congress is required to assemble, determines by two-thirds vote of both Houses that the President is unable to discharge the powers and duties of his office, the Vice President shall continue to discharge the same as Acting President; otherwise, the President shall resume the powers and duties of his office.

[AMENDMENT XXVI][23]

Section 1

The right of citizens of the United States, who are eighteen years of age or older, to vote shall not be denied or abridged by the United States or by any State on account of age.

Section 2

The Congress shall have power to enforce this article by appropriate legislation.

[AMENDMENT XXVII][24]

No law, varying the compensation for the services of the Senators and Representatives, shall take effect, until an election of Representatives shall have intervened.

[21] Adopted in 1964.
[22] Adopted in 1967.
[23] Adopted in 1971.
[24] Adopted in 1992.

PRESIDENTIAL ELECTIONS

Year	Candidates	Parties	Popular Vote	% of Popular Vote	Electoral Vote	% Voter Participation
1789	**George Washington**				69	
	John Adams				34	
	Other candidates				35	
1792	**George Washington**				132	
	John Adams				77	
	George Clinton				50	
	Other candidates				5	
1796	**John Adams**	Federalist			71	
	Thomas Jefferson	Dem.-Rep.			68	
	Thomas Pinckney	Federalist			59	
	Aaron Burr	Dem.-Rep.			30	
	Other candidates				48	
1800	**Thomas Jefferson**	Dem.-Rep.			73	
	Aaron Burr	Dem.-Rep.			73	
	John Adams	Federalist			65	
	Charles C. Pinckney	Federalist			64	
	John Jay	Federalist			1	
1804	**Thomas Jefferson**	Dem.-Rep.			162	
	Charles C. Pinckney	Federalist			14	
1808	**James Madison**	Dem.-Rep.			122	
	Charles C. Pinckney	Federalist			47	
	George Clinton	Dem.-Rep.			6	
1812	**James Madison**	Dem.-Rep.			128	
	DeWitt Clinton	Federalist			89	
1816	**James Monroe**	Dem.-Rep.			183	
	Rufus King	Federalist			34	
1820	**James Monroe**	Dem.-Rep.			231	
	John Quincy Adams	Indep.-Rep.			1	
1824	**John Quincy Adams**	Dem.-Rep.	113,122	31.0	84	26.9
	Andrew Jackson	Dem.-Rep.	151,271	43.0	99	
	Henry Clay	Dem.-Rep.	47,136	13.0	37	
	William H. Crawford	Dem.-Rep.	46,618	13.0	41	
1828	**Andrew Jackson**	Democratic	642,553	56.0	178	57.6
	John Quincy Adams	National Republican	500,897	44.0	83	
1832	**Andrew Jackson**	Democratic	701,780	54.5	219	55.4
	Henry Clay	National Republican	484,205	37.5	49	
	William Wirt	Anti-Masonic }	101,051	8.0	7	
	John Floyd	Democratic }			11	
1836	**Martin Van Buren**	Democratic	764,176	50.9	170	57.8
	William H. Harrison	Whig	550,816	49.1	73	
	Hugh L. White	Whig			26	
	Daniel Webster	Whig			14	
	W. P. Mangum	Whig			11	
1840	**William H. Harrison**	Whig	1,275,390	53.0	234	80.2
	Martin Van Buren	Democratic	1,128,854	47.0	60	

Year	Candidates	Parties	Popular Vote	% of Popular Vote	Electoral Vote	% Voter Participation
1844	**James K. Polk**	Democratic	1,339,494	49.6	170	78.9
	Henry Clay	Whig	1,300,004	48.1	105	
	James G. Birney	Liberty	62,300	2.3		
1848	**Zachary Taylor**	Whig	1,361,393	47.4	163	72.7
	Lewis Cass	Democratic	1,223,460	42.5	127	
	Martin Van Buren	Free Soil	291,263	10.1		
1852	**Franklin Pierce**	Democratic	1,607,510	50.9	254	69.6
	Winfield Scott	Whig	1,386,942	44.1	42	
	John P. Hale	Free Soil	155,825	5.0		
1856	**James Buchanan**	Democratic	1,836,072	45.3	174	78.9
	John C. Fremont	Republican	1,342,345	33.1	114	
	Millard Fillmore	American	871,731	21.6	8	
1860	**Abraham Lincoln**	Republican	1,865,908	39.8	180	81.2
	Stephen A. Douglas	Democratic	1,375,157	29.5	12	
	John C. Breckinridge	Democratic	848,019	18.1	72	
	John Bell	Constitutional Union	590,631	12.6	39	
1864	**Abraham Lincoln**	Republican	2,218,388	55.0	212	73.8
	George B. McClellan	Democratic	1,812,807	45.0	21	
1868	**Ulysses S. Grant**	Republican	3,013,650	52.7	214	78.1
	Horatio Seymour	Democratic	2,708,744	47.3	80	
1872	**Ulysses S. Grant**	Republican	3,598,235	55.6	286	71.3
	Horace Greeley	Democratic	2,834,761	43.9	66	
1876	**Rutherford B. Hayes**	Republican	4,034,311	48.0	185	81.8
	Samuel J. Tilden	Democratic	4,288,546	51.0	184	
1880	**James A. Garfield**	Republican	4,446,158	48.5	214	79.4
	Winfield S. Hancock	Democratic	4,444,260	48.1	155	
	James B. Weaver	Greenback-Labor	308,578	3.4		
1884	**Grover Cleveland**	Democratic	4,874,621	48.5	219	77.5
	James G. Blaine	Republican	4,848,936	48.2	182	
	Benjamin F. Butler	Greenback-Labor	175,370	1.8		
	John P. St. John	Prohibition	150,369	1.5		
1888	**Benjamin Harrison**	Republican	5,443,892	47.9	233	79.3
	Grover Cleveland	Democratic	5,534,488	48.6	168	
	Clinton B. Fisk	Prohibition	249,506	2.2		
	Anson J. Streeter	Union Labor	146,935	1.3		
1892	**Grover Cleveland**	Democratic	5,551,883	46.1	277	74.7
	Benjamin Harrison	Republican	5,179,244	43.0	145	
	James B. Weaver	People's	1,029,846	8.5	22	
	John Bidwell	Prohibition	264,133	2.2		
1896	**William McKinley**	Republican	7,108,480	52.0	271	79.3
	William J. Bryan	Democratic	6,511,495	48.0	176	
1900	**William McKinley**	Republican	7,218,039	51.7	292	73.2
	William J. Bryan	Democratic; Populist	6,358,345	45.5	155	
	John C. Wooley	Prohibition	208,914	1.5		
1904	**Theodore Roosevelt**	Republican	7,626,593	57.4	336	65.2
	Alton B. Parker	Democratic	5,082,898	37.6	140	
	Eugene V. Debs	Socialist	402,283	3.0		
	Silas C. Swallow	Prohibition	258,536	1.9		

Year	Candidates	Parties	Popular Vote	% of Popular Vote	Electoral Vote	% Voter Participation
1908	**William H. Taft**	Republican	7,676,258	51.6	321	65.4
	William J. Bryan	Democratic	6,406,801	43.1	162	
	Eugene V. Debs	Socialist	420,793	2.8		
	Eugene W. Chafin	Prohibition	253,840	1.7		
1912	**Woodrow Wilson**	Democratic	6,293,152	42.0	435	58.8
	Theodore Roosevelt	Progressive	4,119,207	28.0	88	
	William H. Taft	Republican	3,484,980	24.0	8	
	Eugene V. Debs	Socialist	900,672	6.0		
	Eugene W. Chafin	Prohibition	206,275	1.4		
1916	**Woodrow Wilson**	Democratic	9,126,300	49.4	277	61.6
	Charles E.. Hughes	Republican	8,546,789	46.2	254	
	A. L. Benson	Socialist	585,113	3.2		
	J. Frank Hanly	Prohibition	220,506	1.2		
1920	**Warren G. Harding**	Republican	16,153,115	60.4	404	49.2
	James M. Cox	Democratic	9,133,092	34.2	127	
	Eugene V. Debs	Socialist	919,799	3.4		
	P. P. Christensen	Farmer-Labor	265,411	1.0		
1924	**Calvin Coolidge**	Republican	15,719,921	54.0	382	48.9
	John W. Davis	Democratic	8,386,704	28.8	136	
	Robert M. La Follette	Progressive	4,831,289	16.6	13	
1928	**Herbert C. Hoover**	Republican	21,437,277	58.2	444	56.9
	Alfred E. Smith	Democratic	15,007,698	40.9	87	
1932	**Franklin D. Roosevelt**	Democratic	22,829,501	57.4	472	56.9
	Herbert C. Hoover	Republican	15,760,684	39.7	59	
	Norman Thomas	Socialist	881,951	2.2		
1936	**Franklin D. Roosevelt**	Democratic	27,757,333	60.8	523	61.0
	Alfred M. Landon	Republican	16,684,231	36.5	8	
	William Lemke	Union	882,479	1.9		
1940	**Franklin D. Roosevelt**	Democratic	27,313,041	54.8	449	62.5
	Wendell L. Wilkie	Republican	22,348,480	44.8	82	
1944	**Franklin D. Roosevelt**	Democratic	25,612,610	53.5	432	55.9
	Thomas E. Dewey	Republican	22,117,617	46.0	99	
1948	**Harry S Truman**	Democratic	24,179,345	50.0	303	53.0
	Thomas E. Dewey	Republican	21,991,291	46.0	189	
	J. Strom Thurmond	States' Rights	1,169,021	2.0	39	
	Henry A. Wallace	Progressive	1,157,172	2.0		
1952	**Dwight D. Eisenhower**	Republican	33,936,234	55.1	442	63.3
	Adlai E. Stevenson	Democratic	27,314,992	44.4	89	
1956	**Dwight D. Eisenhower**	Republican	35,590,472	57.6	457	60.6
	Adlai E. Stevenson	Democratic	26,022,752	42.1	73	
1960	**John F. Kennedy**	Democratic	34,226,731	49.7	303	62.8
	Richard M. Nixon	Republican	34,108,157	49.6	219	
	Harry F. Byrd	Independent	501,643		15	
1964	**Lyndon B. Johnson**	Democratic	43,129,566	61.1	486	61.7
	Barry M. Goldwater	Republican	27,178,188	38.5	52	
1968	**Richard M. Nixon**	Republican	31,785,480	44.0	301	60.6
	Hubert H. Humphrey	Democratic	31,275,166	42.7	191	
	George C. Wallace	American Independent	9,906,473	13.5	46	

Year	Candidates	Parties	Popular Vote	% of Popular Vote	Electoral Vote	% Voter Participation
1972	**Richard M. Nixon**	Republican	47,169,911	60.7	520	55.2
	George S. McGovern	Democratic	29,170,383	37.5	17	
	John G. Schmitz	American	1,099,482	1.4		
1976	**Jimmy Carter**	Democratic	40,830,763	50.1	297	53.5
	Gerald R. Ford	Republican	39,147,793	48.0	240	
1980	**Ronald Reagan**	Republican	43,904,153	51.0	489	52.6
	Jimmy Carter	Democratic	35,483,883	41.0	49	
	John B. Anderson	Independent	5,719,437	7.0	0	
	Ed Clark	Libertarian	920,859	1.0	0	
1984	**Ronald Reagan**	Republican	54,455,075	58.8	525	53.3
	Walter Mondale	Democratic	37,577,185	40.5	13	
1988	**George H. W. Bush**	Republican	48,886,097	53.9	426	48.6
	Michael Dukakis	Democratic	41,809,074	46.1	111	
1992	**William J. Clinton**	Democratic	44,908,254	43.0	370	55.9
	George H. W. Bush	Republican	39,102,343	37.4	168	
	H. Ross Perot	Independent	19,741,065	18.9	0	
1996	**William J. Clinton**	Democratic	45,590,703	49.3	379	49
	Robert Dole	Republican	37,816,307	40.7	159	
	H. Ross Perot	Reform	8,085,294	8.4	0	
2000	**George W. Bush**	Republican	50,456,062	47.9	271	51.2
	Al Gore	Democratic	50,996,582	48.4	266	
	Ralph Nader	Green	2,858,843	2.7	0	
2004	**George W. Bush**	Republican	62,048,610	50.7	286	60.7
	John F. Kerry	Democrat	59,028,444	48.3	251	
	Ralph Nader	Independent	465,650	0.4	0	
2008	**Barack Obama**	Democratic	65,070,487	53	365	63.0
	John McCain	Republican	57,154,810	46	173	
2012	**Barack Obama**	Democrat	65,899,660	51.0	332	58.9
	Mitt Romney	Republican	60,929,152	47.2	206	

GLOSSARY

A

abolitionists Radical opponents of slavery, vilified throughout the country for their views on emancipation and racial equality.

abstract expressionists A small group of loosely affiliated artists in the 1940s and 1950s who transformed the art establishment by making monumental, abstract works that they believed expressed the artist's inner psyche.

Acadian diaspora The dispersion of French-speaking colonists from eastern Canada after the French and Indian War, which led to the formation of a Cajun community and culture in Louisiana.

adelantado Spanish term for "advance men" who organized conquest expeditions to foreign lands on behalf of the monarchy.

affirmative action The policy of advancing the educational and employment opportunities of members of groups that traditionally had been oppressed, exploited, and abandoned.

affluence gap The relative difference, which increased dramatically during the Gilded Age, the 1920s, and the late twentieth century, between society's wealthiest stratum and the average wealth of the majority.

African slave trade The term that historians commonly use to designate the long-distance commerce in human laborers from sub-Saharan Africa, especially between 1500 and 1800.

agricultural revolution The major shift in subsistence among North Americans, beginning around the tenth century, as many native societies turned to planting corn and legumes for their principal food sources.

al-Qaeda The loose coalition of radical Islamists who have waged terrorist warfare against the United States since the 1990s.

amalgamationists Antebellum term meaning advocates of interracial sex and reproduction, used to disparage abolitionists.

American dream The popular perception dating from the Gilded Age that any individual in the United States who works hard and shows initiative will prosper and be happy.

American Renaissance Term used by literary critics for the period in which many works of American literature now considered masterpieces (including a number in the early 1850s) were produced.

American way The idea, first promoted by big business at the 1939 World's Fair, that the ideal society was one in which government played a limited role in the economy and where responsible corporations provided jobs, good wages, advanced technology, and consumer choice.

anarchism A diverse set of political philosophies—originating in Early Modern Europe, adopted in Gilded Age America, and resurgent in the anti-globalization and Occupy movements—that advocates the dissolution of the state and the creation of stateless societies made up of voluntary egalitarian associations.

Antifederalists Opponents of ratifying the U.S. Constitution.

anti-miscegenation laws Laws under which most states in the nineteenth century prohibited interracial marriage and in some cases interracial sex.

assembly line A manufacturing process by which parts are sequentially added to the product, whether by humans, automated machines, or a combination of humans and machines.

attack ads A new kind of electoral advertisement that began appearing in the 1980s and that emphasized the negative attributes of the opposing candidate rather than the positive attributes or policy positions of the preferred candidate.

avant-garde French term, literally meaning "advance guard" and entering American English after World War II, referring to innovative and experimental art, people, ideas, and ways of life.

B

baby boomers Americans born between 1946 and 1964, a period in which the national birthrate temporarily rebounded from the historic low of the 1930s.

balance of power The general principle, dating back to Early Modern Europe and still influential today, that international peace prevails only when rival states or alliances are equally powerful.

ballot initiative A Progressive Era reform, still in force in twenty-four states and the District of Columbia, that enables citizens to force a public vote on a particular issue provided that they gather a certain number of voters' signatures.

bank notes The various notes of private banks before the Civil War, which could serve as currency promising to pay the bearer a certain quantity of specie (silver or gold).

Benevolent Empire A network of national Protestant organizations in the early republic that were committed to the spread of Christianity and to various philanthropic goals.

bicameral Having two legislative chambers, typically one higher than the other.

Bill of Rights Conventional name for the first ten amendments to the U.S. Constitution.

biotechnology The use of science and technology to improve biological systems, industry, and agriculture; came into prominence in the 2000s.

Black Codes Laws passed immediately after the Civil War by Confederate legislatures seeking to return the freedpeople to a condition akin to slavery.

blackface minstrelsy An extraordinarily popular brand of theatrical entertainment in nineteenth-century America, featuring performers wearing burnt cork or black paint on their faces.

blue-collar strategy The largely successful attempt by the Republican Party, beginning around 1968, to court historically Democratic union voters by stressing cultural issues and themes, such as patriotism, traditional gender roles, and hostility to the counterculture.

bodily self-control A cultural ideal, central to many antebellum reform causes, that valued suppressing violent impulses and bodily appetites.

Bolshevik Revolution Overthrow of Russia's provisional government in 1917 by communist workers' associations, culminating in the establishment of the Union of Soviet Socialist Republics (USSR) in 1922.

boosters Civic-minded businessmen who promoted the prospects and fortunes of rival frontier cities in the nineteenth century, typically where they lived and owned property.

braceros The Mexican workers or "helping hands" invited into the United States during World War II in order to fill the labor shortage caused by military conscription.

broad construction Approach to constitutional interpretation that favors granting the federal government any powers consistent with its general charge as long as those powers are not explicitly restricted by the Constitution (*see* **strict construction**).

broker state The term that historians use to describe the form of government that emerged from the New Deal: a state that mediated between and distributed resources among different interest groups.

Burned-Over District Name given to the area in western New York, along the Erie Canal route, where religious revivals were particularly influential during the Second Great Awakening.

Bushwhackers Pro-Confederate guerrillas who operated in Missouri and eastern Kansas during the Civil War.

busing Court-ordered programs that transported schoolchildren from one part of a city to another to achieve racial desegregation.

C

Californios Hispanic population of Mexican California, born before the United States acquired the region.

camp followers Women who attach themselves to military units, often serving as nurses, cooks, and laundresses.

camp meeting Outdoor, multiday mass revival held in a rural area.

carpetbaggers Derisive name for white northerners who moved South during Reconstruction to take up farming or start a small business and who often carried their belongings in a bag made of carpet.

chain stores Retail outlets that operated under the same brand and management and that helped spread mass consumption from the 1920s onward.

chattel slavery Labor system in which human beings are held and exchanged as movable property.

checks and balances The idea that various kinds of political equilibrium would prevent any one branch of government or political interest from seizing too much power under a new constitution.

circuit riders Itinerant Methodist preachers sent around the country to evangelize, especially in sparsely settled regions.

civilization program U.S. initiative to convert Indians to European ways of living, including private property, agriculture, literacy, and European gender roles.

Cold War The military, economic, cultural, psychological, and political rivalry between the United States and the Soviet Union following World War II.

Columbian exchange Scholarly term for the massive transfer of people, animals, plants, microbes, commodities, ideas, and information across the Atlantic Ocean in the decades following Columbus's voyages.

Comanchería Name given to the region dominated by Comanche Indians during the eighteenth and early nineteenth centuries, extending from western Kansas through much of New Mexico.

commercial mining enterprises Large-scale underground mining operations that replaced placer miners with heavy equipment and wage laborers.

common schools Publicly supported, tuition-free schools that proliferated in the North during the 1840s.

congressional caucus Nominating process in the early republic in which congressmen from the same party designated presidential candidates.

Congressional Reconstruction The phase of Reconstruction during which Congress rather the president directed the reconstruction of the South.

conservative nationalism The term that historians use to describe the belief, briefly popularized during the Spanish-American War and influential after World War II, that all nations pursue their own national interest and that maintaining U.S. military power is vital to the nation's self-interest.

consumer rights A new set of rights that consumer advocacy groups first defined and demanded in the 1890s, such as the customer's right to safety and to full, truthful product information.

containment The foundation of U.S. foreign policy during the Cold War (1947–1989); the strategy of confining communism to the Soviet Union and blocking the expansion of Soviet influence and power.

contrabands Name given to fugitive slaves who escaped to Union camps during the Civil War and were declared freed from their masters on the model of enemy property captured during war.

Copperheads Name given to Democrats in the North who sought to end the Civil War.

counterculture Sociological term for the unconventional attitudes, desires, values, and ways of life that many U.S. youths adopted in the second half of the 1960s.

"the country" Name that prosperous Gilded Age urbanites gave rural areas in which resorts, spas, and inns were replacing working farms.

court-packing President Franklin D. Roosevelt's controversial plan (never implemented) to appoint up to six additional Supreme Court justices so as to expand the number of pro–New Deal liberals on the bench.

Covenant Chain A system of diplomatic negotiation between British colonies and Indian groups during the first half of the eighteenth century, led by New York and the Iroquois League.

coverture The long-standing legal doctrine that subsumed a married woman's identity to that of her husband.

creole Term applied to people of foreign ancestry born in colonial territory, such as the children of Europeans or Africans in North American colonies.

cruising A form of socializing that emerged in the 1950s in which teens drove around town in small groups with no single destination in mind and for the purpose of having fun; later adapted to refer to the practice of walking the streets in search of a casual sexual partner.

Crusades A series of religiously motivated military expeditions by European Christians in the medieval era to seize control of Jerusalem and other lands held by non-Christians.

cult of domesticity The term that historians use for the popular celebration, mostly in antebellum northern middle-class culture, of the ideal home as a morally nourishing female-dominated sphere.

culture wars Term coined in the 1980s to describe the clash of value systems that characterized that decade but that has also accompanied most other periods of rapid economic and political change.

D

de facto segregation Separate and unequal treatment of minorities, especially African Americans, despite the absence of racial segregation laws.

debt assumption A new government's taking on of financial obligations incurred by earlier (or other) governments.

decolonization The process by which colonial peoples in Asia, Africa, the Middle East, and the Caribbean demanded and won their independence from European rule in the three decades following World War II.

Deists Adherents of a religious outlook (but not an organized church or denomination) that sees evidence of God in the natural world rather than in special acts of divine revelation and intervention.

deregulation The abolition or suspension of regulations, after 1980, that were designed to stabilize the economy and protect consumers, workers, and the environment but that business considered cumbersome, costly, or ineffective.

deskilling The subdivision of craft labor into smaller components, at least some of which require less skill.

détente From the French word for relaxation, a policy of easing tense political relations, especially between the United States and the Soviet Union in the 1970s.

diaspora A geographically dispersed community linked by a shared identification with or attachment to a distant homeland.

digital divide The gap between people with access to the Internet and all it has to offer and those without access.

Digital Revolution The mass digitization of information and widespread adoption of the Internet and cellular phones.

dollar diplomacy Term coined by Theodore Roosevelt to describe President William Howard Taft's policy of pursuing U.S business interests overseas and gaining access to foreign markets by extending loans to foreign governments.

downsizing Term used to describe corporations' reduction in their workforce size in the 1980s and 1990s.

Dust Bowl The long drought of the 1930s that afflicted much of the United States, especially Oklahoma, Kansas, and northern Texas; also used to refer to the areas stricken by the drought conditions.

E

eight-hour day The length of the workday demanded by workers and unions in the Gilded Age and Progressive Era; became standard for workers in many industries during the New Deal.

empire of goods Term used by recent historians to describe the way consumption linked dispersed colonial populations to one another and to the British Empire during the eighteenth century.

enclosure movement Trend in England around 1700 toward fencing off pastures and converting land traditionally held in common into exclusive private property.

encomienda The exploitative labor regime that Spanish conquerors imposed on native populations in the Americas.

energy crisis A shortage of energy resources that precipitates a social or political problem by making it difficult or expensive to light and heat homes and businesses or to fuel transportation vehicles.

English Civil War Violent political conflict in the 1640s that divided English society and deposed the English monarchy.

Enlightenment A broad European intellectual movement in the seventeenth and eighteenth centuries, promoting reason, the scientific method, religious skepticism, and the exchange of new ideas.

"the establishment" Critical term popularized in the 1960s that referred to long-standing social conventions, entrenched elites, and political and cultural institutions.

ethnic revival The rise of ethnic pride movements in the 1970s, especially among the descendants of eastern and southern European immigrants.

Exodusters Name given to African Americans in 1879 who, in response to the defeat of Reconstruction, embarked on what they called a Great Exodus from the South to Kansas.

expansionist The name that Gilded Age and early Progressive Era advocates of U.S. empire-building preferred because of the popular association of imperialism with unpopular European monarchies.

F

Fair Deal The name that Harry Truman used to describe and promote his plans to extend the New Deal.

farming frontier American farmers' westward migration onto the Great Plains and elsewhere, sped by federal distribution of western lands after the Civil War.

Federalists In the 1780s, the proponents of the new national constitution and a stronger federal government. A decade later, a national political party that championed strong central government.

Fifth Freedom The idea that, in addition to President Franklin D. Roosevelt's fundamental Four Freedoms, there was the freedom of economic choice: that is, the freedom to undertake economic actions—including buying and selling—without government regulation.

filibusters Unauthorized expeditions by private armies into foreign lands, either for profit or for political ideals such as U.S. expansionism.

final solution The Nazi regime's name for the Holocaust's deadliest phase, from 1942 to 1945, during which it carried out the execution of 12 million Jews, communists, Poles, Slavs, Roma (gypsies), gays, Jehovah's Witnesses, and other minorities.

fire-eaters Name given to southern defenders of slavery who adopted increasingly intransigent and belligerent postures in the 1850s.

fireside chats President Franklin D. Roosevelt's publicity technique of using the new medium of radio to bypass the conventional news media (the press) and communicate directly with voters.

first hundred days The period immediately following a president's first inauguration, which, beginning with Franklin D. Roosevelt, has been held by voters and the news media to be a crucial period for establishing the president's priorities, leadership style, and legislative agenda.

Five Civilized Tribes Designation applied to those Indian groups in the Southeast (Creeks, Cherokees, Chickasaws, Choctaws, and Seminoles) that appeared to have embraced key aspects of white American culture, including settled agriculture and literacy.

flapper A young woman who openly transgressed the gender and class conventions of the 1920s through her dress, comportment, use of makeup, and assertive sexuality.

Fordism The economic system, named after auto manufacturer Henry Ford and dominant from 1945 to the 1970s, that paired mass production with mass consumption by ensuring that industrial workers were optimally efficient and well paid (so as to enable them to purchase consumer goods).

forty-niners Term for gold seekers during the California gold rush.

Four Freedoms The universal freedoms defined by President Franklin D. Roosevelt in a 1941 speech: freedoms of worship and of speech, and freedoms from fear and from economic want.

free enterprise Libertarian economist Friedrich Hayek's name for the business sector, which, he argued in the 1940s, was the origin and guarantor of freedom itself and should therefore be free of almost all legal constraints.

free silver A political slogan coined by farmers and mining companies of the late Gilded Age who called for the unlimited minting of silver coins, which would have reduced farmers' debts and increased mining profits.

free trade zone A designated area of a foreign country, increasingly common in the late twentieth century, in which American and other companies are permitted to land, reconfigure, manufacture, and reexport goods without paying taxes or export duties.

freedom suits Legal petitions for freedom presented by enslaved African Americans during the revolutionary era to colonial or state courts.

freehold A form of land ownership (common in the modern West) in which an individual can buy, sell, bequeath, or exchange the land at will.

frontier thesis Historians' name for the popular theory, advanced by Frederick Jackson Turner in 1893, that the experience of westward expansion freed Americans from outdated European customs and instilled in them a love of democracy.

fundamentalism The Protestant belief system and religious movement dating from the late nineteenth century that rejected liberal (modernist) Christianity and the secularization of American culture and asserted that every word in the Bible is true.

G

gang system A method of labor management, used on tobacco plantations, for example, in which enslaved laborers work together in teams under the scrutiny of a foreman or an overseer (*see* **task system**).

Generation X The generation of Americans that followed the baby boomers and defined themselves as distinct from hippies, the counterculture, and mass protest movements.

gentry Members of an economically privileged and socially refined class.

gerrymandering The practice, common but increasingly controversial in the Gilded Age, of setting electoral districts to the advantage of one's own party.

Gilded Age Term coined by Mark Twain and Charles Dudley Warner, and later adopted by historians, to describe the period 1865–1895.

globalization A complex and controversial process, under way since the 1960s but intensifying since 1980, by which certain national barriers, particularly those constraining money, goods, and ideas, are lowered or disassembled.

gold standard The monetary system in operation in the United States between 1879 and 1971, under which paper notes were convertible into a predetermined quantity of gold.

gradual abolition Process by which slavery ended legally in many northern states, typically by laws that declared children born to slaves after a certain date to be free and that liberated those already enslaved once they reached a particular age.

Grangers A farmers' movement founded after the Civil War that protested corporate monopolization of railroads and grain storage facilities and provided alternative cooperative services.

Great Awakening Historians' name for a series of religious revivals and pietist movements in various British American colonies in the second quarter of the eighteenth century.

Great Migration The movement between 1910 and 1970 of over six million African Americans out of the South into the cities of the West, Midwest, and Northeast.

Great Puritan Migration Historians' name for the movement of tens of thousands of Puritans from England to the American colonies (mostly New England and the Caribbean) from the late 1620s to 1640.

greenback Name of the paper currency first issued during the Civil War (by the Union) to stabilize the economy.

grid design The use of rectilinear patterns in land subdivision and city planning.

growth liberalism The theory behind Lyndon B. Johnson's War on Poverty (1964–1968) that government-funded education and vocational training programs would get the unemployed back to work and out of poverty and dependence.

Gullah A patois (blended language) developed by slaves in parts of the South Carolina Lowcountry, with many African words and linguistic features.

H

Harlem Renaissance The diverse cultural movement of the 1920s, centered in Harlem, New York, in which African American writers, musicians, and artists defied racism and embraced black pride.

hiring-out system The practice, common in southern cities, of renting out one's slave to another white employer in return for wages.

honor A cultural ideal cited by historians and anthropologists as central to the values of elite whites in the antebellum South.

Hoovervilles Shantytowns that unemployed Americans set up during the Great Depression on the periphery of cities, typically alongside rail lines and near city dumps; satirically named after President Herbert Hoover.

humanitarian crisis Term used to describe an event in which mass death or suffering is thought to be under way or imminent yet avoidable, provided that governments, relief agencies, and/or citizens take action.

I

illegal alien A category, originating with the Chinese Exclusion Act (1882) and reinforced by the National Origins Act (1924), denoting a person who has entered the United States illegally.

immediatism The radical ideology of American abolitionists who favored the immediate and uncompensated emancipation of all slaves.

impressment The forced conscription of men into naval service, a practice the British were frequently accused of carrying out on American ships in the early nineteenth century.

industrialization The reorganization of an economy and a society as it turns toward large-scale manufacturing, typically involving the specialization, subdivision, and mechanization of traditional production processes.

internal improvements Government-subsidized projects, such as roads and canals, designed to facilitate economic development and bind a country together.

international human rights movement An informal network of dissident political groups in different countries and of nongovernmental organizations that seek to hold governments and other entities accountable to universal standards of human rights; a concept that drew increasing power and prestige after the 1970s.

internationalists The name given to those commentators and policymakers, particularly during the 1930s, who criticized isolationism and argued that the United States should play an active role in international relations.

Internet piracy Originally, in the 2000s, the music industry's term for the unauthorized duplication and sale over the Internet of copyrighted music; subsequently used to describe the illegal Internet duplication of any and all copyrighted material.

iron curtain Popular term, coined by British prime minister Winston Churchill in 1946, to describe the ideological barrier and physical boundary between Soviet-dominated Europe and Western Europe.

isolationism The policy or attitude, popular before and after World War I and again during the Great Depression, that the United States should not get involved in other nations' conflicts or enter into international alliances.

J

Jacksonian Democracy Common but potentially misleading scholarly term for the culture of mass political participation that President Andrew Jackson both championed and symbolized.

Jayhawkers Unionist military outfits in Kansas that conducted raids across the Missouri border during the Civil War.

Jim Crow Name of both a standard dance and a stock character on the blackface stage.

Jim Crow laws Collective term for the legal system of racial segregation and discrimination that characterized the South between the late nineteenth century and the mid-1960s.

jingoism Pejorative term for a form of extreme patriotism, first identified in connection with British imperialism in the 1870s and later popularized in the United States by critics of U.S. expansionism.

judicial review The practice of judges' assessing the constitutional validity of acts by the executive and legislative branches of government.

K

Keynesianism The branch of economics, developed by John Maynard Keynes and applied in the United States in 1933–1980, in which government stabilized the economy by actively stimulating consumer demand and investing directly in the housing sector, agriculture, industry, interstate transportation, and science and technology.

L

land speculation Buying or owning land with the intention of selling it at a profit.

Latin Christendom The dominant religious community of western Europe in the medieval period, spread across much of the continent and unified under the authority of a pope in Rome.

League of the Iroquois A powerful political bloc of Indian nations that formed in the region south of Lake Ontario before the arrival of Europeans in North America.

League of Nations First intergovernmental organization, operating from 1919 to 1946, to promote peace and a system of collective security based on negotiation and arbitration.

liberal (modernist) Christianity Diverse body of thought that gained popularity among urban Protestants in the late nineteenth and early twentieth centuries and that emphasized the importance of active interpretation in the reading of scripture.

libertarianism A body of thought, initially influential among a small segment of the American business elite in the 1950s, holding that individuals own themselves and have a moral right to acquire property in things and that the state should simply keep the peace and protect private property.

limited war An armed conflict, such as the Korean and Iraq wars, in which the combatants do not seek the total destruction of the enemy or expend all their military, economic, and cultural resources.

literacy test A test administered to African Americans in the Jim Crow era (1889–1965) for the purpose of disqualifying them from registering to vote.

Loyalists Name adopted by colonists who favored rapprochement with Great Britain and the maintenance of colonial relations during the Revolutionary era.

lynching The illegal but unpunished execution of African Americans that served, between 1880 and the 1930s, to enforce blacks' subordinate status in southern society.

M

manifest destiny Popular ideology from the 1840s maintaining that the United States was divinely ordained to expand to the Pacific Ocean.

manumission The legal emancipation of a slave by his or her owner.

marching clubs Voluntary organizations of the Gilded Age, usually urban and affiliated with a major party, that whipped up voters' fervor and passion for politics by staging numerous preelection parades.

mass consumption An economic and cultural system, which took root in the nineteenth century and became dominant in the twentieth century, that produces an ever wider array of commercial goods and services and promotes the idea that personal happiness can be attained through the acquisition of material goods.

McCarthyism Originally Senator Joseph McCarthy's policy of identifying and purging from government and the culture industries persons suspected of being communist, but subsequently any form of persecutory investigation that has the effect of stifling free speech or that is motivated chiefly by partisan politics.

meetinghouse In New England colonial towns, the central building where religious services and public affairs were conducted.

mercantilism Term coined by economists in the eighteenth century for the belief that a nation's military and political well-being depended on an active regulation of international trade, generally toward such goals as increasing exports, decreasing imports, and securing a net influx of gold and silver.

merger and integration The process by which two or more companies combine to form a larger whole.

Middle Colonies Conventional term for the English colonies on the Atlantic seaboard that lay between New England and the Chesapeake (New York, New Jersey, Pennsylvania, and Delaware).

Middle Passage The forced transatlantic journey of African captives bound for slavery in the Americas.

military-industrial complex Dwight D. Eisenhower's disparaging name for the tight-knit relationship that emerged between some branches of industry and the Department of Defense in the 1950s.

militiamen Members of locally governed military units during the Revolutionary War, typically serving for short periods.

millennialism The belief in the imminent arrival of a thousand-year reign of Christ that will usher in the Last Judgment, or more generally an anticipation of imminent apocalyptic change.

Millerites Name given to the adherents of William Miller's millennialist prophecies in the 1840s.

mining frontier Miners' eastward movement in the second half of the nineteenth century from California to newly discovered ore deposits in Nevada, Montana, Idaho, Colorado, and elsewhere.

Mississippian civilization Term used by archaeologists and historians to describe a shared culture and a network of political influence, centered in Cahokia near present-day St. Louis, linking a broad range of Indian groups in the Midwest and Southeast.

modern corporation A large, hierarchical business enterprise, staffed by salaried and waged employees and owned by stockholders, that came to play a dominant and sometimes controversial role in the American economy after 1865.

modern Republicanism An approach to government, championed by Dwight D. Eisenhower in the 1950s, that followed a conciliatory middle path between New Deal liberalism and conservative Republicanism and that promoted the interests both of corporations and middle-class Americans.

monopoly The term that critics of big business used in the nineteenth and early twentieth centuries to describe companies that were free to charge high prices because they had no or only a few competitors.

moral drama A new kind of reform-minded theatrical entertainment, deemed respectable for women and children, introduced in American cities in the mid-nineteenth century.

moundbuilding A type of massive earthworks construction used by numerous indigenous North American groups for ceremonial and political purposes many centuries before European contact.

muckrakers The name that President Theodore Roosevelt gave journalists of the Progressive Era who investigated and publicized governmental corruption, dangerous living and working conditions, and the ruthlessness of certain leading businessmen.

N

nationalization A controversial strategy, popular among postcolonial peoples after World War II and frequently opposed by the U.S. government, for returning ownership of national resources such as land and oil deposits to the people, usually through a government takeover.

nation-state A political unit claiming sovereignty over a distinct territory with a shared ethnic or historical identity, as distinguished from an individual city-state or an empire governing diverse lands.

nativists Advocates of the interests and privileges of native-born citizens and supporters of immigration restriction.

natural rights Basic individual rights that many eighteenth-century pamphleteers, orators, and theorists believed to emanate from nature or God rather than from tradition or government.

Navigation Acts A series of laws imposed by England's Parliament, beginning in 1651, regulating the commerce and shipping of its colonies.

neocolonialism An arrangement by which business and government in the developed world exercised economic, cultural, political, or technological influence over a developing country; critics condemned such policies as a new kind of colonialism.

neoconservatism Late-twentieth-century intellectual and political movement that rejected the liberalism and leftism of the 1960s and revived and updated the political, economic, and social conservatism of the early and mid-twentieth century.

New Deal President Franklin D. Roosevelt's collective name for the reforms he pushed through Congress during the Depression era and that historians later distinguished as the First New Deal (1933–1935) and Second New Deal (1935–1936).

New Economy Term coined in the 1990s to describe the changing economy, which was increasingly service oriented and based on digital technologies.

New Federalism The conservative judicial philosophy, increasingly influential in the late twentieth century, holding that the courts should compel the federal government to devolve as much regulatory power as possible to the states.

nonaligned movement An alliance of developing countries, founded in the 1950s and still active today, whose members were committed to steering an independent "middle path" through the Cold War and resisted pressure to align themselves with either the United States or the Soviet Union.

nonconsumption A strategy of broad consumer boycotts of British-made goods by colonists opposed to Parliament's taxation and regulation.

nonimportation agreements Boycotts of British imports by colonial merchants seeking to reverse Parliament's taxation and regulation.

nonresistance Abolitionist doctrine of disavowing all violence, including the coercive powers of the state.

nuclear brinksmanship A negotiating tactic adopted under President Dwight D. Eisenhower by which the United States refused to back down in a Cold War crisis even if it meant taking the nation to the brink of nuclear war.

nuclear family The most common family unit between the end of World War II and 1970, composed of two married, heterosexual parents and their children.

O

Open Door Name of the foreign affairs policy, first articulated in 1899, that all major powers should have trading rights with China and respect China's administrative and territorial integrity.

open range A large area of western prairie on which cattle ranged freely after the Civil War.

Overland Trail Land route across the Rocky Mountains, traversed by tens of thousands of Americans every year from the mid-1840s through the 1860s.

P

pan-Indian An outlook that minimized the differences among Indian villages and nations and asserted the common political interest and identity of all Native Americans.

Paris Commune A revolutionary alliance between middle and working classes that briefly ruled Paris, France, in 1871 and was subsequently portrayed in the mainstream American press as proof that the world's laboring classes were organized and dangerous.

paternalism A form of labor discipline and ideology associated with slaveholders who knew their slaves intimately, took an active and meddlesome interest in their lives, and regarded them as childlike inferiors who needed care and protection.

patriarch A male head-of-household who wields broad authority over household members, including women, children, relatives, and other dependents.

penny press Cheap daily urban newspapers pitched to a mass readership.

pictorial magazines Mass-circulation weeklies in the Civil War era that featured engravings and drawings.

pietism Religious movements that stress rigorous personal observance and intense prayer experience.

Pilgrims Radical religious dissenters in seventeenth-century England who favored separating themselves from the corrupting influence of the Anglican Church and from English society.

placer mining Sifting sand and gravel in search of gold and other precious metals.

Plains bison A near-extinct species of bison common on the Great Plains before the 1870s and of great spiritual and economic importance to Plains Indians.

plantation A large farm engaged in commercial agricultural production, typically worked by enslaved laborers.

pluralist nationalism The belief, widely promoted by government and the culture industries during World War II, that the United States is made up of people from many ethnic and religious backgrounds who nevertheless constitute one unified people.

political abolitionists Historians' term for antislavery activists who favored participating in the political process in order to achieve their goals.

political clubs Voluntary societies of the nineteenth century, often organized along ethnic lines and always partisan, that initiated members into the democratic process and campaigned on the party's behalf.

political machine A hierarchical political organization, influential in the nineteenth and early twentieth centuries, that controlled enough votes through a system of rewards and incentives to maintain control over city, county, or state government.

Popular Front The broad coalition of anti-fascist leftist groups, including American organizations, that fought the spread of fascism in Spain in the 1930s.

popular sovereignty The principle that the legal status of slavery in a western territory or a new state should be determined by a vote of that territory's inhabitants.

Populists A political movement, made up mostly of rural and small-town Americans in the 1890s, that demanded that the supposed interests of the people be put first in politics and the economy.

praying towns Special villages in New England where Indians who embraced Christianity were gathered in the mid-seventeenth century.

preparedness The proposition, initially promoted by Theodore Roosevelt and eventually embraced by Woodrow Wilson during World War I, that the nation ought to mobilize its military and people in preparation for war.

producers The identity that many workers and farmers assumed in the Gilded Age as a way of distinguishing themselves from alleged nonproducers such as bankers, lawyers, and gamblers.

progressive idealism Historians' term for the view, popular among middle-class social reformers in the Progressive Era, that the United States has a special, even divine, mission to improve the world, chiefly by ending war and spreading American-style democracy.

Prohibition The period from 1920 to 1933 during which it was a federal crime to produce, sell, or transport alcohol.

proprietary colony A type of English colony in the Americas entrusted to the control of an individual or a group to whom the monarch granted special authority (*see* **royal colony**).

proslavery ideology New beliefs and claims in the antebellum era that chattel slavery, at least for African Americans, was a blessing rather than a necessary evil.

protective tariffs Taxes on foreign imports, typically passed along to consumers, designed to make domestic goods more attractive.

Protestant Reformation Religious movement in sixteenth-century northern Europe that rejected the authority of the pope and ignited a revolution in Christian thought and practice.

Puritans Radical Protestants in seventeenth-century England who opposed the Anglican Church.

Q

quadroon balls Formal social gatherings in New Orleans at which elite white men cultivated intimate relationships with free women of color.

quitrent Small perpetual taxes paid by landholders in the colonies to the colonial proprietors or to the English government.

R

radical feminism An ideology that emerged from the women's rights movement in the 1970s that celebrates distinctively female worlds and values and stresses the paramount significance of sexism as a form of social oppression.

Radical Republicans Faction of the Republican Party during Reconstruction that pursued full rights for freedpeople and advocated against the rapid readmission of the Confederate states to the union.

ranching frontier The movement of ranching north from Texas and west Louisiana to Colorado and the Great Plains after the Civil War.

Reaganomics The name given to Ronald Reagan's economic policy, which emphasized lower taxes, less federal spending, and fewer regulations for business and assumed that the accumulation of wealth among the richest Americans would eventually trickle down to the less affluent classes in the form of more employment and higher wages.

real estate covenant A written agreement, typical of the early and mid-twentieth century, by which a white home purchaser promised to sell or rent his or her property only to another white person, thereby excluding African Americans and other minorities from the neighborhood or suburb.

recall A special election, called by voters and initiated in several states during the Progressive Era, whereby citizens can force a governor, a mayor, or another elected official to step down.

Reconstruction governments The state governments elected by the multiracial electorates that Reconstruction made possible between 1866 and 1877.

Red Scare Originally a reference to the alleged spread of communism and worker radicalism in the United States after communists seized power in Russia in 1917; now denotes episodes of intensive anti-communist scare-mongering that took place in 1919–1920 and 1947–1957.

redlining The institutional practice, common in mid-twentieth-century cities, of either withholding home mortgages, insurance, health care, and other resources from residents in minority-intensive neighborhoods or overcharging them for such services.

referendum A Progressive Era reform that enabled citizens in some states, provided they had gathered enough signatures for a petition, to invalidate a state or city law through a popular vote.

Regulars Full-time soldiers in a professional, hierarchical army.

Regulators Name adopted by various rural Revolutionary-era protest movements claiming the right to use violence against the government in order to redress wrongs and express broadly shared grievances.

repatriation The forcible return of persons presumed to be foreigners to their alleged homeland, most controversially carried out against almost a half-million Mexican nationals and U.S. citizens of Mexican descent during the Great Depression.

Republicans National political party in the early republic, led by Thomas Jefferson, that called for a restrained national government with modest expenditures; often called Jeffersonian Republicans to distinguish them from the later Republican Party.

Restoration The period in English history initiated by the return of the Stuart monarchy to power in 1660.

royal colony A type of English colony in the Americas directly controlled by the monarch.

S

Sabbatarianism A movement to enforce Sabbath observance.

scalawags Derisive name that Southern Democrats used during Reconstruction to refer to white Southern Republicans.

scientific management An approach to industrial production popularized by Frederick Winslow Taylor in the Progressive Era, by which the physical motions of laborers were measured, analyzed, and optimized with the objective of accelerating production.

secession commissioners Advocates of secession from the Deep South who traveled to other southern states to lobby them to join the Confederacy.

Second Empire Term used by historians of art and architecture to describe the blend of traditional and new styles that flourished in mid-nineteenth-century France under Emperor Napoleon III and that elite and middle-class Americans replicated in the Gilded Age.

Second Great Awakening Historians' term for a series of religious revivals in different parts of the United States, climaxing between 1825 and 1835 in the Northeast.

Second Party System The highly organized national political competition between Whigs and Democrats during the second quarter of the nineteenth century.

self-determination Term coined in the World War I era to describe the right of a people to form their own independent state.

sensational literature Genre of popular fiction featuring entertaining, titillating, and sometimes outrageous stories of adventure, crime, sex, and corruption.

sentimental literature Genre of popular fiction that explored and celebrated the private feelings of the characters and focused on domestic settings and family relationships.

separate spheres The nineteenth-century doctrine that men and women, because of their fundamentally different natures, ought to perform different social roles and occupy different kinds of social spaces.

service economy An economy in which businesses provide services, such as travel and financial and technical advice, rather than goods; eclipsed traditional manufacturing as the United States' dominant economic form after 1970.

sexual revolution The rejection of conventional sexual norms and practices, particularly the prohibition on extramarital sex, most strongly associated with the counterculture and radical political movements of the late 1960s and 1970s.

sit-in A protest tactic popularized by the civil rights movement of the early 1960s, in which activists integrated lunch counters, bus terminals, and other public spaces by physically occupying them.

slave codes Special laws regulating the status and conduct of slaves, first instituted in the second half of the seventeenth century.

slave narratives Examples of a literary genre in which former slaves recounted their lives in print as a means of dramatizing the horrors and injustice of slavery.

slave patrols Police forces staffed by white men and established by southern states to enforce racial hierarchy and protect against slave rebellions.

Slave Power Term used by critics of slavery to suggest that slaveholders were rigging the political system for their own benefit and undermining the freedom of white Americans.

slave societies Societies that depend primarily or heavily on the labor of chattel slaves (*see* **societies with slaves**).

social work Term that middle-class social reformers coined in the Progressive Era to describe their poor-relief activity and imbue it with professional status.

societies with slaves Societies in which slavery exists but other labor systems predominate.

southern strategy Republican Party strategy, originating in 1960 and implemented effectively by Richard Nixon's presidential campaign in 1968, to bring white working-class northerners and segregationist southern Democrats into the Republican fold.

speakeasy An unlicensed saloon that illegally sold alcohol and became prominent in the 1920s under Prohibition.

spirituals Sacred songs created by enslaved African American Christians.

spoils system The practice and policy of awarding government jobs and resources to one's partisan supporters.

stagflation Economic term developed in the 1970s to describe the convergence of inflation, stagnation, and high unemployment.

states' rights The ideology and slogan that advocated the right of individual states to resist intervention by the federal government.

street theater Rallies, processions, parades, demonstrations, and riots in public space—typically following established ritual—designed to dramatize and reinforce a political cause.

strict construction Approach to constitutional interpretation that favors limiting the federal government to those powers explicitly enumerated in the Constitution.

supply-side economics The theory, popular among conservatives from the 1980s onward but derided by most economists, that economic growth is best achieved by stimulating production through tax cuts and deregulation.

T

task system A method of labor management in which enslaved laborers are assigned quotas of work to complete in a certain time.

teetotaler Term coined by antebellum temperance reformers for someone who had signed a pledge of total abstinence from alcohol.

tenement A substandard and typically overcrowded form of urban rental housing that arose with industrialization in the nineteenth century and in which the poor, particularly immigrants, lived and sometimes worked.

Tories Name of a royalist political party in England, used by colonial Whigs to describe their local political opponents (those who remained loyal to Britain).

Trail of Tears Historians' term for the forced migration of Cherokee Indians from their homeland to Oklahoma in the mid-1830s.

tramping Popular among laborers of the Gilded Age and Great Depression eras, the practice of hitching a ride on a train for free, usually in search of work.

trench warfare A type of warfare, employed on a mass scale in World War I, in which troops create fighting lines in the form of trenches and which came to connote any kind of protracted conflict characterized by little progress.

Tsenacommacah Indian name for the tidewater region of the Chesapeake, where settlers would establish the first lasting English colony in the Americas.

U

Underground Railroad A secret network of people, routes, and safe houses that aided fugitive slaves attempting to escape the South during the antebellum era.

universal manhood suffrage A political ideal of granting all adult white men the right to vote.

urban frontier A network of cities established west of the Appalachian Mountains in the early national period that encouraged and facilitated westward migration and economic development.

urban gentrification The migration, beginning in the 1980s, of wealthy people from the suburbs to the cities, which pushed rents up and poorer residents out.

urban renewal Official name for a series of urban development schemes undertaken in the 1950s and 1960s in which slums were bulldozed to make way for expressways, skyscrapers, civic centers, and middle-class apartment blocks at the expense of poor (typically, African American) residents, who were compelled to relocate.

urbanization The process by which increasing proportions of a population come to live in cities.

utopian communities Idealistic ventures to form societies of like-minded people who would live harmoniously and according to novel theories of the good life.

V

vagrancy laws State laws from the nineteenth century under which a person who could not show proof of a permanent abode (home) or, in some cases, steady employment, could be fined or imprisoned.

vertical integration A business structure, pioneered by Andrew Carnegie in the nineteenth century and adopted by many corporations after 1980, in which the corporation takes control of every step of the business, from production to finishing and distribution.

voluntarism An idea championed by Herbert Hoover in the 1920s and Great Depression that the federal government, rather than legislating solutions, should work collaboratively with big business, the states, and voluntary relief organizations to solve the nation's problems.

voluntary associations An array of social organizations, including charity groups, fraternal orders, and benevolent societies, that became central vehicles of reform activity in the antebellum North.

W

wage and price controls Economic policies, introduced during times of inflation (in the United States, notably in the 1970s), in which the government restricts what laborers will receive for their work and what can be charged for goods and services.

wage slavery A rhetorical metaphor that compares wage labor to chattel slavery for a variety of political purposes.

Waltham-Lowell system An innovative system of textile production in the early nineteenth century that employed single women and housed them in tightly regulated dormitories.

wampum Shells from whelks or quahog clams, strung together in beads and used as currency in North America after 1600 in commercial exchanges between European colonists and Indians.

war collectivism The action by which the federal government, during the two world wars, worked with industry, agriculture, labor unions, consumers, and the culture industries to channel all available resources into the war effort.

War Hawks Republican proponents of invading British Canada in 1811–1812, mostly from western states.

war on drugs Term coined by President Ronald Reagan in the 1980s to promote what became a thirty-year process of stiffening drug sentences for users and targeting the illegal drug trade at home and overseas.

war on terror An ongoing conflict, which began in 2001, with al-Qaeda and its suspected affiliates.

welfare queens Stereotype for poor, single, urban, African American mothers, whom the Reagan reelection campaign targeted in the hope of attracting the white working-class vote in 1984.

Whigs Name of an English political party, adopted by colonial critics of Britain's imperial policies in the 1760s and 1770s.

white man's burden Originally the title of a poem by English poet Rudyard Kipling, a phrase that came to denote the controversial view that white peoples had an obligation to tutor and uplift supposedly more "backward" peoples of color and that this goal could best be achieved through colonization.

women's liberation A diverse movement arising out of the radical political movements and counterculture of the late 1960s and that variously demanded equal opportunity, rights, wages, respect, and sexual enjoyment for women.

women's rights New political movement in the antebellum period designed to secure certain forms of legal and political equality for women.

women's suffrage Women's legal right to vote.

Y

yellow journalism Critical term coined in the 1890s to describe sensationalist newspaper stories that had little or no factual basis and that were designed by rival publishers Joseph Pulitzer and William Randolph Hearst to boost sales.

yeoman farmer A free agricultural landowner, typically without slaves or many dependents outside the family.

Young America Name adopted in the late 1840s by both the expansionist wing of the Democratic Party and a nationalist literary movement.

PHOTO CREDITS

FRONT END SHEET

Historical photo of school children at their desks: © Dynamic Graphics/Jupiterimages RF; Teenage boy using laptop outdoors: © Comstock Images/Getty Images RF.

FRONT MATTER

Page vii(left): Michael Elias, London, U.K., 2013; p. vii(right): Dore Bowen Solomon, San Francisco, 2013; Contents Chapter 1: © Glow Images RF; 2: Courtesy National Gallery of Art, Washington; 3: © World History Archive/Alamy; 5: © eidon photographers/Demotix/Corbis; 6: © Geoffrey Clements/Corbis; 7: © Marek Zuk/Alamy; 8: © Francis G. Mayer/Corbis; 9: © Lebrecht Music and Arts Photo Library/Alamy; 10: Library of Congress, Prints & Photographs Division [LC-USZ61-1448]; 12: © The Granger Collection, New York; 13: © Image Asset Management Ltd./Alamy; 14: Library of Congress, Prints & Photographs Division [LC-USZ62-79305]; 15: Library of Congress, Prints & Photographs Division [LC-DIG-ppmsca-12615]; 16: © North Wind Picture Archives/Alamy; 17: © Union Station, Ogden, UT; 19: © The Granger Collection, New York; 20: Library of Congress, Prints & Photographs Division [LC-USZ62-9981]; 21: © The Granger Collection, New York; 22: Library of Congress, Prints & Photographs Division [LC-USZC4-2426]; 23: © FPG/Getty Images; 24: © JHPhoto/Alamy; 25: Courtesy of the Army Art Collection, US Army Center of Military History; 26: © Pictorial Press Ltd./Alamy; 27: © J.R. Eyerman/*Life Magazine*/Time & Life Pictures/Getty Images; 28(Star Trek): © CBS via Getty Images; (television set): © Ingram Publishing/Alamy RF; 29: NASA; 30: © David J. & Janice L. Frent Collection/Corbis; 31: © Michael S. Yamashita/Corbis.

CHAPTER 1

Opener: © Aldo Tutino/Art Resource, NY; p. 4: © Peter Visscher/Getty Images RF; p. 5: © John Doebley; p. 7(top): © Glow Images RF; p. 7(bottom): NPS Photo/Martha Smith; p. 8: © Ira Block/National Geographic Creative; p. 10: © Lloyd K. Townsend/Cahokia Mounds State Historic Site; p. 11: © Ira Block/National Geographic Creative; p. 14: © Antoine Verard/The Bridgeman Art Library/Getty Images; p. 15: © Courtesy of Museum of Maritimo (Barcelona)/Ramon Manent/Corbis; p. 16(top): © V&A Images, London/Art Resource, NY; p. 16(bottom): Library of Congress, Prints & Photographs Division [LCPPa31406]; p. 17: © Max Milligan/AWL Images/Getty Images; p. 18: Library of Congress, Prints & Photographs Division [LC-DIG-pga-02716]; p. 21: © North Wind Picture Archives/Alamy; p. 22: © Dorling Kindersley/Getty Images RF; p. 23: © FALKENSTEINFOTO/Alamy; p. 24: © Bettmann/Corbis; p. 25: © Science Source; p. 26(left): © Matson Museum of Anthropology, Pennsylvania State University; p. 26(right): © North Wind Picture Archives/Alamy; p. 27: © Andreas-Ludwig Kruger/The Bridgeman Art Library/Getty Images; p. 29(top): © John Doebley; p. 29(middle): © V&A Images, London/Art Resource, NY; p. 29(bottom): © FALKENSTEINFOTO/Alamy.

CHAPTER 2

Opener: © Virginia Historical Society, Richmond, Virginia, USA/The Bridgeman Art Library; p. 32: Courtesy National Gallery of Art, Washington; p. 33(top): © Royalty-Free/Corbis; p. 33(bottom): © Witold Skrypczak/Lonely Planet Images/Getty Images; p. 34: National Archives & Records Administration [79-AA-A03]; p. 35: © Photo by The British Library/Robana via Getty Images; p. 36: © Vanessa Muros; p. 38: © Photo by Field Museum Library/Getty Images; p. 40(top): © INTERFOTO/Alamy; p. 40(bottom): © Bettmann/Corbis; p. 43: ©TopFoto/The Image Works; p. 44(both): © Robert Dechert Collection/Rare Book and Manuscript Library/University of Pennsylvania; p. 45(top): © North Wind Picture Archives/Alamy; p. 45(bottom): © Corbis; p. 47(top): Courtesy of Historic St. Luke's Church, photo by Kevin Lanpher; p. 47(bottom): © Peter Newark American Pictures/The Bridgeman Art Library; p. 49: © Culver Pictures/The Art Archive at Art Resource, NY; p. 50: © Della Huff/Alamy; p. 51: Library of Congress, Prints & Photographs Division [HABS MASS, 12-HING,5–25]; p. 52(top): © Burstein Collection/Corbis; p. 52(bottom): © SuperStock/Getty Images; p. 55: Mashantucket Pequot Museum and Research Center, Archives & Special Collections; p. 56: © The Granger Collection, New York; p. 57(bottom left): © Photo by The British Library/Robana via Getty Images; p. 57(top right): © Della Huff/Alamy.

CHAPTER 3

Opener(slave chains): © Chicago History Museum/The Bridgeman Art Library; (background): © Hemera Technologies RF; p. 60: © The Granger Collection, New York; p. 62: © G. Bramati/The Bridgeman Art Library/Getty Images; p. 63: © The New York Public Library/Art Resource, NY; p. 67(top): Courtesy of the John Carter Brown Library at Brown University; p. 67(bottom): © Mary Evans Picture Library/The Image Works; p. 68(Monticello shell): © Thomas Jefferson Foundation at Monticello; p. 68(modern shells): © Matthew Ward/Getty Images; p. 69: © The Bridgeman Art Library/Getty Images; p. 70: © Photo by Fotosearch/Getty Images; p. 71(top): © National Maritime Museum, London/The Image Works; p. 71(bottom left): From: Glassie, Henry H., *Folk Housing in Middle Virginia: A Structural Analysis of Historic Artifacts*. Knoxville: University of Tennessee Press, 1975; p. 71(bottom right): Library of Congress, Prints & Photographs Division [HABS VA,16-LONI.V,1D–1]; p. 72: © Christie's Images/The Bridgeman Art Library; p. 73: © World History Archive/Alamy; p. 74(both): © Virginia Historical Society; p. 75: © SSPL/The Image Works; p. 76: Photographs in the Carol M. Highsmith Archive, Library of Congress, Prints & Photographs Division [LC-DIG-highsm-03712]; p. 77: © North Wind Picture Archives/The Image Works; p. 78(top): Courtesy of the Peabody Museum of Archaeology and Ethnology, Harvard University, number 41–72-10/20 (60741527), www.peabody.harvard.edu; p. 78(bottom right): © Photo by Fotosearch/Getty Images; p. 79: © North Wind Picture Archives/The Image Works.

CHAPTER 4

Opener: © Museum of the City of New York/Corbis; p. 82: © Alex Cao/Getty Images RF; p. 85(top): © The Granger Collection, New York; p. 85(bottom): © Philadelphia History Museum at the Atwater Kent/Courtesy of Historical Society of Pennsylvania Collection/The Bridgeman Art Library; p. 87: © Division of Home and Community Life, National Museum of American History, Smithsonian Institution; p. 88: © Jessica Linker; p. 89: © Niday Picture Library/Alamy; p. 93: © National Museum of American History, Smithsonian Institution; p. 94(right): © The Metropolitan Museum of Art/Art Resource, NY; p. 94(bottom): © Manchester City Galleries; p. 95(left): © North Wind Picture Archives/Alamy; p. 95(right): Library of Congress, Prints & Photographs Division [HABS DEL,1-DOV,5–8]; p. 96(top): © The Warner House Association; p. 96(bottom): © Historic Map Works LLC/Getty Images; p. 97(top left): Library of Congress, Prints & Photographs Division, [HABS 166021pv]; p. 97(top right): Terraced gardens, Carter's Grove, Virginia, image # T1994–479 © The Colonial Williamsburg Foundation; p. 97(right): © Virginia Historical Society, Richmond, Virginia, USA/The Bridgeman Art Library; p. 99(top): © North Wind Picture Archives/Alamy; p. 99(bottom): Courtesy The

New-York Historical Society; p. 100: © The Art Gallery Collection/Alamy; p. 101(bottom left): © Niday Picture Library/Alamy; p. 101(top right): © North Wind Picture Archives/Alamy.

CHAPTER 5

Opener: © Private Collection/The Bridgeman Art Library; p. 104: © Ingram Publishing/SuperStock RF; p. 105: © eidon photographers/Demotix/Corbis; p. 106(top): *Sir William Johnson (1715–1774)*. John Wollaston (1736–1767) 1750–1752. Oil on canvas, ht. 30 1/16" × w. 25". Albany Institute of History & Art, gift of Laura Munsell Tremaine in memory of her father, Joel Munsell, 1922.2; p. 106(bottom): © The Granger Collection, New York; p. 108: © Peter Newark American Pictures/The Bridgeman Art Library; p. 110: © Hulton-Deutsch Collection/Corbis; p. 111: "Indigenes Du Mexique Voyage De" J. Luis Berlandier. Plate XIII "Cados" 4016.336.19. © Gilcrease Museum, Tulsa OK; p. 112: © Peter Newark American Pictures/The Bridgeman Art Library; p. 113(top): Collections of Old Sturbridge Village; p. 113(bottom): © The Metropolitan Museum of Art/Art Resource, NY; p. 114: © Museum Associates/LACMA/Art Resource, NY; p. 115: Library of Congress, Prints & Photographs Division [LC-USZC4-5315]; p. 118: Library of Congress, Prints & Photographs Division [LC-USZ62-120704]; p. 122: Courtesy of Louisiana State Museum, Gift of Mr. and Mrs. Donald W. Smith; p. 123: William L. Clements Library, University of Michigan; p. 125: Courtesy City of Brantford; p. 126: © The Granger Collection, New York; p. 127(top): Library of Congress, Prints & Photographs Division [LC-USZC4-5315]; p. 127(bottom): Library of Congress, Prints & Photographs Division [LC-USZ62-120704].

CHAPTER 6

Opener: © Private Collection/Picture Research Consultants & Archives; p. 130: © Geoffrey Clements/Corbis; p. 131: © Corbis; p. 133: Courtesy of the Bostonian Society; p. 135: *Boy's Suit*, Isle of Wight County, Virginia, 1780–1790, cotton, accession # 1964-174, image # DS1984-515 © The Colonial Williamsburg Foundation. Museum Purchase; p. 136: © Peter Newark Pictures/The Bridgeman Art Library; p. 137: Courtesy National Gallery of Art, Washington, D.C.; p. 138(top): © The Bridgeman Art Library/Getty Images; p. 138(bottom): © North Wind Picture Archives/Alamy; p. 139: Library of Congress, Prints & Photographs Division [LC-USZC4-5280]; p. 140: © The Granger Collection, New York; p. 141: Detail of *Miss Hallam as Imogen* by Charles Willson Peale, Annapolis, Maryland, 1771, oil on canvas, accession # 1956–296, image # TC1994-10 © The Colonial Williamsburg Foundation. Museum Purchase; p. 142: © The Bridgeman Art Library/Alamy; p. 144: © The Granger Collection, New York; p. 145: This image is available from the United States Library of Congress's Rare Book and Special Collections Division under the digital ID rbpe.1780180; p. 148: © Stocktrek Images, Inc./Alamy RF; p. 151: © The Trustees of the British Museum/Art Resource, NY; p. 153: © Peter Newark Pictures/The Bridgeman Art Library; p. 154: Massachusetts Archives Collection. v. 212: p.132, Petition from Prince Hall and others, January 13, 1777. SC1/series 45X. Massachusetts Archives, Boston, MA. Courtesy Massachusetts Archives; p. 155: © Image Asset Management Ltd./Alamy; p. 157(top): © Corbis; p. 157(middle): © North Wind Picture Archives/Alamy; p. 157(bottom): © Stocktrek Images, Inc./Alamy RF.

CHAPTER 7

Opener: William L. Clements Library, University of Michigan; p. 160: Library of Congress, Prints & Photographs Division [LC-DIG-pga-03091]; p. 161: Photographs in the Carol M. Highsmith Archive, Library of Congress, Prints & Photographs Division [LC-DIG-highsm-15716]; pp. 162(top, bottom), 166(top, bottom): © North Wind Picture Archives/Alamy; p. 167(left): © Bettmann/Corbis; p. 167(right): Library of Congress, Geography & Map Division, Washington [G3290 1550 .M8]; p. 169: © Division of Home and Community Life, National Museum of American History, Smithsonian Institution; p. 172: Photographs in the Carol M. Highsmith Archive, Library of Congress, Prints & Photographs Division [LC-DIG-highsm-12311]; p. 175: © Marek Zuk/Alamy; p. 176(top): John Singleton Copley, American, 1738–1815. *Mrs. James Warren (Mercy Otis)*, about 1763. Oil on canvas. 126.05 × 100.33 cm (49 5/8 × 39 1/2 in.) Museum of Fine Arts, Boston. Bequest of Winslow Warren, 31.212. Photograph © 2014 Museum of Fine Arts, Boston; p. 176(bottom): © Jon Helgason/Alamy RF; p. 177(top): Library of Congress, Prints & Photographs Division [LC-USZ62-45589]; p. 177(bottom): © Division of Home and Community Life, National Museum of American History, Smithsonian Institution; p. 178: Library of Congress, Prints & Photographs Division [LC-DIG-pga-03236]; p. 179: Susanna Rowson Papers, 1770–1879, in the Clifton Waller Barrett Library, Accession #7379–7379-c, Special Collections, University of Virginia Library, Charlottesville, VA; p. 180: Library of Congress, Prints & Photographs Division [LC-DIG-ppmsca-13641]; p. 181(left): Courtesy of the Maryland Historical Society, item ID #SVF; p. 181(middle): © Lebrecht Music and Arts Photo Library/Alamy; p. 181(right): © Evan D. Kalish; p. 182(top, bottom): © North Wind Picture Archives/Alamy.

CHAPTER 8

Opener: © Private Collection/The Bridgeman Art Library; p. 186: © Division of Home and Community Life, National Museum of American History, Smithsonian Institution; p. 188(left): © The Metropolitan Museum of Art/Art Resource, NY; p. 188(right): © Christie's Images/Corbis; p. 190(left): © The Philadelphia Museum of Art/Art Resource, NY; p. 190(right): © Picture History/Newscom; p. 191: © Bettmann/Corbis; p. 193: © AFP PHOTO/Paul J. Richards/Newscom; p. 196: Library of Congress, Prints & Photographs Division [LC-DIG-ppmsca-31832]; p. 197: © The Granger Collection, New York; p. 199(top): Library of Congress, Manuscript Division [LC-us0074]; p. 199(bottom): Library of Congress, Geography & Map Division [G3850 1792 .L4]; p. 200(top): Library of Congress, Prints & Photographs Division [LC-USZ62-48766]; p. 200(bottom): Library of Congress, Prints & Photographs Division [LC-USZ62-68175]; p. 202(top): © The Granger Collection, New York; p. 202(bottom): © J. Charles Riecks; p. 203: © The Granger Collection, New York; p. 204(top): © Francis G. Mayer/Corbis; p. 204(bottom): Library of Congress, Geography & Map Division [G3804. N4:2M3 1811 .B7]; p. 207: © Peter Newark American Pictures/The Bridgeman Art Library; p. 208: © Picture History/Newscom; p. 209: © SOTK2011/Alamy; p. 211(top): © Christie's Images/Corbis; p. 211(middle): © Bettmann/Corbis; p. 211(bottom): © SOTK2011/Alamy.

CHAPTER 9

Opener: Wisconsin Historical Society, WHi-42292; p. 214: Library of Congress, Prints & Photographs Division [LC-DIG-pga-01891]; p. 215: © North Wind Picture Archives/Alamy; p. 216: © Tom Till/Alamy; p. 218: © The Granger Collection, New York; p. 220: Library of Congress, Prints & Photographs Division [LC-USZC4-4555]; p. 221: © SuperStock/SuperStock; p. 222: Library of Congress, Prints & Photographs Division [LC-DIG-ppmsca-10755]; p. 223: Courtesy of the State Archives of Florida; p. 226: Courtesy of the Maryland Historical Society, item ID #1899.3.1; p. 228: © The Granger Collection, New York; p. 229: © Collection of the New-York Historical Society, USA/The Bridgeman Art Library; p. 230: © Fotosearch/Stringer/Getty Images; p. 232(left): © North Wind Picture Archives/AP Photo; p. 232(right): *Cherokee Singing Book*. Printed for the American Board of Commissioners for Foreign Missions. Boston: Alonzo P. Kenrich, 1846. Division of Rare and Manuscript Collections, Cornell University Library; p. 234: © Lebrecht Music and Arts Photo Library/Alamy; p. 235: © Picture History/Newscom; p. 236: © The New York Public Library/Art Resource, NY; p. 237: © Archive Photos/Getty Images; p. 238(bottom left): © North Wind Picture

Archives/Alamy; p. 238(top right): © SuperStock/SuperStock; p. 238(right): © Lebrecht Music and Arts Photo Library/Alamy.

CHAPTER 10

Opener: © Gift of Mrs. Samuel T. Carson/The Bridgeman Art Library; p. 242: Library of Congress, Prints & Photographs Division [LC-USZC4-970]; p. 244: Library of Congress, Prints & Photographs Division [LC_001da]; p. 245: Courtesy of Smithsonian National Postal Museum; p. 247: © Fotosearch/Stringer/Getty Images; p. 248: © RI Currency; p. 249: © Wadsworth Atheneum Museum of Art/Art Resource, NY; p. 251(left): Library of Congress, Prints & Photographs Division [LC-USZ61-1449]; p. 251(right): Library of Congress, Prints & Photographs Division [LC-USZ61-1448]; p. 251(bottom): © North Wind Picture Archives/The Image Works; p. 252(top): © Burstein Collection/Corbis; p. 252(bottom): © National Portrait Gallery, Smithsonian Institution/Art Resource, NY; p. 253: © The Philadelphia Print Shop of Philadelphia, PA and Denver, CO. www.philaprintshop.com; p. 255: © akg-images/The Image Works; p. 257: Library of Congress, Prints & Photographs Division [LC-DIG-pga-03183]; p. 259: Library of Congress, Prints & Photographs Division [LC-USZ61-372]; p. 260: © The Museum of the City of New York/Art Resource, NY; p. 262: © The Granger Collection, New York; p. 263: © The New York Public Library/Art Resource, NY; p. 264: Courtesy of the Church History Library, Salt Lake City, Utah; p. 266(top): Library of Congress, Prints & Photographs Division [LC_001da]; p. 266(middle): © Fotosearch/Stringer/Getty Images; p. 266(bottom): Library of Congress, Prints & Photographs Division [LC-USZ61-372].

CHAPTER 11

Opener: Courtesy, Georgia Archives, Vanishing Georgia Collection, dgh001; p. 270: © Corbis; p. 273: © The Historic New Orleans Collection, acc. No. 1975.93.2; p. 274(top): © The Historic New Orleans Collection/The Bridgeman Art Library; p. 274(bottom): © The Granger Collection, New York; p. 275: © Snark/Art Resource, NY; p. 276: © Philip Gould/Corbis; p. 277: © Everett Collection/Newscom; p. 278: Image courtesy of *Documenting the American South*, The University of North Carolina at Chapel Hill Libraries; p. 279: Library of Congress, Prints & Photographs Division [LC-USZC4-4659]; p. 280: © Schomburg Center, NYPL/Art Resource, NY; p. 281: © Corbis; p. 283: © The Granger Collection, New York; p. 285: © Yale Center for British Art, Paul Mellon Collection, USA/The Bridgeman Art Library; p. 286: Courtesy of Troy-Bumpas Inn Bed and Breakfast, Greensboro, NC; p. 288: Library of Congress, Prints & Photographs Division [LC-USZ62-9916]; p. 289: © Corbis; p. 292: Library of Congress, Prints & Photographs Division [LC-USZ62-123830]; p. 293: © The New York Public Library/Art Resource, NY; p. 294: © Chicago History Museum, USA/The Bridgeman Art Library; p. 295(top): © The Granger Collection, New York; p. 295(bottom): Library of Congress, Prints & Photographs Division [LC-USZ62-123830].

CHAPTER 12

Opener: © The Granger Collection, New York; p. 298: Library of Congress, Prints & Photographs Division [LC-USZC4-10005]; p. 299: Library of Congress, Prints & Photographs Division [LC-USZ62-116399]; p. 301: © Corbis; p. 302: Library of Congress, Prints & Photographs Division [LC-DIG-pga-02824]; pp. 303, 304(top): © The Granger Collection, New York; p. 304(bottom): John Hopkins University, Levy Sheet Music Collection, Box 099, Item 055; p. 305: Library of Congress, Prints & Photographs Division [LC-USZ62-123830]; p. 306: Library of Congress, Prints & Photographs Division [LC-USZ62-44265]; p. 307(top): © The Granger Collection, New York; p. 307(bottom): © American Antiquarian Society, Worcester, Massachusetts, USA/The Bridgeman Art Library; p. 308: © North Wind Picture Archives/Alamy; p. 309: © Cincinnati Museum Center. Detail of image, color overlay added; p. 310: © The Metropolitan Museum of Art/Art Resource, NY; p. 311: © The Granger Collection, New York; p. 312: © North Wind Picture Archives; p. 313(both): © The Granger Collection, New York; p. 314: © MPI/Getty Images; p. 315: The Library Company of Philadelphia; p. 317: Courtesy of Canadiana.org; p. 319(top): Library of Congress, Prints & Photographs Division [LC-USZ62-116399]; p. 319(bottom): © MPI/Getty Images.

CHAPTER 13

Opener: © The Granger Collection, New York; p. 322: Library of Congress, Prints & Photographs Division [LC-USZC4-4438]; p. 327: Library of Congress, Prints & Photographs Division [LC-DIG-pga-03889]; p. 328: © Herbert Orth/Time & Life Pictures/Getty Images; p. 333(top): © Image Asset Management Ltd./Alamy; p. 333(bottom): © Dave Porter/Alamy; p. 334 (top): © Dorothy Sloan Rare Books; p. 334(bottom): Courtesy of the Bancroft Library, University of California, Berkeley; p. 335(left): Library of Congress, Geography & Map Division, Washington [G4364.S5A35 1847 .B6]; p. 335 (right): Library of Congress, Prints & Photographs Division [LC-USZC4-7421]; p. 336: Western History Collections, University of Oklahoma, Phillips 1476; p. 337: Library of Congress, Prints & Photographs Division [LC-USZ62-108416]; p. 338: Library of Congress, Geography & Map Division, Washington [G4344.S3A3 1870 .K6]; p. 339: By permission of the Folger Shakespeare Library; p. 340: © Museum of the City of New York/Corbis; p. 341: John Hopkins University, Levy Sheet Music Collection, Box 018, Item 044; p. 342: © Lebrecht/The Image Works; p. 343: © Look and Learn/Peter Jackson Collection/The Bridgeman Art Library; p. 344: © Free Library, Philadelphia, PA, USA/The Bridgeman Art Library; p. 345: © North Wind Picture Archives/Alamy; p. 346: Library of Congress, Prints & Photographs Division [LC-DIG-ppmsca-08978]; p. 348: © bygone/Alamy; p. 349(bottom left): © Image Asset Management Ltd./Alamy; p. 349(top right): By permission of the Folger Shakespeare Library.

CHAPTER 14

Opener: © 2014 Philbrook Museum of Art, Inc., Tulsa, Oklahoma; p. 352: Courtesy of the Trustees of the Boston Public Library/Rare Books; p. 355: © The Granger Collection, New York; p. 356: © Culver Pictures/The Art Archive at Art Resource, NY; p. 357: Library of Congress, Prints & Photographs Division [LC-USZ62-107753]; p. 358: © akg/De Agostini Pic. Lib.; p. 359: © 19th era 2/Alamy RF; p. 360: © PAINTING/Alamy; p. 362(top): © The Granger Collection, New York; p. 362(bottom): Currier Museum of Art, Manchester, New Hampshire. Gift of Henry Melville Fuller, 1974.34; p. 367: © The Granger Collection, New York; p. 368: © Hulton Archive/Getty Images; p. 370: Library of Congress, Prints & Photographs Division [LC-USZ62-79305]; p. 371: © Picture History/Newscom; p. 372: © The Granger Collection, New York; p. 374: © Culver Pictures/The Art Archive at Art Resource, NY; p. 375: © Peter Horree/Alamy; p. 376: Library of Congress, Prints & Photographs Division [LC-USZC2-2564]; p. 378(top): Courtesy of the Trustees of the Boston Public Library/Rare Books; p. 378(bottom): © PAINTING/Alamy.

CHAPTER 15

Opener: Library of Congress, Prints & Photographs Division [LC-DIG-ppmsca-36863]; p. 382: Library of Congress, Prints & Photographs Division [LC-DIG-ds-00293]; p. 386: © The Granger Collection, New York; p. 387(top, bottom): © Civil War Archive/The Bridgeman Art Library; p. 390: © North Wind/North Wind Picture Archives; p. 391: © MPI/Getty Images; p. 392: © North Wind Picture Archives/Alamy; p. 396: © ClassicStock.com/SuperStock; p. 397(top): © Medford Historical Society Collection/Corbis; p. 397(bottom): © Thinkstock/Getty Images RF; p. 398: The Library Company of Philadelphia; p. 399: © Fotosearch/Getty Images; p. 401: © American Antiquarian Society; p. 402(top):

© Smithsonian American Art Museum, Washington, DC/Art Resource, NY; p. 402(bottom): Library of Congress, Prints & Photographs Division [LC-DIG-ppmsca-12561]; p. 403(top): Library of Congress, Prints & Photographs Division [LC-DIG-ppmsca-12615]; p. 403(bottom): Library of Congress, Prints & Photographs Division [LC-USP6-2415-A]; p. 409: Library of Congress, Prints & Photographs Division [LC-USZ62-96391]; p. 410: Library of Congress, Prints & Photographs Division [LC-USZ62-3855]; p. 411: From the Lincoln Financial Foundation Collection, courtesy of the Indiana State Museum and Allen County Public Library; p. 412(top): © North Wind/North Wind Picture Archives; p. 412(middle): © North Wind Picture Archives/Alamy; p. 412(bottom): Library of Congress, Prints & Photographs Division [LC-USZ62-3855].

CHAPTER 16

Opener: © The Granger Collection, New York; p. 416: Library of Congress, Prints & Photographs Division [LC-B8171-152-A]; p. 417: © Bettmann/Corbis; p. 418: © Pictorial Press Ltd./Alamy; p. 420: © Hulton Collection/Getty Images; p. 421: Courtesy North Carolina Museum of History; p. 424: Papers, 1865, Accession #6060, University of Virginia Library, Charlottesville, VA; p. 425: National Archives and Records Administration [111-B-1458]; p. 426: Library of Congress, Prints & Photographs Division [LC-USZ62-40764]; p. 427: © North Wind Picture Archives/Alamy; p. 428: Library of Congress, Prints & Photographs Division [LC-USZC4-5947]; p. 429(top): Library of Congress, Prints & Photographs Division [LC-USZ62-125422]; p. 429(bottom): © J.R. Bale Balefire C/agefotostock RF; p. 430: © Image Asset Management Ltd./SuperStock; p. 432: Library of Congress, Prints & Photographs Division [LC-DIG-ppmsca-11008]; p. 433: © Corbis; p. 435: Chicago History Museum, CHi-29053; p. 436 (left): Library of Congress, Prints & Photographs Division [LC-USZ62-102256]; p. 436(right): Courtesy American Social History Project; p. 437: Library of Congress, Prints & Photographs Division [LC-USZ62-58277]; p. 438: © The Granger Collection, New York; p. 439: © The Historic New Orleans Collection, acc. no. 89-098-RL; p. 441: U.S. Senate Collection; p. 442(top): © Hulton Collection/Getty Images; p. 442(middle): National Archives and Records Administration [111-B-1458]; p. 442(bottom): U.S. Senate Collection.

CHAPTER 17

Opener: Tom Lea, *Design for The Western Frontier, 1st Phase, 1830–1860, 1935.* Casein Tempera. © Tom Lea Institute; p. 446: © Peter Newark American Pictures/The Bridgeman Art Library; p. 448: Courtesy of Michael D. Schroeder at The Gilbert Munger Web Site; p. 449(top): Courtesy of Reynolda House Museum of American Art, Winston-Salem, North Carolina; p. 449(bottom): National Archives and Records Administration [77-KS-P-13]; p. 450: © Union Station, Ogden, UT; p. 451: © The Art Gallery Collection/Alamy; p. 453: © Gift of Mrs. Jacob D. Cox/The Bridgeman Art Library; p. 454: © Bettmann/Corbis; p. 455: © INTERFOTO/agefotostock; p. 456: © Glasshouse Images/Alamy; p. 457: © Corbis; p. 461: © David Henderson/Corbis RF; p. 462: Sharlot Hall Museum; p. 463: Library of Congress, Prints & Photographs Division [LC-DIG-pga-00435]; pp. 464, 465: © The Granger Collection, New York; p. 466: © Bill Manns/The Art Archive at Art Resource, NY; p. 468: Courtesy of The Huntington Library, Rare Books Department, RB471218; p. 470(bottom left): © Gift of Mrs. Jacob D. Cox/The Bridgeman Art Library; p. 470(top right): © Union Station, Ogden, UT; p. 470(right): © The Granger Collection, New York.

CHAPTER 18

Opener: © The Granger Collection, New York; p. 474: Library of Congress, Prints & Photographs Division [LC-DIG-ppmsca-02957]; p. 476: © The Museum of the City of New York/Art Resource, NY; p. 477: © Sears Roebuck and Co./AP Photo; p. 478: Library of Congress, Prints & Photographs Division [LC-USZC2-3252]; p. 479(left): Library of Congress, Prints & Photographs Division [LC-DIG-pga-02434]; p. 479(right): William L. Clements Library, University of Michigan; p. 480: © Bettmann/Corbis; p. 481: © Buyenlarge/Getty Images; p. 483: © Collection of the New-York Historical Society, USA/The Bridgeman Art Library; p. 485: Library of Congress, Prints & Photographs Division [LC-USZC4-3936]; p. 486: Library of Congress, Prints & Photographs Division [LC-USZ62-119782]; p. 489: © Amoret Tanner/Alamy; p. 490: The Library Company of Philadelphia; p. 491: © The New York Public Library/Art Resource, NY; p. 492: Library of Congress, Prints & Photographs Division [LC-USZ62-16348]; p. 493: Library of Congress, Prints & Photographs Division [LC-USZ62-63945]; p. 495: © The New York Public Library/Art Resource, NY; p. 496: Library of Congress, Prints & Photographs Division [LC-USZ62-55171]; p. 497: Library of Congress, Prints & Photographs Division [LC-USZC4-4698]; p. 499(bottom left): Library of Congress, Prints & Photographs Division [LC-DIG-ppmsca-02957]; p. 499(top right): © Sears Roebuck and Co./AP Photo.

CHAPTER 19

Opener: Library of Congress, Prints & Photographs Division [LC-DIG-ppmsca-19299]; p. 502: © Corbis; p. 503: © The Granger Collection, New York; p. 505: © HarpWeek, LLC; p. 506: © The Granger Collection, New York; p. 507: © Culver Pictures/The Art Archive at Art Resource, NY; p. 508: Courtesy Mary Mark Ockerbloom; p. 509: © Everett Collection/Newscom; p. 511: Special Collections & University Archives, University of Illinois at Chicago Library, JAMC_0000_0147_0882; p. 512: © Warshaw Collection of Business Americana, Archives Center, National Museum of American History, Smithsonian Institution; p. 514: Library of Congress, Prints & Photographs Division [LC-USZ62-121654]; p. 516: © The Granger Collection, New York; p. 517: Library of Congress, Prints & Photographs Division [LC-DIG-ppmsca-28325]; p. 519: Library of Congress, Prints & Photographs Division [LC-USZ62-120765]; p. 521: © North Wind Picture Archives/Alamy; p. 523: Library of Congress, Prints & Photographs Division [LC-US2C4-5126]; p. 524: © The Granger Collection, New York; p. 526(left): Courtesy The Newberry Library, Chicago. Call# MMS Pullman, Box 9, Fl. 110; p. 526(right): © The Granger Collection, New York; p. 527: © Fotosearch/Getty Images; p. 528: © Schomburg Center, NYPL/Art Resource, NY; p. 531(top): © The Granger Collection, New York; p. 531(middle): © North Wind Picture Archives/Alamy; p. 531 (bottom): © Schomburg Center, NYPL/Art Resource, NY.

CHAPTER 20

Opener: © Bettmann/Corbis; p. 534: Library of Congress, Prints & Photographs Division [LC-DIG-ggbain-17937]; p. 535: © Roger-Viollet/The Image Works; p. 537: © Bettmann/Corbis; p. 538: Courtesy of the American Labor Museum/Botto House National Landmark; p. 541: Silicon Valley Historical Association; p. 542: © Bettmann/Corbis; p. 543: Library of Congress, Prints & Photographs Division [LC-USZ62-121061]; p. 544: © Bettmann/Corbis; p. 545: © American Stock/Getty Images; p. 546: © Gianni Dagli Orti/The Art Archive at Art Resource, NY; p. 547: Library of Congress, Prints & Photographs Division [LC-USZ62-100109]; p. 548: © Mary Evans Picture Library/The Image Works; p. 550: Library of Congress, Prints & Photographs Division [LC-USZ62-16767]; p. 551: Courtesy, California Historical Society, FN-19319/CHS2010.222; p. 552: © The Granger Collection, New York; p. 553: From: Florence Kelley, "Aims and Principles of the Consumers' League," *American Journal of Sociology*, 5(3):289-304, illustration p. 299, (Nov., 1899), published by The University of Chicago Press; p. 555: © Science Source; p. 556: Birmingham, Ala. Public Library Archives; p. 561: Library of Congress, Prints & Photographs Division [LC-USZ62-9981]; p. 562 (top): © Bettmann/Corbis; p. 562(bottom): © Gianni Dagli Orti/The Art Archive at Art Resource, NY; p. 563: Courtesy of the American Labor Museum/Botto House National Landmark.

CHAPTER 21

Opener: Library of Congress, Prints & Photographs Division [LC-DIG-ppmsca-28945]; p. 566: © Circus World Museum, Baraboo, Wisconsin; p. 569: Photo courtesy of the Presbyterian Heritage Center at Montreat. William Henry Sheppard (far right), whom the peoples of Congo called the "black white man"; p. 570: © Underwood & Underwood/Corbis; p. 572: Library of Congress, Prints & Photographs Division [LC-USZ62-80003]; p. 573: Image courtesy of Independence Seaport Museum (Philadelphia, PA); p. 575: Library of Congress, Prints & Photographs Division [LC-USZ62-26149]; p. 576: © The Granger Collection, New York; p. 578(top): Library of Congress, Motion Picture Broadcasting & Recorded Sound Division [FLA 5963]; p. 578(bottom): © The Granger Collection, New York; p. 579: Library of Congress, Prints & Photographs Division [LC-USZ62-63679]; p. 582: © Corbis; p. 584: National Archives and Records Administration [111-SC-83648]; p. 585: Library of Congress, Prints & Photographs Division [LC-USZ62-111761]; p. 587: Collection of the Australian National Maritime Museum, Object no. 00050217; p. 590: © Atlas Archive/The Image Works; p. 592: © Mary Evans Picture Library/Science Source; p. 594(left): Library of Congress, Prints & Photographs Division [LC-USZ62-80003]; p. 594 (bottom left): © The Granger Collection, New York; p. 594(right): © Mary Evans Picture Library/Science Source.

CHAPTER 22

Opener: © The Granger Collection, New York; p. 598: © Corbis; p. 601: © Bettmann/Corbis; p. 603: © Swim Ink 2, LLC/Corbis; p. 604: © WW/Alamy; p. 606: Library of Congress, Prints & Photographs Division [LC-USZC4-10234]; p. 607: Library of Congress, Prints & Photographs Division [LC-USZC2-1351]; p. 609: © The Film Company/AF archive/Alamy; p. 611: Library of Congress, Prints & Photographs Division [LC-USZC4-1539]; p. 612: © Corbis; p. 613: © Giraudon/The Bridgeman Art Library; p. 614: Library of Congress, Prints & Photographs Division [LC-USZC4-2426]; p. 615: © Corbis; p. 617: Library of Congress, Prints & Photographs Division [LC-USZ62-31799]; p. 620: © Time & Life Pictures/Getty Images; p. 621: Library of Congress, Prints & Photographs Division [LC-DIG-ppmsca-13425]; p. 622: © Harris Lewine Collection/AP Photo; p. 623: Library of Congress, Prints & Photographs Division [LC-DIG-ds-00894]; pp. 624, 627(top): © Bettmann/Corbis; p. 627(middle): Library of Congress, Prints & Photographs Division [LC-USZC4-10234]; p. 627(bottom): Library of Congress, Prints & Photographs Division [LC-USZC4-2426].

CHAPTER 23

Opener: © Bettmann/Corbis; p. 630: Library of Congress, Prints & Photographs Division [LC-USZ62-136527]; p. 631: Library of Congress, Prints & Photographs Division [LC-DIG-hec-42099]; p. 633: © Transcendental Graphics/Getty Images; p. 634: © Bettmann/Corbis; p. 635: © MBR KRT/Newscom; p. 636: © FPG/Getty Images; p. 637: Image courtesy University of Minnesota Libraries; p. 639: © Planet News Archive/SSPL/Getty Images; p. 640: © Mark Rucker/Transcendental Graphics/Getty Images; p. 641(top): Library of Congress, Prints & Photographs Division [LC-USZ62-22847]; p. 641(bottom): © ClassicStock/Corbis; p. 642: © NY Daily News via Getty Images; p. 643: © David Pollack/Corbis; p. 645: Courtesy: Everett Collection; p. 649: © Education Images/UIG/Getty Images; p. 651: Library of Congress, Prints & Photographs Division [LC-DIG-npcc-06624]; pp. 654, 656: © Corbis; pp. 657, 658(bottom left): © Bettmann/Corbis; p. 658(top right): © Education Images/UIG/Getty Images; p. 658(right): Library of Congress, Prints & Photographs Division [LC-DIG-npcc-06624].

CHAPTER 24

Opener: © Margaret Bourke-White/Time & Life Pictures/Getty Images; p. 662: © Smithsonian American Art Museum, Washington, DC/Art Resource, NY; pp. 665, 666, 668, 669, 671: © Bettmann/Corbis; p. 672: Missouri Valley Special Collections, Kansas City Public Library, Kansas City, Missouri; p. 674: Library of Congress, Prints & Photographs Division [LC-USZC2-662]; p. 675: Courtesy of the Archives and Records Services Division, Mississippi Department of Archives and History; p. 676: © Nickolas Muray/George Eastman House/Getty Images; p. 677(top): © Universal Images Group/Getty Images; p. 677(bottom): © JHPhoto/Alamy; p. 678(left): © Corbis; p. 678(right): Courtesy: Everett Collection; p. 679: © David Pollack/Corbis; p. 680: © The Granger Collection, New York; p. 682: © David J. & Janice L. Frent Collection/Corbis; p. 684: Library of Congress, Prints & Photographs Division [LC-DIG-fsa-8b29516]; p. 686: © Corbis; p. 691(top): © Bettmann/Corbis; p. 691(middle): © Corbis; p. 691(bottom): Library of Congress, Prints & Photographs Division [LC-DIG-fsa-8b29516].

CHAPTER 25

Opener: Library of Congress, Prints & Photographs Division [LC-USZC4-12529]; p. 694: © INTERFOTO/Alamy; p. 697: © Bettmann/Corbis; p. 698: © J.A. Hampton/Topical Press Agency/Getty Images; p. 699: © Zoonar/S. Nezhinkiy/agefotostock RF; p. 700: © Getty Images; p. 701: National Archives and Records Administration [179-WP-12]; p. 702: National Archives and Records Administration [NWDNS-44-PA-24]; p. 704: Courtesy of the Bancroft Library, University of California, Berkeley; p. 707: Naval History and Heritage Command, Washington, DC; p. 708: © Lake County Museum/Corbis; p. 709: Library of Congress, Prints & Photographs Division [LC-USF34-011543-D]; p. 710: © Terry Smith Images/Alamy; p. 711: © Getty Images; p. 712: © picture-alliance/Newscom; p. 713: © Pictorial Press Ltd./Alamy; p. 714: © akg-images/Newscom; p. 718: Courtesy of the Army Art Collection, US Army Center of Military History; p. 720: © Roger Viollet/Getty Images; p. 722(top): © J.A. Hampton/Topical Press Agency/Getty Images; p. 722(bottom): © Zoonar/S. Nezhinkiy/agefotostock RF; p. 723: © Terry Smith Images/Alamy.

CHAPTER 26

Opener: © Three Lions/Hulton Archive/Getty Images; p. 726: © Pictorial Press Ltd./Alamy; p. 727: Library of Congress, Prints & Photographs Division [LC-USZC4-6144]; p. 728: © Pictorial Press Ltd./Alamy; p. 730: © AP Photo; p. 735: © Time & Life Pictures/Getty Images; p. 736: © Culinary Institute of America; p. 737: Courtesy of the State Museum of Pennsylvania, Pennsylvania Historical and Museum Commission; p. 738: The J. Paul Getty Museum, Los Angeles. William A. Garnett, *Finished Housing, Lakewood, California, 1950*, Gelatin silver print © Estate of William A. Garnett; p. 739: © SuperStock/Getty Images; p. 740: © Jeff Morgan 06/Alamy; p. 742: © Walter Sanders/Time & Life Pictures/Getty Images; p. 743: National Archives and Records Administration II RG 195 Entry 39 Folder "Greater Detroit, MI" Box 21. Image provided by LaDale Winling, www.urbanoasis.org; p. 744(top): © Atlanta Journal-Constitution, Guy Hayes/AP Photo; p. 744(bottom): Used with permission from the Afro-American Newspapers Archives and Research Center; p. 747: Photograph by William Dellenback. Courtesy of The Kinsey Institute for Research in Sex, Gender, and Reproduction; p. 749: © Time & Life Pictures/Getty Images; p. 751: © AF archive/Alamy; p. 752: © Time & Life Pictures/Getty Images; p. 753: © Bettmann/Corbis; p. 754(top): Library of Congress, Prints & Photographs Division [LC-USZC4-6144]; p. 754(middle): © Time & Life Pictures/Getty Images; p. 754(bottom): © AF archive/Alamy.

CHAPTER 27

Opener: © Private Collection/Picture Research Consultants & Archives; p. 758: © PhotoEdit/Alamy; p. 760: Courtesy: Everett Collection; p. 761: © Hulton Archive/Getty Images; p. 762: © J.R. Eyerman/*Life Magazine*/Time & Life Pictures/Getty Images; p. 763: © Bettmann/

Corbis; p. 764: © William Gottlieb/Corbis; p. 766: © Corbis; p. 768: © Everett Collection/ Newscom; p. 771: © ZUMA Press, Inc./Alamy; p. 773: © Bettmann/Corbis; p. 774: © Columbia Pictures/Getty Images; p. 775: © Paul Hoeffler/ Redferns/Getty Images; p. 776: © Allen Ginsberg/Corbis; p. 778: © Mug Shot/Alamy; p. 779: © Bettmann/Corbis; p. 781: © ullstein bild/The Image Works; p. 784: © Paul Schutzer/Time & Life Pictures/Getty Images; p. 785(top): © J.R. Eyerman/*Life Magazine*/Time & Life Pictures/ Getty Images; p. 785(bottom): © ZUMA Press, Inc./Alamy.

CHAPTER 28

Opener: © Bettmann/Corbis; p. 788: © CBS via Getty Images; p. 789: Robert Knudsen, White House/John F. Kennedy Presidential Library and Museum; p. 790: © Pictorial Press Ltd./Alamy; p. 795: © Jack Moebes/Corbis; p. 797: © Bill Hudson, file/AP Photo; p. 798: © Bob Parent/ Getty Images; p. 799: Library of Congress, Prints & Photographs Division [LC-USZ62-120412]; p. 803: © Everett Collection/Newscom; p. 806: © Three Lions/Getty Images; p. 807: Library of Congress, Prints & Photographs Division [LC-USZ62-119478]; p. 808: © Bettmann/Corbis; p. 809: © Duke Downey/*San Francisco Chronicle*/ Corbis; p. 811: © Donne Bryant/Art Resource, NY; p. 812: © Elliott Landy/Corbis; p. 813: © Imagno/Getty Images; p. 815: © Bettmann/ Corbis; p. 817: © Henry Diltz/Corbis; p. 818(top): Robert Knudsen, White House/John F. Kennedy Presidential Library and Museum; p. 818(middle): © Bob Parent/Getty Images; p. 818(bottom): © Pictorial Press Ltd./Alamy; p. 819: © Donne Bryant/Art Resource, NY.

CHAPTER 29

Opener(Polaroid picture): © ClassicStock/Corbis; (background): © Nick Koudis/Getty Images RF; p. 822: © Idols/Photoshot; p. 823: © Str/FILE UPI Photo Service/Newscom; p. 824: © Fred Waters/AP Photo; p. 825: © United Archives GmbH/Alamy; p. 826: © Moviestore collection Ltd./Alamy; p. 829: © Dave Pickoff/AP Photo; p. 830: © Michael Ochs Archives/Getty Images; p. 831: © Spencer Jones/AP Photo; pp. 832, 834: © Bettmann/Corbis; p. 837: © Edie Baskin/ NBC/NBCU Photo Bank/Getty Images; p. 838: National Archives and Records Administration [412-DA-13037]; p. 840: © Brand X Pictures/ PunchStock RF; p. 841: © Fred Jewell/AP Photo; p. 842: © Bettmann/Corbis; p. 844: © Charles Tasnadi/AP Photo; p. 845: © Bettmann/Corbis; p. 847: NASA; p. 848: © Str/FILE UPI Photo Service/Newscom; p. 849(top): © United Archives GmbH/Alamy; p. 849(bottom): © Bettmann/ Corbis.

CHAPTER 30

Opener: © Boris Roessler/dpa/Corbis; p. 852: © Timothy Fadek/Corbis; p. 853: © Joe Klein/ ZUMAPRESS.com/Newscom; p. 855: © David J. & Janice L. Frent Collection/Corbis; p. 858: © MCA/Universal/Courtesy: Everett Collection; p. 860: Photo courtesy of the Exxon Valdez Oil Spill Trustee Council; p. 862: © Wally McNamee/ Corbis; p. 863: PHOTOGRAPH BY NORMAN SEEFF; p. 864: © Jeff Greenberg "0 people images"/Alamy; p. 865: © AP Photo; p. 866: © ClassicStock/Alamy; p. 867: © James Keyser/ Time & Life Pictures/Getty Images; p. 868: © United Archives GmbH/Alamy; p. 869: © Blank Archives/Getty Images; p. 871: © David Hume Kennerly/Getty Images; p. 872(top): © Susan Steinkamp/Corbis; p. 872(bottom): © The New York Public Library/Art Resource, NY; p. 873: © SuperStock/Alamy; p. 878: © Peter Turnley/ Corbis; p. 879: © David J. & Janice L. Frent Collection/Corbis; p. 880(top): © MCA/Universal/ Courtesy: Everett Collection; p. 880(bottom): © Blank Archives/Getty Images.

CHAPTER 31

Opener(crowd of people): © Nicole Bengiveno/ The New York Times Photo Archives; (hand holding camera): © Photodisc/Getty Images RF; p. 884: © Leslie Close/AP Photo; p. 885: © Reed Saxon, File/AP Photo; p. 889: © Susan Weems, File/AP Photo; p. 890: © Michael S. Yamashita/ Corbis; p. 891: © David Bookstaver/AP Photo; p. 892: © Peter Turnley/Corbis; p. 895(top): © Chris Harrison, Carnegie Mellon University; p. 895(bottom right): © Najlah Feanny/Corbis SABA; p. 896: Photo by: Tony Gonzalez/Everett Collection; p. 897: © Mark Lennihan/AP Photo; p. 901: © UPI Photo/Kamenko Pajic/Newscom; p. 903: © J. Scott Applewhite, File/AP Photo; p. 904: © AP Photo, File; p. 905: U.S. Navyphoto by Photographer's Mate Airman Jeremy L. Grisham; p. 906: © Lance Iversen/*San Francisco Chronicle*/Corbis; p. 909: © Saul Loeb, Pool/AP Photo; p. 911: © Reed Saxon, File/AP Photo; p. 912(top): © Najlah Feanny/Corbis SABA; p. 912(bottom): © AP Photo, File.

INDEX

Page numbers with *m* refer to maps.

A

B

D

F

H

I

I

L

M

N

Q

R

S

U

X

Y

Z